1997 COMIC BOOK CHECKLIST & PRICE GUIDE

1961 - PRESENT

3RD EDITION

D1309017

MAGGIE THOMPSON &
BRENT FRANKENHOFF

Published by

 **krause
publications**

700 E. State Street • Iola, WI 54990-0001
Telephone: 715/445-2214

Please call or write for our free catalog.
Our toll-free number to place an order or obtain a free catalog is 800-258-0929
or please use our regular business telephone 715-445-2214
for editorial comment and further information.

Library of Congress Catalog Number: 94-77503

ISBN: 0-87341-466-7

Printed in the United States of America

Contents

Acknowledgments

As always, there are so many people to thank that we're bound to miss a few on this page. To anyone who should be thanked but isn't (you know who you are): We are sorry, and you know we couldn't have done any of this without you.

Thanks to Cliff Biggers, Larry Hancock, Mike Tiefenbacher, James E. McGinnis, and John Weber II for their invaluable help with pricing and title information each year (especially Cliff's who provides massive last-minute pricing input). Thanks, too, to Jack Abramowitz, Craig Shutt, and Greg Myers, who provided information for several of our background features.

Thanks to all the publishers who came through with additional information (not to mention additions and corrections) on their respective titles. Thanks also to the readers of our previous editions who have been providing additional data on their favorite titles, data we didn't have or didn't know existed. See our introduction for information on how you can be part of these acknowledgments next year.

Thanks to our own behind-the-scenes people, including computer genius Steve Duberstein (who performed his usual magic on the data, transforming it into information that could be designed); Bonnie Tetzlaff, Patsy Morrison, and Rajean Civik for designing the price guide (and discovering that the price listings took 556 of the projected 560 total pages, leading to the addition of 16 pages so that we could bring you background features, the introduction, and these acknowledgments); Allen West for designing the covers; Book Department Copy Editor Melissa Warden for jumping in at the last minute to catch all those last-minute things one finds when a project's on its way out the door; the photo-scanning department and book production department; such others as Greg Loescher and Pat Klug; the entire comics and records department at Krause Publications and everyone else at KP (especially Kim Pichler) for being understanding and helpful when we were in the home stretch of sending this book to the printer.

A special thanks to *Comic Buyer's Guide* Associate Editors Michael Dean and John Jackson Miller, who provided copious amounts of background information from their collections, and Associate Editor Joyce Greenholdt, who assisted in the design of the background feature pages.

Most of all, we acknowledge the work of Don Thompson, who nursed this project through the last 11 years of his life. We miss you, Don.

And we thank you all.

Introduction

By Maggie Thompson

This checklist and price guide is intended to function in a number of fashions. You can use it as a "have" list, in which you maintain an inventory of the comics you're collecting. (Make an "X" in the box for each one you have. If you want, you can circle the condition indicated — or use your own symbols indicating what you please in the open box. You can then see at a glance what is left of a title you might want to collect.)

You can use it as a guide to show prices you can expect to pay for items, if you find them in comics shops throughout the country. (You may find much higher prices for specific items in top condition from mail-order and auction house sales. Those vendors can reach a national audience for select hard-to-find items and, thus, can realize higher prices.)

Whether you're buying or selling comic books, one of the most important factors in setting the price is condition of the material. A scuffed, torn "reading copy" (that is, one that is suitable for reading but not for getting high prices at resale) will bring only a fraction of the price of a copy of the same issue in the same shape in which it came off the newsstand. Picky collectors will even go through all the copies on the newsstand so as to buy the one in best condition. (Even a so-called "news-stand mint" copy of *Fantastic Four* #1 may have what is called "Marvel chipping," since many of those early-'60s issues were badly cut by the printer.)

On the other hand, beat-up copies can provide bargains for collectors whose primary focus is reading the comic-book story. The same goes for reprints of comics which would otherwise be hard to find.

In addition to new character background features similar to the ones we ran last year, we have brought in modified versions of features we run in both *Comics Buyer's Guide* and its monthly *Comic Buyer's Guide Price Guide*: *Didja know?*, *How's That Again?*, and *Flashback*. You'll find them at the end of each letter where space was available.

Are There Any Questions?

Readers have been kind enough to ask many questions about our price guide. To help you make best use of this volume, we're answering many of them here (and we're providing answers to questions you didn't ask us, too, in an attempt to give you more information than you can possibly use).

?

Why do we need a *price* guide at all? Why not just provide a comprehensive guide to what's available?

We've spent more than a dozen years trying to produce an indication of back-issue prices that reflect what a consumer can expect to pay in a comics shop, if he's looking — for example — for that issue that will complete his run of the two DC series of *Shade the Changing Man*. The collector will find that even the highest-priced issue in the best condition probably won't cost more than about $10 — and that's the sort of information that can motivate a casual reader to become a collector.

Moreover, *Comics Buyer's Guide* tries to provide helpful information to people who purchase it in order to have a (yes) guide to buying comics. Pricing information is just one part of what we offer. (And, by the way, I am increasingly intrigued by the even *more* detailed information you'll find in this book — where we provide original cover date and price information wherever we can locate it.)

?

Why can't I find the title in your list?

We're working constantly to (a) increase the listings themselves and (b) increase the information on the listings we already provide.

Check out what we have included and — if you have what we want and we're not listing it — please let us know the details!

We need to know the information as given in the indicia of the issue (that's the tiny print, usually on the first few pages, that gives the publishing information): the full title, the number, and the issue month and year — and the U.S. price given on the cover. If you find work by a creator on our abbreviations list and we haven't noted it in this guide, please include that information. If there's a significant event (especially as given in the abbreviations list), please include that, too.

This is an annual volume designed to consolidate our information — but **Comics Buyer's Guide** runs updated portions on a monthly basis (with commentary on the preceding month's sales activity and previews of upcoming material), and we're trying to add to the data constantly.

Check, too, on whether you're looking up the title as it appears in the indicia. In some cases, we refer you to the complete title (which may not occur to you immediately). For example, we list *Anne Rice's The Vampire Lestat*, not *The Vampire Lestat*; we list *Don Pendleton's Mack Bolan: The Executioner*, not *The Executioner*.

Many Marvel titles have adjectives. *Hulk*, for example, is listed as *The Incredible Hulk*.

?

What's in this book?

This Silver Age price guide began as a quarterly update of activity in the comics field as reflected in prices comics shops were likely to charge. Moreover, the focus was pretty much limited to Silver Age super-hero titles: in fact, Silver Age super-hero titles *that were being published when the price guide began.*

This meant that such titles as OMAC, which was a Silver Age title that starred a super-hero but was not still being published by 1983, didn't get listed.

It also meant that so-called "funny animal" titles, "war" titles, and the like were not included.

Once the listings were begun (not by **Comics Buyer's Guide** staff, incidentally; the material was started for another publication), however, Don Thompson took over the compilation. From that point, every effort was made to include every issue of every comic book received in the office. However, since the entries were not on a database and had to be compressed as much as possible to fit the space available, annotation, dates, and original prices were not usually part of the listing.

On the other hand (and because of Don's care, once he took over the project), material has been listed from the beginning in the **CBG** listings which was often overlooked by other reference publishers. *Concrete* and *Teenage Mutant Ninja Turtles*, for example, were first listed in **CBG**'s price listings.

And now we're continuing to fill in the blanks that remain whenever we get the information.

?

What is this "Silver Age" you keep referring to?

Comic-book collectors divide the history of comics into the "Golden Age" and the "Silver Age." "Golden Age" indicates the first era of comic-book production — which occurred in the '30s and '40s. It was a time of incredible creation in the field — when such characters as Superman and Batman first appeared. It's the era *before* material in this price guide was published.

"Silver Age" is used to indicate a period of comic-book production of slightly less (nostalgic?) luster than that of the Golden Age. It is usually considered to have begun with the publication of the first revival of a '40s super-hero: the appearance of The Flash in *Showcase* #4 (Sep-Oct 1956). However, that was a lone appearance at the time, so this price guide begins to catalog most titles at the time Marvel entered the field — with the publication of *Fantastic Four* #1 (1961).

?

This guide lists a #8 and a #10. What happened to #9?

We haven't seen a copy. There was a time when collectors could assume that numbers would run in normal sequence, when no numbers were skipped, and when there were no special numbers to trick completists. That's not the case in the field any more, and what we need from those who want to help add to information is confirmation that an item has been actually been published. (This guide *does* include information on material that was published but not widely distributed. Eternity's *Uncensored Mouse* #2, for example, was pulled from distribution after legal problems with The Walt Disney Company — but copies *do* exist. So few transactions involve it, however, that retailers have not established an exceptional price for the item at this point.)

?

So do you own all these comics?

No, many publishers and collectors have helped us over the years by sending photocopies of indicia, records of publication, annotations, and the like — all of which has permitted us to provide collectors with increasing information every year. What we cannot do — and *do* not do — is pull information from other price guides or from announcements of what is scheduled for publication. The former would not be proper; the latter leads to errors — the sort of errors that have been known to become imbedded in some price guides' information files.

This is also why the information sometimes seems inconsistent. Every effort has been made to make the notations consistent, but this list of more than 75,000 comics is so long that this can be an arduous task. Nevertheless, we're slowly whittling away at problems between weekly issues of **Comics Buyer's Guide** and the assorted other projects we take on.

?

This title switched publishers. Why wasn't that information noted?

Chances are the publishers involved didn't give us the information.

?

I tried to sell my comics to a retailer, but he wouldn't even offer me 10% of

the prices you list. Is he trying to cheat me? Are your prices wrong?

Remember, our prices are based on what a shop will charge its customers. And a shop has a huge overhead — and needs to tailor its stock to the interest shown by its customers in that sort of product. If no one locally is buying comics starring Muggy-Doo, Boy Cat, it doesn't matter that *Muggy-Doo, Boy Cat* is bringing high prices elsewhere in the country.

Also, a comic book which is in our price guide at its original price may be showing no movement in most comics shops — which means a retailer isn't usually interested in devoting store space to it, no matter *how* nice it is or *how* much you're discounting it.

?

I'm a publisher, and I'd be willing to buy a hundred copies of my first issue at the price you list. I'm out of copies, I get calls from all over America, and those would-be buyers would pay 10 times the price you give here for out-of-print issues from my line of comics.

This is the flip side to the guy who was trying to sell his comics to that retailer in the previous question; a publisher like you hears from faithful followers living across the nation. The comics shop deals with a market of one community or smaller. You're dealing with a narrow, focused market of aficionados of your product who are looking for the specific issues they're missing. As a result, you, as a publisher who may maintain back-issue files for sale, may get far higher prices for that material than readers will find in this checklist. It doesn't mean you're ripping off your fans; it means fans looking to buy that material are competing for it out of a nationwide pool.

?

Can I just order the back-issue comics I want from *Comics Buyer's Guide*?

This price guide is just that: a guide to the average back-issue prices comics shops are likely to charge their customers. We maintain no back-issue stock for sale; we leave that to comics shops that specialize in back issues. (Start with your local shops. You'll be able to check out the variety of material available and take a look in advance at what you're buying.)

Comics Buyer's Guide itself is primarily the weekly newspaper of the comic-book field. As such it carries ads from many, many retailers across the country; you can check those advertisements for the specific back issues that you're looking for. You can even take out a "wants" ad to locate particular items, if that appeals to you. A free sample copy is available from *Comics Buyer's Guide* Sample Copy, 700 E. State St., Iola, WI 54990.

Finally —

We'd like to hear from you about this guide: additions, corrections, and comments. Write: Maggie Thompson, **CBG 1997 Checklist and Price Guide**, 700 E. State St., Iola, WI 54990.

Maggie Thompson, August 23, 1996

Top 10 Comics

Although you will find the complete price listings for the more than 75,000 comics in our database on the following pages, we thought you might like to see what the 10 most valuable comics were. In addition to their ranking, we've added the rest of the price guide information of the issues in near-mint condition in expanded form.

Showcase #4 © 1956 National Comics Publications, Inc. (DC)

Amazing Fantasy #15 © 1962 Marvel

$25,000

1. *Showcase* #4 (Carmine Infantino-Joe Kubert, origin and first Silver Age appearance of The Flash, Oct 56)

$24,000

2. *Amazing Fantasy* #15 (Steve Ditko, origin and first appearance of Spider-Man, Aug 62)

$18,500

3. *Amazing Spider-Man* #1 (Steve Ditko, origin of Spider-Man retold, Mar 63)

$17,000

4. *Fantastic Four* #1 (Jack Kirby, origin and first appearance of The Fantastic Four)

$9500

5. *Incredible Hulk* #1 (Jack Kirby, origin and first appearance of The Hulk)

$6200

6. *Showcase* #8 (Carmine Infantino, Flash story, origin of Captain Cold, Jun 57)

$5250

7. *X-Men* (first series) #1 (Jack Kirby, origin and first appearance of X-Men, first appearance of Magneto)

$4800

8. *The Flash* #105 (Carmine Infantino, origin of Flash retold)

$4500

9. *Brave and the Bold* #28 (introduction of The Justice League of America, origin of Snapper Carr)

10. *Showcase* #22 (Gil Kane, origin and first appearance of Green Lantern, Oct 59)

From left to right: *Amazing Spider-Man* #1 © 1963 Marvel, *Fantastic Four* #1 © 1961 Marvel, and *Incredible Hulk* #1 © 1962 Marvel

Photo Grading Guide

MINT: This is a perfect comic book. Its cover has a full luster, with its edges sharp and its pages like new. There are no signs of wear or aging. It is not imperfectly printed or marked off-center. "Mint" means just what it says.

NEAR MINT: This is a nearly perfect comic book. Its cover shows barely perceptible signs of wear. Its spine is tight, and its cover has only minor loss of luster and only minor printing defects. Some discoloration is acceptable in older comics - as are signs of aging. A "Near Mint" comic book is the standard on which this price guide is based.

VERY FINE: This is a nice comic book with beginning signs of wear. There can be slight creases and wrinkles at the staples, but it is a flat, clean issue with definite signs of being read a few times. There is some loss of the original gloss, but it is in general an attractive comic book.

FINE: This comic book's cover is worn but flat and clean with no defacement. There is no cover writing or tape repair. Stress lines around the staples and more rounded corners are permitted. It is a good-looking issue at first glance.

VERY GOOD: Most of the original gloss is gone from this well-read issue. There are minor markings, discoloration, and/or heavier stress lines around the staples and spine. The cover may have minor tears and/or corner creases, and spine-rolling is permissable. These comics have problems but are nice.

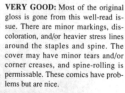

GOOD: This is a very worn comic book with nothing missing. Creases, minor tears, rolled spine, and cover flaking are permissible - but there is no tape or browned pages. Older Golden Age comic books often come in this condition.

POOR: This issue is damaged and generally considered unsuitable for collecting. It may, however, still contain readable stories.

When comics are compared with the Photo Grading Guide, it's easy to see there are many comics which fall between categories in something of an infinite gradation. For example, a "Fair" condition comic book (which falls between "Good" and "Poor") may have a soiled, slightly damaged cover, a badly rolled spine, cover flaking, corners gone, tears, and the like. It is an issue with multiple problems but it is intact - and some collectors enjoy collecting in this grade for the fun of it. Tape may be present; tape is always considered a defect.

The condition of comic book is a vital factor in determining the price of a comic book. A "Fair" issue would be worth about 10% of the price given in our price guide section. A "Good" issue would be worth about 20% of our price. A "fine" issue would be worth about 60% of our price. And a "Mint" copy would be worth 120% of our price.

Guide to Defects

Stamped arrival date and **off-center cover** and **off-center stapling.** Minor defects. Some will not call it "Mint"; some will.

Writing defacing cover. Marking can include filling in light areas or childish scribbling. No better than "Good."

Subscription crease. Comic books sent by mail were often folded down the middle, leaving a permanent crease. Definitely no better than "Very Good"; probably no better than "Good."

Rusty staple. Caused by dampness during storage, rust stains around staples may be minor - or more apparent. Couldn't be better than "Very Good."

Chunk missing. Actual piece missing. Couldn't be better than "Fair."

Water damage. Varies from simple page-warping to staining shown here. Less damage than this could be "Very Good"; this is no better than "Good."

Multiple folds and wrinkles. No better than "Fair" condition.

Stains. Can vary widely, depending on cause. These look like mud - but food, grease, and the like also stain. No better than "Good."

Tape. Extreme example of tape damage. Used to show *why* tape shouldn't be used on a comic book - or *any* book - for repairs. *All* tape (even so-called "magic" tape) ages badly - as does rubber cement. *Any* tape means "Fair," at best.

Rolled Spine. Caused by folding back each page while reading - rather than opening the comic book flat. Repeated folding permanently bent the spine. *May* be corrected, but the issue is no better than "Very Good."

The problem of grading comics accurately is one which seems to have an easy solution. Theoretically, given a set of grading rules, determining the condition of a comic book should be simple. Unfortunately, flaws vary from item to item, and it can be difficult to pin one label on a particular issue.

The examples shown here represent specific defects listed in each case. The condition of the individual issue as a whole is not necessarily that of the specific defect. (For example, the copy with stamped arrival date, off-center staple is *not* in mint condition aside from those defects.)

Abbreviations

AA— Alfredo Alcala
AAd— Art Adams
AF— Al Feldstein
AM— Al Milgrom
AMo— Alan Moore
AN— Alex Nino
AR— Alex Raymond
AT— Angelo Torres
ATh— Alex Toth
AW— Al Williamson
BA— Brent Anderson
BB— Brian Bolland
BE— Bill Elder
BEv— Bill Everett
BG— Butch Guice
BH— Bob Hall
BK— Bernie Krigstein
BL— Bob Layton
BMc— Bob McLeod
BO— Bob Oksner
BS— Barry Smith
BSz— Bill Sienkiewicz
BT— Bryan Talbot
BW— Basil Wolverton
BWa— Bill Ward
BWi— Bob Wiacek
BWr— Berni Wrightson
CB— Carl Barks
CCB— C.C. Beck
CI— Carmine Infantino
CR— P. Craig Russell
CS— Curt Swan
CV— Charles Vess
DA— Dan Adkins
DC— Dave Cockrum
DD— Dick Dillin
DaG— Dave Gibbons
DG— Dick Giordano
DGr— Dan Green
DH— Don Heck
DN— Don Newton
DP— Don Perlin
DR— Don Rosa
DS— Dan Spiegle
DSt— Dave Stevens
EC— Ernie Colon
EL— Erik Larsen
FB— Frank Brunner
FF— Frank Frazetta
FG— Floyd Gottfredson
FGu— Fred Guardineer
FH— Fred Hembeck
FM— Frank Miller
FMc— Frank McLaughlin
FR— Frank Robbins
FS— Frank Springer
FT— Frank Thorne
GC— Gene Colan
GD— Gene Day
GE— George Evans

GI— Graham Ingels
GK— Gil Kane
GM— Gray Morrow
GP— George Perez
GT— George Tuska
HC— Howard Chaykin
HK— Harvey Kurtzman
HN— Howard Nostrand
HT— Herb Trimpe
IN— Irv Novick
JA— Jim Aparo
JAb— Jack Abel
JB— John Buscema
JBy— John Byrne
JCr— Johnny Craig
JD— Jayson Disbrow
JDu— Jan Duursema
JJ— Jeff Jones
JK— Jack Kirby
JKa— Jack Kamen
JKu— Joe Kubert
JL— Jose Luis Garcia Lopez
JLee— Jim Lee
JM— Jim Mooney
JO— Joe Orlando
JOy— Jerry Ordway
JR— John Romita
JR2— John Romita Jr.
JS— John Stanley
JSa— Joe Staton
JSe— John Severin
JSh— Jim Sherman
JSn— Jim Starlin
JSo— Jim Steranko
JSt— Joe Sinnott
KG— Keith Giffen
KGa— Kerry Gammill
KJ— Klaus Janson
KN— Kevin Nowlan
KP— Keith Pollard
KS— Kurt Schaffenberger
LMc— Luke McDonnell
MA— Murphy Anderson
MB— Matt Baker
MD— Mort Drucker
MG— Michael Golden
MGr— Mike Grell
MGu— Mike Gustovich
MK— Mike Kaluta
MM— Mort Meskin
MN— Mike Nasser
MP— Mike Ploog
MR— Marshall Rogers
MW— Matt Wagner
MZ— Mike Zeck
NA— Neal Adams
NC— Nick Cardy
NG— Neil Gaiman
NR— Nestor Redondo
PB— Pat Broderick

PG— Paul Gulacy
PM— Pete Morisi
PS— Paul Smith
RA— Ross Andru
RB— Rich Buckler
RBy— Reggie Byers
RCo— Rich Corben
RE— Ric Estrada
RH— Russ Heath
RHo— Richard Howell
RK— Roy Krenkel
RL— Rob Liefeld
RM— Russ Manning
RMo— Ruben Moreira
RP— Rudy Palais
RT— Romeo Tanghal
SA— Sergio Aragones
SB— Sal Buscema
SD— Steve Ditko
S&K— Simon & Kirby
SR— Steve Rude
SRB— Stephen R. Bissette
S&S— Siegel & Shuster
TA— Terry Austin
TD— Tony DeZuniga
TMc— Todd McFarlane
TP— Tom Palmer
TS— Tom Sutton
TVE— Trevor Von Eeden
TY— Tom Yeates
VM— Val Mayerik
WE— Will Eisner
WH— Wayne Howard
WK— Walt Kelly
WP— Wendy Pini
WS— Walter Simonson
WW— Wally Wood
•••••
A - Appearance of
BM - Batman
C - Cameo of
(c) - cover
D - Death of
GA - Green Arrow
I - Introduction of
(i) - inks
J - Joining of
L - Leaving of
M or W - Wedding of
N - New costume
nn - no number
O - Origin of
(p) - pencils
R - Revival of
rep. - reprint
SpM - Spider-Man
Thg - Thing
tpb - trade paperback
V - versus
WW - Wonder Woman
1 - first appearance of

Miscellaneous

	ORIG.	GOOD	FINE	N-MINT

!GAG!
HARRIER

	ORIG.	GOOD	FINE	N-MINT
❏ 1		0.39	1.17	1.95
❏ 2		0.39	1.17	1.95
❏ 3		0.39	1.17	1.95
❏ 4, magazine		0.59	1.77	2.95
❏ 5, magazine		0.59	1.77	2.95
❏ 6, magazine		0.59	1.77	2.95
❏ 7, magazine		0.59	1.77	2.95

.357!
MU PRESS

	ORIG.	GOOD	FINE	N-MINT
❏ 1, b&w		0.45	1.35	2.25

1,001 NIGHTS OF BACCHUS, THE
DARK HORSE

	ORIG.	GOOD	FINE	N-MINT
❏ 0, 93, nn;b&w;one-shot; ECampbell	3.95	0.79	2.37	3.95

100 DEGREES IN THE SHADE
EROS COMIX

	ORIG.	GOOD	FINE	N-MINT
❏ 1, adult; b&w		0.50	1.50	2.50
❏ 2, adult; b&w		0.50	1.50	2.50
❏ 3, adult; b&w		0.50	1.50	2.50
❏ 4, adult; b&w		0.50	1.50	2.50

101 DALMATIANS
DISNEY

	ORIG.	GOOD	FINE	N-MINT
❏ 0, nn movie		0.50	1.50	2.50

13 ASSASSIN COMICS MODULE
TSR INC.

	ORIG.	GOOD	FINE	N-MINT
❏ 1		0.59	1.77	2.95
❏ 2		0.59	1.77	2.95
❏ 3		0.59	1.77	2.95
❏ 4		0.59	1.77	2.95
❏ 5, Search for Maggie Darr		0.59	1.77	2.95
❏ 6, Search for Maggie Darr		0.59	1.77	2.95
❏ 7, Search for Maggie Darr		0.59	1.77	2.95
❏ 8, Search for Maggie Darr		0.59	1.77	2.95

1963 BOOK FIVE: HORUS, LORD OF LIGHT
IMAGE

	ORIG.	GOOD	FINE	N-MINT
❏ 0, AMo(w)	1.95	0.39	1.17	1.95

1963 BOOK FOUR: TALES FROM BEYOND

	ORIG.	GOOD	FINE	N-MINT
❏ 0, AMo(w)	1.95	0.39	1.17	1.95

1963 BOOK ONE: MYSTERY INCORPORATED

	ORIG.	GOOD	FINE	N-MINT
❏ 0, Apr 93, AMo(w)	1.95	0.39	1.17	1.95

1963 BOOK SIX: TOMORROW SYNDICATE

	ORIG.	GOOD	FINE	N-MINT
❏ 0, AMo(w)	1.95	0.39	1.17	1.95

1963 BOOK THREE: TALES OF THE UNCANNY

	ORIG.	GOOD	FINE	N-MINT
❏ 0, AMo(w)	1.95	0.39	1.17	1.95

1963 BOOK TWO: NO ONE ESCAPES…THE FURY

	ORIG.	GOOD	FINE	N-MINT
❏ 0, May 93, AMo(w)	1.95	0.39	1.17	1.95

1ST FOLIO
PACIFIC

	ORIG.	GOOD	FINE	N-MINT
❏ 1, Mar 84, Joe Kubert School	1.50	0.30	0.90	1.50

2 LIVE CREW COMICS
EROS COMIX

	ORIG.	GOOD	FINE	N-MINT
❏ 1, adult; b&w		0.59	1.77	2.95

2-HEADED GIANT
A IS A

	ORIG.	GOOD	FINE	N-MINT
❏ 1, Oct 95, b&w anthology	2.95	0.59	1.77	2.95

2000 A.D. MONTHLY
EAGLE

	ORIG.	GOOD	FINE	N-MINT
❏ 1		0.20	0.60	1.00
❏ 2		0.20	0.60	1.00
❏ 3		0.20	0.60	1.00
❏ 4		0.20	0.60	1.00
❏ 5		0.20	0.60	1.00
❏ 6		0.20	0.60	1.00

2000 A.D. MONTHLY (2nd series)

	ORIG.	GOOD	FINE	N-MINT
❏ 1		0.25	0.75	1.25
❏ 2		0.25	0.75	1.25
❏ 3, (moves to Quality Comics)		0.25	0.75	1.25

2000 A.D. PRESENTS (was Eagle title)
FLEETWAY/QUALITY

	ORIG.	GOOD	FINE	N-MINT
❏ 4		0.25	0.75	1.25
❏ 5		0.25	0.75	1.25
❏ 6		0.25	0.75	1.25
❏ 7		0.25	0.75	1.25
❏ 8		0.25	0.75	1.25
❏ 9		0.25	0.75	1.25
❏ 10		0.25	0.75	1.25
❏ 11		0.25	0.75	1.25
❏ 12		0.30	0.90	1.50
❏ 13		0.25	0.75	1.25
❏ 14		0.25	0.75	1.25
❏ 15		0.25	0.75	1.25
❏ 16		0.25	0.75	1.25
❏ 17		0.25	0.75	1.25
❏ 18		0.25	0.75	1.25
❏ 19		0.25	0.75	1.25
❏ 20		0.25	0.75	1.25
❏ 21		0.25	0.75	1.25
❏ 22		0.25	0.75	1.25
❏ 23		0.25	0.75	1.25
❏ 24		0.25	0.75	1.25
❏ 25, (becomes 2000 AD Showcase)		0.25	0.75	1.25

2000 AD SHOWCASE

	ORIG.	GOOD	FINE	N-MINT
❏ 3	2.95	0.59	1.77	2.95
❏ 4, Axa	2.95	0.59	1.77	2.95
❏ 5, Axa	2.95	0.59	1.77	2.95
❏ 6, Strontium Dogs	2.95	0.59	1.77	2.95
❏ 7, Strontium Dogs	2.95	0.59	1.77	2.95
❏ 8	2.95	0.59	1.77	2.95
❏ 9	2.95	0.59	1.77	2.95
❏ 10	2.95	0.59	1.77	2.95
❏ 11	2.95	0.59	1.77	2.95

2000 AD SHOWCASE (was 2000 AD Presents)

	ORIG.	GOOD	FINE	N-MINT
❏ 26		0.30	0.90	1.50
❏ 27, 27 and 28 are one issue		0.30	0.90	1.50
❏ 29, 29 and 30 are one issue; I:Zenith		0.30	0.90	1.50
❏ 31, Zenith		0.30	0.90	1.50
❏ 32, Zenith		0.30	0.90	1.50
❏ 33, Zenith		0.30	0.90	1.50
❏ 34, Zenith		0.30	0.90	1.50
❏ 35, Zenith		0.30	0.90	1.50
❏ 36, Zenith		0.30	0.90	1.50
❏ 37, Zenith		0.30	0.90	1.50
❏ 38, Zenith		0.30	0.90	1.50
❏ 39, Zenith		0.30	0.90	1.50
❏ 40, Zenith		0.30	0.90	1.50
❏ 41, Zenith		0.30	0.90	1.50
❏ 42, Zenith		0.30	0.90	1.50
❏ 43, Zenith		0.30	0.90	1.50
❏ 44, Zenith		0.30	0.90	1.50
❏ 45, Zenith		0.35	1.05	1.75
❏ 46		0.35	1.05	1.75
❏ 47		0.35	1.05	1.75
❏ 48		0.35	1.05	1.75
❏ 49		0.35	1.05	1.75
❏ 50		0.35	1.05	1.75
❏ 51		0.35	1.05	1.75
❏ 52		0.35	1.05	1.75
❏ 53		0.35	1.05	1.75
❏ 54		0.35	1.05	1.75

	ORIG.	GOOD	FINE	N-MINT

2000 MANIACS
AIRCEL

	ORIG.	GOOD	FINE	N-MINT
☐ 1, b&w;movie		0.50	1.50	2.50
☐ 2, b&w;movie		0.50	1.50	2.50
☐ 3, b&w;movie		0.50	1.50	2.50

2001 NIGHTS
VIZ

	ORIG.	GOOD	FINE	N-MINT
☐ 1, b&w		0.79	2.37	3.95
☐ 2, b&w		0.79	2.37	3.95
☐ 3, b&w		0.79	2.37	3.95
☐ 4, b&w		0.79	2.37	3.95
☐ 5, b&w		0.75	2.25	3.75
☐ 6, b&w		0.85	2.55	4.25
☐ 7, b&w		0.85	2.55	4.25
☐ 8, b&w		0.85	2.55	4.25
☐ 9, b&w		0.85	2.55	4.25
☐ 10, b&w		0.85	2.55	4.25

2001: A SPACE ODYSSEY
MARVEL

	ORIG.	GOOD	FINE	N-MINT
☐ 1, Dec 76, JK	0.30	1.60	4.80	8.00
☐ 2, JK	0.30	1.00	3.00	5.00
☐ 3, JK	0.30	1.00	3.00	5.00
☐ 4, JK	0.30	0.80	2.40	4.00
☐ 5, JK	0.30	0.80	2.40	4.00
☐ 6, JK	0.30	0.80	2.40	4.00
☐ 7, JK	0.30	0.80	2.40	4.00
☐ 8, JK	0.30	0.80	2.40	4.00
☐ 9, JK	0.30	0.80	2.40	4.00
☐ 10, JK	0.30	0.80	2.40	4.00

2010

	ORIG.	GOOD	FINE	N-MINT
☐ 1, movie	0.75	0.20	0.60	1.00
☐ 2, movie	0.75	0.20	0.60	1.00

2099 A.D.

	ORIG.	GOOD	FINE	N-MINT
☐ 1, May 95, enhanced cover	3.95	0.79	2.37	3.95

2099 A.D. APOCALYPSE

☐ 1, Dec 95, enhanced wraparound cover continues in
2099 A.D. Genesis #1;D: Punisher 2099, Hulk 2099

	ORIG.	GOOD	FINE	N-MINT
	4.95	0.99	2.97	4.95

2099 A.D. GENESIS

☐ 1, Jan 96, A:Daredevil 2099; I:X-Nation 2099 and
Fantastic Four 2099; enhanced wraparound cover

	ORIG.	GOOD	FINE	N-MINT
	4.95	0.99	2.97	4.95

2099 SPECIAL: WORLD OF DOOM

	ORIG.	GOOD	FINE	N-MINT
☐ 1, May 95	2.25	0.45	1.35	2.25

2099 UNLIMITED

	ORIG.	GOOD	FINE	N-MINT
☐ 1	3.95	1.00	3.00	5.00
☐ 2	3.95	0.79	2.37	3.95
☐ 3	3.95	0.79	2.37	3.95
☐ 4	3.95	0.79	2.37	3.95
☐ 5, Jul 94	3.95	0.79	2.37	3.95
☐ 6, Aug 94	3.95	0.79	2.37	3.95
☐ 7, Nov 94	3.95	0.79	2.37	3.95
☐ 8, Apr 95	3.95	0.79	2.37	3.95
☐ 9, Jul 95	3.95	0.79	2.37	3.95
☐ 10, Oct 95	3.95	0.79	2.37	3.95

21
IMAGE

	ORIG.	GOOD	FINE	N-MINT
☐ 1, Feb 96	2.50	0.50	1.50	2.50
☐ 2, Mar 96	2.50	0.50	1.50	2.50

3 DIMENSIONAL DNAGENTS
ECLIPSE

☐ 1, Jan 86, really *3 Dimensional DNAgents*

	ORIG.	GOOD	FINE	N-MINT
	2.25	0.45	1.35	2.25

3-D ADVENTURE COMICS
STATS ETC.

	ORIG.	GOOD	FINE	N-MINT
☐ 1	1.50	0.30	0.90	1.50

3-D ALIEN TERROR
ECLIPSE

	ORIG.	GOOD	FINE	N-MINT
☐ 1		0.50	1.50	2.50

3-D EXOTIC BEAUTIES
3-D ZONE

	ORIG.	GOOD	FINE	N-MINT
☐ 0, nn;L.B. Cole		0.70	2.10	3.50

3-D HEROES
BLACKTHORNE

	ORIG.	GOOD	FINE	N-MINT
☐ 1		0.40	1.20	2.00

3-D HOLLYWOOD
3-D ZONE

	ORIG.	GOOD	FINE	N-MINT
☐ 1, paper dolls		0.59	1.77	2.95

3-D SPACE ZOMBIES
3-D ZONE

	ORIG.	GOOD	FINE	N-MINT
☐ 0, nn	3.95	0.79	2.37	3.95

3-D SUBSTANCE

	ORIG.	GOOD	FINE	N-MINT
☐ 0, nn SD		0.59	1.77	2.95
☐ 2, SD		0.79	2.37	3.95

3-D THREE STOOGES
ECLIPSE

	ORIG.	GOOD	FINE	N-MINT
☐ 1		0.50	1.50	2.50
☐ 2		0.50	1.50	2.50
☐ 3		0.50	1.50	2.50

3-D TRUE CRIME
3-D ZONE

	ORIG.	GOOD	FINE	N-MINT
☐ 1, 92, Jack Cole art	3.95	0.79	2.37	3.95

3-D ZONE, THE

	ORIG.	GOOD	FINE	N-MINT
☐ 1, WW		0.50	1.50	2.50
☐ 2, Wolverton		0.50	1.50	2.50
☐ 3, LBCole,JD		0.50	1.50	2.50
☐ 4, Electric Fear		0.50	1.50	2.50
☐ 5, Krazy Kat		0.50	1.50	2.50
☐ 6, Rat Fink		0.50	1.50	2.50
☐ 7, JKu,Hollywood		0.50	1.50	2.50
☐ 8, JKu,High Seas		0.50	1.50	2.50
☐ 9, Red Mask		0.50	1.50	2.50
☐ 10, AW;Jet		0.50	1.50	2.50
☐ 11, Matt Fox		0.50	1.50	2.50
☐ 12, Presidents		0.50	1.50	2.50
☐ 13, Flash Gordon		0.50	1.50	2.50
☐ 14, Tyranostar		0.50	1.50	2.50
☐ 15, HK;humor		0.50	1.50	2.50
☐ 16, DS;space vixens		0.50	1.50	2.50
☐ 17, Kamen;Feldstein;WW;FF		0.50	1.50	2.50
☐ 18, Wolverton		0.50	1.50	2.50
☐ 19, Cracked		0.50	1.50	2.50
☐ 20, Atomic Sub		0.50	1.50	2.50

39 SCREAMS, THE
THUNDER BAAS

	ORIG.	GOOD	FINE	N-MINT
☐ 1		0.40	1.20	2.00
☐ 2		0.40	1.20	2.00
☐ 3		0.40	1.20	2.00
☐ 4		0.40	1.20	2.00
☐ 5		0.40	1.20	2.00
☐ 6		0.40	1.20	2.00

3x3 EYES
INNOVATION

	ORIG.	GOOD	FINE	N-MINT
☐ 1, b&w;Japanese		0.45	1.35	2.25
☐ 2, b&w;Japanese		0.45	1.35	2.25
☐ 3, b&w;Japanese		0.45	1.35	2.25
☐ 4, b&w;Japanese		0.45	1.35	2.25
☐ 5, b&w;Japanese		0.45	1.35	2.25

3x3 EYES: CURSE OF THE GESU (mini-series)
DARK HORSE/MANGA

	ORIG.	GOOD	FINE	N-MINT
☐ 1, Oct 95, b&w	2.95	0.59	1.77	2.95
☐ 2, Nov 95, b&w	2.95	0.59	1.77	2.95
☐ 3, Dec 95, b&w	2.95	0.59	1.77	2.95
☐ 4, Jan 96, b&w	2.95	0.59	1.77	2.95
☐ 5, Feb 96, b&w;final issue	2.95	0.59	1.77	2.95

	ORIG.	GOOD	FINE	N-MINT
☐ 2 .... 1.95		0.39	1.17	1.95
☐ 3 .... 1.95		0.39	1.17	1.95
☐ 4 .... 1.95		0.39	1.17	1.95
☐ 5 .... 1.95		0.39	1.17	1.95
☐ 6 .... 1.95		0.39	1.17	1.95
☐ 7 .... 1.95		0.39	1.17	1.95
☐ 8 .... 1.95		0.39	1.17	1.95
☐ 9 .... 1.95		0.39	1.17	1.95
☐ 10 .... 1.95		0.39	1.17	1.95
☐ 11 .... 1.95		0.39	1.17	1.95
☐ 12 .... 1.95		0.39	1.17	1.95
☐ 13 .... 1.95		0.39	1.17	1.95
☐ 14 .... 1.95		0.39	1.17	1.95
☐ 15 .... 1.95		0.39	1.17	1.95
☐ 16 .... 1.95		0.39	1.17	1.95
☐ 17 .... 1.95		0.39	1.17	1.95
☐ 18 .... 1.95		0.39	1.17	1.95

80 PAGE GIANT MAGAZINE

DC

	ORIG.	GOOD	FINE	N-MINT
☐ 1, Aug 64	0.25	60.00	180.00	300.00
☐ 2, 64, Jimmy Olsen.........	0.25	40.00	120.00	200.00
☐ 3, Lois Lane	0.25	35.00	105.00	175.00
☐ 4, Oct 64, Flash..............	0.25	32.00	96.00	160.00
☐ 5, Batman	0.25	32.00	96.00	160.00
☐ 6, Jan 65, Superman	0.25	25.00	75.00	125.00
☐ 7, Feb 65, Sgt. Rock	0.25	25.00	75.00	125.00
☐ 8, Mar 65, Secret Origins				
....	0.25	55.00	165.00	275.00
☐ 9, Apr 65, Flash;reprint Flash of Two Worlds				
....	0.25	28.00	84.00	140.00
☐ 10, May 65, Superman ...	0.25	24.00	72.00	120.00
☐ 11, Jun 65, Superman	0.25	22.00	66.00	110.00
☐ 12, Jul 65, Batman..........	0.25	22.00	66.00	110.00
☐ 13, Aug 65, Jimmy Olsen	0.25	22.00	66.00	110.00
☐ 14, Sep 65, Lois Lane	0.25	22.00	66.00	110.00
☐ 15, Oct 65, Batman/Superman				
....	0.25	22.00	66.00	110.00

80 Page Giant

80 Page Giant Magazine #9 ©1965 National Periodical Publications Inc. (DC)

The number of pages in comics has changed over the years. During the Golden Age, 64 pages was the biggest usual size for a dime comic book. For a short time in the 1950s, Dell advertised "52 pages, all comics!" on the covers of its comics, a practice that required the use of the inside front, inside back, and back covers for entertainment. Eventually Dell dropped the "all comics" pledge to add subscription forms and eventually, other advertising.

Golden Age anthologies contained new stories, but most would have no unifying theme, something that DC addressed when it came out with its *80 Page Giant* series in the 1960s. The comics sported a square spine and, while they often contained reprint material, did have a common theme. The format spawned its own title, as shown above. *80 Page Giant* ran for 15 issues in 1964 and 1965 and retailed for 25¢. The 80 Page Giant format was also used for a number of DC annuals and individual issues of various titles. It is often necessary to check the indicia of the individual comic book to determine if it is an 80 Page Giant or an issue of *80 Page Giant*.

In the 1970s, DC took the next step in the evolution of its 80 Page Giant format with the *DC 100-Page Super-Spectacular*. As can be inferred from its name, the square-spined comics were 100 pages long, often containing one or more original stories and a number of reprints. Often the main story and the reprints would have a unifying theme, but not always. *DC 100-Page Super-Spectacular* ran for 18 issues and then the format was used for individual issues of various comics, beginning with *Shazam!* #8. The 100-page comics first retailed for 50¢ each and then were priced at 60¢ each.

Marvel also experimented with the longer format in its annuals and specials of the 1960s and its "Giant-Size" series of the 1970s.

After DC cut back on its titles in the mid-'70s in what many termed the "DC Implosion," it came out with Dollar Comics. *Superman's Pal, Jimmy Olsen* became *Superman Family* and was one of the few ongoing titles in the format, as well as one of the few to contain all-new material. After the demise of the Dollar Comic format, DC's annuals and specials were the only form in which longer stories than the average 22 to 23-page story could appear.

The last DC comic book to sport the 80 Page Giant logo was published in 1988. *Action Comics* #600 celebrated Superman's 50th anniversary and contained all-new material. The cover was an homage to Superman's 25th anniversary cover from 25 years earlier, with a gold statue of the Man of Steel replacing the earlier silver one.

While fondly remembered, DC's 80 Page Giants and 100 Page Super-Spectaculars are somewhat hard to find in higher grades, due to the tendency of the square spines to split over time and from repeated readings.

A

	ORIG.	GOOD	FINE	N-MINT

A TOUCH OF SILK, A TASTE OF LEATHER
BONEYARD
	ORIG.	GOOD	FINE	N-MINT
❏ 0, Mar 94, b&w	2.95	0.59	1.77	2.95

A VERY MU CHRISTMAS
MU PRESS
	ORIG.	GOOD	FINE	N-MINT
❏ 0, Nov 92	2.95	0.59	1.77	2.95

A*K*Q*J
FANTAGRAPHICS
	ORIG.	GOOD	FINE	N-MINT
❏ 1, Captain Jack;b&w		0.55	1.65	2.75

A-BOMB
ANTARCTIC
	ORIG.	GOOD	FINE	N-MINT
❏ 1, Dec 93, adult;b&w	2.95	0.59	1.77	2.95
❏ 2, Mar 94, adult;b&w	2.95	0.59	1.77	2.95
❏ 3, Jun 94, adult;b&w	2.95	0.59	1.77	2.95
❏ 4, Sep 94, adult;b&w	2.95	0.59	1.77	2.95
❏ 5, Dec 94, adult;b&w	2.95	0.59	1.77	2.95
❏ 6, Mar 95, adult;b&w	2.95	0.59	1.77	2.95
❏ 7, Jun 95, adult;b&w	2.95	0.59	1.77	2.95
❏ 8, Sep 95, adult;b&w	2.95	0.59	1.77	2.95
❏ 9, Nov 95, adult;b&w	2.95	0.59	1.77	2.95

A-OK
	ORIG.	GOOD	FINE	N-MINT
❏ 1, Sep 92, b&w	2.50	0.50	1.50	2.50
❏ 2, Nov 92, b&w	2.50	0.50	1.50	2.50
❏ 3, Jan 93, b&w	2.50	0.50	1.50	2.50
❏ 4, Feb 93, b&w	2.50	0.50	1.50	2.50

A.B.C. WARRIORS
FLEETWAY/QUALITY
	ORIG.	GOOD	FINE	N-MINT
❏ 1, b&w		0.39	1.17	1.95
❏ 2, b&w		0.39	1.17	1.95
❏ 3, b&w		0.39	1.17	1.95
❏ 4, b&w		0.39	1.17	1.95
❏ 5, b&w		0.39	1.17	1.95
❏ 6, b&w		0.39	1.17	1.95
❏ 7, b&w		0.39	1.17	1.95
❏ 8, b&w		0.39	1.17	1.95

A.B.C. WARRIORS: KHRONICLES OF KHAOS
	ORIG.	GOOD	FINE	N-MINT
❏ 4	2.95	0.59	1.77	2.95

A.K.A. GOLDFISH: ACE
CALIBER
	ORIG.	GOOD	FINE	N-MINT
❏ 0, 94, b&w	3.95	0.79	2.37	3.95

A.K.A. GOLDFISH: JACK
	ORIG.	GOOD	FINE	N-MINT
❏ 0, 95, b&w	3.95	0.79	2.37	3.95

A.K.A. GOLDFISH: JOKER
	ORIG.	GOOD	FINE	N-MINT
❏ 0, 94, b&w	3.50	0.70	2.10	3.50

A.K.A. GOLDFISH: QUEEN
	ORIG.	GOOD	FINE	N-MINT
❏ 0, 95, b&w	2.95	0.59	1.77	2.95

A.R.M.
ADVENTURE
	ORIG.	GOOD	FINE	N-MINT
❏ 1, b&w		0.50	1.50	2.50
❏ 2, b&w		0.50	1.50	2.50
❏ 3, b&w		0.50	1.50	2.50

A1
ATOMEKA
	ORIG.	GOOD	FINE	N-MINT
❏ 1, 89, BWS,DaG,AMo, BSz, BB	9.95	1.99	5.97	9.95
❏ 2, 89, BWS,DaG,AMo, BB, MW	9.95	1.99	5.97	9.95
❏ 3, 90, BB(c)	5.95	1.19	3.57	5.95
❏ 4, 90, BSz;Moebius	5.95	1.19	3.57	5.95
❏ 5, 91, Stout;JKu	7.95	1.59	4.77	7.95
❏ 6, 92	4.95	0.99	2.97	4.95

EPIC
	ORIG.	GOOD	FINE	N-MINT
❏ 1	5.95	1.19	3.57	5.95
❏ 2	5.95	1.19	3.57	5.95
❏ 3	5.95	1.19	3.57	5.95
❏ 4	5.95	1.19	3.57	5.95

A1 TRUE LIFE BIKINI CONFIDENTIAL, THE
ATOMEKA
	ORIG.	GOOD	FINE	N-MINT
❏ 1, b&w;BB		0.20	0.60	1.00

AARDWOLF
AARDWOLF
	ORIG.	GOOD	FINE	N-MINT
❏ 1, Dec 94, b&w	2.95	0.59	1.77	2.95

ABC WARRIORS
FLEETWAY/QUALITY
	ORIG.	GOOD	FINE	N-MINT
❏ 1	2.95	0.59	1.77	2.95
❏ 2	2.95	0.59	1.77	2.95
❏ 3	2.95	0.59	1.77	2.95

ABSOLUTE ZERO
ANTARCTIC
	ORIG.	GOOD	FINE	N-MINT
❏ 1, Feb 95, b&w	3.50	0.70	2.10	3.50
❏ 2, May 95, b&w	2.95	0.59	1.77	2.95
❏ 3, Aug 95, b&w	2.95	0.59	1.77	2.95

ABSURD ART OF J.J. GRANDVILLE, THE
TOME PRESS
	ORIG.	GOOD	FINE	N-MINT
❏ 1, b&w		0.50	1.50	2.50

ABYSS, THE
DARK HORSE
	ORIG.	GOOD	FINE	N-MINT
❏ 1, Aug 89, movie;color	2.25	0.45	1.35	2.25
❏ 2, Sep 89, movie;color	2.25	0.45	1.35	2.25

AC ANNUAL
AC
	ORIG.	GOOD	FINE	N-MINT
❏ 1, 90, b&w	3.95	0.79	2.37	3.95
❏ 2, b&w	3.95	1.00	3.00	5.00
❏ 3	3.95	0.79	2.37	3.95
❏ 4	3.95	0.79	2.37	3.95

ACCIDENT MAN
DARK HORSE
	ORIG.	GOOD	FINE	N-MINT
❏ 1, 93, HC(c)	2.50	0.50	1.50	2.50
❏ 2, 93, HC(c)	2.50	0.50	1.50	2.50
❏ 3, 93, HC(c)	2.50	0.50	1.50	2.50

ACCIDENTAL DEATH, AN
FANTAGRAPHICS
	ORIG.	GOOD	FINE	N-MINT
❏ 0, nn b&w	3.50	0.70	2.10	3.50

ACE
HARRIER
	ORIG.	GOOD	FINE	N-MINT
❏ 1, b&w		0.39	1.17	1.95

ACE COMICS PRESENTS
ACE
	ORIG.	GOOD	FINE	N-MINT
❏ 1, May 87, JC	1.75	0.35	1.05	1.75
❏ 2, Jul 87, Jack Bradbury	1.75	0.35	1.05	1.75
❏ 3, Sep 87, Klaus Nordling	1.75	0.35	1.05	1.75
❏ 4, Nov 87, Lou Fine	1.75	0.35	1.05	1.75

ACES
ECLIPSE
	ORIG.	GOOD	FINE	N-MINT
❏ 1, b&w mag	2.95	0.59	1.77	2.95
❏ 2, b&w mag	2.95	0.59	1.77	2.95
❏ 3, b&w mag	2.95	0.59	1.77	2.95
❏ 4, b&w mag	2.95	0.59	1.77	2.95
❏ 5, b&w mag	2.95	0.59	1.77	2.95

ACHILLES STORM/RAZMATAZ
AJA BLU
	ORIG.	GOOD	FINE	N-MINT
❏ 1, adult;b&w	2.25	0.60	1.80	3.00
❏ 2, adult;b&w	2.25	0.45	1.35	2.25

ACK THE BARBARIAN
INNOVATION
	ORIG.	GOOD	FINE	N-MINT
❏ 1, b&w		0.45	1.35	2.25

ACME
FANDOM HOUSE
	ORIG.	GOOD	FINE	N-MINT
❏ 1, b&w		0.60	1.80	3.00
❏ 2, b&w		0.60	1.80	3.00
❏ 3, b&w		0.60	1.80	3.00

	ORIG.	GOOD	FINE	N-MINT
☐ 4, b&w		0.60	1.80	3.00
☐ 5, b&w		0.60	1.80	3.00
☐ 6, b&w		0.60	1.80	3.00
☐ 7, b&w		0.60	1.80	3.00
☐ 8, b&w		0.60	1.80	3.00
☐ 9, b&w		0.60	1.80	3.00

ACME NOVELTY LIBRARY
FANTAGRAPHICS

	ORIG.	GOOD	FINE	N-MINT
☐ 1	4.50	1.00	3.00	5.00
☐ 3, Aut 94	3.95	0.79	2.37	3.95

ACTION COMICS
DC

	ORIG.	GOOD	FINE	N-MINT
☐ 0, Oct 94	1.50	0.30	0.90	1.50
☐ 1, 16-pg. r. (1988)	0.50	0.20	0.60	1.00
☐ 230, Jul 57	0.10	35.00	105.00	175.00
☐ 231, Aug 57	0.10	35.00	105.00	175.00
☐ 232, Sep 57	0.10	35.00	105.00	175.00
☐ 233, Oct 57	0.10	35.00	105.00	175.00
☐ 234, Nov 57	0.10	35.00	105.00	175.00
☐ 235, Dec 57	0.10	35.00	105.00	175.00
☐ 236, Jan 58	0.10	35.00	105.00	175.00
☐ 237, Feb 58	0.10	35.00	105.00	175.00
☐ 238, Mar 58	0.10	35.00	105.00	175.00
☐ 239, Apr 58	0.10	35.00	105.00	175.00
☐ 240, May 58	0.10	35.00	105.00	175.00
☐ 241, Jun 58	0.10	40.00	120.00	200.00
☐ 242, Jul 58, O,1:Brainiac		160.00	480.00	800.00
☐ 243, Aug 58	0.10	25.00	75.00	125.00
☐ 244, Sep 58	0.10	25.00	75.00	125.00
☐ 245, Oct 58	0.10	25.00	75.00	125.00
☐ 246, Nov 58	0.10	25.00	75.00	125.00
☐ 247, Dec 58	0.10	25.00	75.00	125.00
☐ 248, Jan 59	0.10	25.00	75.00	125.00
☐ 249, Feb 59	0.10	25.00	75.00	125.00
☐ 250, Mar 59	0.10	25.00	75.00	125.00
☐ 251, Apr 59, Legion; Tommy Tomorrow	0.10	25.00	75.00	125.00
☐ 252, May 59, O,1:Supergirl		250.00	750.00	1250.00
☐ 253, Jun 59, Supergirl	0.10	80.00	240.00	400.00
☐ 254, Jul 59, Bizarro		40.00	120.00	200.00
☐ 255, Aug 59, 1: Bizarro Lois	0.10	20.00	60.00	100.00
☐ 256, Sep 59	0.10	16.00	48.00	80.00
☐ 257, Oct 59	0.10	16.00	48.00	80.00
☐ 258, Nov 59	0.10	16.00	48.00	80.00
☐ 259, Dec 59	0.10	16.00	48.00	80.00
☐ 260, Jan 60	0.10	16.00	48.00	80.00
☐ 261, Feb 60, O: Streaky		20.00	60.00	100.00
☐ 262, Mar 60		10.00	30.00	50.00
☐ 263, Apr 60		10.00	30.00	50.00
☐ 264, May 60		10.00	30.00	50.00
☐ 265, Jun 60		10.00	30.00	50.00
☐ 266, Jul 60		10.00	30.00	50.00
☐ 267, Aug 60, Legion; J:Chameleon Boy, Colossa Boy, Invisible Kid, Supergirl	0.10	64.00	192.00	320.00
☐ 268, Sep 60	0.10	8.00	24.00	40.00
☐ 269, Oct 60	0.10	8.00	24.00	40.00
☐ 270, Nov 60	0.10	8.00	24.00	40.00
☐ 271, Dec 60	0.10	8.00	24.00	40.00
☐ 272, Jan 61	0.10	8.00	24.00	40.00
☐ 273, Feb 61	0.10	8.00	24.00	40.00
☐ 274, Mar 61	0.10	8.00	24.00	40.00
☐ 275, Apr 61	0.10	8.00	24.00	40.00
☐ 276, May 61, Legion;J: Triplicate Girl, Phantom Girl, Brainiac 5, Shrinking Violet, Bouncing Boy		16.00	48.00	80.00
☐ 277, Jun 61	0.10	6.00	18.00	30.00
☐ 278, Jul 61	0.10	6.00	18.00	30.00
☐ 279, Aug 61	0.10	6.00	18.00	30.00

	ORIG.	GOOD	FINE	N-MINT
☐ 280, Sep 61	0.10	6.00	18.00	30.00
☐ 281, Oct 61	0.10	6.00	18.00	30.00
☐ 282, Nov 61	0.10	6.00	18.00	30.00
☐ 283, Dec 61, Legion of Super-Villains	0.12	9.60	28.80	48.00
☐ 284, Jan 62, Mon-El	0.12	8.80	26.40	44.00
☐ 285, Feb 62, NA;A: Legion	0.12	10.00	30.00	50.00
☐ 286, Mar 62, Legion of Super-Villains	0.12	5.00	15.00	25.00
☐ 287, Apr 62, Legion	0.12	4.00	12.00	20.00
☐ 288, May 62, Mon-El	0.12	4.00	12.00	20.00
☐ 289, Jun 62, Legion	0.12	4.00	12.00	20.00
☐ 290, Jul 62, Legion	0.12	4.00	12.00	20.00
☐ 291, Aug 62, NA	0.12	3.00	9.00	15.00
☐ 292, Sep 62, Superhorse	0.12	3.00	9.00	15.00
☐ 293, Oct 62, O:Superhorse	0.12	3.60	10.80	18.00
☐ 294, Nov 62	0.12	3.00	9.00	15.00
☐ 295, Dec 62	0.12	3.00	9.00	15.00
☐ 296, Jan 63	0.12	3.00	9.00	15.00
☐ 297, Feb 63	0.12	3.00	9.00	15.00
☐ 298, Mar 63	0.12	3.00	9.00	15.00
☐ 299, Apr 63	0.12	3.00	9.00	15.00
☐ 300, May 63	0.12	5.00	15.00	25.00
☐ 301, Jun 63	0.12	2.40	7.20	12.00
☐ 302, Jul 63	0.12	2.40	7.20	12.00
☐ 303, Aug 63	0.12	2.40	7.20	12.00
☐ 304, Sep 63	0.12	2.40	7.20	12.00
☐ 305, Oct 63	0.12	2.40	7.20	12.00
☐ 306, Nov 63	0.12	2.40	7.20	12.00
☐ 307, Dec 63	0.12	2.40	7.20	12.00
☐ 308, Jan 64	0.12	2.40	7.20	12.00
☐ 309, Feb 64, NA;Legion	0.12	2.80	8.40	14.00
☐ 310, Mar 64	0.12	2.00	6.00	10.00
☐ 311, Apr 64	0.12	2.00	6.00	10.00
☐ 312, May 64	0.12	2.00	6.00	10.00
☐ 313, Jun 64	0.12	2.00	6.00	10.00
☐ 314, Jul 64	0.12	2.00	6.00	10.00
☐ 315, Aug 64	0.12	2.00	6.00	10.00
☐ 316, Sep 64	0.12	2.00	6.00	10.00
☐ 317, Oct 64	0.12	2.00	6.00	10.00
☐ 318, Nov 64	0.12	2.00	6.00	10.00
☐ 319, Dec 64	0.12	2.00	6.00	10.00
☐ 320, Jan 65	0.12	2.00	6.00	10.00
☐ 321, Feb 65	0.12	2.00	6.00	10.00
☐ 322, Mar 65	0.12	2.00	6.00	10.00
☐ 323, Apr 65	0.12	2.00	6.00	10.00
☐ 324, May 65	0.12	2.00	6.00	10.00
☐ 325, Jun 65	0.12	2.00	6.00	10.00
☐ 326, Jul 65	0.12	2.00	6.00	10.00
☐ 327, Aug 65, Imaginary story: Three Generations of Superman	0.12	2.00	6.00	10.00
☐ 328, Sep 65	0.12	2.00	6.00	10.00
☐ 329, Oct 65	0.12	2.00	6.00	10.00
☐ 330, Nov 65	0.12	2.00	6.00	10.00
☐ 331, Dec 65	0.12	2.00	6.00	10.00
☐ 332, Jan 66	0.12	2.00	6.00	10.00
☐ 333, Feb 66	0.12	2.00	6.00	10.00
☐ 334, Mar 66, O:Supergirl; giant	0.25	2.00	6.00	10.00
☐ 335, Mar 66	0.12	1.40	4.20	7.00
☐ 336, Apr 66	0.12	1.40	4.20	7.00
☐ 337, May 66	0.12	1.40	4.20	7.00
☐ 338, Jun 66	0.12	1.40	4.20	7.00
☐ 339, Jul 66	0.12	1.40	4.20	7.00
☐ 340, Aug 66	0.12	1.40	4.20	7.00
☐ 341, Sep 66	0.12	1.20	3.60	6.00
☐ 342, Oct 66	0.12	1.20	3.60	6.00
☐ 343, Nov 66	0.12	1.20	3.60	6.00
☐ 344, Dec 66	0.12	1.20	3.60	6.00

	ORIG.	GOOD	FINE	N-MINT
345, Jan 67 ....0.12	1.20	3.60	6.00
346, Feb 67 ....0.12	1.20	3.60	6.00
347, Apr 67, Supergirl giant			
.....................0.25	2.00	6.00	10.00
348, Mar 67 ....0.12	1.00	3.00	5.00
349, Apr 67 ....0.12	1.00	3.00	5.00
350, May 67 ....0.12	1.00	3.00	5.00
351, Jun 67 ....0.12	1.00	3.00	5.00
352, Jul 67 ....0.12	1.00	3.00	5.00
353, Aug 67 ....0.12	1.00	3.00	5.00
354, Sep 67 ....0.12	1.00	3.00	5.00
355, Oct 67 ....0.12	1.00	3.00	5.00
356, Nov 67 ....0.12	1.00	3.00	5.00
357, Dec 67 ....0.12	1.00	3.00	5.00
358, Jan 68 ....0.12	1.00	3.00	5.00
359, Feb 68 ....0.12	1.00	3.00	5.00
360, Mar 68, Supergirl; giant			
.....................0.25	1.20	3.60	6.00
361, Apr 68 ....0.12	1.00	3.00	5.00
362, May 68 ....0.12	0.80	2.40	4.00
363, Jun 68 ....0.12	0.80	2.40	4.00
364, Jul 68 ....0.12	0.80	2.40	4.00
365, Aug 68 ....0.12	0.80	2.40	4.00
366, Sep 68 ....0.12	0.80	2.40	4.00
367, Oct 68 ....0.12	0.80	2.40	4.00
368, Nov 68 ....0.12	0.80	2.40	4.00
369, Dec 68 ....0.12	0.80	2.40	4.00
370, Jan 69 ....0.12	0.80	2.40	4.00
371, Feb 69 ....0.12	0.80	2.40	4.00
372, Mar 69 ....0.12	0.80	2.40	4.00
373, Apr 69, NA giant; Supergirl			
.....................0.25	1.20	3.60	6.00
374, Mar 69 ....0.12	0.80	2.40	4.00
375, Apr 69 ....0.12	0.80	2.40	4.00
376, May 69 ....0.12	0.80	2.40	4.00
377, Jun 69, LSH 0.15	1.10	3.30	5.50
378, Jul 69, LSH 0.15	1.10	3.30	5.50
379, Aug 69, LSH...........0.15	1.10	3.30	5.50
380, Sep 69, LSH...........0.15	1.10	3.30	5.50
381, Oct 69, LSH............0.15	1.10	3.30	5.50
382, Nov 69, LSH...........0.15	1.10	3.30	5.50
383, Dec 69, LSH...........0.15	1.10	3.30	5.50
384, Jan 70, LSH 0.15	1.10	3.30	5.50
385, Feb 70, LSH 0.15	1.10	3.30	5.50
386, Mar 70, LSH...........0.15	1.10	3.30	5.50
387, Apr 70, LSH............0.15	1.10	3.30	5.50
388, May 70, LSH 0.15	1.10	3.30	5.50
389, Jun 70, LSH 0.15	1.10	3.30	5.50
390, Jul 70, LSH 0.15	1.10	3.30	5.50
391, Aug 70, LSH...........0.15	1.10	3.30	5.50
392, Sep 70, LSH...........0.15	1.10	3.30	5.50
393, Oct 70 ....0.15	0.80	2.40	4.00
394, Nov 70 ....0.15	0.80	2.40	4.00
395, Dec 70 ....0.15	0.80	2.40	4.00
396, Jan 71 ....0.15	0.80	2.40	4.00
397, Feb 71 ....0.15	0.80	2.40	4.00
398, Mar 71 ....0.15	0.80	2.40	4.00
399, Apr 71 ....0.15	0.80	2.40	4.00
400, May 71 ....0.15	0.80	2.40	4.00
401, Jun 71 ....0.15	0.80	2.40	4.00
402, Jul 71 ....0.15	0.80	2.40	4.00
403, Aug 71 ....0.25	0.80	2.40	4.00
404, Sep 71 ....0.25	0.80	2.40	4.00
405, Oct 71 ....0.25	0.80	2.40	4.00
406, Nov 71 ....0.25	0.80	2.40	4.00
407, Dec 71 ....0.25	0.80	2.40	4.00
408, Jan 72 ....0.25	0.80	2.40	4.00
409, Feb 72 ....0.25	0.80	2.40	4.00
410, Feb 72 ....0.25	0.80	2.40	4.00
411, Apr 72 ....0.25	0.80	2.40	4.00
412, May 72 ....0.25	0.80	2.40	4.00
413, Jun 72 ....0.25	0.80	2.40	4.00
414, Jul 72.....................0.20	0.80	2.40	4.00
415, Aug 72.....................0.20	0.80	2.40	4.00
416, Sep 72.....................0.20	0.80	2.40	4.00
417, Oct 72.....................0.20	0.80	2.40	4.00
418, Nov 72.....................0.20	0.80	2.40	4.00
419, Dec 72.....................0.20	0.80	2.40	4.00
420, Jan 73.....................0.20	1.20	3.60	6.00
421, Feb 73, Green Arrow begins			
.....................0.20	1.60	4.80	8.00
422, Mar 73.....................0.20	0.60	1.80	3.00
423, Apr 73.....................0.20	0.60	1.80	3.00
424, Jun 73, CS/MA/DG; GA			
.....................0.20	0.60	1.80	3.00
425, Jul 73, CS/MA,NA, DG			
.....................0.20	0.60	1.80	3.00
426, Aug 73.....................0.20	0.40	1.20	2.00
427, Sep 73.....................0.20	0.40	1.20	2.00
428, Oct 73.....................0.20	0.40	1.20	2.00
429, Nov 73.....................0.20	0.40	1.20	2.00
430, Dec 73.....................0.20	0.40	1.20	2.00
431, Jan 74.....................0.20	0.40	1.20	2.00
432, Feb 74.....................0.20	0.40	1.20	2.00
433, Mar 74.....................0.20	0.40	1.20	2.00
434, Apr 74.....................0.20	0.40	1.20	2.00
435, May 74.....................0.20	0.40	1.20	2.00
436, Jun 74.....................0.20	0.40	1.20	2.00
437, Jul 74, CI;GA; 100 pgs			
.....................0.60	0.80	2.40	4.00
438, Aug 74, CS 0.20	0.40	1.20	2.00
439, Sep 74, CS.............0.20	0.40	1.20	2.00
440, Oct 74, CS 1:MGr Green Arrow			
.....................0.20	1.20	3.60	6.00
441, Nov 74, CS; A: Flash0.20	0.40	1.20	2.00
442, Dec 74, CS.............0.20	0.40	1.20	2.00
443, Jan 75, JLA; 100 pgs			
.....................0.60	0.80	2.40	4.00
444, Feb 75.....................0.25	0.40	1.20	2.00
445, Mar 75.....................0.25	0.40	1.20	2.00
446, Apr 75.....................0.25	0.40	1.20	2.00
447, May 75.....................0.25	0.40	1.20	2.00
448, Jun 75 ....0.25	0.40	1.20	2.00
449, Jul 75, JK;GA giant 0.50	0.80	2.40	4.00
450, Aug 75.....................0.25	0.40	1.20	2.00
451, Sep 75.....................0.25	0.40	1.20	2.00
452, Oct 75.....................0.25	0.40	1.20	2.00
453, Nov 75.....................0.25	0.40	1.20	2.00
454, Dec 75, last Atom ...0.25	0.40	1.20	2.00
455, Jan 76.....................0.25	0.40	1.20	2.00
456, Feb 76.....................0.25	0.40	1.20	2.00
457, Mar 76.....................0.30	0.40	1.20	2.00
458, Apr 76, CS/MGr GA 0.30	0.40	1.20	2.00
459, May 76.....................0.30	0.40	1.20	2.00
460, Jun 76.....................0.30	0.40	1.20	2.00
461, Jul 76.....................0.30	0.40	1.20	2.00
462, Aug 76.....................0.30	0.40	1.20	2.00
463, Sep 76.....................0.30	0.40	1.20	2.00
464, Oct 76.....................0.30	0.40	1.20	2.00
465, Nov 76.....................0.30	0.40	1.20	2.00
466, Dec 76.....................0.30	0.40	1.20	2.00
467, Jan 77.....................0.30	0.40	1.20	2.00
468, Feb 77.....................0.30	0.40	1.20	2.00
469, Mar 77.....................0.30	0.40	1.20	2.00
470, Apr 77.....................0.30	0.40	1.20	2.00
471, May 77.....................0.30	0.40	1.20	2.00
472, Jun 77.....................0.30	0.40	1.20	2.00
473, Jul 77.....................0.35	0.40	1.20	2.00
474, Aug 77.....................0.35	0.40	1.20	2.00
475, Sep 77.....................0.35	0.40	1.20	2.00
476, Oct 77.....................0.35	0.40	1.20	2.00
477, Nov 77.....................0.35	0.40	1.20	2.00
478, Dec 77.....................0.35	0.40	1.20	2.00
479, Jan 78.....................0.35	0.40	1.20	2.00

	ORIG.	GOOD	FINE	N-MINT
480, Feb 78	0.35	0.40	1.20	2.00
481, Mar 78	0.35	0.40	1.20	2.00
482, Apr 78	0.35	0.40	1.20	2.00
483, May 78	0.35	0.40	1.20	2.00
484, Jun 78	0.35	0.40	1.20	2.00
485, Jul 78	0.35	0.40	1.20	2.00
486, Aug 78	0.35	0.40	1.20	2.00
487, Sep 78	0.50	0.40	1.20	2.00
488, Oct 78	0.50	0.40	1.20	2.00
489, Nov 78	0.50	0.40	1.20	2.00
490, Dec 78	0.40	0.40	1.20	2.00
491, Jan 79	0.40	0.40	1.20	2.00
492, Feb 79	0.40	0.40	1.20	2.00
493, Mar 79	0.40	0.40	1.20	2.00
494, Apr 79	0.40	0.40	1.20	2.00
495, May 79	0.40	0.40	1.20	2.00
496, Jun 79	0.40	0.40	1.20	2.00
497, Jul 79	0.40	0.40	1.20	2.00
498, Aug 79	0.40	0.40	1.20	2.00
499, Sep 79	0.40	0.40	1.20	2.00
500, Oct 79, Superman's life	1.00	0.60	1.80	3.00
501, Nov 79	0.40	0.45	1.35	2.25
502, Dec 79	0.40	0.45	1.35	2.25
503, Jan 80	0.40	0.45	1.35	2.25
504, Feb 80	0.40	0.45	1.35	2.25
505, Mar 80	0.40	0.45	1.35	2.25
506, Apr 80	0.40	0.45	1.35	2.25
507, May 80	0.40	0.45	1.35	2.25
508, Jun 80	0.40	0.45	1.35	2.25
509, Jul 80, JSn	0.40	0.45	1.35	2.25
510, Aug 80	0.40	0.45	1.35	2.25
511, Sep 80	0.50	0.45	1.35	2.25
512, Oct 80	0.50	0.45	1.35	2.25
513, Nov 80	0.50	0.45	1.35	2.25
514, Dec 80	0.50	0.45	1.35	2.25
515, Jan 81	0.50	0.45	1.35	2.25
516, Feb 81	0.50	0.45	1.35	2.25
517, Mar 81	0.50	0.45	1.35	2.25
518, Apr 81	0.50	0.45	1.35	2.25
519, May 81	0.50	0.45	1.35	2.25
520, Jun 81	0.50	0.45	1.35	2.25
521, Jul 81	0.50	0.45	1.35	2.25
522, Aug 81	0.50	0.45	1.35	2.25
523, Sep 81	0.50	0.45	1.35	2.25
524, Oct 81	0.60	0.45	1.35	2.25
525, Nov 81	0.60	0.45	1.35	2.25
526, Dec 81	0.60	0.45	1.35	2.25
527, Jan 82	0.60	0.45	1.35	2.25
528, Feb 82	0.60	0.45	1.35	2.25
529, Mar 82	0.60	0.45	1.35	2.25
530, Apr 82	0.60	0.45	1.35	2.25
531, May 82	0.60	0.45	1.35	2.25
532, Jun 82	0.60	0.45	1.35	2.25
533, Jul 82	0.60	0.45	1.35	2.25
534, Aug 82	0.60	0.45	1.35	2.25
535, Sep 82, Omega Man	0.60	0.45	1.35	2.25
536, Oct 82, Omega Man	0.60	0.45	1.35	2.25
537, Nov 82	0.60	0.45	1.35	2.25
538, Dec 82	0.60	0.45	1.35	2.25
539, Jan 83, GK;Flash, Atom	0.60	0.45	1.35	2.25
540, Feb 83, CS	0.60	0.45	1.35	2.25
541, Mar 83, CS	0.60	0.45	1.35	2.25
542, Apr 83, CS	0.60	0.45	1.35	2.25
543, May 83, CS	0.60	0.45	1.35	2.25
544, Jun 83, 45th anniv.	1.50	0.45	1.35	2.25
545, Jul 83	1.50	0.45	1.35	2.25
546, Aug 83	1.50	0.45	1.35	2.25
547, Sep 83	1.50	0.45	1.35	2.25

	ORIG.	GOOD	FINE	N-MINT
548, Oct 83	1.50	0.45	1.35	2.25
549, Nov 83	1.50	0.45	1.35	2.25
550, Dec 83	0.75	0.45	1.35	2.25
551, Jan 84	0.75	0.45	1.35	2.25
552, Feb 84, Animal Man	0.75	1.00	3.00	5.00
553, Mar 84, Animal Man	0.75	1.00	3.00	5.00
554, Apr 84	0.75	0.40	1.20	2.00
555, May 84	0.75	0.40	1.20	2.00
556, Jun 84	0.75	0.40	1.20	2.00
557, Jul 84	0.75	0.40	1.20	2.00
558, Aug 84	0.75	0.40	1.20	2.00
559, Sep 84	0.75	0.40	1.20	2.00
560, Oct 84	0.75	0.40	1.20	2.00
561, Nov 84	0.75	0.40	1.20	2.00
562, Dec 84	0.75	0.40	1.20	2.00
563, Jan 85	0.75	0.40	1.20	2.00
564, Feb 85	0.75	0.40	1.20	2.00
565, Mar 85	0.75	0.40	1.20	2.00
566, Apr 85	0.75	0.40	1.20	2.00
567, May 85	0.75	0.40	1.20	2.00
568, Jun 85	0.75	0.40	1.20	2.00
569, Jul 85	0.75	0.40	1.20	2.00
570, Aug 85	0.75	0.40	1.20	2.00
571, Sep 85	0.75	0.40	1.20	2.00
572, Oct 85	0.75	0.40	1.20	2.00
573, Nov 85	0.75	0.40	1.20	2.00
574, Dec 85	0.75	0.40	1.20	2.00
575, Jan 86	0.75	0.40	1.20	2.00
576, Feb 86	0.75	0.40	1.20	2.00
577, Mar 86	0.75	0.40	1.20	2.00
578, Apr 86	0.75	0.40	1.20	2.00
579, May 86	0.75	0.40	1.20	2.00
580, Jun 86	0.75	0.40	1.20	2.00
581, Jul 86	0.75	0.40	1.20	2.00
582, Aug 86	0.75	0.40	1.20	2.00
583, Sep 86, AMo	0.75	1.20	3.60	6.00
584, Jan 87, JBy,DG	0.75	0.40	1.20	2.00
585, Feb 87, JBy,DG	0.75	0.40	1.20	2.00
586, Mar 87, JBy, DG Legends	0.75	0.40	1.20	2.00
587, Apr 87, JBy,DG	0.75	0.40	1.20	2.00
588, May 87, JBy,DG	0.75	0.40	1.20	2.00
589, Jun 87, JBy,DG	0.75	0.40	1.20	2.00
590, Jul 87, JBy,DG	0.75	0.40	1.20	2.00
591, Aug 87, JBy,DG Superboy	0.75	0.50	1.50	2.50
592, Sep 87, JBy,DG	0.75	0.40	1.20	2.00
593, Oct 87, JBy,DG	0.75	0.40	1.20	2.00
594, Nov 87, JBy A:Batman; Booster Gold	0.75	0.40	1.20	2.00
595, Dec 87, JBy A:Batman; J'onn J'onzz	0.75	0.40	1.20	2.00
596, Jan 88, JBy; Millennium	0.75	0.40	1.20	2.00
597, Feb 88, JBy	0.75	0.40	1.20	2.00
598, Mar 88, JBy I:Checkmate	0.75	0.50	1.50	2.50
599, Apr 88, RA/JBy A:Metal Men; Bonus Book #1	0.75	0.40	1.20	2.00
600, May 88, JBy,GP (becomes *Action Comics Weekly*)	2.50	0.80	2.40	4.00
643, Jul 89, GP (was Action Comics Weekly)	0.75	0.20	0.60	1.00
644, Aug 89, GP	0.75	0.20	0.60	1.00
645, Sep 89, GP	0.75	0.20	0.60	1.00
646, Oct 89, GP	0.75	0.20	0.60	1.00
647, Nov 89, GP(c) O:Brainiac	0.75	0.20	0.60	1.00
648, Dec 89, GP(c)	0.75	0.20	0.60	1.00
649, Jan 90, GP(c)	0.75	0.20	0.60	1.00

	ORIG.	GOOD	FINE	N-MINT
❏ 650, Feb 90, JO,GP 1.50		0.30	0.90	1.50
❏ 651, Mar 90, Krypton Man				
.... 0.75		0.20	0.60	1.00
❏ 652, Apr 90, Krypton Man				
.... 0.75		0.20	0.60	1.00
❏ 653, May 90 .... 0.75		0.15	0.45	0.75
❏ 654, Jun 90, Batman...... 0.75		0.15	0.45	0.75
❏ 655, Jul 90 .... 0.75		0.15	0.45	0.75
❏ 656, Aug 90 .... 0.75		0.15	0.45	0.75
❏ 657, Sep 90, Toyman..... 0.75		0.15	0.45	0.75
❏ 658, Oct 90, CS.............. 0.75		0.20	0.60	1.00
❏ 659, Nov 90 .... 0.75		0.80	2.40	4.00
❏ 660, Dec 90 .... 0.75		0.20	0.60	1.00
❏ 661, Jan 91, Plastic Man1.00		0.20	0.60	1.00
❏ 662, Feb 91, Clark tells Lois				
.... 1.00		1.20	3.60	6.00
❏ 663, Mar 91 .... 1.00		0.20	0.60	1.00
❏ 664, Apr 91 .... 1.00		0.20	0.60	1.00
❏ 665, May 91 .... 1.00		0.20	0.60	1.00
❏ 666, Jun 91 .... 1.00		0.20	0.60	1.00
❏ 667, Jul 91 .... 1.75		0.35	1.05	1.75
❏ 668, Aug 91 .... 1.00		0.20	0.60	1.00
❏ 669, Sep 91 .... 1.00		0.20	0.60	1.00
❏ 670, Oct 91 .... 1.00		0.20	0.60	1.00
❏ 671, Nov 91, Superman blackout				
.... 1.00		0.20	0.60	1.00
❏ 672, Dec 91 .... 1.00		0.20	0.60	1.00
❏ 673, Jan 92 .... 1.00		0.20	0.60	1.00
❏ 674, Apr 92, Supergirl.... 1.00		0.40	1.20	2.00
❏ 675, Mar 92, Panic in Sky				
.... 1.00		0.20	0.60	1.00
❏ 676, Apr 92 .... 1.00		0.20	0.60	1.00
❏ 677, May 92 .... 1.00		0.20	0.60	1.00
❏ 678, Jun 92, O:Luthor.... 1.00		0.20	0.60	1.00
❏ 679, Jul 92 .... 1.00		0.20	0.60	1.00
❏ 680, Aug 92 .... 1.25		0.25	0.75	1.25
❏ 681, Sep 92 .... 1.25		0.25	0.75	1.25
❏ 682, Oct 92 .... 1.25		0.25	0.75	1.25
❏ 683, Nov 92 .... 1.25		0.80	2.40	4.00
❏ 684, Dec 92, Doomsday. 1.25		0.80	2.40	4.00
❏ 685, Jan 93, Superman funeral				
.... 1.25		0.80	2.40	4.00
❏ 686, Feb 93, Superman funeral				
I.. 1.25		0.70	2.10	3.50
❏ 687, Jun 93, 1:alien Superman				
.... 1.50		0.60	1.80	3.00
❏ 687, Jun 93, 1:alien Superman, die-cut cover				
.... 1.95		0.60	1.80	3.00
❏ 688, Jul 93, Reign of Supermen				
.... 1.50		0.60	1.80	3.00
❏ 689, Reign of Supermen 1.50		1.20	3.60	6.00
❏ 690, Reign of Supermen 1.50		0.60	1.80	3.00
❏ 691, Reign of Supermen 1.50		0.80	2.40	4.00
❏ 692, Clark Kent returns .. 1.50		0.60	1.80	3.00
❏ 693 .... 1.50		0.40	1.20	2.00
❏ 694 .... 1.50		0.30	0.90	1.50
❏ 695, A:Lobo 1.50		0.30	0.90	1.50
❏ 695, A:Lobo;enhanced cover				
.... 2.50		0.50	1.50	2.50
❏ 696, R: Doomsday 1.50		0.30	0.90	1.50
❏ 697, Bizarro 1.50		0.30	0.90	1.50
❏ 698 .... 1.50		0.30	0.90	1.50
❏ 699, May 94 .... 1.50		0.30	0.90	1.50
❏ 700, Jun 94, M:Pete Ross, Lana Lang; Fall of				
Metropolis........ 2.95		0.59	1.77	2.95
❏ 700, platinum..................		4.00	12.00	20.00
❏ 701, Jul 94, The Fall of Metropolis				
.... 1.50		0.30	0.90	1.50
❏ 702, Aug 94 .... 1.50		0.30	0.90	1.50
❏ 703, Sep 94, Zero Hour.. 1.50		0.30	0.90	1.50
❏ 704, Nov 94, V: Eradictor and The Outsiders. Dead				
Again.......................... 1.50		0.30	0.90	1.50

	ORIG.	GOOD	FINE	N-MINT
❏ 705, Dec 94, Dead Again1.50		0.30	0.90	1.50
❏ 706, Jan 95................... 1.50		0.30	0.90	1.50
❏ 707, Feb 95................... 1.50		0.30	0.90	1.50
❏ 708, Mar 95, A: Mister Miracle				
.... 1.50		0.30	0.90	1.50
❏ 709, Apr 95, V:Guy Gardner				
.... 1.50		0.30	0.90	1.50
❏ 710, Jun 95, "Death of Clark Kent"				
.... 1.95		0.39	1.17	1.95
❏ 711, Jul 95, "Death of Clark Kent";D: Kenny Braverman				
(Conduit) 1.95		0.39	1.17	1.95
❏ 712, Aug 95................... 1.95		0.39	1.17	1.95
❏ 713, Sep 95 .... 1.95		0.39	1.17	1.95
❏ 714, Oct 95, A:Joker....... 1.95		0.39	1.17	1.95
❏ 715, Nov 95, V:Parasite ..1.95		0.39	1.17	1.95
❏ 716, Dec 95, "Trial of Superman"				
.... 1.95		0.39	1.17	1.95
❏ 717, Jan 96, "Trial of Superman"				
.... 1.95		0.39	1.17	1.95
❏ 719, Mar 96, A:Batman...1.95		0.39	1.17	1.95
❏ 720, Apr 96, Lois ends engagement				
.... 1.95		0.39	1.17	1.95
❏ 721, May 96.................. 1.95		0.39	1.17	1.95
❏ 722, Jun 96 .... 1.95		0.39	1.17	1.95

ACTION COMICS ANNUAL

	ORIG.	GOOD	FINE	N-MINT
❏ 1, Oct 87, AAd,DG...........1.25		0.35	1.05	1.75
❏ 2, Jul 89, JO,GP,CS 1.75		0.35	1.05	1.75
❏ 3, Sep 91, Armageddon 2001				
.... 2.00		0.40	1.20	2.00
❏ 4, 92, Eclipso.................2.50		0.50	1.50	2.50
❏ 5, 93, Bloodlines; 1: Loose Cannon				
.... 2.50		0.50	1.50	2.50
❏ 6, 94 ....2.95		0.59	1.77	2.95
❏ 7, 95, "Year One"............3.95		0.79	2.37	3.95

ACTION COMICS WEEKLY (was Action Comics)

	ORIG.	GOOD	FINE	N-MINT
❏ 601, Aug 88, Superman,Blackhawk, Green Lantern,				
Deadman, Wild Dog, Secret Six				
.... 1.50		0.30	0.90	1.50
❏ 602, Aug 88, Superman, Blackhawk, Green Lantern,				
Deadman, Wild Dog, Secret Six				
.... 1.50		0.30	0.90	1.50
❏ 603, Aug 88, Superman, Blackhawk, Green Lantern,				
Deadman, Wild Dog, Secret Six				
.... 1.50		0.30	0.90	1.50
❏ 604, Aug 88, Superman, Blackhawk, Green Lantern,				
Deadman, Wild Dog, Secret Six				
.... 1.50		0.30	0.90	1.50
❏ 605, Aug 88, Superman, Blackhawk, Green Lantern,				
Deadman, Wild Dog, Secret Six				
.... 1.50		0.30	0.90	1.50
❏ 606, Sep 88, Superman, Blackhawk, Green Lantern,				
Deadman, Wild Dog, Secret Six				
.... 1.50		0.30	0.90	1.50
❏ 607, Sep 88, Superman, Blackhawk, Green Lantern,				
Deadman, Wild Dog, Secret Six				
.... 1.50		0.30	0.90	1.50
❏ 608, Sep 88 ....1.50		0.30	0.90	1.50
❏ 609, Sep 88, BB(c) Black Canary				
.... 1.50		0.30	0.90	1.50
❏ 610, Sep 88..................1.50		0.30	0.90	1.50
❏ 611, Oct 88....................1.50		0.30	0.90	1.50
❏ 612, Oct 88....................1.50		0.30	0.90	1.50
❏ 613, Oct 88....................1.50		0.30	0.90	1.50
❏ 614, Oct 88....................1.50		0.30	0.90	1.50
❏ 615, Oct 88....................1.50		0.30	0.90	1.50
❏ 616, Nov 88...................1.50		0.30	0.90	1.50
❏ 617, Nov 88...................1.50		0.30	0.90	1.50
❏ 618, Nov 88...................1.50		0.30	0.90	1.50
❏ 619, Nov 88...................1.50		0.30	0.90	1.50
❏ 620, Dec 88 ....1.50		0.30	0.90	1.50
❏ 621, Dec 88 ....1.50		0.30	0.90	1.50

	ORIG.	GOOD	FINE	N-MINT
❑ 622, Dec 88..................1.50		0.30	0.90	1.50
❑ 623, Dec 88..................1.50		0.30	0.90	1.50
❑ 624, Dec 88..................1.50		0.30	0.90	1.50
❑ 625, Dec 88..................1.50		0.30	0.90	1.50
❑ 626, Dec 88..................1.50		0.30	0.90	1.50
❑ 627, Dec 88..................1.50		0.30	0.90	1.50
❑ 628, Jan 89...................1.50		0.30	0.90	1.50
❑ 629, Jan 89...................1.50		0.30	0.90	1.50
❑ 630, Jan 89...................1.50		0.30	0.90	1.50
❑ 631, Jan 89...................1.50		0.30	0.90	1.50
❑ 632, Jan 89...................1.50		0.30	0.90	1.50
❑ 633, Jan 89...................1.50		0.30	0.90	1.50
❑ 634, Jan 89...................1.50		0.30	0.90	1.50
❑ 635, Jan 89, crossover ..1.50		0.30	0.90	1.50
❑ 636, Jan 89, 1:new Phantom Lady				
..................................1.50		0.30	0.90	1.50
❑ 637, Jan 89, 1:Hero Hotline				
..................................1.50		0.30	0.90	1.50
❑ 638, Feb 89, JK/TA(c) 1.50		0.30	0.90	1.50
❑ 639, Feb 89...................1.50		0.30	0.90	1.50
❑ 640, Feb 89...................1.50		0.30	0.90	1.50
❑ 641, Feb 89...................1.50		0.30	0.90	1.50
❑ 642, Mar 89, (becomes Action Comics)				
..................................1.50		0.30	0.90	1.50

ACTION FORCE
LIGHTNING

	ORIG.	GOOD	FINE	N-MINT
❑ 1, Jan 87		0.35	1.05	1.75

MARVEL UK

	ORIG.	GOOD	FINE	N-MINT
❑ 1, (reprinted in U.S. as G.I. Joe European Missions)				
..................................1.00		0.20	0.60	1.00
❑ 2 ....1.00		0.20	0.60	1.00
❑ 3 ....1.00		0.20	0.60	1.00
❑ 4 ....1.00		0.20	0.60	1.00
❑ 5 ....1.00		0.20	0.60	1.00
❑ 6 ....1.00		0.20	0.60	1.00
❑ 7 ....1.00		0.20	0.60	1.00
❑ 8 ....1.00		0.20	0.60	1.00
❑ 9 ....1.00		0.20	0.60	1.00
❑ 10 ....1.00		0.20	0.60	1.00
❑ 11 ....1.00		0.20	0.60	1.00
❑ 12 ....1.00		0.20	0.60	1.00
❑ 13 ....1.00		0.20	0.60	1.00
❑ 14 ....1.00		0.20	0.60	1.00
❑ 15 ....1.00		0.20	0.60	1.00
❑ 16 ....1.00		0.20	0.60	1.00
❑ 17 ....1.00		0.20	0.60	1.00
❑ 18 ....1.00		0.20	0.60	1.00
❑ 19 ....1.00		0.20	0.60	1.00
❑ 20 ....1.00		0.20	0.60	1.00
❑ 21 ....1.00		0.20	0.60	1.00
❑ 22 ....1.00		0.20	0.60	1.00
❑ 23 ....1.00		0.20	0.60	1.00

ACTION FORCE HOLIDAY SPECIAL (1987)

	ORIG.	GOOD	FINE	N-MINT
❑ 0, nn..............................1.50		0.30	0.90	1.50

ACTION GIRL COMICS
SLAVE LABOR

	ORIG.	GOOD	FINE	N-MINT
❑ 1, Oct 94, b&w...............2.50		0.50	1.50	2.50
❑ 3, Apr 95, b&w...............2.50		0.50	1.50	2.50

ADAM & EVE A.D.
BAM

	ORIG.	GOOD	FINE	N-MINT
❑ 1 ....1.50		0.30	0.90	1.50
❑ 2 ....1.50		0.30	0.90	1.50
❑ 3 ....1.50		0.30	0.90	1.50
❑ 4 ....1.50		0.30	0.90	1.50
❑ 5 ....1.50		0.30	0.90	1.50
❑ 6 ....1.50		0.30	0.90	1.50
❑ 7 ....1.50		0.30	0.90	1.50
❑ 8 ....1.50		0.30	0.90	1.50
❑ 9 ....1.50		0.30	0.90	1.50
❑ 10 ....1.50		0.30	0.90	1.50

ADAM STRANGE
DC

	ORIG.	GOOD	FINE	N-MINT
❑ 1, Mar 90......................3.95		0.79	2.37	3.95
❑ 2, May 90......................3.95		0.79	2.37	3.95
❑ 3, Jul 90........................3.95		0.79	2.37	3.95

ADOLESCENT BLACK BELT HAMSTERS CLASSICS
PARODY

	ORIG.	GOOD	FINE	N-MINT
❑ 5, b&w............................		0.50	1.50	2.50

ADOLESCENT BLACK BELT HAMSTERS GOLD EDITION

	ORIG.	GOOD	FINE	N-MINT
❑ 1, b&w............................		0.59	1.77	2.95

ADOLESCENT RADIOACTIVE BLACK BELT HAMSTERS
ECLIPSE

	ORIG.	GOOD	FINE	N-MINT
❑ 1, b&w............................		0.70	2.10	3.50
❑ 1, (reprint)		0.30	0.90	1.50
❑ 2		0.40	1.20	2.00
❑ 3		0.30	0.90	1.50
❑ 4		0.30	0.90	1.50
❑ 5		0.30	0.90	1.50
❑ 6		0.30	0.90	1.50
❑ 7, D:Bruce......................		0.30	0.90	1.50
❑ 8		0.30	0.90	1.50
❑ 9, last.............................		0.40	1.20	2.00

PARODY PRESS

	ORIG.	GOOD	FINE	N-MINT
❑ 1 ....2.50		0.50	1.50	2.50
❑ 2 ....2.50		0.50	1.50	2.50
❑ 3 ....2.50		0.50	1.50	2.50
❑ 4 ....2.50		0.50	1.50	2.50
❑ 5 ....2.50		0.50	1.50	2.50

ADOLESCENT RADIOACTIVE BLACK BELT HAMSTERS 3-D
ECLIPSE

	ORIG.	GOOD	FINE	N-MINT
❑ 1		0.40	1.20	2.00
❑ 2		0.40	1.20	2.00
❑ 3		0.50	1.50	2.50
❑ 4		0.50	1.50	2.50

ADOLESCENT RADIOACTIVE BLACK BELT HAMSTERS MASSACRE THE JAPANESE INVASION

	ORIG.	GOOD	FINE	N-MINT
❑ 1, b&w............................		0.50	1.50	2.50

ADOLESCENT RADIOACTIVE BLACK BELT HAMSTERS: THE LOST TREASURES
PARODY

	ORIG.	GOOD	FINE	N-MINT
❑ 1, b&w...........................2.95		0.59	1.77	2.95

ADULT ACTION FANTASY FEATURING: TAWNY'S TALES
LOUISIANA LEISURE

	ORIG.	GOOD	FINE	N-MINT
❑ 1, adult 2.50		0.50	1.50	2.50
❑ 2, adult 2.50		0.50	1.50	2.50

ADVANCED DUNGEONS & DRAGONS ANNUAL
DC

	ORIG.	GOOD	FINE	N-MINT
❑ 1		0.79	2.37	3.95

ADVANCED DUNGEONS AND DRAGONS

	ORIG.	GOOD	FINE	N-MINT
❑ 1		2.40	7.20	12.00
❑ 2, JDu		2.00	6.00	10.00
❑ 3		1.40	4.20	7.00
❑ 4		1.40	4.20	7.00
❑ 5		1.40	4.20	7.00
❑ 6		1.00	3.00	5.00
❑ 7		1.00	3.00	5.00
❑ 8		1.00	3.00	5.00
❑ 9		1.00	3.00	5.00
❑ 10		1.00	3.00	5.00
❑ 11		0.40	1.20	2.00
❑ 12		0.40	1.20	2.00
❑ 13		0.40	1.20	2.00
❑ 14		0.40	1.20	2.00
❑ 15		0.40	1.20	2.00
❑ 16		0.40	1.20	2.00
❑ 17		0.40	1.20	2.00

	ORIG.	GOOD	FINE	N-MINT
❑ 18	0.40	1.20	2.00
❑ 19	0.40	1.20	2.00
❑ 20	0.40	1.20	2.00
❑ 21	0.40	1.20	2.00
❑ 22	0.40	1.20	2.00
❑ 23	0.40	1.20	2.00
❑ 24	0.40	1.20	2.00
❑ 25	0.40	1.20	2.00
❑ 26	0.40	1.20	2.00
❑ 27	0.40	1.20	2.00
❑ 28	0.40	1.20	2.00
❑ 29	0.40	1.20	2.00
❑ 30	0.40	1.20	2.00
❑ 31	0.40	1.20	2.00
❑ 32	0.40	1.20	2.00
❑ 33	0.40	1.20	2.00
❑ 34	0.40	1.20	2.00
❑ 35	0.40	1.20	2.00
❑ 36	0.40	1.20	2.00

ADVENTURE

	ORIG.	GOOD	FINE	N-MINT
❑ 247, Apr 58, 1&O: Legion of Super-Heroes, Cosmic Boy, Saturn Girl, Lightning Lad;J: Superboy		840.00	2520.00	4200.00
❑ 248, May 58, GA	0.10	40.00	120.00	200.00
❑ 249, Jun 58, GA	0.10	35.00	105.00	175.00
❑ 250, Jul 58, GA	0.10	35.00	105.00	175.00
❑ 251, Aug 58, GA	0.10	35.00	105.00	175.00
❑ 252, Sep 58, GA	0.10	35.00	105.00	175.00
❑ 253, Oct 58, GA	0.10	36.00	108.00	180.00
❑ 254, Nov 58, GA	0.10	28.00	84.00	140.00
❑ 255, Dec 58, GA	0.10	28.00	84.00	140.00
❑ 256, Jan 59, JK;O:GA	0.10	120.00	360.00	600.00
❑ 257, Feb 59	0.10	24.00	72.00	120.00
❑ 258, Mar 59	0.10	24.00	72.00	120.00
❑ 259, Apr 59	0.10	20.00	60.00	100.00
❑ 260, May 59, O:Aquaman	0.10	115.00	345.00	575.00
❑ 261, Jun 59	0.10	18.00	54.00	90.00
❑ 262, Jul 59	0.10	18.00	54.00	90.00
❑ 263, Aug 59	0.10	18.00	54.00	90.00
❑ 264, Sep 59	0.10	18.00	54.00	90.00
❑ 265, Oct 59	0.10	18.00	54.00	90.00
❑ 266, Nov 59	0.10	18.00	54.00	90.00
❑ 267, Dec 59, Legion	0.10	110.00	330.00	550.00
❑ 268, Jan 60	0.10	16.00	48.00	80.00
❑ 269, Feb 60, 1:Aqualad	0.10	25.00	75.00	125.00
❑ 270, Mar 60	0.10	12.00	36.00	60.00
❑ 271, Apr 60	0.10	12.00	36.00	60.00
❑ 272, May 60	0.10	12.00	36.00	60.00
❑ 273, Jun 60	0.10	12.00	36.00	60.00
❑ 274, Jul 60	0.10	12.00	36.00	60.00
❑ 275, Aug 60	0.10	12.00	36.00	60.00
❑ 276, Sep 60, 1: Sun Boy	0.10	16.00	48.00	80.00
❑ 277, Oct 60	0.10	10.00	30.00	50.00
❑ 278, Nov 60	0.10	10.00	30.00	50.00
❑ 279, Dec 60	0.10	10.00	30.00	50.00
❑ 280, Jan 61	0.10	10.00	30.00	50.00
❑ 281, Feb 61	0.10	10.00	30.00	50.00
❑ 282, Mar 61, 1&O: Starboy	0.10	20.00	60.00	100.00
❑ 283, Apr 61, 1: Phantom Zone	0.10	12.00	36.00	60.00
❑ 284, May 61	0.10	5.00	15.00	25.00
❑ 285, Jun 61, 1:Bizarro World	0.10	14.00	42.00	70.00
❑ 286, Jul 61, 1:Bizarro Mxyzptlk	10.00	30.00	50.00	
❑ 287, Aug 61	0.10	5.00	15.00	25.00
❑ 288, Sep 61	0.10	5.00	15.00	25.00
❑ 289, Oct 61	0.10	5.00	15.00	25.00

	ORIG.	GOOD	FINE	N-MINT
❑ 290, Nov 61, O&J: Sun Boy	0.10	12.00	36.00	60.00
❑ 291, Dec 61, Superboy	0.12	6.00	18.00	30.00
❑ 292, Jan 62, Superboy	0.12	6.00	18.00	30.00
❑ 293, Feb 62, O&1:Mon-El		8.00	24.00	40.00
❑ 294, Mar 62, Superboy	0.12	6.00	18.00	30.00
❑ 295, Apr 62, Superboy	0.12	6.00	18.00	30.00
❑ 296, May 62, Superboy	0.12	6.00	18.00	30.00
❑ 297, Jun 62, Superboy	0.12	6.00	18.00	30.00
❑ 298, Jul 62, Superboy	0.12	6.00	18.00	30.00
❑ 299, Aug 62, Superboy	0.10	6.00	18.00	30.00
❑ 300, Sep 62, J:Mon-El, Legion	0.12	75.00	225.00	375.00
❑ 301, Oct 62, O:Bouncing Boy	0.12	27.00	81.00	135.00
❑ 302, Nov 62, Legion	0.12	20.00	60.00	100.00
❑ 303, Dec 62, Legion; J:Matter-Eater Lad	0.12	16.00	48.00	80.00
❑ 304, Jan 63, Legion	0.12	16.00	48.00	80.00
❑ 305, Feb 63, Legion	0.12	16.00	48.00	80.00
❑ 306, Mar 63, Legion	0.12	13.00	39.00	65.00
❑ 307, Apr 63, Legion; J:Element Lad	0.12	13.00	39.00	65.00
❑ 308, May 63, Legion; J:Light Lass	0.12	13.00	39.00	65.00
❑ 309, Jun 63, Legion	0.12	13.00	39.00	65.00
❑ 310, Jul 63, Legion	0.12	13.00	39.00	65.00
❑ 311, Aug 63, Legion	0.12	8.00	24.00	40.00
❑ 312, Sep 63, Legion	0.12	8.00	24.00	40.00
❑ 313, Oct 63, Legion	0.12	8.00	24.00	40.00
❑ 314, Nov 63, Legion	0.12	8.00	24.00	40.00
❑ 315, Dec 63, Legion	0.12	8.00	24.00	40.00
❑ 316, Jan 64, Legion	0.12	8.00	24.00	40.00
❑ 317, Feb 64, Legion; J:Dream Girl	0.12	8.00	24.00	40.00
❑ 318, Mar 64, Legion	0.12	8.00	24.00	40.00
❑ 319, Apr 64, Legion	0.12	8.00	24.00	40.00
❑ 320, May 64, Legion	0.12	8.00	24.00	40.00
❑ 321, Jun 64, Legion	0.12	6.00	18.00	30.00
❑ 322, Jul 64, Legion	0.12	6.00	18.00	30.00
❑ 323, Aug 64, Legion	0.12	6.00	18.00	30.00
❑ 324, Sep 64, Legion	0.12	6.00	18.00	30.00
❑ 325, Oct 64, Legion	0.12	6.00	18.00	30.00
❑ 326, Nov 64, Legion	0.12	6.00	18.00	30.00
❑ 327, Dec 64, 1&J: Timber Wolf	0.12	6.00	18.00	30.00
❑ 328, Jan 65, Legion	0.12	6.00	18.00	30.00
❑ 329, Feb 65, Legion	0.12	6.00	18.00	30.00
❑ 330, Mar 65, Legion	0.12	6.00	18.00	30.00
❑ 331, Apr 65, Legion	0.12	4.40	13.20	22.00
❑ 332, May 65, Legion	0.12	4.40	13.20	22.00
❑ 333, Jun 65, Legion	0.12	4.40	13.20	22.00
❑ 334, Jul 65, Legion	0.12	4.40	13.20	22.00
❑ 335, Aug 65, Legion	0.12	4.40	13.20	22.00
❑ 336, Sep 65, Legion	0.12	4.40	13.20	22.00
❑ 337, Oct 65, Legion	0.12	4.40	13.20	22.00
❑ 338, Nov 65, Legion	0.12	4.40	13.20	22.00
❑ 339, Dec 65, Legion	0.12	4.40	13.20	22.00
❑ 340, Jan 66, Legion	0.12	4.40	13.20	22.00
❑ 341, Feb 66, Legion	0.12	2.80	8.40	14.00
❑ 342, Mar 66, Legion	0.12	2.80	8.40	14.00
❑ 343, Apr 66, Legion	0.12	2.80	8.40	14.00
❑ 344, May 66, Legion	0.12	2.80	8.40	14.00
❑ 345, Jun 66, Legion	0.12	2.80	8.40	14.00
❑ 346, Jul 66, 1&J:Karate Kid. Princess Projectra, Ferro Lad	0.12	3.00	9.00	15.00
❑ 347, Aug 66, Legion	0.12	1.60	4.80	8.00
❑ 348, Sep 66	0.12	1.80	5.40	9.00
❑ 349, Oct 66	0.12	1.80	5.40	9.00
❑ 350, Nov 66, Legion	0.12	1.60	4.80	8.00

	ORIG.	GOOD	FINE	N-MINT
351, Dec 66, 1:White Witch	0.12	1.60	4.80	8.00
352, Jan 67, Legion	0.12	2.40	7.20	12.00
353, Feb 67, D:Ferro Lad	0.12	2.00	6.00	10.00
354, Mar 67, Legion	0.12	1.60	4.80	8.00
355, Apr 67, Legion	0.12	1.60	4.80	8.00
356, May 67, Legion	0.12	1.60	4.80	8.00
357, Jun 67, Legion	0.12	1.60	4.80	8.00
358, Jul 67, Legion	0.12	1.60	4.80	8.00
359, Aug 67, Legion	0.12	1.60	4.80	8.00
360, Sep 67, Legion	0.12	1.60	4.80	8.00
361, Oct 67, Legion	0.12	1.60	4.80	8.00
362, Nov 67, Legion	0.12	1.60	4.80	8.00
363, Dec 67, Legion	0.12	1.60	4.80	8.00
364, Jan 65, Legion	0.12	1.60	4.80	8.00
365, Feb 68, NA; 1:Shadow Lass	0.12	1.70	5.10	8.50
366, Mar 68, Legion	0.12	1.60	4.80	8.00
367, Apr 68, Legion	0.12	1.60	4.80	8.00
368, May 68, Legion	0.12	1.60	4.80	8.00
369, Jun 68, Legion	0.12	1.60	4.80	8.00
370, Jul 68, Legion	0.12	1.60	4.80	8.00
371, Aug 68, NA;Legion	0.12	1.60	4.80	8.00
372, Sep 68, NA;Legion	0.12	1.60	4.80	8.00
373, Oct 68, Legion	0.12	1.60	4.80	8.00
374, Nov 68, Legion	0.12	1.60	4.80	8.00
375, Dec 68, NA; 1:Quantum Queen	0.12	1.60	4.80	8.00
376, Jan 69, Legion	0.12	1.60	4.80	8.00
377, Feb 69, Legion	0.12	1.60	4.80	8.00
378, Mar 69, Legion	0.12	1.60	4.80	8.00
379, Apr 69, Legion	0.12	1.60	4.80	8.00
380, Apr 69, Legion	0.12	1.60	4.80	8.00
381, Jun 69, Supergirl begins	0.15	0.80	2.40	4.00
382, Jul 69	0.15	0.60	1.80	3.00
383, Aug 69	0.15	0.60	1.80	3.00
384, Sep 69	0.15	0.60	1.80	3.00
385, Oct 69	0.15	0.60	1.80	3.00
386, Nov 69	0.15	0.60	1.80	3.00
387, Dec 69	0.15	0.60	1.80	3.00
388, Jan 70	0.15	0.60	1.80	3.00
389, Feb 70	0.15	0.60	1.80	3.00
390, Apr 70, giant	0.25	2.00	6.00	10.00
391, Mar 70	0.15	0.45	1.35	2.25
392, Apr 70	0.15	0.45	1.35	2.25
393, May 70	0.15	0.45	1.35	2.25
394, Jun 70	0.15	0.45	1.35	2.25
395, Jul 70	0.15	0.45	1.35	2.25
396, Aug 70	0.15	0.45	1.35	2.25
397, Sep 70	0.15	0.45	1.35	2.25
398, Oct 70	0.15	0.45	1.35	2.25
399, Nov 70	0.15	0.45	1.35	2.25
400, Dec 70	0.15	0.45	1.35	2.25
401, Jan 71	0.15	0.35	1.05	1.75
402, Feb 71	0.15	0.35	1.05	1.75
403, Apr 71, giant	0.25	1.00	3.00	5.00
404, Mar 71	0.15	0.35	1.05	1.75
405, Apr 71	0.15	0.35	1.05	1.75
406, May 71	0.15	0.35	1.05	1.75
407, Jun 71	0.15	0.35	1.05	1.75
408, Jul 71	0.15	0.35	1.05	1.75
409, Aug 71	0.25	0.35	1.05	1.75
410, Sep 71	0.25	0.35	1.05	1.75
411, Oct 71	0.25	0.35	1.05	1.75
412, Nov 71, Animal Man rep.	0.25	1.00	3.00	5.00
413, Dec 71	0.25	0.25	0.75	1.25
414, Jan 72	0.25	0.70	2.10	3.50
415, Feb 72, Animal Man rep.	0.25	1.00	3.00	5.00
416, Mar 72, all-women issue	0.50	0.35	1.05	1.75
417, Mar 72, Frazetta art	0.25	0.50	1.50	2.50
418, Apr 72, Black Canary	0.25	0.30	0.90	1.50
419, May 72, Black Canary	0.25	0.30	0.90	1.50
420, Jun 72, Animal Man rep.	0.25	0.70	2.10	3.50
421, Jul 72, Animal Man rep.	0.20	0.70	2.10	3.50
422, Aug 72	0.20	0.30	0.90	1.50
423, Sep 72	0.20	0.30	0.90	1.50
424, Oct 72	0.20	0.30	0.90	1.50
425, Jan 73, ATh;O: Capt. Fear	0.20	0.40	1.20	2.00
426, Mar 73	0.20	0.20	0.60	1.00
427, May 73	0.20	2.00	6.00	10.00
428, Aug 73	0.20	1.20	3.60	6.00
429, Oct 73	0.20	1.00	3.00	5.00
430, Dec 73	0.20	1.00	3.00	5.00
431, Feb 74, JA/ATh; Spectre	0.20	0.60	1.80	3.00
432, Apr 74	0.20	0.60	1.80	3.00
433, Jun 74	0.20	0.60	1.80	3.00
434, Aug 74	0.20	0.60	1.80	3.00
435, Oct 74	0.20	0.60	1.80	3.00
436, Dec 74	0.20	0.60	1.80	3.00
437, Feb 75	0.25	0.60	1.80	3.00
438, Apr 75	0.25	0.60	1.80	3.00
439, Jun 75	0.25	0.60	1.80	3.00
440, Aug 75	0.25	0.60	1.80	3.00
441, Oct 75	0.25	0.40	1.20	2.00
442, Dec 75	0.25	0.40	1.20	2.00
443, Feb 76	0.25	0.40	1.20	2.00
444, Apr 76	0.30	0.40	1.20	2.00
445, Jun 76	0.30	0.40	1.20	2.00
446, Aug 76	0.30	0.40	1.20	2.00
447, Oct 76	0.30	0.40	1.20	2.00
448, Nov 76	0.30	0.40	1.20	2.00
449, Jan 77	0.30	0.40	1.20	2.00
450, Mar 77	0.30	0.40	1.20	2.00
451, May 77	0.30	0.40	1.20	2.00
452, Jul 77	0.35	0.40	1.20	2.00
453, Sep 77	0.35	0.20	0.60	1.00
454, Nov 77	0.35	0.20	0.60	1.00
455, Jan 78	0.35	0.20	0.60	1.00
456, Mar 78	0.35	0.20	0.60	1.00
457, May 78	0.35	0.20	0.60	1.00
458, Jul 78	0.35	0.20	0.60	1.00
459, Sep 78, JA/DN/JSa	1.00	0.25	0.75	1.25
460, Nov 78, SA/DN/JSa	1.00	0.30	0.90	1.50
461, Jan 79, JA/DN/JSa;D:JSA	1.00	0.30	0.90	1.50
462, Mar 79, JSa/JL/DG;D:E-2 Batman	1.00	0.30	0.90	1.50
463, May 79, JSa/FMc/JL/DH	1.00	0.25	0.75	1.25
464, Jul 79, Deadman	1.00	0.30	0.90	1.50
465, Sep 79	1.00	0.25	0.75	1.25
466, Nov 79	1.00	0.25	0.75	1.25
467, Jan 80	0.40	0.35	1.05	1.75
468, Feb 80	0.40	0.35	1.05	1.75
469, Mar 80	0.40	0.35	1.05	1.75
470, Apr 80	0.40	0.35	1.05	1.75
471, May 80	0.40	0.35	1.05	1.75
472, Jun 80	0.40	0.35	1.05	1.75
473, Jul 80	0.40	0.35	1.05	1.75
474, Aug 80	0.40	0.35	1.05	1.75
475, Sep 80	0.50	0.35	1.05	1.75
476, Oct 80	0.50	0.35	1.05	1.75
477, Nov 80	0.50	0.35	1.05	1.75

	ORIG.	GOOD	FINE	N-MINT
☐ 478, Dec 80	0.50	0.35	1.05	1.75
☐ 479, Mar 81	0.50	0.35	1.05	1.75
☐ 480, Apr 81	0.50	0.35	1.05	1.75
☐ 481, May 81	0.50	0.35	1.05	1.75
☐ 482, Jun 81	0.50	0.35	1.05	1.75
☐ 483, Jul 81	0.50	0.35	1.05	1.75
☐ 484, Aug 81	0.50	0.35	1.05	1.75
☐ 485, Sep 81	0.50	0.35	1.05	1.75
☐ 486, Oct 81	0.60	0.35	1.05	1.75
☐ 487, Nov 81	0.60	0.35	1.05	1.75
☐ 488, Dec 81	0.60	0.35	1.05	1.75
☐ 489, Jan 82	0.60	0.35	1.05	1.75
☐ 490, Feb 82	0.60	0.35	1.05	1.75
☐ 491, Sep 82, digest size begins	0.95	0.20	0.60	1.00
☐ 492, Oct 82	1.25	0.25	0.75	1.25
☐ 493, Nov 82	1.25	0.25	0.75	1.25
☐ 494, Dec 82	1.25	0.25	0.75	1.25
☐ 495, Jan 83	1.25	0.25	0.75	1.25
☐ 496, Feb 83	1.25	0.25	0.75	1.25
☐ 497, Mar 83	1.25	0.25	0.75	1.25
☐ 498, Apr 83	1.25	0.25	0.75	1.25
☐ 499, May 83	1.25	0.25	0.75	1.25
☐ 500, Jun 83	1.25	0.25	0.75	1.25
☐ 501, Jul 83	1.25	0.25	0.75	1.25
☐ 502, Aug 83	1.25	0.25	0.75	1.25
☐ 503, Sep 83	1.25	0.25	0.75	1.25

ADVENTURE INTO FEAR
(see Fear)
MARVEL

ADVENTURE OF THE KARATE PIG, NINJA FLOUNDER AND THE 4-D MONKEY
DR. LEUNG'S

		GOOD	FINE	N-MINT
☐ 1		0.36	1.08	1.80
☐ 2		0.36	1.08	1.80
☐ 3		0.36	1.08	1.80
☐ 4		0.36	1.08	1.80
☐ 5		0.36	1.08	1.80

ADVENTURE STRIP DIGEST
WCG

	ORIG.	GOOD	FINE	N-MINT
☐ 1, Aug 94, b&w	2.00	0.40	1.20	2.00
☐ 2, Apr 95, b&w	2.50	0.50	1.50	2.50

ADVENTURERS
AIRCEL

		GOOD	FINE	N-MINT
☐ 1, regular cover		1.00	3.00	5.00
☐ 1, skeleton cover		3.00	9.00	15.00
☐ 2, (moves to Adventure Publications)		0.80	2.40	4.00

ADVENTURERS (was Aircel title)
ADVENTURE

		GOOD	FINE	N-MINT
☐ 0		0.30	0.90	1.50
☐ 1, reprint		0.30	0.90	1.50
☐ 3		0.30	0.90	1.50
☐ 4		0.30	0.90	1.50
☐ 5		0.30	0.90	1.50
☐ 6		0.30	0.90	1.50
☐ 7		0.30	0.90	1.50
☐ 8		0.30	0.90	1.50
☐ 9		0.35	1.05	1.75
☐ 10		0.35	1.05	1.75

ADVENTURERS BOOK II

	ORIG.	GOOD	FINE	N-MINT
☐ 0, b&w		0.39	1.17	1.95
☐ 1, 'limited' cover		0.39	1.17	1.95
☐ 1, 'regular' cover		0.39	1.17	1.95
☐ 2		0.39	1.17	1.95
☐ 3		0.39	1.17	1.95
☐ 4		0.39	1.17	1.95
☐ 5		0.39	1.17	1.95
☐ 6		0.39	1.17	1.95
☐ 7, Mar 89, b&w	1.95	0.39	1.17	1.95

ADVENTURERS BOOK III

		GOOD	FINE	N-MINT
☐ 1, limited cover		0.45	1.35	2.25
☐ 1, regular cover		0.45	1.35	2.25
☐ 2		0.45	1.35	2.25
☐ 3		0.45	1.35	2.25
☐ 4		0.45	1.35	2.25
☐ 5		0.45	1.35	2.25
☐ 6		0.45	1.35	2.25

ADVENTURES IN READING STARRING: THE AMAZING SPIDER-MAN
MARVEL

		GOOD	FINE	N-MINT
☐ 1, Sep 90, giveaway		0.20	0.60	1.00

ADVENTURES IN THE MYSTWOOD
BLACKTHORNE

		GOOD	FINE	N-MINT
☐ 1		0.40	1.20	2.00

ADVENTURES INTO THE UNKNOWN!
A-PLUS

		GOOD	FINE	N-MINT
☐ 1, FF,AW b&w rep.		0.50	1.50	2.50
☐ 2, FF(c) reprints		0.50	1.50	2.50
☐ 3, AW;reprints		0.50	1.50	2.50
☐ 4, reprints		0.50	1.50	2.50

ADVENTURES OF B.O.C.
INVASION

	ORIG.	GOOD	FINE	N-MINT
☐ 1	1.50	0.30	0.90	1.50
☐ 2	1.50	0.30	0.90	1.50
☐ 3	1.50	0.30	0.90	1.50

ADVENTURES OF BARON MUNCHAUSEN
NOW

	ORIG.	GOOD	FINE	N-MINT
☐ 1, Jul 89, movie	1.75	0.35	1.05	1.75
☐ 2, Aug 89, movie	1.75	0.35	1.05	1.75
☐ 3, Sep 89, movie	1.75	0.35	1.05	1.75
☐ 4, Oct 89, movie	1.75	0.35	1.05	1.75

ADVENTURES OF BAYOU BILLY, THE
ARCHIE

	ORIG.	GOOD	FINE	N-MINT
☐ 1, Sep 89, O:Bayou Billy	1.00	0.20	0.60	1.00
☐ 2	1.00	0.20	0.60	1.00
☐ 3	1.00	0.20	0.60	1.00
☐ 4	1.00	0.20	0.60	1.00
☐ 5, Jun 90	1.00	0.20	0.60	1.00

ADVENTURES OF CAPTAIN AMERICA
MARVEL

	ORIG.	GOOD	FINE	N-MINT
☐ 1, Sep 91, O: Capt. America	4.95	1.20	3.60	6.00
☐ 2, Nov 91, O: Capt. America	4.95	0.99	2.97	4.95
☐ 3, Dec 91, O: Capt. America	4.95	0.99	2.97	4.95
☐ 4, Jan 92, O: Capt. America	4.95	0.99	2.97	4.95

ADVENTURES OF CAPTAIN JACK
FANTAGRAPHICS

	ORIG.	GOOD	FINE	N-MINT
☐ 1, b&w	2.00	0.40	1.20	2.00
☐ 2, b&w	2.00	0.40	1.20	2.00
☐ 3, b&w	2.00	0.40	1.20	2.00
☐ 4, b&w	2.00	0.40	1.20	2.00
☐ 5, b&w	2.00	0.40	1.20	2.00
☐ 6, b&w	2.00	0.40	1.20	2.00
☐ 7, b&w	2.00	0.40	1.20	2.00
☐ 8, b&w	2.00	0.40	1.20	2.00
☐ 9, b&w	2.00	0.40	1.20	2.00
☐ 10, b&w	2.00	0.40	1.20	2.00
☐ 11, b&w	2.00	0.40	1.20	2.00
☐ 12, b&w	2.00	0.40	1.20	2.00

ADVENTURES OF CHRISSIE CLAUS
HERO

	ORIG.	GOOD	FINE	N-MINT
☐ 1, May 91, b&w	2.95	0.59	1.77	2.95
☐ 2, b&w	2.95	0.59	1.77	2.95

	ORIG.	GOOD	FINE	N-MINT

ADVENTURES OF CHUK THE BARBARIC
WHITE WOLF
	ORIG.	GOOD	FINE	N-MINT
❏ 1		0.25	0.75	1.25
❏ 2		0.25	0.75	1.25

ADVENTURES OF CYCLOPS AND PHOENIX
MARVEL
	ORIG.	GOOD	FINE	N-MINT
❏ 1, May 94	2.95	0.59	1.77	2.95
❏ 2, Jun 94	2.95	0.59	1.77	2.95
❏ 3, Jul 94	2.95	0.59	1.77	2.95
❏ 4, Aug 94	2.95	0.59	1.77	2.95

ADVENTURES OF DR. GRAVES
A-PLUS
	GOOD	FINE	N-MINT
❏ 1, b&w;reprints	0.50	1.50	2.50

ADVENTURES OF FELIX THE CAT
HARVEY
	GOOD	FINE	N-MINT
❏ 1	0.25	0.75	1.25

ADVENTURES OF FORD FAIRLANE, THE
DC
	GOOD	FINE	N-MINT
❏ 1, movie tie-in	0.30	0.90	1.50
❏ 2, movie tie-in	0.30	0.90	1.50
❏ 3, movie tie-in	0.30	0.90	1.50
❏ 4, movie tie-in	0.30	0.90	1.50

ADVENTURES OF HUCKLEBERRY FINN
ETERNITY
	ORIG.	GOOD	FINE	N-MINT
❏ 0, paperback strips	2.59	7.77	12.95

ADVENTURES OF KOOL-AID MAN
MARVEL
	GOOD	FINE	N-MINT
❏ 0, nn;giveaway	0.20	0.60	1.00

ADVENTURES OF LUTHER ARKWRIGHT
DARK HORSE
	ORIG.	GOOD	FINE	N-MINT
❏ 1, 90, BT;b&w	1.95	0.39	1.17	1.95
❏ 2, 90, BT;b&w	1.95	0.39	1.17	1.95
❏ 3, 90, BT;b&w	1.95	0.39	1.17	1.95
❏ 4, 90, BT;b&w	1.95	0.39	1.17	1.95
❏ 5, 90, BT;b&w	1.95	0.39	1.17	1.95
❏ 6, 90, BT;b&w	1.95	0.39	1.17	1.95
❏ 7, 90, BT;b&w	1.95	0.39	1.17	1.95
❏ 8, 90, BT;b&w	1.95	0.39	1.17	1.95
❏ 9, BT;trading cards	1.95	0.39	1.17	1.95
VALKYRIE
	ORIG.	GOOD	FINE	N-MINT
❏ 1, Oct 87	2.00	0.40	1.20	2.00
❏ 2, Dec 87	2.00	0.40	1.20	2.00
❏ 3, Feb 88	2.00	0.40	1.20	2.00
❏ 4, Apr 88	2.00	0.40	1.20	2.00
❏ 5, Jun 88	2.00	0.40	1.20	2.00
❏ 6	2.00	0.40	1.20	2.00
❏ 7, Oct 88	2.00	0.40	1.20	2.00
❏ 8, Dec 88	2.00	0.40	1.20	2.00
❏ 9	2.00	0.40	1.20	2.00

ADVENTURES OF MISTY
FORBIDDEN FRUIT
	ORIG.	GOOD	FINE	N-MINT
❏ 1, adult;b&w	2.95	0.59	1.77	2.95
❏ 2, adult;b&w	2.95	0.59	1.77	2.95
❏ 3, adult;b&w	2.95	0.59	1.77	2.95
❏ 4, adult;b&w	2.95	0.59	1.77	2.95
❏ 5, adult;b&w	2.95	0.59	1.77	2.95
❏ 6, adult;b&w	2.95	0.59	1.77	2.95
❏ 7, adult;b&w	2.95	0.59	1.77	2.95
❏ 8, adult;b&w	2.95	0.59	1.77	2.95
❏ 11, adult;b&w	2.95	0.70	2.10	3.50
❏ 12, adult;b&w	2.95	0.70	2.10	3.50

ADVENTURES OF MONKEY, THE
WOMP
	ORIG.	GOOD	FINE	N-MINT
❏ 1, Jul 95, b&w	1.50	0.30	0.90	1.50

ADVENTURES OF MR. PYRIDINE
FANTAGRAPHICS
	GOOD	FINE	N-MINT
❏ 1, b&w	0.50	1.50	2.50

ADVENTURES OF QUICK BUNNY
MARVEL
	ORIG.	GOOD	FINE	N-MINT
❏ 0, nn;giveaway				

ADVENTURES OF ROMA
FORBIDDEN FRUIT
	ORIG.	GOOD	FINE	N-MINT
❏ 1, adult;b&w	0.70	2.10	3.50	

ADVENTURES OF SPENCER SPOOK
ACE
	GOOD	FINE	N-MINT
❏ 1	0.39	1.17	1.95
❏ 2	0.39	1.17	1.95
❏ 3	0.39	1.17	1.95
❏ 4	0.39	1.17	1.95
❏ 5	0.39	1.17	1.95
❏ 6	0.39	1.17	1.95

ADVENTURES OF SPIDER-MAN
MARVEL
	ORIG.	GOOD	FINE	N-MINT
❏ 1, Apr 96, animated series adaptations; (was *Spider-Man Adventures*)	0.99	0.20	0.59	0.99
❏ 2, May 96, V:Hammerhead	0.99	0.20	0.59	0.99
❏ 3, Jun 96, V:Mr. Sinister; A:X-Men	0.99	0.20	0.59	0.99

ADVENTURES OF SUPERBOY (was Superboy)
DC
	ORIG.	GOOD	FINE	N-MINT
❏ 19, Aug 91	1.25	0.20	0.60	1.00
❏ 20, Oct 91	1.25	0.20	0.60	1.00
❏ 21, Nov 91	1.25	0.25	0.75	1.25
❏ 22, Dec 91	1.25	0.20	0.60	1.00

ADVENTURES OF SUPERMAN ANNUAL, THE
	ORIG.	GOOD	FINE	N-MINT
❏ 1, Sep 87	1.25	0.25	0.75	1.25
❏ 2, Aug 90, L.E.G.I.O.N. '90	2.00	0.40	1.20	2.00
❏ 3, Oct 91, Armageddo 2001	2.00	0.40	1.20	2.00
❏ 4, 92, Eclipso	2.50	0.50	1.50	2.50
❏ 5, Bloodlines	2.50	0.50	1.50	2.50
❏ 6, 94, "Elseworlds"; concludes in *Superboy Annual #1* (1994)	2.95	0.59	1.77	2.95
❏ 7, 95, "Year One"; V:Kalibak	3.95	0.79	2.37	3.95
❏ 8, 96, "Legends of the Dead Earth"; Elseworlds	2.95	0.59	1.77	2.95

ADVENTURES OF SUPERMAN, THE
(formerly Superman)
	ORIG.	GOOD	FINE	N-MINT
❏ 0, Oct 94, came between #516 and 517	1.50	0.40	1.20	2.00
❏ 424, Jan 87, JOy	0.75	0.35	1.05	1.75
❏ 425, Feb 87, JOy	0.75	0.35	1.05	1.75
❏ 426, Mar 87, JOy; Legends	0.75	0.20	0.60	1.00
❏ 427, Apr 87, JOy	0.75	0.20	0.60	1.00
❏ 428, May 87, JOy	0.75	0.20	0.60	1.00
❏ 429, Jun 87, JOy	0.75	0.20	0.60	1.00
❏ 430, Jul 87, JOy	0.75	0.20	0.60	1.00
❏ 431, Aug 87, JOy(c)	0.75	0.20	0.60	1.00
❏ 432, Sep 87, JOy	0.75	0.20	0.60	1.00
❏ 433, Oct 87, JOy	0.75	0.20	0.60	1.00
❏ 434, Nov 87, JOy	0.75	0.20	0.60	1.00
❏ 435, Dec 87, JOy	0.75	0.20	0.60	1.00
❏ 436, Jan 88, JOy; Millennium	0.75	0.20	0.60	1.00
❏ 437, Feb 88, JOy; Millennium	0.75	0.20	0.60	1.00
❏ 438, Mar 88, JOy O:Brainiac	0.75	0.20	0.60	1.00
❏ 439, Apr 88, JOy	0.75	0.20	0.60	1.00
❏ 440, May 88, JOy	0.75	0.20	0.60	1.00
❏ 441, Jun 88, JOy	0.75	0.20	0.60	1.00
❏ 442, Jul 88, JOy	0.75	0.20	0.60	1.00
❏ 443, Aug 88, JOy	0.75	0.20	0.60	1.00

	ORIG.	GOOD	FINE	N-MINT
444, Sep 88, JOy	0.75	0.20	0.60	1.00
445, Oct 88, JOy	0.75	0.20	0.60	1.00
446, Nov 88, JOy	0.75	0.20	0.60	1.00
447, Dec 88, JOy	0.75	0.20	0.60	1.00
448, Dec 88, JOy	0.75	0.20	0.60	1.00
449, Jan 89, Invasion!	0.75	0.20	0.60	1.00
450, Jan 89, Invasion!	0.75	0.20	0.60	1.00
451, Feb 89	0.75	0.20	0.60	1.00
452, Mar 89	0.75	0.20	0.60	1.00
453, Apr 89	0.75	0.20	0.60	1.00
454, May 89	0.75	0.20	0.60	1.00
455, Jun 89	0.75	0.20	0.60	1.00
456, Jul 89	0.75	0.20	0.60	1.00
457, Aug 89	0.75	0.20	0.60	1.00
458, Sep 89	0.75	0.20	0.60	1.00
459, Oct 89	0.75	0.20	0.60	1.00
460, Nov 89	0.75	0.20	0.60	1.00
461, Dec 89	0.75	0.20	0.60	1.00
462, Jan 90	0.75	0.20	0.60	1.00
463, Feb 90, A:Flash	0.75	0.15	0.45	0.75
464, Mar 90, Krypton Man	0.75	0.15	0.45	0.75
465, Apr 90, Krypton Man	0.75	0.15	0.45	0.75
466, May 90	0.75	0.15	0.45	0.75
467, Jun 90, Batman	0.75	0.30	0.90	1.50
468, Jul 90	0.75	0.15	0.45	0.75
469, Aug 90	0.75	0.15	0.45	0.75
470, Sep 90	0.75	0.15	0.45	0.75
471, Oct 90	0.75	0.15	0.45	0.75
472, Nov 90	0.75	0.80	2.40	4.00
473, Dec 90	0.75	0.20	0.60	1.00
474, Jan 91	1.00	0.20	0.60	1.00
475, Feb 91, Batman, Flash, Wonder Woman	1.00	0.30	0.90	1.50
476, Mar 91	1.00	0.20	0.60	1.00
477, Apr 91	1.00	0.20	0.60	1.00
478, May 91	1.00	0.20	0.60	1.00
479, Jun 91	1.00	0.20	0.60	1.00
480, Jul 91	1.75	0.35	1.05	1.75
481, Aug 91	1.00	0.20	0.60	1.00
482, Sep 91	1.00	0.20	0.60	1.00
483, Oct 91	1.00	0.20	0.60	1.00
484, Nov 91, Blackout	1.00	0.20	0.60	1.00
485, Dec 91, Blackout	1.00	0.20	0.60	1.00
486, Jan 92	1.00	0.20	0.60	1.00
487, Feb 92	1.00	0.20	0.60	1.00
488, Mar 92, Panic in Sky	1.00	0.30	0.90	1.50
489, Apr 92, Panic in Sky	1.00	0.20	0.60	1.00
490, May 92	1.00	0.20	0.60	1.00
491, Jun 92	1.00	0.20	0.60	1.00
492, Jul 92	1.00	0.20	0.60	1.00
493, Aug 92	1.25	0.25	0.75	1.25
494, Sep 92	1.25	0.25	0.75	1.25
495, Oct 92	1.25	0.25	0.75	1.25
496, Nov 92, Mxyzptlk	1.25	1.40	4.20	7.00
497, Dec 92, Doomsday	1.25	0.80	2.40	4.00
498, Jan 93, Superman funeral	1.25	1.40	4.20	7.00
499, Feb 93, Superman funeral	1.25	0.70	2.10	3.50
500, Jun 93, begins return from dead	2.50	0.60	1.80	3.00
500, Jun 93, begins return from dead; translucent cover; trading card		0.60	1.80	3.00
500, platinum edition .,....	7.00	21.00		35.00
501, Jun 93, 1:Superboy	1.50	0.60	1.80	3.00
501, Jun 93, 1:Superboy;die-cut cover	1.95	0.39	1.17	1.95
502	1.50	0.30	0.90	1.50
503	1.50	0.60	1.80	3.00

	ORIG.	GOOD	FINE	N-MINT
504	1.50	0.80	2.40	4.00
505, Oct 93	1.50	1.00	3.00	5.00
505, Oct 93, foil cover	2.50	0.50	1.50	2.50
505, Oct 93, with postcard	1.50	0.30	0.90	1.50
506	1.50	0.30	0.90	1.50
507	1.50	0.30	0.90	1.50
508, Challengers	1.50	0.30	0.90	1.50
509	1.50	0.30	0.90	1.50
510, Bizarro	1.50	0.30	0.90	1.50
511, Apr 94	1.50	0.30	0.90	1.50
512, May 94	1.50	0.30	0.90	1.50
513, Jun 94	1.50	0.30	0.90	1.50
514, Jul 94	1.50	0.30	0.90	1.50
515, Aug 94	1.50	0.30	0.90	1.50
516, Sep 94	1.50	0.30	0.90	1.50
517, Nov 94, Dead Again	1.50	0.30	0.90	1.50
518, Dec 94, Dead Again	1.50	0.30	0.90	1.50
519, Jan 95, Dead Again.	1.50	0.30	0.90	1.50
520, Feb 95	1.50	0.30	0.90	1.50
521, Mar 95	1.50	0.30	0.90	1.50
522, Apr 95, R: Metropolis	1.50	0.30	0.90	1.50
523, May 95, Death of Clark Kent	1.50	0.30	0.90	1.50
524, Jun 95, "Death of Clark Kent"	1.95	0.39	1.17	1.95
525, Jul 95	1.95	0.39	1.17	1.95
526, Aug 95, Bloodsport vs. Bloodsport	1.95	0.39	1.17	1.95
527, Sep 95, Alpha-Centurion returns	1.95	0.39	1.17	1.95
528, Oct 95	1.95	0.39	1.17	1.95
529, Nov 95, "Trial of Superman"	1.95	0.39	1.17	1.95
530, Dec 95, "Trial of Superman/Underworld Unleashed";SCU vs. Hellgrammite	1.95	0.39	1.17	1.95
531, Jan 96	1.95	0.39	1.17	1.95
532, Feb 96, Return of Lori Lemaris	1.95	0.39	1.17	1.95
533, Mar 96, A:Impulse	1.95	0.39	1.17	1.95
534, May 96	1.95	0.39	1.17	1.95
535, Jun 96	1.95	0.39	1.17	1.95

ADVENTURES OF THE FLY
ARCHIE/RED CIRCLE

	ORIG.	GOOD	FINE	N-MINT
19, May 62	0.12	11.00	33.00	55.00
20, Jul 62	0.12	10.00	30.00	50.00
22, Oct 62	0.12	7.20	21.60	36.00
23, Nov 62	0.12	7.20	21.60	36.00
24, Feb 63	0.12	6.00	18.00	30.00
30, Oct 64	0.12	6.00	18.00	30.00
31, May 65, becomes Fly Man	0.12	6.00	18.00	30.00

ADVENTURES OF THE JAGUAR

	ORIG.	GOOD	FINE	N-MINT
1, Sep 61	0.10	40.00	120.00	200.00
2, Oct 61	0.10	20.00	60.00	100.00
3, Nov 61	0.10	16.00	48.00	80.00
4	0.12	10.00	30.00	50.00
5	0.12	10.00	30.00	50.00
6	0.12	10.00	30.00	50.00
7, Jul 62	0.12	7.00	21.00	35.00
8, Aug 62	0.12	7.00	21.00	35.00
9, Sep 62	0.12	7.00	21.00	35.00
10	0.12	7.00	21.00	35.00
11	0.12	5.00	15.00	25.00
12, May 63	0.12	5.00	15.00	25.00
13, Aug 63	0.12	5.00	15.00	25.00
14	0.12	5.00	15.00	25.00
15, Nov 63	0.12	5.00	15.00	25.00

	ORIG.	GOOD	FINE	N-MINT

ADVENTURES OF THE MAD HUNDA DAY DAY, THE
THAUMATURGE
	ORIG.	GOOD	FINE	N-MINT
❏ 1, Win 95, b&w	2.00	0.40	1.20	2.00

ADVENTURES OF THE MASK
DARK HORSE
	ORIG.	GOOD	FINE	N-MINT
❏ 1, Jan 96, adapts animated series	2.50	0.50	1.50	2.50
❏ 2, Feb 96, adapts animated series; V:Walter	2.50	0.50	1.50	2.50

ADVENTURES OF THE OUTSIDERS
(was Batman and the Outsiders)
DC
	ORIG.	GOOD	FINE	N-MINT
❏ 32, Apr 86	0.75	0.20	0.60	1.00
❏ 33, May 86	0.75	0.20	0.60	1.00
❏ 34, Jun 86	0.75	0.20	0.60	1.00
❏ 35, Jul 86	0.75	0.20	0.60	1.00
❏ 36, Aug 86	0.75	0.20	0.60	1.00
❏ 37, Sep 86	0.75	0.20	0.60	1.00
❏ 38, Oct 86	0.75	0.20	0.60	1.00
❏ 39, Nov 86		0.20	0.60	1.00
❏ 40, Dec 86		0.20	0.60	1.00
❏ 41, Jan 87		0.20	0.60	1.00
❏ 42, Feb 87		0.20	0.60	1.00
❏ 43, Mar 87		0.20	0.60	1.00
❏ 44, Apr 87		0.20	0.60	1.00
❏ 45, May 87		0.20	0.60	1.00
❏ 46, Jun 87		0.20	0.60	1.00

ADVENTURES OF THE SCREAMER BROTHERS
SUPERSTAR
	ORIG.	GOOD	FINE	N-MINT
❏ 1, b&w		0.30	0.90	1.50
❏ 2, color		0.39	1.17	1.95
❏ 3, color		0.39	1.17	1.95

ADVENTURES OF THE SUPER MARIO BROS.
VALIANT
	ORIG.	GOOD	FINE	N-MINT
❏ 1		0.30	0.90	1.50
❏ 2		0.30	0.90	1.50
❏ 3		0.30	0.90	1.50
❏ 4		0.30	0.90	1.50
❏ 5		0.30	0.90	1.50
❏ 6		0.30	0.90	1.50
❏ 7		0.30	0.90	1.50
❏ 8		0.30	0.90	1.50
❏ 9		0.30	0.90	1.50

ADVENTURES OF THE THING
MARVEL
	ORIG.	GOOD	FINE	N-MINT
❏ 1, reprint	1.25	0.25	0.75	1.25
❏ 2, reprint	1.25	0.25	0.75	1.25
❏ 3, reprint	1.25	0.25	0.75	1.25
❏ 4, reprint	1.25	0.25	0.75	1.25

ADVENTURES OF THE VITAL MAN
CORNERSTONE
	ORIG.	GOOD	FINE	N-MINT
❏ 1, b&w (moves to Budgie Press)		0.40	1.20	2.00

ADVENTURES OF THE VITAL MAN
(was Cornerstone)
BUDGIE
	ORIG.	GOOD	FINE	N-MINT
❏ 2, b&w		0.40	1.20	2.00
❏ 3, b&w		0.40	1.20	2.00
❏ 4, b&w		0.40	1.20	2.00

ADVENTURES OF THE X-MEN
MARVEL
	ORIG.	GOOD	FINE	N-MINT
❏ 1, 96, Wolverine vs. Hulk	0.99	0.20	0.59	0.99
❏ 2, May 96	0.99	0.20	0.59	0.99
❏ 3, Jun 96, V:Mr. Sinister;A:SpM	0.99	0.20	0.59	0.99

ADVENTURES OF ZOT! IN DIMENSION 10 1/2, THE
ECLIPSE
	ORIG.	GOOD	FINE	N-MINT
❏ 14, Sep 87	2.00	0.40	1.20	2.00

ADVENTURES ON THE FRINGE
FANTAGRAPHICS
	ORIG.	GOOD	FINE	N-MINT
❏ 1, b&w		0.45	1.35	2.25
❏ 2, b&w		0.45	1.35	2.25
❏ 3, b&w		0.45	1.35	2.25
❏ 4, b&w		0.45	1.35	2.25
❏ 5, b&w		0.45	1.35	2.25

AEON FOCUS
AEON
	ORIG.	GOOD	FINE	N-MINT
❏ 1, Mar 94, "Justin Hampton's Twitch"; b&w	2.75	0.55	1.65	2.75
❏ 2, Jun 94, "Colin Upton's Other Other Even Bigger Than Slightly Smaller That Got Bigger Big Thing"; b&w	2.75	0.55	1.65	2.75
❏ 3, Oct 94, "Filthy Habits"; b&w	2.95	0.59	1.77	2.95
❏ 4, Nov 94, "Ward Sutton's Ink Blot";b&w	2.95	0.59	1.77	2.95

AESOP'S DESECRETED MORALS
MAGNECOM
	ORIG.	GOOD	FINE	N-MINT
❏ 1	2.95	0.59	1.77	2.95

AESOP'S FABLES
FANTAGRAPHICS
	ORIG.	GOOD	FINE	N-MINT
❏ 1, Spr 91, b&w (no number on cover)	2.50	0.50	1.50	2.50
❏ 2, b&w	2.50	0.50	1.50	2.50
❏ 3, b&w	2.50	0.50	1.50	2.50

AETOS THE EAGLE
ORPHAN UNDERGROUND
	ORIG.	GOOD	FINE	N-MINT
❏ 1, Sep 94, b&w	2.50	0.50	1.50	2.50

AFTER APOCALYPSE
PARAGRAPHICS
	ORIG.	GOOD	FINE	N-MINT
❏ 1, (Mark Bagley art)		0.60	1.80	3.00

AFTERMATH
PINNACLE
	ORIG.	GOOD	FINE	N-MINT
❏ 1, sequel to Messiah		0.30	0.90	1.50

AGAINST BLACKSHARD 3-D
SIRIUS
	ORIG.	GOOD	FINE	N-MINT
❏ 1		0.30	0.90	1.50

AGE OF APOCALYPSE: THE CHOSEN
MARVEL
	ORIG.	GOOD	FINE	N-MINT
❏ 0, Apr 95, one-shot	2.50	0.50	1.50	2.50

AGE OF INNOCENCE: THE REBIRTH OF IRON MAN
MARVEL
	ORIG.	GOOD	FINE	N-MINT
❏ 0, Feb 96, nn;one-shot; retells O:Iron Man, Pepper Potts, Happy Hogan	2.50	0.50	1.50	2.50

AGE OF REPTILES
DARK HORSE
	ORIG.	GOOD	FINE	N-MINT
❏ 1, 93	2.50	0.50	1.50	2.50
❏ 2, 93	2.50	0.50	1.50	2.50
❏ 3, Feb 94	2.50	0.50	1.50	2.50
❏ 4, 94	2.50	0.50	1.50	2.50

AGENT LIBERTY SPECIAL
DC
	ORIG.	GOOD	FINE	N-MINT
❏ 1, 92, O:Agent Liberty	2.00	0.40	1.20	2.00

AGENT THREE-ZERO
GALAXINOVELS
	ORIG.	GOOD	FINE	N-MINT
❏ 1, trading card,poster	3.95	0.79	2.37	3.95

AGENT UNKNOWN
RENEGADE
	ORIG.	GOOD	FINE	N-MINT
❏ 1, b&w		0.40	1.20	2.00
❏ 2, b&w		0.40	1.20	2.00
❏ 3, b&w		0.40	1.20	2.00

AGENTS OF LAW
DARK HORSE
	ORIG.	GOOD	FINE	N-MINT
❏ 1, Mar 95	2.50	0.50	1.50	2.50
❏ 2, 95	2.50	0.50	1.50	2.50
❏ 3, 95	2.50	0.50	1.50	2.50

	ORIG.	GOOD	FINE	N-MINT
☐ 4, 95	2.50	0.50	1.50	2.50
☐ 5, 95	2.50	0.50	1.50	2.50
☐ 6, Sep 95, V:Predators; final issue				
	2.50	0.50	1.50	2.50

AIDA-ZEE
NATE BUTLER

	ORIG.	GOOD	FINE	N-MINT
☐ 1, JD,KGa,MA,NR		0.30	0.90	1.50

AIR FIGHTERS CLASSICS
ECLIPSE

	ORIG.	GOOD	FINE	N-MINT
☐ 1, Nov 87	3.95	0.79	2.37	3.95
☐ 2, Jan 88	3.95	0.79	2.37	3.95

AIR RAIDERS
STAR

	ORIG.	GOOD	FINE	N-MINT
☐ 1	1.00	0.20	0.60	1.00
☐ 2, (Becomes Marvel Comic)				
	1.00	0.20	0.60	1.00

AIR RAIDERS (Was Star Comic)
MARVEL

	ORIG.	GOOD	FINE	N-MINT
☐ 3	1.00	0.20	0.60	1.00
☐ 4	1.00	0.20	0.60	1.00
☐ 5	1.00	0.20	0.60	1.00

AIRBOY
ECLIPSE

	ORIG.	GOOD	FINE	N-MINT
☐ 1, Jul 86	0.50	0.60	1.80	3.00
☐ 2, Jul 86	0.50	0.40	1.20	2.00
☐ 3, Aug 86	0.50	0.40	1.20	2.00
☐ 4, Aug 86	0.50	0.40	1.20	2.00
☐ 5, Sep 86, DSt(c)	0.50	1.20	3.60	6.00
☐ 6, Sep 86	0.50	0.20	0.60	1.00
☐ 7, Oct 86	0.50	0.20	0.60	1.00
☐ 8, Oct 86	0.50	0.20	0.60	1.00
☐ 9, Nov 86	1.25	0.25	0.75	1.25
☐ 10, Nov 86	1.25	0.25	0.75	1.25
☐ 11, Dec 86	1.25	0.25	0.75	1.25
☐ 12, Dec 86	1.25	0.25	0.75	1.25
☐ 13, Jan 87	1.25	0.25	0.75	1.25
☐ 14, Jan 87	1.25	0.25	0.75	1.25
☐ 15, Feb 87	1.25	0.25	0.75	1.25
☐ 16, Feb 87	1.25	0.25	0.75	1.25
☐ 17, Mar 87	1.25	0.25	0.75	1.25
☐ 18, Mar 87	1.25	0.25	0.75	1.25
☐ 19, Apr 87, rats	1.25	0.25	0.75	1.25
☐ 20, Apr 87, rats	1.25	0.25	0.75	1.25
☐ 21, May 87, GE(c)	1.25	0.25	0.75	1.25
☐ 22, May 87	1.25	0.25	0.75	1.25
☐ 23, Jun 87	1.25	0.25	0.75	1.25
☐ 24, Jun 87	1.25	0.25	0.75	1.25
☐ 25, Jul 87	1.25	0.25	0.75	1.25
☐ 26, Jul 87	1.25	0.25	0.75	1.25
☐ 27, Aug 87	1.25	0.25	0.75	1.25
☐ 28, Aug 87	1.25	0.25	0.75	1.25
☐ 29, Sep 87	1.25	0.25	0.75	1.25
☐ 30, Sep 87	1.25	0.25	0.75	1.25
☐ 31, Oct 87	1.25	0.25	0.75	1.25
☐ 32, Oct 87	1.25	0.25	0.75	1.25
☐ 33, Nov 87	1.75	0.35	1.05	1.75
☐ 34, Dec 87	1.75	0.35	1.05	1.75
☐ 35, Jan 88	1.75	0.35	1.05	1.75
☐ 36, Feb 88	1.75	0.35	1.05	1.75
☐ 37, Mar 88	1.75	0.35	1.05	1.75
☐ 38, Apr 88	1.75	0.35	1.05	1.75
☐ 39, May 88	1.75	0.35	1.05	1.75
☐ 40, Jun 88	1.75	0.35	1.05	1.75
☐ 41, Jul 88	1.75	0.35	1.05	1.75
☐ 42, Aug 88	1.95	0.39	1.17	1.95
☐ 43, Sep 88	1.95	0.39	1.17	1.95
☐ 44, Oct 88	1.95	0.39	1.17	1.95
☐ 45, Nov 88	1.95	0.39	1.17	1.95
☐ 46, Jan 89, Airboy Diary	1.95	0.39	1.17	1.95
☐ 47, Mar 89, Airboy Diary	1.95	0.39	1.17	1.95
☐ 48, Apr 89, Airboy Diary	1.95	0.39	1.17	1.95

	ORIG.	GOOD	FINE	N-MINT
☐ 49, Jun 89, Airboy Diary				
	1.95	0.39	1.17	1.95
☐ 50, Oct 89, JKu(c)		0.99	2.97	4.95

AIRBOY MEETS THE PROWLER

	ORIG.	GOOD	FINE	N-MINT
☐ 1, Dec 87	1.95	0.39	1.17	1.95

AIRBOY VERSUS THE AIRMAIDENS

	ORIG.	GOOD	FINE	N-MINT
☐ 1, Jul 88		0.39	1.17	1.95

AIRBOY-MR. MONSTER SPECIAL

	ORIG.	GOOD	FINE	N-MINT
☐ 1, Aug 87		0.35	1.05	1.75

AIRFIGHTERS MEET SGT. STRIKE SPECIAL

	ORIG.	GOOD	FINE	N-MINT
☐ 1, Jan 88		0.39	1.17	1.95

AIRLOCK
ECLECTUS

	ORIG.	GOOD	FINE	N-MINT
☐ 1, b&w		0.45	1.35	2.25
☐ 2		0.50	1.50	2.50
☐ 3		0.50	1.50	2.50

AIRMAIDENS SPECIAL
ECLIPSE

	ORIG.	GOOD	FINE	N-MINT
☐ 1, Aug 87	1.75	0.35	1.05	1.75

AIRMAN
MALIBU

	ORIG.	GOOD	FINE	N-MINT
☐ 1		0.39	1.17	1.95

AIRTIGHT GARAGE
EPIC

	ORIG.	GOOD	FINE	N-MINT
☐ 1, Moebius	2.50	0.50	1.50	2.50
☐ 2, Moebius	2.50	0.50	1.50	2.50
☐ 3, Moebius	2.50	0.50	1.50	2.50
☐ 4, Moebius	2.50	0.50	1.50	2.50

AIRWAVES
CALIBER

	ORIG.	GOOD	FINE	N-MINT
☐ 1, b&w	2.50	0.50	1.50	2.50
☐ 2, b&w	2.50	0.50	1.50	2.50
☐ 3, b&w	2.50	0.50	1.50	2.50
☐ 4, b&w	2.50	0.50	1.50	2.50

AKIKO ON THE PLANET SMOO
SIRIUS ENTERTAINMENT

	ORIG.	GOOD	FINE	N-MINT
☐ 1, Dec 95, b&w	3.95	1.20	3.60	6.00

AKIRA
EPIC

	ORIG.	GOOD	FINE	N-MINT
☐ 1, Sep 88, 1st printing	3.50	4.40	13.20	22.00
☐ 1, 2nd printing	3.95	1.00	3.00	5.00
☐ 2, 1st printing	3.50	3.00	9.00	15.00
☐ 2, 2nd printing	3.95	0.70	2.10	3.50
☐ 3	3.50	2.40	7.20	12.00
☐ 4	3.50	2.40	7.20	12.00
☐ 5	3.50	2.40	7.20	12.00
☐ 6	3.50	1.60	4.80	8.00
☐ 7	3.50	1.60	4.80	8.00
☐ 8	3.50	1.60	4.80	8.00
☐ 9	3.50	1.60	4.80	8.00
☐ 10	3.50	1.60	4.80	8.00
☐ 11	3.50	1.20	3.60	6.00
☐ 12	3.50	1.20	3.60	6.00
☐ 13	3.50	1.20	3.60	6.00
☐ 14	3.50	1.20	3.60	6.00
☐ 15	3.50	1.40	4.20	7.00
☐ 16	3.50	1.40	4.20	7.00
☐ 17	3.95	1.40	4.20	7.00
☐ 18	3.95	1.40	4.20	7.00
☐ 19	3.95	1.40	4.20	7.00
☐ 20	3.95	1.40	4.20	7.00
☐ 21	3.95	1.40	4.20	7.00
☐ 22	3.95	1.40	4.20	7.00
☐ 23	3.95	1.40	4.20	7.00
☐ 24	3.95	1.40	4.20	7.00
☐ 25	3.95	1.40	4.20	7.00
☐ 26	3.95	1.40	4.20	7.00
☐ 27	3.95	1.40	4.20	7.00
☐ 28	3.95	1.40	4.20	7.00

	ORIG.	GOOD	FINE	N-MINT
❑ 29 ....3.95	1.40	4.20	7.00
❑ 30 ....3.95	1.40	4.20	7.00
❑ 31 ....3.95	1.20	3.60	6.00
❑ 32 ....3.95	1.20	3.60	6.00
❑ 33 ....3.95	1.20	3.60	6.00

ALADDIN
DISNEY

	ORIG.	GOOD	FINE	N-MINT
❑ 0, movie adaptation; newsstand	0.59	1.77	2.95
❑ 0, movie adaptation; Prestige format			
....	0.99	2.97	4.95

ALBEDO
THOUGHTS & IMAGES

	ORIG.	GOOD	FINE	N-MINT
❑ 0, 1st printing		22.00	66.00	110.00
❑ 0, 2nd printing		18.00	54.00	90.00
❑ 0, 3rd printing 0.50	1.00	3.00	5.00
❑ 1		18.00	54.00	90.00
❑ 2		12.00	36.00	60.00
❑ 3		4.00	12.00	20.00
❑ 4		2.40	7.20	12.00
❑ 5		1.40	4.20	7.00
❑ 6		1.40	4.20	7.00
❑ 7 ....2.00	0.80	2.40	4.00
❑ 8 ....2.00	0.60	1.80	3.00
❑ 9 ....2.00	0.60	1.80	3.00
❑ 10 ....2.00	0.60	1.80	3.00
❑ 11 ....2.00	0.60	1.80	3.00
❑ 12 ....2.00	0.60	1.80	3.00
❑ 13 ....2.00	0.60	1.80	3.00
❑ 14 ....2.00	0.60	1.80	3.00

ALBEDO (Volume 2) (formerly Thoughts & Images)
ANTARCTIC

	ORIG.	GOOD	FINE	N-MINT
❑ 1, Jun 91, b&w 2.50	0.50	1.50	2.50
❑ 2, Sep 91, b&w 2.50	0.50	1.50	2.50
❑ 3, Dec 91, b&w 2.50	0.50	1.50	2.50
❑ 4, Mar 92, b&w 2.50	0.50	1.50	2.50
❑ 5, Jun 92, b&w 2.50	0.50	1.50	2.50
❑ 6, Sep 92, b&w 2.50	0.50	1.50	2.50
❑ 7, Dec 92, b&w 2.50	0.50	1.50	2.50
❑ 8, Mar 93, b&w 2.50	0.50	1.50	2.50
❑ 9, Jun 93, b&w 2.50	0.50	1.50	2.50
❑ 10, Oct 93, b&w 2.75	0.55	1.65	2.75

ALBEDO (Volume 3)

	ORIG.	GOOD	FINE	N-MINT
❑ 1, Feb 94 ....2.95	0.59	1.77	2.95
❑ 2, Oct 94 ....2.95	0.59	1.77	2.95
❑ 3, Feb 95 ....2.95	0.59	1.77	2.95

ALBEDO COLOR SPECIAL

	ORIG.	GOOD	FINE	N-MINT
❑ 1, Jul 93, color 2.95	0.59	1.77	2.95

ALEX
FANTAGRAPHICS

	ORIG.	GOOD	FINE	N-MINT
❑ 1, b&w 2.95	0.59	1.77	2.95
❑ 2, Apr 94, b&w 2.95	0.59	1.77	2.95
❑ 3, Jul 94, b&w 2.95	0.59	1.77	2.95
❑ 4, Oct 94, b&w 2.95	0.59	1.77	2.95
❑ 5, Nov 94, b&w 2.95	0.59	1.77	2.95

ALEX NINO'S NIGHTMARE
INNOVATION

	ORIG.	GOOD	FINE	N-MINT
❑ 1 ....1.95	0.39	1.17	1.95
❑ 2 ....1.95	0.39	1.17	1.95

ALF
MARVEL

	ORIG.	GOOD	FINE	N-MINT
❑ 1, TV series 1.00	0.60	1.80	3.00
❑ 2 ....1.00	0.40	1.20	2.00
❑ 3 ....1.00	0.40	1.20	2.00
❑ 4 ....1.00	0.30	0.90	1.50
❑ 5 ....1.00	0.30	0.90	1.50
❑ 6 ....1.00	0.20	0.60	1.00
❑ 7 ....1.00	0.20	0.60	1.00
❑ 8 ....1.00	0.20	0.60	1.00
❑ 9 ....1.00	0.20	0.60	1.00
❑ 10 ....1.00	0.20	0.60	1.00

	ORIG.	GOOD	FINE	N-MINT
❑ 11 ....1.00	0.20	0.60	1.00
❑ 12 ....1.00	0.20	0.60	1.00
❑ 13 ....1.00	0.20	0.60	1.00
❑ 14 ....1.00	0.20	0.60	1.00
❑ 15 ....1.00	0.20	0.60	1.00
❑ 16 ....1.00	0.20	0.60	1.00
❑ 17 ....1.00	0.20	0.60	1.00
❑ 18 ....1.00	0.20	0.60	1.00
❑ 19 ....1.00	0.20	0.60	1.00
❑ 20 ....1.00	0.20	0.60	1.00
❑ 21 ....1.00	0.20	0.60	1.00
❑ 22, X-Men parody 1.00	0.40	1.20	2.00
❑ 23 ....1.00	0.20	0.60	1.00
❑ 24 ....1.00	0.20	0.60	1.00
❑ 25 ....1.00	0.20	0.60	1.00
❑ 26 ....1.00	0.20	0.60	1.00
❑ 27 ....1.00	0.20	0.60	1.00
❑ 28 ....1.00	0.20	0.60	1.00
❑ 29, "3-D" cover 1.00	0.20	0.60	1.00
❑ 30 ....1.00	0.20	0.60	1.00
❑ 31 ....1.00	0.20	0.60	1.00
❑ 32 ....1.00	0.20	0.60	1.00
❑ 33 ....1.00	0.20	0.60	1.00
❑ 34 ....1.00	0.20	0.60	1.00
❑ 35 ....1.00	0.20	0.60	1.00
❑ 36 ....1.00	0.20	0.60	1.00
❑ 37 ....1.00	0.20	0.60	1.00
❑ 38 ....1.00	0.20	0.60	1.00
❑ 39 ....1.00	0.20	0.60	1.00
❑ 40 ....1.00	0.20	0.60	1.00
❑ 41 ....1.00	0.20	0.60	1.00
❑ 42 ....1.00	0.20	0.60	1.00
❑ 43 ....1.00	0.20	0.60	1.00
❑ 44, X-Men parody 1.00	0.20	0.60	1.00
❑ 45 ....1.00	0.20	0.60	1.00
❑ 46 ....1.00	0.20	0.60	1.00
❑ 47 ....1.00	0.20	0.60	1.00
❑ 48 ....1.00	0.20	0.60	1.00
❑ 49 ....1.00	0.20	0.60	1.00
❑ 50 ....1.75	0.35	1.05	1.75

ALF ANNUAL

	ORIG.	GOOD	FINE	N-MINT
❑ 1, Evolutionary War 1.75	0.35	1.05	1.75
❑ 2, BSz(c) 2.00	0.40	1.20	2.00
❑ 3, TMNT parody 2.00	0.40	1.20	2.00

ALF COMICS MAGAZINE

	ORIG.	GOOD	FINE	N-MINT
❑ 1, digest 1.50	0.30	0.90	1.50
❑ 2, digest 1.50	0.30	0.90	1.50

ALF HOLIDAY SPECIAL

	ORIG.	GOOD	FINE	N-MINT
❑ 1 ....1.75	0.35	1.05	1.75
❑ 2 ....2.00	0.40	1.20	2.00

ALF SPRING SPECIAL

	ORIG.	GOOD	FINE	N-MINT
❑ 1 ....1.75	0.35	1.05	1.75

ALFRED HARVEY'S BLACK CAT
LORNE-HARVEY

	ORIG.	GOOD	FINE	N-MINT
❑ 1, 95, color and b&w; reprints Black Cat and Sad Sack strips; text feature on Alfred Harvey			
.......................3.50	0.70	2.10	3.50

ALFRED HARVEY'S BLACK CAT (THE ORIGINS)

	ORIG.	GOOD	FINE	N-MINT
❑ 1, 95 ....3.50	0.70	2.10	3.50

ALFRED HITCHCOCK'S PSYCHO
INNOVATION

	ORIG.	GOOD	FINE	N-MINT
❑ 1, movie adaptation 2.50	0.50	1.50	2.50
❑ 2, movie adaptation	0.50	1.50	2.50
❑ 3	0.50	1.50	2.50

ALIAS:
NOW

	ORIG.	GOOD	FINE	N-MINT
❑ 1, Jul 90 ....1.75	0.35	1.05	1.75
❑ 2, Aug 90 ....1.75	0.35	1.05	1.75
❑ 3, Sep 90 ....1.75	0.35	1.05	1.75
❑ 4, Oct 90 ....1.75	0.35	1.05	1.75
❑ 5, Nov 90 ....1.75	0.35	1.05	1.75

	ORIG.	GOOD	FINE	N-MINT

ALICE COOPER: THE LAST TEMPTATION OF ALICE
MARVEL

	ORIG.	GOOD	FINE	N-MINT
❑ 1, 94, direct edition	1.60	4.80	8.00	
❑ 1, 94, Sony edition	1.20	3.60	6.00	
❑ 2, 94	1.20	3.60	6.00	

ALIEN 3
DARK HORSE

	ORIG.	GOOD	FINE	N-MINT
❑ 1, 92, movie adaptation	2.50	0.50	1.50	2.50
❑ 2, 92, movie adaptation	2.50	0.50	1.50	2.50
❑ 3, 92, movie adaptation	2.50	0.50	1.50	2.50

ALIEN DUCKLINGS
BLACKTHORNE

	GOOD	FINE	N-MINT
❑ 1	0.35	1.05	1.75
❑ 2	0.35	1.05	1.75
❑ 3	0.35	1.05	1.75
❑ 4	0.35	1.05	1.75

ALIEN ENCOUNTERS
ECLIPSE

	GOOD	FINE	N-MINT
❑ 1	0.35	1.05	1.75
❑ 2	0.35	1.05	1.75
❑ 3	0.35	1.05	1.75
❑ 4	0.35	1.05	1.75
❑ 5	0.35	1.05	1.75
❑ 6	0.35	1.05	1.75
❑ 7	0.35	1.05	1.75
❑ 8	0.35	1.05	1.75
❑ 9	0.35	1.05	1.75
❑ 10	0.35	1.05	1.75
❑ 11	0.40	1.20	2.00
❑ 12	0.40	1.20	2.00
❑ 13	0.40	1.20	2.00
❑ 14	0.40	1.20	2.00

FANTACO

	ORIG.	GOOD	FINE	N-MINT
❑ 1, 80	1.25	0.25	0.75	1.25

ALIEN FIRE
KITCHEN SINK

	ORIG.	GOOD	FINE	N-MINT
❑ 1, Jan 87, b&w	2.00	0.40	1.20	2.00
❑ 2, May 87, b&w	2.00	0.40	1.20	2.00
❑ 3, May 87, b&w	2.00	0.40	1.20	2.00

ALIEN FIRE: PASS IN THUNDER

	ORIG.	GOOD	FINE	N-MINT
❑ 0, May 95, nn;b&w; squarebound	6.95	1.39	4.17	6.95

ALIEN LEGION
EPIC

	ORIG.	GOOD	FINE	N-MINT
❑ 1, TA	2.00	0.80	2.40	4.00
❑ 2	1.50	0.60	1.80	3.00
❑ 3	1.50	0.60	1.80	3.00
❑ 4	1.50	0.60	1.80	3.00
❑ 5	1.50	0.60	1.80	3.00
❑ 6	1.50	0.40	1.20	2.00
❑ 7	1.50	0.40	1.20	2.00
❑ 8	1.50	0.40	1.20	2.00
❑ 9	1.50	0.40	1.20	2.00
❑ 10	1.50	0.40	1.20	2.00
❑ 11	1.50	0.40	1.20	2.00
❑ 12	1.50	0.40	1.20	2.00
❑ 13	1.50	0.40	1.20	2.00
❑ 14	1.50	0.40	1.20	2.00
❑ 15	1.50	0.40	1.20	2.00
❑ 16	1.50	0.40	1.20	2.00
❑ 17	1.50	0.40	1.20	2.00
❑ 18	1.75	0.40	1.20	2.00
❑ 19	1.75	0.40	1.20	2.00
❑ 20	1.75	0.40	1.20	2.00

ALIEN LEGION (Volume Two)

	ORIG.	GOOD	FINE	N-MINT
❑ 1	1.25	0.40	1.20	2.00
❑ 2	1.25	0.25	0.75	1.25
❑ 3	1.25	0.25	0.75	1.25
❑ 4	1.25	0.25	0.75	1.25
❑ 5	1.25	0.25	0.75	1.25

	ORIG.	GOOD	FINE	N-MINT
❑ 6	1.25	0.25	0.75	1.25
❑ 7	1.25	0.25	0.75	1.25
❑ 8	1.50	0.30	0.90	1.50
❑ 9	1.50	0.30	0.90	1.50
❑ 10	1.50	0.30	0.90	1.50
❑ 11	1.50	0.30	0.90	1.50
❑ 12	1.50	0.30	0.90	1.50
❑ 13	1.50	0.30	0.90	1.50
❑ 14	1.50	0.30	0.90	1.50
❑ 15	1.50	0.30	0.90	1.50
❑ 16	1.50	0.30	0.90	1.50
❑ 17	1.50	0.30	0.90	1.50
❑ 18	1.50	0.30	0.90	1.50

ALIEN LEGION: BINARY DEEP

	ORIG.	GOOD	FINE	N-MINT
❑ 0, nn	3.50	0.70	2.10	3.50

ALIEN LEGION: ON THE EDGE

	ORIG.	GOOD	FINE	N-MINT
❑ 1	4.50	0.90	2.70	4.50
❑ 2	4.50	0.90	2.70	4.50
❑ 3	4.50	0.90	2.70	4.50

ALIEN LEGION: ONE PLANET AT A TIME

	ORIG.	GOOD	FINE	N-MINT
❑ 1	4.95	0.99	2.97	4.95
❑ 2	4.95	0.99	2.97	4.95
❑ 3	4.95	0.99	2.97	4.95

ALIEN LEGION: TENANTS OF HELL

	ORIG.	GOOD	FINE	N-MINT
❑ 1	4.50	0.90	2.70	4.50
❑ 2	4.50	0.90	2.70	4.50

ALIEN NATION
DC

	GOOD	FINE	N-MINT
❑ 1, movie	1.00	3.00	5.00

ALIEN NATION: A BREED APART (mini-series)
ADVENTURE

	ORIG.	GOOD	FINE	N-MINT
❑ 1, Nov 90, b&w; movie/TV	2.50	0.50	1.50	2.50
❑ 2, Dec 90, b&w; movie/TV	2.50	0.50	1.50	2.50
❑ 3, Jan 91, b&w; movie/TV	2.50	0.50	1.50	2.50
❑ 4, Mar 91, b&w; movie/TV	2.50	0.50	1.50	2.50

ALIEN NATION: THE FIRSTCOMERS (mini-series)

	ORIG.	GOOD	FINE	N-MINT
❑ 1, May 91, b&w	2.50	0.50	1.50	2.50
❑ 2, Jun 91, b&w	2.50	0.50	1.50	2.50
❑ 3, Jul 91, b&w	2.50	0.50	1.50	2.50
❑ 4, Aug 91, b&w	2.50	0.50	1.50	2.50

ALIEN NATION: THE LOST EPISODE
MALIBU

	ORIG.	GOOD	FINE	N-MINT
❑ 0, 92, nn;adapts second season opener;b&w; one-shot;squarebound	4.95	0.99	2.97	4.95

ALIEN NATION: THE PUBLIC ENEMY (mini-series)
ADVENTURE

	ORIG.	GOOD	FINE	N-MINT
❑ 1, Dec 91, b&w	2.50	0.50	1.50	2.50
❑ 2, Jan 92, b&w	2.50	0.50	1.50	2.50
❑ 3, Feb 92, b&w	2.50	0.50	1.50	2.50
❑ 4, Mar 92, b&w	2.50	0.50	1.50	2.50

ALIEN NATION: THE SKIN TRADE (mini-series)

	ORIG.	GOOD	FINE	N-MINT
❑ 1, Mar 91, b&w	2.50	0.50	1.50	2.50
❑ 2, Apr 91, b&w	2.50	0.50	1.50	2.50
❑ 3, May 91, b&w	2.50	0.50	1.50	2.50
❑ 4, Jun 91, b&w	2.50	0.50	1.50	2.50

ALIEN NATION: THE SPARTANS (mini-series)

	ORIG.	GOOD	FINE	N-MINT
❑ 1, 90, b&w;movie/TV	2.50	0.80	2.40	4.00
❑ 1, limited		1.60	4.80	8.00
❑ 2, 90, b&w		0.50	1.50	2.50
❑ 3, 90, b&w		0.50	1.50	2.50
❑ 4, 90, b&w		0.50	1.50	2.50

	ORIG.	GOOD	FINE	N-MINT

ALIEN SEX/MONSTER LUST
EROS COMIX
	ORIG.	GOOD	FINE	N-MINT
☐ 1, adult;b&w		0.50	1.50	2.50

ALIEN WORLDS
BLACKTHORNE
☐ 1, b&w		1.19	3.57	5.95

PACIFIC
☐ 0, 3-D 1 AAd		0.60	1.80	3.00
☐ 1, Dec 82, AW/VM/NR....	1.50	0.30	0.90	1.50
☐ 2, May 83, DSt	1.50	1.00	3.00	5.00
☐ 3, Jul 83.......................	1.50	0.30	0.90	1.50
☐ 4, Sep 83, DSt	1.50	1.00	3.00	5.00
☐ 5	1.50	0.30	0.90	1.50
☐ 6	1.50	0.30	0.90	1.50
☐ 7	1.50	0.30	0.90	1.50

ALIEN WORLDS (former Pacific title)
ECLIPSE
☐ 8	1.50	0.30	0.90	1.50
☐ 9, FB.............................	1.50	0.30	0.90	1.50

ALIENS
DARK HORSE
☐ 1, May 88, b&w; 1st printing				
....	1.95	6.40	19.20	32.00
☐ 1, 2nd printing	1.95	0.80	2.40	4.00
☐ 1, 3rd printing	1.95	0.60	1.80	3.00
☐ 1, 4th printing	1.95	0.39	1.17	1.95
☐ 2, Sep 88, 1st printing ...	1.95	4.40	13.20	22.00
☐ 2, 2nd printing	1.95	0.60	1.80	3.00
☐ 2, 3rd printing	1.95	0.39	1.17	1.95
☐ 3, Jan 89, 1st printing....	1.95	2.40	7.20	12.00
☐ 3, 2nd printing	1.95	0.39	1.17	1.95
☐ 4, Mar 89	1.95	2.00	6.00	10.00
☐ 5, Jun 89	1.95	2.00	6.00	10.00
☐ 6, Jul 89	1.95	2.00	6.00	10.00

ALIENS (Volume 2)
☐ 1, Aug 89, color; 1st printing				
....	2.25	3.60	10.80	18.00
☐ 2, Dec 89.......................	2.25	2.40	7.20	12.00
☐ 3, 90.............................	2.25	2.00	6.00	10.00
☐ 4, May 90	2.25	2.00	6.00	10.00

ALIENS VS. PREDATOR
☐ 0, 90, b&w	2.50	2.00	6.00	10.00
☐ 1, 90, color....................	2.50	2.40	7.20	12.00
☐ 2, 90.............................	2.50	1.60	4.80	8.00
☐ 3, 90.............................	2.50	1.20	3.60	6.00
☐ 4, 90.............................	2.50	1.20	3.60	6.00

ALIENS VS. PREDATOR: BOOTY
☐ 0, Jan 96, nn;one-shot ...	2.50	0.50	1.50	2.50

ALIENS VS. PREDATOR: DUEL (mini-series)
☐ 1, Mar 95	2.50	0.50	1.50	2.50

ALIENS VS. PREDATOR: WAR (mini-series)
☐ 2, Jun 95	2.50	0.50	1.50	2.50
☐ 3, Jul 95.......................	2.50	0.50	1.50	2.50
☐ 4, Aug 95	2.50	0.50	1.50	2.50

ALIENS/PREDATOR: THE DEADLIEST OF THE SPECIES (mini-series)
☐ 1, 93.............................	2.50	0.50	1.50	2.50
☐ 2, 93.............................	2.50	0.50	1.50	2.50
☐ 3, 93.............................	2.50	0.50	1.50	2.50
☐ 4, 94.............................	2.50	0.50	1.50	2.50
☐ 5, Mar 94	2.50	0.50	1.50	2.50
☐ 6, May 94	2.50	0.50	1.50	2.50
☐ 7, Aug 94	2.50	0.50	1.50	2.50
☐ 8, Oct 94	2.50	0.50	1.50	2.50
☐ 9, Dec 94.......................	2.50	0.50	1.50	2.50
☐ 10, Feb 95	2.50	0.50	1.50	2.50
☐ 11, May 95	2.50	0.50	1.50	2.50
☐ 12, Aug 95, final issue ...	2.50	0.50	1.50	2.50

ALIENS: BERSERKER (mini-series)
☐ 1, Jan 95........................	2.50	0.50	1.50	2.50
☐ 2, Feb 95	2.50	0.50	1.50	2.50
☐ 3, Mar 95	2.50	0.50	1.50	2.50
☐ 4, Apr 95........................	2.50	0.50	1.50	2.50

ALIENS: COLONIAL MARINES (mini-series)
☐ 1, 93.............................	2.50	0.50	1.50	2.50
☐ 2, 93.............................	2.50	0.50	1.50	2.50
☐ 3, 93.............................	2.50	0.50	1.50	2.50
☐ 4, 93.............................	2.50	0.50	1.50	2.50
☐ 5, 93.............................	2.50	0.50	1.50	2.50
☐ 6, 93.............................	2.50	0.50	1.50	2.50
☐ 7, 93.............................	2.50	0.50	1.50	2.50
☐ 8	2.50	0.50	1.50	2.50
☐ 9	2.50	0.50	1.50	2.50
☐ 10	2.50	0.50	1.50	2.50
☐ 11	2.50	0.50	1.50	2.50
☐ 12	2.50	0.50	1.50	2.50

ALIENS: EARTH ANGEL
☐ 0, Aug 94	2.95	0.59	1.77	2.95

ALIENS: EARTH WAR (mini-series)
☐ 1, Jun 90, color	2.50	1.20	3.60	6.00
☐ 2, Jul 90, color...............	2.50	0.80	2.40	4.00
☐ 3, Sep 90, color	2.50	0.60	1.80	3.00
☐ 4, Oct 90, color..............	2.50	0.60	1.80	3.00

ALIENS: GENOCIDE (mini-series)
☐ 1	2.50	0.50	1.50	2.50
☐ 2	2.50	0.50	1.50	2.50
☐ 3	2.50	0.50	1.50	2.50
☐ 4	2.50	0.50	1.50	2.50

ALIENS: HIVE (mini-series)
☐ 1	2.50	0.80	2.40	4.00
☐ 2	2.50	0.60	1.80	3.00
☐ 3	2.50	0.50	1.50	2.50
☐ 4	2.50	0.50	1.50	2.50

ALIENS: LABYRINTH (mini-series)
☐ 1	2.50	0.50	1.50	2.50
☐ 2	2.50	0.50	1.50	2.50
☐ 3	2.50	0.50	1.50	2.50
☐ 4	2.50	0.50	1.50	2.50

ALIENS: MONDO HEAT
☐ 0, Feb 96, nn;one-shot....	2.50	0.50	1.50	2.50

ALIENS: MONDO PEST
☐ 0, Apr 95, reprints story from *Dark Horse Comics* #22-24...........................	2.95	0.59	1.77	2.95

ALIENS: MUSIC OF THE SPEARS (mini-series)
☐ 1, Jan 94........................	2.50	0.50	1.50	2.50
☐ 2, Feb 94	2.50	0.50	1.50	2.50
☐ 3, Mar 94	2.50	0.50	1.50	2.50
☐ 4, Apr 94........................	2.50	0.50	1.50	2.50

ALIENS: NEWT'S TALE
☐ 1	4.95	0.99	2.97	4.95

ALIENS: ROGUE (mini-series)
☐ 1	2.50	0.50	1.50	2.50
☐ 2	2.50	0.50	1.50	2.50
☐ 3	2.50	0.50	1.50	2.50
☐ 4	2.50	0.50	1.50	2.50

ALIENS: SACRIFICE
☐ 0, nn	4.95	0.99	2.97	4.95

ALIENS: SALVATION
☐ 0, nn	4.95	0.99	2.97	4.95

ALIENS: STRONGHOLD (mini-series)
☐ 1, May 94	2.50	0.50	1.50	2.50
☐ 2, Jun 94	2.50	0.50	1.50	2.50
☐ 3, Jul 94........................	2.50	0.50	1.50	2.50
☐ 4, Sep 94	2.50	0.50	1.50	2.50

	ORIG.	GOOD	FINE	N-MINT

ALISTER THE SLAYER
MIDNIGHT PRESS

	ORIG.	GOOD	FINE	N-MINT
❑ 1, Oct 95	2.50	0.50	1.50	2.50

ALL ABOUT COLLECTING COMIC BOOKS
MARVEL

	ORIG.	GOOD	FINE	N-MINT
❑ 0, 89, giveaway		0.20	0.60	1.00

ALL HALLOW'S EVE
INNOVATION

	ORIG.	GOOD	FINE	N-MINT
❑ 1		0.99	2.97	4.95

ALL NEW ADVENTURES OF THE MIGHTY CRUSADERS
ARCHIE/RED CIRCLE

	ORIG.	GOOD	FINE	N-MINT
❑ 1, Mar 83	1.00	0.20	0.60	1.00
❑ 2, May 83	1.00	0.20	0.60	1.00
❑ 3, Jul 83	1.00	0.20	0.60	1.00

ALL NEW COLLECTOR'S EDITION
DC

	ORIG.	GOOD	FINE	N-MINT
❑ 53	2.00	0.40	1.20	2.00
❑ 54, Jan 78	2.00	0.40	1.20	2.00
❑ 55, Feb 78	2.00	0.40	1.20	2.00
❑ 56, Apr 78	2.00	0.40	1.20	2.00
❑ 57	2.00	0.40	1.20	2.00
❑ 58, Jun 78	2.00	0.40	1.20	2.00
❑ 60, Feb 79	2.00	0.40	1.20	2.00
❑ 62, Mar 79	2.50	0.50	1.50	2.50

ALL NEW EXILES, THE
MALIBU/ULTRAVERSE

	ORIG.	GOOD	FINE	N-MINT
❑ 0		0.80	2.40	4.00
❑ 0, Sep 95, Infinity; "Black September"				
	1.50	0.30	0.90	1.50
❑ 0, Sep 95, Infinity;"Black September"; alternate cover				
	1.50	0.30	0.90	1.50
❑ 1, Oct 95, contains *UltraForce* Vol. 2 #1				
	1.50	0.30	0.90	1.50
❑ 2, Nov 95, flip book with The Phoenix Resurrection Pt. 5	1.50	0.30	0.90	1.50
❑ 3, Dec 95	1.50	0.30	0.90	1.50
❑ 4, Jan 96, V:UltraForce	1.50	0.30	0.90	1.50
❑ 5, Feb 96	2.50	0.50	1.50	2.50
❑ 6, Mar 96	1.50	0.30	0.90	1.50
❑ 7, Apr 96	1.50	0.30	0.90	1.50

ALL SHOOK UP
RIP OFF

	ORIG.	GOOD	FINE	N-MINT
❑ 0, Jun 90, nn b&w; earthquake				
	3.50	0.70	2.10	3.50

ALL-STAR COMICS
DC

	ORIG.	GOOD	FINE	N-MINT
❑ 58, Feb 76, regrouping of JSA;J: Power Girl				
	0.25	1.00	3.00	5.00
❑ 59, Apr 76, Brain Wave	0.25	0.50	1.50	2.50
❑ 60, Jun 76, KG/WW	0.30	0.50	1.50	2.50
❑ 61, Aug 76, KG/WW	0.30	0.50	1.50	2.50
❑ 62, Oct 76, KG/WW	0.30	0.50	1.50	2.50
❑ 63, Dec 76, KG/WW	0.30	0.50	1.50	2.50
❑ 64, Feb 77, WW	0.30	0.30	0.90	1.50
❑ 65, Apr 77, WW	0.30	0.30	0.90	1.50
❑ 66, Jun 77, JSa/BL	0.30	0.35	1.05	1.75
❑ 67, Aug 77, JSa/BL	0.35	0.35	1.05	1.75
❑ 68, Oct 77, JSa/BL	0.35	0.35	1.05	1.75
❑ 69, Dec 77, JSa/BL	0.35	0.35	1.05	1.75
❑ 70, Feb 78, JSa/BL; Huntress				
	0.35	0.30	0.90	1.50
❑ 71, Apr 78, JSa/BL	0.35	0.30	0.90	1.50
❑ 72, Jun 78, J:Huntress	0.35	0.30	0.90	1.50
❑ 73, Aug 78, JSa	0.35	0.30	0.90	1.50
❑ 74, Oct 78, JSa	0.50	0.30	0.90	1.50

ALL-STAR INDEX, THE
ECLIPSE/INDEPENDENT

	ORIG.	GOOD	FINE	N-MINT
❑ 1, Feb 87		0.40	1.20	2.00

ALL-STAR SQUADRON
DC

	ORIG.	GOOD	FINE	N-MINT
❑ 1, Sep 81, A&I:Danette Reilly (Firebrand II)				
	0.50	0.50	1.50	2.50
❑ 2, Oct 81, RB/JOy	0.60	0.40	1.20	2.00
❑ 3, Nov 81, RB/JOy	0.60	0.35	1.05	1.75
❑ 4, Dec 81, RB/JOy	0.60	0.35	1.05	1.75
❑ 5, Jan 82, RB/JOy	0.60	0.35	1.05	1.75
❑ 6, Feb 82	0.60	0.35	1.05	1.75
❑ 7, Mar 82	0.60	0.35	1.05	1.75
❑ 8, Apr 82	0.60	0.35	1.05	1.75
❑ 9, May 82	0.60	0.35	1.05	1.75
❑ 10, Jun 82	0.60	0.35	1.05	1.75
❑ 11, Jul 82	0.60	0.35	1.05	1.75
❑ 12, Aug 82	0.60	0.35	1.05	1.75
❑ 13, Sep 82	0.60	0.35	1.05	1.75
❑ 14, Oct 82	0.60	0.35	1.05	1.75
❑ 15, Nov 82	0.60	0.35	1.05	1.75
❑ 16, Dec 82	0.60	0.35	1.05	1.75
❑ 17, Jan 83	0.60	0.35	1.05	1.75
❑ 18, Feb 83	0.60	0.35	1.05	1.75
❑ 19, Mar 83	0.60	0.35	1.05	1.75
❑ 20, Apr 83	0.60	0.35	1.05	1.75
❑ 21, May 83	0.60	0.35	1.05	1.75
❑ 22, Jun 83	0.60	0.35	1.05	1.75
❑ 23, Jul 83	0.60	0.35	1.05	1.75
❑ 24, Aug 83, I:Infinity Inc.	0.60	0.40	1.20	2.00
❑ 25, Sep 83, I:Infinity Inc.	0.60	0.40	1.20	2.00
❑ 26, Oct 83	0.60	0.30	0.90	1.50
❑ 27, Nov 83	0.60	0.30	0.90	1.50
❑ 28, Dec 83	0.75	0.30	0.90	1.50
❑ 29, Jan 84	0.75	0.30	0.90	1.50
❑ 30, Feb 84	0.75	0.30	0.90	1.50
❑ 31, Mar 84	0.75	0.30	0.90	1.50
❑ 32, Apr 84	0.75	0.30	0.90	1.50
❑ 33, May 84	0.75	0.30	0.90	1.50
❑ 34, Jun 84	0.75	0.30	0.90	1.50
❑ 35, Jul 84	0.75	0.30	0.90	1.50
❑ 36, Aug 84	0.75	0.30	0.90	1.50
❑ 37, Sep 84	0.75	0.30	0.90	1.50
❑ 38, Oct 84	0.75	0.30	0.90	1.50
❑ 39, Nov 84	0.75	0.30	0.90	1.50
❑ 40, Dec 84	0.75	0.30	0.90	1.50
❑ 41, Jan 85	0.75	0.30	0.90	1.50
❑ 42, Feb 85	0.75	0.30	0.90	1.50
❑ 43, Mar 85	0.75	0.30	0.90	1.50
❑ 44, Apr 85	0.75	0.30	0.90	1.50
❑ 45, May 85	0.75	0.30	0.90	1.50
❑ 46, Jun 85	0.75	0.30	0.90	1.50
❑ 47, Jul 85, TMc	0.75	1.20	3.60	6.00
❑ 48, Aug 85	0.75	0.30	0.90	1.50
❑ 49, Sep 85	0.75	0.30	0.90	1.50
❑ 50, Oct 85, Crisis	0.75	0.30	0.90	1.50
❑ 51, Nov 85, Crisis	0.75	0.30	0.90	1.50
❑ 52, Dec 85, Crisis	0.75	0.30	0.90	1.50
❑ 53, Jan 86, Crisis	0.75	0.30	0.90	1.50
❑ 54, Feb 86, Crisis	0.75	0.30	0.90	1.50
❑ 55, Mar 86, Crisis	0.75	0.30	0.90	1.50
❑ 56, Apr 86, Crisis	0.75	0.30	0.90	1.50
❑ 57, May 86, Crisis	0.75	0.30	0.90	1.50
❑ 58, Jun 86	0.75	0.30	0.90	1.50
❑ 59, Jul 86	0.75	0.30	0.90	1.50
❑ 60, Aug 86	0.75	0.30	0.90	1.50
❑ 61, Sep 86	0.75	0.30	0.90	1.50
❑ 62, Oct 86	0.75	0.30	0.90	1.50
❑ 63, Nov 86	0.75	0.30	0.90	1.50
❑ 64, Dec 86	0.75	0.30	0.90	1.50
❑ 65, Jan 87	0.75	0.30	0.90	1.50
❑ 66, Feb 87	0.75	0.30	0.90	1.50
❑ 67, Mar 87	0.75	0.30	0.90	1.50

	ORIG.	GOOD	FINE	N-MINT

ALL-STAR SQUADRON ANNUAL

	ORIG.	GOOD	FINE	N-MINT
❑ 1, Nov 82, JOy;O:Atom .. 1.00		0.30	0.90	1.50
❑ 2, Nov 83, A:Infinity Inc.;D: Cyclotron				
.................................1.00		0.30	0.90	1.50
❑ 3, Sep 84, WB;JOy; DN;KG;GP				
.................................1.25		0.25	0.75	1.25

ALL-STAR WESTERN

	ORIG.	GOOD	FINE	N-MINT
❑ 1, Sep 70......................0.15		2.00	6.00	10.00
❑ 2, Nov 70 ....0.15		1.00	3.00	5.00
❑ 3, Jan 71 ....0.15		0.80	2.40	4.00
❑ 4, Mar 71 ....0.15		0.80	2.40	4.00
❑ 5, May 71 ....0.15		0.80	2.40	4.00
❑ 6, Jul 71 ....0.15		0.80	2.40	4.00
❑ 7, Sep 71 ....0.25		0.80	2.40	4.00
❑ 8, Nov 71 ....0.25		0.80	2.40	4.00
❑ 9, Jan 72 ....0.25		0.80	2.40	4.00
❑ 10, Mar 72, (first Jonah Hex)				
.................................0.25		20.00	60.00	100.00
❑ 11, May 72, (becomes *Weird Western Tales*)				
.................................0.25		11.00	33.00	55.00

ALLEY OOP
DRAGON LADY

	ORIG.	GOOD	FINE	N-MINT
❑ 1, O:Oop, Dinny................		1.19	3.57	5.95
❑ 2, time machine		1.39	4.17	6.95
❑ 3, Hercules........................		1.59	4.77	7.95

ALLIANCE, THE
IMAGE

	ORIG.	GOOD	FINE	N-MINT
❑ 2, Sep 95........................2.50		0.50	1.50	2.50

ALLY
ALLY-WINSOR

	ORIG.	GOOD	FINE	N-MINT
❑ 1, Fal 95, b&w................2.95		0.59	1.77	2.95

ALONE IN THE SHADE SPECIAL
ALCHEMY

	ORIG.	GOOD	FINE	N-MINT
❑ 0, nn b&w		0.40	1.20	2.00

ALPHA FLIGHT
MARVEL

	ORIG.	GOOD	FINE	N-MINT
❑ 1, Aug 83, JBy;1:Puck, Marrina				
.................................1.00		1.60	4.80	8.00
❑ 2, Sep 83, JBy................0.60		0.80	2.40	4.00
❑ 3, Oct 83, JBy................0.60		0.60	1.80	3.00
❑ 4, Nov 83, JBy................0.60		0.60	1.80	3.00
❑ 5, Dec 83, JBy................0.60		0.60	1.80	3.00
❑ 6, Jan 84, JBy;all-white issue				
.................................0.60		0.60	1.80	3.00
❑ 7, Feb 84, JBy................0.60		0.60	1.80	3.00
❑ 8, Mar 84, JBy................0.60		0.50	1.50	2.50
❑ 9, Apr 84, JBy;A:Thing ... 0.60		0.50	1.50	2.50
❑ 10, May 84, JBy 0.60		0.50	1.50	2.50
❑ 11, Jun 84, JBy 0.60		0.50	1.50	2.50
❑ 12, Jul 84, JBy; D:Guardian				
.................................0.60		0.60	1.80	3.00
❑ 13, Aug 84, Wolverine.... 0.60		2.80	8.40	14.00
❑ 14, Sep 84......................0.60		0.35	1.05	1.75
❑ 15, Oct 84, A:Sub-Mariner				
.................................0.60		0.35	1.05	1.75
❑ 16, Nov 84, A:Sub-Mariner				
.................................0.60		0.35	1.05	1.75
❑ 17, Dec 84, A:Wolverine JBy				
.................................0.60		2.00	6.00	10.00
❑ 18, Jan 85, JBy 0.60		0.50	1.50	2.50
❑ 19, Feb 85, JBy; 1:Talisman				
.................................0.60		0.50	1.50	2.50
❑ 20, Mar 85, JBy..............0.60		0.50	1.50	2.50
❑ 21, Apr 85, JBy 0.65		0.50	1.50	2.50
❑ 22, May 85, JBy 0.65		0.50	1.50	2.50
❑ 23, Jun 85, JBy 0.65		0.50	1.50	2.50
❑ 24, Jul 85, JBy 1.25		0.50	1.50	2.50
❑ 25, Aug 85, JBy..............0.65		0.50	1.50	2.50
❑ 26, Sep 85, JBy..............0.65		0.50	1.50	2.50
❑ 27, Oct 85, JBy 0.65		0.50	1.50	2.50

	ORIG.	GOOD	FINE	N-MINT
❑ 28, Nov 85, JBy Secret Wars II				
.................................0.65		0.50	1.50	2.50
❑ 29, Dec 85 ....0.65		0.50	1.50	2.50
❑ 30, Jan 86......................0.65		0.50	1.50	2.50
❑ 31, Feb 86......................0.75		0.50	1.50	2.50
❑ 32, Mar 86......................0.75		0.50	1.50	2.50
❑ 33, Apr 86, Wolverine.....0.75		1.60	4.80	8.00
❑ 34, May 86, Wolverine...0.75		1.60	4.80	8.00
❑ 35, Jun 86, Wolverine.....0.75		0.40	1.20	2.00
❑ 36, Jul 86, Wolverine......0.75		0.40	1.20	2.00
❑ 37, Aug 86, Wolverine.....0.75		0.40	1.20	2.00
❑ 38, Sep 86, Wolverine ...0.75		0.40	1.20	2.00
❑ 39, Oct 86, Wolverine.....0.75		0.40	1.20	2.00
❑ 40, Nov 86, Wolverine.....0.75		0.40	1.20	2.00
❑ 41, Dec 86, Wolverine....0.75		0.40	1.20	2.00
❑ 42, Jan 87, Wolverine.....0.75		0.40	1.20	2.00
❑ 43, Feb 87, Wolverine.....0.75		0.40	1.20	2.00
❑ 44, Mar 87, Wolverine.....0.75		0.40	1.20	2.00
❑ 45, Apr 87, Wolverine.....0.75		0.40	1.20	2.00
❑ 46, May 87, Wolverine.....0.75		0.40	1.20	2.00
❑ 47, Jun 87, Wolverine.....0.75		0.40	1.20	2.00
❑ 48, Jul 87, Wolverine......0.75		0.40	1.20	2.00
❑ 49, Aug 87, Wolverine.....0.75		0.40	1.20	2.00
❑ 50, Sep 87 ....1.25		0.50	1.50	2.50
❑ 51, Oct 87, JL (first Marvel)				
.................................0.75		3.00	9.00	15.00
❑ 52, Nov 87, Wolverine 1.00		1.60	4.80	8.00
❑ 53, Dec 87, Wolverine 1.00		1.60	4.80	8.00
❑ 54, Jan 88......................1.00		0.80	2.40	4.00
❑ 55, Feb 88......................1.00		0.80	2.40	4.00
❑ 56, Mar 88......................1.00		0.80	2.40	4.00
❑ 57, Apr 88......................1.00		0.80	2.40	4.00
❑ 58, May 88......................1.00		0.80	2.40	4.00
❑ 59, Jun 88......................1.00		0.80	2.40	4.00
❑ 60, Jul 88......................1.25		0.80	2.40	4.00
❑ 61, Aug 88......................1.25		0.40	1.20	2.00
❑ 62, Sep 88......................1.25		0.40	1.20	2.00
❑ 63, Oct 88......................1.25		0.40	1.20	2.00
❑ 64, Nov 88......................1.25		0.40	1.20	2.00
❑ 65, Dec 88......................1.50		0.40	1.20	2.00
❑ 66, Jan 89......................1.50		0.40	1.20	2.00
❑ 67, Feb 89......................1.50		0.40	1.20	2.00
❑ 68, Mar 89......................1.50		0.40	1.20	2.00
❑ 69, Apr 89......................1.50		0.40	1.20	2.00
❑ 70, May 89......................1.50		0.40	1.20	2.00
❑ 71, Jun 89......................1.50		0.40	1.20	2.00
❑ 72, Jul 89......................1.50		0.40	1.20	2.00
❑ 73, Aug 89......................1.50		0.40	1.20	2.00
❑ 74, Sep 89......................1.50		0.40	1.20	2.00
❑ 75, Oct 89......................1.95		0.39	1.17	1.95
❑ 76, Nov 89......................1.50		0.30	0.90	1.50
❑ 77, Nov 89......................1.95		0.39	1.17	1.95
❑ 78, Dec 89......................1.50		0.30	0.90	1.50
❑ 79, Dec 89, Acts of Vengeance				
.................................1.50		0.50	1.50	2.50
❑ 80, Jan 90, Acts of Vengeance				
.................................1.50		0.50	1.50	2.50
❑ 81, Feb 90......................1.50		0.30	0.90	1.50
❑ 82, Mar 90......................1.50		0.30	0.90	1.50
❑ 83, Apr 90......................1.50		0.30	0.90	1.50
❑ 84, May 90......................1.50		0.30	0.90	1.50
❑ 85, Jun 90......................1.50		0.30	0.90	1.50
❑ 86, Jul 90......................1.50		0.30	0.90	1.50
❑ 87, Aug 90, Wolverine ...1.50		1.20	3.60	6.00
❑ 88, Sep 90, Wolverine 1.50		0.80	2.40	4.00
❑ 89, Oct 90, Guardian returns; Wolverine				
.................................1.50		0.80	2.40	4.00
❑ 90, Nov 90......................1.50		0.60	1.80	3.00
❑ 91, Dec 90, Dr. Doom.....1.50		0.30	0.90	1.50
❑ 92, Jan 91......................1.50		0.30	0.90	1.50
❑ 93, Feb 91......................1.50		0.30	0.90	1.50
❑ 94, Mar 91, Fantastic 4 ...1.50		0.30	0.90	1.50

	ORIG.	GOOD	FINE	N-MINT
❏ 95, Apr 91 .... 1.50		0.30	0.90	1.50
❏ 96, May 91 .... 1.50		0.30	0.90	1.50
❏ 97, Jun 91 .... 1.50		0.30	0.90	1.50
❏ 98, Jul 91 .... 1.50		0.30	0.90	1.50
❏ 99, Aug 91 .... 1.50		0.30	0.90	1.50
❏ 100, Sep 91 .... 2.00		0.40	1.20	2.00
❏ 101, Oct 91 .... 1.50		0.30	0.90	1.50
❏ 102, Nov 91 .... 1.50		0.30	0.90	1.50
❏ 103, Dec 91 .... 1.50		0.30	0.90	1.50
❏ 104, Jan 92 .... 1.50		0.30	0.90	1.50
❏ 105, Feb 92 .... 1.75		0.35	1.05	1.75
❏ 106, Mar 92, Northstar admits he's gay; 1st printing				
.... 1.75		1.00	3.00	5.00
❏ 106, Mar 92, 2nd printing 1.75		0.60	1.80	3.00
❏ 107, Apr 92 .... 1.75		0.35	1.05	1.75
❏ 108, May 92 .... 1.75		0.35	1.05	1.75
❏ 109, Jun 92 .... 1.75		0.35	1.05	1.75
❏ 110, Jul 92 .... 1.75		0.35	1.05	1.75
❏ 111, Aug 92 .... 1.75		0.35	1.05	1.75
❏ 112, Sep 92 .... 1.75		0.35	1.05	1.75
❏ 113, Oct 92 .... 1.75		0.35	1.05	1.75
❏ 114, Nov 92 .... 1.75		0.35	1.05	1.75
❏ 115, Dec 92 .... 1.75		0.35	1.05	1.75
❏ 116, Jan 93 .... 1.75		0.35	1.05	1.75
❏ 117, Feb 93 .... 1.75		0.35	1.05	1.75
❏ 118, Mar 93 .... 1.75		0.35	1.05	1.75
❏ 119, Apr 93 .... 1.75		0.35	1.05	1.75
❏ 120, May 93, with poster 2.25		0.45	1.35	2.25
❏ 121, Jun 93 .... 1.75		0.35	1.05	1.75
❏ 122, Jul 93 .... 1.75		0.35	1.05	1.75
❏ 123, Aug 93 .... 1.75		0.35	1.05	1.75
❏ 124, Sep 93 .... 1.75		0.35	1.05	1.75
❏ 125, Oct 93 .... 1.75		0.35	1.05	1.75
❏ 126, Nov 93 .... 1.75		0.35	1.05	1.75
❏ 127, Dec 93 .... 1.75		0.35	1.05	1.75
❏ 128, Jan 94 .... 1.75		0.35	1.05	1.75
❏ 129, Feb 94 .... 1.75		0.35	1.05	1.75

ALPHA FLIGHT ANNUAL

	ORIG.	GOOD	FINE	N-MINT
❏ 1, Sep 86 .... 1.25		0.25	0.75	1.25
❏ 2, Dec 87 .... 1.25		0.25	0.75	1.25

ALPHA FLIGHT SPECIAL

	ORIG.	GOOD	FINE	N-MINT
❏ 0, nn (1992) 2.50		0.50	1.50	2.50

ALPHA FLIGHT SPECIAL (1991)

	ORIG.	GOOD	FINE	N-MINT
❏ 1, Jul 91, reprint 1.50		0.30	0.90	1.50
❏ 2, Aug 91, reprint 1.50		0.30	0.90	1.50
❏ 3, Sep 91, reprint 1.50		0.30	0.90	1.50
❏ 4, Oct 91, reprint 2.00		0.40	1.20	2.00

ALPHA ILLUSTRATED
ALPHA PRODUCTIONS

	ORIG.	GOOD	FINE	N-MINT
❏ 0, Apr 94, b&w;free				
❏ 1, b&w		0.70	2.10	3.50

ALPHA TEAM OMEGA
FANTASY GRAPHICS

	ORIG.	GOOD	FINE	N-MINT
❏ 1		0.25	0.75	1.25

ALPHA TRACK
FANTASY GENERAL

	ORIG.	GOOD	FINE	N-MINT
❏ 1		0.20	0.60	1.00
❏ 2		0.20	0.60	1.00

ALPHA WAVE
DARKLINE

	ORIG.	GOOD	FINE	N-MINT
❏ 1		0.35	1.05	1.75

ALTER EGO (mini-series)
FIRST

	ORIG.	GOOD	FINE	N-MINT
❏ 1, May 86 .... 1.25		0.25	0.75	1.25
❏ 2, Jul 86 .... 1.25		0.25	0.75	1.25
❏ 3, Sep 86 .... 1.25		0.25	0.75	1.25
❏ 4, Nov 86 .... 1.25		0.25	0.75	1.25

ALTERNATE HEROES
PRELUDE

	ORIG.	GOOD	FINE	N-MINT
❏ 1		0.39	1.17	1.95

ALTERNATIVE COMICS
REVOLUTIONARY

	ORIG.	GOOD	FINE	N-MINT
❏ 1, Jan 94, b&w; Pearl Jam/Cure/REM				
.... 2.50		0.50	1.50	2.50

ALVIN AND THE CHIPMUNKS
HARVEY

	ORIG.	GOOD	FINE	N-MINT
❏ 1 .... 1.25		0.25	0.75	1.25
❏ 2 .... 1.50		0.30	0.90	1.50
❏ 3 .... 1.50		0.30	0.90	1.50
❏ 4 .... 1.50		0.30	0.90	1.50
❏ 5 .... 1.50		0.30	0.90	1.50

AMAZING ADVENTURES
MARVEL

	ORIG.	GOOD	FINE	N-MINT
❏ 1, Aug 70, JK/JB; Inhumans				
.... 0.15		4.00	12.00	20.00
❏ 2 .... 0.15		1.60	4.80	8.00
❏ 3 .... 0.15		1.60	4.80	8.00
❏ 4 .... 0.15		1.60	4.80	8.00
❏ 5, NA 0.15		1.20	3.60	6.00
❏ 6, NA 0.15		1.20	3.60	6.00
❏ 7, NA 0.15		1.20	3.60	6.00
❏ 8, NA 0.15		1.60	4.80	8.00
❏ 9 .... 0.20		1.00	3.00	5.00
❏ 10 .... 0.20		1.00	3.00	5.00
❏ 11, O:new Beast 0.20		3.60	10.80	18.00
❏ 12 .... 0.20		2.00	6.00	10.00
❏ 13 .... 0.20		2.00	6.00	10.00
❏ 14 .... 0.20		2.00	6.00	10.00
❏ 15 .... 0.20		2.00	6.00	10.00
❏ 16 .... 0.20		2.00	6.00	10.00
❏ 17 .... 0.20		2.00	6.00	10.00
❏ 18, May 73, HC/NA;I: Killraven				
.... 0.20		3.00	9.00	15.00
❏ 19, Killraven 0.20		0.80	2.40	4.00
❏ 20, Killraven 0.20		0.80	2.40	4.00
❏ 21, Killraven 0.20		0.80	2.40	4.00
❏ 22, Killraven 0.20		0.80	2.40	4.00
❏ 23, Killraven 0.20		0.80	2.40	4.00
❏ 24, Killraven 0.25		0.80	2.40	4.00
❏ 25, Killraven 0.25		0.80	2.40	4.00
❏ 26, Killraven 0.25		0.80	2.40	4.00
❏ 27, CR/JSn 0.25		0.80	2.40	4.00
❏ 28, CR;Killraven 0.25		0.40	1.20	2.00
❏ 29, CR;Killraven 0.25		0.40	1.20	2.00
❏ 30, CR;Killraven 0.25		0.40	1.20	2.00
❏ 31, CR;Killraven 0.25		0.40	1.20	2.00
❏ 32, CR;Killraven 0.25		0.25	0.75	1.25
❏ 33, CR;Killraven 0.25		0.25	0.75	1.25
❏ 34, CR;Killraven 0.25		0.25	0.75	1.25
❏ 35, CR;Killraven 0.25		0.40	1.20	2.00
❏ 36, CR;Killraven 0.25		0.40	1.20	2.00
❏ 37, CR;O:Old Skull 0.25		0.25	0.75	1.25
❏ 38, CR;Killraven 0.30		0.40	1.20	2.00
❏ 39, CR;Killraven 0.30		0.40	1.20	2.00

AMAZING ADVENTURES (1988)

	ORIG.	GOOD	FINE	N-MINT
❏ 1, Jul 88, squarebound ... 4.95		0.99	2.97	4.95

AMAZING ADVENTURES (2nd series)

	ORIG.	GOOD	FINE	N-MINT
❏ 1, rep. X-Men #1 .... 0.40		0.25	0.75	1.25
❏ 2, Jan 80, all X-Men rep.. 0.40		0.20	0.60	1.00
❏ 3, Feb 80, all X-Men rep....		0.20	0.60	1.00
❏ 4, Mar 80, all X-Men rep...		0.20	0.60	1.00
❏ 5, Apr 80, all X-Men rep....		0.20	0.60	1.00
❏ 6, May 80, all X-Men rep. .		0.20	0.60	1.00
❏ 7, Jun 80, all X-Men rep. ..		0.20	0.60	1.00
❏ 8, Jul 80, all X-Men rep. ...		0.20	0.60	1.00
❏ 9, Aug 80, all X-Men rep...		0.20	0.60	1.00
❏ 10, Sep 80, all X-Men rep.		0.20	0.60	1.00

	ORIG.	GOOD	FINE	N-MINT

☐ 11, Oct 80, all X-Men rep.
..................................0.50 0.20 0.60 1.00
☐ 12, Nov 80, all X-Men rep.
..................................0.50 0.20 0.60 1.00
☐ 13, Dec 80, all X-Men rep
..................................0.50 0.20 0.60 1.00
☐ 14, Jan 81, all X-Men rep.
..................................0.50 0.20 0.60 1.00

AMAZING ADVENTURES OF ACE INTERNATIONAL, THE
STARHEAD
☐ 1, Nov 93, b&w.............2.95 0.59 1.77 2.95

AMAZING COMICS PREMIERE
AMAZING
☐ 1 .... 0.39 1.17 1.95
☐ 2 .... 0.39 1.17 1.95
☐ 3 .... 0.39 1.17 1.95
☐ 4 .... 0.39 1.17 1.95
☐ 5, Stargrazers.................. 0.39 1.17 1.95

AMAZING CYNICALMAN
ECLIPSE
☐ 1, b&w 0.30 0.90 1.50

AMAZING FANTASY
MARVEL
☐ 15, Aug 62, JK(c);SD; 1&O:SpM
.... 0.12 4800 14400 24000
☐ 16, Dec 95, KB(w);cardstock cover;fills in gaps between
Amazing Fantasy #15 and *Amazing Spider-Man* #1
....3.95 0.79 2.37 3.95
☐ 18, Mar 96, KB(w); cardstock cover
....3.95 0.79 2.37 3.95

AMAZING HIGH ADVENTURE
☐ 1 ....2.00 0.50 1.50 2.50
☐ 2 ....2.00 0.40 1.20 2.00
☐ 3 ....2.00 0.40 1.20 2.00
☐ 4 ....2.00 0.40 1.20 2.00
☐ 5 ....2.00 0.40 1.20 2.00

AMAZING SCARLET SPIDER, THE
☐ 1, Nov 95,;"Virtual Mortality" Part 2 of 4
....1.95 0.39 1.17 1.95
☐ 2, Dec 95, direct edition; "Cyberwar" Part 2 of 4
....1.95 0.39 1.17 1.95
☐ 2, Dec 95, "Cyberwar" Part 2 of 4
....1.50 0.30 0.90 1.50

AMAZING SPIDER-MAN
☐ 1, Mar 63, JK(c);SD;ro: SpM;1:J. Jonah Jameson, Chameleon;A:Fantastic Four
.................................0.12 3700 11100 18500
☐ 2, May 63, SD;1:Vulture, Tinkerer
.... 0.12 550.001650.00 2750.00
☐ 3, Jul 63, SD;1: Dr. Octopus
...........................0.12 310.00 930.00 1550.00
☐ 4, Sep 63, SD;1: Sandman
...........................0.12 250.00 750.00 1250.00
☐ 5, Oct 63, SD;V: Dr. Doom
...........................0.12 220.00 660.00 1100.00
☐ 6, Nov 63, SD;1:Lizard ..0.12 200.00 600.00 1000.00
☐ 7, Dec 63, SD; V:Vulture 0.12 145.00 435.00 725.00
☐ 8, Jan 64, SD;V:Living Brain, Flash Thompson
...........................0.12 145.00 435.00 725.00
☐ 9, Feb 64, SD;1:Electro, Dr. Bromwell
...........................0.12 145.00 435.00 725.00
☐ 10, Mar 64, JK(c);SD; 1:Big Man, Enforcers (Fancy Dan, Ox, Montana) 0.12 145.00 435.00 725.00
☐ 11, Apr 64, SD;V: Dr. Octopus
...........................0.12 88.00 264.00 440.00
☐ 12, May 64, SD;V: Dr. Octopus;Spider-Man unmasked
...........................0.12 88.00 264.00 440.00
☐ 13, Jun 64, SD;1&O: Mysterio
...........................0.12 88.00 264.00 440.00

☐ 14, Jul 64, SD;1:Green Goblin;A:Hulk, Enforcers
.......................0.12 260.00 780.00 1300.00
☐ 15, Aug 64, SD;1&O:Kraven; A:Chameleon
...........................0.12 80.00 240.00 400.00
☐ 16, Sep 64, SD;A:Daredevil; V:Ringmaster and Circus of Crime..........................0.12 32.00 96.00 160.00
☐ 17, Oct 64, SD;V:Green Goblin;A:Torch
...........................0.12 60.00 180.00 300.00
☐ 18, Nov 64, SD;V:Sandman; 1:Ned Leeds
...........................0.12 50.00 150.00 250.00
☐ 19, Dec 64, SD;V:Sandman, Enforcers;A:Torch0.12
...........................50.00 150.00 250.00
☐ 20, Jan 65, SD;1&O: Scorpion
...........................0.12 32.00 96.00 160.00
☐ 21, Feb 65, SD;V:Beetle; A:Torch
...........................0.12 24.00 72.00 120.00
☐ 22, Mar 65, SD;V:Ringmaster and Circus of Crime
...........................0.12 24.00 72.00 120.00
☐ 23, Apr 65, SD;V:Green Goblin
...........................0.12 50.00 150.00 250.00
☐ 24, May 65, SD;V: Mysterio
...........................0.12 24.00 72.00 120.00
☐ 25, Jun 65, SD;1:Spencer Smythe
...........................0.12 24.00 72.00 120.00
☐ 26, Jul 65, SD;1:Patch, Crime-Master;A: Green Goblin
...........................0.12 24.00 72.00 120.00
☐ 27, Aug 65, SD;D: Crime-Master;A: Green Goblin
...........................0.12 24.00 72.00 120.00
☐ 28, Sep 65, SD;1: Molten Man;A:Spencer Smythe; Peter Parker graduates high school
...........................0.12 24.00 72.00 120.00
☐ 29, Oct 65, SD; V:Scorpion
...........................0.12 24.00 72.00 120.00
☐ 30, Nov 65, SD;V:Cat Burglar;1: Master Planner (a.k.a. Dr. Octopus); Ned Leeds proposes to Betty Brant
...........................0.12 24.00 72.00 120.00
☐ 31, Dec 65, SD;1:Harry Osborn, Gwen Stacy, Prof. Warren 0.12 20.00 60.00 100.00
☐ 32, Jan 66, SD;Master Planner revealed as Dr. Octopus
...........................0.12 20.00 60.00 100.00
☐ 33, Feb 66, SD;V: Dr. Octopus (as Master Planner)
...........................0.12 20.00 60.00 100.00
☐ 34, Mar 66, SD;V:Kraven; A:Green Goblin
...........................0.12 20.00 60.00 100.00
☐ 35, Apr 66, SD;V:Molten Man;1:Spider Tracer
...........................0.12 20.00 60.00 100.00
☐ 36, May 66, SD; 1:Looter (later Meteor Man in Marvel Team-Up #33)
☐ 37, Jun 66, SD; V:Professor Mendel Stromm;A:Patch
...........................0.12 20.00 60.00 100.00
☐ 38, Jul 66, SD 0.12 20.00 60.00 100.00
☐ 39, Aug 66, JR; V:Green Goblin; Green Goblin revealed as Norman Osborn 0.12 40.00 120.00 200.00
☐ 40, Sep 66, JR; O:Green Goblin
...........................0.12 55.00 165.00 275.00
☐ 41, Oct 66, JR; 1:Rhino ..0.12 25.00 75.00 125.00
☐ 42, Nov 66, JR; 1:Mary Jane Watson
...........................0.12 25.00 75.00 125.00
☐ 43, Dec 66, JR; V:Rhino;O:Rhino
...........................0.12 10.00 30.00 50.00
☐ 44, Jan 67, JR; V:Lizard..0.12 10.00 30.00 50.00
☐ 45, Feb 67, JR; V:Lizard..0.12 10.00 30.00 50.00
☐ 46, Mar 67, JR; 1:Shocker
...........................0.12 10.00 30.00 50.00
☐ 47, Apr 67, JR; V:Kraven 0.12 10.00 30.00 50.00
☐ 48, May 67, JR; V:second Vulture
...........................0.12 10.00 30.00 50.00
☐ 49, Jun 67, JR; V:Kraven and Vulture
...........................0.12 10.00 30.00 50.00
☐ 50, Jul 67, JR; 1:Kingpin 0.12 75.00 225.00 375.00
☐ 51, Aug 67, JR; 1:Robbie Robertson; V:Kingpin
...........................0.12 30.00 90.00 150.00

	ORIG.	GOOD	FINE	N-MINT

☐ 52, Sep 67, JR; V:Kingpin0.12   11.00   33.00   55.00
☐ 53, Oct 67, JR; V:Dr. Octopus
......................0.12   11.00   33.00   55.00
☐ 54, Nov 67, JR; V:Dr. Octopus
......................0.12   11.00   33.00   55.00
☐ 55, Dec 67, JR; V:Dr. Octopus
......................0.12   11.00   33.00   55.00
☐ 56, Jan 68, JR; 1:Capt. Stacy; V:Dr. Octopus
......................0.12   11.00   33.00   55.00
☐ 57, Feb 68, JR;A:Ka-Zar and Zabu
......................0.12   11.00   33.00   55.00
☐ 58, Mar 68, JR;A:Ka-Zar and Zabu;V:J. Jonah Jameson
and Spencer Smythe....0.12   11.00   33.00   55.00
☐ 59, Apr 68, JR;V:Kingpin (as Brainwasher)
......................0.12   11.00   33.00   55.00
☐ 60, May 68, JR; V:Kingpin
......................0.12   11.00   33.00   55.00
☐ 61, Jun 68, JR; V:Kingpin
......................0.12   8.00   24.00   40.00
☐ 62, Jul 68, JR; A:Medusa0.12   8.00   24.00   40.00
☐ 63, Aug 68, JR; V:both Vultures
......................0.12   8.00   24.00   40.00
☐ 64, Sep 68, JR; V:Vulture0.12   8.00   24.00   40.00
☐ 65, Oct 68, JR 0.12   8.00   24.00   40.00
☐ 66, Nov 68, JR; V:Mysterio
......................0.12   8.00   24.00   40.00
☐ 67, Dec 68, JR; V:Mysterio
......................0.12   8.00   24.00   40.00
☐ 68, Jan 69, JR; V:Kingpin0.12   11.00   33.00   55.00
☐ 69, Feb 69, JR; V:Kingpin0.12   11.00   33.00   55.00
☐ 70, Mar 69, JR; V:Kingpin
......................0.12   11.00   33.00   55.00
☐ 71, Apr 69, JR; A:Quicksilver
......................0.12   7.20   21.60   36.00
☐ 72, May 69, JR; V:Shocker
......................0.12   7.20   21.60   36.00
☐ 73, Jun 69, JR;1:Silvermane, Man-Mountain Marko,
Caesar Cicero;A:Lizard ... 0.12   7.20   21.60   36.00
☐ 74, Jul 69, JR;V:Silvermane, Man-Mountain Marko,
Caesar Cicero 0.12   7.20   21.60   36.00
☐ 75, Aug 69, JR; V:Silvermane, Man-Mountain Marko,
Caesar Cicero 0.15   7.20   21.60   36.00
☐ 76, Sep 69, JR; V:Lizard;A:Torch
......................0.15   7.20   21.60   36.00
☐ 77, Oct 69, JR; V:Lizard;A:Torch
......................0.15   7.20   21.60   36.00
☐ 78, Nov 69, JR; 1:Prowler
......................0.15   7.20   21.60   36.00
☐ 79, Dec 69, JR; V:Prowler
......................0.15   7.20   21.60   36.00
☐ 80, Jan 70, JR; V:Chameleon
......................0.15   7.20   21.60   36.00
☐ 81, Feb 70, JR; 1:Kangaroo
......................0.15   6.00   18.00   30.00
☐ 82, Mar 70, JR; V:Electro0.15   6.00   18.00   30.00
☐ 83, Apr 70, JR;V:Kingpin, Schemer
......................0.15   6.00   18.00   30.00
☐ 84, May 70, JR;V:Kingpin, Schemer
......................0.15   6.00   18.00   30.00
☐ 85, Jun 70, JR;V:Kingpin, Schemer
......................0.15   6.00   18.00   30.00
☐ 86, Jul 70, JR;ro: Black Widow
......................0.15   6.00   18.00   30.00
☐ 87, Aug 70, JR;Peter reveals his secret identity
......................0.15   6.00   18.00   30.00
☐ 88, Sep 70, JR;V: Dr. Octopus
......................0.15   6.00   18.00   30.00
☐ 89, Oct 70, JR(c);GK;V: Dr. Octopus
......................0.15   6.00   18.00   30.00
☐ 90, Nov 70, GK;A: Dr. Octopus;D: Capt. Stacy
......................0.15   6.00   18.00   30.00

☐ 91, Dec 70, JR(c);GK;1: Sam bullit
......................0.15   5.20   15.60   26.00
☐ 92, Jan 71, JR(c); GK;A:Iceman; A:Sam Bullit
......................0.15   5.20   15.60   26.00
☐ 93, Feb 71, JR;A: Prowler
......................0.15   5.20   15.60   26.00
☐ 94, Mar 71, JR/SB; A:Beetle;ro:SpM
......................0.15   6.00   18.00   30.00
☐ 95, Apr 71, JR/SB;SpM goes to London
......................0.15   5.20   15.60   26.00
☐ 96, May 71, GK;drugs;no Comics Code approval;
V:Green Goblin 0.15   8.00   24.00   40.00
☐ 97, Jun 71, JR(c);GK; drugs;no Comics Code
approval;V:Green Goblin.0.15   8.00   24.00   40.00
☐ 98, Jul 71, GK;drugs;no Comics Code approval
......................0.15   8.00   24.00   40.00
☐ 99, Aug 71, GK;A: Johnny Carson
......................0.15   5.20   15.60   26.00
☐ 100, Sep 71, JR(c);GK; A:Green Goblin;Peter grows four
extra arms 0.15   20.00   60.00   100.00
☐ 101, Oct 71, GK;1: Morbius
......................0.15   25.00   75.00   125.00
☐ 101, 1:Morbius;reprint....1.75   0.35   1.05   1.75
☐ 102, Nov 71, GK;O: Morbius;A:Lizard
......................0.25   18.00   54.00   90.00
☐ 103, Dec 71, GK;V: Kraven;A:Ka-Zar and Zabu;1:Gog
......................0.20   4.00   12.00   20.00
☐ 104, Jan 72, GK;V: Kraven;A:Ka-Zar and Zabu;O:Gog
......................0.20   4.00   12.00   20.00
☐ 105, Feb 72, GK; V: Spencer Smythe and Spider Slayer
......................0.20   4.00   12.00   20.00
☐ 106, Mar 72, JR;V: Spencer Smythe and Spider Slayer
......................0.20   4.00   12.00   20.00
☐ 107, Apr 72, JR;V: Spencer Smythe and Spider Slayer
......................0.20   4.00   12.00   20.00
☐ 108, May 72, JR;1: Sha Shan;A:Flash Thompson
......................0.20   4.00   12.00   20.00
☐ 109, Jun 72, JR;A: Dr. Strange
......................0.20   4.00   12.00   20.00
☐ 110, Jul 72, JR;1& O:Gibbon
......................0.20   4.00   12.00   20.00
☐ 111, Aug 72, JR;V:Gibbon, Kraven
......................0.20   4.00   12.00   20.00
☐ 112, Sep 72, JR; V:Dr. Octopus;A:Gibbon
......................0.20   4.00   12.00   20.00
☐ 113, Oct 72, JR/JSn; 1:Hammerhead; V:Dr. Octopus
......................0.20   4.00   12.00   20.00
☐ 114, Nov 72, JR/JSn; O:Hammerhead;1:Dr. Jonas
Harrow......................0.20   4.00   12.00   20.00
☐ 115, Dec 72, JR;V:Hammerhead, Dr. Octopus
......................0.20   4.00   12.00   20.00
☐ 116, Jan 73, JR;1:Smasher (was Man Monster);
V:Richard Raleigh 0.20   4.00   12.00   20.00
☐ 117, Feb 73, JR;reprints story from Spectacular
Spider-Man (magazine) #1 with updates;1:Disruptor;
V:Smasher....................0.20   4.00   12.00   20.00
☐ 118, Mar 73, JR;V: Disruptor, Smasher
......................0.20   4.00   12.00   20.00
☐ 119, Apr 73, JR; V:Hulk in Canada
......................0.20   4.00   12.00   20.00
☐ 120, May 73, JR(c); GK;V:Hulk
......................0.20   4.00   12.00   20.00
☐ 121, Jun 73, JR(c);GK; D:Gwen Stacy; V:Green Goblin
......................0.20   24.00   72.00   120.00
☐ 122, Jul 73, JR(c);GK; D:Green Goblin (Norman
Osborn)......................0.20   24.00   72.00   120.00
☐ 123, Aug 73, JR; A:Luke Cage
......................0.20   3.60   10.80   18.00
☐ 124, Sep 73, JR(c);GK; 1:Man-Wolf
......................0.20   3.60   10.80   18.00
☐ 125, Oct 73, JR(c); RA;O:Man-Wolf
......................0.20   3.60   10.80   18.00

	ORIG.	GOOD	FINE	N-MINT

☐ 126, Nov 73, JR(c);RA; D:Kangaroo;A: Dr. Jonas Harrow 0.20 3.60 10.80 18.00

☐ 127, Dec 73, JR(c);RA; V:third Vulture 0.20 3.60 10.80 18.00

☐ 128, Jan 74, JR(c);RA; O:third Vulture 0.20 3.60 10.80 18.00

☐ 129, Feb 74, GK(c);RA; 1:Punisher, Jackal 0.20 70.00 210.00 350.00

☐ 130, Mar 74, JR(c);RA; 1:Spider-Mobile;V:Hammerhead, Jackal, Dr. Octopus........0.20 2.80 8.40 14.00

☐ 131, Apr 74, GK(c); RA;V:Dr. Octopus, Hammerhead; Hammerhead turned in wraith 0.20 2.80 8.40 14.00

☐ 132, May 74, GK(c);JR; V:Molten Man 0.25 2.80 8.40 14.00

☐ 133, Jun 74, JR(c);RA; V:Molten Man;Molten Man's relationship of Liz Allan revealed 0.25 2.80 8.40 14.00

☐ 134, Jul 74, JR(c);RA; 1:Tarantula; C:Punisher 0.25 8.00 24.00 40.00

☐ 135, Aug 74, JR(c);RA; O:Tarantula; A:Punisher 0.25 9.00 27.00 45.00

☐ 136, Sep 74, JR(c);RA; Harry Osborn becomes second Green Goblin 0.25 8.00 24.00 40.00

☐ 137, Oct 74, GK(c);RA; V:second Green Goblin 0.25 2.80 8.40 14.00

☐ 138, Nov 74, GK(c);RA; O&1:Mindworm;Peter moves in with Flash Thompson.... 0.25 2.80 8.40 14.00

☐ 139, Dec 74, GK(c);RA; 1:Grizzly;A:Jackal 0.25 2.80 8.40 14.00

☐ 140, Jan 75, GK(c);RA; V:Jackal;O:Grizzly 0.25 2.80 8.40 14.00

☐ 141, Feb 75, JR(c);RA; V:second Mysterio; Spider-Mobile sinks in Hudson.. 0.25 2.80 8.40 14.00

☐ 142, Mar 75, JR(c);RA; V:second Mysterio 0.25 2.80 8.40 14.00

☐ 143, Apr 75, GK(c); RA;1:Cyclone 0.25 2.80 8.40 14.00

☐ 144, May 75, GK(c); RA;1:Gwen Stacy clone; V:Cyclone 0.25 2.80 8.40 14.00

☐ 145, Jun 75, GK(c);RA; V:Scorpion 0.25 2.80 8.40 14.00

☐ 146, Jul 75, JR(c);RA; V:Jackal, Scorpion 0.25 2.80 8.40 14.00

☐ 147, Aug 75, JR(c);RA; V:Jackal, Tarantula 0.25 4.00 12.00 20.00

☐ 148, Sep 75, GK(c);RA; V:Jackal, Tarantula 0.25 4.00 12.00 20.00

☐ 149, Oct 75, GK(c); RA;D:Jackal;D(?): Spider-clone 0.25 28.00 84.00 140.00

☐ 150, Nov 75, GK; SpM attempts to determine if he is the clone or the original 0.25 15.00 45.00 75.00

☐ 151, Dec 75, JR; V:Shocker 0.25 12.00 36.00 60.00

☐ 152, Jan 76, GK(c);RA; V:Shocker 0.25 2.40 7.20 12.00

☐ 153, Feb 76, GK(c);RA ... 0.25 2.40 7.20 12.00

☐ 154, Mar 76, JR(c);SB; V:Sandman 0.25 2.40 7.20 12.00

☐ 155, Apr 76, JR(c);SB... 0.25 2.40 7.20 12.00

☐ 156, May 76, JR(c); RA;W:Betty Brant and Ned Leeds;1:Mirage 0.25 2.40 7.20 12.00

☐ 157, Jun 76, JR(c);RA; return of Dr. Octopus 0.25 2.40 7.20 12.00

☐ 158, Jul 76, GK(c);RA; V:Dr. Octopus;Hammerhead regains physical form..... 0.25 2.40 7.20 12.00

☐ 159, Aug 76, GK(c);RA; V:Dr. Octopus, Hammerhead 0.25 2.40 7.20 12.00

☐ 160, Sep 76, GK(c);RA; return of Spider-Mobile; V:Tinkerer 0.30 2.40 7.20 12.00

☐ 161, Oct 76, GK(c);RA; A:Nightcrawler, Punisher 0.30 4.80 14.40 24.00

☐ 162, Nov 76, RA;A:Punisher, Nightcrawler;1:Jigsaw 0.30 8.00 24.00 40.00

☐ 163, Dec 76, DC(c);RA; V:Kingpin 0.30 1.60 4.80 8.00

☐ 164, Jan 77, JR(c);RA; V:Kingpin 0.30 1.60 4.80 8.00

☐ 165, Feb 77, JR(c);RA; V:Stegron 0.30 1.60 4.80 8.00

☐ 166, Mar 77, JR(c);RA; V:Lizard, Stegron 0.30 1.60 4.80 8.00

☐ 167, Apr 77, JR(c);RA;1: Will o' the Wisp 0.30 1.60 4.80 8.00

☐ 168, May 77, RA;V:Will o' the Wisp 0.30 1.60 4.80 8.00

☐ 169, Jun 77, AM(c);RA; J. Jonah Jameson acquires photos showing Spider-Man disposing of clone's(?) body 0.30 1.60 4.80 8.00

☐ 170, Jul 77, RA;V: Dr. Faustus 0.30 1.60 4.80 8.00

☐ 171, Aug 77, RA; A:Nova 0.30 1.60 4.80 8.00

☐ 172, Sep 77, RA;1: Rocket Racer 0.30 1.60 4.80 8.00

☐ 173, Oct 77, RA;V: Molten Man 0.30 1.60 4.80 8.00

☐ 174, Nov 77, RA;V:Hitman; A:Punisher 0.35 4.00 12.00 20.00

☐ 175, Dec 77, RA;V:Hitman; A:Punisher 0.35 4.00 12.00 20.00

☐ 176, Jan 78, RA;1:third Green Goblin 0.35 1.60 4.80 8.00

☐ 177, Feb 78, RA;V:third Green Goblin, Silvermane 0.35 1.60 4.80 8.00

☐ 178, Mar 78, RA;V:third Green Goblin, Silvermane 0.35 1.60 4.80 8.00

☐ 179, Apr 78, RA;V:third Green Goblin, Silvermane 0.35 1.60 4.80 8.00

☐ 180, May 78, RA;V:third Green Goblin, Silvermane; A:second Green Goblin (Harry Osborn) 0.35 1.60 4.80 8.00

☐ 181, Jun 78, GK(c);SB; ro:SpM 0.35 1.40 4.20 7.00

☐ 182, Jul 78, RA;V: Rocket Racer 0.35 1.40 4.20 7.00

☐ 183, Aug 78, RA;V: Rocket Racer, Tinkerer, Big Wheel 0.35 1.40 4.20 7.00

☐ 184, Sep 78, RA;V:second White Dragon 0.35 1.40 4.20 7.00

☐ 185, Oct 78, RA;V: second White Dragon, Dragon Gangs;Peter Parker graduates college 0.35 1.40 4.20 7.00

☐ 186, Nov 78, KP;V: Chameleon 0.35 1.40 4.20 7.00

☐ 187, Dec 78, KP(c);JSn; V:Electro;A:SHIELD, Captain America 0.35 1.40 4.20 7.00

☐ 188, Jan 79, DC(c);KP; V:Jigsaw 0.35 1.40 4.20 7.00

☐ 189, Feb 79, JBy;A: Man-Wolf 0.35 1.40 4.20 7.00

☐ 190, Mar 79, KP(c);JBy; A:Man-Wolf 0.35 1.40 4.20 7.00

☐ 191, Apr 79, AM(c);KP; V:Spencer Smythe and Spider Slayer 0.35 1.40 4.20 7.00

☐ 192, May 79, KP;V: The Fly;D:Spencer Smythe 0.40 1.40 4.20 7.00

☐ 193, Jun 79, KP;V: The Fly 0.40 1.40 4.20 7.00

☐ 194, Jul 79, AM(c); KP;1:Black Cat 0.40 1.40 4.20 7.00

☐ 195, Aug 79, AM(c);KP; O:Black Cat;apparent death of Aunt May 0.40 1.40 4.20 7.00

☐ 196, Sep 79, KP(c);AM; V:Kingpin, Mysterio 0.40 1.40 4.20 7.00

	ORIG.	GOOD	FINE	N-MINT
197, Oct 79, KP; V:Kingpin	0.40	1.40	4.20	7.00
198, Nov 79, KP(c); SB;V:Mysterio	0.40	1.40	4.20	7.00
199, Dec 79, KP(c); SB;V:Mysterio	0.40	1.40	4.20	7.00
200, Jan 80, JR(c);KP; ro:SpM;D:unnamed burglar that shot Uncle Ben;Aunt May revealed to be alive	0.75	6.00	18.00	30.00
201, Feb 80, JR(c);KP; A:Punisher	0.40	5.00	15.00	25.00
202, Mar 80, JR(c);KP; A:Punisher	0.40	5.00	15.00	25.00
203, Apr 80, JR(c);KP; A:Dazzler	0.40	1.00	3.00	5.00
204, May 80, JR2(c);KP; A:Black Cat	0.40	1.00	3.00	5.00
205, Jun 80, AM(c); KP;A:Black Cat	0.40	1.00	3.00	5.00
206, Jul 80, AM(c)	0.40	1.00	3.00	5.00
207, Aug 80, JM;V: Mesmero	0.40	1.00	3.00	5.00
208, Sep 80, JR2/AM; O&1:Fusion	0.50	1.00	3.00	5.00
209, Oct 80, V:Kraven; 1:Calypso	0.50	1.00	3.00	5.00
210, Nov 80, JR2; 1:Madame Web	0.50	1.00	3.00	5.00
211, Dec 80, JR2; A:Sub-Mariner	0.50	1.00	3.00	5.00
212, Jan 81, JR2; 1&O:Hydro-Man	0.50	1.00	3.00	5.00
213, Feb 81, JR2; V:Wizard	0.50	1.00	3.00	5.00
214, Mar 81, JR2; V:Frightful Four; A:Sub-Mariner	0.50	1.00	3.00	5.00
215, Apr 81	0.50	1.00	3.00	5.00
216, May 81	0.50	1.00	3.00	5.00
217, Jun 81	0.50	1.00	3.00	5.00
218, Jul 81	0.50	1.00	3.00	5.00
219, Aug 81	0.50	1.00	3.00	5.00
220, Sep 81, A:Moon Knight	0.50	1.00	3.00	5.00
221, Oct 81	0.50	1.00	3.00	5.00
222, Nov 81	0.50	1.00	3.00	5.00
223, Dec 81	0.50	1.00	3.00	5.00
224, Jan 82	0.60	1.00	3.00	5.00
225, Feb 82	0.60	1.00	3.00	5.00
226, Mar 82, JR2; Black Cat	0.60	1.00	3.00	5.00
227, Apr 82, JR2; Black Cat	0.60	1.00	3.00	5.00
228, May 82, JR2	0.60	1.00	3.00	5.00
229, Jun 82, JR2	0.60	1.00	3.00	5.00
230, Jul 82, JR2	0.60	1.00	3.00	5.00
231, Aug 82, JR2	0.60	1.00	3.00	5.00
232, Sep 82, JR2	0.60	1.00	3.00	5.00
233, Oct 82, JR2	0.60	1.00	3.00	5.00
234, Nov 82	0.60	1.00	3.00	5.00
235, Dec 82	0.60	1.00	3.00	5.00
236, Jan 83	0.60	1.00	3.00	5.00
237, Feb 83	0.60	1.00	3.00	5.00
238, Mar 83, 1:Hobgoblin	0.60	12.00	36.00	60.00
239, Apr 83	0.60	6.00	18.00	30.00
240, May 83	0.60	1.00	3.00	5.00
241, Jun 83	0.60	1.00	3.00	5.00
242, Jul 83	0.60	1.00	3.00	5.00
243, Aug 83	0.60	1.00	3.00	5.00
244, Sep 83	0.60	1.60	4.80	8.00
245, Oct 83	0.60	1.60	4.80	8.00
246, Nov 83	0.60	1.00	3.00	5.00

	ORIG.	GOOD	FINE	N-MINT
247, Dec 83	0.60	1.00	3.00	5.00
248, Jan 84	0.60	1.00	3.00	5.00
249, Feb 84	0.60	1.60	4.80	8.00
250, Mar 84	0.60	2.00	6.00	10.00
251, Apr 84	0.60	1.60	4.80	8.00
252, May 84, new costume	0.60	6.00	18.00	30.00
253, Jun 84, Rose	0.60	2.40	7.20	12.00
254, Jul 84	0.60	1.20	3.60	6.00
255, Aug 84	0.60	1.20	3.60	6.00
256, Sep 84	0.60	1.20	3.60	6.00
257, Oct 84	0.60	1.20	3.60	6.00
258, Nov 84	0.60	1.20	3.60	6.00
259, Dec 84	0.60	1.20	3.60	6.00
260, Jan 85	0.60	1.20	3.60	6.00
261, Feb 85	0.60	1.20	3.60	6.00
262, Mar 85	0.60	1.20	3.60	6.00
263, Apr 85	0.65	1.00	3.00	5.00
264, May 85	0.65	1.00	3.00	5.00
265, Jun 85, 1:Silver Sable	0.65	3.20	9.60	16.00
265, 2nd printing	1.25	0.25	0.75	1.25
266, Jul 85	0.65	1.00	3.00	5.00
267, Aug 85	0.65	1.00	3.00	5.00
268, Sep 85, Secret Wars II	0.65	1.00	3.00	5.00
269, Oct 85	0.65	1.00	3.00	5.00
270, Nov 85	0.65	1.00	3.00	5.00
271, Dec 85	0.65	1.00	3.00	5.00
272, Jan 86	0.65	1.00	3.00	5.00
273, Feb 86, Secret Wars II	0.75	2.00	6.00	10.00
274, Mar 86, Secret Wars II	0.75	1.00	3.00	5.00
275, Apr 86, O:SpM	1.25	1.60	4.80	8.00
276, May 86	0.75	0.80	2.40	4.00
277, Jun 86	0.75	0.80	2.40	4.00
278, Jul 86	0.75	0.50	1.50	2.50
279, Aug 86	0.75	0.80	2.40	4.00
280, Sep 86	0.75	0.80	2.40	4.00
281, Oct 86	0.75	0.80	2.40	4.00
282, Nov 86	0.75	0.80	2.40	4.00
283, Dec 86	0.75	0.80	2.40	4.00
284, Jan 87, A:Punisher	0.75	3.00	9.00	15.00
285, Feb 87, Punisher	0.75	4.00	12.00	20.00
286, Mar 86	0.75	1.60	4.80	8.00
287, Apr 87, Erik Larsen	0.75	2.40	7.20	12.00
288, May 87	0.75	1.60	4.80	8.00
289, Jun 87, Hobgoblin unmasked	1.25	5.60	16.80	28.00
290, Jul 87, proposal	0.75	1.40	4.20	7.00
291, Aug 87	0.75	1.20	3.60	6.00
292, Sep 87	0.75	1.20	3.60	6.00
293, Oct 87, V:Kraven	0.75	2.00	6.00	10.00
294, Nov 87, V:Kraven	0.75	2.00	6.00	10.00
295, Dec 87, BSz(c)	0.75	1.00	3.00	5.00
296, Jan 88, V:Dr. Octopus	0.75	1.00	3.00	5.00
297, Feb 88, V:Dr. Octopus	0.75	1.00	3.00	5.00
298, Mar 88, TMc	0.75	10.00	30.00	50.00
299, Apr 88, TMc	0.75	7.20	21.60	36.00
300, May 88, TMc	1.50	16.00	48.00	80.00
301, Jun 88, TMc	1.00	4.00	12.00	20.00
302, Jul 88, TMc	1.00	4.00	12.00	20.00
303, Aug 88, TMc	1.00	4.00	12.00	20.00
304, Sep 88, TMc	1.00	4.00	12.00	20.00
305, Sep 88, TMc	1.00	4.00	12.00	20.00
306, Oct 88, TMc	1.00	3.00	9.00	15.00
307, Oct 88, TMc	1.00	3.00	9.00	15.00
308, Nov 88, TMc	1.00	3.00	9.00	15.00
309, Nov 88, TMc	1.00	3.00	9.00	15.00

	ORIG.	GOOD	FINE	N-MINT
☐ 310, Dec 88, TMc............ 1.00		3.00	9.00	15.00
☐ 311, Jan 89, TMc Inferno1.00		2.40	7.20	12.00
☐ 312, Feb 89, TMc Inferno1.00		2.40	7.20	12.00
☐ 313, Mar 89, TMc Inferno1.00		2.40	7.20	12.00
☐ 314, Apr 89, TMc 1.00		2.40	7.20	12.00
☐ 315, May 89, TMc 1.00		2.40	7.20	12.00
☐ 316, Jun 89, TMc 1.00		3.60	10.80	18.00
☐ 317, Jul 89, TMc 1.00		3.20	9.60	16.00
☐ 318, Aug 89, TMc 1.00		3.20	9.60	16.00
☐ 319, Sep 89, TMc........... 1.00		2.40	7.20	12.00
☐ 320, Sep 89, TMc........... 1.00		2.00	6.00	10.00
☐ 321, Oct 89, TMc 1.00		2.00	6.00	10.00
☐ 322, Oct 89, TMc 1.00		2.00	6.00	10.00
☐ 323, Nov 89, TMc 1.00		2.00	6.00	10.00
☐ 324, Nov 89, TMc(c) 1.00		2.00	6.00	10.00
☐ 325, Nov 89, TMc 1.00		2.00	6.00	10.00
☐ 326, Dec 89, Acts of Vengeance 1.00		1.00	3.00	5.00
☐ 327, Dec 89, Acts of Vengeance;cosmic Spider-Man 1.00		1.20	3.60	6.00
☐ 328, Jan 90, Acts of Vengeance;TMc;Hulk 1.00		2.40	7.20	12.00
☐ 329, Feb 90, Acts of Vengeance 1.00		1.60	4.80	8.00
☐ 330, Mar 90, Punisher ... 1.00		1.60	4.80	8.00
☐ 331, Apr 90, Punisher.... 1.00		1.60	4.80	8.00
☐ 332, May 90, Venom 1.00		2.00	6.00	10.00
☐ 333, Jun 90, Venom....... 1.00		2.00	6.00	10.00
☐ 334, Jul 90, Sinister Six . 1.00		1.00	3.00	5.00
☐ 335, Jul 90, Sinister Six . 1.00		0.60	1.80	3.00
☐ 336, Aug 90, Sinister Six1.00		0.40	1.20	2.00
☐ 337, Aug 90, Sinister Six1.00		0.40	1.20	2.00
☐ 338, Sep 90, Sinister Six 1.00		0.40	1.20	2.00
☐ 339, Sep 90, Sinister Six 1.00		0.40	1.20	2.00
☐ 340, Oct 90 .... 1.00		0.40	1.20	2.00
☐ 341, Nov 90, Powerless . 1.00		0.40	1.20	2.00
☐ 342, Dec 90, Powerless . 1.00		0.40	1.20	2.00
☐ 343, Jan 91 .... 1.00		0.40	1.20	2.00
☐ 344, Feb 91, Carnage 1.00		2.40	7.20	12.00
☐ 345, Mar 91, Carnage 1.00		3.00	9.00	15.00
☐ 346, Apr 91, Venom....... 1.00		1.60	4.80	8.00
☐ 347, May 91, Venom...... 1.00		1.60	4.80	8.00
☐ 348, Jun 91, Avengers ... 1.00		0.40	1.20	2.00
☐ 349, Jul 91 .... 1.00		0.40	1.20	2.00
☐ 350, Aug 91, V:Dr. Doom 1.50		0.60	1.80	3.00
☐ 351, Sep 91 .... 1.00		0.30	0.90	1.50
☐ 352, Oct 91 .... 1.00		0.30	0.90	1.50
☐ 353, Nov 91 .... 1.00		0.30	0.90	1.50
☐ 354, Nov 91 .... 1.00		0.30	0.90	1.50
☐ 355, Dec 91, Punisher; Moon Knight;others 1.00		0.30	0.90	1.50
☐ 356, Dec 91, Punisher; Moon Knight;others 1.00		0.30	0.90	1.50
☐ 357, Jan 92, Punisher; Moon Knight;others 1.00		0.30	0.90	1.50
☐ 358, Jan 92, Punisher; Moon Knight;others 1.00		0.30	0.90	1.50
☐ 359, Feb 92 .... 1.25		0.30	0.90	1.50
☐ 360, Mar 92 .... 1.25		2.00	6.00	10.00
☐ 361, Apr 92, Carnage 1.25		4.40	13.20	22.00
☐ 361, 2nd printing 1.25		0.80	2.40	4.00
☐ 362, May 92, Carnage 1.25		2.80	8.40	14.00
☐ 362, 2nd printing 1.25		0.25	0.75	1.25
☐ 363, Jun 92, Carnage..... 1.25		2.40	7.20	12.00
☐ 364, Jul 92 .... 1.25		0.40	1.20	2.00
☐ 365, Aug 92, hologram cover 3.95		1.00	3.00	5.00
☐ 366, Sep 92 .... 1.25		0.35	1.05	1.75
☐ 367, Oct 92 .... 1.25		0.35	1.05	1.75
☐ 368, Nov 92 .... 1.25		0.35	1.05	1.75
☐ 369, Nov 92 .... 1.25		0.35	1.05	1.75
☐ 370, Dec 92 ....1.25		0.35	1.05	1.75
☐ 371, Dec 92 ....1.25		0.35	1.05	1.75
☐ 372, Jan 93....................1.25		0.35	1.05	1.75
☐ 373, Jan 93....................1.25		0.35	1.05	1.75
☐ 374, Feb 93....................1.25		0.35	1.05	1.75
☐ 375, Mar 93, foil cover ...3.95		1.00	3.00	5.00
☐ 376, Apr 93....................1.25		0.35	1.05	1.75
☐ 377, May 93...................1.25		0.35	1.05	1.75
☐ 378, Jun 93, Maximum Carnage 1.25		0.35	1.05	1.75
☐ 379, Jul 93, Maximum Carnage 1.25		0.35	1.05	1.75
☐ 380, Aug 93, Maximum Carnage 1.25		0.35	1.05	1.75
☐ 381, Sep 93, V:Hulk........1.25		0.35	1.05	1.75
☐ 382, Oct 93 ....1.25		0.35	1.05	1.75
☐ 383, Nov 93 ....1.25		0.35	1.05	1.75
☐ 384, Dec 93 ....1.25		0.35	1.05	1.75
☐ 385, Jan 94....................1.25		0.35	1.05	1.75
☐ 386, Feb 94....................1.25		0.70	2.10	3.50
☐ 387, Mar 94...................1.25		0.60	1.80	3.00
☐ 388, Apr 94....................2.25		0.50	1.50	2.50
☐ 388, Apr 94, foil cover 2.95		0.59	1.77	2.95
☐ 389, May 94...................1.50		0.30	0.90	1.50
☐ 390, Jun 94 ....1.50		0.30	0.90	1.50
☐ 390, Jun 94, poster, print 2.95		0.59	1.77	2.95
☐ 391, Jul 94.....................1.50		0.30	0.90	1.50
☐ 392, Aug 94 ....1.50		0.30	0.90	1.50
☐ 393, Sep 94 ....1.50		0.30	0.90	1.50
☐ 394, Oct 94 ....1.50		0.70	2.10	3.50
☐ 394, Oct 94, Enhanced cover; flip book 2.95		0.59	1.77	2.95
☐ 395, Nov 94 ....1.50		0.30	0.90	1.50
☐ 396, Dec 94 ....1.50		0.30	0.90	1.50
☐ 397, Jan 95, flip book with illustrated story from *The Ultimate Spider-Man* back-up 2.25		0.45	1.35	2.25
☐ 398, Feb 95....................1.50		0.30	0.90	1.50
☐ 399, Mar 95 ....1.50		0.30	0.90	1.50
☐ 400, Apr 95, enhanced second cover 3.95		0.79	2.37	3.95
☐ 400, Apr 95....................2.95		0.59	1.77	2.95
☐ 400, 95, white cover edition (no ads, back-up story)		4.00	12.00	20.00
☐ 401, May 95 ....1.50		0.30	0.90	1.50
☐ 402, Jun 95 ....1.50		0.30	0.90	1.50
☐ 403, Jul 95.....................1.50		0.30	0.90	1.50
☐ 404, Aug 95, "Maximum Clonage" Part 3 of 6 ....1.50		0.30	0.90	1.50
☐ 405, Sep 95, "Exiled" Part 2 of 4 ....1.50		0.30	0.90	1.50
☐ 406, Oct 95, I:Doctor Octopus II;OverPower cards inserted;(continues in *Amazing Scarlet Spider*) 1.50		0.30	0.90	1.50
☐ 407, Jan 96, A:Sandman, Silver Sable, Human Torch................1.50		0.30	0.90	1.50
☐ 408, Feb 96, "Media Blizzard" Part 2 of 3 ....1.50		0.30	0.90	1.50
☐ 409, Mar 96, "Return of Kaine" Part 3 of 4 ....1.50		0.30	0.90	1.50
☐ 410, Apr 96, "Web of Carnage" Part 2 of 4 ....1.50		0.30	0.90	1.50
☐ 411, May 96, "Blood Brothers" Part 2 of 6 ....1.50		0.30	0.90	1.50
☐ 412, Jun 96, "Blood Brothers" Part 6 of 6 ....1.50		0.30	0.90	1.50

AMAZING SPIDER-MAN 30TH ANNIVERSARY POSTER MAGAZINE

	ORIG.	GOOD	FINE	N-MINT
☐ 0 ....3.95		0.79	2.37	3.95

	ORIG.	GOOD	FINE	N-MINT

AMAZING SPIDER-MAN ANNUAL/SPECIAL

☐ 1, 64, SD;1:Sinister Six (Dr. Octopus, Vulture, Electro, Sandman, Mysterio, Kraven)
.... 0.25 100.00 300.00 500.00

☐ 2, 65, SD;A:Dr. Strange; also reprints *Amazing Spider-Man* #1, 2, and 5 0.25 36.00 108.00 180.00

☐ 3, Nov 66, JR/DH;V:Hulk; A:Avengers, Daredevil
.... 0.25 14.00 42.00 70.00

☐ 4, Nov 67, V:Mysterio and Wizard;A:Torch
.... 0.25 12.00 36.00 60.00

☐ 5, Nov 68, JR;A:Red Skull;fate of Peter Parker's parents revealed 0.25 13.00 39.00 65.00

☐ 6, Nov 69, reprints stories from *Amazing Spider-Man* #8, *Annual* #1, and *Fantastic Four Annual* #1
.... 0.25 2.00 6.00 10.00

☐ 7, Dec 70, JR(c);SD; reprints stories from *Amazing Spider-Man* #1, 2, and 38
.... 0.25 2.00 6.00 10.00

☐ 8, Dec 71, reprints stories from *Amazing Spider-Man* #46 and 50 and *Tales to Astonish* #57
.... 0.25 2.00 6.00 10.00

☐ 9, JR;reprints *Spectacular Spider-Man* (magazine) #2
.... 0.35 1.60 4.80 8.00

☐ 10, Sep 76, GK;O&1: Human Fly
.... 0.50 1.60 4.80 8.00

☐ 11, 77, GK(c);DP 0.50 1.60 4.80 8.00

☐ 12, 78, JBy(c);reprints *Amazing Spider-Man* #119 and 120 .... 0.60 1.20 3.60 6.00

☐ 13, 79, KP(c);JBy/TA; V:Dr. Octopus
.... 0.75 1.20 3.60 6.00

☐ 14, 80, FM;A:Dr. Strange; V:Dr. Doom
.... 0.75 2.40 7.20 12.00

☐ 15, Dec 81, FM; Punisher 0.75 6.00 18.00 30.00

☐ 16, Dec 82, 1:new Captain Marvel
.... 1.00 1.00 3.00 5.00

☐ 17, Dec 83 .... 1.00 0.80 2.40 4.00

☐ 18, Dec 84, W:JJJ 1.00 0.80 2.40 4.00

☐ 19, Nov 85 .... 1.25 0.80 2.40 4.00

☐ 20, Nov 86 .... 1.25 0.80 2.40 4.00

☐ 21, Sep 87, W:SPm direct-sale
.... 1.25 1.40 4.20 7.00

☐ 21, W:SPm newsstand ... 1.25 1.40 4.20 7.00

☐ 22, Sep 88, Evolutionary War;1:Speedball; A:Daredevil
.... 1.75 1.40 4.20 7.00

☐ 23, Sep 89, Atlantis Attacks
.... 2.00 0.80 2.40 4.00

☐ 24, Aug 90, GK;SD; Ant-Man
.... 2.00 0.60 1.80 3.00

☐ 25, Aug 91, Vibranium Vendetta
.... 2.00 0.40 1.20 2.00

☐ 26, 92 .... 2.25 0.45 1.35 2.25

☐ 27, 93, trading card 2.95 0.59 1.77 2.95

☐ 28, 94, Carnage 2.95 0.59 1.77 2.95

AMAZING SPIDER-MAN GIVEAWAYS

☐ 0, nn;child abuse;with New Mutants

☐ 0, nn;Crisis at Cape Canaveral; Aim toothpaste giveaway ....

☐ 0, nn;SpM vs. Dr. Octopus

☐ 1, (two different;both #1).

AMAZING SPIDER-MAN GOLDEN ALL-STAR BOOK
WESTERN PUBLISHING CO

☐ 0, (1977) 0.59

AMAZING SPIDER-MAN MANAGING MATERIALS
MARVEL

☐ 0, nn giveaway 0.20 0.60 1.00

AMAZING SPIDER-MAN SUPER SPECIAL, THE

☐ 1, 95, flip book;two of the stories continue in *Spider-Man Super Special* #1 .... 3.95 0.79 2.37 3.95

AMAZING SPIDER-MAN VS. THE PRODIGY!, THE

☐ 1, Feb 77, Planned Parenthood giveaway;miniature

AMAZING SPIDER-MAN: CHAOS IN CALGARY

☐ 4 .... 1.50 0.60 1.80 3.00

AMAZING SPIDER-MAN: DOUBLE TROUBLE!

☐ 2 .... 1.50 0.60 1.80 3.00

AMAZING SPIDER-MAN: HIT AND RUN!

☐ 3 .... 1.50 0.60 1.80 3.00

AMAZING SPIDER-MAN: SKATING ON THIN ICE!

☐ 1, 90 .... 1.25 0.60 1.80 3.00

AMAZING SPIDER-MAN: SOUL OF THE HUNTER

☐ 0, nn 5.95 1.19 3.57 5.95

AMAZING SPIDER-MAN: THE BIRTH OF A SUPER HERO!, THE

☐ 0, small reprint; was attached to *Eye* magazine

AMAZING STRIP
ANARCTIC

☐ 1, Feb 94, adult;b&w 2.95 0.59 1.77 2.95

☐ 2, Mar 94, adult;b&w 2.95 0.59 1.77 2.95

☐ 3, Apr 94, adult;b&w 2.95 0.59 1.77 2.95

☐ 4, May 94, adult;b&w 2.95 0.59 1.77 2.95

☐ 5, Jun 94, adult;b&w 2.95 0.59 1.77 2.95

☐ 6, Jul 94, adult;b&w 2.95 0.59 1.77 2.95

☐ 7, Aug 94, adult;b&w 2.95 0.59 1.77 2.95

☐ 8, Sep 94, adult;b&w 2.95 0.59 1.77 2.95

☐ 9, Nov 94, adult;b&w 2.95 0.59 1.77 2.95

☐ 10, Dec 94, adult;b&w; final issue
.... 2.95 0.59 1.77 2.95

AMAZING WAHZOO
SOLSON

☐ 1 .... 0.35 1.05 1.75

AMAZING WORLD OF SUPERMAN
DC

☐ 1, 73 .... 2.00 0.40 1.20 2.00

AMAZING X-MEN (mini-series)
MARVEL

☐ 1, Mar 95 .... 1.95 1.80 5.40 9.00

☐ 2, Apr 95 .... 1.95 1.00 3.00 5.00

☐ 3, May 95 .... 1.95 0.80 2.40 4.00

☐ 4, Jun 95 .... 1.95 0.80 2.40 4.00

AMAZON
DC/AMALGAM

☐ 1, Apr 96 .... 1.95 0.39 1.17 1.95

AMAZON ATTACK 3-D
3-D ZONE

☐ 0, nn 0.79 2.37 3.95

AMAZON TAILS
FANTACO

☐ 1 .... 2.95 0.59 1.77 2.95

☐ 2 .... 2.95 0.59 1.77 2.95

☐ 3 .... 2.95 0.59 1.77 2.95

AMAZON WARRIORS
AC

☐ 1, 89, b&w rep. 0.50 1.50 2.50

AMAZON WOMAN
FANTACO

☐ 1 .... 2.95 0.59 1.77 2.95

☐ 2 .... 2.95 0.59 1.77 2.95

☐ 4, 96 .... 2.95 0.59 1.77 2.95

AMAZON, THE
COMICO

☐ 1, Mar 89, mini-series 1.95 0.39 1.17 1.95

☐ 2, Apr 89, mini-series 1.95 0.39 1.17 1.95

☐ 3, May 89, mini-series 1.95 0.39 1.17 1.95

AMAZONS
FANTAGRAPHICS

☐ 1, b&w 0.59 1.77 2.95

	ORIG.	GOOD	FINE	N-MINT

AMBUSH BUG
DC

	ORIG.	GOOD	FINE	N-MINT
☐ 1, Jun 85	0.75	0.40	1.20	2.00
☐ 2, Jul 85	0.75	0.30	0.90	1.50
☐ 3, Aug 85	0.75	0.30	0.90	1.50
☐ 4, Sep 85	0.75	0.30	0.90	1.50

AMBUSH BUG NOTHING SPECIAL

	ORIG.	GOOD	FINE	N-MINT
☐ 1, Sep 92	2.50	0.50	1.50	2.50

AMBUSH BUG STOCKING STUFFER

	ORIG.	GOOD	FINE	N-MINT
☐ 1, Mar 86	1.25	0.25	0.75	1.25

AMERICA VS. THE JUSTICE SOCIETY

	ORIG.	GOOD	FINE	N-MINT
☐ 1, Jan 85, RTh script; ro: JSA	1.50	0.30	0.90	1.50
☐ 2, Feb 85, ro: All-Star Squadron	1.00	0.20	0.60	1.00
☐ 3, Mar 85, ro: Freedom Fighters, Wizard, pre-Crisis Per Degaton	1.00	0.20	0.60	1.00
☐ 4, Apr 85, ro: JSA revival, multiverse (Flash of Two Worlds); D: Prof. Zee and pre-crisis Per Degaton	1.00	0.20	0.60	1.00

AMERICA'S BEST TV COMICS
ABC

	ORIG.
☐ 0, 67, nn;promotional comic published by Marvel for ABC to promote Saturday morning cartoons	0.25

AMERICAN ARTISTS W.O.W. THE WORLD OF WARD
ALLIED

	GOOD	FINE	N-MINT
☐ 1, b&w;Bill Ward, Jack Cole reprints	0.79	2.37	3.95

AMERICAN BOOK, THE
DARK HORSE

	ORIG.	GOOD	FINE	N-MINT
☐ 1, Oct 88, O:American; b&w	1.19	3.57	5.95

AMERICAN FLAGG!
FIRST

	ORIG.	GOOD	FINE	N-MINT
☐ 1, Oct 83, HC	1.00	0.60	1.80	3.00
☐ 2, Nov 83, HC	1.00	0.40	1.20	2.00
☐ 3, Dec 83, HC	1.00	0.40	1.20	2.00
☐ 4, Jan 84, HC	1.00	0.40	1.20	2.00
☐ 5, Feb 84, HC	1.00	0.40	1.20	2.00
☐ 6, Mar 84, HC	1.00	0.30	0.90	1.50
☐ 7, Apr 84, HC	1.00	0.30	0.90	1.50
☐ 8, May 84, HC	1.00	0.30	0.90	1.50
☐ 9, Jun 84, HC	1.00	0.30	0.90	1.50
☐ 10, Jul 84, HC	1.00	0.30	0.90	1.50
☐ 11, Aug 84, HC	1.00	0.30	0.90	1.50
☐ 12, Sep 84, HC	1.00	0.30	0.90	1.50
☐ 13, Oct 84, HC	1.00	0.30	0.90	1.50
☐ 14, Nov 84, PB	1.25	0.25	0.75	1.25
☐ 15, Dec 84, HC	1.25	0.25	0.75	1.25
☐ 16, Jan 85, HC	1.25	0.25	0.75	1.25
☐ 17, Feb 85, HC	1.25	0.25	0.75	1.25
☐ 18, Mar 85, HC	1.25	0.25	0.75	1.25
☐ 19, Apr 85, HC	1.25	0.25	0.75	1.25
☐ 20, May 85, HC	1.25	0.25	0.75	1.25
☐ 21, Jun 85, HC;AMo(w)	1.25	0.25	0.75	1.25
☐ 22, Jul 85, HC;AMo(w)	1.25	0.25	0.75	1.25
☐ 23, Aug 85, HC;AMo(w)	1.25	0.25	0.75	1.25
☐ 24, Sep 85, HC;AMo(w)	1.25	0.25	0.75	1.25
☐ 25, Oct 85, HC;AMo(w)	1.25	0.25	0.75	1.25
☐ 26, Nov 85, HC;AMo(w)	1.25	0.25	0.75	1.25
☐ 27, Dec 85, HC(c); AMo(w)	1.25	0.25	0.75	1.25
☐ 28, Apr 86	1.25	0.25	0.75	1.25
☐ 29, May 86	1.25	0.25	0.75	1.25
☐ 30, Jun 86	1.25	0.25	0.75	1.25
☐ 31, Jul 86	1.25	0.25	0.75	1.25
☐ 32, Aug 86	1.25	0.25	0.75	1.25
☐ 33, Sep 86	1.25	0.25	0.75	1.25
☐ 34	1.25	0.25	0.75	1.25
☐ 35	1.25	0.25	0.75	1.25
☐ 36	1.25	0.25	0.75	1.25
☐ 37	1.25	0.25	0.75	1.25
☐ 38	1.25	0.25	0.75	1.25
☐ 39	1.25	0.25	0.75	1.25
☐ 40	1.25	0.25	0.75	1.25
☐ 41	1.25	0.25	0.75	1.25
☐ 42	1.25	0.25	0.75	1.25
☐ 43	1.25	0.25	0.75	1.25
☐ 44	1.25	0.25	0.75	1.25
☐ 45	1.25	0.25	0.75	1.25
☐ 46, apology		0.25	0.75	1.25
☐ 47		0.35	1.05	1.75
☐ 48		0.35	1.05	1.75
☐ 49		0.35	1.05	1.75
☐ 50		0.35	1.05	1.75

AMERICAN FLAGG! SPECIAL

	ORIG.	GOOD	FINE	N-MINT
☐ 1, Nov 86, HC;Time2	1.75	0.35	1.05	1.75

AMERICAN FREAK: A TALE OF THE UN-MEN
DC/VERTIGO

	ORIG.	GOOD	FINE	N-MINT
☐ 1, 94	1.95	0.39	1.17	1.95
☐ 2, 94	1.95	0.39	1.17	1.95
☐ 3, Apr 94	1.95	0.39	1.17	1.95
☐ 4, May 94	1.95	0.39	1.17	1.95
☐ 5, Jun 94	1.95	0.39	1.17	1.95

AMERICAN HEROES
PERSONALITY

	GOOD	FINE	N-MINT
☐ 1, b&w	0.59	1.77	2.95

AMERICAN PRIMITIVE
3-D ZONE

	GOOD	FINE	N-MINT
☐ 1, b&w;not 3-D	0.50	1.50	2.50

AMERICAN SPECIAL, THE
DARK HORSE

	ORIG.	GOOD	FINE	N-MINT
☐ 1, 90, b&w	2.25	0.45	1.35	2.25

AMERICAN SPLENDOR
PEKAR

	GOOD	FINE	N-MINT
☐ 1	2.00	6.00	10.00
☐ 2	1.00	3.00	5.00
☐ 3	1.00	3.00	5.00
☐ 4	1.00	3.00	5.00
☐ 5	1.00	3.00	5.00
☐ 6	0.60	1.80	3.00
☐ 7	0.60	1.80	3.00
☐ 8	0.60	1.80	3.00
☐ 9	0.60	1.80	3.00
☐ 10	0.60	1.80	3.00
☐ 11	0.60	1.80	3.00
☐ 12	0.60	1.80	3.00
☐ 13	0.70	2.10	3.50
☐ 14	0.70	2.10	3.50
☐ 15, (moves to Dark Horse)	0.70	2.10	3.50

AMERICAN SPLENDOR (was Pekar title)
DARK HORSE

	ORIG.	GOOD	FINE	N-MINT
☐ 17	4.95	0.99	2.97	4.95

AMERICAN SPLENDOR SPECIAL: A STEP OUT OF THE NEST

	ORIG.	GOOD	FINE	N-MINT
☐ 1, Aug 94, b&w	2.95	0.59	1.77	2.95

AMERICAN SPLENDOR: WINDFALL (mini-series)

	ORIG.	GOOD	FINE	N-MINT
☐ 1, 95, b&w	3.95	0.79	2.37	3.95
☐ 2, Oct 95, b&w	3.95	0.79	2.37	3.95

AMERICAN, THE

	ORIG.	GOOD	FINE	N-MINT
☐ 1, Aug 87, b&w	1.50	0.80	2.40	4.00
☐ 2, Oct 87	1.75	0.60	1.80	3.00
☐ 3, Dec 87	1.75	0.35	1.05	1.75
☐ 4, Apr 88	1.75	0.35	1.05	1.75
☐ 5, Jul 88	1.75	0.35	1.05	1.75
☐ 6, Sep 88	1.75	0.35	1.05	1.75
☐ 7, Oct 88	1.75	0.35	1.05	1.75
☐ 8, Feb 89	1.75	0.35	1.05	1.75

	ORIG.	GOOD	FINE	N-MINT

AMERICAN: LOST IN AMERICA, THE

	ORIG.	GOOD	FINE	N-MINT
1, Jul 92	2.50	0.50	1.50	2.50
2, Aug 92	2.50	0.50	1.50	2.50
3, Sep 92	2.50	0.50	1.50	2.50
4, Oct 92	2.50	0.50	1.50	2.50

AMERICOMICS
AC

	GOOD	FINE	N-MINT
1, Apr 83	0.60	1.80	3.00
2, Jun 83	0.40	1.20	2.00
3, Aug 83	0.40	1.20	2.00
4, Oct 83	0.40	1.20	2.00
5, Dec 83	0.35	1.05	1.75
6, Mar 84	0.35	1.05	1.75

AMERICOMICS SPECIAL

	GOOD	FINE	N-MINT
1, Jan 83	0.30	0.90	1.50

AMETHYST
DC

	GOOD	FINE	N-MINT
1, origin	0.30	0.90	1.50
2	0.24	0.72	1.20
3	0.24	0.72	1.20
4	0.24	0.72	1.20
5	0.24	0.72	1.20
6	0.24	0.72	1.20
7	0.24	0.72	1.20
8	0.24	0.72	1.20
9	0.24	0.72	1.20
10, EC	0.20	0.60	1.00
11, EC	0.20	0.60	1.00
12, EC	0.20	0.60	1.00

AMETHYST (2nd series)

	GOOD	FINE	N-MINT
1	0.20	0.60	1.00
2	0.20	0.60	1.00
3	0.20	0.60	1.00
4	0.20	0.60	1.00
5	0.20	0.60	1.00
6	0.20	0.60	1.00
7	0.20	0.60	1.00
8	0.20	0.60	1.00
9	0.20	0.60	1.00
10	0.20	0.60	1.00
11	0.20	0.60	1.00
12	0.20	0.60	1.00
13	0.20	0.60	1.00
14	0.20	0.60	1.00
15	0.20	0.60	1.00
16	0.20	0.60	1.00

AMETHYST (mini-series)

	GOOD	FINE	N-MINT
1, Nov 87	0.25	0.75	1.25
2, Dec 87	0.25	0.75	1.25
3, Jan 88	0.25	0.75	1.25
4, Feb 88	0.25	0.75	1.25

AMETHYST ANNUAL

	GOOD	FINE	N-MINT
1, Sep 84	0.25	0.75	1.25

AMETHYST SPECIAL

	GOOD	FINE	N-MINT
1, Oct 86	0.25	0.75	1.25

AMORA
EROS COMIX

	GOOD	FINE	N-MINT
1, adult;b&w	0.59	1.77	2.95

AMUSING STORIES
RENEGADE

	GOOD	FINE	N-MINT
1, b&w	0.40	1.20	2.00

AN AMERICAN TAIL: FIEVEL GOES WEST
MARVEL

	ORIG.	GOOD	FINE	N-MINT
1, movie	1.00	0.20	0.60	1.00
2, movie	1.00	0.20	0.60	1.00
3, movie	1.00	0.20	0.60	1.00

ANDREW VACHSS' UNDERGROUND
DARK HORSE

	ORIG.	GOOD	FINE	N-MINT
4, May 94, b&w	3.95	0.79	2.37	3.95

ANDROMEDA
SILVER SNAIL

	GOOD	FINE	N-MINT
1	0.40	1.20	2.00
2	0.40	1.20	2.00
3	0.40	1.20	2.00
4	0.40	1.20	2.00
5	0.40	1.20	2.00
6	0.40	1.20	2.00

ANGEL AND THE APE (1968-1969)
DC

	GOOD	FINE	N-MINT
1	7.00	21.00	35.00
2	4.00	12.00	20.00
3	4.00	12.00	20.00
4	4.00	12.00	20.00
5	4.00	12.00	20.00
6	4.00	12.00	20.00
7	4.00	12.00	20.00

ANGEL AND THE APE (1991)

	GOOD	FINE	N-MINT
1, Mar 91, Phil Foglio	0.20	0.60	1.00
2, Apr 91, Phil Foglio	0.20	0.60	1.00
3, May 91, Phil Foglio	0.20	0.60	1.00
4, Jun 91, Phil Foglio	0.20	0.60	1.00

ANGEL LOVE

	GOOD	FINE	N-MINT
1	0.20	0.60	1.00
2	0.20	0.60	1.00
3	0.20	0.60	1.00
4	0.20	0.60	1.00
5	0.20	0.60	1.00
6	0.20	0.60	1.00
7	0.20	0.60	1.00
8	0.20	0.60	1.00

ANGEL LOVE SPECIAL

	GOOD	FINE	N-MINT
1	0.25	0.75	1.25

ANGEL OF DEATH
INNOVATION

	GOOD	FINE	N-MINT
1, b&w	0.45	1.35	2.25
2, b&w	0.45	1.35	2.25
3, b&w	0.45	1.35	2.25
4, b&w	0.45	1.35	2.25

ANGELA
IMAGE

	ORIG.	GOOD	FINE	N-MINT
0, Jun 95, nn;promotional comic offered in conjunction with *Spawn* #25		7.00	21.00	35.00
1, Dec 94, story: NG; A:Spawn	2.25	2.00	6.00	10.00
2, Jan 95, story: NG; A: Spawn	2.25	1.60	4.80	8.00
3	2.25	1.20	3.60	6.00

ANGELA/GLORY: RAGE OF ANGELS

	ORIG.	GOOD	FINE	N-MINT
1, Mar 96	2.50	0.50	1.50	2.50

ANGRY SHADOWS
INNOVATION

	GOOD	FINE	N-MINT
1, b&w	0.99	2.97	4.95

ANGRYMAN
CALIBER

	ORIG.	GOOD	FINE	N-MINT
1	2.50	0.50	1.50	2.50
2	2.50	0.50	1.50	2.50
3	2.50	0.50	1.50	2.50

ICONOGRAFIX

	ORIG.	GOOD	FINE	N-MINT
1, b&w	2.50	0.50	1.50	2.50
2, b&w	2.50	0.50	1.50	2.50
3, b&w	2.50	0.50	1.50	2.50

ANIMA
DC

	ORIG.	GOOD	FINE	N-MINT
0, Oct 94	1.75	0.35	1.05	1.75
1, 94	1.75	0.35	1.05	1.75
2, 94	1.75	0.35	1.05	1.75
3, May 94	1.75	0.35	1.05	1.75
4, Jun 94	1.75	0.35	1.05	1.75

	ORIG.	GOOD	FINE	N-MINT
5, Jul 94	1.75	0.35	1.05	1.75
6, Aug 94	1.95	0.39	1.17	1.95
7, Sep 94	1.95	0.39	1.17	1.95
8, Nov 94	1.95	0.39	1.17	1.95
9, Dec 94	1.95	0.39	1.17	1.95
10, Jan 95	1.95	0.39	1.17	1.95
11, Feb 95	1.95	0.39	1.17	1.95
12, Mar 95	1.95	0.39	1.17	1.95
13, Apr 95	1.95	0.39	1.17	1.95
14, Jun 95	2.25	0.45	1.35	2.25
15, Jul 95	2.25	0.45	1.35	2.25

ANIMAL MAN

	ORIG.	GOOD	FINE	N-MINT
1, Sep 88, Morrison writer; BB(c)	1.25	2.80	8.40	14.00
2, Oct 88, BB(c)	1.25	2.00	6.00	10.00
3, Nov 88, BB(c)	1.25	1.20	3.60	6.00
4, Dec 88, BB(c)	1.25	1.20	3.60	6.00
5, Dec 88, BB(c) Road Runner-Coyote	1.25	2.40	7.20	12.00
6, Jan 89, BB(c) Invasion!	1.25	1.00	3.00	5.00
7, Jan 89, BB(c)	1.25	1.00	3.00	5.00
8, Feb 89, BB(c)	1.25	1.00	3.00	5.00
9, Mar 89, BB(c)	1.25	1.00	3.00	5.00
10, Apr 89, BB(c) A:Vixen	1.25	1.00	3.00	5.00
11, May 89, BB(c) A:Vixen	1.50	1.00	3.00	5.00
12, Jun 89, BB(c) A:Vixen	1.50	1.00	3.00	5.00
13, Jul 89, BB(c)	1.50	0.80	2.40	4.00
14, Aug 89, BB(c)	1.50	0.80	2.40	4.00
15, Sep 89, BB(c)	1.50	0.80	2.40	4.00
16, Oct 89, BB(c)	1.50	0.80	2.40	4.00
17, Nov 89, BB(c)	1.50	0.80	2.40	4.00
18, Dec 89, BB(c)	1.50	0.80	2.40	4.00
19, Jan 90, BB(c)	1.50	0.80	2.40	4.00
20, Feb 90, BB(c)	1.50	0.80	2.40	4.00
21, Mar 90, BB(c)	1.50	0.80	2.40	4.00
22, Apr 90, BB(c)	1.50	0.80	2.40	4.00
23, May 90, BB(c)	1.50	0.80	2.40	4.00
24, Jun 90, BB(c)	1.50	0.80	2.40	4.00
25, Jul 90, BB(c)	1.50	0.80	2.40	4.00
26, Aug 90, BB(c)	1.50	0.80	2.40	4.00
27, Sep 90, Milligan writer; BB(c)	1.50	0.40	1.20	2.00
28, Oct 90, Milligan writer; BB(c)	1.50	0.40	1.20	2.00
29, Nov 90, Milligan writer; BB(c)	1.50	0.40	1.20	2.00
30, Dec 90, Milligan writer; BB(c)	1.50	0.40	1.20	2.00
31, Jan 91, Milligan writer; BB(c)	1.50	0.40	1.20	2.00
32, Feb 91, Milligan writer; BB(c)	1.50	0.40	1.20	2.00
33, Mar 91, Veitch writer; BB(c)	1.50	0.40	1.20	2.00
34, Apr 91, Veitch writer; BB(c)	1.50	0.40	1.20	2.00
35, May 91, Veitch writer; BB(c)	1.50	0.40	1.20	2.00
36, Jun 91, Veitch writer; BB(c)	1.50	0.40	1.20	2.00
37, Jul 91, Veitch writer; BB(c)	1.50	0.40	1.20	2.00
38, Aug 91, Punisher parody;BB(c)	1.50	0.40	1.20	2.00
39, Sep 91	1.50	0.40	1.20	2.00
40, Oct 91	1.50	0.40	1.20	2.00
41, Nov 91	1.75	0.40	1.20	2.00
42, Dec 91	1.50	0.35	1.05	1.75

	ORIG.	GOOD	FINE	N-MINT
43, Jan 92	1.75	0.35	1.05	1.75
44, Feb 92	1.75	0.35	1.05	1.75
45, Mar 92	1.75	0.35	1.05	1.75
46, Apr 92	1.75	0.35	1.05	1.75
47, May 92	1.75	0.35	1.05	1.75
48, Jun 92	1.75	0.35	1.05	1.75
49, Jul 92	1.75	0.35	1.05	1.75
50, Aug 92	2.95	0.59	1.77	2.95
51, Sep 92	1.75	0.35	1.05	1.75
52, Oct 92	1.75	0.35	1.05	1.75
53, Nov 92	1.75	0.35	1.05	1.75
54, Dec 92	1.75	0.35	1.05	1.75
55, Jan 93, BB(c)	1.75	0.35	1.05	1.75
56, Feb 93	3.50	0.70	2.10	3.50

DC/VERTIGO

	ORIG.	GOOD	FINE	N-MINT
57		0.35	1.05	1.75
58		0.35	1.05	1.75
59		0.35	1.05	1.75
60, BB(c)	1.95	0.39	1.17	1.95
61	1.95	0.39	1.17	1.95
62	1.95	0.39	1.17	1.95
63	1.95	0.39	1.17	1.95
64	1.95	0.39	1.17	1.95
65	1.95	0.39	1.17	1.95
66	1.95	0.39	1.17	1.95
67	1.95	0.39	1.17	1.95
68	1.95	0.39	1.17	1.95
69	1.95	0.39	1.17	1.95
70, 94	1.95	0.39	1.17	1.95
71, May 94	1.95	0.39	1.17	1.95
72, Jun 94	1.95	0.39	1.17	1.95
73, Jul 94	1.95	0.39	1.17	1.95
74, Aug 94	1.95	0.39	1.17	1.95
75, Sep 94	1.95	0.39	1.17	1.95
76, Oct 94	1.95	0.39	1.17	1.95
77, Nov 94	1.95	0.39	1.17	1.95
78, Dec 94	1.95	0.39	1.17	1.95
79, Jan 95	1.95	0.39	1.17	1.95
80, Feb 95	1.95	0.39	1.17	1.95
81, Mar 95	1.95	0.39	1.17	1.95
82, Apr 95	1.95	0.39	1.17	1.95
83, May 95	2.25	0.45	1.35	2.25
84, Jun 95	2.25	0.45	1.35	2.25
85, Jul 95	2.25	0.45	1.35	2.25
86, Aug 95	2.25	0.45	1.35	2.25
87, Sep 95	2.25	0.45	1.35	2.25
88, Oct 95	2.25	0.45	1.35	2.25
89, Nov 95, final issue	2.25	0.45	1.35	2.25

ANIMAL MAN ANNUAL

	ORIG.	GOOD	FINE	N-MINT
1, Children's Crusade	3.95	0.79	2.37	3.95

ANIMAL MYSTIC (mini-series)
CRY FOR DAWN

	ORIG.	GOOD	FINE	N-MINT
1		5.00	15.00	25.00
1, limited edition with alternate cover and eight additional pages		8.00	24.00	40.00

SIRIUS ENTERTAINMENT

	ORIG.	GOOD	FINE	N-MINT
1, May 95, second printing with new cover; first printing was by Cry For Dawn;b&w	2.50	0.80	2.40	4.00
2, Jun 94, Was Cry For Dawn series;b&w	2.50	3.60	10.80	18.00
2, May 95, second printing with new cover;b&w	2.50	0.50	1.50	2.50
3, Oct 94, b&w	2.50	1.40	4.20	7.00
4, Aug 95, b&w	3.50	0.70	2.10	3.50
4, 95, b&w;limited edition	10.00	2.00	6.00	10.00

ANIMANIACS
DC

	ORIG.	GOOD	FINE	N-MINT
1, May 95	1.50	0.40	1.20	2.00
2, Jun 95	1.50	0.30	0.90	1.50

	ORIG.	GOOD	FINE	N-MINT
3, Jul 95	1.50	0.30	0.90	1.50
4, Aug 95	1.50	0.30	0.90	1.50
5, Sep 95	1.50	0.30	0.90	1.50
6, Oct 95	1.50	0.30	0.90	1.50
7, Nov 95	1.50	0.30	0.90	1.50
8, Dec 95	1.50	0.30	0.90	1.50
9, Jan 96, "Pulp Fiction" parody cover	1.50	0.30	0.90	1.50
10, Feb 96	1.50	0.30	0.90	1.50
11, Mar 96, Brain duplicates himself	1.50	0.30	0.90	1.50
12, Apr 96	1.50	0.30	0.90	1.50
13, May 96	1.75	0.35	1.05	1.75
14, Jun 96	1.75	0.35	1.05	1.75

ANIMANIACS: A CHRISTMAS SPECIAL

	ORIG.	GOOD	FINE	N-MINT
0, Dec 94	1.50	0.50	1.50	2.50

ANIMAX
STAR

	ORIG.	GOOD	FINE	N-MINT
1	0.75	0.15	0.45	0.75
2	0.75	0.15	0.45	0.75
3	0.75	0.15	0.45	0.75
4	0.75	0.15	0.45	0.75

ANIMISM
CENTURION

	GOOD	FINE	N-MINT
1	0.30	0.90	1.50

ANIVERSE, THE
WEEBEE

	GOOD	FINE	N-MINT
1	0.39	1.17	1.95
2	0.39	1.17	1.95

ANNE RICE'S QUEEN OF THE DAMNED
INNOVATION

	ORIG.	GOOD	FINE	N-MINT
1, 91, Adapts novel; cardstock cover	2.50	0.50	1.50	2.50
2, 92, Adapts novel; cardstock cover	2.50	0.50	1.50	2.50
3, 92, Adapts novel; cardstock cover	2.50	0.50	1.50	2.50
3, 92, Adapts novel; cardstock cover	2.50	0.50	1.50	2.50
4, 92, Adapts novel; cardstock cover	2.50	0.50	1.50	2.50
5, 92, Adapts novel; cardstock cover	2.50	0.50	1.50	2.50
6, 93, Adapts novel; cardstock cover	2.50	0.50	1.50	2.50
7, 93, Adapts novel; cardstock cover	2.50	0.50	1.50	2.50
8, Jul 93, Adapts novel; cardstock cover	2.50	0.50	1.50	2.50
9, Sep 93, Adapts novel; cardstock cover	2.50	0.50	1.50	2.50
10, Nov 93, Adapts novel; cardstock cover	2.50	0.50	1.50	2.50
11, Dec 93, Adapts novel; cardstock cover	2.50	0.50	1.50	2.50

ANNE RICE'S THE VAMPIRE LESTAT

	ORIG.	GOOD	FINE	N-MINT
1, Jan 90, 1st printing	2.50	4.00	12.00	20.00
1, 2nd printing		1.20	3.60	6.00
2, 1st printing	2.50	3.20	9.60	16.00
2, 90, 2nd printing	2.50	0.50	1.50	2.50
3, May 90, 1st printing	2.50	1.60	4.80	8.00
3, 2nd printing		0.50	1.50	2.50
4, Jun 90, Cardstock cover	2.50	1.20	3.60	6.00
5, Sep 90, Cardstock cover	2.50	1.00	3.00	5.00
6, Nov 90, Cardstock cover	2.50	0.80	2.40	4.00
7, Jan 91, Cardstock cover	2.50	0.80	2.40	4.00
8, Mar 91, Cardstock cover	2.50	0.80	2.40	4.00
9, May 91, Cardstock cover	2.50	0.80	2.40	4.00
10, 91, Cardstock cover	2.50	0.80	2.40	4.00
11, 91, Cardstock cover	2.50	0.80	2.40	4.00
12, 91, Cardstock cover;final issue	2.50	0.80	2.40	4.00

ANNEX (mini-series)
MARVEL

	ORIG.	GOOD	FINE	N-MINT
1, Aug 94, Crucible of Power	1.75	0.35	1.05	1.75
2, Sep 94, Crucible of Power	1.75	0.35	1.05	1.75
3, Oct 94, Crucible of Power	1.75	0.35	1.05	1.75
4, Nov 94, Crucible of Power	1.75	0.35	1.05	1.75

ANNIE

	ORIG.	GOOD	FINE	N-MINT
1, Oct 82, movie story	0.60	0.20	0.60	1.00
2, Nov 82, movie story	0.60	0.20	0.60	1.00

ANNIE SPRINKLE IS MISS TIMED
RIP OFF

	ORIG.	GOOD	FINE	N-MINT
1, Sep 91, adult;b&w	2.50	0.50	1.50	2.50
2, Oct 91, adult;b&w	2.50	0.50	1.50	2.50
3, Nov 91, adult;b&w	2.50	0.50	1.50	2.50
4, Dec 91, adult;b&w	2.50	0.50	1.50	2.50

ANT BOY
STEELDRAGON

	GOOD	FINE	N-MINT
1, b&w	0.35	1.05	1.75
2, b&w	0.35	1.05	1.75

ANTARES CIRCLE
ANTARCTIC

	ORIG.	GOOD	FINE	N-MINT
1, b&w	1.95	0.39	1.17	1.95
2, b&w	1.95	0.39	1.17	1.95

ANTHRO
DC

	ORIG.	GOOD	FINE	N-MINT
1, Aug 68	0.12	9.00	27.00	45.00
2, Oct 68	0.12	6.00	18.00	30.00
3, Dec 68	0.12	5.00	15.00	25.00
4, Feb 69	0.12	5.00	15.00	25.00
5, Apr 69	0.12	5.00	15.00	25.00
6, Aug 69	0.12	5.00	15.00	25.00

ANTI SOCIAL FOR THE DISABLED
HELPLESS ANGER

	GOOD	FINE	N-MINT
1, b&w	1.00	3.00	5.00

ANTI SOCIAL JR.

	GOOD	FINE	N-MINT
0, nn b&w;20 pages	0.35	1.05	1.75

ANTI-HITLER COMICS
NEW ENGLAND

	GOOD	FINE	N-MINT
1, b&w reprints	0.55	1.65	2.75
2, b&w reprints	0.55	1.65	2.75

ANTI-SOCIAL
HELPLESS ANGER

	GOOD	FINE	N-MINT
1, b&w	0.40	1.20	2.00
2	0.50	1.50	2.50
3	0.50	1.50	2.50
4	0.55	1.65	2.75

ANTON'S DREKBOOK
EROS COMIX

	GOOD	FINE	N-MINT
1, adult;b&w	0.50	1.50	2.50

ANYTHING GOES
COMICS JOURNAL

	GOOD	FINE	N-MINT
1, color	0.40	1.20	2.00
2, color	0.40	1.20	2.00
3, color	0.40	1.20	2.00
4, color	0.40	1.20	2.00
5, TMNT;b&w	1.00	3.00	5.00
6, b&w	0.40	1.20	2.00

	ORIG.	GOOD	FINE	N-MINT

APACHE DICK
ETERNITY
	ORIG.	GOOD	FINE	N-MINT
☐ 1, adult;b&w		0.45	1.35	2.25
☐ 2, adult;b&w		0.45	1.35	2.25
☐ 3, adult;b&w		0.45	1.35	2.25
☐ 4, adult;b&w		0.45	1.35	2.25

APATHY KAT
EXPRESS/ENTITY
| ☐ 1, 95, b&w | 2.75 | 0.55 | 1.65 | 2.75 |
| ☐ 2, 96, b&w | 2.75 | 0.55 | 1.65 | 2.75 |

APE CITY
ADVENTURE
☐ 1, b&w;Planet of Apes		0.50	1.50	2.50
☐ 2, b&w;Planet of Apes		0.50	1.50	2.50
☐ 3, b&w;Planet of Apes		0.50	1.50	2.50
☐ 4, b&w;Planet of Apes		0.50	1.50	2.50

APE NATION (mini-series)
☐ 1, Feb 91, Alien Nation; Planet of Apes;color

	ORIG.	GOOD	FINE	N-MINT
	2.50	0.50	1.50	2.50
☐ 1, limited edition; Peter Hsu(c)	1.19	3.57	5.95	
☐ 2, Apr 91	2.50	0.50	1.50	2.50
☐ 3, May 91	2.50	0.50	1.50	2.50
☐ 4, Jun 91	2.50	0.50	1.50	2.50

APEX
AZTEC
| ☐ 1, b&w | | 0.40 | 1.20 | 2.00 |

APEX PROJECT, THE
STELLAR
| ☐ 1, b&w | | 0.20 | 0.60 | 1.00 |
| ☐ 2, b&w | | 0.20 | 0.60 | 1.00 |

APOCALYPSE
APOCALYPSE
☐ 1		0.79	2.37	3.95
☐ 2		0.79	2.37	3.95
☐ 3		0.79	2.37	3.95
☐ 4		0.79	2.37	3.95
☐ 5		0.79	2.37	3.95

APOCALYPSE STRIKEFILES
MARVEL
| ☐ 0 | | 1.00 | 3.00 | 5.00 |

APPARITION: ABANDONED, THE
CALIBER
☐ 1, 95, one-shot;prestige format
| | 3.95 | 0.79 | 2.37 | 3.95 |

APPARITION: VISITATIONS, THE
| ☐ 1, Aug 95, one-shot | 2.95 | 0.59 | 1.77 | 2.95 |

APPLESEED BOOK FOUR
ECLIPSE
| ☐ 1, Japanese;b&w | | 0.70 | 2.10 | 3.50 |
| ☐ 2, Japanese;b&w | | 0.70 | 2.10 | 3.50 |

APPLESEED BOOK ONE
☐ 1, Japanese;b&w		2.00	6.00	10.00
☐ 2		1.20	3.60	6.00
☐ 3		1.00	3.00	5.00
☐ 4		1.00	3.00	5.00
☐ 5		1.00	3.00	5.00

APPLESEED BOOK THREE
☐ 1, Japanese;b&w		0.80	2.40	4.00
☐ 2		0.55	1.65	2.75
☐ 3		0.55	1.65	2.75
☐ 4		0.55	1.65	2.75
☐ 5		0.70	2.10	3.50

APPLESEED BOOK TWO
☐ 1, Japanese;b&w		1.40	4.20	7.00
☐ 2		1.00	3.00	5.00
☐ 3		0.60	1.80	3.00
☐ 4		0.60	1.80	3.00
☐ 5		0.60	1.80	3.00

APPLESEED DATABOOK
DARK HORSE
	ORIG.	GOOD	FINE	N-MINT
☐ 1, Apr 94, b&w	3.50	0.70	2.10	3.50
☐ 2, May 94, b&w	3.50	0.70	2.10	3.50

APRIL HORRORS
RIP OFF
| ☐ 1, Sep 93, b&w | 2.95 | 0.59 | 1.77 | 2.95 |

AQUAMAN
DC
☐ 1, Feb 62, 1:Quisp	0.12	110.00	330.00	550.00
☐ 2, Apr 62	0.12	60.00	180.00	300.00
☐ 3, Jun 62	0.12	35.00	105.00	175.00
☐ 4, Aug 62	0.12	20.00	60.00	100.00
☐ 5, Oct 62	0.12	20.00	60.00	100.00
☐ 6, Dec 62	0.12	16.00	48.00	80.00
☐ 7, Feb 63	0.12	16.00	48.00	80.00
☐ 8, Apr 63	0.12	16.00	48.00	80.00
☐ 9, Jun 63	0.12	16.00	48.00	80.00
☐ 10, Aug 63	0.12	16.00	48.00	80.00
☐ 11, Oct 63	0.12	15.00	45.00	75.00
☐ 12, Dec 63	0.12	10.00	30.00	50.00
☐ 13, Feb 64	0.12	10.00	30.00	50.00
☐ 14, Apr 64	0.12	10.00	30.00	50.00
☐ 15, Jun 64	0.12	10.00	30.00	50.00
☐ 16, Aug 64	0.12	10.00	30.00	50.00
☐ 17, Oct 64	0.12	10.00	30.00	50.00
☐ 18, Dec 64	0.12	10.00	30.00	50.00
☐ 19, Feb 65	0.12	10.00	30.00	50.00
☐ 20, Apr 65	0.12	10.00	30.00	50.00
☐ 21, Jun 65	0.12	6.00	18.00	30.00
☐ 22, Aug 65	0.12	6.00	18.00	30.00
☐ 23, Oct 65	0.12	6.00	18.00	30.00
☐ 24, Dec 65	0.12	6.00	18.00	30.00
☐ 25, Feb 66	0.12	6.00	18.00	30.00
☐ 26, Apr 66	0.12	6.00	18.00	30.00
☐ 27, Jun 66	0.12	6.00	18.00	30.00
☐ 28, Aug 66	0.12	6.00	18.00	30.00
☐ 29, Oct 66, 1:Ocean Master				
	0.12	6.00	18.00	30.00
☐ 30, Dec 66	0.12	6.00	18.00	30.00
☐ 31, Feb 67	0.12	4.80	14.40	24.00
☐ 32, Apr 67	0.12	4.80	14.40	24.00
☐ 33, Jun 67, 1:Aqua-Girl	0.12	7.60	22.80	38.00
☐ 34, Aug 67	0.12	4.80	14.40	24.00
☐ 35, Oct 67	0.12	4.80	14.40	24.00
☐ 36, Dec 67	0.12	4.80	14.40	24.00
☐ 37, Feb 68	0.12	4.80	14.40	24.00
☐ 38, Apr 68	0.12	4.80	14.40	24.00
☐ 39, Jun 68	0.12	4.80	14.40	24.00
☐ 40, Aug 68	0.12	3.00	9.00	15.00
☐ 41, Oct 68	0.12	3.00	9.00	15.00
☐ 42, Dec 68	0.12	3.00	9.00	15.00
☐ 43, Feb 69	0.12	3.00	9.00	15.00
☐ 44, Apr 69	0.12	3.00	9.00	15.00
☐ 45, Jun 69	0.12	3.00	9.00	15.00
☐ 46, Aug 69	0.15	3.00	9.00	15.00
☐ 47, Oct 69	0.15	3.00	9.00	15.00
☐ 48, Dec 69, JA;O rep	0.15	3.00	9.00	15.00
☐ 49, Feb 70, JA	0.15	3.00	9.00	15.00
☐ 50, Apr 70, A:Deadman	0.15	3.60	10.80	18.00
☐ 51, Jun 70, A:Deadman	0.15	3.60	10.80	18.00
☐ 52, Aug 70, A:Deadman	0.15	3.60	10.80	18.00
☐ 53, Oct 70, JA	0.15	1.60	4.80	8.00
☐ 54, Dec 70, JA	0.15	1.60	4.80	8.00
☐ 55, Feb 71, JA	0.15	1.60	4.80	8.00
☐ 56, Apr 71, JA	0.15	1.60	4.80	8.00
☐ 57, Aug 77, JA	0.35	1.60	4.80	8.00
☐ 58, Oct 77, JA;O: Aquaman				
	0.35	1.60	4.80	8.00
☐ 59, Dec 77	0.35	1.20	3.60	6.00
☐ 60, Feb 78	0.35	1.20	3.60	6.00

	ORIG.	GOOD	FINE	N-MINT
❏ 61, Apr 78	0.35	1.20	3.60	6.00
❏ 62, Jun 78	0.35	1.20	3.60	6.00
❏ 63, Sep 78	0.35	1.20	3.60	6.00

AQUAMAN (1986 mini-series)

	ORIG.	GOOD	FINE	N-MINT
❏ 1, Feb 86	0.75	1.00	3.00	5.00
❏ 2, Mar 86	0.75	0.60	1.80	3.00
❏ 3, Apr 86	0.75	0.60	1.80	3.00
❏ 4, May 86	0.75	0.60	1.80	3.00

AQUAMAN (1989 mini-series)

	ORIG.	GOOD	FINE	N-MINT
❏ 1, Jun 89	1.00	0.40	1.20	2.00
❏ 2, Jul 89	1.00	0.40	1.20	2.00
❏ 3, Aug 89	1.00	0.40	1.20	2.00
❏ 4, Sep 89	1.00	0.40	1.20	2.00
❏ 5, Oct 89	1.00	0.40	1.20	2.00

AQUAMAN (1991-)

	ORIG.	GOOD	FINE	N-MINT
❏ 1, Dec 91	1.00	0.50	1.50	2.50
❏ 2, Jan 92	1.00	0.40	1.20	2.00
❏ 3, Feb 92	1.00	0.40	1.20	2.00
❏ 4, Mar 92	1.00	0.40	1.20	2.00
❏ 5, Apr 92	1.00	0.40	1.20	2.00
❏ 6, May 92	1.25	0.40	1.20	2.00
❏ 7, Jun 92	1.25	0.40	1.20	2.00
❏ 8, Jul 92	1.25	0.40	1.20	2.00
❏ 9, Aug 92	1.25	0.40	1.20	2.00
❏ 10, Sep 92	1.25	0.40	1.20	2.00
❏ 11, Oct 92	1.25	0.40	1.20	2.00
❏ 12, Nov 92	1.25	0.40	1.20	2.00
❏ 13, Dec 92	1.25	0.40	1.20	2.00

AQUAMAN (1994-)

	ORIG.	GOOD	FINE	N-MINT
❏ 0, Oct 94	1.50	0.30	0.90	1.50
❏ 1, Aug 94	1.50	1.00	3.00	5.00
❏ 2, Sep 94	1.50	0.60	1.80	3.00
❏ 3, Nov 94, V:Superboy	1.50	0.30	0.90	1.50
❏ 4, Dec 94, V:Lobo	1.50	0.30	0.90	1.50
❏ 5, Jan 95	1.50	0.30	0.90	1.50
❏ 7, Mar 95	1.50	0.30	0.90	1.50
❏ 8, Apr 95	1.50	0.30	0.90	1.50
❏ 9, Jun 95	1.75	0.35	1.05	1.75
❏ 10, Jul 95	1.75	0.35	1.05	1.75
❏ 11, Aug 95	1.75	0.35	1.05	1.75
❏ 12, Sep 95, Mera returns	1.75	0.35	1.05	1.75
❏ 13, Oct 95	1.75	0.35	1.05	1.75
❏ 14, Nov 95, "Underworld Unleashed"	1.75	0.35	1.05	1.75
❏ 15, Dec 95	1.75	0.35	1.05	1.75
❏ 16, Jan 96, V:Justice League	1.75	0.35	1.05	1.75
❏ 17, Feb 96	1.75	0.35	1.05	1.75
❏ 18, Mar 96, O:Dolphin	1.75	0.35	1.05	1.75
❏ 19, Apr 96, Aqualad returns	1.75	0.35	1.05	1.75
❏ 20, May 96	1.75	0.35	1.05	1.75
❏ 21, Jun 96	1.75	0.35	1.05	1.75
❏ 22, Jul 96	1.75	0.35	1.05	1.75

AQUAMAN ANNUAL (1994-)

	ORIG.	GOOD	FINE	N-MINT
❏ 1, 95, "Year One";A: Wonder Woman, Superman,	3.50	0.70	2.10	3.50

AQUAMAN SPECIAL (1988)

	ORIG.	GOOD	FINE	N-MINT
❏ 1, Jun 88	1.50	0.30	0.90	1.50

AQUAMAN SPECIAL (1989)

	ORIG.	GOOD	FINE	N-MINT
❏ 0, Apr 89	2.00	0.40	1.20	2.00

AQUAMAN: TIME AND TIDE

	ORIG.	GOOD	FINE	N-MINT
❏ 1	1.50	0.80	2.40	4.00
❏ 2	1.50	0.50	1.50	2.50
❏ 3	1.50	0.40	1.20	2.00
❏ 4	1.50	0.40	1.20	2.00
❏ 5	1.50	0.30	0.90	1.50
❏ 6, Feb 95	1.50	0.30	0.90	1.50

ARABIAN NIGHTS ON THE WORLD OF MAGIC: THE GATHERING (mini-series)
ACCLAIM/ARMADA

	ORIG.	GOOD	FINE	N-MINT
❏ 1, Dec 95	2.50	0.50	1.50	2.50

ARACHNOPHOBIA
HOLLYWOOD

	ORIG.	GOOD	FINE	N-MINT
❏ 0, Sep 90, movie; prestige format DS		1.19	3.57	5.95
❏ 0, Sep 90, comic-book format	0.59	1.77	2.95	

ARAGONES 3-D
3-D ZONE

	ORIG.	GOOD	FINE	N-MINT
❏ 1, SA;paperback	0.99	2.97	4.95	

ARAK
DC

	ORIG.	GOOD	FINE	N-MINT
❏ 1, Sep 81, EC;O:Arak	0.30	0.90	1.50	
❏ 2, EC	0.20	0.60	1.00	
❏ 3, EC	0.20	0.60	1.00	
❏ 4, EC	0.20	0.60	1.00	
❏ 5, EC	0.20	0.60	1.00	
❏ 6, EC	0.20	0.60	1.00	
❏ 7	0.20	0.60	1.00	
❏ 8	0.20	0.60	1.00	
❏ 9	0.20	0.60	1.00	
❏ 10	0.20	0.60	1.00	
❏ 11	0.20	0.60	1.00	
❏ 12	0.20	0.60	1.00	
❏ 13	0.20	0.60	1.00	
❏ 14	0.20	0.60	1.00	
❏ 15	0.20	0.60	1.00	
❏ 16	0.20	0.60	1.00	
❏ 17	0.20	0.60	1.00	
❏ 18	0.20	0.60	1.00	
❏ 19	0.20	0.60	1.00	
❏ 20	0.20	0.60	1.00	
❏ 21	0.20	0.60	1.00	
❏ 22	0.20	0.60	1.00	
❏ 23	0.20	0.60	1.00	
❏ 24	0.20	0.60	1.00	
❏ 25	0.20	0.60	1.00	
❏ 26	0.20	0.60	1.00	
❏ 27	0.20	0.60	1.00	
❏ 28	0.20	0.60	1.00	
❏ 29	0.20	0.60	1.00	
❏ 30	0.20	0.60	1.00	
❏ 31	0.20	0.60	1.00	
❏ 32	0.20	0.60	1.00	
❏ 33	0.20	0.60	1.00	
❏ 34	0.20	0.60	1.00	
❏ 35	0.20	0.60	1.00	
❏ 36	0.20	0.60	1.00	
❏ 37	0.20	0.60	1.00	
❏ 38	0.20	0.60	1.00	
❏ 39	0.20	0.60	1.00	
❏ 40	0.20	0.60	1.00	
❏ 41	0.20	0.60	1.00	
❏ 42	0.20	0.60	1.00	
❏ 43	0.20	0.60	1.00	
❏ 44	0.20	0.60	1.00	
❏ 45	0.20	0.60	1.00	
❏ 46	0.20	0.60	1.00	
❏ 47	0.20	0.60	1.00	
❏ 48	0.20	0.60	1.00	
❏ 49	0.20	0.60	1.00	
❏ 50, Nov 85	0.20	0.60	1.00	

ARAK ANNUAL

	ORIG.	GOOD	FINE	N-MINT
❏ 1	0.25	0.75	1.25	

ARAMIS
COMICS INTERVIEW

	ORIG.	GOOD	FINE	N-MINT
❏ 1, b&w	0.39	1.17	1.95	
❏ 2, b&w	0.39	1.17	1.95	
❏ 3, b&w	0.39	1.17	1.95	

	ORIG.	GOOD	FINE	N-MINT
1, b&w		0.39	1.17	1.95
2, b&w		0.39	1.17	1.95
3, b&w		0.39	1.17	1.95

ARCANA
WELLS & CLARK

	ORIG.	GOOD	FINE	N-MINT
1, 94, b&w	3.00	0.60	1.80	3.00
2, b&w				
3, b&w				
4, Jul 95, b&w	2.25	0.45	1.35	2.25
5, Sep 95, b&w	2.25	0.45	1.35	2.25
6, 96, b&w	2.25	0.45	1.35	2.25
7, 96, b&w	2.25	0.45	1.35	2.25

ARCANA: THE BOOKS OF MAGIC ANNUAL
DC/VERTIGO

	ORIG.	GOOD	FINE	N-MINT
1, Children's Crusade	3.95	1.50	4.50	7.50

ARCANE
ARCANE

	ORIG.	GOOD	FINE	N-MINT
1		0.40	1.20	2.00
2, Fly in My Eye		1.99	5.97	9.95

GRAPHIK

	ORIG.	GOOD	FINE	N-MINT
1, b&w		0.25	0.75	1.25

ARCHANGEL
MARVEL

	ORIG.	GOOD	FINE	N-MINT
1, Feb 96, one-shot; b&w	2.50	0.50	1.50	2.50

ARCHER & ARMSTRONG
VALIANT

	ORIG.	GOOD	FINE	N-MINT
0, Jul 92, BWS	2.50	1.60	4.80	8.00
0, BWS,gold		5.60	16.80	28.00
1, Aug 92, FM(c);BWS Unity	2.50	1.60	4.80	8.00
2, Sep 92, WS(c) Unity	2.50	1.20	3.60	6.00
3, Oct 92	2.50	1.00	3.00	5.00
4, Nov 92	2.50	0.80	2.40	4.00
5, Dec 92	2.50	0.80	2.40	4.00
6, Jan 93	2.50	0.80	2.40	4.00
7, Feb 93	2.50	0.80	2.40	4.00
8, Mar 93	4.50	1.00	3.00	5.00
9, Apr 93	2.50	0.50	1.50	2.50
10, May 93	2.50	0.50	1.50	2.50
11, Jun 93	2.50	0.50	1.50	2.50
12, Jul 93	2.50	0.50	1.50	2.50
13, Jul 93	2.50	0.50	1.50	2.50
14, Jul 93	2.50	0.50	1.50	2.50
15, Jul 93	2.50	0.50	1.50	2.50
16, Jul 93	2.50	0.50	1.50	2.50
17, Jul 93	2.50	0.50	1.50	2.50
18, Jul 93	2.50	0.50	1.50	2.50
19, Jan 94	2.50	0.50	1.50	2.50
20, Mar 94	2.50	0.50	1.50	2.50
21, Apr 94, A:Shadowman	2.50	0.50	1.50	2.50
22, May 94, trading card	2.50	0.50	1.50	2.50
23, Jun 94	2.50	0.50	1.50	2.50
24, Aug 94	2.50	0.50	1.50	2.50
25, Sep 94, A:Eternal Warrior	2.50	0.50	1.50	2.50
26, Oct 94, indicia says August; double issue with *Eternal Warrior #26*	2.75	0.55	1.65	2.75

ARCHIE
ARCHIE

	ORIG.	GOOD	FINE	N-MINT
400, Jun 92	1.25	0.25	0.75	1.25
426, Aug 94	1.50	0.30	0.90	1.50
427, Sep 94	1.50	0.30	0.90	1.50
428, Oct 94	1.50	0.30	0.90	1.50
429, Nov 94, "Love Showdown" Part 1 (of 4)	1.50	0.30	0.90	1.50
430, Dec 94	1.50	0.30	0.90	1.50
431, Jan 95	1.50	0.30	0.90	1.50
432, Feb 95	1.50	0.30	0.90	1.50
433, Mar 95	1.50	0.30	0.90	1.50

	ORIG.	GOOD	FINE	N-MINT
434, Apr 95	1.50	0.30	0.90	1.50
435, May 95	1.50	0.30	0.90	1.50
436, Jun 95	1.50	0.30	0.90	1.50
437, Jul 95	1.50	0.30	0.90	1.50
438, Aug 95	1.50	0.30	0.90	1.50
439, Sep 95	1.50	0.30	0.90	1.50
440, Oct 95	1.50	0.30	0.90	1.50
441, Nov 95	1.50	0.30	0.90	1.50
442, Dec 95, "House of Riverdale" Part 1;continues in *Betty & Veronica #95*	1.50	0.30	0.90	1.50
444, Feb 96	1.50	0.30	0.90	1.50
445, Mar 96	1.50	0.30	0.90	1.50
446, Apr 96	1.50	0.30	0.90	1.50
447, May 96	1.50	0.30	0.90	1.50
449, Jul 96	1.50	0.30	0.90	1.50

ARCHIE 3000

	ORIG.	GOOD	FINE	N-MINT
1, May 89	0.75	0.15	0.45	0.75
2	0.75	0.15	0.45	0.75
3	0.75	0.15	0.45	0.75
4	0.75	0.15	0.45	0.75
5	0.75	0.15	0.45	0.75
6	0.75	0.15	0.45	0.75
7	0.75	0.15	0.45	0.75
8	0.75	0.15	0.45	0.75
9	0.75	0.15	0.45	0.75
10	0.75	0.15	0.45	0.75
11	0.75	0.15	0.45	0.75
12	0.75	0.15	0.45	0.75
13	0.75	0.15	0.45	0.75
14	0.75	0.15	0.45	0.75
15, May 91	0.75	0.15	0.45	0.75

ARCHIE AND FRIENDS

	ORIG.	GOOD	FINE	N-MINT
1, Dec 92	1.25	0.25	0.75	1.25
10, Aug 94	1.50	0.30	0.90	1.50
11, Oct 94	1.50	0.30	0.90	1.50
12, Dec 94	1.50	0.30	0.90	1.50
14, May 95	1.50	0.30	0.90	1.50
15, Aug 95	1.50	0.30	0.90	1.50
16, Nov 95	1.50	0.30	0.90	1.50
17, Feb 96	1.50	0.30	0.90	1.50
18, May 96	1.50	0.30	0.90	1.50
19, Aug 96, X-Men and *E.R.* parodies	1.50	0.30	0.90	1.50

ARCHIE ANNUAL DIGEST MAGAZINE

	ORIG.	GOOD	FINE	N-MINT
66, Jun 95, digest	1.75	0.35	1.05	1.75
67, Oct 95, digest	1.75	0.35	1.05	1.75

ARCHIE AS PUREHEART THE POWERFUL

	ORIG.	GOOD	FINE	N-MINT
1, Sep 66	0.15	12.00	36.00	60.00
2	0.15	8.00	24.00	40.00
3	0.15	6.00	18.00	30.00
4	0.15	6.00	18.00	30.00
5	0.15	6.00	18.00	30.00
6, Nov 67	0.15			

ARCHIE COMICS PRESENTS:
THE LOVE SHOWDOWN COLLECTION

	ORIG.	GOOD	FINE	N-MINT
0, 94, prestige format; reprints stories from *Archie #429*, *Betty #19*, *Betty & Veronica #82*, and *Veronica #39*	4.95	0.99	2.97	4.95

ARCHIE DIGEST MAGAZINE

	ORIG.	GOOD	FINE	N-MINT
131, Dec 94, digest	1.75	0.35	1.05	1.75
133, Apr 95, digest	1.75	0.35	1.05	1.75
134, May 95, digest	1.75	0.35	1.05	1.75
135, Jul 95, digest	1.75	0.35	1.05	1.75
136, Sep 95, digest	1.75	0.35	1.05	1.75
137, Nov 95, digest	1.75	0.35	1.05	1.75
138, Jan 96, digest	1.75	0.35	1.05	1.75
139, Mar 96, digest	1.75	0.35	1.05	1.75
140, Apr 96, digest	1.75	0.35	1.05	1.75

	ORIG.	GOOD	FINE	N-MINT

ARCHIE GIANT SERIES MAGAZINE
☐ 614, Oct 90, Pep Comics; Archie characters meet Archie
Comics staff 1.00   0.20   0.60   1.00

ARCHIE MEETS THE PUNISHER
MARVEL
☐ 1, Aug 94, Archie cover.. 2.95   0.59   1.77   2.95

ARCHIE'S CHRISTMAS STOCKING
ARCHIE
☐ 3, 95.............................. 2.00   0.40   1.20   2.00

ARCHIE'S DOUBLE DIGEST MAGAZINE

#	ORIG.	GOOD	FINE	N-MINT
☐ 75, Nov 94, digest	2.75	0.55	1.65	2.75
☐ 76, Jan 95, digest	2.75	0.55	1.65	2.75
☐ 77, Mar 95, digest	2.75	0.55	1.65	2.75
☐ 78, May 95, digest	2.75	0.55	1.65	2.75
☐ 79, Jul 95, digest	2.75	0.55	1.65	2.75
☐ 80, Aug 95, digest	2.75	0.55	1.65	2.75
☐ 81, Oct 95, digest	2.75	0.55	1.65	2.75
☐ 82, Dec 95, digest	2.75	0.55	1.65	2.75
☐ 83, Feb 96, digest	2.75	0.55	1.65	2.75
☐ 84, Apr 96, digest	2.75	0.55	1.65	2.75
☐ 86, Jul 96, digest	2.75	0.55	1.65	2.75

ARCHIE'S PAL JUGHEAD COMICS

#	ORIG.	GOOD	FINE	N-MINT
☐ 1	1.25	0.25	0.75	1.25
☐ 2	1.25	0.25	0.75	1.25
☐ 3	1.25	0.25	0.75	1.25
☐ 4	1.25	0.25	0.75	1.25
☐ 5	1.25	0.25	0.75	1.25
☐ 6	1.25	0.25	0.75	1.25
☐ 7	1.25	0.25	0.75	1.25
☐ 8	1.25	0.25	0.75	1.25
☐ 9	1.25	0.25	0.75	1.25
☐ 10	1.25	0.25	0.75	1.25
☐ 11	1.25	0.25	0.75	1.25
☐ 12	1.25	0.25	0.75	1.25
☐ 13	1.25	0.25	0.75	1.25
☐ 14	1.25	0.25	0.75	1.25
☐ 15	1.25	0.25	0.75	1.25
☐ 16	1.25	0.25	0.75	1.25
☐ 17	1.25	0.25	0.75	1.25
☐ 18	1.25	0.25	0.75	1.25
☐ 19	1.25	0.25	0.75	1.25
☐ 20	1.25	0.25	0.75	1.25
☐ 21	1.25	0.25	0.75	1.25
☐ 22	1.25	0.25	0.75	1.25
☐ 23	1.25	0.25	0.75	1.25
☐ 24	1.25	0.25	0.75	1.25
☐ 25	1.25	0.25	0.75	1.25
☐ 26	1.25	0.25	0.75	1.25
☐ 27	1.25	0.25	0.75	1.25
☐ 28	1.25	0.25	0.75	1.25
☐ 29	1.25	0.25	0.75	1.25
☐ 30	1.25	0.25	0.75	1.25
☐ 31	1.25	0.25	0.75	1.25
☐ 32	1.25	0.25	0.75	1.25
☐ 33	1.25	0.25	0.75	1.25
☐ 34	1.25	0.25	0.75	1.25
☐ 35	1.25	0.25	0.75	1.25
☐ 36	1.25	0.25	0.75	1.25
☐ 37	1.25	0.25	0.75	1.25
☐ 38	1.25	0.25	0.75	1.25
☐ 39	1.25	0.25	0.75	1.25
☐ 40	1.25	0.25	0.75	1.25
☐ 41	1.25	0.25	0.75	1.25
☐ 42	1.25	0.25	0.75	1.25
☐ 43	1.25	0.25	0.75	1.25
☐ 44	1.25	0.25	0.75	1.25
☐ 45	1.25	0.25	0.75	1.25
☐ 46	1.25	0.25	0.75	1.25
☐ 59, Aug 94	1.50	0.30	0.90	1.50
☐ 60, Sep 94	1.50	0.30	0.90	1.50
☐ 61, Oct 94	1.50	0.30	0.90	1.50

	ORIG.	GOOD	FINE	N-MINT
☐ 62, Nov 94	1.50	0.30	0.90	1.50
☐ 63, Dec 94	1.50	0.30	0.90	1.50
☐ 64, Jan 95	1.50	0.30	0.90	1.50
☐ 66, Mar 95	1.50	0.30	0.90	1.50
☐ 67, Apr 95	1.50	0.30	0.90	1.50
☐ 68, May 95	1.50	0.30	0.90	1.50
☐ 69, Jun 95	1.50	0.30	0.90	1.50
☐ 70, Jul 95	1.50	0.30	0.90	1.50
☐ 71, Aug 95	1.50	0.30	0.90	1.50
☐ 72, Sep 95, Jellybean's real name revealed	1.50	0.30	0.90	1.50
☐ 73, Oct 95	1.50	0.30	0.90	1.50
☐ 74, Nov 95	1.50	0.30	0.90	1.50
☐ 75, Dec 95	1.50	0.30	0.90	1.50
☐ 76, Jan 96, "House of Riverdale" Part 3	1.50	0.30	0.90	1.50
☐ 77, Feb 96	1.50	0.30	0.90	1.50
☐ 78, Mar 96	1.50	0.30	0.90	1.50
☐ 79, Apr 96	1.50	0.30	0.90	1.50
☐ 80, May 96	1.50	0.30	0.90	1.50
☐ 81, Jun 96	1.50	0.30	0.90	1.50

ARCHIE'S PALS 'N' GALS DOUBLE DIGEST

#	ORIG.	GOOD	FINE	N-MINT
☐ 9, Jan 95, digest	2.75	0.55	1.65	2.75
☐ 10, Feb 95, digest	2.75	0.55	1.65	2.75
☐ 11, Apr 95, digest	2.75	0.55	1.65	2.75
☐ 12, Jun 95, digest	2.75	0.55	1.65	2.75
☐ 13, Aug 95, digest	2.75	0.55	1.65	2.75
☐ 14, Oct 95, digest	2.75	0.55	1.65	2.75
☐ 15, Dec 95, digest	2.75	0.55	1.65	2.75
☐ 16, Jan 96, digest	2.75	0.55	1.65	2.75
☐ 17, Mar 96, digest	2.75	0.55	1.65	2.75
☐ 18, May 96, digest	2.75	0.55	1.65	2.75
☐ 19, Jul 96, digest	2.75	0.55	1.65	2.75

ARCHIE'S SPRING BREAK
☐ 1, 96 .... 2.00   0.40   1.20   2.00

ARCHIE'S STORY & GAME DIGEST MAGAZINE

#	ORIG.	GOOD	FINE	N-MINT
☐ 32, Jul 95, digest	1.75	0.35	1.05	1.75
☐ 33, Sep 95, digest	1.75	0.35	1.05	1.75
☐ 34, Mar 96, digest	1.75	0.35	1.05	1.75
☐ 35, May 96, digest	1.75	0.35	1.05	1.75

ARCHIE'S SUPER TEENS

#	ORIG.	GOOD	FINE	N-MINT
☐ 1, 94, poster	2.00	0.40	1.20	2.00
☐ 2, 95	2.00	0.40	1.20	2.00
☐ 3, 95	2.00	0.40	1.20	2.00
☐ 4, 96	2.00	0.40	1.20	2.00

ARCHIE'S VACATION SPECIAL

#	ORIG.	GOOD	FINE	N-MINT
☐ 1, Sum 94, 1994	2.00	0.40	1.20	2.00
☐ 2, Win 95	2.00	0.40	1.20	2.00
☐ 3, Sum 95	2.00	0.40	1.20	2.00

ARCHIE...ARCHIE ANDREWS, WHERE ARE YOU?
DIGEST MAGAZINE

#	ORIG.	GOOD	FINE	N-MINT
☐ 97, Jan 95, digest	1.75	0.35	1.05	1.75
☐ 98, Feb 95, digest	1.75	0.35	1.05	1.75
☐ 99, Apr 95, digest	1.75	0.35	1.05	1.75
☐ 100, Jun 95, digest	1.75	0.35	1.05	1.75
☐ 101, Aug 95, digest	1.75	0.35	1.05	1.75
☐ 102, Oct 95, digest	1.75	0.35	1.05	1.75
☐ 103, Dec 95, digest	1.75	0.35	1.05	1.75
☐ 104, Jan 96, digest	1.75	0.35	1.05	1.75
☐ 105, Mar 96, digest	1.75	0.35	1.05	1.75
☐ 106, May 96, digest	1.75	0.35	1.05	1.75
☐ 107, Aug 96, digest	1.75	0.35	1.05	1.75

ARCTIC COMICS
NICK BURNS
☐ 1, souvenir......................   0.40   1.20   2.00

AREA 88
ECLIPSE
☐ 1 ....   0.80   2.40   4.00
☐ 1, 2nd printing 0.30   0.90   1.50
☐ 2, 1st printing 0.40   1.20   2.00

	ORIG.	GOOD	FINE	N-MINT
❑ 2, 2nd printing		0.30	0.90	1.50
❑ 3		0.30	0.90	1.50
❑ 4		0.30	0.90	1.50
❑ 5		0.30	0.90	1.50
❑ 6		0.30	0.90	1.50
❑ 7		0.30	0.90	1.50
❑ 8		0.30	0.90	1.50
❑ 9		0.30	0.90	1.50
❑ 10		0.30	0.90	1.50
❑ 11		0.30	0.90	1.50
❑ 12		0.30	0.90	1.50
❑ 13		0.30	0.90	1.50
❑ 14		0.30	0.90	1.50
❑ 15		0.30	0.90	1.50
❑ 16		0.30	0.90	1.50
❑ 17		0.30	0.90	1.50
❑ 18		0.30	0.90	1.50
❑ 19		0.30	0.90	1.50
❑ 20		0.30	0.90	1.50
❑ 21		0.30	0.90	1.50
❑ 22		0.30	0.90	1.50
❑ 23		0.30	0.90	1.50
❑ 24		0.30	0.90	1.50
❑ 25		0.30	0.90	1.50
❑ 26		0.30	0.90	1.50
❑ 27		0.30	0.90	1.50
❑ 28		0.30	0.90	1.50
❑ 29		0.30	0.90	1.50
❑ 30		0.30	0.90	1.50
❑ 31		0.30	0.90	1.50
❑ 32		0.30	0.90	1.50
❑ 33		0.30	0.90	1.50
❑ 34		0.30	0.90	1.50
❑ 35		0.30	0.90	1.50
❑ 36		0.30	0.90	1.50

AREA 88 (was Eclipse title)
VIZ

	ORIG.	GOOD	FINE	N-MINT
❑ 37, b&w, Japanese		0.35	1.05	1.75
❑ 38, b&w, Japanese		0.35	1.05	1.75
❑ 39, b&w, Japanese		0.35	1.05	1.75
❑ 40, b&w, Japanese		0.35	1.05	1.75
❑ 41, b&w, Japanese		0.35	1.05	1.75
❑ 42		0.40	1.20	2.00

ARENA
ALCHEMY

	ORIG.	GOOD	FINE	N-MINT
❑ 1, b&w		0.30	0.90	1.50

ARGONAUTS, THE
ALPHA PRODUCTIONS

	ORIG.	GOOD	FINE	N-MINT
❑ 1, b&w	2.50	0.50	1.50	2.50

ETERNITY

	ORIG.	GOOD	FINE	N-MINT
❑ 1, b&w		0.39	1.17	1.95
❑ 2, b&w		0.39	1.17	1.95
❑ 3, b&w		0.39	1.17	1.95
❑ 4, b&w		0.39	1.17	1.95

ARGONAUTS: SYSTEM CRASH
ALPHA PRODUCTIONS

	ORIG.	GOOD	FINE	N-MINT
❑ 1	2.50	0.50	1.50	2.50
❑ 2	2.50	0.50	1.50	2.50

ARGUS
DC

	ORIG.	GOOD	FINE	N-MINT
❑ 1, Apr 95	1.50	0.30	0.90	1.50
❑ 2	1.75	0.35	1.05	1.75
❑ 3, Jul 95	1.75	0.35	1.05	1.75
❑ 4, Aug 95	1.75	0.35	1.05	1.75
❑ 5, Sep 95	1.75	0.35	1.05	1.75
❑ 6, Oct 95, final issue	1.75	0.35	1.05	1.75

ARIANNE
SLAVE LABOR

	ORIG.	GOOD	FINE	N-MINT
❑ 1, b&w		0.50	1.50	2.50
❑ 2		0.59	1.77	2.95

ARIK KHAN
A-PLUS

	ORIG.	GOOD	FINE	N-MINT
❑ 1, b&w, reprints		0.50	1.50	2.50

ANDROMEDA

	ORIG.	GOOD	FINE	N-MINT
❑ 1		0.39	1.17	1.95
❑ 2		0.39	1.17	1.95
❑ 3		0.39	1.17	1.95

ARION
DC

	ORIG.	GOOD	FINE	N-MINT
❑ 1, JDu		0.30	0.90	1.50
❑ 2, JDu		0.20	0.60	1.00
❑ 3, JDu		0.20	0.60	1.00
❑ 4, JDu		0.20	0.60	1.00
❑ 5, JDu		0.20	0.60	1.00
❑ 6, JDu		0.20	0.60	1.00
❑ 7		0.20	0.60	1.00
❑ 8		0.20	0.60	1.00
❑ 9		0.20	0.60	1.00
❑ 10		0.20	0.60	1.00
❑ 11		0.20	0.60	1.00
❑ 12		0.20	0.60	1.00
❑ 13		0.20	0.60	1.00
❑ 14		0.20	0.60	1.00
❑ 15		0.20	0.60	1.00
❑ 16		0.20	0.60	1.00
❑ 17		0.20	0.60	1.00
❑ 18		0.20	0.60	1.00
❑ 19		0.20	0.60	1.00
❑ 20		0.20	0.60	1.00
❑ 21		0.20	0.60	1.00
❑ 22		0.20	0.60	1.00
❑ 23		0.20	0.60	1.00
❑ 24		0.20	0.60	1.00
❑ 25		0.20	0.60	1.00
❑ 26		0.20	0.60	1.00
❑ 27		0.20	0.60	1.00
❑ 28		0.20	0.60	1.00
❑ 29		0.20	0.60	1.00
❑ 30		0.20	0.60	1.00
❑ 31		0.20	0.60	1.00
❑ 32		0.20	0.60	1.00
❑ 33		0.20	0.60	1.00
❑ 34		0.20	0.60	1.00
❑ 35		0.20	0.60	1.00

ARION THE IMMORTAL

	ORIG.	GOOD	FINE	N-MINT
❑ 2		0.30	0.90	1.50
❑ 3		0.30	0.90	1.50
❑ 4		0.30	0.90	1.50
❑ 5		0.30	0.90	1.50
❑ 6		0.30	0.90	1.50

ARISTOCRATIC XTRA-TERRESTRIAL TIME-TRAVELING THIEVES
COMICS INTERVIEW

	ORIG.	GOOD	FINE	N-MINT
❑ 1, Aug 86, one-shot	1.75	0.40	1.20	2.00
❑ 1, 2nd printing		0.35	1.05	1.75

ARISTOCRATIC XTRA-TERRESTRIAL TIME-TRAVELING THIEVES (on-going series)

	ORIG.	GOOD	FINE	N-MINT
❑ 1, Feb 87, b&w	1.75	0.35	1.05	1.75
❑ 2, Apr 87, b&w	1.75	0.35	1.05	1.75
❑ 3, Jun 87, b&w	1.75	0.35	1.05	1.75
❑ 4, Aug 87, b&w	1.75	0.35	1.05	1.75
❑ 5, Oct 87, b&w	1.75	0.35	1.05	1.75
❑ 6, Dec 87, b&w	1.75	0.35	1.05	1.75
❑ 7, Feb 88, b&w	1.75	0.35	1.05	1.75
❑ 8, Apr 88, b&w	1.75	0.35	1.05	1.75
❑ 9, Jun 88, b&w	1.75	0.35	1.05	1.75
❑ 10, Aug 88, b&w	1.95	0.39	1.17	1.95
❑ 11, Oct 88, b&w	1.95	0.39	1.17	1.95
❑ 12, Dec 88, final issue; b&w	1.95	0.39	1.17	1.95

	ORIG.	GOOD	FINE	N-MINT

ARLINGTON HAMMER IN: "GET ME TO THE CHURCH ON TIME"
ONE SHOT

	ORIG.	GOOD	FINE	N-MINT
❑ 0, 95, nn;comic for sale at conventions only	2.50	0.50	1.50	2.50

ARMAGEDDON 2001
DC

	ORIG.	GOOD	FINE	N-MINT
❑ 1, May 91, 1st printing I:Waverider	2.00	1.00	3.00	5.00
❑ 1, May 91, 2nd printing....		0.40	1.20	2.00
❑ 1, May 91, 3rd printing, silver		0.40	1.20	2.00
❑ 2, Oct 91	2.00	0.60	1.80	3.00

ARMAGEDDON FACTOR
AC

	ORIG.	GOOD	FINE	N-MINT
❑ 1, Jun 87		0.39	1.17	1.95
❑ 2, Aug 87		0.39	1.17	1.95
❑ 3		0.39	1.17	1.95

ARMAGEDDON FACTOR: THE CONCLUSION, THE

	ORIG.	GOOD	FINE	N-MINT
❑ 0, 90, nn b&w		0.79	2.37	3.95

ARMAGEDDON: ALIEN AGENDA
DC

	ORIG.	GOOD	FINE	N-MINT
❑ 1, Nov 91	1.00	0.20	0.60	1.00
❑ 2, Dec 91	1.00	0.20	0.60	1.00
❑ 3, Jan 92	1.00	0.20	0.60	1.00
❑ 4, Feb 92	1.00	0.20	0.60	1.00

ARMAGEDDON: INFERNO

	ORIG.	GOOD	FINE	N-MINT
❑ 1, Apr 92	1.00	0.20	0.60	1.00
❑ 2, May 92	1.00	0.20	0.60	1.00
❑ 3, Jun 92	1.00	0.20	0.60	1.00
❑ 4, Jul 92;JSA returns	1.00	0.20	0.60	1.00

ARMAGEDDONQUEST
STARHEAD

	ORIG.	GOOD	FINE	N-MINT
❑ 1, 94, adult;b&w	3.95	0.79	2.37	3.95
❑ 2, 94, adult;b&w	3.95	0.79	2.37	3.95

ARMED & DANGEROUS
KITCHEN SINK

	ORIG.	GOOD	FINE	N-MINT
❑ 0, Jul 95, nn;magazine-sized graphic novel	9.95	1.99	5.97	9.95

ARMED & DANGEROUS (mini-series)
ACCLAIM/ARMADA

	ORIG.	GOOD	FINE	N-MINT
❑ 1, Apr 96, b&w	2.95	0.59	1.77	2.95
❑ 2, May 96, b&w	2.95	0.59	1.77	2.95
❑ 3, Jun 96, b&w	2.95	0.59	1.77	2.95

ARMITAGE
FLEETWAY/QUALITY

	ORIG.	GOOD	FINE	N-MINT
❑ 1	2.95	0.59	1.77	2.95
❑ 2	2.95	0.59	1.77	2.95

ARMOR
CONTINUITY

	ORIG.	GOOD	FINE	N-MINT
❑ 1	2.00	0.40	1.20	2.00
❑ 1		0.40	1.20	2.00
❑ 2		0.40	1.20	2.00
❑ 3		0.40	1.20	2.00
❑ 4		0.40	1.20	2.00
❑ 5		0.40	1.20	2.00
❑ 6		0.40	1.20	2.00
❑ 7		0.40	1.20	2.00
❑ 8		0.40	1.20	2.00
❑ 9		0.40	1.20	2.00
❑ 10		0.40	1.20	2.00
❑ 11		0.40	1.20	2.00
❑ 12		0.40	1.20	2.00
❑ 2, trading card	2.50	0.50	1.50	2.50
❑ 3	2.50	0.50	1.50	2.50
❑ 4, Jul 88	2.50	0.50	1.50	2.50
❑ 5, Dec 88	2.50	0.50	1.50	2.50
❑ 6, Apr 89	2.50	0.50	1.50	2.50

ARMOR DEATHWATCH 2000

	ORIG.	GOOD	FINE	N-MINT
❑ 1, 2 trading cards, foil cover	2.50	0.50	1.50	2.50

ARMORINES
VALIANT

	ORIG.	GOOD	FINE	N-MINT
❑ 1, Jun 94	2.25	0.45	1.35	2.25
❑ 2, Aug 94	2.25	0.45	1.35	2.25
❑ 3, Sep 94	2.25	0.45	1.35	2.25
❑ 4, Oct 94	2.25	0.45	1.35	2.25
❑ 5, Nov 94	2.25	0.45	1.35	2.25
❑ 7, Jan 95	2.25	0.45	1.35	2.25
❑ 8, Feb 95	2.25	0.45	1.35	2.25
❑ 9, Mar 95	2.25	0.45	1.35	2.25
❑ 10, Apr 95	2.25	0.45	1.35	2.25
❑ 11, May 95	2.25	0.45	1.35	2.25

ARMY OF DARKNESS
DARK HORSE

	ORIG.	GOOD	FINE	N-MINT
❑ 1, movie adaptation	2.50	0.50	1.50	2.50
❑ 2, movie adaptation	2.50	0.50	1.50	2.50
❑ 3, movie adaptation	2.50	0.50	1.50	2.50

ARMY SURPLUS KOMIKZ FEATURING CUTEY BUNNY
QUAGMIRE

	ORIG.	GOOD	FINE	N-MINT
❑ 1		1.00	3.00	5.00
❑ 2		0.30	0.90	1.50
❑ 3		0.30	0.90	1.50
❑ 4, (moves to Eclipse)		0.30	0.90	1.50

ARMY SURPLUS KOMIKZ FEATURING CUTEY BUNNY
(was Joshua Quagmire Enterprises title)
ECLIPSE

	ORIG.	GOOD	FINE	N-MINT
❑ 5, b&w		0.30	0.90	1.50

ARRGH!
MARVEL

	ORIG.	GOOD	FINE	N-MINT
❑ 1, Dec 74, TS,RTh	0.25	0.50	1.50	2.50
❑ 2, Feb 75, TS,RTh	0.25	0.40	1.20	2.00
❑ 3, May 75, AA(c),RTh	0.25	0.40	1.20	2.00
❑ 4, Jul 75, RTh	0.25	0.40	1.20	2.00
❑ 5, Sep 75, RA(c), Mike Esposito	0.25	0.40	1.20	2.00

ARROW, THE
MALIBU

	ORIG.	GOOD	FINE	N-MINT
❑ 1		0.39	1.17	1.95

ARROWMAN
PARODY PRESS

	ORIG.	GOOD	FINE	N-MINT
❑ 1, b&w	2.50	0.50	1.50	2.50

ART D'ECCO
FANTAGRAPHICS

	ORIG.	GOOD	FINE	N-MINT
❑ 1, b&w		0.50	1.50	2.50
❑ 2, b&w		0.50	1.50	2.50
❑ 3		0.55	1.65	2.75

ART IN SHAMBLES
MAX HOPPER

	ORIG.	GOOD	FINE	N-MINT
❑ 1, b&w		0.50	1.50	2.50

ART OF AUBREY BEARDSLEY, THE
TOME PRESS

	ORIG.	GOOD	FINE	N-MINT
❑ 1, b&w		0.59	1.77	2.95

ART OF HEATH ROBINSON

	ORIG.	GOOD	FINE	N-MINT
❑ 1, b&w		0.59	1.77	2.95

ART OF HOMAGE STUDIOS, THE
IMAGE

	ORIG.	GOOD	FINE	N-MINT
❑ 1	4.95	0.99	2.97	4.95

ART OF MUCHA
TOME PRESS

	ORIG.	GOOD	FINE	N-MINT
❑ 1, 92	2.95	0.59	1.77	2.95

	ORIG.	GOOD	FINE	N-MINT

ARTEMIS: REQUIEM
DC
❏ 1, Jun 96	1.75	0.35	1.05	1.75
❏ 2, Jul 96	1.75	0.35	1.05	1.75

ARTHUR SEX
AIRCEL
❏ 1, adult, b&w	2.50	0.50	1.50	2.50
❏ 2, adult, b&w	2.50	0.50	1.50	2.50
❏ 3, adult, b&w	2.50	0.50	1.50	2.50
❏ 4, adult, b&w	2.50	0.50	1.50	2.50
❏ 5, adult, b&w	2.50	0.50	1.50	2.50
❏ 6, adult, b&w	2.50	0.50	1.50	2.50
❏ 7, adult, b&w	2.50	0.50	1.50	2.50
❏ 8, adult, b&w	2.50	0.50	1.50	2.50

ARTHUR, KING OF BRITAIN
TOME
❏ 1, b&w	2.95	0.59	1.77	2.95
❏ 2, b&w	2.95	0.59	1.77	2.95
❏ 3, b&w	2.95	0.59	1.77	2.95
❏ 4, b&w	2.95	0.59	1.77	2.95
❏ 5, b&w	3.95	0.79	2.37	3.95

ARTILLERY ONE-SHOT
RED BULLET
❏ 1, 95, b&w	2.50	0.50	1.50	2.50

ARTISTIC COMICS
KITCHEN SINK
❏ 0, Aug 95, nn;adults only; b&w;new printing; squarebound	4.95	0.99	2.97	4.95

ARTISTIC LICENTIOUSNESS
STARHEAD
❏ 1, adult, b&w		0.50	1.50	2.50

ASH
EVENT
❏ 1, Nov 94	2.50	3.60	10.80	18.00
❏ 2	2.50	2.40	7.20	12.00
❏ 3, May 95	2.50	1.20	3.60	6.00
❏ 4	2.50	1.00	3.00	5.00
❏ 5, Sep 95, Outer cover by the Hildebrandt brothers	2.50	0.60	1.80	3.00

ASHES
CALIBER
❏ 1, b&w	2.50	0.50	1.50	2.50
❏ 2, b&w	2.50	0.50	1.50	2.50
❏ 3, b&w	2.50	0.50	1.50	2.50
❏ 4, b&w	2.50	0.50	1.50	2.50
❏ 5, b&w	2.50	0.50	1.50	2.50

ASHLEY DUST
KNIGHT PRESS
❏ 2, Dec 94, b&w	2.95	0.59	1.77	2.95

ASKANI'SON
MARVEL
❏ 2, Apr 96, cardstock wraparound cover	2.95	0.59	1.77	2.95
❏ 3, Apr 96, cardstock wraparound cover	2.95	0.59	1.77	2.95
❏ 4, May 96, cardstock wraparound cover; final issue	2.95	0.59	1.77	2.95

ASSASSINS
DC/AMALGAM
❏ 1, Apr 96	1.95	0.39	1.17	1.95

ASSASSINS INC.
SILVERLINE
❏ 1		0.39	1.17	1.95
❏ 2		0.39	1.17	1.95

ASTER
EXPRESS/ENTITY
❏ 0, 95	2.95	0.80	2.40	4.00
❏ 1, Oct 94, b&w	2.95	0.70	2.10	3.50
❏ 1, b&w;gold edition	2.00	6.00	10.00	

	ORIG.	GOOD	FINE	N-MINT
❏ 2, Nov 94, enhanced cardstock cover	2.95	0.59	1.77	2.95
❏ 3, Jan 95, enhanced cover	2.95	0.59	1.77	2.95
❏ 3, Jan 95, enhanced cover; alternate cover with "#3a," but just "#3" in indicia	2.95	0.59	1.77	2.95

ASTER ASHCAN PREVIEW
❏ 0, 94, no cover price, b&w preview of upcoming series, small size		0.50	1.50	2.50

ASTER: THE LAST CELESTIAL KNIGHT (Vol. 2)
❏ 1, 95, enhanced wraparound cover	3.75	0.75	2.25	3.75

ASTONISH!
WEHNER
❏ 1, b&w		0.40	1.20	2.00

ASTONISHING TALES
MARVEL
❏ 1, Aug 70, JK/WW, Ka-Zar, Dr. Doom	0.15	4.80	14.40	24.00
❏ 2, Oct 70, JK/WW, Ka-Zar/Dr. Doom	0.15	3.60	10.80	18.00
❏ 3, Dec 70, Ka-Zar, Dr. Doom	0.15	3.00	9.00	15.00
❏ 4, Feb 71, Ka-Zar, Dr. Doom	0.15	3.00	9.00	15.00
❏ 5, Apr 71, Ka-Zar, Dr. Doom	0.15	3.00	9.00	15.00
❏ 6, Jun 71, Ka-Zar, Dr. Doom	0.15	3.00	9.00	15.00
❏ 7, Aug 71, Ka-Zar/Dr. Doom	0.15	2.00	6.00	10.00
❏ 8, Oct 71, Ka-Zar/Dr. Doom	0.25	2.00	6.00	10.00
❏ 9, Dec 71, Ka-Zar/Dr. Doom	0.20	2.00	6.00	10.00
❏ 10, Feb 72, SB/BS, Ka-Zar/Dr. Doom	0.20	1.60	4.80	8.00
❏ 11, Apr 72	0.20	1.20	3.60	6.00
❏ 12, Jun 72	0.20	1.20	3.60	6.00
❏ 13, Aug 72	0.20	0.60	1.80	3.00
❏ 14, Oct 72	0.20	0.60	1.80	3.00
❏ 15, Dec 72	0.20	0.60	1.80	3.00
❏ 16, Feb 73	0.20	0.60	1.80	3.00
❏ 17, Apr 73	0.20	0.60	1.80	3.00
❏ 18, Jun 73	0.20	0.60	1.80	3.00
❏ 19, Aug 73	0.20	0.60	1.80	3.00
❏ 20, Oct 73	0.20	0.60	1.80	3.00
❏ 21	0.25	0.60	1.80	3.00
❏ 22	0.25	0.60	1.80	3.00
❏ 23	0.25	0.60	1.80	3.00
❏ 24	0.25	0.60	1.80	3.00
❏ 25, Aug 74, RB, O:Deathlok	0.25	18.00	54.00	90.00
❏ 26, Deathlok	0.25	7.00	21.00	35.00
❏ 27, Deathlok	0.25	6.00	18.00	30.00
❏ 28, Feb 75, Deathlok	0.25	6.00	18.00	30.00
❏ 29, 1:Guardians of Galaxy	0.25	5.20	15.60	26.00
❏ 30, Jun 75, RB/KP Deathlok	0.25	3.20	9.60	16.00
❏ 31, Aug 75, Deathlok	0.25	3.20	9.60	16.00
❏ 32, Deathlok	0.25	3.20	9.60	16.00
❏ 33, Jan 76, Deathlok	0.25	3.20	9.60	16.00
❏ 34, Deathlok	0.25	3.20	9.60	16.00
❏ 35, Deathlok	0.25	3.20	9.60	16.00
❏ 36, Jul 76, Deathlok	0.25	3.20	9.60	16.00

ASTONISHING X-MEN (mini-series)
❏ 1, Mar 95	1.95	1.60	4.80	8.00
❏ 2, Apr 95	1.95	1.00	3.00	5.00
❏ 3, May 95	1.95	0.80	2.40	4.00
❏ 4, Jun 95	1.95	0.80	2.40	4.00

ASYLUM
MAXIMUM

	ORIG.	GOOD	FINE	N-MINT
1, Dec 95, flipbook with Beanworld back-up	2.95	0.59	1.77	2.95
1, Dec 95, alternate cover; flipbook with Beanworld back-up	2.95	0.59	1.77	2.95
2, Jan 96	2.95	0.59	1.77	2.95
3, Apr 96	2.95	0.59	1.77	2.95

MILLENNIUM

	ORIG.	GOOD	FINE	N-MINT
1	2.50	0.50	1.50	2.50
2	2.50	0.50	1.50	2.50
3, HC	4.95	0.99	2.97	4.95

NEW COMICS

	GOOD	FINE	N-MINT
1, b&w	0.39	1.17	1.95
2	0.45	1.35	2.25

ATARI FORCE
DC

	ORIG.	GOOD	FINE	N-MINT
1, Jan 84, JL	0.75	0.35	1.05	1.75
2, Feb 84	0.75	0.25	0.75	1.25
3, Mar 84	0.75	0.25	0.75	1.25
4, Apr 84	0.75	0.20	0.60	1.00
5, May 84	0.75	0.20	0.60	1.00
6, Jun 84	0.75	0.20	0.60	1.00
7, Jul 84	0.75	0.20	0.60	1.00
8, Aug 84	0.75	0.20	0.60	1.00
9, Sep 84	0.75	0.20	0.60	1.00
10, Oct 84	0.75	0.20	0.60	1.00
11, Nov 84	0.75	0.20	0.60	1.00
12, Dec 84	0.75	0.20	0.60	1.00
13, Jan 85	0.75	0.20	0.60	1.00
14, Feb 85	0.75	0.20	0.60	1.00
15, Mar 85	0.75	0.20	0.60	1.00
16, Apr 85	0.75	0.20	0.60	1.00
17, May 85	0.75	0.20	0.60	1.00
18, Jun 85	0.75	0.20	0.60	1.00
19, Jul 85	0.75	0.20	0.60	1.00
20, Aug 85	0.75	0.20	0.60	1.00

ATARI SPECIAL

	ORIG.	GOOD	FINE	N-MINT
1, 86	2.00	0.40	1.20	2.00

ATLANTIS CHRONICLES (mini-series)

	GOOD	FINE	N-MINT
1, Mar 90	1.20	3.60	6.00
2, Apr 90	1.00	3.00	5.00
3, May 90	0.80	2.40	4.00
4, Jun 90	0.80	2.40	4.00
5, Jul 90	0.80	2.40	4.00
6, Aug 90	0.80	2.40	4.00
7, Sep 90, O:Aquaman	0.80	2.40	4.00

ATLAS
DARK HORSE

	ORIG.	GOOD	FINE	N-MINT
1	2.50	0.50	1.50	2.50
2, Apr 94	2.50	0.50	1.50	2.50
4, Aug 94	2.50	0.50	1.50	2.50

ATOM & HAWKMAN, THE
DC

	ORIG.	GOOD	FINE	N-MINT
39, Nov 68	0.12	7.00	21.00	35.00
40, Jan 69	0.12	5.60	16.80	28.00
41, Mar 69	0.12	5.60	16.80	28.00
42, May 69	0.12	5.60	16.80	28.00
43, Jul 69	0.12	5.60	16.80	28.00
44, Sep 69	0.12	5.60	16.80	28.00
45, Nov 69	0.12	5.60	16.80	28.00

ATOM SPECIAL

	ORIG.	GOOD	FINE	N-MINT
2, 95	2.95	0.59	1.77	2.95

ATOM SPECIAL, THE (1993)

	ORIG.	GOOD	FINE	N-MINT
1	2.50	0.50	1.50	2.50

ATOM, THE

	ORIG.	GOOD	FINE	N-MINT
1, Jul 62, MA/GK 1:Plant Master	0.12	120.00	360.00	600.00
2, Sep 62, MA/GK	0.12	52.00	156.00	260.00

	ORIG.	GOOD	FINE	N-MINT
3, Nov 62, MA/GK, 1:Chronos	0.12	32.00	96.00	160.00
4, Jan 63, MA/GK	0.12	18.00	54.00	90.00
5, Mar 63, MA/GK	0.12	18.00	54.00	90.00
6, May 63, MA/GK	0.12	13.00	39.00	65.00
7, Jul 63, MA/GK Hawkman	0.12	32.00	96.00	160.00
8, Sep 63, MA/GK	0.12	11.00	33.00	55.00
9, Nov 63, MA/GK	0.12	11.00	33.00	55.00
10, Jan 64, MA/GK	0.12	11.00	33.00	55.00
11, Mar 64, MA/GK	0.12	8.00	24.00	40.00
12, May 64, MA/GK	0.12	8.00	24.00	40.00
13, Jul 64	0.12	8.00	24.00	40.00
14, Sep 64	0.12	8.00	24.00	40.00
15, Nov 64	0.12	8.00	24.00	40.00
16, Jan 65, MA/GK	0.12	6.00	18.00	30.00
17, Mar 65, MA/GK	0.12	6.00	18.00	30.00
18, May 65, MA/GK	0.12	6.00	18.00	30.00
19, Jul 65, MA/GK	0.12	6.00	18.00	30.00
20, Sep 65, MA/GK	0.12	6.00	18.00	30.00
21, Nov 65	0.12	4.00	12.00	20.00
22, Jan 66	0.12	4.00	12.00	20.00
23, Mar 66	0.12	4.00	12.00	20.00
24, May 66	0.12	4.00	12.00	20.00
25, Jul 66	0.12	4.00	12.00	20.00
26, Sep 66	0.12	4.00	12.00	20.00
27, Nov 66	0.12	4.00	12.00	20.00
28, Jan 67	0.12	4.00	12.00	20.00
29, Mar 67, Earth-2 Atom	0.12	10.00	30.00	50.00
30, May 67	0.12	5.80	17.40	29.00
31, Jul 67	0.12	4.80	14.40	24.00
32, Sep 67	0.12	4.80	14.40	24.00
33, Nov 67	0.12	4.80	14.40	24.00
34, Jan 68	0.12	4.80	14.40	24.00
35, Mar 68	0.12	4.80	14.40	24.00
36, May 68	0.12	4.80	14.40	24.00
37, Jul 68	0.12	4.80	14.40	24.00
38, Sep 68	0.12	4.80	14.40	24.00

ATOMIC AGE
EPIC

	GOOD	FINE	N-MINT
1	0.90	2.70	4.50
2	0.90	2.70	4.50
3	0.90	2.70	4.50
4	0.90	2.70	4.50

ATOMIC AGE TRUCKSTOP WAITRESS
EROS COMIX

	GOOD	FINE	N-MINT
1, adult, b&w	0.45	1.35	2.25

ATOMIC MAN
BLACKTHORNE

	GOOD	FINE	N-MINT
1, Dec 86, b&w	0.35	1.05	1.75
2, Feb 87, b&w	0.35	1.05	1.75
3, Apr 87, b&w	0.35	1.05	1.75

ATOMIC MOUSE
A-PLUS

	GOOD	FINE	N-MINT
1, (#3 on cover)b&w	0.20	0.60	1.00

ATTACK OF THE AMAZON GIRLS
FANTACO

	ORIG.	GOOD	FINE	N-MINT
0, nn	4.95	0.99	2.97	4.95

ATTACK OF THE MUTANT MONSTERS
A-PLUS

	GOOD	FINE	N-MINT
1, SD, b&w reprints	0.50	1.50	2.50

ATTITUDE LAD
ICONOGRAFIX

	ORIG.	GOOD	FINE	N-MINT
1, b&w	2.95	0.59	1.77	2.95

AV IN 3-D
AARDVARK-VANAHEIM

	GOOD	FINE	N-MINT
1	0.40	1.20	2.00

	ORIG.	GOOD	FINE	N-MINT

AVALON
HARRIER

	ORIG.	GOOD	FINE	N-MINT
1, O:Diana		0.39	1.17	1.95
2		0.39	1.17	1.95
3		0.39	1.17	1.95
4		0.39	1.17	1.95
5		0.39	1.17	1.95
6		0.39	1.17	1.95
7		0.39	1.17	1.95
8		0.39	1.17	1.95
9		0.39	1.17	1.95
10		0.39	1.17	1.95
11		0.39	1.17	1.95
12		0.39	1.17	1.95
13		0.39	1.17	1.95
14		0.39	1.17	1.95

AVANT GUARD: HEROES AT THE FUTURE'S EDGE
DAY ONE

	ORIG.	GOOD	FINE	N-MINT
1, Mar 94, b&w	2.50	0.50	1.50	2.50

AVATAR
DC

	ORIG.	GOOD	FINE	N-MINT
1		1.19	3.57	5.95
2		1.19	3.57	5.95
3		1.19	3.57	5.95

AVENGELYNE
MAXIMUM

	ORIG.	GOOD	FINE	N-MINT
1, May 95, RL	2.50	0.80	2.40	4.00
2, Jun 95	2.50	0.60	1.80	3.00
3, Jul 95	2.50	0.50	1.50	2.50

AVENGELYNE (Vol. 2)

	ORIG.	GOOD	FINE	N-MINT
1, Apr 96	2.95	0.59	1.77	2.95
1, Apr 96, alternate cover (photo wraparound)	2.95	0.59	1.77	2.95

AVENGELYNE DEADLY SINS (mini-series)

	ORIG.	GOOD	FINE	N-MINT
1, Feb 95	2.95	0.59	1.77	2.95
1, Feb 95, alternate cover (photo)	2.95	0.59	1.77	2.95
2, Mar 95	2.95	0.59	1.77	2.95

AVENGELYNE SWIMSUIT

	ORIG.	GOOD	FINE	N-MINT
1, Aug 95, pin-ups, both drawn and photographed	2.95	0.59	1.77	2.95
1, Aug 95, pin-ups, both drawn and photographed; alternate cover	2.95	0.59	1.77	2.95

AVENGELYNE/GLORY

	ORIG.	GOOD	FINE	N-MINT
1, Sep 95, wraparound enhanced cover	3.95	0.79	2.37	3.95

AVENGELYNE: POWER

	ORIG.	GOOD	FINE	N-MINT
1, Jan 96, red background cover	2.50	0.50	1.50	2.50
1, Jan 96, blue background cover	2.50	0.50	1.50	2.50

AVENGERS
MARVEL

	ORIG.	GOOD	FINE	N-MINT
1, Sep 63, JK, origin	0.12	440.00	1320.00	2200.00
2, Nov 63, JK, Space Phantom	0.12	130.00	390.00	650.00
3, Jan 64, JK	0.12	100.00	300.00	500.00
4, Mar 64, JK, Capt. America	0.12	296.00	888.00	1480.00
5, May 64, JK, Hulk leaves	0.12	50.00	150.00	250.00
6, Jul 64, JK	0.12	40.00	120.00	200.00
7, Aug 64, JK	0.12	40.00	120.00	200.00
8, Sep 64, JK	0.12	40.00	120.00	200.00
9, Oct 64, JK, D:Wonder Man	0.12	50.00	150.00	250.00
10, Nov 64, JK, I:Hercules	0.12	36.00	108.00	180.00
11, Dec 64, JK, SpM	0.12	18.00	54.00	90.00

	ORIG.	GOOD	FINE	N-MINT
12, Jan 65, JK	0.12	18.00	54.00	90.00
13, Feb 65, JK	0.12	18.00	54.00	90.00
14, Mar 65, JK	0.12	18.00	54.00	90.00
15, Apr 65, JK	0.12	18.00	54.00	90.00
16, May 65, JK	0.12	15.00	45.00	75.00
17, Jun 65, JK	0.12	10.00	30.00	50.00
18, Jul 65, JK	0.12	10.00	30.00	50.00
19, Aug 65, JK	0.12	10.00	30.00	50.00
20, Sep 65, JK/DH	0.12	7.00	21.00	35.00
21, Oct 65, JK/DH	0.12	7.00	21.00	35.00
22, Nov 65, JK/DH	0.12	7.00	21.00	35.00
23, Dec 65, JK/DH	0.12	6.00	18.00	30.00
24, Jan 66, JK/DH	0.12	6.00	18.00	30.00
25, Feb 66, JK/DH	0.12	6.00	18.00	30.00
26, Mar 66, JK/DH	0.12	6.00	18.00	30.00
27, Apr 66, JK/DH	0.12	6.00	18.00	30.00
28, May 66, JK/DH	0.12	6.00	18.00	30.00
29, Jun 66, JK/DH	0.12	6.00	18.00	30.00
30, Jul 66, JK/DH	0.12	6.00	18.00	30.00
31, Aug 66, JK/DH	0.12	6.00	18.00	30.00
32, Sep 66	0.12	4.00	12.00	20.00
33, Oct 66, DH	0.12	4.00	12.00	20.00
34, Nov 66	0.12	4.00	12.00	20.00
35, Dec 66	0.12	4.00	12.00	20.00
36, Jan 67	0.12	4.00	12.00	20.00
37, Feb 67	0.12	4.00	12.00	20.00
38, Mar 67	0.12	4.00	12.00	20.00
39, Apr 67	0.12	4.00	12.00	20.00
40, May 67	0.12	4.00	12.00	20.00
41, Jun 67	0.12	2.40	7.20	12.00
42, Jul 67	0.12	2.40	7.20	12.00
43, Aug 67	0.12	2.40	7.20	12.00
44, Sep 67	0.12	2.40	7.20	12.00
45, Oct 67	0.12	2.40	7.20	12.00
46, Nov 67	0.12	2.40	7.20	12.00
47, Dec 67	0.12	2.40	7.20	12.00
48, Jan 68	0.12	2.40	7.20	12.00
49, Feb 68	0.12	2.40	7.20	12.00
50, Mar 68	0.12	2.40	7.20	12.00
51, Apr 68	0.12	2.40	7.20	12.00
52, May 68	0.12	2.40	7.20	12.00
53, Jun 68, JB, X-Men	0.12	3.00	9.00	15.00
54, Jul 68, JB	0.12	2.40	7.20	12.00
55, Aug 68, JB	0.12	2.40	7.20	12.00
56, Sep 68, JB	0.12	2.40	7.20	12.00
57, Oct 68, JB, 1:Vision	0.12	8.00	24.00	40.00
58, Nov 68, JB, O:Vision	0.12	6.00	18.00	30.00
59, Dec 68, JB	0.12	2.00	6.00	10.00
60, Jan 69, JB	0.12	2.00	6.00	10.00
61, Feb 69, JB	0.12	2.00	6.00	10.00
62, Mar 69	0.12	2.00	6.00	10.00
63, Apr 69	0.12	2.00	6.00	10.00
64, May 69	0.12	2.00	6.00	10.00
65, Jun 69	0.12	2.00	6.00	10.00
66, Jul 69, BS	0.15	2.80	8.40	14.00
67, Aug 69, BS	0.15	2.80	8.40	14.00
68, Sep 69	0.15	2.00	6.00	10.00
69, Oct 69	0.15	2.00	6.00	10.00
70, Nov 69	0.15	2.00	6.00	10.00
71, Dec 69, SB/SB, 1:Invaders	0.15	2.40	7.20	12.00
72, Jan 70	0.15	2.00	6.00	10.00
73, Feb 70	0.15	2.00	6.00	10.00
74, Mar 70	0.15	2.00	6.00	10.00
75, Apr 70	0.15	2.00	6.00	10.00
76, May 70	0.15	2.00	6.00	10.00
77, Jun 70	0.15	2.00	6.00	10.00
78, Jul 70	0.15	2.00	6.00	10.00
79, Aug 70	0.15	2.00	6.00	10.00
80, Sep 70	0.15	2.00	6.00	10.00
81, Oct 70	0.15	2.00	6.00	10.00
82, Nov 70	0.15	2.00	6.00	10.00

	ORIG.	GOOD	FINE	N-MINT
83, Dec 70, JB, 1:Valkyrie	0.15	2.00	6.00	10.00
84, Jan 71, JB	0.15	1.60	4.80	8.00
85, Feb 71, JB	0.15	1.60	4.80	8.00
86, Mar 71, JB	0.15	1.60	4.80	8.00
87, Apr 71, O:Black Panther	0.15	1.60	4.80	8.00
88, May 71, SB	0.15	1.60	4.80	8.00
89, Jun 71, SB	0.15	1.60	4.80	8.00
90, Jul 71, SB	0.15	1.60	4.80	8.00
91, Aug 71, SB	0.15	1.60	4.80	8.00
92, Sep 71, SB, NA(c)	0.15	1.60	4.80	8.00
93, Nov 71, NA	0.25	8.00	24.00	40.00
94, Dec 71, NA, 52 pages	0.20	4.80	14.40	24.00
95, Jan 72, NA	0.20	4.00	12.00	20.00
96, Feb 72, NA	0.20	4.00	12.00	20.00
97, Mar 72, SB/BEv/GK	0.20	2.40	7.20	12.00
98, Apr 72, BS	0.20	3.00	9.00	15.00
99, May 72, BS	0.20	3.00	9.00	15.00
100, Jun 72, BS	0.20	6.00	18.00	30.00
101, Jul 72	0.20	1.20	3.60	6.00
102, Aug 72	0.20	1.20	3.60	6.00
103, Sep 72	0.20	1.20	3.60	6.00
104, Oct 72	0.20	1.20	3.60	6.00
105, Nov 72	0.20	1.20	3.60	6.00
106, Dec 72	0.20	1.20	3.60	6.00
107, JS, DC	0.20	1.20	3.60	6.00
107, Jan 73	0.20	1.20	3.60	6.00
108, Feb 73	0.20	1.20	3.60	6.00
109, Mar 73	0.20	1.20	3.60	6.00
110, Apr 73, DH, X-Men	0.20	2.40	7.20	12.00
111, May 73, DH, X-Men	0.20	2.40	7.20	12.00
112, Jun 73, DH, 1:Mantis	0.20	2.00	6.00	10.00
113, Jul 73, Silver Surfer	0.20	2.00	6.00	10.00
114, Aug 73, Silver Surfer	0.20	2.00	6.00	10.00
115, Sep 73, Silver Surfer	0.20	2.00	6.00	10.00
116, Oct 73, Silver Surfer	0.20	2.00	6.00	10.00
117, Nov 73, Silver Surfer	0.20	2.00	6.00	10.00
118, Dec 73, Silver Surfer	0.20	2.00	6.00	10.00
119, Jan 74, Silver Surfer	0.20	2.00	6.00	10.00
120, Feb 74, DH/JSn	0.20	1.20	3.60	6.00
121, Mar 74	0.20	1.20	3.60	6.00
122, Apr 74	0.20	1.20	3.60	6.00
123, May 74	0.25	1.20	3.60	6.00
124, Jun 74	0.25	1.20	3.60	6.00
125, Jul 74	0.25	1.20	3.60	6.00
126, Aug 74	0.25	1.20	3.60	6.00
127, Sep 74	0.25	1.20	3.60	6.00
128, Oct 74	0.25	1.20	3.60	6.00
129, Nov 74	0.25	1.20	3.60	6.00
130, Dec 74	0.25	1.00	3.00	5.00
131, Jan 75, SB	0.25	1.00	3.00	5.00
132, Feb 75, SB	0.25	1.00	3.00	5.00
133, Mar 75, SB	0.25	1.00	3.00	5.00
134, Apr 75	0.25	1.00	3.00	5.00
135, May 75	0.25	1.00	3.00	5.00
136, Jun 75	0.25	1.00	3.00	5.00
137, Jul 75	0.25	1.00	3.00	5.00
138, Aug 75	0.25	1.00	3.00	5.00
139, Sep 75	0.25	1.00	3.00	5.00
140, Oct 75	0.25	1.00	3.00	5.00
141, Nov 75, Squadron Sinister	0.25	1.00	3.00	5.00
142, Dec 75	0.25	0.80	2.40	4.00
143, Jan 76	0.25	0.80	2.40	4.00
144, Feb 76	0.25	0.80	2.40	4.00
145, Mar 76	0.25	0.80	2.40	4.00
146, Apr 76	0.25	0.80	2.40	4.00
147, May 76	0.25	0.80	2.40	4.00
148, Jun 76	0.25	0.80	2.40	4.00
149, Jul 76	0.25	0.80	2.40	4.00
150, Aug 76, GP	0.25	0.80	2.40	4.00
151, Sep 76	0.30	0.80	2.40	4.00
152, Oct 76	0.30	0.80	2.40	4.00
153, Nov 76	0.30	0.80	2.40	4.00
154, Dec 76	0.30	0.80	2.40	4.00
155, Jan 77	0.30	0.80	2.40	4.00
156, Feb 77	0.30	0.80	2.40	4.00
157, Mar 77	0.30	0.80	2.40	4.00
158, Apr 77	0.30	0.80	2.40	4.00
159, May 77	0.30	0.80	2.40	4.00
160, Jun 77	0.30	0.80	2.40	4.00
161, Jul 77, JBy/GP	0.30	0.60	1.80	3.00
162, Aug 77, JBy/GP	0.30	0.60	1.80	3.00
163, Sep 77, JBy/GP	0.30	0.60	1.80	3.00
164, Oct 77, JBy/GP	0.30	1.10	3.30	5.50
165, Nov 77, JBy	0.35	1.10	3.30	5.50
166, Dec 77, JBy	0.35	1.10	3.30	5.50
167, Jan 78, JBy	0.35	1.10	3.30	5.50
168, Feb 78, JBy	0.35	1.10	3.30	5.50
169, Mar 78, JBy	0.35	1.10	3.30	5.50
170, Apr 78, JBy	0.35	1.10	3.30	5.50
171, May 78, JBy	0.35	1.10	3.30	5.50
172, Jun 78	0.35	0.60	1.80	3.00
173, Jul 78	0.35	0.60	1.80	3.00
174, Aug 78	0.35	0.60	1.80	3.00
175, Sep 78	0.35	0.60	1.80	3.00
176, Oct 78	0.35	0.60	1.80	3.00
177, Nov 78	0.35	0.60	1.80	3.00
178, Dec 78, JBy	0.35	1.10	3.30	5.50
179, Jan 79	0.35	0.60	1.80	3.00
180, Feb 79	0.35	0.60	1.80	3.00
181, Mar 79, JBy/GP/TA, new team	0.35	1.00	3.00	5.00
182, Apr 79	0.35	0.60	1.80	3.00
183, May 79	0.40	0.60	1.80	3.00
184, Jun 79	0.40	0.60	1.80	3.00
185, Jul 79	0.40	0.60	1.80	3.00
186, Aug 79	0.40	0.60	1.80	3.00
187, Sep 79	0.40	0.60	1.80	3.00
188, Oct 79	0.40	0.60	1.80	3.00
189, Nov 79	0.40	0.60	1.80	3.00
190, Dec 79, JBy, Daredevil	0.40	0.70	2.10	3.50
191, Jan 80, JBy/GP	0.40	0.60	1.80	3.00
192, Feb 80	0.40	0.30	0.90	1.50
193, Mar 80	0.40	0.30	0.90	1.50
194, Apr 80	0.40	0.30	0.90	1.50
195, May 80	0.40	0.30	0.90	1.50
196, Jun 80	0.40	0.30	0.90	1.50
197, Jul 80	0.40	0.30	0.90	1.50
198, Aug 80	0.40	0.30	0.90	1.50
199, Sep 80	0.50	0.30	0.90	1.50
200, Oct 80, GP L:Ms. Marvel	0.75	0.60	1.80	3.00
201, Nov 80	0.50	0.40	1.20	2.00
202, Dec 80, V:Ultron	0.50	0.40	1.20	2.00
203, Jan 81	0.50	0.40	1.20	2.00
204, Feb 81, A:Yellow Claw	0.50	0.40	1.20	2.00
205, Mar 81, A:Yellow Claw	0.50	0.40	1.20	2.00
206, Apr 81	0.50	0.40	1.20	2.00

	ORIG.	GOOD	FINE	N-MINT
207, May 81 ....0.50		0.40	1.20	2.00
208, Jun 81 ....0.50		0.40	1.20	2.00
209, Jul 81 ....0.50		0.40	1.20	2.00
210, Aug 81, GC/DG 0.50		0.40	1.20	2.00
211, Sep 81, GC/DG, Moon Knight, Dazzler 0.50		0.40	1.20	2.00
212, Oct 81 ....0.50		0.40	1.20	2.00
213, Nov 81, Yellowjacket's court martial 0.50		0.40	1.20	2.00
214, Dec 81, A:Ghost Rider 0.50		0.40	1.20	2.00
215, Jan 82, A:Silver Surfer 0.60		0.40	1.20	2.00
216, Feb 82 ....0.60		0.40	1.20	2.00
217, Mar 82, Yellowjacket jailed 0.60		0.40	1.20	2.00
218, Apr 82 ....0.60		0.40	1.20	2.00
219, May 82, A:Drax 0.60		0.40	1.20	2.00
220, Jun 82, A:Drax 0.60		0.40	1.20	2.00
221, Jul 82, Wolverine on cover only 0.60		1.40	4.20	7.00
222, Aug 82, V:Masters of Evil 0.60		0.40	1.20	2.00
223, Sep 82, A:Ant-Man. 0.60		0.40	1.20	2.00
224, Oct 82, Tony Stark/Wasp romance 0.60		0.40	1.20	2.00
225, Nov 82, A:Black Knight 0.60		0.40	1.20	2.00
226, Dec 82, A:Black Knight 0.60		0.40	1.20	2.00
227, Jan 83, A:Captain Marvel II 0.60		0.40	1.20	2.00
228, Feb 83, Trial of Yellowjacket 0.60		0.40	1.20	2.00
229, Mar 83 ....0.60		0.40	1.20	2.00
230, Apr 83 ....0.60		0.40	1.20	2.00
231, May 83 ....0.60		0.40	1.20	2.00
232, Jun 83, A:Starfox ...0.60		0.40	1.20	2.00
233, Jul 83 ....0.60		0.40	1.20	2.00
234, Aug 83 ....0.60		0.40	1.20	2.00
235, Sep 83 ....0.60		0.40	1.20	2.00
236, Oct 83, SpM 0.60		0.40	1.20	2.00
237, Nov 83, SpM 0.60		0.40	1.20	2.00
238, Dec 83 ....0.60		0.40	1.20	2.00
239, Jan 84, A:David Letterman 0.60		0.40	1.20	2.00
240, Feb 84, A:Spider-Woman 0.60		0.40	1.20	2.00
241, Mar 84, A:Spider-Woman 0.60		0.40	1.20	2.00
242, Apr 84 ....0.60		0.40	1.20	2.00
243, May 84 ....0.60		0.40	1.20	2.00
244, Jun 84, V:Dire Wraiths 0.60		0.40	1.20	2.00
245, Jul 84, V:Dire Wraiths 0.60		0.40	1.20	2.00
246, Aug 84, A:Sersi 0.60		0.40	1.20	2.00
247, Sep 84, A:Uni-Mind 0.60		0.40	1.20	2.00
248, Oct 84, A:Eternals .. 0.60		0.40	1.20	2.00
249, Nov 84, A:Fantastic Four 0.60		0.40	1.20	2.00
250, Dec 84, Maelstrom. 1.00		0.40	1.20	2.00
251, Jan 85 ....0.60		0.40	1.20	2.00
252, Feb 85 ....0.60		0.40	1.20	2.00
253, Mar 85 ....0.60		0.40	1.20	2.00
254, Apr 85 ....0.65		0.40	1.20	2.00
255, May 85 ....0.65		0.40	1.20	2.00
256, Jun 85, Savage Land 0.65		0.40	1.20	2.00
257, Jul 85 ....0.65		0.40	1.20	2.00
258, Aug 85, SpM vs. Firelord 0.65		0.40	1.20	2.00

	ORIG.	GOOD	FINE	N-MINT
259, Sep 85, V:Skrulls 0.65		0.40	1.20	2.00
260, Oct 85, Secret Wars II 0.65		0.40	1.20	2.00
261, Nov 85, Secret Wars II 0.65		0.40	1.20	2.00
262, Dec 85, A:Sub-Mariner 0.65		0.40	1.20	2.00
263, Jan 86, X-Factor 0.65		0.80	2.40	4.00
264, Feb 86 ....0.75		0.40	1.20	2.00
265, Mar 86, Secret Wars II 0.75		0.40	1.20	2.00
266, Apr 86, Secret Wars II 0.75		0.40	1.20	2.00
267, May 86, V:Kang 0.75		0.40	1.20	2.00
268, Jun 86, V:Kang 0.75		0.40	1.20	2.00
269, Jul 86, V:Kang 0.75		0.40	1.20	2.00
270, Aug 86, A:Namor 0.75		0.40	1.20	2.00
271, Sep 86 ....0.75		0.40	1.20	2.00
272, Oct 86, A:Alpha Flight 0.75		0.40	1.20	2.00
273, Nov 86 ....0.75		0.40	1.20	2.00
274, Dec 86 ....0.75		0.40	1.20	2.00
275, Jan 87 ....0.75		0.40	1.20	2.00
276, Feb 87 ....0.75		0.40	1.20	2.00
277, Mar 87 ....0.75		0.40	1.20	2.00
278, Apr 87 ....0.75		0.40	1.20	2.00
279, May 87 ....0.75		0.40	1.20	2.00
280, Jun 87 ....0.75		0.40	1.20	2.00
281, Jul 87 ....0.75		0.40	1.20	2.00
282, Aug 87 ....0.75		0.40	1.20	2.00
283, Sep 87 ....0.75		0.40	1.20	2.00
284, Oct 87 ....0.75		0.40	1.20	2.00
285, Nov 87 ....0.75		0.40	1.20	2.00
286, Dec 87 ....0.75		0.40	1.20	2.00
287, Jan 88 ....0.75		0.40	1.20	2.00
288, Feb 88 ....0.75		0.40	1.20	2.00
289, Mar 88 ....0.75		0.40	1.20	2.00
290, Apr 88 ....0.75		0.40	1.20	2.00
291, May 88 ....1.00		0.40	1.20	2.00
292, Jun 88 ....1.00		0.40	1.20	2.00
293, Jul 88, D:Marrina 1.00		0.40	1.20	2.00
294, Aug 88, L:Capt. Marvel 1.00		0.40	1.20	2.00
295, Sep 88 ....1.00		0.40	1.20	2.00
296, Oct 88 ....1.00		0.40	1.20	2.00
297, Nov 88, L:Thor, Black Knight,She-Hulk; D:Dr. Druid 1.00		0.40	1.20	2.00
298, Dec 88, Inferno 1.00		0.40	1.20	2.00
299, Jan 89, Inferno 1.00		0.40	1.20	2.00
300, Feb 89, new team, Inferno 1.75		0.40	1.20	2.00
301, Mar 89 ....1.00		0.40	1.20	2.00
302, Apr 89 ....1.00		0.40	1.20	2.00
303, May 89 ....1.00		0.40	1.20	2.00
304, Jun 89 ....1.00		0.40	1.20	2.00
305, Jul 89, JBy(c) 1.00		0.30	0.90	1.50
306, Aug 89 ....1.00		0.30	0.90	1.50
307, Sep 89 ....1.00		0.30	0.90	1.50
308, Oct 89 ....1.00		0.30	0.90	1.50
309, Nov 89 ....1.00		0.30	0.90	1.50
310, Nov 89 ....1.00		0.30	0.90	1.50
311, Dec 89, Acts of Vengeance 1.00		0.30	0.90	1.50
312, Dec 89, Acts of Vengeance 1.00		0.30	0.90	1.50
313, Jan 90, Acts of Vengeance 1.00		0.30	0.90	1.50
314, Feb 90, SpM 1.00		0.60	1.80	3.00
315, Mar 90, SpM 1.00		0.60	1.80	3.00
316, Apr 90, SpM 1.00		0.50	1.50	2.50
317, May 90, SpM 1.00		0.50	1.50	2.50
318, Jun 90, SpM 1.00		0.50	1.50	2.50

	ORIG.	GOOD	FINE	N-MINT
319, Jul 90, Crossing Line	1.00	0.30	0.90	1.50
320, Aug 90, Crossing Line	1.00	0.30	0.90	1.50
321, Aug 90, Crossing Line	1.00	0.30	0.90	1.50
322, Sep 90, Crossing Line	1.00	0.30	0.90	1.50
323, Sep 90, Crossing Line	1.00	0.30	0.90	1.50
324, Oct 90, Crossing Line	1.00	0.30	0.90	1.50
325, Oct 90	1.00	0.20	0.60	1.00
326, Nov 90	1.00	1.00	3.00	5.00
327, Dec 90	1.00	0.20	0.60	1.00
328, Jan 91, O:Rage	1.00	0.60	1.80	3.00
329, Feb 91	1.00	0.30	0.90	1.50
330, Mar 91	1.00	0.30	0.90	1.50
331, Apr 91	1.00	0.30	0.90	1.50
332, May 91	1.00	0.30	0.90	1.50
333, Jun 91	1.00	0.30	0.90	1.50
334, Jul 91	1.00	0.30	0.90	1.50
335, Aug 91	1.00	0.30	0.90	1.50
336, Aug 91	1.00	0.30	0.90	1.50
337, Sep 91	1.00	0.30	0.90	1.50
338, Sep 91	1.00	0.30	0.90	1.50
339, Oct 91	1.00	0.30	0.90	1.50
340, Oct 91	1.00	0.30	0.90	1.50
341, Nov 91	1.00	0.30	0.90	1.50
342, Dec 91	1.00	0.30	0.90	1.50
343	1.00	0.30	0.90	1.50
344	1.25	0.30	0.90	1.50
345, Galactic Storm	1.25	0.30	0.90	1.50
346, Galactic Storm	1.25	0.30	0.90	1.50
347, Storm ends	1.75	0.35	1.05	1.75
348	1.25	0.25	0.75	1.25
349	1.25	0.25	0.75	1.25
350	2.50	0.50	1.50	2.50
351	1.25	0.25	0.75	1.25
352	1.25	0.25	0.75	1.25
353	1.25	0.25	0.75	1.25
354	1.25	0.25	0.75	1.25
355	1.25	0.25	0.75	1.25
356	1.25	0.25	0.75	1.25
357	1.25	0.25	0.75	1.25
358	1.25	0.25	0.75	1.25
359	1.25	0.25	0.75	1.25
360, foil cover	2.95	0.80	2.40	4.00
361	1.25	0.25	0.75	1.25
362	1.25	0.25	0.75	1.25
363, silver embossed cover	2.95	0.59	1.77	2.95
364	1.25	0.25	0.75	1.25
365	1.25	0.25	0.75	1.25
366, sculpted foil cover	3.95	0.79	2.37	3.95
367	1.25	0.25	0.75	1.25
368	1.25	0.25	0.75	1.25
369, sculpted foil cover	2.95	0.59	1.77	2.95
370, 94	1.25	0.25	0.75	1.25
371, 94	1.25	0.25	0.75	1.25
372, 94	1.25	0.25	0.75	1.25
373, Apr 94	1.25	0.25	0.75	1.25
374, May 94, cards	1.50	0.30	0.90	1.50
375, Jun 94	2.00	0.40	1.20	2.00
375, Jun 94, poster	2.50	0.50	1.50	2.50
376, Jul 94	1.50	0.30	0.90	1.50
377, Aug 94	1.50	0.30	0.90	1.50
378, Sep 94	1.50	0.30	0.90	1.50
379, Oct 94	1.50	0.30	0.90	1.50
380, Nov 94	1.50	1.20	3.60	6.00
381, Dec 94	1.50	0.40	1.20	2.00
382, Jan 95	1.50	0.40	1.20	2.00

	ORIG.	GOOD	FINE	N-MINT
383, Feb 95	1.50	0.40	1.20	2.00
384, Mar 95	1.50	0.40	1.20	2.00
385, Apr 95	1.50	1.00	3.00	5.00
386, May 95	1.50	0.40	1.20	2.00
387, Jun 95	1.50	0.80	2.40	4.00
388, Jul 95, Taking A.I.M. Part 4 of 4	1.50	0.80	2.40	4.00
389, Aug 95	1.50	0.80	2.40	4.00
390, Sep 95	1.50	0.80	2.40	4.00
391, Oct 95	1.50	1.00	3.00	5.00
392, Nov 95, Mantis returns	1.50	1.00	3.00	5.00
393, Dec 95	1.50	1.00	3.00	5.00
394, Jan 96	1.50	1.00	3.00	5.00
395, Feb 96, D:Tony Stark	1.50	0.30	0.90	1.50
396, Mar 96	1.50	0.30	0.90	1.50
397, Apr 96	1.50	0.30	0.90	1.50
397, Apr 96	1.50	0.30	0.90	1.50
398, May 96	1.50	0.30	0.90	1.50
399, Jun 96	1.50	0.30	0.90	1.50

AVENGERS ANNIVERSARY MAGAZINE

	ORIG.	GOOD	FINE	N-MINT
1	3.95	0.79	2.37	3.95

AVENGERS ANNUAL

	ORIG.	GOOD	FINE	N-MINT
1, Sep 67, DH	0.25	7.20	21.60	36.00
2, Sep 68	0.25	3.00	9.00	15.00
3, Sep 69	0.25	3.00	9.00	15.00
4, 71, reprint	0.25	0.60	1.80	3.00
5, 72, reprint	0.25	0.60	1.80	3.00
6, 76, GP	0.50	0.50	1.50	2.50
7, Nov 77, JSn, Warlock	0.60	1.50	4.50	7.50
8, Jan 79, GP; A:Ms. Marvel	0.60	0.60	1.80	3.00
9, Oct 79, DN	0.60	0.60	1.80	3.00
10, Nov 81, MG;X-Men; O&1:Rogue	0.75	0.60	1.80	3.00
11, Dec 82	1.00	0.20	0.60	1.00
12, Jan 84	1.00	0.20	0.60	1.00
13, Nov 84, JBy	1.00	0.30	0.90	1.50
14, Nov 85, JBy	1.25	0.30	0.90	1.50
15, Oct 86	1.25	0.25	0.75	1.25
16, Oct 87	1.25	0.25	0.75	1.25
17, Nov 88, Evolutionary War	1.75	0.40	1.20	2.00
18, Oct 89, Atlantis Attacks	1.75	0.60	1.80	3.00
19, Sep 90, Terminus	2.00	0.40	1.20	2.00
20, Sep 91, Subterranean Wars	2.00	0.40	1.20	2.00
21	2.25	0.45	1.35	2.25
22, trading card	2.95	0.59	1.77	2.95
23, 94	2.95	0.59	1.77	2.95

AVENGERS COLLECTOR'S EDITION

	ORIG.	GOOD	FINE	N-MINT
0		0.40	1.20	2.00

AVENGERS LOG

	ORIG.	GOOD	FINE	N-MINT
1	1.95	0.39	1.17	1.95

AVENGERS SPOTLIGHT (was Solo Avengers)

	ORIG.	GOOD	FINE	N-MINT
21, Aug 89	0.75	0.20	0.60	1.00
22, Sep 89	1.00	0.20	0.60	1.00
23, Oct 89	1.00	0.20	0.60	1.00
24, Nov 89	1.00	0.20	0.60	1.00
25, Nov 89	1.00	0.20	0.60	1.00
26, Dec 89, Acts of Vengeance	1.00	0.20	0.60	1.00
27, Dec 89, Acts of Vengeance	1.00	0.20	0.60	1.00
28, Jan 90, Acts of Vengeance	1.00	0.20	0.60	1.00
29, Feb 90, Acts of Vengeance	1.00	0.20	0.60	1.00

	ORIG.	GOOD	FINE	N-MINT
❏ 30, Mar 90, new Hawkeye costume				
..............1.00	0.20	0.60	1.00
❏ 31, Apr 90......................1.00	0.20	0.60	1.00
❏ 32, May 90......................1.00	0.20	0.60	1.00
❏ 33, Jun 90......................1.00	0.20	0.60	1.00
❏ 34, Jul 90......................1.00	0.20	0.60	1.00
❏ 35, Aug 90......................1.00	0.20	0.60	1.00
❏ 36, Sep 90......................1.00	0.20	0.60	1.00
❏ 37, Oct 90......................1.00	0.20	0.60	1.00
❏ 38, Nov 90......................1.00	0.20	0.60	1.00
❏ 39, Dec 90......................1.00	0.20	0.60	1.00
❏ 40, Jan 91......................1.00	0.20	0.60	1.00

AVENGERS STRIKE FILE

	ORIG.	GOOD	FINE	N-MINT
❏ 1 ....1.75	0.35	1.05	1.75

AVENGERS UNPLUGGED

	ORIG.	GOOD	FINE	N-MINT
❏ 1, Oct 95......................0.99	0.20	0.59	0.99
❏ 2, Dec 95......................0.99	0.20	0.59	0.99
❏ 3, Jan 96......................0.99	0.20	0.59	0.99
❏ 4, Apr 96......................0.99	0.20	0.59	0.99
❏ 5, Jun 96, A:Captain Marvel				
..............0.99	0.20	0.59	0.99

AVENGERS WEST COAST
(was West Coast Avengers)

	ORIG.	GOOD	FINE	N-MINT
❏ 48, Sep 89......................1.00	0.20	0.60	1.00
❏ 49, Oct 89 ....1.00	0.20	0.60	1.00
❏ 50, Nov 89, Golden Age Human Torch returns				
..............1.00	0.20	0.60	1.00
❏ 51, Nov 89 ....1.00	0.20	0.60	1.00
❏ 52, Dec 89......................1.00	0.20	0.60	1.00
❏ 53, Dec 89, Acts of Vengeance				
..............1.00	0.20	0.60	1.00
❏ 54, Jan 90, Acts of Vengeance				
..............1.00	0.20	0.60	1.00
❏ 55, Feb 90, Acts of Vengeance				
..............1.00	0.20	0.60	1.00
❏ 56, Mar 90, JBy..............1.00	0.20	0.60	1.00
❏ 57, Apr 90, JBy 1.00	0.20	0.60	1.00
❏ 58, May 90......................1.00	0.20	0.60	1.00
❏ 59, Jun 90......................1.00	0.20	0.60	1.00
❏ 60, Jul 90......................1.00	0.20	0.60	1.00
❏ 61, Aug 90......................1.00	0.20	0.60	1.00
❏ 62, Sep 90......................1.00	0.20	0.60	1.00
❏ 63, Oct 90......................1.00	0.20	0.60	1.00
❏ 64, Nov 90 ....1.00	0.20	0.60	1.00
❏ 65, Dec 90......................1.00	0.20	0.60	1.00
❏ 66, Jan 91......................1.00	0.20	0.60	1.00
❏ 67, Feb 91......................1.00	0.20	0.60	1.00
❏ 68, Mar 91 ....1.00	0.20	0.60	1.00
❏ 69, Apr 91......................1.00	0.20	0.60	1.00
❏ 70, May 91......................1.00	0.20	0.60	1.00
❏ 71, Jun 91......................1.00	0.20	0.60	1.00
❏ 72, Jul 91......................1.00	0.20	0.60	1.00
❏ 73, Aug 91......................1.00	0.20	0.60	1.00
❏ 74, Sep 91......................1.00	0.20	0.60	1.00
❏ 75, Oct 91......................1.50	0.30	0.90	1.50
❏ 76, Nov 91 ....1.00	0.20	0.60	1.00
❏ 77, Dec 91......................1.00	0.20	0.60	1.00
❏ 78 ....1.00	0.20	0.60	1.00
❏ 79 ....1.25	0.25	0.75	1.25
❏ 80, Galactic Storm ..1.25	0.25	0.75	1.25
❏ 81, Galactic Storm 1.25	0.25	0.75	1.25
❏ 82, Galactic Storm 1.25	0.25	0.75	1.25
❏ 83 ....1.25	0.25	0.75	1.25
❏ 84, O:Spider Woman......1.25	0.25	0.75	1.25
❏ 85 ....1.25	0.25	0.75	1.25
❏ 86 ....1.25	0.25	0.75	1.25
❏ 87 ....1.25	0.25	0.75	1.25
❏ 88 ....1.25	0.25	0.75	1.25
❏ 89 ....1.25	0.25	0.75	1.25
❏ 90 ....1.25	0.25	0.75	1.25
❏ 91 ....1.25	0.25	0.75	1.25

	ORIG.	GOOD	FINE	N-MINT
❏ 92 ....1.25	0.25	0.75	1.25
❏ 93 ....1.25	0.25	0.75	1.25
❏ 94 ....1.25	0.25	0.75	1.25
❏ 95 ....1.25	0.25	0.75	1.25
❏ 96 ....1.25	0.25	0.75	1.25
❏ 97 ....1.25	0.25	0.75	1.25
❏ 98 ....1.25	0.25	0.75	1.25
❏ 99 ....1.25	0.25	0.75	1.25
❏ 100, sculpted foil cover ..3.95	1.00	3.00	5.00
❏ 101 ....1.25	1.20	3.60	6.00
❏ 102, final issue 1.25	0.60	1.80	3.00

AVENGERS WEST COAST ANNUAL
(was West Coast Avengers Annual)

	ORIG.	GOOD	FINE	N-MINT
❏ 4, Nov 89, Atlantis Attacks				
..............2.00	0.40	1.20	2.00
❏ 5, Sep 90, Terminus Factor				
..............2.00	0.40	1.20	2.00
❏ 6, Oct 91, Subterranean Wars				
..............2.00	0.40	1.20	2.00
❏ 7 ....2.25	0.45	1.35	2.25
❏ 8, trading card 2.95	0.59	1.77	2.95

AVENGERS/ULTRAFORCE
MARVEL

	ORIG.	GOOD	FINE	N-MINT
❏ 1, Oct 95, enhanced cardstock cover;continues in				
UltraForce/Avengers #1 ..3.95	0.79	2.37	3.95

AVENGERS: THE CROSSING (mini-series)

	ORIG.	GOOD	FINE	N-MINT
❏ 1, Sep 95, enhanced wraparound cover				
..............4.95	1.40	4.20	7.00

AVENGERS: THE TERMINATRIX OBJECTIVE

	ORIG.	GOOD	FINE	N-MINT
❏ 1, foil cover..............2.50	0.50	1.50	2.50
❏ 2 ....1.25	0.25	0.75	1.25
❏ 3 ....1.25	0.25	0.75	1.25
❏ 4 ....1.25	0.25	0.75	1.25

AVENGERS: TIMESLIDE

	ORIG.	GOOD	FINE	N-MINT
❏ 0, Feb 96, nn;one-shot; enhanced wraparound cardstock				
cover..............4.95	0.99	2.97	4.95

AVENUE D
FANTAGRAPHICS

	ORIG.	GOOD	FINE	N-MINT
❏ 1, adult, b&w	0.70	2.10	3.50

AVENUE X
INNOVATION

	ORIG.	GOOD	FINE	N-MINT
❏ 1	0.50	1.50	2.50

AVIATRIX
FORBIDDEN FRUIT

	ORIG.	GOOD	FINE	N-MINT
❏ 1, adult, b&w	0.59	1.77	2.95
❏ 2, adult, b&w	0.59	1.77	2.95
❏ 3, adult, b&w	0.59	1.77	2.95

AXA
ECLIPSE

	ORIG.	GOOD	FINE	N-MINT
❏ 1	0.35	1.05	1.75
❏ 2	0.35	1.05	1.75

AXED FILES
EXPRESS/PARODY

	ORIG.	GOOD	FINE	N-MINT
❏ 1, 95, b&w..............2.50	0.50	1.50	2.50

AXEL PRESSBUTTON
ECLIPSE

	ORIG.	GOOD	FINE	N-MINT
❏ 1	0.30	0.90	1.50
❏ 2	0.35	1.05	1.75
❏ 3	0.35	1.05	1.75
❏ 4, (becomes Pressbutton)	0.35	1.05	1.75

AZ
COMICO

	ORIG.	GOOD	FINE	N-MINT
❏ 1, b&w..............	0.60	1.80	3.00
❏ 2, b&w..............	0.40	1.20	2.00

AZRAEL
DC

	ORIG.	GOOD	FINE	N-MINT
❏ 1, Feb 95..............1.95	1.40	4.20	7.00
❏ 2, Mar 95......................1.95	1.00	3.00	5.00

	ORIG.	GOOD	FINE	N-MINT
☐ 3, Apr 95 .... 1.95		0.80	2.40	4.00
☐ 4, May 95 .... 1.95		0.70	2.10	3.50
☐ 5, Jun 95 .... 1.95		0.70	2.10	3.50
☐ 6, Jul 95 .... 1.95		0.50	1.50	2.50
☐ 7, Aug 95 .... 1.95		0.50	1.50	2.50
☐ 8, Sep 95 .... 1.95		0.50	1.50	2.50
☐ 9, Oct 95 .... 1.95		0.50	1.50	2.50
☐ 10, Nov 95, "Underworld Unleashed"				
.... 1.95		0.50	1.50	2.50
☐ 11, Dec 95 .... 1.95		0.39	1.17	1.95
☐ 12, Jan 96 .... 1.95		0.39	1.17	1.95
☐ 13, Feb 96 .... 1.95		0.39	1.17	1.95
☐ 14, Mar 96 .... 1.95		0.39	1.17	1.95
☐ 15, Mar 96, "Contagion" Part 4				
.... 1.95		0.39	1.17	1.95
☐ 16, Apr 96, "Contagion" Part 10				
.... 1.95		0.39	1.17	1.95
☐ 17, May 96 .... 1.95		0.39	1.17	1.95
☐ 18, Jun 96 .... 1.95		0.39	1.17	1.95

AZRAEL ANNUAL

	ORIG.	GOOD	FINE	N-MINT
☐ 1, 95, "Year One" 3.95		0.79	2.37	3.95

AZTEC ACE
ECLIPSE

	ORIG.	GOOD	FINE	N-MINT
☐ 1, Mar 84		0.50	1.50	2.50
☐ 2, Apr 84		0.35	1.05	1.75
☐ 3, Jun 84		0.35	1.05	1.75
☐ 4, Jul 84		0.35	1.05	1.75
☐ 5, Jul 84		0.35	1.05	1.75
☐ 6, Aug 84		0.35	1.05	1.75
☐ 7, Oct 84		0.35	1.05	1.75
☐ 8, Dec 84		0.35	1.05	1.75
☐ 9, Jan 85		0.35	1.05	1.75
☐ 10, Feb 85		0.35	1.05	1.75
☐ 11, Mar 85		0.35	1.05	1.75
☐ 12, Apr 85		0.35	1.05	1.75
☐ 13, May 85		0.35	1.05	1.75
☐ 14, Jun 85		0.35	1.05	1.75
☐ 15, Sep 85		0.35	1.05	1.75

AZTEC ANTHROPOMORPHIC AMAZONS
ANTARCTIC

	ORIG.	GOOD	FINE	N-MINT
☐ 1, Mar 94, b&w 2.75		0.55	1.65	2.75

All-Star Squadron

First appearance: *Justice League of America* #193.

"Retroactive continuity" is a concept that explores what happened "off-stage" when a hero or villain changed — in costume, powers, or identity — from one appearance to the next with little or no explanation. For example, Dr. Fate's helmet changed in the '40s from one that covered his whole face to one that only obscured half of it.

Roy Thomas, an avid Golden Age fan, wrote a number of stories — years after the original stories were published — to try to explain these changes and make them agree with later stories. This was especially evident in DC's *All-Star Squadron* series.

Thomas' first bit of retroactive continuity was to explain why the Golden Age heroes didn't prevent the Japanese bombing of Pearl Harbor. He did this by having the major powerhouses of the day — Superman, Wonder Woman, Batman and Robin, and most of rest of the Justice Society of America — captured by the time-traveling villain Per Degaton and rendered unconscious while the events of Dec. 7, 1941, unfolded. The heroes were released and Degaton and his villainous crew defeated by a group of what could be best described as "second-stringers" including Robotman, Johnny Quick, Liberty Belle, Plastic Man, and The Shining Knight, assembled by President Roosevelt into The All-Star Squadron.

Thomas went on to establish why the Justice Society, *et al.*, didn't invade Japan and Europe immediately after the United States declared war on the Axis powers. The explanation involved the use of the Spear of Destiny (which played a part in the origin of the JSA) and the Holy Grail to create a sphere of influence that covered the Axis' front lines and would turn the mightiest heroes to the Axis cause if they crossed those lines.

The group eventually grew to include the JSA, The Seven Soldiers of Victory, and other Golden Age heroes. In *All-Star Squadron Annual* #3, Thomas explained why many Golden Age heroes had not aged as rapidly as the rest of their age group, leaving many of the heroes still fighting crime in the 1980s.

During the Crisis on Infinite Earths, Thomas began a storyline based on the originally planned ending for *Crisis* with a number of heroes migrating to other Earths, only to have those changes scrapped by the final ending of *Crisis*. The heroes who had migrated were "returned" to the one remaining Earth, and a number of heroes who had dopplegangers, such as the Golden Age Superman, Wonder Woman, Batman, and Robin, were removed. Although most of these heroes "died" before or during Crisis, many fans consider *All-Star Squadron* #60 their "final" appearance, at least in print, since it was published well after *Crisis* #12.

The series concluded with a set of origin stories for Robotman, Liberty Belle, The Shining Knight, and Johnny Quick. The All-Star Squadron breathed again for a short time in *The Young All-Stars*, but the group took a backseat to the adventures of the youthful heroes who were the headliners of the new series.

Partial checklist

B

	ORIG.	GOOD	FINE	N-MINT

B********U
FANTAGRAPHICS
	ORIG.	GOOD	FINE	N-MINT
❑ 0, Oct 94, b&w	3.25	0.65	1.95	3.25

B-BAR-B RIDERS
AC
❑ 1, FF				

B-MOVIE PRESENTS
B-MOVIE
		GOOD	FINE	N-MINT
❑ 1		0.30	0.90	1.50
❑ 2		0.30	0.90	1.50
❑ 3		0.30	0.90	1.50
❑ 4		0.30	0.90	1.50

BABE (mini-series)
DARK HORSE/LEGEND
	ORIG.	GOOD	FINE	N-MINT
❑ 1, Jul 94	2.50	0.50	1.50	2.50
❑ 2, Aug 94	2.50	0.50	1.50	2.50
❑ 3, Sep 94	2.50	0.50	1.50	2.50
❑ 4, Oct 94	2.50	0.50	1.50	2.50

BABE 2 (mini-series)
	ORIG.	GOOD	FINE	N-MINT
❑ 1, Mar 95	2.50	0.50	1.50	2.50
❑ 2, Apr 95	2.50	0.50	1.50	2.50

BABEWATCH
EXPRESS/PARODY
	ORIG.	GOOD	FINE	N-MINT
❑ 1, 95, (DD);cardstock cover;b&w	2.95	0.59	1.77	2.95
❑ 1, 95, b&w	2.50	0.50	1.50	2.50
❑ 1, 95, A;b&w	2.50	0.50	1.50	2.50

BABY HUEY
HARVEY
	ORIG.	GOOD	FINE	N-MINT
❑ 1	1.25	0.25	0.75	1.25
❑ 2	1.25	0.25	0.75	1.25
❑ 3	1.25	0.25	0.75	1.25
❑ 4	1.25	0.25	0.75	1.25
❑ 5	1.25	0.25	0.75	1.25
❑ 6	1.25	0.25	0.75	1.25
❑ 7	1.25	0.25	0.75	1.25
❑ 8	1.50	0.30	0.90	1.50
❑ 9	1.50	0.30	0.90	1.50

BABY HUEY DIGEST
	ORIG.	GOOD	FINE	N-MINT
❑ 1	1.75	0.35	1.05	1.75

BABY HUEY IN 3-D
BLACKTHORNE
		GOOD	FINE	N-MINT
❑ 1		0.50	1.50	2.50

BABY, YOU'RE REALLY SOMETHING!
EROS COMIX
		GOOD	FINE	N-MINT
❑ 1, FF, b&w, reprints		0.50	1.50	2.50

BABYLON 5
DC
	ORIG.	GOOD	FINE	N-MINT
❑ 1, Jan 95	1.95	1.00	3.00	5.00
❑ 2, Feb 95	1.95	0.80	2.40	4.00
❑ 3, Mar 95	1.95	0.60	1.80	3.00
❑ 4, Apr 95	1.95	0.60	1.80	3.00
❑ 5, Jun 95	2.50	0.60	1.80	3.00
❑ 6, Jul 95	2.50	0.60	1.80	3.00
❑ 7, Aug 95	2.50	0.50	1.50	2.50
❑ 8, Sep 95	2.50	0.50	1.50	2.50
❑ 9, Oct 95	2.50	0.50	1.50	2.50
❑ 10, Nov 95	2.50	0.50	1.50	2.50
❑ 11, Dec 95, final issue	2.50	0.50	1.50	2.50

BABYLON CRUSH (mini-series)
BONEYARD
	ORIG.	GOOD	FINE	N-MINT
❑ 1, May 95, b&w;cardstock cover	2.95	0.59	1.77	2.95

BACCHUS
HARRIER
		GOOD	FINE	N-MINT
❑ 1		1.60	4.80	8.00
❑ 2		1.00	3.00	5.00

BACK TO THE FUTURE
HARVEY
	ORIG.	GOOD	FINE	N-MINT
❑ 1, Sep 91	1.25	0.25	0.75	1.25
❑ 2, Nov 91	1.25	0.25	0.75	1.25
❑ 3	1.25	0.25	0.75	1.25
❑ 4	1.25	0.25	0.75	1.25

BACKLASH
IMAGE
	ORIG.	GOOD	FINE	N-MINT
❑ 1, Nov 94, issue has two covers, one inside the other	1.95	0.80	2.40	4.00
❑ 1, Nov 94	1.95	0.60	1.80	3.00
❑ 2, Dec 94	1.95	0.39	1.17	1.95
❑ 3, Jan 95	2.50	0.50	1.50	2.50
❑ 4, Feb 95	2.50	0.50	1.50	2.50
❑ 6, Mar 95	2.50	0.50	1.50	2.50
❑ 7, Apr 95	2.50	0.50	1.50	2.50
❑ 8, May 95, "WildStorm Rising" Part 8;bound-in trading cards	2.50	0.50	1.50	2.50
❑ 10, Jul 95, cover says "Aug", indicia says "Jul"	2.50	0.50	1.50	2.50
❑ 11, Aug 95	2.50	0.50	1.50	2.50
❑ 13, Nov 95	2.50	0.50	1.50	2.50
❑ 14, Nov 95, indicia says "Nov";cover says "Dec"	2.50	0.50	1.50	2.50
❑ 15, Dec 95, indicia says "Dec";cover says "Jan"	2.50	0.50	1.50	2.50
❑ 16, Jan 96, indicia says "Jan";cover says "Feb"	2.50	0.50	1.50	2.50
❑ 17, Feb 96	2.50	0.50	1.50	2.50
❑ 18, Mar 96	2.50	0.50	1.50	2.50
❑ 19, Apr 96, "Fire from Heaven" Part 2	2.50	0.50	1.50	2.50

BAD COMICS
CAT-HEAD
		GOOD	FINE	N-MINT
❑ 1, b&w		0.55	1.65	2.75

BAD COMPANY
FLEETWAY/QUALITY
		GOOD	FINE	N-MINT
❑ 1, O:Bad Company		0.30	0.90	1.50
❑ 2		0.30	0.90	1.50
❑ 3		0.30	0.90	1.50
❑ 4		0.30	0.90	1.50
❑ 5		0.30	0.90	1.50
❑ 6		0.30	0.90	1.50
❑ 7		0.30	0.90	1.50
❑ 8		0.30	0.90	1.50
❑ 9		0.30	0.90	1.50
❑ 10		0.30	0.90	1.50
❑ 11		0.30	0.90	1.50
❑ 12		0.30	0.90	1.50
❑ 13		0.30	0.90	1.50
❑ 14		0.30	0.90	1.50
❑ 15		0.30	0.90	1.50
❑ 16		0.35	1.05	1.75
❑ 17		0.35	1.05	1.75
❑ 18		0.35	1.05	1.75
❑ 19		0.35	1.05	1.75

BAD EGGS (mini-series)
ACCLAIM/ARMADA
	ORIG.	GOOD	FINE	N-MINT
❑ 1, Jun 96	2.95	0.59	1.77	2.95
❑ 2, Jul 96	2.95	0.59	1.77	2.95
❑ 3, Aug 96	2.95	0.59	1.77	2.95

BAD GIRLS OF BLACKOUT
BLACKOUT
	ORIG.	GOOD	FINE	N-MINT
❑ 0, 95	3.50	0.70	2.10	3.50

BAD GIRLS OF BLACKOUT ANNUAL
BLACK OUT
	ORIG.	GOOD	FINE	N-MINT
❑ 1, 95	3.50	0.70	2.10	3.50

	ORIG.	GOOD	FINE	N-MINT

BAD MEAT
EROS COMIX

	ORIG.	GOOD	FINE	N-MINT
1, adult, b&w		0.45	1.35	2.25
2		0.55	1.65	2.75

BAD NEWS
FANTAGRAPHICS

	GOOD	FINE	N-MINT
3, b&w	0.70	2.10	3.50

BADAXE
ADVENTURE

	GOOD	FINE	N-MINT
1, b&w	0.45	1.35	2.25
2, b&w	0.45	1.35	2.25
3, b&w	0.45	1.35	2.25

BADE BIKER
MIRAGE

	GOOD	FINE	N-MINT
1	0.30	0.90	1.50
2	0.30	0.90	1.50
3	0.30	0.90	1.50
4	0.30	0.90	1.50

BADGE
VANGUARD

	ORIG.	GOOD	FINE	N-MINT
1, 81	2.95	0.59	1.77	2.95

BADGER
CAPITAL

	GOOD	FINE	N-MINT
1, Oct 83	1.60	4.80	8.00
2, Feb 84	1.20	3.60	6.00
3, Mar 84	1.00	3.00	5.00
4, Apr 84, (moves to First)	1.00	3.00	5.00

BADGER (former Capital title)
FIRST

	GOOD	FINE	N-MINT
5, May 85	0.50	1.50	2.50
6, Jul 85	0.50	1.50	2.50
7, Sep 85	0.50	1.50	2.50
8, Nov 85	0.50	1.50	2.50
9, Jan 86	0.50	1.50	2.50
10, Mar 86	0.50	1.50	2.50
11, May 86	0.35	1.05	1.75
12, Jun 86	0.35	1.05	1.75
13, Jul 86	0.35	1.05	1.75
14, Aug 86	0.35	1.05	1.75
15, Sep 86	0.35	1.05	1.75
16, Oct 86	0.35	1.05	1.75
17, Nov 86	0.35	1.05	1.75
18, Dec 86	0.35	1.05	1.75
19, Jan 87	0.35	1.05	1.75
20, Feb 87	0.35	1.05	1.75
21, Mar 87	0.35	1.05	1.75
22, Apr 87	0.35	1.05	1.75
23, May 87	0.35	1.05	1.75
24, Jun 87	0.35	1.05	1.75
25, Jul 87	0.35	1.05	1.75
26, Aug 87, Roach Wrangler	0.35	1.05	1.75
27, Sep 87, Roach Wrangler	0.35	1.05	1.75
28, Oct 87	0.35	1.05	1.75
29, Nov 87	0.35	1.05	1.75
30, Dec 87	0.35	1.05	1.75
31, Jan 88	0.35	1.05	1.75
32, Feb 88	0.35	1.05	1.75
33, Mar 88	0.35	1.05	1.75
34, Apr 88	0.35	1.05	1.75
35, May 88	0.35	1.05	1.75
36, Jun 88	0.35	1.05	1.75
37, Jul 88	0.35	1.05	1.75
38, Aug 88	0.35	1.05	1.75
39, Sep 88	0.35	1.05	1.75
40, Oct 88	0.35	1.05	1.75
41, Nov 88	0.39	1.17	1.95
42, Dec 88	0.39	1.17	1.95
43, Jan 89	0.39	1.17	1.95
44, Feb 89	0.39	1.17	1.95
45, Mar 89	0.39	1.17	1.95

	GOOD	FINE	N-MINT
46, Apr 89	0.39	1.17	1.95
47, May 89	0.39	1.17	1.95
48, Jun 89	0.39	1.17	1.95
49, Jul 89	0.39	1.17	1.95
50, Aug 89	0.79	2.37	3.95
51, Sep 89	0.39	1.17	1.95
52, Oct 89, Tim Vigil	0.90	2.70	4.50
53, Nov 89, Tim Vigil	0.90	2.70	4.50
54, Dec 89, Tim Vigil	0.90	2.70	4.50
55, Jan 90	0.39	1.17	1.95
56, Feb 90	0.39	1.17	1.95
57, Mar 90	0.39	1.17	1.95
58, Apr 90	0.39	1.17	1.95
59, May 90	0.39	1.17	1.95
60, Jun 90	0.39	1.17	1.95
61, Jul 90	0.39	1.17	1.95
62, Aug 90	0.39	1.17	1.95
63, Sep 90	0.39	1.17	1.95
64, Oct 90	0.45	1.35	2.25
65, Nov 90	0.45	1.35	2.25
66, Dec 90	0.45	1.35	2.25
67, Jan 91	0.45	1.35	2.25
68, Feb 91	0.45	1.35	2.25
69, Mar 91	0.45	1.35	2.25
70, Apr 91	0.45	1.35	2.25

BADGER (former Capital title) (Volume 2)

	ORIG.	GOOD	FINE	N-MINT
1, May 91, Badger Bedlam	0.99	2.97	4.95	

BADGER GOES BERSERK!

	GOOD	FINE	N-MINT
1, Sep 89	0.39	1.17	1.95
2, Oct 89	0.39	1.17	1.95
3, Nov 89	0.39	1.17	1.95
4, Dec 89	0.39	1.17	1.95

BADGER: SHATTERED MIRROR (mini-series)
DARK HORSE

	ORIG.	GOOD	FINE	N-MINT
1, Jul 94	2.50	0.50	1.50	2.50
2, Aug 94	2.50	0.50	1.50	2.50
3, Sep 94	2.50	0.50	1.50	2.50
4, Oct 94	2.50	0.50	1.50	2.50

BADGER: ZEN POP FUNNY-ANIMAL VERSION (mini-series)

	ORIG.	GOOD	FINE	N-MINT
1, Jul 94	2.50	0.50	1.50	2.50
2, Aug 94	2.50	0.50	1.50	2.50

BADLANDS

	ORIG.	GOOD	FINE	N-MINT
1, b&w	2.25	0.80	2.40	4.00
2, b&w	2.25	0.60	1.80	3.00
3, b&w	2.25	0.60	1.80	3.00
4, b&w	2.25	0.60	1.80	3.00
5, b&w	2.25	0.60	1.80	3.00
6, b&w	2.25	0.60	1.80	3.00

BADROCK
IMAGE

	ORIG.	GOOD	FINE	N-MINT
1, Mar 95, B;RL	1.75	0.50	1.50	2.50
1, Mar 95, A;BL	1.75	0.35	1.05	1.75
1, Mar 95, C;BL	1.75	0.35	1.05	1.75

BADROCK & COMPANY (mini-series)

	ORIG.	GOOD	FINE	N-MINT
1, Sep 94, A;San Diego Comic-Con edition	2.50	0.50	1.50	2.50
1, Sep 94	2.50	0.50	1.50	2.50
2, Oct 94	2.50	0.50	1.50	2.50
3, Nov 94	2.50	0.50	1.50	2.50
4, Dec 94	2.50	0.50	1.50	2.50
5, Jan 95	2.50	0.50	1.50	2.50
6, Feb 95, (indicia says October 1994)	2.50	0.50	1.50	2.50

BADROCK ANNUAL

	ORIG.	GOOD	FINE	N-MINT
1, Jul 95	2.95	0.59	1.77	2.95

BAKER STREET
CALIBER

	ORIG.	GOOD	FINE	N-MINT
1, Mar 89, b&w	1.95	1.60	4.80	8.00

	ORIG.	GOOD	FINE	N-MINT
☐ 2	1.95	1.00	3.00	5.00
☐ 3	1.95	0.80	2.40	4.00
☐ 4	1.95	0.39	1.17	1.95
☐ 5	2.50	0.60	1.80	3.00
☐ 6	2.50	0.60	1.80	3.00
☐ 7	2.50	0.60	1.80	3.00
☐ 8	2.50	0.60	1.80	3.00
☐ 9	2.50	0.60	1.80	3.00
☐ 10	2.50	0.60	1.80	3.00

BAKER STREET GRAFFITI

	ORIG.	GOOD	FINE	N-MINT
☐ 1, b&w	2.50	0.50	1.50	2.50

BAKER STREET SKETCHBOOK

	ORIG.	GOOD	FINE	N-MINT
☐ 1	3.95	1.00	3.00	5.00

BALANCE OF POWER
MU PRESS

	ORIG.	GOOD	FINE	N-MINT
☐ 1, b&w		0.40	1.20	2.00
☐ 2		0.45	1.35	2.25
☐ 3, Mar 91	2.50	0.50	1.50	2.50
☐ 4, Jul 91	2.50	0.50	1.50	2.50

BALDER THE BRAVE
MARVEL

	ORIG.	GOOD	FINE	N-MINT
☐ 1, Nov 85	0.75	0.40	1.20	2.00
☐ 2, Jan 86	0.75	0.20	0.60	1.00
☐ 3, Mar 86	0.75	0.20	0.60	1.00
☐ 4, May 86	0.75	0.20	0.60	1.00

BALLISTIC
IMAGE

	ORIG.	GOOD	FINE	N-MINT
☐ 1, Sep 95	2.50	0.50	1.50	2.50

BALLISTIC ACTION

	ORIG.	GOOD	FINE	N-MINT
☐ 1, May 96, pin-ups	2.95	0.59	1.77	2.95

BALLISTIC IMAGERY

	ORIG.	GOOD	FINE	N-MINT
☐ 1, Jan 96, anthology	2.50	0.50	1.50	2.50

BALLOONATIKS
BEST

	ORIG.	GOOD	FINE	N-MINT
☐ 1, b&w		0.99	2.97	4.95

BALLOONATIKS, THE

	ORIG.	GOOD	FINE	N-MINT
☐ 1		0.50	1.50	2.50

BAMBI AND HER FRIENDS
FRIENDLY

	ORIG.	GOOD	FINE	N-MINT
☐ 1, adult, b&w		0.50	1.50	2.50
☐ 2, adult, b&w		0.50	1.50	2.50
☐ 3, adult, b&w		0.50	1.50	2.50
☐ 4, adult, b&w		0.50	1.50	2.50
☐ 5, adult, b&w		0.50	1.50	2.50
☐ 6		0.59	1.77	2.95
☐ 7		0.59	1.77	2.95
☐ 8		0.59	1.77	2.95
☐ 9		0.59	1.77	2.95

BANG GANG
EROS COMIX

	ORIG.	GOOD	FINE	N-MINT
☐ 1, adult, b&w		0.50	1.50	2.50

BAOH
VIZ

	ORIG.	GOOD	FINE	N-MINT
☐ 1, b&w, Japanese		0.59	1.77	2.95
☐ 2, b&w, Japanese		0.59	1.77	2.95
☐ 3, b&w, Japanese		0.59	1.77	2.95
☐ 4, b&w, Japanese		0.59	1.77	2.95
☐ 5, b&w, Japanese		0.59	1.77	2.95
☐ 6, b&w, Japanese		0.59	1.77	2.95
☐ 7, b&w, Japanese		0.59	1.77	2.95
☐ 8, b&w, Japanese		0.59	1.77	2.95

BAR SINISTER
WINDJAMMER/ACCLAIM

	ORIG.	GOOD	FINE	N-MINT
☐ 1, Jun 95, MGr	2.50	0.50	1.50	2.50

BARABBAS
SLAVE LABOR

	ORIG.	GOOD	FINE	N-MINT
☐ 1		0.30	0.90	1.50
☐ 2		0.30	0.90	1.50

BARB WIRE
DARK HORSE

	ORIG.	GOOD	FINE	N-MINT
☐ 1, Apr 94	2.00	0.80	2.40	4.00
☐ 2, May 94	2.00	0.60	1.80	3.00
☐ 3, Jun 94	2.00	0.40	1.20	2.00
☐ 4, Aug 94	2.00	0.40	1.20	2.00
☐ 5, Sep 94	2.50	0.50	1.50	2.50
☐ 6, Oct 94	2.50	0.50	1.50	2.50
☐ 7, Nov 94	2.50	0.50	1.50	2.50
☐ 8, Jan 95	2.50	0.50	1.50	2.50
☐ 9, Feb 95	2.50	0.50	1.50	2.50

BARB WIRE MOVIE SPECIAL

	ORIG.	GOOD	FINE	N-MINT
☐ 0, May 96, nn;adapts movie	3.95	0.79	2.37	3.95

BARBARIAN, THE
CONQUEST

	ORIG.	GOOD	FINE	N-MINT
☐ 0, Conan parody, b&w		0.59	1.77	2.95

BARBARIANS, THE
ATLAS/SEABOARD

	ORIG.	GOOD	FINE	N-MINT
☐ 1, Jun 75	0.25	0.20	0.60	1.00

BARBARIC TALES
PYRAMID

	ORIG.	GOOD	FINE	N-MINT
☐ 1		0.30	0.90	1.50
☐ 2		0.30	0.90	1.50

BARBARIENNE
EROS

	ORIG.	GOOD	FINE	N-MINT
☐ 2, adult, b&w		0.50	1.50	2.50
☐ 3, adult, b&w		0.50	1.50	2.50

HARRIER

	ORIG.	GOOD	FINE	N-MINT
☐ 1		0.39	1.17	1.95
☐ 2		0.39	1.17	1.95
☐ 3		0.39	1.17	1.95
☐ 4		0.39	1.17	1.95
☐ 5		0.39	1.17	1.95
☐ 6, vs. Cuirass		0.39	1.17	1.95
☐ 7, vs. Cuirass		0.39	1.17	1.95
☐ 8, vs. Cuirass		0.39	1.17	1.95

BARBI TWINS ADVENTURES, THE
TOPPS

	ORIG.	GOOD	FINE	N-MINT
☐ 1, Jul 95	2.50	0.50	1.50	2.50
☐ 1, Jul 95, flip-book;A:Razor	2.50	0.50	1.50	2.50

BARBIE
MARVEL

	ORIG.	GOOD	FINE	N-MINT
☐ 1, with door hanger	1.00	1.60	4.80	8.00
☐ 1, with membership card	1.00	1.60	4.80	8.00
☐ 2	1.00	1.00	3.00	5.00
☐ 3	1.00	0.80	2.40	4.00
☐ 4	1.00	0.80	2.40	4.00
☐ 5	1.00	0.80	2.40	4.00
☐ 6	1.00	0.60	1.80	3.00
☐ 7	1.00	0.60	1.80	3.00
☐ 8	1.00	0.60	1.80	3.00
☐ 9	1.00	0.60	1.80	3.00
☐ 10	1.00	0.60	1.80	3.00
☐ 11	1.00	0.40	1.20	2.00
☐ 12	1.00	0.40	1.20	2.00
☐ 13	1.00	0.40	1.20	2.00
☐ 14	1.25	0.40	1.20	2.00
☐ 15	1.25	0.40	1.20	2.00
☐ 16	1.25	0.40	1.20	2.00
☐ 17	1.25	0.40	1.20	2.00
☐ 18	1.25	0.40	1.20	2.00
☐ 19	1.25	0.40	1.20	2.00
☐ 20	1.25	0.40	1.20	2.00
☐ 21	1.25	0.40	1.20	2.00
☐ 22	1.25	0.40	1.20	2.00
☐ 23	1.25	0.40	1.20	2.00
☐ 24	1.25	0.40	1.20	2.00
☐ 25	1.25	0.40	1.20	2.00

	ORIG.	GOOD	FINE	N-MINT
❏ 26	1.25	0.40	1.20	2.00
❏ 27	1.25	0.40	1.20	2.00
❏ 28	1.25	0.40	1.20	2.00
❏ 29	1.25	0.40	1.20	2.00
❏ 30	1.25	0.40	1.20	2.00
❏ 31	1.25	0.25	0.75	1.25
❏ 32	1.25	0.25	0.75	1.25
❏ 33	1.25	0.25	0.75	1.25
❏ 34	1.25	0.25	0.75	1.25
❏ 35	1.25	0.25	0.75	1.25
❏ 36	1.25	0.25	0.75	1.25
❏ 37	1.25	0.25	0.75	1.25
❏ 38	1.25	0.25	0.75	1.25
❏ 39	1.25	0.25	0.75	1.25
❏ 40, 94	1.25	0.25	0.75	1.25
❏ 41, May 94	1.25	0.25	0.75	1.25
❏ 42, Jun 94	1.50	0.30	0.90	1.50
❏ 43, Jul 94	1.50	0.30	0.90	1.50
❏ 44, Aug 94	1.50	0.30	0.90	1.50
❏ 45, Sep 94	1.50	0.30	0.90	1.50
❏ 46, Oct 94	1.50	0.30	0.90	1.50
❏ 47, Nov 94	1.50	0.30	0.90	1.50
❏ 48, Dec 94	1.50	0.30	0.90	1.50
❏ 49, Jan 95	1.50	0.30	0.90	1.50
❏ 50, Feb 95	2.25	0.45	1.35	2.25
❏ 51, Mar 95	1.50	0.30	0.90	1.50
❏ 52, Apr 95	1.50	0.30	0.90	1.50
❏ 53, May 95, final issue	1.50	0.30	0.90	1.50
❏ 54, Jun 95	1.50	0.30	0.90	1.50
❏ 55, Jul 95	1.50	0.30	0.90	1.50
❏ 56, Aug 95	1.50	0.30	0.90	1.50
❏ 57, Sep 95	1.50	0.30	0.90	1.50
❏ 58, Oct 95	1.50	0.30	0.90	1.50
❏ 59, Nov 95	1.50	0.30	0.90	1.50
❏ 60, Dec 95	1.50	0.30	0.90	1.50
❏ 61, Jan 96	1.50	0.30	0.90	1.50
❏ 62, Feb 96	1.50	0.30	0.90	1.50
❏ 63, Mar 96, final issue	1.50	0.30	0.90	1.50

BARBIE FASHION

	ORIG.	GOOD	FINE	N-MINT
❏ 1, with doorknob hanger	1.00	1.60	4.80	8.00
❏ 2	1.00	1.00	3.00	5.00
❏ 3	1.00	0.80	2.40	4.00
❏ 4	1.00	0.80	2.40	4.00
❏ 5	1.00	0.80	2.40	4.00
❏ 6	1.00	0.60	1.80	3.00
❏ 7	1.00	0.60	1.80	3.00
❏ 8	1.00	0.60	1.80	3.00
❏ 9	1.00	0.60	1.80	3.00
❏ 10	1.00	0.60	1.80	3.00
❏ 11	1.00	0.40	1.20	2.00
❏ 12	1.00	0.40	1.20	2.00
❏ 13	1.00	0.40	1.20	2.00
❏ 14	1.00	0.40	1.20	2.00
❏ 15	1.00	0.40	1.20	2.00
❏ 16	1.00	0.40	1.20	2.00
❏ 17	1.00	0.40	1.20	2.00
❏ 18	1.00	0.40	1.20	2.00
❏ 19	1.00	0.40	1.20	2.00
❏ 20	1.00	0.40	1.20	2.00
❏ 21	1.00	0.40	1.20	2.00
❏ 22	1.00	0.40	1.20	2.00
❏ 23	1.00	0.40	1.20	2.00
❏ 24	1.00	0.40	1.20	2.00
❏ 25	1.00	0.40	1.20	2.00
❏ 26	1.00	0.40	1.20	2.00
❏ 27	1.00	0.40	1.20	2.00
❏ 28	1.00	0.40	1.20	2.00
❏ 29	1.00	0.40	1.20	2.00
❏ 30	1.00	0.40	1.20	2.00
❏ 31	1.25	0.25	0.75	1.25
❏ 32	1.25	0.25	0.75	1.25

	ORIG.	GOOD	FINE	N-MINT
❏ 33	1.25	0.25	0.75	1.25
❏ 34	1.25	0.25	0.75	1.25
❏ 35	1.25	0.25	0.75	1.25
❏ 36	1.25	0.25	0.75	1.25
❏ 37	1.25	0.25	0.75	1.25
❏ 38	1.25	0.25	0.75	1.25
❏ 39	1.25	0.25	0.75	1.25
❏ 40, 94	1.25	0.25	0.75	1.25
❏ 41, May 94	1.25	0.25	0.75	1.25
❏ 42, Jun 94	1.50	0.30	0.90	1.50
❏ 43, Jul 94	1.50	0.30	0.90	1.50
❏ 44, Aug 94	1.50	0.30	0.90	1.50
❏ 45, Sep 94	1.50	0.30	0.90	1.50
❏ 46, Oct 94	1.50	0.30	0.90	1.50
❏ 47, Nov 94	1.50	0.30	0.90	1.50
❏ 48, Dec 94	1.50	0.30	0.90	1.50
❏ 49, Jan 95	1.50	0.30	0.90	1.50
❏ 50, Feb 95	2.25	0.45	1.35	2.25
❏ 51, Mar 95	1.50	0.30	0.90	1.50
❏ 52, Apr 95	1.50	0.30	0.90	1.50
❏ 53, May 95, final issue	1.50	0.30	0.90	1.50

BARF
REVOLUTIONARY

	ORIG.	GOOD	FINE	N-MINT
❏ 1, Apr 90, b&w	1.95	0.39	1.17	1.95
❏ 2, Jun 90, b&w	2.50	0.50	1.50	2.50
❏ 3, Sep 90, b&w	2.50	0.50	1.50	2.50

BARNEY THE INVISIBLE TURTLE
AMAZING

		GOOD	FINE	N-MINT
❏ 1		0.39	1.17	1.95

BARRON STOREY'S WATCH ANNUAL (Vol. 2)
VANGUARD

	ORIG.	GOOD	FINE	N-MINT
❏ 1, 96, b&w anthology;squarebound	5.95	1.19	3.57	5.95

BART SIMPSON'S TREEHOUSE OF HORROR
BONGO

	ORIG.	GOOD	FINE	N-MINT
❏ 1, 95, Halloween stories by Mike Allred, James Robinson, and Jeff Smith	2.95	0.59	1.77	2.95

BARTMAN

	ORIG.	GOOD	FINE	N-MINT
❏ 1, 93, silver cover	2.95	1.00	3.00	5.00
❏ 2, 94	1.95	0.70	2.10	3.50
❏ 3, 94, trading card	2.25	0.80	2.40	4.00
❏ 4, 95	2.25	0.60	1.80	3.00
❏ 5, 95, I&1:Lisa the Conjuror and The Great Maggeena	2.25	0.45	1.35	2.25
❏ 6, 95, O&1:Bart Dog	2.25	0.45	1.35	2.25

BASEBALL CLASSICS
PERSONALITY

		GOOD	FINE	N-MINT
❏ 1		0.59	1.77	2.95
❏ 2		0.59	1.77	2.95

BASEBALL COMICS
KITCHEN SINK

		GOOD	FINE	N-MINT
❏ 1, May 91, WE, trading cards	0.79	2.37	3.95	
❏ 2, WE cards		0.59	1.77	2.95

PERSONALITY

		GOOD	FINE	N-MINT
❏ 1		0.59	1.77	2.95
❏ 2		0.59	1.77	2.95

BASEBALL GREATS
DARK HORSE

	ORIG.	GOOD	FINE	N-MINT
❏ 1, Jimmy Piersall, with cards	2.95	0.59	1.77	2.95
❏ 2	2.95	0.59	1.77	2.95
❏ 3, 2 trading cards	2.95	0.59	1.77	2.95

BASEBALL LEGENDS
REVOLUTIONARY

	ORIG.	GOOD	FINE	N-MINT
❏ 1, Mar 92, b&w, Babe Ruth	2.50	0.50	1.50	2.50
❏ 2, Apr 92, b&w, Ty Cobb	2.50	0.50	1.50	2.50
❏ 3, May 92, b&w, Ted Williams	2.50	0.50	1.50	2.50

	ORIG.	GOOD	FINE	N-MINT
☐ 4, Jun 92, b&w, Mickey Mantle 2.50		0.55	1.65	2.75
☐ 5, Jul 92, b&w, Joe DiMaggio 2.50		0.55	1.65	2.75
☐ 6, Aug 92, b&w, Jackie Robinson 2.50		0.55	1.65	2.75
☐ 7, Sep 92, b&w, Sandy Koufax 2.50		0.55	1.65	2.75
☐ 8, Oct 92, b&w, Willie Mays 2.50		0.55	1.65	2.75
☐ 9, Nov 92, b&w, Honus Wagner 2.50		0.55	1.65	2.75
☐ 10, Dec 92, color, Roberto Clemente 2.75		0.55	1.65	2.75
☐ 11, Jan 93, color, Yogi Berra 2.75		0.55	1.65	2.75
☐ 12, Feb 93, color, Billy Martin 2.75		0.55	1.65	2.75
☐ 13, Mar 93, color, Hank Aaron 2.95		0.59	1.77	2.95
☐ 14, Apr 93, b&w, Carl Yastrzemski 2.95		0.59	1.77	2.95
☐ 15, May 93, b&w, Satchel Paige 2.95		0.59	1.77	2.95
☐ 16, Jun 93, b&w, Johnny Bench 2.95		0.59	1.77	2.95
☐ 17, Jul 93, b&w, Shoeless Joe Jackson 2.95		0.59	1.77	2.95
☐ 18, Aug 93, b&w, Lou Gehrig 2.95		0.59	1.77	2.95
☐ 19, Sep 93, b&w, Casey Stengel 2.95		0.59	1.77	2.95

BASEBALL SLUGGERS
PERSONALITY

	GOOD	FINE	N-MINT
☐ 1, b&w	0.59	1.77	2.95
☐ 2, b&w	0.59	1.77	2.95
☐ 3, b&w	0.59	1.77	2.95
☐ 4, b&w	0.59	1.77	2.95

BASEBALL SUPERSTARS
REVOLUTIONARY

	ORIG.	GOOD	FINE	N-MINT
☐ 1, Nov 91, Nolan Ryan	2.50	0.50	1.50	2.50
☐ 2, Feb 92, Bo Jackson	2.50	0.55	1.65	2.75
☐ 3, Mar 92, Ken Griffey Jr.	2.50	0.55	1.65	2.75
☐ 4, Apr 92, Pete Rose	2.50	0.55	1.65	2.75
☐ 5, May 92, Rickey Henderson 2.50		0.55	1.65	2.75
☐ 6, Jun 92, Jose Canseco	2.50	0.55	1.65	2.75
☐ 7, Jul 92, Cal Ripkin Jr.	2.50	0.55	1.65	2.75
☐ 8, Aug 92, Carlton Fisk	2.50	0.55	1.65	2.75
☐ 9, Sep 92, George Brett	2.50	0.55	1.65	2.75
☐ 10, Oct 92, Darryl Strawberry 2.50		0.55	1.65	2.75
☐ 11, Nov 92, Frank Thomas 2.50		0.55	1.65	2.75
☐ 12, Dec 92, color, Ryne Sandberg 2.75		0.55	1.65	2.75
☐ 13, Jan 93, color, Kirby Puckett 2.75		0.55	1.65	2.75
☐ 14, Feb 93, color, Roberto & Sandi Alomar 2.75		0.55	1.65	2.75
☐ 15, Mar 93, color, Roger Clemens 2.95		0.59	1.77	2.95
☐ 16, Apr 93, b&w, Mark McGuire 2.95		0.59	1.77	2.95
☐ 17, May 93, b&w, Avery/Glavine 2.95		0.59	1.77	2.95
☐ 18, Jun 93, b&w, Dennis Eckersley 2.95		0.59	1.77	2.95
☐ 19, Jul 93, b&w, Dave Winfield 2.95		0.59	1.77	2.95
☐ 20, Aug 93, b&w, Jim Abbott 2.95		0.59	1.77	2.95

BASEBALL THRILLS 3-D
3-D ZONE

	GOOD	FINE	N-MINT
☐ 0, nn	0.59	1.77	2.95

BASIL WOLVERTON'S FANTASTIC FABLES
DARK HORSE

	ORIG.	GOOD	FINE	N-MINT
☐ 1, b&w reprints	2.50	0.50	1.50	2.50

BASIL WOLVERTON'S GATEWAY TO HORROR

	ORIG.	GOOD	FINE	N-MINT
☐ 1, Aug 87, BW b&w	1.75	0.35	1.05	1.75

BASIL WOLVERTON'S PLANET OF TERROR

	ORIG.	GOOD	FINE	N-MINT
☐ 1, Jul 87, BW	1.75	0.35	1.05	1.75

BAT LASH
DC

	ORIG.	GOOD	FINE	N-MINT
☐ 1, Nov 68	0.12	2.40	7.20	12.00
☐ 2, Jan 69	0.12	1.60	4.80	8.00
☐ 3, Mar 69	0.12	1.60	4.80	8.00
☐ 4, May 69	0.12	1.60	4.80	8.00
☐ 5, Jul 69	0.12	1.60	4.80	8.00
☐ 6, Sep 69	0.12	1.60	4.80	8.00
☐ 7, Nov 69	0.12	1.60	4.80	8.00

BAT, THE
ADVENTURE

	GOOD	FINE	N-MINT
☐ 1, b&w	0.50	1.50	2.50

APPLE

	GOOD	FINE	N-MINT
☐ 1, b&w	0.45	1.35	2.25

BATBABE
SPOOF

	GOOD	FINE	N-MINT
☐ 2	0.50	1.50	2.50

BATCH
CALIBER

	ORIG.	GOOD	FINE	N-MINT
☐ 1, b&w	2.95	0.59	1.77	2.95

BATGIRL SPECIAL
DC

	ORIG.	GOOD	FINE	N-MINT
☐ 1, Jul 88	1.50	1.60	4.80	8.00

BATHING MACHINE
C&T

	GOOD	FINE	N-MINT
☐ 1, b&w	0.50	1.50	2.50
☐ 2	0.30	0.90	1.50
☐ 3	0.30	0.90	1.50

BATMAN
DC

	ORIG.	GOOD	FINE	N-MINT
☐ 0, Oct 94	1.50	0.60	1.80	3.00
☐ 110, Sep 57	0.10	56.00	168.00	280.00
☐ 111, Oct 57		45.00	135.00	225.00
☐ 112, Dec 57		45.00	135.00	225.00
☐ 113, Feb 58		45.00	135.00	225.00
☐ 114, Mar 58		45.00	135.00	225.00
☐ 115, Apr 58		45.00	135.00	225.00
☐ 116, Jun 58	0.10	40.00	120.00	200.00
☐ 117, Jul 58	0.10	40.00	120.00	200.00
☐ 118, Sep 58	0.10	40.00	120.00	200.00
☐ 119, Oct 58	0.10	40.00	120.00	200.00
☐ 120, Dec 58	0.10	40.00	120.00	200.00
☐ 121, Feb 59		32.00	96.00	160.00
☐ 122, Mar 59		32.00	96.00	160.00
☐ 123, Apr 59		36.00	108.00	180.00
☐ 124, Jun 59		28.00	84.00	140.00
☐ 125, Aug 59	0.10	28.00	84.00	140.00
☐ 126, Sep 59	0.10	28.00	84.00	140.00
☐ 127, Oct 59	0.10	28.00	84.00	140.00
☐ 128, Dec 59	0.10	28.00	84.00	140.00
☐ 129, Feb 60	0.10	28.00	84.00	140.00
☐ 130, Mar 60	0.10	28.00	84.00	140.00
☐ 131, Apr 60, I:2nd Batman	17.00	51.00	85.00
☐ 132, Jun 60	0.10	16.00	48.00	80.00
☐ 133, Aug 60	0.10	16.00	48.00	80.00

	ORIG.	GOOD	FINE	N-MINT
☐ 134, Sep 60	0.10	16.00	48.00	80.00
☐ 135, Oct 60	0.10	16.00	48.00	80.00
☐ 136, Dec 60	0.10	16.00	48.00	80.00
☐ 137, Feb 61	0.10	16.00	48.00	80.00
☐ 138, Mar 61	0.10	16.00	48.00	80.00
☐ 139, Apr 61, I:old Batgirl..		18.00	54.00	90.00
☐ 140, Jun 61, Joker		17.00	51.00	85.00
☐ 141, Aug 61		12.00	36.00	60.00
☐ 142, Sep 61	0.10	12.00	36.00	60.00
☐ 143, Oct 61	0.10	12.00	36.00	60.00
☐ 144, Dec 61	0.12	12.00	36.00	60.00
☐ 145, Feb 62	0.12	12.00	36.00	60.00
☐ 146, Mar 62	0.12	12.00	36.00	60.00
☐ 147, May 62	0.12	12.00	36.00	60.00
☐ 148, Jul 62	0.12	12.00	36.00	60.00
☐ 149, Aug 62	0.12	12.00	36.00	60.00
☐ 150, Oct 62	0.12	12.00	36.00	60.00
☐ 151, Nov 62	0.12	10.00	30.00	50.00
☐ 152, Dec 62, Joker	0.12	10.00	30.00	50.00
☐ 153, Feb 63	0.12	10.00	30.00	50.00
☐ 154, Mar 63	0.12	10.00	30.00	50.00
☐ 155, Apr 63, Penguin	0.12	50.00	150.00	250.00
☐ 156, Jun 63	0.12	10.00	30.00	50.00
☐ 157, Aug 63	0.12	10.00	30.00	50.00
☐ 158, Sep 63	0.12	10.00	30.00	50.00
☐ 159, Nov 63	0.12	10.00	30.00	50.00
☐ 160, Dec 63	0.12	10.00	30.00	50.00
☐ 161, Feb 64	0.12	10.00	30.00	50.00
☐ 162, Mar 64	0.12	10.00	30.00	50.00
☐ 163, May 64	0.12	10.00	30.00	50.00
☐ 164, Jun 64	0.12	15.00	45.00	75.00
☐ 165, Aug 64		8.00	24.00	40.00
☐ 166, Sep 64	0.12	8.00	24.00	40.00
☐ 167, Nov 64	0.12	8.00	24.00	40.00
☐ 168, Dec 64	0.12	8.00	24.00	40.00
☐ 169, Feb 65	0.12	8.00	24.00	40.00
☐ 170, Mar 65	0.12	8.00	24.00	40.00
☐ 171, May 65, CI, Riddler	0.12	48.00	144.00	240.00
☐ 172, Jun 65	0.12	6.00	18.00	30.00
☐ 173, Aug 65	0.12	6.00	18.00	30.00
☐ 174, Sep 65	0.12	6.00	18.00	30.00
☐ 175, Nov 65	0.12	6.00	18.00	30.00
☐ 176, Dec 65	0.25	6.00	18.00	30.00
☐ 177, Dec 65	0.12	6.00	18.00	30.00
☐ 178, Feb 66	0.12	6.00	18.00	30.00
☐ 179, Mar 66	0.12	6.00	18.00	30.00
☐ 180, May 66	0.12	6.00	18.00	30.00
☐ 181, Jun 66	0.12	4.80	14.40	24.00
☐ 182, Aug 66	0.25	4.80	14.40	24.00
☐ 183, Aug 66	0.12	4.80	14.40	24.00
☐ 184, Sep 66	0.12	4.80	14.40	24.00
☐ 185, Nov 66	0.25	4.80	14.40	24.00
☐ 186, Nov 66	0.12	4.80	14.40	24.00
☐ 187, Jan 67	0.25	4.80	14.40	24.00
☐ 188, Dec 66	0.12	4.80	14.40	24.00
☐ 189, Feb 67	0.12	18.00	54.00	90.00
☐ 190, Mar 67	0.12	4.80	14.40	24.00
☐ 191, May 67	0.12	4.80	14.40	24.00
☐ 192, Jun 67	0.12	4.80	14.40	24.00
☐ 193, Aug 67	0.25	4.80	14.40	24.00
☐ 194, Aug 67	0.12	4.80	14.40	24.00
☐ 195, Sep 67	0.12	4.80	14.40	24.00
☐ 196, Nov 67	0.12	4.80	14.40	24.00
☐ 197, Dec 67	0.12	10.00	30.00	50.00
☐ 198, Feb 68	0.25	4.80	14.40	24.00
☐ 199, Feb 68	0.12	4.80	14.40	24.00
☐ 200, Mar 68, NA, O:retold				
	0.12	20.00	60.00	100.00
☐ 201, May 68, Joker	0.12	4.80	14.40	24.00
☐ 202, Jun 68	0.12	2.00	6.00	10.00
☐ 203, Aug 68	0.25	2.00	6.00	10.00
☐ 204, Aug 68	0.12	2.00	6.00	10.00
☐ 205, Sep 68	0.12	2.00	6.00	10.00
☐ 206, Nov 68	0.12	2.00	6.00	10.00
☐ 207, Dec 68	0.12	2.00	6.00	10.00
☐ 208, Feb 69	0.25	2.00	6.00	10.00
☐ 209, Feb 69	0.12			
☐ 209, Feb 69	0.12	2.00	6.00	10.00
☐ 210, Mar 69	0.12	2.00	6.00	10.00
☐ 211, May 69	0.12	2.00	6.00	10.00
☐ 212, Jun 69	0.12	2.00	6.00	10.00
☐ 213, Aug 69, Joker reprint				
	0.25	5.60	16.80	28.00
☐ 214, Aug 69	0.15	4.00	12.00	20.00
☐ 215, Sep 69	0.15	3.00	9.00	15.00
☐ 216, Nov 69	0.15	3.00	9.00	15.00
☐ 217, Dec 69	0.15	3.00	9.00	15.00
☐ 218, Feb 70	0.25	3.00	9.00	15.00
☐ 219, Feb 70, NA	0.15	5.00	15.00	25.00
☐ 220, Mar 70, NA	0.15	1.60	4.80	8.00
☐ 221, May 70, NA	0.15	1.60	4.80	8.00
☐ 222, Jun 70, NA, Beatles				
	0.15	3.00	9.00	15.00
☐ 223, Aug 70, MA, giant	0.25	2.00	6.00	10.00
☐ 224, Aug 70, NA	0.15	1.60	4.80	8.00
☐ 225, Sep 70, NA	0.15	1.60	4.80	8.00
☐ 226, Nov 70, NA	0.15	1.60	4.80	8.00
☐ 227, Dec 70, NA	0.15	1.60	4.80	8.00
☐ 228, Feb 71, MA, giant	0.25	2.00	6.00	10.00
☐ 229, Feb 71	0.15	1.60	4.80	8.00
☐ 230, Mar 71	0.15	1.60	4.80	8.00
☐ 231, May 71	0.15	1.60	4.80	8.00
☐ 232, Jun 71, NA/DG, I:Ra's al Ghul, O:Batman				
	0.15	4.40	13.20	22.00
☐ 233, Aug 71, giant	0.25	1.60	4.80	8.00
☐ 234, Aug 71, NA/CI 1:Silver Age Two-Face				
	0.25	7.20	21.60	36.00
☐ 235, Sep 71, CI	0.25	1.60	4.80	8.00
☐ 236, Nov 71, NA	0.25	1.60	4.80	8.00
☐ 237, Dec 71, NA	0.25	5.00	15.00	25.00
☐ 238, Jan 72, NA/JC/JKu, giant				
	0.50	1.60	4.80	8.00
☐ 239, Feb 72, NA/RB	0.25	1.60	4.80	8.00
☐ 240, Mar 72, NA/RB	0.25	1.60	4.80	8.00
☐ 241, May 72, NA/RB	0.25	1.60	4.80	8.00
☐ 242, Jun 72, RB/MK	0.25	1.60	4.80	8.00
☐ 243, Aug 72, NA/DG Ra's al Ghul				
	0.20	4.40	13.20	22.00
☐ 244, Sep 72, NA/DG Ra's al Ghul				
	0.20	4.40	13.20	22.00
☐ 245, Oct 72, NA, IN/DG, IN/FMC				
	0.20	4.40	13.20	22.00
☐ 246, Dec 72	0.20	1.00	3.00	5.00
☐ 247, Feb 73	0.20	1.00	3.00	5.00
☐ 248, Apr 73	0.20	1.60	4.80	8.00
☐ 249, Jun 73	0.20	1.60	4.80	8.00
☐ 250, Jul 73	0.20	1.60	4.80	8.00
☐ 251, Sep 73, NA, Joker	0.20	4.80	14.40	24.00
☐ 252, Sep 73, 100 pgs.	0.20	1.00	3.00	5.00
☐ 253, Nov 73, 100 pgs.	0.20	1.00	3.00	5.00
☐ 254, Feb 74, NA/GK, 100 pgs.				
	0.50	1.40	4.20	7.00
☐ 255, Apr 74, GK/CI/NA/DG				
	0.50	2.00	6.00	10.00
☐ 256, Jun 74	0.60	0.80	2.40	4.00
☐ 257, Aug 74	0.60	0.80	2.40	4.00
☐ 258, Oct 74	0.60	0.80	2.40	4.00
☐ 259, Dec 74	0.60	0.80	2.40	4.00
☐ 260, Feb 75, Joker	0.60	1.20	3.60	6.00
☐ 261, Mar 75	0.60	0.80	2.40	4.00
☐ 262, Apr 75	0.50	0.80	2.40	4.00
☐ 263, May 75	0.25	0.80	2.40	4.00
☐ 264, Jun 75	0.25	0.80	2.40	4.00
☐ 265, Jul 75	0.25	0.80	2.40	4.00

	ORIG.	GOOD	FINE	N-MINT
266, Aug 75	0.25	0.80	2.40	4.00
267, Sep 75	0.25	0.80	2.40	4.00
268, Oct 75	0.25	0.80	2.40	4.00
269, Nov 75	0.25	0.80	2.40	4.00
270, Dec 75	0.25	0.80	2.40	4.00
271, Jan 76	0.25	0.80	2.40	4.00
272, Feb 76	0.25	0.80	2.40	4.00
273, Mar 76	0.25	0.80	2.40	4.00
274, Apr 76	0.30	0.80	2.40	4.00
275, May 76	0.30	0.80	2.40	4.00
276, Jun 76	0.30	0.80	2.40	4.00
277, Jul 76	0.30	0.80	2.40	4.00
278, Aug 76	0.30	0.80	2.40	4.00
279, Sep 76	0.30	0.80	2.40	4.00
280, Oct 76	0.30	0.80	2.40	4.00
281, Nov 76	0.30	0.80	2.40	4.00
282, Dec 76	0.30	0.80	2.40	4.00
283, Jan 77	0.30	0.80	2.40	4.00
284, Feb 77	0.30	0.80	2.40	4.00
285, Mar 77	0.30	0.80	2.40	4.00
286, Apr 77, Joker	0.30	1.20	3.60	6.00
287, May 77	0.30	0.80	2.40	4.00
288, Jun 77	0.35	0.80	2.40	4.00
289, Jul 77	0.35	0.80	2.40	4.00
290, Aug 77	0.35	0.80	2.40	4.00
291, Sep 77, Joker	0.35	1.20	3.60	6.00
292, Oct 77	0.35	0.80	2.40	4.00
293, Nov 77	0.35	0.80	2.40	4.00
294, Dec 77, Joker	0.35	1.20	3.60	6.00
295, Jan 78	0.35	0.80	2.40	4.00
296, Feb 78	0.35	0.80	2.40	4.00
297, Mar 78	0.35	0.80	2.40	4.00
298, Apr 78	0.35	0.80	2.40	4.00
299, May 78	0.35	0.80	2.40	4.00
300, Jun 78	0.60	2.00	6.00	10.00
301, Jul 78	0.35	0.60	1.80	3.00
302, Aug 78	0.35	0.60	1.80	3.00
303, Sep 78	0.50	0.60	1.80	3.00
304, Oct 78	0.50	0.60	1.80	3.00
305, Nov 78	0.50	0.60	1.80	3.00
306, Dec 78	0.40	0.60	1.80	3.00
307, Jan 79	0.40	0.60	1.80	3.00
308, Feb 79	0.40	0.60	1.80	3.00
309, Mar 79	0.40	0.60	1.80	3.00
310, Apr 79	0.40	0.60	1.80	3.00
311, May 79	0.40	0.60	1.80	3.00
312, Jun 79	0.40	0.60	1.80	3.00
313, Jul 79	0.40	0.60	1.80	3.00
314, Aug 79	0.40	0.60	1.80	3.00
315, Sep 79	0.40	0.60	1.80	3.00
316, Oct 79	0.40	0.60	1.80	3.00
317, Nov 79	0.40	0.60	1.80	3.00
318, Dec 79	0.40	0.60	1.80	3.00
319, Jan 80	0.40	0.60	1.80	3.00
320, Feb 80	0.40	0.60	1.80	3.00
321, Mar 80, Joker	0.40	1.00	3.00	5.00
322, Apr 80	0.40	0.60	1.80	3.00
323, May 80	0.40	0.60	1.80	3.00
324, Jun 80	0.40	0.60	1.80	3.00
325, Jul 80	0.40	0.60	1.80	3.00
326, Aug 80	0.40	0.60	1.80	3.00
327, Sep 80	0.50	0.60	1.80	3.00
328, Oct 80	0.50	0.60	1.80	3.00
329, Nov 80	0.50	0.60	1.80	3.00
330, Dec 80	0.50	0.60	1.80	3.00
331, Jan 81	0.50	0.60	1.80	3.00
332, Feb 81	0.50	0.60	1.80	3.00
333, Mar 81	0.50	0.60	1.80	3.00
334, Apr 81	0.50	0.60	1.80	3.00
335, May 81	0.50	0.60	1.80	3.00
336, Jun 81	0.50	0.60	1.80	3.00
337, Jul 81	0.50	0.60	1.80	3.00

	ORIG.	GOOD	FINE	N-MINT
338, Aug 81	0.50	0.60	1.80	3.00
339, Sep 81	0.50	0.60	1.80	3.00
340, Oct 81	0.60	0.60	1.80	3.00
341, Nov 81	0.60	0.60	1.80	3.00
342, Dec 81	0.60	0.60	1.80	3.00
343, Jan 82	0.60	0.60	1.80	3.00
344, Feb 82	0.60	0.60	1.80	3.00
345, Mar 82	0.60	0.60	1.80	3.00
346, Apr 82	0.60	0.60	1.80	3.00
347, May 82	0.60	0.60	1.80	3.00
348, Jun 82	0.60	0.60	1.80	3.00
349, Jul 82	0.60	0.60	1.80	3.00
350, Aug 82	0.60	0.60	1.80	3.00
351, Sep 82	0.60	0.60	1.80	3.00
352, Oct 82	0.60	0.60	1.80	3.00
353, Nov 82, Joker	0.60	1.00	3.00	5.00
354, Dec 82	0.60	0.60	1.80	3.00
355, Jan 83	0.60	0.60	1.80	3.00
356, Feb 83	0.60	0.60	1.80	3.00
357, Mar 83, Jason Todd	0.60	2.00	6.00	10.00
358, Apr 83	0.60	0.60	1.80	3.00
359, May 83, Joker	0.60	0.60	1.80	3.00
360, Jun 83	0.60	0.60	1.80	3.00
361, Jul 83	0.60	0.60	1.80	3.00
362, Aug 83	0.60	0.60	1.80	3.00
363, Sep 83	0.60	0.60	1.80	3.00
364, Oct 83	0.60	0.60	1.80	3.00
365, Nov 83	0.60	0.60	1.80	3.00
366, Dec 83, Joker, Jason Todd	0.75	2.80	8.40	14.00
367, Jan 84	0.75	0.60	1.80	3.00
368, Feb 84, DN/AA I:new Robin	0.75	2.40	7.20	12.00
369, Mar 84	0.75	0.60	1.80	3.00
370, Apr 84	0.75	0.60	1.80	3.00
371, May 84	0.75	0.60	1.80	3.00
372, Jun 84	0.75	0.60	1.80	3.00
373, Jul 84	0.75	0.60	1.80	3.00
374, Aug 84	0.75	0.60	1.80	3.00
375, Sep 84	0.75	0.60	1.80	3.00
376, Oct 84	0.75	0.60	1.80	3.00
377, Nov 84	0.75	0.60	1.80	3.00
378, Dec 84	0.75	0.60	1.80	3.00
379, Jan 85	0.75	0.60	1.80	3.00
380, Feb 85	0.75	0.60	1.80	3.00
381, Mar 85	0.75	0.60	1.80	3.00
382, Apr 85	0.75	0.60	1.80	3.00
383, May 85	0.75	0.60	1.80	3.00
384, Jun 85	0.75	0.60	1.80	3.00
385, Jul 85	0.75	0.60	1.80	3.00
386, Aug 85	0.75	0.60	1.80	3.00
387, Sep 85	0.75	0.60	1.80	3.00
388, Oct 85	0.75	0.60	1.80	3.00
389, Nov 85	0.75	0.60	1.80	3.00
390, Dec 85	0.75	0.60	1.80	3.00
391, Jan 86	0.75	0.60	1.80	3.00
392, Feb 86	0.75	0.60	1.80	3.00
393, Mar 86	0.75	0.60	1.80	3.00
394, Apr 86	0.75	0.60	1.80	3.00
395, May 86	0.75	0.60	1.80	3.00
396, Jun 86	0.75	0.60	1.80	3.00
397, Jul 86	0.75	0.60	1.80	3.00
398, Aug 86	0.75	0.60	1.80	3.00
399, Sep 86	0.75	0.60	1.80	3.00
400, Oct 86	0.75	5.00	15.00	25.00
401, Nov 86	0.75	0.80	2.40	4.00
402, Dec 86	0.75	0.80	2.40	4.00
403, Jan 87	0.75	0.80	2.40	4.00
404, Feb 87, FM script, O:retold	0.75	2.00	6.00	10.00
405, Mar 87, FM script	0.75	1.20	3.60	6.00

	ORIG.	GOOD	FINE	N-MINT
406, Apr 87, FM script ...	0.75	1.20	3.60	6.00
407, May 87, FM script ..	0.75	1.20	3.60	6.00
408, Jun 87	0.75	0.60	1.80	3.00
409, Jul 87	0.75	0.60	1.80	3.00
410, Aug 87	0.75	0.60	1.80	3.00
411, Sep 87	0.75	0.60	1.80	3.00
412, Oct 87	0.75	0.60	1.80	3.00
413, Nov 87	0.75	0.60	1.80	3.00
414, Dec 87, Millennium	0.75	0.60	1.80	3.00
415, Jan 88, Millennium	0.75	0.60	1.80	3.00
416, Feb 88, JA A:Nightwing	0.75	0.60	1.80	3.00
417, Mar 88, MZ(c) V:KGBeast	0.75	4.00	12.00	20.00
418, Apr 88, MZ(c) V:KGBeast	0.75	3.00	9.00	15.00
419, May 88, MZ(c) V:KGBeast	0.75	3.00	9.00	15.00
420, Jun 88, MZ(c) V:KGBeast	0.75	3.00	9.00	15.00
421, Jul 88	0.75	0.60	1.80	3.00
422, Aug 88	0.75	0.60	1.80	3.00
423, Sep 88, TMc(c)	0.75	0.60	1.80	3.00
424, Oct 88	0.75	0.60	1.80	3.00
425, Nov 88	0.75	0.60	1.80	3.00
426, Dec 88, Death in Family	1.50	3.60	10.80	18.00
427, Dec 88, D:Robin, newsstand	1.50	2.40	7.20	12.00
427, 88, D:Robin, direct sale	1.50	3.00	9.00	15.00
428, Jan 89, Robin declared dead	0.75	1.40	4.20	7.00
429, Jan 89	0.75	1.20	3.60	6.00
430, Feb 89	0.75	0.60	1.80	3.00
431, Mar 89	0.75	0.60	1.80	3.00
432, Apr 89	0.75	0.25	0.75	1.25
433, May 89, JBy;"Many Deaths of the Batman"	0.75	0.80	2.40	4.00
434, Jun 89, JBy;"Many Deaths of the Batman"	0.75	0.50	1.50	2.50
435, Jul 89, JBy;"Many Deaths of the Batman"	0.75	0.50	1.50	2.50
436, Aug 89	0.75	1.00	3.00	5.00
437, Aug 89, Year 3	0.75	0.40	1.20	2.00
438, Sep 89, Year 3	1.00	0.40	1.20	2.00
439, Sep 89, Year 3	1.00	0.40	1.20	2.00
440, Oct 89, "A Lonely Place of Dying"	1.00	1.00	3.00	5.00
441, Nov 89, "A Lonely Place of Dying"	1.00	1.00	3.00	5.00
442, Dec 89, "A Lonely Place of Dying";1:Robin III	1.00	1.60	4.80	8.00
443, Jan 90	1.00	0.30	0.90	1.50
444, Feb 90	1.00	0.30	0.90	1.50
445, Mar 90	1.00	0.30	0.90	1.50
446, Apr 90	1.00	0.30	0.90	1.50
447, May 90	1.00	0.30	0.90	1.50
448, Jun 90, Penguin	1.00	0.30	0.90	1.50
449, Jun 90, Penguin	1.00	0.30	0.90	1.50
450, Jul 90	1.00	0.30	0.90	1.50
451, Jul 90, Joker	1.00	0.30	0.90	1.50
452, Aug 90, Riddler	1.00	0.60	1.80	3.00
453, Aug 90, Riddler	1.00	0.60	1.80	3.00
454, Sep 90, Riddler	1.00	0.60	1.80	3.00
455, Oct 90	1.00	1.00	3.00	5.00
456, Nov 90	1.00	1.00	3.00	5.00
457, Dec 90, 1:new Robin costume	1.00	1.40	4.20	7.00
457, Dec 90, with #000 on indicia	1.00	2.40	7.20	12.00

	ORIG.	GOOD	FINE	N-MINT
457, Dec 90, 2nd printing	1.00	0.20	0.60	1.00
458, Jan 91	1.00	0.20	0.60	1.00
459, Feb 91	1.00	0.20	0.60	1.00
460, Mar 91, Catwoman	1.00	0.20	0.60	1.00
461, Apr 91, Catwoman	1.00	0.20	0.60	1.00
462, May 91	1.00	0.20	0.60	1.00
463, Jun 91	1.00	0.20	0.60	1.00
464, Jul 91	1.00	0.20	0.60	1.00
465, Jul 91, Robin	1.00	0.40	1.20	2.00
466, Aug 91, Robin	1.00	0.20	0.60	1.00
467, Aug 91, Robin	1.00	0.20	0.60	1.00
468, Sep 91, Robin	1.00	0.20	0.60	1.00
469, Sep 91, Robin	1.00	0.20	0.60	1.00
470, Oct 91, War of Gods	1.00	0.20	0.60	1.00
471, Nov 91	1.00	0.20	0.60	1.00
472, Dec 91	1.00	0.20	0.60	1.00
473, Jan 92	1.00	0.20	0.60	1.00
474, Feb 92	1.00	0.20	0.60	1.00
475, Mar 92	1.00	0.20	0.60	1.00
476, Apr 92	1.00	0.20	0.60	1.00
477, May 92	1.25	0.25	0.75	1.25
478, May 92	1.25	0.25	0.75	1.25
479, Jun 92	1.25	0.25	0.75	1.25
480, Jun 92	1.25	0.25	0.75	1.25
481, Jul 92	1.25	0.25	0.75	1.25
482, Jul 92	1.25	0.25	0.75	1.25
483, Aug 92	1.25	0.25	0.75	1.25
484, Sep 92	1.25	0.25	0.75	1.25
485, Oct 92	1.25	0.25	0.75	1.25
486, Nov 92	1.25	0.25	0.75	1.25
487, Dec 92	1.25	0.25	0.75	1.25
488, Jan 93	1.25	4.00	12.00	20.00
489, Feb 93	1.25	4.00	12.00	20.00
490, Mar 93	1.25	3.00	9.00	15.00
491, Apr 93, "Knightfall" prequel	1.25	3.00	9.00	15.00
492, May 93, "Knightfall" Part 1, first printing	1.25	3.00	9.00	15.00
492, "Knightfall", second printing	1.25	0.60	1.80	3.00
492, platinum edition		8.00	24.00	40.00
493, May 93, "Knightfall" Part 3	1.25	1.80	5.40	9.00
494, Jun 93, "Knightfall" Part 5	1.25	1.20	3.60	6.00
495, Jun 93, "Knightfall" Part 7	1.25	1.00	3.00	5.00
496, Jul 93, "Knightfall" Part 9	1.25	1.00	3.00	5.00
497, Jul 93, "Knightfall" Part 11, Batman crippled (first printing), partial overlay outer cover	1.25	2.40	7.20	12.00
497, Jul 93, "Knightfall" Part 11, Batman crippled (second printing)	1.25	0.25	0.75	1.25
498, "Knightfall"	1.25	0.25	0.75	1.25
499, "Knightfall"	1.25	0.25	0.75	1.25
500, Azrael vs. Bane, with poster	2.50	1.00	3.00	5.00
500, diecut,2-level cover, Azrael vs. Bane	3.95	0.79	2.37	3.95
501, Nov 93, Knightquest	1.50	0.30	0.90	1.50
502, Dec 93, Knightquest	1.50	0.30	0.90	1.50
503, Jan 94, Knightquest	1.50	0.30	0.90	1.50
504, Feb 94, Knightquest	1.50	0.30	0.90	1.50
505, Mar 94, Knightquest	1.50	0.30	0.90	1.50

	ORIG.	GOOD	FINE	N-MINT

❏ 506, Apr 94, Knightquest
................................1.50 0.30 0.90 1.50
❏ 507, May 94, Knightquest
................................1.50 0.30 0.90 1.50
❏ 508, Jun 94, Knightquest
................................1.50 0.30 0.90 1.50
❏ 509, Jul 94, KnightEnd... 1.50 0.60 1.80 3.00
❏ 510, Aug 94 .... 1.50 0.30 0.90 1.50
❏ 511, Sep 94.................. 1.50 0.30 0.90 1.50
❏ 512, Nov 94.................. 1.50 0.30 0.90 1.50
❏ 513, Dec 94.................. 1.50 0.30 0.90 1.50
❏ 514, Jan 95.................. 1.50 0.30 0.90 1.50
❏ 515, Feb 95, Return of Bruce Wayne as Batman
................................1.50 0.50 1.50 2.50
❏ 515, Feb 95, Return of Bruce Wayne as Batman;
enhanced cover 2.50 0.80 2.40 4.00
❏ 516, Mar 95.................. 1.50 0.30 0.90 1.50
❏ 517, Apr 95 .... 1.50 0.30 0.90 1.50
❏ 518, May 95, V:Black Mask
................................1.50 0.30 0.90 1.50
❏ 519, Jun 95.................. 1.95 0.39 1.17 1.95
❏ 520, Jul 95.................. 1.95 0.39 1.17 1.95
❏ 521, Aug 95, V:Killer Croc1.95 0.39 1.17 1.95
❏ 522, Sep 95, V:Killer Croc,Swamp Thing
................................1.95 0.39 1.17 1.95
❏ 523, Oct 95, V:Scarecrow
................................1.95 0.39 1.17 1.95
❏ 524, Nov 95 .... 1.95 0.39 1.17 1.95
❏ 525, Dec 95, "Underworld Unleashed";V:Mr. Freeze
................................1.95 0.39 1.17 1.95
❏ 526, Jan 96.................. 1.95 0.39 1.17 1.95
❏ 527, Feb 96, V:Two-Face 1.95 0.39 1.17 1.95
❏ 528, Mar 96.................. 1.95 0.39 1.17 1.95
❏ 529, Apr 96, "Contagion" Part 9
................................1.95 0.39 1.17 1.95
❏ 530, May 96, "The Deadman Connection";
glow-in-the-dark cover... 2.50 0.50 1.50 2.50
❏ 530, May 96, "The Deadman Connection"
................................1.95 0.39 1.17 1.95
❏ 531, Jun 96, "The Deadman Connection"
................................1.95 0.39 1.17 1.95
❏ 531, Jun 96, "The Deadman Connection";
glow-in-the-dark cover... 2.50 0.50 1.50 2.50

BATMAN 3-D

❏ 0, nn, 1990 JBy............. 9.95 1.99 5.97 9.95

BATMAN ADVENTURES ANNUAL, THE

❏ 1, 94............................ 2.95 0.59 1.77 2.95
❏ 2, 95, A:The Demon 3.50 0.70 2.10 3.50

BATMAN ADVENTURES HOLIDAY SPECIAL, THE

❏ 1, Jan 95 .... 2.95 0.59 1.77 2.95

BATMAN ADVENTURES, THE

❏ 1, Oct 92, TV cartoon version
................................1.25 1.60 4.80 8.00
❏ 1, silver edition 1.95 0.39 1.17 1.95
❏ 2, Nov 92 .... 1.25 1.00 3.00 5.00
❏ 3, Dec 92, Joker............ 1.25 0.80 2.40 4.00
❏ 4, Jan 93, Robin............ 1.25 0.80 2.40 4.00
❏ 5, Feb 93.................. 1.25 0.80 2.40 4.00
❏ 6, Mar 93.................. 1.25 0.60 1.80 3.00
❏ 7, Apr 93, trading card ... 1.25 1.60 4.80 8.00
❏ 7, Apr 93, without card .. 1.25 0.40 1.20 2.00
❏ 8, May 93.................. 1.25 0.50 1.50 2.50
❏ 9, Jun 93.................. 1.25 0.50 1.50 2.50
❏ 10 .... 1.25 0.50 1.50 2.50
❏ 11 .... 1.25 0.50 1.50 2.50
❏ 12, Batgirl 1.25 0.50 1.50 2.50
❏ 13 .... 1.25 0.25 0.75 1.25
❏ 14, Robin 1.25 0.25 0.75 1.25
❏ 15 .... 1.25 0.25 0.75 1.25
❏ 16, 94, Joker 1.50 0.30 0.90 1.50
❏ 17, 94.................. 1.50 0.30 0.90 1.50

❏ 18, 94, Batgirl-Robin 1.50 0.30 0.90 1.50
❏ 19, 94 .... 1.50 0.30 0.90 1.50
❏ 20, May 94.................. 1.50 0.30 0.90 1.50
❏ 21, Jun 94 .... 1.50 0.30 0.90 1.50
❏ 22, Jul 94.................. 1.50 0.30 0.90 1.50
❏ 23, Aug 94 .... 1.50 0.30 0.90 1.50
❏ 24, Sep 94 .... 1.50 0.30 0.90 1.50
❏ 25, Oct 94, A:Superman .2.50 0.50 1.50 2.50
❏ 26, Nov 94.................. 1.50 0.30 0.90 1.50
❏ 27, Dec 94 .... 1.50 0.30 0.90 1.50
❏ 28, Jan 95.................. 1.50 0.30 0.90 1.50
❏ 29, Feb 95.................. 1.50 0.30 0.90 1.50
❏ 30, Mar 95.................. 1.50 0.30 0.90 1.50
❏ 31, Apr 95.................. 1.50 0.30 0.90 1.50
❏ 32 .... 1.50 0.30 0.90 1.50
❏ 33, Jul 95.................. 1.75 0.35 1.05 1.75
❏ 34, Aug 95 .... 1.75 0.35 1.05 1.75
❏ 35, Sep 95 .... 1.75 0.35 1.05 1.75
❏ 36, Oct 95, final issue;(becomes *Batman and Robin
Adventures, The*) 1.75 0.35 1.05 1.75

BATMAN ADVENTURES: MAD LOVE, THE

❏ 0, nn;A:Joker;O:Harley Quinn
................................3.95 2.20 6.60 11.00
❏ 0, 94, nn;prestige format;A:Joker;O:Harley Quinn
................................4.95 0.99 2.97 4.95

BATMAN AND ROBIN ADVENTURES, THE

❏ 1, Nov 95, (was *Batman Adventures, The*);based on
animated series 1.75 0.35 1.05 1.75
❏ 2, Dec 95 .... 1.75 0.35 1.05 1.75
❏ 3, Jan 96, V:Riddler 1.75 0.35 1.05 1.75
❏ 4, Feb 96, V:Penguin.... 1.75 0.35 1.05 1.75
❏ 5, Mar 96, V:Joker 1.75 0.35 1.05 1.75
❏ 6, May 96.................. 1.75 0.35 1.05 1.75
❏ 7, Jun 96, V:Scarface...... 1.75 0.35 1.05 1.75

BATMAN AND THE OUTSIDERS

❏ 1, Aug 83, O:Geo-Force ..0.60 0.80 2.40 4.00
❏ 2, Sep 83 .... 0.60 0.60 1.80 3.00
❏ 3, Oct 83, JA.................. 0.60 0.50 1.50 2.50
❏ 4, Nov 83, JA.................. 0.60 0.50 1.50 2.50
❏ 5, Dec 83, JA, A: Teen Titans
................................0.75 0.50 1.50 2.50
❏ 6, Jan 84.................. 0.75 0.40 1.20 2.00
❏ 7, Feb 84.................. 0.75 0.40 1.20 2.00
❏ 8, Mar 84.................. 0.75 0.40 1.20 2.00
❏ 9, Apr 84.................. 0.75 0.40 1.20 2.00
❏ 10, May 84 .... 0.75 0.40 1.20 2.00
❏ 11, Jun 84 .... 0.75 0.40 1.20 2.00
❏ 12, Jul 84.................. 0.75 0.40 1.20 2.00
❏ 13, Aug 84 .... 0.75 0.40 1.20 2.00
❏ 14, Oct 84 .... 0.75 0.35 1.05 1.75
❏ 15, Nov 84 .... 0.75 0.35 1.05 1.75
❏ 16, Dec 84 .... 0.75 0.35 1.05 1.75
❏ 17, Jan 85.................. 0.75 0.35 1.05 1.75
❏ 18, Feb 85.................. 0.75 0.35 1.05 1.75
❏ 19, Mar 85.................. 0.75 0.35 1.05 1.75
❏ 20, Apr 85.................. 0.75 0.35 1.05 1.75
❏ 21, May 85.................. 0.75 0.35 1.05 1.75
❏ 22, Jun 85.................. 0.75 0.35 1.05 1.75
❏ 23, Jul 85.................. 0.75 0.35 1.05 1.75
❏ 24, Aug 85 .... 0.75 0.35 1.05 1.75
❏ 25, Sep 85 .... 0.75 0.35 1.05 1.75
❏ 26, Oct 85 .... 0.75 0.35 1.05 1.75
❏ 27, Nov 85 .... 0.75 0.35 1.05 1.75
❏ 28, Dec 85 .... 0.75 0.35 1.05 1.75
❏ 29, Jan 86.................. 0.75 0.35 1.05 1.75
❏ 30, Feb 86.................. 0.75 0.35 1.05 1.75
❏ 31, Mar 86.................. 0.75 0.35 1.05 1.75
❏ 32, Apr 86, (becomes *Adventures of the Outsiders*)
................................0.75 0.35 1.05 1.75

BATMAN AND THE OUTSIDERS ANNUAL

❏ 1, Sep 84, FM(c)............. 1.25 0.30 0.90 1.50
❏ 2, Sep 85, JA 1.25 0.25 0.75 1.25

	ORIG.	GOOD	FINE	N-MINT

BATMAN ANNUAL

	ORIG.	GOOD	FINE	N-MINT
1, CS		80.00	240.00	400.00
2		56.00	168.00	280.00
3		36.00	108.00	180.00
4, Win 63	0.25	20.00	60.00	100.00
5, Sum 63	0.25	16.00	48.00	80.00
6, Win 64	0.25	13.00	39.00	65.00
7		13.00	39.00	65.00
8, Oct 82, A:Ra's al Ghul	1.00	1.00	3.00	5.00
9, Jul 85, JOy, AN, PS	1.25	0.60	1.80	3.00
10, Aug 86	1.25	0.60	1.80	3.00
11, Jul 87, Alan Moore	1.25	1.00	3.00	5.00
12, Aug 88, MWK(c)	1.50	0.60	1.80	3.00
13, May 89	1.75	0.60	1.80	3.00
14, Jun 90, O:Two-Face	2.00	0.40	1.20	2.00
15, Jun 91, 1st printing Armageddon 2001	2.00	1.00	3.00	5.00
15, Jun 91, 2nd printing		0.40	1.20	2.00
15, 3rd printing, silver		0.40	1.20	2.00
16, 92, Eclipso	2.50	0.50	1.50	2.50
17, 93, Bloodlines	2.50	0.50	1.50	2.50
18, 94, Elseworlds	2.95	0.59	1.77	2.95
19, 95, "Year One";ro: Scarecrow	3.95	0.79	2.37	3.95

BATMAN BLACK AND WHITE

	ORIG.	GOOD	FINE	N-MINT
1, Jun 96, b&w anthology;JLee(c)	2.95	0.59	1.77	2.95
2, Jul 96, b&w anthology;FM(c)	2.95	0.59	1.77	2.95

BATMAN CHRONICLES, THE

	ORIG.	GOOD	FINE	N-MINT
1, Sum 95	2.95	0.59	1.77	2.95
2, Fal 95	2.95	0.59	1.77	2.95
3, Win 96	2.95	0.59	1.77	2.95
4, Spr 96, "Contagion"	2.95	0.59	1.77	2.95

BATMAN FAMILY, THE

	ORIG.	GOOD	FINE	N-MINT
1, Oct 75	0.50	2.60	7.80	13.00
2, Dec 75	0.50	1.40	4.20	7.00
3, Feb 76	0.50	1.20	3.60	6.00
4, Apr 76	0.50	1.20	3.60	6.00
5, Jun 76	0.50	1.20	3.60	6.00
6, Aug 76	0.50	1.40	4.20	7.00
7, Sep 76	0.50	1.10	3.30	5.50
8, Nov 76	0.50	1.10	3.30	5.50
9, Jan 77	0.50	1.10	3.30	5.50
10, Mar 77	0.50	1.10	3.30	5.50
11, May 77	0.50	1.00	3.00	5.00
12, Jul 77	0.60	1.00	3.00	5.00
13, Sep 77	0.60	1.00	3.00	5.00
14, Oct 77	0.60	1.00	3.00	5.00
15, Dec 77	0.60	1.00	3.00	5.00
16, Feb 78	0.60	1.00	3.00	5.00
17, Apr 78	1.00	1.10	3.30	5.50
18, Jun 78	1.00	1.00	3.00	5.00
19, Aug 78	1.00	1.00	3.00	5.00
20, Oct 78	1.00	1.00	3.00	5.00

BATMAN FOREVER: THE OFFICIAL COMIC ADAPTATION OF THE WARNER BROS. MOTION PICTURE

	ORIG.	GOOD	FINE	N-MINT
0, 95, nn;movie adaptation;prestige format	5.95	1.19	3.57	5.95
0, 95, nn;movie adaptation	3.95	0.79	2.37	3.95

BATMAN GALLERY, THE

	ORIG.	GOOD	FINE	N-MINT
1, NA, FM, DG, CI, MA, GP, BB, TMc, JKu, WS		0.59	1.77	2.95

BATMAN SPECIAL

	ORIG.	GOOD	FINE	N-MINT
1, 84, MG	1.25	0.25	0.75	1.25

BATMAN VERSUS PREDATOR (with Dark Horse)

	ORIG.	GOOD	FINE	N-MINT
1, prestige format, trading cards, Batman on front cover		1.80	5.40	9.00
1, prestige format, trading cards, Predator on front, Batman on back cover		1.80	5.40	9.00
1, newsstand	1.95	1.00	3.00	5.00
2, prestige, pin-ups	4.95	1.40	4.20	7.00
2, newsstand	1.95	0.80	2.40	4.00
3, prestige	4.95	1.40	4.20	7.00
3, newsstand	1.95	0.80	2.40	4.00
4, newsstand, trading cards	1.95	0.39	1.17	1.95

BATMAN VERSUS PREDATOR II: BLOODMATCH (mini-series)
DC/DARK HORSE

	ORIG.	GOOD	FINE	N-MINT
1, 94, Crossover;no year in indicia	2.50	0.50	1.50	2.50
2, 94, Crossover	2.50	0.50	1.50	2.50
3, 94, Crossover	2.50	0.50	1.50	2.50
4, 94, Crossover	2.50	0.50	1.50	2.50

BATMAN VERSUS THE INCREDIBLE HULK
DC

	ORIG.	GOOD	FINE	N-MINT
0, oversized;(DC Special Series #27)	2.50	0.50	1.50	2.50

BATMAN/GRENDEL
DC/COMICO

	ORIG.	GOOD	FINE	N-MINT
1, MW	4.95	0.99	2.97	4.95
2	4.95	0.99	2.97	4.95

BATMAN/HOUDINI: THE DEVIL'S WORKSHOP
DC

	ORIG.	GOOD	FINE	N-MINT
0, nn	3.95	0.79	2.37	3.95

BATMAN/JUDGE DREDD: JUDGMENT ON GOTHAM

	ORIG.	GOOD	FINE	N-MINT
0, nn;Simon Bisley		1.40	4.20	7.00

BATMAN/JUDGE DREDD: VENDETTA IN GOTHAM

	ORIG.	GOOD	FINE	N-MINT
0, nn	5.95	1.19	3.57	5.95

BATMAN/PUNISHER: LAKE OF FIRE
DC/MARVEL

	ORIG.	GOOD	FINE	N-MINT
0, 94	4.95	0.99	2.97	4.95

BATMAN/SPAWN: WAR DEVIL
DC

	ORIG.	GOOD	FINE	N-MINT
0, 94, nn	4.95	0.99	2.97	4.95

BATMAN: A WORD TO THE WISE

	ORIG.	GOOD	FINE	N-MINT
0, 92, nn (DC giveaway)		0.25	0.75	1.25

BATMAN: BROTHERHOOD OF THE BAT

	ORIG.	GOOD	FINE	N-MINT
0, 95, Elseworlds;prestige format one-shot	5.95	1.19	3.57	5.95

BATMAN: CASTLE OF THE BAT

	ORIG.	GOOD	FINE	N-MINT
0, 94, prestige format	5.95	1.19	3.57	5.95

BATMAN: DARK ALLEGIANCES

	ORIG.	GOOD	FINE	N-MINT
0, 96, Elseworlds;prestige format one-shot	5.95	1.19	3.57	5.95

BATMAN: DARK KNIGHT GALLERY

	ORIG.	GOOD	FINE	N-MINT
1, Jan 96, pin-ups	3.50	0.70	2.10	3.50

BATMAN: GHOSTS LEGENDS OF THE DARK KNIGHT HALLOWEEN SPECIAL

	ORIG.	GOOD	FINE	N-MINT
0, 95, nn;prestige format one-shot	4.95	0.99	2.97	4.95

BATMAN: GOTHAM NIGHTS (mini-series)

	ORIG.	GOOD	FINE	N-MINT
1, Mar 92	1.25	0.25	0.75	1.25
2, Apr 92	1.25	0.25	0.75	1.25
3, May 92	1.25	0.25	0.75	1.25
4, Jun 92	1.25	0.25	0.75	1.25

BATMAN: GOTHAM NIGHTS II (mini-series)

	ORIG.	GOOD	FINE	N-MINT
1, Mar 95	1.95	0.39	1.17	1.95
2, Apr 95	1.95	0.39	1.17	1.95
3, May 95	1.95	0.39	1.17	1.95
4, Jun 95	1.95	0.39	1.17	1.95

	ORIG.	GOOD	FINE	N-MINT

BATMAN: IN DARKEST KNIGHT

☐ 0, 94, prestige format one-shot;Elseworlds;Bruce Wayne as Green Lantern............ 4.95 / 1.60 / 4.80 / 8.00

BATMAN: JUDGMENT ON GOTHAM

☐ 0, 91, nn...................... 5.95 / 1.19 / 3.57 / 5.95

BATMAN: KNIGHTGALLERY

☐ 0, 95, Elseworlds one-shot;Batman costume designs; leads into *Batman: Brotherhood of the Bat* .... 3.50 / 0.70 / 2.10 / 3.50

BATMAN: LEGENDS OF THE DARK KNIGHT
(was Legends of the Dark Knight)

#	ORIG.	GOOD	FINE	N-MINT
☐ 0, Oct 94	1.95	0.39	1.17	1.95
☐ 37, Sep 92	1.75	0.35	1.05	1.75
☐ 38, Oct 92	1.75	0.35	1.05	1.75
☐ 39, Nov 92, BT	1.75	0.35	1.05	1.75
☐ 40, Dec 92, BT	1.75	0.35	1.05	1.75
☐ 41, Jan 93	1.75	0.35	1.05	1.75
☐ 42, Feb 93, PCR	1.75	0.35	1.05	1.75
☐ 43, Mar 93, PCR	1.75	0.35	1.05	1.75
☐ 44, Apr 93	1.75	0.35	1.05	1.75
☐ 45, May 93	1.75	0.35	1.05	1.75
☐ 46, Jun 93	1.75	0.35	1.05	1.75
☐ 47	1.75	0.35	1.05	1.75
☐ 48	1.75	0.35	1.05	1.75
☐ 49	1.75	0.35	1.05	1.75
☐ 50, foil cover, Joker	3.95	1.50	4.50	7.50
☐ 51	1.75	0.35	1.05	1.75
☐ 52	1.75	0.35	1.05	1.75
☐ 53	1.75	0.35	1.05	1.75
☐ 54	1.75	0.35	1.05	1.75
☐ 55	1.75	0.35	1.05	1.75
☐ 56	1.75	0.35	1.05	1.75
☐ 57	1.75	0.35	1.05	1.75
☐ 58	1.75	0.35	1.05	1.75
☐ 59, 94, Knightquest........	1.75	0.35	1.05	1.75
☐ 60, May 94, Knightquest	1.75	0.35	1.05	1.75
☐ 61, Jun 94	1.75	0.35	1.05	1.75
☐ 62, Jul 94	1.75	0.35	1.05	1.75
☐ 63, Aug 94	1.75	0.35	1.05	1.75
☐ 64, Sep 94	1.95	0.39	1.17	1.95
☐ 65, Nov 94	1.95	0.39	1.17	1.95
☐ 66, Dec 94......................	1.95	0.39	1.17	1.95
☐ 67, Jan 95	1.95	0.39	1.17	1.95
☐ 68, Feb 95	1.95	0.39	1.17	1.95
☐ 69, Mar 95	1.95	0.39	1.17	1.95
☐ 70, Apr 95	1.95	0.39	1.17	1.95

☐ 71, May 95, "Werewolf" Part 1 of 3 .... 1.95 / 0.39 / 1.17 / 1.95

☐ 72, Jun 95, "Werewolf" Part 2 of 3 .... 1.95 / 0.39 / 1.17 / 1.95

☐ 73, Jul 95, "Werewolf" Part 3 of 3 .... 1.95 / 0.39 / 1.17 / 1.95

☐ 74, Aug 95, "Engines" Part 1 of 2 .... 1.95 / 0.39 / 1.17 / 1.95

☐ 75, Sep 95, "Engines" Part 2 of 2 .... 1.95 / 0.39 / 1.17 / 1.95

☐ 76, Oct 95, "The Sleeping" Part 1 of 3 .... 1.95 / 0.39 / 1.17 / 1.95

☐ 77, Nov 95, "The Sleeping" Part 2 of 3 .... 1.95 / 0.39 / 1.17 / 1.95

☐ 78, Dec 95, "The Sleeping" Part 3 of 3 .... 1.95 / 0.39 / 1.17 / 1.95

☐ 79, Jan 96, "Favorite Things" .... 1.95 / 0.39 / 1.17 / 1.95

☐ 80, Feb 96, "Idols" Part 1 of 3 .... 1.95 / 0.39 / 1.17 / 1.95

☐ 81, Mar 96, "Idols" Part 2 of 3 .... 1.95 / 0.39 / 1.17 / 1.95

☐ 82, May 96, "Idols" Part 3 of 3 .... 1.95 / 0.39 / 1.17 / 1.95

☐ 83, Jun 96, "Infected" Part 1 of 2 .... 1.95 / 0.39 / 1.17 / 1.95

BATMAN: LEGENDS OF THE DARK KNIGHT ANNUAL

☐ 1, Dec 91, JA, DS, MG ....3.95 / 0.79 / 2.37 / 3.95

☐ 2, 92, Wedding: James Gordon .... 3.50 / 0.70 / 2.10 / 3.50

☐ 3, 93, Bloodlines............. 3.50 / 0.70 / 2.10 / 3.50

☐ 4, 94, Elseworlds............. 3.50 / 0.70 / 2.10 / 3.50

☐ 5, 95, "Year One";"Wings";ro:Man-Bat .... 3.95 / 0.79 / 2.37 / 3.95

BATMAN: LEGENDS OF THE DARK KNIGHT HALLOWEEN SPECIAL

☐ 1 .... 6.95 / 1.39 / 4.17 / 6.95

BATMAN: LEGENDS OF THE DARK KNIGHT: JAZZ (mini-series)

☐ 1, Apr 95...................... 2.50 / 0.50 / 1.50 / 2.50

☐ 2, May 95...................... 2.50 / 0.50 / 1.50 / 2.50

☐ 3, Jun 95 .... 2.50 / 0.50 / 1.50 / 2.50

BATMAN: MADNESS A LEGENDS OF THE DARK KNIGHT HALLOWEEN SPECIAL

☐ 0, 94, prestige format one-shot .... 4.95 / 0.99 / 2.97 / 4.95

BATMAN: MANBAT (mini-series)

☐ 1, Oct 95, Elseworlds;prestige format .... 4.95 / 0.99 / 2.97 / 4.95

☐ 2, Nov 95, Elseworlds;prestige format .... 4.95 / 0.99 / 2.97 / 4.95

☐ 3, Dec 95, Elseworlds;prestige format .... 4.95 / 0.99 / 2.97 / 4.95

BATMAN: MASK OF THE PHANTASM

☐ 0, digest-sized;no cover price;packaged as set with movie video cassette .... 1.00 / 3.00 / 5.00

BATMAN: MASK OF THE PHANTASM-THE ANIMATED MOVIE

☐ 0, nn newsstand .... 2.95 / 0.59 / 1.77 / 2.95

☐ 0, nn slick paper .... 4.95 / 0.99 / 2.97 / 4.95

BATMAN: MITEFALL

☐ 0, 95, prestige format one-shot .... 4.95 / 0.99 / 2.97 / 4.95

BATMAN: RIDDLER - THE RIDDLE FACTORY

☐ 0, 95, nn;prestige format;cover forms diptych with *Batman: Two-Face - Crime and Punishment* .... 4.95 / 0.99 / 2.97 / 4.95

BATMAN: RUN, RIDDLER, RUN

☐ 1, 92 .... 4.95 / 0.99 / 2.97 / 4.95

☐ 2, 92 .... 4.95 / 0.99 / 2.97 / 4.95

☐ 3, 92 .... 4.95 / 0.99 / 2.97 / 4.95

BATMAN: SCAR OF THE BAT

☐ 0, 96, MAC;Elseworlds;prestige format;Batman becomes an Untouchable............... 4.95 / 0.99 / 2.97 / 4.95

BATMAN: SEDUCTION OF THE GUN

☐ 1, Feb 93...................... 2.50 / 0.50 / 1.50 / 2.50

BATMAN: SHADOW OF THE BAT

#	ORIG.	GOOD	FINE	N-MINT
☐ 0, Oct 94	1.95	0.39	1.17	1.95
☐ 1, Jun 92	1.50	1.00	3.00	5.00
☐ 1, collector's set		0.80	2.40	4.00
☐ 2, Jul 92......................	1.50	0.80	2.40	4.00
☐ 3, Aug 92	1.50	0.50	1.50	2.50
☐ 4, Sep 92	1.50	0.50	1.50	2.50
☐ 5, Oct 92......................	1.50	0.50	1.50	2.50
☐ 6, Nov 92	1.50	0.40	1.20	2.00
☐ 7, Dec 92	1.50	0.40	1.20	2.00
☐ 8, Jan 93	1.75	0.40	1.20	2.00
☐ 9, Feb 93......................	1.75	0.40	1.20	2.00
☐ 10, Mar 93	1.75	0.40	1.20	2.00

	ORIG.	GOOD	FINE	N-MINT
11, Apr 93 .... 1.75	0.40	1.20	2.00
12, May 93 .... 1.75	0.40	1.20	2.00
13, Jun 93 .... 1.75	0.40	1.20	2.00
14, Jul 93 .... 1.75	0.40	1.20	2.00
15 .... 1.75	0.40	1.20	2.00
16, Scarecrow 1.75	0.50	1.50	2.50
17 .... 1.75	0.35	1.05	1.75
18, "Knightfall" 1.75	0.35	1.05	1.75
19, Knightquest 1.75	0.35	1.05	1.75
20, Knightquest 1.75	0.35	1.05	1.75
21, Knightquest 1.75	0.35	1.05	1.75
22, Knightquest 1.75	0.35	1.05	1.75
23, 94, Knightquest 1.75	0.35	1.05	1.75
24, 94, Knightquest 1.75	0.35	1.05	1.75
25, 94, Knightquest 1.75	0.35	1.05	1.75
26, 94, Knightquest 1.75	0.35	1.05	1.75
27, May 94, Knightquest 1.75	0.35	1.05	1.75
28, Jun 94, Knightquest . 1.75	0.35	1.05	1.75
29, Jul 94, Knights End Part 2 .... 2.95	0.59	1.77	2.95
30, Aug 94 .... 1.95	0.80	2.40	4.00
31, Sep 94, Zero Hour;R: Alfred as detective 1.95	0.39	1.17	1.95
32, Nov 94 .... 1.95	0.39	1.17	1.95
33, Dec 94 .... 1.95	0.39	1.17	1.95
34, Jan 95 .... 1.95	0.39	1.17	1.95
35, Feb 95 .... 1.95	0.39	1.17	1.95
35, Feb 95, enhanced cover 2.95	0.59	1.77	2.95
36, Mar 95, A:Black Canary 1.95	0.39	1.17	1.95
37, Apr 95 .... 1.95	0.39	1.17	1.95
38, May 95 .... 1.95	0.39	1.17	1.95
39, Jun 95 .... 1.95	0.39	1.17	1.95
40, Jul 95 .... 1.95	0.39	1.17	1.95
41, Aug 95 .... 1.95	0.39	1.17	1.95
42, Sep 95 .... 1.95	0.39	1.17	1.95
43, Oct 95 .... 1.95	0.39	1.17	1.95
44, Nov 95 .... 1.95	0.39	1.17	1.95
45, Dec 95, Wayne Manor history 1.95	0.39	1.17	1.95
46, Jan 96 .... 1.95	0.39	1.17	1.95
47, Feb 96 .... 1.95	0.39	1.17	1.95
48, Mar 96, "Contagion" Part 1;trading card bound in 1.95	0.39	1.17	1.95
49, Apr 96, "Contagion" Part 7 .... 1.95	0.39	1.17	1.95
50, May 96 .... 1.95	0.39	1.17	1.95
51, Jun 96 .... 1.95	0.39	1.17	1.95
52, Jul 96 .... 1.95	0.39	1.17	1.95

BATMAN: SHADOW OF THE BAT ANNUAL

	ORIG.	GOOD	FINE	N-MINT
1, 93, Bloodlines 3.50	0.70	2.10	3.50
2, 94 .... 3.95	0.79	2.37	3.95
3, 95, "Year One";ro: Poison Ivy 3.95	0.79	2.37	3.95

BATMAN: SWORD OF AZRAEL

	ORIG.	GOOD	FINE	N-MINT
1, Oct 92 .... 1.75	4.40	13.20	22.00
1, silver edition 1.95	0.39	1.17	1.95
2, Nov 92 .... 1.75	3.20	9.60	16.00
2, silver edition 1.95	0.39	1.17	1.95
3, Dec 92 .... 1.75	3.20	9.60	16.00
3, silver edition 1.95	0.39	1.17	1.95
4, Jan 93 .... 1.75	3.20	9.60	16.00
4, silver edition 1.95	0.39	1.17	1.95

BATMAN: THE BLUE, THE GREY, AND THE BAT

	ORIG.	GOOD	FINE	N-MINT
0, 92 .... 5.95	1.19	3.57	5.95

BATMAN: THE CULT

	ORIG.	GOOD	FINE	N-MINT
1, Aug 88, BWr/JSn 3.50	3.20	9.60	16.00
2, Sep 88, BWr/JSn 3.50	2.80	8.40	14.00
3, Oct 88, BWr/JSn 3.50	2.40	7.20	12.00
4, Nov 88, BWr/JSn 3.50	2.40	7.20	12.00

BATMAN: THE DARK KNIGHT RETURNS

	ORIG.	GOOD	FINE	N-MINT
1, 86, FM 2.95	8.00	24.00	40.00
1, second printing	2.40	7.20	12.00
1, third printing	1.60	4.80	8.00
2, 86, FM 2.95	3.60	10.80	18.00
2, second printing	1.40	4.20	7.00
2, third printing	0.80	2.40	4.00
3, 86, FM 2.95	2.00	6.00	10.00
3, second printing	0.80	2.40	4.00
4, 86, FM 2.95	1.60	4.80	8.00

BATMAN: THE KILLING JOKE

	ORIG.	GOOD	FINE	N-MINT
1, Jul 88, AMo, BB;V:Joker;ro: Joker;first printing; prestige format 3.50	4.00	12.00	20.00
1, second printing	1.00	3.00	5.00

BATMAN: THE OFFICIAL COMIC ADAPTATION OF THE WARNER BROS. MOTION PICTURE

	ORIG.	GOOD	FINE	N-MINT
0, Jun 89, prestige format	1.80	5.40	9.00
0, newsstand format	1.20	3.60	6.00

BATMAN: THE ULTIMATE EVIL (mini-series)

	ORIG.	GOOD	FINE	N-MINT
1, 95, adapts Andrew Vachss novel;prestige format 5.95	1.19	3.57	5.95
2, 95, adapts Andrew Vachss novel;prestige format 5.95	1.19	3.57	5.95

BATMAN: THE VENGEANCE OF BANE II

	ORIG.	GOOD	FINE	N-MINT
0, 95, nn;one-shot 3.95	0.79	2.37	3.95

BATMAN: TWO-FACE - CRIME AND PUNISHMENT

	ORIG.	GOOD	FINE	N-MINT
0, 95, nn;prestige format one-shot;cover forms diptych with *Batman: Riddler - The Riddle Factory* 4.95	0.99	2.97	4.95

BATMAN: TWO-FACE STRIKES TWICE!

	ORIG.	GOOD	FINE	N-MINT
1 .... 4.95	0.99	2.97	4.95
2 .... 4.95	0.99	2.97	4.95

BATMAN: VENGEANCE OF BANE SPECIAL

	ORIG.	GOOD	FINE	N-MINT
1, 93 .... 2.50	4.40	13.20	22.00

BATS, CATS & CADILLACS
NOW

	ORIG.	GOOD	FINE	N-MINT
1, Oct 90 .... 1.75	0.35	1.05	1.75
2, Nov 90 .... 1.75	0.35	1.05	1.75

BATTLE ANGEL ALITA
VIZ

	ORIG.	GOOD	FINE	N-MINT
1, 92 .... 2.75	1.80	5.40	9.00
2, 92	1.20	3.60	6.00
3, 92 .... 2.75	0.80	2.40	4.00
4, 92 .... 2.75	0.80	2.40	4.00
5, 92 .... 2.75	0.80	2.40	4.00
6, 92 .... 2.75	0.80	2.40	4.00
7, 92 .... 2.75	0.80	2.40	4.00
8, 93 .... 2.75	0.80	2.40	4.00
9, 93 .... 2.75	0.80	2.40	4.00

BATTLE ANGEL ALITA, PART FOUR

	ORIG.	GOOD	FINE	N-MINT
1, 95, b&w 2.75	0.55	1.65	2.75
2, 95, b&w 2.75	0.55	1.65	2.75
3, 95, b&w 2.75	0.55	1.65	2.75
5, 95, b&w 2.75	0.55	1.65	2.75
6, 95, b&w 2.75	0.55	1.65	2.75

BATTLE ANGEL ALITA, PART THREE

	ORIG.	GOOD	FINE	N-MINT
1, b&w 2.75	0.55	1.65	2.75
2, b&w 2.75	0.55	1.65	2.75
3, b&w 2.75	0.55	1.65	2.75
4, b&w 2.75	0.55	1.65	2.75
5, 94, b&w 2.75	0.55	1.65	2.75
6, 94, b&w 2.75	0.55	1.65	2.75
7, 94, b&w 2.75	0.55	1.65	2.75
8, 94, b&w 2.75	0.55	1.65	2.75
9, 94, b&w 2.75	0.55	1.65	2.75
10, 94, b&w 2.75	0.55	1.65	2.75
11, 94, b&w 2.75	0.55	1.65	2.75
12, 94, b&w 2.75	0.55	1.65	2.75
13, 94, b&w 2.75	0.55	1.65	2.75

	ORIG.	GOOD	FINE	N-MINT

BATTLE ANGEL ALITA, PART TWO

	ORIG.	GOOD	FINE	N-MINT
❏ 1, 93, b&w	2.75	1.00	3.00	5.00
❏ 2, b&w	2.75	0.70	2.10	3.50
❏ 3, b&w	2.75	0.60	1.80	3.00
❏ 4, b&w	2.75	0.60	1.80	3.00
❏ 5, b&w	2.75	0.60	1.80	3.00
❏ 6, b&w	2.75	0.60	1.80	3.00
❏ 7, b&w	2.75	0.60	1.80	3.00

BATTLE ARMOR
ETERNITY

	GOOD	FINE	N-MINT
❏ 1, b&w, game tie-in	0.39	1.17	1.95
❏ 2, b&w, game tie-in	0.39	1.17	1.95
❏ 3, b&w, game tie-in	0.39	1.17	1.95

BATTLE AXE
COMICS INTERVIEW

	GOOD	FINE	N-MINT
❏ 1, b&w	0.50	1.50	2.50

BATTLE BEASTS
BLACKTHORNE

	GOOD	FINE	N-MINT
❏ 1, b&w	0.30	0.90	1.50
❏ 2, b&w	0.30	0.90	1.50
❏ 3, b&w	0.30	0.90	1.50
❏ 4	0.35	1.05	1.75

BATTLE BINDER PLUS
ANTARCTIC

	ORIG.	GOOD	FINE	N-MINT
❏ 1, Nov 94, adult;b&w	3.50	0.70	2.10	3.50
❏ 2, Dec 94, adult;b&w	2.95	0.59	1.77	2.95
❏ 3, Jan 95, adult;b&w	2.95	0.59	1.77	2.95
❏ 4, Feb 95, adult;b&w	2.95	0.59	1.77	2.95
❏ 5, Mar 95, adult;b&w	2.95	0.59	1.77	2.95
❏ 6, Apr 95, adult;b&w;final issue	2.95	0.59	1.77	2.95

BATTLE FOR A 3-D WORLD
3-D COSMIC

❏ 1, 82, no cover price;JK ...				

BATTLE GROUP PEIPER
TOME PRESS

	ORIG.	GOOD	FINE	N-MINT
❏ 1, b&w	2.95	0.59	1.77	2.95

BATTLE OF THE ULTRA-BROTHERS
VIZ

	ORIG.	GOOD	FINE	N-MINT
❏ 1	4.95	0.99	2.97	4.95
❏ 2	4.95	0.99	2.97	4.95
❏ 3, 94	4.95	0.99	2.97	4.95
❏ 4, 94	4.95	0.99	2.97	4.95
❏ 5	4.95	0.99	2.97	4.95

BATTLE TO THE DEATH
ETERNITY

	GOOD	FINE	N-MINT
❏ 2	0.39	1.17	1.95
❏ 3	0.39	1.17	1.95
#### IMPERIAL			
❏ 1, b&w	0.36	1.08	1.80

BATTLEFORCE
BLACKTHORNE

	GOOD	FINE	N-MINT
❏ 1, color	0.35	1.05	1.75
❏ 2, b&w	0.35	1.05	1.75

BATTLESTAR GALACTICA
MAXIMUM

	ORIG.	GOOD	FINE	N-MINT
❏ 1, 95	2.50	0.80	2.40	4.00
❏ 2, Aug 95	2.50	0.60	1.80	3.00
❏ 3, Sep 95	2.50	0.50	1.50	2.50
❏ 4, Nov 95	2.50	0.50	1.50	2.50

BATTLESTAR GALACTICA: STARBUCK
(mini-series)

	ORIG.	GOOD	FINE	N-MINT
❏ 3, Mar 96	2.95	0.59	1.77	2.95

BATTLESTAR GALACTICA: THE ENEMY WITHIN
(mini-series)

	ORIG.	GOOD	FINE	N-MINT
❏ 1, Nov 95	2.50	0.50	1.50	2.50
❏ 3, Feb 96	2.95	0.59	1.77	2.95
❏ 3, Feb 96, alternate cover	2.95	0.59	1.77	2.95

BATTLESTAR: GALACTICA
MARVEL

	ORIG.	GOOD	FINE	N-MINT
❏ 1	0.35	0.60	1.80	3.00
❏ 2	0.35	0.40	1.20	2.00
❏ 3	0.40	0.30	0.90	1.50
❏ 4	0.40	0.30	0.90	1.50
❏ 5	0.40	0.30	0.90	1.50
❏ 6	0.40	0.30	0.90	1.50
❏ 7	0.40	0.30	0.90	1.50
❏ 8	0.40	0.30	0.90	1.50
❏ 9	0.40	0.30	0.90	1.50
❏ 10	0.40	0.30	0.90	1.50
❏ 11	0.40	0.20	0.60	1.00
❏ 12	0.40	0.20	0.60	1.00
❏ 13	0.40	0.20	0.60	1.00
❏ 14	0.40	0.20	0.60	1.00
❏ 15	0.40	0.20	0.60	1.00
❏ 16	0.40	0.20	0.60	1.00
❏ 17	0.40	0.20	0.60	1.00
❏ 18	0.40	0.20	0.60	1.00
❏ 19	0.50	0.20	0.60	1.00
❏ 20	0.50	0.20	0.60	1.00
❏ 21	0.50	0.20	0.60	1.00
❏ 22	0.50	0.20	0.60	1.00
❏ 23	0.50	0.20	0.60	1.00

BATTLESTONE
IMAGE

	ORIG.	GOOD	FINE	N-MINT
❏ 1, Nov 94, two covers	2.50	0.50	1.50	2.50
❏ 2, Dec 94	2.50	0.50	1.50	2.50

BATTLETECH
BLACKTHORNE

	GOOD	FINE	N-MINT
❏ 1, color	0.35	1.05	1.75
❏ 2, b&w	0.35	1.05	1.75
❏ 3, b&w	0.35	1.05	1.75
❏ 4, b&w	0.35	1.05	1.75
❏ 5, b&w	0.35	1.05	1.75
❏ 6, b&w	0.35	1.05	1.75

BATTLETECH IN 3-D

	GOOD	FINE	N-MINT
❏ 1	0.50	1.50	2.50

BATTLETIDE
MARVEL

	ORIG.	GOOD	FINE	N-MINT
❏ 1, Death's Head II, Killpower	1.75	0.35	1.05	1.75
❏ 2	1.75	0.35	1.05	1.75
❏ 3	1.75	0.35	1.05	1.75
❏ 4	1.75	0.35	1.05	1.75

BATTLETIDE II

	ORIG.	GOOD	FINE	N-MINT
❏ 1	2.95	0.59	1.77	2.95
❏ 2	1.75	0.35	1.05	1.75
❏ 3	1.75	0.35	1.05	1.75
❏ 4	1.75	0.35	1.05	1.75

BATTLEZONES: DREAM TEAM 2
MALIBU

	ORIG.	GOOD	FINE	N-MINT
❏ 1, Mar 96, pin-ups of battles between Malibu and Marvel characters	3.95	0.79	2.37	3.95

BATTRON
NEC

	GOOD	FINE	N-MINT
❏ 1, b&w	0.55	1.65	2.75
❏ 2, b&w	0.55	1.65	2.75

BEACH PARTY
ETERNITY

	GOOD	FINE	N-MINT
❏ 1, b&w pin-ups	0.50	1.50	2.50

BEAST WARRIORS OF SHAOLIN
PIED PIPER

	GOOD	FINE	N-MINT
❏ 1, b&w	0.39	1.17	1.95
❏ 2, b&w	0.39	1.17	1.95
❏ 3, b&w	0.39	1.17	1.95

BEATLES EXPERIENCE (8 issue series)
REVOLUTIONARY

	ORIG.	GOOD	FINE	N-MINT
❏ 1, Mar 91, b&w	2.50	1.60	4.80	8.00

	ORIG.	GOOD	FINE	N-MINT
2, May 91, b&w	2.50	1.00	3.00	5.00
3, Jul 91, b&w	2.50	0.60	1.80	3.00
4, Sep 91, b&w	2.50	0.60	1.80	3.00
5, Nov 91, b&w	2.50	0.60	1.80	3.00
6, Jan 92, b&w	2.50	0.60	1.80	3.00
7, Mar 92, b&w	2.50	0.60	1.80	3.00
8, May 92	2.50	0.60	1.80	3.00

BEATLES, THE
PERSONALITY

	ORIG.	GOOD	FINE	N-MINT
1, b&w		1.00	3.00	5.00
1, limited edition, b&w		1.60	4.80	8.00
2, b&w		0.80	2.40	4.00

BEAUTIES & BARBARIANS
AC

	ORIG.	GOOD	FINE	N-MINT
1, WW				

BEAUTIFUL STORIES FOR UGLY CHILDREN
PIRANHA

	ORIG.	GOOD	FINE	N-MINT
1		0.60	1.80	3.00
2, b&w		0.60	1.80	3.00
3, b&w		0.60	1.80	3.00
4, b&w		0.60	1.80	3.00
5, b&w		0.60	1.80	3.00
6		0.50	1.50	2.50
7		0.50	1.50	2.50
8		0.40	1.20	2.00
9		0.40	1.20	2.00
10		0.40	1.20	2.00
11		0.40	1.20	2.00
12		0.50	1.50	2.50
13		0.50	1.50	2.50
14		0.50	1.50	2.50
15		0.50	1.50	2.50
16		0.50	1.50	2.50
17		0.50	1.50	2.50
18		0.50	1.50	2.50
19		0.50	1.50	2.50
20		0.50	1.50	2.50
21		0.50	1.50	2.50
22		0.50	1.50	2.50
23		0.50	1.50	2.50
24		0.50	1.50	2.50
25		0.50	1.50	2.50
26		0.50	1.50	2.50
27		0.50	1.50	2.50
28		0.50	1.50	2.50

BEAUTY AND THE BEAST
DISNEY

	ORIG.	GOOD	FINE	N-MINT
0, nn, movie adaptation		0.50	1.50	2.50
0, nn, squarebound		0.99	2.97	4.95

INNOVATION

	ORIG.	GOOD	FINE	N-MINT
1, TV series	2.50	0.50	1.50	2.50
2, TV series	2.50	0.50	1.50	2.50
3, TV series	2.50	0.50	1.50	2.50
4, TV series	2.50	0.50	1.50	2.50
5	2.50	0.50	1.50	2.50
6	2.50	0.50	1.50	2.50

MARVEL

	ORIG.	GOOD	FINE	N-MINT
1, Dec 84, DP	0.75	0.30	0.90	1.50
2, Feb 85, DP	0.75	0.20	0.60	1.00
3, Apr 85, DP	0.75	0.20	0.60	1.00
4, Jun 85, DP	0.75	0.20	0.60	1.00

BEAUTY AND THE BEAST: NIGHT OF BEAUTY
FIRST

	ORIG.	GOOD	FINE	N-MINT
0, 90, pb, WP	5.95	1.19	3.57	5.95

BEAUTY AND THE BEAST: PORTRAIT OF LOVE

	ORIG.	GOOD	FINE	N-MINT
0, 89, pb, WP	5.95	1.19	3.57	5.95

BEAUTY OF THE BEASTS
MU PRESS

	ORIG.	GOOD	FINE	N-MINT
1, Nov 91, b&w	2.50	0.50	1.50	2.50
2, b&w	2.50	0.50	1.50	2.50

BEAVIS & BUTT-HEAD
MARVEL

	ORIG.	GOOD	FINE	N-MINT
1, 94	1.95	1.00	3.00	5.00
2, 94	1.95	0.60	1.80	3.00
3, May 94	1.95	0.39	1.17	1.95
4, Jun 94	1.95	0.39	1.17	1.95
5, Jul 94	1.95	0.39	1.17	1.95
6, Aug 94	1.95	0.39	1.17	1.95
7, Sep 94	1.95	0.39	1.17	1.95
8, Oct 94	1.95	0.39	1.17	1.95
9, Nov 94	1.95	0.39	1.17	1.95
10, Dec 94	1.95	0.39	1.17	1.95
11, Jan 95	1.95	0.39	1.17	1.95
12, Feb 95	1.95	0.39	1.17	1.95
13, Mar 95	1.95	0.39	1.17	1.95
14, Apr 95	1.95	0.39	1.17	1.95
15, May 95	1.95	0.39	1.17	1.95
16, Jun 95	1.95	0.39	1.17	1.95
17, Jul 95	1.95	0.39	1.17	1.95
18, Aug 95	1.95	0.39	1.17	1.95
19, Sep 95	1.95	0.39	1.17	1.95
20, Oct 95	1.95	0.39	1.17	1.95
21, Nov 95	1.95	0.39	1.17	1.95
22, Dec 95	1.95	0.39	1.17	1.95
23, Jan 96	1.50	0.30	0.90	1.50
24, Feb 96	1.95	0.39	1.17	1.95
25, Mar 96	1.95	0.39	1.17	1.95
26, Apr 96	1.95	0.39	1.17	1.95
27, May 96	1.95	0.39	1.17	1.95
28, Jun 96, final issue	1.95	0.39	1.17	1.95

BEDLAM!
ECLIPSE

	ORIG.	GOOD	FINE	N-MINT
1		0.35	1.05	1.75
2		0.35	1.05	1.75

BEER NUTZ
TUNDRA

	ORIG.	GOOD	FINE	N-MINT
1		0.59	1.77	2.95
2		0.40	1.20	2.00
3, b&w		0.45	1.35	2.25

BEETHOVEN
HARVEY

	ORIG.	GOOD	FINE	N-MINT
1, 94	1.50	0.30	0.90	1.50
2, 94	1.50	0.30	0.90	1.50
3, Jul 94	1.50	0.30	0.90	1.50

BEETLE BAILEY

	ORIG.	GOOD	FINE	N-MINT
1	1.25	0.25	0.75	1.25
2	1.25	0.25	0.75	1.25
3	1.25	0.25	0.75	1.25
4	1.25	0.25	0.75	1.25
5	1.25	0.25	0.75	1.25
6	1.50	0.30	0.90	1.50
7	1.50	0.30	0.90	1.50
8	1.50	0.30	0.90	1.50

BEETLE BAILEY BIG BOOK

	ORIG.	GOOD	FINE	N-MINT
2		0.39	1.17	1.95

BEETLE BAILEY GIANT SIZE

	ORIG.	GOOD	FINE	N-MINT
2		0.45	1.35	2.25

BEETLEJUICE

	ORIG.	GOOD	FINE	N-MINT
1	1.50	0.25	0.75	1.25
2	1.50	0.25	0.75	1.25

BEETLEJUICE: CRIMEBUSTERS ON THE HAUNT

	ORIG.	GOOD	FINE	N-MINT
1		0.30	0.90	1.50

BELLA DONNA
PINNACLE

	ORIG.	GOOD	FINE	N-MINT
1, b&w		0.35	1.05	1.75

BENZANGO OBSCURO
STARHEAD

	ORIG.	GOOD	FINE	N-MINT
1	2.75	0.55	1.65	2.75

BERNI WRIGHTSON MASTER OF MACABRE
PACIFIC

	ORIG.	GOOD	FINE	N-MINT
❏ 1, BWr	1.50	0.30	0.90	1.50
❏ 2, BWr	1.50	0.30	0.90	1.50
❏ 3, BWr	1.50	0.30	0.90	1.50
❏ 4, BWr (moves to Eclipse)	1.50	0.30	0.90	1.50

BERNI WRIGHTSON MASTER OF MACABRE
(former Pacific title)
ECLIPSE

	ORIG.	GOOD	FINE	N-MINT
❏ 5, BWr	1.50	0.30	0.90	1.50

BERZERKER
GAUNTLET

	ORIG.	GOOD	FINE	N-MINT
❏ 1, RL,EL,Medina	2.95	0.79	2.37	3.95
❏ 2	2.95	0.59	1.77	2.95
❏ 3	2.95	0.59	1.77	2.95
❏ 4	2.95	0.59	1.77	2.95
❏ 5	2.95	0.59	1.77	2.95

BERZERKERS
IMAGE

	ORIG.	GOOD	FINE	N-MINT
❏ 1, Aug 95	2.50	0.50	1.50	2.50
❏ 1, Aug 95, alternate cover	2.50	0.50	1.50	2.50
❏ 2, Sep 95	2.50	0.50	1.50	2.50
❏ 3, Oct 95	2.50	0.50	1.50	2.50

BESET BY DEMONS
TUNDRA

	ORIG.	GOOD	FINE	N-MINT
❏ 0		0.79	2.37	3.95

BEST OF BARRON STOREY'S W.A.T.C.H.
MAGAZINE
VANGUARD

	ORIG.	GOOD	FINE	N-MINT
❏ 1, Dec 93	2.95	0.59	1.77	2.95

BEST OF DC, THE
DC

	ORIG.	GOOD	FINE	N-MINT
❏ 1, Sep 79	0.95	0.40	1.20	2.00
❏ 2, Nov 79	0.95	0.40	1.20	2.00
❏ 3, Jan 80	0.95	0.40	1.20	2.00
❏ 4, Mar 80	0.95	0.40	1.20	2.00
❏ 5, May 80	0.95	0.40	1.20	2.00
❏ 6, Jul 80	0.95	0.40	1.20	2.00
❏ 7, Sep 80	0.95	0.40	1.20	2.00
❏ 8, Nov 80	0.95	0.40	1.20	2.00
❏ 9, Jan 81	0.95	0.40	1.20	2.00
❏ 10, Mar 81	0.95	0.40	1.20	2.00
❏ 11, Apr 81	0.95	0.40	1.20	2.00
❏ 12, May 81	0.95	0.40	1.20	2.00
❏ 13, Jun 81	0.95	0.40	1.20	2.00
❏ 14, Jul 81	0.95	0.40	1.20	2.00
❏ 15, Aug 81	0.95	0.40	1.20	2.00
❏ 16, Sep 81	0.95	0.40	1.20	2.00
❏ 17, Oct 81	0.95	0.40	1.20	2.00
❏ 18, Nov 81	0.95	0.40	1.20	2.00
❏ 19, Dec 81	0.95	0.40	1.20	2.00
❏ 20, Jan 82	0.95	0.40	1.20	2.00
❏ 21, Feb 82	0.95	0.40	1.20	2.00
❏ 22, Mar 82	0.95	0.40	1.20	2.00
❏ 23, Apr 82	1.25	0.40	1.20	2.00
❏ 24, May 82	0.95	0.40	1.20	2.00
❏ 25, Jun 82	0.95	0.40	1.20	2.00
❏ 26, Jul 82	0.95	0.40	1.20	2.00
❏ 27, Aug 82	0.95	0.40	1.20	2.00
❏ 28, Sep 82		0.40	1.20	2.00
❏ 29, Oct 82		0.40	1.20	2.00
❏ 30, Nov 82	1.25	0.40	1.20	2.00
❏ 31, Dec 82	1.25	0.40	1.20	2.00
❏ 32		0.40	1.20	2.00
❏ 33		0.40	1.20	2.00
❏ 34		0.40	1.20	2.00
❏ 35		0.40	1.20	2.00
❏ 36		0.40	1.20	2.00

	ORIG.	GOOD	FINE	N-MINT
❏ 37		0.40	1.20	2.00
❏ 38		0.40	1.20	2.00
❏ 39		0.40	1.20	2.00
❏ 40		0.40	1.20	2.00
❏ 41		0.40	1.20	2.00
❏ 42		0.40	1.20	2.00
❏ 43		0.40	1.20	2.00
❏ 44		0.40	1.20	2.00
❏ 45		0.40	1.20	2.00
❏ 46		0.40	1.20	2.00
❏ 47		0.40	1.20	2.00
❏ 48		0.40	1.20	2.00
❏ 49		0.40	1.20	2.00
❏ 50		0.40	1.20	2.00
❏ 51		0.40	1.20	2.00
❏ 52		0.40	1.20	2.00
❏ 53		0.40	1.20	2.00
❏ 54		0.40	1.20	2.00
❏ 55		0.40	1.20	2.00
❏ 56		0.40	1.20	2.00
❏ 57		0.40	1.20	2.00
❏ 58, Mar 85	1.50	0.40	1.20	2.00

BEST OF FURRLOUGH
ANTARCTIC

	ORIG.	GOOD	FINE	N-MINT
❏ 1, Jan 95, b&w	3.95	0.79	2.37	3.95

BEST OF HORROR AND SCIENCE FICTION
WEBSTER

	ORIG.	GOOD	FINE	N-MINT
❏ 1, BW,FF,SD		0.40	1.20	2.00

BEST OF NORTHSTAR, THE
NORTHSTAR

	ORIG.	GOOD	FINE	N-MINT
❏ 1, b&w		0.39	1.17	1.95

BEST OF THE BRAVE AND THE BOLD, THE
DC

	ORIG.	GOOD	FINE	N-MINT
❏ 1, Oct 88, NA, JKu rep.		0.50	1.50	2.50
❏ 2, Nov 88, NA, JKu rep.		0.50	1.50	2.50
❏ 3, Dec 88, NA, JKu rep.		0.50	1.50	2.50
❏ 4, Dec 88, NA, JKu rep.		0.50	1.50	2.50
❏ 5, Jan 89, NA, JKu rep.		0.50	1.50	2.50
❏ 6, Jan 89, NA, JKu rep.		0.50	1.50	2.50

BEST OF THE BRITISH INVASION
REVOLUTIONARY

	ORIG.	GOOD	FINE	N-MINT
❏ 1, Sep 93, b&w	2.50	0.50	1.50	2.50
❏ 2, Jan 94, b&w	2.50	0.50	1.50	2.50

BEST OF TRIBUNE CO.
DRAGON LADY

	ORIG.	GOOD	FINE	N-MINT
❏ 1		0.59	1.77	2.95
❏ 2		0.59	1.77	2.95
❏ 3		0.59	1.77	2.95
❏ 4, (becomes *Thrilling Adventure Strips*)		0.59	1.77	2.95

BETA SEXUS (mini-series)
FANTAGRAPHICS/EROS

	ORIG.	GOOD	FINE	N-MINT
❏ 1, adult, b&w	2.75	0.55	1.65	2.75
❏ 2, Jul 94, adult, b&w	2.75	0.55	1.65	2.75

BETTY
ARCHIE

	ORIG.	GOOD	FINE	N-MINT
❏ 1, Sep 92	1.25	0.25	0.75	1.25
❏ 2	1.25	0.25	0.75	1.25
❏ 3	1.25	0.25	0.75	1.25
❏ 4	1.25	0.25	0.75	1.25
❏ 5	1.25	0.25	0.75	1.25
❏ 6	1.25	0.25	0.75	1.25
❏ 7	1.25	0.25	0.75	1.25
❏ 8	1.25	0.25	0.75	1.25
❏ 9	1.25	0.25	0.75	1.25
❏ 10	1.25	0.25	0.75	1.25
❏ 11	1.25	0.25	0.75	1.25
❏ 12	1.25	0.25	0.75	1.25
❏ 13	1.25	0.25	0.75	1.25
❏ 14	1.25	0.25	0.75	1.25

	ORIG.	GOOD	FINE	N-MINT
☐ 15	1.25	0.25	0.75	1.25
☐ 16	1.25	0.25	0.75	1.25
☐ 17, Sep 94	1.50	0.30	0.90	1.50
☐ 18, Oct 94	1.50	0.30	0.90	1.50
☐ 19, Nov 94, "Love Showdown"	1.50	0.30	0.90	1.50
☐ 20, Dec 94	1.50	0.30	0.90	1.50
☐ 21, Jan 95	1.50	0.30	0.90	1.50
☐ 22, Feb 95	1.50	0.30	0.90	1.50
☐ 23, Mar 95	1.50	0.30	0.90	1.50
☐ 24, Apr 95	1.50	0.30	0.90	1.50
☐ 25, May 95	1.50	0.30	0.90	1.50
☐ 26, Jun 95	1.50	0.30	0.90	1.50
☐ 27, Jul 95	1.50	0.30	0.90	1.50
☐ 28, Aug 95	1.50	0.30	0.90	1.50
☐ 29, Sep 95	1.50	0.30	0.90	1.50
☐ 30, Oct 95	1.50	0.30	0.90	1.50
☐ 31, Nov 95	1.50	0.30	0.90	1.50
☐ 32, Dec 95	1.50	0.30	0.90	1.50
☐ 33, Jan 96	1.50	0.30	0.90	1.50
☐ 34, Feb 96	1.50	0.30	0.90	1.50
☐ 35, Mar 96	1.50	0.30	0.90	1.50
☐ 36, Apr 96	1.50	0.30	0.90	1.50
☐ 39, Jul 96	1.50	0.30	0.90	1.50

BETTY & VERONICA (Volume 2)

	ORIG.	GOOD	FINE	N-MINT
☐ 1, Jun 87	0.75	0.15	0.45	0.75
☐ 2	0.75	0.15	0.45	0.75
☐ 3	0.75	0.15	0.45	0.75
☐ 4	0.75	0.15	0.45	0.75
☐ 5	0.75	0.15	0.45	0.75
☐ 6	0.75	0.15	0.45	0.75
☐ 7	0.75	0.15	0.45	0.75
☐ 8	0.75	0.15	0.45	0.75
☐ 9	0.75	0.15	0.45	0.75
☐ 10	0.75	0.15	0.45	0.75
☐ 11	0.75	0.15	0.45	0.75
☐ 12	0.75	0.15	0.45	0.75
☐ 13	0.75	0.15	0.45	0.75
☐ 14	0.75	0.15	0.45	0.75
☐ 15	0.75	0.15	0.45	0.75
☐ 16	0.75	0.15	0.45	0.75
☐ 17	0.75	0.15	0.45	0.75
☐ 18	0.75	0.15	0.45	0.75
☐ 19	0.75	0.15	0.45	0.75
☐ 20	0.75	0.15	0.45	0.75
☐ 21		0.20	0.60	1.00
☐ 22		0.20	0.60	1.00
☐ 23		0.20	0.60	1.00
☐ 24		0.20	0.60	1.00
☐ 25		0.20	0.60	1.00
☐ 26		0.20	0.60	1.00
☐ 27		0.20	0.60	1.00
☐ 28		0.20	0.60	1.00
☐ 29		0.20	0.60	1.00
☐ 30		0.20	0.60	1.00
☐ 31		0.20	0.60	1.00
☐ 32		0.20	0.60	1.00
☐ 33		0.20	0.60	1.00
☐ 34		0.20	0.60	1.00
☐ 35		0.20	0.60	1.00
☐ 36		0.20	0.60	1.00
☐ 37		0.20	0.60	1.00
☐ 38		0.20	0.60	1.00
☐ 39		0.20	0.60	1.00
☐ 40		0.20	0.60	1.00
☐ 41		0.20	0.60	1.00
☐ 42		0.20	0.60	1.00
☐ 43		0.20	0.60	1.00
☐ 44		0.20	0.60	1.00
☐ 45		0.20	0.60	1.00
☐ 46		0.20	0.60	1.00

	ORIG.	GOOD	FINE	N-MINT
☐ 47		0.20	0.60	1.00
☐ 48		0.20	0.60	1.00
☐ 49		0.20	0.60	1.00
☐ 50		0.20	0.60	1.00
☐ 51		0.20	0.60	1.00
☐ 52		0.20	0.60	1.00
☐ 53		0.20	0.60	1.00
☐ 54		0.20	0.60	1.00
☐ 55		0.20	0.60	1.00
☐ 56		0.20	0.60	1.00
☐ 57		0.20	0.60	1.00
☐ 58		0.20	0.60	1.00
☐ 59		0.20	0.60	1.00
☐ 60		0.20	0.60	1.00
☐ 61		0.20	0.60	1.00
☐ 62		0.20	0.60	1.00
☐ 63		0.20	0.60	1.00
☐ 64		0.20	0.60	1.00
☐ 65		0.20	0.60	1.00
☐ 66		0.20	0.60	1.00
☐ 67		0.20	0.60	1.00
☐ 68		0.20	0.60	1.00
☐ 69		0.20	0.60	1.00
☐ 70		0.20	0.60	1.00
☐ 71		0.20	0.60	1.00
☐ 72		0.20	0.60	1.00
☐ 73		0.20	0.60	1.00
☐ 74		0.20	0.60	1.00
☐ 75		0.20	0.60	1.00
☐ 76		0.20	0.60	1.00
☐ 77		0.20	0.60	1.00
☐ 78, Aug 94	1.50	0.30	0.90	1.50
☐ 79, Sep 94	1.50	0.30	0.90	1.50
☐ 80, Oct 94	1.50	0.30	0.90	1.50
☐ 81, Nov 94	1.50	0.30	0.90	1.50
☐ 82, Dec 94, "Love Showdown"	1.50	0.30	0.90	1.50
☐ 83, Jan 95	1.50	0.30	0.90	1.50
☐ 84, Feb 95	1.50	0.30	0.90	1.50
☐ 85, Mar 95	1.50	0.30	0.90	1.50
☐ 87, May 95	1.50	0.30	0.90	1.50
☐ 88, Jun 95	1.50	0.30	0.90	1.50
☐ 89, Jul 95	1.50	0.30	0.90	1.50
☐ 90, Aug 95	1.50	0.30	0.90	1.50
☐ 91, Sep 95	1.50	0.30	0.90	1.50
☐ 92, Oct 95	1.50	0.30	0.90	1.50
☐ 93, Nov 95	1.50	0.30	0.90	1.50
☐ 94, Dec 95	1.50	0.30	0.90	1.50
☐ 95, Jan 96, "House of Riverdale" Part 2;concludes in Archie's Pal, Jughead #76	1.50	0.30	0.90	1.50
☐ 96, Feb 96	1.50	0.30	0.90	1.50
☐ 97, Mar 96	1.50	0.30	0.90	1.50
☐ 98, Apr 96	1.50	0.30	0.90	1.50
☐ 99, May 96	1.50	0.30	0.90	1.50
☐ 100, Jun 96	1.50	0.30	0.90	1.50
☐ 102, Aug 96	1.50	0.30	0.90	1.50

BETTY & VERONICA ANNUAL DIGEST MAGAZINE

	ORIG.	GOOD	FINE	N-MINT
☐ 12, Jan 95, digest	1.75	0.35	1.05	1.75
☐ 13, Sep 95, digest	1.75	0.35	1.05	1.75
☐ 14, Feb 96, digest	1.75	0.35	1.05	1.75
☐ 15, Jul 96, digest	1.75	0.35	1.05	1.75

BETTY & VERONICA SUMMER FUN

	ORIG.	GOOD	FINE	N-MINT
☐ 1, Sum 94	2.00	0.40	1.20	2.00

BETTY AND VERONICA DIGEST MAGAZINE

	ORIG.	GOOD	FINE	N-MINT
☐ 72, Jan 95, digest	1.75	0.35	1.05	1.75
☐ 73, Mar 95, digest	1.75	0.35	1.05	1.75
☐ 74, Apr 95, digest	1.75	0.35	1.05	1.75
☐ 75, Jun 95, digest	1.75	0.35	1.05	1.75
☐ 76, Aug 95, digest	1.75	0.35	1.05	1.75
☐ 77, Oct 95, digest	1.75	0.35	1.05	1.75

	ORIG.	GOOD	FINE	N-MINT
78, Dec 95, digest 1.75	0.35	1.05	1.75
79, Feb 96, digest 1.75	0.35	1.05	1.75
80, Apr 96, digest 1.75	0.35	1.05	1.75
81, Jun 96, digest 1.75	0.35	1.05	1.75
82, Jul 96, digest 1.75	0.35	1.05	1.75

BETTY AND VERONICA DOUBLE DIGEST

	ORIG.	GOOD	FINE	N-MINT
1, digest		0.55	1.65	2.75
2, digest		0.55	1.65	2.75
3, digest		0.55	1.65	2.75
4, digest		0.55	1.65	2.75
5, digest		0.55	1.65	2.75
6, digest		0.55	1.65	2.75
7, digest		0.55	1.65	2.75
8, digest		0.55	1.65	2.75
9, digest		0.55	1.65	2.75
10, digest		0.55	1.65	2.75
11, digest		0.55	1.65	2.75
12, digest		0.55	1.65	2.75
13, digest		0.55	1.65	2.75
14, digest		0.55	1.65	2.75
15, digest		0.55	1.65	2.75
16, digest		0.55	1.65	2.75
17, digest		0.55	1.65	2.75
18, digest		0.55	1.65	2.75
19, digest		0.55	1.65	2.75
20, digest		0.55	1.65	2.75
21, digest		0.55	1.65	2.75
22, digest		0.55	1.65	2.75
23, digest		0.55	1.65	2.75
24, digest		0.55	1.65	2.75
25, digest		0.55	1.65	2.75
26, digest		0.55	1.65	2.75
27, digest		0.55	1.65	2.75
28, digest		0.55	1.65	2.75
29, digest		0.55	1.65	2.75
30, digest		0.55	1.65	2.75
31, digest		0.55	1.65	2.75
32, digest		0.55	1.65	2.75
33, digest		0.55	1.65	2.75
34, digest		0.55	1.65	2.75
35, digest		0.55	1.65	2.75
36, digest		0.55	1.65	2.75
37, digest		0.55	1.65	2.75
38, digest		0.55	1.65	2.75
39, digest		0.55	1.65	2.75
40, digest		0.55	1.65	2.75
41, digest		0.55	1.65	2.75
42, digest		0.55	1.65	2.75
43, digest		0.55	1.65	2.75
44, digest		0.55	1.65	2.75
45, digest		0.55	1.65	2.75
46, digest		0.55	1.65	2.75
47, digest		0.55	1.65	2.75
48, Dec 94, digest 2.75	0.55	1.65	2.75
50, Apr 95, digest 2.75	0.55	1.65	2.75
51, Jun 95, digest 2.75	0.55	1.65	2.75
52, Aug 95, digest 2.75	0.55	1.65	2.75
53, Sep 95, digest 2.75	0.55	1.65	2.75
55, Jan 96, digest 2.75	0.55	1.65	2.75
56, Mar 96, digest 2.75	0.55	1.65	2.75
57, Apr 96, digest 2.75	0.55	1.65	2.75

BETTY AND VERONICA SPECTACULAR

	ORIG.	GOOD	FINE	N-MINT
1, Oct 92 .... 1.25	0.25	0.75	1.25
2 .... 1.25	0.25	0.75	1.25
3 .... 1.25	0.25	0.75	1.25
4 .... 1.25	0.25	0.75	1.25
5 .... 1.25	0.25	0.75	1.25
10, Sep 94 .... 1.50	0.30	0.90	1.50
11, Nov 94 .... 1.50	0.30	0.90	1.50
12, Jan 95 .... 1.50	0.30	0.90	1.50
13, Feb 95 .... 1.50	0.30	0.90	1.50

	ORIG.	GOOD	FINE	N-MINT
14, Apr 95 .... 1.50	0.30	0.90	1.50
15, Jul 95 .... 1.50	0.30	0.90	1.50
16, Oct 95 .... 1.50	0.30	0.90	1.50
17, Jan 96 .... 1.50	0.30	0.90	1.50
18, Apr 96 .... 1.50	0.30	0.90	1.50
19, Jul 96 .... 1.50	0.30	0.90	1.50

BETTY BEING BAD
EROS COMIX

	ORIG.	GOOD	FINE	N-MINT
0, no photos of Betty Page		0.70	2.10	3.50

BETTY BOOP IN 3-D
BLACKTHORNE

	ORIG.	GOOD	FINE	N-MINT
1		0.50	1.50	2.50

BETTY BOOP'S BIG BREAK
FIRST

	ORIG.	GOOD	FINE	N-MINT
0, nn		1.19	3.57	5.95

BETTY IN BONDAGE
SHUNGA

	ORIG.	GOOD	FINE	N-MINT
1, adult, b&w		0.60	1.80	3.00
2, adult, b&w		0.60	1.80	3.00
3, adult, b&w		0.60	1.80	3.00
4, adult, b&w		0.60	1.80	3.00

BETTY PAGE 3-D COMICS
3-D ZONE

	ORIG.	GOOD	FINE	N-MINT
1		0.79	2.37	3.95

BETTY PAGE IN JUNGLE LAND
CONQUEST

	ORIG.	GOOD	FINE	N-MINT
0, pin-up photos		0.99	2.97	4.95

BETTY PAGE "CAPTURED JUNGLE GIRL" 3-D
3-D ZONE

	ORIG.	GOOD	FINE	N-MINT
1, photos		0.79	2.37	3.95

BETTY PAGES, THE
PURE IMAGINATION

	ORIG.	GOOD	FINE	N-MINT
1, DSt, Ward, photos		2.00	6.00	10.00
1, reprint		1.00	3.00	5.00
2		1.00	3.00	5.00
3		1.00	3.00	5.00
4		1.00	3.00	5.00
5		0.90	2.70	4.50
6		0.90	2.70	4.50

BETTY'S DIARY
ARCHIE

	ORIG.	GOOD	FINE	N-MINT
1, Apr 86 .... 0.75	0.15	0.45	0.75
2 .... 0.75	0.15	0.45	0.75
3 .... 0.75	0.15	0.45	0.75
4 .... 0.75	0.15	0.45	0.75
5 .... 0.75	0.15	0.45	0.75
6 .... 0.75	0.15	0.45	0.75
7 .... 0.75	0.15	0.45	0.75
8 .... 0.75	0.15	0.45	0.75
9 .... 0.75	0.15	0.45	0.75
10 .... 0.75	0.15	0.45	0.75
11 .... 0.75	0.15	0.45	0.75
12 .... 0.75	0.15	0.45	0.75
13 .... 0.75	0.15	0.45	0.75
14 .... 0.75	0.15	0.45	0.75
15 .... 0.75	0.15	0.45	0.75
16 .... 0.75	0.15	0.45	0.75
17 .... 0.75	0.15	0.45	0.75
18 .... 0.75	0.15	0.45	0.75
19 .... 0.75	0.15	0.45	0.75
20 .... 0.75	0.15	0.45	0.75
21 .... 0.75	0.15	0.45	0.75
22 .... 0.75	0.15	0.45	0.75
23 .... 0.75	0.15	0.45	0.75
24 .... 0.75	0.15	0.45	0.75
25 .... 0.75	0.15	0.45	0.75
26 .... 0.75	0.15	0.45	0.75
27 .... 0.75	0.15	0.45	0.75
28 .... 0.75	0.15	0.45	0.75
29 .... 0.75	0.15	0.45	0.75

	ORIG.	GOOD	FINE	N-MINT
30 .... 0.75		0.15	0.45	0.75
31 .... 0.75		0.15	0.45	0.75
32 .... 0.75		0.15	0.45	0.75
33 .... 0.75		0.15	0.45	0.75
34 .... 0.75		0.15	0.45	0.75
35 .... 0.75		0.15	0.45	0.75
36 .... 0.75		0.15	0.45	0.75
37 .... 0.75		0.15	0.45	0.75
38 .... 0.75		0.15	0.45	0.75
39 .... 0.75		0.15	0.45	0.75
40 .... 0.75		0.15	0.45	0.75

BEWARE THE CREEPER
DC

	ORIG.	GOOD	FINE	N-MINT
1, Jun 68 .... 0.12		13.00	39.00	65.00
2, Aug 68 .... 0.12		10.00	30.00	50.00
3, Oct 68 .... 0.12		7.00	21.00	35.00
4, Dec 68 .... 0.12		7.00	21.00	35.00
5, Feb 69 .... 0.12		7.00	21.00	35.00
6, Apr 69 .... 0.12		7.00	21.00	35.00

BEYOND HUMAN
BATTLELINE

	ORIG.	GOOD	FINE	N-MINT
0, Mar 95, b&w 3.50		0.70	2.10	3.50

BEYOND MARS
BLACKTHORNE

	ORIG.	GOOD	FINE	N-MINT
0, book 1-3		0.40	1.20	2.00
1		1.39	4.17	6.95
2		1.39	4.17	6.95

BEZANGO OBSCURO
STARHEAD

	ORIG.	GOOD	FINE	N-MINT
1, 94, b&w 2.75		0.55	1.65	2.75

BIG
DARK HORSE

	ORIG.	GOOD	FINE	N-MINT
1, Mar 89, adaptation 2.00		0.40	1.20	2.00

BIG BAD BLOOD OF DRACULA
APPLE

	ORIG.	GOOD	FINE	N-MINT
1, b&w, rep:BWr		0.55	1.65	2.75
2		0.59	1.77	2.95

BIG BANG COMICS
CALIBER/BIG BANG

	ORIG.	GOOD	FINE	N-MINT
1, Spr 94 .... 1.95		0.39	1.17	1.95
2, Sum 94 .... 1.95		0.39	1.17	1.95
3, 94 .... 1.95		0.39	1.17	1.95
4, 95 .... 1.95		0.39	1.17	1.95

BIG BANG COMICS (Vol. 2)
IMAGE

	ORIG.	GOOD	FINE	N-MINT
1, May 96 .... 1.95		0.39	1.17	1.95

BIG BLACK KISS
VORTEX

	ORIG.	GOOD	FINE	N-MINT
1, Sep 89, HC, adult, reprint 3.75		0.75	2.25	3.75
2, Oct 89, HC, adult, reprint 3.75		0.75	2.25	3.75
3, Nov 89, HC, adult, reprint 3.75		0.75	2.25	3.75

BIG DOG FUNNIES
RIP OFF

	ORIG.	GOOD	FINE	N-MINT
0, Jun 92, nn 2.50		0.50	1.50	2.50

BIG EDSEL BAND
ACE

	ORIG.	GOOD	FINE	N-MINT
1		0.35	1.05	1.75

BIG GUY AND RUSTY THE BOY ROBOT, THE
(mini-series)
DARK HORSE

	ORIG.	GOOD	FINE	N-MINT
1, Jul 95, over-sized 4.95		0.99	2.97	4.95
2, Aug 95, over-sized;final issue 4.95		0.99	2.97	4.95

BIG MONSTER FIGHT
KIDGANG COMICS

	ORIG.	GOOD	FINE	N-MINT
0, 95, b&w 2.50		0.50	1.50	2.50

BIG MOUTH
STARHEAD

	ORIG.	GOOD	FINE	N-MINT
1, b&w 2.95		0.59	1.77	2.95
2, b&w 2.95		0.59	1.77	2.95

BIG NUMBERS
MAD LOVE

	ORIG.	GOOD	FINE	N-MINT
1		1.10	3.30	5.50
2		1.10	3.30	5.50

BIG PRIZE, THE
ETERNITY

	ORIG.	GOOD	FINE	N-MINT
1, b&w		0.39	1.17	1.95
2, b&w		0.39	1.17	1.95

BIG TOP BONDAGE
EROS

	ORIG.	GOOD	FINE	N-MINT
1, adult, b&w		0.50	1.50	2.50

BIKER MICE FROM MARS
MARVEL

	ORIG.	GOOD	FINE	N-MINT
1 .... 1.50		0.30	0.90	1.50
2 .... 1.50		0.30	0.90	1.50
3 .... 1.50		0.30	0.90	1.50

BIKINI BATTLE 3-D
3-D ZONE

	ORIG.	GOOD	FINE	N-MINT
0, nn Crumb, adult		0.79	2.37	3.95

BILL & TED'S EXCELLENT COMIC BOOK
MARVEL

	ORIG.	GOOD	FINE	N-MINT
1, ED 1.00		0.20	0.60	1.00
2, ED 1.00		0.20	0.60	1.00
3, ED 1.25		0.25	0.75	1.25
4, ED 1.25		0.25	0.75	1.25
5, ED 1.25		0.25	0.75	1.25
6, ED 1.25		0.25	0.75	1.25
7, Jun 92, ED 1.25		0.25	0.75	1.25
8, Jul 92, ED 1.25		0.25	0.75	1.25
9, Aug 92, ED 1.25		0.25	0.75	1.25
10, Sep 92, ED 1.25		0.25	0.75	1.25
11, ED 1.25		0.25	0.75	1.25
12, ED 1.25		0.25	0.75	1.25

BILL THE BULL: BURNT CAIN
BONEYARD

	ORIG.	GOOD	FINE	N-MINT
1, b&w		0.50	1.50	2.50
2, b&w		0.50	1.50	2.50

BILL THE BULL:
ONE SHOT, ONE BOURBON, ONE BEER

	ORIG.	GOOD	FINE	N-MINT
1, Dec 94, b&w 2.95		0.59	1.77	2.95
2, Mar 95, b&w;indicia says Mar 94, a misprint 2.95		0.59	1.77	2.95

BILL THE CLOWN
SLAVE LABOR

	ORIG.	GOOD	FINE	N-MINT
1, b&w		0.50	1.50	2.50

BILLI 99
DARK HORSE

	ORIG.	GOOD	FINE	N-MINT
1, 91, b&w 3.50		0.70	2.10	3.50
2, 91, b&w 3.50		0.70	2.10	3.50
3, 91, b&w 3.50		0.70	2.10	3.50
4, 91, b&w 3.95		0.79	2.37	3.95

BILLY COLE
CULT

	ORIG.	GOOD	FINE	N-MINT
1, Jun 94, b&w 2.75		0.55	1.65	2.75

BILLY NGUYEN
CALIBER

	ORIG.	GOOD	FINE	N-MINT
1, b&w 2.95		0.59	1.77	2.95

BILLY NGUYEN, PRIVATE EYE
ATTITUDE

	ORIG.	GOOD	FINE	N-MINT
1 .... 2.00		0.40	1.20	2.00
2 .... 2.00		0.40	1.20	2.00
3 .... 2.00		0.40	1.20	2.00

	ORIG.	GOOD	FINE	N-MINT

BILLY RAY CYRUS
MARVEL MUSIC
☐ 0, 95, nn;prestige format

.................................5.95 1.19 3.57 5.95

BIO 90
BULLET
☐ 1, b&w 0.50 1.50 2.50

BIO-BOOSTER ARMOR GUYVER
VIZ
☐ 7, 94, b&w 2.75 0.55 1.65 2.75
☐ 8, 94, b&w 2.75 0.55 1.65 2.75
☐ 9, 94, b&w 2.75 0.55 1.65 2.75
☐ 10, 94, b&w 2.75 0.55 1.65 2.75
☐ 11, 94, b&w 2.75 0.55 1.65 2.75

BIO-BOOSTER ARMOR GUYVER, PART THREE
☐ 1, 95, b&w 2.75 0.55 1.65 2.75
☐ 2, 95, b&w 2.75 0.55 1.65 2.75

BIO-BOOSTER ARMOR GUYVER, PART TWO
☐ 2, 94, b&w 2.75 0.55 1.65 2.75
☐ 3, 94, b&w 2.75 0.55 1.65 2.75
☐ 4, 95, b&w 2.75 0.55 1.65 2.75
☐ 5, 95, b&w 2.75 0.55 1.65 2.75

BIOLOGIC SHOW, THE
FANTAGRAPHICS
☐ 0, Oct 94, b&w magazine-sized comic book with
cardstock cover............. 2.95 0.59 1.77 2.95
☐ 1, Jan 95, b&w.............. 2.75 0.55 1.65 2.75

BIONEERS
MIRAGE
☐ 1, Aug 94 .... 2.75 0.55 1.65 2.75

BIRD, THE
ENTERTAINMENT
☐ 1, O:Bird............................. 0.30 0.90 1.50

BIRDLAND
EROS COMIX
☐ 1, adult, b&w 0.39 1.17 1.95
☐ 2 .... 0.45 1.35 2.25
☐ 3 .... 0.45 1.35 2.25

BIRDLAND VOL. 2
☐ 1, Jun 94, b&w 2.95 0.59 1.77 2.95

BIRTHRIGHT (also Critters #47-49)
FANTAGRAPHICS
☐ 1, b&w 0.40 1.20 2.00
☐ 2, b&w 0.40 1.20 2.00
☐ 3, b&w 0.40 1.20 2.00

BIRTHRITE
CONGRESS
☐ 1 .... 0.50 1.50 2.50
☐ 2 .... 0.50 1.50 2.50

BISHOP (mini-series)
MARVEL
☐ 1, Dec 94, enhanced cover

.............................2.95 0.59 1.77 2.95
☐ 2, Jan 95, enhanced cover

.............................2.95 0.59 1.77 2.95
☐ 3, Feb 95, enhanced cover

.............................2.95 0.59 1.77 2.95
☐ 4, Mar 95, enhanced cover

.............................2.95 0.59 1.77 2.95

BISLEY'S SCRAPBOOK
ATOMEKA
☐ 0, nn.............................. 2.50 0.50 1.50 2.50

BIZARRE 3-D ZONE
BLACKTHORNE
☐ 1, Jul 86 .... 2.25 0.45 1.35 2.25

BIZARRE ADVENTURES
MARVEL
☐ 34, (was b&w magazine)

.................................2.00 0.40 1.20 2.00

BIZARRE ADVENTURES (b&w magazine)
☐ 25, Mar 81, (was *Marvel Preview*) Black Widow

.................................1.25 0.25 0.75 1.25
☐ 26, May 81, Kull............1.25 0.25 0.75 1.25
☐ 27, Jul 81, X-Men 1.25 0.25 0.75 1.25
☐ 28, Oct 81, Elektra 1.50 0.30 0.90 1.50
☐ 29, Dec 81, Stephen King

.................................1.50 0.30 0.90 1.50
☐ 30, Paradox 1.50 0.30 0.90 1.50
☐ 31 ....1.50 0.30 0.90 1.50
☐ 32, Aug 82, Thor............1.50 0.30 0.90 1.50
☐ 33, (becomes comic book) Dracula, Zombie

.................................1.50 0.30 0.90 1.50

BIZARRE HEROES
FIASCO
☐ 14, Oct 95, (was *Don Simpson's Bizarre Heroes*);b&w

.................................2.95 0.59 1.77 2.95

KITCHEN SINK
☐ 1, May 90, b&w, parody ... 0.50 1.50 2.50

BLAB!
☐ 8, Sum 95, odd-sized anthology;Chris Ware (c)

.................................16.95 3.39 10.17 16.95

BLACK & WHITE
IMAGE
☐ 1, Oct 94 ....1.95 0.39 1.17 1.95
☐ 2, Nov 94 ....1.95 0.39 1.17 1.95
☐ 3, Jan 95 ....1.95 0.39 1.17 1.95

BLACK & WHITE (second series)
☐ 1, Feb 96 ....2.50 0.50 1.50 2.50

BLACK AXE
MARVEL
☐ 1 ....1.75 0.35 1.05 1.75
☐ 2 ....1.75 0.35 1.05 1.75
☐ 3 ....1.75 0.35 1.05 1.75
☐ 4 ....1.75 0.35 1.05 1.75
☐ 5 ....1.75 0.35 1.05 1.75
☐ 6 ....1.75 0.35 1.05 1.75
☐ 7 ....1.75 0.35 1.05 1.75

BLACK BOOK
COMICO
☐ 1, 87, AAd......................1.50 0.30 0.90 1.50

BLACK CANARY
DC
☐ 1, Nov 91 ....1.75 0.35 1.05 1.75
☐ 2, Dec 91 ....1.75 0.35 1.05 1.75
☐ 3, Jan 92 ....1.75 0.35 1.05 1.75
☐ 4, Feb 92 ....1.75 0.35 1.05 1.75

BLACK CANARY (2nd series)
☐ 1, Jan 93 ....1.75 0.35 1.05 1.75
☐ 2, Feb 93 ....1.75 0.35 1.05 1.75
☐ 3, Mar 93 ....1.75 0.35 1.05 1.75
☐ 4, Apr 93 ....1.75 0.35 1.05 1.75
☐ 5, May 93 ....1.75 0.35 1.05 1.75
☐ 6, Jun 93 ....1.75 0.35 1.05 1.75
☐ 7 ....1.75 0.35 1.05 1.75
☐ 8, The Ray 1.75 0.35 1.05 1.75
☐ 9 ....1.75 0.35 1.05 1.75
☐ 10 ....1.75 0.35 1.05 1.75
☐ 11 ....1.75 0.35 1.05 1.75
☐ 12 ....1.75 0.35 1.05 1.75

BLACK CANARY/ORACLE: BIRDS OF PREY
☐ 1, 96, one-shot 3.95 0.79 2.37 3.95

BLACK CAT (was Original Black Cat)
RECOLLECTIONS
☐ 8, b&w reprints................. 0.40 1.20 2.00
☐ 10, b&w reprints............1.00 0.20 0.60 1.00

	ORIG.	GOOD	FINE	N-MINT

BLACK CAT COMICS
LORNE-HARVEY

	ORIG.	GOOD	FINE	N-MINT
☐ 10, 93, b&w	1.00	0.20	0.60	1.00

BLACK CONDOR
DC

	ORIG.	GOOD	FINE	N-MINT
☐ 1, Jun 92, O:Black Condor	1.25	0.25	0.75	1.25
☐ 2, Jul 92	1.25	0.25	0.75	1.25
☐ 3, Aug 92	1.25	0.25	0.75	1.25
☐ 4, Sep 92	1.25	0.25	0.75	1.25
☐ 5, Oct 92	1.25	0.25	0.75	1.25
☐ 6, Nov 92	1.25	0.25	0.75	1.25
☐ 7, Dec 92	1.25	0.25	0.75	1.25
☐ 8, Jan 93	1.25	0.25	0.75	1.25
☐ 9, Feb 93	1.25	0.25	0.75	1.25
☐ 10, Mar 93, The Ray	1.25	0.25	0.75	1.25
☐ 11, Apr 93	1.25	0.25	0.75	1.25
☐ 12, May 93, Batman	1.25	0.25	0.75	1.25

BLACK CROSS SPECIAL
DARK HORSE

	ORIG.	GOOD	FINE	N-MINT
☐ 1, Jan 88, b&w	2.95	0.59	1.77	2.95
☐ 1, second printing	2.95	0.59	1.77	2.95

BLACK DIAMOND
AC

	ORIG.	GOOD	FINE	N-MINT
☐ 1, May 83		0.40	1.20	2.00
☐ 2, Jul 83		0.40	1.20	2.00
☐ 3, Dec 83		0.40	1.20	2.00
☐ 4, Feb 84		0.40	1.20	2.00
☐ 5, May 84		0.40	1.20	2.00

BLACK DRAGON
EPIC

	ORIG.	GOOD	FINE	N-MINT
☐ 1		0.60	1.80	3.00
☐ 2		0.40	1.20	2.00
☐ 3		0.40	1.20	2.00
☐ 4		0.40	1.20	2.00
☐ 5		0.40	1.20	2.00
☐ 6		0.40	1.20	2.00

BLACK FLAG
IMAGE

	ORIG.	GOOD	FINE	N-MINT
☐ 1, Jun 94, b&w	1.95	0.39	1.17	1.95

MAXIMUM PRESS

	ORIG.	GOOD	FINE	N-MINT
☐ 0, Jul 95	2.50	0.50	1.50	2.50
☐ 1, Jan 95	2.50	0.50	1.50	2.50
☐ 2, Feb 95	2.50	0.50	1.50	2.50
☐ 3, Mar 95	2.50	0.50	1.50	2.50
☐ 4, Apr 95, cover has black background	2.50	0.50	1.50	2.50
☐ 4, Apr 95, cover has white background	2.50	0.50	1.50	2.50

BLACK HOLE
KITCHEN SINK

	ORIG.	GOOD	FINE	N-MINT
☐ 2, Nov 95, b&w;cardstock cover	3.50	0.70	2.10	3.50

BLACK HOOD
ARCHIE/RED CIRCLE

	ORIG.	GOOD	FINE	N-MINT
☐ 1, Jun 83, ATh/GM	1.00	0.40	1.20	2.00
☐ 2, Aug 83, ATh/GM	1.00	0.30	0.90	1.50
☐ 3, Oct 83, ATh/GM	1.00	0.30	0.90	1.50

BLACK HOOD ANNUAL, THE
DC/IMPACT

	ORIG.	GOOD	FINE	N-MINT
☐ 1, trading card		0.50	1.50	2.50

BLACK HOOD, THE

	ORIG.	GOOD	FINE	N-MINT
☐ 1, Dec 91	1.00	0.20	0.60	1.00
☐ 2, Jan 92	1.00	0.20	0.60	1.00
☐ 3, Feb 92	1.00	0.20	0.60	1.00
☐ 4, Mar 92	1.00	0.20	0.60	1.00
☐ 5, Apr 92	1.00	0.20	0.60	1.00
☐ 6, May 92	1.00	0.20	0.60	1.00
☐ 7, Jun 92	1.25	0.25	0.75	1.25
☐ 8, Aug 92	1.25	0.25	0.75	1.25
☐ 9, Sep 92	1.25	0.25	0.75	1.25
☐ 10, Oct 92	1.25	0.25	0.75	1.25
☐ 11, Nov 92, 1:Fox	1.25	0.25	0.75	1.25
☐ 12, Dec 92, O:Black Hood	1.25	0.25	0.75	1.25

BLACK KISS
VORTEX

	ORIG.	GOOD	FINE	N-MINT
☐ 1, HC, adult, first printing	1.60	4.80	8.00
☐ 1, HC second printing	0.25	0.75	1.25
☐ 2, HC first printing	1.20	3.60	6.00
☐ 2, HC second printing	0.25	0.75	1.25
☐ 3, HC first printing	0.80	2.40	4.00
☐ 4, HC first printing	0.80	2.40	4.00
☐ 5, HC	0.25	0.75	1.25
☐ 6, HC	0.25	0.75	1.25
☐ 7, HC	0.25	0.75	1.25
☐ 8, HC	0.25	0.75	1.25
☐ 9, HC	0.25	0.75	1.25
☐ 10, HC	0.25	0.75	1.25
☐ 11, HC	0.30	0.90	1.50
☐ 12, HC	0.30	0.90	1.50

BLACK KNIGHT
MARVEL

	ORIG.	GOOD	FINE	N-MINT
☐ 1, Jun 90, O:Black Knight	1.50	0.30	0.90	1.50
☐ 2, Jul 90, Capt. Britain	1.50	0.30	0.90	1.50
☐ 3, Aug 90, Dr. Strange, 1:new Valkyrie	1.50	0.30	0.90	1.50
☐ 4, Sep 90, Dr. Strange, Valkyrie	1.50	0.30	0.90	1.50

BLACK LIGHTNING
DC

	ORIG.	GOOD	FINE	N-MINT
☐ 1, Apr 77	0.30	0.80	2.40	4.00
☐ 2, May 77	0.30	0.50	1.50	2.50
☐ 3, Jul 77	0.35	0.50	1.50	2.50
☐ 4, Sep 77	0.35	0.50	1.50	2.50
☐ 5, Nov 77	0.35	0.50	1.50	2.50
☐ 6, Jan 78	0.35	0.40	1.20	2.00
☐ 7, Mar 78	0.35	0.40	1.20	2.00
☐ 8, Apr 78	0.35	0.40	1.20	2.00
☐ 9, May 78	0.35	0.40	1.20	2.00
☐ 10, Jul 78	0.35	0.40	1.20	2.00
☐ 11, Sep 78	0.50	0.50	1.50	2.50

BLACK LIGHTNING (1995-)

	ORIG.	GOOD	FINE	N-MINT
☐ 1, Feb 95	1.95	0.39	1.17	1.95
☐ 2, Mar 95	1.95	0.39	1.17	1.95
☐ 3, Apr 95	1.95	0.39	1.17	1.95
☐ 4, May 95	1.95	0.39	1.17	1.95
☐ 5, Jun 95	1.95	0.39	1.17	1.95
☐ 6, Jul 95	2.75	0.55	1.65	2.75
☐ 7, Aug 95, A:Gangbuster	2.25	0.45	1.35	2.25
☐ 8, Sep 95	2.25	0.45	1.35	2.25
☐ 9, Oct 95	2.25	0.45	1.35	2.25
☐ 10, Nov 95	2.25	0.45	1.35	2.25
☐ 11, Dec 95	2.25	0.45	1.35	2.25
☐ 12, Jan 96	2.25	0.45	1.35	2.25
☐ 13, Feb 96, final issue	2.25	0.45	1.35	2.25

BLACK MAGIC
ECLIPSE

	ORIG.	GOOD	FINE	N-MINT
☐ 1, Japanese, b&w		1.00	3.00	5.00
☐ 2		0.70	2.10	3.50
☐ 3		0.70	2.10	3.50
☐ 4		0.70	2.10	3.50

BLACK MIST
CALIBER

	ORIG.	GOOD	FINE	N-MINT
☐ 1, 94, b&w	2.95	0.59	1.77	2.95
☐ 2, 94, b&w	2.95	0.59	1.77	2.95
☐ 3, 94, b&w	2.95	0.59	1.77	2.95
☐ 4, 94, b&w	2.95	0.59	1.77	2.95

	ORIG.	GOOD	FINE	N-MINT

BLACK OPS
IMAGE

	ORIG.	GOOD	FINE	N-MINT
1, Jan 96	2.50	0.50	1.50	2.50
2, Feb 96	2.50	0.50	1.50	2.50
3, Mar 96	2.50	0.50	1.50	2.50
4, Apr 96	2.50	0.50	1.50	2.50

BLACK ORCHID (mini-series)
DC

	ORIG.	GOOD	FINE	N-MINT
1, Jan 89, Gaiman, McKean	2.40	7.20		12.00
1, Gaiman, McKean, platinum edition	9.00	27.00		45.00
2, Jan 89, Gaiman, McKean	1.95	2.00	6.00	10.00
3, Feb 89, Gaiman, McKean	1.95	2.00	6.00	10.00

BLACK ORCHID (ongoing)
DC/VERTIGO

	ORIG.	GOOD	FINE	N-MINT
1	1.95	0.39	1.17	1.95
2	1.95	0.39	1.17	1.95
3	1.95	0.39	1.17	1.95
4	1.95	0.39	1.17	1.95
5	1.95	0.39	1.17	1.95
6	1.95	0.39	1.17	1.95
7	1.95	0.39	1.17	1.95
8	1.95	0.39	1.17	1.95
9, May 94	1.95	0.39	1.17	1.95
10, Jun 94	1.95	0.39	1.17	1.95
11, Jul 94	1.95	0.39	1.17	1.95
12, Aug 94	1.95	0.39	1.17	1.95
13, Sep 94	1.95	0.39	1.17	1.95
15, Nov 94	1.95	0.39	1.17	1.95
16, Dec 94	1.95	0.39	1.17	1.95
17, Jan 95	1.95	0.39	1.17	1.95
18, Feb 95	1.95	0.39	1.17	1.95
19, Mar 95	1.95	0.39	1.17	1.95
20, Apr 95	1.95	0.39	1.17	1.95
21, May 95	1.95	0.39	1.17	1.95

BLACK ORCHID ANNUAL (ongoing)

	ORIG.	GOOD	FINE	N-MINT
1, Children's Crusade	3.95	0.79	2.37	3.95

BLACK PANTHER (1976-1978)
MARVEL

	ORIG.	GOOD	FINE	N-MINT
1, Jan 77	0.30	2.40	7.20	12.00
2, Mar 77	0.30	1.20	3.60	6.00
3, May 77	0.30	0.80	2.40	4.00
4, Jul 77	0.30	0.80	2.40	4.00
5, Sep 77	0.30	0.80	2.40	4.00
6, Nov 77	0.35	0.80	2.40	4.00
7, Jan 78	0.35	0.80	2.40	4.00
8, Mar 78	0.35	0.80	2.40	4.00
9, May 78	0.35	0.80	2.40	4.00
10, Jul 78	0.35	0.80	2.40	4.00
11, Sep 78	0.35	0.60	1.80	3.00
12, Nov 78	0.35	0.60	1.80	3.00
13, Jan 79	0.35	0.60	1.80	3.00
14, Mar 79	0.35	0.60	1.80	3.00
15, May 79	0.35	0.60	1.80	3.00

BLACK PANTHER (mini-series)

	ORIG.	GOOD	FINE	N-MINT
1, Jul 88	1.25	0.25	0.75	1.25
2, Aug 88	1.25	0.25	0.75	1.25
3, Sep 88	1.25	0.25	0.75	1.25
4, Oct 88	1.25	0.25	0.75	1.25

BLACK PANTHER: PANTHER'S PREY (mini-series)

	ORIG.	GOOD	FINE	N-MINT
1, May 91	4.95	0.99	2.97	4.95
2, Jun 91	4.95	0.99	2.97	4.95
3, Aug 91	4.95	0.99	2.97	4.95
4, Oct 91	4.95	0.99	2.97	4.95

BLACK PHANTOM
AC

	ORIG.	GOOD	FINE	N-MINT
1, b&w		0.50	1.50	2.50
2		0.50	1.50	2.50
3, b&w		0.55	1.65	2.75

BLACK SABBATH
ROCK-IT/MALIBU

	ORIG.	GOOD	FINE	N-MINT
1, Feb 94	3.95	0.79	2.37	3.95

BLACK SCORPION
SPECIAL STUDIO

	ORIG.	GOOD	FINE	N-MINT
1, b&w		0.55	1.65	2.75
2, b&w		0.55	1.65	2.75
3, b&w		0.55	1.65	2.75

BLACK SEPTEMBER
MALIBU/ULTRAVERSE

	ORIG.	GOOD	FINE	N-MINT
0, Sep 95, Infinity;events affect the Infinity issues of the other Ultraverse titles	1.50	0.30	0.90	1.50

BLACK TERROR, THE
ECLIPSE

	ORIG.	GOOD	FINE	N-MINT
1, Oct 89		0.99	2.97	4.95
2, Mar 90		0.99	2.97	4.95
3, Jun 90		0.99	2.97	4.95

BLACK ZEPPELIN
RENEGADE

	ORIG.	GOOD	FINE	N-MINT
1, b&w		0.34	1.02	1.70
2, b&w		0.34	1.02	1.70
3, b&w		0.34	1.02	1.70
4, b&w		0.34	1.02	1.70
5		0.40	1.20	2.00

BLACKBALL COMICS
BLACKBALL

	ORIG.	GOOD	FINE	N-MINT
1, Mar 94	3.00	0.60	1.80	3.00

BLACKHAWK
DC

	ORIG.	GOOD	FINE	N-MINT
164, Sep 61, O:retold		10.00	30.00	50.00
165, Oct 61		6.40	19.20	32.00
166, Nov 61	0.10	6.40	19.20	32.00
167, Dec 61	0.12	6.40	19.20	32.00
168, Jan 62	0.12	6.40	19.20	32.00
169, Feb 62		6.40	19.20	32.00
170, Mar 62	0.12	6.40	19.20	32.00
171, Apr 62	0.12	6.40	19.20	32.00
172, May 62		6.40	19.20	32.00
173, Jun 62		6.40	19.20	32.00
174, Jul 62	0.12	6.40	19.20	32.00
175, Aug 62	0.12	6.40	19.20	32.00
176, Sep 62	0.12	6.40	19.20	32.00
177, Oct 62	0.12	6.40	19.20	32.00
178, Nov 62		6.40	19.20	32.00
179, Dec 62	0.12	6.40	19.20	32.00
180, Jan 63		6.40	19.20	32.00
181, Feb 63		4.80	14.40	24.00
182, Mar 63	0.12	4.80	14.40	24.00
183, Apr 63		4.80	14.40	24.00
184, May 63	0.12	4.80	14.40	24.00
185, Jun 63	0.12	4.80	14.40	24.00
186, Jul 63		4.80	14.40	24.00
187, Aug 63	0.12	4.80	14.40	24.00
188, Sep 63	0.12	4.80	14.40	24.00
189, Oct 63, O:retold		4.80	14.40	24.00
190, Nov 63	0.12	4.80	14.40	24.00
191, Dec 63	0.12	4.00	12.00	20.00
192, Jan 64		4.00	12.00	20.00
193, Feb 64	0.12	4.00	12.00	20.00
194, Mar 64		4.00	12.00	20.00
195, Apr 64	0.12	4.00	12.00	20.00
196, May 64	0.12	4.00	12.00	20.00
197, Jun 64, new look	0.12	4.00	12.00	20.00
198, O:retold		4.00	12.00	20.00
199, Aug 64	0.12	4.00	12.00	20.00
200, Sep 64	0.12	4.00	12.00	20.00
201, Oct 64	0.12	3.00	9.00	15.00
202, Nov 64	0.12	3.00	9.00	15.00
203, Dec 64, O:Chop-Chop	0.12	3.00	9.00	15.00

	ORIG.	GOOD	FINE	N-MINT
204, Jan 65	0.12	3.00	9.00	15.00
205, Feb 65	0.12	3.00	9.00	15.00
206, Mar 65	0.12	3.00	9.00	15.00
207, Apr 65	0.12	3.00	9.00	15.00
208, May 65	0.12	3.00	9.00	15.00
209, Jun 65	0.12	3.00	9.00	15.00
210, Jul 65	0.12	3.00	9.00	15.00
211, Aug 65	0.12	2.00	6.00	10.00
212, Sep 65	0.12	1.20	3.60	10.00
213, Oct 65	0.12	1.20	3.60	10.00
214, Nov 65	0.12	1.20	3.60	10.00
215, Dec 65	0.12	1.20	3.60	10.00
216, Jan 66	0.12	1.20	3.60	10.00
217, Feb 66	0.12	1.20	3.60	10.00
218, Mar 66	0.12	1.20	3.60	10.00
219, Apr 66	0.12	1.20	3.60	10.00
220, May 66	0.12	1.20	3.60	10.00
221, Jun 66	0.12	1.20	3.60	10.00
222, Jul 66	0.12	1.20	3.60	10.00
223, Aug 66	0.12	1.20	3.60	10.00
224, Sep 66	0.12	1.20	3.60	10.00
225, Oct 66	0.12	1.20	3.60	10.00
226, Nov 66	0.12	1.20	3.60	10.00
227, Dec 66	0.12	1.20	3.60	10.00
228, Jan 67	0.12	1.20	3.60	10.00
229, Feb 67	0.12	1.20	3.60	10.00
230, Mar 67	0.12	1.20	3.60	10.00
231, Apr 67	0.12	1.20	3.60	10.00
232, May 67	0.12	1.20	3.60	10.00
233, Jun 67	0.12	1.20	3.60	10.00
234, Jul 67	0.12	1.20	3.60	10.00
235, Aug 67	0.12	1.20	3.60	10.00
236, Sep 67	0.12	1.20	3.60	10.00
237, Nov 67	0.12	1.20	3.60	10.00
238, Jan 68	0.12	1.20	3.60	10.00
239, Mar 68	0.12	1.20	3.60	10.00
240, May 68	0.12	1.20	3.60	10.00
241, Jul 68	0.12	1.20	3.60	10.00
242, Sep 68	0.12	1.20	3.60	10.00
243, Nov 68	0.12	1.20	3.60	10.00
244, Feb 76	0.25	0.40	1.20	2.00
245, Apr 76	0.30	0.40	1.20	2.00
246, Jun 76	0.30	0.40	1.20	2.00
247, Aug 76	0.30	0.40	1.20	2.00
248, Sep 76	0.30	0.40	1.20	2.00
249, Nov 76	0.30	0.40	1.20	2.00
250, Jan 77	0.30	0.40	1.20	2.00
251, Oct 82	0.60	0.20	0.60	1.00
252, Nov 82	0.60	0.20	0.60	1.00
253, Dec 82	0.60	0.20	0.60	1.00
254, Jan 83	0.60	0.20	0.60	1.00
255, Feb 83	0.60	0.20	0.60	1.00
256, Mar 83	0.60	0.20	0.60	1.00
257, Apr 83	0.60	0.20	0.60	1.00
258, May 83	0.60	0.20	0.60	1.00
259, Jun 83	0.60	0.20	0.60	1.00
260, Jul 83	0.60	0.20	0.60	1.00
261, Aug 83	0.60	0.20	0.60	1.00
262, Sep 93	0.60	0.20	0.60	1.00
263, Oct 83	0.60	0.20	0.60	1.00
264, Nov 83	0.60	0.20	0.60	1.00
265, Dec 83	0.75	0.20	0.60	1.00
266, Jan 84	0.75	0.20	0.60	1.00
267, Feb 84	0.75	0.20	0.60	1.00
268, Mar 84	0.75	0.20	0.60	1.00
269, Apr 84	0.75	0.20	0.60	1.00
270, May 84	0.75	0.20	0.60	1.00
271, Jul 84	0.75	0.20	0.60	1.00
272, Sep 84	0.75	0.20	0.60	1.00
273, Nov 84	0.75	0.20	0.60	1.00

	ORIG.	GOOD	FINE	N-MINT
BLACKHAWK (2nd series)				
1		0.30	0.90	1.50
2		0.30	0.90	1.50
3		0.30	0.90	1.50
4		0.30	0.90	1.50
5		0.30	0.90	1.50
6		0.30	0.90	1.50
7, WE rep.		0.50	1.50	2.50
8		0.30	0.90	1.50
9		0.30	0.90	1.50
10		0.30	0.90	1.50
11		0.30	0.90	1.50
12		0.35	1.05	1.75
13		0.35	1.05	1.75
14		0.35	1.05	1.75
15		0.35	1.05	1.75
16		0.35	1.05	1.75
BLACKHAWK (mini-series)				
1, Mar 88, HC;prestige format;no mature readers advisory	2.95	0.59	1.77	2.95
2, Apr 88, HC;prestige format	2.95	0.59	1.77	2.95
3, May 88, HC;prestige format	2.95	0.59	1.77	2.95
BLACKHAWK ANNUAL				
1, May 89		0.59	1.77	2.95
BLACKHAWK SPECIAL				
1		0.70	2.10	3.50
BLACKMASK				
1	4.95	0.99	2.97	4.95
2	4.95	0.99	2.97	4.95
3	4.95	0.99	2.97	4.95
BLACKMOON				
U.S.COMICS				
1		0.30	0.90	1.50
2		0.30	0.90	1.50
3		0.35	1.05	1.75
BLACKSTAR				
IMPERIAL				
1		0.36	1.08	1.80
2		0.36	1.08	1.80
BLACKTHORNE'S 3 IN 1				
BLACKTHORNE				
1		0.35	1.05	1.75
2		0.35	1.05	1.75
BLACKTHORNE'S HARVEY FLIP BOOK				
1, Sad Sack, Stumbo, b&w		0.40	1.20	2.00
BLACKWULF				
MARVEL				
1, Jun 94, embossed	2.50	0.50	1.50	2.50
2, Jul 94	1.50	0.30	0.90	1.50
3, Aug 94	1.50	0.30	0.90	1.50
4, Sep 94	1.50	0.30	0.90	1.50
5, Oct 94	1.50	0.30	0.90	1.50
6, Nov 94	1.50	0.30	0.90	1.50
7, Dec 94	1.50	0.30	0.90	1.50
8, Jan 95	1.50	0.30	0.90	1.50
9, Feb 95	1.50	0.30	0.90	1.50
10, Mar 95	1.50	0.30	0.90	1.50
BLADE OF SHURIKEN				
ETERNITY				
1		0.39	1.17	1.95
2		0.39	1.17	1.95
3		0.39	1.17	1.95
4		0.39	1.17	1.95
5		0.39	1.17	1.95
BLADE RUNNER				
MARVEL				
1, AW movie	0.60	0.20	0.60	1.00
2, AW movie	0.60	0.20	0.60	1.00

	ORIG.	GOOD	FINE	N-MINT

BLADE: THE VAMPIRE-HUNTER

	ORIG.	GOOD	FINE	N-MINT
☐ 1, Jul 94	2.95	0.59	1.77	2.95
☐ 2, Aug 94	1.95	0.39	1.17	1.95
☐ 3, Sep 94	1.95	0.39	1.17	1.95
☐ 4, Oct 94	1.95	0.39	1.17	1.95
☐ 5, Nov 94	1.95	0.39	1.17	1.95
☐ 6, Dec 94	1.95	0.39	1.17	1.95
☐ 7, Jan 95	1.95	0.39	1.17	1.95
☐ 8, Feb 95	1.95	0.39	1.17	1.95
☐ 9, Mar 95	1.95	0.39	1.17	1.95
☐ 10, Apr 95, final issue	1.95	0.39	1.17	1.95

BLADESMEN, THE
BLUE COMET

	ORIG.	GOOD	FINE	N-MINT
☐ 1, b&w		0.40	1.20	2.00
☐ 2		0.45	1.35	2.25

BLANCHE GOES TO HOLLYWOOD
DARK HORSE

	ORIG.	GOOD	FINE	N-MINT
☐ 0, 93, nn;b&w	2.95	0.59	1.77	2.95

BLANCHE GOES TO NEW YORK

	ORIG.	GOOD	FINE	N-MINT
☐ 0, 92, nn;b&w	2.95	0.59	1.77	2.95

BLARNEY
DISCOVERY

	ORIG.	GOOD	FINE	N-MINT
☐ 1, 95, b&w;cardstock cover	2.95	0.59	1.77	2.95

BLASTERS SPECIAL
DC

	ORIG.	GOOD	FINE	N-MINT
☐ 1, May 89	2.00	0.40	1.20	2.00

BLAZE
MARVEL

	ORIG.	GOOD	FINE	N-MINT
☐ 1, Aug 94, silver enhanced cover	2.95	0.59	1.77	2.95
☐ 2, Sep 94	1.95	0.39	1.17	1.95
☐ 3, Oct 94	1.95	0.39	1.17	1.95
☐ 4, Nov 94	1.95	0.39	1.17	1.95
☐ 5, Dec 94	1.95	0.39	1.17	1.95
☐ 6, Jan 95	1.95	0.39	1.17	1.95
☐ 7, Feb 95	1.95	0.39	1.17	1.95
☐ 8, Mar 95	1.95	0.39	1.17	1.95
☐ 9, Apr 95	1.95	0.39	1.17	1.95
☐ 10, May 95	1.95	0.39	1.17	1.95
☐ 11, Jun 95	1.95	0.39	1.17	1.95
☐ 12, Jul 95, final issue	1.95	0.39	1.17	1.95

BLAZE: LEGACY OF BLOOD

	ORIG.	GOOD	FINE	N-MINT
☐ 1	1.75	0.35	1.05	1.75
☐ 2	1.75	0.35	1.05	1.75
☐ 3	1.75	0.35	1.05	1.75
☐ 4	1.75	0.35	1.05	1.75

BLAZING COMBAT
APPLE

	ORIG.	GOOD	FINE	N-MINT
☐ 1	4.50	0.90	2.70	4.50
☐ 2, b&w reprints	4.50	0.90	2.70	4.50

BLAZING COMBAT: WORLD WAR I AND WORLD WAR II

	ORIG.	GOOD	FINE	N-MINT
☐ 1, reprints	3.75	0.75	2.25	3.75
☐ 2, Jun 94, reprints	3.75	0.75	2.25	3.75

BLAZING WESTERN
AC

	ORIG.	GOOD	FINE	N-MINT
☐ 1, b&w		0.50	1.50	2.50

BLEEDING HEART
FANTAGRAPHICS

	ORIG.	GOOD	FINE	N-MINT
☐ 1, b&w	2.50	0.50	1.50	2.50
☐ 2, b&w	2.50	0.50	1.50	2.50
☐ 3, b&w	2.50	0.50	1.50	2.50
☐ 4, b&w	2.50	0.50	1.50	2.50
☐ 5, b&w	2.50	0.50	1.50	2.50

BLIP
MARVEL

	ORIG.	GOOD	FINE	N-MINT
☐ 1, video game mag. in comic-book format/size	1.00	0.20	0.60	1.00
☐ 2	1.00	0.20	0.60	1.00
☐ 3	1.00	0.20	0.60	1.00
☐ 4	1.00	0.20	0.60	1.00
☐ 5	1.00	0.20	0.60	1.00
☐ 6	1.00	0.20	0.60	1.00

BLIP AND THE C.C.A.D.S.
AMAZING

	ORIG.	GOOD	FINE	N-MINT
☐ 1		0.39	1.17	1.95
☐ 2		0.39	1.17	1.95

BLITE
FANTAGRAPHICS

	ORIG.	GOOD	FINE	N-MINT
☐ 1, b&w		0.45	1.35	2.25

BLITZ
NIGHTWYND

	ORIG.	GOOD	FINE	N-MINT
☐ 1, b&w		0.50	1.50	2.50
☐ 2, b&w		0.50	1.50	2.50

BLONDE, THE
EROS COMIX

	ORIG.	GOOD	FINE	N-MINT
☐ 1, adult, b&w		0.50	1.50	2.50
☐ 2, adult, b&w		0.50	1.50	2.50
☐ 3, adult, b&w		0.50	1.50	2.50

BLONDE: BONDAGE PALACE

	ORIG.	GOOD	FINE	N-MINT
☐ 1, adult, b&w	2.95	0.59	1.77	2.95
☐ 2, adult, b&w	2.95	0.59	1.77	2.95
☐ 3, adult, b&w	2.95	0.59	1.77	2.95
☐ 5, May 94, adult, b&w	2.95	0.59	1.77	2.95

BLOOD
FANTACO

	ORIG.	GOOD	FINE	N-MINT
☐ 1, b&w	3.95	0.79	2.37	3.95

BLOOD & KISSES

	ORIG.	GOOD	FINE	N-MINT
☐ 1, 93, b&w	3.95	0.79	2.37	3.95
☐ 2, 94, b&w	3.95	0.79	2.37	3.95

BLOOD & ROSES
SKY

	ORIG.	GOOD	FINE	N-MINT
☐ 1	2.25	0.45	1.35	2.25

BLOOD & ROSES ADVENTURES
KNIGHT PRESS

	ORIG.	GOOD	FINE	N-MINT
☐ 1, May 95, b&w	2.95	0.59	1.77	2.95

BLOOD AND SHADOWS (mini-series)
DC/VERTIGO

	ORIG.	GOOD	FINE	N-MINT
☐ 1, 96, prestige format	5.95	1.19	3.57	5.95
☐ 2, 96, prestige format	5.95	1.19	3.57	5.95
☐ 3, 96, prestige format	5.95	1.19	3.57	5.95

BLOOD AND THUNDER
CONQUEST

	ORIG.	GOOD	FINE	N-MINT
☐ 1, b&w		0.59	1.77	2.95

BLOOD AND WATER
SLAVE LABOR

	ORIG.	GOOD	FINE	N-MINT
☐ 1, b&w		0.79	2.37	3.95

BLOOD CLUB
KITCHEN SINK

	ORIG.	GOOD	FINE	N-MINT
☐ 0, nn, color		1.19	3.57	5.95

BLOOD FEAST
ETERNITY

	ORIG.	GOOD	FINE	N-MINT
☐ 1, graphic cover, b&w		0.50	1.50	2.50
☐ 1, tame cover		0.50	1.50	2.50
☐ 2		0.50	1.50	2.50

BLOOD GOTHIC
FANTACO

	ORIG.	GOOD	FINE	N-MINT
☐ 1	4.95	0.99	2.97	4.95
☐ 2	4.95	0.99	2.97	4.95

BLOOD IS THE HARVEST
ECLIPSE

	ORIG.	GOOD	FINE	N-MINT
☐ 1, b&w		0.50	1.50	2.50
☐ 2, b&w		0.50	1.50	2.50
☐ 3, b&w		0.50	1.50	2.50
☐ 4, b&w		0.50	1.50	2.50

	ORIG.	GOOD	FINE	N-MINT

BLOOD JUNKIES
ETERNITY

	ORIG.	GOOD	FINE	N-MINT
1, b&w		0.50	1.50	2.50
2, b&w		0.50	1.50	2.50

BLOOD N' GUTS
AIRCEL

	ORIG.	GOOD	FINE	N-MINT
1, b&w		0.50	1.50	2.50
2, b&w		0.50	1.50	2.50
3, b&w		0.50	1.50	2.50

BLOOD OF DRACULA
APPLE

	ORIG.	GOOD	FINE	N-MINT
1, b&w		0.35	1.05	1.75
2, b&w		0.35	1.05	1.75
3, b&w		0.35	1.05	1.75
4, b&w		0.35	1.05	1.75
5, b&w		0.35	1.05	1.75
6		0.39	1.17	1.95
7		0.39	1.17	1.95
8		0.39	1.17	1.95
9		0.39	1.17	1.95
10		0.39	1.17	1.95
11		0.39	1.17	1.95
12		0.39	1.17	1.95
13		0.39	1.17	1.95
13, BW		0.45	1.35	2.25
14, BW		0.45	1.35	2.25
15, flexidisc		0.75	2.25	3.75
16, BW		0.45	1.35	2.25
17, BW		0.45	1.35	2.25
18, BW		0.45	1.35	2.25
19, BW		0.45	1.35	2.25

BLOOD OF THE INNOCENT
WARP

	ORIG.	GOOD	FINE	N-MINT
1		0.40	1.20	2.00
2		0.40	1.20	2.00
3		0.40	1.20	2.00
4		0.40	1.20	2.00

BLOOD PACK (mini-series)
DC

	ORIG.	GOOD	FINE	N-MINT
1, Mar 95	1.50	0.30	0.90	1.50
2, Apr 95	1.50	0.30	0.90	1.50
3, May 95	1.50	0.30	0.90	1.50
4, Jun 95	1.50	0.30	0.90	1.50

BLOOD SWORD DYNASTY
JADEMAN

	ORIG.	GOOD	FINE	N-MINT
1	1.25	0.25	0.75	1.25
2	1.25	0.25	0.75	1.25
3	1.25	0.25	0.75	1.25
4	1.25	0.25	0.75	1.25
5	1.25	0.25	0.75	1.25
6	1.25	0.25	0.75	1.25
7	1.25	0.25	0.75	1.25
8	1.25	0.25	0.75	1.25
9	1.25	0.25	0.75	1.25
10	1.25	0.25	0.75	1.25
11	1.25	0.25	0.75	1.25
12	1.25	0.25	0.75	1.25
13	1.25	0.25	0.75	1.25
14	1.25	0.25	0.75	1.25
15	1.25	0.25	0.75	1.25
16	1.25	0.25	0.75	1.25
17	1.25	0.25	0.75	1.25
18	1.25	0.25	0.75	1.25
19	1.25	0.25	0.75	1.25
20	1.25	0.25	0.75	1.25
21	1.25	0.25	0.75	1.25
22	1.25	0.25	0.75	1.25
23	1.25	0.25	0.75	1.25
24	1.25	0.25	0.75	1.25
25	1.25	0.25	0.75	1.25
26	1.25	0.25	0.75	1.25
27	1.25	0.25	0.75	1.25
28	1.25	0.25	0.75	1.25
29	1.25	0.25	0.75	1.25

BLOOD SWORD, THE

	ORIG.	GOOD	FINE	N-MINT
1	1.95	0.39	1.17	1.95
2	1.95	0.39	1.17	1.95
3	1.95	0.39	1.17	1.95
4	1.95	0.39	1.17	1.95
5	1.95	0.39	1.17	1.95
6	1.95	0.39	1.17	1.95
7	1.95	0.39	1.17	1.95
8	1.95	0.39	1.17	1.95
9	1.95	0.39	1.17	1.95
10	1.95	0.39	1.17	1.95
11	1.95	0.39	1.17	1.95
12	1.95	0.39	1.17	1.95
13	1.95	0.39	1.17	1.95
14	1.95	0.39	1.17	1.95
15	1.95	0.39	1.17	1.95
16	1.95	0.39	1.17	1.95
17	1.95	0.39	1.17	1.95
18	1.95	0.39	1.17	1.95
19	1.95	0.39	1.17	1.95
20	1.95	0.39	1.17	1.95
21	1.95	0.39	1.17	1.95
22	1.95	0.39	1.17	1.95
23	1.95	0.39	1.17	1.95
24	1.95	0.39	1.17	1.95
25	1.95	0.39	1.17	1.95
26	1.95	0.39	1.17	1.95
27	1.95	0.39	1.17	1.95
28	1.95	0.39	1.17	1.95
29	1.95	0.39	1.17	1.95
30	1.95	0.39	1.17	1.95
31	1.95	0.39	1.17	1.95
32	1.95	0.39	1.17	1.95
33	1.95	0.39	1.17	1.95
34	1.95	0.39	1.17	1.95
35	1.95	0.39	1.17	1.95
36	1.95	0.39	1.17	1.95
37	1.95	0.39	1.17	1.95
38	1.95	0.39	1.17	1.95
39	1.95	0.39	1.17	1.95
40	1.95	0.39	1.17	1.95
41	1.95	0.39	1.17	1.95
42	1.95	0.39	1.17	1.95

BLOOD SYNDICATE
DC/MILESTONE

	ORIG.	GOOD	FINE	N-MINT
1, Apr 93	1.50	0.70	2.10	3.50
1, Apr 93, poster, trading card	2.95	0.59	1.77	2.95
2, May 93	1.50	0.40	1.20	2.00
3, Jun 93	1.50	0.30	0.90	1.50
4, Jul 93	1.50	0.30	0.90	1.50
5, Aug 93	1.50	0.30	0.90	1.50
6, Sep 93	1.50	0.30	0.90	1.50
7, Oct 93	1.50	0.30	0.90	1.50
8, Nov 93	1.50	0.30	0.90	1.50
9, Dec 93	1.50	0.30	0.90	1.50
10, Jan 94, Shadow War	2.50	0.50	1.50	2.50
11, Feb 94	1.50	0.30	0.90	1.50
12, Mar 94	1.50	0.30	0.90	1.50
13, Apr 94	1.50	0.30	0.90	1.50
14, May 94	1.50	0.30	0.90	1.50
15, Jun 94	1.50	0.30	0.90	1.50
16, Jul 94	1.50	0.45	1.35	2.25
17, Aug 94	1.75	0.40	1.20	2.00
18, Sep 94	1.75	0.35	1.05	1.75
19, Oct 94	1.75	0.35	1.05	1.75
20, Nov 94	1.75	0.35	1.05	1.75

	ORIG.	GOOD	FINE	N-MINT
☐ 21, Dec 94	1.75	0.35	1.05	1.75
☐ 22, Jan 95	1.75	0.35	1.05	1.75
☐ 23, Feb 95	1.75	0.35	1.05	1.75
☐ 24, Mar 95	1.75	0.35	1.05	1.75
☐ 25, Apr 95, extra-sized	2.95	0.59	1.77	2.95
☐ 26, May 95	1.75	0.35	1.05	1.75
☐ 27, Jun 95	1.75	0.35	1.05	1.75
☐ 28, Jul 95	2.50	0.50	1.50	2.50
☐ 29, Aug 95	0.99	0.20	0.59	0.99
☐ 30, Sep 95	2.50	0.50	1.50	2.50
☐ 31, Oct 95	2.50	0.50	1.50	2.50
☐ 32, Nov 95	2.50	0.50	1.50	2.50
☐ 33, Dec 95	0.99	0.20	0.59	0.99
☐ 34, Jan 96	2.50	0.50	1.50	2.50
☐ 35, Feb 96, final issue	3.50	0.70	2.10	3.50

BLOOD WULF (mini-series)
IMAGE

	ORIG.	GOOD	FINE	N-MINT
☐ 1, Feb 95	2.50	0.50	1.50	2.50
☐ 1, Feb 95, alternate cover	2.50	0.50	1.50	2.50
☐ 2, Mar 95	2.50	0.50	1.50	2.50
☐ 3, Apr 95	2.50	0.50	1.50	2.50
☐ 4, May 95	2.50	0.50	1.50	2.50

BLOOD: A TALE
EPIC

	ORIG.	GOOD	FINE	N-MINT
☐ 1	3.25	1.00	3.00	5.00
☐ 2	3.25	0.80	2.40	4.00
☐ 3	3.25	0.80	2.40	4.00
☐ 4	3.25	0.80	2.40	4.00

BLOODBATH
DC

	ORIG.	GOOD	FINE	N-MINT
☐ 1	3.50	0.70	2.10	3.50
☐ 2, Dec 93	3.50	0.70	2.10	3.50

BLOODBROTHERS
ETERNITY

	ORIG.	GOOD	FINE	N-MINT
☐ 1, b&w		0.39	1.17	1.95
☐ 2, b&w		0.39	1.17	1.95
☐ 3, b&w		0.39	1.17	1.95
☐ 4, b&w		0.39	1.17	1.95

BLOODFIRE
LIGHTNING

	ORIG.	GOOD	FINE	N-MINT
☐ 1, Mar 93, promotional copy, b&w	3.50	2.00	6.00	10.00
☐ 1, Jun 93, red foil	3.50	0.70	2.10	3.50
☐ 1, Jun 93, platinum	3.50	0.70	2.10	3.50
☐ 2, Jul 93	2.95	1.60	4.80	8.00
☐ 3, Aug 93	2.95	1.00	3.00	5.00
☐ 4, Sep 93	2.95	1.00	3.00	5.00
☐ 5, Oct 93, trading card	2.95	0.59	1.77	2.95
☐ 6, Nov 93	2.95	0.59	1.77	2.95
☐ 7, Dec 93	2.95	0.59	1.77	2.95
☐ 8, Jan 94, O:Prodigal	2.95	0.59	1.77	2.95
☐ 9, Feb 94	2.95	0.59	1.77	2.95
☐ 10, Mar 94	2.95	0.59	1.77	2.95

BLOODFIRE/HELLINA

	ORIG.	GOOD	FINE	N-MINT
☐ 1, Aug 95	3.00	0.60	1.80	3.00
☐ 1, Aug 95, nude edition	9.95	1.99	5.97	9.95

BLOODLETTING
FANTACO

	ORIG.	GOOD	FINE	N-MINT
☐ 1	2.95	0.59	1.77	2.95

BLOODLETTING (mini-series)

	ORIG.	GOOD	FINE	N-MINT
☐ 1	3.95	0.79	2.37	3.95
☐ 2	3.95	0.79	2.37	3.95

BLOODLINES
AIRCEL

	ORIG.	GOOD	FINE	N-MINT
☐ 1, 87	1.70			

VORTEX

	ORIG.	GOOD	FINE	N-MINT
☐ 5		0.35	1.05	1.75
☐ 6		0.35	1.05	1.75

BLOODLINES (was Aircel title)
BLACKBURN

	ORIG.	GOOD	FINE	N-MINT
☐ 2		0.34	1.02	1.70

BLOODPOOL
IMAGE

	ORIG.	GOOD	FINE	N-MINT
☐ 1, Aug 95	2.50	0.50	1.50	2.50
☐ 1, Aug 95, alternate cover	2.50	0.50	1.50	2.50
☐ 2, Sep 95	2.50	0.50	1.50	2.50
☐ 3, Oct 95	2.50	0.50	1.50	2.50

BLOODPOOL SPECIAL

	ORIG.	GOOD	FINE	N-MINT
☐ 1, Mar 96	2.50	0.50	1.50	2.50

BLOODSCENT
COMICO

	ORIG.	GOOD	FINE	N-MINT
☐ 1, GC		0.40	1.20	2.00

BLOODSEED
MARVEL

	ORIG.	GOOD	FINE	N-MINT
☐ 1	1.95	0.39	1.17	1.95
☐ 2, nudity	1.95	0.39	1.17	1.95

BLOODSHED LIMITED EDITION
DAMAGE!

	ORIG.	GOOD	FINE	N-MINT
☐ 1, 94, b&w;no cover price				

BLOODSHOT
ACCLAIM/VALIANT

	ORIG.	GOOD	FINE	N-MINT
☐ 29, Jun 95	2.25	0.45	1.35	2.25
☐ 30, Jul 95, NB	2.25	0.45	1.35	2.25
☐ 31, Jul 95, NB	2.25	0.45	1.35	2.25
☐ 32, Aug 95	2.25	0.45	1.35	2.25
☐ 33, Aug 95	2.25	0.45	1.35	2.25
☐ 34, Sep 95, NB	2.50	0.50	1.50	2.50
☐ 35, Sep 95, NB	2.50	0.50	1.50	2.50
☐ 36, Oct 95, MGr	2.50	0.50	1.50	2.50
☐ 37, Oct 95	2.50	0.50	1.50	2.50
☐ 38, Nov 95	2.50	0.50	1.50	2.50
☐ 39, Nov 95	2.50	0.50	1.50	2.50
☐ 40, Dec 95	2.50	0.50	1.50	2.50
☐ 41, Dec 95	2.50	0.50	1.50	2.50
☐ 42, Jan 96	2.50	0.50	1.50	2.50
☐ 43, Jan 96	2.50	0.50	1.50	2.50
☐ 45, Mar 96	2.50	0.50	1.50	2.50
☐ 46, Apr 96	2.50	0.50	1.50	2.50
☐ 48, May 96	2.50	0.50	1.50	2.50
☐ 49, Jun 96	2.50	0.50	1.50	2.50

VALIANT

	ORIG.	GOOD	FINE	N-MINT
☐ 0, chromium cover	3.50	0.70	2.10	3.50
☐ 0, gold		3.60	10.80	18.00
☐ 1, Feb 93, chromium cover	3.50	1.60	4.80	8.00
☐ 2, Mar 93	2.50	0.80	2.40	4.00
☐ 3, Apr 93	2.25	0.60	1.80	3.00
☐ 4, May 93	2.25	0.60	1.80	3.00
☐ 5, Jun 93	2.25	0.60	1.80	3.00
☐ 6, Jul 93	2.25	1.60	4.80	8.00
☐ 7, Aug 93	2.25	1.20	3.60	6.00
☐ 8	2.25	0.45	1.35	2.25
☐ 9	2.25	0.45	1.35	2.25
☐ 10	2.25	0.45	1.35	2.25
☐ 11	2.25	0.45	1.35	2.25
☐ 12	2.25	0.45	1.35	2.25
☐ 13, Feb 94	2.25	0.45	1.35	2.25
☐ 14, Mar 94	2.25	0.45	1.35	2.25
☐ 15, Apr 94	2.25	0.45	1.35	2.25
☐ 16, May 94, trading card	2.25	0.45	1.35	2.25
☐ 17, Jun 94, A: H.A.R.D. Corps	2.25	0.45	1.35	2.25
☐ 18, Aug 94	2.25	0.45	1.35	2.25
☐ 19, Sep 94	2.25	0.45	1.35	2.25
☐ 20, Oct 94, Chaos Effect	2.25	0.45	1.35	2.25
☐ 21, Nov 94	2.25	0.50	1.50	2.50
☐ 22		0.50	1.50	2.50

	ORIG.	GOOD	FINE	N-MINT
23		0.50	1.50	2.50
24		0.50	1.50	2.50
25		0.50	1.50	2.50
26, Apr 95	2.25	0.45	1.35	2.25
27, May 95	2.25	0.45	1.35	2.25
28, May 95	2.25	0.45	1.35	2.25

BLOODSHOT LAST STAND
ACCLAIM/VALIANT

	ORIG.	GOOD	FINE	N-MINT
0, Mar 96, one-shot;cardstock cover	5.95	1.19	3.57	5.95

BLOODSHOT YEARBOOK
VALIANT

	ORIG.	GOOD	FINE	N-MINT
1, 94	3.95	0.79	2.37	3.95

BLOODSTRIKE
IMAGE

	ORIG.	GOOD	FINE	N-MINT
1, Apr 93, RL, fading blood cover	2.95	0.59	1.77	2.95
2, Jun 93	1.95	0.39	1.17	1.95
3, Jul 93	1.95	0.39	1.17	1.95
4, Oct 93	1.95	0.39	1.17	1.95
5, Nov 93	1.95	0.39	1.17	1.95
6, Dec 93	1.95	0.39	1.17	1.95
7, Jan 94	1.95	0.39	1.17	1.95
8, Feb 94	1.95	0.39	1.17	1.95
9, Mar 94, Extreme Prejudice	1.95	0.39	1.17	1.95
10, Apr 94, Extreme Prejudice	1.95	0.39	1.17	1.95
11, Jul 94	1.95	0.39	1.17	1.95
12, Aug 94	1.95	0.39	1.17	1.95
13, Aug 94	2.50	0.50	1.50	2.50
14, Sep 94	2.50	0.50	1.50	2.50
15, Oct 94	1.95	0.39	1.17	1.95
16, Nov 94	2.50	0.50	1.50	2.50
17, Dec 94	1.95	0.39	1.17	1.95
18, Jan 95, Extreme Sacrifice;polybagged w/ trading card	2.50	0.50	1.50	2.50
19, Feb 95, Extreme Sacrifice Aftermath;polybagged	2.50	0.50	1.50	2.50
20, Mar 95	2.50	0.50	1.50	2.50
21, Apr 95	2.50	0.50	1.50	2.50
22, May 95	2.50	0.50	1.50	2.50
25, May 94	1.95	0.39	1.17	1.95

BLOODSTRIKE: ASSASSIN

	ORIG.	GOOD	FINE	N-MINT
0, Oct 95	2.50	0.50	1.50	2.50
1, Jun 95	2.50	0.50	1.50	2.50
1, Jun 95, A;alternate cover	2.50	0.50	1.50	2.50
2, Jul 95	2.50	0.50	1.50	2.50
3, Aug 95	2.50	0.50	1.50	2.50

BLOODSUCKER
EROS

	ORIG.	GOOD	FINE	N-MINT
1, adult, b&w		0.50	1.50	2.50

BLOODTHIRST: THE TERMINUS OPTION
ALPHA PRODUCTIONS

	ORIG.	GOOD	FINE	N-MINT
1, b&w		0.70	2.10	3.50

BLOODWING
ETERNITY

	ORIG.	GOOD	FINE	N-MINT
1, b&w		0.39	1.17	1.95
2, b&w		0.39	1.17	1.95
3, b&w		0.39	1.17	1.95
4, b&w		0.39	1.17	1.95
5, b&w		0.39	1.17	1.95

BLOODWULF (mini-series)
IMAGE

	ORIG.	GOOD	FINE	N-MINT
1, Feb 95, DG2;five different covers	2.50	0.50	1.50	2.50
2, Mar 95	2.50	0.50	1.50	2.50
3, Apr 95	2.50	0.50	1.50	2.50
4, May 95	2.50	0.50	1.50	2.50

BLOODWULF SUMMER SPECIAL

	ORIG.	GOOD	FINE	N-MINT
1, Aug 95, A:Supreme	2.50	0.50	1.50	2.50

BLOODY BONES & BLACKEYED PEAS
GALAXY

	ORIG.	GOOD	FINE	N-MINT
1		0.20	0.60	1.00

BLOODYHOT
PARODY PRESS

	ORIG.	GOOD	FINE	N-MINT
1	2.50	0.50	1.50	2.50

BLUE BEETLE
DC

	ORIG.	GOOD	FINE	N-MINT
1, Jun 86	0.75	0.60	1.80	3.00
2, Jul 86	0.75	0.40	1.20	2.00
3, Aug 86	0.75	0.40	1.20	2.00
4, Sep 86	0.75	0.40	1.20	2.00
5, Oct 86	0.75	0.40	1.20	2.00
6, Nov 86	0.75	0.40	1.20	2.00
7, Dec 86	0.75	0.40	1.20	2.00
8, Jan 87	0.75	0.40	1.20	2.00
9, Feb 87, Legends	0.75	0.30	0.90	1.50
10, Mar 87, Legends	0.75	0.30	0.90	1.50
11, Apr 87, Teen Titans	0.75	0.30	0.90	1.50
12, May 87, Teen Titans	0.75	0.30	0.90	1.50
13, Jun 87, Teen Titans	0.75	0.30	0.90	1.50
14, Jul 87	0.75	0.20	0.60	1.00
15, Aug 87	0.75	0.20	0.60	1.00
16, Sep 87	0.75	0.20	0.60	1.00
17, Oct 87	0.75	0.20	0.60	1.00
18, Nov 87	1.00	0.20	0.60	1.00
19, Dec 87	1.00	0.20	0.60	1.00
20, Jan 88, Millennium	1.00	0.20	0.60	1.00
21, Feb 88, Millennium	1.00	0.20	0.60	1.00
22, Mar 88	1.00	0.20	0.60	1.00
23, Apr 88	1.00	0.20	0.60	1.00
24, May 88	1.00	0.20	0.60	1.00

BLUE BULLETEER
AC

	ORIG.	GOOD	FINE	N-MINT
1, 89, b&w, O:Blue Bulleteer		0.45	1.35	2.25

BLUE DEVIL
DC

	ORIG.	GOOD	FINE	N-MINT
1, Jun 84, O:Blue Devil	0.75	0.30	0.90	1.50
2, Jul 84	0.75	0.20	0.60	1.00
3, Aug 84	0.75	0.20	0.60	1.00
4, Sep 84	0.75	0.20	0.60	1.00
5, Oct 84	0.75	0.20	0.60	1.00
6, Nov 84	0.75	0.20	0.60	1.00
7, Dec 84	0.75	0.20	0.60	1.00
8, Jan 85	0.75	0.20	0.60	1.00
9, Feb 85	0.75	0.20	0.60	1.00
10, Mar 85	0.75	0.20	0.60	1.00
11, Apr 85	0.75	0.20	0.60	1.00
12, May 85	0.75	0.20	0.60	1.00
13, Jun 85	0.75	0.20	0.60	1.00
14, Jul 85	0.75	0.20	0.60	1.00
15, Aug 85	0.75	0.20	0.60	1.00
16, Sep 85	0.75	0.20	0.60	1.00
17, Oct 85, Crisis	0.75	0.20	0.60	1.00
18, Nov 85, Crisis	0.75	0.20	0.60	1.00
19, Dec 85	0.75	0.20	0.60	1.00
20, Jan 86	0.75	0.20	0.60	1.00
21, Feb 86	0.75	0.20	0.60	1.00
22, Mar 86	0.75	0.20	0.60	1.00
23, Apr 86	0.75	0.20	0.60	1.00
24, May 86	0.75	0.20	0.60	1.00
25, Jun 86	0.75	0.20	0.60	1.00
26, Jul 86	0.75	0.20	0.60	1.00
27, Aug 86	0.75	0.20	0.60	1.00
28, Sep 86	0.75	0.20	0.60	1.00
29, Oct 86	0.75	0.20	0.60	1.00
30, Nov 86	1.25	0.25	0.75	1.25
31, Dec 86	1.25	0.25	0.75	1.25

	ORIG.	GOOD	FINE	N-MINT

BLUE DEVIL ANNUAL
	ORIG.	GOOD	FINE	N-MINT
❑ 1, Nov 85	1.25	0.25	0.75	1.25

BLUE LILY, THE
DARK HORSE
	ORIG.	GOOD	FINE	N-MINT
❑ 1, 93	3.95	0.79	2.37	3.95
❑ 2, 93	3.95	0.79	2.37	3.95

BLUE MOON
MU PRESS
	ORIG.	GOOD	FINE	N-MINT
❑ 1, b&w	2.50	0.50	1.50	2.50
❑ 2, b&w	2.50	0.50	1.50	2.50
❑ 3, Feb 93, b&w	2.50	0.50	1.50	2.50
❑ 4, May 93, b&w	2.50	0.50	1.50	2.50
❑ 5, Dec 93, b&w;(moves to Aeon)	2.50	0.50	1.50	2.50

BLUE MOON (Vol. 2)
AEON
	ORIG.	GOOD	FINE	N-MINT
❑ 1, Aug 94, (was Mu series);b&w	2.95	0.59	1.77	2.95

BLUE RIBBON
ARCHIE
	ORIG.	GOOD	FINE	N-MINT
❑ 1, Nov 83	1.50	0.30	0.90	1.50
❑ 2, Nov 83	1.50	0.30	0.90	1.50
❑ 3, Dec 83	1.50	0.30	0.90	1.50
❑ 4, Jan 84	1.00	0.20	0.60	1.00
❑ 5, Feb 84	0.75	0.15	0.45	0.75
❑ 6, Mar 84	0.75	0.15	0.45	0.75
❑ 7, Apr 84	0.75	0.15	0.45	0.75
❑ 8, May 84	0.75	0.15	0.45	0.75
❑ 9, Jun 84	0.75	0.15	0.45	0.75
❑ 10, Jul 84	0.75	0.15	0.45	0.75
❑ 11, Aug 84	0.75	0.15	0.45	0.75
❑ 12, Sep 84	0.75	0.15	0.45	0.75
❑ 13, Oct 84	0.75	0.15	0.45	0.75
❑ 14, Dec 84	0.75	0.15	0.45	0.75

BLUEBEARD
SLAVE LABOR
	ORIG.	GOOD	FINE	N-MINT
❑ 1, b&w	2.95	0.59	1.77	2.95

BO JACKSON VS. MICHAEL JORDAN
CELEBRITY
	ORIG.	GOOD	FINE	N-MINT
❑ 1		0.59	1.77	2.95
❑ 2		0.59	1.77	2.95

BOB MARLEY, TALE OF THE TUFF GONG,
BOOK ONE: IRON
MARVEL MUSIC
	ORIG.	GOOD	FINE	N-MINT
❑ 0, 94, prestige format	5.95	1.19	3.57	5.95

BOB POWELL'S TIMELESS TALES
ECLIPSE
	ORIG.	GOOD	FINE	N-MINT
❑ 1, b&w	2.00	0.40	1.20	2.00

BOB RUMBA'S STAND UP COMIX
GREY
	ORIG.	GOOD	FINE	N-MINT
❑ 1, b&w	2.50	0.50	1.50	2.50

BOB STEELE WESTERN
AC
	ORIG.	GOOD	FINE	N-MINT
❑ 1, reprint, b&w		0.55	1.65	2.75

BOB'S FAVORITE COMICS
(really "Bob's" Favorite Comics)
RIP OFF
	ORIG.	GOOD	FINE	N-MINT
❑ 1, Mar 90, b&w;adult	2.50	0.50	1.50	2.50
❑ 1, b&w;adult;second printing	2.50	0.50	1.50	2.50
❑ 1, Jun 92, b&w;adult;third printing	2.50	0.50	1.50	2.50

BOB, THE GALACTIC BUM (mini-series)
DC
	ORIG.	GOOD	FINE	N-MINT
❑ 1, Feb 95	1.95	0.39	1.17	1.95
❑ 2, Mar 95	1.95	0.39	1.17	1.95
❑ 3, Apr 95	1.95	0.39	1.17	1.95
❑ 4, Jun 95	1.95	0.39	1.17	1.95

BODY COUNT
AIRCEL
	ORIG.	GOOD	FINE	N-MINT
❑ 1, b&w		0.45	1.35	2.25
❑ 2, b&w		0.45	1.35	2.25
❑ 3, b&w		0.45	1.35	2.25
❑ 4, b&w		0.45	1.35	2.25

MARVEL
	ORIG.	GOOD	FINE	N-MINT
❑ 1, free		0.60	1.80	3.00

BODYCOUNT (mini-series)
IMAGE
	ORIG.	GOOD	FINE	N-MINT
❑ 1, Mar 96	2.50	0.50	1.50	2.50
❑ 2, Apr 96	2.50	0.50	1.50	2.50

BODYGUARD
AIRCEL
	ORIG.	GOOD	FINE	N-MINT
❑ 0, pb		1.99	5.97	9.95
❑ 1, adult		0.50	1.50	2.50
❑ 2, adult		0.50	1.50	2.50
❑ 3, adult		0.50	1.50	2.50

BOFFO LAFFS
PARAGRAPHICS
	ORIG.	GOOD	FINE	N-MINT
❑ 1, first hologram cover		0.40	1.20	2.00
❑ 2		0.30	0.90	1.50
❑ 3		0.39	1.17	1.95
❑ 4		0.39	1.17	1.95
❑ 5		0.39	1.17	1.95

BOGIE MAN, THE
FAT MAN
	ORIG.	GOOD	FINE	N-MINT
❑ 1, b&w		0.39	1.17	1.95
❑ 2, b&w		0.39	1.17	1.95
❑ 3, b&w		0.39	1.17	1.95
❑ 4, b&w		0.39	1.17	1.95

BOGIE MAN: CHINATOON, THE
ATOMEKA
	ORIG.	GOOD	FINE	N-MINT
❑ 1, b&w	2.95	0.59	1.77	2.95
❑ 2, b&w	2.95	0.59	1.77	2.95
❑ 3, b&w	2.95	0.59	1.77	2.95
❑ 4, b&w	2.95	0.59	1.77	2.95

BOLD ADVENTURE
PACIFIC
	ORIG.	GOOD	FINE	N-MINT
❑ 1		0.25	0.75	1.25
❑ 2		0.30	0.90	1.50
❑ 3		0.30	0.90	1.50

BOLT & STARFORCE SIX
AC
	ORIG.	GOOD	FINE	N-MINT
❑ 1, Jul 84		0.35	1.05	1.75

BOLT SPECIAL
	ORIG.	GOOD	FINE	N-MINT
❑ 1, 84		0.30	0.90	1.50

BOMARC
NIGHTWYND
	ORIG.	GOOD	FINE	N-MINT
❑ 1, b&w		0.50	1.50	2.50
❑ 2, b&w		0.50	1.50	2.50
❑ 3, b&w		0.50	1.50	2.50

BOMBAST
TOPPS
	ORIG.	GOOD	FINE	N-MINT
❑ 1, Apr 93, JK(c), Savage Dragon, trading card	2.95	0.59	1.77	2.95

BONDAGE FAIRIES
ANTARCTIC
	ORIG.	GOOD	FINE	N-MINT
❑ 1, Mar 94, adult;b&w	2.95	2.00	6.00	10.00
❑ 1, May 94, adult;b&w;second printing	2.95	1.20	3.60	6.00
❑ 1, Aug 94, adult;b&w;third printing	2.95	0.59	1.77	2.95
❑ 1, Jan 95, adult;b&w;fourth printing	2.95	0.59	1.77	2.95
❑ 2, Apr 94, adult;b&w	2.95	1.20	3.60	6.00
❑ 2, Jun 94, adult;b&w;second printing	2.95	0.59	1.77	2.95

	ORIG.	GOOD	FINE	N-MINT
2, Oct 94, adult;b&w;third printing				
....2.95		0.59	1.77	2.95
2, Apr 95, adult;b&w;fourth printing				
....2.95		0.59	1.77	2.95
3, May 94, adult;b&w.....2.95		1.00	3.00	5.00
3, Sep 94, adult;b&w;second printing				
....2.95		0.59	1.77	2.95
3, Dec 94, adult;b&w;third printing				
....2.95		0.59	1.77	2.95
4, Jun 94, adult;b&w.. 2.95		0.59	1.77	2.95
4, Nov 94, adult;b&w;second printing				
....2.95		0.59	1.77	2.95
4, Jan 95, adult;b&w;third printing				
....2.95		0.59	1.77	2.95
5, Jul 94, adult;b&w.....2.95		0.59	1.77	2.95
5, Nov 94, adult;b&w;second printing				
....2.95		0.59	1.77	2.95
5, Feb 95, adult;b&w;third printing				
....2.95		0.59	1.77	2.95
6, Aug 94, adult;b&w.. 2.95		0.59	1.77	2.95
6, Feb 95, adult;b&w;second printing				
....2.95		0.59	1.77	2.95

BONE
CARTOON BOOKS

	ORIG.	GOOD	FINE	N-MINT
1, Jul 91, 1st printing;b&w				
....2.95		50.00	150.00	250.00
1, second printing;b&w. 2.95		4.00	12.00	20.00
1, third printing;b&w...... 2.95		2.40	7.20	12.00
2, Sep 91, 1st printing;b&w				
....2.95		30.00	90.00	150.00
2, second printing;b&w.. 2.95		2.40	7.20	12.00
3, Dec 91, 1st printing;b&w				
....2.95		20.00	60.00	100.00
3, second printing;b&w.. 2.95		1.00	3.00	5.00
4, Mar 92, 1st printing;b&w				
....2.95		12.00	36.00	60.00
5, Jun 92, b&w 2.95		10.00	30.00	50.00
6, Nov 92, b&w 2.95		10.00	30.00	50.00
6, second printing;b&w. 2.95		0.59	1.77	2.95
7, Dec 92, b&w 2.95		6.40	19.20	32.00
7, second printing;b&w. 2.95		0.59	1.77	2.95
8, Feb 93, b&w 2.95		6.40	19.20	32.00
8, second printing;b&w.. 2.95		0.59	1.77	2.95
9, b&w 2.95		3.00	9.00	15.00
10, b&w 2.95		1.60	4.80	8.00
11, b&w 2.95		0.80	2.40	4.00
12, b&w 2.95		0.80	2.40	4.00
13, Mar 94, b&w............2.95		0.70	2.10	3.50
14, May 94, b&w............2.95		0.70	2.10	3.50
15, b&w 2.95		0.70	2.10	3.50
16, b&w 2.95		0.70	2.10	3.50
17, b&w 2.95		0.70	2.10	3.50
18, Apr 95, b&w............2.95		0.59	1.77	2.95
19, Jun 95, b&w 2.95		0.59	1.77	2.95
20, b&w;(becomes Image title)				
....2.95		0.59	1.77	2.95

IMAGE

	ORIG.	GOOD	FINE	N-MINT
1, Jan 96, b&w;reprints Cartoon Books issue				
....2.95		0.59	1.77	2.95
4, Apr 96, b&w;reprints Cartoon Books issue				
....2.95		0.59	1.77	2.95
5, May 96, b&w;reprints Cartoon Books issue				
....2.95		0.59	1.77	2.95
6, Jun 96, b&w;reprints Cartoon Books issue				
....2.95		0.59	1.77	2.95
7, Jul 96, b&w;reprints Cartoon Books issue				
....2.95		0.59	1.77	2.95
21, b&w;(was Cartoon Books title)				
....2.95		0.59	1.77	2.95
22, Feb 96, b&w............2.95		0.59	1.77	2.95

	ORIG.	GOOD	FINE	N-MINT
23, May 96, b&w;1:Baby Rat Creature				
....2.95		0.59	1.77	2.95
24, Jun 96 ....2.95		0.59	1.77	2.95

BONE SAW
TUNDRA

	ORIG.	GOOD	FINE	N-MINT
1, b&w, adult..................		2.99	8.97	14.95

BONE SOURCEBOOK
IMAGE

	ORIG.	GOOD	FINE	N-MINT
1, Nov 95, promotional handout;no cover price;b&w				
....		0.40	1.20	2.00

BONE SPECIAL EDITION
HERO

	ORIG.	GOOD	FINE	N-MINT
0, nn		0.40	1.20	2.00

BONES
MALIBU

	ORIG.	GOOD	FINE	N-MINT
1		0.39	1.17	1.95
2		0.39	1.17	1.95
3		0.39	1.17	1.95
4		0.39	1.17	1.95

BOOF
ICONOGRAPHIX

	ORIG.	GOOD	FINE	N-MINT
1, b&w............................2.50		0.50	1.50	2.50

IMAGE

	ORIG.	GOOD	FINE	N-MINT
1, Jul 94........................1.95		0.39	1.17	1.95
2, Aug 94 ....1.95		0.39	1.17	1.95
3, Sep 94.......................1.95		0.39	1.17	1.95
4, Oct 94........................1.95		0.39	1.17	1.95
6, Dec 94.......................1.95		0.39	1.17	1.95

BOOF AND THE BRUISE CREW

	ORIG.	GOOD	FINE	N-MINT
1, Jul 94........................1.95		0.39	1.17	1.95
2, Aug 94 ....1.95		0.39	1.17	1.95
3, Sep 94.......................1.95		0.39	1.17	1.95
4, Oct 94........................1.95		0.39	1.17	1.95
6, Dec 94.......................1.95		0.39	1.17	1.95

BOOGIEMAN, THE
RION

	ORIG.	GOOD	FINE	N-MINT
1, b&w............................		0.30	0.90	1.50

BOOK OF BALLADS AND SAGAS, THE
GREEN MAN PRESS

	ORIG.	GOOD	FINE	N-MINT
1, 95, b&w......................2.95		0.59	1.77	2.95

BOOK OF NIGHT, THE
DARK HORSE

	ORIG.	GOOD	FINE	N-MINT
1, Jul 87, CV;b&w..........1.50		0.30	0.90	1.50
2, Aug 87, CV;b&w 1.50		0.30	0.90	1.50
3, Sep 87, CV;b&w 1.75		0.35	1.05	1.75

BOOK OF REDFOX, THE
HARRIER

	ORIG.	GOOD	FINE	N-MINT
1		1.39	4.17	6.95

BOOK OF THE DEAD
MARVEL

	ORIG.	GOOD	FINE	N-MINT
1, reprints 1.75		0.35	1.05	1.75
2, reprints 1.75		0.35	1.05	1.75
3, reprints 1.75		0.35	1.05	1.75
4, reprints 1.75		0.35	1.05	1.75

BOOK OF THOTH, THE
CIRCLE STUDIOS

	ORIG.	GOOD	FINE	N-MINT
1, Jun 95 ....2.50		0.50	1.50	2.50

BOOKS OF MAGIC, THE (1990-91 mini-series)
DC

	ORIG.	GOOD	FINE	N-MINT
1, Dec 90, NG, John Bolton				
....3.95		2.40	7.20	12.00
2, Jan 91, NG, Scott Hampton				
....3.95		2.00	6.00	10.00
3, Feb 91, NG, CV 3.95		1.40	4.20	7.00
4, Mar 91, NG, Paul Johnson				
....3.95		1.40	4.20	7.00

BOOKS OF MAGIC, THE (1994-)

	ORIG.	GOOD	FINE	N-MINT
1, May 94, platinum..........		4.00	12.00	20.00

	ORIG.	GOOD	FINE	N-MINT
DC/VERTIGO				
❑ 1, May 94	1.95	0.60	1.80	3.00
❑ 2, Jun 94	1.95	0.50	1.50	2.50
❑ 3, Jul 94	1.95	0.50	1.50	2.50
❑ 4, Aug 94	1.95	1.00	3.00	5.00
❑ 5, Sep 94	1.95	0.60	1.80	3.00
❑ 6, Oct 94	1.95	0.39	1.17	1.95
❑ 7, Nov 94	1.95	0.39	1.17	1.95
❑ 8, Dec 94	1.95	0.39	1.17	1.95
❑ 9, Jan 95	1.95	0.39	1.17	1.95
❑ 10, Feb 95	1.95	0.39	1.17	1.95
❑ 11, Mar 95	1.95	0.39	1.17	1.95
❑ 12, Apr 95	1.95	0.39	1.17	1.95
❑ 13	1.95	0.39	1.17	1.95
❑ 14, Jul 95	2.50	0.50	1.50	2.50
❑ 15, Aug 95	2.50	0.50	1.50	2.50
❑ 16, Sep 95	2.50	0.50	1.50	2.50
❑ 17, Oct 95	2.50	0.50	1.50	2.50
❑ 18, Nov 95	2.50	0.50	1.50	2.50
❑ 19, Dec 95	2.50	0.50	1.50	2.50
❑ 20, Jan 96	2.50	0.50	1.50	2.50
❑ 22, Mar 96	2.50	0.50	1.50	2.50
❑ 23, Apr 96	2.50	0.50	1.50	2.50
❑ 24, May 96	2.50	0.50	1.50	2.50
❑ 25, Jun 96	2.50	0.50	1.50	2.50
BOOM BOOM				
AEON				
❑ 1, 94, b&w	2.50	0.50	1.50	2.50
❑ 2, Sep 94, b&w	2.50	0.50	1.50	2.50
BOONDOGGLE				
KNIGHT PRESS				
❑ 1, Mar 95, b&w	2.95	0.59	1.77	2.95
❑ 3, Nov 95, b&w	2.95	0.59	1.77	2.95
BOOSTER GOLD				
DC				
❑ 1, Feb 86, DJ	0.75	0.50	1.50	2.50
❑ 2, Mar 86, DJ	0.75	0.40	1.20	2.00
❑ 3, Apr 86, DJ	0.75	0.40	1.20	2.00
❑ 4, May 86, DJ	0.75	0.40	1.20	2.00
❑ 5, Jun 86, DJ	0.75	0.40	1.20	2.00
❑ 6, Jul 86, DJ	0.75	0.30	0.90	1.50
❑ 7, Aug 86, DJ	0.75	0.30	0.90	1.50
❑ 8, Sep 86, DJ;A:Legion	0.75	0.30	0.90	1.50
❑ 9, Oct 86, DJ;A:Legion	0.75	0.30	0.90	1.50
❑ 10, Nov 86, DJ		0.30	0.90	1.50
❑ 11, Dec 86, DJ		0.30	0.90	1.50
❑ 12, Jan 87, DJ		0.30	0.90	1.50
❑ 13, Feb 87, DJ		0.30	0.90	1.50
❑ 14, Mar 87, DJ		0.30	0.90	1.50
❑ 15, Apr 87, DJ		0.30	0.90	1.50
❑ 16, May 87, DJ		0.30	0.90	1.50
❑ 17, Jun 87, DJ		0.30	0.90	1.50
❑ 18, Jul 87, DJ		0.30	0.90	1.50
❑ 19, Aug 87, DJ		0.30	0.90	1.50
❑ 20, Sep 87, DJ		0.30	0.90	1.50
❑ 21, Oct 87, DJ		0.30	0.90	1.50
❑ 22, Nov 87, DJ;A:Justice League		0.30	0.90	1.50
❑ 23, Dec 87, DJ;A:Superman		0.30	0.90	1.50
❑ 24, Jan 88, DJ;Millennium	1.00	0.30	0.90	1.50
❑ 25, Feb 88, DJ;Millennium;final issue	1.00	0.30	0.90	1.50
BORDER WORLDS				
KITCHEN SINK				
❑ 1, Jul 86	1.95	0.40	1.20	2.00
❑ 2, Sep 86	1.95	0.40	1.20	2.00
❑ 3, Nov 86	1.95	0.40	1.20	2.00
❑ 4, Jan 87	1.95	0.40	1.20	2.00
❑ 5, Apr 87	1.95	0.40	1.20	2.00
❑ 6, Jun 87	1.95	0.40	1.20	2.00

	ORIG.	GOOD	FINE	N-MINT
❑ 7, Aug 87, pages 4-5 transposed		0.40	1.20	2.00
❑ 7, 87, corrected		0.40	1.20	2.00
BORDER WORLDS: MAROONED				
❑ 1, adult, b&w		0.40	1.20	2.00
BORDERGUARD				
ETERNITY				
❑ 1		0.39	1.17	1.95
❑ 2		0.39	1.17	1.95
BORIS THE BEAR				
DARK HORSE				
❑ 1, 86	1.50	1.50	4.50	7.50
❑ 1, reprint	1.50	0.40	1.20	2.00
❑ 2	1.50	0.60	1.80	3.00
❑ 3	1.50	0.30	0.90	1.50
❑ 4, 2 diff. covers	1.50	0.30	0.90	1.50
❑ 5	1.50	0.30	0.90	1.50
❑ 6	1.50	0.30	0.90	1.50
❑ 7	1.50	0.30	0.90	1.50
❑ 8	1.50	0.40	1.20	2.00
❑ 9	1.50	0.30	0.90	1.50
❑ 10, May 87	1.50	0.30	0.90	1.50
❑ 11	1.50	0.30	0.90	1.50
❑ 12, Jul 87, (moves to Nicotat)	1.75	0.35	1.05	1.75
BORIS THE BEAR (was Dark Horse title)				
NICOTAT				
❑ 13		0.30	0.90	1.50
❑ 14		0.30	0.90	1.50
❑ 15		0.30	0.90	1.50
❑ 16		0.30	0.90	1.50
❑ 17		0.30	0.90	1.50
❑ 18		0.30	0.90	1.50
❑ 19		0.35	1.05	1.75
❑ 20		0.35	1.05	1.75
❑ 21		0.35	1.05	1.75
❑ 22		0.39	1.17	1.95
❑ 23		0.39	1.17	1.95
❑ 24		0.39	1.17	1.95
❑ 25		0.39	1.17	1.95
❑ 26		0.39	1.17	1.95
❑ 27		0.39	1.17	1.95
❑ 28		0.39	1.17	1.95
❑ 29		0.39	1.17	1.95
❑ 30	2.25	0.45	1.35	2.25
❑ 31	2.25	0.45	1.35	2.25
❑ 32	2.25	0.45	1.35	2.25
❑ 33	2.25	0.45	1.35	2.25
❑ 34	2.25	0.45	1.35	2.25
BORIS THE BEAR INSTANT COLOR CLASSICS				
DARK HORSE				
❑ 1, Jul 87	1.75	0.35	1.05	1.75
❑ 2, Aug 87	1.75	0.35	1.05	1.75
❑ 3, Sep 87	1.95	0.39	1.17	1.95
BORIS' ADVENTURE MAGAZINE				
NICOTAT				
❑ 1, b&w		0.40	1.20	2.00
BORN TO BE WILD				
ECLIPSE				
❑ 0, nn b&w, BSz(c), TA,TMc	2.19	6.57	10.95	
BORN TO KILL				
AIRCEL				
❑ 1, b&w		0.50	1.50	2.50
❑ 2, b&w		0.50	1.50	2.50
❑ 3, b&w		0.50	1.50	2.50
BOSTON BOMBERS				
CALIBER				
❑ 1, 90, b&w	2.50	0.50	1.50	2.50
❑ 2, b&w	2.50	0.50	1.50	2.50
❑ 3, b&w	2.50	0.50	1.50	2.50
❑ 4, b&w	2.50	0.50	1.50	2.50

	ORIG.	GOOD	FINE	N-MINT

BOULEVARD OF BROKEN DREAMS
FANTAGRAPHICS
☐ 0, nn.....................3.95 0.79 2.37 3.95

BOUNTY
CALIBER
☐ 1, b&w.....................2.50 0.50 1.50 2.50
☐ 2, b&w.....................2.50 0.50 1.50 2.50
☐ 3, b&w.....................2.50 0.50 1.50 2.50

BOX
EROS COMIX
☐ 1, adult, b&w................... 0.45 1.35 2.25
☐ 2, adult, b&w................... 0.45 1.35 2.25
☐ 3, adult, b&w................... 0.45 1.35 2.25
☐ 4, adult, b&w................... 0.45 1.35 2.25
☐ 5, adult, b&w................... 0.45 1.35 2.25
☐ 6, adult, b&w................... 0.45 1.35 2.25

BOY AND HIS 'BOT, A
NOW
☐ 1, Jan 87.....................1.95 0.39 1.17 1.95

BOY COMMANDOS
DC
☐ 1, Oct 73.....................0.20 0.20 0.60 1.00
☐ 2, Dec 73.....................0.20 0.20 0.60 1.00

BOZO
INNOVATION
☐ 1, some reprint 1.39 4.17 6.95

BOZO IN 3-D
BLACKTHORNE
☐ 1 .... 0.50 1.50 2.50
☐ 2 .... 0.50 1.50 2.50

BOZZ CHRONICLES
EPIC
☐ 1 ....1.50 0.30 0.90 1.50
☐ 2 ....1.50 0.30 0.90 1.50
☐ 3 ....1.50 0.30 0.90 1.50
☐ 4 ....1.50 0.30 0.90 1.50
☐ 5 ....1.50 0.30 0.90 1.50
☐ 6 ....1.50 0.30 0.90 1.50

BRAGADE
PARODY PRESS
☐ 1 ....2.50 0.50 1.50 2.50

BRAIN BAT 3-D
3-D ZONE
☐ 1, 92.....................3.95 0.79 2.37 3.95

BRAIN CAPERS
FANTAGRAPHICS
☐ 1 ....3.95 0.79 2.37 3.95

BRAINGLO
PSI COMICS
☐ 1, 87.....................1.75 0.35 1.05 1.75

BRAM STOKER'S DRACULA
TOPPS
☐ 1, movie adaptation, bagged w/cards
.....................1.60 4.80 8.00
☐ 1, no cover price, red foil cover
.....................1.60 4.80 8.00
☐ 2, movie adaptation, bagged w/cards
.....................1.20 3.60 6.00
☐ 3, movie adaptation, bagged w/cards
.....................1.00 3.00 5.00
☐ 4, movie adaptation, bagged w/cards
.....................1.00 3.00 5.00

BRAT PACK
KING HELL
☐ 1, Aug 90, b&w.............2.95 0.80 2.40 4.00
☐ 1, second printing 0.59 1.77 2.95
☐ 2, Nov 90 ....2.95 0.59 1.77 2.95
☐ 3, Jan 91 ....2.95 0.59 1.77 2.95
☐ 4, Mar 91 ....2.95 0.59 1.77 2.95
☐ 5, May 91 ....2.95 0.59 1.77 2.95

BRATS BIZARRE
EPIC
☐ 1, 94 ....2.50 0.50 1.50 2.50
☐ 2, Jun 94 ....2.50 0.50 1.50 2.50
☐ 3, Jul 94, trading card.....2.50 0.50 1.50 2.50
☐ 4, Aug 94 ....2.50 0.50 1.50 2.50

BRAVE AND THE BOLD
DC
☐ 1, JKu, Viking Prince 0.10 400.00 1200.00 2000.00
☐ 2 ....0.10 170.00 510.00 850.00
☐ 3 ....0.10 110.00 330.00 550.00
☐ 4 ....0.10 110.00 330.00 550.00
☐ 5 ....0.10 110.00 330.00 550.00
☐ 6, Robin Hood 0.10 60.00 180.00 300.00
☐ 7, Robin Hood 0.10 60.00 180.00 300.00
☐ 8, Robin Hood 0.10 60.00 180.00 300.00
☐ 9, Robin Hood 0.10 60.00 180.00 300.00
☐ 10, Robin Hood 0.10 60.00 180.00 300.00
☐ 11, JKu 0.10 55.00 165.00 275.00
☐ 12, JKu 0.10 55.00 165.00 275.00
☐ 13, Sep 57, JKu 0.10 55.00 165.00 275.00
☐ 14, JKu 0.10 55.00 165.00 275.00
☐ 15, JKu 0.10 55.00 165.00 275.00
☐ 16, JKu 0.10 55.00 165.00 275.00
☐ 17, JKu 0.10 55.00 165.00 275.00
☐ 18, JKu 0.10 55.00 165.00 275.00
☐ 19, JKu 0.10 55.00 165.00 275.00
☐ 20, JKu 0.10 55.00 165.00 275.00
☐ 21, JKu 0.10 55.00 165.00 275.00
☐ 22, JKu 0.10 55.00 165.00 275.00
☐ 23, Viking Prince 0.10 75.00 225.00 375.00
☐ 24, Viking Prince 0.10 55.00 165.00 275.00
☐ 25, Sep 59, Suicide Squad
.....................0.10 120.00 360.00 600.00
☐ 26, Nov 59, Suicide Squad
.....................0.10 60.00 180.00 300.00
☐ 27, Suicide Squad...........0.10 60.00 180.00 300.00
☐ 28, I:JLA, O:Snapper Carr
.....................0.10 900.00 2700.00 4500.00
☐ 29, May 60, JLA.............0.10 500.00 1500.00 2500.00
☐ 30, Jul 60, JLA.............0.10 400.00 1200.00 2000.00
☐ 31, Sep 60, Cave Carson.0.10 60.00 180.00 300.00
☐ 32, Cave Carson.............0.10 30.00 90.00 150.00
☐ 33, Jan 61, Cave Carson .0.10 30.00 90.00 150.00
☐ 34, Mar 61, JKu, O:Hawkman
.....................0.10 350.00 1050.00 1750.00
☐ 35, May 61, JKu, Hawkman
.....................0.10 120.00 360.00 600.00
☐ 36, Jul 61, JKu, Hawkman
.....................0.10 100.00 300.00 500.00
☐ 37, Sep 61, Suicide Squad
.....................0.10 40.00 120.00 200.00
☐ 38, Nov 61, Suicide Squad
.....................0.10 40.00 120.00 200.00
☐ 39, Jan 62, Suicide Squad
.....................0.10 40.00 120.00 200.00
☐ 40, Mar 62, Cave Carson
.....................0.12 25.00 75.00 125.00
☐ 41, May 62, Cave Carson
.....................0.12 25.00 75.00 125.00
☐ 42, Jul 62, JKu, Hawkman
.....................0.12 72.00 216.00 360.00
☐ 43, Sep 62, JKu, Hawkman
.....................0.12 70.00 210.00 350.00
☐ 44, Nov 62, JKu, Hawkman
.....................0.12 60.00 180.00 300.00
☐ 45, Jan 63, CI, Strange Sports
.....................0.12 10.00 30.00 50.00
☐ 46, Mar 63, CI, Strange Sports
.....................0.12 10.00 30.00 50.00

	ORIG.	GOOD	FINE	N-MINT
☐ 47, May 63, CI, Strange Sports	0.12	10.00	30.00	50.00
☐ 48, Jul 63, CI, Strange Sports	0.12	10.00	30.00	50.00
☐ 49, Sep 63, CI, Strange Sports	0.12	10.00	30.00	50.00
☐ 50, Nov 63, Green Arrow	0.12	35.00	105.00	175.00
☐ 51, Jan 64, Aquaman	0.12	40.00	120.00	200.00
☐ 52, Mar 64, JKu, Sgt. Rock	0.12	24.00	72.00	120.00
☐ 53, May 64, ATh, Atom & Flash	0.12	10.00	30.00	50.00
☐ 54, Jul 64, 1:Teen Titans	0.12	50.00	150.00	250.00
☐ 55, Sep 64, Metal Men ...	0.12	6.00	18.00	30.00
☐ 56, Nov 64, Flash	0.12	6.00	18.00	30.00
☐ 57, Jan 65, I&O: Metamorpho	0.12	30.00	90.00	150.00
☐ 58, Mar 65, RF, Metamorpho	0.12	12.00	36.00	60.00
☐ 59, May 65, Batman	0.12	15.00	45.00	75.00
☐ 60, Jul 65, Teen Titans ...	0.12	15.00	45.00	75.00
☐ 61, Sep 65, MA, Starman	0.12	5.00	15.00	25.00
☐ 62, Nov 65, MA, Starman	0.12	5.00	15.00	25.00
☐ 63, Jan 66, Supergirl......	0.12	2.00	6.00	10.00
☐ 64, Mar 66, Batman/Eclipso	0.12	7.00	21.00	35.00
☐ 65, May 66, Doom Patrol	0.12	1.60	4.80	8.00
☐ 66, Jul 66, Metamorpho.	0.12	1.60	4.80	8.00
☐ 67, Sep 66, CI, Batman/Flash	0.12	1.60	4.80	8.00
☐ 68, Nov 66, BM/Metamorpho	0.12	6.00	18.00	30.00
☐ 69, Jan 67, BM/Green Lantern	0.12	2.80	8.40	14.00
☐ 70, Mar 67, Batman/Hawkman	0.12	2.80	8.40	14.00
☐ 71, May 67, BM/Green Arrow	0.12	3.20	9.60	16.00
☐ 72, Jul 67, CI, Spectre....	0.12	2.00	6.00	10.00
☐ 73, Sep 67, Aquaman & Atom (Batman in all)	0.12	2.00	6.00	10.00
☐ 74, Nov 67, Metal Men ...	0.12	2.00	6.00	10.00
☐ 75, Jan 68, Spectre	0.12	2.00	6.00	10.00
☐ 76, Mar 68, Plastic Man .	0.12	2.00	6.00	10.00
☐ 77, May 68, Atom	0.12	2.00	6.00	10.00
☐ 78, Jul 68, Wonder Woman	0.12	2.00	6.00	10.00
☐ 79, Sep 68, NA, Deadman	0.12	4.40	13.20	22.00
☐ 80, Nov 68, NA, Creeper	0.12	4.00	12.00	20.00
☐ 81, Jan 69, NA, Flash	0.12	4.00	12.00	20.00
☐ 82, Mar 69, NA, O:Ocean Master	0.12	4.00	12.00	20.00
☐ 83, May 69, NA, Titans...	0.12	6.00	18.00	30.00
☐ 84, Jul 69, NA, Sgt. Rock	0.12	4.00	12.00	20.00
☐ 85, Sep 69, NA, Green Arrow	0.15	4.00	12.00	20.00
☐ 86, Nov 69, NA, Deadman	0.15	4.00	12.00	20.00
☐ 87, Jan 70, Wonder Woman	0.15	1.60	4.80	8.00
☐ 88, Mar 70, Wildcat...	0.15	1.60	4.80	8.00
☐ 89, May 70, Phantom Stranger	0.15	1.60	4.80	8.00
☐ 90, Jul 70, Adam Strange	0.15	1.60	4.80	8.00
☐ 91, Sep 70, Black Canary	0.15	1.60	4.80	8.00
☐ 92, Nov 70, Bat Squad	0.15	1.60	4.80	8.00
☐ 93, Jan 71, NA, House of Mystery	0.15	3.60	10.80	18.00
☐ 94, Mar 71, Titans	0.15	1.20	3.60	6.00
☐ 95, May 71, Plastic Man .	0.15	1.20	3.60	6.00
☐ 96, Jul 71, Sgt. Rock	0.15	1.20	3.60	6.00
☐ 97, Sep 71, NC(i), Wildcat	0.25	1.20	3.60	6.00
☐ 98, Nov 71, Phantom Stranger	0.25	1.20	3.60	6.00
☐ 99, Jan 72, NC, Flash......	0.25	1.20	3.60	6.00
☐ 100, Mar 72, NA, Green Arrow	0.25	3.60	10.80	18.00
☐ 101, May 72, Metamorpho	0.25	1.00	3.00	5.00
☐ 102, Jul 72, NA, Titans ...	0.25	1.00	3.00	5.00
☐ 103, Oct 72, Metal Men ..	0.20	1.00	3.00	5.00
☐ 104, Dec 72, JA, Deadman	0.20	1.00	3.00	5.00
☐ 105, Feb 73, JA, Wonder Woman	0.20	1.00	3.00	5.00
☐ 106, Apr 73, JA, Green Arrow	0.20	1.00	3.00	5.00
☐ 107, Jul 73, Black Canary	0.20	1.00	3.00	5.00
☐ 108, Sep 73, JA, Sgt. Rock	0.20	1.00	3.00	5.00
☐ 109, Nov 73, JA, Demon	0.20	1.00	3.00	5.00
☐ 110, Jan 74, JA, Wildcat.	0.20	1.00	3.00	5.00
☐ 111, Mar 74, JA, Joker ...	0.20	2.00	6.00	10.00
☐ 112, May 74, Mr. Miracle, 100 pgs.	0.60	1.50	4.50	7.50
☐ 113, Jul 74, JA, Metal Men, 100 pgs.	0.60	1.50	4.50	7.50
☐ 114, Sep 74, JA, Aquaman, 100 pgs.	0.60	1.50	4.50	7.50
☐ 115, Nov 74, JA, O:Viking Prince, 100 pgs.	0.60	1.50	4.50	7.50
☐ 116, Jan 75, JA, Spectre, 100 pgs.	0.60	1.50	4.50	7.50
☐ 117, Mar 75, JA, Sgt. Rock, 100 pgs.	0.60	1.50	4.50	7.50
☐ 118, Apr 75, JA, Wildcat, Joker	0.25	1.20	3.60	6.00
☐ 119, Jun 75, JA, Man-Bat	0.25	1.00	3.00	5.00
☐ 120, Jul 75, JA, Kamandi, 68 pgs.	0.50	1.00	3.00	5.00
☐ 121, Sep 75, JA, Metal Men	0.25	1.00	3.00	5.00
☐ 122, Oct 75, Swamp Thing	0.25	1.00	3.00	5.00
☐ 123, Dec 75, JA, Plastic Man/Metamorpho	0.25	1.00	3.00	5.00
☐ 124, Jan 76, JA, Sgt. Rock	0.25	1.00	3.00	5.00
☐ 125, Mar 76, JA, Flash....	0.25	1.00	3.00	5.00
☐ 126, Apr 76, JA, Aquaman	0.30	1.00	3.00	5.00
☐ 127, Jun 76, JA, Wildcat	0.30	1.00	3.00	5.00
☐ 128, Jul 76, JA, Mr. Miracle	0.30	1.00	3.00	5.00
☐ 129, Sep 76, Green Arrow, Joker	0.30	1.40	4.20	7.00
☐ 130, Oct 76, Green Arrow, Joker	0.30	1.40	4.20	7.00
☐ 131, Dec 76, JA, Wonder Woman	0.30	1.00	3.00	5.00

	ORIG.	GOOD	FINE	N-MINT
☐ 132, Feb 77, JA, Kung Fu Fighter	0.30	1.00	3.00	5.00
☐ 133, Apr 77, JA, Deadman	0.30	1.00	3.00	5.00
☐ 134, May 77, JA, Green Lantern	0.30	1.00	3.00	5.00
☐ 135, Jul 77, JA, Metal Men	0.35	1.00	3.00	5.00
☐ 136, Sep 77, Metal Men/GA	0.35	1.00	3.00	5.00
☐ 137, Oct 77, Demon	0.35	1.00	3.00	5.00
☐ 138, Nov 77, JA, Mr. Miracle	0.35	1.00	3.00	5.00
☐ 139, Jan 78, JA, Hawkman	0.35	1.00	3.00	5.00
☐ 140, Mar 78, JA, Wonder Woman	0.35	1.00	3.00	5.00
☐ 141, May 78, Black Canary, Joker	0.35	1.00	3.00	5.00
☐ 142, Jul 78, JA, Aquaman	0.35	1.00	3.00	5.00
☐ 143, Sep 78, JA, O:Human Target	0.50	1.00	3.00	5.00
☐ 144, Nov 78, JA, Green Arrow	0.50	1.00	3.00	5.00
☐ 145, Dec 78, JA, Phantom Stranger	0.40	1.00	3.00	5.00
☐ 146, Jan 79, JA, E-2 Batman	0.40	1.00	3.00	5.00
☐ 147, Feb 79, JA, A:Dr. Light	0.40	1.00	3.00	5.00
☐ 148, Mar 79, Plastic Man	0.40	1.00	3.00	5.00
☐ 149, Apr 79, JA, Teen Titans	0.40	1.00	3.00	5.00
☐ 150, May 79, JA, Superman	0.40	1.00	3.00	5.00
☐ 151, Jun 79, JA, Flash	0.40	0.75	2.25	3.75
☐ 152, Jul 79, JA, Atom	0.40	0.75	2.25	
☐ 153, Aug 79, DN, Red Tornado	0.40	0.75	2.25	3.75
☐ 154, Sep 79, JA, Metamorpho	0.40	0.75	2.25	3.75
☐ 155, Oct 79, JA, Green Lantern	0.40	0.75	2.25	3.75
☐ 156, Nov 79, DN, Dr. Fate	0.40	0.75	2.25	3.75
☐ 157, Dec 79, JA, Kamandi	0.40	0.75	2.25	3.75
☐ 158, Jan 80, JA, Wonder Woman	0.40	0.75	2.25	3.75
☐ 159, Feb 80, JA, Ra's al Ghul	0.40	0.75	2.25	3.75
☐ 160, Mar 80, JA, Supergirl	0.40	0.75	2.25	3.75
☐ 161, Apr 80, JA, Adam Strange	0.40	0.75	2.25	3.75
☐ 162, May 80, JA, Sgt. Rock	0.40	0.75	2.25	3.75
☐ 163, Jun 80, DG, Black Lightning	0.40	0.75	2.25	3.75
☐ 164, Jul 80, JL, Hawkman	0.40	0.75	2.25	3.75
☐ 165, Aug 80, DN, Man-Bat	0.40	0.75	2.25	3.75
☐ 166, Sep 80, DS/TA, I:Nemesis	0.40	0.75	2.25	3.75
☐ 167, Oct 80, DC/DA, Blackhawk	0.50	0.75	2.25	3.75
☐ 168, Nov 80, JA, Green Arrow	0.50	0.75	2.25	3.75
☐ 169, Dec 80, JA, Zatanna	0.50	0.75	2.25	3.75

	ORIG.	GOOD	FINE	N-MINT
☐ 170, Jan 81, JA, Nemesis	0.50	0.75	2.25	3.75
☐ 171, Feb 81, JL/GC, Scalphunter	0.50	0.75	2.25	3.75
☐ 172, Mar 81, CI, Firestorm	0.50	0.75	2.25	3.75
☐ 173, Apr 81, JA, Guardians	0.50	0.75	2.25	3.75
☐ 174, May 81, JA, Green Lantern	0.50	0.75	2.25	3.75
☐ 175, Jun 81, JA, Lois Lane	0.50	0.75	2.25	3.75
☐ 176, Jul 81, JA, Swamp Thing	0.50	0.75	2.25	3.75
☐ 177, Aug 81, JA, Elongated Man	0.50	0.75	2.25	3.75
☐ 178, Sep 81, JA, Creeper	0.50	0.75	2.25	3.75
☐ 179, Oct 81, EC, Legion	0.60	0.75	2.25	3.75
☐ 180, Nov 81, JA, Spectre;Nemesis	0.60	0.75	2.25	3.75
☐ 181, Dec 81, JA, Hawk & Dove;Nemesis	0.60	0.75	2.25	3.75
☐ 182, Jan 82, JA, E-2 Robin	0.60	0.75	2.25	3.75
☐ 183, Feb 82, CI, Riddler;Nemesis	0.60	0.75	2.25	3.75
☐ 184, Mar 82, JA, Huntress	0.60	0.75	2.25	3.75
☐ 185, Apr 82, Green Lantern	0.60	0.75	2.25	3.75
☐ 186, May 82, JA, Hawkman;Nemesis	0.60	0.75	2.25	3.75
☐ 187, Jun 82, JA, Metal Men;Nemesis	0.60	0.75	2.25	3.75
☐ 188, Jul 82, JA, Rose & Thorn	0.60	0.75	2.25	3.75
☐ 189, Aug 82, JA Thorn;Nemesis	0.60	0.75	2.25	3.75
☐ 190, Sep 82, JA, Adam Strange;Nemesis	0.60	0.75	2.25	3.75
☐ 191, Oct 82, JA, Joker;A:Nemesis	0.60	0.75	2.25	3.75
☐ 192, Nov 82, JA, V:Mr. IQ	0.60	0.75	2.25	3.75
☐ 193, Dec 82, JA, D:Nemesis	0.60	0.75	2.25	3.75
☐ 194, Jan 84, CI, Flash	0.60	0.75	2.25	3.75
☐ 195, Feb 84, JA, I... Vampire	0.60	0.75	2.25	3.75
☐ 196, Mar 84, JA, Ragman	0.60	0.75	2.25	3.75
☐ 197, Apr 84, JS, Catwoman	0.60	0.75	2.25	3.75
☐ 198, May 84, Karate Kid	0.60	0.75	2.25	3.75
☐ 199, Jun 84, RA, Spectre	0.60	0.75	2.25	3.75
☐ 200, Jul 84, JA, giant, 1:Outsiders	1.50	1.20	3.60	6.00

BRAVE AND THE BOLD (beginning 1991)

	ORIG.	GOOD	FINE	N-MINT
☐ 1, Dec 91, Green Arrow, Question, Butcher	1.75	0.35	1.05	1.75
☐ 2, Jan 92, Green Arrow, Question, Butcher	1.75	0.35	1.05	1.75
☐ 3, Feb 92, Green Arrow, Question, Butcher	1.75	0.35	1.05	1.75
☐ 4, Mar 92, Green Arrow, Question, Butcher	1.75	0.35	1.05	1.75
☐ 5, May 92, Green Arrow, Question, Butcher	1.75	0.35	1.05	1.75
☐ 6, Jun 92, Green Arrow, Question, Butcher	1.75	0.35	1.05	1.75

	ORIG.	GOOD	FINE	N-MINT

BRAVESTARR IN 3-D
BLACKTHORNE
	ORIG.	GOOD	FINE	N-MINT
1		0.50	1.50	2.50
2		0.50	1.50	2.50

BRAVO FOR ADVENTURE
DRAGON LADY
	ORIG.	GOOD	FINE	N-MINT
1, ATh		1.19	3.57	5.95

BRAVURA PREVIEW BOOK
MALIBU/BRAVURA
	ORIG.	GOOD	FINE	N-MINT
2, Aug 94	1.50	0.30	0.90	1.50

BREAK THE CHAIN
MARVEL MUSIC
	ORIG.	GOOD	FINE	N-MINT
1, 94, polybagged with KRS-1 cassette tape				
....	6.99	1.40	4.19	6.99

BREAK-THRU
MALIBU
	ORIG.	GOOD	FINE	N-MINT
1, GP	2.50	0.50	1.50	2.50
1, Ultra Ltd., foil logo	2.50	0.50	1.50	2.50
2, Jan 94	2.50	0.50	1.50	2.50

BREAKNECK BLVD.
MOTION
	ORIG.	GOOD	FINE	N-MINT
0, b&w	2.50	0.50	1.50	2.50
1, Jul 94, b&w;1:Blu-J	2.50	0.50	1.50	2.50
2, Sep 94, b&w	2.50	0.50	1.50	2.50
SLAVE LABOR
	ORIG.	GOOD	FINE	N-MINT
1, Jul 95, b&w..............	2.95	0.59	1.77	2.95
2, 95, b&w	2.95	0.59	1.77	2.95

BREATHTAKER
DC
	ORIG.	GOOD	FINE	N-MINT
1, Jul 90.....................		0.99	2.97	4.95
2, Aug 90		0.99	2.97	4.95
3, Sep 90.....................		0.99	2.97	4.95
4, Oct 90		0.99	2.97	4.95

BREED (really 'Breed)
MALIBU/BRAVURA
	ORIG.	GOOD	FINE	N-MINT
1, Jan 94, JSn	2.50	0.60	1.80	3.00
2, Feb 94	2.50	0.50	1.50	2.50
3, Mar 94	2.50	0.50	1.50	2.50
4, Apr 94	2.50	0.50	1.50	2.50
5, May 94	2.50	0.50	1.50	2.50
6, Jun 94......................	2.50	0.50	1.50	2.50

BREED II (really 'Breed) (mini-series)
	ORIG.	GOOD	FINE	N-MINT
1, Nov 94	2.95	0.59	1.77	2.95

BRIAN BOLLAND'S BLACK BOOK
ECLIPSE
	ORIG.	GOOD	FINE	N-MINT
1, BB		0.35	1.05	1.75

BRICKMAN
HARRIER
	ORIG.	GOOD	FINE	N-MINT
1		0.39	1.17	1.95

BRIGADE (mini-series)
IMAGE
	ORIG.	GOOD	FINE	N-MINT
1, RL(c)........................	1.00	3.00	5.00	
1, gold edition	1.95	5.00	15.00	25.00
2, RL(c)........................		0.70	2.10	3.50
3, RL(c)........................	1.95	0.39	1.17	1.95
4, flipside of *Youngblood* #5				
....	2.50	0.50	1.50	2.50

BRIGADE (ongoing)
	ORIG.	GOOD	FINE	N-MINT
0	1.95	0.39	1.17	1.95
1	1.95	0.39	1.17	1.95
2, Jun 93, foil cover	2.95	0.59	1.77	2.95
2, A;alternate cover	2.95	0.59	1.77	2.95
3, Sep 93.....................	1.95	0.39	1.17	1.95
4, Oct 93	1.95	0.39	1.17	1.95
5, Nov 93	1.95	0.39	1.17	1.95
6	1.95	0.39	1.17	1.95
7, Feb 94.....................	1.95	0.39	1.17	1.95
8, Mar 94, Extreme Prejudice				
....	1.95	0.50	1.50	2.50

	ORIG.	GOOD	FINE	N-MINT
9, Apr 94, Extreme Prejudice				
....	1.95	0.50	1.50	2.50
10, Jun 94	1.95	0.50	1.50	2.50
11, Aug 94	2.50	0.50	1.50	2.50
12, Sep 94	2.50	0.50	1.50	2.50
13, Oct 94	1.95	0.39	1.17	1.95
14, Nov 94	1.95	0.39	1.17	1.95
15, Dec 94	2.50	0.50	1.50	2.50
16, Jan 95, polybagged with trading card				
....	2.50	0.50	1.50	2.50
17, Feb 95, Extreme Sacrifice Aftermath				
....	2.50	0.50	1.50	2.50
18, Mar 95	2.50	0.50	1.50	2.50
18, Mar 95, alternate cover				
....	2.50	0.50	1.50	2.50
19, Apr 95, A:Glory	2.50	0.50	1.50	2.50
20, May 95...................	2.50	0.50	1.50	2.50
21, Jun 95, Funeral of Shadowhawk				
....	2.50	0.50	1.50	2.50
22, Jul 95....................	2.50	0.50	1.50	2.50
25, May 94, Images of Tomorrow				
....	1.95	0.39	1.17	1.95

BRIGADE SOURCEBOOK
	ORIG.	GOOD	FINE	N-MINT
1, Aug 94.....................	2.95	0.59	1.77	2.95

BRIK HAUSS
BLACKTHORNE
	ORIG.	GOOD	FINE	N-MINT
1		0.35	1.05	1.75

BRIT-CIT BABES
FLEETWAY/QUALITY
	ORIG.	GOOD	FINE	N-MINT
0, nn, BB(c)	5.95	1.19	3.57	5.95

BROADWAY VIDEO
SPECIAL COLLECTORS EDITION
BROADWAY
	ORIG.	GOOD	FINE	N-MINT
1, Dec 95, cardstock cover;promotional giveaway;				
1150 copies printed				

BROID
ETERNITY
	ORIG.	GOOD	FINE	N-MINT
1, b&w..........................		0.55	1.65	2.75
2		0.45	1.35	2.25
3		0.45	1.35	2.25
4		0.45	1.35	2.25

BRONX
	ORIG.	GOOD	FINE	N-MINT
1, b&w..........................		0.50	1.50	2.50
2, b&w..........................		0.50	1.50	2.50
3, b&w..........................		0.50	1.50	2.50

BROOKLYN DREAMS (mini-series)
DC/PARADOX
	ORIG.	GOOD	FINE	N-MINT
1, 94, digest..................	4.95	0.99	2.97	4.95
2, 95, digest..................	4.95	0.99	2.97	4.95
3, 95, digest..................	4.95	0.99	2.97	4.95
4, 95, digest..................	4.95	0.99	2.97	4.95

BROTHER MAN
BIG CITY
	ORIG.	GOOD	FINE	N-MINT
6	2.00	0.40	1.20	2.00
7	2.00	0.40	1.20	2.00
8	2.00	0.40	1.20	2.00

BROTHER POWER, THE GEEK
DC
	ORIG.	GOOD	FINE	N-MINT
1		10.00	30.00	50.00
2		8.00	24.00	40.00

BROTHERMAN
BIG CITY
	ORIG.	GOOD	FINE	N-MINT
1, b&w..........................		0.40	1.20	2.00
2, b&w..........................		0.40	1.20	2.00
3, b&w..........................		0.40	1.20	2.00
4, b&w..........................		0.40	1.20	2.00
5, b&w..........................		0.40	1.20	2.00
6, b&w..........................		0.40	1.20	2.00

	ORIG.	GOOD	FINE	N-MINT

BRU-HED
SCHISM
❑ 1, ashcan, b&w 2.50	0.50	1.50	2.50

BRU-HED (mini-series)
❑ 1, 94 .... 2.50	0.50	1.50	2.50
❑ 3, 95, b&w 2.50	0.50	1.50	2.50

BRU-HED'S BREATHTAKING BEAUTIES
❑ 1, 95, b&w pin-ups;cardstock cover			
.... 2.50	0.50	1.50	2.50

BRUCE LEE
MALIBU
❑ 1, Jul 94 .... 2.95	0.59	1.77	2.95
❑ 2, Aug 94 .... 2.95	0.59	1.77	2.95
❑ 3, Sep 94 .... 2.95	0.59	1.77	2.95
❑ 4, Oct 94 .... 2.95	0.59	1.77	2.95
❑ 5, Nov 94 .... 2.95	0.59	1.77	2.95
❑ 6, Dec 94 .... 2.95	0.59	1.77	2.95

BRUCE WAYNE: AGENT OF S.H.I.E.L.D.
MARVEL/AMALGAM
❑ 1, Apr 96, one-shot 1.95	0.39	1.17	1.95

BRUISER
ANTHEM
❑ 1 .... 2.45	0.49	1.47	2.45

BRUNNER'S BEAUTIES
EROS
❑ 0, nn, pin-ups, b&w, adult			
.... 4.95	0.99	2.97	4.95

BRUTE FORCE
MARVEL
❑ 1, Aug 90, O:Brute Force			
.... 1.00	0.20	0.60	1.00
❑ 2, Sep 90 .... 1.00	0.20	0.60	1.00
❑ 3, Oct 90 .... 1.00	0.20	0.60	1.00
❑ 4, Nov 90 .... 1.00	0.20	0.60	1.00

BRUTE, THE
ATLAS/ SEABOARD
❑ 1, O:Brute	0.20	0.60	1.00

ATLAS/SEABOARD
❑ 2, Apr 75 .... 0.25	0.20	0.60	1.00
❑ 3, Jul 75 .... 0.25	0.20	0.60	1.00

BUBBLE ECONOMY
EXPRESS/ENTITY
❑ 0, Feb 95, b&w, enhanced cardstock cover (Entity Illustrated Novella #6) 2.95	0.59	1.77	2.95

BUBBLEGUM CRISIS: GRAND MAL (mini-series)
DARK HORSE
❑ 1, Mar 94 .... 2.50	0.50	1.50	2.50
❑ 2, Apr 94 .... 2.50	0.50	1.50	2.50
❑ 3, May 94 .... 2.50	0.50	1.50	2.50
❑ 4, Jun 94 .... 2.50	0.50	1.50	2.50

BUCE N GAR
RAK
❑ 1, b&w	0.35	1.05	1.75
❑ 2, b&w	0.35	1.05	1.75
❑ 3, b&w	0.35	1.05	1.75

BUCK GODOT: ZAP GUN FOR HIRE
PALLIARD PRESS
❑ 1, Foglio, b&w 2.95	0.59	1.77	2.95
❑ 3, Apr 94, b&w 2.95	0.59	1.77	2.95
❑ 4, Aug 94, b&w 2.95	0.59	1.77	2.95
❑ 5, 95, b&w 2.95	0.59	1.77	2.95
❑ 6, 95, b&w 2.95	0.59	1.77	2.95

BUCK ROGERS
MARVEL
❑ 0, (giant movie edition) .. 1.50	0.30	0.90	1.50

BUCK ROGERS COMICS MODULE
TSR INC.
❑ 1	0.59	1.77	2.95

	ORIG.	GOOD	FINE	N-MINT
❑ 2	0.59	1.77	2.95
❑ 3	0.59	1.77	2.95
❑ 4	0.59	1.77	2.95
❑ 5, Black Barney (#5 misnumbered #6)			
....	0.59	1.77	2.95
❑ 6	0.59	1.77	2.95
❑ 7	0.59	1.77	2.95
❑ 8	0.59	1.77	2.95
❑ 9	0.59	1.77	2.95

BUCKAROO BANZAI
MARVEL
❑ 1, Dec 84, movie 0.75	0.20	0.60	1.00
❑ 2, Feb 85, movie 0.75	0.20	0.60	1.00

BUCKY O'HARE
CONTINUITY
❑ 1, MG	0.40	1.20	2.00
❑ 2, MG	0.40	1.20	2.00
❑ 3, MG	0.40	1.20	2.00
❑ 4, MG	0.40	1.20	2.00
❑ 5, MG	0.40	1.20	2.00

BUFFALO WINGS
ANTARCTIC
❑ 1, Sep 93, b&w 2.50	0.50	1.50	2.50
❑ 2, Nov 93, b&w 2.75	0.55	1.65	2.75

BUG
PLANET-X
❑ 1	0.30	0.90	1.50

BUG & STUMP
AAARGH!
❑ 1, b&w, Australian 2.95	0.59	1.77	2.95
❑ 2, b&w, Australian 2.95	0.59	1.77	2.95

BUG HUNTERS, THE
TRIDENT
❑ 0, nn, b&w 5.95	1.19	3.57	5.95

BUGHOUSE
CAT-HEAD
❑ 1, 94, b&w 2.95	0.59	1.77	2.95
❑ 3, Jun 95, b&w 2.50	0.50	1.50	2.50

BUGS BUNNY
DC
❑ 1	0.20	0.60	1.00
❑ 2	0.20	0.60	1.00
❑ 3	0.20	0.60	1.00

BUGS BUNNY & THE LOONEY TUNES MAGAZINE
(was Looney Tunes Magazine)
❑ 11 .... 1.95	0.39	1.17	1.95
❑ 12 .... 1.95	0.39	1.17	1.95
❑ 13 .... 1.95	0.39	1.17	1.95
❑ 14 .... 1.95	0.39	1.17	1.95
❑ 15 .... 1.95	0.39	1.17	1.95
❑ 16, trading cards 1.95	0.39	1.17	1.95
❑ 17, Spr 94 .... 1.95	0.39	1.17	1.95

BUGS BUNNY MONTHLY, THE
❑ 1 .... 1.95	0.39	1.17	1.95
❑ 2 .... 1.95	0.39	1.17	1.95
❑ 3 .... 1.95	0.39	1.17	1.95

BULLET CROW, FOWL OF FORTUNE
ECLIPSE
❑ 1, b&w	0.40	1.20	2.00
❑ 2, b&w	0.40	1.20	2.00

BULLETS AND BRACELETS
MARVEL/AMALGAM
❑ 1, Apr 96 .... 1.95	0.39	1.17	1.95

BULLWINKLE & ROCKY
BLACKTHORNE
❑ 1	0.50	1.50	2.50
❑ 2	0.50	1.50	2.50
❑ 3	0.50	1.50	2.50

	ORIG.	GOOD	FINE	N-MINT

BULLWINKLE & ROCKY 3-D
	ORIG.	GOOD	FINE	N-MINT
☐ 1, Mar 87	2.50	0.50	1.50	2.50

BULLWINKLE AND ROCKY
STAR
	ORIG.	GOOD	FINE	N-MINT
☐ 1	1.00	0.20	0.60	1.00
☐ 2, (becomes Marvel comic)	1.00	0.20	0.60	1.00

BULLWINKLE AND ROCKY (was Star Comic)
MARVEL
	ORIG.	GOOD	FINE	N-MINT
☐ 3	1.00	0.20	0.60	1.00
☐ 4	1.00	0.20	0.60	1.00
☐ 5	1.00	0.20	0.60	1.00
☐ 6	1.00	0.20	0.60	1.00
☐ 7	1.00	0.20	0.60	1.00
☐ 8	1.00	0.20	0.60	1.00
☐ 9	1.00	0.20	0.60	1.00

BULLWINKLE FOR PRESIDENT IN 3-D
BLACKTHORNE
	GOOD	FINE	N-MINT
☐ 1	0.50	1.50	2.50

BURGLAR BILL
TRIDENT
	GOOD	FINE	N-MINT
☐ 1, b&w	0.45	1.35	2.25

BURIED TREASURE
PURE IMAGINATION
	GOOD	FINE	N-MINT
☐ 1, b&w reprints	1.19	3.57	5.95
☐ 2, b&w reprints	1.19	3.57	5.95
☐ 3, b&w reprints (moves to Caliber)	1.19	3.57	5.95

BURIED TREASURE (was Pure Imagination) (Volume 2)
CALIBER
	GOOD	FINE	N-MINT
☐ 1, FF, AW reprints, b&w	0.50	1.50	2.50
☐ 2, reprints Jack Cole, WW, JO, JKu, S&K	0.50	1.50	2.50
☐ 3, reprints Frankenstein, WW, FF	0.50	1.50	2.50
☐ 4, FF	0.50	1.50	2.50

BURRITO
ACCENT!
	ORIG.	GOOD	FINE	N-MINT
☐ 1, Jan 95, b&w	2.50	0.50	1.50	2.50
☐ 2, Apr 95, b&w	2.50	0.50	1.50	2.50
☐ 3, Jul 95, b&w	2.75	0.55	1.65	2.75
☐ 4, Nov 95, b&w	2.75	0.55	1.65	2.75

BUSHIDO
ETERNITY
	GOOD	FINE	N-MINT
☐ 1, b&w	0.39	1.17	1.95
☐ 2, b&w	0.39	1.17	1.95
☐ 3, b&w	0.39	1.17	1.95
☐ 4, b&w	0.39	1.17	1.95

BUSHIDO BLADE OF ZATOICHI WALRUS
SOLSON
	GOOD	FINE	N-MINT
☐ 1	0.40	1.20	2.00

BUSTER
CRISIS
	ORIG.	GOOD	FINE	N-MINT
☐ 1, b&w	2.50	0.50	1.50	2.50
☐ 2, b&w	2.50	0.50	1.50	2.50

BUSTER THE AMAZING BEAR
URSUS STUDIOS
	ORIG.	GOOD	FINE	N-MINT
☐ 5, Nov 94, b&w	2.50	0.50	1.50	2.50

BUTCHER, THE
DC
	GOOD	FINE	N-MINT
☐ 1, May 90	0.50	1.50	2.50
☐ 2, Jun 90	0.50	1.50	2.50
☐ 3, Jul 90	0.50	1.50	2.50
☐ 4, Aug 90	0.50	1.50	2.50
☐ 5, Sep 90	0.50	1.50	2.50

BUTT BISCUIT
FANTAGRAPHICS
	GOOD	FINE	N-MINT
☐ 1, b&w	0.45	1.35	2.25
☐ 2, b&w	0.45	1.35	2.25
☐ 3, b&w	0.45	1.35	2.25

BUTTERSCOTCH
EROS COMIX
	GOOD	FINE	N-MINT
☐ 1, adult, b&w	0.50	1.50	2.50
☐ 2, adult, b&w	0.50	1.50	2.50
☐ 3, adult, b&w	0.50	1.50	2.50

BUZ SAWYER QUARTERLY
DRAGON LADY
	GOOD	FINE	N-MINT
☐ 1	1.19	3.57	5.95
☐ 2	1.19	3.57	5.95
☐ 3	1.19	3.57	5.95

BUZZ
KITCHEN SINK
	GOOD	FINE	N-MINT
☐ 1, b&w	0.59	1.77	2.95
☐ 2, b&w	0.59	1.77	2.95
☐ 3, b&w	0.59	1.77	2.95

BUZZARD
CAT-HEAD
	ORIG.	GOOD	FINE	N-MINT
☐ 1, b&w		0.55	1.65	2.75
☐ 2, b&w		0.55	1.65	2.75
☐ 3, b&w		0.55	1.65	2.75
☐ 4, b&w		0.55	1.65	2.75
☐ 5, b&w		0.55	1.65	2.75
☐ 7, b&w, adult	2.95	0.59	1.77	2.95
☐ 8, b&w, adult	2.95	0.59	1.77	2.95
☐ 9, b&w, adult	2.95	0.59	1.77	2.95
☐ 10, b&w, adult	2.95	0.59	1.77	2.95
☐ 11, 94, b&w, adult	3.25	0.65	1.95	3.25
☐ 12, 94, b&w, adult	3.25	0.65	1.95	3.25
☐ 13, 95, b&w, adult	3.25	0.65	1.95	3.25
☐ 14, 95, b&w, adult, Mark Martin(c)	3.50	0.70	2.10	3.50

BY BIZARRE HANDS
DARK HORSE
	ORIG.	GOOD	FINE	N-MINT
☐ 1, Apr 94, b&w	2.50	0.50	1.50	2.50
☐ 2, May 94, b&w	2.50	0.50	1.50	2.50
☐ 3, 94, b&w	2.50	0.50	1.50	2.50

BY THE TIME I GET TO WAGGA WAGGA
HARRIER
	GOOD	FINE	N-MINT
☐ 1	0.30	0.90	1.50

Didja know?

Following its release in 1988, the first issue of Howard Chaykin's *Black Kiss* was considered to be in mint condition only if it was sealed in the original plastic with the seam across the front cover. However, the plastic was not archival quality and standards have changed in the past few years to the point where the comic book can be carefully removed from the plastic and stored separately.

By the way, the nine-issue Vortex mini-series has been collected in at least two different ways: *Thick Black Kiss* (a single collection of the series) and *Big Black Kiss* (a three-issue mini-series).

C

	ORIG.	GOOD	FINE	N-MINT

C.O.P.S.
DC

	ORIG.	GOOD	FINE	N-MINT
1		0.30	0.90	1.50
2		0.20	0.60	1.00
3		0.20	0.60	1.00
4		0.20	0.60	1.00
5		0.20	0.60	1.00
6		0.20	0.60	1.00
7		0.20	0.60	1.00
8		0.20	0.60	1.00
9		0.20	0.60	1.00
10		0.20	0.60	1.00
11		0.20	0.60	1.00
12		0.20	0.60	1.00
13		0.20	0.60	1.00
14		0.20	0.60	1.00
15		0.20	0.60	1.00

CABINET OF DR. CALIGARI, THE
MONSTER

	ORIG.	GOOD	FINE	N-MINT
1, b&w, movie		0.45	1.35	2.25
2, b&w		0.45	1.35	2.25
3, b&w		0.45	1.35	2.25
2, b&w, movie adaptation		0.45	1.35	2.25

CABLE (mini-series)
MARVEL

	ORIG.	GOOD	FINE	N-MINT
1	2.50	1.20	3.60	6.00
2	2.50	0.80	2.40	4.00
3	2.00	0.40	1.20	2.00

CABLE (ongoing series, 1993-)

	ORIG.	GOOD	FINE	N-MINT
1, foil cover	3.50	1.20	3.60	6.00
2	2.00	0.60	1.80	3.00
3	2.00	0.40	1.20	2.00
4	2.00	0.40	1.20	2.00
5	2.00	0.40	1.20	2.00
6	2.00	0.40	1.20	2.00
7	2.00	0.40	1.20	2.00
8	2.00	0.40	1.20	2.00
9	2.00	0.40	1.20	2.00
10	2.00	0.40	1.20	2.00
11, May 94	2.00	0.40	1.20	2.00
12, Jun 94	2.00	0.40	1.20	2.00
13, Jul 94	2.00	0.40	1.20	2.00
14, Aug 94	2.00	0.40	1.20	2.00
15, Sep 94, Ceremonies of Light	2.00	0.40	1.20	2.00
16, Oct 94	2.00	0.40	1.20	2.00
16, Oct 94, enhanced cover	3.50	0.80	2.40	4.00
17, Nov 94, deluxe	1.95	0.39	1.17	1.95
17, Nov 94	1.50	0.30	0.90	1.50
18, Dec 94, deluxe	1.95	0.39	1.17	1.95
18, Dec 94	1.50	0.30	0.90	1.50
19, Jan 95, deluxe	1.95	0.39	1.17	1.95
19, Jan 95	1.50	0.30	0.90	1.50
20, Feb 95, deluxe	1.95	0.39	1.17	1.95
20, Feb 95	1.50	0.30	0.90	1.50
21, Jul 95	1.95	0.39	1.17	1.95
22, Aug 95	1.95	0.39	1.17	1.95
23, Sep 95	1.95	0.39	1.17	1.95
24, Oct 95, no issue number on cover	1.95	0.39	1.17	1.95
25, Nov 95, enhanced wraparound fold-out cardstock cover	3.95	0.79	2.37	3.95
26, Dec 95	1.95	0.39	1.17	1.95
28, Feb 96	1.95	0.39	1.17	1.95
29, Mar 96	1.95	0.39	1.17	1.95
30, Apr 96, A:X-Man	1.95	0.39	1.17	1.95
31, May 96, V:X-Man	1.95	0.39	1.17	1.95
32, Jun 96	1.95	0.39	1.17	1.95
33, Jul 96	1.95	0.39	1.17	1.95

CABLE TV
PARODY

	ORIG.	GOOD	FINE	N-MINT
1, b&w	2.50	0.50	1.50	2.50

CADAVERA
MONSTER

	ORIG.	GOOD	FINE	N-MINT
1, b&w		0.39	1.17	1.95
2, b&w		0.39	1.17	1.95

CADILLACS & DINOSAURS
EPIC

	ORIG.	GOOD	FINE	N-MINT
1	2.50	0.50	1.50	2.50
2	2.50	0.50	1.50	2.50
3	2.50	0.50	1.50	2.50
4	2.50	0.50	1.50	2.50
5	2.50	0.50	1.50	2.50
6	2.50	0.50	1.50	2.50

TOPPS

	ORIG.	GOOD	FINE	N-MINT
1, DG	2.50	0.50	1.50	2.50
1, DG, foil cover	2.95	0.59	1.77	2.95
2, DG	2.50	0.50	1.50	2.50
3, Apr 94	2.50	0.50	1.50	2.50
3, Apr 94, with poster	2.50	0.50	1.50	2.50

CADILLACS AND DINOSAURS 3-D
KITCHEN SINK

	ORIG.	GOOD	FINE	N-MINT
1, Jul 82	3.95	0.79	2.37	3.95

CAGE
MARVEL

	ORIG.	GOOD	FINE	N-MINT
1, Apr 92	1.50	0.30	0.90	1.50
2, May 92	1.25	0.25	0.75	1.25
3, Punisher	1.25	0.25	0.75	1.25
4, Punisher	1.25	0.25	0.75	1.25
5	1.25	0.25	0.75	1.25
6	1.25	0.25	0.75	1.25
7	1.25	0.25	0.75	1.25
8	1.25	0.25	0.75	1.25
9	1.25	0.25	0.75	1.25
10	1.25	0.25	0.75	1.25
11	1.25	0.25	0.75	1.25
12, Iron Fist	1.75	0.35	1.05	1.75
13	1.25	0.25	0.75	1.25
14	1.25	0.25	0.75	1.25
15	1.25	0.25	0.75	1.25
16	1.25	0.25	0.75	1.25
17	1.25	0.25	0.75	1.25
18	1.25	0.25	0.75	1.25
19	1.25	0.25	0.75	1.25
20	1.25	0.25	0.75	1.25

CAGES
KITCHEN SINK

	ORIG.	GOOD	FINE	N-MINT
8	3.95	0.79	2.37	3.95

TUNDRA

	ORIG.	GOOD	FINE	N-MINT
1, Dave McKean, b&w		0.70	2.10	3.50
2, Dave McKean, b&w		0.70	2.10	3.50
3, Dave McKean, b&w		0.70	2.10	3.50
4	3.95	0.79	2.37	3.95
5	3.95	0.79	2.37	3.95
6	3.95	0.79	2.37	3.95
7	3.95	0.79	2.37	3.95

CAIN
HARRIS

	ORIG.	GOOD	FINE	N-MINT
1, 93, trading card	2.95	0.80	2.40	4.00
2, BSt(c), two alternate covers	2.95	0.59	1.77	2.95

CALCULATED RISK
GENESIS

	ORIG.	GOOD	FINE	N-MINT
1, b&w		0.60	1.80	3.00

CALIBER CHRISTMAS, A
CALIBER

	ORIG.	GOOD	FINE	N-MINT
1, Crow, sampler	3.95	12.00	36.00	60.00

	ORIG.	GOOD	FINE	N-MINT
CALIBER PRESENTS				
1, 89, Crow, b&w	1.95	25.00	75.00	125.00
2, b&w	1.95	0.39	1.17	1.95
3, b&w	1.95	0.39	1.17	1.95
4, b&w	1.95	0.39	1.17	1.95
5, b&w	1.95	0.39	1.17	1.95
6, b&w	1.95	0.39	1.17	1.95
7, b&w	1.95	0.39	1.17	1.95
8, b&w	1.95	0.39	1.17	1.95
9	2.50	0.50	1.50	2.50
10	2.95	0.59	1.77	2.95
11, misnumbered #12	2.95	0.59	1.77	2.95
12	2.95	0.59	1.77	2.95
13	2.95	0.59	1.77	2.95
14	2.95	0.59	1.77	2.95
15, 64 pages	3.50	0.70	2.10	3.50
16, 64 pages	3.50	0.70	2.10	3.50
17, 64 pages	3.50	0.70	2.10	3.50
18, 64 pages	3.50	0.70	2.10	3.50
19, 64 pages	3.50	0.70	2.10	3.50
20, 64 pages	3.50	0.70	2.10	3.50
21, 64 pages	3.50	0.70	2.10	3.50
22, 64 pages	3.50	0.70	2.10	3.50
23, 64 pages	3.50	0.70	2.10	3.50
24, 64 pages	3.50	0.70	2.10	3.50
CALIBER PRESENTS: CINDERELLA ON FIRE				
0, 94, nn;b&w	2.95	0.59	1.77	2.95
CALIBER PRESENTS: GENERATOR COMICS				
0, 94, nn;b&w	2.95	0.59	1.77	2.95
CALIBER PRESENTS: HYBRID STORIES				
0, nn, b&w	2.95	0.59	1.77	2.95
CALIBER PRESENTS: PETIT MAL				
0, nn;b&w	2.95	0.59	1.77	2.95
CALIBER PRESENTS: ROMANTIC TALES				
0, 95, nn;b&w	2.95	0.59	1.77	2.95
CALIBER PRESENTS: SEPULCHER OPUS				
0, 93, nn;b&w	2.95	0.59	1.77	2.95
CALIBER PRESENTS: SUB-ATOMIC SHOCK				
0, nn;b&w	2.95	0.59	1.77	2.95
CALIBRATIONS				
1, b&w	2.95	0.59	1.77	2.95
CALIFORNIA GIRLS				
ECLIPSE				
1, b&w		0.40	1.20	2.00
2, b&w		0.40	1.20	2.00
3, b&w		0.40	1.20	2.00
4, b&w		0.40	1.20	2.00
5, b&w		0.40	1.20	2.00
6, b&w		0.40	1.20	2.00
7, b&w		0.40	1.20	2.00
8, b&w		0.40	1.20	2.00
CALIFORNIA RAISINS IN 3-D				
BLACKTHORNE				
1		0.50	1.50	2.50
2		0.50	1.50	2.50
3		0.50	1.50	2.50
4		0.50	1.50	2.50
5		0.50	1.50	2.50
CALIGARI 2050				
MONSTER				
1, b&w		0.45	1.35	2.25
2, b&w		0.45	1.35	2.25
3, b&w		0.45	1.35	2.25
CAMELOT 3000				
DC				
1, Dec 82, BB, O:Arthur, Merlin	1.00	0.60	1.80	3.00
2, Jan 83, BB	1.00	0.50	1.50	2.50

	ORIG.	GOOD	FINE	N-MINT
3, Feb 83, BB	1.00	0.50	1.50	2.50
4, Mar 83, BB	1.00	0.30	0.90	1.50
5, Apr 83, BB	1.00	0.30	0.90	1.50
6, Jul 83, BB	1.00	0.30	0.90	1.50
7, Aug 83, BB	1.00	0.30	0.90	1.50
8, Sep 83, BB	1.00	0.30	0.90	1.50
9, Dec 83, BB	1.00	0.30	0.90	1.50
10, Mar 83, BB	1.00	0.30	0.90	1.50
11, Jul 84, BB	1.00	0.30	0.90	1.50
12, Apr 85, BB	1.00	0.50	1.50	2.50
CAMELOT ETERNAL				
CALIBER				
1, b&w	2.50	0.50	1.50	2.50
2, b&w	2.50	0.50	1.50	2.50
3, b&w	2.50	0.50	1.50	2.50
4, b&w	2.50	0.50	1.50	2.50
5, b&w	2.50	0.50	1.50	2.50
6, b&w	2.50	0.50	1.50	2.50
7, b&w	2.50	0.50	1.50	2.50
8, b&w	2.50	0.50	1.50	2.50
CAMP CANDY				
MARVEL				
1	1.00	0.20	0.60	1.00
2	1.00	0.20	0.60	1.00
3	1.00	0.20	0.60	1.00
4	1.00	0.20	0.60	1.00
5	1.00	0.20	0.60	1.00
6	1.00	0.20	0.60	1.00
7	1.00	0.20	0.60	1.00
CANADIAN COMICS CAVALCADE				
ARTWORX				
1, Dan Day, Peter Hsu, Chester Brown, Arn Saba, Dean Motter, Ty Templeton, b&w		0.40	1.20	2.00
CANADIAN NINJA				
QUEBEC				
1		0.30	0.90	1.50
CANADIAN ROCK SPECIAL				
REVOLUTIONARY				
1, Apr 94, b&w, Rush	2.50	0.50	1.50	2.50
CANDIDE REVEALED				
EROS COMIX				
1, adult, b&w		0.45	1.35	2.25
CANNIBALIS				
RAGING RHINO				
1, adult, b&w	2.95	0.59	1.77	2.95
CANNON				
EROS COMIX				
1, Feb 91, WW b&w	2.75	0.55	1.65	2.75
2, Mar 91, WW b&w	2.75	0.55	1.65	2.75
3, Apr 91, WW	2.75	0.59	1.77	2.95
4, May 91, WW	2.75	0.59	1.77	2.95
5, Jun 91, WW	2.75	0.59	1.77	2.95
6, Jul 91, WW	2.75	0.59	1.77	2.95
7, Aug 91, WW	2.75	0.59	1.77	2.95
8, Sep 91, WW	2.95	0.59	1.77	2.95
CAP'N OATMEAL				
ALL AMERICAN				
1, b&w		0.45	1.35	2.25
CAP'N QUICK & A FOOZLE				
ECLIPSE				
1, Jul 84, MR		0.30	0.90	1.50
2, Mar 85, MR (becomes *The Foozle*)		0.30	0.90	1.50
CAPE CITY				
DIMENSION X				
1, b&w	2.75	0.55	1.65	2.75
2, b&w	2.75	0.55	1.65	2.75

	ORIG.	GOOD	FINE	N-MINT

CAPT. HOLO AND HIS ADVENTURES IN THE HOLOGRAPHIC DIMENSION IN 3-D
BLACKTHORNE
	ORIG.	GOOD	FINE	N-MINT
1, hologram cover............		0.50	1.50	2.50

CAPT. SAVAGE (was Captain Savage)
MARVEL
15, Jul 69, DAy	0.12	0.70	2.10	3.50
16, Sep 69, DAy.............	0.12	0.70	2.10	3.50
17, Nov 69, DAy.............	0.12	0.70	2.10	3.50
18, Jan 70, DAy.............	0.12	0.70	2.10	3.50
19, Mar 70, DAy ;final issue				
....	0.12	0.70	2.10	3.50

CAPT. SAVAGE AND HIS LEATHERNECK RAIDERS
1, Jan 68, DAy; O:Captain Savage and his Leatherneck Raiders........................	0.12	3.60	10.80	18.00
2, Mar 68, DAy; V:Baron Strucker				
....	0.12	2.40	7.20	12.00
3, May 68, DAy; V:Baron Strucker and Hydra				
....	0.12	1.40	4.20	7.00
4, Jul 68, DAy; V:Baron Strucker				
....	0.12	1.40	4.20	7.00
5, Aug 68, DAy	0.12	1.40	4.20	7.00
6, Sep 68, DAy; A:Izzy Cohen				
....	0.12	1.00	3.00	5.00
7, Oct 68, DAy; A: Ben Grimm				
....	0.12	1.60	4.80	8.00
8, Nov 68, DAy; (becomes *Captain Savage*)				
....	0.12	1.00	3.00	5.00

CAPT. STORM
DC
1, Jun 64......................	0.12	3.60	10.80	18.00
2, Aug 64	0.12	2.00	6.00	10.00
3	0.12	2.00	6.00	10.00
4	0.12	2.00	6.00	10.00
5	0.12	2.00	6.00	10.00
6	0.12	2.00	6.00	10.00
7	0.12	2.00	6.00	10.00
8	0.12	2.00	6.00	10.00
9	0.12	2.00	6.00	10.00
10	0.12	2.00	6.00	10.00
11	0.12	2.00	6.00	10.00
12, Apr 66	0.12	2.00	6.00	10.00
13	0.12	2.00	6.00	10.00
14	0.12	2.00	6.00	10.00
15	0.12	2.00	6.00	10.00
16	0.12	2.00	6.00	10.00
17	0.12	2.00	6.00	10.00
18	0.12	2.00	6.00	10.00

CAPT. VICTORY SPECIAL
PACIFIC
| 1 .... | | 0.30 | 0.90 | 1.50 |

CAPTAIN ACTION
DC
1, Nov 68, WW, O:Capt. Action				
....	0.12	7.20	21.60	36.00
2, Jan 69, WW,GK....	0.12	5.00	15.00	25.00
3, Mar 69, WW,GK.........	0.12	5.00	15.00	25.00
4, May 69......................	0.12	4.40	13.20	22.00
5, Jul 69, WW,GK...........	0.12	4.40	13.20	22.00
KARL ART
| 0, 95, preview of ongoing series | | | | |
| .... | 1.95 | 0.39 | 1.17 | 1.95 |

CAPTAIN AMERICA (was Tales of Suspense)
MARVEL
100, Apr 68, JK, A:Avengers				
....	0.12	68.00	204.00	340.00
101, May 68, JK, I:4th Sleeper				
....	0.12	16.00	48.00	80.00
102, Jun 68, JK.............	0.12	8.00	24.00	40.00
103, Jul 68, JK...............	0.12	8.00	24.00	40.00

	ORIG.	GOOD	FINE	N-MINT
104, Aug 68, JK; V:Red Skull				
....	0.12	8.00	24.00	40.00
105, Sep 68, JK; V:Batroc				
....	0.12	8.00	24.00	40.00
106, Oct 68, JK.............	0.12	8.00	24.00	40.00
107, Nov 68, JK.............	0.12	8.00	24.00	40.00
108, Dec 68, JK.............	0.12	8.00	24.00	40.00
109, Jan 69, JK, O:retold	0.12	15.00	45.00	75.00
110, Feb 69, JSo............	0.12	8.80	26.40	44.00
111, Mar 69, JSo	0.12	8.80	26.40	44.00
112, Apr 69, JK/GT, album				
....	0.12	2.00	6.00	10.00
113, May 69, JSo, Avengers				
....	0.12	8.80	26.40	44.00
114, Jun 69	0.12	2.00	6.00	10.00
115, Jul 69.....................	0.12	2.00	6.00	10.00
116, Aug 69...................	0.15	2.00	6.00	10.00
117, Sep 69, GC/JSt, I:Falcon				
....	0.15	2.40	7.20	12.00
118, Oct 69, GC/JSt, A:Falcon				
....	0.15	1.50	4.50	7.50
119, Nov 69, GC/JSt, A:Falcon				
....	0.15	1.50	4.50	7.50
120, Dec 69, GC/JSt, A:Falcon				
....	0.15	1.50	4.50	7.50
121, Jan 70, GC	0.15	1.20	3.60	6.00
122, Feb 70, GC	0.15	1.20	3.60	6.00
123, Mar 70, GC	0.15	1.20	3.60	6.00
124, Apr 70, GC	0.15	1.20	3.60	6.00
125, May 70, GC.............	0.15	1.20	3.60	6.00
126, Jun 70, GC..............	0.15	1.20	3.60	6.00
127, Jul 70, GC...............	0.15	1.20	3.60	6.00
128, Aug 70, GC.............	0.15	1.20	3.60	6.00
129, Sep 70, GC.............	0.15	1.20	3.60	6.00
130, Oct 70, GC.............	0.15	1.20	3.60	6.00
131, Nov 70, GC	0.15	1.20	3.60	6.00
132, Dec 70, GC.............	0.15	1.20	3.60	6.00
133, Jan 71, GC..............	0.15	1.20	3.60	6.00
134, Feb 71, GC	0.15	1.20	3.60	6.00
135, Mar 71, GC	0.15	1.20	3.60	6.00
136, Apr 71, GC	0.15	1.20	3.60	6.00
137, May 71, GC/BEv, A:SpM				
....	0.15	3.40	10.20	17.00
138, Jun 71, JR, A:SpM..	0.15	3.40	10.20	17.00
139, Jul 71.....................	0.15	1.00	3.00	5.00
140, Aug 71...................	0.15	1.00	3.00	5.00
141, Sep 71...................	0.15	1.00	3.00	5.00
142, Oct 71...................	0.15	1.00	3.00	5.00
143, Nov 71...................	0.25	1.00	3.00	5.00
144, Dec 71	0.20	1.00	3.00	5.00
145, Jan 72...................	0.20	1.00	3.00	5.00
146, Feb 72...................	0.20	1.00	3.00	5.00
147, Mar 72...................	0.20	1.00	3.00	5.00
148, Apr 72...................	0.20	1.00	3.00	5.00
149, May 72...................	0.20	1.00	3.00	5.00
150, Jun 72	0.20	1.00	3.00	5.00
151, Jul 72.....................	0.20	1.00	3.00	5.00
152, Aug 72...................	0.20	1.00	3.00	5.00
153, Sep 72, V:Red Skull				
....	0.20	1.00	3.00	5.00
154, Oct 72...................	0.20	1.60	4.80	8.00
155, Nov 72...................	0.20	1.00	3.00	5.00
156, Dec 72	0.20	1.00	3.00	5.00
157, Jan 73...................	0.20	1.00	3.00	5.00
158, Feb 73...................	0.20	1.00	3.00	5.00
159, Mar 73...................	0.20	1.00	3.00	5.00
160, Apr 73...................	0.20	1.00	3.00	5.00
161, May 73...................	0.20	1.00	3.00	5.00
162, Jun 73	0.20	1.00	3.00	5.00
163, Jul 73.....................	0.20	1.00	3.00	5.00
164, Aug 73...................	0.20	1.00	3.00	5.00
165, Sep 73	0.20	1.00	3.00	5.00

	ORIG.	GOOD	FINE	N-MINT
❑ 166, Oct 73	0.20	1.00	3.00	5.00
❑ 167, Nov 73	0.20	1.00	3.00	5.00
❑ 168, Dec 73	0.20	1.00	3.00	5.00
❑ 169, Jan 74	0.20	1.00	3.00	5.00
❑ 170, Feb 74	0.20	1.00	3.00	5.00
❑ 171, Mar 74	0.20	1.00	3.00	5.00
❑ 172, Apr 74, SB; A:Banshee	0.20	1.60	4.80	8.00
❑ 173, May 74, SB X-Men	0.25	2.00	6.00	10.00
❑ 174, Jun 74, SB X-Men	0.25	2.00	6.00	10.00
❑ 175, Jul 74, SB X-Men	0.25	2.00	6.00	10.00
❑ 176, Aug 74, SB	0.25	1.60	4.80	8.00
❑ 177, Sep 74, SB, recalls origin and quits	0.25	0.80	2.40	4.00
❑ 178, Oct 74, SB	0.25	0.80	2.40	4.00
❑ 179, Nov 74, SB	0.25	0.80	2.40	4.00
❑ 180, Dec 74, SB; O:Nomad	0.25	0.80	2.40	4.00
❑ 181, Jan 75	0.25	0.80	2.40	4.00
❑ 182, Feb 75	0.25	0.80	2.40	4.00
❑ 183, Mar 75	0.25	2.00	6.00	10.00
❑ 184, Apr 75	0.25	0.80	2.40	4.00
❑ 185, May 75	0.25	0.80	2.40	4.00
❑ 186, Jun 75	0.25	0.80	2.40	4.00
❑ 187, Jul 75	0.25	0.80	2.40	4.00
❑ 188, Aug 75	0.25	0.80	2.40	4.00
❑ 189, Sep 75	0.25	0.80	2.40	4.00
❑ 190, Oct 75	0.25	0.80	2.40	4.00
❑ 191, Nov 75	0.25	0.80	2.40	4.00
❑ 192, Dec 75	0.25	0.80	2.40	4.00
❑ 193, Jan 76, JK	0.25	0.80	2.40	4.00
❑ 194, Feb 76, JK	0.25	0.80	2.40	4.00
❑ 195, Mar 76, JK	0.25	0.80	2.40	4.00
❑ 196, Apr 76, JK	0.25	0.80	2.40	4.00
❑ 197, May 76, JK	0.25	0.80	2.40	4.00
❑ 198, Jun 76, JK	0.25	0.80	2.40	4.00
❑ 199, Jul 76, JK	0.25	0.80	2.40	4.00
❑ 200, Aug 76, JK	0.25	1.20	3.60	6.00
❑ 201, Sep 76, JK	0.30	1.00	3.00	5.00
❑ 202, Oct 76, JK	0.30	1.00	3.00	5.00
❑ 203, Nov 76, JK	0.30	1.00	3.00	5.00
❑ 204, Dec 76, JK	0.30	1.00	3.00	5.00
❑ 205, Jan 77, JK	0.30	1.00	3.00	5.00
❑ 206, Feb 77, JK	0.30	1.00	3.00	5.00
❑ 207, Mar 77, JK	0.30	1.00	3.00	5.00
❑ 208, Apr 77, JK	0.30	1.00	3.00	5.00
❑ 209, May 77, JK	0.30	1.00	3.00	5.00
❑ 210, Jun 77, JK	0.30	1.00	3.00	5.00
❑ 211, Jul 77, JK	0.30	1.00	3.00	5.00
❑ 212, Aug 77, JK	0.30	1.00	3.00	5.00
❑ 213, Sep 77, JK	0.30	1.00	3.00	5.00
❑ 214, Oct 77, JK	0.30	1.00	3.00	5.00
❑ 215, Nov 77, GK	0.35	1.00	3.00	5.00
❑ 216, Dec 77, GK	0.35	1.00	3.00	5.00
❑ 217, Jan 78, JB	0.35	1.00	3.00	5.00
❑ 218, Feb 78, SB	0.35	1.00	3.00	5.00
❑ 219, Mar 78, SB	0.35	1.00	3.00	5.00
❑ 220, Apr 78, GK	0.35	1.00	3.00	5.00
❑ 221, May 78, GK	0.35	1.00	3.00	5.00
❑ 222, Jun 78	0.35	1.00	3.00	5.00
❑ 223, Jul 78, JBy	0.35	1.00	3.00	5.00
❑ 224, Aug 78, MZ	0.35	1.00	3.00	5.00
❑ 225, Sep 78	0.35	1.00	3.00	5.00
❑ 226, Oct 78	0.35	1.00	3.00	5.00
❑ 227, Nov 78	0.35	1.00	3.00	5.00
❑ 228, Dec 78	0.35	1.00	3.00	5.00
❑ 229, Jan 79	0.35	1.00	3.00	5.00
❑ 230, Feb 79	0.35	1.00	3.00	5.00
❑ 231, Mar 79	0.35	1.00	3.00	5.00
❑ 232, Apr 79	0.35	1.00	3.00	5.00
❑ 233, May 79	0.40	1.00	3.00	5.00
❑ 234, Jun 79, A:Daredevil	0.40	1.00	3.00	5.00

	ORIG.	GOOD	FINE	N-MINT
❑ 235, Jul 79, A:Daredevil	0.40	1.00	3.00	5.00
❑ 236, Aug 79	0.40	1.00	3.00	5.00
❑ 237, Sep 79	0.40	1.00	3.00	5.00
❑ 238, Oct 79, JBy	0.40	1.00	3.00	5.00
❑ 239, Nov 79, JBy	0.40	1.00	3.00	5.00
❑ 240, Dec 79	0.40	1.00	3.00	5.00
❑ 241, Jan 80, Punisher, FM	0.40	5.20	15.60	26.00
❑ 242, Feb 80	0.40	1.00	3.00	5.00
❑ 243, Mar 80, GP	0.40	1.00	3.00	5.00
❑ 244, Apr 80, FM	0.40	1.00	3.00	5.00
❑ 245, May 80, FM	0.40	1.00	3.00	5.00
❑ 246, Jun 80, GP	0.40	1.00	3.00	5.00
❑ 247, Jul 80, JBy	0.40	1.20	3.60	6.00
❑ 248, Aug 80, JBy	0.40	1.20	3.60	6.00
❑ 249, Sep 80, JBy	0.50	1.20	3.60	6.00
❑ 250, Oct 80, JBy	0.50	1.20	3.60	6.00
❑ 251, Nov 80, JBy	0.50	1.20	3.60	6.00
❑ 252, Dec 80, JBy	0.50	1.20	3.60	6.00
❑ 253, Jan 81, JBy	0.50	1.20	3.60	6.00
❑ 254, Feb 81, JBy	0.50	0.80	2.40	4.00
❑ 255, Mar 81, JBy,FM; 40th anniv.	0.50	1.20	3.60	6.00
❑ 256, Apr 81	0.50	0.80	2.40	4.00
❑ 257, May 81	0.50	0.80	2.40	4.00
❑ 258, Jun 81, MZ	0.50	0.80	2.40	4.00
❑ 259, Jul 81, MZ	0.50	0.80	2.40	4.00
❑ 260, Aug 81	0.50	0.80	2.40	4.00
❑ 261, Sep 81, MZ	0.50	0.80	2.40	4.00
❑ 262, Oct 81, MZ	0.50	0.80	2.40	4.00
❑ 263, Nov 81, MZ	0.50	1.00	3.00	5.00
❑ 264, Dec 81, MZ, X-Men	0.50	1.00	3.00	5.00
❑ 265, Jan 82, MZ	0.60	0.80	2.40	4.00
❑ 266, Feb 82, MZ	0.60	0.80	2.40	4.00
❑ 267, Mar 82, MZ	0.60	0.80	2.40	4.00
❑ 268, Apr 82, MZ	0.60	0.80	2.40	4.00
❑ 269, May 82, I:Team America, MZ	0.60	0.80	2.40	4.00
❑ 270, Jun 82, MZ	0.60	0.80	2.40	4.00
❑ 271, Jul 82	0.60	0.80	2.40	4.00
❑ 272, Aug 82, MZ	0.60	0.80	2.40	4.00
❑ 273, Sep 82, MZ	0.60	0.80	2.40	4.00
❑ 274, Oct 82, MZ	0.60	0.80	2.40	4.00
❑ 275, Nov 82, MZ	0.60	0.80	2.40	4.00
❑ 276, Dec 82, MZ	0.60	0.80	2.40	4.00
❑ 277, Jan 83, MZ	0.60	0.80	2.40	4.00
❑ 278, Feb 83, MZ	0.60	0.80	2.40	4.00
❑ 279, Mar 83, MZ	0.60	0.80	2.40	4.00
❑ 280, Apr 83, MZ	0.60	0.80	2.40	4.00
❑ 281, May 83, MZ	0.60	0.80	2.40	4.00
❑ 282, Jun 83, 1:new Nomad, MZ	0.60	2.40	7.20	12.00
❑ 282, MZ, reprint, silver ink	1.75	0.60	1.80	3.00
❑ 283, Jul 83, MZ	0.60	0.60	1.80	3.00
❑ 284, Aug 83, MZ	0.60	0.60	1.80	3.00
❑ 285, Sep 83, MZ	0.60	0.60	1.80	3.00
❑ 286, Oct 83, MZ	0.60	0.60	1.80	3.00
❑ 287, Nov 83, MZ	0.60	0.60	1.80	3.00
❑ 288, Dec 83, MZ	0.60	0.60	1.80	3.00
❑ 289, Jan 84, MZ	0.60	0.60	1.80	3.00
❑ 290, Feb 84, JBy	0.60	0.60	1.80	3.00
❑ 291, Mar 84, JBy	0.60	0.60	1.80	3.00
❑ 292, Apr 84	0.60	0.60	1.80	3.00
❑ 293, May 84	0.60	0.60	1.80	3.00
❑ 294, Jun 84	0.60	0.60	1.80	3.00
❑ 295, Jul 84	0.60	0.60	1.80	3.00
❑ 296, Aug 84	0.60	0.60	1.80	3.00
❑ 297, Sep 84	0.60	0.60	1.80	3.00
❑ 298, Oct 84	0.60	0.60	1.80	3.00
❑ 299, Nov 84	0.60	0.60	1.80	3.00

	ORIG.	GOOD	FINE	N-MINT
300, Dec 84, anniversary, MZ				
..............................0.60		1.40	4.20	7.00
301, Jan 85 ....0.60		0.40	1.20	2.00
302, Feb 85 ....0.60		0.40	1.20	2.00
303, Mar 85 ....0.60		0.40	1.20	2.00
304, Apr 85 ....0.65		0.40	1.20	2.00
305, May 85 ....0.65		0.40	1.20	2.00
306, Jun 85 ....0.65		0.40	1.20	2.00
307, Jul 85 ....0.65		0.40	1.20	2.00
308, Aug 85, Secret Wars II, JBy				
..............................0.65		0.60	1.80	3.00
309, Sep 85 ....0.65		0.40	1.20	2.00
310, Oct 85 ....0.65		0.40	1.20	2.00
311, Nov 85 ....0.65		0.40	1.20	2.00
312, Dec 85 ....0.65		0.40	1.20	2.00
313, Jan 86, JBy 0.65		0.40	1.20	2.00
314, Feb 86 ....0.75		0.40	1.20	2.00
315, Mar 86 ....0.75		0.40	1.20	2.00
316, Apr 86 ....0.75		0.40	1.20	2.00
317, May 86 ....0.75		0.40	1.20	2.00
318, Jun 86 ....0.75		0.40	1.20	2.00
319, Jul 86 ....0.75		0.40	1.20	2.00
320, Aug 86 ....0.75		0.40	1.20	2.00
321, Sep 86, MZ 0.75		0.40	1.20	2.00
322, Oct 86 ....0.75		0.40	1.20	2.00
323, Nov 86, MZ 0.75		0.40	1.20	2.00
324, Dec 86, MZ 0.75		0.40	1.20	2.00
325, Jan 87, MZ 0.75		0.40	1.20	2.00
326, Feb 87, MZ 0.75		0.40	1.20	2.00
327, Mar 87, MZ 0.75		0.40	1.20	2.00
328, Apr 87, MZ 0,75		0.40	1.20	2.00
329, May 87, MZ............0.75		0.40	1.20	2.00
330, Jun 87, MZ; A:D-Man				
..............................0.75		0.40	1.20	2.00
331, Jul 87, MZ..............0.75		0.40	1.20	2.00
332, Aug 87, CA fired, MZ				
..............................0.75		1.60	4.80	8.00
333, Sep 87, new CA, MZ0.75		1.20	3.60	6.00
334, Oct 87, new Bucky, MZ				
..............................0.75		1.00	3.00	5.00
335, Nov 87 ....0.75		1.00	3.00	5.00
336, Dec 87, MZ 0.75		0.40	1.20	2.00
337, Jan 88, 1:The Captain, MZ				
..............................0.75		0.40	1.20	2.00
338, Feb 88 ....0.75		0.40	1.20	2.00
339, Mar 88, Fall of Mutants				
..............................0.75		0.40	1.20	2.00
340, Apr 88 ....0.75		0.40	1.20	2.00
341, May 88, A:Iron Man0.75		0.40	1.20	2.00
342, Jun 88 ....0.75		0.40	1.20	2.00
343, Jul 88 ....0.75		0.40	1.20	2.00
344, Aug 88, giant.........1.50		0.80	2.40	4.00
345, Sep 88 ....0.75		0.40	1.20	2.00
346, Oct 88 ....0.75		0.40	1.20	2.00
347, Nov 88 ....0.75		0.40	1.20	2.00
348, Dec 88, V:Flag Smasher				
..............................0.75		0.40	1.20	2.00
349, Jan 89 ....0.75		0.40	1.20	2.00
350, Feb 89, double-sized				
..............................1.75		0.80	2.40	4.00
351, Mar 89, A:Nick Fury0.75		0.40	1.20	2.00
352, Apr 89, A:Soviet Super Soldiers				
..............................0.75		0.50	1.50	2.50
353, May 89, A:Soviet Super Soldiers				
..............................0.75		0.50	1.50	2.50
354, Jun 89 ....0.75		0.50	1.50	2.50
355, Jul 89 ....0.75		0.50	1.50	2.50
356, Aug 89 ....0.75		0.50	1.50	2.50
357, Sep 89, "Bloodstone Hunt";CBG Fan Awards parody				
ballot..............................1.00		0.50	1.50	2.50
358, Sep 89..................1.00		0.50	1.50	2.50
359, Oct 89 ....1.00		0.50	1.50	2.50

	ORIG.	GOOD	FINE	N-MINT
360, Oct 89..................1.00		0.50	1.50	2.50
361, Nov 89..................1.00		0.50	1.50	2.50
362, Nov 89..................1.00		0.50	1.50	2.50
363, Nov 89..................1.00		0.50	1.50	2.50
364, Dec 89..................1.00		0.50	1.50	2.50
365, Dec 89, Acts of Vengeance				
..............................1.00		0.40	1.20	2.00
366, Jan 90, Acts of Vengeance				
..............................1.00		0.40	1.20	2.00
367, Feb 90, Acts of Vengeance				
..............................1.00		0.40	1.20	2.00
368, Mar 90..................1.00		0.40	1.20	2.00
369, Apr 90..................1.00		0.40	1.20	2.00
370, May 90..................1.00		0.40	1.20	2.00
371, Jun 90..................1.00		0.40	1.20	2.00
372, Jul 90, Streets of Poison				
..............................1.00		0.30	0.90	1.50
373, Jul 90, Streets of Poison				
..............................1.00		0.30	0.90	1.50
374, Aug 90, Streets of Poison				
..............................1.00		0.30	0.90	1.50
375, Aug 90, Streets of Poison				
..............................1.00		0.30	0.90	1.50
376, Sep 90, Streets of Poison				
..............................1.00		0.30	0.90	1.50
377, Sep 90, Streets of Poison				
..............................1.00		0.30	0.90	1.50
378, Oct 90, Streets of Poison				
..............................1.00		0.30	0.90	1.50
379, Nov 90..................1.00		0.30	0.90	1.50
380, Dec 90..................1.00		0.30	0.90	1.50
381, Jan 91..................1.00		0.30	0.90	1.50
382, Feb 91..................1.00		0.30	0.90	1.50
383, Mar 91, 50th anniv. 2.00		0.70	2.10	3.50
384, Apr 91, Jack Frost...1.00		0.30	0.90	1.50
385, May 91..................1.00		0.30	0.90	1.50
386, Jun 91..................1.00		0.30	0.90	1.50
387, Jul 91, Superia Stratagem				
..............................1.00		0.30	0.90	1.50
388, Jul 91, Superia Stratagem				
..............................1.00		0.30	0.90	1.50
389, Aug 91, Superia Stratagem				
..............................1.00		0.30	0.90	1.50
390, Aug 91, Superia Stratagem				
..............................1.00		0.30	0.90	1.50
391, Sep 91, Superia Stratagem				
..............................1.00		0.30	0.90	1.50
392, Sep 91, Superia Stratagem				
..............................1.00		0.30	0.90	1.50
393, Oct 91..................1.00		0.30	0.90	1.50
394, Nov 91..................1.00		0.30	0.90	1.50
395, Dec 91..................1.00		0.30	0.90	1.50
396, Jan 92..................1.00		0.30	0.90	1.50
397, Feb 92..................1.25		0.30	0.90	1.50
398, Mar 92, Galactic Storm				
..............................1.25		0.30	0.90	1.50
399, Apr 92, Galactic Storm				
..............................1.25		0.30	0.90	1.50
400, May 92, Galactic Storm;reprint of *Avengers* #4;80				
pages..........................2.25		1.00	3.00	5.00
401 ....1.25		0.25	0.75	1.25
402 ....1.25		0.25	0.75	1.25
403 ....1.25		0.25	0.75	1.25
404 ....1.25		0.25	0.75	1.25
405 ....1.25		0.25	0.75	1.25
406 ....1.25		0.25	0.75	1.25
407 ....1.25		0.25	0.75	1.25
408 ....1.25		0.25	0.75	1.25
409 ....1.25		0.25	0.75	1.25
410 ....1.25		0.25	0.75	1.25
411 ....1.25		0.25	0.75	1.25
412 ....1.25		0.25	0.75	1.25

	ORIG.	GOOD	FINE	N-MINT
❑ 413, Mar 93 .... 1.25		0.25	0.75	1.25
❑ 414, Apr 93, Savage Land				
.... 1.25		0.25	0.75	1.25
❑ 415, May 93 .... 1.25		0.25	0.75	1.25
❑ 416, Jun 93 .... 1.25		0.25	0.75	1.25
❑ 417, Jul 93 .... 1.25		0.25	0.75	1.25
❑ 418, Aug 93 .... 1.25		0.25	0.75	1.25
❑ 419, Sep 93 .... 1.25		0.25	0.75	1.25
❑ 420, Oct 93 .... 1.25		0.25	0.75	1.25
❑ 421, Nov 93 .... 1.25		0.25	0.75	1.25
❑ 422, Dec 93 .... 1.25		0.25	0.75	1.25
❑ 423, Jan 94 .... 1.25		0.25	0.75	1.25
❑ 424, Feb 94 .... 1.25		0.25	0.75	1.25
❑ 425, Mar 94, Fighting Chance				
.... 1.75		0.35	1.05	1.75
❑ 425, Mar 94, Fighting Chance, foil cover				
.... 2.95		0.59	1.77	2.95
❑ 426, Apr 94, Fighting Chance				
.... 1.25		0.25	0.75	1.25
❑ 427, May 94 .... 1.50		0.30	0.90	1.50
❑ 428, Jun 94 .... 1.50		0.30	0.90	1.50
❑ 429, Jul 94 .... 1.50		0.30	0.90	1.50
❑ 430, Aug 94 .... 1.50		0.30	0.90	1.50
❑ 431, Sep 94 .... 1.50		0.30	0.90	1.50
❑ 432, Oct 94 .... 1.50		0.30	0.90	1.50
❑ 433, Nov 94 .... 1.50		0.30	0.90	1.50
❑ 434, Dec 94 .... 1.50		0.30	0.90	1.50
❑ 435, Jan 95 .... 1.50		0.30	0.90	1.50
❑ 436, Feb 95 .... 1.50		0.30	0.90	1.50
❑ 437, Mar 95 .... 1.50		0.30	0.90	1.50
❑ 438, Apr 95 .... 1.50		0.30	0.90	1.50
❑ 439, May 95 .... 1.50		0.30	0.90	1.50
❑ 440, Jun 95 .... 1.50		0.30	0.90	1.50
❑ 441, Jul 95, "Taking A.I.M." Part 3 of 4				
.... 1.50		0.30	0.90	1.50
❑ 442, Aug 95 .... 1.50		0.30	0.90	1.50
❑ 443, Sep 95, (becomes *Steve Rogers, Captain America*)				
.... 1.50		0.30	0.90	1.50
❑ 450, Apr 96, (was *Steve Rogers, Captain America*);Cap's American citizenship is revoked				
.... 1.50		0.30	0.90	1.50
❑ 451, May 96 .... 1.50		0.30	0.90	1.50
❑ 452, Jun 96 .... 1.50		0.30	0.90	1.50
❑ 453, Jul 96, Cap's citizenship restored				
.... 1.50		0.30	0.90	1.50

CAPTAIN AMERICA AND THE CAMPBELL KIDS

	ORIG.	GOOD	FINE	N-MINT
❑ 0, giveaway		0.40	1.20	2.00

CAPTAIN AMERICA ANNUAL

	ORIG.	GOOD	FINE	N-MINT
❑ 1, reprint 0.25		1.40	4.20	7.00
❑ 2, reprint 0.25		1.00	3.00	5.00
❑ 3, JK 0.50		0.60	1.80	3.00
❑ 4, JK 0.50		0.60	1.80	3.00
❑ 5, 81 .... 0.75		0.60	1.80	3.00
❑ 6, 82, Four Caps 1.00		0.60	1.80	3.00
❑ 7, 83, Cosmic Cube 1.00		0.60	1.80	3.00
❑ 8, 86, Wolverine 1.25		3.00	9.00	15.00
❑ 9, 90, Terminus Factor ... 2.00		0.40	1.20	2.00
❑ 10, 91, Von Strucker 2.00		0.40	1.20	2.00
❑ 11, 92, V:Kang 2.25		0.45	1.35	2.25
❑ 12, 93, trading card 2.95		0.59	1.77	2.95
❑ 13, 94 .... 2.95		0.59	1.77	2.95

CAPTAIN AMERICA ASHCAN EDITION

	ORIG.	GOOD	FINE	N-MINT
❑ 0, no indicia 0.75		0.15	0.45	0.75

CAPTAIN AMERICA GOES TO WAR AGAINST DRUGS

	ORIG.	GOOD	FINE	N-MINT
❑ 0, giveaway		0.20	0.60	1.00

CAPTAIN AMERICA SPECIAL EDITION

	ORIG.	GOOD	FINE	N-MINT
❑ 1, reprint of Steranko issues				
.... 2.00		0.40	1.20	2.00
❑ 2, reprint of Steranko issues				
.... 2.00		0.40	1.20	2.00

CAPTAIN AMERICA/NICK FURY: BLOOD TRUCE

	ORIG.	GOOD	FINE	N-MINT
❑ 0, Feb 95, prestige format one-shot				
.... 5.95		1.19	3.57	5.95

CAPTAIN AMERICA: DRUG WAR

	ORIG.	GOOD	FINE	N-MINT
❑ 1 .... 2.00		0.40	1.20	2.00

CAPTAIN AMERICA: MEDUSA EFFECT

	ORIG.	GOOD	FINE	N-MINT
❑ 1 .... 2.95		0.59	1.77	2.95

CAPTAIN AMERICA: THE MOVIE SPECIAL

	ORIG.	GOOD	FINE	N-MINT
❑ 0, nn 3.50		0.70	2.10	3.50

CAPTAIN ATOM
DC

	ORIG.	GOOD	FINE	N-MINT
❑ 1, Mar 87 .... 1.00		0.60	1.80	3.00
❑ 2, Apr 87 .... 0.75		0.40	1.20	2.00
❑ 3, May 87 .... 0.75		0.40	1.20	2.00
❑ 4, Jun 87 .... 0.75		0.40	1.20	2.00
❑ 5, Jul 87, A:Firestorm 0.75		0.40	1.20	2.00
❑ 6, Aug 87 .... 0.75		0.40	1.20	2.00
❑ 7, Sep 87 .... 0.75		0.40	1.20	2.00
❑ 8, Oct 87 .... 0.75		0.40	1.20	2.00
❑ 9, Nov 87 .... 0.75		0.40	1.20	2.00
❑ 10, Dec 87 .... 0.75		0.40	1.20	2.00
❑ 11, Jan 88, Millennium ... 0.75		0.20	0.60	1.00
❑ 12, Feb 88 .... 0.75		0.20	0.60	1.00
❑ 13, Mar 88 .... 0.75		0.20	0.60	1.00
❑ 14, Apr 88 .... 0.75		0.20	0.60	1.00
❑ 15, May 88 .... 0.75		0.20	0.60	1.00
❑ 16, Jun 88, A:JLI 0.75		0.40	1.20	2.00
❑ 17, Jul 88, A:Swamp Thing				
.... 1.00		0.20	0.60	1.00
❑ 18, Aug 88 .... 1.00		0.20	0.60	1.00
❑ 19, Sep 88 .... 1.00		0.20	0.60	1.00
❑ 20, Oct 88, A:Blue Beetle 1.00		0.20	0.60	1.00
❑ 21, Nov 88 .... 1.00		0.20	0.60	1.00
❑ 22, Dec 88 .... 1.00		0.20	0.60	1.00
❑ 23, 88 .... 1.00		0.20	0.60	1.00
❑ 24, 88, Invasion! 1.00		0.20	0.60	1.00
❑ 25, 88, Invasion! 1.00		0.20	0.60	1.00
❑ 26, Feb 89, O:Captain Atom				
.... 1.00		0.20	0.60	1.00
❑ 27, Mar 89, O:Captain Atom				
.... 1.00		0.20	0.60	1.00
❑ 28, Apr 89, O:Captain Atom				
.... 1.00		0.20	0.60	1.00
❑ 29, May 89 .... 1.00		0.20	0.60	1.00
❑ 30, Jun 89, Janus Directive				
.... 1.00		0.20	0.60	1.00
❑ 31, Jul 89 .... 1.00		0.20	0.60	1.00
❑ 32, Aug 89 .... 1.00		0.20	0.60	1.00
❑ 33, Sep 89, Batman 1.00		0.20	0.60	1.00
❑ 34, Oct 89 .... 1.00		0.20	0.60	1.00
❑ 35, Nov 89 .... 1.00		0.20	0.60	1.00
❑ 36, Dec 89 .... 1.00		0.20	0.60	1.00
❑ 37, Jan 90 .... 1.00		0.20	0.60	1.00
❑ 38, Feb 90 .... 1.00		0.20	0.60	1.00
❑ 39, Mar 90 .... 1.00		0.20	0.60	1.00
❑ 40, Apr 90 .... 1.00		0.20	0.60	1.00
❑ 41, May 90 .... 1.00		0.20	0.60	1.00
❑ 42, Jun 90 .... 1.00		0.20	0.60	1.00
❑ 43, Jul 90 .... 1.00		0.20	0.60	1.00
❑ 44, Aug 90 .... 1.00		0.20	0.60	1.00
❑ 45, Sep 90 .... 1.00		0.20	0.60	1.00
❑ 46, Oct 90, Superman 1.00		0.20	0.60	1.00
❑ 47, Nov 90 .... 1.00		0.20	0.60	1.00
❑ 48, Dec 90 .... 1.00		0.20	0.60	1.00
❑ 49, Jan 91 .... 1.00		0.20	0.60	1.00

	ORIG.	GOOD	FINE	N-MINT
50, Feb 91 ...... 2.00		0.40	1.20	2.00
51, Mar 91 ...... 1.00		0.20	0.60	1.00
52, Apr 91 ...... 1.00		0.20	0.60	1.00
53, May 91 ...... 1.00		0.20	0.60	1.00
54, Jun 91 ...... 1.00		0.20	0.60	1.00
55, Jul 91 ...... 1.00		0.20	0.60	1.00
56, Aug 91 ...... 1.00		0.20	0.60	1.00
57, Sep 91 ...... 1.00		0.20	0.60	1.00

CAPTAIN ATOM ANNUAL

	ORIG.	GOOD	FINE	N-MINT
1, 88 ...... 1.25		0.25	0.75	1.25
2, 88 ...... 1.50		0.30	0.90	1.50

CAPTAIN BRITAIN (second series, 1985/86)
MARVEL UK

	ORIG.	GOOD	FINE	N-MINT
1 ...... 1.75		0.35	1.05	1.75
2 ...... 1.75		0.35	1.05	1.75
3 ...... 1.75		0.35	1.05	1.75
4 ...... 1.75		0.35	1.05	1.75
5 ...... 1.75		0.35	1.05	1.75
6 ...... 1.75		0.35	1.05	1.75
7 ...... 1.75		0.35	1.05	1.75
8 ...... 1.75		0.35	1.05	1.75
9 ...... 1.75		0.35	1.05	1.75
10 ...... 1.75		0.35	1.05	1.75
11 ...... 1.75		0.35	1.05	1.75
12 ...... 1.75		0.35	1.05	1.75
13 ...... 1.75		0.35	1.05	1.75
14 ...... 1.75		0.35	1.05	1.75

CAPTAIN CANUCK
COMELY

	ORIG.	GOOD	FINE	N-MINT
1				
2				
3				
4				
5				
6				
7				
8				
9				
10				
11				
12				
13				
14				

SEMPLE

	ORIG.	GOOD	FINE	N-MINT
0, English 0.95		0.19	0.57	0.95
0, French 0.95		0.19	0.57	0.95
1 ...... 1.95		0.39	1.17	1.95
1, gold, trading cards 2.95		0.59	1.77	2.95

CAPTAIN CANUCK REBORN

	ORIG.	GOOD	FINE	N-MINT
1, Jan 94 ...... 2.50		0.50	1.50	2.50
2, Jul 94 ...... 2.50		0.50	1.50	2.50

CAPTAIN CANUCK SUMMER SPECIAL
COMELY

	ORIG.	GOOD	FINE	N-MINT
1, 80 ...... 0.95		0.19	0.57	0.95

CAPTAIN CARROT
DC

	ORIG.	GOOD	FINE	N-MINT
1, A:Superman, Starro 0.25		0.75	1.25	
2, AA		0.20	0.60	1.00
3		0.20	0.60	1.00
4		0.20	0.60	1.00
5		0.20	0.60	1.00
6		0.20	0.60	1.00
7		0.20	0.60	1.00
8		0.20	0.60	1.00
9		0.20	0.60	1.00
10		0.20	0.60	1.00
11		0.20	0.60	1.00
12, 1:AAd art		0.40	1.20	2.00
13		0.20	0.60	1.00
14, Justa Lotta Animals ...		0.20	0.60	1.00
15, Justa Lotta Animals ...		0.20	0.60	1.00

	ORIG.	GOOD	FINE	N-MINT
16		0.20	0.60	1.00
17		0.20	0.60	1.00
18		0.20	0.60	1.00
19		0.20	0.60	1.00
20		0.20	0.60	1.00

CAPTAIN CONFEDERACY
EPIC

	ORIG.	GOOD	FINE	N-MINT
1, Nov 91 ...... 1.95		0.39	1.17	1.95
2, Dec 91 ...... 1.95		0.39	1.17	1.95
3, Jan 92 ...... 1.95		0.39	1.17	1.95
4, Feb 92 ...... 1.95		0.39	1.17	1.95

STEELDRAGON

	ORIG.	GOOD	FINE	N-MINT
1, 86, b&w 1.50		1.00	3.00	5.00
2, 86, b&w 1.50		1.00	3.00	5.00
3, 86, b&w 1.50		0.40	1.20	2.00
4, 87, b&w 1.50		0.40	1.20	2.00
5, 87, b&w 1.50		0.40	1.20	2.00
6, Sum 87, b&w 1.50		0.40	1.20	2.00
7, Aut 87, b&w 1.75		0.40	1.20	2.00
8, Wtr 87, b&w 1.75		0.40	1.20	2.00
9, Spr 88, b&w 1.75		0.40	1.20	2.00
10, Jun 88, b&w 1.75		0.40	1.20	2.00
11, Jun 88, b&w 1.75		0.40	1.20	2.00
12, Oct 88, b&w 1.75		0.40	1.20	2.00

CAPTAIN CONFEDERACY SPECIAL EDITION

	ORIG.	GOOD	FINE	N-MINT
1, Sum 87, rep:O 1.75		0.35	1.05	1.75
2, Sum 87, rep:O 1.75		0.35	1.05	1.75

CAPTAIN CRAFTY
CONCEPTION

	ORIG.	GOOD	FINE	N-MINT
2, Win 94, b&w 2.50		0.50	1.50	2.50

CAPTAIN ELECTRON
BCSI

	ORIG.	GOOD	FINE	N-MINT
1, JD, color		0.45	1.35	2.25

CAPTAIN EO 3-D
ECLIPSE

	ORIG.	GOOD	FINE	N-MINT
0, nn		0.70	2.10	3.50
1, Aug 87, giant size (11x17") 6.95		1.39	4.17	6.95

CAPTAIN FORTUNE
RIP OFF

	ORIG.	GOOD	FINE	N-MINT
1, 93, b&w;adult 2.95		0.59	1.77	2.95

CAPTAIN GLORY
TOPPS

	ORIG.	GOOD	FINE	N-MINT
0, Apr 93, JK,SD, trading card 2.95		0.59	1.77	2.95

CAPTAIN HARLOCK
ETERNITY

	ORIG.	GOOD	FINE	N-MINT
1, b&w		0.60	1.80	3.00
2		0.39	1.17	1.95
3		0.39	1.17	1.95
4		0.39	1.17	1.95
5		0.39	1.17	1.95
6		0.39	1.17	1.95
7		0.39	1.17	1.95
8		0.39	1.17	1.95
9		0.39	1.17	1.95
10		0.39	1.17	1.95
11		0.39	1.17	1.95
12		0.45	1.35	2.25
13		0.45	1.35	2.25

CAPTAIN HARLOCK CHRISTMAS SPECIAL

	ORIG.	GOOD	FINE	N-MINT
1, b&w		0.50	1.50	2.50

CAPTAIN HARLOCK: DEATHSHADOW RISING

	ORIG.	GOOD	FINE	N-MINT
1, b&w		0.45	1.35	2.25
2, b&w		0.45	1.35	2.25
3, b&w		0.45	1.35	2.25
4, b&w		0.45	1.35	2.25
5, b&w		0.45	1.35	2.25
6, b&w		0.45	1.35	2.25

	ORIG.	GOOD	FINE	N-MINT

CAPTAIN HARLOCK: THE FALL OF THE EMPIRE

	ORIG.	GOOD	FINE	N-MINT
☐ 1, b&w		0.50	1.50	2.50
☐ 2, b&w		0.50	1.50	2.50
☐ 3, b&w		0.50	1.50	2.50
☐ 4, b&w		0.50	1.50	2.50

CAPTAIN HARLOCK: THE MACHINE PEOPLE

	ORIG.	GOOD	FINE	N-MINT
☐ 1, b&w	2.50	0.50	1.50	2.50
☐ 2, b&w	2.50	0.50	1.50	2.50
☐ 3, b&w	2.50	0.50	1.50	2.50

CAPTAIN JOHNER & THE ALIENS (mini-series)
VALIANT

	ORIG.	GOOD	FINE	N-MINT
☐ 1, May 95, cardstock cover	2.95	0.59	1.77	2.95

CAPTAIN JUSTICE
MARVEL

	ORIG.	GOOD	FINE	N-MINT
☐ 1, TV show	1.25	0.25	0.75	1.25
☐ 2, TV show	1.25	0.25	0.75	1.25

CAPTAIN MARVEL

	ORIG.	GOOD	FINE	N-MINT
☐ 1, May 68, GC	0.12	14.00	42.00	70.00
☐ 2, GC, V:Skrull	0.12	4.80	14.40	24.00
☐ 3, GC	0.12	3.20	9.60	16.00
☐ 4, GC	0.12	3.20	9.60	16.00
☐ 5, DH	0.12	2.00	6.00	10.00
☐ 6, DH	0.12	2.00	6.00	10.00
☐ 7, DH	0.12	2.00	6.00	10.00
☐ 8, DH	0.12	2.00	6.00	10.00
☐ 9, DH	0.12	2.00	6.00	10.00
☐ 10, DH	0.12	2.00	6.00	10.00
☐ 11, BS(c)	0.12	2.00	6.00	10.00
☐ 12	0.12	1.40	4.20	7.00
☐ 13	0.12	1.40	4.20	7.00
☐ 14	0.12	1.40	4.20	7.00
☐ 15	0.15	1.40	4.20	7.00
☐ 16	0.15	1.40	4.20	7.00
☐ 17, Oct 69, GK/DA, new costume, O:Rick Jones retold	0.15	2.40	7.20	12.00
☐ 18, Nov 69	0.15	1.20	3.60	6.00
☐ 19, Dec 69	0.15	1.20	3.60	6.00
☐ 20, Jun 70	0.15	1.20	3.60	6.00
☐ 21, Aug 70	0.15	1.20	3.60	6.00
☐ 22, Sep 72	0.20	1.20	3.60	6.00
☐ 23, Nov 72	0.20	1.20	3.60	6.00
☐ 24, Jan 73	0.20	1.20	3.60	6.00
☐ 25, Mar 73, JSn	0.20	7.20	21.60	36.00
☐ 26, May 73	0.20	6.00	18.00	30.00
☐ 27, Jul 73	0.20	5.00	15.00	25.00
☐ 28, Sep 73, JSn/AM	0.20	5.00	15.00	25.00
☐ 29, Nov 73, JSn/AM	0.20	2.00	6.00	10.00
☐ 30, Jan 74, JSn/AM	0.20	5.00	15.00	25.00
☐ 31, Mar 74	0.20	3.00	9.00	15.00
☐ 32, May 74	0.25	3.00	9.00	15.00
☐ 33, Jul 74	0.25	3.00	9.00	15.00
☐ 34, Sep 74, JSn/JAb, I:Nitro	0.25	1.00	3.00	5.00
☐ 35, Nov 74, AA, Ant-Man	0.25	1.00	3.00	5.00
☐ 36, JSn, Watcher	0.25	3.60	10.80	18.00
☐ 37	0.25	0.40	1.20	2.00
☐ 38	0.25	0.40	1.20	2.00
☐ 39	0.25	0.40	1.20	2.00
☐ 40	0.25	0.40	1.20	2.00
☐ 41	0.25	0.40	1.20	2.00
☐ 42	0.25	0.40	1.20	2.00
☐ 43	0.25	0.40	1.20	2.00
☐ 44	0.25	0.40	1.20	2.00
☐ 45	0.25	0.40	1.20	2.00
☐ 46	0.30	0.40	1.20	2.00
☐ 47	0.30	0.40	1.20	2.00
☐ 48	0.30	0.40	1.20	2.00
☐ 49	0.30	0.40	1.20	2.00
☐ 50	0.30	0.40	1.20	2.00
☐ 51	0.30	0.40	1.20	2.00
☐ 52	0.30	0.40	1.20	2.00
☐ 53	0.35	0.40	1.20	2.00
☐ 54	0.35	0.40	1.20	2.00
☐ 55	0.35	0.40	1.20	2.00
☐ 56	0.35	0.40	1.20	2.00
☐ 57	0.35	0.40	1.20	2.00
☐ 58	0.35	0.40	1.20	2.00
☐ 59	0.35	0.40	1.20	2.00
☐ 60	0.35	0.40	1.20	2.00
☐ 61	0.35	0.40	1.20	2.00
☐ 62	0.40	0.40	1.20	2.00

CAPTAIN MARVEL (1989)

	ORIG.	GOOD	FINE	N-MINT
☐ 1, 89, one-shot	1.50	0.30	0.90	1.50

CAPTAIN MARVEL (1994)

	ORIG.	GOOD	FINE	N-MINT
☐ 1, 94	1.75	0.35	1.05	1.75

CAPTAIN MARVEL (1995-)

	ORIG.	GOOD	FINE	N-MINT
☐ 1, Dec 95, enhanced cardstock cover	2.95	0.59	1.77	2.95
☐ 2, Jan 96	1.95	0.39	1.17	1.95
☐ 3, Feb 96	1.95	0.39	1.17	1.95
☐ 4, Mar 96	1.95	0.39	1.17	1.95
☐ 5, Apr 96	1.95	0.39	1.17	1.95
☐ 6, May 96	1.95	0.39	1.17	1.95

CAPTAIN N THE GAME MASTER
VALIANT

	ORIG.	GOOD	FINE	N-MINT
☐ 1		0.39	1.17	1.95
☐ 2		0.39	1.17	1.95
☐ 3		0.39	1.17	1.95
☐ 4		0.39	1.17	1.95

CAPTAIN NAUTICUS & THE OCEAN FORCE
EXPRESS/ENTITY

	ORIG.	GOOD	FINE	N-MINT
☐ 1, May 94	2.95	0.59	1.77	2.95
☐ 1, Oct 94, limited promotional edition	2.95	0.59	1.77	2.95
☐ 2, Dec 94, for The National Maritime Center Authority	2.95	0.59	1.77	2.95

CAPTAIN OBLIVION
HARRIER

	ORIG.	GOOD	FINE	N-MINT
☐ 1		0.39	1.17	1.95

CAPTAIN PARAGON
AC

	ORIG.	GOOD	FINE	N-MINT
☐ 1		0.30	0.90	1.50
☐ 2		0.30	0.90	1.50
☐ 3		0.30	0.90	1.50
☐ 4		0.30	0.90	1.50

CAPTAIN PARAGON & SENTINELS OF JUSTICE

	ORIG.	GOOD	FINE	N-MINT
☐ 1		0.35	1.05	1.75
☐ 2		0.35	1.05	1.75
☐ 3		0.35	1.05	1.75
☐ 4, (becomes *Sentinels of Justice*)	0.35	1.05	1.75	

CAPTAIN PHIL
STEELDRAGON

	ORIG.	GOOD	FINE	N-MINT
☐ 1		0.30	0.90	1.50

CAPTAIN PLANET AND THE PLANETEERS
MARVEL

	ORIG.	GOOD	FINE	N-MINT
☐ 1, NA(c) tv	1.00	0.20	0.60	1.00
☐ 2	1.00	0.20	0.60	1.00
☐ 3	1.00	0.20	0.60	1.00
☐ 4	1.00	0.20	0.60	1.00
☐ 5	1.25	0.25	0.75	1.25
☐ 6	1.25	0.25	0.75	1.25
☐ 7	1.25	0.25	0.75	1.25
☐ 8	1.25	0.25	0.75	1.25
☐ 9	1.25	0.25	0.75	1.25
☐ 10	1.25	0.25	0.75	1.25
☐ 11	1.25	0.25	0.75	1.25
☐ 12	1.25	0.25	0.75	1.25

	ORIG.	GOOD	FINE	N-MINT

CAPTAIN POWER
AND THE SOLDIERS OF THE FUTURE
CONTINUITY

	ORIG.	GOOD	FINE	N-MINT
☐ 1, direct-sale cover, Captain Power kneeling		0.40	1.20	2.00
☐ 1, newsstand cover, Captain Power standing		0.80	2.40	4.00
☐ 2		0.40	1.20	2.00

CAPTAIN SAVAGE
(was Capt. Savage and his Leatherneck Raiders)
MARVEL

	ORIG.	GOOD	FINE	N-MINT
☐ 9, Dec 68, DAy	0.12	1.00	3.00	5.00
☐ 10, Jan 69, DAy	0.12	1.00	3.00	5.00
☐ 11, Feb 69, DAy	0.12	0.70	2.10	3.50
☐ 12, Mar 69, DAy	0.12	0.70	2.10	3.50
☐ 13, 69, DAy	0.12	0.70	2.10	3.50
☐ 14, 69, DAy;(becomes *Capt. Savage*)	0.12	0.70	2.10	3.50

CAPTAIN STERNN: RUNNING OUT OF TIME
(mini-series)
KITCHEN SINK

	ORIG.	GOOD	FINE	N-MINT
☐ 1, BW, b&w	4.95	0.99	2.97	4.95
☐ 2, BW, b&w	4.95	0.99	2.97	4.95
☐ 3, 94, BW	4.95	0.99	2.97	4.95
☐ 4, May 94, BW	4.95	0.99	2.97	4.95
☐ 5, Sep 94, BW	4.95	0.99	2.97	4.95

CAPTAIN STORM
DC

	GOOD	FINE	N-MINT
☐ 1, O:Capt. Storm	5.00	15.00	25.00
☐ 2	3.00	9.00	15.00
☐ 3	2.40	7.20	12.00
☐ 4	2.40	7.20	12.00
☐ 5	2.40	7.20	12.00
☐ 6	2.00	6.00	10.00
☐ 7	2.00	6.00	10.00
☐ 8	2.00	6.00	10.00
☐ 9	2.00	6.00	10.00
☐ 10	2.00	6.00	10.00
☐ 11	2.00	6.00	10.00
☐ 12	2.00	6.00	10.00
☐ 13	2.00	6.00	10.00
☐ 14	2.00	6.00	10.00
☐ 15	2.00	6.00	10.00
☐ 16	2.00	6.00	10.00
☐ 17	2.00	6.00	10.00
☐ 18	2.00	6.00	10.00

CAPTAIN TAX TIME
PAUL HAYNES COMICS

	ORIG.	GOOD	FINE	N-MINT
☐ 1	3.50	0.70	2.10	3.50

CAPTAIN THUNDER AND BLUE BOLT
HERO

	GOOD	FINE	N-MINT
☐ 1	0.39	1.17	1.95
☐ 2	0.39	1.17	1.95
☐ 3	0.39	1.17	1.95
☐ 4	0.39	1.17	1.95
☐ 5	0.39	1.17	1.95
☐ 6	0.39	1.17	1.95
☐ 7	0.39	1.17	1.95
☐ 8, I:King's Gambit	0.39	1.17	1.95
☐ 9	0.39	1.17	1.95
☐ 10	0.39	1.17	1.95

CAPTAIN THUNDER AND BLUE BOLT (Volume 2)

	GOOD	FINE	N-MINT
☐ 1	0.70	2.10	3.50
☐ 2	0.70	2.10	3.50

CAPTAIN VICTORY
PACIFIC

	ORIG.	GOOD	FINE	N-MINT
☐ 1, JK	0.40	1.20	2.00
☐ 2, JK	0.30	0.90	1.50
☐ 3, JK, I:Ms. Mystic	0.30	0.90	1.50
☐ 4, JK	0.20	0.60	1.00

	ORIG.	GOOD	FINE	N-MINT
☐ 5, JK		0.20	0.60	1.00
☐ 6, JK		0.20	0.60	1.00
☐ 7, JK		0.20	0.60	1.00
☐ 8, JK		0.20	0.60	1.00
☐ 9, JK		0.20	0.60	1.00
☐ 10, JK		0.20	0.60	1.00
☐ 11, JK		0.20	0.60	1.00
☐ 12, JK		0.20	0.60	1.00
☐ 13, JK		0.20	0.60	1.00

CAPTAIN WINGS COMPACT COMICS
AC

	ORIG.	GOOD	FINE	N-MINT
☐ 1, reprints	3.95	0.79	2.37	3.95
☐ 2, reprints	3.95	0.79	2.37	3.95

CAPTAIN'S JOLTING TALES
ONE SHOT

	ORIG.	GOOD	FINE	N-MINT
☐ 1, b&w		0.59	1.77	2.95
☐ 2, b&w	3.50	0.70	2.10	3.50
☐ 3, trading card	3.50	0.70	2.10	3.50
☐ 3, Dec 92, signed "special collector addition [sic]"; b&w	3.50	0.70	2.10	3.50
☐ 4	3.50	0.70	2.10	3.50

CAR WARRIORS
EPIC

	ORIG.	GOOD	FINE	N-MINT
☐ 1	2.25	0.45	1.35	2.25
☐ 2	2.25	0.45	1.35	2.25
☐ 3	2.25	0.45	1.35	2.25
☐ 4	2.25	0.45	1.35	2.25

CARAVAN KIDD
DARK HORSE

	ORIG.	GOOD	FINE	N-MINT
☐ 1, 92, Japanese, b&w	2.50	0.50	1.50	2.50
☐ 2, 92, Japanese, b&w	2.50	0.50	1.50	2.50
☐ 3, 92, Japanese, b&w	2.50	0.50	1.50	2.50
☐ 4, 92, Japanese, b&w	2.50	0.50	1.50	2.50
☐ 5, 92, Japanese, b&w	2.50	0.50	1.50	2.50
☐ 6, 92, Japanese, b&w	2.50	0.50	1.50	2.50
☐ 7, 92, Japanese, b&w	2.50	0.50	1.50	2.50
☐ 8, 92, Japanese, b&w	2.50	0.50	1.50	2.50
☐ 9, 92, Japanese, b&w	2.50	0.50	1.50	2.50
☐ 10, 92, Japanese, b&w	2.50	0.50	1.50	2.50

CARAVAN KIDD, PART THREE

	ORIG.	GOOD	FINE	N-MINT
☐ 1, May 94, b&w	2.50	0.50	1.50	2.50
☐ 2, Jun 94, b&w	2.50	0.50	1.50	2.50
☐ 3, Jul 94, b&w	2.50	0.50	1.50	2.50
☐ 4, Aug 94, b&w	2.50	0.50	1.50	2.50
☐ 5, Sep 94, b&w	2.50	0.50	1.50	2.50
☐ 6, Oct 94, b&w	2.50	0.50	1.50	2.50
☐ 7, Nov 94, b&w	2.95	0.59	1.77	2.95
☐ 8, Dec 94, b&w	2.95	0.59	1.77	2.95

CARAVAN KIDD, PART TWO

	ORIG.	GOOD	FINE	N-MINT
☐ 1	2.50	0.50	1.50	2.50
☐ 2, Jun 93	2.50	0.50	1.50	2.50
☐ 3, Jul 93	2.95	0.59	1.77	2.95
☐ 4, Aug 93	2.50	0.50	1.50	2.50
☐ 5	2.50	0.50	1.50	2.50
☐ 6	2.50	0.50	1.50	2.50
☐ 7	2.50	0.50	1.50	2.50
☐ 8	2.50	0.50	1.50	2.50
☐ 9, Mar 94	2.50	0.50	1.50	2.50
☐ 10, Apr 94	2.50	0.50	1.50	2.50

CARE BEARS
STAR

	ORIG.	GOOD	FINE	N-MINT
☐ 1	0.65	0.15	0.45	0.75
☐ 2	0.65	0.15	0.45	0.75
☐ 3	0.65	0.15	0.45	0.75
☐ 4	0.75	0.15	0.45	0.75
☐ 5	0.75	0.15	0.45	0.75
☐ 6	0.75	0.15	0.45	0.75
☐ 7	0.75	0.15	0.45	0.75
☐ 8	0.75	0.15	0.45	0.75
☐ 9	0.75	0.15	0.45	0.75

	ORIG.	GOOD	FINE	N-MINT
❑ 10	0.75	0.15	0.45	0.75
❑ 11	1.00	0.20	0.60	1.00
❑ 12	1.00	0.20	0.60	1.00
❑ 13, A:Madballs	1.00	0.20	0.60	1.00
❑ 14, (becomes Marvel comic)	1.00	0.20	0.60	1.00

CARE BEARS (was Star Comic)
MARVEL

	ORIG.	GOOD	FINE	N-MINT
❑ 15	1.00	0.20	0.60	1.00
❑ 16	1.00	0.20	0.60	1.00
❑ 17	1.00	0.20	0.60	1.00
❑ 18	1.00	0.20	0.60	1.00
❑ 19	1.00	0.20	0.60	1.00
❑ 20	1.00	0.20	0.60	1.00

CARL AND LARRY CHRISTMAS SPECIAL
COMICS INTERVIEW

	GOOD	FINE	N-MINT
❑ 1, b&w	0.45	1.35	2.25

CARMILLA
AIRCEL

	GOOD	FINE	N-MINT
❑ 1, adult, b&w	0.50	1.50	2.50
❑ 2, adult, b&w	0.50	1.50	2.50
❑ 3, adult, b&w	0.50	1.50	2.50
❑ 4, adult, b&w	0.50	1.50	2.50
❑ 5, adult, b&w	0.50	1.50	2.50
❑ 6, adult, b&w	0.50	1.50	2.50

CARNAGE
ETERNITY

	GOOD	FINE	N-MINT
❑ 1	0.39	1.17	1.95

CARNAL COMICS
REVOLUTIONARY

	ORIG.	GOOD	FINE	N-MINT
❑ 1, Mar 94, Sarah Jane Hamilton	2.50	0.50	1.50	2.50
❑ 2, Apr 94, Sarah Jane Hamilton	2.50	0.50	1.50	2.50

CARNEYS, THE
ARCHIE

	ORIG.	GOOD	FINE	N-MINT
❑ 1, Sum 94	2.00	0.40	1.20	2.00

CARTOON HISTORY OF THE UNIVERSE
(Deluxe Edition)
RIP OFF

	ORIG.	GOOD	FINE	N-MINT
❑ 1, 87, b&w	2.50	0.50	1.50	2.50
❑ 2, b&w	2.50	0.50	1.50	2.50
❑ 3, b&w	2.50	0.50	1.50	2.50
❑ 4, b&w	2.50	0.50	1.50	2.50
❑ 5, b&w	2.50	0.50	1.50	2.50
❑ 6, b&w	2.50	0.50	1.50	2.50
❑ 7, b&w	2.50	0.50	1.50	2.50
❑ 8, b&w	2.95	0.59	1.77	2.95
❑ 9, b&w	2.95	0.59	1.77	2.95

CARTOON QUARTERLY
GLADSTONE

	ORIG.	GOOD	FINE	N-MINT
❑ 1, Mickey Mouse	1.00	3.00	5.00	

CARTUNE LAND
MAGIC CARPET

	GOOD	FINE	N-MINT
❑ 1, b&w	0.30	0.90	1.50
❑ 2, b&w	0.30	0.90	1.50

CASANOVA
AIRCEL

	GOOD	FINE	N-MINT
❑ 1, adult, b&w	0.50	1.50	2.50
❑ 2, adult, b&w	0.50	1.50	2.50
❑ 3, adult, b&w	0.50	1.50	2.50
❑ 4, adult, b&w	0.50	1.50	2.50
❑ 5, adult, b&w	0.50	1.50	2.50
❑ 6, adult, b&w	0.50	1.50	2.50
❑ 7, adult, b&w	0.50	1.50	2.50
❑ 8, adult, b&w	0.50	1.50	2.50
❑ 9	0.59	1.77	2.95
❑ 10	0.59	1.77	2.95

CASE MORGAN, GUMSHOE PRIVATE EYE
FORBIDDEN FRUIT

	ORIG.	GOOD	FINE	N-MINT
❑ 1, adult, b&w	2.95	0.59	1.77	2.95
❑ 2, adult, b&w	2.95	0.59	1.77	2.95
❑ 3, adult, b&w	2.95	0.59	1.77	2.95
❑ 4, adult, b&w	2.95	0.59	1.77	2.95
❑ 5, adult, b&w	2.95	0.59	1.77	2.95
❑ 6, adult, b&w	2.95	0.59	1.77	2.95
❑ 7, adult, b&w	2.95	0.59	1.77	2.95
❑ 8, adult, b&w	2.95	0.59	1.77	2.95
❑ 9, adult, b&w	2.95	0.59	1.77	2.95
❑ 10, adult, b&w	2.95	0.59	1.77	2.95
❑ 11, adult, b&w		0.70	2.10	3.50

CASE OF BLIND FEAR, A
ETERNITY

	GOOD	FINE	N-MINT
❑ 1, b&w, Sherlock Holmes, Invisible Man	0.39	1.17	1.95
❑ 2, b&w, Sherlock Holmes, Invisible Man	0.39	1.17	1.95
❑ 3, b&w, Sherlock Holmes, Invisible Man	0.39	1.17	1.95
❑ 4, b&w, Sherlock Holmes, Invisible Man	0.39	1.17	1.95

CASES OF SHERLOCK HOLMES
(was Renegade title)
NORTHSTAR

	ORIG.	GOOD	FINE	N-MINT
❑ 16, b&w		0.45	1.35	2.25
❑ 17, b&w		0.45	1.35	2.25
❑ 18, b&w		0.45	1.35	2.25
❑ 20, 90	2.25	0.45	1.35	2.25

CASES OF SHERLOCK HOLMES, THE
RENEGADE

	GOOD	FINE	N-MINT
❑ 1, b&w	0.34	1.02	1.70
❑ 2, b&w	0.34	1.02	1.70
❑ 3	0.40	1.20	2.00
❑ 4	0.40	1.20	2.00
❑ 5	0.40	1.20	2.00
❑ 6	0.40	1.20	2.00
❑ 7	0.40	1.20	2.00
❑ 8	0.40	1.20	2.00
❑ 9	0.40	1.20	2.00
❑ 10	0.40	1.20	2.00
❑ 11	0.40	1.20	2.00
❑ 12	0.40	1.20	2.00
❑ 13	0.40	1.20	2.00
❑ 14	0.40	1.20	2.00
❑ 15, (moves to Northstar)	0.40	1.20	2.00

CASEY JONES & RAPHAEL
MIRAGE

	ORIG.	GOOD	FINE	N-MINT
❑ 1, Oct 94	2.75	0.55	1.65	2.75

CASEY JONES: "NORTH BY DOWNEAST"

	ORIG.	GOOD	FINE	N-MINT
❑ 1, May 94	2.75	0.55	1.65	2.75
❑ 2, Jul 94, final issue	2.75	0.55	1.65	2.75

CASPER 3-D
BLACKTHORNE

	ORIG.	GOOD	FINE	N-MINT
❑ 1, Win 88	2.50	0.50	1.50	2.50

CASPER ADVENTURE DIGEST
HARVEY

	ORIG.	GOOD	FINE	N-MINT
❑ 1, Oct 92, digest	1.75	0.35	1.05	1.75
❑ 2, Dec 92, digest	1.75	0.35	1.05	1.75
❑ 3, Jan 93, digest	1.75	0.35	1.05	1.75
❑ 4, Apr 93, digest	1.75	0.35	1.05	1.75
❑ 5, Jul 93, digest	1.75	0.35	1.05	1.75
❑ 6, Oct 93, digest	1.75	0.35	1.05	1.75
❑ 7, digest	1.75	0.35	1.05	1.75
❑ 8, digest	1.75	0.35	1.05	1.75

CASPER AND FRIENDS

	GOOD	FINE	N-MINT
❑ 1	0.25	0.75	1.25
❑ 2	0.25	0.75	1.25
❑ 3	0.25	0.75	1.25

	ORIG.	GOOD	FINE	N-MINT
❏ 4		0.25	0.75	1.25
❏ 5		0.25	0.75	1.25

CASPER BIG BOOK

	ORIG.	GOOD	FINE	N-MINT
❏ 1		0.39	1.17	1.95
❏ 2		0.39	1.17	1.95
❏ 3		0.39	1.17	1.95

CASPER DIGEST MAGAZINE

	ORIG.	GOOD	FINE	N-MINT
❏ 1, digest	1.75	0.35	1.05	1.75
❏ 2, digest	1.75	0.35	1.05	1.75
❏ 3, digest	1.75	0.35	1.05	1.75
❏ 4, digest	1.75	0.35	1.05	1.75
❏ 9, Sep 89, digest	1.75	0.35	1.05	1.75
❏ 10, Feb 90, digest; "Thanksgiving Parade Special"				
....	1.75	0.35	1.05	1.75
❏ 11, May 90, digest	1.75	0.35	1.05	1.75
❏ 12, Jul 90, digest	1.75	0.35	1.05	1.75
❏ 13, Aug 90, digest..........	1.75	0.35	1.05	1.75

CASPER DIGEST MAGAZINE (Vol. 2)

	ORIG.	GOOD	FINE	N-MINT
❏ 1, digest	1.75	0.35	1.05	1.75
❏ 2, digest	1.75	0.35	1.05	1.75
❏ 3, digest	1.75	0.35	1.05	1.75
❏ 4, Jul 92, digest; indicia says "Casper Digest"				
....	1.75	0.35	1.05	1.75
❏ 5, Nov 92, digest	1.75	0.35	1.05	1.75
❏ 6, Feb 93, digest	1.75	0.35	1.05	1.75
❏ 7, May 93, digest	1.75	0.35	1.05	1.75
❏ 8, Aug 93, digest	1.75	0.35	1.05	1.75
❏ 9, Nov 93, digest...........	1.75	0.35	1.05	1.75
❏ 10, Feb 94, digest	1.75	0.35	1.05	1.75
❏ 11, May 94, digest	1.75	0.35	1.05	1.75
❏ 12, Jul 94, digest	1.75	0.35	1.05	1.75
❏ 13, Aug 94, digest..........	1.75	0.35	1.05	1.75
❏ 14, Nov 94, digest..........	1.75	0.35	1.05	1.75

CASPER ENCHANTED TALES DIGEST

	ORIG.	GOOD	FINE	N-MINT
❏ 1, May 92, digest	1.75	0.35	1.05	1.75
❏ 2, Sep 92, digest	1.75	0.35	1.05	1.75
❏ 3, digest	1.75	0.35	1.05	1.75
❏ 4, Jun 93, digest	1.75	0.35	1.05	1.75
❏ 5, Sep 93, digest	1.75	0.35	1.05	1.75
❏ 6, Dec 93, digest	1.75	0.35	1.05	1.75
❏ 7, digest	1.75	0.35	1.05	1.75
❏ 8, Jun 94, digest	1.75	0.35	1.05	1.75
❏ 9, 94, digest..................	1.75	0.35	1.05	1.75
❏ 10, Oct 94, digest...........	1.75	0.35	1.05	1.75

CASPER GHOSTLAND

	ORIG.	GOOD	FINE	N-MINT
❏ 1		0.25	0.75	1.25

CASPER GIANT SIZE

	ORIG.	GOOD	FINE	N-MINT
❏ 1	2.25	0.45	1.35	2.25
❏ 2	2.25	0.45	1.35	2.25
❏ 3	2.25	0.45	1.35	2.25
❏ 4	2.25	0.45	1.35	2.25

CASPER THE FRIENDLY GHOST

	ORIG.	GOOD	FINE	N-MINT
❏ 1	1.25	0.25	0.75	1.25
❏ 2	1.25	0.25	0.75	1.25
❏ 3	1.25	0.25	0.75	1.25
❏ 4	1.25	0.25	0.75	1.25
❏ 5	1.25	0.25	0.75	1.25
❏ 6	1.25	0.25	0.75	1.25
❏ 7	1.25	0.25	0.75	1.25
❏ 8	1.25	0.25	0.75	1.25
❏ 9	1.25	0.25	0.75	1.25
❏ 10	1.25	0.25	0.75	1.25
❏ 11	1.25	0.25	0.75	1.25
❏ 12	1.25	0.25	0.75	1.25
❏ 13	1.25	0.25	0.75	1.25
❏ 14	1.25	0.25	0.75	1.25
❏ 15	1.50	0.30	0.90	1.50
❏ 16	1.50	0.30	0.90	1.50
❏ 17	1.50	0.30	0.90	1.50
❏ 18	1.50	0.30	0.90	1.50

	ORIG.	GOOD	FINE	N-MINT
❏ 19	1.50	0.30	0.90	1.50
❏ 20	1.50	0.30	0.90	1.50
❏ 21	1.50	0.30	0.90	1.50
❏ 22	1.50	0.30	0.90	1.50
❏ 23	1.50	0.30	0.90	1.50
❏ 24, Jul 94.....................	1.50	0.30	0.90	1.50
❏ 25, Aug 94	1.50	0.30	0.90	1.50
❏ 26, Sep 94	1.50	0.30	0.90	1.50
❏ 27, Oct 94	1.50	0.30	0.90	1.50
❏ 28, Nov 94	1.50	0.30	0.90	1.50

CASUAL HEROES
IMAGE

	ORIG.	GOOD	FINE	N-MINT
❏ 1, Apr 96........................	2.25	0.45	1.35	2.25

CAT & MOUSE
AIRCEL

	ORIG.	GOOD	FINE	N-MINT
❏ 1, Mar 90, b&w..............		0.70	2.10	3.50
❏ 2, Apr 90........................		0.60	1.80	3.00
❏ 3, May 90.......................		0.60	1.80	3.00
❏ 4, Jun 90		0.60	1.80	3.00
❏ 11, Jan 91......................		0.45	1.35	2.25
❏ 12, Feb 91, D:Nail		0.45	1.35	2.25
❏ 13, Mar 91......................		0.45	1.35	2.25
❏ 14, Apr 91......................		0.45	1.35	2.25
❏ 15, May 91.....................		0.45	1.35	2.25
❏ 16, Jun 91		0.45	1.35	2.25
❏ 17, Aug 91		0.45	1.35	2.25
❏ 18, Sep 91		0.45	1.35	2.25

EF GRAPHICS

	ORIG.	GOOD	FINE	N-MINT
❏ 1, Jan 89, part color		0.40	1.20	2.00

CAT AND MOUSE
SILVERLINE

	ORIG.	GOOD	FINE	N-MINT
❏ 1		0.35	1.05	1.75

CAT CLAW
ETERNITY

	ORIG.	GOOD	FINE	N-MINT
❏ 1, Sep 90, O:Cat Claw, b&w	0.50	1.50	2.50	
❏ 1, 2nd printing		0.50	1.50	2.50
❏ 2, Nov 90		0.50	1.50	2.50
❏ 3, Jan 91........................		0.50	1.50	2.50
❏ 4, Feb 91........................		0.50	1.50	2.50
❏ 5, Apr 91........................		0.50	1.50	2.50
❏ 6, Jun 91		0.50	1.50	2.50
❏ 7		0.50	1.50	2.50
❏ 8		0.50	1.50	2.50
❏ 9		0.50	1.50	2.50

CAT TALES

	ORIG.	GOOD	FINE	N-MINT
❏ 0, 3-D, Felix, b&w............		0.59	1.77	2.95
❏ 1, 3-D, Felix, b&w............		0.59	1.77	2.95

CAT, THE
AIRCEL

	ORIG.	GOOD	FINE	N-MINT
❏ 1, adult, b&w		0.50	1.50	2.50
❏ 2, adult, b&w		0.50	1.50	2.50

MARVEL

	ORIG.	GOOD	FINE	N-MINT
❏ 1, Nov 72.......................	0.20	3.00	9.00	15.00
❏ 2	0.20	2.00	6.00	10.00
❏ 3	0.20	2.00	6.00	10.00
❏ 4	0.20	2.00	6.00	10.00

CATALYST: AGENTS OF CHANGE
DARK HORSE

	ORIG.	GOOD	FINE	N-MINT
❏ 1, Feb 94........................	2.00	0.40	1.20	2.00
❏ 2, Mar 94.......................	2.00	0.40	1.20	2.00
❏ 3, Apr 94........................	2.00	0.40	1.20	2.00
❏ 4, May 94.......................	2.00	0.40	1.20	2.00
❏ 5, 94	2.00	0.40	1.20	2.00
❏ 6, Aug 94	2.00	0.40	1.20	2.00
❏ 7, Sep 94	2.00	0.40	1.20	2.00

CATFIGHT
INSOMNIA

	ORIG.	GOOD	FINE	N-MINT
❏ 1, Mar 95, b&w...............	2.75	0.55	1.65	2.75

	ORIG.	GOOD	FINE	N-MINT

CATMAN
AC
	ORIG.	GOOD	FINE	N-MINT
1, reprints	5.95	1.19	3.57	5.95

CATSEYE
MANIC PRESS
	ORIG.	GOOD	FINE	N-MINT
1	2.50	0.50	1.50	2.50
2	2.50	0.50	1.50	2.50
3	2.50	0.50	1.50	2.50
4	2.50	0.50	1.50	2.50
5	2.50	0.50	1.50	2.50
6	2.50	0.50	1.50	2.50
7	2.50	0.50	1.50	2.50
8	2.50	0.50	1.50	2.50

CATSEYE AGENCY
RIP OFF
	ORIG.	GOOD	FINE	N-MINT
1, Sep 92, b&w	2.50	0.50	1.50	2.50
2, Oct 92, b&w	2.50	0.50	1.50	2.50

CATTLE BRAIN
ITCHY EYEBALL
	ORIG.	GOOD	FINE	N-MINT
1, b&w	2.75	0.55	1.65	2.75
2, b&w	2.75	0.55	1.65	2.75
3, b&w	2.75	0.55	1.65	2.75

CATWOMAN (mini-series)
DC
	ORIG.	GOOD	FINE	N-MINT
1, Feb 89	1.50	2.80	8.40	14.00
2, Mar 89	1.50	1.80	5.40	9.00
3, Apr 89	1.50	1.20	3.60	6.00
4, May 89	1.50	1.20	3.60	6.00

CATWOMAN (ongoing)
	ORIG.	GOOD	FINE	N-MINT
0, Oct 94	1.50	1.00	3.00	5.00
1, O:Catwoman		1.60	4.80	8.00
2	1.50	2.40	7.20	12.00
3	1.50	2.00	6.00	10.00
4	1.50	2.00	6.00	10.00
5	1.50	0.50	1.50	2.50
6	1.50	0.30	0.90	1.50
7, Knightquest	1.50	0.30	0.90	1.50
8	1.50	0.30	0.90	1.50
9	1.50	0.30	0.90	1.50
10, May 94	1.50	0.30	0.90	1.50
11, Jun 94	1.50	0.30	0.90	1.50
12, Jul 94	1.50	1.00	3.00	5.00
13, Aug 94, "KnightsEnd" Aftermath	1.50	0.30	0.90	1.50
14, Sep 94	1.50	0.30	0.90	1.50
15, Nov 94	1.50	0.30	0.90	1.50
16, Dec 94	1.50	0.30	0.90	1.50
17, Jan 95	1.50	0.30	0.90	1.50
18, Feb 95	1.50	0.30	0.90	1.50
19, Mar 95	1.50	0.30	0.90	1.50
20, Apr 95	1.50	0.30	0.90	1.50
21	1.95	0.39	1.17	1.95
22, Jul 95	1.95	0.39	1.17	1.95
23, Aug 95	1.95	0.39	1.17	1.95
24, Sep 95	1.95	0.39	1.17	1.95
25, Oct 95	2.95	0.59	1.77	2.95
26, Nov 95	1.95	0.39	1.17	1.95
27, Dec 95	1.95	0.39	1.17	1.95
28, Jan 96	1.95	0.39	1.17	1.95
29, Feb 96	1.95	0.39	1.17	1.95
30, Mar 96	1.95	0.39	1.17	1.95
31, Mar 96, "Contagion" Part 5	1.95	0.39	1.17	1.95
32, Apr 96, "Contagion" Part 9	1.95	0.39	1.17	1.95
33, May 96	1.95	0.39	1.17	1.95
34, Jun 96	1.95	0.39	1.17	1.95

CATWOMAN ANNUAL
	ORIG.	GOOD	FINE	N-MINT
1, 94, Elseworlds	2.95	0.59	1.77	2.95
2, 95, "Year One"	3.95	0.79	2.37	3.95

	ORIG.	GOOD	FINE	N-MINT
3, 96, "Legends of the Dead Earth"	2.95	0.59	1.77	2.95

CAVE GIRL
AC
	ORIG.	GOOD	FINE	N-MINT
1, reprint;O:Cave Girl		0.59	1.77	2.95

CAVEWOMAN
BASEMENT
	ORIG.	GOOD	FINE	N-MINT
1, b&w	2.95	0.59	1.77	2.95

CBS PRESENTS ACTION ZONE
	ORIG.	GOOD	FINE	N-MINT
1, no indicia; free				

CECIL KUNKLE
RENEGADE
	ORIG.	GOOD	FINE	N-MINT
1, b&w		0.34	1.02	1.70

CECIL KUNKLE (Volume 2)
DARKLINE
	ORIG.	GOOD	FINE	N-MINT
1		0.70	2.10	3.50
2, (moves to Renegade)		0.70	2.10	3.50

CECIL KUNKLE (Volume 2, was Darkline)
RENEGADE
	ORIG.	GOOD	FINE	N-MINT
3, b&w, Santa cover		0.40	1.20	2.00

CELESTIAL MECHANICS
INNOVATION
	ORIG.	GOOD	FINE	N-MINT
1, b&w		0.55	1.65	2.75
2, b&w		0.55	1.65	2.75
3, b&w		0.55	1.65	2.75

CELESTINE
IMAGE
	ORIG.	GOOD	FINE	N-MINT
1, May 96	2.50	0.50	1.50	2.50
1, May 96, alternate cover	2.50	0.50	1.50	2.50

CENTRIFUGAL BUMBLE-PUPPY
FANTAGRAPHICS
	ORIG.	GOOD	FINE	N-MINT
1, b&w		0.45	1.35	2.25
2, b&w		0.45	1.35	2.25
3, b&w		0.45	1.35	2.25
4, b&w		0.45	1.35	2.25
5, b&w		0.45	1.35	2.25
6, b&w		0.45	1.35	2.25
8		0.50	1.50	2.50

CENTURIONS
DC
	ORIG.	GOOD	FINE	N-MINT
1		0.20	0.60	1.00
2		0.20	0.60	1.00
3		0.20	0.60	1.00
4		0.20	0.60	1.00

CENTURY: DISTANTS SONS
MARVEL
	ORIG.	GOOD	FINE	N-MINT
1, Feb 96	2.95	0.59	1.77	2.95

CEREAL KILLINGS
FANTAGRAPHICS
	ORIG.	GOOD	FINE	N-MINT
1, b&w		0.50	1.50	2.50
2, b&w		0.45	1.35	2.25
3, b&w		0.45	1.35	2.25
4, b&w	2.50	0.50	1.50	2.50
5, b&w	2.50	0.50	1.50	2.50

CEREBUS
AARDVARK-VANAHEIM
	ORIG.	GOOD	FINE	N-MINT
1, 77, genuine	1.00	70.00	210.00	350.00
1, counterfeit		10.00	30.00	50.00
2, 78	1.00	25.00	75.00	125.00
3	1.00	20.00	60.00	100.00
4	1.00	20.00	60.00	100.00
5, Aug 78	1.00	20.00	60.00	100.00
6, Oct 78	1.00	16.00	48.00	80.00
7, Dec 78	1.00	16.00	48.00	80.00
8, Feb 79	1.00	12.00	36.00	60.00
9, Apr 79	1.00	12.00	36.00	60.00
10, Jun 79	1.00	12.00	36.00	60.00
11, Aug 79	1.00	12.00	36.00	60.00

	ORIG.	GOOD	FINE	N-MINT
☐ 12, Oct 79 ...... 1.00		8.00	24.00	40.00
☐ 13, Dec 79 ...... 1.00		8.00	24.00	40.00
☐ 14, Mar 80 ...... 1.00		8.00	24.00	40.00
☐ 15, Apr 80 ...... 1.00		8.00	24.00	40.00
☐ 16, May 80 ...... 1.25		8.00	24.00	40.00
☐ 17, Jun 80 ...... 1.25		8.00	24.00	40.00
☐ 18, Jul 80 ...... 1.25		8.00	24.00	40.00
☐ 19, Aug 80 ...... 1.25		8.00	24.00	40.00
☐ 20, Sep 80 ...... 1.25		8.00	24.00	40.00
☐ 21, Oct 80 ...... 1.25		12.00	36.00	60.00
☐ 22, Nov 80, no cover price		5.00	15.00	25.00
☐ 23, Dec 80 ...... 1.50		3.00	9.00	15.00
☐ 24, Jan 81 ...... 1.50		3.00	9.00	15.00
☐ 25, Mar 81 ...... 1.50		3.00	9.00	15.00
☐ 26, May 81 ...... 1.50		3.00	9.00	15.00
☐ 27, Jun 81 ...... 1.50		3.00	9.00	15.00
☐ 28, Jul 81 ...... 1.50		3.00	9.00	15.00
☐ 29, Aug 81 ...... 1.50		3.00	9.00	15.00
☐ 30, Sep 81 ...... 1.50		3.00	9.00	15.00
☐ 31, Oct 81 ...... 1.50		3.00	9.00	15.00
☐ 32, Nov 81 ...... 1.50		2.00	6.00	10.00
☐ 33, Dec 81 ...... 1.50		2.00	6.00	10.00
☐ 34, Jan 82 ...... 1.50		2.00	6.00	10.00
☐ 35, Feb 82 ...... 1.50		2.00	6.00	10.00
☐ 36, Mar 82 ...... 1.50		2.00	6.00	10.00
☐ 37, Apr 82 ...... 1.50		2.00	6.00	10.00
☐ 38, May 82 ...... 1.50		2.00	6.00	10.00
☐ 39, Jun 82 ...... 1.50		2.00	6.00	10.00
☐ 40, Jul 82 ...... 1.50		2.00	6.00	10.00
☐ 41, Aug 82 ...... 1.50		1.60	4.80	8.00
☐ 42, Sep 82 ...... 1.50		1.60	4.80	8.00
☐ 43, Oct 82 ...... 1.50		1.60	4.80	8.00
☐ 44, Nov 82 ...... 1.50		1.60	4.80	8.00
☐ 45, Dec 82 ...... 1.50		1.60	4.80	8.00
☐ 46, Jan 83 ...... 1.40		1.60	4.80	8.00
☐ 47, Feb 83 ...... 1.40		1.60	4.80	8.00
☐ 48, Mar 83 ...... 1.40		1.60	4.80	8.00
☐ 49, Apr 83 ...... 1.40		1.60	4.80	8.00
☐ 50, May 83 ...... 1.40		1.60	4.80	8.00
☐ 51, Jun 83 ...... 1.40		5.00	15.00	25.00
☐ 52, Jul 83 ...... 1.40		1.20	3.60	6.00
☐ 53, Aug 83 ...... 1.40		1.20	3.60	6.00
☐ 54, Sep 83 ...... 1.40		1.20	3.60	6.00
☐ 55, Oct 83 ...... 1.40		1.20	3.60	6.00
☐ 57, Dec 83 ...... 1.40		1.20	3.60	6.00
☐ 58, Jan 84 ...... 1.70		1.20	3.60	6.00
☐ 59, Feb 84 ...... 1.70		1.00	3.00	5.00
☐ 60, Mar 84 ...... 1.70		1.00	3.00	5.00
☐ 61, Apr 84, Flaming Carrot				
...... 1.70		2.00	6.00	10.00
☐ 62, May 84, Flaming Carrot				
...... 1.70		2.00	6.00	10.00
☐ 63, Jun 84 ...... 1.70		0.80	2.40	4.00
☐ 64, Jul 84 ...... 1.70		0.80	2.40	4.00
☐ 65, Aug 84 ...... 1.70		0.80	2.40	4.00
☐ 66, Sep 84 ...... 1.70		0.80	2.40	4.00
☐ 67, Oct 84 ...... 1.70		0.80	2.40	4.00
☐ 68, Nov 84 ...... 1.70		0.80	2.40	4.00
☐ 69, Dec 84 ...... 1.70		0.80	2.40	4.00
☐ 70, Jan 85 ...... 1.70		0.80	2.40	4.00
☐ 71, Feb 85 ...... 1.70		1.00	3.00	5.00
☐ 72, Mar 85 ...... 1.70		1.00	3.00	5.00
☐ 73, Apr 85 ...... 1.70		1.00	3.00	5.00
☐ 74, May 85 ...... 1.70		1.00	3.00	5.00
☐ 75, Jun 85 ...... 1.70		1.00	3.00	5.00
☐ 76, Jul 85 ...... 1.70		1.00	3.00	5.00
☐ 77, Aug 85 ...... 1.70		1.00	3.00	5.00
☐ 78, Sep 85 ...... 1.70		1.00	3.00	5.00
☐ 79, Oct 85 ...... 1.70		1.00	3.00	5.00
☐ 80, Nov 85 ...... 1.70		1.00	3.00	5.00
☐ 81, Dec 85 ...... 1.70		1.00	3.00	5.00
☐ 82, Jan 86 ...... 1.70		1.00	3.00	5.00

	ORIG.	GOOD	FINE	N-MINT
☐ 83, Feb 86 ...... 1.70		1.00	3.00	5.00
☐ 84, Mar 86 ...... 1.70		1.00	3.00	5.00
☐ 85, Apr 86 ...... 1.70		1.00	3.00	5.00
☐ 86, May 86 ...... 1.70		1.00	3.00	5.00
☐ 87, Jun 86 ...... 1.70		1.00	3.00	5.00
☐ 88, Jul 86 ...... 1.70		1.00	3.00	5.00
☐ 89, Aug 86 ...... 1.70		1.00	3.00	5.00
☐ 90, Sep 86 ...... 1.70		1.00	3.00	5.00
☐ 91, Oct 86 ...... 1.70		1.00	3.00	5.00
☐ 92, Nov 86 ...... 1.70		1.00	3.00	5.00
☐ 93, Dec 86 ...... 1.70		1.00	3.00	5.00
☐ 94, Jan 87 ...... 1.70		1.00	3.00	5.00
☐ 95, Feb 87 ...... 1.70		1.00	3.00	5.00
☐ 96, Mar 87 ...... 1.70		1.00	3.00	5.00
☐ 97, Apr 87 ...... 1.70		1.00	3.00	5.00
☐ 98, May 87 ...... 1.70		1.00	3.00	5.00
☐ 99, Jun 87 ...... 1.70		1.00	3.00	5.00
☐ 100, Jul 87 ...... 1.70		1.00	3.00	5.00
☐ 101, Aug 87 ...... 1.70		1.00	3.00	5.00
☐ 102, Sep 87 ...... 1.70		1.00	3.00	5.00
☐ 103, Oct 87 ...... 1.70		1.00	3.00	5.00
☐ 104, Nov 87, A:Flaming Carrot				
...... 1.70		1.00	3.00	5.00
☐ 105, Dec 87 ...... 1.70		0.70	2.10	3.50
☐ 106, Jan 88 ...... 2.00		0.70	2.10	3.50
☐ 107, Feb 88 ...... 2.00		0.70	2.10	3.50
☐ 108, Mar 88 ...... 2.00		0.70	2.10	3.50
☐ 109, Apr 88 ...... 2.00		0.70	2.10	3.50
☐ 110, May 88 ...... 2.00		0.70	2.10	3.50
☐ 111, Jun 88 ...... 2.00		0.70	2.10	3.50
☐ 112, Jul 88, /113; double issue		0.70	2.10	3.50
☐ 114, Sep 88 ...... 2.00		0.70	2.10	3.50
☐ 115, Oct 88 ...... 2.00		0.70	2.10	3.50
☐ 116, Nov 88 ...... 2.00		0.70	2.10	3.50
☐ 117, Dec 88 ...... 2.00		0.70	2.10	3.50
☐ 118, Jan 89 ...... 2.00		0.70	2.10	3.50
☐ 119, Feb 89 ...... 2.00		0.70	2.10	3.50
☐ 120, Mar 89 ...... 2.00		0.70	2.10	3.50
☐ 121, Apr 89 ...... 2.00		0.70	2.10	3.50
☐ 122, May 89 ...... 2.00		0.70	2.10	3.50
☐ 123, Jun 89 ...... 2.00		0.70	2.10	3.50
☐ 124, Jul 89 ...... 2.00		0.70	2.10	3.50
☐ 125, Aug 89 ...... 2.00		0.70	2.10	3.50
☐ 126, Sep 89 ...... 2.00		0.70	2.10	3.50
☐ 127, Oct 89 ...... 2.00		0.70	2.10	3.50
☐ 128, Nov 89 ...... 2.00		0.70	2.10	3.50
☐ 129, Dec 89 ...... 2.00		0.70	2.10	3.50
☐ 130, Jan 90 ...... 2.00		0.70	2.10	3.50
☐ 131, Feb 90 ...... 2.00		0.70	2.10	3.50
☐ 132, Mar 90 ...... 2.00		0.70	2.10	3.50
☐ 133, Apr 90 ...... 2.00		0.70	2.10	3.50
☐ 134, May 90 ...... 2.00		0.70	2.10	3.50
☐ 135, Jun 90 ...... 2.00		0.70	2.10	3.50
☐ 136, Jul 90 ...... 2.00		0.70	2.10	3.50
☐ 137, Aug 90 ...... 2.25		0.70	2.10	3.50
☐ 138, Sep 90 ...... 2.25		0.70	2.10	3.50
☐ 139, Oct 90, Melmoth 2.25		0.70	2.10	3.50
☐ 140, Nov 90, Melmoth 2.25		0.70	2.10	3.50
☐ 141, Dec 90, Melmoth 2.25		0.70	2.10	3.50
☐ 142, Jan 91, Melmoth 2.25		0.70	2.10	3.50
☐ 143, Feb 91, Melmoth 2.25		0.70	2.10	3.50
☐ 144, Mar 91, Melmoth 2.25		0.70	2.10	3.50
☐ 145, Apr 91, Melmoth 2.25		0.70	2.10	3.50
☐ 146, May 91, Melmoth 2.25		0.70	2.10	3.50
☐ 147, Jun 91, Melmoth 2.25		0.70	2.10	3.50
☐ 148, Jul 91, Melmoth 2.25		0.70	2.10	3.50
☐ 149, Aug 91, Melmoth 2.25		0.70	2.10	3.50
☐ 150, Sep 91, Melmoth 2.25		0.70	2.10	3.50
☐ 151, Oct 91, Mothers & Daughters				
...... 2.25		0.45	1.35	2.25
☐ 152, Nov 91, Mothers & Daughters				
...... 2.25		0.45	1.35	2.25

	ORIG.	GOOD	FINE	N-MINT
153, Dec 91, Mothers & Daughters				
........2.25		0.45	1.35	2.25
154, Jan 92, Mothers & Daughters				
........2.25		0.45	1.35	2.25
155, Feb 92, Mothers & Daughters				
........2.25		0.45	1.35	2.25
156, Mar 92, Mothers & Daughters				
........2.25		0.45	1.35	2.25
157, Apr 92, Mothers & Daughters				
........2.25		0.45	1.35	2.25
158, May 92 ....2.25		0.45	1.35	2.25
159, Jun 92 ....2.25		0.45	1.35	2.25
160, Jul 92 ....2.25		0.45	1.35	2.25
161, Aug 92, Bone 2.25		3.00	9.00	15.00
162, Sep 92 ....2.25		0.45	1.35	2.25
163, Oct 92 ....2.25		0.45	1.35	2.25
164, Nov 92 ....2.25		0.45	1.35	2.25
165, Dec 92 ....2.25		0.45	1.35	2.25
166, Jan 93 ....2.25		0.45	1.35	2.25
167, Feb 93 ....2.25		0.45	1.35	2.25
168, Mar 93 ....2.25		0.45	1.35	2.25
169, Apr 93 ....2.25		0.45	1.35	2.25
170, May 93 ....2.25		0.45	1.35	2.25
171, Jun 93 ....2.25		0.45	1.35	2.25
172, Jul 93 ....2.25		0.45	1.35	2.25
173, Aug 93 ....2.25		0.45	1.35	2.25
174, Sep 93 ....2.25		0.45	1.35	2.25
175, Oct 93 ....2.25		0.45	1.35	2.25
176, Nov 93 ....2.25		0.45	1.35	2.25
177, Dec 93 ....2.25		0.45	1.35	2.25
178, Jan 94 ....2.25		0.45	1.35	2.25
179, Feb 94 ....2.25		0.45	1.35	2.25
180, Mar 94 ....2.25		0.45	1.35	2.25
181, Apr 94 ....2.25		0.45	1.35	2.25
182, May 94, b&w 2.25		0.45	1.35	2.25
183, Jun 94, b&w 2.25		0.45	1.35	2.25
184, Jul 94, b&w........2.25		0.45	1.35	2.25
185, Aug 94, b&w 2.25		0.45	1.35	2.25
186, Sep 94, b&w 2.25		0.45	1.35	2.25
187, Oct 94, b&w........2.25		0.45	1.35	2.25
194, May 95, "Mothers & Daughters" Part 44; b&w				
........2.25		0.45	1.35	2.25
195, Jun 95, "Mothers & Daughters" Part 45; b&w				
2.25........		0.45	1.35	2.25
196, Jul 95, "Mothers & Daughters" Part 46; b&w				
........2.25		0.45	1.35	2.25
197, Aug 95, "Mothers & Daughters" Part 47; b&w				
........2.25		0.45	1.35	2.25
199, Oct 95, "Mothers & Daughters" Part 49; b&w				
........2.25		0.45	1.35	2.25
200, Nov 95, "Mothers & Daughters" Part 50; b&w;"Patty				
Cake" back-up 2.25		0.45	1.35	2.25
201, Dec 95, "Guys" Part 1;b&w				
........2.25		0.45	1.35	2.25
203, Feb 96, "Guys" Part 3;b&w				
........2.25		0.45	1.35	2.25
204, Mar 96, "Guys" Part 4;b&w				
........2.25		0.45	1.35	2.25

CEREBUS BI-WEEKLY

	ORIG.	GOOD	FINE	N-MINT
1, b&w reprints		0.25	0.75	1.25
2, b&w reprints		0.25	0.75	1.25
3, b&w reprints		0.25	0.75	1.25
4, b&w reprints		0.25	0.75	1.25
5, b&w reprints		0.25	0.75	1.25
6, b&w reprints		0.25	0.75	1.25
7, b&w reprints		0.25	0.75	1.25
8, b&w reprints		0.25	0.75	1.25
9, b&w reprints		0.25	0.75	1.25
10, b&w reprints		0.25	0.75	1.25
11, b&w reprints		0.25	0.75	1.25
12, b&w reprints		0.25	0.75	1.25

	ORIG.	GOOD	FINE	N-MINT
13, b&w reprints........		0.25	0.75	1.25
14, b&w reprints........		0.25	0.75	1.25
15, b&w reprints........		0.25	0.75	1.25
16, b&w reprints........		0.25	0.75	1.25
17, b&w reprints........		0.25	0.75	1.25
18, b&w reprints........		0.25	0.75	1.25
19, b&w reprints........		0.25	0.75	1.25
20, b&w reprints........		0.25	0.75	1.25
21, b&w reprints........		0.25	0.75	1.25
22, b&w reprints........		0.25	0.75	1.25
23, b&w reprints........		0.25	0.75	1.25
24, b&w reprints........		0.25	0.75	1.25
25, b&w reprints........		0.25	0.75	1.25

CEREBUS HIGH SOCIETY

	GOOD	FINE	N-MINT
1, b&w reprints........	0.34	1.02	1.70
2, b&w reprints........	0.34	1.02	1.70
3, b&w reprints........	0.34	1.02	1.70
4, b&w reprints........	0.34	1.02	1.70
5, b&w reprints........	0.34	1.02	1.70
6, b&w reprints........	0.34	1.02	1.70
7, b&w reprints........	0.34	1.02	1.70
8, b&w reprints........	0.34	1.02	1.70
9, b&w reprints........	0.34	1.02	1.70
10, b&w reprints........	0.34	1.02	1.70
11, b&w reprints........	0.40	1.20	2.00
12, b&w reprints........	0.40	1.20	2.00
13, b&w reprints........	0.40	1.20	2.00
14, b&w reprints........	0.40	1.20	2.00
15, b&w reprints........	0.40	1.20	2.00
16, b&w reprints........	0.40	1.20	2.00
17, b&w reprints........	0.40	1.20	2.00
18, b&w reprints........	0.40	1.20	2.00
19, b&w reprints........	0.40	1.20	2.00
20, b&w reprints........	0.40	1.20	2.00
21, b&w reprints........	0.40	1.20	2.00
22, b&w reprints........	0.40	1.20	2.00
23, b&w reprints........	0.40	1.20	2.00
24, b&w reprints........	0.40	1.20	2.00
25, b&w reprints........	0.40	1.20	2.00

CEREBUS JAM

	GOOD	FINE	N-MINT
1	1.60	4.80	8.00

CEREBUS NUMBER ZERO

	ORIG.	GOOD	FINE	N-MINT
0, reprints, b&w........2.25		0.45	1.35	2.25

CEREBUS: CHURCH AND STATE

	GOOD	FINE	N-MINT
1, b&w reprints........	0.40	1.20	2.00
2, b&w reprints........	0.40	1.20	2.00
3, b&w reprints........	0.40	1.20	2.00
4, b&w reprints........	0.40	1.20	2.00
5, b&w reprints........	0.40	1.20	2.00
6, b&w reprints........	0.40	1.20	2.00
7, b&w reprints........	0.40	1.20	2.00
8, b&w reprints........	0.40	1.20	2.00
9, b&w reprints........	0.40	1.20	2.00
10, b&w reprints........	0.40	1.20	2.00
11, b&w reprints........	0.40	1.20	2.00
12, b&w reprints........	0.40	1.20	2.00
13, b&w reprints........	0.40	1.20	2.00
14, b&w reprints........	0.40	1.20	2.00
15, b&w reprints........	0.40	1.20	2.00
16, b&w reprints........	0.40	1.20	2.00
17, b&w reprints........	0.40	1.20	2.00
18, b&w reprints........	0.40	1.20	2.00
19, b&w reprints........	0.40	1.20	2.00
20, b&w reprints........	0.40	1.20	2.00
21, b&w reprints........	0.40	1.20	2.00
22, b&w reprints........	0.40	1.20	2.00
23, b&w reprints........	0.40	1.20	2.00
24, b&w reprints........	0.40	1.20	2.00
25, b&w reprints........	0.40	1.20	2.00
26, b&w reprints........	0.40	1.20	2.00
27, b&w reprints........	0.40	1.20	2.00

	ORIG.	GOOD	FINE	N-MINT
☐ 28, b&w reprints.............	0.40	1.20	2.00
☐ 29, b&w reprints.............	0.40	1.20	2.00

CHAIN GANG WAR
DC

	ORIG.	GOOD	FINE	N-MINT
☐ 1, foil embossed cover...	2.50	0.50	1.50	2.50
☐ 2	1.75	0.35	1.05	1.75
☐ 3	1.75	0.35	1.05	1.75
☐ 4	1.75	0.35	1.05	1.75
☐ 5	2.50	0.50	1.50	2.50
☐ 6	1.75	0.35	1.05	1.75
☐ 7	1.75	0.35	1.05	1.75
☐ 8	1.75	0.35	1.05	1.75
☐ 9	1.75	0.35	1.05	1.75
☐ 10	1.75	0.35	1.05	1.75
☐ 11, May 94	1.75	0.35	1.05	1.75
☐ 12, last issue	1.75	0.35	1.05	1.75

CHAINGANG
NORTHSTAR

	GOOD	FINE	N-MINT
☐ 1, b&w	0.80	2.40	4.00
☐ 2	0.50	1.50	2.50

CHAINS OF CHAOS
HARRIS

	ORIG.	GOOD	FINE	N-MINT
☐ 1, Nov 94	2.95	0.80	2.40	4.00
☐ 2, Dec 94......................	2.95	0.59	1.77	2.95
☐ 3, Jan 95	2.95	0.59	1.77	2.95

CHAKAN
RAK

	GOOD	FINE	N-MINT
☐ 1, b&w	0.80	2.40	4.00

CHALLENGERS OF THE UNKNOWN (1958-1978)
DC

	ORIG.	GOOD	FINE	N-MINT
☐ 1, JK................................		370.00	1110.00	1850.00
☐ 2, JK................................		180.00	540.00	900.00
☐ 3, JK................................		120.00	360.00	600.00
☐ 4, JK/WW		100.00	300.00	500.00
☐ 5, JK/WW		100.00	300.00	500.00
☐ 6, JK/WW		80.00	240.00	400.00
☐ 7, JK/WW		80.00	240.00	400.00
☐ 8, JK/WW		85.00	255.00	425.00
☐ 9, JK...............................		70.00	210.00	350.00
☐ 10, JK.............................		70.00	210.00	350.00
☐ 11		20.00	60.00	100.00
☐ 12		20.00	60.00	100.00
☐ 13, May 60	0.10	20.00	60.00	100.00
☐ 14, 60............................	0.10	20.00	60.00	100.00
☐ 15, Sep 60.....................	0.10	20.00	60.00	100.00
☐ 16, Nov 60	0.10	13.00	39.00	65.00
☐ 17	0.10	13.00	39.00	65.00
☐ 18	0.10	13.00	39.00	65.00
☐ 19, May 61	0.10	13.00	39.00	65.00
☐ 20, 61............................	0.10	13.00	39.00	65.00
☐ 21, Sep 61.....................	0.10	10.00	30.00	50.00
☐ 22, Nov 61	0.10	10.00	30.00	50.00
☐ 23, Jan 62	0.12	10.00	30.00	50.00
☐ 24, Mar 62	0.12	10.00	30.00	50.00
☐ 25, May 62.....................	0.12	10.00	30.00	50.00
☐ 26, Jul 62.......................	0.12	10.00	30.00	50.00
☐ 27, Sep 62.....................	0.12	10.00	30.00	50.00
☐ 28, Nov 62	0.12	10.00	30.00	50.00
☐ 29, Jan 63	0.12	10.00	30.00	50.00
☐ 30, Mar 63	0.12	10.00	30.00	50.00
☐ 31, May 63	0.12	6.00	18.00	30.00
☐ 32, Jul 63.......................	0.12	6.00	18.00	30.00
☐ 33, Sep 63.....................	0.12	6.00	18.00	30.00
☐ 34, Nov 63	0.12	6.00	18.00	30.00
☐ 35, Jan 64	0.12	6.00	18.00	30.00
☐ 36, Mar 64	0.12	6.00	18.00	30.00
☐ 37, May 64.....................	0.12	6.00	18.00	30.00
☐ 38, Jul 64.......................	0.12	6.00	18.00	30.00
☐ 39, Sep 64.....................	0.12	6.00	18.00	30.00
☐ 40, Nov 64	0.12	6.00	18.00	30.00
☐ 41, Jan 65	0.12	2.40	7.20	12.00

	ORIG.	GOOD	FINE	N-MINT
☐ 42, Mar 65	0.12	2.40	7.20	12.00
☐ 43, May 65......................	0.12	2.40	7.20	12.00
☐ 44, Jul 65.......................	0.12	2.40	7.20	12.00
☐ 45, Sep 65......................	0.12	2.40	7.20	12.00
☐ 46, Nov 65......................	0.12	2.40	7.20	12.00
☐ 47, Jan 66......................	0.12	2.40	7.20	12.00
☐ 48, Mar 66	0.12	2.40	7.20	12.00
☐ 49, May 66......................	0.12	2.40	7.20	12.00
☐ 50, Jul 66.......................	0.12	2.40	7.20	12.00
☐ 51, Sep 66	0.12	2.40	7.20	12.00
☐ 52, Nov 66	0.12	2.40	7.20	12.00
☐ 53, Jan 67	0.12	2.40	7.20	12.00
☐ 54, Mar 67	0.12	2.40	7.20	12.00
☐ 55, May 67.....................	0.12	2.40	7.20	12.00
☐ 56, Jul 67.......................	0.12	2.40	7.20	12.00
☐ 57, Sep 67.....................	0.12	2.40	7.20	12.00
☐ 58, Nov 67	0.12	2.40	7.20	12.00
☐ 59, Jan 68	0.12	2.40	7.20	12.00
☐ 60, Mar 68	0.12	2.40	7.20	12.00
☐ 61, May 68.....................	0.12	2.00	6.00	10.00
☐ 62, Jul 68.......................	0.12	2.00	6.00	10.00
☐ 63, Sep 68.....................	0.12	2.00	6.00	10.00
☐ 64, Nov 68	0.12	2.00	6.00	10.00
☐ 65, Jan 69	0.12	2.00	6.00	10.00
☐ 66, Mar 69	0.12	2.00	6.00	10.00
☐ 67, May 69.....................	0.12	2.00	6.00	10.00
☐ 68, Jul 69.......................	0.12	2.00	6.00	10.00
☐ 69, Sep 69.....................	0.15	2.00	6.00	10.00
☐ 70, Nov 69	0.15	2.00	6.00	10.00
☐ 71, Jan 70......................	0.15	1.20	3.60	6.00
☐ 72, Mar 70......................	0.15	1.20	3.60	6.00
☐ 73, May 70......................	0.15	1.20	3.60	6.00
☐ 74, Jul 70.......................	0.15	2.40	7.20	12.00
☐ 75, Sep 70.....................	0.15	1.20	3.60	6.00
☐ 76, Nov 70	0.15	1.20	3.60	6.00
☐ 77, Jan 71......................	0.15	1.20	3.60	6.00
☐ 78, Feb 73......................	0.20	0.40	1.20	2.00
☐ 79, Apr 73......................	0.20	0.40	1.20	2.00
☐ 80, Jul 73.......................	0.20	0.40	1.20	2.00
☐ 81, Jun 77	0.20	0.40	1.20	2.00
☐ 82, Aug 77	0.20	0.40	1.20	2.00
☐ 83, Oct 77	0.20	0.40	1.20	2.00
☐ 84, Dec 77	0.20	0.40	1.20	2.00
☐ 85, Feb 78......................	0.20	0.40	1.20	2.00
☐ 86, Apr 78.......................	0.20	0.40	1.20	2.00
☐ 87, Jul 78, KG.................	0.35	0.40	1.20	2.00

CHALLENGERS OF THE UNKNOWN
(1991 mini-series)

	ORIG.	GOOD	FINE	N-MINT
☐ 1, Mar 91, new O:Challengers	0.35	1.05	1.75
☐ 2, Apr 91........................	0.35	1.05	1.75
☐ 3, May 91.......................	0.35	1.05	1.75
☐ 4, Jun 91	0.35	1.05	1.75
☐ 5, Jul 91.........................	0.35	1.05	1.75
☐ 6, Aug 91	0.35	1.05	1.75
☐ 7, Sep 91	0.35	1.05	1.75
☐ 8, Oct 91	0.35	1.05	1.75

CHAMBER OF CHILLS
MARVEL

	ORIG.	GOOD	FINE	N-MINT
☐ 1	0.20	1.00	3.00	5.00
☐ 2	0.20	0.70	2.10	3.50
☐ 3	0.20	0.70	2.10	3.50
☐ 4	0.20	0.70	2.10	3.50
☐ 5	0.20	0.30	0.90	1.50
☐ 6	0.20	0.30	0.90	1.50
☐ 7	0.20	0.30	0.90	1.50

CHAMBER OF DARKNESS

	ORIG.	GOOD	FINE	N-MINT
☐ 1	0.15	6.40	19.20	32.00
☐ 2	0.15	3.00	9.00	15.00
☐ 3, Feb 69.......................	0.15	3.00	9.00	15.00
☐ 4, Apr 69, B.W. Smith.....	0.15	9.60	28.80	48.00
☐ 5	0.15	1.20	3.60	6.00

	ORIG.	GOOD	FINE	N-MINT
❑ 6 .... 0.15		1.20	3.60	6.00
❑ 7, Wrighton 0.15		4.00	12.00	20.00
❑ 8, (becomes *Monsters on the Prowl*)				
.... 0.15		1.20	3.60	6.00

CHAMPION OF KATARA
CRACK O'DAWN

❑ 1		0.30	0.90	1.50

MU PRESS

❑ 2, Apr 92 .... 2.50		0.50	1.50	2.50

CHAMPION OF KATARA, THE (Vol. 2)

❑ 1, Jan 92, b&w 2.50		0.50	1.50	2.50

CHAMPION OF KATARA, THE: DUM-DUMS & DRAGONS (mini-series)
MU

❑ 1, Jun 95, b&w 2.95		0.59	1.77	2.95
❑ 2, Jul 95, b&w 2.95		0.59	1.77	2.95
❑ 3, Aug 95, b&w 2.95		0.59	1.77	2.95

CHAMPION, THE
SPECIAL STUDIO

❑ 1, b&w		0.50	1.50	2.50

CHAMPIONS
ECLIPSE

❑ 1, Jun 86, 1:Flare		0.25	0.75	1.25
❑ 2, Sep 86.......................		0.25	0.75	1.25
❑ 3, Oct 86		0.25	0.75	1.25
❑ 4, Nov 86		0.25	0.75	1.25
❑ 5, Feb 87, O:Flare		0.25	0.75	1.25
❑ 6, Feb 87		0.25	0.75	1.25

MARVEL

❑ 1, DH, I&O 0.25		2.00	6.00	10.00
❑ 2 .... 0.25		0.60	1.80	3.00
❑ 3 .... 0.25		0.60	1.80	3.00
❑ 4 .... 0.25		0.60	1.80	3.00
❑ 5, DH, C:Ghost Rider...... 0.25		1.20	3.60	6.00
❑ 6 .... 0.25		0.30	0.90	1.50
❑ 7 .... 0.25		0.30	0.90	1.50
❑ 8, GK 0.30		0.30	0.90	1.50
❑ 9, GK 0.30		0.30	0.90	1.50
❑ 10, Jan 77, DC 0.30		0.30	0.90	1.50
❑ 11, JBy......................... 0.30		0.60	1.80	3.00
❑ 12, JBy......................... 0.30		0.60	1.80	3.00
❑ 13, JBy......................... 0.30		0.60	1.80	3.00
❑ 14, JBy......................... 0.30		0.60	1.80	3.00
❑ 15, JBy......................... 0.30		0.60	1.80	3.00
❑ 16, BH, Dr. Doom........... 0.35		0.30	0.90	1.50
❑ 17, GT/JBy, Sentinels..... 0.35		0.60	1.80	3.00

CHAMPIONS (second series)
HERO

❑ 1, Sep 87....................... 1.95		0.39	1.17	1.95
❑ 2, Oct 87 .... 1.95		0.39	1.17	1.95
❑ 3, Nov 87 .... 1.95		0.39	1.17	1.95
❑ 4, Dec 87....................... 1.95		0.39	1.17	1.95
❑ 5, Jan 88........................ 1.95		0.39	1.17	1.95
❑ 6, Feb 88 .... 1.95		0.39	1.17	1.95
❑ 7, Mar 88 .... 1.95		0.39	1.17	1.95
❑ 8, May 88, O:Foxbat 1.95		0.39	1.17	1.95
❑ 9, Jun 88, (also was *Flare #0*)				
.... 1.95		0.39	1.17	1.95
❑ 10, Jul 88....................... 1.95		0.39	1.17	1.95
❑ 11, Sep 88...................... 1.95		0.39	1.17	1.95
❑ 12, Oct 88 .... 1.95		0.39	1.17	1.95
❑ 15, b&w 3.95		0.79	2.37	3.95

CHAMPIONS ANNUAL

❑ 1, Dec 88, O:Giant...........		0.55	1.65	2.75
❑ 2		0.90	2.70	4.50

CHAMPIONS CLASSICS

❑ 1, reprints		0.18	0.54	0.90
❑ 13, b&w reprint.............. 3.95		0.79	2.37	3.95
❑ 14, b&w reprint.............. 3.95		0.79	2.37	3.95

	ORIG.	GOOD	FINE	N-MINT
CHAMPIONS CLASSICS/FLARE ADVENTURES				
❑ 2, flip-format......................		0.59	1.77	2.95
❑ 3, flip-format......................		0.59	1.77	2.95
❑ 4, flip-format......................		0.70	2.10	3.50
❑ 5, flip-format......................		0.70	2.10	3.50
❑ 6, flip-format......................		0.70	2.10	3.50
❑ 7, flip-format......................		0.70	2.10	3.50

CHANGE COMMANDER GOKU
ANTARCTIC

❑ 1, Oct 93, b&w...............2.95		0.59	1.77	2.95
❑ 2, Nov 93, b&w...............2.95		0.59	1.77	2.95
❑ 3, Dec 93, b&w...............2.95		0.59	1.77	2.95
❑ 4, Jan 94.......................2.95		0.59	1.77	2.95
❑ 5, Feb 94.......................2.95		0.59	1.77	2.95

CHAPEL
IMAGE

❑ 1, Feb 95.......................2.50		0.80	2.40	4.00
❑ 2, Mar 95 ....2.50		0.60	1.80	3.00
❑ 2, Mar 95, alternate cover				
.................................2.50		0.50	1.50	2.50

CHAPEL (Vol. 2)

❑ 1, Aug 95 ....2.50		0.50	1.50	2.50
❑ 2, Sep 95 ....2.50		0.50	1.50	2.50
❑ 3, Cot 95 ....2.50		0.50	1.50	2.50
❑ 4, Nov 95, "Babewatch"...2.50		0.50	1.50	2.50
❑ 5, Dec 95, V:Spawn 2.50		0.50	1.50	2.50
❑ 6, Feb 96, A:Spawn.........2.50		0.50	1.50	2.50
❑ 7, Apr 96, V:Shadowhawk				
.................................2.50		0.50	1.50	2.50

CHARLEMAGNE
DEFIANT

❑ 0, Feb 94, giveaway		2.00	6.00	10.00
❑ 1, Mar 94, O:Charlemagne				
.................................3.25		0.65	1.95	3.25
❑ 2, Apr 94.......................2.50		0.50	1.50	2.50
❑ 3 ....2.50		0.50	1.50	2.50
❑ 4, Jun 94 ....3.25		0.65	1.95	3.25

CHARLES BURNS' MODERN HORROR SKETCHBOOK
KITCHEN SINK

❑ 0, 94, nn 6.95		1.39	4.17	6.95

CHARLIE CHAN
ETERNITY

❑ 1, Mar 89, b&w strip rep.1.95		0.39	1.17	1.95
❑ 2, Mar 89, b&w strip rep.1.95		0.39	1.17	1.95
❑ 3, Apr 89, b&w strip rep. 1.95		0.39	1.17	1.95
❑ 4, May 89, b&w strip rep.				
.................................1.95		0.39	1.17	1.95
❑ 5, Jul 89........................2.25		0.45	1.35	2.25
❑ 6, Aug 89		0.45	1.35	2.25

CHARLIE THE CAVEMAN
FANTASY GENERAL

❑ 1, b&w...........................		0.34	1.02	1.70

CHASER PLATOON
AIRCEL

❑ 1, b&w		0.45	1.35	2.25
❑ 2, b&w		0.45	1.35	2.25
❑ 3, b&w		0.45	1.35	2.25
❑ 4, b&w		0.45	1.35	2.25
❑ 5, b&w		0.45	1.35	2.25
❑ 6, b&w		0.45	1.35	2.25

CHEAPSKIN
EROS COMIX

❑ 1, adult, b&w		0.59	1.77	2.95

CHECK-UP
FANTAGRAPHICS

❑ 1, b&w............................		0.55	1.65	2.75

	ORIG.	GOOD	FINE	N-MINT

CHECKMATE!
DC

	ORIG.	GOOD	FINE	N-MINT
1		0.50	1.50	2.50
2		0.50	1.50	2.50
3		0.50	1.50	2.50
4		0.50	1.50	2.50
5		0.50	1.50	2.50
6		0.50	1.50	2.50
7		0.50	1.50	2.50
8		0.50	1.50	2.50
9		0.50	1.50	2.50
10		0.50	1.50	2.50
11, Invasion!		0.25	0.75	1.25
12, Invasion!		0.25	0.75	1.25
13		0.30	0.90	1.50
14		0.30	0.90	1.50
15, Janus		0.30	0.90	1.50
16, Janus		0.30	0.90	1.50
17, Janus		0.30	0.90	1.50
18, Janus		0.30	0.90	1.50
19		0.30	0.90	1.50
20		0.30	0.90	1.50
21		0.30	0.90	1.50
22		0.30	0.90	1.50
23		0.30	0.90	1.50
24		0.30	0.90	1.50
25		0.30	0.90	1.50
26		0.30	0.90	1.50
27		0.30	0.90	1.50
28		0.30	0.90	1.50
29		0.30	0.90	1.50
30		0.30	0.90	1.50
31		0.40	1.20	2.00
32		0.40	1.20	2.00
33		0.40	1.20	2.00

CHEERLEADERS FROM HELL
CALIBER

	ORIG.	GOOD	FINE	N-MINT
1, b&w	2.50	0.50	1.50	2.50

CHEESE HEADS, THE
TRAGEDY STRIKES

	ORIG.	GOOD	FINE	N-MINT
1, b&w		0.50	1.50	2.50
2, b&w		0.50	1.50	2.50
1, second edition, b&w		0.59	1.77	2.95
3		0.59	1.77	2.95
4		0.59	1.77	2.95
5		0.59	1.77	2.95

CHEETA POP, SCREAM QUEEN
ANTARCTIC

	ORIG.	GOOD	FINE	N-MINT
1, May 94, adult, b&w	2.95	0.59	1.77	2.95
2, Nov 94, adult, b&w	2.95	0.59	1.77	2.95
3, Jan 95, adult, b&w	2.95	0.59	1.77	2.95
4, Mar 95, adult;b&w	2.95	0.59	1.77	2.95
5, May 95, adult;b&w; (becomes Fantagraphics title)	2.95	0.59	1.77	2.95

CHEQUE, MATE, THE
FANTAGRAPHICS

	ORIG.	GOOD	FINE	N-MINT
0, nn b&w		0.70	2.10	3.50

CHERRY
KITCHEN SINK

	ORIG.	GOOD	FINE	N-MINT
14, Feb 93, (was Last Gasp); adults;b&w;O:Cherry	2.95	0.59	1.77	2.95
15, Nov 93, adults;b&w	2.95	0.59	1.77	2.95
16, Nov 94, adults;b&w	2.95	0.59	1.77	2.95
17, Apr 95, adults;b&w; TMNT parody	2.95	0.59	1.77	2.95
18, Oct 95, adults;b&w	2.95	0.59	1.77	2.95

LAST GASP

	ORIG.	GOOD	FINE	N-MINT
3, 86, (was Cherry Poptart); adults;b&w;indica says Cherry (nee Poptart)	2.50	0.50	1.50	2.50
4, 87, adults;b&w	2.50	0.50	1.50	2.50

	ORIG.	GOOD	FINE	N-MINT
5, 87, adults;b&w	2.50	0.50	1.50	2.50
6, 88, adults;b&w	2.50	0.50	1.50	2.50
7, 88, adults;b&w	2.50	0.50	1.50	2.50
8, 89, Oz parody "Land of Woz";adults;b&w	2.50	0.50	1.50	2.50
9, 90, adults;b&w	2.50	0.50	1.50	2.50
10, 90, adults;b&w	2.50	0.50	1.50	2.50
11, 90, adults;b&w; 3-D issue	3.50	0.70	2.10	3.50
12, Sum 91, adults;b&w	2.95	0.59	1.77	2.95
13, 92, adults;b&w; (moves to Kitchen Sink)	2.95	0.59	1.77	2.95

CHERRY POPTART

	ORIG.	GOOD	FINE	N-MINT
1, 82, adults;b&w	2.50	0.50	1.50	2.50
2, 85, adults;b&w (becomes Cherry)	2.50	0.50	1.50	2.50

CHERRY'S JUBILEE
CHERRY/KITCHEN SINK

	ORIG.	GOOD	FINE	N-MINT
3, adult;b&w;(was Cherry/Tundra title)	2.95	0.59	1.77	2.95
4, 94, adult, b&w	2.95	0.59	1.77	2.95

CHERRY/TUNDRA

	ORIG.	GOOD	FINE	N-MINT
1, adult;b&w		0.59	1.77	2.95
2, adult;b&w;(becomes Cherry/Kitchen Sink title)		0.59	1.77	2.95

CHERYL BLOSSOM (2nd mini-series)
ARCHIE

	ORIG.	GOOD	FINE	N-MINT
1, Jul 96	1.50	0.30	0.90	1.50

CHERYL BLOSSOM (mini-series)

	ORIG.	GOOD	FINE	N-MINT
1, Sep 95	1.50	0.30	0.90	1.50
2, Oct 95	1.50	0.30	0.90	1.50
3, Nov 95	1.50	0.30	0.90	1.50

CHERYL BLOSSOM SPECIAL

	ORIG.	GOOD	FINE	N-MINT
1, 95	2.00	0.40	1.20	2.00
2, 95	2.00	0.40	1.20	2.00
3, 95	2.00	0.40	1.20	2.00

CHEVAL NOIR
DARK HORSE

	ORIG.	GOOD	FINE	N-MINT
1, Aug 89, DSt(c) b&w	3.50	0.70	2.10	3.50
2	3.50	0.70	2.10	3.50
3	3.50	0.70	2.10	3.50
4	3.50	0.70	2.10	3.50
5	3.50	0.70	2.10	3.50
6	3.50	0.70	2.10	3.50
2, Oct 89, DSt(c) b&w	3.50	0.70	2.10	3.50
7, DSt(c)	3.50	0.70	2.10	3.50
8	3.50	0.70	2.10	3.50
9	3.50	0.90	2.70	4.50
10	3.50	0.70	2.10	3.50
11	3.50	0.90	2.70	4.50
12	3.50	0.79	2.37	3.95
13	3.50	0.90	2.70	4.50
14	3.50	0.99	2.97	4.95
15	3.50	0.90	2.70	4.50
16, trading cards	3.50	0.75	2.25	3.75
17, trading cards	3.50	0.90	2.70	4.50
18, trading cards	3.50	0.79	2.37	3.95
19, trading cards	3.50	0.79	2.37	3.95
20	3.50	0.90	2.70	4.50
21	3.50	0.79	2.37	3.95
22	3.50	0.90	2.70	4.50
23	3.50	0.79	2.37	3.95
24	3.50	0.75	2.25	3.75
25	3.50	0.79	2.37	3.95
26	3.50	0.79	2.37	3.95
27	2.95	0.59	1.77	2.95
28	2.95	0.59	1.77	2.95
32	2.95	0.59	1.77	2.95
33	2.95	0.59	1.77	2.95
34	2.95	0.59	1.77	2.95

	ORIG.	GOOD	FINE	N-MINT
35	2.95	0.59	1.77	2.95
36	2.95	0.59	1.77	2.95
37	2.95	0.59	1.77	2.95
38	2.95	0.59	1.77	2.95
39	2.95	0.59	1.77	2.95
40	2.95	0.59	1.77	2.95
41	2.95	0.59	1.77	2.95
42	2.95	0.59	1.77	2.95
43	2.95	0.59	1.77	2.95
44, Jul 93	2.95	0.59	1.77	2.95
45, Aug 93	2.95	0.59	1.77	2.95
46	2.95	0.59	1.77	2.95
47	2.95	0.59	1.77	2.95
48	2.95	0.59	1.77	2.95
49	2.95	0.59	1.77	2.95
50	2.95	0.59	1.77	2.95

CHIAROSCURO (mini-series)
DC/VERTIGO

	ORIG.	GOOD	FINE	N-MINT
1, Jul 95	2.50	0.50	1.50	2.50
2, Aug 95	2.50	0.50	1.50	2.50
3, Sep 95	2.95	0.59	1.77	2.95
4, Oct 95	2.95	0.59	1.77	2.95
5, Nov 95	2.95	0.59	1.77	2.95
6, Dec 95	2.95	0.59	1.77	2.95
7, Jan 96	2.95	0.59	1.77	2.95
8, Feb 96	2.95	0.59	1.77	2.95
9, Mar 96	2.95	0.59	1.77	2.95
10, Apr 96, final issue	2.95	0.59	1.77	2.95

CHILD'S PLAY 2
INNOVATION

	GOOD	FINE	N-MINT
1, movie adaptation	0.50	1.50	2.50
2, movie adaptation	0.50	1.50	2.50
3, movie adaptation	0.50	1.50	2.50

CHILD'S PLAY 3

	ORIG.	GOOD	FINE	N-MINT
1, movie	2.50	0.50	1.50	2.50
2, movie	2.50	0.50	1.50	2.50
3, movie	2.50	0.50	1.50	2.50
4, movie	2.50	0.50	1.50	2.50

CHILD'S PLAY: THE SERIES

	GOOD	FINE	N-MINT
1	0.50	1.50	2.50
2	0.50	1.50	2.50
3	0.50	1.50	2.50
4	0.50	1.50	2.50
5	0.50	1.50	2.50

CHILDREN OF FIRE
FANTAGOR

	GOOD	FINE	N-MINT
1, Corben, color	0.40	1.20	2.00
2, Corben, color	0.40	1.20	2.00
3, Corben, color	0.40	1.20	2.00

CHILDREN OF THE NIGHT
NIGHTWYND

	GOOD	FINE	N-MINT
1, b&w	0.50	1.50	2.50
2, b&w	0.50	1.50	2.50
3, b&w	0.50	1.50	2.50
4, b&w	0.50	1.50	2.50

CHILDREN OF THE VOYAGER
MARVEL

	ORIG.	GOOD	FINE	N-MINT
1, foil	2.95	0.59	1.77	2.95
2	1.95	0.39	1.17	1.95
3	1.95	0.39	1.17	1.95
4	1.95	0.39	1.17	1.95

CHILDREN'S CRUSADE, THE
DC/VERTIGO

	ORIG.	GOOD	FINE	N-MINT
1	3.95	1.20	3.60	6.00
2	2.95	0.70	2.10	3.50

CHILLER
EPIC

	ORIG.	GOOD	FINE	N-MINT
1	7.95	1.59	4.77	7.95
2	7.95	1.59	4.77	7.95

CHINA SEA
NIGHTWYND

	GOOD	FINE	N-MINT
1, b&w	0.50	1.50	2.50
2, b&w	0.50	1.50	2.50
3, b&w	0.50	1.50	2.50
4, b&w	0.50	1.50	2.50

CHINAGO AND OTHER STORIES
TOME PRESS

	ORIG.	GOOD	FINE	N-MINT
1, b&w	2.50	0.50	1.50	2.50

CHIP 'N' DALE
W.D.

	GOOD	FINE	N-MINT
0, nn Secret Casebook	0.70	2.10	3.50

CHIP 'N' DALE RESCUE RANGERS
DISNEY

	ORIG.	GOOD	FINE	N-MINT
1, O:Rescue Rangers	1.50	0.30	0.90	1.50
2, O:Rescue Rangers	1.50	0.30	0.90	1.50
3	1.50	0.30	0.90	1.50
4	1.50	0.30	0.90	1.50
5	1.50	0.30	0.90	1.50
6	1.50	0.30	0.90	1.50
7	1.50	0.30	0.90	1.50
8	1.50	0.30	0.90	1.50
9	1.50	0.30	0.90	1.50
10	1.50	0.30	0.90	1.50
11	1.50	0.30	0.90	1.50
12	1.50	0.30	0.90	1.50
13	1.50	0.30	0.90	1.50
14	1.50	0.30	0.90	1.50
15	1.50	0.30	0.90	1.50
16	1.50	0.30	0.90	1.50
17	1.50	0.30	0.90	1.50
18	1.50	0.30	0.90	1.50
19	1.50	0.30	0.90	1.50

CHIPS AND VANILLA
KITCHEN SINK

	GOOD	FINE	N-MINT
1, b&w	0.35	1.05	1.75

CHIRON
HAMMAC

	GOOD	FINE	N-MINT
1, b&w	0.40	1.20	2.00
2, b&w	0.40	1.20	2.00

CHIRON (was Hammac title)
ALPHA PRODUCTIONS

	GOOD	FINE	N-MINT
3, b&w	0.39	1.17	1.95

CHOICES
ANGRY ISIS

	GOOD	FINE	N-MINT
0, nn	0.80	2.40	4.00

CHOPPER: EARTH, WIND & FIRE
FLEETWAY/QUALITY

	ORIG.	GOOD	FINE	N-MINT
1	2.95	0.59	1.77	2.95
2	2.95	0.59	1.77	2.95

CHRISTIAN COMICS & GAMES MAGAZINE
AIDA-ZEE

	ORIG.	GOOD	FINE	N-MINT
0, 95, b&w	3.50	0.70	2.10	3.50

CHRISTMAS WITH SUPERSWINE
FANTAGRAPHICS

	GOOD	FINE	N-MINT
1, b&w	0.40	1.20	2.00

CHRISTMAS WITH THE SUPER-HEROES
DC

	ORIG.	GOOD	FINE	N-MINT
1, Jan 89, FM, CS, MA, DG reprints		0.59	1.77	2.95
2, Dec 89, JBy, GM, DG new	2.95	0.59	1.77	2.95

CHROMA-TICK
NEW ENGLAND

	ORIG.	GOOD	FINE	N-MINT
1, color, trading cards		0.79	2.37	3.95
2, color, trading cards		0.79	2.37	3.95
3, reprints, color		0.70	2.10	3.50
4, color		0.59	1.77	2.95
6, color	3.50	0.70	2.10	3.50

	ORIG.	GOOD	FINE	N-MINT
CHROMIUM MAN, THE				
TRIUMPHANT				
☐ 0, Apr 94	2.50	0.50	1.50	2.50
☐ 1, 93, ashcan edition	2.50	1.00	3.00	5.00
☐ 1	2.50	0.50	1.50	2.50
☐ 2	2.50	0.50	1.50	2.50
☐ 3	2.50	0.50	1.50	2.50
☐ 4, Unleashed!	2.50	0.50	1.50	2.50
☐ 5, Unleashed!	2.50	0.50	1.50	2.50
☐ 6	2.50	0.50	1.50	2.50
☐ 7	2.50	0.50	1.50	2.50
☐ 8, Mar 94	2.50	0.50	1.50	2.50
☐ 9, Mar 94	2.50	0.50	1.50	2.50
☐ 10, May 94	2.50	0.50	1.50	2.50
CHROMIUM MAN: VIOLENT PAST				
☐ 1	2.50	0.50	1.50	2.50
☐ 2, 94	2.50	0.50	1.50	2.50
CHRONIC APATHY				
ILLITERATURE PRESS				
☐ 1, Aug 95, b&w	2.95	0.59	1.77	2.95
☐ 2, Sep 95, b&w	2.95	0.59	1.77	2.95
☐ 3, Oct 95, b&w	2.95	0.59	1.77	2.95
☐ 4, Dec 95, b&w	2.95	0.59	1.77	2.95
CHRONIC IDIOCY				
CALIBER				
☐ 1, b&w	2.50	0.50	1.50	2.50
☐ 2, b&w	2.50	0.50	1.50	2.50
☐ 3, b&w	2.50	0.50	1.50	2.50
CHRONICLES OF CORUM				
FIRST				
☐ 1		0.35	1.05	1.75
☐ 2		0.35	1.05	1.75
☐ 3		0.35	1.05	1.75
☐ 4		0.35	1.05	1.75
☐ 5		0.35	1.05	1.75
☐ 6		0.35	1.05	1.75
☐ 7		0.35	1.05	1.75
☐ 8		0.35	1.05	1.75
☐ 9		0.35	1.05	1.75
☐ 10		0.35	1.05	1.75
☐ 11		0.35	1.05	1.75
☐ 12		0.39	1.17	1.95
CHRONICLES OF CRIME AND MYSTERY:				
SHERLOCK HOLMES				
NORTHSTAR				
☐ 1, b&w		0.45	1.35	2.25
CHRONICLES OF PANDA KHAN				
ABACUS				
☐ 1		0.30	0.90	1.50
☐ 2		0.40	1.20	2.00
☐ 3		0.40	1.20	2.00
☐ 4		0.40	1.20	2.00
CHUCK NORRIS				
STAR				
☐ 1, Jan 87, SD	0.75	0.15	0.45	0.75
☐ 2, Mar 87, SD	0.75	0.15	0.45	0.75
☐ 3, May 87, SD	0.75	0.15	0.45	0.75
☐ 4, Jul 87	0.75	0.20	0.60	1.00
CHUK THE BARBARIC (was White Wolf)				
AVATAR				
☐ 3, no color cover		0.25	0.75	1.25
CHURCH AND STATE				
AARDVARK-VANAHEIM				
☐ 0, graphic novel		7.00	21.00	35.00
CINDER AND ASHE				
DC				
☐ 1, May 88	1.75	0.35	1.05	1.75
☐ 2, Jun 88	1.75	0.35	1.05	1.75
☐ 3, Jul 88	1.75	0.35	1.05	1.75
☐ 4, Aug 88	1.75	0.35	1.05	1.75

	ORIG.	GOOD	FINE	N-MINT
CIRCLE WEAVE, THE: APPRENTICE TO A GOD				
ABALONE PRESS				
☐ 1, 95, b&w	2.00	0.40	1.20	2.00
☐ 2, 95, b&w	2.00	0.40	1.20	2.00
CIRCUS WORLD				
HAMMAC				
☐ 1, b&w		0.50	1.50	2.50
CLANDESTINE				
MARVEL				
☐ 1, Oct 94, enhanced cover				
	2.95	0.59	1.77	2.95
☐ 2, Nov 94	2.50	0.50	1.50	2.50
☐ 3, Dec 94	2.50	0.50	1.50	2.50
☐ 4, Jan 95	2.50	0.50	1.50	2.50
☐ 5, Feb 95	2.50	0.50	1.50	2.50
☐ 6, Mar 95	2.50	0.50	1.50	2.50
☐ 7, Apr 95	2.50	0.50	1.50	2.50
☐ 8, May 95	2.50	0.50	1.50	2.50
☐ 9, Jun 95	2.50	0.50	1.50	2.50
☐ 10, Jul 95	2.50	0.50	1.50	2.50
☐ 11, Aug 95	2.50	0.50	1.50	2.50
☐ 12, Sep 95, final issue	2.50	0.50	1.50	2.50
CLANDESTINE PREVIEW, THE				
☐ 1, Oct 94	1.50	0.30	0.90	1.50
CLASH				
DC				
☐ 1, Dec 91		0.99	2.97	4.95
☐ 2		0.99	2.97	4.95
☐ 3		0.99	2.97	4.95
CLASSIC ADVENTURE STRIPS				
DRAGON LADY				
☐ 1		0.59	1.77	2.95
☐ 2		0.59	1.77	2.95
☐ 3		0.59	1.77	2.95
☐ 4		0.59	1.77	2.95
☐ 5		0.59	1.77	2.95
☐ 6		0.59	1.77	2.95
☐ 7		0.59	1.77	2.95
☐ 8		0.59	1.77	2.95
☐ 9		0.59	1.77	2.95
☐ 10		0.59	1.77	2.95
☐ 11		0.59	1.77	2.95
☐ 12		0.59	1.77	2.95
CLASSIC COMICS AND CROSSWORDS				
TRADER				
☐ 1, strip reprints, b&w		0.15	0.45	0.75
☐ 2, strip reprints, b&w		0.15	0.45	0.75
☐ 3, strip reprints, b&w		0.15	0.45	0.75
☐ 4, strip reprints, b&w		0.15	0.45	0.75
☐ 5, strip reprints, b&w		0.15	0.45	0.75
☐ 6, strip reprints, b&w		0.15	0.45	0.75
☐ 7, strip reprints, b&w		0.15	0.45	0.75
☐ 8, strip reprints, b&w		0.15	0.45	0.75
☐ 9, strip reprints, b&w		0.15	0.45	0.75
☐ 10, strip reprints, b&w		0.15	0.45	0.75
☐ 11, strip reprints, b&w		0.15	0.45	0.75
☐ 12, strip reprints, b&w		0.15	0.45	0.75
☐ 13, strip reprints, b&w		0.15	0.45	0.75
☐ 14, strip reprints, b&w		0.15	0.45	0.75
☐ 15, strip reprints, b&w		0.15	0.45	0.75
☐ 16, strip reprints, b&w		0.15	0.45	0.75
☐ 17, strip reprints, b&w		0.15	0.45	0.75
CLASSIC COMICS AND CROSSWORDS (Volume I)				
☐ 1, b&w strip reprints	2.50	0.50	1.50	2.50
☐ 2, b&w strip reprints	2.50	0.50	1.50	2.50
☐ 3, b&w strip reprints	2.50	0.50	1.50	2.50
☐ 4, b&w strip reprints	2.50	0.50	1.50	2.50
☐ 5, b&w strip reprints	2.50	0.50	1.50	2.50
☐ 6, b&w strip reprints	2.50	0.50	1.50	2.50
☐ 7, b&w strip reprints	2.50	0.50	1.50	2.50

	ORIG.	GOOD	FINE	N-MINT
❑ 8, b&w strip reprints...... 2.50		0.50	1.50	2.50
❑ 9, b&w strip reprints........		0.75	2.25	3.75

CLASSIC GIRLS
ETERNITY

	ORIG.	GOOD	FINE	N-MINT
❑ 1, b&w reprints................		0.50	1.50	2.50
❑ 2, b&w reprints................		0.50	1.50	2.50
❑ 3, b&w reprints................		0.50	1.50	2.50
❑ 4, b&w reprints................		0.50	1.50	2.50

CLASSIC PUNISHER
MARVEL

	ORIG.	GOOD	FINE	N-MINT
❑ 1, Dec 89, prestige format; b&w 4.95		0.99	2.97	4.95

CLASSIC STAR WARS
DARK HORSE

	ORIG.	GOOD	FINE	N-MINT
❑ 1, 92, AW, strip reprints. 2.50		0.50	1.50	2.50
❑ 2, 92, AW, strip reprints. 2.50		0.50	1.50	2.50
❑ 3, 92, AW, strip reprints. 2.50		0.50	1.50	2.50
❑ 4, 92, AW, strip reprints. 2.50		0.50	1.50	2.50
❑ 5, 92, AW, strip reprints. 2.50		0.50	1.50	2.50
❑ 6, 92, AW, strip reprints. 2.50		0.50	1.50	2.50
❑ 7, 92, AW, strip reprints. 2.50		0.50	1.50	2.50
❑ 8, AW, trading card 2.50		0.50	1.50	2.50
❑ 9, AW, strip reprints....... 2.50		0.50	1.50	2.50
❑ 10, strip reprints 2.50		0.50	1.50	2.50
❑ 11, strip reprints 2.50		0.50	1.50	2.50
❑ 12, strip reprints 2.50		0.50	1.50	2.50
❑ 13, AW, reprints............. 2.50		0.50	1.50	2.50
❑ 14, AW, reprints............. 2.50		0.50	1.50	2.50
❑ 15, strip reprints 2.50		0.50	1.50	2.50
❑ 16, strip reprints 2.50		0.50	1.50	2.50
❑ 17, Mar 94, strip reprints 2.50		0.50	1.50	2.50
❑ 18, Apr 94, AW 2.50		0.50	1.50	2.50
❑ 19, May 94, AW 2.50		0.50	1.50	2.50
❑ 20, Jun 94, AW; final issue 3.50		0.70	2.10	3.50

CLASSIC STAR WARS: A NEW HOPE

	ORIG.	GOOD	FINE	N-MINT
❑ 1, Jun 94, prestige format; reprints Marvel's *Star Wars* #1-3; movie adaptation .. 3.95		0.79	2.37	3.95
❑ 2, Jul 94, prestige format; reprints Marvel's *Star Wars* #4-6; movie adaptation .. 3.95		0.79	2.37	3.95

CLASSIC STAR WARS: RETURN OF THE JEDI

	ORIG.	GOOD	FINE	N-MINT
❑ 1, Oct 94, polybagged with trading card 3.50		0.70	2.10	3.50

CLASSIC STAR WARS: THE EARLY ADVENTURES

	ORIG.	GOOD	FINE	N-MINT
❑ 1, Aug 94 .... 2.50		0.50	1.50	2.50
❑ 2, Sep 94...................... 2.50		0.50	1.50	2.50
❑ 3, Oct 94....................... 2.50		0.50	1.50	2.50
❑ 4, Nov 94...................... 2.50		0.50	1.50	2.50
❑ 5, Dec 94...................... 2.50		0.50	1.50	2.50
❑ 6, Jan 95 .... 2.50		0.50	1.50	2.50
❑ 7, Feb 95 .... 2.50		0.50	1.50	2.50

CLASSIC STAR WARS: THE EMPIRE STRIKES BACK

	ORIG.	GOOD	FINE	N-MINT
❑ 1, Aug 94, prestige format 3.95		0.79	2.37	3.95
❑ 2, Sep 94, prestige format 3.95		0.79	2.37	3.95

CLASSIC STAR WARS: THE VANDELHEIM MISSION

	ORIG.	GOOD	FINE	N-MINT
❑ 0, Mar 95 .... 2.50		0.50	1.50	2.50

CLASSIC X-MEN
MARVEL

	ORIG.	GOOD	FINE	N-MINT
❑ 1, Sep 86, AAd(c) 1.00		1.40	4.20	7.00
❑ 2, Oct 86, AAd(c) 1.00		0.80	2.40	4.00
❑ 3, Nov 86, AAd(c) 1.00		0.80	2.40	4.00
❑ 4, Dec 86, AAd(c).......... 1.00		0.60	1.80	3.00
❑ 5, Jan 87, AAd(c) 1.00		0.60	1.80	3.00
❑ 6, Feb 87, AAd(c) 1.00		0.60	1.80	3.00
❑ 7, Mar 87, AAd(c) 1.00		0.60	1.80	3.00
❑ 8, Apr 87, AAd(c) 1.00		0.60	1.80	3.00
❑ 9, May 87, AAd(c) 1.00		0.60	1.80	3.00
❑ 10, Jun 87, AAd(c) 1.00		0.60	1.80	3.00

	ORIG.	GOOD	FINE	N-MINT
❑ 11, Jul 87........................ 1.00		0.60	1.80	3.00
❑ 12, Aug 87, AAd(c) 1.00		0.60	1.80	3.00
❑ 13, Sep 87, AAd(c) 1.00		0.60	1.80	3.00
❑ 14, Oct 87, AAd(c) 1.00		0.60	1.80	3.00
❑ 15, Nov 87, AAd(c) 1.00		0.60	1.80	3.00
❑ 16, Dec 87, AAd(c) 1.00		0.60	1.80	3.00
❑ 17, Jan 88...................... 1.00		0.60	1.80	3.00
❑ 18, Feb 88, AAd(c) 1.00		0.60	1.80	3.00
❑ 19, Mar 88, AAd(c) 1.00		0.60	1.80	3.00
❑ 20, Apr 88, AAd(c) 1.00		0.60	1.80	3.00
❑ 21, May 88, AAd(c)......... 1.00		0.60	1.80	3.00
❑ 22, Jun 88, AAd(c) 1.00		0.60	1.80	3.00
❑ 23, Jul 88, AAd(c) 1.00		0.60	1.80	3.00
❑ 24, Aug 88...................... 1.00		0.60	1.80	3.00
❑ 25, Sep 88...................... 1.00		0.60	1.80	3.00
❑ 26, Oct 88...................... 1.25		0.50	1.50	2.50
❑ 27, Nov 88...................... 1.25		0.50	1.50	2.50
❑ 28, Dec 88...................... 1.25		0.50	1.50	2.50
❑ 29, Jan 89...................... 1.25		0.50	1.50	2.50
❑ 30, Feb 89...................... 1.25		0.50	1.50	2.50
❑ 31, Mar 89...................... 1.25		0.50	1.50	2.50
❑ 32, Apr 89...................... 1.25		0.50	1.50	2.50
❑ 33, May 89...................... 1.25		0.50	1.50	2.50
❑ 34, Jun 89...................... 1.25		0.50	1.50	2.50
❑ 35, Jul 89........................ 1.25		0.50	1.50	2.50
❑ 36, Aug 89...................... 1.25		0.50	1.50	2.50
❑ 37, Sep 89...................... 1.25		0.50	1.50	2.50
❑ 38, Oct 89...................... 1.25		0.50	1.50	2.50
❑ 39, Nov 89...................... 1.25		0.50	1.50	2.50
❑ 40, Nov 89...................... 1.25		0.50	1.50	2.50
❑ 41, Dec 89...................... 1.25		0.50	1.50	2.50
❑ 42, Dec 89...................... 1.25		0.50	1.50	2.50
❑ 43, Jan 90...................... 1.75		0.40	1.20	2.00
❑ 44, Feb 90...................... 1.25		0.25	0.75	1.25
❑ 45, Mar 90...................... 1.25		0.25	0.75	1.25

CLASSICS ILLUSTRATED
FIRST

	ORIG.	GOOD	FINE	N-MINT
❑ 1, Raven, Gahan Wilson....		0.75	2.25	3.75
❑ 2, Great Expectations, Rick Geary		0.75	2.25	3.75
❑ 3, Through the Looking Glass, Kyle Baker		0.75	2.25	3.75
❑ 4, Moby Dick, BSz		0.75	2.25	3.75
❑ 5, Hamlet, Tom Mandrake		0.75	2.25	3.75
❑ 6, Scarlet Letter, PCR/Jill Thompson		0.75	2.25	3.75
❑ 7, Count of Monte Cristo, DS		0.75	2.25	3.75
❑ 8, Dr. Jekyll & Mr. Hyde, JK Snyder		0.75	2.25	3.75
❑ 9, Tom Sawyer, Mike Ploog		0.75	2.25	3.75
❑ 10, Call of the Wild, Ricardo Villagran		0.75	2.25	3.75
❑ 11, Rip Van Winkle, Jeffrey Busch		0.75	2.25	3.75
❑ 12, Island of Dr. Moreau, Eric Vincent		0.75	2.25	3.75
❑ 13, Wuthering Heights, Rick Geary		0.75	2.25	3.75
❑ 14, Fall of the House of Usher, PCR & Jay Geldhof		0.75	2.25	3.75
❑ 15, Gift of Magi, Gary Gianni		0.75	2.25	3.75
❑ 16, Christmas Carol, Joe Staton		0.75	2.25	3.75
❑ 17, Treasure Island, Pat Boyette		0.75	2.25	3.75
❑ 18, Jungle, Peter Kuper		0.79	2.37	3.95
❑ 19, Secret Agent, John K. Snyder III		0.79	2.37	3.95
❑ 20, Invisible Man, Rick Geary		0.79	2.37	3.95
❑ 21, Cyrano de Bergerac, Kyle Baker		0.79	2.37	3.95
❑ 22, Jungle Books, Jeffrey Busch		0.79	2.37	3.95
❑ 23, Robinson Crusoe, Pat Boyette		0.79	2.37	3.95

	ORIG.	GOOD	FINE	N-MINT
☐ 24, Rime of Ancient Mariner, Dean Motter				
		0.79	2.37	3.95
☐ 25, Ivanhoe, Harris & Lago		0.79	2.37	3.95
☐ 26, Aesop's Fables, Eric Vincent	0.79	2.37	3.95	
☐ 27, Jungle, Peter Kuper....		0.79	2.37	3.95

CLAW THE UNCONQUERED
DC

	ORIG.	GOOD	FINE	N-MINT
☐ 1, Jun 75	0.25	0.50	1.50	2.50
☐ 2, Aug 75	0.25	0.30	0.90	1.50
☐ 3, Oct 75	0.25	0.30	0.90	1.50
☐ 4, Dec 75	0.25	0.30	0.90	1.50
☐ 5, Feb 76	0.25	0.30	0.90	1.50
☐ 6, Apr 76	0.25	0.30	0.90	1.50
☐ 7, Jun 76	0.30	0.30	0.90	1.50
☐ 8, Aug 76	0.30	0.30	0.90	1.50
☐ 9, Oct 76	0.30	0.30	0.90	1.50
☐ 10, May 78	0.35	0.30	0.90	1.50
☐ 11, Jul 78	0.35	0.30	0.90	1.50
☐ 12, Sep 78	0.35	0.30	0.90	1.50

CLAWS
CONQUEST

	ORIG.	GOOD	FINE	N-MINT
☐ 1, b&w	2.95	0.59	1.77	2.95

CLEOPATRA
RIP OFF

	ORIG.	GOOD	FINE	N-MINT
☐ 0, Feb 92, nn adult, b&w	2.50	0.50	1.50	2.50

CLIFFHANGER COMICS
AC

	ORIG.	GOOD	FINE	N-MINT
☐ 1, 89, b&w reprints		0.50	1.50	2.50
☐ 1, A;b&w;new and reprint		0.55	1.65	2.75
☐ 2, Aug 90, A;b&w; new and reprint				
		0.55	1.65	2.75
☐ 2, 89, b&w reprints		0.50	1.50	2.50

CLIMAXXX
AIRCEL

	ORIG.	GOOD	FINE	N-MINT
☐ 1, adult, color		0.70	2.10	3.50
☐ 2, adult, color		0.70	2.10	3.50
☐ 3, adult, color		0.70	2.10	3.50
☐ 4, adult, color		0.70	2.10	3.50

CLINT
TRIGON.

	ORIG.	GOOD	FINE	N-MINT
☐ 1		0.50	1.50	2.50
☐ 2		0.50	1.50	2.50

CLINT: THE HAMSTER TRIUMPHANT
ECLIPSE

	ORIG.	GOOD	FINE	N-MINT
☐ 1, b&w		0.30	0.90	1.50
☐ 2, b&w		0.30	0.90	1.50

CLIVE BARKER'S BOOK OF THE DAMNED
EPIC

	ORIG.	GOOD	FINE	N-MINT
☐ 1	4.95	0.99	2.97	4.95
☐ 2	4.95	0.99	2.97	4.95
☐ 3	4.95	0.99	2.97	4.95
☐ 4	4.95	0.99	2.97	4.95

CLIVE BARKER'S BOOK OF THE DAMNED II

	ORIG.	GOOD	FINE	N-MINT
☐ 0	4.95	0.99	2.97	4.95

CLIVE BARKER'S BOOK OF THE DAMNED III

	ORIG.	GOOD	FINE	N-MINT
☐ 0		0.99	2.97	4.95

CLIVE BARKER'S HELLRAISER

	ORIG.	GOOD	FINE	N-MINT
☐ 1	4.95	1.00	3.00	5.00
☐ 2	4.95	1.00	3.00	5.00
☐ 3	4.95	1.00	3.00	5.00
☐ 4	4.95	1.00	3.00	5.00
☐ 5	5.95	1.19	3.57	5.95
☐ 6	5.95	1.19	3.57	5.95
☐ 7	5.95	1.19	3.57	5.95
☐ 8	5.95	1.19	3.57	5.95
☐ 9	5.95	1.19	3.57	5.95
☐ 10	4.50	0.90	2.70	4.50
☐ 11	4.50	0.90	2.70	4.50
☐ 12	4.50	0.90	2.70	4.50
☐ 13	4.95	0.99	2.97	4.95
☐ 14	4.95	0.99	2.97	4.95
☐ 15	4.95	0.99	2.97	4.95
☐ 16, NG	4.95	0.99	2.97	4.95
☐ 17, NG	4.95	0.99	2.97	4.95
☐ 18, NG	4.95	0.99	2.97	4.95
☐ 19, NG	4.95	0.99	2.97	4.95
☐ 20, NG	4.95	0.99	2.97	4.95

CLIVE BARKER'S HELLRAISER DARK HOLIDAY SPECIAL

	ORIG.	GOOD	FINE	N-MINT
☐ 1	4.95	0.99	2.97	4.95

CLIVE BARKER'S HELLRAISER SUMMER SPECIAL

	ORIG.	GOOD	FINE	N-MINT
☐ 1	5.95	1.19	3.57	5.95

CLIVE BARKER'S NIGHTBREED

	ORIG.	GOOD	FINE	N-MINT
☐ 1	1.95	0.80	2.40	4.00
☐ 2	1.95	0.60	1.80	3.00
☐ 3	1.95	0.60	1.80	3.00
☐ 4	1.95	0.60	1.80	3.00
☐ 5	2.25	0.45	1.35	2.25
☐ 6	2.25	0.45	1.35	2.25
☐ 7	2.25	0.45	1.35	2.25
☐ 8	2.25	0.45	1.35	2.25
☐ 9	2.25	0.45	1.35	2.25
☐ 10	2.25	0.45	1.35	2.25
☐ 11	2.25	0.45	1.35	2.25
☐ 12	2.25	0.45	1.35	2.25
☐ 13, Rawhead Rex	2.25	0.45	1.35	2.25
☐ 14	2.25	0.45	1.35	2.25
☐ 15	2.25	0.45	1.35	2.25
☐ 16	2.25	0.45	1.35	2.25
☐ 17	2.25	0.45	1.35	2.25
☐ 18	2.25	0.45	1.35	2.25
☐ 19	2.25	0.45	1.35	2.25
☐ 20	2.50	0.50	1.50	2.50
☐ 21	2.50	0.50	1.50	2.50
☐ 22	2.50	0.50	1.50	2.50
☐ 23	2.50	0.50	1.50	2.50
☐ 24	2.50	0.50	1.50	2.50
☐ 25	2.50	0.50	1.50	2.50

CLIVE BARKER'S THE HARROWERS
MARVEL

	ORIG.	GOOD	FINE	N-MINT
☐ 1, glow cover	2.95	0.59	1.77	2.95

CLOAK & DAGGER (2nd series)

	ORIG.	GOOD	FINE	N-MINT
☐ 1, Jul 85, TA	0.65	0.30	0.90	1.50
☐ 2, Sep 85, TA	0.65	0.20	0.60	1.00
☐ 3, Nov 85, TA	0.65	0.20	0.60	1.00
☐ 4, Jan 86, TA Secret Wars II				
	0.65	0.20	0.60	1.00
☐ 5, Mar 85, TA	0.75	0.20	0.60	1.00
☐ 6, May 85, TA	0.75	0.20	0.60	1.00
☐ 7, Jul 85, TA	0.75	0.20	0.60	1.00
☐ 8, Sep 85, TA	0.75	0.20	0.60	1.00
☐ 9, Nov 85, TA	0.75	0.20	0.60	1.00
☐ 10, Jan 86, TA	0.75	0.20	0.60	1.00
☐ 11, Mar 86, TA	1.25	0.25	0.75	1.25

CLOAK & DAGGER (mini-series)

	ORIG.	GOOD	FINE	N-MINT
☐ 1, Oct 83, TA, I: Det. O'Reilly				
	0.60	0.50	1.50	2.50
☐ 2, Nov 83, TA	0.60	0.30	0.90	1.50
☐ 3, Dec 83, TA	0.60	0.30	0.90	1.50
☐ 4, Jan 84, TA	0.60	0.30	0.90	1.50

CLOAK AND DAGGER
(was Mutant Misadventures of Cloak and Dagger)

	ORIG.	GOOD	FINE	N-MINT
☐ 14, Oct 90	1.50	0.30	0.90	1.50
☐ 15, Dec 90	1.50	0.30	0.90	1.50
☐ 16, Feb 91	1.50	0.30	0.90	1.50
☐ 17, Apr 91, SpM	1.50	0.30	0.90	1.50
☐ 18, Jun 91, SpM, Ghost Rider				
	1.50	0.30	0.90	1.50
☐ 19, Aug 91, O:retold	2.50	0.50	1.50	2.50

	ORIG.	GOOD	FINE	N-MINT

CLONEZONE SPECIAL
DARK HORSE

	ORIG.	GOOD	FINE	N-MINT
☐ 1, 89, b&w		0.40	1.20	2.00

CLOWN: NOBODY'S LAUGHING NOW, THE
FLEETWAY/QUALITY

| ☐ 0, nn | 4.95 | 0.99 | 2.97 | 4.95 |

COBALT 60
TUNDRA

| ☐ 1 | | 0.99 | 2.97 | 4.95 |
| ☐ 2 | | 0.99 | 2.97 | 4.95 |

COBALT BLUE
INNOVATION

| ☐ 1, Sep 89, MGu | | 0.39 | 1.17 | 1.95 |
| ☐ 2, Oct 89, MGu | | 0.39 | 1.17 | 1.95 |

POWER

| ☐ 1, Jan 78, MGu | | 1.20 | 3.60 | 6.00 |

COBRA
VIZ

☐ 1, b&w, Japanese		0.59	1.77	2.95
☐ 2, b&w, Japanese		0.59	1.77	2.95
☐ 3, b&w, Japanese		0.59	1.77	2.95
☐ 4, b&w, Japanese		0.59	1.77	2.95
☐ 5, b&w, Japanese		0.59	1.77	2.95
☐ 6, b&w, Japanese		0.59	1.77	2.95
☐ 7		0.65	1.95	3.25
☐ 8		0.65	1.95	3.25
☐ 9		0.65	1.95	3.25
☐ 10		0.65	1.95	3.25
☐ 11		0.65	1.95	3.25
☐ 12		0.65	1.95	3.25

CODA
CODA

☐ 1		0.40	1.20	2.00
☐ 2		0.40	1.20	2.00
☐ 3		0.40	1.20	2.00
☐ 4		0.40	1.20	2.00

CODENAME DANGER
LODESTONE

☐ 1, Aug 85	1.50	0.30	0.90	1.50
☐ 2, Oct 85	1.50	0.30	0.90	1.50
☐ 3, Jan 86	1.50	0.30	0.90	1.50
☐ 4, May 86	1.50	0.30	0.90	1.50

CODENAME: GENETIX
MARVEL

☐ 1	1.75	0.35	1.05	1.75
☐ 2	1.75	0.35	1.05	1.75
☐ 3	1.75	0.35	1.05	1.75
☐ 4	1.75	0.35	1.05	1.75

CODENAME: NINJA
SOLSON

| ☐ 1, b&w | | 0.20 | 0.60 | 1.00 |

CODENAME: SPITFIRE
(was Spitfire and the Troubleshooters)
MARVEL

☐ 10, Jul 87	0.75	0.20	0.60	1.00
☐ 11, Aug 87	0.75	0.20	0.60	1.00
☐ 12, Sep 87	0.75	0.20	0.60	1.00
☐ 13, Oct 87	0.75	0.20	0.60	1.00

CODENAME: STRIKEFORCE
SPECTRUM

| ☐ 1, Jun 84 | | 0.20 | 0.60 | 1.00 |

CODENAME: STRYKEFORCE
IMAGE

☐ 0, Jun 95, indicia says "Jun";cover says "Jul"				
	2.50	0.50	1.50	2.50
☐ 2, Mar 94	1.95	0.39	1.17	1.95
☐ 3, Apr 94	1.95	0.39	1.17	1.95
☐ 4, Jun 94	1.95	0.39	1.17	1.95
☐ 5, Jul 94	1.95	0.39	1.17	1.95
☐ 6, Aug 94	1.95	0.39	1.17	1.95
☐ 8, Nov 94	1.95	0.39	1.17	1.95
☐ 9, Dec 94	1.95	0.39	1.17	1.95
☐ 10, Jan 95	1.95	0.39	1.17	1.95
☐ 11, Mar 95	1.95	0.39	1.17	1.95
☐ 12, Apr 95	1.95	0.39	1.17	1.95
☐ 13, May 95	2.25	0.45	1.35	2.25
☐ 14, Aug 95	2.25	0.45	1.35	2.25

CODY STARBUCK
STAR*REACH

| ☐ 1, HC | | 0.40 | 1.20 | 2.00 |

COFFIN BLOOD
MONSTER

| ☐ 1, b&w | | 0.79 | 2.37 | 3.95 |

COLD BLOODED
NORTHSTAR

| ☐ 1, b&w | 2.95 | 0.59 | 1.77 | 2.95 |

COLD BLOODED CHAMELEON COMMANDOS
BLACKTHORNE

☐ 1		0.35	1.05	1.75
☐ 2		0.35	1.05	1.75
☐ 3		0.35	1.05	1.75
☐ 4		0.35	1.05	1.75
☐ 5		0.35	1.05	1.75

COLE BLACK (Volume 2)
HARTBERG

☐ 1		0.30	0.90	1.50
☐ 2		0.30	0.90	1.50
☐ 3		0.30	0.90	1.50

COLIN UPTON'S BIG THING
UPTON

| ☐ 1, b&w, adult | | 0.65 | 1.95 | 3.25 |

COLIN UPTON'S OTHER BIG THING
FANTAGRAPHICS

☐ 1, b&w		0.55	1.65	2.75
☐ 2		0.45	1.35	2.25
☐ 3		0.45	1.35	2.25

COLLECTION
ETERNITY

| ☐ 1 | | 0.59 | 1.77 | 2.95 |

COLLECTOR'S DRACULA, THE
MILLENNIUM

| ☐ 1, 94 | 3.95 | 0.79 | 2.37 | 3.95 |
| ☐ 2, 94 | 3.95 | 0.79 | 2.37 | 3.95 |

COLLECTORS GUIDE TO THE ULTRAVERSE
MALIBU/ULTRAVERSE

| ☐ 1, Aug 94 | 0.99 | 0.20 | 0.59 | 0.99 |

COLLIER'S
FANTAGRAPHICS

| ☐ 1, b&w | | 0.55 | 1.65 | 2.75 |
| ☐ 2, b&w | | 0.65 | 1.95 | 3.25 |

COLORS IN BLACK (mini-series)
DARK HORSE

☐ 1, Mar 95	2.95	0.59	1.77	2.95
☐ 2	2.95	0.59	1.77	2.95
☐ 3	2.95	0.59	1.77	2.95
☐ 4	2.95	0.59	1.77	2.95

COLOSSUS: GOD'S COUNTRY
MARVEL

| ☐ 0, 94, one-shot, prestige format | | | | |
| | 6.95 | 1.39 | 4.17 | 6.95 |

COLOUR OF MAGIC
INNOVATION

☐ 1		0.50	1.50	2.50
☐ 2		0.50	1.50	2.50
☐ 3		0.50	1.50	2.50
☐ 4		0.50	1.50	2.50

	ORIG.	GOOD	FINE	N-MINT

COLT
KZ COMICS
	ORIG.	GOOD	FINE	N-MINT
☐ 1	0.19	0.57	0.95	
☐ 2	0.19	0.57	0.95	
☐ 3	0.19	0.57	0.95	
☐ 4	0.19	0.57	0.95	

COLT SPECIAL
AC
☐ 1, Aug 85		0.30	0.90	1.50

COLUMBUS
DARK HORSE
☐ 1, 92, b&w	2.50	0.50	1.50	2.50

COMBAT
IMAGE
☐ 1, Jan 96	2.50	0.50	1.50	2.50
☐ 2, Jan 96	2.50	0.50	1.50	2.50

COMBAT KELLY AND HIS DEADLY DOZEN
MARVEL
☐ 1, Jun 72, DAy;Combat Kelly becomes leader of Dum-Dum Dugan's Deadly Dozen (from *Sgt. Fury #98*)

	ORIG.	GOOD	FINE	N-MINT
	0.20	0.40	1.20	2.00
☐ 2, Aug 72, DAy	0.20	0.20	0.60	1.00

☐ 3, Oct 72, DAy; O:Combat Kelly

	ORIG.	GOOD	FINE	N-MINT
	0.20	0.20	0.60	1.00

☐ 4, Dec 72, DAy;A:Sgt. Fury and his Howling Commandos

	ORIG.	GOOD	FINE	N-MINT
	0.20	0.20	0.60	1.00
☐ 5, Feb 73, DAy	0.20	0.20	0.60	1.00
☐ 6, Apr 73, DAy	0.20	0.20	0.60	1.00
☐ 7, Jun 73, DAy	0.20	0.20	0.60	1.00
☐ 8, Aug 73, DAy	0.20	0.20	0.60	1.00

☐ 9, Oct 73, DAy;D:Deadly Dozen;L:Combat Kelly; final issue

	ORIG.	GOOD	FINE	N-MINT
	0.20	0.20	0.60	1.00

COMET ANNUAL, THE
IMPACT
☐ 1, 92, trading card	2.50	0.50	1.50	2.50

COMET MAN, THE
MARVEL
☐ 1, Feb 87	1.00	0.20	0.60	1.00
☐ 2, Mar 87	1.00	0.20	0.60	1.00
☐ 3, Apr 87	1.00	0.20	0.60	1.00
☐ 4, May 87	1.00	0.20	0.60	1.00
☐ 5, Jun 87	1.00	0.20	0.60	1.00
☐ 6, Jul 87	1.00	0.20	0.60	1.00

COMET TALES
ROCKET
☐ 1		0.20	0.60	1.00
☐ 2		0.20	0.60	1.00
☐ 3		0.20	0.60	1.00

COMET, THE
ARCHIE/RED CIRCLE
☐ 1, Oct 83, CI	1.00	0.20	0.60	1.00
☐ 2, Dec 83, CI	1.00	0.20	0.60	1.00

IMPACT
☐ 1, Jul 91, O:Comet	1.00	0.20	0.60	1.00
☐ 2, Aug 91, 1:Applejack	1.00	0.20	0.60	1.00
☐ 3, Sep 91	1.00	0.20	0.60	1.00
☐ 4, Oct 91	1.00	0.20	0.60	1.00
☐ 5, Nov 91	1.00	0.20	0.60	1.00
☐ 6, Dec 91, 1:Hangman	1.00	0.20	0.60	1.00

☐ 7, Jan 92, 1:Bob Phantom

	ORIG.	GOOD	FINE	N-MINT
	1.00	0.20	0.60	1.00
☐ 8, Feb 92	1.00	0.20	0.60	1.00
☐ 9, Mar 92	1.00	0.20	0.60	1.00
☐ 10, Apr 92, trading card	1.00	0.20	0.60	1.00
☐ 11, May 92	1.00	0.20	0.60	1.00
☐ 12, Jun 92	1.00	0.20	0.60	1.00
☐ 13, Jul 92	1.00	0.20	0.60	1.00
☐ 14, Aug 92	1.25	0.25	0.75	1.25
☐ 15, Sep 92	1.25	0.25	0.75	1.25
☐ 16, Oct 92	1.25	0.25	0.75	1.25

	ORIG.	GOOD	FINE	N-MINT
☐ 17, Nov 92	1.25	0.25	0.75	1.25
☐ 18, Dec 92	1.25	0.25	0.75	1.25

COMIC BOOK CONFIDENTIAL
SPHINX
☐ 0, 88, nn;giveaway promo for documentary film of same name

COMIC RELIEF
PAGE ONE
☐ 1, strips,b&w	2.50	1.60	4.80	8.00
☐ 2, strips,b&w	2.50	1.00	3.00	5.00
☐ 3, strips,b&w	2.50	1.00	3.00	5.00
☐ 4, strips,b&w	2.50	1.00	3.00	5.00
☐ 5, Outland	2.50	1.00	3.00	5.00
☐ 6, Outland	2.50	0.60	1.80	3.00
☐ 7, Outland	2.50	0.60	1.80	3.00
☐ 8, Outland	2.50	0.60	1.80	3.00
☐ 9, Outland	2.50	0.60	1.80	3.00
☐ 10, Outland	2.50	0.60	1.80	3.00
☐ 11, Outland	2.50	0.50	1.50	2.50
☐ 12, Outland	2.50	0.50	1.50	2.50
☐ 13, Outland	2.50	0.50	1.50	2.50
☐ 14, Outland	2.50	0.50	1.50	2.50
☐ 15	2.95	0.59	1.77	2.95
☐ 16	2.95	0.59	1.77	2.95
☐ 17	2.95	0.59	1.77	2.95
☐ 18	2.95	0.59	1.77	2.95
☐ 19	2.95	0.59	1.77	2.95
☐ 20	2.95	0.59	1.77	2.95
☐ 21	2.95	0.59	1.77	2.95
☐ 22	2.95	0.59	1.77	2.95
☐ 23	2.95	0.59	1.77	2.95
☐ 24	2.95	0.59	1.77	2.95
☐ 25	2.95	0.59	1.77	2.95
☐ 26	2.95	0.59	1.77	2.95
☐ 27	2.95	0.59	1.77	2.95
☐ 28	2.95	0.59	1.77	2.95
☐ 29	2.95	0.59	1.77	2.95
☐ 30	2.95	0.59	1.77	2.95
☐ 31	2.95	0.59	1.77	2.95

☐ 32, uncensored Doonesbury

	ORIG.	GOOD	FINE	N-MINT
	2.95	0.59	1.77	2.95
☐ 33	2.95	0.59	1.77	2.95
☐ 34	2.95	0.59	1.77	2.95
☐ 35	2.95	0.59	1.77	2.95
☐ 36	2.95	0.59	1.77	2.95
☐ 37	2.95	0.59	1.77	2.95
☐ 40	3.50	0.70	2.10	3.50
☐ 41	3.50	0.70	2.10	3.50
☐ 42	3.50	0.70	2.10	3.50
☐ 43	3.50	0.70	2.10	3.50
☐ 44	3.50	0.70	2.10	3.50
☐ 45	3.50	0.70	2.10	3.50
☐ 46	3.50	0.70	2.10	3.50
☐ 47	3.50	0.70	2.10	3.50
☐ 48	3.50	0.70	2.10	3.50
☐ 49	3.50	0.70	2.10	3.50
☐ 50	3.50	0.70	2.10	3.50
☐ 51	3.50	0.70	2.10	3.50
☐ 52	3.50	0.70	2.10	3.50
☐ 53	3.95	0.79	2.37	3.95
☐ 54	3.95	0.79	2.37	3.95
☐ 55	3.95	0.79	2.37	3.95
☐ 56	3.95	0.79	2.37	3.95
☐ 57	3.95	0.79	2.37	3.95
☐ 58	3.95	0.79	2.37	3.95
☐ 59	3.95	0.79	2.37	3.95
☐ 60	3.95	0.79	2.37	3.95
☐ 61	3.95	0.79	2.37	3.95

☐ 62, Apr 94, b&w strip reprints

	ORIG.	GOOD	FINE	N-MINT
	3.95	0.79	2.37	3.95

	ORIG.	GOOD	FINE	N-MINT
❏ 63, May 94, b&w strip reprints 3.95		0.79	2.37	3.95
❏ 67, Sep 94, b&w strip reprints 3.95		0.79	2.37	3.95
❏ 68, Oct 94, b&w strip reprints 3.95		0.79	2.37	3.95
❏ 69, b&w strip reprints.... 3.95		0.79	2.37	3.95
❏ 70, b&w strip reprints.... 3.95		0.79	2.37	3.95
❏ 71, b&w strip reprints.... 3.95		0.79	2.37	3.95
❏ 72, Feb 95, b&w strip reprints 3.95		0.79	2.37	3.95
❏ 75, May 95, b&w strip reprints 3.95		0.79	2.37	3.95

COMIC STRIP SHOWCASE
ARCADIA

	ORIG.	GOOD	FINE	N-MINT
❏ 1, Lone Ranger	1.59	4.77	7.95	
❏ 2, Polly & Her Pals	1.59	4.77	7.95	
❏ 3, Skyroads, Flyin' Jenny .	1.59	4.77	7.95	
❏ 4, Capt. Midnight	1.59	4.77	7.95	

COMICO CHRISTMAS SPECIAL
COMICO

	ORIG.	GOOD	FINE	N-MINT
❏ 1, DSt(c), SR	0.50	1.50	2.50	

COMICO COLLECTION

	ORIG.	GOOD	FINE	N-MINT
❏ 1, 10 comics & *Grendel: Devil's Vagary*	1.99	5.97	9.95	

COMICS & STORIES (mini-series)
DARK HORSE

	ORIG.	GOOD	FINE	N-MINT
❏ 1, Apr 96, Tex Avery inspired stories 2.95		0.59	1.77	2.95

COMICS 101 PRESENTS
CHEAP THRILLS

❏ 0, Aug 94, nn;no cover price; b&w anthology;two covers, one inside the other ....

COMICS ARTISTS SHOWCASE
SHOWCASE

	ORIG.	GOOD	FINE	N-MINT
❏ 1	0.20	0.60	1.00	

COMICS EXPRESS
COMICS INTERVIEW

	ORIG.	GOOD	FINE	N-MINT
❏ 3, b&w strip rep. (was Eclipse)	0.79	2.37	3.95	
❏ 4, b&w strip rep.	0.79	2.37	3.95	
❏ 5, b&w strip rep.	0.79	2.37	3.95	
❏ 6, b&w strip rep.	0.79	2.37	3.95	
❏ 7, b&w strip rep.	0.79	2.37	3.95	
❏ 8, Pogo added	0.79	2.37	3.95	
❏ 9, Pogo added	0.79	2.37	3.95	
❏ 10, Pogo added	0.79	2.37	3.95	
❏ 11, Pogo added	0.79	2.37	3.95	
❏ 12, Pogo added	0.79	2.37	3.95	
❏ 13, Pogo added	0.79	2.37	3.95	
❏ 14, Pogo added	0.79	2.37	3.95	
❏ 15, Pogo added	0.79	2.37	3.95	
❏ 16, Pogo added	0.79	2.37	3.95	
❏ 17, Pogo added	0.79	2.37	3.95	
❏ 18, Pogo added	0.79	2.37	3.95	
❏ 19, Pogo added	0.79	2.37	3.95	
❏ 20, Pogo added	0.79	2.37	3.95	
❏ 21, Pogo added	0.79	2.37	3.95	
❏ 22, Pogo added	0.79	2.37	3.95	
❏ 23, Pogo added	0.79	2.37	3.95	
❏ 24, Pogo added	0.79	2.37	3.95	
❏ 25, Pogo added	0.79	2.37	3.95	
❏ 26, Pogo added	0.79	2.37	3.95	

ECLIPSE

	ORIG.	GOOD	FINE	N-MINT
❏ 1, b&w, strips	0.59	1.77	2.95	
❏ 2, b&w, strips (moves to Comics Interview)	0.59	1.77	2.95	

COMICS REVIEW
MANUSCRIPT

	ORIG.	GOOD	FINE	N-MINT
❏ 1	0.70	2.10	3.50	
❏ 2	0.40	1.20	2.00	

	ORIG.	GOOD	FINE	N-MINT
❏ 3	0.40	1.20	2.00	
❏ 4	0.40	1.20	2.00	
❏ 5	0.40	1.20	2.00	
❏ 6	0.40	1.20	2.00	
❏ 7	0.40	1.20	2.00	
❏ 8	0.40	1.20	2.00	
❏ 9	0.40	1.20	2.00	
❏ 10	0.40	1.20	2.00	
❏ 11	0.40	1.20	2.00	
❏ 12	0.40	1.20	2.00	
❏ 13	0.50	1.50	2.50	
❏ 14	0.50	1.50	2.50	
❏ 15	0.50	1.50	2.50	
❏ 16	0.50	1.50	2.50	
❏ 17	0.50	1.50	2.50	
❏ 18	0.70	2.10	3.50	
❏ 19	0.70	2.10	3.50	
❏ 20	0.70	2.10	3.50	
❏ 21	0.70	2.10	3.50	
❏ 22	0.70	2.10	3.50	
❏ 23	0.70	2.10	3.50	
❏ 24	0.70	2.10	3.50	
❏ 25	0.70	2.10	3.50	
❏ 26, DG(c) 1:Modesty Blaise	0.79	2.37	3.95	
❏ 27, 1:Phantom	0.79	2.37	3.95	
❏ 28	0.79	2.37	3.95	
❏ 29, TY(c)	0.79	2.37	3.95	
❏ 30, Caniff tribute (becomes *Comics Revue*)	0.79	2.37	3.95	

COMICS REVUE (was Comics Interview title)

	ORIG.	GOOD	FINE	N-MINT
❏ 101, 94, b&w; reprints comic strips 5.95		1.19	3.57	5.95
❏ 105, 95, b&w; reprints comic strips 5.95		1.19	3.57	5.95
❏ 106, 95, b&w; reprints comic strips 5.95		1.19	3.57	5.95
❏ 113, 95, b&w; reprints comic strips 5.95		1.19	3.57	5.95

COMICS REVUE (was Manuscript)
COMICS INTERVIEW

	ORIG.	GOOD	FINE	N-MINT
❏ 31	0.79	2.37	3.95	
❏ 32	0.79	2.37	3.95	
❏ 33	0.79	2.37	3.95	
❏ 34	0.79	2.37	3.95	
❏ 35	0.79	2.37	3.95	
❏ 36	0.79	2.37	3.95	
❏ 37	0.79	2.37	3.95	
❏ 38, WS(c)	0.99	2.97	4.95	
❏ 39	0.99	2.97	4.95	
❏ 40	0.99	2.97	4.95	
❏ 41, Batman begins	0.99	2.97	4.95	
❏ 42, Calvin and Hobbes begins	0.99	2.97	4.95	
❏ 43	0.99	2.97	4.95	
❏ 44	0.99	2.97	4.95	
❏ 45	0.99	2.97	4.95	
❏ 46	0.99	2.97	4.95	
❏ 47	0.99	2.97	4.95	
❏ 48	0.99	2.97	4.95	
❏ 49	0.99	2.97	4.95	
❏ 50	0.99	2.97	4.95	
❏ 51, TMc(c)	0.99	2.97	4.95	
❏ 52	0.99	2.97	4.95	
❏ 53	0.99	2.97	4.95	
❏ 54	0.99	2.97	4.95	
❏ 55	0.99	2.97	4.95	
❏ 56	0.99	2.97	4.95	
❏ 57	0.99	2.97	4.95	
❏ 58, TMNT added	0.99	2.97	4.95	
❏ 59, TMc(c)	0.99	2.97	4.95	
❏ 60	0.99	2.97	4.95	
❏ 61, Bloom County ends	0.99	2.97	4.95	

	ORIG.	GOOD	FINE	N-MINT
62, Latigo ends		0.99	2.97	4.95
63		0.99	2.97	4.95
64		0.99	2.97	4.95
65		0.99	2.97	4.95
66, 1:Judge Dredd		0.99	2.97	4.95
67		0.99	2.97	4.95
68		0.99	2.97	4.95
69		0.99	2.97	4.95
70		0.99	2.97	4.95
71, Krazy Kat begins		0.99	2.97	4.95
72		0.99	2.97	4.95
73		0.99	2.97	4.95
74		0.99	2.97	4.95
75		0.99	2.97	4.95
76		0.99	2.97	4.95
77		0.99	2.97	4.95
78		0.99	2.97	4.95
79, CVess(c)		1.19	3.57	5.95
80, b&w strips	5.95	1.19	3.57	5.95
81, b&w strips	5.95	1.19	3.57	5.95
82, b&w strips	5.95	1.19	3.57	5.95
83, b&w strips	5.95	1.19	3.57	5.95
84, b&w strips	5.95	1.19	3.57	5.95
85, b&w strips	5.95	1.19	3.57	5.95
86, b&w strips	5.95	1.19	3.57	5.95
87, O:Daredevil	5.95	1.19	3.57	5.95
88	5.95	1.19	3.57	5.95
89	5.95	1.19	3.57	5.95
90	5.95	1.19	3.57	5.95
91	5.95	1.19	3.57	5.95
92	5.95	1.19	3.57	5.95
93	5.95	1.19	3.57	5.95
94	5.95	1.19	3.57	5.95
95, 94	5.95	1.19	3.57	5.95
96, 94	5.95	1.19	3.57	5.95
97, 94	5.95	1.19	3.57	5.95
98, 94	5.95	1.19	3.57	5.95
100, 94, b&w; returns to Manuscript Press	6.95	1.39	4.17	6.95

COMICS REVUE ANNUAL
MANUSCRIPT

	ORIG.	GOOD	FINE	N-MINT
1		0.70	2.10	3.50
2		0.99	2.97	4.95

COMICS REVUE ANNUAL (was Manuscript)
COMICS INTERVIEW

	ORIG.	GOOD	FINE	N-MINT
2		0.99	2.97	4.95

COMICS REVUE PRESENTS MODESTY BLAISE
MANUSCRIPT

	ORIG.	GOOD	FINE	N-MINT
1, comic strip	5.95	1.19	3.57	5.95
4, comic strip	5.95	1.19	3.57	5.95
5, 95, b&w magazine; strip reprints	5.95	1.19	3.57	5.95

COMICS' GREATEST WORLD
DARK HORSE

	ORIG.	GOOD	FINE	N-MINT
1, preview copy; 1500 printed	1.00	0.20	0.60	1.00

COMICS' GREATEST WORLD-ARCADIA

	ORIG.	GOOD	FINE	N-MINT
0, 93, collected edition		15.00	45.00	75.00
1, Jun 93, X;limited edition for Heroes World Distribution;enhanced cardstock cover; no cover price	4.00	12.00	20.00	
1, 93, X	1.00	0.20	0.60	1.00
2, 93, Pit Bulls	1.00	0.20	0.60	1.00
3, Jun 93, Ghost	1.00	0.20	0.60	1.00
4, 93, Monster;continues in Comics' Greatest World-Golden City	1.00	0.20	0.60	1.00

COMICS' GREATEST WORLD-CINNABAR FLATS

	ORIG.	GOOD	FINE	N-MINT
0, 93, collected edition		15.00	45.00	75.00
1, 93, Division 13	1.00	0.20	0.60	1.00

	ORIG.	GOOD	FINE	N-MINT
1, Aug 93, Division 13; limited edition for American Distribution;enhanced cover				
1, Aug 93, Division 13; limited edition;cardstock cover;no cover price				
2, 93, Hero Zero	1.00	0.20	0.60	1.00
3, 93, King Tiger	1.00	0.20	0.60	1.00
4, 93, Out of the Vortex; continues in Comics' Greatest World-Out of the Vortex	1.00	0.20	0.60	1.00

COMICS' GREATEST WORLD-GOLDEN CITY

	ORIG.	GOOD	FINE	N-MINT
0, 93, collected edition; no cover price		15.00	45.00	75.00
1, Jul 93, Rebel;JO(c)	1.00	0.20	0.60	1.00
1, Rebel;JO(c);limited edition for Heroes World Distribution;enhanced cardstock cover		4.00	12.00	20.00
2, Mecha	1.00	0.20	0.60	1.00
3, Jul 93, Titan;WS(c)	1.00	0.20	0.60	1.00
4, Aug 93, Catalyst; continues in Comics' Greatest World-Steel Harbor	1.00	0.20	0.60	1.00

COMICS' GREATEST WORLD-OUT OF THE VORTEX

	ORIG.	GOOD	FINE	N-MINT
1, Oct 93, foil embossed cover	2.00	0.40	1.20	2.00
2	2.00	0.40	1.20	2.00
3	1.00	0.20	0.60	1.00
4	1.00	0.20	0.60	1.00

COMICS' GREATEST WORLD-STEEL HARBOR

	ORIG.	GOOD	FINE	N-MINT
0, 93, collected edition		15.00	45.00	75.00
1, Aug 93, Barb Wire	1.00	0.20	0.60	1.00
2, 93, The Machine	1.00	0.20	0.60	1.00
3, Aug 93, Wolf Gang	1.00	0.20	0.60	1.00
4, Aug 93, Motorhead; continues in Comics' Greatest World-Cinnabar Flats	1.00	0.20	0.60	1.00

COMING OF APHRODITE
HERO

	ORIG.	GOOD	FINE	N-MINT
1, b&w		0.79	2.37	3.95

COMMAND REVIEW
ANTARCTIC

	ORIG.	GOOD	FINE	N-MINT
4, Jan 94, (former Thoughts & Images title)	4.95	0.99	2.97	4.95

THOUGHTS & IMAGES

	ORIG.	GOOD	FINE	N-MINT
1, b&w		1.60	4.80	8.00
2, b&w		1.00	3.00	5.00
3, b&w		1.00	3.00	5.00

COMMUNION
EROS COMIX

	ORIG.	GOOD	FINE	N-MINT
1, adult, b&w		0.55	1.65	2.75

COMPLETE CHEECH WIZARD
RIP OFF

	ORIG.	GOOD	FINE	N-MINT
1, Oct 86, Vaughn Bode; b&w	2.25	0.50	1.50	2.50
2, Jan 87, Vaughn Bode; b&w	2.25	0.50	1.50	2.50
3, May 87, Vaughn Bode; b&w and color	2.50	0.50	1.50	2.50
4, Nov 87, Vaughn Bode; b&w and color	2.50	0.50	1.50	2.50

COMPLETE MAX COLLINS/RICK FLETCHER DICK TRACY
DRAGON LADY

	ORIG.	GOOD	FINE	N-MINT
1		1.19	3.57	5.95
2		1.19	3.57	5.95
3		1.19	3.57	5.95

COMPLETE POGO COMICS, THE
ECLIPSE

	ORIG.	GOOD	FINE	N-MINT
1, WK, reprints		1.79	5.37	8.95
2, WK, reprints		1.79	5.37	8.95
3, WK, reprints		1.79	5.37	8.95
4, WK, reprints		1.79	5.37	8.95

COMPLETELY BAD BOYS
FANTAGRAPHICS

	ORIG.	GOOD	FINE	N-MINT
❑ 1, b&w		0.50	1.50	2.50

CONAN
MARVEL

	ORIG.	GOOD	FINE	N-MINT
❑ 1, Aug 95, Cardstock cover	2.95	0.59	1.77	2.95
❑ 2, Sep 95, Cardstock cover	2.95	0.59	1.77	2.95
❑ 3, Oct 95, Cardstock cover	2.95	0.59	1.77	2.95
❑ 4, Nov 95, Cardstock cover;A:Rune	2.95	0.59	1.77	2.95
❑ 5, Dec 95, Cardstock cover	2.95	0.59	1.77	2.95
❑ 6, Jan 96, Cardstock cover	2.95	0.59	1.77	2.95
❑ 7, Feb 96	2.95	0.59	1.77	2.95
❑ 8, Mar 96, Cardstock cover	2.95	0.59	1.77	2.95
❑ 9, Apr 96, Cardstock cover	2.95	0.59	1.77	2.95
❑ 10, May 96, Cardstock cover	2.95	0.59	1.77	2.95
❑ 11, Jun 96, Cardstock cover	2.95	0.59	1.77	2.95

CONAN CLASSIC

	ORIG.	GOOD	FINE	N-MINT
❑ 1, Jun 94, reprint	1.50	0.30	0.90	1.50
❑ 2, Jul 94, reprint	1.50	0.30	0.90	1.50
❑ 3, Aug 94	1.50	0.30	0.90	1.50
❑ 4, Sep 94	1.50	0.30	0.90	1.50
❑ 5, Oct 94	1.50	0.30	0.90	1.50
❑ 6, Nov 94	1.50	0.30	0.90	1.50
❑ 7, Dec 94	1.50	0.30	0.90	1.50
❑ 8, Jan 95	1.50	0.30	0.90	1.50
❑ 9, Feb 95	1.50	0.30	0.90	1.50
❑ 10, Mar 95	1.50	0.30	0.90	1.50
❑ 11, Apr 95	1.50	0.30	0.90	1.50

CONAN SAGA

	ORIG.	GOOD	FINE	N-MINT
❑ 1, BWS b&w, reprints	2.00	1.00	3.00	5.00
❑ 2	2.00	0.80	2.40	4.00
❑ 3	2.00	0.80	2.40	4.00
❑ 4	2.00	0.80	2.40	4.00
❑ 5	2.00	0.80	2.40	4.00
❑ 6	2.00	0.60	1.80	3.00
❑ 7	2.00	0.60	1.80	3.00
❑ 8	2.00	0.60	1.80	3.00
❑ 9	2.00	0.60	1.80	3.00
❑ 10	2.00	0.60	1.80	3.00
❑ 11	2.00	0.60	1.80	3.00
❑ 12	2.00	0.60	1.80	3.00
❑ 13	2.00	0.60	1.80	3.00
❑ 14	2.00	0.60	1.80	3.00
❑ 15	2.00	0.60	1.80	3.00
❑ 16	2.00	0.60	1.80	3.00
❑ 17	2.00	0.60	1.80	3.00
❑ 18	2.00	0.60	1.80	3.00
❑ 19	2.00	0.60	1.80	3.00
❑ 20	2.00	0.60	1.80	3.00
❑ 21	2.00	0.40	1.20	2.00
❑ 22	2.00	0.40	1.20	2.00
❑ 23	2.00	0.40	1.20	2.00
❑ 24	2.00	0.40	1.20	2.00
❑ 25	2.00	0.40	1.20	2.00
❑ 26	2.00	0.40	1.20	2.00
❑ 27	2.00	0.40	1.20	2.00
❑ 28, b&w, reprints	2.25	0.45	1.35	2.25
❑ 29, b&w, reprints	2.25	0.45	1.35	2.25
❑ 30, b&w, reprints	2.25	0.45	1.35	2.25
❑ 31, b&w, reprints	2.25	0.45	1.35	2.25
❑ 32, b&w, reprints	2.25	0.45	1.35	2.25
❑ 33, b&w, reprints	2.25	0.45	1.35	2.25
❑ 34, b&w, reprints	2.25	0.45	1.35	2.25
❑ 35, b&w, reprints	2.25	0.45	1.35	2.25
❑ 36, b&w, reprints	2.25	0.45	1.35	2.25
❑ 37, b&w, reprints	2.25	0.45	1.35	2.25
❑ 38, b&w, reprints	2.25	0.45	1.35	2.25
❑ 39, b&w, reprints	2.25	0.45	1.35	2.25
❑ 40, b&w, reprints	2.25	0.45	1.35	2.25
❑ 41, b&w, reprints	2.25	0.45	1.35	2.25
❑ 42, b&w, reprints	2.25	0.45	1.35	2.25
❑ 43, b&w, reprints	2.25	0.45	1.35	2.25
❑ 44, b&w, reprints	2.25	0.45	1.35	2.25
❑ 45, b&w, reprints	2.25	0.45	1.35	2.25
❑ 46, b&w, reprints	2.25	0.45	1.35	2.25
❑ 47, b&w, reprints	2.25	0.45	1.35	2.25
❑ 48, b&w, reprints	2.25	0.45	1.35	2.25
❑ 49, b&w, reprints	2.25	0.45	1.35	2.25
❑ 50, b&w, reprints	2.25	0.45	1.35	2.25
❑ 51, b&w, reprints	2.25	0.45	1.35	2.25
❑ 52, b&w, reprints	2.25	0.45	1.35	2.25
❑ 53, b&w, reprints	2.25	0.45	1.35	2.25
❑ 54, b&w, reprints	2.25	0.45	1.35	2.25
❑ 55, b&w, reprints	2.25	0.45	1.35	2.25
❑ 56, b&w, reprints	2.25	0.45	1.35	2.25
❑ 57, b&w, reprints	2.25	0.45	1.35	2.25
❑ 58, b&w, reprints	2.25	0.45	1.35	2.25
❑ 59, b&w, reprints	2.25	0.45	1.35	2.25
❑ 60, b&w, reprints	2.25	0.45	1.35	2.25
❑ 61, b&w, reprints	2.25	0.45	1.35	2.25
❑ 62, b&w, reprints	2.25	0.45	1.35	2.25
❑ 63, b&w, reprints	2.25	0.45	1.35	2.25
❑ 64, b&w, reprints	2.25	0.45	1.35	2.25
❑ 65, b&w, reprints	2.25	0.45	1.35	2.25
❑ 66, b&w, reprints	2.25	0.45	1.35	2.25
❑ 67, b&w, reprints	2.25	0.45	1.35	2.25
❑ 68, b&w, reprints	2.25	0.45	1.35	2.25
❑ 69, b&w, reprints	2.25	0.45	1.35	2.25
❑ 70, b&w, reprints	2.25	0.45	1.35	2.25
❑ 71, b&w, reprints	2.25	0.45	1.35	2.25
❑ 72, b&w, reprints	2.25	0.45	1.35	2.25
❑ 73, b&w, reprints	2.25	0.45	1.35	2.25
❑ 74, b&w, reprints	2.25	0.45	1.35	2.25
❑ 75, poster, handbook	3.95	0.79	2.37	3.95
❑ 76, b&w, reprints	2.25	0.45	1.35	2.25
❑ 77, b&w, reprints	2.25	0.45	1.35	2.25
❑ 78, b&w, reprints	2.25	0.45	1.35	2.25
❑ 79, b&w, reprints	2.25	0.45	1.35	2.25
❑ 80, b&w, reprints	2.25	0.45	1.35	2.25
❑ 81, b&w, reprints	2.25	0.45	1.35	2.25
❑ 82, b&w, reprints	2.25	0.45	1.35	2.25
❑ 83, b&w, reprints	3.00	0.60	1.80	3.00
❑ 84, b&w, reprints	2.25	0.45	1.35	2.25
❑ 85, b&w, reprints	2.25	0.45	1.35	2.25
❑ 86, May 94, b&w, reprints	2.25	0.45	1.35	2.25
❑ 87, Jun 94, b&w, reprints	2.25	0.45	1.35	2.25
❑ 88, Jul 94, b&w, reprints	2.25	0.45	1.35	2.25
❑ 89, Aug 94, b&w, reprints	2.25	0.45	1.35	2.25
❑ 90, Sep 94, b&w, reprints	2.25	0.45	1.35	2.25
❑ 91, Oct 94, b&w, reprints	2.25	0.45	1.35	2.25
❑ 92, Nov 94, b&w, reprints	2.25	0.45	1.35	2.25
❑ 93, Dec 94, b&w, reprints	2.25	0.45	1.35	2.25
❑ 94, Jan 95, b&w, reprints	2.25	0.45	1.35	2.25
❑ 95, Feb 95, b&w, reprints	2.25	0.45	1.35	2.25

	ORIG.	GOOD	FINE	N-MINT
❑ 96, Mar 95, b&w, reprints				
.... 2.25	0.45	1.35	2.25
❑ 97, Apr 95, b&w, reprints				
.... 2.25	0.45	1.35	2.25

CONAN THE ADVENTURER

	ORIG.	GOOD	FINE	N-MINT
❑ 1, Jun 94, foil embossed	2.50	0.60	1.80	3.00
❑ 2, Jul 94 .... 1.50	0.30	0.90	1.50
❑ 3, Aug 94 .... 1.50	0.30	0.90	1.50
❑ 4, Sep 94 .... 1.50	0.30	0.90	1.50
❑ 5, Oct 94 .... 1.50	0.30	0.90	1.50
❑ 6, Nov 94 .... 1.50	0.30	0.90	1.50
❑ 7, Dec 94........................ 1.50	0.30	0.90	1.50
❑ 8, Jan 95 .... 1.50	0.30	0.90	1.50
❑ 9, Feb 95 .... 1.50	0.30	0.90	1.50
❑ 10, Mar 95 .... 1.50	0.30	0.90	1.50
❑ 11, Apr 95 .... 1.50	0.30	0.90	1.50
❑ 12, May 95 .... 1.50	0.30	0.90	1.50
❑ 13, Jun 95 .... 1.50	0.30	0.90	1.50
❑ 14, Jul 95, Final issue 1.50	0.30	0.90	1.50

CONAN THE BARBARIAN

	ORIG.	GOOD	FINE	N-MINT
❑ 1, Oct 70, BS, O:Conan A:Kull				
.... 0.15	40.00	120.00	200.00
❑ 2, Dec 70, BS, Howard story				
.... 0.15	20.00	60.00	100.00
❑ 3, Feb 71, BS/TS, low dist.				
.... 0.15	20.00	60.00	100.00
❑ 4, Apr 71, BS/TS 0.15	12.00	36.00	60.00
❑ 5, May 71, BS/TS 0.15	12.00	36.00	60.00
❑ 6, Jun 71, BS 0.15	7.20	21.60	36.00
❑ 7, Jul 71, BS 0.15	7.20	21.60	36.00
❑ 8, Aug 71, BS 0.15	7.20	21.60	36.00
❑ 9, Aug 71, BS 0.15	7.20	21.60	36.00
❑ 10, Oct 71, BS, grant...... 0.25	8.00	24.00	40.00
❑ 11, Nov 71, BS, grant..... 0.25	8.00	24.00	40.00
❑ 12, Dec 71, BS 0.20	7.00	21.00	35.00
❑ 13, Jan 72, BS................ 0.20	7.00	21.00	35.00
❑ 14, Mar 72, BS, A:Elric.... 0.20	8.00	24.00	40.00
❑ 15, May 72, BS, A:Elric .. 0.20	8.00	24.00	40.00
❑ 16, Jul 72, BS/TS, rep.... 0.20	4.00	12.00	20.00
❑ 17, Aug 72, GK.............. 0.20	2.40	7.20	12.00
❑ 18, Aug 72, GK.............. 0.20	2.40	7.20	12.00
❑ 19, Oct 72, BS............... 0.20	4.00	12.00	20.00
❑ 20, Nov 72, BS............... 0.20	4.00	12.00	20.00
❑ 21, Dec 72, BS 0.20	4.00	12.00	20.00
❑ 22, Jan 73, BS................ 0.20	4.00	12.00	20.00
❑ 23, Feb 73, GK/BS/TS 1:Red Sonja				
.... 0.20	6.80	20.40	34.00
❑ 24, Mar 73, BS, Red Sonja				
.... 0.20	5.00	15.00	25.00
❑ 25, Apr 73, JB/GK/TS, mirrors				
.... 0.20	2.40	7.20	12.00
❑ 26, May 73, JB.............. 0.20	1.00	3.00	5.00
❑ 27, Jun 73, JB................ 0.20	1.00	3.00	5.00
❑ 28, Jul 73, JB/GK/TS...... 0.20	1.10	3.30	5.50
❑ 29, Aug 73, JB/GK/TS 0.20	1.10	3.30	5.50
❑ 30, Sep 73, JB/GK/TS 0.20	1.10	3.30	5.50
❑ 31, Oct 73 .... 0.20	0.70	2.10	3.50
❑ 32, Nov 73 .... 0.20	0.70	2.10	3.50
❑ 33, Dec 73...................... 0.20	0.70	2.10	3.50
❑ 34, Jan 74 .... 0.20	0.70	2.10	3.50
❑ 35, Feb 74 .... 0.20	0.70	2.10	3.50
❑ 36, Mar 74 .... 0.20	0.70	2.10	3.50
❑ 37, Apr 74, TS/NA......... 0.20	1.30	3.90	6.50
❑ 38, May 74...................... 0.25	0.50	1.50	2.50
❑ 39, Jun 74....................... 0.25	0.50	1.50	2.50
❑ 40, Jul 74........................ 0.25	0.50	1.50	2.50
❑ 41, Aug 74, JB/GK.......... 0.25	0.45	1.35	2.25
❑ 42, Sep 74, JB/GK.......... 0.25	0.45	1.35	2.25
❑ 43, Oct 74, JB/GK 0.25	0.45	1.35	2.25
❑ 44, Nov 74 .... 0.25	1.00	3.00	5.00
❑ 45, Dec 74...................... 0.25	1.00	3.00	5.00

	ORIG.	GOOD	FINE	N-MINT
❑ 46, Jan 75.......................0.25	0.45	1.35	2.25
❑ 47, Feb 75.......................0.25	0.45	1.35	2.25
❑ 48, Mar 75.......................0.25	0.45	1.35	2.25
❑ 49, Apr 75.......................0.25	0.45	1.35	2.25
❑ 50, May 75.......................0.25	0.45	1.35	2.25
❑ 51, Jun 75 ....0.25	0.40	1.20	2.00
❑ 52, Jul 75.......................0.25	0.40	1.20	2.00
❑ 53, Aug 75 ....0.25	0.40	1.20	2.00
❑ 54, Sep 75 ....0.25	0.40	1.20	2.00
❑ 55, Oct 75.......................0.25	0.40	1.20	2.00
❑ 56, Nov 75 ....0.25	0.40	1.20	2.00
❑ 57, Dec 75.......................0.25	0.40	1.20	2.00
❑ 58, Jan 76.......................0.25	0.60	1.80	3.00
❑ 59, Feb 76.......................0.25	0.60	1.80	3.00
❑ 60, Mar 76.......................0.25	0.40	1.20	2.00
❑ 61, Apr 76.......................0.25	0.40	1.20	2.00
❑ 62, May 76.......................0.25	0.40	1.20	2.00
❑ 63, Jun 76.......................0.25	0.40	1.20	2.00
❑ 64, Jul 76.......................0.25	0.40	1.20	2.00
❑ 65, Aug 76, JB/GK 0.25	0.35	1.05	1.75
❑ 66, Sep 76, JB/GK 0.30	0.35	1.05	1.75
❑ 67, Oct 76, JB/GK, Red Sonja				
....0.30	0.40	1.20	2.00
❑ 68, Nov 76, JB/GK, Red Sonja				
....0.30	0.40	1.20	2.00
❑ 69, Dec 76.......................0.30	0.35	1.05	1.75
❑ 70, Jan 77.......................0.30	0.35	1.05	1.75
❑ 71, Feb 77.......................0.30	0.30	0.90	1.50
❑ 72, Mar 77.......................0.30	0.30	0.90	1.50
❑ 73, Apr 77.......................0.30	0.30	0.90	1.50
❑ 74, May 77.......................0.30	0.30	0.90	1.50
❑ 75, Jun 77.......................0.30	0.30	0.90	1.50
❑ 76, Jul 77.......................0.30	0.30	0.90	1.50
❑ 77, Aug 77.......................0.30	0.30	0.90	1.50
❑ 80, Nov 77.......................0.35	0.30	0.90	1.50
❑ 81, Dec 77.......................0.35	0.30	0.90	1.50
❑ 82, Jan 78.......................0.35	0.30	0.90	1.50
❑ 83, Feb 78.......................0.35	0.25	0.75	1.25
❑ 84, Mar 78.......................0.35	0.25	0.75	1.25
❑ 85, Apr 78.......................0.35	0.25	0.75	1.25
❑ 86, May 78.......................0.35	0.25	0.75	1.25
❑ 87, Jun 78.......................0.35	0.25	0.75	1.25
❑ 88, Jul 78.......................0.35	0.25	0.75	1.25
❑ 89, Aug 78.......................0.35	0.25	0.75	1.25
❑ 90, Sep 78.......................0.35	0.25	0.75	1.25
❑ 91, Oct 78.......................0.35	0.25	0.75	1.25
❑ 92, Nov 78.......................0.35	0.25	0.75	1.25
❑ 93, Dec 78.......................0.35	0.25	0.75	1.25
❑ 94, Jan 79, JB.................0.35	0.30	0.90	1.50
❑ 95, Feb 79, JB.................0.35	0.30	0.90	1.50
❑ 96, Mar 79, JB.................0.35	0.30	0.90	1.50
❑ 97, Apr 79, JB.................0.35	0.30	0.90	1.50
❑ 98, JB 0.40	0.30	0.90	1.50
❑ 99, JB 0.40	0.30	0.90	1.50
❑ 98, May 79, JB.................0.40	0.30	0.90	1.50
❑ 99, Jun 79, JB 0.40	0.30	0.90	1.50
❑ 100, Jul 79, JB/TS, D:Belit				
....0.60	0.60	1.80	3.00
❑ 101, Aug 79, JB...............0.40	0.30	0.90	1.50
❑ 102, Sep 79, JB...............0.40	0.30	0.90	1.50
❑ 103, Oct 79, JB...............0.40	0.30	0.90	1.50
❑ 104, Nov 79, JB...............0.40	0.30	0.90	1.50
❑ 105, Dec 79, JB...............0.40	0.30	0.90	1.50
❑ 106, Jan 80, JB...............0.40	0.30	0.90	1.50
❑ 107, Feb 80, JB...............0.40	0.30	0.90	1.50
❑ 108, Mar 80, JB...............0.40	0.30	0.90	1.50
❑ 109, Apr 80, JB...............0.40	0.30	0.90	1.50
❑ 110, May 80, JB...............0.40	0.30	0.90	1.50
❑ 111, Jun 80, JB...............0.40	0.30	0.90	1.50
❑ 112, Jul 80, JB...............0.40	0.30	0.90	1.50
❑ 113, Aug 80, JB...............0.40	0.30	0.90	1.50
❑ 114, Sep 80, JB 0.50	0.30	0.90	1.50

	ORIG.	GOOD	FINE	N-MINT
❑ 115, Oct 80, JB, 10th anniv.	0.75	0.40	1.20	2.00
❑ 116, Nov 80, JB/NA, rep.	0.50	0.30	0.90	1.50
❑ 117	0.50	0.25	0.75	1.25
❑ 118	0.50	0.25	0.75	1.25
❑ 119	0.50	0.25	0.75	1.25
❑ 120	0.50	0.25	0.75	1.25
❑ 121	0.50	0.25	0.75	1.25
❑ 122	0.50	0.25	0.75	1.25
❑ 123	0.50	0.25	0.75	1.25
❑ 124	0.50	0.25	0.75	1.25
❑ 125	0.50	0.25	0.75	1.25
❑ 126	0.50	0.25	0.75	1.25
❑ 127	0.50	0.20	0.60	1.00
❑ 128	0.50	0.20	0.60	1.00
❑ 129	0.50	0.20	0.60	1.00
❑ 130	0.60	0.20	0.60	1.00
❑ 131	0.60	0.20	0.60	1.00
❑ 132	0.60	0.20	0.60	1.00
❑ 133	0.60	0.20	0.60	1.00
❑ 134	0.60	0.20	0.60	1.00
❑ 135	0.60	0.20	0.60	1.00
❑ 136	0.60	0.20	0.60	1.00
❑ 137	0.60	0.20	0.60	1.00
❑ 138	0.60	0.20	0.60	1.00
❑ 139	0.60	0.20	0.60	1.00
❑ 140	0.60	0.20	0.60	1.00
❑ 141	0.60	0.20	0.60	1.00
❑ 142	0.60	0.20	0.60	1.00
❑ 143	0.60	0.20	0.60	1.00
❑ 144	0.60	0.20	0.60	1.00
❑ 145	0.60	0.20	0.60	1.00
❑ 146	0.60	0.20	0.60	1.00
❑ 147	0.60	0.20	0.60	1.00
❑ 148	0.60	0.20	0.60	1.00
❑ 149	0.60	0.20	0.60	1.00
❑ 150	0.60	0.20	0.60	1.00
❑ 151	0.60	0.20	0.60	1.00
❑ 152	0.60	0.20	0.60	1.00
❑ 153	0.60	0.20	0.60	1.00
❑ 154	0.60	0.20	0.60	1.00
❑ 155	0.60	0.20	0.60	1.00
❑ 156	0.60	0.20	0.60	1.00
❑ 157	0.60	0.20	0.60	1.00
❑ 158	0.60	0.20	0.60	1.00
❑ 159	0.60	0.20	0.60	1.00
❑ 160	0.60	0.20	0.60	1.00
❑ 161	0.60	0.20	0.60	1.00
❑ 162	0.60	0.20	0.60	1.00
❑ 163	0.60	0.20	0.60	1.00
❑ 164	0.60	0.20	0.60	1.00
❑ 165	0.60	0.20	0.60	1.00
❑ 166	0.60	0.20	0.60	1.00
❑ 167	0.60	0.20	0.60	1.00
❑ 168	0.60	0.20	0.60	1.00
❑ 169	0.65	0.20	0.60	1.00
❑ 170	0.65	0.20	0.60	1.00
❑ 171	0.65	0.20	0.60	1.00
❑ 172	0.65	0.20	0.60	1.00
❑ 173	0.65	0.20	0.60	1.00
❑ 174	0.65	0.20	0.60	1.00
❑ 175	0.65	0.20	0.60	1.00
❑ 176	0.65	0.20	0.60	1.00
❑ 177	0.65	0.20	0.60	1.00
❑ 178	0.65	0.20	0.60	1.00
❑ 179	0.75	0.20	0.60	1.00
❑ 180	0.75	0.20	0.60	1.00
❑ 181	0.75	0.20	0.60	1.00
❑ 182	0.75	0.20	0.60	1.00
❑ 183	0.75	0.20	0.60	1.00
❑ 184	0.75	0.20	0.60	1.00
❑ 185	0.75	0.20	0.60	1.00

	ORIG.	GOOD	FINE	N-MINT
❑ 186	0.75	0.20	0.60	1.00
❑ 187	0.75	0.20	0.60	1.00
❑ 188	0.75	0.20	0.60	1.00
❑ 189	0.75	0.20	0.60	1.00
❑ 190	0.75	0.20	0.60	1.00
❑ 191	0.75	0.20	0.60	1.00
❑ 192	0.75	0.20	0.60	1.00
❑ 193	0.75	0.20	0.60	1.00
❑ 194	1.00	0.20	0.60	1.00
❑ 195	1.00	0.20	0.60	1.00
❑ 196	1.00	0.20	0.60	1.00
❑ 197	1.00	0.20	0.60	1.00
❑ 198	1.00	0.20	0.60	1.00
❑ 199	1.00	0.20	0.60	1.00
❑ 200	1.50	0.30	0.90	1.50
❑ 201	1.00	0.20	0.60	1.00
❑ 202	1.00	0.20	0.60	1.00
❑ 203	1.00	0.20	0.60	1.00
❑ 204	1.00	0.20	0.60	1.00
❑ 205	1.00	0.20	0.60	1.00
❑ 206	1.00	0.20	0.60	1.00
❑ 207	1.00	0.20	0.60	1.00
❑ 208	1.00	0.20	0.60	1.00
❑ 209	1.00	0.20	0.60	1.00
❑ 210	1.00	0.20	0.60	1.00
❑ 211	1.00	0.20	0.60	1.00
❑ 212	1.00	0.20	0.60	1.00
❑ 213	1.00	0.20	0.60	1.00
❑ 214	1.00	0.20	0.60	1.00
❑ 215	1.00	0.20	0.60	1.00
❑ 216	1.00	0.20	0.60	1.00
❑ 217	1.00	0.20	0.60	1.00
❑ 218	1.00	0.20	0.60	1.00
❑ 219	1.00	0.20	0.60	1.00
❑ 220	1.00	0.20	0.60	1.00
❑ 221	1.00	0.20	0.60	1.00
❑ 222	1.00	0.20	0.60	1.00
❑ 223	1.00	0.20	0.60	1.00
❑ 224	1.00	0.20	0.60	1.00
❑ 225	1.00	0.20	0.60	1.00
❑ 226	1.00	0.20	0.60	1.00
❑ 227	1.00	0.20	0.60	1.00
❑ 228	1.00	0.20	0.60	1.00
❑ 229	1.00	0.20	0.60	1.00
❑ 230	1.00	0.20	0.60	1.00
❑ 231	1.00	0.20	0.60	1.00
❑ 232, starts over	1.00	0.20	0.60	1.00
❑ 233	1.00	0.20	0.60	1.00
❑ 234	1.00	0.20	0.60	1.00
❑ 235	1.00	0.20	0.60	1.00
❑ 236	1.00	0.20	0.60	1.00
❑ 237	1.00	0.20	0.60	1.00
❑ 238	1.00	0.20	0.60	1.00
❑ 239	1.00	0.20	0.60	1.00
❑ 240	1.00	0.20	0.60	1.00
❑ 241, TMc(c)	1.00	0.80	2.40	4.00
❑ 242, JLee(c)	1.00	0.50	1.50	2.50
❑ 243, Red Sonja	1.00	0.20	0.60	1.00
❑ 244, Red Sonja	1.00	0.20	0.60	1.00
❑ 245, Red Sonja	1.00	0.20	0.60	1.00
❑ 246, Red Sonja	1.00	0.20	0.60	1.00
❑ 247, Red Sonja	1.00	0.20	0.60	1.00
❑ 248, Red Sonja	1.00	0.20	0.60	1.00
❑ 249, Red Sonja	1.00	0.20	0.60	1.00
❑ 250	1.50	0.30	0.90	1.50
❑ 251	1.00	0.20	0.60	1.00
❑ 252	1.00	0.20	0.60	1.00
❑ 253	1.25	0.25	0.75	1.25
❑ 254	1.25	0.25	0.75	1.25
❑ 255	1.25	0.25	0.75	1.25
❑ 256	1.25	0.25	0.75	1.25
❑ 257	1.25	0.25	0.75	1.25

	ORIG.	GOOD	FINE	N-MINT
☐ 258	1.25	0.25	0.75	1.25
☐ 259	1.25	0.25	0.75	1.25
☐ 260	1.25	0.25	0.75	1.25
☐ 261	1.25	0.25	0.75	1.25
☐ 262	1.25	0.25	0.75	1.25
☐ 263	1.25	0.25	0.75	1.25
☐ 264	1.25	0.25	0.75	1.25
☐ 265	1.25	0.25	0.75	1.25
☐ 266	1.25	0.25	0.75	1.25
☐ 267	1.25	0.25	0.75	1.25
☐ 268	1.25	0.25	0.75	1.25
☐ 269	1.25	0.25	0.75	1.25
☐ 270	1.25	0.25	0.75	1.25
☐ 271	1.25	0.25	0.75	1.25
☐ 272	1.25	0.25	0.75	1.25
☐ 273	1.25	0.25	0.75	1.25
☐ 274	1.25	0.25	0.75	1.25
☐ 275, last issue	2.50	0.50	1.50	2.50

CONAN THE BARBARIAN KING-SIZE/ANNUAL

	ORIG.	GOOD	FINE	N-MINT
☐ 1, 73, BS	0.35	2.00	6.00	10.00
☐ 2, 76, BS	0.50	0.60	1.80	3.00
☐ 3, 77, A:Kull	0.60	0.40	1.20	2.00
☐ 4, 78	0.60	0.30	0.90	1.50
☐ 5, 79	0.75	0.30	0.90	1.50
☐ 6, 81	0.75	0.30	0.90	1.50
☐ 7	1.00	0.25	0.75	1.25
☐ 8	1.00	0.25	0.75	1.25
☐ 9	1.00	0.25	0.75	1.25
☐ 10	1.25	0.25	0.75	1.25
☐ 11	1.25	0.25	0.75	1.25

CONAN THE BARBARIAN MOVIE SPECIAL

	ORIG.	GOOD	FINE	N-MINT
☐ 1, JB	0.60	0.20	0.60	1.00
☐ 2, JB	0.60	0.20	0.60	1.00

CONAN THE BARBARIAN SPECIAL

	ORIG.	GOOD	FINE	N-MINT
☐ 1, reprint	2.50	0.50	1.50	2.50

CONAN THE DESTROYER MOVIE SPECIAL

	ORIG.	GOOD	FINE	N-MINT
☐ 1	0.75	0.30	0.90	1.50
☐ 2	0.75	0.30	0.90	1.50

CONAN THE KING (formerly King Conan)

	ORIG.	GOOD	FINE	N-MINT
☐ 21	1.00	0.20	0.60	1.00
☐ 22	1.00	0.20	0.60	1.00
☐ 23	1.00	0.20	0.60	1.00
☐ 24	1.00	0.20	0.60	1.00
☐ 25	1.00	0.20	0.60	1.00
☐ 26	1.00	0.20	0.60	1.00
☐ 27	1.00	0.20	0.60	1.00
☐ 28	1.25	0.25	0.75	1.25
☐ 29	1.25	0.25	0.75	1.25
☐ 30	1.25	0.25	0.75	1.25
☐ 31	1.25	0.25	0.75	1.25
☐ 32	1.25	0.25	0.75	1.25
☐ 33	1.25	0.25	0.75	1.25
☐ 34	1.25	0.25	0.75	1.25
☐ 35	1.25	0.25	0.75	1.25
☐ 36	1.25	0.25	0.75	1.25
☐ 37	1.25	0.25	0.75	1.25
☐ 38	1.25	0.25	0.75	1.25
☐ 39	1.25	0.25	0.75	1.25
☐ 40	1.25	0.25	0.75	1.25
☐ 41	1.25	0.25	0.75	1.25
☐ 42	1.25	0.25	0.75	1.25
☐ 43	1.25	0.25	0.75	1.25
☐ 44	1.25	0.25	0.75	1.25
☐ 45	1.25	0.25	0.75	1.25
☐ 46	1.50	0.30	0.90	1.50
☐ 47	1.50	0.30	0.90	1.50
☐ 48	1.50	0.30	0.90	1.50
☐ 49	1.50	0.30	0.90	1.50
☐ 50	1.50	0.30	0.90	1.50
☐ 51	1.50	0.30	0.90	1.50

	ORIG.	GOOD	FINE	N-MINT
☐ 52	1.50	0.30	0.90	1.50
☐ 53	1.50	0.30	0.90	1.50
☐ 54	1.50	0.30	0.90	1.50
☐ 55	1.50	0.30	0.90	1.50

CONAN THE SAVAGE

	ORIG.	GOOD	FINE	N-MINT
☐ 2, Sep 95, b&w magazine	2.95	0.59	1.77	2.95
☐ 3, Oct 95, b&w magazine	2.95	0.59	1.77	2.95
☐ 4, Nov 95, b&w magazine; V:Rune;indicia gives title as "Conan"	2.95	0.59	1.77	2.95
☐ 5, Dec 95, b&w magazine	2.95	0.59	1.77	2.95
☐ 6, Jan 96, b&w magazine	2.95	0.59	1.77	2.95
☐ 7, Feb 96, b&w magazine	2.95	0.59	1.77	2.95
☐ 8, Mar 96, b&w magazine	2.95	0.59	1.77	2.95
☐ 9, Apr 96, b&w magazine	2.95	0.59	1.77	2.95
☐ 10, May 96, b&w magazine	2.95	0.59	1.77	2.95

CONAN VS. RUNE

	ORIG.	GOOD	FINE	N-MINT
☐ 1, Nov 95, BWS; one-shot	2.95	0.59	1.77	2.95

CONCRETE
DARK HORSE

	ORIG.	GOOD	FINE	N-MINT
☐ 1, Mar 87, PC	1.50	2.00	6.00	10.00
☐ 2, Jun 87, PC	1.50	1.20	3.60	6.00
☐ 3, Aug 87, O:Concrete, PC	1.50	0.80	2.40	4.00
☐ 4, Oct 87, O:Concrete, PC	1.75	0.80	2.40	4.00
☐ 5, Dec 87, PC	1.75	0.80	2.40	4.00
☐ 6, Feb 88, PC	1.75	0.50	1.50	2.50
☐ 7, Apr 88, PC	1.75	0.50	1.50	2.50
☐ 8, Jun 88, PC	1.75	0.50	1.50	2.50
☐ 9, Sep 88, PC	1.75	0.50	1.50	2.50
☐ 10, 88, PC	1.75	0.50	1.50	2.50

CONCRETE CELEBRATES EARTH DAY

	ORIG.	GOOD	FINE	N-MINT
☐ 1, Apr 90, Moebius;PC	3.50	1.00	3.00	5.00

CONCRETE COLOR SPECIAL

	ORIG.	GOOD	FINE	N-MINT
☐ 1, Feb 89, PC, Elizabeth Chadwick, rep. in color	2.95	0.59	1.77	2.95

CONCRETE: A NEW LIFE

	ORIG.	GOOD	FINE	N-MINT
☐ 1, Oct 89, O:Concrete, PC, b&w reprint	2.95	0.59	1.77	2.95

CONCRETE: ECLECTICA

	ORIG.	GOOD	FINE	N-MINT
☐ 1, Apr 93	2.95	0.59	1.77	2.95
☐ 2, May 93	2.95	0.59	1.77	2.95

CONCRETE: FRAGILE CREATURE

	ORIG.	GOOD	FINE	N-MINT
☐ 1, Jun 91, PC, color	2.50	0.50	1.50	2.50
☐ 2, 91, PC, color	2.50	0.50	1.50	2.50
☐ 3, Aug 91, PC, color	2.50	0.50	1.50	2.50
☐ 4, Feb 92, PC, color	2.50	0.50	1.50	2.50

CONCRETE: KILLER SMILE (mini-series)
DARK HORSE/LEGEND

	ORIG.	GOOD	FINE	N-MINT
☐ 1, Jul 94	2.95	0.59	1.77	2.95
☐ 2, Aug 94	2.95	0.59	1.77	2.95
☐ 3, Sep 94	2.95	0.59	1.77	2.95
☐ 4, Oct 94	2.95	0.59	1.77	2.95

CONCRETE: LAND & SEA
DARK HORSE

	ORIG.	GOOD	FINE	N-MINT
☐ 1, Feb 89, PC, b&w reprint	2.95	0.59	1.77	2.95

CONCRETE: ODD JOBS

	ORIG.	GOOD	FINE	N-MINT
☐ 1, Jul 90, PC, b&w reprint	3.50	0.70	2.10	3.50

CONCRETE: THINK LIKE A MOUNTAIN
DARK HORSE/LEGEND

	ORIG.	GOOD	FINE	N-MINT
☐ 0, 96, nn;promotional giveaway for mini-series;b&w				
☐ 1, Mar 96, "Green Fire"	2.95	0.59	1.77	2.95

	ORIG.	GOOD	FINE	N-MINT
❏ 2, Apr 96 .... 2.95		0.59	1.77	2.95
❏ 3, May 96, "Arms and Boxes"				
.... 2.95		0.59	1.77	2.95

CONEHEADS (mini-series)
MARVEL

	ORIG.	GOOD	FINE	N-MINT
❏ 1, Jun 94 .... 1.75		0.35	1.05	1.75
❏ 2, Jul 94 .... 1.75		0.35	1.05	1.75
❏ 3, Aug 94 .... 1.75		0.35	1.05	1.75
❏ 4, Sep 94 .... 1.75		0.35	1.05	1.75

CONGORILLA
DC

	ORIG.	GOOD	FINE	N-MINT
❏ 1, Nov 92 .... 1.75		0.35	1.05	1.75
❏ 2, Dec 92 .... 1.75		0.35	1.05	1.75
❏ 3, Jan 93 .... 1.75		0.35	1.05	1.75
❏ 4, Feb 93 .... 1.75		0.35	1.05	1.75

CONQUEROR
HARRIER

	GOOD	FINE	N-MINT
❏ 1	0.20	0.60	1.00
❏ 2	0.20	0.60	1.00
❏ 3	0.20	0.60	1.00
❏ 4	0.20	0.60	1.00
❏ 5	0.20	0.60	1.00
❏ 6	0.20	0.60	1.00
❏ 7	0.20	0.60	1.00
❏ 8	0.20	0.60	1.00
❏ 9	0.20	0.60	1.00

CONQUEROR OF THE BARREN EARTH
DC

	ORIG.	GOOD	FINE	N-MINT
❏ 1, Feb 83 .... 0.75		0.20	0.60	1.00
❏ 2, Mar 83 .... 0.75		0.20	0.60	1.00
❏ 3, Apr 83 .... 0.75		0.20	0.60	1.00
❏ 4, May 83 .... 0.75		0.20	0.60	1.00

CONQUEROR SPECIAL
HARRIER

	GOOD	FINE	N-MINT
❏ 1	0.39	1.17	1.95

CONQUEROR UNIVERSE

	GOOD	FINE	N-MINT
❏ 1	0.20	0.60	1.00

CONSERVATION CORPS
ARCHIE

	ORIG.	GOOD	FINE	N-MINT
❏ 1, Aug 93 .... 1.25		0.25	0.75	1.25
❏ 2 .... 1.25		0.25	0.75	1.25
❏ 3, Nov 93 .... 1.25		0.25	0.75	1.25

CONSPIRACY COMICS
REVOLUTIONARY

	ORIG.	GOOD	FINE	N-MINT
❏ 1, Oct 91, M. Monroe 2.50		0.50	1.50	2.50
❏ 2, Feb 92, b&w, JFK 2.50		0.50	1.50	2.50
❏ 3, Jul 92, b&w, RFK 2.50		0.50	1.50	2.50

CONSTELLATION GRAPHICS
STAGES

	GOOD	FINE	N-MINT
❏ 1	0.30	0.90	1.50
❏ 2	0.30	0.90	1.50

CONTAMINATED ZONE
BRAVE NEW WORDS

	GOOD	FINE	N-MINT
❏ 1, b&w	0.50	1.50	2.50
❏ 2, b&w	0.50	1.50	2.50
❏ 3, b&w	0.50	1.50	2.50

CONTEMPORARY BIO-GRAPHICS
REVOLUTIONARY

	ORIG.	GOOD	FINE	N-MINT
❏ 1, Dec 91, b&w, Stan Lee 2.50		0.50	1.50	2.50
❏ 2, Apr 92, b&w, Boris Yeltsin				
.... 2.50		0.50	1.50	2.50
❏ 3, May 92, b&w, Gene Roddenberry				
.... 2.50		0.50	1.50	2.50
❏ 4, Jun 92, Pee Wee Herman				
.... 2.50		0.50	1.50	2.50
❏ 5, Sep 92, b&w, David Lynch				
.... 2.50		0.50	1.50	2.50
❏ 6, Oct 92, Ross Perot 2.50		0.50	1.50	2.50

	ORIG.	GOOD	FINE	N-MINT
❏ 7, Dec 92, b&w, Spike Lee				
.... 2.50		0.50	1.50	2.50
❏ 8, Jun 93, b&w, Image story				
.... 2.50		0.50	1.50	2.50

CONTENDER COMICS SPECIAL
CONTENDER

	GOOD	FINE	N-MINT
❏ 1, 94, b&w			

CONTRACTORS
ECLIPSE

	GOOD	FINE	N-MINT
❏ 1, Ken Macklin, b&w	0.40	1.20	2.00

CONVOCATIONS--A MAGIC:
THE GATHERING GALLERY
ACCLAIM/ARMADA

	ORIG.	GOOD	FINE	N-MINT
❏ 1, Jan 95, pin-ups;reproduces covers from several Magic				
mini-series 2.50		0.50	1.50	2.50

COOL WORLD
DC

	GOOD	FINE	N-MINT
❏ 1	0.35	1.05	1.75
❏ 2	0.35	1.05	1.75
❏ 3	0.35	1.05	1.75
❏ 4	0.35	1.05	1.75

COOL WORLD MOVIE ADAPTATION

	GOOD	FINE	N-MINT
❏ 0, nn	0.70	2.10	3.50

COPS: THE JOB
MARVEL

	ORIG.	GOOD	FINE	N-MINT
❏ 1 .... 1.25		0.25	0.75	1.25
❏ 2 .... 1.25		0.25	0.75	1.25
❏ 3 .... 1.25		0.25	0.75	1.25
❏ 4 .... 1.25		0.25	0.75	1.25

CORBAN THE BARBEARIAN
ME COMIX

	GOOD	FINE	N-MINT
❏ 1	0.30	0.90	1.50
❏ 2	0.30	0.90	1.50

CORBEN SPECIAL
PACIFIC

	GOOD	FINE	N-MINT
❏ 1	0.30	0.90	1.50

CORBO
SWORD IN STONE

	GOOD	FINE	N-MINT
❏ 1	0.35	1.05	1.75

CORMAC MAC ART
DARK HORSE

	GOOD	FINE	N-MINT
❏ 1, b&w	0.39	1.17	1.95
❏ 2, b&w	0.39	1.17	1.95
❏ 3, b&w	0.39	1.17	1.95
❏ 4, b&w	0.39	1.17	1.95

CORTEZ AND THE FALL OF THE AZTECS
TOME

	ORIG.	GOOD	FINE	N-MINT
❏ 1, b&w 2.95		0.59	1.77	2.95

CORUM: THE BULL AND THE SPEAR
FIRST

	GOOD	FINE	N-MINT
❏ 1	0.39	1.17	1.95
❏ 2	0.39	1.17	1.95
❏ 3	0.39	1.17	1.95
❏ 4	0.39	1.17	1.95

COSMIC BOOK, THE
ACE

	GOOD	FINE	N-MINT
❏ 1, WW,ATh	0.39	1.17	1.95

COSMIC BOY
DC

	ORIG.	GOOD	FINE	N-MINT
❏ 1, Dec 86, Legends 0.75		0.30	0.90	1.50
❏ 2, Jan 87, Legends 0.75		0.30	0.90	1.50
❏ 3, Feb 87, Legends 0.75		0.30	0.90	1.50
❏ 4, Mar 87, Legends 0.75		0.30	0.90	1.50

COSMIC HEROES
ETERNITY

	GOOD	FINE	N-MINT
❏ 1, b&w, Buck Rogers	0.39	1.17	1.95
❏ 2, b&w, Buck Rogers	0.39	1.17	1.95
❏ 3, b&w, Buck Rogers	0.39	1.17	1.95

	ORIG.	GOOD	FINE	N-MINT
☐ 4, b&w, Buck Rogers......	0.39	1.17	1.95	
☐ 5, b&w, Buck Rogers......	0.39	1.17	1.95	
☐ 6, b&w, Buck Rogers......	0.39	1.17	1.95	
☐ 7	0.45	1.35	2.25	
☐ 8	0.45	1.35	2.25	
☐ 9	0.59	1.77	2.95	
☐ 10	0.70	2.10	3.50	
☐ 11	0.79	2.37	3.95	

COSMIC KLITI
EROS COMIX

	ORIG.	GOOD	FINE	N-MINT
☐ 1, b&w, GM....................	0.45	1.35	2.25	

COSMIC ODYSSEY
DC

	ORIG.	GOOD	FINE	N-MINT
☐ 1, Nov 88, A:Superman, Batman V:Darkseid				
.... 3.50	1.20	3.60	6.00	
☐ 2, Dec 88...................... 3.50	1.00	3.00	5.00	
☐ 3, Dec 88...................... 3.50	1.00	3.00	5.00	
☐ 4, Jan 89...................... 3.50	1.00	3.00	5.00	

COSMIC POWERS
MARVEL

	ORIG.	GOOD	FINE	N-MINT
☐ 1, Mar 94, Thanos... 2.50	0.60	1.80	3.00	
☐ 2, Apr 94, Terrax........... 2.50	0.50	1.50	2.50	
☐ 3, May 94, Jack of Hearts & Ganymede				
.... 2.50	0.50	1.50	2.50	
☐ 4, Jun 94, Legacy.......... 2.50	0.50	1.50	2.50	
☐ 5, Jul 94, Morg 2.50	0.50	1.50	2.50	
☐ 6, Aug 94 .... 2.50	0.50	1.50	2.50	

COSMIC POWERS UNLIMITED

	ORIG.	GOOD	FINE	N-MINT
☐ 1, May 95...................... 3.95	0.79	2.37	3.95	
☐ 2, Aug 95, no issue number on cover				
.... 3.95	0.79	2.37	3.95	
☐ 3, Dec 95...................... 3.95	0.79	2.37	3.95	
☐ 4, Feb 96...................... 3.95	0.79	2.37	3.95	
☐ 5, May 96...................... 3.95	0.79	2.37	3.95	

COSMIC STELLER REBELLERS
HAMMAC

	ORIG.	GOOD	FINE	N-MINT
☐ 1, b&w	0.30	0.90	1.50	
☐ 2, b&w	0.30	0.90	1.50	

COSMOS
MICMAC

	ORIG.	GOOD	FINE	N-MINT
☐ 1	0.40	1.20	2.00	

COUGAR, THE
ATLAS/ SEABOARD

	ORIG.	GOOD	FINE	N-MINT
☐ 1, Apr 75 .... 0.25	0.20	0.60	1.00	
☐ 2, Jul 75, O:Cougar 0.25	0.20	0.60	1.00	

COUNT DUCKULA
MARVEL

	ORIG.	GOOD	FINE	N-MINT
☐ 1, O:Count Duckula 1.00	0.20	0.60	1.00	
☐ 2 .... 1.00	0.20	0.60	1.00	
☐ 3, 1:Danger Mouse.......... 1.00	0.20	0.60	1.00	
☐ 4, Danger Mouse............. 1.00	0.20	0.60	1.00	
☐ 5, Danger Mouse............. 1.00	0.20	0.60	1.00	
☐ 6, Danger Mouse............. 1.00	0.20	0.60	1.00	
☐ 7, Danger Mouse............. 1.00	0.20	0.60	1.00	
☐ 8, Geraldo Rivera 1.00	0.20	0.60	1.00	
☐ 9 .... 1.00	0.20	0.60	1.00	
☐ 10 .... 1.00	0.20	0.60	1.00	
☐ 11 .... 1.00	0.20	0.60	1.00	
☐ 12 .... 1.00	0.20	0.60	1.00	
☐ 13 .... 1.00	0.20	0.60	1.00	
☐ 14 .... 1.00	0.20	0.60	1.00	
☐ 15 .... 1.00	0.20	0.60	1.00	

COUNTERPARTS
TUNDRA

	ORIG.	GOOD	FINE	N-MINT
☐ 1, b&w	0.59	1.77	2.95	
☐ 2, b&w	0.59	1.77	2.95	

COUPLE OF WINOS, A
FANTAGRAPHICS

	ORIG.	GOOD	FINE	N-MINT
☐ 1, b&w	0.45	1.35	2.25	

COUTOO
DARK HORSE

	ORIG.	GOOD	FINE	N-MINT
☐ 0, 94, nn;one-shot;b&w....				

COYOTE
EPIC

	ORIG.	GOOD	FINE	N-MINT
☐ 1, Apr 83...................... 1.50	0.30	0.90	1.50	
☐ 2, Jun 83 .... 1.50	0.30	0.90	1.50	
☐ 3, Sep 83 .... 1.50	0.30	0.90	1.50	
☐ 4, Jan 84...................... 1.50	0.30	0.90	1.50	
☐ 5, Apr 84...................... 1.50	0.30	0.90	1.50	
☐ 6, Jun 84 .... 1.50	0.30	0.90	1.50	
☐ 7, Jul 84....................... 1.50	0.30	0.90	1.50	
☐ 8, Oct 84....................... 1.50	0.30	0.90	1.50	
☐ 9, Dec 84...................... 1.50	0.30	0.90	1.50	
☐ 10, Jan 85..................... 1.50	0.30	0.90	1.50	
☐ 11, Mar 85, TMc 1.50	1.20	3.60	6.00	
☐ 12, May 85, TMc............ 1.50	0.80	2.40	4.00	
☐ 13, Jul 85, TMc.............. 1.50	0.80	2.40	4.00	
☐ 14, Sep 85, A:Badger......1.50	1.20	3.60	6.00	
☐ 15, Nov 85..................... 1.50	0.30	0.90	1.50	
☐ 16, Jan 86..................... 1.50	0.30	0.90	1.50	

CRABBS
CAT-HEAD

	ORIG.	GOOD	FINE	N-MINT
☐ 1, b&w............................ 3.75	0.75	2.25	3.75	

CRACK BUSTERS
SHOWCASE

	ORIG.	GOOD	FINE	N-MINT
☐ 1	0.39	1.17	1.95	
☐ 2	0.39	1.17	1.95	

CRAP
FANTAGRAPHICS

	ORIG.	GOOD	FINE	N-MINT
☐ 1, b&w............................ 2.50	0.50	1.50	2.50	
☐ 2, b&w............................ 2.50	0.50	1.50	2.50	
☐ 3, b&w............................ 2.50	0.50	1.50	2.50	
☐ 4, b&w............................ 2.50	0.50	1.50	2.50	
☐ 5, Aug 94, b&w.............. 2.50	0.50	1.50	2.50	

CRASH DUMMIES
HARVEY

	ORIG.	GOOD	FINE	N-MINT
☐ 1 .... 1.50	0.30	0.90	1.50	
☐ 2 .... 1.50	0.30	0.90	1.50	
☐ 3 .... 1.50	0.30	0.90	1.50	

CRASH RYAN
EPIC

	ORIG.	GOOD	FINE	N-MINT
☐ 1, Oct 84....................... 1.50	0.30	0.90	1.50	
☐ 2, Nov 84...................... 1.50	0.30	0.90	1.50	
☐ 3, Dec 84...................... 1.50	0.30	0.90	1.50	
☐ 4, Jan 85...................... 1.50	0.30	0.90	1.50	

CRASH TEST DUMMIES
HARVEL

	ORIG.	GOOD	FINE	N-MINT
☐ 1 .... 1.50	0.30	0.90	1.50	
☐ 2 .... 1.50	0.30	0.90	1.50	
☐ 3 .... 1.50	0.30	0.90	1.50	

CRAZY (black-and-white magazine)
MARVEL

	ORIG.	GOOD	FINE	N-MINT
☐ 1 .... 0.40	2.00	6.00	10.00	
☐ 2 .... 0.40	1.20	3.60	6.00	
☐ 3 .... 0.40	1.00	3.00	5.00	
☐ 4 .... 0.40	1.00	3.00	5.00	
☐ 5 .... 0.40	1.00	3.00	5.00	
☐ 6 .... 0.40	0.60	1.80	3.00	
☐ 7 .... 0.40	0.60	1.80	3.00	
☐ 8 .... 0.50	0.60	1.80	3.00	
☐ 9 .... 0.50	0.60	1.80	3.00	
☐ 10 .... 0.50	0.60	1.80	3.00	
☐ 11 .... 0.50	0.60	1.80	3.00	
☐ 12 .... 0.50	0.60	1.80	3.00	
☐ 13 .... 0.50	0.60	1.80	3.00	
☐ 14 .... 0.50	0.60	1.80	3.00	
☐ 15 .... 0.50	0.60	1.80	3.00	
☐ 16 .... 0.50	0.40	1.20	2.00	
☐ 17 .... 0.50	0.40	1.20	2.00	

	ORIG.	GOOD	FINE	N-MINT
☐ 18	0.50	0.40	1.20	2.00
☐ 19	0.50	0.40	1.20	2.00
☐ 20		0.40	1.20	2.00
☐ 21		0.30	0.90	1.50
☐ 22		0.30	0.90	1.50
☐ 23		0.30	0.90	1.50
☐ 24		0.30	0.90	1.50
☐ 25		0.30	0.90	1.50
☐ 26		0.30	0.90	1.50
☐ 27		0.30	0.90	1.50
☐ 28		0.30	0.90	1.50
☐ 29		0.30	0.90	1.50
☐ 30		0.30	0.90	1.50
☐ 31		0.30	0.90	1.50
☐ 32		0.30	0.90	1.50
☐ 33		0.30	0.90	1.50
☐ 34		0.30	0.90	1.50
☐ 35		0.30	0.90	1.50
☐ 36		0.30	0.90	1.50
☐ 37		0.30	0.90	1.50
☐ 38		0.30	0.90	1.50
☐ 39		0.30	0.90	1.50
☐ 40		0.30	0.90	1.50
☐ 41		0.30	0.90	1.50
☐ 42		0.30	0.90	1.50
☐ 43		0.30	0.90	1.50
☐ 44		0.30	0.90	1.50
☐ 45		0.30	0.90	1.50
☐ 46		0.30	0.90	1.50
☐ 47		0.30	0.90	1.50
☐ 48		0.30	0.90	1.50
☐ 49		0.30	0.90	1.50
☐ 50		0.30	0.90	1.50
☐ 51		0.30	0.90	1.50
☐ 52		0.30	0.90	1.50
☐ 53		0.30	0.90	1.50
☐ 54		0.30	0.90	1.50
☐ 55		0.30	0.90	1.50
☐ 56		0.30	0.90	1.50
☐ 57		0.30	0.90	1.50
☐ 58		0.30	0.90	1.50
☐ 59		0.30	0.90	1.50
☐ 60		0.30	0.90	1.50
☐ 61		0.30	0.90	1.50
☐ 62		0.30	0.90	1.50
☐ 63		0.30	0.90	1.50
☐ 64		0.30	0.90	1.50
☐ 65		0.30	0.90	1.50
☐ 66, Sep 80, Empire Strikes Back parody		0.30	0.90	1.50
☐ 67		0.30	0.90	1.50
☐ 68		0.30	0.90	1.50
☐ 69		0.30	0.90	1.50
☐ 70		0.30	0.90	1.50
☐ 71		0.30	0.90	1.50
☐ 72		0.30	0.90	1.50
☐ 73		0.30	0.90	1.50
☐ 74		0.30	0.90	1.50
☐ 75		0.30	0.90	1.50
☐ 76		0.30	0.90	1.50
☐ 77		0.30	0.90	1.50
☐ 78		0.30	0.90	1.50
☐ 79		0.30	0.90	1.50
☐ 80	0.90	0.30	0.90	1.50
☐ 81	0.90	0.30	0.90	1.50
☐ 82	1.25	0.30	0.90	1.50
☐ 83, Feb 81, Raiders of the Lost Ark parody				
	0.90	0.30	0.90	1.50
☐ 84	0.90	0.30	0.90	1.50
☐ 85	1.25	0.30	0.90	1.50
☐ 86	0.90	0.30	0.90	1.50
☐ 87	0.90	0.30	0.90	1.50

	ORIG.	GOOD	FINE	N-MINT
☐ 88	0.90	0.30	0.90	1.50
☐ 89	0.90	0.30	0.90	1.50
☐ 90	0.90	0.30	0.90	1.50
☐ 91, Oct 82, Blade Runner parody				
	1.25	0.30	0.90	1.50
☐ 92, Dec 82, Star Trek II parody				
	1.25	0.30	0.90	1.50
☐ 93	1.25	0.30	0.90	1.50
☐ 94	1.25	0.30	0.90	1.50

CRAZY BOB
BLACKBIRD

	ORIG.	GOOD	FINE	N-MINT
☐ 1, b&w		0.55	1.65	2.75
☐ 2, b&w	2.00	0.40	1.20	2.00

CRAZYMAN
CONTINUITY

	ORIG.	GOOD	FINE	N-MINT
☐ 1		0.79	2.37	3.95
☐ 2, BB/NA(c)		0.50	1.50	2.50

CRAZYMAN (1992)

	ORIG.	GOOD	FINE	N-MINT
☐ 1, diecut issue	2.50	0.50	1.50	2.50
☐ 2	2.50	0.50	1.50	2.50
☐ 3	2.50	0.50	1.50	2.50
☐ 4	2.50	0.50	1.50	2.50

CREATURE FEATURES
MOJO

	ORIG.	GOOD	FINE	N-MINT
☐ 0, 94, b&w, prestige format one-shot				
	4.95	0.99	2.97	4.95

CREATURES OF THE ID
CALIBER

	ORIG.	GOOD	FINE	N-MINT
☐ 1, b&w;Allred,Mireault	2.95	0.59	1.77	2.95

CREATURES ON THE LOOSE
(was Tower of Shadows)
MARVEL

	ORIG.	GOOD	FINE	N-MINT
☐ 10, Mar 71, first King Kull story				
	0.15	3.60	10.80	18.00
☐ 11, reprints		0.20	0.60	1.00
☐ 12, reprints		0.20	0.60	1.00
☐ 13, reprints		0.20	0.60	1.00
☐ 14, reprints	0.20	0.20	0.60	1.00
☐ 15, reprints	0.20	0.20	0.60	1.00
☐ 16, Mar 72, Zullivan of Mars				
	0.20	0.50	1.50	2.50
☐ 17, May 72, Zullivan of Mars				
	0.20	0.50	1.50	2.50
☐ 18, Jul 72, Zullivan of Mars				
	0.20	0.50	1.50	2.50
☐ 19, Sep 72, Zullivan of Mars				
	0.20	0.50	1.50	2.50
☐ 20, Nov 72, Zullivan of Mars				
	0.20	0.50	1.50	2.50
☐ 21, Jan 73, Zullivan of Mars				
	0.20	0.50	1.50	2.50
☐ 22, Thongon	0.20	0.80	2.40	4.00
☐ 23, Thongon	0.20	0.40	1.20	2.00
☐ 24, Thongon	0.20	0.40	1.20	2.00
☐ 25, Thongon	0.20	0.40	1.20	2.00
☐ 26, Thongon	0.20	0.40	1.20	2.00
☐ 27, Thongon	0.20	0.40	1.20	2.00
☐ 28, Thongon	0.20	0.40	1.20	2.00
☐ 29, Thongon	0.25	0.40	1.20	2.00
☐ 30, Man-wolf	0.25	0.80	2.40	4.00
☐ 31, Man-wolf	0.25	0.30	0.90	1.50
☐ 32, Man-wolf	0.25	0.30	0.90	1.50
☐ 33, Man-wolf	0.25	0.30	0.90	1.50
☐ 34, Man-wolf	0.25	0.30	0.90	1.50
☐ 35, Man-wolf	0.25	0.30	0.90	1.50
☐ 36, Man-wolf	0.25	0.30	0.90	1.50
☐ 37, Man-wolf	0.25	0.30	0.90	1.50

	ORIG.	GOOD	FINE	N-MINT

CREED
HALL OF HEROES
	ORIG.	GOOD	FINE	N-MINT
❑ 1		3.60	10.80	18.00
❑ 2		2.40	7.20	12.00

LIGHTNING
	ORIG.	GOOD	FINE	N-MINT
❑ 1, Sep 95, really CreeD; collector's edition; enhanced cover	3.00	0.80	2.40	4.00
❑ 1, Sep 95, really CreeD...	3.00	0.60	1.80	3.00
❑ 2, Jan 96	3.00	0.60	1.80	3.00
❑ 2, Jan 96, B; alternate cover	3.00	0.60	1.80	3.00

CREEPSVILLE
GO-GO
	ORIG.	GOOD	FINE	N-MINT
❑ 1, b&w, trading cards		0.59	1.77	2.95
❑ 2, b&w, trading cards		0.59	1.77	2.95
❑ 3		0.45	1.35	2.25
❑ 4		0.45	1.35	2.25
❑ 5		0.45	1.35	2.25

CREEPY
DARK HORSE
	ORIG.	GOOD	FINE	N-MINT
❑ 1, 92, b&w				
❑ 2, 92, b&w				
❑ 3, 92, b&w				
❑ 4, 92, b&w				

HARRIS
	ORIG.	GOOD	FINE	N-MINT
❑ 1, 92, b&w	3.95	0.79	2.37	3.95
❑ 2, 92, b&w	3.95	0.79	2.37	3.95
❑ 3, 92, b&w	3.95	0.79	2.37	3.95
❑ 4, 92, b&w	3.95	0.79	2.37	3.95

CREEPY 1993 FEARBOOK
	ORIG.	GOOD	FINE	N-MINT
❑ 0, 93, nn, AAd	3.95	0.79	2.37	3.95

CREEPY TALES
PINNACLE
	ORIG.	GOOD	FINE	N-MINT
❑ 1		0.35	1.05	1.75

CRIME CLASSICS
ETERNITY
	ORIG.	GOOD	FINE	N-MINT
❑ 1, Jul 88, b&w, Shadow		0.39	1.17	1.95
❑ 2, Aug 88, b&w, Shadow		0.39	1.17	1.95
❑ 3, Sep 88, b&w, Shadow		0.39	1.17	1.95
❑ 4, Jan 89, b&w, Shadow		0.39	1.17	1.95
❑ 5, Feb 89, b&w, Shadow		0.39	1.17	1.95
❑ 6, Mar 89, b&w, Shadow		0.39	1.17	1.95
❑ 7, Apr 89, b&w, Shadow		0.39	1.17	1.95
❑ 8, May 89, b&w, Shadow		0.39	1.17	1.95
❑ 9, Jun 89, b&w, Shadow		0.39	1.17	1.95
❑ 10, Aug 89, b&w, Shadow		0.39	1.17	1.95
❑ 11, Sep 89, b&w, Shadow		0.39	1.17	1.95
❑ 12, Oct 89		0.45	1.35	2.25
❑ 13, Nov 89		0.45	1.35	2.25

CRIME SUSPENSTORIES
EC/GEMSTONE
	ORIG.	GOOD	FINE	N-MINT
❑ 1, EC reprints	1.50	0.30	0.90	1.50
❑ 2, reprints JC,GI,JK	1.50	0.30	0.90	1.50
❑ 3, reprints JC,HK, WW,GI	1.50	0.30	0.90	1.50
❑ 4, reprints:JC,JK,JD,GI	2.00	0.40	1.20	2.00
❑ 5, reprints:JC,JK,JD,GI	2.00	0.40	1.20	2.00
❑ 6, reprints:JC,JK,GI	2.00	0.40	1.20	2.00
❑ 7, May 94, reprints: JC,JK,JD,GI	2.00	0.40	1.20	2.00
❑ 8, reprints	2.00	0.40	1.20	2.00
❑ 9, reprints	2.00	0.40	1.20	2.00
❑ 10, reprints	2.00	0.40	1.20	2.00
❑ 11, reprints	2.00	0.40	1.20	2.00
❑ 12, reprints	2.00	0.40	1.20	2.00

CRIME-SMASHER SPECIAL EDITION
BLUE COMET
	ORIG.	GOOD	FINE	N-MINT
❑ 1, 87		0.36	1.08	1.80

CRIMEBUSTER
AC
	ORIG.	GOOD	FINE	N-MINT
❑ 0, 95	2.95	0.59	1.77	2.95

CRIMEBUSTER CLASSICS
	ORIG.	GOOD	FINE	N-MINT
❑ 1	3.50	0.70	2.10	3.50

CRIMSON AVENGER
DC
	ORIG.	GOOD	FINE	N-MINT
❑ 1, Jun 88	1.00	0.20	0.60	1.00
❑ 2, Jul 88	1.00	0.20	0.60	1.00
❑ 3, Aug 88	1.00	0.20	0.60	1.00
❑ 4, Sep 88	1.00	0.20	0.60	1.00

CRIMSON DREAMS
CRIMSON
	ORIG.	GOOD	FINE	N-MINT
❑ 1		0.40	1.20	2.00
❑ 2		0.40	1.20	2.00
❑ 3		0.40	1.20	2.00
❑ 4		0.40	1.20	2.00
❑ 5		0.40	1.20	2.00
❑ 6		0.40	1.20	2.00
❑ 7		0.40	1.20	2.00
❑ 8		0.40	1.20	2.00
❑ 9		0.40	1.20	2.00
❑ 10		0.40	1.20	2.00
❑ 11		0.40	1.20	2.00

CRIMSON LETTERS
ADVENTURE
	ORIG.	GOOD	FINE	N-MINT
❑ 1, Adventurers b&w		0.45	1.35	2.25

CRISIS ON INFINITE EARTHS
DC
	ORIG.	GOOD	FINE	N-MINT
❑ 1, Apr 85, GP;D:Crime Syndicate, Alex Luthor	0.75	2.20	6.60	11.00
❑ 2, May 85, GP	0.75	1.30	3.90	6.50
❑ 3, Jun 85, GP;D:Losers, Nighthawk, Kid Psycho	0.75	1.00	3.00	5.00
❑ 4, Jul 85, GP;I:Lady Quark, Dr. Light D:Lord Volt, Liana, The Monitor	0.75	1.00	3.00	5.00
❑ 5, Aug 85, GP	0.75	1.00	3.00	5.00
❑ 6, Sep 85, GP; I:New Wildcat	0.75	1.00	3.00	5.00
❑ 7, Oct 85, GP;D:Supergirl; double-size	1.25	2.00	6.00	10.00
❑ 8, Nov 85, GP;D:Flash	0.75	2.40	7.20	12.00
❑ 9, Dec 85, GP; D:Alexi Luthor	0.75	1.50	4.50	7.50
❑ 10, Jan 86, GP;D:Psimon, Starman 3, Immortal Man, Aquagirl, Icicle, Maaldor, Mirror Master, Shaggy Man, Chemo	0.75	1.00	3.00	5.00
❑ 11, Feb 86, GP; D:Angle-Man	0.75	1.00	3.00	5.00
❑ 12, Mar 86, GP;I:Wally West as Flash;D:Sunburst, Dove, Bandit, Clayface 2, Lori Lemaris, Earth-2 Green Arrow	1.25	1.00	3.00	5.00

CRITICAL ERROR
DARK HORSE
	ORIG.	GOOD	FINE	N-MINT
❑ 0, 92, nn;JBy		0.50	1.50	2.50

CRITICAL MASS
EPIC
	ORIG.	GOOD	FINE	N-MINT
❑ 1, BSz,GM	4.95	0.99	2.97	4.95
❑ 2	4.95	0.99	2.97	4.95
❑ 3	4.95	0.99	2.97	4.95
❑ 4	4.95	0.99	2.97	4.95
❑ 5	4.95	0.99	2.97	4.95
❑ 6	4.95	0.99	2.97	4.95
❑ 7	5.95	1.19	3.57	5.95

CRITTERS
FANTAGRAPHICS
	ORIG.	GOOD	FINE	N-MINT
❑ 1, b&w, Usagi Yojimbo	3.00	9.00	15.00	
❑ 2, Captain Jack debut	1.20	3.60	6.00	
❑ 3, Usagi Yojimbo	2.00	6.00	10.00	
❑ 4	0.60	1.80	3.00	

	ORIG.	GOOD	FINE	N-MINT
❑ 5		0.60	1.80	3.00
❑ 6, Usagi		2.00	6.00	10.00
❑ 7, Usagi		2.00	6.00	10.00
❑ 8		0.60	1.80	3.00
❑ 9		0.60	1.80	3.00
❑ 10		0.60	1.80	3.00
❑ 11		0.70	2.10	3.50
❑ 12		0.40	1.20	2.00
❑ 13		0.40	1.20	2.00
❑ 14, Usagi Yojimbo		0.40	1.20	2.00
❑ 15		0.40	1.20	2.00
❑ 16		0.40	1.20	2.00
❑ 17		0.40	1.20	2.00
❑ 18		0.40	1.20	2.00
❑ 19		0.40	1.20	2.00
❑ 20		0.40	1.20	2.00
❑ 21		0.40	1.20	2.00
❑ 22		0.40	1.20	2.00
❑ 22, parody cover		0.40	1.20	2.00
❑ 23, AMO flexidisc		0.79	2.37	3.95
❑ 24		0.40	1.20	2.00
❑ 25		0.40	1.20	2.00
❑ 26		0.40	1.20	2.00
❑ 27		0.40	1.20	2.00
❑ 28		0.40	1.20	2.00
❑ 29		0.40	1.20	2.00
❑ 30		0.40	1.20	2.00
❑ 31		0.40	1.20	2.00
❑ 32		0.40	1.20	2.00
❑ 33		0.40	1.20	2.00
❑ 34		0.40	1.20	2.00
❑ 35		0.40	1.20	2.00
❑ 36		0.40	1.20	2.00
❑ 37		0.40	1.20	2.00
❑ 38, Usagi Yojimbo		0.40	1.20	2.00
❑ 39, Fission Chicken		0.40	1.20	2.00
❑ 40, Gnuff		0.40	1.20	2.00
❑ 41, Platypus		0.40	1.20	2.00
❑ 42, Captain Jack		0.40	1.20	2.00
❑ 43		0.40	1.20	2.00
❑ 44		0.40	1.20	2.00
❑ 45		0.40	1.20	2.00
❑ 46		0.40	1.20	2.00
❑ 47		0.40	1.20	2.00
❑ 48		0.40	1.20	2.00
❑ 49		0.40	1.20	2.00
❑ 50		0.99	2.97	4.95

CRITTURS
MU PRESS

	ORIG.	GOOD	FINE	N-MINT
❑ 0, Nov 92	2.50	0.50	1.50	2.50

CROMWELL STONE
DARK HORSE

	ORIG.	GOOD	FINE	N-MINT
❑ 0, 92, nn;b&w				

CROSS (mini-series)

	ORIG.	GOOD	FINE	N-MINT
❑ 0, Oct 95	2.95	0.59	1.77	2.95
❑ 1, Nov 95	2.95	0.59	1.77	2.95
❑ 2, Dec 95	2.95	0.59	1.77	2.95
❑ 3, Jan 96	2.95	0.59	1.77	2.95
❑ 4, Feb 96	2.95	0.59	1.77	2.95

CROSSFIRE
ECLIPSE

	ORIG.	GOOD	FINE	N-MINT
❑ 1, May 84, DS	1.50	0.30	0.90	1.50
❑ 2, Jun 84, DS	1.50	0.30	0.90	1.50
❑ 3, Jul 84, DS	1.50	0.30	0.90	1.50
❑ 4, Aug 84, DS	1.50	0.30	0.90	1.50
❑ 5, Sep 84, DS	1.50	0.30	0.90	1.50
❑ 6, Nov 84, DS	1.50	0.30	0.90	1.50
❑ 7, Dec 84, DS	1.50	0.30	0.90	1.50
❑ 8, Jan 85, DS	1.50	0.35	1.05	1.75
❑ 9, Mar 85, DS	1.50	0.35	1.05	1.75
❑ 10, Apr 85, DS	1.50	0.35	1.05	1.75

	ORIG.	GOOD	FINE	N-MINT
❑ 11, May 85, DS	1.50	0.35	1.05	1.75
❑ 12, Jun 85, DS, DSt: Marilyn Monroe cover				
	1.50	0.50	1.50	2.50
❑ 13, Jul 85, DS	1.75	0.35	1.05	1.75
❑ 14, Aug 85, DS	1.75	0.35	1.05	1.75
❑ 15, Oct 85, DS	1.75	0.35	1.05	1.75
❑ 16, Jan 86, DS	1.75	0.35	1.05	1.75
❑ 17, Mar 86, DS	1.75	0.35	1.05	1.75
❑ 18, Jan 87, DS b&w	2.00	0.40	1.20	2.00
❑ 19, Feb 87, DS b&w	2.00	0.40	1.20	2.00
❑ 20, Mar 87, DS b&w	2.00	0.40	1.20	2.00
❑ 21, Apr 87, DS b&w	2.00	0.40	1.20	2.00
❑ 22, Jun 87, DS b&w	2.00	0.40	1.20	2.00
❑ 23, Jul 87, DS b&w	2.00	0.40	1.20	2.00
❑ 24, Aug 87, DS b&w	2.00	0.40	1.20	2.00
❑ 25, Oct 87, DS b&w	2.00	0.40	1.20	2.00
❑ 26, Feb 88, DS b&w	2.00	0.40	1.20	2.00

CROSSFIRE & RAINBOW

	ORIG.	GOOD	FINE	N-MINT
❑ 1, Jun 86	1.25	0.25	0.75	1.25
❑ 2, Jul 86	1.25	0.25	0.75	1.25
❑ 3, Aug 86	1.25	0.25	0.75	1.25
❑ 4, Sep 86, DSt(c)	1.25	0.80	2.40	4.00

CROSSROADS
FIRST

	ORIG.	GOOD	FINE	N-MINT
❑ 1, Jul 88, Sable, Whisper	1.00	3.00	5.00	
❑ 2, Agu 88, Sable, Badger	0.80	2.40	4.00	
❑ 3, Sep 88, Badger, Luther Ironheart				
		0.65	1.95	3.25
❑ 4, Oct 88, Grimjack, Judah	0.65	1.95	3.25	
❑ 5, Nov 88, Grimjack, Nexus, Dreadstar				
		0.65	1.95	3.25

CROW OF THE BEAR CLAN
BLACKTHORNE

	ORIG.	GOOD	FINE	N-MINT
❑ 1		0.30	0.90	1.50
❑ 2		0.30	0.90	1.50
❑ 3		0.30	0.90	1.50
❑ 4		0.35	1.05	1.75
❑ 5		0.35	1.05	1.75
❑ 6		0.35	1.05	1.75

CROW, THE
CALIBER

	ORIG.	GOOD	FINE	N-MINT
❑ 1, Feb 89, b&w, 1st printing (10,000 print run)				
	1.95	25.00	75.00	125.00
❑ 1, 2nd printing (5000 print run)				
	1.95	5.00	15.00	25.00
❑ 1, 3rd printing (5000 print run)				
	1.95	1.20	3.60	6.00
❑ 2, Mar 89, 1st printing (7000 print run)				
	1.95	15.00	45.00	75.00
❑ 2, Dec 89, 2nd printing (5000 print run)				
	1.95	2.80	8.40	14.00
❑ 2, Jun 90, 3rd printing (5000 print run)				
	1.95	1.00	3.00	5.00
❑ 3, 1st printing (5000 print run)				
	1.95	10.00	30.00	50.00
❑ 3, 2nd printing (5000 print run)				
	1.95	1.00	3.00	5.00
❑ 4, only printing (12,000 print run)				
	1.95	7.20	21.60	36.00

TUNDRA

	ORIG.	GOOD	FINE	N-MINT
❑ 1, Jan 92, b&w; prestige format				
	4.95	3.00	9.00	15.00
❑ 2, 92, b&w; prestige format				
	4.95	2.80	8.40	14.00
❑ 3, May 92, b&w; prestige format				
	4.95	2.80	8.40	14.00
❑ 4		4.00	12.00	20.00

CROW, THE: DEAD TIME (mini-series)
KITCHEN SINK

	ORIG.	GOOD	FINE	N-MINT
❑ 1, Jan 96, b&w	2.95	0.59	1.77	2.95

	ORIG.	GOOD	FINE	N-MINT
CRUCIAL FICTION				
FANTAGRAPHICS				
❏ 1, b&w		0.50	1.50	2.50
❏ 2, b&w		0.45	1.35	2.25
❏ 3, b&w		0.45	1.35	2.25
CRUCIBLE				
DC/IMPACT				
❏ 1, Feb 93	0.99	0.25	0.75	1.25
❏ 2, Mar 93	1.25	0.25	0.75	1.25
❏ 3, Apr 93	1.25	0.25	0.75	1.25
❏ 4, May 93	1.25	0.25	0.75	1.25
❏ 5	1.25	0.25	0.75	1.25
❏ 6	1.25	0.25	0.75	1.25
CRUEL & UNUSUAL PUNISHMENT				
STARHEAD				
❏ 1, Nov 93, adult;b&w	2.75	0.55	1.65	2.75
❏ 2, Oct 94, adult;b&w	2.95	0.59	1.77	2.95
CRUEL WORLD				
FANTAGRAPHICS				
❏ 1, b&w	3.50	0.70	2.10	3.50
CRUSADERS				
GUILD				
❏ 1, 82, (becomes *Southern Knights*)				
		4.00	12.00	20.00
CRUSADERS, THE				
DC/IMPACT				
❏ 1, May 92, trading cards	1.00	0.20	0.60	1.00
❏ 2, Jun 92	1.00	0.20	0.60	1.00
❏ 3, Jul 92	1.00	0.20	0.60	1.00
❏ 4, Aug 92	1.00	0.20	0.60	1.00
❏ 5, Sep 92	1.00	0.20	0.60	1.00
❏ 6, Oct 92	1.00	0.20	0.60	1.00
❏ 7, Nov 92	1.00	0.20	0.60	1.00
❏ 8, Dec 92	1.00	0.20	0.60	1.00
CRUSH				
AEON				
❏ 1, Nov 95, cardstock cover;b&w				
	2.95	0.59	1.77	2.95
❏ 2, Dec 95, cardstock cover;b&w				
	2.95	0.59	1.77	2.95
❏ 3, Jan 96, cardstock cover;b&w				
	2.95	0.59	1.77	2.95
❏ 4, Feb 96, cardstock cover;b&w				
	2.95	0.59	1.77	2.95
CRUSH, THE				
IMAGE				
❏ 2, Apr 96	2.25	0.45	1.35	2.25
❏ 3, May 96	2.25	0.45	1.35	2.25
❏ 4, Jun 96	2.25	0.45	1.35	2.25
❏ 5, Jul 96	2.25	0.45	1.35	2.25
CRY FOR DAWN				
CRY FOR DAWN				
❏ 1, adult;b&w;first printing	35.00	105.00	175.00	
❏ 1, 2nd printing	10.00	30.00	50.00	
❏ 1, 3rd printing	6.00	18.00	30.00	
❏ 2	16.00	48.00	80.00	
❏ 2, 2nd printing	1.00	3.00	5.00	
❏ 3	9.60	28.80	48.00	
❏ 4	6.00	18.00	30.00	
❏ 5	5.00	15.00	25.00	
❏ 6, b&w	3.20	9.60	16.00	
❏ 7, b&w	3.20	9.60	16.00	
❏ 8, b&w	2.00	6.00	10.00	
❏ 9, b&w	2.00	6.00	10.00	
CRYING FREEMAN				
VIZ				
❏ 1, b&w, Japanese	1.20	3.60	6.00	
❏ 2		0.80	2.40	4.00
❏ 3		0.70	2.10	3.50
❏ 4		0.70	2.10	3.50

	ORIG.	GOOD	FINE	N-MINT
❏ 5		0.70	2.10	3.50
❏ 6		0.70	2.10	3.50
❏ 7		0.70	2.10	3.50
❏ 8		0.70	2.10	3.50
CRYING FREEMAN (Part Five)				
❏ 1, 92, b&w	2.75	0.55	1.65	2.75
❏ 2, 92, b&w	2.75	0.55	1.65	2.75
❏ 3, 93, b&w	2.75	0.55	1.65	2.75
❏ 4, 93, b&w	2.75	0.55	1.65	2.75
❏ 5, 93, b&w	2.75	0.55	1.65	2.75
❏ 6, 93, b&w	2.75	0.55	1.65	2.75
❏ 7, 93, b&w	2.75	0.55	1.65	2.75
❏ 8, 93, b&w	2.75	0.55	1.65	2.75
❏ 9, 93, b&w	2.75	0.55	1.65	2.75
❏ 10, 93, b&w	2.75	0.55	1.65	2.75
❏ 11, 93, b&w	2.75	0.55	1.65	2.75
CRYING FREEMAN (Part Four)				
❏ 1		0.99	2.97	4.95
❏ 2		0.99	2.97	4.95
❏ 3		0.99	2.97	4.95
❏ 4		0.55	1.65	2.75
❏ 5		0.55	1.65	2.75
❏ 6		0.55	1.65	2.75
❏ 7		0.55	1.65	2.75
CRYING FREEMAN (Part Three)				
❏ 1, color		0.99	2.97	4.95
❏ 2, color		0.99	2.97	4.95
❏ 3, color		0.99	2.97	4.95
❏ 4, color		0.99	2.97	4.95
❏ 5, color		0.99	2.97	4.95
❏ 6, color		0.99	2.97	4.95
❏ 7, color		0.99	2.97	4.95
❏ 8, color		0.99	2.97	4.95
❏ 9, color		0.99	2.97	4.95
❏ 10, color		0.99	2.97	4.95
CRYING FREEMAN (Part Two)				
❏ 1, b&w, Japanese		0.70	2.10	3.50
❏ 2, b&w, Japanese		0.70	2.10	3.50
❏ 3, b&w, Japanese		0.70	2.10	3.50
❏ 4		0.75	2.25	3.75
❏ 5		0.79	2.37	3.95
❏ 6		0.79	2.37	3.95
❏ 7		0.79	2.37	3.95
❏ 8		0.79	2.37	3.95
❏ 9		0.79	2.37	3.95
CRYPT				
IMAGE				
❏ 1, Aug 95	2.50	0.50	1.50	2.50
❏ 2, Oct 95	2.50	0.50	1.50	2.50
CRYPT, THE				
AAAARGH!				
❏ 1		0.39	1.17	1.95
CRYPTIC TALES				
SHOWCASE				
❏ 1		0.39	1.17	1.95
CUD				
FANTAGRAPHICS				
❏ 1, b&w	2.25	0.45	1.35	2.25
❏ 2, b&w,adult	2.50	0.50	1.50	2.50
❏ 3, b&w,adult	2.50	0.50	1.50	2.50
❏ 4, b&w,adult	2.50	0.50	1.50	2.50
❏ 5, b&w,adult	2.50	0.50	1.50	2.50
❏ 6, b&w,adult	2.50	0.50	1.50	2.50
❏ 7, Aug 94, b&w;adult	2.50	0.50	1.50	2.50
CUD COMICS				
DARK HORSE				
❏ 1, Nov 95, b&w	2.95	0.59	1.77	2.95
❏ 2, Jan 96, b&w	2.95	0.59	1.77	2.95
❏ 3, Mar 96, b&w	2.95	0.59	1.77	2.95

	ORIG.	GOOD	FINE	N-MINT

CUIRASS
HARRIER

	ORIG.	GOOD	FINE	N-MINT
1, b&w		0.39	1.17	1.95

CULTURAL JET LAG
FANTAGRAPHICS

1, b&w		0.50	1.50	2.50

CURIO SHOPPE, THE
PHOENIX PRESS

1, Mar 95, b&w	2.50	0.50	1.50	2.50

CURSE OF DREADWOLF
LIGHTNING

1, Sep 94, b&w	2.75	0.55	1.65	2.75

CURSE OF THE SHE-CAT
AC

1, Feb 89, b&w		0.50	1.50	2.50

CURSE OF THE WEIRD
MARVEL

1, reprints	1.25	0.25	0.75	1.25
2, reprints	1.25	0.25	0.75	1.25
3, reprints	1.25	0.25	0.75	1.25
4, reprints	1.25	0.25	0.75	1.25

CURSE OF THE ZOMBIE

4, reprints	1.25	0.25	0.75	1.25

CUTTING EDGE

1, Dec 95, continued from *The Incredible Hulk* #436; continues in *The Incredible Hulk* #437

	2.95	0.59	1.77	2.95

CYBER 7
ECLIPSE

1, Japanese, b&w		0.40	1.20	2.00
2, Japanese, b&w		0.40	1.20	2.00
3, Japanese, b&w		0.40	1.20	2.00
4, Japanese, b&w		0.40	1.20	2.00
5, Japanese, b&w		0.40	1.20	2.00
6, Japanese, b&w		0.40	1.20	2.00
7, Japanese, b&w		0.40	1.20	2.00

CYBER 7 BOOK TWO

1, Japanese, b&w		0.40	1.20	2.00
2, Japanese, b&w		0.40	1.20	2.00
3, Japanese, b&w		0.40	1.20	2.00
4, Japanese, b&w		0.40	1.20	2.00
5, Japanese, b&w		0.40	1.20	2.00
6, Japanese, b&w		0.40	1.20	2.00
7, Japanese, b&w		0.40	1.20	2.00
8, Japanese, b&w		0.40	1.20	2.00
9, Japanese, b&w		0.40	1.20	2.00
10, Japanese, b&w		0.40	1.20	2.00

CYBER CITY: PART ONE (mini-series)
CPM COMICS

1, Sep 95, adapts anime.	2.95	0.59	1.77	2.95
2, Sep 95, adapts anime.	2.95	0.59	1.77	2.95

CYBER CITY: PART TWO (mini-series)

1, Oct 95, adapts anime .	2.95	0.59	1.77	2.95

CYBER REALITY COMIX
WONDER COMIX

1, Fal 94	3.95	0.79	2.37	3.95

CYBERCOM: HEART OF THE BLUE MESA
MATRIX

1, b&w		0.40	1.20	2.00

CYBERCRUSH
FLEETWAY/QUALITY

1		0.39	1.17	1.95
2		0.39	1.17	1.95
3		0.39	1.17	1.95
4		0.39	1.17	1.95
5		0.39	1.17	1.95
6		0.39	1.17	1.95
7		0.39	1.17	1.95
8		0.39	1.17	1.95
9		0.39	1.17	1.95
10		0.39	1.17	1.95
11		0.39	1.17	1.95
12		0.39	1.17	1.95
13		0.39	1.17	1.95
14		0.39	1.17	1.95

CYBERCRUSH: ROBOTS IN REVOLT

8		0.39	1.17	1.95

CYBERFARCE
PARODY

1, b&w	2.50	0.50	1.50	2.50

CYBERFORCE
IMAGE

0, Sep 93	1.95	0.39	1.17	1.95
1	1.95	2.00	6.00	10.00
2, Jan 94	1.95	0.80	2.40	4.00
3	1.95	0.39	1.17	1.95
4, foil cover	2.50	0.50	1.50	2.50

CYBERFORCE (Volume 2)

1, Nov 93	1.95	0.39	1.17	1.95
2	1.95	0.39	1.17	1.95
4, Apr 94	1.95	0.39	1.17	1.95
5, Jun 94	1.95	0.39	1.17	1.95
6, Jul 94	1.95	0.39	1.17	1.95
7, Sep 94	1.95	0.39	1.17	1.95
9, Dec 94	1.95	0.39	1.17	1.95
10, Feb 95	1.95	0.39	1.17	1.95
11, Mar 95	1.95	0.39	1.17	1.95
12, Apr 95	1.95	0.39	1.17	1.95
13, Jun 95	2.25	0.45	1.35	2.25
14, Jul 95	2.25	0.45	1.35	2.25
18, Jan 96	2.25	0.45	1.35	2.25
19, Feb 96	2.50	0.50	1.50	2.50
20, Mar 96	2.50	0.50	1.50	2.50
21, May 96	2.50	0.50	1.50	2.50
22, May 96	2.50	0.50	1.50	2.50
23, Jun 96	2.50	0.50	1.50	2.50

CYBERFORCE ANNUAL

1, Mar 95, 1995	2.50	0.50	1.50	2.50

CYBERFORCE ORIGINS: CYBLADE

1, Jan 95	2.50	0.50	1.50	2.50

CYBERFORCE UNIVERSE SOURCEBOOK

1, Aug 94	2.50	0.50	1.50	2.50

CYBERFORCE, STRYKE FORCE: OPPOSING FORCES

1, Sep 95	2.50	0.50	1.50	2.50

CYBERFROG
HARRIS

1, Feb 96	2.95	0.59	1.77	2.95

CYBERHAWKS
PYRAMID

1, b&w		0.36	1.08	1.80
2, b&w		0.36	1.08	1.80

CYBERLUST
AIRCEL

1, adult, b&w		0.59	1.77	2.95
2, adult, b&w		0.59	1.77	2.95
3, adult, b&w		0.59	1.77	2.95

CYBERNARY
IMAGE

3, Jan 96	2.50	0.50	1.50	2.50
4, Feb 96	2.50	0.50	1.50	2.50
5, Mar 96	2.50	0.50	1.50	2.50

CYBERPUNK
INNOVATION

1		0.39	1.17	1.95
2		0.39	1.17	1.95

	ORIG.	GOOD	FINE	N-MINT
CYBERPUNK BOOK TWO				
☐ 1		0.45	1.35	2.25
☐ 2		0.45	1.35	2.25
CYBERPUNK: THE SERAPHIM FILES				
☐ 1		0.50	1.50	2.50
☐ 2		0.50	1.50	2.50
CYBERPUNX				
IMAGE				
☐ 1, Mar 96	2.50	0.50	1.50	2.50
☐ 1, Mar 96, alternate cover				
	2.50	0.50	1.50	2.50
☐ 1, Mar 96, other alternate cover				
	2.50	0.50	1.50	2.50
CYBERRAD				
CONTINUITY				
☐ 1		0.40	1.20	2.00
☐ 2		0.40	1.20	2.00
☐ 3		0.40	1.20	2.00
☐ 4		0.40	1.20	2.00
☐ 5, glow cover		1.40	4.20	7.00
☐ 6, foldout poster		0.40	1.20	2.00
☐ 7		0.40	1.20	2.00
CYBERRAD (Volume Two)				
☐ 1, hologram cover		0.59	1.77	2.95
CYBERRAD: DEATHWATCH 2000				
☐ 1, trading card	2.50	0.50	1.50	2.50
☐ 2, Jul 93, trading card	2.50	0.50	1.50	2.50
CYBERSPACE 3000				
MARVEL				
☐ 1, glowing cover	2.95	0.59	1.77	2.95
☐ 2	1.75	0.35	1.05	1.75
☐ 3	1.75	0.35	1.05	1.75
☐ 4	1.75	0.35	1.05	1.75
☐ 5	1.75	0.35	1.05	1.75
☐ 6	1.75	0.35	1.05	1.75
☐ 7	1.75	0.35	1.05	1.75
☐ 8	1.75	0.35	1.05	1.75
CYBERSUIT ARKADYNE (mini-series)				
IANUS				
☐ 1, b&w		0.50	1.50	2.50
☐ 2, b&w		0.50	1.50	2.50
☐ 3, Jun 92, b&w	2.50	0.50	1.50	2.50

	ORIG.	GOOD	FINE	N-MINT
☐ 4	2.50	0.50	1.50	2.50
☐ 5	2.50	0.50	1.50	2.50
☐ 6	2.50	0.50	1.50	2.50
CYBERZONE				
JET-BLACK GRAFIKS				
☐ 1, Jul 94, b&w	2.50	0.50	1.50	2.50
☐ 2, Sep 94, b&w	2.50	0.50	1.50	2.50
☐ 3, Dec 94, b&w	2.50	0.50	1.50	2.50
☐ 4, Mar 95, b&w	2.50	0.50	1.50	2.50
☐ 5, May 95, b&w	2.50	0.50	1.50	2.50
☐ 6, Sep 95, b&w	2.50	0.50	1.50	2.50
CYBLADE/SHI: THE BATTLE FOR INDEPENDENTS				
IMAGE/CRUSADE				
☐ 1, 95, crossover;concludes in *Shi/Cyblade: The Battle for Independents #2*	2.95	0.80	2.40	4.00
CYBORG GERBILS				
TRIGON				
☐ 1		0.50	1.50	2.50
☐ 2		0.50	1.50	2.50
CYBRID				
MAXIMUM				
☐ 1, Jul 95	2.95	0.59	1.77	2.95
CYCOPS				
COMICS INTERVIEW				
☐ 1, Stelfreeze art, b&w		1.20	3.60	6.00
☐ 2, Stelfreeze art, b&w		0.80	2.40	4.00
☐ 3, Stelfreeze art, b&w		0.80	2.40	4.00
CYLINDERHEAD				
SLAVE LABOR				
☐ 1, b&w		0.39	1.17	1.95
CYNTHIA PETAL'S REALLY FANTASTIC ALIEN SEX FRENZY				
EROS				
☐ 1, b&w, adult		0.79	2.37	3.95
CZAR CHASM				
C&T				
☐ 1, b&w		0.40	1.20	2.00
☐ 2, b&w		0.40	1.20	2.00

Captain Marvel

First appearance: *Marvel Super-Heroes #12* (Dec 67)

During the years that Fawcett's Captain Marvel was lingering in limbo (see our *Shazam!* entry for information on Captain Marvel and the Marvel Family), Marvel Comics introduced its own Captain. Mar-Vell was a Kree warrior sent to Earth to scout it for a possible invasion. Originally attired in green and white, with a finned helmet and a ringed planet for an emblem, Marvel's costume changed to red and blue with a yellow starburst. While the costume didn't resemble the Fawcett Captain Marvel's, it did lead to confusion for fans of both Captains who couldn't then differentiate between "the one in green" and "the one in red."

Marvel's Captain came closer to Fawcett's Captain when he was banished to The Negative Zone, from which he could be freed only by exchanging places with former Hulk sidekick Rick Jones when Jones slammed together a pair of wristbands, known as Nega-Bands.

Mar-Vell succumbed to cancer in the *Death of Captain Marvel* graphic novel. The name passed to a black woman with light-based powers. Before his death, Mar-Vell fathered a son who took the name Legacy but later changed it to Captain Marvel.

One final note: The adventures of an android version of Captain Marvel — not related to either the Fawcett or Marvel versions — were published by M.F. Enterprises in 1966. The character shouted "Split!" to send his body parts flying in various directions and "Xam!" to bring them back.

D

	ORIG.	GOOD	FINE	N-MINT
D.P.7				
MARVEL				
❑ 1, Nov 86	0.75	0.40	1.20	2.00
❑ 2, Dec 86	0.75	0.40	1.20	2.00
❑ 3, Jan 87	0.75	0.40	1.20	2.00
❑ 4, Feb 87	0.75	0.40	1.20	2.00
❑ 5, Mar 87	0.75	0.40	1.20	2.00
❑ 6, Apr 87	0.75	0.40	1.20	2.00
❑ 7, May 87	0.75	0.40	1.20	2.00
❑ 8, Jun 87	0.75	0.40	1.20	2.00
❑ 9, Jul 87	0.75	0.40	1.20	2.00
❑ 10, Aug 87	0.75	0.40	1.20	2.00
❑ 11, Sep 87	0.75	0.40	1.20	2.00
❑ 12, Oct 87	0.75	0.40	1.20	2.00
❑ 13, Nov 87	0.75	0.40	1.20	2.00
❑ 14, Dec 87	0.75	0.40	1.20	2.00
❑ 15, Jan 88	0.75	0.40	1.20	2.00
❑ 16, Feb 88	0.75	0.40	1.20	2.00
❑ 17, Mar 88	0.75	0.40	1.20	2.00
❑ 18, Apr 88	0.75	0.40	1.20	2.00
❑ 19, May 88	1.25	0.25	0.75	1.25
❑ 20, Jun 88	1.25	0.25	0.75	1.25
❑ 21, Jul 88	1.25	0.25	0.75	1.25
❑ 22, Aug 88	1.25	0.25	0.75	1.25
❑ 23, Sep 88, A:Psi-Force	1.25	0.25	0.75	1.25
❑ 24, Oct 88	1.25	0.25	0.75	1.25
❑ 25, Nov 88, A:Nightmask	1.25	0.25	0.75	1.25
❑ 26, Dec 88	1.50	0.30	0.90	1.50
❑ 27, Jan 89	1.50	0.30	0.90	1.50
❑ 28, Feb 89	1.50	0.30	0.90	1.50
❑ 29, Mar 89	1.50	0.30	0.90	1.50
❑ 30, Apr 89, I:Capt. Manhattan				
	1.50	0.40	1.20	2.00
❑ 31, May 89	1.50	0.40	1.20	2.00
❑ 32, Jun 89	1.50	0.40	1.20	2.00
D.P.7 ANNUAL				
❑ 1, Nov 87, O:D.P.7	1.25	0.25	0.75	1.25
DADAVILLE				
CALIBER				
❑ 1, b&w	2.95	0.59	1.77	2.95
DAEMON MASK				
AMAZING				
❑ 1		0.39	1.17	1.95
DAFFY QADDAFI				
COMICS UNLIMITED				
❑ 1, b&w	0.35	1.05	1.75	
DAI KAMIKAZE!				
NOW				
❑ 1, Jun 87, 1st printing	3.00	0.60	1.80	3.00
❑ 1, Sep 87, 2nd printing	1.75	0.35	1.05	1.75
❑ 2, Jul 87	1.50	0.30	0.90	1.50
❑ 3, Aug 87	1.50	0.30	0.90	1.50
❑ 4, Oct 87	1.50	0.30	0.90	1.50
❑ 5, Nov 87	1.75	0.35	1.05	1.75
❑ 6, Dec 87	1.75	0.35	1.05	1.75
❑ 7, Jan 88	1.75	0.35	1.05	1.75
❑ 8, Feb 88	1.75	0.35	1.05	1.75
❑ 9, Apr 88	1.75	0.35	1.05	1.75
❑ 10, Apr 88	1.75	0.35	1.05	1.75
❑ 11, Jun 88	1.75	0.35	1.05	1.75
❑ 12, Jul 88	1.75	0.35	1.05	1.75
DAIKAZU				
GROUND ZERO				
❑ 1, b&w, 1st printings		0.30	0.90	1.50
❑ 2, b&w, 1st printings		0.30	0.90	1.50
❑ 1, 2nd printings		0.30	0.90	1.50
❑ 2, 2nd printings		0.30	0.90	1.50
❑ 3, b&w		0.30	0.90	1.50

	ORIG.	GOOD	FINE	N-MINT
❑ 4, b&w		0.30	0.90	1.50
❑ 5, b&w		0.30	0.90	1.50
❑ 6, b&w		0.30	0.90	1.50
❑ 7, b&w		0.30	0.90	1.50
❑ 8		0.35	1.05	1.75
DAILY PLANET INVASION! EXTRA				
DC				
❑ 1, "newspaper"		0.40	1.20	2.00
DAKOTA NORTH				
MARVEL				
❑ 1, Jun 86	0.75	0.20	0.60	1.00
❑ 2, Aug 86	0.75	0.20	0.60	1.00
❑ 3, Oct 86	0.75	0.20	0.60	1.00
❑ 4, Dec 86	0.75	0.20	0.60	1.00
❑ 5, Feb 87	0.75	0.20	0.60	1.00
DALGODA				
FANTAGRAPHICS				
❑ 1, Aug 84	2.25	0.45	1.35	2.25
❑ 2, Dec 84	1.50	0.30	0.90	1.50
❑ 3, Feb 85	1.50	0.30	0.90	1.50
❑ 4, Apr 85	1.50	0.30	0.90	1.50
❑ 5, Jun 85	2.00	0.40	1.20	2.00
❑ 6, Oct 85	2.00	0.40	1.20	2.00
❑ 7, Jan 86	2.00	0.40	1.20	2.00
❑ 8, Apr 86	2.00	0.40	1.20	2.00
DAMAGE				
DC				
❑ 0, Oct 94	1.95	0.39	1.17	1.95
❑ 1, Apr 94	1.75	0.35	1.05	1.75
❑ 2, May 94	1.75	0.35	1.05	1.75
❑ 3, Jun 94	1.75	0.35	1.05	1.75
❑ 4, Jul 94	1.75	0.35	1.05	1.75
❑ 5, Aug 94	1.95	0.39	1.17	1.95
❑ 6, Sep 94	1.95	0.39	1.17	1.95
❑ 7, Nov 94	1.95	0.39	1.17	1.95
❑ 8, Dec 94	1.95	0.39	1.17	1.95
❑ 9, Jan 95	1.95	0.39	1.17	1.95
❑ 10, Feb 95	1.95	0.39	1.17	1.95
❑ 11, Mar 95	1.95	0.39	1.17	1.95
❑ 12, Apr 95	1.95	0.39	1.17	1.95
❑ 13, Jun 95, "Picking Up the Pieces" Part 1 of 3				
	1.95	0.39	1.17	1.95
❑ 14, Jul 95, "Picking Up the Pieces" Part 2 of 3				
	2.25	0.45	1.35	2.25
❑ 15, Aug 95, "Picking Up the Pieces" Part 3 of 3				
	2.25	0.45	1.35	2.25
❑ 16, Sep 95, "The Siege of the Zi Charam" Part 4 of 5	2.25	0.45	1.35	2.25
❑ 17, Oct 95	2.25	0.45	1.35	2.25
❑ 18, Nov 95	2.25	0.45	1.35	2.25
❑ 19, Dec 95	2.25	0.45	1.35	2.25
❑ 20, Jan 96	2.25	0.45	1.35	2.25
DAMAGE CONTROL				
MARVEL				
❑ 1, May 89, SpM, Thor	1.00	0.60	1.80	3.00
❑ 2, Jun 89, Dr. Doom	1.00	0.40	1.20	2.00
❑ 3, Jul 89, Iron Man	1.00	0.40	1.20	2.00
❑ 4, Aug 89, Wolverine, Inferno				
	1.00	0.40	1.20	2.00
DAMAGE CONTROL (Volume 2)				
❑ 1, Dec 89, Capt. America, Thor				
	1.00	0.40	1.20	2.00
❑ 2, Dec 89, Punisher	1.00	0.40	1.20	2.00
❑ 3, Jan 90, She-Hulk	1.00	0.30	0.90	1.50
❑ 4, Feb 90, Thor, Capt. America, Punisher, SHIELD				
	1.00	0.40	1.20	2.00
DAMAGE CONTROL (Volume 3)				
❑ 1, Jun 91, KBaker, SpM	1.25	0.25	0.75	1.25

	ORIG.	GOOD	FINE	N-MINT
❏ 2, Jul 91, Hulk	1.25	0.25	0.75	1.25
❏ 3, Aug 91, Galactus	1.25	0.25	0.75	1.25
❏ 4, Sep 91	1.25	0.25	0.75	1.25

DAME PATROL
SPOOF

	ORIG.	GOOD	FINE	N-MINT
❏ 1, b&w	2.95	0.59	1.77	2.95

DAMLOG
PYRAMID

	GOOD	FINE	N-MINT
❏ 1, b&w	0.36	1.08	1.80

DAMNATION
FANTAGRAPHICS

	ORIG.	GOOD	FINE	N-MINT
❏ 1, Sum 94, b&w magazine	2.95	0.59	1.77	2.95

DAN PANIC FUNNIES
PANIC

	GOOD	FINE	N-MINT
❏ 1	0.35	1.05	1.75

DAN TURNER: ACE IN THE HOLE
ETERNITY

	GOOD	FINE	N-MINT
❏ 1, b&w	0.50	1.50	2.50

DAN TURNER: DARK STAR OF DEATH

	GOOD	FINE	N-MINT
❏ 1, 91, b&w	0.50	1.50	2.50

DAN TURNER: HOMICIDE HUNCH

	GOOD	FINE	N-MINT
❏ 1, Jul 91, b&w	0.50	1.50	2.50

DAN TURNER: STAR CHAMBER

	GOOD	FINE	N-MINT
❏ 1, Sep 91, b&w	0.50	1.50	2.50

DANCE OF DEATH
TOME PRESS

	ORIG.	GOOD	FINE	N-MINT
❏ 1, b&w	2.95	0.59	1.77	2.95

DANCE OF LIFEY DEATH, THE
DARK HORSE

	ORIG.	GOOD	FINE	N-MINT
❏ 0, 94, nn	3.95	0.79	2.37	3.95

DANCES WITH DEMONS
MARVEL

	ORIG.	GOOD	FINE	N-MINT
❏ 1, foil cover	2.95	0.59	1.77	2.95
❏ 2	1.95	0.39	1.17	1.95
❏ 3	1.95	0.39	1.17	1.95
❏ 4	1.95	0.39	1.17	1.95

DANGER COMICS
DANGER COMICS

	ORIG.	GOOD	FINE	N-MINT
❏ 1, b&w	2.25	0.45	1.35	2.25
❏ 2, b&w	2.25	0.45	1.35	2.25

DANGER COMIX
DANGER GRAPHIX

	ORIG.	GOOD	FINE	N-MINT
❏ 1	2.25	0.45	1.35	2.25

DANGER TRAIL
DC

	ORIG.	GOOD	FINE	N-MINT
❏ 1, Apr 93, CI	1.50	0.30	0.90	1.50
❏ 2, May 93, CI	1.50	0.30	0.90	1.50
❏ 3, Jun 93	1.50	0.30	0.90	1.50
❏ 4, Jul 93	1.50	0.30	0.90	1.50

DANGER UNLIMITED
DARK HORSE/LEGEND

	ORIG.	GOOD	FINE	N-MINT
❏ 1, Feb 94, JBY	2.00	0.40	1.20	2.00
❏ 2, Mar 94, JBY	2.50	0.50	1.50	2.50
❏ 3, Apr 94, JBY	2.50	0.50	1.50	2.50
❏ 4, May 94	2.50	0.50	1.50	2.50

DANGEROUS TIMES
EVOLUTION

	ORIG.	GOOD	FINE	N-MINT
❏ 1, MWK(c) b&w		0.35	1.05	1.75
❏ 2	1.95	0.39	1.17	1.95
❏ 3	1.95	0.39	1.17	1.95
❏ 4	1.95	0.39	1.17	1.95
❏ 6, b&w	2.25	0.45	1.35	2.25

DANGLE
CAT-HEAD

	GOOD	FINE	N-MINT
❏ 1, b&w	0.55	1.65	2.75

DANSE
BLACKTHORNE

	GOOD	FINE	N-MINT
❏ 1	0.40	1.20	2.00

DANTE'S INFERNO
TOME PRESS

	ORIG.	GOOD	FINE	N-MINT
❏ 1, GDore, b&w	3.50	0.70	2.10	3.50
❏ 2, GDore, b&w	3.50	0.70	2.10	3.50

DAPIEK ABSAROKA: THE KILLER OF CROWS

	GOOD	FINE	N-MINT
❏ 1, b&w	0.50	1.50	2.50

DARE
MONSTER

	GOOD	FINE	N-MINT
❏ 1, reprint	0.55	1.65	2.75
❏ 2, reprint	0.55	1.65	2.75
❏ 3, reprint	0.50	1.50	2.50

DARE THE IMPOSSIBLE
FLEETWAY/QUALITY

	ORIG.	GOOD	FINE	N-MINT
❏ 1	1.95	0.39	1.17	1.95
❏ 2	1.95	0.39	1.17	1.95
❏ 3	1.95	0.39	1.17	1.95
❏ 4	1.95	0.39	1.17	1.95
❏ 5	1.95	0.39	1.17	1.95
❏ 6	1.95	0.39	1.17	1.95
❏ 7	1.95	0.39	1.17	1.95
❏ 8	1.95	0.39	1.17	1.95
❏ 9	1.95	0.39	1.17	1.95
❏ 10	1.95	0.39	1.17	1.95
❏ 11	1.95	0.39	1.17	1.95
❏ 12	1.95	0.39	1.17	1.95
❏ 13	1.95	0.39	1.17	1.95
❏ 14	1.95	0.39	1.17	1.95
❏ 15	1.95	0.39	1.17	1.95

DAREDEVIL
MARVEL

	ORIG.	GOOD	FINE	N-MINT
❏ 1, BEv, O:DD	0.12	300.00	900.00	1500.00
❏ 2, JO, V:Electro	0.12	130.00	390.00	650.00
❏ 3, JO, O:Owl	0.12	70.00	210.00	350.00
❏ 4, JO, V:Killgrave	0.12	40.00	120.00	200.00
❏ 5, WW, V:Masked Matador	0.12	25.00	75.00	125.00
❏ 6, WW, V:Fellowship of Fear	0.12	20.00	60.00	100.00
❏ 7, WW, 1:red costume	0.12	52.00	156.00	260.00
❏ 8, WW	0.12	16.00	48.00	80.00
❏ 9, WW	0.12	16.00	48.00	80.00
❏ 10, WW	0.12	16.00	48.00	80.00
❏ 11	0.12	11.00	33.00	55.00
❏ 12	0.12	11.00	33.00	55.00
❏ 13	0.12	11.00	33.00	55.00
❏ 14	0.12	11.00	33.00	55.00
❏ 15	0.12	11.00	33.00	55.00
❏ 16	0.12	8.00	24.00	40.00
❏ 17, SpM	0.12	8.00	24.00	40.00
❏ 18, JR, Gladiator	0.12	9.60	28.80	48.00
❏ 19, JR, Gladiator	0.12	8.00	24.00	40.00
❏ 20, GC, V:Owl	0.12	6.00	18.00	30.00
❏ 21, GC, V:Owl	0.12	6.00	18.00	30.00
❏ 22, GC	0.12	6.00	18.00	30.00
❏ 23, GC	0.12	6.00	18.00	30.00
❏ 24, GC	0.12	6.00	18.00	30.00
❏ 25, GC	0.12	6.00	18.00	30.00
❏ 26, GC	0.12	6.00	18.00	30.00
❏ 27, GC	0.12	6.00	18.00	30.00
❏ 28, GC	0.12	6.00	18.00	30.00
❏ 29, GC	0.12	6.00	18.00	30.00
❏ 30, GC, A:Thor	0.12	7.20	21.60	36.00
❏ 31, Aug 67, GC, Cobra	0.12	4.00	12.00	20.00
❏ 32, Sep 67, GC	0.12	4.00	12.00	20.00
❏ 33, Oct 67, GC	0.12	4.00	12.00	20.00
❏ 34, Nov 67, GC	0.12	4.00	12.00	20.00
❏ 35, Dec 67, GC	0.12	4.00	12.00	20.00

Daredevil

Daredevil #191 ©1982 Marvel Comics Group

First appearance: *Daredevil* #1, April 1964, Marvel Comics Group.

Two years after Marvel's successful introduction of Spider-Man, Stan Lee created Daredevil in much the same mold. The hero was, again, an alienated loner who turned to crimefighting after an accident involving radiation invested him with modest super-powers. Both Spidey and DD swung, Batman-like, from building to building and suffered from complicated personal lives between battles.

The son of a prizefighter, young Matt Murdock gained his powers when he was struck on the head by a radioactive canister after pushing an elderly man from the path of an oncoming truck. The accident left him blind, but the radiation enhanced his other senses and given him an additional "radar sense." Frank Miller's retelling of Daredevil's origin in the 1993 mini-series *Daredevil the Man without Fear* downplayed the radiation and emphasized Murdock's Zen training at the hands of a blind mentor named Stick. Daredevil turned to crimefighting after the death of his father at the hands of a criminal. Like Spider-Man, Daredevil was not cut out for cosmic menaces and tended to concentrate on crime bosses and costumed bank robbers.

Following Lee's usual formula, *Daredevil's* supporting cast formed a love triangle. Murdock, who went into practice as a trial attorney, secretly loved and was secretly loved by his secretary, Karen Page. Murdock did not reveal his feelings, considering his blindness to be a barrier to any relationship. Meanwhile, his law partner Foggy Nelson secretly loved Page and suffered an inferiority complex with respect to Murdock. Needless to say, the office was thick with thought balloons.

To begin with, *Daredevil* was more sober and brooding than its *Amazing* predecessor, but the protagonist was revamped with issue #7; his yellow-and-red costume was replaced with a jazzier, bright red outfit, and DD himself became jauntier, developing Spidey's ability to wisecrack under pressure. The schizophrenia between the somber Murdock and his daring, wiseacre alter ego came to a head in a 16-issue sequence (1967-68) in which Matt invented a hip brother Mike to play the role of Daredevil's civilian identity and divert suspicion from himself. In issue #41, he engineered Mike's (and Daredevil's) apparent death, leaving the public to wonder about the identity of the "new" Daredevil." In issue #57 in 1969, Murdock revealed to Page that he was Daredevil. After enduring the frustrations of a super-hero's girlfriend, Page departed in

1970 to pursue a career as an actress in California. In 1971, Daredevil moved to San Francisco and began a long love affair/partnership with Russian expatriate heroine The Black Widow, her image appearing across from his on the title logo. Second billing wasn't enough for her, however, and four years later she left the series.

In issue #161 in 1988, Frank Miller introduced the popular Elektra, who would be a formidable opponent and love interest for Daredevil for the next 13 issues. Like Daredevil, Elektra, an assassin with ninja skills, had lost her father to criminals. Their tumultuous relationship came to an end in 1982 with her death. The same year, another *femme fatale* was introduced in the form of Typhoid Mary. Mary's schizophrenic love/hate pursuit of DD would continue off and on for many years.

Meanwhile, Page had self-destructed in L.A. Strung out and jobless, she sold Daredevil out to The Kingpin, precipitating the six-issue story arc "Fall from Grace," drawn by David Mazzucchelli. This story, along with the Elektra storyline, established themes of spiritual trial and redemption that writer Ann Nocenti and artist John Romita Jr. continued to explore in a series of encounters between DD and Mephisto in the early 1990s. Writers like D.G. Chichester and Gregory Wright returned DD to the streets, embroiling him in gang wars and even outfitting him with body armor.

Currently, the series seems to have come full circle, with DD returning to his Matt Murdock identity, his armorless costume, his old law practice with Foggy Nelson, and his erstwhile heartthrob, Karen Page.

Partial Checklist:

Daredevil #7	Introduction of red costume
Daredevil #25 (Feb 67)	Introduction of Mike Murdock
Daredevil #41 (Jun 68)	Mike's death
Daredevil #81 (Nov 71)	Black Widow enters series
Daredevil #124 (Aug 75)	Black Widow exits
Daredevil #168 (Jan 81)	Introduction of Elektra
Daredevil #181 (Apr 82)	Death of Elektra
Daredevil #320-325	"Fall from Grace"

	ORIG.	GOOD	FINE	N-MINT
36, Jan 68, GC	0.12	4.00	12.00	20.00
37, f‡È 68, GC; V:Dr. Doom	0.12	4.00	12.00	20.00
38, Mar 68, GC	0.12	4.00	12.00	20.00
39, Apr 68, GC	0.12	4.00	12.00	20.00
40, May 68, GC	0.12	4.00	12.00	20.00
41, Jun 68, D:Mike Murdock	0.12	4.00	12.00	20.00
42, Jul 68, GC	0.12	4.00	12.00	20.00
43, Aug 68, GC	0.12	4.00	12.00	20.00
44, Sep 68, GC	0.12	4.00	12.00	20.00
45, Oct 68, GC	0.12	4.00	12.00	20.00
46, Nov 68, GC	0.12	4.00	12.00	20.00
47, Dec 68, GC	0.12	4.00	12.00	20.00
48, Jan 69, GC	0.12	4.00	12.00	20.00
49, Feb 69, GC	0.12	4.00	12.00	20.00
50, Mar 69, BS	0.12	4.00	12.00	20.00
51, BS	0.12	4.00	12.00	20.00
52, BS	0.12	4.00	12.00	20.00
53, GC, O:DD	0.12	4.00	12.00	20.00
54, GC	0.15	2.00	6.00	10.00
55, GC	0.15	2.00	6.00	10.00
56, GC	0.15	2.00	6.00	10.00
57, GC	0.15	2.00	6.00	10.00
58, GC	0.15	2.00	6.00	10.00
59, GC	0.15	2.00	6.00	10.00
60, GC	0.15	2.00	6.00	10.00
61, GC	0.15	2.00	6.00	10.00
62, GC, O:Nighthawk	0.15	2.00	6.00	10.00
63, GC	0.15	2.00	6.00	10.00
64, GC	0.15	2.00	6.00	10.00
65, GC	0.15	2.00	6.00	10.00
66, GC	0.15	2.00	6.00	10.00
67, GC	0.15	2.00	6.00	10.00
68, GC	0.15	2.00	6.00	10.00
69, GC	0.15	2.00	6.00	10.00
70, GC	0.15	2.00	6.00	10.00
71, GC	0.15	2.00	6.00	10.00
72, GC	0.15	2.00	6.00	10.00
73, GC	0.15	2.00	6.00	10.00
74, GC	0.15	2.00	6.00	10.00
75, GC	0.15	2.00	6.00	10.00
76, GC	0.15	2.00	6.00	10.00
77, GC	0.15	2.00	6.00	10.00
78, GC	0.15	2.00	6.00	10.00
79, GC	0.15	2.00	6.00	10.00
80, GC	0.15	2.00	6.00	10.00
81, GC, giant	0.25	2.00	6.00	10.00
82, Dec 71, GC	0.20	2.00	6.00	10.00
83, Jan 72, BS, V:Mr. Hyde	0.20	2.00	6.00	10.00
84, Feb 72	0.20	2.00	6.00	10.00
85	0.20	2.00	6.00	10.00
86	0.20	2.00	6.00	10.00
87	0.20	2.00	6.00	10.00
88	0.20	2.00	6.00	10.00
89	0.20	2.00	6.00	10.00
90	0.20	2.00	6.00	10.00
91	0.20	2.00	6.00	10.00
92	0.20	2.00	6.00	10.00
93	0.20	2.00	6.00	10.00
94	0.20	2.00	6.00	10.00
95	0.20	2.00	6.00	10.00
96	0.20	2.00	6.00	10.00
97	0.20	2.00	6.00	10.00
98	0.20	2.00	6.00	10.00
99	0.20	2.00	6.00	10.00
100, GC, anniversary	0.20	4.80	14.40	24.00
101	0.20	1.00	3.00	5.00
102	0.20	1.00	3.00	5.00
103	0.20	1.00	3.00	5.00
104	0.20	1.00	3.00	5.00
105, O:Moondragon	0.20	1.00	3.00	5.00
106, DH, A:Black Widow	0.20	1.00	3.00	5.00
107, SB, A:Capt. Marvel	0.20	1.00	3.00	5.00
108	0.20	1.00	3.00	5.00
109	0.25	1.00	3.00	5.00
110	0.25	1.00	3.00	5.00
111	0.25	1.00	3.00	5.00
112	0.25	1.00	3.00	5.00
113	0.25	1.00	3.00	5.00
114, 1:Death Stalker	0.25	1.00	3.00	5.00
115	0.25	1.00	3.00	5.00
116	0.25	1.00	3.00	5.00
117	0.25	1.00	3.00	5.00
118	0.25	1.00	3.00	5.00
119	0.25	1.00	3.00	5.00
120	0.25	1.00	3.00	5.00
121	0.25	1.00	3.00	5.00
122	0.25	1.00	3.00	5.00
123	0.25	1.00	3.00	5.00
124, GC/KJ, 1:Copperhead	0.25	1.00	3.00	5.00
125, KJ	0.25	1.00	3.00	5.00
126, KJ	0.25	1.00	3.00	5.00
127, KJ	0.25	1.00	3.00	5.00
128, KJ	0.25	1.00	3.00	5.00
129, KJ	0.25	1.00	3.00	5.00
130, KJ	0.25	1.00	3.00	5.00
131, KJ, O:Bullseye	0.25	5.00	15.00	25.00
132	0.25	1.00	3.00	5.00
133	0.25	1.00	3.00	5.00
134	0.25	1.00	3.00	5.00
135	0.25	1.00	3.00	5.00
136	0.25	1.00	3.00	5.00
137, Sep 76, JB	0.30	1.00	3.00	5.00
138, Oct 76, JBy, A:Ghost Rider	0.30	2.00	6.00	10.00
139, Nov 76, SB	0.30	1.00	3.00	5.00
140, Dec 76, SB	0.30	1.00	3.00	5.00
141, Jan 77, GK	0.30	1.00	3.00	5.00
142, Feb 77, JB	0.30	1.00	3.00	5.00
143, Mar 77	0.30	1.00	3.00	5.00
144, Apr 77	0.30	1.00	3.00	5.00
145, May 77	0.30	1.00	3.00	5.00
146, Jun 77, GK	0.30	1.00	3.00	5.00
147, Jul 77, GK, KJ	0.30	1.00	3.00	5.00
148, Sep 77, GK, KJ	0.30	1.00	3.00	5.00
149, Nov 77, KJ, CI	0.35	1.00	3.00	5.00
150, Jan 78, KJ, CI I:Paladin	0.35	1.00	3.00	5.00
151, Mar 78, GK, KJ	0.35	1.00	3.00	5.00
151, May 78, CI, KJ	0.35	1.00	3.00	5.00
153, Jul 78	0.35	1.00	3.00	5.00
154, Sep 78	0.35	1.00	3.00	5.00
155, Nov 78	0.35	1.00	3.00	5.00
156, Jan 79	0.35	1.00	3.00	5.00
157, Mar 79	0.35	1.00	3.00	5.00
158, May 79, FM, V:Deathstalker	0.40	8.00	24.00	40.00
159, Jul 79, FM, V:Bullseye	0.40	6.00	18.00	30.00
160, Sep 79, FM, V:Bullseye	0.40	3.20	9.60	16.00
161, Nov 79, FM, V:Bullseye	0.40	3.20	9.60	16.00
162, Jan 80, SD	0.40	0.80	2.40	4.00
163, Mar 80, FM	0.40	2.40	7.20	12.00
164, May 80, FM	0.40	2.40	7.20	12.00
165, Jul 80, FM	0.40	2.40	7.20	12.00
166, Sep 80, FM	0.50	2.40	7.20	12.00
167, Nov 80, FM	0.50	2.40	7.20	12.00
168, Jan 81, FM, O&1:Elektra	0.50	8.00	24.00	40.00

	ORIG.	GOOD	FINE	N-MINT
☐ 169, Mar 81, FM, V:Bullseye				
............................0.50		3.00	9.00	15.00
☐ 170, May 81, FM, V:Bullseye				
............................0.50		3.00	9.00	15.00
☐ 171, Jun 81, FM............0.50		1.60	4.80	8.00
☐ 172, Jul 81, FM.............0.50		1.60	4.80	8.00
☐ 173, Aug 81, FM............0.50		1.60	4.80	8.00
☐ 174, Sep 81, FM.............0.50		2.40	7.20	12.00
☐ 175, Oct 81, FM.............0.50		2.40	7.20	12.00
☐ 176, Nov 81, FM, A:Elektra				
............................0.50		2.00	6.00	10.00
☐ 177, Dec 81, FM............0.50		1.00	3.00	5.00
☐ 178, Jan 82, FM............0.60		1.00	3.00	5.00
☐ 179, Feb 82, FM.............0.60		1.00	3.00	5.00
☐ 180, Mar 82, FM 0.60		1.00	3.00	5.00
☐ 181, Apr 82, FM, V:Bullseye, D:Elektra				
............................1.00		3.00	9.00	15.00
☐ 182, May 82, FM, V:Punisher				
............................0.60		2.80	8.40	14.00
☐ 183, Jun 82, FM, V:Punisher				
............................0.60		2.80	8.40	14.00
☐ 184, Jul 82, FM, V:Punisher				
............................0.60		2.80	8.40	14.00
☐ 185, Aug 82, FM 0.60		0.60	1.80	3.00
☐ 186, Sep 82, FM.............0.60		0.60	1.80	3.00
☐ 187, Oct 82, FM 0.60		0.60	1.80	3.00
☐ 188, Nov 82, FM.............0.60		0.60	1.80	3.00
☐ 189, Dec 82, FM.............0.60		0.60	1.80	3.00
☐ 190, Jan 83, FM; A:Elektra				
............................1.00		0.60	1.80	3.00
☐ 191, Feb 83, FM 0.60		0.60	1.80	3.00
☐ 192, Mar 83, KJ 0.60		0.40	1.20	2.00
☐ 193, Apr 83, KJ 0.60		0.40	1.20	2.00
☐ 194, May 83, KJ.............0.60		0.40	1.20	2.00
☐ 195, Jun 83, KJ 0.60		0.40	1.20	2.00
☐ 196, Jun 83, KJ, A:Wolverine				
............................0.60		2.00	6.00	10.00
☐ 197, Aug 83, V:Bullseye . 0.60		1.00	3.00	5.00
☐ 198, Sep 83.................0.60		0.40	1.20	2.00
☐ 199, Oct 83.................0.60		0.40	1.20	2.00
☐ 200, Nov 83 ....0.60		0.40	1.20	2.00
☐ 201, Dec 83.................0.60		0.40	1.20	2.00
☐ 202, Jan 84 ....0.60		0.40	1.20	2.00
☐ 203, Feb 84 ....0.60		0.40	1.20	2.00
☐ 204, Mar 84 ....0.60		0.40	1.20	2.00
☐ 205, Apr 84 ....0.60		0.40	1.20	2.00
☐ 206, May 84.................0.60		0.40	1.20	2.00
☐ 207, Jun 84 ....0.60		0.40	1.20	2.00
☐ 208, Jul 84...................0.60		0.25	0.75	1.25
☐ 209, Aug 84 ....0.60		0.25	0.75	1.25
☐ 210, Sep 84.................0.60		0.25	0.75	1.25
☐ 211, Oct 84 ....0.60		0.25	0.75	1.25
☐ 212, Nov 84.................0.60		0.25	0.75	1.25
☐ 213, Dec 84.................0.60		0.25	0.75	1.25
☐ 214, Jan 85 ....0.60		0.25	0.75	1.25
☐ 215, Feb 85 ....0.60		0.25	0.75	1.25
☐ 216, Mar 85 ....0.60		0.25	0.75	1.25
☐ 217, Apr 85 ....0.65		0.25	0.75	1.25
☐ 218, May 85 ....0.65		0.25	0.75	1.25
☐ 219, Jun 85, FM.............0.65		1.00	3.00	5.00
☐ 220, Jul 85...................0.65		0.25	0.75	1.25
☐ 221, Aug 85 ....0.65		0.25	0.75	1.25
☐ 222, Sep 85.................0.65		0.25	0.75	1.25
☐ 223, Oct 85, Secret Wars II				
............................0.65		0.25	0.75	1.25
☐ 224, Nov 85 ....0.65		0.25	0.75	1.25
☐ 225, Dec 85.................0.65		0.25	0.75	1.25
☐ 226, Jan 86, FM 0.65		1.40	4.20	7.00
☐ 227, Feb 86, FM writer, Kingpin				
............................0.75		1.60	4.80	8.00
☐ 228, Mar 86, FM writer .. 0.75		1.20	3.60	6.00
☐ 229, Apr 86, FM writer ... 0.75		1.20	3.60	6.00
☐ 230, May 86, FM writer...0.75		1.20	3.60	6.00
☐ 231, Jun 86, FM writer ...0.75		1.20	3.60	6.00
☐ 232, Jul 86, FM writer.....0.75		1.20	3.60	6.00
☐ 233, Aug 86, FM writer ...0.75		1.20	3.60	6.00
☐ 234, Sep 86 ....0.75		0.80	2.40	4.00
☐ 235, Oct 86 ....0.75		0.80	2.40	4.00
☐ 236, Nov 86 ....0.75		0.80	2.40	4.00
☐ 237, Dec 86 ....0.75		0.80	2.40	4.00
☐ 238, Jan 87, Mutant Massacre				
............................0.75		0.80	2.40	4.00
☐ 239, Feb 87, AAd(c)........0.75		0.70	2.10	3.50
☐ 240, Mar 87, TMc...........0.75		0.40	1.20	2.00
☐ 241, Apr 87, TMc...........0.75		0.40	1.20	2.00
☐ 242, May 87...................0.75		0.40	1.20	2.00
☐ 243, Jun 87 ....0.75		0.40	1.20	2.00
☐ 244, Jul 87...................0.75		0.40	1.20	2.00
☐ 245, Aug 87, A:Black Panther				
............................0.75		0.40	1.20	2.00
☐ 246, Sep 87 ....0.75		0.40	1.20	2.00
☐ 247, Oct 87 ....0.75		0.40	1.20	2.00
☐ 248, Nov 87, A:Wolverine0.75		2.40	7.20	12.00
☐ 249, Dec 87, A:Wolverine0.75		2.40	7.20	12.00
☐ 250, Jan 88...................0.75		0.20	0.60	1.00
☐ 251, Feb 88...................0.75		0.20	0.60	1.00
☐ 252, Mar 88, Fall of Mutants				
............................1.25		0.25	0.75	1.25
☐ 253, Apr 88, Typhoid Mary				
............................0.75		2.40	7.20	12.00
☐ 254, May 88, Typhoid Mary				
............................0.75		2.80	8.40	14.00
☐ 255, Jun 88, Typhoid Mary				
............................0.75		2.40	7.20	12.00
☐ 256, Jul 88...................0.75		0.80	2.40	4.00
☐ 257, Aug 88, A:Punisher.0.75		4.80	14.40	24.00
☐ 258, Sep 88, 1:Bengal.....0.75		0.30	0.90	1.50
☐ 259, Oct 88 ....0.75		0.30	0.90	1.50
☐ 260, Nov 88, giant 1.50		0.30	0.90	1.50
☐ 261, Dec 88, A:Human Torch				
............................0.75		0.30	0.90	1.50
☐ 262, Jan 89, Inferno 0.75		0.30	0.90	1.50
☐ 263, Feb 89, Inferno 0.75		0.30	0.90	1.50
☐ 264, Mar 89 ....0.75		0.30	0.90	1.50
☐ 265, Apr 89, Inferno 0.75		0.30	0.90	1.50
☐ 266, May 89...................0.75		0.30	0.90	1.50
☐ 267, Jun 89 ....0.75		0.30	0.90	1.50
☐ 268, Jul 89 ....0.75		0.30	0.90	1.50
☐ 269, Aug 89 ....0.75		0.30	0.90	1.50
☐ 270, Sep 89, SpM...........1.00		0.80	2.40	4.00
☐ 271, Oct 89 ....1.00		0.20	0.60	1.00
☐ 272, Nov 89, 1:Shotgun..1.00		0.20	0.60	1.00
☐ 273, Nov 89 ....1.00		0.20	0.60	1.00
☐ 274, Dec 89 ....1.00		0.20	0.60	1.00
☐ 275, Dec 89, Acts of Vengeance				
............................1.00		0.30	0.90	1.50
☐ 276, Jan 90, Acts of Vengeance				
............................1.00		0.30	0.90	1.50
☐ 277, Feb 90...................1.00		0.30	0.90	1.50
☐ 278, Mar 90 ....1.00		0.30	0.90	1.50
☐ 279, Apr 90 ....1.00		0.30	0.90	1.50
☐ 280, May 90...................1.00		0.30	0.90	1.50
☐ 281, Jun 90 ....1.00		0.30	0.90	1.50
☐ 282, Jul 90...................1.00		0.30	0.90	1.50
☐ 283, Aug 90, Capt. America				
............................1.00		0.30	0.90	1.50
☐ 284, Sep 90 ....1.00		0.30	0.90	1.50
☐ 285, Oct 90...................1.00		0.30	0.90	1.50
☐ 286, Nov 90 ....1.00		0.30	0.90	1.50
☐ 287, Dec 90 ....1.00		0.30	0.90	1.50
☐ 288, Jan 91 ....1.00		0.30	0.90	1.50
☐ 289, Feb 91 ....1.00		0.30	0.90	1.50
☐ 290, Mar 91 ....1.00		0.30	0.90	1.50
☐ 291, Apr 91...................1.00		0.30	0.90	1.50

	ORIG.	GOOD	FINE	N-MINT
☐ 292, May 91, Punisher.... 1.00		0.40	1.20	2.00
☐ 293, Jun 91, Punisher.... 1.00		0.40	1.20	2.00
☐ 294, Jul 91 .... 1.00		0.20	0.60	1.00
☐ 295, Aug 91 .... 1.00		0.20	0.60	1.00
☐ 296, Sep 91.................. 1.00		0.20	0.60	1.00
☐ 297, Oct 91 .... 1.00		0.20	0.60	1.00
☐ 298, Nov 91 .... 1.00		0.20	0.60	1.00
☐ 299, Dec 91.................. 1.00		0.20	0.60	1.00
☐ 300, fall of Kingpin.. 2.00		0.70	2.10	3.50
☐ 301, V:Owl 1.25		0.25	0.75	1.25
☐ 302, V:Owl 1.25		0.25	0.75	1.25
☐ 303, V:Owl 1.25		0.25	0.75	1.25
☐ 304 .... 1.25		0.25	0.75	1.25
☐ 305 .... 1.25		0.25	0.75	1.25
☐ 306 .... 1.25		0.25	0.75	1.25
☐ 307 .... 1.25		0.25	0.75	1.25
☐ 308 .... 1.25		0.25	0.75	1.25
☐ 309 .... 1.25		0.25	0.75	1.25
☐ 310 .... 1.25		0.25	0.75	1.25
☐ 311 .... 1.25		0.25	0.75	1.25
☐ 312 .... 1.25		0.25	0.75	1.25
☐ 313 .... 1.25		0.25	0.75	1.25
☐ 314 .... 1.25		0.25	0.75	1.25
☐ 315 .... 1.25		0.25	0.75	1.25
☐ 316 .... 1.25		0.25	0.75	1.25
☐ 317 .... 1.25		0.25	0.75	1.25
☐ 318 .... 1.25		0.25	0.75	1.25
☐ 319, first printing (white) 1.25		3.60	10.80	18.00
☐ 319, second printing (black)				
.... 1.25		0.60	1.80	3.00
☐ 320 .... 1.25		3.20	9.60	16.00
☐ 321, Fall from Grace....... 2.00		1.20	3.60	6.00
☐ 321, Fall from Grace, glow in the dark cover				
.... 2.00		1.60	4.80	8.00
☐ 322 .... 1.25		0.80	2.40	4.00
☐ 323 .... 1.25		0.80	2.40	4.00
☐ 324 .... 1.25		0.80	2.40	4.00
☐ 325, poster.................... 2.50		0.50	1.50	2.50
☐ 326, Mar 94 .... 1.25		0.25	0.75	1.25
☐ 327, Apr 94 .... 1.25		0.25	0.75	1.25
☐ 328, May 94 .... 1.25		0.25	0.75	1.25
☐ 329, Jun 94 .... 1.50		0.30	0.90	1.50
☐ 330, Jul 94, Gambit........ 1.50		0.30	0.90	1.50
☐ 331, Aug 94 .... 1.50		0.30	0.90	1.50
☐ 332, Sep 94.................. 1.50		0.30	0.90	1.50
☐ 333, Oct 94 .... 1.50		0.30	0.90	1.50
☐ 334, Nov 94 .... 1.50		0.30	0.90	1.50
☐ 335, Dec 94.................. 1.50		0.30	0.90	1.50
☐ 336, Jan 95 .... 1.50		0.30	0.90	1.50
☐ 337, Feb 95 .... 1.50		0.30	0.90	1.50
☐ 338, Mar 95 .... 1.50		0.30	0.90	1.50
☐ 339, Apr 95 .... 1.50		0.30	0.90	1.50
☐ 340, May 95 .... 1.50		0.30	0.90	1.50
☐ 341, Jun 95 .... 1.50		0.30	0.90	1.50
☐ 342, Jul 95 .... 1.50		0.30	0.90	1.50
☐ 343, Aug 95 .... 1.50		0.30	0.90	1.50
☐ 344, Sep 95, Yellow and red-costumed Daredevil returns 1.95		0.39	1.17	1.95
☐ 345, Oct 95, Red-costumed Daredevil returns; OverPower card inserted 1.95		0.39	1.17	1.95
☐ 346, Nov 95 .... 1.95		0.39	1.17	1.95
☐ 347, Dec 95, Identity of both Daredevils revealed 1.95		0.39	1.17	1.95
☐ 348, Dec 95.................. 1.95		0.39	1.17	1.95
☐ 349, Feb 96 .... 1.95		0.39	1.17	1.95
☐ 350, Mar 96, double-sized				
.... 3.50		0.70	2.10	3.50
☐ 351, Apr 96 .... 1.95		0.39	1.17	1.95
☐ 352, May 96 .... 1.95		0.39	1.17	1.95
☐ 353, Jun 96, V:Mr. Hyde 1.95		0.39	1.17	1.95
☐ 354, Jul 96, A:SpM 1.50		0.30	0.90	1.50

	ORIG.	GOOD	FINE	N-MINT
DAREDEVIL ANNUAL				
☐ 1, GC.............................. 0.25		4.40	13.20	22.00
☐ 2, reprint........................ 0.25		1.60	4.80	8.00
☐ 3, reprint........................ 0.25		1.60	4.80	8.00
☐ 4, Oct 76, reprint 0.50		1.00	3.00	5.00
☐ 4, Sep 89, (misnumbered) Atlantis Attacks				
.... 2.00		1.00	3.00	5.00
☐ 6, Jun 90, Lifeform 2.00		0.40	1.20	2.00
☐ 7, Jun 91 .... 2.00		0.40	1.20	2.00
☐ 8 .... 2.25		0.45	1.35	2.25
☐ 9, trading card 2.95		0.59	1.77	2.95
☐ 10, 94 .... 2.95		0.59	1.77	2.95
DAREDEVIL: MAN WITHOUT FEAR (mini-series)				
☐ 1, Oct 93, FM(w), JRjr,AW				
.... 2.95		1.50	4.50	7.50
☐ 2, Nov 93, FM(w), JRjr,AW				
.... 2.95		1.20	3.60	6.00
☐ 3, Dec 93, FM(w); JRjr,AW				
.... 2.95		1.00	3.00	5.00
☐ 4, Jan 94, FM(w); JRjr,AW				
.... 2.95		1.00	3.00	5.00
☐ 5, Feb 94, FM(w); JRjr,AW				
.... 2.95		1.00	3.00	5.00
DARERAT/TADPOLE				
MIGHTY PUMPKIN				
☐ 1, 87, Batman parody 1.95		0.39	1.17	1.95
DARK ADVENTURES				
DARKLINE				
☐ 1		0.25	0.75	1.25
☐ 2		0.35	1.05	1.75
☐ 3		0.30	0.90	1.50
☐ 4, I:Terror Knight............		0.25	0.75	1.25
DARK ANGEL (formerly Hell's Angel)				
MARVEL				
☐ 6 .... 1.75		0.35	1.05	1.75
☐ 7 .... 1.75		0.35	1.05	1.75
☐ 8 .... 1.75		0.35	1.05	1.75
☐ 9 .... 1.75		0.35	1.05	1.75
☐ 10 .... 1.75		0.35	1.05	1.75
☐ 11 .... 1.75		0.35	1.05	1.75
☐ 12 .... 1.75		0.35	1.05	1.75
☐ 13 .... 1.75		0.35	1.05	1.75
☐ 14 .... 1.75		0.35	1.05	1.75
☐ 15 .... 1.75		0.35	1.05	1.75
☐ 16 .... 1.75		0.35	1.05	1.75
DARK COMICS				
IMPERIAL				
☐ 1		0.36	1.08	1.80
DARK CONVENTION BOOK, THE				
CONTINUM				
☐ 1 .... 1.95		0.80	2.40	4.00
DARK CRYSTAL				
MARVEL				
☐ 1, movie........................ 0.60		0.20	0.60	1.00
☐ 2, movie........................ 0.60		0.20	0.60	1.00
DARK DOMINION				
DEFIANT				
☐ 1 .... 2.50		0.50	1.50	2.50
☐ 2 .... 2.50		0.50	1.50	2.50
☐ 3, Dec 93 .... 2.50		0.50	1.50	2.50
☐ 4, Jan 94 .... 2.50		0.50	1.50	2.50
☐ 5, Feb 94 .... 2.50		0.50	1.50	2.50
☐ 6, Mar 94 .... 2.50		0.50	1.50	2.50
☐ 7, Apr 94 .... 2.50		0.50	1.50	2.50
☐ 8, May 94 .... 2.50		0.50	1.50	2.50
☐ 9, Jun 94 .... 2.50		0.50	1.50	2.50
DARK FANTASY				
APPLE				
☐ 1, b&w..........................		0.55	1.65	2.75

	ORIG.	GOOD	FINE	N-MINT

DARK GUARD
MARVEL

	ORIG.	GOOD	FINE	N-MINT
1, foil cover	2.25	0.45	1.35	2.25
2	1.75	0.35	1.05	1.75
3	1.75	0.35	1.05	1.75
4	1.75	0.35	1.05	1.75

DARK HORSE CLASSICS
DARK HORSE

	ORIG.	GOOD	FINE	N-MINT
1, 92, Last of the Mohicans;b&w		0.79	2.37	3.95
1, May 96, reprints "Predator: Rite of Passage" and "Predator: The Pride at Nghasa"	2.95	0.59	1.77	2.95
2, 92, 20,000 Leagues; b&w		0.79	2.37	3.95

DARK HORSE COMICS

	ORIG.	GOOD	FINE	N-MINT
1, 92	2.50	0.50	1.50	2.50
2, 92	2.50	0.50	1.50	2.50
3, 92	2.50	0.50	1.50	2.50
4, 92	2.50	0.50	1.50	2.50
5, 92	2.50	0.50	1.50	2.50
6, 92	2.50	0.50	1.50	2.50
7	2.50	1.00	3.00	5.00
8	2.50	3.60	10.80	18.00
9	2.50	2.00	6.00	10.00
10, Predator,Godzilla,X, James Bond	2.50	1.60	4.80	8.00
11, Predator,Godzilla,X, James Bond	2.50	0.80	2.40	4.00
12, Predator,Godzilla,X, James Bond	2.50	0.80	2.40	4.00
13, Predator,Godzilla,X, James Bond	2.50	0.80	2.40	4.00
14	2.50	0.50	1.50	2.50
15	2.50	0.50	1.50	2.50
16	2.50	0.50	1.50	2.50
17	2.50	0.50	1.50	2.50
18, Feb 94	2.50	0.50	1.50	2.50
19, Mar 94	2.50	0.50	1.50	2.50
20, Apr 94	2.50	0.50	1.50	2.50
21, May 94	2.50	0.50	1.50	2.50
23, Jul 94	2.50	0.50	1.50	2.50
24, Aug 94	2.50	0.50	1.50	2.50
25, Sep 94, flip book	2.50	0.50	1.50	2.50

DARK HORSE DOWN UNDER

	ORIG.	GOOD	FINE	N-MINT
1, Jun 94, b&w	2.50	0.50	1.50	2.50
2, Aug 94, b&w	2.50	0.50	1.50	2.50
3, Oct 94, b&w	2.50	0.50	1.50	2.50

DARK HORSE FUTURES

	ORIG.	GOOD	FINE	N-MINT
0, 1991, ads		0.20	0.60	1.00

DARK HORSE PRESENTS

	ORIG.	GOOD	FINE	N-MINT
1, 86, I:Concrete, 1st printing	2.25	2.80	8.40	14.00
1, (2nd printing)	2.25	0.45	1.35	2.25
1, reprint, green border	2.25	0.45	1.35	2.25
1, reprint, silver border	2.25	0.45	1.35	2.25
2	2.25	1.60	4.80	8.00
3, Nov 86	1.50	1.40	4.20	7.00
4, Jan 87	1.50	1.20	3.60	6.00
5, Feb 87	1.50	1.20	3.60	6.00
6, Apr 87	1.50	1.00	3.00	5.00
7, May 87	1.50	1.00	3.00	5.00
8, Jun 87	1.50	1.00	3.00	5.00
9, Jul 87	2.25	1.00	3.00	5.00
10, Sep 87	1.75	0.80	2.40	4.00
11, Oct 87	2.25	0.45	1.35	2.25
12, Nov 87	1.75	0.80	2.40	4.00
13, Dec 87	1.75	0.35	1.05	1.75
14, Jan 87	1.75	0.80	2.40	4.00
15, Feb 88	1.75	0.35	1.05	1.75
16, Mar 88	1.75	0.80	2.40	4.00
17, Apr 88	1.75	0.35	1.05	1.75
18, Jun 88	1.75	0.80	2.40	4.00
19, Jul 88	1.75	0.35	1.05	1.75
20, Aug 88, Concrete, Flaming Carrot, Mr. Monster	2.95	1.60	4.80	8.00
21, Aug 88	1.75	0.35	1.05	1.75
22, Sep 88, b&w; 1:Duckman	1.75	1.00	3.00	5.00
23, Oct 88	1.75	0.35	1.05	1.75
24, Nov 88, Aliens	1.75	4.80	14.40	24.00
25, Dec 88	1.75	0.40	1.20	2.00
26, Jan 89	1.75	0.40	1.20	2.00
27, Feb 89	1.75	0.40	1.20	2.00
28, Mar 89, Concrete, Mr. Monster	2.95	0.59	1.77	2.95
29, Apr 89	1.75	0.40	1.20	2.00
30, May 89	1.75	0.40	1.20	2.00
31, Jul 89, b&w; Duckman	1.75	0.80	2.40	4.00
32, Jul 89	3.50	0.70	2.10	3.50
33, Aug 89		0.45	1.35	2.25
34, Aug 89, Aliens		2.40	7.20	12.00
35, Sep 89, Predator		2.40	7.20	12.00
36, Oct 89, Aliens v. Predator		3.20	9.60	16.00
37, Nov 89		0.39	1.17	1.95
38, Apr 90, Concrete	1.95	0.39	1.17	1.95
39, May 90	1.95	0.39	1.17	1.95
40, 90, MW	2.95	0.59	1.77	2.95
41, 90	2.95	0.59	1.77	2.95
42, 90, Aliens		0.80	2.40	4.00
43, 90, Aliens		0.80	2.40	4.00
44, 90		0.39	1.17	1.95
45, 90, MW		0.39	1.17	1.95
46, 90, Predator		1.00	3.00	5.00
47, Dec 90, monsters		0.39	1.17	1.95
48, Jan 91, trading cards		0.39	1.17	1.95
49, Feb 91, trading cards		0.39	1.17	1.95
50, Apr 91, trading cards		0.39	1.17	1.95
51, Jun 91, FM	1.95	2.00	6.00	10.00
52, Jul 91, FM		1.60	4.80	8.00
53, Aug 91, FM		1.60	4.80	8.00
54, Sep 91, FM,JBy,GM		2.40	7.20	12.00
55, Oct 91, FM, JBy		2.00	6.00	10.00
56, Nov 91, FM, JBy, Aliens		1.60	4.80	8.00
57, Dec 91, FM, JBy 1:Next Men		1.60	4.80	8.00
58, Jan 92, FM		1.00	3.00	5.00
59, Feb 92, FM		1.00	3.00	5.00
60, Mar 92, FM		1.00	3.00	5.00
61, Apr 92, FM		1.00	3.00	5.00
65, Sep 92		0.45	1.35	2.25
66, Oct 92, Concrete		0.45	1.35	2.25
67, Nov 92		0.79	2.37	3.95
69, Feb 93	2.25	0.45	1.35	2.25
70, Mar 93	2.25	0.45	1.35	2.25
71, Apr 93	2.25	0.45	1.35	2.25
72, Apr 93	2.25	0.45	1.35	2.25
73, Jun 93	2.25	0.45	1.35	2.25
74, Jun 93	2.25	0.45	1.35	2.25
75, Jul 93	2.25	0.45	1.35	2.25
76, Aug 93	2.25	0.45	1.35	2.25
77, Sep 93	2.25	0.45	1.35	2.25
78, Oct 93	2.25	0.45	1.35	2.25
79, Nov 93	2.25	0.45	1.35	2.25
80, Dec 93	2.25	1.00	3.00	5.00
81, Jan 94	2.25	0.45	1.35	2.25
82, Apr 94	2.25	0.45	1.35	2.25
83	2.25	0.45	1.35	2.25
84, Apr 94	2.50	0.50	1.50	2.50
85, May 94	2.50	0.50	1.50	2.50
86, Jun 94, b&w	2.50	0.50	1.50	2.50
87, Jul 94, b&w	2.50	0.50	1.50	2.50
88, Aug 94, Hellboy; b&w	2.50	0.60	1.80	3.00

	ORIG.	GOOD	FINE	N-MINT
☐ 89, Sep 94, Hellboy; b&w	2.50	0.50	1.50	2.50
☐ 90, Oct 94, b&w	2.50	0.50	1.50	2.50
☐ 91, Nov 94, b&w	2.50	0.50	1.50	2.50
☐ 92, b&w;A:Too Much Coffee Man				
	0.80	2.40	4.00	
☐ 93, Jan 95, b&w;A:Too Much Coffee Man				
	2.50	0.80	2.40	4.00
☐ 94, Feb 95, b&w	2.50	0.50	1.50	2.50
☐ 95, Mar 95, b&w;A:Too Much Coffee Man				
	2.50	0.80	2.40	4.00
☐ 96, 95	2.50	0.50	1.50	2.50
☐ 97, 95	2.50	0.50	1.50	2.50
☐ 98, 95	2.50	0.50	1.50	2.50
☐ 99, 95	2.50	0.50	1.50	2.50
☐ 100, Aug 95, -1;FM (c) and story;b&w				
	2.50	0.50	1.50	2.50
☐ 100, Aug 95, -2;Hellboy cover and story;b&w				
	2.50	0.50	1.50	2.50
☐ 100, Aug 95, -3;Concrete cover and story;b&w				
	2.50	0.50	1.50	2.50
☐ 100, Aug 95, -4;Dave Gibbons (c);Martha Washington story;b&w	2.50	0.50	1.50	2.50
☐ 100, Aug 95, -5;Mike and Laura Allred cover;b&w				
	2.50	0.50	1.50	2.50
☐ 101, Sep 95, b&w; A:Aliens				
	2.50	0.50	1.50	2.50
☐ 102, Oct 95, b&w	2.50	0.50	1.50	2.50
☐ 103, Nov 95, b&w; JK centerfold				
	2.95	0.59	1.77	2.95
☐ 104, Dec 95, b&w	2.95	0.59	1.77	2.95
☐ 105, Jan 96, b&w	2.95	0.59	1.77	2.95
☐ 106, Feb 96, b&w; Big Blown Baby				
	2.95	0.59	1.77	2.95
☐ 108, Apr 96, The Ninth Gland;b&w				
	2.95	0.59	1.77	2.95
☐ 109, May 96, The One Trick Rip Off				
	2.95	0.59	1.77	2.95

DARK HORSE PRESENTS ALIENS

	ORIG.	GOOD	FINE	N-MINT
☐ 0, Platinum		6.00	18.00	30.00
☐ 1, 92, color reprints		0.99	2.97	4.95

DARK HORSE PRESENTS FIFTH ANNIVERSARY SPECIAL (1991)

	ORIG.	GOOD	FINE	N-MINT
☐ 0, Apr 91, FM, MW, Concrete, b&w				
	9.95	1.99	5.97	9.95

DARK REGIONS
WHITE WOLF

	ORIG.	GOOD	FINE	N-MINT
☐ 1		0.35	1.05	1.75
☐ 2		0.35	1.05	1.75
☐ 3		0.35	1.05	1.75

DARK SHADOWS
INNOVATION

	ORIG.	GOOD	FINE	N-MINT
☐ 1, TV series		0.50	1.50	2.50
☐ 2, TV series		0.50	1.50	2.50
☐ 3, TV series		0.50	1.50	2.50
☐ 4, TV series		0.50	1.50	2.50

DARK SHADOWS (Book Three)

	ORIG.	GOOD	FINE	N-MINT
☐ 1, Nov 93	2.50	0.50	1.50	2.50

DARK SHADOWS (Book Two)

	ORIG.	GOOD	FINE	N-MINT
☐ 1, Sum 93	2.50	0.50	1.50	2.50
☐ 2, Sum 93, indicia says #1 and contains the same information as the first issue's				
	2.50	0.50	1.50	2.50
☐ 3, Jun 93	2.50	0.50	1.50	2.50
☐ 4, Jul 93	2.50	0.50	1.50	2.50

DARK TALES OF DAILY HORROR
ANTARCTIC

	ORIG.	GOOD	FINE	N-MINT
☐ 1, Feb 94, b&w	2.95	0.59	1.77	2.95

DARK VISIONS
PYRAMID

	ORIG.	GOOD	FINE	N-MINT
☐ 1		0.34	1.02	1.70
☐ 2		0.34	1.02	1.70

DARK WOLF
ETERNITY

	ORIG.	GOOD	FINE	N-MINT
☐ 1, b&w		0.39	1.17	1.95
☐ 2, b&w		0.39	1.17	1.95
☐ 3, b&w		0.39	1.17	1.95
☐ 4, b&w		0.39	1.17	1.95
☐ 5, b&w		0.39	1.17	1.95
☐ 6, b&w		0.39	1.17	1.95
☐ 7, b&w		0.39	1.17	1.95
☐ 8, b&w		0.39	1.17	1.95
☐ 9, b&w		0.39	1.17	1.95
☐ 10, b&w		0.39	1.17	1.95
☐ 11, b&w		0.39	1.17	1.95
☐ 12, b&w		0.39	1.17	1.95
☐ 13, b&w		0.39	1.17	1.95
☐ 14, b&w		0.39	1.17	1.95

MALIBU

	ORIG.	GOOD	FINE	N-MINT
☐ 1		0.39	1.17	1.95
☐ 2		0.39	1.17	1.95
☐ 3		0.39	1.17	1.95
☐ 4		0.39	1.17	1.95

DARK WOLF ANNUAL
ETERNITY

	ORIG.	GOOD	FINE	N-MINT
☐ 1, b&w		0.45	1.35	2.25

DARK, THE
AUGUST HOUSE

	ORIG.	GOOD	FINE	N-MINT
☐ 1, Jan 95, enhanced cover				
	2.50	0.50	1.50	2.50

DARK, THE (volume 1)
CONTINUM

	ORIG.	GOOD	FINE	N-MINT
☐ 1, Mark Bright(p);Dan Panosian,Scott Hanna(i)				
	2.00	1.20	3.60	6.00
☐ 2, Larry Stroman(p);Rick Bryant,Dan Panosian(i)				
	2.25	0.80	2.40	4.00
☐ 3, Mark Bright(p);Jerry Acerno,Robert Campanella, Dan Panosian, Scott Hanna(i)				
	2.50	0.60	1.80	3.00
☐ 4, GP(c);Mark Bright(p); Jerry Acerno(i)				
	2.50	0.60	1.80	3.00

DARK, THE (volume 2)

	ORIG.	GOOD	FINE	N-MINT
☐ 1, May 93, red foil cover; Bart Sears(c)				
	1.95	2.00	6.00	10.00
☐ 1, 93, blue foil cover, Bart Sears(c), (second printing)				
	1.95	2.00	6.00	10.00
☐ 1, May 93	1.95	0.39	1.17	1.95
☐ 2	1.95	0.80	2.40	4.00
☐ 3, foil cover; GP, Chris Gossett(c)				
	1.95	0.60	1.80	3.00
☐ 4	1.95	0.60	1.80	3.00
☐ 5	1.95	0.39	1.17	1.95
☐ 6	1.95	0.39	1.17	1.95
☐ 7, Jul 94	1.95	0.39	1.17	1.95

DARKER IMAGE
IMAGE

	ORIG.	GOOD	FINE	N-MINT
☐ 0, b&w		8.00	24.00	40.00
☐ 1, trading card	2.50	0.50	1.50	2.50

DARKEWOOD
AIRCEL

	ORIG.	GOOD	FINE	N-MINT
☐ 1, color		0.40	1.20	2.00
☐ 2, color		0.40	1.20	2.00
☐ 3, color		0.40	1.20	2.00
☐ 4, color		0.40	1.20	2.00
☐ 5, color		0.40	1.20	2.00

DARKFORCE
OMEGA 7

	ORIG.	GOOD	FINE	N-MINT
☐ 1	2.50	0.50	1.50	2.50
☐ 2	2.50	0.50	1.50	2.50

DARKHAWK
MARVEL

	ORIG.	GOOD	FINE	N-MINT
☐ 1, Mar 91	1.00	0.80	2.40	4.00

	ORIG.	GOOD	FINE	N-MINT
❏ 2, Apr 91, SpM............... 1.00		0.60	1.80	3.00
❏ 3, May 91, SpM.............. 1.00		0.50	1.50	2.50
❏ 4, Jun 91......................... 1.00		0.50	1.50	2.50
❏ 5, Jul 91.......................... 1.00		0.50	1.50	2.50
❏ 6, Aug 91, Daredevil, Capt. America				
.... 1.00		0.30	0.90	1.50
❏ 7, Sep 91......................... 1.00		0.30	0.90	1.50
❏ 8, Oct 91 .... 1.00		0.30	0.90	1.50
❏ 9, Nov 91, Punisher 1.00		0.30	0.90	1.50
❏ 10, Dec 91...................... 1.00		0.30	0.90	1.50
❏ 11 .... 1.00		0.30	0.90	1.50
❏ 12 .... 1.25		0.30	0.90	1.50
❏ 13, Venom 1.25		0.60	1.80	3.00
❏ 14, Venom 1.25		0.60	1.80	3.00
❏ 15 .... 1.25		0.30	0.90	1.50
❏ 16 .... 1.25		0.30	0.90	1.50
❏ 17 .... 1.25		0.30	0.90	1.50
❏ 18 .... 1.25		0.30	0.90	1.50
❏ 19 .... 1.25		0.30	0.90	1.50
❏ 20 .... 1.25		0.30	0.90	1.50
❏ 21 .... 1.25		0.30	0.90	1.50
❏ 22 .... 1.25		0.30	0.90	1.50
❏ 23 .... 1.25		0.30	0.90	1.50
❏ 24 .... 1.25		0.30	0.90	1.50
❏ 25, foil cover 2.95		0.60	1.80	3.00
❏ 26 .... 1.25		0.30	0.90	1.50
❏ 27 .... 1.25		0.30	0.90	1.50
❏ 28 .... 1.25		0.30	0.90	1.50
❏ 29 .... 1.25		0.30	0.90	1.50
❏ 30 .... 1.25		0.30	0.90	1.50
❏ 31 .... 1.25		0.30	0.90	1.50
❏ 32 .... 1.25		0.30	0.90	1.50
❏ 33 .... 1.25		0.30	0.90	1.50
❏ 34 .... 1.25		0.30	0.90	1.50
❏ 35 .... 1.25		0.30	0.90	1.50
❏ 36 .... 1.25		0.30	0.90	1.50
❏ 37 .... 1.25		0.30	0.90	1.50
❏ 38 .... 1.25		0.30	0.90	1.50
❏ 39, May 94 .... 1.50		0.30	0.90	1.50
❏ 40, Jun 94....................... 1.50		0.30	0.90	1.50
❏ 41, Jul 94 .... 1.50		0.30	0.90	1.50
❏ 42, Aug 94...................... 1.50		0.30	0.90	1.50
❏ 43, Sep 94....................... 1.50		0.30	0.90	1.50
❏ 44, Oct 94 .... 1.50		0.30	0.90	1.50
❏ 45, Nov 94 .... 1.50		0.30	0.90	1.50
❏ 47, Jan 95 .... 1.50		0.30	0.90	1.50
❏ 48, Feb 95....................... 1.50		0.30	0.90	1.50
❏ 49, Mar 95....................... 1.50		0.30	0.90	1.50
❏ 50, Apr 95, final issue 2.50		0.50	1.50	2.50

DARKHAWK ANNUAL

	ORIG.	GOOD	FINE	N-MINT
❏ 1 .... 2.25		0.45	1.35	2.25
❏ 2, trading card................ 2.95		0.59	1.77	2.95
❏ 3, 94................................ 2.95		0.59	1.77	2.95

DARKHOLD

	ORIG.	GOOD	FINE	N-MINT
❏ 1, Midnight Sons, polybagged, poster				
.... 2.75		0.70	2.10	3.50
❏ 2 .... 1.75		0.35	1.05	1.75
❏ 3 .... 1.75		0.60	1.80	3.00
❏ 4 .... 1.75		0.35	1.05	1.75
❏ 5 .... 1.75		0.35	1.05	1.75
❏ 6 .... 1.75		0.35	1.05	1.75
❏ 7 .... 1.75		0.35	1.05	1.75
❏ 8 .... 1.75		0.35	1.05	1.75
❏ 9 .... 1.75		0.35	1.05	1.75
❏ 10 .... 1.75		0.35	1.05	1.75
❏ 11 .... 1.75		0.35	1.05	1.75
❏ 12 .... 1.75		0.35	1.05	1.75
❏ 13 .... 1.75		0.35	1.05	1.75
❏ 14 .... 1.75		0.35	1.05	1.75
❏ 15 .... 1.75		0.35	1.05	1.75
❏ 16 .... 1.75		0.35	1.05	1.75

DARKLON THE MYSTIC
PACIFIC

	ORIG.	GOOD	FINE	N-MINT
❏ 1		0.30	0.90	1.50

DARKMAN
MARVEL

	ORIG.	GOOD	FINE	N-MINT
❏ 1, Sep 90, b&w mag, movie				
.... 2.25		0.45	1.35	2.25
❏ 1, Oct 90, comic book.....1.50		0.20	0.60	1.00
❏ 2, Nov 90, comic book....1.50		0.20	0.60	1.00
❏ 3, Dec 90, comic book....1.50		0.20	0.60	1.00

DARKMAN (1993 ongoing series)

	ORIG.	GOOD	FINE	N-MINT
❏ 1 ....3.95		0.79	2.37	3.95
❏ 2 ....2.95		0.59	1.77	2.95
❏ 3 ....2.95		0.59	1.77	2.95
❏ 4 ....2.95		0.59	1.77	2.95
❏ 5 ....2.95		0.59	1.77	2.95
❏ 6 ....2.95		0.59	1.77	2.95

DARKSEED AND OTHER DEFAMATIONS
BONEYARD

	ORIG.	GOOD	FINE	N-MINT
❏ 0, adult, b&w 3.95		0.79	2.37	3.95

DARKSEID VS. GALACTUS: THE HUNGER
DC/MARVEL

	ORIG.	GOOD	FINE	N-MINT
❏ 0, 95, JBy;prestige format; one-shot				
.... 4.95		0.99	2.97	4.95

DARKSIDE
DARKLINE

	ORIG.	GOOD	FINE	N-MINT
❏ 1		0.30	0.90	1.50

DARKSTAR
REBEL

	ORIG.	GOOD	FINE	N-MINT
❏ 1, b&w............................		0.45	1.35	2.25
❏ 2, b&w............................		0.45	1.35	2.25

DARKSTARS, THE
DC

	ORIG.	GOOD	FINE	N-MINT
❏ 0, Oct 94 ....1.95		0.39	1.17	1.95
❏ 1, Oct 92 ....1.75		1.00	3.00	5.00
❏ 2, Nov 92 ....1.75		0.70	2.10	3.50
❏ 3, Dec 92 ....1.75		0.70	2.10	3.50
❏ 4, Jan 93 ....1.75		1.00	3.00	5.00
❏ 5, Feb 93 ....1.75		0.50	1.50	2.50
❏ 6, Mar 93 ....1.75		0.50	1.50	2.50
❏ 7, Apr 93.........................1.75		0.35	1.05	1.75
❏ 8, May 93........................1.75		0.35	1.05	1.75
❏ 9, Jun 93 ....1.75		0.35	1.05	1.75
❏ 10, Jun 93 ....1.75		0.35	1.05	1.75
❏ 11, Trinity 1.75		0.35	1.05	1.75
❏ 12, Trinity 1.75		0.35	1.05	1.75
❏ 13 ....1.75		0.35	1.05	1.75
❏ 14 ....1.75		0.35	1.05	1.75
❏ 15 ....1.75		0.35	1.05	1.75
❏ 16 ....1.75		0.35	1.05	1.75
❏ 17 ....1.75		0.35	1.05	1.75
❏ 18 ....1.75		0.35	1.05	1.75
❏ 19, Flash 1.75		0.35	1.05	1.75
❏ 20, May 94, Flash 1.75		0.35	1.05	1.75
❏ 21, Jun 94 ....1.75		0.35	1.05	1.75
❏ 22, Jul 94........................1.95		0.39	1.17	1.95
❏ 23, Aug 94......................1.95		0.39	1.17	1.95
❏ 24, Sep 94......................1.95		0.39	1.17	1.95
❏ 25, Nov 94......................1.95		0.39	1.17	1.95
❏ 26, Dec 94......................1.95		0.39	1.17	1.95
❏ 27, Jan 95.......................1.95		0.39	1.17	1.95
❏ 28, Feb 95.......................1.95		0.39	1.17	1.95
❏ 29, Mar 95.......................1.95		0.39	1.17	1.95
❏ 30, Apr 95.......................1.95		0.39	1.17	1.95
❏ 31, Jun 95.......................2.25		0.45	1.35	2.25
❏ 32, Jul 95........................2.25		0.45	1.35	2.25
❏ 33, Aug 95......................2.25		0.45	1.35	2.25
❏ 34, Sep 95, "The Siege of the Zi Charam" Part 3 of 5				
.... 2.25		0.45	1.35	2.25
❏ 35, Oct 95.......................2.25		0.45	1.35	2.25

	ORIG.	GOOD	FINE	N-MINT
36, Nov 95, A:Flash........	2.25	0.45	1.35	2.25
37, Dec 95, V:Guy Gardner				
....	2.25	0.45	1.35	2.25
38, Jan 96, final issue	2.25	0.45	1.35	2.25

DARKWING DUCK
DISNEY

	ORIG.	GOOD	FINE	N-MINT
1	1.50	0.30	0.90	1.50
2	1.50	0.30	0.90	1.50
3	1.50	0.30	0.90	1.50
4	1.50	0.30	0.90	1.50

DARQUE PASSAGES
VALIANT

		GOOD	FINE	N-MINT
1		0.40	1.20	2.00

DART (mini-series)
IMAGE

	ORIG.	GOOD	FINE	N-MINT
1, 96...............................	2.50	0.50	1.50	2.50
1, 96, alternate cover	2.50	0.50	1.50	2.50
2, Apr 96	2.50	0.50	1.50	2.50

DARTMAN
NORTHEASTERN PRESS

	ORIG.	GOOD	FINE	N-MINT
1	2.00	0.40	1.20	2.00

DATA 6
ARTIST'S UNLIMITED

	ORIG.	GOOD	FINE	N-MINT
1	1.95	0.39	1.17	1.95

DAUGHTERS OF TIME 3-D
3-D ZONE

		GOOD	FINE	N-MINT
0, nn SD(c),KS		0.79	2.37	3.95

DAVE COOPER'S PRESSED TONGUE
FANTAGRAPHICS

	ORIG.	GOOD	FINE	N-MINT
3, Dec 94, b&w	2.95	0.59	1.77	2.95

DAVID CHELSEA IN LOVE
ECLIPSE

		GOOD	FINE	N-MINT
1, b&w		0.70	2.10	3.50
2, b&w		0.70	2.10	3.50
3, b&w		0.70	2.10	3.50
4, b&w		0.70	2.10	3.50

DAWN (mini-series)
SIRIUS ENTERTAINMENT

	ORIG.	GOOD	FINE	N-MINT
1, Jul 95	2.95	1.60	4.80	8.00
1, 95, blacklight edition	10.00	2.00	6.00	10.00
2, Sep 95	2.95	0.80	2.40	4.00
2, 95, Mystery Book	10.00	2.00	6.00	10.00
3, 96..............................	2.95	0.59	1.77	2.95
4, 96..............................	2.95	0.59	1.77	2.95

DAY BROTHERS PRESENT
CALIBER

	ORIG.	GOOD	FINE	N-MINT
1, reprints	2.50	0.50	1.50	2.50
2, reprints	2.50	0.50	1.50	2.50
3, reprints	2.50	0.50	1.50	2.50
4, reprints	2.50	0.50	1.50	2.50

DAYS OF DARKNESS
APPLE

		GOOD	FINE	N-MINT
1, b&w		0.55	1.65	2.75
2, b&w		0.55	1.65	2.75
3, b&w		0.55	1.65	2.75
4, b&w		0.55	1.65	2.75
5, b&w		0.55	1.65	2.75

DAYS OF WRATH

	ORIG.	GOOD	FINE	N-MINT
1, b&w	2.75	0.55	1.65	2.75
2, b&w	2.75	0.55	1.65	2.75
3, b&w	2.75	0.55	1.65	2.75
4, Jun 94, b&w	2.75	0.55	1.65	2.75

DAYTONA 500 STORY
VORTEX

		GOOD	FINE	N-MINT
1, color...........................		0.40	1.20	2.00

DAZZLER
MARVEL

	ORIG.	GOOD	FINE	N-MINT
1, Mar 81, JR2, direct	0.50	0.50	1.50	2.50

	ORIG.	GOOD	FINE	N-MINT
2, Apr 81, JR2/AA, X-Men				
......................................0.50		0.40	1.20	2.00
3, May 81......................0.50		0.20	0.60	1.00
4, Jun 81.......................0.50		0.20	0.60	1.00
5, Jul 81........................0.50		0.20	0.60	1.00
6, Aug 81.......................0.50		0.20	0.60	1.00
7, Sep 81.......................0.50		0.20	0.60	1.00
8, Oct 81........................0.50		0.20	0.60	1.00
9, Nov 81.......................0.50		0.20	0.60	1.00
10, Dec 81 ....0.50		0.20	0.60	1.00
11, Jan 82......................0.60		0.20	0.60	1.00
12, Feb 82......................0.60		0.20	0.60	1.00
13, Mar 82......................0.60		0.20	0.60	1.00
14, Apr 82......................0.60		0.20	0.60	1.00
15, May 82, FS/BSz 0.60		0.30	0.90	1.50
16, Jun 82, FS/BSz 0.60		0.30	0.90	1.50
17, Jul 82, FS, Angel.......0.60		0.20	0.60	1.00
18, Aug 82, FS/BSz, FF ...0.60		0.30	0.90	1.50
19, Sep 82 ....0.60		0.20	0.60	1.00
20, Oct 82......................0.60		0.20	0.60	1.00
21, Nov 82, giant 1.00		0.20	0.60	1.00
22, Dec 82 ....0.60		0.20	0.60	1.00
23, Jan 83......................0.60		0.20	0.60	1.00
24, Feb 83......................0.60		0.20	0.60	1.00
25, Mar 83......................0.60		0.20	0.60	1.00
26, May 83......................0.60		0.20	0.60	1.00
27, Jul 83.......................0.60		0.20	0.60	1.00
28, Sep 83 ....0.60		0.20	0.60	1.00
29, Nov 83......................0.60		0.20	0.60	1.00
30, Jan 84......................0.60		0.20	0.60	1.00
31, Mar 84......................0.60		0.20	0.60	1.00
32, Jun 84.......................0.60		0.20	0.60	1.00
33, Aug 84......................0.60		0.20	0.60	1.00
34, Oct 84......................0.60		0.20	0.60	1.00
35, Jan 85......................0.60		0.20	0.60	1.00
36, Mar 85......................0.60		0.20	0.60	1.00
37, May 85......................0.65		0.20	0.60	1.00
38, Jul 85.......................0.65		0.90	2.70	4.50
39, Sep 85 ....0.65		0.20	0.60	1.00
40, Nov 85, Secret Wars II				
......................................0.65		0.35	1.05	1.75
41, Jan 86......................0.65		0.20	0.60	1.00
42, Mar 86......................0.75		0.20	0.60	1.00

DC 100-PAGE SUPER SPECTACULAR
DC

		GOOD	FINE	N-MINT
4, really DC-4;Weird Mystery Tales				
....		1.00	3.00	5.00
5, really DC-5;Love Stories		1.00	3.00	5.00
6, 71, really DC-6; World's Greatest Super-Heroes;				
reprints *JLA #21-22*........0.50		1.00	3.00	5.00
7, really DC-7;Superman.0.50		1.00	3.00	5.00
8, really DC-8;Batman.....0.50		1.00	3.00	5.00
9, really DC-9; Sgt. Rock 0.50		1.00	3.00	5.00
10, really DC-10; Supergirl				
......................................0.50		1.00	3.00	5.00
11, really DC-11;Flash.....0.50		1.00	3.00	5.00
12, really DC-12; Superboy				
......................................0.50		1.00	3.00	5.00
13, really DC-13; Superman				
......................................0.50		1.00	3.00	5.00
14, Feb 73, really DC-14; Batman				
......................................0.50		1.60	4.80	8.00
15, Mar 73, really DC-15; Superboy				
......................................0.50		0.80	2.40	4.00
16, 73, really DC-16; Sgt. Rock				
......................................0.50		0.80	2.40	4.00
17, Jun 73, really DC-17; JLA/JSA				
......................................0.50		0.80	2.40	4.00
18, Jul 73, really DC-18; Superman				
......................................0.50		0.80	2.40	4.00

	ORIG.	GOOD	FINE	N-MINT
19, Aug 73, really DC-19; Tarzan	0.50	0.80	2.40	4.00
20, Sep 73, really DC-20; Batman	0.50	0.80	2.40	4.00
21, Oct 73, really DC-21; Superboy	0.50	0.80	2.40	4.00
22, Nov 73, really DC-22; Flash;Super Specs become part of individual series beginning with *Shazam!* #8	0.50	0.80	2.40	4.00

DC CHALLENGE

	ORIG.	GOOD	FINE	N-MINT
1, Nov 85	1.25	0.80	2.40	4.00
2, Dec 85	1.25	0.40	1.20	2.00
3, Jan 86	1.25	0.40	1.20	2.00
4, Feb 86	1.25	0.40	1.20	2.00
5, Mar 86	1.25	0.40	1.20	2.00
6, Apr 86	1.25	0.40	1.20	2.00
7, May 86	1.25	0.40	1.20	2.00
8, Jun 86	1.25	0.40	1.20	2.00
9, Jul 86	1.25	0.40	1.20	2.00
10, Aug 86	1.25	0.40	1.20	2.00
11, Sep 86	1.25	0.40	1.20	2.00
12, Oct 86	1.25	0.40	1.20	2.00

DC COMICS PRESENTS (All have Superman)

	ORIG.	GOOD	FINE	N-MINT
1, Jul 78, JL/DA, Flash	0.35	0.60	1.80	3.00
2, Sep 78, JL/DA, Flash..	0.50	0.40	1.20	2.00
3, Oct 78, JL, Adam Strange	0.50	0.40	1.20	2.00
4, Dec 78, JL, Metal Men	0.40	0.40	1.20	2.00
5, Jan 79, MA, Aquaman	0.40	0.40	1.20	2.00
6, Feb 79, CS, Green Lantern	0.40	0.35	1.05	1.75
7, Mar 79, DD, Red Tornado	0.40	0.35	1.05	1.75
8, Apr 79, MA, Swamp Thing	0.40	0.40	1.20	2.00
9, May 79, JSa, WW	0.40	0.35	1.05	1.75
10, Jun 79, JSa, Sgt. Rock	0.40	0.35	1.05	1.75
11, Jul 79, JSa, Hawkman	0.40	0.25	0.75	1.25
12, Aug 79, RB/DG, Mr. Miracle	0.40	0.25	0.75	1.25
13, Sep 79, DD/DG, Legion	0.40	0.50	1.50	2.50
14, Oct 79, DD/DG, Superboy	0.40	0.25	0.75	1.25
15, Nov 79, JSa, Atom	0.40	0.25	0.75	1.25
16, Dec 79, Black Lightning	0.40	0.25	0.75	1.25
17, Jan 80, JL, Firestorm	0.40	0.30	0.90	1.50
18, Feb 80, DD, Zatanna.	0.40	0.25	0.75	1.25
19, Mar 80, JSa, Batgirl .	0.40	0.25	0.75	1.25
20, Apr 80, JL, Green Arrow	0.40	0.30	0.90	1.50
21, May 80, JSa, Elongated Man	0.40	0.20	0.60	1.00
22, Jun 80, Capt. Comet	0.40	0.20	0.60	1.00
23, Jul 80, JSa, Dr. Fate.	0.40	0.20	0.60	1.00
24, Aug 80, JL, Deadman	0.40	0.20	0.60	1.00
25, Sep 80, Phantom Stranger	0.50	0.20	0.60	1.00
26, Oct 80, GP/JSn, I:New Teen Titans, GL	0.50	3.20	9.60	16.00
27, Nov 80, JSn, I:Mongul	0.50	0.20	0.60	1.00
28, Dec 80, JSn, Mongul	0.50	0.20	0.60	1.00
29, Jan 81, JSn/RT, Spectre	0.50	0.40	1.20	2.00
30, Feb 81, CS, Black Canary	0.50	0.20	0.60	1.00
31, Mar 81, JL/DG, Robin	0.50	0.50	1.50	2.50
32, Apr 81, WW	0.50	0.20	0.60	1.00
33, May 81, Capt. Marvel	0.50	0.20	0.60	1.00
34, Jun 81, Marvel Family	0.50	0.20	0.60	1.00
35, Jul 81, CS, Man-Bat..	0.50	0.20	0.60	1.00
36, Aug 81, JSn, Starman	0.50	0.20	0.60	1.00
37, Sep 81, JSn/RT, Hawkgirl	0.50	0.20	0.60	1.00
38, Oct 81, D:Crimson Avenger	0.60	0.20	0.60	1.00
39, Nov 81, JSn, A:Toyman	0.60	0.20	0.60	1.00
40, Dec 81, Metamorpho	0.60	0.20	0.60	1.00
41, Jan 82, Joker, I:new WW	0.60	0.60	1.80	3.00
42, Feb 82, Unknown Soldier	0.60	0.20	0.60	1.00
43, Mar 82, CS, Legion	0.60	0.20	0.60	1.00
44, Apr 82, Dial 'H' for Hero	0.60	0.20	0.60	1.00
45, May 82, RB, Firestorm	0.60	0.20	0.60	1.00
46, Jun 82, I:Global Guardians	0.60	0.20	0.60	1.00
47, Jul 82, I:Masters of Universe	0.60	0.20	0.60	1.00
48, Aug 82, Aquaman	0.60	0.20	0.60	1.00
49, Sep 82, RB, Capt. Marvel	0.60	0.20	0.60	1.00
50, Oct 82, CS, Clark Kent	0.60	0.20	0.60	1.00
51, Nov 82, FMc, Atom	0.60	0.60	1.80	3.00
52, Dec 82, KG, Doom Patrol, 1:Ambush Bug	0.60	0.60	1.80	3.00
53, Jan 83, H. of Mystery, I:Atari Force	0.60	0.20	0.60	1.00
54, Feb 83, DN, GA, Black Canary	0.60	0.20	0.60	1.00
55, Mar 83, Air Wave A:Superboy, Parasite	0.60	0.20	0.60	1.00
56, Apr 83, CS, Power Girl	0.60	0.20	0.60	1.00
57, May 83, Atomic Knights	0.60	0.20	0.60	1.00
58, Jun 83, CS, Robin, Elongated Man	0.60	0.40	1.20	2.00
59, Jul 83, KG, LSH, Ambush Bug	0.60	0.50	1.50	2.50
60, Aug 83	0.60	0.20	0.60	1.00
61, Sep 83	0.60	0.20	0.60	1.00
62, Oct 83	0.60	0.20	0.60	1.00
63, Nov 83, DS, Amethyst	0.60	0.20	0.60	1.00
64, Dec 83, Kamandi	0.75	0.20	0.60	1.00
65, Jan 84, Madame Xanadu	0.75	0.20	0.60	1.00
66, Feb 84, JKu, Demon .	0.75	0.20	0.60	1.00
67, Mar 84, Santa Claus .	0.75	0.20	0.60	1.00
68, Apr 84, CS/MA, Vixen	0.75	0.20	0.60	1.00
69, May 84, IN, Blackhawk	0.75	0.20	0.60	1.00
70, Jun 84, Metal Men	0.75	0.20	0.60	1.00
71, Jul 84, CS, Bizarro	0.75	0.40	1.20	2.00
72, Aug 84, Phantom Stranger, Joker	0.75	0.60	1.80	3.00
73, Sep 84, Flash	0.75	0.20	0.60	1.00
74, Oct 84, Hawkman	0.75	0.20	0.60	1.00
75, Nov 84, Arion	0.75	0.20	0.60	1.00
76, Dec 84	0.75	0.20	0.60	1.00

	ORIG.	GOOD	FINE	N-MINT
❑ 77, Jan 85, Animal Man . 0.75		1.20	3.60	6.00
❑ 78, Feb 85, Animal Man . 0.75		1.20	3.60	6.00
❑ 79, Mar 85 .... 0.75		0.20	0.60	1.00
❑ 80, Apr 85 .... 0.75		0.20	0.60	1.00
❑ 81, May 85 .... 0.75		0.20	0.60	1.00
❑ 82, Jun 85 .... 0.75		0.20	0.60	1.00
❑ 83, Jul 85 .... 0.75		0.20	0.60	1.00
❑ 84, Aug 85 .... 0.75		0.20	0.60	1.00
❑ 85, Sep 85, Alan Moore Swamp Thing				
.... 0.75		1.00	3.00	5.00
❑ 86, Oct 85, Crisis 0.75		0.20	0.60	1.00
❑ 87, Nov 85, Crisis 1.25		0.25	0.75	1.25
❑ 88, Dec 85, Crisis........... 0.75		0.20	0.60	1.00
❑ 89, Jan 86 .... 0.75		0.20	0.60	1.00
❑ 90, Feb 86 .... 0.75		0.20	0.60	1.00
❑ 91, Mar 86 .... 0.75		0.20	0.60	1.00
❑ 92, Apr 86 .... 0.75		0.20	0.60	1.00
❑ 93, May 86 .... 0.75		0.20	0.60	1.00
❑ 94, Jun 86 .... 0.75		0.20	0.60	1.00
❑ 95, Jul 86 .... 0.75		0.20	0.60	1.00
❑ 96, Aug 86 .... 0.75		0.20	0.60	1.00
❑ 97, Sep 86..................... 1.25		0.25	0.75	1.25

DC COMICS PRESENTS ANNUAL

	ORIG.	GOOD	FINE	N-MINT
❑ 1, Oct 82, RB, Superman & E-2 Superman				
.... 1.00		0.50	1.50	2.50
❑ 2, Jul 83, O&1:Superwoman				
.... 1.00		0.35	1.05	1.75
❑ 3, Sep 84, Dr. Sivana gains the Shazam! powers				
.... 1.25		0.35	1.05	1.75
❑ 4, Oct 85, A:Superwoman				
.... 1.25		0.35	1.05	1.75

DC GRAPHIC NOVEL

	GOOD	FINE	N-MINT
❑ 1, JL, Star Raiders	1.19	3.57	5.95
❑ 2, Warlords	1.19	3.57	5.95
❑ 3, EC, Medusa Chain........	1.19	3.57	5.95
❑ 4, JK, Hunger Dogs..........	1.19	3.57	5.95
❑ 5, Me and Joe Priest	1.19	3.57	5.95
❑ 6, Metalzoic....................	1.39	4.17	6.95
❑ 7, Space Clusters	1.19	3.57	5.95

DC SAMPLER

	GOOD	FINE	N-MINT
❑ 1, Sep 83.......................	0.20	0.60	1.00
❑ 2, Sep 84.......................	0.20	0.60	1.00
❑ 3, 85..............................	0.20	0.60	1.00

DC SCIENCE FICTION GRAPHIC NOVEL

	GOOD	FINE	N-MINT
❑ 1, Hell on Earth	1.19	3.57	5.95
❑ 2, Nightwings..................	1.19	3.57	5.95
❑ 3, Frost and Fire	1.19	3.57	5.95
❑ 4, Merchants Venus.........	1.19	3.57	5.95
❑ 5, Demon with a Glass Hand	1.19	3.57	5.95
❑ 6, Magic Goes Away.........	1.19	3.57	5.95

DC SILVER AGE CLASSICS

	ORIG.	GOOD	FINE	N-MINT
❑ 92, *Action Comics #252*, reprint O:Supergirl				
.... 1.00		0.20	0.60	1.00
❑ 92, *Adventure 247*, reprint O:Legion				
.... 1.00		0.20	0.60	1.00
❑ 92, *Brave & Bold 28*, reprint 1:JLA				
.... 1.00		0.20	0.60	1.00
❑ 92, *Detective 225*, reprint 1:J'onn J'onzz				
.... 1.00		0.20	0.60	1.00
❑ 92, *Detective 327*, reprint 1:new Batman				
.... 1.00		0.20	0.60	1.00
❑ 92, *Green Lantern 76*, reprint O:GL/GA team				
		0.20	0.60	1.00
❑ 92, *House of Secrets*, reprint 1:Swamp Thing				
		0.20	0.60	1.00
❑ 92, *Showcase 4*, reprint O:Flash				
.... 1.00		0.20	0.60	1.00
❑ 92, *Showcase 22*, reprint O:Green Lantern				
.... 1.00		0.20	0.60	1.00
❑ 92, *Sugar and Spike 99*....		0.40	1.20	2.00

DC SPECIAL (all reprint)

	ORIG.	GOOD	FINE	N-MINT
❑ 1, Dec 68, CI, Flash/BM/Adam Strange				
.................................0.25		0.80	2.40	4.00
❑ 2, teen.............................		0.60	1.80	3.00
❑ 3, Jun 69, GA, Black Canary				
.................................0.25		0.70	2.10	3.50
❑ 4		0.60	1.80	3.00
❑ 5, Dec 69 ....0.25		0.60	1.80	3.00
❑ 6, Mar 70 ....0.25		0.60	1.80	3.00
❑ 7, Jun 70 ....0.25		0.60	1.80	3.00
❑ 8, Sep 70 ....0.25		0.60	1.80	3.00
❑ 9, Dec 70 ....0.25		0.60	1.80	3.00
❑ 10, Feb 71......................0.25		0.60	1.80	3.00
❑ 11, Apr 71......................0.25		0.60	1.80	3.00
❑ 12, Jun 71......................0.25		0.60	1.80	3.00
❑ 13, Aug 71......................0.25		0.60	1.80	3.00
❑ 14, Oct 71......................0.25		0.60	1.80	3.00
❑ 15, Dec 71, O:G.A. Plastic Man				
.................................0.25		0.70	2.10	3.50
❑ 16, Spr 75......................0.50		0.60	1.80	3.00
❑ 17, Sum 75.....................0.50		0.60	1.80	3.00
❑ 18, Nov 75.....................0.50		0.60	1.80	3.00
❑ 19, Jan 76......................0.50		0.60	1.80	3.00
❑ 20, Mar 76, Green Lantern				
.................................0.50		0.70	2.10	3.50
❑ 21, May 76.....................0.50		0.60	1.80	3.00
❑ 22, Jul 76.......................0.50		0.60	1.80	3.00
❑ 23, Sep 76 ....0.50		0.60	1.80	3.00
❑ 24, Oct 76......................0.50		0.60	1.80	3.00
❑ 25, Dec 76......................0.50		0.60	1.80	3.00
❑ 26, Feb 77......................0.50		0.60	1.80	3.00
❑ 27, Apr 77......................0.50		0.60	1.80	3.00
❑ 28, Jun 77, DN, disasters; new Legion story				
.................................0.60		0.60	1.80	3.00
❑ 29, Aug 77, JSa/BL, origin JSA				
.................................0.60		0.60	1.80	3.00

DC SPECIAL BLUE RIBBON DIGEST

	ORIG.	GOOD	FINE	N-MINT
❑ 1, Apr 80......................0.95		0.50	1.50	2.50
❑ 2, Jun 80 ....0.95		0.50	1.50	2.50
❑ 3, Aug 80......................0.95		0.50	1.50	2.50
❑ 4, Oct 80.......................0.95		0.50	1.50	2.50
❑ 5, Dec 80......................0.95		0.50	1.50	2.50
❑ 6, 81............................0.95		0.50	1.50	2.50
❑ 7, Mar 81......................0.95		0.50	1.50	2.50
❑ 8, Apr 81.......................0.95		0.50	1.50	2.50
❑ 9, May 81......................0.95		0.50	1.50	2.50
❑ 10, Jun 81......................0.95		0.50	1.50	2.50
❑ 11, Jul 81.......................0.95		0.50	1.50	2.50
❑ 12, Aug 81.....................0.95		0.50	1.50	2.50
❑ 13, Sep 81.....................0.95		0.50	1.50	2.50
❑ 14, Oct 81......................0.95		0.50	1.50	2.50
❑ 15, Nov 81.....................0.95		0.50	1.50	2.50
❑ 16, Dec 81......................0.95		0.50	1.50	2.50
❑ 17, Jan 82......................0.95		0.50	1.50	2.50
❑ 18, Feb 82......................0.95		0.50	1.50	2.50
❑ 19, Mar 82.....................0.95		0.50	1.50	2.50
❑ 20, Apr 82......................0.95		0.50	1.50	2.50
❑ 21, May 82.....................0.95		0.50	1.50	2.50
❑ 22, Jun 82 ....0.95		0.50	1.50	2.50
❑ 23, Jul 82.......................0.95		0.50	1.50	2.50

DC SPECIAL SERIES

	ORIG.	GOOD	FINE	N-MINT
❑ 1, Sep 77, MN/JR/DD/IN/FMc, Five Star				
.................................0.77		0.80	2.40	4.00
❑ 2, Sep 77, BWr, Swamp Thing rep.				
.................................0.60		0.70	2.10	3.50
❑ 3, Oct 77, JKu, Sgt. Rock0.60		0.65	1.95	3.25
❑ 4, Oct 77, Unexpected Annual	0.60	0.60	1.80	3.00
❑ 5, Nov 77, Superman, Luthor, C:Brainiac				
.................................1.00		0.65	1.95	3.25
❑ 6, Nov 77, JLA...............0.60		0.60	1.80	3.00
❑ 7, Dec 77, Ghosts		0.60	1.80	3.00

	ORIG.	GOOD	FINE	N-MINT

☐ 8, Feb 78, DG, Brave & Bold
.................0.60 0.65 1.95 3.25
☐ 9, Mar 78, SD/RH/DAy, Wonder Woman
.................1.00 0.60 1.80 3.00
☐ 10, Apr 78, MN, Super-Heroes
.................0.60 0.60 1.80 3.00
☐ 11, May 78, JG/GL/KS/MA/IN/WW, Flash
.................1.00 0.70 2.10 3.50
☐ 12, Jun 78, Secrets of Haunted House
.... 0.60 1.80 3.00
☐ 13, Jul 78, Sgt. Rock...... 1.00 0.60 1.80 3.00
☐ 14, Jul 78, Swamp Thing rep.
.................0.60 0.70 2.10 3.50
☐ 15, Aug 78, BM, Ra's al Ghul
.................1.00 0.65 1.95 3.25
☐ 16, Sep 78, RH, D:Jonah Hex
.................1.00 0.60 1.80 3.00
☐ 17, Sep 79, Swamp Thing rep.
.................1.00 0.60 1.80 3.00
☐ 18, Oct 79, digest Sgt. Rock
.................0.95 0.60 1.80 3.00
☐ 19, Oct 79, digest, O:WW0.95 0.70 2.10 3.50
☐ 20, Jan 80, Swamp Thing rep.
.................1.00 0.60 1.80 3.00
☐ 21, Mar 80, FM, BM, Legion
.................1.00 2.00 6.00 10.00
☐ 22, Sep 80, G.I. Combat... 0.40 1.20 2.00
☐ 23, Feb 81, digest Flash . 0.75 0.70 2.10 3.50
☐ 24, Feb 81, Superman II Photo Album
.................0.75 0.60 1.80 3.00
☐ 25, Sep 81, RA/RT, Superman's Fortress
.................2.95 0.70 2.10 3.50
☐ 26, Sep 81, JL/GL/DG 2.50 0.70 2.10 3.50
☐ 27, Dec 81, Batman vs. Incredible Hulk; oversized
.................2.50 0.60 1.80 3.00

DC SPOTLIGHT
☐ 1, Sep 85, JL(c) 0.20 0.60 1.00

DC SUPER STARS
☐ 1, Mar 76, Teen Titans rep.
.................0.50 0.50 1.50 2.50
☐ 2, Apr 76, Space 0.50 0.20 0.60 1.00
☐ 3, May 76, CS, Superman
.................0.50 0.50 1.50 2.50
☐ 4, Jun 76 .... 0.50 0.20 0.60 1.00
☐ 5, Jul 76 .... 0.50 0.20 0.60 1.00
☐ 6, Aug 76 .... 0.50 0.20 0.60 1.00
☐ 7, Sep 76 .... 0.50 0.20 0.60 1.00
☐ 8, Oct 76 .... 0.50 0.20 0.60 1.00
☐ 9, Nov 76 .... 0.50 0.20 0.60 1.00
☐ 10, Dec 76 .... 0.50 0.20 0.60 1.00
☐ 11, Jan 77 .... 0.50 0.20 0.60 1.00
☐ 12, Feb 77 .... 0.50 0.20 0.60 1.00
☐ 13, Mar 77 .... 0.50 0.20 0.60 1.00
☐ 14, May 77 .... 0.50 0.20 0.60 1.00
☐ 15, Jul 77 .... 0.50 0.20 0.60 1.00
☐ 16, Sep 77, DN/BL, 1:Star Hunters
.................0.60 0.30 0.90 1.50
☐ 17, Nov 77, JSa/BL, MGr, Secret Origins, I:Huntress;
Legion story.................. 0.60 1.20 3.60 6.00
☐ 18, Jan 78, Deadman/Phantom Stranger
.................0.60 0.25 0.75 1.25

DC VERSUS MARVEL (mini-series)
☐ 1, 96, crossover with Marvel;continues in *Marvel versus DC #2*; cardstock cover. 3.95 0.79 2.37 3.95
☐ 4, 96, final issue;cardstock cover;continued from *Marvel versus DC #3* 3.95 0.79 2.37 3.95

DEAD CLOWN
MALIBU
☐ 1 .... 2.50 0.50 1.50 2.50
☐ 2 .... 2.50 0.50 1.50 2.50
☐ 3, Feb 94 .... 2.50 0.50 1.50 2.50

DEAD HEAT, THE
ALL AMERICAN
☐ 1, b&w.......................... 0.39 1.17 1.95

DEAD IN THE WEST
DARK HORSE
☐ 1, 93, adult;b&w 3.95 0.79 2.37 3.95
☐ 2, Mar 94, adult;b&w......3.95 0.79 2.37 3.95

DEAD MEAT
FLEETWAY/QUALITY
☐ 1 ....2.95 0.59 1.77 2.95
☐ 2 ....2.95 0.59 1.77 2.95

DEAD MUSE, THE
FANTAGRAPHICS
☐ 0, nn b&w anthology 0.79 2.37 3.95

DEAD OF NIGHT
MARVEL
☐ 1, reprints 0.20 0.40 1.20 2.00
☐ 2, reprints 0.20 0.20 0.60 1.00
☐ 3, reprints 0.20 0.20 0.60 1.00
☐ 4, reprints 0.20 0.20 0.60 1.00
☐ 5, reprints 0.20 0.20 0.60 1.00
☐ 6, reprints 0.20 0.20 0.60 1.00
☐ 7, reprints 0.20 0.20 0.60 1.00
☐ 8, reprints 0.20 0.20 0.60 1.00
☐ 9, reprints 0.20 0.20 0.60 1.00
☐ 10, reprints 0.20 0.20 0.60 1.00
☐ 11, I:Scarecrow 0.25 0.60 1.80 3.00

DEAD WALKERS
AIRCEL
☐ 1, "gross" cover 0.50 1.50 2.50
☐ 1, "not-so-gross" cover.... 0.50 1.50 2.50
☐ 2 .... 0.50 1.50 2.50
☐ 3 .... 0.50 1.50 2.50
☐ 4 .... 0.50 1.50 2.50

DEAD, THE
ARROW
☐ 1, two different covers....2.25 0.45 1.35 2.25

DEADBEATS
CLAYPOOL
☐ 1, b&w..........................2.50 0.50 1.50 2.50
☐ 2, b&w..........................2.50 0.50 1.50 2.50
☐ 3, b&w..........................2.50 0.50 1.50 2.50
☐ 4, Oct 93, b&w...............2.50 0.50 1.50 2.50
☐ 5, Sep 93, b&w...............2.50 0.50 1.50 2.50
☐ 7, Jun 94, b&w...............2.50 0.50 1.50 2.50
☐ 11, Mar 95, b&w.............2.50 0.50 1.50 2.50
☐ 12, May 95, b&w.............2.50 0.50 1.50 2.50
☐ 13, Jul 95, b&w 2.50 0.50 1.50 2.50
☐ 14, Sep 95, b&w 2.50 0.50 1.50 2.50
☐ 15, Nov 95, b&w 2.50 0.50 1.50 2.50
☐ 16, Jan 96, b&w 2.50 0.50 1.50 2.50

DEADFACE
HARRIER
☐ 1 .... 1.20 3.60 6.00
☐ 2 .... 1.00 3.00 5.00
☐ 3 .... 1.00 3.00 5.00
☐ 4 .... 1.00 3.00 5.00
☐ 5 .... 1.00 3.00 5.00
☐ 6 .... 0.80 2.40 4.00
☐ 7 .... 0.80 2.40 4.00
☐ 8 .... 0.80 2.40 4.00

DEADFACE: DOING THE ISLANDS WITH BACCHUS
DARK HORSE
☐ 1, 91, b&w...................... 0.59 1.77 2.95
☐ 2, 91, b&w...................... 0.59 1.77 2.95
☐ 3, 91, b&w...................... 0.59 1.77 2.95

DEADFACE: EARTH, WATER, AIR, FIRE
☐ 1, 92, b&w...................... 0.50 1.50 2.50
☐ 2, 92, b&w...................... 0.50 1.50 2.50

	ORIG.	GOOD	FINE	N-MINT
☐ 3, 92, b&w		0.50	1.50	2.50
☐ 4, 92, b&w		0.50	1.50	2.50

DEADFISH BEDEVILED
ALL AMERICAN

☐ 1, b&w		0.45	1.35	2.25

DEADLIEST CREATURE ON EARTH … MAN, THE
NICOTAT

☐ 1, b&w		0.40	1.20	2.00

DEADLIEST HEROES OF KUNG FU, THE
MARVEL

☐ 1, (b&w mag)	1.00	0.20	0.60	1.00

DEADLINE USA
DARK HORSE

☐ 1, 91, b&w;reprints		1.99	5.97	9.95
☐ 2, 91, b&w;reprints		1.99	5.97	9.95
☐ 3, 91, b&w;reprints		1.99	5.97	9.95
☐ 4		0.79	2.37	3.95
☐ 5	3.95	0.79	2.37	3.95
☐ 6	3.95	0.79	2.37	3.95
☐ 7	3.95	0.79	2.37	3.95
☐ 8	3.95	0.79	2.37	3.95

DEADLY DUO, THE
IMAGE

☐ 2, Dec 94	2.50	0.50	1.50	2.50
☐ 3, Jan 95	2.50	0.50	1.50	2.50

DEADLY DUO, THE (second series)

☐ 2, Aug 95	2.50	0.50	1.50	2.50

DEADLY FOES OF SPIDER-MAN
MARVEL

☐ 1, May 91	1.00	0.80	2.40	4.00
☐ 2, Jun 91, SpM	1.00	0.50	1.50	2.50
☐ 3, Jul 91, SpM	1.00	0.50	1.50	2.50
☐ 4, Aug 91, SpM	1.00	0.50	1.50	2.50

DEADLY HANDS OF KUNG FU (b&w mag)

☐ 1	0.75	0.15	0.45	0.75
☐ 2	0.75	0.15	0.45	0.75
☐ 3	0.75	0.15	0.45	0.75
☐ 4	0.75	0.15	0.45	0.75
☐ 5	0.75	0.15	0.45	0.75
☐ 6	0.75	0.15	0.45	0.75
☐ 7	0.75	0.15	0.45	0.75
☐ 8	0.75	0.15	0.45	0.75
☐ 9	0.75	0.15	0.45	0.75
☐ 10	0.75	0.15	0.45	0.75
☐ 11	0.75	0.15	0.45	0.75
☐ 12	0.75	0.15	0.45	0.75
☐ 13	0.75	0.15	0.45	0.75
☐ 14	0.75	0.15	0.45	0.75
☐ 15	1.25	0.25	0.75	1.25
☐ 16	1.00	0.20	0.60	1.00
☐ 17	1.00	0.20	0.60	1.00
☐ 18	1.00	0.20	0.60	1.00
☐ 19	1.00	0.20	0.60	1.00
☐ 20	1.00	0.20	0.60	1.00
☐ 21	1.00	0.20	0.60	1.00
☐ 22	1.00	0.20	0.60	1.00
☐ 23	1.00	0.20	0.60	1.00
☐ 24	1.00	0.20	0.60	1.00
☐ 25	1.00	0.20	0.60	1.00
☐ 26	1.00	0.20	0.60	1.00
☐ 27	1.00	0.20	0.60	1.00
☐ 28, Sep 76	1.00	0.20	0.60	1.00
☐ 29, Oct 76	1.00	0.20	0.60	1.00
☐ 30, Nov 76	1.00	0.20	0.60	1.00
☐ 31, Dec 76	1.00	0.20	0.60	1.00
☐ 32, Jan 77	1.00	0.20	0.60	1.00
☐ 33, Feb 77	1.00	0.20	0.60	1.00

DEADLY HANDS OF KUNG FU SPECIAL (b&w mag)

☐ 1	1.00	0.20	0.60	1.00

	ORIG.	GOOD	FINE	N-MINT

DEADMAN (mini-series)
DC

☐ 1, Mar 86, JL	0.75	0.20	0.60	1.00
☐ 2, Apr 86, JL	0.75	0.20	0.60	1.00
☐ 3, Apr 86, JL	0.75	0.20	0.60	1.00
☐ 4, Jun 86, JL	0.75	0.20	0.60	1.00

DEADMAN (reprint)

☐ 1, May 85, CI,NA	1.75	0.40	1.20	2.00
☐ 2, Jun 85, NA	1.75	0.35	1.05	1.75
☐ 3, Jul 85, NA	1.75	0.35	1.05	1.75
☐ 4, Aug 85, NA	1.75	0.35	1.05	1.75
☐ 5, Sep 85, NA	1.75	0.35	1.05	1.75
☐ 6, Oct 85, NA	1.75	0.35	1.05	1.75
☐ 7, Nov 85, NA	1.75	0.35	1.05	1.75

DEADMAN: EXORCISM

☐ 1		0.99	2.97	4.95
☐ 2		0.99	2.97	4.95

DEADMAN: LOVE AFTER DEATH

☐ 1, Dec 89		0.79	2.37	3.95
☐ 2, Jan 90		0.79	2.37	3.95

DEADPOOL
MARVEL

☐ 1, embossed cover	2.50	1.00	3.00	5.00
☐ 2	2.00	0.80	2.40	4.00
☐ 3	2.00	0.60	1.80	3.00
☐ 4	2.00	0.60	1.80	3.00

DEADPOOL (series 2, 1994)

☐ 2, Sep 94	2.50	0.50	1.50	2.50
☐ 3, Oct 94	2.50	0.50	1.50	2.50
☐ 4, Nov 94	2.50	0.50	1.50	2.50

DEADSHOT
DC

☐ 1, Nov 88, O:Deadshot	1.00	0.20	0.60	1.00
☐ 2, Dec 88	1.00	0.20	0.60	1.00
☐ 3, Dec 88	1.00	0.20	0.60	1.00
☐ 4, Jan 89	1.00	0.20	0.60	1.00

DEADTIME STORIES
NEW COMICS

☐ 1, SRB, AAd b&w		0.35	1.05	1.75

DEADWORLD
ARROW

☐ 1, b&w		1.20	3.60	6.00
☐ 2		1.00	3.00	5.00
☐ 3		0.60	1.80	3.00
☐ 4		0.60	1.80	3.00
☐ 5		0.60	1.80	3.00
☐ 6		0.60	1.80	3.00
☐ 7		0.60	1.80	3.00
☐ 8		0.60	1.80	3.00
☐ 9		0.60	1.80	3.00

CALIBER

☐ 10, b&w	2.50	0.50	1.50	2.50
☐ 11, b&w	2.50	0.50	1.50	2.50
☐ 12, b&w	2.50	0.50	1.50	2.50
☐ 13, b&w	2.50	0.50	1.50	2.50
☐ 14, b&w	2.50	0.50	1.50	2.50
☐ 15, b&w	2.50	0.50	1.50	2.50
☐ 16, b&w	2.50	0.50	1.50	2.50
☐ 17, b&w	2.50	0.50	1.50	2.50
☐ 18, b&w	2.50	0.50	1.50	2.50
☐ 19, b&w	2.50	0.50	1.50	2.50
☐ 20, b&w	2.50	0.50	1.50	2.50
☐ 21, b&w	2.50	0.50	1.50	2.50
☐ 22, b&w	2.50	0.50	1.50	2.50
☐ 23, b&w	2.50	0.50	1.50	2.50
☐ 24, b&w	2.50	0.50	1.50	2.50
☐ 25, b&w	2.50	0.50	1.50	2.50
☐ 26, b&w	3.50	0.70	2.10	3.50

	ORIG.	GOOD	FINE	N-MINT

DEADWORLD (Volume 2)

	ORIG.	GOOD	FINE	N-MINT
❏ 1, 93, b&w	5.95	1.19	3.57	5.95
❏ 2, b&w	2.95	0.59	1.77	2.95
❏ 3, b&w	2.95	0.59	1.77	2.95
❏ 4, b&w	2.95	0.59	1.77	2.95
❏ 5, b&w	2.95	0.59	1.77	2.95
❏ 6, b&w	2.95	0.59	1.77	2.95
❏ 7, b&w	2.95	0.59	1.77	2.95
❏ 8, b&w	2.95	0.59	1.77	2.95
❏ 9, b&w	2.95	0.59	1.77	2.95
❏ 10, b&w	2.95	0.59	1.77	2.95
❏ 11, b&w	2.95	0.59	1.77	2.95
❏ 12, b&w	2.95	0.59	1.77	2.95
❏ 13, b&w	2.95	0.59	1.77	2.95
❏ 14, b&w	2.95	0.59	1.77	2.95
❏ 15, b&w	2.95	0.59	1.77	2.95

DEADWORLD ARCHIVES

	ORIG.	GOOD	FINE	N-MINT
❏ 1, b&w	2.50	0.50	1.50	2.50
❏ 2, b&w	2.50	0.50	1.50	2.50
❏ 3, b&w	2.50	0.50	1.50	2.50

DEADWORLD: BITS AND PIECES

	ORIG.	GOOD	FINE	N-MINT
❏ 1, reprints, b&w	2.95	0.59	1.77	2.95

DEADWORLD: TO KILL A KING

	ORIG.	GOOD	FINE	N-MINT
❏ 1	2.95	0.59	1.77	2.95
❏ 1, limited edition	5.95	1.19	3.57	5.95
❏ 2	2.95	0.59	1.77	2.95
❏ 3	2.95	0.59	1.77	2.95

DEATH & TAXES: THE REAL COSTS OF LIVING
PARODY

	ORIG.	GOOD	FINE	N-MINT
❏ 1, b&w	2.50	0.50	1.50	2.50

DEATH CRAZED TEENAGE SUPERHEROES
ARF!ARF!

	GOOD	FINE	N-MINT
❏ 1	0.30	0.90	1.50
❏ 2	0.30	0.90	1.50

DEATH DREAMS OF DRACULA
APPLE

	GOOD	FINE	N-MINT
❏ 1, b&w	0.50	1.50	2.50
❏ 2, b&w	0.50	1.50	2.50
❏ 3, b&w	0.50	1.50	2.50
❏ 4, b&w	0.50	1.50	2.50

DEATH GALLERY
DC/VERTIGO

	ORIG.	GOOD	FINE	N-MINT
❏ 1, portraits	2.95	1.60	4.80	8.00

DEATH HAWK
ADVENTURE

	GOOD	FINE	N-MINT
❏ 1, b&w	0.39	1.17	1.95
❏ 2, b&w	0.39	1.17	1.95
❏ 3, b&w	0.39	1.17	1.95

DEATH HUNT
ETERNITY

	GOOD	FINE	N-MINT
❏ 1, b&w	0.39	1.17	1.95

DEATH METAL
MARVEL

	ORIG.	GOOD	FINE	N-MINT
❏ 1	1.95	0.39	1.17	1.95
❏ 2	1.95	0.39	1.17	1.95
❏ 3	1.95	0.39	1.17	1.95
❏ 4	1.95	0.39	1.17	1.95

DEATH METAL VS. GENETIX

	ORIG.	GOOD	FINE	N-MINT
❏ 1, two trading cards	2.95	0.59	1.77	2.95
❏ 2, two trading cards	2.95	0.59	1.77	2.95

DEATH OF SUPERBABE
SPOOF

	ORIG.	GOOD	FINE	N-MINT
❏ 1, b&w	3.95	0.79	2.37	3.95

DEATH RACE 2020
ROGER CORMAN'S COSMIC COMICS

	ORIG.	GOOD	FINE	N-MINT
❏ 5, Aug 95	2.50	0.50	1.50	2.50

DEATH RATTLE (Vol. 3)
KITCHEN SINK

	ORIG.	GOOD	FINE	N-MINT
❏ 1, Dec 95, b&w	2.95	0.59	1.77	2.95
❏ 2, Dec 95, b&w	2.95	0.59	1.77	2.95

DEATH RATTLE (Volume 2)

	ORIG.	GOOD	FINE	N-MINT
❏ 1, color		0.40	1.20	2.00
❏ 2, color		0.40	1.20	2.00
❏ 3, color		0.40	1.20	2.00
❏ 4, color		0.40	1.20	2.00
❏ 5, color		0.40	1.20	2.00
❏ 6, b&w		0.40	1.20	2.00
❏ 7, b&w		0.40	1.20	2.00
❏ 8, 1:Xenozoic		0.40	1.20	2.00
❏ 9		0.40	1.20	2.00
❏ 10, AW,FF,WW		0.40	1.20	2.00
❏ 11		0.40	1.20	2.00
❏ 12		0.40	1.20	2.00
❏ 13, Nov 87	2.00	0.40	1.20	2.00
❏ 14		0.40	1.20	2.00
❏ 15		0.40	1.20	2.00
❏ 16		0.40	1.20	2.00
❏ 17		0.40	1.20	2.00
❏ 18, FM(c)		0.40	1.20	2.00

DEATH SHRIKE
BRAINSTORM

	ORIG.	GOOD	FINE	N-MINT
❏ 1, Jul 93, b&w	2.95	0.59	1.77	2.95

DEATH TALKS ABOUT LIFE
DC/VERTIGO

	ORIG.	GOOD	FINE	N-MINT
❏ 0, 16-page booklet about AIDS	0.60	1.80	3.00

DEATH WARMED OVER
CAT-HEAD

	GOOD	FINE	N-MINT
❏ 1, adult, b&w	0.55	1.65	2.75

DEATH WRECK
MARVEL

	ORIG.	GOOD	FINE	N-MINT
❏ 1	1.95	0.39	1.17	1.95
❏ 2	1.95	0.39	1.17	1.95
❏ 3	1.95	0.39	1.17	1.95
❏ 4	1.95	0.39	1.17	1.95
❏ 5	1.95	0.39	1.17	1.95
❏ 6	1.95	0.39	1.17	1.95
❏ 7	1.95	0.39	1.17	1.95

DEATH'S HEAD

	ORIG.	GOOD	FINE	N-MINT
❏ 1, Dec 88	1.75	0.60	1.80	3.00
❏ 2, Jan 89	1.75	0.39	1.17	1.95
❏ 3, Feb 89	1.75	0.39	1.17	1.95
❏ 4, Mar 89	1.75	0.39	1.17	1.95
❏ 5, Apr 89	1.75	0.39	1.17	1.95
❏ 6, May 89	1.75	0.39	1.17	1.95
❏ 7, Jun 89	1.75	0.39	1.17	1.95
❏ 8, Jul 89, Doctor Who	1.75	0.39	1.17	1.95
❏ 9, Aug 89, Fantastic 4	1.75	0.39	1.17	1.95
❏ 10, Sep 89, Iron Man of 2020	1.75	0.39	1.17	1.95

DEATH'S HEAD II

	ORIG.	GOOD	FINE	N-MINT
❏ 1, 1st printing	1.75	0.50	1.50	2.50
❏ 1, 2nd printing	1.75	0.35	1.05	1.75
❏ 2, 1st printing	1.75	0.39	1.17	1.95
❏ 2, 2nd printing	1.75	0.35	1.05	1.75
❏ 3	1.75	0.39	1.17	1.95
❏ 4	1.75	0.39	1.17	1.95
❏ 5	1.75	0.39	1.17	1.95
❏ 6	1.75	0.39	1.17	1.95
❏ 9	1.95	0.39	1.17	1.95
❏ 10	1.95	0.39	1.17	1.95
❏ 11	1.95	0.39	1.17	1.95
❏ 12	1.95	0.39	1.17	1.95
❏ 13	1.95	0.39	1.17	1.95
❏ 14, foil cover	2.95	0.59	1.77	2.95
❏ 15	1.95	0.39	1.17	1.95
❏ 16	1.95	0.39	1.17	1.95

	ORIG.	GOOD	FINE	N-MINT

DEATH'S HEAD II & THE ORIGIN OF DIE CUT
	ORIG.	GOOD	FINE	N-MINT
☐ 1, foil cover	2.95	0.59	1.77	2.95
☐ 2	1.75	0.35	1.05	1.75

DEATH'S HEAD II (ongoing series)
	ORIG.	GOOD	FINE	N-MINT
☐ 1	1.75	0.35	1.05	1.75
☐ 2	1.75	0.35	1.05	1.75
☐ 3	1.75	0.35	1.05	1.75
☐ 4	1.75	0.35	1.05	1.75
☐ 5	1.75	0.35	1.05	1.75
☐ 6	1.95	0.39	1.17	1.95
☐ 7	1.95	0.39	1.17	1.95
☐ 8	1.95	0.39	1.17	1.95
☐ 9	1.95	0.39	1.17	1.95
☐ 10	1.95	0.39	1.17	1.95

DEATH'S HEAD II (volume 2)
	ORIG.	GOOD	FINE	N-MINT
☐ 1		1.00	3.00	5.00

DEATH'S HEAD II GOLD
	ORIG.	GOOD	FINE	N-MINT
☐ 1	3.95	0.79	2.37	3.95

DEATH'S HEAD II/KILLPOWER-BATTLETIDE
	ORIG.	GOOD	FINE	N-MINT
☐ 1		0.45	1.35	2.25
☐ 2		0.35	1.05	1.75
☐ 3		0.35	1.05	1.75
☐ 4		0.35	1.05	1.75

DEATH'S-HEAD
CRYSTAL
	ORIG.	GOOD	FINE	N-MINT
☐ 1		0.39	1.17	1.95

DEATH3
MARVEL
	ORIG.	GOOD	FINE	N-MINT
☐ 1, foil cover	2.95	0.59	1.77	2.95
☐ 2	1.75	0.35	1.05	1.75
☐ 3	1.75	0.35	1.05	1.75
☐ 4	1.75	0.35	1.05	1.75

DEATH: THE HIGH COST OF LIVING
DC/VERTIGO
	ORIG.	GOOD	FINE	N-MINT
☐ 1, platinum edition	10.00	30.00	50.00	
☐ 1	1.95	2.80	8.40	14.00
☐ 2	1.95	2.40	7.20	12.00
☐ 3, with error	1.95	1.40	4.20	7.00
☐ 3, regular edition	1.95	1.40	4.20	7.00

DEATHBLOW
IMAGE
	ORIG.	GOOD	FINE	N-MINT
☐ 1, Apr 93, JLee	2.50	0.80	2.40	4.00
☐ 2, Aug 93	1.75	0.60	1.80	3.00
☐ 3	1.75	0.50	1.50	2.50
☐ 4, Apr 94	1.75	0.50	1.50	2.50
☐ 5, May 94	1.95	0.50	1.50	2.50
☐ 6, variant cover		1.00	3.00	5.00
☐ 6, Jun 94	1.95	0.39	1.17	1.95
☐ 7, Jul 94	1.95	0.39	1.17	1.95
☐ 8, Aug 94	1.95	0.39	1.17	1.95
☐ 10, Nov 94	2.50	0.50	1.50	2.50
☐ 11, Dec 94	2.50	0.50	1.50	2.50
☐ 12, Jan 95	2.50	0.50	1.50	2.50
☐ 14, Mar 95	2.50	0.50	1.50	2.50
☐ 15, Apr 95	2.50	0.50	1.50	2.50
☐ 16, May 95, "WildStorm Rising" Part 6;bound-in trading cards	2.50	0.50	1.50	2.50
☐ 17, Jun 95	2.50	0.50	1.50	2.50
☐ 20, Oct 95	2.50	0.50	1.50	2.50
☐ 22, Dec 95	2.50	0.50	1.50	2.50
☐ 23, Jan 96	2.50	0.50	1.50	2.50
☐ 24, Feb 96, A:Grifter	2.50	0.50	1.50	2.50
☐ 25, Mar 96	2.50	0.50	1.50	2.50
☐ 26, Mar 96, "Fire from Heaven" Prelude 3	2.50	0.50	1.50	2.50
☐ 27, Apr 96, "Fire from Heaven" Part 8	2.50	0.50	1.50	2.50

DEATHBLOW & CYBERNARY
	ORIG.	GOOD	FINE	N-MINT
☐ 4, Apr 94	1.75	0.35	1.05	1.75

DEATHLOK (mini-series)
MARVEL
	ORIG.	GOOD	FINE	N-MINT
☐ 1, Jul 90, O:Deathlok	3.95	2.00	6.00	10.00
☐ 2, Aug 90	3.95	1.60	4.80	8.00
☐ 3, Sep 90	3.95	1.60	4.80	8.00
☐ 4, Oct 90	3.95	1.60	4.80	8.00

DEATHLOK (starting July '91)
	ORIG.	GOOD	FINE	N-MINT
☐ 1, Jul 91	1.75	1.20	3.60	6.00
☐ 2, Aug 91	1.75	0.60	1.80	3.00
☐ 3, Sep 91, Dr. Doom	1.75	0.50	1.50	2.50
☐ 4, Oct 91	1.75	0.35	1.05	1.75
☐ 5, Nov 91	1.75	0.35	1.05	1.75
☐ 6, Dec 91, Punisher	1.75	0.35	1.05	1.75
☐ 7, Punisher	1.75	0.35	1.05	1.75
☐ 8	1.75	0.35	1.05	1.75
☐ 9, Ghost Rider	1.75	0.35	1.05	1.75
☐ 10	1.75	0.35	1.05	1.75
☐ 11	1.75	0.35	1.05	1.75
☐ 12	1.75	0.35	1.05	1.75
☐ 13	1.75	0.35	1.05	1.75
☐ 14	1.75	0.35	1.05	1.75
☐ 15	1.75	0.35	1.05	1.75
☐ 16	1.75	0.35	1.05	1.75
☐ 17	1.75	0.35	1.05	1.75
☐ 18	1.75	0.45	1.35	2.25
☐ 19, foil cover	2.25	0.45	1.35	2.25
☐ 20	1.75	0.35	1.05	1.75
☐ 21	1.75	0.35	1.05	1.75
☐ 22	1.75	0.35	1.05	1.75
☐ 23	1.75	0.35	1.05	1.75
☐ 24	1.75	0.35	1.05	1.75
☐ 25, foil cover	2.95	0.59	1.77	2.95
☐ 26	1.75	0.35	1.05	1.75
☐ 27	1.75	0.35	1.05	1.75
☐ 28	1.75	0.35	1.05	1.75
☐ 29	1.75	0.35	1.05	1.75
☐ 30	1.75	0.35	1.05	1.75
☐ 31	1.75	0.35	1.05	1.75
☐ 32	1.75	0.35	1.05	1.75
☐ 33	1.75	0.35	1.05	1.75
☐ 34, Apr 94	1.75	0.35	1.05	1.75

DEATHLOK ANNUAL
	ORIG.	GOOD	FINE	N-MINT
☐ 1	2.50	0.50	1.50	2.50
☐ 2, trading card	2.95	0.59	1.77	2.95

DEATHLOK SPECIAL
	ORIG.	GOOD	FINE	N-MINT
☐ 1, May 91, reprint	2.00	0.80	2.40	4.00
☐ 2, Jun 91, reprint	2.00	0.60	1.80	3.00
☐ 3, Jun 91, reprint	2.00	0.60	1.80	3.00
☐ 4, Jun 91, reprint	2.00	0.60	1.80	3.00

DEATHMARK
LIGHTNING
	ORIG.	GOOD	FINE	N-MINT
☐ 1, Dec 94, b&w	2.95	0.59	1.77	2.95

DEATHMATE
IMAGE/VALIANT
	ORIG.	GOOD	FINE	N-MINT
☐ 0, Yellow	4.95	1.00	3.00	5.00
☐ 0, Blue	4.95	1.00	3.00	5.00
☐ 0, Black	4.95	2.00	6.00	10.00
☐ 0, Red	4.95	1.40	4.20	7.00
☐ 0, Yellow (gold edition)		5.00	15.00	25.00
☐ 0, Red (gold edition)		5.00	15.00	25.00
☐ 0, Black (gold edition)		5.00	15.00	25.00
☐ 0, Blue (gold edition)		5.00	15.00	25.00

DEATHMATE EPILOGUE
	ORIG.	GOOD	FINE	N-MINT
☐ 0	2.95	0.60	1.80	3.00
☐ 0, Gold		4.00	12.00	20.00

DEATHMATE PROLOGUE
	ORIG.	GOOD	FINE	N-MINT
☐ 0, Gold	4.95	4.00	12.00	20.00
☐ 0, crossover	2.95	0.60	1.80	3.00

	ORIG.	GOOD	FINE	N-MINT

DEATHRACE 2020
COSMIC

	ORIG.	GOOD	FINE	N-MINT
❑ 1, Apr 95, sequel to Corman film	2.50	0.50	1.50	2.50

DEATHROW
HEROIC/BLUE COMET

	ORIG.	GOOD	FINE	N-MINT
❑ 1, Sep 93, b&w	3.50	0.70	2.10	3.50

DEATHSTROKE
DC

	ORIG.	GOOD	FINE	N-MINT
❑ 50, Aug 95, (was *Deathstroke, the Hunted*)	3.50	0.70	2.10	3.50
❑ 51, Sep 95	2.25	0.45	1.35	2.25
❑ 52, Oct 95, A:Hawkman	2.25	0.45	1.35	2.25
❑ 53, Nov 95	2.25	0.45	1.35	2.25
❑ 54, Dec 95	2.25	0.45	1.35	2.25
❑ 55, Jan 96	2.25	0.45	1.35	2.25
❑ 56, Feb 96	2.25	0.45	1.35	2.25
❑ 57, Mar 96	2.25	0.45	1.35	2.25
❑ 58, Apr 96, V:Joker	2.25	0.45	1.35	2.25
❑ 59, May 96	2.25	0.45	1.35	2.25
❑ 60, Jun 96	2.25	0.45	1.35	2.25

DEATHSTROKE ANNUAL

	ORIG.	GOOD	FINE	N-MINT
❑ 4, 95, "Year One"; (was *Deathstroke, the Terminator Annual*)	3.95	0.79	2.37	3.95

DEATHSTROKE, THE HUNTED
(was Deathstroke, the Terminator)

	ORIG.	GOOD	FINE	N-MINT
❑ 0, Oct 94	1.95	0.39	1.17	1.95
❑ 41, Nov 94	1.95	0.39	1.17	1.95
❑ 42, Dec 94	1.95	0.39	1.17	1.95
❑ 43, Jan 95	1.95	0.39	1.17	1.95
❑ 44, Feb 95	1.95	0.39	1.17	1.95
❑ 45, Mar 95	1.95	0.39	1.17	1.95
❑ 46, Apr 95	1.95	0.39	1.17	1.95
❑ 47, May 95	1.95	0.39	1.17	1.95
❑ 48, Jun 95	2.25	0.45	1.35	2.25
❑ 49, Jul 95, (becomes *Deathstroke*)	2.25	0.45	1.35	2.25

DEATHSTROKE, THE TERMINATOR

	ORIG.	GOOD	FINE	N-MINT
❑ 1, Aug 91, 1st printing	1.75	1.60	4.80	8.00
❑ 1, 2nd printing		0.60	1.80	3.00
❑ 2, Sep 91	1.75	1.00	3.00	5.00
❑ 3, Oct 91	1.75	0.60	1.80	3.00
❑ 4, Nov 91	1.75	0.60	1.80	3.00
❑ 5, Dec 91	1.75	0.60	1.80	3.00
❑ 6, Jan 92	1.75	0.60	1.80	3.00
❑ 7, Feb 92, Batman	1.75	0.50	1.50	2.50
❑ 8, Mar 92, Batman	1.75	0.50	1.50	2.50
❑ 9, Apr 92, Batman	1.75	0.50	1.50	2.50
❑ 10, Jun 92, Vigilante	1.75	0.50	1.50	2.50
❑ 11, Jun 92, Vigilante	1.75	0.50	1.50	2.50
❑ 12, Jul 92	1.75	0.35	1.05	1.75
❑ 13, Aug 92	1.75	0.35	1.05	1.75
❑ 14, Sep 92	1.75	0.35	1.05	1.75
❑ 15, Oct 92	1.75	0.35	1.05	1.75
❑ 16, Nov 92	1.75	0.35	1.05	1.75
❑ 17, Dec 92	1.75	0.35	1.05	1.75
❑ 18, Jan 93	1.75	0.35	1.05	1.75
❑ 19, Feb 93	1.75	0.35	1.05	1.75
❑ 20, Mar 93	1.75	0.35	1.05	1.75
❑ 21, Apr 93	1.75	0.35	1.05	1.75
❑ 22, May 93	1.75	0.35	1.05	1.75
❑ 23, May 93	1.75	0.35	1.05	1.75
❑ 24, Jun 93	1.75	0.35	1.05	1.75
❑ 25, Jun 93	1.75	0.35	1.05	1.75
❑ 26, Jul 93	1.75	0.35	1.05	1.75
❑ 27, Aug 93	1.75	0.35	1.05	1.75
❑ 28, Sep 93	1.75	0.35	1.05	1.75
❑ 29, Oct 93	1.75	0.35	1.05	1.75
❑ 30, Nov 93	1.75	0.35	1.05	1.75
❑ 31, Dec 93	1.75	0.35	1.05	1.75

	ORIG.	GOOD	FINE	N-MINT
❑ 32, Jan 94	1.75	0.35	1.05	1.75
❑ 33, Feb 94	1.75	0.35	1.05	1.75
❑ 34, Mar 94	1.75	0.35	1.05	1.75
❑ 35, Apr 94	1.75	0.35	1.05	1.75
❑ 36, May 94	1.75	0.35	1.05	1.75
❑ 37, Jun 94	1.75	0.35	1.05	1.75
❑ 38, Jul 94	1.95	0.39	1.17	1.95
❑ 39, Aug 94	1.95	0.39	1.17	1.95
❑ 40, Sep 94, (becomes *Deathstroke, the Hunted*)	1.95	0.39	1.17	1.95

DEATHSTROKE, THE TERMINATOR ANNUAL

	ORIG.	GOOD	FINE	N-MINT
❑ 1, 92, Eclipso	3.50	0.70	2.10	3.50
❑ 2, 93, Bloodlines	3.50	0.70	2.10	3.50
❑ 3, 94, (becomes *Deathstroke Annual*)	3.95	0.79	2.37	3.95

DEATHWATCH
HARRIER

	ORIG.	GOOD	FINE	N-MINT
❑ 1		0.39	1.17	1.95

DEATHWISH (mini-series)
MILESTONE/DC

	ORIG.	GOOD	FINE	N-MINT
❑ 1, Dec 94	2.50	0.50	1.50	2.50
❑ 2, Jan 95	2.50	0.50	1.50	2.50
❑ 3, Feb 95	2.50	0.50	1.50	2.50
❑ 4, Mar 95	2.50	0.50	1.50	2.50

DEATHWORLD
ADVENTURE

	ORIG.	GOOD	FINE	N-MINT
❑ 1, b&w		0.50	1.50	2.50
❑ 2, b&w		0.50	1.50	2.50
❑ 3, b&w		0.50	1.50	2.50
❑ 4, Feb 91, b&w	2.50	0.50	1.50	2.50

DEATHWORLD BOOK II

	ORIG.	GOOD	FINE	N-MINT
❑ 1, b&w		0.50	1.50	2.50
❑ 2, b&w		0.50	1.50	2.50
❑ 3, b&w		0.50	1.50	2.50
❑ 4, b&w		0.50	1.50	2.50

DEATHWORLD BOOK III

	ORIG.	GOOD	FINE	N-MINT
❑ 1, b&w		0.50	1.50	2.50
❑ 2, b&w		0.50	1.50	2.50
❑ 3, b&w		0.50	1.50	2.50
❑ 4, b&w		0.50	1.50	2.50

DEBBIE DOES COMICS
AIRCEL

	ORIG.	GOOD	FINE	N-MINT
❑ 1, adult, b&w		0.59	1.77	2.95

DEBBIE DOES DALLAS

	ORIG.	GOOD	FINE	N-MINT
❑ 1, 1st printing		0.60	1.80	3.00
❑ 1, 2nd printing		0.50	1.50	2.50
❑ 2, adult, b&w		0.50	1.50	2.50
❑ 3, adult, b&w		0.50	1.50	2.50
❑ 4, adult, b&w		0.50	1.50	2.50
❑ 5, adult, b&w		0.50	1.50	2.50
❑ 6, adult, b&w		0.50	1.50	2.50
❑ 7, adult, b&w		0.50	1.50	2.50
❑ 8, adult, b&w		0.50	1.50	2.50
❑ 9, adult, b&w		0.50	1.50	2.50
❑ 10, adult, b&w		0.50	1.50	2.50
❑ 12, adult, b&w	2.95	0.59	1.77	2.95
❑ 13, adult, b&w	2.95	0.59	1.77	2.95
❑ 14, adult, b&w	2.95	0.59	1.77	2.95
❑ 15, adult, b&w	2.95	0.59	1.77	2.95
❑ 16, adult, b&w	2.95	0.59	1.77	2.95
❑ 17, adult, b&w	2.95	0.59	1.77	2.95
❑ 18, adult, b&w	2.95	0.59	1.77	2.95

DEBBIE DOES DALLAS 3-D

	ORIG.	GOOD	FINE	N-MINT
❑ 1, adult		0.79	2.37	3.95

DECORATOR, THE
EROS

	ORIG.	GOOD	FINE	N-MINT
❑ 1, adult, b&w		0.50	1.50	2.50

	ORIG.	GOOD	FINE	N-MINT

DEEP DIMENSION HORROR
AC
☐ 1, Simulated 3-D; b&w reprints

	ORIG.	GOOD	FINE	N-MINT
	2.95	0.59	1.77	2.95

DEEP, THE
MARVEL
| ☐ 1, Nov 77, movie | 0.60 | 0.20 | 0.60 | 1.00 |

DEEPEST DIMENSION
REVOLUTIONARY
| ☐ 1, Jun 93 | 2.50 | 0.50 | 1.50 | 2.50 |
| ☐ 2, Aug 93 | 2.50 | 0.50 | 1.50 | 2.50 |

DEFCON 4
IMAGE
| ☐ 1, Feb 96, wraparound cover | 2.50 | 0.50 | 1.50 | 2.50 |
| ☐ 2, Mar 96 | 2.50 | 0.50 | 1.50 | 2.50 |

DEFENDERS
MARVEL
☐ 1, Aug 72, SB, Hulk	0.20	12.00	36.00	60.00
☐ 2, Oct 72, SB, Silver Surfer	0.20	6.40	19.20	32.00
☐ 3, Dec 72, SB/JM, Silver Surfer	0.20	3.60	10.80	18.00
☐ 4, Feb 73, SB/FMc	0.20	2.80	8.40	14.00
☐ 5, Apr 73, SB/FMc	0.20	2.80	8.40	14.00
☐ 6, Jun 73, SB/FMc	0.20	2.80	8.40	14.00
☐ 7, Aug 73, SB, A:Hawkeye	0.20	2.40	7.20	12.00
☐ 8, Sep 73, Avengers	0.20	2.40	7.20	12.00
☐ 9, Oct 73, Avengers	0.20	2.40	7.20	12.00
☐ 10, Nov 73, Avengers	0.20	2.40	7.20	12.00
☐ 11, Dec 73, Avengers	0.20	1.60	4.80	8.00
☐ 12, Feb 74	0.20	1.60	4.80	8.00
☐ 13, May 74	0.25	1.60	4.80	8.00
☐ 14, Jul 74	0.25	1.60	4.80	8.00
☐ 15, Sep 74	0.25	1.60	4.80	8.00
☐ 16, Oct 74	0.25	1.60	4.80	8.00
☐ 17, Nov 74	0.25	1.60	4.80	8.00
☐ 18, Dec 74	0.25	1.60	4.80	8.00
☐ 19, Jan 75	0.25	1.60	4.80	8.00
☐ 20, Feb 75, SB, Thing	0.25	1.60	4.80	8.00
☐ 21, Mar 75, SB	0.25	1.60	4.80	8.00
☐ 22, Apr 75, SB	0.25	1.60	4.80	8.00
☐ 23, May 75, SB	0.25	1.60	4.80	8.00
☐ 24, Jun 75, Daredevil	0.25	1.60	4.80	8.00
☐ 25, Jul 75, Daredevil	0.25	1.60	4.80	8.00
☐ 26, Aug 75	0.25	2.00	6.00	10.00
☐ 27, Sep 75	0.25	2.00	6.00	10.00
☐ 28, Oct 75	0.25	2.00	6.00	10.00
☐ 29, Nov 75	0.25	2.00	6.00	10.00
☐ 30, Dec 75	0.25	1.00	3.00	5.00
☐ 31, Jan 76	0.25	0.80	2.40	4.00
☐ 32, Feb 76, O:Nighthawk	0.25	0.80	2.40	4.00
☐ 33, Mar 76	0.25	0.80	2.40	4.00
☐ 34, Apr 76	0.25	0.80	2.40	4.00
☐ 35, May 76	0.25	0.80	2.40	4.00
☐ 36, Jun 76	0.25	0.80	2.40	4.00
☐ 37, Jul 76, SB/KJ	0.25	0.80	2.40	4.00
☐ 38, Aug 76, SB/KJ	0.25	0.80	2.40	4.00
☐ 39, Sep 76, SB/KJ	0.30	0.80	2.40	4.00
☐ 40, Oct 76, SB/KJ	0.30	0.80	2.40	4.00
☐ 41, Nov 76, SB/KJ	0.30	0.80	2.40	4.00
☐ 42, Dec 76, KG/KJ	0.30	0.80	2.40	4.00
☐ 43, Jan 77, KG/KJ	0.30	0.80	2.40	4.00
☐ 44, Feb 77, KG/KJ	0.30	0.80	2.40	4.00
☐ 45, Mar 77, KG/KJ	0.30	0.80	2.40	4.00
☐ 46, Apr 77, KG/KJ	0.30	0.80	2.40	4.00
☐ 47, May 77, KG/KJ, Moon Knight	0.30	1.00	3.00	5.00
☐ 48, Jun 77, KG	0.30	0.80	2.40	4.00
☐ 49, Jul 77, KG	0.30	0.80	2.40	4.00
☐ 50, Aug 77, KG	0.30	0.80	2.40	4.00

	ORIG.	GOOD	FINE	N-MINT
☐ 51, Sep 77, KG, Moon Knight	0.30	0.60	1.80	3.00
☐ 52, Oct 77, KG, Hulk V:Sub-Mariner	0.30	0.60	1.80	3.00
☐ 53, Nov 77, MG	0.35	0.60	1.80	3.00
☐ 54, Dec 77, MG	0.35	0.60	1.80	3.00
☐ 55, Jan 78	0.35	0.60	1.80	3.00
☐ 56, Feb 78	0.35	0.60	1.80	3.00
☐ 57, Mar 78	0.35	0.60	1.80	3.00
☐ 58, Apr 78	0.35	0.60	1.80	3.00
☐ 59, May 78	0.35	0.60	1.80	3.00
☐ 60, Jun 78	0.35	0.60	1.80	3.00
☐ 61, Jul 78	0.35	0.60	1.80	3.00
☐ 62, Aug 78	0.35	0.60	1.80	3.00
☐ 63, Sep 78	0.35	0.60	1.80	3.00
☐ 64, Oct 78	0.35	0.60	1.80	3.00
☐ 65, Nov 78	0.35	0.60	1.80	3.00
☐ 66, Dec 78	0.35	0.60	1.80	3.00
☐ 67, Jan 79	0.35	0.60	1.80	3.00
☐ 68, Feb 79	0.35	0.60	1.80	3.00
☐ 69, Mar 79	0.35	0.60	1.80	3.00
☐ 70, Apr 79	0.35	0.60	1.80	3.00
☐ 71, May 79	0.40	0.60	1.80	3.00
☐ 72, Jun 79	0.40	0.60	1.80	3.00
☐ 73, Jul 79, Foolkiller	0.40	1.00	3.00	5.00
☐ 74, Aug 79, Foolkiller	0.40	1.00	3.00	5.00
☐ 75, Sep 79, Foolkiller	0.40	1.00	3.00	5.00
☐ 76, Oct 79	0.40	0.60	1.80	3.00
☐ 77, Nov 79	0.40	0.60	1.80	3.00
☐ 78, Dec 79	0.40	0.60	1.80	3.00
☐ 79, Jan 80	0.40	0.60	1.80	3.00
☐ 80, Feb 80	0.40	0.60	1.80	3.00
☐ 81, Mar 80	0.40	0.60	1.80	3.00
☐ 82, Apr 80	0.40	0.60	1.80	3.00
☐ 83, May 80	0.40	0.60	1.80	3.00
☐ 84, Jun 80	0.40	0.60	1.80	3.00
☐ 85, Jul 80	0.40	0.60	1.80	3.00
☐ 86, Aug 80	0.40	0.60	1.80	3.00
☐ 87, Sep 80	0.50	0.60	1.80	3.00
☐ 88, Oct 80	0.50	0.60	1.80	3.00
☐ 89, Nov 80	0.50	0.60	1.80	3.00
☐ 90, Dec 80, DP/JSt, Daredevil	0.50	0.60	1.80	3.00
☐ 91, Jan 81, DP/JSt, Daredevil	0.50	0.60	1.80	3.00
☐ 92, Feb 81, DP/JSt	0.50	0.60	1.80	3.00
☐ 93, Mar 81, DP/JSt	0.50	0.60	1.80	3.00
☐ 94, Apr 81, DP/JSt	0.50	0.60	1.80	3.00
☐ 95, May 81, DP/JSt	0.50	0.60	1.80	3.00
☐ 96, Jun 81, DP/JSt	0.50	0.60	1.80	3.00
☐ 97, Jul 81, DP/JSt	0.50	0.60	1.80	3.00
☐ 98, Aug 81, DP/JSt	0.50	0.60	1.80	3.00
☐ 99, Sep 81, DP/JSt, conflict	0.50	0.60	1.80	3.00
☐ 100, Oct 81, DP/JSt, giant	0.75	1.00	3.00	5.00
☐ 101, Nov 81, DP/JSt, Silver Surfer	0.50	0.40	1.20	2.00
☐ 102, Dec 81, DP/JSt	0.50	0.40	1.20	2.00
☐ 103, Jan 82, DP/JSt	0.60	0.40	1.20	2.00
☐ 104, Feb 82, DP/JSt	0.60	0.40	1.20	2.00
☐ 105, Mar 82, DP/JSt	0.60	0.40	1.20	2.00
☐ 106, Apr 82, DP, Daredevil	0.60	0.40	1.20	2.00
☐ 107, May 82, DP/JSt, Enchantress	0.60	0.40	1.20	2.00
☐ 108, Jun 82	0.60	0.40	1.20	2.00
☐ 109, Jul 82	0.60	0.40	1.20	2.00
☐ 110, Aug 82	0.60	0.40	1.20	2.00
☐ 111, Sep 82	0.60	0.40	1.20	2.00
☐ 112, Oct 82	0.60	0.40	1.20	2.00
☐ 113, Nov 82	0.60	0.40	1.20	2.00

	ORIG.	GOOD	FINE	N-MINT
❏ 114, Dec 82	0.60	0.40	1.20	2.00
❏ 115, Jan 83	0.60	0.40	1.20	2.00
❏ 116, Feb 83	0.60	0.40	1.20	2.00
❏ 117, Mar 83	0.60	0.40	1.20	2.00
❏ 118, Apr 83	0.60	0.40	1.20	2.00
❏ 119, May 83	0.60	0.40	1.20	2.00
❏ 120, Jun 83	0.60	0.40	1.20	2.00
❏ 121, Jul 83	0.60	0.40	1.20	2.00
❏ 122, Aug 83	0.60	0.40	1.20	2.00
❏ 123, Sep 83	0.60	0.40	1.20	2.00
❏ 124, Oct 83	0.60	0.40	1.20	2.00
❏ 125, Nov 83	1.00	0.40	1.20	2.00
❏ 126, Dec 83	0.60	0.40	1.20	2.00
❏ 127, Jan 84	0.60	0.40	1.20	2.00
❏ 128, Feb 84	0.60	0.40	1.20	2.00
❏ 129, Mar 84, V:New Mutants	0.60	0.40	1.20	2.00
❏ 130, Apr 84	0.60	0.40	1.20	2.00
❏ 131, May 84	0.60	0.40	1.20	2.00
❏ 132, Jun 84	0.60	0.40	1.20	2.00
❏ 133, Jul 84	0.60	0.40	1.20	2.00
❏ 134, Aug 84	0.60	0.40	1.20	2.00
❏ 135, Sep 84	0.60	0.40	1.20	2.00
❏ 136, Oct 84	0.60	0.40	1.20	2.00
❏ 137, Nov 84	0.60	0.40	1.20	2.00
❏ 138, Dec 84	0.60	0.40	1.20	2.00
❏ 139, Jan 85, (becomes *The New Defenders*)	0.60	0.40	1.20	2.00

DEFENDERS ANNUAL

	ORIG.	GOOD	FINE	N-MINT
❏ 1, Nov 76, JSn, O:Hulk	0.50	0.60	1.80	3.00
❏ 2, GK/KJ, Son of Satan	0.50	0.40	1.20	2.00
❏ 3	0.50	0.80	2.40	4.00
❏ 4	0.50	0.80	2.40	4.00
❏ 5, DH, Guardians	0.50	0.40	1.20	2.00

DEFENDERS OF DYNATRON CITY

	ORIG.	GOOD	FINE	N-MINT
❏ 1	1.25	0.25	0.75	1.25
❏ 2	1.25	0.25	0.75	1.25
❏ 3	1.25	0.25	0.75	1.25
❏ 4	1.25	0.25	0.75	1.25
❏ 5	1.25	0.25	0.75	1.25
❏ 6	1.25	0.25	0.75	1.25

DEFENDERS OF EARTH

	ORIG.	GOOD	FINE	N-MINT
❏ 4, Jul 87, (was Star title)	1.00	0.20	0.60	1.00

STAR

	ORIG.	GOOD	FINE	N-MINT
❏ 1, Jan 87, Flash Gordon, Mandrake, Phantom	0.75	0.15	0.45	0.75
❏ 2, Mar 87, Flash Gordon, Mandrake, Phantom	0.75	0.15	0.45	0.75
❏ 3, May 87, Flash Gordon, Mandrake, Phantom; (becomes Marvel title)	0.75	0.15	0.45	0.75

DEFENSELESS DEAD, THE
ADVENTURE

		GOOD	FINE	N-MINT
❏ 1, b&w, Larry Niven story		0.50	1.50	2.50
❏ 2, b&w, Larry Niven story		0.50	1.50	2.50
❏ 3, b&w, Larry Niven story		0.50	1.50	2.50

DEFIANT GENESIS
DEFIANT

		GOOD	FINE	N-MINT
❏ 1, Oct 93, no cover price		1.00	3.00	5.00

DEJA VU
FANTACO

	ORIG.	GOOD	FINE	N-MINT
❏ 1, 82, BWr,MK	2.95	0.59	1.77	2.95

DELIRIUM
METRO

		GOOD	FINE	N-MINT
❏ 1		0.40	1.20	2.00

DELTA SQUADRON
ANDERPOL

		GOOD	FINE	N-MINT
❏ 1		0.40	1.20	2.00

DELTA TENN
ENTERTAINMENT

		GOOD	FINE	N-MINT
❏ 1		0.30	0.90	1.50
❏ 2		0.30	0.90	1.50
❏ 3		0.30	0.90	1.50
❏ 4		0.30	0.90	1.50
❏ 5		0.30	0.90	1.50
❏ 6		0.30	0.90	1.50
❏ 7		0.30	0.90	1.50
❏ 8, (moves to Big City)		0.30	0.90	1.50

DELTA TENN (was Entertainment Comic)
BIG CITY

		GOOD	FINE	N-MINT
❏ 9, b&w		0.30	0.90	1.50
❏ 10, b&w		0.30	0.90	1.50

DEMI ADVENTURE SPECIAL
RIP OFF PRESS

	ORIG.	GOOD	FINE	N-MINT
❏ 1, 95, adults;b&w; cardstock cover	5.95	1.19	3.57	5.95

DEMI THE DEMONESS (was Revolutionary title)
RIP OFF

	ORIG.	GOOD	FINE	N-MINT
❏ 1, Mar 93, adult;b&w	2.95	0.59	1.77	2.95
❏ 2, Nov 93, adult;b&w	2.95	0.59	1.77	2.95
❏ 3, Mar 95, adult;b&w	2.95	0.59	1.77	2.95

DEMOLITION MAN
DC

	ORIG.	GOOD	FINE	N-MINT
❏ 1, movie adaptation	1.75	0.35	1.05	1.75
❏ 2, movie adaptation	1.75	0.35	1.05	1.75
❏ 3	1.75	0.35	1.05	1.75
❏ 4	1.75	0.35	1.05	1.75

DEMON ANNUAL, THE

		GOOD	FINE	N-MINT
❏ 1, Eclipso		0.60	1.80	3.00
❏ 2	3.50	0.70	2.10	3.50

DEMON DREAMS
PACIFIC

		GOOD	FINE	N-MINT
❏ 1		0.30	0.90	1.50
❏ 2		0.30	0.90	1.50

DEMON DREAMS OF DR. DREW
AC

	ORIG.	GOOD	FINE	N-MINT
❏ 1, reprints	2.95	0.59	1.77	2.95

DEMON HUNTER
AIRCEL

		GOOD	FINE	N-MINT
❏ 1, b&w		0.39	1.17	1.95
❏ 2, b&w		0.39	1.17	1.95
❏ 3, b&w		0.39	1.17	1.95
❏ 4, b&w		0.39	1.17	1.95

ATLAS/ SEABOARD

	ORIG.	GOOD	FINE	N-MINT
❏ 1, Sep 75	0.25	0.20	0.60	1.00

DEMON WARRIOR
EASTERN

		GOOD	FINE	N-MINT
❏ 1, b&w		0.30	0.90	1.50
❏ 2, b&w		0.30	0.90	1.50
❏ 3, b&w		0.30	0.90	1.50
❏ 4, b&w		0.30	0.90	1.50

DEMON'S BLOOD
ODYSSEY

		GOOD	FINE	N-MINT
❏ 1		0.34	1.02	1.70

DEMON'S TAILS
ADVENTURE

	ORIG.	GOOD	FINE	N-MINT
❏ 1, b&w	2.50	0.50	1.50	2.50
❏ 2, b&w	2.50	0.50	1.50	2.50
❏ 3, b&w	2.50	0.50	1.50	2.50
❏ 4, b&w	2.50	0.50	1.50	2.50

DEMON, THE (1972-)
DC

	ORIG.	GOOD	FINE	N-MINT
❏ 1, Sep 72	0.20	1.20	3.60	6.00
❏ 2, Oct 72	0.20	0.60	1.80	3.00
❏ 3, Nov 72, Batman	0.20	0.60	1.80	3.00
❏ 4, Dec 72	0.20	0.50	1.50	2.50
❏ 5, Jan 73	0.20	0.50	1.50	2.50

	ORIG.	GOOD	FINE	N-MINT
❏ 6, Feb 73	0.20	0.50	1.50	2.50
❏ 7, Mar 73	0.20	0.50	1.50	2.50
❏ 8, Apr 73	0.20	0.50	1.50	2.50
❏ 9, Jun 73	0.20	0.50	1.50	2.50
❏ 10, Jul 73	0.20	0.50	1.50	2.50
❏ 11, Aug 73	0.20	0.60	1.80	3.00
❏ 12, Sep 73	0.20	0.50	1.50	2.50
❏ 13, Oct 73	0.20	0.40	1.20	2.00
❏ 14, Nov 73	0.20	0.40	1.20	2.00
❏ 15, Dec 73	0.20	0.40	1.20	2.00
❏ 16, Jan 74	0.20	0.30	0.90	1.50

DEMON, THE (1987 mini-series)

	ORIG.	GOOD	FINE	N-MINT
❏ 1, Jan 87, MW	0.75	0.80	2.40	4.00
❏ 2, Feb 87, MW	0.75	0.60	1.80	3.00
❏ 3, Mar 87, MW	0.75	0.60	1.80	3.00
❏ 4, Apr 87, MW	0.75	0.60	1.80	3.00

DEMON, THE (1990-)

	ORIG.	GOOD	FINE	N-MINT
❏ 0, Oct 94	1.95	0.39	1.17	1.95
❏ 1	1.50	0.30	0.90	1.50
❏ 2	1.50	0.30	0.90	1.50
❏ 3, Batman	1.50	0.30	0.90	1.50
❏ 4	1.50	0.30	0.90	1.50
❏ 5	1.50	0.30	0.90	1.50
❏ 6	1.50	0.30	0.90	1.50
❏ 7	1.50	0.30	0.90	1.50
❏ 8, Batman	1.50	0.30	0.90	1.50
❏ 9	1.50	0.30	0.90	1.50
❏ 10	1.50	0.30	0.90	1.50
❏ 11	1.50	0.30	0.90	1.50
❏ 12, Lobo	1.50	0.30	0.90	1.50
❏ 13, Lobo	1.50	0.30	0.90	1.50
❏ 14, Lobo	1.50	0.30	0.90	1.50
❏ 15, Lobo	1.50	0.30	0.90	1.50
❏ 16	1.50	0.30	0.90	1.50
❏ 17, War of Gods	1.50	0.30	0.90	1.50
❏ 18	1.50	0.30	0.90	1.50
❏ 19, poster	2.50	0.50	1.50	2.50
❏ 20	1.50	0.30	0.90	1.50
❏ 21	1.50	0.30	0.90	1.50
❏ 22	1.50	0.30	0.90	1.50
❏ 23, Robin	1.50	0.30	0.90	1.50
❏ 24, Robin	1.50	0.30	0.90	1.50
❏ 25	1.50	0.30	0.90	1.50
❏ 26	1.50	0.30	0.90	1.50
❏ 27	1.50	0.30	0.90	1.50
❏ 28, Superman	1.75	0.35	1.05	1.75
❏ 29	1.75	0.35	1.05	1.75
❏ 30	1.75	0.35	1.05	1.75
❏ 31	1.75	0.35	1.05	1.75
❏ 32	1.75	0.35	1.05	1.75
❏ 33	1.75	0.35	1.05	1.75
❏ 34, Lobo	1.75	0.35	1.05	1.75
❏ 35, Lobo	1.75	0.35	1.05	1.75
❏ 36	1.75	0.35	1.05	1.75
❏ 37	1.75	0.35	1.05	1.75
❏ 38	1.75	0.35	1.05	1.75
❏ 39	1.75	0.35	1.05	1.75
❏ 40	1.75	0.35	1.05	1.75
❏ 41	1.75	0.35	1.05	1.75
❏ 42	1.75	0.35	1.05	1.75
❏ 43	1.75	0.35	1.05	1.75
❏ 44	1.75	0.35	1.05	1.75
❏ 45	1.75	0.35	1.05	1.75
❏ 46	1.75	0.35	1.05	1.75
❏ 47, May 94	1.75	0.35	1.05	1.75
❏ 48, Jun 94	1.75	0.35	1.05	1.75
❏ 49, Jul 94	1.95	0.39	1.17	1.95
❏ 50, Aug 94	2.95	0.59	1.77	2.95
❏ 51, Sep 94	1.95	0.39	1.17	1.95
❏ 52, Nov 94	1.95	0.39	1.17	1.95
❏ 53, Dec 94	1.95	0.39	1.17	1.95

	ORIG.	GOOD	FINE	N-MINT
❏ 54, Jan 95	1.95	0.39	1.17	1.95
❏ 55, Feb 95	1.95	0.39	1.17	1.95
❏ 56, Mar 95	1.95	0.39	1.17	1.95
❏ 57, Apr 95	1.95	0.39	1.17	1.95
❏ 58, May 95, final issue	1.95	0.39	1.17	1.95

DEMONBLADE
NEW COMICS

	ORIG.	GOOD	FINE	N-MINT
❏ 1, b&w		0.39	1.17	1.95

DEMONIC TOYS
ETERNITY

	ORIG.	GOOD	FINE	N-MINT
❏ 1		0.50	1.50	2.50
❏ 2		0.50	1.50	2.50
❏ 3		0.50	1.50	2.50
❏ 4		0.50	1.50	2.50

DEMONIQUE (mini-series)
LONDON NIGHT

	ORIG.	GOOD	FINE	N-MINT
❏ 1, Oct 94, b&w	3.00	0.60	1.80	3.00

DEMONS & DARK ELVES
WEIRDWORX

	ORIG.	GOOD	FINE	N-MINT
❏ 1, b&w	2.95	0.59	1.77	2.95

DEN
FANTAGOR

	ORIG.	GOOD	FINE	N-MINT
❏ 1, Corben, color		0.40	1.20	2.00
❏ 2, Corben, color		0.40	1.20	2.00
❏ 3, Corben, color		0.40	1.20	2.00
❏ 4, Corben, color		0.40	1.20	2.00
❏ 5, Corben, color		0.40	1.20	2.00
❏ 6, Corben, color		0.40	1.20	2.00
❏ 7, Corben, color		0.40	1.20	2.00
❏ 8, Corben, color		0.40	1.20	2.00
❏ 9, Corben, color		0.40	1.20	2.00
❏ 10, Corben, color		0.40	1.20	2.00

DENIZENS OF DEEP CITY
KITCHEN SINK

	ORIG.	GOOD	FINE	N-MINT
❏ 1, b&w		0.40	1.20	2.00
❏ 2, b&w		0.40	1.20	2.00
❏ 3, b&w		0.40	1.20	2.00
❏ 4, b&w		0.40	1.20	2.00
❏ 5, b&w		0.40	1.20	2.00
❏ 6, b&w		0.40	1.20	2.00
❏ 7, b&w		0.40	1.20	2.00
❏ 8, b&w		0.40	1.20	2.00

DENNIS THE MENACE
MARVEL

	ORIG.	GOOD	FINE	N-MINT
❏ 1	0.50	0.40	1.20	2.00
❏ 2	0.50	0.30	0.90	1.50

DENNIS THE MENACE COMICS DIGEST

	ORIG.	GOOD	FINE	N-MINT
❏ 1	1.25	0.25	0.75	1.25
❏ 2	1.25	0.25	0.75	1.25
❏ 3	1.25	0.25	0.75	1.25

DESERT PEACH
3-D ZONE

	ORIG.	GOOD	FINE	N-MINT
❏ 1, b&w		2.40	7.20	12.00
❏ 2, b&w		1.60	4.80	8.00
❏ 3, b&w		1.20	3.60	6.00

DESERT PEACH (was from Mu Press)
AEON

	ORIG.	GOOD	FINE	N-MINT
❏ 19, b&w	4.95	0.99	2.97	4.95
❏ 20, Sep 93, b&w; aka *Desert Peach: Fever Dream*	4.95	0.99	2.97	4.95
❏ 21, Jun 94, b&w	4.95	0.99	2.97	4.95
❏ 22, Nov 94, b&w	4.95	0.99	2.97	4.95
❏ 23, Jun 95, b&w;a.k.a. *The Desert Peach: Visions*	2.95	0.59	1.77	2.95
❏ 24, Sep 95, b&w; a.k.a. *The Desert Peach: Ups and Downs*	2.95	0.59	1.77	2.95

	ORIG.	GOOD	FINE	N-MINT

DESERT PEACH (was Thoughts & Images)
MU PRESS

	ORIG.	GOOD	FINE	N-MINT
4, Mar 90, b&w	2.00	1.00	3.00	5.00
5, b&w		0.80	2.40	4.00
6, b&w		0.80	2.40	4.00
7		0.80	2.40	4.00
8		0.80	2.40	4.00
9		0.80	2.40	4.00
10		0.80	2.40	4.00
11		0.60	1.80	3.00
12		0.60	1.80	3.00
13		0.60	1.80	3.00
14		0.60	1.80	3.00
15		0.60	1.80	3.00
16		0.50	1.50	2.50
17, b&w		0.79	2.37	3.95
18, b&w (moves to Aeon)		0.50	1.50	2.50

DESERT STORM JOURNAL
APPLE

	GOOD	FINE	N-MINT
1, Hussein on cover	0.55	1.65	2.75
1, Schwartzkopf on cover.	0.55	1.65	2.75
2, b&w	0.55	1.65	2.75
3, b&w	0.55	1.65	2.75
4, b&w	0.55	1.65	2.75
5, b&w	0.55	1.65	2.75
6, b&w	0.55	1.65	2.75
7, b&w	0.55	1.65	2.75
8, b&w	0.55	1.65	2.75

DESTROY!!
ECLIPSE

	GOOD	FINE	N-MINT
1, Nov 86, b&w, oversize.	0.99	2.97	4.95
1	0.50	1.50	2.50
2	0.50	1.50	2.50
3	0.50	1.50	2.50

DESTROYER DUCK

	GOOD	FINE	N-MINT
1, Feb 82, JK,SA 1:Groo...	5.00	15.00	25.00
2, Jan 83, JK	0.30	0.90	1.50
3, Jun 83, JK	0.30	0.90	1.50
4, Oct 83, JK	0.30	0.90	1.50
5, Dec 83	0.30	0.90	1.50
6, Mar 84	0.30	0.90	1.50
7, May 84	0.30	0.90	1.50

DESTROYER, THE
VALIANT

	ORIG.	GOOD	FINE	N-MINT
1, Apr 95, cover says "#0"	2.95	0.59	1.77	2.95

DESTROYER, THE (Volume 1)
MARVEL

	ORIG.	GOOD	FINE	N-MINT
1, Nov 89, (b&w mag)	2.25	0.45	1.35	2.25
2, Dec 89, (b&w mag)	2.25	0.45	1.35	2.25
3, Dec 89, (b&w mag)	2.25	0.45	1.35	2.25
4, Jan 90, (b&w mag)	2.25	0.45	1.35	2.25
5, Feb 90, (b&w mag)	2.25	0.45	1.35	2.25
6, Mar 90, (b&w mag)	2.25	0.45	1.35	2.25

DESTROYER, THE (Volume 2)

	ORIG.	GOOD	FINE	N-MINT
1, Mar 91, color	1.95	0.39	1.17	1.95

DESTROYER, THE (Volume 3)

	ORIG.	GOOD	FINE	N-MINT
1, Dec 91, color	1.95	0.39	1.17	1.95
2, color	1.95	0.39	1.17	1.95
3, color	1.95	0.39	1.17	1.95
4, color	1.95	0.39	1.17	1.95

DESTRUCTOR
ATLAS/ SEABOARD

	ORIG.	GOOD	FINE	N-MINT
1, Feb 75, WW, SD O:Destructor	0.25	0.20	0.60	1.00
2, Apr 75, WW, SD	0.25	0.20	0.60	1.00
3, Jun 75	0.25	0.20	0.60	1.00
4, Aug 75	0.25	0.20	0.60	1.00

DESTRUCTOR, THE
ATLAS

	ORIG.	GOOD	FINE	N-MINT
1, Feb 75	0.25	0.20	0.60	1.00

DETECTIVE COMICS
DC

	ORIG.	GOOD	FINE	N-MINT
0, Oct 94	1.50	0.30	0.90	1.50
225, O&1:J'onn J'onzz	0.10	960.00	2880.00	4800.00
226	0.10	240.00	720.00	1200.00
227	0.10	84.00	252.00	420.00
228	0.10	84.00	252.00	420.00
229	0.10	84.00	252.00	420.00
230, Martian Manhunter	0.10	150.00	450.00	750.00
231, O:M. Manhunter	0.10	48.00	144.00	240.00
232	0.10	45.00	135.00	225.00
233, O:Batwoman	0.10	200.00	600.00	1000.00
234	0.10	40.00	120.00	200.00
235	0.10	80.00	240.00	400.00
236	0.10	44.00	132.00	220.00
237	0.10	30.00	90.00	150.00
238	0.10	30.00	90.00	150.00
239	0.10	30.00	90.00	150.00
240	0.10	30.00	90.00	150.00
241	0.10	28.00	84.00	140.00
242	0.10	28.00	84.00	140.00
243	0.10	28.00	84.00	140.00
244	0.10	28.00	84.00	140.00
245	0.10	28.00	84.00	140.00
246	0.10	28.00	84.00	140.00
247	0.10	28.00	84.00	140.00
248	0.10	28.00	84.00	140.00
249	0.10	28.00	84.00	140.00
250	0.10	28.00	84.00	140.00
251	0.10	25.00	75.00	125.00
252	0.10	25.00	75.00	125.00
253	0.10	25.00	75.00	125.00
254	0.10	25.00	75.00	125.00
255	0.10	25.00	75.00	125.00
256	0.10	25.00	75.00	125.00
257	0.10	25.00	75.00	125.00
258	0.10	25.00	75.00	125.00
259	0.10	25.00	75.00	125.00
260	0.10	25.00	75.00	125.00
261	0.10	24.00	72.00	120.00
262	0.10	24.00	72.00	120.00
263	0.10	24.00	72.00	120.00
264	0.10	24.00	72.00	120.00
265, O:Batman retold	0.10	48.00	144.00	240.00
266	0.10	20.00	60.00	100.00
267, O:Bat-Mite	0.10	30.00	90.00	150.00
268	0.10	18.00	54.00	90.00
269	0.10	18.00	54.00	90.00
270	0.10	18.00	54.00	90.00
271	0.10	18.00	54.00	90.00
272	0.10	18.00	54.00	90.00
273	0.10	18.00	54.00	90.00
274	0.10	18.00	54.00	90.00
275, Jan 60	0.10	18.00	54.00	90.00
276	0.10	18.00	54.00	90.00
277	0.10	18.00	54.00	90.00
278	0.10	18.00	54.00	90.00
279	0.10	18.00	54.00	90.00
280, Jun 60	0.10	18.00	54.00	90.00
281, Jul 60	0.10	12.00	36.00	60.00
282, Aug 60	0.10	12.00	36.00	60.00
283, Sep 60	0.10	12.00	36.00	60.00
284, Oct 60	0.10	12.00	36.00	60.00
285, Nov 60	0.10	12.00	36.00	60.00
286, Dec 60	0.10	12.00	36.00	60.00
287, Jan 61	0.10	12.00	36.00	60.00
288, Feb 61	0.10	12.00	36.00	60.00
289, Mar 61	0.10	12.00	36.00	60.00

	ORIG.	GOOD	FINE	N-MINT
290, Apr 61	0.10	12.00	36.00	60.00
291, May 61	0.10	12.00	36.00	60.00
292, Jun 61	0.10	12.00	36.00	60.00
293, Jul 61	0.10	12.00	36.00	60.00
294, Aug 61	0.10	12.00	36.00	60.00
295, Sep 61	0.10	12.00	36.00	60.00
296, Oct 61	0.10	12.00	36.00	60.00
297, Nov 61	0.10	12.00	36.00	60.00
298, Dec 61, I:Clayface	0.12	18.00	54.00	90.00
299, Jan 62	0.12	8.00	24.00	40.00
300, Feb 62	0.12	8.00	24.00	40.00
301, Mar 62	0.12	5.00	15.00	25.00
302, Apr 62	0.12	5.00	15.00	25.00
303, May 62	0.12	5.00	15.00	25.00
304, May 62	0.12	5.00	15.00	25.00
305, Jul 62	0.12	5.00	15.00	25.00
306, Aug 62	0.12	5.00	15.00	25.00
307, Sep 62	0.12	5.00	15.00	25.00
308, Oct 62	0.12	5.00	15.00	25.00
309, Oct 62	0.12	5.00	15.00	25.00
310, Dec 62	0.12	5.00	15.00	25.00
311, Jan 63	0.12	5.00	15.00	25.00
312, Feb 63	0.12	5.00	15.00	25.00
313, Mar 63	0.12	5.00	15.00	25.00
314, Apr 63	0.12	5.00	15.00	25.00
315, May 63	0.12	5.00	15.00	25.00
316, Jun 63	0.12	5.00	15.00	25.00
317, Jul 63	0.12	5.00	15.00	25.00
318, Aug 63	0.12	5.00	15.00	25.00
319, Sep 63	0.12	5.00	15.00	25.00
320, Oct 63	0.12	5.00	15.00	25.00
321, Nov 63	0.12	5.00	15.00	25.00
322, Dec 63	0.12	5.00	15.00	25.00
323, Jan 64	0.12	5.00	15.00	25.00
324, Feb 64	0.12	5.00	15.00	25.00
325, Mar 64	0.12	5.00	15.00	25.00
326, Apr 64	0.12	5.00	15.00	25.00
327, May 64, CI, 25th ann., symbol change	0.12	11.00	33.00	55.00
328, Jun 64, D:Alfred	0.12	8.00	24.00	40.00
329, Jul 64	0.12	4.00	12.00	20.00
330, Aug 64	0.12	4.00	12.00	20.00
331, Sep 64	0.12	4.00	12.00	20.00
332, Oct 64, Joker	0.12	6.00	18.00	30.00
333, Nov 64	0.12	4.00	12.00	20.00
334, Dec 64, Joker	0.12	6.00	18.00	30.00
334, Dec 64, Joker	0.12	6.00	18.00	30.00
335, Jan 65, Joker	0.12	6.00	18.00	30.00
336, Feb 65, Joker	0.12	6.00	18.00	30.00
337, Mar 65, Joker	0.12	6.00	18.00	30.00
338, Apr 65, Joker	0.12	6.00	18.00	30.00
339, May 65, Joker	0.12	6.00	18.00	30.00
340, Jun 65, Joker	0.12	6.00	18.00	30.00
341, Jul 65, Joker	0.12	5.00	15.00	25.00
342, Aug 65	0.12	3.20	9.60	16.00
343, Sep 65	0.12	2.80	8.40	14.00
344, Oct 65	0.12	2.80	8.40	14.00
345, Nov 65	0.12	2.80	8.40	14.00
346, Dec 65	0.12	2.80	8.40	14.00
347, Jan 66	0.12	2.80	8.40	14.00
348, Feb 66	0.12	2.80	8.40	14.00
349, Mar 66	0.12	2.80	8.40	14.00
350, Apr 66	0.12	2.80	8.40	14.00
351, May 66	0.12	2.80	8.40	14.00
352, Jun 66	0.12	2.80	8.40	14.00
353, Jul 66	0.12	2.80	8.40	14.00
354, Aug 66	0.12	2.80	8.40	14.00
355, Sep 66	0.12	2.80	8.40	14.00
356, Oct 66	0.12	2.80	8.40	14.00
357, Nov 66	0.12	2.80	8.40	14.00
358, Dec 66	0.12	2.80	8.40	14.00

	ORIG.	GOOD	FINE	N-MINT
359, Jan 67, I:new Batgir I	0.12	13.00	39.00	65.00
360, Feb 67	0.12	2.00	6.00	10.00
361, Mar 67	0.12	2.00	6.00	10.00
362, Apr 67	0.12	2.00	6.00	10.00
363, May 67	0.12	2.00	6.00	10.00
364, Jun 67	0.12	2.00	6.00	10.00
365, Jul 67, Joker	0.12	2.40	7.20	12.00
366, Aug 67	0.12	2.00	6.00	10.00
367, Sep 67	0.12	2.00	6.00	10.00
368, Oct 67	0.12	2.00	6.00	10.00
369, Nov 67, CA, Elongated Man	0.12	3.60	10.80	18.00
370, Dec 67, BK/GK, Elongated Man	0.12	2.00	6.00	10.00
371, Jan 68	0.12	7.60	22.80	38.00
372, Feb 68	0.12	2.00	6.00	10.00
373, Mar 68	0.12	2.00	6.00	10.00
374, Apr 68	0.12	2.00	6.00	10.00
375, May 68	0.12	2.00	6.00	10.00
376, Jun 68	0.12	2.00	6.00	10.00
377, Jul 68	0.12	2.00	6.00	10.00
378, Aug 68	0.12	2.00	6.00	10.00
379, Sep 68	0.12	2.00	6.00	10.00
380, Oct 68	0.12	2.00	6.00	10.00
381, Nov 68	0.12	2.00	6.00	10.00
382, Dec 68	0.12	2.00	6.00	10.00
383, Jan 69	0.12	2.00	6.00	10.00
384, Feb 69	0.12	2.00	6.00	10.00
385, Mar 69	0.12	2.00	6.00	10.00
386, Apr 69	0.12	2.00	6.00	10.00
387, May 69	0.12	2.00	6.00	10.00
388, Jun 69, Joker	0.15	3.00	9.00	15.00
389, Jul 69	0.15	4.40	13.20	22.00
390, Aug 69	0.15	2.00	6.00	10.00
391, Sep 69	0.15	3.20	9.60	16.00
392, Oct 69	0.15	2.00	6.00	10.00
393, Nov 69	0.15	2.00	6.00	10.00
394, Dec 69	0.15	2.00	6.00	10.00
395, Jan 70, NA/DG/GK/MA	0.15	3.00	9.00	15.00
396, Feb 70, GK, NA(c) Batgirl	0.15	2.80	8.40	14.00
397, Mar 70	0.15	3.00	9.00	15.00
398, Apr 70	0.15	1.20	3.60	6.00
399, May 70	0.15	1.20	3.60	6.00
400, Jun 70, NA/GC, I&O:Man-Bat	0.15	6.00	18.00	30.00
401, Jul 70	0.15	3.00	9.00	15.00
402, Aug 70	0.15	3.00	9.00	15.00
403, Sep 70, GK, NA(c) Robin	0.15	0.90	2.70	4.50
404, Oct 70, NA/DG/GK, Batgirl	0.15	5.00	15.00	25.00
405, Nov 70	0.15	2.40	7.20	12.00
406, Dec 70	0.15	0.90	2.70	4.50
407, Jan 71	0.15	3.00	9.00	15.00
408, Feb 71	0.15	3.00	9.00	15.00
409, Mar 71, IN/DG, NA(c),	0.15	0.90	2.70	4.50
410, Apr 71, NA/DG/DH, Batgirl	0.15	2.40	7.20	12.00
411, May 71	0.15	0.90	2.70	4.50
412, Jun 71	0.15	0.90	2.70	4.50
413, Jul 71	0.15	0.90	2.70	4.50
414, Aug 71	0.15	0.90	2.70	4.50
415, Sep 71	0.25	0.90	2.70	4.50
416, Oct 71	0.25	0.90	2.70	4.50
417, Nov 71	0.25	0.90	2.70	4.50
418, Dec 71	0.25	0.90	2.70	4.50
419, Jan 72	0.25	0.90	2.70	4.50
420, Feb 72	0.25	0.90	2.70	4.50

	ORIG.	GOOD	FINE	N-MINT
❏ 421, Mar 72 ....0.25		0.75	2.25	3.75
❏ 422, Apr 72 ....0.25		0.75	2.25	3.75
❏ 423, May 72..................0.25		0.75	2.25	3.75
❏ 424, Jun 72...................0.25		0.75	2.25	3.75
❏ 425, Jul 72 ....0.20		0.75	2.25	3.75
❏ 426, Aug 72 ....0.20		0.75	2.25	3.75
❏ 427, Sep 72..................0.20		0.75	2.25	3.75
❏ 428, Oct 72 ....0.20		0.75	2.25	3.75
❏ 429, Nov 72 ....0.20		0.75	2.25	3.75
❏ 430, Dec 72..................0.20		0.75	2.25	3.75
❏ 431, Jan 73 ....0.20		0.75	2.25	3.75
❏ 432, Feb 73 ....0.20		0.75	2.25	3.75
❏ 433, Mar 73 ....0.20		0.75	2.25	3.75
❏ 434, Apr 73 ....0.20		0.75	2.25	3.75
❏ 435, Jul 73....................0.20		0.75	2.25	3.75
❏ 436, Sep 73..................0.20		0.75	2.25	3.75
❏ 437, Nov 73, JA, WS, I:Manhunter				
......................0.20		2.00	6.00	10.00
❏ 438, Jan 74, WS, Manhunter				
......................0.50		1.20	3.60	6.00
❏ 439, Mar 74, WS, Manhunter				
......................0.50		1.20	3.60	6.00
❏ 440, May 74, WS, Manhunter				
......................0.60		1.20	3.60	6.00
❏ 441, Jul 74, WS, Manhunter				
......................0.60		1.20	3.60	6.00
❏ 442, Sep 74, WS, Manhunter				
......................0.60		1.20	3.60	6.00
❏ 443, Nov 74, WS, D:Manhunter				
......................0.60		1.50	4.50	7.50
❏ 444, Jan 75 ....0.60		0.95	2.85	4.75
❏ 445, Mar 75 ....0.60		0.95	2.85	4.75
❏ 446, Apr 75 ....0.25		0.95	2.85	4.75
❏ 447, May 75 ....0.25		0.95	2.85	4.75
❏ 448, Jun 75...................0.25		0.95	2.85	4.75
❏ 449, Jul 75 ....0.25		0.95	2.85	4.75
❏ 450, Aug 75 ....0.25		0.95	2.85	4.75
❏ 451, Sep 75..................0.25		0.95	2.85	4.75
❏ 452, Oct 75 ....0.25		0.95	2.85	4.75
❏ 453, Nov 75 ....0.25		0.95	2.85	4.75
❏ 454, Dec 75..................0.25		0.60	1.80	3.00
❏ 455, Jan 76 ....0.25		0.60	1.80	3.00
❏ 456, Feb 76 ....0.25		0.60	1.80	3.00
❏ 457, Mar 76 ....0.30		0.60	1.80	3.00
❏ 458, Apr 76 ....0.30		0.60	1.80	3.00
❏ 459, May 76 ....0.30		0.60	1.80	3.00
❏ 460, Jun 76...................0.30		0.60	1.80	3.00
❏ 461, Jul 76 ....0.30		0.60	1.80	3.00
❏ 462, Aug 76 ....0.30		0.60	1.80	3.00
❏ 463, Sep 76..................0.30		0.60	1.80	3.00
❏ 464, Oct 76 ....0.30		0.60	1.80	3.00
❏ 465, Nov 76, TA, Elongated Man				
......................0.30		0.60	1.80	3.00
❏ 466, Dec 76, MR/TA.......0.30		1.60	4.80	8.00
❏ 467, Jan 77, MR/TA 0.30		1.60	4.80	8.00
❏ 468, Mar 77, MR/TA 0.30		1.60	4.80	8.00
❏ 469, May 77, WS/AM, MR 1:Dr. Phosphorus				
......................0.30		1.60	4.80	8.00
❏ 470, Jun 77, WS/AM, MR0.35		1.60	4.80	8.00
❏ 471, Aug 77, MR............0.35		2.00	6.00	10.00
❏ 472, Sep 77, MR 0.35		2.00	6.00	10.00
❏ 473, Oct 77, MR..............0.35		2.00	6.00	10.00
❏ 474, Dec 77, MR 0.35		2.00	6.00	10.00
❏ 475, Feb 78, MR, Joker..0.35		3.00	9.00	15.00
❏ 476, Mar 78, MR, Joker.0.35		3.00	9.00	15.00
❏ 477, May 78, MR 0.35		1.60	4.80	8.00
❏ 478, Jul 78, MR 0.35		1.60	4.80	8.00
❏ 479, Sep 78, MR 0.50		1.60	4.80	8.00
❏ 480, Nov 78, DN/MA 0.50		0.30	0.90	1.50
❏ 481, Dec 78, JSn/CR/DN/DA/MR				
......................1.00		1.00	3.00	5.00

	ORIG.	GOOD	FINE	N-MINT
❏ 482, Feb 79, JSn/CR/HC/DG				
......................1.00		0.60	1.80	3.00
❏ 483, Apr 79, DN/DA/MG/DG				
......................1.00		0.50	1.50	2.50
❏ 484, Jun 79 ....1.00		0.55	1.65	2.75
❏ 485, Aug 79 ....1.00		0.55	1.65	2.75
❏ 486, Oct 79...................1.00		0.55	1.65	2.75
❏ 487, Dec 79 ....1.00		0.55	1.65	2.75
❏ 488, Feb 80...................1.00		0.55	1.65	2.75
❏ 489, Apr 80...................1.00		0.55	1.65	2.75
❏ 490, May 80..................1.00		0.55	1.65	2.75
❏ 491, Jun 80 ....1.00		0.55	1.65	2.75
❏ 492, Jul 80.....................1.00		0.55	1.65	2.75
❏ 493, Aug 80 ....1.00		0.55	1.65	2.75
❏ 494, Sep 80 ....1.00		0.55	1.65	2.75
❏ 495, Oct 80 ....1.00		0.55	1.65	2.75
❏ 496, Nov 80...................0.50		0.55	1.65	2.75
❏ 497, Dec 80 ....0.50		0.55	1.65	2.75
❏ 498, Jan 81....................0.50		0.55	1.65	2.75
❏ 499, Feb 81...................0.50		0.55	1.65	2.75
❏ 500, Mar 81, DG/CI/WS/TY/JKu, A:Deadman, Slam Bradley, Hawkman, Robin				
......................1.50		1.00	3.00	5.00
❏ 501, Apr 81....................0.50		0.60	1.80	3.00
❏ 502, May 81...................0.50		0.60	1.80	3.00
❏ 503, Jun 81, JSn 0.50		0.60	1.80	3.00
❏ 504, Jul 81, JSn, Joker...0.50		1.00	3.00	5.00
❏ 505, Aug 81 ....0.50		0.60	1.80	3.00
❏ 506, Sep 81 ....0.50		0.60	1.80	3.00
❏ 507, Oct 81....................0.60		0.60	1.80	3.00
❏ 508, Nov 81...................0.60		0.60	1.80	3.00
❏ 509, Dec 81 ....0.60		0.60	1.80	3.00
❏ 510, Jan 82....................0.60		0.60	1.80	3.00
❏ 511, Feb 82...................0.60		0.60	1.80	3.00
❏ 512, Mar 82...................0.60		0.60	1.80	3.00
❏ 513, Apr 82....................0.60		0.60	1.80	3.00
❏ 514, May 82...................0.60		0.60	1.80	3.00
❏ 515, Jun 82 ....0.60		0.60	1.80	3.00
❏ 516, Jul 82.....................0.60		0.60	1.80	3.00
❏ 517, Aug 82 ....0.60		0.60	1.80	3.00
❏ 518, Sep 82 ....0.60		0.60	1.80	3.00
❏ 519, Oct 82....................0.60		0.60	1.80	3.00
❏ 520, Nov 82...................0.60		0.60	1.80	3.00
❏ 521, Dec 82 ....0.60		0.60	1.80	3.00
❏ 522, Jan 83....................0.60		0.60	1.80	3.00
❏ 523, Feb 83...................0.60		0.60	1.80	3.00
❏ 524, Mar 83...................0.60		1.00	3.00	5.00
❏ 525, Apr 83....................0.60		0.60	1.80	3.00
❏ 526, May 83, DN/AA, 500th A:Batman				
......................1.50		2.40	7.20	12.00
❏ 527, Jun 83 ....0.60		0.30	0.90	1.50
❏ 528, Jul 83.....................0.60		0.30	0.90	1.50
❏ 529, Aug 83 ....0.60		0.30	0.90	1.50
❏ 530, Sep 83 ....0.60		0.30	0.90	1.50
❏ 531, Oct 83....................0.60		0.30	0.90	1.50
❏ 532, Nov 83, Joker 0.60		0.60	1.80	3.00
❏ 533, Dec 83 ....0.75		0.30	0.90	1.50
❏ 534, Jan 84....................0.75		0.30	0.90	1.50
❏ 535, Feb 84...................0.75		0.30	0.90	1.50
❏ 536, Mar 84...................0.75		0.30	0.90	1.50
❏ 537, Apr 84....................0.75		0.30	0.90	1.50
❏ 538, May 84...................0.75		0.30	0.90	1.50
❏ 539, Jun 84 ....0.75		0.30	0.90	1.50
❏ 540, Jul 84.....................0.75		0.30	0.90	1.50
❏ 541, Aug 84 ....0.75		0.30	0.90	1.50
❏ 542, Sep 84 ....0.75		0.30	0.90	1.50
❏ 543, Oct 84....................0.75		0.30	0.90	1.50
❏ 544, Nov 84...................0.75		0.30	0.90	1.50
❏ 545, Dec 84 ....0.75		0.30	0.90	1.50
❏ 546, Jan 85....................0.75		0.30	0.90	1.50
❏ 547, Feb 85...................0.75		0.30	0.90	1.50
❏ 548, Mar 85...................0.75		0.30	0.90	1.50

	ORIG.	GOOD	FINE	N-MINT
549, Apr 85 ....0.75	0.30	0.90	1.50
549, Apr 85 ....0.75	0.30	0.90	1.50
550, May 85 ....0.75	0.30	0.90	1.50
551, Jun 85 ....0.75	0.30	0.90	1.50
552, Jul 85 ....0.75	0.30	0.90	1.50
553, Aug 85 ....0.75	0.30	0.90	1.50
554, Sep 85 ....0.75	0.30	0.90	1.50
555, Oct 85 ....0.75	0.30	0.90	1.50
556, Nov 85 ....0.75	0.30	0.90	1.50
557, Dec 85...................0.75	0.30	0.90	1.50
558, Jan 86 ....0.75	0.30	0.90	1.50
559, Feb 86 ....0.75	0.30	0.90	1.50
560, Mar 86 ....0.75	0.30	0.90	1.50
561, Apr 86 ....0.75	0.30	0.90	1.50
562, May 86 ....0.75	0.30	0.90	1.50
563, Jun 86 ....0.75	0.30	0.90	1.50
564, Jul 86 ....0.75	0.30	0.90	1.50
565, Aug 86 ....0.75	0.30	0.90	1.50
566, Sep 86 ....0.75	0.30	0.90	1.50
567, Oct 86, JSn 0.75	0.30	0.90	1.50
568, Nov 86 ....0.75	0.30	0.90	1.50
569, Dec 86, Joker 0.75	0.60	1.80	3.00
570, Jan 87 ....0.75	0.30	0.90	1.50
571, Feb 87 ....0.75	0.30	0.90	1.50
572, Mar 87, 50th anniv. 1.25	0.50	1.50	2.50
573, Apr 87 ....0.75	0.30	0.90	1.50
574, May 87 ....0.75	0.30	0.90	1.50
575, Jun 87, Year Two ... 0.75	3.00	9.00	15.00
576, Jul 87, TMc, Year Two			
....................0.75	2.80	8.40	14.00
577, Aug 87, TMc, Year Two			
....................0.75	2.80	8.40	14.00
578, Sep 87, TMc, Year Two			
....................0.75	2.80	8.40	14.00
579, Oct 87, V:Two-Face 0.75	0.30	0.90	1.50
580, Nov 87, V:Two-Face0.75	0.30	0.90	1.50
581, Dec 87, V:Two-Face0.75	0.30	0.90	1.50
582, Jan 88, Millennium 0.75	0.30	0.90	1.50
583, Feb 88 ....0.75	0.30	0.90	1.50
584, Mar 88 ....0.75	0.30	0.90	1.50
585, Apr 88...................0.75	0.30	0.90	1.50
586, May 88..................0.75	0.30	0.90	1.50
587, Jun 88...................0.75	0.30	0.90	1.50
588, Jul 88.....................0.75	0.30	0.90	1.50
589, Aug 88, Bonus Book #5			
....................0.75	0.30	0.90	1.50
590, Sep 88...................0.75	0.30	0.90	1.50
591, Oct 88 ....0.75	0.30	0.90	1.50
592, Nov 88 ....0.75	0.30	0.90	1.50
593, Dec 88...................0.75	0.30	0.90	1.50
594, Dec 88...................0.75	0.30	0.90	1.50
595, Jan 89, Bonus Book, Invasion!			
....................0.75	0.30	0.90	1.50
596, Jan 89....................0.75	0.30	0.90	1.50
597, Feb 89....................0.75	0.30	0.90	1.50
598, Mar 89, giant.......... 2.95	2.00	6.00	10.00
599, Apr 89....................0.75	1.40	4.20	7.00
600, May 89...................2.95	2.00	6.00	10.00
601, Jun 89....................0.75	0.40	1.20	2.00
602, Jul 89.....................0.75	0.40	1.20	2.00
603, Aug 89 ....0.75	0.40	1.20	2.00
604, Sep 89, Mud Pack.. 1.00	0.50	1.50	2.50
605, Sep 89, Mud Pack.. 1.00	0.50	1.50	2.50
606, Oct 89, Mud Pack... 1.00	0.50	1.50	2.50
607, Oct 89, Mud Pack... 1.00	0.50	1.50	2.50
608, Nov 89 ....1.00	0.40	1.20	2.00
609, Dec 89...................1.00	0.40	1.20	2.00
610, Jan 90, Penguin 1.00	0.40	1.20	2.00
611, Feb 90, Penguin ... 1.00	0.40	1.20	2.00
612, Mar 90, Catman, Catwoman			
....................1.00	0.40	1.20	2.00
613, Apr 90....................1.00	0.40	1.20	2.00

	ORIG.	GOOD	FINE	N-MINT
614, May 90...................1.00	0.40	1.20	2.00
615, Jun 90, Penguin......1.00	0.40	1.20	2.00
616, Jun 90 ....1.00	0.40	1.20	2.00
617, Jul 90, Joker...........1.00	0.60	1.80	3.00
618, Jul 90.....................1.00	0.20	0.60	1.00
619, Aug 90 ....1.00	0.20	0.60	1.00
620, Aug 90 ....1.00	0.20	0.60	1.00
621, Sep 90 ....1.00	0.20	0.60	1.00
622, Oct 90, Sprang (c) ..1.00	0.20	0.60	1.00
623, Nov 90, Sprang (c) .1.00	0.20	0.60	1.00
624, Dec 90, Sprang (c) .1.00	0.20	0.60	1.00
625, Jan 91 ....1.00	0.20	0.60	1.00
626, Feb 91...................1.00	0.20	0.60	1.00
627, Mar 91, Batman's 600th appearance in *Detective*;			
giant;retells 1:Batman.....2.95	0.59	1.77	2.95
628, Apr 91....................1.00	0.20	0.60	1.00
629, May 91...................1.00	0.20	0.60	1.00
630, Jun 91 ....1.00	0.20	0.60	1.00
631, Jul 91.....................1.00	0.20	0.60	1.00
632, Jul 91.....................1.00	0.20	0.60	1.00
633, Aug 91 ....1.00	0.20	0.60	1.00
634, Aug 91 ....1.00	0.20	0.60	1.00
635, Sep 91 ....1.00	0.20	0.60	1.00
636, Sep 91 ....1.00	0.20	0.60	1.00
637, Oct 91 ....1.00	0.20	0.60	1.00
638, Nov 91 ....1.00	0.20	0.60	1.00
639, Dec 91...................1.00	0.20	0.60	1.00
640, Jan 92....................1.00	0.20	0.60	1.00
641, Feb 92...................1.00	0.20	0.60	1.00
642, Mar 92....................1.00	0.20	0.60	1.00
643, Apr 92....................1.00	0.20	0.60	1.00
644, May 92...................1.00	0.20	0.60	1.00
645, Jun 92 ....1.25	0.25	0.75	1.25
646, Jul 92.....................1.25	0.25	0.75	1.25
647, Aug 92 ....1.25	0.25	0.75	1.25
648, Aug 92 ....1.25	0.25	0.75	1.25
649, Sep 92 ....1.25	0.25	0.75	1.25
650, Sep 92 ....1.25	0.25	0.75	1.25
651, Oct 92 ....1.25	0.25	0.75	1.25
652, Oct 92 ....1.25	0.25	0.75	1.25
653, Nov 92 ....1.25	0.25	0.75	1.25
654, Dec 92...................1.25	0.25	0.75	1.25
655, Jan 93....................1.25	0.25	0.75	1.25
656, Feb 93...................1.25	0.25	0.75	1.25
657, Mar 93....................1.25	2.40	7.20	12.00
658, Apr 93....................1.25	2.00	6.00	10.00
659, May 93, "Knightfall" Part 2;first printing			
....................1.25	2.40	7.20	12.00
659, May 93, "Knightfall" Part 2;second printing			
....................1.25	0.25	0.75	1.25
660, May 93, "Knightfall".1.25	1.80	5.40	9.00
661, Jun 93, "Knightfall"..1.25	1.00	3.00	5.00
662, Jun 93, "Knightfall"..1.25	1.00	3.00	5.00
663, Jul 93, "Knightfall" Part 10			
....................1.25	0.60	1.80	3.00
664, "Knightfall" 1.25	0.25	0.75	1.25
665, "Knightfall" 1.25	0.25	0.75	1.25
666, "Knightfall" 1.25	0.50	1.50	2.50
667 ....1.25	0.25	0.75	1.25
668, Knightquest 1.25	0.25	0.75	1.25
669, Knightquest 1.25	0.25	0.75	1.25
670, Knightquest 1.25	0.25	0.75	1.25
671, Knightquest 1.50	0.30	0.90	1.50
672, Knightquest 1.50	0.30	0.90	1.50
673, Knightquest 1.50	0.30	0.90	1.50
674, May 94, Knightquest			
....................1.50	0.30	0.90	1.50
675, Jun 94, Knightquest1.50	0.40	1.20	2.00
675, Jun 94, Knightquest,platinum			
....................2.95	5.00	15.00	25.00
675, Jun 94, no cover price; premium edition			
676, Jul 94.....................2.50	0.50	1.50	2.50
677, Aug 94 ....1.50	0.30	0.90	1.50

	ORIG.	GOOD	FINE	N-MINT
☐ 678, Sep 94.....................1.50		0.30	0.90	1.50
☐ 679, Nov 94 ....1.50		0.30	0.90	1.50
☐ 680, Dec 94.....................1.50		0.30	0.90	1.50
☐ 681, Jan 95 ....1.50		0.30	0.90	1.50
☐ 682, Feb 95 ....1.50		0.30	0.90	1.50
☐ 682, Feb 95, enhanced cover				
....2.50		0.50	1.50	2.50
☐ 684, Apr 95.....................1.50		0.30	0.90	1.50
☐ 685, May 95.....................1.50		0.30	0.90	1.50
☐ 686, Jun 95.....................1.95		0.39	1.17	1.95
☐ 687, Jul 95.....................1.95		0.39	1.17	1.95
☐ 688, Aug 95.....................1.95		0.39	1.17	1.95
☐ 689, Sep 95.....................1.95		0.39	1.17	1.95
☐ 690, Oct 95 ....1.95		0.39	1.17	1.95
☐ 691, Nov 95, "Underworld Unleashed"				
....1.95		0.39	1.17	1.95
☐ 692, Dec 95, "Underworld Unleashed"				
....1.95		0.39	1.17	1.95
☐ 693, Jan 96, 1:Allergent.1.95		0.39	1.17	1.95
☐ 694, Feb 96.....................1.95		0.39	1.17	1.95
☐ 695, Mar 96, "Contagion" Part 2				
....1.95		0.39	1.17	1.95
☐ 696, Apr 96, "Contagion" Part 8				
....1.95		0.39	1.17	1.95
☐ 697, Jun 96.....................1.95		0.39	1.17	1.95

DETECTIVE COMICS ANNUAL

	ORIG.	GOOD	FINE	N-MINT
☐ 1, Sep 88, V:Penguin 1.50		1.00	3.00	5.00
☐ 2, Sep 89.....................2.00		0.40	1.20	2.00
☐ 3, Nov 90 ....2.00		0.40	1.20	2.00
☐ 4, Oct 91, Armageddon 2001				
....2.00		0.40	1.20	2.00
☐ 5, 92, Eclipso 2.00		0.40	1.20	2.00
☐ 6, Bloodlines 2.50		0.50	1.50	2.50
☐ 7, 94, Elseworlds 2.95		0.59	1.77	2.95
☐ 8, 95, "Year One"; ro:Riddler				
....3.95		0.79	2.37	3.95

DETECTIVES, INC.
ECLIPSE

	ORIG.	GOOD	FINE	N-MINT
☐ 1, Apr 85, MR		0.35	1.05	1.75
☐ 2, Apr 85, MR		0.35	1.05	1.75

DETECTIVES, INC. (second series)

	ORIG.	GOOD	FINE	N-MINT
☐ 1, GC,sepia......................		0.35	1.05	1.75
☐ 2, GC,sepia......................		0.35	1.05	1.75
☐ 3, GC,sepia......................		0.35	1.05	1.75

DETECTIVES, THE
ALPHA PRODUCTIONS

	ORIG.	GOOD	FINE	N-MINT
☐ 1, Apr 93, b&w...............4.95		0.99	2.97	4.95

DETROIT! MURDER CITY COMIX
KENT MYERS

	ORIG.	GOOD	FINE	N-MINT
☐ 1, b&w 2.50		0.50	1.50	2.50
☐ 2, b&w 2.50		0.50	1.50	2.50
☐ 3, b&w 2.50		0.50	1.50	2.50

DEVIL CHEF
DARK HORSE

	ORIG.	GOOD	FINE	N-MINT
☐ 0, 94, b&w 2.50		0.50	1.50	2.50

DEVIL DINOSAUR
MARVEL

	ORIG.	GOOD	FINE	N-MINT
☐ 1, JK..............................0.35		2.00	6.00	10.00
☐ 2, JK..............................0.35		1.20	3.60	6.00
☐ 3, JK..............................0.35		1.00	3.00	5.00
☐ 4, JK..............................0.35		1.00	3.00	5.00
☐ 5, JK..............................0.35		1.00	3.00	5.00
☐ 6, JK..............................0.35		0.80	2.40	4.00
☐ 7, JK..............................0.35		0.80	2.40	4.00
☐ 8, JK..............................0.35		0.80	2.40	4.00
☐ 9, JK..............................0.35		0.80	2.40	4.00

DEVILINA
ATLAS/ SEABOARD

	ORIG.	GOOD	FINE	N-MINT
☐ 1, Jan 75, b&w mag.......0.75		0.50	1.50	2.50
☐ 2, Jun 75, b&w mag.......0.75		0.50	1.50	2.50

DEVLIN
MAXIMUM

	ORIG.	GOOD	FINE	N-MINT
☐ 1, Apr 96.......................2.50		0.50	1.50	2.50

DIARY OF A DOMINATRIX
EROS

	ORIG.	GOOD	FINE	N-MINT
☐ 1, adult, b&w 2.95		0.59	1.77	2.95

DIARY OF EMILY K., THE

	ORIG.	GOOD	FINE	N-MINT
☐ 1, adult, b&w		0.50	1.50	2.50

DIATOM
PHOTOGRAPHICS

	ORIG.	GOOD	FINE	N-MINT
☐ 1, Apr 95, b&w fumetti book;prestige format				
....4.95		0.99	2.97	4.95

DICK TRACY
DISNEY

	ORIG.	GOOD	FINE	N-MINT
☐ 1, prestige, Kyle Baker......		0.99	2.97	4.95
☐ 2, prestige, Kyle Baker......		0.99	2.97	4.95
☐ 2, newsstand, Baker..........		0.59	1.77	2.95
☐ 3, movie, Kyle Baker.........		1.19	3.57	5.95
☐ 3, newsstand, Baker		0.59	1.77	2.95

DICK TRACY ADVENTURES
GLADSTONE

	ORIG.	GOOD	FINE	N-MINT
☐ 1, Sep 91, JSt(c) B.B. Eyes		0.99	2.97	4.95

HAMILTON

	ORIG.	GOOD	FINE	N-MINT
☐ 1, b&w..............................		0.79	2.37	3.95

DICK TRACY IN 3-D
BLACKTHORNE

	ORIG.	GOOD	FINE	N-MINT
☐ 1, Jul 86...........................		0.40	1.20	2.00

DICK TRACY MONTHLY

	ORIG.	GOOD	FINE	N-MINT
☐ 1		0.40	1.20	2.00
☐ 2		0.40	1.20	2.00
☐ 3		0.40	1.20	2.00
☐ 4		0.40	1.20	2.00
☐ 5		0.40	1.20	2.00
☐ 6		0.40	1.20	2.00
☐ 7		0.40	1.20	2.00
☐ 8		0.40	1.20	2.00
☐ 9		0.40	1.20	2.00
☐ 10		0.40	1.20	2.00
☐ 11		0.40	1.20	2.00
☐ 12		0.40	1.20	2.00
☐ 13		0.40	1.20	2.00
☐ 14		0.40	1.20	2.00
☐ 15		0.40	1.20	2.00
☐ 16		0.40	1.20	2.00
☐ 17		0.40	1.20	2.00
☐ 18		0.40	1.20	2.00
☐ 19		0.40	1.20	2.00
☐ 20		0.40	1.20	2.00
☐ 21		0.40	1.20	2.00
☐ 22		0.40	1.20	2.00
☐ 23		0.40	1.20	2.00
☐ 24		0.40	1.20	2.00
☐ 25, (becomes *Dick Tracy Weekly*)				
....		0.40	1.20	2.00

DICK TRACY SPECIAL

	ORIG.	GOOD	FINE	N-MINT
☐ 1, Jan 88, O:Tracy............		0.59	1.77	2.95
☐ 2, Mar 88, O:Tracy...........		0.59	1.77	2.95
☐ 3, 88, O:Tracy		0.59	1.77	2.95

DICK TRACY WEEKLY (was Dick Tracy Monthly)

	ORIG.	GOOD	FINE	N-MINT
☐ 26, Jan 88.......................		0.40	1.20	2.00
☐ 27, Jan 88.......................		0.40	1.20	2.00
☐ 28, Jan 88.......................		0.40	1.20	2.00
☐ 29, Jan 88.......................		0.40	1.20	2.00
☐ 30, Feb 88.......................		0.40	1.20	2.00
☐ 31, Feb 88.......................		0.40	1.20	2.00
☐ 32, Feb 88.......................		0.40	1.20	2.00
☐ 33, Feb 88.......................		0.40	1.20	2.00
☐ 34, Mar 88.......................		0.40	1.20	2.00
☐ 35, Mar 88.......................		0.40	1.20	2.00

	ORIG.	GOOD	FINE	N-MINT
❏ 36, Mar 88		0.40	1.20	2.00
❏ 37, Mar 88		0.40	1.20	2.00
❏ 38, Jun 88		0.40	1.20	2.00
❏ 39, Jun 88		0.40	1.20	2.00
❏ 40, Jun 88		0.40	1.20	2.00
❏ 41, Jun 88		0.40	1.20	2.00
❏ 42, Jul 88		0.40	1.20	2.00
❏ 43, Jul 88		0.40	1.20	2.00
❏ 44, Jul 88		0.40	1.20	2.00
❏ 45, Jul 88		0.40	1.20	2.00
❏ 46, Aug 88		0.40	1.20	2.00
❏ 47, Aug 88		0.40	1.20	2.00
❏ 48, Aug 88		0.40	1.20	2.00
❏ 49, Aug 88		0.40	1.20	2.00
❏ 50, Sep 88		0.40	1.20	2.00
❏ 51, Sep 88		0.40	1.20	2.00
❏ 52, Sep 88		0.40	1.20	2.00
❏ 53, Sep 88		0.40	1.20	2.00
❏ 54, Oct 88		0.40	1.20	2.00
❏ 55, Oct 88		0.40	1.20	2.00
❏ 56, Oct 88		0.40	1.20	2.00
❏ 57, Oct 88		0.40	1.20	2.00
❏ 58, Oct 88		0.40	1.20	2.00
❏ 59, Oct 88		0.40	1.20	2.00
❏ 60, Nov 88		0.40	1.20	2.00
❏ 61, Nov 88		0.40	1.20	2.00
❏ 62, Nov 88		0.40	1.20	2.00
❏ 63, Nov 88		0.40	1.20	2.00
❏ 64, Nov 88		0.40	1.20	2.00
❏ 65, Nov 88		0.40	1.20	2.00
❏ 66, Dec 88		0.40	1.20	2.00
❏ 67, Dec 88		0.40	1.20	2.00
❏ 68, Dec 88		0.40	1.20	2.00
❏ 69, Dec 88		0.40	1.20	2.00
❏ 70, Jan 89		0.40	1.20	2.00
❏ 71, Jan 89		0.40	1.20	2.00
❏ 72, Jan 89		0.40	1.20	2.00
❏ 73, Jan 89		0.40	1.20	2.00
❏ 74, Feb 89		0.40	1.20	2.00
❏ 75, Feb 89		0.40	1.20	2.00
❏ 76, Feb 89		0.40	1.20	2.00
❏ 77, Feb 89		0.40	1.20	2.00
❏ 78, Mar 89		0.40	1.20	2.00
❏ 79, Mar 89		0.40	1.20	2.00
❏ 80, Mar 89		0.40	1.20	2.00
❏ 81, Mar 89		0.40	1.20	2.00
❏ 82, Apr 89		0.40	1.20	2.00
❏ 83, Apr 89		0.40	1.20	2.00
❏ 84, Apr 89		0.40	1.20	2.00
❏ 85, Apr 89		0.40	1.20	2.00
❏ 86, May 89		0.40	1.20	2.00
❏ 87, May 89		0.40	1.20	2.00
❏ 88, May 89		0.40	1.20	2.00
❏ 89, May 89		0.40	1.20	2.00
❏ 90, Jun 89		0.40	1.20	2.00
❏ 91, Jun 89		0.40	1.20	2.00
❏ 92, Jun 89		0.40	1.20	2.00
❏ 93, Jun 89		0.40	1.20	2.00
❏ 94, Aug 89		0.40	1.20	2.00
❏ 95, Aug 89		0.40	1.20	2.00
❏ 96, Aug 89		0.40	1.20	2.00
❏ 97, Aug 89, 1:Moon Maid		0.40	1.20	2.00
❏ 98, Sep 89		0.40	1.20	2.00
❏ 99, Sep 89		0.40	1.20	2.00

DICK TRACY: THE EARLY YEARS

	ORIG.	GOOD	FINE	N-MINT
❏ 1, Aug 87		1.39	4.17	6.95
❏ 2, Oct 87		1.39	4.17	6.95
❏ 3, Apr 88		1.39	4.17	6.95
❏ 4, 88		0.59	1.77	2.95

DICK TRACY: THE "UNPRINTED" STORIES

	ORIG.	GOOD	FINE	N-MINT
❏ 1, Sep 87		0.59	1.77	2.95
❏ 2, Nov 87		0.59	1.77	2.95
❏ 3, Jan 88		0.59	1.77	2.95
❏ 4, Jun 88, D:Flattop Jr.		0.99	2.97	4.95

DIE CUT
MARVEL

	ORIG.	GOOD	FINE	N-MINT
❏ 1, diecut cover	2.50	0.50	1.50	2.50
❏ 2	1.75	0.35	1.05	1.75
❏ 3	1.75	0.35	1.05	1.75
❏ 4	1.75	0.35	1.05	1.75

DIE CUT VS. G-FORCE

	ORIG.	GOOD	FINE	N-MINT
❏ 1, foil cover	2.75	0.55	1.65	2.75
❏ 2, foil cover	2.75	0.55	1.65	2.75

DIEBOLD
SILENT PARTNERS

	ORIG.	GOOD	FINE	N-MINT
❏ 1, 94, b&w	2.95	0.59	1.77	2.95
❏ 2, 95, b&w	2.95	0.59	1.77	2.95

DIFFERENT BEAT COMICS
FANTAGRAPHICS

	ORIG.	GOOD	FINE	N-MINT
❏ 1, b&w	3.50	0.70	2.10	3.50

DIGGERS, THE
C&T

	ORIG.	GOOD	FINE	N-MINT
❏ 1, b&w		0.30	0.90	1.50

DIGITEK
MARVEL

	ORIG.	GOOD	FINE	N-MINT
❏ 1	1.95	0.39	1.17	1.95
❏ 2	1.95	0.39	1.17	1.95
❏ 3	2.25	0.45	1.35	2.25
❏ 4	2.25	0.45	1.35	2.25

DIK SKYCAP
RIP OFF

	ORIG.	GOOD	FINE	N-MINT
❏ 1, Dec 91, b&w	2.50	0.50	1.50	2.50
❏ 2, May 92, b&w	2.50	0.50	1.50	2.50

DILEMMA PRESENTS
DILEMMA

	ORIG.	GOOD	FINE	N-MINT
❏ 1, Oct 94, b&w	2.50	0.50	1.50	2.50
❏ 2, 95, b&w flip book	2.50	0.50	1.50	2.50
❏ 3, Apr 95, b&w flip book.	2.50	0.50	1.50	2.50

DILTON'S STRANGE SCIENCE
ARCHIE

	ORIG.	GOOD	FINE	N-MINT
❏ 1, May 89	0.75	0.15	0.45	0.75
❏ 2	0.75	0.15	0.45	0.75
❏ 3	0.75	0.15	0.45	0.75
❏ 4	0.75	0.15	0.45	0.75
❏ 5, May 90	0.75	0.15	0.45	0.75

DIMENSION 5
EDGE

	ORIG.	GOOD	FINE	N-MINT
❏ 1, Oct 95, adults;b&w	3.95	0.79	2.37	3.95

DIMENSION X
KARL ART

	ORIG.	GOOD	FINE	N-MINT
❏ 1, b&w		0.70	2.10	3.50

DIMENSION Z
PYRAMID

	ORIG.	GOOD	FINE	N-MINT
❏ 1		0.34	1.02	1.70
❏ 2		0.34	1.02	1.70

DINGLEDORFS, THE
SKYLIGHT

	ORIG.	GOOD	FINE	N-MINT
❏ 1, b&w	2.75	0.55	1.65	2.75

DINKY ON THE ROAD
BLIND BAT PRESS

	ORIG.	GOOD	FINE	N-MINT
❏ 1, Jun 94, b&w	1.95	0.39	1.17	1.95

DINO ISLAND
MIRAGE

	ORIG.	GOOD	FINE	N-MINT
❏ 1	2.75	0.55	1.65	2.75
❏ 2	2.75	0.55	1.65	2.75

	ORIG.	GOOD	FINE	N-MINT

DINO-RIDERS
MARVEL
	ORIG.	GOOD	FINE	N-MINT
❏ 1 .... 1.00	0.20	0.60	1.00
❏ 2 .... 1.00	0.20	0.60	1.00
❏ 3 .... 1.00	0.20	0.60	1.00

DINOSAUR BOP
MONSTER
	GOOD	FINE	N-MINT
❏ 1, b&w	0.50	1.50	2.50
❏ 2, b&w	0.50	1.50	2.50

DINOSAUR ISLAND
	GOOD	FINE	N-MINT
❏ 1, b&w	0.45	1.35	2.25

DINOSAUR MANSION (mini-series)
EDGE
	ORIG.	GOOD	FINE	N-MINT
❏ 1, b&w;no indicia 2.95	0.59	1.77	2.95

DINOSAUR REX
UPSHOT
	GOOD	FINE	N-MINT
❏ 1, color	0.40	1.20	2.00
❏ 2, b&w	0.40	1.20	2.00
❏ 3, b&w	0.40	1.20	2.00

DINOSAURS
HOLLYWOOD
	GOOD	FINE	N-MINT
❏ 1, TV based	0.59	1.77	2.95
❏ 2, TV based	0.59	1.77	2.95

DINOSAURS ATTACK!
ECLIPSE
	GOOD	FINE	N-MINT
❏ 1, color, trading cards	0.79	2.37	3.95

DINOSAURS FOR HIRE
ETERNITY
	GOOD	FINE	N-MINT
❏ 1, (1st printing) b&w	0.60	1.80	3.00
❏ 1, (2nd printing)	0.39	1.17	1.95
❏ 2	0.39	1.17	1.95
❏ 3	0.39	1.17	1.95
❏ 4	0.39	1.17	1.95
❏ 5	0.39	1.17	1.95
❏ 6	0.39	1.17	1.95
❏ 7	0.39	1.17	1.95
❏ 8	0.39	1.17	1.95
❏ 9	0.39	1.17	1.95

MALIBU
	ORIG.	GOOD	FINE	N-MINT
❏ 1 .... 1.95	0.39	1.17	1.95
❏ 2 .... 1.95	0.39	1.17	1.95
❏ 3 .... 1.95	0.39	1.17	1.95
❏ 4 .... 1.95	0.39	1.17	1.95
❏ 5 .... 2.50	0.50	1.50	2.50
❏ 6 .... 2.50	0.50	1.50	2.50
❏ 7 .... 2.50	0.50	1.50	2.50
❏ 8 .... 2.50	0.50	1.50	2.50
❏ 9 .... 2.50	0.50	1.50	2.50
❏ 10 .... 2.50	0.50	1.50	2.50
❏ 11 .... 2.50	0.50	1.50	2.50
❏ 12, Feb 94 .... 2.50	0.50	1.50	2.50

DINOSAURS FOR HIRE 3-D
ETERNITY
	GOOD	FINE	N-MINT
❏ 1, 3-D	0.59	1.77	2.95

DINOSAURS FOR HIRE FALL CLASSIC
	GOOD	FINE	N-MINT
❏ 1, b&w, Elvis	0.45	1.35	2.25

DINOSAURS: A CELEBRATION
EPIC
	ORIG.	GOOD	FINE	N-MINT
❏ 1, Horns and heavy armor 4.95	0.99	2.97	4.95
❏ 2, Bone heads and Duck-bills 4.95	0.99	2.97	4.95
❏ 3, Egg stealers and Earth shakers 4.95	0.99	2.97	4.95
❏ 4, Terrible claws and tyrants 4.95	0.99	2.97	4.95

DIRE WOLVES: A CHRONICLE OF THE DEADWORLD
CALIBER
	ORIG.	GOOD	FINE	N-MINT
❏ 0, 94, b&w 3.95	0.79	2.37	3.95

DIRECTORY TO A NONEXISTENT UNIVERSE
ECLIPSE
	GOOD	FINE	N-MINT
❏ 1	0.40	1.20	2.00

DIRTY PAIR
	GOOD	FINE	N-MINT
❏ 1, b&w	0.80	2.40	4.00
❏ 2, b&w	0.60	1.80	3.00
❏ 3, b&w	0.70	2.10	3.50
❏ 4, b&w	0.70	2.10	3.50

VIZ
	ORIG.	GOOD	FINE	N-MINT
❏ 1, 94, To Kill a Computer 4.95	0.99	2.97	4.95
❏ 4, 94, Come Out, Come Out, Assassin 4.95	0.99	2.97	4.95
❏ 5, 94, Address for Danger 4.95	0.99	2.97	4.95

DIRTY PAIR II
ECLIPSE
	GOOD	FINE	N-MINT
❏ 1, b&w	0.40	1.20	2.00
❏ 2, b&w	0.40	1.20	2.00
❏ 3, misnumbered #1	0.40	1.20	2.00
❏ 4	0.40	1.20	2.00
❏ 5	0.40	1.20	2.00

DIRTY PAIR III
	GOOD	FINE	N-MINT
❏ 1, b&w	0.40	1.20	2.00
❏ 2, b&w	0.40	1.20	2.00
❏ 3	0.45	1.35	2.25
❏ 4	0.45	1.35	2.25
❏ 5	0.45	1.35	2.25

DIRTY PAIR, THE: FATAL BUT NOT SERIOUS (mini-series)
DARK HORSE/MANGA
	ORIG.	GOOD	FINE	N-MINT
❏ 1, Jul 95 .... 2.95	0.59	1.77	2.95
❏ 2, Aug 95 .... 2.95	0.59	1.77	2.95
❏ 3, Sep 95 .... 2.95	0.59	1.77	2.95
❏ 4, Oct 95 .... 2.95	0.59	1.77	2.95
❏ 5, Nov 95 .... 2.95	0.59	1.77	2.95

DIRTY PAIR: SIM HELL
DARK HORSE
	ORIG.	GOOD	FINE	N-MINT
❏ 1, 93, b&w 2.50	0.70	2.10	3.50
❏ 2, 93, b&w 2.50	0.70	2.10	3.50
❏ 3, 93, b&w 2.50	0.70	2.10	3.50
❏ 4, 93, b&w 2.50	0.70	2.10	3.50

DIRTY PICTURES
AIRCEL
	GOOD	FINE	N-MINT
❏ 1, b&w, adult	0.50	1.50	2.50
❏ 2, b&w, adult	0.50	1.50	2.50
❏ 3, b&w, adult	0.50	1.50	2.50

DISHMAN
ECLIPSE
	GOOD	FINE	N-MINT
❏ 1, O:Dishman, b&w	0.50	1.50	2.50

DISNEY ADVENTURES
DISNEY
	GOOD	FINE	N-MINT
❏ 1, undistributed	1.00	3.00	5.00
❏ 1, digest	0.39	1.17	1.95
❏ 2, digest	0.39	1.17	1.95
❏ 3, digest	0.39	1.17	1.95
❏ 4, digest	0.39	1.17	1.95
❏ 5, digest	0.39	1.17	1.95
❏ 6, digest	0.39	1.17	1.95
❏ 7, digest	0.39	1.17	1.95
❏ 8, digest	0.39	1.17	1.95
❏ 9, Rocketeer comic	0.39	1.17	1.95
❏ 9, Space Mickey	0.39	1.17	1.95
❏ 10	0.39	1.17	1.95
❏ 11	0.39	1.17	1.95
❏ 12	0.39	1.17	1.95

	ORIG.	GOOD	FINE	N-MINT

DISNEY MAGAZINE PUBLISHING
☐ 0, Aug 94, digest-sized magazine

	ORIG.	GOOD	FINE	N-MINT
	2.50	0.50	1.50	2.50

DISNEY ADVENTURES (Volume 2)
DISNEY

	ORIG.	GOOD	FINE	N-MINT
1, (#13)		0.39	1.17	1.95
2, (#14)		0.39	1.17	1.95
3, (#15)		0.39	1.17	1.95
4, (#16)		0.39	1.17	1.95
5, (#17)		0.39	1.17	1.95
6, (#18)		0.39	1.17	1.95
7, (#19)		0.39	1.17	1.95
8, (#20)		0.39	1.17	1.95
9, (#21)		0.39	1.17	1.95
10, (#22)		0.39	1.17	1.95
11, (#23)		0.39	1.17	1.95
12, (#24)		0.39	1.17	1.95

DISNEY ADVENTURES (Volume 3)

	ORIG.	GOOD	FINE	N-MINT
1, (#25)		0.39	1.17	1.95
2, (#26)		0.39	1.17	1.95
3, (#27)		0.39	1.17	1.95
4, (#28)		0.39	1.17	1.95
5, (#29)		0.39	1.17	1.95
6, (#30)		0.39	1.17	1.95
7, (#31)	2.50	0.50	1.50	2.50
8, (#32)	2.50	0.50	1.50	2.50
9, (#33)	2.50	0.50	1.50	2.50
10, (#34)	2.50	0.50	1.50	2.50
11, (#35)	2.50	0.50	1.50	2.50
12, (#36)	2.50	0.50	1.50	2.50

DISNEY ADVENTURES (Volume 4)

	ORIG.	GOOD	FINE	N-MINT
1, (#37)	2.50	0.50	1.50	2.50
2, (#38)	2.50	0.50	1.50	2.50
3, (#39)	2.50	0.50	1.50	2.50
4, (#40)	2.50	0.50	1.50	2.50
5, (#41)	2.50	0.50	1.50	2.50
6, Apr 94, (#42) color Bone				
	2.50	0.60	1.80	3.00

DISNEY AFTERNOON
MARVEL

	ORIG.	GOOD	FINE	N-MINT
1, Nov 94	1.50	0.30	0.90	1.50
2, Dec 94	1.50	0.30	0.90	1.50
3, Jan 95	1.50	0.30	0.90	1.50
4, Feb 95	1.50	0.30	0.90	1.50
5, Mar 95	1.50	0.30	0.90	1.50
6, Apr 95	1.50	0.30	0.90	1.50
7, May 95	1.50	0.30	0.90	1.50
8, Jun 95	1.50	0.30	0.90	1.50
9, Jul 95	1.50	0.30	0.90	1.50
10, Aug 95, final issue	1.50	0.30	0.90	1.50

DISNEY COMIC HITS

	ORIG.	GOOD	FINE	N-MINT
1, Oct 95, Pocahontas	1.50	0.30	0.90	1.50
2, Nov 95, Timon and Pumbaa				
	1.50	0.30	0.90	1.50
3, Dec 95, Pocahontas	1.50	0.30	0.90	1.50
4, Jan 96, Adapts *Toy Story*				
	2.50	0.50	1.50	2.50
5, Feb 96	1.50	0.30	0.90	1.50
6, Mar 96	1.50	0.30	0.90	1.50
7, Apr 96	1.50	0.30	0.90	1.50
8, May 96	1.50	0.30	0.90	1.50

DISNEY MOVIE BOOK
DISNEY
☐ 1, Roger Rabbit in "Tummy Trouble"

	ORIG.	GOOD	FINE	N-MINT
		1.59	4.77	7.95

DISNEY'S ALADDIN

	ORIG.	GOOD	FINE	N-MINT
1	2.00	0.40	1.20	2.00

MARVEL

	ORIG.	GOOD	FINE	N-MINT
1, Oct 94	1.50	0.30	0.90	1.50
2, Nov 94	1.50	0.30	0.90	1.50
3, Dec 94	1.50	0.30	0.90	1.50
4, Jan 95	1.50	0.30	0.90	1.50
5, Feb 95	1.50	0.30	0.90	1.50
6, Mar 95	1.50	0.30	0.90	1.50
7, Apr 95	1.50	0.30	0.90	1.50
8, May 95	1.50	0.30	0.90	1.50
9, Jun 95	1.50	0.30	0.90	1.50
10, Jul 95	1.50	0.30	0.90	1.50
11, Aug 95	1.50	0.30	0.90	1.50

DISNEY'S BEAUTY AND THE BEAST
DISNEY

	ORIG.	GOOD	FINE	N-MINT
1, Sep 94	1.50	0.30	0.90	1.50
2, Oct 94	1.50	0.30	0.90	1.50
3, Nov 94	1.50	0.30	0.90	1.50
4, Dec 94	1.50	0.30	0.90	1.50
5, Jan 95	1.50	0.30	0.90	1.50
6, Feb 95	1.50	0.30	0.90	1.50
7, Mar 95	1.50	0.30	0.90	1.50
8, Apr 95	1.50	0.30	0.90	1.50
9, May 95	1.50	0.30	0.90	1.50
10, Jun 95	1.50	0.30	0.90	1.50
11, Jul 95	1.50	0.30	0.90	1.50
12, Aug 95	1.50	0.30	0.90	1.50
12, Sep 95	1.50	0.30	0.90	1.50

DISNEY'S COLOSSAL COMICS

	ORIG.	GOOD	FINE	N-MINT
1	2.00	0.40	1.20	2.00

DISNEY'S COLOSSAL COMICS COLLECTION

	ORIG.	GOOD	FINE	N-MINT
1, digest		0.39	1.17	1.95
2, digest		0.39	1.17	1.95
3, digest		0.39	1.17	1.95
4, digest		0.39	1.17	1.95
5, digest		0.39	1.17	1.95
6, digest		0.39	1.17	1.95
7, digest		0.39	1.17	1.95
8, digest		0.39	1.17	1.95
9, digest		0.39	1.17	1.95
10, digest		0.39	1.17	1.95

DISNEY'S COMICS IN 3-D
☐ 1, 92, CB, FG, Don Rosa

	ORIG.	GOOD	FINE	N-MINT
	2.95	0.59	1.77	2.95

DISNEY'S NEW ADVENTURES OF BEAUTY AND THE BEAST

	ORIG.	GOOD	FINE	N-MINT
1	2.00	0.40	1.20	2.00

DISNEY'S POCAHONTAS
MARVEL
☐ 1, Jul 95, movie adaptation; prestige format one-shot

	ORIG.	GOOD	FINE	N-MINT
	4.95	0.99	2.97	4.95

DISNEY'S RESCUERS DOWN UNDER
DISNEY

	ORIG.	GOOD	FINE	N-MINT
1, 90	2.95	0.59	1.77	2.95

DISNEY'S THE LION KING
MARVEL

	ORIG.	GOOD	FINE	N-MINT
1, Jul 94	2.50	0.50	1.50	2.50

DISNEY'S THE LITTLE MERMAID

	ORIG.	GOOD	FINE	N-MINT
1, Sep 94	1.50	0.30	0.90	1.50
2, Oct 94	1.50	0.30	0.90	1.50
3, Nov 94	1.50	0.30	0.90	1.50
4, Dec 94	1.50	0.30	0.90	1.50
5, Jan 95	1.50	0.30	0.90	1.50
6, Feb 95	1.50	0.30	0.90	1.50
7, Mar 95	1.50	0.30	0.90	1.50
8, Apr 95	1.50	0.30	0.90	1.50
9, May 95	1.50	0.30	0.90	1.50
10, Jun 95	1.50	0.30	0.90	1.50
11, Jul 95	1.50	0.30	0.90	1.50
12, Aug 95	1.50	0.30	0.90	1.50

DISNEYLAND BIRTHDAY PARTY
GLADSTONE

	ORIG.	GOOD	FINE	N-MINT
1		1.00	3.00	5.00
1, (digest)		3.00	9.00	15.00

	ORIG.	GOOD	FINE	N-MINT

DISOBEDIENT DAISY
EROS

	ORIG.	GOOD	FINE	N-MINT
1, Aug 95, adults;b&w ... 2.95		0.59	1.77	2.95

DISTANT SOIL, A
ARIA

	ORIG.	GOOD	FINE	N-MINT
1, 91, b&w;first printing. 1.75		0.35	1.05	1.75
1, 92, b&w; second printing				
.... 1.75		0.35	1.05	1.75
1, 93, b&w;third printing 1.75		0.35	1.05	1.75
1, 95, b&w; fourth printing				
.... 1.75		0.35	1.05	1.75
2, 92, b&w;first printing. 1.75		0.35	1.05	1.75
2, 93, b&w; second printing				
.... 1.75		0.35	1.05	1.75
3, 93, b&w;first printing. 1.75		0.35	1.05	1.75
3, 93, b&w; second printing				
.... 1.75		0.35	1.05	1.75
4, 93, b&w;first printing. 1.75		0.35	1.05	1.75
4, 95, b&w; second printing				
.... 1.75		0.35	1.05	1.75
5, 93, b&w 1.75		0.35	1.05	1.75
6, 93, b&w 1.75		0.35	1.05	1.75
7, 94, b&w 1.75		0.35	1.05	1.75
8, Jun 94, b&w 1.75		0.35	1.05	1.75
9, 94, b&w 2.50		0.50	1.50	2.50
10, 94, b&w 2.50		0.50	1.50	2.50
11, 94, b&w 2.50		0.50	1.50	2.50
12, Nov 95, b&w 2.50		0.50	1.50	2.50

WARP

	ORIG.	GOOD	FINE	N-MINT
1		0.30	0.90	1.50
2		0.30	0.90	1.50
3		0.30	0.90	1.50
4		0.30	0.90	1.50
5		0.30	0.90	1.50
6		0.30	0.90	1.50
7		0.30	0.90	1.50
8		0.30	0.90	1.50
9		0.30	0.90	1.50

DIVA
STARHEAD

	ORIG.	GOOD	FINE	N-MINT
1, Nov 93, adult;b&w 3.95		0.79	2.37	3.95
2, 94, adult;b&w 3.95		0.79	2.37	3.95

DIVA GRAFIX & STORIES

	ORIG.	GOOD	FINE	N-MINT
1 .... 3.95		0.79	2.37	3.95

DIVAS
CALIBER

	ORIG.	GOOD	FINE	N-MINT
1, b&w 2.50		0.50	1.50	2.50
2, b&w 2.50		0.50	1.50	2.50
3, b&w 2.50		0.50	1.50	2.50
4, b&w 2.50		0.50	1.50	2.50

DIVISION 13
DARK HORSE

	ORIG.	GOOD	FINE	N-MINT
1, Sep 94 .... 2.50		0.50	1.50	2.50
2, Oct 94 .... 2.50		0.50	1.50	2.50
3, Dec 94 .... 2.50		0.50	1.50	2.50

DJANGO & ANGEL
CALIBER

	ORIG.	GOOD	FINE	N-MINT
1, b&w		0.50	1.50	2.50
2, b&w		0.50	1.50	2.50
3, b&w		0.50	1.50	2.50
4, b&w		0.50	1.50	2.50
5, b&w		0.50	1.50	2.50

DNAGENTS
ECLIPSE

	ORIG.	GOOD	FINE	N-MINT
1, Mar 83		0.50	1.50	2.50
2, Apr 83		0.35	1.05	1.75
3, May 83		0.35	1.05	1.75
4, Jul 83		0.35	1.05	1.75
5, Aug 83		0.35	1.05	1.75
6, Oct 83		0.30	0.90	1.50
7, Nov 83		0.30	0.90	1.50
8, Jan 84		0.30	0.90	1.50
9, Feb 84		0.30	0.90	1.50
10, Mar 84		0.30	0.90	1.50
11, May 84		0.30	0.90	1.50
12, May 84		0.30	0.90	1.50
13, Jun 84		0.30	0.90	1.50
14, Jul 84		0.30	0.90	1.50
15, Aug 84		0.30	0.90	1.50
16, Sep 84		0.30	0.90	1.50
17, Dec 84		0.30	0.90	1.50
18, Jan 85		0.30	0.90	1.50
19, Feb 85		0.30	0.90	1.50
20, Mar 85		0.30	0.90	1.50
21, Apr 85		0.30	0.90	1.50
22, May 85		0.30	0.90	1.50
23, Jun 85		0.30	0.90	1.50
24, Jul 85, DSt(c) (becomes *New DNAgents*)				
....		1.40	4.20	7.00

DNAGENTS SPECIAL
ANTARCTIC

	ORIG.	GOOD	FINE	N-MINT
1, Apr 94, 8 pages in color				
.... 3.50		0.70	2.10	3.50

DNAGENTS SUPER SPECIAL

	ORIG.	GOOD	FINE	N-MINT
1, Apr 94, b&w 3.50		0.70	2.10	3.50

DOC SAMSON
MARVEL

	ORIG.	GOOD	FINE	N-MINT
1, Jan 96 .... 1.95		0.39	1.17	1.95
2, Feb 96 .... 1.95		0.39	1.17	1.95
3, Mar 96, V:Punisher 1.95		0.39	1.17	1.95
4, Apr 96, A:Polaris 1.95		0.39	1.17	1.95

DOC SAVAGE
DC

	ORIG.	GOOD	FINE	N-MINT
1, Nov 88 .... 1.75		0.35	1.05	1.75
2, Dec 88 .... 1.75		0.35	1.05	1.75
3, Dec 88 .... 1.75		0.35	1.05	1.75
4, Jan 89 .... 1.75		0.35	1.05	1.75
5, Jan 89 .... 1.75		0.35	1.05	1.75
6, Mar 89 .... 1.75		0.35	1.05	1.75
7, Apr 89 .... 1.75		0.35	1.05	1.75
8, May 89 .... 1.75		0.35	1.05	1.75
9, Jun 89 .... 1.75		0.35	1.05	1.75
10, Jul 89 .... 1.75		0.35	1.05	1.75
11, Aug 89 .... 1.75		0.35	1.05	1.75
12, Sep 89 .... 1.75		0.35	1.05	1.75
13, Oct 89 .... 2.00		0.40	1.20	2.00
14, Nov 89 .... 2.00		0.40	1.20	2.00
15, Dec 89 .... 2.00		0.40	1.20	2.00
16, Jan 90 .... 2.00		0.40	1.20	2.00
17, Feb 90, Shadow 2.00		0.40	1.20	2.00
18, Mar 90, Shadow 2.00		0.40	1.20	2.00
19, May 90, Air Lord 2.00		0.40	1.20	2.00
20, Jun 90, Air Lord 2.00		0.40	1.20	2.00
21, Jul 90, Air Lord 2.00		0.40	1.20	2.00
22, Aug 90 .... 2.00		0.40	1.20	2.00
23, Sep 90 .... 2.00		0.40	1.20	2.00
24, Oct 90 .... 2.00		0.40	1.20	2.00

MARVEL

	ORIG.	GOOD	FINE	N-MINT
1, Oct 72 .... 0.20		0.50	1.50	2.50
2, Dec 72 .... 0.20		0.30	0.90	1.50
3, Feb 73 .... 0.20		0.30	0.90	1.50
4, Apr 73 .... 0.20		0.30	0.90	1.50
5, Jun 73 .... 0.20		0.30	0.90	1.50
6, Aug 73 .... 0.20		0.30	0.90	1.50
7, Oct 73 .... 0.20		0.30	0.90	1.50
8, Jan 74 .... 0.20		0.30	0.90	1.50

DOC SAVAGE (b&w mag)

	ORIG.	GOOD	FINE	N-MINT
1, Aug 75 .... 1.00		0.20	0.60	1.00
2, Oct 75 .... 1.00		0.20	0.60	1.00
3, Jan 76 .... 1.00		0.20	0.60	1.00

	ORIG.	GOOD	FINE	N-MINT
☐ 4, Apr 76	1.00	0.20	0.60	1.00
☐ 5, Jul 76	1.00	0.20	0.60	1.00
☐ 6, Oct 76	1.00	0.20	0.60	1.00
☐ 7, Jan 77	1.00	0.20	0.60	1.00
☐ 8, Spr 77	1.00	0.20	0.60	1.00

DOC SAVAGE (mini-series)
DC

	ORIG.	GOOD	FINE	N-MINT
☐ 1, Nov 87, AnK/AdK	1.75	0.35	1.05	1.75
☐ 2, Dec 87, AnK/AdK	1.75	0.35	1.05	1.75
☐ 3, Jan 88, AnK/AdK	1.75	0.35	1.05	1.75
☐ 4, Feb 88, AnK/AdK	1.75	0.35	1.05	1.75

DOC SAVAGE ANNUAL

	ORIG.	GOOD	FINE	N-MINT
☐ 1, Aug 89		0.70	2.10	3.50

DOC SAVAGE: CURSE OF THE FIRE GOD (mini-series)
DARK HORSE

	ORIG.	GOOD	FINE	N-MINT
☐ 1, Sep 95	2.95	0.59	1.77	2.95
☐ 2, Oct 95	2.95	0.59	1.77	2.95
☐ 3, Nov 95	2.95	0.59	1.77	2.95
☐ 4, Dec 95	2.95	0.59	1.77	2.95

DOC SAVAGE: DEVIL'S THOUGHTS
MILLENNIUM

	ORIG.	GOOD	FINE	N-MINT
☐ 1		0.50	1.50	2.50
☐ 2		0.50	1.50	2.50
☐ 3		0.50	1.50	2.50

DOC SAVAGE: DOOM DYNASTY

	ORIG.	GOOD	FINE	N-MINT
☐ 1, color		0.50	1.50	2.50
☐ 2, color		0.50	1.50	2.50

DOC SAVAGE: THE MAN OF BRONZE

	ORIG.	GOOD	FINE	N-MINT
☐ 1, Dec 91, color		0.50	1.50	2.50
☐ 2, Doug Wildey (c)		0.50	1.50	2.50
☐ 3		0.50	1.50	2.50
☐ 4		0.50	1.50	2.50

DOC SAVAGE: THE MANUAL OF BRONZE

	ORIG.	GOOD	FINE	N-MINT
☐ 1, Aug 92	2.50	0.50	1.50	2.50

DOC WEIRD'S THRILL BOOK
PURE IMAGINATION

	ORIG.	GOOD	FINE	N-MINT
☐ 1, FF,AW,ATh,Bob Powell, Mike Peppe,Virgil Finlay	1.75	0.35	1.05	1.75
☐ 2, WW,Jack Cole		0.35	1.05	1.75
☐ 3, WW		0.40	1.20	2.00

DOCTOR BANG
RIP OFF

	ORIG.	GOOD	FINE	N-MINT
☐ 1, Feb 92, b&w	2.50	0.50	1.50	2.50

DOCTOR BOOGIE
MEDIA ARTS

	ORIG.	GOOD	FINE	N-MINT
☐ 1		0.20	0.60	1.00

DOCTOR CHAOS
TRIUMPHANT

	ORIG.	GOOD	FINE	N-MINT
☐ 1, Unleashed!	2.50	0.50	1.50	2.50
☐ 2, Unleashed!	2.50	0.50	1.50	2.50
☐ 3	2.50	0.50	1.50	2.50
☐ 4, 94	2.50	0.50	1.50	2.50
☐ 5, Mar 94	2.50	0.50	1.50	2.50
☐ 6, Mar 94	2.50	0.50	1.50	2.50

DOCTOR FATE (1987 mini-series)
DC

	ORIG.	GOOD	FINE	N-MINT
☐ 1, Jul 87, KG	1.50	0.30	0.90	1.50
☐ 2, Aug 87, KG	1.50	0.30	0.90	1.50
☐ 3, Sep 87, KG	1.50	0.30	0.90	1.50
☐ 4, Oct 87, KG	1.50	0.30	0.90	1.50

DOCTOR FATE (beginning 1988)

	ORIG.	GOOD	FINE	N-MINT
☐ 1, Dec 88	1.25	0.50	1.50	2.50
☐ 2, Jan 89	1.25	0.40	1.20	2.00
☐ 3, Jan 89	1.25	0.40	1.20	2.00
☐ 4, Feb 89		0.40	1.20	2.00
☐ 5, Apr 89		0.40	1.20	2.00
☐ 6, May 89		0.35	1.05	1.75

	ORIG.	GOOD	FINE	N-MINT
☐ 7, Jun 89		0.35	1.05	1.75
☐ 8, Jul 89		0.35	1.05	1.75
☐ 9, Aug 89		0.35	1.05	1.75
☐ 10, Sep 89		0.35	1.05	1.75
☐ 11, Nov 89		0.35	1.05	1.75
☐ 12, Dec 89		0.35	1.05	1.75
☐ 13, Jan 90		0.35	1.05	1.75
☐ 14, Feb 90		0.35	1.05	1.75
☐ 15, Mar 90, A:JLI		0.30	0.90	1.50
☐ 16, Apr 90		0.30	0.90	1.50
☐ 17, May 90		0.30	0.90	1.50
☐ 18, Jun 90		0.30	0.90	1.50
☐ 19, Jul 90		0.30	0.90	1.50
☐ 20, Aug 90		0.30	0.90	1.50
☐ 21, Oct 90		0.30	0.90	1.50
☐ 22, Nov 90		0.30	0.90	1.50
☐ 23, Dec 90		0.30	0.90	1.50
☐ 24, Jan 91		0.30	0.90	1.50
☐ 25, Feb 91		0.30	0.90	1.50
☐ 26, Mar 91		0.30	0.90	1.50
☐ 27, Apr 91		0.30	0.90	1.50
☐ 28, May 91		0.30	0.90	1.50
☐ 29, Jun 91		0.30	0.90	1.50
☐ 30, Jul 91		0.30	0.90	1.50
☐ 31, Aug 91		0.30	0.90	1.50
☐ 32, Sep 91, War of Gods		0.35	1.05	1.75
☐ 33, Oct 91, War of Gods		0.35	1.05	1.75
☐ 34, Nov 91		0.35	1.05	1.75
☐ 35, Dec 91		0.35	1.05	1.75
☐ 36		0.35	1.05	1.75
☐ 37		0.35	1.05	1.75
☐ 38		0.35	1.05	1.75
☐ 39		0.35	1.05	1.75
☐ 40		0.35	1.05	1.75
☐ 41		0.35	1.05	1.75

DOCTOR FATE ANNUAL

	ORIG.	GOOD	FINE	N-MINT
☐ 1, Nov 89		0.59	1.77	2.95

DOCTOR FAUSTUS
ANARCHY

	ORIG.	GOOD	FINE	N-MINT
☐ 1, b&w	2.95	0.59	1.77	2.95
☐ 1, ashcan, b&w		0.60	1.80	3.00

DOCTOR FRANKENSTEIN'S HOUSE OF 3-D
3-D ZONE

	ORIG.	GOOD	FINE	N-MINT
☐ 1, 92, oversized	3.95	0.79	2.37	3.95

DOCTOR GORPON
ETERNITY

	ORIG.	GOOD	FINE	N-MINT
☐ 1, b&w		0.50	1.50	2.50
☐ 2, b&w		0.50	1.50	2.50
☐ 3, b&w		0.50	1.50	2.50

DOCTOR STRANGE (1974-1987)
MARVEL

	ORIG.	GOOD	FINE	N-MINT
☐ 1, DG/FB	0.25	4.00	12.00	20.00
☐ 2, DG/FB, A:Defenders	0.25	2.40	7.20	12.00
☐ 3, FB/DG, A:Dormammu	0.25	1.20	3.60	6.00
☐ 4, DG/FB	0.25	1.20	3.60	6.00
☐ 5, DG/FB	0.25	1.20	3.60	6.00
☐ 6, GC	0.25	0.40	1.20	2.00
☐ 7, GC	0.25	0.40	1.20	2.00
☐ 8, GC	0.25	0.40	1.20	2.00
☐ 9, GC	0.25	0.40	1.20	2.00
☐ 10, GC	0.25	0.40	1.20	2.00
☐ 11, GC	0.25	0.40	1.20	2.00
☐ 12, GC	0.25	0.40	1.20	2.00
☐ 13, GC	0.25	0.40	1.20	2.00
☐ 14, GC	0.25	0.30	0.90	1.50
☐ 15, GC	0.25	0.30	0.90	1.50
☐ 16, GC	0.25	0.30	0.90	1.50
☐ 17, Aug 76, GC	0.25	0.30	0.90	1.50
☐ 18, Sep 76, GC	0.30	0.30	0.90	1.50

	ORIG.	GOOD	FINE	N-MINT
❑ 19, Oct 76, GC/AA, I:Xander				
............................0.30	0.40	1.20	2.00	
❑ 20, Dec 76......................0.30	0.30	0.90	1.50	
❑ 21, Feb 77........................0.30	0.30	0.90	1.50	
❑ 22, Apr 77........................0.30	0.30	0.90	1.50	
❑ 23, Jun 77........................0.30	0.30	0.90	1.50	
❑ 24, Aug 77.......................0.30	0.30	0.90	1.50	
❑ 25, Oct 77........................0.30	0.40	1.20	2.00	
❑ 26, Dec 77.......................0.35	0.40	1.20	2.00	
❑ 27, Feb 78.......................0.35	0.20	0.60	1.00	
❑ 28, Apr 78........................0.35	0.20	0.60	1.00	
❑ 29, Jun 78........................0.35	0.20	0.60	1.00	
❑ 30, Aug 78.......................0.35	0.20	0.60	1.00	
❑ 31, Oct 78........................0.35	0.20	0.60	1.00	
❑ 32, Dec 78.......................0.35	0.20	0.60	1.00	
❑ 33, Feb 79.......................0.35	0.20	0.60	1.00	
❑ 34, Apr 79........................0.35	0.20	0.60	1.00	
❑ 35, Jun 79........................0.40	0.20	0.60	1.00	
❑ 36, Aug 79.......................0.40	0.20	0.60	1.00	
❑ 37, Oct 79........................0.40	0.20	0.60	1.00	
❑ 38, Dec 79.......................0.40	0.20	0.60	1.00	
❑ 39, Feb 80.......................0.40	0.20	0.60	1.00	
❑ 40, Apr 80........................0.40	0.20	0.60	1.00	
❑ 41, Jun 80........................0.40	0.20	0.60	1.00	
❑ 42, Aug 80.......................0.40	0.20	0.60	1.00	
❑ 43, Oct 80........................0.50	0.20	0.60	1.00	
❑ 44, Dec 80.......................0.50	0.20	0.60	1.00	
❑ 45, Feb 81.......................0.50	0.20	0.60	1.00	
❑ 46, Apr 81........................0.50	0.20	0.60	1.00	
❑ 47, Jun 81........................0.50	0.20	0.60	1.00	
❑ 48, Aug 81, A:Brother Voodoo				
............................0.50	0.30	0.90	1.50	
❑ 49, Oct 81, A:Baron Mordo				
............................0.50	0.25	0.75	1.25	
❑ 50, Dec 81, A:Baron Mordo				
............................0.50	0.25	0.75	1.25	
❑ 51, Feb 82.......................0.60	0.20	0.60	1.00	
❑ 52, Apr 82........................0.60	0.20	0.60	1.00	
❑ 53, Jun 82........................0.60	0.20	0.60	1.00	
❑ 54, Aug 82, PS...............0.60	0.25	0.75	1.25	
❑ 55, Oct 82, PS................0.60	0.25	0.75	1.25	
❑ 56, Dec 82, PS 0.60	0.25	0.75	1.25	
❑ 57, Feb 83.......................0.60	0.20	0.60	1.00	
❑ 58, Apr 83........................0.60	0.20	0.60	1.00	
❑ 59, Jun 83........................0.60	0.20	0.60	1.00	
❑ 60, Aug 83, A:Dracula 0.60	0.20	0.60	1.00	
❑ 61, Oct 83, A:Dracula 0.60	0.20	0.60	1.00	
❑ 62, Dec 83.......................0.60	0.20	0.60	1.00	
❑ 63, Feb 84.......................0.60	0.20	0.60	1.00	
❑ 64, Apr 84........................0.60	0.20	0.60	1.00	
❑ 65, Jun 84........................0.60	0.20	0.60	1.00	
❑ 66, Aug 84 ....0.60	0.20	0.60	1.00	
❑ 67, Oct 84........................0.60	0.20	0.60	1.00	
❑ 68, Dec 84.......................0.60	0.20	0.60	1.00	
❑ 69, Feb 85.......................0.60	0.20	0.60	1.00	
❑ 70, Apr 85........................0.65	0.20	0.60	1.00	
❑ 71, Jun 85........................0.65	0.20	0.60	1.00	
❑ 72, Aug 85.......................0.65	0.20	0.60	1.00	
❑ 73, Oct 85........................0.65	0.20	0.60	1.00	
❑ 74, Dec 85, Secret Wars II				
............................0.65	0.20	0.60	1.00	
❑ 75, Feb 86.......................0.75	0.20	0.60	1.00	
❑ 76, Apr 86........................0.75	0.20	0.60	1.00	
❑ 77, Jun 86........................0.75	0.20	0.60	1.00	
❑ 78, Aug 86.......................0.75	0.20	0.60	1.00	
❑ 79, Oct 86........................0.75	0.20	0.60	1.00	
❑ 80, Dec 86.......................0.75	0.20	0.60	1.00	
❑ 81, Feb 87.......................0.75	0.20	0.60	1.00	

DOCTOR STRANGE (was Strange Tales)

	ORIG.	GOOD	FINE	N-MINT
❑ 169, Jun 68, DA, O:Dr. Strange				
............................0.12	16.00	48.00	80.00	

	ORIG.	GOOD	FINE	N-MINT
❑ 170, Jul 68......................0.12	10.00	30.00	50.00	
❑ 171, Aug 68.....................0.12	6.00	18.00	30.00	
❑ 172, Sep 68.....................0.12	6.00	18.00	30.00	
❑ 173, Oct 68......................0.12	6.00	18.00	30.00	
❑ 174 ....0.12	6.00	18.00	30.00	
❑ 175, Dec 68.....................0.12	6.00	18.00	30.00	
❑ 176, Jan 69.....................0.12	6.00	18.00	30.00	
❑ 177, Feb 69.....................0.12	6.00	18.00	30.00	
❑ 178, Mar 69.....................0.12	6.00	18.00	30.00	
❑ 179, Apr 69......................0.12	6.00	18.00	30.00	
❑ 180, May 69.....................0.12	6.00	18.00	30.00	
❑ 181, Jul 69......................0.12	6.00	18.00	30.00	
❑ 182 ....0.15	6.00	18.00	30.00	
❑ 183 ....0.15	6.00	18.00	30.00	
❑ 182, Sep 69.....................0.12	6.00	18.00	30.00	
❑ 183, Nov 69.....................0.12	6.00	18.00	30.00	

DOCTOR STRANGE ANNUAL

	ORIG.	GOOD	FINE	N-MINT
❑ 1, Feb 77........................0.50	1.00	3.00	5.00	
❑ 2, 92 ....2.25	0.45	1.35	2.25	
❑ 3, 93, trading card 2.95	0.59	1.77	2.95	

DOCTOR STRANGE CLASSICS

	ORIG.	GOOD	FINE	N-MINT
❑ 1, Mar 84, SD rep. 0.30	0.30	0.90	1.50	
❑ 2, Apr 84, SD rep. 0.30	0.30	0.90	1.50	
❑ 3, May 84, AAd (c).........0.30	0.30	0.90	1.50	
❑ 4, Jun 84 ....0.30	0.30	0.90	1.50	

DOCTOR STRANGE SPECIAL EDITION

	ORIG.	GOOD	FINE	N-MINT
❑ 1, Mar 83 ....2.50	0.50	1.50	2.50	

DOCTOR STRANGE VS. DRACULA

	ORIG.	GOOD	FINE	N-MINT
❑ 1, reprints 1.75	0.35	1.05	1.75	

DOCTOR STRANGE, SORCERER SUPREME

	ORIG.	GOOD	FINE	N-MINT
❑ 81, Sep 95, (was Doctor Strange: Sorcerer Supreme)				
............................1.95	0.39	1.17	1.95	
❑ 82, Oct 95.......................1.95	0.39	1.17	1.95	
❑ 83, Nov 95.......................1.95	0.39	1.17	1.95	
❑ 84, Dec 95, A:Mordo.......1.95	0.39	1.17	1.95	
❑ 85, Jan 96.......................1.95	0.39	1.17	1.95	
❑ 86, Feb 96.......................1.95	0.39	1.17	1.95	
❑ 87, Mar 96, D:Mordo 1.95	0.39	1.17	1.95	
❑ 89, May 96, "Fall of the Tempo" Part 2 of 2				
............................1.95	0.39	1.17	1.95	

DOCTOR STRANGE/GHOST RIDER SPECIAL

	ORIG.	GOOD	FINE	N-MINT
❑ 1, Apr 91, rep: Dr. Strange #28				
............................1.50	0.30	0.90	1.50	

DOCTOR STRANGE: SORCERER SUPREME
(beginning 1988)

	ORIG.	GOOD	FINE	N-MINT
❑ 1, Nov 88........................1.25	0.80	2.40	4.00	
❑ 2, Jan 89, Inferno 1.50	0.60	1.80	3.00	
❑ 3, Mar 89........................1.50	0.40	1.20	2.00	
❑ 4, May 89........................1.50	0.40	1.20	2.00	
❑ 5, Jul 89.........................1.50	0.40	1.20	2.00	
❑ 6, Aug 89........................1.50	0.40	1.20	2.00	
❑ 7, Sep 89........................1.50	0.40	1.20	2.00	
❑ 8, Oct 89.........................1.50	0.40	1.20	2.00	
❑ 9, Nov 89........................1.50	0.40	1.20	2.00	
❑ 10, Dec 89......................1.50	0.40	1.20	2.00	
❑ 11, Dec 89, Acts of Vengeance				
............................1.50	1.00	3.00	5.00	
❑ 12, Dec 89, Acts of Vengeance				
............................1.50	0.40	1.20	2.00	
❑ 13, Jan 90, Acts of Vengeance				
............................1.50	0.40	1.20	2.00	
❑ 14, Feb 90, vampires 1.50	0.60	1.80	3.00	
❑ 15, Mar 90, vampires......1.50	1.60	4.80	8.00	
❑ 16, Apr 90, vampires 1.50	0.30	0.90	1.50	
❑ 17, May 90, vampires 1.50	0.30	0.90	1.50	
❑ 18, Jun 90, vampires 1.50	0.30	0.90	1.50	
❑ 19, Jul 90, GC 1.50	0.30	0.90	1.50	
❑ 20, Aug 90......................1.50	0.30	0.90	1.50	
❑ 21, Sep 90 ....1.50	0.30	0.90	1.50	
❑ 22, Oct 90.......................1.50	0.30	0.90	1.50	

	ORIG.	GOOD	FINE	N-MINT
❏ 23, Nov 90	1.50	0.30	0.90	1.50
❏ 24, Dec 90	1.50	0.30	0.90	1.50
❏ 25, Jan 91	1.50	0.30	0.90	1.50
❏ 26, Feb 91, werewolf	1.50	0.30	0.90	1.50
❏ 27, Mar 91, werewolf	1.50	0.30	0.90	1.50
❏ 28, Apr 91, Ghost Rider	1.50	1.60	4.80	8.00
❏ 29, May 91	1.75	0.35	1.05	1.75
❏ 30, Jun 91	1.75	0.35	1.05	1.75
❏ 31, Jul 91, Infinity Gauntlet	1.75	0.60	1.80	3.00
❏ 32, Aug 91, Infinity Gauntlet	1.75	0.35	1.05	1.75
❏ 33, Sep 91, Infinity Gauntlet	1.75	0.35	1.05	1.75
❏ 34, Oct 91, Infinity Gauntlet	1.75	0.35	1.05	1.75
❏ 35, Nov 91, Infinity Gauntlet	1.75	0.35	1.05	1.75
❏ 36, Dec 91, Infinity Gauntlet	1.75	0.35	1.05	1.75
❏ 37	1.75	0.35	1.05	1.75
❏ 38	1.75	0.35	1.05	1.75
❏ 39	1.75	0.35	1.05	1.75
❏ 40	1.75	0.35	1.05	1.75
❏ 41, Wolverine	1.75	0.35	1.05	1.75
❏ 42, Galactus	1.75	0.35	1.05	1.75
❏ 43	1.75	0.35	1.05	1.75
❏ 44	1.75	0.35	1.05	1.75
❏ 45	1.75	0.35	1.05	1.75
❏ 46	1.75	0.35	1.05	1.75
❏ 47	1.75	0.35	1.05	1.75
❏ 48	1.75	0.35	1.05	1.75
❏ 49	1.75	0.35	1.05	1.75
❏ 50, foil cover	2.95	0.59	1.77	2.95
❏ 51	1.75	0.35	1.05	1.75
❏ 52	1.75	0.35	1.05	1.75
❏ 53	1.75	0.35	1.05	1.75
❏ 54	1.75	0.35	1.05	1.75
❏ 55	1.75	0.35	1.05	1.75
❏ 56	1.75	0.35	1.05	1.75
❏ 57	1.75	0.35	1.05	1.75
❏ 58, Oct 93	1.75	0.35	1.05	1.75
❏ 59, Nov 93	1.75	0.35	1.05	1.75
❏ 60, Dec 93	1.75	0.60	1.80	3.00
❏ 61, Jan 94	1.75	0.35	1.05	1.75
❏ 62, Feb 94	1.75	0.35	1.05	1.75
❏ 63, Mar 94	1.75	0.35	1.05	1.75
❏ 64, Apr 94	1.75	0.35	1.05	1.75
❏ 65, May 94	1.95	0.39	1.17	1.95
❏ 66, Jun 94	1.95	0.39	1.17	1.95
❏ 67, Jul 94	1.95	0.39	1.17	1.95
❏ 68, Aug 94	1.95	0.39	1.17	1.95
❏ 69, Sep 94	1.95	0.39	1.17	1.95
❏ 70, Oct 94	1.95	0.39	1.17	1.95
❏ 71, Nov 94	1.95	0.39	1.17	1.95
❏ 72, Dec 94	1.95	0.39	1.17	1.95
❏ 73, Jan 95	1.95	0.39	1.17	1.95
❏ 74, Feb 95	1.95	0.39	1.17	1.95
❏ 75, Mar 95, enhanced cover	3.50	0.70	2.10	3.50
❏ 75, Mar 95	2.50	0.50	1.50	2.50
❏ 76, Apr 95	1.95	0.39	1.17	1.95
❏ 77, May 95	1.95	0.39	1.17	1.95
❏ 78, Jun 95	1.95	0.39	1.17	1.95
❏ 79, Jul 95	1.95	0.39	1.17	1.95
❏ 80, Aug 95, (becomes *Doctor Strange, Sorcerer Supreme*)	1.95	0.39	1.17	1.95

DOCTOR STRANGE: SORCERER SUPREME ANNUAL

	ORIG.	GOOD	FINE	N-MINT
❏ 1	2.00	0.45	1.35	2.25
❏ 2	2.25	0.45	1.35	2.25

	ORIG.	GOOD	FINE	N-MINT
❏ 3	2.95	0.59	1.77	2.95
❏ 4, 94	2.95	0.59	1.77	2.95

DOCTOR STRANGE: SORCERER SUPREME ASHCAN

	ORIG.	GOOD	FINE	N-MINT
❏ 0, b&w; no indicia	0.75	0.15	0.45	0.75

DOCTOR STRANGEFATE
DC/AMALGAM

	ORIG.	GOOD	FINE	N-MINT
❏ 1, Apr 96	1.95	0.39	1.17	1.95

DOCTOR WHO
MARVEL

	ORIG.	GOOD	FINE	N-MINT
❏ 1, BBC TV series	1.50	0.40	1.20	2.00
❏ 2	1.50	0.30	0.90	1.50
❏ 3	1.50	0.30	0.90	1.50
❏ 4	1.50	0.30	0.90	1.50
❏ 5	1.50	0.30	0.90	1.50
❏ 6	1.50	0.30	0.90	1.50
❏ 7	1.50	0.30	0.90	1.50
❏ 8	1.50	0.30	0.90	1.50
❏ 9	1.50	0.30	0.90	1.50
❏ 10	1.50	0.30	0.90	1.50
❏ 11	1.50	0.30	0.90	1.50
❏ 12	1.50	0.30	0.90	1.50
❏ 13	1.50	0.30	0.90	1.50
❏ 14	1.50	0.30	0.90	1.50
❏ 15	1.50	0.30	0.90	1.50
❏ 16	1.50	0.30	0.90	1.50
❏ 17	1.50	0.30	0.90	1.50
❏ 18	1.50	0.30	0.90	1.50
❏ 19	1.50	0.30	0.90	1.50
❏ 20	1.50	0.30	0.90	1.50
❏ 21	1.50	0.30	0.90	1.50
❏ 22	1.50	0.30	0.90	1.50
❏ 23	1.50	0.30	0.90	1.50

DOCTOR WHO 10TH ANNIVERSARY SPECIAL 1979-1989
MARVEL UK

	ORIG.	GOOD	FINE	N-MINT
❏ 0	7.95	1.59	4.77	7.95

DOCTOR WHO AUTUMN SPECIAL

	ORIG.	GOOD	FINE	N-MINT
❏ 0, (1987)	5.95	1.19	3.57	5.95

DOCTOR WHO CLASSIC COMICS
MARVEL

	ORIG.	GOOD	FINE	N-MINT
❏ 15	4.95	0.99	2.97	4.95
❏ 16	4.95	0.99	2.97	4.95
❏ 17, Mar 94	4.95	0.99	2.97	4.95

MARVEL UK

	ORIG.	GOOD	FINE	N-MINT
❏ 1	4.95	0.99	2.97	4.95
❏ 2	4.95	0.99	2.97	4.95
❏ 3	4.95	0.99	2.97	4.95
❏ 4	4.95	0.99	2.97	4.95
❏ 5	4.95	0.99	2.97	4.95
❏ 6	4.95	0.99	2.97	4.95
❏ 7	4.95	0.99	2.97	4.95
❏ 8	2.50	0.50	1.50	2.50
❏ 12	4.95	0.99	2.97	4.95
❏ 13	4.95	0.99	2.97	4.95
❏ 14	4.95	0.99	2.97	4.95

DOCTOR WHO COLLECTED COMICS

	ORIG.	GOOD	FINE	N-MINT
❏ 0, nn	5.95	1.19	3.57	5.95

DOCTOR WHO HOLIDAY SPECIAL

	ORIG.	GOOD	FINE	N-MINT
❏ 0, (1992)	4.50	0.90	2.70	4.50

DOCTOR WHO MAGAZINE
(was Doctor Who Monthly)

	ORIG.	GOOD	FINE	N-MINT
❏ 96	2.00	0.40	1.20	2.00
❏ 97	2.00	0.40	1.20	2.00
❏ 98	2.00	0.40	1.20	2.00
❏ 99	2.00	0.40	1.20	2.00
❏ 100	2.00	0.40	1.20	2.00
❏ 101	2.00	0.40	1.20	2.00
❏ 102	2.00	0.40	1.20	2.00

	ORIG.	GOOD	FINE	N-MINT
❑ 103	2.00	0.40	1.20	2.00
❑ 104	2.25	0.45	1.35	2.25
❑ 105	2.25	0.45	1.35	2.25
❑ 106	2.25	0.45	1.35	2.25
❑ 107	2.25	0.45	1.35	2.25
❑ 108	3.00	0.60	1.80	3.00
❑ 109	2.25	0.45	1.35	2.25
❑ 110	2.25	0.45	1.35	2.25
❑ 111	2.25	0.45	1.35	2.25
❑ 112	2.25	0.45	1.35	2.25
❑ 113	2.25	0.45	1.35	2.25
❑ 114	3.00	0.60	1.80	3.00
❑ 115	2.75	0.55	1.65	2.75
❑ 116	2.75	0.55	1.65	2.75
❑ 117	2.75	0.55	1.65	2.75
❑ 118	2.75	0.55	1.65	2.75
❑ 119	2.75	0.55	1.65	2.75
❑ 120	3.75	0.75	2.25	3.75
❑ 121	2.75	0.55	1.65	2.75
❑ 122	2.75	0.55	1.65	2.75
❑ 123	2.75	0.55	1.65	2.75
❑ 124	2.75	0.55	1.65	2.75
❑ 125	2.95	0.59	1.77	2.95
❑ 126	2.95	0.59	1.77	2.95
❑ 127	4.50	0.90	2.70	4.50
❑ 128	2.95	0.59	1.77	2.95
❑ 129	2.95	0.59	1.77	2.95
❑ 130	2.95	0.59	1.77	2.95
❑ 131	3.50	0.70	2.10	3.50
❑ 132	3.50	0.70	2.10	3.50
❑ 133	3.50	0.70	2.10	3.50
❑ 134	3.50	0.70	2.10	3.50
❑ 135	3.75	0.75	2.25	3.75
❑ 136	3.75	0.75	2.25	3.75
❑ 137	3.75	0.75	2.25	3.75
❑ 138	3.75	0.75	2.25	3.75
❑ 139	4.75	0.95	2.85	4.75
❑ 140	4.75	0.95	2.85	4.75
❑ 141	4.75	0.95	2.85	4.75
❑ 142	4.75	0.95	2.85	4.75
❑ 143	4.75	0.95	2.85	4.75
❑ 144	4.75	0.95	2.85	4.75
❑ 145	4.75	0.95	2.85	4.75
❑ 146	4.75	0.95	2.85	4.75
❑ 147	4.75	0.95	2.85	4.75
❑ 148	4.75	0.95	2.85	4.75
❑ 149	4.75	0.95	2.85	4.75
❑ 150	5.95	1.19	3.57	5.95
❑ 151	5.95	1.19	3.57	5.95
❑ 152	3.25	0.65	1.95	3.25
❑ 153	4.95	0.99	2.97	4.95
❑ 154	4.95	0.99	2.97	4.95
❑ 155	4.95	0.99	2.97	4.95
❑ 156	4.95	0.99	2.97	4.95
❑ 157	2.95	0.59	1.77	2.95
❑ 158	2.95	0.59	1.77	2.95
❑ 159	2.95	0.59	1.77	2.95
❑ 160				
❑ 161	3.95	0.79	2.37	3.95
❑ 162	3.95	0.79	2.37	3.95
❑ 163				
❑ 164	3.95	0.79	2.37	3.95
❑ 165	3.95	0.79	2.37	3.95
❑ 166	3.95	0.79	2.37	3.95
❑ 167, (with record)	5.50	1.10	3.30	5.50
❑ 168	3.95	0.79	2.37	3.95
❑ 169	3.95	0.79	2.37	3.95
❑ 170	3.95	0.79	2.37	3.95
❑ 171	3.95	0.79	2.37	3.95
❑ 172	3.95	0.79	2.37	3.95
❑ 173	3.95	0.79	2.37	3.95
❑ 174	4.50	0.90	2.70	4.50

	ORIG.	GOOD	FINE	N-MINT
❑ 175	3.95	0.79	2.37	3.95
❑ 176	3.95	0.79	2.37	3.95
❑ 177	3.95	0.79	2.37	3.95
❑ 178	3.95	0.79	2.37	3.95
❑ 179	3.95	0.79	2.37	3.95
❑ 180	4.50	0.90	2.70	4.50
❑ 181	4.50	0.90	2.70	4.50
❑ 182	4.50	0.90	2.70	4.50
❑ 183	4.50	0.90	2.70	4.50
❑ 184, (postcards)	4.50	0.90	2.70	4.50
❑ 185, (postcards)	4.50	0.90	2.70	4.50
❑ 186, (postcards)	4.50	0.90	2.70	4.50
❑ 187, (postcards)	4.50	0.90	2.70	4.50
❑ 188, (postcards)	4.50	0.90	2.70	4.50
❑ 189, (postcards)	4.50	0.90	2.70	4.50
❑ 195, (postcards)				
❑ 196, (postcards)	4.95	0.99	2.97	4.95
❑ 197	4.95	0.99	2.97	4.95
❑ 198	4.95	0.99	2.97	4.95
❑ 199	4.95	0.99	2.97	4.95
❑ 200	4.95	0.99	2.97	4.95

DOCTOR WHO SUMMER SPECIAL

	ORIG.	GOOD	FINE	N-MINT
❑ 0, 1985	3.95	0.79	2.37	3.95
❑ 0, 1986	3.50	0.70	2.10	3.50
❑ 0, 1991	4.50	0.90	2.70	4.50

DOCTOR WHO WINTER SPECIAL

	ORIG.	GOOD	FINE	N-MINT
❑ 0, 1985	2.50	0.50	1.50	2.50
❑ 0, 1985	3.00	0.60	1.80	3.00
❑ 0, 1986	3.75	0.75	2.25	3.75
❑ 0, 1991	4.50	0.90	2.70	4.50
❑ 0, 1992	4.50	0.90	2.70	4.50

DOCTOR WHO YEARBOOK (hardcover)

	ORIG.	GOOD	FINE	N-MINT
❑ 0, 1992	8.95	1.79	5.37	8.95
❑ 0, 1993	8.95	1.79	5.37	8.95

DOCTOR ZERO
EPIC

	ORIG.	GOOD	FINE	N-MINT
❑ 1, Apr 88, BSz(c)	1.25	0.30	0.90	1.50
❑ 2, Jun 88, BSz(c)	1.25	0.30	0.90	1.50
❑ 3, Aug 88	1.25	0.30	0.90	1.50
❑ 4, Oct 88	1.50	0.30	0.90	1.50
❑ 5, Dec 88	1.50	0.30	0.90	1.50
❑ 6, Feb 89	1.50	0.30	0.90	1.50
❑ 7, Apr 89	1.50	0.30	0.90	1.50
❑ 8, Jun 89	1.50	0.30	0.90	1.50

DODEKAIN
ANTARCTIC

	ORIG.	GOOD	FINE	N-MINT
❑ 1, Nov 94, b&w	2.95	0.59	1.77	2.95
❑ 2, Dec 94, b&w	2.95	0.59	1.77	2.95
❑ 3, Jan 95, b&w	2.95	0.59	1.77	2.95
❑ 4, Feb 95, b&w	2.95	0.59	1.77	2.95
❑ 5, Mar 95, b&w	2.95	0.59	1.77	2.95
❑ 6, Apr 95, b&w	2.95	0.59	1.77	2.95
❑ 7, May 95, b&w	2.95	0.59	1.77	2.95
❑ 8, Jun 95, b&w; final issue	2.95	0.59	1.77	2.95

DOG
REBEL

	ORIG.	GOOD	FINE	N-MINT
❑ 1, b&w		0.45	1.35	2.25
❑ 2, b&w		0.45	1.35	2.25

DOG BOY
FANTAGRAPHICS

	ORIG.	GOOD	FINE	N-MINT
❑ 1		0.35	1.05	1.75
❑ 2		0.35	1.05	1.75
❑ 3		0.35	1.05	1.75
❑ 4		0.35	1.05	1.75
❑ 5		0.35	1.05	1.75
❑ 6		0.35	1.05	1.75
❑ 7		0.35	1.05	1.75
❑ 8		0.35	1.05	1.75
❑ 9		0.35	1.05	1.75

	ORIG.	GOOD	FINE	N-MINT

DOG MOON
DC/VERTIGO
	ORIG.	GOOD	FINE	N-MINT
❑ 0, 96, nn;one-shot	6.95	1.39	4.17	6.95

DOG SOUP
DOG SOUP
		GOOD	FINE	N-MINT
❑ 1, b&w		0.50	1.50	2.50

DOG T.A.G.S.: TRAINED ANIMAL GUN SQUADRON
BUGGED OUT
	ORIG.	GOOD	FINE	N-MINT
❑ 1, Jun 93, b&w	1.95	0.39	1.17	1.95

DOGS OF WAR
DEFIANT
	ORIG.	GOOD	FINE	N-MINT
❑ 1, Apr 94	2.50	0.50	1.50	2.50
❑ 3, Jun 94	2.50	0.50	1.50	2.50

DOIN' TIME WITH OJ
BONEYARD
	ORIG.	GOOD	FINE	N-MINT
❑ 0, Dec 94, b&w	2.95	0.59	1.77	2.95

DOJINSHI
ANTARCTIC
	ORIG.	GOOD	FINE	N-MINT
❑ 1, Oct 92, b&w	2.95	0.59	1.77	2.95
❑ 2, Dec 92, b&w	2.95	0.59	1.77	2.95
❑ 3, Feb 93, b&w	2.95	0.59	1.77	2.95
❑ 4, Apr 93, b&w	2.95	0.59	1.77	2.95

DOLL
RIP OFF
	ORIG.	GOOD	FINE	N-MINT
❑ 1, Feb 89, b&w;adult	2.50	0.50	1.50	2.50
❑ 2, Mar 89, b&w;adult	2.50	0.50	1.50	2.50
❑ 3, May 89, b&w;adult	2.50	0.50	1.50	2.50
❑ 4, Feb 90, b&w;adult	2.50	0.50	1.50	2.50
❑ 5, Mar 91, b&w;adult	2.50	0.50	1.50	2.50
❑ 6, May 91, b&w;adult	2.50	0.50	1.50	2.50
❑ 7, Jun 91, b&w;adult	2.50	0.50	1.50	2.50
❑ 8, Sep 92, b&w, adult	2.95	0.59	1.77	2.95

DOLLMAN
ETERNITY
	ORIG.	GOOD	FINE	N-MINT
❑ 1, Nov 91, movie tie-in, color		0.50	1.50	2.50
❑ 2, movie tie-in, color		0.50	1.50	2.50
❑ 3, movie tie-in, color		0.50	1.50	2.50
❑ 4, movie tie-in, color		0.50	1.50	2.50

DOMINION
ECLIPSE
		GOOD	FINE	N-MINT
❑ 1, b&w, Japanese		0.80	2.40	4.00
❑ 2, b&w, Japanese		0.60	1.80	3.00
❑ 3, b&w, Japanese		0.60	1.80	3.00
❑ 4, b&w, Japanese		0.40	1.20	2.00
❑ 5, b&w, Japanese		0.40	1.20	2.00
❑ 6, b&w, Japanese		0.40	1.20	2.00

DOMINION: CONFLICT 1 (mini-series)
DARK HORSE/MANGA
	ORIG.	GOOD	FINE	N-MINT
❑ 2, Apr 96, b&w	2.95	0.59	1.77	2.95
❑ 3, May 96, b&w	2.95	0.59	1.77	2.95

DOMINION: PHANTOM OF THE AUDIENCE
DARK HORSE
	ORIG.	GOOD	FINE	N-MINT
❑ 0, 94, nn	2.50	0.50	1.50	2.50

DOMINIQUE: FAMILY MATTERS
CALIBER
	ORIG.	GOOD	FINE	N-MINT
❑ 1, 94, b&w	2.95	0.59	1.77	2.95

DOMINIQUE: KILLZONE
	ORIG.	GOOD	FINE	N-MINT
❑ 1, 95, b&w;one-shot	2.95	0.59	1.77	2.95

DOMINIQUE: PROTECT & SERVE
	ORIG.	GOOD	FINE	N-MINT
❑ 1, 95, b&w one-shot	2.95	0.59	1.77	2.95

DOMINIQUE: WHITE KNUCKLE DRIVE
	ORIG.	GOOD	FINE	N-MINT
❑ 1, 94, b&w, one-shot	2.95	0.59	1.77	2.95

DOMINO CHANCE
CHANCE
	ORIG.	GOOD	FINE	N-MINT
❑ 1, 1st printing;b&w	1.50	1.20	3.60	6.00
❑ 1, 2nd printing;b&w	1.50	0.30	0.90	1.50
❑ 2, b&w	1.50	0.30	0.90	1.50
❑ 3, b&w	1.50	0.30	0.90	1.50

	ORIG.	GOOD	FINE	N-MINT
❑ 4, b&w	1.50	0.30	0.90	1.50
❑ 5, b&w	1.50	0.30	0.90	1.50
❑ 6, b&w	1.50	0.30	0.90	1.50
❑ 7, 1:Gizmo;b&w	1.50	1.00	3.00	5.00
❑ 8, 2:Gizmo;b&w	1.50	0.60	1.80	3.00
❑ 9, b&w	1.50	0.30	0.90	1.50

DOMINO CHANCE: ROACH EXTRAORDINAIRE
AMAZING
		GOOD	FINE	N-MINT
❑ 1		0.39	1.17	1.95

DOMINO LADY
EROS COMIX
		GOOD	FINE	N-MINT
❑ 1, Dec 90, adult, b&w		0.39	1.17	1.95
❑ 2, Jan 91, adult, b&w		0.39	1.17	1.95

DOMINO LADY'S JUNGLE ADVENTURE
EROS
		GOOD	FINE	N-MINT
❑ 1, adult, b&w		0.50	1.50	2.50

DON MARTIN MAGAZINE
WELSH
	ORIG.	GOOD	FINE	N-MINT
❑ 1, poster	2.50	0.50	1.50	2.50
❑ 2, poster	2.50	0.50	1.50	2.50
❑ 3	2.50	0.50	1.50	2.50

DON PENDLETON'S MACK BOLAN: THE EXECUTIONER
INNOVATION
	ORIG.	GOOD	FINE	N-MINT
❑ 1, "indestructible" cover	3.95	0.79	2.37	3.95
❑ 1, black outer cover with red X	3.50	0.70	2.10	3.50
❑ 1, Jul 93, Enhanced cardstock cover; adapts "War Against the Mafia"	2.95	0.59	1.77	2.95
❑ 2, Aug 93, Adapts "War Against the Mafia"	2.50	0.50	1.50	2.50
❑ 3, Nov 93, Adapts "War Against the Mafia"	2.50	0.50	1.50	2.50

DON SIMPSON'S BIZARRE HEROES
FIASCO
	ORIG.	GOOD	FINE	N-MINT
❑ 0, Dec 94, b&w	2.95	0.59	1.77	2.95
❑ 1, May 94, b&w	2.95	0.59	1.77	2.95
❑ 2, Jun 94, b&w	2.95	0.59	1.77	2.95
❑ 3, Jul 94, b&w	2.95	0.59	1.77	2.95
❑ 4, Aug 94, b&w	2.95	0.59	1.77	2.95
❑ 5, Sep 94, b&w	2.95	0.59	1.77	2.95
❑ 6, Oct 94, b&w	2.95	0.59	1.77	2.95
❑ 7, Nov 94, b&w	2.95	0.59	1.77	2.95
❑ 8, Dec 94, b&w; (becomes *Bizarre Heroes*)	2.95	0.59	1.77	2.95

DON WINSLOW TROUBLE SHOOTER
AC
		GOOD	FINE	N-MINT
❑ 1, 91, reprints, b&w		0.55	1.65	2.75

DONALD AND MICKEY (was Mickey and Donald)
GLADSTONE
	ORIG.	GOOD	FINE	N-MINT
❑ 19, Sep 93	1.50	0.30	0.90	1.50
❑ 20, Nov 93, CB reprint; 64 pages	2.95	0.59	1.77	2.95
❑ 21, Jan 94, CB (reprint), WVH	1.50	0.30	0.90	1.50
❑ 22, Mar 94, CB reprint	1.50	0.30	0.90	1.50
❑ 23, May 94, CB reprint	1.50	0.30	0.90	1.50
❑ 24, Jul 94, CB reprint	1.50	0.30	0.90	1.50
❑ 25, Sep 94, 64 pages	2.95	0.59	1.77	2.95
❑ 26, Nov 94, newsstand distribution by Marvel	1.50	0.30	0.90	1.50
❑ 27, Jan 95	1.50	0.30	0.90	1.50
❑ 28, Mar 95	1.50	0.30	0.90	1.50
❑ 29, May 95	1.50	0.30	0.90	1.50
❑ 30, Jul 95	1.50	0.30	0.90	1.50

DONALD AND SCROOGE
DISNEY
		GOOD	FINE	N-MINT
❑ 0, nn, Don Rosa reprints	1.79	5.37	8.95

	ORIG.	GOOD	FINE	N-MINT

DONALD DUCK
GLADSTONE

	ORIG.	GOOD	FINE	N-MINT
☐ 246, CB		1.60	4.80	8.00
☐ 247, Nov 86, CB	0.75	1.00	3.00	5.00
☐ 248, Nov 86, CB	0.75	1.00	3.00	5.00
☐ 249, Jan 87, CB	0.75	1.00	3.00	5.00
☐ 250, rep: 1st CB comic		1.00	3.00	5.00
☐ 251, Mar 87, CB	0.75	0.80	2.40	4.00
☐ 252, CB		0.40	1.20	2.00
☐ 253, May 87, CB	0.75	0.40	1.20	2.00
☐ 254		0.80	2.40	4.00
☐ 255, Jul 87	0.95	0.40	1.20	2.00
☐ 256, Jul 87	0.95	0.40	1.20	2.00
☐ 257, CB forest fire		0.60	1.80	3.00
☐ 258, Oct 87, CB	0.95	0.40	1.20	2.00
☐ 259, Nov 87, CB	0.95	0.40	1.20	2.00
☐ 260, Dec 87, CB	0.95	0.40	1.20	2.00
☐ 261, Dec 87, CB	0.95	0.40	1.20	2.00
☐ 262, Mar 88, CB	0.95	0.40	1.20	2.00
☐ 263, Jun 88, CB	0.95	0.40	1.20	2.00
☐ 264, Jul 88, CB	0.95	0.40	1.20	2.00
☐ 265, Aug 88	0.95	0.60	1.80	3.00
☐ 266, Sep 88	0.95	0.40	1.20	2.00
☐ 267, Oct 88	0.95	0.40	1.20	2.00
☐ 268, Oct 88	0.95	0.40	1.20	2.00
☐ 269, Oct 88	0.95	0.40	1.20	2.00
☐ 270, Oct 88	0.95	0.40	1.20	2.00
☐ 271, Oct 88	0.95	0.40	1.20	2.00
☐ 272, Oct 88	0.95	0.40	1.20	2.00
☐ 273, Oct 88	0.95	0.40	1.20	2.00
☐ 274, Oct 88	0.95	0.40	1.20	2.00
☐ 275, CB,WK Donocchio		0.40	1.20	2.00
☐ 276, CB		0.40	1.20	2.00
☐ 277, CB		0.40	1.20	2.00
☐ 278, CB, Don Rosa		1.60	4.80	8.00
☐ 279, CB		0.80	2.40	4.00
☐ 280, Sep 93	1.50	0.30	0.90	1.50
☐ 281, Nov 93	1.50	0.30	0.90	1.50
☐ 282, Jan 94, CB reprint	1.50	0.30	0.90	1.50
☐ 283, Mar 94, Don Rosa	1.50	0.50	1.50	2.50
☐ 284, May 94, CB reprint; Al Taliaferro	1.50	0.30	0.90	1.50
☐ 285, Jul 94, CB reprint; Al Taliaferro	1.50	0.30	0.90	1.50
☐ 286, Sep 94, Donald Duck's 60th	2.95	0.59	1.77	2.95
☐ 287, Nov 94	1.50	0.30	0.90	1.50
☐ 288, Jan 95	1.50	0.30	0.90	1.50
☐ 289, Mar 95	1.50	0.30	0.90	1.50
☐ 290, May 95	1.50	0.30	0.90	1.50
☐ 291, Jul 95	1.50	0.30	0.90	1.50
☐ 292, Sep 95	1.50	0.30	0.90	1.50
☐ 293, Nov 95	1.50	0.30	0.90	1.50
☐ 294, Jan 96, CB reprint; "The Persistent Postman"	1.50	0.30	0.90	1.50

DONALD DUCK & MICKEY MOUSE

	ORIG.	GOOD	FINE	N-MINT
☐ 1, Sep 95, newsprint cover	1.50	0.30	0.90	1.50
☐ 2, Nov 95, newsprint cover	1.50	0.30	0.90	1.50

DONALD DUCK ADVENTURES
DISNEY

	ORIG.	GOOD	FINE	N-MINT
☐ 1, Jun 90, Don Rosa	1.50	1.20	3.60	6.00
☐ 2, CB, Wm. Van Horn		0.30	0.90	1.50
☐ 3, Wm. Van Horn		0.30	0.90	1.50
☐ 4, CB, Van Horn		0.30	0.90	1.50
☐ 5, Van Horn		0.30	0.90	1.50
☐ 6, Van Horn		0.30	0.90	1.50
☐ 7, Van Horn		0.30	0.90	1.50
☐ 8, Van Horn		0.30	0.90	1.50

	ORIG.	GOOD	FINE	N-MINT
☐ 9, CB, reprint of 1: Uncle Scrooge		0.30	0.90	1.50
☐ 10, Van Horn		0.30	0.90	1.50
☐ 11, Mad #1 cover parody		0.30	0.90	1.50
☐ 12	1.50	0.30	0.90	1.50
☐ 13, Van Horn		0.30	0.90	1.50
☐ 14, CB		0.30	0.90	1.50
☐ 15, Van Horn		0.30	0.90	1.50
☐ 16	1.50	0.30	0.90	1.50
☐ 17, CB	1.50	0.30	0.90	1.50
☐ 18, Van Horn		0.30	0.90	1.50
☐ 19, Van Horn		0.30	0.90	1.50
☐ 20, Van Horn		0.30	0.90	1.50
☐ 21, CB, golden Christmas tree		0.30	0.90	1.50
☐ 22, Mar 92, DR	1.50	0.30	0.90	1.50
☐ 23, CB	1.50	0.30	0.90	1.50
☐ 24, May 92, DR	1.50	0.30	0.90	1.50
☐ 25, map piece		0.30	0.90	1.50
☐ 26, CB, map piece		0.30	0.90	1.50
☐ 27, CB, map piece		0.30	0.90	1.50
☐ 28, CB		0.30	0.90	1.50
☐ 29, CB		0.30	0.90	1.50
☐ 30, CB		0.30	0.90	1.50
☐ 31, CB		0.30	0.90	1.50
☐ 32, CB		0.30	0.90	1.50
☐ 33		0.30	0.90	1.50
☐ 34, Mar 93, DR	1.50	0.30	0.90	1.50
☐ 35, CB reprints		0.30	0.90	1.50
☐ 36, CB reprints		0.30	0.90	1.50
☐ 37, Jun 93, CB reprints, DR	1.50	0.30	0.90	1.50

GLADSTONE

	ORIG.	GOOD	FINE	N-MINT
☐ 1, Nov 87, CB	0.95	1.00	3.00	5.00
☐ 2, CB		0.60	1.80	3.00
☐ 3, CB;"Lost in the Andes"		0.60	1.80	3.00
☐ 4, CB		0.60	1.80	3.00
☐ 5, Jul 88, CB, DR	0.95	1.00	3.00	5.00
☐ 6, Aug 88, CB	0.95	0.40	1.20	2.00
☐ 7, Aug 88, CB	0.95	0.40	1.20	2.00
☐ 8, Oct 88, CB, DR	0.95	1.00	3.00	5.00
☐ 9, CB		0.40	1.20	2.00
☐ 10, CB		0.40	1.20	2.00
☐ 11, CB		0.40	1.20	2.00
☐ 12, May 89, CB,DR; "Return to Plain Awful"	1.50	1.00	3.00	5.00
☐ 13, DR(c), CB		0.40	1.20	2.00
☐ 14, CB		0.40	1.20	2.00
☐ 15, CB		0.40	1.20	2.00
☐ 16, CB		0.40	1.20	2.00
☐ 17, CB		0.40	1.20	2.00
☐ 18, CB		0.40	1.20	2.00
☐ 19, CB		0.80	2.40	4.00
☐ 20, CB		0.80	2.40	4.00
☐ 21, Aug 93, DR(c), CB reprint	1.50	0.30	0.90	1.50
☐ 22, Oct 93, CB reprint; "The Pixalated Parrot"	1.50	0.30	0.90	1.50
☐ 23, Dec 93, DR(c)	1.50	0.30	0.90	1.50
☐ 24, Feb 94, WVH; "The Black Moon"	1.50	0.30	0.90	1.50
☐ 25, Apr 94	1.50	0.30	0.90	1.50
☐ 26, Jun 94, CB reprint; 64 pages	2.95	0.59	1.77	2.95
☐ 27, Aug 94	1.50	0.30	0.90	1.50
☐ 28, Oct 94, CB reprint; "Sheriff of Bullet Valley"; cover uses portion of Barks painting	1.50	0.30	0.90	1.50
☐ 29, Dec 94, newsstand distribution by Marvel	1.50	0.30	0.90	1.50
☐ 30, Feb 95, CB reprint; "Christmas for Shacktown"; 64 pages	2.95	0.59	1.77	2.95
☐ 31, Apr 95	1.50	0.30	0.90	1.50

	ORIG.	GOOD	FINE	N-MINT
32, Jun 95	1.50	0.30	0.90	1.50
33, Aug 95, CB reprint; "The Golden Helmet"				
	1.95	0.39	1.17	1.95
34, Oct 95, first newsprint cover				
	1.50	0.30	0.90	1.50
35, Dec 95	1.50	0.30	0.90	1.50
36, Feb 96	1.50	0.30	0.90	1.50

DONALD DUCK DIGEST

	ORIG.	GOOD	FINE	N-MINT
1		0.70	2.10	3.50
2		0.60	1.80	3.00
3		0.60	1.80	3.00
4		0.60	1.80	3.00
5		0.40	1.20	2.00

DONATELLO
MIRAGE

	ORIG.	GOOD	FINE	N-MINT
1		1.40	4.20	7.00

DONIELLE: ENSLAVED AT SEA
RAGING RHINO

	ORIG.	GOOD	FINE	N-MINT
1, adult, b&w	2.95	0.59	1.77	2.95
2, adult, b&w	2.95	0.59	1.77	2.95
3, adult, b&w	2.95	0.59	1.77	2.95
4, adult, b&w	2.95	0.59	1.77	2.95

DOOFER
FANTAGRAPHICS

	ORIG.	GOOD	FINE	N-MINT
1, b&w		0.55	1.65	2.75

DOOFUS

	ORIG.	GOOD	FINE	N-MINT
1, Dec 94, b&w	2.75	0.55	1.65	2.75

DOOM 2099
MARVEL

	ORIG.	GOOD	FINE	N-MINT
1, silver cover	1.75	0.45	1.35	2.25
2	1.25	0.25	0.75	1.25
3	1.25	0.25	0.75	1.25
4	1.25	0.25	0.75	1.25
5	1.25	0.25	0.75	1.25
6	1.25	0.25	0.75	1.25
7	1.25	0.25	0.75	1.25
8	1.25	0.25	0.75	1.25
9	1.25	0.25	0.75	1.25
10	1.25	0.25	0.75	1.25
11	1.25	0.25	0.75	1.25
12	1.25	0.25	0.75	1.25
13	1.25	0.25	0.75	1.25
14	1.25	0.25	0.75	1.25
15	1.25	0.25	0.75	1.25
16	1.25	0.25	0.75	1.25
17, May 94	1.50	0.30	0.90	1.50
18, May 94, poster	1.50	0.30	0.90	1.50
19, Jul 94	1.50	0.30	0.90	1.50
20, Aug 94	1.50	0.30	0.90	1.50
21, Sep 94	1.50	0.30	0.90	1.50
22, Oct 94	1.50	0.30	0.90	1.50
23, Nov 94	1.50	0.30	0.90	1.50
24, Dec 94	1.50	0.30	0.90	1.50
25, Jan 95, enhanced cover				
	2.95	0.59	1.77	2.95
26, Feb 95	1.50	0.30	0.90	1.50
27, Mar 95	1.50	0.30	0.90	1.50
28, Apr 95	1.50	0.30	0.90	1.50
29, May 95, enhanced acetate overlay cover				
	3.50	0.70	2.10	3.50
29, May 95	1.95	0.39	1.17	1.95
30, Jun 95	1.95	0.39	1.17	1.95
31, Jul 95	1.95	0.39	1.17	1.95
32, Aug 95	1.95	0.39	1.17	1.95
33, Sep 95	1.95	0.39	1.17	1.95
34, Oct 95	1.95	0.39	1.17	1.95
35, Nov 95	1.95	0.39	1.17	1.95
36, Dec 95	1.95	0.39	1.17	1.95
37, Jan 96	1.95	0.39	1.17	1.95
38, Feb 96	1.95	0.39	1.17	1.95

	ORIG.	GOOD	FINE	N-MINT
39, Mar 96	1.95	0.39	1.17	1.95
40, Apr 96, Doom 2099 comes to present				
	1.95	0.39	1.17	1.95
41, May 96, V:Namor, Daredevil				
	1.95	0.39	1.17	1.95
42, Jun 96, V:FF	1.95	0.39	1.17	1.95
43, Jul 96	1.95	0.39	1.17	1.95

DOOM FORCE
DC

	ORIG.	GOOD	FINE	N-MINT
1, X-Force parody		0.59	1.77	2.95

DOOM PATROL

	ORIG.	GOOD	FINE	N-MINT
1, Oct 87	0.75	0.40	1.20	2.00
2, Nov 87	0.75	0.35	1.05	1.75
3, Dec 87	0.75	0.35	1.05	1.75
4, Jan 88	0.75	0.35	1.05	1.75
5, Feb 88	0.75	0.35	1.05	1.75
6, Mar 88	0.75	0.35	1.05	1.75
7, Apr 88	0.75	0.35	1.05	1.75
8, May 88, AAd(ci)	0.75	0.35	1.05	1.75
9, Jun 88, Bonus Book	0.75	0.35	1.05	1.75
10, Jul 88, A:Superman	0.75	0.20	0.60	1.00
11, Aug 88	1.00	0.20	0.60	1.00
12, Sep 88	1.00	0.20	0.60	1.00
13, Oct 88	1.00	0.20	0.60	1.00
14, Nov 88, A:Power Girl	1.00	0.20	0.60	1.00
15, Dec 88	1.00	0.20	0.60	1.00
16, Dec 88	1.00	0.20	0.60	1.00
17, Jan 89, D:Celsius, Invasion!				
	1.00	0.20	0.60	1.00
18, Jan 89, Invasion!	1.00	0.20	0.60	1.00
19, Feb 89, 1: Grant Morrison				
	1.50	1.40	4.20	7.00
20, Mar 89	1.50	1.00	3.00	5.00
21, Apr 89	1.50	1.00	3.00	5.00
22, May 89	1.50	1.00	3.00	5.00
23, Jun 89	1.50	1.00	3.00	5.00
24, Jul 89	1.50	1.00	3.00	5.00
25, Aug 89	1.50	1.00	3.00	5.00
26, Sep 89	1.50	1.00	3.00	5.00
27, Nov 89	1.50	1.00	3.00	5.00
28, Dec 89	1.50	0.80	2.40	4.00
29, Jan 90, Superman, JLI				
	1.50	1.00	3.00	5.00
30, Feb 90	1.50	0.50	1.50	2.50
31, Apr 90	1.50	0.50	1.50	2.50
32, May 90	1.50	0.50	1.50	2.50
33, Jun 90	1.50	0.30	0.90	1.50
34, Jul 90	1.50	0.30	0.90	1.50
35, Aug 90	1.50	0.30	0.90	1.50
36, Sep 90	1.50	0.30	0.90	1.50
37, Oct 90	1.50	0.30	0.90	1.50
38, Nov 90	1.50	0.30	0.90	1.50
39, Dec 90	1.50	0.30	0.90	1.50
40, Jan 91	1.50	0.30	0.90	1.50
41, Feb 91	1.50	0.30	0.90	1.50
42, Mar 91	1.50	0.30	0.90	1.50
43, Apr 91		0.30	0.90	1.50
44, May 91		0.30	0.90	1.50
45, Jul 91		0.30	0.90	1.50
46, Aug 91		0.30	0.90	1.50
47, Sep 91		0.30	0.90	1.50
48, Oct 91		0.30	0.90	1.50
49, Nov 91		0.30	0.90	1.50
50, Dec 91		0.50	1.50	2.50
51		0.30	0.90	1.50
52		0.30	0.90	1.50
53, Mar 92, Fantastic 4 parody				
	1.50	0.30	0.90	1.50
54, photo cover		0.30	0.90	1.50
55		0.30	0.90	1.50
56		0.30	0.90	1.50

	ORIG.	GOOD	FINE	N-MINT
57		0.50	1.50	2.50
58		0.30	0.90	1.50
59		0.30	0.90	1.50
60		0.30	0.90	1.50

DC/VERTIGO

	ORIG.	GOOD	FINE	N-MINT
61	1.75	0.35	1.05	1.75
62	1.75	0.35	1.05	1.75
63	1.75	0.35	1.05	1.75
64	1.75	0.35	1.05	1.75
65	1.75	0.35	1.05	1.75
66	1.75	0.35	1.05	1.75
67	1.95	0.39	1.17	1.95
68	1.95	0.39	1.17	1.95
69	1.95	0.39	1.17	1.95
70	1.95	0.39	1.17	1.95
71	1.95	0.39	1.17	1.95
72	1.95	0.39	1.17	1.95
73	1.95	0.39	1.17	1.95
74	1.95	0.39	1.17	1.95
75	1.95	0.39	1.17	1.95
76	1.95	0.39	1.17	1.95
77, Apr 94	1.95	0.39	1.17	1.95
78, May 94	1.95	0.39	1.17	1.95
79, Jun 94	1.95	0.39	1.17	1.95
80, Jul 94	1.95	0.39	1.17	1.95
81, Aug 94	1.95	0.39	1.17	1.95
82, Sep 94	1.95	0.39	1.17	1.95
83, Oct 94	1.95	0.39	1.17	1.95
84, Nov 94	1.95	0.39	1.17	1.95
85, Dec 94	1.95	0.39	1.17	1.95
86, Jan 95	1.95	0.39	1.17	1.95
87, Feb 95, final issue	1.95	0.39	1.17	1.95

DOOM PATROL (formerly My Greatest Adventure)
DC

	ORIG.	GOOD	FINE	N-MINT
86, BP		16.00	48.00	80.00
87, BP		12.00	36.00	60.00
88		10.00	30.00	50.00
89		10.00	30.00	50.00
90		10.00	30.00	50.00
91		10.00	30.00	50.00
92		10.00	30.00	50.00
93		10.00	30.00	50.00
94		10.00	30.00	50.00
95		10.00	30.00	50.00
96		10.00	30.00	50.00
97		10.00	30.00	50.00
98		10.00	30.00	50.00
99		10.00	30.00	50.00
100, BP		9.60	28.80	48.00
101, BP		4.00	12.00	20.00
102, BP		4.00	12.00	20.00
103, BP		4.00	12.00	20.00
104, BP		4.00	12.00	20.00
105, BP		4.00	12.00	20.00
106, BP		4.00	12.00	20.00
107, BP		4.00	12.00	20.00
108, BP		4.00	12.00	20.00
109, BP		4.00	12.00	20.00
110, BP		4.00	12.00	20.00
111, BP		4.00	12.00	20.00
112, BP		4.00	12.00	20.00
113, BP		4.00	12.00	20.00
114, BP		4.00	12.00	20.00
115, BP		4.00	12.00	20.00
116, BP		4.00	12.00	20.00
117, BP		4.00	12.00	20.00
118, BP		4.00	12.00	20.00
119, BP		4.00	12.00	20.00
120, BP		4.00	12.00	20.00
121, JO, D:Doom Patrol		10.00	30.00	50.00
122, rep.		0.80	2.40	4.00
123, rep.		0.80	2.40	4.00
124, rep.		0.80	2.40	4.00

DOOM PATROL AND SUICIDE SQUAD SPECIAL

	ORIG.	GOOD	FINE	N-MINT
1, Feb 88	1.50	0.30	0.90	1.50

DOOM PATROL ANNUAL

	ORIG.	GOOD	FINE	N-MINT
1, Jan 89	1.50	0.30	0.90	1.50
2, Children's Crusade	3.95	0.79	2.37	3.95

DOOM'S IV (mini-series)
IMAGE

	ORIG.	GOOD	FINE	N-MINT
1, Jul 94	2.50	0.80	2.40	4.00
2, Aug 94	2.50	0.50	1.50	2.50
3, Sep 94	2.50	0.50	1.50	2.50
4, Oct 94	2.50	0.50	1.50	2.50

DOOMSDAY ANNUAL
DC

	ORIG.	GOOD	FINE	N-MINT
1, 95	3.95	0.79	2.37	3.95

DOOMSDAY SQUAD
FANTAGRAPHICS

	ORIG.	GOOD	FINE	N-MINT
1, Aug 86, JBy	2.00	0.40	1.20	2.00
2, JBy	2.00	0.40	1.20	2.00
3, JBy	2.00	0.40	1.20	2.00
4, JBy	2.00	0.40	1.20	2.00
5, JBy	2.00	0.40	1.20	2.00
6, JBy	2.00	0.40	1.20	2.00
7, JBy	2.00	0.40	1.20	2.00

DOOMSDAY+1
CHARLTON

	ORIG.	GOOD	FINE	N-MINT
1, 75		1.00	3.00	5.00
2		0.60	1.80	3.00
3		0.60	1.80	3.00
4		0.60	1.80	3.00
5		0.60	1.80	3.00
6		0.60	1.80	3.00

DOOR MAN
CULT PRESS

	ORIG.	GOOD	FINE	N-MINT
1, ashcan		1.00	3.00	5.00
2, b&w	2.95	0.59	1.77	2.95

DOORWAY TO NIGHTMARE
DC

	ORIG.	GOOD	FINE	N-MINT
1, Feb 78	0.35	0.07	0.21	0.35
2, Apr 78	0.35	0.07	0.21	0.35
3, Jun 78	0.35	0.07	0.21	0.35
4, Aug 78	0.35	0.07	0.21	0.35
5, Oct 78	0.50	0.10	0.30	0.50

DORK HOUSE COMICS
PARODY PRESS

	ORIG.	GOOD	FINE	N-MINT
0	2.50	0.50	1.50	2.50

DORKIER IMAGES

	ORIG.	GOOD	FINE	N-MINT
1, gold, silver blue edition	2.95	0.59	1.77	2.95
1, standard edition	2.50	0.50	1.50	2.50

DOUBLE DRAGON
MARVEL

	ORIG.	GOOD	FINE	N-MINT
1	1.00	0.20	0.60	1.00
2	1.00	0.20	0.60	1.00
3	1.00	0.20	0.60	1.00
4	1.00	0.20	0.60	1.00
5	1.00	0.20	0.60	1.00
6	1.00	0.20	0.60	1.00

DOUBLE EDGE: OMEGA

	ORIG.	GOOD	FINE	N-MINT
0, Oct 95, D:Nick Fury; enhanced wraparound cover	4.95	0.99	2.97	4.95

DOUBLE IMPACT
HIGH IMPACT

0, 95, nn;no cover price;no indicia;gray polybag; preview of *Double Impact* #3 and 4;San Diego Comic-Con ed.

	ORIG.	GOOD	FINE	N-MINT

☐ 0, 95, nn;no cover price;no indicia;black polybag; letters pages and pin-ups;limited to 5000
☐ 4, Sep 95, no cover price;no information on cover whatsoever

DR. ANDY
ALLIANCE

	ORIG.	GOOD	FINE	N-MINT
☐ 1, Aug 94, b&w	2.50	0.50	1.50	2.50

DR. GIGGLES
DARK HORSE

		GOOD	FINE	N-MINT
☐ 1, 92, movie		0.50	1.50	2.50
☐ 2, 92, movie		0.50	1.50	2.50

DR. RADIUM, MAN OF SCIENCE
SLAVE LABOR

	ORIG.	GOOD	FINE	N-MINT
☐ 1, b&w	2.50	0.50	1.50	2.50
☐ 2, b&w	2.50	0.50	1.50	2.50
☐ 3	2.95	0.59	1.77	2.95

DR. WEIRD SPECIAL
CALIBER/BIG BANG

	ORIG.	GOOD	FINE	N-MINT
☐ 1, Feb 94, b&w	3.95	0.79	2.37	3.95

DR. ZOMB'S HOUSE OF FREAKS
STARHEAD

	ORIG.	GOOD	FINE	N-MINT
☐ 1, b&w	2.75	0.55	1.65	2.75

DRACULA
ETERNITY

		GOOD	FINE	N-MINT
☐ 1, 1st printing		0.70	2.10	3.50
☐ 1, 2nd printing		0.50	1.50	2.50
☐ 2, b&w		0.50	1.50	2.50
☐ 3, b&w		0.50	1.50	2.50
☐ 4, b&w		0.50	1.50	2.50

DRACULA 3-D
3-D ZONE

		GOOD	FINE	N-MINT
☐ 0, nn		0.79	2.37	3.95

DRACULA IN HELL
APPLE

		GOOD	FINE	N-MINT
☐ 1, adult, b&w		0.50	1.50	2.50
☐ 2, adult, b&w		0.50	1.50	2.50

DRACULA LIVES! (b&w mag)
MARVEL

	ORIG.	GOOD	FINE	N-MINT
☐ 1	0.75	0.15	0.45	0.75
☐ 2, 73	0.75	0.15	0.45	0.75
☐ 3	0.75	0.15	0.45	0.75
☐ 4	0.75	0.15	0.45	0.75
☐ 5	0.75	0.15	0.45	0.75
☐ 6	0.75	0.15	0.45	0.75
☐ 7	0.75	0.15	0.45	0.75
☐ 8	0.75	0.15	0.45	0.75
☐ 9	0.75	0.15	0.45	0.75
☐ 10	0.75	0.15	0.45	0.75
☐ 11	0.75	0.15	0.45	0.75
☐ 12	0.75	0.15	0.45	0.75
☐ 13	0.75	0.15	0.45	0.75

DRACULA LIVES! ANNUAL (b&w mag)

		GOOD	FINE	N-MINT
☐ 1	1.25	0.25	0.75	1.25

DRACULA VERSUS ZORRO (Volume 2)
TOPPS

	ORIG.	GOOD	FINE	N-MINT
☐ 1, Apr 94	5.95	1.19	3.57	5.95

DRACULA VS. ZORRO

	ORIG.	GOOD	FINE	N-MINT
☐ 1, TY	2.95	0.80	2.40	4.00

DRACULA'S DAUGHTER
EROS

		GOOD	FINE	N-MINT
☐ 1, adult, b&w		0.50	1.50	2.50

DRACULA: RETURN OF THE IMPALER
SLAVE LABOR

	ORIG.	GOOD	FINE	N-MINT
☐ 1, Jul 93	2.95	0.59	1.77	2.95
☐ 2, Jul 93	2.95	0.59	1.77	2.95

DRACULA: THE LADY IN THE TOMB
ETERNITY

		GOOD	FINE	N-MINT
☐ 1, b&w		0.50	1.50	2.50

DRACULA: THE SUICIDE CLUB
ADVENTURE

		GOOD	FINE	N-MINT
☐ 1, b&w		0.50	1.50	2.50
☐ 2, b&w		0.50	1.50	2.50
☐ 3, b&w		0.50	1.50	2.50
☐ 4, b&w		0.50	1.50	2.50

DRACULA: VLAD THE IMPALER
TOPPS

	ORIG.	GOOD	FINE	N-MINT
☐ 1, trading cards	2.95	0.59	1.77	2.95
☐ 2, trading cards	2.95	0.59	1.77	2.95
☐ 3, trading cards	2.95	0.59	1.77	2.95

DRACULINA'S COZY COFFIN
DRACULINA

	ORIG.	GOOD	FINE	N-MINT
☐ 1, 94, b&w; no indicia	2.50	0.50	1.50	2.50
☐ 2, 94, b&w; no indicia	2.50	0.50	1.50	2.50

DRAFT, THE
MARVEL

	ORIG.	GOOD	FINE	N-MINT
☐ 1, Jul 88, D.P.7, Nightmask	3.50	0.70	2.10	3.50

DRAGON
COMICS INTERVIEW

		GOOD	FINE	N-MINT
☐ 1, Aug 87, weekly		0.35	1.05	1.75
☐ 2, Aug 87, weekly		0.35	1.05	1.75
☐ 3, Aug 87, weekly		0.35	1.05	1.75
☐ 4, Aug 87, weekly		0.35	1.05	1.75

DRAGON LADY
DRAGON LADY PRESS

		GOOD	FINE	N-MINT
☐ 1, King of Mounted		1.39	4.17	6.95
☐ 2, Red Ryder		1.39	4.17	6.95
☐ 3, Capt. Easy		1.19	3.57	5.95
☐ 4, AW,Secret Agent X-9		1.19	3.57	5.95
☐ 5, Brick Bradford		1.19	3.57	5.95
☐ 6, ATh(c) Secret Agent X-9		1.19	3.57	5.95
☐ 7, Capt. Easy		1.19	3.57	5.95
☐ 8, ATh(c) Terry		1.19	3.57	5.95

DRAGON LINES
EPIC

	ORIG.	GOOD	FINE	N-MINT
☐ 1, embossed cover	2.50	0.50	1.50	2.50
☐ 2	1.95	0.39	1.17	1.95
☐ 3	1.95	0.39	1.17	1.95
☐ 4	1.95	0.39	1.17	1.95

DRAGON LINES: WAY OF THE WARRIOR

	ORIG.	GOOD	FINE	N-MINT
☐ 1	2.25	0.45	1.35	2.25
☐ 2	2.25	0.45	1.35	2.25

DRAGON OF THE VALKYR
RAK

	ORIG.	GOOD	FINE	N-MINT
☐ 1, b&w	1.75	0.35	1.05	1.75
☐ 2		0.40	1.20	2.00
☐ 3		0.40	1.20	2.00

DRAGON QUEST
SILVERWOLF

		GOOD	FINE	N-MINT
☐ 1, Tim Vigil b&w		2.40	7.20	12.00
☐ 2, Tim Vigil		1.60	4.80	8.00

DRAGON'S CLAWS
MARVEL

	ORIG.	GOOD	FINE	N-MINT
☐ 1	1.25	0.40	1.20	2.00
☐ 2	1.50	0.30	0.90	1.50
☐ 3		0.30	0.90	1.50
☐ 4		0.30	0.90	1.50
☐ 5	1.75	0.35	1.05	1.75
☐ 6	1.75	0.35	1.05	1.75
☐ 7	1.75	0.35	1.05	1.75
☐ 8	1.75	0.35	1.05	1.75
☐ 9	1.75	0.35	1.05	1.75
☐ 10	1.75	0.35	1.05	1.75

DRAGON'S STAR
MATRIX

		GOOD	FINE	N-MINT
☐ 1		0.35	1.05	1.75
☐ 2		0.35	1.05	1.75
☐ 3		0.35	1.05	1.75

	ORIG.	GOOD	FINE	N-MINT

DRAGON'S TEETH
DRAGON'S TEETH
	ORIG.	GOOD	FINE	N-MINT
1, b&w		0.59	1.77	2.95

DRAGON, THE (mini-series)
IMAGE
	ORIG.	GOOD	FINE	N-MINT
1, Apr 96	0.99	0.20	0.59	0.99
2, Apr 96	2.50	0.50	1.50	2.50
3, May 96	0.99	0.20	0.59	0.99

DRAGONFIRE (Volume I)
NIGHTWYND
	GOOD	FINE	N-MINT
1, b&w	0.50	1.50	2.50
2, b&w	0.50	1.50	2.50
3, b&w	0.50	1.50	2.50
4, b&w	0.50	1.50	2.50

DRAGONFIRE (Volume II)
	GOOD	FINE	N-MINT
1, b&w	0.50	1.50	2.50
2, b&w	0.50	1.50	2.50
3, b&w	0.50	1.50	2.50
4, b&w	0.50	1.50	2.50

DRAGONFIRE: THE CLASSIFIED FILES
	GOOD	FINE	N-MINT
1, b&w	0.50	1.50	2.50
2, b&w	0.50	1.50	2.50
3, b&w	0.50	1.50	2.50
4, b&w	0.50	1.50	2.50

DRAGONFIRE: UFO WARS
	GOOD	FINE	N-MINT
1, b&w	0.50	1.50	2.50
2, b&w	0.50	1.50	2.50
3, b&w	0.50	1.50	2.50

DRAGONFLIGHT
ECLIPSE
	GOOD	FINE	N-MINT
1, Anne McCaffrey	0.99	2.97	4.95
2, Anne McCaffrey	0.99	2.97	4.95
3, Anne McCaffrey	0.99	2.97	4.95

DRAGONFLY
AC
	GOOD	FINE	N-MINT
1, Aug 85	0.60	1.80	3.00
2, 85	0.35	1.05	1.75
3, 86	0.35	1.05	1.75
4, 86	0.35	1.05	1.75
5, 86	0.35	1.05	1.75
6, Feb 87	0.35	1.05	1.75
7, Jul 87	0.35	1.05	1.75
8, 87	0.39	1.17	1.95

DRAGONFORCE
AIRCEL
	GOOD	FINE	N-MINT
1, b&w	0.39	1.17	1.95
2, b&w	0.39	1.17	1.95
3, b&w	0.39	1.17	1.95
4, b&w	0.39	1.17	1.95
5, b&w	0.39	1.17	1.95
6, b&w	0.39	1.17	1.95
7, b&w	0.39	1.17	1.95
8, b&w	0.39	1.17	1.95
9, b&w	0.39	1.17	1.95
10, b&w	0.39	1.17	1.95
11, b&w	0.39	1.17	1.95
12, b&w	0.39	1.17	1.95
13, b&w	0.39	1.17	1.95

DRAGONFORCE CHRONICLES
	GOOD	FINE	N-MINT
1, rep. b&w	0.59	1.77	2.95
2, rep. b&w	0.59	1.77	2.95
3, rep. b&w	0.59	1.77	2.95
4, rep. b&w	0.59	1.77	2.95
5, rep. b&w	0.59	1.77	2.95

DRAGONLANCE
DC
	GOOD	FINE	N-MINT
1	1.60	4.80	8.00
2	1.20	3.60	6.00
3	1.00	3.00	5.00

	ORIG.	GOOD	FINE	N-MINT
4		1.00	3.00	5.00
5		1.00	3.00	5.00
6		0.80	2.40	4.00
7		0.80	2.40	4.00
8		0.80	2.40	4.00
9		0.80	2.40	4.00
10		0.80	2.40	4.00
11		0.60	1.80	3.00
12		0.60	1.80	3.00
13		0.60	1.80	3.00
14		0.60	1.80	3.00
15		0.60	1.80	3.00
16		0.60	1.80	3.00
17		0.60	1.80	3.00
18		0.60	1.80	3.00
19		0.60	1.80	3.00
20		0.60	1.80	3.00
21		0.60	1.80	3.00
22		0.60	1.80	3.00
23		0.60	1.80	3.00
24		0.60	1.80	3.00
25		0.40	1.20	2.00
26		0.40	1.20	2.00
27		0.40	1.20	2.00
28		0.40	1.20	2.00
29		0.40	1.20	2.00
30		0.40	1.20	2.00
31		0.40	1.20	2.00
32		0.40	1.20	2.00
33		0.40	1.20	2.00
34		0.40	1.20	2.00

DRAGONLANCE SAGA
TSR INC.
	GOOD	FINE	N-MINT
1, TY	1.99	5.97	9.95
2, TY	1.99	5.97	9.95
3, TY	1.99	5.97	9.95

DRAGONLANCE SAGA (was TSR series)
DC
	GOOD	FINE	N-MINT
4	1.99	5.97	9.95
5	1.99	5.97	9.95

DRAGONRING
AIRCEL
	GOOD	FINE	N-MINT
1	0.40	1.20	2.00
2	0.40	1.20	2.00
3	0.30	0.90	1.50
4	0.30	0.90	1.50
5	0.30	0.90	1.50
6	0.30	0.90	1.50

DRAGONRING (color)
	GOOD	FINE	N-MINT
1	0.40	1.20	2.00
2	0.40	1.20	2.00
3	0.40	1.20	2.00
4	0.40	1.20	2.00
5	0.40	1.20	2.00
6	0.40	1.20	2.00
7	0.40	1.20	2.00
8	0.40	1.20	2.00
9, Dale Keown	0.80	2.40	4.00
10, Dale Keown	0.80	2.40	4.00
11, Dale Keown	0.80	2.40	4.00
12, Dale Keown	0.80	2.40	4.00
13, Dale Keown	0.80	2.40	4.00
14, Dale Keown	0.80	2.40	4.00
15	0.40	1.20	2.00

DRAGONROK SAGA, THE
HANTHERCRAFT
	ORIG.	GOOD	FINE	N-MINT
1, b&w, Tandra	2.50	0.50	1.50	2.50
2, b&w, Tandra	2.50	0.50	1.50	2.50
3, 94, b&w	2.50	0.50	1.50	2.50

	ORIG.	GOOD	FINE	N-MINT

DRAGONS IN THE MOON
AIRCEL

	ORIG.	GOOD	FINE	N-MINT
☐ 1, Oct 90, b&w............... 2.50		0.50	1.50	2.50
☐ 2, Oct 90, b&w............... 2.50		0.50	1.50	2.50
☐ 3, Oct 90, b&w............... 2.50		0.50	1.50	2.50
☐ 4, Oct 90, b&w............... 2.50		0.50	1.50	2.50

DRAGONSLAYER
MARVEL

	ORIG.	GOOD	FINE	N-MINT
☐ 1, movie story 0.50		0.20	0.60	1.00
☐ 2, movie story 0.50		0.20	0.60	1.00

DRAGONSTRIKE

	ORIG.	GOOD	FINE	N-MINT
☐ 1 .... 1.25		0.25	0.75	1.25

DRAMA
SIRIUS ENTERTAINMENT

	ORIG.	GOOD	FINE	N-MINT
☐ 0, Jun 95, nn;one-shot... 2.95		2.00	6.00	10.00
☐ 0, 95, one-shot;signed and numbered by Joseph Michael Linsner;limited to 1400 copies				
.... 15.00		3.00	9.00	15.00

DRAWN & QUARTERLY
DRAWN & QUARTERLY

	ORIG.	GOOD	FINE	N-MINT
☐ 1, b&w		1.00	3.00	5.00

DREAD OF NIGHT
HAMILTON

	ORIG.	GOOD	FINE	N-MINT
☐ 1, b&w		0.79	2.37	3.95
☐ 2, b&w		0.79	2.37	3.95

DREADLANDS
EPIC

	ORIG.	GOOD	FINE	N-MINT
☐ 1 .... 3.95		0.79	2.37	3.95
☐ 2 .... 3.95		0.79	2.37	3.95
☐ 3 .... 3.95		0.79	2.37	3.95
☐ 4 .... 3.95		0.79	2.37	3.95

DREADSTAR

	ORIG.	GOOD	FINE	N-MINT
☐ 1, Nov 82, JSn 1.50		0.70	2.10	3.50
☐ 2, Jan 83, JSn, Willow ... 1.50		0.60	1.80	3.00
☐ 3, Mar 83, JSn, Lord Papal				
.... 1.50		0.50	1.50	2.50
☐ 4, May 83, JSn............... 1.50		0.45	1.35	2.25
☐ 5, Jul 83, JSn................. 1.50		0.45	1.35	2.25
☐ 6, Sep 83, JSn............... 1.50		0.40	1.20	2.00
☐ 7, Nov 83, JSn 1.50		0.40	1.20	2.00
☐ 8, Jan 84, JSn 1.50		0.40	1.20	2.00
☐ 9, Mar 84, JSn 1.50		0.40	1.20	2.00
☐ 10, Apr 84, JSn 1.50		0.40	1.20	2.00
☐ 11, Jun 84, JSn............. 1.50		0.40	1.20	2.00
☐ 12, Jul 84, JSn............... 1.50		0.40	1.20	2.00
☐ 13, Aug 84, JSn............. 1.50		0.40	1.20	2.00
☐ 14, Oct 84, JSn 1.50		0.40	1.20	2.00
☐ 15, Nov 84, JSn 1.50		0.40	1.20	2.00
☐ 16, Dec 84, JSn............. 1.50		0.30	0.90	1.50
☐ 17, Feb 85, JSn............. 1.50		0.30	0.90	1.50
☐ 18, Apr 85, JSn 1.50		0.30	0.90	1.50
☐ 19, Jun 85, JSn............. 1.50		0.30	0.90	1.50
☐ 20, Aug 85, JSn 1.50		0.35	1.05	1.75
☐ 21, Oct 85, JSn 1.50		0.35	1.05	1.75
☐ 22, Dec 85, JSn............. 1.50		0.35	1.05	1.75
☐ 23, Feb 86, JSn............. 1.50		0.35	1.05	1.75
☐ 24, Apr 86, JSn 1.50		0.35	1.05	1.75
☐ 25, Jun 86, JSn............. 1.50		0.35	1.05	1.75
☐ 26, Aug 86, JSn (moves to First)				
.... 1.50		0.35	1.05	1.75

DREADSTAR & COMPANY

	ORIG.	GOOD	FINE	N-MINT
☐ 1, reprints 0.75		0.20	0.60	1.00
☐ 2, reprints 0.75		0.20	0.60	1.00
☐ 3, reprints 0.75		0.20	0.60	1.00
☐ 4, reprints 0.75		0.20	0.60	1.00
☐ 5, reprints 0.75		0.20	0.60	1.00
☐ 6, reprints 0.75		0.20	0.60	1.00

DREADSTAR (former Epic title)
FIRST

	ORIG.	GOOD	FINE	N-MINT
☐ 27, Nov 86...................... 1.75		0.35	1.05	1.75
☐ 28, Jan 87....................... 1.75		0.35	1.05	1.75
☐ 29, Mar 87...................... 1.75		0.35	1.05	1.75
☐ 30, May 87...................... 1.75		0.35	1.05	1.75
☐ 31, Jul 87........................ 1.75		0.35	1.05	1.75
☐ 32, Sep 87...................... 1.75		0.35	1.05	1.75
☐ 33, Nov 87...................... 1.75		0.35	1.05	1.75
☐ 34, Jan 88....................... 1.75		0.35	1.05	1.75
☐ 35, Jan 88....................... 1.75		0.35	1.05	1.75
☐ 36, Jan 88....................... 1.75		0.35	1.05	1.75
☐ 37, Jan 88....................... 1.75		0.35	1.05	1.75
☐ 38, Jan 88....................... 1.75		0.35	1.05	1.75
☐ 39, Crossroads		0.39	1.17	1.95
☐ 40		0.39	1.17	1.95
☐ 41		0.39	1.17	1.95
☐ 42		0.39	1.17	1.95
☐ 43		0.39	1.17	1.95
☐ 44		0.39	1.17	1.95
☐ 45		0.39	1.17	1.95
☐ 46		0.39	1.17	1.95
☐ 47		0.39	1.17	1.95
☐ 48		0.39	1.17	1.95
☐ 49		0.39	1.17	1.95
☐ 50		0.79	2.37	3.95
☐ 51		0.39	1.17	1.95
☐ 52		0.39	1.17	1.95
☐ 53		0.39	1.17	1.95
☐ 54		0.39	1.17	1.95
☐ 55		0.39	1.17	1.95
☐ 56		0.39	1.17	1.95
☐ 57		0.39	1.17	1.95
☐ 58		0.39	1.17	1.95
☐ 59		0.45	1.35	2.25
☐ 60		0.45	1.35	2.25
☐ 61		0.45	1.35	2.25
☐ 62		0.45	1.35	2.25
☐ 63		0.45	1.35	2.25
☐ 64		0.45	1.35	2.25

DREADSTAR (mini-series)
MALIBU/BRAVURA

	ORIG.	GOOD	FINE	N-MINT
☐ 1, Apr 94, P.David(w); EC				
.... 2.50		0.50	1.50	2.50
☐ 2, May 94, P.David(w); EC				
.... 2.50		0.50	1.50	2.50
☐ 3, Jun 94, P.David(w); EC				
.... 2.50		0.50	1.50	2.50
☐ 4, Sep 94, P.David(w); EC				
.... 2.50		0.50	1.50	2.50
☐ 5, Oct 94, P.David(w); EC				
.... 2.50		0.50	1.50	2.50
☐ 6, P.David(w);EC; final issue				
.... 2.50		0.50	1.50	2.50

DREADSTAR ANNUAL
EPIC

	ORIG.	GOOD	FINE	N-MINT
☐ 1, JSn 2.00		0.60	1.80	3.00

DREAMERY, THE
ECLIPSE

	ORIG.	GOOD	FINE	N-MINT
☐ 1, b&w..............................		0.40	1.20	2.00
☐ 2, b&w..............................		0.40	1.20	2.00
☐ 3, b&w..............................		0.40	1.20	2.00
☐ 4, b&w..............................		0.40	1.20	2.00
☐ 5, b&w..............................		0.40	1.20	2.00
☐ 6, b&w..............................		0.40	1.20	2.00
☐ 7, b&w..............................		0.40	1.20	2.00
☐ 8, b&w..............................		0.40	1.20	2.00
☐ 9, b&w..............................		0.40	1.20	2.00
☐ 10, b&w............................		0.40	1.20	2.00
☐ 11, b&w............................		0.40	1.20	2.00
☐ 12, b&w............................		0.40	1.20	2.00

	ORIG.	GOOD	FINE	N-MINT
13, b&w		0.40	1.20	2.00
14, b&w		0.40	1.20	2.00

DREAMING, THE
DC/VERTIGO

	ORIG.	GOOD	FINE	N-MINT
1, Jun 96, "The Goldie Factor" Part 1				
	2.50	0.50	1.50	2.50

DREAMS 'N' SCHEMES OF COL. KILGORE
SPECIAL STUDIO

	GOOD	FINE	N-MINT
1, b&w	0.50	1.50	2.50
2, b&w	0.50	1.50	2.50

DREAMS OF A DOG
RIP OFF

	ORIG.	GOOD	FINE	N-MINT
1, May 90, b&w	2.00	0.40	1.20	2.00
2, Jun 92, b&w	2.50	0.50	1.50	2.50

DREAMS OF EVERYMAN

	ORIG.	GOOD	FINE	N-MINT
0, Jun 92, nn	2.50	0.50	1.50	2.50

DREAMTIME (mini-series)
BLIND BAT PRESS

	ORIG.	GOOD	FINE	N-MINT
1, May 95, b&w	2.50	0.50	1.50	2.50
2, 95, b&w;no indicia	2.50	0.50	1.50	2.50

DREDD BY BISLEY
FLEETWAY/QUALITY

	ORIG.	GOOD	FINE	N-MINT
0, nn	5.95	1.60	4.80	8.00

DREDD RULES!

	ORIG.	GOOD	FINE	N-MINT
1	2.95	0.59	1.77	2.95
2	2.95	0.59	1.77	2.95
3	2.95	0.59	1.77	2.95
4	2.95	0.59	1.77	2.95
5	2.95	0.59	1.77	2.95
6	2.95	0.59	1.77	2.95
7	2.95	0.59	1.77	2.95
8	2.95	0.59	1.77	2.95
9	2.95	0.59	1.77	2.95
10	2.95	0.59	1.77	2.95
11	2.95	0.59	1.77	2.95
12	2.95	0.59	1.77	2.95
13	2.95	0.59	1.77	2.95
14	2.95	0.59	1.77	2.95
15	2.95	0.59	1.77	2.95
16	2.95	0.59	1.77	2.95
17	2.95	0.59	1.77	2.95
18	2.95	0.59	1.77	2.95
19	2.95	0.59	1.77	2.95
20	2.95	0.59	1.77	2.95

DRIFTER
BRAINSTORM

	ORIG.	GOOD	FINE	N-MINT
1, b&w	2.95	0.59	1.77	2.95

DRIFTERS
INFINITY

	GOOD	FINE	N-MINT
1	0.34	1.02	1.70

DRIFTERS, THE
CORNERSTONE

	GOOD	FINE	N-MINT
1, b&w	0.40	1.20	2.00

DROIDS
STAR

	ORIG.	GOOD	FINE	N-MINT
1, Star Wars	0.75	0.15	0.45	0.75
2, Star Wars	0.75	0.15	0.45	0.75
3, Star Wars	0.75	0.15	0.45	0.75
4, Star Wars	0.75	0.15	0.45	0.75
5, Star Wars	0.75	0.15	0.45	0.75
6, Star Wars	0.75	0.15	0.45	0.75
7, Star Wars	0.75	0.15	0.45	0.75
8, Star Wars	1.00	0.20	0.60	1.00

DROOPY (mini-series)
DARK HORSE

	ORIG.	GOOD	FINE	N-MINT
1, Oct 95, Screwball Squirrel back-up				
	2.50	0.50	1.50	2.50

	ORIG.	GOOD	FINE	N-MINT
2, Nov 95, Wolf and Red back-up				
	2.50	0.50	1.50	2.50
3, Dec 95, Screwball Squirrel back-up; final issue				
	2.50	0.50	1.50	2.50

DROWNED GIRL, THE
PIRANHA

	GOOD	FINE	N-MINT
0, pb, color	1.19	3.57	5.95

DRUG WARS
PIONEER

	GOOD	FINE	N-MINT
1, MGr(c)	0.39	1.17	1.95

DRUID
MARVEL

	ORIG.	GOOD	FINE	N-MINT
1, May 95	2.50	0.50	1.50	2.50
2, Jun 95	1.95	0.39	1.17	1.95
3, Jul 95	1.95	0.39	1.17	1.95
4, Aug 95, Final issue	1.95	0.39	1.17	1.95

DRUNKEN FIST
JADEMAN

	GOOD	FINE	N-MINT
1	0.39	1.17	1.95
2	0.39	1.17	1.95
3	0.39	1.17	1.95
4	0.39	1.17	1.95
5	0.39	1.17	1.95
6	0.39	1.17	1.95
7	0.39	1.17	1.95
8	0.39	1.17	1.95
9	0.39	1.17	1.95
10	0.39	1.17	1.95
11	0.39	1.17	1.95
12	0.39	1.17	1.95
13	0.39	1.17	1.95
14	0.39	1.17	1.95
15	0.39	1.17	1.95
16	0.39	1.17	1.95
17	0.39	1.17	1.95
18	0.39	1.17	1.95
19	0.39	1.17	1.95
20	0.39	1.17	1.95
21	0.39	1.17	1.95
22	0.39	1.17	1.95
23	0.39	1.17	1.95
24	0.39	1.17	1.95
25	0.39	1.17	1.95
26	0.39	1.17	1.95
27	0.39	1.17	1.95
28	0.39	1.17	1.95
29	0.39	1.17	1.95
30	0.39	1.17	1.95
31	0.39	1.17	1.95
32	0.39	1.17	1.95
33	0.39	1.17	1.95
34	0.39	1.17	1.95
35	0.39	1.17	1.95
36	0.39	1.17	1.95
37	0.39	1.17	1.95
38	0.39	1.17	1.95
39	0.39	1.17	1.95
40	0.39	1.17	1.95
41	0.39	1.17	1.95
42	0.39	1.17	1.95

DRY ROT
ZOLTON

	ORIG.	GOOD	FINE	N-MINT
1, 94, b&w	2.95	0.59	1.77	2.95

DUCK AND COVER
CAT-HEAD

	GOOD	FINE	N-MINT
1, b&w	0.40	1.20	2.00
2, b&w	0.40	1.20	2.00

	ORIG.	GOOD	FINE	N-MINT

DUCKBOTS
BLACKTHORNE

	ORIG.	GOOD	FINE	N-MINT
☐ 1		0.35	1.05	1.75
☐ 2		0.35	1.05	1.75

DUCKMAN
DARK HORSE

	ORIG.	GOOD	FINE	N-MINT
☐ 1, b&w		0.39	1.17	1.95
☐ 2, b&w		0.39	1.17	1.95

DUCKMAN SPECIAL

	ORIG.	GOOD	FINE	N-MINT
☐ 0, Apr 90, nn;one-shot; b&w				
.... 1.95		0.39	1.17	1.95

DUCKTALES
DISNEY

	ORIG.	GOOD	FINE	N-MINT
☐ 1 .... 1.50		0.50	1.50	2.50
☐ 2 .... 1.50		0.40	1.20	2.00
☐ 3 .... 1.50		0.30	0.90	1.50
☐ 4 .... 1.50		0.30	0.90	1.50
☐ 5 .... 1.50		0.30	0.90	1.50
☐ 6 .... 1.50		0.30	0.90	1.50
☐ 7 .... 1.50		0.30	0.90	1.50
☐ 8		0.30	0.90	1.50
☐ 9		0.30	0.90	1.50
☐ 10		0.30	0.90	1.50
☐ 11		0.30	0.90	1.50
☐ 12		0.30	0.90	1.50
☐ 13		0.30	0.90	1.50
☐ 14		0.30	0.90	1.50
☐ 15		0.30	0.90	1.50
☐ 16		0.30	0.90	1.50
☐ 17 .... 1.50		0.30	0.90	1.50

GLADSTONE

	ORIG.	GOOD	FINE	N-MINT
☐ 1, CB		1.20	3.60	6.00
☐ 2		0.80	2.40	4.00
☐ 3		0.40	1.20	2.00
☐ 4		0.40	1.20	2.00
☐ 5		0.40	1.20	2.00
☐ 6		0.40	1.20	2.00
☐ 7		0.40	1.20	2.00
☐ 8		0.40	1.20	2.00
☐ 9, CB		0.60	1.80	3.00
☐ 10, CB		0.60	1.80	3.00
☐ 11, CB		0.60	1.80	3.00
☐ 12, CB		0.80	2.40	4.00
☐ 13, CB		0.80	2.40	4.00

W.D.

	ORIG.	GOOD	FINE	N-MINT
☐ 0, nn Dime after Dime		0.70	2.10	3.50

DUCKTALES: THE MOVIE
DISNEY

	ORIG.	GOOD	FINE	N-MINT
☐ 1, adaptation		1.19	3.57	5.95

DUNE
MARVEL

	ORIG.	GOOD	FINE	N-MINT
☐ 1, movie 0.75		0.30	0.90	1.50
☐ 2, movie 0.75		0.30	0.90	1.50
☐ 3, movie 0.75		0.30	0.90	1.50

DUNGEONEERS, THE
SILVERWOLF

	ORIG.	GOOD	FINE	N-MINT
☐ 1		0.30	0.90	1.50

	ORIG.	GOOD	FINE	N-MINT
☐ 2		0.30	0.90	1.50
☐ 3		0.30	0.90	1.50
☐ 4		0.30	0.90	1.50

DUPLEX PLANET ILLUSTRATED
FANTAGRAPHICS

	ORIG.	GOOD	FINE	N-MINT
☐ 1, b&w 2.95		0.59	1.77	2.95
☐ 2 .... 2.50		0.50	1.50	2.50
☐ 3 .... 2.50		0.50	1.50	2.50
☐ 4 .... 2.50		0.50	1.50	2.50
☐ 5 .... 2.95		0.59	1.77	2.95
☐ 7, b&w 2.50		0.50	1.50	2.50
☐ 8, May 94, b&w 2.50		0.50	1.50	2.50
☐ 9, Jul 94, b&w 2.50		0.50	1.50	2.50
☐ 10, Sep 94, b&w 2.50		0.50	1.50	2.50

DURANGO KID, THE
AC

	ORIG.	GOOD	FINE	N-MINT
☐ 1, reprint, some color		0.50	1.50	2.50
☐ 2, b&w;FF		0.55	1.65	2.75

DUTCH DECKER AND THE VOODOO QUEEN
CALIBER

	ORIG.	GOOD	FINE	N-MINT
☐ 1, b&w 2.50		0.50	1.50	2.50

DYNAMIC CLASSICS
DC

	ORIG.	GOOD	FINE	N-MINT
☐ 1, Sep 78 .... 0.50		0.10	0.30	0.50

DYNAMO
TOWER

	ORIG.	GOOD	FINE	N-MINT
☐ 1, Aug 66, WW 0.25		12.00	36.00	60.00
☐ 2, Oct 66, WW 0.25		8.50	25.50	42.50
☐ 3, Mar 67, WW 0.25		6.00	18.00	30.00
☐ 4, Jun 67, WW 0.25		6.00	18.00	30.00

DYNAMO JOE
FIRST

	ORIG.	GOOD	FINE	N-MINT
☐ 1		0.25	0.75	1.25
☐ 2		0.25	0.75	1.25
☐ 3		0.25	0.75	1.25
☐ 4		0.25	0.75	1.25
☐ 5		0.25	0.75	1.25
☐ 6		0.25	0.75	1.25
☐ 7		0.25	0.75	1.25
☐ 8		0.25	0.75	1.25
☐ 9		0.25	0.75	1.25
☐ 10		0.25	0.75	1.25
☐ 11		0.25	0.75	1.25
☐ 12		0.35	1.05	1.75
☐ 13		0.35	1.05	1.75
☐ 14		0.35	1.05	1.75
☐ 15		0.35	1.05	1.75

DYNAMO JOE SPECIAL

	ORIG.	GOOD	FINE	N-MINT
☐ 1		0.35	1.05	1.75

Dracula

Bram Stoker's creation Dracula has provided public-domain inspiration for various comic-book incarnations. Probably the company most committed to the character has been Marvel Comics, which published 70 issues of the *Tomb of Dracula* (Apr 72-Aug 79) color comic book, as well as 13 issues of the black-and-white *Dracula Lives* magazine. Other Dracula series (some outside the scope of this book) were published by Warren (1979), Apple (1987-90, and Topps (1993, 1995). One of the stranger uses of the character was Dell's super-hero *Dracula* (Nov 66-Mar 67). The super-hero series began with issue #2 and continued until #4. Here, Count Dracula was a scientist who developed a serum that allowed him to transform into a bat, a power that had its advantages but, as he noted, left him prey to any "small boy with a BB gun."

E

	ORIG.	GOOD	FINE	N-MINT
E-MAN				
ALPHA				
❑ 1 ....2.75	0.55	1.65	2.75
CHARLTON				
❑ 1, 73...............................	3.60	10.80	18.00
❑ 2, 73...............................	2.40	7.20	12.00
❑ 3, 73...............................	2.40	7.20	12.00
❑ 4, 73...............................	2.40	7.20	12.00
❑ 5, 73...............................	2.40	7.20	12.00
❑ 6	1.60	4.80	8.00
❑ 7	1.60	4.80	8.00
❑ 8	1.60	4.80	8.00
❑ 9	1.60	4.80	8.00
❑ 10	1.60	4.80	8.00
COMICO				
❑ 1, Sep 88...............2.75	0.55	1.65	2.75
FIRST				
❑ 1, Apr 83, JSa 1.00	0.30	0.90	1.50
❑ 2, Jun 83, JSa 1.00	0.25	0.75	1.25
❑ 3, Jun 83, JSa 1.00	0.25	0.75	1.25
❑ 4, Jul 83, JSa 1.00	0.25	0.75	1.25
❑ 5, Aug 83, JSa 1.00	0.25	0.75	1.25
❑ 6, Sep 83, JSa 1.00	0.25	0.75	1.25
❑ 7, Oct 83, JSa 1.00	0.25	0.75	1.25
❑ 8, Nov 83, JSa 1.00	0.25	0.75	1.25
❑ 9, Dec 83, JSa...... 1.00	0.25	0.75	1.25
❑ 10, Jan 84, JSa 1.00	0.25	0.75	1.25
❑ 11, Feb 84, JSa 1.00	0.25	0.75	1.25
❑ 12, Mar 84, JSa...... 1.00	0.25	0.75	1.25
❑ 13, Apr 84, JSa 1.00	0.25	0.75	1.25
❑ 14, May 84, JSa 1.00	0.25	0.75	1.25
❑ 15, Jun 84, JSa 1.00	0.25	0.75	1.25
❑ 16, Jul 84, JSa 1.00	0.25	0.75	1.25
❑ 17, Aug 84, JSa...... 1.00	0.25	0.75	1.25
❑ 18, Sep 84, JSa 1.00	0.25	0.75	1.25
❑ 19, Oct 84, JSa 1.00	0.25	0.75	1.25
❑ 20, Nov 84, JSa...... 1.25	0.25	0.75	1.25
❑ 21, Dec 84, JSa...... 1.25	0.25	0.75	1.25
❑ 22, Feb 85, JSa...... 1.25	0.25	0.75	1.25
❑ 23, Apr 85, JSa 1.25	0.25	0.75	1.25
❑ 24, Jun 85, JSa 1.25	0.25	0.75	1.25
❑ 25, Aug 85, JSa...... 1.25	0.25	0.75	1.25
E-MAN (Volume 2)				
COMICO				
❑ 1, Jan 90 ....2.50	0.50	1.50	2.50
❑ 2, Feb 90 ....2.50	0.50	1.50	2.50
❑ 3, Mar 90 ....2.50	0.50	1.50	2.50
E-MAN (Volume 3, was at First)				
❑ 1, Apr 83, JSn..................	0.55	1.65	2.75
E-MAN (Volume 4)				
❑ 1, Sep 89, JSn..................	0.50	1.50	2.50
❑ 2, JSn..................	0.50	1.50	2.50
❑ 3, JSn..................	0.50	1.50	2.50
E-MAN RETURNS				
ALPHA PRODUCTIONS				
❑ 1, 94, b&w 2.75	0.55	1.65	2.75
EAGLE				
COMIC ZONE				
❑ 1, b&w	0.55	1.65	2.75
❑ 2, b&w	0.55	1.65	2.75
❑ 3, b&w	0.55	1.65	2.75
CRYSTAL				
❑ 1	1.00	3.00	5.00
❑ 1, limited edition	2.00	6.00	10.00
❑ 2	0.30	0.90	1.50
❑ 3	0.30	0.90	1.50
❑ 4	0.30	0.90	1.50
❑ 5	0.30	0.90	1.50

	ORIG.	GOOD	FINE	N-MINT
❑ 6	0.30	0.90	1.50
❑ 7	0.35	1.05	1.75
❑ 8	0.35	1.05	1.75
❑ 9	0.35	1.05	1.75
❑ 10	0.35	1.05	1.75
❑ 11	0.35	1.05	1.75
❑ 12	0.50	1.50	2.50
❑ 13	0.39	1.17	1.95
❑ 14	0.39	1.17	1.95
❑ 15	0.39	1.17	1.95
❑ 16, (moves to Apple)	0.39	1.17	1.95
EAGLE (was Crystal title)				
APPLE				
❑ 17, b&w............................	0.39	1.17	1.95
❑ 18, b&w............................	0.39	1.17	1.95
❑ 19, b&w............................	0.39	1.17	1.95
❑ 20, b&w............................	0.39	1.17	1.95
❑ 21, b&w............................	0.39	1.17	1.95
❑ 22, b&w............................	0.39	1.17	1.95
❑ 23	0.45	1.35	2.25
EARTH 4 (Volume 2)				
CONTINUITY				
❑ 1 ....2.50	0.50	1.50	2.50
❑ 2 ....2.50	0.50	1.50	2.50
❑ 3 ....2.50	0.50	1.50	2.50
EARTH 4: DEATHWATCH 2000 PRELUDE				
❑ 1, trading cards 2.50	0.50	1.50	2.50
❑ 2, trading card 2.50	0.50	1.50	2.50
❑ 3, trading card 2.50	0.50	1.50	2.50
❑ 4 ....2.50	0.50	1.50	2.50
EARTH C.O.R.E.				
INDEPENDENT				
❑ 1, 94 ....1.95	0.39	1.17	1.95
EARTHLORE				
ETERNITY				
❑ 1	0.36	1.08	1.80
❑ 2	0.36	1.08	1.80
EARTHWORM JIM				
MARVEL				
❑ 1, Dec 95, based on video game				
...................................2.25	0.45	1.35	2.25
❑ 2, Jan 96...................2.25	0.45	1.35	2.25
❑ 3, Feb 96...................2.25	0.45	1.35	2.25
EAST MEETS WEST				
INNOVATION				
❑ 1, Apr 90, DSt..................	0.50	1.50	2.50
EASTER STORY, THE				
MARVEL/NELSON				
❑ 0, nn 2.99	0.60	1.79	2.99
EATERS, THE				
DC/VERTIGO				
❑ 1, 95, one-shot 4.95	0.99	2.97	4.95
EB'NN (former Crowquill title)				
NOW				
❑ 3, Jun 86 ....1.50	0.30	0.90	1.50
❑ 4, Aug 86 ....1.50	0.30	0.90	1.50
❑ 5, Nov 86, MW(c) 1.50	0.30	0.90	1.50
❑ 6, Jan 87, Jim Engel 1.50	0.30	0.90	1.50
EB'NN THE RAVEN				
CROWQUILL				
❑ 1	0.80	2.40	4.00
❑ 2, (moves to Now Comics)	0.60	1.80	3.00
EC CLASSICS				
COCHRAN				
❑ 1, rep. 4.95	0.99	2.97	4.95
❑ 2, rep. 4.95	0.99	2.97	4.95
❑ 3, rep. 4.95	0.99	2.97	4.95

	ORIG.	GOOD	FINE	N-MINT
❑ 4, rep. 4.95	0.99	2.97	4.95
❑ 5, rep. 4.95	0.99	2.97	4.95
❑ 6, rep. 4.95	0.99	2.97	4.95
❑ 7, rep. 4.95	0.99	2.97	4.95
❑ 8, rep. 4.95	0.99	2.97	4.95
❑ 9, rep. 4.95	0.99	2.97	4.95
❑ 10, rep. 4.95	0.99	2.97	4.95
❑ 11, rep. 4.95	0.99	2.97	4.95
❑ 12, rep. 4.95	0.99	2.97	4.95

ECHO OF FUTUREPAST
CONTINUITY

	GOOD	FINE	N-MINT
❑ 1, NA..................................	0.59	1.77	2.95
❑ 2, NA..................................	0.59	1.77	2.95
❑ 3, NA..................................	0.59	1.77	2.95
❑ 4, NA..................................	0.59	1.77	2.95
❑ 5, NA..................................	0.59	1.77	2.95
❑ 6, NA..................................	0.59	1.77	2.95
❑ 7, NA..................................	0.59	1.77	2.95
❑ 8, NA..................................	0.59	1.77	2.95
❑ 9, NA..................................	0.59	1.77	2.95

ECLIPSE MAGAZINE
ECLIPSE

	ORIG.	GOOD	FINE	N-MINT
❑ 1, May 81, PG(c),MR, 1:Ms. Tree, Foozle b&w			
....2.95	1.20	3.60	6.00
❑ 2, Jul 81, MG(c), 1:Coyote			
....2.95	0.80	2.40	4.00
❑ 3, Nov 81, 1:Ragamuffins			
....2.95	0.60	1.80	3.00
❑ 4, Jan 82 ....2.95	0.60	1.80	3.00
❑ 5, Mar 82, MK(c)...........2.95	0.60	1.80	3.00
❑ 6, Jul 82, PG(c)..............2.95	0.60	1.80	3.00
❑ 7, Nov 82, 1:Masked Man			
....2.95	0.60	1.80	3.00
❑ 8, Jan 83, MR(c) 2.95	0.60	1.80	3.00

ECLIPSE MONTHLY

	ORIG.	GOOD	FINE	N-MINT
❑ 1, Aug 83, SD, KJ,MR,TR			
....2.00	0.40	1.20	2.00
❑ 2, Sep 83, GC, KJ,MR,TR2.00	0.40	1.20	2.00
❑ 3, Oct 83 ....2.00	0.30	0.90	1.50
❑ 4, Jan 84 ....1.50	0.30	0.90	1.50
❑ 5, Feb 84 ....1.50	0.30	0.90	1.50
❑ 6, Mar 84 ....1.50	0.30	0.90	1.50
❑ 7, Apr 84 ....1.50	0.30	0.90	1.50
❑ 8, May 84 ....1.50	0.30	0.90	1.50
❑ 9, Jun 84 ....1.75	0.30	0.90	1.50
❑ 10, Jul 84 ....1.75	0.30	0.90	1.50

ECLIPSO
DC

	ORIG.	GOOD	FINE	N-MINT
❑ 1, Nov 92 ....1.25	0.25	0.75	1.25
❑ 2 ....1.25	0.25	0.75	1.25
❑ 3 ....1.25	0.25	0.75	1.25
❑ 4 ....1.25	0.25	0.75	1.25
❑ 5 ....1.25	0.25	0.75	1.25
❑ 6 ....1.25	0.25	0.75	1.25
❑ 7 ....1.25	0.25	0.75	1.25
❑ 8 ....1.25	0.25	0.75	1.25
❑ 9 ....1.25	0.25	0.75	1.25
❑ 10 ....1.75	0.35	1.05	1.75
❑ 11 ....1.25	0.25	0.75	1.25
❑ 12 ....1.25	0.25	0.75	1.25
❑ 13 ....1.25	0.25	0.75	1.25
❑ 14 ....1.25	0.25	0.75	1.25
❑ 15 ....1.25	0.25	0.75	1.25
❑ 16 ....1.50	0.30	0.90	1.50
❑ 17 ....1.50	0.30	0.90	1.50
❑ 18 ....1.50	0.30	0.90	1.50

ECLIPSO ANNUAL

	ORIG.	GOOD	FINE	N-MINT
❑ 1, Bloodlines 2.50	0.50	1.50	2.50

ECLIPSO: THE DARKNESS WITHIN

	ORIG.	GOOD	FINE	N-MINT
❑ 1, Jul 92, plastic diamond glued to cover			
....2.50	0.60	1.80	3.00
❑ 1, Jul 92.........................2.50	0.60	1.80	3.00
❑ 2, Jul 92.........................2.50	0.50	1.50	2.50

ECTOKID
MARVEL

	ORIG.	GOOD	FINE	N-MINT
❑ 1, foil cover....................2.50	0.50	1.50	2.50
❑ 2 ....1.75	0.35	1.05	1.75
❑ 3 ....1.75	0.35	1.05	1.75
❑ 4 ....1.75	0.35	1.05	1.75
❑ 5 ....1.75	0.35	1.05	1.75
❑ 6 ....1.75	0.35	1.05	1.75
❑ 7 ....1.75	0.35	1.05	1.75
❑ 8 ....1.75	0.35	1.05	1.75
❑ 9, May 94........................1.75	0.35	1.05	1.75

ECTOKID UNLEASHED!

	ORIG.	GOOD	FINE	N-MINT
❑ 1, Oct 94.........................2.95	0.59	1.77	2.95

ED "BIG DADDY" ROTH'S RAT FINK COMIX
STARHEAD

	GOOD	FINE	N-MINT
❑ 1	0.40	1.20	2.00

EDDY CURRENT
MAD DOG

	GOOD	FINE	N-MINT
❑ 1, b&w.............................	0.80	2.40	4.00
❑ 2, b&w.............................	0.60	1.80	3.00
❑ 3, b&w.............................	0.60	1.80	3.00
❑ 4, b&w.............................	0.40	1.20	2.00
❑ 5, b&w.............................	0.40	1.20	2.00
❑ 6, b&w.............................	0.40	1.20	2.00
❑ 7, b&w.............................	0.40	1.20	2.00
❑ 8, b&w.............................	0.40	1.20	2.00
❑ 9, b&w.............................	0.40	1.20	2.00
❑ 10, b&w...........................	0.40	1.20	2.00
❑ 11, b&w...........................	0.40	1.20	2.00
❑ 12, b&w...........................	0.40	1.20	2.00

EDEN MATRIX, THE
ADHESIVE

	ORIG.	GOOD	FINE	N-MINT
❑ 1, 94 ....2.95	0.59	1.77	2.95

EDGAR ALLAN POE
ETERNITY

	GOOD	FINE	N-MINT
❑ 1, Tell-Tale Heart b&w	0.39	1.17	1.95
❑ 1, Pit & Pendulum b&w	0.39	1.17	1.95
❑ 1, Red Death b&w.............	0.39	1.17	1.95
❑ 1, Black Cat b&w	0.39	1.17	1.95
❑ 1, Rue Morgue b&w	0.39	1.17	1.95

EDGAR RICE BURROUGHS' TARZAN: A TALE OF MUGAMBI
DARK HORSE

	ORIG.	GOOD	FINE	N-MINT
❑ 0, Jun 95, nn;one-shot ...2.95	0.59	1.77	2.95

EDGAR RICE BURROUGHS' TARZAN: THE LOST ADVENTURE (mini-series)

	ORIG.	GOOD	FINE	N-MINT
❑ 1, Jan 95, b&w, squarebound			
....2.95	0.59	1.77	2.95
❑ 2, Feb 95, b&w, prestige format			
....2.95	0.59	1.77	2.95
❑ 3, Mar 95, b&w, prestige format			
....2.95	0.59	1.77	2.95
❑ 4, Apr 95, b&w, prestige format			
....2.95	0.59	1.77	2.95

EDGE (mini-series)
BRAVURA/MALIBU

	ORIG.	GOOD	FINE	N-MINT
❑ 1, Jul 94.........................2.50	0.50	1.50	2.50
❑ 2, Aug 94........................2.50	0.50	1.50	2.50

EDGE OF CHAOS
PACIFIC

	GOOD	FINE	N-MINT
❑ 1, GM...............................	0.25	0.75	1.25
❑ 2, GM...............................	0.20	0.60	1.00
❑ 3, GM...............................	0.20	0.60	1.00

	ORIG.	GOOD	FINE	N-MINT

EEK! THE CAT
HAMILTON

	ORIG.	GOOD	FINE	N-MINT
❑ 1, Feb 94, TV show	1.95	0.39	1.17	1.95
❑ 2, Mar 94, TV show	1.95	0.39	1.17	1.95
❑ 3, Apr 94, TV show	1.95	0.39	1.17	1.95

EGYPT (mini-series)
DC/VERTIGO

	ORIG.	GOOD	FINE	N-MINT
❑ 1, Aug 95	2.50	0.70	2.10	3.50
❑ 2, Sep 95	2.50	0.50	1.50	2.50
❑ 3, Oct 95	2.50	0.50	1.50	2.50
❑ 4, Nov 95	2.50	0.50	1.50	2.50
❑ 5, Dec 95	2.50	0.50	1.50	2.50
❑ 6, Jan 96	2.50	0.50	1.50	2.50
❑ 7, Feb 96, final issue	2.50	0.50	1.50	2.50

EIGHTBALL
FANTAGRAPHICS

	ORIG.	GOOD	FINE	N-MINT
❑ 1, b&w	3.00	9.00	15.00	
❑ 2, b&w	1.60	4.80	8.00	
❑ 3, b&w	1.00	3.00	5.00	
❑ 4, b&w	2.50	1.00	3.00	5.00
❑ 5, b&w	2.50	1.00	3.00	5.00
❑ 6, b&w	2.50	0.50	1.50	2.50
❑ 7, b&w	2.50	0.70	2.10	3.50
❑ 8, b&w	2.50	0.70	2.10	3.50
❑ 9, b&w	2.50	0.70	2.10	3.50
❑ 10, b&w	2.50	0.70	2.10	3.50
❑ 11, b&w	2.75	0.60	1.80	3.00
❑ 12, Nov 93, b&w	2.75	0.60	1.80	3.00
❑ 13, b&w	2.75	0.60	1.80	3.00
❑ 14, b&w	2.75	0.60	1.80	3.00
❑ 15, b&w	2.75	0.60	1.80	3.00
❑ 16, Nov 95, b&w; cardstock cover	3.95	0.79	2.37	3.95

EL DIABLO
DC

	ORIG.	GOOD	FINE	N-MINT
❑ 1, Aug 89	2.50	0.50	1.50	2.50
❑ 2, Sep 89	1.50	0.30	0.90	1.50
❑ 3, Oct 89	1.50	0.30	0.90	1.50
❑ 4, Dec 89	1.50	0.30	0.90	1.50
❑ 5, Jan 90	1.50	0.30	0.90	1.50
❑ 6, Feb 90	1.50	0.30	0.90	1.50
❑ 7, Mar 90	1.75	0.30	0.90	1.50
❑ 8, Apr 90	1.75	0.30	0.90	1.50
❑ 9, May 90	1.75	0.30	0.90	1.50
❑ 10, Jun 90	1.75	0.30	0.90	1.50
❑ 11, Jul 90	1.75	0.30	0.90	1.50
❑ 12, Aug 90, GA:Vigilante	2.00	0.40	1.20	2.00
❑ 13, Sep 90	2.00	0.40	1.20	2.00
❑ 14, Oct 90	2.00	0.40	1.20	2.00
❑ 15, Dec 90	2.00	0.40	1.20	2.00
❑ 16, Jan 91	2.00	0.40	1.20	2.00

EL GATO
AZTECA

	ORIG.	GOOD	FINE	N-MINT
❑ 1, b&w	2.00	0.40	1.20	2.00

EL SALVADOR: A HOUSE DIVIDED
ECLIPSE

	ORIG.	GOOD	FINE	N-MINT
❑ 1, b&w		0.50	1.50	2.50

ELECTRIC FEAR
SPARKS

	ORIG.	GOOD	FINE	N-MINT
❑ 1		0.25	0.75	1.25
❑ 2		0.25	0.75	1.25

ELECTRIC UNDERTOW
MARVEL

	ORIG.	GOOD	FINE	N-MINT
❑ 1, Strikeforce: Morituri	3.95	0.79	2.37	3.95
❑ 2, Strikeforce: Morituri	3.95	0.79	2.37	3.95
❑ 3, Strikeforce: Morituri	3.95	0.79	2.37	3.95
❑ 4, Strikeforce: Morituri	3.95	0.79	2.37	3.95
❑ 5, Strikeforce: Morituri	3.95	0.79	2.37	3.95

ELECTRIC WARRIOR
DC

	ORIG.	GOOD	FINE	N-MINT
❑ 1		0.40	1.20	2.00
❑ 2		0.30	0.90	1.50
❑ 3		0.30	0.90	1.50
❑ 4		0.30	0.90	1.50
❑ 5		0.30	0.90	1.50
❑ 6		0.30	0.90	1.50
❑ 7		0.30	0.90	1.50
❑ 8		0.30	0.90	1.50
❑ 9		0.30	0.90	1.50
❑ 10		0.30	0.90	1.50
❑ 11		0.30	0.90	1.50
❑ 12		0.30	0.90	1.50
❑ 13		0.30	0.90	1.50
❑ 14		0.30	0.90	1.50
❑ 15		0.30	0.90	1.50
❑ 16		0.30	0.90	1.50
❑ 17		0.30	0.90	1.50
❑ 18		0.30	0.90	1.50

ELEKTRA (mini-series)
MARVEL

	ORIG.	GOOD	FINE	N-MINT
❑ 1, Mar 95, enhanced cover	2.95	0.80	2.40	4.00
❑ 2, Apr 95, enhanced cover	2.95	0.59	1.77	2.95
❑ 3, May 95, enhanced cover	2.95	0.59	1.77	2.95
❑ 4, Jun 95, enhanced cover	2.95	0.59	1.77	2.95

ELEKTRA SAGA

	ORIG.	GOOD	FINE	N-MINT
❑ 0, tpb	5.00	15.00	25.00	
❑ 1, Feb 84, FM rep. Daredevil	2.00	1.50	4.50	7.50
❑ 2, Mar 84, FM rep. Daredevil	2.00	1.20	3.60	6.00
❑ 3, Apr 84, FM rep. Daredevil	2.00	1.20	3.60	6.00
❑ 4, May 84, FM rep. Daredevil	2.00	1.20	3.60	6.00

ELEKTRA: ASSASSIN
EPIC

	ORIG.	GOOD	FINE	N-MINT
❑ 1, Aug 86, FM,BSz	1.50	1.80	5.40	9.00
❑ 2, Sep 86, FM,BSz	1.50	1.50	4.50	7.50
❑ 3, Oct 86, FM,BSz	1.50	1.20	3.60	6.00
❑ 4, Nov 86, FM,BSz	1.50	1.20	3.60	6.00
❑ 5, Dec 86, FM,BSz	1.50	1.20	3.60	6.00
❑ 6, Jan 87, FM,BSz	1.50	1.20	3.60	6.00
❑ 7, Feb 87, FM,BSz	1.75	1.20	3.60	6.00
❑ 8, Mar 87, FM,BSz	1.75	1.20	3.60	6.00

ELEMENTALS
COMICO

	ORIG.	GOOD	FINE	N-MINT
❑ 1		1.60	4.80	8.00
❑ 2		1.20	3.60	6.00
❑ 3		1.00	3.00	5.00
❑ 4		0.80	2.40	4.00
❑ 5		0.80	2.40	4.00
❑ 6		0.40	1.20	2.00
❑ 7		0.40	1.20	2.00
❑ 8		0.40	1.20	2.00
❑ 9		0.40	1.20	2.00
❑ 10		0.40	1.20	2.00
❑ 11		0.50	1.50	2.50
❑ 12		0.50	1.50	2.50
❑ 13		0.50	1.50	2.50
❑ 14		0.50	1.50	2.50
❑ 15		0.50	1.50	2.50
❑ 16		0.50	1.50	2.50
❑ 17		0.50	1.50	2.50
❑ 18		0.50	1.50	2.50
❑ 19		0.50	1.50	2.50

	ORIG.	GOOD	FINE	N-MINT
20		0.50	1.50	2.50
21		0.50	1.50	2.50
22		0.50	1.50	2.50
23		0.35	1.05	1.75
24		0.35	1.05	1.75
25		0.35	1.05	1.75
26		0.35	1.05	1.75
27		0.35	1.05	1.75
28		0.35	1.05	1.75
29		0.35	1.05	1.75

ELEMENTALS (Vol. 3)

	ORIG.	GOOD	FINE	N-MINT
3, May 96	2.95	0.59	1.77	2.95

ELEMENTALS (Volume 2)

	ORIG.	GOOD	FINE	N-MINT
1, Mar 89		0.39	1.17	1.95
2, Apr 89		0.39	1.17	1.95
3, May 89		0.39	1.17	1.95
4, Jun 89	2.50	0.50	1.50	2.50
5, Jul 89	2.50	0.50	1.50	2.50
6, Aug 89	2.50	0.50	1.50	2.50
7, Sep 89	2.50	0.50	1.50	2.50
8, Oct 89	2.50	0.50	1.50	2.50
9, Nov 89	2.50	0.50	1.50	2.50
10, Dec 89	2.50	0.50	1.50	2.50
11, Jan 90	2.50	0.50	1.50	2.50
12, Feb 90	2.50	0.50	1.50	2.50
13, Mar 90	2.50	0.50	1.50	2.50
14, Apr 90	2.50	0.50	1.50	2.50
15, May 90	2.50	0.50	1.50	2.50
16, Apr 91	2.50	0.50	1.50	2.50
17, May 91	2.50	0.50	1.50	2.50
18, Jun 91	2.50	0.50	1.50	2.50
19, Aug 91	2.50	0.50	1.50	2.50
20, Oct 91	2.50	0.50	1.50	2.50
21, Nov 91	2.50	0.50	1.50	2.50
22, Dec 91	2.50	0.50	1.50	2.50
23	2.50	0.50	1.50	2.50
24	2.50	0.50	1.50	2.50
25	2.50	0.50	1.50	2.50
26	2.50	0.50	1.50	2.50

ELEMENTALS LINGERIE

	ORIG.	GOOD	FINE	N-MINT
1, May 96, pin-ups	2.95	0.59	1.77	2.95

ELEMENTALS SEX SPECIAL

	ORIG.	GOOD	FINE	N-MINT
1, Oct 91, adult		0.59	1.77	2.95
2, adult		0.59	1.77	2.95
3, adult		0.59	1.77	2.95
4, adult		0.59	1.77	2.95

ELEMENTALS SEXY LINGERIE SPECIAL

	ORIG.	GOOD	FINE	N-MINT
1, with poster		1.19	3.57	5.95
1, without poster		0.59	1.77	2.95

ELEMENTALS SPECIAL

	ORIG.	GOOD	FINE	N-MINT
1, Mar 86		0.39	1.17	1.95
2, Jan 89		0.39	1.17	1.95

ELEMENTALS: THE VAMPIRES REVENGE

	ORIG.	GOOD	FINE	N-MINT
1, Jun 96	2.95	0.59	1.77	2.95

ELEVEN OR ONE: AN ANGRY CHRIST COMIC
SIRIUS ENTERTAINMENT

	ORIG.	GOOD	FINE	N-MINT
0, Apr 95, nn;reprints new story from *Angry Christ Comics* tpb	2.95	0.59	1.77	2.95

ELF WARRIOR
ADVENTURE

	ORIG.	GOOD	FINE	N-MINT
1		0.39	1.17	1.95
2		0.39	1.17	1.95
3		0.39	1.17	1.95

ELF-THING
ECLIPSE

	ORIG.	GOOD	FINE	N-MINT
1, b&w		0.30	0.90	1.50

ELFHEIM (Volume I)
NIGHTWYND

	ORIG.	GOOD	FINE	N-MINT
1, b&w		0.50	1.50	2.50
2, b&w		0.50	1.50	2.50
3, b&w		0.50	1.50	2.50
4, b&w		0.50	1.50	2.50

ELFHEIM (Volume II)

	ORIG.	GOOD	FINE	N-MINT
1, b&w		0.50	1.50	2.50
2, b&w		0.50	1.50	2.50
3, b&w		0.50	1.50	2.50
4, b&w		0.50	1.50	2.50

ELFHEIM (Volume III)

	ORIG.	GOOD	FINE	N-MINT
1, b&w		0.50	1.50	2.50
2, b&w		0.50	1.50	2.50
3, b&w		0.50	1.50	2.50
4, b&w		0.50	1.50	2.50

ELFHEIM (Volume IV)

	ORIG.	GOOD	FINE	N-MINT
1, b&w		0.50	1.50	2.50
2, b&w		0.50	1.50	2.50

ELFIN ROMANCE
MT. WILSON

	ORIG.	GOOD	FINE	N-MINT
1, Feb 94, b&w	1.25	0.25	0.75	1.25
2, Apr 94, b&w	1.25	0.25	0.75	1.25
3, Apr 94, b&w	1.25	0.25	0.75	1.25
4, Jun 94, b&w	2.00	0.40	1.20	2.00
6, Oct 94, b&w	1.75	0.35	1.05	1.75

ELFLORD
AIRCEL

	ORIG.	GOOD	FINE	N-MINT
1, b&w; 1st printing	1.20	3.60	6.00	
1, 2nd printing	0.40	1.20	2.00	
2, 1st printing	1.00	3.00	5.00	
2, 2nd printing	0.40	1.20	2.00	
3		0.40	1.20	2.00
4		0.40	1.20	2.00
5		0.34	1.02	1.70
6		0.34	1.02	1.70
7		0.34	1.02	1.70
8		0.34	1.02	1.70

ELFLORD (Volume 2)

	ORIG.	GOOD	FINE	N-MINT
1, color		0.40	1.20	2.00
2, color		0.40	1.20	2.00
3, color		0.40	1.20	2.00
4, color		0.40	1.20	2.00
5, color		0.40	1.20	2.00
6, color		0.40	1.20	2.00
7, color		0.40	1.20	2.00
8, color		0.40	1.20	2.00
9, color		0.40	1.20	2.00
10, color		0.40	1.20	2.00
11, color		0.40	1.20	2.00
12, color		0.40	1.20	2.00
13, color		0.40	1.20	2.00
14, color		0.40	1.20	2.00
16, color		0.40	1.20	2.00
17, color		0.40	1.20	2.00
18, color		0.40	1.20	2.00
19, color		0.40	1.20	2.00
20, color		0.40	1.20	2.00
21, color; double-sized		0.99	2.97	4.95
22, color		0.40	1.20	2.00
23, b&w		0.39	1.17	1.95
24, b&w		0.39	1.17	1.95
25, b&w		0.39	1.17	1.95
26, b&w		0.39	1.17	1.95
27, b&w		0.39	1.17	1.95
28, b&w		0.39	1.17	1.95
29, b&w		0.39	1.17	1.95
30, b&w		0.39	1.17	1.95
31, b&w		0.39	1.17	1.95

ELFLORD CHRONICLES

	ORIG.	GOOD	FINE	N-MINT
1, b&w, reprint		0.50	1.50	2.50
2, b&w, reprint		0.50	1.50	2.50
3, b&w, reprint		0.50	1.50	2.50

	ORIG.	GOOD	FINE	N-MINT
❏ 4, b&w, reprint...............		0.50	1.50	2.50
❏ 5, b&w, reprint...............		0.50	1.50	2.50
❏ 6, b&w, reprint...............		0.50	1.50	2.50
❏ 7, b&w, reprint...............		0.55	1.65	2.75
❏ 8		0.50	1.50	2.50

ELFLORE (Volume I)
NIGHTWYND

	ORIG.	GOOD	FINE	N-MINT
❏ 1, b&w		0.50	1.50	2.50
❏ 2, b&w		0.50	1.50	2.50
❏ 3, b&w		0.50	1.50	2.50
❏ 4, b&w		0.50	1.50	2.50

ELFLORE (Volume II)

	ORIG.	GOOD	FINE	N-MINT
❏ 1, b&w		0.50	1.50	2.50
❏ 2, b&w		0.50	1.50	2.50
❏ 3, b&w		0.50	1.50	2.50
❏ 4, b&w		0.50	1.50	2.50

ELFLORE (Volume III)

	ORIG.	GOOD	FINE	N-MINT
❏ 1, b&w		0.50	1.50	2.50
❏ 2, b&w		0.50	1.50	2.50
❏ 3, b&w		0.50	1.50	2.50
❏ 4, b&w		0.50	1.50	2.50

ELFQUEST
EPIC

	ORIG.	GOOD	FINE	N-MINT
❏ 1, WP 0.75		1.00	3.00	5.00
❏ 2, WP 0.75		0.60	1.80	3.00
❏ 3, WP 0.75		0.60	1.80	3.00
❏ 4, WP 0.75		0.60	1.80	3.00
❏ 5, WP 0.75		0.60	1.80	3.00
❏ 6, WP 0.75		0.40	1.20	2.00
❏ 7, WP 0.75		0.40	1.20	2.00
❏ 8, WP 0.75		0.40	1.20	2.00
❏ 9, WP 0.75		0.40	1.20	2.00
❏ 10, WP 0.75		0.40	1.20	2.00
❏ 11, WP 0.75		0.40	1.20	2.00
❏ 12, WP 0.75		0.40	1.20	2.00
❏ 13, WP 0.75		0.40	1.20	2.00
❏ 14, WP 0.75		0.40	1.20	2.00
❏ 15, WP 0.75		0.40	1.20	2.00
❏ 16, WP 0.75		0.40	1.20	2.00
❏ 17, WP 0.75		0.40	1.20	2.00
❏ 18, WP 0.75		0.40	1.20	2.00
❏ 19, WP 0.75		0.40	1.20	2.00
❏ 20, WP 0.75		0.40	1.20	2.00
❏ 21, WP 0.75		0.40	1.20	2.00
❏ 22, WP 1.00		0.40	1.20	2.00
❏ 23, WP 1.00		0.40	1.20	2.00
❏ 24, WP 1.00		0.40	1.20	2.00
❏ 25, WP 1.00		0.40	1.20	2.00
❏ 26, WP 1.00		0.40	1.20	2.00
❏ 27, WP 1.00		0.40	1.20	2.00
❏ 28, WP 1.00		0.40	1.20	2.00
❏ 29, WP 1.00		0.40	1.20	2.00
❏ 30, WP 1.00		0.40	1.20	2.00
❏ 31, WP 1.00		0.40	1.20	2.00
❏ 32, WP 1.00		0.40	1.20	2.00

WARP

	ORIG.	GOOD	FINE	N-MINT
❏ 1, Apr 79, (1st printing) . 1.00		12.00	36.00	60.00
❏ 1, (2nd printing)............ 1.25		2.00	6.00	10.00
❏ 1, (3rd printing) 1.50		1.00	3.00	5.00
❏ 2, Aug 78, (1st printing). 1.00		6.00	18.00	30.00
❏ 2, (2nd printing)............ 1.25		1.00	3.00	5.00
❏ 2, (3rd printing) 1.50		0.60	1.80	3.00
❏ 3, Dec 78, (1st printing). 1.00		4.00	12.00	20.00
❏ 3, (2nd printing)............ 1.25		1.00	3.00	5.00
❏ 3, (3rd printing) 1.50		0.60	1.80	3.00
❏ 4, Apr 79, (1st printing) . 1.00		4.00	12.00	20.00
❏ 4, (2nd printing)............ 1.25		1.00	3.00	5.00
❏ 4, (3rd printing) 1.50		0.60	1.80	3.00
❏ 5, Aug 79, (1st printing). 1.00		4.00	12.00	20.00
❏ 5, (2nd printing)............ 1.25		1.00	3.00	5.00
❏ 5, (3rd printing) 1.50		0.60	1.80	3.00

	ORIG.	GOOD	FINE	N-MINT
❏ 6, Jan 80, (1st printing)..1.25		2.40	7.20	12.00
❏ 6, (2nd printing) 1.50		0.80	2.40	4.00
❏ 7, May 80, (1st printing).1.25		2.40	7.20	12.00
❏ 7, (2nd printing) 1.50		0.80	2.40	4.00
❏ 8, Sep 80, (1st printing) .1.25		2.40	7.20	12.00
❏ 8, (2nd printing) 1.50		0.80	2.40	4.00
❏ 9, Feb 81, (1st printing)..1.25		2.40	7.20	12.00
❏ 9, (2nd printing) 1.50		0.80	2.40	4.00
❏ 10, Jun 81 ....1.50		1.60	4.80	8.00
❏ 11, Oct 81 ....1.50		1.60	4.80	8.00
❏ 12, Feb 82......................1.50		1.60	4.80	8.00
❏ 13, Jun 82 ....1.50		1.60	4.80	8.00
❏ 14, Oct 82......................1.50		1.60	4.80	8.00
❏ 15, Feb 83......................1.50		1.60	4.80	8.00
❏ 16, Jun 83, I:Distant Soil 1.50		1.60	4.80	8.00
❏ 17, Oct 83, Elf orgy........1.50		1.60	4.80	8.00
❏ 18, Feb 84......................1.50		1.60	4.80	8.00
❏ 19, Jun 84 ....1.50		1.60	4.80	8.00
❏ 20, Oct 84......................1.50		1.60	4.80	8.00
❏ 21, Feb 85, all letters 1.50		1.60	4.80	8.00

ELFQUEST (1989 reprint series)

	ORIG.	GOOD	FINE	N-MINT
❏ 1, May 89, b&w 1.50		0.30	0.90	1.50
❏ 2, Jun 89, b&w 1.50		0.30	0.90	1.50
❏ 3, Jul 89, b&w 1.50		0.30	0.90	1.50
❏ 4, Aug 89, b&w..............1.50		0.30	0.90	1.50

ELFQUEST GATHERUM
FATHER TREE

	ORIG.	GOOD	FINE	N-MINT
❏ 1		1.79	5.37	8.95
❏ 2		1.79	5.37	8.95

ELFQUEST: BLOOD OF TEN CHIEFS
WARP

	ORIG.	GOOD	FINE	N-MINT
❏ 1, Aug 93, color 2.00		0.60	1.80	3.00
❏ 2, Sep 93, color 2.00		0.40	1.20	2.00
❏ 3, Nov 93, color 2.00		0.40	1.20	2.00
❏ 4, Jan 94, color 2.00		0.40	1.20	2.00
❏ 5, Mar 94, color.............2.25		0.45	1.35	2.25
❏ 6, May 94, color.............2.25		0.45	1.35	2.25
❏ 7, Jun 94, color 2.25		0.45	1.35	2.25
❏ 8, Jul 94, color...............2.25		0.45	1.35	2.25
❏ 9, Aug 94, color 2.25		0.45	1.35	2.25
❏ 10, Sep 94, color 2.25		0.45	1.35	2.25
❏ 11, Oct 94, color 2.25		0.45	1.35	2.25
❏ 12, Nov 94, color 2.25		0.45	1.35	2.25
❏ 13, Dec 94, color 2.25		0.45	1.35	2.25
❏ 14, Jan 95, color 2.25		0.45	1.35	2.25
❏ 15, Feb 95, color............2.25		0.45	1.35	2.25
❏ 16, Apr 95, color............2.25		0.45	1.35	2.25
❏ 17, May 95, color...........2.50		0.50	1.50	2.50
❏ 18, Jun 95, color 2.50		0.50	1.50	2.50
❏ 19, Aug 95, color;contains Elfquest timeline				
................................2.50		0.50	1.50	2.50
❏ 20, Sep 95, final issue 2.50		0.50	1.50	2.50

ELFQUEST: HIDDEN YEARS

	ORIG.	GOOD	FINE	N-MINT
❏ 1, May 92, color.............2.00		0.60	1.80	3.00
❏ 2, Jul 92, color...............2.00		0.40	1.20	2.00
❏ 3, Sep 92, color 2.00		0.40	1.20	2.00
❏ 4, Nov 92, color 2.00		0.40	1.20	2.00
❏ 5, Jan 93, color 2.00		0.40	1.20	2.00
❏ 6, Mar 93, color.............2.00		0.40	1.20	2.00
❏ 7, May 93, color.............2.00		0.40	1.20	2.00
❏ 8, Jul 93, color...............2.00		0.40	1.20	2.00
❏ 9, Sep 93, color 2.00		0.40	1.20	2.00
❏ 9, Nov 93, 1/2 holiday special				
................................2.95		0.59	1.77	2.95
❏ 10, Jan 94, color............2.00		0.40	1.20	2.00
❏ 11, Mar 94, color............2.25		0.45	1.35	2.25
❏ 12, Apr 94, color............2.25		0.45	1.35	2.25
❏ 13, May 94, color............2.25		0.45	1.35	2.25
❏ 14, Jun 94, color 2.25		0.45	1.35	2.25
❏ 15, Jul 94, color.............3.50		0.70	2.10	3.50
❏ 16, Aug 94, color............2.25		0.45	1.35	2.25

	ORIG.	GOOD	FINE	N-MINT
❏ 17, Oct 94, color 2.25		0.45	1.35	2.25
❏ 19, Jan 95, color............ 2.25		0.45	1.35	2.25
❏ 20, Apr 95, color............ 2.50		0.50	1.50	2.50
❏ 21, May 95, color............ 2.50		0.50	1.50	2.50
❏ 23, Aug 95, color;contains Elfquest timeline				
.... 2.50		0.50	1.50	2.50
❏ 24, Sep 95.......................... 2.50		0.50	1.50	2.50
❏ 25, Oct 95, b&w 2.25		0.45	1.35	2.25
❏ 26, Dec 95, b&w............ 2.25		0.45	1.35	2.25

ELFQUEST: JINK

	ORIG.	GOOD	FINE	N-MINT
❏ 1, Nov 94, color 2.25		0.45	1.35	2.25
❏ 2, Dec 94, color............ 2.25		0.45	1.35	2.25
❏ 3, Jan 95, color 2.25		0.45	1.35	2.25
❏ 4, Apr 95, color............ 2.50		0.50	1.50	2.50
❏ 5, May 95, color............ 2.50		0.50	1.50	2.50
❏ 6, Jul 95, color;contains Elfquest world map				
.... 2.50		0.50	1.50	2.50
❏ 7, Aug 95, color;contains Elfquest timeline				
.... 2.50		0.50	1.50	2.50
❏ 8, Oct 95, b&w 2.25		0.45	1.35	2.25
❏ 9, Nov 95, b&w............ 2.25		0.45	1.35	2.25
❏ 10, Dec 95, b&w............ 2.25		0.45	1.35	2.25
❏ 11, Jan 96, b&w............ 2.25		0.45	1.35	2.25

ELFQUEST: KAHVI (mini-series)

	ORIG.	GOOD	FINE	N-MINT
❏ 1, Oct 95, b&w............ 2.25		0.45	1.35	2.25
❏ 2, Nov 95, b&w............ 2.25		0.45	1.35	2.25
❏ 3, Dec 95, b&w............ 2.25		0.45	1.35	2.25

ELFQUEST: KINGS OF THE BROKEN WHEEL

	ORIG.	GOOD	FINE	N-MINT
❏ 1, Jun 90, b&w 2.00		0.80	2.40	4.00
❏ 2, Aug 90 .... 2.00		0.40	1.20	2.00
❏ 3, Sep 90.......................... 2.00		0.40	1.20	2.00
❏ 4, Oct 90 .... 2.00		0.40	1.20	2.00
❏ 5, Feb 91 .... 2.00		0.40	1.20	2.00
❏ 6, May 91 .... 2.00		0.40	1.20	2.00
❏ 7, Aug 91 .... 2.00		0.40	1.20	2.00
❏ 8, Nov 91 .... 2.00		0.40	1.20	2.00
❏ 9, Feb 92 .... 2.00		0.40	1.20	2.00

ELFQUEST: NEW BLOOD

	ORIG.	GOOD	FINE	N-MINT
❏ 1, Aug 92, JBY 3.95		0.79	2.37	3.95
❏ 2, Oct 92, color 2.00		0.40	1.20	2.00
❏ 3, Dec 92, color............ 2.00		0.40	1.20	2.00
❏ 4, Feb 93, color 2.00		0.40	1.20	2.00
❏ 5, Apr 93, color 2.00		0.40	1.20	2.00
❏ 6, Jun 93, color............ 2.00		0.40	1.20	2.00
❏ 7, Jul 93, color............ 2.00		0.40	1.20	2.00
❏ 8, Aug 93, color 2.00		0.40	1.20	2.00
❏ 9, Sep 93, color............ 2.00		0.40	1.20	2.00
❏ 10, Oct 93, color 2.00		0.40	1.20	2.00
❏ 11, Nov 93, color 2.00		0.40	1.20	2.00
❏ 12, Dec 93, color............ 2.00		0.40	1.20	2.00
❏ 13, Jan 94, color............ 2.00		0.40	1.20	2.00
❏ 14, Feb 94, color 2.25		0.45	1.35	2.25
❏ 15, Mar 94, color 2.25		0.45	1.35	2.25
❏ 16, Apr 94, color 2.25		0.45	1.35	2.25
❏ 17, May 94, color............ 2.25		0.45	1.35	2.25
❏ 18, Jun 94, color............ 2.25		0.45	1.35	2.25
❏ 19, Jul 94, color............ 2.25		0.45	1.35	2.25
❏ 20, Aug 94, color 2.25		0.45	1.35	2.25
❏ 21, Sep 94, color............ 2.25		0.45	1.35	2.25
❏ 22, Oct 94, color 2.25		0.45	1.35	2.25
❏ 23, Nov 94, color 2.25		0.45	1.35	2.25
❏ 24, Dec 94, color............ 2.25		0.45	1.35	2.25
❏ 25, Jan 95, color............ 2.25		0.45	1.35	2.25
❏ 26, Feb 95, color............ 2.25		0.45	1.35	2.25
❏ 27, Apr 95, color............ 2.50		0.50	1.50	2.50
❏ 28, May 95, color............ 2.50		0.50	1.50	2.50
❏ 30, Aug 95, color;contains Elfquest timeline				
.... 2.50		0.50	1.50	2.50
❏ 31, Sep 95, color............ 2.50		0.50	1.50	2.50
❏ 32, Oct 95, b&w 2.25		0.45	1.35	2.25
❏ 33, Nov 95, b&w............ 2.25		0.45	1.35	2.25
❏ 34, Dec 95, b&w............ 2.25		0.45	1.35	2.25

ELFQUEST: NEW BLOOD '93 SUMMER SPECIAL

	ORIG.	GOOD	FINE	N-MINT
❏ 1, Aug 93, JBy, color 3.95		0.79	2.37	3.95

ELFQUEST: SHARDS

	ORIG.	GOOD	FINE	N-MINT
❏ 1, Aug 94, color.............2.25		0.45	1.35	2.25
❏ 2, Sep 94, color 2.25		0.45	1.35	2.25
❏ 3, Oct 94, color.............2.25		0.45	1.35	2.25
❏ 4, Nov 94, color.............2.25		0.45	1.35	2.25
❏ 5, Dec 94, color 2.25		0.45	1.35	2.25
❏ 6, Jan 95, color.............2.25		0.45	1.35	2.25
❏ 7, Mar 95, color.............2.50		0.50	1.50	2.50
❏ 8, May 95, color 2.50		0.50	1.50	2.50
❏ 9, Jun 95, color 2.50		0.50	1.50	2.50
❏ 10, Aug 95, color;contains Elfquest timeline				
....2.50		0.50	1.50	2.50
❏ 11, Sep 95, color 2.50		0.50	1.50	2.50
❏ 12, Oct 95, b&w.............2.25		0.45	1.35	2.25
❏ 13, Dec 95, b&w.............2.25		0.45	1.35	2.25

ELFQUEST: SHARDS/ELFQUEST: HIDDEN YEARS

	ORIG.	GOOD	FINE	N-MINT
❏ 0, 94, ashcan preview, San Diego Comic-Con premium				
....0.50		0.10	0.30	0.50

ELFQUEST: SIEGE AT BLUE MOUNTAIN
WARP/APPLE

	ORIG.	GOOD	FINE	N-MINT
❏ 1, Mar 87, WP/JSa b&w .1.75		1.20	3.60	6.00
❏ 2, May 87, WP/JSa 1st printing				
....1.75		1.00	3.00	5.00
❏ 2, 2nd printing		0.60	1.80	3.00
❏ 3, Jul 87, WP/JSa 1.75		0.60	1.80	3.00
❏ 3, 2nd printing		0.50	1.50	2.50
❏ 4, Sep 87, WP/JSa...........1.75		0.60	1.80	3.00
❏ 5, Nov 87, WP/JSa...........1.75		0.60	1.80	3.00
❏ 6, Aug 88, WP/JSa...........1.95		0.50	1.50	2.50
❏ 7, Oct 88, WP/JSa...........1.95		0.50	1.50	2.50
❏ 8, Dec 88, WP/JSa...........1.95		0.50	1.50	2.50

ELFQUEST: THE REBELS
WARP

	ORIG.	GOOD	FINE	N-MINT
❏ 1, Nov 94, color 2.25		0.45	1.35	2.25
❏ 2, Dec 94, color 2.25		0.45	1.35	2.25
❏ 3, Jan 95, color.............2.25		0.45	1.35	2.25
❏ 4, Mar 95, color.............2.50		0.50	1.50	2.50
❏ 5, Apr 95, color.............2.50		0.50	1.50	2.50
❏ 6, Jun 95, color 2.50		0.50	1.50	2.50
❏ 7, Jul 95, color;contains Elfquest world map				
....2.50		0.50	1.50	2.50
❏ 8, Sep 95, color 2.50		0.50	1.50	2.50
❏ 9, Oct 95, b&w.............2.25		0.45	1.35	2.25
❏ 10, Nov 95, b&w.............2.25		0.45	1.35	2.25
❏ 11, Jan 96, b&w.............2.25		0.45	1.35	2.25

ELFQUEST: TWO-SPEAR (mini-series)

	ORIG.	GOOD	FINE	N-MINT
❏ 1, Oct 95, b&w.............2.25		0.45	1.35	2.25
❏ 2, Nov 95, b&w.............2.25		0.45	1.35	2.25
❏ 3, Dec 95, b&w.............2.25		0.45	1.35	2.25

ELFQUEST: WAVEDANCERS

	ORIG.	GOOD	FINE	N-MINT
❏ 1, color 2.00		0.40	1.20	2.00
❏ 2, color 2.25		0.45	1.35	2.25
❏ 3, Apr 94, color.............2.25		0.45	1.35	2.25
❏ 4, Jun 94, color 2.25		0.45	1.35	2.25
❏ 5, Aug 94, color.............2.25		0.45	1.35	2.25
❏ 6, Oct 94, color.............2.25		0.45	1.35	2.25

ELFTREK
DIMENSION

	ORIG.	GOOD	FINE	N-MINT
❏ 1, parody:Star Trek, Elfquest		0.35	1.05	1.75
❏ 2, parody:Star Trek, Elfquest		0.35	1.05	1.75

ELIMINATOR
ETERNITY

	ORIG.	GOOD	FINE	N-MINT
❏ 1, b&w.............................		0.50	1.50	2.50
❏ 2, b&w.............................		0.50	1.50	2.50

ELONGATED MAN
DC

	ORIG.	GOOD	FINE	N-MINT
❏ 1, Jan 92.......................1.00		0.20	0.60	1.00

	ORIG.	GOOD	FINE	N-MINT
2, Feb 92 ....1.00	0.20	0.60	1.00
3, Mar 92 ....1.00	0.20	0.60	1.00
4, Apr 92 ....1.00	0.20	0.60	1.00

ELRIC
PACIFIC

		GOOD	FINE	N-MINT
1, CR		0.60	1.80	3.00
2, CR		0.50	1.50	2.50
3, CR		0.50	1.50	2.50
4, CR		0.50	1.50	2.50
5, CR		0.50	1.50	2.50
6, CR (see First Comics) ..		0.50	1.50	2.50

ELRIC: BANE OF THE BLACK SWORD
FIRST

		GOOD	FINE	N-MINT
1		0.35	1.05	1.75
2		0.39	1.17	1.95
3		0.39	1.17	1.95
4		0.39	1.17	1.95
5		0.39	1.17	1.95
6		0.39	1.17	1.95

ELRIC: SAILOR ON SEAS OF FATE

		GOOD	FINE	N-MINT
1		0.35	1.05	1.75
2		0.35	1.05	1.75
3		0.35	1.05	1.75
4		0.35	1.05	1.75
5		0.35	1.05	1.75
6		0.35	1.05	1.75
7		0.35	1.05	1.75

ELRIC: THE VANISHING TOWER

		GOOD	FINE	N-MINT
1, JDu		0.35	1.05	1.75
2, JDu		0.35	1.05	1.75
3, JDu		0.35	1.05	1.75
4, JDu		0.35	1.05	1.75
5, JDu		0.35	1.05	1.75
6, JDu		0.35	1.05	1.75

ELRIC: WEIRD OF THE WHITE WOLF

		GOOD	FINE	N-MINT
1, CR		0.40	1.20	2.00
2, CR		0.35	1.05	1.75
3, CR		0.35	1.05	1.75
4, CR		0.35	1.05	1.75
5, CR		0.35	1.05	1.75

ELSEWHERE PRINCE, THE
EPIC

	ORIG.	GOOD	FINE	N-MINT
1, Moebius 1.95	0.39	1.17	1.95
2, Moebius 1.95	0.39	1.17	1.95
3, Moebius 1.95	0.39	1.17	1.95
4, Moebius 1.95	0.39	1.17	1.95
5, Moebius 1.95	0.39	1.17	1.95
6, Moebius 1.95	0.39	1.17	1.95

ELVEN
MALIBU/ULTRAVERSE

	ORIG.	GOOD	FINE	N-MINT
0, Oct 94 ....2.95	0.59	1.77	2.95

ELVIRA'S HOUSE OF MYSTERY
DC

		GOOD	FINE	N-MINT
1		0.25	0.75	1.25
2		0.20	0.60	1.00
3		0.20	0.60	1.00
4		0.20	0.60	1.00
5		0.20	0.60	1.00
6		0.20	0.60	1.00
7		0.20	0.60	1.00
8		0.20	0.60	1.00
9		0.20	0.60	1.00
10		0.20	0.60	1.00
11, Jan 87, DSt(c); final issue 1.25	2.00	6.00	10.00

ELVIRA'S HOUSE OF MYSTERY SPECIAL

		GOOD	FINE	N-MINT
1		0.25	0.75	1.25

ELVIRA, MISTRESS OF THE DARK
CLAYPOOL

	ORIG.	GOOD	FINE	N-MINT
1, May 93, b&w 2.50	0.50	1.50	2.50
2, b&w 2.50	0.50	1.50	2.50
3, b&w 2.50	0.50	1.50	2.50
4, b&w 2.50	0.50	1.50	2.50
5 ....1.50	0.30	0.90	1.50
6 ....1.50	0.30	0.90	1.50
7 ....1.50	0.30	0.90	1.50
8, Dec 93, b&w 2.50	0.50	1.50	2.50
9, Jan 94, b&w 2.50	0.50	1.50	2.50
10, Feb 94, b&w 2.50	0.50	1.50	2.50
11, Mar 94, b&w 2.50	0.50	1.50	2.50
13, May 94, b&w 2.50	0.50	1.50	2.50
14, 94, b&w 2.50	0.50	1.50	2.50
15, Jul 94, b&w 2.50	0.50	1.50	2.50
24, Apr 95, b&w 2.50	0.50	1.50	2.50
25, May 95, b&w 2.50	0.50	1.50	2.50
26, Jun 95, b&w 2.50	0.50	1.50	2.50
27, Jul 95, b&w 2.50	0.50	1.50	2.50
28, Aug 95, b&w 2.50	0.50	1.50	2.50
29, Sep 95, b&w 2.50	0.50	1.50	2.50
30, Oct 95, b&w 2.50	0.50	1.50	2.50
31, Nov 95, b&w 2.50	0.50	1.50	2.50
32, Dec 95, b&w 2.50	0.50	1.50	2.50
33, Jan 96, b&w 2.50	0.50	1.50	2.50
34, Feb 96, b&w 2.50	0.50	1.50	2.50

ELVIS MANDIBLE, THE
PIRANHA

		GOOD	FINE	N-MINT
0, nn;b&w;one-shot		0.70	2.10	3.50

ELVIS PRESLEY EXPERIENCE, THE (7 issue series)
REVOLUTIONARY

	ORIG.	GOOD	FINE	N-MINT
1, Aug 92, b&w 2.50	0.50	1.50	2.50
2, Oct 92, b&w 2.50	0.50	1.50	2.50
3, Jan 93, b&w 2.50	0.50	1.50	2.50
4, Feb 93, b&w 2.50	0.50	1.50	2.50
5, Jul 93, b&w 2.50	0.50	1.50	2.50
6, Aug 93, b&w 2.50	0.50	1.50	2.50
7, Apr 94, b&w 2.50	0.50	1.50	2.50

ELVIS SHRUGGED

	ORIG.	GOOD	FINE	N-MINT
1, Feb 92, b&w, Dave Garcia 0.25	0.50	1.50	2.50
2, Aug 92, b&w, Dave Garcia 0.25	0.50	1.50	2.50
3, Apr 92, b&w, Dave Garcia 3.95	0.79	2.37	3.95

ELVIS SHRUGGED GRAPHIC NOVEL

	ORIG.	GOOD	FINE	N-MINT
0, Dec 93, b&w 9.95	1.99	5.97	9.95

EMBLEM
ANTARCTIC

	ORIG.	GOOD	FINE	N-MINT
1, May 94, adult;b&w 3.50	0.70	2.10	3.50
2, Jun 94, adult;b&w 2.95	0.59	1.77	2.95
3, Jul 94, adult;b&w 2.95	0.59	1.77	2.95
5, Oct 94, adult;b&w 2.95	0.59	1.77	2.95
6, Nov 94, adult;b&w 2.95	0.59	1.77	2.95
7, Dec 94, adult;b&w 2.95	0.59	1.77	2.95
8, Feb 95, adult;b&w 2.95	0.59	1.77	2.95

EMERALDAS
ETERNITY

		GOOD	FINE	N-MINT
1, b&w		0.45	1.35	2.25
2, b&w		0.45	1.35	2.25
3, b&w		0.45	1.35	2.25
4, b&w		0.45	1.35	2.25

EMMA DAVENPORT
LOHMAN HILLS

	ORIG.	GOOD	FINE	N-MINT
1, Apr 95, b&w 2.75	0.55	1.65	2.75
2, Jun 95, b&w 2.75	0.55	1.65	2.75
3, Aug 95, b&w 2.75	0.55	1.65	2.75
4, b&w 2.75	0.55	1.65	2.75
5, b&w 2.75	0.55	1.65	2.75
6, Feb 96, b&w 2.75	0.55	1.65	2.75

	ORIG.	GOOD	FINE	N-MINT

EMPIRE
ETERNITY
	ORIG.	GOOD	FINE	N-MINT
❏ 1	0.39	1.17	1.95	
❏ 2	0.39	1.17	1.95	
❏ 3	0.39	1.17	1.95	
❏ 4	0.39	1.17	1.95	

EMPIRE LANES
KEYLINE
		GOOD	FINE	N-MINT
❏ 1		0.59	1.77	2.95

NORTHERN LIGHTS
		GOOD	FINE	N-MINT
❏ 1		0.35	1.05	1.75
❏ 2		0.35	1.05	1.75
❏ 3		0.35	1.05	1.75
❏ 4		0.35	1.05	1.75

EMPTY LOVE STORIES
SLAVE LABOR
	ORIG.	GOOD	FINE	N-MINT
❏ 1, Nov 94, b&w	2.95	0.59	1.77	2.95

ENCHANTED VALLEY
BLACKTHORNE
		GOOD	FINE	N-MINT
❏ 1		0.35	1.05	1.75
❏ 2		0.35	1.05	1.75

ENCHANTED WORLDS
BLACKMORE
	ORIG.	GOOD	FINE	N-MINT
❏ 1, 94, b&w	2.75	0.55	1.65	2.75

ENCHANTER
ECLIPSE
		GOOD	FINE	N-MINT
❏ 1, b&w		0.40	1.20	2.00
❏ 2, b&w		0.40	1.20	2.00
❏ 3, b&w		0.40	1.20	2.00

ENCHANTER: APOCALYPSE MOON
EXPRESS/ENTITY
	ORIG.	GOOD	FINE	N-MINT
❏ 1, 95, illustrated novella;b&w	2.95	0.59	1.77	2.95

ENCHANTER: PRELUDE TO APOCALYPSE
EXPRESS PRESS
	ORIG.	GOOD	FINE	N-MINT
❏ 1, b&w	2.50	0.50	1.50	2.50
❏ 2, b&w	2.50	0.50	1.50	2.50
❏ 3, b&w	2.50	0.50	1.50	2.50

ENEMY (mini-series)
DARK HORSE
	ORIG.	GOOD	FINE	N-MINT
❏ 1, May 94	2.50	0.50	1.50	2.50
❏ 2, Jun 94	2.50	0.50	1.50	2.50
❏ 3, Jul 94	2.50	0.50	1.50	2.50
❏ 4, Aug 94	2.50	0.50	1.50	2.50
❏ 5, Sep 94	2.50	0.50	1.50	2.50

ENEMY ACE SPECIAL
DC
		GOOD	FINE	N-MINT
❏ 1, Oct 90, JKu, reprints		0.20	0.60	1.00

ENIGMA
DC/VERTIGO
	ORIG.	GOOD	FINE	N-MINT
❏ 1	2.50	0.50	1.50	2.50
❏ 2	2.50	0.50	1.50	2.50
❏ 3	2.50	0.50	1.50	2.50
❏ 4	2.50	0.50	1.50	2.50
❏ 5	2.50	0.50	1.50	2.50
❏ 6	2.50	0.50	1.50	2.50
❏ 7	2.50	0.50	1.50	2.50
❏ 8	2.50	0.50	1.50	2.50

ENTROPY TALES
ENTROPY
		GOOD	FINE	N-MINT
❏ 1		0.30	0.90	1.50
❏ 2		0.30	0.90	1.50
❏ 3		0.30	0.90	1.50
❏ 4		0.30	0.90	1.50

ENTS
MANIC PRESS
	ORIG.	GOOD	FINE	N-MINT
❏ 1, b&w	2.50	0.50	1.50	2.50
❏ 2, b&w	2.50	0.50	1.50	2.50
❏ 3, b&w	2.50	0.50	1.50	2.50

EPIC
EPIC
	ORIG.	GOOD	FINE	N-MINT
❏ 1	4.95	0.99	2.97	4.95
❏ 2	4.95	0.99	2.97	4.95
❏ 3	4.95	0.99	2.97	4.95
❏ 4	4.95	0.99	2.97	4.95

EPIC ILLUSTRATED
	ORIG.	GOOD	FINE	N-MINT
❏ 1, Spr 80, (magazine); 1:Dreadstar	2.00	0.40	1.20	2.00
❏ 2, Sum 80, (magazine)	2.00	0.40	1.20	2.00
❏ 3, Aut 80, (magazine)	2.00	0.40	1.20	2.00
❏ 4, Wtr 80, (magazine)	2.00	0.40	1.20	2.00
❏ 5, Apr 81, (magazine)	2.00	0.40	1.20	2.00
❏ 6, Jun 81, (magazine)	2.00	0.40	1.20	2.00
❏ 7, Aug 81, (magazine)	2.00	0.40	1.20	2.00
❏ 8, Oct 81, (magazine)	2.00	0.40	1.20	2.00
❏ 9, Dec 81, (magazine)	2.00	0.40	1.20	2.00
❏ 10, Feb 82, (magazine)	2.00	0.40	1.20	2.00
❏ 11, Apr 82, (magazine)	2.50	0.50	1.50	2.50
❏ 12, Jun 82, (magazine)	2.50	0.50	1.50	2.50
❏ 13, Aug 82, (magazine)	2.50	0.50	1.50	2.50
❏ 14, Oct 82, (magazine)	2.50	0.50	1.50	2.50
❏ 15, Dec 82, (magazine)	2.50	0.50	1.50	2.50
❏ 16, Feb 83, (magazine)	2.50	0.50	1.50	2.50
❏ 17, Apr 83, (magazine)	2.50	0.50	1.50	2.50
❏ 18, Jun 83, (magazine)	2.50	0.50	1.50	2.50
❏ 19, Aug 83, (magazine)	2.50	0.50	1.50	2.50
❏ 20, Oct 83, (magazine)	2.50	0.50	1.50	2.50
❏ 21, Dec 83, (magazine)	2.50	0.50	1.50	2.50
❏ 22, Feb 84, (magazine)	2.50	0.50	1.50	2.50
❏ 23, Apr 84, (magazine)	2.50	0.50	1.50	2.50
❏ 24, Jun 84, (magazine)	2.50	0.50	1.50	2.50
❏ 25, Aug 84, (magazine)	2.50	0.50	1.50	2.50
❏ 26, Oct 84, (magazine)	2.50	0.50	1.50	2.50
❏ 27, Dec 84, (magazine)	2.50	0.50	1.50	2.50
❏ 28, Feb 85, (magazine)	2.50	0.50	1.50	2.50
❏ 29, Apr 85, (magazine)	2.50	0.50	1.50	2.50
❏ 30, Jun 85, (magazine)	2.50	0.50	1.50	2.50
❏ 31, Aug 85, (magazine)	2.50	0.50	1.50	2.50
❏ 32, Oct 85, (magazine)	2.50	0.50	1.50	2.50
❏ 33, Dec 85, (magazine)	2.50	0.50	1.50	2.50
❏ 34, Feb 86, (magazine); final issue	2.50	0.50	1.50	2.50

EPIC LITE
	ORIG.	GOOD	FINE	N-MINT
❏ 1	3.95	0.79	2.37	3.95

EPISODE GUIDES, THE
CELEBRITY
		GOOD	FINE	N-MINT
❏ 1, index to Star Trek		1.19	3.57	5.95

EPSILON WAVE (was Independent title)
ELITE
		GOOD	FINE	N-MINT
❏ 5		0.35	1.05	1.75
❏ 6		0.35	1.05	1.75
❏ 7, Aug 86		0.35	1.05	1.75
❏ 8		0.35	1.05	1.75

EPSILON WAVE, THE
INDEPENDENT
		GOOD	FINE	N-MINT
❏ 1, Oct 85		0.30	0.90	1.50
❏ 2, Dec 85		0.30	0.90	1.50
❏ 3, Feb 86		0.30	0.90	1.50
❏ 4, Apr 86, (moves to Elite)		0.30	0.90	1.50

EQUINE THE UNCIVILIZED
GRAPHXPRESS
		GOOD	FINE	N-MINT
❏ 1, b&w		0.20	0.60	1.00
❏ 2		0.40	1.20	2.00
❏ 3		0.40	1.20	2.00
❏ 4		0.40	1.20	2.00
❏ 5		0.40	1.20	2.00
❏ 6		0.40	1.20	2.00

	ORIG.	GOOD	FINE	N-MINT

EQUINOX CHRONICLES
INNOVATION
	ORIG.	GOOD	FINE	N-MINT
❏ 1, b&w		0.45	1.35	2.25
❏ 2, b&w		0.45	1.35	2.25

ERADICATORS, THE
SILVERWOLF
	ORIG.	GOOD	FINE	N-MINT
❏ 1		0.30	0.90	1.50
❏ 2		0.30	0.90	1.50
❏ 3		0.30	0.90	1.50
❏ 4		0.30	0.90	1.50

ERIC PRESTON IS THE FLAME
B-MOVIE
	ORIG.	GOOD	FINE	N-MINT
❏ 1		0.19	0.57	0.95

ERNIE
KITCHEN SINK
	ORIG.	GOOD	FINE	N-MINT
❏ 1, comics		0.40	1.20	2.00

EROS FORUM
EROS
	ORIG.	GOOD	FINE	N-MINT
❏ 1, adult only, b&w		0.50	1.50	2.50
❏ 3, adult only, b&w	2.95	0.59	1.77	2.95

EROS HAWK III
FANTAGRAPHICS/EROS
	ORIG.	GOOD	FINE	N-MINT
❏ 0, Jul 94, b&w	2.75	0.55	1.65	2.75

EROTIC FABLES & FAERIE TALES
EROS COMIX
	ORIG.	GOOD	FINE	N-MINT
❏ 1, adult, b&w		0.50	1.50	2.50
❏ 2, adult, b&w		0.50	1.50	2.50

EROTIC ORBITS
COMAX
	ORIG.	GOOD	FINE	N-MINT
❏ 1, b&w, adult		0.59	1.77	2.95

EROTIC TALES
AIRCEL
	ORIG.	GOOD	FINE	N-MINT
❏ 1, adult, b&w		0.59	1.77	2.95
❏ 2, adult, b&w		0.59	1.77	2.95
❏ 3, adult, b&w		0.59	1.77	2.95

EROTIC WORLDS OF FRANK THORNE, THE
EROS COMIX
	ORIG.	GOOD	FINE	N-MINT
❏ 1, sexy cover, adult		0.59	1.77	2.95
❏ 1, violent cover, adult		0.59	1.77	2.95
❏ 2		0.50	1.50	2.50
❏ 3		0.50	1.50	2.50
❏ 4		0.50	1.50	2.50
❏ 5		0.50	1.50	2.50
❏ 6		0.50	1.50	2.50

EROTICOM
CALIBER
	ORIG.	GOOD	FINE	N-MINT
❏ 1	2.50	0.50	1.50	2.50

EROTICOM II
	ORIG.	GOOD	FINE	N-MINT
❏ 0, 94, b&w	2.95	0.59	1.77	2.95

EROTIQUE
AIRCEL
	ORIG.	GOOD	FINE	N-MINT
❏ 1, adult, b&w		0.50	1.50	2.50

ERSATZ PEACH
AEON
	ORIG.	GOOD	FINE	N-MINT
❏ 0, Jul 95, nn;multiple interpretations of The Desert Peach by various artists	7.95	1.59	4.77	7.95

ESCAPE TO THE STARS
SOLSON
	ORIG.	GOOD	FINE	N-MINT
❏ 1		0.35	1.05	1.75

ESCAPE VELOCITY
ESCAPE VELOCITY
	ORIG.	GOOD	FINE	N-MINT
❏ 1		0.30	0.90	1.50
❏ 2		0.30	0.90	1.50

ESPERS
ECLIPSE
	ORIG.	GOOD	FINE	N-MINT
❏ 1, Jul 86		0.35	1.05	1.75
❏ 2, Sep 86		0.35	1.05	1.75
❏ 3, Nov 86		0.35	1.05	1.75

	ORIG.	GOOD	FINE	N-MINT
❏ 4, Feb 87		0.35	1.05	1.75
❏ 5, Apr 87		0.35	1.05	1.75

ETC
PIRANHA
	ORIG.	GOOD	FINE	N-MINT
❏ 1, color		0.90	2.70	4.50
❏ 2, color		0.90	2.70	4.50
❏ 3, color		0.90	2.70	4.50
❏ 4, color		0.90	2.70	4.50
❏ 5, color		0.90	2.70	4.50

ETERNAL THIRST (was Hammac title)
ALPHA PRODUCTIONS
	ORIG.	GOOD	FINE	N-MINT
❏ 3, b&w		0.39	1.17	1.95
❏ 4, b&w		0.39	1.17	1.95
❏ 5, b&w		0.39	1.17	1.95

ETERNAL WARRIOR
ACCLAIM/VALIANT
	ORIG.	GOOD	FINE	N-MINT
❏ 34, Jun 95	2.25	0.50	1.50	2.50
❏ 35, Jul 95	2.50	0.50	1.50	2.50
❏ 36, Jul 95	2.50	0.50	1.50	2.50
❏ 37, Aug 95	2.50	0.50	1.50	2.50
❏ 38, Aug 95	2.50	0.50	1.50	2.50
❏ 39, Sep 95	2.50	0.50	1.50	2.50
❏ 40, Sep 95	2.50	0.50	1.50	2.50
❏ 41, Oct 95	2.50	0.50	1.50	2.50
❏ 42, Oct 95	2.50	0.50	1.50	2.50
❏ 43, Nov 95	2.50	0.50	1.50	2.50
❏ 44, Nov 95	2.50	0.50	1.50	2.50
❏ 45, Dec 95	2.50	0.50	1.50	2.50
❏ 46, Dec 95	2.50	0.50	1.50	2.50
❏ 47, Jan 96	2.50	0.50	1.50	2.50
❏ 48, Jan 96	2.50	0.50	1.50	2.50
❏ 49, Feb 96	2.50	0.50	1.50	2.50
❏ 50, Mar 96	2.50	0.50	1.50	2.50

VALIANT
	ORIG.	GOOD	FINE	N-MINT
❏ 1, Aug 92, FM(c) Unity	2.25	1.20	3.60	6.00
❏ 1, gold edition		5.00	15.00	25.00
❏ 1, gold logo		6.00	18.00	30.00
❏ 2, Sep 92, WS(c) Unity	2.25	1.00	3.00	5.00
❏ 3, Oct 92	2.25	1.00	3.00	5.00
❏ 4, Nov 92	2.25	2.00	6.00	10.00
❏ 5, Dec 92	2.25	1.40	4.20	7.00
❏ 6, Jan 93	2.25	1.00	3.00	5.00
❏ 7, Feb 93	2.25	1.00	3.00	5.00
❏ 8, Mar 93, combined with Archer & Armstrong #8	4.50	1.60	4.80	8.00
❏ 9, Apr 93	2.25	0.45	1.35	2.25
❏ 10, May 93	2.25	0.45	1.35	2.25
❏ 11, Jun 93	2.25	0.45	1.35	2.25
❏ 12, Jul 93	2.25	0.45	1.35	2.25
❏ 13, Aug 93	2.25	0.45	1.35	2.25
❏ 14, Aug 93	2.25	0.45	1.35	2.25
❏ 15, Aug 93	2.25	0.45	1.35	2.25
❏ 16, Aug 93	2.25	0.45	1.35	2.25
❏ 17, Aug 93	2.25	0.45	1.35	2.25
❏ 18, Aug 93	2.25	0.45	1.35	2.25
❏ 19, Aug 93	2.25	0.45	1.35	2.25
❏ 20, Aug 93	2.25	0.45	1.35	2.25
❏ 21, Aug 93	2.25	0.45	1.35	2.25
❏ 22, Aug 93	2.25	0.45	1.35	2.25
❏ 23, Jun 94	2.25	0.45	1.35	2.25
❏ 24, Aug 94	2.25	0.45	1.35	2.25
❏ 25, Sep 94	2.25	0.45	1.35	2.25
❏ 26, Oct 94, indicia says August; double issue with Archer & Armstrong #26	2.75	0.55	1.65	2.75
❏ 27, Nov 94	2.25	0.45	1.35	2.25
❏ 31, Mar 95	2.25	0.45	1.35	2.25
❏ 32, Apr 95	2.25	0.45	1.35	2.25
❏ 33, May 95	1.95	0.39	1.17	1.95

	ORIG.	GOOD	FINE	N-MINT

ETERNAL WARRIOR FIST AND STEEL (mini-series)
ACCLAIM/VALIANT

	ORIG.	GOOD	FINE	N-MINT
❑ 1, May 96, A:Geomancer 2.50		0.50	1.50	2.50
❑ 2, Jun 96, A:Geomancer. 2.50		0.50	1.50	2.50

ETERNAL WARRIOR SPECIAL

❑ 1, Feb 96, Eternal Warrior in WW II
.... 2.50 — 0.50 — 1.50 — 2.50

ETERNAL WARRIOR YEARBOOK
VALIANT

	ORIG.	GOOD	FINE	N-MINT
❑ 1 .... 3.95		0.79	2.37	3.95
❑ 2, 94, 1994; cardstock cover 3.95		0.79	2.37	3.95

ETERNALS
MARVEL

	ORIG.	GOOD	FINE	N-MINT
❑ 1, JK 0.25		0.20	0.60	1.00
❑ 2, JK 0.25		0.20	0.60	1.00
❑ 3, Sep 76, JK 0.30		0.20	0.60	1.00
❑ 4, Oct 76, JK 0.30		0.20	0.60	1.00
❑ 5, Nov 76, JK 0.30		0.20	0.60	1.00
❑ 6, Dec 76, JK 0.30		0.20	0.60	1.00
❑ 7, Jan 77, JK 0.30		0.20	0.60	1.00
❑ 8, Feb 77, JK 0.30		0.20	0.60	1.00
❑ 9, Mar 77, JK 0.30		0.20	0.60	1.00
❑ 10, Apr 77, JK 0.30		0.20	0.60	1.00
❑ 11, May 77, JK 0.30		0.20	0.60	1.00
❑ 12, Jun 77, JK 0.30		0.20	0.60	1.00
❑ 13, Jul 77, JK 0.30		0.20	0.60	1.00
❑ 14, Aug 77, JK 0.30		0.20	0.60	1.00
❑ 15, Sep 77, JK 0.30		0.20	0.60	1.00
❑ 16, Oct 77, JK 0.30		0.20	0.60	1.00
❑ 17, Nov 77, JK 0.35		0.20	0.60	1.00
❑ 18, Dec 77, JK 0.35		0.20	0.60	1.00
❑ 19, Jan 78, JK 0.35		0.20	0.60	1.00

ETERNALS (maxi-series)

	ORIG.	GOOD	FINE	N-MINT
❑ 1, Oct 85 .... 1.25		0.25	0.75	1.25
❑ 2, Nov 85 .... 0.75		0.20	0.60	1.00
❑ 3, Dec 85 .... 0.75		0.20	0.60	1.00
❑ 4, Jan 86 .... 0.75		0.20	0.60	1.00
❑ 5, Feb 86 .... 0.75		0.20	0.60	1.00
❑ 6, Mar 86 .... 0.75		0.20	0.60	1.00
❑ 7, Apr 86 .... 0.75		0.20	0.60	1.00
❑ 8, May 86 .... 0.75		0.20	0.60	1.00
❑ 9, Jun 86 .... 0.75		0.20	0.60	1.00
❑ 10, Jul 86 .... 0.75		0.20	0.60	1.00
❑ 11, Aug 86 .... 0.75		0.20	0.60	1.00
❑ 12, Sep 86 .... 1.25		0.25	0.75	1.25

ETERNALS ANNUAL

❑ 1, Oct 77, JK .... — 2.10 — 6.30 — 10.50

ETERNALS: THE HEROD FACTOR

❑ 1, Nov 91 .... 2.50 — 0.50 — 1.50 — 2.50

ETERNITY SMITH
RENEGADE

	ORIG.	GOOD	FINE	N-MINT
❑ 1, Sep 86, color 1.25		0.25	0.75	1.25
❑ 2, Nov 86 .... 1.50		0.30	0.90	1.50
❑ 3, Jan 87 .... 1.50		0.30	0.90	1.50
❑ 4, Mar 87 .... 1.50		0.30	0.90	1.50
❑ 5, May 87 .... 1.50		0.30	0.90	1.50

ETERNITY SMITH (second series)
HERO

	ORIG.	GOOD	FINE	N-MINT
❑ 1, Sep 87		0.39	1.17	1.95
❑ 2, Oct 87		0.39	1.17	1.95
❑ 3, Nov 87		0.39	1.17	1.95
❑ 4, Dec 87		0.39	1.17	1.95
❑ 5, Jan 88		0.39	1.17	1.95
❑ 6, Feb 88		0.39	1.17	1.95
❑ 7, Apr 88		0.39	1.17	1.95
❑ 8, Jun 88		0.39	1.17	1.95
❑ 9, Aug 88, A:Walter Koenig		0.39	1.17	1.95

ETERNITY TRIPLE ACTION
ETERNITY

	ORIG.	GOOD	FINE	N-MINT
❑ 1, b&w 2.50		0.50	1.50	2.50
❑ 2, b&w 2.50		0.50	1.50	2.50
❑ 3, b&w 2.50		0.50	1.50	2.50

EUDAEMON, THE
DARK HORSE

	ORIG.	GOOD	FINE	N-MINT
❑ 1, Aug 93 .... 2.50		0.50	1.50	2.50
❑ 2, 93 .... 2.50		0.50	1.50	2.50
❑ 3, 93 .... 2.50		0.50	1.50	2.50

EUGENUS
EUGENUS

	ORIG.	GOOD	FINE	N-MINT
❑ 1, b&w 3.50		0.70	2.10	3.50
❑ 2, b&w 3.50		0.70	2.10	3.50
❑ 3 .... 2.50		0.50	1.50	2.50

EVANGELINE
COMICO

	ORIG.	GOOD	FINE	N-MINT
❑ 1		0.80	2.40	4.00
❑ 2		0.60	1.80	3.00

FIRST

	ORIG.	GOOD	FINE	N-MINT
❑ 1		0.35	1.05	1.75
❑ 2		0.35	1.05	1.75
❑ 3		0.35	1.05	1.75
❑ 4		0.35	1.05	1.75
❑ 5		0.35	1.05	1.75
❑ 6		0.35	1.05	1.75
❑ 7		0.35	1.05	1.75
❑ 8		0.35	1.05	1.75
❑ 9		0.35	1.05	1.75
❑ 10		0.39	1.17	1.95
❑ 11		0.39	1.17	1.95
❑ 12		0.39	1.17	1.95

EVANGELINE SPECIAL
LODESTONE

	ORIG.	GOOD	FINE	N-MINT
❑ 1		0.40	1.20	2.00

EVEL KNIEVEL
MARVEL

	ORIG.	GOOD	FINE	N-MINT
❑ 0, giveaway		0.60	1.80	3.00

EVIL ERNIE
CHAOS!

	ORIG.	GOOD	FINE	N-MINT
❑ 0				
❑ 0, platinum edition				

ETERNITY

	ORIG.	GOOD	FINE	N-MINT
❑ 1, b&w		25.00	75.00	125.00
❑ 2, b&w		20.00	60.00	100.00
❑ 3, b&w		12.00	36.00	60.00
❑ 4, b&w		10.00	30.00	50.00
❑ 5, b&w		10.00	30.00	50.00

EVIL ERNIE VS. THE SUPER HEROES
CHAOS!

	ORIG.	GOOD	FINE	N-MINT
❑ 1, Aug 95, one-shot 2.95		0.59	1.77	2.95
❑ 1, no cover price; premium edition (10,000 copies); enhanced cover				

EVIL ERNIE: REVENGE (mini-series)

	ORIG.	GOOD	FINE	N-MINT
❑ 0		2.00	6.00	10.00
❑ 1				
❑ 1, "Master of Annihilation" premium edition				
❑ 2		1.00	3.00	5.00
❑ 3, Jan 95 .... 2.50		0.80	2.40	4.00
❑ 4, Feb 95 .... 2.50		0.80	2.40	4.00

EVIL ERNIE: STRAIGHT TO HELL (mini-series)

	ORIG.	GOOD	FINE	N-MINT
❑ 2, Dec 95 .... 2.95		0.59	1.77	2.95
❑ 5, May 96, final issue 2.95		0.59	1.77	2.95

EVIL ERNIE: THE RESURRECTION

	ORIG.	GOOD	FINE	N-MINT
❑ 1		2.40	7.20	12.00
❑ 1, gold edition				
❑ 2		2.00	6.00	10.00
❑ 3		2.00	6.00	10.00
❑ 4		1.60	4.80	8.00

	ORIG.	GOOD	FINE	N-MINT

EWOKS
STAR

	ORIG.	GOOD	FINE	N-MINT
1, Star Wars	0.65	0.60	1.80	3.00
2, Star Wars	0.65	0.40	1.20	2.00
3, Star Wars	0.65	0.40	1.20	2.00
4, Star Wars	0.65	0.40	1.20	2.00
5, Star Wars	0.65	0.40	1.20	2.00
6, Star Wars	0.75	0.30	0.90	1.50
7, Star Wars	0.75	0.30	0.90	1.50
8, Star Wars	0.75	0.30	0.90	1.50
9, Star Wars	0.75	0.30	0.90	1.50
10, Star Wars	0.75	0.30	0.90	1.50
11, Star Wars	0.75	0.30	0.90	1.50
12, Star Wars	0.75	0.30	0.90	1.50
13, Star Wars	0.75	0.30	0.90	1.50
14, Star Wars	1.00	0.30	0.90	1.50

EX-MUTANTS
ETERNITY

	ORIG.	GOOD	FINE	N-MINT
1	1.80	1.00	3.00	5.00
2		0.39	1.17	1.95
3		0.39	1.17	1.95
4		0.39	1.17	1.95
5		0.39	1.17	1.95
6		0.39	1.17	1.95
7		0.39	1.17	1.95
8		0.39	1.17	1.95
9		0.39	1.17	1.95
10		0.39	1.17	1.95
11		0.39	1.17	1.95
12		0.39	1.17	1.95
13		0.39	1.17	1.95
14		0.39	1.17	1.95
15, (moves to Amazing Comics)	0.39	1.17	1.95

MALIBU

	ORIG.	GOOD	FINE	N-MINT
1, O:Ex-Mutants	1.95	0.39	1.17	1.95
1, shiny cover, O:Ex-Mutants	0.50	1.50	2.50
2	1.95	0.39	1.17	1.95
3	1.95	0.39	1.17	1.95
4	1.95	0.39	1.17	1.95
5	1.95	0.39	1.17	1.95
6	1.95	0.39	1.17	1.95
7	1.95	0.39	1.17	1.95
8	1.95	0.39	1.17	1.95
9	1.95	0.39	1.17	1.95
10	1.95	0.39	1.17	1.95
11	2.25	0.45	1.35	2.25
12	2.25	0.45	1.35	2.25
13	2.25	0.45	1.35	2.25
14, Genesis	2.25	0.45	1.35	2.25
15, Genesis	2.50	0.50	1.50	2.50
16, Feb 94, Genesis	2.50	0.50	1.50	2.50
17, Mar 94, Genesis	2.50	0.50	1.50	2.50
18, Apr 94, Genesis; final issue	2.50	0.50	1.50	2.50

EX-MUTANTS (former Amazing Comics title)
PIED PIPER

	ORIG.	GOOD	FINE	N-MINT
6		0.39	1.17	1.95
7		0.39	1.17	1.95
8		0.39	1.17	1.95

EX-MUTANTS (former Eternity title)
AMAZING

	ORIG.	GOOD	FINE	N-MINT
1, reprint		0.40	1.20	2.00
2		0.60	1.80	3.00
3		0.36	1.08	1.80
4		0.39	1.17	1.95
5, (moves to Pied Piper Comics)	0.39	1.17	1.95

EX-MUTANTS (former Pied Piper title)
ETERNITY

	ORIG.	GOOD	FINE	N-MINT
6, reprints		0.39	1.17	1.95
7, reprints		0.39	1.17	1.95

EX-MUTANTS ANNUAL

	ORIG.	GOOD	FINE	N-MINT
1		0.39	1.17	1.95

EX-MUTANTS GRAPHIC NOVEL

	ORIG.	GOOD	FINE	N-MINT
1, b&w		1.39	4.17	6.95
2, Gods or Men		1.59	4.77	7.95

EX-MUTANTS PIN-UP BOOK

	ORIG.	GOOD	FINE	N-MINT
1		0.39	1.17	1.95

EX-MUTANTS WINTER SPECIAL

	ORIG.	GOOD	FINE	N-MINT
1, b&w		0.39	1.17	1.95

EX-MUTANTS: THE SPECIAL EDITION
AMAZING

	ORIG.	GOOD	FINE	N-MINT
1		0.45	1.35	2.25

EXCALIBUR
MARVEL

	ORIG.	GOOD	FINE	N-MINT
1, Oct 88	1.50	2.40	7.20	12.00
2, Nov 88	1.50	1.60	4.80	8.00
3, Dec 88	1.50	1.00	3.00	5.00
4, Jan 89	1.50	1.00	3.00	5.00
5, Feb 89	1.50	1.00	3.00	5.00
6, Mar 89, Inferno	1.50	0.60	1.80	3.00
7, Apr 89, Inferno	1.50	0.60	1.80	3.00
8, May 89	1.50	0.50	1.50	2.50
9, Jun 89	1.50	0.50	1.50	2.50
10, Jul 89	1.50	0.50	1.50	2.50
11, Aug 89	1.50	0.50	1.50	2.50
12, Sep 89	1.50	0.50	1.50	2.50
13, Oct 89	1.50	0.50	1.50	2.50
14, Nov 89	1.50	0.50	1.50	2.50
15, Nov 89	1.50	0.50	1.50	2.50
16, Dec 89	1.50	0.50	1.50	2.50
17, Dec 89	1.50	0.50	1.50	2.50
18, Jan 90	1.50	0.50	1.50	2.50
19, Feb 90	1.50	0.50	1.50	2.50
20, Mar 90	1.50	0.50	1.50	2.50
21, Apr 90	1.50	0.50	1.50	2.50
22, May 90	1.50	0.50	1.50	2.50
23, Jun 90	1.50	0.50	1.50	2.50
24, Jul 90	1.75	0.50	1.50	2.50
25, Aug 90	1.75	0.50	1.50	2.50
26, Aug 90	1.75	0.40	1.20	2.00
27, Aug 90	1.75	0.40	1.20	2.00
28, Sep 90	1.75	0.40	1.20	2.00
29, Sep 90	1.75	0.40	1.20	2.00
30, Oct 90	1.75	0.40	1.20	2.00
31, Nov 90	1.75	0.40	1.20	2.00
32, Dec 90, with $1.50 price	1.50	0.40	1.20	2.00
32, with $1.75 price	1.75	0.40	1.20	2.00
33, Jan 91	1.75	0.40	1.20	2.00
34, Feb 91	1.75	0.40	1.20	2.00
35, Mar 91	1.75	0.40	1.20	2.00
36, Apr 91, Outlaws	1.75	0.40	1.20	2.00
37, May 91	1.75	0.40	1.20	2.00
38, Jun 91	1.75	0.40	1.20	2.00
39, Jul 91	1.75	0.40	1.20	2.00
40, Aug 91	1.75	0.40	1.20	2.00
41, Sep 91	1.75	0.40	1.20	2.00
42, Oct 91	1.75	0.40	1.20	2.00
43, Nov 91	1.75	0.40	1.20	2.00
44, Nov 91	1.75	0.40	1.20	2.00
45, Dec 91	1.75	0.40	1.20	2.00
46, Dec 91	1.75	0.40	1.20	2.00
47	1.75	0.40	1.20	2.00
48	1.75	0.40	1.20	2.00
49	1.75	0.40	1.20	2.00
50, May 92	2.75	0.55	1.65	2.75
51	1.75	0.40	1.20	2.00
52, A:X-Men	1.75	0.35	1.05	1.75
53	1.75	0.35	1.05	1.75
54	1.75	0.35	1.05	1.75

	ORIG.	GOOD	FINE	N-MINT
☐ 55 ....1.75		0.35	1.05	1.75
☐ 56 ....1.75		0.35	1.05	1.75
☐ 57 ....1.75		0.35	1.05	1.75
☐ 58 ....1.75		0.35	1.05	1.75
☐ 59 ....1.75		0.35	1.05	1.75
☐ 60 ....1.75		0.35	1.05	1.75
☐ 61 ....1.75		0.35	1.05	1.75
☐ 62 ....1.75		0.35	1.05	1.75
☐ 63, Mar 93 ....1.75		0.35	1.05	1.75
☐ 64, Apr 93 ....1.75		0.35	1.05	1.75
☐ 65, May 93 ....1.75		0.35	1.05	1.75
☐ 66, Jun 93 ....1.75		0.35	1.05	1.75
☐ 67, Jul 93 ....1.75		0.35	1.05	1.75
☐ 68, Aug 93 ....1.75		0.35	1.05	1.75
☐ 69, Sep 93 ....1.75		0.35	1.05	1.75
☐ 70, Oct 93 ....1.75		0.35	1.05	1.75
☐ 71, Nov 93, hologram 3.95		1.20	3.60	6.00
☐ 72, Dec 93................1.75		0.35	1.05	1.75
☐ 73, Jan 94 ....1.75		0.35	1.05	1.75
☐ 74, Feb 94 ....1.75		0.35	1.05	1.75
☐ 75, Mar 94, foil cover..... 3.50		0.70	2.10	3.50
☐ 75, Mar 94 ....2.25		0.45	1.35	2.25
☐ 76, Apr 94 ....2.25		0.45	1.35	2.25
☐ 77, May 94................1.95		0.39	1.17	1.95
☐ 78, Jun 94................1.95		0.39	1.17	1.95
☐ 79, Jul 94.................1.95		0.39	1.17	1.95
☐ 80, Aug 94................1.95		0.39	1.17	1.95
☐ 81, Sep 94................1.95		0.39	1.17	1.95
☐ 82, Oct 94, enhanced cover				
...........................3.50		0.70	2.10	3.50
☐ 82, 94.....................2.50		0.50	1.50	2.50
☐ 83, Nov 94, deluxe edition				
...........................1.95		0.39	1.17	1.95
☐ 84, Dec 94................1.50		0.30	0.90	1.50
☐ 84, Dec 94, deluxe edition				
...........................1.95		0.39	1.17	1.95
☐ 85, Jan 95, deluxe edition				
...........................1.95		0.39	1.17	1.95
☐ 85, Jan 95.................1.50		0.30	0.90	1.50
☐ 86, Feb 95.................1.50		0.30	0.90	1.50
☐ 86, Feb 95, deluxe edition				
...........................1.95		0.39	1.17	1.95
☐ 87, Jul 95.................1.95		0.39	1.17	1.95
☐ 88, Aug 95 ....1.95		0.39	1.17	1.95
☐ 89, Sep 95................1.95		0.39	1.17	1.95
☐ 90, Oct 95, OverPower cards inserted				
...........................1.95		0.39	1.17	1.95
☐ 91, Nov 95 ....1.95		0.39	1.17	1.95
☐ 92, Dec 95................1.95		0.39	1.17	1.95
☐ 93, Jan 96 ....1.95		0.39	1.17	1.95
☐ 94, Feb 96................1.95		0.39	1.17	1.95
☐ 95, Mar 96 ....1.95		0.39	1.17	1.95
☐ 96, Apr 96 ....1.95		0.39	1.17	1.95
☐ 97, May 96................1.95		0.39	1.17	1.95
☐ 98, Jun 96................1.95		0.39	1.17	1.95
☐ 99, Jul 96.................1.95		0.39	1.17	1.95

EXCALIBUR ANNUAL

	ORIG.	GOOD	FINE	N-MINT
☐ 1, trading card...............2.95		0.59	1.77	2.95
☐ 2, 94.........................2.95		0.59	1.77	2.95

EXCALIBUR SPECIAL: SWORD IS DRAWN

	ORIG.	GOOD	FINE	N-MINT
☐ 1, 88, 1st printing;I&1:Excalibur				
...........................3.25		3.60	10.80	18.00

EXCALIBUR: THE POSSESSION

	ORIG.	GOOD	FINE	N-MINT
☐ 0, Jul 91 ....2.95		0.59	1.77	2.95

EXILE EARTH
RIVER CITY

	ORIG.	GOOD	FINE	N-MINT
☐ 1 ....1.95		0.39	1.17	1.95
☐ 2, 94.........................1.95		0.39	1.17	1.95

EXILES
ALPHA PRODUCTIONS

	ORIG.	GOOD	FINE	N-MINT
☐ 1, b&w.....................		0.39	1.17	1.95

MALIBU

	ORIG.	GOOD	FINE	N-MINT
☐ 1 ....1.95		1.60	4.80	8.00
☐ 1, hologram		12.00	36.00	60.00
☐ 2 ....1.95		0.80	2.40	4.00
☐ 3, Oct 93, Rune,BWS......2.50		0.80	2.40	4.00
☐ 4, Nov 93, D: Exiles, final issue				
...........................1.95		1.00	3.00	5.00

EXODUS REVELATION
EXODUS

	ORIG.	GOOD	FINE	N-MINT
☐ 1, Nov 94, b&w;no cover price				

EXOSQUAD
TOPPS

	ORIG.	GOOD	FINE	N-MINT
☐ 0, Jan 94...................1.00		0.20	0.60	1.00

EXOTIC FANTASY
EROS

	ORIG.	GOOD	FINE	N-MINT
☐ 1, sketches, adult, b&w ..4.95		0.99	2.97	4.95
☐ 2, sketches, adult, b&w ..4.95		0.99	2.97	4.95
☐ 3, sketches, adult, b&w ..4.95		0.99	2.97	4.95

EXOTICA
CRY FOR DAWN

	ORIG.	GOOD	FINE	N-MINT
☐ 1, adult, b&w..............		0.80	2.40	4.00

EXPERIENCE, THE
AIRCEL

	ORIG.	GOOD	FINE	N-MINT
☐ 1, adult, b&w..................		0.65	1.95	3.25

EXPLORERS
EXPLORER

	ORIG.	GOOD	FINE	N-MINT
☐ 1, 95, b&w................2.95		0.59	1.77	2.95
☐ 2, 95, b&w................2.95		0.59	1.77	2.95

EXPLORERS OF THE UNKNOWN
ARCHIE

	ORIG.	GOOD	FINE	N-MINT
☐ 1, Jun 90 ....1.00		0.20	0.60	1.00
☐ 2 ....1.00		0.20	0.60	1.00
☐ 3 ....1.00		0.20	0.60	1.00
☐ 4 ....1.00		0.20	0.60	1.00
☐ 5 ....1.00		0.20	0.60	1.00
☐ 6 ....1.00		0.20	0.60	1.00

EXPOSE
CRACKED PEPPER

	ORIG.	GOOD	FINE	N-MINT
☐ 1, Dec 93, b&w.............2.50		0.50	1.50	2.50

EXQUISITE CORPSE
DARK HORSE

	ORIG.	GOOD	FINE	N-MINT
☐ 1, 90		0.50	1.50	2.50
☐ 2, 90		0.50	1.50	2.50
☐ 3, 90		0.50	1.50	2.50

EXTINCT!
NEW ENGLAND

	ORIG.	GOOD	FINE	N-MINT
☐ 1, b&w reprints...............		0.70	2.10	3.50
☐ 2, b&w reprints...............		0.70	2.10	3.50

EXTREME
IMAGE

	ORIG.	GOOD	FINE	N-MINT
☐ 0		3.00	9.00	15.00

EXTREME DESTROYER EPILOGUE

	ORIG.	GOOD	FINE	N-MINT
☐ 1, Jan 96.................2.50		0.50	1.50	2.50

EXTREME DESTROYER PROLOGUE

	ORIG.	GOOD	FINE	N-MINT
☐ 1, Jan 96, bagged with card				
...........................2.50		0.50	1.50	2.50

EXTREME JUSTICE
DC

	ORIG.	GOOD	FINE	N-MINT
☐ 1, Feb 95.................1.50		0.30	0.90	1.50
☐ 2, Mar 95.................1.50		0.30	0.90	1.50
☐ 3, Apr 95.................1.50		0.30	0.90	1.50
☐ 4, May 95.................1.50		0.30	0.90	1.50
☐ 5, Jun 95.................1.75		0.35	1.05	1.75
☐ 6, Jul 95.................1.75		0.35	1.05	1.75
☐ 7, Aug 95.................1.75		0.35	1.05	1.75

	ORIG.	GOOD	FINE	N-MINT
☐ 8, Sep 95	1.75	0.35	1.05	1.75
☐ 9, Oct 95	1.75	0.35	1.05	1.75
☐ 10, Nov 95	1.75	0.35	1.05	1.75
☐ 11, Dec 95	1.75	0.35	1.05	1.75
☐ 12, Jan 96	1.75	0.35	1.05	1.75
☐ 13, Feb 96	1.75	0.35	1.05	1.75
☐ 14, Mar 96	1.75	0.35	1.05	1.75
☐ 15, Apr 96	1.75	0.35	1.05	1.75
☐ 16, May 96	1.75	0.35	1.05	1.75
☐ 17, Jun 96	1.75	0.35	1.05	1.75

EXTREME SACRIFICE
IMAGE

	ORIG.	GOOD	FINE	N-MINT
☐ 1, Jan 95, polybagged with trading card	2.50	0.50	1.50	2.50

EXTREME SACRIFICE EPILOGUE

	ORIG.	GOOD	FINE	N-MINT
☐ 2, Jan 95	2.50	0.50	1.50	2.50

EXTREME SACRIFICE PRELUDE

	ORIG.	GOOD	FINE	N-MINT
☐ 1, Jan 95	2.50	0.50	1.50	2.50

EXTREME SUPER CHRISTMAS SPECIAL

	ORIG.	GOOD	FINE	N-MINT
☐ 1, Dec 94	2.95	0.59	1.77	2.95

EXTREME TOUR BOOK

	ORIG.	GOOD	FINE	N-MINT
☐ 1		2.40	7.20	12.00

EXTREMELY SILLY
ANTARCTIC

	GOOD	FINE	N-MINT
☐ 1	1.00	3.00	5.00

EXTREMELY SILLY (Volume 2)

	GOOD	FINE	N-MINT
☐ 1	0.25	0.75	1.25

EXTREMES OF VIOLET
BLACKOUT

	ORIG.	GOOD	FINE	N-MINT
☐ 2, 95	2.95	0.59	1.77	2.95

EXTREMIST, THE
DC/VERTIGO

	ORIG.	GOOD	FINE	N-MINT
☐ 1	1.95	0.39	1.17	1.95
☐ 1, platinum edition		8.00	24.00	40.00
☐ 2, Oct 93	1.95	0.39	1.17	1.95
☐ 3	1.95	0.39	1.17	1.95
☐ 4	1.95	0.39	1.17	1.95

EYE OF MONGOMBO, THE
FANTAGRAPHICS

	GOOD	FINE	N-MINT
☐ 1, b&w	0.40	1.20	2.00
☐ 2, b&w	0.40	1.20	2.00
☐ 3, b&w	0.40	1.20	2.00
☐ 4, b&w	0.40	1.20	2.00
☐ 5, b&w	0.40	1.20	2.00
☐ 6, b&w	0.40	1.20	2.00

EYEBALL KID
DARK HORSE

	GOOD	FINE	N-MINT
☐ 1, 92, b&w	0.45	1.35	2.25
☐ 2, 92, b&w	0.45	1.35	2.25
☐ 3, 92, b&w	0.45	1.35	2.25

EYEBEAM
DOUBLE DIAMOND

	GOOD	FINE	N-MINT
☐ 1, b&w strip reprints	0.50	1.50	2.50
☐ 2, b&w strip reprints	0.50	1.50	2.50
☐ 3, b&w strip reprints	0.50	1.50	2.50
☐ 4, b&w strip reprints	0.50	1.50	2.50
☐ 5, b&w strip reprints	0.50	1.50	2.50

Enemy Ace

Star Spangled War Stories #138 ©1968 National Periodical Publications Inc.

World War I German flying ace Hans Von Hammer made his debut in DC's *Our Army at War* #151 (Feb 65). Like *Our Army at War*'s Sgt. Rock, Von Hammer was the creation of writer Robert Kanigher and artist Joe Kubert. After three issues backing up Rock and Easy Co. (#151, 153, and 155), Von Hammer's Enemy Ace series was given a full-length tryout in *Showcase* #58 (Sep-Oct 65).

When Enemy Ace finally returned to the skies three years later, he had enough support to take over *Star-Spangled War Stories*. Beginning with issue #138, the cover title became *Star-Spangled War Stories Presents Enemy Ace* (though the indicia title was unchanged). Full-length Enemy Ace stories continued until issue #150.

The series was characterized by an unrelenting grimness and attention to detail in both script and art. Kubert's trademark panel-layout techniques worked to advantage here, with panoramic aerial dogfights surrounding inset close-ups of the pilot's face. Kanigher's scripts followed a strict formula: Von Hammer, a dour loner (called The Killing Machine by his fellow pilots), only came alive in the air, where he saluted his British and French enemies as they went down in flames. On the ground, Von Hammer's only friend was a wild black wolf who accompanied him on hunting trips in the Black Forest. Periodically wounded, Von Hammer would be nursed by beautiful angels of mercy, but any budding romance was always squelched by his icy demeanor.

Some of Von Hammer's more colorful opponents included The Hangman, St. George, and The Harpy (The Hangman's sister). SSWS #139 (Jun-Jul 68) included a brief flashback of Von Hammer's youth, where he was seen learning fighting skills and a rigid code of honor in his ancestral home near the Black Forest. In SSWS #149 (Feb-Mar 70), the origin of the dueling scar on Von Hammer's face was revealed in another flashback.

F

	ORIG.	GOOD	FINE	N-MINT
F-3 BANDIT				
ANTARCTIC				
☐ 1, Jan 95, mini-poster.... 2.95		0.59	1.77	2.95
☐ 2, Mar 95, trading card .. 2.95		0.59	1.77	2.95
☐ 3, May 95, trading card.. 2.95		0.59	1.77	2.95
☐ 4, Jul 95, trading card.... 2.95		0.59	1.77	2.95
☐ 5, Sep 95, trading card... 2.95		0.59	1.77	2.95
FABULOUS FURRY FREAK BROTHERS				
RIP OFF				
☐ 0, 95, multiple printings on all issues;orig. price reflects most recent printing (1995)				
.... 2.95		0.59	1.77	2.95
☐ 1, b&w		0.50	1.50	2.50
☐ 2, b&w		0.50	1.50	2.50
☐ 3, b&w		0.50	1.50	2.50
☐ 4, b&w		0.50	1.50	2.50
☐ 5, b&w		0.50	1.50	2.50
☐ 6, b&w		0.50	1.50	2.50
☐ 7, 82, b&w 2.50		0.50	1.50	2.50
☐ 8, color...........................		0.50	1.50	2.50
☐ 9, color...........................		0.50	1.50	2.50
☐ 10, color.........................		0.50	1.50	2.50
☐ 11, color.........................		0.50	1.50	2.50
☐ 12, b&w		0.59	1.77	2.95
FACE				
DC/VERTIGO				
☐ 1, Jan 95 .... 4.95		0.99	2.97	4.95
FACTOR X (mini-series)				
MARVEL				
☐ 1, Mar 95 .... 1.95		1.00	3.00	5.00
☐ 2, Apr 95 .... 1.95		0.70	2.10	3.50
☐ 3, May 95 .... 1.95		0.50	1.50	2.50
☐ 4, Jun 95 .... 1.95		0.50	1.50	2.50
FACTUAL ILLUSION				
BLACKMORE				
☐ 0, nn, b&w; cover says "Factual Illusions," while indicia says "Factual Illusion".... 2.50		0.50	1.50	2.50
FACULTY FUNNIES				
ARCHIE				
☐ 1, Jun 89...................... 0.75		0.15	0.45	0.75
☐ 2 .... 0.75		0.15	0.45	0.75
☐ 3 .... 0.75		0.15	0.45	0.75
☐ 4 .... 0.75		0.15	0.45	0.75
☐ 5 .... 0.75		0.15	0.45	0.75
FAFHRD AND THE GRAY MOUSER				
EPIC				
☐ 1, Oct 90, MM, AW 4.50		0.90	2.70	4.50
☐ 2, MM, AW.................... 4.50		0.90	2.70	4.50
☐ 3, MM, AW.................... 4.50		0.90	2.70	4.50
☐ 4, MM, AW.................... 4.50		0.90	2.70	4.50
FAILED UNIVERSE				
BLACKTHORNE				
☐ 1		0.35	1.05	1.75
FAITH OF THE FOE				
FANDOM HOUSE				
☐ 1, Howarth,b&w..............		0.90	2.70	4.50
FALCON				
MARVEL				
☐ 1 .... 0.60		0.25	0.75	1.25
☐ 2 .... 0.60		0.20	0.60	1.00
☐ 3 .... 0.60		0.20	0.60	1.00
☐ 4 .... 0.60		0.20	0.60	1.00
FALL, THE				
CALIBER				
☐ 1, b&w 2.95		0.59	1.77	2.95

	ORIG.	GOOD	FINE	N-MINT
FALLEN ANGEL ON THE WORLD OF MAGIC: THE GATHERING				
ACCLAIM/ARMADA				
☐ 0, May 96, prestige format one-shot;polybagged with Fallen Angel card 5.95		1.19	3.57	5.95
FALLEN ANGELS				
MARVEL				
☐ 1, Apr 87......................0.75		1.00	3.00	5.00
☐ 2, May 87.....................0.75		0.70	2.10	3.50
☐ 3, Jun 87......................0.75		0.60	1.80	3.00
☐ 4, Jul 87.......................0.75		0.60	1.80	3.00
☐ 5, Aug 87, D:Don 0.75		0.60	1.80	3.00
☐ 6, Sep 87......................0.75		0.50	1.50	2.50
☐ 7, Oct 87......................0.75		0.50	1.50	2.50
☐ 8, Nov 87......................0.75		0.50	1.50	2.50
FALLEN EMPIRES ON THE WORLD OF MAGIC: THE GATHERING				
ACCLAIM/ARMADA				
☐ 0, 95, nn;collects mini-series;prestige format; polybagged with pack of Fallen Empires cards				
....4.95		0.99	2.97	4.95
FALLEN EMPIRES ON THE WORLD OF MAGIC: THE GATHERING (mini-series)				
☐ 1, Sep 95, polybagged with pack of Fallen Empires cards............................2.75		0.55	1.65	2.75
☐ 2, Oct 95, polybagged with sheet of creature tokens 2.75		0.55	1.65	2.75
FAMILY MAN (mini-series)				
DC/PARADOX				
☐ 1, 95, digest;b&w 4.95		0.99	2.97	4.95
☐ 2, 95, digest;b&w 4.95		0.99	2.97	4.95
☐ 3, 95, digest;b&w 4.95		0.99	2.97	4.95
FAMOUS FIRST EDITION				
DC				
☐ 4, Nov 74.......................1.00		1.00	3.00	5.00
☐ 5, Jan 75.......................1.00		1.00	3.00	5.00
☐ 6, May 75.......................1.00		1.00	3.00	5.00
☐ 7, Jul 75.......................1.00		1.00	3.00	5.00
☐ 8, Sep 75 ....1.00		1.00	3.00	5.00
☐ 26 ....1.00		1.00	3.00	5.00
☐ 28 ....1.00		1.00	3.00	5.00
☐ 30 ....1.00		1.00	3.00	5.00
☐ 61, Mar 79.....................1.00		1.00	3.00	5.00
FANA				
COMAX				
☐ 1, b&w, adult..................		0.59	1.77	2.95
FANA THE JUNGLE GIRL				
☐ 1, b&w............................		0.59	1.77	2.95
FANG				
CONQUEST				
☐ 1, b&w............................2.95		0.59	1.77	2.95
SIRIUS ENTERTAINMENT				
☐ 1, Feb 95.......................2.95		0.59	1.77	2.95
☐ 2, Apr 95.......................2.95		0.59	1.77	2.95
☐ 3, Jun 95 ....2.95		0.59	1.77	2.95
TANGRAM				
☐ 0, nn, 1992 b&w..............		0.59	1.77	2.95
FANNY				
FANNY				
☐ 3, b&w............................3.95		0.79	2.37	3.95
FANNY HILL				
SHUNGA				
☐ 1, adult, b&w..................		0.50	1.50	2.50
FANTASCI				
APPLE				
☐ 1, b&w............................		0.30	0.90	1.50
☐ 2, b&w............................		0.30	0.90	1.50

	ORIG.	GOOD	FINE	N-MINT
☐ 3, b&w	0.30	0.90	1.50
☐ 4	0.35	1.05	1.75
☐ 5	0.35	1.05	1.75
☐ 6	0.35	1.05	1.75
☐ 7	0.35	1.05	1.75
☐ 8	0.35	1.05	1.75
☐ 9	0.39	1.17	1.95

FANTASTIC ADVENTURES
ACE

	ORIG.	GOOD	FINE	N-MINT
☐ 1, Mar 87	0.35	1.05	1.75
☐ 2, Jun 87	0.35	1.05	1.75
☐ 3, Oct 87	0.35	1.05	1.75

FANTASTIC FORCE
MARVEL

	ORIG.	GOOD	FINE	N-MINT
☐ 1, Nov 94, enhanced cover	2.50	0.50	1.50	2.50
☐ 2, Dec 94	1.75	0.35	1.05	1.75
☐ 3, Jan 95	1.75	0.35	1.05	1.75
☐ 4, Feb 95	1.75	0.35	1.05	1.75
☐ 5, Mar 95	1.75	0.35	1.05	1.75
☐ 6, Apr 95	1.75	0.35	1.05	1.75
☐ 7, May 95	1.75	0.35	1.05	1.75
☐ 8, Jun 95	1.75	0.35	1.05	1.75
☐ 9, Jul 95	1.75	0.35	1.05	1.75
☐ 10, Aug 95	1.75	0.35	1.05	1.75
☐ 11, Sep 95	1.75	0.35	1.05	1.75
☐ 12, Oct 95	1.75	0.35	1.05	1.75
☐ 13, Nov 95, J:She-Hulk	1.75	0.35	1.05	1.75
☐ 14, Dec 95	1.75	0.35	1.05	1.75
☐ 15, Jan 96, cover says "Jan 95";indicia says "Jan 96"	1.75	0.35	1.05	1.75
☐ 16, Feb 96	1.75	0.35	1.05	1.75
☐ 17, Mar 96	1.75	0.35	1.05	1.75
☐ 18, Apr 96, final issue	1.75	0.35	1.05	1.75

FANTASTIC FOUR

	ORIG.	GOOD	FINE	N-MINT
☐ 1, Nov 61, JK, 1&O:FF	0.10	3400	10200	17000
☐ 2, Jan 62, JK, 1:Skrulls; ro:FF	0.10	600.00	1800.00	3000.00
☐ 3, Mar 62, JK, 1:Miracle Man, Baxter Building, Fantasti-Car, Pogo Plane, Fantasti-Copter, FF costumes	0.12	400.00	1200.00	2000.00
☐ 4, May 62, JK, R:Sub-Mariner	0.12	500.00	1500.00	2500.00
☐ 5, Jul 62, JK, 1:Dr. Doom	0.12	520.00	1560.00	2600.00
☐ 6, Sep 62, JK;Dr. Doom and Sub-Mariner team-up; 1:Yancy Street Gang	0.12	320.00	960.00	1600.00
☐ 7, Oct 62, JK;1:Kurrgo	0.12	100.00	300.00	500.00
☐ 8, Nov 62, JK; 1:Puppet Master, Alicia Masters	0.12	100.00	300.00	500.00
☐ 9, Dec 62, JK; A:Sub-Mariner	0.12	100.00	300.00	500.00
☐ 10, Jan 63, JK;V:Dr. Doom; A:Stan Lee and JK	0.12	100.00	300.00	500.00
☐ 11, Feb 63, JK; 1:Willie Lumpkin, Impossible Man	0.12	60.00	180.00	300.00
☐ 12, Mar 63, JK;V:Hulk	0.12	170.00	510.00	850.00
☐ 13, Apr 63, JK;1:Watcher, Red Ghost	0.12	40.00	120.00	200.00
☐ 14, May 63, JK; V:Sub-Mariner, Puppet Master	0.12	45.00	135.00	225.00
☐ 15, Jun 63, JK; 1:Mad Thinker, Mad Thinker's Android	0.12	36.00	108.00	180.00
☐ 16, Jul 63, JK;A:Ant Man, The Wasp;V:Dr. Doom	0.12	36.00	108.00	180.00
☐ 17, Aug 63, JK; V:Dr. Doom;A:Ant Man	0.12	36.00	108.00	180.00
☐ 18, Sep 63, JK; O&1:Super-Skrull	0.12	36.00	108.00	180.00
☐ 19, Oct 63, JK; O&1:Rama-Tut	0.12	36.00	108.00	180.00

	ORIG.	GOOD	FINE	N-MINT
☐ 20, Nov 63, JK; V:Molecule Man; A:Watcher	0.12	36.00	108.00	180.00
☐ 21, Dec 63, JK; O&1:Hate-Monger; A:Nick Fury	0.12	25.00	75.00	125.00
☐ 22, Jan 64, JK; V:Mole Man	0.12	25.00	75.00	125.00
☐ 23, Feb 64, JK; V:Dr. Doom	0.12	25.00	75.00	125.00
☐ 24, Mar 64, JK	0.12	25.00	75.00	125.00
☐ 25, Apr 64, JK; V:Hulk;A:Avengers, Rick Jones	0.12	65.00	195.00	325.00
☐ 26, May 64, JK; V:Hulk;A:Avengers, Rick Jones	0.12	65.00	195.00	325.00
☐ 27, Jun 64, JK; V:Sub-Mariner; A:Dr. Strange	0.12	24.00	72.00	120.00
☐ 28, Jul 64, JK; V:Mad Thinker, Puppet Master; A:X-Men	0.12	40.00	120.00	200.00
☐ 29, Aug 64, JK; V:Red Ghost;A:Watcher	0.12	18.00	54.00	90.00
☐ 30, Sep 64, JK; V:Diablo	0.12	18.00	54.00	90.00
☐ 31, Oct 64, JK; V:Mole Man;A:Avengers	0.12	11.00	33.00	55.00
☐ 32, Nov 64, JK; V:Super-Skrull	0.12	11.00	33.00	55.00
☐ 33, Dec 64, JK; A:Sub-Mariner	0.12	11.00	33.00	55.00
☐ 34, Jan 65, JK	0.12	11.00	33.00	55.00
☐ 35, Feb 65, JK;V:Diablo, Dragon Man	0.12	11.00	33.00	55.00
☐ 36, Mar 65, JK; O&1:Frightful Four; 1:Medusa	0.12	11.00	33.00	55.00
☐ 37, Apr 65, JK	0.12	11.00	33.00	55.00
☐ 38, May 65, JK;V:Frightful Four;Paste-Pot Pete becomes Trapster	0.12	11.00	33.00	55.00
☐ 39, Jun 65, JK;V:Dr. Doom; A:Daredevil	0.12	11.00	33.00	55.00
☐ 40, Jul 65, JK; V:Dr. Doom; A:Daredevil	0.12	11.00	33.00	55.00
☐ 41, Aug 65, JK; V:Frightful Four	0.12	12.00	36.00	60.00
☐ 42, Sep 65, JK; V:Frightful Four	0.12	12.00	36.00	60.00
☐ 43, Oct 65, JK; V:Frightful Four, Dr. Doom	0.12	12.00	36.00	60.00
☐ 44, Nov 65, JK; 1:Gorgon;A:Dragon Man, Medusa	0.12	10.00	30.00	50.00
☐ 45, Dec 65, JK; 1:Inhumans;V:Dragon Man, Maximus;A:Sandman, Trapster	0.12	9.60	28.80	48.00
☐ 46, Jan 66, JK; A:Inhumans	0.12	9.60	28.80	48.00
☐ 47, Feb 66, JK;V:Maximus; A:Inhumans	0.12	8.80	26.40	44.00
☐ 48, Mar 66, JK;1:Silver Surfer, Galactus; A:Inhumans	0.12	150.00	450.00	750.00
☐ 49, Apr 66, JK;V:Galactus; A:Silver Surfer, Watcher	0.12	35.00	105.00	175.00
☐ 50, May 66, JK; V:Galactus;A:Silver Surfer, Watcher;1:Wyatt Wingfoot	0.12	80.00	240.00	400.00
☐ 51, Jun 66, JK	0.12	7.20	21.60	36.00
☐ 52, Jul 66, JK; 1:Black Panther	0.12	16.00	48.00	80.00
☐ 53, Aug 66, JK; O:Black Panther;1:Klaw	0.12	7.20	21.60	36.00
☐ 54, Sep 66, JK; A:Black Panther	0.12	7.20	21.60	36.00
☐ 55, Oct 66, JK;Thing vs. Silver Surfer	0.12	15.00	45.00	75.00
☐ 56, Nov 66, JK;V:Klaw	0.12	7.20	21.60	36.00
☐ 57, Dec 66, JK;V:Dr. Doom, Sandman, Wizard; A:Inhumans	0.12	7.20	21.60	36.00

The Flash

First appearance: (Jay Garrick) *Flash Comics* #1, January 1940 (DC).

Although super-speeders have been with us from the times of the Greeks' Hermes, it was 1940 before a super-hero entered the scene whose sole power was immense speed.

The first Flash, Jay Garrick, was a chemistry student experimenting with "hard water." Overcome by fumes from a spilled beaker of the liquid, Garrick awoke to find that inhaling the fumes overnight had given him super-speed. In lieu of a mask, he subconsciously maintained a wave of vibrations over his face to obscure it.

In addition to appearing in *Flash Comics* and *All-Flash*, Garrick was also a member of the Justice Society of America, whose exploits were covered in *All-Star Comics*. The Flash, with many of his Golden Age contemporaries, disappeared from newsstands in the early '50s.

In 1956, DC Editor Julius Schwartz decided to try a revival of the super-hero and picked The Flash as the first subject. This Flash was police scientist Barry Allen, who gained super-speed through a bath of chemicals struck by lightning. Allen based his costumed identity on the exploits of Garrick, whom Allen had read about in comic books. As a counterpoint to his super-speed exploits as The Flash, Allen was notoriously slow and often late for dates with his *fiancée* (later wife), Iris.

After tryouts in *Showcase*, Allen graduated to his own title, which took up the numbering of the earlier *Flash Comics*, with issue #105.

Five issues later, in *The Flash* #110, Iris' nephew, Wally West, was introduced. While The Flash was showing Wally the wall of chemicals that had been struck by lightning to give him super-speed, lightning struck again, imparting the same powers to the boy, whom the media dubbed "Kid Flash."

In *The Flash* #123, a speed demonstration for a group of school children sent Allen hurtling through a dimensional barrier to a duplicate Earth where he found himself in Keystone City, the home of Jay Garrick. The issue paved the way for the return of Golden Age versions of Silver Age heroes and laid the groundwork for the entire DC multiverse.

Eventually, Allen travelled to the 30th century to live with Iris, who was revealed to be a time traveller. When Allen was killed during "Crisis on Infinite Earths," West took Allen's

The Silver Age Flash and the Golden Age Flash (from left to right) as they appeared on the cover of 80 Page Giant #9 © 1965 National Periodical Publications, Inc. (DC)

empty costume and the "Flash" name to honor Allen's memory.

Iris eventually returned to the present to ask West's help in training her grandson, Bart Allen, in the proper use of his super-speed. As Impulse, Bart moved to the South with his mentor, super-speedster Max Mercury.

All DC's super-speedsters, from Garrick to Bart Allen, possess an invisible aura that prevents friction burn from their super-swift passage through the air destroying their clothes or skin. The effects of the aura was diminished in the 1990-91 CBS television show, which featured police scientist Barry Allen (played by John Wesley Shipp).

All three Flashes, as well as Impulse, have a top speed of 186,000 miles per second (the speed of light). They also have absolute control over their individual molecules and can use this ability to vibrate between the molecules of solid objects without damage.

In addition to Max Mercury, DC's other super-speedsters include Johnny Quick and his daughter, who invoke a mathematical formula to attain super-speed in addition to limited flying ability. It was recently revealed that all the super-speedsters tap into a force of nature known as "the speed-force" from which they draw their powers. Johnny Quick became part of "the speed-force" on a recent mission.

While The Flash was created in the Golden Age of comics, this price guide only covers appearances from the Silver Age to the present, including the following (listed chronologically):

Partial Checklist:

Showcase #4 (Sept-Oct 56) ....1st appearance of Silver Age Flash (Barry Allen)
The Flash #105 (Feb-Mar 59)..1st appearance of Mirror Master
The Flash #110 (Jan 60) ....Wally West becomes Kid Flash
The Flash #123 (Sep 61)..................................Reintroduces Golden Age Flash; 1st mention of Earth-2
The Flash #137 (Jun 63) ....1st Silver Age appearance of the Justice Society of America
The Flash #165 (Nov 66) ....Barry Allen marries Iris West
Superman #199 (Aug 67) ....1st Superman-Flash race
Crisis on Infinite Earths #12 (Mar 86) ....1st Wally West as Flash

	ORIG.	GOOD	FINE	N-MINT
☐ 58, Jan 67, JK;V:Dr. Doom; A:Silver Surfer, Lockjaw	0.12	7.20	21.60	36.00
☐ 59, Feb 67, JK;V:Dr. Doom; A:Silver Surfer, Inhumans	0.12	7.20	21.60	36.00
☐ 60, Mar 67, JK; V:Dr. Doom;A:Silver Surfer, Inhumans, Watcher, Black Panther.	0.12	7.20	21.60	36.00
☐ 61, Apr 67, JK;V:Sandman; A:Silver Surfer, Inhumans	0.12	7.20	21.60	36.00
☐ 62, May 67, JK;1:Blastaar; A:Sandman	0.12	5.00	15.00	25.00
☐ 63, Jun 67, JK;V:Blastaar, Sandman	0.12	5.00	15.00	25.00
☐ 64, Jul 67, JK	0.12	5.00	15.00	25.00
☐ 65, Aug 67, JK;1:Ronan the Accuser, Kree Supreme Intelligence	0.12	5.00	15.00	25.00
☐ 66, Sep 67, JK;1:Him;A:Crystal	0.12	18.00	54.00	90.00
☐ 67, Oct 67, JK;A:Him	0.12	20.00	60.00	100.00
☐ 68, Nov 67, JK; V:Mad Thinker	0.12	5.00	15.00	25.00
☐ 69, Dec 67, JK; V:Mad Thinker	0.12	5.00	15.00	25.00
☐ 70, Jan 68, JK; V:Mad Thinker	0.12	5.00	15.00	25.00
☐ 71, Feb 68, JK; V:Mad Thinker	0.12	5.00	15.00	25.00
☐ 72, Mar 68, JK; A:Silver Surfer	0.12	6.00	18.00	30.00
☐ 73, Apr 68, JK;V:Dr. Doom; A:Daredevil, SpM, Thor	0.12	3.20	9.60	16.00
☐ 74, May 68, JK;A: Silver Surfer;V:Galactus	0.12	4.40	13.20	22.00
☐ 75, Jun 68, JK;A:Silver Surfer;V:Galactus	0.12	4.40	13.20	22.00
☐ 76, Jul 68, JK;A:Silver Surfer;V:Galactus, Psycho-Man	0.12	4.40	13.20	22.00
☐ 77, Aug 68, JK;A:Silver Surfer;V:Galactus, Psycho-Man	0.12	4.40	13.20	22.00
☐ 78, Sep 68, JK; V:Wizard	0.12	3.20	9.60	16.00
☐ 79, Oct 68, JK; V:Mad Thinker	0.12	3.20	9.60	16.00
☐ 80, Nov 68, JK	0.12	3.20	9.60	16.00
☐ 81, Dec 68, JK;V:Wizard	0.12	3.20	9.60	16.00
☐ 82, Jan 69, JK; V:Maximus	0.12	3.20	9.60	16.00
☐ 83, Feb 69, JK; V:Maximus	0.12	3.20	9.60	16.00
☐ 84, Mar 69, JK; V:Dr. Doom	0.12	3.20	9.60	16.00
☐ 85, Apr 69, JK; V:Dr. Doom	0.12	3.20	9.60	16.00
☐ 86, May 69, JK; V:Dr. Doom	0.12	3.20	9.60	16.00
☐ 87, Jun 69, JK; V:Dr. Doom	0.12	3.20	9.60	16.00
☐ 88, Jul 69, JK; V:Mole Man	0.12	3.20	9.60	16.00
☐ 89, Aug 69, JK; V:Mole Man	0.15	3.20	9.60	16.00
☐ 90, Sep 69, JK; V:Mole Man	0.15	3.20	9.60	16.00
☐ 91, Oct 69, JK;1:Torgo	0.15	3.20	9.60	16.00
☐ 92, Nov 69, JK;V:Torgo	0.15	3.20	9.60	16.00
☐ 93, Dec 69, JK;V:Torgo	0.15	3.20	9.60	16.00
☐ 94, Jan 70, JK;1:Agatha Harkness;V:Wizard, Sandman, Trapster	0.15	3.20	9.60	16.00
☐ 95, Feb 70, JK; 1:Monocle	0.15	3.20	9.60	16.00
☐ 96, Mar 70, JK; V:Mad Thinker	0.15	3.20	9.60	16.00
☐ 97, Apr 70, JK	0.15	3.20	9.60	16.00
☐ 98, May 70, JK; C:Neil Armstrong	0.15	3.20	9.60	16.00

	ORIG.	GOOD	FINE	N-MINT
☐ 99, Jun 70, JK; A:Inhumans	0.15	3.20	9.60	16.00
☐ 100, Jul 70, JK;anniversary; V:Lots of villains	0.15	8.00	24.00	40.00
☐ 101, Aug 70, JK	0.15	2.00	6.00	10.00
☐ 102, Sep 70, JK;JR(c); V:Magneto; A:Sub-Mariner	0.15	2.00	6.00	10.00
☐ 103, Oct 70, JR;V:Magneto; A:Sub-Mariner	0.15	2.00	6.00	10.00
☐ 104, Nov 70, JR;V:Magneto; A:Sub-Mariner	0.15	2.00	6.00	10.00
☐ 105, Dec 70, JR	0.15	2.00	6.00	10.00
☐ 106, Jan 71, JR	0.15	2.00	6.00	10.00
☐ 107, Feb 71, JB	0.15	2.00	6.00	10.00
☐ 108, Mar 71, JB,JK	0.15	2.00	6.00	10.00
☐ 109, Apr 71, JB; V:Annihilus;D:Janus	0.15	2.00	6.00	10.00
☐ 110, May 71, JB; V:Annihilus	0.15	2.00	6.00	10.00
☐ 111, Jun 71, JB	0.15	2.00	6.00	10.00
☐ 112, Jul 71, JB; Thing vs. Hulk	0.15	3.60	10.80	18.00
☐ 113, Aug 71, JB; 1:Overmind	0.15	1.60	4.80	8.00
☐ 114, Sep 71, JB; V:Overmind	0.15	1.60	4.80	8.00
☐ 115, Oct 71, JB;1:Eternals; O:Overmind	0.15	1.60	4.80	8.00
☐ 116, Nov 71, JB; O:Stranger	0.25	1.60	4.80	8.00
☐ 117, Dec 71, JB; V:Diablo	0.20	1.60	4.80	8.00
☐ 118, Jan 72, JB;A:Crystal; V:Diablo	0.20	1.60	4.80	8.00
☐ 119, Feb 72, JB;V:Klaw; A:Black Panther	0.20	1.60	4.80	8.00
☐ 120, Mar 72, JB;V:Air-Walker Automaton	0.20	1.60	4.80	8.00
☐ 121, Apr 72, JB;V:Air-Walker Automaton	0.20	2.00	6.00	10.00
☐ 122, May 72, JB;V:Galactus; A:Silver Surfer	0.20	1.60	4.80	8.00
☐ 123, Jun 72, JB; A:Silver Surfer; V:Galactus	0.20	1.60	4.80	8.00
☐ 124, Jul 72, JB	0.20	1.60	4.80	8.00
☐ 125, Aug 72, JB	0.20	1.60	4.80	8.00
☐ 126, Sep 72, JB;ro:FF	0.20	1.60	4.80	8.00
☐ 127, Oct 72, JB; V:Mole Man	0.20	1.60	4.80	8.00
☐ 128, Nov 72, JB;V:Mole Man, Tyrannus	0.20	1.60	4.80	8.00
☐ 129, Dec 72, JB;1:Thundra; A:Medusa	0.20	1.80	5.40	9.00
☐ 130, Jan 73, JB; V:Thundra, Wizard, Sandman, Trapster	0.20	1.00	3.00	5.00
☐ 131, Feb 73, JB(c);RA; V:Maximus	0.20	1.00	3.00	5.00
☐ 132, Mar 73, JB; V:Maximus	0.20	1.00	3.00	5.00
☐ 133, Apr 73, JB(c); V:Thundra, Wizard, Trapster, Sandman	0.20	1.00	3.00	5.00
☐ 134, May 73, JB; V:Dragon Man	0.20	1.00	3.00	5.00
☐ 135, Jun 73, JB; V:Dragon Man	0.20	1.00	3.00	5.00
☐ 136, Jul 73, JB; V:Shaper of Worlds	0.20	1.00	3.00	5.00
☐ 137, Aug 73, JB; V:Shaper of Worlds	0.20	1.00	3.00	5.00
☐ 138, Sep 73, JB; V:Miracle Man	0.20	1.00	3.00	5.00
☐ 139, Oct 73, JB; V:Miracle Man	0.20	1.00	3.00	5.00

	ORIG.	GOOD	FINE	N-MINT

❑ 140, Nov 73, RB(c);JB; V:Annihilus
.................0.20   1.00   3.00   5.00

❑ 141, Dec 73, JR(c);JB; V:Annihilus
.................0.20   1.00   3.00   5.00

❑ 142, Jan 74, RB; V:Dr. Doom;1:Darkoth the Death-Demon.................0.20   1.00   3.00   5.00

❑ 143, Feb 74, GK(c);RB; V:Dr. Doom
.................0.20   1.00   3.00   5.00

❑ 144, Mar 74, RB; V:Dr. Doom
.................0.20   1.00   3.00   5.00

❑ 145, Apr 74, GK(c);RA ... 0.20   1.00   3.00   5.00

❑ 146, May 74, GK(c);RA .. 0.25   1.00   3.00   5.00

❑ 147, Jun 74, RB 0.25   1.00   3.00   5.00

❑ 148, Jul 74, RB; V:Frightful Four
.................0.25   1.00   3.00   5.00

❑ 149, Aug 74, RB............. 0.25   1.00   3.00   5.00

❑ 150, Sep 74, GK(c); RB;W:Crystal and Quicksilver; A:Avengers, Inhumans.. 0.25   1.40   4.20   7.00

❑ 151, Oct 74, RB; 1:Mahkizmo
.................0.25   0.60   1.80   3.00

❑ 152, Nov 74, RB............. 0.25   0.60   1.80   3.00

❑ 153, Dec 74, GK(c);RB; V:Mahkizmo
.................0.25   0.60   1.80   3.00

❑ 154, Jan 75, GK(c) 0.25   0.60   1.80   3.00

❑ 155, Feb 75, RB;A:Surfer; V:Dr. Doom
.................0.25   1.00   3.00   5.00

❑ 156, Mar 75, RB;A:Surfer; V:Dr. Doom
.................0.25   1.00   3.00   5.00

❑ 157, Apr 75, RB;A:Surfer; V:Dr. Doom
.................0.25   1.00   3.00   5.00

❑ 158, May 75, RB; V:Xemu
.................0.25   0.45   1.35   2.25

❑ 159, Jun 75, RB;V:Xemu; A:Inhumans
.................0.25   0.60   1.80   3.00

❑ 160, Jul 75, GK(c);JB; V:Arkon
.................0.25   0.60   1.80   3.00

❑ 161, Aug 75, RB............. 0.25   0.60   1.80   3.00

❑ 162, Sep 75, RB............. 0.25   0.60   1.80   3.00

❑ 163, Oct 75, RB............. 0.25   0.60   1.80   3.00

❑ 164, Nov 75, JK(c);GP; A:Crusader (a.k.a. Marvel Boy)
.................0.25   0.60   1.80   3.00

❑ 165, Dec 75, GP;ro: Crusader (a.k.a. Marvel Boy)
.................0.25   0.60   1.80   3.00

❑ 166, Jan 76, RB(c);GP; V:Hulk
.................0.25   0.60   1.80   3.00

❑ 167, Feb 76, JK(c);GP; V:Hulk
.................0.25   0.60   1.80   3.00

❑ 168, Mar 76, RB;Thing replaced by Luke Cage, Power Man..................... 0.25   0.60   1.80   3.00

❑ 169, Apr 76, RB; A:Luke Cage
.................0.25   0.60   1.80   3.00

❑ 170, May 76, GP; A:Luke Cage
.................0.25   0.60   1.80   3.00

❑ 171, Jun 76, JK(c);RB;GP; V:Galactus
.................0.25   0.60   1.80   3.00

❑ 172, Jul 76, JK(c);GP; V:Galactus
.................0.25   0.60   1.80   3.00

❑ 173, Aug 76, JK(c);JB; V:Galactus;A:High Evolutionary
.................0.25   0.60   1.80   3.00

❑ 174, Sep 76, JK(c);JB; V:Galactus
.................0.30   0.60   1.80   3.00

❑ 175, Oct 76, JK(c);JB; V:Galactus
.................0.30   0.60   1.80   3.00

❑ 176, Nov 76, JK(c);GP; V:Wizard, Sandman, Trapster;A:Impossible Man
.................0.30   0.60   1.80   3.00

❑ 177, Dec 76, JK(c);GP; V:Brute, Wizard, Trapster, Sandman...................... 0.30   0.60   1.80   3.00

❑ 178, Jan 77, JR(c);GP; V:Brute, Wizard, Trapster, Sandman...................... 0.30   0.60   1.80   3.00

❑ 179, Feb 77, AM(c); V:Reed Richards of Counter-Earth, Annihilus, Mad Thinker . 0.30   0.60   1.80   3.00

❑ 180, Mar 77, JK(c);reprints FF #101
.................0.30   0.60   1.80   3.00

❑ 181, Apr 77, JK(c); V:Annihilus, Reed Richards of Counter-Earth, Mad Thinker
.................0.30   0.60   1.80   3.00

❑ 182, May 77, SB;V:Annihilus, Reed Richards of Counter-Earth, Mad Thinker 0.30   0.60   1.80   3.00

❑ 183, Jun 77, GP(c);SB; V:Annihilus, Brute, Mad Thinker
.................0.30   0.60   1.80   3.00

❑ 184, Jul 77, GP; A:Impossible Man, Thundra, Tigra
.................0.30   0.60   1.80   3.00

❑ 185, Aug 77, GP 0.30   0.60   1.80   3.00

❑ 186, Sep 77, GP............0.30   0.60   1.80   3.00

❑ 187, Oct 77, GP; A:Impossible Man; V:Molecule Man, Klaw.................0.30   0.60   1.80   3.00

❑ 188, Nov 77, GP; A:Impossible Man; V:Molecule Man, Klaw.................0.35   0.60   1.80   3.00

❑ 189, Dec 77, KP(c);reprints FF Annual #4
.................0.35   0.60   1.80   3.00

❑ 190, Jan 78, JK(c);SB;Thing recounts FF's career
.................0.35   0.60   1.80   3.00

❑ 191, Feb 78, GP;V:Plunderer; A:Thundra
.................0.35   0.60   1.80   3.00

❑ 192, Mar 78, GP 0.35   0.60   1.80   3.00

❑ 193, Apr 78, KP;V:Diablo; O:Darketh the Death-Demon
.................0.35   0.60   1.80   3.00

❑ 194, May 78, GP(c);KP; V:Diablo;A:Darkoth, Impossible Man 0.35   0.60   1.80   3.00

❑ 195, Jun 78, GP(c);KP; A:Sub-Mariner
.................0.35   0.60   1.80   3.00

❑ 196, Jul 78, GP(c);KP 0.35   0.60   1.80   3.00

❑ 197, Aug 78, GP(c);KP; V:Dr. Doom, Red Ghost
.................0.35   0.60   1.80   3.00

❑ 198, Sep 78, JB(c); KP;V:Dr. Doom
.................0.35   0.60   1.80   3.00

❑ 199, Oct 78....................0.35   0.60   1.80   3.00

❑ 200, Nov 78, KP, V:Dr. Doom
.................0.60   1.00   3.00   5.00

❑ 201, Dec 78, KP.............0.35   0.60   1.80   3.00

❑ 202, Jan 79, KP.............0.35   0.60   1.80   3.00

❑ 203, Feb 79, KP 0.35   0.60   1.80   3.00

❑ 204, Mar 79...................0.35   0.60   1.80   3.00

❑ 205, Apr 79...................0.35   0.60   1.80   3.00

❑ 206, May 79...................0.40   0.60   1.80   3.00

❑ 207, Jun 79...................0.40   0.60   1.80   3.00

❑ 208, Jul 79, SB, A:Nova.0.40   1.00   3.00   5.00

❑ 209, Aug 79, JBy, 1:Herbie
.................0.40   0.70   2.10   3.50

❑ 210, Sep 79, JBy 0.40   0.60   1.80   3.00

❑ 211, Oct 79, JBy 0.40   0.60   1.80   3.00

❑ 212, Nov 79, JBy 0.40   0.60   1.80   3.00

❑ 213, Dec 79, JBy 0.40   0.60   1.80   3.00

❑ 214, Jan 80, JBy 0.40   0.60   1.80   3.00

❑ 215, Feb 80, JBy 0.40   0.60   1.80   3.00

❑ 216, Mar 80, JBy 0.40   0.60   1.80   3.00

❑ 217, Apr 80, JBy, A:Dazzler
.................0.40   1.00   3.00   5.00

❑ 218, May 80....................0.40   0.60   1.80   3.00

❑ 219, Jun 80 ....0.40   0.60   1.80   3.00

❑ 220, Jul 80......................0.40   0.60   1.80   3.00

❑ 221, Aug 80....................0.40   0.60   1.80   3.00

❑ 222, Sep 80, BS..............0.50   0.60   1.80   3.00

❑ 223, Oct 80, BS...............0.50   0.60   1.80   3.00

❑ 224, Nov 80, BS..............0.50   0.60   1.80   3.00

❑ 225, Dec 80, BS..............0.50   0.60   1.80   3.00

❑ 226, Jan 81, BS 0.50   0.60   1.80   3.00

❑ 227, Feb 81, BS 0.50   0.60   1.80   3.00

❑ 228, Mar 81, BS..............0.50   0.60   1.80   3.00

❑ 229, Apr 81, BS...............0.50   0.60   1.80   3.00

❑ 230, May 81, BS 0.50   0.60   1.80   3.00

❑ 231, Jun 81, BS 0.50   0.60   1.80   3.00

❑ 232, Jul 81, JBy..............0.50   1.00   3.00   5.00

❑ 233, Aug 81, JBy 0.50   0.50   1.50   2.50

	ORIG.	GOOD	FINE	N-MINT
❏ 234, Sep 81, JBy	0.50	0.50	1.50	2.50
❏ 235, Oct 81, JBy	0.50	0.50	1.50	2.50
❏ 236, Nov 81, JBy, V:Dr. Doom				
	1.00	0.60	1.80	3.00
❏ 237, Dec 81, JBy	0.50	0.50	1.50	2.50
❏ 238, Jan 82, JBy	0.60	0.45	1.35	2.25
❏ 239, Feb 82, JBy	0.60	0.45	1.35	2.25
❏ 240, Mar 82, JBy, 1:Luna				
	0.60	0.45	1.35	2.25
❏ 241, Apr 82, JBy, A:Black Panther				
	0.60	0.45	1.35	2.25
❏ 242, May 82, JBy, A:Daredevil				
	0.60	0.50	1.50	2.50
❏ 243, Jun 82, JBy	0.60	0.50	1.50	2.50
❏ 244, Jul 82, JBy	0.60	0.50	1.50	2.50
❏ 245, Aug 82, JBy	0.60	0.50	1.50	2.50
❏ 246, Sep 82, JBy	0.60	0.50	1.50	2.50
❏ 247, Oct 82, JBy	0.60	0.50	1.50	2.50
❏ 248, Nov 82, JBy	0.60	0.50	1.50	2.50
❏ 249, Dec 82, JBy	0.60	0.50	1.50	2.50
❏ 250, Jan 83, JBy, A:Captain America				
	1.00	0.50	1.50	2.50
❏ 251, Feb 83, JBy, Negative Zone				
	0.60	0.40	1.20	2.00
❏ 252, Mar 83, JBy, new format				
	0.60	0.40	1.20	2.00
❏ 253, Apr 83, JBy	0.60	0.40	1.20	2.00
❏ 254, May 83, JBy	0.60	0.40	1.20	2.00
❏ 255, Jun 83, JBy	0.60	0.40	1.20	2.00
❏ 256, Jul 83, JBy	0.60	0.40	1.20	2.00
❏ 257, Aug 83, JBy	0.60	0.40	1.20	2.00
❏ 258, Sep 83, JBy	0.60	0.40	1.20	2.00
❏ 259, Oct 83, JBy	0.60	0.40	1.20	2.00
❏ 260, Nov 83, JBy, Silver Surfer, Dr. Doom				
	0.60	0.40	1.20	2.00
❏ 261, Dec 83, JBy	0.60	0.40	1.20	2.00
❏ 262, Jan 84, JBy	0.60	0.40	1.20	2.00
❏ 263, Feb 84, JBy	0.60	0.40	1.20	2.00
❏ 264, Mar 84, JBy	0.60	0.40	1.20	2.00
❏ 265, Apr 84, JBy	0.60	0.40	1.20	2.00
❏ 266, May 84, JBy	0.60	0.40	1.20	2.00
❏ 267, Jun 84, JBy	0.60	0.40	1.20	2.00
❏ 268, Jul 84, JBy	0.60	0.40	1.20	2.00
❏ 269, Aug 84, JBy	0.60	0.40	1.20	2.00
❏ 270, Sep 84, JBy	0.60	0.40	1.20	2.00
❏ 271, Oct 84, JBy	0.60	0.40	1.20	2.00
❏ 272, Nov 84, JBy	0.60	0.40	1.20	2.00
❏ 273, Dec 84, JBy	0.60	0.40	1.20	2.00
❏ 274, Jan 85, JBy	0.60	0.40	1.20	2.00
❏ 275, Feb 85, JBy	0.60	0.40	1.20	2.00
❏ 276, Mar 85, JBy	0.60	0.40	1.20	2.00
❏ 277, Apr 85, JBy	0.65	0.40	1.20	2.00
❏ 278, May 85, JBy	0.65	0.40	1.20	2.00
❏ 279, Jun 85, JBy	0.65	0.40	1.20	2.00
❏ 280, Jul 85, JBy	0.65	0.40	1.20	2.00
❏ 281, Aug 85, JBy	0.65	0.40	1.20	2.00
❏ 282, Sep 85, JBy Secret Wars II				
	0.65	0.40	1.20	2.00
❏ 283, Oct 85, JBy	0.65	0.40	1.20	2.00
❏ 284, Nov 85, JBy	0.65	0.40	1.20	2.00
❏ 285, Dec 85, JBy Secret Wars II				
	0.65	0.40	1.20	2.00
❏ 286, Jan 86, JBy, X-Factor				
	0.65	0.80	2.40	4.00
❏ 287, Feb 86, JBy	0.75	0.40	1.20	2.00
❏ 288, Mar 86, JBy Secret Wars II				
	0.75	0.40	1.20	2.00
❏ 289, Apr 86	0.75	0.30	0.90	1.50
❏ 290, May 86	0.75	0.30	0.90	1.50
❏ 291, Jun 86	0.75	0.30	0.90	1.50
❏ 292, Jul 86	0.75	0.30	0.90	1.50
❏ 293, Aug 86	0.75	0.30	0.90	1.50
❏ 294, Sep 86	0.75	0.30	0.90	1.50

	ORIG.	GOOD	FINE	N-MINT
❏ 295, Nov 86	0.75	0.30	0.90	1.50
❏ 296, Nov 86	1.50	0.30	0.90	1.50
❏ 297, Dec 86	0.75	0.30	0.90	1.50
❏ 298, Jan 87	0.75	0.30	0.90	1.50
❏ 299, Feb 87	0.75	0.30	0.90	1.50
❏ 300, Mar 87, M:Torch, Alicia				
	0.75	0.30	0.90	1.50
❏ 301, Apr 87	0.75	0.30	0.90	1.50
❏ 302, May 87	0.75	0.30	0.90	1.50
❏ 303, Jun 87	0.75	0.30	0.90	1.50
❏ 304, Jul 87	0.75	0.30	0.90	1.50
❏ 305, Aug 87	0.75	0.30	0.90	1.50
❏ 306, Sep 87	0.75	0.30	0.90	1.50
❏ 307, Oct 87	0.75	0.30	0.90	1.50
❏ 308, Nov 87, I:Fasaud	0.75	0.30	0.90	1.50
❏ 309, Dec 87	0.75	0.30	0.90	1.50
❏ 310, Jan 88	0.75	0.30	0.90	1.50
❏ 311, Feb 88	0.75	0.30	0.90	1.50
❏ 312, Mar 88, Fall of Mutants				
	0.75	0.30	0.90	1.50
❏ 313, Apr 88	0.75	0.30	0.90	1.50
❏ 314, May 88	0.75	0.30	0.90	1.50
❏ 315, Jun 88	0.75	0.30	0.90	1.50
❏ 316, Jul 88	0.75	0.30	0.90	1.50
❏ 317, Aug 88	0.75	0.30	0.90	1.50
❏ 318, Sep 88, Dr. Doom	0.75	0.30	0.90	1.50
❏ 319, Oct 88, Dr. Doom v. Beyonder				
	1.50	0.30	0.90	1.50
❏ 320, Nov 88, Thing vs. Hulk				
	0.75	0.30	0.90	1.50
❏ 321, Dec 88, Ms. Marvel vs. She-Hulk				
	0.75	0.30	0.90	1.50
❏ 322, Jan 89, Inferno	0.75	0.30	0.90	1.50
❏ 323, Feb 89, Inferno	0.75	0.30	0.90	1.50
❏ 324, Mar 89, Inferno	0.75	0.30	0.90	1.50
❏ 325, Apr 89	0.75	0.30	0.90	1.50
❏ 326, May 89	0.75	0.30	0.90	1.50
❏ 327, Jun 89	0.75	0.30	0.90	1.50
❏ 328, Jul 89	0.75	0.30	0.90	1.50
❏ 329, Aug 89	0.75	0.30	0.90	1.50
❏ 330, Sep 89	1.00	0.30	0.90	1.50
❏ 331, Oct 89	1.00	0.30	0.90	1.50
❏ 332, Nov 89	1.00	0.30	0.90	1.50
❏ 333, Nov 89	1.00	0.30	0.90	1.50
❏ 334, Dec 89, Acts of Vengeance				
	1.00	0.30	0.90	1.50
❏ 335, Dec 89, Acts of Vengeance				
	1.00	0.30	0.90	1.50
❏ 336, Jan 90, Acts of Vengeance				
	1.00	0.30	0.90	1.50
❏ 337, Feb 90, WS	1.00	0.80	2.40	4.00
❏ 338, Mar 90, WS	1.00	0.40	1.20	2.00
❏ 339, Apr 90, WS	1.00	0.30	0.90	1.50
❏ 340, May 90, WS	1.00	0.30	0.90	1.50
❏ 341, Jun 90, WS	1.00	0.30	0.90	1.50
❏ 342, Jul 90	1.00	0.30	0.90	1.50
❏ 343, Aug 90, WS	1.00	0.30	0.90	1.50
❏ 344, Sep 90, WS	1.00	0.30	0.90	1.50
❏ 345, Oct 90, WS	1.00	0.30	0.90	1.50
❏ 346, Nov 90	1.00	0.30	0.90	1.50
❏ 347, Dec 90, WS,AAd Spider-Man, Hulk, Ghost Rider, Wolverine (1st printing)	1.00	2.00	6.00	10.00
❏ 347, Dec 90, (2nd printing)				
	1.00	0.80	2.40	4.00
❏ 348, Jan 91, WS,AAd Spider-Man, Hulk, Ghost Rider, Wolverine (1st printing)	1.00	1.40	4.20	7.00
❏ 348, Jan 91, (2nd printing)				
	1.00	0.80	2.40	4.00
❏ 349, Feb 91, WS,AAd Spider-Man, Hulk, Ghost Rider, Wolverine; Punisher cameo				
	1.00	1.00	3.00	5.00
❏ 350, Mar 91, WS, Return:Thing				
	1.50	0.30	0.90	1.50

	ORIG.	GOOD	FINE	N-MINT
❑ 351, Apr 91 .... 1.00		0.20	0.60	1.00
❑ 352, May 91, WS 1.00		0.20	0.60	1.00
❑ 353, Jun 91, WS 1.00		0.20	0.60	1.00
❑ 354, Jul 91, WS 1.00		0.20	0.60	1.00
❑ 355, Aug 91 .... 1.00		0.20	0.60	1.00
❑ 356, Sep 91, Alicia is Skrull				
.... 1.00		0.20	0.60	1.00
❑ 357, Oct 91 .... 1.00		0.20	0.60	1.00
❑ 358, Nov 91, die-cut cover				
.... 2.50		1.40	4.20	7.00
❑ 359, Dec 91................... 1.00		0.20	0.60	1.00
❑ 360 .... 1.00		0.20	0.60	1.00
❑ 361, Dr. Doom 1.25		0.25	0.75	1.25
❑ 362 .... 1.25		0.25	0.75	1.25
❑ 363 .... 1.25		0.25	0.75	1.25
❑ 364 .... 1.25		0.25	0.75	1.25
❑ 365 .... 1.25		0.25	0.75	1.25
❑ 367 .... 1.25		0.25	0.75	1.25
❑ 368 .... 1.25		0.25	0.75	1.25
❑ 369 .... 1.25		0.25	0.75	1.25
❑ 370 .... 1.25		0.25	0.75	1.25
❑ 371, white embossed cover				
.... 2.00		2.00	6.00	10.00
❑ 371, second printing, red embossed cover				
.... 2.00		0.80	2.40	4.00
❑ 372 .... 1.25		0.25	0.75	1.25
❑ 373 .... 1.25		0.25	0.75	1.25
❑ 374 .... 1.25		0.25	0.75	1.25
❑ 375, foil cover 2.95		0.80	2.40	4.00
❑ 376 .... 1.25		0.25	0.75	1.25
❑ 377 .... 1.25		0.25	0.75	1.25
❑ 378 .... 1.25		0.25	0.75	1.25
❑ 379 .... 1.25		0.25	0.75	1.25
❑ 380 .... 1.25		0.60	1.80	3.00
❑ 381, "D":Reed Richards .. 1.25		2.00	6.00	10.00
❑ 382 .... 1.25		0.80	2.40	4.00
❑ 383 .... 1.25		0.25	0.75	1.25
❑ 384 .... 1.25		0.25	0.75	1.25
❑ 385 .... 1.25		0.25	0.75	1.25
❑ 386 .... 1.25		0.25	0.75	1.25
❑ 387, Apr 94, diecut cover 2.95		0.59	1.77	2.95
❑ 387, Apr 94 .... 1.25		0.25	0.75	1.25
❑ 388, May 94, cards 1.50		0.30	0.90	1.50
❑ 389, Jun 94 .... 1.50		0.30	0.90	1.50
❑ 391, Aug 94 .... 1.50		0.30	0.90	1.50
❑ 392, Sep 94.................. 1.50		0.30	0.90	1.50
❑ 393, Oct 94 .... 1.50		0.30	0.90	1.50
❑ 394, Nov 94, polybagged with 16-page *Marvel Action Hour* preview, acetate print, and other items				
.... 2.95		0.59	1.77	2.95
❑ 394, Nov 94 .... 1.50		0.30	0.90	1.50
❑ 395, Dec 94................... 1.50		0.30	0.90	1.50
❑ 396, Jan 95 .... 1.50		0.30	0.90	1.50
❑ 397, Feb 95 .... 1.50		0.30	0.90	1.50
❑ 398, Mar 95, enhanced cover				
.... 2.50		0.50	1.50	2.50
❑ 398, Mar 95 .... 1.50		0.30	0.90	1.50
❑ 399, Apr 95, enhanced cardstock cover				
.... 2.50		0.50	1.50	2.50
❑ 399, Apr 95 .... 1.50		0.30	0.90	1.50
❑ 400, May 95, enhanced cover				
.... 3.95		0.79	2.37	3.95
❑ 401, Jun 95................... 1.50		0.30	0.90	1.50
❑ 402, Jul 95, "Atlantis Rising"				
.... 1.50		0.30	0.90	1.50
❑ 403, Aug 95 .... 1.50		0.30	0.90	1.50
❑ 404, Sep 95.................. 1.50		0.30	0.90	1.50
❑ 405, Oct 95, The Thing becomes human;A:Zarko, Iron Man 2020,Green Goblin,Red Raven, Young Allies,Conan 1.50		0.30	0.90	1.50
❑ 406, Nov 95, Return of Dr. Doom				
.... 1.50		0.30	0.90	1.50

	ORIG.	GOOD	FINE	N-MINT
❑ 407, Dec 95, Return of Reed Richards				
.... 1.50		0.40	1.20	2.00
❑ 408, Jan 96................... 1.50		0.30	0.90	1.50
❑ 409, Feb 96, The Thing's face is healed				
.... 1.50		0.30	0.90	1.50
❑ 410, Mar 96, retells origin of Kristoff				
.... 1.50		0.30	0.90	1.50
❑ 411, Apr 96, V:Black Bolt				
.... 1.50		0.30	0.90	1.50

FANTASTIC FOUR 2099

	ORIG.	GOOD	FINE	N-MINT
❑ 1, Jan 96, enhanced wraparound cover				
.... 3.95		0.79	2.37	3.95
❑ 2, Feb 96...................... 1.95		0.39	1.17	1.95
❑ 3, Mar 96 .... 1.95		0.39	1.17	1.95
❑ 4, Apr 96, A:Spider-Man 2099				
.... 1.95		0.39	1.17	1.95
❑ 5, May 96, A:Dr. Strange 1.95		0.39	1.17	1.95

FANTASTIC FOUR ANNUAL/SPECIAL

	ORIG.	GOOD	FINE	N-MINT
❑ 1, 63, JK;ro:FF; V:Sub-Mariner;ro: Sub-Mariner;A:SpM				
.... 0.25		120.00	360.00	600.00
❑ 2, 64, ro:Dr. Doom; 1:Boris				
.... 0.25		70.00	210.00	350.00
❑ 3, 65, W:Sue and Reed; guest appearances too numerous to list 0.25		36.00	108.00	180.00
❑ 4, Nov 66, I:Quasimodo; R:Golden Age Human Torch; reprints *FF* #25 and 26... 0.25		7.20	21.60	36.00
❑ 5, Nov 67, JK;A:Inhumans, Black Panther; 1:Psycho-Man 0.25		6.00	18.00	30.00
❑ 6, Nov 68, JK;1:Franklin Richards, Annihilus				
.... 0.25		5.00	15.00	25.00
❑ 7, Nov 69, JK;reprints *FF* #1, *FF Annual* #2				
.... 0.25		2.40	7.20	12.00
❑ 8, Dec 70, JK;reprints *FF Annual* #1				
.... 0.25		1.40	4.20	7.00
❑ 9, Dec 71, JK;reprints stories from *FF* #43, *Annual* #3, and *Strange Tales* #131				
.... 0.25		1.40	4.20	7.00
❑ 10, 73, JK;reprints stories from *FF Annual* #3 and 4				
.... 0.35		1.40	4.20	7.00
❑ 11, 76, JK(c);JB; V:Invaders				
.... 0.50		1.00	3.00	5.00
❑ 12, 78, Invaders.............. 0.60		1.00	3.00	5.00
❑ 13, 78 .... 0.60		0.60	1.80	3.00
❑ 14, 79 .... 0.75		0.60	1.80	3.00
❑ 15, 80, GP, Skrulls.......... 0.75		0.40	1.20	2.00
❑ 16, 81, JBy 0.75		0.40	1.20	2.00
❑ 17, 83, JBy 1.00		0.40	1.20	2.00
❑ 18, 84, Kree-Skrull War .. 1.00		0.40	1.20	2.00
❑ 19, 85, JBy 1.25		0.40	1.20	2.00
❑ 20, 87 .... 1.25		0.40	1.20	2.00
❑ 21, 88, Evolutionary War 1.75		0.40	1.20	2.00
❑ 22, 89, Atlantis Attacks ... 2.00		0.80	2.40	4.00
❑ 23, 90, Future Present 2.00		0.40	1.20	2.00
❑ 24, 91, Guardians of Galaxy				
.... 2.00		0.40	1.20	2.00
❑ 25 .... 2.25		0.45	1.35	2.25
❑ 26, trading card 2.95		0.59	1.77	2.95
❑ 27, 94 .... 2.95		0.59	1.77	2.95

FANTASTIC FOUR ROAST

	ORIG.	GOOD	FINE	N-MINT
❑ 1, May 82, FH/MG/FM/JB/MA/TA				
.... 1.00		0.40	1.20	2.00

FANTASTIC FOUR SPECIAL

	ORIG.	GOOD	FINE	N-MINT
❑ 1, May 84...................... 2.00		0.40	1.20	2.00

FANTASTIC FOUR UNLIMITED

	ORIG.	GOOD	FINE	N-MINT
❑ 1 .... 3.95		0.79	2.37	3.95
❑ 2 .... 3.95		0.79	2.37	3.95
❑ 3 .... 3.95		0.79	2.37	3.95
❑ 4 .... 3.95		0.79	2.37	3.95
❑ 5 .... 3.95		0.79	2.37	3.95
❑ 6, Jun 94 .... 3.95		0.79	2.37	3.95

	ORIG.	GOOD	FINE	N-MINT
☐ 7, Sep 94	3.95	0.79	2.37	3.95
☐ 8, Dec 94	3.95	0.79	2.37	3.95
☐ 9, Mar 95	3.95	0.79	2.37	3.95
☐ 10, Jul 95	3.95	0.79	2.37	3.95
☐ 11, Sep 95	3.95	0.79	2.37	3.95
☐ 12, Dec 95	3.95	0.79	2.37	3.95

FANTASTIC FOUR UNPLUGGED

	ORIG.	GOOD	FINE	N-MINT
☐ 1, Sep 95	0.99	0.20	0.59	0.99
☐ 2, Nov 95, reading of Reed Richards' will				
	0.99	0.20	0.59	0.99
☐ 3, Jan 96	0.99	0.20	0.59	0.99
☐ 4, Mar 96	0.99	0.20	0.59	0.99
☐ 5, May 96	0.99	0.20	0.59	0.99
☐ 6, Jul 96	0.99	0.20	0.59	0.99

FANTASTIC FOUR VS. THE X-MEN

	ORIG.	GOOD	FINE	N-MINT
☐ 1, Feb 87	1.50	1.60	4.80	8.00
☐ 2, Mar 87	1.50	1.20	3.60	6.00
☐ 3, Apr 87	1.50	1.20	3.60	6.00
☐ 4, May 87	1.50	1.20	3.60	6.00

FANTASTIC FOUR: ATLANTIS RISING

	ORIG.	GOOD	FINE	N-MINT
☐ 1, Jun 95, acetate outer cover				
	3.95	0.79	2.37	3.95
☐ 2, Jul 95, acetate outer cover				
	3.95	0.79	2.37	3.95

FANTASTIC FOUR: ATLANTIS RISING COLLECTOR'S PREVIEW

	ORIG.	GOOD	FINE	N-MINT
☐ 1, May 95	2.25	0.45	1.35	2.25

FANTASTIC PANIC
ANTARCTIC

	ORIG.	GOOD	FINE	N-MINT
☐ 1, Aug 93, b&w	2.75	0.55	1.65	2.75
☐ 2, Oct 93, b&w	2.75	0.55	1.65	2.75
☐ 3, Dec 93, b&w	2.75	0.55	1.65	2.75
☐ 4, Feb 94, b&w	2.75	0.55	1.65	2.75
☐ 5, Apr 94, b&w	2.75	0.55	1.65	2.75
☐ 6, Jun 94, b&w	2.75	0.55	1.65	2.75
☐ 7, Aug 94, b&w	2.75	0.55	1.65	2.75
☐ 8, Oct 94, b&w	2.75	0.55	1.65	2.75

FANTASTIC VOYAGES OF SINDBAD
GOLD KEY

	ORIG.	GOOD	FINE	N-MINT
☐ 1, Oct 65, pin-up on back cover				
	0.12	3.00	9.00	15.00

FANTASTIC WORLDS
FLASHBACK COMICS

	ORIG.	GOOD	FINE	N-MINT
☐ 1, Sep 95, b&w	2.95	0.59	1.77	2.95

FANTASY FEATURES
AC

	ORIG.	GOOD	FINE	N-MINT
☐ 1		0.35	1.05	1.75
☐ 2		0.39	1.17	1.95

FANTASY GIRLS
COMAX

	ORIG.	GOOD	FINE	N-MINT
☐ 1, b&w, adult		0.50	1.50	2.50

FANTASY MASTERPIECES
MARVEL

	ORIG.	GOOD	FINE	N-MINT
☐ 1, JK/DH/SD	0.12	7.00	21.00	35.00
☐ 2, JK/SD/DH	0.12	3.00	9.00	15.00
☐ 3	0.25	6.00	18.00	30.00
☐ 4	0.25	4.40	13.20	22.00
☐ 5	0.25	4.40	13.20	22.00
☐ 6	0.25	3.20	9.60	16.00
☐ 7	0.25	3.20	9.60	16.00
☐ 8	0.25	3.20	9.60	16.00
☐ 9	0.25	3.20	9.60	16.00
☐ 10	0.25	3.20	9.60	16.00
☐ 11, (becomes *Marvel Super-Heroes* 1967-1982)				
	0.25	3.20	9.60	16.00

FANTASY MASTERPIECES (Volume 2)

	ORIG.	GOOD	FINE	N-MINT
☐ 1, Dec 79, Silver Surfer rep.				
	0.75	0.40	1.20	2.00
☐ 2, Jan 80	0.75	0.20	0.60	1.00

	ORIG.	GOOD	FINE	N-MINT
☐ 3, Feb 80	0.75	0.20	0.60	1.00
☐ 4, Mar 80	0.75	0.20	0.60	1.00
☐ 5, Apr 80	0.75	0.20	0.60	1.00
☐ 6, May 80	0.75	0.20	0.60	1.00
☐ 7, Jun 80	0.75	0.20	0.60	1.00
☐ 8, Jul 80	0.75	0.20	0.60	1.00
☐ 9, Aug 80	0.75	0.20	0.60	1.00
☐ 10, Sep 80	0.75	0.20	0.60	1.00
☐ 11, Oct 80	0.75	0.20	0.60	1.00
☐ 12, Nov 80	0.75	0.20	0.60	1.00
☐ 13, Dec 80	0.75	0.20	0.60	1.00
☐ 14, Jan 81	0.50	0.20	0.60	1.00

FANTASY QUARTERLY
INDEPENDENT PUB. SYND.

	ORIG.	GOOD	FINE	N-MINT
☐ 1, Spr 78, b&w;1:Elfquest; back-up story with art by Dave Sim	1.00	10.00	30.00	50.00

FAREWELL TO WEAPONS
EPIC

	ORIG.	GOOD	FINE	N-MINT
☐ 0, nn	2.25	0.45	1.35	2.25

FASHION IN ACTION SUMMER SPECIAL
ECLIPSE

	ORIG.	GOOD	FINE	N-MINT
☐ 1		0.35	1.05	1.75

FASHION IN ACTION WINTER SPECIAL

	ORIG.	GOOD	FINE	N-MINT
☐ 1		0.40	1.20	2.00

FAST FORWARD
PIRANHA

	ORIG.	GOOD	FINE	N-MINT
☐ 1, phobias		0.99	2.97	4.95
☐ 2		0.99	2.97	4.95
☐ 3		0.99	2.97	4.95

FASTLANE ILLUSTRATED
FASTLANE

	ORIG.	GOOD	FINE	N-MINT
☐ 1, Sep 94, b&w	2.50	0.50	1.50	2.50
☐ 2, Jun 95, b&w	2.50	0.50	1.50	2.50

FAT DOG MENDOZA
DARK HORSE

	ORIG.	GOOD	FINE	N-MINT
☐ 1, 92, b&w	2.50	0.50	1.50	2.50

FAT FREDDY'S CAT
RIP OFF

	ORIG.	GOOD	FINE	N-MINT
☐ 0, multiple printings, both digest and comic-book sized				
☐ 1, b&w		0.40	1.20	2.00
☐ 2, b&w		0.40	1.20	2.00
☐ 3, b&w		0.40	1.20	2.00
☐ 4, b&w		0.40	1.20	2.00
☐ 5, b&w		0.40	1.20	2.00
☐ 6, b&w		0.40	1.20	2.00
☐ 7, b&w	2.95	0.59	1.77	2.95

FAT FREDDY'S COMICS & STORIES

	ORIG.	GOOD	FINE	N-MINT
☐ 1, Dec 83	2.00	0.40	1.20	2.00
☐ 2, Dec 86	2.00	0.40	1.20	2.00

FAT NINJA, THE
SILVERWOLF

	ORIG.	GOOD	FINE	N-MINT
☐ 1, b&w		0.30	0.90	1.50
☐ 2, b&w		0.30	0.90	1.50
☐ 3, b&w		0.30	0.90	1.50
☐ 4, b&w		0.30	0.90	1.50
☐ 5, b&w		0.30	0.90	1.50

FATALE
BROADWAY

	ORIG.	GOOD	FINE	N-MINT
☐ 1, Sep 95, giveaway preview edition;b&w				
☐ 1, Jan 96, enhanced cardstock cover				
	2.50	0.90	2.70	4.50
☐ 2	2.50	0.70	2.10	3.50

FATE
DC

	ORIG.	GOOD	FINE	N-MINT
☐ 0, Oct 94	1.95	0.39	1.17	1.95
☐ 1, Nov 94	1.95	0.39	1.17	1.95
☐ 2, Dec 94	1.95	0.39	1.17	1.95
☐ 3, Jan 95	1.95	0.39	1.17	1.95
☐ 4, Feb 95	1.95	0.39	1.17	1.95

	ORIG.	GOOD	FINE	N-MINT
❏ 5, Mar 95 .... 1.95		0.39	1.17	1.95
❏ 6, Apr 95 .... 1.95		0.39	1.17	1.95
❏ 7, May 95 .... 1.95		0.39	1.17	1.95
❏ 8, Jun 95 .... 2.25		0.45	1.35	2.25
❏ 9, Jul 95 .... 2.25		0.45	1.35	2.25
❏ 10, Aug 95 .... 2.25		0.45	1.35	2.25
❏ 11, Sep 95 .... 2.25		0.45	1.35	2.25
❏ 12, Oct 95 .... 2.25		0.45	1.35	2.25
❏ 13, Nov 95, "Underworld Unleashed"				
.... 2.25		0.45	1.35	2.25
❏ 14, Dec 95 .... 2.25		0.45	1.35	2.25
❏ 15, Jan 96 .... 2.25		0.45	1.35	2.25
❏ 16, Feb 96 .... 2.25		0.45	1.35	2.25
❏ 17, Mar 96 .... 2.25		0.45	1.35	2.25
❏ 18, May 96 .... 2.25		0.45	1.35	2.25
❏ 19, Jun 96 .... 2.25		0.45	1.35	2.25
❏ 20, Jul 96, "The Hand of Fate" Part 1 of 3				
.... 2.25		0.45	1.35	2.25

FATHER & SON
KITCHEN SINK

	ORIG.	GOOD	FINE	N-MINT
❏ 1, Jul 95, b&w 2.75		0.55	1.65	2.75
❏ 2, Sep 95, b&w 2.75		0.55	1.65	2.75
❏ 3, Dec 95, b&w 2.75		0.55	1.65	2.75
❏ 4, Jan 96, b&w 2.75		0.55	1.65	2.75

FATHOM
COMICO

	GOOD	FINE	N-MINT
❏ 1, May 87	0.30	0.90	1.50
❏ 2, Jun 87	0.30	0.90	1.50
❏ 3, Jul 87	0.30	0.90	1.50

FATT FAMILY, THE
SIDE SHOW

	GOOD	FINE	N-MINT
❏ 1, b&w	0.59	1.77	2.95

FAUNA REBELLION, THE
FANTAGRAPHICS

	GOOD	FINE	N-MINT
❏ 1, b&w	0.40	1.20	2.00
❏ 2, b&w	0.40	1.20	2.00
❏ 3, b&w	0.40	1.20	2.00

FAUST
NORTHSTAR

	ORIG.	GOOD	FINE	N-MINT
❏ 1, 1st printing, adult b&w	7.00	21.00	35.00	
❏ 1, 2nd printing, adult b&w	1.00	3.00	5.00	
❏ 2, 1st printing, adult b&w	4.40	13.20	22.00	
❏ 2, 2nd printing, adult b&w	0.60	1.80	3.00	
❏ 3, adult b&w	3.20	9.60	16.00	
❏ 4, adult b&w	2.00	6.00	10.00	
❏ 5, adult b&w	1.20	3.60	6.00	
❏ 6, adult b&w	1.00	3.00	5.00	
❏ 7, adult b&w (moves to Rebel)	1.00	3.00	5.00	

FAUST (was Northstar)
REBEL

	ORIG.	GOOD	FINE	N-MINT
❏ 1, Volume 2 .... 2.25		0.45	1.35	2.25
❏ 2, Volume 2 .... 2.25		0.45	1.35	2.25
❏ 3, Volume 2 .... 2.25		0.45	1.35	2.25
❏ 8, adult, b&w		0.45	1.35	2.25
❏ 9, adult, b&w		0.45	1.35	2.25

FAZE ONE FAZERS
AC

	GOOD	FINE	N-MINT
❏ 1, 86	0.80	2.40	4.00
❏ 2, 86	0.40	1.20	2.00
❏ 3, 86	0.40	1.20	2.00
❏ 4, 86	0.40	1.20	2.00

FEAR (ADVENTURE INTO FEAR)
MARVEL

	ORIG.	GOOD	FINE	N-MINT
❏ 1, science fiction, giant rep.				
.... 0.25		0.30	0.90	1.50
❏ 2, science fiction, giant rep.				
.... 0.25		0.25	0.75	1.25
❏ 3, science fiction, giant rep.				
.... 0.25		0.25	0.75	1.25
❏ 4, science fiction, giant rep.				
.... 0.25		0.25	0.75	1.25
❏ 5, science fiction, giant rep.				
.... 0.25		0.25	0.75	1.25
❏ 6, science fiction, giant rep.				
.... 0.25		0.25	0.75	1.25
❏ 7, science fiction, reprints				
.... 0.20		0.25	0.75	1.25
❏ 8, science fiction, reprints				
.... 0.20		0.25	0.75	1.25
❏ 9, science fiction, reprints				
.... 0.20		0.25	0.75	1.25
❏ 10, HC, Man-Thing 0.20		1.40	4.20	7.00
❏ 11, Man-Thing 0.20		0.60	1.80	3.00
❏ 12, Man-Thing 0.20		0.60	1.80	3.00
❏ 13, Man-Thing 0.20		0.30	0.90	1.50
❏ 14, Man-Thing 0.20		0.30	0.90	1.50
❏ 15, Man-Thing 0.20		0.30	0.90	1.50
❏ 16, Man-Thing 0.20		0.30	0.90	1.50
❏ 17, Man-Thing 0.20		0.30	0.90	1.50
❏ 18, Man-Thing 0.20		0.30	0.90	1.50
❏ 19, Man-Thing, 1:Howard the Duck				
.... 0.20		2.00	6.00	10.00
❏ 20, Feb 74, PG, Morbius 0.20		3.20	9.60	16.00
❏ 21, Morbius 0.20		1.60	4.80	8.00
❏ 22, Morbius 0.25		1.50	4.50	7.50
❏ 23, CR, 1st Russell art, Morbius				
.... 0.25		1.20	3.60	6.00
❏ 24, Morbius 0.25		1.20	3.60	6.00
❏ 25, Morbius 0.25		1.20	3.60	6.00
❏ 26, Morbius 0.25		1.20	3.60	6.00
❏ 27, Morbius 0.25		1.20	3.60	6.00
❏ 28, Morbius 0.25		1.20	3.60	6.00
❏ 29, Morbius 0.25		1.20	3.60	6.00
❏ 30, Morbius 0.25		1.20	3.60	6.00
❏ 31, Morbius 0.25		1.20	3.60	6.00

FEAR BOOK
ECLIPSE

	ORIG.	GOOD	FINE	N-MINT
❏ 1, 86, SRB 1.75		0.35	1.05	1.75

FEAR IS HELL
C&T

	GOOD	FINE	N-MINT
❏ 1, b&w	0.30	0.90	1.50

FELICIA HARDY: THE BLACK CAT
MARVEL

	ORIG.	GOOD	FINE	N-MINT
❏ 1, Jul 94 .... 1.50		0.30	0.90	1.50
❏ 2, Aug 94 .... 1.50		0.30	0.90	1.50
❏ 3, Sep 94 .... 1.50		0.30	0.90	1.50
❏ 4, Oct 94, final issue 1.50		0.30	0.90	1.50

FELIX THE CAT
HARVEY

	GOOD	FINE	N-MINT
❏ 1	0.25	0.75	1.25
❏ 2	0.25	0.75	1.25
❏ 3	0.25	0.75	1.25
❏ 4	0.25	0.75	1.25
❏ 5	0.25	0.75	1.25
❏ 6	0.25	0.75	1.25
❏ 7	0.25	0.75	1.25

FELIX THE CAT AND FRIENDS
FELIX

	GOOD	FINE	N-MINT
❏ 1	0.39	1.17	1.95

FELIX THE CAT BIG BOOK
HARVEY

	GOOD	FINE	N-MINT
❏ 1	0.39	1.17	1.95

FELIX THE CAT DIGEST MAGAZINE

	GOOD	FINE	N-MINT
❏ 1	0.35	1.05	1.75

FEM 5
EXPRESS/PARODY

	ORIG.	GOOD	FINE	N-MINT
❏ 1, 96, four cover variants				
.... 2.95		0.59	1.77	2.95
❏ 2, 96 .... 2.95		0.59	1.77	2.95

	ORIG.	GOOD	FINE	N-MINT

FEM FANTASTIQUE
AC

	ORIG.	GOOD	FINE	N-MINT
1, Jul 88, b&w		0.39	1.17	1.95

FEMFORCE

	ORIG.	GOOD	FINE	N-MINT
1, 85, color		0.80	2.40	4.00
2, 85, color		0.60	1.80	3.00
3, 85, color		0.60	1.80	3.00
4, 86, color		0.60	1.80	3.00
5, 86, color		0.35	1.05	1.75
6, Feb 87, color		0.35	1.05	1.75
7, May 87, color		0.35	1.05	1.75
8, Jul 87, color		0.35	1.05	1.75
9, Aug 87, color		0.39	1.17	1.95
10, 87, color		0.39	1.17	1.95
11, Mar 88, color		0.39	1.17	1.95
12, May 88, color		0.39	1.17	1.95
13, May 88, color		0.39	1.17	1.95
14, 88, color		0.39	1.17	1.95
15, Aug 88, color		0.39	1.17	1.95
16, 88		0.45	1.35	2.25
17, Jan 89		0.45	1.35	2.25
18, 89		0.45	1.35	2.25
19, Apr 89		0.45	1.35	2.25
20, 89, b&w		0.50	1.50	2.50
21, 89, b&w		0.50	1.50	2.50
22, 89, b&w		0.50	1.50	2.50
23, 89, b&w		0.50	1.50	2.50
24, Apr 90, b&w		0.50	1.50	2.50
25, May 90, b&w		0.50	1.50	2.50
26, Jun 90, b&w		0.50	1.50	2.50
27, Jul 90, b&w		0.50	1.50	2.50
28, Aug 90, b&w		0.50	1.50	2.50
29, Sep 90, b&w		0.50	1.50	2.50
30, Nov 90, b&w		0.50	1.50	2.50
31, Dec 90		0.55	1.65	2.75
32, Jan 91		0.55	1.65	2.75
33, Feb 91		0.55	1.65	2.75
34, Mar 91		0.55	1.65	2.75
35, Apr 91		0.55	1.65	2.75
36, May 91		0.59	1.77	2.95
37, Jun 91		0.55	1.65	2.75
38, Jul 91		0.55	1.65	2.75
39, Aug 91		0.55	1.65	2.75
40, Sep 91		0.55	1.65	2.75
41, Oct 91		0.55	1.65	2.75
42, Nov 91		0.55	1.65	2.75
43, Dec 91		0.55	1.65	2.75
44		0.55	1.65	2.75
45		0.55	1.65	2.75
46		0.55	1.65	2.75
47		0.55	1.65	2.75
48		0.55	1.65	2.75
49		0.55	1.65	2.75
50, contains flexidisc, color	0.59	1.77	2.95	
51	2.75	0.55	1.65	2.75
52	2.75	0.55	1.65	2.75
53	2.75	0.55	1.65	2.75
54	2.75	0.55	1.65	2.75
55	2.75	0.55	1.65	2.75
56	2.75	0.55	1.65	2.75
57, color	2.75	0.55	1.65	2.75
58	2.75	0.55	1.65	2.75
59	2.75	0.55	1.65	2.75
60	2.75	0.55	1.65	2.75
61	2.75	0.55	1.65	2.75
62	2.75	0.55	1.65	2.75
63	2.95	0.59	1.77	2.95
64	2.95	0.59	1.77	2.95
65	2.95	0.59	1.77	2.95
66	2.95	0.59	1.77	2.95
67	2.95	0.59	1.77	2.95
68	2.95	0.59	1.77	2.95
69	2.95	0.59	1.77	2.95
70	2.95	0.59	1.77	2.95
71, 94	2.95	0.59	1.77	2.95
80, 95, V:Iron Jaw	2.95	0.59	1.77	2.95
82, 95, "Twilight's Last Gleaming" Part 1				
	2.95	0.59	1.77	2.95
84, 95, "The Death of Joan Wayne"				
	2.95	0.59	1.77	2.95
85, 95	2.95	0.59	1.77	2.95
86, 95	2.95	0.59	1.77	2.95
87, 95, 10th Anniversary issue;A:AC staff				
	3.50	0.70	2.10	3.50

FEMFORCE FRIGHTBOOK

	ORIG.	GOOD	FINE	N-MINT
1, b&w		0.59	1.77	2.95

FEMFORCE IN THE HOUSE OF HORROR

	ORIG.	GOOD	FINE	N-MINT
1, 89, b&w		0.50	1.50	2.50

FEMFORCE PIN UP PORTFOLIO

	ORIG.	GOOD	FINE	N-MINT
1		0.59	1.77	2.95
2		0.59	1.77	2.95
3, 91		0.79	2.37	3.95
4, Dec 91		1.00	3.00	5.00

FEMFORCE SPECIAL

	ORIG.	GOOD	FINE	N-MINT
1, Nov 84		0.30	0.90	1.50

FEMFORCE UP CLOSE

	ORIG.	GOOD	FINE	N-MINT
1, Nightveil, color		0.55	1.65	2.75
2, Stardust		0.55	1.65	2.75
3, Dragonfly		0.55	1.65	2.75
4, O:She Cat	2.95	0.59	1.77	2.95
5, Blue Bulleteer	2.95	0.59	1.77	2.95
6, Ms. Victory	2.95	0.59	1.77	2.95
7, Ms. Victory	2.95	0.59	1.77	2.95
8, Tara/Garganta	2.95	0.59	1.77	2.95
9, Synn	2.95	0.59	1.77	2.95
10, Yankee Girl;b&w	2.95	0.59	1.77	2.95
11, Nightveil;b&w	2.95	0.59	1.77	2.95

FEMFORCE: NIGHT OF THE DEMON

	ORIG.	GOOD	FINE	N-MINT
0, 90, nn b&w		0.55	1.65	2.75

FEMFORCE: OUT OF THE ASYLUM SPECIAL

	ORIG.	GOOD	FINE	N-MINT
1, Aug 87, b&w		0.50	1.50	2.50

FEMME NOIR
CAT-HEAD

	ORIG.	GOOD	FINE	N-MINT
1		0.35	1.05	1.75
2		0.35	1.05	1.75

FENRY
RAVEN

	ORIG.	GOOD	FINE	N-MINT
1	6.95	1.39	4.17	6.95

FERRET, THE
MALIBU

	ORIG.	GOOD	FINE	N-MINT
1	1.95	0.39	1.17	1.95
1, die-cut	2.50	0.50	1.50	2.50
2	2.50	0.50	1.50	2.50
3	2.50	0.50	1.50	2.50
4	2.25	0.45	1.35	2.25
5	2.25	0.45	1.35	2.25
6	2.25	0.45	1.35	2.25
7	2.25	0.45	1.35	2.25
8	2.25	0.45	1.35	2.25
9, Jan 94	2.50	0.50	1.50	2.50
10, Feb 94	2.50	0.50	1.50	2.50

FEUD
EPIC

	ORIG.	GOOD	FINE	N-MINT
1, Jul 93, Embossed cardstock cover				
	2.50	0.50	1.50	2.50
2, Aug 93	1.95	0.39	1.17	1.95
3, Sep 93	1.95	0.39	1.17	1.95
4, Oct 93	1.95	0.39	1.17	1.95

	ORIG.	GOOD	FINE	N-MINT

FEVER
WONDER COMIX
- 1, 95, b&w anthology..... 1.95   0.39   1.17   1.95

FIFTIES TERROR
ETERNITY
- 1, b&w rep 0.39   1.17   1.95
- 2, b&w rep 0.39   1.17   1.95
- 3, b&w rep 0.39   1.17   1.95
- 4, b&w rep 0.39   1.17   1.95
- 5, b&w rep 0.39   1.17   1.95
- 6, b&w rep 0.39   1.17   1.95

FIGHT MAN
MARVEL
- 1 .... 2.00   0.40   1.20   2.00

FIGHTING AMERICAN
DC
- 1, 94.............................. 1.50   0.30   0.90   1.50
- 2, 94.............................. 1.50   0.30   0.90   1.50
- 3, 94.............................. 1.50   0.30   0.90   1.50
- 4, May 94...................... 1.50   0.30   0.90   1.50
- 5, Jun 94....................... 1.50   0.30   0.90   1.50
- 6, Jul 94......................... 1.50   0.30   0.90   1.50

HARVEY
- 1, Oct 66 .... 0.25   4.00   12.00   20.00

FIGHTING FEM CLASSICS
FORBIDDEN FRUIT
- 1, adult b&w 0.70   2.10   3.50

FIGHTING FEMS
- 1, adult, b&w 0.70   2.10   3.50
- 2, adult, b&w 0.70   2.10   3.50

FIGMENTS
BLACKTHORNE
- 1 ....   0.35   1.05   1.75
- 2 ....   0.35   1.05   1.75

FIGMENTS UNLIMITED
GRAPHIK
- 1 .... 1.25   0.25   0.75   1.25
- 2 .... 1.25   0.25   0.75   1.25

FILES OF MS. TREE, THE
RENEGADE
- 1, Jun 84, b&w 1.40   4.20   7.00
- 2, Sep 85, b&w 1.40   4.20   7.00
- 3, b&w 1.40   4.20   7.00

FILIBUSTING COMICS
FANTAGRAPHICS
- 1, Jan 95, b&w.............. 2.75   0.55   1.65   2.75

FINAL CYCLE, THE
DRAGON'S TEETH
- 1, b&w 0.35   1.05   1.75
- 2, b&w 0.35   1.05   1.75
- 3, b&w 0.35   1.05   1.75
- 4, b&w 0.35   1.05   1.75

FINAL MAN, THE
C&T
- 1, b&w 0.30   0.90   1.50

FINAL TABOO
AIRCEL
- 1, adult, b&w 0.50   1.50   2.50
- 2, adult, b&w 0.50   1.50   2.50

FINN
FLEETWAY/QUALITY
- 1 .... 2.95   0.59   1.77   2.95
- 2 .... 2.95   0.59   1.77   2.95
- 3 .... 2.95   0.59   1.77   2.95
- 4 .... 2.95   0.59   1.77   2.95

FIRE
CALIBER
- 1, b&w 2.95   0.59   1.77   2.95
- 2, b&w 2.95   0.59   1.77   2.95

FIRE FROM HEAVEN
IMAGE
- 1, Mar 96 .... 2.50   0.50   1.50   2.50

FIRE SALE
RIP OFF
- 1, Dec 89, b&w;benefit ... 2.50   0.50   1.50   2.50

FIRE TEAM
AIRCEL
- 1, b&w 0.50   1.50   2.50
- 2, b&w 0.50   1.50   2.50
- 3, b&w 0.50   1.50   2.50
- 4, b&w 0.50   1.50   2.50
- 5, b&w 0.50   1.50   2.50
- 6, b&w 0.50   1.50   2.50

FIREARM
MALIBU/ULTRAVERSE
- 0, with videotape 2.99   8.97   14.95
- 1 .... 1.95   0.39   1.17   1.95
- 2, Rune,BWS 2.50   0.50   1.50   2.50
- 3 .... 1.95   0.39   1.17   1.95
- 4, Dec 93, Break-Thru..... 1.95   0.39   1.17   1.95
- 5, Jan 94........................ 1.95   0.39   1.17   1.95
- 6, Feb 94........................ 1.95   0.39   1.17   1.95
- 7, Mar 94........................ 1.95   0.39   1.17   1.95
- 8, May 94........................ 1.95   0.39   1.17   1.95
- 9, Jun 94......................... 1.95   0.39   1.17   1.95
- 10, Jul 94......................... 1.95   0.39   1.17   1.95
- 12, Aug 94....................... 1.95   0.39   1.17   1.95
- 13, Sep 94 .... 1.95   0.39   1.17   1.95

FIREBRAND
DC
- 1, Feb 96........................ 1.75   0.35   1.05   1.75
- 2, Mar 96........................ 1.75   0.35   1.05   1.75
- 3, Apr 96......................... 1.75   0.35   1.05   1.75
- 4, May 96........................ 1.75   0.35   1.05   1.75
- 5, Jun 96 .... 1.75   0.35   1.05   1.75

FIRESTAR
MARVEL
- 1, Mar 86........................ 0.75   0.80   2.40   4.00
- 2, Apr 86, AAd(c)............ 0.75   1.60   4.80   8.00
- 3, May 86........................ 0.75   0.80   2.40   4.00
- 4, Jun 86 .... 0.75   0.80   2.40   4.00

FIRESTORM
DC
- 1, Mar 78, AM/JR, I&O:Firestorm
  .... 0.35   0.40   1.20   2.00
- 2, Apr 78......................... 0.35   0.20   0.60   1.00
- 3, Jun 78 .... 0.35   0.20   0.60   1.00
- 4, Aug 78........................ 0.35   0.20   0.60   1.00

FIRESTORM ANNUAL
(was Fury of Firestorm Annual)
- 5, Oct 87, Suicide Squad
  .... 0.35   0.25   0.75   1.25

FIRESTORM, THE NUCLEAR MAN
(was Fury of Firestorm)
- 65, A:Green Lantern; new Firestorm
  ....   0.20   0.60   1.00
- 66 ....   0.20   0.60   1.00
- 67, Jan 88, Millennium ... 0.75   0.20   0.60   1.00
- 68, Feb 88, Millennium ... 0.75   0.20   0.60   1.00
- 69, Mar 88...................... 0.75   0.20   0.60   1.00
- 70 ....   0.20   0.60   1.00
- 71 ....   0.20   0.60   1.00
- 72 ....   0.20   0.60   1.00
- 73 ....   0.20   0.60   1.00
- 74 ....   0.20   0.60   1.00
- 75 ....   0.20   0.60   1.00
- 76 ....   0.20   0.60   1.00
- 77 ....   0.20   0.60   1.00
- 78 ....   0.20   0.60   1.00

	ORIG.	GOOD	FINE	N-MINT
❑ 79		0.20	0.60	1.00
❑ 80, 88, Invasion!	1.00	0.20	0.60	1.00
❑ 81, Jan 89, Invasion!	1.00	0.20	0.60	1.00
❑ 82		0.20	0.60	1.00
❑ 83		0.20	0.60	1.00
❑ 84		0.20	0.60	1.00
❑ 85, new Firestorm		0.20	0.60	1.00
❑ 86, Janus		0.20	0.60	1.00
❑ 87		0.20	0.60	1.00
❑ 88		0.20	0.60	1.00
❑ 89		0.20	0.60	1.00
❑ 90		0.20	0.60	1.00
❑ 91		0.20	0.60	1.00
❑ 92		0.20	0.60	1.00
❑ 93, Jan 90		0.20	0.60	1.00
❑ 94, Feb 90		0.20	0.60	1.00
❑ 95, Mar 90		0.20	0.60	1.00
❑ 96, Apr 90		0.20	0.60	1.00
❑ 97, May 90		0.20	0.60	1.00
❑ 98, Jun 90		0.20	0.60	1.00
❑ 99, Jul 90		0.20	0.60	1.00
❑ 100, Aug 90, final issue		0.59	1.77	2.95

FIRKIN (was Last Gasp)
KNOCKABOUT

	ORIG.	GOOD	FINE	N-MINT
❑ 6, adult, b&w		0.50	1.50	2.50

FIRST ADVENTURES
FIRST

	ORIG.	GOOD	FINE	N-MINT
❑ 1		0.25	0.75	1.25
❑ 2		0.25	0.75	1.25
❑ 3		0.25	0.75	1.25
❑ 4		0.25	0.75	1.25
❑ 5		0.25	0.75	1.25

FIRST FOLIO
PACIFIC

❑ 0, (see 1st Folio) ....

FIRST ISSUE SPECIAL
DC

	ORIG.	GOOD	FINE	N-MINT
❑ 1, Apr 75, JK, Atlas	0.25	1.50	4.50	7.50
❑ 2, May 75, Green Team	0.25	0.40	1.20	2.00
❑ 3, Jun 75, Metamorpho	0.25	0.80	2.40	4.00
❑ 4, Jul 75, Lady Cop	0.25	0.40	1.20	2.00
❑ 5, Aug 75, JK, Manhunter				
	0.25	1.50	4.50	7.50
❑ 6, Sep 75, JK, Dingbats	0.25	1.20	3.60	6.00
❑ 7, Oct 75, SD, Creeper	0.25	0.40	1.20	2.00
❑ 8, Nov 75, MGr, Warlord	0.25	3.00	9.00	15.00
❑ 9, Dec 75, WS, Dr. Fate	0.25	0.60	1.80	3.00
❑ 10, Jan 76, Outsiders	0.25	0.40	1.20	2.00
❑ 11, Feb 76, Code Name: Assassin				
	0.25	0.40	1.20	2.00
❑ 12, Mar 76, new Starman				
	0.30	1.20	3.60	6.00
❑ 13, Apr 76, New Gods	0.30	1.00	3.00	5.00

FIRST KINGDOM
BUD PLANT

	ORIG.	GOOD	FINE	N-MINT
❑ 1		0.40	1.20	2.00
❑ 2		0.40	1.20	2.00
❑ 3		0.40	1.20	2.00
❑ 4		0.40	1.20	2.00
❑ 5		0.40	1.20	2.00
❑ 6		0.40	1.20	2.00
❑ 7		0.40	1.20	2.00
❑ 8		0.40	1.20	2.00
❑ 9		0.40	1.20	2.00
❑ 10		0.40	1.20	2.00
❑ 11		0.40	1.20	2.00
❑ 12		0.40	1.20	2.00
❑ 13		0.40	1.20	2.00
❑ 14		0.40	1.20	2.00
❑ 15		0.40	1.20	2.00
❑ 16		0.40	1.20	2.00

	ORIG.	GOOD	FINE	N-MINT
❑ 17		0.40	1.20	2.00
❑ 18		0.40	1.20	2.00
❑ 19		0.40	1.20	2.00
❑ 20		0.40	1.20	2.00
❑ 21		0.40	1.20	2.00
❑ 22		0.40	1.20	2.00
❑ 23		0.40	1.20	2.00
❑ 24		0.40	1.20	2.00

FIRST SIX-PACK
FIRST

	ORIG.	GOOD	FINE	N-MINT
❑ 1, sampler		0.10	0.30	0.50
❑ 2, sampler		0.10	0.30	0.50

FISH POLICE
FISHWRAP

	ORIG.	GOOD	FINE	N-MINT
❑ 1		5.00	15.00	25.00
❑ 1, (2nd printing)		0.30	0.90	1.50
❑ 2		3.00	9.00	15.00
❑ 3		0.60	1.80	3.00
❑ 4		0.30	0.90	1.50
❑ 5		0.30	0.90	1.50
❑ 6		0.30	0.90	1.50
❑ 7		0.30	0.90	1.50
❑ 8		0.30	0.90	1.50
❑ 9		0.30	0.90	1.50
❑ 10		0.30	0.90	1.50
❑ 11		0.30	0.90	1.50

MARVEL

	ORIG.	GOOD	FINE	N-MINT
❑ 1, reprint	1.25	0.25	0.75	1.25
❑ 2, reprint	1.25	0.25	0.75	1.25
❑ 3, reprint	1.25	0.25	0.75	1.25
❑ 4, reprint	1.25	0.25	0.75	1.25
❑ 5, reprint	1.25	0.25	0.75	1.25
❑ 6, reprint	1.25	0.25	0.75	1.25

FISH POLICE (Volume 2; was Fishwrap title)
COMICO

	ORIG.	GOOD	FINE	N-MINT
❑ 5		0.35	1.05	1.75
❑ 6		0.35	1.05	1.75
❑ 7		0.35	1.05	1.75
❑ 8		0.35	1.05	1.75
❑ 9		0.35	1.05	1.75
❑ 10		0.35	1.05	1.75
❑ 11		0.35	1.05	1.75
❑ 12		0.35	1.05	1.75
❑ 13		0.35	1.05	1.75
❑ 14		0.35	1.05	1.75
❑ 15		0.35	1.05	1.75
❑ 16		0.35	1.05	1.75
❑ 17, (becomes Apple title)		0.50	1.50	2.50

FISH POLICE (was Comico title)
APPLE

	ORIG.	GOOD	FINE	N-MINT
❑ 0		0.50	1.50	2.50
❑ 18, b&w		0.45	1.35	2.25
❑ 19, b&w		0.45	1.35	2.25
❑ 20, b&w		0.45	1.35	2.25
❑ 21, b&w		0.45	1.35	2.25
❑ 22, b&w		0.45	1.35	2.25
❑ 23, b&w		0.45	1.35	2.25
❑ 24, b&w		0.45	1.35	2.25
❑ 25, b&w		0.45	1.35	2.25
❑ 26, b&w		0.45	1.35	2.25

FISH POLICE SPECIAL
COMICO

	ORIG.	GOOD	FINE	N-MINT
❑ 1		0.50	1.50	2.50

FISH SCHTICKS
APPLE

	ORIG.	GOOD	FINE	N-MINT
❑ 1, b&w	2.75	0.55	1.65	2.75
❑ 2, b&w	2.75	0.55	1.65	2.75
❑ 3, b&w	2.75	0.55	1.65	2.75
❑ 4, b&w	2.75	0.55	1.65	2.75
❑ 5, b&w	2.75	0.55	1.65	2.75

	ORIG.	GOOD	FINE	N-MINT
❏ 6, b&w 2.75		0.55	1.65	2.75

FISSION CHICKEN
FANTAGRAPHICS

	ORIG.	GOOD	FINE	N-MINT
❏ 1, b&w		0.40	1.20	2.00
❏ 2, b&w		0.40	1.20	2.00
❏ 3, b&w		0.40	1.20	2.00
❏ 4, b&w		0.40	1.20	2.00

FISSION CHICKEN: PLAN NINE FROM VORTOX
MU PRESS

	ORIG.	GOOD	FINE	N-MINT
❏ 0, Jul 94 .... 3.95		0.79	2.37	3.95

FIST OF GOD
ETERNITY

	ORIG.	GOOD	FINE	N-MINT
❏ 1		0.39	1.17	1.95
❏ 2		0.39	1.17	1.95
❏ 3		0.39	1.17	1.95
❏ 4		0.39	1.17	1.95

FIST OF THE NORTH STAR
VIZ

	ORIG.	GOOD	FINE	N-MINT
❏ 1, b&w, Japanese............		0.59	1.77	2.95
❏ 2, b&w, Japanese............		0.59	1.77	2.95
❏ 3, b&w, Japanese............		0.59	1.77	2.95
❏ 4, b&w, Japanese............		0.59	1.77	2.95
❏ 5, O:Fist.......................		0.65	1.95	3.25
❏ 6		0.59	1.77	2.95
❏ 7		0.59	1.77	2.95
❏ 8		0.59	1.77	2.95

FLAME TWISTERS
BROWN STUDY

	ORIG.	GOOD	FINE	N-MINT
❏ 1, Oct 94, b&w............. 2.50		0.50	1.50	2.50
❏ 2, Mar 95, b&w............. 2.50		0.50	1.50	2.50

FLAMING CARROT
AARDVARK-VANAHEIM

	ORIG.	GOOD	FINE	N-MINT
❏ 1		7.00	21.00	35.00
❏ 2		4.00	12.00	20.00
❏ 3		2.00	6.00	10.00
❏ 4		1.60	4.80	8.00
❏ 5		1.60	4.80	8.00
❏ 6, (moves to Renegade Press)		1.60	4.80	8.00

KILIAN

	ORIG.	GOOD	FINE	N-MINT
❏ 1, magazine....................		8.00	24.00	40.00

FLAMING CARROT
(former Aardvark Vanaheim title)
RENEGADE

	ORIG.	GOOD	FINE	N-MINT
❏ 7, b&w		1.00	3.00	5.00
❏ 8, b&w		1.00	3.00	5.00
❏ 9, b&w		1.00	3.00	5.00
❏ 10, b&w		1.00	3.00	5.00
❏ 11		1.00	3.00	5.00
❏ 12		1.00	3.00	5.00
❏ 13		1.00	3.00	5.00
❏ 14		1.00	3.00	5.00
❏ 15, b&w 2.00		1.00	3.00	5.00
❏ 16		1.00	3.00	5.00
❏ 17, b&w; (moves to Dark Horse)				
.... 2.00		1.00	3.00	5.00

FLAMING CARROT (was Renegade title)
DARK HORSE

	ORIG.	GOOD	FINE	N-MINT
❏ 18, 88, b&w		0.80	2.40	4.00
❏ 19, b&w		0.80	2.40	4.00
❏ 20, b&w		0.80	2.40	4.00
❏ 21, b&w		0.80	2.40	4.00
❏ 22, b&w 2.00		0.80	2.40	4.00
❏ 23, b&w		0.80	2.40	4.00
❏ 24		0.59	1.77	2.95
❏ 25, TMNT, trading cards ..		0.45	1.35	2.25
❏ 26, TMNT		0.45	1.35	2.25
❏ 27, TMc(c) TMNT........... 2.25		0.45	1.35	2.25
❏ 28		0.45	1.35	2.25
❏ 29, b&w		0.50	1.50	2.50

	ORIG.	GOOD	FINE	N-MINT
❏ 30, b&w		0.50	1.50	2.50
❏ 31, Oct 94, b&w; A:Herbie				
.... 2.50		0.50	1.50	2.50

FLARE
HERO

	ORIG.	GOOD	FINE	N-MINT
❏ 1, 52 pages......................		1.00	3.00	5.00
❏ 2, 52 pages......................		0.55	1.65	2.75
❏ 3, 52 pages......................		0.55	1.65	2.75

FLARE (Volume 2)

	ORIG.	GOOD	FINE	N-MINT
❏ 1		0.59	1.77	2.95
❏ 2		0.59	1.77	2.95
❏ 3, 1:Britannia		0.59	1.77	2.95
❏ 4		0.70	2.10	3.50
❏ 5, Eternity Smith..............		0.70	2.10	3.50
❏ 6, I:Tigress.....................		0.70	2.10	3.50
❏ 7		0.79	2.37	3.95
❏ 8, b&w.........................3.50		0.70	2.10	3.50
❏ 9, b&w.........................3.50		0.70	2.10	3.50
❏ 10, b&w.........................3.50		0.70	2.10	3.50
❏ 11, b&w.........................2.95		0.59	1.77	2.95
❏ 12, Jun 93 ....3.95		0.79	2.37	3.95
❏ 13, Aug 93 ....3.95		0.79	2.37	3.95
❏ 14 ....3.95		0.79	2.37	3.95
❏ 15 ....3.95		0.79	2.37	3.95
❏ 16 ....2.95		0.59	1.77	2.95

FLARE ADVENTURES

	ORIG.	GOOD	FINE	N-MINT
❏ 1, reprints........................		0.18	0.54	0.90
❏ 8, b&w		0.79	2.37	3.95

FLARE ADVENTURES/CHAMPIONS CLASSICS

	ORIG.	GOOD	FINE	N-MINT
❏ 2, flip-format....................		0.59	1.77	2.95
❏ 3, flip-format....................		0.59	1.77	2.95
❏ 4, b&w, flip-format		0.70	2.10	3.50
❏ 5, b&w, flip-format		0.70	2.10	3.50
❏ 6, b&w, flip-format		0.70	2.10	3.50
❏ 7, b&w, flip-format		0.70	2.10	3.50
❏ 9, b&w, flip-format 3.95		0.79	2.37	3.95
❏ 10, b&w, flip-format 3.95		0.79	2.37	3.95
❏ 11, b&w, flip-format 3.95		0.79	2.37	3.95
❏ 12, b&w, flip-format 3.95		0.79	2.37	3.95
❏ 13, b&w, flip-format 3.95		0.79	2.37	3.95

FLARE ANNUAL

	ORIG.	GOOD	FINE	N-MINT
❏ 1, b&w..........................		0.90	2.70	4.50

FLARE FIRST EDITION

	ORIG.	GOOD	FINE	N-MINT
❏ 1, contents will vary.........		0.70	2.10	3.50
❏ 2, contents will vary.........		0.70	2.10	3.50
❏ 3, b&w..........................		0.70	2.10	3.50
❏ 4, b&w..........................		0.90	2.70	4.50
❏ 5, b&w..........................		0.90	2.70	4.50
❏ 6, b&w.......................3.95		0.79	2.37	3.95
❏ 7, b&w.......................3.95		0.79	2.37	3.95
❏ 8, b&w.......................3.95		0.79	2.37	3.95
❏ 9, Sparkplug 3.95		0.79	2.37	3.95

FLARE FIRST EDITION/CHAMPIONS CLASSICS

	ORIG.	GOOD	FINE	N-MINT
❏ 10 ....3.95		0.79	2.37	3.95
❏ 11 ....3.95		0.79	2.37	3.95

FLASH
DC

	ORIG.	GOOD	FINE	N-MINT
❏ 0, Oct 94......................1.50		0.60	1.80	3.00
❏ 1, Jun 87, Wally West.....0.75		2.40	7.20	12.00
❏ 2, Jul 87......................0.75		1.60	4.80	8.00
❏ 3, Aug 87......................0.75		1.00	3.00	5.00
❏ 4, Sep 87......................0.75		0.80	2.40	4.00
❏ 5, Oct 87......................0.75		0.80	2.40	4.00
❏ 6, Nov 87......................0.75		0.80	2.40	4.00
❏ 7, Dec 87......................0.75		0.80	2.40	4.00
❏ 8, Jan 88, Millennium 0.75		0.80	2.40	4.00
❏ 9, Feb 88, Millennium 0.75		0.80	2.40	4.00
❏ 10, May 88......................0.75		0.80	2.40	4.00
❏ 11, Apr 88......................0.75		0.80	2.40	4.00

	ORIG.	GOOD	FINE	N-MINT
☐ 12, May 88, Bonus Book #2 ....0.75	0.80	2.40	4.00
☐ 13, Jun 88, V:Vandal Savage 0.75	1.00	3.00	5.00
☐ 14, Jul 88, V:Vandal Savage 0.75	1.00	3.00	5.00
☐ 15, Aug 88	0.75	0.60	1.80	3.00
☐ 16, Sep 88	0.75	0.60	1.80	3.00
☐ 17, Oct 88	1.00	0.60	1.80	3.00
☐ 18, Nov 88	1.00	0.60	1.80	3.00
☐ 19, Dec 88, Bonus Book	1.00	0.60	1.80	3.00
☐ 20, 88	1.00	0.60	1.80	3.00
☐ 21, 88, Invasion!	1.00	0.48	1.44	2.40
☐ 22, Jan 89, Invasion!	1.00	0.48	1.44	2.40
☐ 23, Feb 89	1.00	0.50	1.50	2.50
☐ 24, Mar 89	1.00	0.50	1.50	2.50
☐ 25, Apr 89	1.00	0.50	1.50	2.50
☐ 26, May 89	1.00	0.50	1.50	2.50
☐ 27, Jun 89	1.00	0.50	1.50	2.50
☐ 28, Jul 89	1.00	0.50	1.50	2.50
☐ 29, Aug 89	1.00	0.50	1.50	2.50
☐ 30, Sep 89	1.00	0.50	1.50	2.50
☐ 31, Oct 89	1.00	0.50	1.50	2.50
☐ 32, Nov 89	1.00	0.50	1.50	2.50
☐ 33, Dec 89	1.00	0.50	1.50	2.50
☐ 34, Jan 90	1.00	0.50	1.50	2.50
☐ 35, Feb 90	1.00	0.50	1.50	2.50
☐ 36, Mar 90	1.00	0.50	1.50	2.50
☐ 37, Apr 90	1.00	0.50	1.50	2.50
☐ 38, May 90	1.00	0.50	1.50	2.50
☐ 39, Jun 90	1.00	0.50	1.50	2.50
☐ 40, Jul 90	1.00	0.50	1.50	2.50
☐ 41, Aug 90	1.00	0.30	0.90	1.50
☐ 42, Sep 90	1.00	0.30	0.90	1.50
☐ 43, Oct 90	1.00	0.30	0.90	1.50
☐ 44, Nov 90	1.00	0.30	0.90	1.50
☐ 45, Dec 90	1.00	0.30	0.90	1.50
☐ 46, Jan 91	1.00	0.30	0.90	1.50
☐ 47, Feb 91	1.00	0.30	0.90	1.50
☐ 48, Mar 91	1.00	0.30	0.90	1.50
☐ 49, Apr 91	1.00	0.30	0.90	1.50
☐ 50, May 91	1.75	1.20	3.60	6.00
☐ 51, Jun 91	1.00	0.35	1.05	1.75
☐ 52, Jul 91	1.00	0.20	0.60	1.00
☐ 53, Aug 91, Superman	1.00	0.20	0.60	1.00
☐ 54, Sep 91	1.00	0.20	0.60	1.00
☐ 55, Oct 91, War of Gods	1.00	0.20	0.60	1.00
☐ 56, Nov 91, Icicle story	1.00	0.20	0.60	1.00
☐ 57, Dec 91, Icicle story	1.00	0.20	0.60	1.00
☐ 58, Jan 92	1.00	0.20	0.60	1.00
☐ 59, Feb 92	1.00	0.20	0.60	1.00
☐ 60, Mar 92	1.00	0.20	0.60	1.00
☐ 61, Apr 92	1.00	0.20	0.60	1.00
☐ 62, May 92, 65 O:retold	1.00	0.20	0.60	1.00
☐ 63, May 92, 65 O:retold	1.00	0.20	0.60	1.00
☐ 64, Jun 92, 65 O:retold	1.00	0.20	0.60	1.00
☐ 65, Jun 92, 65 O:retold	1.00	0.20	0.60	1.00
☐ 66, Jul 92, Aquaman	1.25	0.25	0.75	1.25
☐ 67, Aug 92	1.25	0.25	0.75	1.25
☐ 68, Sep 92	1.25	0.25	0.75	1.25
☐ 69, Oct 92, Green Lantern 1.25	0.25	0.75	1.25
☐ 70, Nov 92	1.25	0.25	0.75	1.25
☐ 71, Dec 92	1.25	0.25	0.75	1.25
☐ 72, Jan 93	1.25	0.40	1.20	2.00
☐ 73, Feb 93	1.25	0.80	2.40	4.00
☐ 74, Mar 93	1.25	0.50	1.50	2.50
☐ 75, Arp 93	1.25	0.50	1.50	2.50
☐ 76, May 93	1.25	0.50	1.50	2.50
☐ 76, Jun 93	1.25	0.50	1.50	2.50
☐ 78, Jul 93	1.25	0.50	1.50	2.50
☐ 79	2.50	0.60	1.80	3.00

	ORIG.	GOOD	FINE	N-MINT
☐ 80, foil cover	2.50	0.50	1.50	2.50
☐ 80, regular cover	1.25	0.25	0.75	1.25
☐ 81	1.25	0.25	0.75	1.25
☐ 82	1.25	0.25	0.75	1.25
☐ 83	1.25	0.25	0.75	1.25
☐ 84	1.25	0.25	0.75	1.25
☐ 85	1.50	0.30	0.90	1.50
☐ 86	1.50	0.30	0.90	1.50
☐ 87	1.50	0.30	0.90	1.50
☐ 88	1.50	0.30	0.90	1.50
☐ 89	1.50	0.30	0.90	1.50
☐ 90, May 94	1.50	0.30	0.90	1.50
☐ 91, Jun 94	1.50	0.30	0.90	1.50
☐ 92, Jul 94	1.50	3.00	9.00	15.00
☐ 93, Aug 94	1.50	1.60	4.80	8.00
☐ 94, Sep 94	1.50	1.20	3.60	6.00
☐ 95, Nov 94	1.50	0.50	1.50	2.50
☐ 96, Dec 94	1.50	0.40	1.20	2.00
☐ 97, Jan 95	1.50	0.30	0.90	1.50
☐ 98, Feb 95	1.50	0.30	0.90	1.50
☐ 99, Mar 95	1.50	0.30	0.90	1.50
☐ 100, Apr 95	2.50	0.50	1.50	2.50
☐ 100, Apr 95, enhanced cover 3.50	0.70	2.10	3.50
☐ 101, May 95	1.75	0.35	1.05	1.75
☐ 102, Jun 95	1.75	0.35	1.05	1.75
☐ 103, Jul 95	1.75	0.35	1.05	1.75
☐ 104, Aug 95	1.75	0.35	1.05	1.75
☐ 105, Sep 95, V:Mirror Master 1.75	0.35	1.05	1.75
☐ 106, Oct 95, return of Frances Kane 1.75	0.35	1.05	1.75
☐ 107, Nov 95, "Underworld Unleashed";A:Captain Marvel 1.75	0.35	1.05	1.75
☐ 108, Dec 95, "Dead Heat" Part 1 of 6 ....1.75	0.35	1.05	1.75
☐ 109, Jan 96, "Dead Heat" Part 2 of 6;continues in *Impulse* #10 ....1.75	0.35	1.05	1.75
☐ 110, Feb 96, "Dead Heat" Part 4 of 6;continues in *Impulse* #11 ....1.75	0.35	1.05	1.75
☐ 111, Mar 96, "Dead Heat" Finale 1.75	0.35	1.05	1.75
☐ 112, Apr 96, A:John Fox	1.75	0.35	1.05	1.75
☐ 113, May 96, "Race Against Time" Part 1 ....1.75	0.35	1.05	1.75
☐ 114, Jun 96, "Race Against Time" Part 2;A:Don and Dawn Allen 1.75	0.35	1.05	1.75

FLASH ANNUAL

	ORIG.	GOOD	FINE	N-MINT
☐ 1, 87	1.25	0.80	2.40	4.00
☐ 2, 88	1.50	0.30	0.90	1.50
☐ 3, 89	1.75	0.35	1.05	1.75
☐ 4, 91, Armageddon 2001 ....2.00	0.40	1.20	2.00
☐ 5, 92, Eclipso	2.50	0.50	1.50	2.50
☐ 6, Bloodlines	2.50	0.50	1.50	2.50
☐ 7, 94	2.95	0.59	1.77	2.95
☐ 8, 95, "Year One"	3.50	0.70	2.10	3.50

FLASH GORDON

	GOOD	FINE	N-MINT
☐ 1	0.25	0.75	1.25
☐ 2	0.25	0.75	1.25
☐ 3	0.25	0.75	1.25
☐ 4	0.25	0.75	1.25
☐ 5	0.25	0.75	1.25
☐ 6	0.25	0.75	1.25
☐ 7	0.25	0.75	1.25
☐ 8	0.25	0.75	1.25
☐ 9	0.25	0.75	1.25

	ORIG.	GOOD	FINE	N-MINT

MARVEL

☐ 1, Jun 95, cardstock wraparound cover
.... 2.95 | 0.59 | 1.77 | 2.95

☐ 2, Jul 95, Final issue; wraparound cardstock cover
.... 2.95 | 0.59 | 1.77 | 2.95

FLASH SPECIAL
DC

☐ 1, 90, JKu(c), CI; 1:John Fox; 3 Flashes
.... 2.95 | 1.00 | 3.00 | 5.00

FLASH TV SPECIAL, THE

☐ 1, 91 .... 3.95 | 0.79 | 2.37 | 3.95

FLASH, THE

Issue	ORIG.	GOOD	FINE	N-MINT
☐ 105, CI, O:Flash	0.10	960.00	2880.00	4800.00
☐ 106, CI, O:Pied Piper	0.10	280.00	840.00	1400.00
☐ 107, CI	0.10	140.00	420.00	700.00
☐ 108, Sep 59, CI	0.10	120.00	360.00	600.00
☐ 109, Nov 59, CI	0.10	100.00	300.00	500.00
☐ 110, Jan 60, CI/MA, I:Kid Flash	0.10	230.00	690.00	1150.00
☐ 111, Mar 60, CI	0.10	65.00	195.00	325.00
☐ 112, May 60, CI, I:Elongated Man	0.10	100.00	300.00	500.00
☐ 113, Jul 60, CI	0.10	52.00	156.00	260.00
☐ 114, Aug 60, CI	0.10	48.00	144.00	240.00
☐ 115, Sep 60, CI	0.10	40.00	120.00	200.00
☐ 116, Nov 60, CI	0.10	40.00	120.00	200.00
☐ 117, Dec 60, CI	0.10	40.00	120.00	200.00
☐ 118, Feb 61, CI	0.10	40.00	120.00	200.00
☐ 119, Mar 61, CI, W:Elongated Man	0.10	108.00	180.00	
☐ 120, May 61, CI	0.10	30.00	90.00	150.00
☐ 121, Jun 61, CI	0.10	26.00	78.00	130.00
☐ 122, Aug 61, CI	0.10	26.00	78.00	130.00
☐ 123, Sep 61, I, I:Earth 2	0.10	180.00	540.00	900.00
☐ 124, Nov 61, CI	0.10	13.00	39.00	65.00
☐ 125, Dec 61, CI, 1:cosmic treadmil	0.12	13.00	39.00	65.00
☐ 126, Feb 62, CI	0.12	13.00	39.00	65.00
☐ 127, Mar 62, CI	0.12	13.00	39.00	65.00
☐ 128, May 62, CI, O/1: Abra Kadabra	0.12	13.00	39.00	65.00
☐ 129, Jun 62, CI Golden Age Flash	0.12	45.00	135.00	225.00
☐ 130, Aug 62, CI	0.12	10.00	30.00	50.00
☐ 131, Sep 62, CI	0.12	10.00	30.00	50.00
☐ 132, Nov 62, CI	0.12	10.00	30.00	50.00
☐ 133, Dec 62, CI	0.12	10.00	30.00	50.00
☐ 134, Feb 63, CI	0.12	10.00	30.00	50.00
☐ 135, Mar 63, CI	0.12	10.00	30.00	50.00
☐ 136, May 63, CI	0.12	10.00	30.00	50.00
☐ 137, Jun 63, CI, Vandal Savage	0.12	45.00	135.00	225.00
☐ 138, Sep 63, CI	0.12	10.00	30.00	50.00
☐ 139, Sep 63, CI	0.12	14.00	42.00	70.00
☐ 140, Nov 63, CI	0.12	10.00	30.00	50.00
☐ 141, Dec 63, CI	0.12	7.20	21.60	36.00
☐ 142, Feb 63, CI	0.12	7.20	21.60	36.00
☐ 143, Mar 64, CI	0.12	7.20	21.60	36.00
☐ 144, May 64, CI	0.12	7.20	21.60	36.00
☐ 145, Jun 64, CI	0.12	7.20	21.60	36.00
☐ 146, Aug 64, CI	0.12	7.20	21.60	36.00
☐ 147, Sep 64, CI	0.12	7.20	21.60	36.00
☐ 148, Nov 64, CI	0.12	7.20	21.60	36.00
☐ 149, Dec 64, CI	0.12	7.20	21.60	36.00
☐ 150, Feb 65, CI	0.12	7.20	21.60	36.00
☐ 151, Mar 65, CI	0.12	4.00	12.00	20.00
☐ 152, May 65, CI	0.12	4.00	12.00	20.00
☐ 153, Jun 65, CI	0.12	4.00	12.00	20.00
☐ 154, Aug 65, CI	0.12	4.00	12.00	20.00
☐ 155, Sep 65, CI	0.12	4.00	12.00	20.00
☐ 156, Nov 65, CI	0.12	4.00	12.00	20.00
☐ 157, Dec 65, CI	0.12	4.00	12.00	20.00
☐ 158, Feb 65, CI	0.12	4.00	12.00	20.00
☐ 159, Mar 65, CI	0.12	4.00	12.00	20.00
☐ 160, Apr 65, CI	0.25	4.00	12.00	20.00
☐ 161, May 66, CI	0.12	4.00	12.00	20.00
☐ 162, Jun 66, CI	0.12	4.00	12.00	20.00
☐ 163, Aug 66, CI	0.12	4.00	12.00	20.00
☐ 164, Sep 66, CI	0.12	4.00	12.00	20.00
☐ 165, Nov 66, CI	0.12	4.00	12.00	20.00
☐ 166, Dec 66, CI	0.12	4.00	12.00	20.00
☐ 167, Feb 67, CI, O:Flash, I:Mopee	0.12	5.20	15.60	26.00
☐ 168, Mar 67	0.12	4.00	12.00	20.00
☐ 169, May 67	0.25	4.00	12.00	20.00
☐ 170, Jun 67	0.12	4.00	12.00	20.00
☐ 171, Jun 67	0.12	4.00	12.00	20.00
☐ 172, Aug 67	0.12	4.00	12.00	20.00
☐ 173, Sep 67	0.12	4.00	12.00	20.00
☐ 174, Nov 67	0.12	4.00	12.00	20.00
☐ 175, Dec 67	0.12	10.00	30.00	50.00
☐ 176, Feb 68	0.12	2.40	7.20	12.00
☐ 177, Mar 68	0.12	2.40	7.20	12.00
☐ 178, May 68	0.25	2.40	7.20	12.00
☐ 179, May 68	0.12	2.40	7.20	12.00
☐ 180, Jun 68	0.12	2.40	7.20	12.00
☐ 181, Aug 68	0.12	2.40	7.20	12.00
☐ 182, Sep 68	0.12	2.40	7.20	12.00
☐ 183, Nov 68	0.12	2.40	7.20	12.00
☐ 184, Dec 68	0.12	2.40	7.20	12.00
☐ 185, Feb 69	0.12	2.40	7.20	12.00
☐ 186, Mar 69	0.12	2.40	7.20	12.00
☐ 187, May 69	0.25	2.40	7.20	12.00
☐ 188, May 69	0.12	2.40	7.20	12.00
☐ 189, Jun 69	0.12	2.40	7.20	12.00
☐ 190, Aug 69	0.15	2.40	7.20	12.00
☐ 191, Sep 69	0.15	2.40	7.20	12.00
☐ 192, Nov 69	0.15	2.40	7.20	12.00
☐ 193, Dec 69	0.15	2.40	7.20	12.00
☐ 194, Feb 70	0.15	2.40	7.20	12.00
☐ 195, Mar 70	0.15	2.40	7.20	12.00
☐ 196, May 70	0.25	2.40	7.20	12.00
☐ 197, May 70	0.15	2.40	7.20	12.00
☐ 198, Jun 70	0.15	2.40	7.20	12.00
☐ 199, Aug 70	0.15	2.40	7.20	12.00
☐ 200, Sep 70	0.15	3.20	9.60	16.00
☐ 201, Nov 70	0.15	1.20	3.60	6.00
☐ 202, Dec 70	0.15	1.20	3.60	6.00
☐ 203, Feb 71	0.15	1.20	3.60	6.00
☐ 204, Mar 71	0.15	1.20	3.60	6.00
☐ 205, May 71, giant	0.25	2.00	6.00	10.00
☐ 206, May 71	0.15	1.20	3.60	6.00
☐ 207, Jun 71	0.15	1.20	3.60	6.00
☐ 208, Aug 71	0.25	1.20	3.60	6.00
☐ 209, Sep 71	0.25	1.20	3.60	6.00
☐ 210, Dec 71	0.25	1.20	3.60	6.00
☐ 211, Dec 71	0.25	1.20	3.60	6.00
☐ 212, Feb 72	0.25	1.20	3.60	6.00
☐ 213, Mar 72	0.25	1.20	3.60	6.00
☐ 214, Apr 72, CI, O:Metal Men	0.50	1.60	4.80	8.00
☐ 215, May 72	0.25	1.00	3.00	5.00
☐ 216, Jun 72	0.25	1.00	3.00	5.00
☐ 217, Sep 72, NA, A:Green Arrow	0.20	2.00	6.00	10.00
☐ 218, Nov 72, NA	0.20	2.00	6.00	10.00
☐ 219, Jan 73, NA, L:Green Arrow	0.20	2.00	6.00	10.00
☐ 220, Mar 73	0.20	0.60	1.80	3.00
☐ 221, May 73	0.20	0.60	1.80	3.00
☐ 222, Aug 73	0.20	0.60	1.80	3.00
☐ 223, Oct 73, NA	0.20	1.00	3.00	5.00
☐ 224, Dec 73	0.20	0.50	1.50	2.50

	ORIG.	GOOD	FINE	N-MINT
225, Feb 74 ....0.20	0.50	1.50	2.50
226, Apr 74, NA, A:Capt. Cold				
...................0.20	1.00	3.00	5.00
227, Jun 74 ....0.20	0.50	1.50	2.50
228, Aug 74 ....0.20	0.50	1.50	2.50
229, Oct 74 ....0.60	0.50	1.50	2.50
230, Dec 74 ....0.20	0.50	1.50	2.50
231, Feb 75 ....0.25	0.50	1.50	2.50
232, Apr 75 ....0.60	0.50	1.50	2.50
233, May 75 ....0.25	0.40	1.20	2.00
234, Jun 75 ....0.25	0.40	1.20	2.00
235, Aug 75 ....0.25	0.40	1.20	2.00
236, Sep 75 ....0.25	0.40	1.20	2.00
237, Nov 75 ....0.25	0.40	1.20	2.00
238, Dec 75 ....0.25	0.40	1.20	2.00
239, Feb 76 ....0.25	0.40	1.20	2.00
240, Mar 76 ....0.30	0.40	1.20	2.00
241, May 76 ....0.30	0.40	1.20	2.00
242, Jun 76 ....0.30	0.40	1.20	2.00
243, Aug 76 ....0.30	0.40	1.20	2.00
244, Sep 76 ....0.30	0.40	1.20	2.00
245, Nov 76 ....0.30	0.40	1.20	2.00
246, Jan 77 ....0.30	0.40	1.20	2.00
247, Mar 77 ....0.30	0.40	1.20	2.00
248, Apr 77 ....0.30	0.40	1.20	2.00
249, May 77 ....0.30	0.40	1.20	2.00
250, Jun 77 ....0.35	0.40	1.20	2.00
251, Aug 77 ....0.35	0.40	1.20	2.00
252, Sep 77 ....0.35	0.40	1.20	2.00
253, Sep 77 ....0.35	0.40	1.20	2.00
254, Oct 77 ....0.35	0.40	1.20	2.00
255, Nov 77 ....0.35	0.40	1.20	2.00
256, Dec 77 ....0.35	0.40	1.20	2.00
257, Jan 78 ....0.35	0.40	1.20	2.00
258, Feb 78 ....0.35	0.40	1.20	2.00
259, Mar 78 ....0.35	0.40	1.20	2.00
259, Mar 78 ....0.35	0.40	1.20	2.00
260, Apr 78 ....0.35	0.40	1.20	2.00
261, May 78 ....0.35	0.40	1.20	2.00
262, Jun 78 ....0.35	0.40	1.20	2.00
263, Jul 78 ....0.35	0.40	1.20	2.00
264, Aug 78 ....0.35	0.40	1.20	2.00
265, Sep 78 ....0.50	0.40	1.20	2.00
266, Oct 78 ....0.50	0.40	1.20	2.00
267, Nov 78 ....0.50	0.40	1.20	2.00
268, Dec 78 ....0.40	0.40	1.20	2.00
269, Jan 79 ....0.40	0.40	1.20	2.00
270, Mar 79 ....0.40	0.40	1.20	2.00
271, Mar 79, RB 0.40	0.40	1.20	2.00
272, Apr 79, RB 0.40	0.40	1.20	2.00
273, May 79, RB 0.40	0.40	1.20	2.00
274, Jun 79, RB 0.40	0.40	1.20	2.00
275, Jul 79, D:Iris West . 0.40	0.75	2.25	3.75
276, Aug 79, A:JLA 0.40	0.60	1.80	3.00
277, Sep 79, A:JLA 0.40	0.60	1.80	3.00
278, Oct 79 ....0.40	0.60	1.80	3.00
279, Nov 79 ....0.40	0.60	1.80	3.00
280, Dec 79 ....0.40	0.60	1.80	3.00
281, Jan 80 ....0.40	0.60	1.80	3.00
282, Feb 80 ....0.40	0.60	1.80	3.00
283, Mar 80 ....0.40	0.60	1.80	3.00
284, Apr 80 ....0.40	0.60	1.80	3.00
285, May 80 ....0.40	0.60	1.80	3.00
286, Jun 80 ....0.40	0.60	1.80	3.00
287, Jul 80 ....0.40	0.60	1.80	3.00
288, Aug 80 ....0.40	0.60	1.80	3.00
289, Sep 80, DH/GP, 1st Perez DC art				
...................0.50	0.80	2.40	4.00
290, Oct 80, GP, A:Firestorm				
...................0.50	0.60	1.80	3.00
291, Nov 80 ....0.50	0.60	1.80	3.00
292, Dec 80 ....0.50	0.60	1.80	3.00

	ORIG.	GOOD	FINE	N-MINT
293, Jan 81 ....0.50	0.60	1.80	3.00
294, Feb 81 ....0.50	0.60	1.80	3.00
295, Mar 81 ....0.50	0.60	1.80	3.00
296, Apr 81 ....0.50	0.60	1.80	3.00
297, May 81 ....0.50	0.60	1.80	3.00
298, Jun 81 ....0.50	0.60	1.80	3.00
299, Jul 81 ....0.50	0.60	1.80	3.00
300, Aug 81, CI, C:New Teen Titans, O:Flash				
...................1.00	1.00	3.00	5.00
301, Sep 81 ....0.50	0.60	1.80	3.00
302, Oct 81 ....0.60	0.60	1.80	3.00
303, Nov 81 ....0.60	0.60	1.80	3.00
304, Dec 81 ....0.60	0.60	1.80	3.00
305, Jan 82 ....0.60	0.60	1.80	3.00
306, Feb 82, CI/KG 0.60	1.00	3.00	5.00
307, Mar 82, CI/KG 0.60	0.80	2.40	4.00
308, Apr 82, CI/KG 0.60	0.80	2.40	4.00
309, May 82, CI/KG 0.60	0.80	2.40	4.00
310, Jun 82, CI/KG 0.60	0.80	2.40	4.00
311, Jul 82, CI/KG 0.60	0.80	2.40	4.00
312, Aug 82, CI/KG 0.60	0.80	2.40	4.00
313, Sep 82, CI/KG 0.60	0.80	2.40	4.00
314, Oct 82 ....0.60	0.70	2.10	3.50
315, Nov 82 ....0.60	0.70	2.10	3.50
316, Dec 82 ....0.60	0.70	2.10	3.50
317, Jan 83 ....0.60	0.70	2.10	3.50
318, Feb 83 ....0.60	0.70	2.10	3.50
319, Mar 83 ....0.60	0.70	2.10	3.50
320, Apr 83 ....0.60	0.70	2.10	3.50
321, May 83 ....0.60	0.70	2.10	3.50
322, Jun 83 ....0.60	0.70	2.10	3.50
323, Jul 83 ....0.60	0.70	2.10	3.50
324, Aug 83 ....0.60	0.70	2.10	3.50
325, Sep 83 ....0.60	0.70	2.10	3.50
326, Oct 83 ....0.60	0.70	2.10	3.50
327, Nov 83 ....0.60	0.70	2.10	3.50
328, Dec 83 ....0.75	0.70	2.10	3.50
329, Jan 84 ....0.75	0.70	2.10	3.50
330, Feb 84 ....0.75	0.70	2.10	3.50
331, Mar 84 ....0.75	0.70	2.10	3.50
332, Apr 84 ....0.75	0.70	2.10	3.50
333, May 84 ....0.75	0.70	2.10	3.50
334, Jun 84 ....0.75	0.70	2.10	3.50
335, Jul 84 ....0.75	0.70	2.10	3.50
336, Aug 84 ....0.75	0.70	2.10	3.50
337, Sep 84 ....0.75	0.70	2.10	3.50
338, Oct 84 ....0.75	0.70	2.10	3.50
339, Nov 84 ....0.75	0.70	2.10	3.50
340, Dec 84 ....0.75	0.70	2.10	3.50
341, Jan 85 ....0.75	0.70	2.10	3.50
342, Feb 85 ....0.75	0.70	2.10	3.50
343, Mar 85 ....0.75	0.70	2.10	3.50
344, Apr 85 ....0.75	0.70	2.10	3.50
345, May 85 ....0.75	0.70	2.10	3.50
346, Jun 85 ....0.75	0.70	2.10	3.50
347, Jul 85 ....0.75	0.70	2.10	3.50
348, Aug 85 ....0.75	0.70	2.10	3.50
349, Sep 85 ....0.75	0.70	2.10	3.50
350, Oct 85, last issue 1.25	2.00	6.00	10.00

FLASHMARKS
FANTAGRAPHICS

		GOOD	FINE	N-MINT
1, b&w		0.59	1.77	2.95

FLAXEN: ALTER EGO
CALIBER

	ORIG.	GOOD	FINE	N-MINT
1, Mar 95 ....2.95	0.59	1.77	2.95

FLESH
FLEETWAY/QUALITY

	ORIG.	GOOD	FINE	N-MINT
1 ....2.95	0.59	1.77	2.95
2 ....2.95	0.59	1.77	2.95

	ORIG.	GOOD	FINE	N-MINT

FLESH & BONES
UPSHOT

	ORIG.	GOOD	FINE	N-MINT
☐ 1, 86, color	2.00	0.40	1.20	2.00
☐ 2, 86, color	2.00	0.40	1.20	2.00
☐ 3, 86, color	2.00	0.40	1.20	2.00
☐ 4, 86, color	2.00	0.40	1.20	2.00

FLESH CRAWLERS
KITCHEN SINK

	ORIG.	GOOD	FINE	N-MINT
☐ 1	2.50	0.50	1.50	2.50

FLESH GORDON
AIRCEL

	GOOD	FINE	N-MINT
☐ 3	0.59	1.77	2.95

FLEX MENTALLO (mini-series)
DC/VERTIGO

	ORIG.	GOOD	FINE	N-MINT
☐ 1, Jun 96	2.50	0.50	1.50	2.50

FLINT ARMBUSTER JR. SPECIAL
ALCHEMY

	GOOD	FINE	N-MINT
☐ 0, nn b&w	0.59	1.77	2.95

FLINTSTONE KIDS (was Star Comic)
MARVEL

	ORIG.	GOOD	FINE	N-MINT
☐ 5	1.00	0.20	0.60	1.00
☐ 6	1.00	0.20	0.60	1.00
☐ 7	1.00	0.20	0.60	1.00
☐ 8	1.00	0.20	0.60	1.00
☐ 9	1.00	0.20	0.60	1.00
☐ 10	1.00	0.20	0.60	1.00
☐ 11	1.00	0.20	0.60	1.00

FLINTSTONE KIDS, THE
STAR

	ORIG.	GOOD	FINE	N-MINT
☐ 1	1.00	0.20	0.60	1.00
☐ 2	1.00	0.20	0.60	1.00
☐ 3	1.00	0.20	0.60	1.00
☐ 4, (becomes Marvel comic)	1.00	0.20	0.60	1.00

FLINTSTONES 3-D
BLACKTHORNE

	GOOD	FINE	N-MINT
☐ 1	0.50	1.50	2.50
☐ 2	0.50	1.50	2.50
☐ 3	0.50	1.50	2.50
☐ 4	0.50	1.50	2.50

FLINTSTONES BIG BOOK
HARVEY

	GOOD	FINE	N-MINT
☐ 2	0.39	1.17	1.95

FLINTSTONES BIG BOOK, THE

	GOOD	FINE	N-MINT
☐ 1	0.39	1.17	1.95

FLINTSTONES DOUBLEVISION, THE

	ORIG.	GOOD	FINE	N-MINT
☐ 0, Sep 94, polybagged with double vision glasses; adaptation of movie	2.95	0.59	1.77	2.95

FLINTSTONES GIANT SIZE

	ORIG.	GOOD	FINE	N-MINT
☐ 2	2.25	0.45	1.35	2.25
☐ 3	2.25	0.45	1.35	2.25

FLINTSTONES, THE
ARCHIE

	ORIG.	GOOD	FINE	N-MINT
☐ 1, Sep 95	1.50	0.30	0.90	1.50
☐ 2, Oct 95	1.50	0.30	0.90	1.50
☐ 3, Nov 95	1.50	0.30	0.90	1.50
☐ 5, Jan 96	1.50	0.30	0.90	1.50
☐ 6, Feb 96	1.50	0.30	0.90	1.50
☐ 7, Mar 96	1.50	0.30	0.90	1.50
☐ 8, Apr 96	1.50	0.30	0.90	1.50
☐ 9, May 96	1.50	0.30	0.90	1.50
☐ 10, Jun 96	1.50	0.30	0.90	1.50
☐ 12, Aug 96	1.50	0.30	0.90	1.50

HARVEY

	ORIG.	GOOD	FINE	N-MINT
☐ 1	1.25	0.25	0.75	1.25
☐ 2	1.25	0.25	0.75	1.25
☐ 3	1.25	0.25	0.75	1.25
☐ 4	1.25	0.25	0.75	1.25
☐ 5	1.25	0.25	0.75	1.25

	ORIG.	GOOD	FINE	N-MINT
☐ 6	1.50	0.30	0.90	1.50
☐ 7	1.50	0.30	0.90	1.50
☐ 8	1.50	0.30	0.90	1.50
☐ 9	1.50	0.30	0.90	1.50
☐ 10	1.50	0.30	0.90	1.50
☐ 11	1.50	0.30	0.90	1.50
☐ 12	1.50	0.30	0.90	1.50
☐ 13	1.50	0.30	0.90	1.50

MARVEL

	ORIG.	GOOD	FINE	N-MINT
☐ 1	0.30	0.40	1.20	2.00
☐ 2	0.30	0.20	0.60	1.00
☐ 3	0.30	0.20	0.60	1.00
☐ 4	0.30	0.20	0.60	1.00
☐ 5	0.35	0.20	0.60	1.00
☐ 6	0.35	0.20	0.60	1.00
☐ 7	0.35	0.20	0.60	1.00
☐ 8	0.35	0.20	0.60	1.00
☐ 9	0.35	0.20	0.60	1.00

FLOATERS
DARK HORSE

	ORIG.	GOOD	FINE	N-MINT
☐ 1, 93, b&w	2.50	0.50	1.50	2.50
☐ 2, 93, b&w	2.50	0.50	1.50	2.50
☐ 3, 93, b&w	2.50	0.50	1.50	2.50
☐ 4, 93, b&w	2.50	0.50	1.50	2.50

FLOOD RELIEF
MALIBU

	GOOD	FINE	N-MINT
☐ 1, Ultraverse Red Cross giveaway	1.60	4.80	8.00

FLOWERS ON THE RAZOR WIRE
BONEYARD

	ORIG.	GOOD	FINE	N-MINT
☐ 4, Nov 94, b&w	2.95	0.59	1.77	2.95

FLY ANNUAL
IMPACT

	ORIG.	GOOD	FINE	N-MINT
☐ 1, 92, trading card	2.50	0.50	1.50	2.50

FLY, THE
ARCHIE/RED CIRCLE

	ORIG.	GOOD	FINE	N-MINT
☐ 1, May 83	1.00	0.20	0.60	1.00
☐ 2, Jul 83	1.00	0.20	0.60	1.00
☐ 3, Oct 83	1.00	0.20	0.60	1.00
☐ 4, Dec 83	1.00	0.20	0.60	1.00
☐ 5, Feb 84	0.75	0.15	0.45	0.75
☐ 6, Apr 84	0.75	0.15	0.45	0.75
☐ 7, Jun 84	0.75	0.15	0.45	0.75
☐ 8, Aug 84	0.75	0.15	0.45	0.75
☐ 9, Oct 84	0.75	0.15	0.45	0.75

IMPACT

	ORIG.	GOOD	FINE	N-MINT
☐ 1, Aug 91, O:The Fly	1.00	0.20	0.60	1.00
☐ 2, Sep 91	1.00	0.20	0.60	1.00
☐ 3, Oct 91	1.00	0.20	0.60	1.00
☐ 4, Nov 91	1.00	0.20	0.60	1.00
☐ 4, Dec 91	1.00	0.20	0.60	1.00
☐ 5, Dec 91	1.00	0.20	0.60	1.00
☐ 6, Jan 92, 1:Blackjack	1.00	0.20	0.60	1.00
☐ 7, Feb 92	1.00	0.20	0.60	1.00
☐ 8, Mar 92	1.00	0.20	0.60	1.00
☐ 9, Apr 92, 1:Fireball, trading card	1.00	0.20	0.60	1.00
☐ 10, May 92	1.00	0.20	0.60	1.00
☐ 11, Jun 92	1.25	0.20	0.60	1.00
☐ 12, Jul 92	1.25	0.20	0.60	1.00
☐ 13, Aug 92, I: Tremor	1.25	0.25	0.75	1.25
☐ 14, Sep 92	1.25	0.25	0.75	1.25
☐ 15, Oct 92	1.25	0.25	0.75	1.25
☐ 16, Nov 92	1.25	0.25	0.75	1.25
☐ 17, Dec 92	1.25	0.25	0.75	1.25

FOCUS
DC

	GOOD	FINE	N-MINT
☐ 1, Sum 87, GP,BSz	0.20	0.60	1.00

	ORIG.	GOOD	FINE	N-MINT

FOODANG
AUGUST HOUSE
☐ 1, Jan 95, enhanced cover; oversized trading card
.... 2.50 | 0.50 | 1.50 | 2.50

CONTINUM
☐ 1, Jul 94, b&w .... 1.95 | 0.39 | 1.17 | 1.95

FOOFUR
STAR
☐ 1 .... 1.00 | 0.20 | 0.60 | 1.00
☐ 2 .... 1.00 | 0.20 | 0.60 | 1.00
☐ 3 .... 1.00 | 0.20 | 0.60 | 1.00
☐ 4, (becomes Marvel comic)
.... 1.00 | 0.20 | 0.60 | 1.00

FOOFUR (was Star Comic)
MARVEL
☐ 5 .... 1.00 | 0.20 | 0.60 | 1.00
☐ 6 .... 1.00 | 0.20 | 0.60 | 1.00

FOOLKILLER
☐ 1 .... 1.75 | 0.35 | 1.05 | 1.75
☐ 2 .... 1.75 | 0.35 | 1.05 | 1.75
☐ 3 .... 1.75 | 0.35 | 1.05 | 1.75
☐ 4 .... 1.75 | 0.35 | 1.05 | 1.75
☐ 5 .... 1.75 | 0.35 | 1.05 | 1.75
☐ 6 .... 1.75 | 0.35 | 1.05 | 1.75
☐ 7 .... 1.75 | 0.35 | 1.05 | 1.75
☐ 8, SpM .... 1.75 | 0.35 | 1.05 | 1.75
☐ 9 .... 1.75 | 0.35 | 1.05 | 1.75
☐ 10 .... 1.75 | 0.35 | 1.05 | 1.75

FOOT SOLDIERS, THE
DARK HORSE
☐ 1, Jan 96 .... 2.95 | 0.59 | 1.77 | 2.95
☐ 2, Feb 96 .... 2.95 | 0.59 | 1.77 | 2.95

FOOTBALL HEROES
PERSONALITY
☐ 1, b&w .... | 0.59 | 1.77 | 2.95
☐ 2, b&w .... | 0.59 | 1.77 | 2.95

FOOZLE, THE (was Cap'n Quick & Foozle)
ECLIPSE
☐ 3, MR .... | 0.30 | 0.90 | 1.50

FOR YOUR EYES ONLY
MARVEL
☐ 1, movie .... 0.50 | 0.20 | 0.60 | 1.00
☐ 2, movie .... 0.50 | 0.20 | 0.60 | 1.00

FORBIDDEN 3-D
3-D ZONE
☐ 0, 93, nn,3-D version with glasses
.... 3.95 | 0.79 | 2.37 | 3.95
☐ 0, 93, nn,non 3-D version
.... 3.95 | 0.79 | 2.37 | 3.95

FORBIDDEN FRANKENSTEIN
EROS COMIX
☐ 1, adult, b&w .... | 0.45 | 1.35 | 2.25
☐ 2, adult, b&w .... | 0.45 | 1.35 | 2.25

FORBIDDEN PLANET
INNOVATION
☐ 1, movie adaptation ...... 2.50 | 0.50 | 1.50 | 2.50
☐ 2, movie adaptation ...... 2.50 | 0.50 | 1.50 | 2.50
☐ 3, movie adaptation ...... 2.50 | 0.50 | 1.50 | 2.50
☐ 4, movie adaptation ...... 2.50 | 0.50 | 1.50 | 2.50

FORBIDDEN WORLDS
A-PLUS
☐ 1, SD b&w, reprints .... | 0.50 | 1.50 | 2.50

FORCE OF BUDDHA'S PALM, THE
JADEMAN
☐ 1 .... | 0.39 | 1.17 | 1.95
☐ 2 .... | 0.39 | 1.17 | 1.95
☐ 3 .... | 0.39 | 1.17 | 1.95
☐ 4 .... | 0.39 | 1.17 | 1.95
☐ 5 .... | 0.39 | 1.17 | 1.95

☐ 6 .... | 0.39 | 1.17 | 1.95
☐ 7 .... | 0.39 | 1.17 | 1.95
☐ 8 .... | 0.39 | 1.17 | 1.95
☐ 9 .... | 0.39 | 1.17 | 1.95
☐ 10 .... | 0.39 | 1.17 | 1.95
☐ 11 .... | 0.39 | 1.17 | 1.95
☐ 12 .... | 0.39 | 1.17 | 1.95
☐ 13 .... | 0.39 | 1.17 | 1.95
☐ 14 .... | 0.39 | 1.17 | 1.95
☐ 15 .... | 0.39 | 1.17 | 1.95
☐ 16 .... | 0.39 | 1.17 | 1.95
☐ 17 .... | 0.39 | 1.17 | 1.95
☐ 18 .... | 0.39 | 1.17 | 1.95
☐ 19 .... | 0.39 | 1.17 | 1.95
☐ 20 .... | 0.39 | 1.17 | 1.95
☐ 21 .... | 0.39 | 1.17 | 1.95
☐ 22 .... | 0.39 | 1.17 | 1.95
☐ 23 .... | 0.39 | 1.17 | 1.95
☐ 24 .... | 0.39 | 1.17 | 1.95
☐ 25 .... | 0.39 | 1.17 | 1.95
☐ 26 .... | 0.39 | 1.17 | 1.95
☐ 27 .... | 0.39 | 1.17 | 1.95
☐ 28 .... | 0.39 | 1.17 | 1.95
☐ 29 .... | 0.39 | 1.17 | 1.95
☐ 30 .... | 0.39 | 1.17 | 1.95
☐ 31 .... | 0.39 | 1.17 | 1.95
☐ 32 .... | 0.39 | 1.17 | 1.95
☐ 33 .... | 0.39 | 1.17 | 1.95
☐ 34 .... | 0.39 | 1.17 | 1.95
☐ 35 .... | 0.39 | 1.17 | 1.95
☐ 36 .... | 0.39 | 1.17 | 1.95
☐ 37 .... | 0.39 | 1.17 | 1.95
☐ 38 .... | 0.39 | 1.17 | 1.95
☐ 39 .... | 0.39 | 1.17 | 1.95
☐ 40 .... | 0.39 | 1.17 | 1.95
☐ 41 .... | 0.39 | 1.17 | 1.95
☐ 42 .... | 0.39 | 1.17 | 1.95

FORCE WORKS
MARVEL
☐ 0, ashcan .... | 0.40 | 1.20 | 2.00
☐ 1, Jul 94, pull-apart cover
.... 3.95 | 0.80 | 2.40 | 4.00
☐ 2, Aug 94 .... 1.50 | 0.30 | 0.90 | 1.50
☐ 3, Sep 94 .... 1.50 | 0.30 | 0.90 | 1.50
☐ 4, Oct 94 .... 1.50 | 0.30 | 0.90 | 1.50
☐ 5, Nov 94 .... 1.50 | 0.30 | 0.90 | 1.50
☐ 6, Dec 94 .... 1.50 | 0.30 | 0.90 | 1.50
☐ 7, Jan 95 .... 1.50 | 0.30 | 0.90 | 1.50
☐ 8, Feb 95 .... 1.50 | 0.30 | 0.90 | 1.50
☐ 9, Mar 95 .... 1.50 | 0.30 | 0.90 | 1.50
☐ 10, Apr 95 .... 1.50 | 0.30 | 0.90 | 1.50
☐ 11, May 95 .... 1.50 | 0.30 | 0.90 | 1.50
☐ 12, Jun 95, flip book with War Machine: Brothers in Arms
Part 1 back-up .... 2.50 | 0.50 | 1.50 | 2.50
☐ 13, Jul 95 .... 1.50 | 0.30 | 0.90 | 1.50
☐ 14, Aug 95 .... 1.50 | 0.30 | 0.90 | 1.50
☐ 15, Sep 95 .... 1.50 | 0.30 | 0.90 | 1.50
☐ 16, Oct 95 .... 1.50 | 0.30 | 0.90 | 1.50
☐ 17, Nov 95 .... 1.50 | 0.30 | 0.90 | 1.50
☐ 18, Dec 95 .... 1.50 | 0.30 | 0.90 | 1.50
☐ 19, Jan 96 .... 1.50 | 0.30 | 0.90 | 1.50
☐ 20, Feb 96 .... 1.50 | 0.30 | 0.90 | 1.50
☐ 21, Mar 96 .... 1.50 | 0.30 | 0.90 | 1.50
☐ 22, Apr 96, final issue ..... 1.50 | 0.30 | 0.90 | 1.50

FORE/PUNK
PARODY PRESS
☐ 1, punk cover .... 2.50 | 0.50 | 1.50 | 2.50
☐ 1, fore cover .... 2.50 | 0.50 | 1.50 | 2.50

FOREVER NOW
ENTERTAINMENT
☐ 1 .... | 0.30 | 0.90 | 1.50
☐ 2 .... | 0.30 | 0.90 | 1.50

	ORIG.	GOOD	FINE	N-MINT

FOREVER PEOPLE (1971-1972 series)
DC

	ORIG.	GOOD	FINE	N-MINT
❑ 1, Mar 71, JK, O:Forever People 0.15		9.00	27.00	45.00
❑ 2, May 71, JK 0.15		4.00	12.00	20.00
❑ 3, Jul 71, JK 0.15		3.60	10.80	18.00
❑ 4, Sep 71, JK 0.25		3.60	10.80	18.00
❑ 5, Nov 71, JK 0.25		3.60	10.80	18.00
❑ 6, Jan 72, JK 0.25		2.20	6.60	11.00
❑ 7, Mar 72, JK 0.25		2.20	6.60	11.00
❑ 8, May 72, JK 0.25		2.20	6.60	11.00
❑ 9, Jul 72, JK 0.25		2.20	6.60	11.00
❑ 10, Jul 72, JK 0.20		2.20	6.60	11.00
❑ 11, Nov 72, JK 0.20		2.20	6.60	11.00

FOREVER PEOPLE (1988 mini-series)

		GOOD	FINE	N-MINT
❑ 1		0.25	0.75	1.25
❑ 2		0.25	0.75	1.25
❑ 3		0.25	0.75	1.25
❑ 4		0.25	0.75	1.25
❑ 5		0.25	0.75	1.25
❑ 6		0.25	0.75	1.25

FORGOTTEN REALMS

		GOOD	FINE	N-MINT
❑ 1		0.40	1.20	2.00
❑ 2		0.30	0.90	1.50
❑ 3		0.30	0.90	1.50
❑ 4		0.30	0.90	1.50
❑ 5		0.30	0.90	1.50
❑ 6		0.30	0.90	1.50
❑ 7		0.30	0.90	1.50
❑ 8		0.30	0.90	1.50
❑ 9		0.30	0.90	1.50
❑ 10		0.30	0.90	1.50
❑ 11		0.30	0.90	1.50
❑ 12		0.30	0.90	1.50
❑ 13		0.30	0.90	1.50
❑ 14		0.30	0.90	1.50
❑ 15		0.30	0.90	1.50
❑ 16		0.35	1.05	1.75
❑ 17		0.35	1.05	1.75
❑ 18		0.35	1.05	1.75
❑ 19		0.35	1.05	1.75
❑ 20		0.35	1.05	1.75
❑ 21		0.35	1.05	1.75
❑ 22		0.35	1.05	1.75
❑ 23		0.35	1.05	1.75
❑ 24		0.35	1.05	1.75
❑ 25		0.35	1.05	1.75

FORGOTTEN REALMS ANNUAL

		GOOD	FINE	N-MINT
❑ 1, GK(c)		0.59	1.77	2.95

FOTON EFFECT, THE
ACED

	ORIG.	GOOD	FINE	N-MINT
❑ 1, (becomes CA Comics title)	0.30	0.90	1.50

CA

	ORIG.	GOOD	FINE	N-MINT
❑ 2	1.50	0.30	0.90	1.50
❑ 3	1.50	0.30	0.90	1.50

FOUR STAR BATTLE TALES
DC

	ORIG.	GOOD	FINE	N-MINT
❑ 1, Feb 73	0.20	0.04	0.12	0.20
❑ 2, 73	0.20	0.04	0.12	0.20
❑ 3, 73	0.20	0.04	0.12	0.20
❑ 4, 73	0.20	0.04	0.12	0.20
❑ 5, Nov 73	0.20	0.04	0.12	0.20

FOX COMICS
FANTAGRAPHICS

		GOOD	FINE	N-MINT
❑ 24, b&w		0.59	1.77	2.95
❑ 25, b&w		0.59	1.77	2.95
❑ 26, b&w		0.59	1.77	2.95

FOX COMICS LEGENDS SERIES

		GOOD	FINE	N-MINT
❑ 2, Elvis b&w		0.50	1.50	2.50

FOX COMICS SPECIAL

		GOOD	FINE	N-MINT
❑ 1, b&w, Australian	0.59	1.77	2.95

FOXFIRE
MALIBU/ULTRAVERSE

	ORIG.	GOOD	FINE	N-MINT
❑ 1, Feb 96	1.50	0.30	0.90	1.50
❑ 2, Mar 96, V:UltraForce	1.50	0.30	0.90	1.50

NIGHTWYND

		GOOD	FINE	N-MINT
❑ 1, b&w		0.50	1.50	2.50
❑ 2, b&w		0.50	1.50	2.50
❑ 3, b&w		0.50	1.50	2.50

FRAGGLE ROCK
MARVEL

	ORIG.	GOOD	FINE	N-MINT
❑ 1, rep.	1.00	0.20	0.60	1.00
❑ 2, rep.	1.00	0.20	0.60	1.00
❑ 3, rep.	1.00	0.20	0.60	1.00
❑ 4, rep.	1.00	0.20	0.60	1.00
❑ 5, rep.	1.00	0.20	0.60	1.00

STAR

	ORIG.	GOOD	FINE	N-MINT
❑ 1	0.65	0.13	0.39	0.65
❑ 2	0.65	0.13	0.39	0.65
❑ 3	0.65	0.13	0.39	0.65
❑ 4	0.65	0.13	0.39	0.65
❑ 5	0.65	0.13	0.39	0.65
❑ 6	0.65	0.13	0.39	0.65
❑ 7	0.75	0.15	0.45	0.75
❑ 8	0.75	0.15	0.45	0.75

FRAGMENTS
SCREAMING CAT

		GOOD	FINE	N-MINT
❑ 1		0.35	1.05	1.75

FRANCIS, BROTHER OF THE UNIVERSE
MARVEL

	ORIG.	GOOD	FINE	N-MINT
❑ 1	0.75	0.15	0.45	0.75

FRANK
NEMESIS

	ORIG.	GOOD	FINE	N-MINT
❑ 1	1.75	0.35	1.05	1.75
❑ 2	1.75	0.35	1.05	1.75
❑ 3, newsstand	1.75	0.35	1.05	1.75
❑ 3, direct sale	2.50	0.50	1.50	2.50
❑ 4, Jul 94, newsstand	1.75	0.35	1.05	1.75

FRANK FRAZETTA'S THUN'DA TALES
FANTAGRAPHICS

		GOOD	FINE	N-MINT
❑ 1, reprints		0.40	1.20	2.00

FRANK FRAZETTA'S UNTAMED LOVE

		GOOD	FINE	N-MINT
❑ 1, reprints		0.40	1.20	2.00

FRANK IN THE RIVER
TUNDRA

		GOOD	FINE	N-MINT
❑ 1		0.59	1.77	2.95

FRANK THE UNICORN
FRAGMENTS WEST

		GOOD	FINE	N-MINT
❑ 1, b&w		0.40	1.20	2.00
❑ 2, b&w		0.40	1.20	2.00
❑ 3, b&w		0.40	1.20	2.00
❑ 4, b&w		0.40	1.20	2.00
❑ 5, b&w		0.40	1.20	2.00
❑ 6, b&w		0.40	1.20	2.00
❑ 7, b&w		0.40	1.20	2.00
❑ 8, b&w		0.40	1.20	2.00
❑ 9, b&w		0.40	1.20	2.00

FRANK ZAPPA: VIVA LA BIZARRE
REVOLUTIONARY

	ORIG.	GOOD	FINE	N-MINT
❑ 1, Feb 94, b&w	2.50	0.50	1.50	2.50

FRANKENSTEIN
ETERNITY

		GOOD	FINE	N-MINT
❑ 1, b&w		0.39	1.17	1.95
❑ 2, b&w		0.39	1.17	1.95
❑ 3, b&w		0.39	1.17	1.95

MARVEL

	ORIG.	GOOD	FINE	N-MINT
❑ 1	0.20	2.40	7.20	12.00
❑ 2	0.20	1.60	4.80	8.00

	ORIG.	GOOD	FINE	N-MINT
3	0.20	1.60	4.80	8.00
4	0.20	1.60	4.80	8.00
5	0.20	1.60	4.80	8.00
6	0.20	1.00	3.00	5.00
7	0.20	1.00	3.00	5.00
8	0.20	1.40	4.20	7.00
9	0.20	1.40	4.20	7.00
10	0.25	1.00	3.00	5.00
11	0.25	0.80	2.40	4.00
12	0.25	0.80	2.40	4.00
13	0.25	0.80	2.40	4.00
14	0.25	0.80	2.40	4.00
15	0.25	0.80	2.40	4.00
16	0.25	0.80	2.40	4.00
17	0.25	0.80	2.40	4.00
18	0.25	0.80	2.40	4.00

FREAK FORCE
IMAGE

	ORIG.	GOOD	FINE	N-MINT
1		0.70	2.10	3.50
2		0.60	1.80	3.00
3		0.60	1.80	3.00
4	1.95	0.39	1.17	1.95
5, Apr 94	1.95	0.39	1.17	1.95
6, Jun 94	1.95	0.39	1.17	1.95
7, Jul 94	1.95	0.39	1.17	1.95
8, Aug 94	1.95	0.39	1.17	1.95
9, Sep 94	2.50	0.50	1.50	2.50
10, Oct 94	2.50	0.50	1.50	2.50
12, Dec 94	2.50	0.50	1.50	2.50
13, Jan 95	2.50	0.50	1.50	2.50
13, Jan 95, alternate cover	2.50	0.50	1.50	2.50
14, Feb 95	2.50	0.50	1.50	2.50
15, Mar 95	2.50	0.50	1.50	2.50
16, Apr 95	2.50	0.50	1.50	2.50
17, Jun 95	2.50	0.50	1.50	2.50

FREAK-OUT ON INFANT EARTHS
BLACKTHORNE

	GOOD	FINE	N-MINT
1	0.40	1.20	2.00
2	0.40	1.20	2.00

FREAKS
MONSTER

	GOOD	FINE	N-MINT
1, movie, b&w	0.45	1.35	2.25
2, movie, b&w	0.45	1.35	2.25
3, movie, b&w	0.45	1.35	2.25

FREAKS' AMOUR
DARK HORSE

	GOOD	FINE	N-MINT
1, 92, b&w	0.79	2.37	3.95
2, 92, b&w	0.79	2.37	3.95
3, 92, b&w	0.79	2.37	3.95

FRED & BIANCA CENSORSHIP SUCKS SPECIAL
COMICS INTERVIEW

	GOOD	FINE	N-MINT
1, reprint, b&w	0.45	1.35	2.25

FRED & BIANCA MOTHER'S DAY MASSACRE

	GOOD	FINE	N-MINT
1, reprint;b&w	0.45	1.35	2.25

FRED & BIANCA VALENTINE'S DAY MASSACRE

	GOOD	FINE	N-MINT
1, reprint, b&w	0.45	1.35	2.25

FRED HEMBECK DESTROYS THE MARVEL UNIVERSE
MARVEL

	ORIG.	GOOD	FINE	N-MINT
1, D:everyone	1.50	0.30	0.90	1.50

FRED HEMBECK SELLS THE MARVEL UNIVERSE

	ORIG.	GOOD	FINE	N-MINT
1, TA(c,i)	1.25	0.25	0.75	1.25

FREDDY KRUEGER'S NIGHTMARE ON ELM STREET

	ORIG.	GOOD	FINE	N-MINT
1, O:Freddy Krueger, b&w mag	2.25	0.45	1.35	2.25
2, b&w mag	2.25	0.45	1.35	2.25

FREDDY'S DEAD: THE FINAL NIGHTMARE
INNOVATION

	GOOD	FINE	N-MINT
1, movie	0.50	1.50	2.50
2, movie	0.50	1.50	2.50
3, movie	0.50	1.50	2.50

FREDDY'S DEAD: THE FINAL NIGHTMARE 3-D

	GOOD	FINE	N-MINT
1, part 3-D	0.50	1.50	2.50

FREDERIC REMINGTON: THE MAN WHO PAINTED THE WEST
TOME PRESS

	GOOD	FINE	N-MINT
1, b&w	0.59	1.77	2.95

FREE LAUGHS
DESCHAINE

	GOOD	FINE	N-MINT
1, b&w	0.20	0.60	1.00

FREEDOM FIGHTERS
DC

	ORIG.	GOOD	FINE	N-MINT
1, Apr 76	0.25	0.50	1.50	2.50
2, Jun 76	0.30	0.30	0.90	1.50
3, Aug 76	0.30	0.30	0.90	1.50
4, Oct 76	0.30	0.30	0.90	1.50
5, Dec 76	0.30	0.30	0.90	1.50
6, Feb 77	0.30	0.20	0.60	1.00
7, Apr 77	0.30	0.20	0.60	1.00
8, Jun 77	0.30	0.20	0.60	1.00
9, Aug 77	0.35	0.20	0.60	1.00
10, Oct 77	0.35	0.20	0.60	1.00
11, Dec 77	0.35	0.20	0.60	1.00
12, Feb 78	0.35	0.20	0.60	1.00
13, Apr 78	0.35	0.20	0.60	1.00
14, Jun 78	0.35	0.20	0.60	1.00
15, Aug 78	0.35	0.20	0.60	1.00

FREEJACK
NOW

	ORIG.	GOOD	FINE	N-MINT
1, Apr 92, movie, direct	2.50	0.50	1.50	2.50
1, Apr 92, newsstand	1.95	0.39	1.17	1.95
2, May 92, newsstand	1.95	0.39	1.17	1.95
2, May 92, direct-sale	2.50	0.50	1.50	2.50
3, Jun 92, newsstand	1.95	0.39	1.17	1.95
3, Jun 92, direct-sale	2.50	0.50	1.50	2.50

FREEX
MALIBU/ULTRAVERSE

	ORIG.	GOOD	FINE	N-MINT
1, Jul 93	1.95	0.60	1.80	3.00
1, hologram cover		5.00	15.00	25.00
1, Ultra Ltd	1.95	1.00	3.00	5.00
2, Aug 93	1.95	0.50	1.50	2.50
3, Sep 93	1.95	0.50	1.50	2.50
4, Rune, BWS	2.50	0.50	1.50	2.50
5, 93	1.95	0.39	1.17	1.95
6, Break-Thru	1.95	0.39	1.17	1.95
7	1.95	0.39	1.17	1.95
8, Feb 94	1.95	0.39	1.17	1.95
9, Mar 94	1.95	0.39	1.17	1.95
10, Apr 94	1.95	0.39	1.17	1.95
11, May 94	1.95	0.39	1.17	1.95
12, Aug 94	1.95	0.39	1.17	1.95
13, Sep 94	1.95	0.39	1.17	1.95

FRENCH ICE
RENEGADE

	ORIG.	GOOD	FINE	N-MINT
1, b&w		0.40	1.20	2.00
2, Apr 87, b&w	2.00	0.40	1.20	2.00
3, May 87, b&w	2.00	0.40	1.20	2.00
4, Jun 87, b&w	2.00	0.40	1.20	2.00
5, Jul 87, b&w	2.00	0.40	1.20	2.00
6, Sep 87, b&w	2.00	0.40	1.20	2.00
7, Oct 87, b&w	2.00	0.40	1.20	2.00
8, Nov 87, b&w	2.00	0.40	1.20	2.00
9, Dec 87, b&w	2.00	0.40	1.20	2.00
10, Jan 88, b&w	2.00	0.40	1.20	2.00
11, Feb 88, b&w	2.00	0.40	1.20	2.00
12, Mar 88, b&w	2.00	0.40	1.20	2.00
13, Apr 88, b&w	2.00	0.40	1.20	2.00

	ORIG.	GOOD	FINE	N-MINT

FRENCH TICKLERS
KITCHEN SINK

	ORIG.	GOOD	FINE	N-MINT
1, Oct 89, b&w	2.00	0.40	1.20	2.00
2, Oct 89, b&w	2.00	0.40	1.20	2.00
3, Oct 89, b&w	2.00	0.40	1.20	2.00

FRENZY
INDEPENDENT

	ORIG.	GOOD	FINE	N-MINT
1, 94	1.00	0.20	0.60	1.00
1, 94, A	1.00	0.20	0.60	1.00

FRIENDS
RENEGADE

	GOOD	FINE	N-MINT
1, b&w	0.40	1.20	2.00
2, b&w	0.40	1.20	2.00
3, b&w	0.40	1.20	2.00

FRIENDS OF MAXX
IMAGE

	ORIG.	GOOD	FINE	N-MINT
1, Apr 96, Dude Japan	2.95	0.59	1.77	2.95

FRIGHT
ATLAS/ SEABOARD

	ORIG.	GOOD	FINE	N-MINT
1, Jun 75, O:Son of Dracula	0.25	0.20	0.60	1.00

ETERNITY

	GOOD	FINE	N-MINT
1, b&w, rep.	0.39	1.17	1.95
2, b&w, rep.	0.39	1.17	1.95
3, b&w, rep.	0.39	1.17	1.95
4, b&w, rep.	0.39	1.17	1.95
5, b&w, rep.	0.39	1.17	1.95
6, b&w, rep.	0.39	1.17	1.95
7, b&w, rep.	0.39	1.17	1.95
8, b&w, rep.	0.39	1.17	1.95
9, b&w, rep.	0.39	1.17	1.95
10, b&w, rep.	0.39	1.17	1.95
11, b&w, rep.	0.39	1.17	1.95
12, b&w, rep.	0.39	1.17	1.95

FRIGHT NIGHT
NOW

	ORIG.	GOOD	FINE	N-MINT
1, Oct 88, movie tie-in	1.75	0.35	1.05	1.75
2, Nov 88, movie tie-in	1.75	0.35	1.05	1.75
3, Dec 88, movie tie-in	1.75	0.35	1.05	1.75
4, Feb 89, movie tie-in	1.75	0.35	1.05	1.75
5, Mar 89, movie tie-in	1.75	0.35	1.05	1.75
6, Apr 89, movie tie-in	1.75	0.35	1.05	1.75
7, May 89, Comics Code	1.75	0.35	1.05	1.75
8, Jun 89, Comics Code	1.75	0.35	1.05	1.75
9, Jul 89, Comics Code	1.75	0.35	1.05	1.75
10, Aug 89, Comics Code	1.75	0.35	1.05	1.75
11, Sep 89	1.75	0.35	1.05	1.75
12, Oct 89	1.75	0.35	1.05	1.75
13, Nov 89	1.75	0.35	1.05	1.75
14, Dec 89	1.75	0.35	1.05	1.75
15, Jan 90	1.75	0.35	1.05	1.75
16, Feb 90	1.75	0.35	1.05	1.75
17, Mar 90	1.75	0.35	1.05	1.75
18, Apr 90	1.75	0.35	1.05	1.75
19, May 90	1.75	0.35	1.05	1.75
20, Jun 90	1.75	0.35	1.05	1.75
21, Jul 90	1.75	0.35	1.05	1.75
22, Aug 90	1.75	0.35	1.05	1.75

FRIGHT NIGHT 1993 HALLOWEEN ANNUAL

	ORIG.	GOOD	FINE	N-MINT
0, nn, 3-D	2.95	0.59	1.77	2.95

FRIGHT NIGHT 3-D

	ORIG.	GOOD	FINE	N-MINT
0, Fal 92, Dracula	2.95	0.59	1.77	2.95
0, Win 93, Brainbats	2.95	0.59	1.77	2.95
1, Jun 92	2.95	0.59	1.77	2.95

FRINGE
CALIBER

	ORIG.	GOOD	FINE	N-MINT
1, b&w	2.50	0.50	1.50	2.50
2, b&w	2.50	0.50	1.50	2.50
3, b&w	2.50	0.50	1.50	2.50
4, b&w	2.50	0.50	1.50	2.50
5, b&w	2.50	0.50	1.50	2.50
6, b&w	2.50	0.50	1.50	2.50
7, b&w	2.50	0.50	1.50	2.50
8, b&w	2.50	0.50	1.50	2.50

FROM BEYOND THE UNKNOWN
DC

	ORIG.	GOOD	FINE	N-MINT
1, Nov 69	0.15	1.00	3.00	5.00
2, Jan 70	0.15	0.70	2.10	3.50
3, Mar 70	0.15	0.70	2.10	3.50
4, May 70	0.15	0.70	2.10	3.50
5, Jul 70	0.15	0.70	2.10	3.50
6, Sep 70	0.15	0.40	1.20	2.00
7, Nov 70	0.25	0.40	1.20	2.00
8, Jan 71	0.25	0.40	1.20	2.00
9, Mar 71	0.25	0.40	1.20	2.00
10, May 71	0.25	0.40	1.20	2.00
11, Jul 71	0.25	0.40	1.20	2.00
12, Sep 71	0.25	0.40	1.20	2.00
13, Nov 71	0.25	0.40	1.20	2.00
14, Jan 72	0.25	0.40	1.20	2.00
15, Mar 72	0.25	0.40	1.20	2.00
16, May 72	0.25	0.40	1.20	2.00
17, Jul 72	0.25	0.40	1.20	2.00
18, Sep 72	0.20	0.40	1.20	2.00
19, Nov 72	0.20	0.40	1.20	2.00
20, Jan 73	0.20	0.40	1.20	2.00
21, Mar 73	0.20	0.40	1.20	2.00
22, May 73	0.20	0.40	1.20	2.00
23, Aug 73	0.20	0.40	1.20	2.00
24, Oct 73	0.20	0.40	1.20	2.00
25, Dec 73	0.20	0.40	1.20	2.00

FROM BEYONDE
STUDIO INSIDIO

	GOOD	FINE	N-MINT
1, b&w	0.45	1.35	2.25

FROM HELL
KITCHEN SINK

	ORIG.	GOOD	FINE	N-MINT
2, b&w, adult; 1st printing	4.95	2.00	6.00	10.00
3, b&w, adult	4.95	1.50	4.50	7.50
4, Mar 94, b&w, adult	4.95	1.20	3.60	6.00
8, Jul 95, b&w	4.95	0.99	2.97	4.95
9, Apr 96, b&w	4.95	0.99	2.97	4.95

TUNDRA

	ORIG.	GOOD	FINE	N-MINT
1, AMo, Eddie Campbell, b&w;first printing	4.95	2.40	7.20	12.00
1, AMo, Eddie Campbell, b&w;second printing	4.95	1.40	4.20	7.00
2	4.95	0.99	2.97	4.95

FROM THE DARKNESS
ADVENTURE

	GOOD	FINE	N-MINT
1	0.80	2.40	4.00
2	0.80	2.40	4.00
3, b&w	0.50	1.50	2.50
4, b&w	0.50	1.50	2.50

FROM THE DARKNESS BOOK II: BLOOD VOWS
CRY FOR DAWN

	GOOD	FINE	N-MINT
1, adult, b&w	0.50	1.50	2.50
2, adult, b&w	0.50	1.50	2.50
3, adult, b&w	0.50	1.50	2.50

FROM THE DARKNESS: BLOOD VOWS

	GOOD	FINE	N-MINT
1, b&w, adult	0.50	1.50	2.50
2, b&w, adult	0.50	1.50	2.50

FRONTIERS '86 PRESENTS
FRONTIERS

	GOOD	FINE	N-MINT
1, Crusaders	0.30	0.90	1.50
2, Crusaders	0.30	0.90	1.50

	ORIG.	GOOD	FINE	N-MINT

FRONTLINE COMBAT
EC/GEMSTONE
	ORIG.	GOOD	FINE	N-MINT
❏ 1, 95, reprints;JSe;HK; Jack Davis;RH;WW	2.00	0.40	1.20	2.00

FROST
CALIBER
	ORIG.	GOOD	FINE	N-MINT
❏ 1, b&w	1.95	0.39	1.17	1.95

FROST: THE DYING BREED
	ORIG.	GOOD	FINE	N-MINT
❏ 1, b&w	2.95	0.59	1.77	2.95
❏ 2, b&w	2.95	0.59	1.77	2.95
❏ 3, b&w	2.95	0.59	1.77	2.95

FUGITOID
MIRAGE
	ORIG.	GOOD	FINE	N-MINT
❏ 1	2.00	6.00	10.00	

FULL THROTTLE
AIRCEL
	ORIG.	GOOD	FINE	N-MINT
❏ 1, b&w		0.59	1.77	2.95
❏ 2, b&w		0.59	1.77	2.95

FUN AND GAMES MAGAZINE
MARVEL
	ORIG.	GOOD	FINE	N-MINT
❏ 1	0.50	0.20	0.60	1.00
❏ 2	0.50	0.20	0.60	1.00
❏ 3	0.50	0.20	0.60	1.00
❏ 4	0.50	0.20	0.60	1.00
❏ 5	0.50	0.20	0.60	1.00
❏ 6	0.50	0.20	0.60	1.00
❏ 7	0.50	0.20	0.60	1.00
❏ 8	0.50	0.20	0.60	1.00
❏ 9	0.50	0.20	0.60	1.00
❏ 10	0.50	0.20	0.60	1.00
❏ 11	0.50	0.20	0.60	1.00
❏ 12	0.50	0.20	0.60	1.00
❏ 13	0.50	0.20	0.60	1.00

FUN BOYS SPRING SPECIAL
TUNDRA
	ORIG.	GOOD	FINE	N-MINT
❏ 0, nn b&w		0.39	1.17	1.95

FUN HOUSE
MN DESIGN
	ORIG.	GOOD	FINE	N-MINT
❏ 0, nn photos, color	1.30	3.90	6.50	

FUNNY STUFF STOCKING STUFFER
DC
	ORIG.	GOOD	FINE	N-MINT
❏ 1		0.25	0.75	1.25

FUNNYTIME FEATURES
EENIEWEENIE
	ORIG.	GOOD	FINE	N-MINT
❏ 1, Jul 94, b&w	2.50	0.50	1.50	2.50
❏ 1, 94, b&w;second printing	2.50	0.50	1.50	2.50
❏ 2, 94, b&w	2.50	0.50	1.50	2.50
❏ 3, 94, b&w	2.50	0.50	1.50	2.50
❏ 4, 95, b&w	2.50	0.50	1.50	2.50
❏ 5, 95, b&w	2.50	0.50	1.50	2.50

FURRLOUGH
ANTARCTIC
	ORIG.	GOOD	FINE	N-MINT
❏ 1, Nov 91, b&w	2.50	0.50	1.50	2.50
❏ 2, Feb 92, b&w	2.50	0.50	1.50	2.50
❏ 3, May 92, b&w	2.50	0.50	1.50	2.50
❏ 4, Jul 92, b&w	2.50	0.50	1.50	2.50
❏ 5, Nov 92, b&w	2.50	0.50	1.50	2.50
❏ 6, Jan 93, b&w	2.50	0.50	1.50	2.50
❏ 7, Mar 93, b&w	2.50	0.50	1.50	2.50
❏ 8, May 93, b&w	2.50	0.50	1.50	2.50
❏ 9, Jul 93, b&w	2.50	0.50	1.50	2.50
❏ 10, Sep 93, b&w	2.50	0.50	1.50	2.50
❏ 11, Nov 93, b&w	2.75	0.55	1.65	2.75
❏ 12, Dec 93, b&w	2.75	0.55	1.65	2.75
❏ 13, Jan 94, b&w	2.75	0.55	1.65	2.75
❏ 14, Feb 94, b&w	2.75	0.55	1.65	2.75
❏ 15, Mar 94, b&w	2.75	0.55	1.65	2.75
❏ 16, Apr 94, b&w	2.75	0.55	1.65	2.75
❏ 17, May 94, b&w	2.75	0.55	1.65	2.75
❏ 18, Jun 94, b&w	2.75	0.55	1.65	2.75
❏ 19, Jul 94, b&w	2.75	0.55	1.65	2.75
❏ 20, Aug 94, b&w	2.75	0.55	1.65	2.75
❏ 22, Oct 94, b&w	2.75	0.55	1.65	2.75
❏ 23, Nov 94, b&w	3.50	0.70	2.10	3.50
❏ 24, Dec 94, b&w	2.75	0.55	1.65	2.75
❏ 25, Jan 95, b&w	2.75	0.55	1.65	2.75
❏ 26, Feb 95, b&w	2.75	0.55	1.65	2.75
❏ 27, Mar 95, b&w	2.75	0.55	1.65	2.75
❏ 28, Apr 95, b&w	2.75	0.55	1.65	2.75
❏ 29, May 95, b&w	2.75	0.55	1.65	2.75
❏ 30, Jun 95, b&w	2.75	0.55	1.65	2.75
❏ 31, Jul 95, b&w	2.75	0.55	1.65	2.75
❏ 32, Aug 95, b&w	2.75	0.55	1.65	2.75
❏ 33, Sep 95, b&w	2.75	0.55	1.65	2.75
❏ 34, Oct 95, b&w	2.75	0.55	1.65	2.75
❏ 35, Nov 95, b&w;fourth anniversary special	3.50	0.70	2.10	3.50

FURTHER ADVENTURES OF INDIANA JONES, THE
MARVEL
	ORIG.	GOOD	FINE	N-MINT
❏ 1, Jan 83, JBy/TA	0.60	0.30	0.90	1.50
❏ 2, Feb 83, JBy/TA	0.60	0.20	0.60	1.00
❏ 3, Mar 83	0.60	0.20	0.60	1.00
❏ 4	0.60	0.20	0.60	1.00
❏ 5	0.60	0.20	0.60	1.00
❏ 6	0.60	0.20	0.60	1.00
❏ 7	0.60	0.20	0.60	1.00
❏ 8	0.60	0.20	0.60	1.00
❏ 9	0.60	0.20	0.60	1.00
❏ 10	0.60	0.20	0.60	1.00
❏ 11	0.60	0.20	0.60	1.00
❏ 12	0.60	0.20	0.60	1.00
❏ 13	0.60	0.20	0.60	1.00
❏ 14	0.60	0.20	0.60	1.00
❏ 15	0.60	0.20	0.60	1.00
❏ 16	0.60	0.20	0.60	1.00
❏ 17	0.60	0.20	0.60	1.00
❏ 18	0.60	0.20	0.60	1.00
❏ 19	0.60	0.20	0.60	1.00
❏ 20	0.60	0.20	0.60	1.00
❏ 21	0.60	0.20	0.60	1.00
❏ 22	0.60	0.20	0.60	1.00
❏ 23	0.60	0.20	0.60	1.00
❏ 24	0.60	0.20	0.60	1.00
❏ 25, SD	0.60	0.20	0.60	1.00
❏ 26, SD	0.60	0.20	0.60	1.00
❏ 27, SD	0.60	0.20	0.60	1.00
❏ 28, SD	0.65	0.20	0.60	1.00
❏ 29, SD	0.65	0.20	0.60	1.00
❏ 30, SD	0.65	0.20	0.60	1.00
❏ 31, SD	0.65	0.20	0.60	1.00
❏ 32, SD	0.65	0.20	0.60	1.00
❏ 33	0.65	0.20	0.60	1.00
❏ 34	0.75	0.20	0.60	1.00

FURTHER ADVENTURES OF NYOKA THE JUNGLE GIRL, THE
AC
	ORIG.	GOOD	FINE	N-MINT
❏ 1		0.39	1.17	1.95
❏ 2		0.39	1.17	1.95
❏ 3, b&w		0.45	1.35	2.25
❏ 4, b&w		0.45	1.35	2.25
❏ 5		0.50	1.50	2.50

FURTHER ADVENTURES OF YOUNG JEFFY DAHMER
BONEYARD
	ORIG.	GOOD	FINE	N-MINT
❏ 1, adult, b&w		0.55	1.65	2.75

FURTHER FATTENING ADVENTURES OF PUDGE, GIRL BLIMP, THE
STAR*REACH
	ORIG.	GOOD	FINE	N-MINT
❏ 1, large size		0.60	1.80	3.00

	ORIG.	GOOD	FINE	N-MINT
☐ 1, comic size		0.60	1.80	3.00
☐ 2, comic size		0.60	1.80	3.00
☐ 3, comic size		0.60	1.80	3.00

FURY
MARVEL

	ORIG.	GOOD	FINE	N-MINT
☐ 1, May 94, O: S.H.I.E.L.D.	2.95	0.59	1.77	2.95

FURY OF FIRESTORM
DC

	ORIG.	GOOD	FINE	N-MINT
☐ 1, Jun 82, PB, I:Black Bison	0.60	0.50	1.50	2.50
☐ 2, Jul 82, PB	0.60	0.40	1.20	2.00
☐ 3, Aug 82, PB	0.60	0.40	1.20	2.00
☐ 4, Sep 82, PB	0.60	0.40	1.20	2.00
☐ 5, Oct 82	0.60	0.30	0.90	1.50
☐ 6, Nov 82	0.60	0.30	0.90	1.50
☐ 7, Dec 82	0.60	0.30	0.90	1.50
☐ 8, Jan 83	0.60	0.30	0.90	1.50
☐ 9, Feb 83	0.60	0.30	0.90	1.50
☐ 10, Mar 83	0.60	0.30	0.90	1.50
☐ 11, Apr 83	0.60	0.30	0.90	1.50
☐ 12, May 83	0.60	0.30	0.90	1.50
☐ 13, Jun 83	0.60	0.30	0.90	1.50
☐ 14, Jul 83	0.60	0.30	0.90	1.50
☐ 15, Aug 83	0.60	0.30	0.90	1.50
☐ 16, Sep 83	0.60	0.30	0.90	1.50
☐ 17, Oct 83	0.60	0.30	0.90	1.50
☐ 18		0.20	0.60	1.00
☐ 19		0.20	0.60	1.00
☐ 20		0.20	0.60	1.00
☐ 21		0.20	0.60	1.00
☐ 22, I:Blue Devil		0.50	1.50	2.50
☐ 23		0.20	0.60	1.00
☐ 24, Jun 84	0.75	0.20	0.60	1.00
☐ 25		0.20	0.60	1.00
☐ 26		0.20	0.60	1.00
☐ 27		0.20	0.60	1.00
☐ 28		0.20	0.60	1.00
☐ 29		0.20	0.60	1.00
☐ 30		0.20	0.60	1.00
☐ 31		0.20	0.60	1.00
☐ 32		0.20	0.60	1.00
☐ 33		0.20	0.60	1.00
☐ 34		0.20	0.60	1.00
☐ 35		0.20	0.60	1.00
☐ 36		0.20	0.60	1.00
☐ 37		0.20	0.60	1.00
☐ 38		0.20	0.60	1.00
☐ 39		0.20	0.60	1.00
☐ 40		0.20	0.60	1.00
☐ 41, Crisis		0.20	0.60	1.00
☐ 42, Crisis		0.20	0.60	1.00
☐ 43		0.20	0.60	1.00
☐ 44		0.20	0.60	1.00
☐ 45		0.20	0.60	1.00
☐ 46		0.20	0.60	1.00
☐ 47		0.20	0.60	1.00
☐ 48		0.20	0.60	1.00
☐ 49		0.20	0.60	1.00
☐ 50		0.20	0.60	1.00
☐ 51		0.20	0.60	1.00
☐ 52		0.20	0.60	1.00
☐ 53		0.20	0.60	1.00
☐ 54		0.20	0.60	1.00
☐ 55, Legends		0.20	0.60	1.00
☐ 56, Legends		0.20	0.60	1.00
☐ 57		0.20	0.60	1.00
☐ 58		0.20	0.60	1.00
☐ 59		0.20	0.60	1.00
☐ 60		0.20	0.60	1.00
☐ 61, regular cover		0.20	0.60	1.00

	ORIG.	GOOD	FINE	N-MINT
☐ 61, alternate cover	14.00	42.00	70.00	
☐ 62		0.20	0.60	1.00
☐ 63, Capt. Atom		0.20	0.60	1.00
☐ 64, Suicide Squad (Becomes *Firestorm, the Nuclear Man*)		0.20	0.60	1.00

FURY OF FIRESTORM ANNUAL

	ORIG.	GOOD	FINE	N-MINT
☐ 1		0.20	0.60	1.00
☐ 2		0.25	0.75	1.25
☐ 3		0.25	0.75	1.25
☐ 4, (becomes *Firestorm Annual*)		0.25	0.75	1.25

FURY OF HELLINA
LIGHTNING

	ORIG.	GOOD	FINE	N-MINT
☐ 1, Jan 95, b&w	2.75	0.55	1.65	2.75

FURY OF S.H.I.E.L.D. (mini-series)
MARVEL

	ORIG.	GOOD	FINE	N-MINT
☐ 1, Apr 95, Enhanced cardstock cover	2.50	0.50	1.50	2.50
☐ 2, May 95	1.95	0.39	1.17	1.95
☐ 3, Jun 95	1.95	0.39	1.17	1.95
☐ 4, Jul 95, Polybagged with decoder	2.50	0.50	1.50	2.50

FURY/BLACK WIDOW: DEATH DUTY

	ORIG.	GOOD	FINE	N-MINT
☐ 0, Feb 95, prestige format	5.95	1.19	3.57	5.95

FUSION
ECLIPSE

	ORIG.	GOOD	FINE	N-MINT
☐ 1, b&w		0.40	1.20	2.00
☐ 2, b&w		0.40	1.20	2.00
☐ 3, b&w		0.40	1.20	2.00
☐ 4, b&w		0.40	1.20	2.00
☐ 5, b&w		0.40	1.20	2.00
☐ 6, b&w		0.40	1.20	2.00
☐ 7, b&w		0.40	1.20	2.00
☐ 8, b&w		0.40	1.20	2.00
☐ 9, b&w		0.40	1.20	2.00
☐ 10, b&w		0.40	1.20	2.00
☐ 11, b&w		0.40	1.20	2.00
☐ 12, b&w		0.40	1.20	2.00
☐ 13, b&w		0.40	1.20	2.00
☐ 14, b&w		0.40	1.20	2.00
☐ 15, b&w		0.40	1.20	2.00
☐ 16, b&w		0.40	1.20	2.00
☐ 17, b&w		0.40	1.20	2.00

FUTURAMA
SLAVE LABOR

	ORIG.	GOOD	FINE	N-MINT
☐ 1, b&w		0.35	1.05	1.75
☐ 2, b&w		0.35	1.05	1.75
☐ 3, b&w		0.35	1.05	1.75

FUTURE BEAT
OASIS

	ORIG.	GOOD	FINE	N-MINT
☐ 1		0.40	1.20	2.00
☐ 2		0.40	1.20	2.00

FUTURE COURSE
REOCCURRING IMAGES

	ORIG.	GOOD	FINE	N-MINT
☐ 1	2.95	0.59	1.77	2.95

FUTURETECH
MUSHROOM

	ORIG.	GOOD	FINE	N-MINT
☐ 1, Feb 95, b&w (second printing; first printing published by BlackLine Studios, Oct. '94)	3.50	0.70	2.10	3.50

FUTURIANS
LODESTONE

	ORIG.	GOOD	FINE	N-MINT
☐ 1, Oct 85	1.50	0.40	1.20	2.00
☐ 2, Dec 85	1.50	0.40	1.20	2.00
☐ 3, Apr 86	1.50	0.40	1.20	2.00

G

	ORIG.	GOOD	FINE	N-MINT
G'N'R'S GREATEST HITS				
REVOLUTIONARY				
☐ 1, Oct 93, b&w	2.50	0.50	1.50	2.50
G-8 AND HIS BATTLE ACES				
BLAZING				
☐ 1, color, includes *Spider's Web* #1				
		0.30	0.90	1.50
G-MEN				
CALIBER				
☐ 1, b&w	2.50	0.50	1.50	2.50
G.I. COMBAT				
DC				
☐ 44		13.00	39.00	65.00
☐ 45		6.50	19.50	32.50
☐ 46		3.40	10.20	17.00
☐ 47		3.40	10.20	17.00
☐ 48		3.40	10.20	17.00
☐ 49		3.40	10.20	17.00
☐ 50		3.40	10.20	17.00
☐ 51		1.30	3.90	6.50
☐ 52		1.30	3.90	6.50
☐ 53		1.30	3.90	6.50
☐ 54		1.30	3.90	6.50
☐ 55		1.30	3.90	6.50
☐ 56		1.30	3.90	6.50
☐ 57		1.30	3.90	6.50
☐ 58		1.30	3.90	6.50
☐ 59		1.30	3.90	6.50
☐ 60		1.30	3.90	6.50
☐ 61		1.30	3.90	6.50
☐ 62		1.30	3.90	6.50
☐ 63		1.30	3.90	6.50
☐ 64		1.30	3.90	6.50
☐ 65		1.30	3.90	6.50
☐ 66		1.30	3.90	6.50
☐ 67, I:Tank Killer		2.60	7.80	13.00
☐ 68		1.30	3.90	6.50
☐ 69		1.30	3.90	6.50
☐ 70		1.30	3.90	6.50
☐ 71		1.30	3.90	6.50
☐ 72		1.30	3.90	6.50
☐ 73		1.30	3.90	6.50
☐ 74		1.30	3.90	6.50
☐ 75		1.30	3.90	6.50
☐ 76		1.30	3.90	6.50
☐ 77		1.30	3.90	6.50
☐ 78		1.30	3.90	6.50
☐ 79		1.30	3.90	6.50
☐ 80		1.30	3.90	6.50
☐ 81		1.30	3.90	6.50
☐ 82		1.30	3.90	6.50
☐ 83, I:Big & Little Al		1.60	4.80	8.00
☐ 84		1.30	3.90	6.50
☐ 85		1.30	3.90	6.50
☐ 86		1.30	3.90	6.50
☐ 87, I:Haunted Tank		24.00	72.00	120.00
☐ 88		18.00	54.00	90.00
☐ 89		12.00	36.00	60.00
☐ 90		12.00	36.00	60.00
☐ 91		8.00	24.00	40.00
☐ 92		8.00	24.00	40.00
☐ 93		8.00	24.00	40.00
☐ 94		8.00	24.00	40.00
☐ 95		8.00	24.00	40.00
☐ 96		8.00	24.00	40.00
☐ 97		8.00	24.00	40.00
☐ 98, Mar 63	0.12	8.00	24.00	40.00
☐ 99		8.00	24.00	40.00
☐ 100		6.00	18.00	30.00

	ORIG.	GOOD	FINE	N-MINT
☐ 101, Sep 63	0.12	6.00	18.00	30.00
☐ 102, Nov 63	0.12	6.00	18.00	30.00
☐ 103	0.12	6.00	18.00	30.00
☐ 104	0.12	6.00	18.00	30.00
☐ 105, May 64	0.12	6.00	18.00	30.00
☐ 106		6.00	18.00	30.00
☐ 107		6.00	18.00	30.00
☐ 108		8.00	24.00	40.00
☐ 109		5.00	15.00	25.00
☐ 110		5.00	15.00	25.00
☐ 111		5.00	15.00	25.00
☐ 112		5.00	15.00	25.00
☐ 113		5.00	15.00	25.00
☐ 114, O:Haunted Tank		14.00	42.00	70.00
☐ 115		2.40	7.20	12.00
☐ 116		2.40	7.20	12.00
☐ 117		2.40	7.20	12.00
☐ 118		2.40	7.20	12.00
☐ 119		2.40	7.20	12.00
☐ 120		2.40	7.20	12.00
☐ 121		2.40	7.20	12.00
☐ 122		2.40	7.20	12.00
☐ 123		2.40	7.20	12.00
☐ 124		2.40	7.20	12.00
☐ 125		2.40	7.20	12.00
☐ 126		2.40	7.20	12.00
☐ 127		2.40	7.20	12.00
☐ 128		2.40	7.20	12.00
☐ 129		2.40	7.20	12.00
☐ 130		2.40	7.20	12.00
☐ 131		2.40	7.20	12.00
☐ 132		2.40	7.20	12.00
☐ 133		2.40	7.20	12.00
☐ 134		2.40	7.20	12.00
☐ 135		2.40	7.20	12.00
☐ 136		2.40	7.20	12.00
☐ 137		2.00	6.00	10.00
☐ 138, Nov 69, I:Losers	0.15	2.40	7.20	12.00
☐ 139		0.80	2.40	4.00
☐ 140		0.80	2.40	4.00
☐ 141		0.80	2.40	4.00
☐ 142		0.80	2.40	4.00
☐ 143		0.80	2.40	4.00
☐ 144		0.80	2.40	4.00
☐ 145		0.80	2.40	4.00
☐ 146		0.80	2.40	4.00
☐ 147		0.80	2.40	4.00
☐ 148		0.80	2.40	4.00
☐ 149		0.80	2.40	4.00
☐ 150, Nov 71		0.20	0.60	1.00
☐ 151		0.20	0.60	1.00
☐ 152, Mar 72		0.20	0.60	1.00
☐ 153		0.20	0.60	1.00
☐ 154		0.20	0.60	1.00
☐ 155		0.20	0.60	1.00
☐ 156		0.20	0.60	1.00
☐ 157		0.20	0.60	1.00
☐ 158		0.20	0.60	1.00
☐ 159		0.20	0.60	1.00
☐ 160		0.20	0.60	1.00
☐ 161		0.20	0.60	1.00
☐ 162		0.20	0.60	1.00
☐ 163		0.20	0.60	1.00
☐ 164		0.20	0.60	1.00
☐ 165		0.20	0.60	1.00
☐ 166		0.20	0.60	1.00
☐ 167		0.20	0.60	1.00
☐ 168		0.20	0.60	1.00
☐ 169		0.20	0.60	1.00
☐ 170		0.20	0.60	1.00

	ORIG.	GOOD	FINE	N-MINT
❑ 171		0.20	0.60	1.00
❑ 172		0.20	0.60	1.00
❑ 173		0.20	0.60	1.00
❑ 174		0.20	0.60	1.00
❑ 175		0.20	0.60	1.00
❑ 176		0.20	0.60	1.00
❑ 177		0.20	0.60	1.00
❑ 178		0.20	0.60	1.00
❑ 179		0.20	0.60	1.00
❑ 180		0.20	0.60	1.00
❑ 181		0.20	0.60	1.00
❑ 182		0.20	0.60	1.00
❑ 183		0.20	0.60	1.00
❑ 184		0.20	0.60	1.00
❑ 185		0.20	0.60	1.00
❑ 186		0.20	0.60	1.00
❑ 187		0.20	0.60	1.00
❑ 188		0.20	0.60	1.00
❑ 189		0.20	0.60	1.00
❑ 190		0.20	0.60	1.00
❑ 191		0.20	0.60	1.00
❑ 192		0.20	0.60	1.00
❑ 193		0.20	0.60	1.00
❑ 194, Sep 76		0.20	0.60	1.00
❑ 195, Oct 76		0.20	0.60	1.00
❑ 196, Nov 76		0.20	0.60	1.00
❑ 197, Dec 76		0.20	0.60	1.00
❑ 197, Jan 77		0.20	0.60	1.00
❑ 199, Feb 77		0.20	0.60	1.00
❑ 200, Mar 77		0.20	0.60	1.00
❑ 201, Apr 77		0.20	0.60	1.00
❑ 202, Jun 77		0.20	0.60	1.00
❑ 203, Aug 77		0.20	0.60	1.00
❑ 204, Oct 77		0.20	0.60	1.00
❑ 205, Dec 77		0.20	0.60	1.00
❑ 206, Feb 78		0.20	0.60	1.00
❑ 207, Apr 78		0.20	0.60	1.00
❑ 208, Jun 78		0.20	0.60	1.00
❑ 209, Aug 78		0.20	0.60	1.00
❑ 210, Oct 78		0.20	0.60	1.00
❑ 211, Dec 78		0.20	0.60	1.00
❑ 212, Feb 78		0.20	0.60	1.00
❑ 213, Apr 78		0.20	0.60	1.00
❑ 214, Jun 78		0.20	0.60	1.00
❑ 215, Aug 78		0.20	0.60	1.00
❑ 216, Oct 78		0.20	0.60	1.00
❑ 217, Dec 79		0.20	0.60	1.00
❑ 218, Feb 80		0.20	0.60	1.00
❑ 219, Apr 80		0.20	0.60	1.00
❑ 220, Jun 80		0.20	0.60	1.00
❑ 221, Aug 80		0.20	0.60	1.00
❑ 222, Oct 80		0.20	0.60	1.00
❑ 223, Nov 80		0.20	0.60	1.00
❑ 224, Dec 80		0.20	0.60	1.00
❑ 225, Jan 81		0.20	0.60	1.00
❑ 226, Feb 81		0.20	0.60	1.00
❑ 227, Mar 81		0.20	0.60	1.00
❑ 228, Apr 81		0.20	0.60	1.00
❑ 229, May 81		0.20	0.60	1.00
❑ 230, Jun 81		0.20	0.60	1.00
❑ 231, Jul 81		0.20	0.60	1.00
❑ 232, Aug 81		0.20	0.60	1.00
❑ 233, Sep 81		0.20	0.60	1.00
❑ 234, Oct 81		0.20	0.60	1.00
❑ 235, Nov 81		0.20	0.60	1.00
❑ 236, Dec 81		0.20	0.60	1.00
❑ 237, Jan 82		0.20	0.60	1.00
❑ 238, Feb 82		0.20	0.60	1.00
❑ 239, Mar 82		0.20	0.60	1.00
❑ 240, Apr 82		0.20	0.60	1.00
❑ 241, May 82		0.20	0.60	1.00
❑ 242, Jun 82		0.20	0.60	1.00
❑ 243, Jul 82		0.20	0.60	1.00
❑ 244, Aug 82, I:Mercenaries		0.20	0.60	1.00
❑ 245, Sep 82		0.20	0.60	1.00
❑ 246, Oct 82		0.20	0.60	1.00
❑ 247, Nov 82		0.20	0.60	1.00
❑ 248, Dec 82		0.20	0.60	1.00
❑ 249, Jan 83		0.20	0.60	1.00
❑ 250, Feb 83		0.20	0.60	1.00
❑ 251, Mar 83		0.20	0.60	1.00
❑ 252, Apr 83		0.20	0.60	1.00
❑ 253, May 83		0.20	0.60	1.00
❑ 254, Jun 83		0.20	0.60	1.00
❑ 255, Jul 83		0.20	0.60	1.00
❑ 256, Aug 83		0.20	0.60	1.00
❑ 257, Sep 83		0.20	0.60	1.00
❑ 258, Oct 83		0.20	0.60	1.00
❑ 259, Nov 83		0.20	0.60	1.00
❑ 260, Dec 83		0.20	0.60	1.00
❑ 261, Jan 84		0.20	0.60	1.00
❑ 262, Feb 84		0.20	0.60	1.00
❑ 263, Mar 84		0.20	0.60	1.00
❑ 264, Apr 84		0.20	0.60	1.00
❑ 265, May 84		0.20	0.60	1.00
❑ 266, Jun 84		0.20	0.60	1.00
❑ 267, Jul 84		0.20	0.60	1.00
❑ 268, Aug 84		0.20	0.60	1.00
❑ 269, Sep 84		0.20	0.60	1.00
❑ 270, Oct 84		0.20	0.60	1.00
❑ 271, Nov 84		0.20	0.60	1.00
❑ 272, Dec 84		0.20	0.60	1.00
❑ 273, Jan 85		0.20	0.60	1.00
❑ 274, Feb 85		0.20	0.60	1.00
❑ 275, Mar 85		0.20	0.60	1.00
❑ 276, Apr 85		0.20	0.60	1.00
❑ 277, May 85		0.20	0.60	1.00
❑ 278, Jul 85		0.20	0.60	1.00
❑ 279, Sep 85		0.20	0.60	1.00
❑ 280, Nov 85		0.20	0.60	1.00
❑ 281, Jan 86		0.20	0.60	1.00
❑ 282, Mar 86		0.20	0.60	1.00
❑ 283, May 86		0.20	0.60	1.00
❑ 284, Jul 86		0.20	0.60	1.00
❑ 285, Sep 86		0.20	0.60	1.00
❑ 286, Nov 86		0.20	0.60	1.00
❑ 287, Jan 87		0.20	0.60	1.00
❑ 288, Mar 87		0.20	0.60	1.00

G.I. JACK RABBITS
EXCALIBUR

	ORIG.	GOOD	FINE	N-MINT
❑ 1		0.30	0.90	1.50

G.I. JOE AND THE TRANSFORMERS
MARVEL

	ORIG.	GOOD	FINE	N-MINT
❑ 1, Jan 87	0.75	0.20	0.60	1.00
❑ 2, Feb 87	0.75	0.20	0.60	1.00
❑ 3, Mar 87	0.75	0.20	0.60	1.00
❑ 4, Apr 87	0.75	0.20	0.60	1.00

G.I. JOE COMICS MAGAZINE

	ORIG.	GOOD	FINE	N-MINT
❑ 1, Dec 86, digest	1.50	0.30	0.90	1.50
❑ 2, Feb 87, digest	1.50	0.30	0.90	1.50
❑ 3, Apr 87, digest	1.50	0.30	0.90	1.50
❑ 4, Jun 87, digest	1.50	0.30	0.90	1.50
❑ 5, Aug 87, digest	1.50	0.30	0.90	1.50
❑ 6, Oct 87, digest	1.50	0.30	0.90	1.50
❑ 7, Dec 87, digest	1.50	0.30	0.90	1.50
❑ 8, Feb 88, digest	1.50	0.30	0.90	1.50
❑ 9, Apr 88, digest	1.50	0.30	0.90	1.50
❑ 10, Jun 88, digest	1.50	0.30	0.90	1.50
❑ 11, Aug 88, digest	1.50	0.30	0.90	1.50
❑ 12, Oct 88, digest	1.50	0.30	0.90	1.50
❑ 13, Dec 88, digest	1.50	0.30	0.90	1.50

G.I. JOE EUROPEAN MISSIONS

	ORIG.	GOOD	FINE	N-MINT
❑ 1, Jun 88	1.50	0.30	0.90	1.50

	ORIG.	GOOD	FINE	N-MINT
2, Jul 88 ...... 1.50	0.30	0.90	1.50
3, Aug 88 ...... 1.50	0.30	0.90	1.50
4, Sep 88 ...... 1.50	0.30	0.90	1.50
5, Oct 88 ...... 1.50	0.30	0.90	1.50
6, Nov 88 ...... 1.50	0.30	0.90	1.50
7, Dec 88 ...... 1.50	0.30	0.90	1.50
8, Jan 89 ...... 1.50	0.30	0.90	1.50
9, Feb 89 ...... 1.50	0.30	0.90	1.50
10, Mar 89 ...... 1.50	0.30	0.90	1.50
11, Apr 89 ...... 1.50	0.30	0.90	1.50
12, May 89 ...... 1.75	0.35	1.05	1.75
13, Jun 89 ...... 1.75	0.35	1.05	1.75
14, Jul 89 ...... 1.75	0.35	1.05	1.75
15, Aug 89 ...... 1.75	0.35	1.05	1.75

G.I. JOE IN 3-D
BLACKTHORNE

	ORIG.	GOOD	FINE	N-MINT
1, Jul 87		0.50	1.50	2.50
2, Oct 87		0.50	1.50	2.50
3, Jan 88		0.50	1.50	2.50
4, Apr 88		0.50	1.50	2.50
5, Jul 88		0.50	1.50	2.50
6, 88		0.40	1.20	2.00

G.I. JOE ORDER OF BATTLE
MARVEL

	ORIG.	GOOD	FINE	N-MINT
1, Dec 86 ...... 1.25	0.25	0.75	1.25
2, Jan 87, Rocky Balboa. 1.25	0.60	1.80	3.00
3, Feb 87 ...... 1.25	0.25	0.75	1.25
4, Mar 87 ...... 1.25	0.25	0.75	1.25

G.I. JOE SPECIAL MISSIONS

	ORIG.	GOOD	FINE	N-MINT
1, Oct 86 ...... 0.75	0.20	0.60	1.00
2, Dec 86 ...... 0.75	0.20	0.60	1.00
3, Feb 87 ...... 0.75	0.20	0.60	1.00
4, Apr 87 ...... 0.75	0.20	0.60	1.00
5, Jun 87 ...... 1.00	0.20	0.60	1.00
6, Aug 87 ...... 1.00	0.20	0.60	1.00
7, Oct 87 ...... 1.00	0.20	0.60	1.00
8, Dec 87 ...... 1.00	0.20	0.60	1.00
9, Feb 88 ...... 1.00	0.20	0.60	1.00
10, Apr 88 ...... 1.00	0.20	0.60	1.00
11, Jun 88 ...... 1.00	0.20	0.60	1.00
12, Aug 88 ...... 1.00	0.20	0.60	1.00
13, Sep 88 ...... 1.00	0.20	0.60	1.00
14, Oct 88 ...... 1.00	0.20	0.60	1.00
15, Nov 88 ...... 1.00	0.20	0.60	1.00
16, Dec 88 ...... 1.00	0.20	0.60	1.00
17, Jan 89 ...... 1.00	0.20	0.60	1.00
18, Feb 89 ...... 1.00	0.20	0.60	1.00
19, Mar 89 ...... 1.00	0.20	0.60	1.00
20, Apr 89 ...... 1.00	0.20	0.60	1.00
21, May 89 ...... 1.00	0.20	0.60	1.00
22, Jun 89 ...... 1.00	0.20	0.60	1.00
23, Jul 89 ...... 1.00	0.20	0.60	1.00
24, Aug 89 ...... 1.00	0.20	0.60	1.00
25, Sep 89 ...... 1.00	0.20	0.60	1.00
26, Oct 89 ...... 1.00	0.20	0.60	1.00
27, Nov 89 ...... 1.00	0.20	0.60	1.00
28, Nov 89 ...... 1.00	0.20	0.60	1.00

G.I. JOE YEARBOOK

	ORIG.	GOOD	FINE	N-MINT
1, Mar 85 ...... 1.50	0.80	2.40	4.00
2, Mar 86 ...... 1.50	0.60	1.80	3.00
3, Mar 87 ...... 1.50	0.30	0.90	1.50
4, Feb 88 ...... 1.50	0.30	0.90	1.50

G.I. JOE: A REAL AMERICAN HERO

	ORIG.	GOOD	FINE	N-MINT
1, Jun 82 ...... 1.50	1.60	4.80	8.00
2, Aug 82 ...... 0.60	2.00	6.00	10.00
3, Sep 82, HT/JAb 0.60	0.80	2.40	4.00
4, Oct 82, HT/JAb 0.60	0.80	2.40	4.00
5, Nov 82, HT/JAb 0.60	0.80	2.40	4.00
6, Dec 82, HT 0.60	0.80	2.40	4.00
7, Jan 83, HT 0.60	0.80	2.40	4.00

	ORIG.	GOOD	FINE	N-MINT
8, Feb 83, HT 0.60	0.80	2.40	4.00
9, Mar 83 ...... 0.60	0.80	2.40	4.00
10, Apr 83 ...... 0.60	0.80	2.40	4.00
11, May 83 ...... 0.60	0.60	1.80	3.00
12, Jun 83 ...... 0.60	0.60	1.80	3.00
13, Jul 83 ...... 0.60	0.60	1.80	3.00
14, Aug 83 ...... 0.60	0.60	1.80	3.00
15, Sep 83 ...... 0.60	0.60	1.80	3.00
16, Oct 83 ...... 0.60	0.60	1.80	3.00
17, Nov 83 ...... 0.60	0.60	1.80	3.00
18, Dec 83 ...... 0.60	0.60	1.80	3.00
19, Jan 84 ...... 0.60	0.60	1.80	3.00
20, Feb 84 ...... 0.60	0.60	1.80	3.00
21, Mar 84, "silent" issue 0.60	1.20	3.60	6.00
22, Apr 84 ...... 0.60	0.70	2.10	3.50
23, May 84 ...... 0.60	0.70	2.10	3.50
24, Jun 84 ...... 0.60	0.70	2.10	3.50
25, Jul 84 ...... 0.60	0.70	2.10	3.50
26, Aug 84 ...... 0.60	1.00	3.00	5.00
27, Sep 84 ...... 0.60	1.00	3.00	5.00
28, Oct 84 ...... 0.60	0.60	1.80	3.00
29, Nov 84 ...... 0.60	0.60	1.80	3.00
30, Dec 84 ...... 0.60	0.60	1.80	3.00
31, Jan 85 ...... 0.60	0.60	1.80	3.00
32, Feb 85 ...... 0.60	0.60	1.80	3.00
33, Mar 85 ...... 0.60	0.60	1.80	3.00
34, Apr 85 ...... 0.75	0.60	1.80	3.00
35, May 85 ...... 0.75	0.60	1.80	3.00
36, Jun 85 ...... 0.75	0.50	1.50	2.50
37, Jul 85 ...... 0.75	0.50	1.50	2.50
38, Aug 85 ...... 0.75	0.50	1.50	2.50
39, Sep 85 ...... 0.75	0.50	1.50	2.50
40, Oct 85 ...... 0.75	0.50	1.50	2.50
41, Nov 85 ...... 0.75	0.50	1.50	2.50
42, Dec 85 ...... 0.75	0.50	1.50	2.50
43, Jan 86 ...... 0.75	0.60	1.80	3.00
44, Feb 86 ...... 0.75	0.25	0.75	1.25
45, Mar 86 ...... 0.75	0.25	0.75	1.25
46, Apr 86 ...... 0.75	0.25	0.75	1.25
47, May 86 ...... 0.75	0.25	0.75	1.25
48, Jun 86 ...... 0.75	0.25	0.75	1.25
49, Jul 86 ...... 0.75	0.25	0.75	1.25
50, Aug 86 ...... 1.25	0.60	1.80	3.00
51, Sep 86 ...... 0.75	0.20	0.60	1.00
52, Oct 86 ...... 0.75	0.20	0.60	1.00
53, Nov 86 ...... 0.75	0.20	0.60	1.00
54, Dec 86 ...... 0.75	0.20	0.60	1.00
55, Jan 87 ...... 0.75	0.20	0.60	1.00
56, Feb 87 ...... 0.75	0.20	0.60	1.00
57, Mar 87 ...... 0.75	0.20	0.60	1.00
58, Apr 87 ...... 0.75	0.20	0.60	1.00
59, May 87 ...... 1.00	0.20	0.60	1.00
60, Jun 87, TMc 1.00	1.00	3.00	5.00
61, Jul 87 ...... 1.00	0.20	0.60	1.00
62, Aug 87 ...... 1.00	0.20	0.60	1.00
63, Sep 87 ...... 1.00	0.20	0.60	1.00
64, Oct 87 ...... 1.00	0.20	0.60	1.00
65, Nov 87 ...... 1.00	0.20	0.60	1.00
66, Dec 87 ...... 1.00	0.20	0.60	1.00
67, Jan 88 ...... 1.00	0.20	0.60	1.00
68, Feb 88 ...... 1.00	0.20	0.60	1.00
69, Mar 88 ...... 1.00	0.20	0.60	1.00
70, Apr 88 ...... 1.00	0.20	0.60	1.00
71, May 88 ...... 1.00	0.20	0.60	1.00
72, Jun 88 ...... 1.00	0.20	0.60	1.00
73, Jul 88 ...... 1.00	0.20	0.60	1.00
74, Aug 88 ...... 1.00	0.20	0.60	1.00
75, Sep 88 ...... 1.00	0.20	0.60	1.00
76, Sep 88 ...... 1.00	0.20	0.60	1.00
77, Oct 88 ...... 1.00	0.20	0.60	1.00
78, Oct 88 ...... 1.00	0.20	0.60	1.00

	ORIG.	GOOD	FINE	N-MINT
79, Nov 88 .... 1.00	0.20	0.60	1.00
80, Nov 88 .... 1.00	0.20	0.60	1.00
81, Dec 88..................... 1.00	0.20	0.60	1.00
82, Jan 89 .... 1.00	0.20	0.60	1.00
83, Feb 89 .... 1.00	0.20	0.60	1.00
84, Mar 89 .... 1.00	0.20	0.60	1.00
85, Apr 89 .... 1.00	0.20	0.60	1.00
86, May 89 .... 1.00	0.20	0.60	1.00
87, Jun 89 .... 1.00	0.20	0.60	1.00
88, Jul 89 .... 1.00	0.20	0.60	1.00
89, Aug 89 .... 1.00	0.20	0.60	1.00
90, Sep 89 .... 1.00	0.20	0.60	1.00
91, Oct 89 .... 1.00	0.20	0.60	1.00
92, Nov 89 .... 1.00	0.20	0.60	1.00
93, Nov 89 .... 1.00	0.20	0.60	1.00
94, Dec 89 .... 1.00	0.20	0.60	1.00
95, Dec 89..................... 1.00	0.50	1.50	2.50
96, Jan 90 .... 1.00	0.20	0.60	1.00
97, Feb 90 .... 1.00	0.20	0.60	1.00
98, Mar 90 .... 1.00	0.20	0.60	1.00
99, Apr 90 .... 1.00	0.20	0.60	1.00
100, May 90..................... 1.50	0.30	0.90	1.50
101, Jun 90..................... 1.00	0.20	0.60	1.00
102, Jul 90 .... 1.00	0.20	0.60	1.00
103, Aug 90 .... 1.00	0.20	0.60	1.00
104, Sep 90 .... 1.00	0.20	0.60	1.00
105, Oct 90 .... 1.00	0.20	0.60	1.00
106, Nov 90 .... 1.00	0.20	0.60	1.00
107, Dec 90..................... 1.00	0.20	0.60	1.00
108, Jan 91, Dossiers begin 1.00	0.20	0.60	1.00
109, Feb 91 .... 1.00	0.20	0.60	1.00
110, Mar 91 .... 1.00	0.20	0.60	1.00
111, Apr 91 .... 1.00	0.20	0.60	1.00
112, May 91 .... 1.00	0.20	0.60	1.00
113, Jun 91 .... 1.00	0.20	0.60	1.00
114, Jul 91, I:Metal-Head 1.00	0.20	0.60	1.00
115, Aug 91 .... 1.00	0.20	0.60	1.00
116, Sep 91 .... 1.00	0.20	0.60	1.00
117, Oct 91 .... 1.00	0.20	0.60	1.00
118, Nov 91 .... 1.00	0.20	0.60	1.00
119, Dec 91 .... 1.00	0.20	0.60	1.00
120 .... 1.00	0.20	0.60	1.00
121 .... 1.25	0.25	0.75	1.25
122 .... 1.25	0.25	0.75	1.25
123 .... 1.25	0.25	0.75	1.25
124 .... 1.25	0.25	0.75	1.25
125 .... 1.25	0.25	0.75	1.25
126 .... 1.25	0.25	0.75	1.25
127 .... 1.25	0.25	0.75	1.25
128 .... 1.25	0.25	0.75	1.25
129 .... 1.25	0.25	0.75	1.25
130 .... 1.25	0.25	0.75	1.25
131 .... 1.25	0.25	0.75	1.25
132 .... 1.25	0.25	0.75	1.25
133 .... 1.25	0.25	0.75	1.25
134 .... 1.25	0.25	0.75	1.25
135, trading card........... 1.75	0.35	1.05	1.75
136, trading card........... 1.75	0.35	1.05	1.75
137, trading card........... 1.75	0.35	1.05	1.75
138, trading card........... 1.75	0.35	1.05	1.75
139, Transformers 1.25	0.25	0.75	1.25
140 .... 1.25	0.25	0.75	1.25
141 .... 1.25	0.25	0.75	1.25
142 .... 1.25	0.25	0.75	1.25
143 .... 1.25	0.25	0.75	1.25
144 .... 1.25	0.25	0.75	1.25
145 .... 1.25	0.25	0.75	1.25
146 .... 1.25	0.25	0.75	1.25
147 .... 1.25	0.25	0.75	1.25
148, May 94 .... 1.25	0.25	0.75	1.25

	ORIG.	GOOD	FINE	N-MINT
149, Jun 94 ....1.25	0.25	0.75	1.25
150, Jul 94.....................2.00	0.40	1.20	2.00
151, Aug 94 ....1.25	0.25	0.75	1.25
152, Sep 94 ....1.25	0.25	0.75	1.25
153, Oct 94...................1.50	0.30	0.90	1.50
154, Nov 94...................1.50	0.30	0.90	1.50
155, Dec 94, final issue ..1.50	0.30	0.90	1.50

G.I. MUTANTS
ETERNITY

		GOOD	FINE	N-MINT
1		0.39	1.17	1.95
2		0.39	1.17	1.95
3		0.39	1.17	1.95
4		0.39	1.17	1.95

G.I. RAMBOT
WONDER COLOR

		GOOD	FINE	N-MINT
1		0.39	1.17	1.95

GABRIEL
CALIBER

		GOOD	FINE	N-MINT
1, 95, b&w;one-shot; prestige format 3.95	0.79	2.37	3.95

GAIJIN

		GOOD	FINE	N-MINT
1, b&w...............	0.70	2.10	3.50

MATRIX

		GOOD	FINE	N-MINT
1		0.35	1.05	1.75

GAJIT GANG, THE
AMAZING

		GOOD	FINE	N-MINT
1		0.39	1.17	1.95

GALACTIC GUARDIANS (mini-series)
MARVEL

		GOOD	FINE	N-MINT
1, Jul 94.....................1.50	0.30	0.90	1.50
2, Aug 94.....................1.50	0.30	0.90	1.50
3, Sep 94.....................1.50	0.30	0.90	1.50
4, Oct 94.....................1.50	0.30	0.90	1.50

GALAXINA
AIRCEL

		GOOD	FINE	N-MINT
1, adult, b&w	0.59	1.77	2.95
2, adult, b&w	0.59	1.77	2.95
3, adult, b&w	0.59	1.77	2.95

GALAXY GIRL
DYNAMIC

		GOOD	FINE	N-MINT
1, b&w...............	0.50	1.50	2.50

GALL FORCE: ETERNAL STORY (mini-series)
CPM COMICS

		GOOD	FINE	N-MINT
1, Mar 95.....................2.95	0.59	1.77	2.95
2, May 95.....................2.95	0.59	1.77	2.95
3, Jul 95.....................2.95	0.59	1.77	2.95
4, Sep 95.....................2.95	0.59	1.77	2.95

GAMBIT
ETERNITY

		GOOD	FINE	N-MINT
1, b&w...............	0.39	1.17	1.95

ORACLE

		GOOD	FINE	N-MINT
1		0.40	1.20	2.00
2		0.40	1.20	2.00

GAMBIT & THE X-TERNALS (mini-series)
MARVEL

		GOOD	FINE	N-MINT
1, Mar 95.....................1.95	1.00	3.00	5.00
2, Apr 95.....................1.95	0.70	2.10	3.50
3, May 95.....................1.95	0.50	1.50	2.50
4, Jun 95 ....1.95	0.50	1.50	2.50

GAMBIT (mini-series)

		GOOD	FINE	N-MINT
1, foil cover.....................2.50	1.20	3.60	6.00
1, Gold edition	5.00	15.00	25.00
2 ....2.00	0.80	2.40	4.00
3 ....2.00	0.80	2.40	4.00
4 ....2.00	0.80	2.40	4.00

GAME BOY
VALIANT

		GOOD	FINE	N-MINT
1		0.39	1.17	1.95

	ORIG.	GOOD	FINE	N-MINT
❑ 2		0.39	1.17	1.95
❑ 3		0.39	1.17	1.95
❑ 4		0.39	1.17	1.95

GAMMARAUDERS
DC

	ORIG.	GOOD	FINE	N-MINT
❑ 1		0.25	0.75	1.25
❑ 2		0.25	0.75	1.25
❑ 3		0.25	0.75	1.25
❑ 4		0.25	0.75	1.25
❑ 5		0.25	0.75	1.25
❑ 6		0.25	0.75	1.25
❑ 7		0.40	1.20	2.00
❑ 8		0.40	1.20	2.00
❑ 9		0.40	1.20	2.00
❑ 10		0.40	1.20	2.00

GANTAR: THE LAST NABU
TARGET

	ORIG.	GOOD	FINE	N-MINT
❑ 1		0.35	1.05	1.75
❑ 2		0.35	1.05	1.75

GARGOYLE
MARVEL

	ORIG.	GOOD	FINE	N-MINT
❑ 1	0.75	0.25	0.75	1.25
❑ 2	0.75	0.20	0.60	1.00
❑ 3	0.75	0.20	0.60	1.00
❑ 4	0.75	0.20	0.60	1.00

GARGOYLES

	ORIG.	GOOD	FINE	N-MINT
❑ 1, Feb 95, enhanced cover	2.50	0.50	1.50	2.50
❑ 2, Mar 95	1.50	0.30	0.90	1.50
❑ 3, Apr 95	1.50	0.30	0.90	1.50
❑ 4, May 95	1.50	0.30	0.90	1.50
❑ 5, Jun 95	1.50	0.30	0.90	1.50
❑ 6, Jul 95	1.50	0.30	0.90	1.50
❑ 7, Aug 95	1.50	0.30	0.90	1.50
❑ 8, Sep 95	1.50	0.30	0.90	1.50
❑ 9, Oct 95	1.50	0.30	0.90	1.50
❑ 10, Nov 95	1.50	0.30	0.90	1.50
❑ 11, Dec 95, final issue	1.50	0.30	0.90	1.50

GATEKEEPER
GATEKEEPER

	ORIG.	GOOD	FINE	N-MINT
❑ 1		0.50	1.50	2.50

GATES OF EDEN
FANTACO

	ORIG.	GOOD	FINE	N-MINT
❑ 1, 82, MK,JBy,JS, FH,CR	3.50	0.70	2.10	3.50

GATES OF PANDRAGON
IANUS

	ORIG.	GOOD	FINE	N-MINT
❑ 1, b&w		0.45	1.35	2.25

GAUNTLET
AIRCEL

	ORIG.	GOOD	FINE	N-MINT
❑ 1, adult, b&w	2.95	0.59	1.77	2.95
❑ 2, adult, b&w	2.95	0.59	1.77	2.95
❑ 3, adult, b&w	2.95	0.59	1.77	2.95
❑ 4, adult, b&w	2.95	0.59	1.77	2.95
❑ 5, adult, b&w	2.95	0.59	1.77	2.95
❑ 6, adult, b&w	2.95	0.59	1.77	2.95
❑ 7, adult, b&w	2.95	0.59	1.77	2.95
❑ 8, adult, b&w	2.95	0.59	1.77	2.95

GAY COMICS
BOB ROSS

	ORIG.	GOOD	FINE	N-MINT
❑ 10, adult, b&w		0.40	1.20	2.00
❑ 11, adult, b&w		0.40	1.20	2.00
❑ 16, b&w, adult	2.95	0.59	1.77	2.95
❑ 17, b&w, adult	2.95	0.59	1.77	2.95
❑ 18, b&w, adult	2.95	0.59	1.77	2.95
❑ 19, b&w, adult	2.95	0.59	1.77	2.95
❑ 20, super-heroes, adult	2.95	0.59	1.77	2.95

GEN OF HIROSHIMA
EDUCOMICS

	ORIG.	GOOD	FINE	N-MINT
❑ 1, Jan 80	1.50	0.30	0.90	1.50
❑ 2, 81	2.00	0.40	1.20	2.00

GEN13 (1994 mini-series)
IMAGE

	ORIG.	GOOD	FINE	N-MINT
❑ 0, Sep 94	2.50	1.60	4.80	8.00
❑ 1, first printing		9.00	27.00	45.00
❑ 1, second printing		2.00	6.00	10.00
❑ 2		7.60	22.80	38.00
❑ 3, Apr 94	1.95	5.00	15.00	25.00
❑ 4, May 94	1.95	3.60	10.80	18.00
❑ 5		2.00	6.00	10.00

GEN13 (1995- ongoing series)

	ORIG.	GOOD	FINE	N-MINT
❑ 1, Mar 95, A- Charge! (13 diff. covers)	2.95	2.80	8.40	14.00
❑ 1, Mar 95, B- Thumbs Up (13 diff. covers)	2.95	2.80	8.40	14.00
❑ 1, Mar 95, C- Li'l GEN13 (13 diff. covers)	2.95	4.40	13.20	22.00
❑ 1, Mar 95, D- Barbari-GEN (13 diff. covers)	2.95	4.40	13.20	22.00
❑ 1, Mar 95, E- Your Friendly Neighborhood Grunge (13 diff. covers)	2.95	4.40	13.20	22.00
❑ 1, Mar 95, F- Gen13 Goes Madison Avenue (13 diff. covers)	2.95	4.40	13.20	22.00
❑ 1, Mar 95, G- Lin-GEN-re (13 diff. covers)	2.95	4.40	13.20	22.00
❑ 1, Mar 95, H- GEN-et Jackson (13 diff. covers)	2.95	4.40	13.20	22.00
❑ 1, Mar 95, I- That's the Way We Became the GEN13 (13 diff. covers)	2.95	4.40	13.20	22.00
❑ 1, Mar 95, J- All Dolled Up (13 diff. covers)	2.95	4.40	13.20	22.00
❑ 1, Mar 95, K- Verti-GEN (13 diff. covers)	2.95	4.40	13.20	22.00
❑ 1, Mar 95, L- Picto-Fiction (13 diff. covers)	2.95	4.40	13.20	22.00
❑ 1, Mar 95, M- Do-It-Yourself-Cover (13 diff. covers)	2.95	4.40	13.20	22.00
❑ 2		1.40	4.20	7.00
❑ 3		1.00	3.00	5.00
❑ 4		2.50	0.80	2.40	4.00
❑ 5, Oct 95	2.50	0.80	2.40	4.00
❑ 7, Jan 96, indicia says "Jan";cover says "Dec"	2.50	0.50	1.50	2.50
❑ 8, Feb 96	2.50	0.50	1.50	2.50
❑ 9, Mar 96	2.50	0.50	1.50	2.50
❑ 10, Apr 96, "Fire from Heaven" Part 3	2.50	0.50	1.50	2.50

GEN13 (Volume 2)

	ORIG.	GOOD	FINE	N-MINT
❑ 1, Jun 94	2.50	0.50	1.50	2.50

GEN13 COLLECTORS EDITION

	ORIG.	GOOD	FINE	N-MINT
❑ 0, 1st		60.00	180.00	300.00
❑ 0, 2nd		45.00	135.00	225.00
❑ 0, 3rd		40.00	120.00	200.00
❑ 0, 4th		35.00	105.00	175.00

GEN13 RAVE

	ORIG.	GOOD	FINE	N-MINT
❑ 1, Mar 95	1.50	1.20	3.60	6.00

GEN13: ORDINARY HEROES

	ORIG.	GOOD	FINE	N-MINT
❑ 1, Feb 96	2.50	0.50	1.50	2.50

GENE DOG
MARVEL

	ORIG.	GOOD	FINE	N-MINT
❑ 1, four trading cards	2.75	0.55	1.65	2.75
❑ 2	1.75	0.35	1.05	1.75
❑ 3	1.75	0.35	1.05	1.75
❑ 4	1.75	0.35	1.05	1.75

GENE RODDENBERRY'S LOST UNIVERSE
TEKNO

	ORIG.	GOOD	FINE	N-MINT
❑ 1, Apr 95	1.95	0.39	1.17	1.95

	ORIG.	GOOD	FINE	N-MINT
☐ 2, May 95 .... 1.95	0.39	1.17	1.95
☐ 3, Jun 95 .... 1.95	0.39	1.17	1.95
☐ 4, Jul 95 .... 1.95	0.39	1.17	1.95
☐ 5, Aug 95 .... 1.95	0.39	1.17	1.95
☐ 6, Sep 95 .... 1.95	0.39	1.17	1.95
☐ 7, Oct 95 .... 1.95	0.39	1.17	1.95

GENE RODDENBERRY'S XANDER IN LOST UNIVERSE

	ORIG.	GOOD	FINE	N-MINT
☐ 0, Nov 95 .... 2.25	0.45	1.35	2.25
☐ 1, Dec 95 .... 2.25	0.45	1.35	2.25
☐ 2, Dec 95 .... 2.25	0.45	1.35	2.25
☐ 3, 95 .... 2.25	0.45	1.35	2.25
☐ 4, Jan 96 .... 2.25	0.45	1.35	2.25
☐ 5, Feb 96 .... 2.25	0.45	1.35	2.25
☐ 7, Apr 96 .... 2.25	0.45	1.35	2.25

GENERATION NEXT (mini-series)
MARVEL

	ORIG.	GOOD	FINE	N-MINT
☐ 1, Mar 95 .... 1.95	1.00	3.00	5.00
☐ 2, Apr 95 .... 1.95	0.70	2.10	3.50
☐ 3, May 95 .... 1.95	0.50	1.50	2.50
☐ 4, Jun 95 .... 1.95	0.50	1.50	2.50

GENERATION X

	ORIG.	GOOD	FINE	N-MINT
☐ 1, Nov 94, enhanced cover			
.... 3.95	1.60	4.80	8.00
☐ 2, Dec 94, deluxe edition 1.95	1.00	3.00	5.00
☐ 2, Dec 94 .... 1.50	0.60	1.80	3.00
☐ 3, Jan 95, deluxe edition 1.95	0.39	1.17	1.95
☐ 3, Jan 95 .... 1.50	0.30	0.90	1.50
☐ 4, Feb 95 .... 1.50	0.30	0.90	1.50
☐ 4, Feb 95, deluxe edition 1.95	0.39	1.17	1.95
☐ 5, Jul 95 .... 1.95	0.39	1.17	1.95
☐ 6, Aug 95 .... 1.95	0.39	1.17	1.95
☐ 7, Sep 95 .... 1.95	0.39	1.17	1.95
☐ 8, Oct 95 .... 1.95	0.39	1.17	1.95
☐ 9, Nov 95 .... 1.95	0.39	1.17	1.95
☐ 10, Dec 95 .... 1.95	0.39	1.17	1.95
☐ 11, Jan 96 .... 1.95	0.39	1.17	1.95
☐ 12, Feb 96 .... 1.95	0.39	1.17	1.95
☐ 13, Mar 96 .... 1.95	0.39	1.17	1.95
☐ 14, Apr 96 .... 1.95	0.39	1.17	1.95
☐ 15, May 96 .... 1.95	0.39	1.17	1.95
☐ 16, Jun 96 .... 1.95	0.39	1.17	1.95

GENERATION X '95

	ORIG.	GOOD	FINE	N-MINT
☐ 1, 95, wraparound cover 3.95	0.79	2.37	3.95

GENERATION X COLLECTORS' PREVIEW

	ORIG.	GOOD	FINE	N-MINT
☐ 1, Oct 94 .... 1.75	0.60	1.80	3.00

GENERIC COMIC
MARVEL

	ORIG.	GOOD	FINE	N-MINT
☐ 1 .... 0.60	0.20	0.60	1.00

GENESIS
MALIBU

	ORIG.	GOOD	FINE	N-MINT
☐ 0, Oct 93, foil cover 3.50	0.70	2.10	3.50

GENETIX
MARVEL

	ORIG.	GOOD	FINE	N-MINT
☐ 1, four trading cards 2.75	0.55	1.65	2.75
☐ 2 .... 1.75	0.35	1.05	1.75
☐ 3 .... 1.75	0.35	1.05	1.75
☐ 4 .... 1.75	0.35	1.05	1.75
☐ 5 .... 1.75	0.35	1.05	1.75
☐ 6 .... 1.75	0.35	1.05	1.75

GENOCIDE
RENEGADE TRIBE

	ORIG.	GOOD	FINE	N-MINT
☐ 1, Aug 94, second printing			
.... 2.95	0.59	1.77	2.95

GENOCYBER
VIZ

	ORIG.	GOOD	FINE	N-MINT
☐ 1, Japanese, b&w 2.75	0.55	1.65	2.75
☐ 2, Japanese, b&w 2.75	0.55	1.65	2.75
☐ 3, Japanese, b&w 2.75	0.55	1.65	2.75

	ORIG.	GOOD	FINE	N-MINT
☐ 4, Japanese, b&w 2.75	0.55	1.65	2.75
☐ 5, Japanese, b&w 2.75	0.55	1.65	2.75

GENSAGA
EXPRESS/ENTITY

	ORIG.	GOOD	FINE	N-MINT
☐ 1, 95 .... 2.50	0.50	1.50	2.50

GENUS
ANTARCTIC

	ORIG.	GOOD	FINE	N-MINT
☐ 1, May 93, adult;b&w 2.95	0.59	1.77	2.95
☐ 2, Sep 93, adult;b&w 2.95	0.59	1.77	2.95
☐ 3, Nov 93, adult;b&w 2.95	0.59	1.77	2.95
☐ 4, Jan 94, adult;b&w 2.95	0.59	1.77	2.95
☐ 5, Mar 94, adult;b&w 2.95	0.59	1.77	2.95
☐ 6, May 94, adult;b&w 2.95	0.59	1.77	2.95
☐ 7, Jul 94, adult;b&w 2.95	0.59	1.77	2.95
☐ 8, Sep 94, adult;b&w 2.95	0.59	1.77	2.95
☐ 9, Nov 94, adult;b&w 2.95	0.59	1.77	2.95
☐ 10, Jan 95, adult;b&w 3.50	0.70	2.10	3.50
☐ 11, Mar 95, adult;b&w 2.95	0.59	1.77	2.95
☐ 12, May 95, adult;b&w 2.95	0.59	1.77	2.95
☐ 13, Jul 95, adult;b&w 2.95	0.59	1.77	2.95
☐ 14, Sep 95, adult;b&w 2.95	0.59	1.77	2.95
☐ 15, Nov 95, adult;b&w 2.95	0.59	1.77	2.95

GEOMANCER
ACCLAIM/VALIANT

	ORIG.	GOOD	FINE	N-MINT
☐ 8, Jun 95, final issue.......2.25	0.45	1.35	2.25

VALIANT

	ORIG.	GOOD	FINE	N-MINT
☐ 1	1.00	3.00	5.00
☐ 2, Dec 94 .... 2.25	0.45	1.35	2.25
☐ 3	0.50	1.50	2.50
☐ 4, Feb 95 .... 2.25	0.45	1.35	2.25
☐ 5, Mar 95 .... 2.25	0.45	1.35	2.25
☐ 6, Apr 95 .... 2.25	0.45	1.35	2.25
☐ 7, May 95 .... 2.25	0.45	1.35	2.25

GERIATRIC GANGRENE JUJITSU GERBILS
PLANET-X

	ORIG.	GOOD	FINE	N-MINT
☐ 1	0.30	0.90	1.50
☐ 2	0.30	0.90	1.50

GERIATRICMAN
C&T

	ORIG.	GOOD	FINE	N-MINT
☐ 1, b&w	0.35	1.05	1.75

GESTALT
NEW ENGLAND

	ORIG.	GOOD	FINE	N-MINT
☐ 1, b&w 1.95	0.39	1.17	1.95

GET ALONG GANG
STAR

	ORIG.	GOOD	FINE	N-MINT
☐ 1 .... 0.65	0.13	0.39	0.65
☐ 2 .... 0.65	0.13	0.39	0.65
☐ 3 .... 0.65	0.13	0.39	0.65
☐ 4 .... 0.65	0.13	0.39	0.65
☐ 5 .... 0.65	0.13	0.39	0.65
☐ 6 .... 0.65	0.13	0.39	0.65

GET LOST
NEW COMICS

	ORIG.	GOOD	FINE	N-MINT
☐ 1, b&w reprint	0.39	1.17	1.95
☐ 2, b&w reprint	0.39	1.17	1.95
☐ 3, BB(c) b&w reprint.........	0.39	1.17	1.95

GHETTO BITCH
EROS

	ORIG.	GOOD	FINE	N-MINT
☐ 1, adult, b&w 2.75	0.55	1.65	2.75

GHOST
DARK HORSE

	ORIG.	GOOD	FINE	N-MINT
☐ 1	0.80	2.40	4.00
☐ 5, Aug 95, V:Predator 2.50	0.50	1.50	2.50
☐ 6, Sep 95 .... 2.50	0.50	1.50	2.50
☐ 7, Oct 95 .... 2.50	0.50	1.50	2.50
☐ 8, Nov 95 .... 2.50	0.50	1.50	2.50
☐ 9, Dec 95 .... 2.50	0.50	1.50	2.50
☐ 10, Jan 96 .... 2.50	0.50	1.50	2.50
☐ 11, Feb 96 .... 2.50	0.50	1.50	2.50

	ORIG.	GOOD	FINE	N-MINT

☐ 12, Mar 96, preview of *Ghost/Hellboy* crossover

	2.50	0.50	1.50	2.50
☐ 13, Apr 96	2.50	0.50	1.50	2.50
☐ 14, May 96	2.50	0.50	1.50	2.50

GHOST AND THE SHADOW

☐ 0, Dec 95, nn;one-shot	2.95	0.59	1.77	2.95

GHOST IN THE SHELL (mini-series)
DARK HORSE/MANGA

☐ 1, Mar 95, b&w&color, cardstock cover

	3.95	0.79	2.37	3.95

☐ 2, Apr 95, b&w&color, cardstock cover

	3.95	0.79	2.37	3.95

☐ 4, Jun 95, b&w&color, cardstock cover

	3.95	0.79	2.37	3.95

☐ 5, Jul 95, b&w&color, cardstock cover

	3.95	0.79	2.37	3.95

☐ 6, Aug 95, b&w&color, cardstock cover

	3.95	0.79	2.37	3.95

☐ 7, Sep 95, b&w&color, cardstock cover

	3.95	0.79	2.37	3.95

☐ 8, Oct 95, b&w;cardstock cover;final issue

	3.95	0.79	2.37	3.95

GHOST RIDER (1973-1983)
MARVEL

☐ 1, GK, A:Son of Satan	0.20	10.00	30.00	50.00
☐ 2	0.20	6.00	18.00	30.00
☐ 3	0.20	5.00	15.00	25.00
☐ 4	0.20	5.00	15.00	25.00
☐ 5	0.20	5.00	15.00	25.00
☐ 6	0.25	3.20	9.60	16.00
☐ 7	0.25	3.20	9.60	16.00
☐ 8	0.25	3.20	9.60	16.00
☐ 9	0.25	3.20	9.60	16.00
☐ 10	0.25	3.20	9.60	16.00
☐ 11, GK/KJ/SB, A:Hulk	0.25	3.20	9.60	16.00
☐ 12	0.25	2.00	6.00	10.00
☐ 13	0.25	2.00	6.00	10.00
☐ 14	0.25	2.00	6.00	10.00
☐ 15	0.25	2.00	6.00	10.00
☐ 16	0.25	2.00	6.00	10.00
☐ 17	0.25	2.00	6.00	10.00
☐ 18	0.25	2.00	6.00	10.00
☐ 19	0.25	2.00	6.00	10.00

☐ 20, Oct 76, GK/KJ/JBy, A:Daredevil

	0.30	3.00	9.00	15.00
☐ 21, Dec 76	0.30	1.20	3.60	6.00
☐ 22, Feb 77	0.30	1.20	3.60	6.00
☐ 23, Apr 77	0.30	1.20	3.60	6.00
☐ 24, Jun 77	0.30	1.20	3.60	6.00
☐ 25, Aug 77	0.30	1.20	3.60	6.00
☐ 26, Oct 77	0.30	1.20	3.60	6.00
☐ 27, Dec 77	0.35	1.20	3.60	6.00
☐ 28, Feb 78	0.35	1.20	3.60	6.00
☐ 29, Apr 78	0.35	1.20	3.60	6.00
☐ 30, Jun 78	0.35	1.20	3.60	6.00
☐ 31, Aug 78	0.35	1.20	3.60	6.00
☐ 32, Oct 78	0.35	1.20	3.60	6.00
☐ 33, Dec 78	0.35	1.20	3.60	6.00
☐ 34, Feb 79	0.35	1.20	3.60	6.00
☐ 35, Apr 79	0.35	1.20	3.60	6.00
☐ 36, Jun 79	0.40	1.20	3.60	6.00
☐ 37, Aug 79	0.40	1.20	3.60	6.00
☐ 38, Oct 79	0.40	1.20	3.60	6.00
☐ 39, Dec 79	0.40	1.20	3.60	6.00
☐ 40, Jan 80	0.40	1.20	3.60	6.00
☐ 41, Feb 80	0.40	1.00	3.00	5.00
☐ 42, Mar 80	0.40	1.00	3.00	5.00
☐ 43, Apr 80	0.40	1.00	3.00	5.00
☐ 44, May 80	0.40	1.00	3.00	5.00
☐ 45, Jun 80	0.40	1.00	3.00	5.00
☐ 46, Jul 80	0.40	1.00	3.00	5.00

	ORIG.	GOOD	FINE	N-MINT
☐ 47, Aug 80	0.40	1.00	3.00	5.00
☐ 48, Sep 80	0.50	1.00	3.00	5.00
☐ 49, Oct 80	0.50	1.00	3.00	5.00

☐ 50, Nov 80, DP, A:Night Rider

	0.75	1.40	4.20	7.00
☐ 51, Dec 80	0.50	0.80	2.40	4.00
☐ 52, Jan 81	0.50	0.80	2.40	4.00
☐ 53, Feb 81	0.50	0.80	2.40	4.00
☐ 54, Mar 81	0.50	0.80	2.40	4.00
☐ 55, Apr 81	0.50	0.80	2.40	4.00
☐ 56, May 81	0.50	0.80	2.40	4.00
☐ 57, Jun 81	0.50	0.80	2.40	4.00
☐ 58, Jul 81	0.50	0.80	2.40	4.00
☐ 59, Aug 81	0.50	0.80	2.40	4.00
☐ 60, Sep 81	0.50	0.80	2.40	4.00
☐ 61, Oct 81	0.50	0.80	2.40	4.00
☐ 62, Nov 81	0.50	0.80	2.40	4.00
☐ 63, Dec 81	0.50	0.80	2.40	4.00
☐ 64, Jan 82	0.60	0.80	2.40	4.00
☐ 65, Feb 82	0.60	0.80	2.40	4.00
☐ 66, Mar 82	0.60	0.80	2.40	4.00
☐ 67, Apr 82	0.60	0.80	2.40	4.00
☐ 68, May 82	0.60	0.80	2.40	4.00
☐ 69, Jun 82	0.60	0.80	2.40	4.00
☐ 70, Jul 82	0.60	0.80	2.40	4.00
☐ 71, Aug 82	0.60	0.80	2.40	4.00
☐ 72, Sep 82	0.60	0.80	2.40	4.00
☐ 73, Oct 82	0.60	0.80	2.40	4.00
☐ 74, Nov 82	0.60	0.80	2.40	4.00
☐ 75, Dec 82	0.60	0.80	2.40	4.00
☐ 76, Jan 83	0.60	0.80	2.40	4.00
☐ 77, Feb 83	0.60	0.80	2.40	4.00
☐ 78, Mar 83	0.60	0.80	2.40	4.00
☐ 79, Apr 83	0.60	0.80	2.40	4.00
☐ 80, May 83	0.60	0.80	2.40	4.00
☐ 81, D:Ghost Rider	0.60	2.40	7.20	12.00

GHOST RIDER (Volume 2, began 1990)

☐ 1, May 90, O, 1st printing	1.95	3.60	10.80	18.00

☐ 1, Sep 90, O, 2nd printing

	1.95	2.00	6.00	10.00
☐ 2, Jun 90	1.50	2.80	8.40	14.00
☐ 3, Jul 90	1.50	2.80	8.40	14.00
☐ 4, Aug 90	1.50	3.60	10.80	18.00

☐ 5, Sep 90, Punisher, 1st printing

	1.50	3.00	9.00	15.00
☐ 5, Sep 90, 2nd printing	1.50	2.00	6.00	10.00
☐ 6, Oct 90, Punisher	1.50	2.00	6.00	10.00
☐ 7, Nov 90	1.50	1.20	3.60	6.00
☐ 8, Dec 90	1.50	1.20	3.60	6.00
☐ 9, Jan 91, X-Factor	1.50	1.00	3.00	5.00
☐ 10, Feb 91	1.50	0.80	2.40	4.00
☐ 11, Mar 91	1.50	0.80	2.40	4.00
☐ 12, Apr 91, Dr. Strange	1.50	0.30	0.90	1.50
☐ 13, May 91	1.50	0.30	0.90	1.50
☐ 14, Jun 91, Johnny Blaze	1.50	0.30	0.90	1.50

☐ 15, Jul 91, glowing cover 1st printing

	1.75	2.00	6.00	10.00
☐ 15, 2nd printing	1.75	1.40	4.20	7.00

☐ 16, Aug 91, SpM, Hobgoblin

	1.75	0.70	2.10	3.50

☐ 17, Sep 91, SpM, Hobgoblin

	1.75	0.70	2.10	3.50
☐ 18, Oct 91	1.75	0.60	1.80	3.00
☐ 19, Nov 91	1.75	0.60	1.80	3.00
☐ 20, Dec 91	1.75	0.60	1.80	3.00
☐ 21	1.75	0.60	1.80	3.00
☐ 22	1.75	0.60	1.80	3.00
☐ 23	1.75	0.60	1.80	3.00
☐ 24	1.75	0.60	1.80	3.00
☐ 25, pop-up	2.75	0.55	1.65	2.75
☐ 26, X-Men	1.75	0.35	1.05	1.75

	ORIG.	GOOD	FINE	N-MINT
27, X-Men	1.75	0.50	1.50	2.50
28, poster	2.50	1.00	3.00	5.00
29, Wolverine	2.50	0.50	1.50	2.50
30	2.50	0.50	1.50	2.50
31, poster	2.50	0.50	1.50	2.50
32	1.75	0.35	1.05	1.75
33	1.75	0.35	1.05	1.75
34	1.75	0.35	1.05	1.75
35	1.75	0.35	1.05	1.75
36	1.75	0.35	1.05	1.75
37	1.75	0.35	1.05	1.75
38	1.75	0.35	1.05	1.75
39	1.75	0.35	1.05	1.75
40, black cover	2.25	0.45	1.35	2.25
41	1.75	0.35	1.05	1.75
42	1.75	0.35	1.05	1.75
43	1.75	0.35	1.05	1.75
44	1.75	0.60	1.80	3.00
45	1.75	0.35	1.05	1.75
46	1.75	0.35	1.05	1.75
47	1.75	0.35	1.05	1.75
48	1.75	0.35	1.05	1.75
49, May 94	1.75	0.35	1.05	1.75
50, Jun 94, die-cut cover	2.50	0.50	1.50	2.50
50, Jun 94, foil cover	2.95	0.59	1.77	2.95
51, Jul 94	1.95	0.39	1.17	1.95
52, Aug 94	1.95	0.39	1.17	1.95
53, Sep 94	1.95	0.39	1.17	1.95
54, Oct 94	1.95	0.39	1.17	1.95
55, Nov 94	1.95	0.39	1.17	1.95
56, Dec 94	1.95	0.39	1.17	1.95
57, Jan 95	1.95	0.39	1.17	1.95
58, Feb 95	1.95	0.39	1.17	1.95
59, Mar 95	1.95	0.39	1.17	1.95
60, Apr 95	1.95	0.39	1.17	1.95
61, May 95	2.50	0.50	1.50	2.50
62, Jun 95, "In Chains" Part 1 of 4	1.95	0.39	1.17	1.95
63, Jul 95, "In Chains" Part 2 of 4	1.95	0.39	1.17	1.95
64, Aug 95, "In Chains" Part 3 of 4	1.95	0.39	1.17	1.95
65, Sep 95, "In Chains" Part 4 of 4; "Over the Edge"	1.95	0.39	1.17	1.95
66, Oct 95, D:Blackout	1.95	0.39	1.17	1.95
67, Nov 95, A:Gambit	1.95	0.39	1.17	1.95
68, Dec 95, A:Gambit, Wolverine	1.95	0.39	1.17	1.95
69, Jan 96	1.95	0.39	1.17	1.95
70, Feb 96	1.95	0.39	1.17	1.95
71, Mar 96	1.95	0.39	1.17	1.95
73, May 96	1.95	0.39	1.17	1.95
74, Jun 96	1.95	0.39	1.17	1.95

GHOST RIDER 2099

	ORIG.	GOOD	FINE	N-MINT
1, May 94, foil cover	2.25	0.45	1.35	2.25
1, May 94	1.50	0.30	0.90	1.50
2, Jun 94	1.50	0.30	0.90	1.50
3, Jul 94	1.50	0.30	0.90	1.50
4, Aug 94	1.50	0.30	0.90	1.50
5, Sep 94	1.50	0.30	0.90	1.50
6, Oct 94	1.50	0.30	0.90	1.50
7, Nov 94	1.50	0.30	0.90	1.50
8, Dec 94	1.50	0.30	0.90	1.50
9, Jan 95	1.50	0.30	0.90	1.50
10, Feb 95	1.50	0.30	0.90	1.50
11, Mar 95	1.50	0.30	0.90	1.50
12, Apr 95	1.50	0.30	0.90	1.50
13, May 95	1.95	0.39	1.17	1.95
14, Jun 95	1.95	0.39	1.17	1.95
15, Jul 95, I: Heartbreaker	1.95	0.39	1.17	1.95

	ORIG.	GOOD	FINE	N-MINT
16, Aug 95	1.95	0.39	1.17	1.95
17, Sep 95	1.95	0.39	1.17	1.95
18, Oct 95	1.95	0.39	1.17	1.95
19, Nov 95	1.95	0.39	1.17	1.95
20, Dec 95	1.95	0.39	1.17	1.95
21, Jan 96	1.95	0.39	1.17	1.95
22, Feb 96	1.95	0.39	1.17	1.95
24, Apr 96	1.95	0.39	1.17	1.95
25, May 96, wraparound cover;double-sized final issue	2.95	0.59	1.77	2.95

GHOST RIDER AND CABLE

	ORIG.	GOOD	FINE	N-MINT
1	3.95	0.79	2.37	3.95

GHOST RIDER AND THE MIDNIGHT SONS MAGAZINE

	ORIG.	GOOD	FINE	N-MINT
1	3.95	0.79	2.37	3.95

GHOST RIDER ANNUAL

	ORIG.	GOOD	FINE	N-MINT
1, trading card	2.95	0.59	1.77	2.95
2, 94	2.95	0.59	1.77	2.95

GHOST RIDER POSTER MAGAZINE

	ORIG.	GOOD	FINE	N-MINT
1	4.95	0.99	2.97	4.95

GHOST RIDER, THE

	ORIG.	GOOD	FINE	N-MINT
1, 67	0.12	4.80	14.40	24.00
2, 67	0.12	2.80	8.40	14.00
3, 67	0.12	2.80	8.40	14.00
4, 67	0.12	2.00	6.00	10.00
5, 67	0.12	2.00	6.00	10.00
6, 67	0.12	2.00	6.00	10.00
7, 67	0.12	2.00	6.00	10.00

GHOST RIDER/BLAZE: SPIRITS OF VENGEANCE

	ORIG.	GOOD	FINE	N-MINT
1, poster	2.75	0.70	2.10	3.50
2	1.75	0.35	1.05	1.75
3	1.75	0.35	1.05	1.75
4	1.75	0.35	1.05	1.75
5, Venom	1.75	0.35	1.05	1.75
6	1.75	0.35	1.05	1.75
7	1.75	0.35	1.05	1.75
8	1.75	0.35	1.05	1.75
9	1.75	0.35	1.05	1.75
10	1.75	0.35	1.05	1.75
11	1.75	0.35	1.05	1.75
12, glowing cover	2.75	0.55	1.65	2.75
13, black cover	2.50	0.50	1.50	2.50
14	1.75	0.35	1.05	1.75
15	1.75	0.35	1.05	1.75
16	1.75	0.35	1.05	1.75
17	1.75	0.60	1.80	3.00
18	1.75	0.35	1.05	1.75
19	1.75	0.35	1.05	1.75
20	1.75	0.35	1.05	1.75
21	1.75	0.35	1.05	1.75
22, May 94	1.95	0.39	1.17	1.95
23, Jun 94, last issue	1.95	0.39	1.17	1.95

GHOST RIDER/WOLVERINE/PUNISHER: THE DARK DESIGN

	ORIG.	GOOD	FINE	N-MINT
0, Dec 94, prestige format, foldout covers	5.95	1.19	3.57	5.95

GHOST RIDER: CROSSROADS

	ORIG.	GOOD	FINE	N-MINT
1, Dec 95, one-shot; enhanced wraparound cardstock cover	3.95	0.79	2.37	3.95

GHOST SPECIAL
DARK HORSE

	ORIG.	GOOD	FINE	N-MINT
1, Jul 94	3.95	1.20	3.60	6.00

GHOSTBUSTERS
FIRST

	ORIG.	GOOD	FINE	N-MINT
1		0.25	0.75	1.25
2		0.25	0.75	1.25
3		0.25	0.75	1.25
4		0.25	0.75	1.25

	ORIG.	GOOD	FINE	N-MINT

GHOSTBUSTERS II
NOW

	ORIG.	GOOD	FINE	N-MINT
1, Oct 89, movie	1.95	0.39	1.17	1.95
2, Nov 89, movie	1.95	0.39	1.17	1.95
3, Dec 89, movie	1.95	0.39	1.17	1.95

GHOSTDANCING (mini-series)
DC/VERTIGO

	ORIG.	GOOD	FINE	N-MINT
1, Mar 95	1.95	0.39	1.17	1.95
2, Apr 95	1.95	0.39	1.17	1.95
3, Jun 95	2.50	0.50	1.50	2.50
4, Jul 95	2.50	0.50	1.50	2.50
5, Aug 95	2.50	0.50	1.50	2.50
6, Sep 95	2.50	0.50	1.50	2.50

GHOSTS OF DRACULA
ETERNITY

	GOOD	FINE	N-MINT
1, b&w	0.50	1.50	2.50
2, b&w	0.50	1.50	2.50
3, b&w	0.50	1.50	2.50
4, b&w	0.50	1.50	2.50
5, b&w	0.50	1.50	2.50

GHOUL GALLERY
AC

	ORIG.	GOOD	FINE	N-MINT
1, reprints	2.95	0.59	1.77	2.95
2, reprints	2.95	0.59	1.77	2.95

GHOULS
ETERNITY

	GOOD	FINE	N-MINT
1, b&w rep.	0.45	1.35	2.25

GI JOE (mini-series)
DARK HORSE

	ORIG.	GOOD	FINE	N-MINT
1, Dec 95	1.95	0.39	1.17	1.95
2, Jan 96	1.95	0.39	1.17	1.95
3, Mar 96	1.95	0.39	1.17	1.95
4, Apr 96, final issue	1.95	0.39	1.17	1.95

GIANT SIZE FREEX
MALIBU/ULTRAVERSE

	ORIG.	GOOD	FINE	N-MINT
1, Jul 94	2.50	0.50	1.50	2.50

GIANT SIZE MANTRA

	ORIG.	GOOD	FINE	N-MINT
1, Jul 94, (indicia says "Vol. 1, Number 11")	2.50	0.50	1.50	2.50

GIANT SIZE OFFICIAL PRINCE VALIANT
PIONEER

	GOOD	FINE	N-MINT
1, b&w, Hal Foster	0.79	2.37	3.95

GIANT SIZE PROTOTYPE
MALIBU/ULTRAVERSE

	ORIG.	GOOD	FINE	N-MINT
1, Oct 94	2.50	0.50	1.50	2.50

GIANT-SIZE AVENGERS
MARVEL

	ORIG.	GOOD	FINE	N-MINT
1, RB, rep.	0.50	1.20	3.60	6.00
2, DC, rep.	0.50	0.80	2.40	4.00
3, DC, rep.	0.50	0.80	2.40	4.00
4, DH W:Vision & Scarlet Witch	0.50	0.80	2.40	4.00
5, rep.	0.50	0.30	0.90	1.50

GIANT-SIZE CAPTAIN AMERICA

	ORIG.	GOOD	FINE	N-MINT
1, rep:O	0.50	1.20	3.60	6.00

GIANT-SIZE CAPTAIN MARVEL

	ORIG.	GOOD	FINE	N-MINT
1, rep.	0.50	1.20	3.60	6.00

GIANT-SIZE CHILLERS (1974)

	ORIG.	GOOD	FINE	N-MINT
1, Dracula;1:Lilith (becomes Giant-Size Dracula)	0.35	1.20	3.60	6.00

GIANT-SIZE CHILLERS (1975)

	ORIG.	GOOD	FINE	N-MINT
1	0.50	0.40	1.20	2.00
2	0.50	0.40	1.20	2.00
3	0.50	0.40	1.20	2.00

GIANT-SIZE CONAN

	ORIG.	GOOD	FINE	N-MINT
1, Sep 74, GK/TS/BB	0.50	1.80	5.40	9.00
2, Dec 74, GK/TS/BS	0.50	1.20	3.60	6.00
3, Apr 75	0.50	0.40	1.20	2.00

	ORIG.	GOOD	FINE	N-MINT
4, Jun 75	0.50	0.40	1.20	2.00
5, Jun 75	0.50	0.40	1.20	2.00

GIANT-SIZE CREATURES

	ORIG.	GOOD	FINE	N-MINT
1, (becomes Giant-Size Werewolf by Night)	0.35	0.80	2.40	4.00

GIANT-SIZE DAREDEVIL

	ORIG.	GOOD	FINE	N-MINT
1	0.50	1.20	3.60	6.00

GIANT-SIZE DEFENDERS

	ORIG.	GOOD	FINE	N-MINT
1, Jul 74, Silver Surfer	0.50	2.00	6.00	10.00
2, Oct 74	0.50	1.20	3.60	6.00
3, Jan 75	0.50	1.20	3.60	6.00
4, Apr 75	0.50	1.20	3.60	6.00
5, Jul 75	0.50	1.20	3.60	6.00

GIANT-SIZE DOC SAVAGE

	ORIG.	GOOD	FINE	N-MINT
1, movie	0.50	0.60	1.80	3.00

GIANT-SIZE DOCTOR STRANGE

	ORIG.	GOOD	FINE	N-MINT
1	0.50	1.20	3.60	6.00

GIANT-SIZE DRACULA (was Giant-Size Chillers)

	ORIG.	GOOD	FINE	N-MINT
2	0.50	1.00	3.00	5.00
3	0.50	1.00	3.00	5.00
4	0.50	1.00	3.00	5.00
5, JBy	0.50	0.60	1.80	3.00

GIANT-SIZE FANTASTIC FOUR
(was Giant-Size Super-Stars)

	ORIG.	GOOD	FINE	N-MINT
2, Aug 74, GK(c);JB; V:Tempus;A:Willie Lumpkin; also reprints FF #13	0.50	1.50	4.50	7.50
3, Nov 74, RB; also reprints FF #21	0.50	1.50	4.50	7.50
4, Feb 75, RB(c);JB; A:Madrox	0.50	1.50	4.50	7.50
5, May 75, reprints FF Annual #5 and FF #15	0.50	1.50	4.50	7.50
6, Oct 75, reprints FF Annual #6;final issue	0.50	1.50	4.50	7.50

GIANT-SIZE HULK

	ORIG.	GOOD	FINE	N-MINT
1, reprint	0.50	1.60	4.80	8.00

GIANT-SIZE INVADERS

	ORIG.	GOOD	FINE	N-MINT
1, Jun 74, O&1:Invaders, rep. O:Sub-Mariner	0.50	1.20	3.60	6.00

GIANT-SIZE IRON MAN

	ORIG.	GOOD	FINE	N-MINT
1, reprint	0.50	0.40	1.20	2.00

GIANT-SIZE KID COLT

	ORIG.	GOOD	FINE	N-MINT
1	0.50	0.60	1.80	3.00
2	0.50	0.20	0.60	1.00
3	0.50	0.20	0.60	1.00

GIANT-SIZE MAN-THING

	ORIG.	GOOD	FINE	N-MINT
1, SD/JK	0.50	1.00	3.00	5.00
2	0.50	0.60	1.80	3.00
3	0.50	0.60	1.80	3.00
4, FB, 1:Howard the Duck	0.50	1.40	4.20	7.00
5, FB, Howard the Duck	0.50	1.00	3.00	5.00

GIANT-SIZE MARVEL TRIPLE ACTION

	ORIG.	GOOD	FINE	N-MINT
1, reprints	0.50	0.60	1.80	3.00
2, reprints	0.50	0.20	0.60	1.00

GIANT-SIZE MASTER OF KUNG FU

	ORIG.	GOOD	FINE	N-MINT
1, CR/PG	0.50	1.40	4.20	7.00
2	0.50	1.00	3.00	5.00
3	0.50	1.00	3.00	5.00
4, JK, Yellow Claw	0.50	1.20	3.60	6.00

GIANT-SIZE MINI COMICS
ECLIPSE

	GOOD	FINE	N-MINT
1, b&w	0.30	0.90	1.50
2, b&w	0.30	0.90	1.50
3, b&w	0.30	0.90	1.50
4, b&w	0.30	0.90	1.50

	ORIG.	GOOD	FINE	N-MINT

GIANT-SIZE POWER MAN
MARVEL

❑ 1 .... 0.50 1.20 3.60 6.00

GIANT-SIZE SPIDER-MAN

❑ 1, Jul 74, JR(c);RA; A:Dracula;reprints story from *Strange Tales Annual #2*
.... 0.50 3.60 10.80 18.00

❑ 2, Oct 74, GK/JR(c);RA; A:Shang-Chi;reprints story from *Amazing Spider-Man Annual #3*
.... 0.50 1.20 3.60 6.00

❑ 3, Jan 75, GK(c);RA; A:Doc Savage;also reprints story from *Amazing Spider-Man #16*
.... 0.50 1.20 3.60 6.00

❑ 4, Apr 75, GK(c);RA; A:Punisher
.... 0.50 12.00 36.00 60.00

❑ 5, Jul 75, GK(c);RA; V:Lizard;A:Man-Thing
.... 0.50 1.00 3.00 5.00

❑ 6, 75, reprints *Amazing Spider-Man Annual #4*
.... 0.50 1.00 3.00 5.00

GIANT-SIZE SUPER-HEROES FEATURING SPIDER-MAN

❑ 1, Jun 74, GK;SpM, Man-Wolf, Morbius
.... 0.35 8.00 24.00 40.00

GIANT-SIZE SUPER-STARS

❑ 1, May 74, RB;Fantastic 4, Hulk (becomes *Giant-Size Fantastic Four*) 0.35 2.00 6.00 10.00

GIANT-SIZE SUPER-VILLAIN TEAM-UP

❑ 1 .... 0.50 1.60 4.80 8.00

❑ 2, Dr. Doom, Sub-Mariner
.... 0.50 1.00 3.00 5.00

GIANT-SIZE THOR

❑ 1, GK, rep...................... 0.50 1.00 3.00 5.00

GIANT-SIZE WEREWOLF BY NIGHT
(was Giant-Size Creatures)

❑ 2, SD, Frankenstein rep.. 0.50 0.60 1.80 3.00
❑ 3, GK.............................. 0.50 0.40 1.20 2.00
❑ 4, GK.............................. 0.50 0.40 1.20 2.00
❑ 5, GK.............................. 0.50 0.40 1.20 2.00

GIANT-SIZE X-MEN

❑ 1, Mar 75, GK/DC 1&O: New X-Men
.... 0.50 70.00 210.00 350.00

❑ 2, Nov 75, GK/KJ rep. 0.50 4.00 12.00 20.00

GIDEON HAWK
BIG SHOT

❑ 2, Mar 95, b&w 2.00 0.40 1.20 2.00
❑ 3, Jun 95, b&w 2.00 0.40 1.20 2.00

GILGAMESH II (mini-series)
DC

❑ 1, 89, Starlin;O:Gilgamesh; prestige format
.... 3.95 0.79 2.37 3.95

❑ 2, 89, Starlin; prestige format
.... 3.95 0.79 2.37 3.95

❑ 3, 89, Starlin; prestige format
.... 3.95 0.79 2.37 3.95

❑ 4, 89, Starlin; prestige format
.... 3.95 0.79 2.37 3.95

GIN-RYU
BELIEVE IN YOURSELF

❑ 1, Mar 95 .... 2.75 0.55 1.65 2.75
❑ 2, May 95 .... 2.75 0.55 1.65 2.75

GINGER FOX
COMICO

❑ 1, Sep 88...................... 0.35 1.05 1.75
❑ 2, Oct 88 .... 0.35 1.05 1.75
❑ 3, Nov 88 .... 0.35 1.05 1.75
❑ 4, Dec 88...................... 0.35 1.05 1.75

GIRL, THE
RIP OFF

❑ 1, Feb 91, adult;b&w; first printing
.... 2.50 0.50 1.50 2.50

❑ 1, Oct 92, adult;b&w; second printing
.... 2.50 0.50 1.50 2.50

❑ 2, May 91, adult;b&w.... 2.50 0.50 1.50 2.50
❑ 3, Aug 91, adult;b&w.... 2.50 0.50 1.50 2.50
❑ 4, Dec 91, adult;b&w 2.50 0.50 1.50 2.50

GIRL: THE RULE OF DARKNESS
CRY FOR DAWN

❑ 1, adult, b&w 0.50 1.50 2.50

GIRLHERO
HIGH DRIVE

❑ 1, Aug 93, b&w............. 3.00 0.60 1.80 3.00
❑ 2, Feb 94, b&w 2.95 0.59 1.77 2.95
❑ 3, Jul 94, b&w 2.95 0.59 1.77 2.95

GIRLS OF NINJA HIGH SCHOOL
ANTARCTIC

❑ 1, 91, b&w...................... 0.75 2.25 3.75
❑ 2, 92, b&w...................... 0.75 2.25 3.75
❑ 3, 93, b&w.............. 3.95 0.79 2.37 3.95
❑ 4, Apr 94, b&w 3.95 0.79 2.37 3.95
❑ 5, Apr 95, 1995 Annual... 4.50 0.90 2.70 4.50

GIRLSQUAD X
FANTACO

❑ 1, b&w.................. 2.95 0.59 1.77 2.95

GIVE ME LIBERTY
DARK HORSE

❑ 1, Jun 90, FM(writer), DG
.... 4.95 2.00 6.00 10.00

❑ 2, Sep 90, FM(w), DG.... 4.95 1.60 4.80 8.00
❑ 3, Dec 90, FM(w), DG..... 4.95 1.60 4.80 8.00
❑ 4, Apr 91, FM(w), DG..... 4.95 1.60 4.80 8.00

GIZMO
CHANCE

❑ 1 .... 1.00 3.00 5.00

MIRAGE

❑ 1 .... 0.60 1.80 3.00
❑ 2 .... 0.30 0.90 1.50
❑ 3 .... 0.30 0.90 1.50
❑ 4 .... 0.30 0.90 1.50
❑ 5 .... 0.30 0.90 1.50
❑ 6 .... 0.30 0.90 1.50

GIZMO AND THE FUGITOID

❑ 1, b&w.............................. 0.35 1.05 1.75
❑ 2, b&w.............................. 0.35 1.05 1.75

GLOBAL FORCE
SILVERLINE

❑ 1, color 0.39 1.17 1.95

GLORY
IMAGE

❑ 0, Feb 96........................ 2.50 0.80 2.40 4.00
❑ 1, Mar 95........................ 2.50 0.50 1.50 2.50
❑ 1, Mar 95, alternate cover
.... 2.50 0.50 1.50 2.50

❑ 2, Apr 95........................ 2.50 0.50 1.50 2.50
❑ 3, May 95........................ 2.50 0.50 1.50 2.50
❑ 4, Jun 95 .... 2.50 0.50 1.50 2.50
❑ 5, Aug 95, polybagged with trading card
.... 2.50 0.50 1.50 2.50

❑ 6, Sep 95 .... 2.50 0.50 1.50 2.50
❑ 7, Oct 95........................ 2.50 0.50 1.50 2.50
❑ 8, Nov 95, "Babewatch" 2.50 0.50 1.50 2.50
❑ 9, Dec 95, "Extreme Destroyer" Part 5 of 9; polybagged with Glory card 2.50 0.50 1.50 2.50
❑ 10, Mar 96, A:Angela 2.50 0.50 1.50 2.50

	ORIG.	GOOD	FINE	N-MINT

GLORY & FRIENDS BIKINI FEST
	ORIG.	GOOD	FINE	N-MINT
1, Sep 95, pin-ups	2.50	0.50	1.50	2.50
1, Sep 95, pin-ups; alternate cover				
	2.50	0.50	1.50	2.50

GLORY & FRIENDS CHRISTMAS SPECIAL
	ORIG.	GOOD	FINE	N-MINT
1, Dec 95	2.50	0.50	1.50	2.50

GLORY & FRIENDS LINGERIE SPECIAL
	ORIG.	GOOD	FINE	N-MINT
1, Sep 95, pin-ups	2.95	0.59	1.77	2.95
1, Sep 95, pin-ups; alternate cover (photo)				
	2.95	0.59	1.77	2.95

GLORY/AVENGELYNE
	ORIG.	GOOD	FINE	N-MINT
1, Oct 95, wraparound enhanced cover;no title				
information on cover	3.95	0.79	2.37	3.95

GNATRAT: THE DARK GNAT RETURNS
PRELUDE
	ORIG.	GOOD	FINE	N-MINT
1		0.60	1.80	3.00

GNATRAT: THE MOVIE
INNOVATION
	ORIG.	GOOD	FINE	N-MINT
1, Batman parody, b&w		0.45	1.35	2.25

GO-GO BOY ASHCAN
MERMAID
	ORIG.	GOOD	FINE	N-MINT
0, b&w, no cover price				

GO-MAN!
CALIBER
	ORIG.	GOOD	FINE	N-MINT
1, b&w	2.50	0.50	1.50	2.50
2, b&w	2.50	0.50	1.50	2.50
3, b&w	2.50	0.50	1.50	2.50
4, b&w	2.50	0.50	1.50	2.50

GOBBLEDYGOOK
MIRAGE
	ORIG.	GOOD	FINE	N-MINT
1		1.20	3.60	6.00

GOBLIN MARKET
TOME PRESS
	ORIG.	GOOD	FINE	N-MINT
1, poem, b&w	2.50	0.50	1.50	2.50

GOD'S HAMMER
CALIBER
	ORIG.	GOOD	FINE	N-MINT
1, b&w	2.50	0.50	1.50	2.50
2, b&w	2.50	0.50	1.50	2.50
3, b&w	2.50	0.50	1.50	2.50

GODDESS
TWILIGHT TWINS
	ORIG.	GOOD	FINE	N-MINT
1, b&w, Zolastraya		0.40	1.20	2.00

GODDESS (mini-series)
DC/VERTIGO
	ORIG.	GOOD	FINE	N-MINT
1, Jun 95	2.95	0.80	2.40	4.00
2, Jul 95	2.95	0.59	1.77	2.95
3, Aug 95	2.95	0.59	1.77	2.95
4, Sep 95	2.95	0.59	1.77	2.95
4, Oct 95	2.95	0.59	1.77	2.95
6, Nov 95	2.95	0.59	1.77	2.95
7, Dec 95	2.95	0.59	1.77	2.95
8, Jan 96, final issue	2.95	0.59	1.77	2.95

GODS FOR HIRE
HOT
	ORIG.	GOOD	FINE	N-MINT
1, Dec 86		0.30	0.90	1.50
2, Jan 87		0.35	1.05	1.75

GODZILLA
MARVEL
	ORIG.	GOOD	FINE	N-MINT
1, Aug 77	0.30	1.50	4.50	7.50
2, Sep 77	0.30	1.00	3.00	5.00
3, Oct 77	0.30	0.70	2.10	3.50
4, Nov 77, V:Batragon	0.35	0.70	2.10	3.50
5, Dec 77	0.35	0.70	2.10	3.50
6, Jan 78	0.35	0.70	2.10	3.50
7, Feb 78, V:Red Ronin	0.35	0.70	2.10	3.50
8, Mar 78, V:Red Ronin	0.35	0.70	2.10	3.50
9, Apr 78	0.35	0.70	2.10	3.50
10, May 78	0.35	0.70	2.10	3.50

	ORIG.	GOOD	FINE	N-MINT
11, Jun 78	0.35	0.60	1.80	3.00
12, Jul 78	0.35	0.60	1.80	3.00
13, Aug 78	0.35	0.60	1.80	3.00
14, Sep 78	0.35	0.60	1.80	3.00
15, Oct 78	0.35	0.60	1.80	3.00
16, Nov 78	0.35	0.60	1.80	3.00
17, Dec 78, Godzilla shrunk by Henry Pym's gas				
	0.35	0.60	1.80	3.00
18, Jan 79	0.35	0.60	1.80	3.00
19, Feb 79	0.35	0.60	1.80	3.00
20, Mar 79	0.35	0.60	1.80	3.00
21, Apr 79	0.35	0.60	1.80	3.00
22, May 79	0.40	0.60	1.80	3.00
23, Jun 79	0.40	0.60	1.80	3.00
24, Jul 79, V:Avengers, Fantastic Four;A:SpM;				
final issue	0.40	0.60	1.80	3.00

GODZILLA (1995-)
DARK HORSE
	ORIG.	GOOD	FINE	N-MINT
0, May 95, reprints and expands story from *Dark Horse Comics* #10 and 11				
	2.50	0.50	1.50	2.50
1, Jun 95	2.50	0.50	1.50	2.50
2, Jul 95	2.50	0.50	1.50	2.50
3, Aug 95, V:Bagorah, the Bat Monster				
	2.50	0.50	1.50	2.50
4, Sep 95, V:Bagorah, the Bat Monster				
	2.50	0.50	1.50	2.50
5, Oct 95, "Target: Godzilla" Part 1				
	2.50	0.50	1.50	2.50
6, Nov 95, "Target: Godzilla" Part 2				
	2.50	0.50	1.50	2.50
7, Dec 95, "Target: Godzilla" Part 3				
	2.50	0.50	1.50	2.50
8, Jan 96, "Target: Godzilla" Part 4				
	2.50	0.50	1.50	2.50
9, Mar 96, "Lost in Time" Part 1				
	2.50	0.50	1.50	2.50
10, Apr 96, "Lost in Time" Part 2;Godzilla vs. Spanish Armada	2.50	0.50	1.50	2.50
11, May 96, Godzilla travels through time to sink the Titanic	2.50	0.50	1.50	2.50

GODZILLA (mini-series)
	ORIG.	GOOD	FINE	N-MINT
1, Jul 87, b&w manga movie adaptation				
		1.00	3.00	5.00
2, 88, b&w manga movie adaptation				
		0.60	1.80	3.00
3, 88, b&w manga movie adaptation				
		0.60	1.80	3.00
4, 88, b&w manga movie adaptation				
		0.60	1.80	3.00
5, 88, b&w manga movie adaptation				
		0.60	1.80	3.00
6, 88, b&w manga movie adaptation				
		0.60	1.80	3.00

GODZILLA COLOR SPECIAL
	ORIG.	GOOD	FINE	N-MINT
1, 92		0.70	2.10	3.50

GODZILLA VERSUS HERO ZERO
	ORIG.	GOOD	FINE	N-MINT
1, Jul 95	2.50	0.50	1.50	2.50

GODZILLA VS. BARKLEY
	ORIG.	GOOD	FINE	N-MINT
0, 93, nn	2.95	0.59	1.77	2.95

GODZILLA, KING OF THE MONSTERS SPECIAL
	ORIG.	GOOD	FINE	N-MINT
1, Aug 87		0.30	0.90	1.50
1, misprinted cover; fewer than 100				
		5.00	15.00	25.00

GOJIN
ANTARCTIC
	ORIG.	GOOD	FINE	N-MINT
1, Apr 95	3.50	0.70	2.10	3.50
2, Jun 95	2.95	0.59	1.77	2.95

	ORIG.	GOOD	FINE	N-MINT

	ORIG.	GOOD	FINE	N-MINT

☐ 3, Aug 95 .... 2.95 | 0.59 | 1.77 | 2.95
☐ 3, Aug 95, alternate cover
.... 2.95 | 0.59 | 1.77 | 2.95

GOLD DIGGER (Volume 1)

☐ 1, Sep 92, b&w .... 2.50 | 0.50 | 1.50 | 2.50
☐ 2, Nov 92, b&w .... 2.50 | 0.50 | 1.50 | 2.50
☐ 3, Jan 93, b&w .... 2.50 | 0.50 | 1.50 | 2.50
☐ 4, Mar 93, b&w .... 2.50 | 0.50 | 1.50 | 2.50

GOLD DIGGER (Volume 2, 1993-)

☐ 1, Jul 93, b&w .... 2.50 | 0.50 | 1.50 | 2.50
☐ 2, Aug 93, b&w .... 2.50 | 0.50 | 1.50 | 2.50
☐ 3, Sep 93, b&w .... 2.50 | 0.50 | 1.50 | 2.50
☐ 4, Oct 93, b&w .... 2.75 | 0.55 | 1.65 | 2.75
☐ 5, Nov 93, b&w;(has "issue #0" on cover. Production
mistake.) .... 2.75 | 0.55 | 1.65 | 2.75
☐ 6, Dec 93, b&w .... 2.75 | 0.55 | 1.65 | 2.75
☐ 7, Jan 94, b&w .... 2.75 | 0.55 | 1.65 | 2.75
☐ 8, Feb 94, b&w .... 2.75 | 0.55 | 1.65 | 2.75
☐ 9, Mar 94, b&w .... 2.75 | 0.55 | 1.65 | 2.75
☐ 10, Apr 94, b&w .... 2.75 | 0.55 | 1.65 | 2.75
☐ 11, May 94, b&w .... 2.75 | 0.55 | 1.65 | 2.75
☐ 12, Jun 94, b&w .... 2.75 | 0.55 | 1.65 | 2.75
☐ 13, Jul 94, b&w .... 2.75 | 0.55 | 1.65 | 2.75
☐ 14, Aug 94, b&w .... 2.75 | 0.55 | 1.65 | 2.75
☐ 15, Sep 94, b&w .... 2.75 | 0.55 | 1.65 | 2.75
☐ 16, Oct 94, b&w .... 2.75 | 0.55 | 1.65 | 2.75
☐ 17, Nov 94, b&w .... 2.75 | 0.55 | 1.65 | 2.75
☐ 18, Dec 94, b&w .... 2.75 | 0.55 | 1.65 | 2.75
☐ 19, Feb 95, b&w .... 2.75 | 0.55 | 1.65 | 2.75
☐ 20, Apr 95, b&w .... 2.75 | 0.55 | 1.65 | 2.75
☐ 21, May 95, b&w .... 2.75 | 0.55 | 1.65 | 2.75
☐ 22, Jun 95, b&w .... 2.75 | 0.55 | 1.65 | 2.75
☐ 23, Jul 95, b&w .... 2.75 | 0.55 | 1.65 | 2.75
☐ 24, Aug 95, b&w .... 2.75 | 0.55 | 1.65 | 2.75
☐ 25, Oct 95, b&w .... 2.75 | 0.55 | 1.65 | 2.75

GOLD DIGGER ANNUAL

☐ 1, Sep 95 .... 3.95 | 0.79 | 2.37 | 3.95

GOLD DIGGER MANGAZINE SPECIAL

☐ 1, Mar 94 .... 2.75 | 0.55 | 1.65 | 2.75

GOLDEN AGE, THE (mini-series)
DC

☐ 1, 93, Elseworlds; prestige format
.... 4.95 | 3.20 | 9.60 | 16.00
☐ 2, 93, Elseworlds; prestige format;O:Dynaman
.... 4.95 | 2.00 | 6.00 | 10.00
☐ 3, Elseworlds; prestige format
.... 4.95 | 1.60 | 4.80 | 8.00
☐ 4, 94, Elseworlds;prestige format;D:Dynaman,
Ultra-Humanite,Miss America,Doll Man, Hawkman,etc.
.... 4.95 | 1.60 | 4.80 | 8.00

GOLDEN DRAGON
SYNCHRONICITY

☐ 1 .... | | 0.30 | 0.90 | 1.50

GOLDEN WARRIOR ICZER ONE
ANTARCTIC

☐ 1, Apr 94, b&w .... 2.95 | 0.59 | 1.77 | 2.95
☐ 2, May 94, b&w .... 2.95 | 0.59 | 1.77 | 2.95
☐ 3, Jun 94, b&w .... 2.95 | 0.59 | 1.77 | 2.95
☐ 4, Jul 94, b&w .... 2.95 | 0.59 | 1.77 | 2.95
☐ 5, Aug 94, b&w; final issue
.... 2.95 | 0.59 | 1.77 | 2.95

GOLDYN 3-D
BLACKTHORNE

☐ 1 .... | | 0.40 | 1.20 | 2.00

GONAD THE BARBARIAN
ETERNITY

☐ 1 .... | | 0.39 | 1.17 | 1.95

GOOD GIRL ART QUARTERLY
AC

☐ 1, Jul 90, new & reprints .. | | 0.70 | 2.10 | 3.50
☐ 2, Oct 90, Fall '90 .... | | 0.79 | 2.37 | 3.95
☐ 3, Jan 91, Win '91 .... | | 0.79 | 2.37 | 3.95
☐ 4, Apr 91, Spr '91 .... | | 0.79 | 2.37 | 3.95
☐ 5, Aug 91, Sum '91 .... | | 0.79 | 2.37 | 3.95
☐ 6, Nov 91, Fall '91 .... | | 0.79 | 2.37 | 3.95
☐ 7, Win '92 .... 3.95 | 0.79 | 2.37 | 3.95
☐ 8, Spr '92 .... 3.95 | 0.79 | 2.37 | 3.95
☐ 9, Sum '92 .... 3.95 | 0.79 | 2.37 | 3.95
☐ 10, Fall '92 .... 3.95 | 0.79 | 2.37 | 3.95
☐ 11, Win '93 .... 3.95 | 0.79 | 2.37 | 3.95
☐ 12, Spr '93 .... 3.95 | 0.79 | 2.37 | 3.95
☐ 13, Sum '93 .... 3.95 | 0.79 | 2.37 | 3.95
☐ 14, Fall '93 .... 3.95 | 0.79 | 2.37 | 3.95
☐ 15, Win '94 .... 3.95 | 0.79 | 2.37 | 3.95
☐ 16 .... 3.95 | 0.79 | 2.37 | 3.95
☐ 17 .... 3.95 | 0.79 | 2.37 | 3.95
☐ 18 .... 3.95 | 0.79 | 2.37 | 3.95

GOOD GIRLS
FANTAGRAPHICS

☐ 1, b&w .... 2.00 | 0.40 | 1.20 | 2.00
☐ 2 .... | | 0.40 | 1.20 | 2.00
☐ 3 .... | | 0.40 | 1.20 | 2.00
☐ 4 .... | | 0.40 | 1.20 | 2.00

GOOD GIRLS (was Fantagraphics)
RIP OFF

☐ 6, Jun 91, b&w .... 2.00 | 0.40 | 1.20 | 2.00

GOOD GUYS, THE
DEFIANT

☐ 1, Nov 93, O:Good Guys .3.50 | 0.70 | 2.10 | 3.50
☐ 2 .... 2.50 | 0.50 | 1.50 | 2.50
☐ 3, Jan 94 .... 2.50 | 0.50 | 1.50 | 2.50
☐ 4, Feb 94 .... 3.25 | 0.65 | 1.95 | 3.25
☐ 5 .... 2.50 | 0.50 | 1.50 | 2.50
☐ 6, Apr 94 .... 2.50 | 0.50 | 1.50 | 2.50

GOOFY ADVENTURES
DISNEY

☐ 1 .... | | 0.30 | 0.90 | 1.50
☐ 2 .... | | 0.30 | 0.90 | 1.50
☐ 3 .... | | 0.30 | 0.90 | 1.50
☐ 4 .... | | 0.30 | 0.90 | 1.50
☐ 5 .... | | 0.30 | 0.90 | 1.50
☐ 6 .... | | 0.30 | 0.90 | 1.50
☐ 7, Three Musketeers .... 1.50 | 0.30 | 0.90 | 1.50
☐ 8 .... | | 0.30 | 0.90 | 1.50
☐ 9, James Bond parody ...... | | 0.30 | 0.90 | 1.50
☐ 10 .... | | 0.30 | 0.90 | 1.50
☐ 11 .... | | 0.30 | 0.90 | 1.50
☐ 12 .... | | 0.30 | 0.90 | 1.50
☐ 13 .... | | 0.30 | 0.90 | 1.50
☐ 14 .... | | 0.30 | 0.90 | 1.50
☐ 15 .... | | 0.30 | 0.90 | 1.50
☐ 16, Sherlock Holmes parody
.... 1.50 | 0.30 | 0.90 | 1.50
☐ 17 .... | | 0.30 | 0.90 | 1.50

GORE SHRIEK
FANTACO

☐ 1, 86, b&w;1st Greg Capullo story
.... 1.50 | 0.30 | 0.90 | 1.50
☐ 2, b&w;Greg Capullo .... 1.50 | 0.30 | 0.90 | 1.50
☐ 3, b&w;Greg Capullo .... | | 0.59 | 1.77 | 2.95
☐ 4, b&w;Greg Capullo(c) .... | | | |
☐ 5 .... | | 0.70 | 2.10 | 3.50
☐ 6 .... | | 0.70 | 2.10 | 3.50
☐ 6, 1/2 .... 2.50 | 0.50 | 1.50 | 2.50

GORE SHRIEK (Volume 2)

☐ 1, b&w .... | | 0.50 | 1.50 | 2.50
☐ 2, b&w .... | | 0.50 | 1.50 | 2.50

	ORIG.	GOOD	FINE	N-MINT
☐ 3, b&w		0.50	1.50	2.50
☐ 2, 90, 1/2	1.50	0.30	0.90	1.50

GORE SHRIEK ANNUAL
☐ 1, b&w		0.99	2.97	4.95

GORE SHRIEK DELECTUS
☐ 0, nn	8.95	1.79	5.37	8.95

GORGANA'S GHOUL GALLERY
AC
☐ 1, b&w	2.95	0.59	1.77	2.95
☐ 2, 94	2.95	0.59	1.77	2.95

GOTCHA!
RIP OFF
☐ 1, Sep 91, adult, b&w	2.50	0.50	1.50	2.50

GOTHAM BY GASLIGHT: AN ALTERNATIVE HISTORY OF THE BATMAN
DC
☐ 0, 89, prestige format one-shot;first Elseworlds story;Victorian-era Batman;MMi;CR

	3.95	0.79	2.37	3.95

GOTHIC NIGHTS (mini-series)
REBEL
☐ 1, 95, b&w	2.00	0.40	1.20	2.00

GRAFIK MUZIK
(was Slave Labor as Graphique Musique)
CALIBER
☐ 1, b&w;Mike Allred	3.50	0.70	2.10	3.50
☐ 2, Mike Allred	2.50	0.50	1.50	2.50
☐ 3, Mike Allred	2.50	0.50	1.50	2.50
☐ 4, Mike Allred	2.50	0.50	1.50	2.50

GRAMMAR PATROL, THE
CASTEL PUBLICATIONS
☐ 1, 93	2.00	0.40	1.20	2.00

GRAPHIC
FANTACO
☐ 1	3.95	0.79	2.37	3.95

GRAPHIC HEROES IN HOUSE OF CARDS
GRAPHIC STAFFING
☐ 0, 95, nn;personalized promotional piece for temporary graphics employees ....

GRAPHIC STORY MONTHLY
FANTAGRAPHICS
☐ 1, b&w		0.59	1.77	2.95
☐ 2, b&w		0.59	1.77	2.95
☐ 3, b&w		0.59	1.77	2.95
☐ 4, b&w		0.59	1.77	2.95
☐ 5, b&w		0.59	1.77	2.95
☐ 6, b&w		0.59	1.77	2.95
☐ 7		0.70	2.10	3.50

GRAPHIQUE MUSIQUE
SLAVE LABOR
☐ 1		0.59	1.77	2.95
☐ 2		0.59	1.77	2.95
☐ 3, b&w (moves to Caliber as *Grafik Muzik*)				
		0.59	1.77	2.95

GRASS GREEN'S WILDMAN
MEGATON
☐ 1		0.30	0.90	1.50
☐ 2		0.30	0.90	1.50

GRATEFUL DEAD (Volume 2)
KITCHEN SINK
☐ 1, comic-book size	3.95	0.79	2.37	3.95

GRATEFUL DEAD COMIX
☐ 1, color		2.00	6.00	10.00
☐ 2, color		1.60	4.80	8.00
☐ 3, color		1.20	3.60	6.00
☐ 4, color		1.20	3.60	6.00
☐ 5, color		1.20	3.60	6.00
☐ 6, color		1.20	3.60	6.00
☐ 7, color		1.20	3.60	6.00

GRATEFUL DEAD COMIX (Volume 2)
☐ 2, Apr 94	3.95	0.79	2.37	3.95

GRAVE TALES
HAMILTON
☐ 1, Oct 91, b&w	3.95	0.79	2.37	3.95
☐ 2, b&w		0.79	2.37	3.95
☐ 3, b&w		0.79	2.37	3.95

GRAVESTONE
MALIBU
☐ 1	2.25	0.45	1.35	2.25
☐ 2	2.25	0.45	1.35	2.25
☐ 3, Genesis	2.25	0.45	1.35	2.25
☐ 4	2.25	0.45	1.35	2.25
☐ 5, Genesis	2.25	0.45	1.35	2.25
☐ 6, Genesis	2.25	0.45	1.35	2.25
☐ 7, Feb 94, Genesis, last issue				
	2.25	0.45	1.35	2.25

GRAY MORROW'S PRIVATE COMMISSIONS
FORBIDDEN FRUIT
☐ 1, adult, b&w		0.59	1.77	2.95
☐ 2, adult, b&w		0.59	1.77	2.95

GREAT AMERICAN WESTERN PRESENTS SUNSET CARSON
AC
☐ 1, DAy		1.00	3.00	5.00

GREAT AMERICAN WESTERN, THE
☐ 1		0.35	1.05	1.75
☐ 2		0.59	1.77	2.95
☐ 3		0.59	1.77	2.95
☐ 4		0.70	2.10	3.50

GREAT GALAXIES!
ZUB
☐ 0, 94, b&w	2.95	0.59	1.77	2.95
☐ 1, 94, b&w	2.50	0.50	1.50	2.50
☐ 2, 94, b&w	2.50	0.50	1.50	2.50
☐ 3, 94, b&w	2.50	0.50	1.50	2.50

GREAT MORONS IN HISTORY
REVOLUTIONARY
☐ 1, Oct 93, b&w, Dan Quayle				
	2.50	0.50	1.50	2.50

GREATEST AMERICAN COMIC BOOK
OCEAN
☐ 1, parody: Batman, SpM		0.51	1.53	2.55

GREATEST DIGGS OF ALL TIME!
RIP OFF
☐ 0, Feb 91, nn;b&w	2.00	0.40	1.20	2.00

GREEENLOCK
AIRCEL
☐ 1, b&w		0.50	1.50	2.50

GREEN ARROW
DC
☐ 0, Oct 94	1.95	0.50	1.50	2.50
☐ 1, Feb 88, MGr(c)	1.00	1.20	3.60	6.00
☐ 2, Mar 88, MGr(c)	1.00	0.80	2.40	4.00
☐ 3, Apr 88, MGr(c)	1.00	0.60	1.80	3.00
☐ 4, May 88, MGr(c)	1.00	0.60	1.80	3.00
☐ 5, Jun 88	1.00	0.40	1.20	2.00
☐ 6, Jul 88	1.00	0.40	1.20	2.00
☐ 7, Aug 88	1.00	0.40	1.20	2.00
☐ 8, Sep 88	1.00	0.40	1.20	2.00
☐ 9, Oct 88	1.00	0.40	1.20	2.00
☐ 10, Nov 88, MGr(c)	1.00	0.40	1.20	2.00
☐ 11, Dec 88, MGr(c)	1.00	0.40	1.20	2.00
☐ 12, Dec 88, MGr(c)	1.00	0.40	1.20	2.00
☐ 13, Jan 89	1.25	0.40	1.20	2.00
☐ 14, Jan 89	1.25	0.40	1.20	2.00
☐ 15, Feb 89	1.25	0.40	1.20	2.00
☐ 16, Mar 89	1.25	0.40	1.20	2.00
☐ 17, Apr 89	1.25	0.40	1.20	2.00

	ORIG.	GOOD	FINE	N-MINT
18, May 89	1.25	0.40	1.20	2.00
19, Jun 89	1.25	0.40	1.20	2.00
20, Jul 89	1.25	0.40	1.20	2.00
21, Aug 89	1.25	0.40	1.20	2.00
22, Aug 89	1.25	0.40	1.20	2.00
23, Sep 89	1.25	0.40	1.20	2.00
24, Sep 89	1.25	0.40	1.20	2.00
25, Oct 89	1.25	0.40	1.20	2.00
26, Nov 89	1.25	0.40	1.20	2.00
27, Dec 89	1.25	0.40	1.20	2.00
28, Jan 90	1.25	0.40	1.20	2.00
29, Feb 90	1.25	0.40	1.20	2.00
30, Mar 90	1.20	0.25	0.75	1.25
31, Apr 90	1.20	0.25	0.75	1.25
32, May 90	1.20	0.25	0.75	1.25
33, Jun 90	1.20	0.25	0.75	1.25
34, Jul 90	1.20	0.25	0.75	1.25
35, Aug 90, Black Arrow	1.25	0.25	0.75	1.25
36, Sep 90, Black Arrow	1.25	0.25	0.75	1.25
37, Sep 90, Black Arrow	1.25	0.25	0.75	1.25
38, Oct 90, Black Arrow	1.25	0.25	0.75	1.25
39, Nov 90	1.25	0.25	0.75	1.25
40, Dec 90	1.25	0.25	0.75	1.25
41, Dec 90	1.25	0.25	0.75	1.25
42, Jan 91	1.25	0.25	0.75	1.25
43, Feb 91	1.25	0.25	0.75	1.25
44, Mar 91	1.25	0.25	0.75	1.25
45, Apr 91	1.25	0.25	0.75	1.25
46, May 91	1.25	0.25	0.75	1.25
47, Jun 91	1.50	0.25	0.75	1.25
48, Jun 91	1.50	0.30	0.90	1.50
49, Jul 91	1.50	0.30	0.90	1.50
50, Aug 91	2.50	0.50	1.50	2.50
51, Aug 91	1.50	0.30	0.90	1.50
52, Sep 91	1.50	0.30	0.90	1.50
53, Oct 91	1.50	0.30	0.90	1.50
54, Nov 91	1.50	0.30	0.90	1.50
55, Dec 91	1.50	0.30	0.90	1.50
56, Jan 92	1.50	0.30	0.90	1.50
57, Feb 92	1.25	0.30	0.90	1.50
58, Mar 92	1.25	0.30	0.90	1.50
59, Apr 92	1.25	0.30	0.90	1.50
60, May 92	1.25	0.30	0.90	1.50
61, May 92	1.50	0.30	0.90	1.50
62, Jun 92	1.50	0.30	0.90	1.50
63, Jun 92	1.50	0.30	0.90	1.50
64, Jul 92	1.50	0.30	0.90	1.50
65, Aug 92	1.50	0.30	0.90	1.50
66, Sep 92	1.50	0.30	0.90	1.50
67, Oct 92	1.50	0.30	0.90	1.50
68, Nov 92	1.50	0.30	0.90	1.50
69, Dec 92	1.75	0.35	1.05	1.75
70, Jan 93	1.75	0.35	1.05	1.75
71, Feb 93	1.75	0.35	1.05	1.75
72, Mar 93	1.75	0.35	1.05	1.75
73, Apr 93	1.75	0.35	1.05	1.75
74, May 93	1.75	0.35	1.05	1.75
75, Jun 93	2.50	0.50	1.50	2.50
76, Jul 93	1.75	0.35	1.05	1.75
77, Aug 93	1.75	0.35	1.05	1.75
78, Sep 93	1.75	0.35	1.05	1.75
79, Oct 93	1.75	0.35	1.05	1.75
80, Nov 93	1.75	0.35	1.05	1.75
81, Dec 93	1.75	0.35	1.05	1.75
82, Jan 94	1.75	0.35	1.05	1.75
83, Feb 94	1.75	0.35	1.05	1.75
84, Mar 94	1.75	0.35	1.05	1.75
85, Apr 94	1.75	0.35	1.05	1.75
86, May 94, Catwoman	1.75	0.35	1.05	1.75
87, Jun 94	1.75	0.35	1.05	1.75
88, Jul 94	1.95	0.39	1.17	1.95
89, Aug 94	1.95	0.39	1.17	1.95

	ORIG.	GOOD	FINE	N-MINT
90, Sep 94	1.95	0.39	1.17	1.95
91, Nov 94	1.95	0.39	1.17	1.95
92, Dec 94	1.95	0.39	1.17	1.95
93, Jan 95	1.95	0.39	1.17	1.95
94, Feb 95	1.95	0.39	1.17	1.95
95, Mar 95	1.95	0.39	1.17	1.95
96, Apr 95, "Where Angels Fear to Tread" Part 1 of 5	1.95	0.39	1.17	1.95
97, Jun 95, "Where Angels Fear to Tread" Part 2 of 5	2.25	0.45	1.35	2.25
98, Jul 95, "Where Angels Fear to Tread" Part 3 of 5	2.25	0.45	1.35	2.25
99, Aug 95, "Where Angels Fear to Tread" Part 4 of 5	2.25	0.45	1.35	2.25
100, Sep 95, "Where Angels Fear to Tread" Part 5 of 5; enhanced cover	3.95	0.79	2.37	3.95
101, Oct 95, D:Oliver Queen	2.25	0.45	1.35	2.25
102, Nov 95	2.25	0.45	1.35	2.25
103, Dec 95	2.25	0.45	1.35	2.25
104, Jan 96	2.25	0.45	1.35	2.25
105, Feb 96	2.25	0.45	1.35	2.25
106, Mar 96	2.25	0.45	1.35	2.25
107, Apr 96	2.25	0.45	1.35	2.25
108, May 96, A:Thorn	2.25	0.45	1.35	2.25
109, Jun 96	2.25	0.45	1.35	2.25

GREEN ARROW (mini-series)

	ORIG.	GOOD	FINE	N-MINT
1, May 83, DG	0.60	0.40	1.20	2.00
2, Jun 83, DG	0.60	0.30	0.90	1.50
3, Jul 83, DG	0.60	0.30	0.90	1.50
4, Aug 83, DG	0.60	0.30	0.90	1.50

GREEN ARROW ANNUAL

	ORIG.	GOOD	FINE	N-MINT
1, Sep 88, A:Batman	2.00	0.40	1.20	2.00
2, Aug 89, A:Question	2.50	0.50	1.50	2.50
3, Dec 90, A:Question	2.50	0.50	1.50	2.50
4, Jun 91, Robin Hood; 50th Anniversary	2.95	0.59	1.77	2.95
5, 92, Eclipso, Batman	3.00	0.60	1.80	3.00
6, Bloodlines	3.50	0.70	2.10	3.50
7, 95, "Year One"	3.95	0.79	2.37	3.95

GREEN ARROW: THE LONGBOW HUNTERS

	ORIG.	GOOD	FINE	N-MINT
1, Aug 87, MGr; prestige format	2.95	3.00	9.00	15.00
1, (2nd printing)		2.00	6.00	10.00
2, Sep 87, prestige format	2.95	2.00	6.00	10.00
3, Oct 87, MGr; prestige format	2.95	1.60	4.80	8.00

GREEN ARROW: THE WONDER YEAR

	ORIG.	GOOD	FINE	N-MINT
1, Feb 93	1.75	0.25	0.75	1.25
2, Mar 93	1.75	0.25	0.75	1.25
3, Apr 93	1.75	0.35	1.05	1.75
4, May 93	1.75	0.35	1.05	1.75

GREEN CANDLES (mini-series)
DC/PARADOX

	ORIG.	GOOD	FINE	N-MINT
1, 95, digest	5.95	1.19	3.57	5.95
3, 95	5.95	1.19	3.57	5.95

GREEN GOBLIN
MARVEL

	ORIG.	GOOD	FINE	N-MINT
1, Oct 95, enhanced cardstock cover	2.95	0.59	1.77	2.95
2, Nov 95, V:Rhino	1.95	0.39	1.17	1.95
3, Dec 95, V:Scarlet Spider	1.95	0.39	1.17	1.95
4, Jan 96	1.95	0.39	1.17	1.95
5, Feb 96	1.95	0.39	1.17	1.95
6, Mar 96, A:Daredevil	1.95	0.39	1.17	1.95
7, Apr 96	1.95	0.39	1.17	1.95
8, May 96	1.95	0.39	1.17	1.95
10, Jul 96	1.95	0.39	1.17	1.95

	ORIG.	GOOD	FINE	N-MINT

GREEN HORNET
NOW

	ORIG.	GOOD	FINE	N-MINT
❏ 1, Nov 89, JSo(c) O:Green Hornet I				
............2.95		2.00	6.00	10.00
❏ 1, Apr 90, reprint, perfect bound				
............3.95		0.79	2.37	3.95
❏ 2, Dec 89............1.75		1.40	4.20	7.00
❏ 3, Jan 90............1.75		0.70	2.10	3.50
❏ 4, Feb 90, SR(c)............1.75		0.70	2.10	3.50
❏ 5, Mar 90 ....1.75		0.70	2.10	3.50
❏ 6, Apr 90 ....1.75		0.70	2.10	3.50
❏ 7, May 90, BSz(c) 1:new Kato				
............1.75		0.60	1.80	3.00
❏ 8, Jun 90............1.75		0.35	1.05	1.75
❏ 9, Jul 90............1.75		0.35	1.05	1.75
❏ 10, Aug 90............1.75		0.35	1.05	1.75
❏ 11, Sep 90............1.75		0.35	1.05	1.75
❏ 12, Oct 90............1.75		0.35	1.05	1.75
❏ 13, Nov 90 ....1.75		0.35	1.05	1.75
❏ 14, Feb 91 ....1.75		0.35	1.05	1.75

GREEN HORNET (Volume 2, ongoing)

	ORIG.	GOOD	FINE	N-MINT
❏ 1, Sep 91............1.95		0.39	1.17	1.95
❏ 2, Oct 91............1.95		0.39	1.17	1.95
❏ 3, Nov 91............1.95		0.39	1.17	1.95
❏ 4, Dec 91............1.95		0.39	1.17	1.95
❏ 5, Jan 92............1.95		0.39	1.17	1.95
❏ 6, Feb 92............1.95		0.39	1.17	1.95
❏ 7, Mar 92............1.95		0.39	1.17	1.95
❏ 8, Apr 92............1.95		0.39	1.17	1.95
❏ 9, May 92............1.95		0.39	1.17	1.95
❏ 10, Jun 92............1.95		0.39	1.17	1.95
❏ 11, Jul 92............1.95		0.39	1.17	1.95
❏ 12, Aug 92, bagged, with button				
............2.50		0.50	1.50	2.50
❏ 13, Sep 92............1.95		0.39	1.17	1.95
❏ 14, Oct 92............1.95		0.39	1.17	1.95
❏ 15, Nov 92............1.95		0.39	1.17	1.95
❏ 16, Dec 92............1.95		0.39	1.17	1.95
❏ 17, Jan 93............1.95		0.39	1.17	1.95
❏ 18, Feb 93............1.95		0.39	1.17	1.95
❏ 19, Mar 93............1.95		0.39	1.17	1.95
❏ 20, Apr 93............1.95		0.39	1.17	1.95
❏ 21, May 93............1.95		0.39	1.17	1.95
❏ 22, Jun 93, newsstand, trading card				
............2.95		0.59	1.77	2.95
❏ 22, Jun 93, direct sale, trading card				
............2.95		0.59	1.77	2.95
❏ 23, Jul 93, hologram trading card				
............2.95		0.59	1.77	2.95
❏ 24, Aug 93 ....1.95		0.59	1.17	1.95
❏ 25, Sep 93............1.95		0.59	1.77	2.95
❏ 26, Oct 93............2.95		0.59	1.77	2.95
❏ 27, Nov 93, trading card 2.95		0.59	1.77	2.95
❏ 28, Dec 93............1.95		0.39	1.17	1.95
❏ 29, Jan 94 ....1.95		0.39	1.17	1.95

GREEN HORNET 1992 ANNUAL

	ORIG.	GOOD	FINE	N-MINT
❏ 1, Dec 92............2.50		0.50	1.50	2.50

GREEN HORNET ANNIVERSARY SPECIAL

	ORIG.	GOOD	FINE	N-MINT
❏ 1, bagged, with button		0.50	1.50	2.50
❏ 2		0.39	1.17	1.95
❏ 3		0.39	1.17	1.95

GREEN HORNET: DARK TOMORROW (mini-series)

	ORIG.	GOOD	FINE	N-MINT
❏ 1, Jun 93............2.50		0.50	1.50	2.50
❏ 2, Jul 93............2.50		0.50	1.50	2.50
❏ 3, Aug 93 ....2.50		0.50	1.50	2.50

GREEN HORNET: SOLITARY SENTINEL
(mini-series)

	ORIG.	GOOD	FINE	N-MINT
❏ 1, Dec 92............2.50		0.50	1.50	2.50
❏ 2, Jan 93............2.50		0.50	1.50	2.50
❏ 3, Feb 93............2.50		0.50	1.50	2.50

GREEN LANTERN
DC

	ORIG.	GOOD	FINE	N-MINT
❏ 1, Aug 60, GK; O:Green Lantern				
....		550.00	1650.00	2750.00
❏ 2, Oct 60, GK;1:Pieface 0.10		140.00	420.00	700.00
❏ 3, Dec 60, GK............0.10		80.00	240.00	400.00
❏ 4, Feb 61, GK............0.10		60.00	180.00	300.00
❏ 5, Apr 61, GK............0.10		60.00	180.00	300.00
❏ 6, Jun 61, GK............0.10		48.00	144.00	240.00
❏ 7, Aug 61, GK............0.10		40.00	120.00	200.00
❏ 8, Oct 61, GK............0.10		35.00	105.00	175.00
❏ 9, Dec 61, GK............0.10		35.00	105.00	175.00
❏ 10, Jan 62, GK............0.12		35.00	105.00	175.00
❏ 11, Mar 62, GK 0.12		35.00	105.00	175.00
❏ 12, Apr 62, GK............0.12		35.00	105.00	175.00
❏ 13, Jun 62, GK;Flash......0.12		48.00	144.00	240.00
❏ 14, Jul 62, GK............0.12		25.00	75.00	125.00
❏ 15, Sep 62, GK............0.12		25.00	75.00	125.00
❏ 16, Oct 62, GK; O:Star Sapphire				
............0.12		28.00	84.00	140.00
❏ 17, Dec 62, GK............0.12		22.00	66.00	110.00
❏ 18, Jan 63, GK............0.12		22.00	66.00	110.00
❏ 19, Mar 63, GK............0.12		22.00	66.00	110.00
❏ 20, Apr 63, GK............0.12		28.00	84.00	140.00
❏ 21, Jun 63, GK; O:Dr. Polaris				
............0.12		20.00	60.00	100.00
❏ 22, Jul 63, GK............0.12		20.00	60.00	100.00
❏ 23, Sep 63, GK............0.12		20.00	60.00	100.00
❏ 24, Oct 63, GK............0.12		20.00	60.00	100.00
❏ 25, Dec 63, GK............0.12		20.00	60.00	100.00
❏ 26, Jan 64, GK............0.12		20.00	60.00	100.00
❏ 27, Mar 64, GK............0.12		20.00	60.00	100.00
❏ 28, Apr 64, GK............0.12		20.00	60.00	100.00
❏ 29, Jun 64, GK, 1:Black Hand				
............0.12		20.00	60.00	100.00
❏ 30, Jul 64, GK............0.12		20.00	60.00	100.00
❏ 31, Sep 64, GK............0.12		15.00	45.00	75.00
❏ 32, Oct 64, GK............0.12		15.00	45.00	75.00
❏ 33, Dec 64, GK............0.12		15.00	45.00	75.00
❏ 34, Jan 65, GK............0.12		15.00	45.00	75.00
❏ 35, Mar 65, GK 0.12		15.00	45.00	75.00
❏ 36, Apr 65, GK 0.12		15.00	45.00	75.00
❏ 37, Jun 65, GK............0.12		15.00	45.00	75.00
❏ 38, Jul 65, GK............0.12		15.00	45.00	75.00
❏ 39, Sep 65, GK............0.12		15.00	45.00	75.00
❏ 40, Oct 65, O:Guardians .0.12		60.00	180.00	300.00
❏ 41, Dec 65, GK, A:Star Sapphire				
............0.12		7.20	21.60	36.00
❏ 42, Jan 66, GK............0.12		7.20	21.60	36.00
❏ 43, Mar 66, GK............0.12		7.20	21.60	36.00
❏ 44, Apr 66, GK............0.12		7.20	21.60	36.00
❏ 45, Jun 66, GK, I:Prince Peril				
............0.12		9.60	28.80	48.00
❏ 46, Jul 66, GK............0.12		7.20	21.60	36.00
❏ 47, Sep 66, GK............0.12		7.20	21.60	36.00
❏ 48, Oct 66, GK............0.12		7.20	21.60	36.00
❏ 49, Dec 66, GK............0.12		7.20	21.60	36.00
❏ 50, Jan 67, GK............0.12		7.20	21.60	36.00
❏ 51, Mar 67............0.12		5.00	15.00	25.00
❏ 52, Apr 67............0.12		5.00	15.00	25.00
❏ 53, Jun 67............0.12		5.00	15.00	25.00
❏ 54, Jul 67............0.12		5.00	15.00	25.00
❏ 55, Sep 67 ....0.12		5.00	15.00	25.00
❏ 56, Oct 67 ....0.12		5.00	15.00	25.00
❏ 57, Dec 67 ....0.12		5.00	15.00	25.00
❏ 58, Jan 68............0.12		5.00	15.00	25.00
❏ 59, Mar 68, 1:Guy Gardner				
............0.12		32.00	96.00	160.00
❏ 60, Apr 68............0.12		3.20	9.60	16.00
❏ 61, Jun 68............0.12		3.20	9.60	16.00
❏ 62, Jul 68............0.12		3.20	9.60	16.00
❏ 63, Sep 68 ....0.12		3.20	9.60	16.00

	ORIG.	GOOD	FINE	N-MINT			ORIG.	GOOD	FINE	N-MINT
☐ 64, Oct 68	0.12	3.20	9.60	16.00	☐ 129, Jun 80, JSa	0.40	0.40	1.20	2.00
☐ 65, Dec 68	0.12	3.20	9.60	16.00	☐ 130, Jun 80, JSa	0.40	0.40	1.20	2.00
☐ 66, Jan 69	0.12	3.20	9.60	16.00	☐ 131, Aug 80, JSa	0.40	0.40	1.20	2.00
☐ 67, Mar 69	0.12	3.20	9.60	16.00	☐ 132, Sep 80, JSa	0.50	0.40	1.20	2.00
☐ 68, Apr 69	0.12	3.20	9.60	16.00	☐ 133, Oct 80, JSa, A:Dr. Polaris				
☐ 69, Jun 69	0.12	3.20	9.60	16.00		0.50	0.40	1.20	2.00
☐ 70, Jul 69, GK	0.15	3.20	9.60	16.00	☐ 134, Nov 80, JSa, A:Dr. Polaris				
☐ 71, Sep 69, GK	0.15	3.20	9.60	16.00		0.50	0.40	1.20	2.00
☐ 72, Oct 69, GK	0.15	3.20	9.60	16.00	☐ 135, Dec 80, JSa, A:Dr. Polaris				
☐ 73, Dec 69, GK	0.15	3.20	9.60	16.00		0.50	0.40	1.20	2.00
☐ 74, Jan 70, GK	0.15	3.20	9.60	16.00	☐ 136, Jan 81, JSa	0.50	0.40	1.20	2.00
☐ 75, Mar 70, GK	0.15	3.20	9.60	16.00	☐ 137, Feb 81, JSa	0.50	0.40	1.20	2.00
☐ 76, Apr 70, NA, A:GA	0.15	16.00	48.00	80.00	☐ 138, Mar 81, JSa	0.50	0.40	1.20	2.00
☐ 77, Jun 70, NA, A:GA	0.15	9.00	27.00	45.00	☐ 139, Apr 81, JSa	0.50	0.40	1.20	2.00
☐ 78, Jul 70, NA, A:GA	0.15	6.00	18.00	30.00	☐ 140, May 81, JSa	0.50	0.40	1.20	2.00
☐ 79, Sep 70, NA, A:GA	0.15	6.00	18.00	30.00	☐ 141, Jun 81, JSa, I:Omega Men				
☐ 80, Oct 70, NA, A:GA	0.15	6.00	18.00	30.00		0.50	0.40	1.20	2.00
☐ 81, Dec 70, NA, A:GA	0.15	4.40	13.20	22.00	☐ 142, Jul 81, JSa, A:Omega Men				
☐ 82, Mar 71, NA, A:GA	0.15	4.40	13.20	22.00		0.50	0.40	1.20	2.00
☐ 83, May 71, NA, A:GA	0.15	4.40	13.20	22.00	☐ 143, Aug 81, JSa, A:Omega Men				
☐ 84, Jul 71, NA/BWr, GA.	0.15	4.40	13.20	22.00		0.50	0.40	1.20	2.00
☐ 85, Sep 71, NA, drugs, GA					☐ 144, Sep 81, JSa, C:Omega Men				
	0.25	6.00	18.00	30.00		0.50	0.40	1.20	2.00
☐ 86, Nov 71, NA, drugs, G					☐ 145, Oct 81, JSa	0.60	0.40	1.20	2.00
A	0.25	6.00	18.00	30.00	☐ 146, Nov 81, JSa	0.60	0.40	1.20	2.00
☐ 87, Jan 72, GK/NA, A:GA, Guy Gardner cameo					☐ 147, Dec 81, JSa	0.60	0.40	1.20	2.00
	0.25	4.40	13.20	22.00	☐ 148, Jan 82, JSa	0.60	0.40	1.20	2.00
☐ 88, Mar 72, GK, A:GA	0.25	1.20	3.60	6.00	☐ 149, Feb 82, JSa	0.60	0.40	1.20	2.00
☐ 89, May 72, NA, A:GA	0.25	4.00	12.00	20.00	☐ 150, Mar 82, JSa, anniversary				
☐ 90, Sep 76, MGr, A:GA	0.30	1.20	3.60	6.00		1.00	0.40	1.20	2.00
☐ 91, Nov 76, MGr	0.30	0.80	2.40	4.00	☐ 151, Apr 82	0.60	0.40	1.20	2.00
☐ 92, Dec 76, MGr	0.30	0.80	2.40	4.00	☐ 152, May 82	0.60	0.40	1.20	2.00
☐ 93, Feb 77, MGr	0.30	0.80	2.40	4.00	☐ 153, Jun 82	0.60	0.40	1.20	2.00
☐ 94, Apr 77, MGr	0.30	0.80	2.40	4.00	☐ 154, Jul 82	0.60	0.40	1.20	2.00
☐ 95, Jun 77, MGr	0.35	0.80	2.40	4.00	☐ 155, Aug 82	0.60	0.40	1.20	2.00
☐ 96, Aug 77, MGr	0.35	0.80	2.40	4.00	☐ 156, Sep 82	0.60	0.40	1.20	2.00
☐ 97, Oct 77, MGr	0.35	0.80	2.40	4.00	☐ 157, Oct 82	0.60	0.40	1.20	2.00
☐ 98, Nov 77, MGr	0.35	0.80	2.40	4.00	☐ 158, Nov 82	0.60	0.40	1.20	2.00
☐ 99, Dec 77, MGr	0.35	0.80	2.40	4.00	☐ 159, Dec 82	0.60	0.40	1.20	2.00
☐ 100, Jan 78, MGr, I:Air Wave					☐ 160, Jan 83, Omega Men	0.60	0.40	1.20	2.00
	0.60	1.00	3.00	5.00	☐ 161, Feb 83, Omega Men	0.60	0.40	1.20	2.00
☐ 101, Feb 78, McGinty	0.60	1.20	3.60	6.00	☐ 162, Mar 83, KP	0.60	0.40	1.20	2.00
☐ 102, Mar 78, MGr, A:GA.	0.60	0.60	1.80	3.00	☐ 163, Apr 83, KP	0.60	0.40	1.20	2.00
☐ 103, Apr 78, MGr, A:GA	0.60	0.60	1.80	3.00	☐ 164, May 83, KP	0.60	0.40	1.20	2.00
☐ 104, May 78, MGr, A:GA	0.60	0.60	1.80	3.00	☐ 165, Jun 83, KP	0.60	0.40	1.20	2.00
☐ 105, Jun 78, MGr, A:GA.	0.60	0.60	1.80	3.00	☐ 166, Jul 83	0.60	0.40	1.20	2.00
☐ 106, Jul 78, MGr, A:GA.	0.60	0.60	1.80	3.00	☐ 167, Aug 83	0.60	0.40	1.20	2.00
☐ 107, Aug 78, MGr, A:GA	0.60	0.60	1.80	3.00	☐ 168, Sep 83	0.60	0.40	1.20	2.00
☐ 108, Sep 78, MGr,A:GA; Golden Age Green Lantern					☐ 169, Oct 83	0.60	0.40	1.20	2.00
back-up	0.50	0.60	1.80	3.00	☐ 170, Nov 83	0.60	0.40	1.20	2.00
☐ 109, Oct 78, MGr, A:GA; Golden Age Green Lantern					☐ 171, Dec 83	0.75	0.40	1.20	2.00
back-up	0.50	0.60	1.80	3.00	☐ 172, Jan 84	0.75	0.40	1.20	2.00
☐ 110, Nov 78, MGr,A:GA.	0.50	0.60	1.80	3.00	☐ 173, Feb 84	0.75	0.40	1.20	2.00
☐ 111, Dec 78, MGr, A:GA.	0.40	0.60	1.80	3.00	☐ 174, Mar 84	0.75	0.40	1.20	2.00
☐ 112, Jan 79	0.40	0.40	1.20	2.00	☐ 175, Apr 84	0.75	0.40	1.20	2.00
☐ 113, Feb 79	0.40	0.40	1.20	2.00	☐ 176, May 84	0.75	0.40	1.20	2.00
☐ 114, Mar 79	0.40	0.40	1.20	2.00	☐ 177, Jun 84	0.75	0.40	1.20	2.00
☐ 115, Apr 79	0.40	0.40	1.20	2.00	☐ 178, Jul 84	0.75	0.40	1.20	2.00
☐ 116, May 79, Guy Gardner					☐ 179, Aug 84	0.75	0.40	1.20	2.00
	0.40	4.00	12.00	20.00	☐ 180, Sep 84	0.75	0.40	1.20	2.00
☐ 117, Jun 79	0.40	0.40	1.20	2.00	☐ 181, Oct 84, Hal Jordan quits as Green Lantern				
☐ 118, Jul 79	0.40	0.40	1.20	2.00		0.75	0.40	1.20	2.00
☐ 119, Aug 79	0.40	0.40	1.20	2.00	☐ 182, Nov 84, John Stewart becomes new Green Lantern;				
☐ 120, Sep 79	0.40	0.40	1.20	2.00	retells origin	0.75	0.40	1.20	2.00
☐ 121, Oct 79	0.40	0.40	1.20	2.00	☐ 183, Dec 84	0.75	0.40	1.20	2.00
☐ 122, Nov 79	0.40	0.40	1.20	2.00	☐ 184, Jan 85, reprints origin of Guy Gardner				
☐ 123, Dec 79	0.40	0.40	1.20	2.00		0.75	0.40	1.20	2.00
☐ 124, Jan 80	0.40	0.40	1.20	2.00	☐ 185, Feb 85	0.75	0.40	1.20	2.00
☐ 125, Feb 80	0.40	0.40	1.20	2.00	☐ 186, Mar 85	0.75	0.40	1.20	2.00
☐ 126, Mar 80	0.40	0.40	1.20	2.00	☐ 187, Apr 85	0.75	0.40	1.20	2.00
☐ 127, Apr 80, JSa	0.40	0.40	1.20	2.00	☐ 188, May 85	0.75	0.40	1.20	2.00
☐ 128, May 80, JSa	0.40	0.40	1.20	2.00	☐ 189, Jun 85	0.75	0.40	1.20	2.00

	ORIG.	GOOD	FINE	N-MINT
☐ 190, Jul 85	0.75	0.40	1.20	2.00
☐ 191, Aug 85	0.75	0.40	1.20	2.00
☐ 192, Sep 85	0.75	0.40	1.20	2.00
☐ 193, Oct 85	0.75	0.40	1.20	2.00
☐ 194, Nov 85, Crisis, Guy Gardner returns				
	0.75	2.00	6.00	10.00
☐ 195, Dec 85, Crisis, Guy Gardner is GL				
	0.75	2.80	8.40	14.00
☐ 196, Jan 86, Crisis	0.75	0.40	1.20	2.00
☐ 197, Feb 86, Crisis; Guy Gardner vs. John Stewart				
	0.75	0.40	1.20	2.00
☐ 198, Mar 86, Crisis	0.75	0.40	1.20	2.00
☐ 199, Apr 86, Crisis; Hal Jordan returns as GL				
	0.75	0.40	1.20	2.00
☐ 200, May 86, Crisis; Guardians join Zamarons				
	1.25	0.40	1.20	2.00
☐ 201, Jun 86, Crisis aftermath				
	0.75	0.40	1.20	2.00
☐ 202, Jul 86,	0.75	0.40	1.20	2.00
☐ 203, Aug 86, O:Ch'p	0.75	0.40	1.20	2.00
☐ 204, Sep 86,	0.75	0.40	1.20	2.00
☐ 205, Oct 86, (becomes *Green Lantern Corps*)				
	0.75	0.40	1.20	2.00

GREEN LANTERN (beginning 1990)

	ORIG.	GOOD	FINE	N-MINT
☐ 0, Oct 94	1.50	0.30	0.90	1.50
☐ 1, Jun 90	1.00	1.20	3.60	6.00
☐ 2, Jul 90	1.00	1.00	3.00	5.00
☐ 3, Aug 90	1.00	0.60	1.80	3.00
☐ 4, Sep 90	1.00	0.60	1.80	3.00
☐ 5, Oct 90	1.00	0.60	1.80	3.00
☐ 6, Nov 90	1.00	0.40	1.20	2.00
☐ 7, Dec 90	1.00	0.40	1.20	2.00
☐ 8, Jan 91	1.00	0.40	1.20	2.00
☐ 9, Feb 91	1.00	0.40	1.20	2.00
☐ 10, Mar 91	1.00	0.40	1.20	2.00
☐ 11, Apr 91	1.00	0.40	1.20	2.00
☐ 12, May 91	1.00	0.40	1.20	2.00
☐ 13, Jun 91	1.75	0.35	1.05	1.75
☐ 14, Jul 91	1.00	0.20	0.60	1.00
☐ 15, Aug 91	1.00	0.20	0.60	1.00
☐ 16, Sep 91	1.00	0.20	0.60	1.00
☐ 17, Oct 91	1.00	0.20	0.60	1.00
☐ 18, Nov 91	1.00	0.20	0.60	1.00
☐ 19, Dec 91, 50th anniv., GK(c)				
	1.75	0.35	1.05	1.75
☐ 20, Jan 92	1.00	0.20	0.60	1.00
☐ 21, Feb 92	1.00	0.20	0.60	1.00
☐ 22, Mar 92	1.00	0.20	0.60	1.00
☐ 23, Apr 92	1.00	0.20	0.60	1.00
☐ 24, May 92	1.00	0.20	0.60	1.00
☐ 25, Jun 92, Jordan-Gardner fight				
	1.75	0.35	1.05	1.75
☐ 26, Jul 92	1.00	0.20	0.60	1.00
☐ 27, Aug 92	1.25	0.25	0.75	1.25
☐ 28, Sep 92	1.25	0.25	0.75	1.25
☐ 29, Sep 92	1.25	0.25	0.75	1.25
☐ 30, Oct 92, Flash	1.25	0.25	0.75	1.25
☐ 31, Oct 92, Flash	1.25	0.25	0.75	1.25
☐ 32, Nov 92	1.25	0.25	0.75	1.25
☐ 33, Nov 92	1.25	0.25	0.75	1.25
☐ 34, Dec 92	1.25	0.25	0.75	1.25
☐ 35, Jan 93	1.25	0.25	0.75	1.25
☐ 36, Feb 93	1.25	0.25	0.75	1.25
☐ 37, Mar 93	1.25	0.25	0.75	1.25
☐ 38, Apr 93, Adam Strange				
	1.25	0.25	0.75	1.25
☐ 39, May 93	1.25	0.25	0.75	1.25
☐ 40, May 93	1.25	0.25	0.75	1.25
☐ 41, Jun 93	1.25	0.25	0.75	1.25
☐ 42, Jun 93	1.25	0.25	0.75	1.25
☐ 43, Jul 93	1.25	0.25	0.75	1.25

	ORIG.	GOOD	FINE	N-MINT
☐ 44	1.25	0.25	0.75	1.25
☐ 45	1.25	0.25	0.75	1.25
☐ 46, Reign of Supermen	1.25	2.00	6.00	10.00
☐ 47, Green Arrow	1.25	0.60	1.80	3.00
☐ 48, Emerald Twilight	1.50	2.40	7.20	12.00
☐ 49, Emerald Twilight	1.50	1.60	4.80	8.00
☐ 50, Emerald Twilight, glow cover				
	2.95	2.00	6.00	10.00
☐ 51, May 94	1.50	0.60	1.80	3.00
☐ 52, Jun 94, V:Mongul	1.50	0.60	1.80	3.00
☐ 53, Jul 94, Superman	1.50	0.30	0.90	1.50
☐ 54, Aug 94	1.50	0.30	0.90	1.50
☐ 55, Sep 94, "Zero Hour"; V:Alan Scott				
	1.50	0.30	0.90	1.50
☐ 56, Nov 94	1.50	0.30	0.90	1.50
☐ 57, Dec 94	1.50	0.30	0.90	1.50
☐ 58, Jan 95	1.50	0.30	0.90	1.50
☐ 59, Feb 95	1.50	0.30	0.90	1.50
☐ 60, Mar 95	1.50	0.30	0.90	1.50
☐ 61, Apr 95	1.50	0.30	0.90	1.50
☐ 62, May 95	1.50	0.30	0.90	1.50
☐ 63, Jun 95, "Parallax View" Part 1 of 2				
	1.75	0.35	1.05	1.75
☐ 64, Jul 95, "Parallax View" Part 2 of 2				
	1.75	0.35	1.05	1.75
☐ 65, Aug 95, "The Siege of the Zi Charam" Part 2 of 5; continues in Darkstars #34				
	1.75	0.35	1.05	1.75
☐ 66, Sep 95, teams with Flash				
	1.75	0.35	1.05	1.75
☐ 67, Oct 95	1.75	0.35	1.05	1.75
☐ 68, Nov 95, "Underworld Unleashed"				
	1.75	0.35	1.05	1.75
☐ 69, Dec 95, "Underworld Unleashed"				
	1.75	0.35	1.05	1.75
☐ 70, Jan 96, A:John Stewart				
	1.75	0.35	1.05	1.75
☐ 71, Feb 96, "Hero Quest" Part 1 of 3;A:Batman, Robin, Sentinel	1.75	0.35	1.05	1.75
☐ 72, Mar 96, "Hero Quest" Part 2 of 3; A:Captain Marvel				
	1.75	0.35	1.05	1.75
☐ 73, Apr 96, "Hero Quest" Part 3 of 3; A:Wonder Woman				
	1.75	0.35	1.05	1.75
☐ 74, Jun 96	1.75	0.35	1.05	1.75

GREEN LANTERN ANNUAL

	ORIG.	GOOD	FINE	N-MINT
☐ 1, 92, "Eclipso: The Darkness Within"				
	2.50	0.50	1.50	2.50
☐ 2, 93, "Bloodlines: Outbreak";O:Nightblade				
	2.50	0.50	1.50	2.50
☐ 3, 94, Elseworlds	2.95	0.59	1.77	2.95
☐ 4, 95, "Year One";Kyle and Hal switch places				
	3.50	0.70	2.10	3.50
☐ 5, 96, "Legends of the Dead Earth"				
	2.95	0.59	1.77	2.95

GREEN LANTERN CORPS (was Green Lantern)

	ORIG.	GOOD	FINE	N-MINT
☐ 206, Nov 86	0.75	0.20	0.60	1.00
☐ 207, Dec 86, Legends	0.75	0.20	0.60	1.00
☐ 208, Jan 87	0.75	0.20	0.60	1.00
☐ 209, Feb 87	0.75	0.20	0.60	1.00
☐ 210, Mar 87	0.75	0.20	0.60	1.00
☐ 211, Apr 87	0.75	0.20	0.60	1.00
☐ 212, May 87	0.75	0.20	0.60	1.00
☐ 213, Jun 87	0.75	0.20	0.60	1.00
☐ 214, Jul 87	0.75	0.20	0.60	1.00
☐ 215, Aug 87	0.75	0.20	0.60	1.00
☐ 216, Sep 87	0.75	0.20	0.60	1.00
☐ 217, Oct 87	0.75	0.20	0.60	1.00
☐ 218, Nov 87	0.75	0.20	0.60	1.00
☐ 219, Dec 87	0.75	0.20	0.60	1.00
☐ 220, Jan 88, Millennium	0.75	0.20	0.60	1.00
☐ 221, Feb 88, Millennium	0.75	0.20	0.60	1.00

	ORIG.	GOOD	FINE	N-MINT
222, Mar 88 .... 0.75		0.20	0.60	1.00
223, Apr 88 .... 0.75		0.20	0.60	1.00
224, May 88, GK 1.50		0.30	0.90	1.50

GREEN LANTERN CORPS QUARTERLY

	ORIG.	GOOD	FINE	N-MINT
1, Sum 92 .... 2.50		0.50	1.50	2.50
2, Aut 92 .... 2.50		0.50	1.50	2.50
3, Wtr 92 .... 2.50		0.50	1.50	2.50
4, Spr 93, Alan Scott vs. Solomon Grundy				
.... 2.50		0.50	1.50	2.50
5, Sum 93, O&1:Adam ... 2.50		0.50	1.50	2.50
6, Aut 93, Alan Scott vs. New Harlequin				
.... 2.95		0.59	1.77	2.95
7, Win 93 .... 2.95		0.59	1.77	2.95
8, Spr 94, Jack Chance vs. Lobo				
.... 2.95		0.59	1.77	2.95

GREEN LANTERN SPECIAL

	ORIG.	GOOD	FINE	N-MINT
1, Dec 88.....................		0.30	0.90	1.50
2, 89............................ 1.50		0.30	0.90	1.50

GREEN LANTERN/ GREEN ARROW

	ORIG.	GOOD	FINE	N-MINT
1, Oct 93, NA reprints 2.00		0.60	1.80	3.00
2, Nov 83, NA/DG reprints				
.... 2.00		0.40	1.20	2.00
3, Dec 83, NA/DG reprints				
.... 2.00		0.40	1.20	2.00
4, Jan 84, NA/DG reprints				
.... 2.00		0.40	1.20	2.00
5, Feb 84, NA/DG reprints				
.... 2.00		0.40	1.20	2.00
6, Mar 84, NA/DG reprints				
.... 2.00		0.40	1.20	2.00
7, Apr 84, NA/DG reprints				
.... 2.50		0.40	1.20	2.00

GREEN LANTERN/SILVER SURFER: UNHOLY ALLIANCES

	ORIG.	GOOD	FINE	N-MINT
0, 95, nn;one-shot crossover with Marvel; A:Thanos, Terrax, Parallax, Cyborg Superman; prestige format				
.... 4.95		0.99	2.97	4.95

GREEN LANTERN: EMERALD DAWN

	ORIG.	GOOD	FINE	N-MINT
0, Apr 91, reprint.............		0.99	2.97	4.95
1, Dec 89, O:Green Lantern				
.... 1.00		2.80	8.40	14.00
2, Jan 90 .... 1.00		2.00	6.00	10.00
3, Feb 90 .... 1.00		1.60	4.80	8.00
4, Mar 90 .... 1.00		1.60	4.80	8.00
5, Apr 90 .... 1.00		1.20	3.60	6.00
6, May 90 .... 1.00		1.20	3.60	6.00

GREEN LANTERN: EMERALD DAWN II

	ORIG.	GOOD	FINE	N-MINT
1, Apr 91 .... 1.00		0.80	2.40	4.00
2, May 91 .... 1.00		0.50	1.50	2.50
3, Jun 91 .... 1.00		0.20	0.60	1.00
4, Jul 91 .... 1.00		0.20	0.60	1.00
5, Aug 91 .... 1.00		0.20	0.60	1.00
6, Sep 91 .... 1.00		0.20	0.60	1.00

GREEN LANTERN: GANTHET'S TALE

	ORIG.	GOOD	FINE	N-MINT
0, 92, one-shot;prestige format;JBy,Larry Niven; enhanced cover............. 5.95		1.19	3.57	5.95

GREEN LANTERN: MOSAIC

	ORIG.	GOOD	FINE	N-MINT
1, Jun 92 .... 1.25		0.25	0.75	1.25
2, Jul 92 .... 1.25		0.25	0.75	1.25
3, Aug 92 .... 1.25		0.25	0.75	1.25
4, Sep 92 .... 1.25		0.25	0.75	1.25
5, Oct 92 .... 1.25		0.25	0.75	1.25
6, Nov 92 .... 1.25		0.25	0.75	1.25
7, Dec 92 .... 1.25		0.25	0.75	1.25
8, Jan 93 .... 1.25		0.25	0.75	1.25
9, Feb 93 .... 1.25		0.25	0.75	1.25
10, Mar 93 .... 1.25		0.25	0.75	1.25
11, Apr 93 .... 1.25		0.25	0.75	1.25
12, May 93 .... 1.25		0.25	0.75	1.25
13, Jun 93 .... 1.25		0.25	0.75	1.25

	ORIG.	GOOD	FINE	N-MINT
14, Jul 93..................... 1.25		0.25	0.75	1.25
15 .... 1.25		0.25	0.75	1.25
16 .... 1.25		0.25	0.75	1.25
17 .... 1.25		0.25	0.75	1.25
18 .... 1.25		0.25	0.75	1.25

GREEN SKULL, THE KNOWN ASSOCIATES

	ORIG.	GOOD	FINE	N-MINT
0, 95, nn;one-shot 2.50		0.50	1.50	2.50

GREEN-GREY SPONGE-SUIT SUSHI TURTLES
MIRAGE

	ORIG.	GOOD	FINE	N-MINT
1, 90, color;Mark Martin parody;cardstock cover				
..................................3.33		0.67	2.00	3.33

GREENHAVEN
AIRCEL

	ORIG.	GOOD	FINE	N-MINT
1, color		0.40	1.20	2.00
2, color		0.40	1.20	2.00
3, color		0.40	1.20	2.00

GREGORY
PIRANHA PRESS

	ORIG.	GOOD	FINE	N-MINT
3, 93 ....4.95		0.99	2.97	4.95

GREGORY III

	ORIG.	GOOD	FINE	N-MINT
0, Platinum		10.00	30.00	50.00

GREGORY IV: FAT BOY

	ORIG.	GOOD	FINE	N-MINT
0, b&w..........................4.95		0.99	2.97	4.95

GRENDEL (black-and-white)
COMICO

	ORIG.	GOOD	FINE	N-MINT
1, MW..............................		8.00	24.00	40.00
2, MW..............................		6.00	18.00	30.00
3, MW..............................		6.00	18.00	30.00

GRENDEL (color)

	ORIG.	GOOD	FINE	N-MINT
1, 1st printing		1.00	3.00	5.00
1, 2nd printing		0.30	0.90	1.50
2		0.60	1.80	3.00
3		0.60	1.80	3.00
4, DSt(c)		0.60	1.80	3.00
5		0.60	1.80	3.00
6		0.60	1.80	3.00
7		0.60	1.80	3.00
8		0.60	1.80	3.00
9		0.60	1.80	3.00
10		0.60	1.80	3.00
11		0.60	1.80	3.00
12, D:Grendel..................		0.60	1.80	3.00
13, new Grendel...............		0.60	1.80	3.00
14, new Grendel...............		0.60	1.80	3.00
15, new Grendel...............		0.60	1.80	3.00
16, Mage begins		0.70	2.10	3.50
17		0.50	1.50	2.50
18, MW............................		0.50	1.50	2.50
19, MW............................		0.50	1.50	2.50
20		0.50	1.50	2.50
21		0.50	1.50	2.50
22		0.50	1.50	2.50
23		0.50	1.50	2.50
24		0.50	1.50	2.50
25		0.50	1.50	2.50
26		0.50	1.50	2.50
27		0.50	1.50	2.50
28		0.50	1.50	2.50
29		0.50	1.50	2.50
30		0.50	1.50	2.50
31		0.50	1.50	2.50
32		0.50	1.50	2.50
33		0.59	1.77	2.95
34		0.50	1.50	2.50
35		0.50	1.50	2.50
36		0.50	1.50	2.50
37		0.50	1.50	2.50
38		0.50	1.50	2.50
39		0.50	1.50	2.50

	ORIG.	GOOD	FINE	N-MINT

GRENDEL CLASSICS (mini-series)
DARK HORSE
☐ 1, Jul 95, cardstock cover

.... 3.95   0.79   2.37   3.95
☐ 2, Aug 95, cardstock cover; final issue

.... 3.95   0.79   2.37   3.95

GRENDEL CYCLE
☐ 0, Oct 95, nn;background information on the various
series including a timeline; prestige format

.... 5.95   1.19   3.57   5.95

GRENDEL IN DEVIL BY THE DEED
☐ 0, 93, nn...................... 3.95   0.79   2.37   3.95

GRENDEL TALES
☐ 1 .... 2.95   0.59   1.77   2.95
☐ 2 .... 2.95   0.59   1.77   2.95
☐ 3 .... 2.95   0.59   1.77   2.95
☐ 4 .... 2.95   0.59   1.77   2.95
☐ 5 .... 2.95   0.59   1.77   2.95
☐ 6 .... 2.95   0.59   1.77   2.95

GRENDEL TALES: DEVIL'S CHOICES (mini-series)
☐ 1, Mar 95 .... 2.95   0.59   1.77   2.95
☐ 2, Apr 95 .... 2.95   0.59   1.77   2.95
☐ 3, May 95 .... 2.95   0.59   1.77   2.95
☐ 4, Jun 95...................... 2.95   0.59   1.77   2.95

GRENDEL TALES: DEVIL'S HAMMER
☐ 1, Feb 94 .... 2.95   0.59   1.77   2.95
☐ 2, Mar 94 .... 2.95   0.59   1.77   2.95
☐ 3, Apr 94...................... 2.95   0.59   1.77   2.95

GRENDEL TALES: DEVILS AND DEATHS
(mini-series)
☐ 1, Oct 94 .... 2.95   0.59   1.77   2.95
☐ 2, Nov 94 .... 2.95   0.59   1.77   2.95

GRENDEL TALES: FOUR DEVILS, ONE HELL
☐ 1, Aug 93 .... 2.95   0.59   1.77   2.95
☐ 2, 93............................. 2.95   0.59   1.77   2.95
☐ 3, 93............................. 2.95   0.59   1.77   2.95
☐ 4 .... 2.95   0.59   1.77   2.95
☐ 5 .... 2.95   0.59   1.77   2.95
☐ 6 .... 2.95   0.59   1.77   2.95

GRENDEL TALES: HOMECOMING (mini-series)
☐ 1, Dec 94, cardstock cover

.... 2.95   0.59   1.77   2.95
☐ 2, Jan 95, cardstock cover

.... 2.95   0.59   1.77   2.95
☐ 3, Feb 95, cardstock cover

.... 2.95   0.59   1.77   2.95

GRENDEL TALES: THE DEVIL IN OUR MIDST
(mini-series)
☐ 1, May 94 .... 2.95   0.59   1.77   2.95
☐ 2, Jun 94...................... 2.95   0.59   1.77   2.95
☐ 3, Jul 94....................... 2.95   0.59   1.77   2.95
☐ 4, Aug 94..................... 2.95   0.59   1.77   2.95
☐ 5, Sep 94...................... 2.95   0.59   1.77   2.95

GRENDEL TALES: THE DEVIL MAY CARE
(mini-series)
☐ 1, Dec 95, cardstock cover

.... 2.95   0.59   1.77   2.95
☐ 2, Jan 96, cardstock cover

.... 2.95   0.59   1.77   2.95
☐ 3, Feb 96, cardstock cover

.... 2.95   0.59   1.77   2.95
☐ 4, Mar 96, cardstock cover

.... 2.95   0.59   1.77   2.95
☐ 5, Apr 96, cardstock cover

.... 2.95   0.59   1.77   2.95

GRENDEL: DEVIL QUEST
☐ 0, Nov 95, nn;one-shot; prestige format

.... 4.95   0.99   2.97   4.95

GRENDEL: DEVIL'S VAGARY
COMICO
☐ 1, 16-pg. b&w&red.......... 1.00   3.00   5.00

GRENDEL: WAR CHILD
DARK HORSE
☐ 1, 92, MW, Bisley(c) 0.80   2.40   4.00
☐ 2, 92............................2.50   0.50   1.50   2.50
☐ 3, 92............................2.50   0.50   1.50   2.50
☐ 4, 92............................2.50   0.50   1.50   2.50
☐ 5, 92............................2.50   0.50   1.50   2.50
☐ 6, 92............................2.50   0.50   1.50   2.50
☐ 7, 92............................2.50   0.50   1.50   2.50
☐ 8, 92............................2.50   0.50   1.50   2.50
☐ 9, 92............................2.50   0.50   1.50   2.50
☐ 10 ....3.50   0.70   2.10   3.50

GREY
VIZ
☐ 1, b&w, Japanese 0.65   1.95   3.25
☐ 2, b&w, Japanese 0.65   1.95   3.25
☐ 3, b&w, Japanese 0.65   1.95   3.25
☐ 4, b&w, Japanese 0.65   1.95   3.25
☐ 5, b&w, Japanese 0.65   1.95   3.25
☐ 6, b&w, Japanese 0.65   1.95   3.25
☐ 7, b&w, Japanese 0.65   1.95   3.25
☐ 8, b&w, Japanese 0.65   1.95   3.25
☐ 9, b&w, Japanese 0.65   1.95   3.25

GREY LEGACY
FRAGILE ELITE
☐ 1, b&w......................2.75   0.55   1.65   2.75

GREYLORE
SIRIUS
☐ 1, Dec 85 ....1.50   0.40   1.20   2.00
☐ 2, Jan 86...................1.50   0.40   1.20   2.00
☐ 3, Jan 86...................1.50   0.40   1.20   2.00
☐ 4, Jan 86...................1.50   0.40   1.20   2.00
☐ 5, Jan 86...................1.50   0.40   1.20   2.00

GREYMATTER
ALAFFINITY
☐ 1 ....2.95   0.59   1.77   2.95
☐ 2 ....2.95   0.59   1.77   2.95
☐ 3 ....2.95   0.59   1.77   2.95

GRIFFIN, THE
DC
☐ 1, Nov 91 .... 1.20   3.60   6.00
☐ 2, Dec 91 .... 1.00   3.00   5.00
☐ 3 .... 1.00   3.00   5.00
☐ 4 .... 1.00   3.00   5.00
☐ 5 .... 1.00   3.00   5.00
☐ 6 .... 1.00   3.00   5.00

SLAVE LABOR
☐ 1, Sep 88, b&w............... 1.20   3.60   6.00
☐ 2, Nov 88........................ 1.00   3.00   5.00
☐ 3, Jan 89........................ 1.00   3.00   5.00

GRIFFITH OBSERVATORY
FANTAGRAPHICS
☐ 0, nn 4.95   0.99   2.97   4.95

GRIFTER
IMAGE
☐ 1, May 95, "WildStorm Rising" Chapter 5; bound-in
trading cards 2.50   0.50   1.50   2.50
☐ 2, Jun 95 ....2.50   0.50   1.50   2.50
☐ 3, Jul 95, indicia says "Jul";cover says "Aug"

.................................2.50   0.50   1.50   2.50
☐ 5, Oct 95, indicia says "Oct";cover says "Jun"

.................................2.50   0.50   1.50   2.50
☐ 6, Nov 95 ....2.50   0.50   1.50   2.50
☐ 7, Dec 95 ....2.50   0.50   1.50   2.50
☐ 8, Jan 96........................2.50   0.50   1.50   2.50

	ORIG.	GOOD	FINE	N-MINT
☐ 9, Feb 96, "City of Angels" Part 3 of 4				
	2.50	0.50	1.50	2.50
☐ 10, Mar 96, "City of Angels" Part 4 of 4				
	2.50	0.50	1.50	2.50

GRIFTER/BADROCK

	ORIG.	GOOD	FINE	N-MINT
☐ 1, Oct 95	2.50	0.50	1.50	2.50
☐ 1, Oct 95, alternate cover	2.50	0.50	1.50	2.50
☐ 2, Nov 95, flipbook with Badrock #2A				
	2.50	0.50	1.50	2.50

GRIFTER/SHI

	ORIG.	GOOD	FINE	N-MINT
☐ 1, Mar 96, crossover with Crusade				
	2.95	0.59	1.77	2.95

GRIFTER: ONE SHOT

	ORIG.	GOOD	FINE	N-MINT
☐ 1, Jan 95	4.95	1.00	3.00	5.00

GRIM GHOST, THE
ATLAS/ SEABOARD

	ORIG.	GOOD	FINE	N-MINT
☐ 1, Jan 75, O:Grim Ghost	0.25	0.20	0.60	1.00
☐ 2, Mar 75	0.25	0.20	0.60	1.00
☐ 3, Jul 75	0.25	0.20	0.60	1.00

GRIMJACK
FIRST

	GOOD	FINE	N-MINT
☐ 1	0.60	1.80	3.00
☐ 2	0.40	1.20	2.00
☐ 3	0.40	1.20	2.00
☐ 4	0.25	0.75	1.25
☐ 5	0.25	0.75	1.25
☐ 6	0.25	0.75	1.25
☐ 7	0.25	0.75	1.25
☐ 8	0.25	0.75	1.25
☐ 9	0.25	0.75	1.25
☐ 10	0.25	0.75	1.25
☐ 11	0.25	0.75	1.25
☐ 12	0.25	0.75	1.25
☐ 13	0.25	0.75	1.25
☐ 14	0.25	0.75	1.25
☐ 15	0.25	0.75	1.25
☐ 16	0.25	0.75	1.25
☐ 17	0.25	0.75	1.25
☐ 18	0.25	0.75	1.25
☐ 19	0.25	0.75	1.25
☐ 20	0.25	0.75	1.25
☐ 21	0.25	0.75	1.25
☐ 22	0.25	0.75	1.25
☐ 23	0.25	0.75	1.25
☐ 24	0.25	0.75	1.25
☐ 25	0.25	0.75	1.25
☐ 26, Mutant Turtles	1.20	3.60	6.00
☐ 27	0.25	0.75	1.25
☐ 28	0.25	0.75	1.25
☐ 29	0.25	0.75	1.25
☐ 30, Dynamo Joe	0.25	0.75	1.25
☐ 31	0.25	0.75	1.25
☐ 32	0.25	0.75	1.25
☐ 33	0.25	0.75	1.25
☐ 34	0.25	0.75	1.25
☐ 35	0.25	0.75	1.25
☐ 36, D:Grimjack	0.25	0.75	1.25
☐ 37	0.25	0.75	1.25
☐ 38	0.25	0.75	1.25
☐ 39	0.35	1.05	1.75
☐ 40	0.35	1.05	1.75
☐ 41	0.35	1.05	1.75
☐ 42	0.35	1.05	1.75
☐ 43	0.35	1.05	1.75
☐ 44	0.35	1.05	1.75
☐ 45	0.35	1.05	1.75
☐ 46	0.35	1.05	1.75
☐ 47	0.35	1.05	1.75
☐ 48	0.35	1.05	1.75
☐ 49	0.35	1.05	1.75
☐ 50	0.35	1.05	1.75
☐ 51	0.35	1.05	1.75
☐ 52, Crossroads	0.39	1.17	1.95
☐ 53	0.39	1.17	1.95
☐ 54	0.39	1.17	1.95
☐ 55, new Grimjack	0.80	2.40	4.00
☐ 56	0.60	1.80	3.00
☐ 57	0.60	1.80	3.00
☐ 58	0.60	1.80	3.00
☐ 59	0.60	1.80	3.00
☐ 60	0.60	1.80	3.00
☐ 61	0.39	1.17	1.95
☐ 62	0.39	1.17	1.95
☐ 63	0.39	1.17	1.95
☐ 64	0.39	1.17	1.95
☐ 65	0.39	1.17	1.95
☐ 66, Demon Wars	0.39	1.17	1.95
☐ 67, Demon Wars	0.39	1.17	1.95
☐ 68, Demon Wars	0.39	1.17	1.95
☐ 69, Demon Wars	0.39	1.17	1.95
☐ 70	0.39	1.17	1.95
☐ 71	0.39	1.17	1.95
☐ 72	0.39	1.17	1.95
☐ 73	0.39	1.17	1.95
☐ 74	0.39	1.17	1.95
☐ 75	1.19	3.57	5.95
☐ 76	0.45	1.35	2.25
☐ 77	0.45	1.35	2.25
☐ 78	0.45	1.35	2.25
☐ 79	0.45	1.35	2.25
☐ 80	0.45	1.35	2.25
☐ 81	0.45	1.35	2.25

GRIMJACK CASEFILES

	GOOD	FINE	N-MINT
☐ 1, Truman, reprint	0.39	1.17	1.95
☐ 2, Truman, reprint	0.39	1.17	1.95
☐ 3, Truman, reprint	0.39	1.17	1.95
☐ 4, Truman, reprint	0.39	1.17	1.95
☐ 5, Truman, reprint	0.39	1.17	1.95

GRINGO
CALIBER

	ORIG.	GOOD	FINE	N-MINT
☐ 1, b&w	1.95	0.39	1.17	1.95

GRIPS
SILVERWOLF

	GOOD	FINE	N-MINT
☐ 1, Tim Vigil	3.00	9.00	15.00
☐ 2, Tim Vigil	2.40	7.20	12.00
☐ 3, Tim Vigil	2.00	6.00	10.00
☐ 4, Tim Vigil	2.00	6.00	10.00

GRIPS (Volume 2)
GREATER MERCURY

	GOOD	FINE	N-MINT
☐ 1	0.40	1.20	2.00

GRIT BATH
FANTAGRAPHICS

	ORIG.	GOOD	FINE	N-MINT
☐ 1, b&w	2.50	0.50	1.50	2.50
☐ 3, Aug 94, no cover price				

GROO CHRONICLES, THE
EPIC

	ORIG.	GOOD	FINE	N-MINT
☐ 1, SA, reprints, squarebound				
	3.50	1.20	3.60	6.00
☐ 2, SA, reprints, squarebound				
	3.50	1.00	3.00	5.00
☐ 3, SA, reprints, squarebound				
	3.50	1.00	3.00	5.00
☐ 4, SA, reprints, squarebound				
	3.50	0.80	2.40	4.00
☐ 5, SA, reprints, squarebound				
	3.50	0.80	2.40	4.00
☐ 6, SA, reprints, squarebound				
	3.50	0.80	2.40	4.00

Gorillas on Parade

There was a period in DC Comics' history when at least one of its titles each month would cover-feature a gorilla.

According to Julius Schwartz, the catalyst came from "Evolution Plus!" in *Strange Adventures* #8 (May 51). In that cover story, a man ended up in a gorilla's body and landed behind bars at the zoo. The cover showed him holding out a chalkboard with the message, "Ruth — Please believe me! I am the victim of a terrible scientific experiment! Ralph."

A few months after the issue came out, Schwartz's boss, Irwin Donenfeld, came into Schwartz's office and showed him that sales had jumped 25% on that issue.

They guessed it was because of the gorilla on the cover, Schwartz said. So they put another gorilla on one of their covers. "It did very well, too."

So what would any good publisher do if a gorilla on the cover goosed his sales? You got it. Schwartz said that soon DC was publishing one cover nearly every month featuring a gorilla.

Donenfeld discovered something else: Sales also shot up when fire and/or jail cells were pictured. He kept a small card listing these elements to remind himself to feature them or some variation as much as possible. (After all, that first cover had had two of the three key ingredients.)

"It drove us nuts," Schwartz said. "It's hard enough to come up with cover ideas. But to have to feature gorillas, jail cells, or fire really made it tough!"

Needless to say, by the time The Silver Age rolled around, the gorilla craze was in full roar. Virtually every hero got his or her share of gorilla encounters. DC even had two gorilla

Secret Origins #40 ©1989 DC Comics.

heroes: Sam Simeon of *Angel and the Ape* and Congorilla, the alter ego of the shape-changing Congo Bill.

By now, it's safe to say the craze has died down. But primate protaganists are still appearing in modern comics, including Art Adams' erudite gorilla from another dimension, Axwell Tiberius, appearing in *Monkeyman and O'Brien* published by Dark Horse Comics' Legend imprint, and the bio-engineered apes of the science-fiction series *Grease Monkey* from Kitchen Sink Press.

Partial Checklist of DC Gorillas

Batman stories:	The Gorilla Boss of Gotham City, Karmak, The Living Beast Bomb
Brave & Bold's Strange Sports Stories:	The Gorilla Wonders of the Diamond
Doom Patrol stories:	Monsieur Mallah
Flash stories:	Grodd the Super Gorilla, Solovar
Jerry Lewis:	Priscilla the Gorilla
Superman family stories:	Titano, The Giant Super-Ape, King Krypton, the Gorilla of Steel, Bruna, the Bride of Jungle Jimmy
Tomahawk:	Mikora, The Gorilla Ranger
Wonder Woman:	The Gorilla King of Amazon Island.

	ORIG.	GOOD	FINE	N-MINT

GROO SPECIAL
ECLIPSE
1, Oct 84, SA	2.00	4.80	14.40	24.00

GROO THE WANDERER
EPIC
0, (see Sergio Aragones Groo the Wanderer)				

PACIFIC
1, Dec 82, SA	1.00	6.00	18.00	30.00
2, Feb 83, SA	1.00	5.00	15.00	25.00
3, Apr 83, SA	1.00	3.60	10.80	18.00
4, Sep 83, SA	1.00	3.60	10.80	18.00
5, Oct 83, SA	1.00	3.60	10.80	18.00
6, Dec 83, SA	1.00	3.60	10.80	18.00
7, Feb 84, SA	1.00	3.60	10.80	18.00
8, Apr 84, SA	1.00	3.60	10.80	18.00

GROOTLORE
FANTAGRAPHICS
1, b&w		0.40	1.20	2.00
2, b&w		0.40	1.20	2.00

GROOTLORE (Volume 2)
1, b&w		0.40	1.20	2.00
2, b&w		0.40	1.20	2.00
3		0.45	1.35	2.25

GROUND POUND
BLACKTHORNE
1		0.40	1.20	2.00

GROUND ZERO
ETERNITY
1, b&w		0.50	1.50	2.50
2, b&w		0.50	1.50	2.50

GRUN
HARRIER
1		0.39	1.17	1.95
2		0.39	1.17	1.95
3		0.39	1.17	1.95
4		0.39	1.17	1.95

GRUNTS
MIRAGE
1		0.40	1.20	2.00

GUARDIAN, THE
SPECTRUM
1, Mar 84		0.20	0.60	1.00
2, Jun 84		0.20	0.60	1.00

GUARDIANS OF METROPOLIS
DC
1, Nov 94	1.50	0.30	0.90	1.50
2, Dec 94	1.50	0.30	0.90	1.50
3, Jan 95	1.50	0.30	0.90	1.50
4, Feb 95	1.50	0.30	0.90	1.50

GUARDIANS OF THE GALAXY
MARVEL
1, Jun 90	1.00	1.40	4.20	7.00
2, Jul 90	1.00	1.00	3.00	5.00
3, Aug 90	1.00	0.60	1.80	3.00
4, Sep 90	1.00	0.60	1.80	3.00
5, Oct 90	1.00	0.60	1.80	3.00
6, Nov 90	1.00	0.40	1.20	2.00
7, Dec 90	1.00	0.40	1.20	2.00
8, Jan 91	1.00	0.40	1.20	2.00
9, Feb 91	1.00	0.40	1.20	2.00
10, Mar 91	1.00	0.40	1.20	2.00
11, Apr 91	1.00	0.40	1.20	2.00
12, May 91	1.00	0.40	1.20	2.00
13, Jun 91, Ghost Rider	1.00	1.00	3.00	5.00
14, Jul 91, Ghost Rider	1.00	1.00	3.00	5.00
15, Aug 91	1.00	0.40	1.20	2.00
16, Sep 91	1.50	0.40	1.20	2.00
17, Oct 91	1.00	0.40	1.20	2.00
18, Nov 91	1.00	0.40	1.20	2.00
19, Dec 91	1.00	0.40	1.20	2.00
20	1.00	0.40	1.20	2.00
21	1.25	0.30	0.90	1.50
22	1.25	0.30	0.90	1.50
23	1.25	0.25	0.75	1.25
24	1.25	0.25	0.75	1.25
25, foil cover	2.50	1.00	3.00	5.00
26	1.25	0.25	0.75	1.25
27	1.25	0.25	0.75	1.25
28	1.25	0.25	0.75	1.25
29	1.25	0.25	0.75	1.25
30	1.25	0.25	0.75	1.25
31	1.25	0.25	0.75	1.25
32	1.25	0.25	0.75	1.25
33	1.25	0.25	0.75	1.25
34	1.25	0.25	0.75	1.25
35, sculpted cover	2.95	0.59	1.77	2.95
36	1.25	0.25	0.75	1.25
37	1.25	0.25	0.75	1.25
38	1.25	0.25	0.75	1.25
39, sculpted foil cover	2.95	0.59	1.77	2.95
40	1.25	0.25	0.75	1.25
41	1.25	0.25	0.75	1.25
42	1.25	0.25	0.75	1.25
43	1.25	0.25	0.75	1.25
44	1.25	0.25	0.75	1.25
45	1.25	0.25	0.75	1.25
46	1.25	0.25	0.75	1.25
47	1.25	0.25	0.75	1.25
48, May 94	1.50	0.30	0.90	1.50
49, Jun 94	1.50	0.30	0.90	1.50
50, Jul 94, foil embossed cover	2.95	0.59	1.77	2.95
50, Jul 94	2.00	0.40	1.20	2.00
51, Aug 94	1.50	0.30	0.90	1.50
52, Sep 94	1.50	0.30	0.90	1.50
53, Oct 94	1.50	0.30	0.90	1.50
54, Nov 94	1.50	0.30	0.90	1.50
55, Dec 94	1.50	0.30	0.90	1.50
56, Jan 95	1.50	0.30	0.90	1.50
57, Feb 95	1.50	0.30	0.90	1.50
58, Mar 95	1.50	0.30	0.90	1.50
59, Apr 95	1.50	0.30	0.90	1.50
60, May 95	1.50	0.30	0.90	1.50
61, Jun 95	1.50	0.30	0.90	1.50
62, Jul 95, Final issue	2.50	0.50	1.50	2.50

GUARDIANS OF THE GALAXY ANNUAL
1, Jul 91, Korvac Quest	2.00	0.40	1.20	2.00
2	2.25	0.45	1.35	2.25
3, trading card	2.95	0.59	1.77	2.95
4, 94	2.95	0.59	1.77	2.95

GUMBY 3-D
BLACKTHORNE
1		0.50	1.50	2.50
2		0.50	1.50	2.50
3		0.50	1.50	2.50
4		0.50	1.50	2.50
5		0.50	1.50	2.50
6		0.50	1.50	2.50
7		0.50	1.50	2.50

GUMBY'S SUMMER FUN SPECIAL
COMICO
1, AAd		0.80	2.40	4.00

GUMBY'S WINTER FUN SPECIAL
1, AAd		0.50	1.50	2.50

GUN FURY
AIRCEL
1, b&w		0.39	1.17	1.95
2, b&w		0.39	1.17	1.95
3, b&w		0.39	1.17	1.95

	ORIG.	GOOD	FINE	N-MINT
❏ 4, b&w		0.39	1.17	1.95
❏ 5, b&w		0.39	1.17	1.95
❏ 6, b&w		0.39	1.17	1.95
❏ 7, b&w		0.39	1.17	1.95
❏ 8, b&w		0.39	1.17	1.95
❏ 9, b&w		0.39	1.17	1.95
❏ 10, b&w		0.39	1.17	1.95

GUN FURY RETURNS

	ORIG.	GOOD	FINE	N-MINT
❏ 1, b&w		0.45	1.35	2.25
❏ 2, b&w		0.45	1.35	2.25
❏ 3, b&w		0.45	1.35	2.25
❏ 4, b&w		0.45	1.35	2.25

GUN RUNNER
MARVEL

	ORIG.	GOOD	FINE	N-MINT
❏ 1, four cards	2.75	0.55	1.65	2.75
❏ 2	1.75	0.35	1.05	1.75
❏ 3	1.75	0.35	1.05	1.75
❏ 4	1.75	0.35	1.05	1.75
❏ 5	1.75	0.35	1.05	1.75
❏ 6	1.75	0.35	1.05	1.75

GUNFIGHTERS IN HELL
REBEL

	ORIG.	GOOD	FINE	N-MINT
❏ 3, 94, b&w	2.25	0.45	1.35	2.25

GUNFIRE
DC

	ORIG.	GOOD	FINE	N-MINT
❏ 0, Oct 94	1.95	0.39	1.17	1.95
❏ 1, May 94	1.75	0.35	1.05	1.75
❏ 2, Jun 94	1.75	0.35	1.05	1.75
❏ 3, Jul 94	1.75	0.35	1.05	1.75
❏ 4, Aug 94	1.75	0.35	1.05	1.75
❏ 5		0.35	1.05	1.75
❏ 6, Nov 94	1.95	0.39	1.17	1.95
❏ 7, Dec 94	1.95	0.39	1.17	1.95
❏ 8, Jan 95	1.95	0.39	1.17	1.95
❏ 9, Feb 95	1.95	0.39	1.17	1.95
❏ 10, Mar 95	1.95	0.39	1.17	1.95
❏ 11, Apr 95	1.95	0.39	1.17	1.95
❏ 12, May 95	1.95	0.39	1.17	1.95
❏ 13, Jun 95	2.25	0.45	1.35	2.25

GUNHED
VIZ

	ORIG.	GOOD	FINE	N-MINT
❏ 1, Japanese, color		1.40	4.20	7.00
❏ 2, Japanese, color		1.40	4.20	7.00
❏ 3, Japanese, color		1.40	4.20	7.00

GUNS OF SHAR-PEI
CALIBER

	ORIG.	GOOD	FINE	N-MINT
❏ 1, b&w		0.59	1.77	2.95
❏ 2, b&w		0.59	1.77	2.95
❏ 3, b&w		0.59	1.77	2.95

GUNSMITH CATS (mini-series)
DARK HORSE/MANGA

	ORIG.	GOOD	FINE	N-MINT
❏ 5, Sep 95, b&w	2.95	0.59	1.77	2.95
❏ 6, Oct 95, b&w	2.95	0.59	1.77	2.95
❏ 7, Nov 95, b&w	2.95	0.59	1.77	2.95
❏ 8, Dec 95, b&w	2.95	0.59	1.77	2.95
❏ 9, Jan 96, b&w	2.95	0.59	1.77	2.95
❏ 10, Feb 96, b&w; final issue				
	2.95	0.59	1.77	2.95

GUY GARDNER
DC

	ORIG.	GOOD	FINE	N-MINT
❏ 1, Oct 92	1.25	0.40	1.20	2.00
❏ 2, Nov 92	1.25	0.30	0.90	1.50
❏ 3, Dec 92	1.25	0.30	0.90	1.50
❏ 4, Jan 93	1.25	0.25	0.75	1.25
❏ 5, Feb 93	1.25	0.25	0.75	1.25
❏ 6, Mar 93	1.25	0.25	0.75	1.25

	ORIG.	GOOD	FINE	N-MINT
❏ 7, Apr 93	1.25	0.25	0.75	1.25
❏ 8, May 93	1.25	0.25	0.75	1.25
❏ 9, Jun 93	1.25	0.25	0.75	1.25
❏ 10, Jun 93	1.25	0.25	0.75	1.25
❏ 11	1.25	0.40	1.20	2.00
❏ 12	1.25	0.35	1.05	1.75
❏ 13	1.25	0.35	1.05	1.75
❏ 14	1.25	0.35	1.05	1.75
❏ 15	1.50	0.30	0.90	1.50
❏ 16, (becomes *Guy Gardner: Warrior*)				
	1.50	0.30	0.90	1.50

GUY GARDNER REBORN

	ORIG.	GOOD	FINE	N-MINT
❏ 1, 92, JSt	4.95	1.20	3.60	6.00
❏ 2, 92	4.95	0.99	2.97	4.95
❏ 3, 92	4.95	0.99	2.97	4.95

GUY GARDNER: WARRIOR (was Guy Gardner)

	ORIG.	GOOD	FINE	N-MINT
❏ 0, Oct 94	1.50	0.30	0.90	1.50
❏ 17	1.50	0.30	0.90	1.50
❏ 18	1.50	0.30	0.90	1.50
❏ 19	1.50	0.30	0.90	1.50
❏ 20, May 94	1.50	0.30	0.90	1.50
❏ 21, Jun 94	1.50	0.30	0.90	1.50
❏ 22, Jul 94	1.50	0.30	0.90	1.50
❏ 23, Aug 94	1.50	0.30	0.90	1.50
❏ 24, Sep 94	1.50	0.30	0.90	1.50
❏ 25, Nov 94	2.50	0.50	1.50	2.50
❏ 26, Dec 94	1.50	0.30	0.90	1.50
❏ 27, Jan 95	1.50	0.30	0.90	1.50
❏ 28, Feb 95	1.50	0.30	0.90	1.50
❏ 29, Mar 95	1.50	0.30	0.90	1.50
❏ 29, May 95, enhanced foldout cover				
	2.95	0.59	1.77	2.95
❏ 30, Apr 95	1.50	0.30	0.90	1.50
❏ 31, Jun 95	1.75	0.35	1.05	1.75
❏ 32, Jul 95	1.75	0.35	1.05	1.75
❏ 33, Aug 95	1.75	0.35	1.05	1.75
❏ 34, Sep 95	1.75	0.35	1.05	1.75
❏ 35, Oct 95	1.75	0.35	1.05	1.75
❏ 36, Nov 95, "Underworld Unleashed"				
	1.75	0.35	1.05	1.75
❏ 37, Dec 95, "Underworld Unleashed"				
	1.75	0.35	1.05	1.75
❏ 38, Jan 96	1.75	0.35	1.05	1.75
❏ 39, Feb 96	1.75	0.35	1.05	1.75
❏ 40, Mar 96	1.75	0.35	1.05	1.75
❏ 41, Apr 96	1.75	0.35	1.05	1.75
❏ 42, May 96, Guy becomes a woman				
	1.75	0.35	1.05	1.75
❏ 43, Jun 96	1.75	0.35	1.05	1.75

GUY GARDNER: WARRIOR ANNUAL

	ORIG.	GOOD	FINE	N-MINT
❏ 1, 95, "Year One"	3.50	0.70	2.10	3.50

GUYVER
VIZ

	ORIG.	GOOD	FINE	N-MINT
❏ 1	2.75	0.55	1.65	2.75
❏ 2	2.75	0.55	1.65	2.75
❏ 3	2.75	0.55	1.65	2.75
❏ 4	2.75	0.55	1.65	2.75
❏ 5	2.75	0.55	1.65	2.75
❏ 6	2.75	0.55	1.65	2.75

GYRO COMICS
RIP OFF

	ORIG.	GOOD	FINE	N-MINT
❏ 1, b&w;Mark Bode		0.40	1.20	2.00
❏ 2, b&w;Mark Bode		0.40	1.20	2.00
❏ 3, b&w;Mark Bode		0.40	1.20	2.00

H

	ORIG.	GOOD	FINE	N-MINT
H-BOMB				
ANTARCTIC				
☐ 1, Apr 93, adult only, b&w				
................................2.95	0.59	1.77	2.95	
H.A.R.D. CORPS				
VALIANT				
☐ 1, Dec 92....................2.50	1.00	3.00	5.00	
☐ 1, gold...........................	3.60	10.80	18.00	
☐ 2, Jan 93.....................2.25	0.60	1.80	3.00	
☐ 3, Feb 93.....................2.25	0.60	1.80	3.00	
☐ 4, Apr 93......................2.25	0.45	1.35	2.25	
☐ 5, Apr 93, Bloodshot......2.25	0.80	2.40	4.00	
☐ 6, May 93.....................2.25	0.45	1.35	2.25	
☐ 7, Jun 93......................2.25	0.45	1.35	2.25	
☐ 8, Jul 93.......................2.25	0.45	1.35	2.25	
☐ 9, Aug 93.....................2.25	0.45	1.35	2.25	
☐ 10, Sep 93....................2.25	0.45	1.35	2.25	
☐ 11, Oct 93.....................2.25	0.45	1.35	2.25	
☐ 12, Nov 93....................2.25	0.45	1.35	2.25	
☐ 13, Dec 93....................2.25	0.45	1.35	2.25	
☐ 14, Jan 94.....................2.25	0.45	1.35	2.25	
☐ 15, Feb 94....................2.25	0.45	1.35	2.25	
☐ 16, Mar 94....................2.25	0.45	1.35	2.25	
☐ 17, Apr 94.....................2.25	0.45	1.35	2.25	
☐ 18, May 94, trading card 2.25	0.45	1.35	2.25	
☐ 19, Jun 94.....................2.25	0.45	1.35	2.25	
☐ 20, Jul 94, A:Harbinger..2.25	0.45	1.35	2.25	
☐ 21, Sep 94....................2.25	0.45	1.35	2.25	
☐ 22, Oct 94.....................2.25	0.45	1.35	2.25	
☐ 23, Nov 94, Chaos Effect 2.25	0.45	1.35	2.25	
☐ 28, Apr 95.....................2.50	0.50	1.50	2.50	
☐ 29, May 95....................2.25	0.45	1.35	2.25	
☐ 30, Jun 95, final issue....2.25	0.45	1.35	2.25	
H.P. LOVECRAFT'S CTHULHU				
MILLENNIUM				
☐ 1 ....2.50	0.50	1.50	2.50	
☐ 1, trading cards.............3.50	0.70	2.10	3.50	
☐ 2, trading cards...............	0.50	1.50	2.50	
H.P. LOVECRAFT'S CTHULHU:				
THE WHISPER IN DARKNESS				
☐ 0, nn.............................6.95	1.39	4.17	6.95	
HACKER FILES, THE				
DC				
☐ 1 ....1.95	0.39	1.17	1.95	
☐ 2 ....1.95	0.39	1.17	1.95	
☐ 3 ....1.95	0.39	1.17	1.95	
☐ 4 ....1.95	0.39	1.17	1.95	
☐ 5 ....1.95	0.39	1.17	1.95	
☐ 6 ....1.95	0.39	1.17	1.95	
☐ 7 ....1.95	0.39	1.17	1.95	
☐ 8 ....1.95	0.39	1.17	1.95	
☐ 9 ....1.95	0.39	1.17	1.95	
☐ 10 ....1.95	0.39	1.17	1.95	
☐ 11 ....1.95	0.39	1.17	1.95	
☐ 12 ....1.95	0.39	1.17	1.95	
HAIRBAT				
SCREAMING RICE				
☐ 1, b&w 2.50	0.60	1.80	3.00	
☐ 2, b&w 2.50	0.50	1.50	2.50	
☐ 3, b&w 2.50	0.50	1.50	2.50	
HALL OF FAME				
J.C.				
☐ 1	0.20	0.60	1.00	
☐ 2	0.20	0.60	1.00	
☐ 3	0.20	0.60	1.00	
HALL OF HEROES				
HALL OF HEROES				
☐ 1, b&w 2.50	0.50	1.50	2.50	

	ORIG.	GOOD	FINE	N-MINT
HALLOWEEN HORROR				
ECLIPSE				
☐ 1	0.35	1.05	1.75	
HALLOWEEN TERROR				
ETERNITY				
☐ 1, b&w..........................	0.50	1.50	2.50	
HALO JONES				
FLEETWAY/QUALITY				
☐ 1, AMo..........................	0.25	0.75	1.25	
☐ 2, AMo..........................	0.25	0.75	1.25	
☐ 3, AMo..........................	0.25	0.75	1.25	
☐ 4, AMo..........................	0.25	0.75	1.25	
☐ 5, AMo..........................	0.25	0.75	1.25	
☐ 6, AMo..........................	0.25	0.75	1.25	
☐ 7, AMo..........................	0.25	0.75	1.25	
☐ 8, AMo..........................	0.25	0.75	1.25	
☐ 9, AMo..........................	0.25	0.75	1.25	
☐ 10, AMo........................	0.25	0.75	1.25	
☐ 11, Alan Moore	0.30	0.90	1.50	
☐ 12, Alan Moore	0.30	0.90	1.50	
HAMMER OF GOD				
FIRST				
☐ 1	0.39	1.17	1.95	
☐ 2	0.39	1.17	1.95	
☐ 3	0.39	1.17	1.95	
☐ 4	0.39	1.17	1.95	
HAMMER OF GOD: BUTCH (mini-series)				
DARK HORSE				
☐ 1, May 94.....................2.50	0.50	1.50	2.50	
☐ 2, Jul 94.......................2.50	0.50	1.50	2.50	
☐ 3, Aug 94, final issue 2.50	0.50	1.50	2.50	
HAMMER OF GOD: PENTATHLON				
☐ 0, 94, nn 2.50	0.50	1.50	2.50	
HAMMER OF GOD: SWORD OF JUSTICE				
FIRST				
☐ 1	0.99	2.97	4.95	
☐ 2	0.99	2.97	4.95	
HAMMERLOCKE				
DC				
☐ 1	0.50	1.50	2.50	
☐ 2 ....1.75	0.35	1.05	1.75	
☐ 3 ....1.75	0.35	1.05	1.75	
☐ 4 ....1.75	0.35	1.05	1.75	
☐ 5 ....1.75	0.35	1.05	1.75	
☐ 6 ....1.75	0.35	1.05	1.75	
☐ 7 ....1.75	0.35	1.05	1.75	
☐ 8 ....1.75	0.35	1.05	1.75	
☐ 9 ....1.75	0.35	1.05	1.75	
HAMSTER VICE				
BLACKTHORNE				
☐ 1	0.40	1.20	2.00	
☐ 2	0.40	1.20	2.00	
☐ 3	0.40	1.20	2.00	
☐ 4	0.40	1.20	2.00	
☐ 5	0.40	1.20	2.00	
☐ 6	0.40	1.20	2.00	
☐ 7	0.40	1.20	2.00	
☐ 8	0.40	1.20	2.00	
ETERNITY				
☐ 1, b&w..........................	0.39	1.17	1.95	
☐ 2, b&w..........................	0.39	1.17	1.95	
HAMSTER VICE 3-D				
BLACKTHORNE				
☐ 1	0.50	1.50	2.50	
☐ 2	0.50	1.50	2.50	

	ORIG.	GOOD	FINE	N-MINT
HAND OF FATE				
ECLIPSE				
☐ 1, Feb 88, color	0.35	1.05	1.75	
☐ 2, Mar 88, color	0.35	1.05	1.75	
☐ 3, Apr 88, b&w	0.40	1.20	2.00	
HAND SHADOWS				
DOYAN				
☐ 1	0.30	0.90	1.50	
☐ 2	0.30	0.90	1.50	
HANDS OF THE DRAGON				
ATLAS/ SEABOARD				
☐ 1, Jun 75	0.25	0.20	0.60	1.00
HANDS OFF!				
WARD SUTTON				
☐ 0, 94, b&w, one-shot	2.95	0.59	1.77	2.95
HANNA-BARBERA ALL-STARS				
ARCHIE				
☐ 1, Oct 95, anthology	1.50	0.30	0.90	1.50
☐ 2, Dec 95, anthology	1.50	0.30	0.90	1.50
☐ 3, Feb 96, anthology	1.50	0.30	0.90	1.50
☐ 4, Apr 96, anthology	1.50	0.30	0.90	1.50
HANNA-BARBERA BIG BOOK				
HARVEY				
☐ 1	0.39	1.17	1.95	
☐ 3	2.50	0.50	1.50	2.50
HANNA-BARBERA PRESENTS				
ARCHIE				
☐ 1, Nov 95, Atom Ant and Secret Squirrel				
	1.50	0.30	0.90	1.50
☐ 2, Jan 96, Wacky Races	1.50	0.30	0.90	1.50
☐ 3, Mar 96, Yogi Bear	1.50	0.30	0.90	1.50
☐ 4, May 96, Quick Draw McGraw and Magilla Gorilla				
	1.50	0.30	0.90	1.50
☐ 5, Jul 96, A Pup Named Scooby-Doo				
	1.50	0.30	0.90	1.50
HANNA-BARBERA PRESENTS ALL-NEW COMICS				
HARVEY				
☐ 0, giveaway promo	0.60	1.80	3.00	
HAP HAZARD				
FANDOM HOUSE				
☐ 1, b&w	0.40	1.20	2.00	
HAPPY				
WONDER COMICS				
☐ 1, b&w	0.40	1.20	2.00	
HAPPY BIRTHDAY GNATRAT				
DIMENSION				
☐ 1	0.39	1.17	1.95	
HAPPY BIRTHDAY MARTHA WASHINGTON				
DARK HORSE				
☐ 0, Mar 95, cardstock cover				
	2.95	0.59	1.77	2.95
HAR*HAR				
FANTAGRAPHICS				
☐ 1, b&w	2.25	0.45	1.35	2.25
☐ 2, b&w	2.25	0.45	1.35	2.25
HARBINGER				
VALIANT				
☐ 0, Feb 93		7.60	22.80	38.00
☐ 1, Jan 92, O:Harbinger	1.95	5.00	15.00	25.00
☐ 2, Feb 92	1.95	4.00	12.00	20.00
☐ 3, Mar 92	1.95	3.20	9.60	16.00
☐ 4, Apr 92	1.95	4.00	12.00	20.00
☐ 5, May 92	2.50	3.00	9.00	15.00
☐ 6, Jun 92	2.50	3.00	9.00	15.00
☐ 7, Jul 92	2.25	2.40	7.20	12.00
☐ 8, Aug 92, FM(c) Unity	2.50	1.60	4.80	8.00
☐ 9, Sep 92, WS(c) Unity	2.50	1.60	4.80	8.00
☐ 10, Oct 92, 1:H.A.R.D Corps				
	2.50	1.60	4.80	8.00

	ORIG.	GOOD	FINE	N-MINT
☐ 11, Nov 92	2.50	1.20	3.60	6.00
☐ 12, Dec 92	2.50	1.00	3.00	5.00
☐ 13, Jan 93, Dark Knight cover				
	2.50	1.00	3.00	5.00
☐ 14, Feb 93	2.50	1.00	3.00	5.00
☐ 15, Mar 93	2.50	1.00	3.00	5.00
☐ 16, Apr 93	2.50	0.50	1.50	2.50
☐ 17, May 93	2.50	0.50	1.50	2.50
☐ 18, Jun 93	2.50	0.50	1.50	2.50
☐ 19, Jul 93	2.50	0.50	1.50	2.50
☐ 20, Aug 93	2.50	0.50	1.50	2.50
☐ 21, Aug 93	2.50	0.50	1.50	2.50
☐ 22, Aug 93	2.50	0.50	1.50	2.50
☐ 23, Aug 93	2.50	0.50	1.50	2.50
☐ 24, Aug 93	2.50	0.50	1.50	2.50
☐ 25, Aug 93	2.50	0.50	1.50	2.50
☐ 26, Feb 94	2.50	0.50	1.50	2.50
☐ 27, Mar 94	2.50	0.50	1.50	2.50
☐ 28, Apr 94	2.50	0.50	1.50	2.50
☐ 29, May 94, trading card	2.50	0.50	1.50	2.50
☐ 30, Jun 94, A: H.A.R.D.Corps				
	2.50	0.50	1.50	2.50
☐ 31, Aug 94, A:H.A.R.D.Corps				
	2.50	0.50	1.50	2.50
☐ 32, Sep 94, A: Eternal Warrior				
	2.50	0.50	1.50	2.50
☐ 33, Oct 94, A: Dr. Eclipse	2.50	0.50	1.50	2.50
☐ 34, Nov 94, Chaos Effect	2.50	0.50	1.50	2.50
☐ 37, Feb 95	2.50	0.50	1.50	2.50
☐ 38, Mar 95	2.50	0.50	1.50	2.50
☐ 39, Apr 95	2.50	0.50	1.50	2.50
☐ 40, May 95	2.50	0.50	1.50	2.50
HARBINGER FILES				
☐ 1, Aug 94, O:Harada	2.50	0.50	1.50	2.50
☐ 2, Feb 95	2.50	0.50	1.50	2.50
HARD BOILED				
DARK HORSE				
☐ 1, Sep 90, FM(w) GD	4.95	1.50	4.50	7.50
☐ 2, Dec 90, FM(w) GD	5.95	1.20	3.60	6.00
☐ 3, Mar 92	5.95	1.20	3.60	6.00
HARD LOOKS				
☐ 1, b&w		0.50	1.50	2.50
☐ 2, b&w		0.50	1.50	2.50
☐ 3, b&w		0.50	1.50	2.50
☐ 4, b&w		0.50	1.50	2.50
☐ 5, b&w		0.50	1.50	2.50
☐ 6, b&w	2.95	0.59	1.77	2.95
☐ 7, b&w	2.95	0.59	1.77	2.95
☐ 8, b&w	2.95	0.59	1.77	2.95
☐ 9, b&w	2.95	0.59	1.77	2.95
☐ 10, b&w	3.50	0.70	2.10	3.50
HARD ROCK				
REVOLUTIONARY				
☐ 1, Mar 92, b&w, Metallica, early				
	2.50	0.50	1.50	2.50
☐ 2, Apr 92, b&w, Motley Crue				
	2.50	0.50	1.50	2.50
☐ 3, May 92, b&w, Jane's Addiction				
	2.50	0.50	1.50	2.50
☐ 4, Jun 92, b&w, Nirvana	2.50	0.50	1.50	2.50
☐ 5, Jul 92, b&w, KISS on tour				
	2.50	0.50	1.50	2.50
☐ 6, Sep 92, b&w, Def Leppard II				
	2.50	0.50	1.50	2.50
☐ 7, Oct 92, b&w, Red Hot Chili Peppers				
	2.50	0.50	1.50	2.50
☐ 8, Nov 92, b&w, Soundgarden/Pearl Jam				
	2.50	0.50	1.50	2.50
☐ 9, Dec 92, b&w, Queen II				
	2.50	0.50	1.50	2.50

	ORIG.	GOOD	FINE	N-MINT
10, Jan 93, b&w, Birth of Punk				
.....2.50	0.50	1.50	2.50
11, Feb 93, b&w, Pantera				
.....2.50	0.50	1.50	2.50
12, Mar 93, b&w, Hendrix				
.....2.50	0.50	1.50	2.50
13, Apr 93, b&w, Dead Kennedys				
.....2.50	0.50	1.50	2.50
14, May 93, b&w, Van Halen II				
.....2.50	0.50	1.50	2.50
15, Jun 93, b&w, Megadeath/Motorhead				
.....2.50	0.50	1.50	2.50
16, Jul 93, b&w, Joan Jett/Lita Ford				
.....2.50	0.50	1.50	2.50
17, never published..........				
18, Sep 93, b&w, Queensryche II				
.....2.50	0.50	1.50	2.50
19, Oct 93, b&w, Tesla/Spirit/UKJ				
.....2.50	0.50	1.50	2.50
20, Nov 93, b&w, Ratt/P-Funk/Sweet				
.....2.50	0.50	1.50	2.50

HARDBALL
AIRCEL

	ORIG.	GOOD	FINE	N-MINT
1, adult, b&w		0.59	1.77	2.95
2, adult, b&w		0.59	1.77	2.95
3, adult, b&w		0.59	1.77	2.95
4, adult, b&w		0.59	1.77	2.95

HARDCASE
MALIBU/ULTRAVERSE

	ORIG.	GOOD	FINE	N-MINT
1	1.95	0.80	2.40	4.00
1, Ultra Ltd., silver cover	1.95	0.39	1.17	1.95
1, hologram cover...........	8.00	24.00	40.00	
2, trading card........	1.95	1.40	4.20	7.00
3	1.95	0.60	1.80	3.00
4, Sep 93	1.95	0.60	1.80	3.00
5, Rune, BWS........	2.50	0.50	1.50	2.50
6, Nov 93	1.95	0.39	1.17	1.95
7, Dec 93, Break-Thru	1.95	0.39	1.17	1.95
8, Jan 94, A:Solution......	1.95	0.39	1.17	1.95
9, Feb 94	1.95	0.39	1.17	1.95
10, Mar 94........	1.95	0.39	1.17	1.95
12, May 94........	1.95	0.39	1.17	1.95
13, Jun 94	1.95	0.39	1.17	1.95
14, Jul 94	1.95	0.39	1.17	1.95
15, Aug 94	1.95	0.39	1.17	1.95
16, Oct 94, (contains *Ultraverse Premiere* #7)				
.....3.50	0.70	2.10	3.50

HARDKORR
AIRCEL

	ORIG.	GOOD	FINE	N-MINT
1, adult, b&w		0.50	1.50	2.50
2, adult, b&w		0.50	1.50	2.50
3, adult, b&w		0.50	1.50	2.50
4, adult, b&w		0.50	1.50	2.50

HARDWARE
DC/MILESTONE

	ORIG.	GOOD	FINE	N-MINT
1, Apr 93, newsstand	1.50	0.30	0.90	1.50
1, Apr 93, bagged, trading card, poster				
.....2.95	0.59	1.77	2.95
1, Apr 93, platinum	9.00	27.00	45.00	
1, Apr 93, silver edition....	5.00	15.00	25.00	
2, May 93........	1.50	0.30	0.90	1.50
3, May 93........	1.50	0.30	0.90	1.50
4, Jun 93	1.50	0.30	0.90	1.50
5, Jul 93	1.50	0.30	0.90	1.50
6, Aug 93........	1.50	0.30	0.90	1.50
7, Sep 93........	1.50	0.30	0.90	1.50
8, Oct 93	1.50	0.30	0.90	1.50
9, Nov 93	1.50	0.30	0.90	1.50
10, Dec 93........	1.50	0.30	0.90	1.50
11, Jan 94, Shadow War	1.50	0.30	0.90	1.50
12, Feb 94	1.50	0.30	0.90	1.50

	ORIG.	GOOD	FINE	N-MINT
13, Mar 94........	1.50	0.30	0.90	1.50
14, Apr 94........	1.50	0.30	0.90	1.50
15, May 94........	1.50	0.30	0.90	1.50
16, Jun 94	2.50	0.50	1.50	2.50
16, Jun 94, foldout cover				
.....3.95	0.79	2.37	3.95
17, Jul 94, Worlds Collide				
.....1.50	0.45	1.35	2.25
18, Aug 94........	1.75	0.35	1.05	1.75
19, Sep 94	1.75	0.35	1.05	1.75
20, Oct 94........	1.75	0.35	1.05	1.75
21, Nov 94........	1.75	0.35	1.05	1.75
22, Dec 94........	1.75	0.35	1.05	1.75
23, Jan 95........	1.75	0.35	1.05	1.75
24, Feb 95........	1.75	0.35	1.05	1.75
25, Mar 95........	2.95	0.59	1.77	2.95
26, Apr 95........	1.75	0.35	1.05	1.75
27, May 95........	1.75	0.35	1.05	1.75
28, Jun 95	1.75	0.35	1.05	1.75
29, Jul 95, cover has both .99 and 2.50 cover price				
.....2.50	0.50	1.50	2.50
30, Aug 95........	2.50	0.50	1.50	2.50
31, Sep 95, D:Edwin Alva				
.....2.50	0.50	1.50	2.50
32, Oct 95........	2.50	0.50	1.50	2.50
33, Nov 95, HC(c)	2.50	0.50	1.50	2.50
34, Dec 95........	2.50	0.50	1.50	2.50
35, Jan 96........	2.50	0.50	1.50	2.50
36, Feb 96........	2.50	0.50	1.50	2.50
37, Mar 96........	2.50	0.50	1.50	2.50
38, Apr 96........	2.50	0.50	1.50	2.50
39, May 96........	2.50	0.50	1.50	2.50
40, Jun 96	2.50	0.50	1.50	2.50

HARI KARI
BLACK OUT

	ORIG.	GOOD	FINE	N-MINT
0, 95, indicia says "#0 #1"				
.....2.95	0.59	1.77	2.95
1, 95	2.95	0.59	1.77	2.95

HARLAN ELLISON'S DREAM CORRIDOR
DARK HORSE

	ORIG.	GOOD	FINE	N-MINT
1, Mar 95........	2.95	0.59	1.77	2.95
2, Apr 95........	2.95	0.59	1.77	2.95
3, May 95........	2.95	0.59	1.77	2.95
4, Jun 95, cardstock cover				
.....2.95	0.59	1.77	2.95
5, Aug 95, cardstock cover				
.....2.95	0.59	1.77	2.95
6, Sep 95	2.95	0.59	1.77	2.95

HARLAN ELLISON'S DREAM CORRIDOR SPECIAL

	ORIG.	GOOD	FINE	N-MINT
0, Jan 95, prestige format				
.....4.95	0.99	2.97	4.95
0, Sep 95, prestige format;second printing				
.....4.95	0.99	2.97	4.95

HARLEM HEROES
FLEETWAY/QUALITY

	ORIG.	GOOD	FINE	N-MINT
1, b&w........	1.95	0.39	1.17	1.95
2, b&w........	1.95	0.39	1.17	1.95
3, b&w........	1.95	0.39	1.17	1.95
4, b&w........	1.95	0.39	1.17	1.95
5, b&w........	1.95	0.39	1.17	1.95
6, b&w........	1.95	0.39	1.17	1.95

HARLEQUIN
CALIBER

	ORIG.	GOOD	FINE	N-MINT
0, nn, b&w........	2.95	0.59	1.77	2.95

HARLEY RIDER
HUNGNESS

	ORIG.	GOOD	FINE	N-MINT
1, GM........		0.40	1.20	2.00

	ORIG.	GOOD	FINE	N-MINT

HARRIER PREVIEW
HARRIER
	ORIG.	GOOD	FINE	N-MINT
☐ 1, 1:Cuirass, Night Bird....	0.39	1.17	1.95	

HARRIERS (mini-series)
EXPRESS/ENTITY
	ORIG.	GOOD	FINE	N-MINT
☐ 1, 95, Enhanced cover....	2.95	0.59	1.77	2.95
☐ 2, 95..............................	2.50	0.50	1.50	2.50
☐ 3, 95..............................	2.50	0.50	1.50	2.50

HARROWERS: RAIDERS OF THE ABYSS, THE
EPIC
	ORIG.	GOOD	FINE	N-MINT
☐ 1	2.50	0.50	1.50	2.50
☐ 2	2.50	0.50	1.50	2.50
☐ 3	2.50	0.50	1.50	2.50
☐ 4	2.50	0.50	1.50	2.50
☐ 5	2.50	0.50	1.50	2.50
☐ 6, May 94	2.50	0.50	1.50	2.50

HARRY THE COP
SLAVE LABOR
	ORIG.	GOOD	FINE	N-MINT
☐ 1, b&w		0.59	1.77	2.95

HARSH REALM
HARRIS
	ORIG.	GOOD	FINE	N-MINT
☐ 1, 94, color....................	2.95	0.59	1.77	2.95
☐ 2, 94, color....................	2.95	0.59	1.77	2.95
☐ 3, 94, color....................	2.95	0.59	1.77	2.95
☐ 4, 94, color....................	2.95	0.59	1.77	2.95
☐ 5, 94, color....................	2.95	0.59	1.77	2.95

HARTE OF DARKNESS
ETERNITY
	ORIG.	GOOD	FINE	N-MINT
☐ 1, b&w		0.50	1.50	2.50
☐ 2, b&w		0.50	1.50	2.50
☐ 3, b&w		0.50	1.50	2.50
☐ 4, b&w		0.50	1.50	2.50

HATE
FANTAGRAPHICS
	ORIG.	GOOD	FINE	N-MINT
☐ 1, b&w		1.60	4.80	8.00
☐ 2		1.00	3.00	5.00
☐ 3		1.00	3.00	5.00
☐ 4		1.00	3.00	5.00
☐ 4, 2nd printing		0.40	1.20	2.00
☐ 5		0.80	2.40	4.00
☐ 6		0.60	1.80	3.00
☐ 7		0.60	1.80	3.00
☐ 8		0.60	1.80	3.00
☐ 9		0.60	1.80	3.00
☐ 10		0.60	1.80	3.00
☐ 11	2.50	0.50	1.50	2.50
☐ 12	2.50	0.50	1.50	2.50
☐ 13	2.50	0.50	1.50	2.50
☐ 14	2.50	0.50	1.50	2.50
☐ 15, Spr 94	2.50	0.50	1.50	2.50
☐ 16, color story.................	2.95	0.59	1.77	2.95
☐ 20, Sep 95, color and b&w				
....	2.95	0.59	1.77	2.95

HAUNT OF FEAR
COCHRAN
	ORIG.	GOOD	FINE	N-MINT
☐ 1, reprints, O:Old Witch Ingels, Kamen, Check, Davis, WW, JO........................	2.00	0.40	1.20	2.00
☐ 2, reprints, Ingels, Kamen, Davis, WW	2.00	0.40	1.20	2.00
☐ 3, reprints, Ingels, Kamen, Davis, WW	2.00	0.40	1.20	2.00
☐ 4, reprints, Ingels, Kamen, Davis, WW	2.00	0.40	1.20	2.00
☐ 5, reprints, Ingels, Kamen, Davis, WW	2.00	0.40	1.20	2.00

HAUNT OF FEAR, THE
EC/GEMSTONE
	ORIG.	GOOD	FINE	N-MINT
☐ 1, EC reprints	1.50	0.30	0.90	1.50
☐ 2, EC reprints, JC,WW, GI,JK				
....	1.50	0.30	0.90	1.50
☐ 3, reprints	1.50	0.30	0.90	1.50
☐ 4, reprints:AF(c),GI,JK, JD,WW				
....	2.00	0.40	1.20	2.00
☐ 5, reprints:JC,GI,WW,JD.	2.00	0.40	1.20	2.00
☐ 6, reprints:JC(c),GI,WW, JK,JD				
....	2.00	0.40	1.20	2.00
☐ 7, May 94, r:GI,JD, JK,JC				
....	2.00	0.40	1.20	2.00
☐ 8, reprints	2.00	0.40	1.20	2.00
☐ 9, reprints	2.00	0.40	1.20	2.00
☐ 10, reprints	2.00	0.40	1.20	2.00
☐ 11, reprints	2.00	0.40	1.20	2.00
☐ 12, reprints	2.00	0.40	1.20	2.00

GLADSTONE
	ORIG.	GOOD	FINE	N-MINT
☐ 1, May 91, reprint, Ingels, Evans, Davis, Kamen, Feldstein, Wood, Williamson, Orlando				
....	2.00	0.40	1.20	2.00
☐ 2, Jul 91, reprint, Craig, Ingels, Wood, Davis, Frazetta, Crandall, Orlando.........	2.00	0.40	1.20	2.00

HAUNT OF HORROR, THE (b&w comics mag)
MARVEL
	ORIG.	GOOD	FINE	N-MINT
☐ 1	0.75	0.15	0.45	0.75
☐ 2	0.75	0.15	0.45	0.75
☐ 3	0.75	0.15	0.45	0.75
☐ 4	0.75	0.15	0.45	0.75
☐ 5	0.75	0.15	0.45	0.75

HAUNT OF HORROR, THE (digest; not comics)
	ORIG.	GOOD	FINE	N-MINT
☐ 0, June 1973..................	0.75	0.15	0.45	0.75
☐ 0, August 1973	0.75	0.15	0.45	0.75

HAVOK & WOLVERINE: MELTDOWN
EPIC
	ORIG.	GOOD	FINE	N-MINT
☐ 1, Jan 88........................	3.50	2.80	8.40	14.00
☐ 2, Feb 88........................	3.50	2.40	7.20	12.00
☐ 3, Mar 88........................	3.50	2.00	6.00	10.00
☐ 4, Apr 88........................	3.50	2.00	6.00	10.00

HAWK AND DOVE
DC
	ORIG.	GOOD	FINE	N-MINT
☐ 1, Aug 68.........................		10.00	30.00	50.00
☐ 2, Oct 68.........................		7.20	21.60	36.00
☐ 3, Dec 68.........................		5.00	15.00	25.00
☐ 4, Feb 69.........................		5.00	15.00	25.00
☐ 5, Mar 69.........................		5.00	15.00	25.00
☐ 6, Jun 69		5.00	15.00	25.00

HAWK AND DOVE (mini-series)
	ORIG.	GOOD	FINE	N-MINT
☐ 1, Oct 88........................	1.00	2.00	6.00	10.00
☐ 2, Nov 88........................	1.00	1.20	3.60	6.00
☐ 3, Dec 88........................	1.00	1.20	3.60	6.00
☐ 4, Dec 88........................	1.00	1.00	3.00	5.00
☐ 5, Jan 89, O:Dove	1.00	1.00	3.00	5.00

HAWK AND DOVE (third series)
	ORIG.	GOOD	FINE	N-MINT
☐ 1, Jun 89	1.00	0.40	1.20	2.00
☐ 2, Jul 89	1.00	0.30	0.90	1.50
☐ 3, Aug 89	1.00	0.30	0.90	1.50
☐ 4, Sep 89	1.00	0.30	0.90	1.50
☐ 5, Oct 89	1.00	0.20	0.60	1.00
☐ 6, Nov 89	1.00	0.20	0.60	1.00
☐ 7, Dec 89	1.00	0.20	0.60	1.00
☐ 8, Jan 90........................	1.00	0.20	0.60	1.00
☐ 9, Feb 90........................	1.00	0.20	0.60	1.00
☐ 10, Mar 90......................	1.00	0.20	0.60	1.00
☐ 11, Apr 90.......................	1.00	0.20	0.60	1.00
☐ 12, May 90......................	1.00	0.20	0.60	1.00
☐ 13, Jun 90	1.00	0.20	0.60	1.00
☐ 14, Jul 90........................	1.00	0.20	0.60	1.00
☐ 15, Aug 90......................	1.00	0.20	0.60	1.00
☐ 16, Sep 90	1.00	0.20	0.60	1.00
☐ 17, Oct 90.......................	1.00	0.20	0.60	1.00

	ORIG.	GOOD	FINE	N-MINT
☐ 18, Nov 90 .... 1.00		0.20	0.60	1.00
☐ 19, Dec 90..................... 1.00		0.20	0.60	1.00
☐ 20, Jan 91 .... 1.00		0.20	0.60	1.00
☐ 21, Feb 91 .... 1.00		0.20	0.60	1.00
☐ 22, Mar 91 .... 1.00		0.20	0.60	1.00
☐ 23, Apr 91 .... 1.00		0.20	0.60	1.00
☐ 24, May 91 .... 1.00		0.20	0.60	1.00
☐ 25, Jun 91 .... 2.00		0.40	1.20	2.00
☐ 26, Aug 92, O:retold....... 1.25		0.25	0.75	1.25
☐ 27, Sep 91 .... 1.25		0.25	0.75	1.25
☐ 28, Oct 91, War of Gods 2.00		0.40	1.20	2.00

HAWK AND DOVE ANNUAL

	ORIG.	GOOD	FINE	N-MINT
☐ 1, Oct 90, Titans West......		0.40	1.20	2.00
☐ 2, Sep 91, Armageddon 2001		0.40	1.20	2.00

HAWKEYE
MARVEL

	ORIG.	GOOD	FINE	N-MINT
☐ 1, Sep 83 .... 0.60		0.30	0.90	1.50
☐ 2, Oct 83 .... 0.60		0.20	0.60	1.00
☐ 3, Nov 83 .... 0.60		0.20	0.60	1.00
☐ 4, Dec 83..................... 0.60		0.20	0.60	1.00

HAWKEYE (Volume 2)

	ORIG.	GOOD	FINE	N-MINT
☐ 1 .... 1.75		0.35	1.05	1.75
☐ 2 .... 1.75		0.35	1.05	1.75
☐ 3 .... 1.75		0.35	1.05	1.75
☐ 4, Apr 94 .... 1.75		0.35	1.05	1.75

HAWKMAN
DC

	ORIG.	GOOD	FINE	N-MINT
☐ 1, May 64, MA............... 0.12		85.00	255.00	425.00
☐ 2, Jul 64, MA................. 0.12		36.00	108.00	180.00
☐ 3, Sep 64, MA 0.12		24.00	72.00	120.00
☐ 4, Nov 64, MA............... 0.12		24.00	72.00	120.00
☐ 5, Jan 65, MA............... 0.12		24.00	72.00	120.00
☐ 5, Jan 65, MA............... 0.12		16.00	48.00	80.00
☐ 6, Mar 65, MA............... 0.12		9.60	28.80	48.00
☐ 7, May 65, MA............... 0.12		9.60	28.80	48.00
☐ 8, Jul 65, MA................. 0.12		9.60	28.80	48.00
☐ 9, Sep 65, MA 0.12		9.60	28.80	48.00
☐ 10, Nov 65, MA............... 0.12		9.60	28.80	48.00
☐ 11, Jan 66, MA............... 0.12		7.00	21.00	35.00
☐ 12, Mar 66, MA............... 0.12		7.00	21.00	35.00
☐ 13, May 66, MA............... 0.12		7.00	21.00	35.00
☐ 14, Jul 66, MA............... 0.12		7.00	21.00	35.00
☐ 15, Sep 66, MA 0.12		7.00	21.00	35.00
☐ 16, Nov 66 .... 0.12		2.80	8.40	14.00
☐ 17, Jan 67..................... 0.12		4.80	14.40	24.00
☐ 18, Mar 67 .... 0.12		9.00	27.00	45.00
☐ 19, May 67..................... 0.12		7.60	22.80	38.00
☐ 20, Jul 67 .... 0.12		4.80	14.40	24.00
☐ 21, Sep 67..................... 0.12		4.80	14.40	24.00
☐ 22, Nov 67..................... 0.12		4.80	14.40	24.00
☐ 23, Jan 68..................... 0.12		4.80	14.40	24.00
☐ 24, Mar 68..................... 0.12		4.80	14.40	24.00
☐ 25, May 68..................... 0.12		4.80	14.40	24.00
☐ 26, Jul 68..................... 0.12		4.80	14.40	24.00
☐ 27, Sep 68..................... 0.12		4.80	14.40	24.00

HAWKMAN (2nd series)

	ORIG.	GOOD	FINE	N-MINT
☐ 1, Aug 86 .... 0.75		0.40	1.20	2.00
☐ 2, Sep 86..................... 0.75		0.35	1.05	1.75
☐ 3, Oct 86 .... 0.75		0.35	1.05	1.75
☐ 4, Nov 86..................... 0.75		0.35	1.05	1.75
☐ 5, Dec 86..................... 0.75		0.35	1.05	1.75
☐ 6, Jan 87 .... 0.75		0.35	1.05	1.75
☐ 7, Feb 87 .... 0.75		0.35	1.05	1.75
☐ 8, Mar 87 .... 0.75		0.35	1.05	1.75
☐ 9, Apr 87 .... 0.75		0.35	1.05	1.75
☐ 10, May 87..................... 0.75		0.35	1.05	1.75
☐ 11, Jun 87..................... 0.75		0.35	1.05	1.75

	ORIG.	GOOD	FINE	N-MINT
☐ 12, Jul 87.....................0.75		0.35	1.05	1.75
☐ 13, Aug 87.....................0.75		0.35	1.05	1.75
☐ 14, Sep 87.....................0.75		0.35	1.05	1.75
☐ 15, Oct 87.....................0.75		0.35	1.05	1.75
☐ 16, Nov 87.....................1.00		0.35	1.05	1.75
☐ 17, Dec 87.....................1.00		0.35	1.05	1.75

HAWKMAN (3rd series)

	ORIG.	GOOD	FINE	N-MINT
☐ 0, Oct 94.....................1.95		0.39	1.17	1.95
☐ 1, foil cover.....................2.50		1.00	3.00	5.00
☐ 2 ....1.75		0.60	1.80	3.00
☐ 3 ....1.75		0.35	1.05	1.75
☐ 4 ....1.75		0.35	1.05	1.75
☐ 5 ....1.75		0.35	1.05	1.75
☐ 6 ....1.75		0.35	1.05	1.75
☐ 7, Mongrel.....................1.75		0.35	1.05	1.75
☐ 8, Mongrel.....................1.75		0.35	1.05	1.75
☐ 9, May 94.....................1.75		0.35	1.05	1.75
☐ 10, Jun 94.....................1.75		0.35	1.05	1.75
☐ 11, Jul 94.....................1.75		0.35	1.05	1.75
☐ 12, Aug 94.....................1.95		0.39	1.17	1.95
☐ 13, Sep 94.....................1.95		0.39	1.17	1.95
☐ 14, Nov 94.....................1.95		0.39	1.17	1.95
☐ 15, Dec 94.....................1.95		0.39	1.17	1.95
☐ 16, Jan 95.....................1.95		0.39	1.17	1.95
☐ 17, Feb 95.....................1.95		0.39	1.17	1.95
☐ 18, Mar 95.....................1.95		0.39	1.17	1.95
☐ 19, Apr 95.....................1.95		0.39	1.17	1.95
☐ 20, May 95.....................1.95		0.39	1.17	1.95
☐ 21, Jun 95.....................2.25		0.45	1.35	2.25
☐ 22, Jul 95.....................2.25		0.45	1.35	2.25
☐ 23, Aug 95.....................2.25		0.45	1.35	2.25
☐ 24, Sep 95.....................2.25		0.45	1.35	2.25
☐ 25, Oct 95.....................2.25		0.45	1.35	2.25
☐ 26, Nov 95, "Underworld Unleashed"				
.....................2.25		0.45	1.35	2.25
☐ 27, Dec 95, "Underworld Unleashed"				
.....................2.25		0.45	1.35	2.25
☐ 28, Jan 96, V:Dr. Polaris 2.25		0.45	1.35	2.25
☐ 29, Feb 96.....................2.25		0.45	1.35	2.25
☐ 30, Mar 96.....................2.25		0.45	1.35	2.25
☐ 31, Apr 96.....................2.25		0.45	1.35	2.25
☐ 32, Jun 96 ....2.25		0.45	1.35	2.25

HAWKMAN ANNUAL

	ORIG.	GOOD	FINE	N-MINT
☐ 1, Bloodlines.....................3.50		0.70	2.10	3.50
☐ 2, 95, "Year One".............3.95		0.79	2.37	3.95

HAWKMAN SPECIAL

	ORIG.	GOOD	FINE	N-MINT
☐ 1, Mar 86.....................1.25		0.25	0.75	1.25

HAWKMOON: JEWEL IN THE SKULL
FIRST

	ORIG.	GOOD	FINE	N-MINT
☐ 1		0.35	1.05	1.75
☐ 2		0.35	1.05	1.75
☐ 3		0.35	1.05	1.75
☐ 4		0.35	1.05	1.75

HAWKMOON: MAD GOD'S AMULET

	ORIG.	GOOD	FINE	N-MINT
☐ 1		0.35	1.05	1.75
☐ 2		0.35	1.05	1.75
☐ 3		0.35	1.05	1.75
☐ 4		0.35	1.05	1.75

HAWKMOON: THE RUNESTAFF

	ORIG.	GOOD	FINE	N-MINT
☐ 1		0.35	1.05	1.75
☐ 2		0.35	1.05	1.75
☐ 3		0.39	1.17	1.95
☐ 4		0.39	1.17	1.95

HAWKMOON: THE SWORD OF THE DAWN

	ORIG.	GOOD	FINE	N-MINT
☐ 1		0.35	1.05	1.75
☐ 2		0.35	1.05	1.75
☐ 3		0.35	1.05	1.75
☐ 4		0.35	1.05	1.75

	ORIG.	GOOD	FINE	N-MINT

HAWKWORLD (beginning 1990)
DC

	ORIG.	GOOD	FINE	N-MINT
☐ 1, Jun 90	1.50	1.60	4.80	8.00
☐ 2, Jul 90	1.50	1.20	3.60	6.00
☐ 3, Aug 90	1.50	1.20	3.60	6.00
☐ 4, Sep 90	1.50	1.20	3.60	6.00
☐ 5, Oct 90	1.50	1.20	3.60	6.00
☐ 6, Dec 90	1.50	0.30	0.90	1.50
☐ 7, Jan 91	1.50	0.30	0.90	1.50
☐ 8, Feb 91	1.50	0.30	0.90	1.50
☐ 9, Mar 91	1.50	0.30	0.90	1.50
☐ 10, Apr 91	1.50	0.30	0.90	1.50
☐ 11, May 91	1.50	0.30	0.90	1.50
☐ 12, Jun 91	1.50	0.30	0.90	1.50
☐ 13, Jul 91	1.50	0.30	0.90	1.50
☐ 14, Aug 91	1.50	0.30	0.90	1.50
☐ 15, Sep 91, War of Gods	1.50	0.30	0.90	1.50
☐ 16, Oct 91, War of Gods	1.50	0.30	0.90	1.50
☐ 17, Nov 91	1.50	0.30	0.90	1.50
☐ 18, Dec 91	1.50	0.30	0.90	1.50
☐ 19, Jan 92	1.50	0.30	0.90	1.50
☐ 20, Feb 92	1.50	0.30	0.90	1.50
☐ 21, Mar 92	1.25	0.30	0.90	1.50
☐ 22, Apr 92	1.50	0.30	0.90	1.50
☐ 23, May 92	1.50	0.30	0.90	1.50
☐ 24, Jul 92	1.50	0.30	0.90	1.50
☐ 25, Aug 92	1.50	0.30	0.90	1.50
☐ 26, Sep 92	1.50	0.30	0.90	1.50
☐ 27, Oct 92	1.75	0.35	1.05	1.75
☐ 28, Nov 92	1.75	0.35	1.05	1.75
☐ 29, Dec 92	1.75	0.35	1.05	1.75
☐ 30, Jan 93	1.75	0.35	1.05	1.75
☐ 31, Feb 93	1.75	0.35	1.05	1.75
☐ 32, Mar 93	1.75	0.35	1.05	1.75

HAWKWORLD (mini-series)

	ORIG.	GOOD	FINE	N-MINT
☐ 1, Aug 89, Tim Truman O:Hawkman	3.95	1.60	4.80	8.00
☐ 2, Sep 89, Truman	3.95	1.20	3.60	6.00
☐ 3, Oct 89, Truman	3.95	1.20	3.60	6.00

HAWKWORLD ANNUAL

	ORIG.	GOOD	FINE	N-MINT
☐ 1, Dec 90, A:Flash	2.95	0.59	1.77	2.95
☐ 2, Aug 91, Armageddon Factor	2.95	1.20	3.60	6.00
☐ 2, Aug 91, 2nd printing, silver		0.59	1.77	2.95
☐ 3, 92, Eclipso	2.95	0.59	1.77	2.95

HAYWIRE

	ORIG.	GOOD	FINE	N-MINT
☐ 1, Oct 88		0.25	0.75	1.25
☐ 2, Nov 88		0.25	0.75	1.25
☐ 3, Dec 88		0.25	0.75	1.25
☐ 4, Dec 88		0.25	0.75	1.25
☐ 5, Jan 89		0.25	0.75	1.25
☐ 6, Jan 89		0.25	0.75	1.25
☐ 7, Mar 89		0.30	0.90	1.50
☐ 8, Apr 89		0.30	0.90	1.50
☐ 9, May 89		0.30	0.90	1.50
☐ 10, Jun 89		0.30	0.90	1.50
☐ 11, Jul 89		0.30	0.90	1.50
☐ 12, Aug 89		0.30	0.90	1.50
☐ 13, Sep 89		0.30	0.90	1.50

HAZARD!
MOTION

	ORIG.	GOOD	FINE	N-MINT
☐ 1, b&w;"Breakneck Blvd."	2.50	0.50	1.50	2.50

RECKLESS VISION

	ORIG.	GOOD	FINE	N-MINT
☐ 1, b&w;first "Breakneck Blvd." story	2.50	0.50	1.50	2.50

	ORIG.	GOOD	FINE	N-MINT

HE IS JUST A RAT
EXCLAIM! BRAND COMICS

	ORIG.	GOOD	FINE	N-MINT
☐ 1, b&w	2.75	0.55	1.65	2.75
☐ 2, b&w	2.75	0.55	1.65	2.75
☐ 3, Spr 96, b&w	2.75	0.55	1.65	2.75

HE SAID/SHE SAID
FIRST AMENDMENT

	ORIG.	GOOD	FINE	N-MINT
☐ 1, adult, b&w	3.00	0.60	1.80	3.00
☐ 2, adult, b&w	3.00	0.60	1.80	3.00
☐ 3, adult, b&w	3.00	0.60	1.80	3.00
☐ 5, adult;b&w;OJ trial		3.60	10.80	18.00

HEADLESS HORSEMAN
ETERNITY

	ORIG.	GOOD	FINE	N-MINT
☐ 1, b&w		0.45	1.35	2.25
☐ 2, b&w		0.45	1.35	2.25

HEADMAN
INNOVATION

	ORIG.	GOOD	FINE	N-MINT
☐ 1		0.50	1.50	2.50

HEARTBREAKERS (mini-series)
DARK HORSE

	ORIG.	GOOD	FINE	N-MINT
☐ 1, Apr 96	2.95	0.59	1.77	2.95
☐ 2, May 96	2.95	0.59	1.77	2.95

HEATHCLIFF
STAR

	ORIG.	GOOD	FINE	N-MINT
☐ 1	0.65	0.13	0.39	0.65
☐ 2	0.65	0.13	0.39	0.65
☐ 3	0.65	0.13	0.39	0.65
☐ 4	0.65	0.13	0.39	0.65
☐ 5	0.65	0.13	0.39	0.65
☐ 6	0.65	0.13	0.39	0.65
☐ 7	0.75	0.15	0.45	0.75
☐ 8	0.75	0.15	0.45	0.75
☐ 9	0.75	0.15	0.45	0.75
☐ 10	0.75	0.15	0.45	0.75
☐ 11	0.75	0.15	0.45	0.75
☐ 12	0.75	0.15	0.45	0.75
☐ 13	0.75	0.15	0.45	0.75
☐ 14	0.75	0.15	0.45	0.75
☐ 15	0.75	0.15	0.45	0.75
☐ 16	1.00	0.20	0.60	1.00
☐ 17	1.00	0.20	0.60	1.00
☐ 18	1.00	0.20	0.60	1.00
☐ 19	1.00	0.20	0.60	1.00
☐ 20	1.00	0.20	0.60	1.00
☐ 21	1.00	0.20	0.60	1.00
☐ 22, (becomes Marvel comic)	1.00	0.20	0.60	1.00

HEATHCLIFF (was Star Comic)
MARVEL

	ORIG.	GOOD	FINE	N-MINT
☐ 23	1.00	0.20	0.60	1.00
☐ 24	1.00	0.20	0.60	1.00
☐ 25	1.00	0.20	0.60	1.00
☐ 26	1.00	0.20	0.60	1.00
☐ 27	1.00	0.20	0.60	1.00
☐ 28	1.00	0.20	0.60	1.00
☐ 29	1.00	0.20	0.60	1.00
☐ 30	1.00	0.20	0.60	1.00
☐ 31	1.00	0.20	0.60	1.00
☐ 32	1.00	0.20	0.60	1.00
☐ 33	1.00	0.20	0.60	1.00
☐ 34	1.00	0.20	0.60	1.00
☐ 35	1.00	0.20	0.60	1.00
☐ 36	1.00	0.20	0.60	1.00
☐ 37	1.00	0.20	0.60	1.00
☐ 38	1.00	0.20	0.60	1.00
☐ 39	1.00	0.20	0.60	1.00
☐ 40	1.00	0.20	0.60	1.00
☐ 41	1.00	0.20	0.60	1.00
☐ 42	1.00	0.20	0.60	1.00
☐ 43	1.00	0.20	0.60	1.00

	ORIG.	GOOD	FINE	N-MINT
44	1.00	0.20	0.60	1.00
45	1.00	0.20	0.60	1.00
46	1.00	0.20	0.60	1.00
47, Batman parody	1.00	0.20	0.60	1.00
48	1.00	0.20	0.60	1.00
49	1.00	0.20	0.60	1.00
50, giant	1.50	0.30	0.90	1.50
51	1.00	0.20	0.60	1.00
52	1.00	0.20	0.60	1.00
53	1.00	0.20	0.60	1.00
54	1.00	0.20	0.60	1.00
55	1.00	0.20	0.60	1.00
56	1.00	0.20	0.60	1.00

HEATHCLIFF ANNUAL
STAR

	ORIG.	GOOD	FINE	N-MINT
1, (becomes Marvel comic)	1.25	0.25	0.75	1.25

HEATHCLIFF'S FUNHOUSE

	ORIG.	GOOD	FINE	N-MINT
1	1.00	0.20	0.60	1.00
2	1.00	0.20	0.60	1.00
3	1.00	0.20	0.60	1.00
4	1.00	0.20	0.60	1.00
5, (becomes Marvel comic)	1.00	0.20	0.60	1.00

HEATHCLIFF'S FUNHOUSE (was Star Comic)
MARVEL

	ORIG.	GOOD	FINE	N-MINT
6	1.00	0.20	0.60	1.00
7	1.00	0.20	0.60	1.00
8	1.00	0.20	0.60	1.00
9	1.00	0.20	0.60	1.00
10	1.00	0.20	0.60	1.00

HEATSEEKER
FANTACO

	ORIG.	GOOD	FINE	N-MINT
0, nn	5.95	1.19	3.57	5.95

HEAVY HITTERS ANNUAL
EPIC

	ORIG.	GOOD	FINE	N-MINT
1	3.75	0.75	2.25	3.75

HEAVY METAL MONSTERS
3-D ZONE

	ORIG.	GOOD	FINE	N-MINT
2, 93, (3-D)	3.95	0.79	2.37	3.95

REVOLUTIONARY

	ORIG.	GOOD	FINE	N-MINT
1, Jan 92, b&w	2.50	0.50	1.50	2.50

HECK!
RIP OFF

	ORIG.	GOOD	FINE	N-MINT
1, b&w;tpb	7.95	1.59	4.77	7.95

HECKLER, THE
DC

	ORIG.	GOOD	FINE	N-MINT
1, Sep 92	1.25	0.25	0.75	1.25
2, Sep 92	1.25	0.25	0.75	1.25
3, Nov 92	1.25	0.25	0.75	1.25
4	1.25	0.25	0.75	1.25
5	1.25	0.25	0.75	1.25
6	1.25	0.25	0.75	1.25

HELL'S ANGEL
MARVEL

	ORIG.	GOOD	FINE	N-MINT
1, O:Hell's Angel, A:X-Men	1.75	0.35	1.05	1.75
2	1.75	0.35	1.05	1.75
3	1.75	0.35	1.05	1.75
4	1.75	0.35	1.05	1.75
5, (becomes Dark Angel)	1.75	0.35	1.05	1.75

HELLBENDER
ETERNITY

	ORIG.	GOOD	FINE	N-MINT
1, b&w, Shuriken		0.45	1.35	2.25

HELLBLAZER
DC

	ORIG.	GOOD	FINE	N-MINT
1, Jan 88		4.40	13.20	22.00
2, Feb 88		2.40	7.20	12.00
3, Mar 88		1.60	4.80	8.00

	ORIG.	GOOD	FINE	N-MINT
4, Apr 88	1.60	4.80		8.00
5, May 88	1.60	4.80		8.00
6, Jun 88	1.20	3.60		6.00
7, Jul 88	1.20	3.60		6.00
8, Aug 88	1.20	3.60		6.00
9, Sep 88	1.00	3.00		5.00
10, Oct 88	1.00	3.00		5.00
11, Nov 88	1.00	3.00		5.00
12, Dec 88	1.00	3.00		5.00
13, Dec 88	1.00	3.00		5.00
14, Jan 89	1.00	3.00		5.00
15, Jan 89	1.00	3.00		5.00
16, Feb 89	1.00	3.00		5.00
17, Apr 89	1.00	3.00		5.00
18, May 89	1.00	3.00		5.00
19, Jun 89	1.60	4.80		8.00
20, Jul 89	1.00	3.00		5.00
21, Aug 89	0.60	1.80		3.00
22, Sep 89	0.60	1.80		3.00
23, Oct 89	0.60	1.80		3.00
24, Nov 89	0.60	1.80		3.00
25, Jan 90	0.60	1.80		3.00
26, Feb 90	0.50	1.50		2.50
27, Mar 90	0.50	1.50		2.50
28, Apr 90	0.50	1.50		2.50
29, May 90	0.50	1.50		2.50
30, Jun 90	0.50	1.50		2.50
31, Jul 90	0.50	1.50		2.50
32, Aug 90	0.50	1.50		2.50
33, Sep 90	0.50	1.50		2.50
34, Oct 90	0.50	1.50		2.50
35, Nov 90	0.50	1.50		2.50
36, Dec 90	0.50	1.50		2.50
37, Jan 91	0.50	1.50		2.50
38, Feb 91	0.50	1.50		2.50
39, Mar 91	0.50	1.50		2.50
40, Apr 91	0.50	1.50		2.50
41, MA 91	2.00	6.00		10.00
42, Jun 91	1.60	4.80		8.00
43, Jul 91	1.60	4.80		8.00
44, Aug 91	1.60	4.80		8.00
45, Sep 91	1.60	4.80		8.00
46, Oct 91	1.60	4.80		8.00
47, Nov 91	1.00	3.00		5.00
48, Dec 91	1.00	3.00		5.00
49	1.00	3.00		5.00
50	1.00	3.00		5.00
51	0.70	2.10		3.50
52	0.70	2.10		3.50
53	0.70	2.10		3.50
54	0.70	2.10		3.50
55	0.70	2.10		3.50
56	0.70	2.10		3.50
57	0.70	2.10		3.50
58	0.70	2.10		3.50
59	0.70	2.10		3.50
60	1.70	5.10		8.50
61	1.00	3.00		5.00
62, Death on AIDS	1.75	0.50	1.50	2.50

DC/VERTIGO

	ORIG.	GOOD	FINE	N-MINT
63	1.75	0.50	1.50	2.50
64	1.75	0.50	1.50	2.50
65	1.75	0.50	1.50	2.50
66	1.95	0.50	1.50	2.50
67	1.95	0.39	1.17	1.95
68	1.95	0.39	1.17	1.95
69	1.95	0.39	1.17	1.95
70	1.95	0.39	1.17	1.95
71	1.95	0.39	1.17	1.95
72	1.95	0.39	1.17	1.95
73	1.95	0.39	1.17	1.95
74	1.95	0.39	1.17	1.95

	ORIG.	GOOD	FINE	N-MINT
75 .... 2.95		0.59	1.77	2.95
76 .... 1.95		0.39	1.17	1.95
77, May 94 .... 1.95		0.39	1.17	1.95
78, Jun 94 .... 1.95		0.39	1.17	1.95
79, Jul 94 .... 1.95		0.39	1.17	1.95
80, Aug 94 .... 1.95		0.39	1.17	1.95
81, Sep 94 .... 1.95		0.39	1.17	1.95
82, Oct 94 .... 1.95		0.39	1.17	1.95
83, Nov 94 .... 1.95		0.39	1.17	1.95
84, Dec 94 .... 1.95		0.39	1.17	1.95
85, Jan 95 .... 1.95		0.39	1.17	1.95
86, Feb 95 .... 1.95		0.39	1.17	1.95
87, Mar 95 .... 1.95		0.39	1.17	1.95
88, Apr 95 .... 1.95		0.39	1.17	1.95
89, May 95 .... 2.25		0.45	1.35	2.25
90, Jun 95 .... 2.25		0.45	1.35	2.25
91, Jul 95 .... 2.25		0.45	1.35	2.25
92, Aug 95, "Critical Mass" Part 1 of 5				
.... 2.25		0.45	1.35	2.25
93, Sep 95, "Critical Mass" Part 2 of 5				
.... 2.25		0.45	1.35	2.25
94, Oct 95, "Critical Mass" Part 3 of 5				
.... 2.25		0.45	1.35	2.25
95, Nov 95, "Critical Mass" Part 4 of 5				
.... 2.25		0.45	1.35	2.25
96, Dec 95, "Critical Mass" Part 5 of 5				
.... 2.25		0.45	1.35	2.25
97, Jan 96 .... 2.25		0.45	1.35	2.25
98, Feb 96 .... 2.25		0.45	1.35	2.25
99, Mar 96 .... 2.25		0.45	1.35	2.25
100, Apr 96 .... 3.50		0.70	2.10	3.50
101, May 96 .... 2.25		0.45	1.35	2.25
102, Jun 96, "Difficult Beginnings" Part 1 of 3				
.... 2.25		0.45	1.35	2.25

HELLBLAZER ANNUAL
DC

	ORIG.	GOOD	FINE	N-MINT
1, Oct 89		1.00	3.00	5.00

HELLBLAZER SPECIAL
DC/VERTIGO

	ORIG.	GOOD	FINE	N-MINT
1 .... 3.95		0.79	2.37	3.95

HELLBOY, THE CORPSE AND THE IRON SHOES
DARK HORSE/LEGEND

	ORIG.	GOOD	FINE	N-MINT
0, 96, nn;collects the story serialized in *Advance Comics* #75-82 ...... 2.95		0.59	1.77	2.95

HELLBOY: SEED OF DESTRUCTION

	ORIG.	GOOD	FINE	N-MINT
1, Mar 94 .... 2.50		1.40	4.20	7.00
2, Apr 94 .... 2.50		1.00	3.00	5.00
3, May 94 .... 2.50		1.00	3.00	5.00
4, Jun 94 .... 2.50		1.00	3.00	5.00

HELLBOY: THE WOLVES OF SAINT AUGUST

	ORIG.	GOOD	FINE	N-MINT
0, 95, nn;one-shot; prestige format;collects the story from Dark Horse Presents #88-91 .... 4.95		0.99	2.97	4.95

HELLHOUND: THE REDEMPTION QUEST
EPIC

	ORIG.	GOOD	FINE	N-MINT
1 .... 2.25		0.45	1.35	2.25
2 .... 2.25		0.45	1.35	2.25
3 .... 2.25		0.45	1.35	2.25
4 .... 2.25		0.45	1.35	2.25

HELLHOUNDS
DARK HORSE

	ORIG.	GOOD	FINE	N-MINT
1, 94, Japanese, b&w 2.50		0.50	1.50	2.50
2, 94 .... 2.95		0.59	1.77	2.95

HELLHOUNDS: PANZER CORPS

	ORIG.	GOOD	FINE	N-MINT
1, 94, b&w 2.50		0.50	1.50	2.50
2, 94, b&w 2.50		0.50	1.50	2.50
3, Apr 94, b&w 2.50		0.50	1.50	2.50
4, May 94, b&w 2.50		0.50	1.50	2.50
5, Jun 94, b&w 2.50		0.50	1.50	2.50
6, Jul 94, b&w 2.50		0.50	1.50	2.50

HELLINA
LIGHTNING

	ORIG.	GOOD	FINE	N-MINT
1, Sep 94, b&w 2.75		1.00	3.00	5.00

HELLINA/CATFIGHT

	ORIG.	GOOD	FINE	N-MINT
1, Oct 95, b&w 2.75		0.55	1.65	2.75

HELLINA/DOUBLE IMPACT

	ORIG.	GOOD	FINE	N-MINT
1, Feb 96, crossover with High Impact 3.00		0.60	1.80	3.00
1, Feb 96, B;alternate cover; crossover with High Impact 3.00		0.60	1.80	3.00
1, Feb 96, crossover with High Impact; polybagged nude cover............................... 9.95		1.99	5.97	9.95

HELLINA: KISS OF DEATH

	ORIG.	GOOD	FINE	N-MINT
1, Jul 95, b&w 2.75		0.55	1.65	2.75
1, Jul 95, b&w; nude edition 9.95		1.99	5.97	9.95

HELLINA: WICKED WAYS

	ORIG.	GOOD	FINE	N-MINT
1, Nov 95, cover version A;b&w 2.75		0.55	1.65	2.75
1, Nov 95, cover version B;polybagged;b&w 3.00		0.60	1.80	3.00
1, Nov 95, cover version C; nude cover;polybagged; b&w............................. 9.95		1.99	5.97	9.95

HELLRAISER III: HELL ON EARTH
EPIC

	ORIG.	GOOD	FINE	N-MINT
1, movie......................... 4.95		0.99	2.97	4.95

HELLRAISER/NIGHTBREED: JIHAD

	ORIG.	GOOD	FINE	N-MINT
1 .... 4.50		0.90	2.70	4.50
2 .... 4.50		0.90	2.70	4.50

HELLRAISER: SPRING SLAUGHTER

	ORIG.	GOOD	FINE	N-MINT
1, 94 .... 6.95		1.39	4.17	6.95

HELLSHOCK
IMAGE

	ORIG.	GOOD	FINE	N-MINT
1, Jul 94, Jae Lee 1.95		0.39	1.17	1.95
2, Aug 94, Jae Lee 1.95		0.39	1.17	1.95
4, Nov 94, Jae Lee 1.95		0.39	1.17	1.95

MARVEL

	ORIG.	GOOD	FINE	N-MINT
0, ashcan		0.40	1.20	2.00

HELLSPOCK
EXPRESS/PARODY

	ORIG.	GOOD	FINE	N-MINT
1, 94, b&w, one-shot...... 2.95		0.59	1.77	2.95

HELLSTORM: PRINCE OF LIES
MARVEL

	ORIG.	GOOD	FINE	N-MINT
1 .... 2.95		0.80	2.40	4.00
2 .... 2.00		0.50	1.50	2.50
3 .... 2.00		0.50	1.50	2.50
4 .... 2.00		0.50	1.50	2.50
5 .... 2.00		0.40	1.20	2.00
6 .... 2.00		0.40	1.20	2.00
7 .... 2.00		0.40	1.20	2.00
8 .... 2.00		0.40	1.20	2.00
9 .... 2.00		0.40	1.20	2.00
10 .... 2.00		0.40	1.20	2.00
11 .... 2.00		0.40	1.20	2.00
12 .... 2.00		0.40	1.20	2.00
13, Apr 94 .... 2.00		0.40	1.20	2.00
14, May 94......................... 2.00		0.40	1.20	2.00
15, Jun 94 .... 2.00		0.40	1.20	2.00
16, Jul 94............................ 2.00		0.40	1.20	2.00
17, Aug 94 .... 2.00		0.40	1.20	2.00
18, Sep 94 .... 2.00		0.40	1.20	2.00
19, Oct 94 .... 2.00		0.40	1.20	2.00
20, Nov 94 .... 2.00		0.40	1.20	2.00
21, Dec 94 .... 2.00		0.40	1.20	2.00

HELYUN
SLAVE LABOR

	ORIG.	GOOD	FINE	N-MINT
0, nn b&w..........................		1.39	4.17	6.95

	ORIG.	GOOD	FINE	N-MINT

HELYUN: BONES OF THE BACKWOODS

	ORIG.	GOOD	FINE	N-MINT
☐ 0, nn b&w		0.59	1.77	2.95

HEMBECK
FANTACO

	ORIG.	GOOD	FINE	N-MINT
☐ 1, Best of Dateline		0.50	1.50	2.50
☐ 2, Hembeck 1980		0.50	1.50	2.50
☐ 3, Abbott & Costello Meet Bride of Hembeck		0.25	0.75	1.25
☐ 4, Bah, Hembeck!		0.25	0.75	1.25
☐ 5, Hembeck File		0.50	1.50	2.50
☐ 6, Jimmy Olsen's Pal		0.45	1.35	2.25
☐ 7, Dial H for Hembeck		0.39	1.17	1.95

HEMP FOR VICTORY
STARHEAD

	ORIG.	GOOD	FINE	N-MINT
☐ 0, Sep 93, b&w;based on 1943 USDA film	2.50	0.50	1.50	2.50

HEPCATS
DOUBLE DIAMOND

	ORIG.	GOOD	FINE	N-MINT
☐ 1, b&w	2.00	0.40	1.20	2.00
☐ 1, special edition;b&w	2.00	0.40	1.20	2.00
☐ 2, b&w	2.00	0.40	1.20	2.00
☐ 3, b&w	2.00	0.40	1.20	2.00
☐ 4, b&w	2.00	0.40	1.20	2.00
☐ 5, b&w	2.00	0.40	1.20	2.00
☐ 6, b&w	2.00	0.40	1.20	2.00
☐ 7, b&w	2.25	0.45	1.35	2.25
☐ 8, b&w	2.25	0.45	1.35	2.25
☐ 9, b&w	2.25	0.45	1.35	2.25
☐ 10, b&w		0.50	1.50	2.50

HERBIE
A-PLUS

	ORIG.	GOOD	FINE	N-MINT
☐ 1, 90, b&w, reprints ACG series	2.50	0.50	1.50	2.50
☐ 2, 90, b&w, reprints ACG series	2.50	0.50	1.50	2.50
☐ 3, 90, b&w, reprints ACG series	2.50	0.50	1.50	2.50
☐ 4, 91, b&w, reprints ACG series	2.50	0.50	1.50	2.50
☐ 5, 91, b&w, reprints ACG series	2.50	0.50	1.50	2.50
☐ 6, 91, b&w, reprints ACG series	2.50	0.50	1.50	2.50

DARK HORSE

	ORIG.	GOOD	FINE	N-MINT
☐ 1, 92, JBY		0.50	1.50	2.50
☐ 2, 92, reprints		0.50	1.50	2.50

HERCULES PRINCE OF POWER
MARVEL

	ORIG.	GOOD	FINE	N-MINT
☐ 1, BL	0.60	0.40	1.20	2.00
☐ 2, BL	0.60	0.20	0.60	1.00
☐ 3, BL	0.60	0.20	0.60	1.00
☐ 4, BL	0.60	0.20	0.60	1.00

HERCULES PRINCE OF POWER (2nd series)

	ORIG.	GOOD	FINE	N-MINT
☐ 1, BL	0.60	0.30	0.90	1.50
☐ 2	0.60	0.20	0.60	1.00
☐ 3	0.60	0.20	0.60	1.00
☐ 4	0.60	0.20	0.60	1.00

HERCULES PROJECT
MONSTER

	ORIG.	GOOD	FINE	N-MINT
☐ 1, b&w		0.39	1.17	1.95
☐ 2, b&w		0.39	1.17	1.95

HERCULES UNBOUND
DC

	ORIG.	GOOD	FINE	N-MINT
☐ 1, Nov 75	0.25	0.30	0.90	1.50
☐ 2, Jan 76	0.25	0.25	0.75	1.25
☐ 3, Mar 76	0.25	0.25	0.75	1.25
☐ 4, May 76	0.30	0.25	0.75	1.25
☐ 5, Jul 76	0.30	0.25	0.75	1.25
☐ 6, Sep 76	0.30	0.25	0.75	1.25
☐ 7, Nov 76	0.30	0.25	0.75	1.25

	ORIG.	GOOD	FINE	N-MINT
☐ 8, Jan 77	0.30	0.25	0.75	1.25
☐ 9, Mar 77	0.30	0.25	0.75	1.25
☐ 10, May 77	0.30	0.25	0.75	1.25
☐ 11, Jul 77	0.35	0.25	0.75	1.25
☐ 12, Sep 77	0.35	0.25	0.75	1.25

HERMES VS. THE EYEBALL KID (mini-series)
DARK HORSE

	ORIG.	GOOD	FINE	N-MINT
☐ 1, Dec 94, b&w	2.95	0.59	1.77	2.95
☐ 2, Jan 95, b&w	2.95	0.59	1.77	2.95
☐ 3, Feb 95, b&w	2.95	0.59	1.77	2.95

HERO
MARVEL

	ORIG.	GOOD	FINE	N-MINT
☐ 1, May 90	1.50	0.30	0.90	1.50
☐ 2, Jun 90	1.50	0.30	0.90	1.50
☐ 3, Jul 90	1.50	0.30	0.90	1.50
☐ 4, Aug 90	1.50	0.30	0.90	1.50
☐ 5, Sep 90	1.50	0.30	0.90	1.50
☐ 6, Oct 90	1.50	0.30	0.90	1.50

HERO ALLIANCE
INNOVATION

	ORIG.	GOOD	FINE	N-MINT
☐ 1, Sep 89	1.75	0.35	1.05	1.75
☐ 2, Oct 89	1.75	0.35	1.05	1.75
☐ 3, Dec 89		0.39	1.17	1.95
☐ 4, Feb 90		0.39	1.17	1.95
☐ 5, Mar 90		0.39	1.17	1.95
☐ 6, Apr 90		0.39	1.17	1.95
☐ 7, May 90		0.39	1.17	1.95
☐ 8, Jul 90		0.39	1.17	1.95
☐ 9, Sep 90		0.39	1.17	1.95
☐ 10, Oct 90		0.39	1.17	1.95
☐ 11, Nov 90		0.39	1.17	1.95
☐ 12, Dec 90		0.39	1.17	1.95
☐ 13, Mar 91		0.39	1.17	1.95
☐ 14, Apr 91		0.39	1.17	1.95
☐ 15, May 91		0.39	1.17	1.95
☐ 16, Jun 91		0.39	1.17	1.95
☐ 17, Jul 91		0.50	1.50	2.50

WONDER COLOR

	ORIG.	GOOD	FINE	N-MINT
☐ 1, May 87	1.95	0.39	1.17	1.95

HERO ALLIANCE & JUSTICE MACHINE: IDENTITY CRISIS
INNOVATION

	ORIG.	GOOD	FINE	N-MINT
☐ 1, Oct 90		0.55	1.65	2.75

HERO ALLIANCE ANNUAL

	ORIG.	GOOD	FINE	N-MINT
☐ 1, Sep 90		0.55	1.65	2.75

HERO ALLIANCE QUARTERLY

	ORIG.	GOOD	FINE	N-MINT
☐ 1, Sep 91		0.55	1.65	2.75
☐ 2, Dec 91		0.55	1.65	2.75
☐ 3		0.55	1.65	2.75
☐ 4		0.55	1.65	2.75

HERO ALLIANCE SPECIAL

	ORIG.	GOOD	FINE	N-MINT
☐ 1		0.50	1.50	2.50

HERO ALLIANCE: END OF THE GOLDEN AGE

	ORIG.	GOOD	FINE	N-MINT
☐ 1, Jul 89	1.75	0.35	1.05	1.75
☐ 2, Jul 89	1.75	0.35	1.05	1.75
☐ 3, Aug 89	1.75	0.35	1.05	1.75

HERO FOR HIRE
MARVEL

	ORIG.	GOOD	FINE	N-MINT
☐ 1, GT/JR, O:Power Man, 1:Luke Cage	0.20	5.20	15.60	26.00
☐ 2	0.20	2.40	7.20	12.00
☐ 3	0.20	1.60	4.80	8.00
☐ 4	0.20	1.60	4.80	8.00
☐ 5	0.20	1.60	4.80	8.00
☐ 6	0.20	1.00	3.00	5.00
☐ 7	0.20	1.00	3.00	5.00
☐ 8	0.20	1.00	3.00	5.00
☐ 9	0.20	1.00	3.00	5.00
☐ 10	0.20	1.00	3.00	5.00

	ORIG.	GOOD	FINE	N-MINT
❑ 11	0.20	1.00	3.00	5.00
❑ 12	0.20	1.00	3.00	5.00
❑ 13	0.20	1.00	3.00	5.00
❑ 14	0.20	1.00	3.00	5.00
❑ 15	0.20	1.00	3.00	5.00
❑ 16, (becomes *Power Man*)	0.20	1.00	3.00	5.00

HERO GRAPHICS SUPER-SPECTACULAR
HERO
❑ 1, contents vary; front cover misprinted on back (front cover appeared on Southern Knights #35) ... 0.79 2.37 3.95

HERO HOTLINE
DC

	GOOD	FINE	N-MINT
❑ 1, Apr 89	0.35	1.05	1.75
❑ 2, May 89	0.35	1.05	1.75
❑ 3, Jun 89	0.35	1.05	1.75
❑ 4, Jul 89	0.35	1.05	1.75
❑ 5, Aug 89	0.35	1.05	1.75
❑ 6, Sep 89	0.35	1.05	1.75

HERO SANDWICH
SLAVE LABOR

	GOOD	FINE	N-MINT
❑ 1	0.30	0.90	1.50
❑ 2	0.30	0.90	1.50
❑ 3	0.30	0.90	1.50
❑ 4	0.35	1.05	1.75
❑ 5	0.35	1.05	1.75
❑ 6	0.35	1.05	1.75
❑ 7	0.45	1.35	2.25
❑ 8	0.50	1.50	2.50
❑ 9	0.50	1.50	2.50

HERO ZERO
DARK HORSE
❑ 0, Sep 94 ... 2.50 0.50 1.50 2.50

HEROES
BLACKBIRD

	GOOD	FINE	N-MINT
❑ 1	1.00	3.00	5.00
❑ 2	0.35	1.05	1.75
❑ 3	0.35	1.05	1.75
❑ 4, comic book size	0.40	1.20	2.00
❑ 5, comic book size	0.40	1.20	2.00
❑ 6, comic book size	0.40	1.20	2.00

DC/MILESTONE
❑ 1, May 96 ... 2.50 0.50 1.50 2.50
❑ 2, Jun 96, V:Shadow Cabinet ... 2.50 0.50 1.50 2.50

HEROES AGAINST HUNGER
DC
❑ 1, Aug 86 ... 1.50 1.00 3.00 5.00

HEROES FOR HOPE
MARVEL
❑ 1, Dec 85 ... 1.50 0.80 2.40 4.00

HEROES FROM WORDSMITH
SPECIAL STUDIO
❑ 1, b&w ... 0.50 1.50 2.50

HEROES OF ROCK 'N FIRE
WONDER COMIX
❑ 1 ... 0.39 1.17 1.95

HEROIC
LIGHTNING
❑ 1 ... 0.35 1.05 1.75

HEROINES INC.
AVATAR
❑ 1, b&w ... 0.35 1.05 1.75

HEROMAN
DIMENSION
❑ 1 ... 0.35 1.05 1.75

HERU, SON OF AUSAR
ANIA
❑ 1 ... 1.95 0.39 1.17 1.95

HEX
DC

	ORIG.	GOOD	FINE	N-MINT
❑ 1		1.00	3.00	5.00
❑ 2	1.00	0.70	2.10	3.50
❑ 3	1.00	0.70	2.10	3.50
❑ 4	1.00	0.70	2.10	3.50
❑ 5	1.00	0.70	2.10	3.50
❑ 6	1.00	0.60	1.80	3.00
❑ 7	1.00	0.60	1.80	3.00
❑ 8	1.00	0.60	1.80	3.00
❑ 9	1.00	0.60	1.80	3.00
❑ 10	1.00	0.60	1.80	3.00
❑ 11	1.00	0.40	1.20	2.00
❑ 12	1.00	0.40	1.20	2.00
❑ 13	1.00	0.40	1.20	2.00
❑ 14	1.00	0.40	1.20	2.00
❑ 15, KG		0.40	1.20	2.00
❑ 16, KG		0.40	1.20	2.00
❑ 17, KG		0.40	1.20	2.00
❑ 18, KG		0.40	1.20	2.00

HEY, BOSS!
VISIONARY
❑ 1 ... 0.30 0.90 1.50

HIDEO LI FILES, THE
RAGING RHINO
❑ 1, adult, b&w ... 2.95 0.59 1.77 2.95

HIGH SHINING BRASS
APPLE
❑ 1, b&w ... 0.55 1.65 2.75
❑ 2, b&w ... 0.55 1.65 2.75
❑ 3, b&w ... 0.55 1.65 2.75
❑ 4 ... 0.59 1.77 2.95

HIGHWAY 61
VORTEX
❑ 0, nn movie adaptation ... 2.39 7.17 11.95

HILLY ROSE
ASTRO
❑ 2, Jul 95, b&w ... 2.95 0.59 1.77 2.95
❑ 3, Oct 95, b&w ... 2.95 0.59 1.77 2.95
❑ 5, Feb 96, b&w ... 2.95 0.59 1.77 2.95

HILLY ROSE'S SPACE ADVENTURES
❑ 1, May 95, b&w; (becomes *Hilly Rose*) ... 2.95 0.59 1.77 2.95

HISTORY OF THE DC UNIVERSE
DC
❑ 1, Sep 86, GP ... 2.95 1.20 3.60 6.00
❑ 2, Nov 86, GP ... 2.95 1.00 3.00 5.00

HIT THE BEACH
ANTARCTIC
❑ 1, Jul 93, b&w ... 2.95 0.59 1.77 2.95
❑ 1, Jul 93, gold foil, deluxe edition ... 4.95 0.99 2.97 4.95
❑ 2, Jul 94, b&w ... 2.95 0.59 1.77 2.95
❑ 3, Jul 95, b&w ... 2.95 0.59 1.77 2.95

HITCHHIKER'S GUIDE TO THE GALAXY, THE
DC
❑ 1 ... 4.95 0.99 2.97 4.95
❑ 2 ... 4.95 0.99 2.97 4.95
❑ 3 ... 4.95 0.99 2.97 4.95

HITMAN
❑ 1, Apr 96 ... 2.25 0.45 1.35 2.25
❑ 2, Jun 96, V:Joker ... 2.25 0.45 1.35 2.25
❑ 3, Jul 96 ... 2.25 0.45 1.35 2.25

	ORIG.	GOOD	FINE	N-MINT

HITOMI AND HER GIRL COMMANDOS
ANTARCTIC
☐ 1, Apr 92, b&w............ 2.50	0.50	1.50	2.50
☐ 2, Jun 92, b&w 2.50	0.50	1.50	2.50
☐ 3, Aug 92, b&w............ 2.50	0.50	1.50	2.50
☐ 4, Oct 92, b&w............ 2.50	0.50	1.50	2.50

HITOMI AND HER GIRL COMMANDOS II
☐ 1, Aug 93, b&w............ 2.50	0.50	1.50	2.50
☐ 2, Oct 93, b&w............ 2.75	0.55	1.65	2.75
☐ 3, Dec 93, b&w............ 2.75	0.55	1.65	2.75
☐ 4, Feb 94, b&w............ 2.75	0.55	1.65	2.75
☐ 5, Apr 94, b&w............ 2.75	0.55	1.65	2.75
☐ 6, Jul 94, b&w............ 2.75	0.55	1.65	2.75
☐ 7, Nov 94, b&w............ 2.75	0.55	1.65	2.75
☐ 8, Mar 95, b&w............ 2.75	0.55	1.65	2.75
☐ 9, May 95, b&w............ 2.75	0.55	1.65	2.75

HOBBIT, THE
ECLIPSE
☐ 1, 89, prestige format; adapts Tolkien novel				
.... 4.95	3.00	9.00	15.00
☐ 2 .... 4.95	1.60	4.80	8.00
☐ 3 .... 4.95	1.60	4.80	8.00

HOCKEY MASTERS
REVOLUTIONARY
☐ 1, Dec 93, b&w 2.95	0.59	1.77	2.95

HOKUM & HEX
MARVEL
☐ 1, foil cover 2.50	0.50	1.50	2.50
☐ 2 .... 1.75	0.35	1.05	1.75
☐ 3 .... 1.75	0.35	1.05	1.75
☐ 4 .... 1.75	0.35	1.05	1.75
☐ 5 .... 1.75	0.35	1.05	1.75
☐ 6 .... 1.75	0.35	1.05	1.75
☐ 7 .... 1.75	0.35	1.05	1.75
☐ 8 .... 1.75	0.35	1.05	1.75
☐ 9, May 94 .... 1.75	0.35	1.05	1.75

HOLIDAY OUT
RENEGADE
☐ 1, b&w	0.40	1.20	2.00
☐ 2, b&w	0.40	1.20	2.00
☐ 3, b&w	0.40	1.20	2.00

HOLLYWOOD SUPERSTARS
EPIC
☐ 1, Nov 90, DS............ 2.95	0.59	1.77	2.95
☐ 2, Jan 91, DS 2.25	0.45	1.35	2.25
☐ 3, Feb 91, DS 2.25	0.45	1.35	2.25
☐ 4, Mar 91, DS............ 2.25	0.45	1.35	2.25
☐ 5, Apr 91, DS 2.25	0.45	1.35	2.25

HOLO BROTHERS
MONSTER
☐ 1, b&w	0.39	1.17	1.95
☐ 2, b&w	0.39	1.17	1.95
☐ 3	0.45	1.35	2.25
☐ 4	0.45	1.35	2.25
☐ 5	0.45	1.35	2.25
☐ 6	0.45	1.35	2.25
☐ 7	0.45	1.35	2.25
☐ 8	0.45	1.35	2.25
☐ 9	0.45	1.35	2.25
☐ 10	0.45	1.35	2.25

HOLO. BROTHERS SPECIAL
FANTAGRAPHICS
☐ 1, O:Holo. Brothers	0.45	1.35	2.25

HOLY CROSS
☐ 0, b&w 4.95	0.99	2.97	4.95
☐ 2, Oct 94, b&w 2.95	0.59	1.77	2.95

HOMELANDS ON THE WORLS OF MAGIC: THE GATHERING
ACCLAIM/ARMADA
☐ 0, 95, nn;one-shot; prestige format;polybagged with Homelands card............ 5.95	1.19	3.57	5.95

HOMICIDE
DARK HORSE
☐ 1, 90, b&w	0.39	1.17	1.95

HOMO PATROL
HELPLESS ANGER
☐ 0, nn b&w, adult	0.70	2.10	3.50

HONEYMOONERS
LODESTONE
☐ 1	0.30	0.90	1.50

HONEYMOONERS, THE
TRIAD
☐ 1	0.40	1.20	2.00
☐ 2	0.40	1.20	2.00
☐ 3, Christmas	0.70	2.10	3.50
☐ 4	0.40	1.20	2.00
☐ 5	0.40	1.20	2.00
☐ 6	0.40	1.20	2.00
☐ 7	0.40	1.20	2.00
☐ 8	0.40	1.20	2.00
☐ 9	0.40	1.20	2.00
☐ 10	0.40	1.20	2.00
☐ 11	0.40	1.20	2.00
☐ 12, Aug 89 .... 2.00	0.40	1.20	2.00

HONK!
FANTAGRAPHICS
☐ 1	0.45	1.35	2.25
☐ 2	0.45	1.35	2.25
☐ 3	0.45	1.35	2.25
☐ 4	0.45	1.35	2.25
☐ 5	0.45	1.35	2.25

HONKO THE CLOWN
C&T
☐ 1, b&w	0.40	1.20	2.00

HONOR AMONG THIEVES
GATEWAY
☐ 1	0.30	0.90	1.50

HOOD, THE
SOUTH CENTRAL
☐ 1, b&w 2.75	0.55	1.65	2.75

HOODOO
3-D ZONE
☐ 1, b&w	0.50	1.50	2.50

HOOK
MARVEL
☐ 0, nn bookshelf 5.95	1.19	3.57	5.95
☐ 0, nn magazine 2.95	0.59	1.77	2.95
☐ 1, movie 1.00	0.20	0.60	1.00
☐ 2, movie 1.00	0.20	0.60	1.00
☐ 3, movie 1.00	0.20	0.60	1.00
☐ 4, movie 1.00	0.20	0.60	1.00

HOON, THE
EENIEWEENIE
☐ 1, Jun 95, b&w 2.50	0.50	1.50	2.50

HORDE
SWING SHIFT
☐ 1, b&w	0.40	1.20	2.00

HORNY BIKER SLUTS
LAST GASP
☐ 5, adult, b&w	0.59	1.77	2.95

HORNY COMIX & STORIES
RIP OFF
☐ 1, Apr 91, adult;b&w 2.50	0.50	1.50	2.50
☐ 2, Jul 91, adult;b&w 2.50	0.50	1.50	2.50

	ORIG.	GOOD	FINE	N-MINT
❏ 3, Dec 91, adult;b&w 2.50		0.50	1.50	2.50
❏ 4, May 92, adult;b&w 2.50		0.50	1.50	2.50

HOROBI BOOK ONE
VIZ

	GOOD	FINE	N-MINT
❏ 1, b&w Japanese..............	0.75	2.25	3.75
❏ 2, b&w Japanese..............	0.75	2.25	3.75
❏ 3, b&w Japanese..............	0.75	2.25	3.75
❏ 4, b&w Japanese..............	0.75	2.25	3.75
❏ 5, b&w Japanese..............	0.75	2.25	3.75
❏ 6, b&w Japanese..............	0.75	2.25	3.75
❏ 7, b&w Japanese..............	0.75	2.25	3.75
❏ 8, b&w Japanese..............	0.75	2.25	3.75

HOROBI BOOK TWO

	GOOD	FINE	N-MINT
❏ 1, b&w Japanese..............	0.85	2.55	4.25
❏ 2, b&w Japanese..............	0.85	2.55	4.25
❏ 3, b&w Japanese..............	0.85	2.55	4.25
❏ 4, b&w Japanese..............	0.85	2.55	4.25
❏ 5, b&w Japanese..............	0.85	2.55	4.25
❏ 6, b&w Japanese..............	0.85	2.55	4.25
❏ 7, b&w Japanese..............	0.85	2.55	4.25

HORROR IN THE DARK
FANTAGOR

	GOOD	FINE	N-MINT
❏ 1, adult, b&w	0.40	1.20	2.00
❏ 2, adult, b&w	0.40	1.20	2.00
❏ 3, adult, b&w	0.40	1.20	2.00
❏ 4, adult, b&w	0.40	1.20	2.00

HORRORIST, THE (mini-series)
DC/VERTIGO

	ORIG.	GOOD	FINE	N-MINT
❏ 1, Dec 95, A:John Constantine ;prestige format 5.95		1.19	3.57	5.95
❏ 2, Jan 96, A:John Constantine; prestige format 5.95		1.19	3.57	5.95

HORRORS OF THE HAUNTER
AC

	ORIG.	GOOD	FINE	N-MINT
❏ 1, b&w reprints 2.95		0.59	1.77	2.95

HORSE
SLAVE LABOR

	GOOD	FINE	N-MINT
❏ 1, b&w	0.59	1.77	2.95

HORSEMAN
CRUSADE

	ORIG.	GOOD	FINE	N-MINT
❏ 1, Mar 96 .... 2.95		0.59	1.77	2.95

HOT 'N COLD HEROES
A-PLUS

	GOOD	FINE	N-MINT
❏ 1, 90, JBy 1:Hellsing, b&w	0.50	1.50	2.50
❏ 2, Mar 91, reprints O:Nemesis, Magicman	0.50	1.50	2.50

HOT SHOTS
HOT

	GOOD	FINE	N-MINT
❏ 1, color..........................	0.39	1.17	1.95

HOT SHOTS: AVENGERS
MARVEL

	ORIG.	GOOD	FINE	N-MINT
❏ 0, Oct 95, one-shot; pin-ups 2.95		0.59	1.77	2.95

HOT SHOTS: X-MEN

	ORIG.	GOOD	FINE	N-MINT
❏ 0, Jan 96, nn;pin-ups 2.95		0.59	1.77	2.95

HOT STUFF
HARVEY

	ORIG.	GOOD	FINE	N-MINT
❏ 1 .... 1.25		0.25	0.75	1.25
❏ 2 .... 1.25		0.25	0.75	1.25
❏ 3 .... 1.25		0.25	0.75	1.25
❏ 4 .... 1.25		0.25	0.75	1.25
❏ 5 .... 1.25		0.25	0.75	1.25
❏ 6 .... 1.25		0.25	0.75	1.25
❏ 7 .... 1.25		0.25	0.75	1.25
❏ 8 .... 1.25		0.25	0.75	1.25
❏ 9 .... 1.50		0.30	0.90	1.50
❏ 10 .... 1.50		0.30	0.90	1.50
❏ 11 .... 1.50		0.30	0.90	1.50
❏ 12 .... 1.50		0.30	0.90	1.50

HOT STUFF BIG BOOK

	GOOD	FINE	N-MINT
❏ 1	0.39	1.17	1.95
❏ 2	0.39	1.17	1.95

HOT STUFF DIGEST

	ORIG.	GOOD	FINE	N-MINT
❏ 1		0.45	1.35	2.25
❏ 2		0.45	1.35	2.25
❏ 3 .... 1.75		0.35	1.05	1.75
❏ 4 .... 1.75		0.35	1.05	1.75
❏ 5 .... 1.75		0.35	1.05	1.75

HOT STUFF GIANT SIZE

	ORIG.	GOOD	FINE	N-MINT
❏ 1 .... 2.25		0.45	1.35	2.25
❏ 2 .... 2.25		0.45	1.35	2.25
❏ 3 .... 2.25		0.45	1.35	2.25

HOT STUFF SIZZLERS

	GOOD	FINE	N-MINT
❏ 1	0.25	0.75	1.25

HOT WHEELS
DC

	ORIG.	GOOD	FINE	N-MINT
❏ 1, Apr 70 .... 0.15		4.80	14.40	24.00
❏ 2, Jun 70 .... 0.15		3.60	10.80	18.00
❏ 3, Aug 70 .... 0.15		4.80	14.40	24.00
❏ 4, Oct 70 .... 0.15		3.60	10.80	18.00
❏ 5, Dec 70 .... 0.15		3.60	10.80	18.00
❏ 6, Feb 71 .... 0.15		5.60	16.80	28.00

HOTSPUR
ECLIPSE

	GOOD	FINE	N-MINT
❏ 1	0.40	1.20	2.00
❏ 2	0.40	1.20	2.00
❏ 3	0.40	1.20	2.00

HOUSE II: THE SECOND STORY
MARVEL

	ORIG.	GOOD	FINE	N-MINT
❏ 1, Oct 87, movie adapt.... 2.00		0.40	1.20	2.00

HOUSE OF FRIGHTENSTEIN
AC

	ORIG.	GOOD	FINE	N-MINT
❏ 1, b&w reprints 2.95		0.59	1.77	2.95

HOUSE OF MYSTERY
DC

	GOOD	FINE	N-MINT
❏ 100	3.60	10.80	18.00
❏ 101	2.40	7.20	12.00
❏ 102	2.40	7.20	12.00
❏ 103	2.40	7.20	12.00
❏ 104	2.40	7.20	12.00
❏ 105	2.40	7.20	12.00
❏ 106	2.40	7.20	12.00
❏ 107	2.40	7.20	12.00
❏ 108	2.40	7.20	12.00
❏ 109	2.40	7.20	12.00
❏ 110	2.40	7.20	12.00
❏ 111	2.40	7.20	12.00
❏ 112	2.40	7.20	12.00
❏ 113	2.40	7.20	12.00
❏ 114	2.40	7.20	12.00
❏ 115	2.40	7.20	12.00
❏ 116	2.40	7.20	12.00
❏ 117	2.40	7.20	12.00
❏ 118	2.40	7.20	12.00
❏ 119	2.40	7.20	12.00
❏ 120	2.40	7.20	12.00
❏ 121	1.60	4.80	8.00
❏ 122	1.60	4.80	8.00
❏ 123	1.60	4.80	8.00
❏ 124	1.60	4.80	8.00
❏ 125	1.60	4.80	8.00
❏ 126	1.60	4.80	8.00
❏ 127	1.60	4.80	8.00
❏ 128	1.60	4.80	8.00
❏ 129	1.60	4.80	8.00
❏ 130	1.60	4.80	8.00
❏ 131	1.60	4.80	8.00
❏ 132	1.60	4.80	8.00
❏ 133	1.60	4.80	8.00

	ORIG.	GOOD	FINE	N-MINT
☐ 134		1.60	4.80	8.00
☐ 135		1.60	4.80	8.00
☐ 136		1.60	4.80	8.00
☐ 137		1.60	4.80	8.00
☐ 138		1.60	4.80	8.00
☐ 139		1.60	4.80	8.00
☐ 140		1.60	4.80	8.00
☐ 141		1.60	4.80	8.00
☐ 142		1.60	4.80	8.00
☐ 143, J'onn J'onzz		28.00	84.00	140.00
☐ 144		15.00	45.00	75.00
☐ 145		10.00	30.00	50.00
☐ 146		10.00	30.00	50.00
☐ 147		10.00	30.00	50.00
☐ 148		10.00	30.00	50.00
☐ 149, ATh		11.00	33.00	55.00
☐ 150		7.20	21.60	36.00
☐ 151		7.20	21.60	36.00
☐ 152		7.20	21.60	36.00
☐ 153		7.20	21.60	36.00
☐ 154		7.20	21.60	36.00
☐ 155		7.20	21.60	36.00
☐ 156, O:Dial 'H' for Hero		13.00	39.00	65.00
☐ 157		5.60	16.80	28.00
☐ 158		5.60	16.80	28.00
☐ 159		5.60	16.80	28.00
☐ 160		5.60	16.80	28.00
☐ 161		5.60	16.80	28.00
☐ 162		5.60	16.80	28.00
☐ 163		5.60	16.80	28.00
☐ 164		5.60	16.80	28.00
☐ 165		5.60	16.80	28.00
☐ 166		5.60	16.80	28.00
☐ 167		5.60	16.80	28.00
☐ 168		5.60	16.80	28.00
☐ 169		5.60	16.80	28.00
☐ 170		5.60	16.80	28.00
☐ 171		5.60	16.80	28.00
☐ 172		5.60	16.80	28.00
☐ 173		5.60	16.80	28.00
☐ 174, NA		1.20	3.60	6.00
☐ 175, NA		1.20	3.60	6.00
☐ 176, NA		1.20	3.60	6.00
☐ 177, NA		1.20	3.60	6.00
☐ 178, Feb 69, NA	0.12	2.00	6.00	10.00
☐ 179, Apr 69, NA/JO, 1st Wrightson DC art				
	0.12	3.00	9.00	15.00
☐ 180, NA,BWr		1.20	3.60	6.00
☐ 181, Aug 69, NA,BWr	0.15	1.20	3.60	6.00
☐ 182, Oct 69, NA,WH,AT	0.15	0.50	1.50	2.50
☐ 183, Dec 69, NA, BWr,WW				
	0.15	1.20	3.60	6.00
☐ 184, Feb 70, NA,GK, WW,AT,BWr				
	0.15	0.60	1.80	3.00
☐ 185, Apr 70, NA,BWr, WW				
	0.15	0.60	1.80	3.00
☐ 186, Jun 70, NA,BWr	0.15	0.80	2.40	4.00
☐ 187, Aug 70, NA/WH/AT	0.15	0.30	0.90	1.50
☐ 188, Oct 70, NA/BWr	0.15	0.50	1.50	2.50
☐ 189, NA/AT		0.50	1.50	2.50
☐ 190, Feb 71, NA/AT	0.15	0.50	1.50	2.50
☐ 191, Apr 71, NA	0.15	0.70	2.10	3.50
☐ 192, Jun 71, NA,GM	0.15	0.50	1.50	2.50
☐ 193, BWr		0.45	1.35	2.25
☐ 194, Sep 71, BWr	0.25	0.70	2.10	3.50
☐ 195, Oct 71, BWr		8.40	25.20	42.00
☐ 196, Nov 71, NA	0.25	0.50	1.50	2.50
☐ 197, Dec 71, NA		0.50	1.50	2.50
☐ 198, Jan 72		0.40	1.20	2.00
☐ 199, Feb 72, NA,JK,WW		0.60	1.80	3.00
☐ 200, Mar 72		0.40	1.20	2.00
☐ 201, Apr 72	0.25	0.40	1.20	2.00
☐ 202, May 72	0.25	0.40	1.20	2.00
☐ 203, Jun 72		0.40	1.20	2.00
☐ 204, Jul 72, AN,BWr	0.20	0.70	2.10	3.50
☐ 205		0.40	1.20	2.00
☐ 206		0.40	1.20	2.00
☐ 207, JSn,BWr,JSt,NR		0.60	1.80	3.00
☐ 208		0.40	1.20	2.00
☐ 209, AA,BWr		0.40	1.20	2.00
☐ 210		0.40	1.20	2.00
☐ 211, AA,BWr,NR		0.40	1.20	2.00
☐ 212, AN		0.40	1.20	2.00
☐ 213, BWr		0.40	1.20	2.00
☐ 214, BWr		0.40	1.20	2.00
☐ 215		0.40	1.20	2.00
☐ 216		0.40	1.20	2.00
☐ 217, BWr		0.40	1.20	2.00
☐ 218		0.40	1.20	2.00
☐ 219		0.40	1.20	2.00
☐ 220		0.40	1.20	2.00
☐ 221, Jan 74, BWr/MK	0.20	0.60	1.80	3.00
☐ 222		0.40	1.20	2.00
☐ 223		0.40	1.20	2.00
☐ 224, giant, AN/BWr, NA, Phantom Stranger				
		0.80	2.40	4.00
☐ 225, giant, AN		0.40	1.20	2.00
☐ 226, giant, NR		0.60	1.80	3.00
☐ 227, giant, NR		0.60	1.80	3.00
☐ 228, giant, NA/NR/AT		0.70	2.10	3.50
☐ 229, giant		0.80	2.40	4.00
☐ 230		0.40	1.20	2.00
☐ 231		0.20	0.60	1.00
☐ 232		0.20	0.60	1.00
☐ 233		0.20	0.60	1.00
☐ 234		0.20	0.60	1.00
☐ 235		0.20	0.60	1.00
☐ 236, SD/BWr/NA		0.40	1.20	2.00
☐ 237		0.20	0.60	1.00
☐ 238		0.20	0.60	1.00
☐ 239		0.20	0.60	1.00
☐ 240		0.20	0.60	1.00
☐ 241		0.20	0.60	1.00
☐ 242		0.20	0.60	1.00
☐ 243		0.20	0.60	1.00
☐ 244		0.20	0.60	1.00
☐ 245		0.20	0.60	1.00
☐ 246		0.20	0.60	1.00
☐ 247		0.20	0.60	1.00
☐ 248		0.20	0.60	1.00
☐ 249		0.20	0.60	1.00
☐ 250		0.20	0.60	1.00
☐ 251, NA/WW, giant		0.20	0.60	1.00
☐ 252, NA/AN, giant		0.25	0.75	1.25
☐ 253, NA/AN, giant		0.30	0.90	1.50
☐ 254, NA/SD/WH, giant		0.40	1.20	2.00
☐ 255, BWr giant		0.25	0.75	1.25
☐ 256, BWr giant		0.25	0.75	1.25
☐ 257, MG, giant		0.30	0.90	1.50
☐ 258, SD, giant		0.25	0.75	1.25
☐ 259, DN/MG, giant		0.30	0.90	1.50
☐ 260		0.20	0.60	1.00
☐ 261		0.20	0.60	1.00
☐ 262		0.20	0.60	1.00
☐ 263		0.20	0.60	1.00
☐ 264		0.20	0.60	1.00
☐ 265		0.20	0.60	1.00
☐ 266		0.20	0.60	1.00
☐ 267		0.20	0.60	1.00
☐ 268		0.20	0.60	1.00
☐ 269		0.20	0.60	1.00
☐ 270		0.20	0.60	1.00
☐ 271		0.20	0.60	1.00
☐ 272		0.20	0.60	1.00

	ORIG.	GOOD	FINE	N-MINT
273		0.20	0.60	1.00
274, JO		0.20	0.60	1.00
275		0.20	0.60	1.00
276		0.20	0.60	1.00
277		0.20	0.60	1.00
278		0.20	0.60	1.00
279		0.20	0.60	1.00
280		0.20	0.60	1.00
281		0.20	0.60	1.00
282, JSn		0.20	0.60	1.00
283		0.20	0.60	1.00
284		0.20	0.60	1.00
285		0.20	0.60	1.00
286		0.20	0.60	1.00
287		0.20	0.60	1.00
288		0.20	0.60	1.00
289		0.20	0.60	1.00
290, Mar 81		0.20	0.60	1.00
291, Apr 81		0.20	0.60	1.00
292, May 81		0.20	0.60	1.00
293, Jun 81		0.20	0.60	1.00
294, Jul 81		0.20	0.60	1.00
295, Aug 81		0.20	0.60	1.00
296, Sep 81		0.20	0.60	1.00
297, Oct 81		0.20	0.60	1.00
298, Nov 81		0.20	0.60	1.00
299, Dec 81		0.20	0.60	1.00
300, Jan 82		0.20	0.60	1.00
301, Feb 82		0.20	0.60	1.00
302, Mar 82		0.20	0.60	1.00
303, Apr 82		0.20	0.60	1.00
304, May 82		0.20	0.60	1.00
305, Jun 82		0.20	0.60	1.00
306, Jul 82		0.20	0.60	1.00
307, Aug 82		0.20	0.60	1.00
308, Sep 82		0.20	0.60	1.00
309, Oct 82		0.20	0.60	1.00
310, Nov 82		0.20	0.60	1.00
311, Dec 82		0.20	0.60	1.00
312, Jan 83		0.20	0.60	1.00
313, Feb 83		0.20	0.60	1.00
314, Mar 83		0.20	0.60	1.00
315, Apr 83		0.20	0.60	1.00
316, May 83		0.20	0.60	1.00
317, Jun 83		0.20	0.60	1.00
318, Jul 83		0.20	0.60	1.00
319, Aug 83		0.20	0.60	1.00
320, Sep 83		0.20	0.60	1.00
321, Oct 83		0.20	0.60	1.00

HOUSE OF SECRETS

	ORIG.	GOOD	FINE	N-MINT
1, MD		72.00	216.00	360.00
2		30.00	90.00	150.00
3		25.00	75.00	125.00
4, JK		15.00	45.00	75.00
5		10.00	30.00	50.00
6		10.00	30.00	50.00
7		10.00	30.00	50.00
8, JK		15.00	45.00	75.00
9		10.00	30.00	50.00
10		10.00	30.00	50.00
11		10.00	30.00	50.00
12, JK		12.00	36.00	60.00
13		6.00	18.00	30.00
14		6.00	18.00	30.00
15		6.00	18.00	30.00
16		6.00	18.00	30.00
17		6.00	18.00	30.00
18		6.00	18.00	30.00
19		6.00	18.00	30.00
20		6.00	18.00	30.00
21		6.00	18.00	30.00

	ORIG.	GOOD	FINE	N-MINT
22, MM		6.00	18.00	30.00
23, O:Mark Merlin		7.20	21.60	36.00
24		3.60	10.80	18.00
25		3.60	10.80	18.00
26		3.60	10.80	18.00
27		3.60	10.80	18.00
28		3.60	10.80	18.00
29		3.60	10.80	18.00
30		3.60	10.80	18.00
31		3.60	10.80	18.00
32		3.60	10.80	18.00
33		3.60	10.80	18.00
34		3.60	10.80	18.00
35		3.60	10.80	18.00
36		3.60	10.80	18.00
37		3.60	10.80	18.00
38		3.60	10.80	18.00
39		3.60	10.80	18.00
40		3.60	10.80	18.00
41		3.60	10.80	18.00
42		3.60	10.80	18.00
43		3.60	10.80	18.00
44		3.60	10.80	18.00
45		3.60	10.80	18.00
46		3.60	10.80	18.00
47		3.60	10.80	18.00
48		3.60	10.80	18.00
49		3.60	10.80	18.00
50		3.60	10.80	18.00
51		2.00	6.00	10.00
52		2.00	6.00	10.00
53		2.00	6.00	10.00
54		2.00	6.00	10.00
55		2.00	6.00	10.00
56		2.00	6.00	10.00
57		2.00	6.00	10.00
58		2.00	6.00	10.00
59		2.00	6.00	10.00
60		2.00	6.00	10.00
61, 1:Eclipso		32.00	96.00	160.00
62		8.00	24.00	40.00
63		8.00	24.00	40.00
64		8.00	24.00	40.00
65		8.00	24.00	40.00
66		8.00	24.00	40.00
67		8.00	24.00	40.00
68		6.00	18.00	30.00
69		6.00	18.00	30.00
70		6.00	18.00	30.00
71		6.00	18.00	30.00
72		6.00	18.00	30.00
73		6.00	18.00	30.00
74		6.00	18.00	30.00
75		6.00	18.00	30.00
76, Jan 66, A:Eclipso	0.12	6.00	18.00	30.00
77		6.00	18.00	30.00
78		6.00	18.00	30.00
79		6.00	18.00	30.00
80		6.00	18.00	30.00
81, NA(c), 1:mystery format		0.70	2.10	3.50
82, NA		0.70	2.10	3.50
83, Jan 70, ATh	0.15	0.70	2.10	3.50
84, NA(c)		0.70	2.10	3.50
85, May 70, NA	0.15	0.70	2.10	3.50
86, NA(c), GM		0.70	2.10	3.50
87, NA(c), MK, BWr		0.70	2.10	3.50
88		0.70	2.10	3.50
89		0.70	2.10	3.50
90, Mar 71, NA/GM/RB 1st Buckler DC art	0.15	0.80	2.40	4.00
91, NA/MA/WW		0.70	2.10	3.50

	ORIG.	GOOD	FINE	N-MINT
❑ 92, Jul 71, BWr, I:Swamp Thing				
.................................0.15		75.00	225.00	375.00
❑ 93, JA/BWr..................		0.30	0.90	1.50
❑ 94, BWr/ATh		0.60	1.80	3.00
❑ 95		0.20	0.60	1.00
❑ 96		0.30	0.90	1.50
❑ 97		0.30	0.90	1.50
❑ 98		0.30	0.90	1.50
❑ 99		0.20	0.60	1.00
❑ 100		0.20	0.60	1.00
❑ 101		0.20	0.60	1.00
❑ 102		0.20	0.60	1.00
❑ 103		0.20	0.60	1.00
❑ 104		0.20	0.60	1.00
❑ 105		0.20	0.60	1.00
❑ 106		0.20	0.60	1.00
❑ 107		0.20	0.60	1.00
❑ 108		0.20	0.60	1.00
❑ 109		0.20	0.60	1.00
❑ 110		0.20	0.60	1.00
❑ 111		0.20	0.60	1.00
❑ 112		0.20	0.60	1.00
❑ 113		0.20	0.60	1.00
❑ 114		0.20	0.60	1.00
❑ 115		0.20	0.60	1.00
❑ 116		0.20	0.60	1.00
❑ 117, AA/AN		0.25	0.75	1.25
❑ 118		0.20	0.60	1.00
❑ 119		0.20	0.60	1.00
❑ 120		0.20	0.60	1.00
❑ 121		0.20	0.60	1.00
❑ 122		0.20	0.60	1.00
❑ 123, Sep 74, ATh 0.20		0.25	0.75	1.25
❑ 124		0.20	0.60	1.00
❑ 125		0.20	0.60	1.00
❑ 126		0.20	0.60	1.00
❑ 127		0.20	0.60	1.00
❑ 128		0.20	0.60	1.00
❑ 129		0.20	0.60	1.00
❑ 130		0.20	0.60	1.00
❑ 131		0.20	0.60	1.00
❑ 132		0.20	0.60	1.00
❑ 133		0.20	0.60	1.00
❑ 134		0.20	0.60	1.00
❑ 135		0.20	0.60	1.00
❑ 136		0.20	0.60	1.00
❑ 137		0.20	0.60	1.00
❑ 138		0.20	0.60	1.00
❑ 139		0.20	0.60	1.00
❑ 140		0.20	0.60	1.00
❑ 141, O:Patchwork Man.....		0.60	1.80	3.00
❑ 142		0.20	0.60	1.00
❑ 143		0.20	0.60	1.00
❑ 144		0.20	0.60	1.00
❑ 145		0.20	0.60	1.00
❑ 146		0.20	0.60	1.00
❑ 147		0.20	0.60	1.00
❑ 148		0.20	0.60	1.00
❑ 149		0.20	0.60	1.00
❑ 150, Mar 78 .... 0.35		0.20	0.60	1.00
❑ 151, MK/MG....................		0.20	0.60	1.00
❑ 152		0.20	0.60	1.00
❑ 153		0.20	0.60	1.00
❑ 154		0.20	0.60	1.00

HOW TO DRAW FELIX THE CAT AND HIS FRIENDS
FELIX

	ORIG.	GOOD	FINE	N-MINT
❑ 1, b&w		0.45	1.35	2.25

HOWARD CHAYKIN'S AMERICAN FLAGG!
FIRST

	ORIG.	GOOD	FINE	N-MINT
❑ 1		0.35	1.05	1.75
❑ 2		0.35	1.05	1.75

	ORIG.	GOOD	FINE	N-MINT
❑ 3		0.35	1.05	1.75
❑ 4		0.35	1.05	1.75
❑ 5		0.35	1.05	1.75
❑ 6		0.35	1.05	1.75
❑ 7		0.35	1.05	1.75
❑ 8		0.35	1.05	1.75
❑ 9		0.39	1.17	1.95
❑ 10		0.39	1.17	1.95
❑ 11		0.39	1.17	1.95
❑ 12		0.39	1.17	1.95

HOWARD THE DUCK
MARVEL

	ORIG.	GOOD	FINE	N-MINT
❑ 1, FB, A:SpM..............0.25		1.60	4.80	8.00
❑ 2, FB 0.25		0.80	2.40	4.00
❑ 3 ....0.25		0.50	1.50	2.50
❑ 4 ....0.25		0.50	1.50	2.50
❑ 5, Sep 76 ....0.30		0.50	1.50	2.50
❑ 6, Nov 76 ....0.30		0.50	1.50	2.50
❑ 7, Dec 76 ....0.30		0.50	1.50	2.50
❑ 8, Jan 77....................0.30		0.50	1.50	2.50
❑ 9, Feb 77....................0.30		0.50	1.50	2.50
❑ 10, Mar 77..................0.30		0.50	1.50	2.50
❑ 11, Apr 77...................0.30		0.50	1.50	2.50
❑ 12, May 77..................0.30		1.00	3.00	5.00
❑ 13, Jun 77 ....0.30		1.00	3.00	5.00
❑ 14, Jul 77....................0.30		1.00	3.00	5.00
❑ 15, Aug 77 ....0.30		0.50	1.50	2.50
❑ 16, Sep 77 ....0.30		0.50	1.50	2.50
❑ 17, Oct 77...................0.30		0.50	1.50	2.50
❑ 18, Nov 77 ....0.35		0.50	1.50	2.50
❑ 19, Dec 77 ....0.35		0.50	1.50	2.50
❑ 20, Jan 78...................0.35		0.50	1.50	2.50
❑ 21, Feb 78...................0.35		0.40	1.20	2.00
❑ 22, Mar 78...................0.35		0.40	1.20	2.00
❑ 23, Apr 78....................0.35		0.40	1.20	2.00
❑ 24, May 78...................0.35		0.40	1.20	2.00
❑ 25, Jun 78 ....0.35		0.40	1.20	2.00
❑ 26, Jul 78.....................0.35		0.40	1.20	2.00
❑ 27, Sep 78 ....0.35		0.40	1.20	2.00
❑ 28, Nov 78 ....0.35		0.40	1.20	2.00
❑ 29, Jan 79...................0.35		0.40	1.20	2.00
❑ 30, Mar 79...................0.35		0.40	1.20	2.00
❑ 31, May 79...................0.40		0.40	1.20	2.00
❑ 32, Jan 86...................0.65		0.40	1.20	2.00
❑ 33, Sep 86 ....1.50		0.40	1.20	2.00

HOWARD THE DUCK (b&w mag)

	ORIG.	GOOD	FINE	N-MINT
❑ 1, Oct 79, contains nudity				
.................................1.00		0.20	0.60	1.00
❑ 2, Dec 79 ....1.25		0.25	0.75	1.25
❑ 3, Feb 80....................1.25		0.25	0.75	1.25
❑ 4, Mar 80....................1.25		0.25	0.75	1.25
❑ 5, May 80....................1.25		0.25	0.75	1.25
❑ 6, Jul 80......................1.25		0.25	0.75	1.25
❑ 7, Sep 80 ....1.25		0.25	0.75	1.25
❑ 8, Nov 80, Batman parody				
.................................1.25		0.25	0.75	1.25
❑ 9, Mar 81.....................1.25		0.25	0.75	1.25

HOWARD THE DUCK (movie adaptation)

	ORIG.	GOOD	FINE	N-MINT
❑ 1, Dec 86, movie............0.75		0.20	0.60	1.00
❑ 2, Jan 87, movie 0.75		0.20	0.60	1.00
❑ 3, Feb 87, movie 0.75		0.20	0.60	1.00

HOWARD THE DUCK ANNUAL

	ORIG.	GOOD	FINE	N-MINT
❑ 1, Oct 77.........................0.50		0.20	0.60	1.00

	ORIG.	GOOD	FINE	N-MINT

HOWL
ETERNITY
	ORIG.	GOOD	FINE	N-MINT
1, b&w rep.		0.45	1.35	2.25
2, b&w rep.		0.45	1.35	2.25

HUCKLEBERRY HOUND & QUICK DRAW MCGRAW GIANT-SIZE FLIP BOOK
HARVEY
	ORIG.	GOOD	FINE	N-MINT
1	2.25	0.45	1.35	2.25

HUGGA BUNCH
STAR
	ORIG.	GOOD	FINE	N-MINT
1	0.75	0.15	0.45	0.75
2	0.75	0.15	0.45	0.75
3	0.75	0.15	0.45	0.75
4	0.75	0.15	0.45	0.75
5	1.00	0.20	0.60	1.00
6	1.00	0.20	0.60	1.00

HUGO
FANTAGRAPHICS
	ORIG.	GOOD	FINE	N-MINT
1		0.40	1.20	2.00
2		0.40	1.20	2.00
3		0.40	1.20	2.00

HULK 2099
MARVEL
	ORIG.	GOOD	FINE	N-MINT
1, Dec 94	2.50	0.50	1.50	2.50
2, Jan 95	1.50	0.30	0.90	1.50
3, Feb 95	1.50	0.30	0.90	1.50
4, Mar 95	1.50	0.30	0.90	1.50
5, Apr 95	1.50	0.30	0.90	1.50
6, May 95	1.50	0.30	0.90	1.50
7, Jun 95	1.95	0.39	1.17	1.95
8, Jul 95	1.95	0.39	1.17	1.95
9, Aug 95	1.95	0.39	1.17	1.95
10, Sep 95, final issue; continued in *2099 A.D. Apocalypse* #1	1.95	0.39	1.17	1.95

HULK, THE (color mag)
	ORIG.	GOOD	FINE	N-MINT
10, Aug 78, (was *Rampaging Hulk*)	1.50	0.30	0.90	1.50
11, Oct 78	1.50	0.30	0.90	1.50
12, Dec 78	1.50	0.30	0.90	1.50
13, Feb 79	1.50	0.30	0.90	1.50
14, Apr 79	1.50	0.30	0.90	1.50
15, Jun 79	1.50	0.30	0.90	1.50
16, Aug 79	1.50	0.30	0.90	1.50
17, Oct 79	1.50	0.30	0.90	1.50
18, Dec 79	1.50	0.30	0.90	1.50
19, Feb 80	1.50	0.30	0.90	1.50
20, Apr 80	1.50	0.30	0.90	1.50
21, Jun 80	1.50	0.30	0.90	1.50
22, Aug 80	1.50	0.30	0.90	1.50
23, Oct 80	1.50	0.30	0.90	1.50
24, Dec 80	1.50	0.30	0.90	1.50
25, Feb 81	1.50	0.30	0.90	1.50
26, Apr 81	1.50	0.30	0.90	1.50
27, Jun 81	1.50	0.30	0.90	1.50

HUMAN FLY, THE
	ORIG.	GOOD	FINE	N-MINT
1, Sep 77	0.30	0.40	1.20	2.00
2, Oct 77	0.30	0.30	0.90	1.50
3, Nov 77	0.35	0.30	0.90	1.50
4, Dec 77	0.35	0.30	0.90	1.50
5, Jan 78	0.35	0.30	0.90	1.50
6, Feb 78	0.35	0.20	0.60	1.00
7, Mar 78	0.35	0.20	0.60	1.00
8, Apr 78	0.35	0.20	0.60	1.00
9, May 78	0.35	0.20	0.60	1.00
10, Jun 78	0.35	0.20	0.60	1.00
11, Jul 78	0.35	0.20	0.60	1.00
12, Aug 78	0.35	0.20	0.60	1.00
13, Sep 78	0.35	0.20	0.60	1.00
14, Oct 78	0.35	0.20	0.60	1.00
15, Nov 78	0.35	0.20	0.60	1.00

	ORIG.	GOOD	FINE	N-MINT
16, Dec 78	0.35	0.20	0.60	1.00
17, Jan 79	0.35	0.20	0.60	1.00
18, Feb 79	0.35	0.20	0.60	1.00
19, Mar 79	0.35	0.20	0.60	1.00

HUMAN GARGOYLES
ETERNITY
	ORIG.	GOOD	FINE	N-MINT
1, b&w		0.39	1.17	1.95
2, b&w		0.39	1.17	1.95
3, b&w		0.39	1.17	1.95
4, b&w		0.39	1.17	1.95

HUMAN HEAD COMIX
ICONOGRAFIX
	ORIG.	GOOD	FINE	N-MINT
1, b&w	2.50	0.50	1.50	2.50

HUMAN POWERHOUSE
PURE IMAGINATION
	ORIG.	GOOD	FINE	N-MINT
1, b&w,BW		0.40	1.20	2.00

HUMAN TORCH, THE
MARVEL
	ORIG.	GOOD	FINE	N-MINT
1, reprints	0.25	0.20	0.60	1.00
2, reprints	0.25	0.20	0.60	1.00
3, reprints	0.25	0.20	0.60	1.00
4, reprints	0.25	0.20	0.60	1.00
5, reprints	0.25	0.20	0.60	1.00
6, reprints	0.25	0.20	0.60	1.00
7, reprints	0.25	0.20	0.60	1.00
8, reprints	0.25	0.20	0.60	1.00

HUMOR ON THE CUTTING...EDGE
EDGE
	ORIG.	GOOD	FINE	N-MINT
1, 93, b&w	2.95	0.59	1.77	2.95
2, 94, b&w	2.95	0.59	1.77	2.95
3, 94, b&w	2.95	0.59	1.77	2.95
4, 94, b&w	2.95	0.59	1.77	2.95

HUNT FOR BLACK WIDOW, THE
FLEETWAY/QUALITY
	ORIG.	GOOD	FINE	N-MINT
1, Judge Dredd	2.95	0.59	1.77	2.95

HUNTER'S HEART (mini-series)
DC/PARADOX
	ORIG.	GOOD	FINE	N-MINT
1, 95, digest;b&w	5.95	1.19	3.57	5.95
2, 95, digest;b&w	5.95	1.19	3.57	5.95

HUNTRESS, THE
DC
	ORIG.	GOOD	FINE	N-MINT
1, Apr 89, O:Huntress	1.00	0.20	0.60	1.00
2, May 89	1.00	0.20	0.60	1.00
3, Jun 89	1.00	0.20	0.60	1.00
4, Jul 89	1.00	0.20	0.60	1.00
5, Aug 89	1.00	0.20	0.60	1.00
6, Sep 89	1.00	0.20	0.60	1.00
7, Oct 89	1.00	0.20	0.60	1.00
8, Nov 89	1.00	0.20	0.60	1.00
9, Dec 89	1.00	0.20	0.60	1.00
10, Jan 90	1.00	0.20	0.60	1.00
11, Feb 90	1.00	0.20	0.60	1.00
12, Mar 90	1.00	0.20	0.60	1.00
13, Apr 90	1.00	0.20	0.60	1.00
14, May 90	1.00	0.20	0.60	1.00
15, Jun 90	1.25	0.20	0.60	1.00
16, Jul 90	1.25	0.20	0.60	1.00
17, Aug 90, Batman	1.25	0.25	0.75	1.25
18, Sep 90, Batman	1.25	0.25	0.75	1.25
19, Oct 90, Batman	1.25	0.25	0.75	1.25

HUNTRESS, THE (1994-)
	ORIG.	GOOD	FINE	N-MINT
1, Jun 94	1.50	0.30	0.90	1.50
2, Jul 94	1.50	0.30	0.90	1.50
3, Aug 94	1.50	0.30	0.90	1.50
4, Sep 94	1.50	0.30	0.90	1.50

HUP
LAST GASP
	ORIG.	GOOD	FINE	N-MINT
1, 87, RCrumb,b&w	2.50	0.50	1.50	2.50

	ORIG.	GOOD	FINE	N-MINT
HURRICANE GIRLS				
ANTARCTIC				
☐ 1, Jul 95, b&w 2.95		0.59	1.77	2.95
☐ 2, Sep 95, b&w 2.95		0.59	1.77	2.95
☐ 3, Nov 95, b&w 2.95		0.59	1.77	2.95
HUTCH OWEN'S WORKING HARD				
NEW HAT				
☐ 0, 94, b&w 3.95		0.79	2.37	3.95
HY-BREED, THE				
DIVISION				
☐ 4, 95, b&w 2.90		0.58	1.74	2.90
☐ 5, 95, b&w 2.50		0.50	1.50	2.50
HYBRIDS				
CONTINUITY				
☐ 1 .... 2.50		0.50	1.50	2.50
HYBRIDS: DEATHWATCH 2000				
☐ 0, red foil cover				
☐ 1, trading cards 2.50		0.50	1.50	2.50
☐ 2, trading card 2.50		0.50	1.50	2.50
☐ 3, trading card 2.50		0.50	1.50	2.50
HYBRIDS: THE ORIGIN				
☐ 1 .... 2.50		0.50	1.50	2.50
☐ 2 .... 2.50		0.50	1.50	2.50
☐ 3 .... 2.50		0.50	1.50	2.50
☐ 4 .... 2.50		0.50	1.50	2.50
☐ 5 .... 2.50		0.50	1.50	2.50

	ORIG.	GOOD	FINE	N-MINT
HYDE-25				
HARRIS				
☐ 0, Apr 95 .... 2.95		0.59	1.77	2.95
HYENA				
KITCHEN SINK				
☐ 4 .... 3.95		0.79	2.37	3.95
TUNDRA				
☐ 1, b&w 3.95		0.79	2.37	3.95
☐ 2, b&w 3.95		0.79	2.37	3.95
☐ 3, b&w 3.95		0.79	2.37	3.95
HYPERKIND				
MARVEL/RAZORLINE				
☐ 1, foil cover 2.50		0.50	1.50	2.50
☐ 2 .... 1.75		0.35	1.05	1.75
☐ 3 .... 1.75		0.35	1.05	1.75
☐ 4 .... 1.75		0.35	1.05	1.75
☐ 5 .... 1.75		0.35	1.05	1.75
☐ 6 .... 1.75		0.35	1.05	1.75
☐ 7 .... 1.75		0.35	1.05	1.75
☐ 8 .... 1.75		0.35	1.05	1.75
☐ 9, May 94 .... 1.75		0.35	1.05	1.75
HYPERKIND UNLEASHED!				
MARVEL				
☐ 1, Aug 94 .... 2.95		0.59	1.77	2.95

Herbie

First Appearance: *Forbidden Worlds* #73.

Comic books have produced a lot of strange heroes but few, if any, are stranger than Herbie Popnecker. Created by writer-editor Richard Hughes and artist Ogden Whitney, Herbie first appeared in 1960 in the ACG supernatural anthology title *Forbidden Worlds*. After four other sporadic appearances (#94, #110, #114, #116), he was given his own title in 1964.

Initially, the rotund, super-powered preadolescent had no secret identity and wore no costume beyond the standard nerd attire of glasses, necktie, and shirt and pants stretched just short of bursting. He was shaped like a large beach ball, sported a bowl-shaped haircut, and had a serious lollipop addiction. His command of the English language just a notch above Tarzan's, Herbie spoke entirely in sentence fragments.

He evinced an unflappable cool at all times, his eyelids never motivated to rise above the halfway point. His vast supply of lollipops functioned much like Popeye's spinach, maintaining the laconic youth's extra-human strength and other powers, as well as serving as a weapon for "bopping" miscreants. Herbie did not so much defy gravity as ignore it, calmly strolling through the air, as though he couldn't be bothered by the laws of science.

In *Herbie* #8 (Mar 65), Herbie decided to become a more conventional costumed super-hero, and, despite flunking out of the American Hero School, he soon gave birth to a new identity as The Fat Fury. His new costume consisted of longjohns, a face-mask, a cape, and a plumber's helper. The Fat Fury allowed Herbie to experience the traditional super-hero dichotomy, in which his exasperated parents regarded him as a "little fat nothing" while admiring the exploits of The Fat Fury.

The Herbie stories occasionally saw cameo appearances by The Grim Reaper, Magicman, and other characters from Hughes' other anthology title *Unknown Worlds*. Herbie returned the favor with a cameo of his own in *Unknown Worlds* #20 (Dec-Jan 62-63). The series continued, with regular appearances by The Fat Fury, until issue #23 (Feb 67). Throughout the ACG run, Whitney provided the art, and Hughes wrote the scripts under the name "Shane O'Shea."

While these earlier appearances are outside the scope of this book, Herbie's modern appearances began in 1990, when A-Plus published six issues of black-and-white reprints of Herbie stories. In 1992, Dark Horse published two color issues of *Herbie* mixing ACG reprints with new material by John Byrne. A surreal team-up between Herbie and Bob Burden's Flaming Carrot appeared in *Flaming Carrot* #31 (Oct 94). Herbie made a cameo appearance in the *normalman-Megaton Man Special* (Aug 94).

I

	ORIG.	GOOD	FINE	N-MINT
I AM LEGEND				
ECLIPSE				
1, b&w, Matheson............	1.19	3.57	5.95	
2	1.19	3.57	5.95	
3	1.19	3.57	5.95	
4	1.19	3.57	5.95	
I BEFORE E				
FANTAGRAPHICS				
1, b&w, Sam Kieth 3.95	0.79	2.37	3.95	
1, May 94, second printing				
.... 3.95	0.79	2.37	3.95	
2, b&w, Sam Kieth 3.95	0.79	2.37	3.95	
I LOVE LUCY				
ETERNITY				
1, b&w strip rep.	0.59	1.77	2.95	
2, b&w strip rep.	0.59	1.77	2.95	
3, b&w strip rep.	0.59	1.77	2.95	
4, b&w strip rep.	0.59	1.77	2.95	
5, b&w strip rep.	0.59	1.77	2.95	
6, b&w strip rep.	0.59	1.77	2.95	
I LOVE LUCY BOOK TWO				
1, b&w strip reprints.......	0.59	1.77	2.95	
2, b&w strip reprints.......	0.59	1.77	2.95	
3, b&w strip reprints.......	0.59	1.77	2.95	
4, b&w strip reprints.......	0.59	1.77	2.95	
5, b&w strip reprints.......	0.59	1.77	2.95	
6, b&w strip reprints.......	0.59	1.77	2.95	
I LOVE LUCY IN 3-D				
1	0.79	2.37	3.95	
I LOVE LUCY IN FULL COLOR				
1, comic book rep.	1.19	3.57	5.95	
I SAW IT				
EDUCOMICS				
0, Hiroshima, b&w...........	0.40	1.20	2.00	
I WANT TO BE YOUR DOG				
EROS COMIX				
1, adult, b&w	0.39	1.17	1.95	
2, adult, b&w	0.39	1.17	1.95	
3, adult, b&w	0.39	1.17	1.95	
4, adult, b&w	0.39	1.17	1.95	
5	0.45	1.35	2.25	
I, LUSIPHUR				
MULEHIDE				
1, b&w	12.00	36.00	60.00	
2, b&w	8.00	24.00	40.00	
3, b&w	8.00	24.00	40.00	
4, b&w	7.20	21.60	36.00	
5, b&w	7.20	21.60	36.00	
6, b&w	6.00	18.00	30.00	
7, b&w	6.00	18.00	30.00	
8, b&w	4.40	13.20	22.00	
9, b&w	4.40	13.20	22.00	
10, (becomes *Poison Elves*);b&w				
....	4.40	13.20	22.00	
I.F.S. ZONE				
KHB				
1, b&w 1.25	0.25	0.75	1.25	
2, b&w 1.25	0.25	0.75	1.25	
3, b&w 1.25	0.25	0.75	1.25	
4, b&w 1.25	0.25	0.75	1.25	
ICARUS				
AIRCEL				
1	0.40	1.20	2.00	
2	0.40	1.20	2.00	
3	0.40	1.20	2.00	
4	0.40	1.20	2.00	
5	0.40	1.20	2.00	

	ORIG.	GOOD	FINE	N-MINT
ICE AGE ON THE WORLD OF MAGIC: THE GATHERING				
ACCLAIM/ARMADA				
1, 95, prestige format collection of first two issues; polybagged with sheet of counters				
.... 4.95	0.99	2.97	4.95	
2, 95, prestige format collection of issues #3 and 4; polybagged with sheet of counters				
.... 4.95	0.99	2.97	4.95	
ICE AGE ON THE WORLD OF MAGIC: THE GATHERING (mini-series)				
1, 95, bound-in Magic card (Chub Toad)				
.... 2.50	0.50	1.50	2.50	
2, Aug 95, bound-in Chub Toad card from Ice Age				
.... 2.50	0.50	1.50	2.50	
3, Sep 95, polybagged with sheet of creature tokens				
.... 2.50	0.50	1.50	2.50	
4, Oct 95, polybagged with sheet of creature tokens				
.... 2.50	0.50	1.50	2.50	
ICEMAN				
MARVEL				
1, Dec 84....................... 0.75	0.60	1.80	3.00	
2, Feb 85....................... 0.75	0.40	1.20	2.00	
3, Apr 85........................ 0.75	0.40	1.20	2.00	
4, Jun 85........................ 0.75	0.40	1.20	2.00	
ICICLE				
HERO				
1	0.99	2.97	4.95	
2, b&w...........................	0.70	2.10	3.50	
3, b&w...........................	0.70	2.10	3.50	
4, b&w, A: Chrissie Claus .	0.70	2.10	3.50	
5, b&w........................... 3.95	0.79	2.37	3.95	
ICON				
DC/MILESTONE				
1, May 93....................... 1.50	0.40	1.20	2.00	
1, May 93, poster, trading card				
.... 2.95	1.00	3.00	5.00	
2, Jun 93 .... 1.50	0.60	1.80	3.00	
3, Jul 93......................... 1.50	0.40	1.20	2.00	
4, Aug 93........................ 1.50	0.40	1.20	2.00	
5, Sep 93 .... 1.50	0.40	1.20	2.00	
6, Oct 93........................ 1.50	0.30	0.90	1.50	
7, Nov 93........................ 1.50	0.30	0.90	1.50	
8, Dec 93........................ 1.50	0.30	0.90	1.50	
9, Jan 94, Shadow War... 1.50	0.30	0.90	1.50	
10, Feb 94...................... 1.50	0.30	0.90	1.50	
11, Mar 94 .... 1.50	0.30	0.90	1.50	
12, Apr 94...................... 1.50	0.30	0.90	1.50	
13, May 94..................... 1.50	0.30	0.90	1.50	
14, Jun 94...................... 1.50	0.30	0.90	1.50	
15, Jul 94, Worlds Collide;Superboy				
.... 1.75	0.50	1.50	2.50	
16, Aug 94...................... 1.75	0.45	1.35	2.25	
17, Sep 94...................... 1.75	0.35	1.05	1.75	
18, Oct 94...................... 1.75	0.35	1.05	1.75	
19, Nov 94...................... 1.75	0.35	1.05	1.75	
20, Dec 94...................... 1.75	0.35	1.05	1.75	
21, Jan 95...................... 1.75	0.35	1.05	1.75	
22, Feb 95...................... 1.75	0.35	1.05	1.75	
23, Mar 95 .... 1.75	0.35	1.05	1.75	
24, Apr 95...................... 1.75	0.35	1.05	1.75	
25, May 95..................... 2.95	0.59	1.77	2.95	
26, Jun 95 .... 1.75	0.35	1.05	1.75	
27, Jul 95....................... 2.50	0.50	1.50	2.50	
28, Aug 95...................... 2.50	0.50	1.50	2.50	
29, Sep 95...................... 2.50	0.50	1.50	2.50	
30, Oct 95, Funeral of Buck Wild				
.... 2.50	0.50	1.50	2.50	
31, Nov 95...................... 0.99	0.20	0.59	0.99	

	ORIG.	GOOD	FINE	N-MINT
☐ 32, Dec 95	2.50	0.50	1.50	2.50
☐ 33, Jan 96	2.50	0.50	1.50	2.50
☐ 34, Feb 96	2.50	0.50	1.50	2.50
☐ 35, Mar 96	2.50	0.50	1.50	2.50
☐ 36, Apr 96	2.50	0.50	1.50	2.50

ICON DEVIL
SPIDER

		GOOD	FINE	N-MINT
☐ 1		0.32	0.96	1.60
☐ 2		0.32	0.96	1.60

ICON DEVIL (Volume 2)

		GOOD	FINE	N-MINT
☐ 2, b&w		0.45	1.35	2.25

ICONOGRAFIX SPECIAL
ICONOGRAFIX

	ORIG.	GOOD	FINE	N-MINT
☐ 1, b&w	2.50	0.50	1.50	2.50

ID
EROS COMIX

		GOOD	FINE	N-MINT
☐ 1, adult, b&w, Crumb		0.50	1.50	2.50
☐ 2, adult, b&w, Crumb		0.50	1.50	2.50
☐ 3, adult, b&w, Crumb		0.50	1.50	2.50

IDIOTLAND
FANTAGRAPHICS

	ORIG.	GOOD	FINE	N-MINT
☐ 1, b&w	2.95	0.59	1.77	2.95
☐ 2, b&w	2.50	0.50	1.50	2.50
☐ 3, b&w	2.50	0.50	1.50	2.50
☐ 4, b&w	2.50	0.50	1.50	2.50
☐ 5, b&w	2.50	0.50	1.50	2.50
☐ 6, Aug 94, b&w	2.50	0.50	1.50	2.50

IDOL
EPIC

	ORIG.	GOOD	FINE	N-MINT
☐ 1, 92	2.95	0.59	1.77	2.95
☐ 2, 92	2.95	0.59	1.77	2.95
☐ 3, 92	2.95	0.59	1.77	2.95

ILIAD II
MICMAC

		GOOD	FINE	N-MINT
☐ 1, b&w		0.34	1.02	1.70
☐ 2, b&w		0.34	1.02	1.70
☐ 3, b&w		0.34	1.02	1.70

ILLEGAL ALIENS
ECLIPSE

		GOOD	FINE	N-MINT
☐ 0, nn b&w		0.50	1.50	2.50

ILLUMINATOR
MARVEL/ NELSON

	ORIG.	GOOD	FINE	N-MINT
☐ 1	4.99	1.00	2.99	4.99
☐ 2	4.99	1.00	2.99	4.99
☐ 3	2.95	0.59	1.77	2.95

ILLUMINATUS
EYE-N-APPLE

		GOOD	FINE	N-MINT
☐ 1, (moves to Rip Off Press)		0.40	1.20	2.00

ILLUMINATUS!
RIP OFF

	ORIG.	GOOD	FINE	N-MINT
☐ 1, Oct 90, b&w	2.50	0.50	1.50	2.50
☐ 2, Dec 90, b&w	2.50	0.50	1.50	2.50
☐ 3, Apr 91, b&w	2.50	0.50	1.50	2.50

ILLUSTRATED CLASSEX
COMIC ZONE

		GOOD	FINE	N-MINT
☐ 1, adult, b&w		0.55	1.65	2.75

ILLUSTRATED DORE: BOOK OF GENESIS
TOME PRESS

		GOOD	FINE	N-MINT
☐ 1, Dore, b&w		0.50	1.50	2.50

ILLUSTRATED DORE: BOOK OF THE APOCRYPHA

		GOOD	FINE	N-MINT
☐ 1, b&w		0.50	1.50	2.50

IMAGE
IMAGE

		GOOD	FINE	N-MINT
☐ 0,		7.00	21.00	35.00

IMAGE 0

☐ 0, 93				

IMAGE PLUS

	ORIG.	GOOD	FINE	N-MINT
☐ 1	2.25	0.45	1.35	2.25

IMAGES OF OMAHA
KITCHEN SINK

		GOOD	FINE	N-MINT
☐ 1, adult, b&w		0.79	2.37	3.95
☐ 2, adult, b&w		0.79	2.37	3.95

IMAGES OF SHADOWHAWK
IMAGE

	ORIG.	GOOD	FINE	N-MINT
☐ 1	1.95	0.39	1.17	1.95
☐ 2, Oct 93	1.95	0.39	1.17	1.95
☐ 3	1.95	0.39	1.17	1.95

IMAGI-MATION
IMAGI-MATION

		GOOD	FINE	N-MINT
☐ 1, Gnatman		0.35	1.05	1.75

IMMORTAL COMBAT
EXPRESS/ENTITY

	ORIG.	GOOD	FINE	N-MINT
☐ 0, Feb 95, cardstock cover; Entity Illustrated Novella #5	2.95	0.59	1.77	2.95

IMMORTAL DR. FATE
DC

	ORIG.	GOOD	FINE	N-MINT
☐ 1, Jan 85, WS, KG	1.25	0.35	1.05	1.75
☐ 2, Feb 85, KG	1.25	0.25	0.75	1.25
☐ 3, Mar 85, KG	1.25	0.25	0.75	1.25

IMMORTALIS
MARVEL

	ORIG.	GOOD	FINE	N-MINT
☐ 1	1.95	0.39	1.17	1.95
☐ 2	1.95	0.39	1.17	1.95
☐ 3	1.95	0.39	1.17	1.95

IMMORTALS, THE
COMICS BY DAY

		GOOD	FINE	N-MINT
☐ 1		0.20	0.60	1.00

IMP-UNITY
SPOOF

		GOOD	FINE	N-MINT
☐ 0, parody, b&w		0.59	1.77	2.95

IMPACT COMICS WHO'S WHO
IMPACT

		GOOD	FINE	N-MINT
☐ 1		0.99	2.97	4.95
☐ 2		0.99	2.97	4.95
☐ 3, trading cards		0.99	2.97	4.95

IMPACT WINTER SPECIAL

	ORIG.	GOOD	FINE	N-MINT
☐ 1, 91, Shield, Comet, Fly, Jaguar, Web	2.50	0.50	1.50	2.50

IMPOSSIBLE MAN SUMMER VACATION SPECTACULAR
MARVEL

	ORIG.	GOOD	FINE	N-MINT
☐ 1, Aug 90	2.00	0.40	1.20	2.00
☐ 2, Aug 91	2.00	0.40	1.20	2.00

IMPULSE
DC

	ORIG.	GOOD	FINE	N-MINT
☐ 1, Apr 95	1.50	1.20	3.60	6.00
☐ 2, May 95	1.50	0.70	2.10	3.50
☐ 3, Jun 95	1.75	0.60	1.80	3.00
☐ 4, Jul 95	1.75	0.60	1.80	3.00
☐ 5, Aug 95	1.75	0.60	1.80	3.00
☐ 6, Sep 95, Child abuse	1.75	0.35	1.05	1.75
☐ 7, Oct 95	1.75	0.35	1.05	1.75
☐ 8, Nov 95, "Underworld Unleashed"; V:Blockbuster	1.75	0.35	1.05	1.75
☐ 9, Dec 95, A:Xs	1.75	0.35	1.05	1.75
☐ 10, Jan 96, "Dead Heat" Part 3 of 6;continues in Flash #110	1.75	0.35	1.05	1.75
☐ 11, Feb 96, "Dead Heat" Part 5 of 6; D:Johnny Quick	1.75	0.35	1.05	1.75
☐ 12, Mar 96	1.75	0.35	1.05	1.75
☐ 13, May 96	1.75	0.35	1.05	1.75
☐ 14, Jun 96, V:Trickster, White Lightning	1.75	0.35	1.05	1.75

	ORIG.	GOOD	FINE	N-MINT

IN THE DAYS OF THE ACE ROCK 'N' ROLL CLUB
FANTAGRAPHICS

	ORIG.	GOOD	FINE	N-MINT
❏ 0, nn b&w	4.95	0.99	2.97	4.95

IN THIN AIR
TOME PRESS

	ORIG.	GOOD	FINE	N-MINT
❏ 1, b&w;version a	2.95	0.59	1.77	2.95
❏ 1, b&w;version b	2.95	0.59	1.77	2.95

IN-COUNTRY NAM
SURVIVAL ARTS

	ORIG.	GOOD	FINE	N-MINT
❏ 1		0.39	1.17	1.95
❏ 2		0.39	1.17	1.95

INCOMPLETE DEATH'S HEAD, THE
MARVEL

	ORIG.	GOOD	FINE	N-MINT
❏ 1, reprints	2.95	0.59	1.77	2.95
❏ 2	1.75	0.35	1.05	1.75
❏ 3	1.75	0.35	1.05	1.75
❏ 4	1.75	0.35	1.05	1.75
❏ 5	1.75	0.35	1.05	1.75
❏ 6	1.75	0.35	1.05	1.75
❏ 7	1.75	0.35	1.05	1.75
❏ 8	1.75	0.35	1.05	1.75
❏ 9	1.75	0.35	1.05	1.75
❏ 10	1.75	0.35	1.05	1.75
❏ 11	1.75	0.35	1.05	1.75
❏ 12	2.50	0.50	1.50	2.50

INCREDIBLE HULK

	ORIG.	GOOD	FINE	N-MINT
❏ 1, JK, I:Hulk	0.12	1900.00	5700.00	9500.00
❏ 2, JK/SD, O:retold	0.12	500.00	1500.00	2500.00
❏ 3, JK, O:retold	0.12	300.00	900.00	1500.00
❏ 4, JK	0.12	200.00	600.00	1000.00
❏ 5	0.12	200.00	600.00	1000.00
❏ 6	0.12	270.00	810.00	1350.00

INCREDIBLE HULK (was Tales to Astonish)

	ORIG.	GOOD	FINE	N-MINT
❏ 102, O:retold	0.12	36.00	108.00	180.00
❏ 103, I:Space Parasite	0.12	10.00	30.00	50.00
❏ 104	0.12	8.00	24.00	40.00
❏ 105	0.12	8.00	24.00	40.00
❏ 106, HT	0.12	6.00	18.00	30.00
❏ 107, HT	0.12	6.00	18.00	30.00
❏ 108, HT	0.12	6.00	18.00	30.00
❏ 109, HT	0.12	6.00	18.00	30.00
❏ 110, HT	0.12	6.00	18.00	30.00
❏ 111, HT/DA	0.12	2.40	7.20	12.00
❏ 112, HT/DA	0.12	2.40	7.20	12.00
❏ 113, HT/DA	0.12	2.40	7.20	12.00
❏ 114, HT/DA	0.12	2.40	7.20	12.00
❏ 115	0.12	2.00	6.00	10.00
❏ 116	0.12	2.00	6.00	10.00
❏ 117	0.12	2.00	6.00	10.00
❏ 118	0.15	2.00	6.00	10.00
❏ 119	0.15	2.00	6.00	10.00
❏ 120	0.15	2.00	6.00	10.00
❏ 121	0.15	2.00	6.00	10.00
❏ 122, HT, A:Thing	0.15	2.00	6.00	10.00
❏ 123	0.15	1.00	3.00	5.00
❏ 124	0.15	1.00	3.00	5.00
❏ 125	0.15	1.00	3.00	5.00
❏ 126	0.15	1.00	3.00	5.00
❏ 127	0.15	1.00	3.00	5.00
❏ 128	0.15	1.00	3.00	5.00
❏ 129	0.15	1.00	3.00	5.00
❏ 130	0.15	1.00	3.00	5.00
❏ 131, HT, Iron Man	0.15	0.60	1.80	3.00
❏ 132, HT/JSe, V:Hydra	0.15	0.60	1.80	3.00
❏ 133	0.15	0.60	1.80	3.00
❏ 134	0.15	0.60	1.80	3.00
❏ 135	0.15	0.60	1.80	3.00
❏ 136	0.15	0.60	1.80	3.00
❏ 137	0.15	0.60	1.80	3.00
❏ 138	0.15	0.60	1.80	3.00

	ORIG.	GOOD	FINE	N-MINT
❏ 139	0.15	0.60	1.80	3.00
❏ 140	0.15	0.80	2.40	4.00
❏ 141	0.15	0.80	2.40	4.00
❏ 142	0.15	0.60	1.80	3.00
❏ 143	0.15	0.60	1.80	3.00
❏ 144	0.15	0.60	1.80	3.00
❏ 145, HT/JSe;O:retold; giant	0.25	0.80	2.40	4.00
❏ 146, HT/JSe	0.20	0.60	1.80	3.00
❏ 147, HT/JSe	0.20	0.60	1.80	3.00
❏ 148, HT/JSe	0.20	0.60	1.80	3.00
❏ 149, HT/JSe	0.20	0.60	1.80	3.00
❏ 150, HT/JSe, I:Viking	0.20	1.00	3.00	5.00
❏ 151	0.20	0.60	1.80	3.00
❏ 152	0.20	0.60	1.80	3.00
❏ 153	0.20	0.60	1.80	3.00
❏ 154	0.20	0.60	1.80	3.00
❏ 155	0.20	0.60	1.80	3.00
❏ 156	0.20	0.60	1.80	3.00
❏ 157	0.20	0.60	1.80	3.00
❏ 158	0.20	0.60	1.80	3.00
❏ 159	0.20	0.60	1.80	3.00
❏ 160	0.20	0.60	1.80	3.00
❏ 161, HT, V:Beast	0.20	0.80	2.40	4.00
❏ 162, HT, T:Wendigo	0.20	0.90	2.70	4.50
❏ 163, HT	0.20	0.60	1.80	3.00
❏ 164, HT	0.20	0.60	1.80	3.00
❏ 165, HT	0.20	0.60	1.80	3.00
❏ 166, HT	0.20	0.60	1.80	3.00
❏ 167, HT	0.20	0.60	1.80	3.00
❏ 168, HT	0.20	0.60	1.80	3.00
❏ 169, HT	0.20	0.60	1.80	3.00
❏ 170, HT	0.20	0.60	1.80	3.00
❏ 171, HT	0.20	0.60	1.80	3.00
❏ 172, HT, X-Men	0.20	4.00	12.00	20.00
❏ 173, HT, V:Cobalt Man	0.20	0.30	0.90	1.50
❏ 174, HT	0.20	0.50	1.50	2.50
❏ 175, HT	0.25	0.50	1.50	2.50
❏ 176, HT	0.25	0.80	2.40	4.00
❏ 177, HT	0.25	0.80	2.40	4.00
❏ 178, HT	0.25	3.60	10.80	18.00
❏ 179, HT, Missing Link	0.25	0.30	0.90	1.50
❏ 180, HT, 1:Wolverine	0.25	20.00	60.00	100.00
❏ 181, HT, A:Wolverine	0.25	78.00	234.00	390.00
❏ 182, I:Crackajack	0.25	16.00	48.00	80.00
❏ 183	0.25	0.40	1.20	2.00
❏ 184	0.25	0.40	1.20	2.00
❏ 185	0.25	0.40	1.20	2.00
❏ 186	0.25	0.40	1.20	2.00
❏ 187	0.25	0.40	1.20	2.00
❏ 188	0.25	0.40	1.20	2.00
❏ 189	0.25	0.40	1.20	2.00
❏ 190	0.25	0.40	1.20	2.00
❏ 191	0.25	0.40	1.20	2.00
❏ 192	0.25	0.40	1.20	2.00
❏ 193	0.25	0.40	1.20	2.00
❏ 194	0.25	0.40	1.20	2.00
❏ 195	0.25	0.40	1.20	2.00
❏ 196	0.25	0.40	1.20	2.00
❏ 197	0.25	0.40	1.20	2.00
❏ 198	0.25	0.40	1.20	2.00
❏ 199	0.25	0.40	1.20	2.00
❏ 200, SB/JSt, Surfer	0.25	4.40	13.20	22.00
❏ 201, SB/JSt	0.25	0.60	1.80	3.00
❏ 202, SB/JSt	0.25	0.60	1.80	3.00
❏ 203, Sep 76, SB/JSt	0.25	0.60	1.80	3.00
❏ 204, Oct 76, HT/JSt, I:Kronus	0.30	0.60	1.80	3.00
❏ 205, Nov 76	0.30	0.60	1.80	3.00
❏ 206, Dec 76	0.30	0.60	1.80	3.00
❏ 207, Jan 77	0.30	0.60	1.80	3.00
❏ 208, Feb 77	0.30	0.60	1.80	3.00

	ORIG.	GOOD	FINE	N-MINT
209, Mar 77	0.30	0.60	1.80	3.00
210, Apr 77	0.30	0.60	1.80	3.00
211, May 77	0.30	0.60	1.80	3.00
212, Jun 77	0.30	0.60	1.80	3.00
213, Jul 77	0.30	0.60	1.80	3.00
214, Aug 77, SB, Jack of Hearts	0.30	0.60	1.80	3.00
215, Sep 77	0.30	0.60	1.80	3.00
216, Oct 77	0.30	0.60	1.80	3.00
217, Nov 77	0.35	0.60	1.80	3.00
218, Dec 77	0.35	0.60	1.80	3.00
219, Jan 78	0.35	0.60	1.80	3.00
220, Feb 78	0.35	0.60	1.80	3.00
221, Mar 78	0.35	0.60	1.80	3.00
222, Apr 78, JSn/AA	0.35	0.60	1.80	3.00
223, May 78	0.35	0.60	1.80	3.00
224, Jun 78	0.35	0.60	1.80	3.00
225, Jul 78	0.35	0.60	1.80	3.00
226, Aug 78	0.35	0.60	1.80	3.00
227, Sep 78, Doc Samson	0.35	0.60	1.80	3.00
228, Oct 78, O&1:Moonstone	0.35	0.60	1.80	3.00
229, Nov 78	0.35	0.60	1.80	3.00
230, Dec 78	0.35	0.60	1.80	3.00
231, Jan 79	0.35	0.60	1.80	3.00
232, Feb 79, SB	0.35	0.60	1.80	3.00
233, Mar 79, SB	0.35	0.60	1.80	3.00
234, Apr 79, SB	0.35	0.60	1.80	3.00
235, May 79, SB	0.40	0.60	1.80	3.00
236, Jun 79, SB	0.40	0.60	1.80	3.00
237, Jul 79, SB	0.40	0.60	1.80	3.00
238, Aug 79, SB	0.40	0.60	1.80	3.00
239, Sep 79, SB	0.40	0.60	1.80	3.00
240, Oct 79, SB	0.40	0.60	1.80	3.00
241, Nov 79, SB	0.40	0.60	1.80	3.00
242, Dec 79, SB	0.40	0.60	1.80	3.00
243, Jan 80, SB; A:Power Man and Iron Fist	0.40	0.60	1.80	3.00
244, Feb 80, SB	0.40	0.60	1.80	3.00
245, Mar 80, SB	0.40	0.60	1.80	3.00
246, Apr 80, SB	0.40	0.60	1.80	3.00
247, May 80, SB; A:Jarella	0.40	0.60	1.80	3.00
248, Jun 80, SB; V:Gardener	0.40	0.60	1.80	3.00
249, Jul 80, SB	0.40	0.60	1.80	3.00
250, Aug 80, SB, Silver Surfer, giant	0.75	0.80	2.40	4.00
251, Sep 80	0.50	0.40	1.20	2.00
252, Oct 80	0.50	0.40	1.20	2.00
253, Nov 80	0.50	0.40	1.20	2.00
254, Dec 80, O&1:U-Foes	0.50	0.40	1.20	2.00
255, Jan 81	0.50	0.40	1.20	2.00
256, Feb 81	0.50	0.40	1.20	2.00
257, Mar 81	0.50	0.40	1.20	2.00
258, Apr 81	0.50	0.40	1.20	2.00
259, May 81, SB	0.50	0.40	1.20	2.00
260, Jun 81, SB	0.50	0.40	1.20	2.00
261, Jul 81, SB	0.50	0.40	1.20	2.00
262, Aug 81, SB	0.50	0.40	1.20	2.00
263, Sep 81, SB	0.50	0.40	1.20	2.00
264, Oct 81, SB	0.50	0.40	1.20	2.00
265, Nov 81, SB	0.50	0.40	1.20	2.00
266, Dec 81, SB	0.50	0.40	1.20	2.00
267, Jan 82, SB	0.60	0.40	1.20	2.00
268, Feb 82, SB	0.60	0.40	1.20	2.00
269, Mar 82, SB	0.60	0.40	1.20	2.00
270, Apr 82, SB	0.60	0.40	1.20	2.00
271, May 82, SB	0.60	0.40	1.20	2.00
272, Jun 82, SB	0.60	0.40	1.20	2.00
273, Jul 82, SB, Alpha Flight	0.60	0.60	1.80	3.00
274, Aug 82, SB	0.60	0.40	1.20	2.00
275, Sep 82, SB	0.60	0.40	1.20	2.00
276, Oct 82, SB	0.60	0.40	1.20	2.00
277, Nov 82, SB; V:U-Foes	0.60	0.40	1.20	2.00
278, Dec 82, SB;Hulk granted amnesty	0.60	0.40	1.20	2.00
279, Jan 83, SB	0.60	0.40	1.20	2.00
280, Feb 83, SB	0.60	0.40	1.20	2.00
281, Mar 83, SB	0.60	0.40	1.20	2.00
282, Apr 83, SB	0.60	0.40	1.20	2.00
283, May 83, SB; A:Avengers	0.60	0.40	1.20	2.00
284, Jun 83, SB	0.60	0.40	1.20	2.00
285, Jul 83, SB	0.60	0.40	1.20	2.00
286, Aug 83, SB	0.60	0.40	1.20	2.00
287, Sep 83, SB	0.60	0.40	1.20	2.00
288, Oct 83, SB; V:Modok	0.60	0.40	1.20	2.00
289, Nov 83, SB; V:A.I.M.	0.60	0.40	1.20	2.00
290, Dec 83, SB	0.60	0.40	1.20	2.00
291, Jan 84, SB	0.60	0.40	1.20	2.00
292, Feb 84, SB	0.60	0.40	1.20	2.00
293, Mar 84, SB	0.60	0.40	1.20	2.00
294, Apr 84, SB	0.60	0.40	1.20	2.00
295, May 84, SB	0.60	0.40	1.20	2.00
296, Jun 84, SB	0.60	0.40	1.20	2.00
297, Jul 84, SB	0.60	0.40	1.20	2.00
298, Aug 84, SB	0.60	0.40	1.20	2.00
299, Sep 84, SB	0.60	0.40	1.20	2.00
300, Oct 84, SB A:SpM, giant	1.00	1.20	3.60	6.00
301, Nov 84, SB	0.60	0.30	0.90	1.50
302, Dec 84, SB	0.60	0.30	0.90	1.50
303, Jan 85, SB	0.60	0.30	0.90	1.50
304, Feb 85, SB	0.60	0.30	0.90	1.50
305, Mar 85, SB	0.60	0.30	0.90	1.50
306, Apr 85, SB	0.65	0.30	0.90	1.50
307, May 85, SB	0.65	0.30	0.90	1.50
308, Jun 85, SB	0.65	0.30	0.90	1.50
309, Jul 85, SB	0.65	0.30	0.90	1.50
310, Aug 85, SB	0.65	0.30	0.90	1.50
311, Sep 85, SB	0.65	0.30	0.90	1.50
312, Oct 85, Secret Wars II	0.65	0.30	0.90	1.50
313, Nov 85, Alpha Flight	0.65	0.20	0.60	1.00
314, Dec 85, JBy	0.65	1.00	3.00	5.00
315, Jan 86, JBy	0.65	0.60	1.80	3.00
316, Feb 86, JBy	0.75	0.60	1.80	3.00
317, Mar 86, JBy	0.75	0.60	1.80	3.00
318, Apr 86, JBy	0.75	0.60	1.80	3.00
319, May 86, JBy; W:Bruce Banner and Betty Ross	0.75	0.60	1.80	3.00
320, Jun 86	0.75	0.60	1.80	3.00
321, Jul 86	0.75	0.65	1.95	3.25
322, Aug 86	0.75	0.65	1.95	3.25
323, Sep 86	0.75	0.65	1.95	3.25
324, Oct 86, Hulk seen as gray	0.75	2.40	7.20	12.00
326, Dec 86	0.75	0.65	1.95	3.25
327, Jan 87	0.75	0.65	1.95	3.25
328, Feb 87	0.75	0.65	1.95	3.25
329, Mar 87	0.75	0.65	1.95	3.25
330, Apr 87, TMc	0.75	5.60	16.80	28.00
331, May 87, TMc Hulk turns gray	0.75	3.60	10.80	18.00
332, Jun 87, TMc	0.75	2.40	7.20	12.00
333, Jul 87, TMc	0.75	2.40	7.20	12.00

	ORIG.	GOOD	FINE	N-MINT
334, Aug 87, TMc	0.75	2.40	7.20	12.00
335, Sep 87, TMc	0.75	2.40	7.20	12.00
336, Oct 87, TMc A:X-Factor	0.75	2.00	6.00	10.00
337, Nov 87, TMc A:X-Factor	0.75	2.00	6.00	10.00
338, Dec 87, TMc	0.75	2.00	6.00	10.00
339, Jan 88, TMc	0.75	2.00	6.00	10.00
340, Feb 88, TMc A:Wolverine	0.75	10.00	30.00	50.00
341, Mar 88, TMc V:Man-Bull	0.75	2.00	6.00	10.00
342, Apr 88, TMc	0.75	2.00	6.00	10.00
343, Mar 88, TMc	0.75	2.00	6.00	10.00
344, Jun 88, TMc	0.75	2.00	6.00	10.00
345, Jul 88, TMc	1.50	2.00	6.00	10.00
346, Aug 88, TMc	0.75	2.00	6.00	10.00
347, Sep 88	0.75	0.40	1.20	2.00
348, Oct 88	0.75	0.40	1.20	2.00
349, Nov 88, A:SpM	0.75	0.40	1.20	2.00
350, Dec 88, Hulk vs. Thing	0.75	0.80	2.40	4.00
351, Jan 89	0.75	0.60	1.80	3.00
352, Feb 89	0.75	0.60	1.80	3.00
353, Mar 89	0.75	0.60	1.80	3.00
354, Apr 89	0.75	0.60	1.80	3.00
355, May 89	0.75	0.60	1.80	3.00
356, Jun 89	0.75	0.60	1.80	3.00
357, Jul 89	0.75	0.60	1.80	3.00
358, Aug 89	0.75	0.60	1.80	3.00
359, Sep 89	1.00	0.60	1.80	3.00
360, Oct 89	1.00	0.60	1.80	3.00
361, Nov 89, Iron Man	1.00	0.40	1.20	2.00
362, Nov 89	1.00	0.40	1.20	2.00
363, Dec 89, Acts of Vengeance	1.00	0.40	1.20	2.00
364, Dec 89, WS(c) Countdown	1.00	0.60	1.80	3.00
365, Jan 90, WS(c) Countdown	1.00	0.60	1.80	3.00
366, Feb 90, WS(c); Countdown;V:Leader	1.00	0.60	1.80	3.00
367, Mar 90, WS(c) Countdown	1.00	4.40	13.20	22.00
368, Apr 90	1.00	2.40	7.20	12.00
369, May 90	1.00	2.40	7.20	12.00
370, Jun 90, Dr. Strange, Sub-Mariner	1.00	1.60	4.80	8.00
371, Jul 90, Dr. Strange, Sub-Mariner	1.00	1.60	4.80	8.00
372, Aug 90, Green Hulk returns	1.00	4.00	12.00	20.00
373, Sep 90	1.00	1.20	3.60	6.00
374, Oct 90	1.00	1.20	3.60	6.00
375, Nov 90	1.00	1.20	3.60	6.00
376, Dec 90	1.00	1.20	3.60	6.00
377, Jan 91, 1:new Hulk, 1st printing	1.00	4.40	13.20	22.00
377, Jan 91, 2nd printing	1.00	0.60	1.80	3.00
377, Jan 91, 3rd printing	1.75	0.35	1.05	1.75
378, Feb 91, Rhino as Santa	1.00	0.60	1.80	3.00
379, Mar 91	1.00	1.20	3.60	6.00
380, Apr 91	1.00	1.20	3.60	6.00
381, May 91	1.00	1.20	3.60	6.00
382, Jun 91	1.00	1.20	3.60	6.00
383, Jul 91, Infinity Gauntlet	1.00	1.00	3.00	5.00
384, Aug 91, Infinity Gauntlet	1.00	1.00	3.00	5.00
385, Sep 91, Infinity Gauntlet	1.00	1.00	3.00	5.00

	ORIG.	GOOD	FINE	N-MINT
386, Oct 91, Infinity Gauntlet	1.00	1.00	3.00	5.00
387, Nov 91, Infinity Gauntlet	1.00	1.00	3.00	5.00
388, Dec 91, 1:Speedfreek	1.00	0.60	1.80	3.00
389	1.00	0.50	1.50	2.50
390	1.25	0.50	1.50	2.50
391, X-Factor	1.25	0.50	1.50	2.50
392	1.25	0.50	1.50	2.50
393, green foil cover	2.50	2.00	6.00	10.00
395	1.25	0.60	1.80	3.00
396	1.25	0.60	1.80	3.00
397	1.25	0.60	1.80	3.00
398	1.25	0.60	1.80	3.00
399	1.25	0.60	1.80	3.00
400, shiny cover	2.50	1.20	3.60	6.00
401	1.25	0.25	0.75	1.25
402	1.25	0.25	0.75	1.25
403, V:Juggernaut	1.25	0.25	0.75	1.25
404	1.25	0.25	0.75	1.25
405	1.25	0.25	0.75	1.25
406, A:Captain America				
407	1.25	0.25	0.75	1.25
408	1.25	0.25	0.75	1.25
409	1.25	0.25	0.75	1.25
410	1.25	0.25	0.75	1.25
411, Nov 93	1.25	0.25	0.75	1.25
412, Dec 93	1.25	0.25	0.75	1.25
413, Jan 94	1.25	0.25	0.75	1.25
414, Feb 94	1.25	0.25	0.75	1.25
415, Mar 94	1.25	0.25	0.75	1.25
416, Apr 94	1.25	0.25	0.75	1.25
417, May 94	1.50	0.30	0.90	1.50
418, Jun 94	1.50	0.30	0.90	1.50
418, Jun 94, enhanced cover	2.50	0.50	1.50	2.50
419, Jul 94	1.50	0.30	0.90	1.50
420, Aug 94	1.50	0.30	0.90	1.50
421, Sep 94	1.50	0.30	0.90	1.50
422, Oct 94	1.50	0.30	0.90	1.50
423, Nov 94	1.50	0.30	0.90	1.50
424, Dec 94	1.50	0.30	0.90	1.50
425, Jan 95	2.25	0.45	1.35	2.25
425, Jan 95, enhanced cover	3.50	1.00	3.00	5.00
426, Feb 95, deluxe edition	1.95	0.39	1.17	1.95
426, Feb 95	1.50	0.30	0.90	1.50
427, Mar 95	1.95	0.39	1.17	1.95
428, Apr 95	1.95	0.39	1.17	1.95
429, May 95	1.95	0.39	1.17	1.95
430, Jun 95	1.95	0.39	1.17	1.95
431, Jul 95, V: Abomination	1.95	0.39	1.17	1.95
432, Aug 95, V: Abomination	1.95	0.39	1.17	1.95
433, Sep 95, "Over the Edge";A:Punisher, Nick Fury	1.95	0.39	1.17	1.95
434, Oct 95, Funeral of Nick Fury;A:Howling Commandoes;OverPower cards inserted	1.95	0.39	1.17	1.95
435, Nov 95, V:Rhino;" Casey at the Bat" tribute	1.95	0.39	1.17	1.95
436, Dec 95, "Ghosts of the Future" Part 1 of 5; continued in *Cutting Edge* #1	1.95	0.39	1.17	1.95
437, Jan 96, "Ghosts of the Future" Part 2 of 5	1.95	0.39	1.17	1.95
438, Feb 96, "Ghosts of the Future" Part 3 of 5	1.95	0.39	1.17	1.95
439, Mar 96, "Ghosts of the Future" Part 4 of 5	1.95	0.39	1.17	1.95

	ORIG.	GOOD	FINE	N-MINT

☐ 440, Apr 96, "Ghosts of the Future" Part 5 of 5; V:Thor
....1.95 0.39 1.17 1.95
☐ 441, May 96, Pulp Fiction tribute cover
....1.95 0.39 1.17 1.95

INCREDIBLE HULK AND WOLVERINE
☐ 1, Oct 86, reprint............ 2.00 0.40 1.20 2.00

INCREDIBLE HULK ANNUAL/SPECIAL
☐ 1, Steranko cover........... 0.25 8.40 25.20 42.00
☐ 2, reprint 0.25 4.80 14.40 24.00
☐ 3, reprint 0.25 2.00 6.00 10.00
☐ 4 .... 0.50 1.20 3.60 6.00
☐ 5, Oct 76 .... 0.50 1.20 3.60 6.00
☐ 6, Nov 77, HT, Dr. Strange
....0.60 1.00 3.00 5.00
☐ 7, Dec 78, JBy/BL;SpM .. 0.60 2.00 6.00 10.00
☐ 8, Dec 79, Alpha Flight ... 0.75 0.40 1.20 2.00
☐ 9, Sep 80......................... 0.75 0.40 1.20 2.00
☐ 10, Sep 81, Captain Universe
....0.75 0.40 1.20 2.00
☐ 11, Oct 82, First Frank Miller Marvel pencils
....1.00 0.40 1.20 2.00
☐ 12, Aug 83 .... 1.00 0.20 0.60 1.00
☐ 13, Nov 84 .... 1.00 0.20 0.60 1.00
☐ 14, Dec 85...................... 1.25 0.25 0.75 1.25
☐ 15, Oct 86...................... 1.25 0.25 0.75 1.25
☐ 16, Jul 90, Lifeform........ 2.00 0.40 1.20 2.00
☐ 17, Aug 91, Subterranean
....2.00 0.40 1.20 2.00
☐ 18 .... 2.25 0.45 1.35 2.25
☐ 19, 1:Lazarus, trading card
....2.95 0.59 1.77 2.95
☐ 20, 94.............................. 2.95 0.59 1.77 2.95

INCREDIBLE HULK POSTER MAGAZINE
☐ 1, tv show 1.50 0.79 2.37 3.95
☐ 1, comics 3.95 0.79 2.37 3.95

INCREDIBLE HULK VS. QUASIMODO
☐ 1, Mar 83 .... 0.60 0.60 1.80 3.00

INCREDIBLE HULK VS. VENOM
☐ 0, 94.................................2.50 0.50 1.50 2.50

INCREDIBLE HULK: FUTURE IMPERFECT
(mini-series)
☐ 1, GP;prestige format..... 5.95 2.00 6.00 10.00
☐ 2, GP;prestige format..... 5.95 2.00 6.00 10.00

INCUBUS
PALLIARD PRESS
☐ 1, adult only, b&w.......... 2.95 0.59 1.77 2.95
☐ 2, adult only, b&w.......... 2.95 0.59 1.77 2.95

INDIANA JONES AND THE ARMS OF GOLD
DARK HORSE
☐ 1, Feb 94 .... 2.50 0.50 1.50 2.50
☐ 2, Mar 94 .... 2.50 0.50 1.50 2.50
☐ 3, Apr 94 .... 2.50 0.50 1.50 2.50
☐ 4, May 94 .... 2.50 0.50 1.50 2.50
☐ 6, Apr 94 .... 2.50 0.50 1.50 2.50

INDIANA JONES AND THE FATE OF ATLANTIS
☐ 1, Mar 91, 1st printing ... 2.50 0.80 2.40 4.00
☐ 1, 2nd printing 0.50 1.50 2.50
☐ 2, May 91, trading cards 2.50 0.50 1.50 2.50
☐ 3, Jul 91 .... 2.50 0.50 1.50 2.50
☐ 4, Sep 91......................... 2.50 0.50 1.50 2.50

INDIANA JONES AND THE GOLDEN FLEECE
☐ 1, Jun 94......................... 2.50 0.50 1.50 2.50
☐ 2, Jul 94 .... 2.50 0.50 1.50 2.50

INDIANA JONES AND THE IRON PHOENIX
(mini-series)
☐ 1, Dec 94......................... 2.50 0.50 1.50 2.50
☐ 2, Jan 95......................... 2.50 0.50 1.50 2.50
☐ 3, Feb 95......................... 2.50 0.50 1.50 2.50
☐ 4, Mar 95 .... 2.50 0.50 1.50 2.50

INDIANA JONES AND THE LAST CRUSADE
MARVEL
☐ 1, Aug 89, b&w mag......... 0.59 1.77 2.95
☐ 1, Oct 89, comic book.....1.00 0.20 0.60 1.00
☐ 2, Oct 89, comic book.....1.00 0.20 0.60 1.00
☐ 3, Nov 89, comic book....1.00 0.20 0.60 1.00
☐ 4, Nov 89, comic book....1.00 0.20 0.60 1.00

INDIANA JONES AND THE SARGASSO PIRATES
DARK HORSE
☐ 1, Dec 95 ....2.50 0.50 1.50 2.50
☐ 2, Jan 96.........................2.50 0.50 1.50 2.50
☐ 3, Feb 96.........................2.50 0.50 1.50 2.50
☐ 4, Mar 96, final issue 2.50 0.50 1.50 2.50

INDIANA JONES AND THE SHRINE
OF THE SEA DEVIL
☐ 1, Sep 94, one-shot 2.50 0.50 1.50 2.50

INDIANA JONES AND THE TEMPLE OF DOOM
MARVEL
☐ 1, Sep 84, movie.............0.75 0.20 0.60 1.00
☐ 2, Oct 84, movie 0.75 0.20 0.60 1.00
☐ 3, Nov 84, movie 0.75 0.20 0.60 1.00

INDIANA JONES: THUNDER IN THE ORIENT
DARK HORSE
☐ 1 ....2.50 0.50 1.50 2.50
☐ 2 ....2.50 0.50 1.50 2.50
☐ 3 ....2.50 0.50 1.50 2.50
☐ 4 ....2.50 0.50 1.50 2.50
☐ 5, Mar 94 ....2.50 0.50 1.50 2.50
☐ 6, Apr 94.........................2.50 0.50 1.50 2.50

INDUSTRIAL GOTHIC (mini-series)
DC/VERTIGO
☐ 1, Dec 95 ....2.50 0.50 1.50 2.50
☐ 2, Jan 96.........................2.50 0.50 1.50 2.50
☐ 3, Feb 96.........................2.50 0.50 1.50 2.50
☐ 4, Mar 96 ....2.50 0.50 1.50 2.50
☐ 5, Apr 96, final issue.......2.50 0.50 1.50 2.50

INDUSTRIAL STRENGTH PREVIEW
SILVER SKULL
☐ 1, b&w............................1.50 0.30 0.90 1.50

INEDIBLE ADVENTURES OF CLINT THE CARROT
HOT LEG
☐ 1, Mar 94, b&w...............2.50 0.50 1.50 2.50

INFECTIOUS
FANTACO
☐ 0, KEastman;one-shot ...3.95 0.79 2.37 3.95

INFERIOR FIVE, THE
DC
☐ 1, Apr 67.........................0.12 11.00 33.00 55.00
☐ 2, Jun 67 ....0.12 6.60 19.80 33.00
☐ 3, Aug 67 ....0.12 5.00 15.00 25.00
☐ 4, Oct 67.........................0.12 5.00 15.00 25.00
☐ 5, Dec 67 ....0.12 5.00 15.00 25.00
☐ 6, Feb 68.........................0.12 3.60 10.80 18.00
☐ 7, Apr 68.........................0.12 3.60 10.80 18.00
☐ 8, Jun 68 ....0.12 3.60 10.80 18.00
☐ 9, Aug 68 ....0.12 3.60 10.80 18.00
☐ 10, Oct 68.......................0.12 3.60 10.80 18.00
☐ 11, Sep 72, reprints *Showcase #62*
....0.20 3.00 9.00 15.00
☐ 12, Nov 72, reprints *Showcase #63*
....0.20 3.00 9.00 15.00

INFERNO
AIRCEL
☐ 1, adult, b&w 0.50 1.50 2.50
☐ 2, adult, b&w 0.50 1.50 2.50
☐ 3, adult, b&w 0.50 1.50 2.50
☐ 4, adult, b&w 0.50 1.50 2.50

CALIBER
☐ 1, Aug 95, b&w...............2.95 0.59 1.77 2.95

	ORIG.	GOOD	FINE	N-MINT

INFINITY CRUSADE, THE
MARVEL

	ORIG.	GOOD	FINE	N-MINT
☐ 1, foil cover	3.50	0.70	2.10	3.50
☐ 2	2.50	0.50	1.50	2.50
☐ 3	2.50	0.50	1.50	2.50
☐ 4	2.50	0.50	1.50	2.50
☐ 5	2.50	0.50	1.50	2.50

INFINITY GAUNTLET

	ORIG.	GOOD	FINE	N-MINT
☐ 1, Jul 91, GP, Thanos, Surfer, SpM, Avengers	2.50	1.40	4.20	7.00
☐ 2, Aug 91, GP, Thanos, Surfer, SpM, Avengers	2.50	1.00	3.00	5.00
☐ 3, Sep 91, GP, Thanos, Surfer, SpM, Avengers	2.50	1.00	3.00	5.00
☐ 4, Oct 91, GP, Thanos, Surfer, SpM, Avengers	2.50	1.00	3.00	5.00
☐ 5, Nov 91, GP(c) Ron Lim	2.50	1.00	3.00	5.00
☐ 6, Dec 91, GP(c) Ron Lim	2.50	1.00	3.00	5.00

INFINITY WAR

	ORIG.	GOOD	FINE	N-MINT
☐ 1	2.50	1.00	3.00	5.00
☐ 2	2.50	0.60	1.80	3.00
☐ 3	2.50	0.60	1.80	3.00
☐ 4	2.50	0.60	1.80	3.00
☐ 5	2.50	0.60	1.80	3.00
☐ 6	2.50	0.60	1.80	3.00

INFINITY, INC.
DC

	ORIG.	GOOD	FINE	N-MINT
☐ 1, Mar 84, JOy, O:Infinity Inc	1.25	0.80	2.40	4.00
☐ 2, May 84, JOy, origin ends	1.25	0.60	1.80	3.00
☐ 3, Jun 84	1.25	0.40	1.20	2.00
☐ 4, Jul 84	1.25	0.40	1.20	2.00
☐ 5, Aug 84	1.25	0.40	1.20	2.00
☐ 6, Sep 84, JOy	1.25	0.25	0.75	1.25
☐ 7, Oct 84, JOy	1.25	0.25	0.75	1.25
☐ 8, Nov 84	1.25	0.20	0.60	1.00
☐ 9, Dec 84	1.25	0.20	0.60	1.00
☐ 10, Jan 85	1.25	0.20	0.60	1.00
☐ 11, Feb 85	1.25	0.25	0.75	1.25
☐ 12, Mar 85	1.25	0.25	0.75	1.25
☐ 13, Apr 85	1.25	0.25	0.75	1.25
☐ 14, May 85, TMc	1.25	1.40	4.20	7.00
☐ 15, Jun 85, TMc	1.25	1.00	3.00	5.00
☐ 16, Jul 85, TMc	1.25	1.00	3.00	5.00
☐ 17, Aug 85, TMc	1.25	1.00	3.00	5.00
☐ 18, Sep 85, TMc, Crisis	1.25	1.00	3.00	5.00
☐ 19, Oct 85, TMc, Crisis	1.25	1.00	3.00	5.00
☐ 20, Nov 85, TMc, Crisis	1.25	1.00	3.00	5.00
☐ 21, Dec 85, TMc, Crisis	1.50	1.00	3.00	5.00
☐ 22, Jan 86, TMc, Crisis	1.50	1.00	3.00	5.00
☐ 23, Feb 86, TMc, Crisis	1.50	1.00	3.00	5.00
☐ 24, Mar 86, TMc, Crisis	1.50	1.00	3.00	5.00
☐ 25, Apr 86, TMc, Crisis	1.50	1.00	3.00	5.00
☐ 26, May 86, TMc, Crisis	1.50	1.00	3.00	5.00
☐ 27, Jun 86, TMc, Crisis	1.50	1.00	3.00	5.00
☐ 28, Jul 86, TMc	1.50	1.00	3.00	5.00
☐ 29, Jul 86, TMc	1.50	1.00	3.00	5.00
☐ 30, Sep 86, TMc	1.50	1.00	3.00	5.00
☐ 31, Oct 86, TMc	1.50	1.00	3.00	5.00
☐ 32, Nov 86, TMc	1.50	1.00	3.00	5.00
☐ 33, Dec 86, TMc	1.50	1.00	3.00	5.00
☐ 34, Jan 87, TMc	1.50	1.00	3.00	5.00
☐ 35, Feb 87, TMc	1.50	1.00	3.00	5.00
☐ 36, Mar 87, TMc	1.50	1.00	3.00	5.00
☐ 37, Apr 87, TMc	1.50	1.00	3.00	5.00
☐ 38, May 87	1.50	0.30	0.90	1.50
☐ 39, Jun 87	1.50	0.30	0.90	1.50
☐ 40, Jul 87	1.50	0.30	0.90	1.50
☐ 41, Aug 87	1.50	0.30	0.90	1.50
☐ 42, Sep 87	1.50	0.30	0.90	1.50
☐ 43, Oct 87	1.50	0.30	0.90	1.50
☐ 44, Nov 87	1.50	0.30	0.90	1.50
☐ 45, Dec 87, A:Titans	1.50	0.30	0.90	1.50
☐ 46, Jan 88, Millennium	1.75	0.35	1.05	1.75
☐ 47, Feb 88, Millennium	1.75	0.35	1.05	1.75
☐ 48, Mar 88, O:Nuklon	1.75	0.35	1.05	1.75
☐ 49, Apr 88	1.75	0.35	1.05	1.75
☐ 50, May 88	2.50	0.50	1.50	2.50
☐ 51, Jun 88, D:Skyman	1.75	0.35	1.05	1.75
☐ 52, Jul 88	1.75	0.35	1.05	1.75
☐ 53, Aug 88, final issue	1.75	0.35	1.05	1.75

INFINITY, INC. ANNUAL

	ORIG.	GOOD	FINE	N-MINT
☐ 1, Nov 85, TMc;Crisis; O:Jade and Obsidian	2.00	0.40	1.20	2.00
☐ 2, Jul 88, crossover with *Young All-Stars Annual #1*	2.00	0.40	1.20	2.00

INHUMANOIDS
STAR

	ORIG.	GOOD	FINE	N-MINT
☐ 1, Jan 87	0.75	0.15	0.45	0.75
☐ 2, Mar 87	0.75	0.15	0.45	0.75
☐ 3, May 87	0.75	0.15	0.45	0.75
☐ 4, Jul 87	1.00	0.20	0.60	1.00

INHUMANS
MARVEL

	ORIG.	GOOD	FINE	N-MINT
☐ 1, GP, V:Blastaar	0.12	0.60	1.80	3.00
☐ 2	0.12	0.30	0.90	1.50
☐ 3	0.12	0.30	0.90	1.50
☐ 4	0.12	0.30	0.90	1.50
☐ 5	0.30	0.30	0.90	1.50
☐ 6	0.30	0.30	0.90	1.50
☐ 7, Oct 76	0.30	0.20	0.60	1.00
☐ 8, Dec 76	0.30	0.20	0.60	1.00
☐ 9, Feb 77	0.30	0.20	0.60	1.00
☐ 10, Apr 77	0.30	0.20	0.60	1.00
☐ 11, Jun 77	0.30	0.20	0.60	1.00
☐ 12, Aug 77	0.30	0.20	0.60	1.00

INHUMANS SPECIAL

	ORIG.	GOOD	FINE	N-MINT
☐ 1, Apr 90	1.50	0.30	0.90	1.50

INHUMANS: THE GREAT REFUGE

	ORIG.	GOOD	FINE	N-MINT
☐ 1, May 95	2.95	0.59	1.77	2.95

INNER CIRCLE (mini-series)
MUSHROOM

	ORIG.	GOOD	FINE	N-MINT
☐ 0, Feb 95, 0.1	2.50	0.50	1.50	2.50

INNER-CITY PRODUCTS
HYPE

	ORIG.	GOOD	FINE	N-MINT
☐ 1, b&w	2.00	0.40	1.20	2.00

INNERCIRCLE (mini-series)
MUSHROOM

	ORIG.	GOOD	FINE	N-MINT
☐ 1, Feb 95, (numbered as 0.1)	2.50	0.50	1.50	2.50

INNOCENT BYSTANDER
OLLIE OLLIE! OXEN FREE PRESS

	ORIG.	GOOD	FINE	N-MINT
☐ 1, 95, b&w	2.50	0.50	1.50	2.50

INNOVATION PREVIEW SPECIAL
INNOVATION

	ORIG.	GOOD	FINE	N-MINT
☐ 1, Jun 89, sampler		0.20	0.60	1.00

INNOVATION SPECTACULAR

	ORIG.	GOOD	FINE	N-MINT
☐ 1, Dec 90		0.59	1.77	2.95
☐ 2, Jan 91		0.59	1.77	2.95

INNOVATION SUMMER FUN SPECIAL

	ORIG.	GOOD	FINE	N-MINT
☐ 1		0.70	2.10	3.50

INOVATORS
DARK MOON

	ORIG.	GOOD	FINE	N-MINT
☐ 1, Apr 95	2.50	0.50	1.50	2.50

	ORIG.	GOOD	FINE	N-MINT

INSANE
DARK HORSE
	ORIG.	GOOD	FINE	N-MINT
❑ 1, Dec 87		0.35	1.05	1.75
❑ 2		0.35	1.05	1.75

INSOMNIA
FANTAGRAPHICS
	ORIG.	GOOD	FINE	N-MINT
❑ 0, nn	2.95	0.59	1.77	2.95

INSTANT PIANO
DARK HORSE
	ORIG.	GOOD	FINE	N-MINT
❑ 1, Aug 94, b&w	3.95	0.79	2.37	3.95
❑ 2, Dec 94, b&w	3.95	0.79	2.37	3.95
❑ 3, Feb 95, b&w	3.95	0.79	2.37	3.95
❑ 4, Jun 95, b&w	3.95	0.79	2.37	3.95

INTENSE!
PURE IMAGINATION
	ORIG.	GOOD	FINE	N-MINT
❑ 2, BW,b&w reprints	3.00	0.60	1.80	3.00

INTERACTIVE COMICS
ADVENTURE
	ORIG.	GOOD	FINE	N-MINT
❑ 0, nn b&w		0.99	2.97	4.95
❑ 0, nn Saves World		0.99	2.97	4.95

INTERFACE
EPIC
	ORIG.	GOOD	FINE	N-MINT
❑ 1, Dec 89	1.95	0.39	1.17	1.95
❑ 2, Feb 90	1.95	0.39	1.17	1.95
❑ 3, Apr 90	1.95	0.39	1.17	1.95
❑ 4, Jun 90	1.95	0.39	1.17	1.95
❑ 5, Aug 90	1.95	0.39	1.17	1.95
❑ 6, Oct 90	2.25	0.45	1.35	2.25
❑ 7, Nov 90	2.25	0.45	1.35	2.25
❑ 8, Dec 90	2.25	0.45	1.35	2.25

INTERNATIONAL COWGIRL MAGAZINE
ICONOGRAFIX
	ORIG.	GOOD	FINE	N-MINT
❑ 1, b&w	2.95	0.59	1.77	2.95
❑ 2, b&w	2.95	0.59	1.77	2.95

INTERPLANETARY LIZARDS OF THE TEXAS PLAINS
LEADBELLY
	ORIG.	GOOD	FINE	N-MINT
❑ 0,	2.50	0.50	1.50	2.50
❑ 1, b&w		0.40	1.20	2.00
❑ 2, b&w		0.40	1.20	2.00
❑ 8, b&w	2.50	0.50	1.50	2.50

INTERVIEW WITH THE VAMPIRE
INNOVATION
	ORIG.	GOOD	FINE	N-MINT
❑ 1	2.50	0.50	1.50	2.50
❑ 2	2.50	0.50	1.50	2.50
❑ 3	2.50	0.50	1.50	2.50
❑ 4	2.50	0.50	1.50	2.50
❑ 5	2.50	0.50	1.50	2.50
❑ 6	2.50	0.50	1.50	2.50
❑ 7	2.50	0.50	1.50	2.50
❑ 8	2.50	0.50	1.50	2.50
❑ 9	2.50	0.50	1.50	2.50
❑ 10	2.50	0.50	1.50	2.50
❑ 11	2.50	0.50	1.50	2.50
❑ 12	2.50	0.50	1.50	2.50

INTRAZINE
BRAINSTORM
	ORIG.	GOOD	FINE	N-MINT
❑ 1, Mar 93, b&w	2.95	0.59	1.77	2.95
❑ 2, Apr 93, b&w	2.95	0.59	1.77	2.95

INTRUDER COMICS MODULE
TSR INC.
	ORIG.	GOOD	FINE	N-MINT
❑ 1		0.59	1.77	2.95
❑ 2		0.59	1.77	2.95
❑ 3		0.59	1.77	2.95
❑ 4		0.59	1.77	2.95
❑ 5, Intruder II		0.59	1.77	2.95
❑ 6, Intruder II		0.59	1.77	2.95
❑ 7, Intruder II		0.59	1.77	2.95
❑ 8, Intruder II		0.59	1.77	2.95
❑ 9, Intruder II		0.59	1.77	2.95

INVADERS ANNUAL, THE
MARVEL
	ORIG.	GOOD	FINE	N-MINT
❑ 1, 77	0.50	1.00	3.00	5.00

INVADERS FROM HOME
PIRANHA
	ORIG.	GOOD	FINE	N-MINT
❑ 1, color		0.50	1.50	2.50
❑ 2, color		0.50	1.50	2.50
❑ 3, color		0.50	1.50	2.50
❑ 4, color, John Blair Moore	2.50	0.50	1.50	2.50
❑ 5, color, John Blair Moore	2.50	0.50	1.50	2.50
❑ 6, color, John Blair Moore	2.50	0.50	1.50	2.50

INVADERS FROM MARS
ETERNITY
	ORIG.	GOOD	FINE	N-MINT
❑ 1, movie, b&w		0.50	1.50	2.50
❑ 2, movie, b&w		0.50	1.50	2.50
❑ 3, movie, b&w		0.50	1.50	2.50

INVADERS FROM MARS (Book II)
	ORIG.	GOOD	FINE	N-MINT
❑ 1, b&w, sequel		0.50	1.50	2.50
❑ 2, b&w, sequel		0.50	1.50	2.50
❑ 3, b&w, sequel		0.50	1.50	2.50

INVADERS, THE
MARVEL
	ORIG.	GOOD	FINE	N-MINT
❑ 1, Aug 75	0.25	2.00	6.00	10.00
❑ 2, Oct 75	0.25	1.40	4.20	7.00
❑ 3, Nov 75	0.25	1.20	3.60	6.00
❑ 4, Jan 76	0.25	1.20	3.60	6.00
❑ 5, Mar 76	0.25	1.20	3.60	6.00
❑ 6, May 76	0.25	0.80	2.40	4.00
❑ 7, Jul 76	0.25	0.80	2.40	4.00
❑ 8, Sep 76	0.30	0.80	2.40	4.00
❑ 9, Oct 76	0.30	0.80	2.40	4.00
❑ 10, Nov 76	0.30	0.80	2.40	4.00
❑ 11, Dec 76	0.30	0.80	2.40	4.00
❑ 12, Jan 77	0.30	0.80	2.40	4.00
❑ 13, Feb 77	0.30	0.80	2.40	4.00
❑ 14, Mar 77	0.30	0.80	2.40	4.00
❑ 15, Apr 77	0.30	0.80	2.40	4.00
❑ 16, May 77	0.30	0.80	2.40	4.00
❑ 17, Jun 77	0.30	0.80	2.40	4.00
❑ 18, Jul 77	0.30	0.80	2.40	4.00
❑ 19, Aug 77	0.30	0.80	2.40	4.00
❑ 20, Sep 77	0.30	1.20	3.60	6.00
❑ 21, Oct 77	0.30	0.60	1.80	3.00
❑ 22, Nov 77	0.35	0.60	1.80	3.00
❑ 23, Dec 77	0.35	0.60	1.80	3.00
❑ 24, Jan 78	0.35	0.60	1.80	3.00
❑ 25, Feb 78	0.35	0.60	1.80	3.00
❑ 26, Mar 78	0.35	0.60	1.80	3.00
❑ 27, Apr 78	0.35	0.60	1.80	3.00
❑ 28, May 78	0.35	0.60	1.80	3.00
❑ 29, Jun 78	0.35	0.60	1.80	3.00
❑ 30, Jul 78	0.35	0.60	1.80	3.00
❑ 31, Aug 78	0.35	0.60	1.80	3.00
❑ 32, Sep 78	0.35	0.60	1.80	3.00
❑ 33, Oct 78	0.35	0.60	1.80	3.00
❑ 34, Nov 78	0.35	0.60	1.80	3.00
❑ 35, Dec 78	0.35	0.60	1.80	3.00
❑ 36, Jan 79	0.35	0.60	1.80	3.00
❑ 37, Feb 79	0.35	0.60	1.80	3.00
❑ 38, Mar 79	0.35	0.60	1.80	3.00
❑ 39, Apr 79	0.35	0.60	1.80	3.00
❑ 40, May 79	0.40	0.60	1.80	3.00
❑ 41, Sep 79, giant	0.60	0.60	1.80	3.00

INVADERS, THE (mini-series)
	ORIG.	GOOD	FINE	N-MINT
❑ 1, May 93	1.75	0.35	1.05	1.75
❑ 2, Jun 93	1.75	0.35	1.05	1.75
❑ 3, Jul 93	1.75	0.35	1.05	1.75
❑ 4, Aug 93	1.75	0.35	1.05	1.75

	ORIG.	GOOD	FINE	N-MINT

INVASION '55
APPLE

		GOOD	FINE	N-MINT
❑ 1, b&w		0.45	1.35	2.25
❑ 2, b&w		0.45	1.35	2.25
❑ 3, b&w		0.45	1.35	2.25

INVASION OF THE MIND SAPPERS
FANTAGRAPHICS

	ORIG.	GOOD	FINE	N-MINT
❑ 0, Jan 96, nn;cardstock cover;b&w	8.95	1.79	5.37	8.95

INVASION!
DC

	ORIG.	GOOD	FINE	N-MINT
❑ 1, Jan 89, TMc	2.95	1.20	3.60	6.00
❑ 2, Feb 89, TMc	2.95	1.00	3.00	5.00
❑ 3, Mar 89	2.95	1.00	3.00	5.00

INVERT
CALIBER

	ORIG.	GOOD	FINE	N-MINT
❑ 0, nn b&w	2.95	0.59	1.77	2.95

INVINCIBLE FOUR OF KUNG FU & NINJA
DR. LEUNG'S

		GOOD	FINE	N-MINT
❑ 1		0.36	1.08	1.80
❑ 2		0.36	1.08	1.80
❑ 3		0.36	1.08	1.80
❑ 4		0.36	1.08	1.80
❑ 5		0.36	1.08	1.80

INVISIBLES, THE
DC/VERTIGO

	ORIG.	GOOD	FINE	N-MINT
❑ 1, Sep 94	2.95	0.59	1.77	2.95
❑ 2, Oct 94	1.95	0.39	1.17	1.95
❑ 3, Nov 94	1.95	0.39	1.17	1.95
❑ 4, Dec 94	1.95	0.39	1.17	1.95
❑ 5, Jan 95, There are at least four cover variants, denoted "A" through "D."	1.95	0.39	1.17	1.95
❑ 6, Feb 95	1.95	0.39	1.17	1.95
❑ 7, Mar 95	1.95	0.39	1.17	1.95
❑ 8, Apr 95	1.95	0.39	1.17	1.95
❑ 9, Jun 95	2.50	0.50	1.50	2.50
❑ 10, Jul 95	2.50	0.50	1.50	2.50
❑ 11, Aug 95	2.50	0.50	1.50	2.50
❑ 12, Sep 95	2.50	0.50	1.50	2.50
❑ 13, Oct 95	2.50	0.50	1.50	2.50
❑ 14, Nov 95	2.50	0.50	1.50	2.50
❑ 15, Dec 95	2.50	0.50	1.50	2.50
❑ 16, Jan 96	2.50	0.50	1.50	2.50
❑ 17, Feb 96	2.50	0.50	1.50	2.50
❑ 18, Mar 96	2.50	0.50	1.50	2.50
❑ 19, Apr 96	2.50	0.50	1.50	2.50
❑ 20, May 96	2.50	0.50	1.50	2.50
❑ 21, Jun 96	2.50	0.50	1.50	2.50

INVISOWORLD
ETERNITY

		GOOD	FINE	N-MINT
❑ 1		0.39	1.17	1.95

IO
INVICTUS

	ORIG.	GOOD	FINE	N-MINT
❑ 1, Oct 94	2.25	0.45	1.35	2.25
❑ 3, Win 95, b&w ashcan	2.25	0.45	1.35	2.25

IRON DEVIL, THE
EROS

	ORIG.	GOOD	FINE	N-MINT
❑ 1, adult, b&w	2.95	0.59	1.77	2.95
❑ 2, adult, b&w	2.95	0.59	1.77	2.95

IRON FIST
MARVEL

	ORIG.	GOOD	FINE	N-MINT
❑ 1, JBy	0.25	12.00	36.00	60.00
❑ 2, JBy	0.25	4.00	12.00	20.00
❑ 3, JBy	0.25	4.00	12.00	20.00
❑ 4, JBy	0.25	4.00	12.00	20.00
❑ 5, JBy	0.25	4.00	12.00	20.00
❑ 6, JBy	0.25	4.00	12.00	20.00
❑ 7, Sep 76, JBy	0.30	4.00	12.00	20.00
❑ 8, Oct 76, JBy	0.30	4.00	12.00	20.00
❑ 9, Nov 76, JBy	0.30	4.00	12.00	20.00
❑ 10, Dec 76, JBy	0.30	4.00	12.00	20.00
❑ 11, Feb 77, JBy	0.30	4.00	12.00	20.00
❑ 12, Apr 77, JBy	0.30	4.00	12.00	20.00
❑ 13, Jun 77, JBy	0.30	4.00	12.00	20.00
❑ 14, Aug 77, JBy 1:Sabretooth	0.30	35.00	105.00	175.00
❑ 15, Oct 77, JBy, A:Wolverine	0.30	15.00	45.00	75.00

IRON MAN

	ORIG.	GOOD	FINE	N-MINT
❑ 1, JCr/GC	0.12	76.00	228.00	380.00
❑ 2, JCr, I:Demolisher	0.12	16.00	48.00	80.00
❑ 3, JCr	0.12	10.00	30.00	50.00
❑ 4, JCr	0.12	10.00	30.00	50.00
❑ 5, JCr	0.12	10.00	30.00	50.00
❑ 6, JCr/GT	0.12	7.00	21.00	35.00
❑ 7, JCr/GT	0.12	7.00	21.00	35.00
❑ 8, JCr/GT	0.12	7.00	21.00	35.00
❑ 9, JCr/GT	0.12	7.00	21.00	35.00
❑ 10, JCr/GT	0.12	7.00	21.00	35.00
❑ 11	0.12	5.00	15.00	25.00
❑ 12	0.12	5.00	15.00	25.00
❑ 13	0.12	5.00	15.00	25.00
❑ 14	0.12	5.00	15.00	25.00
❑ 15	0.12	5.00	15.00	25.00
❑ 16	0.15	4.00	12.00	20.00
❑ 17	0.15	4.00	12.00	20.00
❑ 18	0.15	4.00	12.00	20.00
❑ 19	0.15	4.00	12.00	20.00
❑ 20	0.15	4.00	12.00	20.00
❑ 21	0.15	2.40	7.20	12.00
❑ 22	0.15	2.40	7.20	12.00
❑ 23	0.15	2.40	7.20	12.00
❑ 24	0.15	2.40	7.20	12.00
❑ 25	0.15	2.40	7.20	12.00
❑ 26	0.15	2.40	7.20	12.00
❑ 27	0.15	2.40	7.20	12.00
❑ 28	0.15	2.40	7.20	12.00
❑ 29	0.15	2.40	7.20	12.00
❑ 30	0.15	2.40	7.20	12.00
❑ 31	0.15	2.00	6.00	10.00
❑ 32	0.15	2.00	6.00	10.00
❑ 33	0.15	2.00	6.00	10.00
❑ 34	0.15	2.00	6.00	10.00
❑ 35	0.15	2.00	6.00	10.00
❑ 36	0.15	2.00	6.00	10.00
❑ 37	0.15	2.00	6.00	10.00
❑ 38	0.15	2.00	6.00	10.00
❑ 39	0.15	2.00	6.00	10.00
❑ 40	0.15	2.00	6.00	10.00
❑ 41	0.15	2.00	6.00	10.00
❑ 42	0.15	2.00	6.00	10.00
❑ 43, GT/JM, A:Midas	0.25	2.00	6.00	10.00
❑ 44, GT	0.20	1.60	4.80	8.00
❑ 45, GT	0.20	1.60	4.80	8.00
❑ 46, GT	0.20	1.60	4.80	8.00
❑ 47, Jun 72, BS/JM, O:retold	0.20	3.00	9.00	15.00
❑ 48	0.20	1.60	4.80	8.00
❑ 49	0.20	1.60	4.80	8.00
❑ 50	0.20	1.60	4.80	8.00
❑ 51	0.20	1.60	4.80	8.00
❑ 52	0.20	1.60	4.80	8.00
❑ 53	0.20	1.60	4.80	8.00
❑ 54	0.20	1.60	4.80	8.00
❑ 55, Feb 73, JSn, I:Destroyer, Thanos	0.20	13.00	39.00	65.00
❑ 56, Mar 73, JSn, I:Fangor	0.20	2.40	7.20	12.00
❑ 57, Apr 73	0.20	1.20	3.60	6.00
❑ 58, May 73, V:Mandarin	0.20	1.20	3.60	6.00
❑ 59, Jun 73	0.20	1.20	3.60	6.00

	ORIG.	GOOD	FINE	N-MINT
☐ 60, Jul 73	0.20	1.20	3.60	6.00
☐ 61, Aug 73	0.20	1.20	3.60	6.00
☐ 62, Sep 73	0.20	1.20	3.60	6.00
☐ 63, Oct 73	0.20	1.20	3.60	6.00
☐ 64, Nov 73, survey	0.20	1.20	3.60	6.00
☐ 65, Dec 73	0.20	1.20	3.60	6.00
☐ 66, Feb 74, A:Thor;Marvel Value Stamp A80				
	0.20	1.20	3.60	6.00
☐ 67, Apr 74, A:Sunfire	0.20	1.20	3.60	6.00
☐ 68, Jun 74, GT;O:retold; A:Sunfire				
	0.25	2.00	6.00	10.00
☐ 69, Aug 74, GT	0.25	1.20	3.60	6.00
☐ 70, Sep 74, GT	0.25	1.20	3.60	6.00
☐ 71, Nov 74, GT	0.25	1.20	3.60	6.00
☐ 72, Jan 75, GT/NA; comic con				
	0.25	1.20	3.60	6.00
☐ 73, Mar 75	0.25	1.20	3.60	6.00
☐ 74, May 75, V:Modok	0.25	1.20	3.60	6.00
☐ 75, Jun 75	0.25	1.20	3.60	6.00
☐ 76, Jul 75	0.25	1.20	3.60	6.00
☐ 77, Aug 75	0.25	1.20	3.60	6.00
☐ 78, Sep 75	0.25	1.20	3.60	6.00
☐ 79, Oct 75	0.25	1.20	3.60	6.00
☐ 80, Nov 75, JK(c)	0.25	1.20	3.60	6.00
☐ 81, Dec 75, Marvel Value Stamp				
	0.25	1.20	3.60	6.00
☐ 82, Jan 76, repeats letter column from #81; Marvel Value Stamp B2	0.25	1.20	3.60	6.00
☐ 83, Feb 76, V:Red Ghost; Marvel Value Stamp B16				
	0.25	1.20	3.60	6.00
☐ 84, Mar 76, Marvel Value Stamp B56				
	0.25	1.20	3.60	6.00
☐ 85, Apr 76	0.25	1.20	3.60	6.00
☐ 86, May 76, V:Blizzard; Marvel Value Stamp B84				
	0.25	1.20	3.60	6.00
☐ 87, Jun 76, Marvel Value Stamp				
	0.25	1.20	3.60	6.00
☐ 88, Jul 76, Marvel Value Stamp 66				
	0.25	1.20	3.60	6.00
☐ 89, Aug 76, A:Daredevil	0.25	1.20	3.60	6.00
☐ 90, Sep 76	0.30	1.20	3.60	6.00
☐ 91, Oct 76	0.30	1.20	3.60	6.00
☐ 92, Nov 76, V:Melter	0.30	1.20	3.60	6.00
☐ 93, Dec 76	0.30	1.20	3.60	6.00
☐ 94, Jan 77	0.30	1.20	3.60	6.00
☐ 95, Feb 77	0.30	1.20	3.60	6.00
☐ 96, Mar 77	0.30	1.20	3.60	6.00
☐ 97, Apr 77	0.30	1.20	3.60	6.00
☐ 98, May 77	0.30	1.20	3.60	6.00
☐ 99, Jun 77	0.30	1.20	3.60	6.00
☐ 100, Jul 77, GT/JSn(c), Mandarin				
	0.30	3.00	9.00	15.00
☐ 101, Aug 77	0.30	0.80	2.40	4.00
☐ 102, Sep 77	0.30	0.80	2.40	4.00
☐ 103, Oct 77	0.30	0.80	2.40	4.00
☐ 104, Nov 77	0.35	0.80	2.40	4.00
☐ 105, Dec 77, A:Jack of Hearts				
	0.35	0.80	2.40	4.00
☐ 106, Jan 78	0.35	0.80	2.40	4.00
☐ 107, Feb 78	0.35	0.80	2.40	4.00
☐ 108, Mar 78, CI	0.35	0.80	2.40	4.00
☐ 109, Apr 78	0.35	0.80	2.40	4.00
☐ 110, May 78, A:Jack of Hearts				
	0.35	0.80	2.40	4.00
☐ 111, Jun 78, Wundagore	0.35	0.80	2.40	4.00
☐ 112, Jul 78	0.35	0.80	2.40	4.00
☐ 113, Aug 78	0.35	0.80	2.40	4.00
☐ 114, Sep 78	0.35	0.80	2.40	4.00
☐ 115, Oct 78	0.35	0.80	2.40	4.00
☐ 116, Nov 78, BL/JR2; First David Michelinie written issue	0.35	0.80	2.40	4.00
☐ 117, Dec 78, BL/JR2; 1:Beth Cabe				
	0.35	1.40	4.20	7.00
☐ 118, Jan 79, JBy/BL	0.35	1.00	3.00	5.00
☐ 119, Feb 79, BL/JR2, alcoholism				
	0.35	1.20	3.60	6.00
☐ 120, Mar 79, A:Sub-Mariner				
	0.35	1.20	3.60	6.00
☐ 121, Apr 79, A:Sub-Mariner				
	0.35	1.20	3.60	6.00
☐ 122, May 79, A:Sub-Mariner				
	0.40	1.20	3.60	6.00
☐ 123, Jun 79	0.40	1.20	3.60	6.00
☐ 124, Jul 79	0.40	1.20	3.60	6.00
☐ 125, Aug 79	0.40	1.20	3.60	6.00
☐ 126, Sep 79, V:Justin Hammer				
	0.40	1.20	3.60	6.00
☐ 127, Oct 79	0.40	1.20	3.60	6.00
☐ 128, Nov 79, BL/JR2, alcoholism				
	0.40	1.00	3.00	5.00
☐ 129, Dec 79, V:Dreadnought				
	0.40	0.60	1.80	3.00
☐ 130, Jan 80	0.40	0.60	1.80	3.00
☐ 131, Feb 80, A:Hulk	0.40	0.60	1.80	3.00
☐ 132, Mar 80, A:Hulk	0.40	0.60	1.80	3.00
☐ 133, Apr 80, A:Hulk	0.40	0.60	1.80	3.00
☐ 134, May 80	0.40	0.60	1.80	3.00
☐ 135, Jun 80	0.40	0.60	1.80	3.00
☐ 136, Jul 80	0.40	0.60	1.80	3.00
☐ 137, Aug 80	0.40	0.60	1.80	3.00
☐ 138, Sep 80	0.50	0.60	1.80	3.00
☐ 139, Oct 80	0.50	0.60	1.80	3.00
☐ 140, Nov 80	0.50	0.60	1.80	3.00
☐ 141, Dec 80	0.50	0.60	1.80	3.00
☐ 142, Jan 81	0.50	0.60	1.80	3.00
☐ 143, Feb 81	0.50	0.60	1.80	3.00
☐ 144, Mar 81	0.50	0.60	1.80	3.00
☐ 145, Apr 81	0.50	0.60	1.80	3.00
☐ 146, May 81	0.50	0.60	1.80	3.00
☐ 147, Jun 81	0.50	0.60	1.80	3.00
☐ 148, Jul 81	0.50	0.60	1.80	3.00
☐ 149, Aug 81	0.50	0.60	1.80	3.00
☐ 150, Sep 81	0.75	0.60	1.80	3.00
☐ 151, Oct 81	0.50	0.40	1.20	2.00
☐ 152, Nov 81	0.50	0.40	1.20	2.00
☐ 153, Dec 81	0.50	0.40	1.20	2.00
☐ 154, Jan 82	0.60	0.40	1.20	2.00
☐ 155, Feb 82	0.60	0.40	1.20	2.00
☐ 156, Mar 82	0.60	0.40	1.20	2.00
☐ 157, Apr 82	0.60	0.40	1.20	2.00
☐ 158, May 82	0.60	0.40	1.20	2.00
☐ 159, Jun 82, PS, Diablo	0.60	0.40	1.20	2.00
☐ 160, Jul 82, Serpent Squad				
	0.60	0.40	1.20	2.00
☐ 161, Aug 82, Moon Knight				
	0.60	0.40	1.20	2.00
☐ 162, Sep 82	0.60	0.40	1.20	2.00
☐ 163, Oct 82	0.60	0.40	1.20	2.00
☐ 164, Nov 82	0.60	0.40	1.20	2.00
☐ 165, Dec 82	0.60	0.40	1.20	2.00
☐ 166, Jan 83	0.60	0.40	1.20	2.00
☐ 167, Feb 83, LMc, alcoholism				
	0.60	0.40	1.20	2.00
☐ 168, Mar 83, LMc, Machine Man				
	0.60	0.40	1.20	2.00
☐ 169, Apr 83, LMc;new Iron Man				
	0.60	2.40	7.20	12.00
☐ 170, May 83	0.60	0.80	2.40	4.00
☐ 171, Jun 83	0.60	0.40	1.20	2.00
☐ 172, Jul 83	0.60	0.40	1.20	2.00
☐ 173, Aug 83, LMc	0.60	0.40	1.20	2.00
☐ 174, Sep 83, LMc	0.60	0.40	1.20	2.00
☐ 175, Oct 83, LMc	0.60	0.40	1.20	2.00

	ORIG.	GOOD	FINE	N-MINT
❑ 176, Nov 83, LMc	0.60	0.40	1.20	2.00
❑ 177, Dec 83, LMc	0.60	0.40	1.20	2.00
❑ 178, Jan 84, LMc	0.60	0.40	1.20	2.00
❑ 179, Feb 84, LMc	0.60	0.40	1.20	2.00
❑ 180, Mar 84, LMc	0.60	0.40	1.20	2.00
❑ 181, Apr 84, LMc	0.60	0.40	1.20	2.00
❑ 182, May 84, LMc	0.60	0.40	1.20	2.00
❑ 183, Jun 84, LMc	0.60	0.40	1.20	2.00
❑ 184, Jul 84, LMc	0.60	0.40	1.20	2.00
❑ 185, Aug 84, LMc	0.60	0.40	1.20	2.00
❑ 186, Sep 84	0.60	0.40	1.20	2.00
❑ 187, Oct 84	0.60	0.40	1.20	2.00
❑ 188, Nov 84	0.60	0.40	1.20	2.00
❑ 189, Dec 84	0.60	0.40	1.20	2.00
❑ 190, Jan 85	0.60	0.40	1.20	2.00
❑ 191, Feb 85, LMc old Iron Man	0.60	0.40	1.20	2.00
❑ 192, Mar 85	0.60	0.40	1.20	2.00
❑ 193, Apr 85	0.65	0.40	1.20	2.00
❑ 194, May 85	0.65	0.40	1.20	2.00
❑ 195, Jun 85	0.65	0.40	1.20	2.00
❑ 196, Jul 85	0.65	0.40	1.20	2.00
❑ 197, Aug 85, Secret Wars II	0.65	0.40	1.20	2.00
❑ 198, Sep 85	0.65	0.40	1.20	2.00
❑ 199, Oct 85	0.65	0.40	1.20	2.00
❑ 200, Nov 85	1.25	1.20	3.60	6.00
❑ 201, Dec 85	0.60	0.20	0.60	1.00
❑ 202, Jan 86	0.60	0.20	0.60	1.00
❑ 203, Feb 86	0.75	0.20	0.60	1.00
❑ 204, Mar 86	0.75	0.20	0.60	1.00
❑ 205, Apr 86	0.75	0.20	0.60	1.00
❑ 206, May 86	0.75	0.20	0.60	1.00
❑ 207, Jun 86	0.75	0.20	0.60	1.00
❑ 208, Jul 86	0.75	0.20	0.60	1.00
❑ 209, Aug 86	0.75	0.20	0.60	1.00
❑ 210, Sep 86	0.75	0.20	0.60	1.00
❑ 211, Oct 86	0.75	0.20	0.60	1.00
❑ 212, Nov 86	0.75	0.20	0.60	1.00
❑ 213, Dec 86	0.75	0.20	0.60	1.00
❑ 214, Jan 87	0.75	0.20	0.60	1.00
❑ 215, Feb 87	0.75	0.20	0.60	1.00
❑ 216, Mar 87	0.75	0.20	0.60	1.00
❑ 217, Apr 87	0.75	0.20	0.60	1.00
❑ 218, May 87	0.75	0.20	0.60	1.00
❑ 219, Jun 87	0.75	0.20	0.60	1.00
❑ 220, Jul 87, D:Spymaster	0.75	0.20	0.60	1.00
❑ 221, Aug 87	0.75	0.20	0.60	1.00
❑ 222, Sep 87	0.75	0.20	0.60	1.00
❑ 223, Oct 87	0.75	0.20	0.60	1.00
❑ 224, Nov 87	0.75	0.20	0.60	1.00
❑ 225, Dec 87, Armor Wars	1.25	1.20	3.60	6.00
❑ 226, Jan 88, Armor Wars	0.75	0.80	2.40	4.00
❑ 227, Feb 88, Armor Wars	0.75	0.80	2.40	4.00
❑ 228, Mar 88, Armor Wars	0.75	0.80	2.40	4.00
❑ 229, Apr 88, Armor Wars	0.75	0.80	2.40	4.00
❑ 230, May 88, Armor Wars	0.75	0.80	2.40	4.00
❑ 231, Jun 88, Armor Wars	0.75	0.80	2.40	4.00
❑ 232, Jul 88, BWS, Flexographic	0.75	0.60	1.80	3.00
❑ 232, BWS, offset	0.75	0.60	1.80	3.00
❑ 233, Aug 88, A:Ant-Man	0.75	0.20	0.60	1.00
❑ 234, Sep 88, A:SpM	0.75	0.20	0.60	1.00
❑ 235, Oct 88	0.75	0.20	0.60	1.00
❑ 236, Nov 88	0.75	0.20	0.60	1.00
❑ 237, Dec 88	0.75	0.20	0.60	1.00
❑ 238, Jan 89	0.75	0.20	0.60	1.00
❑ 239, Feb 89	0.75	0.20	0.60	1.00
❑ 240, Mar 89	0.75	0.20	0.60	1.00
❑ 241, Apr 89	0.75	0.20	0.60	1.00
❑ 242, May 89, Stark shot	0.75	0.50	1.50	2.50
❑ 243, Jun 89, Stark crippled	0.75	0.50	1.50	2.50
❑ 244, Jul 89	1.50	0.30	0.90	1.50
❑ 245, Aug 89	0.75	0.30	0.90	1.50
❑ 246, Sep 89	1.00	0.20	0.60	1.00
❑ 247, Oct 89	1.00	0.20	0.60	1.00
❑ 248, Nov 89, Stark cured	1.00	0.20	0.60	1.00
❑ 249, Nov 89, Dr. Doom	1.00	0.20	0.60	1.00
❑ 250, Dec 89, Dr. Doom, Acts	1.50	0.30	0.90	1.50
❑ 251, Dec 89, Acts of Vengeance	1.00	0.20	0.60	1.00
❑ 252, Jan 90, Acts of Vengeance	1.00	0.20	0.60	1.00
❑ 253, Feb 90, JBy(c)	1.00	0.20	0.60	1.00
❑ 254, Mar 90	1.00	0.20	0.60	1.00
❑ 255, Apr 90	1.00	0.20	0.60	1.00
❑ 256, May 90	1.00	0.20	0.60	1.00
❑ 257, Jun 90	1.00	0.20	0.60	1.00
❑ 258, Jul 90	1.00	0.60	1.80	3.00
❑ 259, Aug 90, Armor Wars II	1.00	0.40	1.20	2.00
❑ 260, Sep 90, Armor Wars II	1.00	0.40	1.20	2.00
❑ 261, Oct 90, Armor Wars II	1.00	0.40	1.20	2.00
❑ 262, Nov 90, Armor Wars II	1.00	0.40	1.20	2.00
❑ 263, Dec 90, Armor Wars II	1.00	0.40	1.20	2.00
❑ 264, Jan 91, Armor Wars II	1.00	0.40	1.20	2.00
❑ 265, Feb 91, Armor Wars II	1.00	0.40	1.20	2.00
❑ 266, Mar 91, Armor Wars II	1.00	0.40	1.20	2.00
❑ 267, Apr 91	1.00	0.20	0.60	1.00
❑ 268, May 91, O:retold	1.00	0.20	0.60	1.00
❑ 269, Jun 91	1.00	0.20	0.60	1.00
❑ 270, Jul 91	1.00	0.20	0.60	1.00
❑ 271, Aug 91	1.00	0.20	0.60	1.00
❑ 272, Sep 91	1.00	0.20	0.60	1.00
❑ 273, Oct 91	1.00	0.20	0.60	1.00
❑ 274, Nov 91	1.00	0.20	0.60	1.00
❑ 275, Dec 91	1.50	0.30	0.90	1.50
❑ 276	1.00	0.20	0.60	1.00
❑ 277	1.25	0.25	0.75	1.25
❑ 278, Galactic Storm	1.25	0.25	0.75	1.25
❑ 279, Galactic Storm	1.25	0.25	0.75	1.25
❑ 280	1.25	0.25	0.75	1.25
❑ 281	1.25	0.25	0.75	1.25
❑ 282	1.25	0.25	0.75	1.25
❑ 283	1.25	0.25	0.75	1.25
❑ 284	1.25	1.60	4.80	8.00
❑ 285	1.25	0.25	0.75	1.25
❑ 286	1.25	0.25	0.75	1.25
❑ 287	1.25	0.25	0.75	1.25
❑ 288, silver foil cover	2.50	0.80	2.40	4.00
❑ 289	1.25	0.25	0.75	1.25
❑ 290, foil cover	2.95	0.59	1.77	2.95
❑ 291, Apr 93	1.25	0.25	0.75	1.25
❑ 292, May 93	1.25	0.25	0.75	1.25
❑ 293, Jun 93	1.25	0.25	0.75	1.25
❑ 294, Jul 93	1.25	0.25	0.75	1.25
❑ 295, Aug 93	1.25	0.25	0.75	1.25
❑ 296, Sep 93	1.25	0.25	0.75	1.25

	ORIG.	GOOD	FINE	N-MINT
☐ 297, Oct 93 .... 1.25	0.25	0.75	1.25
☐ 298, Nov 93 .... 1.25	0.25	0.75	1.25
☐ 299, Dec 93, LK 1.25	0.25	0.75	1.25
☐ 300, Jan 94 .... 2.50	0.50	1.50	2.50
☐ 300, Jan 94, foil cover ... 3.95	0.79	2.37	3.95
☐ 301, Feb 94 .... 1.25	0.25	0.75	1.25
☐ 302, Mar 94 .... 1.25	0.25	0.75	1.25
☐ 303, Apr 94 .... 1.25	0.25	0.75	1.25
☐ 304, May 94 .... 1.50	0.30	0.90	1.50
☐ 305, Jun 94 .... 1.50	0.30	0.90	1.50
☐ 306, Jul 94 .... 1.50	0.30	0.90	1.50
☐ 307, Aug 94 .... 1.50	0.30	0.90	1.50
☐ 308, Sep 94................... 1.50	0.30	0.90	1.50
☐ 309, Oct 94 .... 1.50	0.30	0.90	1.50
☐ 310, Nov 94 .... 1.50	0.30	0.90	1.50
☐ 310, Nov 94, polybagged with 16-page preview, acetate print, and other items.... 2.95	0.59	1.77	2.95
☐ 311, Dec 94 .... 1.50	0.30	0.90	1.50
☐ 312, Jan 95 .... 2.25	0.45	1.35	2.25
☐ 313, Feb 95 .... 1.50	0.30	0.90	1.50
☐ 314, Mar 95 .... 1.50	0.30	0.90	1.50
☐ 315, Apr 95 .... 1.50	0.30	0.90	1.50
☐ 316, May 95 .... 1.50	0.30	0.90	1.50
☐ 317, Jun 95, flip book with War Machine: Brothers in Arms part 3 back-up 2.50	0.50	1.50	2.50
☐ 318, Jul 95 .... 1.50	0.30	0.90	1.50
☐ 319, Aug 95, origin retold 1.50	0.30	0.90	1.50
☐ 320, Sep 95................... 1.50	0.30	0.90	1.50
☐ 321, Oct 95, OverPower cards inserted 1.50	0.30	0.90	1.50
☐ 322, Nov 95 .... 1.50	0.30	0.90	1.50
☐ 323, Dec 95................... 1.50	0.30	0.90	1.50
☐ 324, Jan 96 .... 1.50	0.30	0.90	1.50
☐ 325, Feb 96, wraparound cover 2.95	0.59	1.77	2.95
☐ 326, Mar 96 .... 1.95	0.39	1.17	1.95
☐ 327, Apr 96, reading of Tony Stark's will; V:Frostbite 1.95	0.39	1.17	1.95
☐ 328, May 96 .... 1.50	0.30	0.90	1.50
☐ 329, Jun 96 .... 1.50	0.30	0.90	1.50

IRON MAN 2020
| ☐ 0, 94, one-shot............. 5.95 | 1.19 | 3.57 | 5.95 |

IRON MAN AND SUB-MARINER
| ☐ 1, GC,JCr.................... 0.12 | 36.00 | 108.00 | 180.00 |

IRON MAN ANNUAL
☐ 1, reprint...................... 0.25	3.00	9.00	15.00
☐ 2, reprint...................... 0.25	1.60	4.80	8.00
☐ 3 .... 0.50	0.80	2.40	4.00
☐ 4, Aug 77 .... 0.50	0.80	2.40	4.00
☐ 5, Nov 82 .... 1.00	0.80	2.40	4.00
☐ 6, Nov 83 .... 1.00	0.60	1.80	3.00
☐ 7, Oct 84, West Coast Avengers 1.00	0.40	1.20	2.00
☐ 8, Oct 86...................... 1.25	0.40	1.20	2.00
☐ 9, Dec 87...................... 1.25	0.40	1.20	2.00
☐ 10, Sep 89, Atlantis Attacks 2.00	0.40	1.20	2.00
☐ 11, Sep 90, Terminus Factor 2.00	0.40	1.20	2.00
☐ 12, Sep 91, Subterranean Wars 2.00	0.40	1.20	2.00
☐ 13 .... 2.25	0.45	1.35	2.25
☐ 14, trading card............. 2.95	0.59	1.77	2.95
☐ 15, 94............................ 2.95	0.59	1.77	2.95

IRON MAN COLLECTORS' PREVIEW
| ☐ 1, Nov 94 .... 1.95 | 0.39 | 1.17 | 1.95 |

IRON MANUAL, THE
| ☐ 1 .... 1.75 | 0.35 | 1.05 | 1.75 |

IRON MARSHAL
JADEMAN
☐ 1	0.35	1.05	1.75
☐ 2	0.35	1.05	1.75
☐ 3	0.35	1.05	1.75
☐ 4	0.35	1.05	1.75
☐ 5	0.35	1.05	1.75
☐ 6	0.35	1.05	1.75
☐ 7	0.35	1.05	1.75
☐ 8	0.35	1.05	1.75
☐ 9	0.35	1.05	1.75
☐ 10	0.35	1.05	1.75
☐ 11	0.35	1.05	1.75
☐ 12	0.35	1.05	1.75
☐ 13	0.35	1.05	1.75
☐ 14	0.35	1.05	1.75
☐ 15	0.35	1.05	1.75
☐ 16	0.35	1.05	1.75
☐ 17	0.35	1.05	1.75
☐ 18	0.35	1.05	1.75
☐ 19	0.35	1.05	1.75

IRON SAGA'S ANTHOLOGY
IRON SAGA
| ☐ 1 .... | 0.35 | 1.05 | 1.75 |

IRONHAND OF ALMURIC
DARK HORSE
☐ 1, 91, b&w......................	0.40	1.20	2.00
☐ 2, 91, b&w......................	0.40	1.20	2.00
☐ 3, 91, b&w......................	0.40	1.20	2.00
☐ 4, 91, b&w......................	0.40	1.20	2.00

IRONJAW
ATLAS/ SEABOARD
☐ 1, Jan 75, NA(c)............. 0.25	0.20	0.60	1.00
☐ 2, Mar 75, NA(c)............. 0.25	0.20	0.60	1.00
☐ 3, May 75....................... 0.25	0.20	0.60	1.00
☐ 4, Jul 75, O:Ironjaw 0.25	0.20	0.60	1.00

IRONWOLF
DC
| ☐ 1, HC............................. | 0.40 | 1.20 | 2.00 |

IRONWOOD
EROS COMIX
☐ 1, adult, b&w	0.39	1.17	1.95
☐ 2, adult, b&w	0.45	1.35	2.25
☐ 3, adult, b&w	0.45	1.35	2.25
☐ 4, adult, b&w	0.45	1.35	2.25
☐ 5, adult, b&w	0.45	1.35	2.25
☐ 6, adult, b&w	0.45	1.35	2.25
☐ 7, adult, b&w 2.50	0.50	1.50	2.50
☐ 8, adult, b&w 2.50	0.50	1.50	2.50
☐ 9, adult, b&w 2.50	0.50	1.50	2.50

FANTAGRAPHICS/EROS
| ☐ 10, Sep 94, adult, b&w ... 2.75 | 0.55 | 1.65 | 2.75 |

ISAAC ASIMOV'S I-BOTS
TEKNO
☐ 1, Dec 95, GP................. 1.95	0.39	1.17	1.95
☐ 2, Dec 95 .... 1.95	0.39	1.17	1.95
☐ 4, Feb 96....................... 2.25	0.45	1.35	2.25
☐ 5, Mar 96....................... 2.25	0.45	1.35	2.25

ISIS
DC
☐ 1, Oct 76........................	0.20	0.60	1.00
☐ 2, 76..............................	0.20	0.60	1.00
☐ 3, 77..............................	0.20	0.60	1.00
☐ 4, 77..............................	0.20	0.60	1.00
☐ 5, 77..............................	0.20	0.60	1.00
☐ 6, 77..............................	0.20	0.60	1.00
☐ 7, 77..............................	0.20	0.60	1.00
☐ 8, Dec 77.......................	0.20	0.60	1.00

	ORIG.	GOOD	FINE	N-MINT
ISLAND OF DR. MOREAU, THE				
MARVEL				
☐ 1, Oct 77, movie	0.50	0.20	0.60	1.00
ISMET				
CANIS				
☐ 1		0.25	0.75	1.25
☐ 2		0.25	0.75	1.25
☐ 3		0.25	0.75	1.25
☐ 4		0.25	0.75	1.25
☐ 5		0.25	0.75	1.25
IT! THE TERROR FROM BEYOND SPACE				
MILLENNIUM				
☐ 1		0.50	1.50	2.50
☐ 2		0.50	1.50	2.50
IT'S ONLY A MATTER OF LIFE AND DEATH				
FANTAGRAPHICS				
☐ 1, b&w		0.79	2.37	3.95
IT'S SCIENCE WITH DR. RADIUM				
SLAVE LABOR				
☐ 1, Sep 86	1.50	0.30	0.90	1.50
☐ 2		0.30	0.90	1.50
☐ 3		0.30	0.90	1.50

	ORIG.	GOOD	FINE	N-MINT
☐ 4		0.30	0.90	1.50
☐ 5		0.30	0.90	1.50
☐ 6		0.30	0.90	1.50
☐ 7		0.35	1.05	1.75
ITCHY & SCRATCHY COMICS				
BONGO				
☐ 1, 93	2.25	1.00	3.00	5.00
☐ 2, 94	1.95	0.50	1.50	2.50
☐ 3, 94	2.25	0.45	1.35	2.25
ITCHY & SCRATCHY: HOLIDAY HI-JINX SPECIAL				
☐ 1, 94	1.95	0.39	1.17	1.95
ITCHY PLANET				
FANTAGRAPHICS				
☐ 1, b&w		0.45	1.35	2.25
☐ 2, b&w		0.45	1.35	2.25
☐ 3, b&w		0.45	1.35	2.25
IT'S SCIENCE WITH DR. RADIUM SPECIAL				
SLAVE LABOR				
☐ 1, b&w		0.59	1.77	2.95

Infinity, Inc.

First appearance: *All-Star Squadron* #25.

Many teens rebel against their parents' wishes, but what do you do when the teen-agers in question have super-powers?

That was one of the questions writer Roy Thomas addressed when he created *Infinity, Inc.* for DC. Thomas took the idea of an aging Justice Society of America that had settled down and produced progeny. That group of special children come together to form their own super-hero team after being denied membership in the JSA.

One of the youngest members of the JSA — The Star-Spangled Kid — left the JSA to help form and guide the new group. The "Inc." part of the name came from The Star-Spangled Kid's dream of using the team for commercial purposes. The Huntress and Power Girl were also associated with the group at various times.

The main group's other members were:

• Jade and Obsidian — The children of Green Lantern Alan Scott and Rose Forrest, the original Thorn, Jade had a green power pulse with characteristics like Green Lantern's ring, while Obsidian could become a shadow and show criminals their dark sides.

• Nuklon — Albert Rothstein was The Atom's godson and had nuclear-powered strength.

• Fury — Before the events of *Crisis on Infinite Earths*, Hippolyta Trevor was the daughter of Wonder Woman and Steve Trevor, whereas after *Crisis* her mother was the Golden Age Fury. Her post-*Crisis* father's identity was never revealed.

• Silver Scarab — Hector Hall was the son of Carter and Shiera Hall, Hawkman and Hawkwoman.

• Northwind — Norda Cantrell was a half-

breed from Feithera, a race of birdlike humanoids who live in the Arctic. The Halls were his godparents.

• Brainwave, Jr. — The son of the original Brainwave's powers were limited at first to telekinesis and telepathy, but he later acquired his father's ability to project realistic illusions.

During the Crisis, Hourman's son, Dr. Mid-Nite's assistant, and Wildcat's goddaughter took up the mantles of their respective predecessors and joined the group.

The group's antithesis was a group known as Helix. The mothers of Helix members had been experimented on while carrying the unborn children. This resulted in a team of super-powered beings who turned bad after kidnapping Fury. The most memorable member of the group was Mr. Bones, a skeletal creature who spoke in rhyme and possessed a cyanide touch.

During the series' run, the group crossed over with The Outsiders, The Young All-Stars, and The All-Star Squadron.

Both The Silver Scarab and The Star-Spangled Kid died during the series' run. The Scarab came back as The Sandman (the one from the mid-'70s, not Morpheus) and took Fury into the Dream Dimension with him. Hippolyta Trevor eventually became part of *The Sandman's* cast and played a part in Morpheus' death.

The remainder of the team went its separate ways when the series folded with issue #53. Nuklon and Obsidian eventually joined the Justice League, while Jade teamed with her father for a few adventures. The new Dr. Mid-Nite and Wildcat were killed by Eclipso, while young Hourman was dying of cancer in the short-lived *Justice Society of America* series.

J

	ORIG.	GOOD	FINE	N-MINT

J.R. WILLIAMS' FUN HOUSE
STARHEAD

	ORIG.	GOOD	FINE	N-MINT
❏ 1, Nov 93, adult;b&w	3.95	0.79	2.37	3.95

JAB
ADHESIVE

❏ 3, bullet hole	2.50	0.50	1.50	2.50

FUNNY PAPERS

❏ 1, b&w		0.50	1.50	2.50
❏ 2, b&w		0.50	1.50	2.50

JAB VOL. 2
CUMMINGS DESIGN GROUP

❏ 3, Aut 94, b&w	2.95	0.59	1.77	2.95

JACK FROST
AMAZING

❏ 1		0.39	1.17	1.95
❏ 2		0.39	1.17	1.95

JACK HUNTER
BLACKTHORNE

❏ 1, Mar 88, JKu(c)		0.25	0.75	1.25

JACK KIRBY'S SECRET CITY SAGA
TOPPS

❏ 0, WS, foil cover				
❏ 1, trading cards	2.95	0.59	1.77	2.95
❏ 2, JBy,BSz, trading cards	2.95	0.59	1.77	2.95
❏ 3, trading cards	2.95	0.59	1.77	2.95
❏ 4, trading cards	2.95	0.59	1.77	2.95

JACK KIRBY'S TEENAGENTS

❏ 1, three trading cards	2.95	0.59	1.77	2.95
❏ 2, trading cards	2.95	0.59	1.77	2.95
❏ 3, trading cards, A:Liberty Project				
	2.95	0.59	1.77	2.95
❏ 4, Nov 93, cards, Zorro preview				
	2.95	0.59	1.77	2.95

JACK LONDON'S KOOLAU THE LEPER
TOME PRESS

❏ 1, b&w		0.50	1.50	2.50

JACK OF HEARTS
MARVEL

❏ 1, Jan 84	0.60	0.30	0.90	1.50
❏ 2, Feb 84	0.60	0.20	0.60	1.00
❏ 3, Mar 84	0.60	0.20	0.60	1.00
❏ 4, Apr 84	0.60	0.20	0.60	1.00

JACK THE RIPPER
ETERNITY

❏ 1, b&w		0.45	1.35	2.25
❏ 2, b&w		0.45	1.35	2.25
❏ 3, b&w		0.45	1.35	2.25

JACKAROO, THE

❏ 1, Feb 90, b&w, Australian	0.45	1.35	2.25
❏ 2, Mar 90, b&w, Australian	0.45	1.35	2.25
❏ 3, Apr 90, b&w, Australian	0.45	1.35	2.25

JACQUE'S VOICE OF DOOM
DOOMED COMICS

❏ 1, 95, b&w;strip reprints				
	1.50	0.30	0.90	1.50

JACQUELYN THE RIPPER
FANTAGRAPHICS

❏ 2, Oct 94, b&w	2.95	0.59	1.77	2.95

JADEMAN COLLECTION
JADEMAN

❏ 1		0.50	1.50	2.50
❏ 2		0.50	1.50	2.50

JADEMAN KUNG FU SPECIAL

❏ 1		0.30	0.90	1.50

JAGUAR ANNUAL, THE
IMPACT

❏ 1, 92	2.50	0.50	1.50	2.50

JAGUAR GOD
VEROTIK

❏ 3, Mar 96	2.95	0.59	1.77	2.95

JAGUAR, THE
IMPACT

❏ 1, Aug 91, O:Jaguar	1.00	0.20	0.60	1.00
❏ 2, Sep 91	1.00	0.20	0.60	1.00
❏ 3, Oct 91	1.00	0.20	0.60	1.00
❏ 4, Nov 91	1.00	0.20	0.60	1.00
❏ 5, Dec 91	1.00	0.20	0.60	1.00
❏ 6, Jan 92	1.00	0.20	0.60	1.00
❏ 7, Mar 92	1.00	0.20	0.60	1.00
❏ 8, Apr 92	1.00	0.20	0.60	1.00
❏ 9, May 92, trading card	1.00	0.20	0.60	1.00
❏ 10, Jun 92	1.00	0.20	0.60	1.00
❏ 11, Jul 92	1.00	0.20	0.60	1.00
❏ 12, Aug 92	1.25	0.25	0.75	1.25
❏ 13, Sep 92	1.25	0.25	0.75	1.25
❏ 14, Oct 92	1.25	0.25	0.75	1.25

JAKE THRASH
AIRCEL

❏ 1, color		0.40	1.20	2.00
❏ 2, color		0.40	1.20	2.00

JAKE THRASH BOOK

❏ 1, b&w		0.79	2.37	3.95

JAM QUACKY
JQ PRODUCTIONS

❏ 1, b&w		0.40	1.20	2.00

JAM SPECIAL, THE
MATRIX

❏ 1		0.50	1.50	2.50

JAM SUPER COOL COLOR-INJECTED TURBO ADVENTURE FROM HELL
COMICO

❏ 1		0.50	1.50	2.50

JAM, THE
CALIBER

❏ 9, Aug 95, b&w	2.95	0.59	1.77	2.95

DARK HORSE

❏ 6	2.50	0.50	1.50	2.50
❏ 7, Mar 94, b&w	2.50	0.50	1.50	2.50
❏ 8, Feb 95, b&w;(becomes Caliber title)				
	2.50	0.50	1.50	2.50

SLAVE LABOR

❏ 1, b&w		0.39	1.17	1.95
❏ 2, b&w		0.39	1.17	1.95
❏ 3, b&w		0.39	1.17	1.95
❏ 4		0.45	1.35	2.25
❏ 5, (becomes Dark Horse title)	0.45	1.35	2.25

TUNDRA

❏ 1, color		0.59	1.77	2.95
❏ 2, color		0.59	1.77	2.95
❏ 3, color		0.59	1.77	2.95

JAMES BOND 007/GOLDENEYE (mini-series)
TOPPS

❏ 1, Jan 96, movie adaptation				
	2.95	0.59	1.77	2.95

JAMES BOND 007: A SILENT ARMAGEDDON (mini-series)
DARK HORSE

❏ 1, Mar 93	2.95	0.59	1.77	2.95
❏ 2, May 93	2.95	0.59	1.77	2.95

	ORIG.	GOOD	FINE	N-MINT

JAMES BOND 007: SERPENT'S TOOTH
(mini-series)

	ORIG.	GOOD	FINE	N-MINT
1, Jul 92, Paul Gulacy 2.95		0.99	2.97	4.95
2, Aug 92, Paul Gulacy ... 2.95		0.99	2.97	4.95
3, Feb 93 .... 4.95		0.99	2.97	4.95

JAMES BOND 007: SHATTERED HELIX
(mini-series)

	ORIG.	GOOD	FINE	N-MINT
1, Jun 94 .... 2.50		0.50	1.50	2.50
2, Jul 94 .... 2.50		0.50	1.50	2.50

JAMES BOND 007: THE QUASIMODO GAMBIT
(mini-series)

	ORIG.	GOOD	FINE	N-MINT
1, Jan 95, cardstock cover				
.... 3.95		0.79	2.37	3.95
2, Feb 95, cardstock cover				
.... 3.95		0.79	2.37	3.95
3, May 95, cardstock cover				
.... 3.95		0.79	2.37	3.95

JAMES BOND JR.
MARVEL

	ORIG.	GOOD	FINE	N-MINT
1, TV cartoon 1.00		0.25	0.75	1.25
2, TV cartoon 1.25		0.25	0.75	1.25
3, TV cartoon 1.25		0.25	0.75	1.25
4, TV cartoon 1.25		0.25	0.75	1.25
5, TV cartoon 1.25		0.25	0.75	1.25
6, TV cartoon 1.25		0.25	0.75	1.25
8 .... 1.25		0.25	0.75	1.25
9 .... 1.25		0.25	0.75	1.25
10 .... 1.25		0.25	0.75	1.25
11 .... 1.25		0.25	0.75	1.25
12 .... 1.25		0.25	0.75	1.25

JAMES BOND: PERMISSION TO DIE
ECLIPSE

	ORIG.	GOOD	FINE	N-MINT
1, Jul 91 .... 3.95		0.79	2.37	3.95
2, Aug 91 .... 3.95		0.79	2.37	3.95
3, Sep 91 .... 4.95		0.99	2.97	4.95

JANE BOND: THUNDERBALLS
EROS COMIX

	ORIG.	GOOD	FINE	N-MINT
1, adult, b&w		0.50	1.50	2.50

JANE DOE
RAGING RHINO

	ORIG.	GOOD	FINE	N-MINT
1, 93, "Androgyne Anger Extreme;" adult; b&w				
.... 2.95		0.59	1.77	2.95
2, 93, "Slice by Slice;" adult; b&w				
.... 2.95		0.59	1.77	2.95
3, 94, adult; b&w 2.95		0.59	1.77	2.95

JANX
ES GRAPHICS

	ORIG.	GOOD	FINE	N-MINT
1		0.20	0.60	1.00
2		0.20	0.60	1.00

JAR OF FOOLS PART ONE
PENNY DREADFUL

	ORIG.	GOOD	FINE	N-MINT
0, Jun 94, nn;b&w 5.95		1.19	3.57	5.95

JASON AND THE ARGONAUTS
TOME PRESS

	ORIG.	GOOD	FINE	N-MINT
1, b&w 2.50		0.50	1.50	2.50
2, b&w 2.50		0.50	1.50	2.50
3, b&w 2.50		0.50	1.50	2.50
4, b&w 2.50		0.50	1.50	2.50
5, b&w 2.50		0.50	1.50	2.50

JASON GOES TO HELL: THE FINAL FRIDAY
TOPPS

	ORIG.	GOOD	FINE	N-MINT
1, glowing cover, trading cards				
.... 2.95		0.59	1.77	2.95
2, three trading cards..... 2.95		0.59	1.77	2.95
3, trading cards............. 2.95		0.59	1.77	2.95

JASON MONARCH
ORACLE

	ORIG.	GOOD	FINE	N-MINT
1, b&w		0.40	1.20	2.00

JASON VS. LEATHERFACE (mini-series)
TOPPS

	ORIG.	GOOD	FINE	N-MINT
1, Oct 95 .... 2.95		0.59	1.77	2.95
2, Nov 95 .... 2.95		0.59	1.77	2.95

JAVA TOWN
SLAVE LABOR

	ORIG.	GOOD	FINE	N-MINT
1, b&w		0.59	1.77	2.95
4, Jul 95, b&w 2.95		0.59	1.77	2.95
5, Nov 95, b&w............ 2.95		0.59	1.77	2.95

JAX AND THE HELL HOUND
BLACKTHORNE

	ORIG.	GOOD	FINE	N-MINT
1		0.35	1.05	1.75
2		0.35	1.05	1.75
3		0.35	1.05	1.75

JAZZ AGE CHRONICLES
CALIBER

	ORIG.	GOOD	FINE	N-MINT
1, b&w 2.50		0.50	1.50	2.50
2, b&w 2.50		0.50	1.50	2.50
3, b&w 2.50		0.50	1.50	2.50
4, b&w 2.50		0.50	1.50	2.50
5, b&w 2.50		0.50	1.50	2.50
6, b&w 2.50		0.50	1.50	2.50

EF GRAPHICS

	ORIG.	GOOD	FINE	N-MINT
1		0.30	0.90	1.50
2		0.30	0.90	1.50
3		0.30	0.90	1.50

JCP FEATURES
J.C.

	ORIG.	GOOD	FINE	N-MINT
1, Feb 81, THUNDER Agents, rep:S&K,NA,DG				
.... 2.00		1.00	3.00	5.00

JEFFERY DAHMER: AN UNAUTHORIZED BIOGRAPHY OF A SERIAL KILLER
BONEYARD PRESS

	ORIG.	GOOD	FINE	N-MINT
0 .... 2.50		0.50	1.50	2.50

JEMM, SON OF SATURN
DC

	ORIG.	GOOD	FINE	N-MINT
1, Sep 84, GC/KJ		0.30	0.90	1.50
2, Oct 84		0.20	0.60	1.00
3, Nov 84		0.20	0.60	1.00
4, Dec 84		0.20	0.60	1.00
5, Jan 85		0.20	0.60	1.00
6, Feb 85		0.20	0.60	1.00
7, Mar 85		0.20	0.60	1.00
8, Apr 85		0.20	0.60	1.00
9, May 85		0.20	0.60	1.00
10, Jun 85		0.20	0.60	1.00
11, Jul 85		0.20	0.60	1.00
12, Aug 85		0.20	0.60	1.00

JEREMIAH: A FISTFUL OF SAND
ADVENTURE

	ORIG.	GOOD	FINE	N-MINT
1, b&w..............................		0.50	1.50	2.50
2, b&w..............................		0.50	1.50	2.50

JEREMIAH: BIRDS OF PREY
ADVENTURE

	ORIG.	GOOD	FINE	N-MINT
1, b&w..............................		0.50	1.50	2.50
2, b&w..............................		0.50	1.50	2.50

JEREMIAH: THE HEIRS

	ORIG.	GOOD	FINE	N-MINT
1, b&w..............................		0.50	1.50	2.50
2, b&w..............................		0.50	1.50	2.50

JERRY IGER'S FAMOUS FEATURES
PACIFIC

	ORIG.	GOOD	FINE	N-MINT
1, Jul 84, Flamingo		0.30	0.90	1.50

JERRY IGER'S GOLDEN FEATURES
BLACKTHORNE

	ORIG.	GOOD	FINE	N-MINT
1, 86		0.40	1.20	2.00
2, 86		0.40	1.20	2.00
3, Jun 86		0.40	1.20	2.00
4, Aug 86		0.40	1.20	2.00
5, Oct 86		0.40	1.20	2.00
6		0.40	1.20	2.00

	ORIG.	GOOD	FINE	N-MINT

JESSE JAMES
AC
	ORIG.	GOOD	FINE	N-MINT
❏ 1, reprint, b&w;JKu.........	0.79	2.37	3.95	

JETSONS BIG BOOK, THE
HARVEY
	ORIG.	GOOD	FINE	N-MINT
❏ 1 .... 1.95	0.39	1.17	1.95	
❏ 2 .... 1.95	0.39	1.17	1.95	
❏ 3 .... 1.95	0.39	1.17	1.95	

JETSONS GIANT SIZE
	ORIG.	GOOD	FINE	N-MINT
❏ 2 .... 2.25	0.45	1.35	2.25	
❏ 3 .... 2.25	0.45	1.35	2.25	

JETSONS, THE
ARCHIE
	ORIG.	GOOD	FINE	N-MINT
❏ 1, Sep 95, A:The Flintstones				
.... 1.50	0.30	0.90	1.50	
❏ 2, Oct 95 .... 1.50	0.30	0.90	1.50	
❏ 3, Nov 95 .... 1.50	0.30	0.90	1.50	
❏ 4, Dec 95...................... 1.50	0.30	0.90	1.50	
❏ 5, Jan 96 .... 1.50	0.30	0.90	1.50	
❏ 6, Feb 96 .... 1.50	0.30	0.90	1.50	
❏ 7, Mar 96 .... 1.50	0.30	0.90	1.50	
❏ 8, Apr 96 .... 1.50	0.30	0.90	1.50	

HARVEY
	ORIG.	GOOD	FINE	N-MINT
❏ 1 .... 1.25	0.25	0.75	1.25	
❏ 2 .... 1.25	0.25	0.75	1.25	
❏ 3 .... 1.25	0.25	0.75	1.25	
❏ 4 .... 1.25	0.25	0.75	1.25	
❏ 5 .... 1.50	0.30	0.90	1.50	

JEZEBEL JADE
COMICO
	ORIG.	GOOD	FINE	N-MINT
❏ 1, Oct 88 .... 2.00	0.40	1.20	2.00	
❏ 2, Nov 88 .... 2.00	0.40	1.20	2.00	
❏ 3, Dec 88...................... 2.00	0.40	1.20	2.00	

JIM
FANTAGRAPHICS
	ORIG.	GOOD	FINE	N-MINT
❏ 1	0.45	1.35	2.25	
❏ 2	0.45	1.35	2.25	
❏ 3	0.45	1.35	2.25	
❏ 4	0.45	1.35	2.25	

JIM (Volume 2)
	ORIG.	GOOD	FINE	N-MINT
❏ 1, Dec 93, b&w 2.95	0.59	1.77	2.95	

JIM LEE'S WILDC.A.T.S
IMAGE
	ORIG.	GOOD	FINE	N-MINT
❏ 1, Apr 95, No cover price; informational comic for San Diego Police Dept......				

JIMBO
BONGO/ZONGO
	ORIG.	GOOD	FINE	N-MINT
❏ 1, 95, b&w;adults........... 2.95	0.59	1.77	2.95	
❏ 2, 95, b&w;adults........... 2.95	0.59	1.77	2.95	
❏ 3, 95, indicia says "#2" ... 2.95	0.59	1.77	2.95	

JIZZ
FANTAGRAPHICS
	ORIG.	GOOD	FINE	N-MINT
❏ 1, b&w, adult	0.40	1.20	2.00	
❏ 2, b&w, adult	0.40	1.20	2.00	
❏ 3, b&w, adult	0.40	1.20	2.00	
❏ 4, b&w, adult	0.40	1.20	2.00	
❏ 5	0.45	1.35	2.25	
❏ 6	0.45	1.35	2.25	
❏ 7	0.45	1.35	2.25	
❏ 8	0.50	1.50	2.50	
❏ 9	0.59	1.77	2.95	
❏ 10, b&w	0.50	1.50	2.50	

JLX
DC/AMALGAM
	ORIG.	GOOD	FINE	N-MINT
❏ 1, Apr 96 .... 1.95	0.39	1.17	1.95	

JOE DIMAGGIO
CELEBRITY
	ORIG.	GOOD	FINE	N-MINT
❏ 1, trading cards................	1.39	4.17	6.95	

	ORIG.	GOOD	FINE	N-MINT

JOE KUBERT'S TOR
EPIC
	ORIG.	GOOD	FINE	N-MINT
❏ 1, large size 5.95	1.19	3.57	5.95	
❏ 2, large size 5.95	1.19	3.57	5.95	
❏ 3, large size 5.95	1.19	3.57	5.95	
❏ 4, large size 5.95	1.19	3.57	5.95	

JOE SINN
CALIBER
	ORIG.	GOOD	FINE	N-MINT
❏ 1, b&w 2.95	0.59	1.77	2.95	
❏ 1, limited edition 5.95	1.19	3.57	5.95	
❏ 2, b&w 2.95	0.59	1.77	2.95	

JOHN BOLTON HALLS OF HORROR
ECLIPSE
	ORIG.	GOOD	FINE	N-MINT
❏ 1 .... 1.75	0.50	1.50	2.50	
❏ 2 .... 1.75	0.50	1.50	2.50	

JOHN BYRNE'S NEXT MEN
DARK HORSE
	ORIG.	GOOD	FINE	N-MINT
❏ 0, Feb 92 .... 2.50	1.20	3.60	6.00	
❏ 1, Jan 92 .... 2.50	1.60	4.80	8.00	
❏ 2, Mar 92 .... 2.50	1.00	3.00	5.00	
❏ 3, Apr 92 .... 2.50	1.00	3.00	5.00	
❏ 4, May 92 .... 2.50	0.80	2.40	4.00	
❏ 5, Jun 92 .... 2.50	0.80	2.40	4.00	
❏ 6, Jul 92 .... 2.50	0.60	1.80	3.00	
❏ 7, Sep 92 .... 2.50	0.60	1.80	3.00	
❏ 8, Oct 92 .... 2.50	0.60	1.80	3.00	
❏ 9, Nov 92 .... 2.50	0.50	1.50	2.50	
❏ 10, Dec 92 .... 2.50	0.50	1.50	2.50	
❏ 11, Jan 93 .... 2.50	0.50	1.50	2.50	
❏ 12, Feb 93 .... 2.50	0.50	1.50	2.50	
❏ 13, Mar 93 .... 2.50	0.50	1.50	2.50	
❏ 14, Apr 93, JBy 2.50	0.50	1.50	2.50	
❏ 15 .... 2.50	0.50	1.50	2.50	
❏ 16 .... 2.50	0.50	1.50	2.50	
❏ 17, Aug 93 .... 2.50	0.50	1.50	2.50	
❏ 18 .... 2.50	0.50	1.50	2.50	
❏ 19, "Faith" part 1 of 4 ...... 2.50	0.70	2.10	3.50	
❏ 20, "Faith" part 2 of 4 ...... 2.50	0.50	1.50	2.50	
❏ 21, Dec 93, "Faith" part 3 of 4;A:Hellboy				
.... 2.50	0.80	2.40	4.00	
❏ 22, "Faith" part 4 of 4 ...... 2.50	0.50	1.50	2.50	
❏ 23, Mar 94, "Power" part 1 of 4				
.... 2.50	0.50	1.50	2.50	
❏ 24, Apr 94, "Power" part 2 of 4				
.... 2.50	0.50	1.50	2.50	
❏ 25, May 94, "Power" part 3 of 4				
.... 2.50	0.50	1.50	2.50	
❏ 26, Jun 94, "Power" part 4 of 4				
.... 2.50	0.50	1.50	2.50	
❏ 27, Aug 94, "Lies" part 1 of 4				
.... 2.50	0.50	1.50	2.50	
❏ 28, Sep 94, "Lies" part 2 of 4				
.... 2.50	0.50	1.50	2.50	
❏ 29, Oct 94, "Lies" part 3 of 4				
.... 2.50	0.50	1.50	2.50	
❏ 30, Dec 94, "Lies" part 4 of 4				
.... 2.50	0.50	1.50	2.50	

JOHN CARTER OF MARS
MARVEL
	ORIG.	GOOD	FINE	N-MINT
❏ 1 .... 0.30	0.80	2.40	4.00	
❏ 2 .... 0.30	0.60	1.80	3.00	
❏ 3 .... 0.30	0.60	1.80	3.00	
❏ 4 .... 0.30	0.60	1.80	3.00	
❏ 5 .... 0.30	0.40	1.20	2.00	
❏ 6 .... 0.35	0.40	1.20	2.00	
❏ 7 .... 0.35	0.40	1.20	2.00	
❏ 8 .... 0.35	0.40	1.20	2.00	
❏ 9 .... 0.35	0.40	1.20	2.00	
❏ 10 .... 0.35	0.40	1.20	2.00	
❏ 11 .... 0.35	0.30	0.90	1.50	
❏ 12 .... 0.35	0.30	0.90	1.50	

	ORIG.	GOOD	FINE	N-MINT
❏ 13	0.35	0.30	0.90	1.50
❏ 14	0.35	0.30	0.90	1.50
❏ 15	0.35	0.30	0.90	1.50
❏ 16	0.35	0.30	0.90	1.50
❏ 17	0.35	0.30	0.90	1.50
❏ 18, FM	0.35	0.60	1.80	3.00
❏ 19	0.35	0.30	0.90	1.50
❏ 20	0.35	0.30	0.90	1.50
❏ 21	0.35	0.30	0.90	1.50
❏ 22	0.35	0.30	0.90	1.50
❏ 23	0.35	0.30	0.90	1.50
❏ 24	0.40	0.30	0.90	1.50
❏ 25	0.40	0.30	0.90	1.50
❏ 26	0.40	0.30	0.90	1.50
❏ 27	0.40	0.30	0.90	1.50
❏ 28	0.40	0.30	0.90	1.50

JOHN CARTER OF MARS ANNUAL

	ORIG.	GOOD	FINE	N-MINT
❏ 1	0.50	0.60	1.80	3.00
❏ 2	0.60	0.40	1.20	2.00
❏ 3	0.60	0.40	1.20	2.00

JOHN DIXON'S AIR HAWK MAGAZINE
COMICOZ

	GOOD	FINE	N-MINT
❏ 1, Australian	1.20	3.60	6.00
❏ 2	1.00	3.00	5.00
❏ 3	0.50	1.50	2.50
❏ 4	0.50	1.50	2.50
❏ 5	0.50	1.50	2.50
❏ 6	0.40	1.20	2.00

JOHN JAKES' MULLKON EMPIRE
TEKNO

	ORIG.	GOOD	FINE	N-MINT
❏ 1, Sep 95	1.95	0.39	1.17	1.95
❏ 2, Oct 95	1.95	0.39	1.17	1.95
❏ 3, Nov 95	1.95	0.39	1.17	1.95
❏ 4, Dec 95	1.95	0.39	1.17	1.95
❏ 6, Jan 96	2.25	0.45	1.35	2.25

JOHN LAW
ECLIPSE

	ORIG.	GOOD	FINE	N-MINT
❏ 1, Apr 83, WE	1.50	0.40	1.20	2.00

JOHNNY ATOMIC
ETERNITY

	GOOD	FINE	N-MINT
❏ 1, b&w	0.50	1.50	2.50
❏ 2, b&w	0.50	1.50	2.50
❏ 3, b&w	0.50	1.50	2.50

JOHNNY DYNAMITE (mini-series)
DARK HORSE

	ORIG.	GOOD	FINE	N-MINT
❏ 1, Sep 94, b&w&red	2.95	0.59	1.77	2.95
❏ 2, Oct 94, b&w&red	2.95	0.59	1.77	2.95
❏ 3, Nov 94, b&w&red	2.95	0.59	1.77	2.95
❏ 4, Dec 94, b&w&red	2.95	0.59	1.77	2.95

JOHNNY GAMBIT
HOT

	GOOD	FINE	N-MINT
❏ 1	0.35	1.05	1.75

JOHNNY HAZARD
PIONEER

	GOOD	FINE	N-MINT
❏ 1, HC(c) b&w	0.40	1.20	2.00

JOHNNY HAZARD QUARTERLY
DRAGON LADY

	GOOD	FINE	N-MINT
❏ 1, ATh(c)	1.19	3.57	5.95
❏ 2, ATh(c)	1.19	3.57	5.95
❏ 3, ATh(c)	1.19	3.57	5.95
❏ 4, ATh(c)	1.19	3.57	5.95

JOHNNY NEMO
ECLIPSE

	GOOD	FINE	N-MINT
❏ 1	0.55	1.65	2.75
❏ 2	0.55	1.65	2.75
❏ 3	0.55	1.65	2.75

JOHNNY THUNDER
DC

	ORIG.	GOOD	FINE	N-MINT
❏ 1, Mar 73	0.20	0.80	2.40	4.00

	ORIG.	GOOD	FINE	N-MINT
❏ 2, May 73	0.20	0.50	1.50	2.50
❏ 3, Aug 73	0.20	0.50	1.50	2.50

JOKER, THE

	ORIG.	GOOD	FINE	N-MINT
❏ 1, May 75	0.25	3.20	9.60	16.00
❏ 2, Jul 75	0.25	2.40	7.20	12.00
❏ 3, Oct 75	0.25	2.00	6.00	10.00
❏ 4, Dec 75, V:Green Arrow	0.25	2.00	6.00	10.00
❏ 5, Feb 76	0.25	2.00	6.00	10.00
❏ 6, Apr 76	0.25	2.00	6.00	10.00
❏ 7, Jun 76	0.30	2.00	6.00	10.00
❏ 8, Aug 76	0.30	2.00	6.00	10.00
❏ 9, Sep 76	0.30	2.00	6.00	10.00

JOLLY JACK STARJUMPER SUMMER OF '92 ONE-SHOT, THE
CONQUEST

	GOOD	FINE	N-MINT
❏ 0, nn, b&w	0.59	1.77	2.95

JON SABLE, FREELANCE
FIRST

	ORIG.	GOOD	FINE	N-MINT
❏ 1, Jun 83, MGr	1.00	0.80	2.40	4.00
❏ 2, Jul 83, MGr	1.00	0.50	1.50	2.50
❏ 3, Aug 83, MGr	1.00	0.50	1.50	2.50
❏ 4, Sep 83, MGr	1.00	0.50	1.50	2.50
❏ 5, Oct 83, MGr	1.00	0.40	1.20	2.00
❏ 6, Nov 83, MGr	1.00	0.20	0.60	1.00
❏ 7, Dec 83, MGr	1.00	0.20	0.60	1.00
❏ 8, Jan 84, MGr	1.00	0.20	0.60	1.00
❏ 9, Feb 84, MGr	1.00	0.20	0.60	1.00
❏ 10, Mar 84, MGr	1.00	0.20	0.60	1.00
❏ 11, Apr 84, MGr	1.00	0.20	0.60	1.00
❏ 12, May 84, MGr	1.00	0.20	0.60	1.00
❏ 13, Jun 84, MGr	1.00	0.20	0.60	1.00
❏ 14, Jul 84, MGr	1.00	0.20	0.60	1.00
❏ 15, Aug 84, MGr	1.00	0.20	0.60	1.00
❏ 16, Sep 84, MGr	1.00	0.20	0.60	1.00
❏ 17, Oct 84, MGr	1.00	0.20	0.60	1.00
❏ 18, Oct 84, MGr	1.25	0.25	0.75	1.25
❏ 19, Dec 84, MGr	1.25	0.25	0.75	1.25
❏ 20, Jan 85, MGr	1.25	0.25	0.75	1.25
❏ 21, Feb 85, MGr	1.25	0.25	0.75	1.25
❏ 22, Mar 85, MGr	1.25	0.25	0.75	1.25
❏ 23, Apr 85, MGr	1.25	0.25	0.75	1.25
❏ 24, May 85, MGr	1.25	0.25	0.75	1.25
❏ 25, Jun 85, MGr	1.25	0.25	0.75	1.25
❏ 26, Jul 85, MGr	1.25	0.25	0.75	1.25
❏ 27, Aug 85, MGr	1.25	0.25	0.75	1.25
❏ 28, Sep 85, MGr	1.25	0.25	0.75	1.25
❏ 29, Oct 85, MGr	1.25	0.25	0.75	1.25
❏ 30, Nov 85, MGr	1.25	0.25	0.75	1.25
❏ 31, Dec 85, MGr	1.25	0.25	0.75	1.25
❏ 32, Jan 86, MGr	1.25	0.25	0.75	1.25
❏ 33, Feb 86, MGr	1.25	0.35	1.05	1.75
❏ 34, Mar 86, MGr	1.75	0.35	1.05	1.75
❏ 35, Apr 86, MGr	1.75	0.35	1.05	1.75
❏ 36, May 86, MGr	1.75	0.35	1.05	1.75
❏ 37, Jun 86, MGr	1.75	0.35	1.05	1.75
❏ 38, Jul 86, MGr	1.75	0.35	1.05	1.75
❏ 39, Aug 86, MGr	1.75	0.35	1.05	1.75
❏ 40, Sep 86, MGr	1.75	0.35	1.05	1.75
❏ 41, Oct 86, MGr	1.75	0.35	1.05	1.75
❏ 42, Nov 86, MGr	1.75	0.35	1.05	1.75
❏ 43, Dec 86, MGr	1.75	0.35	1.05	1.75
❏ 44, Jan 87, MGr(c)	1.75	0.35	1.05	1.75
❏ 45, Mar 87, MGr(c)	1.75	0.35	1.05	1.75
❏ 46, Apr 87, MGr(c)	1.75	0.35	1.05	1.75
❏ 47, May 87, MGr(c)	1.75	0.35	1.05	1.75
❏ 48, Jun 87, MGr(c)	1.75	0.35	1.05	1.75
❏ 49, Jul 87, MGr(c)	1.75	0.35	1.05	1.75
❏ 50, Aug 87, MGr(c)	1.75	0.35	1.05	1.75
❏ 51, Sep 87, MGr(c)	1.75	0.35	1.05	1.75
❏ 52, Oct 87, MGr(c)	1.75	0.35	1.05	1.75

	ORIG.	GOOD	FINE	N-MINT
☐ 53, Nov 87, MGr(c) 1.75		0.35	1.05	1.75
☐ 54, Dec 87, MGr(c) 1.75		0.35	1.05	1.75
☐ 55, Jan 88, MGr(c) 1.75		0.35	1.05	1.75
☐ 56, Feb 88, MGr(c) (becomes Sable)				
.... 1.75		0.35	1.05	1.75

JONAH HEX
DC

	ORIG.	GOOD	FINE	N-MINT
☐ 1, Apr 77 .... 0.30		9.60	28.80	48.00
☐ 2, Jun 77 .... 0.30		6.00	18.00	30.00
☐ 3, Aug 77 .... 0.35		4.00	12.00	20.00
☐ 4, Sep 77 .... 0.35		4.00	12.00	20.00
☐ 5, Sep 77 .... 0.35		4.00	12.00	20.00
☐ 6		2.40	7.20	12.00
☐ 7		2.40	7.20	12.00
☐ 8		2.40	7.20	12.00
☐ 9		2.40	7.20	12.00
☐ 10		2.40	7.20	12.00
☐ 11		2.00	6.00	10.00
☐ 12		2.00	6.00	10.00
☐ 13		2.00	6.00	10.00
☐ 14		2.00	6.00	10.00
☐ 15		2.00	6.00	10.00
☐ 21		1.20	3.60	6.00
☐ 22		1.20	3.60	6.00
☐ 23		1.20	3.60	6.00
☐ 24		1.20	3.60	6.00
☐ 25		1.20	3.60	6.00
☐ 26		1.20	3.60	6.00
☐ 27		1.20	3.60	6.00
☐ 28		1.20	3.60	6.00
☐ 29		1.20	3.60	6.00
☐ 30		1.20	3.60	6.00
☐ 31		1.00	3.00	5.00
☐ 32, Jan 80 .... 0.40		1.00	3.00	5.00
☐ 33		1.00	3.00	5.00
☐ 34		1.00	3.00	5.00
☐ 35		1.00	3.00	5.00
☐ 36		1.00	3.00	5.00
☐ 37		1.00	3.00	5.00
☐ 38		1.00	3.00	5.00
☐ 39		1.00	3.00	5.00
☐ 40		1.00	3.00	5.00
☐ 41		1.00	3.00	5.00
☐ 42		1.00	3.00	5.00
☐ 43		1.00	3.00	5.00
☐ 44		1.00	3.00	5.00
☐ 45		1.00	3.00	5.00
☐ 46		1.00	3.00	5.00
☐ 47		1.00	3.00	5.00
☐ 48		1.00	3.00	5.00
☐ 49		1.00	3.00	5.00
☐ 50		1.00	3.00	5.00
☐ 51		0.80	2.40	4.00
☐ 52		0.80	2.40	4.00
☐ 53		0.80	2.40	4.00
☐ 54		0.80	2.40	4.00
☐ 55		0.80	2.40	4.00
☐ 56		0.80	2.40	4.00
☐ 57		0.80	2.40	4.00
☐ 58		0.80	2.40	4.00
☐ 59		0.80	2.40	4.00
☐ 60		0.80	2.40	4.00
☐ 61		0.80	2.40	4.00
☐ 62		0.80	2.40	4.00
☐ 63		0.80	2.40	4.00
☐ 64		0.80	2.40	4.00
☐ 65		0.80	2.40	4.00
☐ 66		0.80	2.40	4.00
☐ 67		0.80	2.40	4.00
☐ 68		0.80	2.40	4.00
☐ 69		0.80	2.40	4.00

	ORIG.	GOOD	FINE	N-MINT
☐ 70		0.80	2.40	4.00
☐ 71		0.80	2.40	4.00
☐ 72		0.80	2.40	4.00
☐ 73		0.80	2.40	4.00
☐ 74		0.80	2.40	4.00
☐ 75		0.80	2.40	4.00
☐ 76		0.80	2.40	4.00
☐ 77		0.80	2.40	4.00
☐ 78		0.80	2.40	4.00
☐ 79		0.80	2.40	4.00
☐ 80		0.80	2.40	4.00
☐ 81		0.80	2.40	4.00
☐ 82		0.80	2.40	4.00
☐ 83		0.80	2.40	4.00
☐ 84		0.80	2.40	4.00
☐ 85		0.80	2.40	4.00
☐ 86		0.80	2.40	4.00
☐ 87		0.80	2.40	4.00
☐ 88		0.80	2.40	4.00
☐ 89		0.80	2.40	4.00
☐ 90		0.80	2.40	4.00
☐ 91		0.80	2.40	4.00
☐ 92		0.80	2.40	4.00

JONAH HEX AND OTHER WESTERN TALES

	ORIG.	GOOD	FINE	N-MINT
☐ 1, Oct 79 .... 0.95		0.60	1.80	3.00
☐ 2, Dec 79 .... 0.95		1.00	3.00	5.00
☐ 3, Feb 80 .... 0.95		0.40	1.20	2.00

JONAH HEX: RIDERS OF THE WORM AND SUCH
(mini-series)
DC/VERTIGO

	ORIG.	GOOD	FINE	N-MINT
☐ 1, Mar 95 .... 2.95		0.59	1.77	2.95
☐ 2, Apr 95 .... 2.95		0.59	1.77	2.95
☐ 3, May 95 .... 2.95		0.59	1.77	2.95
☐ 4, Jun 95 .... 2.95		0.59	1.77	2.95
☐ 5, Jul 95 .... 2.95		0.59	1.77	2.95

JONAH HEX: TWO-GUN MOJO

	ORIG.	GOOD	FINE	N-MINT
☐ 1 .... 2.95		1.60	4.80	8.00
☐ 1, platinum		3.60	10.80	18.00
☐ 2 .... 1.95		1.20	3.60	6.00
☐ 3 .... 1.95		1.00	3.00	5.00
☐ 4 .... 2.95		1.00	3.00	5.00
☐ 5 .... 2.95		1.00	3.00	5.00

JONATHAN FOX
MARIAH GRAPHICS

	ORIG.	GOOD	FINE	N-MINT
☐ 1 .... 2.00		0.40	1.20	2.00

JONES TOUCH
EROS

	ORIG.	GOOD	FINE	N-MINT
☐ 1, adult 2.75		0.55	1.65	2.75

JONNI THUNDER
DC

	ORIG.	GOOD	FINE	N-MINT
☐ 1, Feb 85, DG, origin 0.75		0.20	0.60	1.00
☐ 2, Apr 85, DG 0.75		0.20	0.60	1.00
☐ 3, Jun 85, DG 0.75		0.20	0.60	1.00
☐ 4, Aug 85, DG 0.75		0.20	0.60	1.00

JONNY DEMON
DARK HORSE

	ORIG.	GOOD	FINE	N-MINT
☐ 1, May 94 .... 2.50		0.50	1.50	2.50
☐ 2, Jun 94 .... 2.50		0.50	1.50	2.50
☐ 3, Jul 94 .... 2.50		0.50	1.50	2.50

JONNY QUEST
COMICO

	ORIG.	GOOD	FINE	N-MINT
☐ 1, Jun 86 .... 1.50		1.60	4.80	8.00
☐ 2, Jul 86 .... 1.50		1.20	3.60	6.00
☐ 3, Aug 86, DSt(c) 1.50		1.00	3.00	5.00
☐ 4, Sep 86 .... 1.50		1.00	3.00	5.00
☐ 5, Oct 86, DSt(c) 1.50		1.00	3.00	5.00
☐ 6, Nov 86 .... 1.50		0.80	2.40	4.00
☐ 7, Dec 86 .... 1.50		0.80	2.40	4.00
☐ 8, Jan 87 .... 1.50		0.80	2.40	4.00
☐ 9, Feb 87 .... 1.50		0.80	2.40	4.00

	ORIG.	GOOD	FINE	N-MINT
10, Mar 87 .... 1.50		0.80	2.40	4.00
11, Apr 87, BSz(c).......... 1.50		0.60	1.80	3.00
12, May 87 .... 1.50		0.60	1.80	3.00
13, Jun 87, CI 1.50		0.60	1.80	3.00
14, Jul 87 .... 1.50		0.60	1.80	3.00
15, Aug 87 .... 1.75		0.60	1.80	3.00
16, Sep 87 .... 1.75		0.60	1.80	3.00
17, Oct 87 .... 1.75		0.60	1.80	3.00
18, Nov 87 .... 1.75		0.60	1.80	3.00
19, Dec 87 .... 1.75		0.60	1.80	3.00
20, Jan 88 .... 1.75		0.60	1.80	3.00
21, Feb 88 .... 1.75		0.60	1.80	3.00
22, Mar 88 .... 1.75		0.60	1.80	3.00
23, Apr 88 .... 1.75		0.60	1.80	3.00
24, May 88 .... 1.75		0.60	1.80	3.00
25, Jun 88 .... 1.75		0.60	1.80	3.00
26, Jul 88 .... 1.75		0.60	1.80	3.00
27, Aug 88 .... 1.75		0.60	1.80	3.00
28, Sep 88 .... 1.75		0.60	1.80	3.00
29, Oct 88 .... 1.75		0.60	1.80	3.00
30, Nov 88 .... 1.75		0.60	1.80	3.00
31, Dec 88 .... 1.75		0.60	1.80	3.00

JONNY QUEST CLASSICS

	ORIG.	GOOD	FINE	N-MINT
1, May 87, Doug Wildey . 2.00		0.40	1.20	2.00
2, Jun 87, Doug Wildey .. 2.00		0.40	1.20	2.00
3, Jul 87, Doug Wildey ... 2.00		0.40	1.20	2.00

JONNY QUEST SPECIAL

	ORIG.	GOOD	FINE	N-MINT
1, Sep 88 .... 1.95		0.39	1.17	1.95
2, Oct 88 .... 1.95		0.39	1.17	1.95

JONTAR RETURNS
MILLER

	GOOD	FINE	N-MINT
1, b&w	0.40	1.20	2.00
2, b&w	0.40	1.20	2.00
3, b&w	0.40	1.20	2.00
4, b&w	0.40	1.20	2.00

JOSIE
ARCHIE

	GOOD	FINE	N-MINT
17, (was *She's Josie*)	1.20	3.60	6.00
18	1.20	3.60	6.00
19	1.20	3.60	6.00
20	1.20	3.60	6.00
21	1.00	3.00	5.00
22	1.00	3.00	5.00
23	1.00	3.00	5.00
24	1.00	3.00	5.00
25	1.00	3.00	5.00
26	1.00	3.00	5.00
27	1.00	3.00	5.00
28	1.00	3.00	5.00
29	1.00	3.00	5.00
30	1.00	3.00	5.00
31	1.00	3.00	5.00
32	1.00	3.00	5.00
33	1.00	3.00	5.00
34	1.00	3.00	5.00
35	1.00	3.00	5.00
36	1.00	3.00	5.00
37	1.00	3.00	5.00
38	1.00	3.00	5.00
39	1.00	3.00	5.00
40	1.00	3.00	5.00
41	1.00	3.00	5.00
42	1.00	3.00	5.00
43	1.00	3.00	5.00
44, (becomes *Josie & the Pussycats*)			
....	1.00	3.00	5.00

JOSIE & THE PUSSYCATS

	GOOD	FINE	N-MINT
45, (was *Josie*)	0.80	2.40	4.00
46	0.80	2.40	4.00
47	0.80	2.40	4.00

	ORIG.	GOOD	FINE	N-MINT
48		0.80	2.40	4.00
49		0.80	2.40	4.00
50		0.80	2.40	4.00
51		0.80	2.40	4.00
52		0.80	2.40	4.00
53		0.80	2.40	4.00
54		0.80	2.40	4.00
55		0.80	2.40	4.00
56		0.80	2.40	4.00
57		0.80	2.40	4.00
58		0.80	2.40	4.00
59		0.80	2.40	4.00
60		0.80	2.40	4.00
61		0.60	1.80	3.00
62		0.60	1.80	3.00
63		0.60	1.80	3.00
64		0.60	1.80	3.00
65		0.60	1.80	3.00
66		0.60	1.80	3.00
67		0.60	1.80	3.00
68		0.60	1.80	3.00
69		0.60	1.80	3.00
70		0.60	1.80	3.00
71		0.60	1.80	3.00
72		0.60	1.80	3.00
73		0.60	1.80	3.00
74		0.60	1.80	3.00
75		0.60	1.80	3.00
76		0.40	1.20	2.00
77		0.40	1.20	2.00
78		0.40	1.20	2.00
79		0.40	1.20	2.00
80		0.40	1.20	2.00
81		0.40	1.20	2.00
82		0.40	1.20	2.00
83		0.40	1.20	2.00
84		0.40	1.20	2.00
85		0.40	1.20	2.00
86		0.40	1.20	2.00
87		0.40	1.20	2.00
88		0.40	1.20	2.00
89		0.40	1.20	2.00
90		0.40	1.20	2.00
91		0.40	1.20	2.00
92		0.40	1.20	2.00
93		0.40	1.20	2.00
94		0.40	1.20	2.00
95		0.40	1.20	2.00
96		0.40	1.20	2.00
97		0.40	1.20	2.00
98		0.40	1.20	2.00
99		0.40	1.20	2.00
100		0.40	1.20	2.00
101		0.40	1.20	2.00
102		0.40	1.20	2.00
103		0.40	1.20	2.00
104		0.40	1.20	2.00
105		0.40	1.20	2.00
106		0.40	1.20	2.00

JOSIE & THE PUSSYCATS (1993-)

	ORIG.	GOOD	FINE	N-MINT
1 ....2.00		0.40	1.20	2.00
2 ....2.00		0.40	1.20	2.00

JOURNEY
AARDVARK-VANAHEIM

	ORIG.	GOOD	FINE	N-MINT
1, Mar 83 .... 1.60		2.40	7.20	12.00
2		1.60	4.80	8.00
3		1.60	4.80	8.00
4		1.60	4.80	8.00
5		1.00	3.00	5.00
6		1.00	3.00	5.00
7		1.00	3.00	5.00

	ORIG.	GOOD	FINE	N-MINT
☐ 8		1.00	3.00	5.00
☐ 9		1.00	3.00	5.00
☐ 10		1.00	3.00	5.00
☐ 11		1.00	3.00	5.00
☐ 12		1.00	3.00	5.00
☐ 13		1.00	3.00	5.00
☐ 14, (moves to Fantagraphics)		1.00	3.00	5.00

JOURNEY (former Aardvark-Vanaheim title)
FANTAGRAPHICS

	ORIG.	GOOD	FINE	N-MINT
☐ 15		0.40	1.20	2.00
☐ 16		0.40	1.20	2.00
☐ 17		0.40	1.20	2.00
☐ 18		0.40	1.20	2.00
☐ 19		0.40	1.20	2.00
☐ 20		0.40	1.20	2.00
☐ 21		0.40	1.20	2.00
☐ 22		0.40	1.20	2.00
☐ 23		0.40	1.20	2.00
☐ 24		0.40	1.20	2.00
☐ 25		0.40	1.20	2.00
☐ 26		0.40	1.20	2.00
☐ 27		0.40	1.20	2.00

JOURNEY INTO MYSTERY
MARVEL

	ORIG.	GOOD	FINE	N-MINT
☐ 1	0.10	320.00	960.00	1600.00
☐ 2	0.10	120.00	360.00	600.00
☐ 3	0.10	100.00	300.00	500.00
☐ 4	0.10	80.00	240.00	400.00
☐ 5	0.10	80.00	240.00	400.00
☐ 6	0.10	60.00	180.00	300.00
☐ 7	0.10	60.00	180.00	300.00
☐ 8	0.10	48.00	144.00	240.00
☐ 9	0.10	48.00	144.00	240.00
☐ 10	0.10	48.00	144.00	240.00
☐ 11	0.10	40.00	120.00	200.00
☐ 12	0.10	40.00	120.00	200.00
☐ 13	0.10	40.00	120.00	200.00
☐ 14	0.10	40.00	120.00	200.00
☐ 15	0.10	40.00	120.00	200.00
☐ 16	0.10	40.00	120.00	200.00
☐ 17	0.10	40.00	120.00	200.00
☐ 18	0.10	40.00	120.00	200.00
☐ 19	0.10	40.00	120.00	200.00
☐ 20	0.10	40.00	120.00	200.00
☐ 21	0.10	45.00	135.00	225.00
☐ 22	0.10	30.00	90.00	150.00
☐ 23	0.10	20.00	60.00	100.00
☐ 24	0.10	20.00	60.00	100.00
☐ 25	0.10	20.00	60.00	100.00
☐ 26	0.10	20.00	60.00	100.00
☐ 27	0.10	20.00	60.00	100.00
☐ 28	0.10	20.00	60.00	100.00
☐ 29	0.10	20.00	60.00	100.00
☐ 30	0.10	20.00	60.00	100.00
☐ 31	0.10	20.00	60.00	100.00
☐ 32	0.10	20.00	60.00	100.00
☐ 33	0.10	20.00	60.00	100.00
☐ 34	0.10	20.00	60.00	100.00
☐ 35	0.10	18.00	54.00	90.00
☐ 36	0.10	18.00	54.00	90.00
☐ 37	0.10	18.00	54.00	90.00
☐ 38	0.10	18.00	54.00	90.00
☐ 39	0.10	20.00	60.00	100.00
☐ 40	0.10	18.00	54.00	90.00
☐ 41	0.10	15.00	45.00	75.00
☐ 42	0.10	15.00	45.00	75.00
☐ 43	0.10	15.00	45.00	75.00
☐ 44	0.10	15.00	45.00	75.00
☐ 45	0.10	15.00	45.00	75.00
☐ 46	0.10	15.00	45.00	75.00
☐ 47	0.10	15.00	45.00	75.00

	ORIG.	GOOD	FINE	N-MINT
☐ 48	0.10	15.00	45.00	75.00
☐ 49	0.10	15.00	45.00	75.00
☐ 50	0.10	15.00	45.00	75.00
☐ 51	0.10	12.00	36.00	60.00
☐ 52	0.10	12.00	36.00	60.00
☐ 53	0.10	12.00	36.00	60.00
☐ 54	0.10	12.00	36.00	60.00
☐ 55	0.10	12.00	36.00	60.00
☐ 56	0.10	12.00	36.00	60.00
☐ 57	0.10	12.00	36.00	60.00
☐ 58	0.10	12.00	36.00	60.00
☐ 59	0.10	12.00	36.00	60.00
☐ 60	0.10	12.00	36.00	60.00
☐ 61	0.10	12.00	36.00	60.00
☐ 62	0.10	18.00	54.00	90.00
☐ 63	0.10	12.00	36.00	60.00
☐ 64	0.10	12.00	36.00	60.00
☐ 65	0.10	12.00	36.00	60.00
☐ 66	0.10	12.00	36.00	60.00
☐ 67	0.10	12.00	36.00	60.00
☐ 68	0.10	12.00	36.00	60.00
☐ 69	0.10	12.00	36.00	60.00
☐ 70	0.10	12.00	36.00	60.00
☐ 71	0.10	12.00	36.00	60.00
☐ 72	0.10	12.00	36.00	60.00
☐ 73	0.10	12.00	36.00	60.00
☐ 74	0.10	12.00	36.00	60.00
☐ 75	0.10	12.00	36.00	60.00
☐ 76	0.12	10.00	30.00	50.00
☐ 77	0.12	10.00	30.00	50.00
☐ 78	0.12	10.00	30.00	50.00
☐ 79	0.12	10.00	30.00	50.00
☐ 80	0.12	10.00	30.00	50.00
☐ 81	0.12	10.00	30.00	50.00
☐ 82	0.12	10.00	30.00	50.00
☐ 83, JK/SD, O:I:Thor	0.12	720.00	2160.00	3600.00
☐ 84, JK/SD/DH, I:Executioner	0.12	170.00	510.00	850.00
☐ 85, JK/SD, 1:Loki	0.12	100.00	300.00	500.00
☐ 86, JK/SD/DH, 1:Odin	0.12	64.00	192.00	320.00
☐ 87, JK/SD	0.12	28.00	84.00	140.00
☐ 88, JK/SD	0.12	28.00	84.00	140.00
☐ 89, JK/SD	0.12	28.00	84.00	140.00
☐ 90, SD, 1:Carbon-Copy	0.12	16.00	48.00	80.00
☐ 91, JSt/SD, 1:Sandu	0.12	14.00	42.00	70.00
☐ 92, JSt/SD, Loki	0.12	18.00	54.00	90.00
☐ 93, JK/SD, 1:Radioactive Man	0.12	18.00	54.00	90.00
☐ 94, JSt/SD, Loki	0.12	14.00	42.00	70.00
☐ 95, JSt/SD, Merlin	0.12	12.00	36.00	60.00
☐ 96, JSt/SD, Merlin	0.12	12.00	36.00	60.00
☐ 97, JK	0.12	16.00	48.00	80.00
☐ 98, JK	0.12	16.00	48.00	80.00
☐ 99, JK	0.12	16.00	48.00	80.00
☐ 100, JK	0.12	16.00	48.00	80.00
☐ 101, JK, Iron Man, Giant Man	0.12	9.00	27.00	45.00
☐ 102, JK	0.12	9.00	27.00	45.00
☐ 103, JK	0.12	9.00	27.00	45.00
☐ 104, JK, giants	0.12	9.00	27.00	45.00
☐ 105, JK, Hyde, Cobra	0.12	9.00	27.00	45.00
☐ 106, JK, O:Balder	0.12	9.00	27.00	45.00
☐ 107, JK, I:Grey Gargoyle	0.12	9.00	27.00	45.00
☐ 108, JK, Dr. Strange	0.12	9.00	27.00	45.00
☐ 109, JK, Magneto	0.12	12.00	36.00	60.00
☐ 110, JK, Hyde-Cobra-Loki	0.12	9.00	27.00	45.00
☐ 111, JK, Hyde-Cobra-Loki	0.12	8.00	24.00	40.00
☐ 112, JK, Hulk	0.12	20.00	60.00	100.00
☐ 113, JK, Grey Gargoyle	0.12	8.00	24.00	40.00

	ORIG.	GOOD	FINE	N-MINT
☐ 114, JK, 1:Absorbing Man				
.... 0.12	8.00	24.00	40.00
☐ 115, JK, O:Loki 0.12	8.00	24.00	40.00
☐ 116, JK, Loki, Daredevil . 0.12	8.00	24.00	40.00
☐ 117, JK, Loki................. 0.12	8.00	24.00	40.00
☐ 118, JK, 1st Destroyer ... 0.12	8.00	24.00	40.00
☐ 119, JK........................ 0.12	8.00	24.00	40.00
☐ 120, JK........................ 0.12	8.00	24.00	40.00
☐ 121, JK........................ 0.12	8.00	24.00	40.00
☐ 122, JK........................ 0.12	8.00	24.00	40.00
☐ 123, JK........................ 0.12	8.00	24.00	40.00
☐ 124, JK........................ 0.12	8.00	24.00	40.00
☐ 125, JK (becomes *Thor*) 0.12	8.00	24.00	40.00

JOURNEY INTO MYSTERY
(second series, beginning 1972)

	ORIG.	GOOD	FINE	N-MINT
☐ 1, Oct 72........................ 0.20	0.20	0.60	1.00
☐ 2 .... 0.20	0.20	0.60	1.00
☐ 3 .... 0.20	0.20	0.60	1.00
☐ 4 .... 0.20	0.20	0.60	1.00
☐ 5 .... 0.20	0.20	0.60	1.00
☐ 6 .... 0.20	0.20	0.60	1.00
☐ 7 .... 0.20	0.20	0.60	1.00
☐ 8 .... 0.20	0.20	0.60	1.00
☐ 9 .... 0.20	0.20	0.60	1.00
☐ 10 .... 0.20	0.20	0.60	1.00
☐ 11 .... 0.25	0.20	0.60	1.00
☐ 12 .... 0.25	0.20	0.60	1.00
☐ 13 .... 0.25	0.20	0.60	1.00
☐ 14 .... 0.25	0.20	0.60	1.00
☐ 15 .... 0.25	0.20	0.60	1.00
☐ 16 .... 0.25	0.20	0.60	1.00
☐ 17 .... 0.25	0.20	0.60	1.00
☐ 18 .... 0.25	0.20	0.60	1.00
☐ 19 .... 0.25	0.20	0.60	1.00

JOURNEY INTO MYSTERY KING-SIZE ANNUAL
(1965)

	ORIG.	GOOD	FINE	N-MINT
☐ 1, 65, JK, I:Hercules (becomes *Thor Annual*)				
.... 0.25	20.00	60.00	100.00

JOURNEY: WARDRUMS
FANTAGRAPHICS

	ORIG.	GOOD	FINE	N-MINT
☐ 1	0.40	1.20	2.00
☐ 2	0.40	1.20	2.00

JUDGE DREDD
EAGLE

	ORIG.	GOOD	FINE	N-MINT
☐ 1, Nov 83, BB................. 1.00	2.80	8.40	14.00
☐ 2, BB	2.00	6.00	10.00
☐ 3, BB	1.60	4.80	8.00
☐ 4, BB	1.60	4.80	8.00
☐ 5	1.20	3.60	6.00
☐ 6	1.20	3.60	6.00
☐ 7	1.20	3.60	6.00
☐ 8	1.20	3.60	6.00
☐ 9	1.20	3.60	6.00
☐ 10	1.20	3.60	6.00
☐ 11	0.80	2.40	4.00
☐ 12	0.80	2.40	4.00
☐ 13	0.80	2.40	4.00
☐ 14	0.80	2.40	4.00
☐ 15	0.80	2.40	4.00
☐ 16	0.80	2.40	4.00
☐ 17	0.80	2.40	4.00
☐ 18	0.80	2.40	4.00
☐ 19	0.80	2.40	4.00
☐ 20	0.80	2.40	4.00
☐ 21	0.40	1.20	2.00
☐ 22	0.40	1.20	2.00
☐ 23	0.40	1.20	2.00
☐ 24	0.40	1.20	2.00
☐ 25	0.40	1.20	2.00
☐ 26	0.40	1.20	2.00
☐ 27	0.40	1.20	2.00

	ORIG.	GOOD	FINE	N-MINT
☐ 28		0.40	1.20	2.00
☐ 29		0.40	1.20	2.00
☐ 30		0.40	1.20	2.00
☐ 31		0.40	1.20	2.00
☐ 32, (moves to Quality Comics)		0.40	1.20	2.00

JUDGE DREDD (1994-)
DC

	ORIG.	GOOD	FINE	N-MINT
☐ 1, Aug 94 .... 1.95	1.00	3.00	5.00
☐ 2, Sep 94 .... 1.95	0.70	2.10	3.50
☐ 3, Oct 94 .... 1.95	0.39	1.17	1.95
☐ 4, Nov 94 .... 1.95	0.39	1.17	1.95
☐ 5, Dec 94 .... 1.95	0.39	1.17	1.95
☐ 6, Jan 95 .... 1.95	0.39	1.17	1.95
☐ 7, Feb 95 .... 1.95	0.39	1.17	1.95
☐ 8, Mar 95 .... 1.95	0.39	1.17	1.95
☐ 9, Apr 95 .... 1.95	0.39	1.17	1.95
☐ 10, May 95 .... 1.95	0.39	1.17	1.95
☐ 11, Jun 95 .... 2.25	0.45	1.35	2.25
☐ 12, Jul 95.......................... 2.25	0.45	1.35	2.25
☐ 13, Aug 95 .... 2.25	0.45	1.35	2.25
☐ 14, Sep 95 .... 2.25	0.45	1.35	2.25
☐ 15, Oct 95 .... 2.25	0.45	1.35	2.25
☐ 16, Nov 95 .... 2.25	0.45	1.35	2.25
☐ 17, Dec 95 .... 2.25	0.45	1.35	2.25
☐ 18, Jan 96........................ 2.25	0.45	1.35	2.25

JUDGE DREDD (second series)
FLEETWAY/QUALITY

	ORIG.	GOOD	FINE	N-MINT
☐ 1		0.40	1.20	2.00
☐ 2		0.40	1.20	2.00
☐ 3		0.40	1.20	2.00
☐ 4		0.40	1.20	2.00
☐ 5		0.40	1.20	2.00
☐ 6		0.40	1.20	2.00
☐ 7		0.40	1.20	2.00
☐ 8		0.40	1.20	2.00
☐ 9		0.40	1.20	2.00
☐ 10		0.40	1.20	2.00
☐ 11		0.40	1.20	2.00
☐ 12		0.40	1.20	2.00
☐ 13		0.40	1.20	2.00
☐ 14		0.40	1.20	2.00
☐ 15		0.40	1.20	2.00
☐ 16		0.40	1.20	2.00
☐ 17		0.40	1.20	2.00
☐ 18		0.40	1.20	2.00
☐ 19		0.40	1.20	2.00
☐ 20		0.40	1.20	2.00
☐ 21, 21 and 22 are one issue		0.40	1.20	2.00
☐ 23, 23 and 24 are one issue		0.40	1.20	2.00
☐ 25		0.40	1.20	2.00
☐ 26		0.40	1.20	2.00
☐ 27		0.40	1.20	2.00
☐ 28		0.40	1.20	2.00
☐ 29		0.40	1.20	2.00
☐ 30		0.40	1.20	2.00
☐ 31		0.40	1.20	2.00
☐ 32		0.40	1.20	2.00
☐ 33		0.40	1.20	2.00
☐ 34		0.40	1.20	2.00
☐ 35		0.40	1.20	2.00
☐ 36		0.40	1.20	2.00
☐ 37		0.40	1.20	2.00
☐ 38		0.40	1.20	2.00
☐ 39		0.35	1.05	1.75
☐ 40		0.35	1.05	1.75
☐ 41		0.35	1.05	1.75
☐ 42		0.35	1.05	1.75
☐ 43		0.35	1.05	1.75
☐ 44		0.35	1.05	1.75
☐ 45		0.35	1.05	1.75
☐ 46		0.35	1.05	1.75

	ORIG.	GOOD	FINE	N-MINT
❑ 47		0.35	1.05	1.75
❑ 48		0.35	1.05	1.75
❑ 49		0.35	1.05	1.75
❑ 50		0.35	1.05	1.75
❑ 51		0.35	1.05	1.75
❑ 52		0.35	1.05	1.75
❑ 53		0.35	1.05	1.75
❑ 54		0.35	1.05	1.75
❑ 55		0.35	1.05	1.75
❑ 56		0.35	1.05	1.75
❑ 57		0.35	1.05	1.75
❑ 58		0.35	1.05	1.75
❑ 59		0.35	1.05	1.75
❑ 60		0.35	1.05	1.75
❑ 61, (becomes *Judge Dredd Classics*)		0.35	1.05	1.75

JUDGE DREDD (was Eagle title)

	ORIG.	GOOD	FINE	N-MINT
❑ 33		0.40	1.20	2.00
❑ 34		0.40	1.20	2.00
❑ 35		0.40	1.20	2.00

JUDGE DREDD CLASSICS

	ORIG.	GOOD	FINE	N-MINT
❑ 62	1.95	0.39	1.17	1.95
❑ 63	1.95	0.39	1.17	1.95
❑ 64	1.95	0.39	1.17	1.95
❑ 65	1.95	0.39	1.17	1.95
❑ 66	1.95	0.39	1.17	1.95
❑ 67	1.95	0.39	1.17	1.95
❑ 68	1.95	0.39	1.17	1.95
❑ 69	1.95	0.39	1.17	1.95
❑ 70	1.95	0.39	1.17	1.95
❑ 71	1.95	0.39	1.17	1.95
❑ 72	1.95	0.39	1.17	1.95
❑ 73	1.95	0.39	1.17	1.95
❑ 74	1.95	0.39	1.17	1.95
❑ 75	1.95	0.39	1.17	1.95
❑ 76	1.95	0.39	1.17	1.95
❑ 77	1.95	0.39	1.17	1.95

JUDGE DREDD MOVIE ADAPTATION
DC

	ORIG.	GOOD	FINE	N-MINT
❑ 0, 95, nn;prestige format; adapts movie	5.95	1.19	3.57	5.95

JUDGE DREDD THE EARLY CASES
EAGLE

	ORIG.	GOOD	FINE	N-MINT
❑ 1		0.60	1.80	3.00
❑ 2		0.60	1.80	3.00
❑ 3		0.60	1.80	3.00
❑ 4		0.60	1.80	3.00
❑ 5		0.60	1.80	3.00
❑ 6		0.60	1.80	3.00

JUDGE DREDD'S CRIME FILE

	ORIG.	GOOD	FINE	N-MINT
❑ 1		0.60	1.80	3.00
❑ 2		0.60	1.80	3.00
❑ 3		0.60	1.80	3.00
❑ 4		0.60	1.80	3.00
❑ 5		0.60	1.80	3.00
❑ 6		0.60	1.80	3.00

FLEETWAY/QUALITY

	ORIG.	GOOD	FINE	N-MINT
❑ 1, BB(c)		1.19	3.57	5.95
❑ 2, BB(c)		1.19	3.57	5.95
❑ 3, BB(c)		1.19	3.57	5.95
❑ 4, BB(c)		1.19	3.57	5.95

JUDGE DREDD: AMERICA

	ORIG.	GOOD	FINE	N-MINT
❑ 1	2.95	0.59	1.77	2.95
❑ 2	2.95	0.59	1.77	2.95

JUDGE DREDD: EMERALD ISLE

	ORIG.	GOOD	FINE	N-MINT
❑ 0, nn	4.95	0.99	2.97	4.95

JUDGE DREDD: JUDGE CHILD QUEST
EAGLE

	ORIG.	GOOD	FINE	N-MINT
❑ 1		0.60	1.80	3.00

	ORIG.	GOOD	FINE	N-MINT
❑ 2		0.60	1.80	3.00
❑ 3		0.60	1.80	3.00
❑ 4		0.60	1.80	3.00
❑ 5		0.60	1.80	3.00

JUDGE DREDD: LEGENDS OF THE LAW
DC

	ORIG.	GOOD	FINE	N-MINT
❑ 1, Dec 94	1.95	0.39	1.17	1.95
❑ 2, Jan 95	1.95	0.39	1.17	1.95
❑ 3, Feb 95	1.95	0.39	1.17	1.95
❑ 4, Mar 95	1.95	0.39	1.17	1.95
❑ 5, Apr 95	1.95	0.39	1.17	1.95
❑ 6, May 95	1.95	0.39	1.17	1.95
❑ 7, Jun 95	2.25	0.45	1.35	2.25
❑ 8, Jul 95, "Fall from Grace" Part 1 of 3;JBy	2.25	0.45	1.35	2.25
❑ 9, Aug 95, "Fall from Grace" Part 2 of 3;JBy	2.25	0.45	1.35	2.25
❑ 10, Sep 95, "Fall from Grace" Part 3 of 3;JBy	2.25	0.45	1.35	2.25
❑ 11, Oct 95, "Dredd of Knight" Part 1 of 3	2.25	0.45	1.35	2.25
❑ 12, Nov 95, "Dredd of Knight" Part 2 of 3	2.25	0.45	1.35	2.25
❑ 13, Dec 95, "Dredd of Knight" Part 3 of 3;final issue	2.25	0.45	1.35	2.25

JUDGE DREDD: THE MEGAZINE
FLEETWAY

	ORIG.	GOOD	FINE	N-MINT
❑ 1, color		0.99	2.97	4.95

FLEETWAY/QUALITY

	ORIG.	GOOD	FINE	N-MINT
❑ 1		0.99	2.97	4.95
❑ 2		0.99	2.97	4.95

JUDGMENT DAY
LIGHTNING

	ORIG.	GOOD	FINE	N-MINT
❑ 1, Aug 93, promotional copy, platinum	3.50	1.20	3.60	6.00
❑ 1, Sep 93, red foil cover	3.50	7.00	21.00	35.00
❑ 1, Aug 93, promotional copy, metallic ink	3.50	1.20	3.60	6.00
❑ 1, Sep 93, gold foil cover	3.50	7.00	21.00	35.00
❑ 1, Sep 93, purple foil cover	3.50	7.00	21.00	35.00
❑ 1, Sep 93, misprint	3.50	7.00	21.00	35.00
❑ 2, Oct 93, trading card	2.95	0.80	2.40	4.00
❑ 3, Nov 93, O:X-Treme	2.95	0.59	1.77	2.95
❑ 4, Dec 93	2.95	0.59	1.77	2.95
❑ 5, Jan 94	2.95	0.59	1.77	2.95
❑ 6, Feb 94, O:Salubrio	2.95	0.59	1.77	2.95
❑ 7, Mar 94, O:Safeguard	2.95	0.59	1.77	2.95
❑ 8, Apr 94	2.95	0.59	1.77	2.95

JUDO JOE
ACE

	ORIG.	GOOD	FINE	N-MINT
❑ 1, Mar 87, b&w, reprints		0.35	1.05	1.75

JUGHEAD AS CAPTAIN HERO
ARCHIE

	ORIG.	GOOD	FINE	N-MINT
❑ 4, Apr 67	0.12	1.60	4.80	8.00

JUGHEAD JONES DIGEST MAGAZINE, THE

	ORIG.	GOOD	FINE	N-MINT
❑ 92, Dec 94, digest	1.75	0.35	1.05	1.75
❑ 93, Feb 95, digest	1.75	0.35	1.05	1.75
❑ 94, Apr 95, digest	1.75	0.35	1.05	1.75
❑ 95, Jun 95, digest	1.75	0.35	1.05	1.75
❑ 96, Aug 95, digest	1.75	0.35	1.05	1.75
❑ 97, Oct 95, digest	1.75	0.35	1.05	1.75
❑ 98, Nov 95, digest	1.75	0.35	1.05	1.75
❑ 99, Feb 96, digest	1.75	0.35	1.05	1.75
❑ 100, May 96, digest; A:Nathan Jones	1.75	0.35	1.05	1.75

JUGHEAD WITH ARCHIE DIGEST MAGAZINE

	ORIG.	GOOD	FINE	N-MINT
❑ 122, Jan 95, digest	1.75	0.35	1.05	1.75
❑ 123, May 95, digest	1.75	0.35	1.05	1.75

	ORIG.	GOOD	FINE	N-MINT
124, Aug 95, digest........ 1.75	0.35	1.05	1.75
125, Oct 95, digest......... 1.75	0.35	1.05	1.75
126, Jan 96, digest 1.75	0.35	1.05	1.75

JUGHEAD'S BABY TALES

	ORIG.	GOOD	FINE	N-MINT
2, Win 94 .... 2.00	0.40	1.20	2.00

JUGHEAD'S DINER

	ORIG.	GOOD	FINE	N-MINT
1, Apr 90........................ 1.00	0.20	0.60	1.00
2 .... 1.00	0.20	0.60	1.00
3 .... 1.00	0.20	0.60	1.00
4 .... 1.00	0.20	0.60	1.00
5 .... 1.00	0.20	0.60	1.00
6 .... 1.00	0.20	0.60	1.00
7 .... 1.00	0.20	0.60	1.00

JUGHEAD'S DOUBLE DIGEST

	ORIG.	GOOD	FINE	N-MINT
27, Dec 93, digest.......... 2.75	0.55	1.65	2.75
29, Mar 95, digest.......... 2.75	0.55	1.65	2.75
30, May 95, digest.......... 2.75	0.55	1.65	2.75
31, Jul 95, digest 2.75	0.55	1.65	2.75
32, Sep 95, digest.......... 2.75	0.55	1.65	2.75
33, Nov 95, digest.......... 2.75	0.55	1.65	2.75
34, Jan 96, digest 2.75	0.55	1.65	2.75
35, Feb 96, digest 2.75	0.55	1.65	2.75
36, Apr 96, digest 2.75	0.55	1.65	2.75
37, Jun 96, digest 2.75	0.55	1.65	2.75
38, Aug 96, digest.......... 2.75	0.55	1.65	2.75

JUGHEAD'S PAL HOT DOG

	ORIG.	GOOD	FINE	N-MINT
1, Jan 90 .... 1.00	0.20	0.60	1.00
2 .... 1.00	0.20	0.60	1.00
3 .... 1.00	0.20	0.60	1.00
4 .... 1.00	0.20	0.60	1.00
5 .... 1.00	0.20	0.60	1.00

JUGHEAD'S TIME POLICE

	ORIG.	GOOD	FINE	N-MINT
1, Jul 90........................ 1.00	0.20	0.60	1.00
2 .... 1.00	0.20	0.60	1.00
3 .... 1.00	0.20	0.60	1.00
4 .... 1.00	0.20	0.60	1.00
5 .... 1.00	0.20	0.60	1.00
6 .... 1.00	0.20	0.60	1.00

JUMPER
ZAV

	ORIG.	GOOD	FINE	N-MINT
1, b&w		0.60	1.80	3.00
2, b&w		0.60	1.80	3.00

JUN
DISNEY

	ORIG.	GOOD	FINE	N-MINT
1, 90 .... 1.50	1.00	3.00	5.00

JUNGLE ACTION
MARVEL

	ORIG.	GOOD	FINE	N-MINT
1, reprints 0.20	0.30	0.90	1.50
2, reprints 0.20	0.20	0.60	1.00
3, reprints 0.20	0.20	0.60	1.00
4, reprints 0.20	0.20	0.60	1.00
5, Black Panther............. 0.20	0.20	0.60	1.00
6, Sep 73, Black Panther 0.20	0.20	0.60	1.00
7, Nov 73, Black Panther 0.20	0.20	0.60	1.00
8, Jan 74, Black Panther 0.20	0.20	0.60	1.00
9, May 74, Black Panther 0.25	0.20	0.60	1.00
10, Jul 74, Black Panther 0.25	0.20	0.60	1.00
11, Sep 74, Black Panther 0.25	0.20	0.60	1.00
12, Nov 74, Black Panther 0.25	0.20	0.60	1.00
13, Jan 75, Black Panther 0.25	0.20	0.60	1.00
14, Mar 75, Black Panther 0.25	0.20	0.60	1.00
15, May 75, Black Panther 0.25 .... 0.20	0.60	1.00

	ORIG.	GOOD	FINE	N-MINT
16, Jul 75, Black Panther 0.25	0.20	0.60	1.00
17, Sep 75, Black Panther 0.25	0.20	0.60	1.00
18, Nov 75, Black Panther 0.25	0.20	0.60	1.00
19, Jan 76, Black Panther 0.25	0.20	0.60	1.00
20, Mar 76, Black Panther 0.25	0.20	0.60	1.00
21, May 76, Black Panther 0.25	0.20	0.60	1.00
22, Jul 76, Black Panther 0.25	0.20	0.60	1.00
23, Sep 76, Black Panther 0.30	0.20	0.60	1.00
24, Nov 76, Black Panther 0.30	0.20	0.60	1.00

JUNGLE BOOK, THE
DISNEY

	ORIG.	GOOD	FINE	N-MINT
1, movie, squarebound	1.19	3.57	5.95
1, movie, saddle-stitched..	0.59	1.77	2.95

JUNGLE COMICS
BLACKTHORNE

	ORIG.	GOOD	FINE	N-MINT
1, May 88, O:Sheena, Kaanga b&w	0.40	1.20	2.00
2, 88	0.40	1.20	2.00
3, 88	0.40	1.20	2.00

JUNGLE GIRLS
AC

	ORIG.	GOOD	FINE	N-MINT
1, Aug 88, b&w...............	0.39	1.17	1.95
2, 89	0.45	1.35	2.25
3	0.55	1.65	2.75
4	0.55	1.65	2.75
5	0.55	1.65	2.75
6, Matt Baker reprints	0.59	1.77	2.95
7, Matt Baker reprints	0.59	1.77	2.95
8, b&w.........................2.95	0.59	1.77	2.95
9, b&w.........................2.95	0.59	1.77	2.95
10, b&w.......................2.95	0.59	1.77	2.95
11, b&w.......................2.95	0.59	1.77	2.95
12, b&w.......................2.95	0.59	1.77	2.95
13, b&w.......................2.95	0.59	1.77	2.95
14, b&w.......................2.95	0.59	1.77	2.95
15, b&w.......................2.95	0.59	1.77	2.95
16, b&w.......................2.95	0.59	1.77	2.95

JUNGLE GIRLS!
ETERNITY

	ORIG.	GOOD	FINE	N-MINT
8	0.59	1.77	2.95

JUNGLE LOVE
AIRCEL

	ORIG.	GOOD	FINE	N-MINT
1, adult, b&w	0.59	1.77	2.95
2, adult, b&w	0.59	1.77	2.95
3, adult, b&w	0.59	1.77	2.95

JUNIOR CARROT PATROL
DARK HORSE

	ORIG.	GOOD	FINE	N-MINT
1, b&w.............................	0.40	1.20	2.00
2, b&w.............................	0.40	1.20	2.00

JUNIOR WOODCHUCKS
DISNEY

	ORIG.	GOOD	FINE	N-MINT
1, CB...............................	0.30	0.90	1.50
2	0.30	0.90	1.50
3	0.30	0.90	1.50
4	0.30	0.90	1.50

JUNKER
FLEETWAY/QUALITY

	ORIG.	GOOD	FINE	N-MINT
1 ....2.95	0.59	1.77	2.95

JURASSIC LARK DELUXE EDITION
PARODY PRESS

	ORIG.	GOOD	FINE	N-MINT
1, b&w..........................2.95	0.59	1.77	2.95

	ORIG.	GOOD	FINE	N-MINT

JURASSIC PARK
TOPPS

	ORIG.	GOOD	FINE	N-MINT
0, GK/GP(c) movie adaptation, trading cards (came packed with tpb of #1-4) 2.50	2.80	8.40	14.00
0, without tpb...................	1.20	3.60	6.00
1, DC(c);movie adaptation 2.50	1.50	4.50	7.50
2 ....2.50	0.60	1.80	3.00
2, trading cards.............2.95	0.80	2.40	4.00
3 ....2.50	0.60	1.80	3.00
3, trading cards.............2.95	0.80	2.40	4.00
4 ....2.50	0.60	1.80	3.00
4, hologram card............2.95	0.80	2.40	4.00

JURASSIC PARK: RAPTOR (mini-series)

1, trading cards, *Zorro* #0 ....2.95	0.59	1.77	2.95
2, Dec 93, cards.............2.95	0.59	1.77	2.95

JURASSIC PARK: RAPTORS ATTACK (mini-series)

1 ....2.50	0.50	1.50	2.50
2, Apr 94 ....2.50	0.50	1.50	2.50
3, May 94 ....2.50	0.50	1.50	2.50
4, Jun 94.......................2.50	0.50	1.50	2.50

JUST IMAGINE COMICS & STORIES
JUST IMAGINE

1	0.40	1.20	2.00
2	0.40	1.20	2.00
3	0.40	1.20	2.00
4	0.40	1.20	2.00
5	0.40	1.20	2.00
6	0.40	1.20	2.00
7	0.40	1.20	2.00
8	0.40	1.20	2.00
9	0.40	1.20	2.00
10	0.40	1.20	2.00
11	0.40	1.20	2.00

JUST IMAGINE'S SPECIAL

1, gophers......................	0.30	0.90	1.50

JUST TWISTED
NECROMICS

1	0.40	1.20	2.00

JUSTICE
ANTARCTIC

1, May 94, b&w.............3.50	0.70	2.10	3.50

MARVEL

	ORIG.	GOOD	FINE	N-MINT
1, Nov 86 ....0.75	0.20	0.60	1.00
2, Dec 86.......................0.75	0.20	0.60	1.00
3, Jan 87 ....0.75	0.20	0.60	1.00
4, Feb 87 ....0.75	0.20	0.60	1.00
5, Mar 87 ....0.75	0.20	0.60	1.00
6, Apr 87 ....0.75	0.20	0.60	1.00
7, May 87 ....0.75	0.20	0.60	1.00
8, Jun 87 ....0.75	0.20	0.60	1.00
9, Jul 87 ....0.75	0.20	0.60	1.00
10, Aug 87 ....0.75	0.20	0.60	1.00
11, Sep 87......................0.75	0.20	0.60	1.00
12, Oct 87 ....0.75	0.20	0.60	1.00
13, Nov 87......................0.75	0.20	0.60	1.00
14, Dec 87......................0.75	0.20	0.60	1.00
15, Jan 88......................0.75	0.20	0.60	1.00
16, Feb 88......................0.75	0.20	0.60	1.00
17, Mar 88......................0.75	0.20	0.60	1.00
18, Apr 88.......................0.75	0.20	0.60	1.00
19, May 88......................1.25	0.25	0.75	1.25
20, Jun 88.......................1.25	0.25	0.75	1.25
21, Jul 88.......................1.25	0.25	0.75	1.25
22, Aug 88 ....1.25	0.25	0.75	1.25
23, Sep 88......................1.25	0.25	0.75	1.25
24, Oct 88 ....1.25	0.25	0.75	1.25
25, Nov 88......................1.25	0.25	0.75	1.25
26, Dec 88......................1.50	0.30	0.90	1.50

	ORIG.	GOOD	FINE	N-MINT
27, Jan 89......................1.50	0.30	0.90	1.50
28, Feb 89......................1.50	0.30	0.90	1.50
29, Mar 89......................1.50	0.30	0.90	1.50
30, Apr 89.......................1.50	0.30	0.90	1.50
31, May 89......................1.50	0.30	0.90	1.50
32, Jun 89 ....1.50	0.30	0.90	1.50

JUSTICE BRIGADE
TCB COMICS

1, b&w...........................1.50	0.30	0.90	1.50
2, b&w...........................1.50	0.30	0.90	1.50
3, b&w...........................1.50	0.30	0.90	1.50
4, b&w...........................1.50	0.30	0.90	1.50
5, b&w...........................1.50	0.30	0.90	1.50
6, b&w...........................1.50	0.30	0.90	1.50
7, b&w...........................1.50	0.30	0.90	1.50
8, b&w...........................1.50	0.30	0.90	1.50

JUSTICE LEAGUE
DC

1, May 87......................0.75	2.40	7.20	12.00
2, Jun 87 ....0.75	2.00	6.00	10.00
3, Jul 87.......................0.75	1.60	4.80	8.00
3, Jul 87, alternate cover ..	15.00	45.00	75.00
4, Aug 87, J:Booster Gold 0.75	1.20	3.60	6.00
5, Sep 87 ....0.75	1.00	3.00	5.00
6, Oct 87, (becomes *Justice League International*) 0.75	1.00	3.00	5.00

JUSTICE LEAGUE AMERICA
(was Justice League International)

0, Oct 94, J:Nuklon, Obsidian 1.50	0.30	0.90	1.50
26, May 89......................0.75	0.40	1.20	2.00
27, Jun 89 ....0.75	0.40	1.20	2.00
28, Jul 89.......................0.75	0.40	1.20	2.00
29, Aug 89 ....1.00	0.40	1.20	2.00
30, Sep 89 ....1.00	0.40	1.20	2.00
31, Oct 89, JLE/JLA........1.00	0.50	1.50	2.50
32, Nov 89, JLE/JLA 1.00	0.50	1.50	2.50
33, Dec 89......................1.00	0.30	0.90	1.50
34, Jan 90......................1.00	0.30	0.90	1.50
35, Feb 90......................1.00	0.30	0.90	1.50
36, Mar 90......................1.00	0.30	0.90	1.50
37, Apr 90.......................1.00	0.30	0.90	1.50
38, May 90......................1.00	0.30	0.90	1.50
39, Jun 90 ....1.00	0.30	0.90	1.50
40, Jul 90.......................1.00	0.30	0.90	1.50
41, Aug 90 ....1.00	0.30	0.90	1.50
42, Sep 90 ....1.00	0.30	0.90	1.50
43, Oct 90 ....1.00	0.30	0.90	1.50
44, Nov 90......................1.00	0.30	0.90	1.50
45, Jan 90......................1.00	0.30	0.90	1.50
46, Jan 91......................1.00	0.30	0.90	1.50
47, Feb 91......................1.00	0.30	0.90	1.50
48, Mar 91......................1.00	0.30	0.90	1.50
49, Apr 91.......................1.00	0.30	0.90	1.50
50, May 91......................1.75	0.50	1.50	2.50
51, Jun 91 ....1.00	0.20	0.60	1.00
52, Jul 91.......................1.00	0.20	0.60	1.00
53, Aug 91 ....1.00	0.20	0.60	1.00
54, Sep 91 ....1.00	0.20	0.60	1.00
55, Oct 91 ....1.00	0.20	0.60	1.00
56, Nov 91......................1.00	0.20	0.60	1.00
57, Dec 91 ....1.00	0.20	0.60	1.00
58, Jan 92......................1.00	0.20	0.60	1.00
59, Feb 92......................1.00	0.20	0.60	1.00
60, Apr 92.......................1.00	0.20	0.60	1.00
61, Apr 92, new JLA 1.00	0.20	0.60	1.00
62, May 92......................1.00	0.20	0.60	1.00
63, Jun 92 ....1.25	0.25	0.75	1.25
64, Jul 92.......................1.25	0.25	0.75	1.25
65, Aug 92 ....1.25	0.25	0.75	1.25

	ORIG.	GOOD	FINE	N-MINT
66, Sep 92	1.25	0.25	0.75	1.25
67, Oct 92	1.25	0.25	0.75	1.25
68, Nov 92	1.25	0.25	0.75	1.25
69, Dec 92, Doomsday	1.25	8.00	24.00	40.00
70, Jan 93, Funeral, cover wrapper	1.25	5.60	16.80	28.00
71, Feb 93, black cover wrapper, Wonder Woman, Ray, Agent Liberty, Black Condor join	1.25	0.25	0.75	1.25
72, Mar 93	1.25	0.25	0.75	1.25
73, Apr 93	1.25	0.25	0.75	1.25
74, May 93	1.25	0.25	0.75	1.25
75, Jun 93	1.25	0.25	0.75	1.25
76, Jul 93	1.25	0.25	0.75	1.25
77		0.25	0.75	1.25
78		0.25	0.75	1.25
79		0.25	0.75	1.25
80		0.25	0.75	1.25
81		0.25	0.75	1.25
82		0.25	0.75	1.25
83	1.50	0.30	0.90	1.50
84	1.50	0.30	0.90	1.50
85	1.50	0.30	0.90	1.50
86	1.50	0.30	0.90	1.50
87	1.50	0.30	0.90	1.50
88, May 94	1.50	0.30	0.90	1.50
89, Jun 94	1.50	0.30	0.90	1.50
90, Jul 94	1.50	0.30	0.90	1.50
91, Aug 94	1.50	0.30	0.90	1.50
92, Sep 94	1.50	0.30	0.90	1.50
93, Nov 94	1.50	0.30	0.90	1.50
94, Dec 94	1.50	0.30	0.90	1.50
95, Jan 95	1.50	0.30	0.90	1.50
96, Feb 95	1.50	0.30	0.90	1.50
97, Mar 95	1.50	0.30	0.90	1.50
98, Apr 95	1.50	0.30	0.90	1.50
99, May 95	1.50	0.30	0.90	1.50
100, Jun 95	2.95	0.59	1.77	2.95
101, Jul 95	1.75	0.35	1.05	1.75
102, Aug 95	1.75	0.35	1.05	1.75
103, Sep 95	1.75	0.35	1.05	1.75
104, Oct 95	1.75	0.35	1.05	1.75
105, Nov 95, "Underworld Unleashed"	1.75	0.35	1.05	1.75
106, Dec 95, "Underworld Unleashed"	1.75	0.35	1.05	1.75
107, Jan 96	1.75	0.35	1.05	1.75
108, Feb 96	1.75	0.35	1.05	1.75
109, Mar 96	1.75	0.35	1.05	1.75
110, Apr 96, A:El Diablo	1.75	0.35	1.05	1.75
111, Jun 96	1.75	0.35	1.05	1.75

JUSTICE LEAGUE AMERICA ANNUAL
(was Justice League Annual)

	ORIG.	GOOD	FINE	N-MINT
4, 90		0.40	1.20	2.00
5, 91, Armageddon 2001	2.00	0.40	1.20	2.00
5, 2nd printing, silver		0.40	1.20	2.00
6, 92, Eclipso	2.50	0.50	1.50	2.50
7, Bloodlines	2.50	0.50	1.50	2.50
8, 94	2.95	0.59	1.77	2.95
9, 95, "Year One"	3.50	0.70	2.10	3.50

JUSTICE LEAGUE ANNUAL

	ORIG.	GOOD	FINE	N-MINT
1, 87	1.25	0.80	2.40	4.00
2, 88, V:Joker	1.50	1.20	3.60	6.00
3, 89, (becomes Justice League America Annual)	1.75	0.35	1.05	1.75

JUSTICE LEAGUE EUROPE

	ORIG.	GOOD	FINE	N-MINT
1, Apr 89	0.75	2.40	7.20	12.00
2, May 89	0.75	1.20	3.60	6.00
3, Jun 89	0.75	0.80	2.40	4.00
4, Jul 89	0.75	0.60	1.80	3.00

	ORIG.	GOOD	FINE	N-MINT
5, Aug 89	0.75	0.60	1.80	3.00
6, Sep 89	0.75	0.60	1.80	3.00
7, Oct 89, JLA/JLE	1.00	0.60	1.80	3.00
8, Nov 89, JLA/JLE	1.00	0.60	1.80	3.00
9, Dec 89	1.00	0.40	1.20	2.00
10, Jan 90	1.00	0.40	1.20	2.00
11, Feb 90	1.00	0.40	1.20	2.00
12, Mar 90	1.00	0.40	1.20	2.00
13, Apr 90	1.00	0.40	1.20	2.00
14, May 90	1.00	0.40	1.20	2.00
15, Jun 90	1.00	0.40	1.20	2.00
16, Jun 90	1.00	0.30	0.90	1.50
17, Aug 90	1.00	0.30	0.90	1.50
18, Sep 90	1.00	0.30	0.90	1.50
19, Oct 90	1.00	0.30	0.90	1.50
20, Nov 90	1.00	0.30	0.90	1.50
21, Dec 90	1.00	0.30	0.90	1.50
22, Jan 91	1.00	0.30	0.90	1.50
23, Feb 91	1.00	0.30	0.90	1.50
24, Mar 91	1.00	0.30	0.90	1.50
25, Apr 91	1.00	0.30	0.90	1.50
26, May 91	1.00	0.20	0.60	1.00
27, Jun 91	1.00	0.20	0.60	1.00
28, Jul 91	1.00	0.20	0.60	1.00
29, Aug 91	1.00	0.20	0.60	1.00
30, Sep 91	1.00	0.20	0.60	1.00
31, Oct 91	1.00	0.20	0.60	1.00
32, Nov 91	1.00	0.20	0.60	1.00
33, Dec 91	1.00	0.20	0.60	1.00
34, Jan 92	1.00	0.20	0.60	1.00
35, Feb 92	1.00	0.20	0.60	1.00
36, Mar 92	1.00	0.20	0.60	1.00
37, Apr 92	1.00	0.20	0.60	1.00
38, May 92	1.00	0.20	0.60	1.00
39, Jun 92	1.25	0.25	0.75	1.25
40, Jul 92	1.25	0.25	0.75	1.25
41, Aug 92	1.25	0.25	0.75	1.25
42, Sep 92, J:WW	1.25	0.25	0.75	1.25
43, Oct 92	1.25	0.25	0.75	1.25
44, Oct 92	1.25	0.25	0.75	1.25
45, Dec 92	1.25	0.25	0.75	1.25
46, Jan 93	1.25	0.25	0.75	1.25
47, Feb 93	1.25	0.25	0.75	1.25
48, Mar 93	1.25	0.25	0.75	1.25
49, Apr 93	1.25	0.25	0.75	1.25
50, May 93, (becomes Justice League International)	2.50	0.50	1.50	2.50

JUSTICE LEAGUE EUROPE ANNUAL

	ORIG.	GOOD	FINE	N-MINT
1, 90, Global Guardians		0.60	1.80	3.00
2, 91, Armageddon 2001		0.40	1.20	2.00
3, 92, Eclipso		0.50	1.50	2.50

JUSTICE LEAGUE INTERNATIONAL
(was Justice League Europe)

	ORIG.	GOOD	FINE	N-MINT
51, Jun 93	1.25	0.25	0.75	1.25
52	1.25	0.25	0.75	1.25
53	1.25	0.25	0.75	1.25
54	1.25	0.25	0.75	1.25
55	1.25	0.25	0.75	1.25
56	1.25	0.25	0.75	1.25
57	1.25	0.25	0.75	1.25
58	1.25	0.25	0.75	1.25
59	1.50	0.30	0.90	1.50
60	1.50	0.30	0.90	1.50
61	1.50	0.30	0.90	1.50
62	1.50	0.30	0.90	1.50
63	1.50	0.30	0.90	1.50
64, May 94	1.50	0.30	0.90	1.50
65, Jun 94	1.50	0.30	0.90	1.50
66, Jul 94	1.50	0.30	0.90	1.50
67, Aug 94	1.50	0.30	0.90	1.50
68, Sep 94	1.50	0.30	0.90	1.50

	ORIG.	GOOD	FINE	N-MINT

JUSTICE LEAGUE INTERNATIONAL
(was Justice League)

❑ 7, Nov 87, L:Captain Marvel J:Capt. Atom, Rocket Red
................1.25 1.00 3.00 5.00
❑ 8, Dec 87.....................0.75 0.60 1.80 3.00
❑ 9, Jan 88, Millennium 0.75 0.40 1.20 2.00
❑ 10, Feb 88, Millennium ..0.75 0.40 1.20 2.00
❑ 11, Mar 88.....................0.75 0.40 1.20 2.00
❑ 12, Apr 88.....................0.75 0.40 1.20 2.00
❑ 13, May 88, A:Suicide Squad
................0.75 0.40 1.20 2.00
❑ 14, Jun 88.....................0.75 0.20 0.60 1.00
❑ 15, Jul 88.....................0.75 0.20 0.60 1.00
❑ 16, Aug 88.....................0.75 0.20 0.60 1.00
❑ 17, Sep 88.....................0.75 0.20 0.60 1.00
❑ 18, Oct 88, Lobo, Bonus Book
................0.75 1.60 4.80 8.00
❑ 19, Nov 88, Lobo 0.75 1.60 4.80 8.00
❑ 20, Dec 88.....................0.75 0.20 0.60 1.00
❑ 21, 88.....................0.75 0.20 0.60 1.00
❑ 22, 88, Invasion! 0.75 0.20 0.60 1.00
❑ 23, Jan 89, Invasion! 0.75 0.20 0.60 1.00
❑ 24, Feb 89, I:JL Europe, Bonus Book
................1.50 0.30 0.90 1.50
❑ 25, Apr 89, (becomes *Justice League America*)
................0.75 0.20 0.60 1.00

JUSTICE LEAGUE INTERNATIONAL ANNUAL
❑ 4, Bloodlines 2.50 0.50 1.50 2.50
❑ 5, Jun 94, Elseworlds.....2.95 0.59 1.77 2.95

JUSTICE LEAGUE INTERNATIONAL SPECIAL
❑ 1, Mr. Miracle..................0.30 0.90 1.50
❑ 2, 91, Huntress 2.95 0.59 1.77 2.95

JUSTICE LEAGUE OF AMERICA
❑ 1, I:Despero 650.00 1950.00 3250.00
❑ 2, A:Merlin 160.00 480.00 800.00
❑ 3, Mar 61, 1:Kanjar Ro... 0.10 130.00 390.00 650.00
❑ 4, J:Green Arrow............. 95.00 285.00 475.00
❑ 5, Jul 61 .... 0.10 65.00 195.00 325.00
❑ 6, Sep 61 .... 0.10 45.00 135.00 225.00
❑ 7, Nov 61 .... 0.10 45.00 135.00 225.00
❑ 8, Jan 62 .... 0.12 45.00 135.00 225.00
❑ 9, O:JLA..................... 84.00 252.00 420.00
❑ 10, Mar 62, I:Felix Faust. 0.12 45.00 135.00 225.00
❑ 11, May 62 .... 0.12 33.00 99.00 165.00
❑ 12, Jun 62 .... 0.12 33.00 99.00 165.00
❑ 13, Aug 62 .... 0.12 33.00 99.00 165.00
❑ 14, Sep 62 .... 0.12 33.00 99.00 165.00
❑ 15, Nov 62 .... 0.12 33.00 99.00 165.00
❑ 16, Dec 62 .... 0.12 28.00 84.00 140.00
❑ 17, Feb 63 .... 0.12 28.00 84.00 140.00
❑ 18, Mar 63 .... 0.12 28.00 84.00 140.00
❑ 19, May 63 .... 0.12 28.00 84.00 140.00
❑ 20, Jun 63 .... 0.12 28.00 84.00 140.00
❑ 21, Aug 63, R:JSA.......... 0.12 60.00 180.00 300.00
❑ 22, Sep 63, R:JSA.......... 0.12 60.00 180.00 300.00
❑ 23, Nov 63 .... 0.12 20.00 60.00 100.00
❑ 24, Dec 63 .... 0.12 20.00 60.00 100.00
❑ 25, Feb 64 .... 0.12 20.00 60.00 100.00
❑ 26, Mar 64 .... 0.12 20.00 60.00 100.00
❑ 27, May 64 .... 0.12 20.00 60.00 100.00
❑ 28, Jun 64 .... 0.12 20.00 60.00 100.00
❑ 29, Aug 64, "Crisis on Earth-Three" Part 1; 1&
I:Crime Syndicate, Earth-3;A:Justice Society
................0.12 20.00 60.00 100.00
❑ 30, Sep 64 .... 0.12 20.00 60.00 100.00
❑ 31, Nov 64, J:Hawkman . 0.12 28.00 84.00 140.00
❑ 32, Dec 64 .... 0.12 12.00 36.00 60.00
❑ 33, Feb 65 .... 0.12 12.00 36.00 60.00
❑ 34, Mar 65 .... 0.12 12.00 36.00 60.00
❑ 35, May 65 .... 0.12 12.00 36.00 60.00
❑ 36, Jun 65 .... 0.12 12.00 36.00 60.00

	ORIG.	GOOD	FINE	N-MINT

❑ 37, Aug 65, A:JSA 0.12 15.00 45.00 75.00
❑ 38, Sep 65, A:JSA..........0.12 15.00 45.00 75.00
❑ 39, Nov 65, 80 page giant;reprints *Brave and the Bold*
#28, 30, and *Justice League of America* #5
................0.25 11.00 33.00 55.00
❑ 40, Nov 65, social issue..0.12 9.00 27.00 45.00
❑ 41, Dec 65 ....0.12 6.00 18.00 30.00
❑ 42, Feb 66.....................0.12 6.00 18.00 30.00
❑ 43, Mar 66.....................0.12 6.00 18.00 30.00
❑ 44, May 66.....................0.12 6.00 18.00 30.00
❑ 45, Jun 66.....................0.12 6.00 18.00 30.00
❑ 46, Aug 66.....................0.12 8.00 24.00 40.00
❑ 47, Sep 66.....................0.12 5.60 16.80 28.00
❑ 48, Dec 66.....................0.12 5.60 16.80 28.00
❑ 49, Nov 66.....................0.12 5.60 16.80 28.00
❑ 50, Dec 66.....................0.12 5.60 16.80 28.00
❑ 51, Feb 67.....................0.12 4.00 12.00 20.00
❑ 52, Mar 67.....................0.12 4.00 12.00 20.00
❑ 53, May 67.....................0.12 4.00 12.00 20.00
❑ 54, Jun 67.....................0.12 4.00 12.00 20.00
❑ 55, Aug 67.....................0.12 4.00 12.00 20.00
❑ 56, Sep 67.....................0.12 4.00 12.00 20.00
❑ 57, Nov 67.....................0.12 4.00 12.00 20.00
❑ 58, Dec 67, reprint..........0.25 4.00 12.00 20.00
❑ 59, Dec 67.....................0.12 4.00 12.00 20.00
❑ 60, Feb 67.....................0.12 4.00 12.00 20.00
❑ 61, Mar 67.....................0.12 2.40 7.20 12.00
❑ 62, May 67.....................0.12 2.40 7.20 12.00
❑ 63, Jun 67.....................0.12 2.40 7.20 12.00
❑ 64, Aug 67, DP; R:Red Tornado
................0.12 2.40 7.20 12.00
❑ 65, Sep 67, DP; V:T.O.Morrow
................0.12 2.40 7.20 12.00
❑ 66, Nov 67, DP 0.12 2.40 7.20 12.00
❑ 67, Dec 67, reprint..........0.25 2.40 7.20 12.00
❑ 68, Dec 67, DD...............0.12 2.40 7.20 12.00
❑ 69, Feb 68, DD...............0.12 2.40 7.20 12.00
❑ 70, Mar 68, DD 0.12 2.40 7.20 12.00
❑ 71, May 68, DD...............0.12 2.00 6.00 10.00
❑ 72, Jun 68, DD...............0.12 2.00 6.00 10.00
❑ 73, Aug 68, DD 0.15 2.00 6.00 10.00
❑ 74, Sep 68, DD;D:Larry Lance;A:Justice Society;
Black Canary goes to Earth-1
................0.15 2.00 6.00 10.00
❑ 75, Nov 68, DD 0.15 2.00 6.00 10.00
❑ 76, Dec 68, DD 0.25 2.00 6.00 10.00
❑ 77, Dec 68, DD 0.15 2.00 6.00 10.00
❑ 78, Feb 70, DD...............0.15 2.00 6.00 10.00
❑ 79, Mar 70, DD 0.15 2.00 6.00 10.00
❑ 80, May 70, DD...............0.15 2.00 6.00 10.00
❑ 81, Jun 70, DD...............0.15 2.00 6.00 10.00
❑ 82, Aug 70, DD 0.15 2.00 6.00 10.00
❑ 83, Sep 70, DD 0.15 2.00 6.00 10.00
❑ 84, Nov 70, DD 0.15 2.00 6.00 10.00
❑ 85, Dec 70, reprint..........0.25 2.00 6.00 10.00
❑ 86, Dec 70, DD 0.15 1.20 3.60 6.00
❑ 87, Feb 71, DD...............0.15 1.20 3.60 6.00
❑ 88, Mar 71, DD 0.15 1.60 4.80 8.00
❑ 89, May 71, DD...............0.15 1.60 4.80 8.00
❑ 90, Jun 71, DD...............0.15 1.60 4.80 8.00
❑ 91, Aug 71, DD 0.25 1.60 4.80 8.00
❑ 92, Sep 71, DD 0.25 1.60 4.80 8.00
❑ 93, Nov 71, reprint..........0.35 1.20 3.60 6.00
❑ 94, Nov 71, DD, NA A:Deadman
................0.25 3.00 9.00 15.00
❑ 95, Dec 71, DD 0.25 1.00 3.00 5.00
❑ 96, Feb 72, DD...............0.25 1.00 3.00 5.00
❑ 97, Mar 72, DD, O:JLA...0.25 1.00 3.00 5.00
❑ 98, May 72, DD, A:Sargon
................0.25 1.00 3.00 5.00
❑ 99, Jun 72, DD, A:Sargon
................0.25 1.00 3.00 5.00

	ORIG.	GOOD	FINE	N-MINT
❏ 100, Aug 72, DD, A:7 Soldiers	0.20	1.00	3.00	5.00
❏ 101, Sep 72, DD	0.20	1.20	3.60	6.00
❏ 102, Oct 72, DD	0.20	1.20	3.60	6.00
❏ 103, Dec 72, DD/DG	0.20	1.00	3.00	5.00
❏ 104, Feb 73, DD/DG	0.20	1.00	3.00	5.00
❏ 105, May 73, DD/DG	0.20	1.00	3.00	5.00
❏ 106, Aug 73, DD/DG	0.20	1.00	3.00	5.00
❏ 107, Oct 73, DD/DG, I:Freedom Fighters	0.20	1.00	3.00	5.00
❏ 108, Dec 73, DD/DG, A:JSA	0.20	1.00	3.00	5.00
❏ 109, Feb 74, DD/DG	0.20	1.00	3.00	5.00
❏ 110, Apr 74, DD/DG , 100 pgs.	0.50	1.00	3.00	5.00
❏ 111, Jun 74, DD/DG	0.60	1.00	3.00	5.00
❏ 112, Aug 74, DD/DG	0.60	1.00	3.00	5.00
❏ 113, Oct 74, DD/DG	0.60	1.00	3.00	5.00
❏ 114, Dec 74, DD/DG	0.60	1.00	3.00	5.00
❏ 115, Feb 75, DD/DG	0.60	1.00	3.00	5.00
❏ 116, Mar 75, DD/DG, 100 pgs.	0.60	1.00	3.00	5.00
❏ 117, Apr 75, DD/FMc	0.25	0.60	1.80	3.00
❏ 118, May 75, DD/FMc	0.25	0.60	1.80	3.00
❏ 119, Jun 75, DD/FMc	0.25	0.60	1.80	3.00
❏ 120, Jul 75, DD/FMc	0.25	0.60	1.80	3.00
❏ 121, Aug 75, DD/FMc	0.25	0.60	1.80	3.00
❏ 122, Sep 75, DD/FMc	0.25	0.60	1.80	3.00
❏ 123, Oct 75, DD/FMc	0.25	0.60	1.80	3.00
❏ 124, Nov 75, DD/FMc	0.25	0.60	1.80	3.00
❏ 125, Dec 75, DD/FMc	0.25	0.60	1.80	3.00
❏ 126, Jan 76, DD/FMc, Joker	0.26	0.70	2.10	3.50
❏ 127, Feb 76, DD/FMc	0.25	0.60	1.80	3.00
❏ 128, Mar 76, DD/FMc	0.25	0.60	1.80	3.00
❏ 129, Apr 76, DD/FMc	0.30	0.60	1.80	3.00
❏ 130, May 76, DD/FMc	0.30	0.60	1.80	3.00
❏ 131, Jun 76, DD/FMc	0.30	0.60	1.80	3.00
❏ 132, Jul 76, DD/FMc	0.30	0.60	1.80	3.00
❏ 133, Aug 76, DD/FMc	0.30	0.60	1.80	3.00
❏ 134, Sep 76, DD/FMc	0.30	0.60	1.80	3.00
❏ 135, Oct 76, DD/FMc	0.30	0.60	1.80	3.00
❏ 136, Nov 76, DD/FMc, Joker	0.30	1.00	3.00	5.00
❏ 137, Dec 76, DD/FMc, double size	0.30	0.60	1.80	3.00
❏ 138, Jan 77, DD/FMc, double size	0.30	0.60	1.80	3.00
❏ 139, Feb 77, DD/FMc, double size	0.50	0.60	1.80	3.00
❏ 140, Mar 77, DD/FMc, A:Manhunter	0.50	0.40	1.20	2.00
❏ 141, Apr 77, DD/FMc, A:Manhunter	0.50	0.40	1.20	2.00
❏ 142, May 77, DD/FMc	0.50	0.40	1.20	2.00
❏ 143, Jun 77, DD/FMc	0.60	0.40	1.20	2.00
❏ 144, Jul 77, DD/FMc	0.60	0.40	1.20	2.00
❏ 145, Aug 77, DD/FMc	0.60	0.40	1.20	2.00
❏ 146, Sep 77, DD/FMc	0.60	0.40	1.20	2.00
❏ 147, Oct 77, DD/FMc	0.60	0.40	1.20	2.00
❏ 148, Nov 77, DD/FMc	0.60	0.40	1.20	2.00
❏ 149, Dec 77, DD/FMc	0.60	0.40	1.20	2.00
❏ 150, Jan 78, DD/FMc	0.60	0.40	1.20	2.00
❏ 151, Feb 78, DD/FMc	0.60	0.40	1.20	2.00
❏ 152, Mar 78, DD/FMc	0.60	0.40	1.20	2.00
❏ 153, Apr 78, DD/FMc	0.60	0.40	1.20	2.00
❏ 154, May 78, DD/FMc	0.60	0.40	1.20	2.00
❏ 155, Jun 78, DD/FMc	0.60	0.40	1.20	2.00
❏ 156, Jul 78, DD/FMc	0.60	0.40	1.20	2.00
❏ 157, Aug 78, DD/FMc	0.60	0.40	1.20	2.00
❏ 158, Sep 78, DD/FMc	0.60	0.40	1.20	2.00
❏ 159, Oct 78, DD/FMc	0.60	0.40	1.20	2.00

	ORIG.	GOOD	FINE	N-MINT
❏ 160, Nov 78, DD/FMc	0.60	0.40	1.20	2.00
❏ 161, Dec 78, DD/FMc	0.40	0.40	1.20	2.00
❏ 162, Jan 79, DD/FMc	0.40	0.40	1.20	2.00
❏ 163, Feb 79, DD/FMc	0.40	0.40	1.20	2.00
❏ 164, Mar 79, DD/FMc	0.40	0.40	1.20	2.00
❏ 165, Apr 79, DD/FMc	0.40	0.40	1.20	2.00
❏ 166, May 79, DD/FMc	0.40	0.40	1.20	2.00
❏ 167, Jun 79, DD/FMc	0.40	0.40	1.20	2.00
❏ 168, Jul 79, DD/FMc	0.40	0.40	1.20	2.00
❏ 169, Aug 79, DD/FMc	0.40	0.40	1.20	2.00
❏ 170, Sep 79, DD/FMc	0.40	0.40	1.20	2.00
❏ 171, Oct 79, DD/FMc	0.40	0.40	1.20	2.00
❏ 172, Nov 79, DD/FMc	0.40	0.40	1.20	2.00
❏ 173, Dec 79, DD/FMc	0.40	0.40	1.20	2.00
❏ 174, Jan 80, DD/FMc	0.40	0.40	1.20	2.00
❏ 175, Feb 80, DD/FMc	0.40	0.40	1.20	2.00
❏ 176, Mar 80, DD/FMc	0.40	0.40	1.20	2.00
❏ 177, Apr 80, DD/FMc	0.40	0.40	1.20	2.00
❏ 178, May 80, DD/FMc/JSn	0.40	0.40	1.20	2.00
❏ 179, Jun 80, DD/FMc/JSn	0.40	0.40	1.20	2.00
❏ 180, Jul 80, DD/FMc/JSn	0.40	0.40	1.20	2.00
❏ 181, Aug 80	0.40	0.40	1.20	2.00
❏ 182, Sep 80	0.50	0.40	1.20	2.00
❏ 183, Oct 80, DD/FMc/JSn, Darkseid	0.50	0.40	1.20	2.00
❏ 184, Nov 80, DD/FMc, Darkseid	0.50	0.40	1.20	2.00
❏ 185, Dec 80, DD/FMc/JSn, Darkseid	0.50	0.40	1.20	2.00
❏ 186, Jan 81, GP/FMc	0.50	0.40	1.20	2.00
❏ 187, Feb 81	0.50	0.40	1.20	2.00
❏ 188, Mar 81	0.50	0.40	1.20	2.00
❏ 189, Apr 81	0.50	0.40	1.20	2.00
❏ 190, May 81	0.50	0.40	1.20	2.00
❏ 191, Jun 81	0.50	0.40	1.20	2.00
❏ 192, Jul 81, GP	0.50	0.40	1.20	2.00
❏ 193, Aug 81, GP 1:All-Star Squadron	0.50	0.40	1.20	2.00
❏ 194, Sep 81, GP	0.50	0.40	1.20	2.00
❏ 195, Oct 81, GP	0.60	0.40	1.20	2.00
❏ 196, Nov 81, GP	0.60	0.40	1.20	2.00
❏ 197, Dec 81, GP	0.60	0.40	1.20	2.00
❏ 198, Jan 82, DH	0.60	0.40	1.20	2.00
❏ 199, Feb 82, DH	0.60	0.40	1.20	2.00
❏ 200, Mar 82, GP/DG/GK/ CI/JKu/BB-PB/TA	1.50	0.80	2.40	4.00
❏ 201, Apr 82, DH	0.60	0.35	1.05	1.75
❏ 202, May 82, DH	0.60	0.35	1.05	1.75
❏ 203, Jun 82, DH	0.60	0.35	1.05	1.75
❏ 204, Jul 82, DH	0.60	0.35	1.05	1.75
❏ 205, Aug 82, DH	0.60	0.35	1.05	1.75
❏ 206, Sep 82, DH/RT	0.60	0.35	1.05	1.75
❏ 207, Oct 82	0.60	0.35	1.05	1.75
❏ 208, Nov 82	0.60	0.35	1.05	1.75
❏ 209, Dec 82	0.60	0.35	1.05	1.75
❏ 210, Jan 83	0.60	0.35	1.05	1.75
❏ 211, Feb 83	0.60	0.35	1.05	1.75
❏ 212, Mar 83	0.60	0.35	1.05	1.75
❏ 213, Apr 83	0.60	0.35	1.05	1.75
❏ 214, May 83	0.60	0.35	1.05	1.75
❏ 215, Jun 83	0.60	0.35	1.05	1.75
❏ 216, Jul 83	0.60	0.35	1.05	1.75
❏ 217, Aug 83	0.60	0.35	1.05	1.75
❏ 218, Sep 83	0.60	0.35	1.05	1.75
❏ 219, Oct 83	0.60	0.35	1.05	1.75
❏ 220, Nov 83	0.60	0.35	1.05	1.75
❏ 221, Dec 83	0.75	0.35	1.05	1.75
❏ 222, Jan 84	0.75	0.35	1.05	1.75
❏ 223, Feb 84	0.75	0.35	1.05	1.75

	ORIG.	GOOD	FINE	N-MINT
224, Mar 84	0.75	0.35	1.05	1.75
225, Apr 84	0.75	0.35	1.05	1.75
226, May 84	0.75	0.35	1.05	1.75
227, Jun 84	0.75	0.35	1.05	1.75
228, Jul 84	0.75	0.35	1.05	1.75
229, Aug 84	0.75	0.35	1.05	1.75
230, Sep 84	0.75	0.35	1.05	1.75
231, Oct 84	0.75	0.35	1.05	1.75
232, Nov 84	0.75	0.35	1.05	1.75
233, Dec 84	0.75	0.35	1.05	1.75
234, Jan 85	0.75	0.35	1.05	1.75
235, Feb 85	0.75	0.35	1.05	1.75
236, Mar 85	0.75	0.35	1.05	1.75
237, Apr 85	0.75	0.35	1.05	1.75
238, May 85	0.75	0.35	1.05	1.75
239, Jun 85	0.75	0.35	1.05	1.75
240, Jul 85	0.75	0.35	1.05	1.75
241, Aug 85	0.75	0.35	1.05	1.75
242, Sep 85	0.75	0.35	1.05	1.75
243, Oct 85	0.75	0.35	1.05	1.75
244, Nov 85	0.75	0.35	1.05	1.75
245, Dec 85, Crisis	0.75	0.35	1.05	1.75
246, Jan 86	0.75	0.35	1.05	1.75
247, Feb 86	0.75	0.35	1.05	1.75
248, Mar 86	0.75	0.35	1.05	1.75
249, Apr 86	0.75	0.35	1.05	1.75
250, May 86	0.75	0.35	1.05	1.75
251, Jun 86	0.75	0.35	1.05	1.75
252, Jul 86	0.75	0.35	1.05	1.75
253, Aug 86	0.75	0.35	1.05	1.75
254, Sep 86	0.75	0.35	1.05	1.75
255, Oct 86	0.75	0.35	1.05	1.75
256, Nov 86	0.75	0.35	1.05	1.75
257, Dec 86	0.75	0.35	1.05	1.75
258, Jan 87, Legends, D:Vibe	0.75	0.35	1.05	1.75
259, Feb 87, Legends, L:Gypsy	0.75	0.35	1.05	1.75
260, Mar 87, Legends, D:Steel	0.75	0.35	1.05	1.75
261, Apr 87, end of JLA	0.75	0.35	1.05	1.75

JUSTICE LEAGUE OF AMERICA ANNUAL
	ORIG.	GOOD	FINE	N-MINT
1, Oct 83	1.00	0.25	0.75	1.25
2, Oct 84	1.25	0.25	0.75	1.25
3, Nov 85, Crisis	1.25	0.30	0.90	1.50

JUSTICE LEAGUE OF AMERICA INDEX
(was Official Index to...)
ECLIPSE/INDEPENDENT
		GOOD	FINE	N-MINT
8		0.40	1.20	2.00

JUSTICE LEAGUE QUARTERLY
DC
	ORIG.	GOOD	FINE	N-MINT
1, Dec 90	2.95	0.59	1.77	2.95
2, Mar 91	2.95	0.59	1.77	2.95
3, Jun 91	2.95	0.59	1.77	2.95
4, Sep 91	2.95	0.59	1.77	2.95
5, Dec 91	2.95	0.59	1.77	2.95
6, Spr 92	2.95	0.59	1.77	2.95
7, Sum 92	3.50	0.79	2.37	3.95
8, Aut 92	3.50	0.70	2.10	3.50
9, Win 92	3.50	0.70	2.10	3.50
10, Spr 93	3.50	0.70	2.10	3.50
11, Sum 93	3.50	0.70	2.10	3.50
12, Aut 93	3.50	0.70	2.10	3.50
13, Win 93	3.50	0.70	2.10	3.50
14, Spr 94	3.50	0.70	2.10	3.50
15, Sum 94	3.50	0.70	2.10	3.50
16, Sep 94	3.50	0.70	2.10	3.50
17, Win 94	3.50	0.70	2.10	3.50

JUSTICE LEAGUE SPECTACULAR
	ORIG.	GOOD	FINE	N-MINT
1, Superman cover, O:new teams	1.50	0.30	0.90	1.50
1, Green Lantern cover, O:new teams	1.50	0.30	0.90	1.50

JUSTICE LEAGUE TASK FORCE
	ORIG.	GOOD	FINE	N-MINT
0, Oct 94	1.50	0.30	0.90	1.50
1, "membership" card	1.25	0.25	0.75	1.25
2	1.25	0.25	0.75	1.25
3	1.25	0.25	0.75	1.25
4	1.25	0.25	0.75	1.25
5	1.25	0.80	2.40	4.00
6	1.25	0.40	1.20	2.00
7, transsexual J'onn J'onzz	1.25	0.40	1.20	2.00
8	1.50	0.30	0.90	1.50
9	1.50	0.30	0.90	1.50
10	1.50	0.30	0.90	1.50
11	1.50	0.30	0.90	1.50
12, May 94	1.50	0.30	0.90	1.50
13, Jun 94	1.50	0.30	0.90	1.50
14, Jul 94	1.50	0.30	0.90	1.50
15, Aug 94	1.50	0.30	0.90	1.50
16, Sep 94	1.50	0.30	0.90	1.50
17, Nov 94	1.50	0.30	0.90	1.50
18, Dec 94	1.50	0.30	0.90	1.50
19, Jan 95	1.50	0.30	0.90	1.50
20, Feb 95	1.50	0.30	0.90	1.50
21, Mar 95	1.50	0.30	0.90	1.50
22, Apr 95	1.50	0.30	0.90	1.50
23, May 95	1.50	0.30	0.90	1.50
24, Jun 95	1.75	0.35	1.05	1.75
25, Jul 95	1.75	0.35	1.05	1.75
26, Aug 95	1.75	0.35	1.05	1.75
27, Sep 95	1.75	0.35	1.05	1.75
28, Oct 95	1.75	0.35	1.05	1.75
29, Nov 95	1.75	0.35	1.05	1.75
30, Dec 95, "Underworld Unleashed"	1.75	0.35	1.05	1.75
31, Jan 96	1.75	0.35	1.05	1.75
32, Feb 96	1.75	0.35	1.05	1.75
33, Mar 96	1.75	0.35	1.05	1.75
34, May 96	1.75	0.35	1.05	1.75
35, Jun 96, A:Warlord	1.75	0.35	1.05	1.75

JUSTICE MACHINE
COMICO
		GOOD	FINE	N-MINT
1, Jan 87, MGu		0.30	0.90	1.50
2, Feb 87, MGu		0.30	0.90	1.50
3, Mar 87, MGu		0.30	0.90	1.50
4, Apr 87, MGu		0.30	0.90	1.50
5, May 87, MGu		0.30	0.90	1.50
6, Jun 87, MGu		0.30	0.90	1.50
7, Jul 87, MGu		0.30	0.90	1.50
8, Aug 87, MGu,D:Demon.		0.30	0.90	1.50
9, Sep 87, MGu		0.30	0.90	1.50
10, Oct 87, MGu		0.30	0.90	1.50
11, Nov 87, MGu		0.30	0.90	1.50
12, Dec 87, MGu		0.30	0.90	1.50
13, Jan 88, MGu		0.30	0.90	1.50
14, Feb 88, MGu		0.30	0.90	1.50
15, Mar 88		0.35	1.05	1.75
16, Apr 88		0.35	1.05	1.75
17, May 88		0.35	1.05	1.75
18, Jun 88		0.35	1.05	1.75
19, Jul 88		0.35	1.05	1.75
20, Aug 88		0.35	1.05	1.75
21, Sep 88		0.35	1.05	1.75
22, Oct 88		0.35	1.05	1.75
23, Nov 88		0.35	1.05	1.75
24, Dec 88		0.35	1.05	1.75
25, Jan 89		0.35	1.05	1.75

	ORIG.	GOOD	FINE	N-MINT
☐ 26, Feb 89	0.39	1.17	1.95
☐ 27, Mar 89	0.39	1.17	1.95
☐ 28, Apr 89	0.39	1.17	1.95
☐ 29, May 89	0.39	1.17	1.95

MILLENNIUM

		GOOD	FINE	N-MINT
☐ 1		0.50	1.50	2.50

NOBLE

		GOOD	FINE	N-MINT
☐ 1, 81, JBy(c),MGu		5.00	15.00	25.00
☐ 2, 81, TA(c),MGu		3.00	9.00	15.00
☐ 3, Jun 81, MGu		2.00	6.00	10.00
☐ 4, 82, MGu		1.50	4.50	7.50
☐ 5, Nov 83, MGu		1.50	4.50	7.50

JUSTICE MACHINE & ELEMENTALS
COMICO

		GOOD	FINE	N-MINT
☐ 1, May 86		0.40	1.20	2.00
☐ 2, Jun 86		0.40	1.20	2.00
☐ 3, Jul 86		0.40	1.20	2.00
☐ 4, Aug 86		0.40	1.20	2.00

JUSTICE MACHINE ANNUAL

		GOOD	FINE	N-MINT
☐ 1, Jun 89		0.50	1.50	2.50

TEXAS

		GOOD	FINE	N-MINT
☐ 1, Jan 84, THUNDER Agents, 1:Elementals				
		2.00	6.00	10.00

JUSTICE MACHINE SUMMER SPECTACULAR
INNOVATION

		GOOD	FINE	N-MINT
☐ 1, Aug 90		0.55	1.65	2.75

JUSTICE MACHINE, THE
MILLENNIUM

		GOOD	FINE	N-MINT
☐ 1		0.50	1.50	2.50
☐ 2		0.50	1.50	2.50

JUSTICE MACHINE, THE (was Comico title)
INNOVATION

		GOOD	FINE	N-MINT
☐ 1, Apr 90		0.39	1.17	1.95
☐ 2, May 90		0.39	1.17	1.95
☐ 3, Jul 90		0.39	1.17	1.95
☐ 4, Sep 90		0.39	1.17	1.95
☐ 5, Nov 90		0.39	1.17	1.95
☐ 6, Jan 91		0.45	1.35	2.25
☐ 7, Apr 91		0.45	1.35	2.25

JUSTICE SOCIETY OF AMERICA (mini-series)
DC

	ORIG.	GOOD	FINE	N-MINT
☐ 1, Apr 91, Flash	1.00	0.40	1.20	2.00
☐ 2, May 91, Black Canary	1.00	0.20	0.60	1.00
☐ 3, Jun 91, Green Lantern	1.00	0.20	0.60	1.00
☐ 4, Jul 91, Hawkman	1.00	0.20	0.60	1.00

	ORIG.	GOOD	FINE	N-MINT
☐ 5, Aug 91, Flash, Hawkman				
	1.00	0.20	0.60	1.00
☐ 6, Sep 91, GL, BC	1.00	0.20	0.60	1.00
☐ 7, Oct 91, GL, BC, Hawkman, Flash				
	1.00	0.20	0.60	1.00
☐ 8, Nov 91, GL, BC, Hawkman, Flash				
	1.00	0.20	0.60	1.00

JUSTICE SOCIETY OF AMERICA
(ongoing series, begins 1992)

	ORIG.	GOOD	FINE	N-MINT
☐ 1, Aug 92	1.25	0.25	0.75	1.25
☐ 2, Sep 92	1.25	0.25	0.75	1.25
☐ 3, Oct 92	1.25	0.25	0.75	1.25
☐ 4, Nov 92	1.25	0.25	0.75	1.25
☐ 5, Dec 92	1.25	0.25	0.75	1.25
☐ 6, Jan 93	1.25	0.25	0.75	1.25
☐ 7, Feb 93	1.25	0.25	0.75	1.25
☐ 8, Mar 93	1.25	0.25	0.75	1.25
☐ 9, Apr 93	1.25	0.25	0.75	1.25
☐ 10, May 93	1.25	0.25	0.75	1.25

JUSTICE, INC.

	ORIG.	GOOD	FINE	N-MINT
☐ 1, Jun 75	0.25	0.79	2.37	3.95
☐ 2, Aug 75	0.25	0.79	2.37	3.95
☐ 3, Oct 75	0.25	0.79	2.37	3.95
☐ 4, Dec 75	0.25	0.79	2.37	3.95

JUSTICE: FOUR BALANCE (mini-series)
MARVEL

	ORIG.	GOOD	FINE	N-MINT
☐ 1, Sep 94	1.75	0.35	1.05	1.75
☐ 2, Oct 94	1.75	0.35	1.05	1.75
☐ 3, Nov 94	1.75	0.35	1.05	1.75
☐ 4, Dec 94	1.75	0.35	1.05	1.75

JUSTY
VIZ

		GOOD	FINE	N-MINT
☐ 1, b&w, Japanese		0.35	1.05	1.75
☐ 2, b&w, Japanese		0.35	1.05	1.75
☐ 3, b&w, Japanese		0.35	1.05	1.75
☐ 4, b&w, Japanese		0.35	1.05	1.75
☐ 5, b&w, Japanese		0.35	1.05	1.75
☐ 6, b&w, Japanese		0.35	1.05	1.75
☐ 7, b&w, Japanese		0.35	1.05	1.75
☐ 8, b&w, Japanese		0.35	1.05	1.75
☐ 9, b&w, Japanese		0.35	1.05	1.75

Didja know?

Journey into Mystery began as a science-fiction and fantasy anthology for its first 82 issues. Thor was introduced in issue #83 in 1962. The series' title was changed to *Thor* with issue #126 and continued *Journey into Mystery*'s numbering. Since then, the title has changed to *The Mighty Thor* and back again to *Thor*.

A second *Journey into Mystery* series began in 1972, and the first issue is shown at right.

Journey into Mystery #83 © 1962 Atlas Magazines, Inc. (Marvel)

Journey into Mystery #1 © 1972 Magazine Management Co., Inc. (Marvel)

K

	ORIG.	GOOD	FINE	N-MINT
KA-ZAR (1970)				
MARVEL				
❏ 1, giant	0.25	1.20	3.60	6.00
❏ 2, giant	0.25	1.00	3.00	5.00
❏ 3, giant	0.25	1.00	3.00	5.00
KA-ZAR (1972)				
❏ 1, O:Savage Land	0.20	0.60	1.80	3.00
❏ 2, DH	0.20	0.40	1.20	2.00
❏ 3, DH	0.25	0.40	1.20	2.00
❏ 4, DH	0.25	0.40	1.20	2.00
❏ 5, DH	0.25	0.40	1.20	2.00
❏ 6, JB	0.25	0.30	0.90	1.50
❏ 7, JB	0.25	0.30	0.90	1.50
❏ 8, JB	0.25	0.30	0.90	1.50
❏ 9, JB	0.25	0.30	0.90	1.50
❏ 10, JB	0.25	0.30	0.90	1.50
❏ 11	0.25	0.20	0.60	1.00
❏ 12	0.25	0.20	0.60	1.00
❏ 13	0.25	0.20	0.60	1.00
❏ 14	0.25	0.20	0.60	1.00
❏ 15	0.25	0.20	0.60	1.00
❏ 16	0.30	0.20	0.60	1.00
❏ 17	0.30	0.20	0.60	1.00
❏ 18	0.30	0.20	0.60	1.00
❏ 19	0.30	0.20	0.60	1.00
❏ 20	0.30	0.20	0.60	1.00
KA-ZAR THE SAVAGE (1981)				
❏ 1, Apr 81, BA, O	0.50	0.30	0.90	1.50
❏ 2, May 81, BA	0.50	0.20	0.60	1.00
❏ 3, Jun 81, BA	0.50	0.20	0.60	1.00
❏ 4, Jul 81, BA	0.50	0.20	0.60	1.00
❏ 5, Aug 81, BA	0.50	0.20	0.60	1.00
❏ 6, Sep 81, BA	0.50	0.20	0.60	1.00
❏ 7, Oct 81, BA	0.50	0.20	0.60	1.00
❏ 8, Nov 81, BA	0.50	0.20	0.60	1.00
❏ 9, Dec 81, BA	0.50	0.20	0.60	1.00
❏ 10, Jan 82, BA, direct distribution	0.75	0.50	1.50	2.50
❏ 11, Feb 82, BA/GK, Zabu	0.75	0.30	0.90	1.50
❏ 12, Mar 82, BA, panel missing	0.75	0.30	0.90	1.50
❏ 12, rep.	0.75	0.40	1.20	2.00
❏ 13, Apr 82, BA	0.75	0.30	0.90	1.50
❏ 14, May 82	0.75	0.20	0.60	1.00
❏ 15, Jun 82	0.75	0.20	0.60	1.00
❏ 16, Jul 82	0.75	0.20	0.60	1.00
❏ 17, Aug 82	0.75	0.20	0.60	1.00
❏ 18, Sep 82	0.75	0.20	0.60	1.00
❏ 19, Oct 82	0.75	0.20	0.60	1.00
❏ 20, Nov 82	0.75	0.20	0.60	1.00
❏ 21, Dec 82	0.75	0.20	0.60	1.00
❏ 22, Jan 83	0.75	0.20	0.60	1.00
❏ 23, Feb 83	0.75	0.20	0.60	1.00
❏ 24, Mar 83	0.75	0.20	0.60	1.00
❏ 25, Apr 83	0.75	0.20	0.60	1.00
❏ 26, May 83	0.75	0.20	0.60	1.00
❏ 27, Aug 83	0.75	0.20	0.60	1.00
❏ 28, Oct 83	0.75	0.20	0.60	1.00
❏ 29, Dec 83	1.00	0.20	0.60	1.00
❏ 30, Feb 84	1.00	0.20	0.60	1.00
❏ 31, Apr 84	1.00	0.20	0.60	1.00
❏ 32, Jun 84	1.00	0.20	0.60	1.00
❏ 33, Aug 84	1.00	0.20	0.60	1.00
❏ 34, Oct 84	1.00	0.20	0.60	1.00
KABUKI GALLERY				
CALIBER				
❏ 1, Aug 95, pin-ups	2.95	0.59	1.77	2.95

	ORIG.	GOOD	FINE	N-MINT
KABUKI: CIRCLE OF BLOOD				
❏ 1, b&w	2.95	1.50	4.50	7.50
❏ 1, Jul 95, b&w;second printing;enhanced cover	2.95	0.59	1.77	2.95
❏ 2, b&w	2.95	0.59	1.77	2.95
❏ 3, Jan 95, b&w	2.95	0.59	1.77	2.95
❏ 4, Jul 95, b&w	2.95	0.59	1.77	2.95
KABUKI: FEAR THE REAPER				
❏ 1, 94	3.50	2.00	6.00	10.00
KAFKA				
RENEGADE				
❏ 1, Apr 87, b&w	2.00	0.40	1.20	2.00
❏ 2, May 87, b&w	2.00	0.40	1.20	2.00
❏ 3, Jun 87, b&w	2.00	0.40	1.20	2.00
❏ 4, Jul 87, b&w	2.00	0.40	1.20	2.00
❏ 5, Aug 87, b&w	2.00	0.40	1.20	2.00
❏ 6, Sep 87, b&w	2.00	0.40	1.20	2.00
KAFKA: THE EXECUTION				
FANTAGRAPHICS				
❏ 1, b&w, Duranona		0.59	1.77	2.95
KAKTUS				
❏ 1, b&w		0.50	1.50	2.50
KALGAN THE GOLDEN				
HARRIER				
❏ 1		0.39	1.17	1.95
KAMANDI AT EARTH'S END				
DC				
❏ 1, Jun 93	1.75	0.50	1.50	2.50
❏ 2	2.25	0.45	1.35	2.25
❏ 3	1.75	0.35	1.05	1.75
❏ 4	1.75	0.35	1.05	1.75
❏ 5	1.75	0.35	1.05	1.75
❏ 6	1.75	0.35	1.05	1.75
KAMANDI, THE LAST BOY ON EARTH				
❏ 1, Nov 72	0.20	10.00	30.00	50.00
❏ 2, Jan 73	0.20	6.40	19.20	32.00
❏ 3, Feb 73	0.20	4.00	12.00	20.00
❏ 4, Mar 73	0.20	4.00	12.00	20.00
❏ 5, Apr 73	0.20	4.00	12.00	20.00
❏ 6, Jun 73	0.20	3.20	9.60	16.00
❏ 7, Jul 73	0.20	3.20	9.60	16.00
❏ 8, Aug 73	0.20	3.20	9.60	16.00
❏ 9, Sep 73	0.20	3.20	9.60	16.00
❏ 10, Oct 73	0.20	3.20	9.60	16.00
❏ 11, Nov 73	0.20	2.00	6.00	10.00
❏ 12, Dec 73	0.20	2.00	6.00	10.00
❏ 13, Jan 74	0.20	2.00	6.00	10.00
❏ 14, Feb 74	0.20	2.00	6.00	10.00
❏ 15, Mar 74	0.20	2.00	6.00	10.00
❏ 16, Apr 74	0.20	2.00	6.00	10.00
❏ 17, May 74	0.20	2.00	6.00	10.00
❏ 18, Jun 74	0.20	2.00	6.00	10.00
❏ 19, Jul 74	0.20	2.00	6.00	10.00
❏ 20, Aug 74	0.20	2.00	6.00	10.00
❏ 21, Sep 74	0.20	1.40	4.20	7.00
❏ 22, Oct 74	0.20	1.40	4.20	7.00
❏ 23, Nov 74	0.20	1.40	4.20	7.00
❏ 24, Dec 74	0.20	1.40	4.20	7.00
❏ 25, Jan 75	0.25	1.40	4.20	7.00
❏ 26, Feb 75	0.25	1.40	4.20	7.00
❏ 27, Mar 75	0.25	1.40	4.20	7.00
❏ 28, Apr 75	0.25	1.40	4.20	7.00
❏ 29, May 75	0.25	1.40	4.20	7.00
❏ 30, Jun 75	0.25	1.40	4.20	7.00
❏ 31, Jul 75	0.25	1.40	4.20	7.00
❏ 32, Aug 75	0.50	1.40	4.20	7.00
❏ 33, Sep 75	0.25	1.40	4.20	7.00
❏ 34, Oct 75	0.25	1.40	4.20	7.00

Kamandi

Kamandi, the Last Boy on Earth #1 © 1972 National Periodical Publications, Inc. (DC)

First appearance: *Kamandi, the Last Boy on Earth* #1, November 1972.

When Jack Kirby came to DC in the early 1970s, he brought along a number of ideas, including The New Gods, Darkseid, the resurrection of The Newsboy Legion, and Kamandi, the Last Boy on Earth.

Kamandi's adventures began when he left the safety of his fallout shelter (known as Command-D, from which the character took his name) to forage for food. While he was gone, his grandfather was attacked by mutated beasts that had quickly swarmed up the evolutionary ladder after the worldwide cataclysm known as The Great Disaster. The beasts had acquired human-like intelligence and the ability to walk upright.

Kamandi's grandfather had shown the boy educational tapes and books during their long stay in the bunker, enabling Kamandi to survive in the outside world. There he found that, while the animals had evolved, humanity had devolved to an animal-like state with the real animals referring to the humans as "animals," often keeping them as pets.

As the series progressed, Kamandi was revealed as a descendant of OMAC (the One Man Army Corps) and his grandfather as either OMAC's offspring or OMAC himself.

Soon, Kamandi met such other human-like survivors of The Great Disaster as Ben Boxer and his friends who had had cyclotronic devices implanted in place of their hearts so that they could survive the deadly radiations generated by The Great Disaster.

After touring the changed geography of the Americas, meeting many other mutated creatures, and discovering the final fate of Superman, Kamandi was told of a site in Australia where he could learn the cause of The Great Disaster.

Over the course of several more issues, he traveled there and, as he was about the learn the cause of The Great Disaster, the series ended abruptly with issue #59.

Issues #60 and 61 had been nearly ready to go to the printer at the time of the series' cancellation. Both issues were photocopied and appeared in *Cancelled Comic Cavalcade* #2, the final issue of a privately circulated (only 35 copies of each issue were made) series. The story was later rewritten and ran in *Brave and the Bold* #157, with Kamandi coming to present-day Gotham City. Batman had made a trip to Kamandi's future in *Brave and the Bold* #120.

After this appearance, Kamandi did not reappear until 1985, when he played a part in *Crisis on Infinite Earths*.

Following the events of *Crisis*, Kamandi's history was altered so that Commander Tomorrow named him Thomas after he found the young boy emerging from the fallout shelter.

The Great Disaster was altered in *Twilight*, a three-issue Elseworlds mini-series, to the point at which genetic tampering, not radiation, was responsible for the rapid evolution of the animals.

In the 1990s, Kamandi was revived for *Kamandi: At Earth's End*, an Elseworlds mini-series that rewrote his origins again and showed another possible future for Superman. That Superman returned in *Superman: At Earth's End*, an Elseworlds one-shot. Elseworlds stories are *not* part of "official" DC continuity.

Partial Checklist

	ORIG.	GOOD	FINE	N-MINT
35, Nov 75 .... 0.25		1.40	4.20	7.00
36, Dec 75 .... 0.25		1.40	4.20	7.00
37, Jan 76 .... 0.25		1.40	4.20	7.00
38, Feb 76 .... 0.25		1.40	4.20	7.00
39, Mar 76 .... 0.25		1.40	4.20	7.00
40, Apr 76 .... 0.30		1.40	4.20	7.00
41, May 76 .... 0.30		0.60	1.80	3.00
42, Jun 76 .... 0.30		0.60	1.80	3.00
43, Jul 76 .... 0.30		0.60	1.80	3.00
44, Aug 76 .... 0.30		0.60	1.80	3.00
45, Sep 76 .... 0.30		0.60	1.80	3.00
46, Oct 76 .... 0.30		0.60	1.80	3.00
47, Nov 76 .... 0.30		0.60	1.80	3.00
48, Jan 77 .... 0.30		0.60	1.80	3.00
49, Mar 77 .... 0.30		0.60	1.80	3.00
50, May 77 .... 0.30		0.60	1.80	3.00
51, Jul 77 .... 0.35		0.60	1.80	3.00
52, Sep 77 .... 0.35		0.60	1.80	3.00
53, Nov 77 .... 0.35		0.60	1.80	3.00
54, Jan 78 .... 0.35		0.60	1.80	3.00
55, Mar 78 .... 0.35		0.60	1.80	3.00
56, May 78 .... 0.35		0.60	1.80	3.00
57, Jul 78 .... 0.35		0.60	1.80	3.00
58, Sep 78 .... 0.35		0.60	1.80	3.00
59, Oct 78 .... 0.50		0.60	1.80	3.00

KAMIKAZE KAT
PIED PIPER

	ORIG.	GOOD	FINE	N-MINT
1		0.39	1.17	1.95

KAPTAIN KEEN & KOMPANY
VORTEX

	GOOD	FINE	N-MINT
1	0.35	1.05	1.75
2	0.35	1.05	1.75
3	0.35	1.05	1.75
4	0.35	1.05	1.75
5	0.35	1.05	1.75
6	0.35	1.05	1.75

KARATE GIRL
EROS COMIX

	GOOD	FINE	N-MINT
1, adult, b&w	0.50	1.50	2.50
2, adult, b&w	0.50	1.50	2.50

KARATE KID
DC

	ORIG.	GOOD	FINE	N-MINT
1, Apr 76 .... 0.25		0.50	1.50	2.50
2, Jun 76 .... 0.30		0.30	0.90	1.50
3, Aug 76 .... 0.30		0.30	0.90	1.50
4, Oct 76 .... 0.30		0.30	0.90	1.50
5, Dec 76 .... 0.30		0.30	0.90	1.50
6, Feb 77 .... 0.30		0.25	0.75	1.25
7, Apr 77, MGr 0.30		0.25	0.75	1.25
8, Jun 77, MGr 0.30		0.25	0.75	1.25
9, Aug 77 .... 0.35		0.25	0.75	1.25
10, Oct 77 .... 0.35		0.25	0.75	1.25
11, Dec 77 .... 0.35		0.25	0.75	1.25
12, Feb 78 .... 0.35		0.25	0.75	1.25
13, Apr 78 .... 0.35		0.25	0.75	1.25
14, Jun 78 .... 0.35		0.25	0.75	1.25
15, Aug 78, final issue ... 0.35		0.25	0.75	1.25

KARATE KREATURES
MA

	GOOD	FINE	N-MINT
1, color	0.40	1.20	2.00
2, color	0.40	1.20	2.00

KATMANDU
ANTARCTIC

	ORIG.	GOOD	FINE	N-MINT
1, Nov 93, b&w;adult 2.75		0.55	1.65	2.75
2, Jan 94, b&w;adult 2.95		0.59	1.77	2.95
3, Apr 94, b&w;adult 2.95		0.59	1.77	2.95
4, Mar 95, b&w;adult 2.75		0.55	1.65	2.75
5, May 95, b&w;adult 2.75		0.55	1.65	2.75

KATO OF THE GREEN HORNET
NOW

	GOOD	FINE	N-MINT
1, Nov 91	0.50	1.50	2.50
2, Dec 91	0.50	1.50	2.50
3	0.50	1.50	2.50
4	0.50	1.50	2.50

KATO OF THE GREEN HORNET II

	ORIG.	GOOD	FINE	N-MINT
1, Nov 92 .... 2.50		0.50	1.50	2.50
2, Dec 92 .... 2.50		0.50	1.50	2.50

KATY KEENE SPECIAL
RED CIRCLE

	GOOD	FINE	N-MINT
1	0.20	0.60	1.00

KEIF LLAMA XENO-TECH
FANTAGRAPHICS

	GOOD	FINE	N-MINT
1, b&w	0.40	1.20	2.00
2, b&w	0.40	1.20	2.00
3, b&w	0.40	1.20	2.00
4, b&w	0.40	1.20	2.00
5, b&w	0.40	1.20	2.00
6, b&w	0.40	1.20	2.00

KEITH LAUMER'S RETIEF
MAD DOG

	ORIG.	GOOD	FINE	N-MINT
1, Apr 87, b&w 1.75		0.60	1.80	3.00
2, Jun 87 .... 1.75		0.40	1.20	2.00
3, Aug 87 .... 1.75		0.40	1.20	2.00
4, Oct 87 .... 1.75		0.40	1.20	2.00
5, Jan 88 .... 1.75		0.40	1.20	2.00
6, Mar 88 .... 1.75		0.40	1.20	2.00

KELVIN MACE
VORTEX

	GOOD	FINE	N-MINT
1	0.60	1.80	3.00
2	0.35	1.05	1.75

KENDRA: LEGACY OF THE BLOOD
PERRYDOG

	GOOD	FINE	N-MINT
1	0.40	1.20	2.00
2	0.40	1.20	2.00

KI-GORR THE KILLER
AC

	ORIG.	GOOD	FINE	N-MINT
1, reprints 3.95		0.79	2.37	3.95

KICKERS, INC.
MARVEL

	ORIG.	GOOD	FINE	N-MINT
1, Nov 86 .... 0.75		0.20	0.60	1.00
2, Dec 86 .... 0.75		0.20	0.60	1.00
3, Jan 87 .... 0.75		0.20	0.60	1.00
4, Feb 87 .... 0.75		0.20	0.60	1.00
5, Mar 87 .... 0.75		0.20	0.60	1.00
6, Apr 87 .... 0.75		0.20	0.60	1.00
7, May 87 .... 0.75		0.20	0.60	1.00
8, Jun 87 .... 0.75		0.20	0.60	1.00
9, Jul 87 .... 0.75		0.20	0.60	1.00
10, Aug 87 .... 0.75		0.20	0.60	1.00
11, Sep 87 .... 0.75		0.20	0.60	1.00
12, Oct 87 .... 0.75		0.20	0.60	1.00

KID 'N PLAY

	ORIG.	GOOD	FINE	N-MINT
1 .... 1.25		0.25	0.75	1.25
2 .... 1.25		0.25	0.75	1.25
3 .... 1.25		0.25	0.75	1.25
4 .... 1.25		0.25	0.75	1.25
5 .... 1.25		0.25	0.75	1.25
6 .... 1.25		0.25	0.75	1.25
7 .... 1.25		0.25	0.75	1.25
8 .... 1.25		0.25	0.75	1.25
9 .... 1.25		0.25	0.75	1.25

KID ANARCHY
FANTAGRAPHICS

	GOOD	FINE	N-MINT
1, b&w	0.50	1.50	2.50
2, b&w	0.55	1.65	2.75
3, b&w	0.55	1.65	2.75

	ORIG.	GOOD	FINE	N-MINT

KID CANNIBAL
ETERNITY
	ORIG.	GOOD	FINE	N-MINT
1		0.50	1.50	2.50
2		0.50	1.50	2.50
3		0.50	1.50	2.50
4		0.50	1.50	2.50

KID ETERNITY
DC
		GOOD	FINE	N-MINT
1, May 91		0.99	2.97	4.95
2, Jul 91		0.99	2.97	4.95
3, Oct 91		0.99	2.97	4.95

DC/VERTIGO
	ORIG.	GOOD	FINE	N-MINT
1	1.95	0.39	1.17	1.95
2	1.95	0.39	1.17	1.95
3	1.95	0.39	1.17	1.95
4	1.95	0.39	1.17	1.95
5	1.95	0.39	1.17	1.95
6	1.95	0.39	1.17	1.95
7	1.95	0.39	1.17	1.95
8	1.95	0.39	1.17	1.95
9	1.95	0.39	1.17	1.95
10	1.95	0.39	1.17	1.95
11	1.95	0.39	1.17	1.95
12, May 94	1.95	0.39	1.17	1.95
13, Jun 94	1.95	0.39	1.17	1.95
14, Jul 94	1.95	0.39	1.17	1.95
15, Aug 94	1.95	0.39	1.17	1.95
16, Sep 94	1.95	0.39	1.17	1.95

KID SUPREME
IMAGE
	ORIG.	GOOD	FINE	N-MINT
1, Mar 96	2.50	0.50	1.50	2.50

KIDZ OF THE KING
KING
	ORIG.	GOOD	FINE	N-MINT
1	2.95	0.59	1.77	2.95
2, May 94	2.95	0.59	1.77	2.95

KIKU SAN
AIRCEL
		GOOD	FINE	N-MINT
1, b&w		0.39	1.17	1.95
2, b&w		0.39	1.17	1.95
3, b&w		0.39	1.17	1.95
4, b&w		0.39	1.17	1.95
5, b&w		0.39	1.17	1.95
6, b&w		0.39	1.17	1.95

KILGORE
RENEGADE
		GOOD	FINE	N-MINT
1, b&w		0.40	1.20	2.00
2, b&w		0.40	1.20	2.00
3, b&w		0.40	1.20	2.00
4, b&w		0.40	1.20	2.00

KILL BARNY
EXPRESS/PARODY
	ORIG.	GOOD	FINE	N-MINT
1, 94, b&w	2.50	0.50	1.50	2.50

KILL BARNY 3
	ORIG.	GOOD	FINE	N-MINT
1, 96, b&w	2.75	0.55	1.65	2.75

KILL IMAGE
BONEYARD
	ORIG.	GOOD	FINE	N-MINT
1, b&w	2.95	0.59	1.77	2.95

KILL YOUR BOYFRIEND
DC/VERTIGO
	ORIG.	GOOD	FINE	N-MINT
1, Jun 95, one-shot	4.95	0.99	2.97	4.95

KILLER
ECLIPSE
		GOOD	FINE	N-MINT
1		0.35	1.05	1.75

KILLER INSTINCT TOUR BOOK
IMAGE
		GOOD	FINE	N-MINT
0		2.00	6.00	10.00

KILLING STROKE
ETERNITY
		GOOD	FINE	N-MINT
1, b&w		0.50	1.50	2.50

	ORIG.	GOOD	FINE	N-MINT
2, b&w		0.50	1.50	2.50
3, b&w		0.50	1.50	2.50
4, b&w		0.50	1.50	2.50

KILLPOWER: THE EARLY YEARS
MARVEL
	ORIG.	GOOD	FINE	N-MINT
1, foil cover	2.95	0.59	1.77	2.95
2	1.75	0.35	1.05	1.75
3	1.75	0.35	1.05	1.75
4	1.75	0.35	1.05	1.75

KILROY IS HERE
CALIBER
	ORIG.	GOOD	FINE	N-MINT
0, 94, b&w;BB(c)	2.95	0.59	1.77	2.95
1, 95, b&w	2.95	0.59	1.77	2.95
2, 95, b&w	2.95	0.59	1.77	2.95
3, 95, b&w	2.95	0.59	1.77	2.95

KILROY: REVELATIONS
	ORIG.	GOOD	FINE	N-MINT
1, 94, b&w;one-shot	2.95	0.59	1.77	2.95

KILROY: THE SHORT STORIES
	ORIG.	GOOD	FINE	N-MINT
1, 95, b&w;one-shot	2.95	0.59	1.77	2.95

KIMBER, PRINCE OF THE FEYLONS
ANTARCTIC
	ORIG.	GOOD	FINE	N-MINT
1, Apr 92, b&w	2.50	0.50	1.50	2.50
2, Jun 92, b&w	2.50	0.50	1.50	2.50

KIMURA
NIGHTWYND
		GOOD	FINE	N-MINT
1, b&w		0.50	1.50	2.50
2, b&w		0.50	1.50	2.50
3, b&w		0.50	1.50	2.50
4, b&w		0.50	1.50	2.50

KINDRED, THE
IMAGE
	ORIG.	GOOD	FINE	N-MINT
1, Mar 94	2.50	2.00	6.00	10.00
2, Apr 94	1.95	1.20	3.60	6.00
3, May 94	1.95	0.70	2.10	3.50
3, May 94, alternate cover	1.95	1.50	4.50	7.50
4, Jul 94	2.50	0.50	1.50	2.50

KING ARTHUR AND THE KNIGHTS OF JUSTICE
MARVEL
	ORIG.	GOOD	FINE	N-MINT
1	1.25	0.25	0.75	1.25
2	1.25	0.25	0.75	1.25
3	1.25	0.25	0.75	1.25

KING CONAN
	ORIG.	GOOD	FINE	N-MINT
1, JB, wife & son	0.75	0.50	1.50	2.50
2, JB	0.75	0.30	0.90	1.50
3, JB	0.75	0.30	0.90	1.50
4	0.75	0.20	0.60	1.00
5	0.75	0.20	0.60	1.00
6	0.75	0.20	0.60	1.00
7, BS	0.75	0.40	1.20	2.00
8, BS	0.75	0.40	1.20	2.00
9	1.00	0.20	0.60	1.00
10	1.00	0.20	0.60	1.00
11	1.00	0.20	0.60	1.00
12	1.00	0.20	0.60	1.00
13	1.00	0.20	0.60	1.00
14	1.00	0.20	0.60	1.00
15	1.00	0.20	0.60	1.00
16	1.00	0.20	0.60	1.00
17	1.00	0.20	0.60	1.00
18	1.00	0.20	0.60	1.00
19, (becomes *Conan the King*)	1.00	0.20	0.60	1.00

KING KONG
GOLD KEY
	ORIG.	GOOD	FINE	N-MINT
0, Sep 68, nn; adapts 1932 film	0.25	2.40	7.20	12.00

	ORIG.	GOOD	FINE	N-MINT
MONSTER				
☐ 1, DSt(c) b&w		0.50	1.50	2.50
☐ 2		0.39	1.17	1.95
☐ 3		0.39	1.17	1.95
☐ 4		0.39	1.17	1.95
☐ 5, Schultz/AW(c)		0.45	1.35	2.25
☐ 6, KSteacy(c)		0.50	1.50	2.50
KING OF THE DEAD				
FANTACO				
☐ 0	1.95	0.39	1.17	1.95
☐ 1	1.95	0.39	1.17	1.95
☐ 2	1.95	0.39	1.17	1.95
☐ 3	1.95	0.39	1.17	1.95
☐ 4	2.95	0.59	1.77	2.95
KINGDOM COME				
DC				
☐ 1, 96, prestige format; Elseworlds				
	4.95	0.99	2.97	4.95
KINGDOM OF THE DWARFS				
COMICO				
☐ 1		0.99	2.97	4.95
KINGS IN DISGUISE				
KITCHEN SINK				
☐ 1, Mar 88, SR(c) b&w	2.00	0.40	1.20	2.00
☐ 2, May 88, Kurtzman(c)	2.00	0.40	1.20	2.00
☐ 3, Jul 88	2.00	0.40	1.20	2.00
☐ 4, Sep 88	2.00	0.40	1.20	2.00
☐ 5, Mar 89	2.00	0.40	1.20	2.00
☐ 6, Sep 89	2.00	0.40	1.20	2.00
KINGS OF THE NIGHT				
DARK HORSE				
☐ 1		0.45	1.35	2.25
☐ 2		0.45	1.35	2.25
KINKI KLITT KOMICS				
RIP OFF				
☐ 1, Apr 92, adult;b&w	2.95	0.59	1.77	2.95
☐ 2, Jun 92, adult;b&w	2.50	0.50	1.50	2.50
KINKY HOOK, THE				
EROS COMIX				
☐ 1, adult, b&w		0.50	1.50	2.50
KIP				
HAMMER & ANVIL				
☐ 1, b&w	2.50	0.50	1.50	2.50
KIRBY KING OF THE SERIALS				
BLACKTHORNE				
☐ 1, Jan 89, b&w		0.40	1.20	2.00
KISS				
PERSONALITY				
☐ 1, b&w		0.59	1.77	2.95
☐ 3, color		0.59	1.77	2.95
KISS & TELL				
PATRICIA BREEN				
☐ 1, Dec 95, "The Cage";b&w; magazine-sized				
	2.75	0.55	1.65	2.75
KISS OF DEATH				
ACME				
☐ 1		0.40	1.20	2.00
KISS PRE-HISTORY				
REVOLUTIONARY				
☐ 1, Apr 93, b&w	2.50	1.00	3.00	5.00
☐ 2, May 93, b&w	2.50	0.80	2.40	4.00
☐ 3, Jul 93, b&w	2.50	0.80	2.40	4.00
KISS: SATAN'S MUSIC?				
CELEBRITY				
☐ 1, trading cards		1.60	4.80	8.00
KISSES				
SPOOF				
☐ 1, b&w		0.59	1.77	2.95

	ORIG.	GOOD	FINE	N-MINT
KISSING CANVAS				
MN DESIGN				
☐ 1, photos, color	1.10	3.30	5.50	
KISSYFUR				
DC				
☐ 1		0.40	1.20	2.00
KITCHEN SINK CLASSICS				
KITCHEN SINK				
☐ 1, Jan 94; reprints *Omaha #0*; adult; b&w				
	3.95	0.79	2.37	3.95
☐ 2, 94, reprints *The People's Comics*, b&w				
	2.95	0.59	1.77	2.95
☐ 3, 94, reprints *Death Rattle #8*, b&w				
	2.95	0.59	1.77	2.95
KITTY PRYDE & WOLVERINE				
MARVEL				
☐ 1, Nov 84, AM	0.75	1.60	4.80	8.00
☐ 2, Dec 84, AM	0.75	1.20	3.60	6.00
☐ 3, Jan 85, AM	0.75	0.80	2.40	4.00
☐ 4, Feb 85, AM	0.75	0.80	2.40	4.00
☐ 5, Mar 85, AM	0.75	0.80	2.40	4.00
☐ 6, Apr 85, AM	0.75	0.80	2.40	4.00
KITZ 'N' KATZ KOMIKS				
PHANTASY				
☐ 1, (moves to Eclipse)		0.80	2.40	4.00
KITZ 'N' KATZ KOMIKS (was Eclipse Comic)				
LAUGHLIN				
☐ 6		0.30	0.90	1.50
KITZ 'N' KATZ KOMIKS (was Phantasy Press)				
ECLIPSE				
☐ 2, b&w		0.30	0.90	1.50
☐ 3, b&w		0.30	0.90	1.50
☐ 4, b&w		0.30	0.90	1.50
☐ 5, (see Laughlin, Bob)		0.40	1.20	2.00
KIWANNI DAUGHTER OF THE DAWN				
C&T				
☐ 1, b&w		0.45	1.35	2.25
KNIGHT WOLF				
FIVE STAR				
☐ 1	2.50	0.50	1.50	2.50
KNIGHTHAWK (mini-series)				
ACCLAIM/WINDJAMMER				
☐ 1, Sep 95	2.50	0.50	1.50	2.50
☐ 4, Oct 95	2.50	0.50	1.50	2.50
☐ 5, Nov 95	2.50	0.50	1.50	2.50
☐ 6, Nov 95, final issue	2.50	0.50	1.50	2.50
KNIGHTMARE				
ANTARCTIC				
☐ 1, Jul 94, b&w	2.75	0.55	1.65	2.75
☐ 2, Sep 94, b&w	2.75	0.55	1.65	2.75
☐ 3, Jan 95, b&w	2.75	0.55	1.65	2.75
☐ 4, Mar 95, b&w	2.75	0.55	1.65	2.75
☐ 5, May 95, b&w	2.75	0.55	1.65	2.75
☐ 6, Jul 95, b&w	2.75	0.55	1.65	2.75
IMAGE				
☐ 0, Aug 95, enhanced wraparound cover				
	3.50	0.70	2.10	3.50
☐ 1, Feb 95	2.50	0.50	1.50	2.50
☐ 2, Mar 95	2.50	0.50	1.50	2.50
☐ 3, Apr 95	2.50	0.50	1.50	2.50
☐ 4, May 95	2.50	0.50	1.50	2.50
☐ 4, May 95, A;alternate cover				
	2.50	0.50	1.50	2.50
☐ 5, Jun 95, flipbook with Warcry back-up				
	2.50	0.50	1.50	2.50
KNIGHTS OF PENDRAGON, THE (1990-1991)				
MARVEL				
☐ 1, Jul 90	1.95	0.39	1.17	1.95
☐ 2, Aug 90	1.95	0.39	1.17	1.95

	ORIG.	GOOD	FINE	N-MINT
3, Oct 90	1.95	0.39	1.17	1.95
4, Oct 90	1.95	0.39	1.17	1.95
5, Nov 90	1.95	0.39	1.17	1.95
6, Dec 90	1.95	0.39	1.17	1.95
7, Jan 91	1.95	0.39	1.17	1.95
8, Feb 91	1.95	0.39	1.17	1.95
9, Mar 91	1.95	0.39	1.17	1.95
10, Apr 91	1.95	0.39	1.17	1.95
11, May 91	1.95	0.39	1.17	1.95
12, Jun 91	1.95	0.39	1.17	1.95
13, Jul 91	1.95	0.39	1.17	1.95
14, Aug 91	1.95	0.39	1.17	1.95
15, Sep 91	1.95	0.39	1.17	1.95
16, Oct 91	1.95	0.39	1.17	1.95
17, Nov 91	1.95	0.39	1.17	1.95

KNIGHTS OF PENDRAGON, THE
(1992) (was Pendragon)

5	1.75	0.35	1.05	1.75
6	1.75	0.35	1.05	1.75
7	1.75	0.35	1.05	1.75
8	1.75	0.35	1.05	1.75
9	1.75	0.35	1.05	1.75
10	1.75	0.35	1.05	1.75
11	1.75	0.35	1.05	1.75
12	1.75	0.35	1.05	1.75
13	1.75	0.35	1.05	1.75
14	1.75	0.35	1.05	1.75
15	1.75	0.35	1.05	1.75

KNIGHTSTRIKE
IMAGE

1, Dec 95, "Extreme Destroyer" Part 6 of 9; polybagged with Sentinel card 2.50 0.50 1.50 2.50

KNUCKLES THE MALEVOLENT NUN
FANTAGRAPHICS

1, b&w		0.45	1.35	2.25
2		0.40	1.20	2.00

KNUCKLES' CHAOTIX
ARCHIE

1, Jan 96 .... 2.00 0.40 1.20 2.00

KOBALT
DC/MILESTONE

1, Jun 94	1.75	0.35	1.05	1.75
2, Jul 94	1.75	0.35	1.05	1.75
3, Aug 94	1.75	0.35	1.05	1.75
4, Sep 94	1.75	0.35	1.05	1.75
5, Oct 94	1.75	0.35	1.05	1.75
6, Nov 94	1.75	0.35	1.05	1.75
7, Dec 94	1.75	0.35	1.05	1.75
8, Jan 95	1.75	0.35	1.05	1.75
9, Feb 95	1.75	0.35	1.05	1.75
10, Mar 95	1.75	0.35	1.05	1.75
11, Apr 95	1.75	0.35	1.05	1.75
12, Jun 95	1.75	0.35	1.05	1.75
13, Jul 95	2.50	0.50	1.50	2.50
14, Jul 95	2.50	0.50	1.50	2.50
15, Aug 95	2.50	0.50	1.50	2.50
16, Sep 95, final issue	2.50	0.50	1.50	2.50

KOBIER AND OSO
GEBHART

1 .... 0.30 0.90 1.50

KOBRA
DC

1, Mar 76, JK	0.25	0.70	2.10	3.50
2, May 76	0.30	0.40	1.20	2.00
3, Jul 76	0.30	0.40	1.20	2.00
4, Sep 76	0.30	0.40	1.20	2.00

	ORIG.	GOOD	FINE	N-MINT
5, Dec 76	0.30	0.40	1.20	2.00
6, Feb 77	0.30	0.40	1.20	2.00
7, Apr 77	0.30	0.40	1.20	2.00

KOMODO AND THE DEFIANTS
VICTORY

1		0.30	0.90	1.50
2		0.30	0.90	1.50

KONG THE UNTAMED
DC

1, Jul 75	0.25	0.20	0.60	1.00
2, Sep 75	0.25	0.20	0.60	1.00
3, Nov 75	0.25	0.20	0.60	1.00
4, Jan 76	0.25	0.20	0.60	1.00
5, Mar 76	0.25	0.20	0.60	1.00

KONNY AND CZU
ANTARCTIC

1, Sep 94, b&w	2.75	0.55	1.65	2.75
2, Nov 94, b&w	2.75	0.55	1.65	2.75
3, Jan 95, b&w	2.75	0.55	1.65	2.75
4, Mar 95, b&w	2.75	0.55	1.65	2.75

KOOSH KINS
ARCHIE

1, Oct 91	1.00	0.20	0.60	1.00
2	1.00	0.20	0.60	1.00
3	1.00	0.20	0.60	1.00

KORAK, SON OF TARZAN
DC

46, Jun 72, first DC	0.25	0.40	1.20	2.00
47, Aug 72	0.20	0.30	0.90	1.50
48, Oct 72	0.20	0.30	0.90	1.50
49, Dec 72	0.20	0.30	0.90	1.50
50, Feb 73	0.20	0.30	0.90	1.50
51, Apr 73	0.20	0.30	0.90	1.50
52, Jul 73	0.20	0.30	0.90	1.50
53, Sep 73	0.20	0.30	0.90	1.50
54, Nov 73	0.20	0.30	0.90	1.50
55, Jan 74	0.20	0.30	0.90	1.50
56, Mar 74	0.20	0.30	0.90	1.50
57, Jun 74	0.20	0.30	0.90	1.50
58, Aug 74	0.20	0.30	0.90	1.50
59, Oct 74 (becomes *Tarzan Family*)	0.20	0.30	0.90	1.50

KREE/SCRULL WAR STARRING THE AVENGERS, THE
MARVEL

1, Sep 83, reprint	2.50	0.50	1.50	2.50
2, Oct 83, reprint	2.50	0.50	1.50	2.50

KREMEN
GREY PRODUCTIONS

1	2.50	0.50	1.50	2.50
2	2.50	0.50	1.50	2.50
3	2.50	0.50	1.50	2.50

KREY
GAUNTLET

1, b&w	2.50	0.50	1.50	2.50
2, b&w	2.50	0.50	1.50	2.50
3, b&w	2.50	0.50	1.50	2.50

KRULL
MARVEL

1, movie	0.60	0.20	0.60	1.00
2, movie	0.60	0.20	0.60	1.00

KRUSTY COMICS (mini-series)
BONGO

1, 95	2.25	0.45	1.35	2.25
2, 95	2.25	0.45	1.35	2.25
3, 95	2.25	0.45	1.35	2.25

	ORIG.	GOOD	FINE	N-MINT

KRYPTON CHRONICLES
DC

☐ 1, Sep 81, CS, A:Superman
.... 0.50 — 0.25 — 0.75 — 1.25

☐ 2, Oct 81, CS, A:Black Flame
.... 0.60 — 0.20 — 0.60 — 1.00

☐ 3, Nov 81, CS, O:name of Kal-El
.... 0.60 — 0.20 — 0.60 — 1.00

KULL AND THE BARBARIANS
MARVEL

	ORIG.	GOOD	FINE	N-MINT
☐ 1, b&w mag	1.00	0.20	0.60	1.00
☐ 2, b&w mag	1.00	0.20	0.60	1.00
☐ 3, b&w mag	1.00	0.20	0.60	1.00

KULL IN 3-D
BLACKTHORNE

	ORIG.	GOOD	FINE	N-MINT
☐ 1		0.50	1.50	2.50
☐ 2		0.50	1.50	2.50

KULL THE CONQUEROR (1971)
MARVEL

☐ 1, Jun 71, WW/RA, O:Kull
.... 0.15 — 1.00 — 3.00 — 5.00

	ORIG.	GOOD	FINE	N-MINT
☐ 2, Sep 71, JSe	0.15	0.80	2.40	4.00
☐ 3, Jul 72, JSe	0.20	0.80	2.40	4.00
☐ 4, Sep 72, JSe	0.20	0.60	1.80	3.00
☐ 5, Nov 72, JSe	0.20	0.60	1.80	3.00
☐ 6, Jan 73	0.20	0.40	1.20	2.00
☐ 7, Mar 73	0.20	0.40	1.20	2.00
☐ 8, May 73	0.20	0.40	1.20	2.00
☐ 9, Jul 73	0.20	0.40	1.20	2.00
☐ 10, Sep 73	0.20	0.40	1.20	2.00
☐ 11, Nov 73	0.20	0.30	0.90	1.50
☐ 12, Nov 73	0.20	0.30	0.90	1.50
☐ 13, Nov 73	0.20	0.30	0.90	1.50
☐ 14, JSn/MP	0.25	0.35	1.05	1.75
☐ 15, SD/MP, rep.	0.25	0.30	0.90	1.50
☐ 16	0.25	0.20	0.60	1.00
☐ 17, AA	0.25	0.20	0.60	1.00
☐ 18, AA	0.30	0.20	0.60	1.00
☐ 19, AA	0.30	0.20	0.60	1.00
☐ 20, AA	0.30	0.20	0.60	1.00
☐ 21	0.30	0.20	0.60	1.00
☐ 22	0.30	0.20	0.60	1.00
☐ 23	0.30	0.20	0.60	1.00
☐ 24	0.35	0.20	0.60	1.00
☐ 25	0.35	0.20	0.60	1.00
☐ 26	0.35	0.20	0.60	1.00
☐ 27	0.35	0.20	0.60	1.00
☐ 28	0.35	0.20	0.60	1.00
☐ 29	0.35	0.20	0.60	1.00

	ORIG.	GOOD	FINE	N-MINT

KULL THE CONQUEROR (1982)

	ORIG.	GOOD	FINE	N-MINT
☐ 1, JB, Brule	2.00	0.50	1.50	2.50
☐ 2, Misareena	2.00	0.40	1.20	2.00

KULL THE CONQUEROR (1983)

	ORIG.	GOOD	FINE	N-MINT
☐ 1, JB, Iraina	1.25	0.30	0.90	1.50
☐ 2, JB	1.25	0.25	0.75	1.25
☐ 3, JB	1.00	0.20	0.60	1.00
☐ 4, JB	1.00	0.20	0.60	1.00
☐ 5	0.60	0.20	0.60	1.00
☐ 6	0.60	0.20	0.60	1.00
☐ 7	0.60	0.20	0.60	1.00
☐ 8	0.60	0.20	0.60	1.00
☐ 9	0.65	0.20	0.60	1.00
☐ 10	0.65	0.20	0.60	1.00

KUNG FU WARRIORS
CFW

	ORIG.	GOOD	FINE	N-MINT
☐ 1		0.45	1.35	2.25
☐ 2		0.45	1.35	2.25
☐ 3		0.45	1.35	2.25
☐ 4		0.45	1.35	2.25
☐ 5		0.45	1.35	2.25
☐ 6		0.45	1.35	2.25
☐ 7		0.45	1.35	2.25
☐ 8		0.45	1.35	2.25
☐ 9		0.45	1.35	2.25
☐ 10		0.45	1.35	2.25
☐ 11		0.45	1.35	2.25
☐ 12		0.45	1.35	2.25
☐ 13		0.45	1.35	2.25
☐ 14		0.45	1.35	2.25
☐ 15		0.45	1.35	2.25

KURT BUSIEK'S ASTRO CITY
IMAGE

	ORIG.	GOOD	FINE	N-MINT
☐ 1, Aug 95, Samaritan	2.25	0.80	2.40	4.00

☐ 2, Sep 95, Silver Agent and Honor Guard
.... 2.25 — 0.60 — 1.80 — 3.00

☐ 3, Oct 95, Jack in the Box
.... 2.25 — 0.45 — 1.35 — 2.25

☐ 4, Nov 95, "Safeguards"; A:First Family, Winged Victory, The Hanged Man .... 2.25 — 0.45 — 1.35 — 2.25

☐ 5, Dec 95, A:Crackerjack, Astro City Irregulars
.... 2.25 — 0.45 — 1.35 — 2.25

	ORIG.	GOOD	FINE	N-MINT
☐ 6, Jan 96	2.25	0.45	1.35	2.25

KYRA
ELSEWHERE

	ORIG.	GOOD	FINE	N-MINT
☐ 1, b&w		0.30	0.90	1.50
☐ 2, b&w		0.30	0.90	1.50
☐ 3, b&w		0.30	0.90	1.50
☐ 4		0.35	1.05	1.75
☐ 5		0.35	1.05	1.75

Kryptonite

Fans listening to the Superman 1940s radio drama were stunned when, at the end of one episode, Superman was mysteriously overcome and fell to the floor stunned. What had happened was that for the first time Superman fans learned of the existence of kryptonite, a radioactive element created in the explosion of Superman's home planet of Krypton. Kryptonite was also used to give Bud Collyer, the actor playing Superman, a vacation from time to time.

In the comics, kryptonite was introduced during the 1940s in *Superman* #61. Eventually, there were multiple versions of the substance, each with its own properties. Green kryptonite (or Green K)

would weaken and eventually kill a Kryptonian, while each separate piece of Red K would have a different effect (most often a mutation) on a Kryptonian. Blue K was only harmful to Bizarro, while White K only killed plant life from any world. Gold K would permanently rob a Kryptonian of his powers and first appeared in an imaginary story. In the early 1970s all kryptonite was turned to iron, but more reached Earth after that point.

Since the revision of Superman's origin in 1986, only two forms of kryptonite have been around: Green K (and only one piece, not the hundreds that were around in the original series) and Red K (created by Mr. Mxyzptlk).

L

	ORIG.	GOOD	FINE	N-MINT

L.E.G.I.O.N. '89
DC

	ORIG.	GOOD	FINE	N-MINT
❑ 1, Feb 89, O:L.E.G.I.O.N. 1.50		0.80	2.40	4.00
❑ 2, Mar 89	1.50	0.60	1.80	3.00
❑ 3, Apr 89	1.50	1.20	3.60	6.00
❑ 4, May 89	1.50	0.80	2.40	4.00
❑ 5, Jun 89	1.50	1.00	3.00	5.00
❑ 6, Jul 89	1.50	0.50	1.50	2.50
❑ 7, Aug 89	1.50	0.50	1.50	2.50
❑ 8, Sep 89	1.50	0.50	1.50	2.50
❑ 9		0.50	1.50	2.50
❑ 10, Dec 89, (becomes *L.E.G.I.O.N. '90*)				
	1.50	0.50	1.50	2.50

L.E.G.I.O.N. '90

	ORIG.	GOOD	FINE	N-MINT
❑ 11, Jan 90	1.50	0.40	1.20	2.00
❑ 12, Feb 90	1.50	0.40	1.20	2.00
❑ 13, Mar 90	1.50	0.40	1.20	2.00
❑ 14, Apr 90	1.50	0.40	1.20	2.00
❑ 15, May 90	1.50	0.40	1.20	2.00
❑ 16, Jun 90	1.50	0.40	1.20	2.00
❑ 17, Jul 90	1.50	0.40	1.20	2.00
❑ 18, Aug 90	1.50	0.40	1.20	2.00
❑ 19, Sep 90	1.50	0.40	1.20	2.00
❑ 20, Oct 90	1.50	0.40	1.20	2.00
❑ 21, Nov 90	1.50	0.40	1.20	2.00
❑ 22, Dec 90, (becomes *L.E.G.I.O.N. '91*)				
	1.50	0.40	1.20	2.00

L.E.G.I.O.N. '90 ANNUAL

	ORIG.	GOOD	FINE	N-MINT
❑ 1, Sep 90, Superman; Vril Dox vs. Brainiac				
	2.95	0.59	1.77	2.95

L.E.G.I.O.N. '91

	ORIG.	GOOD	FINE	N-MINT
❑ 23, Jan 91	2.50	0.50	1.50	2.50
❑ 24, Feb 91	1.50	0.40	1.20	2.00
❑ 25, Mar 91	1.50	0.40	1.20	2.00
❑ 26, Apr 91	1.50	0.40	1.20	2.00
❑ 27, May 91	1.50	0.40	1.20	2.00
❑ 28, Jun 91	1.50	0.40	1.20	2.00
❑ 29, Jul 91	1.50	0.40	1.20	2.00
❑ 30, Aug 91	1.50	0.40	1.20	2.00
❑ 31, Sep 91, Lobo vs. Capt. Marvel				
	1.50	0.60	1.80	3.00
❑ 32, Oct 91	1.50	0.30	0.90	1.50
❑ 33, Nov 91	1.50	0.30	0.90	1.50
❑ 34, Dec 91, (becomes *L.E.G.I.O.N. '92*)				
	1.50	0.30	0.90	1.50

L.E.G.I.O.N. '91 ANNUAL

	ORIG.	GOOD	FINE	N-MINT
❑ 1, Sep 91, Armageddon 2001	0.59	1.77	2.95

L.E.G.I.O.N. '92

	ORIG.	GOOD	FINE	N-MINT
❑ 35, Jan 92	1.50	0.30	0.90	1.50
❑ 36, Feb 92	1.25	0.30	0.90	1.50
❑ 37, Mar 92	1.25	0.30	0.90	1.50
❑ 38, Apr 92	1.25	0.30	0.90	1.50
❑ 39, May 92	1.50	0.30	0.90	1.50
❑ 40, Jun 92	1.50	0.30	0.90	1.50
❑ 41, Jul 92	1.50	0.30	0.90	1.50
❑ 42, Jul 92	1.50	0.30	0.90	1.50
❑ 43, Aug 92	1.50	0.30	0.90	1.50
❑ 44, Aug 92	1.50	0.30	0.90	1.50
❑ 45, Sep 92	1.50	0.30	0.90	1.50
❑ 46, Nov 92	1.50	0.30	0.90	1.50
❑ 47, Dec 92, Lobo vs. Green Lantern (Hal Jordan)				
(becomes *L.E.G.I.O.N. '93*)				
	1.50	0.30	0.90	1.50

L.E.G.I.O.N. '92 ANNUAL

	ORIG.	GOOD	FINE	N-MINT
❑ 3, 93, Eclipso		0.59	1.77	2.95

L.E.G.I.O.N. '93

	ORIG.	GOOD	FINE	N-MINT
❑ 48, Jan 93	1.75	0.35	1.05	1.75
❑ 49, Feb 93	1.75	0.35	1.05	1.75

	ORIG.	GOOD	FINE	N-MINT
❑ 50, Mar 93, L.E.G.I.O.N. '67 back-up				
	3.50	0.70	2.10	3.50
❑ 51, Apr 93	1.75	0.35	1.05	1.75
❑ 52, May 93	1.75	0.35	1.05	1.75
❑ 53, Jun 93	1.75	0.35	1.05	1.75
❑ 54, Jun 93	1.75	0.35	1.05	1.75
❑ 55, Jul 93	1.75	0.35	1.05	1.75
❑ 56, Jul 93	1.75	0.35	1.05	1.75
❑ 57, Aug 93, Trinity	1.75	0.35	1.05	1.75
❑ 58, Sep 93, Trinity	1.75	0.35	1.05	1.75
❑ 59, Oct 93	1.75	0.35	1.05	1.75
❑ 60, Nov 93	1.75	0.35	1.05	1.75
❑ 61, Dec 93, (becomes *L.E.G.I.O.N. '94*)				
	1.75	0.35	1.05	1.75

L.E.G.I.O.N. '93 ANNUAL

	ORIG.	GOOD	FINE	N-MINT
❑ 4, 93, "Bloodlines: Deathstorm"				
	3.50	0.70	2.10	3.50

L.E.G.I.O.N. '94

	ORIG.	GOOD	FINE	N-MINT
❑ 62, 94	1.75	0.35	1.05	1.75
❑ 63, 94	1.75	0.35	1.05	1.75
❑ 64, Mar 94	1.75	0.35	1.05	1.75
❑ 66, May 94	1.75	0.35	1.05	1.75
❑ 67, Jun 94	1.75	0.35	1.05	1.75
❑ 68, Jul 94	1.75	0.35	1.05	1.75
❑ 69, Aug 94	1.75	0.35	1.05	1.75
❑ 70, Sep 94, final issue; story continues in *R.E.B.E.L.S.*				
'94 #0	2.50	0.50	1.50	2.50

L.E.G.I.O.N. '94 ANNUAL

	ORIG.	GOOD	FINE	N-MINT
❑ 5, 94, "Elseworlds"; L.E.G.I.O.N.007				
	3.50	0.70	2.10	3.50

L.I.F.E. BRIGADE
BLUE COMET

	ORIG.	GOOD	FINE	N-MINT
❑ 1		0.40	1.20	2.00
❑ 1, reprint		0.36	1.08	1.80
❑ 2, (becomes *New L.I.F.E. Brigade*)				
		0.36	1.08	1.80

L.T. CAPER
SPOTLIGHT

	ORIG.	GOOD	FINE	N-MINT
❑ 1		0.35	1.05	1.75

LA PACIFICA (mini-series)
DC/PARADOX

	ORIG.	GOOD	FINE	N-MINT
❑ 1, 94, digest;b&w	4.95	0.99	2.97	4.95
❑ 2, 95, digest;b&w	4.95	0.99	2.97	4.95
❑ 3, 95, digest;b&w	4.95	0.99	2.97	4.95

LABOR FORCE
BLACKTHORNE

	ORIG.	GOOD	FINE	N-MINT
❑ 1		0.30	0.90	1.50
❑ 2		0.30	0.90	1.50
❑ 3		0.35	1.05	1.75
❑ 4		0.35	1.05	1.75
❑ 5		0.35	1.05	1.75
❑ 6		0.35	1.05	1.75
❑ 7		0.35	1.05	1.75
❑ 8		0.35	1.05	1.75

LABOURS OF HERCULES, THE
MALAN CLASSICAL ENTERPRISES

	ORIG.	GOOD	FINE	N-MINT
❑ 0, nn Gustave Dore, b&w..		0.59	1.77	2.95

LABYRINTH
MARVEL

	ORIG.	GOOD	FINE	N-MINT
❑ 1, movie	0.75	0.20	0.60	1.00
❑ 2, movie	0.75	0.20	0.60	1.00
❑ 3, movie	0.75	0.20	0.60	1.00

LADY ARCANE
HERO GRAPHICS

	ORIG.	GOOD	FINE	N-MINT
❑ 1		0.99	2.97	4.95
❑ 2, b&w		0.70	2.10	3.50
❑ 3, b&w		0.70	2.10	3.50
❑ 4, b&w	2.95	0.59	1.77	2.95

	ORIG.	GOOD	FINE	N-MINT

LADY CRIME
AC
	ORIG.	GOOD	FINE	N-MINT
☐ 1, b&w, Bob Powell reprints	0.55	1.65	2.75	

LADY DEATH
CHAOS!
	ORIG.	GOOD	FINE	N-MINT
☐ 1	2.75	17.00	51.00	85.00
☐ 1, commemorative edition				
☐ 2, 94	2.75	10.00	30.00	50.00
☐ 3, 94	2.75	6.40	19.20	32.00
☐ 4, 94		2.00	6.00	10.00

LADY DEATH II: BETWEEN HEAVEN & HELL
(mini-series)
	ORIG.	GOOD	FINE	N-MINT
☐ 1		1.20	3.60	6.00
☐ 1, Velvet cover		10.00	30.00	50.00
☐ 1, commemorative edition				
☐ 2, Apr 95	2.75	0.55	1.65	2.75
☐ 3, May 95	2.75	0.55	1.65	2.75
☐ 4, 95				
☐ 4, 95, A;Lady Demon chase cover				

LADY DEATH III: THE ODYSSEY (mini-series)
	ORIG.	GOOD	FINE	N-MINT
☐ 3, Jun 96	2.95	0.59	1.77	2.95

LADY DEATH IN LINGERIE
	ORIG.	GOOD	FINE	N-MINT
☐ 1				
☐ 1, Aug 95, foil-stamped leather premium edition; no cover price;limited to 10,000 copies		20.00	60.00	100.00

LADY DEATH SWIMSUIT SPECIAL
	ORIG.	GOOD	FINE	N-MINT
☐ 1, b&w	2.50	3.00	9.00	15.00
☐ 1, velvet edition		10.00	30.00	50.00

LADY DEATH: THE ODYSSEY - SNEAK PEEK PREVIEW
	ORIG.	GOOD	FINE	N-MINT
☐ 1, Apr 96, promotional piece for mini-series	1.50	0.30	0.90	1.50

LADY PENDRAGON
MAXIMUM
	ORIG.	GOOD	FINE	N-MINT
☐ 1, Mar 96	2.50	0.50	1.50	2.50
☐ 1, Mar 96, alternate cover	2.50	0.50	1.50	2.50

LADY RAWHIDE (mini-series)
TOPPS
	ORIG.	GOOD	FINE	N-MINT
☐ 1, Jul 95	2.95	0.90	2.70	4.50
☐ 2, Sep 95	2.95	0.59	1.77	2.95
☐ 3, Nov 95	2.95	0.59	1.77	2.95

LADY RAWHIDE SPECIAL EDITION
	ORIG.	GOOD	FINE	N-MINT
☐ 1, Jun 95, reprints *Zorro* #2 and 3	3.95	0.79	2.37	3.95

LADY VAMPIRE
BLACKOUT
	ORIG.	GOOD	FINE	N-MINT
☐ 0, 95	2.75	0.55	1.65	2.75

LADY VAMPRE
BLACK OUT
	ORIG.	GOOD	FINE	N-MINT
☐ 0, 95	2.75	0.55	1.65	2.75
☐ 1, 95	2.95	0.59	1.77	2.95

LAFF-A-LYMPICS
MARVEL
	ORIG.	GOOD	FINE	N-MINT
☐ 1	0.35	0.30	0.90	1.50
☐ 2	0.35	0.20	0.60	1.00
☐ 3	0.35	0.20	0.60	1.00
☐ 4	0.35	0.20	0.60	1.00
☐ 5	0.35	0.20	0.60	1.00
☐ 6	0.35	0.20	0.60	1.00
☐ 7	0.35	0.20	0.60	1.00
☐ 8	0.35	0.20	0.60	1.00
☐ 9	0.35	0.20	0.60	1.00
☐ 10	0.35	0.20	0.60	1.00
☐ 11	0.35	0.20	0.60	1.00
☐ 12	0.35	0.20	0.60	1.00
☐ 13	0.35	0.20	0.60	1.00

LAFFIN' GAS
BLACKTHORNE
	ORIG.	GOOD	FINE	N-MINT
☐ 1		0.40	1.20	2.00
☐ 2		0.40	1.20	2.00
☐ 3		0.40	1.20	2.00
☐ 4		0.40	1.20	2.00
☐ 5		0.40	1.20	2.00
☐ 6, 3-D		0.50	1.50	2.50
☐ 7		0.40	1.20	2.00
☐ 8		0.40	1.20	2.00
☐ 9		0.40	1.20	2.00
☐ 10		0.40	1.20	2.00
☐ 11		0.40	1.20	2.00
☐ 12		0.40	1.20	2.00

LANCE BARNES: POST NUKE DICK
EPIC
	ORIG.	GOOD	FINE	N-MINT
☐ 1	2.50	0.50	1.50	2.50
☐ 2	2.50	0.50	1.50	2.50
☐ 3	2.50	0.50	1.50	2.50
☐ 4	2.50	0.50	1.50	2.50

LANCELOT STRONG, THE SHIELD
ARCHIE/RED CIRCLE
	ORIG.	GOOD	FINE	N-MINT
☐ 1, Jun 83	1.00	0.20	0.60	1.00

LANDRA SPECIAL
ALCHEMY
	ORIG.	GOOD	FINE	N-MINT
☐ 0, nn b&w		0.40	1.20	2.00

LANDS OF PRESTER JOHN
NOBLE
	ORIG.	GOOD	FINE	N-MINT
☐ 1, MGu		3.00	9.00	15.00

LANN
EROS COMIX
	ORIG.	GOOD	FINE	N-MINT
☐ 1, adult, b&w		0.50	1.50	2.50

LARS OF MARS 3-D
ECLIPSE
	ORIG.	GOOD	FINE	N-MINT
☐ 1, MA		0.50	1.50	2.50

LASER ERASER & PRESSBUTTON
	ORIG.	GOOD	FINE	N-MINT
☐ 1		0.35	1.05	1.75
☐ 2		0.35	1.05	1.75
☐ 3		0.35	1.05	1.75
☐ 4		0.35	1.05	1.75
☐ 5		0.35	1.05	1.75
☐ 6		0.35	1.05	1.75

LASER ERASER & PRESSBUTTON 3-D
	ORIG.	GOOD	FINE	N-MINT
☐ 1		0.40	1.20	2.00

LASH LaRUE WESTERN
AC
	ORIG.	GOOD	FINE	N-MINT
☐ 1, rep., some color		0.70	2.10	3.50

LASH LaRUE WESTERN ANNUAL
	ORIG.	GOOD	FINE	N-MINT
☐ 1, b&w reprints		0.59	1.77	2.95

LAST AMERICAN, THE
EPIC
	ORIG.	GOOD	FINE	N-MINT
☐ 1	2.25	0.45	1.35	2.25
☐ 2	2.25	0.45	1.35	2.25
☐ 3	2.25	0.45	1.35	2.25
☐ 4	2.25	0.45	1.35	2.25

LAST DEFENDER OF CAMELOT, THE
ZIM
	ORIG.	GOOD	FINE	N-MINT
☐ 0, nn, b&w		0.39	1.17	1.95

LAST DITCH
EDGE
	ORIG.	GOOD	FINE	N-MINT
☐ 1, b&w	2.50	0.50	1.50	2.50

LAST GASP COMICS AND STORIES
LAST GASP ECO-FUNNIES
	ORIG.	GOOD	FINE	N-MINT
☐ 3, 95, b&w anthology	3.95	0.79	2.37	3.95

LAST GENERATION, THE
BLACK TIE
	ORIG.	GOOD	FINE	N-MINT
☐ 1		0.39	1.17	1.95
☐ 2		0.39	1.17	1.95

	ORIG.	GOOD	FINE	N-MINT
❏ 3		0.39	1.17	1.95
❏ 4		0.39	1.17	1.95
❏ 5		0.39	1.17	1.95

LAST KISS
ECLIPSE

	ORIG.	GOOD	FINE	N-MINT
❏ 1, b&w		0.79	2.37	3.95

LAST OF THE VIKING HEROES SUMMER SPECIAL
GENESIS WEST

	ORIG.	GOOD	FINE	N-MINT
❏ 1, Frazetta (c)		0.50	1.50	2.50
❏ 2, TMNT		0.50	1.50	2.50
❏ 3, TMNT		0.50	1.50	2.50

LAST OF THE VIKING HEROES, THE

	ORIG.	GOOD	FINE	N-MINT
❏ 1, JK(c)		0.40	1.20	2.00
❏ 2, GP(c)		0.40	1.20	2.00
❏ 3, JBy(c)		0.35	1.05	1.75
❏ 4, HC(c)		0.35	1.05	1.75
❏ 5, JK/DSt(c)		0.39	1.17	1.95
❏ 5		0.39	1.17	1.95
❏ 6		0.39	1.17	1.95
❏ 7		0.39	1.17	1.95
❏ 8		0.39	1.17	1.95
❏ 9		0.39	1.17	1.95
❏ 10		0.50	1.50	2.50
❏ 11		0.50	1.50	2.50

LAST ONE, THE
DC/VERTIGO

	ORIG.	GOOD	FINE	N-MINT
❏ 1	2.50	0.50	1.50	2.50
❏ 2	2.50	0.50	1.50	2.50
❏ 3	2.50	0.50	1.50	2.50
❏ 4	2.50	0.50	1.50	2.50
❏ 5	2.50	0.50	1.50	2.50
❏ 6	2.50	0.50	1.50	2.50

LAST STARFIGHTER
MARVEL

	ORIG.	GOOD	FINE	N-MINT
❏ 1, Oct 84, movie	0.75	0.20	0.60	1.00
❏ 2, Nov 84, movie	0.75	0.20	0.60	1.00
❏ 3, Dec 84, movie	0.75	0.20	0.60	1.00

LAST TEMPTATION, THE (mini-series)
MARVEL MUSIC

	ORIG.	GOOD	FINE	N-MINT
❏ 1, May 94, cardstock cover				
	4.95	0.99	2.97	4.95
❏ 3, 94, cardstock cover	4.95	0.99	2.97	4.95

LATIGO KID WESTERN
AC

	ORIG.	GOOD	FINE	N-MINT
❏ 1, b&w		0.39	1.17	1.95

LAUGH
ARCHIE

	ORIG.	GOOD	FINE	N-MINT
❏ 1, Jun 87	0.75	0.20	0.60	1.00
❏ 2	0.75	0.20	0.60	1.00
❏ 3	0.75	0.20	0.60	1.00
❏ 4	0.75	0.20	0.60	1.00
❏ 5	0.75	0.20	0.60	1.00
❏ 6	0.75	0.20	0.60	1.00
❏ 7	0.75	0.20	0.60	1.00
❏ 8	0.75	0.20	0.60	1.00
❏ 9	0.75	0.20	0.60	1.00
❏ 10	0.75	0.20	0.60	1.00
❏ 11	0.75	0.20	0.60	1.00
❏ 12	0.75	0.20	0.60	1.00
❏ 13	0.75	0.20	0.60	1.00
❏ 14	0.75	0.20	0.60	1.00
❏ 15	0.75	0.20	0.60	1.00
❏ 16	0.75	0.20	0.60	1.00
❏ 17	0.75	0.20	0.60	1.00
❏ 18	0.75	0.20	0.60	1.00
❏ 19	0.75	0.20	0.60	1.00
❏ 20	0.75	0.20	0.60	1.00
❏ 21	0.75	0.20	0.60	1.00
❏ 22	0.75	0.20	0.60	1.00
❏ 23	0.75	0.20	0.60	1.00

	ORIG.	GOOD	FINE	N-MINT
❏ 24	0.75	0.20	0.60	1.00
❏ 25	0.75	0.20	0.60	1.00
❏ 26	0.75	0.20	0.60	1.00
❏ 27	0.75	0.20	0.60	1.00
❏ 28	0.75	0.20	0.60	1.00
❏ 29	0.75	0.20	0.60	1.00
❏ 30	0.75	0.20	0.60	1.00

LAUGH DIGEST MAGAZINE

	ORIG.	GOOD	FINE	N-MINT
❏ 117, Nov 94, digest	1.75	0.35	1.05	1.75
❏ 118, Jan 95, digest	1.75	0.35	1.05	1.75
❏ 119, Mar 95, digest	1.75	0.35	1.05	1.75
❏ 120, May 95, digest	1.75	0.35	1.05	1.75
❏ 121, Jul 95, digest	1.75	0.35	1.05	1.75
❏ 122, Sep 95, digest	1.75	0.35	1.05	1.75
❏ 123, Nov 95, digest	1.75	0.35	1.05	1.75
❏ 124, Dec 95, digest	1.75	0.35	1.05	1.75
❏ 125, Feb 96, digest	1.75	0.35	1.05	1.75
❏ 126, Apr 96, digest	1.75	0.35	1.05	1.75
❏ 127, May 96, digest	1.75	0.35	1.05	1.75
❏ 128, Jul 96, digest	1.75	0.35	1.05	1.75

LAUNCH
ELSEWHERE

	ORIG.	GOOD	FINE	N-MINT
❏ 1, I:Conscience		0.35	1.05	1.75

LAUNDRYLAND
FANTAGRAPHICS

	ORIG.	GOOD	FINE	N-MINT
❏ 1, b&w		0.45	1.35	2.25
❏ 2, b&w		0.50	1.50	2.50
❏ 3, b&w		0.50	1.50	2.50
❏ 4, b&w		0.50	1.50	2.50

LAUREL & HARDY IN 3-D
BLACKTHORNE

	ORIG.	GOOD	FINE	N-MINT
❏ 1		0.50	1.50	2.50
❏ 2		0.50	1.50	2.50

LAW AND ORDER
MAXIMUM

	ORIG.	GOOD	FINE	N-MINT
❏ 1, Sep 95	2.50	0.50	1.50	2.50
❏ 2, Oct 95	2.50	0.50	1.50	2.50

LAW OF DREDD, THE
FLEETWAY/QUALITY

	ORIG.	GOOD	FINE	N-MINT
❏ 1, Judge Dredd		0.40	1.20	2.00
❏ 2, Judge Dredd		0.40	1.20	2.00
❏ 3, Judge Dredd		0.40	1.20	2.00
❏ 4, Judge Dredd		0.40	1.20	2.00
❏ 5, Judge Dredd		0.40	1.20	2.00
❏ 6, Judge Dredd		0.40	1.20	2.00
❏ 7, Judge Dredd		0.40	1.20	2.00
❏ 8, Judge Dredd		0.40	1.20	2.00
❏ 9		0.35	1.05	1.75
❏ 10		0.35	1.05	1.75
❏ 11		0.35	1.05	1.75
❏ 12		0.35	1.05	1.75
❏ 13		0.35	1.05	1.75
❏ 14		0.35	1.05	1.75
❏ 15		0.35	1.05	1.75
❏ 16		0.35	1.05	1.75
❏ 17		0.35	1.05	1.75
❏ 18		0.35	1.05	1.75
❏ 19		0.35	1.05	1.75
❏ 20		0.35	1.05	1.75
❏ 21		0.35	1.05	1.75
❏ 22		0.35	1.05	1.75
❏ 23		0.35	1.05	1.75
❏ 24		0.35	1.05	1.75
❏ 25		0.35	1.05	1.75
❏ 26		0.35	1.05	1.75
❏ 27		0.35	1.05	1.75
❏ 28		0.35	1.05	1.75
❏ 29		0.35	1.05	1.75
❏ 30		0.35	1.05	1.75
❏ 31		0.39	1.17	1.95

	ORIG.	GOOD	FINE	N-MINT
❑ 32		0.39	1.17	1.95
❑ 33		0.39	1.17	1.95

LAWDOG
EPIC

	ORIG.	GOOD	FINE	N-MINT
❑ 1, embossed cover	2.50	0.50	1.50	2.50
❑ 2	1.95	0.39	1.17	1.95
❑ 3	1.95	0.39	1.17	1.95
❑ 4	1.95	0.39	1.17	1.95
❑ 5	1.95	0.39	1.17	1.95
❑ 6	1.95	0.39	1.17	1.95
❑ 7	1.95	0.39	1.17	1.95
❑ 8, trading card	1.95	0.39	1.17	1.95
❑ 9	1.95	0.39	1.17	1.95
❑ 10	1.95	0.39	1.17	1.95

LAWDOG AND GRIMROD: TERROR AT THE CROSSROADS

	ORIG.	GOOD	FINE	N-MINT
❑ 1	3.50	0.70	2.10	3.50

LAWRENCE & LIM'S EX-MUTANTS MICROSERIES: ERIN
PIED PIPER

	ORIG.	GOOD	FINE	N-MINT
❑ 1, b&w		0.39	1.17	1.95

LAZARUS CHURCHYARD
TUNDRA

	ORIG.	GOOD	FINE	N-MINT
❑ 1		0.90	2.70	4.50
❑ 2		0.90	2.70	4.50
❑ 3		0.99	2.97	4.95

LEAF
NAB

	ORIG.	GOOD	FINE	N-MINT
❑ 1		0.39	1.17	1.95
❑ 1, deluxe		0.99	2.97	4.95

LEAGUE OF CHAMPIONS, THE
HERO

	ORIG.	GOOD	FINE	N-MINT
❑ 1, Dec 90	2.95	0.59	1.77	2.95
❑ 2, Feb 91	2.95	0.59	1.77	2.95
❑ 3, Apr 91	2.95	0.59	1.77	2.95
❑ 4, b&w	3.50	0.70	2.10	3.50
❑ 5, b&w	3.50	0.70	2.10	3.50
❑ 6, b&w	3.50	0.70	2.10	3.50
❑ 7, b&w	3.50	0.70	2.10	3.50
❑ 8, b&w	3.50	0.70	2.10	3.50
❑ 9, b&w	3.50	0.70	2.10	3.50
❑ 10, b&w	3.50	0.70	2.10	3.50
❑ 11, b&w	3.95	0.79	2.37	3.95
❑ 12, Jul 93	2.95	0.59	1.77	2.95

LEAGUE OF JUSTICE
DC

	ORIG.	GOOD	FINE	N-MINT
❑ 1, 96, Elseworlds; prestige format	5.95	1.19	3.57	5.95
❑ 2, 96, Elseworlds; prestige format	5.95	1.19	3.57	5.95

LEATHER & LACE
AIRCEL

	ORIG.	GOOD	FINE	N-MINT
❑ 1, adult, b&w		0.50	1.50	2.50
❑ 1, tame, b&w		0.39	1.17	1.95
❑ 2, tame, b&w		0.39	1.17	1.95
❑ 2, adult, b&w		0.50	1.50	2.50
❑ 3, tame, b&w		0.39	1.17	1.95
❑ 3, adult, b&w		0.50	1.50	2.50
❑ 4, tame, b&w		0.39	1.17	1.95
❑ 4, adult, b&w		0.50	1.50	2.50
❑ 5, tame, b&w		0.39	1.17	1.95
❑ 5, adult, b&w		0.50	1.50	2.50
❑ 6, tame, b&w		0.39	1.17	1.95
❑ 6, adult, b&w		0.50	1.50	2.50
❑ 7, tame, b&w		0.39	1.17	1.95
❑ 7, adult, b&w		0.50	1.50	2.50
❑ 8, tame, b&w		0.39	1.17	1.95
❑ 8, adult, b&w		0.50	1.50	2.50
❑ 9, adult, b&w		0.50	1.50	2.50
❑ 10, adult, b&w		0.50	1.50	2.50

	ORIG.	GOOD	FINE	N-MINT
❑ 11, adult, b&w		0.50	1.50	2.50
❑ 12, adult, b&w		0.50	1.50	2.50
❑ 13, adult, b&w		0.50	1.50	2.50
❑ 14, adult, b&w		0.50	1.50	2.50
❑ 15, adult, b&w		0.50	1.50	2.50
❑ 16, adult, b&w		0.50	1.50	2.50
❑ 17, adult, b&w		0.50	1.50	2.50
❑ 18, adult, b&w		0.50	1.50	2.50
❑ 19, adult, b&w		0.50	1.50	2.50
❑ 20, adult, b&w		0.50	1.50	2.50
❑ 21, adult, b&w		0.50	1.50	2.50
❑ 22, adult, b&w		0.50	1.50	2.50
❑ 23, adult, b&w		0.50	1.50	2.50
❑ 24, adult, b&w		0.50	1.50	2.50
❑ 25, adult, b&w		0.50	1.50	2.50

LEATHER & LACE SUMMER SPECIAL

	ORIG.	GOOD	FINE	N-MINT
❑ 1, adult, b&w		0.50	1.50	2.50

LEATHER & LACE: BLOOD, SEX & TEARS

	ORIG.	GOOD	FINE	N-MINT
❑ 1, adult, b&w		0.59	1.77	2.95
❑ 2, adult, b&w		0.59	1.77	2.95
❑ 3, adult, b&w		0.59	1.77	2.95

LEATHER UNDERWEAR
FANTAGRAPHICS

	ORIG.	GOOD	FINE	N-MINT
❑ 1, b&w		0.50	1.50	2.50

LEATHERFACE
ARPAD

	ORIG.	GOOD	FINE	N-MINT
❑ 1		0.55	1.65	2.75

LED ZEPPELIN
PERSONALITY

	ORIG.	GOOD	FINE	N-MINT
❑ 1, b&w		0.59	1.77	2.95
❑ 2, b&w		0.59	1.77	2.95
❑ 3, b&w		0.59	1.77	2.95
❑ 4, b&w		0.59	1.77	2.95

LED ZEPPELIN EXPERIENCE (mini-series)
REVOLUTIONARY

	ORIG.	GOOD	FINE	N-MINT
❑ 1, Aug 92, b&w	2.50	0.50	1.50	2.50
❑ 2, Oct 92, b&w	2.50	0.50	1.50	2.50
❑ 3, Dec 92, b&w	2.50	0.50	1.50	2.50
❑ 4, Jan 93, b&w	2.50	0.50	1.50	2.50
❑ 5, Feb 93, b&w	2.50	0.50	1.50	2.50

LEGACY
MAJESTIC

	ORIG.	GOOD	FINE	N-MINT
❑ 0,		5.00	15.00	25.00
❑ 0, gold		5.00	15.00	25.00
❑ 1	2.25	0.45	1.35	2.25
❑ 2	2.25	0.45	1.35	2.25

LEGACY OF SUPERMAN
DC

	ORIG.	GOOD	FINE	N-MINT
❑ 1		0.50	1.50	2.50

LEGEND LORE
ARROW

	ORIG.	GOOD	FINE	N-MINT
❑ 1, b&w		0.40	1.20	2.00
❑ 2, b&w		0.40	1.20	2.00

LEGEND OF AQUAMAN
DC

	ORIG.	GOOD	FINE	N-MINT
❑ 1, CS O:Aquaman		0.40	1.20	2.00

LEGEND OF JEDIT OJANEN ON THE WORLD OF MAGIC THE GATHERING, THE (mini-series)
ACCLAIM/ARMADA

	ORIG.	GOOD	FINE	N-MINT
❑ 1, Mar 96, polybagged with card	2.50	0.50	1.50	2.50
❑ 2, Apr 96	2.50	0.50	1.50	2.50

LEGEND OF KAMUI
ECLIPSE

	ORIG.	GOOD	FINE	N-MINT
1, Japanese b&w		0.80	2.40	4.00
1, 2nd printing		0.30	0.90	1.50
2, 1st printing		0.50	1.50	2.50
2, 2nd printing		0.30	0.90	1.50
3		0.30	0.90	1.50
4		0.30	0.90	1.50
5		0.30	0.90	1.50
6		0.30	0.90	1.50
7		0.30	0.90	1.50
8		0.30	0.90	1.50
9		0.30	0.90	1.50
10		0.30	0.90	1.50
11		0.30	0.90	1.50
12		0.30	0.90	1.50
13		0.30	0.90	1.50
14		0.30	0.90	1.50
15		0.30	0.90	1.50
16		0.30	0.90	1.50
17		0.30	0.90	1.50
18, 48 pages		0.39	1.17	1.95
19		0.30	0.90	1.50
20		0.30	0.90	1.50
21		0.30	0.90	1.50
22		0.30	0.90	1.50
23		0.30	0.90	1.50
24		0.30	0.90	1.50
25		0.30	0.90	1.50
26		0.30	0.90	1.50
27		0.30	0.90	1.50
28		0.30	0.90	1.50
29		0.30	0.90	1.50
30		0.30	0.90	1.50
31		0.30	0.90	1.50
32		0.30	0.90	1.50
33		0.30	0.90	1.50
34		0.30	0.90	1.50
35		0.30	0.90	1.50
36		0.30	0.90	1.50
37		0.30	0.90	1.50

LEGEND OF MOTHER SARAH, THE (mini-series)
DARK HORSE/MANGA

	ORIG.	GOOD	FINE	N-MINT
6, Sep 95, b&w	2.95	0.59	1.77	2.95
7, Oct 95, b&w	2.95	0.59	1.77	2.95
8, Nov 95, b&w; final issue	2.95	0.59	1.77	2.95

LEGEND OF MOTHER SARAH, THE: CITY OF THE CHILDREN

	ORIG.	GOOD	FINE	N-MINT
1, Jan 96, b&w	3.95	0.79	2.37	3.95
2, Feb 96, b&w	3.95	0.79	2.37	3.95
3, Mar 96, b&w	3.95	0.79	2.37	3.95
5, May 96, b&w	3.95	0.79	2.37	3.95

LEGEND OF SUPREME (mini-series)
IMAGE

	ORIG.	GOOD	FINE	N-MINT
1, Dec 94	2.50	0.50	1.50	2.50
2, Jan 95	2.50	0.50	1.50	2.50
3, Feb 95	2.50	0.50	1.50	2.50

LEGEND OF THE SHIELD
IMPACT

	ORIG.	GOOD	FINE	N-MINT
1, Jul 91, O:Shield	1.00	0.20	0.60	1.00
2, Aug 91	1.00	0.20	0.60	1.00
3, Sep 91	1.00	0.20	0.60	1.00
4, Oct 91	1.00	0.20	0.60	1.00
5, Nov 91	1.00	0.20	0.60	1.00
6, Dec 91	1.00	0.20	0.60	1.00
7, Jan 92	1.00	0.20	0.60	1.00
8, Feb 92	1.00	0.20	0.60	1.00
9, Mar 92	1.00	0.20	0.60	1.00
10, Apr 92	1.00	0.20	0.60	1.00
11, May 92, trading card	1.00	0.20	0.60	1.00
12, Jun 92	1.25	0.25	0.75	1.25
13, Jul 92	1.25	0.25	0.75	1.25
14, Aug 92	1.25	0.25	0.75	1.25
15, Sep 92	1.25	0.25	0.75	1.25
16, Oct 92	1.25	0.25	0.75	1.25

LEGEND OF THE SHIELD ANNUAL

	ORIG.	GOOD	FINE	N-MINT
1, trading card		0.50	1.50	2.50

LEGEND OF WONDER WOMAN
DC

	ORIG.	GOOD	FINE	N-MINT
1, May 86, KB		0.20	0.60	1.00
2, Jun 86, KB		0.20	0.60	1.00
3, Jul 86, KB		0.20	0.60	1.00
4, Aug 86, KB		0.20	0.60	1.00

LEGEND OF ZELDA, THE
VALIANT

	ORIG.	GOOD	FINE	N-MINT
1		0.39	1.17	1.95
2		0.39	1.17	1.95
3		0.39	1.17	1.95
4		0.39	1.17	1.95

LEGEND OF ZELDA, THE (starting over, 1991)

	ORIG.	GOOD	FINE	N-MINT
1		0.30	0.90	1.50
2		0.30	0.90	1.50
3		0.30	0.90	1.50
4		0.30	0.90	1.50
5		0.30	0.90	1.50

LEGENDS
DC

	ORIG.	GOOD	FINE	N-MINT
1, Nov 86, JBy	0.75	0.40	1.20	2.00
2, Dec 86, JBy	0.75	0.40	1.20	2.00
3, Jan 87, JBy,I:Suicide Squad	0.75	0.30	0.90	1.50
4, Feb 87, JBy	0.75	0.30	0.90	1.50
5, Mar 87, JBy	0.75	0.30	0.90	1.50
6, Apr 87, JBy	0.75	0.30	0.90	1.50

LEGENDS AND FOLKLORE
ZONE

	ORIG.	GOOD	FINE	N-MINT
1, b&w	2.95	0.59	1.77	2.95
2, b&w	2.95	0.59	1.77	2.95

LEGENDS OF ELFINWILD
WEHNER

	ORIG.	GOOD	FINE	N-MINT
1, b&w		0.35	1.05	1.75

LEGENDS OF NASCAR
VORTEX

	ORIG.	GOOD	FINE	N-MINT
1, 90, 1st printing;HT; Bill Elliott	3.00	1.60	4.80	8.00
1, 2nd printing, with cards	3.00	0.60	1.80	3.00
2, hologram; Richard Petty; no indicia	5.00	1.00	3.00	5.00
2, Richard Petty; no indicia	2.00	0.40	1.20	2.00
3, 91, Ken Shrader	2.00	0.40	1.20	2.00
4, 91, DS;Bobby Allison	2.00	0.40	1.20	2.00
5, 91, Sterling Marlin	2.00	0.40	1.20	2.00
6, 91	2.00	0.40	1.20	2.00
7, 91	2.00	0.40	1.20	2.00
8, 91, DH; Benny Parsons	2.00	0.40	1.20	2.00
9, 92, Rusty Wallace	2.00	0.40	1.20	2.00
10, 92, Talladega Story	2.00	0.40	1.20	2.00
11, 92, Morgan Shepherd	2.00	0.40	1.20	2.00

LEGENDS OF THE DARK CLAW
DC/AMALGAM

	ORIG.	GOOD	FINE	N-MINT
1, Apr 96	1.95	0.39	1.17	1.95

LEGENDS OF THE DARK KNIGHT
DC

	ORIG.	GOOD	FINE	N-MINT
1, Nov 89, extra cover (4 different: yellow, blue, orange, pink), poster	1.50	1.40	4.20	7.00

	ORIG.	GOOD	FINE	N-MINT
2, Dec 89	1.50	1.00	3.00	5.00
3, Jan 90	1.00	0.80	2.40	4.00
4, Feb 90	1.50	0.80	2.40	4.00
5, Mar 90	1.50	0.80	2.40	4.00
6, Apr 90, KJ	1.50	0.80	2.40	4.00
7, May 90, KJ	1.50	0.60	1.80	3.00
8, Jun 90, KJ	1.50	0.60	1.80	3.00
9, Jul 90, KJ	1.50	0.60	1.80	3.00
10, Aug 90, KJ	1.50	0.60	1.80	3.00
11, Sep 90, PG/TA	1.50	1.40	4.20	7.00
12, Oct 90, PG/TA	1.50	1.00	3.00	5.00
13, Nov 90, PG/TA	1.50	0.80	2.40	4.00
14, Dec 90, PG/TA	1.50	0.80	2.40	4.00
15, Feb 91, PG/TA	1.50	0.80	2.40	4.00
16, Mar 91	1.50	2.40	7.20	12.00
17, Apr 91	1.50	2.00	6.00	10.00
18, May 91	1.50	2.00	6.00	10.00
19, Jun 91	1.50	2.00	6.00	10.00
20, Jul 91	1.75	2.00	6.00	10.00
21, Aug 91	1.75	0.30	0.90	1.50
22, Sep 91	1.75	0.30	0.90	1.50
23, Oct 91	1.75	0.30	0.90	1.50
24, Nov 91, GK	1.75	0.35	1.05	1.75
25, Dec 91, GK	1.75	0.35	1.05	1.75
26, Jan 92, GK	1.75	0.35	1.05	1.75
27, Feb 92	1.75	0.60	1.80	3.00
28, Mar 92, MW, Two-Face				
	1.75	0.40	1.20	2.00
29, Apr 92, MW, Two-Face				
	1.75	0.40	1.20	2.00
30, May 92, MW, Two-Face				
	1.75	0.40	1.20	2.00
31, Jun 92	1.75	0.35	1.05	1.75
32, Jun 92	1.75	0.35	1.05	1.75
33, Jul 92	1.75	0.35	1.05	1.75
34, Jul 92	1.75	0.35	1.05	1.75
35, Aug 92	1.75	0.35	1.05	1.75
36, Aug 92	1.75	0.35	1.05	1.75
37, Aug 92, (becomes *Batman: Legends of the Dark Knight*)	1.75	0.35	1.05	1.75

LEGENDS OF THE LIVING DEAD
FANTACO

1	3.95	0.79	2.37	3.95

LEGENDS OF THE STARGRAZERS
INNOVATION

		GOOD	FINE	N-MINT
1		0.39	1.17	1.95
2		0.39	1.17	1.95
3		0.39	1.17	1.95
4		0.39	1.17	1.95
5		0.39	1.17	1.95
6		0.39	1.17	1.95

LEGENDS OF THE WORLD'S FINEST (mini-series)
DC

1, WS(w) DBrereton	4.95	0.99	2.97	4.95
2, WS(w) DBrereton	4.95	0.99	2.97	4.95
3, 94, Superman, Batman				
	4.95	0.99	2.97	4.95

LEGION OF MONSTERS, THE
MARVEL

1, b&w, magazine	1.00	0.20	0.60	1.00

LEGION OF NIGHT

1, Nov 91	4.95	0.99	2.97	4.95
2, Dec 91	4.95	0.99	2.97	4.95

LEGION OF STUPID HEROES
BLACKTHORNE

1, b&w, parody		0.35	1.05	1.75

LEGION OF SUBSTITUTE HEROES SPECIAL
DC

1, 85, KG	1.25	0.25	0.75	1.25

	ORIG.	GOOD	FINE	N-MINT

LEGION OF SUPER-HEROES (1973 series)

1, Feb 73, Tommy Tomorrow rep.				
	0.20	1.00	3.00	5.00
2, Mar 73	0.20	0.40	1.20	2.00
3, May 73, V:Computo	0.20	0.40	1.20	2.00
4, Aug 73	0.20	0.40	1.20	2.00

LEGION OF SUPER-HEROES (1984-1989)

1, Aug 84, KG	1.25	0.60	1.80	3.00
2, Sep 84, KG	1.25	0.50	1.50	2.50
3, Oct 84	1.25	0.40	1.20	2.00
4, Nov 84, D:Karate Kid	1.25	0.40	1.20	2.00
5, Dec 84	1.25	0.40	1.20	2.00
6, Jan 85	1.25	0.40	1.20	2.00
7, Feb 85	1.25	0.40	1.20	2.00
8, Mar 85	1.25	0.40	1.20	2.00
9, Apr 85	1.25	0.40	1.20	2.00
10, May 85	1.25	0.40	1.20	2.00
11, Jun 85	1.25	0.40	1.20	2.00
12, Jul 85	1.25	0.40	1.20	2.00
13, Aug 85	1.25	0.40	1.20	2.00
14, Sep 85	1.25	0.40	1.20	2.00
15, Oct 85	1.25	0.40	1.20	2.00
16, Nov 85	1.25	0.40	1.20	2.00
17, Dec 85	1.25	0.40	1.20	2.00
18, Jan 86, Crisis	1.50	0.40	1.20	2.00
19, Feb 86	1.50	0.40	1.20	2.00
20, Mar 86	1.50	0.40	1.20	2.00
21, Apr 86	1.50	0.40	1.20	2.00
22, May 86	1.50	0.40	1.20	2.00
23, Jun 86	1.50	0.40	1.20	2.00
24, Jul 86	1.50	0.40	1.20	2.00
25, Aug 86	1.50	0.40	1.20	2.00
26, Sep 86	1.50	0.40	1.20	2.00
27, Oct 86	1.50	0.40	1.20	2.00
28, Nov 86	1.50	0.40	1.20	2.00
29, Dec 86, V:Starfinger	1.50	0.40	1.20	2.00
30, Jan 87	1.50	0.40	1.20	2.00
31, Feb 87	1.50	0.40	1.20	2.00
32, Mar 87, Universo Project				
	1.50	0.40	1.20	2.00
33, Apr 87, Universo Project				
	1.50	0.40	1.20	2.00
34, May 87, Universo Project				
	1.50	0.40	1.20	2.00
35, Jun 87, Universo Project				
	1.50	0.40	1.20	2.00
36, Jul 87	1.50	0.40	1.20	2.00
37, Aug 87, Superboy	1.50	0.70	2.10	3.50
38, Sep 87, D:Superboy	1.50	0.70	2.10	3.50
39, Oct 87, CS; O:Colossal Boy				
	1.50	0.30	0.90	1.50
40, Nov 87	1.75	0.35	1.05	1.75
41, Dec 87	1.75	0.35	1.05	1.75
42, Jan 88, Millennium	1.75	0.35	1.05	1.75
43, Feb 88, Millennium	1.75	0.35	1.05	1.75
44, Mar 88, O:Quislet	1.75	0.35	1.05	1.75
45, Apr 88, 30th Anniv	2.95	0.59	1.77	2.95
46, May 88	1.75	0.35	1.05	1.75
47, Jun 88	1.75	0.35	1.05	1.75
48, Jul 88	1.75	0.35	1.05	1.75
49, Aug 88	1.75	0.40	1.20	2.00
50, Sep 88, D:1/2 of Duo Damsel, Infinite Man; Mon-El seriously wounded; possible death of Time Trapper	2.50	0.40	1.20	2.00
51, Oct 88, Brainiac Five gives his force-belt to Luornu Durgo Taine (the former Duo Damsel)	1.75	0.40	1.20	2.00
52, Nov 88	1.75	0.40	1.20	2.00
53, Dec 88	1.75	0.40	1.20	2.00
54, Win 88, no month of publication, cover says "Winter"	1.75	0.40	1.20	2.00

	ORIG.	GOOD	FINE	N-MINT
❏ 55, Hol 89, no month of publication, cover says				
"Holiday" 1.75	0.40	1.20	2.00	
❏ 56, Jan 89 .... 1.75	0.40	1.20	2.00	
❏ 57, Feb 89 .... 1.75	0.40	1.20	2.00	
❏ 58, Mar 89, D:Emerald Empress				
.... 1.75	0.40	1.20	2.00	
❏ 59, Apr 89 .... 1.75	0.40	1.20	2.00	
❏ 60, May 89, "The Magic Wars" Part 1 of 4				
.... 1.75	0.40	1.20	2.00	
❏ 61, Jun 89, "The Magic Wars" Part 2 of 4				
.... 1.75	0.40	1.20	2.00	
❏ 62, Jul 89, "The Magic Wars" Part 3 of 4; D:Magnetic Kid				
.... 1.75	0.40	1.20	2.00	
❏ 63, Aug 89, "The Magic Wars" Part 4 of 4; final issue				
.... 1.75	0.40	1.20	2.00	

LEGION OF SUPER-HEROES (beginning 1989)

	ORIG.	GOOD	FINE	N-MINT
❏ 0, Oct 94, Revised Legion origin;continues in *Legion of Super-Heroes* #62 and *Legionnaires* #19				
.... 1.95	0.50	1.50	2.50	
❏ 1, Nov 89, Begins five years after previous series				
.... 1.75	0.60	1.80	3.00	
❏ 2, Dec 89 .... 1.75	0.50	1.50	2.50	
❏ 3, Jan 90 .... 1.75	0.40	1.20	2.00	
❏ 4, Feb 90 .... 1.75	0.40	1.20	2.00	
❏ 5, Mar 90 .... 1.75	0.40	1.20	2.00	
❏ 6, Apr 90 .... 1.75	0.40	1.20	2.00	
❏ 7, May 90 .... 1.75	0.40	1.20	2.00	
❏ 8, Jun 90, origin 1.75	0.40	1.20	2.00	
❏ 9, Jul 90 .... 1.75	0.40	1.20	2.00	
❏ 10, Aug 90 .... 1.75	0.40	1.20	2.00	
❏ 11, Sep 90 .... 1.75	0.40	1.20	2.00	
❏ 12, Oct 90 .... 1.75	0.40	1.20	2.00	
❏ 13, Nov 90, poster 1.75	0.40	1.20	2.00	
❏ 14, Jan 91 .... 1.75	0.40	1.20	2.00	
❏ 15, Feb 91 .... 1.75	0.40	1.20	2.00	
❏ 16, Mar 91 .... 1.75	0.35	1.05	1.75	
❏ 17, Apr 91 .... 1.75	0.35	1.05	1.75	
❏ 18, May 91 .... 1.75	0.35	1.05	1.75	
❏ 19, Jun 91 .... 1.75	0.35	1.05	1.75	
❏ 20, Jul 91 .... 1.75	0.35	1.05	1.75	
❏ 21, Aug 91 .... 1.75	0.35	1.05	1.75	
❏ 22, Sep 91 .... 1.75	0.35	1.05	1.75	
❏ 23, Oct 91, V:Lobo 1.75	0.35	1.05	1.75	
❏ 24, Dec 91 .... 1.75	0.35	1.05	1.75	
❏ 25, Jan 92 .... 1.75	0.35	1.05	1.75	
❏ 26, Feb 92, contains map of Legion headquarters				
.... 1.75	0.35	1.05	1.75	
❏ 27, Mar 92 .... 1.75	0.35	1.05	1.75	
❏ 28, Apr 92 .... 1.75	0.35	1.05	1.75	
❏ 29, May 92 .... 1.75	0.35	1.05	1.75	
❏ 30, Jun 92 .... 1.75	0.35	1.05	1.75	
❏ 31, Jul 92, romance cover				
.... 1.75	0.35	1.05	1.75	
❏ 32, Aug 92 .... 1.75	0.35	1.05	1.75	
❏ 33, Sep 92, fate of Kid Quantum				
.... 1.75	0.35	1.05	1.75	
❏ 34, Oct 92, Timber Wolf mini-series preview				
.... 1.75	0.35	1.05	1.75	
❏ 35, Nov 92, Sun Boy meets Sun Boy				
.... 1.75	0.35	1.05	1.75	
❏ 36, Nov 92 .... 1.75	0.35	1.05	1.75	
❏ 37, Dec 92, Star Boy and Dream Girl return				
.... 1.75	0.35	1.05	1.75	
❏ 38, Dec 92, Earth destroyed				
.... 1.75	0.35	1.05	1.75	
❏ 39, Jan 93 .... 1.75	0.35	1.05	1.75	
❏ 40, Feb 93 .... 1.75	0.35	1.05	1.75	
❏ 41, Mar 93, I:Legionnaires				
.... 1.75	0.35	1.05	1.75	
❏ 42, Apr 93 .... 1.75	0.35	1.05	1.75	

	ORIG.	GOOD	FINE	N-MINT
❏ 43, May 93, White Witch returns				
.... 1.75	0.35	1.05	1.75	
❏ 44, Jun 93, Projectra returns				
.... 1.75	0.35	1.05	1.75	
❏ 45, Jul 93 .... 1.75	0.35	1.05	1.75	
❏ 46, Aug 93 .... 1.75	0.35	1.05	1.75	
❏ 47, Sep 93 .... 1.75	0.35	1.05	1.75	
❏ 48, Oct 93, V:Mordru 1.75	0.35	1.05	1.75	
❏ 49, Nov 93 .... 1.75	0.35	1.05	1.75	
❏ 50, Nov 93, Marriage of Matter-Eater Lad and Saturn				
Queen 3.50	0.70	2.10	3.50	
❏ 51, Dec 93 .... 1.75	0.35	1.05	1.75	
❏ 52, Dec 93, O: Timber Wolf retold				
.... 1.75	0.35	1.05	1.75	
❏ 53, Jan 94 .... 1.75	0.35	1.05	1.75	
❏ 54, Feb 94, die-cut cover 2.95	0.59	1.77	2.95	
❏ 55, Mar 94 .... 1.75	0.35	1.05	1.75	
❏ 56, Apr 94 .... 1.75	0.35	1.05	1.75	
❏ 57, May 94 .... 1.75	0.35	1.05	1.75	
❏ 58, Jun 94 .... 1.75	0.35	1.05	1.75	
❏ 59, Jul 94 .... 1.95	0.39	1.17	1.95	
❏ 60, Aug 94, "End of an Era" Part 3 of 6				
.... 1.95	0.39	1.17	1.95	
❏ 61, Sep 94, "End of an Era" Real Conclusion; "Zero Hour";end of original Legion of Super-Heroes				
.... 1.95	0.39	1.17	1.95	
❏ 62, Nov 94 .... 1.95	0.39	1.17	1.95	
❏ 63, Dec 94, 1:Athramites, new Legion headquarters; Tenzil Kem hired as chef. 1.95	0.39	1.17	1.95	
❏ 64, Jan 95, R:Ultra Boy ... 1.95	0.39	1.17	1.95	
❏ 65, Feb 95 .... 1.95	0.39	1.17	1.95	
❏ 66, Mar 95 .... 1.95	0.39	1.17	1.95	
❏ 67, Apr 95 .... 1.95	0.39	1.17	1.95	
❏ 68, May 95 .... 1.95	0.39	1.17	1.95	
❏ 69, Jun 95 .... 2.25	0.45	1.35	2.25	
❏ 70, Jul 95 .... 2.25	0.45	1.35	2.25	
❏ 71, Aug 95, Trom destroyed				
.... 2.25	0.45	1.35	2.25	
❏ 72, Sep 95 .... 2.25	0.45	1.35	2.25	
❏ 73, Oct 95 .... 2.25	0.45	1.35	2.25	
❏ 74, Nov 95, "Future Tense" Part 2 of 3;A:Superboy, Scavenger;concludes in *Legionnaires* #31				
.... 2.25	0.45	1.35	2.25	
❏ 75, Dec 95, "Underworld Unleashed";A:Chronos				
.... 2.25	0.45	1.35	2.25	
❏ 76, Jan 96, J:Star Boy and Gates				
.... 2.25	0.45	1.35	2.25	
❏ 77, Feb 96 .... 2.25	0.45	1.35	2.25	
❏ 78, Mar 96, O&I:Fatal Five				
.... 2.25	0.45	1.35	2.25	
❏ 79, Apr 96, V:Fatal Five ... 2.25	0.45	1.35	2.25	
❏ 80, May 96 .... 2.25	0.45	1.35	2.25	
❏ 81, Jun 96, Dirk Morgna becomes Sun Boy; Brainiac 5 quits 2.25	0.45	1.35	2.25	

LEGION OF SUPER-HEROES
(formerly Superboy and the Legion of Super-Heroes)

	ORIG.	GOOD	FINE	N-MINT
❏ 259, Jan 80, L:Superboy. 0.40	1.00	3.00	5.00	
❏ 260, Feb 80 .... 0.40	0.60	1.80	3.00	
❏ 261, Mar 80 .... 0.40	0.60	1.80	3.00	
❏ 262, Apr 80 .... 0.40	0.60	1.80	3.00	
❏ 263, May 80 .... 0.40	0.60	1.80	3.00	
❏ 264, Jun 80 .... 0.40	0.60	1.80	3.00	
❏ 265, Jul 80, O:Tyroc 0.40	0.60	1.80	3.00	
❏ 266, Aug 80 .... 0.40	0.40	1.20	2.00	
❏ 267, Sep 80, O:Legion Flight Rings				
.... 0.50	0.40	1.20	2.00	
❏ 268, Oct 80, SD 0.50	0.40	1.20	2.00	
❏ 269, Nov 80, V:Fatal Five				
.... 0.50	0.40	1.20	2.00	
❏ 270, Dec 80, Dark Man's identity revealed				
.... 0.50	0.40	1.20	2.00	

	ORIG.	GOOD	FINE	N-MINT
271, Jan 81, O:Dark Man				
	0.50	0.40	1.20	2.00
272, Feb 81	0.50	0.40	1.20	2.00
273, Mar 81	0.50	0.30	0.90	1.50
274, Apr 81, SD;Ultra Boy becomes pirate				
	0.50	0.30	0.90	1.50
275, May 81	0.50	0.30	0.90	1.50
276, Jun 81	0.50	0.30	0.90	1.50
277, Jul 81	0.50	0.30	0.90	1.50
278, Aug 81, V:Grimbor	0.50	0.30	0.90	1.50
279, Sep 81, Reflecto's identity revealed				
	0.50	0.30	0.90	1.50
280, Oct 81, Superboy rejoins				
	0.60	0.30	0.90	1.50
281, Nov 81, SD; V:Molecule Master				
	0.60	0.20	0.60	1.00
282, Dec 81, Ultra Boy returns;O:Reflecto				
	0.60	0.20	0.60	1.00
283, Jan 82, O:Reflecto	0.60	0.20	0.60	1.00
284, Feb 82	0.60	0.20	0.60	1.00
285, Mar 82, PB 1:Giffen art				
	0.60	1.20	3.60	6.00
286, Apr 82, PB; :Dr. Regulus				
	0.60	0.80	2.40	4.00
287, May 82, KG, V:Kharlak				
	0.60	1.50	4.50	7.50
288, Jun 82, KG	0.60	1.00	3.00	5.00
289, Jul 82, KG	0.60	1.00	3.00	5.00
290, Aug 82, KG; "Great Darkness Saga"				
	0.60	1.00	3.00	5.00
291, Sep 82, KG, Darkseid				
	0.60	0.70	2.10	3.50
292, Oct 82, KG, Darkseid				
	0.60	0.70	2.10	3.50
293, Nov 82, KG, Darkseid				
	0.60	0.70	2.10	3.50
294, Dec 82, KG, Darkseid				
	1.00	0.70	2.10	3.50
295, Jan 83, A:Green Lantern Corps; O?:Universo				
	0.60	0.40	1.20	2.00
296, Feb 83	0.60	0.40	1.20	2.00
297, Mar 83	0.60	0.40	1.20	2.00
298, Apr 83, Amethyst, Princess of Gemworld insert				
	0.60	0.40	1.20	2.00
299, May 83	0.60	0.40	1.20	2.00
300, Jun 83, Tales of the Adult Legion;alternate futures				
	1.50	0.30	0.90	1.50
301, Jul 83	0.60	0.20	0.60	1.00
302, Aug 83, Lightning Lad vs. Lightning Lord				
	0.60	0.20	0.60	1.00
303, Sep 83, V:Emerald Empress				
	0.60	0.20	0.60	1.00
304, Oct 83	0.60	0.20	0.60	1.00
305, Nov 83, Shrinking Violet revealed as Durlan; real Shrinking Violet returns	0.60	0.20	0.60	1.00
306, Dec 83, O:Star Boy	0.75	0.20	0.60	1.00
307, Jan 84	0.75	0.20	0.60	1.00
308, Feb 84	0.75	0.20	0.60	1.00
309, Mar 84	0.75	0.20	0.60	1.00
310, Apr 84	0.75	0.20	0.60	1.00
311, May 84	0.75	0.20	0.60	1.00
312, Jun 84	0.75	0.20	0.60	1.00
313, Jul 84, (becomes Tales of the LSH)				
	0.75	0.20	0.60	1.00

LEGION OF SUPER-HEROES ANNUAL

	ORIG.	GOOD	FINE	N-MINT
1, 82, KG, 1:Invisible Kid II				
	1.00	0.70	2.10	3.50
2, 83, KG;W:Karate Kid and Princess Projectra				
	1.00	0.30	0.90	1.50
3, 84, CS;O:Validus	1.25	0.25	0.75	1.25

LEGION OF SUPER-HEROES ANNUAL (1990-)

	ORIG.	GOOD	FINE	N-MINT
1, 90, O:Glorith, Ultra Boy;ro:Legion				
	3.50	0.70	2.10	3.50
2, 91, O:Valor	3.50	0.70	2.10	3.50
3, 92, Timber Wolf goes to 20th century				
	3.50	0.70	2.10	3.50
4, 93, "Bloodlines: Earthplague";O&1:Jamm				
	3.50	0.70	2.10	3.50
5, 94, "Elseworlds"; Legion in Oz				
	3.50	0.70	2.10	3.50
6, 95, "Year One";ro: Leviathan;O:Kinetix,XS				
	3.95	0.79	2.37	3.95

LEGION OF SUPER-HEROES ANNUAL (direct sale)

	ORIG.	GOOD	FINE	N-MINT
1, Oct 85, KG	2.00	0.40	1.20	2.00
2, Oct 86	2.00	0.50	1.50	2.50
3, 87, O:New Legion of Substitute Heroes				
	2.25	0.45	1.35	2.25
4, 88, O:Starfinger	2.50	0.50	1.50	2.50

LEGION OF SUPER-HEROES INDEX
ECLIPSE/INDEPENDENT

	GOOD	FINE	N-MINT
1	0.40	1.20	2.00
2, Jan 87	0.40	1.20	2.00
3, Feb 87	0.40	1.20	2.00
4, Mar 87	0.40	1.20	2.00
5, May 87	0.40	1.20	2.00

LEGIONNAIRES
DC

	ORIG.	GOOD	FINE	N-MINT
0, Oct 94, revised Legion origin;continues in Legion of Super-Heroes #62 and Legionnaires #19				
	1.50	0.60	1.80	3.00
1, Apr 93, with trading card				
	1.25	1.00	3.00	5.00
2, May 93, V:Fatal Five; covers of issues #2-6 form one image	1.25	0.60	1.80	3.00
3, Jun 93, V:Fatal Five	1.25	0.40	1.20	2.00
4, Jul 93, V:Fatal Five	1.25	0.40	1.20	2.00
5, Aug 93, V:Fatal Five	1.25	0.25	0.75	1.25
6, Sep 93, V:Fatal Five	1.25	0.25	0.75	1.25
7, Oct 93	1.25	0.25	0.75	1.25
8, Nov 93, L:Brainiac 5	1.25	0.25	0.75	1.25
9, Dec 93	1.50	0.30	0.90	1.50
10, Jan 94	1.50	0.30	0.90	1.50
11, Feb 94, J:Kid Quantum				
	1.50	0.30	0.90	1.50
12, Mar 94	1.50	0.30	0.90	1.50
13, Apr 94	1.50	0.30	0.90	1.50
14, May 94	1.50	0.30	0.90	1.50
15, Jun 94	1.50	0.30	0.90	1.50
16, Jul 94, R:Dream Girl	1.50	0.30	0.90	1.50
17, Aug 94, "End of an Era" Conclusion				
	1.50	0.30	0.90	1.50
18, Sep 94, "End of an Era" Part 4 of 6;"Zero Hour"				
	1.50	0.60	1.80	3.00
19, Nov 94	1.50	0.30	0.90	1.50
20, Dec 94, V:Mano	1.50	0.30	0.90	1.50
21, Jan 95, 1:Work Force	1.50	0.30	0.90	1.50
22, Feb 95	1.50	0.30	0.90	1.50
23, Mar 95	1.50	0.30	0.90	1.50
24, Apr 95	1.50	0.30	0.90	1.50
25, May 95	1.50	0.30	0.90	1.50
26, Jun 95	1.75	0.35	1.05	1.75
27, Jul 95	2.25	0.45	1.35	2.25
28, Aug 95, 1:Legion Espionage Squad				
	2.25	0.45	1.35	2.25
29, Sep 95, I: Dirk Morgna				
	2.25	0.45	1.35	2.25
30, Oct 95, Lightning Lad turning point				
	2.25	0.45	1.35	2.25
31, Nov 95, "Future Tense" Part 3 of 3;Superboy made honorary member; Valor released into 30th century				
	2.25	0.45	1.35	2.25

	ORIG.	GOOD	FINE	N-MINT
32, Dec 95, "Underworld Unleashed";A:Chronos;				
	2.25	0.45	1.35	2.25
33, Jan 96	2.25	0.45	1.35	2.25
34, Feb 96	2.25	0.45	1.35	2.25
35, Mar 96, XS returns to 30th century				
	2.25	0.45	1.35	2.25
36, May 96	2.25	0.45	1.35	2.25
37, Jun 96, O:M'onel	2.25	0.45	1.35	2.25

LEGIONNAIRES 3 (mini-series)

	ORIG.	GOOD	FINE	N-MINT
1, Feb 86, V:Time Trapper				
	0.75	0.20	0.60	1.00
2, Mar 86	0.75	0.20	0.60	1.00
3, Apr 86	0.75	0.20	0.60	1.00
4, May 86	0.75	0.20	0.60	1.00

LEGIONNAIRES ANNUAL

	ORIG.	GOOD	FINE	N-MINT
1, 94, "Elseworlds"	2.95	0.59	1.77	2.95
2, 95, D:Apparition;L: Andromeda				
	3.95	0.79	2.37	3.95

LEGIONS OF LUDICROUS HEROES
C&T

	GOOD	FINE	N-MINT
1, b&w	0.40	1.20	2.00

LEJENTIA
OPUS

	GOOD	FINE	N-MINT
1	0.45	1.35	2.25
2	0.45	1.35	2.25

LEMONADE KID
AC

	GOOD	FINE	N-MINT
1, 90, Powell reprints	0.50	1.50	2.50

LENSMAN
ETERNITY

	GOOD	FINE	N-MINT
1, special edition b&w	0.79	2.37	3.95
1, regular b&w	0.45	1.35	2.25
2	0.45	1.35	2.25
3	0.45	1.35	2.25
4	0.45	1.35	2.25
5	0.45	1.35	2.25
6	0.45	1.35	2.25

LENSMAN: GALACTIC PATROL

	GOOD	FINE	N-MINT
1, b&w	0.45	1.35	2.25
2, b&w	0.45	1.35	2.25
3, b&w	0.45	1.35	2.25
4, b&w	0.45	1.35	2.25
5, b&w	0.45	1.35	2.25

LENSMAN: WAR OF THE GALAXIES

	GOOD	FINE	N-MINT
1, b&w	0.45	1.35	2.25
2, b&w	0.45	1.35	2.25
3, b&w	0.45	1.35	2.25
4, b&w	0.45	1.35	2.25
5, b&w	0.45	1.35	2.25
6, b&w	0.45	1.35	2.25
7, b&w	0.45	1.35	2.25

LEONARD NIMOY
CELEBRITY

	GOOD	FINE	N-MINT
1, b&w	1.19	3.57	5.95

LEONARD NIMOY'S PRIMORTALS
TEKNO

	ORIG.	GOOD	FINE	N-MINT
1, Mar 95	1.95	0.39	1.17	1.95
2, Apr 95	1.95	0.39	1.17	1.95
3, May 95	1.95	0.39	1.17	1.95
4, Jun 95	1.95	0.39	1.17	1.95
5, Jul 95	1.95	0.39	1.17	1.95
6, Aug 95	1.95	0.39	1.17	1.95
7, Sep 95	1.95	0.39	1.17	1.95
8, Oct 95	1.95	0.39	1.17	1.95
9, Nov 95	1.95	0.39	1.17	1.95
11, Dec 95	1.95	0.39	1.17	1.95
12, Jan 96	2.25	0.45	1.35	2.25
13, Mar 96	2.25	0.45	1.35	2.25
14, Apr 96	2.25	0.45	1.35	2.25
15, May 96	2.25	0.45	1.35	2.25

LEONARD NIMOY'S PRIMORTALS ORIGINS

	ORIG.	GOOD	FINE	N-MINT
1, 95	2.25	0.45	1.35	2.25

LEONARDO
MIRAGE

	GOOD	FINE	N-MINT
1	1.00	3.00	5.00

LESTER GIRLS: THE LIZARD'S TRAIL
ETERNITY

	GOOD	FINE	N-MINT
1, b&w	0.50	1.50	2.50
2, b&w	0.50	1.50	2.50
3, b&w	0.50	1.50	2.50

LETHAL
IMAGE

	ORIG.	GOOD	FINE	N-MINT
1, Feb 96	2.50	0.50	1.50	2.50

LETHAL FOES OF SPIDER-MAN (mini-series)
MARVEL

	ORIG.	GOOD	FINE	N-MINT
1	1.75	0.35	1.05	1.75
2	1.75	0.35	1.05	1.75
3	1.75	0.35	1.05	1.75
4	1.75	0.35	1.05	1.75

LETHARGIC COMICS
ALPHA

	ORIG.	GOOD	FINE	N-MINT
1, b&w	2.50	0.50	1.50	2.50
2, Feb 94, b&w	2.50	0.50	1.50	2.50
3, Mar 94, b&w	2.50	0.50	1.50	2.50
4, May 94, b&w	2.50	0.50	1.50	2.50
5, Jul 94, b&w	2.50	0.50	1.50	2.50
9, Apr 95, b&w	2.50	0.50	1.50	2.50

LETHARGIC COMICS, WEAKLY
LETHARGIC

	ORIG.	GOOD	FINE	N-MINT
1, b&w	1.95	0.60	1.80	3.00
2, b&w	1.95	0.60	1.80	3.00
3, b&w	1.95	0.60	1.80	3.00
4, b&w	1.75	0.35	1.05	1.75
5, Batman parody, b&w	1.95	0.39	1.17	1.95
6, Batman parody, b&w	1.95	0.39	1.17	1.95
7	2.50	0.50	1.50	2.50
8	2.50	0.50	1.50	2.50
9	2.50	0.50	1.50	2.50
10, Capt. America parody				
	2.25	0.45	1.35	2.25

LETHARGIC COMICS, WEAKLY
(was Lethargic Comics comic)
ALPHA

	ORIG.	GOOD	FINE	N-MINT
12, b&w	2.50	0.50	1.50	2.50

LEX LUTHOR: THE UNAUTHORIZED BIOGRAPHY
DC

	ORIG.	GOOD	FINE	N-MINT
1, Jul 89, O:Luthor	3.95	1.19	3.57	5.95

LIAISONS DELICIEUSES
EROS COMIX

	GOOD	FINE	N-MINT
1, adult, b&w	0.39	1.17	1.95
2, adult, b&w	0.39	1.17	1.95
3	0.45	1.35	2.25
4	0.45	1.35	2.25
5	0.45	1.35	2.25

LIBBY ELLIS
ETERNITY

	GOOD	FINE	N-MINT
1, b&w	0.39	1.17	1.95
2, b&w	0.39	1.17	1.95
3, b&w	0.39	1.17	1.95
4, b&w	0.39	1.17	1.95

MALIBU

	GOOD	FINE	N-MINT
1	0.39	1.17	1.95
2	0.39	1.17	1.95
3	0.39	1.17	1.95
4	0.39	1.17	1.95

LIBERATOR

	GOOD	FINE	N-MINT
1, Dec 87, (becomes Eternity title)			
	0.39	1.17	1.95

	ORIG.	GOOD	FINE	N-MINT

LIBERATOR, THE (was Malibu Comic)
ETERNITY
	ORIG.	GOOD	FINE	N-MINT
2, Feb 88		0.39	1.17	1.95
3, Mar 88		0.39	1.17	1.95
4, Jun 88		0.39	1.17	1.95
5, Oct 88		0.39	1.17	1.95
6, Dec 88		0.39	1.17	1.95

LIBERTINE, THE
EROS COMIX
	GOOD	FINE	N-MINT
1, adult, b&w	0.45	1.35	2.25
2	0.50	1.50	2.50

LIBERTY PROJECT, THE
ECLIPSE
	ORIG.	GOOD	FINE	N-MINT
1, Jun 87	1.75	0.35	1.05	1.75
2, Jul 87		0.35	1.05	1.75
3, Aug 87		0.35	1.05	1.75
4, Sep 87		0.35	1.05	1.75
5, Oct 87		0.35	1.05	1.75
6, Nov 87, A:Valkyrie		0.35	1.05	1.75
7, Dec 87		0.35	1.05	1.75
8, May 88		0.35	1.05	1.75

LIBRA
ETERNITY
	GOOD	FINE	N-MINT
1	0.39	1.17	1.95

LIBRARIAN, THE
FANTAGRAPHICS
	GOOD	FINE	N-MINT
1, b&w	0.55	1.65	2.75

LIFE OF CAPTAIN MARVEL
MARVEL
	ORIG.	GOOD	FINE	N-MINT
1, Aug 85, Baxter rep.	2.00	0.40	1.20	2.00
2, Sep 85, Baxter rep.	2.00	0.40	1.20	2.00
3, Oct 85, Baxter rep.	2.00	0.40	1.20	2.00
4, Nov 85, Baxter rep.	2.00	0.40	1.20	2.00
5, Dec 85, Baxter rep.	2.00	0.40	1.20	2.00

LIFE OF CHRIST, THE
MARVEL/ NELSON
	ORIG.	GOOD	FINE	N-MINT
1	2.99	0.60	1.79	2.99

LIFE OF POPE JOHN-PAUL II
MARVEL
	ORIG.	GOOD	FINE	N-MINT
1, Jan 83, JSt	1.50	0.30	0.90	1.50

LIFE UNDER SANCTIONS
FANTAGRAPHICS
	ORIG.	GOOD	FINE	N-MINT
0, Feb 94, nn b&w	2.95	0.59	1.77	2.95

LIFE, THE UNIVERSE AND EVERYTHING
(mini-series)
DC
	ORIG.	GOOD	FINE	N-MINT
1, 96, adapts the book by Douglas Adams; prestige format	6.95	1.39	4.17	6.95
2, 96, adapts the book by Douglas Adams;prestige format	6.95	1.39	4.17	6.95

LIGHT AND DARKNESS WAR, THE
EPIC
	ORIG.	GOOD	FINE	N-MINT
1	1.95	0.39	1.17	1.95
2	1.95	0.39	1.17	1.95
3	1.95	0.39	1.17	1.95
4	1.95	0.39	1.17	1.95
5	1.95	0.39	1.17	1.95
6	1.95	0.39	1.17	1.95

LIGHT FANTASTIC, THE
INNOVATION
	GOOD	FINE	N-MINT
0, novel adaptation	0.50	1.50	2.50
1	0.50	1.50	2.50
2	0.50	1.50	2.50
3	0.50	1.50	2.50
4	0.50	1.50	2.50

LIPSTICK
RIP OFF
	ORIG.	GOOD	FINE	N-MINT
1, May 92, adult;b&w	2.50	0.50	1.50	2.50

LISA COMICS
BONGO
	ORIG.	GOOD	FINE	N-MINT
1, 95, one-shot; "Lisa in Wordland"	2.25	0.45	1.35	2.25

LITA FORD
ROCK-IT COMICS
	ORIG.	GOOD	FINE	N-MINT
1	4.95	0.99	2.97	4.95

LITTLE ARCHIE DIGEST MAGAZINE
ARCHIE
	ORIG.	GOOD	FINE	N-MINT
14, Aug 95, digest	1.75	0.35	1.05	1.75
15, Oct 95, digest	1.75	0.35	1.05	1.75
16, Jun 96, digest	1.75	0.35	1.05	1.75

LITTLE AUDREY (Volume Two)
HARVEY
	ORIG.	GOOD	FINE	N-MINT
1	1.25	0.25	0.75	1.25
2	1.25	0.25	0.75	1.25
3	1.25	0.25	0.75	1.25
4	1.25	0.25	0.75	1.25
5	1.25	0.25	0.75	1.25
6	1.50	0.30	0.90	1.50
7	1.50	0.30	0.90	1.50
8	1.50	0.30	0.90	1.50

LITTLE DOT (Volume 2)
	ORIG.	GOOD	FINE	N-MINT
1	1.25	0.25	0.75	1.25
2	1.25	0.25	0.75	1.25
3	1.25	0.25	0.75	1.25
4	1.25	0.25	0.75	1.25
5	1.25	0.25	0.75	1.25
6	1.50	0.30	0.90	1.50
7	1.50	0.30	0.90	1.50

LITTLE DOT IN 3-D
BLACKTHORNE
	GOOD	FINE	N-MINT
1	0.50	1.50	2.50

LITTLE DRACULA
HARVEY
	ORIG.	GOOD	FINE	N-MINT
1	1.25	0.25	0.75	1.25
2	1.25	0.25	0.75	1.25
3	1.25	0.25	0.75	1.25

LITTLE GRETA GARBAGE
RIP OFF
	ORIG.	GOOD	FINE	N-MINT
1, Jul 90, adult;b&w	2.50	0.50	1.50	2.50
2, Jun 91, adult;b&w	2.50	0.50	1.50	2.50

LITTLE ITALY
FANTAGRAPHICS
	GOOD	FINE	N-MINT
1, b&w	0.79	2.37	3.95

LITTLE LOTTA
HARVEY
	ORIG.	GOOD	FINE	N-MINT
1	1.25	0.25	0.75	1.25
2	1.25	0.25	0.75	1.25
3	1.25	0.25	0.75	1.25
4	1.25	0.25	0.75	1.25

LITTLE MERMAID
W.D.
	GOOD	FINE	N-MINT
0, nn Under the Sea	0.70	2.10	3.50

LITTLE MERMAID, THE
DISNEY
	GOOD	FINE	N-MINT
1, movie, squarebound	1.19	3.57	5.95
1, movie, stapled	0.50	1.50	2.50

LITTLE MERMAID, THE (mini-series)
	ORIG.	GOOD	FINE	N-MINT
1, Feb 92	1.50	0.30	0.90	1.50
2	1.50	0.30	0.90	1.50
3	1.50	0.30	0.90	1.50
4	1.50	0.30	0.90	1.50

LITTLE MISTER MAN
SLAVE LABOR
	ORIG.	GOOD	FINE	N-MINT
1, Nov 95, b&w	2.95	0.59	1.77	2.95
2, Dec 95, b&w	2.95	0.59	1.77	2.95

	ORIG.	GOOD	FINE	N-MINT

LITTLE MONSTERS
NOW
	ORIG.	GOOD	FINE	N-MINT
❑ 1, Jan 90, movie 1.75		0.35	1.05	1.75
❑ 2, Feb 90, movie 1.75		0.35	1.05	1.75
❑ 3, Mar 90, movie........... 1.75		0.35	1.05	1.75
❑ 4, Apr 90, movie 1.75		0.35	1.05	1.75
❑ 5, May 90, movie 1.75		0.35	1.05	1.75
❑ 6, Jun 90, movie 1.75		0.35	1.05	1.75

LITTLE NEMO IN SLUMBERLAND 3-D
BLACKTHORNE
	GOOD	FINE	N-MINT
❑ 1	0.50	1.50	2.50

LITTLE RONZO IN SLUMBERLAND
SLAVE LABOR
	GOOD	FINE	N-MINT
❑ 1	0.35	1.05	1.75

LITTLE SHOP OF HORRORS
DC
	GOOD	FINE	N-MINT
❑ 1, Mar 87, movie..............	0.40	1.20	2.00

LIVINGSTONE MOUNTAIN
ADVENTURE
	GOOD	FINE	N-MINT
❑ 1, b&w	0.50	1.50	2.50
❑ 2, b&w	0.50	1.50	2.50
❑ 3, b&w	0.50	1.50	2.50
❑ 4, b&w	0.50	1.50	2.50

LIZ AND BETH
EROS COMIX
	GOOD	FINE	N-MINT
❑ 1, adult, b&w	0.45	1.35	2.25
❑ 2, adult, b&w	0.45	1.35	2.25
❑ 3, adult, b&w	0.45	1.35	2.25
❑ 4	0.50	1.50	2.50

LIZ AND BETH (Volume 2)
	GOOD	FINE	N-MINT
❑ 1, adult, b&w	0.50	1.50	2.50
❑ 2, adult, b&w	0.50	1.50	2.50
❑ 3, adult, b&w	0.50	1.50	2.50

LIZ AND BETH (Volume 3)
	ORIG.	GOOD	FINE	N-MINT
❑ 1, adult, b&w 2.50		0.50	1.50	2.50
❑ 2, adult, b&w 2.50		0.50	1.50	2.50
❑ 3, adult, b&w 2.50		0.50	1.50	2.50
❑ 4, adult, b&w 2.50		0.50	1.50	2.50
❑ 5, adult, b&w 2.50		0.50	1.50	2.50
❑ 6, adult, b&w 2.50		0.50	1.50	2.50
❑ 7, adult, b&w 2.50		0.50	1.50	2.50

LIZARD LADY
AIRCEL
	GOOD	FINE	N-MINT
❑ 1, adult, b&w	0.59	1.77	2.95
❑ 2, adult, b&w	0.59	1.77	2.95
❑ 3, adult, b&w	0.59	1.77	2.95
❑ 4, adult, b&w	0.59	1.77	2.95

LIZARDS SUMMER FUN SPECIAL
CALIBER
	ORIG.	GOOD	FINE	N-MINT
❑ 1, b&w 3.50		0.70	2.10	3.50

LLOYD LLEWELLYN
FANTAGRAPHICS
	GOOD	FINE	N-MINT
❑ 1	0.80	2.40	4.00
❑ 2	0.45	1.35	2.25
❑ 3	0.45	1.35	2.25
❑ 4	0.45	1.35	2.25
❑ 5	0.45	1.35	2.25
❑ 6	0.45	1.35	2.25

LLOYD LLEWELLYN SPECIAL
	ORIG.	GOOD	FINE	N-MINT
❑ 1 .... 2.50		0.50	1.50	2.50
❑ 1, second printing 2.95		0.59	1.77	2.95

LOBO (mini-series)
DC
		GOOD	FINE	N-MINT
❑ 1, Nov 90, (1st printing)...		1.20	3.60	6.00
❑ 1, Nov 90, (2nd printing) .		0.60	1.80	3.00
❑ 2, Dec 90........................		0.80	2.40	4.00
❑ 3, Jan 91		0.70	2.10	3.50
❑ 4, Feb 91		0.60	1.80	3.00

LOBO (ongoing series)
	ORIG.	GOOD	FINE	N-MINT
❑ 0, Oct 94.........................1.95		0.39	1.17	1.95
❑ 1, foil cover....................2.95		0.59	1.77	2.95
❑ 5, May 94........................1.75		0.35	1.05	1.75
❑ 6, Jun 94 ....1.75		0.35	1.05	1.75
❑ 7, Jul 94..........................1.75		0.35	1.05	1.75
❑ 8, Aug 94.........................1.75		0.35	1.05	1.75
❑ 9, Sep 94 ....1.95		0.39	1.17	1.95
❑ 10, Nov 94.......................1.95		0.39	1.17	1.95
❑ 11, Dec 94.......................1.95		0.39	1.17	1.95
❑ 12, Jan 95.......................1.95		0.39	1.17	1.95
❑ 13, Feb 95.......................1.95		0.39	1.17	1.95
❑ 14, Mar 95.......................1.95		0.39	1.17	1.95
❑ 15, Apr 95........................1.95		0.39	1.17	1.95
❑ 16, Jun 95........................2.25		0.45	1.35	2.25
❑ 17, Jul 95.........................2.25		0.45	1.35	2.25
❑ 18, Aug 95.......................2.25		0.45	1.35	2.25
❑ 19, Sep 95 ....2.25		0.45	1.35	2.25
❑ 20, Oct 95........................2.25		0.45	1.35	2.25
❑ 21, Nov 95, A:Space Cabby 2.25		0.45	1.35	2.25
❑ 22, Dec 95, "Underworld Unleashed" 2.25		0.45	1.35	2.25
❑ 23, Jan 96.......................2.25		0.45	1.35	2.25
❑ 24, Feb 96.......................2.25		0.45	1.35	2.25
❑ 25, Mar 96.......................2.25		0.45	1.35	2.25
❑ 26, Apr 96........................2.25		0.45	1.35	2.25
❑ 27, May 96.......................2.25		0.45	1.35	2.25
❑ 28, Jun 96, "The Heiress" Part 1 of 4 ....2.25		0.45	1.35	2.25
❑ 29, Jul 96, "The Heiress" Part 2 of 4 ....2.25		0.45	1.35	2.25

LOBO ANNUAL
	ORIG.	GOOD	FINE	N-MINT
❑ 1, Bloodlines.................3.50		0.70	2.10	3.50
❑ 2, 94, Elseworlds 3.50		0.70	2.10	3.50
❑ 3, 95, "Year One"............3.95		0.79	2.37	3.95

LOBO CONVENTION SPECIAL
	ORIG.	GOOD	FINE	N-MINT
❑ 1 ....1.75		0.35	1.05	1.75

LOBO GALLERY, THE: PORTRAITS OF A BASTICH
	ORIG.	GOOD	FINE	N-MINT
❑ 1, Sep 95, pin-ups 3.50		0.70	2.10	3.50

LOBO PARAMILITARY CHRISTMAS SPECIAL
	GOOD	FINE	N-MINT
❑ 1	1.00	3.00	5.00

LOBO'S BACK
	GOOD	FINE	N-MINT
❑ 1	0.60	1.80	3.00
❑ 2	0.30	0.90	1.50
❑ 3	0.30	0.90	1.50
❑ 4	0.30	0.90	1.50

LOBO'S BIG BABE SPRING BREAK SPECIAL
	ORIG.	GOOD	FINE	N-MINT
❑ 0, Spr 95........................1.95		0.39	1.17	1.95

LOBO/DEADMAN: THE BRAVE AND THE BALD
	ORIG.	GOOD	FINE	N-MINT
❑ 0, Feb 95, one-shot.........3.50		0.70	2.10	3.50

LOBO/JUDGE DREDD: PSYCHO BIKERS VS. THE MUTANTS FROM HELL
	ORIG.	GOOD	FINE	N-MINT
❑ 0, 95, nn; prestige format 4.95		0.99	2.97	4.95

LOBO: A CONTRACT ON GAWD
	ORIG.	GOOD	FINE	N-MINT
❑ 1 ....1.75		0.35	1.05	1.75
❑ 2, May 94........................1.75		0.35	1.05	1.75
❑ 3, Jun 94 ....1.75		0.35	1.05	1.75
❑ 4, Jul 94..........................1.75		0.35	1.05	1.75

LOBO: BLAZING CHAIN OF LOVE
	ORIG.	GOOD	FINE	N-MINT
❑ 1 ....1.50		0.30	0.90	1.50

LOBO: BOUNTY HUNTING FOR FUN AND PROFIT
	ORIG.	GOOD	FINE	N-MINT
❑ 0, 95, prestige format 4.95		0.99	2.97	4.95

LOBO: I QUIT
	ORIG.	GOOD	FINE	N-MINT
❑ 1, Dec 95, one-shot; Lobo stops smoking 2.25		0.45	1.35	2.25

	ORIG.	GOOD	FINE	N-MINT

LOBO: IN THE CHAIR

	ORIG.	GOOD	FINE	N-MINT
☐ 1, Aug 94, one-shot	1.95	0.39	1.17	1.95

LOBO: INFANTICIDE

	ORIG.	GOOD	FINE	N-MINT
☐ 1	1.50	0.30	0.90	1.50
☐ 2	1.50	0.30	0.90	1.50
☐ 3	1.50	0.30	0.90	1.50
☐ 4	1.50	0.30	0.90	1.50

LOBO: PORTRAIT OF A VICTIM

	ORIG.	GOOD	FINE	N-MINT
☐ 1	1.75	0.35	1.05	1.75

LOBO: UNAMERICAN GLADIATORS

	ORIG.	GOOD	FINE	N-MINT
☐ 1	1.75	0.35	1.05	1.75
☐ 2	1.75	0.35	1.05	1.75
☐ 3	1.75	0.35	1.05	1.75
☐ 4	1.75	0.35	1.05	1.75

LOBOCOP

	ORIG.	GOOD	FINE	N-MINT
☐ 1	1.95	0.39	1.17	1.95

LOCO VS. PULVERINE
ECLIPSE

	GOOD	FINE	N-MINT
☐ 0, nn, b&w parody	0.50	1.50	2.50

LOGAN'S RUN
ADVENTURE

	GOOD	FINE	N-MINT
☐ 1, b&w	0.45	1.35	2.25
☐ 2, b&w	0.45	1.35	2.25
☐ 3, b&w	0.45	1.35	2.25
☐ 4, b&w	0.45	1.35	2.25
☐ 5, b&w	0.45	1.35	2.25
☐ 6, b&w	0.45	1.35	2.25

MARVEL

	ORIG.	GOOD	FINE	N-MINT
☐ 1, Jan 77, GP, movie	0.30	0.30	0.90	1.50
☐ 2, Feb 77, GP, movie	0.30	0.20	0.60	1.00
☐ 3, Mar 77, GP, movie	0.30	0.20	0.60	1.00
☐ 4, Apr 77, GP, movie	0.30	0.20	0.60	1.00
☐ 5, May 77, GP, movie	0.30	0.20	0.60	1.00
☐ 6, Jun 77, GP, movie	0.30	1.00	3.00	5.00
☐ 7, Jul 77, GP, movie	0.30	0.20	0.60	1.00

LOGAN'S WORLD
ADVENTURE

	GOOD	FINE	N-MINT
☐ 1, b&w	0.50	1.50	2.50
☐ 2, b&w	0.50	1.50	2.50
☐ 3, b&w	0.50	1.50	2.50
☐ 4, b&w	0.50	1.50	2.50
☐ 5, b&w	0.50	1.50	2.50
☐ 6, b&w	0.50	1.50	2.50

LOIS LANE (mini-series)
DC

	ORIG.	GOOD	FINE	N-MINT
☐ 1, Aug 86, GM	1.50	0.30	0.90	1.50
☐ 2, 86, GM	1.50	0.30	0.90	1.50

LOIS LANE ANNUAL

	ORIG.	GOOD	FINE	N-MINT
☐ 1, Sum 62	0.25	40.00	120.00	200.00

LONE RANGER
TOPPS

	ORIG.	GOOD	FINE	N-MINT
☐ 1, 94, foil edition	2.00	6.00	10.00	

LONE WOLF AND CUB
FIRST

	ORIG.	GOOD	FINE	N-MINT
☐ 1, 87, FM(c) 1st printing; b&w;cardstock cover	1.95	1.20	3.60	6.00
☐ 1, FM(c) 2nd printing		0.39	1.17	1.95
☐ 2, FM(c) 1st printing		1.00	3.00	5.00
☐ 2, FM(c) 2nd printing		0.39	1.17	1.95
☐ 3, FM(c)		0.80	2.40	4.00
☐ 4, FM(c)		0.80	2.40	4.00
☐ 5, FM(c)		0.80	2.40	4.00
☐ 6, FM(c) O:Lone Wolf		0.60	1.80	3.00
☐ 7, FM(c) O:Lone Wolf		0.60	1.80	3.00
☐ 8, FM(c)		0.60	1.80	3.00
☐ 9, FM(c)		0.60	1.80	3.00
☐ 10, FM(c)		0.60	1.80	3.00
☐ 11, FM(c)		0.50	1.50	2.50
☐ 12, FM(c)		0.50	1.50	2.50

	ORIG.	GOOD	FINE	N-MINT
☐ 13, BSz(c)		0.50	1.50	2.50
☐ 14, BSz(c)		0.50	1.50	2.50
☐ 15, BSz(c)		0.50	1.50	2.50
☐ 16, BSz(c)		0.50	1.50	2.50
☐ 17, BSz(c)		0.50	1.50	2.50
☐ 18, BSz(c)		0.50	1.50	2.50
☐ 19, BSz(c)		0.50	1.50	2.50
☐ 20, BSz(c)		0.50	1.50	2.50
☐ 21, BSz(c)		0.50	1.50	2.50
☐ 22, BSz(c)		0.50	1.50	2.50
☐ 23, BSz(c)		0.50	1.50	2.50
☐ 24, BSz(c)		0.50	1.50	2.50
☐ 25, MW(c)		0.59	1.77	2.95
☐ 26, MW(c)		0.59	1.77	2.95
☐ 27, MW(c)		0.59	1.77	2.95
☐ 28, MW(c)		0.59	1.77	2.95
☐ 29, MW(c)		0.59	1.77	2.95
☐ 30, MW(c)		0.59	1.77	2.95
☐ 31, MW(c)		0.59	1.77	2.95
☐ 32, MW(c)		0.65	1.95	3.25
☐ 33, MW(c)		0.65	1.95	3.25
☐ 34, MW(c)		0.65	1.95	3.25
☐ 35, MW(c)		0.65	1.95	3.25
☐ 36, MW(c)		0.65	1.95	3.25
☐ 37, Ploog(c)		0.65	1.95	3.25
☐ 38, Ploog(c)		0.65	1.95	3.25
☐ 39, Ploog(c)		0.65	1.95	3.25
☐ 40, Ploog(c)		0.65	1.95	3.25
☐ 41, Ploog(c)		0.65	1.95	3.25
☐ 42, Ploog(c)		0.65	1.95	3.25
☐ 43, Ploog(c)		0.65	1.95	3.25
☐ 44, Ploog(c)		0.65	1.95	3.25
☐ 45, Ploog(c)		0.65	1.95	3.25

LONER
FLEETWAY/QUALITY

	GOOD	FINE	N-MINT
☐ 1, b&w	0.39	1.17	1.95
☐ 2, b&w	0.39	1.17	1.95
☐ 3, b&w	0.39	1.17	1.95
☐ 4, b&w	0.39	1.17	1.95
☐ 5, b&w	0.39	1.17	1.95
☐ 6, b&w	0.39	1.17	1.95
☐ 7, b&w	0.39	1.17	1.95

LONG, HOT SUMMER, THE (mini-series)
DC/MILESTONE

	ORIG.	GOOD	FINE	N-MINT
☐ 1, Jul 95, enhanced cover	2.95	0.59	1.77	2.95
☐ 2, Aug 95	2.50	0.50	1.50	2.50
☐ 3, Sep 95	2.50	0.50	1.50	2.50

LONGSHOT
MARVEL

	ORIG.	GOOD	FINE	N-MINT
☐ 1, Sep 85, AAd	0.75	4.80	14.40	24.00
☐ 2, Oct 85, AAd	0.75	4.00	12.00	20.00
☐ 3, Nov 85, AAd	0.75	3.20	9.60	16.00
☐ 4, Dec 85, AAd	0.75	3.20	9.60	16.00
☐ 5, Jan 86, AAd	0.75	3.20	9.60	16.00
☐ 6, AAd double-size	1.25	3.60	10.80	18.00

LOONEY TUNES
DC

	ORIG.	GOOD	FINE	N-MINT
☐ 1, Apr 94	1.50	0.30	0.90	1.50
☐ 2, May 94	1.50	0.30	0.90	1.50
☐ 3, Jun 94	1.50	0.30	0.90	1.50
☐ 4, Jul 94	1.50	0.30	0.90	1.50
☐ 5, Aug 94	1.50	0.30	0.90	1.50
☐ 6, Sep 94	1.50	0.30	0.90	1.50
☐ 7, Oct 94	1.50	0.30	0.90	1.50
☐ 8, Nov 94	1.50	0.30	0.90	1.50
☐ 9, Dec 94	1.50	0.30	0.90	1.50
☐ 10, Jan 95	1.50	0.30	0.90	1.50
☐ 11, Feb 95	1.50	0.30	0.90	1.50
☐ 12, Mar 95	1.50	0.30	0.90	1.50
☐ 13, Apr 95	1.50	0.30	0.90	1.50

	ORIG.	GOOD	FINE	N-MINT
14, May 95	1.50	0.30	0.90	1.50
15, Jun 95	1.50	0.30	0.90	1.50
16, Jul 95	1.50	0.30	0.90	1.50
17, Aug 95	1.50	0.30	0.90	1.50
18, Sep 95	1.50	0.30	0.90	1.50
19, Oct 95	1.50	0.30	0.90	1.50
20, Nov 95	1.50	0.30	0.90	1.50
21, Feb 96	1.50	0.30	0.90	1.50
22, Apr 96	1.50	0.30	0.90	1.50
23, Jun 96	1.75	0.35	1.05	1.75

LOONEY TUNES MAGAZINE

	GOOD	FINE	N-MINT
1, Bugs Bunny	0.39	1.17	1.95
2, Batman parody	0.39	1.17	1.95
3	0.39	1.17	1.95
4	0.39	1.17	1.95
5	0.39	1.17	1.95
6	0.39	1.17	1.95
7	0.39	1.17	1.95
8	0.39	1.17	1.95
9, (becomes *Bugs Bunny & The Looney Tunes Magazine*)	0.39	1.17	1.95

LOOSE CANNON (mini-series)

	ORIG.	GOOD	FINE	N-MINT
1, Jun 95	1.75	0.35	1.05	1.75
2, Jul 95	1.75	0.35	1.05	1.75
3, Aug 95, V:Eradicator	1.75	0.35	1.05	1.75
4, Sep 95	1.75	0.35	1.05	1.75

LOOSE TEETH
FANTAGRAPHICS

	GOOD	FINE	N-MINT
1, b&w	0.55	1.65	2.75
2, b&w	0.55	1.65	2.75
3, b&w	0.55	1.65	2.75

LORD OF THE DEAD
CONQUEST

	GOOD	FINE	N-MINT
1, b&w	0.59	1.77	2.95

LORD PUMPKIN
MALIBU/ULTRAVERSE

	ORIG.	GOOD	FINE	N-MINT
0, Oct 94	2.50	0.50	1.50	2.50

LORDS
LEGEND

	ORIG.	GOOD	FINE	N-MINT
1, (not Dark Horse imprint)	2.15	0.43	1.29	2.15

LORDS OF THE ULTRA-REALM
DC

	GOOD	FINE	N-MINT
1	0.30	0.90	1.50
2	0.30	0.90	1.50
3	0.30	0.90	1.50
4	0.30	0.90	1.50
5	0.30	0.90	1.50
6	0.30	0.90	1.50

LORDS OF THE ULTRA-REALM SPECIAL

	GOOD	FINE	N-MINT
1	0.45	1.35	2.25

LORELEI
STARWARP

	ORIG.	GOOD	FINE	N-MINT
0, b&w	2.50	0.50	1.50	2.50

LORELEI OF THE RED MIST
CONQUEST

	GOOD	FINE	N-MINT
1, b&w	0.59	1.77	2.95
2, b&w	0.59	1.77	2.95

LOSERS SPECIAL
DC

	ORIG.	GOOD	FINE	N-MINT
1, Sep 85, Crisis	1.25	0.25	0.75	1.25

LOST ANGEL
CALIBER

	ORIG.	GOOD	FINE	N-MINT
1, b&w	2.95	0.70	2.10	3.50

LOST CONTINENT
ECLIPSE

	GOOD	FINE	N-MINT
1, Japanese, b&w	0.70	2.10	3.50
2, Japanese, b&w	0.70	2.10	3.50
3, Japanese, b&w	0.70	2.10	3.50
4, Japanese, b&w	0.70	2.10	3.50
5, Japanese, b&w	0.70	2.10	3.50
6, Japanese, b&w	0.70	2.10	3.50

LOST GIRLS
KITCHEN SINK

	ORIG.	GOOD	FINE	N-MINT
1, Nov 95, AMo(w); oversized; cardstock cover;adults	5.95	1.19	3.57	5.95

LOST IN SPACE
INNOVATION

	ORIG.	GOOD	FINE	N-MINT
1, Aug 91, 1st printing, TV series	2.50	0.70	2.10	3.50
2, Nov 91	2.50	0.50	1.50	2.50
3, Dec 91	2.50	0.50	1.50	2.50
4, Feb 92	2.50	0.50	1.50	2.50
5, Mar 92	2.50	0.50	1.50	2.50
6, May 92	2.50	0.50	1.50	2.50
7, Jun 92	2.50	0.50	1.50	2.50
8, Aug 92	2.50	0.50	1.50	2.50
9, Oct 92	2.50	0.50	1.50	2.50
10, Nov 92	2.50	0.50	1.50	2.50
11, Dec 92	2.50	0.50	1.50	2.50
12	2.50	0.50	1.50	2.50
13, Aug 93, "Voyage to the Bottom of the Soul" Part 1 of 12; enhanced cardstock cover	2.50	0.50	1.50	2.50
13, Aug 93, "Voyage to the Bottom of the Soul" Part 1 of 12; enhanced cardstock cover;gold foil edition	4.95	0.99	2.97	4.95
14, Sep 93, "Voyage to the Bottom of the Soul" Part 2 of 12	2.50	0.50	1.50	2.50
15, Aug 93, "Voyage to the Bottom of the Soul" Part 3 of 12	2.50	0.50	1.50	2.50
16, Sep 93, "Voyage to the Bottom of the Soul" Part 4 of 12	2.50	0.50	1.50	2.50
17, Oct 93, "Voyage to the Bottom of the Soul" Part 5 of 12	2.50	0.50	1.50	2.50
18, Nov 93, "Voyage to the Bottom of the Soul" Part 6 of 12; final issue	2.50	0.50	1.50	2.50

LOST IN SPACE ANNUAL

	ORIG.	GOOD	FINE	N-MINT
1, 92	2.95	0.59	1.77	2.95
2, 93	2.95	0.59	1.77	2.95

LOST IN SPACE SPECIAL EDITION

	GOOD	FINE	N-MINT
1, amended reprint of #1	0.50	1.50	2.50
2	0.50	1.50	2.50

LOST IN SPACE: PROJECT ROBINSON

	ORIG.	GOOD	FINE	N-MINT
1	2.50	0.50	1.50	2.50

LOST IN SPACE: STRANGERS AMONG STRANGERS

	ORIG.	GOOD	FINE	N-MINT
0, reprint	5.95	1.19	3.57	5.95

LOST LAUGHTER
BAD HABIT

	ORIG.	GOOD	FINE	N-MINT
1, b&w	2.50	0.50	1.50	2.50
2, b&w	2.50	0.50	1.50	2.50
3, b&w	2.50	0.50	1.50	2.50
4, b&w	2.50	0.50	1.50	2.50

LOST PLANET
ECLIPSE

	GOOD	FINE	N-MINT
1	0.35	1.05	1.75
2	0.35	1.05	1.75
3	0.35	1.05	1.75
4	0.35	1.05	1.75
5	0.35	1.05	1.75
6	0.35	1.05	1.75

LOUIS VS. ALI
REVOLUTIONARY

	ORIG.	GOOD	FINE	N-MINT
1, Dec 93, b&w	2.95	0.59	1.77	2.95

LOVE & ROCKETS
FANTAGRAPHICS

	GOOD	FINE	N-MINT
1, 1st printing	10.00	30.00	50.00
1, 2nd printing	0.79	2.37	3.95

	ORIG.	GOOD	FINE	N-MINT
☐ 1, 3rd printing		0.79	2.37	3.95
☐ 1, Books		1.99	5.97	9.95
☐ 2, Books		1.99	5.97	9.95
☐ 3, Books		1.99	5.97	9.95
☐ 4, Books		1.99	5.97	9.95
☐ 5, Books		1.99	5.97	9.95
☐ 2, 1st printing		6.00	18.00	30.00
☐ 2, 2nd printing		0.79	2.37	3.95
☐ 3, 1st printing		3.60	10.80	18.00
☐ 3, 2nd printing		0.79	2.37	3.95
☐ 4, 1st printing		3.20	9.60	16.00
☐ 4, 2nd printing		0.79	2.37	3.95
☐ 5, 1st printing		3.20	9.60	16.00
☐ 5, 2nd printing		0.50	1.50	2.50
☐ 6, 1st printing		1.20	3.60	6.00
☐ 6, 2nd printing		0.50	1.50	2.50
☐ 7, 1st printing		1.20	3.60	6.00
☐ 7, 2nd printing		0.50	1.50	2.50
☐ 8, 1st printing		1.20	3.60	6.00
☐ 8, 2nd printing		0.50	1.50	2.50
☐ 9, 1st printing		1.20	3.60	6.00
☐ 9, 2nd printing		0.50	1.50	2.50
☐ 10, 1st printing		1.20	3.60	6.00
☐ 10, 2nd printing		0.59	1.77	2.95
☐ 11, 1st printing		0.80	2.40	4.00
☐ 11, 2nd printing		0.50	1.50	2.50
☐ 12, 1st printing		0.80	2.40	4.00
☐ 12, 2nd printing		0.50	1.50	2.50
☐ 13, 1st printing		0.80	2.40	4.00
☐ 13, 2nd printing		0.50	1.50	2.50
☐ 14, 1st printing		0.80	2.40	4.00
☐ 14, 2nd printing		0.50	1.50	2.50
☐ 15, 2nd printing		0.50	1.50	2.50
☐ 15, 1st printing		0.60	1.80	3.00
☐ 16, 2nd printing		0.50	1.50	2.50
☐ 16, 1st printing		0.60	1.80	3.00
☐ 17		0.60	1.80	3.00
☐ 18		0.60	1.80	3.00
☐ 19		0.60	1.80	3.00
☐ 20		0.60	1.80	3.00
☐ 21		0.45	1.35	2.25
☐ 22		0.45	1.35	2.25
☐ 23		0.45	1.35	2.25
☐ 24		0.45	1.35	2.25
☐ 25		0.45	1.35	2.25
☐ 26		0.45	1.35	2.25
☐ 27		0.45	1.35	2.25
☐ 28		0.45	1.35	2.25
☐ 29, 1st printing		0.45	1.35	2.25
☐ 29, 2nd printing		0.45	1.35	2.25
☐ 30, 1st printing		0.45	1.35	2.25
☐ 30, 2nd printing		0.59	1.77	2.95
☐ 31, 1st printing		0.50	1.50	2.50
☐ 31, 2nd printing		0.50	1.50	2.50
☐ 32		0.50	1.50	2.50
☐ 33		0.50	1.50	2.50
☐ 34		0.50	1.50	2.50
☐ 35		0.55	1.65	2.75
☐ 36		0.55	1.65	2.75
☐ 37		0.55	1.65	2.75
☐ 38		0.55	1.65	2.75
☐ 39		0.55	1.65	2.75
☐ 40	3.50	0.70	2.10	3.50
☐ 41		0.70	2.10	3.50
☐ 42		0.70	2.10	3.50
☐ 43		0.70	2.10	3.50
☐ 44, Mar 94	2.95	0.70	2.10	3.50

LOVE & ROCKETS BONANZA

	ORIG.	GOOD	FINE	N-MINT
☐ 1, b&w rep.		0.59	1.77	2.95
☐ 1, 2nd printing		0.59	1.77	2.95

LOVE BITES
EROS COMIX

	ORIG.	GOOD	FINE	N-MINT
☐ 1, adult, b&w		0.45	1.35	2.25

LOVE FANTASY
RENEGADE

	ORIG.	GOOD	FINE	N-MINT
☐ 1, b&w		0.40	1.20	2.00

LOVE LETTERS IN THE HAND
EROS COMIX

	ORIG.	GOOD	FINE	N-MINT
☐ 1, adult, b&w		0.45	1.35	2.25
☐ 2, adult, b&w		0.45	1.35	2.25
☐ 3, adult, b&w		0.50	1.50	2.50

LOVECRAFT
ADVENTURE

	ORIG.	GOOD	FINE	N-MINT
☐ 1, color	2.95	0.59	1.77	2.95
☐ 1, limited edition		1.19	3.57	5.95
☐ 2		0.59	1.77	2.95
☐ 3		0.59	1.77	2.95

LOVELY LADIES
CALIBER

	ORIG.	GOOD	FINE	N-MINT
☐ 1, b&w, pin-ups	3.50	0.70	2.10	3.50

LOWLIFE
AEON

	ORIG.	GOOD	FINE	N-MINT
☐ 4, Feb 94, b&w	2.50	0.50	1.50	2.50

CALIBER

	ORIG.	GOOD	FINE	N-MINT
☐ 1, b&w	2.50	0.70	2.10	3.50
☐ 2, b&w	2.50	0.50	1.50	2.50

LOWLIFE (was Caliber title)
AEON

	ORIG.	GOOD	FINE	N-MINT
☐ 3, b&w	2.50	0.50	1.50	2.50

LUCIFER
TRIDENT

	ORIG.	GOOD	FINE	N-MINT
☐ 1, b&w		0.39	1.17	1.95
☐ 2, b&w		0.39	1.17	1.95
☐ 3, b&w		0.39	1.17	1.95

LUCIFER'S HAMMER
INNOVATION

	ORIG.	GOOD	FINE	N-MINT
☐ 1	2.50	0.50	1.50	2.50
☐ 2	2.50	0.50	1.50	2.50

LUGER
ECLIPSE

	ORIG.	GOOD	FINE	N-MINT
☐ 1, Oct 86		0.35	1.05	1.75
☐ 2, Dec 86		0.35	1.05	1.75
☐ 3, Feb 87		0.35	1.05	1.75

LUGH, LORD OF LIGHT
FLAGSHIP

	ORIG.	GOOD	FINE	N-MINT
☐ 1		0.35	1.05	1.75
☐ 2		0.35	1.05	1.75
☐ 3		0.35	1.05	1.75

LUM URUSEI*YATSURA
VIZ

	ORIG.	GOOD	FINE	N-MINT
☐ 1, b&w, Japanese		0.59	1.77	2.95
☐ 2, b&w, Japanese		0.59	1.77	2.95
☐ 3, b&w, Japanese		0.59	1.77	2.95
☐ 4, b&w, Japanese		0.59	1.77	2.95
☐ 5		0.65	1.95	3.25
☐ 6		0.59	1.77	2.95
☐ 7		0.65	1.95	3.25

LUNATIC BINGE
ETERNITY

	ORIG.	GOOD	FINE	N-MINT
☐ 1		0.39	1.17	1.95

LUNATIC FRINGE
INNOVATION

	ORIG.	GOOD	FINE	N-MINT
☐ 1, Jul 89, O:Lunatic Fringe		0.35	1.05	1.75
☐ 2, 89		0.35	1.05	1.75

LUNATIK (mini-series)
MARVEL

	ORIG.	GOOD	FINE	N-MINT
☐ 1, Dec 95	1.95	0.39	1.17	1.95
☐ 2, Jan 96, V:Avengers	1.95	0.39	1.17	1.95
☐ 3, Feb 96, final issue	1.95	0.39	1.17	1.95

	ORIG.	GOOD	FINE	N-MINT
LURID TALES				
EROS COMIX				
❏ 1, adult, b&w		0.55	1.65	2.75
LUST OF THE NAZI WEASEL WOMEN				
FANTAGRAPHICS				
❏ 1, b&w		0.45	1.35	2.25
❏ 2, b&w		0.45	1.35	2.25
❏ 3, b&w		0.45	1.35	2.25
❏ 4, b&w		0.45	1.35	2.25
LUX AND ALBY SIGN ON AND SAVE THE UNIVERSE				
(mini-series)				
DARK HORSE/ACME				
❏ 1, b&w 2.50		0.50	1.50	2.50
❏ 2, May 93, b&w 2.50		0.50	1.50	2.50
❏ 3, Jun 93, b&w 2.50		0.50	1.50	2.50
❏ 8, Oct 93 .... 2.50		0.50	1.50	2.50
❏ 9, Dec 93 .... 2.50		0.50	1.50	2.50
LUXURA LEATHER SPECIAL				
BRAINSTORM				
❏ 0, Mar 96, nn 2.95		0.59	1.77	2.95
LYCANTHROPE LEO				
VIZ				
❏ 1, 94, b&w 2.95		0.59	1.77	2.95
❏ 2, 94, b&w 2.95		0.59	1.77	2.95
❏ 3, 94, b&w 2.95		0.59	1.77	2.95
❏ 4, 94, b&w 2.95		0.59	1.77	2.95
❏ 5, 94, b&w 2.95		0.59	1.77	2.95
❏ 6, 94, b&w 2.95		0.59	1.77	2.95

	ORIG.	GOOD	FINE	N-MINT
LYCRA WOMAN AND SPANDEX GIRL				
COMIC ZONE				
❏ 1, b&w		0.59	1.77	2.95
LYCRA WOMAN AND SPANDEX GIRL				
CHRISTMAS '77 SPECIAL				
❏ 1, b&w 2.95		0.59	1.77	2.95
LYCRA WOMAN AND SPANDEX GIRL				
HALLOWEEN SPECIAL				
LOST CAUSE				
❏ 1, b&w 2.95		0.59	1.77	2.95
LYCRA WOMAN AND SPANDEX GIRL				
JURASSIC DINOSAUR SPECIAL				
COMIC ZONE				
❏ 1, b&w 2.95		0.59	1.77	2.95
LYCRA WOMAN AND SPANDEX GIRL				
SUMMER VACATION SPECIAL				
❏ 1, b&w 2.95		0.59	1.77	2.95
LYCRA WOMAN AND SPANDEX GIRL				
TIME TRAVEL SPECIAL				
❏ 1, b&w 2.95		0.59	1.77	2.95
LYCRA WOMAN AND SPANDEX GIRL				
VALENTINE SPECIAL				
❏ 1, b&w 2.95		0.59	1.77	2.95

Legion of Super-Heroes

First appearance: *Adventure Comics #247,* April 1958.

One of the longest-lived and largest super-hero teams is The Legion of Super-Heroes, although in their first adventure, its members were more of a fraternity "hazing" Superboy.

In that first story, the trio of Lightning Lad, Cosmic Boy, and Saturn Girl came to Smallville, where they greeted Superboy as Clark Kent when he was in his Superboy costume and vice versa. Fortunately, they did it out of sight and hearing of anyone else, so Superboy's secret was safe.

The group later inducted the 20th-century hero into its membership, and he visited the 30th century on a fairly regular basis, as did Supergirl, Jimmy Olsen, Lana Lang, and Pete Ross (the latter trio were honorary members).

A number of heroes lost their lives throughout the Legion's history, including Lightning Lad (he got better), Ferro Lad, Invisible Kid, and two of Triplicate Girl's three bodies.

Romance was also a big part of the series, with members marrying and being forced to leave the group due to its charter forbidding married couples. The rule was also the basis for several stories, including one in which two couples falsely married to lull the suspicions of an alien invasion force.

The group's headquarters first resembled an upside-down rocket ship, which was later abandonded in favor of more modern digs, which were destroyed and rebuilt several times.

Over the years, the Legion's origin was revealed. The group's three founding members (Lightning Lad, Cosmic Boy, and Saturn Girl) came to Earth from their respective homeworlds on the same freighter. As they left the ship, Saturn Girl detected that one of the passengers, business tycoon R.J. Brande, was in danger. Lightning Lad and Cosmic Boy countered the threat, and Brande was so impressed with the trio's quick thinking that he offered them a job as the founders of a group of teens dedicated to solving catastrophes that the normal authorities were not equipped to handle. He based the group on the heroic legends of Superboy and Supergirl.

Unfortunately, after *Crisis on Infinite Earths,* Superman's revised origin did not have him as Superboy, leaving the Legion's origins hanging in doubt, since they remembered a Superboy being part of their group. The origin was eventually resolved, but at a cost to the fabric of time in the DC universe, which was finally repaired during "Zero Hour" in 1994.

The latest incarnation of the Legion resembles its earlier ones, but with several new members and changes in members more familiar to older fans. The current incarnation of Superboy is an honorary member of the group.

M

	ORIG.	GOOD	FINE	N-MINT

M
ECLIPSE

	ORIG.	GOOD	FINE	N-MINT
☐ 1, Jon J. Muth		0.99	2.97	4.95
☐ 2, Jon J. Muth		0.99	2.97	4.95
☐ 3, Jon J. Muth		0.99	2.97	4.95
☐ 4		1.19	3.57	5.95

M.A.C.H. 1
FLEETWAY/QUALITY

	ORIG.	GOOD	FINE	N-MINT
☐ 1, b&w		0.39	1.17	1.95
☐ 2, b&w		0.39	1.17	1.95
☐ 3, b&w		0.39	1.17	1.95
☐ 4, b&w		0.39	1.17	1.95
☐ 5, b&w		0.39	1.17	1.95
☐ 6, b&w		0.39	1.17	1.95
☐ 7, b&w		0.39	1.17	1.95
☐ 8, b&w		0.39	1.17	1.95
☐ 9, b&w		0.39	1.17	1.95

M.D. GEIST (mini-series)
CPM COMICS

	ORIG.	GOOD	FINE	N-MINT
☐ 1, Jun 95	2.95	0.59	1.77	2.95
☐ 2, Jul 95	2.95	0.59	1.77	2.95
☐ 3, Aug 95	2.95	0.59	1.77	2.95

MACABRE
LIGHTHOUSE

	ORIG.	GOOD	FINE	N-MINT
☐ 1, b&w		0.40	1.20	2.00
☐ 2, b&w		0.40	1.20	2.00
☐ 3, b&w		0.40	1.20	2.00

MACABRE (Volume 2)

	ORIG.	GOOD	FINE	N-MINT
☐ 1		0.40	1.20	2.00
☐ 2		0.40	1.20	2.00

MACHINE MAN (1978-1981)
MARVEL

	ORIG.	GOOD	FINE	N-MINT
☐ 1, Apr 78, JK	0.35	0.40	1.20	2.00
☐ 2, May 78	0.35	0.30	0.90	1.50
☐ 3, Jun 78	0.35	0.25	0.75	1.25
☐ 4, Jul 78	0.35	0.25	0.75	1.25
☐ 5, Aug 78	0.35	0.25	0.75	1.25
☐ 6, Sep 78	0.35	0.20	0.60	1.00
☐ 7, Oct 78	0.35	0.20	0.60	1.00
☐ 8, Nov 78	0.35	0.20	0.60	1.00
☐ 9, Dec 78	0.35	0.20	0.60	1.00
☐ 10, Aug 79	0.40	0.20	0.60	1.00
☐ 11, Oct 79	0.40	0.20	0.60	1.00
☐ 12, Dec 79	0.40	0.20	0.60	1.00
☐ 13, Feb 80	0.40	0.20	0.60	1.00
☐ 14, Apr 80	0.40	0.20	0.60	1.00
☐ 15, Jun 80	0.40	0.20	0.60	1.00
☐ 16, Aug 80	0.40	0.20	0.60	1.00
☐ 17, Oct 80	0.50	0.20	0.60	1.00
☐ 18, Dec 80, A:Alpha Flight	0.50	1.00	3.00	5.00

MACHINE MAN (1984-1985)

	ORIG.	GOOD	FINE	N-MINT
☐ 1, Oct 84, HT/BS	0.75	0.60	1.80	3.00
☐ 2, Nov 84, HT/BS	0.75	0.40	1.20	2.00
☐ 3, Dec 84, HT/BS	0.75	0.40	1.20	2.00
☐ 4, Jan 85, HT/BS	0.75	0.40	1.20	2.00

MACHINE MAN 2020

	ORIG.	GOOD	FINE	N-MINT
☐ 1, Aug 94	2.00	0.40	1.20	2.00
☐ 2, Sep 94	2.00	0.40	1.20	2.00

MACHINE, THE
DARK HORSE

	ORIG.	GOOD	FINE	N-MINT
☐ 1, Nov 94	2.50	0.50	1.50	2.50
☐ 2, Dec 94	2.50	0.50	1.50	2.50
☐ 3, Jan 95	2.50	0.50	1.50	2.50
☐ 4, Feb 95	2.50	0.50	1.50	2.50

MACK THE KNIFE: MONOCHROME MEMORIES
CALIBER

	ORIG.	GOOD	FINE	N-MINT
☐ 1, b&w	2.50	0.50	1.50	2.50

MACKENZIE QUEEN
MATRIX

	ORIG.	GOOD	FINE	N-MINT
☐ 1		0.30	0.90	1.50
☐ 2		0.30	0.90	1.50
☐ 3		0.30	0.90	1.50
☐ 4		0.30	0.90	1.50
☐ 5		0.30	0.90	1.50

MACROSS
COMICO

	ORIG.	GOOD	FINE	N-MINT
☐ 1, (becomes *Robotech the Macross Saga*)		3.00	9.00	15.00

MACROSS II
VIZ

	ORIG.	GOOD	FINE	N-MINT
☐ 1, Japanese, b&w	2.75	0.55	1.65	2.75
☐ 2, Japanese, b&w	2.75	0.55	1.65	2.75
☐ 3, Japanese, b&w	2.75	0.55	1.65	2.75
☐ 4, Japanese, b&w	2.75	0.55	1.65	2.75
☐ 5, Japanese, b&w	2.75	0.55	1.65	2.75
☐ 6, Japanese, b&w	2.75	0.55	1.65	2.75
☐ 7, Japanese, b&w	2.75	0.55	1.65	2.75
☐ 8, Japanese, b&w	2.75	0.55	1.65	2.75
☐ 9, Japanese, b&w	2.75	0.55	1.65	2.75
☐ 10, Japanese, b&w	2.75	0.55	1.65	2.75

MACROSS II: THE MICRON CONSPIRACY

	ORIG.	GOOD	FINE	N-MINT
☐ 1, 94, b&w	2.75	0.55	1.65	2.75
☐ 2, 94, b&w	2.75	0.55	1.65	2.75
☐ 3, 95, b&w	2.75	0.55	1.65	2.75
☐ 4, 95, b&w	2.75	0.55	1.65	2.75

MAD DOG
MARVEL

	ORIG.	GOOD	FINE	N-MINT
☐ 1, May 93, TV show tie-in	1.25	0.25	0.75	1.25
☐ 2, Jun 93	1.25	0.25	0.75	1.25
☐ 3	1.25	0.25	0.75	1.25
☐ 4	1.25	0.25	0.75	1.25
☐ 5	1.25	0.25	0.75	1.25
☐ 6	1.25	0.25	0.75	1.25

MAD DOG MAGAZINE
BLACKTHORNE

	ORIG.	GOOD	FINE	N-MINT
☐ 1		0.35	1.05	1.75
☐ 2		0.35	1.05	1.75
☐ 3		0.35	1.05	1.75

MAD DOGS
ECLIPSE

	ORIG.	GOOD	FINE	N-MINT
☐ 1		0.50	1.50	2.50
☐ 2		0.50	1.50	2.50

MAD RACCOONS
MU PRESS

	ORIG.	GOOD	FINE	N-MINT
☐ 1, b&w	2.50	0.50	1.50	2.50
☐ 2, b&w	2.50	0.50	1.50	2.50
☐ 3, b&w	2.50	0.50	1.50	2.50
☐ 4, Aug 94, b&w	2.95	0.59	1.77	2.95
☐ 5, Aug 95, b&w; cardstock cover	2.95	0.59	1.77	2.95

MADAME XANADU
DC

	ORIG.	GOOD	FINE	N-MINT
☐ 1, Jul 81, MR, BB		0.40	1.20	2.00

MADBALLS
STAR

	ORIG.	GOOD	FINE	N-MINT
☐ 1	0.75	0.15	0.45	0.75
☐ 2	0.75	0.15	0.45	0.75
☐ 3	0.75	0.15	0.45	0.75
☐ 4	1.00	0.20	0.60	1.00
☐ 5	1.00	0.20	0.60	1.00

	ORIG.	GOOD	FINE	N-MINT
❏ 6 ....1.00		0.20	0.60	1.00
❏ 7 ....1.00		0.20	0.60	1.00
❏ 8, (becomes Marvel Comic)				
..............................1.00		0.20	0.60	1.00

MADBALLS (was Star Comic)
MARVEL

	ORIG.	GOOD	FINE	N-MINT
❏ 9 ....1.00		0.20	0.60	1.00
❏ 10 ....1.00		0.20	0.60	1.00

MADMAN
TUNDRA

	ORIG.	GOOD	FINE	N-MINT
❏ 1, Mar 92, b&w;flip-action corners;prestige format				
..............................3.95		2.20	6.60	11.00
❏ 2, Apr 92 ....3.95		1.60	4.80	8.00
❏ 3, May 92 ....3.95		1.20	3.60	6.00

MADMAN ADVENTURES

	ORIG.	GOOD	FINE	N-MINT
❏ 1 ....2.95		1.60	4.80	8.00
❏ 2 ....2.95		1.00	3.00	5.00
❏ 3 ....2.95		0.80	2.40	4.00

MADMAN COMICS
DARK HORSE

	ORIG.	GOOD	FINE	N-MINT
❏ 1, Apr 94 ....2.95		1.50	4.50	7.50
❏ 2, Jun 94 ....2.95		0.80	2.40	4.00
❏ 3, Aug 94 ....2.95		0.59	1.77	2.95
❏ 4, Oct 94 ....2.95		0.59	1.77	2.95
❏ 5, Jan 95 ....2.95		0.59	1.77	2.95
❏ 6, Mar 95 ....2.95		0.59	1.77	2.95

DARK HORSE/LEGEND

	ORIG.	GOOD	FINE	N-MINT
❏ 8, Jul 95 ....2.95		0.59	1.77	2.95
❏ 9, Oct 95 ....2.95		0.59	1.77	2.95
❏ 10, Jan 96 ....2.95		0.59	1.77	2.95

MADONNA
PERSONALITY

	ORIG.	GOOD	FINE	N-MINT
❏ 1, b&w		0.59	1.77	2.95
❏ 2, b&w		0.59	1.77	2.95

MADONNA SPECIAL
REVOLUTIONARY

	ORIG.	GOOD	FINE	N-MINT
❏ 1, Aug 93, b&w 2.50		0.50	1.50	2.50

MADONNA VS. MARILYN
CELEBRITY

	ORIG.	GOOD	FINE	N-MINT
❏ 1		0.59	1.77	2.95

MADRAVEN HALLOWEEN SPECIAL
HAMILTON

	ORIG.	GOOD	FINE	N-MINT
❏ 0, Oct 95, nn;one-shot; GM;A:Wolff & Byrd; "Hoo-Hah"				
back-up 2.95		0.59	1.77	2.95

MAEL'S RAGE
OMINOUS

	ORIG.	GOOD	FINE	N-MINT
❏ 2, Aug 94 ....2.50		0.50	1.50	2.50
❏ 2, Aug 94, N, cardstock outer cover				
..............................2.50		0.50	1.50	2.50

MAELSTROM
AIRCEL

	ORIG.	GOOD	FINE	N-MINT
❏ 1 ....1.70		0.34	1.02	1.70
❏ 2 ....1.70		0.34	1.02	1.70
❏ 3 ....1.70		0.34	1.02	1.70
❏ 4 ....1.70		0.34	1.02	1.70
❏ 5 ....1.50		0.30	0.90	1.50
❏ 6 ....1.50		0.30	0.90	1.50
❏ 7 ....1.50		0.30	0.90	1.50
❏ 8 ....1.50		0.30	0.90	1.50
❏ 9 ....1.50		0.30	0.90	1.50
❏ 10 ....1.50		0.30	0.90	1.50

MAGE
COMICO

	ORIG.	GOOD	FINE	N-MINT
❏ 1, May 84		1.60	4.80	8.00
❏ 2, Jul 84		1.20	3.60	6.00
❏ 3, Sep 84		1.00	3.00	5.00
❏ 4, Nov 84		1.00	3.00	5.00
❏ 5, Jan 85		1.00	3.00	5.00
❏ 6, Mar 85, Grendel		4.80	14.40	24.00

	ORIG.	GOOD	FINE	N-MINT
❏ 7, May 85........................		2.00	6.00	10.00
❏ 8, Jul 85.........................		0.80	2.40	4.00
❏ 9, Sep 85		0.80	2.40	4.00
❏ 10, Dec 85		0.80	2.40	4.00
❏ 11, Feb 86.......................		0.80	2.40	4.00
❏ 12, Apr 86.......................		0.80	2.40	4.00
❏ 13, Jun 86		0.80	2.40	4.00
❏ 14, Aug 86		0.80	2.40	4.00
❏ 15, Dec 86		1.00	3.00	5.00

MAGEBOOK

	ORIG.	GOOD	FINE	N-MINT
❏ 1, 85		1.60	4.80	8.00
❏ 2, 86		1.60	4.80	8.00

MAGGIE THE CAT
IMAGE

	ORIG.	GOOD	FINE	N-MINT
❏ 1, Jan 96........................2.50		0.50	1.50	2.50
❏ 2, 96 ....2.50		0.50	1.50	2.50

MAGGOTS
HAMILTON

	ORIG.	GOOD	FINE	N-MINT
❏ 1, Nov 91, b&w.............3.95		0.79	2.37	3.95
❏ 2, b&w.........................3.95		0.79	2.37	3.95
❏ 3, b&w.........................3.95		0.79	2.37	3.95

MAGIC: THE GATHERING - ELDER DRAGONS
ACCLAIM/ARMADA

	ORIG.	GOOD	FINE	N-MINT
❏ 2, May 96.......................2.50		0.50	1.50	2.50

MAGIC: THE GATHERING - SHANDALAR
(mini-series)

	ORIG.	GOOD	FINE	N-MINT
❏ 1, Mar 96.......................2.50		0.50	1.50	2.50
❏ 2, Apr 96.......................2.50		0.50	1.50	2.50

MAGIC: THE GATHERING ANTIQUITIES WAR
(mini-series)

	ORIG.	GOOD	FINE	N-MINT
❏ 1, Nov 95, O:Urza and Mishra				
..............................2.50		0.50	1.50	2.50
❏ 2, Dec 95 ....2.50		0.50	1.50	2.50
❏ 3, Jan 96.......................2.50		0.50	1.50	2.50
❏ 4, Feb 96.......................2.50		0.50	1.50	2.50

MAGIC: THE GATHERING WAYFARER (mini-series)

	ORIG.	GOOD	FINE	N-MINT
❏ 1, Nov 95.......................2.50		0.50	1.50	2.50
❏ 2, Dec 95 ....2.50		0.50	1.50	2.50
❏ 3, Jan 96.......................2.50		0.50	1.50	2.50
❏ 4, Feb 96.......................2.50		0.50	1.50	2.50
❏ 5, Mar 96.......................2.50		0.50	1.50	2.50

MAGIC: THE GATHERING-THE SHADOW MAGE

	ORIG.	GOOD	FINE	N-MINT
❏ 1, Dec 95, prestige format collection of first two issues; polybagged with sheet of creature tokens				
..............................4.95		0.99	2.97	4.95
❏ 2, Dec 95, prestige format collection of final two issues; polybagged with sheet of creature tokens				
..............................4.95		0.99	2.97	4.95

MAGIC: THE GATHERING-THE SHADOW MAGE
(mini-series)

	ORIG.	GOOD	FINE	N-MINT
❏ 1, 95, bound-in Fireball card				
..............................2.50		0.50	1.50	2.50
❏ 2, Aug 95, bound-in Blue Elemental card				
..............................2.50		0.50	1.50	2.50
❏ 3, Sep 95, bagged with Magic: The Gathering tokens and counters 2.50		0.50	1.50	2.50
❏ 4, 95, polybagged with sheet of creature tokens				
..............................2.50		0.50	1.50	2.50

MAGICAL NYMPHINI
RIP OFF

	ORIG.	GOOD	FINE	N-MINT
❏ 1, Feb 91, adult;b&w; first printing				
..............................2.50		0.50	1.50	2.50
❏ 1, adult;b&w; second printing				
..............................2.50		0.50	1.50	2.50
❏ 2, Apr 91, adult;b&w; first printing				
..............................2.50		0.50	1.50	2.50
❏ 2, adult;b&w; second printing				
..............................2.50		0.50	1.50	2.50

	ORIG.	GOOD	FINE	N-MINT
3, Aug 91, adult; b&w;first printing				
.................2.50	0.50	1.50	2.50
3, adult;b&w; second printing				
.................2.50	0.50	1.50	2.50
4, Dec 91, adult; b&w;first printing				
.................2.95	0.59	1.77	2.95
4, adult;b&w; second printing				
.................2.95	0.59	1.77	2.95
5, Aug 92, adult;b&w; first printing				
.................2.95	0.59	1.77	2.95
5, adult;b&w; second printing				
.................2.95	0.59	1.77	2.95

MAGICIANS' VILLAGE
MAD MONKEY

1		0.49	1.47	2.45

MAGICMAN
A-PLUS

1, 91, b&w, reprints	0.50	1.50	2.50

MAGIK (mini-series)
MARVEL

1, Dec 83, Illyana & Storm				
.................0.60	0.50	1.50	2.50
2, Jan 84, Illyana & Storm				
.................0.60	0.50	1.50	2.50
3, Feb 84 ....0.60	0.40	1.20	2.00
4, Mar 84 ....0.60	0.40	1.20	2.00

MAGNA-MAN: THE LAST SUPERHERO
COMICS INTERVIEW

1, b&w		0.39	1.17	1.95
2, b&w		0.39	1.17	1.95
3, b&w		0.39	1.17	1.95

MAGNETO
MARVEL

0		1.60	4.80	8.00

MAGNETO AND HIS MAGNETIC MEN
MARVEL/AMALGAM

1, Apr 96 ....1.95	0.39	1.17	1.95

MAGNUS ROBOT FIGHTER
ACCLAIM/VALIANT

49, Jul 95 ....2.50	0.50	1.50	2.50
50, Jul 95 ....2.25	0.50	1.50	2.50
51, Aug 95 ....2.25	0.45	1.35	2.25
52, Aug 95 ....2.25	0.45	1.35	2.25
53, Sep 95 ....2.25	0.45	1.35	2.25
54, Sep 95 ....2.25	0.45	1.35	2.25
55, Oct 95 ....2.50	0.50	1.50	2.50
56, Oct 95 ....2.50	0.50	1.50	2.50
57, Nov 95 ....2.50	0.50	1.50	2.50
58, Nov 95 ....2.50	0.50	1.50	2.50
59, Dec 95 ....2.50	0.50	1.50	2.50
60, Dec 95 ....2.50	0.50	1.50	2.50
61, Jan 96 ....2.50	0.50	1.50	2.50
62, Jan 96, Torque becomes a Psi-Lord				
.................2.50	0.50	1.50	2.50
63, Feb 96 ....2.50	0.50	1.50	2.50
64, Feb 96, final issue 2.50	0.50	1.50	2.50

VALIANT

0, 92, with trading card....	5.00	15.00	25.00
0, without trading card.....	1.80	5.40	9.00
1, May 91, O:Magnus, trading cards				
.................1.75	2.00	6.00	10.00
2, Jul 91, trading cards ..1.75	1.60	4.80	8.00
3, Aug 91, trading cards.1.75	1.00	3.00	5.00
4, Sep 91, trading cards.1.75	1.00	3.00	5.00
5, Oct 91, 1:Rai, trading cards				
.................1.75	1.00	3.00	5.00
6, Nov 91, trading cards.1.75	0.80	2.40	4.00
7, Dec 91, trading cards.1.75	0.80	2.40	4.00
8, Jan 92 ....1.95	0.80	2.40	4.00
9, Feb 92 ....1.95	0.80	2.40	4.00

	ORIG.	GOOD	FINE	N-MINT
10, Mar 92 ....1.95	0.80	2.40	4.00
11, Apr 92 ....1.95	0.70	2.10	3.50
12, May 92, (Turok)........3.25	3.00	9.00	15.00
13, Jun 92 ....2.25	0.70	2.10	3.50
14, Jul 92......................2.25	0.70	2.10	3.50
15, Aug 92, FM(c) Unity.2.25	0.70	2.10	3.50
16, Sep 92, WS(c) Unity.2.25	0.70	2.10	3.50
17, Nov 92 ....2.25	0.70	2.10	3.50
18, Nov 92 ....2.25	0.70	2.10	3.50
19, Dec 92 ....2.25	0.70	2.10	3.50
20, Jan 93......................2.25	0.70	2.10	3.50
21, gold edition................	2.00	6.00	10.00
22, Mar 93......................2.25	0.60	1.80	3.00
21, Feb 93......................2.25	0.60	1.80	3.00
23, Apr 93......................2.25	0.60	1.80	3.00
24, May 93......................2.25	0.60	1.80	3.00
25, Jun 93, silver cover ..2.95	0.60	1.80	3.00
26, Jul 93......................2.25	0.60	1.80	3.00
27, Aug 93......................2.25	0.60	1.80	3.00
28 ....2.25	0.60	1.80	3.00
29 ....2.25	0.60	1.80	3.00
30 ....2.25	0.60	1.80	3.00
31 ....2.25	0.60	1.80	3.00
32 ....2.25	0.60	1.80	3.00
33, Feb 94......................2.25	0.60	1.80	3.00
34, Mar 94......................2.25	0.60	1.80	3.00
35, Apr 94......................2.25	0.60	1.80	3.00
36, May 94, trading card.2.25	0.50	1.50	2.50
37, Jun 94 ....2.25	0.50	1.50	2.50
38, Aug 94......................2.25	0.50	1.50	2.50
39, Sep 94 ....2.25	0.50	1.50	2.50
40, Oct 94......................2.25	0.50	1.50	2.50
41, Nov 94, Chaos Effect				
.................2.25	0.50	1.50	2.50
46, Apr 95......................2.25	0.50	1.50	2.50
47, May 95, War & Remembrance				
.................2.25	0.50	1.50	2.50

MAGNUS ROBOT FIGHTER/NEXUS
VALIANT/DARK HORSE

1 ....2.95	0.59	1.77	2.95
2 ....2.95	0.59	1.77	2.95

MAI, THE PSYCHIC GIRL
ECLIPSE

1, 87, Japanese b&w 1.50	0.60	1.80	3.00
1, 2nd printing..................	0.30	0.90	1.50
2, 1st printing..................	0.40	1.20	2.00
2, 2nd printing..................	0.30	0.90	1.50
3	0.30	0.90	1.50
4	0.30	0.90	1.50
5	0.30	0.90	1.50
6	0.30	0.90	1.50
7	0.30	0.90	1.50
8	0.30	0.90	1.50
9	0.30	0.90	1.50
10	0.30	0.90	1.50
11	0.30	0.90	1.50
12	0.30	0.90	1.50
13	0.30	0.90	1.50
14	0.30	0.90	1.50
15	0.30	0.90	1.50
16	0.30	0.90	1.50
17	0.30	0.90	1.50
18	0.30	0.90	1.50
19	0.30	0.90	1.50
20	0.30	0.90	1.50
21	0.30	0.90	1.50
22	0.30	0.90	1.50
23	0.30	0.90	1.50
24	0.30	0.90	1.50
25	0.30	0.90	1.50
26	0.30	0.90	1.50

	ORIG.	GOOD	FINE	N-MINT
❑ 27		0.30	0.90	1.50
❑ 28		0.30	0.90	1.50

MAINE ZOMBIE LOBSTERMEN
MAINE STREAM COMICS

	ORIG.	GOOD	FINE	N-MINT
❑ 1, b&w		0.50	1.50	2.50
❑ 2, b&w		0.50	1.50	2.50
❑ 3, b&w 3.50		0.70	2.10	3.50

MAISON IKKOKU
VIZ

	ORIG.	GOOD	FINE	N-MINT
❑ 1, b&w 2.95		0.80	2.40	4.00
❑ 2, b&w 2.95		0.59	1.77	2.95
❑ 3, b&w 2.95		0.59	1.77	2.95
❑ 4, b&w 2.95		0.59	1.77	2.95
❑ 5, b&w 2.95		0.59	1.77	2.95
❑ 6, b&w 2.95		0.59	1.77	2.95
❑ 7, b&w 2.95		0.59	1.77	2.95

MAISON IKKOKU, PART FOUR

	ORIG.	GOOD	FINE	N-MINT
❑ 1, 95, b&w 2.95		0.59	1.77	2.95
❑ 2, 95, b&w 2.95		0.59	1.77	2.95
❑ 4, 95, b&w 2.95		0.59	1.77	2.95
❑ 5, 95, b&w 2.95		0.59	1.77	2.95

MAISON IKKOKU, PART THREE

	ORIG.	GOOD	FINE	N-MINT
❑ 1, 94, b&w 2.95		0.59	1.77	2.95
❑ 2, 94, b&w 2.95		0.59	1.77	2.95
❑ 3, 94, b&w 2.95		0.59	1.77	2.95
❑ 4, 94, b&w 2.95		0.59	1.77	2.95
❑ 5, 94, b&w 2.95		0.59	1.77	2.95
❑ 6, 94, b&w 2.95		0.59	1.77	2.95

MAISON IKKOKU, PART TWO

	ORIG.	GOOD	FINE	N-MINT
❑ 1, 94, b&w 2.95		0.59	1.77	2.95
❑ 2, 94, b&w 2.95		0.59	1.77	2.95
❑ 3, 94, b&w 2.95		0.59	1.77	2.95
❑ 4, 94, b&w 2.95		0.59	1.77	2.95
❑ 5, 94, b&w 2.95		0.59	1.77	2.95
❑ 6, 94, b&w 2.95		0.59	1.77	2.95

MAJCANS, THE
P.S.

	ORIG.	GOOD	FINE	N-MINT
❑ 1		0.20	0.60	1.00

MAJOR DAMAGE
INVICTUS

	ORIG.	GOOD	FINE	N-MINT
❑ 1, Oct 94 .... 2.25		0.45	1.35	2.25

MALCOLM X
MILLENNIUM

	ORIG.	GOOD	FINE	N-MINT
❑ 1, 93.............................. 3.95		0.79	2.37	3.95

MALCOLM-10
ONLI STUDIOS

	ORIG.	GOOD	FINE	N-MINT
❑ 1, 92, b&w		0.40	1.20	2.00

MALIBU SIGNATURE SERIES
MALIBU

	ORIG.	GOOD	FINE	N-MINT
❑ 1, autograph book giveaway				

MALICE IN WONDERLAND
EROS

	ORIG.	GOOD	FINE	N-MINT
❑ 1, WW, adult, b&w 2.75		0.55	1.65	2.75

MALLIMALOU
CHANCE

	ORIG.	GOOD	FINE	N-MINT
❑ 1		0.30	0.90	1.50

MAN AGAINST TIME
IMAGE

	ORIG.	GOOD	FINE	N-MINT
❑ 1, May 96 .... 2.25		0.45	1.35	2.25
❑ 3, Jul 96 .... 2.25		0.45	1.35	2.25

MAN FROM ATLANTIS
MARVEL

	ORIG.	GOOD	FINE	N-MINT
❑ 1, Feb 78, TV series, giant				
.... 1.00		0.30	0.90	1.50
❑ 2, Mar 78 .... 0.35		0.20	0.60	1.00
❑ 3, Apr 78 .... 0.35		0.20	0.60	1.00
❑ 4, May 78 .... 0.35		0.20	0.60	1.00
❑ 5, Jun 78 .... 0.35		0.20	0.60	1.00

	ORIG.	GOOD	FINE	N-MINT
❑ 6, Jul 78........................ 0.35		0.20	0.60	1.00
❑ 7, Aug 78 .... 0.35		0.20	0.60	1.00

MAN FROM U.N.C.L.E.:
THE BIRDS OF PREY AFFAIR
MILLENNIUM

	ORIG.	GOOD	FINE	N-MINT
❑ 1 .... 2.95		0.59	1.77	2.95
❑ 2 .... 2.95		0.59	1.77	2.95

MAN FROM UNCLE, THE
ENTERTAINMENT

	ORIG.	GOOD	FINE	N-MINT
❑ 1, Jan 87, b&w 1.50		0.30	0.90	1.50
❑ 2, Feb 87		0.30	0.90	1.50
❑ 3, Apr 87		0.30	0.90	1.50
❑ 4, Aug 87		0.30	0.90	1.50
❑ 5, Dec 87		0.30	0.90	1.50
❑ 6, Feb 88		0.35	1.05	1.75
❑ 7, May 88		0.35	1.05	1.75
❑ 8, Jul 88		0.35	1.05	1.75
❑ 9, Aug 88		0.35	1.05	1.75
❑ 10, Sep 88		0.35	1.05	1.75
❑ 11, Sep 88		0.35	1.05	1.75

MAN IN BLACK
RECOLLECTIONS

	ORIG.	GOOD	FINE	N-MINT
❑ 1, 90		0.40	1.20	2.00
❑ 2, Jul 91.........................		0.40	1.20	2.00

MAN OF RUST
BLACKTHORNE

	ORIG.	GOOD	FINE	N-MINT
❑ 1		0.30	0.90	1.50
❑ 1		0.30	0.90	1.50

MAN OF STEEL
DC

	ORIG.	GOOD	FINE	N-MINT
❑ 1, Oct 86, JBy,DG (direct)				
.... 0.75		0.40	1.20	2.00
❑ 1, JBy (newsstand)		0.40	1.20	2.00
❑ 1, silver edition 1.95		0.39	1.17	1.95
❑ 2, Oct 86, JBy		0.30	0.90	1.50
❑ 2, silver edition 1.95		0.39	1.17	1.95
❑ 3, Nov 86, JBy		0.30	0.90	1.50
❑ 3, silver edition 1.95		0.39	1.17	1.95
❑ 4, Nov 86, JBy		0.30	0.90	1.50
❑ 4, silver edition 1.95		0.39	1.17	1.95
❑ 5, Dec 86, JBy		0.30	0.90	1.50
❑ 5, silver edition 1.95		0.39	1.17	1.95
❑ 6, Dec 86, JBy		0.30	0.90	1.50
❑ 6, silver edition 1.95		0.39	1.17	1.95

MAN OF WAR
ECLIPSE

	ORIG.	GOOD	FINE	N-MINT
❑ 1, Aug 87		0.35	1.05	1.75
❑ 2, Dec 87		0.35	1.05	1.75
❑ 3, Feb 88		0.35	1.05	1.75

MALIBU

	ORIG.	GOOD	FINE	N-MINT
❑ 1 .... 2.50		0.50	1.50	2.50
❑ 2 .... 2.50		0.50	1.50	2.50
❑ 3 .... 2.50		0.50	1.50	2.50
❑ 4 .... 2.50		0.50	1.50	2.50
❑ 5 .... 2.25		0.45	1.35	2.25
❑ 6, POG 2.25		0.45	1.35	2.25
❑ 7 .... 2.25		0.45	1.35	2.25
❑ 8, Feb 94........................ 2.25		0.45	1.35	2.25

MAN WHO WOULD BE KING, THE
TOME

	ORIG.	GOOD	FINE	N-MINT
❑ 0, nn 2.95		0.59	1.77	2.95

MAN-BAT (mini-series)
DC

	ORIG.	GOOD	FINE	N-MINT
❑ 1, Feb 96........................ 2.25		0.45	1.35	2.25
❑ 2, Mar 96, A:Killer Croc .. 2.25		0.45	1.35	2.25
❑ 3, Apr 96, final issue....... 2.25		0.45	1.35	2.25

MAN-BAT VS. BATMAN

	ORIG.	GOOD	FINE	N-MINT
❑ 1, Dec 84, NA/DG reprint ..		1.00	3.00	5.00

	ORIG.	GOOD	FINE	N-MINT

MAN-EATING COW
NEC

	ORIG.	GOOD	FINE	N-MINT
❏ 1, b&w	2.75	0.80	2.40	4.00
❏ 2, b&w	2.75	0.60	1.80	3.00
❏ 3, b&w	2.75	0.60	1.80	3.00
❏ 4, b&w	2.75	0.60	1.80	3.00
❏ 5, b&w	2.75	0.55	1.65	2.75
❏ 6, Aug 93, b&w	2.75	0.55	1.65	2.75
❏ 7, b&w	2.75	0.55	1.65	2.75
❏ 8, Jan 94, b&w	2.75	0.55	1.65	2.75

MAN-FROG
MAD DOG

	ORIG.	GOOD	FINE	N-MINT
❏ 1, b&w		0.40	1.20	2.00
❏ 2, b&w		0.40	1.20	2.00

MAN-THING (1974-1975)
MARVEL

	ORIG.	GOOD	FINE	N-MINT
❏ 1, FB/JM, A: Howard the Duck	0.20	3.00	9.00	15.00
❏ 2	0.20	1.60	4.80	8.00
❏ 3, Foolkiller	0.20	2.00	6.00	10.00
❏ 4, Foolkiller	0.20	1.20	3.60	6.00
❏ 5	0.25	0.60	1.80	3.00
❏ 6, MP	0.25	0.60	1.80	3.00
❏ 7, MP	0.25	0.40	1.20	2.00
❏ 8, MP	0.25	0.40	1.20	2.00
❏ 9, MP	0.25	0.40	1.20	2.00
❏ 10, MP	0.25	0.40	1.20	2.00
❏ 11, MP	0.25	0.40	1.20	2.00
❏ 12	0.25	0.20	0.60	1.00
❏ 13	0.25	0.20	0.60	1.00
❏ 14	0.25	0.20	0.60	1.00
❏ 15	0.25	0.20	0.60	1.00
❏ 16	0.25	0.20	0.60	1.00
❏ 17	0.25	0.20	0.60	1.00
❏ 18	0.25	0.20	0.60	1.00
❏ 19	0.25	0.20	0.60	1.00
❏ 20, JM	0.25	0.20	0.60	1.00
❏ 21	0.25	0.20	0.60	1.00
❏ 22, JM, C:Howard the Duck	0.25	0.30	0.90	1.50

MAN-THING (1979-1981)

	ORIG.	GOOD	FINE	N-MINT
❏ 1, Nov 79	0.40	0.40	1.20	2.00
❏ 2, Jan 80	0.40	0.40	1.20	2.00
❏ 3, Mar 80	0.40	0.20	0.60	1.00
❏ 4, May 80	0.40	0.20	0.60	1.00
❏ 5, Jul 80	0.40	0.20	0.60	1.00
❏ 6, Sep 90	0.50	0.20	0.60	1.00
❏ 7, Nov 90	0.50	0.20	0.60	1.00
❏ 8, Jan 81	0.50	0.20	0.60	1.00
❏ 9, Mar 81	0.50	0.20	0.60	1.00
❏ 10, May 81	0.50	0.20	0.60	1.00
❏ 11, Jul 81	0.50	0.20	0.60	1.00

MANBAT
DC

	ORIG.	GOOD	FINE	N-MINT
❏ 1, Dec 75	0.25	0.05	0.15	0.25
❏ 2, Feb 76	0.25	0.05	0.15	0.25

MANDRAKE
PIONEER

	ORIG.	GOOD	FINE	N-MINT
❏ 1, 89, b&w		0.99	2.97	4.95

MANDRAKE THE MAGICIAN (mini-series)
MARVEL

	ORIG.	GOOD	FINE	N-MINT
❏ 1, Apr 95, cardstock cover	2.95	0.59	1.77	2.95
❏ 2, May 95, cardstock cover	2.95	0.59	1.77	2.95

MANGA VIZION
VIZ

	ORIG.	GOOD	FINE	N-MINT
❏ 2, 95, b&w anthology	4.95	0.99	2.97	4.95
❏ 3, 95, b&w anthology	4.95	0.99	2.97	4.95

MANGA ZEN
ZEN COMICS

	ORIG.	GOOD	FINE	N-MINT
❏ 1, 96, b&w	2.50	0.50	1.50	2.50

MANGAZINE
ANTARCTIC

	ORIG.	GOOD	FINE	N-MINT
❏ 1, 85, (b&w,newsprint cover, first AP book)	1.25	0.60	1.80	3.00
❏ 1, 86, b&w (2nd printing)	1.50	0.30	0.90	1.50
❏ 2		0.60	1.80	3.00
❏ 3		0.30	0.90	1.50
❏ 4		0.30	0.90	1.50
❏ 5		0.30	0.90	1.50

MANGAZINE (Volume 2)

	ORIG.	GOOD	FINE	N-MINT
❏ 1, b&w	3.00	0.60	1.80	3.00
❏ 2, b&w	3.00	0.60	1.80	3.00
❏ 3, b&w		0.35	1.05	1.75
❏ 4, b&w	1.95	0.39	1.17	1.95
❏ 5, b&w	1.95	0.39	1.17	1.95
❏ 6, b&w	1.95	0.39	1.17	1.95
❏ 7, b&w	1.95	0.39	1.17	1.95
❏ 8, b&w	1.95	0.39	1.17	1.95
❏ 9, b&w	1.95	0.39	1.17	1.95
❏ 10, b&w	2.25	0.45	1.35	2.25
❏ 11, b&w	2.25	0.45	1.35	2.25
❏ 12, b&w	2.25	0.45	1.35	2.25
❏ 13, b&w	2.25	0.45	1.35	2.25
❏ 14, b&w	2.95	0.59	1.77	2.95
❏ 15, b&w	2.95	0.59	1.77	2.95
❏ 16, b&w	2.95	0.59	1.77	2.95
❏ 17, Nov 92, b&w	2.95	0.59	1.77	2.95
❏ 18, Dec 92, b&w	2.95	0.59	1.77	2.95
❏ 19, Jan 93, b&w	2.95	0.59	1.77	2.95
❏ 20, Feb 93, b&w	2.95	0.59	1.77	2.95
❏ 21, Mar 93, b&w	2.95	0.59	1.77	2.95
❏ 22, Apr 93, b&w	2.95	0.59	1.77	2.95
❏ 23, May 93, b&w	2.95	0.59	1.77	2.95
❏ 24, Jun 93, b&w	2.95	0.59	1.77	2.95
❏ 25, Jul 93, b&w	3.95	0.79	2.37	3.95
❏ 26, Aug 93, b&w	2.95	0.59	1.77	2.95
❏ 27, Sep 93, b&w	2.95	0.59	1.77	2.95
❏ 28, Oct 93, b&w	2.95	0.59	1.77	2.95
❏ 29, Nov 93, b&w	2.95	0.59	1.77	2.95
❏ 30, Dec 93, b&w	2.95	0.59	1.77	2.95
❏ 31, Jan 94, b&w	2.95	0.59	1.77	2.95
❏ 32, Feb 94, b&w	2.95	0.59	1.77	2.95
❏ 33, May 94, b&w	2.95	0.59	1.77	2.95
❏ 34, Jul 94, b&w	2.95	0.59	1.77	2.95
❏ 35, Sep 94, b&w	2.95	0.59	1.77	2.95
❏ 36, Nov 94, b&w	2.95	0.59	1.77	2.95
❏ 37, Jan 95, b&w	3.95	0.79	2.37	3.95
❏ 38, Mar 95, b&w	2.95	0.59	1.77	2.95
❏ 39, May 95, b&w	2.95	0.59	1.77	2.95
❏ 40, Sep 95, b&w	2.95	0.59	1.77	2.95

MANGLE TANGLE TALES
INNOVATION

	ORIG.	GOOD	FINE	N-MINT
❏ 1, Intro: Ellison		0.59	1.77	2.95

MANHUNTER
DC

	ORIG.	GOOD	FINE	N-MINT
❏ 1, Jul 88, SKi	1.00	0.20	0.60	1.00
❏ 2, Aug 88, SKi		0.20	0.60	1.00
❏ 3, Sep 88, SKi		0.20	0.60	1.00
❏ 4, Oct 88		0.20	0.60	1.00
❏ 5, Nov 88		0.20	0.60	1.00
❏ 6, Dec 88		0.20	0.60	1.00
❏ 7, Dec 88		0.20	0.60	1.00
❏ 8, Jan 89, Invasion!	1.00	0.20	0.60	1.00
❏ 9, Jan 89, Invasion!	1.00	0.20	0.60	1.00
❏ 10, Feb 89		0.20	0.60	1.00
❏ 11, Mar 89		0.20	0.60	1.00
❏ 12, Apr 89		0.20	0.60	1.00

	ORIG.	GOOD	FINE	N-MINT
13, May 89		0.20	0.60	1.00
14, Jun 89, Janus		0.20	0.60	1.00
15, Jul 89		0.20	0.60	1.00
16, Aug 89		0.20	0.60	1.00
17, Sep 89, Batman		0.20	0.60	1.00
18, Oct 89		0.20	0.60	1.00
19, Nov 89		0.20	0.60	1.00
20, Dec 89		0.20	0.60	1.00
21, Jan 90		0.20	0.60	1.00
22, Feb 90		0.20	0.60	1.00
23, Mar 90		0.20	0.60	1.00

MANHUNTER (1994-)

	ORIG.	GOOD	FINE	N-MINT
0, Oct 94	1.95	0.39	1.17	1.95
1, Nov 94	1.95	0.39	1.17	1.95
2, Dec 94	1.95	0.39	1.17	1.95
3, Jan 95	1.95	0.39	1.17	1.95
4, Feb 95	1.95	0.39	1.17	1.95
5, Mar 95	1.95	0.39	1.17	1.95
6, Apr 95	1.95	0.39	1.17	1.95
7, Jun 95	2.25	0.45	1.35	2.25
8, Jul 95	2.25	0.45	1.35	2.25
9, Aug 95	2.25	0.45	1.35	2.25
10, Sep 95	2.25	0.45	1.35	2.25
11, Oct 95	2.25	0.45	1.35	2.25
12, Nov 95, "Underworld Unleashed";final issue	2.25	0.45	1.35	2.25

MANIK
MILLENNIUM

	ORIG.	GOOD	FINE	N-MINT
1, Sep 95, enhanced cardstock cover	2.95	0.59	1.77	2.95

MANIMAL
RENEGADE

	ORIG.	GOOD	FINE	N-MINT
1, Jan 86, b&w		0.34	1.02	1.70

MANOSAURS
EXPRESS/ENTITY

	ORIG.	GOOD	FINE	N-MINT
0, 94	2.95	0.59	1.77	2.95

MANTECH ROBOT WARRIORS
ARCHIE

	ORIG.	GOOD	FINE	N-MINT
1, Sep 84	0.75	0.15	0.45	0.75
2	0.75	0.15	0.45	0.75
3	0.75	0.15	0.45	0.75
4	0.75	0.15	0.45	0.75

MANTRA
MALIBU/ULTRAVERSE

	ORIG.	GOOD	FINE	N-MINT
1, Jul 93, Ultraverse, card	1.95	1.20	3.60	6.00
1, hologram edition		12.00	36.00	60.00
1, Ultra Ltd.	1.95	5.00	15.00	25.00
2	1.95	1.00	3.00	5.00
3, Sep 93	1.95	0.70	2.10	3.50
4, Rune, BWS	2.50	0.60	1.80	3.00
5	1.95	0.50	1.50	2.50
6, Break-Thru	1.95	0.39	1.17	1.95
7	1.95	0.39	1.17	1.95
8, Feb 94	1.95	0.39	1.17	1.95
9, Mar 94	1.95	0.39	1.17	1.95
10, Apr 94, (Ultraverse Premiere #2)	3.50	0.70	2.10	3.50
11, May 94	1.95	0.39	1.17	1.95
12, Jun 94	1.95	0.39	1.17	1.95
13, Aug 94, issue has two different covers	1.95	0.39	1.17	1.95
14, Sep 94	1.95	0.39	1.17	1.95
15, Oct 94	1.95	0.39	1.17	1.95
16, Nov 94	1.95	0.39	1.17	1.95

MANTRA (Vol. 2)

	ORIG.	GOOD	FINE	N-MINT
0, Sep 95, Infinity;alternate cover;O:New Mantra	1.50	0.50	1.50	2.50
0, Sep 95, Infinity;O: New Mantra	1.50	0.30	0.90	1.50

	ORIG.	GOOD	FINE	N-MINT
1, Oct 95, O&1:Coven	1.50	0.30	0.90	1.50
2, Nov 95, flipbook with "The Phoenix Resurrection" Pt. 4	1.50	0.30	0.90	1.50
3, Dec 95, V:Necro Mantra	1.50	0.30	0.90	1.50
4, Jan 96	1.50	0.30	0.90	1.50
5, Feb 96, V:N-ME	1.50	0.30	0.90	1.50
6, Mar 96, A:Rush;Mantra gets new costume	1.50	0.30	0.90	1.50

MANTUS FILES
ETERNITY

	ORIG.	GOOD	FINE	N-MINT
1, b&w		0.50	1.50	2.50
2, b&w		0.50	1.50	2.50
3, b&w		0.50	1.50	2.50
4, b&w		0.50	1.50	2.50

MARA
AIRCEL

	ORIG.	GOOD	FINE	N-MINT
1, adult, b&w		0.50	1.50	2.50
2, adult, b&w		0.50	1.50	2.50
3, adult, b&w		0.50	1.50	2.50
4, adult, b&w		0.59	1.77	2.95

MARA OF THE CELTS SPECIAL
RIP OFF

	ORIG.	GOOD	FINE	N-MINT
1, Sep 93, adult;b&w	2.95	0.59	1.77	2.95

MARC SPECTOR: MOON KNIGHT
MARVEL

	ORIG.	GOOD	FINE	N-MINT
1, Jun 89	1.50	1.00	3.00	5.00
2, Jul 89	1.50	0.80	2.40	4.00
3, Mar 89	1.50	0.60	1.80	3.00
4, Sep 89	1.50	0.60	1.80	3.00
5, Oct 89	1.50	0.60	1.80	3.00
6, Nov 89, Brother Voodoo	1.50	0.30	0.90	1.50
7, Nov 89, Brother Voodoo	1.50	0.30	0.90	1.50
8, Dec 89, Punisher, Acts of Vengeance	1.50	1.60	4.80	8.00
9, Dec 89, Punisher, Acts of Vengeance	1.50	1.60	4.80	8.00
10, Jan 90, Acts of Vengeance	1.50	0.30	0.90	1.50
11, Feb 90	1.50	0.30	0.90	1.50
12, Mar 90	1.50	0.30	0.90	1.50
13, Apr 90	1.50	0.30	0.90	1.50
14, May 90	1.50	0.30	0.90	1.50
15, Jun 90, Trial	1.50	0.30	0.90	1.50
16, Jul 90, Trial	1.50	0.30	0.90	1.50
17, Aug 90, Trial	1.50	0.30	0.90	1.50
18, Sep 90, Trial	1.50	0.30	0.90	1.50
19, Oct 90, SpM, Punisher	1.50	1.60	4.80	8.00
20, Nov 90, SpM, Punisher	1.50	1.40	4.20	7.00
21, Dec 90, SpM, Punisher	1.50	1.00	3.00	5.00
22, Jan 91	1.50	0.30	0.90	1.50
23, Feb 91	1.50	0.30	0.90	1.50
24, Mar 91	1.50	0.30	0.90	1.50
25, Apr 91, Ghost Rider	2.50	0.30	0.90	1.50
26, May 91	1.50	0.30	0.90	1.50
27, Jun 91	1.50	0.30	0.90	1.50
28, Jul 91	1.50	0.30	0.90	1.50
29, Aug 91	1.50	0.30	0.90	1.50
30, Sep 91	1.50	0.30	0.90	1.50
31, Oct 91	1.50	0.30	0.90	1.50
32, Nov 91	1.50	0.30	0.90	1.50
33, Dec 91	1.50	0.30	0.90	1.50
34	1.50	0.30	0.90	1.50
35	1.75	0.35	1.05	1.75
36, Punisher	1.75	0.35	1.05	1.75
37, Punisher	1.75	0.35	1.05	1.75

	ORIG.	GOOD	FINE	N-MINT
☐ 38, Punisher	1.75	0.35	1.05	1.75
☐ 39, Dr. Doom	1.75	0.35	1.05	1.75
☐ 40	1.75	0.35	1.05	1.75
☐ 41	1.75	0.35	1.05	1.75
☐ 42	1.75	0.35	1.05	1.75
☐ 43	1.75	0.35	1.05	1.75
☐ 44	1.75	0.35	1.05	1.75
☐ 45	1.75	0.35	1.05	1.75
☐ 46	1.75	0.35	1.05	1.75
☐ 47	1.75	0.35	1.05	1.75
☐ 48	1.75	0.35	1.05	1.75
☐ 49	1.75	0.35	1.05	1.75
☐ 50, die-cut cover	2.95	0.59	1.77	2.95
☐ 51	1.75	0.35	1.05	1.75
☐ 52	1.75	0.35	1.05	1.75
☐ 53	1.75	0.35	1.05	1.75
☐ 54	1.75	0.35	1.05	1.75
☐ 55	1.75	2.00	6.00	10.00
☐ 56	1.75	1.40	4.20	7.00
☐ 57	1.75	1.00	3.00	5.00
☐ 58	1.75	1.20	3.60	6.00
☐ 59	1.75	0.35	1.05	1.75
☐ 60	1.75	1.00	3.00	5.00

MARCH HARE
LODESTONE

	ORIG.	GOOD	FINE	N-MINT
☐ 1, 86, KG b&w	1.50	0.30	0.90	1.50

MARILYN MONROE-SUICIDE OR MURDER?
REVOLUTIONARY

	ORIG.	GOOD	FINE	N-MINT
☐ 1, Sep 93, b&w	2.50	0.50	1.50	2.50

MARIONETTE, THE
ALPHA PRODUCTIONS

	ORIG.	GOOD	FINE	N-MINT
☐ 1, b&w	2.50	0.50	1.50	2.50
☐ 2, b&w	2.50	0.50	1.50	2.50

MARK HAZZARD: MERC
MARVEL

	ORIG.	GOOD	FINE	N-MINT
☐ 1, Nov 86	0.75	0.20	0.60	1.00
☐ 2, Dec 86	0.75	0.20	0.60	1.00
☐ 3, Jan 87	0.75	0.20	0.60	1.00
☐ 4, Feb 87	0.75	0.20	0.60	1.00
☐ 5, Mar 87	0.75	0.20	0.60	1.00
☐ 6, Apr 87	0.75	0.20	0.60	1.00
☐ 7, May 87	0.75	0.20	0.60	1.00
☐ 9, Jul 87	0.75	0.20	0.60	1.00
☐ 10, Aug 87	0.75	0.20	0.60	1.00
☐ 11, Sep 87	0.75	0.20	0.60	1.00
☐ 12, Oct 87	0.75	0.20	0.60	1.00
☐ 88, Jun 87	0.75	0.20	0.60	1.00

MARK HAZZARD: MERC ANNUAL

	ORIG.	GOOD	FINE	N-MINT
☐ 1, Nov 87, D:Hazzard	1.25	0.25	0.75	1.25

MARK, THE
DARK HORSE

	ORIG.	GOOD	FINE	N-MINT
☐ 1, Sep 87		0.35	1.05	1.75
☐ 2, Dec 87		0.39	1.17	1.95
☐ 3, Aug 88		0.35	1.05	1.75
☐ 4, Sep 88		0.35	1.05	1.75
☐ 5, Nov 88		0.35	1.05	1.75
☐ 6, Jan 89		0.35	1.05	1.75

MARK, THE (1993-)

	ORIG.	GOOD	FINE	N-MINT
☐ 1	2.50	0.50	1.50	2.50
☐ 2	2.50	0.50	1.50	2.50
☐ 3	2.50	0.50	1.50	2.50
☐ 4, Mar 94	2.50	0.50	1.50	2.50

MARKSMAN ANNUAL
HERO

	ORIG.	GOOD	FINE	N-MINT
☐ 1, Dec 88		0.55	1.65	2.75

MARKSMAN, THE

	ORIG.	GOOD	FINE	N-MINT
☐ 1, Jan 88, O:Marksman		0.39	1.17	1.95
☐ 2, Feb 88		0.39	1.17	1.95
☐ 3, Apr 88		0.39	1.17	1.95

	ORIG.	GOOD	FINE	N-MINT
☐ 4, Jun 88		0.39	1.17	1.95
☐ 5, Aug 88		0.39	1.17	1.95

MAROONED
EROS COMIX

	ORIG.	GOOD	FINE	N-MINT
☐ 1, adult, b&w		0.39	1.17	1.95

MARRIED...WITH CHILDREN
NOW

	ORIG.	GOOD	FINE	N-MINT
☐ 1, Jun 90, TV series	1.75	0.60	1.80	3.00
☐ 2, Jul 90	1.75	0.35	1.05	1.75
☐ 3, Aug 90	1.75	0.35	1.05	1.75
☐ 4, Sep 90	1.75	0.35	1.05	1.75
☐ 5, Oct 90	1.75	0.35	1.05	1.75
☐ 6, Nov 90	1.75	0.35	1.05	1.75
☐ 7, Feb 91	1.75	0.35	1.05	1.75

MARRIED...WITH CHILDREN (Volume 2)

	ORIG.	GOOD	FINE	N-MINT
☐ 1, Sep 91	1.95	0.39	1.17	1.95
☐ 2, Oct 91	1.95	0.39	1.17	1.95
☐ 3, Nov 91	1.95	0.39	1.17	1.95
☐ 4, Dec 91	1.95	0.39	1.17	1.95
☐ 5, Jan 92	1.95	0.39	1.17	1.95
☐ 6, Mar 92	1.95	0.39	1.17	1.95
☐ 7, Apr 92	1.95	0.39	1.17	1.95

MARRIED...WITH CHILDREN 1994 ANNUAL

	ORIG.	GOOD	FINE	N-MINT
☐ 0	2.50	0.50	1.50	2.50

MARRIED...WITH CHILDREN 3-D SPECIAL

	ORIG.	GOOD	FINE	N-MINT
☐ 0, Jun 93	2.95	0.59	1.77	2.95

MARRIED...WITH CHILDREN SPECIAL

	ORIG.	GOOD	FINE	N-MINT
☐ 1, Jul 92, with poster		0.39	1.17	1.95

MARRIED...WITH CHILDREN: 2099 (mini-series)

	ORIG.	GOOD	FINE	N-MINT
☐ 1, Jun 93	1.95	0.39	1.17	1.95
☐ 2, Jul 93	1.95	0.39	1.17	1.95
☐ 3, Aug 93	1.95	0.39	1.17	1.95

MARRIED...WITH CHILDREN: FLASHBACK SPECIAL

	ORIG.	GOOD	FINE	N-MINT
☐ 1, Jan 93	1.95	0.39	1.17	1.95
☐ 2, Feb 93	1.95	0.39	1.17	1.95
☐ 3, Mar 93	1.95	0.39	1.17	1.95

MARRIED...WITH CHILDREN: KELLY BUNDY SPECIAL

	ORIG.	GOOD	FINE	N-MINT
☐ 1, Aug 92	1.95	0.39	1.17	1.95
☐ 2, Sep 92	1.95	0.39	1.17	1.95
☐ 3, Oct 92	1.95	0.39	1.17	1.95

MARRIED...WITH CHILDREN: OFF BROADWAY

	ORIG.	GOOD	FINE	N-MINT
☐ 1, Sep 93	1.95	0.39	1.17	1.95

MARRIED...WITH CHILDREN: QUANTUM QUARTET

	ORIG.	GOOD	FINE	N-MINT
☐ 1, Oct 93, parody	1.95	0.39	1.17	1.95
☐ 2, Nov 93, parody	1.95	0.39	1.17	1.95

MARS
FIRST

	ORIG.	GOOD	FINE	N-MINT
☐ 1, Jan 84	1.25	0.25	0.75	1.25
☐ 2, Feb 84	1.25	0.25	0.75	1.25
☐ 3, Mar 84	1.25	0.25	0.75	1.25
☐ 4, Apr 84	1.25	0.25	0.75	1.25
☐ 5, May 84	1.25	0.25	0.75	1.25
☐ 6, Jun 84	1.25	0.25	0.75	1.25
☐ 7, Jul 84	1.25	0.25	0.75	1.25
☐ 8, Aug 84	1.25	0.25	0.75	1.25
☐ 9, Sep 84	1.25	0.25	0.75	1.25
☐ 10, Oct 84	1.25	0.25	0.75	1.25
☐ 11, Nov 84	1.25	0.25	0.75	1.25
☐ 12, Dec 84	1.25	0.25	0.75	1.25

	ORIG.	GOOD	FINE	N-MINT

MARS ATTACKS (mini-series)
TOPPS

	ORIG.	GOOD	FINE	N-MINT
☐ 1, May 94	2.95	1.20	3.60	6.00
☐ 2, Jun 94	2.95	0.80	2.40	4.00
☐ 3	2.95	0.70	2.10	3.50
☐ 4	2.95	0.70	2.10	3.50
☐ 5	2.95	0.70	2.10	3.50

MARS ATTACKS (Vol. 2 ongoing)

	ORIG.	GOOD	FINE	N-MINT
☐ 1, Aug 95, "Counterstrike" Part 1	2.95	1.00	3.00	5.00
☐ 2, Sep 95, "Counterstrike" Part 2	2.95	0.70	2.10	3.50
☐ 3, Oct 95, "Counterstrike" Part 3	2.95	0.59	1.77	2.95
☐ 4, Jan 96, "Counterstrike" Part 4	2.95	0.59	1.77	2.95

MARS ATTACKS!
POCKET

	ORIG.	GOOD	FINE	N-MINT
☐ 1, mini-comics		0.20	0.60	1.00
☐ 2, mini-comics		0.20	0.60	1.00
☐ 3, mini-comics		0.20	0.60	1.00
☐ 4, mini-comics		0.20	0.60	1.00

MARSHAL LAW
EPIC

	ORIG.	GOOD	FINE	N-MINT
☐ 1	1.95	0.80	2.40	4.00
☐ 2	1.95	0.50	1.50	2.50
☐ 3	1.95	0.50	1.50	2.50
☐ 4	1.95	0.50	1.50	2.50
☐ 5	1.95	0.50	1.50	2.50
☐ 6	1.95	0.50	1.50	2.50

MARSHAL LAW: SECRET TRIBUNAL
DARK HORSE

	ORIG.	GOOD	FINE	N-MINT
☐ 1	2.95	0.59	1.77	2.95
☐ 2, Apr 94	2.95	0.59	1.77	2.95

MARTHA SPLATTERHEAD'S WEIRDEST STORIES EVER TOLD
MONSTER

	ORIG.	GOOD	FINE	N-MINT
☐ 1, b&w, adult		0.70	2.10	3.50

MARTHA WASHINGTON GOES TO WAR (mini-series)
DARK HORSE/LEGEND

	ORIG.	GOOD	FINE	N-MINT
☐ 1, May 94	2.95	0.59	1.77	2.95
☐ 2, Jun 94	2.95	0.59	1.77	2.95
☐ 3, Jul 94	2.95	0.59	1.77	2.95
☐ 4, Aug 94	2.95	0.59	1.77	2.95
☐ 5, Nov 94	2.95	0.59	1.77	2.95

MARTHA WASHINGTON: STRANDED IN SPACE

	ORIG.	GOOD	FINE	N-MINT
☐ 0, Nov 95, nn;cardstock cover;A:The Big Guy	2.95	0.59	1.77	2.95

MARTIAN MANHUNTER (mini-series)
DC

	ORIG.	GOOD	FINE	N-MINT
☐ 1, May 88		0.25	0.75	1.25
☐ 2, Jun 88		0.25	0.75	1.25
☐ 3, Jul 88		0.25	0.75	1.25
☐ 4, Aug 88		0.25	0.75	1.25

MARTIAN MANHUNTER: AMERICAN SECRETS (mini-series)

	ORIG.	GOOD	FINE	N-MINT
☐ 1, 92, prestige format	4.95	0.99	2.97	4.95
☐ 2, 92, prestige format	4.95	0.99	2.97	4.95
☐ 3, 93, prestige format	4.95	0.99	2.97	4.95

MARVEL 1994 - THE YEAR IN REVIEW
MARVEL

	ORIG.	GOOD	FINE	N-MINT
☐ 0, 94	2.95	0.59	1.77	2.95

MARVEL ACTION HOUR, FEATURING IRON MAN

	ORIG.	GOOD	FINE	N-MINT
☐ 1, Nov 94, (polybagged with 16-page preview, acetate print, and other items)	2.95	0.59	1.77	2.95
☐ 1, Nov 94	1.50	0.30	0.90	1.50
☐ 2, Dec 94	1.50	0.30	0.90	1.50
☐ 3, Jan 95	1.50	0.30	0.90	1.50
☐ 4, Feb 95	1.50	0.30	0.90	1.50
☐ 5, Mar 95	1.50	0.30	0.90	1.50
☐ 6, Apr 95	1.50	0.30	0.90	1.50
☐ 7, May 95	1.50	0.30	0.90	1.50
☐ 8, Jun 95	1.50	0.30	0.90	1.50

MARVEL ACTION HOUR, FEATURING THE FANTASTIC FOUR

	ORIG.	GOOD	FINE	N-MINT
☐ 1, Nov 94, (polybagged with 16-page preview, acetate print, and other items)	2.95	0.59	1.77	2.95
☐ 1, Nov 94	1.50	0.30	0.90	1.50
☐ 2, Dec 94	1.50	0.30	0.90	1.50
☐ 3, Jan 95	1.50	0.30	0.90	1.50
☐ 4, Feb 95	1.50	0.30	0.90	1.50
☐ 5, Mar 95	1.50	0.30	0.90	1.50
☐ 6, Apr 95	1.50	0.30	0.90	1.50
☐ 7, May 95	1.50	0.30	0.90	1.50
☐ 8, Jun 95	1.50	0.30	0.90	1.50

MARVEL ACTION UNIVERSE

	ORIG.	GOOD	FINE	N-MINT
☐ 1, Jan 89, SM rep.	1.00	0.20	0.60	1.00

MARVEL AGE

	ORIG.	GOOD	FINE	N-MINT
☐ 1, Apr 83	0.25	0.40	1.20	2.00
☐ 2, May 83	0.25	0.20	0.60	1.00
☐ 3, Jun 83	0.25	0.20	0.60	1.00
☐ 4, Jul 83	0.25	0.20	0.60	1.00
☐ 5, Aug 83	0.25	0.20	0.60	1.00
☐ 6, Sep 83	0.25	0.20	0.60	1.00
☐ 7, Oct 83	0.25	0.20	0.60	1.00
☐ 8, Nov 83	0.25	0.20	0.60	1.00
☐ 9, Dec 83	0.25	0.20	0.60	1.00
☐ 10, Jan 84	0.25	0.20	0.60	1.00
☐ 11, Feb 84	0.25	0.20	0.60	1.00
☐ 12, Mar 84	0.25	0.20	0.60	1.00
☐ 13, Apr 84	0.25	0.20	0.60	1.00
☐ 14, May 84	0.25	0.20	0.60	1.00
☐ 15, Jun 84	0.35	0.20	0.60	1.00
☐ 16, Jul 84	0.35	0.20	0.60	1.00
☐ 17, Aug 84	0.35	0.20	0.60	1.00
☐ 18, Sep 84	0.35	0.20	0.60	1.00
☐ 19, Oct 84	0.35	0.20	0.60	1.00
☐ 20, Nov 84	0.35	0.20	0.60	1.00
☐ 21, Dec 84	0.35	0.20	0.60	1.00
☐ 22, Jan 85	0.35	0.20	0.60	1.00
☐ 23, Feb 85	0.35	0.20	0.60	1.00
☐ 24, Mar 85	0.35	0.20	0.60	1.00
☐ 25, Apr 85	0.35	0.20	0.60	1.00
☐ 26, May 85	0.35	0.20	0.60	1.00
☐ 27, Jun 85	0.35	0.20	0.60	1.00
☐ 28, Jul 85	0.35	0.20	0.60	1.00
☐ 29, Aug 85	0.35	0.20	0.60	1.00
☐ 30, Sep 85	0.35	0.20	0.60	1.00
☐ 31, Oct 85	0.35	0.20	0.60	1.00
☐ 32, Nov 85, AAd	0.35	0.20	0.60	1.00
☐ 33, Dec 85	0.35	0.20	0.60	1.00
☐ 34, Jan 86	0.35	0.20	0.60	1.00
☐ 35, Feb 86	0.35	0.20	0.60	1.00
☐ 36, Mar 86	0.35	0.20	0.60	1.00
☐ 37, Apr 86	0.35	0.20	0.60	1.00
☐ 38, May 86	0.35	0.20	0.60	1.00
☐ 39, Jun 86	0.35	0.20	0.60	1.00
☐ 40, Jul 86	0.35	0.20	0.60	1.00
☐ 41, Aug 86	0.50	0.20	0.60	1.00
☐ 42, Sep 86	0.50	0.20	0.60	1.00
☐ 43, Oct 86	0.50	0.20	0.60	1.00
☐ 44, Nov 86	0.50	0.20	0.60	1.00
☐ 45, Dec 86	0.50	0.20	0.60	1.00
☐ 46, Jan 87	0.50	0.20	0.60	1.00
☐ 47, Feb 87	0.50	0.20	0.60	1.00
☐ 48, Mar 87	0.50	0.20	0.60	1.00
☐ 49, Apr 87	0.50	0.20	0.60	1.00
☐ 50, May 87	0.50	0.20	0.60	1.00
☐ 51, Jun 87	0.50	0.20	0.60	1.00

	ORIG.	GOOD	FINE	N-MINT
❏ 52, Jul 87	0.50	0.20	0.60	1.00
❏ 53, Aug 87	0.50	0.20	0.60	1.00
❏ 54, Sep 87, SM wedding	0.50	0.20	0.60	1.00
❏ 55, Oct 87	0.50	0.20	0.60	1.00
❏ 56, Nov 87	0.50	0.20	0.60	1.00
❏ 57, Dec 87	0.50	0.20	0.60	1.00
❏ 58, Jan 88	0.50	0.20	0.60	1.00
❏ 59, Feb 88	0.50	0.20	0.60	1.00
❏ 60, Mar 88	0.50	0.20	0.60	1.00
❏ 61, Apr 88	0.50	0.20	0.60	1.00
❏ 62, May 88	0.50	0.20	0.60	1.00
❏ 63, Jun 88	0.50	0.20	0.60	1.00
❏ 64, Jul 88	0.50	0.20	0.60	1.00
❏ 65, Aug 88	0.50	0.20	0.60	1.00
❏ 66, Sep 88	0.50	0.20	0.60	1.00
❏ 67, Oct 88	0.50	0.20	0.60	1.00
❏ 68, Nov 88	0.50	0.20	0.60	1.00
❏ 69, Dec 88	0.50	0.20	0.60	1.00
❏ 70, Jan 89	0.50	0.20	0.60	1.00
❏ 71, Feb 89	0.50	0.20	0.60	1.00
❏ 72, Mar 89	0.50	0.20	0.60	1.00
❏ 73, Apr 89	0.50	0.20	0.60	1.00
❏ 74, May 89	0.50	0.20	0.60	1.00
❏ 75, Jun 89	0.50	0.20	0.60	1.00
❏ 76, Jul 89	0.50	0.20	0.60	1.00
❏ 77, Aug 89	0.50	0.20	0.60	1.00
❏ 78, Sep 89	0.50	0.20	0.60	1.00
❏ 79, Oct 89	0.75	0.20	0.60	1.00
❏ 80, Nov 89	0.75	0.20	0.60	1.00
❏ 81, Nov 89	0.75	0.20	0.60	1.00
❏ 82, Dec 89	0.75	0.20	0.60	1.00
❏ 83, Dec 89	0.75	0.20	0.60	1.00
❏ 84, Jan 90	0.75	0.20	0.60	1.00
❏ 85, Feb 90	0.75	0.20	0.60	1.00
❏ 86, Mar 90	1.00	0.20	0.60	1.00
❏ 87, Apr 90	1.00	0.20	0.60	1.00
❏ 88, May 90, Guardians of the Galaxy				
	1.00	0.20	0.60	1.00
❏ 89, Jun 90	1.00	0.20	0.60	1.00
❏ 90, Jul 90	1.00	0.20	0.60	1.00
❏ 91, Aug 90	1.00	0.20	0.60	1.00
❏ 92, Sep 90	1.00	0.20	0.60	1.00
❏ 93, Oct 90	1.00	0.20	0.60	1.00
❏ 94, Nov 90	1.00	0.20	0.60	1.00
❏ 95, Dec 90, Capt. America issue				
	1.00	0.20	0.60	1.00
❏ 96, Jan 91	1.00	0.20	0.60	1.00
❏ 97, Feb 91	1.00	0.20	0.60	1.00
❏ 98, Mar 91	1.00	0.20	0.60	1.00
❏ 99, Apr 91	1.00	0.20	0.60	1.00
❏ 100, May 91	1.00	0.20	0.60	1.00
❏ 101, Jun 91	1.00	0.20	0.60	1.00
❏ 102, Jul 91	1.00	0.20	0.60	1.00
❏ 103, Aug 91	1.00	0.20	0.60	1.00
❏ 104, Sep 91	1.00	0.20	0.60	1.00
❏ 105, Oct 91	1.00	0.20	0.60	1.00
❏ 106, Nov 91	1.00	0.20	0.60	1.00
❏ 107, Dec 91	1.00	0.20	0.60	1.00
❏ 108, Jan 92	1.00	0.20	0.60	1.00
❏ 109, Feb 92	1.00	0.20	0.60	1.00
❏ 110, Mar 92	1.00	0.20	0.60	1.00
❏ 111, Apr 92	1.00	0.20	0.60	1.00
❏ 112, May 92	1.00	0.20	0.60	1.00
❏ 113, Jun 92	1.00	0.20	0.60	1.00
❏ 114, Jul 92, Spider-Man's 30th anniversary				
	1.00	0.20	0.60	1.00
❏ 115, Aug 92	1.00	0.20	0.60	1.00
❏ 116, Sep 92, X-Men	1.00	0.20	0.60	1.00
❏ 117, Oct 92, 2099	1.00	0.20	0.60	1.00
❏ 118, Nov 92, with card	1.50	0.30	0.90	1.50
❏ 119, Dec 92	1.00	0.20	0.60	1.00
❏ 120, Jan 93	1.00	0.20	0.60	1.00

	ORIG.	GOOD	FINE	N-MINT
❏ 121, Feb 93, Ren & Stimpy				
	1.00	0.20	0.60	1.00
❏ 122, Mar 93	1.00	0.20	0.60	1.00
❏ 123, Apr 93	1.00	0.20	0.60	1.00
❏ 124, May 93	1.00	0.20	0.60	1.00
❏ 125, Jun 93	1.00	0.20	0.60	1.00
❏ 126, Jul 93	1.00	0.20	0.60	1.00
❏ 127, Aug 93	1.00	0.20	0.60	1.00
❏ 128, Sep 93	1.00	0.20	0.60	1.00
❏ 129, Oct 93	1.00	0.20	0.60	1.00
❏ 130, Nov 93, Marvels; poster;O:Golden Age Human Torch Part 1	1.25	0.80	2.40	4.00
❏ 131, Dec 93, Kuberts/ Excalibur;O:Golden Age Human Torch Part 2	1.00	0.80	2.40	4.00
❏ 132, Jan 94, Force Works/ ClanDestine;O:Golden Age Human Torch Part 3	1.00	0.80	2.40	4.00
❏ 133, Feb 94, X-Wedding/ War Machine;O:Golden Age Human Torch Part 4	1.00	0.80	2.40	4.00
❏ 134, Mar 94	1.00	0.20	0.60	1.00
❏ 135, Apr 94	1.25	0.25	0.75	1.25
❏ 136, May 94	1.25	0.25	0.75	1.25
❏ 137, Jun 94	1.50	0.30	0.90	1.50
❏ 138, Jul 94, remembering Jack Kirby				
	1.25	0.40	1.20	2.00
❏ 139, Aug 94, Batman and the Punisher				
	1.25	0.25	0.75	1.25
❏ 140, Sep 94, final issue	1.25	0.25	0.75	1.25

MARVEL AGE ANNUAL

	ORIG.	GOOD	FINE	N-MINT
❏ 1, Sep 85	0.50	0.30	0.90	1.50
❏ 2, Sep 86	0.50	0.30	0.90	1.50
❏ 3, Sep 87, FH,TA,JBu, MR				
	0.75	0.20	0.60	1.00
❏ 4, Sep 88, Wolverine	0.75	0.20	0.60	1.00

MARVEL AGE PREVIEW

	ORIG.	GOOD	FINE	N-MINT
❏ 1, Apr 90, 1990	1.50	0.30	0.90	1.50
❏ 2, 1992	2.25	0.45	1.35	2.25

MARVEL AND DC PRESENT

	ORIG.	GOOD	FINE	N-MINT
❏ 1, Nov 82, WS/TA, X-Men & Titans				
	2.00	4.80	14.40	24.00

MARVEL CHILLERS

	ORIG.	GOOD	FINE	N-MINT
❏ 1, Modred	0.25	0.80	2.40	4.00
❏ 2, Modred	0.25	0.20	0.60	1.00
❏ 3, Tigra	0.25	0.20	0.60	1.00
❏ 4, Tigra	0.25	0.20	0.60	1.00
❏ 5, Tigra	0.25	0.20	0.60	1.00
❏ 6, Tigra	0.25	0.40	1.20	2.00
❏ 7, Oct 76, Tigra	0.30	0.20	0.60	1.00

MARVEL CLASSIC COMICS

	ORIG.	GOOD	FINE	N-MINT
❏ 1, 76, Dr. Jekyll and Mr. Hyde				
	0.50	0.60	1.80	3.00
❏ 2, The Time Machine	0.50	0.60	1.80	3.00
❏ 3, The Hunchback of Notre Dame				
	0.50	0.60	1.80	3.00
❏ 4, 20,000 Leagues Under the Sea				
	0.50	0.60	1.80	3.00
❏ 5	0.50	0.60	1.80	3.00
❏ 6	0.50	0.60	1.80	3.00
❏ 7	0.50	0.60	1.80	3.00
❏ 8	0.50	0.60	1.80	3.00
❏ 9	0.50	0.60	1.80	3.00
❏ 10	0.50	0.60	1.80	3.00
❏ 11	0.50	0.60	1.80	3.00
❏ 12	0.50	0.60	1.80	3.00
❏ 13	0.50	0.60	1.80	3.00
❏ 14	0.50	0.60	1.80	3.00
❏ 15	0.50	0.60	1.80	3.00
❏ 16	0.50	0.60	1.80	3.00
❏ 17	0.50	0.60	1.80	3.00
❏ 18	0.50	0.60	1.80	3.00
❏ 19	0.50	0.60	1.80	3.00

	ORIG.	GOOD	FINE	N-MINT
❑ 20	0.50	0.60	1.80	3.00
❑ 21	0.50	0.60	1.80	3.00
❑ 22	0.50	0.60	1.80	3.00
❑ 23	0.50	0.60	1.80	3.00
❑ 24	0.50	0.60	1.80	3.00
❑ 25	0.50	0.60	1.80	3.00
❑ 26	0.50	0.60	1.80	3.00
❑ 27	0.60	0.60	1.80	3.00
❑ 28	0.60	0.80	2.40	4.00
❑ 29, Prisoner of Zenda	0.60	0.60	1.80	3.00
❑ 30, The Arabian Nights	0.60	0.60	1.80	3.00
❑ 31	0.60	0.60	1.80	3.00
❑ 32	0.60	0.60	1.80	3.00
❑ 33, 78, The Prince and the Pauper				
	0.60	0.60	1.80	3.00
❑ 34	0.60	0.60	1.80	3.00
❑ 35	0.60	0.60	1.80	3.00
❑ 36	0.60	0.60	1.80	3.00

MARVEL COLLECTOR'S EDITION

	ORIG.	GOOD	FINE	N-MINT
❑ 1, 92, SpM, Wolverine, Ghost Rider, Charleston Chew promotion, $.50 and a candy bar wrapper				
	1.50	0.30	0.90	1.50

MARVEL COLLECTORS' ITEM CLASSICS

	ORIG.	GOOD	FINE	N-MINT
❑ 1, reprints	0.25	10.00	30.00	50.00
❑ 2, reprints	0.25	6.00	18.00	30.00
❑ 3, reprints	0.25	4.00	12.00	20.00
❑ 4, Aug 66, reprints	0.25	4.00	12.00	20.00
❑ 5, reprints	0.25	4.00	12.00	20.00
❑ 6	0.25	2.00	6.00	10.00
❑ 7	0.25	2.00	6.00	10.00
❑ 8	0.25	2.00	6.00	10.00
❑ 9, Jun 67	0.25	2.00	6.00	10.00
❑ 10	0.25	2.00	6.00	10.00
❑ 11, Oct 67	0.25	2.00	6.00	10.00
❑ 12, Dec 67	0.25	2.00	6.00	10.00
❑ 13, Feb 68	0.25	2.00	6.00	10.00
❑ 14	0.25	2.00	6.00	10.00
❑ 15, Jun 68	0.25	2.00	6.00	10.00
❑ 16, Aug 68	0.25	2.00	6.00	10.00
❑ 17, Oct 68	0.25	2.00	6.00	10.00
❑ 18	0.25	2.00	6.00	10.00
❑ 19	0.25	2.00	6.00	10.00
❑ 20	0.25	2.00	6.00	10.00
❑ 21	0.25	2.00	6.00	10.00
❑ 22, Aug 69, reprints (becomes *Marvel's Greatest Comics*)	0.25	1.60	4.80	8.00

MARVEL COMICS PRESENTS

	ORIG.	GOOD	FINE	N-MINT
❑ 1, Sep 88, Wolverine	1.25	2.40	7.20	12.00
❑ 2, Sep 88, Wolverine	1.25	1.20	3.60	6.00
❑ 3, Sep 88, Wolverine	1.25	0.80	2.40	4.00
❑ 4, Oct 88, Wolverine	1.25	0.80	2.40	4.00
❑ 5, Oct 88, Wolverine	1.25	0.80	2.40	4.00
❑ 6, Nov 88, Wolverine	1.25	0.80	2.40	4.00
❑ 7, Nov 88, Wolverine	1.25	0.80	2.40	4.00
❑ 8, Dec 88, Wolverine	1.25	0.80	2.40	4.00
❑ 9, Dec 88, Wolverine	1.25	0.80	2.40	4.00
❑ 10, Jan 89, Wolverine	1.25	0.80	2.40	4.00
❑ 11, Jan 89, Colossus	1.25	0.50	1.50	2.50
❑ 12, Feb 89, Colossus	1.25	0.50	1.50	2.50
❑ 13, Feb 89, Colossus	1.25	0.50	1.50	2.50
❑ 14, Mar 89, Colossus	1.25	0.50	1.50	2.50
❑ 15, Mar 89, Colossus	1.25	0.50	1.50	2.50
❑ 16, Mar 89, Colossus	1.25	0.50	1.50	2.50
❑ 17, Apr 89, Cyclops	1.25	0.80	2.40	4.00
❑ 18, Apr 89, JBy, She-Hulk, Cyclops				
	1.25	0.60	1.80	3.00
❑ 19, May 89, Cyclops	1.25	0.60	1.80	3.00
❑ 20, May 89, Cyclops	1.25	0.60	1.80	3.00
❑ 21, Jun 89, Cyclops	1.25	0.60	1.80	3.00
❑ 22, Jun 89, Cyclops	1.25	0.60	1.80	3.00
❑ 23, Jul 89, Cyclops	1.25	0.60	1.80	3.00

	ORIG.	GOOD	FINE	N-MINT
❑ 24, Jul 89, Cyclops, Havok				
	1.25	0.60	1.80	3.00
❑ 25, Aug 89, Havok	1.25	0.50	1.50	2.50
❑ 26, Aug 89, Havok	1.25	0.50	1.50	2.50
❑ 27, Sep 89, Havok	1.25	0.50	1.50	2.50
❑ 28, Sep 89, Havok	1.25	0.50	1.50	2.50
❑ 29, Sep 89, Havok	1.25	0.50	1.50	2.50
❑ 30, Oct 89, Havok	1.25	0.50	1.50	2.50
❑ 31, Oct 89, Havok, Excalibur				
	1.25	0.80	2.40	4.00
❑ 32, Nov 89, TMc(c) Excalibur				
	1.25	0.80	2.40	4.00
❑ 33, Nov 89, Excalibur	1.25	0.80	2.40	4.00
❑ 34, Nov 89, Excalibur	1.25	0.80	2.40	4.00
❑ 35, Nov 89, Excalibur	1.25	0.60	1.80	3.00
❑ 36, Dec 89, Excalibur	1.25	0.60	1.80	3.00
❑ 37, Dec 89, Excalibur	1.25	0.60	1.80	3.00
❑ 38, Dec 89, Excalibur	1.25	0.60	1.80	3.00
❑ 39, Dec 89, Wolverine	1.25	0.60	1.80	3.00
❑ 40, Dec 89, Wolverine	1.25	0.60	1.80	3.00
❑ 41, Jan 90, Wolverine	1.25	0.60	1.80	3.00
❑ 42, Jan 90, Wolverine	1.25	0.60	1.80	3.00
❑ 43, Feb 90, Wolverine	1.25	0.60	1.80	3.00
❑ 44, Feb 90, Wolverine	1.25	0.60	1.80	3.00
❑ 45, Mar 90, Wolverine	1.25	0.60	1.80	3.00
❑ 46, Mar 90, Wolverine	1.25	0.60	1.80	3.00
❑ 47, Apr 90, Wolverine	1.25	0.60	1.80	3.00
❑ 48, Apr 90, Wolverine, SPM				
	1.25	2.00	6.00	10.00
❑ 49, May 90, Wolverine, SpM				
	1.25	1.20	3.60	6.00
❑ 50, May 90, Wolverine, SpM				
	1.25	1.20	3.60	6.00
❑ 51, Jun 90, Wolverine	1.25	0.50	1.50	2.50
❑ 52, Jun 90, Wolverine	1.25	0.50	1.50	2.50
❑ 53, Jul 90, Wolverine	1.25	0.50	1.50	2.50
❑ 54, Jul 90, Wolverine & Hulk				
	1.25	0.60	1.80	3.00
❑ 55, Jul 90, Wolverine & Hulk				
	1.25	0.40	1.20	2.00
❑ 56, Aug 90, Wolverine & Hulk				
	1.25	0.40	1.20	2.00
❑ 57, Aug 90, Wolverine & Hulk				
	1.25	0.40	1.20	2.00
❑ 58, Sep 90, Wolverine & Hulk				
	1.25	0.40	1.20	2.00
❑ 59, Sep 90, Wolverine & Hulk				
	1.25	0.40	1.20	2.00
❑ 60, Oct 90, Wolverine & Hulk				
	1.25	0.40	1.20	2.00
❑ 61, Oct 90, Wolverine & Hulk				
	1.25	0.40	1.20	2.00
❑ 62, Nov 90, Wolverine	1.25	0.80	2.40	4.00
❑ 63, Nov 90, Wolverine	1.25	0.80	2.40	4.00
❑ 64, Dec 90, Wolverine, Ghost Rider				
	1.25	1.40	4.20	7.00
❑ 65, Dec 90, Wolverine, Ghost Rider				
	1.25	1.00	3.00	5.00
❑ 66, Dec 90, Wolverine, Ghost Rider				
	1.25	0.60	1.80	3.00
❑ 67, Jan 91, Wolverine, Ghost Rider				
	1.25	0.60	1.80	3.00
❑ 68, Jan 91, Wolverine, Ghost Rider				
	1.25	0.60	1.80	3.00
❑ 69, Feb 91, Wolverine, Ghost Rider				
	1.25	0.60	1.80	3.00
❑ 70, Feb 91, Wolverine, Ghost Rider				
	1.25	0.60	1.80	3.00
❑ 71, Mar 91, Wolverine, Ghost Rider				
	1.25	0.60	1.80	3.00
❑ 72, Mar 91, BWS, Weapon X				
	1.25	2.80	8.40	14.00

	ORIG.	GOOD	FINE	N-MINT
❑ 73, Mar 91, BWS, Weapon X				
............................1.25	2.00	6.00	10.00
❑ 74, Apr 91, BWS, Weapon X				
............................1.25	1.60	4.80	8.00
❑ 75, Apr 91, BWS, Weapon X				
............................1.25	1.60	4.80	8.00
❑ 76, May 91, BWS, Weapon X				
............................1.25	1.60	4.80	8.00
❑ 77, May 91, BWS, Weapon X				
............................1.25	0.80	2.40	4.00
❑ 78, Jun 91, BWS, Weapon X				
............................1.25	0.80	2.40	4.00
❑ 79, Jun 91, BWS, Weapon X				
............................1.25	0.80	2.40	4.00
❑ 80, Jul 91, BWS, Weapon X				
............................1.25	0.80	2.40	4.00
❑ 81, Jul 91, BWS, Weapon X				
............................1.25	0.80	2.40	4.00
❑ 82, Aug 91, BWS, Weapon X				
............................1.25	0.80	2.40	4.00
❑ 83, Aug 91, BWS, Weapon X				
............................1.25	0.80	2.40	4.00
❑ 84, Sep 91, BWS, Weapon X				
............................1.25	0.80	2.40	4.00
❑ 85, Sep 91, Wolverine.... 1.25	0.60	1.80	3.00
❑ 86, Oct 91, Wolverine 1.25	0.60	1.80	3.00
❑ 87, Oct 91, Wolverine 1.25	0.60	1.80	3.00
❑ 88, Nov 91, Wolverine.... 1.25	0.60	1.80	3.00
❑ 89, Nov 91, Wolverine.... 1.25	0.60	1.80	3.00
❑ 90, Dec 91, Wolverine.... 1.25	0.60	1.80	3.00
❑ 91, Dec 91, Wolverine.... 1.25	0.60	1.80	3.00
❑ 92, Dec 91, Wolverine.... 1.25	0.60	1.80	3.00
❑ 93, Wolverine................ 1.25	0.60	1.80	3.00
❑ 94, Wolverine................ 1.25	0.60	1.80	3.00
❑ 95, Wolverine................ 1.50	0.60	1.80	3.00
❑ 96, Wolverine................ 1.50	0.60	1.80	3.00
❑ 97, Wolverine................ 1.50	0.60	1.80	3.00
❑ 98, Wolverine................ 1.50	0.60	1.80	3.00
❑ 99, Wolverine................ 1.50	0.60	1.80	3.00
❑ 100, SK;Wolverine;V: Dr. Doom				
............................1.50	1.20	3.60	6.00
❑ 101, Wolverine/Nightcrawler				
............................1.50	0.40	1.20	2.00
❑ 102, Wolverine/Nightcrawler				
............................1.50	0.40	1.20	2.00
❑ 103, Wolverine/Nightcrawler				
............................1.50	0.40	1.20	2.00
❑ 104, Wolverine/Nightcrawler				
............................1.50	0.40	1.20	2.00
❑ 105, Wolverine/Nightcrawler				
............................1.50	0.40	1.20	2.00
❑ 106, Wolverine/Nightcrawler				
............................1.50	0.40	1.20	2.00
❑ 107, Wolverine/Nightcrawler				
............................1.50	0.40	1.20	2.00
❑ 108, Wolverine, Ghost Rider				
............................1.50	0.40	1.20	2.00
❑ 109, Wolverine, Ghost Rider				
............................1.50	0.40	1.20	2.00
❑ 110, Wolverine, Ghost Rider				
............................1.50	0.40	1.20	2.00
❑ 111, Infinity War, Wolverine, Ghost Rider				
............................1.50	0.40	1.20	2.00
❑ 112, Wolverine, Ghost Rider				
............................1.50	0.30	0.90	1.50
❑ 113, Wolverine, Ghost Rider				
............................1.50	0.30	0.90	1.50
❑ 114, Wolverine, Ghost Rider				
............................1.50	0.30	0.90	1.50
❑ 115, Wolverine, Ghost Rider				
............................1.50	0.30	0.90	1.50

	ORIG.	GOOD	FINE	N-MINT
❑ 116, Wolverine, Ghost Rider				
............................1.50	0.30	0.90	1.50
❑ 117, Wolverine, Ghost Rider, Venom				
............................1.50	0.80	2.40	4.00
❑ 118, Wolverine 1.50	0.40	1.20	2.00
❑ 119, Wolverine 1.50	0.40	1.20	2.00
❑ 120, Wolverine 1.50	0.30	0.90	1.50
❑ 121, Wolverine 1.50	0.30	0.90	1.50
❑ 122, Wolverine 1.50	0.30	0.90	1.50
❑ 123, Wolverine 1.50	0.30	0.90	1.50
❑ 124, Wolverine 1.50	0.30	0.90	1.50
❑ 125, Wolverine 1.50	0.30	0.90	1.50
❑ 126, Wolverine 1.50	0.30	0.90	1.50
❑ 127, Wolverine 1.50	0.30	0.90	1.50
❑ 128, Wolverine 1.50	0.30	0.90	1.50
❑ 129, Wolverine 1.50	0.30	0.90	1.50
❑ 130, Wolverine 1.50	0.30	0.90	1.50
❑ 131, Wolverine 1.50	0.30	0.90	1.50
❑ 132, Wolverine 1.50	0.30	0.90	1.50
❑ 133, Wolverine 1.50	0.30	0.90	1.50
❑ 134, Wolverine 1.50	0.30	0.90	1.50
❑ 135, Wolverine 1.50	0.30	0.90	1.50
❑ 136, Wolverine 1.50	0.30	0.90	1.50
❑ 137, Wolverine 1.50	0.30	0.90	1.50
❑ 138, Wolverine 1.50	0.30	0.90	1.50
❑ 139 ....1.50	0.30	0.90	1.50
❑ 140 ....1.50	0.30	0.90	1.50
❑ 141 ....1.50	0.30	0.90	1.50
❑ 142 ....1.50	0.30	0.90	1.50
❑ 143, Ghost Rider 1.75	0.60	1.80	3.00
❑ 144, Ghost Rider 1.75	0.50	1.50	2.50
❑ 145, Ghost Rider 1.75	0.35	1.05	1.75
❑ 146 ....1.75	0.35	1.05	1.75
❑ 147 ....1.75	0.35	1.05	1.75
❑ 148 ....1.50	0.30	0.90	1.50
❑ 149 ....1.50	0.30	0.90	1.50
❑ 150 ....1.50	0.30	0.90	1.50
❑ 151, Apr 94...................1.50	0.30	0.90	1.50
❑ 152, Apr 94...................1.50	0.30	0.90	1.50
❑ 153, May 94...................1.75	0.35	1.05	1.75
❑ 154, May 94...................1.75	0.35	1.05	1.75
❑ 155, May 94...................1.75	0.35	1.05	1.75
❑ 156, Jun 94 ....1.75	0.35	1.05	1.75
❑ 157, Jun 94 ....1.75	0.35	1.05	1.75
❑ 158, Jul 94.....................1.75	0.35	1.05	1.75
❑ 159, Jul 94.....................1.75	0.35	1.05	1.75
❑ 160, Aug 94 ....1.75	0.35	1.05	1.75
❑ 161, Aug 94 ....1.75	0.35	1.05	1.75
❑ 162, Sep 94 ....1.75	0.35	1.05	1.75
❑ 163, Sep 94 ....1.75	0.35	1.05	1.75
❑ 164, Oct 94....................1.75	0.35	1.05	1.75
❑ 165, Oct 94....................1.75	0.35	1.05	1.75
❑ 166, Oct 94....................1.75	0.35	1.05	1.75
❑ 167, Nov 94 ....1.75	0.35	1.05	1.75
❑ 168, Nov 94 ....1.75	0.35	1.05	1.75
❑ 169, Dec 94 ....1.75	0.35	1.05	1.75
❑ 170, Dec 94 ....1.75	0.35	1.05	1.75
❑ 171, Jan 95....................1.75	0.35	1.05	1.75
❑ 172, Jan 95....................1.75	0.35	1.05	1.75
❑ 173, Feb 95....................1.75	0.35	1.05	1.75
❑ 174, Feb 95....................1.75	0.35	1.05	1.75
❑ 175, Mar 95, final issue ..1.75	0.35	1.05	1.75

MARVEL COMICS SUPER SPECIAL (magazine size)

	ORIG.	GOOD	FINE	N-MINT
❑ 1, Sep 77, KISS 1.50	0.30	0.90	1.50
❑ 2, Mar 78, Conan 1.50	0.30	0.90	1.50
❑ 3, Jun 78, Close Encounters				
............................1.50	0.30	0.90	1.50
❑ 4, Aug 78, Beatles (becomes *Marvel Super Special*)				
............................1.50	0.30	0.90	1.50

MARVEL DOUBLE FEATURE

	ORIG.	GOOD	FINE	N-MINT
❑ 1 ....0.20	0.20	0.60	1.00

	ORIG.	GOOD	FINE	N-MINT
❏ 2	0.20	0.20	0.60	1.00
❏ 3	0.20	0.20	0.60	1.00
❏ 4	0.25	0.20	0.60	1.00
❏ 5	0.25	0.20	0.60	1.00
❏ 6	0.25	0.20	0.60	1.00
❏ 7	0.25	0.20	0.60	1.00
❏ 8	0.25	0.20	0.60	1.00
❏ 9	0.25	0.20	0.60	1.00
❏ 10	0.25	0.20	0.60	1.00
❏ 11	0.25	0.20	0.60	1.00
❏ 12	0.25	0.20	0.60	1.00
❏ 13	0.25	0.20	0.60	1.00
❏ 14	0.25	0.20	0.60	1.00
❏ 15	0.25	0.20	0.60	1.00
❏ 16	0.25	0.20	0.60	1.00
❏ 17	0.25	0.20	0.60	1.00
❏ 18	0.30	0.20	0.60	1.00
❏ 19	0.30	0.20	0.60	1.00
❏ 20	0.30	0.20	0.60	1.00
❏ 21	0.30	0.20	0.60	1.00

MARVEL DOUBLE FEATURE...THE AVENGERS/GIANT-MAN

	ORIG.	GOOD	FINE	N-MINT
❏ 380, Nov 94, flip book with Giant-Man back-up	2.50	0.70	2.10	3.50
❏ 381, Dec 94, flip book with Giant-Man back-up	2.50	0.70	2.10	3.50
❏ 382, Jan 95, flip book	2.50	0.70	2.10	3.50

MARVEL DOUBLE FEATURE... THUNDERSTRIKE/CODE BLUE

	ORIG.	GOOD	FINE	N-MINT
❏ 14, Nov 94, flip book with Code Blue back-up	2.50	0.50	1.50	2.50
❏ 15, Dec 94, flip book with Code Blue back-up	2.50	0.50	1.50	2.50
❏ 16, Jan 95, flip book	2.50	0.50	1.50	2.50

MARVEL FANFARE

	ORIG.	GOOD	FINE	N-MINT
❏ 1, Mar 82, MG/TA, SpM/DD	1.25	2.40	7.20	12.00
❏ 2, May 82, MG, SpM/FF	1.25	2.00	6.00	10.00
❏ 3, Jul 82, DC, X-Men	1.25	2.00	6.00	10.00
❏ 4, Sep 82, PS/TA/MG, X-Men; MG, Deathlok	1.25	1.60	4.80	8.00
❏ 5, Nov 82, MR, Dr. Strange/CA	1.25	0.80	2.40	4.00
❏ 6, Jan 83, SpM/Dr. Strange	1.25	0.60	1.80	3.00
❏ 7, Mar 83, Hulk/DD	1.25	0.50	1.50	2.50
❏ 8, May 83	1.50	0.40	1.20	2.00
❏ 9, Jul 83	1.50	0.40	1.20	2.00
❏ 10, Aug 83	1.50	0.40	1.20	2.00
❏ 11, Nov 83	1.50	0.40	1.20	2.00
❏ 12, Jan 84	1.50	0.40	1.20	2.00
❏ 13, Mar 84, AAd (c)	1.50	0.40	1.20	2.00
❏ 14, May 84	1.50	0.40	1.20	2.00
❏ 15, Jul 84, BS, Thing	1.50	0.50	1.50	2.50
❏ 16, Sep 84	1.50	0.40	1.20	2.00
❏ 17, Nov 84	1.50	0.40	1.20	2.00
❏ 18, Jan 85, FM, Capt. America	1.50	1.00	3.00	5.00
❏ 19, Mar 85, JSn, Thing & Hulk	1.50	0.30	0.90	1.50
❏ 20, May 85, JSn, Thing & Hulk	1.50	0.30	0.90	1.50
❏ 21, Jul 85, JSn, Thing & Hulk	1.50	0.30	0.90	1.50
❏ 22, Sep 85, JSn, Thing & Hulk	1.50	0.30	0.90	1.50
❏ 23, Nov 85, JSn, Thing & Hulk	1.50	0.30	0.90	1.50
❏ 24, Jan 86	1.50	0.30	0.90	1.50
❏ 25, Mar 86, Dave Sim pin-up section; "Weirdworld"	1.50	0.30	0.90	1.50

	ORIG.	GOOD	FINE	N-MINT
❏ 26, May 86, "Weirdworld"	1.50	0.30	0.90	1.50
❏ 27, Jul 86, "Weirdworld"	1.50	0.30	0.90	1.50
❏ 28, Sep 86	1.50	0.30	0.90	1.50
❏ 29, Nov 86	1.50	0.30	0.90	1.50
❏ 30, Jan 87	1.50	0.30	0.90	1.50
❏ 31, Mar 87	1.50	0.30	0.90	1.50
❏ 32, May 87	1.50	0.30	0.90	1.50
❏ 33, Jul 87, Wolverine, X-Men	1.50	0.60	1.80	3.00
❏ 34, Sep 87, Warriors 3	1.50	0.30	0.90	1.50
❏ 35, Nov 87, Warriors 3	1.50	0.30	0.90	1.50
❏ 36, Jan 88, Warriors 3	1.50	0.30	0.90	1.50
❏ 37, Mar 88, Warriors 3	1.50	0.30	0.90	1.50
❏ 38, Apr 88, Moon Knight	1.50	0.30	0.90	1.50
❏ 39, Jul 88, Hawkeye, Moon Knight	1.95	0.39	1.17	1.95
❏ 40, Oct 88, Angel, Storm	1.95	0.39	1.17	1.95
❏ 41, Dec 88, DG, Dr. Strange	1.95	0.39	1.17	1.95
❏ 42, Feb 89, SpM	1.95	0.80	2.40	4.00
❏ 43, Apr 89, Sub-Mariner, Torch	1.95	0.39	1.17	1.95
❏ 44, Jun 89, Iron Man	1.95	0.39	1.17	1.95
❏ 45, Aug 89, JBy(c) all pin-ups	1.95	0.39	1.17	1.95
❏ 46, Oct 89, Fantastic Four	1.95	0.39	1.17	1.95
❏ 47, Nov 89, Hulk, SpM	1.95	0.60	1.80	3.00
❏ 48, Dec 89, She-Hulk	1.95	0.39	1.17	1.95
❏ 49, Feb 90, Dr. Strange	1.95	0.39	1.17	1.95
❏ 50, Apr 90, X-Factor	2.25	0.45	1.35	2.25
❏ 51, Jun 90, Silver Surfer	2.95	0.59	1.77	2.95
❏ 52, Aug 90, Black Knight	2.25	0.45	1.35	2.25
❏ 53, Oct 90, Black Knight	2.25	0.45	1.35	2.25
❏ 54, Dec 90, Black Knight	2.25	0.45	1.35	2.25
❏ 55, Feb 91, Power Pack, Wolverine	2.25	0.45	1.35	2.25
❏ 56, Apr 91, Shanna	2.25	0.45	1.35	2.25
❏ 57, Jun 91, Shanna	2.25	0.45	1.35	2.25
❏ 58, Aug 91, Shanna	2.25	0.45	1.35	2.25
❏ 59, Oct 91, Shanna	2.25	0.45	1.35	2.25
❏ 60, WS(i), Denys Cowan, Black Panther, Rogue, Daredevil	2.25	0.45	1.35	2.25

MARVEL FEATURE (1971-1973)

	ORIG.	GOOD	FINE	N-MINT
❏ 1, Dec 71, NA(c), O:Defenders	0.25	15.00	45.00	75.00
❏ 2, Mar 72, BEv, Sub-Mariner rep.	0.25	7.20	21.60	36.00
❏ 3, Jun 72, BEv, Defenders	0.20	6.00	18.00	30.00
❏ 4, Jul 72, Ant-Man	0.20	2.40	7.20	12.00
❏ 5, Sep 72, Ant-Man	0.20	1.20	3.60	6.00
❏ 6, Nov 72, Ant-Man	0.20	1.20	3.60	6.00
❏ 7, Jan 73, Ant-Man	0.20	1.20	3.60	6.00
❏ 8, Mar 73, Ant-Man	0.20	1.20	3.60	6.00
❏ 9, May 73, Ant-Man	0.20	1.20	3.60	6.00
❏ 10, Jul 73, Ant-Man	0.20	1.20	3.60	6.00
❏ 11, Sep 73, Thing	0.20	1.50	4.50	7.50
❏ 12, Nov 73, Thing	0.20	1.50	4.50	7.50

MARVEL FEATURE (1975-1976)

	ORIG.	GOOD	FINE	N-MINT
❏ 1, Nov 75, NA, Red Sonja	0.25	0.50	1.50	2.50
❏ 2, Red Sonja	0.25	0.40	1.20	2.00
❏ 3, Red Sonja	0.25	0.40	1.20	2.00
❏ 4, Red Sonja	0.25	0.40	1.20	2.00
❏ 5, Red Sonja	0.25	0.40	1.20	2.00

	ORIG.	GOOD	FINE	N-MINT
6, Red Sonja	0.30	0.40	1.20	2.00
7, Red Sonja	0.30	0.40	1.20	2.00

MARVEL FRONTIER SPECIAL

	ORIG.	GOOD	FINE	N-MINT
1	2.95	0.59	1.77	2.95

MARVEL FUMETTI BOOK, THE

	ORIG.	GOOD	FINE	N-MINT
1, photos	1.00	0.20	0.60	1.00

MARVEL GUIDE TO COLLECTING COMICS, THE

	ORIG.	GOOD	FINE	N-MINT
1, Sep 82, 1982, no cover price				

MARVEL HOLIDAY SPECIAL

	ORIG.	GOOD	FINE	N-MINT
0, Aad;nn;no cover date or date in indicia	2.25	0.45	1.35	2.25
0, 93, Aad;nn;(for 1992 holiday season)	2.95	0.59	1.77	2.95
0, Jan 94, Aad;nn;(for 1993 holiday season)	2.95	0.59	1.77	2.95
0, 94, nn;(for 1994 holiday season)	2.95	0.59	1.77	2.95

MARVEL ILLUSTRATED: SWIMSUIT ISSUE

	ORIG.	GOOD	FINE	N-MINT
1, Mar 91	3.95	0.79	2.37	3.95

MARVEL MASTERPIECES 2 COLLECTION

	ORIG.	GOOD	FINE	N-MINT
1, Jul 94	2.95	0.59	1.77	2.95
2, Aug 94	2.95	0.59	1.77	2.95
3, Sep 94	2.95	0.59	1.77	2.95

MARVEL MASTERPIECES COLLECTION

	ORIG.	GOOD	FINE	N-MINT
1, Joe Jusko	2.95	0.59	1.77	2.95
2, Joe Jusko	2.95	0.59	1.77	2.95
3, Joe Jusko	2.95	0.59	1.77	2.95
4, Joe Jusko	2.95	0.59	1.77	2.95

MARVEL MILESTONE EDITION: AMAZING FANTASY #15

	ORIG.	GOOD	FINE	N-MINT
0, Mar 92, reprint	2.95	0.59	1.77	2.95

MARVEL MILESTONE EDITION: AMAZING SPIDER-MAN #1

	ORIG.	GOOD	FINE	N-MINT
0, reprint	2.95	0.59	1.77	2.95

MARVEL MILESTONE EDITION: AMAZING SPIDER-MAN #129

	ORIG.	GOOD	FINE	N-MINT
0, reprint;O:Punisher	2.95	0.59	1.77	2.95

MARVEL MILESTONE EDITION: AMAZING SPIDER-MAN #149

	ORIG.	GOOD	FINE	N-MINT
0, Nov 94, reprint; indicia says Marvel Milestone Edition: Amazing Spider-Man #1	2.95	0.59	1.77	2.95

MARVEL MILESTONE EDITION: AMAZING SPIDER-MAN #3

	ORIG.	GOOD	FINE	N-MINT
0, Mar 95, reprint	2.95	0.59	1.77	2.95

MARVEL MILESTONE EDITION: AVENGERS #1

	ORIG.	GOOD	FINE	N-MINT
0, reprint;O:Avengers	2.95	0.59	1.77	2.95

MARVEL MILESTONE EDITION: AVENGERS #16

	ORIG.	GOOD	FINE	N-MINT
0, reprint	2.95	0.59	1.77	2.95

MARVEL MILESTONE EDITION: AVENGERS #4

	ORIG.	GOOD	FINE	N-MINT
0, Mar 95, reprint	2.95	0.59	1.77	2.95

MARVEL MILESTONE EDITION: CAPTAIN AMERICA #1

	ORIG.	GOOD	FINE	N-MINT
0, Mar 95, reprint	3.95	0.79	2.37	3.95

MARVEL MILESTONE EDITION: FANTASTIC FOUR #1

	ORIG.	GOOD	FINE	N-MINT
0, reprint	2.95	0.59	1.77	2.95

MARVEL MILESTONE EDITION: FANTASTIC FOUR #5

	ORIG.	GOOD	FINE	N-MINT
0, reprint	2.95	0.59	1.77	2.95

MARVEL MILESTONE EDITION: GIANT-SIZE X-MEN #1

	ORIG.	GOOD	FINE	N-MINT
0, 91, reprint	3.95	0.79	2.37	3.95

MARVEL MILESTONE EDITION: INCREDIBLE HULK #1

	ORIG.	GOOD	FINE	N-MINT
0, Mar 91, reprint	2.95	0.59	1.77	2.95

MARVEL MILESTONE EDITION: IRON FIST #14

	ORIG.	GOOD	FINE	N-MINT
0, reprint;1:Sabretooth	2.95	0.59	1.77	2.95

MARVEL MILESTONE EDITION: IRON MAN #55

	ORIG.	GOOD	FINE	N-MINT
0, reprint;1:Thanos,Drax, Starfox	2.95	0.59	1.77	2.95

MARVEL MILESTONE EDITION: TALES OF SUSPENSE #39

	ORIG.	GOOD	FINE	N-MINT
0, Nov 94, reprint; O&1:Iron Man	2.95	0.59	1.77	2.95

MARVEL MILESTONE EDITION: X-MEN #1

	ORIG.	GOOD	FINE	N-MINT
0, reprint (first series); O&1:X-Men;1:Magneto	2.95	0.59	1.77	2.95

MARVEL MILESTONE EDITION: X-MEN #28

	ORIG.	GOOD	FINE	N-MINT
0, Nov 94, reprint (first series); indicia says Marvel Milestone Edition: X-Men #1	2.95	0.59	1.77	2.95

MARVEL MILESTONE EDITION: X-MEN #9

	ORIG.	GOOD	FINE	N-MINT
0, reprint	2.95	0.59	1.77	2.95

MARVEL MOVIE PREMIERE

	ORIG.	GOOD	FINE	N-MINT
1, b&w mag	1.00	0.20	0.60	1.00

MARVEL NO-PRIZE BOOK, THE

	ORIG.	GOOD	FINE	N-MINT
1, Jan 83, mistakes	1.00	0.20	0.60	1.00

MARVEL POSTER BOOK

	ORIG.	GOOD	FINE	N-MINT
1, Jan 91, TMc		0.50	1.50	2.50

MARVEL PREMIERE

	ORIG.	GOOD	FINE	N-MINT
1, Apr 72, GK, O:Warlock	0.20	10.00	30.00	50.00
2, May 72, JK, Yellow Claw	0.20	5.00	15.00	25.00
3, Jul 72, BS, Dr. Strange	0.20	5.00	15.00	25.00
4, FB/BS, Dr. Strange	0.20	2.40	7.20	12.00
5, MP/CR, Dr. Strange	0.20	1.40	4.20	7.00
6, MP/FB, Dr. Strange	0.20	1.40	4.20	7.00
7, MP/CR, Dr. Strange	0.20	1.40	4.20	7.00
8, JSn, Dr. Strange	0.20	1.40	4.20	7.00
9, Jul 73, FB, Dr. Strange	0.20	1.40	4.20	7.00
10, NA/FB, Dr. Strange	0.20	1.40	4.20	7.00
11, NA/FB, Dr. Strange	0.20	1.40	4.20	7.00
12, NA/FB, Dr. Strange	0.20	1.40	4.20	7.00
13, Jan 74, NA/FB, Dr. Strange	0.20	1.40	4.20	7.00
14, Mar 74, NA/FB, Dr. Strange	0.20	1.40	4.20	7.00
15, May 74, GK O:Iron Fist	0.25	15.00	45.00	75.00
16, Jul 74, Iron Fist	0.25	7.00	21.00	35.00
17, Sep 74, Iron Fist	0.25	4.80	14.40	24.00
18, Oct 74, Iron Fist	0.25	4.80	14.40	24.00
19, Iron Fist	0.25	4.80	14.40	24.00
20, Jan 75, Iron Fist	0.25	4.80	14.40	24.00
21, Iron Fist	0.25	4.00	12.00	20.00
22, Iron Fist	0.25	4.00	12.00	20.00
23, PB, Iron Fist	0.25	3.00	9.00	15.00
24, PB, Iron Fist	0.25	3.00	9.00	15.00
25, JBy, Iron Fist ends	0.25	6.00	18.00	30.00
26, JK, Hercules	0.25	1.00	3.00	5.00
27, Satana	0.25	1.00	3.00	5.00
28, Legion of Monsters	0.25	2.80	8.40	14.00
29, Apr 76, JK,O:Red Raven, Thin Man, Whizzer, Miss America,Blue Diamond	0.25	0.40	1.20	2.00
30, Jun 76, JK, Liberty Legion	0.25	0.40	1.20	2.00
31, JK, 1:Wood-God	0.25	0.40	1.20	2.00
32, Oct 76, HC, Monark	0.30	0.40	1.20	2.00
33, Dec 76, HC, Monark	0.30	0.40	1.20	2.00

	ORIG.	GOOD	FINE	N-MINT
34, Feb 77, HC, Solomon Kane	0.30	0.40	1.20	2.00
35, Apr 77, 3-D Man	0.30	0.40	1.20	2.00
36, Jun 77, 3-D Man	0.30	0.40	1.20	2.00
37, Aug 77, 3-D Man	0.30	0.40	1.20	2.00
38, Oct 77, Weirdworld	0.30	0.60	1.80	3.00
39, Dec 77, Torpedo	0.35	0.30	0.90	1.50
40, Feb 78, Torpedo	0.35	0.30	0.90	1.50
41, Apr 78, Seeker 3000	0.35	0.30	0.90	1.50
42, Jun 78, Tigra	0.35	0.30	0.90	1.50
43, Aug 78, 1:Paladin	0.35	0.30	0.90	1.50
44, Oct 78, KG, Jack of Hearts	0.35	0.40	1.20	2.00
45, Dec 78, Man-Wolf	0.35	0.30	0.90	1.50
46, Feb 79, GP, War God	0.35	0.30	0.90	1.50
47, Apr 79, JBy, O:new Ant-Man	0.35	0.50	1.50	2.50
48, Jun 79, JBy, Ant-Man	0.40	0.4	1.20	2.00
49, Aug 79, Tigra	0.40	0.20	0.60	1.00
50, Oct 79, Alice Cooper	0.40	1.00	3.00	5.00
51, Dec 79, Black Panther	0.40	0.30	0.90	1.50
52, Feb 80, Black Panther	0.40	0.30	0.90	1.50
53, Apr 80, Black Panther	0.40	0.30	0.90	1.50
54, Jun 80, GD, Caleb Hammer	0.40	0.20	0.60	1.00
55, Aug 80, Wonder Man	0.40	0.60	1.80	3.00
56, Oct 80, TA/HC, Dominic Fortune	0.50	0.30	0.90	1.50
57, Dec 80, WS, Doctor Who	0.50	0.50	1.50	2.50
58, Feb 81, TA/FM, Doctor Who	0.50	0.50	1.50	2.50
59, Apr 81, Doctor Who	0.50	0.40	1.20	2.00
60, Jun 81, WS, Doctor Who	0.50	0.40	1.20	2.00
61, Aug 81, TS, Star Lord	0.50	0.30	0.90	1.50

MARVEL PRESENTS

	ORIG.	GOOD	FINE	N-MINT
1, Bloodstone	0.25	0.40	1.20	2.00
2, Bloodstone	0.25	0.20	0.60	1.00
3, Feb 76, Guardians of the Galaxy	0.25	1.00	3.00	5.00
4, Guardians of the Galaxy	0.25	0.80	2.40	4.00
5, Guardians of the Galaxy	0.25	0.80	2.40	4.00
6, Guardians of the Galaxy	0.25	0.80	2.40	4.00
7, Nov 76, Guardians of the Galaxy	0.30	0.80	2.40	4.00
8, Dec 76, Guardians of the Galaxy;reprints *Silver Surfer* #2	0.30	0.20	0.60	1.00
9, Feb 77, Guardians of the Galaxy;O:Starhawk	0.30	0.80	2.40	4.00
10, Apr 77, Guardians of the Galaxy;O:Starhawk	0.30	0.20	0.60	1.00
11, Jun 77, Guardians of the Galaxy	0.30	0.80	2.40	4.00
12, Aug 77, Guardians of the Galaxy	0.30	0.80	2.40	4.00

MARVEL PREVIEW '93

	ORIG.	GOOD	FINE	N-MINT
0	3.95	0.79	2.37	3.95

MARVEL PREVIEW (b&w mag)

	ORIG.	GOOD	FINE	N-MINT
1, Man-Gods	1.00	1.00	3.00	5.00
2, 75, Punisher	1.00	15.00	45.00	75.00
3, Blade	1.00	3.00	9.00	15.00
4, Jan 76, Star-Lord	1.00	1.20	3.60	6.00
5, Sherlock Holmes	1.00	0.80	2.40	4.00
6, Sherlock Holmes	1.00	0.80	2.40	4.00
7, Sep 76, Satanna	1.00	0.80	2.40	4.00
8, Jan 77, Morbius	1.00	2.00	6.00	10.00
9, Apr 77, Man-God	1.00	0.80	2.40	4.00
10, Jul 77, Thor	1.00	0.80	2.40	4.00
11, Oct 77, Star-Lord	1.00	0.80	2.40	4.00
12, Jan 78, horror	1.00	0.80	2.40	4.00
13, Apr 78, UFO	1.00	0.60	1.80	3.00
14, Aug 78, Star-Lord	1.00	1.00	3.00	5.00
15, Oct 78, Star-Lord	1.00	1.00	3.00	5.00
16, Mar 79, terror	1.00	0.60	1.80	3.00
17, May 79, Blackmark	1.00	0.60	1.80	3.00
18, Aug 79, Star-Lord	1.25	0.80	2.40	4.00
19, Nov 79, Kull	1.25	0.60	1.80	3.00
20, Mar 80, Bizarre Adventures	1.25	0.60	1.80	3.00
21, May 80, Moon Knight	1.25	1.00	3.00	5.00
22, Aug 80, Merlin	1.25	0.60	1.80	3.00
23, Nov 80, Bizarre Adventures	1.25	0.60	1.80	3.00
24, Feb 81, (becomes *Bizarre Adventures*) Paradox	1.25	0.60	1.80	3.00

MARVEL RIOT

	ORIG.	GOOD	FINE	N-MINT
1, Dec 95, one-shot;parodies "Age of Apocalypse"	1.95	0.39	1.17	1.95

MARVEL SAGA

	ORIG.	GOOD	FINE	N-MINT
1, Dec 85	1.00	0.30	0.90	1.50
2, Jan 86	1.00	0.30	0.90	1.50
3, Feb 86	1.00	0.30	0.90	1.50
4, Mar 86	1.00	0.30	0.90	1.50
5, Apr 86	1.00	0.30	0.90	1.50
6, May 86	1.00	0.30	0.90	1.50
7, Jun 86	1.00	0.30	0.90	1.50
8, Jul 86	1.00	0.30	0.90	1.50
9, Aug 86	1.00	0.30	0.90	1.50
10, Sep 86	1.00	0.30	0.90	1.50
11, Oct 86	1.00	0.20	0.60	1.00
12, Nov 86	1.00	0.20	0.60	1.00
13, Dec 86	1.00	0.20	0.60	1.00
14, Jan 87	1.00	0.20	0.60	1.00
15, Feb 87	1.00	0.20	0.60	1.00
16, Mar 87	1.00	0.20	0.60	1.00
17, Apr 87	1.00	0.20	0.60	1.00
18, May 87	1.00	0.20	0.60	1.00
19, Jun 87	1.00	0.20	0.60	1.00
20, Jul 87	1.00	0.20	0.60	1.00
21, Aug 87	1.00	0.20	0.60	1.00
22, Sep 87, O:Mary Jane	1.00	0.20	0.60	1.00
23, Oct 87	1.00	0.20	0.60	1.00
24, Nov 87	1.00	0.20	0.60	1.00
25, Dec 87, O:Silver Surfer	1.00	0.20	0.60	1.00

MARVEL SPECIAL EDITION (tabloid)

	ORIG.	GOOD	FINE	N-MINT
1, Star Wars	1.00	0.20	0.60	1.00
2, Star Wars	1.00	0.20	0.60	1.00
1, Spectacular Spider-Man	1.50	0.30	0.90	1.50
1, Sep 78, Close Encounters of the Third Kind	1.50	0.30	0.90	1.50
3, Star Wars	2.50	0.50	1.50	2.50

MARVEL SPECTACULAR

	ORIG.	GOOD	FINE	N-MINT
1, reprints	0.20	0.20	0.60	1.00
2, reprints	0.20	0.20	0.60	1.00
3, reprints	0.20	0.20	0.60	1.00
4, reprints	0.20	0.20	0.60	1.00
5, reprints	0.20	0.20	0.60	1.00

	ORIG.	GOOD	FINE	N-MINT
☐ 6, reprints 0.20	0.20	0.60	1.00
☐ 7, reprints 0.25	0.20	0.60	1.00
☐ 8, Jul 74, reprints *Thor* #137				
.... 0.25	0.20	0.60	1.00
☐ 9, reprints 0.25	0.20	0.60	1.00
☐ 10, reprints 0.25	0.20	0.60	1.00
☐ 11, reprints 0.25	0.20	0.60	1.00
☐ 12, reprints 0.25	0.20	0.60	1.00
☐ 13, reprints 0.25	0.20	0.60	1.00
☐ 14, reprints 0.25	0.20	0.60	1.00
☐ 15, Jun 75, reprints *Thor* #144				
.... 0.25	0.20	0.60	1.00
☐ 16, reprints 0.25	0.20	0.60	1.00
☐ 17, reprints 0.25	0.20	0.60	1.00
☐ 18, reprints 0.25	0.20	0.60	1.00
☐ 19, reprints 0.25	0.20	0.60	1.00

MARVEL SPOTLIGHT (1971-1977)

	ORIG.	GOOD	FINE	N-MINT
☐ 1, Nov 71, WW/NA, O:Red Wolf				
.... 0.15	4.00	12.00	20.00
☐ 2, 1:Werewolf 0.25	6.00	18.00	30.00
☐ 3, Werewolf 0.20	2.40	7.20	12.00
☐ 4, Werewolf 0.20	2.40	7.20	12.00
☐ 5, SD/MP, 1&O:Ghost Rider				
.... 0.20	20.00	60.00	100.00
☐ 6, Ghost Rider 0.20	11.00	33.00	55.00
☐ 7, Ghost Rider 0.20	8.40	25.20	42.00
☐ 8, Ghost Rider 0.20	8.40	25.20	42.00
☐ 9, Ghost Rider 0.20	8.40	25.20	42.00
☐ 10, Ghost Rider 0.20	8.40	25.20	42.00
☐ 11, Ghost Rider 0.20	8.40	25.20	42.00
☐ 12, SD, 1&O:Son of Satan				
.... 0.20	3.60	10.80	18.00
☐ 13, Son of Satan 0.20	2.00	6.00	10.00
☐ 14, Son of Satan 0.20	2.00	6.00	10.00
☐ 15, Son of Satan 0.25	2.00	6.00	10.00
☐ 16, Son of Satan 0.25	2.00	6.00	10.00
☐ 17, Son of Satan 0.25	2.00	6.00	10.00
☐ 18, Son of Satan 0.25	2.00	6.00	10.00
☐ 19, Son of Satan 0.25	2.00	6.00	10.00
☐ 20, Son of Satan 0.25	2.00	6.00	10.00
☐ 21, Son of Satan 0.25	2.00	6.00	10.00
☐ 22, Son of Satan 0.25	3.00	9.00	15.00
☐ 23, Son of Satan 0.25	1.20	3.60	6.00
☐ 24, Son of Satan 0.25	1.20	3.60	6.00
☐ 25, Sinbad 0.25	0.40	1.20	2.00
☐ 26, Scarecrow 0.25	0.40	1.20	2.00
☐ 27, Sub-Mariner 0.25	0.60	1.80	3.00
☐ 28, Moon Knight 0.25	2.40	7.20	12.00
☐ 29, JK, Moon Knight 0.25	2.00	6.00	10.00
☐ 30, Oct 76, JB, Warriors 3				
.... 0.30	0.20	0.60	1.00
☐ 31, Dec 76, HC/JSn, A:Nick Fury				
.... 0.30	1.40	4.20	7.00
☐ 32, Feb 77, 1:Spider-Woman				
.... 0.30	1.60	4.80	8.00
☐ 33, Apr 77, Deathlok 0.30	1.60	4.80	8.00

MARVEL SPOTLIGHT (1979-1981)

	ORIG.	GOOD	FINE	N-MINT
☐ 1, Jul 79, PB, Capt. Marvel				
.... 0.40	0.20	0.60	1.00
☐ 2, Sep 79, TA/FM(c), Capt. Marvel				
.... 0.40	0.30	0.90	1.50
☐ 3, Nov 79, PB, Capt. Marvel				
.... 0.40	0.30	0.90	1.50
☐ 4, Jan 80, FM(c), SD, Dragon Lord				
.... 0.40	0.25	0.75	1.25
☐ 5, Mar 80, FM(c), SD, Dragon Lord				
.... 0.40	0.25	0.75	1.25
☐ 6, May 80, Star Lord 0.40	0.30	0.90	1.50
☐ 7, Jul 80, Star Lord 0.40	0.30	0.90	1.50
☐ 8, Sep 80, TA/FM, Capt. Marvel				
.... 0.50	0.40	1.20	2.00

	ORIG.	GOOD	FINE	N-MINT
☐ 9, Nov 80, SD Capt. Universe				
.... 0.50	0.30	0.90	1.50
☐ 10, Jan 81, SD Capt. Universe				
.... 0.50	0.30	0.90	1.50
☐ 11, Mar 81, SD Capt. Universe				
.... 0.50	0.30	0.90	1.50

MARVEL SPRING SPECIAL

	ORIG.	GOOD	FINE	N-MINT
☐ 1, Nov 88, Elvira	0.40	1.20	2.00

MARVEL SUPER ACTION (1977-1981)

	ORIG.	GOOD	FINE	N-MINT
☐ 1, May 77, reprints *Captain America* #100				
.... 0.30	0.40	1.20	2.00
☐ 2, Jul 77 .... 0.30	0.20	0.60	1.00
☐ 3, Sep 77 .... 0.30	0.20	0.60	1.00
☐ 4, Nov 77 .... 0.35	0.20	0.60	1.00
☐ 5, Jan 78 .... 0.35	0.20	0.60	1.00
☐ 6, Mar 78 .... 0.35	0.20	0.60	1.00
☐ 7, Apr 78 .... 0.35	0.20	0.60	1.00
☐ 8, Jun 78 .... 0.35	0.20	0.60	1.00
☐ 9, Aug 78 .... 0.35	0.20	0.60	1.00
☐ 10, Oct 78 .... 0.35	0.20	0.60	1.00
☐ 11, Dec 78 .... 0.35	0.20	0.60	1.00
☐ 12, Feb 79 .... 0.35	0.20	0.60	1.00
☐ 13, Apr 79 .... 0.35	0.20	0.60	1.00
☐ 14, Dec 79 .... 0.40	0.20	0.60	1.00
☐ 15, Jan 80 .... 0.40	0.20	0.60	1.00
☐ 16, Feb 80 .... 0.40	0.20	0.60	1.00
☐ 17, Mar 80 .... 0.40	0.20	0.60	1.00
☐ 18, Apr 80 .... 0.40	0.20	0.60	1.00
☐ 19, May 80 .... 0.40	0.20	0.60	1.00
☐ 20, Jun 80 .... 0.40	0.20	0.60	1.00
☐ 21, Jul 80 .... 0.40	0.20	0.60	1.00
☐ 22, Aug 80 .... 0.40	0.20	0.60	1.00
☐ 23, Sep 80 .... 0.50	0.20	0.60	1.00
☐ 24, Oct 80 .... 0.50	0.20	0.60	1.00
☐ 25, Nov 80 .... 0.50	0.20	0.60	1.00
☐ 26, Dec 80 .... 0.50	0.20	0.60	1.00
☐ 27, Jan 81 .... 0.50	0.20	0.60	1.00
☐ 28, Feb 81 .... 0.50	0.20	0.60	1.00
☐ 29, Mar 81 .... 0.50	0.20	0.60	1.00
☐ 30, Apr 81 .... 0.50	0.20	0.60	1.00
☐ 31, May 81 .... 0.50	0.20	0.60	1.00
☐ 32, Jun 81 .... 0.50	0.20	0.60	1.00
☐ 33, Jul 81 .... 0.50	0.20	0.60	1.00
☐ 34, Aug 81 .... 0.50	0.20	0.60	1.00
☐ 35, Sep 81 .... 0.50	0.20	0.60	1.00
☐ 36, Oct 81 .... 0.50	0.20	0.60	1.00
☐ 37, Nov 81 .... 0.50	0.20	0.60	1.00

MARVEL SUPER SPECIAL
(was Marvel Comics Super Special)
(magazine size)

	ORIG.	GOOD	FINE	N-MINT
☐ 5, Dec 78, Jaws 2 ....1.50	0.30	0.90	1.50
☐ 6, Dec 78, Kiss 1.50	0.30	0.90	1.50
☐ 8, Jan 79, Battlestar Galactica, tabloid				
.... 1.50	0.30	0.90	1.50
☐ 9, Feb 79, Conan 1.50	0.30	0.90	1.50
☐ 10, Jun 79, Starlord 1.50	0.30	0.90	1.50
☐ 11, Sep 79, Warriors of Shadow Realm				
.... 1.50	0.30	0.90	1.50
☐ 12, Nov 79, Warriors of Shadow Realm				
.... 1.50	0.30	0.90	1.50
☐ 13, Jan 80, Warriors of Shadow Realm				
.... 1.50	0.30	0.90	1.50
☐ 14, Feb 80, Meteor 1.50	0.30	0.90	1.50
☐ 15, Mar 80, Star Trek: Motion Picture				
.... 1.50	0.30	0.90	1.50
☐ 16, Aug 80, Empire Strikes Back				
.... 2.00	0.40	1.20	2.00
☐ 17, Nov 80, Xanadu 2.00	0.40	1.20	2.00
☐ 18, Sep 81, Raiders of the Lost Ark				
.... 2.50	0.50	1.50	2.50

	ORIG.	GOOD	FINE	N-MINT
❏ 19, Oct 81, For Your Eyes Only				
..............................2.50		0.50	1.50	2.50
❏ 20, Oct 81, Dragonslayer 2.50		0.50	1.50	2.50
❏ 21, Aug 82, Conan movie				
..............................2.50		0.50	1.50	2.50
❏ 22, Sep 82, Bladerunner, comic size				
..............................2.50		0.50	1.50	2.50
❏ 23, Sep 82, Annie..........2.50		0.50	1.50	2.50
❏ 24, Mar 83, Dark Crystal				
..............................2.50		0.50	1.50	2.50
❏ 25, Aug 83, Rock & Rule, comic size				
..............................2.50		0.50	1.50	2.50
❏ 26, Sep 83, Octopussy...2.50		0.50	1.50	2.50
❏ 27, Sep 83, Return of the Jedi				
..............................2.50		0.50	1.50	2.50
❏ 28, Oct 83, Krull.............2.50		0.50	1.50	2.50
❏ 29, Jul 84, Tarzan of the Apes				
..............................2.00		0.40	1.20	2.00
❏ 30, Aug 84, Indiana Jones Temple of Doom				
..............................2.50		0.50	1.50	2.50
❏ 31, Sep 84, The Last Starfighter				
..............................2.50		0.50	1.50	2.50
❏ 32, Oct 84, Muppets Take Manhattan				
..............................2.50		0.50	1.50	2.50
❏ 33, Nov 84, Buckaroo Banzai				
..............................2.50		0.50	1.50	2.50
❏ 34, Nov 84, Sheena........2.50		0.50	1.50	2.50
❏ 35, Dec 84, Conan the Destroyer				
..............................2.50		0.50	1.50	2.50
❏ 36, Apr 85, Dune............2.50		0.50	1.50	2.50
❏ 37, Apr 85, 2010 ....2.00		0.40	1.20	2.00
❏ 38, Nov 85, Red Sonja ...2.00		0.40	1.20	2.00
❏ 39, Mar 85, Santa Claus: the Movie				
..............................2.50		0.50	1.50	2.50
❏ 40, Oct 86, Labyrinth 2.50		0.50	1.50	2.50
❏ 41, Nov 86, Howard the Duck				
..............................2.50		0.50	1.50	2.50

MARVEL SUPER-HEROES (1966)

	ORIG.	GOOD	FINE	N-MINT
❏ 1, reprints 0.25				

MARVEL SUPER-HEROES (1967-1982)
(was Fantasy Masterpieces)

	ORIG.	GOOD	FINE	N-MINT
❏ 12, 1:Captain Marvel, reprints				
..............................0.25		13.00	39.00	65.00
❏ 13, reprints 0.25		8.00	24.00	40.00
❏ 14 ....0.25		18.00	54.00	90.00
❏ 15 ....0.25		2.40	7.20	12.00
❏ 16 ....0.25		2.00	6.00	10.00
❏ 17 ....0.25		2.00	6.00	10.00
❏ 18 ....0.25		4.40	13.20	22.00
❏ 19 ....0.25		2.00	6.00	10.00
❏ 20 ....0.25		4.80	14.40	24.00
❏ 21 ....0.25		0.60	1.80	3.00
❏ 22 ....0.25		0.60	1.80	3.00
❏ 23 ....0.25		0.60	1.80	3.00
❏ 24, Jan 70 ....0.25		0.60	1.80	3.00
❏ 25, Mar 70 ....0.25		0.60	1.80	3.00
❏ 26 ....0.25		0.60	1.80	3.00
❏ 27 ....0.25		0.60	1.80	3.00
❏ 28 ....0.25		0.60	1.80	3.00
❏ 29 ....0.25		0.60	1.80	3.00
❏ 30 ....0.25		0.60	1.80	3.00
❏ 31, Nov 71 ....0.25		0.40	1.20	2.00
❏ 32 ....0.20		0.40	1.20	2.00
❏ 33 ....0.20		0.40	1.20	2.00
❏ 34 ....0.20		0.40	1.20	2.00
❏ 35 ....0.20		0.40	1.20	2.00
❏ 36 ....0.20		0.40	1.20	2.00
❏ 37 ....0.20		0.40	1.20	2.00
❏ 38 ....0.20		0.40	1.20	2.00
❏ 39 ....0.20		0.40	1.20	2.00
❏ 40 ....0.20		0.40	1.20	2.00

	ORIG.	GOOD	FINE	N-MINT
❏ 41 ....0.20		0.40	1.20	2.00
❏ 42 ....0.20		0.40	1.20	2.00
❏ 43 ....0.25		0.20	0.60	1.00
❏ 44 ....0.25		0.20	0.60	1.00
❏ 45 ....0.25		0.20	0.60	1.00
❏ 46 ....0.25		0.20	0.60	1.00
❏ 47 ....0.25		0.20	0.60	1.00
❏ 48 ....0.25		0.20	0.60	1.00
❏ 49 ....0.25		0.20	0.60	1.00
❏ 50 ....0.25		0.20	0.60	1.00
❏ 51 ....0.25		0.20	0.60	1.00
❏ 52 ....0.25		0.20	0.60	1.00
❏ 53 ....0.25		0.20	0.60	1.00
❏ 54 ....0.25		0.20	0.60	1.00
❏ 55, Jan 76, reprints *Tales to Astonish* #101				
..............................0.25		0.20	0.60	1.00
❏ 56 ....0.25		0.20	0.60	1.00
❏ 57 ....0.25		0.20	0.60	1.00
❏ 58 ....0.25		0.20	0.60	1.00
❏ 59 ....0.30		0.20	0.60	1.00
❏ 60 ....0.30		0.20	0.60	1.00
❏ 61 ....0.30		0.20	0.60	1.00
❏ 62 ....0.30		0.20	0.60	1.00
❏ 63, Mar 77, reprints *Incredible Hulk* #109				
..............................0.30		0.20	0.60	1.00
❏ 64 ....0.30		0.20	0.60	1.00
❏ 65 ....0.30		0.20	0.60	1.00
❏ 66, Sep 77, reprints *Incredible Hulk* #112				
..............................0.30		0.20	0.60	1.00
❏ 67, Nov 77, reprints *Incredible Hulk* #113				
..............................0.30		0.20	0.60	1.00
❏ 68 ....0.30		0.20	0.60	1.00
❏ 69 ....0.30		0.20	0.60	1.00
❏ 70 ....0.30		0.20	0.60	1.00
❏ 71, May 78, reprints *Incredible Hulk* #117				
..............................0.30		0.20	0.60	1.00
❏ 72 ....0.35		0.20	0.60	1.00
❏ 73, Aug 78, reprints *Incredible Hulk* #120				
..............................0.35		0.20	0.60	1.00
❏ 74 ....0.35		0.20	0.60	1.00
❏ 75 ....0.35		0.20	0.60	1.00
❏ 76 ....0.35		0.20	0.60	1.00
❏ 77 ....0.35		0.20	0.60	1.00
❏ 78 ....0.35		0.20	0.60	1.00
❏ 79 ....0.35		0.20	0.60	1.00
❏ 80 ....0.35		0.20	0.60	1.00
❏ 81 ....0.35		0.20	0.60	1.00
❏ 82 ....0.35		0.20	0.60	1.00
❏ 83 ....0.35		0.20	0.60	1.00
❏ 84, Oct 79, reprints *Incredible Hulk* #132				
..............................0.35		0.20	0.60	1.00
❏ 85 ....0.35		0.20	0.60	1.00
❏ 86, Jan 80, reprints *Incredible Hulk* #134				
..............................0.35		0.20	0.60	1.00
❏ 87 ....0.35		0.20	0.60	1.00
❏ 88 ....0.35		0.20	0.60	1.00
❏ 89 ....0.35		0.20	0.60	1.00
❏ 90, Aug 80, reprints *Avengers* #88; Harlan Ellison story				
..............................0.35		0.20	0.60	1.00
❏ 91, Sep 80, reprints *Incredible Hulk* #140; "Beast That Shouted Love at the Heart of the Atom" by Harlan Ellison..............0.35		0.20	0.60	1.00
❏ 92 ....0.40		0.20	0.60	1.00
❏ 93 ....0.40		0.20	0.60	1.00
❏ 94 ....0.40		0.20	0.60	1.00
❏ 95 ....0.40		0.20	0.60	1.00
❏ 96 ....0.40		0.20	0.60	1.00
❏ 97 ....0.40		0.20	0.60	1.00
❏ 98 ....0.40		0.20	0.60	1.00
❏ 99 ....0.40		0.20	0.60	1.00
❏ 100 ....0.40		0.20	0.60	1.00
❏ 101 ....0.40		0.20	0.60	1.00

	ORIG.	GOOD	FINE	N-MINT
❏ 102	0.40	0.20	0.60	1.00
❏ 103, Nov 81, reprints *Incredible Hulk* #155				
	0.40	0.20	0.60	1.00
❏ 104	0.40	0.20	0.60	1.00
❏ 105	0.40	0.20	0.60	1.00

MARVEL SUPER-HEROES (1990-)

	ORIG.	GOOD	FINE	N-MINT
❏ 1, 80 pages	2.95	0.59	1.77	2.95
❏ 2, 80 pages	2.95	0.59	1.77	2.95
❏ 3, 80 pages	2.95	0.59	1.77	2.95
❏ 4, 80 pages	2.95	0.59	1.77	2.95
❏ 5, 80 pages	2.95	0.59	1.77	2.95
❏ 6, AAd(c)	2.25	0.45	1.35	2.25
❏ 7	2.25	0.45	1.35	2.25
❏ 8	2.25	0.45	1.35	2.25
❏ 9, Apr 92, A:Cupid	2.50	0.50	1.50	2.50
❏ 10	2.50	0.50	1.50	2.50
❏ 11, Ghost Rider	2.50	0.50	1.50	2.50
❏ 12	2.50	0.50	1.50	2.50
❏ 13, Iron Man	2.75	0.55	1.65	2.75
❏ 14	2.75	0.55	1.65	2.75
❏ 15	2.75	0.55	1.65	2.75

MARVEL SUPER-HEROES CONTEST OF CHAMPIONS (mini-series)

	ORIG.	GOOD	FINE	N-MINT
❏ 1, Jun 82, Alpha Flight	0.25	2.00	6.00	10.00
❏ 2, Jul 82, JR2;X-Men	0.25	1.60	4.80	8.00
❏ 3, Aug 82, JR2;X-Men	0.25	2.00	6.00	10.00

MARVEL SUPER-HEROES MEGAZINE

	ORIG.	GOOD	FINE	N-MINT
❏ 1, Oct 94	2.95	0.59	1.77	2.95
❏ 2, Nov 94	2.95	0.59	1.77	2.95
❏ 3, Dec 94	2.95	0.59	1.77	2.95
❏ 4, Jan 95	2.95	0.59	1.77	2.95
❏ 5, Feb 95	2.95	0.59	1.77	2.95
❏ 6, Mar 95, final issue	2.95	0.59	1.77	2.95

MARVEL SUPER-HEROES SECRET WARS (mini-series)

	ORIG.	GOOD	FINE	N-MINT
❏ 1, MZ, X-Men, Avengers, FF in all				
	0.75	0.80	2.40	4.00
❏ 2, MZ	0.75	0.60	1.80	3.00
❏ 3, MZ	0.75	0.60	1.80	3.00
❏ 4, MZ	0.75	0.60	1.80	3.00
❏ 5, MZ	0.75	0.60	1.80	3.00
❏ 6, MZ	0.75	0.50	1.50	2.50
❏ 7, MZ	0.75	0.50	1.50	2.50
❏ 8, MZ	0.75	0.50	1.50	2.50
❏ 9, MZ	0.75	0.50	1.50	2.50
❏ 10, MZ	0.75	0.50	1.50	2.50
❏ 11, MZ	0.75	0.50	1.50	2.50
❏ 12, MZ	1.00	0.50	1.50	2.50

MARVEL SWIMSUIT SPECIAL

	ORIG.	GOOD	FINE	N-MINT
❏ 1	3.95	0.79	2.37	3.95
❏ 2, 93	4.50	0.90	2.70	4.50
❏ 3, 94	4.50	0.90	2.70	4.50
❏ 4, 95	4.95	0.99	2.97	4.95

MARVEL TAILS

	ORIG.	GOOD	FINE	N-MINT
❏ 1, Nov 83, 1:Peter Porker				
	0.60	0.30	0.90	1.50

MARVEL TALES (reprints)

	ORIG.	GOOD	FINE	N-MINT
❏ 1, Mar 66, O:SpM	0.25	45.00	135.00	225.00
❏ 2, May 66, O:X-Men	0.25	15.00	45.00	75.00
❏ 3, Jul 66, 1:Torch	0.25	8.00	24.00	40.00
❏ 4, Sep 66	0.25	3.60	10.80	18.00
❏ 5, Nov 66	0.25	3.60	10.80	18.00
❏ 6, Jan 67	0.25	3.60	10.80	18.00
❏ 7, Mar 67	0.25	3.60	10.80	18.00
❏ 8, May 67	0.25	3.60	10.80	18.00
❏ 9, Jul 67	0.25	3.60	10.80	18.00
❏ 10, Sep 67	0.25	3.60	10.80	18.00
❏ 11, Nov 67	0.25	3.60	10.80	18.00
❏ 12, Jan 68	0.25	3.60	10.80	18.00
❏ 13, Mar 68, Marvel Boy	0.25	2.40	7.20	12.00

	ORIG.	GOOD	FINE	N-MINT
❏ 14, May 68	0.25	2.00	6.00	10.00
❏ 15, Jul 68	0.25	2.00	6.00	10.00
❏ 16, Sep 68	0.25	1.40	4.20	7.00
❏ 17, Nov 68	0.25	1.40	4.20	7.00
❏ 18, Jan 69	0.25	1.40	4.20	7.00
❏ 19, Mar 69	0.25	1.40	4.20	7.00
❏ 20, May 69	0.25	1.40	4.20	7.00
❏ 21, Jul 69	0.25	1.20	3.60	6.00
❏ 22, Sep 69	0.25	1.20	3.60	6.00
❏ 23, Nov 69	0.25	1.20	3.60	6.00
❏ 24, Jan 70	0.25	1.20	3.60	6.00
❏ 25, Mar 70	0.25	1.20	3.60	6.00
❏ 26	0.25	1.20	3.60	6.00
❏ 27	0.25	1.20	3.60	6.00
❏ 28, Oct 70	0.25	1.20	3.60	6.00
❏ 29, Jan 71, O:Green Goblin				
	0.25	1.20	3.60	6.00
❏ 30	0.25	1.20	3.60	6.00
❏ 31, Jul 71	0.25	1.20	3.60	6.00
❏ 32, Nov 71	0.25	1.20	3.60	6.00
❏ 33, Feb 72	0.25	1.20	3.60	6.00
❏ 34	0.20	1.20	3.60	6.00
❏ 35	0.20	1.20	3.60	6.00
❏ 36, Aug 72	0.20	1.20	3.60	6.00
❏ 37	0.20	1.20	3.60	6.00
❏ 38, Oct 72	0.20	1.20	3.60	6.00
❏ 39, Nov 72	0.20	1.20	3.60	6.00
❏ 40	0.20	1.20	3.60	6.00
❏ 41, Feb 73	0.20	1.20	3.60	6.00
❏ 42	0.20	1.20	3.60	6.00
❏ 43, Jun 73	0.20	1.20	3.60	6.00
❏ 44, Aug 73	0.20	1.20	3.60	6.00
❏ 45	0.20	1.20	3.60	6.00
❏ 46	0.20	1.20	3.60	6.00
❏ 47	0.20	1.20	3.60	6.00
❏ 48	0.20	1.20	3.60	6.00
❏ 49	0.20	1.20	3.60	6.00
❏ 50	0.20	1.20	3.60	6.00
❏ 51	0.25	1.00	3.00	5.00
❏ 52, Aug 74	0.25	1.00	3.00	5.00
❏ 53, Sep 74	0.25	1.00	3.00	5.00
❏ 54, Oct 74	0.25	1.00	3.00	5.00
❏ 55, Nov 74	0.25	1.00	3.00	5.00
❏ 56	0.25	1.00	3.00	5.00
❏ 57	0.25	1.00	3.00	5.00
❏ 58	0.25	1.00	3.00	5.00
❏ 59	0.25	1.00	3.00	5.00
❏ 60	0.25	1.00	3.00	5.00
❏ 61, Sep 75	0.25	1.00	3.00	5.00
❏ 62	0.25	1.00	3.00	5.00
❏ 63	0.25	1.00	3.00	5.00
❏ 64	0.25	1.00	3.00	5.00
❏ 65	0.25	1.00	3.00	5.00
❏ 66	0.25	1.00	3.00	5.00
❏ 67	0.25	1.00	3.00	5.00
❏ 68, Jun 76	0.25	1.00	3.00	5.00
❏ 69, Jul 76	0.25	1.00	3.00	5.00
❏ 70, Aug 76	0.25	1.00	3.00	5.00
❏ 71, Sep 76	0.30	1.00	3.00	5.00
❏ 72, Oct 76	0.30	1.00	3.00	5.00
❏ 73, Nov 76	0.30	1.00	3.00	5.00
❏ 74, Dec 76	0.30	1.00	3.00	5.00
❏ 75, Jan 77	0.30	1.00	3.00	5.00
❏ 76, Feb 77	0.30	1.00	3.00	5.00
❏ 77, Mar 77	0.30	1.00	3.00	5.00
❏ 78, Apr 77	0.30	1.00	3.00	5.00
❏ 79, May 77	0.30	1.00	3.00	5.00
❏ 80, Jun 77	0.30	1.00	3.00	5.00
❏ 81, Jul 77	0.30	1.00	3.00	5.00
❏ 82, Aug 77	0.30	1.00	3.00	5.00
❏ 83, Sep 77	0.30	1.00	3.00	5.00
❏ 84, Oct 77	0.30	1.00	3.00	5.00

	ORIG.	GOOD	FINE	N-MINT
85, Nov 77	0.30	1.00	3.00	5.00
86, Dec 77	0.35	1.00	3.00	5.00
87, Jan 78	0.35	1.00	3.00	5.00
88, Feb 78	0.35	1.00	3.00	5.00
89, Mar 78	0.35	1.00	3.00	5.00
90, Apr 78	0.35	1.00	3.00	5.00
91, May 78	0.35	1.00	3.00	5.00
92, Jun 78	0.35	1.00	3.00	5.00
93, Jul 78	0.35	1.00	3.00	5.00
94, Aug 78	0.35	1.00	3.00	5.00
95, Sep 78	0.35	1.00	3.00	5.00
96, Oct 78	0.35	1.00	3.00	5.00
97, Nov 78	0.35	1.00	3.00	5.00
98, Dec 78, D:Gwen Stacy	0.35	1.20	3.60	6.00
99, Jan 79, D:Green Goblin	0.35	1.20	3.60	6.00
100, Feb 79, TA/SD/GK/MN	0.60	1.20	3.60	6.00
101, Mar 79	0.35	0.40	1.20	2.00
102, Apr 79	0.35	0.40	1.20	2.00
103, May 79	0.35	0.40	1.20	2.00
104, Jun 79	0.35	0.40	1.20	2.00
105, Jul 79	0.35	0.40	1.20	2.00
106, Aug 79, rep. 1:Punisher	0.40	1.00	3.00	5.00
107, Sep 79	0.40	0.40	1.20	2.00
108, Oct 79	0.40	0.40	1.20	2.00
109, Nov 79	0.40	0.40	1.20	2.00
110, Dec 79	0.40	0.40	1.20	2.00
111, Jan 80, Punisher	0.40	1.00	3.00	5.00
112, Feb 80, Punisher	0.40	1.00	3.00	5.00
113, Mar 80	0.40	0.40	1.20	2.00
114, Apr 80	0.40	0.40	1.20	2.00
115, May 80	0.40	0.40	1.20	2.00
116, Jun 80	0.40	0.40	1.20	2.00
117, Jul 80	0.40	0.40	1.20	2.00
118, Aug 80	0.40	0.40	1.20	2.00
119, Sep 80	0.50	0.40	1.20	2.00
120, Oct 80	0.40	0.40	1.20	2.00
121, Nov 80	0.50	0.40	1.20	2.00
122, Dec 80	0.50	0.40	1.20	2.00
123, Jan 81	0.50	0.40	1.20	2.00
124, Feb 81	0.50	0.40	1.20	2.00
125, Mar 81	0.50	0.40	1.20	2.00
126, Apr 81	0.50	0.40	1.20	2.00
127, May 81	0.50	0.40	1.20	2.00
128, Jun 81	0.50	0.40	1.20	2.00
129, Jul 81	0.50	0.40	1.20	2.00
130, Aug 81	0.50	0.40	1.20	2.00
131, Sep 81	0.50	0.40	1.20	2.00
132, Oct 81	0.50	0.40	1.20	2.00
133, Nov 81	0.50	0.40	1.20	2.00
134, Dec 81	0.50	0.40	1.20	2.00
135, Jan 82	0.60	0.40	1.20	2.00
136, Feb 82	0.50	0.40	1.20	2.00
137, Mar 82, 1&O:SpM	0.60	0.80	2.40	4.00
138, Apr 82, *Amazing Spider-Man* #1	0.60	0.80	2.40	4.00
139, May 82		0.40	1.20	2.00
140, Jun 82		0.40	1.20	2.00
141, Jul 82	0.60	0.40	1.20	2.00
142, Aug 82	0.60	0.40	1.20	2.00
143, Sep 82	0.60	0.40	1.20	2.00
144, Oct 82	0.60	0.40	1.20	2.00
145, Nov 82	0.60	0.40	1.20	2.00
146, Dec 82	0.60	0.40	1.20	2.00
147, Jan 83	0.60	0.40	1.20	2.00
148, Feb 83	0.60	0.40	1.20	2.00
149, Mar 83	0.60	0.40	1.20	2.00
150, Apr 83	0.60	0.40	1.20	2.00
151, May 83	0.60	0.40	1.20	2.00

	ORIG.	GOOD	FINE	N-MINT
152, Jun 83	0.60	0.40	1.20	2.00
153, Jul 83	0.60	0.40	1.20	2.00
154, Aug 83	0.60	0.40	1.20	2.00
155, Sep 83	0.60	0.40	1.20	2.00
156, Oct 83	0.60	0.40	1.20	2.00
157, Nov 83	0.60	0.40	1.20	2.00
158, Dec 83	0.60	0.40	1.20	2.00
159, Jan 84	0.60	0.40	1.20	2.00
160, Feb 84	0.60	0.40	1.20	2.00
161, Mar 84	0.60	0.40	1.20	2.00
162, Apr 84	0.60	0.40	1.20	2.00
163, May 84	0.60	0.40	1.20	2.00
164, Jun 84	0.60	0.40	1.20	2.00
165, Jul 84	0.60	0.40	1.20	2.00
166, Aug 84	0.60	0.40	1.20	2.00
167, Sep 84	0.60	0.40	1.20	2.00
168, Oct 84	0.60	0.40	1.20	2.00
169, Nov 84	0.60	0.40	1.20	2.00
170, Dec 84	0.60	0.40	1.20	2.00
171, Jan 85	0.60	0.40	1.20	2.00
172, Feb 85	0.60	0.40	1.20	2.00
173, Mar 85	0.60	0.40	1.20	2.00
174, Apr 85	0.65	0.40	1.20	2.00
175, May 85	0.65	0.40	1.20	2.00
176, Jun 85	0.65	0.40	1.20	2.00
177, Jul 85	0.65	0.40	1.20	2.00
178, Aug 85	0.65	0.40	1.20	2.00
179, Sep 85	0.65	0.40	1.20	2.00
180, Oct 85	0.65	0.40	1.20	2.00
181, Nov 85	0.65	0.40	1.20	2.00
182, Dec 85	0.65	0.40	1.20	2.00
183, Jan 86	0.65	0.40	1.20	2.00
184, Feb 86	0.75	0.40	1.20	2.00
185, Mar 86	0.75	0.40	1.20	2.00
186, Apr 86	0.75	0.40	1.20	2.00
187, May 86	0.75	0.40	1.20	2.00
188, Jun 86	0.75	0.40	1.20	2.00
189, Jul 86	0.75	0.40	1.20	2.00
190, Aug 86	0.75	0.40	1.20	2.00
191, Sep 86	0.75	0.40	1.20	2.00
192, Oct 86	0.75	0.40	1.20	2.00
193, Nov 86	0.75	0.40	1.20	2.00
194, Dec 86	0.75	0.40	1.20	2.00
195, Jan 87	0.75	0.40	1.20	2.00
196, Feb 87	0.75	0.40	1.20	2.00
197, Mar 87	0.75	0.40	1.20	2.00
198, Apr 87	0.75	0.40	1.20	2.00
199, May 87	0.75	0.40	1.20	2.00
200, Jun 87, TMc(c)	1.25	0.60	1.80	3.00
201, Jul 87, TMc(c)	0.75	0.40	1.20	2.00
202, Aug 87, TMc(c)	0.75	0.40	1.20	2.00
203, Sep 87, TMc(c)	0.75	0.40	1.20	2.00
204, Oct 87, TMc(c)	0.75	0.40	1.20	2.00
205, Nov 87, TMc(c)	0.75	0.40	1.20	2.00
206, Dec 87, TMc(c)	0.75	0.40	1.20	2.00
207, Jan 88, TMc(c)	0.75	0.40	1.20	2.00
208, Feb 88, TMc(c)	0.75	0.40	1.20	2.00
209, Mar 88, TMc(c) 1:Punisher	0.75	0.40	1.20	2.00
210, Apr 88, TMc(c) A:Punisher	0.75	0.40	1.20	2.00
211, May 88, TMc(c) A:Punisher	0.75	0.40	1.20	2.00
212, Jun 88, TMc(c) A:Punisher	0.75	0.40	1.20	2.00
213, Jul 88, TMc(c) A:Punisher	0.75	0.40	1.20	2.00
214, Aug 88, TMc(c) A:Punisher	0.75	0.40	1.20	2.00
215, Sep 88, TMc(c) A:Punisher	0.75	0.40	1.20	2.00

	ORIG.	GOOD	FINE	N-MINT
❑ 216, Oct 88, TMc(c) A:Punisher				
.................0.75		0.40	1.20	2.00
❑ 217, Nov 88, TMc(c) A:Punisher				
.................0.75		0.40	1.20	2.00
❑ 218, Dec 88, TMc(c) A:Punisher				
.................0.75		0.40	1.20	2.00
❑ 219, Jan 89, TMc(c) A:Punisher				
.................0.75		0.40	1.20	2.00
❑ 220, Feb 89, TMc(c) A:Punisher				
.................0.75		0.40	1.20	2.00
❑ 221, Mar 89, TMc(c) A:Punisher				
.................0.75		0.40	1.20	2.00
❑ 222, Apr 89, TMc(c) A:Punisher				
.................0.75		0.40	1.20	2.00
❑ 223, May 89, TMc(c)......	0.75	0.40	1.20	2.00
❑ 224, Jun 89, TMc(c)	0.75	0.40	1.20	2.00
❑ 225, Jul 89, TMc(c)........	0.75	0.40	1.20	2.00
❑ 226, Aug 89, TMc(c)	0.75	0.40	1.20	2.00
❑ 227, Sep 89, TMc(c)	1.00	0.40	1.20	2.00
❑ 228, Oct 89, TMc(c)	1.00	0.40	1.20	2.00
❑ 229, Nov 89, TMc(c)	1.00	0.40	1.20	2.00
❑ 230, Nov 89, TMc(c)	1.00	0.40	1.20	2.00
❑ 231, Dec 89, TMc(c)	1.00	0.40	1.20	2.00
❑ 232, Dec 89, TMc(c)	1.00	0.40	1.20	2.00
❑ 233, Jan 90, TMc(c).......	1.00	0.40	1.20	2.00
❑ 234, Feb 90, TMc(c).......	1.00	0.40	1.20	2.00
❑ 235, Mar 90, TMc(c).......	1.00	0.40	1.20	2.00
❑ 236, Apr 90, TMc(c).......	1.00	0.40	1.20	2.00
❑ 237, May 90, TMc(c)......	1.00	0.40	1.20	2.00
❑ 238, Jun 90, TMc(c)	1.00	0.40	1.20	2.00
❑ 239, Jul 90, TMc(c).......	1.00	0.40	1.20	2.00
❑ 240, Aug 90	1.00	0.20	0.60	1.00
❑ 241, Sep 90....................	1.00	0.20	0.60	1.00
❑ 242, Oct 90	1.00	0.20	0.60	1.00
❑ 243, Nov 90	1.00	0.20	0.60	1.00
❑ 244, Dec 90....................	1.00	0.20	0.60	1.00
❑ 245, Jan 91	1.00	0.20	0.60	1.00
❑ 246, Feb 91	1.00	0.20	0.60	1.00
❑ 247, Mar 91	1.00	0.20	0.60	1.00
❑ 248, Apr 91.....................	1.00	0.20	0.60	1.00
❑ 249, May 91	1.00	0.20	0.60	1.00
❑ 250, Jun 91.....................	1.50	0.30	0.90	1.50
❑ 251, Jul 91	1.00	0.20	0.60	1.00
❑ 252, Aug 91	1.00	0.20	0.60	1.00
❑ 253, Sep 91, Moebius(c)	1.50	0.30	0.90	1.50
❑ 254, Oct 91	1.00	0.20	0.60	1.00
❑ 255, Nov 91	1.00	0.20	0.60	1.00
❑ 256, Dec 91	1.00	0.20	0.60	1.00
❑ 257	1.00	0.20	0.60	1.00
❑ 258	1.25	0.25	0.75	1.25
❑ 259	1.25	0.25	0.75	1.25
❑ 260	1.25	0.25	0.75	1.25
❑ 261	1.25	0.25	0.75	1.25
❑ 262, X-Men	1.25	0.25	0.75	1.25
❑ 263	1.25	0.25	0.75	1.25
❑ 264, Aug 92, *Amazing Spider-Man Annual #5*				
.................1.25		0.25	0.75	1.25
❑ 265, Sep 92, *Amazing Spider-Man Annual #5*				
.................1.25		0.25	0.75	1.25
❑ 266	1.25	0.25	0.75	1.25
❑ 267	1.25	0.25	0.75	1.25
❑ 268	1.25	0.25	0.75	1.25
❑ 269	1.25	0.25	0.75	1.25
❑ 270	1.25	0.25	0.75	1.25
❑ 271	1.25	0.25	0.75	1.25
❑ 272	1.25	0.25	0.75	1.25
❑ 273	1.25	0.25	0.75	1.25
❑ 274	1.25	0.25	0.75	1.25
❑ 275	1.25	0.25	0.75	1.25
❑ 276	1.25	0.25	0.75	1.25
❑ 277	1.25	0.25	0.75	1.25
❑ 278	1.25	0.25	0.75	1.25

	ORIG.	GOOD	FINE	N-MINT
❑ 279	1.25	0.25	0.75	1.25
❑ 280	1.25	0.25	0.75	1.25
❑ 281	1.25	0.25	0.75	1.25
❑ 282	1.25	0.25	0.75	1.25
❑ 283	1.25	0.25	0.75	1.25
❑ 284, Aug 94	1.25	0.25	0.75	1.25
❑ 285, May 94...................	1.25	0.25	0.75	1.25
❑ 286, Jun 94, reprint, SpM				
.................1.50		0.30	0.90	1.50
❑ 286, Jun 94, reprint, poster,print				
.................2.95		0.59	1.77	2.95
❑ 287, Jul 94....................	1.25	0.25	0.75	1.25
❑ 288, Aug 94	1.25	0.25	0.75	1.25
❑ 289, Sep 94	1.25	0.25	0.75	1.25
❑ 290, Oct 94.....................	1.50	0.30	0.90	1.50
❑ 291, Nov 94, *Amazing Spider-Man* #283; final issue				
.................1.50		0.30	0.90	1.50

MARVEL TEAM-UP

	ORIG.	GOOD	FINE	N-MINT
❑ 1, Mar 72, GK(c);RA; SpM/Torch;V:Sandman				
.................0.20		10.00	30.00	50.00
❑ 2, May 72, GK(c);RA; SpM/Torch				
.................0.20		6.00	18.00	30.00
❑ 3, Jul 72, GK(c);RA; SpM/Torch				
.................0.20		6.00	18.00	30.00
❑ 4, Sep 72, GK; SpM/X-Men				
.................0.20		8.00	24.00	40.00
❑ 5, Nov 72, GK; SpM/Vision				
.................0.20		1.80	5.40	9.00
❑ 6, Jan 73, GK;SpM/Thing				
.................0.20		1.80	5.40	9.00
❑ 7, GK(c);RA;SpM/Thor....	0.20	1.80	5.40	9.00
❑ 8, Apr 73, JM;SpM/Cat ...	0.20	1.80	5.40	9.00
❑ 9, May 73, JR(c);RA; SpM/Iron Man				
.................0.20		1.80	5.40	9.00
❑ 10, Jun 73, JR(c);JM; SpM/Torch				
.................0.20		1.80	5.40	9.00
❑ 11, Jul 73, JR(c);JM; SpM/Inhumans				
.................0.20		1.20	3.60	6.00
❑ 12, Aug 73, GK(c); RA;SpM/Werewolf				
.................0.20		1.20	3.60	6.00
❑ 13, Sep 73, GK; SpM/Capt. America				
.................0.20		1.20	3.60	6.00
❑ 14, Oct 73, GK; SpM/Sub-Mariner				
.................0.20		1.20	3.60	6.00
❑ 15, Nov 73, GK(c);RA; SpM/Ghost Rider				
.................0.20		2.40	7.20	12.00
❑ 16, Dec 73, GK;SpM/Capt. Marvel;O&1:Basilisk				
.................0.20		2.00	6.00	10.00
❑ 17, Jan 74, GK;SpM/Mr. Fantastic;V:Mole Man, Basilisk				
.................0.20		2.00	6.00	10.00
❑ 18, Feb 74, GK; Torch/Hulk				
.................0.20		2.00	6.00	10.00
❑ 19, Mar 74, GK; SpM/Ka-Zar				
.................0.20		2.00	6.00	10.00
❑ 20, Apr 74, GK(c);SB; SpM/Black Panther				
.................0.20		2.00	6.00	10.00
❑ 21, May 74, GK(c);SB; SpM/Dr. Strange				
.................0.25		1.00	3.00	5.00
❑ 22, Jun 74, JR(c);SB; SpM/Hawkeye				
.................0.25		1.00	3.00	5.00
❑ 23, Jul 74, GK; Torch/Iceman, A:X-Men				
.................0.25		1.80	5.40	9.00
❑ 24, Aug 74, GK(c);JM; SpM/Brother Voodoo				
.................0.25		1.00	3.00	5.00
❑ 25, Sep 74, GK(c);JM; SpM/Daredevil				
.................0.25		1.00	3.00	5.00
❑ 26, Oct 74, GK(c);JM; Torch/Thor				
.................0.25		1.00	3.00	5.00
❑ 27, Nov 74, JSn(c);JM; SpM/Hulk				
.................0.25		1.00	3.00	5.00

	ORIG.	GOOD	FINE	N-MINT

☐ 28, Dec 74, GK(c);JM; SpM/Hercules
.... 0.25 1.00 3.00 5.00

☐ 29, Jan 75, JR(c);JM; Torch/Iron Man
.... 0.25 1.00 3.00 5.00

☐ 30, Feb 75, GK(c); JM;SpM/Falcon
.... 0.25 1.00 3.00 5.00

☐ 31, Mar 75, GK(c); JM;SpM/Iron Fist
.... 0.25 1.00 3.00 5.00

☐ 32, Apr 75, GK(c); SB;Torch/Son of Satan
.... 0.25 1.00 3.00 5.00

☐ 33, May 75, GK(c); SB/VC;SpM/Nighthawk;
V:Meteor Man 0.25 1.00 3.00 5.00

☐ 34, Jun 75, GK(c);SB/VC; SpM/Valkyrie; V:Meteor Man
.... 0.25 1.00 3.00 5.00

☐ 35, Jul 75, GK(c);SB/VC; Torch/Dr. Strange
.... 0.25 1.00 3.00 5.00

☐ 36, Aug 75, SB; SpM/Frankenstein
.... 0.25 1.00 3.00 5.00

☐ 37, Sep 75, SB; SpM/Man-Wolf
.... 0.25 1.00 3.00 5.00

☐ 38, Oct 75, SB; SpM/Beast
.... 0.25 1.00 3.00 5.00

☐ 39, Nov 75, SB; SpM/Torch
.... 0.25 1.00 3.00 5.00

☐ 40, Dec 75, SB;SpM/ Sons of Tiger/Torch
.... 0.25 1.00 3.00 5.00

☐ 41, Jan 76, GK(c);SB; SpM/Scarlet Witch
.... 0.25 1.00 3.00 5.00

☐ 42, Feb 76, SB;SpM/ Scarlet Witch/Vision
.... 0.25 1.00 3.00 5.00

☐ 43, Mar 76, GK(c);SB; SpM/Dr. Doom
.... 0.25 1.00 3.00 5.00

☐ 44, Apr 76, GK(c);SB; SpM/Moondragon
.... 0.25 1.00 3.00 5.00

☐ 45, May 76, GK(c);SB; SpM/Killraven
.... 0.25 1.00 3.00 5.00

☐ 46, Jun 76, RB(c);SB; SpM/Deathlok
.... 0.25 2.00 6.00 10.00

☐ 47, Jul 76, GK(c); SpM/Thing;V:Basilisk
.... 0.25 1.00 3.00 5.00

☐ 48, Jul 76, JR(c);SB; SpM/Iron Man
.... 0.25 1.00 3.00 5.00

☐ 49, Sep 76, JR(c);SB; SpM/Iron Man
.... 0.30 1.00 3.00 5.00

☐ 50, Oct 76, GK(c);SB; SpM/Dr. Strange
.... 0.25 1.00 3.00 5.00

☐ 51, Nov 76, GK(c);SB; SpM/Iron Man
.... 0.30 0.60 1.80 3.00

☐ 52, Dec 76, SB; SpM/Capt. America
.... 0.30 0.60 1.80 3.00

☐ 53, Jan 77, DC(c);JBy; SpM/Hulk, A:X-Men, Woodgod
.... 0.30 2.40 7.20 12.00

☐ 54, Feb 77, GK(c);JBy; SpM/Hulk, A:Woodgod
.... 0.30 1.20 3.60 6.00

☐ 55, Mar 77, DC(c);JBy; SpM/Warlock;V:Gardener
.... 0.30 1.20 3.60 6.00

☐ 56, Apr 77, JR2(c);SB; SpM/Daredevil; V:Electro,
Blizzard 0.30 0.60 1.80 3.00

☐ 57, May 77, DC(c);SB; SpM/Black Widow
.... 0.30 0.60 1.80 3.00

☐ 58, Jun 77, AM(c);SB/DC; SpM/Ghost Rider
.... 0.30 1.20 3.60 6.00

☐ 59, Jul 77, DC(c);JBy; SpM/Yellowjacket/Wasp
.... 0.30 0.70 2.10 3.50

☐ 60, Aug 77, AM(c);JBy; SpM/Wasp, A:Yellowjacket
.... 0.30 0.70 2.10 3.50

☐ 61, Sep 77, RA(c);JBy; SpM/Torch; V:Super-Skrull
.... 0.30 0.70 2.10 3.50

☐ 62, Oct 77, GK(c);JBy; SpM/Ms. Marvel; V:Super-Skrull
.... 0.30 0.70 2.10 3.50

☐ 63, Nov 77, DC(c);JBy; SpM/Iron Fist
.... 0.35 1.00 3.00 5.00

☐ 64, Dec 77, DC(c);JBy; SpM/Daughters of Dragon
.... 0.35 0.70 2.10 3.50

☐ 65, Jan 78, GP(c);JBy; SpM/Capt. Britain
.... 0.35 0.80 2.40 4.00

☐ 66, Feb 78, JBy;SpM/Capt. Britain;V:Arcade
.... 0.35 0.80 2.40 4.00

☐ 67, Mar 78, JBy; SpM/Tigra;V:Kraven
.... 0.35 0.70 2.10 3.50

☐ 68, Apr 78, JBy; SpM/Man-Thing
.... 0.35 0.70 2.10 3.50

☐ 69, May 78, DC(c);JBy; SpM/Havok
.... 0.35 0.80 2.40 4.00

☐ 70, Jun 78, JBy;SpM/Thor; V:Living Monolith
.... 0.35 0.70 2.10 3.50

☐ 71, Jul 78, SpM/Falcon...0.35 0.40 1.20 2.00

☐ 72, Aug 78, JBy(c);JM; SpM/Iron Man
.... 0.35 0.40 1.20 2.00

☐ 73, Sep 78, KP(c); SpM/Daredevil
.... 0.35 0.25 0.75 1.25

☐ 74, Oct 78, DC(c); SpM/Not Ready for Prime Time
Players....................0.35 0.60 1.80 3.00

☐ 75, Nov 78, JBy; SpM/Power Man
.... 0.35 0.60 1.80 3.00

☐ 76, Dec 78, JBy(c);HC; SpM/Dr. Strange
.... 0.35 0.40 1.20 2.00

☐ 77, Jan 79, JR2(c);HC; SpM/Ms. Marvel
.... 0.35 0.40 1.20 2.00

☐ 78, Feb 79, AM(c);DP; SpM/Wonder Man
.... 0.35 0.60 1.80 3.00

☐ 79, Mar 79, JBy; SpM/Red Sonja
.... 0.35 0.40 1.20 2.00

☐ 80, Apr 79, RB(c); SpM/Dr. Strange/Clea
.... 0.35 0.40 1.20 2.00

☐ 81, May 79, AM(c); SpM/Satana
.... 0.40 0.40 1.20 2.00

☐ 82, Jun 79, RB(c);SB; SpM/Black Widow
.... 0.40 0.40 1.20 2.00

☐ 83, Jul 79, RB(c);SB; SpM/Nick Fury
.... 0.40 0.40 1.20 2.00

☐ 84, Aug 79, SB; SpM/Shang-Chi
.... 0.40 0.60 1.80 3.00

☐ 85, Sep 79, AM(c);SB; SpM/Shang-Chi/Nick Fury/
Black Widow.................... 0.40 0.60 1.80 3.00

☐ 86, Oct 79, BMc;SpM/ Guardians of Galaxy
.... 0.40 0.60 1.80 3.00

☐ 87, Nov 79, AM(c);GC; SpM/Black Panther
.... 0.40 0.40 1.20 2.00

☐ 88, Dec 79, RB(c);SB; SpM/Invisible Girl
.... 0.40 0.40 1.20 2.00

☐ 89, Jan 80, RB; SpM/Nightcrawler
.... 0.40 0.60 1.80 3.00

☐ 90, Feb 80, AM(c); SpM/Beast
.... 0.40 0.40 1.20 2.00

☐ 91, Mar 90, RB(c);PB; SpM/Ghost Rider
.... 0.40 0.80 2.40 4.00

☐ 92, Apr 80, AM(c);CI; SpM/Hawkeye
.... 0.40 0.40 1.20 2.00

☐ 93, May 80, DP(c);CI; SpM/Werewolf
.... 0.40 0.40 1.20 2.00

☐ 94, Jun 80, AM(c);MZ; SpM/Shroud
.... 0.40 0.40 1.20 2.00

☐ 95, Jul 80, FM(c); SpM/Mockingbird; 1:Huntress as
Mockingbird 0.40 0.40 1.20 2.00

☐ 96, Aug 80, SpM/Howard the Duck
.... 0.40 0.40 1.20 2.00

☐ 97, Sep 80, CI; Hulk/Spider-Woman
.... 0.50 0.40 1.20 2.00

☐ 98, Oct 80, AM(c); SpM/Black Widow
.... 0.50 0.40 1.20 2.00

☐ 99, Nov 80, FM(c); SpM/Machine Man
.... 0.50 0.40 1.20 2.00

	ORIG.	GOOD	FINE	N-MINT
☐ 100, Dec 80, FM/JBy; SpM/FF, 1:Karma				
...................0.75		2.00	6.00	10.00
☐ 101, Jan 81, SpM/Nighthawk				
...................0.50		0.40	1.20	2.00
☐ 102, Feb 81, FM(c); SpM/Doc Samson				
...................0.50		0.40	1.20	2.00
☐ 103, Mar 81, SpM/Ant-Man				
...................0.50		0.40	1.20	2.00
☐ 104, Apr 81, AM(c); Hulk/Ka-Zar				
...................0.50		0.40	1.20	2.00
☐ 105, May 81, AM(c);CI; Power Man/Iron Fist/Hulk				
...................0.50		0.40	1.20	2.00
☐ 106, Jun 81, FM(c);HT; SpM/Capt. America; V:Scorpion				
...................0.50		0.40	1.20	2.00
☐ 107, Jul 81, HT; SpM/She-Hulk				
...................0.50		0.40	1.20	2.00
☐ 108, Aug 81, HT; SpM/Paladin				
...................0.50		0.40	1.20	2.00
☐ 109, Sep 81, JR2(c);HT; SpM/Dazzler				
...................0.50		0.40	1.20	2.00
☐ 110, Oct 81, BL(c);HT; SpM/Iron Man				
...................0.50		0.40	1.20	2.00
☐ 111, Nov 81, HT; SpM/Devil-Slayer				
...................0.50		0.40	1.20	2.00
☐ 112, Dec 81, HT; SpM/King Kull				
...................0.50		0.40	1.20	2.00
☐ 113, Jan 82, SpM/Quasar				
...................0.60		0.40	1.20	2.00
☐ 114, Feb 82, SpM/Falcon				
...................0.60		0.40	1.20	2.00
☐ 115, Mar 82, SpM/Thor..0.60		0.40	1.20	2.00
☐ 116, Apr 82, SpM/Valkyrie				
...................0.60		0.40	1.20	2.00
☐ 117, May 82, SpM/Wolverine				
...................0.60		0.80	2.40	4.00
☐ 118, Jun 82, SpM/Prof. X				
...................0.60		0.40	1.20	2.00
☐ 119, Jul 82, KGa, SpM/Gargoyle				
...................0.60		0.40	1.20	2.00
☐ 120, Aug 82, KGa, SpM/Dominic Fortune				
...................0.60		0.40	1.20	2.00
☐ 121, Sep 82, KGa, SpM/Torch				
...................0.60		0.40	1.20	2.00
☐ 122, Oct 82, Man-Thing/DD				
...................0.60		0.40	1.20	2.00
☐ 123, Nov 82, Man-Thing/DD				
...................0.60		0.40	1.20	2.00
☐ 124, Dec 82, KGa, SpM/Beast				
...................0.60		0.40	1.20	2.00
☐ 125, Jan 83, KGa, SpM/Tigra				
...................0.60		0.40	1.20	2.00
☐ 126, Feb 83, BH, SpM/Hulk				
...................0.60		0.40	1.20	2.00
☐ 127, Mar 83, KGa, SpM/Watcher				
...................0.60		0.40	1.20	2.00
☐ 128, Apr 83 ....0.60		0.40	1.20	2.00
☐ 129, May 83 ....0.60		0.40	1.20	2.00
☐ 130, Jun 83 ....0.60		0.40	1.20	2.00
☐ 131, Jul 83 ....0.60		0.40	1.20	2.00
☐ 132, Aug 83 ....0.60		0.40	1.20	2.00
☐ 133, Sep 83...................0.60		0.40	1.20	2.00
☐ 134, Oct 83, Jack of Hearts				
...................0.60		0.40	1.20	2.00
☐ 135, Nov 83, Kitty Pryde 0.60		0.40	1.20	2.00
☐ 136, Dec 83, Wonder Man				
...................0.60		0.40	1.20	2.00
☐ 137, Jan 84, Aunt May & Franklin Richards				
...................0.60		0.40	1.20	2.00
☐ 138, Feb 84, Sandman/Nick Fury				
...................0.60		0.40	1.20	2.00
☐ 139, Mar 84, Sandman/Nick Fury				
...................0.60		0.40	1.20	2.00

	ORIG.	GOOD	FINE	N-MINT
☐ 140, Apr 84, Sandman/Nick Fury				
...................0.60		0.40	1.20	2.00
☐ 141, May 84, SpM new costume				
...................0.60		0.40	1.20	2.00
☐ 142, Jun 84, SpM/Capt. Marvel				
...................0.60		0.40	1.20	2.00
☐ 143, Jul 84, SpM/Starfox				
...................0.60		0.40	1.20	2.00
☐ 144, Aug 84, SpM/Moon Knight				
...................0.60		0.40	1.20	2.00
☐ 145, Sep 84, SpM/Iron Man				
...................0.60		0.40	1.20	2.00
☐ 146, Oct 84, SpM...................0.60		0.40	1.20	2.00
☐ 147, Nov 84, SpM/Torch 0.60		0.40	1.20	2.00
☐ 148, Dec 84, SpM/Thor ..0.60		0.40	1.20	2.00
☐ 149, Jan 85...................0.60		0.40	1.20	2.00
☐ 150, Feb 85, SpM/X-Men; final issue				
...................1.00		0.80	2.40	4.00

MARVEL TEAM-UP ANNUAL

	ORIG.	GOOD	FINE	N-MINT
☐ 1, 76, DC(c);SB; SpM/X-Men				
...................0.50		2.40	7.20	12.00
☐ 2, 79, AM(c);SB; SpM/Hulk				
...................0.75		0.40	1.20	2.00
☐ 3, 80, FM(c);HT;Hulk/ Power Man/Iron Fist/				
Machine Man 0.75		0.30	0.90	1.50
☐ 4, 81, FM(c);HT;SpM/ Iron Fist/Power Man/ Daredevil/				
Moon Knight...................0.75		0.50	1.50	2.50
☐ 5, Nov 81, SpM/Thing/ Scarlet Witch				
...................1.00		0.40	1.20	2.00
☐ 6, Oct 83, New Mutants/ Cloak & Dagger				
...................1.00		0.60	1.80	3.00
☐ 7, Oct 84, Alpha Flight 1.00		0.60	1.80	3.00

MARVEL TREASURY EDITION

	ORIG.	GOOD	FINE	N-MINT
☐ 1, SD, SpM 1.50		1.20	3.60	6.00
☐ 2, JK/FF, Silver Surfer.....1.50		0.70	2.10	3.50
☐ 3, Thor 1.50		0.70	2.10	3.50
☐ 4, BS, Conan...................1.50		0.90	2.70	4.50
☐ 5, O:Hulk...................1.50		0.70	2.10	3.50
☐ 6, SD, Dr. Strange...........1.50		0.70	2.10	3.50
☐ 7, JK, Avengers...............1.50		0.90	2.70	4.50
☐ 8, Xmas 1.50		0.90	2.70	4.50
☐ 9, Super-Hero Team-up ..1.50		0.70	2.10	3.50
☐ 10, Thor...................1.50		0.70	2.10	3.50
☐ 11, Nov 76, FF 1.50		0.70	2.10	3.50
☐ 12, Jan 77, Howard the Duck, new stories				
...................1.50		0.70	2.10	3.50
☐ 13, Feb 77, Xmas...........1.50		0.70	2.10	3.50
☐ 14, May 77, SpM 1.50		0.70	2.10	3.50
☐ 15, Sep 77, BS, Conan/Red Sonja				
...................1.50		0.90	2.70	4.50
☐ 16, May 78, Defenders....1.50		0.60	1.80	3.00
☐ 17, Jul 78, Hulk 1.50		0.60	1.80	3.00
☐ 18, Nov 78, SpM, X-Men				
...................2.00		0.70	2.10	3.50
☐ 19, Jan 79, Conan...........2.00		0.90	2.70	4.50
☐ 20, May 79, Hulk 2.00		0.50	1.50	2.50
☐ 21, May 79, FF 2.00		0.50	1.50	2.50
☐ 22, Aug 79, SpM...........2.00		0.50	1.50	2.50
☐ 23, Nov 79, Conan 2.00		0.60	1.80	3.00
☐ 24, Feb 80, Hulk..............2.00		0.50	1.50	2.50
☐ 25, Jun 80, SpM/Hulk.....2.00		0.50	1.50	2.50
☐ 26, Jul 80, Hulk, Wolverine & Hercules				
...................2.00		1.00	3.00	5.00
☐ 27, Sep 80, Hulk/SpM....2.00		0.60	1.80	3.00
☐ 28, Jul 81, SpM/Superman				
...................2.50		2.00	6.00	10.00

MARVEL TREASURY OF OZ

	ORIG.	GOOD	FINE	N-MINT
☐ 1, Land of Oz 1.50		2.00	6.00	10.00

	ORIG.	GOOD	FINE	N-MINT

MARVEL TREASURY SPECIAL

	ORIG.	GOOD	FINE	N-MINT
❏ 1, Giant Super-Hero Holiday Grab Bag				
	1.50	1.00	3.00	5.00
❏ 2, Sep 76, Captain America's Bicentennial Battles				
	1.50	1.00	3.00	5.00

MARVEL TRIPLE ACTION

	ORIG.	GOOD	FINE	N-MINT
❏ 1, reprints	0.25	0.40	1.20	2.00
❏ 2	0.20	0.20	0.60	1.00
❏ 3	0.20	0.20	0.60	1.00
❏ 4	0.20	0.20	0.60	1.00
❏ 5	0.20	0.20	0.60	1.00
❏ 6	0.20	0.20	0.60	1.00
❏ 7	0.20	0.20	0.60	1.00
❏ 8	0.20	0.20	0.60	1.00
❏ 9	0.20	0.20	0.60	1.00
❏ 10	0.20	0.20	0.60	1.00
❏ 11	0.20	0.20	0.60	1.00
❏ 12	0.20	0.20	0.60	1.00
❏ 13	0.20	0.20	0.60	1.00
❏ 14	0.20	0.20	0.60	1.00
❏ 15	0.20	0.20	0.60	1.00
❏ 16	0.20	0.20	0.60	1.00
❏ 17	0.20	0.20	0.60	1.00
❏ 18	0.25	0.20	0.60	1.00
❏ 19	0.25	0.20	0.60	1.00
❏ 20	0.25	0.20	0.60	1.00
❏ 21	0.25	0.20	0.60	1.00
❏ 22, Nov 74	0.25	0.20	0.60	1.00
❏ 23	0.25	0.20	0.60	1.00
❏ 24	0.25	0.20	0.60	1.00
❏ 25	0.25	0.20	0.60	1.00
❏ 26	0.25	0.20	0.60	1.00
❏ 27	0.25	0.20	0.60	1.00
❏ 28	0.25	0.20	0.60	1.00
❏ 29	0.25	0.20	0.60	1.00
❏ 30	0.25	0.20	0.60	1.00
❏ 31, Sep 76	0.30	0.20	0.60	1.00
❏ 32, Nov 76	0.30	0.20	0.60	1.00
❏ 33, Jan 77	0.30	0.20	0.60	1.00
❏ 34, Mar 77	0.30	0.20	0.60	1.00
❏ 35, May 77	0.30	0.20	0.60	1.00
❏ 36, Jul 77	0.30	0.20	0.60	1.00
❏ 37, Sep 77	0.30	0.20	0.60	1.00
❏ 38, Nov 77	0.30	0.20	0.60	1.00
❏ 39, Jan 78	0.30	0.20	0.60	1.00
❏ 40, Mar 78	0.30	0.20	0.60	1.00
❏ 41, Apr 78	0.30	0.20	0.60	1.00
❏ 42, Jun 78	0.30	0.20	0.60	1.00
❏ 43, Aug 78	0.30	0.20	0.60	1.00
❏ 44, Oct 78	0.30	0.20	0.60	1.00
❏ 45, Dec 78	0.30	0.20	0.60	1.00
❏ 46, Feb 79	0.30	0.20	0.60	1.00
❏ 47, Apr 79	0.30	0.20	0.60	1.00

MARVEL TWO-IN-ONE (all have Thing)

	ORIG.	GOOD	FINE	N-MINT
❏ 1, Jan 74, Man-Thing	0.20	3.60	10.80	18.00
❏ 2, Sub-Mariner	0.20	0.80	2.40	4.00
❏ 3, Daredevil, A:Black Widow				
	0.25	0.80	2.40	4.00
❏ 4, Capt. America	0.25	0.80	2.40	4.00
❏ 5, Guardians of Galaxy	0.25	3.00	9.00	15.00
❏ 6, Dr. Strange	0.25	2.00	6.00	10.00
❏ 7, Valkyrie, A:Dr. Strange	0.25	0.60	1.80	3.00
❏ 8, Ghost Rider	0.25	2.00	6.00	10.00
❏ 9, Thor	0.25	0.60	1.80	3.00
❏ 10, Black Widow	0.25	0.60	1.80	3.00
❏ 11, Golem	0.25	0.50	1.50	2.50
❏ 12, Iron Man	0.25	0.50	1.50	2.50
❏ 13, Power Man	0.25	0.50	1.50	2.50
❏ 14, Son of Satan	0.25	0.50	1.50	2.50
❏ 15, Morbius	0.25	0.50	1.50	2.50
❏ 16, Ka-Zar	0.25	0.50	1.50	2.50

	ORIG.	GOOD	FINE	N-MINT
❏ 17, SpM	0.25	0.50	1.50	2.50
❏ 18, SpM	0.25	0.50	1.50	2.50
❏ 19, Sep 76, Tigra	0.30	0.50	1.50	2.50
❏ 20, Oct 76, Liberty Legion;continued from *Marvel Two-In-One Annual* #1	0.30	0.50	1.50	2.50
❏ 21, Nov 76, Doc Savage; A:Torch				
	0.30	0.30	0.90	1.50
❏ 22, Dec 76, Thor & Torch				
	0.30	0.30	0.90	1.50
❏ 23, Jan 77, Thor, Torch	0.30	0.30	0.90	1.50
❏ 24, Feb 77, SB, Black Goliath				
	0.30	0.30	0.90	1.50
❏ 25, Mar 77, Iron Fist	0.30	0.30	0.90	1.50
❏ 26, Apr 77, Nick Fury	0.30	0.30	0.90	1.50
❏ 27, May 77, Deathlok	0.30	0.80	2.40	4.00
❏ 28, Jun 77, Sub-Mariner	0.30	0.30	0.90	1.50
❏ 29, Jul 77, Shang-Chi	0.30	0.30	0.90	1.50
❏ 30, Aug 77, JB, Spider-Woman				
	0.30	0.30	0.90	1.50
❏ 31, Sep 77, Spider-Woman				
	0.30	0.30	0.90	1.50
❏ 32, Oct 77, Invisible Girl	0.30	0.30	0.90	1.50
❏ 33, Nov 77, Mordred	0.35	0.30	0.90	1.50
❏ 34, Dec 77, Nighthawk	0.35	0.25	0.75	1.25
❏ 35, Jan 78, Skull the Slayer				
	0.35	0.25	0.75	1.25
❏ 36, Feb 78, Mr. Fantastic	0.35	0.25	0.75	1.25
❏ 37, Mar 78, Matt Murdock				
	0.35	0.25	0.75	1.25
❏ 38, Apr 78, Daredevil	0.35	0.25	0.75	1.25
❏ 39, May 78, Vision, A:Daredevil				
	0.35	0.25	0.75	1.25
❏ 40, Jun 78, Black Panther				
	0.35	0.25	0.75	1.25
❏ 41, Jul 78, Brother Voodoo				
	0.35	0.25	0.75	1.25
❏ 42, Aug 78, Capt. America				
	0.35	0.25	0.75	1.25
❏ 43, Sep 78, JBy, Man-Thing				
	0.35	0.70	2.10	3.50
❏ 44, Oct 78, GD, Hercules				
	0.35	0.20	0.60	1.00
❏ 45, Nov 78, GD, Capt. Marvel				
	0.35	0.20	0.60	1.00
❏ 46, Dec 78, Hulk	0.35	0.20	0.60	1.00
❏ 47, Jan 79, GD, Yancy Street Gang				
	0.35	0.20	0.60	1.00
❏ 48, Feb 79, Jack of Hearts				
	0.35	0.25	0.75	1.25
❏ 49, Mar 79, GD, Dr. Strange				
	0.35	0.20	0.60	1.00
❏ 50, Apr 79, JBy/JS, 2 Things				
	0.35	0.80	2.40	4.00
❏ 51, May 79, FM/BMc, Beast				
	0.40	1.00	3.00	5.00
❏ 52, Jun 79, Moon Knight				
	0.40	0.50	1.50	2.50
❏ 53, Jul 79, JBy/JS, Quasar				
	0.40	0.60	1.80	3.00
❏ 54, Aug 79, JBy/JS, Deathlok				
	0.40	2.80	8.40	14.00
❏ 55, Sep 79, JBy/JS, Giant Man				
	0.40	0.60	1.80	3.00
❏ 56, Oct 79, GP/GD, Thundar				
	0.40	0.20	0.60	1.00
❏ 57, Nov 79, GP/GD, Wundarr				
	0.40	0.20	0.60	1.00
❏ 58, Dec 79, GP/GD, Aquarian				
	0.40	0.20	0.60	1.00
❏ 59, Jan 80, Torch	0.40	0.20	0.60	1.00
❏ 60, Feb 80, GP/GD, Impossible Man				
	0.40	0.20	0.60	1.00

	ORIG.	GOOD	FINE	N-MINT
❑ 61, Mar 80, GD, Starhawk 0.40		0.25	0.75	1.25
❑ 62, Apr 80, GD, Moondragon 0.40		0.25	0.75	1.25
❑ 63, May 80, GD, Warlock 0.40		0.25	0.75	1.25
❑ 64, Jun 80, GP/GD, Stingray 0.40		0.20	0.60	1.00
❑ 65, Jul 80, GP/GD, Triton	0.40	0.20	0.60	1.00
❑ 66, Aug 80, GD, Scarlet Witch 0.40		0.20	0.60	1.00
❑ 67, Sep 80, Hyperion	0.50	0.20	0.60	1.00
❑ 68, Oct 80, Angel	0.50	0.20	0.60	1.00
❑ 69, Nov 80, Guardians of Galaxy 0.50		0.60	1.80	3.00
❑ 70, Dec 80, Inhumans	0.50	0.20	0.60	1.00
❑ 71, Jan 81, Mr. Fantastic 0.50		0.20	0.60	1.00
❑ 72, Feb 81, Stingray	0.50	0.20	0.60	1.00
❑ 73, Mar 81, Quasar	0.50	0.20	0.60	1.00
❑ 74, Apr 81, Puppet Master 0.50		0.20	0.60	1.00
❑ 75, May 81, Avengers	0.50	0.20	0.60	1.00
❑ 76, Jun 81, Iceman	0.50	0.20	0.60	1.00
❑ 77, Jul 81, Man-Thing	0.50	0.20	0.60	1.00
❑ 78, Aug 81, Wonder Man 0.50		0.20	0.60	1.00
❑ 79, Sep 81, Blue Diamond 0.50		0.20	0.60	1.00
❑ 80, Oct 81, Ghost Rider	0.50	1.00	3.00	5.00
❑ 81, Nov 81, Sub-Mariner	0.50	0.20	0.60	1.00
❑ 82, Dec 81, Capt. America 0.50		0.20	0.60	1.00
❑ 83, Jan 82, Sasquatch	0.60	0.60	1.80	3.00
❑ 84, Feb 82, Alpha Flight	0.60	0.60	1.80	3.00
❑ 85, Mar 82, Giant-Man	0.60	0.20	0.60	1.00
❑ 86, Apr 82, Sandman	0.60	0.20	0.60	1.00
❑ 87, May 82, Ant-Man	0.60	0.20	0.60	1.00
❑ 88, Jun 82, She-Hulk	0.60	0.20	0.60	1.00
❑ 89, Jul 82, Torch	0.60	0.20	0.60	1.00
❑ 90, Aug 82, SpM	0.60	0.20	0.60	1.00
❑ 91, Sep 82, Ghost Rider	0.60	0.80	2.40	4.00
❑ 92, Oct 82, Jocasta	0.60	0.20	0.60	1.00
❑ 93, Nov 82, D:Jocasta	0.60	0.20	0.60	1.00
❑ 94, Dec 82, Power Man	0.60	0.20	0.60	1.00
❑ 95, Jan 83, Living Mummy 0.60		0.20	0.60	1.00
❑ 96, Feb 83	0.60	0.20	0.60	1.00
❑ 97, Mar 83, Iron Man	0.60	0.20	0.60	1.00
❑ 98, Apr 83	0.60	0.20	0.60	1.00
❑ 99, May 83	0.60	0.20	0.60	1.00
❑ 100, Jun 83, Ben Grimm, JBy script 1.00		0.30	0.90	1.50

MARVEL TWO-IN-ONE ANNUAL

	ORIG.	GOOD	FINE	N-MINT
❑ 1	0.50	0.40	1.20	2.00
❑ 2, Dec 77, JSn D:Thanos	0.60	1.00	3.00	5.00
❑ 3, Aug 78	0.60	0.30	0.90	1.50
❑ 4, Oct 79	0.60	0.30	0.90	1.50
❑ 5, Sep 80	0.75	0.30	0.90	1.50
❑ 6, Oct 81	0.75	0.30	0.90	1.50
❑ 7, Oct 82, Champion	1.00	0.30	0.90	1.50

MARVEL VERSUS DC/DC VERSUS MARVEL

	ORIG.	GOOD	FINE	N-MINT
❑ 2, Mar 96, crossover with DC;cardstock cover 3.95		1.40	4.20	7.00
❑ 3, Apr 96, crossover with DC;voting results; cardstock cover	3.95	1.40	4.20	7.00

MARVEL X-MEN COLLECTION, THE

	ORIG.	GOOD	FINE	N-MINT
❑ 1, JLee	2.95	0.59	1.77	2.95
❑ 2, JLee	2.95	0.59	1.77	2.95
❑ 3, JLee	2.95	0.59	1.77	2.95

MARVEL YEAR IN REVIEW

	ORIG.	GOOD	FINE	N-MINT
❑ 1, TMc(c) (1989)	3.95	0.79	2.37	3.95
❑ 2, 1990	3.95	0.79	2.37	3.95
❑ 3, 1991	3.95	0.79	2.37	3.95
❑ 4, 1992	3.95	0.79	2.37	3.95
❑ 5, 1993	3.95	0.79	2.37	3.95

MARVEL'S GREATEST COMICS

	ORIG.	GOOD	FINE	N-MINT
❑ 23, reprints;(was *Marvel Collectors' Item Classics*)	0.25	0.20	0.60	1.00
❑ 24, Dec 69	0.25	0.20	0.60	1.00
❑ 25, Feb 70	0.25	0.20	0.60	1.00
❑ 26	0.25	0.20	0.60	1.00
❑ 27	0.25	0.20	0.60	1.00
❑ 28	0.25	0.20	0.60	1.00
❑ 29	0.25	0.20	0.60	1.00
❑ 30	0.25	0.20	0.60	1.00
❑ 31	0.25	0.20	0.60	1.00
❑ 32	0.25	0.20	0.60	1.00
❑ 33	0.25	0.20	0.60	1.00
❑ 34	0.25	0.20	0.60	1.00
❑ 35	0.20	0.20	0.60	1.00
❑ 36	0.20	0.20	0.60	1.00
❑ 37	0.20	0.20	0.60	1.00
❑ 38	0.20	0.20	0.60	1.00
❑ 39	0.20	0.20	0.60	1.00
❑ 40	0.20	0.20	0.60	1.00
❑ 41	0.20	0.20	0.60	1.00
❑ 42	0.20	0.20	0.60	1.00
❑ 43	0.20	0.20	0.60	1.00
❑ 44	0.20	0.20	0.60	1.00
❑ 45	0.20	0.20	0.60	1.00
❑ 46	0.20	0.20	0.60	1.00
❑ 47	0.20	0.20	0.60	1.00
❑ 48	0.20	0.20	0.60	1.00
❑ 49	0.25	0.20	0.60	1.00
❑ 50	0.25	0.20	0.60	1.00
❑ 51	0.25	0.20	0.60	1.00
❑ 52	0.25	0.20	0.60	1.00
❑ 53	0.25	0.20	0.60	1.00
❑ 54, Jan 75	0.25	0.20	0.60	1.00
❑ 55	0.25	0.20	0.60	1.00
❑ 56	0.25	0.20	0.60	1.00
❑ 57	0.25	0.20	0.60	1.00
❑ 58, Sep 75	0.25	0.20	0.60	1.00
❑ 59	0.25	0.20	0.60	1.00
❑ 60	0.25	0.20	0.60	1.00
❑ 61	0.25	0.20	0.60	1.00
❑ 62	0.25	0.20	0.60	1.00
❑ 63	0.25	0.20	0.60	1.00
❑ 64	0.25	0.20	0.60	1.00
❑ 65, Sep 76	0.30	0.20	0.60	1.00
❑ 66, Oct 76	0.30	0.20	0.60	1.00
❑ 67, Nov 76	0.30	0.20	0.60	1.00
❑ 68, Jan 77	0.30	0.20	0.60	1.00
❑ 69, Mar 77	0.30	0.20	0.60	1.00
❑ 70, May 77	0.30	0.20	0.60	1.00
❑ 71, Jul 77	0.30	0.20	0.60	1.00
❑ 72, Sep 77	0.30	0.20	0.60	1.00
❑ 73, Oct 77	0.30	0.20	0.60	1.00
❑ 74, Nov 77	0.35	0.20	0.60	1.00
❑ 75, Jan 78	0.35	0.20	0.60	1.00
❑ 76, Mar 78	0.35	0.20	0.60	1.00
❑ 77, May 78	0.35	0.20	0.60	1.00
❑ 78, Jul 78	0.35	0.20	0.60	1.00
❑ 79, Sep 78	0.35	0.20	0.60	1.00
❑ 80, Nov 78	0.35	0.20	0.60	1.00
❑ 81, Jan 79	0.35	0.20	0.60	1.00
❑ 82, Mar 79	0.35	0.20	0.60	1.00
❑ 83, Dec 79	0.35	0.20	0.60	1.00
❑ 84, Jan 80	0.35	0.20	0.60	1.00
❑ 85, Feb 80	0.35	0.20	0.60	1.00

	ORIG.	GOOD	FINE	N-MINT
☐ 86, Mar 80	0.35	0.20	0.60	1.00
☐ 87, Apr 80	0.35	0.20	0.60	1.00
☐ 88, May 80	0.40	0.20	0.60	1.00
☐ 89, Jun 80	0.40	0.20	0.60	1.00
☐ 90, Jul 80	0.40	0.20	0.60	1.00
☐ 91, Aug 80	0.40	0.20	0.60	1.00
☐ 92, Sep 80	0.40	0.20	0.60	1.00
☐ 93, Oct 80	0.40	0.20	0.60	1.00
☐ 94, Nov 80	0.40	0.20	0.60	1.00
☐ 95, Dec 80	0.40	0.20	0.60	1.00
☐ 96, Jan 81	0.40	0.20	0.60	1.00

MARVELOUS DRAGON CLAN (mini-series)
LUNAR

	ORIG.	GOOD	FINE	N-MINT
☐ 1, Jul 94, b&w	2.50	0.50	1.50	2.50
☐ 2, Sep 94, b&w	2.50	0.50	1.50	2.50

MARVELS
MARVEL

	ORIG.	GOOD	FINE	N-MINT
☐ 0, Aug 94, collects promo art and Human Torch story from *Marvel Age*	2.95	1.20	3.60	6.00
☐ 1, Jan 94, Torch,Sub-Mariner, Capt. America; wraparound acetate outer cover	4.95	2.00	6.00	10.00
☐ 1, Apr 96, Torch, Sub-Mariner,Capt. America; second printing	2.95	0.59	1.77	2.95
☐ 2, Feb 94, wraparound acetate outer cover	5.95	1.60	4.80	8.00
☐ 2, May 96, second printing	2.95	0.59	1.77	2.95
☐ 3, Mar 94, Coming of Galactus; wraparound acetate outer cover	5.95	1.20	3.60	6.00
☐ 4, Apr 94, Death of Gwen Stacy; wraparound acetate outer cover	5.95	1.20	3.60	6.00

MARVELS: PORTRAITS (mini-series)

	ORIG.	GOOD	FINE	N-MINT
☐ 1, Mar 95	2.95	0.59	1.77	2.95
☐ 2, Apr 95	2.95	0.59	1.77	2.95
☐ 3, May 95	2.95	0.59	1.77	2.95
☐ 4, Jun 95	2.95	0.59	1.77	2.95

MASK (1985-1986)
DC

	GOOD	FINE	N-MINT
☐ 1	0.20	0.60	1.00
☐ 2	0.20	0.60	1.00
☐ 3	0.20	0.60	1.00
☐ 4	0.20	0.60	1.00

MASK (1987)

	GOOD	FINE	N-MINT
☐ 1, CS,KS MA(c)	0.20	0.60	1.00
☐ 2, CS,KS MA(c)	0.20	0.60	1.00
☐ 3, CS,KS MA(c)	0.20	0.60	1.00
☐ 4, CS,KS MA(c)	0.20	0.60	1.00
☐ 5, CS,KS MA(c)	0.20	0.60	1.00
☐ 6, CS,KS MA(c)	0.20	0.60	1.00
☐ 7, CS,KS MA(c)	0.20	0.60	1.00
☐ 8, CS,KS MA(c)	0.20	0.60	1.00

MASK RETURNS, THE
DARK HORSE

	ORIG.	GOOD	FINE	N-MINT
☐ 1, with Mask mask	2.50	1.20	3.60	6.00
☐ 2	2.50	1.00	3.00	5.00
☐ 3	2.50	1.00	3.00	5.00
☐ 4	2.50	1.00	3.00	5.00

MASK, THE

	ORIG.	GOOD	FINE	N-MINT
☐ 0		1.00	3.00	5.00
☐ 1, Jul 94, movie adaptation	2.50	2.80	8.40	14.00
☐ 2, Aug 94, movie adaptation	2.50	1.50	4.50	7.50
☐ 3	2.50	1.50	4.50	7.50
☐ 4	2.50	1.50	4.50	7.50

MASK, THE (1995-)

	ORIG.	GOOD	FINE	N-MINT
☐ 1, Feb 95, "Strikes Back" Part 1 of 5	2.50	0.50	1.50	2.50
☐ 5, Jun 95, "Strikes Back" Part 5 of 5	2.50	0.50	1.50	2.50
☐ 6, Jul 95, "The Hunt for Green October" Part 1 of 4	2.50	0.50	1.50	2.50
☐ 7, Aug 95, "The Hunt for Green October" Part 2 of 4	2.50	0.50	1.50	2.50
☐ 8, Sep 95, "The Hunt for Green October" Part 3 of 4	2.50	0.50	1.50	2.50
☐ 9, Oct 95, "The Hunt for Green October" Part 4 of 4	2.50	0.50	1.50	2.50
☐ 10, Dec 95, "World Tour" Part 1 of 4;A: Hero Zero, King Tiger	2.50	0.50	1.50	2.50
☐ 11, Jan 96, "World Tour" Part 2 of 4;A: Barb Wire, The Machine	2.50	0.50	1.50	2.50
☐ 12, Feb 96, "World Tour" Part 3 of 4;A: X, Ghost, King Tiger	2.50	0.50	1.50	2.50
☐ 13, Mar 96, "World Tour" Part 4 of 4;A: Warmaker, King Tiger, Vortex	2.50	0.50	1.50	2.50
☐ 14, Apr 96, "Southern Discomfort" Part 1 of 4	2.50	0.50	1.50	2.50
☐ 15, May 96, "Southern Discomfort" Part 2 of 4; A:Lt. Kellaway	2.50	0.50	1.50	2.50

MASKED MAN
ECLIPSE

	GOOD	FINE	N-MINT
☐ 1, Dec 84, color	0.35	1.05	1.75
☐ 2, Feb 85, color	0.35	1.05	1.75
☐ 3, Apr 85, color	0.35	1.05	1.75
☐ 4, Jun 85, color	0.35	1.05	1.75
☐ 5, Aug 85, color	0.35	1.05	1.75
☐ 6, Oct 85, color	0.35	1.05	1.75
☐ 7, Dec 85, color	0.35	1.05	1.75
☐ 8, Feb 86, color	0.35	1.05	1.75
☐ 9, Apr 86, color	0.35	1.05	1.75
☐ 10, b&w	0.40	1.20	2.00
☐ 11, b&w	0.40	1.20	2.00
☐ 12, b&w	0.40	1.20	2.00

MASKED RIDER
MARVEL

	ORIG.	GOOD	FINE	N-MINT
☐ 1, Apr 96, based on Saban television series;one-shot; A:Mighty Morphin Power Rangers, Ninja Rangers	2.95	0.59	1.77	2.95

MASQUERADE
MAD MONKEY

	GOOD	FINE	N-MINT
☐ 1	0.79	2.37	3.95
☐ 2	0.79	2.37	3.95

MASQUES
INNOVATION

	GOOD	FINE	N-MINT
☐ 1	0.99	2.97	4.95
☐ 2	0.99	2.97	4.95

MASTER OF KUNG FU
(was Special Marvel Edition)
MARVEL

	ORIG.	GOOD	FINE	N-MINT
☐ 17, JSn, I:Black Jack Tarr	0.20	4.00	12.00	20.00
☐ 18, PG	0.25	2.40	7.20	12.00
☐ 19, PG	0.25	2.00	6.00	10.00
☐ 20, PG	0.25	2.00	6.00	10.00
☐ 21	0.25	1.00	3.00	5.00
☐ 22, PG	0.25	1.00	3.00	5.00
☐ 23	0.25	1.00	3.00	5.00
☐ 24, JSn/WS	0.25	1.00	3.00	5.00
☐ 25, PG	0.25	1.00	3.00	5.00
☐ 26	0.25	1.00	3.00	5.00
☐ 27	0.25	1.00	3.00	5.00
☐ 28	0.25	1.00	3.00	5.00
☐ 29, PG	0.25	1.00	3.00	5.00
☐ 30, PG	0.25	1.00	3.00	5.00
☐ 31, PG	0.25	1.00	3.00	5.00
☐ 32	0.25	0.60	1.80	3.00
☐ 33, PG	0.25	0.60	1.80	3.00
☐ 34, PG	0.25	0.60	1.80	3.00

	ORIG.	GOOD	FINE	N-MINT
☐ 35, PG	0.25	0.60	1.80	3.00
☐ 36	0.25	0.40	1.20	2.00
☐ 37	0.25	0.40	1.20	2.00
☐ 38, PG	0.25	0.40	1.20	2.00
☐ 39, PG	0.25	0.40	1.20	2.00
☐ 40, PG	0.25	0.40	1.20	2.00
☐ 41	0.25	0.40	1.20	2.00
☐ 42, PG	0.25	0.40	1.20	2.00
☐ 43, PG	0.25	0.40	1.20	2.00
☐ 44, Sep 76, PG	0.30	0.40	1.20	2.00
☐ 45, Oct 76, PG	0.30	0.40	1.20	2.00
☐ 46, Nov 76, PG	0.30	0.40	1.20	2.00
☐ 47, Dec 76, PG	0.30	0.40	1.20	2.00
☐ 48, Jan 77, PG	0.30	0.40	1.20	2.00
☐ 49, Feb 77, PG	0.30	0.40	1.20	2.00
☐ 50, Mar 77, PG	0.30	0.40	1.20	2.00
☐ 51, Apr 77, PG	0.30	0.40	1.20	2.00
☐ 52, May 77	0.30	0.20	0.60	1.00
☐ 53, Jun 77	0.30	0.20	0.60	1.00
☐ 54, Jul 77	0.30	0.20	0.60	1.00
☐ 55, Aug 77	0.30	0.20	0.60	1.00
☐ 56, Sep 77	0.30	0.20	0.60	1.00
☐ 57, Oct 77	0.30	0.20	0.60	1.00
☐ 58, Nov 77	0.35	0.20	0.60	1.00
☐ 59, Dec 77	0.35	0.20	0.60	1.00
☐ 60, Jan 78	0.35	0.20	0.60	1.00
☐ 61, Feb 78	0.35	0.20	0.60	1.00
☐ 62, Mar 78	0.35	0.20	0.60	1.00
☐ 63, Apr 78	0.35	0.20	0.60	1.00
☐ 64, May 78	0.35	0.20	0.60	1.00
☐ 65, Jun 78	0.35	0.20	0.60	1.00
☐ 66, Jul 78	0.35	0.20	0.60	1.00
☐ 67, Aug 78	0.35	0.20	0.60	1.00
☐ 68, Sep 78	0.35	0.20	0.60	1.00
☐ 69, Oct 78	0.35	0.20	0.60	1.00
☐ 70, Nov 78	0.35	0.20	0.60	1.00
☐ 71, Dec 78	0.35	0.20	0.60	1.00
☐ 72, Jan 79	0.35	0.20	0.60	1.00
☐ 73, Feb 79	0.35	0.20	0.60	1.00
☐ 74, Mar 79	0.35	0.20	0.60	1.00
☐ 75, Apr 79	0.35	0.20	0.60	1.00
☐ 76, May 79	0.40	0.20	0.60	1.00
☐ 77, Jun 79	0.35	0.20	0.60	1.00
☐ 78, Jul 79	0.35	0.20	0.60	1.00
☐ 79, Aug 79	0.35	0.20	0.60	1.00
☐ 80, Sep 79	0.35	0.20	0.60	1.00
☐ 81, Oct 79	0.35	0.20	0.60	1.00
☐ 82, Nov 79	0.35	0.20	0.60	1.00
☐ 83, Dec 79	0.35	0.20	0.60	1.00
☐ 84, Jan 80	0.35	0.20	0.60	1.00
☐ 85, Feb 80	0.35	0.20	0.60	1.00
☐ 86, Mar 80	0.35	0.20	0.60	1.00
☐ 87, Apr 80	0.35	0.20	0.60	1.00
☐ 88, May 80	0.35	0.20	0.60	1.00
☐ 89, Jun 80	0.35	0.20	0.60	1.00
☐ 90, Jul 80	0.35	0.20	0.60	1.00
☐ 91, Aug 80, GD	0.40	0.40	1.20	2.00
☐ 92, Sep 80, GD	0.50	0.40	1.20	2.00
☐ 93, Oct 80, GD	0.50	0.40	1.20	2.00
☐ 94, Nov 80, GD	0.50	0.40	1.20	2.00
☐ 95, Dec 80, GD	0.50	0.40	1.20	2.00
☐ 96, Jan 81, GD	0.50	0.40	1.20	2.00
☐ 97, Feb 81, GD	0.50	0.40	1.20	2.00
☐ 98, Mar 81, GD	0.50	0.40	1.20	2.00
☐ 99, Apr 81, GD	0.50	0.40	1.20	2.00
☐ 100, May 81, GD	0.75	0.40	1.20	2.00
☐ 101, Jun 81, GD	0.50	0.40	1.20	2.00
☐ 102, Jul 81, GD, 1:Day pencils				
	0.50	0.40	1.20	2.00
☐ 103, Aug 81, GD	0.50	0.40	1.20	2.00
☐ 104, Sep 81	0.50	0.40	1.20	2.00
☐ 105, Oct 81	0.50	0.40	1.20	2.00

	ORIG.	GOOD	FINE	N-MINT
☐ 106, Nov 81, GD, C:Velcro				
	0.50	0.40	1.20	2.00
☐ 107, Dec 81, GD A:Sata	0.50	0.40	1.20	2.00
☐ 108, Jan 82, GD	0.60	0.40	1.20	2.00
☐ 109, Feb 82, GD	0.60	0.40	1.20	2.00
☐ 110, Mar 82, GD	0.60	0.40	1.20	2.00
☐ 111, Apr 82, GD	0.60	0.40	1.20	2.00
☐ 112, May 82, GD	0.60	0.40	1.20	2.00
☐ 113, Jun 82, GD	0.60	0.40	1.20	2.00
☐ 114, Jul 82	0.60	0.40	1.20	2.00
☐ 115, Aug 82, GD	0.60	0.40	1.20	2.00
☐ 116, Sep 82, GD	0.60	0.40	1.20	2.00
☐ 117, Oct 82, GD	0.60	0.40	1.20	2.00
☐ 118, Nov 82, GD, double size				
	1.00	0.40	1.20	2.00
☐ 119, Dec 82, GD	0.60	0.40	1.20	2.00
☐ 120, Jan 83, GD	0.60	0.40	1.20	2.00
☐ 121, Feb 83	0.60	0.40	1.20	2.00
☐ 122, Mar 83	0.60	0.40	1.20	2.00
☐ 123, Apr 83	0.60	0.40	1.20	2.00
☐ 124, May 83	0.60	0.40	1.20	2.00
☐ 125, Jun 83	1.00	0.40	1.20	2.00

MASTER OF KUNG FU ANNUAL

	ORIG.	GOOD	FINE	N-MINT
☐ 1, 76	0.50	0.80	2.40	4.00

MASTER OF KUNG FU: BLEEDING BLACK

	ORIG.	GOOD	FINE	N-MINT
☐ 1, Feb 91	2.95	0.59	1.77	2.95

MASTER, THE
NEW COMICS

	GOOD	FINE	N-MINT
☐ 1, b&w	0.45	1.35	2.25
☐ 2, b&w	0.45	1.35	2.25

MASTERS OF THE UNIVERSE
DC

	GOOD	FINE	N-MINT
☐ 1, GT/AA	0.30	0.90	1.50
☐ 2	0.20	0.60	1.00
☐ 3	0.20	0.60	1.00

STAR

	ORIG.	GOOD	FINE	N-MINT
☐ 1	0.75	0.15	0.45	0.75
☐ 2	0.75	0.15	0.45	0.75
☐ 3	0.75	0.15	0.45	0.75
☐ 4	0.75	0.15	0.45	0.75
☐ 5	0.75	0.15	0.45	0.75
☐ 6	0.75	0.15	0.45	0.75
☐ 7	1.00	0.20	0.60	1.00
☐ 8	1.00	0.20	0.60	1.00
☐ 9	1.00	0.20	0.60	1.00
☐ 10	1.00	0.20	0.60	1.00
☐ 11	1.00	0.20	0.60	1.00
☐ 12	1.00	0.20	0.60	1.00
☐ 13	1.00	0.20	0.60	1.00

MASTERWORKS SERIES OF GREAT COMIC BOOK ARTISTS
DC/SEAGATE

	ORIG.	GOOD	FINE	N-MINT
☐ 1, Spr 83, Frazetta	1.50	0.30	0.90	1.50
☐ 2, Jul 83, Frazetta	1.50	0.30	0.90	1.50
☐ 3, Oct 83, Wrightson	1.50	0.30	0.90	1.50

MATT CHAMPION
METRO

	GOOD	FINE	N-MINT
☐ 1	0.40	1.20	2.00

MAVERICKS
DAGGER

	ORIG.	GOOD	FINE	N-MINT
☐ 1	2.50	0.50	1.50	2.50
☐ 2	2.50	0.50	1.50	2.50

MAX BURGER, P.I.
GRAPHIC IMAGE

	ORIG.	GOOD	FINE	N-MINT
☐ 1, 89, b&w	2.00	0.40	1.20	2.00
☐ 2, 90, b&w	2.50	0.50	1.50	2.50

MAX OF THE REGULATORS
ATLANTIC

	GOOD	FINE	N-MINT
☐ 1	0.20	0.60	1.00
☐ 2	0.20	0.60	1.00

	ORIG.	GOOD	FINE	N-MINT
❑ 3		0.20	0.60	1.00
❑ 4		0.20	0.60	1.00

MAX THE MAGNIFICENT
SLAVE LABOR

	ORIG.	GOOD	FINE	N-MINT
❑ 1, Jul 87, JV 1.50		0.30	0.90	1.50

MAXIMAGE
IMAGE

	ORIG.	GOOD	FINE	N-MINT
❑ 1, Dec 95....................... 2.50		0.60	1.80	3.00
❑ 2, Jan 96, "Extreme Destroyer" Part 2 of 9; polybagged with card..... 2.50		0.50	1.50	2.50
❑ 3, Feb 96 .... 2.50		0.50	1.50	2.50
❑ 4, Mar 96, continued from *Glory* #10 .... 2.50		0.50	1.50	2.50

MAXIMORTAL, THE
TUNDRA

	ORIG.	GOOD	FINE	N-MINT
❑ 1, adult........................... 2.95		0.59	1.77	2.95
❑ 2, adult........................... 2.95		0.59	1.77	2.95
❑ 3, adult........................... 2.95		0.59	1.77	2.95
❑ 4, adult........................... 2.95		0.59	1.77	2.95
❑ 5, May 93 .... 2.95		0.59	1.77	2.95
❑ 6 .... 2.95		0.59	1.77	2.95

MAXIMORTAL, THE (was Tundra title)
KING HELL/KITCHEN SINK

	ORIG.	GOOD	FINE	N-MINT
❑ 7 .... 2.95		0.59	1.77	2.95

MAXWELL MOUSE FOLLIES
RENEGADE

	ORIG.	GOOD	FINE	N-MINT
❑ 1, Feb 86, b&w............... 1.70		0.34	1.02	1.70
❑ 2, Feb 86, b&w............... 1.70		0.34	1.02	1.70
❑ 3, Jun 86, b&w 1.70		0.34	1.02	1.70
❑ 4, Sep 86, b&w 2.00		0.34	1.02	1.70
❑ 5, Dec 86....................... 2.00		0.40	1.20	2.00
❑ 6, Mar 87 .... 2.00		0.40	1.20	2.00

MAXWELL THE MAGIC CAT
ACME

	ORIG.	GOOD	FINE	N-MINT
❑ 1, AMo		0.99	2.97	4.95
❑ 2, AMo		0.99	2.97	4.95
❑ 3, AMo		0.99	2.97	4.95
❑ 4, AMo		1.19	3.57	5.95

MAXX, THE

	ORIG.	GOOD	FINE	N-MINT
❑ 1, Mar 93, SKi 1.95		1.50	4.50	7.50
❑ 1, glow in the dark cover..	6.00	18.00	30.00
❑ 1, /2, SKi	5.00	15.00	25.00
❑ 2, SKi 1.95		1.20	3.60	6.00
❑ 3, SKi 1.95		1.00	3.00	5.00
❑ 4, SKi 1.95		0.80	2.40	4.00
❑ 5, SKi 1.95		0.80	2.40	4.00
❑ 6, SKi 1.95		0.80	2.40	4.00
❑ 7, Mar 94, SKi;A:Pitt	1.00	3.00	5.00
❑ 8, May 94, A:Pitt 1.95		1.00	3.00	5.00
❑ 9, Jun 94, SKi 1.95		0.70	2.10	3.50
❑ 10, Aug 94, SKi............. 1.95		0.70	2.10	3.50
❑ 11, Oct 94, SKi.............. 1.95		0.60	1.80	3.00
❑ 12, Dec 94, SKi 1.95		0.60	1.80	3.00
❑ 13, SKi 1.95		0.60	1.80	3.00
❑ 14, Feb 95, SKi.............. 1.95		0.60	1.80	3.00
❑ 15, Apr 95, SKi (cover says February) 1.95		0.60	1.80	3.00
❑ 18, Aug 95, SKi.............. 1.95		0.60	1.80	3.00
❑ 21, Jan 96, SKi.............. 1.95		0.39	1.17	1.95
❑ 22, Feb 96, SKi.............. 1.95		0.39	1.17	1.95
❑ 23, Mar 96, SKi.............. 1.95		0.39	1.17	1.95

MAYHEM
DARK HORSE

	ORIG.	GOOD	FINE	N-MINT
❑ 1, b&w		0.50	1.50	2.50
❑ 2, b&w		0.50	1.50	2.50
❑ 3, b&w		0.50	1.50	2.50
❑ 4, b&w		0.50	1.50	2.50

MAZE AGENCY ANNUAL
INNOVATION

	ORIG.	GOOD	FINE	N-MINT
❑ 1, Aug 90, Ploog(c) Spirit parody		0.55	1.65	2.75

MAZE AGENCY SPECIAL

	ORIG.	GOOD	FINE	N-MINT
❑ 1, May 90.......................2.75		0.55	1.65	2.75

MAZE AGENCY, THE
COMICO

	ORIG.	GOOD	FINE	N-MINT
❑ 1, Dec 88 ....1.95		0.39	1.17	1.95
❑ 2, Jan 89.........................1.95		0.39	1.17	1.95
❑ 3, Feb 89.........................1.95		0.39	1.17	1.95
❑ 4, Mar 89 ....1.95		0.39	1.17	1.95
❑ 5, Apr 89 ....1.95		0.39	1.17	1.95
❑ 6, May 89.........................1.95		0.39	1.17	1.95
❑ 7, Jun 89, (moves to Innovation) 2.50		0.50	1.50	2.50

MAZE AGENCY, THE (was Comico title)
INNOVATION

	ORIG.	GOOD	FINE	N-MINT
❑ 8, Dec 89 ....1.95		0.39	1.17	1.95
❑ 9, Feb 90, Ellery Queen ...1.95		0.39	1.17	1.95
❑ 10, Apr 90.......................1.95		0.39	1.17	1.95
❑ 11, Apr 90.......................1.95		0.39	1.17	1.95
❑ 12, May 90.......................2.50		0.50	1.50	2.50
❑ 13, Jun 90 ....1.95		0.39	1.17	1.95
❑ 14, Jul 90.........................1.95		0.39	1.17	1.95
❑ 15, Aug 90.......................1.95		0.39	1.17	1.95
❑ 16, Oct 90.......................2.50		0.50	1.50	2.50
❑ 17, Dec 90 ....2.50		0.50	1.50	2.50
❑ 18, Feb 91.......................2.50		0.50	1.50	2.50
❑ 19, Mar 91.......................2.50		0.50	1.50	2.50
❑ 20, May 91.......................2.50		0.50	1.50	2.50
❑ 21, Jun 91 ....2.50		0.50	1.50	2.50
❑ 22, Jul 91 ....2.50		0.50	1.50	2.50
❑ 23, Aug 91 ....2.50		0.50	1.50	2.50

MAZING MAN (really 'Mazing Man)
DC

	ORIG.	GOOD	FINE	N-MINT
❑ 1, Jan 86.........................		0.20	0.60	1.00
❑ 2, Feb 86.........................		0.20	0.60	1.00
❑ 3, Mar 86		0.20	0.60	1.00
❑ 4, Apr 86		0.20	0.60	1.00
❑ 5, May 86.........................		0.20	0.60	1.00
❑ 6, Jun 86		0.20	0.60	1.00
❑ 7, Jul 86...........................		0.20	0.60	1.00
❑ 8, Aug 86.........................		0.20	0.60	1.00
❑ 9, Sep 86.........................		0.20	0.60	1.00
❑ 10, Oct 86		0.20	0.60	1.00
❑ 11, Nov 86		0.20	0.60	1.00
❑ 12, Dec 86, FM(c)		0.20	0.60	1.00

MAZING MAN SPECIAL
(really 'Mazing Man Special)

	ORIG.	GOOD	FINE	N-MINT
❑ 1, Jul 87..........................		0.40	1.20	2.00
❑ 2, Apr 88		0.40	1.20	2.00
❑ 3, Sep 90		0.40	1.20	2.00

ME AND HER
EROS COMIX

	ORIG.	GOOD	FINE	N-MINT
❑ 1, adult, b&w		0.39	1.17	1.95
❑ 2, adult, b&w		0.39	1.17	1.95

ME AND HER SUMMER SPECIAL

	ORIG.	GOOD	FINE	N-MINT
❑ 1, adult, b&w		0.50	1.50	2.50

MEADOWLARK
PARODY PRESS

	ORIG.	GOOD	FINE	N-MINT
❑ 1, b&w, Shadowhawk, silver foil cover parody 2.95		0.59	1.77	2.95

MEAN MACHINE
FLEETWAY/QUALITY

	ORIG.	GOOD	FINE	N-MINT
❑ 1, Judge Dredd 4.95		0.99	2.97	4.95

MEAN, GREEN BONDO MACHINE
MU PRESS

	ORIG.	GOOD	FINE	N-MINT
❑ 0, Jul 92.........................2.50		0.50	1.50	2.50

	ORIG.	GOOD	FINE	N-MINT
MEAT CAKE				
FANTAGRAPHICS				
❏ 1, b&w	2.50	0.50	1.50	2.50
❏ 2, b&w	2.50	0.50	1.50	2.50
❏ 3, 94, b&w	2.50	0.50	1.50	2.50
❏ 5, Nov 95, b&w	2.95	0.59	1.77	2.95
ICONOGRAFIX				
❏ 1, b&w	2.50	0.50	1.50	2.50
MEATFACE THE AMAZING FLESH				
MONSTER				
❏ 1, b&w		0.50	1.50	2.50
MECHA				
DARK HORSE				
❏ 1, color		0.60	1.80	3.00
❏ 2, Aug 87, color		0.60	1.80	3.00
❏ 3, b&w		0.35	1.05	1.75
❏ 4, b&w		0.35	1.05	1.75
❏ 5, b&w		0.35	1.05	1.75
❏ 6		0.30	0.90	1.50
MECHANICS				
FANTAGRAPHICS				
❏ 1, Jaime Hernandez	2.00	0.40	1.20	2.00
❏ 2, Jaime Hernandez	2.00	0.40	1.20	2.00
❏ 3, Jaime Hernandez	2.00	0.40	1.20	2.00
MECHANIMOIDS SPECIAL X ANNIVERSARY				
MU				
❏ 0, 94, b&w; cardstock cover				
	3.50	0.70	2.10	3.50
MECHANOIDS, THE				
CALIBER				
❏ 1, b&w	3.50	0.70	2.10	3.50
❏ 2	3.50	0.70	2.10	3.50
❏ 3	3.50	0.70	2.10	3.50
MECHOVERSE				
AIRBRUSH				
❏ 1		0.30	0.90	1.50
❏ 2		0.30	0.90	1.50
MECHTHINGS				
RENEGADE				
❏ 1, b&w		0.40	1.20	2.00
❏ 2, b&w		0.40	1.20	2.00
❏ 3, b&w		0.40	1.20	2.00
❏ 4, b&w		0.40	1.20	2.00
MEDAL OF HONOR (mini-series)				
DARK HORSE				
❏ 1, Oct 94	2.50	0.50	1.50	2.50
❏ 2, Nov 94	2.50	0.50	1.50	2.50
❏ 3, Dec 94	2.50	0.50	1.50	2.50
❏ 4, Jan 95	2.50	0.50	1.50	2.50
MEDAL OF HONOR SPECIAL				
❏ 0, Apr 94	2.50	0.50	1.50	2.50
MEDIA*STARR				
INNOVATION				
❏ 1, Jul 89		0.39	1.17	1.95
❏ 2, Aug 89		0.39	1.17	1.95
❏ 3, Sep 89		0.39	1.17	1.95
MEDIEVAL SPAWN/WITCHBLADE (mini-series)				
IMAGE				
❏ 1, May 96	2.95	0.59	1.77	2.95
❏ 2, Jun 96	2.95	0.59	1.77	2.95
MEDUSA COMICS				
TRIANGLE				
❏ 1		0.30	0.90	1.50
MEGALITH				
CONTINUITY				
❏ 1, Jul 89		0.40	1.20	2.00
❏ 2, 89		0.40	1.20	2.00
❏ 3, 90		0.40	1.20	2.00
❏ 4, 90		0.40	1.20	2.00

	ORIG.	GOOD	FINE	N-MINT
❏ 5, 91		0.40	1.20	2.00
❏ 6, 91		0.40	1.20	2.00
❏ 7, 91		0.40	1.20	2.00
❏ 8		0.40	1.20	2.00
❏ 9		0.40	1.20	2.00
MEGALITH: DEATHWATCH 2000				
❏ 1, trading cards	2.50	0.50	1.50	2.50
❏ 2, trading cards	2.50	0.50	1.50	2.50
❏ 3, trading cards	2.50	0.50	1.50	2.50
❏ 4, trading cards	2.50	0.50	1.50	2.50
❏ 5, trading cards	2.50	0.50	1.50	2.50
❏ 6, trading cards	2.50	0.50	1.50	2.50
❏ 7	2.50	0.50	1.50	2.50
MEGATON				
MEGATON				
❏ 1		2.80	8.40	14.00
❏ 2		2.00	6.00	10.00
❏ 3		2.80	8.40	14.00
❏ 4		2.40	7.20	12.00
❏ 5		1.60	4.80	8.00
❏ 6		1.60	4.80	8.00
❏ 7		1.00	3.00	5.00
❏ 8		2.00	6.00	10.00
MEGATON HOLIDAY SPECIAL				
EXPRESS/ENTITY				
❏ 1, 94, trading card	2.95	0.59	1.77	2.95
MEGATON MAN				
KITCHEN SINK				
❏ 1, Nov 84, 1st printing		1.40	4.20	7.00
❏ 1, 2nd printing		0.40	1.20	2.00
❏ 2, Feb 85		0.70	2.10	3.50
❏ 3, Apr 85		0.40	1.20	2.00
❏ 4, Jun 85	2.00	0.40	1.20	2.00
❏ 5, Aug 85		0.40	1.20	2.00
❏ 6, Oct 85		0.40	1.20	2.00
❏ 7, Dec 85		0.40	1.20	2.00
❏ 8, Feb 86		0.40	1.20	2.00
❏ 9, Apr 86		0.40	1.20	2.00
❏ 10, Jun 86		0.40	1.20	2.00
MEGATON MAN MEETS				
THE UNCATEGORIZABLE X+THEMS				
❏ 1, Apr 89, X-Men parody, b&w	0.40	1.20	2.00	
MEGAZZAR DUDE				
SLAVE LABOR				
❏ 1, b&w		0.59	1.77	2.95
MELISSA MOORE: BODYGUARD				
DRACULINA				
❏ 1, 95, b&w	2.95	0.59	1.77	2.95
MELODY				
KITCHEN SINK				
❏ 1, b&w, adult		0.40	1.20	2.00
❏ 2, b&w, adult		0.40	1.20	2.00
❏ 3, b&w, adult		0.40	1.20	2.00
❏ 4, b&w, adult		0.40	1.20	2.00
❏ 5, b&w, adult		0.40	1.20	2.00
❏ 6, b&w, adult		0.40	1.20	2.00
❏ 7, b&w, adult		0.45	1.35	2.25
❏ 8, b&w, adult		0.50	1.50	2.50
MELTING POT				
❏ 1, Dec 93	2.95	0.59	1.77	2.95
❏ 2	2.95	0.59	1.77	2.95
❏ 3	2.95	0.59	1.77	2.95
❏ 4, Sep 94	3.50	0.70	2.10	3.50
MELVIS				
CHAMELEON				
❏ 1, Jul 94, 2500 copies				
❏ 2, 94				
❏ 3, 94				
❏ 4, 94				

	ORIG.	GOOD	FINE	N-MINT

MEMENTO MORI
MEMENTO MORI
- 2, Mar 95, b&w anthology; cardstock cover; no cover price ....

MEMORIES
EPIC
- 1, Japanese, b&w .... 2.50 | 0.50 | 1.50 | 2.50

MEMORY MAN
ESP
- 1, 95, b&w .... 2.95 | 0.59 | 1.77 | 2.95

MEN FROM EARTH
FUTURE-FUN
- 1 .... | 0.40 | 1.20 | 2.00

MEN IN BLACK, THE
AIRCEL
- 0, album .... | 1.59 | 4.77 | 7.95
- 1, b&w .... | 0.45 | 1.35 | 2.25
- 2, b&w .... | 0.45 | 1.35 | 2.25
- 3, b&w .... | 0.45 | 1.35 | 2.25

MEN IN BLACK, THE (Book II)
- 1, b&w .... | 0.50 | 1.50 | 2.50
- 2, b&w .... | 0.50 | 1.50 | 2.50
- 3, b&w .... | 0.50 | 1.50 | 2.50

MENDY AND THE GOLEM
MENDY
- 1 .... | 0.40 | 1.20 | 2.00
- 2 .... | 0.40 | 1.20 | 2.00
- 3 .... | 0.40 | 1.20 | 2.00
- 4 .... | 0.40 | 1.20 | 2.00
- 5 .... | 0.40 | 1.20 | 2.00
- 6 .... | 0.40 | 1.20 | 2.00
- 7 .... | 0.40 | 1.20 | 2.00
- 8 .... | 0.40 | 1.20 | 2.00
- 9 .... | 0.40 | 1.20 | 2.00
- 10 .... | 0.40 | 1.20 | 2.00
- 11 .... | 0.40 | 1.20 | 2.00
- 12 .... | 0.40 | 1.20 | 2.00
- 13 .... | 0.40 | 1.20 | 2.00
- 14 .... | 0.40 | 1.20 | 2.00
- 15 .... | 0.40 | 1.20 | 2.00
- 16 .... | 0.40 | 1.20 | 2.00
- 17 .... | 0.40 | 1.20 | 2.00
- 18 .... | 0.40 | 1.20 | 2.00
- 19 .... | 0.40 | 1.20 | 2.00

MEPHISTO VS. ...
MARVEL
- 1, Apr 87, JB, Fantastic Four .... 1.50 | 1.00 | 3.00 | 5.00
- 2, May 87, JB, X-Factor.. 1.50 | 0.60 | 1.80 | 3.00
- 3, Jun 87, JB, X-Men ..... 1.50 | 0.60 | 1.80 | 3.00
- 4, Jul 87, JB, Avengers .. 1.50 | 0.60 | 1.80 | 3.00

MERCHANTS OF DEATH
ECLIPSE
- 1, b&w magazine .... | 0.70 | 2.10 | 3.50
- 2, b&w magazine .... | 0.70 | 2.10 | 3.50
- 3, b&w magazine .... | 0.70 | 2.10 | 3.50
- 4, b&w magazine .... | 0.70 | 2.10 | 3.50

MERCY
DC/VERTIGO
- 0, nn............................... 5.95 | 1.19 | 3.57 | 5.95

MERLIN
ADVENTURE
- 1, b&w .... | 0.50 | 1.50 | 2.50
- 2, b&w .... | 0.50 | 1.50 | 2.50
- 3, b&w .... | 0.50 | 1.50 | 2.50
- 4, b&w .... | 0.50 | 1.50 | 2.50
- 5, b&w .... | 0.50 | 1.50 | 2.50
- 6, b&w .... | 0.50 | 1.50 | 2.50

MERLIN: IDYLLS OF THE KING
- 1, b&w.............................. | 0.50 | 1.50 | 2.50
- 2, b&w.............................. | 0.50 | 1.50 | 2.50

MERLINREALM 3-D
BLACKTHORNE
- 1 .... | 0.40 | 1.20 | 2.00

MERMAID FOREST
VIZ
- 1, 93, b&w .... 2.75 | 0.55 | 1.65 | 2.75
- 2, 94, b&w .... 2.75 | 0.55 | 1.65 | 2.75
- 3, 94, b&w .... 2.75 | 0.55 | 1.65 | 2.75
- 4, 94, b&w .... 2.75 | 0.55 | 1.65 | 2.75

MERMAID'S DREAM
- 1, 94, b&w .... 2.75 | 0.55 | 1.65 | 2.75
- 2, 95, b&w .... 2.75 | 0.55 | 1.65 | 2.75
- 3, 95, b&w .... 2.75 | 0.55 | 1.65 | 2.75

MERMAID'S GAZE
- 2, 95, b&w .... 2.75 | 0.55 | 1.65 | 2.75
- 3, 95, b&w .... 2.75 | 0.55 | 1.65 | 2.75

MERMAID'S PROMISE
- 1, 94, b&w .... 2.75 | 0.55 | 1.65 | 2.75
- 2, 94, b&w .... 2.75 | 0.55 | 1.65 | 2.75

MERMAID'S SCAR
- 1, 94, b&w .... 2.75 | 0.55 | 1.65 | 2.75
- 2, 94, b&w .... 2.75 | 0.55 | 1.65 | 2.75

MESSENGER 29
SEPTEMBER
- 1, b&w.............................. | 0.39 | 1.17 | 1.95

MESSIAH
PINNACLE
- 1, b&w.............................. | 0.30 | 0.90 | 1.50

MESSOZOIC
KITCHEN SINK
- 0, 93, nn .... | 0.59 | 1.77 | 2.95

META-4
FIRST
- 1, Feb 91, O:Meta-4 .... 3.95 | 0.79 | 2.37 | 3.95
- 2, Mar 91 .... | 0.45 | 1.35 | 2.25
- 3, Apr 91 .... | 0.45 | 1.35 | 2.25

METACOPS
MONSTER
- 1, b&w.............................. | 0.39 | 1.17 | 1.95
- 2, b&w.............................. | 0.39 | 1.17 | 1.95

METAL BIKINI
ETERNITY
- 1, b&w.............................. | 0.45 | 1.35 | 2.25
- 2, b&w.............................. | 0.45 | 1.35 | 2.25
- 3, b&w.............................. | 0.45 | 1.35 | 2.25
- 4, b&w.............................. | 0.45 | 1.35 | 2.25
- 5, b&w.............................. | 0.45 | 1.35 | 2.25
- 6, b&w.............................. | 0.45 | 1.35 | 2.25

METAL MEN
DC
- 1 .... | 100.00 | 300.00 | 500.00
- 2 .... | 44.00 | 132.00 | 220.00
- 3 .... | 20.00 | 60.00 | 100.00
- 4 .... | 20.00 | 60.00 | 100.00
- 5 .... | 20.00 | 60.00 | 100.00
- 6 .... | 12.00 | 36.00 | 60.00
- 7 .... | 12.00 | 36.00 | 60.00
- 8 .... | 12.00 | 36.00 | 60.00
- 9 .... | 12.00 | 36.00 | 60.00
- 10 .... | 12.00 | 36.00 | 60.00
- 11 .... | 7.00 | 21.00 | 35.00
- 12 .... | 7.00 | 21.00 | 35.00
- 13 .... | 7.00 | 21.00 | 35.00
- 14 .... | 7.00 | 21.00 | 35.00
- 15 .... | 7.00 | 21.00 | 35.00

	ORIG.	GOOD	FINE	N-MINT
☐ 16		6.00	18.00	30.00
☐ 17		6.00	18.00	30.00
☐ 18		6.00	18.00	30.00
☐ 19		6.00	18.00	30.00
☐ 20		6.00	18.00	30.00
☐ 21		6.00	18.00	30.00
☐ 22		6.00	18.00	30.00
☐ 23		6.00	18.00	30.00
☐ 24		6.00	18.00	30.00
☐ 25		6.00	18.00	30.00
☐ 26		6.00	18.00	30.00
☐ 27, O:Metal Men		7.20	21.60	36.00
☐ 28		3.00	9.00	15.00
☐ 29		3.00	9.00	15.00
☐ 30		3.00	9.00	15.00
☐ 31		3.00	9.00	15.00
☐ 32		3.00	9.00	15.00
☐ 33		3.00	9.00	15.00
☐ 34		3.00	9.00	15.00
☐ 35		3.00	9.00	15.00
☐ 36		3.00	9.00	15.00
☐ 37		3.00	9.00	15.00
☐ 38		3.00	9.00	15.00
☐ 39		3.00	9.00	15.00
☐ 40		3.00	9.00	15.00
☐ 41		3.00	9.00	15.00
☐ 42, reprint		0.80	2.40	4.00
☐ 43, reprint		0.80	2.40	4.00
☐ 44, reprint		0.80	2.40	4.00
☐ 45, May 76, WS	0.30	0.80	2.40	4.00
☐ 46, Jul 76, WS	0.30	0.80	2.40	4.00
☐ 47, Sep 76, WS	0.30	0.80	2.40	4.00
☐ 48, Nov 76, WS	0.30	0.80	2.40	4.00
☐ 49, Jan 77, WS	0.30	0.80	2.40	4.00
☐ 50, Mar 77, WS	0.30	0.80	2.40	4.00
☐ 51, May 77	0.30	0.80	2.40	4.00
☐ 51, May 77, WS	0.30	0.80	2.40	4.00
☐ 52, Jul 77	0.35	0.80	2.40	4.00
☐ 53, Sep 77	0.35	0.80	2.40	4.00
☐ 54, Nov 77	0.35	0.80	2.40	4.00
☐ 55, Jan 78	0.35	0.80	2.40	4.00
☐ 56, Mar 78	0.35	0.80	2.40	4.00

METAL MEN (1993 mini-series)

	ORIG.	GOOD	FINE	N-MINT
☐ 1, foil cover	2.50	1.20	3.60	6.00
☐ 2	1.25	0.60	1.80	3.00
☐ 3	1.25	0.25	0.75	1.25
☐ 4	1.25	0.25	0.75	1.25

METAL MEN OF MARS
SLAVE LABOR

	GOOD	FINE	N-MINT
☐ 1, b&w	0.39	1.17	1.95

METAL MILITIA
EXPRESS/ENTITY

	ORIG.	GOOD	FINE	N-MINT
☐ 1, Aug 95	2.50	0.50	1.50	2.50
☐ 2, 95	2.50	0.50	1.50	2.50
☐ 3, 95	2.50	0.50	1.50	2.50

METALLICA
CELEBRITY

	GOOD	FINE	N-MINT
☐ 1	0.59	1.77	2.95
☐ 1, trading cards	1.39	4.17	6.95

FORBIDDEN FRUIT

	GOOD	FINE	N-MINT
☐ 1, adult, b&w	0.59	1.77	2.95
☐ 2, adult, b&w	0.59	1.77	2.95

ROCK-IT COMICS

	ORIG.	GOOD	FINE	N-MINT
☐ 1	4.95	0.99	2.97	4.95

METALLICA'S GREATEST HITS
REVOLUTIONARY

	ORIG.	GOOD	FINE	N-MINT
☐ 1, Sep 93, b&w	2.50	0.50	1.50	2.50

METAMORPHO
DC

	ORIG.	GOOD	FINE	N-MINT
☐ 1, Aug 65	0.12	20.00	60.00	100.00
☐ 2, Oct 65	0.12	12.00	36.00	60.00
☐ 3, Dec 65	0.12	10.00	30.00	50.00
☐ 4, Feb 66	0.12	10.00	30.00	50.00
☐ 5, Apr 66	0.12	10.00	30.00	50.00
☐ 6, Jun 66	0.12	6.00	18.00	30.00
☐ 7, Aug 66	0.12	6.00	18.00	30.00
☐ 8, Oct 66	0.12	6.00	18.00	30.00
☐ 9, Dec 66	0.12	6.00	18.00	30.00
☐ 10, Feb 67	0.12	8.00	24.00	40.00
☐ 11, Apr 67	0.12	4.00	12.00	20.00
☐ 12, Jun 67	0.12	4.00	12.00	20.00
☐ 13, Aug 67	0.12	4.00	12.00	20.00
☐ 14, Oct 67	0.12	4.00	12.00	20.00
☐ 15, Dec 67	0.12	4.00	12.00	20.00
☐ 16, Feb 68	0.12	4.00	12.00	20.00
☐ 17, Apr 68	0.12	4.00	12.00	20.00

METAMORPHO (1993 mini-series)

	ORIG.	GOOD	FINE	N-MINT
☐ 1	1.50	0.30	0.90	1.50
☐ 2	1.50	0.30	0.90	1.50
☐ 3	1.50	0.30	0.90	1.50
☐ 4	1.50	0.30	0.90	1.50

METAPHYSIQUE
ECLIPSE

	GOOD	FINE	N-MINT
☐ 1, Norm Breyfogle	0.50	1.50	2.50

METEOR MAN
MARVEL

	ORIG.	GOOD	FINE	N-MINT
☐ 1, movie adaptation	2.25	0.45	1.35	2.25

METEOR MAN (series)

	ORIG.	GOOD	FINE	N-MINT
☐ 1	1.25	0.25	0.75	1.25
☐ 2	1.25	0.25	0.75	1.25
☐ 3	1.25	0.25	0.75	1.25
☐ 4	1.25	0.25	0.75	1.25
☐ 5	1.25	0.25	0.75	1.25
☐ 6	1.25	0.25	0.75	1.25

METROPOL
EPIC

	ORIG.	GOOD	FINE	N-MINT
☐ 1	2.95	0.59	1.77	2.95
☐ 2	2.95	0.59	1.77	2.95
☐ 3	2.95	0.59	1.77	2.95
☐ 4	2.95	0.59	1.77	2.95
☐ 5	2.95	0.59	1.77	2.95
☐ 6	2.95	0.59	1.77	2.95
☐ 7	2.95	0.59	1.77	2.95
☐ 8	2.95	0.59	1.77	2.95
☐ 9	2.95	0.59	1.77	2.95
☐ 10	2.95	0.59	1.77	2.95
☐ 11	2.95	0.59	1.77	2.95
☐ 12	2.95	0.59	1.77	2.95

METROPOL A.D.

	ORIG.	GOOD	FINE	N-MINT
☐ 1	3.50	0.70	2.10	3.50
☐ 2	3.50	0.70	2.10	3.50
☐ 3	3.50	0.70	2.10	3.50

METROPOLIS S.C.U. (mini-series)
DC

	ORIG.	GOOD	FINE	N-MINT
☐ 1, Nov 94	1.50	0.30	0.90	1.50
☐ 2, Dec 94	1.50	0.30	0.90	1.50
☐ 3, Jan 95	1.50	0.30	0.90	1.50
☐ 4, Feb 95	1.50	0.30	0.90	1.50

MIAMI MICE COMIC
RIP OFF

	ORIG.	GOOD	FINE	N-MINT
☐ 1, Apr 86, 1st printing		0.70	2.10	3.50
☐ 1, May 86, 2nd printing		0.60	1.80	3.00
☐ 1, May 86, 3rd printing		0.40	1.20	2.00
☐ 2, Jul 86, b&w	2.00	0.40	1.20	2.00
☐ 3, Oct 86, b&w	2.00	0.40	1.20	2.00
☐ 3, b&w;soundsheet	5.00	1.00	3.00	5.00
☐ 4, Jan 87, b&w	2.00	0.40	1.20	2.00

	ORIG.	GOOD	FINE	N-MINT

MICHAELANGELO
MIRAGE

	ORIG.	GOOD	FINE	N-MINT
❑ 1		1.40	4.20	7.00

MICHAELANGELO CHRISTMAS SPECIAL

	ORIG.	GOOD	FINE	N-MINT
❑ 1, b&w		0.35	1.05	1.75

MICKEY & MINNIE
W.D.

	ORIG.	GOOD	FINE	N-MINT
❑ 0, nn Mystery in Mouseton		0.70	2.10	3.50

MICKEY AND DONALD
GLADSTONE

	ORIG.	GOOD	FINE	N-MINT
❑ 1, Mar 88, CB	0.95	1.20	3.60	6.00
❑ 2, CB	0.95	0.60	1.80	3.00
❑ 3, Jul 88, CB	0.95	0.40	1.20	2.00
❑ 4, Aug 88, CB	0.95	0.40	1.20	2.00
❑ 5, Sep 88, WK(c), CB	0.95	0.40	1.20	2.00
❑ 6, Oct 88, CB	0.95	0.40	1.20	2.00
❑ 7, Nov 88, CB	0.95	0.40	1.20	2.00
❑ 8, Dec 88, CB	0.95	0.40	1.20	2.00
❑ 9, Dec 88, CB	0.95	0.40	1.20	2.00
❑ 10, Dec 88, CB	0.95	0.40	1.20	2.00
❑ 11, Dec 88, CB	0.95	0.40	1.20	2.00
❑ 12, Dec 88, CB	0.95	0.40	1.20	2.00
❑ 13, Dec 88, CB	0.95	0.40	1.20	2.00
❑ 14, Dec 88, CB	0.95	0.40	1.20	2.00
❑ 15, Dec 88, CB	0.95	0.40	1.20	2.00
❑ 16, CB, Beanstalk	0.95	0.40	1.20	2.00
❑ 17, CB, FG, Don Rosa	0.95	0.40	1.20	2.00
❑ 18, WK(c), CB, FG	0.95	0.40	1.20	2.00

MICKEY MANTLE
MAGNUM

	ORIG.	GOOD	FINE	N-MINT
❑ 2		0.40	1.20	2.00

MICKEY MOUSE
DISNEY

	ORIG.	GOOD	FINE	N-MINT
❑ 0, nn in Russian		2.00	6.00	10.00

GLADSTONE

	ORIG.	GOOD	FINE	N-MINT
❑ 219, Oct 86, FG	0.75	1.00	3.00	5.00
❑ 220, Nov 86, FG	0.75	3.00	9.00	15.00
❑ 221, Dec 86, FG	0.75	0.80	2.40	4.00
❑ 222, Jan 87, FG	0.75	0.80	2.40	4.00
❑ 223, Feb 87, FG	0.75	0.40	1.20	2.00
❑ 224, Mar 87, FG	0.75	0.40	1.20	2.00
❑ 225, Apr 87, FG	0.75	0.40	1.20	2.00
❑ 226, May 87, FG	0.75	0.40	1.20	2.00
❑ 227, Jun 87, FG	0.95	0.40	1.20	2.00
❑ 228, Jul 87, FG	0.95	0.40	1.20	2.00
❑ 229, Aug 87, FG	0.95	0.40	1.20	2.00
❑ 230, Sep 87, FG	0.95	0.40	1.20	2.00
❑ 231, Oct 87, FG	0.95	0.40	1.20	2.00
❑ 232, Nov 87, FG	0.95	0.40	1.20	2.00
❑ 233, Dec 87, FG	0.95	0.40	1.20	2.00
❑ 234, Jan 88, FG	0.95	0.40	1.20	2.00
❑ 235, Mar 88, FG	0.95	0.40	1.20	2.00
❑ 236, Apr 88, FG	0.95	0.40	1.20	2.00
❑ 237, Jun 88, FG	0.95	0.40	1.20	2.00
❑ 238, Jul 88, FG	0.95	0.40	1.20	2.00
❑ 239, Aug 88, FG	0.95	0.40	1.20	2.00
❑ 240, Sep 88, FG	0.95	0.40	1.20	2.00
❑ 241, Oct 88, FG	0.95	0.40	1.20	2.00
❑ 242, Nov 88, FG	0.95	0.40	1.20	2.00
❑ 243, Dec 88, FG	0.95	0.40	1.20	2.00
❑ 244, Jan 89, FG, 60th anniversary;100 pages	2.95	0.80	2.40	4.00
❑ 245, Mar 89, FG	0.95	0.40	1.20	2.00
❑ 246, Apr 89, FG	0.95	0.40	1.20	2.00
❑ 247, Jun 89, FG	0.95	0.40	1.20	2.00
❑ 248, Jul 89, FG	0.95	0.40	1.20	2.00
❑ 249, Aug 89, FG	0.95	0.40	1.20	2.00
❑ 250, FG		0.40	1.20	2.00
❑ 251, FG		0.40	1.20	2.00
❑ 252, FG		0.40	1.20	2.00
❑ 253, FG		0.40	1.20	2.00
❑ 254, FG		0.40	1.20	2.00
❑ 255		0.80	2.40	4.00
❑ 256		0.80	2.40	4.00

MICKEY MOUSE ADVENTURES
DISNEY

	ORIG.	GOOD	FINE	N-MINT
❑ 1, Jun 90	1.50	0.50	1.50	2.50
❑ 2		0.40	1.20	2.00
❑ 3	1.50	0.30	0.90	1.50
❑ 4	1.50	0.30	0.90	1.50
❑ 5	1.50	0.30	0.90	1.50
❑ 6	1.50	0.30	0.90	1.50
❑ 7	1.50	0.30	0.90	1.50
❑ 8, JBy(c)		0.30	0.90	1.50
❑ 9, Fantasia	1.50	0.30	0.90	1.50
❑ 10	1.50	0.30	0.90	1.50
❑ 11	1.50	0.30	0.90	1.50
❑ 12	1.50	0.30	0.90	1.50
❑ 13	1.50	0.30	0.90	1.50
❑ 14	1.50	0.30	0.90	1.50
❑ 15	1.50	0.30	0.90	1.50
❑ 16, KB	1.50	0.30	0.90	1.50
❑ 17, Dinosaur	1.50	0.30	0.90	1.50
❑ 18, Dinosaur	1.50	0.30	0.90	1.50

MICKEY MOUSE DIGEST
GLADSTONE

	ORIG.	GOOD	FINE	N-MINT
❑ 1		1.00	3.00	5.00
❑ 2		1.20	3.60	6.00
❑ 3		0.60	1.80	3.00
❑ 4		0.40	1.20	2.00
❑ 5		0.40	1.20	2.00

MICKEY SPILLANE'S MIKE DANGER
TEKNO

	ORIG.	GOOD	FINE	N-MINT
❑ 1, Sep 95, MAC	1.95	0.39	1.17	1.95
❑ 2, Oct 95, MAC	1.95	0.39	1.17	1.95
❑ 3, Nov 95, MAC	1.95	0.39	1.17	1.95
❑ 4, Dec 95, MAC	1.95	0.39	1.17	1.95
❑ 6, Jan 96, MAC	2.25	0.45	1.35	2.25
❑ 7, Jan 96, MAC	2.25	0.45	1.35	2.25
❑ 8, Feb 96, MAC	2.25	0.45	1.35	2.25
❑ 9, Mar 96, MAC	2.25	0.45	1.35	2.25

MICRA
COMICS INTERVIEW

	ORIG.	GOOD	FINE	N-MINT
❑ 1, Nov 86	1.75	0.60	1.80	3.00
❑ 2		0.40	1.20	2.00
❑ 3		0.40	1.20	2.00
❑ 4		0.40	1.20	2.00
❑ 5		0.35	1.05	1.75
❑ 6		0.35	1.05	1.75
❑ 7		0.35	1.05	1.75

MICRONAUTS
MARVEL

	ORIG.	GOOD	FINE	N-MINT
❑ 1, Jan 79, MG, O:	0.35	0.40	1.20	2.00
❑ 2, Feb 79, MG	0.35	0.30	0.90	1.50
❑ 3, Mar 79, MG	0.35	0.30	0.90	1.50
❑ 4, Apr 79, MG	0.35	0.30	0.90	1.50
❑ 5, May 79, MG	0.40	0.30	0.90	1.50
❑ 6, Jun 79, MG	0.40	0.30	0.90	1.50
❑ 7, Jul 79, MG	0.40	0.30	0.90	1.50
❑ 8, Aug 79, MG	0.40	0.30	0.90	1.50
❑ 9, Sep 79, MG	0.40	0.30	0.90	1.50
❑ 10, Oct 79, MG	0.40	0.30	0.90	1.50
❑ 11, Nov 79, MG	0.40	0.30	0.90	1.50
❑ 12, Dec 79, MG	0.40	0.30	0.90	1.50
❑ 13, Jan 80	0.40	0.25	0.75	1.25
❑ 14, Feb 80	0.40	0.25	0.75	1.25
❑ 15, Mar 80	0.40	0.25	0.75	1.25
❑ 16, Apr 80	0.40	0.25	0.75	1.25
❑ 17, May 80	0.40	0.25	0.75	1.25
❑ 18, Jun 80	0.40	0.25	0.75	1.25
❑ 19, Jul 80	0.40	0.25	0.75	1.25

	ORIG.	GOOD	FINE	N-MINT
☐ 20, Aug 80	0.40	0.25	0.75	1.25
☐ 21, Sep 80	0.50	0.25	0.75	1.25
☐ 22, Oct 80	0.50	0.25	0.75	1.25
☐ 23, Nov 80	0.50	0.25	0.75	1.25
☐ 24, Dec 80	0.50	0.25	0.75	1.25
☐ 25, Jan 81	0.50	0.25	0.75	1.25
☐ 26, Feb 81, PB	0.50	0.25	0.75	1.25
☐ 27, Mar 81, PB	0.50	0.25	0.75	1.25
☐ 28, Apr 81, PB	0.50	0.25	0.75	1.25
☐ 29, May 81, PB	0.50	0.25	0.75	1.25
☐ 30, Jun 81, PB	0.50	0.25	0.75	1.25
☐ 31, Jul 81, PB Dr. Strange	0.50	0.20	0.60	1.00
☐ 32, Aug 81, PB Dr. Strange	0.50	0.20	0.60	1.00
☐ 33, Sep 81, PB Dr. Strange	0.50	0.20	0.60	1.00
☐ 34, Oct 81, PB Dr. Strange	0.50	0.20	0.60	1.00
☐ 35, Nov 81	0.75	0.40	1.20	2.00
☐ 36, Dec 81	0.50	0.40	1.20	2.00
☐ 37, Jan 81, X-Men	0.60	0.60	1.80	3.00
☐ 38, Feb 82, direct sale	0.75	0.60	1.80	3.00
☐ 39, Mar 82	0.75	0.35	1.05	1.75
☐ 40, Apr 82	0.75	0.35	1.05	1.75
☐ 41, May 82	0.75	0.20	0.60	1.00
☐ 42, Jun 82	0.75	0.20	0.60	1.00
☐ 43, Jul 82	0.75	0.20	0.60	1.00
☐ 44, Aug 82	0.75	0.20	0.60	1.00
☐ 45, Sep 82	0.75	0.20	0.60	1.00
☐ 46, Oct 82	0.75	0.20	0.60	1.00
☐ 47, Nov 82	0.75	0.20	0.60	1.00
☐ 48, Dec 82, BG, 1st Guice	0.75	0.40	1.20	2.00
☐ 49, Jan 83	0.75	0.20	0.60	1.00
☐ 50, Feb 83	0.75	0.20	0.60	1.00
☐ 51, Mar 83	0.75	0.20	0.60	1.00
☐ 52, May 83	0.75	0.20	0.60	1.00
☐ 53, Jul 83	0.75	0.20	0.60	1.00
☐ 54, Sep 83	0.75	0.20	0.60	1.00
☐ 55, Nov 83	0.75	0.20	0.60	1.00
☐ 56, Jan 84	0.75	0.20	0.60	1.00
☐ 57, Mar 84	1.00	0.20	0.60	1.00
☐ 58, May 84	0.75	0.20	0.60	1.00
☐ 59, Aug 84	0.75	0.20	0.60	1.00

MICRONAUTS (2nd Series)

	ORIG.	GOOD	FINE	N-MINT
☐ 1, Oct 84, Makers	0.60	0.30	0.90	1.50
☐ 2, Nov 84	0.60	0.20	0.60	1.00
☐ 3, Dec 84	0.60	0.20	0.60	1.00
☐ 4, Jan 85	0.60	0.20	0.60	1.00
☐ 5, Feb 85	0.60	0.20	0.60	1.00
☐ 6, Mar 85	0.60	0.20	0.60	1.00
☐ 7, Apr 85	0.65	0.20	0.60	1.00
☐ 8, May 85	0.65	0.20	0.60	1.00
☐ 9, Jun 85	0.65	0.20	0.60	1.00
☐ 10, Jul 85	0.65	0.20	0.60	1.00
☐ 11, Aug 85	0.65	0.20	0.60	1.00
☐ 12, Sep 85	0.65	0.20	0.60	1.00
☐ 13, Oct 85	0.65	0.20	0.60	1.00
☐ 14, Nov 85	0.65	0.20	0.60	1.00
☐ 15, Dec 85	0.65	0.20	0.60	1.00
☐ 16, Jan 86, Secret Wars II	0.65	0.20	0.60	1.00
☐ 17, Feb 86	0.75	0.20	0.60	1.00
☐ 18, Mar 86	0.75	0.20	0.60	1.00
☐ 19, Apr 86	0.75	0.20	0.60	1.00
☐ 20, May 86	0.75	0.20	0.60	1.00

MICRONAUTS ANNUAL

	ORIG.	GOOD	FINE	N-MINT
☐ 1, Dec 79, SD	0.75	0.40	1.20	2.00
☐ 2, Oct 80, SD	0.75	0.30	0.90	1.50

MICRONAUTS SPECIAL EDITION

	ORIG.	GOOD	FINE	N-MINT
☐ 1, Dec 83	2.00	0.40	1.20	2.00
☐ 2, Jan 84	2.00	0.40	1.20	2.00
☐ 3, Feb 84	2.00	0.40	1.20	2.00
☐ 4, Mar 84	2.00	0.40	1.20	2.00
☐ 5, Apr 84	2.00	0.40	1.20	2.00

MIDNIGHT EYE
VIZ

		GOOD	FINE	N-MINT
☐ 1, color, Japanese		0.99	2.97	4.95
☐ 2, color, Japanese		0.99	2.97	4.95
☐ 3, color, Japanese		0.99	2.97	4.95
☐ 4, color, Japanese		0.99	2.97	4.95
☐ 5, color, Japanese		0.99	2.97	4.95
☐ 6, color, Japanese		0.99	2.97	4.95

MIDNIGHT MEN
EPIC

	ORIG.	GOOD	FINE	N-MINT
☐ 1, Jun 93, HC, embossed foil cover	2.50	0.50	1.50	2.50
☐ 2, Jul 93, HC	1.95	0.39	1.17	1.95
☐ 3, HC	1.95	0.39	1.17	1.95
☐ 4, HC	1.95	0.39	1.17	1.95

MIDNIGHT SCREAMS
MYSTERY GRAPHIX

		GOOD	FINE	N-MINT
☐ 1		0.50	1.50	2.50
☐ 2		0.50	1.50	2.50

MIDNIGHT SONS UNLIMITED
MARVEL

	ORIG.	GOOD	FINE	N-MINT
☐ 1	3.95	0.79	2.37	3.95
☐ 2	3.95	0.79	2.37	3.95
☐ 3	3.95	0.79	2.37	3.95
☐ 4	3.95	0.79	2.37	3.95
☐ 5	3.95	0.79	2.37	3.95
☐ 6, Jul 94	3.95	0.79	2.37	3.95
☐ 7, Oct 94	3.95	0.79	2.37	3.95
☐ 8, Jan 95	3.95	0.79	2.37	3.95
☐ 9, May 95	3.95	0.79	2.37	3.95

MIDNITE
BLACKTHORNE

		GOOD	FINE	N-MINT
☐ 1		0.35	1.05	1.75
☐ 2		0.35	1.05	1.75
☐ 3		0.35	1.05	1.75

MIDNITE SKULKER
TARGET

		GOOD	FINE	N-MINT
☐ 1		0.30	0.90	1.50
☐ 2		0.30	0.90	1.50
☐ 3		0.30	0.90	1.50
☐ 4		0.35	1.05	1.75
☐ 5		0.35	1.05	1.75
☐ 6		0.35	1.05	1.75
☐ 7		0.35	1.05	1.75

MIDNITE'S QUICKIES
ONE SHOT

	ORIG.	GOOD	FINE	N-MINT
☐ 1, b&w	3.50	0.70	2.10	3.50
☐ 2, 95, b&w	2.95	0.59	1.77	2.95

MIDVALE
MU PRESS

	ORIG.	GOOD	FINE	N-MINT
☐ 1, b&w		0.50	1.50	2.50
☐ 2, Oct 90, b&w	2.00	0.40	1.20	2.00

MIGHTILY MURDERED POWER RINGERS
EXPRESS/PARODY PRESS

	ORIG.	GOOD	FINE	N-MINT
☐ 1, 95, b&w	2.50	0.50	1.50	2.50

MIGHTY ACE, THE
OMEGA 7

	ORIG.	GOOD	FINE	N-MINT
☐ 1	2.00	0.40	1.20	2.00

MIGHTY BOMBSHELLS, THE
ANTARCTIC

	ORIG.	GOOD	FINE	N-MINT
☐ 1, Sep 93, b&w	2.95	0.59	1.77	2.95
☐ 2, Oct 93, b&w	2.75	0.55	1.65	2.75

	ORIG.	GOOD	FINE	N-MINT

MIGHTY COMICS (was Flyman)
ARCHIE

	ORIG.	GOOD	FINE	N-MINT
❏ 40, Nov 66	0.12	3.00	9.00	15.00
❏ 41	0.12	2.00	6.00	10.00
❏ 42	0.12	2.00	6.00	10.00
❏ 43	0.12	2.00	6.00	10.00
❏ 44	0.12	2.00	6.00	10.00
❏ 45	0.12	2.00	6.00	10.00
❏ 46	0.12	2.00	6.00	10.00
❏ 47	0.12	2.00	6.00	10.00
❏ 48	0.12	2.00	6.00	10.00
❏ 49	0.12	2.00	6.00	10.00
❏ 50	0.12	2.00	6.00	10.00

MIGHTY CRUSADERS

	ORIG.	GOOD	FINE	N-MINT
❏ 1, May 91	1.00	0.30	0.90	1.50
❏ 2	1.00	0.30	0.90	1.50
❏ 3	1.00	0.30	0.90	1.50
❏ 4, Nov 83	1.00	0.30	0.90	1.50
❏ 5, Jan 84	1.00	0.20	0.60	1.00
❏ 6, Mar 84	0.75	0.15	0.45	0.75
❏ 7, May 84	0.75	0.15	0.45	0.75
❏ 8, Jul 84	0.75	0.15	0.45	0.75
❏ 9, Sep 84	0.75	0.15	0.45	0.75
❏ 10, Dec 84	0.75	0.15	0.45	0.75
❏ 11, Mar 85	0.75	0.15	0.45	0.75
❏ 12, Jun 85	0.75	0.15	0.45	0.75
❏ 13, Sep 85	0.75	0.15	0.45	0.75

MIGHTY CRUSADERS (1965-)

	ORIG.	GOOD	FINE	N-MINT
❏ 1, Nov 65	0.12	6.00	18.00	30.00
❏ 2	0.12	4.00	12.00	20.00
❏ 3	0.12	3.20	9.60	16.00
❏ 4	0.12	3.20	9.60	16.00
❏ 5	0.12	3.20	9.60	16.00
❏ 6	0.12	3.20	9.60	16.00
❏ 7	0.12	3.20	9.60	16.00

MIGHTY MAGNOR, THE
MALIBU

	ORIG.	GOOD	FINE	N-MINT
❏ 1, 93, SA	1.95	0.39	1.17	1.95
❏ 1, Apr 93, SA, pop-out cover	3.95	0.79	2.37	3.95
❏ 2, SA	1.95	0.39	1.17	1.95
❏ 3, SA	1.95	0.39	1.17	1.95
❏ 4, SA	1.95	0.39	1.17	1.95
❏ 5, SA	1.95	0.39	1.17	1.95
❏ 6, Apr 94, SA, last issue.	1.95	0.39	1.17	1.95

MIGHTY MARVEL WESTERN, THE
MARVEL

	ORIG.	GOOD	FINE	N-MINT
❏ 1	0.25	0.60	1.80	3.00
❏ 2	0.25	0.40	1.20	2.00
❏ 3	0.25	0.40	1.20	2.00
❏ 4	0.25	0.40	1.20	2.00
❏ 5	0.25	0.40	1.20	2.00
❏ 6	0.25	0.30	0.90	1.50
❏ 7	0.25	0.30	0.90	1.50
❏ 8	0.25	0.30	0.90	1.50
❏ 9	0.25	0.30	0.90	1.50
❏ 10	0.25	0.30	0.90	1.50
❏ 11	0.25	0.30	0.90	1.50
❏ 12	0.25	0.30	0.90	1.50
❏ 13	0.25	0.30	0.90	1.50
❏ 14	0.25	0.30	0.90	1.50
❏ 15	0.25	0.30	0.90	1.50
❏ 16	0.25	0.30	0.90	1.50
❏ 17	0.20	0.30	0.90	1.50
❏ 18	0.20	0.30	0.90	1.50
❏ 19	0.20	0.30	0.90	1.50
❏ 20	0.20	0.30	0.90	1.50
❏ 21	0.20	0.20	0.60	1.00
❏ 22	0.20	0.20	0.60	1.00
❏ 23	0.20	0.20	0.60	1.00
❏ 24	0.20	0.20	0.60	1.00
❏ 25	0.20	0.20	0.60	1.00
❏ 26	0.20	0.20	0.60	1.00
❏ 27	0.20	0.20	0.60	1.00
❏ 28	0.20	0.20	0.60	1.00
❏ 29	0.20	0.20	0.60	1.00
❏ 30	0.20	0.20	0.60	1.00
❏ 31	0.20	0.20	0.60	1.00
❏ 32	0.20	0.20	0.60	1.00
❏ 33	0.20	0.20	0.60	1.00
❏ 34	0.25	0.20	0.60	1.00
❏ 35	0.25	0.20	0.60	1.00
❏ 36	0.25	0.20	0.60	1.00
❏ 37	0.25	0.20	0.60	1.00
❏ 38	0.25	0.20	0.60	1.00
❏ 39	0.25	0.20	0.60	1.00
❏ 40	0.25	0.20	0.60	1.00
❏ 41	0.25	0.20	0.60	1.00
❏ 42	0.25	0.20	0.60	1.00
❏ 43	0.25	0.20	0.60	1.00
❏ 44	0.25	0.20	0.60	1.00
❏ 45	0.25	0.20	0.60	1.00
❏ 46	0.25	0.20	0.60	1.00

MIGHTY MITES
ETERNITY

	ORIG.	GOOD	FINE	N-MINT
❏ 1, Oct 86, X-Men parody	1.80	0.36	1.08	1.80
❏ 2, a, 2b Batman parody		0.36	1.08	1.80
❏ 3		0.39	1.17	1.95

MIGHTY MITES (Volume 2)

	GOOD	FINE	N-MINT
❏ 1	0.39	1.17	1.95
❏ 2	0.39	1.17	1.95

MIGHTY MORPHIN POWER RANGERS: THE MOVIE
MARVEL

	ORIG.	GOOD	FINE	N-MINT
❏ 0, Sep 95, nn;movie adaptation;cardstock cover	3.95	0.79	2.37	3.95
❏ 0, Sep 95, nn;movie adaptation	2.95	0.59	1.77	2.95

MIGHTY MOUSE

	ORIG.	GOOD	FINE	N-MINT
❏ 1, Batman parody	1.00	0.20	0.60	1.00
❏ 2	1.00	0.20	0.60	1.00
❏ 3, Bat-Bat, Sub-Mariner parody	1.00	0.20	0.60	1.00
❏ 4, GP(c), Crisis parody	1.00	0.20	0.60	1.00
❏ 5, Crisis parody	1.00	0.20	0.60	1.00
❏ 6, McFarlane parody	1.00	0.20	0.60	1.00
❏ 7, computer art	1.00	0.20	0.60	1.00
❏ 8	1.00	0.20	0.60	1.00
❏ 9	1.00	0.20	0.60	1.00
❏ 10, Letterman parody	1.00	0.20	0.60	1.00

SPOTLIGHT

	GOOD	FINE	N-MINT
❏ 1	0.30	0.90	1.50
❏ 2	0.30	0.90	1.50

MIGHTY MOUSE ADVENTURE MAGAZINE

	GOOD	FINE	N-MINT
❏ 1, b&w	0.40	1.20	2.00

MIGHTY MOUSE AND FRIENDS HOLIDAY SPECIAL

	GOOD	FINE	N-MINT
❏ 1	0.35	1.05	1.75

MIGHTY MUTANIMALS (1992-)
ARCHIE

	ORIG.	GOOD	FINE	N-MINT
❏ 1, Apr 92	1.25	0.25	0.75	1.25
❏ 2	1.25	0.25	0.75	1.25
❏ 3	1.25	0.25	0.75	1.25
❏ 4	1.25	0.25	0.75	1.25
❏ 5	1.25	0.25	0.75	1.25
❏ 6	1.25	0.25	0.75	1.25
❏ 7	1.25	0.25	0.75	1.25
❏ 8	1.25	0.25	0.75	1.25

	ORIG.	GOOD	FINE	N-MINT

MIGHTY MUTANIMALS (mini-series)

	ORIG.	GOOD	FINE	N-MINT
❏ 1, TMNT spin-off	0.25	0.75	1.25
❏ 2, TMNT spin-off	0.25	0.75	1.25
❏ 3, TMNT spin-off	0.25	0.75	1.25

MIGHTY SAMSON
GOLD KEY

	ORIG.	GOOD	FINE	N-MINT
❏ 1, 65, pin-up on back cover	0.12	3.00	9.00	15.00
❏ 2, 65, pin-up on back cover	0.12	3.00	9.00	15.00
❏ 3, Sep 65, pin-up on back cover	0.12	3.00	9.00	15.00
❏ 4, pin-up on back cover	0.12	3.00	9.00	15.00
❏ 5, pin-up on back cover	0.12	3.00	9.00	15.00
❏ 6, Jun 66, pin-up on back cover	0.12	3.00	9.00	15.00
❏ 7, Sep 66, pin-up on back cover	0.12	1.60	4.80	8.00
❏ 8, Dec 66	0.12	1.60	4.80	8.00
❏ 9, Mar 67, In Washington, D.C.	0.12	1.60	4.80	8.00
❏ 10, Jun 67	0.12	1.60	4.80	8.00
❏ 11, Aug 67	0.12	1.20	3.60	6.00
❏ 12, Nov 67	0.12	1.20	3.60	6.00
❏ 13, Feb 68	0.12	1.20	3.60	6.00
❏ 14, May 68	0.12	1.20	3.60	6.00
❏ 15, Aug 68	0.12	1.20	3.60	6.00
❏ 16, Nov 68	0.15	1.20	3.60	6.00
❏ 17, Feb 69	0.15	1.20	3.60	6.00
❏ 18, May 69	0.15	1.20	3.60	6.00
❏ 19, Aug 69, N'Yark floods	0.15	1.20	3.60	6.00
❏ 20, Nov 69	0.15	1.20	3.60	6.00
❏ 21	0.15	1.20	3.60	6.00
❏ 22, Dec 73	0.20	0.80	2.40	4.00
❏ 23, Mar 74	0.20	0.80	2.40	4.00
❏ 24, Jun 74	0.20	0.80	2.40	4.00
❏ 25, Sep 74	0.25	0.60	1.80	3.00
❏ 26, Dec 74	0.25	0.60	1.80	3.00
❏ 27, Mar 75	0.25	0.60	1.80	3.00
❏ 28, Jun 75	0.25	0.60	1.80	3.00
❏ 29, Sep 75	0.25	0.60	1.80	3.00
❏ 30, Dec 75, In Macy's	0.25	0.60	1.80	3.00
❏ 31, Mar 76	0.25	0.40	1.20	2.00
❏ 32, Apr 82, final issue	0.60	0.40	1.20	2.00

MIGHTY THOR ANNUAL, THE (was Thor Annual)
MARVEL

	ORIG.	GOOD	FINE	N-MINT
❏ 14, 89	2.00	0.60	1.80	3.00
❏ 15, 90	2.00	0.50	1.50	2.50
❏ 16, 91		0.50	1.50	2.50
❏ 17, 92	2.25	0.50	1.50	2.50
❏ 18, 93, card	2.95	0.59	1.77	2.95
❏ 19, 94	2.95	0.59	1.77	2.95

MIGHTY THOR, THE (formerly Thor)

	ORIG.	GOOD	FINE	N-MINT
❏ 412, Acts of Vengeance, New Warriors	1.00	4.40	13.20	22.00
❏ 413	1.00	0.20	0.60	1.00
❏ 414	1.00	0.20	0.60	1.00
❏ 413, Jan 90	1.00	0.20	0.60	1.00
❏ 414, Feb 90	1.00	0.20	0.60	1.00
❏ 415, Mar 90, O:Thor revised	1.00	0.20	0.60	1.00
❏ 416, Apr 90	1.00	0.20	0.60	1.00
❏ 417, May 90	1.00	0.20	0.60	1.00
❏ 418, Jun 90	1.00	0.20	0.60	1.00
❏ 419, Jul 90, Black Galaxy	1.00	0.20	0.60	1.00
❏ 420, Aug 90, Black Galaxy	1.00	0.20	0.60	1.00
❏ 421, Aug 90, Black Galaxy	1.00	0.20	0.60	1.00

	ORIG.	GOOD	FINE	N-MINT
❏ 422, Sep 90, Black Galaxy	1.00	0.20	0.60	1.00
❏ 423, Sep 90, Black Galaxy	1.00	0.20	0.60	1.00
❏ 424, Oct 90, Black Galaxy	1.00	0.20	0.60	1.00
❏ 425, Oct 90	1.00	0.20	0.60	1.00
❏ 426, Nov 90	1.00	0.20	0.60	1.00
❏ 427, Dec 90, Excalibur	1.00	0.20	0.60	1.00
❏ 428, Jan 91, Excalibur	1.00	0.20	0.60	1.00
❏ 429, Feb 91, Ghost Rider	1.00	0.80	2.40	4.00
❏ 430, Mar 91, Ghost Rider	1.00	0.60	1.80	3.00
❏ 431, Apr 91	1.00	0.20	0.60	1.00
❏ 432, May 91, JK, D:Loki, 1:new Thor, reprint O:Thor	1.00	0.30	0.90	1.50
❏ 433, Jun 91	1.00	0.20	0.60	1.00
❏ 434, Jul 91	1.00	0.20	0.60	1.00
❏ 435, Aug 91	1.00	0.20	0.60	1.00
❏ 436, Sep 91	1.00	0.20	0.60	1.00
❏ 437, Oct 91	1.00	0.20	0.60	1.00
❏ 438, Nov 91	1.00	0.20	0.60	1.00
❏ 439, Nov 91	1.00	0.20	0.60	1.00
❏ 440, Dec 91	1.00	0.20	0.60	1.00
❏ 441, Dec 91	1.00	0.20	0.60	1.00
❏ 442	1.00	0.20	0.60	1.00
❏ 443	1.00	0.20	0.60	1.00
❏ 444	1.25	0.25	0.75	1.25
❏ 445, Galactic Storm	1.25	0.25	0.75	1.25
❏ 446, Galactic Storm	1.25	0.25	0.75	1.25
❏ 447	1.25	0.25	0.75	1.25
❏ 448, SpM	1.25	0.25	0.75	1.25
❏ 449	1.25	0.25	0.75	1.25
❏ 450, reprints origin of Loki	2.50	0.50	1.50	2.50
❏ 451	1.25	0.25	0.75	1.25
❏ 452	1.25	0.25	0.75	1.25
❏ 453	1.25	0.25	0.75	1.25
❏ 454	1.25	0.25	0.75	1.25
❏ 455	1.25	0.25	0.75	1.25
❏ 456	1.25	0.25	0.75	1.25
❏ 457	1.25	0.25	0.75	1.25
❏ 458	1.25	0.25	0.75	1.25
❏ 459	1.25	0.25	0.75	1.25
❏ 460	1.25	0.25	0.75	1.25
❏ 461	1.25	0.25	0.75	1.25
❏ 462	1.25	0.25	0.75	1.25
❏ 463	1.25	0.25	0.75	1.25
❏ 464	1.25	0.25	0.75	1.25
❏ 465	1.25	0.25	0.75	1.25
❏ 466	1.25	0.25	0.75	1.25
❏ 467	1.25	0.25	0.75	1.25
❏ 468	1.25	0.25	0.75	1.25
❏ 469	1.25	0.25	0.75	1.25
❏ 470	1.25	0.25	0.75	1.25
❏ 471	1.25	0.25	0.75	1.25
❏ 472	1.25	0.25	0.75	1.25
❏ 473, Apr 94	1.25	0.25	0.75	1.25
❏ 474, May 94	1.50	0.30	0.90	1.50
❏ 475, Jun 94, foil cover	2.50	0.50	1.50	2.50
❏ 475, Jun 94	2.00	0.40	1.20	2.00
❏ 476, Jul 94	1.50	0.30	0.90	1.50
❏ 477, Aug 94	1.50	0.30	0.90	1.50
❏ 478, Sep 94	1.50	0.30	0.90	1.50
❏ 479, Oct 94	1.50	0.30	0.90	1.50
❏ 480, Nov 94	1.50	0.30	0.90	1.50
❏ 481, Dec 94	1.50	0.30	0.90	1.50
❏ 482, Jan 95	2.95	0.59	1.77	2.95
❏ 484, Mar 95	1.50	0.30	0.90	1.50
❏ 485, Apr 95	1.50	0.30	0.90	1.50
❏ 486, May 95	1.50	0.30	0.90	1.50
❏ 487, Jun 95	1.50	0.30	0.90	1.50

	ORIG.	GOOD	FINE	N-MINT
❑ 488, Jul 95 .... 1.50	0.30	0.90	1.50
❑ 489, Aug 95, V: Hulk 1.50	0.30	0.90	1.50
❑ 490, Sep 95, V:Absorbing Man;(becomes Thor)			
.... 1.50	0.30	0.90	1.50

MIGHTY TINY
ANTARCTIC

	ORIG.	GOOD	FINE	N-MINT
❑ 1, b&w 1.75	0.35	1.05	1.75
❑ 2, b&w 1.75	0.35	1.05	1.75
❑ 3, b&w 1.75	0.35	1.05	1.75
❑ 4, b&w 1.75	0.35	1.05	1.75
❑ 5 .... 2.50	0.50	1.50	2.50

MIGHTY TINY: THE MOUSE MARINES

	ORIG.	GOOD	FINE	N-MINT
❑ 1, b&w 2.50	0.50	1.50	2.50

MIGHTYGUY
C&T

	GOOD	FINE	N-MINT
❑ 1	0.30	0.90	1.50
❑ 2	0.30	0.90	1.50
❑ 3	0.30	0.90	1.50
❑ 4	0.30	0.90	1.50
❑ 5	0.30	0.90	1.50

MIKE BARON'S THE GROUP LARUE
INNOVATION

	GOOD	FINE	N-MINT
❑ 1	0.39	1.17	1.95
❑ 2	0.39	1.17	1.95
❑ 3	0.39	1.17	1.95

MIKE GRELL'S SABLE
FIRST

	ORIG.	GOOD	FINE	N-MINT
❑ 1, Mar 90, MGr reprint ... 1.75	0.35	1.05	1.75
❑ 2, Apr 90, MGr reprint......	0.35	1.05	1.75
❑ 3, May 90, MGr reprint.....	0.35	1.05	1.75
❑ 4, Jun 90, MGr reprint	0.35	1.05	1.75
❑ 5, Jul 90, MGr reprint.......	0.35	1.05	1.75
❑ 6, Aug 90, MGr reprint.....	0.35	1.05	1.75
❑ 7, Sep 90, MGr reprint	0.35	1.05	1.75
❑ 8, Oct 90, MGr reprint......	0.35	1.05	1.75
❑ 9, Nov 90, MGr reprint.....	0.35	1.05	1.75
❑ 10, Dec 90, MGr reprint ...	0.35	1.05	1.75

MIKE MIST MINUTE MIST-ERIES
ECLIPSE

	ORIG.	GOOD	FINE	N-MINT
❑ 1, Apr 81, b&w 1.50	0.60	1.80	3.00

MIKE REGAN
HARDBOILED

	ORIG.	GOOD	FINE	N-MINT
❑ 1, b&w 2.95	0.59	1.77	2.95

MILK & CHEESE
SLAVE LABOR

	ORIG.	GOOD	FINE	N-MINT
❑ 1, 91, b&w 2.50	4.80	14.40	24.00
❑ 1, 2nd printing	0.50	1.50	2.50

MILK & CHEESE SIX SIX SIX

	ORIG.	GOOD	FINE	N-MINT
❑ 1, Apr 95, b&w............... 2.50	0.50	1.50	2.50

MILK & CHEESE'S FIRST SECOND ISSUE

	ORIG.	GOOD	FINE	N-MINT
❑ 2, b&w 2.50	0.80	2.40	4.00

MILK & CHEESE'S FOURTH #1

	ORIG.	GOOD	FINE	N-MINT
❑ 1, b&w 2.50	1.00	3.00	5.00

MILK & CHEESE'S OTHER NUMBER ONE

	ORIG.	GOOD	FINE	N-MINT
❑ 1, b&w 2.50	1.60	4.80	8.00

MILK & CHEESE'S THIRD #1

	ORIG.	GOOD	FINE	N-MINT
❑ 1, b&w 2.50	1.20	3.60	6.00

MILLENNIUM
DC

	ORIG.	GOOD	FINE	N-MINT
❑ 1, Jan 88...................... 0.75	0.20	0.60	1.00
❑ 2, Jan 88...................... 0.75	0.20	0.60	1.00
❑ 3, Jan 88...................... 0.75	0.20	0.60	1.00
❑ 4, Jan 88...................... 0.75	0.20	0.60	1.00
❑ 5, Feb 88...................... 0.75	0.20	0.60	1.00
❑ 6, Feb 88...................... 0.75	0.20	0.60	1.00
❑ 7, Feb 88...................... 0.75	0.20	0.60	1.00
❑ 8, Feb 88...................... 0.75	0.20	0.60	1.00

MILLENNIUM FEVER (mini-series)
DC/VERTIGO

	ORIG.	GOOD	FINE	N-MINT
❑ 1, Oct 95...................... 2.50	0.50	1.50	2.50
❑ 2, Nov 95...................... 2.50	0.50	1.50	2.50
❑ 3, Dec 95...................... 2.50	0.50	1.50	2.50
❑ 4, Jan 96, final issue....... 2.50	0.50	1.50	2.50

MILLENNIUM INDEX
ECLIPSE

	GOOD	FINE	N-MINT
❑ 1, Mar 88	0.40	1.20	2.00

ECLIPSE/INDEPENDENT

	GOOD	FINE	N-MINT
❑ 2, Mar 88	0.40	1.20	2.00

MINDGAME GALLERY
MINDGAME

	GOOD	FINE	N-MINT
❑ 1, b&w.........................	0.39	1.17	1.95

MINIMUM WAGE
FANTAGRAPHICS

	ORIG.	GOOD	FINE	N-MINT
❑ 1, Jul 95, b&w 9.95	1.99	5.97	9.95

MINIMUM WAGE (Vol. 2)

	ORIG.	GOOD	FINE	N-MINT
❑ 1, Oct 95, b&w............... 2.95	0.59	1.77	2.95
❑ 2, Dec 95, b&w............... 2.95	0.59	1.77	2.95

MINOTAUR (mini-series)
LABYRINTH

	ORIG.	GOOD	FINE	N-MINT
❑ 2, Apr 96, b&w 2.50	0.50	1.50	2.50

MIRACLE SQUAD
UPSHOT

	GOOD	FINE	N-MINT
❑ 1, 86, color	0.40	1.20	2.00
❑ 2, 86, color	0.40	1.20	2.00
❑ 3, 87, b&w......................	0.40	1.20	2.00
❑ 4, 87, b&w......................	0.40	1.20	2.00

MIRACLE SQUAD: BLOOD AND DUST
APPLE

	GOOD	FINE	N-MINT
❑ 1, Jan 89, b&w................	0.39	1.17	1.95
❑ 2, Mar 89, b&w................	0.39	1.17	1.95
❑ 3, May 89, b&w................	0.39	1.17	1.95
❑ 4, Jul 89, b&w.................	0.39	1.17	1.95

MIRACLEMAN
ECLIPSE

	ORIG.	GOOD	FINE	N-MINT
❑ 1, Aug 85...................... 0.75	0.80	2.40	4.00
❑ 2, Oct 85....................... 0.75	0.50	1.50	2.50
❑ 3, Nov 85...................... 0.75	0.40	1.20	2.00
❑ 4, Dec 85...................... 0.75	0.40	1.20	2.00
❑ 5, Jan 86....................... 0.95	0.40	1.20	2.00
❑ 6, Feb 86....................... 0.95	0.40	1.20	2.00
❑ 7, Apr 86....................... 0.95	0.40	1.20	2.00
❑ 8, Jun 86 .... 0.95	0.40	1.20	2.00
❑ 9, Jul 86, birth 0.95	0.40	1.20	2.00
❑ 10, Dec 86 .... 0.95	0.40	1.20	2.00
❑ 11, May 87..................... 1.25	0.40	1.20	2.00
❑ 12, Sep 87 .... 1.25	0.40	1.20	2.00
❑ 13, Nov 87 .... 1.75	0.40	1.20	2.00
❑ 14, Apr 88...................... 1.75	0.40	1.20	2.00
❑ 15, Nov 88..................... 1.75	0.40	1.20	2.00
❑ 16, Dec 89, last Alan Moore	0.39	1.17	1.95
❑ 17, Jun 90, 1st Neil Gaiman	0.39	1.17	1.95
❑ 18, Aug 90......................	0.40	1.20	2.00
❑ 19, Nov 90	0.40	1.20	2.00
❑ 20, Mar 91	0.40	1.20	2.00
❑ 21, Jul 91	0.50	1.50	2.50
❑ 22	0.50	1.50	2.50
❑ 23	0.50	1.50	2.50
❑ 24 .... 2.95	0.59	1.77	2.95

MIRACLEMAN 3-D SPECIAL

	ORIG.	GOOD	FINE	N-MINT
❑ 1, Dec 85 .... 2.25	0.45	1.35	2.25

MIRACLEMAN FAMILY

	GOOD	FINE	N-MINT
❑ 1, May 88, O:Young Miracleman	0.39	1.17	1.95
❑ 2, Sep 88	0.39	1.17	1.95

	ORIG.	GOOD	FINE	N-MINT

MIRACLEMAN: APOCRYPHA

	ORIG.	GOOD	FINE	N-MINT
☐ 1, 90		0.50	1.50	2.50
☐ 2, Aug 90		0.50	1.50	2.50
☐ 3, Apr 91		0.50	1.50	2.50

MIRAGE MINI COMICS
MIRAGE

☐ 1, 12 mini-comics		2.39	7.17	11.95

MIRROR WALKER
NOW

☐ 1, Oct 90	2.95	0.59	1.77	2.95

MISS FURY
ADVENTURE

☐ 1, Nov 91, O:Miss Fury, color	0.50	1.50	2.50	
☐ 1, limited edition	0.99	2.97	4.95	
☐ 2, Dec 91	0.50	1.50	2.50	
☐ 3	0.50	1.50	2.50	
☐ 4	0.50	1.50	2.50	

MISS. VICTORY GOLDEN ANNIVERSARY SPECIAL
AC

☐ 1, Nov 91, rep. 1: Miss Victory;color				
	1.00	3.00	5.00	

MISSING BEINGS SPECIAL
COMICS INTERVIEW

☐ 1, b&w	0.45	1.35	2.25	

MISSION IMPOSSIBLE
MARVEL

☐ 1, May 96, prequel to movie				
	2.95	0.59	1.77	2.95

MISSPENT YOUTHS
BRAVE NEW WORDS

☐ 1, adult, b&w	0.50	1.50	2.50	
☐ 2, adult, b&w	0.50	1.50	2.50	

MISTER E (mini-series)
DC

☐ 1, Jun 91	0.35	1.05	1.75	
☐ 2, Jul 91	0.35	1.05	1.75	
☐ 3, Aug 91	0.35	1.05	1.75	
☐ 4, Sep 91	0.35	1.05	1.75	

MISTER MIRACLE (1971-)

	ORIG.	GOOD	FINE	N-MINT
☐ 1, Apr 71, JK	0.15	5.00	15.00	25.00
☐ 2, Jun 71, JK	0.15	3.00	9.00	15.00
☐ 3, Aug 71, JK	0.15	2.40	7.20	12.00
☐ 4, Oct 71, JK	0.25	2.40	7.20	12.00
☐ 5, Dec 71, JK	0.25	2.40	7.20	12.00
☐ 6, Feb 72, JK	0.25	2.00	6.00	10.00
☐ 7, Apr 72, JK	0.25	2.00	6.00	10.00
☐ 8, Jun 72, JK	0.25	2.00	6.00	10.00
☐ 9, Aug 72, JK	0.20	2.00	6.00	10.00
☐ 10, Oct 72, JK	0.20	2.00	6.00	10.00
☐ 11, Dec 72, JK	0.20	1.60	4.80	8.00
☐ 12, Feb 73, JK	0.20	1.60	4.80	8.00
☐ 13, Apr 73, JK	0.20	1.60	4.80	8.00
☐ 14, Jul 73, JK	0.20	1.60	4.80	8.00
☐ 15, Sep 73, JK	0.20	1.60	4.80	8.00
☐ 16, Nov 73, JK	0.20	1.60	4.80	8.00
☐ 17, Jan 74, JK	0.20	1.60	4.80	8.00
☐ 18, Mar 74, JK	0.20	1.60	4.80	8.00
☐ 19, Sep 77	0.35	0.20	0.60	1.00
☐ 20, Oct 77	0.35	0.20	0.60	1.00
☐ 21, Dec 77	0.35	0.20	0.60	1.00
☐ 22, Feb 78	0.35	0.20	0.60	1.00
☐ 23, Apr 78	0.35	0.20	0.60	1.00
☐ 24, Jun 78	0.35	0.20	0.60	1.00
☐ 25, Sep 78	0.35	0.20	0.60	1.00

MISTER MIRACLE (1989-)

☐ 1, Jan 89	1.00	0.20	0.60	1.00
☐ 2, Feb 89	1.00	0.20	0.60	1.00
☐ 3, Mar 89	1.00	0.20	0.60	1.00
☐ 4, Apr 89	1.00	0.20	0.60	1.00

	ORIG.	GOOD	FINE	N-MINT
☐ 5, Jun 89	1.00	0.20	0.60	1.00
☐ 6, Jul 89	1.00	0.20	0.60	1.00
☐ 7, Aug 89	1.00	0.20	0.60	1.00
☐ 8, Sep 89	1.00	0.20	0.60	1.00
☐ 9, Oct 89	1.00	0.20	0.60	1.00
☐ 10, Nov 89	1.00	0.20	0.60	1.00
☐ 11, Dec 89	1.00	0.20	0.60	1.00
☐ 12, Jan 90	1.00	0.20	0.60	1.00
☐ 13, Mar 90	1.00	0.20	0.60	1.00
☐ 14, Apr 90	1.00	0.20	0.60	1.00
☐ 15, May 90	1.00	0.20	0.60	1.00
☐ 16, Jun 90	1.00	0.20	0.60	1.00
☐ 17, Jul 90	1.00	0.20	0.60	1.00
☐ 18, Aug 90	1.00	0.20	0.60	1.00
☐ 19, Sep 90	1.00	0.20	0.60	1.00
☐ 20, Oct 90	1.00	0.20	0.60	1.00
☐ 21, Nov 90	1.00	0.20	0.60	1.00
☐ 22, Dec 90	1.00	0.20	0.60	1.00
☐ 23, Jan 91	1.00	0.20	0.60	1.00
☐ 24, Feb 91	1.00	0.20	0.60	1.00
☐ 25, Mar 91	1.00	0.20	0.60	1.00
☐ 26, Apr 91	1.00	0.20	0.60	1.00
☐ 27, May 91	1.25	0.25	0.75	1.25
☐ 28, Jun 91	1.25	0.25	0.75	1.25

MISTER MIRACLE (1996-)

☐ 1, Apr 96	1.95	0.39	1.17	1.95
☐ 2, May 96, V:JLA	1.95	0.39	1.17	1.95
☐ 3, Jun 96	1.95	0.39	1.17	1.95

MISTER MIRACLE SPECIAL
MR. PLANET

☐ 1, 87	1.25	0.60	1.80	3.00

MISTER PLANET

☐ 1, b&w		0.60	1.80	3.00
☐ 2, b&w		0.60	1.80	3.00

MISTER X
VORTEX

☐ 1, Jun 84	1.75	0.80	2.40	4.00
☐ 2, Aug 84	1.75	0.80	2.40	4.00
☐ 3		0.40	1.20	2.00
☐ 4		0.40	1.20	2.00
☐ 5		0.40	1.20	2.00
☐ 6		0.40	1.20	2.00
☐ 7		0.40	1.20	2.00
☐ 8		0.40	1.20	2.00
☐ 9		0.35	1.05	1.75
☐ 10, BSz(c)		0.35	1.05	1.75
☐ 11		0.45	1.35	2.25
☐ 12		0.45	1.35	2.25
☐ 13		0.45	1.35	2.25
☐ 14		0.45	1.35	2.25

MISTER X (Volume 2)

☐ 1, b&w		0.40	1.20	2.00
☐ 2, b&w		0.40	1.20	2.00
☐ 3, b&w		0.40	1.20	2.00
☐ 4, b&w		0.40	1.20	2.00
☐ 5, b&w		0.40	1.20	2.00
☐ 6, b&w		0.40	1.20	2.00
☐ 7, b&w		0.40	1.20	2.00
☐ 8, b&w		0.40	1.20	2.00
☐ 9, b&w		0.40	1.20	2.00
☐ 10, b&w		0.40	1.20	2.00
☐ 11, b&w		0.40	1.20	2.00
☐ 12, b&w		0.40	1.20	2.00

MISTRESS OF BONDAGE
EROS

☐ 1, adult, b&w	2.95	0.59	1.77	2.95
☐ 2, adult, b&w	2.95	0.59	1.77	2.95
☐ 3, adult, b&w	2.95	0.59	1.77	2.95

	ORIG.	GOOD	FINE	N-MINT

MISTY
STAR
	ORIG.	GOOD	FINE	N-MINT
❑ 1	0.65	0.15	0.45	0.75
❑ 2	0.65	0.15	0.45	0.75
❑ 3	0.75	0.15	0.45	0.75
❑ 4	0.75	0.15	0.45	0.75
❑ 5	0.75	0.15	0.45	0.75
❑ 6	0.75	0.15	0.45	0.75

MITES
CONTINUM
	GOOD	FINE	N-MINT
❑ 1, b&w	0.25	0.75	1.25
❑ 2	0.35	1.05	1.75

MOBFIRE (mini-series)
DC/VERTIGO
	ORIG.	GOOD	FINE	N-MINT
❑ 1, Dec 94	2.50	0.50	1.50	2.50
❑ 2, Jan 95	2.50	0.50	1.50	2.50
❑ 3, Feb 95	2.50	0.50	1.50	2.50
❑ 4, Mar 95	2.50	0.50	1.50	2.50
❑ 5, Apr 95	2.50	0.50	1.50	2.50
❑ 6, May 95	2.50	0.50	1.50	2.50

MOBILE SUIT GUNDAM 0083
VIZ
	ORIG.	GOOD	FINE	N-MINT
❑ 7, 94	4.95	0.99	2.97	4.95
❑ 11, 94	4.95	0.99	2.97	4.95
❑ 13, 94	4.95	0.99	2.97	4.95

MOD
KITCHEN SINK
	GOOD	FINE	N-MINT
❑ 1, Bob Burden, 1:Advs. in Limbo	2.00	6.00	10.00

MODEL BY DAY
RIP OFF
	ORIG.	GOOD	FINE	N-MINT
❑ 1, Jul 90, adult;b&w	2.50	0.50	1.50	2.50
❑ 2, Oct 90, adult;b&w	2.50	0.50	1.50	2.50

SIRIUS ENTERTAINMENT
	ORIG.	GOOD	FINE	N-MINT
❑ 0, Jul 94, nn;prestige format; reprints the series with new pin-ups by Joseph Michael Linsner and Dark One	5.95	1.19	3.57	5.95

MODERN PULP
SPECIAL STUDIO
	GOOD	FINE	N-MINT
❑ 1, b&w	0.55	1.65	2.75

MODERN ROMANS
EROS COMIX
	GOOD	FINE	N-MINT
❑ 1, adult, b&w	0.45	1.35	2.25
❑ 2, adult, b&w	0.45	1.35	2.25
❑ 3, adult, b&w	0.45	1.35	2.25

MODEST PROPOSAL, A
TOME PRESS
	ORIG.	GOOD	FINE	N-MINT
❑ 1, b&w	2.50	0.50	1.50	2.50
❑ 2, b&w	2.50	0.50	1.50	2.50

MOEBIUS
DARK HORSE
	GOOD	FINE	N-MINT
❑ 0, Horny Goof	2.59	7.77	12.95

MOEBIUS: THE MAN FROM THE CIGURI
	ORIG.	GOOD	FINE	N-MINT
❑ 0, 96, nn;one-shot; smaller than a normal comic book;squarebound; b&w&color	7.95	1.59	4.77	7.95

MONDO 3-D
3-D ZONE
	GOOD	FINE	N-MINT
❑ 0, nn	0.79	2.37	3.95

MONKEY BUSINESS
PARODY
	ORIG.	GOOD	FINE	N-MINT
❑ 1, b&w	2.50	0.50	1.50	2.50

MONOLITH
COMICO
	GOOD	FINE	N-MINT
❑ 1, Oct 91	0.50	1.50	2.50
❑ 2, Nov 91	0.50	1.50	2.50
❑ 3	0.50	1.50	2.50

MONROE
CONQUEST
	ORIG.	GOOD	FINE	N-MINT
❑ 0, b&w, poster, cards	0.99	2.97	4.95

MONSTER BOY
MONSTER
	GOOD	FINE	N-MINT
❑ 1, b&w	0.45	1.35	2.25

MONSTER FRAT HOUSE
ETERNITY
	GOOD	FINE	N-MINT
❑ 1, b&w	0.45	1.35	2.25

MONSTER IN MY POCKET
HARVEY
	GOOD	FINE	N-MINT
❑ 1, Mar 91	0.25	0.75	1.25
❑ 2, May 91, The Exterminator	0.25	0.75	1.25
❑ 3, Jul 91, GK	0.25	0.75	1.25
❑ 4, Sep 91, GK	0.25	0.75	1.25

MONSTER MADNESS (b&w mag; not comics)
MARVEL
	ORIG.	GOOD	FINE	N-MINT
❑ 1	0.60	0.12	0.36	0.60
❑ 2	0.60	0.12	0.36	0.60
❑ 3	0.60	0.12	0.36	0.60

MONSTER MASSACRE SPECIAL
BLACKBALL
	ORIG.	GOOD	FINE	N-MINT
❑ 1, 94	2.50	0.50	1.50	2.50

MONSTER MENACE
MARVEL
	ORIG.	GOOD	FINE	N-MINT
❑ 1, reprints	1.25	0.25	0.75	1.25
❑ 2, reprints	1.25	0.25	0.75	1.25
❑ 3, reprints	1.25	0.25	0.75	1.25
❑ 4, reprints	1.25	0.25	0.75	1.25

MONSTER POSSE
ADVENTURE
	GOOD	FINE	N-MINT
❑ 1, b&w	0.50	1.50	2.50

MONSTERS ATTACK!
GLOBE
	GOOD	FINE	N-MINT
❑ 1, b&w mag	0.40	1.20	2.00
❑ 2, b&w mag	0.40	1.20	2.00
❑ 3	0.45	1.35	2.25
❑ 4	0.45	1.35	2.25
❑ 5, GC, GM, SD, ATh	0.45	1.35	2.25

MONSTERS FROM OUTER SPACE
ADVENTURE
	ORIG.	GOOD	FINE	N-MINT
❑ 1, b&w	2.50	0.50	1.50	2.50
❑ 2, b&w	2.50	0.50	1.50	2.50
❑ 3, b&w	2.50	0.50	1.50	2.50

MONSTERS OF THE MOVIES
(b&w mag; not comics)
MARVEL
	ORIG.	GOOD	FINE	N-MINT
❑ 1	1.00	0.20	0.60	1.00
❑ 2	1.00	0.20	0.60	1.00
❑ 3	1.00	0.20	0.60	1.00
❑ 4	1.00	0.20	0.60	1.00
❑ 5	1.00	0.20	0.60	1.00
❑ 6	1.00	0.20	0.60	1.00
❑ 7	1.00	0.20	0.60	1.00
❑ 8	1.00	0.20	0.60	1.00

MONSTERS OF THE MOVIES ANNUAL
	ORIG.	GOOD	FINE	N-MINT
❑ 1	1.25	0.25	0.75	1.25

MONSTERS ON THE PROWL
(was Chamber of Darkness)
	ORIG.	GOOD	FINE	N-MINT
❑ 9, reprints	0.15	0.25	0.75	1.25
❑ 10, reprints	0.15	0.25	0.75	1.25
❑ 11, reprints	0.15	0.25	0.75	1.25
❑ 12, reprints	0.15	0.25	0.75	1.25
❑ 13	0.25	0.25	0.75	1.25
❑ 14	0.25	0.25	0.75	1.25
❑ 15	0.20	0.25	0.75	1.25
❑ 16, Apr 72, King Kull	0.20	0.40	1.20	2.00
❑ 17	0.20	0.25	0.75	1.25
❑ 18	0.20	0.25	0.75	1.25

	ORIG.	GOOD	FINE	N-MINT
19	0.20	0.25	0.75	1.25
20	0.20	0.25	0.75	1.25
21	0.20	0.25	0.75	1.25
22	0.20	0.25	0.75	1.25
23	0.20	0.25	0.75	1.25
24	0.20	0.25	0.75	1.25
25	0.20	0.25	0.75	1.25
26	0.20	0.25	0.75	1.25
27	0.20	0.25	0.75	1.25
28	0.25	0.25	0.75	1.25
29	0.25	0.25	0.75	1.25
30	0.25	0.25	0.75	1.25

MONSTERS TO LAUGH WITH
(b&w mag; not comics)

	ORIG.	GOOD	FINE	N-MINT
1	0.25	4.00	12.00	20.00
2	0.25	2.40	7.20	12.00
3, (becomes *Monsters Unlimited*)	0.25	2.40	7.20	12.00

MONSTERS UNLEASHED (b&w mag)

	ORIG.	GOOD	FINE	N-MINT
1	0.75	0.15	0.45	0.75
2, Frankenstein	0.75	0.15	0.45	0.75
3, Frankenstein, Man-Thing, Son of Satan	0.75	0.15	0.45	0.75
4, Frankenstein	0.75	0.15	0.45	0.75
5, Frankenstein, Man-Thing	0.75	0.15	0.45	0.75
6, Frankenstein, Werewolf	0.75	0.15	0.45	0.75
7, Frankenstein, Werewolf	0.75	0.15	0.45	0.75
8, Frankenstein, Man-Thing	0.75	0.15	0.45	0.75
9, Frankenstein, Man-Thing, Wendigo	0.75	0.15	0.45	0.75
10, Frankenstein, Tigra...	0.75	0.15	0.45	0.75
11, Gabriel	0.75	0.15	0.45	0.75

MONSTERS UNLEASHED ANNUAL

	ORIG.	GOOD	FINE	N-MINT
1, reprints	1.25	0.25	0.75	1.25

MONSTERS UNLIMITED (b&w mag; not comics)

	ORIG.	GOOD	FINE	N-MINT
4, (was *Monsters to Laugh with*)	0.25	1.60	4.80	8.00
5	0.25	1.60	4.80	8.00
6	0.25	1.60	4.80	8.00
7	0.25	1.60	4.80	8.00

MOON CHILD
FORBIDDEN FRUIT

	ORIG.	GOOD	FINE	N-MINT
1, adult, b&w		0.70	2.10	3.50
2, adult, b&w		0.70	2.10	3.50
3, adult, b&w		0.70	2.10	3.50

MOON KNIGHT (also see Marc Spector, Moon Knight)
MARVEL

	ORIG.	GOOD	FINE	N-MINT
1, Nov 80, BSz, O:Moon Knight	0.50	0.90	2.70	4.50
2, Dec 80, BSz	0.50	0.40	1.20	2.00
3, Jan 81, BSz	0.50	0.40	1.20	2.00
4, Feb 81, BSz	0.50	0.40	1.20	2.00
5, Mar 81, BSz	0.50	0.40	1.20	2.00
6, Apr 81, BSz	0.50	0.40	1.20	2.00
7, May 81, BSz	0.50	0.40	1.20	2.00
8, Jun 81, BSz, V:Moon Kings	0.50	0.45	1.35	2.25
9, Jul 81, BSz, V:Midnight Man	0.50	0.30	0.90	1.50
10, Aug 81, BSz, V:Midnight Man	0.50	0.30	0.90	1.50
11, Sep 81, BSz, V:Creed	0.50	0.45	1.35	2.25
12, Oct 81, BSz	0.50	0.25	0.75	1.25
13, Nov 81, BSz	0.50	0.25	0.75	1.25
14, Dec 81, BSz	0.75	0.25	0.75	1.25

	ORIG.	GOOD	FINE	N-MINT
15, Jan 82, FM (c)/BSz, direct	0.75	0.70	2.10	3.50
16, Feb 82, V:Blacksmith	0.75	0.40	1.20	2.00
17, Mar 82, BSz	0.75	0.30	0.90	1.50
18, Apr 82, BSz, V:Slayers Elite	0.75	0.40	1.20	2.00
19, May 82, BSz, V:Arsenal	0.75	0.30	0.90	1.50
20, Jun 82, BSz, V:Arsenal	0.75	0.30	0.90	1.50
21, Jul 82	0.75	0.25	0.75	1.25
22, Aug 82	0.75	0.25	0.75	1.25
23, Sep 82	0.75	0.25	0.75	1.25
24, Oct 82	0.75	0.25	0.75	1.25
25, Nov 82, BSz	1.00	0.40	1.20	2.00
26, Dec 82	0.75	0.20	0.60	1.00
27, Jan 83	0.75	0.20	0.60	1.00
28, Feb 83	0.75	0.20	0.60	1.00
29, Mar 83	0.75	0.20	0.60	1.00
30, Apr 83	0.75	0.20	0.60	1.00
31, May 83	0.75	0.20	0.60	1.00
32, Jul 83	0.75	0.20	0.60	1.00
33, Sep 83	0.75	0.20	0.60	1.00
34, Nov 83	0.75	0.20	0.60	1.00
35, Jan 84, KN, X-Men	1.00	0.35	1.05	1.75
36, Mar 84	0.75	0.20	0.60	1.00
37, May 84	0.75	0.20	0.60	1.00
38, Jul 84	0.75	0.20	0.60	1.00

MOON KNIGHT (Second Series, 1985)

	ORIG.	GOOD	FINE	N-MINT
1, Jun 85	1.25	0.35	1.05	1.75
2, Aug 85	0.65	0.20	0.60	1.00
3, Sep 85	0.65	0.20	0.60	1.00
4, Oct 85	0.65	0.20	0.60	1.00
5, Nov 85	0.65	0.20	0.60	1.00
6, Dec 85	0.65	0.20	0.60	1.00

MOON KNIGHT SPECIAL

	ORIG.	GOOD	FINE	N-MINT
1, Shang-Chi	2.50	0.50	1.50	2.50

MOON KNIGHT SPECIAL EDITION

	ORIG.	GOOD	FINE	N-MINT
1, Nov 83, BSz, reprints	2.00	0.40	1.20	2.00
2, Dec 83, BSz, reprints	2.00	0.40	1.20	2.00
3, Jan 84, BSz, reprints	2.00	0.40	1.20	2.00

MOON SHOT, THE FLIGHT OF APOLLO 12
PEPPER PIKE GRAPHIX

	ORIG.	GOOD	FINE	N-MINT
0, Jun 94, one-shot	2.95	0.59	1.77	2.95

MOONCHILD
FORBIDDEN FRUIT

	ORIG.	GOOD	FINE	N-MINT
1, adult, b&w		0.59	1.77	2.95
2, adult, b&w		0.59	1.77	2.95

MOONFIGHTING
HARRIER

	ORIG.	GOOD	FINE	N-MINT
1, b&w		0.39	1.17	1.95

MOONSHADOW
EPIC

	ORIG.	GOOD	FINE	N-MINT
1	1.50	1.20	3.60	6.00
2	1.50	1.00	3.00	5.00
3	1.50	1.00	3.00	5.00
4	1.50	1.00	3.00	5.00
5	1.50	1.00	3.00	5.00
6	1.50	0.80	2.40	4.00
7	1.50	0.80	2.40	4.00
8	1.50	0.80	2.40	4.00
9	1.50	0.80	2.40	4.00
10	1.50	0.80	2.40	4.00
11	1.50	0.80	2.40	4.00
12	1.75	0.80	2.40	4.00

MOONSHADOW (mini-series)
DC/VERTIGO

	ORIG.	GOOD	FINE	N-MINT
1, Sep 94	2.25	0.45	1.35	2.25
2, Oct 94	2.25	0.45	1.35	2.25

	ORIG.	GOOD	FINE	N-MINT
☐ 3, Nov 94	2.25	0.45	1.35	2.25
☐ 4, Dec 94	2.25	0.45	1.35	2.25
☐ 5, Jan 95	2.25	0.45	1.35	2.25
☐ 6, Feb 95	2.25	0.45	1.35	2.25
☐ 7, Mar 95	2.25	0.45	1.35	2.25
☐ 8, Apr 95	2.25	0.45	1.35	2.25
☐ 9, May 95	2.25	0.45	1.35	2.25
☐ 10, Jun 95	2.25	0.45	1.35	2.25
☐ 11, Jul 95	2.25	0.45	1.35	2.25
☐ 12, Aug 95, final issue	2.95	0.59	1.77	2.95

MOONSTRUCK
WHITE WOLF

		GOOD	FINE	N-MINT
☐ 1		0.40	1.20	2.00

MOONTRAP
CALIBER

	ORIG.	GOOD	FINE	N-MINT
☐ 1, b&w, movie	1.95	0.50	1.50	2.50

MOONWALKER 3-D
BLACKTHORNE

		GOOD	FINE	N-MINT
☐ 1		0.50	1.50	2.50

MORBIUS REVISITED
MARVEL

	ORIG.	GOOD	FINE	N-MINT
☐ 1, reprint	1.95	0.39	1.17	1.95
☐ 2, reprint	1.95	0.39	1.17	1.95
☐ 3, reprint	1.95	0.39	1.17	1.95
☐ 4, reprint	1.95	0.39	1.17	1.95
☐ 5, reprint	1.95	0.39	1.17	1.95

MORBIUS: THE LIVING VAMPIRE

	ORIG.	GOOD	FINE	N-MINT
☐ 1, poster	2.75	0.80	2.40	4.00
☐ 2	1.75	0.40	1.20	2.00
☐ 3	1.75	0.35	1.05	1.75
☐ 4, SpM	1.75	0.35	1.05	1.75
☐ 5	1.75	0.35	1.05	1.75
☐ 6	1.75	0.35	1.05	1.75
☐ 7	1.75	0.35	1.05	1.75
☐ 8	1.75	0.35	1.05	1.75
☐ 9	1.75	0.35	1.05	1.75
☐ 10	1.75	0.35	1.05	1.75
☐ 11	1.75	0.35	1.05	1.75
☐ 12	2.95	0.59	1.77	2.95
☐ 12, black cover	2.25	0.45	1.35	2.25
☐ 13	1.75	0.35	1.05	1.75
☐ 14	1.75	0.35	1.05	1.75
☐ 15	1.75	0.35	1.05	1.75
☐ 16	1.75	0.35	1.05	1.75
☐ 17	1.75	0.35	1.05	1.75
☐ 18	1.75	0.35	1.05	1.75
☐ 19	1.75	0.35	1.05	1.75
☐ 20	1.75	0.35	1.05	1.75
☐ 21, May 94	1.95	0.39	1.17	1.95
☐ 22, Jun 94	1.95	0.39	1.17	1.95
☐ 23, Jul 94	1.95	0.39	1.17	1.95
☐ 24, Aug 94	1.95	0.39	1.17	1.95
☐ 25, Sep 94	2.50	0.50	1.50	2.50
☐ 26, Oct 94	1.95	0.39	1.17	1.95
☐ 27, Nov 94	1.95	0.39	1.17	1.95
☐ 28, Dec 94	1.95	0.39	1.17	1.95
☐ 29, Jan 95	1.95	0.39	1.17	1.95
☐ 30, Feb 95	1.95	0.39	1.17	1.95
☐ 31, Mar 95	1.95	0.39	1.17	1.95
☐ 32, Apr 95	1.95	0.39	1.17	1.95

MORLOCK 2001
ATLAS/SEABOARD

	ORIG.	GOOD	FINE	N-MINT
☐ 1, Feb 75, O:Morlock	0.25	0.20	0.60	1.00
☐ 2, Apr 75	0.25	0.20	0.60	1.00
☐ 3, Jul 75, SD/BWr O:Midnight Men				
	0.25	0.20	0.60	1.00

MORNINGSTAR
TRIDENT

		GOOD	FINE	N-MINT
☐ 1, b&w		0.50	1.50	2.50

MORPHS
GRAPHXPRESS

		GOOD	FINE	N-MINT
☐ 1		0.40	1.20	2.00
☐ 2		0.40	1.20	2.00
☐ 3		0.40	1.20	2.00
☐ 4		0.40	1.20	2.00

MORRIGAN
DIMENSION X

	ORIG.	GOOD	FINE	N-MINT
☐ 1, b&w	2.75	0.55	1.65	2.75

MORT THE DEAD TEENAGER
MARVEL

	ORIG.	GOOD	FINE	N-MINT
☐ 1	1.75	0.35	1.05	1.75
☐ 2	1.75	0.35	1.05	1.75
☐ 3	1.75	0.35	1.05	1.75
☐ 4	1.75	0.35	1.05	1.75

MORTAL COIL ASHCAN
MERMAID

		GOOD	FINE	N-MINT
☐ 0, b&w, no cover price				

MORTAL KOMBAT
MALIBU

	ORIG.	GOOD	FINE	N-MINT
☐ 1	2.95	0.59	1.77	2.95
☐ 1, variant cover	2.95	1.60	4.80	8.00
☐ 2, Aug 94	2.95	0.59	1.77	2.95
☐ 3, Sep 94	2.95	0.59	1.77	2.95
☐ 4, Oct 94	2.95	0.59	1.77	2.95
☐ 5, Nov 94	2.95	0.59	1.77	2.95

MORTAL KOMBAT SPECIAL EDITION

	ORIG.	GOOD	FINE	N-MINT
☐ 1, Nov 94	2.95	0.59	1.77	2.95

MORTAL KOMBAT: GORO, PRINCE OF PAIN

	ORIG.	GOOD	FINE	N-MINT
☐ 1, Sep 94	2.95	0.59	1.77	2.95
☐ 2, Oct 94	2.95	0.59	1.77	2.95

MORTAR MAN
MARSHALL COMICS

	ORIG.	GOOD	FINE	N-MINT
☐ 1, May 93, b&w	1.95	0.39	1.17	1.95
☐ 2, b&w	1.95	0.39	1.17	1.95
☐ 3	2.50	0.50	1.50	2.50

MORTIGAN GOTH: IMMORTALIS
MARVEL

	ORIG.	GOOD	FINE	N-MINT
☐ 1, foil cover	2.95	0.59	1.77	2.95
☐ 2	1.95	0.39	1.17	1.95
☐ 3	1.95	0.39	1.17	1.95
☐ 4	1.95	0.39	1.17	1.95

MORTY THE DOG
MU PRESS

	ORIG.	GOOD	FINE	N-MINT
☐ 1, digest b&w		0.79	2.37	3.95
☐ 2, Spr 91, digest b&w	3.95	0.79	2.37	3.95

STARHEAD

		GOOD	FINE	N-MINT
☐ 1		0.35	1.05	1.75

MOTHER TERESA OF CALCUTTA
MARVEL

	ORIG.	GOOD	FINE	N-MINT
☐ 1, 84	1.25	0.25	0.75	1.25

MOTHERLESS CHILD
KITCHEN SINK

		GOOD	FINE	N-MINT
☐ 0,		0.59	1.77	2.95

MOTLEY STORIES
DIVISION

	ORIG.	GOOD	FINE	N-MINT
☐ 1, b&w	2.75	0.55	1.65	2.75

MOTORBIKE PUPPIES, THE
DARK ZULU LIES

		GOOD	FINE	N-MINT
☐ 1, color		0.50	1.50	2.50

MOTORHEAD
DARK HORSE

	ORIG.	GOOD	FINE	N-MINT
☐ 1, Aug 95, V:Predator	2.50	0.50	1.50	2.50
☐ 2, Sep 95	2.50	0.50	1.50	2.50
☐ 3, Oct 95	2.50	0.50	1.50	2.50
☐ 4, Nov 95	2.50	0.50	1.50	2.50
☐ 5, Dec 95	2.50	0.50	1.50	2.50
☐ 6, Jan 96	2.50	0.50	1.50	2.50

	ORIG.	GOOD	FINE	N-MINT

MOTORHEAD SPECIAL
☐ 1, Mar 94	3.95	0.79	2.37	3.95

MOTORMOUTH
MARVEL
☐ 1	1.75	0.60	1.80	3.00
☐ 2	1.75	0.40	1.20	2.00
☐ 3, Punisher	1.75	0.35	1.05	1.75
☐ 4	1.75	0.35	1.05	1.75
☐ 5, (becomes Motormouth & Killpower)				
	1.75	0.35	1.05	1.75

MOTORMOUTH & KILLPOWER (was Motormouth)
☐ 6	1.75	0.35	1.05	1.75
☐ 7	1.75	0.35	1.05	1.75
☐ 8	1.75	0.35	1.05	1.75
☐ 9	1.75	0.35	1.05	1.75
☐ 10	1.75	0.35	1.05	1.75
☐ 11	1.75	0.35	1.05	1.75
☐ 12	1.75	0.35	1.05	1.75

MOUNTAIN WORLD
ICICLE RIDGE
☐ 1, b&w		0.40	1.20	2.00

MOVIE STAR NEWS
PURE IMAGINATION
☐ 1, DSt(c) Betty Page photos	1.20	3.60	6.00

MR. CREAM PUFF
BLACKTHORNE
☐ 1		0.35	1.05	1.75

MR. DOOM
PIED PIPER
☐ 1		0.39	1.17	1.95

MR. FIXITT
APPLE
☐ 1, Jan 89, b&w	1.95	0.39	1.17	1.95
☐ 2		0.45	1.35	2.25

HEROIC
☐ 1, b&w, trading card	2.95	0.59	1.77	2.95

MR. JIGSAW SPECIAL
OCEAN
☐ 1, Spr 88, O:Mr. Jigsaw, blue paper				
	1.75	0.35	1.05	1.75

MR. LIZARD 3-D
NOW
☐ 1, May 93, instant Mr. Lizard capsule, 3-D glasses				
	3.50	0.70	2.10	3.50

MR. LIZARD ANNUAL
☐ 1, Sep 93, 1993; Ralph Snart capsule				
	2.95	0.59	1.77	2.95

MR. MONSTER
DARK HORSE
☐ 1, 87, O:Mr. Monster	1.75	0.35	1.05	1.75
☐ 2, Apr 88		0.35	1.05	1.75
☐ 3, Jun 88		0.35	1.05	1.75
☐ 4, Nov 88		0.35	1.05	1.75
☐ 5, Mar 89		0.35	1.05	1.75
☐ 6, Oct 89		0.35	1.05	1.75
☐ 7, Apr 90		0.39	1.17	1.95
☐ 8, Sep 91, D:Mr. Monster.		0.99	2.97	4.95

ECLIPSE
☐ 1		1.00	3.00	5.00
☐ 2, DSt(c)		1.20	3.60	6.00
☐ 3		0.35	1.05	1.75
☐ 4		0.35	1.05	1.75
☐ 5		0.35	1.05	1.75
☐ 6		0.35	1.05	1.75
☐ 7		0.35	1.05	1.75
☐ 8		0.35	1.05	1.75
☐ 9		0.35	1.05	1.75
☐ 10, 6-D		0.35	1.05	1.75

	ORIG.	GOOD	FINE	N-MINT

MR. MONSTER ATTACKS!
TUNDRA
☐ 1, Aug 92	3.95	0.79	2.37	3.95
☐ 2, Sep 92	3.95	0.79	2.37	3.95
☐ 3	3.95	0.79	2.37	3.95

MR. MONSTER'S HI-SHOCK SCHLOCK
ECLIPSE
☐ 1		0.35	1.05	1.75
☐ 2		0.35	1.05	1.75

MR. MONSTER'S HI-VOLTAGE SUPER SCIENCE
☐ 1		0.35	1.05	1.75

MR. MONSTER'S HIGH OCTANE HORROR
☐ 1		0.35	1.05	1.75

MR. MONSTER'S THREE-DIMENSIONAL HI-OCTANE HORROR
☐ 1		0.40	1.20	2.00

MR. MONSTER'S TRIPLE THREAT 3-D
3-D ZONE
☐ 0, 93, nn	3.95	0.79	2.37	3.95

MR. MONSTER'S TRUE CRIME
ECLIPSE
☐ 1, Jack Cole		0.35	1.05	1.75
☐ 2, Jack Cole		0.35	1.05	1.75

MR. MONSTER'S WEIRD TALES OF THE FUTURE
☐ 1, BW		0.35	1.05	1.75

MR. T AND THE T-FORCE
NOW
☐ 1, Jun 93, NA, trading card				
	1.95	0.39	1.17	1.95
☐ 1, Gold, advance		20.00	60.00	100.00
☐ 2, Sep 93, trading card	1.95	0.39	1.17	1.95
☐ 3, Oct 93, trading card	1.95	0.39	1.17	1.95
☐ 4, Nov 93, trading card	1.95	0.39	1.17	1.95
☐ 5, Apr 94, trading card	1.95	0.39	1.17	1.95

MS. ANTI-SOCIAL
HELPLESS ANGER
☐ 0, nn b&w, 16 pages		0.35	1.05	1.75

MS. CYANIDE & ICE
BLACK OUT
☐ 1, 95, Sly & Furious preview				
	2.95	0.59	1.77	2.95

MS. FANTASTIC
CONQUEST
☐ 1, adult, b&w		0.59	1.77	2.95
☐ 2, adult, b&w		0.59	1.77	2.95
☐ 3, adult, b&w		0.59	1.77	2.95
☐ 4, adult, b&w		0.59	1.77	2.95

MS. FANTASTIC CLASSICS
☐ 1, adult, b&w		0.59	1.77	2.95

MS. MARVEL
MARVEL
☐ 1, Jan 77	0.30	1.00	3.00	5.00
☐ 2, Feb 77	0.30	0.70	2.10	3.50
☐ 3, Mar 77	0.30	0.50	1.50	2.50
☐ 4, Apr 77	0.30	0.50	1.50	2.50
☐ 5, May 77	0.30	0.60	1.80	3.00
☐ 6, Jun 77	0.30	0.30	0.90	1.50
☐ 7, Jul 77	0.30	0.30	0.90	1.50
☐ 8, Aug 77	0.30	0.30	0.90	1.50
☐ 9, Sep 77	0.30	0.30	0.90	1.50
☐ 10, Oct 77	0.30	0.30	0.90	1.50
☐ 11, Nov 77	0.35	0.30	0.90	1.50
☐ 12, Dec 77	0.35	0.30	0.90	1.50
☐ 13, Jan 78	0.35	0.30	0.90	1.50
☐ 14, Feb 78	0.35	0.30	0.90	1.50
☐ 15, Mar 78	0.35	0.30	0.90	1.50
☐ 16, Apr 78	0.35	0.30	0.90	1.50
☐ 17, May 78	0.35	0.30	0.90	1.50

	ORIG.	GOOD	FINE	N-MINT
☐ 18, Jun 78.......................0.35	0.30	0.90	1.50
☐ 19, Aug 78 ....0.35	0.30	0.90	1.50
☐ 20, Oct 78 ....0.35	0.40	1.20	2.00
☐ 21, Dec 78......................0.35	0.30	0.90	1.50
☐ 22, Feb 79 ....0.35	0.30	0.90	1.50
☐ 23, Apr 79 ....0.35	0.30	0.90	1.50

MS. MYSTIC
CONTINUITY

	ORIG.	GOOD	FINE	N-MINT
☐ 1, 88, NA,O:Ms. Mystic....	0.40	1.20	2.00
☐ 2, Jun 88, NA	0.40	1.20	2.00
☐ 3, Jan 89, NA	0.40	1.20	2.00
☐ 4, May 89, NA	0.40	1.20	2.00
☐ 5, Aug 90, NA(c), Comics Code	0.40	1.20	2.00
☐ 6, Nov 90, NA(c), Comics Code	0.40	1.20	2.00
☐ 7, 91..............................	0.40	1.20	2.00
☐ 8	0.40	1.20	2.00

PACIFIC

	ORIG.	GOOD	FINE	N-MINT
☐ 1, Oct 82, NA, Origin 1.00	0.40	1.20	2.00
☐ 2, Feb 84, NA 1.50	0.30	0.90	1.50

MS. MYSTIC (Volume 2, 1993)
CONTINUITY

	ORIG.	GOOD	FINE	N-MINT
☐ 1 .... 2.50	0.50	1.50	2.50
☐ 2 .... 2.50	0.50	1.50	2.50
☐ 3 .... 2.50	0.50	1.50	2.50
☐ 4 .... 2.50	0.50	1.50	2.50

MS. MYSTIC: DEATHWATCH 2000

	ORIG.	GOOD	FINE	N-MINT
☐ 1 .... 2.50	0.50	1.50	2.50
☐ 2, trading card................ 2.50	0.50	1.50	2.50
☐ 3, trading card................ 2.50	0.50	1.50	2.50

MS. QUOTED TALES
CHANCE

	ORIG.	GOOD	FINE	N-MINT
☐ 1	0.30	0.90	1.50

MS. TREE
ECLIPSE

	ORIG.	GOOD	FINE	N-MINT
☐ 1	1.00	3.00	5.00
☐ 2	0.60	1.80	3.00
☐ 3	0.60	1.80	3.00
☐ 4, Oct 83	0.40	1.20	2.00
☐ 5, Nov 83	0.40	1.20	2.00
☐ 6, Feb 84	0.40	1.20	2.00
☐ 7, Apr 84	0.40	1.20	2.00
☐ 8, May 84 .... 1.50	0.40	1.20	2.00
☐ 9, Jul 84, (moves to Aardvark-Vanaheim)			
.... 1.75	0.40	1.20	2.00

MS. TREE (former Eclipse title)
AARDVARK-VANAHEIM

	ORIG.	GOOD	FINE	N-MINT
☐ 10, Aug 84 .... 1.70	0.60	1.80	3.00
☐ 11, Sep 84...................... 1.70	0.60	1.80	3.00
☐ 12, Oct 84	0.60	1.80	3.00
☐ 13, Nov 84 .... 1.70	0.60	1.80	3.00
☐ 14, Dec 84 .... 1.70	0.60	1.80	3.00
☐ 15, Jan 85...................... 1.70	0.60	1.80	3.00
☐ 16, Feb 85...................... 1.70	0.60	1.80	3.00
☐ 17, Apr 85	0.60	1.80	3.00
☐ 18, May 85, (moves to Renegade Press)			
....	0.60	1.80	3.00

MS. TREE (was Aardvark-Vanaheim title)
RENEGADE

	ORIG.	GOOD	FINE	N-MINT
☐ 19, Jun 85, b&w 1.70	0.40	1.20	2.00
☐ 20, Jul 85, b&w.............. 1.70	0.40	1.20	2.00
☐ 21, Sep 85, b&w 1.70	0.40	1.20	2.00
☐ 22, Oct 85, b&w 1.70	0.40	1.20	2.00
☐ 23, Nov 85, b&w 1.70	0.40	1.20	2.00
☐ 24, Dec 85, b&w 1.70	0.40	1.20	2.00
☐ 25, Jan 86, b&w 1.70	0.40	1.20	2.00
☐ 26, Feb 86, b&w 1.70	0.40	1.20	2.00
☐ 27, Mar 86, b&w 1.70	0.40	1.20	2.00
☐ 28, Apr 86, b&w 1.70	0.40	1.20	2.00

	ORIG.	GOOD	FINE	N-MINT
☐ 29, May 86, b&w 1.70	0.40	1.20	2.00
☐ 30, Jun 86, b&w 2.00	0.40	1.20	2.00
☐ 31, Jul 86, b&w 2.00	0.40	1.20	2.00
☐ 32, Sep 86, b&w 2.00	0.40	1.20	2.00
☐ 33, Oct 86, b&w 2.00	0.40	1.20	2.00
☐ 34, Nov 86, b&w 2.00	0.40	1.20	2.00
☐ 35, Dec 86, b&w 2.00	0.40	1.20	2.00
☐ 36, Feb 87, b&w 2.00	0.40	1.20	2.00
☐ 37, Mar 87, b&w 2.00	0.40	1.20	2.00
☐ 38, Apr 87, b&w 2.00	0.40	1.20	2.00
☐ 39, May 87, b&w 2.00	0.40	1.20	2.00
☐ 40, Jun 87, b&w 2.00	0.40	1.20	2.00
☐ 41, Oct 87, b&w 2.00	0.40	1.20	2.00
☐ 42, Nov 87, b&w 2.00	0.40	1.20	2.00
☐ 43, Dec 87, b&w 2.00	0.40	1.20	2.00
☐ 44, Feb 88, b&w 2.00	0.40	1.20	2.00
☐ 45, Apr 88, b&w 2.00	0.40	1.20	2.00
☐ 46, May 88, b&w 2.00	0.40	1.20	2.00
☐ 47, Aug 88, b&w 2.00	0.40	1.20	2.00
☐ 48, Nov 88, b&w 2.00	0.40	1.20	2.00
☐ 49, May 89, b&w 2.00	0.40	1.20	2.00
☐ 50, Jun 89, flexidisc, JK..2.75	0.55	1.65	2.75

MS. TREE 3-D

	ORIG.	GOOD	FINE	N-MINT
☐ 1, Aug 85 .... 2.00	0.40	1.20	2.00

MS. TREE QUARTERLY
DC

	ORIG.	GOOD	FINE	N-MINT
☐ 1, Jun 90, MGr, Batman..3.99	0.79	2.37	3.95
☐ 2, Sep 90, Butcher 3.95	0.79	2.37	3.95
☐ 3, Dec 90, Butcher 3.95	0.79	2.37	3.95
☐ 4, Mar 91 .... 3.95	0.79	2.37	3.95
☐ 5, Jun 91 .... 3.95	0.79	2.37	3.95
☐ 6, Sep 91 .... 3.95	0.79	2.37	3.95
☐ 7, Dec 91 .... 3.95	0.79	2.37	3.95
☐ 8, Sum 92...................... 3.95	0.79	2.37	3.95
☐ 9, 92 .... 3.95	0.79	2.37	3.95
☐ 10, 93 .... 3.50	0.79	2.37	3.95

MS. TREE SUMMER SPECIAL
RENEGADE

	ORIG.	GOOD	FINE	N-MINT
☐ 1, Aug 86, b&w 2.00	0.40	1.20	2.00

MS. TREE'S 1950'S THREE-DIMENSIONAL CRIME

	ORIG.	GOOD	FINE	N-MINT
☐ 1, Jul 87, 3-D..................	0.50	1.50	2.50

MS. VICTORY SPECIAL
AC

	ORIG.	GOOD	FINE	N-MINT
☐ 1, 85, color	0.35	1.05	1.75

MUMMY ARCHIVES, THE
MILLENNIUM

	ORIG.	GOOD	FINE	N-MINT
☐ 1 .... 2.50	0.50	1.50	2.50

MUMMY OR RAMSES THE DAMNED, THE

	ORIG.	GOOD	FINE	N-MINT
☐ 1	0.80	2.40	4.00
☐ 2	0.50	1.50	2.50
☐ 3	0.50	1.50	2.50
☐ 4	0.50	1.50	2.50
☐ 5	0.50	1.50	2.50
☐ 6	0.50	1.50	2.50
☐ 7	0.50	1.50	2.50
☐ 8	0.50	1.50	2.50
☐ 9	0.50	1.50	2.50
☐ 10	0.50	1.50	2.50
☐ 11	0.50	1.50	2.50
☐ 12	0.50	1.50	2.50

MUMMY'S CURSE, THE
AIRCEL

	ORIG.	GOOD	FINE	N-MINT
☐ 1, b&w............................	0.45	1.35	2.25
☐ 2, b&w............................	0.45	1.35	2.25
☐ 3, b&w............................	0.45	1.35	2.25
☐ 4, b&w............................	0.45	1.35	2.25

MUMMY, THE
MONSTER

	ORIG.	GOOD	FINE	N-MINT
☐ 1, b&w............................	0.39	1.17	1.95

	ORIG.	GOOD	FINE	N-MINT
☐ 2, b&w		0.39	1.17	1.95
☐ 3, b&w		0.39	1.17	1.95
☐ 4, b&w		0.39	1.17	1.95

MUNDEN'S BAR ANNUAL
FIRST

	ORIG.	GOOD	FINE	N-MINT
☐ 1, BB,SR		0.59	1.77	2.95
☐ 2, TMNT, Omaha		1.19	3.57	5.95

MUPPET BABIES
HARVEY

	ORIG.	GOOD	FINE	N-MINT
☐ 1	1.25	0.25	0.75	1.25
☐ 2	1.25	0.25	0.75	1.25
☐ 3	1.50	0.30	0.90	1.50
☐ 4	1.50	0.30	0.90	1.50
☐ 5	1.50	0.30	0.90	1.50
☐ 6, Aug 94	1.50	0.30	0.90	1.50

STAR

	ORIG.	GOOD	FINE	N-MINT
☐ 1	0.65	0.15	0.45	0.75
☐ 2	0.65	0.15	0.45	0.75
☐ 3	0.65	0.15	0.45	0.75
☐ 4	0.65	0.15	0.45	0.75
☐ 5	0.65	0.15	0.45	0.75
☐ 6	0.65	0.15	0.45	0.75
☐ 7	0.75	0.15	0.45	0.75
☐ 8	0.75	0.15	0.45	0.75
☐ 9	0.75	0.15	0.45	0.75
☐ 10	0.75	0.15	0.45	0.75
☐ 11	0.75	0.15	0.45	0.75
☐ 12	0.75	0.15	0.45	0.75
☐ 13	0.75	0.15	0.45	0.75
☐ 14	1.00	0.20	0.60	1.00
☐ 15	1.00	0.20	0.60	1.00
☐ 16	1.00	0.20	0.60	1.00
☐ 17, (becomes Marvel Comic)	1.00	0.20	0.60	1.00

MUPPET BABIES (Was Star Comic)
MARVEL

	ORIG.	GOOD	FINE	N-MINT
☐ 18	1.00	0.20	0.60	1.00
☐ 19	1.00	0.20	0.60	1.00
☐ 20	1.00	0.20	0.60	1.00
☐ 21	1.00	0.20	0.60	1.00
☐ 22	1.00	0.20	0.60	1.00
☐ 23	1.00	0.20	0.60	1.00
☐ 24	1.00	0.20	0.60	1.00
☐ 25	1.00	0.20	0.60	1.00
☐ 26	1.00	0.20	0.60	1.00

MUPPET BABIES ADVENTURES
HARVEY

	ORIG.	GOOD	FINE	N-MINT
☐ 1		0.25	0.75	1.25

MUPPET BABIES BIG BOOK

	ORIG.	GOOD	FINE	N-MINT
☐ 1		0.39	1.17	1.95

MUPPETS TAKE MANHATTAN
STAR

	ORIG.	GOOD	FINE	N-MINT
☐ 1, movie adaptation	0.60	0.13	0.39	0.65
☐ 2, movie adaptation	0.60	0.13	0.39	0.65
☐ 3, movie adaptation	0.60	0.13	0.39	0.65

MURCIELAGA SHE-BAT
HEROIC

	ORIG.	GOOD	FINE	N-MINT
☐ 1, b&w		0.30	0.90	1.50
☐ 2, b&w		0.59	1.77	2.95

REVOLUTIONARY

	ORIG.	GOOD	FINE	N-MINT
☐ 3, Jul 93, b&w	2.95	0.59	1.77	2.95

MUSIC COMICS
PERSONALITY

	ORIG.	GOOD	FINE	N-MINT
☐ 2, color		0.59	1.77	2.95
☐ 3, color		0.59	1.77	2.95
☐ 4, b&w		0.50	1.50	2.50

MUSIC COMICS ON TOUR

	ORIG.	GOOD	FINE	N-MINT
☐ 1, Beatles, b&w		0.59	1.77	2.95

MUTANT BOOK OF THE DEAD, THE
STARHEAD

	ORIG.	GOOD	FINE	N-MINT
☐ 1, 94, adult;b&w	2.50	0.50	1.50	2.50

MUTANT CHRONICLES
ACCLAIM/ARMADA

	ORIG.	GOOD	FINE	N-MINT
☐ 1, May 96, "Golgotha" Part 1 of 4;cardstock cover; polybagged with Doom Trooper card	2.95	0.59	1.77	2.95
☐ 2, Jun 96, "Golgotha" Part 2 of 4;cardstock cover; polybagged with Doom Trooper card	2.95	0.59	1.77	2.95
☐ 3, Jul 96, "Golgotha" Part 3 of 4;cardstock cover; polybagged with Doom Trooper card	2.95	0.59	1.77	2.95
☐ 4, Aug 96, "Golgotha" Part 4 of 4;cardstock cover; polybagged with Doom Trooper card	2.95	0.59	1.77	2.95

MUTANT MISADVENTURES OF CLOAK & DAGGER
MARVEL

	ORIG.	GOOD	FINE	N-MINT
☐ 1, Oct 88	1.25	0.25	0.75	1.25
☐ 2, Dec 88	1.50	0.30	0.90	1.50
☐ 3, Feb 89	1.50	0.30	0.90	1.50
☐ 4, Apr 89, Inferno	1.50	0.30	0.90	1.50
☐ 5, Jun 89	1.50	0.30	0.90	1.50
☐ 6, Aug 89	1.50	0.30	0.90	1.50
☐ 7, Oct 89	1.50	0.30	0.90	1.50
☐ 8, Dec 89	1.50	0.30	0.90	1.50
☐ 9, Jan 90, Avengers, Acts of Vengeance	2.50	0.50	1.50	2.50
☐ 10, Feb 90	1.50	0.30	0.90	1.50
☐ 11, Apr 90	1.50	0.30	0.90	1.50
☐ 12, Jun 90	1.50	0.30	0.90	1.50
☐ 13, Aug 90, (becomes Cloak & Dagger)	1.50	0.30	0.90	1.50

MUTANT ZONE
AIRCEL

	ORIG.	GOOD	FINE	N-MINT
☐ 1, b&w		0.50	1.50	2.50
☐ 2, b&w		0.50	1.50	2.50
☐ 3, b&w		0.50	1.50	2.50

MUTANTS AND MISFITS
SILVERLINE

	ORIG.	GOOD	FINE	N-MINT
☐ 1, color		0.39	1.17	1.95

MUTANTS VS. ULTRAS: FIRST ENCOUNTERS
MALIBU/ULTRAVERSE

	ORIG.	GOOD	FINE	N-MINT
☐ 1, Nov 95, reprints Prime vs. Hulk, Night Man vs. Wolverine, and Exiles vs. X-Men	6.95	1.39	4.17	6.95

MUTATIS
EPIC

	ORIG.	GOOD	FINE	N-MINT
☐ 1	2.25	0.45	1.35	2.25
☐ 2	2.25	0.45	1.35	2.25
☐ 3	2.25	0.45	1.35	2.25

MY GREATEST ADVENTURE
DC

	ORIG.	GOOD	FINE	N-MINT
☐ 30		6.00	18.00	30.00
☐ 31		6.00	18.00	30.00
☐ 32		6.00	18.00	30.00
☐ 33		6.00	18.00	30.00
☐ 34		6.00	18.00	30.00
☐ 35		6.00	18.00	30.00
☐ 36		6.00	18.00	30.00
☐ 37		6.00	18.00	30.00
☐ 38		6.00	18.00	30.00
☐ 39		6.00	18.00	30.00
☐ 40		6.00	18.00	30.00
☐ 41		6.00	18.00	30.00
☐ 42		6.00	18.00	30.00
☐ 43		6.00	18.00	30.00
☐ 44		6.00	18.00	30.00
☐ 45		6.00	18.00	30.00

	ORIG.	GOOD	FINE	N-MINT
☐ 46		6.00	18.00	30.00
☐ 47		6.00	18.00	30.00
☐ 48		6.00	18.00	30.00
☐ 49		6.00	18.00	30.00
☐ 50		6.00	18.00	30.00
☐ 51		6.00	18.00	30.00
☐ 52		6.00	18.00	30.00
☐ 53		6.00	18.00	30.00
☐ 54		6.00	18.00	30.00
☐ 55		6.00	18.00	30.00
☐ 56		6.00	18.00	30.00
☐ 57		6.00	18.00	30.00
☐ 58		8.00	24.00	40.00
☐ 59		5.00	15.00	25.00
☐ 60, ATh		4.00	12.00	20.00
☐ 61, ATh		4.00	12.00	20.00
☐ 62		3.00	9.00	15.00
☐ 63		3.00	9.00	15.00
☐ 64		3.00	9.00	15.00
☐ 65		3.00	9.00	15.00
☐ 66		3.00	9.00	15.00
☐ 67		3.00	9.00	15.00
☐ 68		3.00	9.00	15.00
☐ 69		3.00	9.00	15.00
☐ 70		3.00	9.00	15.00
☐ 71		3.00	9.00	15.00
☐ 72		3.00	9.00	15.00
☐ 73		3.00	9.00	15.00
☐ 74		3.00	9.00	15.00
☐ 75		3.00	9.00	15.00
☐ 76		3.00	9.00	15.00
☐ 77, ATh		3.00	9.00	15.00
☐ 78		3.00	9.00	15.00
☐ 79		3.00	9.00	15.00
☐ 80, 1:Doom Patrol		70.00	210.00	350.00
☐ 81, Doom Patrol		48.00	144.00	240.00
☐ 82, Doom Patrol		32.00	96.00	160.00
☐ 83, Doom Patrol		28.00	84.00	140.00
☐ 84, Doom Patrol		25.00	75.00	125.00
☐ 85, Doom Patrol (becomes *Doom Patrol*)		20.00	60.00	100.00

MY LOVE (1969-1976)
MARVEL

	ORIG.	GOOD	FINE	N-MINT
☐ 1	0.15	0.40	1.20	2.00
☐ 2	0.15	0.40	1.20	2.00
☐ 3	0.15	0.40	1.20	2.00
☐ 4	0.15	0.40	1.20	2.00
☐ 5	0.15	0.40	1.20	2.00
☐ 6	0.15	0.20	0.60	1.00
☐ 7	0.15	0.20	0.60	1.00
☐ 8	0.15	0.20	0.60	1.00
☐ 9	0.15	0.20	0.60	1.00
☐ 10	0.15	0.20	0.60	1.00
☐ 11	0.15	0.20	0.60	1.00
☐ 12	0.15	0.20	0.60	1.00
☐ 13	0.15	0.20	0.60	1.00
☐ 14	0.15	0.20	0.60	1.00
☐ 15	0.15	0.20	0.60	1.00
☐ 16	0.15	0.20	0.60	1.00
☐ 17	0.15	0.20	0.60	1.00
☐ 18	0.15	0.20	0.60	1.00
☐ 19	0.20	0.20	0.60	1.00
☐ 20	0.20	0.20	0.60	1.00
☐ 21	0.20	0.20	0.60	1.00
☐ 22	0.20	0.20	0.60	1.00
☐ 23	0.20	0.20	0.60	1.00
☐ 24	0.20	0.20	0.60	1.00
☐ 25	0.20	0.20	0.60	1.00
☐ 26	0.20	0.20	0.60	1.00
☐ 27	0.20	0.20	0.60	1.00
☐ 28	0.20	0.20	0.60	1.00
☐ 29	0.20	0.20	0.60	1.00

	ORIG.	GOOD	FINE	N-MINT
☐ 30	0.20	0.20	0.60	1.00
☐ 31	0.20	0.20	0.60	1.00
☐ 32	0.20	0.20	0.60	1.00
☐ 33	0.20	0.20	0.60	1.00
☐ 34	0.20	0.20	0.60	1.00
☐ 35	0.20	0.20	0.60	1.00
☐ 36	0.20	0.20	0.60	1.00
☐ 37	0.20	0.20	0.60	1.00
☐ 38	0.20	0.20	0.60	1.00
☐ 39	0.20	0.20	0.60	1.00

MY NAME IS CHAOS
DC

		GOOD	FINE	N-MINT
☐ 1		0.99	2.97	4.95
☐ 2		0.99	2.97	4.95
☐ 3		0.99	2.97	4.95
☐ 4		0.99	2.97	4.95

MY NAME IS HOLOCAUST (mini-series)
DC/MILESTONE

	ORIG.	GOOD	FINE	N-MINT
☐ 1, May 95	2.50	0.50	1.50	2.50
☐ 2, Jun 95	2.50	0.50	1.50	2.50
☐ 3, Jul 95	2.50	0.50	1.50	2.50
☐ 4, Aug 95	2.50	0.50	1.50	2.50
☐ 5, Sep 95	2.50	0.50	1.50	2.50

MYRON MOOSE FUNNIES
FANTAGRAPHICS

		GOOD	FINE	N-MINT
☐ 1		0.35	1.05	1.75
☐ 2		0.35	1.05	1.75
☐ 3		0.35	1.05	1.75

MYS-TECH WARS
MARVEL

	ORIG.	GOOD	FINE	N-MINT
☐ 1	1.75	0.35	1.05	1.75
☐ 2	1.75	0.35	1.05	1.75
☐ 3	1.75	0.35	1.05	1.75
☐ 4	1.75	0.35	1.05	1.75

MYSTERY IN SPACE
DC

	ORIG.	GOOD	FINE	N-MINT
☐ 53, CI, Adam Strange		300.00	900.00	1500.00
☐ 54, Sep 59, CI	0.10	150.00	450.00	750.00
☐ 55, CI		100.00	300.00	500.00
☐ 56, CI		60.00	180.00	300.00
☐ 57, CI		60.00	180.00	300.00
☐ 58, Mar 60, CI	0.10	60.00	180.00	300.00
☐ 59, May 60, CI	0.10	60.00	180.00	300.00
☐ 60, Jun 60, CI	0.10	60.00	180.00	300.00
☐ 61, Aug 60, CI	0.10	36.00	108.00	180.00
☐ 62, Sep 60, CI	0.10	36.00	108.00	180.00
☐ 63, Nov 60, CI	0.10	36.00	108.00	180.00
☐ 64, Dec 60, CI	0.10	36.00	108.00	180.00
☐ 65, Feb 61, CI	0.10	36.00	108.00	180.00
☐ 66, Mar 61, CI	0.10	36.00	108.00	180.00
☐ 67, May 61, CI	0.10	36.00	108.00	180.00
☐ 68, Jun 61, CI	0.10	36.00	108.00	180.00
☐ 69, Aug 61, CI	0.10	36.00	108.00	180.00
☐ 70, Sep 61, CI	0.10	36.00	108.00	180.00
☐ 71, Nov 61, CI	0.10	24.00	72.00	120.00
☐ 72, Dec 61, CI	0.12	24.00	72.00	120.00
☐ 73, Feb 62, CI	0.12	24.00	72.00	120.00
☐ 74, Mar 62, CI	0.12	24.00	72.00	120.00
☐ 75, May 62, CI;JLA	0.12	48.00	144.00	240.00
☐ 76, Jun 62, CI	0.12	20.00	60.00	100.00
☐ 77, Aug 62, CI	0.12	20.00	60.00	100.00
☐ 78, Sep 62, CI	0.12	20.00	60.00	100.00
☐ 79, Nov 62, CI	0.12	20.00	60.00	100.00
☐ 80, Dec 62, CI	0.12	20.00	60.00	100.00
☐ 81, Feb 63, CI	0.12	10.00	30.00	50.00
☐ 82, Mar 63, CI	0.12	10.00	30.00	50.00
☐ 83, May 63, CI	0.12	10.00	30.00	50.00
☐ 84, Jun 63, CI	0.12	10.00	30.00	50.00
☐ 85, Aug 63, CI	0.12	10.00	30.00	50.00
☐ 86, Sep 63, CI	0.12	10.00	30.00	50.00

	ORIG.	GOOD	FINE	N-MINT
87, Nov 63, CI Hawkman				
.... 0.12		16.00	48.00	80.00
88, Dec 63, CI Hawkman				
.... 0.12		24.00	72.00	120.00
89, Feb 64, CI Hawkman				
.... 0.12		20.00	60.00	100.00
90, Mar 64, CI Hawkman				
.... 0.12		20.00	60.00	100.00
91, May 64, CI....... 0.12		3.00	9.00	15.00
92		3.00	9.00	15.00
93		3.00	9.00	15.00
94		3.00	9.00	15.00
95		3.00	9.00	15.00
96		3.00	9.00	15.00
97		3.00	9.00	15.00
98		3.00	9.00	15.00
99		3.00	9.00	15.00
100		3.00	9.00	15.00
101		3.00	9.00	15.00
102		3.00	9.00	15.00
103		1.00	3.00	5.00
104		1.00	3.00	5.00
105		1.00	3.00	5.00
106		1.00	3.00	5.00
107		1.00	3.00	5.00
108		1.00	3.00	5.00
109		1.00	3.00	5.00
110		1.00	3.00	5.00
111, Sep 80....... 0.50		1.00	3.00	5.00
112, Oct 80....... 0.50		1.00	3.00	5.00
113, Nov 80....... 0.50		1.00	3.00	5.00
114, Dec 80....... 0.50		1.00	3.00	5.00
115, Jan 81 .... 0.50		1.00	3.00	5.00
116, Feb 81 .... 0.50		1.00	3.00	5.00
117, Mar 81 .... 0.50		1.00	3.00	5.00

	ORIG.	GOOD	FINE	N-MINT
MYSTERY MAN, THE				
SLAVE LABOR				
1, b&w.......		0.35	1.05	1.75
2, b&w.......		0.35	1.05	1.75
MYTH CONCEPTIONS				
APPLE				
1, Nov 87, b&w.......	1.75	1.00	3.00	5.00
2, Jan 88, b&w	1.75	1.00	3.00	5.00
3, Mar 88, b&w.......	1.75	1.00	3.00	5.00
4, May 88.......	1.95	0.39	1.17	1.95
5, Jul 88.......	1.95	0.39	1.17	1.95
6, Sep 88.......	1.95	0.39	1.17	1.95
7, Nov 88.......	1.95	0.39	1.17	1.95
8, Jan 89.......	1.95	0.39	1.17	1.95
MYTHADVENTURES				
WARP				
1, Mar 84	1.50	0.30	0.90	1.50
2, Jun 84	1.50	0.30	0.90	1.50
3, Sep 84	1.50	0.30	0.90	1.50
4, Dec 84	1.50	0.30	0.90	1.50
5, Mar 85	1.50	0.30	0.90	1.50
6, Jun 85	1.50	0.30	0.90	1.50
7, Sep 85	1.50	0.30	0.90	1.50
8, Dec 85	1.50	0.30	0.90	1.50
9, Mar 86, (moves to Apple)				
....	1.50	0.30	0.90	1.50
MYTHADVENTURES (former Warp title)				
APPLE				
10, 86, b&w.......	1.50	0.30	0.90	1.50
11, 86, b&w.......	1.50	0.30	0.90	1.50
12, 86	1.75	0.35	1.05	1.75
MYTHOS				
WONDER COMIX				
1		0.30	0.90	1.50
2		0.30	0.90	1.50

Marvelman/Miracleman

Marvelman Family
©1963 L. Miller &
Co. (Hackney) Ltd.

When Fawcett Publications lost the rights to publish the adventures of The Marvel Family in the 1950s (see our *Shazam!* entry for more details), the British publisher decided not to give up so quickly. It produced an independent pastiche of the stories with non-Fawcett characters. Billy Batson aka Captain Marvel became Mike Moran aka Marvelman. Captain Marvel Jr. became Young Marvelman, while the Mary Marvel character was tossed out and replaced with Johnny Bates — Kid Marvelman. Sivana (the Marvel's principal arch-villain) likewise became the evil Gargunza, and the magic word "Shazam" was replaced with the "key harmonic" of the universe (whatever that means), "Kimota" ("atomic" spelled backwards, sort of).

A 1980s revival in the pages of the British magazine *Warrior* was packaged by Eclipse Comics in the United States as *Miracleman*, due to Marvel Comics' objections to the *Marvelman* title. The new continuity established that the 1950s fairy-tale-like tales of the Marvel (Miracle) family were artifically induced dreams and that everything readers had ever known of them was, in fact, a lie. Purists may continue to accept that Marvelman's adventures happened as written in some continuum, even though they were fantasy in another.

Although our price guide does not contain entries for most British publications, including the various Marvelman series and *Warrior*, we do have entries for Eclipse's Miracleman series, including *Miracleman*, *Miracleman 3-D Special*, *Miracleman Family*, and *Miracleman: Apocrypha*.

It should also be noted that both Neil Gaiman and Alan Moore wrote stories for *Miracleman*. Also, the covers of *Miracleman: Apocrypha* were homages to such series as *The Fantastic Four* and *Man of Steel*.

N

	ORIG.	GOOD	FINE	N-MINT

NAIVE INTER-DIMENSIONAL COMMANDO KOALAS
ECLIPSE

	ORIG.	GOOD	FINE	N-MINT
❏ 1, Oct 86, b&w; A:Adolescent Radioactive Black Belt Hamsters 1.50		0.30	0.90	1.50

NAM MAGAZINE, THE (really The 'Nam Magazine)
MARVEL

	ORIG.	GOOD	FINE	N-MINT
❏ 1, Aug 88, b&w rep.	2.00	0.40	1.20	2.00
❏ 2, Sep 88, b&w rep.	2.00	0.40	1.20	2.00
❏ 3, Oct 88, b&w rep.	2.00	0.40	1.20	2.00
❏ 4, Nov 88, b&w rep.	2.00	0.40	1.20	2.00
❏ 5, Dec 88, b&w rep.	2.00	0.40	1.20	2.00
❏ 6, Dec 88, b&w rep.	2.00	0.40	1.20	2.00
❏ 7, Jan 89, b&w rep.	2.00	0.40	1.20	2.00
❏ 8, Feb 89, b&w rep.	2.00	0.40	1.20	2.00
❏ 9, Mar 89, b&w rep.	2.00	0.40	1.20	2.00
❏ 10, Apr 89, b&w rep.	2.00	0.40	1.20	2.00

NAM, THE (really The 'Nam)

	ORIG.	GOOD	FINE	N-MINT
❏ 1, Dec 86, MG, 1st printing	0.75	1.40	4.20	7.00
❏ 1, Dec 86, MG reprint	0.75	0.80	2.40	4.00
❏ 2, Jan 87, MG	0.75	1.00	3.00	5.00
❏ 3, Feb 87	0.75	0.80	2.40	4.00
❏ 4, Mar 87	0.75	0.80	2.40	4.00
❏ 5, Apr 87	0.75	0.80	2.40	4.00
❏ 6, May 87, MG	0.75	0.40	1.20	2.00
❏ 7, Jun 87, MG	0.75	0.40	1.20	2.00
❏ 8, Jul 87, MG	0.75	0.40	1.20	2.00
❏ 9, Aug 87, D:Mike	0.75	0.40	1.20	2.00
❏ 10, Sep 87	0.75	0.40	1.20	2.00
❏ 11, Oct 87	0.75	0.40	1.20	2.00
❏ 12, Nov 87	0.75	0.40	1.20	2.00
❏ 13, Dec 87	0.75	0.40	1.20	2.00
❏ 14, Jan 88	0.75	0.40	1.20	2.00
❏ 15, Feb 88	0.75	0.40	1.20	2.00
❏ 16, Mar 88	0.75	0.40	1.20	2.00
❏ 17, Apr 88	0.75	0.40	1.20	2.00
❏ 18, May 88	1.25	0.30	0.90	1.50
❏ 19, Jun 88		0.30	0.90	1.50
❏ 20, Jul 88		0.30	0.90	1.50
❏ 21, Aug 88		0.30	0.90	1.50
❏ 22, Sep 88		0.30	0.90	1.50
❏ 23, Oct 88		0.30	0.90	1.50
❏ 24, Nov 88		0.30	0.90	1.50
❏ 25, Dec 88		0.30	0.90	1.50
❏ 26, Jan 89	1.50	0.30	0.90	1.50
❏ 27, Feb 89	1.50	0.30	0.90	1.50
❏ 28, Mar 89	1.50	0.30	0.90	1.50
❏ 29, Apr 89	1.50	0.30	0.90	1.50
❏ 30, May 89	1.50	0.30	0.90	1.50
❏ 31, Jun 89	1.50	0.30	0.90	1.50
❏ 32, Jul 89	1.50	0.30	0.90	1.50
❏ 33, Aug 89	1.50	0.30	0.90	1.50
❏ 34, Sep 89	1.50	0.30	0.90	1.50
❏ 35, Oct 89	1.50	0.30	0.90	1.50
❏ 36, Nov 89	1.50	0.30	0.90	1.50
❏ 37, Nov 89	1.50	0.30	0.90	1.50
❏ 38, Dec 89	1.50	0.30	0.90	1.50
❏ 39, Dec 89	1.50	0.30	0.90	1.50
❏ 40, Jan 90	1.50	0.30	0.90	1.50
❏ 41, Feb 90, Capt. America, Thor, Iron Man	1.50	0.40	1.20	2.00
❏ 42, Mar 90	1.50	0.30	0.90	1.50
❏ 43, Apr 90	1.50	0.30	0.90	1.50
❏ 44, May 90	1.50	0.30	0.90	1.50
❏ 45, Jun 90	1.50	0.30	0.90	1.50
❏ 46, Jul 90	1.50	0.30	0.90	1.50
❏ 47, Aug 90	1.50	0.30	0.90	1.50
❏ 48, Sep 90	1.50	0.30	0.90	1.50
❏ 49, Oct 90	1.50	0.30	0.90	1.50

	ORIG.	GOOD	FINE	N-MINT
❏ 50, Nov 90	1.50	0.30	0.90	1.50
❏ 51, Dec 90	1.50	0.30	0.90	1.50
❏ 52, Jan 91, Punisher (1st printing)	1.50	1.60	4.80	8.00
❏ 52, Jan 91, (2nd printing)	1.50	0.30	0.90	1.50
❏ 53, Feb 91, Punisher (1st printing)	1.50	0.80	2.40	4.00
❏ 53, Feb 91, (2nd printing)	1.50	0.30	0.90	1.50
❏ 54, Mar 91	1.50	0.30	0.90	1.50
❏ 55, Apr 91	1.50	0.30	0.90	1.50
❏ 56, May 91	1.50	0.30	0.90	1.50
❏ 57, Jun 91	1.50	0.30	0.90	1.50
❏ 58, Jul 91	1.50	0.30	0.90	1.50
❏ 59, Aug 91	1.50	0.30	0.90	1.50
❏ 60, Sep 91	1.50	0.30	0.90	1.50
❏ 61, Oct 91	1.50	0.30	0.90	1.50
❏ 62, Nov 91	1.50	0.30	0.90	1.50
❏ 63, Dec 91	1.50	0.30	0.90	1.50
❏ 64	1.50	0.30	0.90	1.50
❏ 65	1.75	0.35	1.05	1.75
❏ 66	1.75	0.35	1.05	1.75
❏ 67, Punisher	1.75	0.35	1.05	1.75
❏ 68, Punisher	1.75	0.35	1.05	1.75
❏ 69, Punisher	1.75	0.35	1.05	1.75
❏ 70	1.75	0.35	1.05	1.75
❏ 71	1.75	0.35	1.05	1.75
❏ 72	1.75	0.35	1.05	1.75
❏ 73	1.75	0.35	1.05	1.75
❏ 74	1.75	0.35	1.05	1.75
❏ 75	2.25	0.45	1.35	2.25
❏ 76	1.75	0.35	1.05	1.75
❏ 77	1.75	0.35	1.05	1.75
❏ 78	1.75	0.35	1.05	1.75
❏ 79	1.75	0.35	1.05	1.75
❏ 80	1.75	0.35	1.05	1.75
❏ 81	1.75	0.35	1.05	1.75
❏ 82	1.75	0.35	1.05	1.75
❏ 83	1.75	0.35	1.05	1.75
❏ 84, last issue	1.75	0.35	1.05	1.75

NAMOR THE SUB-MARINER

	ORIG.	GOOD	FINE	N-MINT
❏ 1, Apr 90, JBy, O:Sub-Mariner	1.00	1.00	3.00	5.00
❏ 2, May 90, JBy	1.00	0.80	2.40	4.00
❏ 3, Jun 90, JBy	1.00	0.60	1.80	3.00
❏ 4, Jul 90, JBy	1.00	0.60	1.80	3.00
❏ 5, Aug 90, JBy	1.00	0.60	1.80	3.00
❏ 6, Sep 90, JBy	1.00	0.30	0.90	1.50
❏ 7, Oct 90, JBy	1.00	0.30	0.90	1.50
❏ 8, Nov 90, JBy	1.00	0.30	0.90	1.50
❏ 9, Dec 90, JBy	1.00	0.30	0.90	1.50
❏ 10, Jan 91, JBy	1.00	0.30	0.90	1.50
❏ 11, Feb 91, JBy	1.00	0.30	0.90	1.50
❏ 12, Mar 91, JBy, Torch, Capt. America	1.00	0.30	0.90	1.50
❏ 13, Apr 91, JBy	1.00	0.20	0.60	1.00
❏ 14, May 91, JBy	1.00	0.20	0.60	1.00
❏ 15, Jun 91, JBy	1.00	0.20	0.60	1.00
❏ 16, Jul 91, JBy	1.00	0.20	0.60	1.00
❏ 17, Aug 91, JBy	1.00	0.20	0.60	1.00
❏ 18, Sep 91, JBy	1.00	0.20	0.60	1.00
❏ 19, Oct 91, JBy	1.00	0.20	0.60	1.00
❏ 20, Nov 91, JBy	1.00	0.20	0.60	1.00
❏ 21, Dec 91, JBy	1.00	0.20	0.60	1.00
❏ 22, JBy	1.00	0.20	0.60	1.00
❏ 23, JBy	1.25	0.25	0.75	1.25
❏ 24, JBy Wolverine	1.25	0.25	0.75	1.25
❏ 25, JBy	1.25	0.25	0.75	1.25
❏ 26	1.25	4.80	14.40	24.00

	ORIG.	GOOD	FINE	N-MINT
☐ 27 ....1.25	3.60	10.80	18.00
☐ 28 ....1.25	2.40	7.20	12.00
☐ 29 ....1.25	2.40	7.20	12.00
☐ 30 ....1.25	2.40	7.20	12.00
☐ 31 ....1.25	2.40	7.20	12.00
☐ 32 ....1.25	1.60	4.80	8.00
☐ 33 ....1.25	1.00	3.00	5.00
☐ 34 ....1.25	1.00	3.00	5.00
☐ 35 ....1.25	1.00	3.00	5.00
☐ 36 ....1.25	0.60	1.80	3.00
☐ 37 ....2.00	1.00	3.00	5.00
☐ 38 ....1.25	0.25	0.75	1.25
☐ 39 ....1.25	0.25	0.75	1.25
☐ 40 ....1.25	0.25	0.75	1.25
☐ 41 ....1.25	0.25	0.75	1.25
☐ 42 ....1.25	0.25	0.75	1.25
☐ 43 ....1.25	0.25	0.75	1.25
☐ 44, Geof Isherwood........1.25	0.25	0.75	1.25
☐ 45, Geof Isherwood........1.25	0.25	0.75	1.25
☐ 46, Starblast; Geof Isherwood 1.25	0.25	0.75	1.25
☐ 47, Starblast; Geof Isherwood 1.25	0.25	0.75	1.25
☐ 48, Starblast; Geof Isherwood 1.25	0.25	0.75	1.25
☐ 49, Apr 94 ....1.25	0.25	0.75	1.25
☐ 50, May 94 ....1.75	0.35	1.05	1.75
☐ 50, May 94, foil cover 2.95	0.59	1.77	2.95
☐ 51, Jun 94 ....1.75	0.35	1.05	1.75
☐ 52, Jul 94 ....1.50	0.30	0.90	1.50
☐ 53, Aug 94 ....1.50	0.30	0.90	1.50
☐ 54, Sep 94 ....1.50	0.30	0.90	1.50
☐ 55, Oct 94 ....1.50	0.30	0.90	1.50
☐ 56, Nov 94 ....1.50	0.30	0.90	1.50
☐ 57, Dec 94......................1.50	0.30	0.90	1.50
☐ 58, Jan 95 ....1.50	0.30	0.90	1.50
☐ 59, Feb 95 ....1.95	0.39	1.17	1.95
☐ 60, Mar 95 ....1.95	0.39	1.17	1.95
☐ 61, Apr 95 ....1.50	0.30	0.90	1.50
☐ 62, May 95, final issue ...1.50	0.30	0.90	1.50

NAMOR THE SUB-MARINER ANNUAL

	ORIG.	GOOD	FINE	N-MINT
☐ 1, Sep 91, Subterranean Wars 2.00	0.40	1.20	2.00
☐ 2 ....2.25	0.45	1.35	2.25
☐ 3, card...........................2.95	0.59	1.77	2.95
☐ 4, 94..............................2.95	0.59	1.77	2.95

NASCAR ADVENTURES
VORTEX

	ORIG.	GOOD	FINE	N-MINT
☐ 1, 91, DH; Fred Lorenzen 2.00	0.40	1.20	2.00
☐ 2, 91, Richard Petty 2.00	0.40	1.20	2.00
☐ 5, 92, Ernie Irvan............2.00	0.40	1.20	2.00
☐ 7, 92, Mark Martin 2.00	0.40	1.20	2.00

NATHANIEL DUSK
DC

	ORIG.	GOOD	FINE	N-MINT
☐ 1, Feb 84, GC 1.25	0.30	0.90	1.50
☐ 2, Mar 84 ....1.25	0.25	0.75	1.25
☐ 3, Apr 84........................1.25	0.25	0.75	1.25
☐ 4, May 84 ....1.25	0.25	0.75	1.25

NATHANIEL DUSK II

	ORIG.	GOOD	FINE	N-MINT
☐ 1, Oct 85, GC.................2.00	0.40	1.20	2.00
☐ 2, Nov 85, GC.................2.00	0.40	1.20	2.00
☐ 3, Dec 85, GC.................2.00	0.40	1.20	2.00
☐ 4, Jan 86, GC 2.00	0.40	1.20	2.00

NATURAL INQUIRER
FANTAGRAPHICS

	ORIG.	GOOD	FINE	N-MINT
☐ 1, b&w	0.40	1.20	2.00

NATURE OF THE BEAST
CALIBER

	ORIG.	GOOD	FINE	N-MINT
☐ 1, b&w 2.95	0.59	1.77	2.95
☐ 2, b&w 2.95	0.59	1.77	2.95

NAUGHTY BITS
FANTAGRAPHICS

	ORIG.	GOOD	FINE	N-MINT
☐ 1, Mar 91, adult, b&w.....2.00	2.00	6.00	10.00
☐ 2, adult, b&w...................	1.20	3.60	6.00
☐ 3, adult, b&w...................	1.00	3.00	5.00
☐ 4, adult, b&w...................	1.00	3.00	5.00
☐ 5, adult, b&w...................	1.00	3.00	5.00
☐ 6, Aug 92, adult, b&w.....2.50	0.60	1.80	3.00
☐ 7, adult, b&w.................2.50	0.60	1.80	3.00
☐ 8, adult, b&w.................2.50	0.60	1.80	3.00
☐ 9, adult, b&w.................2.50	0.50	1.50	2.50
☐ 10, adult, b&w................2.50	0.50	1.50	2.50
☐ 11, Jan 94, adult, b&w....2.50	0.50	1.50	2.50
☐ 12, Apr 94, adult, b&w....2.50	0.50	1.50	2.50
☐ 13, Jul 94, adult, b&w 2.50	0.50	1.50	2.50
☐ 14, Oct 94, adult, b&w....2.50	0.50	1.50	2.50
☐ 18, Jan 96, adult, b&w....2.95	0.59	1.77	2.95

NAUSICAA OF THE VALLEY OF WIND
VIZ

	ORIG.	GOOD	FINE	N-MINT
☐ 1, b&w, Japanese	0.65	1.95	3.25
☐ 2, b&w, Japanese	0.65	1.95	3.25
☐ 3, b&w, Japanese	0.65	1.95	3.25
☐ 4, b&w, Japanese	0.65	1.95	3.25
☐ 5, b&w, Japanese	0.65	1.95	3.25
☐ 6, b&w, Japanese	0.65	1.95	3.25
☐ 7, b&w, Japanese	0.65	1.95	3.25

NAUSICAA OF THE VALLEY OF WIND (Part Four)

	ORIG.	GOOD	FINE	N-MINT
☐ 1, 94, b&w.....................2.75	0.55	1.65	2.75
☐ 2, 94, b&w.....................2.75	0.55	1.65	2.75
☐ 3, 94, b&w.....................2.75	0.55	1.65	2.75
☐ 4, 94, b&w.....................2.75	0.55	1.65	2.75

NAUSICAA OF THE VALLEY OF WIND (Part Three)

	ORIG.	GOOD	FINE	N-MINT
☐ 1, b&w.............................3.95	0.79	2.37	3.95
☐ 2, 93, b&w.....................3.95	0.79	2.37	3.95
☐ 3, 93, b&w.....................3.95	0.79	2.37	3.95

NAUSICAA OF THE VALLEY OF WIND (Part Two)

	ORIG.	GOOD	FINE	N-MINT
☐ 1	0.59	1.77	2.95
☐ 2	0.59	1.77	2.95
☐ 3	0.59	1.77	2.95
☐ 4	0.59	1.77	2.95

NAZRAT
IMPERIAL

	ORIG.	GOOD	FINE	N-MINT
☐ 1	0.36	1.08	1.80
☐ 2	0.36	1.08	1.80
☐ 3	0.36	1.08	1.80
☐ 4, (becomes Eternity title).	0.39	1.17	1.95

NAZRAT (was Imperial Comic)
ETERNITY

	ORIG.	GOOD	FINE	N-MINT
☐ 5	0.39	1.17	1.95

NAZZ, THE
DC

	ORIG.	GOOD	FINE	N-MINT
☐ 1, Oct 90, BT..................	0.99	2.97	4.95
☐ 2, Nov 90, BT..................	0.99	2.97	4.95
☐ 3, Dec 90, BT..................	0.99	2.97	4.95
☐ 4, Jan 91, BT	0.99	2.97	4.95

NEAR MYTHS
RIP OFF

	ORIG.	GOOD	FINE	N-MINT
☐ 1, Jul 90, Trina;b&w 2.50	0.50	1.50	2.50

NEAR TO NOW
FANDOM HOUSE

	ORIG.	GOOD	FINE	N-MINT
☐ 1, Howarth,b&w...............	0.40	1.20	2.00
☐ 2, Howarth,b&w...............	0.40	1.20	2.00

NEAT STUFF
FANTAGRAPHICS

	ORIG.	GOOD	FINE	N-MINT
☐ 1, 1st printing	2.00	6.00	10.00
☐ 1, 2nd printing	0.50	1.50	2.50
☐ 2, 1st printing	1.20	3.60	6.00
☐ 2, 2nd printing	0.45	1.35	2.25
☐ 3, 1st printing	0.80	2.40	4.00

	ORIG.	GOOD	FINE	N-MINT
❏ 3, 2nd printing		0.50	1.50	2.50
❏ 4, 1st printing		0.80	2.40	4.00
❏ 4, 2nd printing		0.45	1.35	2.25
❏ 5		0.80	2.40	4.00
❏ 6		0.80	2.40	4.00
❏ 7		0.80	2.40	4.00
❏ 8		0.80	2.40	4.00
❏ 9		0.80	2.40	4.00
❏ 10		0.80	2.40	4.00
❏ 11		0.50	1.50	2.50
❏ 12		0.45	1.35	2.25
❏ 13		0.50	1.50	2.50
❏ 14		0.50	1.50	2.50
❏ 15		0.50	1.50	2.50

NECROMANCER
ANARCHY

	ORIG.	GOOD	FINE	N-MINT
❏ 1, b&w	3.50	0.70	2.10	3.50
❏ 2, b&w	3.50	0.70	2.10	3.50
❏ 3, b&w	3.50	0.70	2.10	3.50
❏ 4, b&w	3.50	0.70	2.10	3.50

NECROMANCER (1993)

	ORIG.	GOOD	FINE	N-MINT
❏ 2, 93, b&w	2.50	0.50	1.50	2.50
❏ 3, 93, b&w	2.50	0.50	1.50	2.50
❏ 4, 93, b&w	2.50	0.50	1.50	2.50

NECROPOLIS
FLEETWAY/QUALITY

	GOOD	FINE	N-MINT
❏ 1, Judge Dredd	0.59	1.77	2.95
❏ 2, Judge Dredd	0.59	1.77	2.95
❏ 3, Judge Dredd	0.59	1.77	2.95
❏ 4	0.59	1.77	2.95
❏ 5	0.59	1.77	2.95
❏ 6	0.59	1.77	2.95
❏ 7	0.59	1.77	2.95
❏ 8	0.59	1.77	2.95
❏ 9	0.59	1.77	2.95

NECROSCOPE
MALIBU

	ORIG.	GOOD	FINE	N-MINT
❏ 1	2.95	0.59	1.77	2.95
❏ 2, bagged with tattoo	2.95	0.59	1.77	2.95
❏ 3	2.95	0.59	1.77	2.95
❏ 4	2.95	0.59	1.77	2.95
❏ 5	2.95	0.59	1.77	2.95

NECROSCOPE BOOK II: WAMPHYRI

	ORIG.	GOOD	FINE	N-MINT
❏ 1	2.95	0.59	1.77	2.95
❏ 2	2.95	0.59	1.77	2.95
❏ 3, Jan 94	2.95	0.59	1.77	2.95

NEGATIVE BURN
CALIBER

	ORIG.	GOOD	FINE	N-MINT
❏ 1, 93, BB, Flaming Carrot, b&w	2.95	1.00	3.00	5.00
❏ 2, 93, b&w	2.95	0.80	2.40	4.00
❏ 3, 93, b&w;Bone	2.95	3.00	9.00	15.00
❏ 4, 93, b&w	2.95	0.59	1.77	2.95
❏ 5, 93, b&w	2.95	0.59	1.77	2.95
❏ 6, 94, b&w	2.95	0.59	1.77	2.95
❏ 7, 94, b&w	2.95	0.59	1.77	2.95
❏ 8, 94, b&w	2.95	0.59	1.77	2.95
❏ 9, 94, b&w;AMo	2.95	0.59	1.77	2.95
❏ 10, 94, b&w;AMo	2.95	0.59	1.77	2.95
❏ 11, 94, b&w	2.95	0.59	1.77	2.95
❏ 12, 94, b&w	2.95	0.59	1.77	2.95
❏ 13, 94, b&w; Strangers in Paradise	3.95	2.40	7.20	12.00
❏ 14, 94, b&w	2.95	0.59	1.77	2.95
❏ 15, 94, b&w	2.95	0.59	1.77	2.95
❏ 16, 94, b&w	2.95	0.59	1.77	2.95
❏ 17, 94, b&w	2.95	0.59	1.77	2.95
❏ 18, 94, b&w	2.95	0.59	1.77	2.95
❏ 19, 95, b&w	2.95	0.59	1.77	2.95
❏ 20, 95, b&w	2.95	0.59	1.77	2.95
❏ 21, 95, b&w	2.95	0.59	1.77	2.95

	ORIG.	GOOD	FINE	N-MINT
❏ 22, 95, b&w	2.95	0.59	1.77	2.95
❏ 23, 95, b&w	2.95	0.59	1.77	2.95
❏ 24, 95, b&w	2.95	0.59	1.77	2.95
❏ 25, 95, b&w	3.95	0.79	2.37	3.95

NEIL & BUZZ IN SPACE AND TIME
FANTAGRAPHICS

	GOOD	FINE	N-MINT
❏ 1, b&w	0.40	1.20	2.00

NEIL GAIMAN'S LADY JUSTICE
TEKNO

	ORIG.	GOOD	FINE	N-MINT
❏ 1, Sep 95	1.95	0.39	1.17	1.95
❏ 2, Oct 95	1.95	0.39	1.17	1.95
❏ 3, Nov 95	1.95	0.39	1.17	1.95
❏ 4, Dec 95, begins new story-arc with new Lady Justice	1.95	0.39	1.17	1.95
❏ 5, Dec 95	1.95	0.39	1.17	1.95
❏ 6, Jan 96	2.25	0.45	1.35	2.25
❏ 7, Jan 96, stand-alone story	2.25	0.45	1.35	2.25
❏ 9, Mar 96	2.25	0.45	1.35	2.25

NEIL GAIMAN'S MR. HERO-THE NEWMATIC MAN

	ORIG.	GOOD	FINE	N-MINT
❏ 1, Mar 95	1.95	0.39	1.17	1.95
❏ 2, Apr 95	1.95	0.39	1.17	1.95
❏ 3, May 95	1.95	0.39	1.17	1.95
❏ 4, Jun 95	1.95	0.39	1.17	1.95
❏ 5, Jul 95	1.95	0.39	1.17	1.95
❏ 6, Aug 95	1.95	0.39	1.17	1.95
❏ 7, Sep 95	1.95	0.39	1.17	1.95
❏ 8, Oct 95	1.95	0.39	1.17	1.95
❏ 9, Nov 95	1.95	0.39	1.17	1.95
❏ 10, Dec 95	1.95	0.39	1.17	1.95
❏ 13, Jan 96	2.25	0.45	1.35	2.25
❏ 14, Feb 96	2.25	0.45	1.35	2.25
❏ 16, Apr 96	2.25	0.45	1.35	2.25

NEIL GAIMAN'S TEKNOPHAGE

	ORIG.	GOOD	FINE	N-MINT
❏ 1, no cover price;enhanced cover; Steel Edition				
❏ 1, Aug 95	1.95	0.39	1.17	1.95
❏ 2, Sep 95	1.95	0.39	1.17	1.95
❏ 3, Oct 95	1.95	0.39	1.17	1.95
❏ 4, Nov 95	1.95	0.39	1.17	1.95
❏ 5, Dec 95	1.95	0.39	1.17	1.95
❏ 7, Jan 96	2.25	0.45	1.35	2.25
❏ 8, Feb 96	2.25	0.45	1.35	2.25
❏ 9, Feb 96	2.25	0.45	1.35	2.25
❏ 10, Mar 96	2.25	0.45	1.35	2.25

NEIL THE HORSE (former Aardvark-Vanaheim title)
RENEGADE

	GOOD	FINE	N-MINT
❏ 11, b&w	0.34	1.02	1.70
❏ 12, b&w	0.34	1.02	1.70
❏ 13	0.40	1.20	2.00
❏ 14, giant	0.60	1.80	3.00
❏ 15, giant	0.60	1.80	3.00

NEIL THE HORSE COMICS AND STORIES
AARDVARK-VANAHEIM

	ORIG.	GOOD	FINE	N-MINT
❏ 1, 83, b&w	1.60	0.40	1.20	2.00
❏ 2, b&w	1.60	0.40	1.20	2.00
❏ 3, b&w	1.60	0.40	1.20	2.00
❏ 4, b&w	1.60	0.40	1.20	2.00
❏ 5, b&w	1.60	0.40	1.20	2.00
❏ 6, b&w	1.60	0.40	1.20	2.00
❏ 7, b&w	1.60	0.40	1.20	2.00
❏ 8, b&w	1.60	0.40	1.20	2.00
❏ 9, b&w	1.60	0.40	1.20	2.00
❏ 10, (moves to Renegade Press)		0.40	1.20	2.00

NEMESIS THE WARLOCK
EAGLE

	GOOD	FINE	N-MINT
❏ 1	0.30	0.90	1.50
❏ 2	0.30	0.90	1.50
❏ 3	0.30	0.90	1.50
❏ 4	0.30	0.90	1.50

	ORIG.	GOOD	FINE	N-MINT
☐ 5		0.30	0.90	1.50
☐ 6		0.30	0.90	1.50
☐ 7		0.30	0.90	1.50

FLEETWAY/QUALITY

	ORIG.	GOOD	FINE	N-MINT
☐ 1, b&w		0.39	1.17	1.95
☐ 2, b&w		0.39	1.17	1.95
☐ 3, b&w		0.39	1.17	1.95
☐ 4, b&w		0.39	1.17	1.95
☐ 5, b&w		0.39	1.17	1.95
☐ 6, b&w		0.39	1.17	1.95
☐ 7, b&w		0.39	1.17	1.95
☐ 8, b&w		0.39	1.17	1.95
☐ 9, b&w		0.39	1.17	1.95
☐ 10, b&w		0.39	1.17	1.95
☐ 11, b&w		0.39	1.17	1.95
☐ 12, b&w		0.39	1.17	1.95
☐ 13, b&w		0.39	1.17	1.95
☐ 14, b&w		0.39	1.17	1.95
☐ 15, b&w		0.39	1.17	1.95
☐ 16, b&w		0.39	1.17	1.95
☐ 17, b&w		0.39	1.17	1.95
☐ 18, b&w		0.39	1.17	1.95
☐ 19, b&w		0.39	1.17	1.95

NEO
EXCALIBUR

	ORIG.	GOOD	FINE	N-MINT
☐ 1, b&w		0.30	0.90	1.50

NEOMEN
SLAVE LABOR

	ORIG.	GOOD	FINE	N-MINT
☐ 1		0.35	1.05	1.75
☐ 2		0.35	1.05	1.75

NEON CITY
INNOVATION

	ORIG.	GOOD	FINE	N-MINT
☐ 1, b&w		0.45	1.35	2.25

NERVE
NERVE

	ORIG.	GOOD	FINE	N-MINT
☐ 1		0.30	0.90	1.50
☐ 2		0.30	0.90	1.50
☐ 3		0.30	0.90	1.50
☐ 4		0.30	0.90	1.50
☐ 5		0.30	0.90	1.50
☐ 6		0.30	0.90	1.50
☐ 7		0.30	0.90	1.50
☐ 8, oversize		0.80	2.40	4.00

NERVOUS REX
BLACKTHORNE

	ORIG.	GOOD	FINE	N-MINT
☐ 1		0.40	1.20	2.00
☐ 2		0.40	1.20	2.00
☐ 3		0.40	1.20	2.00
☐ 4		0.40	1.20	2.00
☐ 5		0.40	1.20	2.00
☐ 6		0.40	1.20	2.00
☐ 7		0.40	1.20	2.00
☐ 8		0.40	1.20	2.00
☐ 9		0.40	1.20	2.00
☐ 10		0.40	1.20	2.00

NESTROBBER
BLUE SKY BLUE

	ORIG.	GOOD	FINE	N-MINT
☐ 1, b&w	1.95	0.39	1.17	1.95
☐ 2, Jun 94, b&w	1.95	0.39	1.17	1.95

NETHERWORLD
AMBITION

	ORIG.	GOOD	FINE	N-MINT
☐ 1, b&w		0.30	0.90	1.50

NETHERWORLDS
ADVENTURE

	ORIG.	GOOD	FINE	N-MINT
☐ 1, Aug 88, b&w	1.95	0.39	1.17	1.95

NEW ADVENTURES OF BEAUTY AND THE BEAST
(mini-series)
DISNEY

	ORIG.	GOOD	FINE	N-MINT
☐ 1	1.50	0.30	0.90	1.50
☐ 2	1.50	0.30	0.90	1.50

NEW ADVENTURES OF CHOLLY AND FLYTRAP
EPIC

	ORIG.	GOOD	FINE	N-MINT
☐ 1	2.50	0.50	1.50	2.50
☐ 2	2.50	0.50	1.50	2.50
☐ 3	2.50	0.50	1.50	2.50

NEW ADVENTURES OF FELIX THE CAT
FELIX

	ORIG.	GOOD	FINE	N-MINT
☐ 1		0.45	1.35	2.25

NEW ADVENTURES OF
RICK O'SHAY AND HIPSHOT
COTTONWOOD

	ORIG.	GOOD	FINE	N-MINT
☐ 1		0.99	2.97	4.95
☐ 2		0.99	2.97	4.95

NEW ADVENTURES OF SHALOMAN
MARK 1

	ORIG.	GOOD	FINE	N-MINT
☐ 0, 95, #X-Y;b&w	2.50	0.50	1.50	2.50
☐ 1, b&w		0.39	1.17	1.95
☐ 2	2.50	0.50	1.50	2.50
☐ 3, O:Shaloman	2.50	0.50	1.50	2.50
☐ 4, 94, b&w	2.50	0.50	1.50	2.50
☐ 5, 94, indicia says "#4"	2.95	0.59	1.77	2.95

NEW ADVENTURES OF SPEED RACER, THE
NOW

	ORIG.	GOOD	FINE	N-MINT
☐ 0, Nov 93, multi-dimensional cover	3.95	0.79	2.37	3.95
☐ 1, Dec 93	1.95	0.39	1.17	1.95
☐ 2	1.95	0.39	1.17	1.95
☐ 3	1.95	0.39	1.17	1.95

NEW ADVENTURES OF SUPERBOY, THE
DC

	ORIG.	GOOD	FINE	N-MINT
☐ 1, Jan 80, KS		0.25	0.75	1.25
☐ 2, Feb 80, KS		0.20	0.60	1.00
☐ 3, Mar 80, KS		0.20	0.60	1.00
☐ 4, Apr 80, KS		0.20	0.60	1.00
☐ 5, May 80, KS		0.20	0.60	1.00
☐ 6, Jun 80, KS		0.20	0.60	1.00
☐ 7, Jul 80, KS		0.20	0.60	1.00
☐ 8, Aug 80, KS		0.20	0.60	1.00
☐ 9, Sep 80, KS		0.20	0.60	1.00
☐ 10, Oct 80, KS		0.20	0.60	1.00
☐ 11, Nov 80, KS		0.20	0.60	1.00
☐ 12, Dec 80, KS		0.20	0.60	1.00
☐ 13, Jan 81, KS		0.20	0.60	1.00
☐ 14, Feb 81, KS		0.20	0.60	1.00
☐ 15, Mar 81, KS		0.20	0.60	1.00
☐ 16, Apr 81, KS		0.20	0.60	1.00
☐ 17, May 81, KS		0.20	0.60	1.00
☐ 18, Jun 81, KS		0.20	0.60	1.00
☐ 19, Jul 81, KS		0.20	0.60	1.00
☐ 20, Aug 81, KS		0.20	0.60	1.00
☐ 21, Sep 81, KS		0.20	0.60	1.00
☐ 22, Oct 81, KS		0.20	0.60	1.00
☐ 23, Nov 81, KS		0.20	0.60	1.00
☐ 24, Dec 81, KS		0.20	0.60	1.00
☐ 25, Jan 82, KS		0.20	0.60	1.00
☐ 26, Feb 82, KS		0.20	0.60	1.00
☐ 27, Mar 82, KS		0.20	0.60	1.00
☐ 28, Apr 82, KS		0.20	0.60	1.00
☐ 29, May 82, KS		0.20	0.60	1.00
☐ 30, Jun 82, KS		0.20	0.60	1.00
☐ 31, Jul 82, KS		0.20	0.60	1.00
☐ 32, Aug 82, KS		0.20	0.60	1.00
☐ 33, Sep 82, KS		0.20	0.60	1.00
☐ 34, Oct 82, KS		0.20	0.60	1.00
☐ 35, Nov 82, KS		0.20	0.60	1.00
☐ 36, Dec 82, KS		0.20	0.60	1.00
☐ 37, Jan 83, KS		0.20	0.60	1.00
☐ 38, Feb 83, KS		0.20	0.60	1.00
☐ 39, Mar 83, KS		0.20	0.60	1.00
☐ 40, Apr 83, KS		0.20	0.60	1.00
☐ 41, May 83, KS		0.20	0.60	1.00

	ORIG.	GOOD	FINE	N-MINT
☐ 42, Jun 83, KS		0.20	0.60	1.00
☐ 43, Jul 83, KS		0.20	0.60	1.00
☐ 44, Aug 83, KS.................		0.20	0.60	1.00
☐ 45, Sep 83, KS		0.20	0.60	1.00
☐ 46, Oct 83, KS.................		0.20	0.60	1.00
☐ 47, Nov 83, KS		0.20	0.60	1.00
☐ 48, Dec 83, KS................		0.20	0.60	1.00
☐ 49, Jan 84, KS.................		0.20	0.60	1.00
☐ 50, Feb 84, KG, KS A:Legion		0.30	0.90	1.50
☐ 51, Mar 84, KS		0.20	0.60	1.00
☐ 52, Apr 84, KS		0.20	0.60	1.00
☐ 53, May 84, KS		0.20	0.60	1.00
☐ 54, Jun 84, KS		0.20	0.60	1.00

NEW AMERICA
ECLIPSE

	ORIG.	GOOD	FINE	N-MINT
☐ 1		0.35	1.05	1.75
☐ 2		0.35	1.05	1.75
☐ 3		0.35	1.05	1.75
☐ 4		0.35	1.05	1.75

NEW ARCHIES, THE
ARCHIE

	ORIG.	GOOD	FINE	N-MINT
☐ 1, Oct 87 .... 0.75		0.40	1.20	2.00
☐ 2		0.30	0.90	1.50
☐ 3		0.30	0.90	1.50
☐ 4		0.30	0.90	1.50
☐ 5		0.30	0.90	1.50
☐ 6		0.30	0.90	1.50
☐ 7		0.30	0.90	1.50
☐ 8		0.30	0.90	1.50
☐ 9		0.30	0.90	1.50
☐ 10		0.30	0.90	1.50
☐ 11		0.25	0.75	1.25
☐ 12		0.25	0.75	1.25
☐ 13		0.25	0.75	1.25
☐ 14		0.25	0.75	1.25
☐ 15		0.25	0.75	1.25
☐ 16		0.25	0.75	1.25
☐ 17		0.25	0.75	1.25
☐ 18		0.25	0.75	1.25
☐ 19		0.25	0.75	1.25
☐ 20		0.25	0.75	1.25
☐ 21		0.25	0.75	1.25
☐ 22		0.25	0.75	1.25

NEW BEGINNING
UNICORN

	ORIG.	GOOD	FINE	N-MINT
☐ 1, b&w		0.30	0.90	1.50
☐ 2, b&w 1.75		0.35	1.05	1.75
☐ 3, b&w 1.75		0.35	1.05	1.75

NEW CREW, THE
PERSONALITY

	ORIG.	GOOD	FINE	N-MINT
☐ 1, b&w		0.59	1.77	2.95
☐ 2, b&w		0.59	1.77	2.95
☐ 3, b&w		0.59	1.77	2.95
☐ 4, b&w		0.59	1.77	2.95
☐ 5, b&w		0.59	1.77	2.95
☐ 6, b&w		0.59	1.77	2.95
☐ 7, b&w		0.59	1.77	2.95
☐ 8, b&w		0.59	1.77	2.95
☐ 9, b&w		0.59	1.77	2.95
☐ 10, b&w		0.59	1.77	2.95

NEW CRIME FILES OF MICHAEL MAUSER, PRIVATE EYE
APPLE

	ORIG.	GOOD	FINE	N-MINT
☐ 1, b&w		0.50	1.50	2.50

NEW DEFENDERS, THE (formerly The Defenders)
MARVEL

	ORIG.	GOOD	FINE	N-MINT
☐ 140, Feb 85 .... 0.60		0.20	0.60	1.00
☐ 141, Mar 85 .... 0.60		0.20	0.60	1.00
☐ 142, Apr 85, AAd(c) 0.65		0.20	0.60	1.00
☐ 143, May 85 .... 0.65		0.20	0.60	1.00

	ORIG.	GOOD	FINE	N-MINT
☐ 144, Jun 85 .... 0.65		0.20	0.60	1.00
☐ 145, Jul 85, A:Johnny Blaze				
.... 0.65		0.20	0.60	1.00
☐ 146, Aug 85 .... 0.65		0.20	0.60	1.00
☐ 147, Sep 85 .... 0.65		0.20	0.60	1.00
☐ 148, Oct 85 .... 0.65		0.20	0.60	1.00
☐ 149, Nov 85 .... 0.65		0.20	0.60	1.00
☐ 150, Dec 85 .... 1.25		0.25	0.75	1.25
☐ 151, Jan 86 .... 0.65		0.20	0.60	1.00
☐ 152, Feb 86, Secret Wars II;final issue				
.... 1.25		0.25	0.75	1.25

NEW DNAgents
ECLIPSE

	ORIG.	GOOD	FINE	N-MINT
☐ 1, Oct 85........................		0.19	0.57	0.95
☐ 2, Nov 85		0.19	0.57	0.95
☐ 3, Nov 85		0.19	0.57	0.95
☐ 4, Dec 85		0.19	0.57	0.95
☐ 5, Jan 86		0.19	0.57	0.95
☐ 6, Feb 86		0.19	0.57	0.95
☐ 7, Apr 86........................		0.19	0.57	0.95
☐ 8, Apr 86........................		0.19	0.57	0.95
☐ 9, Jun 86		0.19	0.57	0.95
☐ 10, Jun 86		0.19	0.57	0.95
☐ 11, Aug 86		0.19	0.57	0.95
☐ 12, Aug 86		0.19	0.57	0.95
☐ 13, Oct 86		0.25	0.75	1.25
☐ 14, Nov 86		0.25	0.75	1.25
☐ 15, Dec 86		0.25	0.75	1.25
☐ 16, Jan 87		0.25	0.75	1.25
☐ 17, Mar 87		0.25	0.75	1.25

NEW FRONTIER, THE
DARK HORSE

	ORIG.	GOOD	FINE	N-MINT
☐ 1, Oct 92, b&w.............. 2.75		0.55	1.65	2.75
☐ 2, Nov 92, b&w.............. 2.75		0.55	1.65	2.75
☐ 3, Dec 92, b&w.............. 2.75		0.55	1.65	2.75

NEW FRONTIERS
EVOLUTION

	ORIG.	GOOD	FINE	N-MINT
☐ 1, 89, b&w.....................		0.20	0.60	1.00

NEW GODS (1984 reprints)
DC

	ORIG.	GOOD	FINE	N-MINT
☐ 1, Jun 84, JK reprints 2.00		0.40	1.20	2.00
☐ 2, Jul 84, JK reprints 2.00		0.40	1.20	2.00
☐ 3, Aug 84, JK reprints..... 2.00		0.40	1.20	2.00
☐ 4, Oct 84, JK reprints..... 2.00		0.40	1.20	2.00
☐ 5, Nov 84, JK reprints.... 2.00		0.40	1.20	2.00
☐ 6, Dec 84, JK reprints.... 2.00		0.40	1.20	2.00

NEW GODS (1995-)

	ORIG.	GOOD	FINE	N-MINT
☐ 1, Oct 95........................ 1.95		0.39	1.17	1.95
☐ 2, Nov 95....................... 1.95		0.39	1.17	1.95
☐ 3, Dec 95....................... 1.95		0.39	1.17	1.95
☐ 4, Jan 96........................ 1.95		0.39	1.17	1.95
☐ 5, Feb 96........................ 1.95		0.39	1.17	1.95
☐ 6, Mar 96....................... 1.95		0.39	1.17	1.95
☐ 7, Apr 96........................ 1.95		0.39	1.17	1.95
☐ 8, Jun 96 .... 1.95		0.39	1.17	1.95
☐ 9, Jul 96......................... 1.95		0.39	1.17	1.95

NEW GODS (beginning 1989)

	ORIG.	GOOD	FINE	N-MINT
☐ 1, Feb 89........................ 1.50		0.30	0.90	1.50
☐ 2, Mar 89....................... 1.50		0.30	0.90	1.50
☐ 3, Apr 89........................ 1.50		0.30	0.90	1.50
☐ 4, May 89....................... 1.50		0.30	0.90	1.50
☐ 5, Jun 89 .... 1.50		0.30	0.90	1.50
☐ 6, Jul 89......................... 1.50		0.30	0.90	1.50
☐ 7, Aug 89....................... 1.50		0.30	0.90	1.50
☐ 8, Sep 89 .... 1.50		0.30	0.90	1.50
☐ 9, Oct 89........................ 1.50		0.30	0.90	1.50
☐ 10, Nov 89...................... 1.50		0.30	0.90	1.50
☐ 11, Dec 89...................... 1.50		0.30	0.90	1.50
☐ 12, Jan 90...................... 1.50		0.30	0.90	1.50
☐ 13, Feb 90...................... 1.50		0.30	0.90	1.50

	ORIG.	GOOD	FINE	N-MINT
☐ 14, Mar 90 ....1.50	0.30	0.90	1.50
☐ 15, Apr 90 ....1.50	0.30	0.90	1.50
☐ 16, May 90 ....1.50	0.30	0.90	1.50
☐ 17, Jun 90 ....1.50	0.30	0.90	1.50
☐ 18, Jul 90 ....1.50	0.30	0.90	1.50
☐ 19, Aug 90 ....1.50	0.30	0.90	1.50
☐ 20, Sep 90 ....1.50	0.30	0.90	1.50
☐ 21, Dec 90 ....1.50	0.30	0.90	1.50
☐ 22, Jan 91 ....1.50	0.30	0.90	1.50
☐ 23, Feb 91 ....1.50	0.30	0.90	1.50
☐ 24, Mar 91 ....1.50	0.30	0.90	1.50
☐ 25, Apr 91 ....1.50	0.30	0.90	1.50
☐ 26, May 91 ....1.50	0.30	0.90	1.50
☐ 27, Jul 91 ....1.50	0.30	0.90	1.50
☐ 28, Aug 91 ....1.50	0.30	0.90	1.50

NEW GODS, THE (1971-1977 series)

	ORIG.	GOOD	FINE	N-MINT
☐ 1, Mar 71, JK 0.15	8.00	24.00	40.00
☐ 2, May 71, JK 0.15	5.00	15.00	25.00
☐ 3, Jul 71, JK 0.15	4.00	12.00	20.00
☐ 4, Sep 71, JK 0.25	4.00	12.00	20.00
☐ 5, Nov 71, JK 0.25	4.00	12.00	20.00
☐ 6, Jan 72, JK 0.25	4.00	12.00	20.00
☐ 7, Mar 72, JK 0.25	4.00	12.00	20.00
☐ 8, May 72, JK 0.25	4.00	12.00	20.00
☐ 9, Jul 72, JK 0.25	3.00	9.00	15.00
☐ 10, Sep 72, JK 0.20	3.00	9.00	15.00
☐ 11, Nov 72, JK 0.20	3.00	9.00	15.00
☐ 12, Jul 77 ....0.35	0.60	1.80	3.00
☐ 13, Aug 77 ....0.35	0.60	1.80	3.00
☐ 14, Oct 77 ....0.35	0.60	1.80	3.00
☐ 15, Dec 77 ....0.35	0.60	1.80	3.00
☐ 16, Feb 78 ....0.35	0.60	1.80	3.00
☐ 17, Apr 78 ....0.35	0.60	1.80	3.00
☐ 18, Jun 78 ....0.35	0.60	1.80	3.00
☐ 19, Aug 78 ....0.35	0.60	1.80	3.00

NEW GUARDIANS, THE

	ORIG.	GOOD	FINE	N-MINT
☐ 1, Sep 88 ....2.00	0.25	0.75	1.25
☐ 2, Oct 88 ....1.25	0.25	0.75	1.25
☐ 3, Nov 88 ....1.25	0.25	0.75	1.25
☐ 4, Dec 88 ....1.25	0.25	0.75	1.25
☐ 5, Dec 88 ....1.25	0.25	0.75	1.25
☐ 6, Jan 89, Invasion! 1.25	0.25	0.75	1.25
☐ 7, Feb 89, Invasion! 1.25	0.25	0.75	1.25
☐ 8, Apr 89 ....1.25	0.25	0.75	1.25
☐ 9, Jun 89 ....1.25	0.25	0.75	1.25
☐ 10, Jul 89 ....1.25	0.25	0.75	1.25
☐ 11, Aug 89 ....1.25	0.25	0.75	1.25
☐ 12, Sep 89 ....1.25	0.25	0.75	1.25

NEW HERO COMICS
RED SPADE

		GOOD	FINE	N-MINT
☐ 1, b&w		0.20	0.60	1.00

NEW HUMANS ANNUAL
ETERNITY

		GOOD	FINE	N-MINT
☐ 1, b&w		0.59	1.77	2.95

NEW HUMANS, THE

		GOOD	FINE	N-MINT
☐ 1, O:New Humans		0.39	1.17	1.95
☐ 2		0.39	1.17	1.95
☐ 3		0.39	1.17	1.95
☐ 4		0.39	1.17	1.95
☐ 5		0.39	1.17	1.95
☐ 6		0.39	1.17	1.95
☐ 7		0.39	1.17	1.95
☐ 8		0.39	1.17	1.95
☐ 9		0.39	1.17	1.95
☐ 10		0.39	1.17	1.95
☐ 11		0.39	1.17	1.95
☐ 12		0.39	1.17	1.95
☐ 13		0.39	1.17	1.95
☐ 14		0.39	1.17	1.95
☐ 15		0.39	1.17	1.95

PIED PIPER

		GOOD	FINE	N-MINT
☐ 1		0.39	1.17	1.95
☐ 2		0.39	1.17	1.95
☐ 3		0.39	1.17	1.95

NEW JUSTICE MACHINE MINI-SERIES
INNOVATION

		GOOD	FINE	N-MINT
☐ 1, Nov 89		0.39	1.17	1.95
☐ 2, Jan 90		0.39	1.17	1.95
☐ 3, Mar 90		0.39	1.17	1.95

NEW KIDS ON THE BLOCK
HARVEY

		GOOD	FINE	N-MINT
☐ 1		0.25	0.75	1.25

NEW KIDS ON THE BLOCK COMIC TOUR '90

		GOOD	FINE	N-MINT
☐ 1		0.25	0.75	1.25

NEW KIDS ON THE BLOCK MAGIC SUMMER TOUR

		GOOD	FINE	N-MINT
☐ 0, nn		0.25	0.75	1.25
☐ 0, nn;limited edition 3.95	0.79	2.37	3.95

NEW KIDS ON THE BLOCK STEP BY STEP

		GOOD	FINE	N-MINT
☐ 0, nn		0.25	0.75	1.25

NEW KIDS ON THE BLOCK: BACKSTAGE PASS

		GOOD	FINE	N-MINT
☐ 1		0.25	0.75	1.25

NEW KIDS ON THE BLOCK: CHILLIN'

		GOOD	FINE	N-MINT
☐ 1		0.25	0.75	1.25

NEW KIDS ON THE BLOCK: VALENTINE GIRL

		GOOD	FINE	N-MINT
☐ 0, nn		0.25	0.75	1.25

NEW L.I.F.E. BRIGADE (was L.I.F.E. Brigade)
BLUE COMET

		GOOD	FINE	N-MINT
☐ 3		0.36	1.08	1.80

NEW MAN
IMAGE

	ORIG.	GOOD	FINE	N-MINT
☐ 1, Jan 96, "Extreme Destroyer" Part 3 of 9;polybagged with card 2.50	0.50	1.50	2.50
☐ 2, Feb 96 ....2.50	0.50	1.50	2.50
☐ 2, Feb 96 ....2.50	0.50	1.50	2.50
☐ 3, Apr 96 ....2.50	0.50	1.50	2.50

NEW MUTANTS
MARVEL

	ORIG.	GOOD	FINE	N-MINT
☐ 1, Mar 83, BMc 0.60	2.40	7.20	12.00
☐ 2, Apr 83, BMc, V:Sentinels 0.60	1.60	4.80	8.00
☐ 3, May 83, BMc, V:Brood 0.60	1.00	3.00	5.00
☐ 4, Jun 83 ....0.60	0.80	2.40	4.00
☐ 5, Jul 83 ....0.60	0.80	2.40	4.00
☐ 6, Aug 83 ....0.60	0.80	2.40	4.00
☐ 7, Sep 83 ....0.60	0.80	2.40	4.00
☐ 8, Oct 83 ....0.60	0.80	2.40	4.00
☐ 9, Nov 83 ....0.60	0.80	2.40	4.00
☐ 10, Dec 83 ....0.60	0.80	2.40	4.00
☐ 11, Jan 84 ....0.60	0.80	2.40	4.00
☐ 12, Feb 84 ....0.60	0.80	2.40	4.00
☐ 13, Mar 84 ....0.60	0.80	2.40	4.00
☐ 14, Apr 84 ....0.60	0.80	2.40	4.00
☐ 15, May 84, SB, X-Men ...0.60	0.80	2.40	4.00
☐ 16, Jun 84 ....0.60	0.80	2.40	4.00
☐ 17, Jul 84 ....0.60	0.80	2.40	4.00
☐ 18, Aug 84, BSz, Moonstar I 0.60	1.60	4.80	8.00
☐ 19, Sep 84, BSz 0.60	0.60	1.80	3.00
☐ 20, Oct 84, BSz 0.60	0.60	1.80	3.00
☐ 21, Nov 84, BSz 1.00	0.60	1.80	3.00
☐ 22, Dec 84, BSz 0.60	0.50	1.50	2.50
☐ 23, Jan 85, BSz 0.60	0.50	1.50	2.50
☐ 24, Feb 85, BSz 0.60	0.50	1.50	2.50
☐ 25, Mar 85, BSz 0.60	1.20	3.60	6.00
☐ 26, Apr 85 ....0.65	1.60	4.80	8.00
☐ 27, May 85 ....0.65	0.80	2.40	4.00
☐ 28, Jun 85 ....0.65	0.80	2.40	4.00
☐ 29, Jul 85 ....0.65	0.50	1.50	2.50

	ORIG.	GOOD	FINE	N-MINT
❑ 30, Aug 85, Secret Wars II				
....0.65		0.50	1.50	2.50
❑ 31, Sep 85.....................0.65		0.50	1.50	2.50
❑ 32, Oct 85 ....0.65		0.50	1.50	2.50
❑ 33, Nov 85 ....0.65		0.50	1.50	2.50
❑ 34, Dec 85.....................0.65		0.50	1.50	2.50
❑ 35, Jan 86 ....0.75		0.50	1.50	2.50
❑ 36, Feb 86, AAd(c), Secret Wars II				
....0.75		0.60	1.80	3.00
❑ 37, Mar 86, Secret Wars II				
....0.75		0.60	1.80	3.00
❑ 38, Apr 86, AAd(c) 0.75		0.60	1.80	3.00
❑ 39, May 86, AAd(c) 0.75		0.60	1.80	3.00
❑ 40, Jun 86 ....0.75		0.60	1.80	3.00
❑ 41, Jul 86 ....0.75		0.60	1.80	3.00
❑ 42, Aug 86 ....0.75		0.60	1.80	3.00
❑ 43, Sep 86.....................0.75		0.60	1.80	3.00
❑ 44, Oct 86 ....0.75		0.60	1.80	3.00
❑ 45, Nov 86 ....0.75		0.60	1.80	3.00
❑ 46, Dec 86, Mutant Massacre				
....0.75		0.60	1.80	3.00
❑ 47, Jan 87 ....0.75		0.60	1.80	3.00
❑ 48, Feb 87 ....0.75		0.60	1.80	3.00
❑ 49, Mar 87 ....0.75		0.60	1.80	3.00
❑ 50, Apr 87 ....1.25		0.60	1.80	3.00
❑ 51, May 87 ....0.75		0.60	1.80	3.00
❑ 52, Jun 87 ....0.75		0.60	1.80	3.00
❑ 53, Jul 87 ....0.75		0.60	1.80	3.00
❑ 54, Aug 87 ....0.75		0.60	1.80	3.00
❑ 55, Sep 87.....................0.75		0.60	1.80	3.00
❑ 56, Oct 87 ....0.75		0.60	1.80	3.00
❑ 57, Nov 87 ....0.75		0.60	1.80	3.00
❑ 58, Dec 87, registration card				
....0.75		1.00	3.00	5.00
❑ 59, Jan 88, Fall of Mutants				
....0.75		1.00	3.00	5.00
❑ 60, Feb 88, Fall, D:Cipher				
....1.25		1.00	3.00	5.00
❑ 61, Mar 88, Fall, new costumes				
....0.75		1.20	3.60	6.00
❑ 62, Apr 88 ....0.75		0.60	1.80	3.00
❑ 63, May 88 ....1.00		0.60	1.80	3.00
❑ 64, Jun 88 ....1.00		0.60	1.80	3.00
❑ 65, Jul 88 ....1.00		0.60	1.80	3.00
❑ 66, Aug 88 ....1.00		0.60	1.80	3.00
❑ 67, Sep 88.....................1.00		0.60	1.80	3.00
❑ 68, Oct 88 ....1.00		0.60	1.80	3.00
❑ 69, Nov 88 ....1.00		0.60	1.80	3.00
❑ 70, Dec 88, Inferno 1.00		0.60	1.80	3.00
❑ 71, Jan 89, Inferno.........1.00		0.60	1.80	3.00
❑ 72, Feb 89, Inferno.........1.00		0.60	1.80	3.00
❑ 73, Mar 89, Inferno 1.50		0.60	1.80	3.00
❑ 74, Apr 89 ....1.00		0.60	1.80	3.00
❑ 75, May 89 ....1.00		0.60	1.80	3.00
❑ 76, Jun 89, Sub-Mariner 1.00		0.60	1.80	3.00
❑ 77, Jul 89 ....1.00		0.60	1.80	3.00
❑ 78, Aug 89 ....1.00		0.60	1.80	3.00
❑ 79, Sep 89.....................1.00		0.60	1.80	3.00
❑ 80, Oct 89 ....1.00		0.60	1.80	3.00
❑ 81, Nov 89 ....1.00		0.60	1.80	3.00
❑ 82, Nov 89 ....1.00		0.60	1.80	3.00
❑ 83, Dec 89.....................1.00		0.60	1.80	3.00
❑ 84, Dec 89, Acts of Vengeance				
....1.00		0.60	1.80	3.00
❑ 85, Jan 90, TMc(c) Acts of Vengeance				
....1.00		0.60	1.80	3.00
❑ 86, Feb 90, TMc(c) Acts of Vengeance				
....1.00		4.40	13.20	22.00
❑ 87, Mar 90, TMc(c) 1:Cable				
....1.00		13.00	39.00	65.00
❑ 88, Apr 90, TMc(c).........1.00		5.00	15.00	25.00
❑ 89, May 90, TMc(c)........1.00		2.40	7.20	12.00

	ORIG.	GOOD	FINE	N-MINT
❑ 90, Jun 90 ....1.00		2.40	7.20	12.00
❑ 91, Jul 90......................1.00		2.40	7.20	12.00
❑ 92, Aug 90.....................1.00		2.40	7.20	12.00
❑ 93, Sep 90, TMc(c).........1.00		5.20	15.60	26.00
❑ 94, Oct 90 ....1.00		2.00	6.00	10.00
❑ 95, Nov 90, X-Tinction....1.00		2.00	6.00	10.00
❑ 96, Dec 90, X-Tinction....1.00		2.80	8.40	14.00
❑ 97, Jan 91, X-Tinction 1.00		2.80	8.40	14.00
❑ 98, Feb 91, I:Deadpool, Gideon, Domino				
....1.00		2.00	6.00	10.00
❑ 99, Mar 91, L:Sunspot....1.00		1.60	4.80	8.00
❑ 100, Apr 91, 1st printing I:X-Force				
....1.50		2.00	6.00	10.00
❑ 100, Apr 91, 2nd printing1.50		0.80	2.40	4.00

NEW MUTANTS ANNUAL/SPECIAL

	ORIG.	GOOD	FINE	N-MINT
❑ 1, 85, AAd......................1.00		1.20	3.60	6.00
❑ 2, 86 ....1.25		0.80	2.40	4.00
❑ 3, 87 ....1.25		0.80	2.40	4.00
❑ 4, 88, Evolutionary War ..1.75		0.80	2.40	4.00
❑ 5, 89, Atlantis Attacks 2.00		0.60	1.80	3.00
❑ 6, 90, Future Present 2.00		0.60	1.80	3.00
❑ 7, 91, Kings of Pain 2.00		0.40	1.20	2.00

NEW MUTANTS SPECIAL EDITION

	ORIG.	GOOD	FINE	N-MINT
❑ 1, Dec 85 ....1.50		0.30	0.90	1.50

NEW MUTANTS SUMMER SPECIAL, THE

	ORIG.	GOOD	FINE	N-MINT
❑ 1, Aug 90.......................2.95		0.59	1.77	2.95

NEW NIGHT OF THE LIVING DEAD
FANTACO

	ORIG.	GOOD	FINE	N-MINT
❑ 0 ....1.95		0.39	1.17	1.95
❑ 1 ....3.95		0.79	2.37	3.95
❑ 2 ....3.95		0.79	2.37	3.95
❑ 3 ....3.95		0.79	2.37	3.95

NEW PARTNERS IN PERIL
BLUE COMET

	ORIG.	GOOD	FINE	N-MINT
❑ 1, b&w............................		0.45	1.35	2.25

NEW POWER STARS, THE

	ORIG.	GOOD	FINE	N-MINT
❑ 1, b&w............................		0.40	1.20	2.00

NEW SHADOWHAWK, THE
IMAGE

	ORIG.	GOOD	FINE	N-MINT
❑ 1, Jun 95 ....2.50		0.50	1.50	2.50
❑ 2, Aug 95 ....2.50		0.50	1.50	2.50
❑ 6, Feb 96.......................2.50		0.50	1.50	2.50
❑ 7, Mar 96.......................2.50		0.50	1.50	2.50

NEW STATESMEN
FLEETWAY/QUALITY

	ORIG.	GOOD	FINE	N-MINT
❑ 1		1.20	3.60	6.00
❑ 2		0.79	2.37	3.95
❑ 3		0.79	2.37	3.95
❑ 4		0.79	2.37	3.95
❑ 5		0.79	2.37	3.95

NEW TALENT SHOWCASE
DC

	ORIG.	GOOD	FINE	N-MINT
❑ 1, Jan 84........................		0.20	0.60	1.00
❑ 2, Feb 84........................		0.20	0.60	1.00
❑ 3, Mar 84........................		0.20	0.60	1.00
❑ 4, Apr 84.........................		0.20	0.60	1.00
❑ 5, May 84........................		0.20	0.60	1.00
❑ 6, Jun 84........................		0.25	0.75	1.25
❑ 7, Jul 84.........................		0.25	0.75	1.25
❑ 8, Aug 84........................		0.25	0.75	1.25
❑ 9, Sep 84		0.25	0.75	1.25
❑ 10, Oct 84.......................		0.25	0.75	1.25
❑ 11, Nov 84.......................		0.25	0.75	1.25
❑ 12, Dec 84......................		0.25	0.75	1.25
❑ 13, Jan 85.......................		0.25	0.75	1.25
❑ 14, Feb 85.......................		0.25	0.75	1.25
❑ 15, Mar 85, (becomes Talent Showcase)				
....		0.25	0.75	1.25

	ORIG.	GOOD	FINE	N-MINT

NEW TEEN TITANS

☐ 1, 83, Keebler/DC GP, drug issue
...... 1.00 0.40 1.20 2.00
☐ 1, Beverage/DC drug issue 0.60 1.80 3.00
☐ 1, IBM/DC drug issue 0.80 2.40 4.00
☐ 2, 83, Keebler/DC, drug issue
...... 1.00 0.40 1.20 2.00

NEW TEEN TITANS (1980-1984 series)

☐ 1, Nov 80, GP/RT, I:Teen Titans
...... 0.50 2.80 8.40 14.00
☐ 2, Dec 80, GP/RT; 1:Terminator
...... 0.50 2.00 6.00 10.00
☐ 3, Jan 81, GP 0.50 1.00 3.00 5.00
☐ 4, Feb 81, GP 0.50 1.00 3.00 5.00
☐ 5, Mar 81, CS/RT, O:Raven I:Trigon
...... 0.50 1.00 3.00 5.00
☐ 6, Apr 81, GP 0.50 0.80 2.40 4.00
☐ 7, May 81, GP/RT, O:Cyborg
...... 0.50 0.80 2.40 4.00
☐ 8, Jun 81, GP/RT............ 0.50 0.80 2.40 4.00
☐ 9, Jul 81, GP/RT............ 0.50 0.80 2.40 4.00
☐ 10, Aug 81, GP/RT, A:Terminator
...... 0.50 2.00 6.00 10.00
☐ 11, Sep 81, GP/RT 0.50 0.60 1.80 3.00
☐ 12, Oct 81, GP/RT........ 0.60 0.60 1.80 3.00
☐ 13, Nov 81, GP/RT, Doom Patrol
...... 0.60 1.00 3.00 5.00
☐ 14, Dec 81, GP/RT, Doom Patrol
...... 0.60 1.00 3.00 5.00
☐ 15, Jan 82, GP/RT, Doom Patrol
...... 0.60 1.00 3.00 5.00
☐ 16, Feb 82, GP/RT, I:Captain Carrot
...... 0.60 0.60 1.80 3.00
☐ 17, Mar 82, GP/RT 0.60 0.60 1.80 3.00
☐ 18, Apr 82, GP/RT 0.60 0.60 1.80 3.00
☐ 19, May 82, GP/RT 0.60 0.60 1.80 3.00
☐ 20, Jun 82, GP/RT........ 0.60 0.60 1.80 3.00
☐ 21, Jul 82, GP/RT, I:Night Force, GC
...... 0.60 0.60 1.80 3.00
☐ 22, Aug 82, GP/RT 0.60 0.55 1.65 2.75
☐ 23, Sep 82, GP/RT 0.60 0.55 1.65 2.75
☐ 24, Oct 82, GP/RT, A:Omega Men
...... 0.60 0.50 1.50 2.50
☐ 25, Nov 82, GP/RT, A:Omega Men
...... 0.60 0.50 1.50 2.50
☐ 26, Dec 82, GP/RT 0.60 0.50 1.50 2.50
☐ 27, Jan 93, GP/RT 0.60 0.50 1.50 2.50
☐ 28, Feb 93, GP/RT........ 0.60 0.50 1.50 2.50
☐ 29, Mar 83, GP/RT 0.60 0.45 1.35 2.25
☐ 30, Apr 83, GP/RT........ 0.60 0.45 1.35 2.25
☐ 31, May 83, GP/RT, Raven insane
...... 0.60 0.30 0.90 1.50
☐ 32, Jun 83, GP/RT........ 0.60 0.25 0.75 1.25
☐ 33, Jul 83, GP/RT.......... 0.60 0.25 0.75 1.25
☐ 34, Aug 83 .... 0.60 0.25 0.75 1.25
☐ 35, Oct 83 .... 0.60 0.25 0.75 1.25
☐ 36, Nov 83, KP............... 0.60 0.25 0.75 1.25
☐ 37, Dec 83, GP, A:Outsiders
...... 0.75 0.30 0.90 1.50
☐ 38, Jan 84, GP, O:Wonder Girl
...... 0.75 0.20 0.60 1.00
☐ 39, Feb 84, GP;Dick Grayson quits as Robin;Wally West retires as Kid Flash .. 0.75 0.30 0.90 1.50
☐ 40, Mar 84, GP (becomes *Tales of the Teen Titans*)
...... 0.75 0.60 1.80 3.00

NEW TEEN TITANS (Direct-sales series)

☐ 1, Aug 84, GP................. 1.25 1.40 4.20 7.00
☐ 2, Oct 84, GP A:Trigon ... 1.25 0.60 1.80 3.00
☐ 3, Nov 84, GP 1.25 0.60 1.80 3.00
☐ 4, Jan 85, GP 1.25 0.60 1.80 3.00
☐ 5, Feb 85, GP 1.25 0.60 1.80 3.00

☐ 6, Mar 85 .... 1.25 0.50 1.50 2.50
☐ 7, Apr 85....................... 1.25 0.50 1.50 2.50
☐ 8, May 85....................... 1.25 0.50 1.50 2.50
☐ 9, Jun 85 .... 1.25 0.50 1.50 2.50
☐ 10, Jul 85...................... 1.25 0.50 1.50 2.50
☐ 11, Aug 85..................... 1.25 0.50 1.50 2.50
☐ 12, Sep 85..................... 1.25 0.50 1.50 2.50
☐ 13, Oct 85, Crisis 1.25 0.40 1.20 2.00
☐ 14, Nov 85, Crisis 1.25 0.40 1.20 2.00
☐ 15, Dec 85 .... 1.50 0.40 1.20 2.00
☐ 16, Jan 86...................... 1.50 0.40 1.20 2.00
☐ 17, Feb 86...................... 1.50 0.40 1.20 2.00
☐ 18, Mar 86...................... 1.50 0.40 1.20 2.00
☐ 19, Apr 86...................... 1.50 0.40 1.20 2.00
☐ 20, May 86...................... 1.50 0.40 1.20 2.00
☐ 21, Jun 86...................... 1.50 0.40 1.20 2.00
☐ 22, Jul 86....................... 1.50 0.40 1.20 2.00
☐ 23, Aug 86...................... 1.50 0.40 1.20 2.00
☐ 24, Oct 86....................... 1.50 0.40 1.20 2.00
☐ 25, Nov 86...................... 1.50 0.40 1.20 2.00
☐ 26, Dec 86...................... 1.50 0.40 1.20 2.00
☐ 27, Jan 87....................... 1.50 0.40 1.20 2.00
☐ 28, Feb 87....................... 1.50 0.40 1.20 2.00
☐ 29, Mar 87...................... 1.50 0.40 1.20 2.00
☐ 30, Apr 87....................... 1.50 0.40 1.20 2.00
☐ 31, May 87, V:Brother Blood; A:Superman, Batman
...... 1.50 0.40 1.20 2.00
☐ 32, Jun 87 .... 1.50 0.40 1.20 2.00
☐ 33, Jul 87....................... 1.50 0.40 1.20 2.00
☐ 34, Aug 87...................... 1.50 0.40 1.20 2.00
☐ 35, Sep 87...................... 1.50 0.40 1.20 2.00
☐ 36, Oct 87....................... 1.50 0.40 1.20 2.00
☐ 37, Nov 87...................... 1.75 0.40 1.20 2.00
☐ 38, Dec 87, A:Infinity Inc.1.75 0.40 1.20 2.00
☐ 39, Jan 88...................... 1.75 0.40 1.20 2.00
☐ 40, Feb 88, V:The Gentleman Ghost,Silver Fog,I.Q.
...... 1.75 0.40 1.20 2.00
☐ 41, Mar 88...................... 1.75 0.40 1.20 2.00
☐ 42, Apr 88...................... 1.75 0.40 1.20 2.00
☐ 43, May 88...................... 1.75 0.40 1.20 2.00
☐ 44, Jun 88 .... 1.75 0.40 1.20 2.00
☐ 45, Jul 88....................... 1.75 0.40 1.20 2.00
☐ 46, Aug 88...................... 1.75 0.40 1.20 2.00
☐ 47, Sep 88, O:Titans 1.75 0.40 1.20 2.00
☐ 48, Oct 88....................... 1.75 0.40 1.20 2.00
☐ 49, Nov 88, (becomes *New Titans*)
...... 1.75 0.40 1.20 2.00

NEW TEEN TITANS ANNUAL (Direct-sale series)

☐ 3, 86, I&1:Danny Chase, Godiva;A:King Faraday; cover indicates '87 Annual, indicia says '86
...... 2.25 0.45 1.35 2.25

NEW TEEN TITANS ANNUAL (Direct-sales series)

☐ 1, 85, A:Superman; V:Vanguard
...... 2.00 0.40 1.20 2.00
☐ 2, 86, JBy;O:Brother Blood; A:Doctor Light
...... 2.50 0.50 1.50 2.50
☐ 4, 88, (becomes *New Titans Annual, The*)
...... 2.50 0.50 1.50 2.50

NEW TEEN TITANS ANNUAL, THE (1980-1984 series)

☐ 1, 82, GP....................... 1.00 0.20 0.60 1.00
☐ 2, 83, GP;I&1:Vigilante; A:Monitor;(becomes *Teen Titans Annual* (1980-1984 series))
...... 1.00 0.20 0.60 1.00

NEW TITANS ANNUAL

☐ 7, Sep 91, (was *New Titans Annual, The*); "Armageddon 2001"; O&1:Team Titans .3.50 0.70 2.10 3.50
☐ 8, 92, "Eclipso: The Darkness Within"
...... 3.50 0.70 2.10 3.50
☐ 9, 93, "Bloodlines: Outbreak";O&1:Anima
...... 3.50 0.70 2.10 3.50

	ORIG.	GOOD	FINE	N-MINT
☐ 10, 94, Elseworlds	3.50	0.70	2.10	3.50
☐ 11, 95..............................	3.95	0.79	2.37	3.95

NEW TITANS ANNUAL, THE

☐ 5, 89, (was *New Teen Titans Annual*)

....	3.50	0.70	2.10	3.50

☐ 6, 90, (becomes *New Titans Annual*)

....	3.50	0.70	2.10	3.50

NEW TITANS, THE (was New Teen Titans)

	ORIG.	GOOD	FINE	N-MINT
☐ 0, Oct 94	1.95	0.39	1.17	1.95

☐ 50, Dec 88, GP;"Who is Wonder Girl" Part 1 of 5; O:Troia

....	1.75	0.40	1.20	2.00

☐ 51, Dec 88, GP;"Who is Wonder Girl" Part 2 of 5

....	1.75	0.40	1.20	2.00

☐ 52, Jan 89, GP;"Who is Wonder Girl" Part 3 of 5

....	1.75	0.40	1.20	2.00

☐ 53, Feb 89, GP;"Who is Wonder Girl" Part 4 of 5

....	1.75	0.40	1.20	2.00

☐ 54, Mar 89, GP;"Who is Wonder Girl" Part 5 of 5

....	1.75	0.40	1.20	2.00
☐ 55, Jun 89, GP	1.75	0.40	1.20	2.00
☐ 56, Jul 89......................	1.75	0.40	1.20	2.00
☐ 57, Aug 89	1.75	0.40	1.20	2.00
☐ 58, Sep 89	1.75	0.40	1.20	2.00
☐ 59, Oct 89	1.75	0.40	1.20	2.00
☐ 60, Nov 89, Tim Drake ...	1.75	1.00	3.00	5.00
☐ 61, Dec 89, Lonely Place	1.75	0.80	2.40	4.00
☐ 62, Jan 90	1.75	0.50	1.50	2.50
☐ 63, Feb 90.....................	1.75	0.40	1.20	2.00
☐ 64, Mar 90	1.75	0.40	1.20	2.00
☐ 65, Apr 90, Robin III	1.75	0.80	2.40	4.00
☐ 66, May 90.....................	1.75	0.40	1.20	2.00
☐ 67, Jul 90.......................	1.75	0.40	1.20	2.00
☐ 68, Jul 90.......................	1.75	0.40	1.20	2.00
☐ 69, Sep 90.....................	1.75	0.40	1.20	2.00
☐ 70, Oct 90	1.75	0.40	1.20	2.00
☐ 71, Nov 90	1.75	0.80	2.40	4.00
☐ 72, Jan 91	1.75	0.80	2.40	4.00
☐ 73, Feb 91	1.75	0.60	1.80	3.00
☐ 74, Mar 91	1.75	0.40	1.20	2.00
☐ 75, Apr 91	1.75	0.40	1.20	2.00
☐ 76, Jun 91......................	1.75	0.40	1.20	2.00
☐ 77, Jul 91.......................	1.75	0.40	1.20	2.00
☐ 78, Aug 91	1.75	0.40	1.20	2.00
☐ 79, Sep 91.....................	1.75	0.40	1.20	2.00
☐ 80, Nov 91	1.75	0.40	1.20	2.00
☐ 81, Dec 91.....................	1.75	0.40	1.20	2.00
☐ 82, Jan 92	1.75	0.40	1.20	2.00
☐ 83, Feb 92, D:Jericho	1.75	0.40	1.20	2.00
☐ 84, Mar 92, D:Raven	1.75	0.35	1.05	1.75
☐ 85, Apr 92......................	1.75	0.35	1.05	1.75
☐ 86, May 92.....................	1.75	0.35	1.05	1.75
☐ 87, Jun 92......................	1.75	0.35	1.05	1.75
☐ 88, Jul 92.......................	1.75	0.35	1.05	1.75
☐ 89, Aug 92	1.75	0.35	1.05	1.75
☐ 90, Sep 92.....................	1.75	0.35	1.05	1.75
☐ 91, Oct 92	1.75	0.35	1.05	1.75

☐ 92, Nov 92, Total Chaos Part 8

....	1.75	0.40	1.20	2.00

☐ 93, Dec 92, follow-up to *Titans Sell-Out Special*

....	1.75	0.40	1.20	2.00
☐ 94, Feb 93	1.75	0.40	1.20	2.00
☐ 95, Mar 93	1.75	0.40	1.20	2.00
☐ 96, Apr 93......................	1.75	0.40	1.20	2.00

☐ 97, May 93, "The Darkening" Part 1

....	1.75	0.40	1.20	2.00

☐ 98, Jun 93, "The Darkening" Part 2

....	1.75	0.40	1.20	2.00
☐ 99, I:Arsenal..................	1.75	0.40	1.20	2.00
☐ 100, foil cover	3.50	0.70	2.10	3.50
☐ 101, Sep 93....................	1.75	0.35	1.05	1.75
☐ 102, Oct 93	1.75	0.35	1.05	1.75

	ORIG.	GOOD	FINE	N-MINT
☐ 103, Nov 93	1.75	0.35	1.05	1.75
☐ 104, Dec 93	1.75	0.35	1.05	1.75
☐ 105, Dec 93	1.75	0.35	1.05	1.75
☐ 106, Jan 94....................	1.75	0.35	1.05	1.75
☐ 107, Jan 94....................	1.75	0.35	1.05	1.75
☐ 108, Feb 94....................	1.75	0.35	1.05	1.75
☐ 109, Mar 94	1.75	0.35	1.05	1.75
☐ 110, May 94...................	1.75	0.35	1.05	1.75
☐ 111, Jun 94....................	1.75	0.35	1.05	1.75
☐ 112, Jul 94.....................	1.95	0.39	1.17	1.95
☐ 113, Aug 94	1.95	0.39	1.17	1.95
☐ 114, Sep 94...................	1.95	0.39	1.17	1.95
☐ 115, Nov 94	1.95	0.39	1.17	1.95
☐ 116, Dec 94	1.95	0.39	1.17	1.95
☐ 117, Jan 95....................	1.95	0.39	1.17	1.95
☐ 118, Feb 95....................	1.95	0.39	1.17	1.95
☐ 119, Mar 95	1.95	0.39	1.17	1.95
☐ 120, Apr 95....................	1.95	0.39	1.17	1.95
☐ 121, May 95...................	1.95	0.39	1.17	1.95
☐ 122, Jun 95....................	2.25	0.45	1.35	2.25
☐ 123, Jul 95.....................	2.25	0.45	1.35	2.25

☐ 124, Aug 95, "The Siege of the Zi Charam" Part 1 of 5

....	2.25	0.45	1.35	2.25

☐ 125, Sep 95, "The Siege of the Zi Charam" Part 5 of 5

....	3.50	0.70	2.10	3.50
☐ 126, Oct 95	2.25	0.45	1.35	2.25
☐ 127, Nov 95, "Meltdown"	2.25	0.45	1.35	2.25
☐ 128, Dec 95, "Meltdown".	2.25	0.45	1.35	2.25
☐ 129, Jan 96, "Meltdown" .	2.25	0.45	1.35	2.25
☐ 130, Feb 96, final issue...	2.25	0.45	1.35	2.25

NEW TRIUMPH FEATURING NORTHGUARD
MATRIX

		GOOD	FINE	N-MINT
☐ 1		0.60	1.80	3.00
☐ 1, 2nd printing		0.35	1.05	1.75
☐ 2		0.30	0.90	1.50
☐ 3		0.30	0.90	1.50
☐ 4		0.30	0.90	1.50
☐ 5		0.30	0.90	1.50

NEW TWO-FISTED TALES, THE
DARK HORSE

	ORIG.	GOOD	FINE	N-MINT
☐ 0, 94, nn	4.95	0.99	2.97	4.95

EC/DARK HORSE

	ORIG.	GOOD	FINE	N-MINT
☐ 1, 93, HK, WE	4.95	0.99	2.97	4.95

NEW WARRIORS
MARVEL

	ORIG.	GOOD	FINE	N-MINT
☐ 1, Jul 90.......................	1.00	2.00	6.00	10.00
☐ 2, Aug 90......................	1.00	1.40	4.20	7.00
☐ 3, Sep 90	1.00	1.00	3.00	5.00
☐ 4, Oct 90	1.00	1.00	3.00	5.00
☐ 5, Nov 90	1.00	1.00	3.00	5.00
☐ 6, Dec 90	1.00	1.00	3.00	5.00
☐ 7, Jan 91, A:Punisher	1.00	1.20	3.60	6.00
☐ 8, Feb 91, A:Punisher	1.00	1.20	3.60	6.00
☐ 9, Mar 91, Punisher	1.00	1.00	3.00	5.00
☐ 10, Apr 91......................	1.00	1.00	3.00	5.00
☐ 11, May 91, Wolverine....	1.00	1.00	3.00	5.00
☐ 12, Jun 91......................	1.00	0.80	2.40	4.00
☐ 13, Jul 91.......................	1.00	0.80	2.40	4.00

☐ 14, Aug 91, Darkhawk, Namor

....	1.00	0.40	1.20	2.00
☐ 15, Sep 91.....................	1.00	0.40	1.20	2.00
☐ 16, Oct 91	1.00	0.40	1.20	2.00
☐ 17, Nov 91, F4................	1.00	0.40	1.20	2.00
☐ 18, Dec 91.....................	1.00	0.40	1.20	2.00
☐ 19	1.00	0.40	1.20	2.00
☐ 20	1.25	0.40	1.20	2.00
☐ 21	1.25	0.40	1.20	2.00
☐ 22	1.25	0.40	1.20	2.00
☐ 23	1.25	0.40	1.20	2.00
☐ 24	1.25	0.40	1.20	2.00
☐ 25	2.50	1.20	3.60	6.00

	ORIG.	GOOD	FINE	N-MINT
❏ 26	1.25	0.25	0.75	1.25
❏ 27	1.25	0.25	0.75	1.25
❏ 28	1.25	0.25	0.75	1.25
❏ 29	1.25	0.25	0.75	1.25
❏ 30	1.25	0.25	0.75	1.25
❏ 31	1.25	0.25	0.75	1.25
❏ 32	1.25	0.25	0.75	1.25
❏ 33	1.25	0.25	0.75	1.25
❏ 34	1.25	0.25	0.75	1.25
❏ 35	1.25	0.25	0.75	1.25
❏ 36	1.25	0.25	0.75	1.25
❏ 37	1.25	0.25	0.75	1.25
❏ 38	1.25	0.25	0.75	1.25
❏ 39	1.25	0.25	0.75	1.25
❏ 40	1.25	0.25	0.75	1.25
❏ 40, foil cover	2.25	0.45	1.35	2.25
❏ 41	1.25	0.25	0.75	1.25
❏ 42	1.25	0.25	0.75	1.25
❏ 43	1.25	0.25	0.75	1.25
❏ 44	1.25	0.25	0.75	1.25
❏ 45	1.25	0.60	1.80	3.00
❏ 46, Apr 94	1.25	0.60	1.80	3.00
❏ 47, May 94	1.50	0.30	0.90	1.50
❏ 48, Jun 94	1.50	0.30	0.90	1.50
❏ 49, Jul 94	1.50	0.30	0.90	1.50
❏ 50, Aug 94	2.00	0.40	1.20	2.00
❏ 50, Aug 94, enhanced cover	2.95	0.59	1.77	2.95
❏ 51, Sep 94	1.50	0.30	0.90	1.50
❏ 52, Oct 94	1.50	0.30	0.90	1.50
❏ 53, Nov 94	1.50	0.30	0.90	1.50
❏ 54, Dec 94	1.50	0.30	0.90	1.50
❏ 55, Jan 95	1.50	0.30	0.90	1.50
❏ 56, Feb 95	1.50	0.30	0.90	1.50
❏ 57, Mar 95	1.50	0.30	0.90	1.50
❏ 58, Apr 95	1.50	0.30	0.90	1.50
❏ 59, May 95	1.50	0.30	0.90	1.50
❏ 60, Jun 95	2.50	0.50	1.50	2.50
❏ 61, Jul 95, "Maximum Clonage" Prologue	1.50	0.30	0.90	1.50
❏ 62, Aug 95, A:Scarlet Spider	1.50	0.30	0.90	1.50
❏ 63, Sep 95	1.50	0.30	0.90	1.50
❏ 64, Oct 95, return of Night Thrasher and Rage	1.50	0.30	0.90	1.50
❏ 65, Nov 95, return of Namorita	1.50	0.30	0.90	1.50
❏ 66, Dec 95	1.50	0.30	0.90	1.50
❏ 67, Jan 96	1.50	0.30	0.90	1.50
❏ 68, Feb 96, "Future Shock" Part 1;A:Guardians of the Galaxy	1.50	0.30	0.90	1.50
❏ 69, Mar 96, "Future Shock" Part 2;D:Speedball	1.50	0.30	0.90	1.50
❏ 70, Apr 96, "Future Shock" Part 3	1.50	0.30	0.90	1.50
❏ 71, May 96, "Future Shock" Part 4; final issue	1.50	0.30	0.90	1.50

NEW WARRIORS ANNUAL

	ORIG.	GOOD	FINE	N-MINT
❏ 1, 91, Kings of Pain	2.00	1.00	3.00	5.00
❏ 2, 92	2.25	0.60	1.80	3.00
❏ 3, 93, trading card	2.95	0.59	1.77	2.95
❏ 4, 94	2.95	0.59	1.77	2.95

NEW WAVE
ECLIPSE

	ORIG.	GOOD	FINE	N-MINT
❏ 1, misprint		0.60	1.80	3.00
❏ 1, Jun 86	0.50	0.10	0.30	0.50
❏ 2, Jul 86		0.10	0.30	0.50
❏ 3, Jul 86		0.10	0.30	0.50
❏ 4, Aug 86		0.10	0.30	0.50
❏ 5, Aug 86		0.10	0.30	0.50
❏ 6, Sep 86		0.10	0.30	0.50
❏ 7, Sep 86		0.10	0.30	0.50
❏ 8, Sep 86		0.10	0.30	0.50
❏ 9, Oct 86		0.30	0.90	1.50
❏ 10, Nov 86		0.30	0.90	1.50
❏ 11, Dec 86		0.30	0.90	1.50
❏ 12, Feb 87		0.30	0.90	1.50
❏ 13, Mar 87		0.30	0.90	1.50

NEW WAVE VS. THE VOLUNTEERS 3-D

	GOOD	FINE	N-MINT
❏ 1, Apr 87	0.50	1.50	2.50
❏ 2, Jun 87	0.50	1.50	2.50

NEW WORLD ORDER
BLAZER

	ORIG.	GOOD	FINE	N-MINT
❏ 1, b&w	2.50	0.50	1.50	2.50
❏ 2, b&w	2.50	0.50	1.50	2.50
❏ 3, b&w	2.50	0.50	1.50	2.50
❏ 4, Aug 93, b&w	2.50	0.50	1.50	2.50
❏ 5, Jan 94, b&w	2.50	0.50	1.50	2.50
❏ 6, May 94, b&w	2.50	0.50	1.50	2.50
❏ 7, Aug 94, b&w	2.50	0.50	1.50	2.50
❏ 8, Feb 95, b&w	2.50	0.50	1.50	2.50

NEW YORK CITY OUTLAWS
OUTLAW

	GOOD	FINE	N-MINT
❏ 1	0.40	1.20	2.00
❏ 2	0.40	1.20	2.00
❏ 3	0.40	1.20	2.00
❏ 4	0.40	1.20	2.00

NEW YORK: YEAR ZERO
ECLIPSE

	GOOD	FINE	N-MINT
❏ 1, b&w	0.40	1.20	2.00
❏ 2, b&w	0.40	1.20	2.00
❏ 3, b&w	0.40	1.20	2.00
❏ 4, b&w	0.40	1.20	2.00

NEWFORCE
IMAGE

	ORIG.	GOOD	FINE	N-MINT
❏ 1, Jan 96, "Extreme Destroyer" Part 8 of 9;polybagged with Kodiak card	2.50	0.50	1.50	2.50
❏ 2, Feb 96	2.50	0.50	1.50	2.50
❏ 3, Mar 96	2.50	0.50	1.50	2.50

NEWMEN

	ORIG.	GOOD	FINE	N-MINT
❏ 1, Apr 94	1.95	0.60	1.80	3.00
❏ 2, May 94	1.95	0.39	1.17	1.95
❏ 3, Jun 94	1.95	0.39	1.17	1.95
❏ 4, Jul 94	1.95	0.39	1.17	1.95
❏ 5, Aug 94	2.50	0.50	1.50	2.50
❏ 6, Sep 94	2.50	0.50	1.50	2.50
❏ 7, Oct 94	2.50	0.50	1.50	2.50
❏ 8, Nov 94	2.50	0.50	1.50	2.50
❏ 9, Dec 94	2.50	0.50	1.50	2.50
❏ 10, Jan 95, polybagged with trading card	2.50	0.50	1.50	2.50
❏ 11, Feb 95, Extreme Sacrifice Aftermath; polybagged	2.50	0.50	1.50	2.50
❏ 12, Mar 95	2.50	0.50	1.50	2.50
❏ 13, Apr 95	2.50	0.50	1.50	2.50
❏ 14, May 95, "Dominion" Part 2 of 4	2.50	0.50	1.50	2.50
❏ 15, Jun 95, "Dominion" Part 3 of 4;no indicia	2.50	0.50	1.50	2.50
❏ 16, Jul 95, "Dominion" Part 4 of 4	2.50	0.50	1.50	2.50
❏ 16, Jul 95, A:"Dominion" Part 4 of 4; alternate cover	2.50	0.50	1.50	2.50
❏ 17, Aug 95	2.50	0.50	1.50	2.50
❏ 18, Sep 95	2.50	0.50	1.50	2.50
❏ 19, Oct 95, "Extreme Destroyer"	2.50	0.50	1.50	2.50
❏ 20, Nov 95, "Babewatch"	2.50	0.50	1.50	2.50

NEWSTIME
DC

	ORIG.	GOOD	FINE	N-MINT
❏ 0, death of Superman magazine	2.95	0.59	1.77	2.95

	ORIG.	GOOD	FINE	N-MINT

NEWSTRALIA
INNOVATION

	ORIG.	GOOD	FINE	N-MINT
1	0.35	1.05	1.75
2	0.39	1.17	1.95
3	0.39	1.17	1.95
4	0.45	1.35	2.25
5, b&w	0.45	1.35	2.25

NEXT MAN
COMICO

	ORIG.	GOOD	FINE	N-MINT
1, Mar 85	0.30	0.90	1.50
2, Apr 85	0.30	0.90	1.50
3, Jun 85	0.30	0.90	1.50
4, Aug 85	0.30	0.90	1.50
5, Oct 85	0.30	0.90	1.50

NEXT NEXUS, THE
FIRST

	ORIG.	GOOD	FINE	N-MINT
1, SR	0.39	1.17	1.95
2, SR	0.39	1.17	1.95
3, SR	0.39	1.17	1.95
4, SR	0.39	1.17	1.95

NEXUS (1st series, b&w)
CAPITAL

	ORIG.	GOOD	FINE	N-MINT
1, 1:Nexus	3.60	10.80	18.00
2	2.40	7.20	12.00
3	2.00	6.00	10.00

NEXUS (2nd series, color)

	ORIG.	GOOD	FINE	N-MINT
1	1.60	4.80	8.00
2	1.20	3.60	6.00
3	1.00	3.00	5.00
4	0.80	2.40	4.00
5	0.80	2.40	4.00
6, (moves to First)	0.80	2.40	4.00

NEXUS (former Capital title)
FIRST

	ORIG.	GOOD	FINE	N-MINT
7	0.50	1.50	2.50
8	0.50	1.50	2.50
9	0.50	1.50	2.50
10	0.50	1.50	2.50
11	0.35	1.05	1.75
12	0.35	1.05	1.75
13	0.35	1.05	1.75
14	0.35	1.05	1.75
15	0.35	1.05	1.75
16	0.35	1.05	1.75
17	0.35	1.05	1.75
18	0.35	1.05	1.75
19	0.35	1.05	1.75
20	0.35	1.05	1.75
21	0.35	1.05	1.75
22	0.35	1.05	1.75
23	0.35	1.05	1.75
24	0.35	1.05	1.75
25	0.35	1.05	1.75
26	0.35	1.05	1.75
27	0.35	1.05	1.75
28	0.35	1.05	1.75
29	0.35	1.05	1.75
30	0.35	1.05	1.75
31	0.35	1.05	1.75
32	0.35	1.05	1.75
33	0.35	1.05	1.75
34	0.35	1.05	1.75
35	0.35	1.05	1.75
36	0.35	1.05	1.75
37	0.35	1.05	1.75
38	0.35	1.05	1.75
39	0.35	1.05	1.75
40	0.35	1.05	1.75
41	0.35	1.05	1.75
42	0.35	1.05	1.75

	ORIG.	GOOD	FINE	N-MINT
43		0.35	1.05	1.75
44		0.35	1.05	1.75
45, A:Badger		0.50	1.50	2.50
46, A:Badger		0.50	1.50	2.50
47, A:Badger		0.50	1.50	2.50
48, A:Badger		0.50	1.50	2.50
49, A:Badger		0.50	1.50	2.50
50, A:Badger, Crossroads.		0.70	2.10	3.50
51		0.39	1.17	1.95
52		0.39	1.17	1.95
53		0.39	1.17	1.95
54		0.39	1.17	1.95
55		0.39	1.17	1.95
56		0.39	1.17	1.95
57		0.39	1.17	1.95
58		0.39	1.17	1.95
59		0.39	1.17	1.95
60		0.39	1.17	1.95
61		0.39	1.17	1.95
62		0.39	1.17	1.95
63		0.39	1.17	1.95
64		0.39	1.17	1.95
65		0.39	1.17	1.95
66		0.39	1.17	1.95
67		0.39	1.17	1.95
68		0.39	1.17	1.95
69		0.39	1.17	1.95
70		0.39	1.17	1.95
71		0.39	1.17	1.95
72		0.39	1.17	1.95
73		0.45	1.35	2.25
74		0.45	1.35	2.25
75		0.45	1.35	2.25
76		0.45	1.35	2.25
77		0.45	1.35	2.25
78		0.45	1.35	2.25
79		0.45	1.35	2.25
80		0.45	1.35	2.25

NEXUS LEGENDS

	ORIG.	GOOD	FINE	N-MINT
1, SR, reprints	0.30	0.90	1.50
2, SR, reprints	0.30	0.90	1.50
3, SR, reprints	0.30	0.90	1.50
4, SR, reprints	0.30	0.90	1.50
5, SR, reprints	0.30	0.90	1.50
6, SR, reprints	0.30	0.90	1.50
7, SR, reprints	0.30	0.90	1.50
8, SR, reprints	0.30	0.90	1.50
9, SR, reprints	0.30	0.90	1.50
10, SR, reprints	0.30	0.90	1.50
11, SR, reprints	0.30	0.90	1.50
12, SR, reprints	0.30	0.90	1.50
13, SR, reprints	0.30	0.90	1.50
14, SR, reprints	0.30	0.90	1.50
15, SR, reprints	0.30	0.90	1.50
16, SR, reprints	0.35	1.05	1.75
17, SR, reprints	0.35	1.05	1.75
18, SR, reprints	0.39	1.17	1.95
19, SR, reprints	0.39	1.17	1.95
20, SR, reprints	0.39	1.17	1.95
21, SR, reprints	0.39	1.17	1.95
22, SR, reprints	0.39	1.17	1.95

NEXUS THE LIBERATOR
DARK HORSE

	ORIG.	GOOD	FINE	N-MINT
1	2.50	0.50	1.50	2.50
2	2.50	0.50	1.50	2.50
3	2.50	0.50	1.50	2.50
4	2.50	0.50	1.50	2.50

NEXUS: ALIEN JUSTICE

	ORIG.	GOOD	FINE	N-MINT
1	3.95	0.79	2.37	3.95
2	3.95	0.79	2.37	3.95
3, SR	3.95	0.79	2.37	3.95

	ORIG.	GOOD	FINE	N-MINT

NEXUS: THE ORIGIN

	ORIG.	GOOD	FINE	N-MINT
☐ 0, nn SR	0.79	2.37	3.95	

NEXUS: THE WAGES OF SIN (mini-series)

☐ 1, Mar 95, cardstock covers	2.95	0.59	1.77	2.95
☐ 2, Apr 95, cardstock cover	2.95	0.59	1.77	2.95
☐ 3, May 95, cardstock cover	2.95	0.59	1.77	2.95

NFL PROACTION VOL. II
MARVEL/NFL PROPERTIES

☐ 3, Nov 94, magazine with bound-in Spider-Man comic book	2.95	0.59	1.77	2.95

NFL SUPERPRO (one-shot, 1990)
MARVEL

☐ 1, O:SuperPro	3.95	1.00	3.00	5.00

NFL SUPERPRO (series, begins 1991)

☐ 1, Oct 91, A:SpM	1.00	0.20	0.60	1.00
☐ 2, Nov 91	1.00	0.20	0.60	1.00
☐ 3, Dec 91	1.00	0.20	0.60	1.00
☐ 4	1.00	0.20	0.60	1.00
☐ 5	1.25	0.25	0.75	1.25
☐ 6	1.25	0.25	0.75	1.25
☐ 7	1.25	0.25	0.75	1.25
☐ 8, Capt. America	1.25	0.25	0.75	1.25
☐ 9	1.25	0.25	0.75	1.25
☐ 10	1.25	0.25	0.75	1.25
☐ 11	1.25	0.25	0.75	1.25
☐ 12	1.25	0.25	0.75	1.25

NICK FURY VS. S.H.I.E.L.D.

☐ 1, Jun 88	3.50	1.60	4.80	8.00
☐ 2, Jul 88, BSz(c)	3.50	1.40	4.20	7.00
☐ 3, Mar 88	3.50	1.20	3.60	6.00
☐ 4, Sep 88	3.50	1.00	3.00	5.00
☐ 5, Oct 88	3.50	1.00	3.00	5.00
☐ 6, Nov 88	3.50	1.00	3.00	5.00

NICK FURY, AGENT OF S.H.I.E.L.D. (1968-1971)

☐ 1, Jun 68	0.12	9.60	28.80	48.00
☐ 2, Jul 68	0.12	7.20	21.60	36.00
☐ 3, Aug 68	0.12	4.80	14.40	24.00
☐ 4	0.12	4.80	14.40	24.00
☐ 5	0.12	4.80	14.40	24.00
☐ 6	0.12	1.60	4.80	8.00
☐ 7	0.12	1.60	4.80	8.00
☐ 8	0.12	0.80	2.40	4.00
☐ 9	0.12	0.80	2.40	4.00
☐ 10	0.12	0.80	2.40	4.00
☐ 11	0.12	0.80	2.40	4.00
☐ 12	0.12	0.80	2.40	4.00
☐ 13	0.12	0.80	2.40	4.00
☐ 14	0.15	0.80	2.40	4.00
☐ 15	0.15	0.80	2.40	4.00
☐ 16	0.25	0.80	2.40	4.00
☐ 17	0.25	0.80	2.40	4.00
☐ 18	0.25	0.80	2.40	4.00

NICK FURY, AGENT OF S.H.I.E.L.D. (1983)

☐ 1, Dec 83, reprints	2.00	0.40	1.20	2.00
☐ 2, Jan 84, reprints	2.00	0.40	1.20	2.00

NICK FURY, AGENT OF S.H.I.E.L.D. (1989-1993)

☐ 1, Sep 89	1.50	0.40	1.20	2.00
☐ 2, Oct 89	1.50	0.30	0.90	1.50
☐ 3, Nov 89	1.50	0.30	0.90	1.50
☐ 4, Nov 89	1.50	0.30	0.90	1.50
☐ 5, Dec 89	1.50	0.30	0.90	1.50
☐ 6, Dec 89	1.50	0.30	0.90	1.50
☐ 7, Jan 90	1.50	0.30	0.90	1.50
☐ 8, Feb 90	1.50	0.30	0.90	1.50
☐ 9, Mar 90	1.50	0.30	0.90	1.50
☐ 10, Apr 90	1.50	0.30	0.90	1.50
☐ 11, May 90	1.50	0.30	0.90	1.50
☐ 12, Jun 90	1.50	0.30	0.90	1.50
☐ 13, Jul 90	1.50	0.30	0.90	1.50
☐ 14, Aug 90	1.50	0.30	0.90	1.50
☐ 15, Sep 90	1.50	0.30	0.90	1.50
☐ 16, Oct 90	1.50	0.30	0.90	1.50
☐ 17, Nov 90	1.50	0.30	0.90	1.50
☐ 18, Dec 90	1.50	0.30	0.90	1.50
☐ 19, Jan 91	1.50	0.30	0.90	1.50
☐ 20, Feb 91	1.50	0.30	0.90	1.50
☐ 21, Mar 91	1.50	0.30	0.90	1.50
☐ 22, Apr 91	1.50	0.30	0.90	1.50
☐ 23, May 91	1.50	0.30	0.90	1.50
☐ 24, Jun 91	1.50	0.30	0.90	1.50
☐ 25, Jul 91	1.50	0.30	0.90	1.50
☐ 26, Aug 91	1.50	0.30	0.90	1.50
☐ 27, Sep 91	1.50	0.30	0.90	1.50
☐ 28, Oct 91	1.50	0.30	0.90	1.50
☐ 29, Nov 91	1.50	0.30	0.90	1.50
☐ 30, Dec 91	1.50	0.30	0.90	1.50
☐ 31	1.50	0.30	0.90	1.50
☐ 32	1.75	0.35	1.05	1.75
☐ 33	1.75	0.35	1.05	1.75
☐ 34	1.75	0.35	1.05	1.75
☐ 35	1.75	0.35	1.05	1.75
☐ 36	1.75	0.35	1.05	1.75
☐ 37	1.75	0.35	1.05	1.75
☐ 38	1.75	0.35	1.05	1.75
☐ 39	1.75	0.35	1.05	1.75
☐ 40	1.75	0.35	1.05	1.75
☐ 41	1.75	0.35	1.05	1.75
☐ 42	1.75	0.35	1.05	1.75
☐ 43	1.75	0.35	1.05	1.75
☐ 44	1.75	0.35	1.05	1.75
☐ 45	1.75	0.35	1.05	1.75
☐ 46	1.75	0.35	1.05	1.75
☐ 47	1.75	0.35	1.05	1.73

NICK HAZARD
HARRIER

☐ 1		0.39	1.17	1.95

NICK RYAN, THE SKULL
ANTARCTIC

☐ 1, Dec 94, b&w	2.75	0.55	1.65	2.75
☐ 2, Jan 95, b&w	2.75	0.55	1.65	2.75
☐ 3, Feb 95, b&w	2.75	0.55	1.65	2.75

NIGHT BRIGADE
WONDER COMIX

☐ 1, b&w		0.39	1.17	1.95

NIGHT FORCE
DC

☐ 1, Aug 82, GC, I:Night Force	0.25	0.75	1.25	
☐ 2, Sep 82, GC	0.20	0.60	1.00	
☐ 3, Oct 82, GC	0.20	0.60	1.00	
☐ 4, Nov 82, GC	0.20	0.60	1.00	
☐ 5, Dec 82, GC	0.20	0.60	1.00	
☐ 6, Jan 83, GC	0.20	0.60	1.00	
☐ 7, Feb 83, GC	0.20	0.60	1.00	
☐ 8, Mar 83, GC	0.20	0.60	1.00	
☐ 9, Apr 83, GC	0.20	0.60	1.00	
☐ 10, May 83, GC	0.20	0.60	1.00	
☐ 11, Jun 83, GC	0.20	0.60	1.00	
☐ 12, Jul 83, GC	0.20	0.60	1.00	
☐ 13, Aug 83, GC	0.60	0.20	0.60	1.00
☐ 14, Sep 83, GC	0.60	0.20	0.60	1.00

NIGHT GLIDER
TOPPS

☐ 1, Apr 93, JK, trading card	2.95	0.59	1.77	2.95

	ORIG.	GOOD	FINE	N-MINT

NIGHT LIFE
STRAWBERRY JAM
	ORIG.	GOOD	FINE	N-MINT
1		0.30	0.90	1.50
2		0.30	0.90	1.50
3		0.30	0.90	1.50
4		0.30	0.90	1.50
5		0.30	0.90	1.50
6		0.30	0.90	1.50
7		0.30	0.90	1.50

NIGHT MAN
MALIBU/ULTRAVERSE
	ORIG.	GOOD	FINE	N-MINT
0, 95, Infinity; alternate cover	0.50	1.50	2.50	
1, Rune, BWS	2.50	0.50	1.50	2.50
2	1.95	0.39	1.17	1.95
3, Dec 93, Break-Thru	1.95	0.39	1.17	1.95
4, Jan 94, O:Firearm	1.95	0.39	1.17	1.95
5, Feb 94	1.95	0.39	1.17	1.95
6, Mar 94	1.95	0.39	1.17	1.95
7, Apr 94	1.95	0.39	1.17	1.95
8, May 94	1.95	0.39	1.17	1.95
9, Jun 94	1.95	0.39	1.17	1.95
10, Jul 94	1.95	0.39	1.17	1.95
11, Aug 94	1.95	0.39	1.17	1.95
12, Sep 94	1.95	0.39	1.17	1.95
13, no indicia	1.95	0.39	1.17	1.95

NIGHT MAN, THE (Vol. 2) (mini-series)
	ORIG.	GOOD	FINE	N-MINT
0, Sep 95, Infinity; "Black September"	1.50	0.30	0.90	1.50
0, Sep 95, Infinity; "Black September";alternate cover	1.50	0.30	0.90	1.50
1, Oct 95	1.50	0.30	0.90	1.50
2, Nov 95, flipbook with "The Phoenix Resurrection" Pt. 2	1.50	0.30	0.90	1.50
3, Dec 95, V:Lord Pumpkin	1.50	0.30	0.90	1.50
4, Dec 95, V:Mangle and Lord Pumpkin;final issue	1.50	0.30	0.90	1.50

NIGHT MAN, THE/GAMBIT (mini-series)
	ORIG.	GOOD	FINE	N-MINT
1, Mar 96	1.95	0.39	1.17	1.95

NIGHT MASTERS
CUSTOM PIC
	ORIG.	GOOD	FINE	N-MINT
1		0.60	1.80	3.00
2		0.30	0.90	1.50
3		0.30	0.90	1.50
4		0.30	0.90	1.50

NIGHT MUSIC
ECLIPSE
	ORIG.	GOOD	FINE	N-MINT
1, Dec 84, CR	1.75	0.40	1.20	2.00
2, Feb 85, CR	1.75	0.35	1.05	1.75
3, Mar 85, CR	1.75	0.35	1.05	1.75
4, Dec 85, Pelleas & Mellisande Part 1;CR	2.00	0.40	1.20	2.00
5, Dec 85, Pelleas & Mellisande Part 2;CR	2.00	0.40	1.20	2.00
6, Salome;CR	1.75	0.35	1.05	1.75
7, CR				
8, 89, Arianne and Bluebeard	3.95	0.79	2.37	3.95
9, 90, The Magic Flute;CR	4.95	0.99	2.97	4.95
10, 90, The Magic Flute;CR	4.95	0.99	2.97	4.95
11, 90, The Magic Flute;CR	4.95	0.99	2.97	4.95

NIGHT NURSE
MARVEL
	ORIG.	GOOD	FINE	N-MINT
1	0.20	0.30	0.90	1.50
2	0.20	0.30	0.90	1.50
3	0.20	0.30	0.90	1.50
4	0.20	0.30	0.90	1.50

NIGHT OF THE LIVING DEAD
FANTACO
	ORIG.	GOOD	FINE	N-MINT
0, 94, b&w	1.95	0.39	1.17	1.95
1, 91, b&w	4.95	0.99	2.97	4.95
2, 91, b&w	4.95	0.99	2.97	4.95
3, b&w	5.95	1.19	3.57	5.95
4, b&w		1.19	3.57	5.95

NIGHT OF THE LIVING DEAD: AFTERMATH
	ORIG.	GOOD	FINE	N-MINT
0		0.39	1.17	1.95

NIGHT OF THE LIVING DEAD: LONDON
	ORIG.	GOOD	FINE	N-MINT
1	5.95	1.19	3.57	5.95
2	5.95	1.19	3.57	5.95

NIGHT OF THE LIVING DEAD: PRELUDE
	ORIG.	GOOD	FINE	N-MINT
1, 91, b&w	1.50	0.30	0.90	1.50

NIGHT STREETS
ARROW
	ORIG.	GOOD	FINE	N-MINT
1		0.30	0.90	1.50
2		0.30	0.90	1.50
3		0.30	0.90	1.50
4		0.30	0.90	1.50
5		0.30	0.90	1.50

NIGHT THRASHER
MARVEL
	ORIG.	GOOD	FINE	N-MINT
1, foil cover	2.95	0.59	1.77	2.95
2	1.75	0.35	1.05	1.75
3	1.75	0.35	1.05	1.75
4	1.75	0.35	1.05	1.75
5	1.75	0.35	1.05	1.75
6	1.75	0.35	1.05	1.75
7	1.75	0.35	1.05	1.75
8	1.75	0.35	1.05	1.75
9	1.75	0.35	1.05	1.75
10, May 94	1.95	0.39	1.17	1.95
11, Jun 94	1.95	0.39	1.17	1.95
12, Jul 94	1.95	0.39	1.17	1.95
13, Aug 94, Lost in the Shadows	1.95	0.39	1.17	1.95
14, Sep 94, Lost in the Shadows	1.95	0.39	1.17	1.95
15, Oct 94	1.95	0.39	1.17	1.95
16, Nov 94	1.95	0.39	1.17	1.95
17, Dec 94	1.95	0.39	1.17	1.95
18, Jan 95	1.95	0.39	1.17	1.95
19, Feb 95	1.95	0.39	1.17	1.95
20, Mar 95	1.95	0.39	1.17	1.95
21, Apr 95	1.95	0.39	1.17	1.95

NIGHT THRASHER: FOUR CONTROL
	ORIG.	GOOD	FINE	N-MINT
1	2.00	0.40	1.20	2.00
2	2.00	0.40	1.20	2.00
3	2.00	0.40	1.20	2.00
4	2.00	0.40	1.20	2.00

NIGHT VISION
ATOMEKA
	ORIG.	GOOD	FINE	N-MINT
0, nn, b&w	2.95	0.59	1.77	2.95
REBEL
	ORIG.	GOOD	FINE	N-MINT
1, b&w		0.70	2.10	3.50

NIGHT WALKER
FLEETWAY/QUALITY
	ORIG.	GOOD	FINE	N-MINT
1	2.95	0.59	1.77	2.95

NIGHT ZERO
	ORIG.	GOOD	FINE	N-MINT
1, b&w		0.39	1.17	1.95
2, b&w		0.39	1.17	1.95
3, b&w		0.39	1.17	1.95
4, b&w		0.39	1.17	1.95

NIGHT'S CHILDREN
FANTACO
	ORIG.	GOOD	FINE	N-MINT
1, b&w		0.70	2.10	3.50
2, b&w		0.70	2.10	3.50
3, b&w		0.70	2.10	3.50
4, b&w	3.50	0.70	2.10	3.50

	ORIG.	GOOD	FINE	N-MINT

NIGHT'S CHILDREN: DOUBLE INDEMNITY
	ORIG.	GOOD	FINE	N-MINT
❑ 0, b&w		1.59	4.77	7.95

NIGHT'S CHILDREN: EXOTIC FANTASIES
	ORIG.	GOOD	FINE	N-MINT
❑ 0, b&w	5.95	1.19	3.57	5.95

NIGHT'S CHILDREN: FOREPLAY
	ORIG.	GOOD	FINE	N-MINT
❑ 1, b&w		0.99	2.97	4.95

NIGHT'S CHILDREN: VAMPYR!
	ORIG.	GOOD	FINE	N-MINT
❑ 1, adult, b&w	3.50	0.70	2.10	3.50
❑ 2, adult, b&w	3.50	0.70	2.10	3.50
❑ 3, adult, b&w	3.50	0.70	2.10	3.50

NIGHTBIRD
HARRIER
	ORIG.	GOOD	FINE	N-MINT
❑ 1, b&w		0.39	1.17	1.95
❑ 2, b&w		0.39	1.17	1.95

NIGHTCAT
MARVEL
	ORIG.	GOOD	FINE	N-MINT
❑ 1, Apr 91, O:Nightcat	3.95	0.79	2.37	3.95

NIGHTCRAWLER
	ORIG.	GOOD	FINE	N-MINT
❑ 1, Nov 85, DC	0.75	1.00	3.00	5.00
❑ 2, Dec 85	0.75	0.70	2.10	3.50
❑ 3, Jan 86	0.75	0.70	2.10	3.50
❑ 4, Feb 86	0.75	0.70	2.10	3.50

NIGHTLINGER
GAUNTLET
	ORIG.	GOOD	FINE	N-MINT
❑ 1, b&w	2.95	0.59	1.77	2.95
❑ 2, b&w	2.95	0.59	1.77	2.95

NIGHTMARE
MARVEL
	ORIG.	GOOD	FINE	N-MINT
❑ 1, Dec 94	1.95	0.39	1.17	1.95
❑ 2, Jan 95	1.95	0.39	1.17	1.95
❑ 3, Feb 95	1.95	0.39	1.17	1.95
❑ 4, Mar 95	1.95	0.39	1.17	1.95

NIGHTMARE ON ELM STREET: THE BEGINNING
INNOVATION
	ORIG.	GOOD	FINE	N-MINT
❑ 1		0.50	1.50	2.50
❑ 2		0.50	1.50	2.50

NIGHTMARES
ECLIPSE
	ORIG.	GOOD	FINE	N-MINT
❑ 1, PG		0.35	1.05	1.75
❑ 2, PG		0.35	1.05	1.75

NIGHTMARES ON ELM STREET
INNOVATION
	ORIG.	GOOD	FINE	N-MINT
❑ 1, Sep 91	2.50	0.50	1.50	2.50
❑ 2		0.50	1.50	2.50
❑ 3		0.50	1.50	2.50
❑ 4		0.50	1.50	2.50
❑ 5		0.50	1.50	2.50
❑ 6		0.50	1.50	2.50

NIGHTMARK
ALPHA PRODUCTIONS
	ORIG.	GOOD	FINE	N-MINT
❑ 1, b&w		0.45	1.35	2.25

NIGHTMARK MYSTERY SPECIAL
ALPHA
	ORIG.	GOOD	FINE	N-MINT
❑ 1, 94, b&w	2.50	0.50	1.50	2.50

NIGHTMARK: BLOOD & HONOR
	ORIG.	GOOD	FINE	N-MINT
❑ 1, Apr 94	2.50	0.50	1.50	2.50

NIGHTMASK
MARVEL
	ORIG.	GOOD	FINE	N-MINT
❑ 1, Nov 86	0.75	0.20	0.60	1.00
❑ 2, Dec 86	0.75	0.20	0.60	1.00
❑ 3, Jan 87	0.75	0.20	0.60	1.00
❑ 4, Feb 87	0.75	0.20	0.60	1.00
❑ 5, Mar 87	0.75	0.20	0.60	1.00
❑ 6, Apr 87	0.75	0.20	0.60	1.00
❑ 7, May 87	0.75	0.20	0.60	1.00
❑ 8, Jun 87	0.75	0.20	0.60	1.00
❑ 9, Jul 87	0.75	0.20	0.60	1.00
❑ 10, Aug 87	0.75	0.20	0.60	1.00
❑ 11, Sep 87	0.75	0.20	0.60	1.00
❑ 12, Oct 87	0.75	0.20	0.60	1.00

NIGHTSTALKERS
	ORIG.	GOOD	FINE	N-MINT
❑ 1, poster	2.75	0.55	1.65	2.75
❑ 2	1.75	0.35	1.05	1.75
❑ 3	1.75	0.35	1.05	1.75
❑ 4	1.75	0.35	1.05	1.75
❑ 5	1.75	0.35	1.05	1.75
❑ 6	1.75	0.35	1.05	1.75
❑ 7	1.75	0.35	1.05	1.75
❑ 8	1.75	0.35	1.05	1.75
❑ 9	1.75	0.35	1.05	1.75
❑ 10	1.75	0.35	1.05	1.75
❑ 11	1.75	0.35	1.05	1.75
❑ 12	1.75	0.35	1.05	1.75
❑ 13	1.75	0.35	1.05	1.75
❑ 14	1.75	0.60	1.80	3.00
❑ 15	1.75	0.35	1.05	1.75
❑ 16	1.75	0.35	1.05	1.75
❑ 17	1.75	0.35	1.05	1.75
❑ 18	1.75	0.35	1.05	1.75

NIGHTVEIL
AC
	ORIG.	GOOD	FINE	N-MINT
❑ 1, Feb 84, color		0.35	1.05	1.75
❑ 2, 85		0.35	1.05	1.75
❑ 3, 85		0.35	1.05	1.75
❑ 4, 85		0.35	1.05	1.75
❑ 5, 86		0.35	1.05	1.75
❑ 6, 86		0.35	1.05	1.75
❑ 7, Mar 87		0.35	1.05	1.75

NIGHTVEIL SPECIAL
	ORIG.	GOOD	FINE	N-MINT
❑ 1, Aug 88		0.39	1.17	1.95

NIGHTVEIL'S CAULDRON OF HORROR
	ORIG.	GOOD	FINE	N-MINT
❑ 1, 89, b&w, reprints		0.50	1.50	2.50
❑ 2, 90		0.59	1.77	2.95
❑ 3, Sep 91		0.59	1.77	2.95

NIGHTVISION
REBEL
	ORIG.	GOOD	FINE	N-MINT
❑ 1, b&w		0.60	1.80	3.00
❑ 2	2.25	0.45	1.35	2.25

NIGHTWATCH
MARVEL
	ORIG.	GOOD	FINE	N-MINT
❑ 1, Apr 94, foil cover	2.95	0.59	1.77	2.95
❑ 1, Apr 94	1.50	0.30	0.90	1.50
❑ 2, May 94	1.50	0.30	0.90	1.50
❑ 3, Jun 94	1.50	0.30	0.90	1.50
❑ 4, Jul 94	1.50	0.30	0.90	1.50
❑ 5, Aug 94	1.50	0.30	0.90	1.50
❑ 6, Sep 94	1.50	0.30	0.90	1.50
❑ 7, Oct 94	1.50	0.30	0.90	1.50
❑ 8, Nov 94	1.50	0.30	0.90	1.50
❑ 9, Dec 94	1.50	0.30	0.90	1.50
❑ 10, Jan 95	1.50	0.30	0.90	1.50
❑ 11, Feb 95	1.50	0.30	0.90	1.50
❑ 12, Mar 95, final issue	1.50	0.30	0.90	1.50

NIGHTWING (mini-series)
DC
	ORIG.	GOOD	FINE	N-MINT
❑ 1, Sep 95	2.25	0.80	2.40	4.00
❑ 2, Oct 95	2.25	0.60	1.80	3.00
❑ 3, Nov 95	2.25	0.45	1.35	2.25
❑ 4, Dec 95	2.25	0.45	1.35	2.25

NIGHTWING: ALFRED'S RETURN
	ORIG.	GOOD	FINE	N-MINT
❑ 1, Jul 95, DG;one-shot	3.50	1.00	3.00	5.00

NIGHTWOLF
ENTROPY
	ORIG.	GOOD	FINE	N-MINT
❑ 1		0.30	0.90	1.50
❑ 2		0.30	0.90	1.50

	ORIG.	GOOD	FINE	N-MINT

NINA'S ALL-TIME GREATEST COLLECTOR'S ITEM CLASSICS
DARK HORSE

	ORIG.	GOOD	FINE	N-MINT
❏ 1, b&w		0.45	1.35	2.25

NINA'S NEW & IMPROVED ALL-TIME GREATEST COLLECTOR'S ITEM CLASSIC COMICS

❏ 1, Feb 94, b&w	2.50	0.50	1.50	2.50

NINE LIVES OF FELIX THE CAT
HARVEY

❏ 1		0.25	0.75	1.25
❏ 2		0.25	0.75	1.25
❏ 3		0.25	0.75	1.25
❏ 4		0.25	0.75	1.25
❏ 5		0.25	0.75	1.25

NINETY-NINE GIRLS
EROS COMIX

❏ 1, adult, b&w		0.45	1.35	2.25

NINJA
ETERNITY

❏ 1		0.36	1.08	1.80
❏ 2		0.36	1.08	1.80
❏ 3		0.36	1.08	1.80
❏ 4		0.36	1.08	1.80
❏ 5		0.39	1.17	1.95
❏ 6		0.39	1.17	1.95
❏ 7		0.39	1.17	1.95
❏ 8		0.39	1.17	1.95
❏ 9		0.39	1.17	1.95
❏ 10		0.39	1.17	1.95
❏ 11		0.39	1.17	1.95
❏ 12		0.39	1.17	1.95
❏ 13		0.39	1.17	1.95

NINJA ELITE
ADVENTURE

❏ 1		0.30	0.90	1.50
❏ 2		0.30	0.90	1.50
❏ 3		0.30	0.90	1.50
❏ 4		0.30	0.90	1.50
❏ 5		0.30	0.90	1.50

NINJA FUNNIES
ETERNITY

❏ 1		0.28	0.84	1.40
❏ 2		0.39	1.17	1.95
❏ 3		0.39	1.17	1.95
❏ 4		0.39	1.17	1.95
❏ 5		0.39	1.17	1.95

NINJA HIGH SCHOOL
ANTARCTIC

	ORIG.	GOOD	FINE	N-MINT
❏ 0, Jan 94, b&w;foil cover edition (500 made)				
	2.75	0.55	1.65	2.75
❏ 0, Jan 94, b&w	2.75	0.55	1.65	2.75
❏ 1		1.60	4.80	8.00
❏ 2		1.00	3.00	5.00
❏ 3		1.00	3.00	5.00
❏ 4, (moves to Eternity)		1.00	3.00	5.00
❏ 40, Jun 94, b&w ;(was Eternity title)				
	2.75	0.55	1.65	2.75
❏ 40, Jun 94, b&w;gold foil logo edition (500 made)				
	2.75	0.55	1.65	2.75
❏ 41, Jul 94, b&w	2.75	0.55	1.65	2.75
❏ 42, Sep 94, b&w	2.75	0.55	1.65	2.75
❏ 43, Nov 94, b&w	2.75	0.55	1.65	2.75
❏ 44, Jan 95, b&w	2.75	0.55	1.65	2.75
❏ 45, Mar 95, b&w	2.75	0.55	1.65	2.75
❏ 46, May 95, b&w	2.75	0.55	1.65	2.75
❏ 47, Jul 95, b&w	2.75	0.55	1.65	2.75
❏ 48, Sep 95, b&w	2.75	0.55	1.65	2.75

NINJA HIGH SCHOOL (was Antarctic title)
ETERNITY

❏ 5, b&w		0.80	2.40	4.00

	ORIG.	GOOD	FINE	N-MINT
❏ 6, 1st printing		0.80	2.40	4.00
❏ 6, 2nd printing		0.39	1.17	1.95
❏ 7		0.60	1.80	3.00
❏ 8		0.60	1.80	3.00
❏ 9		0.60	1.80	3.00
❏ 10		0.60	1.80	3.00
❏ 11		0.50	1.50	2.50
❏ 12		0.50	1.50	2.50
❏ 13		0.50	1.50	2.50
❏ 14		0.50	1.50	2.50
❏ 15		0.50	1.50	2.50
❏ 16, b&w		0.39	1.17	1.95
❏ 17, b&w		0.39	1.17	1.95
❏ 18, b&w		0.39	1.17	1.95
❏ 19, b&w		0.39	1.17	1.95
❏ 20, b&w		0.39	1.17	1.95
❏ 21, b&w		0.39	1.17	1.95
❏ 22, b&w		0.39	1.17	1.95
❏ 23		0.45	1.35	2.25
❏ 24		0.45	1.35	2.25
❏ 25		0.45	1.35	2.25
❏ 26		0.45	1.35	2.25
❏ 27		0.45	1.35	2.25
❏ 28		0.45	1.35	2.25
❏ 29		0.45	1.35	2.25
❏ 30		0.45	1.35	2.25
❏ 31		0.45	1.35	2.25
❏ 32, b&w	2.50	0.50	1.50	2.50
❏ 33, May 92, b&w	2.50	0.50	1.50	2.50
❏ 34, b&w	2.50	0.50	1.50	2.50
❏ 35, b&w	2.50	0.50	1.50	2.50
❏ 36, b&w	2.50	0.50	1.50	2.50
❏ 37, b&w	2.50	0.50	1.50	2.50
❏ 38, b&w	2.50	0.50	1.50	2.50
❏ 39, b&w; (returns to Antarctic)				
	2.50	0.50	1.50	2.50

NINJA HIGH SCHOOL FEATURING SPEED RACER
ETERNITY/NOW

❏ 1, 93	2.95	0.59	1.77	2.95
❏ 2, Dec 93	2.95	0.59	1.77	2.95

NINJA HIGH SCHOOL IN 3-D
ANTARCTIC

❏ 1, Jul 92	3.50	0.70	2.10	3.50

NINJA HIGH SCHOOL IN COLOR
ETERNITY

❏ 1, color	1.95	0.39	1.17	1.95
❏ 2, color	1.95	0.39	1.17	1.95
❏ 3, color	1.95	0.39	1.17	1.95
❏ 4, color	1.95	0.39	1.17	1.95
❏ 5, color	1.95	0.39	1.17	1.95
❏ 6, color	1.95	0.39	1.17	1.95
❏ 7, color	1.95	0.39	1.17	1.95
❏ 8, color	1.95	0.39	1.17	1.95
❏ 9, color	1.95	0.39	1.17	1.95
❏ 10, color	1.95	0.39	1.17	1.95
❏ 11, color	1.95	0.39	1.17	1.95
❏ 12, color	1.95	0.39	1.17	1.95
❏ 13, color	1.95	0.39	1.17	1.95

NINJA HIGH SCHOOL PERFECT MEMORY
ANTARCTIC

❏ 1, background		1.00	3.00	5.00
❏ 2, Nov 93	4.95	0.99	2.97	4.95
❏ 2, Nov 93, platinum				

NINJA HIGH SCHOOL SWIMSUIT SPECIAL

❏ 1, Dec 92, 1992 Annual; two different covers				
	2.95	0.59	1.77	2.95
❏ 2, Dec 93, 1993 Annual	2.95	0.59	1.77	2.95
❏ 3, Dec 94, 1994 Annual	2.95	0.59	1.77	2.95

	ORIG.	GOOD	FINE	N-MINT

NINJA HIGH SCHOOL TALKS ABOUT COMIC BOOK PRINTING
☐ 0, color, giveaway ....

NINJA HIGH SCHOOL TALKS ABOUT SEXUALLY TRANSMITTED DISEASES
☐ 1, color, giveaway 0.20 0.60 1.00

NINJA HIGH SCHOOL YEARBOOK
☐ 1, b&w, 1989 .... 1.20 3.60 6.00
☐ 2, b&w, 1990 .... 1.00 3.00 5.00
☐ 3, b&w, 1991 .... 0.80 2.40 4.00
☐ 4, 8 pages color, 1992 ... 3.95 0.80 2.40 4.00
☐ 5, Oct 93, b&w, 1993..... 3.95 0.80 2.40 4.00
☐ 6, Oct 94, b&w, 1994..... 3.95 0.79 2.37 3.95
☐ 7, Oct 95, b&w, 1995; cover says "Oct. 1994"; indicia says "Oct. 1995" 3.95 0.79 2.37 3.95

NINJA HIGH SCHOOL: THE SPECIAL EDITION
ETERNITY
☐ 1, b&w 0.45 1.35 2.25
☐ 2, b&w 0.45 1.35 2.25
☐ 3, b&w 0.45 1.35 2.25
☐ 4 .... 0.45 1.35 2.25

NINJA SPECIAL
☐ 1, b&w 0.45 1.35 2.25

NINJA-BOTS SUPER SPECIAL
PIED PIPER
☐ 1 .... 0.39 1.17 1.95

NINJAK
ACCLAIM/VALIANT
☐ 16, Jun 95...................... 2.50 0.50 1.50 2.50
☐ 17, Jul 95....................... 2.50 0.50 1.50 2.50
☐ 18, Jul 95....................... 2.50 0.50 1.50 2.50
☐ 19, Aug 95 .... 2.50 0.50 1.50 2.50
☐ 20, Aug 95 .... 2.50 0.50 1.50 2.50
☐ 21, Sep 95 .... 2.50 0.50 1.50 2.50
☐ 22, Sep 95 .... 2.50 0.50 1.50 2.50
☐ 23, Oct 95 .... 2.50 0.50 1.50 2.50
☐ 24, Oct 95 .... 2.50 0.50 1.50 2.50
☐ 25, Nov 95 .... 2.50 0.50 1.50 2.50
☐ 26, Nov 95 .... 2.50 0.50 1.50 2.50

VALIANT
☐ 0, Jun 95........................ 2.50 0.50 1.50 2.50
☐ 0, Jun 95, really #00; cover forms diptych image with #0................................ 2.50 0.50 1.50 2.50
☐ 1, chromium cover......... 3.50 0.80 2.40 4.00
☐ 1, gold........................... 3.50 2.00 6.00 10.00
☐ 2, Mar 94 .... 2.25 0.60 1.80 3.00
☐ 3, Apr 94, JQ.................. 2.25 0.45 1.35 2.25
☐ 4, May 94, trading card .. 2.25 0.45 1.35 2.25
☐ 5, Jun 94, A:X-O Manowar 2.25 0.45 1.35 2.25
☐ 6, Aug 94, A:X-O Manowar 2.25 0.45 1.35 2.25
☐ 7, Sep 94........................ 2.25 0.45 1.35 2.25
☐ 8, Oct 94, Chaos Effect.. 2.25 0.45 1.35 2.25
☐ 9, Nov 94 .... 2.25 0.45 1.35 2.25
☐ 10, Dec 94...................... 2.25 0.45 1.35 2.25
☐ 11, Jan 95....................... 2.25 0.45 1.35 2.25
☐ 12, Feb 95, card 2.25 0.45 1.35 2.25
☐ 13, Mar 95, card 2.25 0.45 1.35 2.25
☐ 14, Apr 95 .... 2.50 0.50 1.50 2.50
☐ 15, May 95, Valiant becomes Acclaim imprint 2.50 0.50 1.50 2.50

NINJAK YEARBOOK
☐ 1, 94, 1994; cardstock cover 3.95 0.79 2.37 3.95

NINJU TSU
SOLSON
☐ 1, b&w 0.40 1.20 2.00

NINTENDO COMICS SYSTEM
VALIANT
☐ 1, anthology.................... 0.99 2.97 4.95
☐ 2, anthology.................... 0.99 2.97 4.95

NINTENDO COMICS SYSTEM (comic book)
☐ 1, Game Boy 0.30 0.90 1.50
☐ 2, Game Boy 0.30 0.90 1.50
☐ 3, Game Boy 0.30 0.90 1.50
☐ 4, Game Boy 0.30 0.90 1.50
☐ 5, Game Boy 0.30 0.90 1.50
☐ 6, Game Boy 0.30 0.90 1.50
☐ 7, Zelda.......................... 0.30 0.90 1.50
☐ 8, Super Mario Bros. 0.30 0.90 1.50
☐ 9, Super Mario Bros. 0.30 0.90 1.50

NIRA X: CYBERANGEL
EXPRESS/ENTITY
☐ 1, Dec 94, cardstock cover 2.95 1.20 3.60 6.00
☐ 2, Feb 95........................ 2.50 0.80 2.40 4.00
☐ 3, Apr 95......................... 2.50 0.50 1.50 2.50
☐ 4, Jun 95......................... 2.50 0.50 1.50 2.50

NIRA X: CYBERANGEL - CYNDER: ENDANGERED SPECIES
☐ 1, 96 .... 2.95 0.59 1.77 2.95
☐ 1, 96, commemorative edition;cardstock cover; limited to 1500 copies............. 12.95 2.59 7.77 12.95

NIRA X: CYBERANGEL ASHCAN EDITION
☐ 1, Sum 94, b&w, no cover price 0.80 2.40 4.00

NIRA X: HEATWAVE SERIES 2
☐ 1, Jul 96, enhanced wraparound cover 3.75 0.75 2.25 3.75
☐ 2, Aug 95........................ 2.50 0.50 1.50 2.50
☐ 3, Sep 95 .... 2.50 0.50 1.50 2.50

NO BUSINESS LIKE SHOW BUSINESS
3-D ZONE
☐ 1, b&w (not 3-D) 0.50 1.50 2.50

NO ESCAPE
MARVEL
☐ 1, Jun 94, movie............. 1.50 0.30 0.90 1.50
☐ 2, Jul 94, movie............. 1.50 0.30 0.90 1.50
☐ 3, Aug 94, movie 1.50 0.30 0.90 1.50

NO GUTS OR GLORY
FANTACO
☐ 1, 91, KEastman b&w 2.95 0.59 1.77 2.95

NOCTURNAL EMISSIONS
VORTEX
☐ 1, b&w, adult 0.50 1.50 2.50

NOCTURNE
AIRCEL
☐ 1, b&w............................. 0.50 1.50 2.50
☐ 2, b&w............................. 0.50 1.50 2.50
☐ 3, b&w............................. 0.50 1.50 2.50

NOCTURNE (mini-series)
MARVEL
☐ 1, Jun 95 .... 1.50 0.30 0.90 1.50
☐ 2, Jul 95, indicia says "Sep 95" 1.50 0.30 0.90 1.50
☐ 3, Aug 95........................ 1.50 0.30 0.90 1.50
☐ 4, Sep 95........................ 1.50 0.30 0.90 1.50

NOG THE PROTECTOR OF THE PYRAMIDES
ONLI STUDIOS
☐ 0, 94, nn 2.00 0.40 1.20 2.00

NOID IN 3-D, THE
BLACKTHORNE
☐ 1 .... 0.50 1.50 2.50
☐ 2 .... 0.50 1.50 2.50

	ORIG.	GOOD	FINE	N-MINT

NOIR
ALPHA
	ORIG.	GOOD	FINE	N-MINT
❑ 1, Win 94, text & comics	3.95	0.79	2.37	3.95

NOIR (VOL. 2)
CREATIVE FORCE
| ❑ 1, Apr 95 | 4.95 | 0.99 | 2.97 | 4.95 |

NOLAN RYAN
CELEBRITY
| ❑ 1 | | 0.59 | 1.77 | 2.95 |

NOLAN RYAN'S 7 NO-HITTERS
REVOLUTIONARY
| ❑ 1, Aug 93, b&w | 2.95 | 0.59 | 1.77 | 2.95 |

NOMAD (1992-)
MARVEL
❑ 1, gatefold cover	2.00	0.50	1.50	2.50
❑ 2	1.75	0.40	1.20	2.00
❑ 3	1.75	0.35	1.05	1.75
❑ 4	1.75	0.35	1.05	1.75
❑ 5	1.75	0.35	1.05	1.75
❑ 6	1.75	0.35	1.05	1.75
❑ 7, Infinity War	1.75	0.35	1.05	1.75
❑ 8	1.75	0.35	1.05	1.75
❑ 9	1.75	0.35	1.05	1.75
❑ 10	1.75	0.35	1.05	1.75
❑ 11	1.75	0.35	1.05	1.75
❑ 12	1.75	0.35	1.05	1.75
❑ 13	1.75	0.35	1.05	1.75
❑ 14	1.75	0.35	1.05	1.75
❑ 15	1.75	0.35	1.05	1.75
❑ 16	1.75	0.35	1.05	1.75
❑ 17	1.75	0.35	1.05	1.75
❑ 18	1.75	0.35	1.05	1.75
❑ 19	1.75	0.35	1.05	1.75
❑ 20	1.75	0.35	1.05	1.75
❑ 21	1.75	0.35	1.05	1.75
❑ 22	1.75	0.35	1.05	1.75
❑ 23	1.75	0.35	1.05	1.75
❑ 24	1.75	0.35	1.05	1.75
❑ 25, May 94	1.75	0.35	1.05	1.75

NOMAD (mini-series)
❑ 1, Nov 90	1.50	0.80	2.40	4.00
❑ 2, Dec 90	1.50	0.60	1.80	3.00
❑ 3, Mar 91	1.50	0.40	1.20	2.00
❑ 4, Feb 91	1.50	0.40	1.20	2.00

NOMAN
TOWER
| ❑ 1, Nov 66, WW | 0.25 | 10.00 | 30.00 | 50.00 |
| ❑ 2, Mar 67, WW | 0.25 | 6.40 | 19.20 | 32.00 |

NORB
MU PRESS
| ❑ 0, Jan 92 | 8.95 | 1.79 | 5.37 | 8.95 |

NORMALMAN
AARDVARK-VANAHEIM
❑ 1, Jan 84, JV		0.50	1.50	2.50
❑ 2, Apr 84, JV		0.40	1.20	2.00
❑ 3, Jun 84, JV		0.40	1.20	2.00
❑ 4, Aug 84, JV		0.40	1.20	2.00
❑ 5, Oct 84, JV		0.40	1.20	2.00
❑ 6, Dec 84, JV		0.40	1.20	2.00
❑ 7, Feb 85, JV		0.40	1.20	2.00
❑ 8, Apr 85, JV	2.00	0.40	1.20	2.00
❑ 9, Jun 85, JV;(moves to Renegade Press)				
	2.00	0.40	1.20	2.00

NORMALMAN (former Aardvark-Vanaheim title)
RENEGADE
❑ 10, Aug 85, JV;color	2.00	0.40	1.20	2.00
❑ 11, Oct 85, JV;color	2.00	0.40	1.20	2.00
❑ 12, Dec 85, JV;color	2.00	0.40	1.20	2.00

NORMALMAN 3-D
| ❑ 1, Feb 86, JV | 2.25 | 0.45 | 1.35 | 2.25 |

NORMALMAN-MEGATON MAN SPECIAL
IMAGE
| ❑ 1, Aug 94, A:Flaming Carrot, Mr. Spook | | | | |
| | 2.50 | 0.50 | 1.50 | 2.50 |

NORTHERN'S HEMISPHERE
NORTHERN'S HEMISPHERE
❑ 5, 93, b&w	2.49	0.50	1.49	2.49
❑ 6, 94, b&w	2.49	0.50	1.49	2.49
❑ 7, 94, b&w	2.49	0.50	1.49	2.49

NORTHERN'S HEMISPHERE UNDISGUISED
| ❑ 0, 95 | 2.50 | 0.50 | 1.50 | 2.50 |

NORTHGUARD: THE MANDES CONCLUSION
CALIBER
❑ 1, Sep 89, b&w	2.50	0.50	1.50	2.50
❑ 2, Oct 89, b&w	2.50	0.50	1.50	2.50
❑ 3, Nov 89, b&w	2.50	0.50	1.50	2.50

NORTHSTAR (mini-series)
MARVEL
❑ 1, Apr 94	1.75	0.35	1.05	1.75
❑ 2, May 94	1.75	0.35	1.05	1.75
❑ 3, Jun 94	1.75	0.35	1.05	1.75
❑ 4, Jul 94	1.75	0.35	1.05	1.75

NORTHWEST CARTOON COOKERY
STARHEAD
| ❑ 0, 95, b&w;recipes from Pacific Northwest cartoonists | | | | |
| | 2.75 | 0.55 | 1.65 | 2.75 |

NOSFERATU
DARK HORSE
| ❑ 1, Druillet, b&w | | 0.79 | 2.37 | 3.95 |
TOME PRESS
| ❑ 1, b&w | | 0.59 | 1.77 | 2.95 |
| ❑ 2, Jul 91, b&w | 2.95 | 0.59 | 1.77 | 2.95 |

NOSFERATU: PLAGUE OF TERROR
MILLENNIUM
❑ 1, b&w, duotone		0.50	1.50	2.50
❑ 2, b&w, duotone		0.50	1.50	2.50
❑ 3, b&w, duotone		0.50	1.50	2.50
❑ 4, b&w, duotone		0.50	1.50	2.50

NOT BRAND ECHH
MARVEL
❑ 1	0.12	7.20	21.60	36.00
❑ 2	0.12	3.60	10.80	18.00
❑ 3	0.12	3.60	10.80	18.00
❑ 4	0.12	3.60	10.80	18.00
❑ 5	0.12	3.60	10.80	18.00
❑ 6	0.12	3.00	9.00	15.00
❑ 7	0.12	3.00	9.00	15.00
❑ 8	0.12	3.00	9.00	15.00
❑ 9	0.25	3.00	9.00	15.00
❑ 10	0.25	3.00	9.00	15.00
❑ 11	0.25	2.40	7.20	12.00
❑ 12	0.25	2.40	7.20	12.00
❑ 13	0.25	2.40	7.20	12.00

NOT QUITE DEAD
RIP OFF
❑ 1, Mar 93, Gilbert Shelton; b&w;first printing				
	2.95	0.59	1.77	2.95
❑ 1, Gilbert Shelton;b&w; second printing				
	2.95	0.59	1.77	2.95
❑ 2, 95, Gilbert Shelton;b&w				
	2.95	0.59	1.77	2.95

NOVA
MARVEL
❑ 1, Sep 76, O:Nova	0.30	2.40	7.20	12.00
❑ 2, Oct 76	0.30	1.60	4.80	8.00
❑ 3, Nov 76	0.30	1.20	3.60	6.00
❑ 4, Dec 76	0.30	1.20	3.60	6.00

	ORIG.	GOOD	FINE	N-MINT
❏ 5, Jan 77	0.30	1.20	3.60	6.00
❏ 6, Feb 77	0.30	1.00	3.00	5.00
❏ 7, Mar 77	0.30	1.00	3.00	5.00
❏ 8, Apr 77	0.30	1.00	3.00	5.00
❏ 9, May 77	0.30	1.00	3.00	5.00
❏ 10, Jun 77	0.30	1.00	3.00	5.00
❏ 11, Jul 77	0.30	0.80	2.40	4.00
❏ 12, Aug 77	0.30	0.80	2.40	4.00
❏ 13, Sep 77	0.30	0.80	2.40	4.00
❏ 14, Oct 77	0.30	0.80	2.40	4.00
❏ 15, Nov 77	0.35	0.80	2.40	4.00
❏ 16, Dec 77	0.35	0.80	2.40	4.00
❏ 17, Jan 78	0.35	0.80	2.40	4.00
❏ 18, Mar 78	0.35	0.80	2.40	4.00
❏ 19, May 78	0.35	0.80	2.40	4.00
❏ 20, Jul 78	0.35	0.80	2.40	4.00
❏ 21, Sep 78	0.35	0.80	2.40	4.00
❏ 22, Nov 78	0.35	0.80	2.40	4.00
❏ 23, Jan 79	0.35	0.80	2.40	4.00
❏ 24, Mar 79	0.35	0.80	2.40	4.00
❏ 25, May 79	0.40	0.80	2.40	4.00

NOVA (1993-)

	ORIG.	GOOD	FINE	N-MINT
❏ 1, foil cover	2.95	0.59	1.77	2.95
❏ 1	2.25	0.45	1.35	2.25
❏ 2	1.75	0.35	1.05	1.75
❏ 3	1.75	0.35	1.05	1.75
❏ 4	1.75	0.35	1.05	1.75
❏ 5, May 94	1.95	0.39	1.17	1.95
❏ 6, Jun 94	1.95	0.39	1.17	1.95
❏ 7, Jul 94	1.95	0.39	1.17	1.95
❏ 8, Aug 94	1.95	0.39	1.17	1.95
❏ 9, Sep 94	1.95	0.39	1.17	1.95
❏ 10, Oct 94	1.95	0.39	1.17	1.95
❏ 11, Nov 94	1.95	0.39	1.17	1.95
❏ 12, Dec 94	1.95	0.39	1.17	1.95
❏ 13, Jan 95	1.95	0.39	1.17	1.95
❏ 14, Feb 95	1.95	0.39	1.17	1.95
❏ 15, Mar 95	1.95	0.39	1.17	1.95
❏ 16, Apr 95	1.95	0.39	1.17	1.95
❏ 17, May 95	1.95	0.39	1.17	1.95
❏ 18, Jun 95	1.95	0.39	1.17	1.95

NOW COMICS PREVIEW
NOW

	ORIG.	GOOD	FINE	N-MINT
❏ 1, 1:Ralph Snart, Syphons, Valor Thunderstar, Vector	0.20	0.60	1.00	

NOW HEPESVILLE
CALIBER

	ORIG.	GOOD	FINE	N-MINT
❏ 1, 95, b&w;one-shot	3.50	0.70	2.10	3.50

NOW WHAT?!
NOW

	ORIG.	GOOD	FINE	N-MINT
❏ 1		0.10	0.30	0.50
❏ 2		0.10	0.30	0.50
❏ 3		0.10	0.30	0.50
❏ 4		0.10	0.30	0.50
❏ 5		0.10	0.30	0.50
❏ 6		0.10	0.30	0.50

	ORIG.	GOOD	FINE	N-MINT
❏ 7		0.10	0.30	0.50
❏ 8		0.10	0.30	0.50
❏ 9		0.10	0.30	0.50
❏ 10		0.10	0.30	0.50
❏ 11		0.10	0.30	0.50

NOW, ON A MORE SERIOUS NOTE...
DAWN

❏ 0, Sum 94, b&w;no cover price

NOWHERESVILLE
CALIBER

	ORIG.	GOOD	FINE	N-MINT
❏ 1, 95, b&w	3.50	0.70	2.10	3.50

Nth MAN
MARVEL

	ORIG.	GOOD	FINE	N-MINT
❏ 1, Aug 89	1.00	0.20	0.60	1.00
❏ 2, Sep 89	1.00	0.20	0.60	1.00
❏ 3, Oct 89	1.00	0.20	0.60	1.00
❏ 4, Nov 89	1.00	0.20	0.60	1.00
❏ 5, Nov 89	1.00	0.20	0.60	1.00
❏ 6, Dec 89	1.00	0.20	0.60	1.00
❏ 7, Dec 89	1.00	0.20	0.60	1.00
❏ 8, Jan 90	1.00	0.20	0.60	1.00
❏ 9, Feb 90	1.00	0.20	0.60	1.00
❏ 10, Mar 90	1.00	0.20	0.60	1.00
❏ 11, Apr 90	1.00	0.20	0.60	1.00
❏ 12, May 90	1.00	0.20	0.60	1.00
❏ 13, Jun 90	1.00	0.20	0.60	1.00
❏ 14, Jul 90	1.00	0.20	0.60	1.00
❏ 15, Aug 90	1.00	0.20	0.60	1.00
❏ 16, Sep 90	1.00	0.20	0.60	1.00

NUANCE
MAGNETIC INK

	ORIG.	GOOD	FINE	N-MINT
❏ 1, b&w		0.55	1.65	2.75
❏ 2, b&w		0.55	1.65	2.75
❏ 3, b&w		0.55	1.65	2.75

NULL PATROL
ESCAPE VELOCITY

	ORIG.	GOOD	FINE	N-MINT
❏ 1		0.30	0.90	1.50

NUMIDIAN FORCE
KAMITE

	ORIG.	GOOD	FINE	N-MINT
❏ 4	2.00	0.40	1.20	2.00

NURTURE THE DEVIL
FANTAGRAPHICS

	ORIG.	GOOD	FINE	N-MINT
❏ 2, Jul 94, b&w	2.50	0.50	1.50	2.50
❏ 3, Dec 94, b&w	2.50	0.50	1.50	2.50

NUT RUNNERS
RIP OFF

	ORIG.	GOOD	FINE	N-MINT
❏ 1, Sep 91, b&w	2.50	0.50	1.50	2.50
❏ 2, Jan 92, b&w	2.50	0.50	1.50	2.50

NYGHT SCHOOL
BRAINSTORM

	ORIG.	GOOD	FINE	N-MINT
❏ 2, adult, b&w	2.95	0.59	1.77	2.95

Nick Fury

Nick Fury's career has taken him from army sergeant to secret agent to the head of S.H.I.E.L.D. But who got him started on one of the longest careers in comics?

"The Name Is Bass — Sergeant Bass!" he boomed on the splash page of *Sgt. Fury and His Howling Commandos* #62 (Jan 69).

As his origin story opens in 1941, Nick Fury has enlisted because he was "outta work and starvin' to death," as he puts it. Otherwise, "I'd have never joined up in the first place! But I don't figure a couple a years with these Boy Scouts is gonna do me any harm!"

Needless to say, our boy Fury doesn't take to soldiering right off the bat, leading to a variety of slugfests which show how tough Fury really is. But Bass stays on Fury's back, because he knows Fury has The Right Stuff.

O

	ORIG.	GOOD	FINE	N-MINT

O.J.'S BIG BUST OUT
BONEYARD
☐ 0, Mar 95, b&w	2.95	0.59	1.77	2.95

OBLIVION
COMICO
☐ 3, May 96	2.95	0.59	1.77	2.95

OBLIVION CITY
SLAVE LABOR
☐ 1, b&w		0.50	1.50	2.50
☐ 2, b&w		0.50	1.50	2.50
☐ 3, b&w		0.50	1.50	2.50
☐ 4, b&w		0.50	1.50	2.50
☐ 5, b&w		0.50	1.50	2.50
☐ 6, b&w		0.50	1.50	2.50
☐ 7		0.59	1.77	2.95
☐ 8		0.59	1.77	2.95
☐ 9		0.79	2.37	3.95

OBNOXIO THE CLOWN
MARVEL
☐ 1, Apr 83, X-Men	0.60	0.20	0.60	1.00

OCEAN COMICS
OCEAN
☐ 1, b&w		0.35	1.05	1.75

OF MIND AND SOUL
RAGE
☐ 1, 94, b&w	2.25	0.45	1.35	2.25

OF MYTHS AND MEN
BLACKTHORNE
☐ 1, b&w		0.35	1.05	1.75
☐ 2, b&w		0.35	1.05	1.75

OFFCASTES
EPIC
☐ 1, embossed cover	2.50	0.50	1.50	2.50
☐ 2	1.95	0.39	1.17	1.95
☐ 3	1.95	0.39	1.17	1.95

OFFERINGS
CRY FOR DAWN
☐ 1, adult, b&w		0.55	1.65	2.75
☐ 2, adult, b&w	2.50	0.50	1.50	2.50

OFFICIAL BUZ SAWYER
PIONEER
☐ 1, Aug 88, b&w, Roy Crane				
		0.40	1.20	2.00
☐ 2, Sep 88, b&w, Roy Crane				
		0.40	1.20	2.00
☐ 3, Oct 88, b&w, Roy Crane				
		0.40	1.20	2.00
☐ 4, Nov 88, b&w, Roy Crane				
		0.40	1.20	2.00
☐ 5, Dec 88, b&w, Roy Crane				
		0.40	1.20	2.00

OFFICIAL CRISIS CROSSOVER INDEX
ECLIPSE/INDEPENDENT
☐ 1, Jun 86		0.25	0.75	1.25

OFFICIAL CRISIS INDEX
☐ 1, Mar 86		0.25	0.75	1.25

OFFICIAL DOOM PATROL INDEX
☐ 1, Feb 86		0.30	0.90	1.50
☐ 2, Feb 86		0.30	0.90	1.50

OFFICIAL HANDBOOK OF THE CONAN UNIVERSE
MARVEL
☐ 1	1.25	0.25	0.75	1.25

OFFICIAL HANDBOOK OF THE CONAN UNIVERSE
(1993)
☐ 0, no number or price, sold with *Conan Saga* #75

OFFICIAL HANDBOOK OF THE MARVEL UNIVERSE
☐ 1, Jan 83	1.00	1.20	3.60	6.00
☐ 2, Feb 83	1.00	0.90	2.70	4.50
☐ 3, Mar 83	1.00	0.80	2.40	4.00
☐ 4, Apr 83	1.00	0.70	2.10	3.50
☐ 5, May 83	1.00	0.70	2.10	3.50
☐ 6, Jun 83	1.00	0.60	1.80	3.00
☐ 7, Jul 83	1.00	0.60	1.80	3.00
☐ 8, Aug 83	1.00	0.60	1.80	3.00
☐ 9, Sep 83	1.00	0.60	1.80	3.00
☐ 10, Oct 83	1.00	0.60	1.80	3.00
☐ 11, Nov 83	1.00	0.60	1.80	3.00
☐ 12, Dec 83	1.00	0.60	1.80	3.00
☐ 13, Jan 84	1.00	0.50	1.50	2.50
☐ 14, Mar 84	1.00	0.80	2.40	4.00
☐ 15, May 84	1.00	0.80	2.40	4.00
☐ 20	1.00	0.90	2.70	4.50
☐ 21	1.00	0.90	2.70	4.50
☐ 22	1.00	0.90	2.70	4.50
☐ 23	1.00	0.90	2.70	4.50
☐ 24	1.00	0.90	2.70	4.50
☐ 25	1.00	0.90	2.70	4.50

OFFICIAL HANDBOOK OF THE MARVEL UNIVERSE
(2nd series)
☐ 1	1.50	0.80	2.40	4.00
☐ 2	1.50	0.60	1.80	3.00
☐ 3	1.50	0.60	1.80	3.00
☐ 4	1.50	0.60	1.80	3.00
☐ 5	1.50	0.60	1.80	3.00
☐ 6	1.50	0.60	1.80	3.00
☐ 7	1.50	0.60	1.80	3.00
☐ 8	1.50	0.60	1.80	3.00
☐ 9	1.50	0.60	1.80	3.00
☐ 10	1.50	0.60	1.80	3.00
☐ 11	1.50	0.50	1.50	2.50
☐ 12	1.50	0.50	1.50	2.50
☐ 13	1.50	0.50	1.50	2.50
☐ 14	1.50	0.50	1.50	2.50
☐ 15	1.50	0.50	1.50	2.50
☐ 16	1.50	0.50	1.50	2.50
☐ 17	1.50	0.50	1.50	2.50
☐ 18	1.50	0.50	1.50	2.50
☐ 19	1.50	0.50	1.50	2.50
☐ 20	1.50	0.50	1.50	2.50

OFFICIAL HANDBOOK OF THE
MARVEL UNIVERSE MASTER EDITION (looseleaf)
☐ 1, Dec 90	3.95	0.79	2.37	3.95
☐ 2, Jan 91	3.95	0.79	2.37	3.95
☐ 3, Feb 91	3.95	0.79	2.37	3.95
☐ 4, Mar 91	3.95	0.79	2.37	3.95
☐ 5, Apr 91	3.95	0.79	2.37	3.95
☐ 6, May 91	3.95	0.79	2.37	3.95
☐ 7, Jun 91	3.95	0.79	2.37	3.95
☐ 8, Jul 91	3.95	0.79	2.37	3.95
☐ 9, Aug 91	3.95	0.79	2.37	3.95
☐ 10, Sep 91	3.95	0.79	2.37	3.95
☐ 11, Oct 91	3.95	0.79	2.37	3.95
☐ 12, Nov 91	4.50	0.90	2.70	4.50
☐ 13, Dec 91	4.50	0.90	2.70	4.50
☐ 14	4.50	0.90	2.70	4.50
☐ 15	4.50	0.90	2.70	4.50
☐ 16	4.50	0.90	2.70	4.50
☐ 17	4.50	0.90	2.70	4.50
☐ 18	4.50	0.90	2.70	4.50
☐ 19	4.50	0.90	2.70	4.50
☐ 20	4.50	0.90	2.70	4.50
☐ 21	4.50	0.90	2.70	4.50
☐ 22	4.50	0.90	2.70	4.50
☐ 23	4.50	0.90	2.70	4.50
☐ 24	4.50	0.90	2.70	4.50

	ORIG.	GOOD	FINE	N-MINT
❑ 25	4.50	0.90	2.70	4.50
❑ 26	4.50	0.90	2.70	4.50
❑ 27	4.50	0.90	2.70	4.50
❑ 28	4.95	0.99	2.97	4.95
❑ 29	4.95	0.99	2.97	4.95
❑ 30	4.95	0.99	2.97	4.95
❑ 31	4.95	0.99	2.97	4.95
❑ 32	4.95	0.99	2.97	4.95
❑ 33	4.95	0.99	2.97	4.95
❑ 34	4.95	0.99	2.97	4.95
❑ 35	4.95	0.99	2.97	4.95
❑ 36	4.95	0.99	2.97	4.95

OFFICIAL HANDBOOK OF THE MARVEL UNIVERSE UPDATE '89

	ORIG.	GOOD	FINE	N-MINT
❑ 1, Jul 89	1.50	0.30	0.90	1.50
❑ 2, Aug 89	1.50	0.30	0.90	1.50
❑ 3, Sep 89	1.50	0.30	0.90	1.50
❑ 4, Oct 89	1.50	0.30	0.90	1.50
❑ 5, Nov 89	1.50	0.30	0.90	1.50
❑ 6, Nov 89	1.50	0.30	0.90	1.50
❑ 7, Dec 89	1.50	0.30	0.90	1.50
❑ 8, Dec 89	1.50	0.30	0.90	1.50

OFFICIAL HAWKMAN INDEX
ECLIPSE/INDEPENDENT

	GOOD	FINE	N-MINT
❑ 1, Nov 86	0.40	1.20	2.00
❑ 2, Dec 86	0.40	1.20	2.00

OFFICIAL HOW TO DRAW G.I. JOE
BLACKTHORNE

	GOOD	FINE	N-MINT
❑ 1, Nov 87	0.40	1.20	2.00
❑ 2, Jan 88	0.40	1.20	2.00

OFFICIAL HOW TO DRAW ROBOTECH

	GOOD	FINE	N-MINT
❑ 1	0.40	1.20	2.00
❑ 2	0.40	1.20	2.00
❑ 3	0.40	1.20	2.00
❑ 4	0.40	1.20	2.00
❑ 5	0.40	1.20	2.00
❑ 6	0.40	1.20	2.00
❑ 7	0.40	1.20	2.00
❑ 8	0.40	1.20	2.00
❑ 9	0.40	1.20	2.00
❑ 10	0.40	1.20	2.00
❑ 11	0.40	1.20	2.00
❑ 12	0.40	1.20	2.00
❑ 13	0.40	1.20	2.00
❑ 14	0.40	1.20	2.00

OFFICIAL HOW TO DRAW TRANSFORMERS

	GOOD	FINE	N-MINT
❑ 1, Sep 87	0.40	1.20	2.00
❑ 2, Nov 87	0.40	1.20	2.00
❑ 3, Jan 88	0.40	1.20	2.00
❑ 4, Mar 88	0.40	1.20	2.00

OFFICIAL JOHNNY HAZARD
PIONEER

	GOOD	FINE	N-MINT
❑ 1, Aug 88, b&w strips	0.40	1.20	2.00

OFFICIAL JUNGLE JIM

	GOOD	FINE	N-MINT
❑ 1, Jun 88, b&w, AR	0.40	1.20	2.00
❑ 2, Jul 88, b&w, AR	0.40	1.20	2.00
❑ 3, Aug 88, b&w, AR	0.40	1.20	2.00
❑ 4, Sep 88, b&w, AR	0.40	1.20	2.00
❑ 5, Oct 88, b&w, AR	0.40	1.20	2.00
❑ 6, Nov 88, b&w, AR	0.40	1.20	2.00
❑ 7, Dec 88, b&w, AR	0.40	1.20	2.00
❑ 8, Jan 89, b&w, AR	0.40	1.20	2.00
❑ 9, Feb 89, b&w, AR	0.40	1.20	2.00
❑ 10, Apr 89	0.50	1.50	2.50
❑ 11, Apr 89	0.50	1.50	2.50
❑ 12, 89	0.50	1.50	2.50
❑ 13, 89	0.50	1.50	2.50
❑ 14, 89	0.50	1.50	2.50
❑ 15, 89	0.50	1.50	2.50
❑ 16	0.50	1.50	2.50

OFFICIAL JUNGLE JIM ANNUAL, THE

	GOOD	FINE	N-MINT
❑ 1, Jan 89, b&w, AR	0.79	2.37	3.95

OFFICIAL JUSTICE LEAGUE OF AMERICA INDEX
ECLIPSE/INDEPENDENT

	GOOD	FINE	N-MINT
❑ 1, Apr 86	0.30	0.90	1.50
❑ 2, Apr 86	0.30	0.90	1.50
❑ 3, May 86	0.30	0.90	1.50
❑ 4, May 86	0.30	0.90	1.50
❑ 5, Oct 86	0.40	1.20	2.00
❑ 6, Nov 86	0.40	1.20	2.00
❑ 7, Jan 87, (becomes *Justice League of America Index*)	0.40	1.20	2.00

OFFICIAL MANDRAKE
PIONEER

	GOOD	FINE	N-MINT
❑ 1, Jun 88, b&w	0.40	1.20	2.00
❑ 2, Jul 88, b&w	0.40	1.20	2.00
❑ 3, Aug 88, b&w	0.40	1.20	2.00
❑ 4, Sep 88, b&w	0.40	1.20	2.00
❑ 5, Oct 88, b&w	0.40	1.20	2.00
❑ 6, Nov 88, b&w	0.40	1.20	2.00
❑ 7, Dec 88, b&w	0.40	1.20	2.00
❑ 8, Jan 89, b&w	0.40	1.20	2.00
❑ 9, Feb 89, b&w	0.40	1.20	2.00
❑ 10, Apr 89	0.50	1.50	2.50
❑ 11, Apr 89	0.50	1.50	2.50
❑ 12, 89	0.50	1.50	2.50
❑ 13, 89	0.50	1.50	2.50
❑ 14, 89	0.50	1.50	2.50
❑ 15, 89	0.50	1.50	2.50

OFFICIAL MARVEL INDEX TO MARVEL TEAM-UP
MARVEL

	ORIG.	GOOD	FINE	N-MINT
❑ 1, Jan 86	1.25	0.25	0.75	1.25
❑ 2, Feb 86	1.25	0.25	0.75	1.25
❑ 3, May 86	1.25	0.25	0.75	1.25
❑ 4, Jul 86	1.25	0.25	0.75	1.25
❑ 5, Oct 86	1.25	0.25	0.75	1.25
❑ 6, Jul 87	1.25	0.25	0.75	1.25

OFFICIAL MARVEL INDEX TO THE AMAZING SPIDER-MAN

	ORIG.	GOOD	FINE	N-MINT
❑ 1, Apr 85	1.25	0.30	0.90	1.50
❑ 2, May 85	1.25	0.25	0.75	1.25
❑ 3, Jun 85	1.25	0.25	0.75	1.25
❑ 4, Jul 85	1.25	0.25	0.75	1.25
❑ 5, Aug 85	1.25	0.25	0.75	1.25
❑ 6, Sep 85	1.25	0.25	0.75	1.25
❑ 7, Oct 85	1.25	0.25	0.75	1.25
❑ 8, Nov 85	1.25	0.25	0.75	1.25
❑ 9, Dec 85	1.25	0.25	0.75	1.25

OFFICIAL MARVEL INDEX TO THE AVENGERS

	ORIG.	GOOD	FINE	N-MINT
❑ 1, Jun 87	2.95	0.59	1.77	2.95
❑ 2, Aug 87	2.95	0.59	1.77	2.95
❑ 3, Oct 87	2.95	0.59	1.77	2.95
❑ 4, Dec 87	2.95	0.59	1.77	2.95
❑ 5, Apr 88	2.95	0.59	1.77	2.95
❑ 6, Jun 88	2.95	0.59	1.77	2.95
❑ 7, Aug 88	2.95	0.59	1.77	2.95

OFFICIAL MARVEL INDEX TO THE AVENGERS (1994)

	ORIG.	GOOD	FINE	N-MINT
❑ 1, Oct 94	1.95	0.39	1.17	1.95
❑ 2, Nov 94	1.95	0.39	1.17	1.95
❑ 3, Dec 94	1.95	0.39	1.17	1.95
❑ 4, Jan 95	1.95	0.39	1.17	1.95
❑ 5, Feb 95	1.95	0.39	1.17	1.95
❑ 6, Mar 95	1.95	0.39	1.17	1.95

OFFICIAL MARVEL INDEX TO THE FANTASTIC FOUR

	ORIG.	GOOD	FINE	N-MINT
❑ 1, Dec 85	1.25	0.25	0.75	1.25
❑ 2, Jan 86	1.25	0.25	0.75	1.25
❑ 3, Feb 86	1.25	0.25	0.75	1.25
❑ 4, Mar 86	1.25	0.25	0.75	1.25

	ORIG.	GOOD	FINE	N-MINT
5, Apr 86 ....1.25	0.25	0.75	1.25
6, May 86 ....1.25	0.25	0.75	1.25
7, Jun 86 ....1.25	0.25	0.75	1.25
8, Jul 86 ....1.25	0.25	0.75	1.25
9, Aug 86 ....1.25	0.25	0.75	1.25
10, Sep 86 ....1.25	0.25	0.75	1.25
11, Oct 86 ....1.25	0.25	0.75	1.25
12, Jan 87 ....1.25	0.25	0.75	1.25

OFFICIAL MARVEL INDEX TO THE X-MEN

1, May 87 ....2.95	0.59	1.77	2.95
2, Jul 87 ....2.95	0.59	1.77	2.95
3, Sep 87 ....2.95	0.59	1.77	2.95
4, Nov 87 ....2.95	0.59	1.77	2.95
5, Mar 88 ....2.95	0.59	1.77	2.95
6, May 88 ....2.95	0.59	1.77	2.95
7, Jul 88 ....2.95	0.59	1.77	2.95

OFFICIAL MARVEL INDEX TO THE X-MEN (Volume 2)

1 ....1.95	0.39	1.17	1.95
2, May 94 ....1.95	0.39	1.17	1.95
3, Jun 94 ....1.95	0.39	1.17	1.95
4, Jul 94 ....1.95	0.39	1.17	1.95
5, Aug 94 ....1.95	0.39	1.17	1.95

OFFICIAL MODESTY BLAISE ANNUAL
PIONEER

1, 89, O:Modesty, b&w	0.99	2.97	4.95

OFFICIAL MODESTY BLAISE, THE

1, Jul 88, b&w	0.40	1.20	2.00
2, Aug 88, b&w	0.40	1.20	2.00
3, Sep 88, b&w	0.40	1.20	2.00
4, Oct 88, b&w	0.40	1.20	2.00
5, Nov 88, b&w	0.40	1.20	2.00
6, Dec 88, b&w	0.40	1.20	2.00
7, b&w	0.40	1.20	2.00
8, b&w	0.40	1.20	2.00

OFFICIAL PRINCE VALIANT ANNUAL

1, Hal Foster b&w	0.79	2.37	3.95

OFFICIAL PRINCE VALIANT KING SIZE

1, b&w, Foster	0.79	2.37	3.95

OFFICIAL PRINCE VALIANT MONTHLY

1, Jun 89, b&w	0.79	2.37	3.95

OFFICIAL PRINCE VALIANT, THE

1, b&w, Hal Foster	0.40	1.20	2.00
2, b&w, Hal Foster	0.40	1.20	2.00
3, b&w, Hal Foster	0.40	1.20	2.00
4, b&w, Hal Foster	0.40	1.20	2.00
5, b&w, Hal Foster	0.40	1.20	2.00
6, b&w, Hal Foster	0.40	1.20	2.00
7, MGr(c) Foster	0.40	1.20	2.00
8, MGr(c) Foster	0.40	1.20	2.00
9, Foster	0.40	1.20	2.00
10	0.50	1.50	2.50
11	0.50	1.50	2.50
12	0.50	1.50	2.50
13	0.50	1.50	2.50
14	0.50	1.50	2.50
15	0.50	1.50	2.50
16	0.50	1.50	2.50
17	0.50	1.50	2.50
18	0.50	1.50	2.50

OFFICIAL RIP KIRBY

1, Aug 88, b&w, AR 2.00	0.40	1.20	2.00
2, Sep 88, b&w, AR........2.00	0.40	1.20	2.00
3, Oct 88, b&w, AR 2.00	0.40	1.20	2.00
4, Nov 88, b&w, AR; John Bolton(c)			
........................2.00	0.40	1.20	2.00
5, Dec 88, b&w, AR........2.00	0.40	1.20	2.00
6, Jan 89, b&w, AR 2.00	0.40	1.20	2.00

	ORIG.	GOOD	FINE	N-MINT
OFFICIAL SECRET AGENT, THE				
1, Jun 88, AW, b&w..........	0.40	1.20	2.00
2, Jul 88, AW, b&w..........	0.40	1.20	2.00
3, Aug 88, AW, b&w	0.40	1.20	2.00
4, Sep 88, AW, b&w	0.40	1.20	2.00
5, Oct 88, AW, b&w..........	0.40	1.20	2.00
6, Nov 88, AW, b&w	0.40	1.20	2.00
7, Dec 88, AW, b&w	0.40	1.20	2.00

OFFICIAL TEEN TITANS INDEX
INDEPENDENT/ECLIPSE

1, Aug 85	0.30	0.90	1.50
2, Sep 85	0.30	0.90	1.50
3, Oct 85	0.30	0.90	1.50
4, Nov 85	0.30	0.90	1.50
5, Dec 85	0.30	0.90	1.50

OFFICIAL, AUTHORIZED ZEN INTERGALACTIC NINJA SOURCEBOOK
EXPRESS/ENTITY

1, b&w............................3.50	0.70	2.10	3.50

OFFICIAL, AUTHORIZED ZEN INTERGALACTIC NINJA SOURCEBOOK '94 (REVISED EDITION)
EXPRESS

1, 94 ....3.50	0.70	2.10	3.50

OGRE (mini-series)
BLACK DIAMOND

1, Jan 94........................2.95	0.59	1.77	2.95
2, Mar 94 ....2.95	0.59	1.77	2.95
3, May 94........................2.95	0.59	1.77	2.95
4, Jul 94 ....2.95	0.59	1.77	2.95

OH MY GODDESS! (mini-series)
DARK HORSE

1, Aug 94, b&w...............2.50	0.80	2.40	4.00
2, Sep 94, b&w...............2.50	0.60	1.80	3.00
3, Oct 94, b&w................2.50	0.60	1.80	3.00
4, Nov 94, b&w...............2.50	0.50	1.50	2.50
5, Dec 94, b&w...............2.50	0.50	1.50	2.50
6, Jan 95, b&w, final issue			
........................2.50	0.50	1.50	2.50

OH MY GODDESS! II (mini-series)

1, Feb 95, b&w 2.50	0.60	1.80	3.00
2, Mar 95, b&w...............2.50	0.50	1.50	2.50
DARK HORSE/MANGA				
8, Sep 95, final issue;b&w			
........................2.95	0.59	1.77	2.95

OH MY GODDESS! III (mini-series)

1, Nov 95, b&w;cover says"Oh My Goddess! On a Wing and a Prayer" 2.95	0.59	1.77	2.95
2, Dec 95, b&w;cover says "Oh My Goddess! Love Potion #9" 2.95	0.59	1.77	2.95
3, Jan 96, b&w;cover says "Oh My Goddess! Sympathy for the Devil" 2.95	0.59	1.77	2.95
4, Feb 96, b&w;cover says"Oh My Goddess!Mystical Engine"........................2.95	0.59	1.77	2.95
5, Mar 96, b&w;cover says "Oh My Goddess! Valentine Rhapsody" 2.95	0.59	1.77	2.95
6, Apr 96, b&w;cover says"Oh My Goddess!Terrible Master Urd"....................2.95	0.59	1.77	2.95
7, May 96, b&w;cover says"Oh My Goddess!Terrible Master Urd"....................2.95	0.59	1.77	2.95

OINK: HEAVEN'S BUTCHER (mini-series)
KITCHEN SINK

1, Dec 95, cardstock cover			
........................4.95	0.99	2.97	4.95

OKTANE (mini-series)
DARK HORSE

1, Aug 95 ....2.50	0.50	1.50	2.50
2, Sep 95 ....2.50	0.50	1.50	2.50
3, Oct 95 ....2.50	0.50	1.50	2.50
3, Oct 95 ....2.50	0.50	1.50	2.50
4, Nov 95, final issue 2.50	0.50	1.50	2.50

	ORIG.	GOOD	FINE	N-MINT

OLDBLOOD
PARODY PRESS

	ORIG.	GOOD	FINE	N-MINT
❑ 1, first printing 2.50		0.50	1.50	2.50
❑ 1, second printing 2.50		0.50	1.50	2.50

OLYMPIANS, THE
EPIC

	ORIG.	GOOD	FINE	N-MINT
❑ 1 .... 3.95		0.79	2.37	3.95
❑ 2 .... 3.95		0.79	2.37	3.95

OMAC
DC

	ORIG.	GOOD	FINE	N-MINT
❑ 1, Oct 74, JK 0.20		0.79	2.37	3.95
❑ 2, Dec 74, JK.............. 0.20		0.79	2.37	3.95
❑ 3, Feb 75, JK.............. 0.20		0.79	2.37	3.95
❑ 4, Apr 75, JK 0.20		0.79	2.37	3.95
❑ 5, Jun 75, JK 0.20		0.79	2.37	3.95
❑ 6, Aug 75, JK 0.20		0.79	2.37	3.95
❑ 7, Oct 75, JK 0.20		0.79	2.37	3.95
❑ 8, Dec 75, JK.............. 0.20		0.79	2.37	3.95

OMAC: ONE MAN ARMY CORPS (mini-series)

	ORIG.	GOOD	FINE	N-MINT
❑ 1, 91, JBy;b&w;prestige format				
.... 3.95		0.79	2.37	3.95
❑ 2, 91, JBy;b&w;prestige format				
.... 3.95		0.79	2.37	3.95
❑ 3, 91, JBy;b&w;prestige format				
.... 3.95		0.79	2.37	3.95
❑ 4, 92, JBy;b&w;prestige format				
.... 3.95		0.79	2.37	3.95

OMAHA THE CAT DANCER (was SteelDragon)
KITCHEN SINK

	ORIG.	GOOD	FINE	N-MINT
❑ 0, adult, reprints..............		0.40	1.20	2.00
❑ 1, adult, reprints..............		0.50	1.50	2.50
❑ 2, adult, reprints..............		0.50	1.50	2.50
❑ 3, Oct 86, adults;b&w 2.50		0.50	1.50	2.50
❑ 4, adults;b&w................ 2.50		0.50	1.50	2.50
❑ 5, adults;b&w................ 2.50		0.50	1.50	2.50
❑ 6, adults;b&w................ 2.50		0.50	1.50	2.50
❑ 7, adults;b&w................ 2.50		0.50	1.50	2.50
❑ 8, adults;b&w................ 2.50		0.50	1.50	2.50
❑ 9, adults;b&w................ 2.50		0.50	1.50	2.50
❑ 10, adults;b&w................ 2.50		0.50	1.50	2.50
❑ 11, adults;b&w................ 2.50		0.50	1.50	2.50
❑ 12, adults;b&w................ 2.50		0.50	1.50	2.50
❑ 13, adults;b&w................ 2.50		0.50	1.50	2.50
❑ 14, adults;b&w................ 2.50		0.50	1.50	2.50
❑ 15, adults;b&w................ 2.50		0.50	1.50	2.50
❑ 16, adults;b&w................		0.50	1.50	2.50
❑ 17, adults;b&w................		0.50	1.50	2.50
❑ 18, adults;b&w (moves to Fantagraphics)				
....		0.59	1.77	2.95

OMAHA THE CAT DANCER VOL. I
FANTAGRAPHICS

	ORIG.	GOOD	FINE	N-MINT
❑ 11, Dec 88, b&w; reprints the issue originally published by Kitchen Sink 2.95		0.59	1.77	2.95
❑ 12, Jul 89, b&w; reprints the issue originally published by Kitchen Sink 2.95		0.59	1.77	2.95

OMAHA THE CAT DANCER VOL. II

	ORIG.	GOOD	FINE	N-MINT
❑ 1, Jul 94, b&w (was Kitchen Sink title)				
.... 2.50		0.50	1.50	2.50
❑ 2, Aug 94, b&w 2.50		0.50	1.50	2.50
❑ 3, Nov 94, b&w 2.50		0.50	1.50	2.50

OMAHA: CAT DANCER
STEELDRAGON

	ORIG.	GOOD	FINE	N-MINT
❑ 1, preview	2.00	6.00	10.00	
❑ 1	1.00	3.00	5.00	
❑ 1, reprint	0.40	1.20	2.00	
❑ 2, (moves to Kitchen Sink)	0.40	1.20	2.00	

OMAR LENNYX
MAGNECOM

	ORIG.	GOOD	FINE	N-MINT
❑ 1, Blood Seekers, b&w ...2.95		0.59	1.77	2.95

OMEGA ELITE
BLACKTHORNE

	ORIG.	GOOD	FINE	N-MINT
❑ 1, 89, b&w......................		0.70	2.10	3.50

OMEGA MEN
DC

	ORIG.	GOOD	FINE	N-MINT
❑ 1, Apr 83, KG,O:Omega Men				
...........................1.00		0.60	1.80	3.00
❑ 2, May 83, KG, O:Broot...1.00		0.40	1.20	2.00
❑ 3, Jun 83, 1:Lobo 1.00		2.00	6.00	10.00
❑ 4, Jul 83.......................1.00		0.25	0.75	1.25
❑ 5, Aug 83, Lobo.............1.00		1.20	3.60	6.00
❑ 6, Sep 83 ....1.00		0.60	1.80	3.00
❑ 7, Oct 83.......................		0.25	0.75	1.25
❑ 8, Nov 83.......................		0.25	0.75	1.25
❑ 9, Dec 83, Lobo		1.00	3.00	5.00
❑ 10, Jan 84, Lobo.............		1.00	3.00	5.00
❑ 11, Feb 84.......................		0.25	0.75	1.25
❑ 12, Mar 84.......................		0.25	0.75	1.25
❑ 13, Apr 84.......................		0.25	0.75	1.25
❑ 14, May 84.......................		0.25	0.75	1.25
❑ 15, Jun 84		0.25	0.75	1.25
❑ 16, Jul 84.......................		0.25	0.75	1.25
❑ 17, Aug 84.......................		0.25	0.75	1.25
❑ 18, Sep 84		0.25	0.75	1.25
❑ 19, Oct 84, Lobo		1.20	3.60	6.00
❑ 20, Nov 84, Lobo		1.20	3.60	6.00
❑ 21, Dec 84.......................		0.25	0.75	1.25
❑ 22, Jan 85.......................		0.25	0.75	1.25
❑ 23, Feb 85.......................		0.25	0.75	1.25
❑ 24, Mar 85.......................		0.25	0.75	1.25
❑ 25, Apr 85.......................		0.25	0.75	1.25
❑ 26, May 85.......................		0.25	0.75	1.25
❑ 27, Jun 85		0.25	0.75	1.25
❑ 28, Jul 85.......................		0.25	0.75	1.25
❑ 29, Aug 85.......................		0.25	0.75	1.25
❑ 30, Sep 85		0.25	0.75	1.25
❑ 31, Oct 85, Crisis		0.30	0.90	1.50
❑ 32, Nov 85.......................		0.25	0.75	1.25
❑ 33, Dec 85.......................		0.25	0.75	1.25
❑ 34, Jan 86.......................		0.25	0.75	1.25
❑ 35, Feb 86.......................		0.25	0.75	1.25
❑ 36, Mar 86.......................		0.25	0.75	1.25
❑ 37, Apr 86.......................		0.25	0.75	1.25
❑ 38, May 86.......................		0.25	0.75	1.25

OMEGA THE UNKNOWN
MARVEL

	ORIG.	GOOD	FINE	N-MINT
❑ 1 ....0.25		1.20	3.60	6.00
❑ 2 ....0.25		0.60	1.80	3.00
❑ 3 ....0.25		0.60	1.80	3.00
❑ 4, Sep 76 ....0.30		0.60	1.80	3.00
❑ 5, Nov 76 ....0.30		0.60	1.80	3.00
❑ 6, Jan 77.......................0.30		0.60	1.80	3.00
❑ 7, Mar 77.......................0.30		0.60	1.80	3.00
❑ 8, May 77.......................0.30		1.00	3.00	5.00
❑ 9, Jul 77.......................0.30		1.00	3.00	5.00
❑ 10, Oct 77.......................0.30		1.00	3.00	5.00
❑ 11 ....0.30		1.00	3.00	5.00

OMEN
NORTHSTAR

	ORIG.	GOOD	FINE	N-MINT
❑ 1, b&w............................		1.00	3.00	5.00
❑ 2, b&w............................		0.40	1.20	2.00

OMICRON
PYRAMID

	ORIG.	GOOD	FINE	N-MINT
❑ 1, b&w, flexi-disc.............		0.45	1.35	2.25
❑ 2, b&w, flexi-disc.............		0.45	1.35	2.25

	ORIG.	GOOD	FINE	N-MINT

OMNI COMIX
OMNI
☐ 1, Mar 95, magazine-sized comic book; Mar '95 issue of *Omni* inserted 2.95 1.20 3.60 6.00
☐ 2, Apr 95, magazine-sized comic book; insert in Apr. '95 issue of *Omni* with *Omni Comix* #2 cover
.... 3.95 1.00 3.00 5.00
☐ 3, Oct 95, magazine-sized;T.H.U.N.D.E.R. Agents story
.... 4.95 0.99 2.97 4.95

OMNI MEN
BLACKTHORNE
☐ 1, Apr 89, b&w................ 0.70 2.10 3.50

OMNIBUS: MODERN PERVERSITY
BLACKBIRD
☐ 0, nn, b&w, squarebound
.... 3.25 0.65 1.95 3.25

ON A PALE HORSE
INNOVATION
☐ 1 .... 4.95 0.99 2.97 4.95
☐ 2 .... 4.95 0.99 2.97 4.95
☐ 3 .... 4.95 0.99 2.97 4.95
☐ 4 .... 4.95 0.99 2.97 4.95
☐ 5, Dec 93........................ 4.95 0.99 2.97 4.95

ON OUR BUTTS
AEON
☐ 0, Apr 95 .... 2.95 0.59 1.77 2.95

ONE
PACIFIC
☐ 1, b&w (1st Pacific title) .. 0.60 1.80 3.00

ONE MILE UP
ECLIPSE
☐ 1, b&w............................. 0.50 1.50 2.50

ONE, THE
EPIC
☐ 1, Jul 85, Rick Veitch 1.50 0.40 1.20 2.00
☐ 2, Sep 85, Rick Veitch.... 1.50 0.40 1.20 2.00
☐ 3, Nov 85, Rick Veitch.... 1.50 0.40 1.20 2.00
☐ 4, Jan 86, Rick Veitch.... 1.50 0.40 1.20 2.00
☐ 5, Mar 86, Rick Veitch.... 1.50 0.40 1.20 2.00
☐ 6, May 86, Rick Veitch ... 1.50 0.40 1.20 2.00

ONE-ARM SWORDSMAN,
DR. LEUNG'S
☐ 1 .... 0.36 1.08 1.80
☐ 2 .... 0.36 1.08 1.80
☐ 3 .... 0.36 1.08 1.80
☐ 4 .... 0.36 1.08 1.80
☐ 5 .... 0.36 1.08 1.80
☐ 6 .... 0.36 1.08 1.80
☐ 7 .... 0.36 1.08 1.80

ONE-FISTED TALES
SLAVE LABOR
☐ 1, adult, b&w 0.50 1.50 2.50
☐ 2, adult, b&w 0.50 1.50 2.50
☐ 3, adult, b&w 0.50 1.50 2.50
☐ 4, adult, b&w 0.50 1.50 2.50
☐ 5, adult, b&w 0.79 2.37 3.95
☐ 6, adult.............................. 0.59 1.77 2.95
☐ 7, adult, b&w 2.95 0.59 1.77 2.95
☐ 8, adult, b&w 2.95 0.59 1.77 2.95

ONE-SHOT PARODY
MILKY WAY
☐ 1, Xmen 0.30 0.90 1.50

ONE-SHOT WESTERN
CALIBER
☐ 1, b&w.............................. 0.50 1.50 2.50

ONYX OVERLORD
EPIC
☐ 1, Moebius 2.75 0.55 1.65 2.75
☐ 2 .... 2.75 0.55 1.65 2.75

☐ 3 .... 2.75 0.55 1.65 2.75
☐ 4 .... 2.75 0.55 1.65 2.75

OOMBAH, JUNGLE MOON MAN
STRAWBERRY JAM
☐ 1, b&w............................. 0.50 1.50 2.50

OPEN SEASON
RENEGADE
☐ 1, b&w........................... 2.00 0.40 1.20 2.00
☐ 2, b&w........................... 2.00 0.40 1.20 2.00
☐ 3, b&w........................... 2.00 0.40 1.20 2.00
☐ 4, Oct 87, b&w.............. 2.00 0.40 1.20 2.00
☐ 5, Dec 87, b&w.............. 2.00 0.40 1.20 2.00
☐ 6, b&w (moves to Strawberry Jam)
.... 0.40 1.20 2.00

OPEN SEASON (was Renegade title)
STRAWBERRY JAM
☐ 7, 89, b&w..................... 2.00 0.40 1.20 2.00

OPEN SPACE
MARVEL
☐ 1 .... 4.95 1.20 3.60 6.00
☐ 2 .... 4.95 0.99 2.97 4.95
☐ 3 .... 4.95 0.99 2.97 4.95
☐ 4 .... 4.95 0.99 2.97 4.95

OPERATION: KANSAS CITY
MOTION
☐ 1, Win 93, b&w;"Breakneck Blvd." preview
.... 2.50 0.50 1.50 2.50

OPERATION: KNIGHTSTRIKE
IMAGE
☐ 1, May 95........................ 2.50 0.50 1.50 2.50
☐ 2, Jun 95 .... 2.50 0.50 1.50 2.50
☐ 3, Jul 95, A:Bloodstrike... 2.50 0.50 1.50 2.50

OPERATIVE: SCORPIO
BLACKTHORNE
☐ 1, Jan 89, b&w 0.70 2.10 3.50

ORACLE
ORACLE
☐ 1, 1978, GP, b&w 2.00 6.00 10.00

ORACLE PRESENTS
☐ 1, 1986, GP, reprint of *Oracle* #1 b&w
.... 0.60 1.80 3.00
☐ 2, Critter Corps 0.60 1.80 3.00

ORBIT
ECLIPSE
☐ 1, DSt(c), JBolton............ 0.99 2.97 4.95
☐ 2 .... 0.99 2.97 4.95
☐ 3, JBolton, TY 0.99 2.97 4.95

ORIENTAL HEROES
JADEMAN
☐ 1 .... 0.39 1.17 1.95
☐ 2 .... 0.39 1.17 1.95
☐ 3 .... 0.39 1.17 1.95
☐ 4 .... 0.39 1.17 1.95
☐ 5 .... 0.39 1.17 1.95
☐ 6 .... 0.39 1.17 1.95
☐ 7 .... 0.39 1.17 1.95
☐ 8 .... 0.39 1.17 1.95
☐ 9 .... 0.39 1.17 1.95
☐ 10 .... 0.39 1.17 1.95
☐ 11 .... 0.39 1.17 1.95
☐ 12 .... 0.39 1.17 1.95
☐ 13 .... 0.39 1.17 1.95
☐ 14 .... 0.39 1.17 1.95
☐ 15 .... 0.39 1.17 1.95
☐ 16 .... 0.39 1.17 1.95
☐ 17 .... 0.39 1.17 1.95
☐ 18 .... 0.39 1.17 1.95
☐ 19 .... 0.39 1.17 1.95
☐ 20 .... 0.39 1.17 1.95

	ORIG.	GOOD	FINE	N-MINT
21		0.39	1.17	1.95
22		0.39	1.17	1.95
23		0.39	1.17	1.95
24		0.39	1.17	1.95
25		0.39	1.17	1.95
26		0.39	1.17	1.95
27		0.39	1.17	1.95
28		0.39	1.17	1.95
29		0.39	1.17	1.95
30		0.39	1.17	1.95
31		0.39	1.17	1.95
32		0.39	1.17	1.95
33		0.39	1.17	1.95
34		0.39	1.17	1.95
35		0.39	1.17	1.95
36		0.39	1.17	1.95
37		0.39	1.17	1.95
38		0.39	1.17	1.95
39		0.39	1.17	1.95
40		0.39	1.17	1.95
41		0.39	1.17	1.95
42		0.39	1.17	1.95

ORIGIN OF GALACTUS
MARVEL

	ORIG.	GOOD	FINE	N-MINT
0, Feb 96, nn;reprints *Super-Villain Classics* #1	2.50	0.50	1.50	2.50

ORIGIN OF THE DEFIANT UNIVERSE, THE
DEFIANT

	ORIG.	GOOD	FINE	N-MINT
1, Feb 94	1.50	0.30	0.90	1.50

ORIGINAL ASTRO BOY, THE
NOW

	ORIG.	GOOD	FINE	N-MINT
1, Sep 87, Ken Steacy	1.50	0.40	1.20	2.00
2, Oct 87, Ken Steacy	1.50	0.30	0.90	1.50
3, Nov 87, Ken Steacy	1.75	0.35	1.05	1.75
4, Dec 87, Ken Steacy	1.75	0.35	1.05	1.75
5, Jan 88, Ken Steacy	1.75	0.35	1.05	1.75
6, Feb 88, Ken Steacy	1.75	0.35	1.05	1.75
7, Mar 88, Ken Steacy	1.75	0.35	1.05	1.75
8, Apr 88, Ken Steacy	1.75	0.35	1.05	1.75
9, May 88, Ken Steacy	1.75	0.35	1.05	1.75
10, Jun 88, Ken Steacy	1.75	0.35	1.05	1.75
11, Aug 88, Ken Steacy	1.75	0.35	1.05	1.75
12, Sep 88, Ken Steacy	1.75	0.35	1.05	1.75
13, Oct 88, Ken Steacy	1.75	0.35	1.05	1.75
14, Nov 88, Ken Steacy	1.75	0.35	1.05	1.75
15, Jan 89, Ken Steacy	1.75	0.35	1.05	1.75
16, Feb 89, Ken Steacy	1.75	0.35	1.05	1.75
17, Mar 89, Ken Steacy	1.75	0.35	1.05	1.75
18, Apr 89	1.75	0.35	1.05	1.75
19, May 89, Comics Code	1.75	0.35	1.05	1.75
20, Jun 89, . Comics Code	1.75	0.35	1.05	1.75

ORIGINAL BLACK CAT
RECOLLECTIONS

	ORIG.	GOOD	FINE	N-MINT
1, 88, reprints		0.40	1.20	2.00
2, Mar 89, reprints		0.40	1.20	2.00
3, Sep 90, reprints		0.40	1.20	2.00
4, Jun 91, reprints		0.40	1.20	2.00
5, Jul 91, reprints		0.40	1.20	2.00
6, Aug 91, reprints		0.40	1.20	2.00
7, Nov 91, reprints (becomes *Black Cat*)	0.40	1.20	2.00	

ORIGINAL CREW, THE
PERSONALITY

	ORIG.	GOOD	FINE	N-MINT
1, Wm. Shatner		0.59	1.77	2.95
2, b&w		0.59	1.77	2.95
3, b&w		0.59	1.77	2.95
4, b&w		0.59	1.77	2.95
5, b&w		0.59	1.77	2.95
6, b&w		0.59	1.77	2.95

	ORIG.	GOOD	FINE	N-MINT
7, b&w		0.59	1.77	2.95
8, b&w		0.59	1.77	2.95
9, b&w		0.59	1.77	2.95
10, b&w		0.59	1.77	2.95

ORIGINAL DICK TRACY
GLADSTONE

	ORIG.	GOOD	FINE	N-MINT
1, Sep 90, Mrs. Pruneface	1.95	0.39	1.17	1.95
2, Nov 90, Influence	1.95	0.39	1.17	1.95
3, Jan 91, Gargles		0.40	1.20	2.00
4, Mar 91, Itchy		0.40	1.20	2.00
5, May 91, Shoulders		0.40	1.20	2.00

ORIGINAL DOCTOR SOLAR, MAN OF THE ATOM, THE
VALIANT

	ORIG.	GOOD	FINE	N-MINT
1, Apr 95	2.95	0.59	1.77	2.95

ORIGINAL E-MAN
FIRST

	ORIG.	GOOD	FINE	N-MINT
1, Oct 85, reprints	1.75	0.35	1.05	1.75
2, Nov 85, reprints	1.75	0.35	1.05	1.75
3, Dec 85, reprints	1.75	0.35	1.05	1.75
4, Jan 86, reprints	1.75	0.35	1.05	1.75
5, Feb 86, reprints	1.75	0.35	1.05	1.75
6, Mar 86, reprints	1.75	0.35	1.05	1.75
7, Mar 86, reprints	1.75	0.35	1.05	1.75

ORIGINAL GHOST RIDER RIDES AGAIN, THE
MARVEL

	ORIG.	GOOD	FINE	N-MINT
1, Jul 91, reprints	1.50	0.30	0.90	1.50
2, Aug 91, reprints	1.50	0.30	0.90	1.50
3, Sep 91, reprints	1.50	0.30	0.90	1.50
4, Oct 91, reprints	1.50	0.30	0.90	1.50
5, Nov 91, reprints	1.50	0.30	0.90	1.50
6, Dec 91, reprints	1.50	0.30	0.90	1.50
7, reprints	1.50	0.30	0.90	1.50

ORIGINAL GHOST RIDER, THE

	ORIG.	GOOD	FINE	N-MINT
1, O:reprinted	1.75	0.35	1.05	1.75
2, reprints	1.75	0.35	1.05	1.75
3, reprints	1.75	0.35	1.05	1.75
4, reprints	1.75	0.35	1.05	1.75
5, reprints	1.75	0.35	1.05	1.75
6, reprints	1.75	0.35	1.05	1.75
7, reprints	1.75	0.35	1.05	1.75
8, reprints	1.75	0.35	1.05	1.75
9, reprints	1.75	0.35	1.05	1.75
10, reprints	1.75	0.35	1.05	1.75
11, reprints	1.75	0.35	1.05	1.75
12, reprints	1.75	0.35	1.05	1.75
13, reprints	1.75	0.35	1.05	1.75
14, reprints	1.75	0.35	1.05	1.75
15, reprints	1.75	0.35	1.05	1.75
16, reprints	1.75	0.35	1.05	1.75
17, reprints	1.75	0.35	1.05	1.75
18, reprints	1.75	0.35	1.05	1.75
19, reprints	1.75	0.35	1.05	1.75
20, reprints	1.75	0.35	1.05	1.75

ORIGINAL MAN
OMEGA 7

	ORIG.	GOOD	FINE	N-MINT
0	3.50	0.70	2.10	3.50

ORIGINAL SAD SACK
RECOLLECTIONS

	ORIG.	GOOD	FINE	N-MINT
1, b&w, G.Baker		0.40	1.20	2.00

ORIGINAL SHIELD
ARCHIE

	ORIG.	GOOD	FINE	N-MINT
1, Apr 84	0.75	0.20	0.60	1.00
2, Jun 84	0.75	0.15	0.45	0.75
3, Aug 84	0.75	0.15	0.45	0.75
4, Oct 84	0.75	0.15	0.45	0.75

ORIGINAL STREET FIGHTER, THE
ALPHA

	ORIG.	GOOD	FINE	N-MINT
1, b&w	2.50	0.50	1.50	2.50

	ORIG.	GOOD	FINE	N-MINT

ORIGINAL TOM CORBETT
ETERNITY

	ORIG.	GOOD	FINE	N-MINT
1, b&w, strip rep.	0.59	1.77	2.95	
2, b&w, strip rep.	0.59	1.77	2.95	
3, b&w, strip rep.	0.59	1.77	2.95	
4, b&w, strip rep.	0.59	1.77	2.95	
5, b&w, strip rep.	0.59	1.77	2.95	

ORIGINAL TUROK, SON OF STONE, THE
(mini-series)
VALIANT

	ORIG.	GOOD	FINE	N-MINT
1, Apr 95, cardstock cover	2.95	0.59	1.77	2.95
2, May 95, cardstock cover;final issue	2.95	0.59	1.77	2.95

ORION
DARK HORSE

	ORIG.	GOOD	FINE	N-MINT
1, manga, b&w		0.79	2.37	3.95
2, manga, b&w	2.50	0.50	1.50	2.50
3, manga, b&w	2.50	0.50	1.50	2.50
4, manga, b&w	2.50	0.50	1.50	2.50
5, manga, b&w	2.95	0.59	1.77	2.95
6, Jul 93	3.95	0.79	2.37	3.95

ORLAK REDUX
CALIBER

	ORIG.	GOOD	FINE	N-MINT
1, b&w		0.79	2.37	3.95

OTHELLO
TOME

	ORIG.	GOOD	FINE	N-MINT
0, nn b&w	3.50	0.59	1.77	2.95

OTHERS, THE
CORMAC

	ORIG.	GOOD	FINE	N-MINT
1		0.30	0.90	1.50

IMAGE

	ORIG.	GOOD	FINE	N-MINT
0, Mar 95, 16-page preview	1.00	0.20	0.60	1.00
1, Apr 95	2.50	0.50	1.50	2.50

OUR ARMY AT WAR
DC

	ORIG.	GOOD	FINE	N-MINT
125, Dec 62		2.80	8.40	14.00
126		2.80	8.40	14.00
127		2.80	8.40	14.00
128		2.80	8.40	14.00
129		2.80	8.40	14.00
130		2.80	8.40	14.00
131		2.80	8.40	14.00
132		2.80	8.40	14.00
133		2.80	8.40	14.00
134		2.80	8.40	14.00
135		2.80	8.40	14.00
136		2.80	8.40	14.00
137, Dec 63, "Too Many Sergeants"	0.12	2.80	8.40	14.00
138		2.80	8.40	14.00
139		2.80	8.40	14.00
140		2.80	8.40	14.00
141		2.80	8.40	14.00
142		2.80	8.40	14.00
143		2.80	8.40	14.00
144		2.80	8.40	14.00
145		2.80	8.40	14.00
146		2.80	8.40	14.00
147		2.80	8.40	14.00
148, Nov 64	0.12	2.80	8.40	14.00
149, Dec 64	0.12	2.80	8.40	14.00
150, Jan 65	0.12	2.80	8.40	14.00
151, Feb 65, 1:Enemy Ace	0.12	30.00	90.00	150.00
152, Mar 65	0.12	2.80	8.40	14.00
153, Apr 65, 2nd Enemy Ace	0.12	25.00	75.00	125.00
154, May 65	0.12	2.80	8.40	14.00

	ORIG.	GOOD	FINE	N-MINT
155, Jun 65, 3rd Enemy Ace (next appearance is in *Showcase #57*)	0.12	20.00	60.00	100.00
156, Jul 65	0.12	2.80	8.40	14.00
157, Aug 65	0.12	2.80	8.40	14.00
158, Sep 65	0.12	2.80	8.40	14.00
159, Oct 65	0.12	2.80	8.40	14.00
160, Nov 65, "What's the Color of Your Blood?"	0.12	2.80	8.40	14.00
161, Dec 65	0.12	2.80	8.40	14.00
162, Jan 66, A:Viking Prince	0.12	2.80	8.40	14.00
163, A:Viking Prince	0.12	2.80	8.40	14.00
164	0.12	4.00	12.00	20.00
165, Mar 66, V:Iron Major	0.12	2.80	8.40	14.00
166, Apr 66	0.12	2.80	8.40	14.00
167, May 66	0.12	2.80	8.40	14.00
168, Jun 66	0.12	2.80	8.40	14.00
169, Jul 66	0.12	2.80	8.40	14.00
170, Aug 66	0.12	2.80	8.40	14.00
171, Sep 66	0.12	2.80	8.40	14.00
172, Oct 66	0.12	2.80	8.40	14.00
173, Nov 66	0.12	2.80	8.40	14.00
174, Dec 66	0.12	2.80	8.40	14.00
175, Jan 67	0.12	2.80	8.40	14.00
176, Feb 67	0.12	2.80	8.40	14.00
177	0.12	4.00	12.00	20.00
178	0.12	2.80	8.40	14.00
179	0.12	2.80	8.40	14.00
180, May 67	0.12	2.80	8.40	14.00
181, Jun 67	0.12	2.80	8.40	14.00
182, Jul 67	0.12	2.00	6.00	10.00
183, Aug 67	0.12	2.00	6.00	10.00
184, Sep 67	0.12	2.00	6.00	10.00
185, Oct 67	0.12	2.00	6.00	10.00
186, Nov 67	0.12	2.40	7.20	12.00
187, Dec 67	0.12	2.00	6.00	10.00
188	0.12	2.00	6.00	10.00
189	0.12	2.00	6.00	10.00
190	0.12	2.00	6.00	10.00
191, Mar 68	0.12	1.40	4.20	7.00
192, Apr 68	0.12	1.40	4.20	7.00
193, May 68	0.12	1.40	4.20	7.00
194, Jun 68, 1:Unit 3 (kid guerrillas)	0.12	1.40	4.20	7.00
195, Jul 68	0.12	1.40	4.20	7.00
196, Aug 68, "Stop the War,I Want to Get Off"	0.12	1.40	4.20	7.00
197, Sep 68	0.12	1.40	4.20	7.00
198, Oct 68	0.12	1.40	4.20	7.00
199, Nov 68	0.12	1.40	4.20	7.00
200		2.40	7.20	12.00
201		0.80	2.40	4.00
202		0.80	2.40	4.00
203		0.80	2.40	4.00
204		0.80	2.40	4.00
205		0.80	2.40	4.00
206		0.80	2.40	4.00
207		0.80	2.40	4.00
208		0.80	2.40	4.00
209		0.80	2.40	4.00
210		0.80	2.40	4.00
211, Oct 69	0.15	0.80	2.40	4.00
212, Nov 69	0.15	0.80	2.40	4.00
213, Dec 69	0.15	0.80	2.40	4.00
214, Jan 70	0.15	0.80	2.40	4.00
215, Feb 70	0.15	0.80	2.40	4.00
216	0.15	0.80	2.40	4.00
217	0.15	0.80	2.40	4.00
218, Apr 70	0.15	0.80	2.40	4.00
219, May 70	0.15	0.80	2.40	4.00
220, Jun 70	0.15	0.80	2.40	4.00

	ORIG.	GOOD	FINE	N-MINT
☐ 221, Jul 70	0.15	0.80	2.40	4.00
☐ 222, Aug 70	0.15	0.80	2.40	4.00
☐ 223, Sep 70	0.15	0.80	2.40	4.00
☐ 224, Oct 70	0.15	0.80	2.40	4.00
☐ 225, Nov 70	0.15	0.80	2.40	4.00
☐ 226, Dec 70	0.15	0.80	2.40	4.00
☐ 227, Jan 71	0.15	0.80	2.40	4.00
☐ 228	0.15	0.80	2.40	4.00
☐ 229	0.15	0.80	2.40	4.00
☐ 230, Mar 71	0.15	0.80	2.40	4.00
☐ 231, Apr 71	0.15	0.80	2.40	4.00
☐ 232, May 71	0.15	0.80	2.40	4.00
☐ 233, Jun 71	0.15	0.80	2.40	4.00
☐ 234, Jul 71	0.15	0.80	2.40	4.00
☐ 235, Aug 71	0.25	0.80	2.40	4.00
☐ 236, Sep 71	0.25	0.80	2.40	4.00
☐ 237, Oct 71	0.25	0.80	2.40	4.00
☐ 238, Nov 71	0.25	0.80	2.40	4.00
☐ 239, Dec 71	0.25	0.80	2.40	4.00
☐ 240, Jan 72	0.25	0.80	2.40	4.00
☐ 241, Feb 72	0.25	0.80	2.40	4.00
☐ 242	0.25	0.80	2.40	4.00
☐ 243, Mar 72	0.25	0.80	2.40	4.00
☐ 244, Apr 72	0.25	0.80	2.40	4.00
☐ 245, May 72	0.25	0.80	2.40	4.00
☐ 246, Jun 72	0.25	0.80	2.40	4.00
☐ 247, Jul 72	0.20	0.80	2.40	4.00
☐ 248, Aug 72	0.20	0.80	2.40	4.00
☐ 249, Sep 72	0.20	0.80	2.40	4.00
☐ 250, Oct 72	0.20	0.80	2.40	4.00
☐ 251, Nov 72	0.20	0.80	2.40	4.00
☐ 252, Dec 72	0.20	0.80	2.40	4.00
☐ 253, Jan 73	0.20	0.80	2.40	4.00
☐ 254, Feb 73	0.20	0.80	2.40	4.00
☐ 255, Mar 73	0.20	0.80	2.40	4.00
☐ 256, Apr 73	0.20	0.80	2.40	4.00
☐ 257, Jun 73	0.20	0.80	2.40	4.00
☐ 258, Jul 73	0.20	0.80	2.40	4.00
☐ 259, Aug 73	0.20	0.80	2.40	4.00
☐ 260, Sep 73	0.20	0.80	2.40	4.00
☐ 261, Oct 73	0.20	0.80	2.40	4.00
☐ 262, Nov 73	0.20	0.80	2.40	4.00
☐ 263, Dec 73	0.20	0.80	2.40	4.00
☐ 264, Jan 74	0.20	0.80	2.40	4.00
☐ 265, Feb 74	0.20	0.80	2.40	4.00
☐ 266, Mar 74	0.20	0.80	2.40	4.00
☐ 267, Apr 74	0.20	0.80	2.40	4.00
☐ 268, May 74	0.20	0.80	2.40	4.00
☐ 269, Jun 74	0.60	0.80	2.40	4.00
☐ 270, Jul 74		0.80	2.40	4.00
☐ 271, Aug 74	0.20	0.80	2.40	4.00
☐ 272, Sep 74	0.20	0.80	2.40	4.00
☐ 273		0.80	2.40	4.00
☐ 274		0.80	2.40	4.00
☐ 275, Dec 74	0.60	0.80	2.40	4.00
☐ 276, Jan 75		0.80	2.40	4.00
☐ 277, Feb 75	0.25	0.80	2.40	4.00
☐ 278, Mar 75	0.25	0.80	2.40	4.00
☐ 279, Apr 75	0.25	0.80	2.40	4.00
☐ 280, May 75	0.25	0.80	2.40	4.00
☐ 281, Jun 75	0.25	0.80	2.40	4.00
☐ 282, Jul 75	0.25	0.80	2.40	4.00
☐ 283, Aug 75	0.25	0.80	2.40	4.00
☐ 284, Sep 75	0.25	0.80	2.40	4.00
☐ 285, Oct 75	0.25	0.80	2.40	4.00
☐ 286		0.80	2.40	4.00
☐ 287		0.80	2.40	4.00
☐ 288		0.80	2.40	4.00
☐ 289		0.80	2.40	4.00
☐ 290		0.80	2.40	4.00
☐ 291		0.80	2.40	4.00
☐ 292		0.80	2.40	4.00

	ORIG.	GOOD	FINE	N-MINT
☐ 293		0.80	2.40	4.00
☐ 294		0.80	2.40	4.00
☐ 295		0.80	2.40	4.00
☐ 296		0.80	2.40	4.00
☐ 297		0.80	2.40	4.00
☐ 298		0.80	2.40	4.00
☐ 299		0.80	2.40	4.00
☐ 300		0.80	2.40	4.00
☐ 301		0.80	2.40	4.00

OUR FIGHTING FORCES

	ORIG.	GOOD	FINE	N-MINT
☐ 1		140.00	420.00	700.00
☐ 2		172.00	516.00	860.00
☐ 3		60.00	180.00	300.00
☐ 4		50.00	150.00	250.00
☐ 5		45.00	135.00	225.00
☐ 6		33.00	99.00	165.00
☐ 7		33.00	99.00	165.00
☐ 8		33.00	99.00	165.00
☐ 9		33.00	99.00	165.00
☐ 10		33.00	99.00	165.00
☐ 11		20.00	60.00	100.00
☐ 12		20.00	60.00	100.00
☐ 13		20.00	60.00	100.00
☐ 14		20.00	60.00	100.00
☐ 15		20.00	60.00	100.00
☐ 16		20.00	60.00	100.00
☐ 17		20.00	60.00	100.00
☐ 18		20.00	60.00	100.00
☐ 19		20.00	60.00	100.00
☐ 20		16.00	48.00	80.00
☐ 21		16.00	48.00	80.00
☐ 22		16.00	48.00	80.00
☐ 23		16.00	48.00	80.00
☐ 24		16.00	48.00	80.00
☐ 25		16.00	48.00	80.00
☐ 26		12.00	36.00	60.00
☐ 27		12.00	36.00	60.00
☐ 28		12.00	36.00	60.00
☐ 29		12.00	36.00	60.00
☐ 30		12.00	36.00	60.00
☐ 31		11.00	33.00	55.00
☐ 32		11.00	33.00	55.00
☐ 33		11.00	33.00	55.00
☐ 34		11.00	33.00	55.00
☐ 35		11.00	33.00	55.00
☐ 36		11.00	33.00	55.00
☐ 37		11.00	33.00	55.00
☐ 38		11.00	33.00	55.00
☐ 39		11.00	33.00	55.00
☐ 40		11.00	33.00	55.00
☐ 41		16.00	48.00	80.00
☐ 42		11.00	33.00	55.00
☐ 43		11.00	33.00	55.00
☐ 44		11.00	33.00	55.00
☐ 45		48.00	144.00	240.00
☐ 46		24.00	72.00	120.00
☐ 47		13.00	39.00	65.00
☐ 48		13.00	39.00	65.00
☐ 49		13.00	39.00	65.00
☐ 50		13.00	39.00	65.00
☐ 51		7.20	21.60	36.00
☐ 52		7.20	21.60	36.00
☐ 53		7.20	21.60	36.00
☐ 54		7.20	21.60	36.00
☐ 55		6.00	18.00	30.00
☐ 56		6.00	18.00	30.00
☐ 57		6.00	18.00	30.00
☐ 58		6.00	18.00	30.00
☐ 59		6.00	18.00	30.00
☐ 60		6.00	18.00	30.00
☐ 61		4.80	14.40	24.00

	ORIG.	GOOD	FINE	N-MINT
❑ 62		4.80	14.40	24.00
❑ 63		4.80	14.40	24.00
❑ 64		4.00	12.00	20.00
❑ 65		4.00	12.00	20.00
❑ 66		4.00	12.00	20.00
❑ 67		2.00	6.00	10.00
❑ 68		2.00	6.00	10.00
❑ 69		2.00	6.00	10.00
❑ 70		2.00	6.00	10.00
❑ 71		2.00	6.00	10.00
❑ 72		2.00	6.00	10.00
❑ 73		2.00	6.00	10.00
❑ 74		2.00	6.00	10.00
❑ 75		2.00	6.00	10.00
❑ 76		1.60	4.80	8.00
❑ 77		1.60	4.80	8.00
❑ 78, Aug 63	0.12	1.60	4.80	8.00
❑ 79		1.60	4.80	8.00
❑ 80		1.60	4.80	8.00
❑ 81		1.60	4.80	8.00
❑ 82		1.60	4.80	8.00
❑ 83		1.60	4.80	8.00
❑ 84, May 64	0.12	1.60	4.80	8.00
❑ 85		1.60	4.80	8.00
❑ 86		1.60	4.80	8.00
❑ 87		1.60	4.80	8.00
❑ 88		1.60	4.80	8.00
❑ 89		1.60	4.80	8.00
❑ 90		1.60	4.80	8.00
❑ 91		1.60	4.80	8.00
❑ 92		1.60	4.80	8.00
❑ 93		1.60	4.80	8.00
❑ 94		1.60	4.80	8.00
❑ 95		1.60	4.80	8.00
❑ 96		1.60	4.80	8.00
❑ 97		1.60	4.80	8.00
❑ 98		1.60	4.80	8.00
❑ 99		1.60	4.80	8.00
❑ 100		1.60	4.80	8.00
❑ 101		1.00	3.00	5.00
❑ 102		1.00	3.00	5.00
❑ 103		1.00	3.00	5.00
❑ 104		1.00	3.00	5.00
❑ 105		1.00	3.00	5.00
❑ 106		1.00	3.00	5.00
❑ 107		1.00	3.00	5.00
❑ 108		1.00	3.00	5.00
❑ 109		1.00	3.00	5.00
❑ 110		1.00	3.00	5.00
❑ 111		1.00	3.00	5.00
❑ 112		1.00	3.00	5.00
❑ 113		1.00	3.00	5.00
❑ 114, Aug 68	0.12	1.00	3.00	5.00
❑ 115		1.00	3.00	5.00
❑ 116		1.00	3.00	5.00
❑ 117		1.00	3.00	5.00
❑ 118		1.00	3.00	5.00
❑ 119		1.00	3.00	5.00
❑ 120		1.00	3.00	5.00
❑ 121		1.00	3.00	5.00
❑ 122		0.80	2.40	4.00
❑ 123, Feb 70	0.15	0.80	2.40	4.00
❑ 124, Apr 70	0.15	0.80	2.40	4.00
❑ 125, Jun 70	0.15	0.80	2.40	4.00
❑ 126, Aug 70	0.15	0.80	2.40	4.00
❑ 127, Oct 70	0.15	0.80	2.40	4.00
❑ 128, Dec 70	0.15	0.80	2.40	4.00
❑ 129, Feb 71	0.15	0.80	2.40	4.00
❑ 130, Apr 71	0.15	0.80	2.40	4.00
❑ 131, Jun 71	0.15	0.80	2.40	4.00
❑ 132, Aug 71	0.15	0.80	2.40	4.00
❑ 133, Oct 71	0.25	0.80	2.40	4.00

	ORIG.	GOOD	FINE	N-MINT
❑ 134, Dec 71	0.25	0.80	2.40	4.00
❑ 135, Feb 72	0.25	0.80	2.40	4.00
❑ 136, Apr 72	0.25	0.80	2.40	4.00
❑ 137, Jun 72	0.25	0.80	2.40	4.00
❑ 138, Aug 72	0.20	0.80	2.40	4.00
❑ 139, Oct 72	0.20	0.80	2.40	4.00
❑ 140, Dec 72	0.20	0.80	2.40	4.00
❑ 141, Feb 73	0.20	0.80	2.40	4.00
❑ 142, Apr 73	0.20	0.80	2.40	4.00
❑ 143, Jul 73	0.20	0.80	2.40	4.00
❑ 144, Sep 73	0.20	0.80	2.40	4.00
❑ 145, Nov 73	0.20	0.80	2.40	4.00
❑ 146, Jan 74	0.20	0.80	2.40	4.00
❑ 147, Mar 74	0.20	0.80	2.40	4.00
❑ 148, May 74	0.20	0.80	2.40	4.00
❑ 149, Jul 74	0.20	0.80	2.40	4.00
❑ 150, Sep 74	0.20	0.80	2.40	4.00
❑ 151		0.60	1.80	3.00
❑ 152		0.60	1.80	3.00
❑ 153		0.60	1.80	3.00
❑ 154		0.60	1.80	3.00
❑ 155		0.60	1.80	3.00
❑ 156		0.60	1.80	3.00
❑ 157		0.60	1.80	3.00
❑ 158		0.60	1.80	3.00
❑ 159, Sep 75, JK;Losers	0.25	0.60	1.80	3.00
❑ 160, Oct 75, JK;Losers	0.25	0.60	1.80	3.00
❑ 161, Nov 75	0.25	0.60	1.80	3.00
❑ 162, Dec 75, JK;Losers	0.25	0.60	1.80	3.00
❑ 163		0.60	1.80	3.00
❑ 164		0.60	1.80	3.00
❑ 165		0.60	1.80	3.00
❑ 166		0.60	1.80	3.00
❑ 167		0.60	1.80	3.00
❑ 168		0.60	1.80	3.00
❑ 169		0.60	1.80	3.00
❑ 170		0.60	1.80	3.00
❑ 171		0.60	1.80	3.00
❑ 172		0.60	1.80	3.00
❑ 173		0.60	1.80	3.00
❑ 174		0.60	1.80	3.00
❑ 175		0.60	1.80	3.00
❑ 176		0.60	1.80	3.00
❑ 177		0.60	1.80	3.00
❑ 178		0.60	1.80	3.00
❑ 179		0.60	1.80	3.00
❑ 180		0.60	1.80	3.00
❑ 181		0.60	1.80	3.00

OUR LOVE STORY
MARVEL

	ORIG.	GOOD	FINE	N-MINT
❑ 1	0.15	2.00	6.00	10.00
❑ 2	0.15	1.00	3.00	5.00
❑ 3	0.15	1.00	3.00	5.00
❑ 4	0.15	1.00	3.00	5.00
❑ 5, Steranko	0.15	4.00	12.00	20.00
❑ 6	0.15	1.00	3.00	5.00
❑ 7	0.15	1.00	3.00	5.00
❑ 8	0.15	1.00	3.00	5.00
❑ 9	0.15	1.00	3.00	5.00
❑ 10	0.15	1.00	3.00	5.00
❑ 11	0.15	0.60	1.80	3.00
❑ 12	0.15	0.60	1.80	3.00
❑ 13	0.15	0.60	1.80	3.00
❑ 14	0.15	0.60	1.80	3.00
❑ 15	0.15	0.20	0.60	1.00
❑ 16	0.15	0.20	0.60	1.00
❑ 17	0.15	0.20	0.60	1.00
❑ 18	0.20	0.20	0.60	1.00
❑ 19	0.20	0.20	0.60	1.00
❑ 20	0.20	0.20	0.60	1.00
❑ 21	0.20	0.20	0.60	1.00

	ORIG.	GOOD	FINE	N-MINT
22	0.20	0.20	0.60	1.00
23	0.20	0.20	0.60	1.00
24	0.20	0.20	0.60	1.00
25	0.20	0.20	0.60	1.00
26	0.20	0.20	0.60	1.00
27	0.20	0.20	0.60	1.00
28	0.20	0.20	0.60	1.00
29	0.20	0.20	0.60	1.00
30	0.20	0.20	0.60	1.00
31	0.20	0.20	0.60	1.00
32	0.20	0.20	0.60	1.00
33	0.20	0.20	0.60	1.00
34	0.20	0.20	0.60	1.00
35	0.20	0.20	0.60	1.00
36	0.20	0.20	0.60	1.00
37	0.20	0.20	0.60	1.00
38	0.20	0.20	0.60	1.00

OUT OF THE VORTEX
DARK HORSE

	ORIG.	GOOD	FINE	N-MINT
1	2.00	0.40	1.20	2.00
2	2.00	0.40	1.20	2.00
3, Dec 93	2.00	0.40	1.20	2.00
4, Jan 94	2.00	0.40	1.20	2.00
5, Feb 94	2.00	0.40	1.20	2.00
6, Mar 94	2.00	0.40	1.20	2.00
7, Apr 94	2.00	0.40	1.20	2.00
8, May 94	2.00	0.40	1.20	2.00
9, 94	2.00	0.40	1.20	2.00
10, Jul 94	2.00	0.40	1.20	2.00
11, Sep 94	2.50	0.50	1.50	2.50
12, Oct 94, final issue	2.50	0.50	1.50	2.50

OUT OF THIS WORLD
ETERNITY

	GOOD	FINE	N-MINT
1, b&w reprints	0.70	2.10	3.50

OUTBREED 999 (mini-series)
BLACKOUT

	ORIG.	GOOD	FINE	N-MINT
1, May 94	2.95	0.59	1.77	2.95
5, 94	2.95	0.59	1.77	2.95

OUTCAST, THE
ACCLAIM/VALIANT

	ORIG.	GOOD	FINE	N-MINT
1, Dec 95, one-shot	2.50	0.50	1.50	2.50

OUTCASTS
DC

	GOOD	FINE	N-MINT
1	0.35	1.05	1.75
2	0.35	1.05	1.75
3	0.35	1.05	1.75
4	0.35	1.05	1.75
5	0.35	1.05	1.75
6	0.35	1.05	1.75
7	0.35	1.05	1.75
8	0.35	1.05	1.75
9	0.35	1.05	1.75
10	0.35	1.05	1.75
11	0.35	1.05	1.75
12	0.35	1.05	1.75

OUTER EDGE
INNOVATION

	GOOD	FINE	N-MINT
1, b&w	0.50	1.50	2.50

OUTLANDER
MALIBU

	GOOD	FINE	N-MINT
1	0.39	1.17	1.95
2	0.39	1.17	1.95
3	0.39	1.17	1.95
4, (becomes Eternity title)	0.39	1.17	1.95

OUTLANDER (was Malibu title)
ETERNITY

	GOOD	FINE	N-MINT
5	0.39	1.17	1.95
6	0.39	1.17	1.95
7	0.39	1.17	1.95

OUTLANDERS
DARK HORSE

	ORIG.	GOOD	FINE	N-MINT
0		0.55	1.65	2.75
1, b&w manga		0.40	1.20	2.00
2, b&w manga		0.40	1.20	2.00
3, b&w manga		0.40	1.20	2.00
4, b&w manga		0.40	1.20	2.00
5, b&w manga		0.40	1.20	2.00
6, b&w manga		0.40	1.20	2.00
7, b&w manga		0.40	1.20	2.00
8		0.45	1.35	2.25
9		0.45	1.35	2.25
10		0.45	1.35	2.25
11		0.45	1.35	2.25
12		0.45	1.35	2.25
13		0.45	1.35	2.25
14		0.45	1.35	2.25
15		0.45	1.35	2.25
16		0.45	1.35	2.25
17		0.45	1.35	2.25
18		0.45	1.35	2.25
19		0.45	1.35	2.25
20		0.45	1.35	2.25
21		0.45	1.35	2.25
22		0.50	1.50	2.50
23		0.50	1.50	2.50
24		0.50	1.50	2.50
25, trading cards		0.50	1.50	2.50
26, trading cards		0.50	1.50	2.50
27, trading cards		0.59	1.77	2.95
28, trading cards		0.50	1.50	2.50
29, trading cards		0.50	1.50	2.50
30		0.50	1.50	2.50
31		0.50	1.50	2.50
32		0.50	1.50	2.50
33		0.50	1.50	2.50

OUTLANDERS EPILOGUE

	ORIG.	GOOD	FINE	N-MINT
0, Mar 94, nn, b&w	2.50	0.50	1.50	2.50

OUTLANDERS SPECIAL

	ORIG.	GOOD	FINE	N-MINT
1, b&w, manga	2.50	0.50	1.50	2.50

OUTLAWS (mini-series)
DC

	GOOD	FINE	N-MINT
1	0.39	1.17	1.95
2	0.39	1.17	1.95
3	0.39	1.17	1.95
4	0.39	1.17	1.95
5	0.39	1.17	1.95
6	0.39	1.17	1.95
7	0.39	1.17	1.95
8	0.39	1.17	1.95

OUTPOSTS
BLACKTHORNE

	GOOD	FINE	N-MINT
1	0.25	0.75	1.25

OUTSIDERS
DC

	ORIG.	GOOD	FINE	N-MINT
1, Nov 85	1.25	0.30	0.90	1.50
2, Dec 85	1.50	0.30	0.90	1.50
3, Jan 86	1.50	0.30	0.90	1.50
4, Feb 86	1.50	0.30	0.90	1.50
5, Mar 86	1.50	0.30	0.90	1.50
6, Apr 86	1.50	0.30	0.90	1.50
7, May 86	1.50	0.30	0.90	1.50
8, Jun 86	1.50	0.30	0.90	1.50
9, Jul 86	1.50	0.30	0.90	1.50
10, Aug 86	1.50	0.30	0.90	1.50
11, Sep 86	1.50	0.30	0.90	1.50
12, Oct 86	1.50	0.30	0.90	1.50
13, Nov 86	1.50	0.30	0.90	1.50
14, Dec 86	1.50	0.30	0.90	1.50
15, Jan 87	1.50	0.30	0.90	1.50

	ORIG.	GOOD	FINE	N-MINT
❏ 16, Feb 87 .... 1.50		0.30	0.90	1.50
❏ 17, Mar 87, Batman returns				
.... 1.50		0.30	0.90	1.50
❏ 18, Apr 87 .... 1.50		0.30	0.90	1.50
❏ 19, May 87 .... 1.50		0.30	0.90	1.50
❏ 20, Jun 87 .... 1.50		0.30	0.90	1.50
❏ 21, Jul 87 .... 1.50		0.30	0.90	1.50
❏ 22, Aug 87, EC parody ... 1.50		0.30	0.90	1.50
❏ 23, Sep 87 .... 1.50		0.30	0.90	1.50
❏ 24, Oct 87 .... 1.50		0.30	0.90	1.50
❏ 25, Nov 87 .... 1.50		0.30	0.90	1.50
❏ 26, Dec 87 .... 1.50		0.30	0.90	1.50
❏ 27, Jan 88, Millennium .. 1.50		0.30	0.90	1.50
❏ 28, Feb 88, Millennium .. 1.50		0.30	0.90	1.50

OUTSIDERS (1993-)

	ORIG.	GOOD	FINE	N-MINT
❏ 0, Oct 94 .... 1.95		0.39	1.17	1.95
❏ 1, -alpha 1.75		0.50	1.50	2.50
❏ 1, -omega 1.75		0.50	1.50	2.50
❏ 2 .... 1.75		0.35	1.05	1.75
❏ 3 .... 1.75		0.35	1.05	1.75
❏ 4 .... 1.75		0.35	1.05	1.75
❏ 5 .... 1.75		0.35	1.05	1.75
❏ 6, Apr 94 .... 1.75		0.35	1.05	1.75
❏ 7, May 94 .... 1.75		0.35	1.05	1.75
❏ 8, Jun 94 .... 1.75		0.35	1.05	1.75
❏ 9, Jul 94 .... 1.75		0.35	1.05	1.75
❏ 10, Aug 94 .... 1.95		0.39	1.17	1.95
❏ 11, Sep 94 .... 1.95		0.39	1.17	1.95
❏ 12, Nov 94 .... 1.95		0.39	1.17	1.95
❏ 13, Dec 94 .... 1.95		0.39	1.17	1.95
❏ 14, Jan 95 .... 1.95		0.39	1.17	1.95
❏ 15, Feb 95 .... 1.95		0.39	1.17	1.95
❏ 16, Mar 95 .... 1.95		0.39	1.17	1.95
❏ 17, Apr 95 .... 1.95		0.39	1.17	1.95
❏ 18, May 95 .... 1.95		0.39	1.17	1.95
❏ 19, Jun 95 .... 2.25		0.45	1.35	2.25
❏ 20, Jul 95 .... 2.25		0.45	1.35	2.25
❏ 21, Aug 95 .... 2.25		0.45	1.35	2.25
❏ 22, Sep 95 .... 2.25		0.45	1.35	2.25
❏ 23, Oct 95 .... 2.25		0.45	1.35	2.25
❏ 24, Nov 95, final issue ... 2.25		0.45	1.35	2.25

OUTSIDERS ANNUAL

	ORIG.	GOOD	FINE	N-MINT
❏ 1, 86 .... 2.50		0.50	1.50	2.50

OUTSIDERS SPECIAL

	ORIG.	GOOD	FINE	N-MINT
❏ 1, 87, Infinity, Inc. 1.50		0.30	0.90	1.50

OVER THE EDGE
MARVEL

	ORIG.	GOOD	FINE	N-MINT
❏ 1, Nov 95, Daredevil 0.99		0.20	0.59	0.99
❏ 2, Dec 95, Dr. Strange.... 0.99		0.20	0.59	0.99
❏ 3, Jan 96, Hulk 0.99		0.20	0.59	0.99
❏ 4, Feb 96, Ghost Rider ... 0.99		0.20	0.59	0.99
❏ 5, Mar 96, Punisher 0.99		0.20	0.59	0.99

	ORIG.	GOOD	FINE	N-MINT
❏ 6, Apr 96, Daredevil and Black Panther				
.... 0.99		0.20	0.59	0.99
❏ 7, May 96, Dr. Strange .vs. Nightmare				
.... 0.99		0.20	0.59	0.99

OVERLOAD MAGAZINE
ECLIPSE

	ORIG.	GOOD	FINE	N-MINT
❏ 1, b&w		0.30	0.90	1.50

OVERTURE!
ALL AMERICAN

	ORIG.	GOOD	FINE	N-MINT
❏ 1, b&w		0.45	1.35	2.25
❏ 2, b&w		0.45	1.35	2.25

OWLHOOTS
KITCHEN SINK

	ORIG.	GOOD	FINE	N-MINT
❏ 1, two-color		0.50	1.50	2.50
❏ 2, two-color		0.50	1.50	2.50

OX COW O' WAR
SPOOF

	ORIG.	GOOD	FINE	N-MINT
❏ 1, b&w, parody		0.59	1.77	2.95

OZ
CALIBER

	ORIG.	GOOD	FINE	N-MINT
❏ 1, 94, b&w 2.95		0.80	2.40	4.00
❏ 2, b&w 2.95		0.59	1.77	2.95
❏ 3, b&w 2.95		0.59	1.77	2.95
❏ 4, b&w 2.95		0.59	1.77	2.95
❏ 5, b&w 2.95		0.59	1.77	2.95
❏ 6, b&w 2.95		0.59	1.77	2.95
❏ 7, b&w 2.95		0.59	1.77	2.95
❏ 8, b&w 2.95		0.59	1.77	2.95
❏ 9, b&w 2.95		0.59	1.77	2.95
❏ 10, b&w 2.95		0.59	1.77	2.95

OZ SPECIAL: LION

	ORIG.	GOOD	FINE	N-MINT
❏ 1, 95, b&w;continues in *Oz Special: Tin Man*				
.... 2.95		0.59	1.77	2.95

OZ SPECIAL: SCARECROW

	ORIG.	GOOD	FINE	N-MINT
❏ 1, 95, b&w;continues in *Oz Special: Lion*				
.... 2.95		0.59	1.77	2.95

OZ SQUAD
BRAVE NEW WORDS

	ORIG.	GOOD	FINE	N-MINT
❏ 1, Oct 91, b&w 2.50		0.50	1.50	2.50
❏ 2, b&w		0.50	1.50	2.50
❏ 3, b&w		0.50	1.50	2.50

OZ-WONDERLAND WAR
DC

	ORIG.	GOOD	FINE	N-MINT
❏ 1, Jan 86		0.40	1.20	2.00
❏ 2, Feb 86		0.40	1.20	2.00
❏ 3, Mar 86		0.40	1.20	2.00

OZZY OSBOURNE
ROCK-IT COMICS

	ORIG.	GOOD	FINE	N-MINT
❏ 1 .... 4.95		0.99	2.97	4.95

Flashback: 25 years ago

The following Silver Age comic books were advertised for sale by Terry Stroud in the first issue of *The Buyer's Guide*, March 1971:

The Avengers #1 — $4
Daredevil #1 — $2.50
Fantastic Four #1 — $24
Amazing Fantasy #15 — $12

The Amazing Spider-Man #1 — $10.50
The X-Men #1 — $3.50
The Atom #1 — 50¢
The Flash #105 — $4
Green Lantern #1 — $3
Hawkman #1 — 50¢
Justice League of America #1 — $3.50

— Greg W. Myers

P

	ORIG.	GOOD	FINE	N-MINT
P.A.C.				
ARTIFACTS INC.				
❑ 1 ....1.95	0.39	1.17	1.95
P.I.'S, THE				
FIRST				
❑ 1, Jan 85, JSa, Ms. Tree, E-Man				
..............................1.25	0.30	0.90	1.50
❑ 2, Mar 85, JSa...............1.25	0.25	0.75	1.25
❑ 3, May 85, JSa..............1.25	0.25	0.75	1.25
P.J. WARLOCK				
ECLIPSE				
❑ 1, b&w	0.40	1.20	2.00
❑ 2, b&w	0.40	1.20	2.00
❑ 3, b&w	0.40	1.20	2.00
PACIFIC PRESENTS				
PACIFIC				
❑ 1, Oct 82, DSt, Rocketeer; SD, Missing Man				
..............................1.00	0.80	2.40	4.00
❑ 2, Apr 83, DSt, Rocketeer; SD, Missing Man				
..............................1.00	0.80	2.40	4.00
❑ 3, Mar 84, SD, Missing Man				
..............................1.50	0.30	0.90	1.50
❑ 4, Jun 84 ....1.50	0.30	0.90	1.50
PACT, THE				
IMAGE				
❑ 1, 94.............................1.95	0.39	1.17	1.95
❑ 2, Apr 94 ....1.95	0.39	1.17	1.95
❑ 3, Jun 94 ....1.95	0.39	1.17	1.95
PAINTBALL UNIVERSE 2000				
SPLATTOONS				
❑ 1, 95...............................2.95	0.59	1.77	2.95
PAJAMA CHRONICLES				
BLACKTHORNE				
❑ 1	0.35	1.05	1.75
PAL-YAT-CHEE				
ADHESIVE				
❑ 1, b&w 2.50	0.50	1.50	2.50
PALESTINE				
FANTAGRAPHICS				
❑ 1, b&w 2.50	0.50	1.50	2.50
❑ 2, b&w 2.50	0.50	1.50	2.50
❑ 3, b&w 2.50	0.50	1.50	2.50
❑ 4, b&w 2.95	0.59	1.77	2.95
❑ 5 ....2.50	0.50	1.50	2.50
❑ 6				
❑ 7, Sep 94 ....2.95	0.59	1.77	2.95
PANDA KHAN SPECIAL				
ABACUS				
❑ 1, b&w	0.60	1.80	3.00
PANTERA				
MALIBU/ROCK-IT				
❑ 1, Aug 94 ....3.95	0.79	2.37	3.95
PANTHEON				
ARCHER BOOKS & GAMES				
❑ 1, Oct 95, b&w..............2.95	0.59	1.77	2.95
PAPER TALES				
CLG COMICS				
❑ 1, Sum 93, b&w.............2.50	0.50	1.50	2.50
❑ 2, Sum 94, b&w.............2.50	0.50	1.50	2.50
PARADAX				
VORTEX				
❑ 1	0.35	1.05	1.75
❑ 2	0.35	1.05	1.75
PARADIGM				
GAUNTLET				
❑ 1 ....2.95	0.59	1.77	2.95

	ORIG.	GOOD	FINE	N-MINT
PARAGON: DARK APOCALYPSE				
AC				
❑ 1 ....2.95	0.59	1.77	2.95
❑ 2 ....2.95	0.59	1.77	2.95
❑ 3 ....2.95	0.59	1.77	2.95
❑ 4 ....2.95	0.59	1.77	2.95
PARANOIA				
ADVENTURE				
❑ 1, color	0.59	1.77	2.95
❑ 2, color	0.59	1.77	2.95
❑ 3, color	0.59	1.77	2.95
❑ 4, color	0.59	1.77	2.95
❑ 5, color	0.59	1.77	2.95
❑ 6, color	0.59	1.77	2.95
PARDNERS				
COTTONWOOD GRAPHICS				
❑ 1, b&w, Stan Lynde	1.59	4.77	7.95
❑ 2, b&w, Stan Lynde	1.59	4.77	7.95
PARIS THE MAN OF PLASTER				
HARRIER				
❑ 1	0.39	1.17	1.95
❑ 2	0.39	1.17	1.95
❑ 3	0.39	1.17	1.95
❑ 4	0.39	1.17	1.95
❑ 5	0.39	1.17	1.95
❑ 6	0.39	1.17	1.95
PARO-DEE				
PARODY				
❑ 1, b&w............................2.50	0.50	1.50	2.50
PARTICLE DREAMS				
FANTAGRAPHICS				
❑ 1	0.45	1.35	2.25
❑ 2	0.45	1.35	2.25
❑ 3	0.45	1.35	2.25
❑ 4	0.45	1.35	2.25
❑ 5	0.45	1.35	2.25
❑ 6	0.45	1.35	2.25
PARTNERS IN PANDEMONIUM				
CALIBER				
❑ 1, b&w............................2.50	0.50	1.50	2.50
❑ 2, b&w............................2.50	0.50	1.50	2.50
❑ 3, b&w............................2.50	0.50	1.50	2.50
PARTS OF A HOLE				
❑ 0, nn b&w........................2.50	0.50	1.50	2.50
PARTS UNKNOWN				
ECLIPSE				
❑ 1, b&w............................	0.50	1.50	2.50
❑ 2, b&w............................	0.50	1.50	2.50
❑ 3, b&w............................	0.50	1.50	2.50
❑ 4, b&w............................	0.50	1.50	2.50
PARTS UNKNOWN II: THE NEXT INVASION				
❑ 1, Dec 93, b&w................2.95	0.59	1.77	2.95
PARTS UNKNOWN: DARK INTENTIONS				
KNIGHT PRESS				
❑ 0, Aug 95, b&w...............2.95	0.59	1.77	2.95
❑ 1, Mar 95, b&w...............2.95	0.59	1.77	2.95
❑ 2, Jun 95, b&w................2.95	0.59	1.77	2.95
❑ 3, Oct 95, b&w................2.95	0.59	1.77	2.95
PAT SAVAGE, WOMAN OF BRONZE: FAMILY BLOOD SPECIAL				
MILLENNIUM				
❑ 0, nn	0.50	1.50	2.50
PATHWAYS TO FANTASY				
PACIFIC				
❑ 1, BS...............................	0.30	0.90	1.50

	ORIG.	GOOD	FINE	N-MINT

PATRICK RABBIT
CARTOONISTS ACROSS AMERICA

	ORIG.	GOOD	FINE	N-MINT
❑ 7, b&w	2.00	0.40	1.20	2.00

FRAGMENTS WEST

		GOOD	FINE	N-MINT
❑ 1, b&w		0.40	1.20	2.00
❑ 2, b&w		0.40	1.20	2.00
❑ 3, b&w		0.40	1.20	2.00
❑ 4, b&w		0.40	1.20	2.00
❑ 5, b&w		0.40	1.20	2.00
❑ 6, b&w		0.40	1.20	2.00

PATRICK STEWART
CELEBRITY

		GOOD	FINE	N-MINT
❑ 1		0.59	1.77	2.95

PATRICK STEWART VS. WILLIAM SHATNER

		GOOD	FINE	N-MINT
❑ 1, b&w		1.19	3.57	5.95

PATTY CAKE
PERMANENT PRESS

	ORIG.	GOOD	FINE	N-MINT
❑ 1, 94	2.95	0.59	1.77	2.95
❑ 2, 94	2.95	0.59	1.77	2.95

PAUL THE SAMURAI
NEW ENGLAND

	ORIG.	GOOD	FINE	N-MINT
❑ 1, b&w	2.75	0.80	2.40	4.00
❑ 2, b&w	2.75	0.60	1.80	3.00
❑ 3, b&w	2.75	0.55	1.65	2.75
❑ 4, b&w	2.75	0.55	1.65	2.75
❑ 5, b&w	2.75	0.55	1.65	2.75
❑ 6, b&w	2.75	0.55	1.65	2.75

PAYNE
DREAM CATCHER PRESS

	ORIG.	GOOD	FINE	N-MINT
❑ 1, Sep 95, b&w	2.50	0.50	1.50	2.50

PEACEMAKER
DC

	ORIG.	GOOD	FINE	N-MINT
❑ 1, Jan 88	1.25	0.25	0.75	1.25
❑ 2, Feb 88	1.25	0.25	0.75	1.25
❑ 3, Mar 88	1.25	0.25	0.75	1.25
❑ 4, Apr 88	1.25	0.25	0.75	1.25

PEBBLES AND BAMM-BAMM
HARVEY

	ORIG.	GOOD	FINE	N-MINT
❑ 1	1.50	0.30	0.90	1.50
❑ 2	1.50	0.30	0.90	1.50
❑ 3	1.50	0.30	0.90	1.50

PEBBLES AND BAMM-BAMM SUMMER SPECIAL

	ORIG.	GOOD	FINE	N-MINT
❑ 1	2.25	0.45	1.35	2.25

PEDESTRIAN VULGARITY
FANTAGRAPHICS

		GOOD	FINE	N-MINT
❑ 1, b&w		0.50	1.50	2.50

PEEK-A-BOO 3-D
3-D ZONE

		GOOD	FINE	N-MINT
❑ 0, nn Bill Ward		0.79	2.37	3.95

PEEPSHOW
DRAWN & QUARTERLY

	ORIG.	GOOD	FINE	N-MINT
❑ 1, adult, b&w	2.50	0.50	1.50	2.50
❑ 2, adult, b&w	2.50	0.50	1.50	2.50
❑ 3, adult, b&w	2.50	0.50	1.50	2.50
❑ 4, adult, b&w	2.50	0.50	1.50	2.50
❑ 5, adult, b&w	2.95	0.59	1.77	2.95
❑ 6, Apr 94, adult, b&w	2.95	0.59	1.77	2.95

PELLESTAR
ETERNITY

		GOOD	FINE	N-MINT
❑ 1		0.39	1.17	1.95
❑ 2		0.39	1.17	1.95

PENDRAGON
AIRCEL

		GOOD	FINE	N-MINT
❑ 1, b&w		0.59	1.77	2.95
❑ 2, b&w		0.59	1.77	2.95

MARVEL

	ORIG.	GOOD	FINE	N-MINT
❑ 1, Iron Man	1.75	0.35	1.05	1.75
❑ 2	1.75	0.35	1.05	1.75
❑ 3	1.75	0.35	1.05	1.75
❑ 4, (becomes Knights of Pendragon)	1.75	0.35	1.05	1.75

PENDULUM
ADVENTURE

	ORIG.	GOOD	FINE	N-MINT
❑ 1, b&w	2.50	0.50	1.50	2.50
❑ 2, b&w	2.50	0.50	1.50	2.50
❑ 3, b&w	2.50	0.50	1.50	2.50
❑ 4, b&w	2.50	0.50	1.50	2.50

PENDULUM'S ILLUSTRATED STORIES
PENDULUM

		GOOD	FINE	N-MINT
❑ 1, Moby Dick		0.99	2.97	4.95
❑ 2, Treasure Island		0.99	2.97	4.95
❑ 3, Dr. Jekyll		0.99	2.97	4.95
❑ 4, 20,000 Leagues Under the Sea		0.99	2.97	4.95
❑ 5, Midsummer Night's Dream		0.99	2.97	4.95
❑ 6, Christmas Carol		0.99	2.97	4.95

PENGUIN & PENCILGUIN
FRAGMENTS WEST

		GOOD	FINE	N-MINT
❑ 1, b&w		0.40	1.20	2.00
❑ 2, b&w		0.40	1.20	2.00
❑ 3, b&w		0.40	1.20	2.00
❑ 4, b&w		0.40	1.20	2.00
❑ 5, b&w		0.40	1.20	2.00
❑ 6, b&w		0.40	1.20	2.00

PENTACLE: THE SIGN OF THE FIVE
ETERNITY

		GOOD	FINE	N-MINT
❑ 1, b&w		0.45	1.35	2.25
❑ 2, b&w		0.45	1.35	2.25
❑ 3, b&w		0.45	1.35	2.25
❑ 4, b&w		0.45	1.35	2.25

PENTHOUSE COMIX
PENTHOUSE INTERNATIONAL

	ORIG.	GOOD	FINE	N-MINT
❑ 1, Jun 94	4.95	3.80	11.40	19.00
❑ 1, 95, second printing	4.95	0.99	2.97	4.95
❑ 2	4.95	2.40	7.20	12.00
❑ 3	4.95	1.60	4.80	8.00
❑ 4	4.95	1.60	4.80	8.00
❑ 5	4.95	1.60	4.80	8.00
❑ 6, Apr 95	4.95	2.80	8.40	14.00
❑ 7, Jun 95	4.95	0.99	2.97	4.95
❑ 8, Aug 95, adult; magazine-sized comic book	4.95	0.99	2.97	4.95
❑ 9, Sep 95, adult; magazine-sized comic book	4.95	0.99	2.97	4.95
❑ 10, Nov 95, adult; magazine-sized comic book	4.95	0.99	2.97	4.95
❑ 11, Jan 96	4.95	0.99	2.97	4.95
❑ 12, Mar 96, second anniversary issue	4.95	0.99	2.97	4.95

PENTHOUSE MEN'S ADVENTURE COMIX

	ORIG.	GOOD	FINE	N-MINT
❑ 1, May 95, magazine	4.95	0.99	2.97	4.95
❑ 3, Sep 95, magazine	4.95	0.99	2.97	4.95
❑ 4, Nov 95, magazine	4.95	0.99	2.97	4.95
❑ 5, Dec 95, magazine	4.95	0.99	2.97	4.95
❑ 6, Feb 96, magazine	4.95	0.99	2.97	4.95
❑ 7, Apr 96, magazine	4.95	0.99	2.97	4.95

PEREGRINE, THE (mini-series)
ALLIANCE

	ORIG.	GOOD	FINE	N-MINT
❑ 1, b&w	2.50	0.50	1.50	2.50
❑ 2, b&w	2.50	0.50	1.50	2.50

PERG
LIGHTNING

	ORIG.	GOOD	FINE	N-MINT
❑ 1, Oct 93, A:Dreadwolf	3.50	0.80	2.40	4.00
❑ 1, Oct 93, glow cover	3.50	0.70	2.10	3.50
❑ 1, Oct 93, gold edition	3.50	0.70	2.10	3.50
❑ 2, Nov 93, A:Dreadwolf	2.95	0.59	1.77	2.95
❑ 2, Nov 93, platinum	2.95	0.59	1.77	2.95
❑ 3, Dec 93	2.95	0.59	1.77	2.95

	ORIG.	GOOD	FINE	N-MINT
❏ 4, Jan 94, O:Perg 2.95	0.59	1.77	2.95
❏ 4, Jan 94, platinum 2.95	0.59	1.77	2.95
❏ 5, Feb 94 .... 2.95	0.59	1.77	2.95
❏ 6, Mar 94 .... 2.95	0.59	1.77	2.95
❏ 7, Apr 94 .... 2.95	0.59	1.77	2.95
❏ 8, May 94 .... 2.95	0.59	1.77	2.95

PERRAMUS: ESCAPE FROM THE PAST
FANTAGRAPHICS

	GOOD	FINE	N-MINT
❏ 1, b&w	0.70	2.10	3.50
❏ 2, b&w	0.70	2.10	3.50
❏ 3, b&w	0.70	2.10	3.50
❏ 4, b&w	0.70	2.10	3.50

PERSONALITY CLASSICS
PERSONALITY

	GOOD	FINE	N-MINT
❏ 1, John Wayne, b&w........	0.59	1.77	2.95
❏ 2, b&w	0.59	1.77	2.95
❏ 3, b&w	0.59	1.77	2.95
❏ 4, b&w	0.59	1.77	2.95

PERSONALITY COMICS PRESENTS

	GOOD	FINE	N-MINT
❏ 1, b&w, Paulina Porizkova	0.50	1.50	2.50
❏ 2, Traci Lords...................	0.50	1.50	2.50
❏ 3, Schwarzenegger..........	0.50	1.50	2.50
❏ 4, Christina Applegate	0.50	1.50	2.50
❏ 5, Patrick Swayze, Demi Moore			
....	0.59	1.77	2.95
❏ 6, Michael Jordan	0.59	1.77	2.95
❏ 7, b&w	0.59	1.77	2.95
❏ 8, b&w	0.59	1.77	2.95
❏ 9, b&w	0.59	1.77	2.95
❏ 10, b&w	0.59	1.77	2.95
❏ 11, b&w	0.59	1.77	2.95
❏ 12, b&w	0.59	1.77	2.95
❏ 13, b&w	0.59	1.77	2.95
❏ 14, b&w	0.59	1.77	2.95
❏ 15, b&w	0.59	1.77	2.95
❏ 16, b&w	0.59	1.77	2.95
❏ 17, b&w	0.59	1.77	2.95
❏ 18, b&w	0.59	1.77	2.95

PEST
PEST COMICS

	ORIG.	GOOD	FINE	N-MINT
❏ 6, 95, b&w 1.85	0.37	1.11	1.85

PETER CANNON-THUNDERBOLT
DC

	ORIG.	GOOD	FINE	N-MINT
❏ 1, Sep 92 .... 1.25	0.25	0.75	1.25
❏ 2, Oct 92 .... 1.25	0.25	0.75	1.25
❏ 3, Nov 92 .... 1.25	0.25	0.75	1.25
❏ 4, Dec 92 .... 1.25	0.25	0.75	1.25
❏ 5, Jan 93 .... 1.25	0.25	0.75	1.25
❏ 6, Feb 93 .... 1.25	0.25	0.75	1.25
❏ 7, Mar 93 .... 1.25	0.25	0.75	1.25
❏ 8, Apr 93 .... 1.25	0.25	0.75	1.25
❏ 9, May 93, JLA................ 1.50	0.30	0.90	1.50
❏ 10, May 93, JLA............. 1.50	0.30	0.90	1.50
❏ 11, Jul 93 .... 1.50	0.30	0.90	1.50
❏ 12, final issue................. 1.50	0.30	0.90	1.50

PETER KOCK
EROS

	ORIG.	GOOD	FINE	N-MINT
❏ 1, adult, b&w 3.50	0.70	2.10	3.50
❏ 2, adult, b&w 2.75	0.55	1.65	2.75
❏ 3, adult, b&w 2.75	0.55	1.65	2.75
❏ 4, May 94, adult, b&w.... 2.75	0.55	1.65	2.75
❏ 5, Jul 94, adult, b&w.... 2.75	0.55	1.65	2.75
❏ 6, Aug 94, adult, b&w 2.75	0.55	1.65	2.75

PETER PAN
DISNEY

		GOOD	FINE	N-MINT
❏ 1, squarebound................		1.19	3.57	5.95

PETER PAN: RETURN TO NEVER-NEVER LAND
ADVENTURE

	GOOD	FINE	N-MINT
❏ 1, color............................	0.50	1.50	2.50
❏ 2, color............................	0.50	1.50	2.50

PETER PARKER THE SPECTACULAR SPIDER-MAN
(was Spectacular Spider-Man)
MARVEL

	ORIG.	GOOD	FINE	N-MINT
❏ 48, Prowler....................0.50	0.80	2.40	4.00
❏ 49, Dec 80, Prowler........0.50	0.80	2.40	4.00
❏ 50, Jan 81, JR2/JM, Smuggler			
............................0.50	0.80	2.40	4.00
❏ 51, Feb 81, FM(c) 0.50	0.80	2.40	4.00
❏ 52, Mar 81, FM(c)...........0.50	0.80	2.40	4.00
❏ 53, Apr 81, JM/FS, Tinker			
............................0.50	0.80	2.40	4.00
❏ 54, May 81 ....0.50	0.80	2.40	4.00
❏ 55, Jun 81 ....0.50	0.80	2.40	4.00
❏ 56, Jul 81........................0.50	0.80	2.40	4.00
❏ 57, Aug 81 ....0.50	0.80	2.40	4.00
❏ 58, Sep 81, JBy 0.50	1.20	3.60	6.00
❏ 59, Oct 81, JM 0.50	0.80	2.40	4.00
❏ 60, Nov 81, JM/FM(c) O:retold			
............................0.75	1.20	3.60	6.00
❏ 61, Dec 81 ....0.50	0.60	1.80	3.00
❏ 62, Jan 82.......................0.60	0.60	1.80	3.00
❏ 63, Feb 82.......................0.60	0.60	1.80	3.00
❏ 64, Mar 82, I: Cloak & Dagger			
............................0.60	2.80	8.40	14.00
❏ 65, Apr 82.......................0.60	0.60	1.80	3.00
❏ 66, May 82......................0.60	0.60	1.80	3.00
❏ 67, Jun 82.......................0.60	0.60	1.80	3.00
❏ 68, Jul 82........................0.60	0.60	1.80	3.00
❏ 69, Aug 82, Cloak & Dagger			
............................0.60	1.40	4.20	7.00
❏ 70, Sep 82......................0.60	1.40	4.20	7.00
❏ 71, Oct 82.......................0.60	0.50	1.50	2.50
❏ 72, Nov 82......................0.60	0.50	1.50	2.50
❏ 73, Dec 82......................0.60	0.50	1.50	2.50
❏ 74, Jan 83.......................0.60	0.50	1.50	2.50
❏ 75, Feb 83.......................1.00	0.50	1.50	2.50
❏ 76, Mar 83......................0.60	0.50	1.50	2.50
❏ 77, Apr 83.......................0.60	0.50	1.50	2.50
❏ 78, May 83......................0.60	0.50	1.50	2.50
❏ 79, Jun 83 ....0.60	0.50	1.50	2.50
❏ 80, Jul 83........................0.60	0.50	1.50	2.50
❏ 81, Aug 83, Punisher......0.60	3.00	9.00	15.00
❏ 82, Sep 83, Punisher......0.60	3.00	9.00	15.00
❏ 83, Oct 83, Punisher.......0.60	3.00	9.00	15.00
❏ 84, Nov 83......................0.60	0.60	1.80	3.00
❏ 85, Dec 83......................0.60	0.60	1.80	3.00
❏ 86, Jan 84.......................0.60	0.60	1.80	3.00
❏ 87, Feb 84.......................0.60	0.60	1.80	3.00
❏ 88, Mar 84......................0.60	0.60	1.80	3.00
❏ 89, Apr 84.......................0.60	0.60	1.80	3.00
❏ 90, May 84, AM, new costume			
............................0.60	0.50	1.50	2.50
❏ 91, Jun 84 ....0.60	0.50	1.50	2.50
❏ 92, Jul 84........................0.60	0.50	1.50	2.50
❏ 93, Aug 84......................0.60	0.50	1.50	2.50
❏ 94, Sep 84......................0.60	0.50	1.50	2.50
❏ 95, Oct 84.......................0.60	0.50	1.50	2.50
❏ 96, Nov 84......................0.60	0.50	1.50	2.50
❏ 97, Dec 84......................0.60	0.50	1.50	2.50
❏ 98, Jan 85.......................0.60	0.50	1.50	2.50
❏ 99, Feb 85.......................0.60	0.50	1.50	2.50
❏ 100, Mar 85....................1.00	1.00	3.00	5.00
❏ 101, Apr 85.....................0.65	0.50	1.50	2.50
❏ 102, May 85....................0.65	0.50	1.50	2.50
❏ 103, Jun 85 ....0.65	0.50	1.50	2.50
❏ 104, Jul 85......................0.65	0.50	1.50	2.50
❏ 105, Aug 85 ....0.65	0.50	1.50	2.50
❏ 106, Sep 85 ....0.65	0.50	1.50	2.50
❏ 107, Oct 85, D:Jean DeWolff			
............................0.65	0.80	2.40	4.00
❏ 108, Nov 85 ....0.65	0.50	1.50	2.50
❏ 109, Dec 85 ....0.65	0.50	1.50	2.50

	ORIG.	GOOD	FINE	N-MINT
☐ 110, Jan 86	0.65	0.50	1.50	2.50
☐ 111, Feb 86, Secret Wars II				
	0.75	0.50	1.50	2.50
☐ 112, Mar 86	0.75	0.50	1.50	2.50
☐ 113, Apr 86	0.75	0.50	1.50	2.50
☐ 114, May 86	0.75	0.50	1.50	2.50
☐ 115, Jun 86	0.75	0.50	1.50	2.50
☐ 116, Jul 86, Sabretooth	0.75	2.00	6.00	10.00
☐ 117, Aug 86	0.75	0.50	1.50	2.50
☐ 118, Sep 86	0.75	0.50	1.50	2.50
☐ 119, Oct 86, Sabretooth	0.75	1.20	3.60	6.00
☐ 120, Nov 86	0.75	0.50	1.50	2.50
☐ 121, Dec 86	0.75	0.50	1.50	2.50
☐ 122, Jan 87	0.75	0.50	1.50	2.50
☐ 123, Feb 87	0.75	0.50	1.50	2.50
☐ 124, Mar 87	0.75	0.50	1.50	2.50
☐ 125, Apr 87	0.75	0.50	1.50	2.50
☐ 126, May 87	0.75	0.50	1.50	2.50
☐ 127, Jun 87	0.75	0.50	1.50	2.50
☐ 128, Jul 87	0.75	0.50	1.50	2.50
☐ 129, Aug 87	0.75	0.50	1.50	2.50
☐ 130, Sep 87	0.75	0.50	1.50	2.50
☐ 131, Oct 87, Kraven	0.75	1.80	5.40	9.00
☐ 132, Nov 87, Kraven	0.75	1.80	5.40	9.00
☐ 133, Dec 87	0.75	1.80	5.40	9.00
☐ 134, Jan 88, (becomes *The Spectacular Spider-Man*)				
	0.75	1.80	5.40	9.00

PETER PARKER, THE SPECTACULAR SPIDER-MAN
ANNUAL

☐ 4, Nov 84	1.00	0.40	1.20	2.00
☐ 5, Oct 85	1.25	0.30	0.90	1.50
☐ 6, Oct 86, (becomes *The Spectacular Spider-Man Annual*)	1.25	0.30	0.90	1.50

PETER PORKER, THE SPECTACULAR SPIDER-HAM
STAR

☐ 1, May 85	0.65	0.20	0.60	1.00
☐ 2, Jul 85	0.65	0.20	0.60	1.00
☐ 3, Sep 85	0.65	0.20	0.60	1.00
☐ 4, Nov 85	0.65	0.20	0.60	1.00
☐ 5, Jan 86	0.65	0.20	0.60	1.00
☐ 6, Mar 86	0.65	0.20	0.60	1.00
☐ 7, May 86	0.75	0.15	0.45	0.75
☐ 8, Jul 86	0.75	0.15	0.45	0.75
☐ 9, Aug 86	0.75	0.15	0.45	0.75
☐ 10, Sep 86	0.75	0.15	0.45	0.75
☐ 11, Oct 86	0.75	0.15	0.45	0.75
☐ 12, Nov 86	0.75	0.15	0.45	0.75
☐ 13, Jan 87	0.75	0.15	0.45	0.75
☐ 14, Mar 87	0.75	0.15	0.45	0.75
☐ 15, May 87	0.75	0.15	0.45	0.75
☐ 16, Jul 87	1.00	0.20	0.60	1.00
☐ 17, Sep 87	1.00	0.20	0.60	1.00

PETER RABBIT
ETERNITY

☐ 0, pb strip reprints		1.99	5.97	9.95

PETWORKS VS. WILDK.A.T.S
PARODY PRESS

☐ 1	2.50	0.50	1.50	2.50

PHAEDRA
EXPRESS/ENTITY

☐ 0, Sep 94, nn,b&w, cardstock cover; third in series of Entity illustrated novellas with Zen Intergalactic Ninja				
	2.95	0.59	1.77	2.95

PHANTACEA: PHASE ONE
McPHERSON

☐ 1		0.30	0.90	1.50

PHANTASMAGORIA
TOME PRESS

☐ 1, b&w	2.50	0.59	1.77	2.95

	ORIG.	GOOD	FINE	N-MINT

PHANTASY AGAINST HUNGER
TIGER

☐ 1, AAd,JA,GC,JO,JR,BSz...	0.30	0.90	1.50	

PHANTOM 2040 (mini-series)
MARVEL

☐ 1, May 95	1.50	0.30	0.90	1.50
☐ 2, Jun 95	1.50	0.30	0.90	1.50
☐ 3, Jul 95, Poster	1.50	0.30	0.90	1.50
☐ 4, Aug 95, Poster	1.50	0.30	0.90	1.50

PHANTOM FORCE
IMAGE

☐ 1, JK,RL trading card	2.50	0.50	1.50	2.50
☐ 1, ashcan	2.50	5.00	15.00	25.00
☐ 2, Apr 94	3.50	0.70	2.10	3.50

PHANTOM OF FEAR CITY
CLAYPOOL

☐ 1, b&w	2.50	0.50	1.50	2.50
☐ 2, b&w	2.50	0.50	1.50	2.50
☐ 3, b&w	2.50	0.50	1.50	2.50
☐ 4, b&w	2.50	0.50	1.50	2.50
☐ 5, Nov 93	2.50	0.50	1.50	2.50
☐ 6, Jan 94	2.50	0.50	1.50	2.50
☐ 8, Jul 94	2.50	0.50	1.50	2.50
☐ 12, May 95, final issue	2.50	0.50	1.50	2.50

PHANTOM OF THE OPERA
ETERNITY

☐ 1, b&w		0.39	1.17	1.95

INNOVATION

☐ 1		1.39	4.17	6.95

PHANTOM STRANGER
DC

☐ 1, Jun 69	0.12	12.00	36.00	60.00
☐ 2, Aug 69	0.15	8.00	24.00	40.00
☐ 3, Oct 69	0.15	6.00	18.00	30.00
☐ 4, Dec 69, NA	0.15	6.00	18.00	30.00
☐ 5, Feb 70	0.15	6.00	18.00	30.00
☐ 6, Apr 70	0.15	4.80	14.40	24.00
☐ 7, Jun 70	0.15	4.80	14.40	24.00
☐ 8, Aug 70	0.15	4.80	14.40	24.00
☐ 9, Oct 70	0.15	4.80	14.40	24.00
☐ 10, Dec 70	0.15	4.80	14.40	24.00
☐ 11, Feb 71	0.15	3.00	9.00	15.00
☐ 12, Apr 71	0.15	3.00	9.00	15.00
☐ 13, Jun 71	0.15	3.00	9.00	15.00
☐ 14, Aug 71	0.15	3.00	9.00	15.00
☐ 15, Oct 71	0.25	3.00	9.00	15.00
☐ 16, Dec 71	0.25	2.00	6.00	10.00
☐ 17, Feb 72	0.25	2.00	6.00	10.00
☐ 18, Apr 72	0.25	2.00	6.00	10.00
☐ 19, Jun 72	0.25	2.00	6.00	10.00
☐ 20, Aug 72	0.20	2.00	6.00	10.00
☐ 21, Oct 72	0.20	2.00	6.00	10.00
☐ 22, Dec 72	0.20	2.00	6.00	10.00
☐ 23, Feb 73	0.20	2.00	6.00	10.00
☐ 24, Apr 73	0.20	2.00	6.00	10.00
☐ 25, Jul 73	0.20	2.00	6.00	10.00
☐ 26, Sep 73	0.20	2.00	6.00	10.00
☐ 27, Nov 73	0.20	2.00	6.00	10.00
☐ 28, Jan 74	0.20	2.00	6.00	10.00
☐ 29, Mar 74	0.20	2.00	6.00	10.00
☐ 30, May 74	0.20	2.00	6.00	10.00
☐ 31, Jul 74	0.20	2.00	6.00	10.00
☐ 32, Sep 74	0.20	2.00	6.00	10.00
☐ 33, Nov 74	0.20	1.00	3.00	5.00
☐ 34, Jan 75	0.20	1.60	4.80	8.00
☐ 35, Mar 75	0.25	1.60	4.80	8.00
☐ 36, May 75	0.25	1.60	4.80	8.00
☐ 37, Jul 75	0.25	1.60	4.80	8.00
☐ 38, Sep 75	0.25	1.60	4.80	8.00
☐ 39, Nov 75	0.25	1.00	3.00	5.00

	ORIG.	GOOD	FINE	N-MINT
40, Jan 76 ...... 0.25		1.00	3.00	5.00
41, Mar 76 ...... 0.25		1.00	3.00	5.00

PHANTOM STRANGER (mini-series)

	ORIG.	GOOD	FINE	N-MINT
1, Oct 87 ...... 0.75		0.20	0.60	1.00
2, Nov 87 ...... 0.75		0.20	0.60	1.00
3, Dec 87 ...... 0.75		0.20	0.60	1.00
4, Jan 88 ...... 0.75		0.20	0.60	1.00

PHANTOM ZONE

	ORIG.	GOOD	FINE	N-MINT
1, Jan 82, GD/TD 0.60		0.25	0.75	1.25
2, Feb 82, GC/TD 0.60		0.20	0.60	1.00
3, Mar 82, GC/TD 0.60		0.20	0.60	1.00
4, Apr 82, GC/TD 0.60		0.20	0.60	1.00

PHANTOM, THE

		GOOD	FINE	N-MINT
1 ...... 1.50		0.30	0.90	1.50
2 ...... 1.50		0.30	0.90	1.50
3 ...... 1.50		0.30	0.90	1.50
4 ...... 1.50		0.30	0.90	1.50

WOLF

		GOOD	FINE	N-MINT
0, limited edition subscribers' issue 3.50		0.70	2.10	3.50
1 ...... 2.50		0.50	1.50	2.50
2		0.40	1.20	2.00
3		0.40	1.20	2.00
4		0.60	1.80	3.00
5		0.60	1.80	3.00
6		0.45	1.35	2.25
7		0.39	1.17	1.95
8		0.39	1.17	1.95

PHANTOM, THE (mini-series)
DC

		GOOD	FINE	N-MINT
1, O:Phantom		0.25	0.75	1.25
2		0.25	0.75	1.25
3		0.25	0.75	1.25
4		0.25	0.75	1.25

PHANTOM: GHOST WHO WALKS, THE (mini-series)
MARVEL

		GOOD	FINE	N-MINT
1, Feb 95, cardstock cover 2.95		0.59	1.77	2.95
2, Mar 95, cardstock cover 2.95		0.59	1.77	2.95
3, Apr 95, cardstock cover 2.95		0.59	1.77	2.95

PHASE ONE
VICTORY

		GOOD	FINE	N-MINT
1		0.30	0.90	1.50
2		0.30	0.90	1.50
3		0.30	0.90	1.50
4		0.30	0.90	1.50
5		0.30	0.90	1.50

PHAZE
ECLIPSE

		GOOD	FINE	N-MINT
1, BSz(c)		0.45	1.35	2.25
2, PG(c)		0.45	1.35	2.25

PHIGMENTS
AMAZING

		GOOD	FINE	N-MINT
1, b&w (moves to Pied Piper)	0.39	1.17	1.95

PHIGMENTS (former Amazing Comics title)
PIED PIPER

		GOOD	FINE	N-MINT
2		0.39	1.17	1.95

PHILBERT DESANEX' DREAMS
RIP OFF

		GOOD	FINE	N-MINT
1, b&w 2.95		0.59	1.77	2.95

PHILISTINE, THE (mini-series)
ONE-SHOT

		GOOD	FINE	N-MINT
1, Sep 93, b&w 2.50		0.50	1.50	2.50
2, Apr 94, b&w 2.50		0.50	1.50	2.50
3, Sep 94, b&w 2.50		0.50	1.50	2.50

PHOBOS
FLASHPOINT/SAMSON

	ORIG.	GOOD	FINE	N-MINT
1, Sep 94 ...... 2.50		0.50	1.50	2.50

PHOENIX
ATLAS/SEABOARD

	ORIG.	GOOD	FINE	N-MINT
1, Jan 75, O:Phoenix 0.25		0.20	0.60	1.00
2, Mar 75 ...... 0.25		0.20	0.60	1.00
3, Jun 75 ...... 0.25		0.20	0.60	1.00
4, Oct 75 ...... 0.25		0.20	0.60	1.00

PHOENIX RESTAURANT
FANDOM HOUSE

		GOOD	FINE	N-MINT
1, b&w		0.70	2.10	3.50

PHOENIX RESURRECTION, THE: AFTERMATH
MALIBU/ULTRAVERSE

		GOOD	FINE	N-MINT
1, Jan 96, continues in *Foxfire #1* 3.95		0.79	2.37	3.95

PHOENIX RESURRECTION, THE: GENESIS

		GOOD	FINE	N-MINT
1, Dec 95, continues in *The Phoenix Resurrection: Revelations*;wraparound cover 3.95		0.79	2.37	3.95

PHOENIX RESURRECTION, THE: RED SHIFT

		GOOD	FINE	N-MINT
0, Mar 96, collects the seven flipbook chapters plus one new chapter 1.95		0.39	1.17	1.95
0, Dec 95, American Entertainment Edition;collects seven flipbook chapters;no cover price				

PHOENIX RESURRECTION, THE: REVELATIONS

		GOOD	FINE	N-MINT
1, Dec 95, continues in *The Phoenix Resurrection: Aftermath*;wraparound cover 3.95		0.79	2.37	3.95

PHOENIX: THE UNTOLD STORY
MARVEL

		GOOD	FINE	N-MINT
1, X-Men 2.00		2.40	7.20	12.00

PIECE OF STEAK, A
TOME PRESS

		GOOD	FINE	N-MINT
1, b&w 2.50		0.50	1.50	2.50

PIED PIPER OF HAMELIN

		GOOD	FINE	N-MINT
1, b&w 2.95		0.59	1.77	2.95

PIGEON-MAN, THE BIRD-BRAIN
FERRY TAIL STUDIO

		GOOD	FINE	N-MINT
1, b&w 2.50		0.50	1.50	2.50

PIGHEAD
WILLIAMSON

		GOOD	FINE	N-MINT
1, b&w 2.95		0.59	1.77	2.95

PINEAPPLE ARMY
VIZ

		GOOD	FINE	N-MINT
1, b&w, Japanese		0.35	1.05	1.75
2, b&w, Japanese		0.35	1.05	1.75
3, b&w, Japanese		0.35	1.05	1.75
4, b&w, Japanese		0.35	1.05	1.75
5, b&w, Japanese		0.35	1.05	1.75
6, b&w, Japanese		0.35	1.05	1.75
7, b&w, Japanese		0.35	1.05	1.75
8, b&w, Japanese		0.35	1.05	1.75
9, b&w, Japanese		0.35	1.05	1.75
10, b&w, Japanese		0.35	1.05	1.75

PINHEAD
EPIC

		GOOD	FINE	N-MINT
1, foil cover 2.95		0.59	1.77	2.95
2 ...... 2.50		0.50	1.50	2.50
3 ...... 2.50		0.50	1.50	2.50
4 ...... 2.50		0.50	1.50	2.50
5 ...... 2.50		0.50	1.50	2.50
6, May 94 ...... 2.50		0.50	1.50	2.50

PINHEAD VS. MARSHAL LAW: LAW IN HELL

		GOOD	FINE	N-MINT
1, foil cover 2.95		0.59	1.77	2.95
2, foil cover 2.95		0.59	1.77	2.95

	ORIG.	GOOD	FINE	N-MINT

PINK FLOYD
PERSONALITY
	ORIG.	GOOD	FINE	N-MINT
❏ 1, b&w		0.59	1.77	2.95
❏ 2, b&w		0.59	1.77	2.95

PINK FLOYD EXPERIENCE (mini-series)
REVOLUTIONARY
	ORIG.	GOOD	FINE	N-MINT
❏ 1, Jun 91, b&w	2.50	0.50	1.50	2.50
❏ 2, Aug 91, b&w	2.50	0.50	1.50	2.50
❏ 3, Oct 91, b&w	2.50	0.50	1.50	2.50
❏ 4, Dec 91, b&w	2.50	0.50	1.50	2.50
❏ 5, Feb 92, b&w	2.50	0.50	1.50	2.50

PINK PANTHER
HARVEY
	ORIG.	GOOD	FINE	N-MINT
❏ 1	1.50	0.30	0.90	1.50
❏ 2	1.50	0.30	0.90	1.50
❏ 3	1.50	0.30	0.90	1.50
❏ 4	1.50	0.30	0.90	1.50
❏ 5	1.50	0.30	0.90	1.50
❏ 6	1.50	0.30	0.90	1.50
❏ 7	1.50	0.30	0.90	1.50
❏ 8	1.50	0.30	0.90	1.50
❏ 9	1.50	0.30	0.90	1.50

PINK PANTHER SUPER SPECIAL
	ORIG.	GOOD	FINE	N-MINT
❏ 1	2.25	0.45	1.35	2.25

PINKY AND THE BRAIN
DC
	ORIG.	GOOD	FINE	N-MINT
❏ 1, Jul 96, based on animated series				
	1.75	0.35	1.05	1.75

PINKY AND THE BRAIN CHRISTMAS SPECIAL
	ORIG.	GOOD	FINE	N-MINT
❏ 1, Jan 96	1.50	0.30	0.90	1.50

PINOCCHIO AND THE EMPEROR OF THE NIGHT
MARVEL
	ORIG.	GOOD	FINE	N-MINT
❏ 1, movie	1.25	0.25	0.75	1.25

PIRANHA IS LOOSE!
SPECIAL STUDIO
	ORIG.	GOOD	FINE	N-MINT
❏ 1, b&w		0.55	1.65	2.75
❏ 2, b&w		0.55	1.65	2.75

PIRATE CORP$!
SLAVE LABOR
	ORIG.	GOOD	FINE	N-MINT
❏ 1, b&w		0.35	1.05	1.75
❏ 2, b&w		0.35	1.05	1.75
❏ 3		0.50	1.50	2.50
❏ 4		0.50	1.50	2.50

PIRATE CORP$! SPECIAL
	ORIG.	GOOD	FINE	N-MINT
❏ 1, b&w		0.39	1.17	1.95

PIRATE CORPS
ETERNITY
	ORIG.	GOOD	FINE	N-MINT
❏ 1		0.39	1.17	1.95
❏ 2		0.39	1.17	1.95
❏ 3		0.39	1.17	1.95
❏ 4		0.39	1.17	1.95

PIRATE QUEEN, THE
COMAX
	ORIG.	GOOD	FINE	N-MINT
❏ 1, b&w, adult		0.59	1.77	2.95

PIRATES OF DARK WATER
MARVEL
	ORIG.	GOOD	FINE	N-MINT
❏ 1	1.00	0.20	0.60	1.00
❏ 2	1.00	0.20	0.60	1.00
❏ 3	1.00	0.20	0.60	1.00
❏ 4	1.25	0.25	0.75	1.25
❏ 5	1.25	0.25	0.75	1.25
❏ 6	1.25	0.25	0.75	1.25
❏ 7	1.25	0.25	0.75	1.25
❏ 8	1.25	0.25	0.75	1.25
❏ 9	1.25	0.25	0.75	1.25

PISTOLERO
ETERNITY
	ORIG.	GOOD	FINE	N-MINT
❏ 0, one-shot, b&w		0.79	2.37	3.95

PITT
IMAGE
	ORIG.	GOOD	FINE	N-MINT
❏ 1	1.95	0.39	1.17	1.95
❏ 2	1.95	0.39	1.17	1.95
❏ 3	1.95	0.39	1.17	1.95
❏ 4, Apr 94	1.95	0.39	1.17	1.95
❏ 5, Jun 94	1.95	0.39	1.17	1.95
❏ 6, Sep 94	1.95	0.39	1.17	1.95
❏ 7, Dec 94, Dale Keown	1.95	0.39	1.17	1.95
❏ 8, Apr 94, Dale Keown	1.95	0.39	1.17	1.95

PITT, THE
MARVEL
	ORIG.	GOOD	FINE	N-MINT
❏ 1	3.25	0.65	1.95	3.25

PIXY JUNKET
VIZ
	ORIG.	GOOD	FINE	N-MINT
❏ 1, b&w	2.75	0.55	1.65	2.75
❏ 2, b&w	2.75	0.55	1.65	2.75
❏ 3, b&w	2.75	0.55	1.65	2.75
❏ 4, b&w	2.75	0.55	1.65	2.75
❏ 5, b&w	2.75	0.55	1.65	2.75
❏ 6, b&w	2.75	0.55	1.65	2.75

PLACES THAT ARE GONE
AEON
	ORIG.	GOOD	FINE	N-MINT
❏ 1, Jul 94	2.75	0.55	1.65	2.75
❏ 2, Aug 94	2.75	0.55	1.65	2.75

PLAGUE
TOME PRESS
	ORIG.	GOOD	FINE	N-MINT
❏ 1, b&w	2.95	0.59	1.77	2.95

PLAN 9 FROM OUTER SPACE
ETERNITY
	ORIG.	GOOD	FINE	N-MINT
❏ 0, screenplay, photos		0.39	1.17	1.95

PLAN 9 FROM OUTER SPACE: 30 YEARS LATER
	ORIG.	GOOD	FINE	N-MINT
❏ 1, b&w		0.50	1.50	2.50
❏ 2, b&w		0.50	1.50	2.50
❏ 3, b&w		0.50	1.50	2.50

PLANET 29
CALIBER
	ORIG.	GOOD	FINE	N-MINT
❏ 1, b&w	2.50	0.50	1.50	2.50
❏ 2, b&w	2.50	0.50	1.50	2.50

PLANET COMICS
BLACKTHORNE
	ORIG.	GOOD	FINE	N-MINT
❏ 1, Apr 88, DS(c)	2.00	1.00	3.00	5.00
❏ 2, Jun 88, Wm. Stout(c)				
	2.00	0.40	1.20	2.00
❏ 3, Aug 88, Wm. Stout(c)				
	2.00	0.40	1.20	2.00

PLANET OF GEEKS
STARHEAD
	ORIG.	GOOD	FINE	N-MINT
❏ 1, 94, adult;b&w	2.75	0.55	1.65	2.75

PLANET OF THE APES
ADVENTURE
	ORIG.	GOOD	FINE	N-MINT
❏ 1, extra cover in pink, yellow, or green				
		1.00	3.00	5.00
❏ 1, limited		2.40	7.20	12.00
❏ 1, 2nd printing		0.50	1.50	2.50
❏ 2		0.70	2.10	3.50
❏ 3		0.70	2.10	3.50
❏ 4		0.50	1.50	2.50
❏ 5		0.50	1.50	2.50
❏ 6		0.50	1.50	2.50
❏ 7		0.50	1.50	2.50
❏ 8, Christmas		0.50	1.50	2.50
❏ 9		0.50	1.50	2.50
❏ 10		0.50	1.50	2.50
❏ 11		0.50	1.50	2.50
❏ 12		0.50	1.50	2.50
❏ 13		0.50	1.50	2.50
❏ 14		0.50	1.50	2.50
❏ 15		0.50	1.50	2.50

	ORIG.	GOOD	FINE	N-MINT
☐ 16		0.50	1.50	2.50
☐ 17		0.50	1.50	2.50
☐ 18		0.50	1.50	2.50
☐ 19		0.50	1.50	2.50
☐ 20		0.50	1.50	2.50
☐ 21		0.50	1.50	2.50
☐ 22		0.50	1.50	2.50
☐ 23		0.50	1.50	2.50
☐ 24		0.50	1.50	2.50

MARVEL

	ORIG.	GOOD	FINE	N-MINT
☐ 1, Aug 74, b&w magazine;adapts first movie plus new story	1.00	1.00	3.00	5.00
☐ 2, Oct 74, b&w magazine;adapts first movie plus new story	1.00	0.60	1.80	3.00
☐ 3, Dec 74, b&w magazine;adapts first movie plus new stories	1.00	0.60	1.80	3.00
☐ 4, Jan 75, b&w magazine;adapts first movie plus new stories	1.00	0.60	1.80	3.00
☐ 5, Feb 75, b&w magazine;adapts first movie plus new stories	1.00	0.60	1.80	3.00
☐ 6, Mar 75, b&w magazine;concludes first movie adaptations plus new stories	1.00	0.60	1.80	3.00
☐ 7, Apr 75, b&w magazine;begins adaptation of "Beneath the Planet of..... the Apes"	1.00	0.60	1.80	3.00
☐ 8, May 75, b&w magazine;"Beneath the Planet of the Apes"	1.00	0.60	1.80	3.00
☐ 9, Jun 75, "Kingdom of the Apes";"Beneath the Planet of the Apes"	1.00	0.60	1.80	3.00
☐ 10, Jul 75, "Kingdom of the Apes";"Beneath the Planet of the Apes"	1.00	0.60	1.80	3.00
☐ 11, Aug 75, "Kingdom of the Apes";"Beneath the Planet of the Apes"	1.00	0.40	1.20	2.00
☐ 12, Sep 75, "Escape fromthe Planet of the Apes"	1.00	0.40	1.20	2.00
☐ 13, Aug 75, "Escape from the Planet of the Apes"	1.00	0.40	1.20	2.00
☐ 14, Nov 75, "Escape from the Planet of the Apes"	0.75	0.40	1.20	2.00
☐ 15, Dec 75, "Escape from the Planet of the Apes"	0.75	0.40	1.20	2.00
☐ 16, Jan 76, "Escape from the Planet of the Apes"; D:Cornelius,Zira	0.75	0.40	1.20	2.00
☐ 17, Feb 76, "Conquest of the Planet of the Apes"	0.75	0.40	1.20	2.00
☐ 18, Mar 76, "Conquest of the Planet of the Apes"	0.75	0.40	1.20	2.00

PLANET OF THE APES ANNUAL
ADVENTURE

	ORIG.	GOOD	FINE	N-MINT
☐ 1, b&w		0.70	2.10	3.50

PLANET OF THE APES: BLOOD OF THE APES

	ORIG.	GOOD	FINE	N-MINT
☐ 1, b&w		0.50	1.50	2.50
☐ 2, b&w		0.50	1.50	2.50
☐ 3, b&w		0.50	1.50	2.50
☐ 4, b&w		0.50	1.50	2.50

PLANET OF THE APES: FORBIDDEN ZONE

	ORIG.	GOOD	FINE	N-MINT
☐ 3	2.50	0.50	1.50	2.50
☐ 4	2.50	0.50	1.50	2.50

PLANET OF THE APES: SINS OF THE FATHER

	ORIG.	GOOD	FINE	N-MINT
☐ 1, b&w		0.50	1.50	2.50

PLANET OF THE APES: URCHAK'S FOLLY

	ORIG.	GOOD	FINE	N-MINT
☐ 1, b&w		0.50	1.50	2.50
☐ 2, b&w		0.50	1.50	2.50
☐ 3, b&w		0.50	1.50	2.50
☐ 4, b&w		0.50	1.50	2.50

PLANET OF VAMPIRES
ATLAS/SEABOARD

	ORIG.	GOOD	FINE	N-MINT
☐ 1, Feb 75, NA(c)	0.25	0.20	0.60	1.00
☐ 2, Apr 75, NA(c)	0.25	0.20	0.60	1.00
☐ 3, Jul 75	0.25	0.20	0.60	1.00

PLANET TERRY
STAR

	ORIG.	GOOD	FINE	N-MINT
☐ 1	0.65	0.13	0.39	0.65
☐ 2	0.65	0.13	0.39	0.65
☐ 3	0.65	0.13	0.39	0.65
☐ 4	0.65	0.13	0.39	0.65
☐ 5	0.65	0.13	0.39	0.65
☐ 6	0.65	0.13	0.39	0.65
☐ 7	0.65	0.13	0.39	0.65
☐ 8	0.65	0.13	0.39	0.65
☐ 9	0.65	0.13	0.39	0.65
☐ 10	0.65	0.13	0.39	0.65
☐ 11	0.65	0.13	0.39	0.65
☐ 12	0.65	0.13	0.39	0.65

PLANET X REPRINT COMIC
PLANET X

	ORIG.	GOOD	FINE	N-MINT
☐ 1, 87, reprints adaptation of *The Man from Planet X*;no cover price				

PLANET-X
ETERNITY

	ORIG.	GOOD	FINE	N-MINT
☐ 1, b&w		0.50	1.50	2.50

PLASM
DEFIANT

	ORIG.	GOOD	FINE	N-MINT
☐ 0, (in *Diamond Previews*)		0.40	1.20	2.00

PLASMA BABY
CALIBER

	ORIG.	GOOD	FINE	N-MINT
☐ 1, b&w	2.50	0.50	1.50	2.50
☐ 2, b&w	2.50	0.50	1.50	2.50
☐ 3, b&w	2.50	0.50	1.50	2.50

PLASMER
MARVEL

	ORIG.	GOOD	FINE	N-MINT
☐ 1, four trading cards	2.50	0.50	1.50	2.50
☐ 2	1.95	0.39	1.17	1.95
☐ 3	1.95	0.39	1.17	1.95
☐ 4	1.95	0.39	1.17	1.95

PLASTIC FORKS
EPIC

	ORIG.	GOOD	FINE	N-MINT
☐ 1	4.95	0.99	2.97	4.95
☐ 2	4.95	0.99	2.97	4.95
☐ 3	4.95	0.99	2.97	4.95
☐ 4	4.95	0.99	2.97	4.95
☐ 5	4.95	0.99	2.97	4.95

PLASTIC MAN (1966-1977)
DC

	ORIG.	GOOD	FINE	N-MINT
☐ 1, Dec 66, O:Plastic Man	0.12	11.00	33.00	55.00
☐ 2		7.00	21.00	35.00
☐ 3		4.80	14.40	24.00
☐ 4		4.80	14.40	24.00
☐ 5		4.80	14.40	24.00
☐ 6		3.40	10.20	17.00
☐ 7		3.40	10.20	17.00
☐ 8		3.40	10.20	17.00
☐ 9		3.40	10.20	17.00
☐ 10		3.40	10.20	17.00
☐ 11, Mar 76	0.25	2.00	6.00	10.00
☐ 12, May 76	0.30	2.00	6.00	10.00
☐ 13, Jul 76	0.30	2.00	6.00	10.00
☐ 14, Sep 76	0.30	2.00	6.00	10.00
☐ 15, Nov 76	0.30	2.00	6.00	10.00
☐ 16, Mar 77	0.30	2.00	6.00	10.00
☐ 17, May 77	0.30	2.00	6.00	10.00
☐ 18, Jul 77	0.35	2.00	6.00	10.00
☐ 19, Sep 77	0.35	2.00	6.00	10.00
☐ 20, 77 76	0.35	2.00	6.00	10.00

	ORIG.	GOOD	FINE	N-MINT

PLASTIC MAN (mini-series)

	ORIG.	GOOD	FINE	N-MINT
1, Nov 88, Foglio, Barta..	1.00	0.20	0.60	1.00
2, Dec 88, Foglio, Barta..	1.00	0.20	0.60	1.00
3, Jan 89, Foglio, Barta ..	1.00	0.20	0.60	1.00
4, Feb 89, Foglio, Barta ..	1.00	0.20	0.60	1.00

PLASTRON CAFE
MIRAGE

	ORIG.	GOOD	FINE	N-MINT
1, TMNT, b&w	2.25	0.45	1.35	2.25
2, TMNT, b&w	2.25	0.45	1.35	2.25
3	2.25	0.45	1.35	2.25
4	2.25	0.45	1.35	2.25

PLATINUM .44
COMAX

	GOOD	FINE	N-MINT
1, b&w, adult	0.59	1.77	2.95

PLAYGROUND
CALIBER

	ORIG.	GOOD	FINE	N-MINT
1, b&w	2.50	0.50	1.50	2.50

PLAYGROUNDS
FANTAGRAPHICS

	GOOD	FINE	N-MINT
1, b&w	0.40	1.20	2.00

PLOP!
DC

	ORIG.	GOOD	FINE	N-MINT
1, Oct 73	0.20	1.20	3.60	6.00
2, Dec 73	0.20	0.80	2.40	4.00
3, Feb 74	0.20	0.80	2.40	4.00
4, Apr 74	0.20	0.80	2.40	4.00
5, Jun 74	0.20	1.00	3.00	5.00
6, Aug 74	0.20	0.70	2.10	3.50
7, Oct 74	0.20	0.70	2.10	3.50
8, Dec 74	0.20	0.70	2.10	3.50
9, Feb 75	0.25	0.70	2.10	3.50
10, Mar 75	0.25	0.70	2.10	3.50
11, Apr 75	0.25	0.70	2.10	3.50
12, May 75	0.25	0.70	2.10	3.50
13, Jun 75	0.25	0.70	2.10	3.50
14, Jul 75	0.25	0.70	2.10	3.50
15, Aug 75	0.25	0.70	2.10	3.50
16, Sep 75	0.25	0.70	2.10	3.50
17, Oct 75	0.25	0.70	2.10	3.50
18, Dec 75	0.25	0.70	2.10	3.50
19, Feb 76	0.25	0.70	2.10	3.50
20, Apr 76	0.25	0.70	2.10	3.50
21, Jun 76	0.50	1.00	3.00	5.00
22, Aug 76	0.50	1.00	3.00	5.00
23, Oct 76	0.50	0.70	2.10	3.50
24, Dec 76	0.50	1.00	3.00	5.00

POETS PROSPER: RHYME & REVELRY
TOME

	ORIG.	GOOD	FINE	N-MINT
1	3.50	0.70	2.10	3.50

POINT-BLANK
ECLIPSE

	GOOD	FINE	N-MINT
1, b&w	0.59	1.77	2.95
2, b&w	0.59	1.77	2.95

POISON ELVES
SIRIUS ENTERTAINMENT

	ORIG.	GOOD	FINE	N-MINT
1, May 95, (was Mulehide title);b&w	2.50	2.00	6.00	10.00
2, Jun 95, b&w	2.50	1.20	3.60	6.00
3, Jul 95, b&w	2.50	1.00	3.00	5.00
4, Aug 95, b&w	2.50	1.00	3.00	5.00
5, b&w	2.50	1.00	3.00	5.00
6, 95, b&w	2.50	0.60	1.80	3.00
7, 95, b&w	2.50	0.60	1.80	3.00
8, 96, b&w	2.50	0.60	1.80	3.00

POISON ELVES (was I, Lusiphur)
MULEHIDE

	ORIG.	GOOD	FINE	N-MINT
11, b&w	2.50	4.00	12.00	20.00
12, Oct 93, b&w	2.50	4.00	12.00	20.00
13, Dec 93, b&w	2.50	5.00	15.00	25.00
14, Feb 94, b&w	2.50	3.00	9.00	15.00

	ORIG.	GOOD	FINE	N-MINT
15, Apr 94, b&w	2.50	3.00	9.00	15.00
16, Jun 94, b&w	2.50	3.00	9.00	15.00
17, b&w	2.50	2.00	6.00	10.00
18, b&w	2.50	2.00	6.00	10.00
19, b&w	2.50	2.00	6.00	10.00
20, (becomes Sirius title)	2.50	2.00	6.00	10.00

POLICE ACADEMY
MARVEL

	ORIG.	GOOD	FINE	N-MINT
1	1.00	0.20	0.60	1.00
2	1.00	0.20	0.60	1.00
3	1.00	0.20	0.60	1.00
4	1.00	0.20	0.60	1.00
5	1.00	0.20	0.60	1.00
6	1.00	0.20	0.60	1.00

POLICE ACTION
ATLAS/ SEABOARD

	ORIG.	GOOD	FINE	N-MINT
1, Feb 75	0.25	0.20	0.60	1.00
2, Apr 75	0.25	0.20	0.60	1.00
3, Jun 75	0.25	0.20	0.60	1.00

POLIS
BRAVE NEW WORDS

	GOOD	FINE	N-MINT
1, b&w	0.50	1.50	2.50
2, b&w	0.50	1.50	2.50

POLLY AND HER PALS (mini-series)
ETERNITY

	ORIG.	GOOD	FINE	N-MINT
1, Oct 90, b&w, strip reprints	2.95	0.59	1.77	2.95
2, 90, b&w, strip reprints	2.95	0.59	1.77	2.95
3, 90, b&w, strip reprints	2.95	0.59	1.77	2.95
4, 90, b&w, strip reprints	2.95	0.59	1.77	2.95
5, 90, b&w, strip reprints	2.95	0.59	1.77	2.95

POPEYE
HARVEY

	ORIG.	GOOD	FINE	N-MINT
1	1.50	0.30	0.90	1.50
2	1.50	0.30	0.90	1.50
3	1.50	0.30	0.90	1.50
4	1.50	0.30	0.90	1.50
5	1.50	0.30	0.90	1.50
6, Jul 94	1.50	0.30	0.90	1.50

POPEYE SPECIAL
OCEAN

	ORIG.	GOOD	FINE	N-MINT
1, Sum 87, O:Popeye	1.75	0.35	1.05	1.75
2		0.35	1.05	1.75

POPEYE SUMMER SPECIAL
HARVEY

	ORIG.	GOOD	FINE	N-MINT
1	2.25	0.45	1.35	2.25
1	2.25	0.45	1.35	2.25

POPPLES, THE
STAR

	ORIG.	GOOD	FINE	N-MINT
1	0.75	0.15	0.45	0.75
2	0.75	0.15	0.45	0.75
3	0.75	0.15	0.45	0.75
4	1.00	0.20	0.60	1.00

PORT (really 'Port)
SILVERWOLF

	GOOD	FINE	N-MINT
1, b&w	0.30	0.90	1.50
2, b&w	0.30	0.90	1.50

PORTABLE LOWLIFE
AEON

	ORIG.	GOOD	FINE	N-MINT
0, Jul 93, prestige format	4.95	0.99	2.97	4.95

PORTIA PRINZ OF THE GLAMAZONS
ECLIPSE

	GOOD	FINE	N-MINT
1, Dec 86, b&w	0.40	1.20	2.00

	ORIG.	GOOD	FINE	N-MINT
☐ 2, Feb 87, b&w		0.40	1.20	2.00
☐ 3, Apr 87, b&w		0.40	1.20	2.00
☐ 4, Jun 87, b&w		0.40	1.20	2.00
☐ 5, Aug 87, b&w		0.40	1.20	2.00
☐ 6, Oct 87, b&w		0.40	1.20	2.00

POSSIBLEMAN
BLACKTHORNE

	ORIG.	GOOD	FINE	N-MINT
☐ 1		0.35	1.05	1.75
☐ 2		0.35	1.05	1.75

POST BROTHERS (was Vortex title)
RIP OFF

	ORIG.	GOOD	FINE	N-MINT
☐ 19, Apr 91, b&w (was *Those Annoying Post Brothers*)	2.00	0.40	1.20	2.00
☐ 20, Jun 91, b&w	2.50	0.50	1.50	2.50
☐ 21, Aug 91, b&w	2.50	0.50	1.50	2.50
☐ 22, Oct 91, b&w	2.50	0.50	1.50	2.50
☐ 23, Oct 91, b&w	2.50	0.50	1.50	2.50
☐ 24, Dec 91, b&w	2.50	0.50	1.50	2.50
☐ 25, Feb 92, b&w	2.50	0.50	1.50	2.50
☐ 26, Apr 92, b&w	2.50	0.50	1.50	2.50
☐ 27, Jun 92, b&w	2.50	0.50	1.50	2.50
☐ 28, Aug 92, b&w	2.50	0.50	1.50	2.50
☐ 29, Oct 92, b&w	2.50	0.50	1.50	2.50
☐ 30, Dec 92, b&w	2.50	0.50	1.50	2.50
☐ 31, Feb 93, b&w	2.50	0.50	1.50	2.50
☐ 32, Apr 93, b&w	2.50	0.50	1.50	2.50
☐ 33, Jun 93, b&w	2.50	0.50	1.50	2.50
☐ 34, Aug 93, b&w	2.50	0.50	1.50	2.50
☐ 35, Oct 93, b&w	2.50	0.50	1.50	2.50
☐ 36, Dec 93, b&w	2.50	0.50	1.50	2.50
☐ 37, Feb 94, b&w	2.50	0.50	1.50	2.50
☐ 38, Apr 94, b&w	2.50	0.50	1.50	2.50

POWER & GLORY
BRAVURA/MALIBU

	ORIG.	GOOD	FINE	N-MINT
☐ 1, Feb 94, a, HC	2.50	0.60	1.80	3.00
☐ 1, Feb 94, b, HC	2.50	0.60	1.80	3.00
☐ 1, serigraph cover	4.00	12.00	20.00	
☐ 1, blue foil				
☐ 2, Mar 94, HC,adult	2.50	0.50	1.50	2.50
☐ 4, May 94	2.50	0.50	1.50	2.50

POWER COMICS
ECLIPSE

	ORIG.	GOOD	FINE	N-MINT
☐ 1, Mar 88, BB, Dave Gibbons, b&w		0.40	1.20	2.00
☐ 2, May 88, BB, Dave Gibbons, b&w		0.40	1.20	2.00
☐ 3, Jul 88, BB, Dave Gibbons, b&w		0.40	1.20	2.00
☐ 4, Sep 88, BB, Dave Gibbons, b&w		0.40	1.20	2.00

POWER

	ORIG.	GOOD	FINE	N-MINT
☐ 1, Aug 77, 1st printing, 1st Dave Sim Aardvark		4.00	12.00	20.00
☐ 1, 78, 2nd printing		1.20	3.60	6.00
☐ 2, Sep 77, MGu,1:Cobalt Blue		2.00	6.00	10.00
☐ 3, Oct 77		0.40	1.20	2.00
☐ 4, Nov 77		0.40	1.20	2.00
☐ 5, Dec 77, MGu		1.00	3.00	5.00

POWER DEFENSE
MILLER

	ORIG.	GOOD	FINE	N-MINT
☐ 1, b&w	2.50	0.50	1.50	2.50

POWER FACTOR
INNOVATION

	ORIG.	GOOD	FINE	N-MINT
☐ 1, Oct 90		0.39	1.17	1.95
☐ 2, Dec 90		0.45	1.35	2.25
☐ 3, Feb 91		0.45	1.35	2.25

WONDER COLOR

	ORIG.	GOOD	FINE	N-MINT
☐ 1, May 86, (moves to Pied Piper)		0.30	0.90	1.50

POWER FACTOR (former Wonder Color title)
PIED PIPER

	ORIG.	GOOD	FINE	N-MINT
☐ 2, Jun 86		0.39	1.17	1.95

POWER FACTOR SPECIAL
INNOVATION

	ORIG.	GOOD	FINE	N-MINT
☐ 1, Jan 91		0.55	1.65	2.75

POWER GIRL
DC

	ORIG.	GOOD	FINE	N-MINT
☐ 1, Jun 88	1.00	0.20	0.60	1.00
☐ 2, Jul 88	1.00	0.20	0.60	1.00
☐ 3, Aug 88	1.00	0.20	0.60	1.00
☐ 4, Sep 88	1.00	0.20	0.60	1.00

POWER LINE
EPIC

	ORIG.	GOOD	FINE	N-MINT
☐ 1, May 88	1.25	0.25	0.75	1.25
☐ 2, Jul 88	1.25	0.25	0.75	1.25
☐ 3, Sep 88	1.25	0.25	0.75	1.25
☐ 4	1.50	0.30	0.90	1.50
☐ 4, Nov 88	1.25	0.25	0.75	1.25

POWER LORDS
DC

	ORIG.	GOOD	FINE	N-MINT
☐ 1		0.20	0.60	1.00
☐ 2		0.20	0.60	1.00
☐ 3		0.20	0.60	1.00

POWER MAN & IRON FIST (formerly Power Man)
MARVEL

	ORIG.	GOOD	FINE	N-MINT
☐ 50, Apr 78, JBy	0.35	1.60	4.80	8.00
☐ 51, Jun 78	0.35	0.40	1.20	2.00
☐ 52, Aug 78	0.35	0.40	1.20	2.00
☐ 53, Oct 78	0.35	0.40	1.20	2.00
☐ 54, Dec 78, O:Iron Fist	0.35	1.60	4.80	8.00
☐ 55, Feb 79	0.35	0.40	1.20	2.00
☐ 56, Apr 79	0.35	0.40	1.20	2.00
☐ 57, Jun 79, X-Men	0.40	1.60	4.80	8.00
☐ 58, Aug 79, 1:El Aquila	0.40	0.40	1.20	2.00
☐ 59, Oct 79, BL	0.40	0.40	1.20	2.00
☐ 60, Dec 79, BL	0.40	0.40	1.20	2.00
☐ 61, Feb 80, BL	0.40	0.40	1.20	2.00
☐ 62, Apr 80, BL	0.40	0.40	1.20	2.00
☐ 63, Jun 80, BL	0.40	0.40	1.20	2.00
☐ 64, Aug 80, BL	0.40	0.40	1.20	2.00
☐ 65, Oct 80, BL	0.40	0.40	1.20	2.00
☐ 66, Dec 80, FM(c), Sabretooth	0.50	11.00	33.00	55.00
☐ 67, Feb 81	0.50	0.40	1.20	2.00
☐ 68, Apr 81, FM(c)	0.50	0.40	1.20	2.00
☐ 69, May 81	0.50	0.40	1.20	2.00
☐ 70, Jun 81, FM(c)	0.50	0.40	1.20	2.00
☐ 71, Jul 81, FM(c)	0.50	0.40	1.20	2.00
☐ 72, Aug 81, FM(c)	0.50	0.40	1.20	2.00
☐ 73, Sep 81, FM(c)	0.50	0.40	1.20	2.00
☐ 74, Oct 81, FM(c)	0.50	0.40	1.20	2.00
☐ 75, Nov 81, origins	0.75	0.60	1.80	3.00
☐ 76, Dec 81	0.50	0.40	1.20	2.00
☐ 77, Jan 82	0.60	0.40	1.20	2.00
☐ 78, Feb 82	0.60	5.00	15.00	25.00
☐ 79, Mar 82	0.60	0.30	0.90	1.50
☐ 80, Apr 82	0.60	0.30	0.90	1.50
☐ 81, May 82	0.60	0.30	0.90	1.50
☐ 82, Jun 82	0.60	0.30	0.90	1.50
☐ 83, Jul 82	0.60	0.30	0.90	1.50
☐ 84, Aug 82, Sabretooth	0.60	5.20	15.60	26.00
☐ 85, Sep 82	0.60	0.20	0.60	1.00
☐ 86, Oct 82, Moon Knight	0.60	0.60	1.80	3.00
☐ 87, Nov 82, Moon Knight	0.60	0.60	1.80	3.00
☐ 88, Dec 82	0.60	0.20	0.60	1.00
☐ 89, Jan 83	0.60	0.20	0.60	1.00
☐ 90, Feb 83	0.60	0.20	0.60	1.00
☐ 91, Mar 83	0.60	0.20	0.60	1.00

	ORIG.	GOOD	FINE	N-MINT
☐ 92, Apr 83	0.60	0.20	0.60	1.00
☐ 93, May 83	0.60	0.20	0.60	1.00
☐ 94, Jun 83	0.60	0.20	0.60	1.00
☐ 95, Jul 83	0.60	0.20	0.60	1.00
☐ 96, Aug 83	0.60	0.20	0.60	1.00
☐ 97, Sep 83	0.60	0.20	0.60	1.00
☐ 98, Oct 83	0.60	0.20	0.60	1.00
☐ 99, Nov 83	0.60	0.20	0.60	1.00
☐ 100, Dec 83	1.00	0.20	0.60	1.00
☐ 101, Jan 84	0.60	0.20	0.60	1.00
☐ 102, Feb 84	0.60	0.20	0.60	1.00
☐ 103, Mar 84	0.60	0.20	0.60	1.00
☐ 104, Apr 84	0.60	0.20	0.60	1.00
☐ 105, May 84	0.60	0.20	0.60	1.00
☐ 106, Jun 84	0.60	0.20	0.60	1.00
☐ 107, Jul 84	0.60	0.20	0.60	1.00
☐ 108, Aug 84	0.60	0.20	0.60	1.00
☐ 109, Sep 84	0.60	0.20	0.60	1.00
☐ 110, Oct 84	0.60	0.20	0.60	1.00
☐ 111, Nov 84	0.60	0.20	0.60	1.00
☐ 112, Dec 84	0.60	0.20	0.60	1.00
☐ 113, Jan 85	0.60	0.20	0.60	1.00
☐ 114, Feb 85	0.60	0.20	0.60	1.00
☐ 115, Mar 85	0.60	0.20	0.60	1.00
☐ 116, Apr 85	0.65	0.20	0.60	1.00
☐ 117, May 85	0.65	0.20	0.60	1.00
☐ 118, Jul 85	0.65	0.20	0.60	1.00
☐ 119, Sep 85	0.65	0.20	0.60	1.00
☐ 120, Nov 85	0.65	0.20	0.60	1.00
☐ 121, Jan 86, Secret Wars II	0.65	0.20	0.60	1.00
☐ 122, Mar 86	0.75	0.20	0.60	1.00
☐ 123, May 86	0.75	0.20	0.60	1.00
☐ 124, Jul 86	0.75	0.20	0.60	1.00
☐ 125, Sep 86, D:Iron Fist	1.25	1.20	3.60	6.00

POWER MAN (formerly Hero for Hire)

	ORIG.	GOOD	FINE	N-MINT
☐ 17, GT, A:Iron Man	0.20	1.60	4.80	8.00
☐ 18	0.20	0.80	2.40	4.00
☐ 19	0.25	0.80	2.40	4.00
☐ 20	0.25	0.80	2.40	4.00
☐ 21	0.25	0.60	1.80	3.00
☐ 22	0.25	0.60	1.80	3.00
☐ 23	0.25	0.60	1.80	3.00
☐ 24	0.25	0.60	1.80	3.00
☐ 25	0.25	0.60	1.80	3.00
☐ 26	0.25	0.60	1.80	3.00
☐ 27, GP	0.25	0.60	1.80	3.00
☐ 28	0.25	0.60	1.80	3.00
☐ 29	0.25	0.60	1.80	3.00
☐ 30	0.25	0.60	1.80	3.00
☐ 31, NA	0.25	0.60	1.80	3.00
☐ 32	0.25	0.60	1.80	3.00
☐ 33	0.25	0.60	1.80	3.00
☐ 34	0.25	0.60	1.80	3.00
☐ 35, Sep 76	0.30	0.60	1.80	3.00
☐ 36, Oct 76	0.30	0.60	1.80	3.00
☐ 37, Nov 76	0.30	0.60	1.80	3.00
☐ 38, Dec 76	0.30	0.60	1.80	3.00
☐ 39, Jan 77	0.30	0.60	1.80	3.00
☐ 40, Feb 77	0.30	0.60	1.80	3.00
☐ 41, Mar 77	0.30	0.60	1.80	3.00
☐ 42, Apr 77	0.30	0.60	1.80	3.00
☐ 43, May 77	0.30	0.60	1.80	3.00
☐ 44, Jun 77	0.30	0.60	1.80	3.00
☐ 45, Jul 77, JSn, A:Mace	0.30	0.60	1.80	3.00
☐ 46, Aug 77, GT, 1:Zzax	0.30	0.60	1.80	3.00
☐ 47, Oct 77, BS, A:Iron Fist	0.30	1.00	3.00	5.00
☐ 48, Dec 77, JBy, 1:Power Man/Iron Fist	0.35	1.00	3.00	5.00
☐ 49, Feb 78, JBy, A:Iron Fist (becomes *Power Man & Iron Fist*)	0.35	1.00	3.00	5.00

POWER MAN ANNUAL

	ORIG.	GOOD	FINE	N-MINT
☐ 1, Nov 76	0.50	0.60	1.80	3.00

POWER OF SHAZAM!, THE
DC

	ORIG.	GOOD	FINE	N-MINT
☐ 0, 94, tpb, one-shot	9.95	1.99	5.97	9.95
☐ 1, Mar 95	1.50	0.60	1.80	3.00
☐ 2, Apr 95	1.50	0.30	0.90	1.50
☐ 3, May 95	1.75	0.35	1.05	1.75
☐ 4, Jun 95, R:Mary Marvel, Tawky Tawny	1.75	0.35	1.05	1.75
☐ 5, Jul 95	1.75	0.35	1.05	1.75
☐ 6, Aug 95, R:Captain Nazi;Freddy Freeman and grandfather injured	1.75	0.35	1.05	1.75
☐ 7, Sep 95, R:Captain Marvel, Jr.	1.75	0.35	1.05	1.75
☐ 8, Oct 95, CS;A:Bulletman, Spy Smasher, Minuteman	1.75	0.35	1.05	1.75
☐ 9, Nov 95	1.75	0.35	1.05	1.75
☐ 10, Dec 95, O:Shazam, Blaze,Satanus,Rock of Eternity, Black Adam	1.75	0.35	1.05	1.75
☐ 11, Jan 96, R:Ibis, Uncle Marvel,Marvel Family; A:Bulletman	1.75	0.35	1.05	1.75
☐ 12, Feb 96, O:SevenDeadly Foes of Man	1.75	0.35	1.05	1.75
☐ 13, Mar 96	1.75	0.35	1.05	1.75
☐ 14, Apr 96, Captain Marvel Jr. solo story;1:Chain Lightning	1.75	0.35	1.05	1.75
☐ 15, Jun 96	1.75	0.35	1.05	1.75
☐ 16, Jul 96	1.75	0.35	1.05	1.75

POWER OF STRONG MAN
AC

	ORIG.	GOOD	FINE	N-MINT
☐ 1, 89, b&w rep.		0.50	1.50	2.50

POWER OF THE ATOM
DC

	ORIG.	GOOD	FINE	N-MINT
☐ 1, Aug 88	1.00	0.20	0.60	1.00
☐ 2, Sep 88	1.00	0.20	0.60	1.00
☐ 3, Oct 88	1.00	0.20	0.60	1.00
☐ 4, Nov 88, Bonus Book #8	1.00	0.20	0.60	1.00
☐ 5, Dec 88, A:Elongated Man	1.00	0.20	0.60	1.00
☐ 6, Wtr 88	1.00	0.20	0.60	1.00
☐ 7, Hol 88, Invasion!	1.00	0.20	0.60	1.00
☐ 8, Jan 89, Invasion!	1.00	0.20	0.60	1.00
☐ 9, Feb 89, A:JLI	1.00	0.20	0.60	1.00
☐ 10, Mar 89	1.00	0.20	0.60	1.00
☐ 11, Apr 89	1.00	0.20	0.60	1.00
☐ 12, May 89	1.00	0.20	0.60	1.00
☐ 13, Jun 89	1.00	0.20	0.60	1.00
☐ 14, Jul 89	1.00	0.20	0.60	1.00
☐ 15, Aug 89	1.00	0.20	0.60	1.00
☐ 16, Sep 89	1.00	0.20	0.60	1.00
☐ 17, Oct 89	1.00	0.20	0.60	1.00
☐ 18, Nov 89	1.00	0.20	0.60	1.00

POWER PACHYDERMS
MARVEL

	ORIG.	GOOD	FINE	N-MINT
☐ 1, one-shot parody	1.25	0.25	0.75	1.25

POWER PACK

	ORIG.	GOOD	FINE	N-MINT
☐ 1, V: Snarks	1.00	0.60	1.80	3.00
☐ 1, paperback	0.60	1.59	4.77	7.95
☐ 2, Sep 84	0.60	0.40	1.20	2.00
☐ 3, Oct 84	0.60	0.40	1.20	2.00
☐ 4, Nov 84	0.60	0.40	1.20	2.00
☐ 5, Dec 84	0.60	0.40	1.20	2.00
☐ 6, Jan 85	0.60	0.40	1.20	2.00
☐ 7, Feb 85	0.60	0.40	1.20	2.00

	ORIG.	GOOD	FINE	N-MINT
8, Mar 85	0.60	0.40	1.20	2.00
9, Apr 85	0.65	0.40	1.20	2.00
10, May 85	0.65	0.40	1.20	2.00
11, Jun 85	0.65	0.25	0.75	1.25
12, Jul 85, A:X-Men	0.65	0.80	2.40	4.00
13, Aug 85	0.65	0.30	0.90	1.50
14, Sep 85	0.65	0.30	0.90	1.50
15, Oct 85	0.65	0.30	0.90	1.50
16, Nov 85	0.65	0.30	0.90	1.50
17, Dec 85	0.65	0.30	0.90	1.50
18, Jan 86, Secret Wars II				
	0.65	0.30	0.90	1.50
19, Feb 86, Wolverine	1.25	1.40	4.20	7.00
20, Mar 86	0.75	0.30	0.90	1.50
21, Apr 86	0.75	0.30	0.90	1.50
22, May 86	0.75	0.30	0.90	1.50
23, Jun 86	0.75	0.30	0.90	1.50
24, Jul 86	0.75	0.30	0.90	1.50
25, Aug 86	1.25	0.30	0.90	1.50
26, Oct 86	1.00	0.30	0.90	1.50
27, Dec 86, Mutant Massacre				
	1.00	0.80	2.40	4.00
28, Feb 87, A:FF,Avengers				
	1.00	0.30	0.90	1.50
29, Apr 87	1.00	0.30	0.90	1.50
30, Jun 87	1.00	0.30	0.90	1.50
31, Aug 87, I:Trash	1.00	0.30	0.90	1.50
32, Oct 87	1.00	0.30	0.90	1.50
33, Nov 87	1.00	0.30	0.90	1.50
34, Jan 88	1.00	0.30	0.90	1.50
35, Feb 88, Fall of Mutants				
	1.00	0.30	0.90	1.50
36, Apr 88	1.00	0.30	0.90	1.50
37, May 88	1.00	0.30	0.90	1.50
38, Jul 88	1.00	0.30	0.90	1.50
39, Aug 88	1.25	0.30	0.90	1.50
40, Sep 88	1.25	0.30	0.90	1.50
41, Nov 88	1.25	0.30	0.90	1.50
42, Dec 88, Inferno	1.25	0.30	0.90	1.50
43, Jan 89, Inferno	1.50	0.30	0.90	1.50
44, Mar 89, Inferno	1.50	0.30	0.90	1.50
45, Apr 89	1.50	0.30	0.90	1.50
46, May 89, A:Punisher	1.50	0.80	2.40	4.00
47, Jul 89	1.50	0.30	0.90	1.50
48, Sep 89	1.50	0.30	0.90	1.50
49, Oct 89	1.50	0.30	0.90	1.50
50, Nov 89	1.95	0.39	1.17	1.95
51, Dec 89, 1:Numinus	1.50	0.30	0.90	1.50
52, Dec 89	1.50	0.30	0.90	1.50
53, Jan 90, Acts of Vengeance				
	1.50	0.30	0.90	1.50
54, Feb 90	1.50	0.30	0.90	1.50
55, Apr 90	1.50	0.30	0.90	1.50
56, Jun 90	1.50	0.30	0.90	1.50
57, Jul 90	1.50	0.30	0.90	1.50
58, Sep 90, Galactus	1.50	0.30	0.90	1.50
59, Oct 90	1.50	0.30	0.90	1.50
60, Nov 90	1.50	0.30	0.90	1.50
61, Dec 90	1.50	0.30	0.90	1.50
62, Jan 91	1.50	0.30	0.90	1.50

POWER PACK HOLIDAY SPECIAL

	ORIG.	GOOD	FINE	N-MINT
1	2.25	0.45	1.35	2.25

POWER PLAYS
EXTRAVA-GANDT

		GOOD	FINE	N-MINT
1, 83, b&w		0.40	1.20	2.00
3,90, b&w (moves to AC Comics)				
	0.40	1.20	2.00	

POWER PLAYS
(formerly published by Extrava-Gandt)
AC

		GOOD	FINE	N-MINT
1, b&w		0.35	1.05	1.75
2, b&w		0.35	1.05	1.75

POWER, THE
AIRCEL

		GOOD	FINE	N-MINT
1, b&w		0.45	1.35	2.25
2, b&w		0.45	1.35	2.25
3, b&w		0.45	1.35	2.25
4, b&w		0.45	1.35	2.25

POWERLINE
EPIC

		GOOD	FINE	N-MINT
5		0.30	0.90	1.50
6		0.30	0.90	1.50
7		0.30	0.90	1.50
8		0.30	0.90	1.50

POWERS THAT BE
BROADWAY

	ORIG.	GOOD	FINE	N-MINT
1, Nov 95, Fatale and Star Seed				
	2.50	0.50	1.50	2.50
2, Dec 95, Star Seed	2.50	0.50	1.50	2.50
2, Sep 95, giveaway preview edition;Star Seed;b&w				
3, Oct 95, giveaway preview edition;Star Seed;b&w				
3, Jan 96, Star Seed	2.50	0.50	1.50	2.50

PRAIRIE MOON AND OTHER STORIES
DARK HORSE

		GOOD	FINE	N-MINT
0, nn Rick Geary, b&w		0.45	1.35	2.25

PRE-TEEN DIRTY-GENE KUNG-FU KANGAROOS
BLACKTHORNE

		GOOD	FINE	N-MINT
1		0.30	0.90	1.50
2		0.30	0.90	1.50
3		0.35	1.05	1.75

PREACHER
DC/VERTIGO

	ORIG.	GOOD	FINE	N-MINT
1, Apr 95	2.95	7.20	21.60	36.00
2, May 95	2.50	4.80	14.40	24.00
3, Jun 95	2.50	4.80	14.40	24.00
4, Jul 95	2.50	3.20	9.60	16.00
5, Aug 95	2.50	2.80	8.40	14.00
6, Sep 95	2.50	2.40	7.20	12.00
7, Oct 95	2.50	2.00	6.00	10.00
8, Nov 95	2.50	1.60	4.80	8.00
9, Dec 95	2.50	1.20	3.60	6.00
10, Jan 96	2.50	1.20	3.60	6.00
11, Feb 96	2.50	0.80	2.40	4.00
12, Mar 96	2.50	0.50	1.50	2.50
13, Apr 96, "Hunters" Part 1 of 4				
	2.50	0.50	1.50	2.50
14, Jun 96, "Hunters" Part 2 of 4				
	2.50	0.50	1.50	2.50
15, Jul 96, "Hunters" Part 3 of 4				
	2.50	0.50	1.50	2.50

PRECIOUS METAL
ARTS INDUSTRIA

		GOOD	FINE	N-MINT
1, adult, b&w		0.50	1.50	2.50

PREDATOR
DARK HORSE

	ORIG.	GOOD	FINE	N-MINT
1, Jun 89, color, 1st printing				
	2.25	4.80	14.40	24.00
1, 2nd printing		0.45	1.35	2.25
2		2.40	7.20	12.00
3		1.60	4.80	8.00
4		1.20	3.60	6.00

PREDATOR 2
DARK HORSE

		GOOD	FINE	N-MINT
1, movie, trading cards		0.50	1.50	2.50
2, movie, trading cards		0.50	1.50	2.50

PREDATOR VERSUS MAGNUS ROBOT FIGHTER
DARK HORSE/VALIANT

	ORIG.	GOOD	FINE	N-MINT
1, Nov 92	2.95	1.20	3.60	6.00
1, platinum edition		14.00	42.00	70.00
2, 93	2.95	0.59	1.77	2.95

	ORIG.	GOOD	FINE	N-MINT

PREDATOR: BAD BLOOD
DARK HORSE
	ORIG.	GOOD	FINE	N-MINT
❑ 1, Dec 93	2.50	0.50	1.50	2.50
❑ 2, Feb 94	2.50	0.50	1.50	2.50
❑ 3, May 94	2.50	0.50	1.50	2.50
❑ 4, Jun 94	2.50	0.50	1.50	2.50

PREDATOR: BIG GAME
		GOOD	FINE	N-MINT
❑ 1, trading cards		0.50	1.50	2.50
❑ 2, no trading cards		0.50	1.50	2.50
❑ 3, trading cards		0.50	1.50	2.50
❑ 4		0.50	1.50	2.50

PREDATOR: BLOODY SANDS OF TIME
		GOOD	FINE	N-MINT
❑ 1		0.50	1.50	2.50
❑ 2		0.50	1.50	2.50

PREDATOR: COLD WAR
	ORIG.	GOOD	FINE	N-MINT
❑ 1, Sep 91	2.50	0.50	1.50	2.50
❑ 2		0.50	1.50	2.50
❑ 3		0.50	1.50	2.50
❑ 4		0.50	1.50	2.50

PREDATOR: INVADERS FROM THE FOURTH DIMENSION
	ORIG.	GOOD	FINE	N-MINT
❑ 0, Jul 94, one-shot	3.95	0.79	2.37	3.95

PREDATOR: JUNGLE TALES
❑ 0, Mar 95, collects "Predator: Rite of Passage" from *DHC* #1,2; "Predator: The Pride of Nghasa"from *DHC* #10-12

	ORIG.	GOOD	FINE	N-MINT
	2.95	0.59	1.77	2.95

PREDATOR: RACE WAR (mini-series)
	ORIG.	GOOD	FINE	N-MINT
❑ 0	2.50	0.50	1.50	2.50
❑ 1	2.50	0.50	1.50	2.50
❑ 2	2.50	0.50	1.50	2.50
❑ 3	2.50	0.50	1.50	2.50
❑ 4	2.50	0.50	1.50	2.50

PRESERVATION OF OBSCURITY, THE
LUMP OF SQUID
		GOOD	FINE	N-MINT
❑ 1		0.55	1.65	2.75
❑ 2		0.55	1.65	2.75

PRESSBUTTON (formerly Axel Pressbutton)
ECLIPSE
		GOOD	FINE	N-MINT
❑ 5		0.35	1.05	1.75

PRESSED TONGUE
FANTAGRAPHICS
	ORIG.	GOOD	FINE	N-MINT
❑ 1, adult, b&w	2.95	0.59	1.77	2.95

PRESTO KID, THE
AC
		GOOD	FINE	N-MINT
❑ 1, b&w, reprints		0.50	1.50	2.50

PREY
MONSTER
		GOOD	FINE	N-MINT
❑ 1, b&w		0.45	1.35	2.25
❑ 2, b&w		0.45	1.35	2.25
❑ 3, b&w		0.45	1.35	2.25

PREY FOR US SINNERS
FANTACO
	ORIG.	GOOD	FINE	N-MINT
❑ 0, 95	4.95	0.99	2.97	4.95

PREZ
DC
	ORIG.	GOOD	FINE	N-MINT
❑ 1, Aug 73	0.20	1.00	3.00	5.00
❑ 2, 73	0.20	0.60	1.80	3.00
❑ 3, 73	0.20	0.60	1.80	3.00
❑ 4, Feb 74	0.20	0.60	1.80	3.00

PRIMAL
DARK HORSE
	ORIG.	GOOD	FINE	N-MINT
❑ 1	2.50	0.50	1.50	2.50
❑ 2	2.50	0.50	1.50	2.50

PRIMAL FORCE
DC
	ORIG.	GOOD	FINE	N-MINT
❑ 0, Oct 94	1.95	0.39	1.17	1.95
❑ 1, Nov 94	1.95	0.39	1.17	1.95
❑ 2, Dec 94	1.95	0.39	1.17	1.95

	ORIG.	GOOD	FINE	N-MINT
❑ 3, Jan 95	1.95	0.39	1.17	1.95
❑ 4, Feb 95	1.95	0.39	1.17	1.95
❑ 5, Mar 95	1.95	0.39	1.17	1.95
❑ 6, Apr 95	1.95	0.39	1.17	1.95
❑ 7, May 95	1.95	0.39	1.17	1.95
❑ 8, Jun 95	2.25	0.45	1.35	2.25
❑ 9, Jul 95	2.25	0.45	1.35	2.25
❑ 10, Aug 95	2.25	0.45	1.35	2.25
❑ 11, Sep 95	2.25	0.45	1.35	2.25
❑ 12, Oct 95	2.25	0.45	1.35	2.25
❑ 13, Nov 95, "Underworld Unleashed";A:Lord Satanus				
		2.25	0.45	1.35	2.25
❑ 14, Dec 95, final issue	2.25	0.45	1.35	2.25

PRIME
MALIBU/ULTRAVERSE
	ORIG.	GOOD	FINE	N-MINT
❑ 1, Jun 93, Ultraverse	1.95	1.40	4.20	7.00
❑ 1, hologram edition		12.00	36.00	60.00
❑ 1, Ultra Ltd., foil stamped, giveaway				
❑ 2, Ultraverse, trading card				
	1.95	1.60	4.80	8.00
❑ 3	1.95	0.80	2.40	4.00
❑ 4, Sep 93, two different covers				
	1.95	0.80	2.40	4.00
❑ 5, Rune, BWS	2.50	0.70	2.10	3.50
❑ 6	1.95	0.39	1.17	1.95
❑ 7, Break-Thru	1.95	0.39	1.17	1.95
❑ 8	1.95	0.39	1.17	1.95
❑ 9	1.95	0.39	1.17	1.95
❑ 10, Mar 94	1.95	0.39	1.17	1.95
❑ 11, Apr 94	1.95	0.39	1.17	1.95
❑ 12, May 94, (*Ultraverse Premiere #3*)				
	3.50	0.70	2.10	3.50
❑ 13, Jul 94	2.95	0.59	1.77	2.95
❑ 14, Sep 94	1.95	0.39	1.17	1.95
❑ 15, Oct 94	1.95	0.39	1.17	1.95

PRIME (Vol. 2)
	ORIG.	GOOD	FINE	N-MINT
❑ 0, Sep 95, Infinity;alternate cover;"Black September";A:SpM	1.50	0.60	1.80	3.00
❑ 0, Sep 95, Infinity;"Black September";A:SpM				
	1.50	0.30	0.90	1.50
❑ 1, Oct 95, Spider-Prime	1.50	0.70	2.10	3.50
❑ 2, Nov 95, flipbook with "The Phoenix Resurrection" Pt. 1				
	1.50	0.50	1.50	2.50
❑ 3, Dec 95	1.50	0.30	0.90	1.50
❑ 4, Jan 96, Kevin rejoins Prime body				
	1.50	0.30	0.90	1.50
❑ 5, Feb 96	1.50	0.30	0.90	1.50
❑ 6, Mar 96, A:Solitaire	1.50	0.30	0.90	1.50
❑ 7, Apr 96	1.50	0.30	0.90	1.50

PRIME CUTS
FANTAGRAPHICS
		GOOD	FINE	N-MINT
❑ 1		0.70	2.10	3.50
❑ 2		0.70	2.10	3.50
❑ 3		0.70	2.10	3.50
❑ 4		0.70	2.10	3.50
❑ 5		0.70	2.10	3.50
❑ 6		0.70	2.10	3.50
❑ 8		0.79	2.37	3.95
❑ 9		0.79	2.37	3.95
❑ 10		0.79	2.37	3.95

PRIME SLIME TALES
MIRAGE
		GOOD	FINE	N-MINT
❑ 1	1.50	0.30	0.90	1.50
❑ 2, (moves to Now Comics)				
	1.50	0.30	0.90	1.50

PRIME SLIME TALES (former Mirage title)
NOW
		GOOD	FINE	N-MINT
❑ 3, Nov 86	1.50	0.30	0.90	1.50
❑ 4, Jan 87	1.50	0.30	0.90	1.50

	ORIG.	GOOD	FINE	N-MINT

PRIME/CAPTAIN AMERICA
MALIBU/ULTRAVERSE
	ORIG.	GOOD	FINE	N-MINT
☐ 1, Mar 96	3.95	0.79	2.37	3.95

PRIMER
COMICO
		GOOD	FINE	N-MINT
☐ 1, b&w 1:Az, Skrog, Slaughterman		1.00	3.00	5.00
☐ 2, MW,1:Grendel		8.00	24.00	40.00
☐ 3		0.80	2.40	4.00
☐ 4		0.80	2.40	4.00
☐ 5		0.80	2.40	4.00
☐ 6, 1:Evangeline		2.00	6.00	10.00

PRIMER (Vol. 2)
	ORIG.	GOOD	FINE	N-MINT
☐ 1, May 96	2.95	0.59	1.77	2.95

PRIMITIVES
SPARETIME STUDIOS
	ORIG.	GOOD	FINE	N-MINT
☐ 1, Jan 95, b&w	2.50	0.50	1.50	2.50
☐ 2, May 95, b&w	2.50	0.50	1.50	2.50

PRINCE AND THE NEW POWER GENERATION: THREE CHAINS OF GOLD
DC/PIRANHA
	ORIG.	GOOD	FINE	N-MINT
☐ 0, 94, nn	3.50	0.70	2.10	3.50

PRINCE AND THE PAUPER
DISNEY
	ORIG.	GOOD	FINE	N-MINT
☐ 1, movie, squarebound	1.19	3.57	5.95	

PRINCE NAMOR, THE SUB-MARINER
MARVEL
	ORIG.	GOOD	FINE	N-MINT
☐ 1, Sep 84	0.75	0.40	1.20	2.00
☐ 2, Oct 84	0.75	0.20	0.60	1.00
☐ 3, Nov 84	0.75	0.20	0.60	1.00
☐ 4, Dec 84	0.75	0.20	0.60	1.00

PRINCE NIGHTMARE
AAAARGH!
		GOOD	FINE	N-MINT
☐ 1		0.59	1.77	2.95

PRINCE VALIANT (mini-series)
MARVEL
	ORIG.	GOOD	FINE	N-MINT
☐ 1, Dec 94, cardstock cover	3.95	0.79	2.37	3.95
☐ 2, Jan 95, cardstock cover	3.95	0.79	2.37	3.95
☐ 3, Feb 95, cardstock cover	3.95	0.79	2.37	3.95
☐ 4, Mar 95, cardstock cover	3.95	0.79	2.37	3.95

PRINCE VALIANT MONTHLY
PIONEER
		GOOD	FINE	N-MINT
☐ 1, b&w		0.99	2.97	4.95
☐ 2, b&w		0.99	2.97	4.95
☐ 3, 89, b&w		0.99	2.97	4.95
☐ 4, 89, b&w		0.99	2.97	4.95

PRINCE VANDAL
TRIUMPHANT
	ORIG.	GOOD	FINE	N-MINT
☐ 1, Unleashed!	2.50	0.50	1.50	2.50
☐ 2, Unleashed!	2.50	0.50	1.50	2.50
☐ 3	2.50	0.50	1.50	2.50
☐ 4	2.50	0.50	1.50	2.50
☐ 5, 94	2.50	0.50	1.50	2.50
☐ 6, 94	2.50	0.50	1.50	2.50

PRINCE: ALTER EGO
PIRANHA MUSIC
		GOOD	FINE	N-MINT
☐ 1, Dec 91, BB(c)	1.00	3.00	5.00	

PRINCESS KARANAM AND THE DJINN OF THE GREEN JUG
MU PRESS
	ORIG.	GOOD	FINE	N-MINT
☐ 0, nn, b&w	2.50	0.50	1.50	2.50

PRINCESS SALLY (mini-series)
ARCHIE
	ORIG.	GOOD	FINE	N-MINT
☐ 1, Apr 95	1.50	0.30	0.90	1.50
☐ 2, May 95	1.50	0.30	0.90	1.50
☐ 3, Jun 95	1.50	0.30	0.90	1.50

PRIORITY: WHITE HEAT
AC
		GOOD	FINE	N-MINT
☐ 1, Mar 87		0.35	1.05	1.75
☐ 2		0.35	1.05	1.75

PRISONER OF CHILLON
TOME PRESS
	ORIG.	GOOD	FINE	N-MINT
☐ 1, b&w	2.95	0.59	1.77	2.95

PRISONER, THE
DC
	ORIG.	GOOD	FINE	N-MINT
☐ 1, Dec 88, (a);prestige format	3.50	0.70	2.10	3.50
☐ 2, Jan 89, (b);prestige format	3.50	0.70	2.10	3.50
☐ 3, Jan 89, (c);prestige format	3.50	0.70	2.10	3.50
☐ 4, Feb 89, (d);prestige format	3.50	0.70	2.10	3.50

PRIVATE BEACH: FUN AND PERILS IN THE TRUDYVERSE
ANTARCTIC
	ORIG.	GOOD	FINE	N-MINT
☐ 1, Jan 95, b&w	2.75	0.55	1.65	2.75
☐ 2, Mar 95, b&w	2.75	0.55	1.65	2.75
☐ 3, May 95, b&w	2.75	0.55	1.65	2.75

PRIVATE EYES
ETERNITY
		GOOD	FINE	N-MINT
☐ 1, Sep 88, b&w Saint rep.		0.39	1.17	1.95
☐ 2, Nov 88, b&w Saint rep.		0.39	1.17	1.95
☐ 3, Jan 89, b&w Saint rep.		0.39	1.17	1.95
☐ 4, May 89		0.59	1.77	2.95
☐ 5, Aug 89		0.70	2.10	3.50
☐ 6		0.79	2.37	3.95

PRIVATEERS
VANGUARD
		GOOD	FINE	N-MINT
☐ 1		0.30	0.90	1.50
☐ 2		0.30	0.90	1.50

PRO ACTION MAGAZINE
MARVEL/NFL PROPERTIES
	ORIG.	GOOD	FINE	N-MINT
☐ 2, Sep 94	2.95	0.59	1.77	2.95

PRO ACTION MAGAZINE VOL. II
	ORIG.	GOOD	FINE	N-MINT
☐ 1, Jul 94	2.95	0.59	1.77	2.95

PRO WRESTLING'S TRUE FACTS
DAN PETTIGLIO
	ORIG.	GOOD	FINE	N-MINT
☐ 0, Apr 94, nn, b&w	2.95	0.59	1.77	2.95

PROBE
IMPERIAL
		GOOD	FINE	N-MINT
☐ 1		0.36	1.08	1.80
☐ 2, (moves to Eternity)		0.39	1.17	1.95

PROBE (was Imperial Comic)
ETERNITY
		GOOD	FINE	N-MINT
☐ 3		0.39	1.17	1.95

PROFESSIONAL: GOLGO 13, THE
VIZ
		GOOD	FINE	N-MINT
☐ 1, color, Japanese		0.99	2.97	4.95
☐ 2, color, Japanese		0.99	2.97	4.95
☐ 3, color, Japanese		0.99	2.97	4.95

PROFESSOR OM
INNOVATION
		GOOD	FINE	N-MINT
☐ 1, May 90		0.50	1.50	2.50

PROFESSOR XAVIER AND THE X-MEN
MARVEL
	ORIG.	GOOD	FINE	N-MINT
☐ 1, Nov 95, retells origin of team and first mission	0.99	0.20	0.59	0.99
☐ 2, Dec 95, retells first Vanisher story	0.99	0.20	0.59	0.99
☐ 3, Jan 96, retells first Blob story	0.99	0.20	0.59	0.99
☐ 4, Feb 96, retells first meeting with Brotherhood of Evil Mutants	0.99	0.20	0.59	0.99
☐ 5, Mar 96	0.99	0.20	0.59	0.99

	ORIG.	GOOD	FINE	N-MINT
❑ 6, Apr 96 .... 0.99	0.20	0.59	0.99
❑ 7, May 96 .... 0.99	0.20	0.59	0.99
❑ 8, Jun 96 .... 0.99	0.20	0.59	0.99

PROFOLIO
ALCHEMY

		GOOD	FINE	N-MINT
❑ 1, b&w		0.30	0.90	1.50
❑ 2, some color		0.50	1.50	2.50
❑ 3, b&w		0.50	1.50	2.50

PROFOLIO (Volume 3)

		GOOD	FINE	N-MINT
❑ 1		1.19	3.57	5.95

PROGRAM ERROR: BATTLEBOT
PHANTASY

		GOOD	FINE	N-MINT
❑ 1		0.40	1.20	2.00

PROJECT A-KO
MALIBU

	ORIG.	GOOD	FINE	N-MINT
❑ 1, Mar 94 .... 2.95		0.80	2.40	4.00
❑ 2, Apr 94 .... 2.95		0.80	2.40	4.00
❑ 3, May 94 .... 2.95		0.70	2.10	3.50
❑ 4, Jun 94 .... 2.95		0.59	1.77	2.95

PROJECT A-KO 2 (mini-series)
CPM COMICS

	ORIG.	GOOD	FINE	N-MINT
❑ 1, Apr 95 .... 2.95		0.59	1.77	2.95
❑ 2, Jun 95 .... 2.95		0.59	1.77	2.95
❑ 3, Aug 95 .... 2.95		0.59	1.77	2.95

PROJECT A-KO VERSUS (mini-series)
CPM

	ORIG.	GOOD	FINE	N-MINT
❑ 1, Oct 95 .... 2.95		0.59	1.77	2.95

PROJECT HERO
VANGUARD

		GOOD	FINE	N-MINT
❑ 1, Aug 87		0.30	0.90	1.50

PROJECT SEX
EROS COMIX

		GOOD	FINE	N-MINT
❑ 1, adult, b&w		0.50	1.50	2.50

PROJECT X
KITCHEN SINK

❑ 0, nn,Eastman/Bisley, bagged Thump'n Guts, poster,

trading card 4.95	0.99	2.97	4.95

PROJECT, THE
DC/PARADOX PRESS

❑ 1, 96, b&w anthology;digest-sized

.... 5.95	1.19	3.57	5.95

❑ 2, 96, b&w anthology;digest-sized

.... 5.95	1.19	3.57	5.95

PROJECT: DARK MATTER
DIMM COMICS

❑ 1, Apr 96, b&w 2.50	0.50	1.50	2.50

PROM FORMULA, THE
ETERNITY

		GOOD	FINE	N-MINT
❑ 1, color		0.59	1.77	2.95
❑ 2, color		0.59	1.77	2.95

PROMETHEUS' GIFT
CAT-HEAD

		GOOD	FINE	N-MINT
❑ 0, nn, b&w		0.45	1.35	2.25

PROMISE
VIZ

	ORIG.	GOOD	FINE	N-MINT
❑ 0, nn 5.95		1.19	3.57	5.95

PROPELLER MAN
DARK HORSE

	ORIG.	GOOD	FINE	N-MINT
❑ 1 .... 2.95		0.59	1.77	2.95
❑ 2 .... 2.95		0.59	1.77	2.95
❑ 3 .... 2.95		0.59	1.77	2.95
❑ 4 .... 2.95		0.59	1.77	2.95
❑ 5 .... 2.95		0.59	1.77	2.95
❑ 6 .... 2.95		0.59	1.77	2.95
❑ 7 .... 2.95		0.59	1.77	2.95

PROPHET
IMAGE

❑ 0, Jul 94, San Diego Comic-Con edition

	ORIG.	GOOD	FINE	N-MINT
.... 2.50		1.00	3.00	5.00
❑ 1, Boris Vallejo cover 2.50		0.80	2.40	4.00
❑ 2, Nov 93 .... 1.95		0.39	1.17	1.95
❑ 3, Jan 94 .... 1.95		0.39	1.17	1.95
❑ 4, Feb 94 .... 1.95		0.39	1.17	1.95

❑ 4, (S. Platt alternate cover)

.... 1.95	2.00	6.00	10.00

❑ 5, Apr 94 .... 1.95	0.39	1.17	1.95
❑ 6, Jun 94 .... 1.95	0.39	1.17	1.95
❑ 7, Sep 94 .... 2.50	0.50	1.50	2.50

❑ 8, Nov 94, War Games part 2

.... 2.50	0.50	1.50	2.50
❑ 9, Dec 94 .... 2.50	0.50	1.50	2.50

PROPHET (Volume 2)

❑ 1, Aug 95 .... 3.50	0.70	2.10	3.50

❑ 1, Aug 95, enhanced wraparound cover

.... 3.50	1.00	3.00	5.00
❑ 2, Sep 95 .... 2.50	0.50	1.50	2.50

❑ 2, Sep 95, alternate cover

.... 2.50	0.50	1.50	2.50
❑ 3, Nov 95 .... 2.50	0.50	1.50	2.50
❑ 4, Feb 96, A:NewMen 2.50	0.50	1.50	2.50
❑ 5, Feb 96 .... 2.50	0.50	1.50	2.50
❑ 6, Apr 96 .... 2.50	0.50	1.50	2.50

PROPHET ANNUAL

❑ 1, Sep 95, polybagged with PowerCardz

.... 2.50	0.50	1.50	2.50

PROPHET BABEWATCH

❑ 2, Dec 95, Cover says "#1";indicia says "#2"

.... 2.50	0.50	1.50	2.50

PROTECTORS HANDBOOK
MALIBU

		GOOD	FINE	N-MINT
❑ 1		0.50	1.50	2.50

PROTECTORS, THE

❑ 1, O:Protectors	0.39	1.17	1.95

❑ 1, O:Protectors, w/poster, wrapper

.... 2.50	0.50	1.50	2.50
❑ 2, with poster 2.50	0.50	1.50	2.50
❑ 3 .... 2.50	0.50	1.50	2.50
❑ 4 .... 2.50	0.50	1.50	2.50

❑ 5, "bullet hole," embossed cover

.... 2.95	0.59	1.77	2.95
❑ 5, "bullet hole," bagged ... 2.50	0.50	1.50	2.50

❑ 5, "bullet hole," die-cut cover

.... 0.90	2.70	4.50	
❑ 6 .... 2.50	0.50	1.50	2.50
❑ 6, with poster 2.50	0.50	1.50	2.50
❑ 7 .... 2.50	0.50	1.50	2.50
❑ 8 .... 2.50	0.50	1.50	2.50
❑ 9 .... 2.50	0.50	1.50	2.50
❑ 10 .... 2.50	0.50	1.50	2.50
❑ 11 .... 2.50	0.50	1.50	2.50
❑ 13, Genesis 2.25	0.45	1.35	2.25
❑ 14 .... 2.25	0.45	1.35	2.25
❑ 15 .... 2.25	0.45	1.35	2.25
❑ 16, Dec 93 .... 2.25	0.45	1.35	2.25
❑ 17, Jan 94 .... 2.25	0.45	1.35	2.25
❑ 18, Feb 94 .... 2.25	0.45	1.35	2.25
❑ 19, Mar 94 .... 2.50	0.50	1.50	2.50

NEW YORK

❑ 1 .... 1.70	0.34	1.02	1.70
❑ 2 .... 1.70	0.34	1.02	1.70

PROTOTYPE
MALIBU/ULTRAVERSE

❑ 0, Aug 94 .... 2.50	0.50	1.50	2.50
❑ 1, Aug 93, Ultraverse 1.95	0.80	2.40	4.00
❑ 1, hologram	12.00	36.00	60.00

	ORIG.	GOOD	FINE	N-MINT
☐ 2, Sep 93 ....1.95		0.70	2.10	3.50
☐ 3, Oct 93, Rune, BWS 2.50		0.50	1.50	2.50
☐ 4, Nov 93 ....1.95		0.39	1.17	1.95
☐ 5, Dec 93, Break-Thru 1.95		0.39	1.17	1.95
☐ 6, Jan 94 ....1.95		0.39	1.17	1.95
☐ 7, Feb 94 ....1.95		0.39	1.17	1.95
☐ 8, Mar 94 ....1.95		0.39	1.17	1.95
☐ 9, Apr 94 ....1.95		0.39	1.17	1.95
☐ 10, May 94 ....1.95		0.39	1.17	1.95
☐ 11, Jun 94 ....1.95		0.39	1.17	1.95
☐ 12, Jul 94 ....1.95		0.39	1.17	1.95
☐ 13, Aug 94, flipbook with *Ultraverse Premiere #6*				
....3.50		0.70	2.10	3.50
☐ 14, Oct 94 ....1.95		0.39	1.17	1.95
☐ 15, Nov 94 ....1.95		0.39	1.17	1.95

PROWLER
ECLIPSE

	ORIG.	GOOD	FINE	N-MINT
☐ 1, Jul 87 ....1.75		0.35	1.05	1.75
☐ 2, Aug 87 ....1.75		0.35	1.05	1.75
☐ 3, Sep 87 ....1.75		0.35	1.05	1.75
☐ 4, Oct 87 ....1.75		0.35	1.05	1.75

PROWLER (mini-series)
MARVEL

	ORIG.	GOOD	FINE	N-MINT
☐ 1, Nov 94 ....1.75		0.35	1.05	1.75
☐ 2, Dec 94 ....1.75		0.35	1.05	1.75
☐ 3, Jan 95 ....1.75		0.35	1.05	1.75
☐ 4, Feb 95 ....1.75		0.35	1.05	1.75

PROWLER IN "WHITE ZOMBIE"
ECLIPSE

	GOOD	FINE	N-MINT
☐ 1, Oct 88, b&w	0.40	1.20	2.00

PRUDENCE AND CAUTION
DEFIANT

	ORIG.	GOOD	FINE	N-MINT
☐ 1, May 94, English version				
....3.25		0.65	1.95	3.25

PSI-FORCE
MARVEL

	ORIG.	GOOD	FINE	N-MINT
☐ 1, Nov 86 ....0.75		0.35	1.05	1.75
☐ 2, Dec 86 ....0.75		0.35	1.05	1.75
☐ 3, Jan 87 ....0.75		0.35	1.05	1.75
☐ 4, Feb 87 ....0.75		0.35	1.05	1.75
☐ 5, Mar 87 ....0.75		0.35	1.05	1.75
☐ 6, Apr 87 ....0.75		0.35	1.05	1.75
☐ 7, May 87 ....0.75		0.35	1.05	1.75
☐ 8, Jun 87 ....0.75		0.35	1.05	1.75
☐ 9, Jul 87 ....0.75		0.35	1.05	1.75
☐ 10, Aug 87 ....0.75		0.35	1.05	1.75
☐ 11, Sep 87 ....0.75		0.35	1.05	1.75
☐ 12, Oct 87 ....0.75		0.35	1.05	1.75
☐ 13, Nov 87 ....0.75		0.35	1.05	1.75
☐ 14, Dec 87 ....0.75		0.35	1.05	1.75
☐ 15, Jan 88 ....0.75		0.35	1.05	1.75
☐ 16, Feb 88 ....0.75		0.35	1.05	1.75
☐ 17, Mar 88 ....0.75		0.35	1.05	1.75
☐ 18, Apr 88 ....0.75		0.35	1.05	1.75
☐ 19, May 88 ....1.25		0.35	1.05	1.75
☐ 20, Jun 88 ....1.25		0.25	0.75	1.25
☐ 21, Jul 88 ....1.25		0.25	0.75	1.25
☐ 22, Aug 88 ....1.25		0.25	0.75	1.25
☐ 23, Sep 88 ....1.25		0.25	0.75	1.25
☐ 24, Oct 88 ....1.25		0.25	0.75	1.25
☐ 25, Nov 88 ....1.25		0.25	0.75	1.25
☐ 26, Dec 88 ....1.50		0.30	0.90	1.50
☐ 27, Jan 89 ....1.50		0.30	0.90	1.50
☐ 28, Feb 89 ....1.50		0.30	0.90	1.50
☐ 29, Mar 89 ....1.50		0.30	0.90	1.50
☐ 30, Apr 89 ....1.50		0.30	0.90	1.50
☐ 31, May 89 ....1.50		0.30	0.90	1.50
☐ 32, Jun 89 ....1.50		0.30	0.90	1.50

PSI-FORCE ANNUAL

	ORIG.	GOOD	FINE	N-MINT
☐ 1, 87 ....1.25		0.25	0.75	1.25

PSI-JUDGE ANDERSON
FLEETWAY/QUALITY

	GOOD	FINE	N-MINT
☐ 1, b&w	0.39	1.17	1.95
☐ 2, b&w	0.39	1.17	1.95
☐ 3, b&w	0.39	1.17	1.95
☐ 4, b&w	0.39	1.17	1.95
☐ 5, b&w	0.39	1.17	1.95
☐ 6, b&w	0.39	1.17	1.95
☐ 7, b&w	0.39	1.17	1.95
☐ 8, b&w	0.39	1.17	1.95
☐ 9, b&w	0.39	1.17	1.95
☐ 10, b&w	0.39	1.17	1.95
☐ 11, b&w	0.39	1.17	1.95
☐ 12, b&w	0.39	1.17	1.95
☐ 13, b&w	0.39	1.17	1.95
☐ 14, b&w	0.39	1.17	1.95
☐ 15, b&w	0.39	1.17	1.95

PSI-JUDGE ANDERSON: ENGRAMS

	ORIG.	GOOD	FINE	N-MINT
☐ 1, b&w 1.95		0.39	1.17	1.95
☐ 2, b&w 1.95		0.39	1.17	1.95

PSI-JUDGE ANDERSON: PSIFILES

	ORIG.	GOOD	FINE	N-MINT
☐ 1 ....2.95		0.59	1.77	2.95

PSI-LORDS
ACCLAIM/VALIANT

	ORIG.	GOOD	FINE	N-MINT
☐ 10, Jun 95, final issue.....2.25		0.45	1.35	2.25

VALIANT

	ORIG.	GOOD	FINE	N-MINT
☐ 1, Sep 94, Valiant Vision;chromium wrap-around cover				
....3.50		0.70	2.10	3.50
☐ 2, Oct 94, Valiant Vision .2.25		0.45	1.35	2.25
☐ 3, Nov 94, Valiant Vision; Chaos Effect				
....2.25		0.45	1.35	2.25
☐ 4, Dec 94 ....2.25		0.45	1.35	2.25
☐ 5, Jan 95 ....2.25		0.45	1.35	2.25
☐ 6, Feb 95 ....2.25		0.45	1.35	2.25
☐ 7, Mar 95 ....2.25		0.45	1.35	2.25
☐ 8, Apr 95 ....2.25		0.45	1.35	2.25

PSYBA-RATS, THE (mini-series)
DC

	ORIG.	GOOD	FINE	N-MINT
☐ 1, Apr 95 ....2.50		0.50	1.50	2.50
☐ 2, May 95 ....1.50		0.30	0.90	1.50
☐ 3, Jun 95 ....1.50		0.30	0.90	1.50

PSYCHO KILLERS
COMIC ZONE

	GOOD	FINE	N-MINT
☐ 1, b&w	0.55	1.65	2.75
☐ 2, b&w	0.55	1.65	2.75
☐ 3, b&w	0.55	1.65	2.75

PSYCHO, THE
DC

	GOOD	FINE	N-MINT
☐ 1, Sep 91	0.99	2.97	4.95
☐ 2, Oct 91	0.99	2.97	4.95
☐ 3, Dec 91	0.99	2.97	4.95

PSYCHOBLAST
FIRST

	GOOD	FINE	N-MINT
☐ 1, Nov 87	0.35	1.05	1.75
☐ 2, Dec 87	0.35	1.05	1.75
☐ 3, Jan 88	0.35	1.05	1.75
☐ 4, Feb 88	0.35	1.05	1.75
☐ 5, Mar 88	0.35	1.05	1.75
☐ 6, Apr 88	0.35	1.05	1.75
☐ 7, May 88	0.35	1.05	1.75
☐ 8, Jun 88	0.35	1.05	1.75
☐ 9, Jul 88	0.35	1.05	1.75

PSYCHONAUTS
EPIC

	ORIG.	GOOD	FINE	N-MINT
☐ 1 ....4.95		0.99	2.97	4.95
☐ 2 ....4.95		0.99	2.97	4.95
☐ 3 ....4.95		0.99	2.97	4.95
☐ 4 ....4.95		0.99	2.97	4.95

	ORIG.	GOOD	FINE	N-MINT

PTERANOMAN
KITCHEN SINK
	ORIG.	GOOD	FINE	N-MINT
❑ 1, Aug 90, Don Simpson..	0.40	1.20	2.00	

PUBLIC ENEMIES
ETERNITY
| ❑ 1, b&w rep. | 0.79 | 2.37 | 3.95 | |
| ❑ 2, b&w rep. | 0.79 | 2.37 | 3.95 | |

PULP DREAMS
EROS COMIX
| ❑ 1, adult, b&w | 0.50 | 1.50 | 2.50 | |

PUMA BLUES
AARDVARK ONE
❑ 1, Jun 86, 1st printing;b&w;10,000 copies printed				
.... 2.00	0.60	1.80	3.00	
❑ 1, 2nd printing	0.34	1.02	1.70	
❑ 2	0.34	1.02	1.70	
❑ 3	0.34	1.02	1.70	
❑ 4	0.34	1.02	1.70	
❑ 5	0.34	1.02	1.70	
❑ 6	0.34	1.02	1.70	
❑ 7	0.34	1.02	1.70	
❑ 8	0.34	1.02	1.70	
❑ 9	0.34	1.02	1.70	
❑ 10	0.34	1.02	1.70	
❑ 11	0.34	1.02	1.70	
❑ 12	0.34	1.02	1.70	
❑ 13	0.34	1.02	1.70	
❑ 14	0.34	1.02	1.70	
❑ 15	0.34	1.02	1.70	
❑ 16	0.34	1.02	1.70	
❑ 17	0.34	1.02	1.70	
❑ 18, self-published	0.34	1.02	1.70	
❑ 19, self-published	0.34	1.02	1.70	
❑ 20, Alan Moore (self-published) (moves to Mirage)				
	0.34	1.02	1.70	

PUMA BLUES (was Aardvark-One)
MIRAGE
❑ 21, b&w	0.34	1.02	1.70	
❑ 22, b&w	0.34	1.02	1.70	
❑ 23, b&w	0.34	1.02	1.70	

PUMMELER
PARODY PRESS
| ❑ 1, b&w, Punisher parody | | | | |
| .... 2.95 | 0.59 | 1.77 | 2.95 | |

PUMPKINHEAD: THE RITES OF EXORCISM
DARK HORSE
| ❑ 1 .... 2.50 | 0.50 | 1.50 | 2.50 | |
| ❑ 2 .... 2.50 | 0.50 | 1.50 | 2.50 | |

PUNISHER (1995-)
MARVEL
❑ 1, Nov 95, enhanced cardstock cover				
.... 2.95	0.59	1.77	2.95	
❑ 2, Dec 95 .... 1.95	0.39	1.17	1.95	
❑ 3, Dec 95 .... 1.95	0.39	1.17	1.95	
❑ 4, Feb 96, A:Daredevil;V:Jigsaw				
.... 1.95	0.39	1.17	1.95	
❑ 5, Mar 96 .... 1.95	0.39	1.17	1.95	
❑ 6, Apr 96 .... 1.95	0.39	1.17	1.95	
❑ 7, May 96 .... 1.95	0.39	1.17	1.95	
❑ 8, Jun 96 .... 1.95	0.39	1.17	1.95	
❑ 9, Jul 96 .... 1.95	0.39	1.17	1.95	

PUNISHER (mini-series)
❑ 1 .... 1.25	4.00	12.00	20.00	
❑ 2 .... 0.75	2.40	7.20	12.00	
❑ 3 .... 0.75	1.60	4.80	8.00	
❑ 4 .... 0.75	1.60	4.80	8.00	
❑ 5 .... 0.75	1.60	4.80	8.00	

PUNISHER 2099
| ❑ 1, foil cover .... 1.75 | 0.35 | 1.05 | 1.75 | |

	ORIG.	GOOD	FINE	N-MINT
❑ 2 .... 1.25	0.25	0.75	1.25	
❑ 3 .... 1.25	0.25	0.75	1.25	
❑ 4 .... 1.25	0.25	0.75	1.25	
❑ 5 .... 1.25	0.25	0.75	1.25	
❑ 6 .... 1.25	0.25	0.75	1.25	
❑ 7 .... 1.25	0.25	0.75	1.25	
❑ 8 .... 1.25	0.25	0.75	1.25	
❑ 9 .... 1.25	0.25	0.75	1.25	
❑ 10 .... 1.25	0.25	0.75	1.25	
❑ 11 .... 1.25	0.25	0.75	1.25	
❑ 12 .... 1.25	0.25	0.75	1.25	
❑ 13 .... 1.25	0.25	0.75	1.25	
❑ 14 .... 1.25	0.25	0.75	1.25	
❑ 15 .... 1.25	0.25	0.75	1.25	
❑ 16, May 94 .... 1.50	0.30	0.90	1.50	
❑ 17, Jun 94 .... 1.50	0.30	0.90	1.50	
❑ 18, Jul 94 .... 1.50	0.30	0.90	1.50	
❑ 19, Aug 94 .... 1.50	0.30	0.90	1.50	
❑ 20, Sep 94 .... 1.50	0.30	0.90	1.50	
❑ 21, Oct 94 .... 1.50	0.30	0.90	1.50	
❑ 22, Nov 94 .... 1.50	0.30	0.90	1.50	
❑ 23, Dec 94 .... 1.50	0.30	0.90	1.50	
❑ 24, Jan 95 .... 1.50	0.30	0.90	1.50	
❑ 25, Feb 95 .... 2.25	0.45	1.35	2.25	
❑ 25, Feb 95, enhanced cover				
.... 2.95	0.59	1.77	2.95	
❑ 26, Mar 95 .... 1.50	0.30	0.90	1.50	
❑ 27, Apr 95 .... 1.50	0.30	0.90	1.50	
❑ 28, May 95 .... 1.95	0.39	1.17	1.95	
❑ 29, Jun 95 .... 1.95	0.39	1.17	1.95	
❑ 30, Jul 95 .... 1.95	0.39	1.17	1.95	
❑ 31, Aug 95 .... 1.95	0.39	1.17	1.95	
❑ 32, Sep 95 .... 1.95	0.39	1.17	1.95	
❑ 33, Oct 95 .... 1.95	0.39	1.17	1.95	
❑ 34, Nov 95, continues in *2099 A.D. Apocalypse* #1				
.... 1.95	0.39	1.17	1.95	

PUNISHER ANNIVERSARY MAGAZINE, THE
| ❑ 1 .... 4.95 | 0.99 | 2.97 | 4.95 | |

PUNISHER ANNUAL, THE
❑ 1, 88, Evolutionary War .. 1.75	2.00	6.00	10.00	
❑ 2, 89, Atlantis Attacks 2.00	1.60	4.80	8.00	
❑ 3, 90, Lifeform 2.00	0.40	1.20	2.00	
❑ 4, 91, Von Strucker 2.00	0.40	1.20	2.00	
❑ 5 .... 2.25	0.45	1.35	2.25	
❑ 6, trading card 2.95	0.59	1.77	2.95	
❑ 7, 94 .... 2.95	0.59	1.77	2.95	

PUNISHER ARMORY, THE
❑ 1, Jul 90, weapons 1.50	1.60	4.80	8.00	
❑ 2, Jun 91 .... 1.75	0.60	1.80	3.00	
❑ 3	0.60	1.80	3.00	
❑ 4 .... 2.00	0.40	1.20	2.00	
❑ 5 .... 2.00	0.40	1.20	2.00	
❑ 6 .... 2.00	0.40	1.20	2.00	
❑ 7 .... 2.00	0.40	1.20	2.00	
❑ 8 .... 2.00	0.40	1.20	2.00	
❑ 9 .... 2.00	0.40	1.20	2.00	
❑ 10, Nov 94 .... 2.00	0.40	1.20	2.00	

PUNISHER BACK TO SCHOOL SPECIAL, THE
❑ 1 .... 2.95	0.59	1.77	2.95	
❑ 2 .... 2.95	0.59	1.77	2.95	
❑ 3, Oct 94 .... 2.95	0.59	1.77	2.95	

PUNISHER HOLIDAY SPECIAL
❑ 1, foil cover 2.95	0.59	1.77	2.95	
❑ 2 .... 2.95	0.59	1.77	2.95	
❑ 3, Jan 95 .... 2.95	0.59	1.77	2.95	

PUNISHER MAGAZINE
❑ 1, Sep 89, b&w, reprints				
.... 2.25	0.45	1.35	2.25	
❑ 2, Oct 89, b&w,reprints .. 2.25	0.45	1.35	2.25	

	ORIG.	GOOD	FINE	N-MINT
❏ 3, Nov 89, b&w, reprints				
...............2.25		0.45	1.35	2.25
❏ 4, Dec 89, b&w, reprints				
...............2.25		0.45	1.35	2.25
❏ 5, Dec 89, b&w, reprints				
...............2.25		0.45	1.35	2.25
❏ 6, Jan 90, b&w, reprints				
...............2.25		0.45	1.35	2.25
❏ 7, Feb 90, b&w, reprints				
...............2.25		0.45	1.35	2.25
❏ 8, Mar 90, b&w, reprints				
...............2.25		0.45	1.35	2.25
❏ 9, Apr 90, b&w, reprints				
...............2.25		0.45	1.35	2.25
❏ 10, May 90, b&w, reprints				
...............2.25		0.45	1.35	2.25
❏ 11, Jun 90, b&w, reprints				
...............2.25		0.45	1.35	2.25
❏ 12, Jul 90, b&w, reprints				
...............2.25		0.45	1.35	2.25
❏ 13, Aug 90, b&w, reprints				
...............2.25		0.45	1.35	2.25
❏ 14, Sep 90, b&w, reprints				
...............2.25		0.45	1.35	2.25
❏ 15, Oct 90, b&w, reprints				
...............2.25		0.45	1.35	2.25
❏ 16, Nov 90, b&w, reprints				
...............2.25		0.45	1.35	2.25

PUNISHER MEETS ARCHIE, THE

	ORIG.	GOOD	FINE	N-MINT
❏ 1, Aug 94, enhanced cover				
...............3.95		0.79	2.37	3.95

PUNISHER MOVIE SPECIAL

	ORIG.	GOOD	FINE	N-MINT
❏ 0, Jun 90, nn.............5.95		1.19	3.57	5.95

PUNISHER P.O.V.

	ORIG.	GOOD	FINE	N-MINT
❏ 1, BW.............4.95		1.20	3.60	6.00
❏ 2, BW.............4.95		1.20	3.60	6.00
❏ 3, BW.............4.95		1.20	3.60	6.00
❏ 4, BW.............4.95		1.20	3.60	6.00

PUNISHER SUMMER SPECIAL

	ORIG.	GOOD	FINE	N-MINT
❏ 1, Aug 91 ....2.95		0.59	1.77	2.95
❏ 3 ....2.50		0.50	1.50	2.50
❏ 4, Jul 94.............2.95		0.59	1.77	2.95

PUNISHER WAR JOURNAL

	ORIG.	GOOD	FINE	N-MINT
❏ 1, Nov 88 ....1.50		1.50	4.50	7.50
❏ 2, Dec 88, Daredevil.......1.50		1.00	3.00	5.00
❏ 3, Feb 89, Daredevil 1.50		0.60	1.80	3.00
❏ 4, Mar 89 ....1.50		0.60	1.80	3.00
❏ 5, May 89.............1.50		0.60	1.80	3.00
❏ 6, Jun 89, Wolverine......1.50		1.50	4.50	7.50
❏ 7, Jul 89, Wolverine 1.50		0.60	1.80	3.00
❏ 8, Sep 89.............1.50		0.60	1.80	3.00
❏ 9, Oct 89 ....1.50		0.60	1.80	3.00
❏ 10, Nov 89 ....1.50		0.60	1.80	3.00
❏ 11, Dec 89.............1.50		0.40	1.20	2.00
❏ 12, Dec 89, Acts of Vengeance				
...............1.50		0.40	1.20	2.00
❏ 13, Dec 89, Acts of Vengeance				
...............1.50		0.40	1.20	2.00
❏ 14, Jan 90, SpM.............1.50		0.40	1.20	2.00
❏ 15, Feb 90 ....1.50		0.40	1.20	2.00
❏ 16, Mar 90 ....1.50		0.40	1.20	2.00
❏ 17, Apr 90 ....1.50		0.40	1.20	2.00
❏ 18, May 90 ....1.50		0.40	1.20	2.00
❏ 19, Jun 90.............1.50		0.40	1.20	2.00
❏ 20, Jul 90.............1.50		0.40	1.20	2.00
❏ 21, Aug 90 ....1.50		0.40	1.20	2.00
❏ 22, Sep 90 ....1.50		0.40	1.20	2.00
❏ 23, Oct 90 ....1.75		0.40	1.20	2.00
❏ 24, Nov 90 ....1.75		0.40	1.20	2.00
❏ 25, Dec 90.............1.75		0.40	1.20	2.00

	ORIG.	GOOD	FINE	N-MINT
❏ 26, Jan 91.............1.75		0.40	1.20	2.00
❏ 27, Feb 91.............1.75		0.40	1.20	2.00
❏ 28, Mar 91.............1.75		0.40	1.20	2.00
❏ 29, Apr 91.............1.75		0.40	1.20	2.00
❏ 30, May 91, Ghost Rider.1.75		0.40	1.20	2.00
❏ 31, Jun 91 ....1.75		0.40	1.20	2.00
❏ 32, Jul 91.............1.75		0.40	1.20	2.00
❏ 33, Aug 91.............1.75		0.40	1.20	2.00
❏ 34, Sep 91 ....1.75		0.40	1.20	2.00
❏ 35, Oct 91 ....1.75		0.40	1.20	2.00
❏ 36, Nov 91 ....1.75		0.40	1.20	2.00
❏ 37, Dec 91 ....1.75		0.40	1.20	2.00
❏ 38 ....1.75		0.40	1.20	2.00
❏ 39 ....1.75		0.40	1.20	2.00
❏ 40 ....1.75		0.40	1.20	2.00
❏ 41 ....1.75		0.30	0.90	1.50
❏ 42 ....1.75		0.30	0.90	1.50
❏ 43 ....1.75		0.30	0.90	1.50
❏ 44 ....1.75		0.30	0.90	1.50
❏ 45 ....1.75		0.30	0.90	1.50
❏ 46 ....1.75		0.30	0.90	1.50
❏ 47 ....1.75		0.30	0.90	1.50
❏ 48 ....1.75		0.30	0.90	1.50
❏ 49 ....1.75		0.30	0.90	1.50
❏ 50 ....2.95		0.30	0.90	1.50
❏ 51 ....1.75		0.30	0.90	1.50
❏ 52 ....1.75		0.30	0.90	1.50
❏ 53 ....1.75		0.30	0.90	1.50
❏ 54 ....1.75		0.30	0.90	1.50
❏ 55 ....1.75		0.30	0.90	1.50
❏ 56 ....1.75		0.30	0.90	1.50
❏ 57 ....1.75		0.30	0.90	1.50
❏ 58 ....1.75		0.30	0.90	1.50
❏ 59 ....1.75		0.30	0.90	1.50
❏ 60 ....1.75		0.30	0.90	1.50
❏ 61, foil cover.............2.95		0.59	1.77	2.95
❏ 62 ....1.75		0.35	1.05	1.75
❏ 63 ....1.75		0.35	1.05	1.75
❏ 64, diecut cover.............2.95		0.59	1.77	2.95
❏ 65, Apr 94.............1.75		0.35	1.05	1.75
❏ 66, May 94.............1.75		0.35	1.05	1.75
❏ 67, Jun 94 ....1.95		0.39	1.17	1.95
❏ 68, Jul 94.............1.95		0.39	1.17	1.95
❏ 69, Aug 94 ....1.95		0.39	1.17	1.95
❏ 70, Sep 94 ....1.95		0.39	1.17	1.95
❏ 71, Oct 94 ....1.95		0.39	1.17	1.95
❏ 72, Nov 94 ....1.95		0.39	1.17	1.95
❏ 73, Dec 94 ....1.95		0.39	1.17	1.95
❏ 74, Jan 95.............1.95		0.39	1.17	1.95
❏ 75, Feb 95.............2.50		0.50	1.50	2.50
❏ 76, Mar 95.............1.95		0.39	1.17	1.95
❏ 77, Apr 95.............1.95		0.39	1.17	1.95
❏ 78, May 95.............1.95		0.39	1.17	1.95
❏ 79, Jun 95 ....1.95		0.39	1.17	1.95
❏ 80, Jul 95, final issue......1.95		0.39	1.17	1.95

PUNISHER WAR ZONE

	ORIG.	GOOD	FINE	N-MINT
❏ 1, diecut cover.............2.25		0.80	2.40	4.00
❏ 2 ....1.75		0.50	1.50	2.50
❏ 3 ....1.75		0.40	1.20	2.00
❏ 4 ....1.75		0.40	1.20	2.00
❏ 5 ....1.75		0.40	1.20	2.00
❏ 6 ....1.75		0.30	0.90	1.50
❏ 7 ....1.75		0.30	0.90	1.50
❏ 8 ....1.75		0.30	0.90	1.50
❏ 9 ....1.75		0.30	0.90	1.50
❏ 10 ....1.75		0.30	0.90	1.50
❏ 11 ....1.75		0.30	0.90	1.50
❏ 12 ....1.75		0.30	0.90	1.50
❏ 13 ....1.75		0.30	0.90	1.50
❏ 14 ....1.75		0.30	0.90	1.50
❏ 15 ....1.75		0.30	0.90	1.50

	ORIG.	GOOD	FINE	N-MINT
16	1.75	0.30	0.90	1.50
17	1.75	0.30	0.90	1.50
18	1.75	0.30	0.90	1.50
19	1.75	0.30	0.90	1.50
20	1.75	0.30	0.90	1.50
21	1.75	0.35	1.05	1.75
22	1.75	0.35	1.05	1.75
23, foil cover	2.95	0.59	1.77	2.95
24	1.75	0.35	1.05	1.75
25	2.25	0.45	1.35	2.25
26, Apr 94	1.75	0.35	1.05	1.75
27, May 94	1.95	0.39	1.17	1.95
28, Jun 94	1.95	0.39	1.17	1.95
29, Jul 94	1.95	0.39	1.17	1.95
30, Aug 94	1.95	0.39	1.17	1.95
31, Sep 94, River of Blood	1.95	0.39	1.17	1.95
32, Oct 94, River of Blood	1.95	0.39	1.17	1.95
33, Nov 94	1.95	0.39	1.17	1.95
34, Dec 94	1.95	0.39	1.17	1.95
35, Jan 95	1.95	0.39	1.17	1.95
36, Feb 95	1.95	0.39	1.17	1.95
37, Mar 95	1.95	0.39	1.17	1.95
38, Apr 95	1.95	0.39	1.17	1.95
39, May 95	1.95	0.39	1.17	1.95
40, Jun 95	1.95	0.39	1.17	1.95
41, Jul 95, final issue	1.95	0.39	1.17	1.95

PUNISHER WAR ZONE ANNUAL

	ORIG.	GOOD	FINE	N-MINT
1, card	2.95	0.59	1.77	2.95
2, 94	2.95	0.59	1.77	2.95

PUNISHER, THE (ongoing series)

	ORIG.	GOOD	FINE	N-MINT
1, Jul 87	0.75	1.60	4.80	8.00
2, Aug 87	0.75	1.00	3.00	5.00
3, Oct 87	0.75	0.80	2.40	4.00
4, Nov 87	0.75	0.80	2.40	4.00
5, Jan 88	0.75	0.80	2.40	4.00
6, Feb 88	0.75	0.80	2.40	4.00
7, Mar 88	0.75	0.80	2.40	4.00
8, May 88	1.00	1.40	4.20	7.00
9, Jun 88	1.00	1.40	4.20	7.00
10, Aug 88, Daredevil	1.00	2.00	6.00	10.00
11, Sep 88	1.00	0.70	2.10	3.50
12, Oct 88	1.00	0.70	2.10	3.50
13, Nov 88	1.00	0.70	2.10	3.50
14, Dec 88	1.00	0.70	2.10	3.50
15, Jan 89	1.00	0.70	2.10	3.50
16, Feb 89	1.00	0.60	1.80	3.00
17, Mar 89	1.00	0.60	1.80	3.00
18, Apr 89, V:Kingpin	1.00	0.60	1.80	3.00
19, May 89	1.00	0.60	1.80	3.00
20, Jun 89	1.00	0.60	1.80	3.00
21, Jul 89	1.00	0.50	1.50	2.50
22, Aug 89	1.00	0.50	1.50	2.50
23, Sep 89	1.00	0.50	1.50	2.50
24, Oct 89	1.00	0.50	1.50	2.50
25, Nov 89	1.75	0.50	1.50	2.50
26, Nov 89	1.00	0.50	1.50	2.50
27, Dec 89	1.00	0.50	1.50	2.50
28, Dec 89, Acts of Vengeance	1.00	0.50	1.50	2.50
29, Jan 90, Acts of Vengeance	1.00	0.50	1.50	2.50
30, Feb 90	1.00	0.50	1.50	2.50
31, Mar 90	1.00	0.40	1.20	2.00
32, Apr 90	1.00	0.40	1.20	2.00
33, May 90	1.00	0.40	1.20	2.00
34, Jun 90	1.00	0.40	1.20	2.00
35, Jul 90, Jigsaw Puzzle	1.00	0.40	1.20	2.00
36, Aug 90, Jigsaw Puzzle	1.00	0.40	1.20	2.00
37, Aug 90, Jigsaw Puzzle	1.00	0.40	1.20	2.00
38, Sep 90, Jigsaw Puzzle	1.00	0.40	1.20	2.00
39, Sep 90, Jigsaw Puzzle	1.00	0.40	1.20	2.00
40, Oct 90, Jigsaw Puzzle	1.00	0.40	1.20	2.00
41, Oct 90	1.00	0.40	1.20	2.00
42, Nov 90	1.00	0.40	1.20	2.00
43, Dec 90	1.00	0.40	1.20	2.00
44, Jan 91	1.00	0.40	1.20	2.00
45, Feb 91	1.00	0.40	1.20	2.00
46, Mar 91	1.00	0.40	1.20	2.00
47, Apr 91	1.00	0.40	1.20	2.00
48, May 91	1.00	0.40	1.20	2.00
49, Jun 91	1.00	0.40	1.20	2.00
50, Jul 91	1.50	0.60	1.80	3.00
51, Aug 91	1.00	0.40	1.20	2.00
52, Sep 91	1.00	0.40	1.20	2.00
53, Oct 91	1.00	0.40	1.20	2.00
54, Nov 91	1.00	0.40	1.20	2.00
55, Nov 91	1.00	0.40	1.20	2.00
56, Dec 91	1.00	0.40	1.20	2.00
57, Dec 91, photo cover	1.00	0.40	1.20	2.00
58	1.00	0.40	1.20	2.00
59	1.00	0.40	1.20	2.00
60, Cage	1.25	0.40	1.20	2.00
61, Cage	1.25	0.30	0.90	1.50
62	1.25	0.30	0.90	1.50
63	1.25	0.30	0.90	1.50
64	1.25	0.30	0.90	1.50
65	1.25	0.30	0.90	1.50
66	1.25	0.30	0.90	1.50
67	1.25	0.30	0.90	1.50
68	1.25	0.30	0.90	1.50
69	1.25	0.30	0.90	1.50
70	1.25	0.30	0.90	1.50
71	1.25	0.30	0.90	1.50
72	1.25	0.30	0.90	1.50
73	1.25	0.30	0.90	1.50
74	1.25	0.30	0.90	1.50
75, foil cover	2.75	0.30	0.90	1.50
76	1.25	0.30	0.90	1.50
77	1.25	0.30	0.90	1.50
78	1.25	0.30	0.90	1.50
79	1.25	0.30	0.90	1.50
80	1.25	0.30	0.90	1.50
81	1.25	0.30	0.90	1.50
82	1.25	0.30	0.90	1.50
83	1.25	0.30	0.90	1.50
84	1.25	0.30	0.90	1.50
85	1.25	0.30	0.90	1.50
86, foil cover	2.95	0.30	0.90	1.50
87	1.25	0.30	0.90	1.50
88, Mar 94	1.25	0.30	0.90	1.50
89, Apr 94	1.25	0.30	0.90	1.50
90, May 94	1.50	0.30	0.90	1.50
91, Jun 94	1.50	0.30	0.90	1.50
92, Jul 94	1.50	0.30	0.90	1.50
93, Aug 94	1.50	0.30	0.90	1.50
94, Sep 94	1.50	0.30	0.90	1.50
95, Oct 94	1.50	0.30	0.90	1.50
96, Nov 94	1.50	0.30	0.90	1.50
97, Dec 94	1.50	0.30	0.90	1.50
98, Jan 95	1.50	0.30	0.90	1.50
99, Feb 95	1.50	0.30	0.90	1.50
100, Mar 95, enhanced cardstock cover	3.95	0.79	2.37	3.95
100, Mar 95	2.95	0.59	1.77	2.95

	ORIG.	GOOD	FINE	N-MINT
☐ 101, Apr 95 .... 1.50		0.30	0.90	1.50
☐ 102, May 95 .... 1.50		0.30	0.90	1.50
☐ 103, Jun 95 .... 1.50		0.30	0.90	1.50
☐ 104, Jul 95, final issue ... 1.50		0.30	0.90	1.50

PUNISHER/BATMAN: DEADLY KNIGHTS

	ORIG.	GOOD	FINE	N-MINT
☐ 0, Oct 94 .... 4.95		0.99	2.97	4.95

PUNISHER/CAPTAIN AMERICA: BLOOD & GLORY

	ORIG.	GOOD	FINE	N-MINT
☐ 1 .... 5.95		1.19	3.57	5.95
☐ 2 .... 5.95		1.19	3.57	5.95
☐ 3 .... 5.95		1.19	3.57	5.95

PUNISHER: A MAN NAMED FRANK, THE

	ORIG.	GOOD	FINE	N-MINT
☐ 0, Jun 94, one-shot........ 6.95		1.39	4.17	6.95

PUNISHER: EMPTY QUARTER, THE

☐ 0, Nov 94, prestige format one-shot

	ORIG.	GOOD	FINE	N-MINT
.... 6.95		1.39	4.17	6.95

PUNISHER: ORIGIN OF MICRO CHIP

	ORIG.	GOOD	FINE	N-MINT
☐ 1 .... 1.75		0.35	1.05	1.75
☐ 2 .... 1.75		0.35	1.05	1.75

PUNISHER: THE GHOSTS OF INNOCENTS

	ORIG.	GOOD	FINE	N-MINT
☐ 1 .... 5.95		1.19	3.57	5.95
☐ 2 .... 5.95		1.19	3.57	5.95

PUNISHER: YEAR ONE, THE (mini-series)

	ORIG.	GOOD	FINE	N-MINT
☐ 1, Dec 94 .... 2.50		0.50	1.50	2.50
☐ 2, Jan 95 .... 2.50		0.50	1.50	2.50
☐ 3, Feb 95 .... 2.50		0.50	1.50	2.50
☐ 4, Mar 95 .... 2.50		0.50	1.50	2.50

PUNX
ACCLAIM/VALIANT

	ORIG.	GOOD	FINE	N-MINT
☐ 1, Nov 95, KG................. 2.50		0.50	1.50	2.50
☐ 2, Dec 95, KG 2.50		0.50	1.50	2.50
☐ 3, Jan 96, KG 2.50		0.50	1.50	2.50

PUNX (MANGA) SPECIAL

☐ 0, Mar 96, nn;to be read from back to front

	ORIG.	GOOD	FINE	N-MINT
.... 2.50		0.50	1.50	2.50

PUPPET MASTER
ETERNITY

	ORIG.	GOOD	FINE	N-MINT
☐ 1, color		0.50	1.50	2.50
☐ 2, color		0.50	1.50	2.50
☐ 3, color		0.50	1.50	2.50
☐ 4, color		0.50	1.50	2.50

PUPPET MASTER: CHILDREN OF THE PUPPET MASTER

	ORIG.	GOOD	FINE	N-MINT
☐ 1, color		0.50	1.50	2.50
☐ 2, color		0.50	1.50	2.50

PURE IMAGES
PURE IMAGINATION

	ORIG.	GOOD	FINE	N-MINT
☐ 1, S&K,CCBeck some color		0.50	1.50	2.50
☐ 2, S&K, some color		0.50	1.50	2.50
☐ 3, monsters, some color...		0.50	1.50	2.50
☐ 4, monsters, some color...		0.50	1.50	2.50

PURGATORY USA
SLAVE LABOR

	ORIG.	GOOD	FINE	N-MINT
☐ 1, b&w..............................		0.35	1.05	1.75

PURPLE CLAW MYSTERIES
AC

	ORIG.	GOOD	FINE	N-MINT
☐ 1, b&w reprints.............. 2.95		0.59	1.77	2.95

PUSSYCAT
MARVEL

☐ 1, (b&w mag) Wally Wood, Bill Ward

	ORIG.	GOOD	FINE	N-MINT
.... 0.35		5.00	15.00	25.00

Pulp characters in comics

Pulp magazines preceded comic books by decades. The cheaply produced publications often contained one or more stories in a number of genres, including mysteries and suspense. Heroes of the pulps included Tarzan (and other Edgar Rice Burroughs creations), Conan, Doc Savage, The Shadow, G-8, The Spider, and The Avenger. When comics caught on in the late '30s and early '40s, many of these pulp characters either received their own titles or were back-up stories in other characters' comics.

Tarzan, created in 1912, was one of the few major successes in the comics, continuing in both comic books and strips from the '30s to the present day, with a break in the comic books during the 1980s. His adventures were published by Dell (later Gold Key), DC (which continued the Dell/Gold Key numbering), Marvel, Malibu, and, most recently, Dark Horse. Other Burroughs properties, such as John Carter of Mars, have also been adapted for comic books, although not as successfully financially.

Sales of pulp magazines began to decline in the late '40s, as did the sales of comics, and many of the characters disappeared for a number of years. While interest in comics resurged in the early '60s, it wasn't until the late '60s that interest in the pulps similarly resurged with the publication of inexpensive paperback reprints of such characters as Tarzan, Conan, The Shadow, and Doc Savage.

The comics industry took notice of this reader interest and began to acquire the licenses to publish comic-book adventures of some of the better-known and more fondly remembered characters, including Conan (whose first comic-book series began in the early '70s), Doc Savage (who met Spider-Man), and The Shadow (who met Batman).

Unfortunately, most of the series weren't long-lived, but the door was opened for such comic-book versions.

DC had the rights to The Shadow, Doc Savage, and The Avenger in the mid-'80s and produced a series for Doc, a two-issue mini-series for The Avenger, and a number of series for The Shadow.

After the licenses passed from DC, the Doc license was acquired by Millennium for a short time, followed by Dark Horse, who also had The Shadow's license along with a number of Burroughs' licenses.

Q

	ORIG.	GOOD	FINE	N-MINT
Q-UNIT				
HARRIS				
1, 93, trading card..........2.95	0.59	1.77	2.95
QUACK!				
STAR*REACH				
1	0.40	1.20	2.00
2, SA 1.25	0.40	1.20	2.00
3, Dave Sim art 1.25	0.40	1.20	2.00
4	0.40	1.20	2.00
5 ....1.25	0.40	1.20	2.00
6 ....1.25	0.40	1.20	2.00
QUAGMIRE U.S.A.				
ANTARCTIC				
1, Mar 94, b&w..............2.75	0.55	1.65	2.75
2, May 94, b&w..............2.75	0.55	1.65	2.75
3, Jul 94, b&w................2.75	0.55	1.65	2.75
QUALITY SPECIAL				
FLEETWAY/QUALITY				
1, Strontium Dog	0.30	0.90	1.50
2, Midnight Surfer...........	0.30	0.90	1.50
QUANTUM CREEP				
PARODY PRESS				
1, b&w 2.50	0.50	1.50	2.50
QUANTUM LEAP				
INNOVATION				
1, Sep 91, TV series 2.50	0.60	1.80	3.00
2, Dec 91, TV series 2.50	0.50	1.50	2.50
3, Mar 92, TV series;Sam as Santa				
....................................2.50	0.50	1.50	2.50
4, Apr 92, TV series;Sam on game show				
....................................2.50	0.50	1.50	2.50
5, TV series 2.50	0.50	1.50	2.50
6, Sep 92, TV series 2.50	0.50	1.50	2.50
7, Oct 92, TV series........2.50	0.50	1.50	2.50
8, Dec 92, TV series 2.50	0.50	1.50	2.50
9, Feb 93, TV series 2.50	0.50	1.50	2.50
10, Apr 93, TV series 2.50	0.50	1.50	2.50
11, May 93, TV series 2.50	0.50	1.50	2.50
12, Jun 93, TV series 2.50	0.50	1.50	2.50
13, Aug 93, *Time and Space Special* #1; foil-enhanced				
cardstock cover..............2.95	0.59	1.77	2.95
QUASAR				
MARVEL				
1, Oct 89 ....1.00	0.60	1.80	3.00
2, Nov 89 ....1.00	0.50	1.50	2.50
3, Nov 89 ....1.00	0.40	1.20	2.00
4, Dec 89........................1.00	0.40	1.20	2.00
5, Dec 89, Acts of Vengeance				
....................................1.00	0.40	1.20	2.00
6, Jan 90, Acts of Vengeance				
....................................1.00	0.40	1.20	2.00
7, Feb 90, SpM...............1.00	0.60	1.80	3.00
8, Mar 90 ....1.00	0.30	0.90	1.50
9, Apr 90 ....1.00	0.30	0.90	1.50
10, May 90 ....1.00	0.30	0.90	1.50
11, Jun 90, Phoenix 1.00	0.30	0.90	1.50
12, Jul 90........................1.00	0.30	0.90	1.50
13, Aug 90 ....1.00	0.30	0.90	1.50
14, Sep 90, TMc(c) 1.00	0.30	0.90	1.50
15, Oct 90 ....1.00	0.30	0.90	1.50
16, Nov 90, 48 pages 1.50	0.30	0.90	1.50
17, Dec 90......................1.00	0.30	0.90	1.50
18, Jan 91 ....1.50	0.30	0.90	1.50
19, Feb 91 ....1.00	0.30	0.90	1.50
20, Mar 91, F4................1.00	0.30	0.90	1.50
21, Apr 91 ....1.00	0.20	0.60	1.00
22, May 91 ....1.00	0.20	0.60	1.00
23, Jun 91.......................1.00	0.20	0.60	1.00
24, Jul 91........................1.00	0.20	0.60	1.00
25, Aug 91, new costume				
....................................1.00	0.20	0.60	1.00
26, Sep 91, Infinity Gauntlet				
....................................1.00	0.20	0.60	1.00
27, Oct 91, Infinity Gauntlet				
....................................1.00	0.20	0.60	1.00
28, Nov 91 ....1.00	0.20	0.60	1.00
29, Dec 91 ....1.00	0.20	0.60	1.00
30 ....1.00	0.20	0.60	1.00
31, New Universe............1.25	0.25	0.75	1.25
32, Galactic Storm 1.25	0.25	0.75	1.25
33, Galactic Storm 1.25	0.25	0.75	1.25
34, Galactic Storm 1.25	0.25	0.75	1.25
35, Galactic Storm 1.25	0.25	0.75	1.25
38, Infinity War................1.25	0.25	0.75	1.25
39, Infinity War................1.25	0.25	0.75	1.25
40, Infinity War................1.25	0.25	0.75	1.25
41 ....1.25	0.25	0.75	1.25
42 ....1.25	0.25	0.75	1.25
43 ....1.25	0.25	0.75	1.25
44 ....1.25	0.25	0.75	1.25
45 ....1.25	0.25	0.75	1.25
46 ....1.25	0.25	0.75	1.25
47 ....1.25	0.25	0.75	1.25
48 ....1.25	0.25	0.75	1.25
49 ....1.25	0.25	0.75	1.25
50, foil cover...................2.95	0.59	1.77	2.95
51 ....1.25	0.25	0.75	1.25
52 ....1.25	0.25	0.75	1.25
53 ....1.25	0.25	0.75	1.25
54 ....1.25	0.25	0.75	1.25
55 ....1.25	0.25	0.75	1.25
56 ....1.25	0.25	0.75	1.25
57, Apr 94.......................1.25	0.25	0.75	1.25
58, May 94......................1.25	0.25	0.75	1.25
59, Jun 94.......................1.25	0.25	0.75	1.25
60, Jul 94, final issue......1.25	0.25	0.75	1.25
QUASAR SPECIAL EDITION				
1, reprints *Quasar* #32....1.25	0.25	0.75	1.25
2, reprints *Quasar* #33....1.25	0.25	0.75	1.25
3, reprints *Quasar* #34....1.25	0.25	0.75	1.25
QUEEN OF THE DAMNED				
(see Anne Rice's Queen of the Damned)				
INNOVATION				
QUEEN'S GREATEST HITS				
REVOLUTIONARY				
1, Nov 93, b&w..............2.50	0.50	1.50	2.50
QUEST FOR DREAMS LOST				
LITERACY VOLUNTEERS				
1, 87, Turtles, Trollords, b&w				
....................................2.00	0.40	1.20	2.00
QUEST PRESENTS				
QUEST				
1, JD...............................	0.20	0.60	1.00
2	0.25	0.75	1.25
3	0.30	0.90	1.50
QUESTION ANNUAL, THE				
DC				
1, 88, Batman, Green Arrow				
....................................2.50	0.80	2.40	4.00
2, 89, Green Arrow 3.50	0.70	2.10	3.50
QUESTION QUARTERLY				
1, Dec 90 ....2.50	0.50	1.50	2.50
2, May 91 ....2.50	0.50	1.50	2.50
3, Aug 91 ....2.50	0.50	1.50	2.50
4, Nov 91 ....2.95	0.59	1.77	2.95
5, 92 ....2.95	0.59	1.77	2.95

	ORIG.	GOOD	FINE	N-MINT
QUESTION, THE				
☐ 1, Feb 87 .... 1.50		1.00	3.00	5.00
☐ 2, Mar 87 .... 1.50		0.80	2.40	4.00
☐ 3, Apr 87 .... 1.50		0.60	1.80	3.00
☐ 4, May 87 .... 1.50		0.60	1.80	3.00
☐ 5, Jun 87 .... 1.50		0.60	1.80	3.00
☐ 6, Jul 87 .... 1.50		0.60	1.80	3.00
☐ 7, Aug 87 .... 1.50		0.60	1.80	3.00
☐ 8, Sep 87 .... 1.50		0.60	1.80	3.00
☐ 9, Oct 87 .... 1.50		0.60	1.80	3.00
☐ 10, Nov 87 .... 1.50		0.60	1.80	3.00
☐ 11, Dec 87 .... 1.50		0.60	1.80	3.00
☐ 12, Jan 88 .... 1.50		0.60	1.80	3.00
☐ 13, Feb 88 .... 1.75		0.60	1.80	3.00
☐ 14, Mar 88 .... 1.75		0.60	1.80	3.00
☐ 15, Apr 88 .... 1.75		0.60	1.80	3.00
☐ 16, May 88 .... 1.75		0.60	1.80	3.00
☐ 17, Jun 88, Rorschach, Green Arrow				
.... 1.75		0.80	2.40	4.00
☐ 18, Jul 88, Green Arrow . 1.75		0.80	2.40	4.00
☐ 19, Aug 88 .... 1.75		0.60	1.80	3.00
☐ 20, Oct 88 .... 1.75		0.60	1.80	3.00
☐ 21, Nov 88 .... 1.75		0.60	1.80	3.00
☐ 22, Dec 88 .... 1.75		0.60	1.80	3.00

	ORIG.	GOOD	FINE	N-MINT
☐ 23, Wtr 88 .... 1.75		0.60	1.80	3.00
☐ 24, Jan 89 .... 1.75		0.60	1.80	3.00
☐ 25, Feb 89 .... 1.75		0.60	1.80	3.00
☐ 26, Mar 89, A:Riddler 1.75		0.80	2.40	4.00
☐ 27, Jun 89 .... 1.75		0.40	1.20	2.00
☐ 28, Jul 89 .... 1.75		0.40	1.20	2.00
☐ 29, Aug 89 .... 1.75		0.40	1.20	2.00
☐ 30, Sep 89 .... 1.75		0.40	1.20	2.00
☐ 31, Oct 89 .... 1.75		0.40	1.20	2.00
☐ 32, Nov 89 .... 1.75		0.40	1.20	2.00
☐ 33, Dec 89 .... 1.75		0.40	1.20	2.00
☐ 34, Jan 90 .... 1.75		0.40	1.20	2.00
☐ 35, Mar 90 .... 1.75		0.40	1.20	2.00
☐ 36, Apr 90 .... 1.75		0.40	1.20	2.00
QUESTPROBE				
MARVEL				
☐ 1, JR Hulk 0.75		0.20	0.60	1.00
☐ 2, AM/JM SpM 0.75		0.20	0.60	1.00
☐ 3, Thing 0.75		0.20	0.60	1.00
QUIVERS				
CALIBER				
☐ 1, b&w 2.95		0.59	1.77	2.95
☐ 2, b&w 2.95		0.59	1.77	2.95

Quantum Leap

Quantum Leap #5 © 1992 Universal City Studios, Inc. and Innovative Corp. (Innovation)

Many television series have been adapted into comic-book form, although most of the comics series were short-lived at best, *Star Trek* being a notable exception.

In 1992, Innovation began a series based on the NBC television series *Quantum Leap*. The premise of the television show was that Dr. Sam Beckett, a scientist with several Ph.D.s, developed a method of time travel within one's own lifetime. To test his theory, he stepped into the Quantum Leap accelerator and vanished. From there, Beckett "leaped" into various people at various points since the time he was born, which was in the early 1950s. Essentially, Beckett exchanged places with the person, who found him- or herself in the future at Project Quantum Leap. To outside observers in the displaced's own time, Beckett would look like the displaced person. One other side-effect of the leap was that both Beckett and the person he displaced would have their memory messed up. Beckett's friend and colleague, Al, would find Beckett and assist him in the form of a hologram that only Beckett could see and hear.

At the end of each episode of the television series, Beckett would leap out of the person's life and into another person's, usually finding himself in a cliffhanger situation of one sort or another. Due to the idiosyncracies of network television, the situation Beckett found himself in at the end of one week's episode wouldn't always be the situation he found himself in at the beginning of the following week's episode, due to programming changes. Fortunately, this situation didn't affect the comic book, where the situation Beckett found himself in at the end of one issue would be the same one he was in as the next issue opened.

Comic-book fans could appreciate the extra touches the writers of the comic book added, such as Sam and Al conversing about the effects of Leaping when Sam leaped into a desert hermit and waited for something to happen so that he could leap out. The conversation drifted to how the clothes Sam found himself in during each Leap always fit and the only solution the duo could reach was "unstable molecules."

In the series' final issue, Beckett leaped into an alien being on a spaceship orbiting Earth. His mission was to rescue humans the aliens were experimenting on. As Sam would say, "Oh, boy!"

In 1996, Acclaim Comics announced that it had acquired the rights to *Quantum Leap* and that a new comics series would be published.

R

	ORIG.	GOOD	FINE	N-MINT

R.E.B.E.L.S. '94
DC

	ORIG.	GOOD	FINE	N-MINT
❑ 0, Oct 94, continued from *L.E.G.I.O.N. '94* #70				
.... 1.95		0.39	1.17	1.95
❑ 1, Nov 94 .... 1.95		0.39	1.17	1.95
❑ 2, Dec 94, (becomes *R.E.B.E.L.S. '95*)				
.... 1.95		0.39	1.17	1.95

R.E.B.E.L.S. '95

	ORIG.	GOOD	FINE	N-MINT
❑ 3, Jan 95 .... 1.95		0.39	1.17	1.95
❑ 4, Feb 95 .... 1.95		0.39	1.17	1.95
❑ 5, Mar 95 .... 1.95		0.39	1.17	1.95
❑ 6, Apr 95 .... 1.95		0.39	1.17	1.95
❑ 7, May 95 .... 1.95		0.39	1.17	1.95
❑ 8, Jun 95 .... 2.25		0.45	1.35	2.25
❑ 9, Jul 95 .... 2.25		0.45	1.35	2.25
❑ 10, Aug 95 .... 2.25		0.45	1.35	2.25
❑ 11, Sep 95, return of Captain Comet				
.... 2.25		0.45	1.35	2.25
❑ 12, Oct 95 .... 2.25		0.45	1.35	2.25
❑ 13, Nov 95, "Underworld Unleashed"				
.... 2.25		0.45	1.35	2.25
❑ 14, Dec 95, (becomes *R.E.B.E.L.S. '96*)				
.... 2.25		0.45	1.35	2.25

R.E.B.E.L.S. '96

	ORIG.	GOOD	FINE	N-MINT
❑ 15, Jan 96, (was *R.E.B.E.L.S. '95*)				
.... 2.25		0.45	1.35	2.25
❑ 16, Feb 96 .... 2.25		0.45	1.35	2.25
❑ 17, Mar 96, final issue ... 2.25		0.45	1.35	2.25

R.I.P. COMICS MODULE
TSR INC.

	ORIG.	GOOD	FINE	N-MINT
❑ 1		0.59	1.77	2.95
❑ 2		0.59	1.77	2.95
❑ 3		0.59	1.77	2.95
❑ 4		0.59	1.77	2.95
❑ 5, Brasher		0.59	1.77	2.95
❑ 6, Brasher		0.59	1.77	2.95
❑ 7, Brasher		0.59	1.77	2.95
❑ 8, Brasher		0.59	1.77	2.95

R.O.B.O.T. BATTALION 2050
ECLIPSE

	ORIG.	GOOD	FINE	N-MINT
❑ 0, 1 BSz(c),b&w		0.40	1.20	2.00

RABID
FANTACO

	ORIG.	GOOD	FINE	N-MINT
❑ 0, nn 5.95		1.19	3.57	5.95

RABID RACHEL
MILLER

	ORIG.	GOOD	FINE	N-MINT
❑ 1, b&w		0.40	1.20	2.00

RACE OF SCORPIONS
DARK HORSE

	ORIG.	GOOD	FINE	N-MINT
❑ 1, b&w		0.90	2.70	4.50
❑ 2		0.99	2.97	4.95
❑ 3		0.99	2.97	4.95
❑ 4		0.99	2.97	4.95

RACE OF SCORPIONS (1991 mini-series)

	ORIG.	GOOD	FINE	N-MINT
❑ 1, b&w		0.45	1.35	2.25
❑ 2, b&w		0.45	1.35	2.25
❑ 3		0.50	1.50	2.50

RACER X
NOW

	ORIG.	GOOD	FINE	N-MINT
❑ 1, Sep 88 .... 1.75		0.35	1.05	1.75
❑ 2, Oct 88 .... 1.75		0.35	1.05	1.75
❑ 3, Nov 88 .... 1.75		0.35	1.05	1.75
❑ 4, Jan 89 .... 1.75		0.35	1.05	1.75
❑ 5, Feb 89 .... 1.75		0.35	1.05	1.75
❑ 6, Mar 89 .... 1.75		0.35	1.05	1.75
❑ 7, Apr 89 .... 1.75		0.35	1.05	1.75
❑ 8, May 89, Comics Code 1.75		0.35	1.05	1.75

	ORIG.	GOOD	FINE	N-MINT
❑ 9, Jun 89, Comics Code ..1.75		0.35	1.05	1.75
❑ 10, Jul 89, Comics Code .1.75		0.35	1.05	1.75
❑ 11, Aug 89, Comics Code				
.... 1.75		0.35	1.05	1.75

RACER X (Volume Two)

	ORIG.	GOOD	FINE	N-MINT
❑ 1, Sep 89, Chuck Dixon ..1.75		0.35	1.05	1.75
❑ 2, Oct 89, Chuck Dixon ..1.75		0.35	1.05	1.75
❑ 3, Nov 89, Chuck Dixon ..1.75		0.35	1.05	1.75
❑ 4, Dec 89, Chuck Dixon ..1.75		0.35	1.05	1.75
❑ 5, Jan 90, Chuck Dixon ..1.75		0.35	1.05	1.75
❑ 6, Feb 90, Chuck Dixon...1.75		0.35	1.05	1.75
❑ 7, Mar 90, Chuck Dixon...1.75		0.35	1.05	1.75
❑ 8, Apr 90, Chuck Dixon...1.75		0.35	1.05	1.75
❑ 9, May 90, Chuck Dixon ..1.75		0.35	1.05	1.75
❑ 10, Jun 90, Chuck Dixon.1.75		0.35	1.05	1.75

RACER X PREMIERE

	ORIG.	GOOD	FINE	N-MINT
❑ 0, Aug 88, graphic novel .3.50		0.70	2.10	3.50

RACK AND PAIN (mini-series)
DARK HORSE

	ORIG.	GOOD	FINE	N-MINT
❑ 1, Mar 94 .... 2.50		0.50	1.50	2.50
❑ 2, Apr 94 .... 2.50		0.50	1.50	2.50
❑ 3, May 94 .... 2.50		0.50	1.50	2.50
❑ 4, Jun 94 .... 2.50		0.50	1.50	2.50

RADICAL DREAMER
BLACKBALL

	ORIG.	GOOD	FINE	N-MINT
❑ 0, May 94, poster comic .1.99		0.40	1.19	1.99
❑ 1, Jun 94, poster comic ..1.99		0.40	1.19	1.99
❑ 2, 94, poster comic 1.99		0.40	1.19	1.99
❑ 3, 94, poster comic 1.99		0.40	1.19	1.99
❑ 4, Nov 94, foldout comic on cardstock				
.... 2.50		0.50	1.50	2.50

RADICAL DREAMER (Vol. 2)
MARK'S GIANT ECONOMY SIZE

	ORIG.	GOOD	FINE	N-MINT
❑ 1, Jun 95, b&w 2.95		0.59	1.77	2.95
❑ 2, Jul 95, b&w 2.95		0.59	1.77	2.95
❑ 3, Aug 95, b&w 2.95		0.59	1.77	2.95
❑ 4, Sep 95, b&w 2.95		0.59	1.77	2.95
❑ 5, Dec 95, b&w 2.95		0.59	1.77	2.95

RADIO BOY
ECLIPSE

	ORIG.	GOOD	FINE	N-MINT
❑ 1, b&w		0.30	0.90	1.50

RADIOACTIVE MAN
BONGO

	ORIG.	GOOD	FINE	N-MINT
❑ 1, 93, glow cover 2.95		1.00	3.00	5.00
❑ 2, 94, (88) 1.95		0.60	1.80	3.00
❑ 3, 94, (216) 1.95		0.39	1.17	1.95
❑ 4, 94, (412) 2.25		0.45	1.35	2.25
❑ 5, 94, (679) 2.25		0.45	1.35	2.25
❑ 6, 94, (1000) 2.25		0.45	1.35	2.25

RADIOACTIVE MAN 80 PG. COLOSSAL

	ORIG.	GOOD	FINE	N-MINT
❑ 1, 95 .... 4.95		0.99	2.97	4.95

RAGAMUFFINS
ECLIPSE

	ORIG.	GOOD	FINE	N-MINT
❑ 1, Jan 85, GC		0.35	1.05	1.75

RAGGEDYMAN
CULT

	ORIG.	GOOD	FINE	N-MINT
❑ 1, b&w 2.50		0.50	1.50	2.50
❑ 2, b&w 2.50		0.50	1.50	2.50
❑ 3, b&w 2.50		0.50	1.50	2.50
❑ 4, b&w 2.50		0.50	1.50	2.50
❑ 5, Jul 93, b&w 2.50		0.50	1.50	2.50

RAGMAN
DC

	ORIG.	GOOD	FINE	N-MINT
❑ 1, Oct 91 .... 1.50		0.30	0.90	1.50
❑ 2, Nov 91 .... 1.50		0.30	0.90	1.50
❑ 3, Dec 91 .... 1.50		0.30	0.90	1.50
❑ 4, Jan 92 .... 1.50		0.30	0.90	1.50

	ORIG.	GOOD	FINE	N-MINT
☐ 5, Feb 92 ....1.50	0.30	0.90	1.50
☐ 6, Mar 92 ....1.25	0.30	0.90	1.50
☐ 7, Apr 92 ....1.25	0.30	0.90	1.50
☐ 8, May 92......................1.25	0.30	0.90	1.50

RAGMAN (1976-77)

	ORIG.	GOOD	FINE	N-MINT
☐ 1, Sep 76......................0.30	0.60	1.80	3.00
☐ 2, Nov 76 ....0.30	0.40	1.20	2.00
☐ 3, Jan 77 ....0.30	0.40	1.20	2.00
☐ 4, Mar 77 ....0.30	0.40	1.20	2.00
☐ 5, Jul 77 ....0.30	0.40	1.20	2.00

RAGMAN: CRY OF THE DEAD

	ORIG.	GOOD	FINE	N-MINT
☐ 1 ....1.75	0.35	1.05	1.75
☐ 2 ....1.75	0.35	1.05	1.75
☐ 3 ....1.75	0.35	1.05	1.75
☐ 4 ....1.75	0.35	1.05	1.75
☐ 5 ....1.75	0.35	1.05	1.75
☐ 6 ....1.75	0.35	1.05	1.75

RAI
VALIANT

	ORIG.	GOOD	FINE	N-MINT
☐ 0, Nov 92, O:Rai...........2.25	2.00	6.00	10.00
☐ 1, Mar 92 ....1.95	1.60	4.80	8.00
☐ 2, Apr 92 ....1.95	1.00	3.00	5.00
☐ 3, May 92......................1.95	1.60	4.80	8.00
☐ 4, Jun 92 ....1.95	1.60	4.80	8.00
☐ 5, Jul 92 ....2.25	1.00	3.00	5.00
☐ 6, Aug 92, FM(c) Unity... 2.25	0.80	2.40	4.00
☐ 7, Sep 92, WS(c) Unity .. 2.25	0.80	2.40	4.00
☐ 8, Oct 92, (becomes *Rai and the Future Force*)			
...................................2.25	0.80	2.40	4.00

RAI AND THE FUTURE FORCE

	ORIG.	GOOD	FINE	N-MINT
☐ 9, May 93, (was *Rai*) 2.50	0.60	1.80	3.00
☐ 9, Gold	3.20	9.60	16.00
☐ 10, Jun 93.....................2.25	0.45	1.35	2.25
☐ 11, Jul 93.......................2.25	0.45	1.35	2.25
☐ 12, Aug 93 ....2.25	0.45	1.35	2.25
☐ 13, Sep 93.....................2.25	0.45	1.35	2.25
☐ 14, Oct 93 ....2.25	0.45	1.35	2.25
☐ 15, Nov 93 ....2.25	0.45	1.35	2.25
☐ 16, Dec 93.....................2.25	0.45	1.35	2.25
☐ 17, Jan 94......................2.25	0.45	1.35	2.25
☐ 18, Feb 94......................2.25	0.45	1.35	2.25
☐ 19, Mar 94 ....2.25	0.45	1.35	2.25
☐ 20, Apr 94 ....2.25	0.45	1.35	2.25
☐ 21, May 94, trading card 2.25	0.45	1.35	2.25
☐ 22, Jun 94, D:Rai 2.25	0.45	1.35	2.25
☐ 23, Aug 94 ....2.25	0.45	1.35	2.25
☐ 24, Sep 94.....................2.25	0.45	1.35	2.25
☐ 25, Oct 94 ....2.25	0.45	1.35	2.25
☐ 26, Nov 94, Chaos Effect 2.25	0.45	1.35	2.25
☐ 28, Jan 95......................2.25	0.45	1.35	2.25
☐ 31, Apr 95 ....2.25	0.45	1.35	2.25
☐ 32, May 95......................2.25	0.45	1.35	2.25
☐ 33, Jun 95, final issue.... 2.25	0.45	1.35	2.25

RAI COMPANION

☐ 1 ....

RAIDER 3000
GAUNTLET

	ORIG.	GOOD	FINE	N-MINT
☐ 1, b&w 2.95	0.59	1.77	2.95
☐ 2, b&w 2.95	0.59	1.77	2.95

RAIDERS OF THE LOST ARK
MARVEL

	ORIG.	GOOD	FINE	N-MINT
☐ 1, Sep 81, JB/KJ movie.. 0.50	0.30	0.90	1.50
☐ 2, Oct 81, JB/KJ 0.50	0.20	0.60	1.00
☐ 3, Nov 81, JB/KJ 0.50	0.20	0.60	1.00

RAIN
TUNDRA

	ORIG.	GOOD	FINE	N-MINT
☐ 1, b&w	0.39	1.17	1.95
☐ 2, b&w	0.39	1.17	1.95
☐ 3, b&w	0.39	1.17	1.95
☐ 4, b&w	0.39	1.17	1.95

	ORIG.	GOOD	FINE	N-MINT
☐ 5, b&w	0.39	1.17	1.95
☐ 6, b&w	0.39	1.17	1.95

RAINBOW BRITE & THE STAR-STEALER
DC

	ORIG.	GOOD	FINE	N-MINT
☐ 1	0.20	0.60	1.00

RAK
RAK GRAPHICS

	ORIG.	GOOD	FINE	N-MINT
☐ 1, b&w..........................5.00	1.00	3.00	5.00

RALFY ROACH
BUGGED OUT

	ORIG.	GOOD	FINE	N-MINT
☐ 0, Jun 93 ....2.95	0.59	1.77	2.95

RALPH SNART ADVENTURES (mini-series)
NOW

	ORIG.	GOOD	FINE	N-MINT
☐ 1, Jun 86.......................1.00	0.80	2.40	4.00
☐ 2, Jul 86........................1.00	0.80	2.40	4.00
☐ 3, Aug 86......................1.00	0.80	2.40	4.00

RALPH SNART ADVENTURES (Volume 2)

	ORIG.	GOOD	FINE	N-MINT
☐ 1, Nov 86, b&w..............1.25	0.80	2.40	4.00
☐ 2, Dec 86, b&w..............1.25	0.80	2.40	4.00
☐ 3, Jan 87, b&w...............1.50	0.80	2.40	4.00
☐ 4, Feb 87, b&w...............1.50	0.80	2.40	4.00
☐ 5, Mar 87, b&w..............1.50	0.80	2.40	4.00
☐ 6, Apr 87, b&w...............1.50	0.80	2.40	4.00
☐ 7, May 87, b&w..............1.50	0.80	2.40	4.00
☐ 8, Jun 87, color 1.50	0.80	2.40	4.00
☐ 9, Jul 87, color...............1.50	0.80	2.40	4.00

RALPH SNART ADVENTURES (Volume 3)

	ORIG.	GOOD	FINE	N-MINT
☐ 1, Sep 88, color 1.75	0.70	2.10	3.50
☐ 2, Oct 88, color 1.75	0.70	2.10	3.50
☐ 3, Nov 88, color 1.75	0.70	2.10	3.50
☐ 4, Jan 89, color 1.75	0.70	2.10	3.50
☐ 5, Feb 89, color 1.75	0.70	2.10	3.50
☐ 6, Mar 89, color 1.75	0.70	2.10	3.50
☐ 7, Apr 89, color...............1.75	0.70	2.10	3.50
☐ 8, May 89, Comics Code.1.75	0.40	1.20	2.00
☐ 9, Jun 89, Comics Code..1.75	0.40	1.20	2.00
☐ 10, Jul 89, Comics Code.1.75	0.40	1.20	2.00
☐ 11, Aug 89, Comics Code			
..................................1.75	0.40	1.20	2.00
☐ 12, Sep 89, Comics Code1.75	0.40	1.20	2.00
☐ 13, Oct 89,Comics Code.1.75	0.40	1.20	2.00
☐ 14, Nov 89, Comics Code			
..................................1.75	0.40	1.20	2.00
☐ 15, Dec 89, Comics Code1.75	0.40	1.20	2.00
☐ 16, Jan 90, Comics Code1.75	0.40	1.20	2.00
☐ 17, Feb 90, Comics Code1.75	0.40	1.20	2.00
☐ 18, Mar 90, Comics Code			
..................................1.75	0.40	1.20	2.00
☐ 19, Apr 90, Comics Code1.75	0.40	1.20	2.00
☐ 20, May 90, Comics Code			
..................................1.75	0.40	1.20	2.00
☐ 21, Jun 90, Comics Code1.75	0.40	1.20	2.00
☐ 22, Jul 90, Comics Code.1.75	0.40	1.20	2.00
☐ 23, Aug 90, Comics Code			
..................................1.75	0.40	1.20	2.00
☐ 24, Sep 90, 3-D, with glasses			
..................................2.95	0.59	1.77	2.95
☐ 25, Oct 90......................1.75	0.35	1.05	1.75
☐ 26, Nov 90 ....1.75	0.35	1.05	1.75

RALPH SNART ADVENTURES (Volume 4)

	ORIG.	GOOD	FINE	N-MINT
☐ 1, May 92, trading card (two editions; choice of 2 trading cards) 2.50	0.50	1.50	2.50
☐ 2, Jun 92, trading card (two editions; choice of 2 trading cards) 2.50	0.50	1.50	2.50
☐ 3, Jul 92, trading card (two editions; choice of 2 trading cards) 2.50	0.50	1.50	2.50

RALPH SNART ADVENTURES (Volume 5)

	ORIG.	GOOD	FINE	N-MINT
☐ 1, Jul 93, choice of two cards			
..................................2.50	0.50	1.50	2.50

	ORIG.	GOOD	FINE	N-MINT
☐ 2, Aug 93, choice of two cards				
.............................2.50	0.50	1.50	2.50
☐ 3, Sep 93, choice of two cards				
.............................2.50	0.50	1.50	2.50
☐ 4, Oct 93, choice of two cards				
.............................2.50	0.50	1.50	2.50
☐ 5, Nov 93, choice of two cards				
.............................2.50	0.50	1.50	2.50

RALPH SNART ADVENTURES 3-D SPECIAL

	ORIG.	GOOD	FINE	N-MINT
☐ 1, bagged with 12 cards. 3.50	0.70	2.10	3.50
☐ 1, bagged with no cards. 2.95	0.59	1.77	2.95

RALPH SNART: THE LOST ISSUES

	ORIG.	GOOD	FINE	N-MINT
☐ 1, Apr 93 ....2.50	0.50	1.50	2.50
☐ 2, May 93 ....2.50	0.50	1.50	2.50
☐ 3, Jun 93 ....2.50	0.50	1.50	2.50

RAMBLIN' DAWG
EDGE

	ORIG.	GOOD	FINE	N-MINT
☐ 1, Jul 94 ....2.95	0.59	1.77	2.95

RAMBO
BLACKTHORNE

	ORIG.	GOOD	FINE	N-MINT
☐ 1, Oct 88, b&w		0.40	1.20	2.00

RAMBO III IN 3-D

	ORIG.	GOOD	FINE	N-MINT
☐ 1, 88, movie		0.50	1.50	2.50

RAMM
MEGATON

	ORIG.	GOOD	FINE	N-MINT
☐ 1		0.30	0.90	1.50
☐ 2		0.30	0.90	1.50

RAMPAGING HULK, THE (b&w mag)
MARVEL

	ORIG.	GOOD	FINE	N-MINT
☐ 1, Jan 77 ....1.00	0.20	0.60	1.00
☐ 2, Apr 77 ....1.00	0.20	0.60	1.00
☐ 3, Jun 77 ....1.00	0.20	0.60	1.00
☐ 4, Aug 77 ....1.00	0.20	0.60	1.00
☐ 5, Oct 77 ....1.00	0.20	0.60	1.00
☐ 6, Dec 77 ....1.00	0.20	0.60	1.00
☐ 7, Feb 78 ....1.00	0.20	0.60	1.00
☐ 8, Apr 78 ....1.00	0.20	0.60	1.00
☐ 9, Jun 78, (becomes *The Hulk*)				
.............................1.00	0.20	0.60	1.00

RANK & STINKY
PARODY PRESS

	ORIG.	GOOD	FINE	N-MINT
☐ 1, b&w 2.50	0.50	1.50	2.50

RANK & STINKY SPECIAL
EXPRESS/PARODY

	ORIG.	GOOD	FINE	N-MINT
☐ 1, 96, b&w 2.75	0.55	1.65	2.75

RANMA 1/2
VIZ

	ORIG.	GOOD	FINE	N-MINT
☐ 1, Japanese, color	9.60	28.80	48.00
☐ 2, Japanese, color	4.00	12.00	20.00
☐ 3, Japanese, color	2.60	7.80	13.00
☐ 4, Japanese, b&w	1.20	3.60	6.00
☐ 5, Japanese, b&w	1.20	3.60	6.00
☐ 6, Japanese, b&w	1.60	4.80	8.00
☐ 7, Japanese, b&w	1.00	3.00	5.00

RANMA 1/2 (Part 2)

	ORIG.	GOOD	FINE	N-MINT
☐ 1, 93 ....2.95	2.40	7.20	12.00
☐ 2, 93 ....2.95	1.20	3.60	6.00
☐ 3, 93 ....2.95	0.80	2.40	4.00
☐ 4, 93 ....2.95	0.80	2.40	4.00
☐ 5, 93 ....2.95	0.80	2.40	4.00
☐ 6, 93 ....2.95	0.70	2.10	3.50
☐ 7, 93 ....2.95	0.70	2.10	3.50
☐ 8, 93 ....2.95	0.70	2.10	3.50
☐ 9, 93 ....2.95	0.70	2.10	3.50
☐ 10, 93 ....2.95	0.70	2.10	3.50
☐ 11, 93 ....2.95	0.70	2.10	3.50

RANMA 1/2 (Part 3)

	ORIG.	GOOD	FINE	N-MINT
☐ 1, 93, b&w 2.75	1.00	3.00	5.00
☐ 2, 94, b&w 2.75	0.80	2.40	4.00

	ORIG.	GOOD	FINE	N-MINT
☐ 3, 94, b&w 2.75	0.70	2.10	3.50
☐ 4, 94, b&w 2.75	0.70	2.10	3.50
☐ 5, 94, b&w 2.75	0.70	2.10	3.50
☐ 6, 94, b&w 2.75	0.60	1.80	3.00
☐ 7, 94, b&w 2.75	0.60	1.80	3.00
☐ 8, 94, b&w 2.75	0.60	1.80	3.00
☐ 9, 94, b&w 2.75	0.60	1.80	3.00
☐ 10, 94, b&w 2.75	0.60	1.80	3.00
☐ 11, 94, b&w 2.75	0.60	1.80	3.00
☐ 12, 94, b&w 2.75	0.60	1.80	3.00
☐ 13, 94, b&w 2.75	0.60	1.80	3.00

RANMA 1/2 (Part 4)

	ORIG.	GOOD	FINE	N-MINT
☐ 1, 95, b&w 2.75	0.55	1.65	2.75
☐ 2, 95, b&w 2.75	0.55	1.65	2.75
☐ 4, 95, b&w 2.75	0.55	1.65	2.75

RANT (mini-series)
BONEYARD

	ORIG.	GOOD	FINE	N-MINT
☐ 1, Nov 94, b&w 2.95	0.59	1.77	2.95
☐ 2, Feb 95, b&w 2.95	0.59	1.77	2.95

RAPHAEL
MIRAGE

	ORIG.	GOOD	FINE	N-MINT
☐ 1, (1st printing)	2.00	6.00	10.00
☐ 1, (2nd printing)	0.80	2.40	4.00

RAPTAUR
FLEETWAY/QUALITY

	ORIG.	GOOD	FINE	N-MINT
☐ 1, Judge Dredd 2.95	0.59	1.77	2.95
☐ 2, Judge Dredd 2.95	0.59	1.77	2.95

RARE BREED
CHRYSALIS STUDIOS

	ORIG.	GOOD	FINE	N-MINT
☐ 1, Nov 95 ....2.50	0.50	1.50	2.50
☐ 2, Mar 96 ....2.50	0.50	1.50	2.50

RASCALS IN PARADISE (mini-series)
DARK HORSE

	ORIG.	GOOD	FINE	N-MINT
☐ 1, Aug 94, magazine-sized				
.............................3.95	0.79	2.37	3.95
☐ 2, Oct 94, magazine-sized.				
.............................3.95	0.79	2.37	3.95
☐ 3, Dec 94, magazine-sized, final issue				
.............................3.95	0.79	2.37	3.95

RAT FINK COMICS
WORLD OF FANDOM

	ORIG.	GOOD	FINE	N-MINT
☐ 1, b&w		0.50	1.50	2.50
☐ 2, b&w		0.50	1.50	2.50
☐ 3, b&w		0.50	1.50	2.50

RATED X
AIRCEL

	ORIG.	GOOD	FINE	N-MINT
☐ 1, adult, b&w		0.59	1.77	2.95
☐ 2, adult, b&w		0.59	1.77	2.95
☐ 3, adult, b&w		0.59	1.77	2.95

RATED X SPECIAL

	ORIG.	GOOD	FINE	N-MINT
☐ 1, adult, b&w		0.59	1.77	2.95

RATS!
SLAVE LABOR

	ORIG.	GOOD	FINE	N-MINT
☐ 1, b&w		0.50	1.50	2.50

RAVAGE 2099
MARVEL

	ORIG.	GOOD	FINE	N-MINT
☐ 1, foil cover 1.75	0.35	1.05	1.75
☐ 2 ....1.25	0.25	0.75	1.25
☐ 3 ....1.25	0.25	0.75	1.25
☐ 4 ....1.25	0.25	0.75	1.25
☐ 5 ....1.25	0.25	0.75	1.25
☐ 6 ....1.25	0.25	0.75	1.25
☐ 7 ....1.25	0.25	0.75	1.25
☐ 8 ....1.25	0.25	0.75	1.25
☐ 9 ....1.25	0.25	0.75	1.25
☐ 10 ....1.25	0.25	0.75	1.25
☐ 11 ....1.25	0.25	0.75	1.25
☐ 12 ....1.25	0.25	0.75	1.25
☐ 13 ....1.25	0.25	0.75	1.25

	ORIG.	GOOD	FINE	N-MINT
☐ 14	1.25	0.25	0.75	1.25
☐ 15	1.25	0.25	0.75	1.25
☐ 16	1.25	0.25	0.75	1.25
☐ 17	1.25	0.25	0.75	1.25
☐ 18, May 94	1.25	0.25	0.75	1.25
☐ 19, Jun 94	1.50	0.30	0.90	1.50
☐ 20, Jul 94	1.50	0.30	0.90	1.50
☐ 21, Aug 94	1.50	0.30	0.90	1.50
☐ 22, Sep 94	1.50	0.30	0.90	1.50
☐ 23, Oct 94	1.50	0.30	0.90	1.50
☐ 24, Nov 94	1.50	0.30	0.90	1.50
☐ 25, Dec 94	2.25	0.45	1.35	2.25
☐ 25, Dec 94,enhanced cover				
	2.95	0.59	1.77	2.95
☐ 26, Jan 95	1.50	0.30	0.90	1.50
☐ 27, Feb 95	1.50	0.30	0.90	1.50
☐ 28, Mar 95	1.50	0.30	0.90	1.50
☐ 29, Apr 95	1.50	0.30	0.90	1.50
☐ 30, May 95	1.50	0.30	0.90	1.50
☐ 31, Jun 95	1.95	0.39	1.17	1.95
☐ 32, Jul 95	1.95	0.39	1.17	1.95
☐ 33, Aug 95	1.95	0.39	1.17	1.95

RAVEN
RENAISSANCE

	ORIG.	GOOD	FINE	N-MINT
☐ 1, Sep 93	2.50	0.50	1.50	2.50
☐ 2, Nov 93	2.50	0.50	1.50	2.50
☐ 3, Apr 94	2.50	0.50	1.50	2.50
☐ 4, Aug 94	2.75	0.55	1.65	2.75

RAVEN CHRONICLES
CALIBER

	ORIG.	GOOD	FINE	N-MINT
☐ 1, Jul 95, b&w	2.95	0.59	1.77	2.95
☐ 2, 95, b&w	2.95	0.59	1.77	2.95

RAVEN, THE
MALAN CLASSICAL ENTERPRISES

	ORIG.	GOOD	FINE	N-MINT
☐ 0, nn Gustave Dore, b&w.		0.99	2.97	4.95

RAVENS AND RAINBOWS
PACIFIC

	ORIG.	GOOD	FINE	N-MINT
☐ 1, JJ	1.50	0.30	0.90	1.50

RAVER
MALIBU

	ORIG.	GOOD	FINE	N-MINT
☐ 1, foil cover	2.95	0.59	1.77	2.95
☐ 2	1.95	0.39	1.17	1.95

RAW MEDIA MAGS
REBEL

	ORIG.	GOOD	FINE	N-MINT
☐ 1, b&w, adult		1.00	3.00	5.00
☐ 2, b&w, adult		1.00	3.00	5.00
☐ 3, b&w, adult		1.00	3.00	5.00
☐ 4, May 94, b&w, adult	5.00	1.00	3.00	5.00

RAWHIDE KID (1955-1979)
MARVEL

	ORIG.	GOOD	FINE	N-MINT
☐ 1	0.10	60.00	180.00	300.00
☐ 2	0.10	40.00	120.00	200.00
☐ 3	0.10	28.00	84.00	140.00
☐ 4	0.10	28.00	84.00	140.00
☐ 5	0.10	28.00	84.00	140.00
☐ 6	0.10	16.00	48.00	80.00
☐ 7	0.10	16.00	48.00	80.00
☐ 8	0.10	16.00	48.00	80.00
☐ 9	0.10	16.00	48.00	80.00
☐ 10	0.10	16.00	48.00	80.00
☐ 11	0.10	7.20	21.60	36.00
☐ 12	0.10	7.20	21.60	36.00
☐ 13	0.10	7.20	21.60	36.00
☐ 14	0.10	7.20	21.60	36.00
☐ 15	0.10	7.20	21.60	36.00
☐ 16	0.10	7.20	21.60	36.00
☐ 17	0.10	7.20	21.60	36.00
☐ 18	0.10	7.20	21.60	36.00
☐ 19	0.10	7.20	21.60	36.00
☐ 20	0.10	7.20	21.60	36.00

	ORIG.	GOOD	FINE	N-MINT
☐ 21	0.10	7.20	21.60	36.00
☐ 22	0.10	7.20	21.60	36.00
☐ 23	0.10	13.00	39.00	65.00
☐ 24	0.10	6.00	18.00	30.00
☐ 25	0.10	6.00	18.00	30.00
☐ 26	0.10	6.00	18.00	30.00
☐ 27	0.12	6.00	18.00	30.00
☐ 28	0.12	6.00	18.00	30.00
☐ 29	0.12	6.00	18.00	30.00
☐ 30	0.12	6.00	18.00	30.00
☐ 31	0.12	5.20	15.60	26.00
☐ 32	0.12	5.20	15.60	26.00
☐ 33	0.12	5.20	15.60	26.00
☐ 34	0.12	5.20	15.60	26.00
☐ 35	0.12	5.20	15.60	26.00
☐ 36	0.12	5.20	15.60	26.00
☐ 37	0.12	5.20	15.60	26.00
☐ 38	0.12	5.20	15.60	26.00
☐ 39	0.12	5.20	15.60	26.00
☐ 40	0.12	5.20	15.60	26.00
☐ 41	0.12	5.20	15.60	26.00
☐ 42	0.12	5.20	15.60	26.00
☐ 43	0.12	5.20	15.60	26.00
☐ 44	0.12	5.20	15.60	26.00
☐ 45	0.12	5.20	15.60	26.00
☐ 46	0.12	5.20	15.60	26.00
☐ 47	0.12	2.40	7.20	12.00
☐ 48	0.12	2.40	7.20	12.00
☐ 49	0.12	2.40	7.20	12.00
☐ 50	0.12	2.40	7.20	12.00
☐ 51	0.12	2.40	7.20	12.00
☐ 52	0.12	2.40	7.20	12.00
☐ 53	0.12	2.40	7.20	12.00
☐ 54	0.12	2.40	7.20	12.00
☐ 55	0.12	2.40	7.20	12.00
☐ 56	0.12	2.40	7.20	12.00
☐ 57	0.12	2.40	7.20	12.00
☐ 58	0.12	2.40	7.20	12.00
☐ 59	0.12	2.40	7.20	12.00
☐ 60	0.12	2.40	7.20	12.00
☐ 61	0.12	2.40	7.20	12.00
☐ 62	0.12	2.40	7.20	12.00
☐ 63	0.12	2.40	7.20	12.00
☐ 64	0.12	2.40	7.20	12.00
☐ 65	0.12	2.40	7.20	12.00
☐ 66	0.12	2.40	7.20	12.00
☐ 67	0.12	2.40	7.20	12.00
☐ 68	0.12	2.40	7.20	12.00
☐ 69	0.12	2.40	7.20	12.00
☐ 70	0.12	2.40	7.20	12.00
☐ 71	0.15	1.00	3.00	5.00
☐ 72	0.15	1.00	3.00	5.00
☐ 73	0.15	1.00	3.00	5.00
☐ 74	0.15	1.00	3.00	5.00
☐ 75	0.15	1.00	3.00	5.00
☐ 76	0.15	1.00	3.00	5.00
☐ 77	0.15	1.00	3.00	5.00
☐ 78	0.15	1.00	3.00	5.00
☐ 79	0.15	1.00	3.00	5.00
☐ 80	0.15	1.00	3.00	5.00
☐ 81	0.15	1.00	3.00	5.00
☐ 82	0.15	1.00	3.00	5.00
☐ 83	0.15	1.00	3.00	5.00
☐ 84	0.20	1.00	3.00	5.00
☐ 85	0.20	1.00	3.00	5.00
☐ 86	0.20	1.00	3.00	5.00
☐ 87	0.20	1.00	3.00	5.00
☐ 88	0.20	1.00	3.00	5.00
☐ 89	0.20	1.00	3.00	5.00
☐ 90	0.20	1.00	3.00	5.00
☐ 91	0.20	1.00	3.00	5.00
☐ 92	0.20	1.00	3.00	5.00

	ORIG.	GOOD	FINE	N-MINT
❑ 93	0.20	1.00	3.00	5.00
❑ 94	0.20	1.00	3.00	5.00
❑ 95	0.20	1.00	3.00	5.00
❑ 96	0.20	1.00	3.00	5.00
❑ 97	0.25	1.00	3.00	5.00
❑ 98	0.25	1.00	3.00	5.00
❑ 99	0.25	1.00	3.00	5.00
❑ 100	0.25	2.40	7.20	12.00
❑ 101	0.25	1.00	3.00	5.00
❑ 102	0.25	1.00	3.00	5.00
❑ 103	0.25	1.00	3.00	5.00
❑ 104	0.25	1.00	3.00	5.00
❑ 105	0.25	1.00	3.00	5.00
❑ 106	0.25	1.00	3.00	5.00
❑ 107	0.25	1.00	3.00	5.00
❑ 108	0.25	1.00	3.00	5.00
❑ 109	0.25	1.00	3.00	5.00
❑ 110	0.25	1.00	3.00	5.00
❑ 111	0.25	1.00	3.00	5.00
❑ 112	0.25	1.00	3.00	5.00
❑ 113	0.25	1.00	3.00	5.00
❑ 114	0.25	1.00	3.00	5.00
❑ 115	0.25	1.00	3.00	5.00
❑ 116		0.60	1.80	3.00
❑ 117		0.60	1.80	3.00
❑ 118		0.60	1.80	3.00
❑ 119		0.60	1.80	3.00
❑ 120		0.60	1.80	3.00
❑ 121		0.60	1.80	3.00
❑ 122		0.60	1.80	3.00
❑ 123		0.60	1.80	3.00
❑ 124		0.60	1.80	3.00
❑ 125		0.60	1.80	3.00
❑ 126		0.60	1.80	3.00
❑ 127		0.60	1.80	3.00
❑ 128		0.60	1.80	3.00
❑ 129		0.60	1.80	3.00
❑ 130		0.60	1.80	3.00
❑ 131		0.60	1.80	3.00
❑ 132		0.60	1.80	3.00
❑ 133		0.60	1.80	3.00
❑ 134		0.60	1.80	3.00
❑ 135		0.60	1.80	3.00
❑ 136		0.60	1.80	3.00
❑ 137		0.60	1.80	3.00
❑ 138		0.60	1.80	3.00
❑ 139		0.60	1.80	3.00
❑ 140		0.60	1.80	3.00
❑ 141	0.30	0.60	1.80	3.00
❑ 142		0.60	1.80	3.00
❑ 143		0.60	1.80	3.00
❑ 144		0.60	1.80	3.00
❑ 145		0.60	1.80	3.00
❑ 146		0.60	1.80	3.00
❑ 147		0.60	1.80	3.00
❑ 148		0.60	1.80	3.00
❑ 149		0.60	1.80	3.00
❑ 150		0.60	1.80	3.00
❑ 151		0.60	1.80	3.00

RAWHIDE KID (mini-series)

	ORIG.	GOOD	FINE	N-MINT
❑ 1	0.75	0.20	0.60	1.00
❑ 2	0.75	0.20	0.60	1.00
❑ 3	0.75	0.20	0.60	1.00
❑ 4	0.75	0.20	0.60	1.00

RAWHIDE KID SPECIAL

	ORIG.	GOOD	FINE	N-MINT
❑ 1, reprints, 1971	0.25	1.00	3.00	5.00

RAY ANNUAL, THE
DC

	ORIG.	GOOD	FINE	N-MINT
❑ 1, 95	3.95	0.79	2.37	3.95

RAY BRADBURY COMICS
TOPPS

	ORIG.	GOOD	FINE	N-MINT
❑ 1, Feb 93, 3 trading cards	2.95	0.59	1.77	2.95
❑ 2, HK, MW, 3 trading cards	2.95	0.59	1.77	2.95
❑ 3, trading cards	2.95	0.59	1.77	2.95
❑ 4, trading cards	2.95	0.59	1.77	2.95
❑ 5, trading cards	2.95	0.59	1.77	2.95

RAY BRADBURY COMICS SPECIAL EDITION

	ORIG.	GOOD	FINE	N-MINT
❑ 1, 94, Illustrated Man	2.95	0.59	1.77	2.95

RAY BRADBURY COMICS: TRILOGY OF TERROR

	ORIG.	GOOD	FINE	N-MINT
❑ 1, May 94, WW	2.50	0.50	1.50	2.50

RAY, THE (1994-)
DC

	ORIG.	GOOD	FINE	N-MINT
❑ 0, Oct 94	1.95	0.39	1.17	1.95
❑ 1, May 94	1.75	0.35	1.05	1.75
❑ 1, May 94, foil cover	2.95	0.59	1.77	2.95
❑ 2, Jun 94	1.75	0.35	1.05	1.75
❑ 3, Jul 94	1.75	0.35	1.05	1.75
❑ 4, Aug 94	1.95	0.39	1.17	1.95
❑ 5, Sep 94	1.95	0.39	1.17	1.95
❑ 6, Nov 94	1.95	0.39	1.17	1.95
❑ 7, Dec 94	1.95	0.39	1.17	1.95
❑ 8, Jan 95	1.95	0.39	1.17	1.95
❑ 9, Feb 95	1.95	0.39	1.17	1.95
❑ 10, Mar 95	1.95	0.39	1.17	1.95
❑ 11, Apr 95	1.95	0.39	1.17	1.95
❑ 12, May 95	1.95	0.39	1.17	1.95
❑ 13, Jun 95	2.25	0.45	1.35	2.25
❑ 14, Jul 95	2.25	0.45	1.35	2.25
❑ 15, Aug 95	2.25	0.45	1.35	2.25
❑ 16, Sep 95	2.25	0.45	1.35	2.25
❑ 17, Oct 95	2.25	0.45	1.35	2.25
❑ 18, Nov 95, "Underworld Unleashed"	2.25	0.45	1.35	2.25
❑ 19, Dec 95, "Underworld Unleashed"	2.25	0.45	1.35	2.25
❑ 20, Jan 96, A:Golden Age Black Condor	2.25	0.45	1.35	2.25
❑ 21, Feb 96	2.25	0.45	1.35	2.25
❑ 22, Mar 96	2.25	0.45	1.35	2.25
❑ 23, May 96	2.25	0.45	1.35	2.25
❑ 24, Jun 96	2.25	0.45	1.35	2.25

RAY, THE (mini-series)

	ORIG.	GOOD	FINE	N-MINT
❑ 1, Feb 92, O:The Ray	1.00	3.20	9.60	16.00
❑ 2, Mar 92	1.00	2.40	7.20	12.00
❑ 3, Apr 92	1.00	2.00	6.00	10.00
❑ 4, May 92	1.00	2.00	6.00	10.00
❑ 5, Jun 92	1.00	2.00	6.00	10.00
❑ 6, Jul 92	1.00	2.00	6.00	10.00

RAZOR
LONDON NIGHT

	ORIG.	GOOD	FINE	N-MINT
❑ 0, first printing		8.40	25.20	42.00
❑ 0, second printing		1.00	3.00	5.00
❑ 1		7.00	21.00	35.00
❑ 2		5.60	16.80	28.00
❑ 3		3.60	10.80	18.00
❑ 4		3.00	9.00	15.00
❑ 5		2.60	7.80	13.00
❑ 6		1.60	4.80	8.00
❑ 7		1.50	4.50	7.50
❑ 8		1.50	4.50	7.50
❑ 9		1.20	3.60	6.00
❑ 10		2.80	8.40	14.00
❑ 11, Sep 94, b&w	3.00	0.80	2.40	4.00
❑ 12, 95, b&w	3.00	0.80	2.40	4.00

	ORIG.	GOOD	FINE	N-MINT

RAZOR & SHI SPECIAL
	ORIG.	GOOD	FINE	N-MINT
☐ 1, Crossover with Crusade	3.00	9.00		15.00
☐ 1, Crossover with Crusade;platinum edition				
	6.00	18.00		30.00

RAZOR ANNUAL
	ORIG.	GOOD	FINE	N-MINT
☐ 1, A:Shi	10.00	30.00		50.00
☐ 2, 95, b&w	3.00	1.50	4.50	7.50

RAZOR'S EDGE
INNOVATION
	ORIG.	GOOD	FINE	N-MINT
☐ 1, b&w		0.50	1.50	2.50

RAZOR: BURN
LONDON NIGHT
	ORIG.	GOOD	FINE	N-MINT
☐ 1	1.60	4.80		8.00
☐ 2	1.00	3.00		5.00
☐ 3	0.80	2.40		4.00
☐ 4	0.80	2.40		4.00

RAZOR: CRY NO MORE
	ORIG.	GOOD	FINE	N-MINT
☐ 0, 95, nn	3.95	0.79	2.37	3.95

RAZOR: DARK ANGEL/FINAL NAIL
	ORIG.	GOOD	FINE	N-MINT
☐ 1	1.00	3.00		5.00

RAZOR: TORTURE
	ORIG.	GOOD	FINE	N-MINT
☐ 2, 96	3.00	0.60	1.80	3.00

RAZOR: UNCUT
	ORIG.	GOOD	FINE	N-MINT
☐ 18, Dec 95	3.00	0.60	1.80	3.00
☐ 20, 96	3.00	0.60	1.80	3.00

RAZORGUTS
MONSTER
	ORIG.	GOOD	FINE	N-MINT
☐ 1, b&w		0.45	1.35	2.25
☐ 2, b&w		0.45	1.35	2.25
☐ 3, b&w		0.45	1.35	2.25
☐ 4, b&w		0.45	1.35	2.25

RAZORLINE: THE FIRST CUT
MARVEL
	ORIG.	GOOD	FINE	N-MINT
☐ 1, sampler	0.75	0.15	0.45	0.75

RE-ANIMATOR
ADVENTURE
	ORIG.	GOOD	FINE	N-MINT
☐ 1, movie, color		0.59	1.77	2.95
☐ 2, movie, color		0.59	1.77	2.95
☐ 3, movie, color		0.59	1.77	2.95

RE-ANIMATOR: DAWN OF THE RE-ANIMATOR
	ORIG.	GOOD	FINE	N-MINT
☐ 1, b&w		0.50	1.50	2.50
☐ 2		0.59	1.77	2.95
☐ 4		0.50	1.50	2.50

REACTO-MAN
B-MOVIE
	ORIG.	GOOD	FINE	N-MINT
☐ 1		0.30	0.90	1.50
☐ 2		0.30	0.90	1.50
☐ 3, I:Warhead		0.30	0.90	1.50

REACTOR GIRL
TRAGEDY STRIKES
	ORIG.	GOOD	FINE	N-MINT
☐ 1, b&w		0.50	1.50	2.50
☐ 2		0.59	1.77	2.95
☐ 3		0.59	1.77	2.95
☐ 4		0.59	1.77	2.95
☐ 5		0.59	1.77	2.95

REAGAN'S RAIDERS
SOLSON
	ORIG.	GOOD	FINE	N-MINT
☐ 1, RB		0.40	1.20	2.00
☐ 2, RB		0.40	1.20	2.00
☐ 3, RB		0.40	1.20	2.00

REAL GHOSTBUSTERS
NOW
	ORIG.	GOOD	FINE	N-MINT
☐ 1, Aug 88	1.75	0.60	1.80	3.00
☐ 2, Sep 88	1.75	0.35	1.05	1.75
☐ 3, Oct 88	1.75	0.35	1.05	1.75
☐ 4, Nov 88	1.75	0.35	1.05	1.75
☐ 5, Jan 89	1.75	0.35	1.05	1.75
☐ 6, Feb 89	1.75	0.35	1.05	1.75
☐ 7, Mar 89	1.75	0.35	1.05	1.75
☐ 8, Apr 89	1.75	0.35	1.05	1.75
☐ 9, May 89	1.75	0.35	1.05	1.75
☐ 10, Jun 89	1.75	0.35	1.05	1.75
☐ 11, Jul 89	1.75	0.35	1.05	1.75
☐ 12, Aug 89	1.75	0.35	1.05	1.75
☐ 13, Sep 89	1.75	0.35	1.05	1.75
☐ 14, Oct 89	1.75	0.35	1.05	1.75
☐ 15, Nov 89	1.75	0.35	1.05	1.75
☐ 16, Dec 89	1.75	0.35	1.05	1.75
☐ 17, Jan 90	1.75	0.35	1.05	1.75
☐ 18, Feb 90	1.75	0.35	1.05	1.75
☐ 19, Mar 90	1.75	0.35	1.05	1.75
☐ 20, Apr 90	1.75	0.35	1.05	1.75
☐ 21, May 90	1.75	0.35	1.05	1.75
☐ 22, Jun 90	1.75	0.35	1.05	1.75
☐ 23, Jul 90	1.75	0.35	1.05	1.75
☐ 24, Aug 90	1.75	0.35	1.05	1.75
☐ 25, Sep 90	1.75	0.35	1.05	1.75
☐ 26, Oct 90	1.75	0.35	1.05	1.75
☐ 27, Nov 90	1.75	0.35	1.05	1.75
☐ 28, Dec 90	1.75	0.35	1.05	1.75

REAL GHOSTBUSTERS (Volume 2)
	ORIG.	GOOD	FINE	N-MINT
☐ 1, Nov 91	1.75	0.35	1.05	1.75
☐ 2, Dec 91	1.75	0.35	1.05	1.75
☐ 3, Jan 92	1.75	0.35	1.05	1.75
☐ 4, Feb 92	1.75	0.35	1.05	1.75

REAL GHOSTBUSTERS 3-D
	ORIG.	GOOD	FINE	N-MINT
☐ 1, Oct 91, polybagged, w/glasses				
	2.95	0.59	1.77	2.95

REAL GHOSTBUSTERS ANNUAL
	ORIG.	GOOD	FINE	N-MINT
☐ 0, Mar 92, 1992	1.00	0.20	0.60	1.00
☐ 0, Dec 92, 1993, 3-D	2.95	0.59	1.77	2.95

REAL GHOSTBUSTERS SUMMER SPECIAL
	ORIG.	GOOD	FINE	N-MINT
☐ 0, Sum 93, (1993)	2.95	0.59	1.77	2.95

REAL GIRL
FANTAGRAPHICS
	ORIG.	GOOD	FINE	N-MINT
☐ 1, b&w, adult		0.50	1.50	2.50
☐ 2, b&w, adult		0.50	1.50	2.50
☐ 3, b&w adult		0.59	1.77	2.95
☐ 4, b&w adult		0.59	1.77	2.95
☐ 5, b&w adult	3.50	0.70	2.10	3.50
☐ 6, b&w adult	3.50	0.70	2.10	3.50
☐ 7, Aug 94, b&w adult	3.50	0.70	2.10	3.50

REAL LIFE
	ORIG.	GOOD	FINE	N-MINT
☐ 1, b&w		0.50	1.50	2.50

REAL SCHMUCK
STARHEAD
	ORIG.	GOOD	FINE	N-MINT
☐ 1, b&w	2.95	0.59	1.77	2.95

REAL SMUT
EROS
	ORIG.	GOOD	FINE	N-MINT
☐ 1, adult, b&w		0.50	1.50	2.50
☐ 2, adult, b&w		0.50	1.50	2.50
☐ 3, adult, b&w		0.50	1.50	2.50
☐ 4, adult, b&w	2.75	0.55	1.65	2.75
☐ 5, adult, b&w	2.75	0.55	1.65	2.75
☐ 6, adult, b&w	2.50	0.50	1.50	2.50

REAL STUFF
FANTAGRAPHICS
	ORIG.	GOOD	FINE	N-MINT
☐ 1, b&w, adult		0.40	1.20	2.00
☐ 2, b&w, adult		0.40	1.20	2.00
☐ 3, b&w, adult		0.45	1.35	2.25
☐ 4, b&w, adult		0.45	1.35	2.25
☐ 5, b&w, adult		0.45	1.35	2.25
☐ 6, b&w, adult		0.45	1.35	2.25
☐ 7, b&w, adult		0.45	1.35	2.25
☐ 8, b&w, adult		0.45	1.35	2.25
☐ 9, b&w, adult		0.45	1.35	2.25
☐ 10, b&w, adult		0.59	1.77	2.95
☐ 11, b&w, adult	2.50	0.50	1.50	2.50

	ORIG.	GOOD	FINE	N-MINT
❑ 12, b&w, adult	2.50	0.50	1.50	2.50
❑ 13, b&w, adult	2.50	0.50	1.50	2.50
❑ 14, b&w, adult	2.50	0.50	1.50	2.50
❑ 15, b&w, adult	2.50	0.50	1.50	2.50
❑ 16, b&w, adult	2.50	0.50	1.50	2.50
❑ 17, b&w, adult	2.50	0.50	1.50	2.50
❑ 19, Jul 94, b&w, adult	2.50	0.50	1.50	2.50
❑ 20, Oct 94, b&w, adult	2.95	0.59	1.77	2.95

REAL WAR STORIES
ECLIPSE

	ORIG.	GOOD	FINE	N-MINT
❑ 1, BSz(c),BB		0.40	1.20	2.00
❑ 2, BSz		0.99	2.97	4.95

REALM HANDBOOK, THE
CALIBER

	ORIG.	GOOD	FINE	N-MINT
❑ 1	2.95	0.59	1.77	2.95

REALM OF THE DEAD

	ORIG.	GOOD	FINE	N-MINT
❑ 1	2.95	0.59	1.77	2.95
❑ 2	2.95	0.59	1.77	2.95
❑ 3	2.95	0.59	1.77	2.95

REALM, THE
ARROW

	GOOD	FINE	N-MINT
❑ 1	1.00	3.00	5.00
❑ 2	0.80	2.40	4.00
❑ 3	0.60	1.80	3.00
❑ 4, 1:Deadworld	1.60	4.80	8.00
❑ 5	0.30	0.90	1.50
❑ 6	0.30	0.90	1.50
❑ 7	0.30	0.90	1.50
❑ 8	0.30	0.90	1.50
❑ 9	0.30	0.90	1.50
❑ 10	0.30	0.90	1.50
❑ 11	0.30	0.90	1.50
❑ 12, (moves to Caliber)	0.30	0.90	1.50

REALM, THE (Volume 2)
CALIBER

	ORIG.	GOOD	FINE	N-MINT
❑ 1, b&w	2.95	0.59	1.77	2.95
❑ 2, b&w	2.95	0.59	1.77	2.95
❑ 3, b&w	2.95	0.59	1.77	2.95
❑ 4, b&w	2.95	0.59	1.77	2.95
❑ 5, b&w	2.95	0.59	1.77	2.95
❑ 6, b&w	2.95	0.59	1.77	2.95
❑ 7, b&w	2.95	0.59	1.77	2.95
❑ 8, b&w	2.95	0.59	1.77	2.95
❑ 9, b&w	2.95	0.59	1.77	2.95
❑ 10, b&w	2.95	0.59	1.77	2.95
❑ 11, b&w	2.95	0.59	1.77	2.95
❑ 12, b&w	2.95	0.59	1.77	2.95
❑ 13, b&w	2.95	0.59	1.77	2.95

REALM, THE (was an Arrow comic)

	ORIG.	GOOD	FINE	N-MINT
❑ 14, b&w	1.95	0.39	1.17	1.95
❑ 15, b&w	1.95	0.39	1.17	1.95
❑ 16, b&w	1.95	0.39	1.17	1.95
❑ 17	2.50	0.50	1.50	2.50
❑ 18	2.50	0.50	1.50	2.50
❑ 19	2.50	0.50	1.50	2.50
❑ 20, Demonstorm	2.50	0.50	1.50	2.50
❑ 21, Demonstorm	2.50	0.50	1.50	2.50

REBEL SWORD
DARK HORSE

	ORIG.	GOOD	FINE	N-MINT
❑ 1, Oct 94, b&w	2.50	0.50	1.50	2.50
❑ 2, Nov 94, b&w	2.50	0.50	1.50	2.50
❑ 3, Dec 94, b&w	2.50	0.50	1.50	2.50
❑ 4, Jan 95, b&w	2.50	0.50	1.50	2.50
❑ 5, Feb 95, b&w	2.50	0.50	1.50	2.50

RECOLLECTIONS SAMPLER
RECOLLECTIONS

		GOOD	FINE	N-MINT
❑ 1, 16 pages, b&w reprints		0.10	0.30	0.50

RED DOG
ECLIPSE

	ORIG.	GOOD	FINE	N-MINT
❑ 1, PCR		0.40	1.20	2.00

RED DRAGON
COMICO

	ORIG.	GOOD	FINE	N-MINT
❑ 1, Jun 96	2.95	0.59	1.77	2.95

RED HEAT
BLACKTHORNE

		GOOD	FINE	N-MINT
❑ 1, Aug 88, movie, b&w		0.40	1.20	2.00

RED HEAT 3-D

	ORIG.	GOOD	FINE	N-MINT
❑ 1, Jul 88, movie	2.50	0.50	1.50	2.50

RED MOON
MILLENNIUM

	ORIG.	GOOD	FINE	N-MINT
❑ 1, Mar 95, b&w	2.95	0.59	1.77	2.95

RED RAZORS: A DREDDWORLD ADVENTURE
FLEETWAY/QUALITY

	ORIG.	GOOD	FINE	N-MINT
❑ 1	2.95	0.59	1.77	2.95
❑ 2	2.95	0.59	1.77	2.95
❑ 3	2.95	0.59	1.77	2.95

RED SHETLAND
GRAPHXPRESS

		GOOD	FINE	N-MINT
❑ 1, b&w, parody		0.40	1.20	2.00
❑ 2, b&w, parody		0.40	1.20	2.00
❑ 3, b&w, parody		0.40	1.20	2.00
❑ 4, b&w, parody		0.40	1.20	2.00
❑ 5		0.50	1.50	2.50
❑ 6		0.50	1.50	2.50

RED SONJA (1976-1979)
MARVEL

	ORIG.	GOOD	FINE	N-MINT
❑ 1, FT	0.30	0.50	1.50	2.50
❑ 2, FT	0.30	0.35	1.05	1.75
❑ 3, FT	0.30	0.35	1.05	1.75
❑ 4, FT	0.30	0.35	1.05	1.75
❑ 5, FT	0.30	0.35	1.05	1.75
❑ 6	0.35	0.20	0.60	1.00
❑ 7	0.35	0.20	0.60	1.00
❑ 8	0.35	0.20	0.60	1.00
❑ 9	0.35	0.20	0.60	1.00
❑ 10	0.35	0.20	0.60	1.00
❑ 11	0.35	0.20	0.60	1.00
❑ 12	0.35	0.20	0.60	1.00
❑ 13	0.35	0.20	0.60	1.00
❑ 14	0.35	0.20	0.60	1.00
❑ 15	0.40	0.20	0.60	1.00

RED SONJA (1983)

	ORIG.	GOOD	FINE	N-MINT
❑ 1	0.60	0.40	1.20	2.00
❑ 2	0.60	0.30	0.90	1.50

RED SONJA (Vol. 3)

	ORIG.	GOOD	FINE	N-MINT
❑ 1, Aug 83	1.00	0.40	1.20	2.00
❑ 2, 83	1.00	0.30	0.90	1.50
❑ 3, Dec 83	1.00	0.30	0.90	1.50
❑ 4, Feb 84	1.00	0.30	0.90	1.50
❑ 5, Jan 85	0.60	0.30	0.90	1.50
❑ 6, Feb 85	0.60	0.30	0.90	1.50
❑ 7, Mar 85	0.60	0.30	0.90	1.50
❑ 8, Apr 85	0.65	0.30	0.90	1.50
❑ 9, May 85	0.65	0.30	0.90	1.50
❑ 10, Aug 85	0.65	0.30	0.90	1.50
❑ 11, Nov 85	0.65	0.30	0.90	1.50
❑ 12, Feb 86	0.75	0.30	0.90	1.50
❑ 13, 86, final issue	0.75	0.30	0.90	1.50

RED SONJA IN 3-D
BLACKTHORNE

		GOOD	FINE	N-MINT
❑ 1		0.50	1.50	2.50

RED SONJA: SCAVENGER HUNT
MARVEL

	ORIG.	GOOD	FINE	N-MINT
❑ 1, Dec 95, one-shot	2.95	0.59	1.77	2.95

	ORIG.	GOOD	FINE	N-MINT

RED SONJA: THE MOVIE (mini-series)
	ORIG.	GOOD	FINE	N-MINT
❏ 1, Nov 85, movie adaptation 0.75		0.20	0.60	1.00
❏ 2, Dec 85, movie adaptation 0.75		0.20	0.60	1.00

RED TORNADO
DC
	ORIG.	GOOD	FINE	N-MINT
❏ 1, Jul 85, KB 0.75		0.20	0.60	1.00
❏ 2, Aug 85, KB...............0.75		0.20	0.60	1.00
❏ 3, Sep 85, KB 0.75		0.20	0.60	1.00
❏ 4, Oct 85, KB 0.75		0.20	0.60	1.00

RED WOLF
MARVEL
	ORIG.	GOOD	FINE	N-MINT
❏ 1 ....0.20		0.20	0.60	1.00
❏ 2 ....0.20		0.20	0.60	1.00
❏ 3 ....0.20		0.20	0.60	1.00
❏ 4 ....0.20		0.20	0.60	1.00
❏ 5 ....0.20		0.20	0.60	1.00
❏ 6 ....0.20		0.20	0.60	1.00
❏ 7 ....0.20		0.20	0.60	1.00
❏ 8 ....0.20		0.20	0.60	1.00
❏ 9 ....0.20		0.20	0.60	1.00

REDBLADE
DARK HORSE
	ORIG.	GOOD	FINE	N-MINT
❏ 1, gatefold cover 2.50		0.50	1.50	2.50
❏ 2 ....2.50		0.50	1.50	2.50
❏ 3 ....2.50		0.50	1.50	2.50

REDDEVIL
AC
	ORIG.	GOOD	FINE	N-MINT
❏ 1, b&w and red;no indicia 2.95		0.59	1.77	2.95

REDFOX
HARRIER
	ORIG.	GOOD	FINE	N-MINT
❏ 1 ....2.40		7.20	12.00	
❏ 1, (2nd printing)..............0.35		1.05	1.75	
❏ 2 ....2.40		7.20	12.00	
❏ 3 ....1.00		3.00	5.00	
❏ 4 ....0.35		1.05	1.75	
❏ 5 ....0.35		1.05	1.75	
❏ 6 ....0.35		1.05	1.75	
❏ 7 ....0.35		1.05	1.75	
❏ 8 ....0.35		1.05	1.75	
❏ 9, (moves to Valkyrie Press)		0.35	1.05	1.75

REDFOX (was Harrier Comic)
VALKYRIE
	ORIG.	GOOD	FINE	N-MINT
❏ 10		0.40	1.20	2.00
❏ 11		0.40	1.20	2.00
❏ 12		0.40	1.20	2.00
❏ 13		0.40	1.20	2.00
❏ 14		0.40	1.20	2.00
❏ 15		0.40	1.20	2.00
❏ 16		0.40	1.20	2.00
❏ 17		0.40	1.20	2.00
❏ 18		0.40	1.20	2.00
❏ 19		0.40	1.20	2.00
❏ 20		0.40	1.20	2.00

REDMASK OF THE RIO GRANDE
AC
	ORIG.	GOOD	FINE	N-MINT
❏ 1, reprints;color		0.59	1.77	2.95
❏ 2		0.59	1.77	2.95
❏ 3, 3-D effects		0.59	1.77	2.95

REESE'S PIECES
ECLIPSE
	ORIG.	GOOD	FINE	N-MINT
❏ 1		0.35	1.05	1.75
❏ 2		0.35	1.05	1.75

REGGIE'S REVENGE
ARCHIE
	ORIG.	GOOD	FINE	N-MINT
❏ 1, 94................................2.00		0.40	1.20	2.00
❏ 2, Fal 94 ....2.00		0.40	1.20	2.00
❏ 3, Spr 95 ....2.00		0.40	1.20	2.00

REGULATORS
IMAGE
	ORIG.	GOOD	FINE	N-MINT
❏ 1, Jun 95 ....2.50		0.50	1.50	2.50
❏ 3, Aug 95 ....2.50		0.50	1.50	2.50

REID FLEMING
BOSWELL
	ORIG.	GOOD	FINE	N-MINT
❏ 1, 1st printing		2.00	6.00	10.00
❏ 1, 2nd printing (moves to Eclipse)		1.00	3.00	5.00

REID FLEMING, WORLD'S TOUGHEST MILKMAN
(was David Boswell title)
ECLIPSE
	ORIG.	GOOD	FINE	N-MINT
❏ 1, 1st printing;b&w...........		1.00	3.00	5.00
❏ 1, 2nd printing;b&w		0.40	1.20	2.00
❏ 1, 3rd printing;b&w		0.50	1.50	2.50
❏ 1, 4th printing;b&w		0.50	1.50	2.50
❏ 1, 5th printing;b&w		0.80	2.40	4.00
❏ 2, 1st printing;b&w		0.40	1.20	2.00
❏ 2, 2nd printing;b&w		0.40	1.20	2.00
❏ 2, 3rd printing;b&w		0.60	1.80	3.00
❏ 3, b&w...........................		0.60	1.80	3.00
❏ 4, b&w...........................		0.40	1.20	2.00
❏ 5, b&w...........................				

REIGN OF THE DRAGONLORD
ETERNITY
	ORIG.	GOOD	FINE	N-MINT
❏ 1		0.36	1.08	1.80
❏ 2		0.36	1.08	1.80

REIKI WARRIORS
REVOLUTIONARY
	ORIG.	GOOD	FINE	N-MINT
❏ 1, b&w...........................2.95		0.59	1.77	2.95

RELENTLESS PURSUIT
SLAVE LABOR
	ORIG.	GOOD	FINE	N-MINT
❏ 1, b&w...........................		0.35	1.05	1.75
❏ 2, b&w...........................		0.35	1.05	1.75
❏ 3, b&w...........................		0.35	1.05	1.75

REN & STIMPY SHOW
HOLIDAY SPECIAL 1994, THE
MARVEL
	ORIG.	GOOD	FINE	N-MINT
❏ 0, Feb 95, nn..................2.95		0.59	1.77	2.95

REN & STIMPY SHOW SPECIAL
	ORIG.	GOOD	FINE	N-MINT
❏ 2, Jul 94 ....2.95		0.59	1.77	2.95
❏ 3, Oct 94 ....2.95		0.59	1.77	2.95

REN & STIMPY SHOW SPECIAL,
THE: AROUND THE WORLD IN A DAZE
	ORIG.	GOOD	FINE	N-MINT
❏ 0, Jan 96, nn;one-shot...2.95		0.59	1.77	2.95

REN & STIMPY SHOW SPECIAL: EENTERACTIVE
	ORIG.	GOOD	FINE	N-MINT
❏ 0, Jul 95, nn..................2.95		0.59	1.77	2.95

REN & STIMPY SHOW SPECIAL: FOUR SWERKS
	ORIG.	GOOD	FINE	N-MINT
❏ 0, Jan 95, nn..................2.95		0.59	1.77	2.95

REN & STIMPY SHOW SPECIAL:
POWDERED TOAST MAN
	ORIG.	GOOD	FINE	N-MINT
❏ 1, Apr 94 ....2.95		0.59	1.77	2.95

REN & STIMPY SHOW SPECIAL:
POWDERED TOASTMAN'S CEREAL
	ORIG.	GOOD	FINE	N-MINT
❏ 0, Apr 95 ....2.95		0.59	1.77	2.95

REN & STIMPY SHOW SPECIAL: SPORTS
	ORIG.	GOOD	FINE	N-MINT
❏ 0, Oct 95, nn..................2.95		0.59	1.77	2.95

REN & STIMPY SHOW, THE
	ORIG.	GOOD	FINE	N-MINT
❏ 1, Ren scratch&sniff card 2.25		1.60	4.80	8.00
❏ 1, Stimpy scratch&sniff card 2.25		1.20	3.60	6.00
❏ 1, second printing..........2.25		1.00	3.00	5.00
❏ 1, third printing.............2.25		0.60	1.80	3.00
❏ 2 ....1.75		0.80	2.40	4.00
❏ 2, second printing..........1.75		0.40	1.20	2.00
❏ 3 ....1.75		0.80	2.40	4.00
❏ 3, second printing..........1.75		0.40	1.20	2.00

	ORIG.	GOOD	FINE	N-MINT
❑ 4 ....1.75		0.80	2.40	4.00
❑ 5 ....1.75		0.80	2.40	4.00
❑ 6, SpM 1.75		1.20	3.60	6.00
❑ 7, SpM 1.75		0.80	2.40	4.00
❑ 8 ....1.75		0.60	1.80	3.00
❑ 9 ....1.75		0.60	1.80	3.00
❑ 10 ....1.75		0.35	1.05	1.75
❑ 11 ....1.75		0.35	1.05	1.75
❑ 12 ....1.75		0.35	1.05	1.75
❑ 13 ....1.75		0.35	1.05	1.75
❑ 14 ....1.75		0.35	1.05	1.75
❑ 15 ....1.75		0.35	1.05	1.75
❑ 16 ....1.75		0.35	1.05	1.75
❑ 17 ....1.75		0.35	1.05	1.75
❑ 18, May 94, Powdered Toast Man				
..................................1.95		0.39	1.17	1.95
❑ 19, Jun 94.....................1.95		0.39	1.17	1.95
❑ 20, Jul 94......................1.95		0.39	1.17	1.95
❑ 21, Aug 94.....................1.95		0.39	1.17	1.95
❑ 22, Sep 94.....................1.95		0.39	1.17	1.95
❑ 23, Oct 94......................1.95		0.39	1.17	1.95
❑ 24, Nov 94 ....1.95		0.39	1.17	1.95
❑ 25, Dec 94......................1.95		0.39	1.17	1.95
❑ 25, Dec 94, enhanced cover				
..................................2.95		0.59	1.77	2.95
❑ 26, Jan 95 ....1.95		0.39	1.17	1.95
❑ 27, Feb 95 ....1.95		0.39	1.17	1.95
❑ 28, Mar 95 ....1.95		0.39	1.17	1.95
❑ 29, Apr 95 ....1.95		0.39	1.17	1.95
❑ 30, May 95.....................1.95		0.39	1.17	1.95
❑ 31, Jun 95......................1.95		0.39	1.17	1.95
❑ 32, Jul 95......................1.95		0.39	1.17	1.95
❑ 33, Aug 95 ....1.95		0.39	1.17	1.95
❑ 34, Sep 95.....................1.95		0.39	1.17	1.95
❑ 35, Oct 95......................1.95		0.39	1.17	1.95
❑ 36, Nov 95 ....1.95		0.39	1.17	1.95
❑ 37, Dec 95......................1.95		0.39	1.17	1.95
❑ 38, Jan 96 ....1.95		0.39	1.17	1.95
❑ 39, Feb 96 ....1.95		0.39	1.17	1.95
❑ 40, Mar 96 ....1.95		0.39	1.17	1.95
❑ 41, Apr 96 ....1.95		0.39	1.17	1.95
❑ 42, May 96.....................1.95		0.39	1.17	1.95
❑ 43, Jun 96......................1.95		0.39	1.17	1.95
❑ 44, Jul 96, final issue 1.95		0.39	1.17	1.95

REN & STIMPY SHOW, THE: RADIO DAZE

	ORIG.	GOOD	FINE	N-MINT
❑ 1, Nov 95, based on audio release of same name				
..................................1.95		0.39	1.17	1.95

RENEGADE RABBIT
PRINTED MATTER

	GOOD	FINE	N-MINT
❑ 1	0.35	1.05	1.75
❑ 2	0.35	1.05	1.75
❑ 3	0.35	1.05	1.75
❑ 4	0.35	1.05	1.75
❑ 5, Cerebus parody............	0.30	0.90	1.50

RENEGADE ROMANCE
RENEGADE

	GOOD	FINE	N-MINT
❑ 1, b&w	0.70	2.10	3.50
❑ 2, b&w	0.70	2.10	3.50

RENEGADE, THE
RIP OFF

	ORIG.	GOOD	FINE	N-MINT
❑ 1, Aug 91, b&w, adult 2.50		0.50	1.50	2.50

RENEGADE: NIGHT SLAYER

	ORIG.	GOOD	FINE	N-MINT
❑ 0, Dec 93, nn.................2.95		0.59	1.77	2.95

RENEGADES OF JUSTICE, THE (mini-series)
BLUE MASQUE

	ORIG.	GOOD	FINE	N-MINT
❑ 1, 95, b&w 2.50		0.50	1.50	2.50
❑ 2, 95, b&w 2.50		0.50	1.50	2.50

RENEGADES, THE
AGE OF HEROES

	ORIG.	GOOD	FINE	N-MINT
❑ 1		0.20	0.60	1.00
❑ 2		0.20	0.60	1.00

RENFIELD
CALIBER

	ORIG.	GOOD	FINE	N-MINT
❑ 1, 94 ....2.95		0.59	1.77	2.95
❑ 2, 94 ....2.95		0.59	1.77	2.95
❑ 3, 94 ....2.95		0.59	1.77	2.95

RENFIELD: SPECIAL PREVIEW

❑ 0, 94, b&w, no cover price

REQUIEM FOR DRACULA
MARVEL

	ORIG.	GOOD	FINE	N-MINT
❑ 1, reprints 2.00		0.40	1.20	2.00

RESCUEMAN
BEST

	GOOD	FINE	N-MINT
❑ 1, b&w	0.59	1.77	2.95

RESTAURANT AT THE END OF THE UNIVERSE, THE (mini-series)
DC

	ORIG.	GOOD	FINE	N-MINT
❑ 1, 95, prestige format 6.95		1.39	4.17	6.95
❑ 2, 95, prestige format 6.95		1.39	4.17	6.95
❑ 3, 95, prestige format;final issue				
..................................6.95		1.39	4.17	6.95

RETALIATOR, THE
ECLIPSE

	GOOD	FINE	N-MINT
❑ 1, b&w	0.50	1.50	2.50
❑ 2, b&w	0.50	1.50	2.50
❑ 3, b&w	0.50	1.50	2.50
❑ 4, b&w	0.50	1.50	2.50

RETIEF
ADVENTURE

	GOOD	FINE	N-MINT
❑ 1, b&w	0.45	1.35	2.25
❑ 2, b&w	0.45	1.35	2.25
❑ 3, b&w	0.45	1.35	2.25
❑ 4, b&w	0.45	1.35	2.25
❑ 5, b&w	0.45	1.35	2.25
❑ 6, b&w	0.45	1.35	2.25

RETIEF AND THE WARLORDS

	GOOD	FINE	N-MINT
❑ 1, b&w	0.50	1.50	2.50
❑ 2, b&w	0.50	1.50	2.50
❑ 3, b&w	0.50	1.50	2.50
❑ 4, b&w	0.50	1.50	2.50

RETIEF OF THE C.D.T.
MAD DOG

	ORIG.	GOOD	FINE	N-MINT
❑ 1, 88, b&w 2.00		0.40	1.20	2.00

RETIEF: DIPLOMATIC IMMUNITY
ADVENTURE

	GOOD	FINE	N-MINT
❑ 1, b&w	0.50	1.50	2.50
❑ 2, b&w	0.50	1.50	2.50

RETIEF: GRIME AND PUNISHMENT

	GOOD	FINE	N-MINT
❑ 1, b&w	0.50	1.50	2.50

RETIEF: THE GARBAGE INVASION

	GOOD	FINE	N-MINT
❑ 1, b&w	0.50	1.50	2.50

RETIEF: THE GIANT KILLER

	GOOD	FINE	N-MINT
❑ 1, b&w	0.50	1.50	2.50

RETRO 50'S COMIX
EDGE

	ORIG.	GOOD	FINE	N-MINT
❑ 1, 94, b&w 2.95		0.59	1.77	2.95
❑ 2, 94, b&w 2.95		0.59	1.77	2.95

RETROGRADE
ETERNITY

	GOOD	FINE	N-MINT
❑ 1	0.39	1.17	1.95
❑ 2	0.39	1.17	1.95
❑ 3	0.39	1.17	1.95

	ORIG.	GOOD	FINE	N-MINT

RETURN OF DISNEY'S ALADDIN, THE
DISNEY

	ORIG.	GOOD	FINE	N-MINT
❑ 1	1.50	0.30	0.90	1.50
❑ 2	1.50	0.30	0.90	1.50

RETURN OF GIRL SQUAD X
FANTACO

	ORIG.	GOOD	FINE	N-MINT
❑ 0, nn	4.95	0.99	2.97	4.95

RETURN OF HAPPY THE CLOWN, THE
CALIBER

	ORIG.	GOOD	FINE	N-MINT
❑ 1, 95, b&w	3.50	0.70	2.10	3.50
❑ 2, 95, b&w	2.95	0.59	1.77	2.95

RETURN OF LUM-URUSEI YATSURA, THE
VIZ

	ORIG.	GOOD	FINE	N-MINT
❑ 1, 94, b&w	2.95	0.59	1.77	2.95
❑ 2, 95, b&w	2.75	0.55	1.65	2.75
❑ 3, 95, b&w	2.75	0.55	1.65	2.75
❑ 5, 95, b&w	2.95	0.59	1.77	2.95
❑ 6, 95, b&w	2.95	0.59	1.77	2.95

RETURN OF MEGATON MAN, THE
KITCHEN SINK

	ORIG.	GOOD	FINE	N-MINT
❑ 1, color		0.40	1.20	2.00
❑ 2, color		0.40	1.20	2.00
❑ 3, color		0.40	1.20	2.00

RETURN OF THE JEDI
MARVEL

	ORIG.	GOOD	FINE	N-MINT
❑ 1, AW, movie	0.60	0.30	0.90	1.50
❑ 2, AW, movie	0.60	0.30	0.90	1.50
❑ 3, AW	0.60	0.20	0.60	1.00
❑ 4, AW	0.60	0.20	0.60	1.00

RETURN OF THE SKYMAN
ACE

	ORIG.	GOOD	FINE	N-MINT
❑ 1, Sep 87, SD		0.35	1.05	1.75

RETURN TO JURASSIC PARK
TOPPS

	ORIG.	GOOD	FINE	N-MINT
❑ 3, Jun 95, JSa;MGc	2.95	0.59	1.77	2.95
❑ 4, Jul 95, JSa;MGc	2.95	0.59	1.77	2.95
❑ 5, Aug 95	2.95	0.59	1.77	2.95
❑ 6, Sep 95	2.95	0.59	1.77	2.95
❑ 7, Nov 95	2.95	0.59	1.77	2.95
❑ 8, Jan 96	2.95	0.59	1.77	2.95

REVELATIONS
GOLDEN REALM UNLIMITED

	ORIG.	GOOD	FINE	N-MINT
❑ 1		0.55	1.65	2.75

REVELRY IN HELL
EROS COMIX

	ORIG.	GOOD	FINE	N-MINT
❑ 1, adult, b&w		0.50	1.50	2.50

REVENGE OF THE PROWLER
ECLIPSE

	ORIG.	GOOD	FINE	N-MINT
❑ 1, Feb 88	1.75	0.39	1.17	1.95
❑ 2, Mar 88	2.50	0.39	1.17	1.95
❑ 3, Apr 88	1.95	0.39	1.17	1.95
❑ 4, Jun 88	1.95	0.39	1.17	1.95

REVENGERS FEATURING ARMOR/SILVER STREAK
CONTINUITY

	ORIG.	GOOD	FINE	N-MINT
❑ 1, Sep 85	2.00	0.40	1.20	2.00
❑ 2, Jun 86	2.00	0.40	1.20	2.00
❑ 3, Feb 87	2.00	0.40	1.20	2.00

REVENGERS FEATURING MEGALITH

	ORIG.	GOOD	FINE	N-MINT
❑ 1, Apr 85, (1985)	2.00	0.40	1.20	2.00
❑ 1, newsstand (1987)	2.00	0.40	1.20	2.00
❑ 2, Sep 85	2.00	0.40	1.20	2.00
❑ 3, Nov 86	2.00	0.40	1.20	2.00
❑ 4, Mar 88	2.00	0.40	1.20	2.00
❑ 5, Mar 88	2.00	0.40	1.20	2.00
❑ 6, Mar 88	2.00	0.40	1.20	2.00

REVENGERS: HYBRIDS SPECIAL

	ORIG.	GOOD	FINE	N-MINT
❑ 1	4.95	0.99	2.97	4.95

REVOLVER
FLEETWAY

	ORIG.	GOOD	FINE	N-MINT
❑ 1, O:Dan Dare		0.50	1.50	2.50
❑ 2		0.50	1.50	2.50
❑ 3		0.50	1.50	2.50
❑ 4		0.50	1.50	2.50
❑ 5		0.50	1.50	2.50
❑ 6		0.50	1.50	2.50
❑ 7		0.50	1.50	2.50

RENEGADE

	ORIG.	GOOD	FINE	N-MINT
❑ 1, Sci-Fi Adventure		0.34	1.02	1.70
❑ 2, Sci-Fi Adventure		0.34	1.02	1.70
❑ 3, Sci-Fi Adventure		0.34	1.02	1.70
❑ 4, Fantastic Fables		0.34	1.02	1.70
❑ 5, Fantastic Fables		0.34	1.02	1.70
❑ 6, Fantastic Fables		0.34	1.02	1.70
❑ 7, Ditko's World: Static		0.34	1.02	1.70
❑ 8, Ditko's World: Static		0.34	1.02	1.70
❑ 9, Ditko's World: Static		0.34	1.02	1.70
❑ 10, Murder		0.34	1.02	1.70
❑ 11, Murder		0.34	1.02	1.70
❑ 12, Murder		0.34	1.02	1.70

REVOLVER ANNUAL

	ORIG.	GOOD	FINE	N-MINT
❑ 1, ATh(c) b&w		0.40	1.20	2.00

REVOLVING DOORS
BLACKTHORNE

	ORIG.	GOOD	FINE	N-MINT
❑ 1		0.35	1.05	1.75
❑ 2		0.35	1.05	1.75
❑ 3		0.35	1.05	1.75

RHAJ
MU PRESS

	ORIG.	GOOD	FINE	N-MINT
❑ 1, b&w		0.40	1.20	2.00
❑ 2, b&w		0.40	1.20	2.00
❑ 3, b&w		0.40	1.20	2.00
❑ 4		0.45	1.35	2.25

RHUDIPRRT, PRINCE OF FUR

	ORIG.	GOOD	FINE	N-MINT
❑ 1, b&w		0.40	1.20	2.00
❑ 2, b&w		0.40	1.20	2.00
❑ 3		0.45	1.35	2.25
❑ 4, Nov 90	2.50	0.50	1.50	2.50
❑ 5, Jun 91	2.25	0.45	1.35	2.25
❑ 6, Nov 91	2.50	0.50	1.50	2.50
❑ 7, b&w	2.50	0.50	1.50	2.50
❑ 8, Jan 94	2.50	0.50	1.50	2.50

RIB
DILEMMA

	ORIG.	GOOD	FINE	N-MINT
❑ 1, Apr 96, b&w	1.95	0.39	1.17	1.95

RIBIT!
COMICO

	ORIG.	GOOD	FINE	N-MINT
❑ 1, Frank Thorne		0.39	1.17	1.95
❑ 2, Frank Thorne		0.39	1.17	1.95
❑ 3, Frank Thorne		0.39	1.17	1.95
❑ 4, Frank Thorne		0.39	1.17	1.95

RICHARD DRAGON: KUNG FU FIGHTER
DC

	ORIG.	GOOD	FINE	N-MINT
❑ 1, Apr 75	0.25	0.05	0.15	0.25
❑ 2	0.25	0.05	0.15	0.25
❑ 3	0.25	0.05	0.15	0.25
❑ 4	0.25	0.05	0.15	0.25
❑ 5	0.25	0.05	0.15	0.25
❑ 6	0.25	0.05	0.15	0.25
❑ 7	0.25	0.05	0.15	0.25
❑ 8	0.25	0.05	0.15	0.25
❑ 9	0.25	0.05	0.15	0.25
❑ 10	0.25	0.05	0.15	0.25
❑ 11	0.25	0.05	0.15	0.25
❑ 12	0.25	0.05	0.15	0.25
❑ 13	0.25	0.05	0.15	0.25
❑ 14	0.25	0.05	0.15	0.25
❑ 15	0.25	0.05	0.15	0.25

	ORIG.	GOOD	FINE	N-MINT
❑ 16 ....0.25	0.05	0.15	0.25
❑ 17 ....0.25	0.05	0.15	0.25
❑ 18, Nov 77 ....0.25	0.05	0.15	0.25

RICHIE RICH
MARVEL

	ORIG.	GOOD	FINE	N-MINT
❑ 1, Feb 95, movie adaptation			
..........2.95	0.59	1.77	2.95

RICHIE RICH (2nd series)
HARVEY

	ORIG.	GOOD	FINE	N-MINT
❑ 1 ....1.25	0.25	0.75	1.25
❑ 2 ....1.25	0.25	0.75	1.25
❑ 3 ....1.25	0.25	0.75	1.25
❑ 4 ....1.25	0.25	0.75	1.25
❑ 5 ....1.25	0.25	0.75	1.25
❑ 6 ....1.25	0.25	0.75	1.25
❑ 7 ....1.25	0.25	0.75	1.25
❑ 8 ....1.25	0.25	0.75	1.25
❑ 9 ....1.25	0.25	0.75	1.25
❑ 10 ....1.25	0.25	0.75	1.25
❑ 11 ....1.25	0.25	0.75	1.25
❑ 12 ....1.25	0.25	0.75	1.25
❑ 13 ....1.25	0.25	0.75	1.25
❑ 14 ....1.25	0.25	0.75	1.25
❑ 15 ....1.25	0.25	0.75	1.25
❑ 16 ....1.50	0.30	0.90	1.50
❑ 17 ....1.50	0.30	0.90	1.50
❑ 18 ....1.50	0.30	0.90	1.50
❑ 19 ....1.50	0.30	0.90	1.50
❑ 20 ....1.50	0.30	0.90	1.50
❑ 21 ....1.50	0.30	0.90	1.50
❑ 22 ....1.50	0.30	0.90	1.50
❑ 23 ....1.50	0.30	0.90	1.50
❑ 24 ....1.50	0.30	0.90	1.50
❑ 25, Aug 94 ....1.50	0.30	0.90	1.50
❑ 26, Sep 94 ....1.50	0.30	0.90	1.50
❑ 27, Oct 94 ....1.50	0.30	0.90	1.50
❑ 28, Nov 94 ....1.50	0.30	0.90	1.50

RICHIE RICH ADVENTURE DIGEST MAGAZINE

	ORIG.	GOOD	FINE	N-MINT
❑ 1, May 92, digest 1.75	0.35	1.05	1.75
❑ 2, Feb 93, digest 1.75	0.35	1.05	1.75
❑ 3, Jun 93, digest 1.75	0.35	1.05	1.75
❑ 4, Oct 93, digest..........1.75	0.35	1.05	1.75
❑ 5, Feb 94, digest 1.75	0.35	1.05	1.75
❑ 6, Jun 94, digest 1.75	0.35	1.05	1.75

RICHIE RICH AND CASPER IN 3-D
BLACKTHORNE

	GOOD	FINE	N-MINT
❑ 1	0.50	1.50	2.50
❑ 1, Spanish, Burger King ...	0.50	1.50	2.50

RICHIE RICH AND THE NEW KIDS ON THE BLOCK
HARVEY

	GOOD	FINE	N-MINT
❑ 1	0.25	0.75	1.25

RICHIE RICH BIG BOOK

	GOOD	FINE	N-MINT
❑ 2	0.39	1.17	1.95

RICHIE RICH BIG BUCKS

	GOOD	FINE	N-MINT
❑ 1	0.25	0.75	1.25
❑ 2	0.25	0.75	1.25
❑ 3	0.25	0.75	1.25
❑ 4	0.25	0.75	1.25
❑ 5	0.25	0.75	1.25
❑ 6	0.25	0.75	1.25
❑ 7	0.25	0.75	1.25
❑ 8	0.25	0.75	1.25

RICHIE RICH CASH MONEY

	GOOD	FINE	N-MINT
❑ 1	0.25	0.75	1.25
❑ 2	0.25	0.75	1.25

RICHIE RICH DIGEST MAGAZINE

	ORIG.	GOOD	FINE	N-MINT
❑ 1, digest 1.75	0.35	1.05	1.75
❑ 2, digest 1.75	0.35	1.05	1.75
❑ 3, digest 1.75	0.35	1.05	1.75

	ORIG.	GOOD	FINE	N-MINT
❑ 4, digest..........1.75	0.35	1.05	1.75
❑ 5, digest..........1.75	0.35	1.05	1.75
❑ 6, digest..........1.75	0.35	1.05	1.75
❑ 7, digest..........1.75	0.35	1.05	1.75
❑ 8, digest..........1.75	0.35	1.05	1.75
❑ 9, digest..........1.75	0.35	1.05	1.75
❑ 10, digest..........1.75	0.35	1.05	1.75
❑ 11, digest..........1.75	0.35	1.05	1.75
❑ 12, digest..........1.75	0.35	1.05	1.75
❑ 13, digest..........1.75	0.35	1.05	1.75
❑ 14, digest..........1.75	0.35	1.05	1.75
❑ 15, digest..........1.75	0.35	1.05	1.75
❑ 16, digest..........1.75	0.35	1.05	1.75
❑ 17, digest..........1.75	0.35	1.05	1.75
❑ 18, digest..........1.75	0.35	1.05	1.75
❑ 19, digest..........1.75	0.35	1.05	1.75
❑ 20, Apr 90, digest; "Kops 'n' Krooks Special"			
..........1.75	0.35	1.05	1.75
❑ 21, Jun 90, digest..........1.75	0.35	1.05	1.75
❑ 22, Aug 90, digest 1.75	0.35	1.05	1.75
❑ 23, digest..........1.75	0.35	1.05	1.75
❑ 24, digest..........1.75	0.35	1.05	1.75
❑ 25, digest..........1.75	0.35	1.05	1.75
❑ 26, digest..........1.75	0.35	1.05	1.75
❑ 27, digest..........1.75	0.35	1.05	1.75
❑ 28, digest..........1.75	0.35	1.05	1.75
❑ 29, May 91, digest..........1.75	0.35	1.05	1.75
❑ 30, digest..........1.75	0.35	1.05	1.75
❑ 31, digest..........1.75	0.35	1.05	1.75
❑ 32, digest..........1.75	0.35	1.05	1.75
❑ 33, digest..........1.75	0.35	1.05	1.75
❑ 34, Jun 92, digest..........1.75	0.35	1.05	1.75
❑ 35, Sep 92, digest..........1.75	0.35	1.05	1.75
❑ 36, Jan 93, digest..........1.75	0.35	1.05	1.75
❑ 37, May 93, digest..........1.75	0.35	1.05	1.75
❑ 38, Sep 93, digest..........1.75	0.35	1.05	1.75
❑ 39, digest..........1.75	0.35	1.05	1.75
❑ 40, digest..........1.75	0.35	1.05	1.75
❑ 41, Jul 94..........1.75	0.35	1.05	1.75
❑ 42, Oct 94 ....1.75	0.35	1.05	1.75

RICHIE RICH GIANT SIZE

	ORIG.	GOOD	FINE	N-MINT
❑ 1 ....2.25	0.45	1.35	2.25
❑ 2 ....2.25	0.45	1.35	2.25
❑ 3 ....2.25	0.45	1.35	2.25
❑ 4 ....2.25	0.45	1.35	2.25

RICHIE RICH GOLD NUGGETS DIGEST MAGAZINE

	ORIG.	GOOD	FINE	N-MINT
❑ 3, Apr 91, digest 1.75	0.35	1.05	1.75

RICHIE RICH HOLIDAY DIGEST

	ORIG.	GOOD	FINE	N-MINT
❑ 19, 89, digest..........1.75	0.35	1.05	1.75

RICHIE RICH MILLION DOLLAR DIGEST

	ORIG.	GOOD	FINE	N-MINT
❑ 1, digest..........1.75	0.35	1.05	1.75
❑ 2, digest..........1.75	0.35	1.05	1.75
❑ 3, digest..........1.75	0.35	1.05	1.75
❑ 4, digest..........1.75	0.35	1.05	1.75
❑ 5, digest..........1.75	0.35	1.05	1.75
❑ 6, digest..........1.75	0.35	1.05	1.75
❑ 7, digest..........1.75	0.35	1.05	1.75
❑ 8, digest..........1.75	0.35	1.05	1.75
❑ 9, digest..........1.75	0.35	1.05	1.75
❑ 10, digest..........1.75	0.35	1.05	1.75
❑ 11, digest..........1.75	0.35	1.05	1.75
❑ 12, digest..........1.75	0.35	1.05	1.75
❑ 13, Aug 89, digest 1.75	0.35	1.05	1.75
❑ 14, digest..........1.75	0.35	1.05	1.75
❑ 15, digest..........1.75	0.35	1.05	1.75
❑ 16, digest..........1.75	0.35	1.05	1.75
❑ 17, digest..........1.75	0.35	1.05	1.75
❑ 18, digest..........1.75	0.35	1.05	1.75
❑ 19, digest..........1.75	0.35	1.05	1.75
❑ 20, digest..........1.75	0.35	1.05	1.75
❑ 21, digest..........1.75	0.35	1.05	1.75

	ORIG.	GOOD	FINE	N-MINT
❏ 22, digest 1.75	0.35	1.05	1.75
❏ 23, digest 1.75	0.35	1.05	1.75
❏ 24, digest 1.75	0.35	1.05	1.75
❏ 25, digest 1.75	0.35	1.05	1.75
❏ 26, Jul 92, digest 1.75	0.35	1.05	1.75
❏ 27, Nov 92, digest 1.75	0.35	1.05	1.75
❏ 28, Mar 93, digest 1.75	0.35	1.05	1.75
❏ 29, Jul 93, digest 1.75	0.35	1.05	1.75
❏ 30, Nov 93, digest 1.75	0.35	1.05	1.75
❏ 31, Mar 94, digest 1.75	0.35	1.05	1.75
❏ 32, May 94, digest 1.75	0.35	1.05	1.75
❏ 33, Aug 94, digest 1.75	0.35	1.05	1.75
❏ 34, Nov 94, digest 1.75	0.35	1.05	1.75

RICHIE RICH MONEY WORLD DIGEST

	ORIG.	GOOD	FINE	N-MINT
❏ 1, digest 1.75	0.35	1.05	1.75
❏ 2, digest 1.75	0.35	1.05	1.75
❏ 3, Apr 92, digest 1.75	0.35	1.05	1.75
❏ 4, Aug 92, digest 1.75	0.35	1.05	1.75
❏ 5, Dec 92, digest 1.75	0.35	1.05	1.75
❏ 6, Apr 93, digest 1.75	0.35	1.05	1.75
❏ 7, Aug 93, digest 1.75	0.35	1.05	1.75
❏ 8, digest 1.75	0.35	1.05	1.75

RICHIE RICH VACATION DIGEST

	ORIG.	GOOD	FINE	N-MINT
❏ 1, Oct 92, digest 1.75	0.35	1.05	1.75

RICHIE RICH VACATION DIGEST '93 MAGAZINE

	ORIG.	GOOD	FINE	N-MINT
❏ 1, Oct 93, digest 1.75	0.35	1.05	1.75

RICK GEARY'S WONDERS & ODDITIES
DARK HORSE

	GOOD	FINE	N-MINT
❏ 0, nn b&w	0.40	1.20	2.00

RICK RAYGUN
STOP DRAGON

	GOOD	FINE	N-MINT
❏ 1	0.35	1.05	1.75
❏ 2	0.35	1.05	1.75
❏ 3	0.35	1.05	1.75
❏ 4	0.35	1.05	1.75
❏ 5	0.35	1.05	1.75

RIMA, THE JUNGLE GIRL
DC

	ORIG.	GOOD	FINE	N-MINT
❏ 1, May 74 ...... 0.20	0.40	1.20	2.00
❏ 2, Jul 74 ...... 0.20	0.25	0.75	1.25
❏ 3, Sep 74 ...... 0.20	0.25	0.75	1.25
❏ 4, Nov 74 ...... 0.20	0.25	0.75	1.25
❏ 5, Jan 75 ...... 0.20	0.25	0.75	1.25
❏ 6, Mar 75 ...... 0.25	0.25	0.75	1.25
❏ 7, May 75 ...... 0.25	0.25	0.75	1.25

RIME OF THE ANCIENT MARINER, THE
TOME PRESS

	ORIG.	GOOD	FINE	N-MINT
❏ 0, nn, GDore, b&w 3.95	0.79	2.37	3.95

RIMSHOT
RIP OFF

	ORIG.	GOOD	FINE	N-MINT
❏ 1, Jun 90, b&w;adult 2.00	0.40	1.20	2.00
❏ 2, Feb 91, b&w;adult 2.00	0.40	1.20	2.00
❏ 3, Jul 91, b&w;adult 2.50	0.50	1.50	2.50

RING OF ROSES
DARK HORSE

	ORIG.	GOOD	FINE	N-MINT
❏ 1, b&w 2.50	0.50	1.50	2.50
❏ 2, b&w 2.50	0.50	1.50	2.50
❏ 3, b&w 2.50	0.50	1.50	2.50
❏ 4, b&w 2.50	0.50	1.50	2.50

RING OF THE NIBELUNG, THE (mini-series)
DC

	GOOD	FINE	N-MINT
❏ 1, GK;prestige format	1.40	4.20	7.00
❏ 2, GK;prestige format	1.20	3.60	6.00
❏ 3, GK;prestige format	1.00	3.00	5.00
❏ 4, GK;prestige format	1.00	3.00	5.00

RINGO KID (1970-1976)
MARVEL

	ORIG.	GOOD	FINE	N-MINT
❏ 1 ...... 0.15	0.40	1.20	2.00
❏ 2 ...... 0.15	0.20	0.60	1.00

	ORIG.	GOOD	FINE	N-MINT
❏ 3 ...... 0.15	0.20	0.60	1.00
❏ 4 ...... 0.15	0.20	0.60	1.00
❏ 5 ...... 0.15	0.20	0.60	1.00
❏ 6 ...... 0.15	0.20	0.60	1.00
❏ 7 ...... 0.15	0.20	0.60	1.00
❏ 8 ...... 0.15	0.20	0.60	1.00
❏ 9 ...... 0.15	0.20	0.60	1.00
❏ 10 ...... 0.15	0.20	0.60	1.00
❏ 11 ...... 0.15	0.20	0.60	1.00
❏ 12 ...... 0.25	0.20	0.60	1.00
❏ 12 ...... 0.25	0.20	0.60	1.00
❏ 13 ...... 0.20	0.20	0.60	1.00
❏ 14 ...... 0.20	0.20	0.60	1.00
❏ 15 ...... 0.20	0.20	0.60	1.00
❏ 16 ...... 0.20	0.20	0.60	1.00
❏ 17 ...... 0.20	0.20	0.60	1.00
❏ 18 ...... 0.20	0.20	0.60	1.00
❏ 19 ...... 0.20	0.20	0.60	1.00
❏ 20 ...... 0.20	0.20	0.60	1.00
❏ 21 ...... 0.20	0.20	0.60	1.00
❏ 22 ...... 0.20	0.20	0.60	1.00
❏ 23 ...... 0.20	0.20	0.60	1.00
❏ 24 ...... 0.20	0.20	0.60	1.00
❏ 25 ...... 0.20	0.20	0.60	1.00
❏ 26 ...... 0.20	0.20	0.60	1.00
❏ 27 ...... 0.20	0.20	0.60	1.00
❏ 28 ...... 0.20	0.20	0.60	1.00
❏ 29 ...... 0.20	0.20	0.60	1.00
❏ 30 ...... 0.20	0.20	0.60	1.00

RIO AT BAY
DARK HORSE

	ORIG.	GOOD	FINE	N-MINT
❏ 1, Aug 92, Doug Wildey 2.95	0.59	1.77	2.95
❏ 2, Aug 92, Doug Wildey 2.95	0.59	1.77	2.95

RIO AT BAY COLLECTION

	ORIG.	GOOD	FINE	N-MINT
❏ 0, tpb 6.95	1.39	4.17	6.95

RIO KID
ETERNITY

	GOOD	FINE	N-MINT
❏ 1, b&w	0.50	1.50	2.50
❏ 2, b&w	0.50	1.50	2.50
❏ 3, b&w	0.50	1.50	2.50

RION 2990
RION

	GOOD	FINE	N-MINT
❏ 1, b&w	0.30	0.90	1.50
❏ 2, b&w	0.30	0.90	1.50

RIOT GEAR
TRIUMPHANT

	ORIG.	GOOD	FINE	N-MINT
❏ 1, 93, (color, ashcan) 2.50	0.50	1.50	2.50
❏ 1 ...... 2.50	0.65	1.95	3.25
❏ 2 ...... 2.50	0.50	1.50	2.50
❏ 3 ...... 2.50	0.50	1.50	2.50
❏ 4, Unleashed!; D:Captain Tich 2.50	0.50	1.50	2.50
❏ 5, Retribution 2.50	0.50	1.50	2.50
❏ 6, Feb 94, Retribution 2.50	0.50	1.50	2.50
❏ 7, Mar 94 ...... 2.50	0.50	1.50	2.50
❏ 8, Apr 94 ...... 2.50	0.50	1.50	2.50

RIOT GEAR: VIOLENT PAST

	ORIG.	GOOD	FINE	N-MINT
❏ 1, Feb 94 ...... 2.50	0.50	1.50	2.50
❏ 2, Feb 94 ...... 2.50	0.50	1.50	2.50

RIP HUNTER...TIME MASTER
DC

	GOOD	FINE	N-MINT
❏ 1	95.00	285.00	475.00
❏ 2	45.00	135.00	225.00
❏ 3	24.00	72.00	120.00
❏ 4	24.00	72.00	120.00
❏ 5	24.00	72.00	120.00
❏ 6	15.00	45.00	75.00
❏ 7	15.00	45.00	75.00
❏ 8	15.00	45.00	75.00
❏ 9	15.00	45.00	75.00
❏ 10	15.00	45.00	75.00

	ORIG.	GOOD	FINE	N-MINT
❏ 11		12.00	36.00	60.00
❏ 12		12.00	36.00	60.00
❏ 13		12.00	36.00	60.00
❏ 14		12.00	36.00	60.00
❏ 15		12.00	36.00	60.00
❏ 16		10.00	30.00	50.00
❏ 17		10.00	30.00	50.00
❏ 18		10.00	30.00	50.00
❏ 19		10.00	30.00	50.00
❏ 20		10.00	30.00	50.00
❏ 21		9.00	27.00	45.00
❏ 22		9.00	27.00	45.00
❏ 23		9.00	27.00	45.00
❏ 24		9.00	27.00	45.00
❏ 25		9.00	27.00	45.00
❏ 26, Jun 65	0.12	9.00	27.00	45.00
❏ 27		9.00	27.00	45.00
❏ 28		9.00	27.00	45.00
❏ 29		9.00	27.00	45.00

RIP IN TIME
FANTAGOR

	ORIG.	GOOD	FINE	N-MINT
❏ 1, Corben b&w		0.30	0.90	1.50
❏ 2, Corben b&w		0.30	0.90	1.50
❏ 3, Corben b&w		0.30	0.90	1.50
❏ 4, Corben b&w		0.30	0.90	1.50
❏ 5, Corben b&w		0.30	0.90	1.50

RIP OFF COMIX
RIP OFF

	ORIG.	GOOD	FINE	N-MINT
❏ 1, b&w;adult	1.25	0.59	1.77	2.95
❏ 2, b&w;adult	1.50	0.59	1.77	2.95
❏ 3, b&w;adult	1.50	0.59	1.77	2.95
❏ 4, Nov 78, b&w	1.50	0.59	1.77	2.95
❏ 5, Sep 79, b&w	2.00	0.59	1.77	2.95
❏ 6, Mar 80, b&w	2.00	0.59	1.77	2.95
❏ 7, Nov 80, b&w	1.50	0.59	1.77	2.95
❏ 8, May 81, b&w	2.00	0.59	1.77	2.95
❏ 9, Sep 81, b&w	2.00	0.59	1.77	2.95
❏ 10, Mar 82, b&w	2.00	0.59	1.77	2.95
❏ 11, Oct 82, b&w and color;adult	2.95	0.59	1.77	2.95
❏ 12, Apr 83, b&w and color;adult	2.95	0.59	1.77	2.95
❏ 13, never published				
❏ 14, Apr 87,b&w magazine	2.95	0.59	1.77	2.95
❏ 15, Jul 87	2.95	0.59	1.77	2.95
❏ 16, Oct 87	2.95	0.59	1.77	2.95
❏ 17, Jan 88	2.95	0.59	1.77	2.95
❏ 18, Apr 88	2.95	0.59	1.77	2.95
❏ 19, Jul 88	2.95	0.59	1.77	2.95
❏ 20, Oct 88	2.95	0.59	1.77	2.95
❏ 21, Jan 89, 20th Anniversary	3.50	0.70	2.10	3.50
❏ 22, Apr 89	2.95	0.59	1.77	2.95
❏ 23, Jul 89	2.95	0.59	1.77	2.95
❏ 24, Oct 89, San Diego Con	3.25	0.65	1.95	3.25
❏ 25, Jan 90	3.25	0.65	1.95	3.25
❏ 26, Apr 90	3.25	0.65	1.95	3.25
❏ 27, Jul 90	3.25	0.65	1.95	3.25
❏ 28, Oct 90	3.50	0.70	2.10	3.50
❏ 29, Jan 91	3.50	0.70	2.10	3.50
❏ 30, Apr 91	3.50	0.70	2.10	3.50
❏ 31, Mar 92	3.50	0.70	2.10	3.50

RIPCLAW
IMAGE

	ORIG.	GOOD	FINE	N-MINT
❏ 1, Apr 95	2.50	0.50	1.50	2.50
❏ 3, Jul 95	2.50	0.50	1.50	2.50

RIPCLAW (Vol. 2)

	ORIG.	GOOD	FINE	N-MINT
❏ 2, Jan 96	2.50	0.50	1.50	2.50
❏ 3, Feb 96	2.50	0.50	1.50	2.50

	ORIG.	GOOD	FINE	N-MINT
❏ 4, Mar 96	2.50	0.50	1.50	2.50
❏ 5, Apr 96	2.50	0.50	1.50	2.50
❏ 6, Jun 96	2.50	0.50	1.50	2.50

RIPLEY'S BELIEVE IT OR NOT: STRANGE DEATHS
RIPLEY

	ORIG.	GOOD	FINE	N-MINT
❏ 1, Jun 93	2.50	0.50	1.50	2.50

RIPPER
AIRCEL

	ORIG.	GOOD	FINE	N-MINT
❏ 1, b&w, adult		0.50	1.50	2.50
❏ 2, b&w, adult		0.50	1.50	2.50
❏ 3, b&w, adult		0.50	1.50	2.50
❏ 4, b&w, adult		0.50	1.50	2.50
❏ 5, b&w, adult		0.50	1.50	2.50
❏ 6, b&w, adult		0.50	1.50	2.50

RIPTIDE
IMAGE

	ORIG.	GOOD	FINE	N-MINT
❏ 1, Sep 95	2.50	0.50	1.50	2.50
❏ 2, Oct 95	2.50	0.50	1.50	2.50

RIVERDALE HIGH
ARCHIE

	ORIG.	GOOD	FINE	N-MINT
❏ 1, Aug 90	1.00	0.20	0.60	1.00
❏ 2	1.00	0.20	0.60	1.00
❏ 3	1.00	0.20	0.60	1.00
❏ 4	1.00	0.20	0.60	1.00
❏ 5	1.00	0.20	0.60	1.00

RIVIT
BLACKTHORNE

	ORIG.	GOOD	FINE	N-MINT
❏ 1		0.35	1.05	1.75

ROACHMILL

	ORIG.	GOOD	FINE	N-MINT
❏ 1, b&w		0.60	1.80	3.00
❏ 2		0.50	1.50	2.50
❏ 3		0.50	1.50	2.50
❏ 4		0.50	1.50	2.50
❏ 5		0.50	1.50	2.50
❏ 6, (moves to Dark Horse)		0.50	1.50	2.50

ROACHMILL (was Blackthorne)
DARK HORSE

	ORIG.	GOOD	FINE	N-MINT
❏ 1, b&w		0.80	2.40	4.00
❏ 2		0.60	1.80	3.00
❏ 3		0.60	1.80	3.00
❏ 4		0.40	1.20	2.00
❏ 5		0.40	1.20	2.00
❏ 6		0.40	1.20	2.00
❏ 7		0.40	1.20	2.00
❏ 8		0.40	1.20	2.00
❏ 9		0.40	1.20	2.00
❏ 10, trading cards		0.39	1.17	1.95

ROACHMILL BOOK

	ORIG.	GOOD	FINE	N-MINT
❏ 1, b&w, reprints		1.19	3.57	5.95
❏ 2		1.39	4.17	6.95

ROADKILL
LIGHTHOUSE

	ORIG.	GOOD	FINE	N-MINT
❏ 1, b&w		0.40	1.20	2.00
❏ 2, b&w		0.40	1.20	2.00

ROADKILL: A CHRONICLE OF THE DEADWORLD
CALIBER

	ORIG.	GOOD	FINE	N-MINT
❏ 0, nn, text	2.95	0.59	1.77	2.95

ROADWAYS
CULT PRESS

	ORIG.	GOOD	FINE	N-MINT
❏ 1, May 94, b&w	2.75	0.55	1.65	2.75
❏ 2, Jun 94, b&w	2.75	0.55	1.65	2.75

ROARIN' RICK'S RARE BIT FIENDS
KING HELL

	ORIG.	GOOD	FINE	N-MINT
❏ 1, Jul 94, b&w	2.95	0.59	1.77	2.95

ROB HANES
WCG

	ORIG.	GOOD	FINE	N-MINT
❏ 1, Jan 91, b&w	2.50	0.50	1.50	2.50

	ORIG.	GOOD	FINE	N-MINT

ROBBIN' $3000
PARODY

	ORIG.	GOOD	FINE	N-MINT
1, b&w	2.50	0.50	1.50	2.50

ROBIN
DC

	ORIG.	GOOD	FINE	N-MINT
1, Jan 91, 1st printing, w/poster	1.00	1.60	4.80	8.00
1, Jan 91, 2nd printing, no poster		0.70	2.10	3.50
2, Feb 91, 1st printing	1.00	0.80	2.40	4.00
2, Feb 91, 2nd printing		0.20	0.60	1.00
3, Mar 91	1.00	0.50	1.50	2.50
4, Apr 91	1.00	0.50	1.50	2.50
5, May 91	1.00	0.20	0.60	1.00

ROBIN (ongoing series)

	ORIG.	GOOD	FINE	N-MINT
0, Oct 94	1.50	0.30	0.90	1.50
1, embossed cover	2.95	0.80	2.40	4.00
1	1.50	0.30	0.90	1.50
2	1.50	0.30	0.90	1.50
3	1.50	0.30	0.90	1.50
4	1.50	0.30	0.90	1.50
5, Apr 94	1.50	0.30	0.90	1.50
6, May 94	1.50	0.30	0.90	1.50
7, Jun 94, Knightquest	1.50	0.30	0.90	1.50
8, Jul 94	1.50	1.00	3.00	5.00
9, Aug 94	1.50	0.30	0.90	1.50
10, Sep 94, "Zero Hour";Tim Drake Robin teams with Dick Grayson Robin	1.50	0.30	0.90	1.50
11, Nov 94	1.50	0.30	0.90	1.50
12, Dec 94	1.50	0.30	0.90	1.50
13, Jan 95	1.50	0.30	0.90	1.50
14, Feb 95	1.50	0.30	0.90	1.50
14, Feb 95, enhanced cardstock cover	2.50	0.50	1.50	2.50
15, Mar 95	1.50	0.30	0.90	1.50
16, Apr 95	1.50	0.30	0.90	1.50
17, Jun 95	1.95	0.39	1.17	1.95
18, Jul 95	1.95	0.39	1.17	1.95
19, Aug 95, V:Ulysses	1.95	0.39	1.17	1.95
20, Sep 95, V:Ulysses	1.95	0.39	1.17	1.95
21, Oct 95	1.95	0.39	1.17	1.95
22, Nov 95	1.95	0.39	1.17	1.95
23, Dec 95, "Underworld Unleashed";V:Killer Moth a.k.a. Charaxes	1.95	0.39	1.17	1.95
24, Jan 96, "Underworld Unleashed";V:Killer Moth a.k.a. Charaxes	1.95	0.39	1.17	1.95
25, Feb 96	1.95	0.39	1.17	1.95
26, Mar 96	1.95	0.39	1.17	1.95
27, Mar 96, "Contagion" Part 3	1.95	0.39	1.17	1.95
28, Apr 96, "Contagion" Part 11	1.95	0.39	1.17	1.95
29, May 96	1.95	0.39	1.17	1.95
30, Jun 96	1.95	0.39	1.17	1.95

ROBIN 3000

	ORIG.	GOOD	FINE	N-MINT
1, 92, PCR	4.95	0.99	2.97	4.95
2, 92, PCR	4.95	0.99	2.97	4.95

ROBIN ANNUAL

	ORIG.	GOOD	FINE	N-MINT
1, 92, Eclipso	2.50	0.50	1.50	2.50
2, 93, Bloodlines	2.50	0.50	1.50	2.50
3, 94	2.95	0.59	1.77	2.95
5, 96, "Legends of the Dead Earth"	2.95	0.59	1.77	2.95

ROBIN HOOD
ECLIPSE

	ORIG.	GOOD	FINE	N-MINT
1, TT		0.50	1.50	2.50
2, TT		0.50	1.50	2.50
3, TT		0.50	1.50	2.50

ETERNITY

	ORIG.	GOOD	FINE	N-MINT
1, b&w		0.45	1.35	2.25
2, b&w		0.45	1.35	2.25
3, b&w		0.45	1.35	2.25
4, b&w		0.45	1.35	2.25

ROBIN II: THE JOKER'S WILD
DC

	ORIG.	GOOD	FINE	N-MINT
0, set, boxed	8.00	24.00	40.00	
1, newsstand, no hologram	0.20	0.60	1.00	
1, hologram on cover	0.80	2.40	4.00	
1, set of all covers, extra hologram	1.60	4.80	8.00	
2, newsstand, no hologram	0.20	0.60	1.00	
2, holograms	0.40	1.20	2.00	
3, holograms	0.40	1.20	2.00	
4, holograms	0.40	1.20	2.00	
3, 91, newsstand, no hologram	1.00	0.20	0.60	1.00
4, 91, newsstand, no hologram	1.00	0.20	0.60	1.00

ROBIN III: CRY OF THE HUNTRESS

	ORIG.	GOOD	FINE	N-MINT
1, Dec 92, moving cover	1.25	0.50	1.50	2.50
1, newsstand		0.25	0.75	1.25
2, Jan 93, moving cover	1.25	0.50	1.50	2.50
2, newsstand		0.25	0.75	1.25
3, Jan 93, moving cover	1.25	0.50	1.50	2.50
3, newsstand		0.25	0.75	1.25
4, Feb 93, moving cover	1.25	0.50	1.50	2.50
4, newsstand		0.25	0.75	1.25
5, Feb 93, moving cover	1.25	0.50	1.50	2.50
5, newsstand		0.25	0.75	1.25
6, Mar 93, moving cover	1.25	0.50	1.50	2.50
6, newsstand		0.25	0.75	1.25

ROBIN RED AND THE LUTINS
ACE

	ORIG.	GOOD	FINE	N-MINT
1		0.35	1.05	1.75
2		0.35	1.05	1.75

ROBO HUNTER
EAGLE

	ORIG.	GOOD	FINE	N-MINT
1		0.60	1.80	3.00
2		0.40	1.20	2.00
3		0.40	1.20	2.00
4		0.40	1.20	2.00
5		0.40	1.20	2.00

ROBO WARRIORS
CFW

	ORIG.	GOOD	FINE	N-MINT
1, 1: Reiki, Sifu		0.35	1.05	1.75
2, 0: Citation		0.39	1.17	1.95
3, 1: She-Bat, Soliloquy Jones, Soldiers of Reiki		0.39	1.17	1.95
4		0.39	1.17	1.95
5		0.39	1.17	1.95
6		0.39	1.17	1.95
7, 1: Mr. Slimey		0.39	1.17	1.95
8, Reiki becomes Mister No		0.39	1.17	1.95

ROBOCOP
MARVEL

	ORIG.	GOOD	FINE	N-MINT
1, movie adaptation, mag	2.00	0.60	1.80	3.00
1, movie, bookshelf	4.95	0.99	2.97	4.95

ROBOCOP (ongoing series)

	ORIG.	GOOD	FINE	N-MINT
1	1.50	1.60	4.80	8.00
2	1.50	1.00	3.00	5.00
3	1.50	0.60	1.80	3.00
4	1.50	0.60	1.80	3.00
5	1.50	0.30	0.90	1.50
6	1.50	0.30	0.90	1.50
7	1.50	0.30	0.90	1.50
8	1.50	0.30	0.90	1.50
9	1.50	0.30	0.90	1.50

	ORIG.	GOOD	FINE	N-MINT
☐ 10	1.50	0.30	0.90	1.50
☐ 11	1.50	0.30	0.90	1.50
☐ 12	1.50	0.30	0.90	1.50
☐ 13	1.50	0.30	0.90	1.50
☐ 14	1.50	0.30	0.90	1.50
☐ 15	1.50	0.30	0.90	1.50
☐ 16	1.50	0.30	0.90	1.50
☐ 17	1.50	0.30	0.90	1.50
☐ 18	1.50	0.30	0.90	1.50
☐ 19	1.50	0.30	0.90	1.50
☐ 20	1.50	0.30	0.90	1.50
☐ 21	1.50	0.30	0.90	1.50
☐ 22	1.50	0.30	0.90	1.50
☐ 23	1.50	0.30	0.90	1.50

ROBOCOP 2

	ORIG.	GOOD	FINE	N-MINT
☐ 1, bookshelf, movie	4.95	0.99	2.97	4.95
☐ 1, b&w mag, movie	2.25	0.45	1.35	2.25
☐ 1, comic book, movie	1.00	0.20	0.60	1.00
☐ 2, comic book, movie	1.00	0.20	0.60	1.00
☐ 3, comic book, movie	1.00	0.20	0.60	1.00

ROBOCOP 3
DARK HORSE

	ORIG.	GOOD	FINE	N-MINT
☐ 1	2.50	0.50	1.50	2.50
☐ 2	2.50	0.50	1.50	2.50
☐ 3	2.50	0.50	1.50	2.50

ROBOCOP VERSUS TERMINATOR

	ORIG.	GOOD	FINE	N-MINT
☐ 1, 92, FM (w), WS	2.50	0.50	1.50	2.50
☐ 2, FM (w), WS		0.50	1.50	2.50
☐ 3, FM (w), WS		0.50	1.50	2.50
☐ 4, FM (w), WS		0.50	1.50	2.50

ROBOCOP VS. TERMINATOR

	ORIG.	GOOD	FINE	N-MINT
☐ 1, platinum edition	5.00	15.00	25.00

ROBOCOP: MORTAL COILS

	ORIG.	GOOD	FINE	N-MINT
☐ 1	2.50	0.50	1.50	2.50
☐ 2	2.50	0.50	1.50	2.50
☐ 3	2.50	0.50	1.50	2.50

ROBOCOP: PRIME SUSPECT

	ORIG.	GOOD	FINE	N-MINT
☐ 1	2.50	0.50	1.50	2.50
☐ 2	2.50	0.50	1.50	2.50
☐ 3	2.50	0.50	1.50	2.50
☐ 4	2.50	0.50	1.50	2.50

ROBOCOP: ROULETTE

	ORIG.	GOOD	FINE	N-MINT
☐ 1	2.50	0.50	1.50	2.50
☐ 2	2.50	0.50	1.50	2.50
☐ 3, Feb 94	2.50	0.50	1.50	2.50
☐ 4, Mar 94	2.50	0.50	1.50	2.50

ROBOT COMICS
RENEGADE

	ORIG.	GOOD	FINE	N-MINT
☐ 0, b&w		0.40	1.20	2.00

ROBOTECH DEFENDERS
DC

	ORIG.	GOOD	FINE	N-MINT
☐ 1, MA		0.60	1.80	3.00
☐ 2, MA		0.60	1.80	3.00
☐ 3, MA		0.60	1.80	3.00

ROBOTECH GENESIS
ETERNITY

	GOOD	FINE	N-MINT
☐ 1, color, trading cards	0.50	1.50	2.50
☐ 1, limited	1.19	3.57	5.95
☐ 6	0.50	1.50	2.50

ROBOTECH GENESIS: THE LEGEND OF ZOR

	GOOD	FINE	N-MINT
☐ 4, trading cards	0.50	1.50	2.50
☐ 5, trading cards	0.50	1.50	2.50

ROBOTECH II THE SENTINELS SWIMSUIT SPECTACULAR

	GOOD	FINE	N-MINT
☐ 1	0.59	1.77	2.95

ROBOTECH II THE SENTINELS: THE UNTOLD STORY

	ORIG.	GOOD	FINE	N-MINT
☐ 1, b&w	2.50	0.50	1.50	2.50

ROBOTECH II: THE SENTINELS

	ORIG.	GOOD	FINE	N-MINT
☐ 1, b&w		0.60	1.80	3.00
☐ 2		0.39	1.17	1.95
☐ 3, 1st printing		0.39	1.17	1.95
☐ 3, 2nd printing		0.39	1.17	1.95
☐ 4		0.39	1.17	1.95
☐ 5		0.39	1.17	1.95
☐ 6		0.39	1.17	1.95
☐ 7		0.39	1.17	1.95
☐ 8		0.39	1.17	1.95
☐ 9		0.39	1.17	1.95
☐ 10		0.39	1.17	1.95
☐ 11		0.39	1.17	1.95
☐ 12		0.39	1.17	1.95
☐ 13		0.39	1.17	1.95
☐ 14		0.39	1.17	1.95
☐ 15		0.39	1.17	1.95
☐ 16		0.39	1.17	1.95

ROBOTECH II: THE SENTINELS BOOK II

	ORIG.	GOOD	FINE	N-MINT
☐ 1, b&w		0.45	1.35	2.25
☐ 2, b&w		0.45	1.35	2.25
☐ 3, b&w		0.45	1.35	2.25
☐ 4, b&w		0.45	1.35	2.25
☐ 5, b&w		0.45	1.35	2.25
☐ 6, b&w		0.45	1.35	2.25
☐ 7, b&w		0.45	1.35	2.25
☐ 8, b&w		0.45	1.35	2.25
☐ 9, b&w		0.45	1.35	2.25
☐ 10, b&w		0.45	1.35	2.25
☐ 11, b&w		0.45	1.35	2.25
☐ 12, b&w	2.50	0.50	1.50	2.50
☐ 13, b&w	2.50	0.50	1.50	2.50
☐ 14, b&w	2.50	0.50	1.50	2.50
☐ 15, b&w	2.50	0.50	1.50	2.50
☐ 16, b&w	2.50	0.50	1.50	2.50
☐ 17, b&w	2.50	0.50	1.50	2.50
☐ 18, b&w	2.50	0.50	1.50	2.50
☐ 19, b&w	2.50	0.50	1.50	2.50
☐ 20, b&w	2.50	0.50	1.50	2.50

ROBOTECH II: THE SENTINELS BOOK III

	ORIG.	GOOD	FINE	N-MINT
☐ 1, b&w	2.50	0.50	1.50	2.50
☐ 2, b&w	2.50	0.50	1.50	2.50
☐ 3, b&w	2.50	0.50	1.50	2.50
☐ 4, b&w	2.50	0.50	1.50	2.50
☐ 5, b&w	2.50	0.50	1.50	2.50
☐ 6, b&w	2.50	0.50	1.50	2.50

ROBOTECH II: THE SENTINELS CYBERPIRATES

	ORIG.	GOOD	FINE	N-MINT
☐ 1, b&w		0.45	1.35	2.25
☐ 2, b&w		0.45	1.35	2.25
☐ 3, b&w		0.45	1.35	2.25
☐ 4, b&w		0.45	1.35	2.25

ROBOTECH II: THE SENTINELS MALCONTENT UPRISINGS

	ORIG.	GOOD	FINE	N-MINT
☐ 1, b&w		0.39	1.17	1.95
☐ 2, b&w		0.39	1.17	1.95
☐ 3, b&w		0.39	1.17	1.95
☐ 4, b&w		0.39	1.17	1.95
☐ 5, b&w		0.39	1.17	1.95
☐ 6, b&w		0.39	1.17	1.95
☐ 7, b&w		0.39	1.17	1.95
☐ 8, b&w		0.39	1.17	1.95
☐ 9, b&w		0.39	1.17	1.95
☐ 10, b&w		0.39	1.17	1.95
☐ 11, b&w		0.39	1.17	1.95
☐ 12, b&w		0.39	1.17	1.95

ROBOTECH II: THE SENTINELS SCRIPT BOOK

	ORIG.	GOOD	FINE	N-MINT
☐ 1, b&w		1.99	5.97	9.95

MALIBU

	ORIG.	GOOD	FINE	N-MINT
☐ 1, b&w		1.99	5.97	9.95

	ORIG.	GOOD	FINE	N-MINT

ROBOTECH II: THE SENTINELS WEDDING SPECIAL
ETERNITY

	ORIG.	GOOD	FINE	N-MINT
☐ 1, b&w	0.39	1.17	1.95
☐ 2, b&w	0.39	1.17	1.95

ROBOTECH II: THE SENTINELS: THE ILLUSTRATED HANDBOOK

	ORIG.	GOOD	FINE	N-MINT
☐ 1, b&w	0.50	1.50	2.50
☐ 2, b&w	0.50	1.50	2.50
☐ 3, b&w	0.50	1.50	2.50

ROBOTECH IN 3-D
COMICO

	ORIG.	GOOD	FINE	N-MINT
☐ 1	0.50	1.50	2.50

ROBOTECH INVID WAR: AFTERMATH
ETERNITY

	ORIG.	GOOD	FINE	N-MINT
☐ 1, b&w	2.50	0.50	1.50	2.50

ROBOTECH MASTERS
COMICO

	GOOD	FINE	N-MINT
☐ 1	0.50	1.50	2.50
☐ 2	0.30	0.90	1.50
☐ 3	0.30	0.90	1.50
☐ 4	0.30	0.90	1.50
☐ 5	0.30	0.90	1.50
☐ 6	0.30	0.90	1.50
☐ 7	0.30	0.90	1.50
☐ 8	0.30	0.90	1.50
☐ 9	0.30	0.90	1.50
☐ 10	0.30	0.90	1.50
☐ 11	0.30	0.90	1.50
☐ 12	0.30	0.90	1.50
☐ 13	0.30	0.90	1.50
☐ 14	0.30	0.90	1.50
☐ 15	0.30	0.90	1.50
☐ 16	0.30	0.90	1.50
☐ 17	0.30	0.90	1.50
☐ 18	0.30	0.90	1.50
☐ 19	0.30	0.90	1.50
☐ 20	0.30	0.90	1.50
☐ 21	0.30	0.90	1.50
☐ 22	0.30	0.90	1.50
☐ 23	0.30	0.90	1.50

ROBOTECH SPECIAL

	GOOD	FINE	N-MINT
☐ 1, O:Dana Sterling	0.50	1.50	2.50

ROBOTECH THE GRAPHIC NOVEL

	GOOD	FINE	N-MINT
☐ 1	1.19	3.57	5.95

ROBOTECH THE MACROSS SAGA
(formerly Macross)

	GOOD	FINE	N-MINT
☐ 2	1.00	3.00	5.00
☐ 3	0.80	2.40	4.00
☐ 4	0.80	2.40	4.00
☐ 5	0.30	0.90	1.50
☐ 6	0.30	0.90	1.50
☐ 7	0.30	0.90	1.50
☐ 8	0.30	0.90	1.50
☐ 9	0.30	0.90	1.50
☐ 10	0.30	0.90	1.50
☐ 11	0.30	0.90	1.50
☐ 12	0.30	0.90	1.50
☐ 13	0.30	0.90	1.50
☐ 14	0.30	0.90	1.50
☐ 15	0.30	0.90	1.50
☐ 16	0.30	0.90	1.50
☐ 17	0.30	0.90	1.50
☐ 18	0.30	0.90	1.50
☐ 19	0.30	0.90	1.50
☐ 20	0.30	0.90	1.50
☐ 21	0.30	0.90	1.50
☐ 22	0.30	0.90	1.50
☐ 23	0.30	0.90	1.50
☐ 24	0.30	0.90	1.50
☐ 25	0.30	0.90	1.50

	ORIG.	GOOD	FINE	N-MINT
☐ 26		0.35	1.05	1.75
☐ 27		0.35	1.05	1.75
☐ 28		0.35	1.05	1.75
☐ 29		0.35	1.05	1.75
☐ 30		0.35	1.05	1.75
☐ 31		0.35	1.05	1.75
☐ 32		0.35	1.05	1.75
☐ 33		0.35	1.05	1.75
☐ 34		0.35	1.05	1.75
☐ 35		0.35	1.05	1.75
☐ 36, last issue		0.39	1.17	1.95

ROBOTECH THE NEW GENERATION

	GOOD	FINE	N-MINT
☐ 1	0.50	1.50	2.50
☐ 2	0.30	0.90	1.50
☐ 3	0.30	0.90	1.50
☐ 4	0.30	0.90	1.50
☐ 5	0.30	0.90	1.50
☐ 6	0.30	0.90	1.50
☐ 7	0.30	0.90	1.50
☐ 8	0.30	0.90	1.50
☐ 9	0.30	0.90	1.50
☐ 10	0.30	0.90	1.50
☐ 11	0.30	0.90	1.50
☐ 12	0.30	0.90	1.50
☐ 13	0.30	0.90	1.50
☐ 14	0.30	0.90	1.50
☐ 15	0.30	0.90	1.50
☐ 16	0.30	0.90	1.50
☐ 17	0.30	0.90	1.50
☐ 18	0.30	0.90	1.50
☐ 19	0.30	0.90	1.50
☐ 20	0.30	0.90	1.50
☐ 21	0.30	0.90	1.50
☐ 22	0.35	1.05	1.75
☐ 23	0.35	1.05	1.75
☐ 24	0.35	1.05	1.75
☐ 25, last	0.35	1.05	1.75

ROBOTECH: INVID WAR
ETERNITY

	ORIG.	GOOD	FINE	N-MINT
☐ 1, b&w	2.50	0.50	1.50	2.50
☐ 2, b&w	2.50	0.50	1.50	2.50
☐ 3, b&w	2.50	0.50	1.50	2.50
☐ 4, b&w	2.50	0.50	1.50	2.50
☐ 5, b&w	2.50	0.50	1.50	2.50
☐ 6, b&w	2.50	0.50	1.50	2.50
☐ 7, b&w	2.50	0.50	1.50	2.50
☐ 8, b&w	2.50	0.50	1.50	2.50
☐ 9, b&w	2.50	0.50	1.50	2.50
☐ 10, b&w	1.25	0.25	0.75	1.25
☐ 11, b&w	1.25	0.25	0.75	1.25
☐ 12, b&w	1.25	0.25	0.75	1.25
☐ 13, b&w	1.25	0.25	0.75	1.25
☐ 14	2.50	0.50	1.50	2.50
☐ 15	2.50	0.50	1.50	2.50
☐ 16	2.50	0.50	1.50	2.50
☐ 17	2.50	0.50	1.50	2.50
☐ 18	2.50	0.50	1.50	2.50

ROBOTECH: INVID WAR: AFTERMATH

	ORIG.	GOOD	FINE	N-MINT
☐ 1, b&w	2.50	0.50	1.50	2.50
☐ 2, b&w	2.50	0.50	1.50	2.50

ROBOTECH: RETURN TO MACROSS

	ORIG.	GOOD	FINE	N-MINT
☐ 1, b&w	2.50	0.50	1.50	2.50
☐ 2, b&w	2.50	0.50	1.50	2.50
☐ 3, b&w	2.50	0.50	1.50	2.50
☐ 4, b&w	2.50	0.50	1.50	2.50
☐ 5, b&w	2.50	0.50	1.50	2.50
☐ 6, b&w	2.50	0.50	1.50	2.50
☐ 7, b&w	2.50	0.50	1.50	2.50
☐ 8, b&w	2.50	0.50	1.50	2.50
☐ 9, b&w	2.50	0.50	1.50	2.50
☐ 10, Jan 94, b&w	2.50	0.50	1.50	2.50

	ORIG.	GOOD	FINE	N-MINT

ROBOTIX
MARVEL

	ORIG.	GOOD	FINE	N-MINT
❏ 1	0.75	0.40	1.20	2.00

ROCK FANTASY
ROCK FANTASY

	ORIG.	GOOD	FINE	N-MINT
❏ 1, Pink Floyd	1.40	4.20		7.00
❏ 2, Rolling Stones	0.60	1.80		3.00
❏ 3, Led Zeppelin	0.60	1.80		3.00
❏ 4, New Kids on the Block	0.60	1.80		3.00

ROCK HEADS
SOLSON

	ORIG.	GOOD	FINE	N-MINT
❏ 1		0.39	1.17	1.95

ROCK N' ROLL
REVOLUTIONARY

	ORIG.	GOOD	FINE	N-MINT
❏ 1, Jun 89, Guns N' Roses, 1st printing	1.50	1.60	4.80	8.00
❏ 1, Jul 89, 2nd printing	1.50	1.00	3.00	5.00
❏ 1, Aug 89, 3rd printing	1.95	0.39	1.17	1.95
❏ 1, Sep 89, 4th printing	1.95	0.39	1.17	1.95
❏ 1, Oct 89, 5th printing	1.95	0.39	1.17	1.95
❏ 1, Nov 89, 6th printing	1.95	0.39	1.17	1.95
❏ 1, Dec 89, 7th printing, color	1.95	0.39	1.17	1.95
❏ 2, Aug 89, Metallica, 1st printing	1.50	0.80	2.40	4.00
❏ 2, Sep 89, 2nd printing	1.95	0.39	1.17	1.95
❏ 2, Sep 89, 3rd printing	1.95	0.39	1.17	1.95
❏ 2, Sep 89, 4th printing	1.95	0.39	1.17	1.95
❏ 2, Sep 89, 5th printing	1.95	0.39	1.17	1.95
❏ 3, Sep 89, Bon Jovi	1.95	1.20	3.60	6.00
❏ 4, Oct 89, Motley Crue, 1st printing	1.95	0.39	1.17	1.95
❏ 4, Oct 89, 2nd printing	1.95	0.39	1.17	1.95
❏ 5, Nov 89, Def Leppard, 1st printing	1.95	0.39	1.17	1.95
❏ 5, Nov 89, 2nd printing	1.95	0.39	1.17	1.95
❏ 6, Dec 89, Rolling Stones, 1st printing	1.95	0.60	1.80	3.00
❏ 6, Jan 90, 2nd printing	1.95	0.39	1.17	1.95
❏ 6, Jan 90, 3rd printing	1.95	0.39	1.17	1.95
❏ 6, Feb 90, 4th printing	1.95	0.39	1.17	1.95
❏ 7, Jan 90, The Who, 1st printing	1.95	0.39	1.17	1.95
❏ 7, Feb 90, 2nd printing	1.95	0.39	1.17	1.95
❏ 7, Mar 90, 3rd printing	1.95	0.39	1.17	1.95
❏ 8, never published				
❏ 9, Mar 90, Kiss 1st printing	1.95	1.00	3.00	5.00
❏ 9, Apr 90, 2nd printing	1.95	0.39	1.17	1.95
❏ 9, May 90, 3rd printing	1.95	0.39	1.17	1.95
❏ 10, Apr 90, Warrant/Whitesnake	1.95	0.39	1.17	1.95
❏ 10, May 90, 2nd printing	1.95	0.39	1.17	1.95
❏ 11, May 90, Aerosmith	1.95	0.39	1.17	1.95
❏ 12, Jun 90, New Kids on the Block	1.95	1.50	4.50	7.50
❏ 12, Aug 90, 2nd printing	1.95	0.39	1.17	1.95
❏ 13, Jul 90, Led Zeppelin	1.95	0.39	1.17	1.95
❏ 14, Aug 90, Sex Pistols	1.95	0.39	1.17	1.95
❏ 15, Sep 90, Poison, 1st printing, color	1.95	0.39	1.17	1.95
❏ 16, Oct 90, Van Halen, color	1.95	0.39	1.17	1.95
❏ 17, Nov 90, Madonna, color	1.95	0.39	1.17	1.95
❏ 18, Dec 90, Alice Cooper	1.95	0.39	1.17	1.95
❏ 19, Apr 91, Public Enemy/2 Live Crew b&w	2.50	0.50	1.50	2.50
❏ 20, Apr 91, Queensryche b&w	2.50	0.50	1.50	2.50
❏ 21, Feb 91, Prince b&w	2.50	0.50	1.50	2.50
❏ 22, Feb 91, AC/DC, color	2.50	0.50	1.50	2.50
❏ 23, Mar 91, Living Colour b&w	2.50	0.50	1.50	2.50
❏ 24, Mar 91, Anthrax b&w	2.50	0.50	1.50	2.50
❏ 25, May 91, ZZ Top b&w	2.50	0.50	1.50	2.50
❏ 26, May 91, Doors	2.50	0.50	1.50	2.50
❏ 27, Jun 91, Doors	2.50	0.50	1.50	2.50
❏ 28, Jun 91, Ozzy Osbourne/Sabbath	2.50	0.50	1.50	2.50
❏ 29, Jul 91, Ozzy Osbourne/Sabbath	2.50	0.50	1.50	2.50
❏ 30, Jul 91, The Cure	2.50	0.50	1.50	2.50
❏ 31, Aug 91, Vanilla Ice	2.50	0.50	1.50	2.50
❏ 32, Aug 91, Frank Zappa	2.50	0.50	1.50	2.50
❏ 33, Sep 91, Guns 'N Roses II	2.50	0.50	1.50	2.50
❏ 34, Sep 91, Black Crowes	2.50	0.50	1.50	2.50
❏ 35, Oct 91, R.E.M.	2.50	0.50	1.50	2.50
❏ 36, Oct 91, Michael Jackson	2.50	0.50	1.50	2.50
❏ 37, Nov 91, Ice-T	2.50	0.50	1.50	2.50
❏ 38, Nov 91, Rod Stewart	2.50	0.50	1.50	2.50
❏ 39, Dec 91, New Kids on the Block II	2.50	0.50	1.50	2.50
❏ 40, Dec 91, NWA/Ice Cube	2.50	0.50	1.50	2.50
❏ 41, Jan 92, Paula Abdul	2.50	0.50	1.50	2.50
❏ 42, Jan 92, Metallica II	2.50	0.50	1.50	2.50
❏ 43, Feb 92, G'N'R Tour	2.50	0.50	1.50	2.50
❏ 44, Feb 92, Scorpions	2.50	0.50	1.50	2.50
❏ 45, Mar 92, Grateful Dead	2.50	0.50	1.50	2.50
❏ 46, Apr 92, Grateful Dead II	2.50	0.50	1.50	2.50
❏ 47, May 92, Grateful Dead III	2.50	0.50	1.50	2.50
❏ 48, Jun 92, Queen	2.50	0.50	1.50	2.50
❏ 49, Jul 92, Rush	2.50	0.50	1.50	2.50
❏ 50, Aug 92, Bob Dylan	2.50	0.50	1.50	2.50
❏ 51, Sep 92, Bob Dylan II	2.50	0.50	1.50	2.50
❏ 52, Oct 92, Bob Dylan III	2.50	0.50	1.50	2.50
❏ 53, Nov 92, Bruce Springsteen	2.50	0.50	1.50	2.50
❏ 54, Dec 92, U2	2.50	0.50	1.50	2.50
❏ 55, Jan 93, U2 II	2.50	0.50	1.50	2.50
❏ 56, Feb 93, David Bowie	2.50	0.50	1.50	2.50
❏ 57, Mar 93, Aerosmith	2.50	0.50	1.50	2.50
❏ 58, Apr 93, Kate Bush	2.50	0.50	1.50	2.50
❏ 59, May 93, Eric Clapton	2.50	0.50	1.50	2.50
❏ 60, Jun 93, Genesis	2.50	0.50	1.50	2.50
❏ 61, Jul 93, Yes	2.50	0.50	1.50	2.50
❏ 62, Aug 93, Elton John	2.50	0.50	1.50	2.50
❏ 63, Sep 93, Janis Joplin	2.50	0.50	1.50	2.50
❏ 64, Oct 93, '60s San Francisco	2.50	0.50	1.50	2.50
❏ 65, Nov 93, Sci-Fi Space Rockers	2.50	0.50	1.50	2.50

ROCKERS
RIP OFF

	ORIG.	GOOD	FINE	N-MINT
❏ 1, Jul 88, adult;b&w	2.00	0.40	1.20	2.00
❏ 2, Oct 88, adult;b&w	2.00	0.40	1.20	2.00
❏ 3, Jan 89, adult;b&w	2.00	0.40	1.20	2.00
❏ 4, Feb 89, adult;b&w	2.00	0.40	1.20	2.00
❏ 5, May 89, adult;b&w	2.00	0.40	1.20	2.00
❏ 6, Jun 89, adult;b&w	2.00	0.40	1.20	2.00
❏ 7, Sep 89, adult;b&w	2.00	0.40	1.20	2.00
❏ 8, Feb 90, adult;b&w	2.00	0.40	1.20	2.00

	ORIG.	GOOD	FINE	N-MINT

ROCKET RACCOON
MARVEL

	ORIG.	GOOD	FINE	N-MINT
1	0.75	0.25	0.75	1.25
2	0.75	0.20	0.60	1.00
3	0.75	0.20	0.60	1.00
4	0.75	0.20	0.60	1.00

ROCKET RANGER
ADVENTURE

	ORIG.	GOOD	FINE	N-MINT
1, Sep 91, color	2.95	0.59	1.77	2.95
2, Dec 91, b&w		0.59	1.77	2.95
3, b&w		0.59	1.77	2.95
4, b&w		0.59	1.77	2.95
5, b&w		0.59	1.77	2.95

ROCKETEER 3-D COMIC
DISNEY

	ORIG.	GOOD	FINE	N-MINT
0, Jun 91, nn NA, with audiotape		1.00	3.00	5.00

ROCKETEER ADVENTURE MAGAZINE, THE
COMICO

	ORIG.	GOOD	FINE	N-MINT
1, Jul 88, DSt,MK,CV	2.00	1.60	4.80	8.00
2, Jul 89, DSt,MK (moves to Dark Horse)	2.75	1.20	3.60	6.00

DARK HORSE

	ORIG.	GOOD	FINE	N-MINT
3, Jan 95, concludes Comico series	2.95	0.70	2.10	3.50

ROCKETEER SPECIAL
ECLIPSE

	ORIG.	GOOD	FINE	N-MINT
1, Nov 84, DSt	1.50	2.00	6.00	10.00

ROCKETEER, THE
DISNEY

	ORIG.	GOOD	FINE	N-MINT
0, nn DSt(c), RH, movie, squarebound		1.19	3.57	5.95
0, nn DSt(c), RH stapled		0.59	1.77	2.95

ROCKETMAN KING OF THE ROCKET MEN
INNOVATION

	GOOD	FINE	N-MINT
1	0.50	1.50	2.50
2	0.50	1.50	2.50
3	0.50	1.50	2.50
4	0.50	1.50	2.50

ROCKIN' BONES
NEW ENGLAND

	GOOD	FINE	N-MINT
1, b&w	0.55	1.65	2.75
2, b&w	0.55	1.65	2.75
3, b&w	0.55	1.65	2.75

ROCKIN' BONES XMAS SPECIAL

	GOOD	FINE	N-MINT
1	0.55	1.65	2.75

ROCKMEEZ, THE
JZINK COMICS

	GOOD	FINE	N-MINT
1, foil covers	0.50	1.50	2.50
2, foil covers	0.50	1.50	2.50
3, foil covers	0.50	1.50	2.50
4, foil covers	0.50	1.50	2.50

ROCKO'S MODERN LIFE
MARVEL

	ORIG.	GOOD	FINE	N-MINT
1, Jun 94, TV cartoon	1.95	0.39	1.17	1.95
2, Jul 94	1.95	0.39	1.17	1.95
3, Aug 94	1.95	0.39	1.17	1.95
4, Sep 94	1.95	0.39	1.17	1.95
5, Oct 94	1.95	0.39	1.17	1.95
6, Nov 94	1.95	0.39	1.17	1.95
7, Dec 94	1.95	0.39	1.17	1.95

ROCKOLA
MIRAGE

	GOOD	FINE	N-MINT
1	0.30	0.90	1.50

ROCKY HORROR PICTURE SHOW: THE COMIC BOOK
CALIBER

	ORIG.	GOOD	FINE	N-MINT
1, Jul 90, color	2.95	0.59	1.77	2.95

	ORIG.	GOOD	FINE	N-MINT
1, 91, new cover, 2nd printing	2.95	0.59	1.77	2.95
2, Aug 90, color	2.95	0.59	1.77	2.95
3, Sep 90, color	2.95	0.59	1.77	2.95

ROCKY LANE WESTERN
AC

	GOOD	FINE	N-MINT
1, b&w reprints	0.50	1.50	2.50

ROCKY LANE WESTERN ANNUAL

	GOOD	FINE	N-MINT
1, b&w reprints	0.59	1.77	2.95

ROG-2000
PACIFIC

	GOOD	FINE	N-MINT
1, Jby	0.40	1.20	2.00

ROGER FNORD
RIP OFF

	ORIG.	GOOD	FINE	N-MINT
1, Apr 92, adult;b&w	2.50	0.50	1.50	2.50

ROGER RABBIT
DISNEY

	ORIG.	GOOD	FINE	N-MINT
1, Jun 90	1.50	0.80	2.40	4.00
2		0.80	2.40	4.00
3		0.60	1.80	3.00
4		0.60	1.80	3.00
5		0.60	1.80	3.00
6		0.30	0.90	1.50
7		0.30	0.90	1.50
8		0.30	0.90	1.50
9		0.30	0.90	1.50
10		0.30	0.90	1.50
11		0.30	0.90	1.50
12		0.30	0.90	1.50
13		0.30	0.90	1.50
14		0.30	0.90	1.50
15		0.30	0.90	1.50
16		0.30	0.90	1.50
17		0.30	0.90	1.50
18, Nov 91	1.50	0.30	0.90	1.50

W.D.

	GOOD	FINE	N-MINT
0, nn Who Framed Rick Flint?	0.70	2.10	3.50

ROGER RABBIT'S TOONTOWN
DISNEY

	GOOD	FINE	N-MINT
1	0.30	0.90	1.50
2, Winsor McCay tribute	0.30	0.90	1.50
3	0.30	0.90	1.50
4, 1:Winnie Weasel	0.30	0.90	1.50
5	0.30	0.90	1.50

ROGER WILCO
ADVENTURE

	GOOD	FINE	N-MINT
1, color	0.59	1.77	2.95

ROGUE
MONSTER

	GOOD	FINE	N-MINT
1, b&w	0.39	1.17	1.95

ROGUE (mini-series)
MARVEL

	ORIG.	GOOD	FINE	N-MINT
1, Jan 95, enhanced cover	2.95	1.00	3.00	5.00
2, Feb 95,enhanced cover	2.95	0.59	1.77	2.95
3, Mar 95, enhanced cover	2.95	0.59	1.77	2.95
4, Apr 95, enhanced cover	2.95	0.59	1.77	2.95

ROGUE TROOPER
FLEETWAY/QUALITY

	GOOD	FINE	N-MINT
1	0.15	0.45	0.75
2	0.15	0.45	0.75
3	0.15	0.45	0.75
4	0.15	0.45	0.75
5	0.15	0.45	0.75
6	0.30	0.90	1.50
7	0.19	0.57	0.95

	ORIG.	GOOD	FINE	N-MINT
8		0.25	0.75	1.25
9		0.25	0.75	1.25
10		0.25	0.75	1.25
11		0.25	0.75	1.25
12		0.25	0.75	1.25
13		0.25	0.75	1.25
14		0.25	0.75	1.25
15		0.25	0.75	1.25
16		0.25	0.75	1.25
17		0.25	0.75	1.25
18		0.25	0.75	1.25
19		0.25	0.75	1.25
20		0.30	0.90	1.50
21, one issue		0.30	0.90	1.50
23, one issue		0.30	0.90	1.50
25		0.30	0.90	1.50
26		0.30	0.90	1.50
27		0.30	0.90	1.50
28		0.30	0.90	1.50
29		0.30	0.90	1.50
30		0.30	0.90	1.50
31		0.30	0.90	1.50
32		0.30	0.90	1.50
33		0.30	0.90	1.50
34		0.30	0.90	1.50
35		0.30	0.90	1.50
36		0.30	0.90	1.50
37		0.30	0.90	1.50
38		0.30	0.90	1.50
39		0.35	1.05	1.75
40		0.35	1.05	1.75
41		0.35	1.05	1.75
42		0.35	1.05	1.75
43		0.35	1.05	1.75
44		0.35	1.05	1.75
45		0.35	1.05	1.75
46		0.35	1.05	1.75
47		0.35	1.05	1.75
48		0.35	1.05	1.75
49		0.35	1.05	1.75

ROGUE TROOPER (1992-)

	ORIG.	GOOD	FINE	N-MINT
1, O:Rogue Trooper		0.59	1.77	2.95
2		0.59	1.77	2.95
3		0.59	1.77	2.95
4		0.59	1.77	2.95
5		0.59	1.77	2.95
6		0.59	1.77	2.95
7		0.59	1.77	2.95
8		0.59	1.77	2.95
9		0.59	1.77	2.95

ROGUE TROOPER: THE FINAL WARRIOR

	ORIG.	GOOD	FINE	N-MINT
6		0.59	1.77	2.95

ROGUES GALLERY
DC

	ORIG.	GOOD	FINE	N-MINT
1, 96, one-shot;pin-ups	3.50	0.70	2.10	3.50

ROJA FUSION
ANTARCTIC

	ORIG.	GOOD	FINE	N-MINT
1, Apr 95	2.95	0.59	1.77	2.95

ROLLERCOASTERS SPECIAL EDITION
BLUE COMET

	ORIG.	GOOD	FINE	N-MINT
1		0.36	1.08	1.80

ROLLING STONES
PERSONALITY

	ORIG.	GOOD	FINE	N-MINT
1, b&w		0.59	1.77	2.95
2, b&w		0.59	1.77	2.95
3, b&w		0.59	1.77	2.95

ROLLING STONES--VOODOO LOUNGE
MARVEL/MARVEL MUSIC

	ORIG.	GOOD	FINE	N-MINT
0, 95, nn;prestige format one-shot	6.95	1.39	4.17	6.95

ROM
MARVEL

	ORIG.	GOOD	FINE	N-MINT
1, Dec 79, SB, O:Rom	0.40	0.60	1.80	3.00
2, Jan 80, SB,FM(c)	0.40	0.50	1.50	2.50
3, Feb 80, SB,FM(c)	0.40	0.50	1.50	2.50
4, Mar 80, SB	0.40	0.40	1.20	2.00
5, Apr 80, SB	0.40	0.40	1.20	2.00
6, May 90, SB	0.40	0.30	0.90	1.50
7, Jun 90, SB	0.40	0.30	0.90	1.50
8, Jul 90, SB	0.40	0.30	0.90	1.50
9, Aug 90, SB	0.40	0.30	0.90	1.50
10, Sep 90, SB	0.50	0.30	0.90	1.50
11, Oct 90, SB	0.50	0.30	0.90	1.50
12, Nov 90, SB	0.50	0.30	0.90	1.50
13, Dec 80, SB	0.50	0.25	0.75	1.25
14, Jan 81, SB	0.50	0.25	0.75	1.25
15, Feb 81, SB	0.50	0.25	0.75	1.25
16, Mar 81, SB	0.50	0.25	0.75	1.25
17, Apr 81, SB, X-Men	0.50	0.80	2.40	4.00
18, May 81, SB, X-Men	0.50	0.80	2.40	4.00
19, Jun 81, SB/JSt, C:X-Men	0.50	0.30	0.90	1.50
20, Jul 81, SB/JSt	0.50	0.25	0.75	1.25
21, Aug 81, SB/JSt	0.50	0.25	0.75	1.25
22, Sep 81, SB/JSt	0.50	0.25	0.75	1.25
23, Oct 81, SB/JSt	0.50	0.25	0.75	1.25
24, Nov 81, SB/JSt	0.50	0.25	0.75	1.25
25, Dec 81, SB/JSt, double size	0.75	0.30	0.90	1.50
26, Jan 82	0.60	0.25	0.75	1.25
27, Feb 82	0.60	0.25	0.75	1.25
28, Mar 82	0.60	0.25	0.75	1.25
29, Apr 82	0.60	0.25	0.75	1.25
30, May 82	0.60	0.25	0.75	1.25
31, Jun 82	0.60	0.25	0.75	1.25
32, Jul 82	0.60	0.25	0.75	1.25
33, Aug 82	0.60	0.25	0.75	1.25
34, Sep 82	0.60	0.25	0.75	1.25
35, Oct 82	0.60	0.25	0.75	1.25
36, Nov 82	0.60	0.20	0.60	1.00
37, Dec 82	0.60	0.20	0.60	1.00
38, Jan 83	0.60	0.20	0.60	1.00
39, Feb 83	0.60	0.20	0.60	1.00
40, Mar 83	0.60	0.20	0.60	1.00
41, Apr 83	0.60	0.20	0.60	1.00
42, May 83	0.60	0.20	0.60	1.00
43, Jun 83	0.60	0.20	0.60	1.00
44, Jul 83	0.60	0.20	0.60	1.00
45, Aug 83	0.60	0.20	0.60	1.00
46, Sep 83	0.60	0.20	0.60	1.00
47, Oct 83	0.60	0.20	0.60	1.00
48, Nov 83	0.60	0.20	0.60	1.00
49, Dec 83	0.60	0.20	0.60	1.00
50, Jan 84	1.00	0.20	0.60	1.00
51, Feb 84	0.60	0.20	0.60	1.00
52, Mar 84	0.60	0.20	0.60	1.00
53, Apr 84	0.60	0.20	0.60	1.00
54, May 84	0.60	0.20	0.60	1.00
55, Jun 84	0.60	0.20	0.60	1.00
56, Jul 84, Alpha Flight	0.60	0.25	0.75	1.25
57, Aug 84, Alpha Flight	0.60	0.25	0.75	1.25
58, Sep 84, Dire Wraiths	0.60	0.20	0.60	1.00
59, Oct 84, SD	0.60	0.20	0.60	1.00
60, Nov 84, SD	0.60	0.20	0.60	1.00
61, Dec 84, SD	0.60	0.20	0.60	1.00
62, Jan 85, SD	0.60	0.20	0.60	1.00
63, Feb 85, SD	0.60	0.20	0.60	1.00
64, Mar 85	0.60	0.20	0.60	1.00
65, Apr 85	0.65	0.20	0.60	1.00
66, May 85	0.65	0.20	0.60	1.00
67, Jun 85	0.65	0.20	0.60	1.00

	ORIG.	GOOD	FINE	N-MINT
❏ 68, Jul 85	0.65	0.20	0.60	1.00
❏ 69, Aug 85	0.65	0.20	0.60	1.00
❏ 70, Sep 85	0.65	0.20	0.60	1.00
❏ 71, Oct 85	0.65	0.20	0.60	1.00
❏ 72, Nov 85, Secret Wars II				
	0.65	0.20	0.60	1.00
❏ 73, Dec 85	0.75	0.20	0.60	1.00
❏ 74, Jan 86	0.75	0.20	0.60	1.00
❏ 75, Feb 86	0.75	0.20	0.60	1.00

ROM ANNUAL

	ORIG.	GOOD	FINE	N-MINT
❏ 1, 82, Stardust	1.00	0.30	0.90	1.50
❏ 2, 83	1.00	0.25	0.75	1.25
❏ 3, 84	1.00	0.25	0.75	1.25
❏ 4, 85	1.25	0.25	0.75	1.25

RONIN
DC

	ORIG.	GOOD	FINE	N-MINT
❏ 1, Jul 83, FM	2.50	2.80	8.40	14.00
❏ 2, Sep 83, FM	2.50	2.00	6.00	10.00
❏ 3, Nov 83, FM	2.50	2.00	6.00	10.00
❏ 4, Jan 84, FM	2.50	2.00	6.00	10.00
❏ 5, Jan 84, FM	2.50	2.00	6.00	10.00
❏ 6, Aug 84, FM	2.50	3.00	9.00	15.00

ROOK, THE
HARRIS

	ORIG.	GOOD	FINE	N-MINT
❏ 0, Jun 95	2.95	0.59	1.77	2.95

ROOTS OF SWAMP THING
DC

		GOOD	FINE	N-MINT
❏ 1, BWr rep		0.40	1.20	2.00
❏ 2, BWr rep		0.40	1.20	2.00
❏ 3, BWr rep		0.40	1.20	2.00
❏ 4, BWr rep		0.40	1.20	2.00
❏ 5, BWr rep		0.40	1.20	2.00

ROOTS OF THE OPPRESSOR
NORTHSTAR

	ORIG.	GOOD	FINE	N-MINT
❏ 1, b&w	2.95	0.59	1.77	2.95

ROSCOE! THE DAWG, ACE DETECTIVE
RENEGADE

	ORIG.	GOOD	FINE	N-MINT
❏ 1, Jul 87, b&w	2.00	0.40	1.20	2.00
❏ 2, Oct 87, b&w	2.00	0.40	1.20	2.00
❏ 3, Nov 87, b&w	2.00	0.40	1.20	2.00
❏ 4, Jan 88, b&w	2.00	0.40	1.20	2.00

ROSE
HERO

	ORIG.	GOOD	FINE	N-MINT
❏ 1, b&w	3.50	0.70	2.10	3.50
❏ 2, b&w	2.95	0.59	1.77	2.95
❏ 3, b&w	3.95	0.79	2.37	3.95
❏ 4, b&w	3.95	0.79	2.37	3.95
❏ 5, b&w	2.95	0.59	1.77	2.95

ROSE & GUNN
BISHOP

	ORIG.	GOOD	FINE	N-MINT
❏ 3, May 95, b&w	2.95	0.59	1.77	2.95
❏ 4, Jun 95, b&w	2.95	0.59	1.77	2.95
❏ 5, Aug 95, b&w	2.95	0.59	1.77	2.95

ROSE & GUNN CREATOR'S CHOICE

	ORIG.	GOOD	FINE	N-MINT
❏ 1, Sep 95, b&w	2.95	0.59	1.77	2.95

ROUGH RAIDERS
BLUE COMET

		GOOD	FINE	N-MINT
❏ 1		0.36	1.08	1.80
❏ 2		0.36	1.08	1.80
❏ 3		0.36	1.08	1.80

ROUGH RAIDERS ANNUAL

		GOOD	FINE	N-MINT
❏ 1		0.50	1.50	2.50

ROULETTE
CALIBER

	ORIG.	GOOD	FINE	N-MINT
❏ 1, b&w	2.50	0.50	1.50	2.50

ROVERS, THE
MALIBU

		GOOD	FINE	N-MINT
❏ 1		0.39	1.17	1.95
❏ 2		0.39	1.17	1.95
❏ 3		0.39	1.17	1.95
❏ 4		0.39	1.17	1.95
❏ 5, (becomes Eternity title).		0.39	1.17	1.95

ROVERS, THE (was Malibu title)
ETERNITY

		GOOD	FINE	N-MINT
❏ 6, b&w		0.39	1.17	1.95
❏ 7, b&w		0.39	1.17	1.95

ROY ROGERS WESTERN CLASSICS
AC

		GOOD	FINE	N-MINT
❏ 1, reprints, some color		0.59	1.77	2.95
❏ 2, reprints, some color		0.59	1.77	2.95
❏ 3, reprints, some color		0.79	2.37	3.95
❏ 4, reprints, some color		0.79	2.37	3.95
❏ 5, reprints, photos		0.59	1.77	2.95

ROYAL ROY
STAR

		GOOD	FINE	N-MINT
❏ 1	0.65	0.13	0.39	0.65
❏ 2	0.65	0.13	0.39	0.65
❏ 3	0.65	0.13	0.39	0.65
❏ 4	0.65	0.13	0.39	0.65
❏ 5	0.65	0.13	0.39	0.65
❏ 6	0.65	0.13	0.39	0.65

RUBBER BLANKET
RUBBER BLANKET

		GOOD	FINE	N-MINT
❏ 1, b&w		1.15	3.45	5.75

RUBES REVUE, THE
FRAGMENTS WEST

		GOOD	FINE	N-MINT
❏ 1, b&w		0.40	1.20	2.00

RUBY SHAFT'S TALES OF THE UNEXPURGATED
EROS COMIX

		GOOD	FINE	N-MINT
❏ 1, adult, b&w		0.50	1.50	2.50

RUCK BUD WEBSTER AND HIS SCREECHING COMMANDOS
PYRAMID

		GOOD	FINE	N-MINT
❏ 1, b&w		0.32	0.96	1.60

RUINS (mini-series)
MARVEL

	ORIG.	GOOD	FINE	N-MINT
❏ 1, Aug 95, Acetate cover overlaying cardstock inner cover	4.95	0.99	2.97	4.95
❏ 2, Sep 95, Acetate cover overlaying cardstock inner cover	4.95	0.99	2.97	4.95

RUMIC WORLD
VIZ

	ORIG.	GOOD	FINE	N-MINT
❏ 1, 89, Fire Tripper, b&w	3.25	0.65	1.95	3.25
❏ 2, Laughing Target, b&w		0.70	2.10	3.50

RUNE
MALIBU/ULTRAVERSE

	ORIG.	GOOD	FINE	N-MINT
❏ 0, Jan 94, no cover price				
❏ 1, BWS	1.95	0.40	1.20	2.00
❏ 2, Feb 94, BWS	1.95	0.39	1.17	1.95
❏ 3, Mar 94, BWS (includes *Ultraverse Premiere* #1)	3.50	0.70	2.10	3.50
❏ 4, Jun 94	1.95	0.39	1.17	1.95
❏ 5, Sep 94	1.95	0.39	1.17	1.95

RUNE (Vol. 2)

	ORIG.	GOOD	FINE	N-MINT
❏ 0, Sep 95, Infinity;alternate cover;"Black September"	1.50	0.60	1.80	3.00
❏ 0, Sep 95, Infinity;"Black September"	1.50	0.30	0.90	1.50
❏ 1, Oct 95	1.50	0.30	0.90	1.50
❏ 2, Nov 95, flipbook with"The Phoenix Resurrection" Pt. 6	1.50	0.30	0.90	1.50
❏ 3, Dec 95	1.50	0.30	0.90	1.50

	ORIG.	GOOD	FINE	N-MINT
☐ 4, Jan 96	1.50	0.30	0.90	1.50
☐ 5, Feb 96	1.50	0.30	0.90	1.50
☐ 6, Mar 96	1.50	0.30	0.90	1.50

RUNE/SILVER SURFER
MARVEL

	ORIG.	GOOD	FINE	N-MINT
☐ 1, crossover		1.00	3.00	5.00

RUNE/WRATH
MALIBU/ULTRAVERSE

	ORIG.	GOOD	FINE	N-MINT
☐ 1, gold foil ashcan		7.00	21.00	35.00

RUST
ADVENTURE

	ORIG.	GOOD	FINE	N-MINT
☐ 1, O:Rust, color		0.59	1.77	2.95
☐ 1, limited edition		0.99	2.97	4.95
☐ 2		0.59	1.77	2.95
☐ 3, Aug 92, color	2.95	0.59	1.77	2.95
☐ 4		0.59	1.77	2.95

NOW

	ORIG.	GOOD	FINE	N-MINT
☐ 1, Jul 87	1.50	0.30	0.90	1.50
☐ 2, Aug 87	1.50	0.30	0.90	1.50
☐ 3, Sep 87	1.50	0.30	0.90	1.50

	ORIG.	GOOD	FINE	N-MINT
☐ 4, Nov 87	1.50	0.30	0.90	1.50
☐ 5, Dec 87	1.50	0.30	0.90	1.50
☐ 6, Jan 88	1.50	0.30	0.90	1.50
☐ 7, Feb 88	1.75	0.35	1.05	1.75
☐ 8, Mar 88	1.50	0.35	1.05	1.75
☐ 9, Apr 88	1.75	0.35	1.05	1.75
☐ 10, May 88	1.75	0.35	1.05	1.75
☐ 11, Jul 88	1.75	0.35	1.05	1.75
☐ 12, Aug 88, Terminator preview	1.75	0.35	1.05	1.75
☐ 13, Sep 88	1.75	0.35	1.05	1.75

RUST (Volume 2)

	ORIG.	GOOD	FINE	N-MINT
☐ 1, Feb 89	1.75	0.35	1.05	1.75
☐ 2, Mar 89	1.75	0.35	1.05	1.75
☐ 3, Apr 89	1.75	0.35	1.05	1.75
☐ 4, May 89	1.75	0.35	1.05	1.75
☐ 5, Jun 89	1.75	0.35	1.05	1.75
☐ 6, Aug 89	1.75	0.35	1.05	1.75
☐ 7, Sep 89	1.75	0.35	1.05	1.75

The Rocketeer

First appearance: *Starslayer #2*, April 1982.

"Good Girl" artist Dave Stevens' love and appreciation of the late 1930s and early 1940s found its way into *The Rocketeer*, an infrequently appearing series that began as a back-up feature in Pacific Comics' *Starslayer #2*.

Cliff Secord was a barnstorming pilot who discovered a rocket pack in his plane after criminals, fleeing the police, had hidden it there.

Although Stevens didn't have the rights to the actual characters of Doc Savage, Andrew Blodgett "Monk" Mayfair, and Theodore Marley "Ham" Brooks, Stevens' depiction of the rocket pack's inventor was a man who looked a lot like the Man of Bronze and whose associates called him "Doc." The associates bore a strong resemblance to Monk and Ham. In the movie version of the series, the rocket pack's inventor was Howard Hughes.

After getting the rocket pack home, Secord's friend and mechanic, Ambrose Peabody, better known as Peevy (whom Stevens modeled after real-life friend and mentor Doug Wildey) studied the device and instructed Secord in its use.

The rocket pack strapped on the user's back and was turned on and off through the use of a pair of hand throttles. A helmet with a fin on top provided protection, as did a leather jacket and pair of jodhpurs.

After using the pack to rescue his girlfriend Betty (based on '50s pin-up star Bettie Page) from a group of Nazi spies who wanted the rocket pack for use in the pending World War II, Secord found himself at odds with "Doc" and his associates over ownership of the device. Meanwhile, the German spies stole a plane designed by "Doc" and, although warned not to, Secord took off with the rocket pack to recapture the plane. Thousands of feet in the air, the pack ran out of

fuel.

After Pacific folded, The Rocketeer's later adventures (you didn't think Secord perished in his earliest adventure, did you?) were published by Comico in *The Rocketeer Adventure Magazine*, a series which ran only two issues, as ownership of Comico changed. Dark Horse concluded the story in 1995 with issue #3.

Although the star of a series that appeared only sporadically, Stevens' character has appeared on posters, T shirts, tin signs, and other merchandise to the point at which he is better known in those appearances than in comics stories.

This is due to the movie version of the series, produced by Walt Disney Pictures in 1991. In the novelization written by Peter David, Cliff Secord meets George Reeves on a Hollywood movie set, and Reeves is reading a copy of *Action Comics #1*.

S

	ORIG.	GOOD	FINE	N-MINT
S'NOT FOR KIDS				
VORTEX				
☐ 1, b&w		1.39	4.17	6.95
S.A. KING'S NAKED EYE (mini-series)				
ANTARCTIC				
☐ 1, Dec 94, b&w	2.75	0.55	1.65	2.75
☐ 2, Feb 95, b&w	2.75	0.55	1.65	2.75
☐ 3, Apr 95, b&w	2.75	0.55	1.65	2.75
S.H.I.E.L.D. (1973)				
MARVEL				
☐ 1	0.20	0.40	1.20	2.00
☐ 2	0.20	0.40	1.20	2.00
☐ 3	0.20	0.40	1.20	2.00
☐ 4	0.20	0.40	1.20	2.00
☐ 5	0.20	0.40	1.20	2.00
S.O.S.				
FANTAGRAPHICS				
☐ 0, nn b&w, adult		0.55	1.65	2.75
S.T.A.R. CORPS				
DC				
☐ 1	1.50	0.30	0.90	1.50
☐ 2	1.50	0.30	0.90	1.50
☐ 3	1.50	0.30	0.90	1.50
☐ 4	1.50	0.30	0.90	1.50
☐ 5	1.50	0.30	0.90	1.50
☐ 6	1.50	0.30	0.90	1.50
S.T.A.T.				
MAJESTIC				
☐ 1	2.25	0.45	1.35	2.25
☐ 1, foil cover	2.25	0.45	1.35	2.25
SABAN'S MIGHTY MORPHIN POWER RANGERS				
MARVEL				
☐ 1, Nov 95	1.75	0.35	1.05	1.75
☐ 2, Dec 95	1.75	0.35	1.05	1.75
☐ 3, Jan 96	1.75	0.35	1.05	1.75
☐ 4, Feb 96	1.75	0.35	1.05	1.75
☐ 5, Mar 96	1.75	0.35	1.05	1.75
☐ 6, Apr 96	1.75	0.35	1.05	1.75
☐ 7, May 96	1.75	0.35	1.05	1.75
SABAN'S MIGHTY MORPHIN POWER RANGERS:				
NINJA RANGERS				
☐ 1, Dec 95, flip book with VRTroopers back-up				
	1.75	0.35	1.05	1.75
☐ 2, Jan 96, flip book with VR Troopers back-up;Power Rangers cover says "Dec 95"				
	1.75	0.35	1.05	1.75
☐ 3, Feb 96, flip book with VR Troopers back-up				
	1.75	0.35	1.05	1.75
☐ 4, Mar 96, flip book with VR Troopers back-up				
	1.75	0.35	1.05	1.75
☐ 5, Apr 96, flip book with VR Troopers back-up				
	1.75	0.35	1.05	1.75
SABLE (was Jon Sable, Freelance)				
FIRST				
☐ 1, Mar 88	1.75	0.35	1.05	1.75
☐ 2, Apr 88	1.75	0.35	1.05	1.75
☐ 3, May 88	1.75	0.35	1.05	1.75
☐ 4, Jun 88	1.75	0.35	1.05	1.75
☐ 5, Jul 88	1.75	0.35	1.05	1.75
☐ 6, Aug 88	1.75	0.35	1.05	1.75
☐ 7, Sep 88	1.75	0.35	1.05	1.75
☐ 8, Oct 88	1.95	0.39	1.17	1.95
☐ 9, Nov 88	1.95	0.39	1.17	1.95
☐ 10, Dec 88	1.95	0.39	1.17	1.95
☐ 11, Jan 89	1.95	0.39	1.17	1.95
☐ 12, Feb 89	1.95	0.39	1.17	1.95
☐ 13, Mar 89	1.95	0.39	1.17	1.95
☐ 14, Apr 89	1.95	0.39	1.17	1.95

	ORIG.	GOOD	FINE	N-MINT
☐ 15, May 89	1.95	0.39	1.17	1.95
☐ 16, Jun 89	1.95	0.39	1.17	1.95
☐ 17, Jul 89	1.95	0.39	1.17	1.95
☐ 18, Aug 89	1.95	0.39	1.17	1.95
☐ 19, Sep 89	1.95	0.39	1.17	1.95
☐ 20, Oct 89	1.95	0.39	1.17	1.95
☐ 21, Nov 89	1.95	0.39	1.17	1.95
☐ 22, Dec 89	1.95	0.39	1.17	1.95
☐ 23, Jan 90	1.95	0.39	1.17	1.95
☐ 24, Feb 90	1.95	0.39	1.17	1.95
☐ 25, Mar 90	1.95	0.39	1.17	1.95
☐ 26, Apr 90	1.95	0.39	1.17	1.95
☐ 27, May 90	1.95	0.39	1.17	1.95
SABRA BLADE				
DRACULINA				
☐ 1, Dec 94, b&w	2.50	0.50	1.50	2.50
☐ 1, Dec 94, b&w, alternate two-color cover				
	2.50	0.50	1.50	2.50
SABRE				
ECLIPSE				
☐ 1		0.40	1.20	2.00
☐ 2		0.40	1.20	2.00
☐ 3		0.40	1.20	2.00
☐ 4		0.40	1.20	2.00
☐ 5		0.40	1.20	2.00
☐ 6		0.40	1.20	2.00
☐ 7		0.40	1.20	2.00
☐ 8		0.40	1.20	2.00
☐ 9		0.40	1.20	2.00
☐ 10		0.40	1.20	2.00
☐ 11		0.40	1.20	2.00
☐ 12		0.40	1.20	2.00
☐ 13		0.40	1.20	2.00
☐ 14		0.40	1.20	2.00
SABRETOOTH				
MARVEL				
☐ 1, diecut cover	2.95	1.20	3.60	6.00
☐ 2	2.95	1.00	3.00	5.00
☐ 3	2.95	1.00	3.00	5.00
☐ 4	2.95	1.00	3.00	5.00
SABRETOOTH CLASSIC				
☐ 2, Jun 94	1.50	0.30	0.90	1.50
☐ 3, Jul 94	1.50	0.30	0.90	1.50
☐ 4, Aug 94	1.50	0.30	0.90	1.50
☐ 5, Sep 94	1.50	0.30	0.90	1.50
☐ 6, Oct 94	1.50	0.30	0.90	1.50
☐ 7, Nov 94, reprints The Mighty Thor #374				
	1.50	0.30	0.90	1.50
☐ 8, Dec 94	1.50	0.30	0.90	1.50
☐ 9, Jan 95, reprints Uncanny X-Men #212				
	1.50	0.30	0.90	1.50
☐ 10, Feb 95, reprints Uncanny X-Men #213				
	1.50	0.30	0.90	1.50
☐ 11, Mar 95, reprints Daredevil #238				
	1.50	0.30	0.90	1.50
☐ 12, Apr 95, reprints back-up stories from Classic X-Men #10 and Marvel Super-Heroes (no issue # given)				
	1.50	0.30	0.90	1.50
☐ 13, May 95, reprintsUncanny X-Men #219				
	1.50	0.30	0.90	1.50
☐ 14, Jun 95, reprints Uncanny X-Men #221				
	1.50	0.30	0.90	1.50
☐ 15, Jul 95, reprintsuncanny X-Men #222				
	1.50	0.30	0.90	1.50
SABRETOOTH SPECIAL				
☐ 1, 95, enhanced wraparoundcover;one-shot				
	4.95	0.99	2.97	4.95

	ORIG.	GOOD	FINE	N-MINT

SABRINA'S HALLOWEEN SPECTACULAR
ARCHIE
☐ 2, 94, (picks up numbering from *Sabrina's Halloween Spoook-tacular*) .... 2.00 | 0.40 | 1.20 | 2.00

SABRINA'S HALLOWEEN SPOOOK-TACULAR
☐ 1, 93................................ 2.00 | 0.40 | 1.20 | 2.00

SABRINA'S HOLIDAY SPECTACULAR
☐ 2, 94............................... 2.00 | 0.40 | 1.20 | 2.00
☐ 3, 95............................... 2.00 | 0.40 | 1.20 | 2.00

SACHS & VIOLENS
EPIC
☐ 1, GP, embossed cover.. 2.75 | 0.80 | 2.40 | 4.00
☐ 1, platinum...................... 1.60 | 4.80 | 8.00
☐ 2, May 94, GP .... 2.25 | 0.45 | 1.35 | 2.25
☐ 3, Jun 94........................ 2.25 | 0.45 | 1.35 | 2.25
☐ 4, Jul 94......................... 2.25 | 0.45 | 1.35 | 2.25

SAD SACK
RECOLLECTIONS
☐ 290, b&w .... 1.00 | 0.20 | 0.60 | 1.00

SAD SACK AT HOME FOR THE HOLIDAYS
LORNE-HARVEY
☐ 1 .... | 0.40 | 1.20 | 2.00

SAD SACK IN 3-D
BLACKTHORNE
☐ 1 .... | 0.50 | 1.50 | 2.50

SAFEST PLACE IN THE WORLD, THE
DARK HORSE
☐ 0, nn, SD .... 2.50 | 0.50 | 1.50 | 2.50

SAFETY-BELT MAN
SIRIUS ENTERTAINMENT
☐ 1, Jun 94, b&w .... 2.50 | 0.50 | 1.50 | 2.50
☐ 2, Oct 94, b&w.............. 2.50 | 0.50 | 1.50 | 2.50
☐ 3, Feb 95, b&w.............. 2.50 | 0.50 | 1.50 | 2.50
☐ 4, Jun 95, b&w with color centerfold
.... 2.50 | 0.50 | 1.50 | 2.50
☐ 5, 95, b&w .... 2.50 | 0.50 | 1.50 | 2.50
☐ 6, 96, b&w .... 2.50 | 0.50 | 1.50 | 2.50

SAGA OF CRYSTAR, CRYSTAL WARRIOR, THE
MARVEL
☐ 1, Origin........................ 2.00 | 0.40 | 1.20 | 2.00
☐ 2 .... 0.60 | 0.20 | 0.60 | 1.00
☐ 3 .... 0.60 | 0.20 | 0.60 | 1.00
☐ 4 .... 0.60 | 0.20 | 0.60 | 1.00
☐ 5 .... 0.60 | 0.20 | 0.60 | 1.00
☐ 6 .... 0.60 | 0.20 | 0.60 | 1.00
☐ 7 .... 0.60 | 0.20 | 0.60 | 1.00
☐ 8 .... 0.60 | 0.20 | 0.60 | 1.00
☐ 9 .... 0.60 | 0.20 | 0.60 | 1.00
☐ 10 .... 0.60 | 0.20 | 0.60 | 1.00
☐ 11, Alpha Flight.............. 1.00 | 0.20 | 0.60 | 1.00

SAGA OF ELF FACE
EXTER ENTRANCE
☐ 1 .... | 0.20 | 0.60 | 1.00
☐ 2 .... | 0.20 | 0.60 | 1.00

SAGA OF RA'S AL GHUL
DC
☐ 1, Jan 88, NA,DG rep. ...... 1.00 | 3.00 | 5.00
☐ 2, Feb 88, NA,DG rep. ...... 1.00 | 3.00 | 5.00
☐ 3, Mar 88, NA,DG rep....... 1.00 | 3.00 | 5.00
☐ 4, Apr 88, NA,DG rep. ...... 1.00 | 3.00 | 5.00

SAGA OF THE MAN ELF
TRIDENT
☐ 1 .... | 0.45 | 1.35 | 2.25
☐ 2 .... | 0.45 | 1.35 | 2.25
☐ 3 .... | 0.45 | 1.35 | 2.25
☐ 4 .... | 0.45 | 1.35 | 2.25
☐ 5 .... | 0.45 | 1.35 | 2.25

SAGA OF THE ORIGINAL HUMAN TORCH, THE
MARVEL
☐ 1, Apr 90, RB O:Human Torch
.... 1.50 | 0.30 | 0.90 | 1.50
☐ 2, May 90, O:Toro....... 1.50 | 0.30 | 0.90 | 1.50
☐ 3, Jun 90, D:Hitler........... 1.50 | 0.30 | 0.90 | 1.50
☐ 4, Jul 90......................... 1.50 | 0.30 | 0.90 | 1.50

SAGA OF THE REALM
CALIBER
☐ 1, b&w.............................. | 0.50 | 1.50 | 2.50
☐ 2, b&w.............................. | 0.50 | 1.50 | 2.50
☐ 3, b&w.............................. | 0.50 | 1.50 | 2.50

SAGA OF THE SUB-MARINER, THE
MARVEL
☐ 1, Nov 88,O:Sub-Mariner
.... 1.25 | 0.60 | 1.80 | 3.00
☐ 2, Dec 88 .... 1.50 | 0.40 | 1.20 | 2.00
☐ 3, Jan 89........................ 1.50 | 0.40 | 1.20 | 2.00
☐ 4, Feb 89, Human Torch .1.50 | 0.40 | 1.20 | 2.00
☐ 5, Mar 89, Torch, Capt. America, Invaders
.... 1.50 | 0.40 | 1.20 | 2.00
☐ 6, Apr 89, Torch, Capt. America, Invaders
.... 1.50 | 0.40 | 1.20 | 2.00
☐ 7, May 89, Fantastic Four
.... 1.50 | 0.40 | 1.20 | 2.00
☐ 8, Jun 89, F4, Avengers ..1.50 | 0.40 | 1.20 | 2.00
☐ 9, Jul 89, F4, Avengers ...1.50 | 0.40 | 1.20 | 2.00
☐ 10, Aug 89 .... 1.50 | 0.40 | 1.20 | 2.00
☐ 11, Sep 89 .... 1.50 | 0.40 | 1.20 | 2.00
☐ 12, Oct 89...................... 1.50 | 0.40 | 1.20 | 2.00

SAGA OF THE SWAMP THING
DC
☐ 1, May 82, TY .... | 0.60 | 1.80 | 3.00
☐ 2, Jun 82 .... | 0.40 | 1.20 | 2.00
☐ 3, Jul 82.......................... | 0.40 | 1.20 | 2.00
☐ 4, Aug 82 .... | 0.40 | 1.20 | 2.00
☐ 5, Sep 82 .... | 0.40 | 1.20 | 2.00
☐ 6, Oct 82 .... | 0.40 | 1.20 | 2.00
☐ 7, Nov 82 .... | 0.40 | 1.20 | 2.00
☐ 8, Dec 82 .... | 0.40 | 1.20 | 2.00
☐ 9, Jan 83......................... | 0.40 | 1.20 | 2.00
☐ 10, Feb 83....................... | 0.40 | 1.20 | 2.00
☐ 11, Mar 83....................... | 0.40 | 1.20 | 2.00
☐ 12, Apr 83........................ | 0.40 | 1.20 | 2.00
☐ 13, May 83....................... | 0.40 | 1.20 | 2.00
☐ 14, Jun 83 .... | 0.40 | 1.20 | 2.00
☐ 15, Jul 83......................... | 0.40 | 1.20 | 2.00
☐ 16, Aug 83....................... | 0.40 | 1.20 | 2.00
☐ 17, Oct 83........................ | 0.20 | 0.60 | 1.00
☐ 18, Nov 83....................... | 0.20 | 0.60 | 1.00
☐ 19, Dec 83 .... | 0.20 | 0.60 | 1.00
☐ 20, Jan 84, 1:Alan Moore.. | 4.40 | 13.20 | 22.00
☐ 21, Feb 84........................ | 4.40 | 13.20 | 22.00
☐ 22, Mar 84....................... | 3.00 | 9.00 | 15.00
☐ 23, Apr 84........................ | 3.00 | 9.00 | 15.00
☐ 24, May 84....................... | 3.00 | 9.00 | 15.00
☐ 25, Jun 84 .... | 2.00 | 6.00 | 10.00
☐ 26, Jul 84......................... | 2.00 | 6.00 | 10.00
☐ 27, Aug 84....................... | 1.60 | 4.80 | 8.00
☐ 28, Sep 84....................... | 1.60 | 4.80 | 8.00
☐ 29, Oct 84........................ | 1.60 | 4.80 | 8.00
☐ 30, Nov 84....................... | 1.60 | 4.80 | 8.00
☐ 31, Dec 84 .... | 1.60 | 4.80 | 8.00
☐ 32, Jan 85........................ | 1.60 | 4.80 | 8.00
☐ 33, Feb 85........................ | 1.60 | 4.80 | 8.00
☐ 34, Mar 85....................... | 2.00 | 6.00 | 10.00
☐ 35, Apr 85........................ | 0.80 | 2.40 | 4.00
☐ 36, May 85....................... | 0.50 | 1.50 | 2.50
☐ 37, Jun 85,1:John Constantine | 1.40 | 4.20 | 7.00
☐ 38, Jul 85, (becomes *Swamp Thing*)
.... | 0.80 | 2.40 | 4.00

	ORIG.	GOOD	FINE	N-MINT

SAINT SINNER
MARVEL

	ORIG.	GOOD	FINE	N-MINT
❑ 1, foil cover	2.50	0.50	1.50	2.50
❑ 2	1.75	0.35	1.05	1.75
❑ 3	1.75	0.35	1.05	1.75
❑ 4	1.75	0.35	1.05	1.75
❑ 5	1.75	0.35	1.05	1.75
❑ 6	1.75	0.35	1.05	1.75
❑ 7	1.75	0.35	1.05	1.75

SAINTS, THE
SATURN

	ORIG.	GOOD	FINE	N-MINT
❑ 0, Apr 95, b&w	2.50	0.50	1.50	2.50

SALIMBA
BLACKTHORNE

	GOOD	FINE	N-MINT
❑ 1, 89, b&w	0.70	2.10	3.50

SALIMBA 3-D

	GOOD	FINE	N-MINT
❑ 1, Aug 86	0.50	1.50	2.50
❑ 2, Sep 86	0.50	1.50	2.50

SALLY FORTH (mini-series)
EROS

	ORIG.	GOOD	FINE	N-MINT
❑ 1, adult,WW,b&w,reprint	2.95	0.59	1.77	2.95
❑ 2, adult,WW,b&w,reprint	2.95	0.59	1.77	2.95
❑ 3, adult,WW,b&w,reprint	2.95	0.59	1.77	2.95
❑ 4, adult,WW,b&w,reprint	2.95	0.59	1.77	2.95
❑ 5, adult,WW,b&w,reprint .	2.95	0.59	1.77	2.95
❑ 6, Sep 94, adult,b&w,reprint	2.95	0.59	1.77	2.95

SAM & MAX FREELANCE POLICE SPECIAL
COMICO

	GOOD	FINE	N-MINT
❑ 1	0.55	1.65	2.75

SAM & MAX FREELANCE POLICE SPECIAL COLOR COLLECTION
EPIC

	ORIG.	GOOD	FINE	N-MINT
❑ 0, nn, 1992	4.95	0.99	2.97	4.95

SAM & MAX, FREELANCE POLICE

	ORIG.	GOOD	FINE	N-MINT
❑ 0, nn, 1992	2.25	0.45	1.35	2.25

SAM AND MAX, FREELANCE POLICE SPECIAL, THE
FISHWRAP

	ORIG.	GOOD	FINE	N-MINT
❑ 1, 87, b&w	1.75	0.35	1.05	1.75

SAM SLADE, ROBO-HUNTER
FLEETWAY/QUALITY

	ORIG.	GOOD	FINE	N-MINT
❑ 1	0.75	0.15	0.45	0.75
❑ 2	0.75	0.15	0.45	0.75
❑ 3	0.75	0.15	0.45	0.75
❑ 4	0.75	0.15	0.45	0.75
❑ 5	0.75	0.15	0.45	0.75
❑ 6		0.25	0.75	1.25
❑ 7		0.25	0.75	1.25
❑ 8		0.25	0.75	1.25
❑ 9		0.25	0.75	1.25
❑ 10		0.25	0.75	1.25
❑ 11		0.25	0.75	1.25
❑ 12		0.25	0.75	1.25
❑ 13		0.25	0.75	1.25
❑ 14		0.25	0.75	1.25
❑ 15		0.25	0.75	1.25
❑ 16		0.25	0.75	1.25
❑ 17		0.25	0.75	1.25
❑ 18		0.25	0.75	1.25
❑ 19		0.25	0.75	1.25
❑ 20		0.30	0.90	1.50
❑ 21, one issue		0.30	0.90	1.50
❑ 23, one issue		0.30	0.90	1.50
❑ 25		0.30	0.90	1.50
❑ 26		0.30	0.90	1.50

	ORIG.	GOOD	FINE	N-MINT
❑ 27		0.30	0.90	1.50
❑ 28		0.30	0.90	1.50
❑ 29		0.30	0.90	1.50
❑ 30		0.30	0.90	1.50
❑ 31		0.30	0.90	1.50

SAMBU GASSHO (A CHORUS IN THREE PARTS)
BODO GENKI STUDIOS

❑ 0, Aug 94, no cover price;b&w anthology

SAMSON
SAMSON

	ORIG.	GOOD	FINE	N-MINT
❑ 0, 95, 1/2; no indicia	2.50	0.50	1.50	2.50

SAMURAI
AIRCEL

	GOOD	FINE	N-MINT
❑ 1, (1st printing)	1.00	3.00	5.00
❑ 1, (2nd printing)	0.80	2.40	4.00
❑ 1, (3rd printing)	0.60	1.80	3.00
❑ 2	0.80	2.40	4.00
❑ 3	0.60	1.80	3.00
❑ 4	0.60	1.80	3.00
❑ 5	0.34	1.02	1.70
❑ 6	0.34	1.02	1.70
❑ 7	0.34	1.02	1.70
❑ 8	0.34	1.02	1.70
❑ 9	0.34	1.02	1.70
❑ 10	0.34	1.02	1.70
❑ 11	0.34	1.02	1.70
❑ 12	0.34	1.02	1.70
❑ 13, Dale Keown	0.80	2.40	4.00
❑ 14, Dale Keown	0.80	2.40	4.00
❑ 15, Dale Keown	0.80	2.40	4.00
❑ 16, Dale Keown	0.80	2.40	4.00
❑ 17, Dale Keown	0.80	2.40	4.00
❑ 18, Dale Keown	0.80	2.40	4.00
❑ 19	0.34	1.02	1.70
❑ 20	0.34	1.02	1.70
❑ 21	0.34	1.02	1.70
❑ 22	0.34	1.02	1.70
❑ 23	0.34	1.02	1.70

SAMURAI (Volume 2)

	GOOD	FINE	N-MINT
❑ 1, color	0.40	1.20	2.00
❑ 2, color	0.40	1.20	2.00
❑ 3, color	0.40	1.20	2.00

SAMURAI (Volume 3)

	GOOD	FINE	N-MINT
❑ 1, b&w	0.39	1.17	1.95
❑ 2, b&w	0.39	1.17	1.95
❑ 3, b&w	0.39	1.17	1.95
❑ 4, b&w	0.39	1.17	1.95
❑ 5, b&w	0.39	1.17	1.95
❑ 6, b&w	0.39	1.17	1.95
❑ 7, b&w	0.39	1.17	1.95

SAMURAI 7
GAUNTLET

	GOOD	FINE	N-MINT
❑ 1, b&w	0.50	1.50	2.50
❑ 2, b&w	0.50	1.50	2.50
❑ 3, b&w	0.50	1.50	2.50

SAMURAI CAT
EPIC

	ORIG.	GOOD	FINE	N-MINT
❑ 1	2.25	0.45	1.35	2.25
❑ 2	2.25	0.45	1.35	2.25
❑ 3	2.25	0.45	1.35	2.25

SAMURAI FUNNIES
SOLSON

	GOOD	FINE	N-MINT
❑ 1, Texas chainsaw	0.40	1.20	2.00
❑ 2, Samurai 13th	0.40	1.20	2.00

SAMURAI PENGUIN
SLAVE LABOR

	ORIG.	GOOD	FINE	N-MINT
❑ 1, b&w		0.30	0.90	1.50
❑ 2, b&w		0.30	0.90	1.50
❑ 3, b&w	1.50	0.30	0.90	1.50

	ORIG.	GOOD	FINE	N-MINT
4, b&w	1.50	0.30	0.90	1.50
5, b&w	1.50	0.30	0.90	1.50
6, D:Samurai Penguin		0.39	1.17	1.95
7		0.35	1.05	1.75
8		0.35	1.05	1.75

SAMURAI SQUIRREL
SPOTLIGHT
| 1 | | 0.35 | 1.05 | 1.75 |
| 2 | | 0.35 | 1.05 | 1.75 |

SAMURAI: MYSTIC CULT
NIGHTWYND
1, b&w		0.50	1.50	2.50
2, b&w		0.50	1.50	2.50
3, b&w		0.50	1.50	2.50
4, b&w		0.50	1.50	2.50

SAMURAI: VAMPIRE'S HUNT
1, b&w		0.50	1.50	2.50
2, b&w		0.50	1.50	2.50
3, b&w		0.50	1.50	2.50
4, b&w		0.50	1.50	2.50

SAMUREE
CONTINUITY
1, May 87	2.00	0.40	1.20	2.00
2, Aug 87	2.00	0.40	1.20	2.00
3, May 88	2.00	0.40	1.20	2.00
4, Jan 89	2.00	0.40	1.20	2.00
5, Apr 89	2.00	0.40	1.20	2.00
6, Aug 90	2.00	0.40	1.20	2.00
7	2.00	0.40	1.20	2.00
8	2.00	0.40	1.20	2.00
9	2.00	0.40	1.20	2.00

SAMUREE (1995 mini-series)
ACCLAIM/WINDJAMMER
| 1, Oct 95 | 2.50 | 0.50 | 1.50 | 2.50 |
| 2, Nov 95 | 2.50 | 0.50 | 1.50 | 2.50 |

SAMUREE (volume 2, 1993)
CONTINUITY
1, Rise of Magic	2.50	0.50	1.50	2.50
2, Rise of Magic	2.50	0.50	1.50	2.50
3	2.50	0.50	1.50	2.50
4	2.50	0.50	1.50	2.50

SAN DIEGO COMIC-CON COMICS
DARK HORSE
1, con giveaway				
2, Aug 93, con giveaway				
3, Aug 94, con giveaway				

SANCTUARY
VIZ
1, b&w		0.99	2.97	4.95
2, b&w		0.99	2.97	4.95
3		0.99	2.97	4.95
4		0.99	2.97	4.95
5		0.99	2.97	4.95
6		0.99	2.97	4.95
7		0.99	2.97	4.95
8		0.99	2.97	4.95
9		0.99	2.97	4.95

SANCTUARY, PART THREE
1, 94, b&w	3.25	0.65	1.95	3.25
2, 95, b&w	3.25	0.65	1.95	3.25
3, 95, b&w	3.25	0.65	1.95	3.25
5, 95, b&w	3.25	0.65	1.95	3.25
6, 95, b&w	3.25	0.65	1.95	3.25

SANCTUARY, PART TWO
1	4.95	0.99	2.97	4.95
2	4.95	0.99	2.97	4.95
3	4.95	0.99	2.97	4.95
4	4.95	0.99	2.97	4.95
5	4.95	0.99	2.97	4.95

	ORIG.	GOOD	FINE	N-MINT
6	4.95	0.99	2.97	4.95
7	4.95	0.99	2.97	4.95
8	4.95	0.99	2.97	4.95
9, 94	4.95	0.99	2.97	4.95

SANDMADAM
SPOOF
| 1, b&w | 2.95 | 0.59 | 1.77 | 2.95 |

SANDMAN (1974-1976 series)
DC
1, Wtr 74, JK	0.20	1.80	5.40	9.00
2, May 75, JK	0.25	1.00	3.00	5.00
3, Jul 75, JK	0.25	0.80	2.40	4.00
4, Sep 75, JK	0.25	0.80	2.40	4.00
5, Nov 75, JK	0.25	0.60	1.80	3.00
6, Jan 76, JK	0.25	0.60	1.80	3.00

SANDMAN MIDNIGHT THEATRE
DC/VERTIGO
| 0, Sep 95, nn;prestige format;Morpheus meets Wesley Dodds | 6.95 | 1.39 | 4.17 | 6.95 |

SANDMAN MYSTERY THEATRE
1, Apr 93	1.95	0.90	2.70	4.50
2, May 93, MW	1.95	0.80	2.40	4.00
3, Jun 93, MW	1.95	0.80	2.40	4.00
4, Jul 93	1.95	0.80	2.40	4.00
5, Aug 93	1.95	0.80	2.40	4.00
6, Sep 93	1.95	0.70	2.10	3.50
7, Oct 93	1.95	0.70	2.10	3.50
8, Nov 93	1.95	0.70	2.10	3.50
9, Dec 93	1.95	0.70	2.10	3.50
10, Jan 94	1.95	0.70	2.10	3.50
11, Feb 94	1.95	0.60	1.80	3.00
12, Mar 94	1.95	0.60	1.80	3.00
13, Apr 94	1.95	0.60	1.80	3.00
14, May 94	1.95	0.60	1.80	3.00
15, Jun 94	1.95	0.60	1.80	3.00
16, Jul 94	1.95	0.60	1.80	3.00
17, Aug 94	1.95	0.60	1.80	3.00
18, Sep 94	1.95	0.60	1.80	3.00
19, Oct 94	1.95	0.60	1.80	3.00
20, Nov 94	1.95	0.60	1.80	3.00
21, Dec 94	1.95	0.50	1.50	2.50
22, Jan 95	1.95	0.50	1.50	2.50
23, Feb 95	1.95	0.50	1.50	2.50
24, Mar 95	1.95	0.50	1.50	2.50
25, Apr 95	1.95	0.50	1.50	2.50
26, May 95	2.25	0.50	1.50	2.50
27, Jun 95	2.25	0.50	1.50	2.50
28, Jul 95, "Night of theButcher" Part 4 of 4	2.25	0.50	1.50	2.50
29, Aug 95, "The Hourman"Part 1 of 4	2.25	0.60	1.80	3.00
30, Sep 95, "The Hourman"Part 2 of 4	2.25	0.45	1.35	2.25
31, Oct 95, "The Hourman" Part 3 of 4	2.25	0.45	1.35	2.25
32, Nov 95, "The Hourman"Part 4 of 4	2.25	0.45	1.35	2.25
33, Dec 95, "The Python" Part 1 of 4	2.25	0.45	1.35	2.25
34, Jan 96, "The Python" Part 2 of 4	2.25	0.45	1.35	2.25
35, Feb 96, "The Python"Part 3 of 4	2.25	0.45	1.35	2.25
36, Mar 96, "The Python" Part 4 of 4	2.25	0.45	1.35	2.25
37, Apr 96, "The Mist" Part 1 of 4	2.25	0.45	1.35	2.25
38, May 96, "The Mist" Part 2 of 4	2.25	0.45	1.35	2.25
39, Jun 96, "The Mist"Part 3 of 4	2.25	0.45	1.35	2.25

	ORIG.	GOOD	FINE	N-MINT

40, Jul 96, "The Mist" Part 4 of 4
....2.25 0.45 1.35 2.25

SANDMAN MYSTERY THEATRE ANNUAL
1, 94................................3.95 0.79 2.37 3.95

SANDMAN SPECIAL
DC
1, 91, glow cover, BT, Orpheus 1.00 3.00 5.00

SANDMAN, THE (beginning 1989)
1, Jan 89, Neil Gaiman, writer 1:new Sandman
....2.00 16.00 48.00 80.00
2, Feb 89, A:Cain, Abel ... 1.50 10.00 30.00 50.00
3, Mar 89, A:John Constantine 8.00 24.00 40.00
4, Apr 89, A:Demon 8.00 24.00 40.00
5, May 89........................ 8.00 24.00 40.00
6, Jun 89......................... 4.00 12.00 20.00
7, Jul 89......................... 4.00 12.00 20.00
8, with Karen Berger intro, 1000 copies
....36.00 108.00 180.00
8, Aug 89, I&1:Death 12.00 36.00 60.00
9, Sep 89......................... 3.60 10.80 18.00
10, Oct 89 .... 3.60 10.80 18.00
11, Dec 89, Doll's House.. 2.80 8.40 14.00
12, Jan 90, Doll's House.. 2.80 8.40 14.00
13, Feb 90, Doll's House.. 2.80 8.40 14.00
14, Mar 90, Doll's House . 2.80 8.40 14.00
15, Apr 90, Doll's House.. 2.80 8.40 14.00
16, Jun 90, Doll's House.. 2.40 7.20 12.00
17, Jul 90........................ 2.40 7.20 12.00
18, Aug 90 .... 2.40 7.20 12.00
19, Sep 90, CV, pages out of order
....7.00 21.00 35.00
19, CV, properly printed... 2.40 7.20 12.00
20, Oct 90 .... 2.40 7.20 12.00
21, Nov 90 .... 3.00 9.00 15.00
22, Jan 91....................... 5.00 15.00 25.00
23, Feb 91....................... 2.00 6.00 10.00
24, Mar 91....................... 2.00 6.00 10.00
25, Apr 91........................ 2.00 6.00 10.00
26, May 91....................... 2.00 6.00 10.00
27, Jun 91........................ 2.00 6.00 10.00
28, Jul 91......................... 2.00 6.00 10.00
29, Aug 91....................... 1.20 3.60 6.00
30, Sep 91........................ 1.20 3.60 6.00
31, Oct 91 .... 1.20 3.60 6.00
32, Nov 91 .... 1.20 3.60 6.00
33, Dec 91....................... 1.20 3.60 6.00
34 .... 1.20 3.60 6.00
35 .... 1.20 3.60 6.00
36 .... 1.20 3.60 6.00
37 .... 1.20 3.60 6.00
38 .... 1.20 3.60 6.00
39 .... 1.20 3.60 6.00
40 .... 1.20 3.60 6.00
41 .... 1.50 0.60 1.80 3.00
42 .... 1.50 0.60 1.80 3.00
43 .... 1.50 0.60 1.80 3.00
44 .... 1.50 0.60 1.80 3.00
45 .... 1.75 0.50 1.50 2.50
46, Death on AIDS 1.75 0.50 1.50 2.50

DC/VERTIGO
47 .... 1.75 0.50 1.50 2.50
48 .... 1.75 0.50 1.50 2.50
49 .... 1.75 0.50 1.50 2.50
50, CR 2.95 1.00 3.00 5.00
50, CR, Platinum............. 18.00 54.00 90.00
51 .... 1.95 0.45 1.35 2.25
52 .... 1.95 0.45 1.35 2.25
53 .... 1.95 0.45 1.35 2.25
54 .... 1.95 0.45 1.35 2.25
55 .... 1.95 0.45 1.35 2.25
56 .... 1.95 0.39 1.17 1.95
57 .... 1.95 0.39 1.17 1.95
58 .... 1.95 0.39 1.17 1.95
59, Apr 94 .... 1.95 0.39 1.17 1.95
60, Jun 94 .... 1.95 0.39 1.17 1.95
61, Jul 94................ 1.95 0.39 1.17 1.95
62, Aug 94 .... 1.95 0.39 1.17 1.95
63 .... 1.95 0.39 1.17 1.95
64, Nov 94 .... 1.95 0.39 1.17 1.95
65, Dec 94 .... 1.95 0.39 1.17 1.95
66, Jan 95.............. 1.95 0.39 1.17 1.95
67 .... 1.95 0.39 1.17 1.95
68, May 95, "The Kindly Ones"
....1.95 0.39 1.17 1.95
69, Jul 95, "The Kindly Ones"
....2.50 1.00 3.00 5.00
70, Aug 95, "The Wake"...2.50 0.50 1.50 2.50
71, 95, "The Wake"..........2.50 0.50 1.50 2.50
72, Nov 95, "The Wake";"burial" of Dream
....2.50 0.50 1.50 2.50
73, Dec 95, "The Wake";A:Hob Gadling
....2.50 0.50 1.50 2.50
74, Jan 96, "Exiles"..........2.50 0.50 1.50 2.50
75, Mar 96, "The Tempest";A:William Shakespeare;final
issue;contains timeline ...3.95 1.00 3.00 5.00

SANDMAN: A GALLERY OF DREAMS, THE
0, 94, nn 2.95 0.80 2.40 4.00

SANTA CLAWS
ETERNITY
1, b&w................................. 0.59 1.77 2.95

SANTANA
MALIBU/ROCK-IT
1, May 94, magazine.......3.95 0.79 2.37 3.95

SAP TUNES
FANTAGRAPHICS
1, b&w................................. 0.50 1.50 2.50
2, b&w................................. 0.50 1.50 2.50

SAPPHIRE
AIRCEL
1, b&w, adult.................... 0.50 1.50 2.50
2, b&w, adult.................... 0.50 1.50 2.50
3, b&w, adult.................... 0.50 1.50 2.50
4, b&w, adult.................... 0.50 1.50 2.50
5, b&w, adult.................... 0.50 1.50 2.50
6, b&w, adult.................... 0.50 1.50 2.50
7, b&w, adult.................... 0.50 1.50 2.50
8, b&w, adult.................... 0.50 1.50 2.50
9, Sep 90, b&w, adult.....2.50 0.50 1.50 2.50

SATAN'S SIX
TOPPS
1, Apr 93, JK/TMc(c), trading card
....2.95 0.59 1.77 2.95
2, trading cards 2.95 0.59 1.77 2.95
3, trading cards 2.95 0.59 1.77 2.95
4, trading cards 2.95 0.59 1.77 2.95

SATAN'S SIX: HELLSPAWN
2, Jun 94 ....2.50 0.50 1.50 2.50

SATANIKA
VEROTIK
0 ....2.95 1.00 3.00 5.00
1, Jan 95........................2.95 1.50 4.50 7.50

SAVAGE COMBAT TALES
ATLAS/ SEABOARD
1, Feb 75.........................0.25 0.20 0.60 1.00
2, Apr 75..........................0.25 0.20 0.60 1.00
3, Jul 75...........................0.25 0.20 0.60 1.00

SAVAGE DRAGON VS. THE SAVAGE MEGATON MAN, THE
IMAGE
1, EL, gold foil cover.......1.95 0.39 1.17 1.95

	ORIG.	GOOD	FINE	N-MINT

SAVAGE DRAGON, THE (mini-series)

❏ 1, Jul 92, EL;four cover logo variants (bottom of logo is white, blue, green, or yellow)

	ORIG.	GOOD	FINE	N-MINT
	1.95	2.00	6.00	10.00
❏ 2, EL		1.60	4.80	8.00
❏ 3, EL		0.80	2.40	4.00

SAVAGE DRAGON, THE (second series)

	ORIG.	GOOD	FINE	N-MINT
❏ 1	1.95	0.50	1.50	2.50

❏ 2, TMNT (backed with *Vanguard* #0)

	ORIG.	GOOD	FINE	N-MINT
	2.95	0.59	1.77	2.95
❏ 3	1.95	0.39	1.17	1.95
❏ 4	1.95	0.39	1.17	1.95
❏ 5	1.95	0.39	1.17	1.95
❏ 6	1.95	0.39	1.17	1.95
❏ 7	1.95	0.39	1.17	1.95
❏ 8	1.95	0.39	1.17	1.95
❏ 9, Apr 94	1.95	0.39	1.17	1.95
❏ 10, May 94	1.95	0.39	1.17	1.95

❏ 10, May 94, newsstand version, alternate cover

	ORIG.	GOOD	FINE	N-MINT
	1.95	0.39	1.17	1.95
❏ 11, Jul 94	1.95	0.39	1.17	1.95
❏ 12, Aug 94, She Dragon	1.95	0.39	1.17	1.95

❏ 13, Oct 94, Image X month version

	ORIG.	GOOD	FINE	N-MINT
	2.50	0.50	1.50	2.50
❏ 13, Jun 95, EL	1.95	0.39	1.17	1.95
❏ 15, Dec 94, EL	2.50	0.50	1.50	2.50
❏ 16, Jan 95, EL	2.50	0.50	1.50	2.50
❏ 17, Feb 95, EL	2.50	0.50	1.50	2.50

❏ 17, Feb 95, EL;alternate cover;two different interior pages

	ORIG.	GOOD	FINE	N-MINT
	2.50	0.50	1.50	2.50
❏ 18, Mar 95, EL	2.50	0.50	1.50	2.50
❏ 19, Apr 95, EL	2.50	0.50	1.50	2.50
❏ 21, Aug 95, EL	2.50	0.50	1.50	2.50
❏ 23, Oct 95	2.50	0.50	1.50	2.50
❏ 25, Jan 96, double-sized	3.95	0.79	2.37	3.95

❏ 25, Jan 96, double-sized;alternate cover

	ORIG.	GOOD	FINE	N-MINT
	3.95	0.79	2.37	3.95
❏ 26, Mar 96	2.50	0.50	1.50	2.50
❏ 27, Apr 96	2.50	0.50	1.50	2.50

❏ 27, alternate cover only available at WonderCon

	ORIG.	GOOD	FINE	N-MINT
	2.50	0.50	1.50	2.50
❏ 28, May 96, A:Maxx	2.50	0.50	1.50	2.50

SAVAGE DRAGON/TEENAGE MUTANT NINJA TURTLES CROSSOVER
MIRAGE

	ORIG.	GOOD	FINE	N-MINT
❏ 1	2.75	0.55	1.65	2.75

SAVAGE HENRY
CALIBER/ICONOGRAFIX

	ORIG.	GOOD	FINE	N-MINT
❏ 1, b&w	2.95	0.59	1.77	2.95
❏ 2, 94, b&w	2.95	0.59	1.77	2.95
❏ 3, b&w	2.95	0.59	1.77	2.95

VORTEX

	GOOD	FINE	N-MINT
❏ 1	0.35	1.05	1.75
❏ 2	0.35	1.05	1.75
❏ 3	0.35	1.05	1.75
❏ 4	0.35	1.05	1.75
❏ 5	0.35	1.05	1.75
❏ 6	0.35	1.05	1.75
❏ 7	0.35	1.05	1.75
❏ 8	0.35	1.05	1.75
❏ 9	0.35	1.05	1.75
❏ 10	0.35	1.05	1.75
❏ 11	0.40	1.20	2.00
❏ 12	0.40	1.20	2.00
❏ 13, (moves to Rip Off Press)	0.40	1.20	2.00

SAVAGE HENRY (was Vortex title)
RIP OFF

	ORIG.	GOOD	FINE	N-MINT
❏ 14, Mar 91, b&w	2.00	0.40	1.20	2.00
❏ 15, May 91, b&w	2.00	0.40	1.20	2.00
❏ 16, Jul 91, b&w	2.50	0.50	1.50	2.50
❏ 17, Sep 91, b&w	2.50	0.50	1.50	2.50

	ORIG.	GOOD	FINE	N-MINT
❏ 18, Nov 91, b&w	2.50	0.50	1.50	2.50
❏ 19, Jan 92, b&w	2.50	0.50	1.50	2.50
❏ 20, Mar 92, b&w	2.50	0.50	1.50	2.50
❏ 21, May 92, b&w	2.50	0.50	1.50	2.50
❏ 22, Jul 92, b&w	2.50	0.50	1.50	2.50
❏ 23, Sep 92, b&w	2.50	0.50	1.50	2.50
❏ 24, Nov 92, b&w	2.50	0.50	1.50	2.50
❏ 25, Jan 93, b&w	2.50	0.50	1.50	2.50
❏ 26, Mar 93, b&w	2.50	0.50	1.50	2.50
❏ 27, May 93	2.50	0.50	1.50	2.50
❏ 28, Jul 93, b&w	2.50	0.50	1.50	2.50
❏ 29, Sep 93, b&w	2.50	0.50	1.50	2.50
❏ 30, Nov 93, b&w	2.50	0.50	1.50	2.50

SAVAGE HENRY: HEADSTRONG
CALIBER

	ORIG.	GOOD	FINE	N-MINT
❏ 1, 95, b&w	2.95	0.59	1.77	2.95
❏ 2, 95, b&w	2.95	0.59	1.77	2.95
❏ 3, 95, b&w	2.95	0.59	1.77	2.95

SAVAGE NINJA
CADILLAC

	GOOD	FINE	N-MINT
❏ 1	0.20	0.60	1.00

SAVAGE RETURN OF DRACULA
MARVEL

	ORIG.	GOOD	FINE	N-MINT
❏ 1, reprints	2.00	0.40	1.20	2.00

SAVAGE SHE-HULK, THE

	ORIG.	GOOD	FINE	N-MINT
❏ 1, Feb 80, O:	0.40	1.00	3.00	5.00
❏ 2, Mar 80	0.40	0.70	2.10	3.50
❏ 3, Apr 80	0.40	0.70	2.10	3.50
❏ 4, May 80	0.40	0.70	2.10	3.50
❏ 5, Jun 80	0.40	0.70	2.10	3.50
❏ 6, Jul 80	0.40	0.50	1.50	2.50
❏ 7, Aug 80	0.40	0.50	1.50	2.50
❏ 8, Sep 80	0.50	0.50	1.50	2.50
❏ 9, Oct 80	0.50	0.50	1.50	2.50
❏ 10, Nov 80	0.50	0.50	1.50	2.50
❏ 11, Dec 80	0.50	0.40	1.20	2.00
❏ 12, Jan 81	0.50	0.40	1.20	2.00
❏ 13, Feb 81	0.50	0.40	1.20	2.00
❏ 14, Mar 81	0.50	0.40	1.20	2.00
❏ 15, Apr 81	0.50	0.40	1.20	2.00
❏ 16, May 81	0.50	0.40	1.20	2.00
❏ 17, Jun 81	0.50	0.40	1.20	2.00
❏ 18, Jul 81	0.50	0.40	1.20	2.00
❏ 19, Aug 81	0.50	0.40	1.20	2.00
❏ 20, Sep 81	0.50	0.40	1.20	2.00
❏ 21, Oct 81	0.50	0.40	1.20	2.00
❏ 22, Nov 81	0.50	0.40	1.20	2.00
❏ 23, Dec 81	0.50	0.40	1.20	2.00
❏ 24, Jan 82	0.60	0.40	1.20	2.00
❏ 25, Feb 82, double size	1.00	0.40	1.20	2.00

SAVAGE SWORD OF CONAN ANNUAL, THE

	ORIG.	GOOD	FINE	N-MINT
❏ 1, b&w	1.25	0.50	1.50	2.50

SAVAGE SWORD OF CONAN THE BARBARIAN, THE

❏ 175, (was *Savage Sword of Conan, The*)

	ORIG.	GOOD	FINE	N-MINT
	2.25	0.80	2.40	4.00
❏ 176	2.25	0.60	1.80	3.00
❏ 177	2.25	0.60	1.80	3.00
❏ 178	2.25	0.60	1.80	3.00
❏ 179	2.25	0.60	1.80	3.00
❏ 180	2.25	0.60	1.80	3.00
❏ 181	2.25	0.60	1.80	3.00
❏ 182	2.25	0.60	1.80	3.00
❏ 183	2.25	0.60	1.80	3.00
❏ 184	2.25	0.60	1.80	3.00
❏ 185	2.25	0.60	1.80	3.00
❏ 186	2.25	0.60	1.80	3.00
❏ 187	2.25	0.60	1.80	3.00
❏ 188	2.25	0.60	1.80	3.00
❏ 189	2.25	0.60	1.80	3.00
❏ 190	2.25	0.60	1.80	3.00

	ORIG.	GOOD	FINE	N-MINT
☐ 191	2.25	0.45	1.35	2.25
☐ 192	2.25	0.45	1.35	2.25
☐ 193	2.25	0.45	1.35	2.25
☐ 194	2.25	0.45	1.35	2.25
☐ 195	2.25	0.45	1.35	2.25
☐ 196	2.25	0.45	1.35	2.25
☐ 197	2.25	0.45	1.35	2.25
☐ 198	2.25	0.45	1.35	2.25
☐ 199	2.25	0.45	1.35	2.25
☐ 200	2.25	0.45	1.35	2.25
☐ 201	2.25	0.45	1.35	2.25
☐ 202	2.25	0.45	1.35	2.25
☐ 203	2.25	0.45	1.35	2.25
☐ 204	2.25	0.45	1.35	2.25
☐ 205	2.25	0.45	1.35	2.25
☐ 206	2.25	0.45	1.35	2.25
☐ 207	2.25	0.45	1.35	2.25
☐ 208	2.25	0.45	1.35	2.25
☐ 209	2.25	0.45	1.35	2.25
☐ 210	2.25	0.45	1.35	2.25
☐ 211	2.25	0.45	1.35	2.25
☐ 212	2.25	0.45	1.35	2.25
☐ 213	2.25	0.45	1.35	2.25
☐ 214	2.25	0.45	1.35	2.25
☐ 215	2.25	0.45	1.35	2.25
☐ 216	2.25	0.45	1.35	2.25
☐ 217	2.25	0.45	1.35	2.25
☐ 218	2.25	0.45	1.35	2.25
☐ 219	2.25	0.45	1.35	2.25
☐ 220	2.25	0.45	1.35	2.25
☐ 221, May 94, b&w	2.25	0.45	1.35	2.25
☐ 222, Jun 94, b&w	2.25	0.45	1.35	2.25
☐ 223, Jul 94, b&w	2.25	0.45	1.35	2.25
☐ 224, Aug 94, b&w	2.25	0.45	1.35	2.25
☐ 225, Sep 94, b&w	2.25	0.45	1.35	2.25
☐ 226, Oct 94, b&w	2.25	0.45	1.35	2.25
☐ 227, Nov 94, b&w	2.25	0.45	1.35	2.25
☐ 228, Dec 94, b&w	2.25	0.45	1.35	2.25
☐ 229, Jan 95, b&w	2.25	0.45	1.35	2.25
☐ 230, Feb 95, b&w	2.25	0.45	1.35	2.25
☐ 231, Mar 95, b&w	2.25	0.45	1.35	2.25
☐ 232, Apr 95, b&w	2.25	0.45	1.35	2.25
☐ 233, May 95, b&w	2.25	0.45	1.35	2.25
☐ 234, Jun 95, b&w	2.25	0.45	1.35	2.25
☐ 235, Jul 95, b&w;final issue	2.25	0.45	1.35	2.25

SAVAGE SWORD OF CONAN, THE

	ORIG.	GOOD	FINE	N-MINT
☐ 1, Aug 74, O:Blackmark,b&w	1.00	12.00	36.00	60.00
☐ 2, Oct 74	1.00	6.00	18.00	30.00
☐ 3, Dec 74	1.00	3.00	9.00	15.00
☐ 4, Feb 75	3.00	9.00	15.00	
☐ 5, Apr 75	1.00	3.00	9.00	15.00
☐ 6, Jun 75	1.00	1.60	4.80	8.00
☐ 7, Aug 75	1.00	1.60	4.80	8.00
☐ 8, Oct 75	1.00	1.60	4.80	8.00
☐ 9, Dec 75	1.00	1.60	4.80	8.00
☐ 10, Feb 76	1.00	1.60	4.80	8.00
☐ 11, Apr 76	1.00	1.60	4.80	8.00
☐ 12, Jun 76	1.00	1.60	4.80	8.00
☐ 13, Aug 76	1.00	1.60	4.80	8.00
☐ 14, Sep 76	1.00	1.60	4.80	8.00
☐ 15, Oct 76	1.00	1.60	4.80	8.00
☐ 16, Dec 76	1.00	1.60	4.80	8.00
☐ 17, Feb 77	1.00	1.60	4.80	8.00
☐ 18, Apr 77	1.00	1.60	4.80	8.00
☐ 19, Jun 77	1.00	1.60	4.80	8.00
☐ 20, Jul 77	1.00	1.60	4.80	8.00
☐ 21, Aug 77	1.00	1.60	4.80	8.00
☐ 22, Sep 77	1.00	1.60	4.80	8.00
☐ 23, Oct 77	1.00	1.60	4.80	8.00

	ORIG.	GOOD	FINE	N-MINT
☐ 24, Nov 77	1.00	1.60	4.80	8.00
☐ 25, Dec 77	1.00	1.60	4.80	8.00
☐ 26, Jan 78	1.00	1.60	4.80	8.00
☐ 27, Mar 78	1.00	1.60	4.80	8.00
☐ 28, Apr 78	1.00	1.60	4.80	8.00
☐ 29, May 78	1.00	1.60	4.80	8.00
☐ 30, Jun 78	1.00	1.60	4.80	8.00
☐ 31, Jul 78	1.00	1.60	4.80	8.00
☐ 32, Aug 78	1.00	1.60	4.80	8.00
☐ 33, Sep 78	1.00	1.60	4.80	8.00
☐ 34, Oct 78	1.00	1.60	4.80	8.00
☐ 35, Nov 78	1.00	1.60	4.80	8.00
☐ 36, Dec 78	1.00	1.60	4.80	8.00
☐ 37, Feb 79	1.00	1.60	4.80	8.00
☐ 38, Mar 79	1.00	1.60	4.80	8.00
☐ 39, Apr 79	1.00	1.60	4.80	8.00
☐ 40, May 79	1.00	1.60	4.80	8.00
☐ 41, Jun 79	1.00	1.60	4.80	8.00
☐ 42, Jul 79	1.00	1.60	4.80	8.00
☐ 43, Aug 79	1.00	1.60	4.80	8.00
☐ 44, Sep 79	1.00	1.60	4.80	8.00
☐ 45, Oct 79	1.25	1.20	3.60	6.00
☐ 46, Nov 79	1.25	1.20	3.60	6.00
☐ 47, Dec 79	1.25	1.20	3.60	6.00
☐ 48, Jan 80	1.25	1.20	3.60	6.00
☐ 49, Feb 80	1.25	1.20	3.60	6.00
☐ 50, Mar 80	1.25	1.20	3.60	6.00
☐ 51, Apr 80	1.25	1.20	3.60	6.00
☐ 52, May 80	1.25	1.20	3.60	6.00
☐ 53, Jun 80	1.25	1.20	3.60	6.00
☐ 54, Jul 80	1.25	1.20	3.60	6.00
☐ 55, Aug 80	1.25	1.20	3.60	6.00
☐ 56, Sep 80	1.25	1.20	3.60	6.00
☐ 57, Oct 80	1.25	1.20	3.60	6.00
☐ 58, Nov 80	1.25	1.20	3.60	6.00
☐ 59	1.25	1.20	3.60	6.00
☐ 60	1.25	1.20	3.60	6.00
☐ 61	1.25	1.20	3.60	6.00
☐ 62	1.25	1.20	3.60	6.00
☐ 63	1.25	1.20	3.60	6.00
☐ 64	1.25	1.20	3.60	6.00
☐ 65	1.25	1.20	3.60	6.00
☐ 66	1.25	1.20	3.60	6.00
☐ 67	1.25	1.20	3.60	6.00
☐ 68	1.25	1.20	3.60	6.00
☐ 69	1.25	1.20	3.60	6.00
☐ 70	1.25	1.20	3.60	6.00
☐ 71	1.50	1.20	3.60	6.00
☐ 72	1.50	1.20	3.60	6.00
☐ 73	1.50	1.20	3.60	6.00
☐ 74	1.50	1.20	3.60	6.00
☐ 75	1.50	1.20	3.60	6.00
☐ 76	1.50	1.20	3.60	6.00
☐ 77	1.50	1.20	3.60	6.00
☐ 78	1.50	1.20	3.60	6.00
☐ 79	1.50	1.20	3.60	6.00
☐ 80	1.50	1.20	3.60	6.00
☐ 81	1.50	1.20	3.60	6.00
☐ 82	1.50	1.20	3.60	6.00
☐ 83	1.50	1.20	3.60	6.00
☐ 84	1.50	1.20	3.60	6.00
☐ 85	1.50	1.20	3.60	6.00
☐ 86	1.50	1.20	3.60	6.00
☐ 87	1.50	1.20	3.60	6.00
☐ 88	1.50	1.20	3.60	6.00
☐ 89	1.50	1.20	3.60	6.00
☐ 90	1.50	1.20	3.60	6.00
☐ 91	1.50	1.20	3.60	6.00
☐ 92	1.50	1.20	3.60	6.00
☐ 93	1.50	1.20	3.60	6.00
☐ 94	1.50	1.20	3.60	6.00
☐ 95	1.50	1.20	3.60	6.00

	ORIG.	GOOD	FINE	N-MINT
☐ 96	1.50	1.20	3.60	6.00
☐ 97	1.50	1.20	3.60	6.00
☐ 98	1.50	1.20	3.60	6.00
☐ 99	1.50	1.20	3.60	6.00
☐ 100	1.50	1.20	3.60	6.00
☐ 101	1.50	1.00	3.00	5.00
☐ 102	1.50	1.00	3.00	5.00
☐ 103	1.50	1.00	3.00	5.00
☐ 104	1.50	1.00	3.00	5.00
☐ 105	1.50	1.00	3.00	5.00
☐ 106	1.50	1.00	3.00	5.00
☐ 107	1.50	1.00	3.00	5.00
☐ 108	1.50	1.00	3.00	5.00
☐ 109	1.50	1.00	3.00	5.00
☐ 110	1.50	1.00	3.00	5.00
☐ 111	1.50	1.00	3.00	5.00
☐ 112	1.50	1.00	3.00	5.00
☐ 113	1.50	1.00	3.00	5.00
☐ 114	1.50	1.00	3.00	5.00
☐ 115	1.50	1.00	3.00	5.00
☐ 116	1.50	1.00	3.00	5.00
☐ 117	1.50	1.00	3.00	5.00
☐ 118	1.50	1.00	3.00	5.00
☐ 119	1.50	1.00	3.00	5.00
☐ 120	1.50	1.00	3.00	5.00
☐ 121	1.50	1.00	3.00	5.00
☐ 122	1.50	1.00	3.00	5.00
☐ 123	1.50	1.00	3.00	5.00
☐ 124	1.50	1.00	3.00	5.00
☐ 125	1.50	1.00	3.00	5.00
☐ 126	1.50	1.00	3.00	5.00
☐ 127	1.50	1.00	3.00	5.00
☐ 128	1.50	1.00	3.00	5.00
☐ 129	1.50	1.00	3.00	5.00
☐ 130	1.50	1.00	3.00	5.00
☐ 131	1.50	1.00	3.00	5.00
☐ 132	1.50	1.00	3.00	5.00
☐ 133	1.50	1.00	3.00	5.00
☐ 134	1.50	1.00	3.00	5.00
☐ 135	2.00	1.00	3.00	5.00
☐ 136	2.00	1.00	3.00	5.00
☐ 137	2.00	1.00	3.00	5.00
☐ 138	2.00	1.00	3.00	5.00
☐ 139	2.00	1.00	3.00	5.00
☐ 140	2.00	1.00	3.00	5.00
☐ 141	2.00	1.00	3.00	5.00
☐ 142	2.00	1.00	3.00	5.00
☐ 143	2.00	1.00	3.00	5.00
☐ 144	2.00	1.00	3.00	5.00
☐ 145	2.00	1.00	3.00	5.00
☐ 146	2.00	1.00	3.00	5.00
☐ 147	2.00	1.00	3.00	5.00
☐ 148	2.00	1.00	3.00	5.00
☐ 149	2.00	1.00	3.00	5.00
☐ 150	2.00	1.00	3.00	5.00
☐ 151	2.00	0.80	2.40	4.00
☐ 152	2.00	0.80	2.40	4.00
☐ 153	2.00	0.80	2.40	4.00
☐ 154	2.00	0.80	2.40	4.00
☐ 155	2.00	0.80	2.40	4.00
☐ 156	2.00	0.80	2.40	4.00
☐ 157	2.00	0.80	2.40	4.00
☐ 158	2.00	0.80	2.40	4.00
☐ 159	2.00	0.80	2.40	4.00
☐ 160	2.00	0.80	2.40	4.00
☐ 161	2.00	0.80	2.40	4.00
☐ 162	2.00	0.80	2.40	4.00
☐ 163	2.00	0.80	2.40	4.00
☐ 164	2.25	0.80	2.40	4.00
☐ 165	2.25	0.80	2.40	4.00
☐ 166	2.25	0.80	2.40	4.00
☐ 167	2.25	0.80	2.40	4.00

	ORIG.	GOOD	FINE	N-MINT
☐ 168	2.25	0.80	2.40	4.00
☐ 169	2.25	0.80	2.40	4.00
☐ 170	2.25	0.80	2.40	4.00
☐ 171	2.25	0.80	2.40	4.00
☐ 172	2.25	0.80	2.40	4.00
☐ 173	2.25	0.80	2.40	4.00
☐ 174, (becomes *Savage Sword of Conan the Barbarian, The*)	2.25	0.80	2.40	4.00

SAVAGE SWORD OF MIKE
FANDOM HOUSE

	ORIG.	GOOD	FINE	N-MINT
☐ 1, b&w		0.40	1.20	2.00

SAVAGE TALES (1971-1974)
MARVEL

	ORIG.	GOOD	FINE	N-MINT
☐ 1, May 71, BWS, JR, GM b&w mag; Conan, 1&O:Man-Thing	0.50	18.00	54.00	90.00
☐ 2, Oct 73, BWS, AW, FB, GM, BWr	0.75	7.20	21.60	36.00
☐ 3, Feb 74, AW, BWS, JSt, FB	0.75	4.00	12.00	20.00
☐ 4, May 74, NA, GK	0.75	1.60	4.80	8.00
☐ 5, Jul 74, NA, GK	0.75	1.60	4.80	8.00
☐ 6, Sep 74	0.75	0.60	1.80	3.00
☐ 7, Nov 74	0.75	0.60	1.80	3.00
☐ 8, Jan 75	1.00	0.60	1.80	3.00
☐ 9, Mar 75	1.00	0.60	1.80	3.00
☐ 10, May 75	1.00	0.60	1.80	3.00
☐ 11, Jul 75	1.00	0.60	1.80	3.00
☐ 12, Sum 75	1.25	0.60	1.80	3.00

SAVAGE TALES (2nd series)

	ORIG.	GOOD	FINE	N-MINT
☐ 1, Oct 85, b&w mag MG, 1:'Nam	1.50	1.50	4.50	7.50
☐ 2, Dec 85, JSe	1.50	0.30	0.90	1.50
☐ 3	1.50	0.30	0.90	1.50
☐ 4, 'Nam	1.50	0.60	1.80	3.00
☐ 5, Jun 96, JSe	1.50	0.30	0.90	1.50
☐ 6	1.50	0.30	0.90	1.50
☐ 7	1.50	0.30	0.90	1.50
☐ 8	1.50	0.30	0.90	1.50

SAVAGE TALES ANNUAL (1975)

	ORIG.	GOOD	FINE	N-MINT
☐ 1, b&w GK O:Ka-Zar	1.25	0.60	1.80	3.00

SAVAGES
COMAX

	ORIG.	GOOD	FINE	N-MINT
☐ 1, b&w		0.50	1.50	2.50

SAVED BY THE BELL
HARVEY

	ORIG.	GOOD	FINE	N-MINT
☐ 1		0.39	1.17	1.95
☐ 2		0.39	1.17	1.95
☐ 3		0.39	1.17	1.95
☐ 4		0.39	1.17	1.95
☐ 5		0.39	1.17	1.95

SAVIOUR
TRIDENT

	ORIG.	GOOD	FINE	N-MINT
☐ 1, b&w, adult		0.80	2.40	4.00
☐ 2, b&w, adult		0.50	1.50	2.50
☐ 3, b&w, adult		0.50	1.50	2.50
☐ 4, b&w, adult		0.50	1.50	2.50
☐ 5, b&w, adult		0.50	1.50	2.50

SB NINJA HIGH SCHOOL
ANTARCTIC

	ORIG.	GOOD	FINE	N-MINT
☐ 1, Aug 92, b&w	2.95	0.59	1.77	2.95
☐ 1, Aug 92, b&w	4.95	0.99	2.97	4.95
☐ 2, b&w	2.95	0.59	1.77	2.95
☐ 2, b&w;trading card	4.95	0.99	2.97	4.95
☐ 3, Sep 94, b&w	2.75	0.55	1.65	2.75
☐ 3, Sep 94, b&w;trading card	4.95	0.99	2.97	4.95
☐ 4, Feb 95, b&w	2.75	0.55	1.65	2.75
☐ 5, May 95, b&w	2.75	0.55	1.65	2.75
☐ 6, Aug 95, b&w	2.75	0.55	1.65	2.75
☐ 7, Nov 95, b&w	2.75	0.55	1.65	2.75

	ORIG.	GOOD	FINE	N-MINT

SB NINJA HIGH SCHOOL COLLECTION
☐ 0, Jan 94, Vol. 1 .... 6.95		1.39	4.17	6.95

SCAB
FANTACO
☐ 1, b&w		0.70	2.10	3.50
☐ 2, b&w		0.70	2.10	3.50

SCAN
ICONOGRAFIX
☐ 1, Matt Howarth, b&w.... 2.95		0.59	1.77	2.95
☐ 2, Matt Howarth, b&w.... 2.95		0.59	1.77	2.95

SCANDAL SHEET
ARRIBA
☐ 1, b&w		0.50	1.50	2.50

SCARAB
DC/VERTIGO
☐ 1 .... 1.95		0.39	1.17	1.95
☐ 2 .... 1.95		0.39	1.17	1.95
☐ 3 .... 1.95		0.39	1.17	1.95
☐ 4 .... 1.95		0.39	1.17	1.95
☐ 5 .... 1.95		0.39	1.17	1.95
☐ 6, Apr 94 .... 1.95		0.39	1.17	1.95
☐ 7, May 94 .... 1.95		0.39	1.17	1.95
☐ 8, Jun 94 .... 1.95		0.39	1.17	1.95

SCARAMOUCH
INNOVATION
☐ 1, b&w		0.45	1.35	2.25
☐ 2, b&w		0.45	1.35	2.25

SCARLET IN GASLIGHT
ETERNITY
☐ 1, b&w, Sherlock Holmes vs. Dracula				
....		0.80	2.40	4.00
☐ 2		0.60	1.80	3.00
☐ 3		0.60	1.80	3.00
☐ 4		0.60	1.80	3.00

SCARLET KISS: THE VAMPYRE
ALL AMERICAN
☐ 1, b&w		0.59	1.77	2.95

SCARLET SCORPION/DARK SHADE
AC
☐ 1, 95 .... 3.50		0.70	2.10	3.50
☐ 2, 95 .... 3.50		0.70	2.10	3.50

SCARLET SPIDER
MARVEL
☐ 1, Nov 95, "Virtual Mortality"Part 3 of 4				
.... 1.95		0.39	1.17	1.95
☐ 2, Dec 95, "Cyberwar" Part 3 of 4;concludes in				
Spectacular Scarlet Spider #2				
.... 1.95		0.39	1.17	1.95

SCARLET SPIDER UNLIMITED
☐ 1, Nov 95 .... 3.95		0.79	2.37	3.95

SCARLET WITCH
☐ 1 .... 1.75		0.35	1.05	1.75
☐ 2 .... 1.75		0.35	1.05	1.75
☐ 3 .... 1.75		0.35	1.05	1.75
☐ 4 .... 1.75		0.35	1.05	1.75

SCARLET ZOMBIE, THE
COMAX
☐ 1, b&w, adult		0.59	1.77	2.95

SCARLETT
DC
☐ 1		0.59	1.77	2.95
☐ 2		0.59	1.77	2.95
☐ 3 .... 1.75		0.35	1.05	1.75
☐ 4 .... 1.75		0.35	1.05	1.75
☐ 5 .... 1.75		0.35	1.05	1.75
☐ 6 .... 1.75		0.35	1.05	1.75
☐ 7 .... 1.75		0.35	1.05	1.75
☐ 8 .... 1.75		0.35	1.05	1.75

	ORIG.	GOOD	FINE	N-MINT
☐ 9 .... 1.75		0.35	1.05	1.75
☐ 10 .... 1.75		0.35	1.05	1.75
☐ 11 .... 1.75		0.35	1.05	1.75
☐ 12 .... 1.75		0.35	1.05	1.75
☐ 13 .... 1.75		0.35	1.05	1.75
☐ 14 .... 1.75		0.35	1.05	1.75

SCARY BOOK, THE
CALIBER
☐ 1, b&w 2.50		0.50	1.50	2.50
☐ 2, b&w 2.50		0.50	1.50	2.50

SCAVENGERS
FLEETWAY/QUALITY
☐ 1, Judge Dredd		0.25	0.75	1.25
☐ 2, Judge Dredd		0.25	0.75	1.25
☐ 3, Judge Dredd		0.25	0.75	1.25
☐ 3		0.25	0.75	1.25
☐ 4		0.25	0.75	1.25
☐ 5		0.25	0.75	1.25
☐ 6		0.30	0.90	1.50
☐ 7		0.30	0.90	1.50
☐ 8		0.30	0.90	1.50
☐ 9		0.30	0.90	1.50
☐ 10		0.30	0.90	1.50
☐ 11		0.30	0.90	1.50
☐ 12		0.30	0.90	1.50
☐ 13		0.30	0.90	1.50
☐ 14		0.30	0.90	1.50

TRIUMPHANT
☐ 0, Mar 94, 30,000-copy edition; giveaway				
....		0.50	1.50	2.50
☐ 0, Mar 94, 18,000-copy edition				
.... 2.50		0.50	1.50	2.50
☐ 0, Mar 94, 5000-copyedition				
.... 2.50		0.50	1.50	2.50
☐ 1, ashcan edition 2.50		1.00	3.00	5.00
☐ 1, Mar 94, reprint........... 2.50		1.00	3.00	5.00
☐ 3 .... 2.50		0.50	1.50	2.50
☐ 4 .... 2.50		0.50	1.50	2.50
☐ 5, Unleashed!; D:Jack Hanal				
.... 2.50		0.50	1.50	2.50
☐ 6, Unleashed! 2.50		0.50	1.50	2.50
☐ 7 .... 2.50		0.50	1.50	2.50
☐ 8 .... 2.50		0.50	1.50	2.50
☐ 9, Mar 94 .... 2.50		0.50	1.50	2.50
☐ 10, Apr 94 .... 2.50		0.50	1.50	2.50
☐ 11, May 94 .... 2.50		0.50	1.50	2.50

SCHIMIDAR PIN-UP BOOK
ETERNITY
☐ 1, color, unstapled		0.75	2.25	3.75

SCHIZO
ANTARCTIC
☐ 1, Dec 94, b&w;(becomes Fantagraphics title)				
.... 3.50		0.70	2.10	3.50

FANTAGRAPHICS
☐ 2, Jan 96, b&w 3.95		0.79	2.37	3.95

SCIENCE AFFAIR, A
ANTARCTIC
☐ 1, Mar 94, b&w 2.75		0.55	1.65	2.75
☐ 1, Mar 94, gold edition				
☐ 2, May 94, b&w 2.75		0.55	1.65	2.75

SCIENCE FICTION CLASSICS
DRAGON LADY
☐ 1, Twin Earths...............		1.19	3.57	5.95

SCIMIDAR
CFD
☐ 1, 95, b&w 2.95		0.59	1.77	2.95
☐ 3, 95 .... 2.75		0.55	1.65	2.75

ETERNITY
☐ 1, Jun 88, b&w 1.95		0.70	2.10	3.50
☐ 2, b&w		0.80	2.40	4.00

	ORIG.	GOOD	FINE	N-MINT
☐ 3, b&w		0.80	2.40	4.00
☐ 4, hot cover		0.80	2.40	4.00
☐ 4, mild cover		0.60	1.80	3.00

SCIMIDAR BOOK II

	ORIG.	GOOD	FINE	N-MINT
☐ 1, b&w adult, 1st printing		0.80	2.40	4.00
☐ 1, 2nd printing		0.45	1.35	2.25
☐ 2, b&w, adult		0.60	1.80	3.00
☐ 3, b&w, adult		0.60	1.80	3.00
☐ 4, b&w, adult		0.60	1.80	3.00

SCIMIDAR BOOK III

	ORIG.	GOOD	FINE	N-MINT
☐ 1, b&w, adult		0.60	1.80	3.00
☐ 1, 2nd printing		0.50	1.50	2.50
☐ 2, b&w, adult		0.50	1.50	2.50
☐ 3, b&w, adult		0.50	1.50	2.50
☐ 4, b&w, adult		0.50	1.50	2.50

SCIMIDAR BOOK IV: "WILD THING"

	ORIG.	GOOD	FINE	N-MINT
☐ 1, nude cover		0.50	1.50	2.50
☐ 1, clothed cover		0.50	1.50	2.50
☐ 2, b&w, adult		0.50	1.50	2.50
☐ 3, b&w, adult		0.50	1.50	2.50
☐ 4, b&w, adult		0.50	1.50	2.50

SCIMIDAR BOOK V: "LIVING COLOR"

	ORIG.	GOOD	FINE	N-MINT
☐ 1, adult, b&w, nude cover		0.50	1.50	2.50
☐ 1, adult, b&w, clothed cover		0.50	1.50	2.50
☐ 2, b&w, adult		0.50	1.50	2.50
☐ 3, b&w, adult		0.50	1.50	2.50
☐ 4, b&w, adult		0.50	1.50	2.50

SCOOBY-DOO
ARCHIE

	ORIG.	GOOD	FINE	N-MINT
☐ 1, Oct 95	1.50	0.30	0.90	1.50
☐ 2, Nov 95	1.50	0.30	0.90	1.50
☐ 3, Dec 95	1.50	0.30	0.90	1.50
☐ 4, Jan 96	1.50	0.30	0.90	1.50
☐ 5, Feb 96	1.50	0.30	0.90	1.50
☐ 6, Mar 96	1.50	0.30	0.90	1.50
☐ 7, Apr 96	1.50	0.30	0.90	1.50
☐ 8, May 96	1.50	0.30	0.90	1.50

HARVEY

	ORIG.	GOOD	FINE	N-MINT
☐ 1	1.25	0.25	0.75	1.25
☐ 2	1.25	0.25	0.75	1.25
☐ 3	1.25	0.25	0.75	1.25

SCOOBY-DOO BIG BOOK

	ORIG.	GOOD	FINE	N-MINT
☐ 1	1.95	0.39	1.17	1.95
☐ 2	1.95	0.39	1.17	1.95

SCOOBY-DOO GIANT SIZE

	ORIG.	GOOD	FINE	N-MINT
☐ 2	2.25	0.45	1.35	2.25

SCORCHED EARTH
TUNDRA

	ORIG.	GOOD	FINE	N-MINT
☐ 1		0.59	1.77	2.95
☐ 2		0.59	1.77	2.95
☐ 3		0.59	1.77	2.95

SCORCHY
FORBIDDEN FRUIT

	ORIG.	GOOD	FINE	N-MINT
☐ 1, adult, b&w		0.70	2.10	3.50

SCORE, THE
PIRANHA

	ORIG.	GOOD	FINE	N-MINT
☐ 1, adult		0.99	2.97	4.95
☐ 2, adult		0.99	2.97	4.95
☐ 3, adult		0.99	2.97	4.95
☐ 4, adult		0.99	2.97	4.95

SCORPIA
MILLER

	ORIG.	GOOD	FINE	N-MINT
☐ 1		0.50	1.50	2.50
☐ 2		0.50	1.50	2.50

SCORPIO RISING
MARVEL

	ORIG.	GOOD	FINE	N-MINT
☐ 0, Oct 94, prestige format one-shot				
	5.95	1.19	3.57	5.95

SCORPIO ROSE
ECLIPSE

	ORIG.	GOOD	FINE	N-MINT
☐ 1, Jan 83		0.40	1.20	2.00
☐ 2, Oct 83		0.40	1.20	2.00

SCORPION
ANNRUEL STUDIOS

	ORIG.	GOOD	FINE	N-MINT
☐ 1, b&w	2.50	0.50	1.50	2.50

SCORPION CORPS
DAGGER

	ORIG.	GOOD	FINE	N-MINT
☐ 3	2.50	0.50	1.50	2.50

SCORPION MOON
EXPRESS/ENTITY

☐ 0, Oct 94, nn,b&w, cardstock cover; 4th in a series of Entity illustrated novellas with Zen Intergalactic Ninja

	ORIG.	GOOD	FINE	N-MINT
	2.95	0.59	1.77	2.95

SCORPION, THE
ATLAS/SEABOARD

	ORIG.	GOOD	FINE	N-MINT
☐ 1, Feb 75, HC(c)	0.25	0.50	1.50	2.50
☐ 2, Apr 75, MK,BWr,WS	0.25	0.40	1.20	2.00
☐ 3, Jul 75	0.25	0.20	0.60	1.00

SCOUT
ECLIPSE

	ORIG.	GOOD	FINE	N-MINT
☐ 1		0.80	2.40	4.00
☐ 2		0.60	1.80	3.00
☐ 3		0.60	1.80	3.00
☐ 4		0.60	1.80	3.00
☐ 5		0.60	1.80	3.00
☐ 6		0.60	1.80	3.00
☐ 7		0.60	1.80	3.00
☐ 8		0.50	1.50	2.50
☐ 9		0.50	1.50	2.50
☐ 10		0.50	1.50	2.50
☐ 11		0.50	1.50	2.50
☐ 12		0.50	1.50	2.50
☐ 13		0.50	1.50	2.50
☐ 14		0.50	1.50	2.50
☐ 15		0.50	1.50	2.50
☐ 16, 3-D		0.50	1.50	2.50
☐ 17		0.50	1.50	2.50
☐ 18		0.50	1.50	2.50
☐ 19, flexidisc		0.60	1.80	3.00
☐ 20		0.40	1.20	2.00
☐ 21		0.40	1.20	2.00
☐ 22		0.40	1.20	2.00
☐ 23		0.40	1.20	2.00
☐ 24		0.40	1.20	2.00

SCOUT HANDBOOK

	ORIG.	GOOD	FINE	N-MINT
☐ 0, nn		0.35	1.05	1.75

SCOUT: WAR SHAMAN

	ORIG.	GOOD	FINE	N-MINT
☐ 1		0.50	1.50	2.50
☐ 2		0.50	1.50	2.50
☐ 3		0.50	1.50	2.50
☐ 4		0.50	1.50	2.50
☐ 5		0.50	1.50	2.50
☐ 6		0.50	1.50	2.50
☐ 7		0.50	1.50	2.50
☐ 8		0.50	1.50	2.50
☐ 9		0.50	1.50	2.50
☐ 10		0.50	1.50	2.50
☐ 11		0.50	1.50	2.50
☐ 12		0.50	1.50	2.50
☐ 13		0.50	1.50	2.50
☐ 14		0.50	1.50	2.50
☐ 15		0.50	1.50	2.50
☐ 16, D:Scout		0.50	1.50	2.50

SCRAP CITY PACK RATS
OUT OF THE BLUE

	ORIG.	GOOD	FINE	N-MINT
☐ 1, 91, b&w;"Lightning Strikes"				
	1.50	0.30	0.90	1.50
☐ 2, b&w	1.50	0.30	0.90	1.50

	ORIG.	GOOD	FINE	N-MINT
❏ 3, b&w 1.50		0.30	0.90	1.50
❏ 4, b&w 1.75		0.35	1.05	1.75
❏ 5, 93, b&w;"Clam on the Lam"				
.... 1.75		0.35	1.05	1.75

SCRATCH
OUTSIDE

		GOOD	FINE	N-MINT
❏ 1		0.35	1.05	1.75
❏ 2		0.35	1.05	1.75
❏ 3		0.35	1.05	1.75
❏ 4		0.35	1.05	1.75
❏ 5		0.35	1.05	1.75
❏ 6		0.35	1.05	1.75

SCREENPLAY
SLAVE LABOR

		GOOD	FINE	N-MINT
❏ 1, b&w		0.35	1.05	1.75

SCREW COMICS
EROS

		GOOD	FINE	N-MINT
❏ 1, adult, b&w		0.70	2.10	3.50

SCREWBALL SQUIRREL (mini-series)
DARK HORSE

		GOOD	FINE	N-MINT
❏ 1, Jul 95, Wolf & Redback-up				
.... 2.50		0.50	1.50	2.50
❏ 2, Aug 95, Droopy back-up				
.... 2.50		0.50	1.50	2.50
❏ 3, Sep 95, final issue; Wolf & Red back-up				
.... 2.50		0.50	1.50	2.50

SCUD: THE DISPOSABLE ASSASSIN
FIREMAN PRESS

		GOOD	FINE	N-MINT
❏ 1, Feb 94, b&w 2.95		1.60	4.80	8.00
❏ 2, May 94, b&w 2.95		1.00	3.00	5.00
❏ 3, b&w 2.95		1.00	3.00	5.00
❏ 4, b&w 2.95		0.80	2.40	4.00
❏ 5, b&w 2.95		0.80	2.40	4.00

SCUM OF THE EARTH
AIRCEL

		GOOD	FINE	N-MINT
❏ 1, b&w, movie		0.50	1.50	2.50
❏ 2, b&w, movie		0.50	1.50	2.50

SEA DEVILS
DC

		GOOD	FINE	N-MINT
❏ 1, Oct 61 .... 0.10		80.00	240.00	400.00
❏ 2, Dec 61 .... 0.10		44.00	132.00	220.00
❏ 3, Feb 62 .... 0.12		30.00	90.00	150.00
❏ 4, Apr 62 .... 0.12		18.00	54.00	90.00
❏ 5, Jun 62 .... 0.12		18.00	54.00	90.00
❏ 6, Aug 62 .... 0.12		15.00	45.00	75.00
❏ 7, Oct 62 .... 0.12		15.00	45.00	75.00
❏ 8, Dec 62 .... 0.12		15.00	45.00	75.00
❏ 9, Feb 63 .... 0.12		15.00	45.00	75.00
❏ 10, Apr 63 .... 0.12		15.00	45.00	75.00
❏ 11 .... 0.12		7.60	22.80	38.00
❏ 12 .... 0.12		7.60	22.80	38.00
❏ 13 .... 0.12		7.60	22.80	38.00
❏ 14 .... 0.12		7.60	22.80	38.00
❏ 15 .... 0.12		7.60	22.80	38.00
❏ 16 .... 0.12		7.60	22.80	38.00
❏ 17 .... 0.12		7.60	22.80	38.00
❏ 18, Jul 64 .... 0.12		7.60	22.80	38.00
❏ 19 .... 0.12		7.60	22.80	38.00
❏ 20 .... 0.12		7.60	22.80	38.00
❏ 21 .... 0.12		4.80	14.40	24.00
❏ 22 .... 0.12		4.80	14.40	24.00
❏ 23 .... 0.12		4.80	14.40	24.00
❏ 24 .... 0.12		4.80	14.40	24.00
❏ 25 .... 0.12		4.80	14.40	24.00
❏ 26 .... 0.12		4.80	14.40	24.00
❏ 27 .... 0.12		4.80	14.40	24.00
❏ 28 .... 0.12		4.80	14.40	24.00
❏ 29 .... 0.12		4.80	14.40	24.00
❏ 30 .... 0.12		4.80	14.40	24.00
❏ 31 .... 0.12		4.80	14.40	24.00

	ORIG.	GOOD	FINE	N-MINT
❏ 32 .... 0.12		4.80	14.40	24.00
❏ 33 .... 0.12		4.80	14.40	24.00
❏ 34 .... 0.12		4.80	14.40	24.00
❏ 35 .... 0.12		4.80	14.40	24.00

SEADRAGON
ELITE

		GOOD	FINE	N-MINT
❏ 1, May 86		0.35	1.05	1.75
❏ 2, Jun 86		0.35	1.05	1.75
❏ 3, Aug 86		0.35	1.05	1.75
❏ 4		0.35	1.05	1.75
❏ 5		0.35	1.05	1.75
❏ 6		0.35	1.05	1.75

SEAQUEST DSV
NEMESIS

		GOOD	FINE	N-MINT
❏ 1, TV show 2.25		0.45	1.35	2.25

SEBASTIAN
DISNEY

		GOOD	FINE	N-MINT
❏ 1		0.30	0.90	1.50
❏ 2		0.30	0.90	1.50

SEBASTIAN O
DC/VERTIGO

		GOOD	FINE	N-MINT
❏ 1 .... 1.95		0.39	1.17	1.95
❏ 2 .... 1.95		0.39	1.17	1.95
❏ 3 .... 1.95		0.39	1.17	1.95

SECOND CITY
HARRIER

		GOOD	FINE	N-MINT
❏ 1		0.39	1.17	1.95
❏ 2		0.39	1.17	1.95
❏ 3		0.39	1.17	1.95
❏ 4		0.39	1.17	1.95

SECOND LIFE OF DOCTOR MIRAGE, THE
VALIANT

		GOOD	FINE	N-MINT
❏ 1 .... 2.50		0.80	2.40	4.00
❏ 1, gold edition		0.60	1.80	3.00
❏ 2, Dec 93 .... 2.50		0.60	1.80	3.00
❏ 3, 94 .... 2.50		0.60	1.80	3.00
❏ 4, Feb 94 .... 2.50		0.60	1.80	3.00
❏ 5, Mar 94 .... 2.50		0.60	1.80	3.00
❏ 6, Apr 94 .... 2.50		0.50	1.50	2.50
❏ 7, May 94 .... 2.50		0.50	1.50	2.50
❏ 8, Jun 94 .... 2.50		0.50	1.50	2.50
❏ 9, Aug 94 .... 2.50		0.50	1.50	2.50
❏ 10, Sep 94 .... 2.50		0.50	1.50	2.50
❏ 11, Oct 94 .... 2.50		0.50	1.50	2.50
❏ 13, Dec 94 .... 2.50		0.50	1.50	2.50
❏ 17, Apr 95, Building the Perfect Beast pt. 2				
.... 2.50		0.50	1.50	2.50
❏ 18, May 95, Building the Perfect Beast pt. 3 of 3				
.... 2.50		0.50	1.50	2.50

SECRET AGENTS
PERSONALITY

		GOOD	FINE	N-MINT
❏ 1, b&w		0.59	1.77	2.95
❏ 2, b&w		0.59	1.77	2.95
❏ 3, b&w		0.59	1.77	2.95

SECRET DEFENDERS, THE
MARVEL

		GOOD	FINE	N-MINT
❏ 1, foil cover 2.50		0.50	1.50	2.50
❏ 2 .... 1.75		0.35	1.05	1.75
❏ 3 .... 1.75		0.35	1.05	1.75
❏ 4 .... 1.75		0.35	1.05	1.75
❏ 5 .... 1.75		0.35	1.05	1.75
❏ 6 .... 1.75		0.35	1.05	1.75
❏ 7 .... 1.75		0.35	1.05	1.75
❏ 8 .... 1.75		0.35	1.05	1.75
❏ 9 .... 1.75		0.35	1.05	1.75
❏ 10 .... 1.75		0.35	1.05	1.75
❏ 11 .... 1.75		0.35	1.05	1.75
❏ 12, foil cover 2.50		0.50	1.50	2.50
❏ 13 .... 1.75		0.35	1.05	1.75
❏ 14, Apr 94 .... 1.75		0.35	1.05	1.75

	ORIG.	GOOD	FINE	N-MINT
15, May 94 ....1.95	0.39	1.17	1.95
16, Jun 94 ....1.95	0.39	1.17	1.95
17, Jul 94 ....1.95	0.39	1.17	1.95
18, Aug 94 ....1.95	0.39	1.17	1.95
19, Sep 94 ....1.95	0.39	1.17	1.95
20, Oct 94 ....1.95	0.39	1.17	1.95
21, Nov 94 ....1.95	0.39	1.17	1.95
22, Dec 94......................1.95	0.39	1.17	1.95
23, Jan 95 ....1.95	0.39	1.17	1.95
24, Feb 95 ....1.95	0.39	1.17	1.95
25, Mar 95, final issue ... 1.95	0.39	1.17	1.95

SECRET DOORS
DIMENSION

		GOOD	FINE	N-MINT
1, b&w		0.30	0.90	1.50

SECRET ORIGINS (1973 series)
DC

	ORIG.	GOOD	FINE	N-MINT
1, Mar 73 ....0.20	2.00	6.00	10.00
2, May 73 ....0.20	1.00	3.00	5.00
3, Aug 73 ....0.20	1.00	3.00	5.00
4, Oct 73 ....0.20	1.00	3.00	5.00
5, Dec 73......................0.20	1.00	3.00	5.00
6, Feb 74 ....0.20	1.00	3.00	5.00
7, Oct 74 ....0.20	1.00	3.00	5.00

SECRET ORIGINS (1986-)

	ORIG.	GOOD	FINE	N-MINT
1, Apr 86 ....0.75	0.60	1.80	3.00
2, May 86 ....0.75	0.30	0.90	1.50
3, Jun 86 ....0.75	0.30	0.90	1.50
4, Jul 86 ....0.75	0.30	0.90	1.50
5, Aug 86 ....0.75	0.30	0.90	1.50
6, Sep 86, O: GoldenAge Batman				
......................1.25	1.00	3.00	5.00
7, Oct 86 ....1.25	0.30	0.90	1.50
8, Nov 86 ....1.25	0.30	0.90	1.50
9, Dec 86......................1.25	0.30	0.90	1.50
10, Jan 87, Legends.......1.25	0.30	0.90	1.50
11, Feb 87, JOy(c)..........1.25	0.25	0.75	1.25
12, Mar 87 ....1.25	0.25	0.75	1.25
13, Apr 87 ....1.25	0.25	0.75	1.25
14, May 87, Legends......1.25	0.25	0.75	1.25
15, Jun 87 ....1.25	0.25	0.75	1.25
16, Jul 87 ....1.25	0.25	0.75	1.25
17, Aug 87 ....1.25	0.25	0.75	1.25
18, Sep 87......................1.25	0.25	0.75	1.25
19, Oct 87, JK(c),MA .. 1.25	0.25	0.75	1.25
20, Nov 87, O:Batgirl, Dr. Mid-Nite				
......................1.25	0.25	0.75	1.25
21, Dec 87, O:Jonah Hex, Black Condor				
......................1.25	0.25	0.75	1.25
22, Jan 88, Millennium,O:Manhunters				
......................1.25	0.25	0.75	1.25
23, Feb 88, Millennium, O:Guardians, Floronic Man				
......................1.25	0.25	0.75	1.25
24, Mar 88, O:Dr. Fate, Blue Devil				
......................1.25	0.25	0.75	1.25
25, Apr 88, O:Legion, Atom				
......................1.25	0.25	0.75	1.25
26, May 88, O:Black Lightning, Miss America				
......................1.25	0.25	0.75	1.25
27, Jun 88, O:Zatara, Zatanna				
......................1.50	0.25	0.75	1.25
28, Jul 88, O:Midnight, Nightshade				
......................1.50	0.30	0.90	1.50
29, Aug 88, O:Atom, Mr. America, Red Tornado				
......................1.50	0.30	0.90	1.50
30, Sep 88, O:Elongated Man, Plastic Man				
......................1.50	0.30	0.90	1.50
31, Oct 88, O:JSA.......... 1.50	0.30	0.90	1.50
32, Nov 88, O:JLA.......... 1.50	0.60	1.80	3.00
33, Dec 88, O: Mr. Miracle, Green Flame, Icemaiden				
......................1.50	0.30	0.90	1.50

	ORIG.	GOOD	FINE	N-MINT
34, Dec 88, O:Captain Atom, Rocket Red, G'nort				
......................1.50	0.30	0.90	1.50
35, Jan 89, O:Booster Gold, Martian Manhunter, Maxwell Lord......................1.50	0.30	0.90	1.50
36, Jan 89, O:Green Lantern, Poison Ivy				
......................1.50	0.50	1.50	2.50
37, Feb 89, O:Legion of Substitute Heroes, Dr. Light				
......................1.50	0.30	0.90	1.50
38, Mar 89, O:Green Arrow, Speedy				
......................1.50	0.30	0.90	1.50
39, Apr 89, O:Animal Man, Man-Bat				
......................1.50	0.80	2.40	4.00
40, May 89, O:Gorilla Grodd, Congorilla, Det. Chimp				
......................1.50	0.30	0.90	1.50
41, Jun 89, O:Flash villains				
......................1.50	0.60	1.80	3.00
42, Jul 89, O:Phantom Girl, Grim Ghost				
......................1.50	0.30	0.90	1.50
43, Aug 89, O:Hawk, Dove, Cave Carson, Chris KL-99				
......................1.50	0.30	0.90	1.50
44, Sep 89, O:Clayfaces..1.50	1.00	3.00	5.00
45, Oct 89, O:Blackhawk, El Diablo				
......................1.50	0.30	0.90	1.50
46, Dec 89, O: JLA, Titans, LSH HQs				
......................1.75	0.25	0.75	1.25
47, Feb 90, O:Chemical King, Ferro Lad, Karate Kid				
......................1.75	0.35	1.05	1.75
48, Apr 90, O:Ambush Bug, Rex, Trigger Twins, Stanley & Monster....1.75	0.35	1.05	1.75
49, Jun 90, O:Newsboy Legion, Silent Knight, Bouncing Boy 1.75	0.35	1.05	1.75
50, Aug 90, Final issue O:Robin-1, Earth-2, Johnny Thunder (cowboy), Dolphin, Black Canary, Space Museum 3.95	0.79	2.37	3.95

SECRET ORIGINS ANNUAL

	ORIG.	GOOD	FINE	N-MINT
1, 87, JBy(c) O:Doom Patrol				
......................2.00	0.60	1.80	3.00
2, 88, O:Flash.................2.00	0.40	1.20	2.00
3, 89, O:Teen Titans........2.95	0.59	1.77	2.95

SECRET ORIGINS SPECIAL

	ORIG.	GOOD	FINE	N-MINT
1, Oct 89, O:Penguin, Riddler, Two-Face				
......................2.00	1.00	3.00	5.00

SECRET SOCIETY OF SUPER-VILLAINS

	ORIG.	GOOD	FINE	N-MINT
1, Jun 76 ....0.30	0.60	1.80	3.00
2, Aug 76 ....0.30	0.30	0.90	1.50
3, Oct 76 ....0.30	0.30	0.90	1.50
4, Dec 76 ....0.30	0.30	0.90	1.50
5, Feb 77 ....0.30	0.30	0.90	1.50
6, Apr 77 ....0.30	0.30	0.90	1.50
7, Jun 77 ....0.30	0.30	0.90	1.50
8, Aug 77 ....0.35	0.30	0.90	1.50
9, Sep 77 ....0.35	0.30	0.90	1.50
10, Oct 77 ....0.35	0.30	0.90	1.50
11, Dec 77 ....0.35	0.25	0.75	1.25
12, Jan 78......................0.35	0.25	0.75	1.25
13, Mar 78......................0.35	0.25	0.75	1.25
14, May 78......................0.35	0.25	0.75	1.25
15, Jul 78......................0.35	0.25	0.75	1.25

SECRET WARS II
MARVEL

	ORIG.	GOOD	FINE	N-MINT
1, Jul 85, A:X-Men, New Mutants				
......................0.75	0.40	1.20	2.00
2, Aug 85 ....0.75	0.30	0.90	1.50
3, Sep 85 ....0.75	0.30	0.90	1.50
4, Oct 85......................0.75	0.30	0.90	1.50
5, Nov 85 ....0.75	0.30	0.90	1.50
6, Dec 85 ....0.75	0.30	0.90	1.50
7, Jan 86......................0.75	0.30	0.90	1.50
8, Feb 86......................0.75	0.30	0.90	1.50
9, Mar 86, double size 1.25	0.40	1.20	2.00

	ORIG.	GOOD	FINE	N-MINT

SECRET WEAPONS
VALIANT

	ORIG.	GOOD	FINE	N-MINT
1	2.25	0.45	1.35	2.25
2	2.25	0.45	1.35	2.25
3	2.25	0.45	1.35	2.25
4	2.25	0.45	1.35	2.25
5	2.25	0.45	1.35	2.25
1, gold edition	2.00	6.00	10.00	
6, Feb 94	2.25	0.45	1.35	2.25
7, Mar 94	2.25	0.45	1.35	2.25
8, Apr 94	2.25	0.45	1.35	2.25
9, May 94	2.25	0.45	1.35	2.25
10, Jun 94	2.25	0.45	1.35	2.25
11, Aug 94, A:Bloodshot;bagged "top secret"	2.50	0.50	1.50	2.50
12, Sep 94, A:Bloodshot	2.25	0.45	1.35	2.25
13, Oct 94, Chaos Effect	2.25	0.45	1.35	2.25
14, Nov 94	2.25	0.45	1.35	2.25
20, May 95, Rampagept. 2 of 5 (see *Bloodshot* #28)	2.25	0.45	1.35	2.25
21, May 95, Rampagept. 4 of 5	2.25	0.45	1.35	2.25

SECRETS OF DRAWING COMICS
SHOWCASE

	GOOD	FINE	N-MINT
1	0.39	1.17	1.95
2	0.39	1.17	1.95
3	0.39	1.17	1.95
4	0.39	1.17	1.95

SECRETS OF THE LEGION OF SUPER-HEROES
(mini-series)
DC

	ORIG.	GOOD	FINE	N-MINT
1, Jan 81, ro:Legion andits members	0.50	0.20	0.60	1.00
2, Feb 81, ro:Legion andits members	0.50	0.20	0.60	1.00
3, Mar 81, ro:Legion and its members and LegionSubs; final issue	0.50	0.20	0.60	1.00

SECRETS OF THE VALIANT UNIVERSE
VALIANT

	ORIG.	GOOD	FINE	N-MINT
1, May 94, no price listed.				
2, Oct 94, Chaos Effect	2.25	0.45	1.35	2.25

SECRETUM SECRETORUM
TWILIGHT TWINS

	ORIG.	GOOD	FINE	N-MINT
0, Jan 95, b&w	3.50	0.70	2.10	3.50

SECTAURS
MARVEL

	ORIG.	GOOD	FINE	N-MINT
1	0.75	0.30	0.90	1.50
2	0.75	0.25	0.75	1.25
3	0.75	0.20	0.60	1.00
4	0.75	0.20	0.60	1.00
5	0.75	0.20	0.60	1.00
6	0.75	0.20	0.60	1.00
7	0.75	0.20	0.60	1.00
8	0.75	0.20	0.60	1.00

SEDUCTION
ETERNITY

	ORIG.	GOOD	FINE	N-MINT
1, b&w	0.50	1.50	2.50	

SEDUCTION OF THE INNOCENT!
ECLIPSE

	ORIG.	GOOD	FINE	N-MINT
1, ATh,TY,RC	1.75	0.60	1.80	3.00
2, ATh,RMo,MA	1.75	0.35	1.05	1.75
3, ATh	1.75	0.35	1.05	1.75
4, ATh,NC	1.75	0.35	1.05	1.75
5, ATh,TY	1.75	0.35	1.05	1.75
6	1.75	0.35	1.05	1.75

SEDUCTION OF THE INNOCENT! 3-D
	ORIG.	GOOD	FINE	N-MINT
1, DSt(c)	2.25	1.00	3.00	5.00
2, BWr(c),MB,NC,ATh	2.25	0.45	1.35	2.25

SEEKER VENGEANCE
SKY

	ORIG.	GOOD	FINE	N-MINT
1	2.50	0.50	1.50	2.50

SEEKERS INTO THE MYSTERY
DC/VERTIGO

	ORIG.	GOOD	FINE	N-MINT
1, Jan 96	2.50	0.50	1.50	2.50
2, Feb 96	2.50	0.50	1.50	2.50
3, Mar 96	2.50	0.50	1.50	2.50
4, Apr 96	2.50	0.50	1.50	2.50
5, Jun 96	2.50	0.50	1.50	2.50
6, Jul 96	2.50	0.50	1.50	2.50

SEMPER FI'
MARVEL

	ORIG.	GOOD	FINE	N-MINT
1, Dec 88, JSe	0.75	0.20	0.60	1.00
2, Jan 89, JSe	0.75	0.20	0.60	1.00
3, Feb 89, JSe	0.75	0.20	0.60	1.00
4, Mar 89, JSe	0.75	0.20	0.60	1.00
5, Apr 89, JSe	0.75	0.20	0.60	1.00
6, May 89, JSe	0.75	0.20	0.60	1.00
7, Jun 89, JSe	0.75	0.20	0.60	1.00
8, Jul 89, JSe	0.75	0.20	0.60	1.00
9, Aug 89, JSe	0.75	0.20	0.60	1.00

SENSATIONAL SHE-HULK

	ORIG.	GOOD	FINE	N-MINT
1, May 89, JBy	1.50	0.60	1.80	3.00
2, Jun 89, JBy	1.50	0.50	1.50	2.50
3, Jul 89, JBy	1.50	0.50	1.50	2.50
4, Aug 89, JBy A:Blonde Phantom	1.50	0.40	1.20	2.00
5, Sep 89, JBy	1.50	0.40	1.20	2.00
6, Oct 89, JBy	1.50	0.40	1.20	2.00
7, Nov 89, JBy	1.50	0.40	1.20	2.00
8, Nov 89, JBy	1.50	0.40	1.20	2.00
9, Dec 89	1.50	0.30	0.90	1.50
10, Dec 89	1.50	0.30	0.90	1.50
11, Jan 90	1.50	0.30	0.90	1.50
12, Feb 90	1.50	0.30	0.90	1.50
13, Mar 90	1.50	0.30	0.90	1.50
14, Apr 90	1.50	0.30	0.90	1.50
15, May 90	1.50	0.30	0.90	1.50
16, Jun 90	1.50	0.30	0.90	1.50
17, Jul 90	1.50	0.30	0.90	1.50
18, Aug 90	1.50	0.30	0.90	1.50
19, Sep 90	1.50	0.30	0.90	1.50
20, Oct 90	1.50	0.30	0.90	1.50
21, Nov 90, Blonde Phantom	1.50	0.30	0.90	1.50
22, Dec 90, Blonde Phantom	1.50	0.30	0.90	1.50
23, Jan 91, Blonde Phantom	1.50	0.30	0.90	1.50
24, Feb 91, Death's Head	1.50	0.30	0.90	1.50
25, Mar 91, Hercules	1.50	0.30	0.90	1.50
26, Apr 91	1.50	0.30	0.90	1.50
27, May 91,white inside covers	1.50	0.30	0.90	1.50
28, Jun 91	1.50	0.30	0.90	1.50
29, Jul 91	1.50	0.30	0.90	1.50
30, Aug 91	1.50	0.30	0.90	1.50
31, Sep 91, JBy	1.50	0.30	0.90	1.50
32, Oct 91, JBy	1.50	0.30	0.90	1.50
33, Nov 91, JBy	1.50	0.30	0.90	1.50
34, Dec 91, JBy	1.50	0:30	0.90	1.50
35, JBy	1.50	0.30	0.90	1.50
36, JBy	1.75	0.35	1.05	1.75
37, JBy	1.75	0.35	1.05	1.75
38, JBy	1.75	0.35	1.05	1.75
39, JBy	1.75	0.35	1.05	1.75
40, JBy	1.75	0.35	1.05	1.75
41, JBy	1.75	0.35	1.05	1.75
43	1.75	0.35	1.05	1.75
44, JBy	1.75	0.35	1.05	1.75

	ORIG.	GOOD	FINE	N-MINT
❏ 45 ....1.75		0.35	1.05	1.75
❏ 46 ....1.75		0.35	1.05	1.75
❏ 47 ....1.75		0.35	1.05	1.75
❏ 48, JBy 1.75		0.35	1.05	1.75
❏ 49 ....1.75		0.35	1.05	1.75
❏ 50, JBy,DG,FM,WS,TA,WP,HC, foil cover				
.................................2.95		0.59	1.77	2.95
❏ 51 ....1.75		0.35	1.05	1.75
❏ 52 ....1.75		0.35	1.05	1.75
❏ 53 ....1.75		0.35	1.05	1.75
❏ 54 ....1.75		0.35	1.05	1.75
❏ 55 ....1.75		0.35	1.05	1.75
❏ 56 ....1.75		0.35	1.05	1.75
❏ 57 ....1.75		0.35	1.05	1.75
❏ 58 ....1.75		0.35	1.05	1.75
❏ 59 ....1.75		0.35	1.05	1.75
❏ 60 ....1.75		0.35	1.05	1.75

SENSATIONAL SPIDER-MAN

❏ 0, Jan 96, enhanced wraparoundcardstock cover with lenticularanimation card attached;new costume

....................................4.95		0.99	2.97	4.95

❏ 1, Feb 96, "Media Blizzard" Part 1 of 3

....................................1.95		0.39	1.17	1.95

❏ 3, Apr 96, "Web of Carnage" Part 1 of 4

....................................1.95		0.39	1.17	1.95

❏ 4, May 96, "Blood Brothers" Part 1 of 6;Ben Reilly revealed as Spider-Man . 1.95 0.39 1.17 1.95

❏ 5, Jun 96, "Blood Brothers"Part 5 of 6;V:Molten Man

....................................1.95		0.39	1.17	1.95

SENSEI
FIRST

	GOOD	FINE	N-MINT
❏ 1, Aug 89	0.55	1.65	2.75
❏ 2, 89.................................	0.55	1.65	2.75
❏ 3, 89.................................	0.55	1.65	2.75
❏ 4, Dec 89...........................	0.55	1.65	2.75

SENTAI
ANTARCTIC

	ORIG.	GOOD	FINE	N-MINT
❏ 1, Feb 94, b&w 2.95		0.59	1.77	2.95
❏ 2, Apr 94, b&w 2.95		0.59	1.77	2.95
❏ 3, Jul 94, b&w 2.95		0.59	1.77	2.95
❏ 4, Sep 94, b&w 2.95		0.59	1.77	2.95
❏ 5, Nov 94 ....3.95		0.79	2.37	3.95
❏ 6, Feb 95, b&w 2.95		0.59	1.77	2.95
❏ 7, Apr 95, b&w 2.95		0.59	1.77	2.95

SENTINEL
HARRIER

	GOOD	FINE	N-MINT
❏ 1	0.39	1.17	1.95
❏ 2	0.39	1.17	1.95
❏ 3	0.39	1.17	1.95
❏ 4	0.39	1.17	1.95

SENTINELS OF JUSTICE (1994-)
AC

❏ 1, DAy;Avenger ....
❏ 2, Jet Girl ....
❏ 3, Yankee Girl..................

SENTINELS OF JUSTICE
(formerly Captain Paragon
and the Sentinels of Justice)

	GOOD	FINE	N-MINT
❏ 5, 87, O:Capt. Paragon	0.30	0.90	1.50
❏ 6, 87................................	0.30	0.90	1.50

SENTINELS OF JUSTICE COMPACT

	ORIG.	GOOD	FINE	N-MINT
❏ 1 ....3.95		0.79	2.37	3.95
❏ 2 ....3.95		0.79	2.37	3.95
❏ 3 ....3.95		0.79	2.37	3.95

SENTRY SPECIAL
INNOVATION

	GOOD	FINE	N-MINT
❏ 1, Jun 91...........................	0.55	1.65	2.75

SERAPHIM

	GOOD	FINE	N-MINT
❏ 1	0.50	1.50	2.50

SERGIO ARAGONES DESTROYS DC
DC

	ORIG.	GOOD	FINE	N-MINT
❏ 1, Jun 96, one-shot 3.50		0.70	2.10	3.50

SERGIO ARAGONES GROO
IMAGE

	ORIG.	GOOD	FINE	N-MINT
❏ 1, Dec 94, SA 1.95		0.39	1.17	1.95
❏ 2, Jan 95, SA,indicia says issue #1				
..................................1.95		0.39	1.17	1.95
❏ 3, Feb 95, SA 1.95		0.39	1.17	1.95
❏ 4, Mar 95, SA 1.95		0.39	1.17	1.95
❏ 5, Apr 95, SA 1.95		0.39	1.17	1.95
❏ 6, May 95, SA 1.95		0.39	1.17	1.95
❏ 9, Aug 95 ....2.25		0.45	1.35	2.25
❏ 10, Sep 95 ....2.25		0.45	1.35	2.25

SERGIO ARAGONES' GROO THE WANDERER
EPIC

	ORIG.	GOOD	FINE	N-MINT
❏ 1, Mar 85, SA 0.75		3.00	9.00	15.00
❏ 2, Apr 85, SA 0.75		2.00	6.00	10.00
❏ 3, May 85, SA 0.75		2.00	6.00	10.00
❏ 4, Jun 85, SA 0.75		2.00	6.00	10.00
❏ 5, Jul 85, SA 0.75		2.00	6.00	10.00
❏ 6, Aug 85, SA 0.75		1.40	4.20	7.00
❏ 7, Sep 85, SA 0.75		1.40	4.20	7.00
❏ 8, Oct 85, SA 0.75		1.40	4.20	7.00
❏ 9, Nov 85, SA 0.75		1.40	4.20	7.00
❏ 10, Dec 85, SA 0.75		1.40	4.20	7.00
❏ 11, Jan 86, SA 0.75		1.40	4.20	7.00
❏ 12, Feb 86, SA 0.75		1.40	4.20	7.00
❏ 13, Mar 86, SA 0.75		1.40	4.20	7.00
❏ 14, Apr 86, SA 0.75		1.40	4.20	7.00
❏ 15, May 86, SA 0.75		1.40	4.20	7.00
❏ 16, Jun 86, SA 0.75		1.40	4.20	7.00
❏ 17, Jul 86, SA 0.75		1.40	4.20	7.00
❏ 18, Aug 86, SA 0.75		1.40	4.20	7.00
❏ 19, Sep 86, SA 0.75		1.40	4.20	7.00
❏ 20, Oct 86, SA 0.75		1.40	4.20	7.00
❏ 21, Nov 86, SA 0.75		1.20	3.60	6.00
❏ 22, Dec 86, SA 0.75		1.20	3.60	6.00
❏ 23, Jan 87, SA 0.75		1.20	3.60	6.00
❏ 24, Feb 87, SA 0.75		1.20	3.60	6.00
❏ 25, Mar 87, SA 0.75		1.20	3.60	6.00
❏ 26, Apr 87, SA 0.75		1.20	3.60	6.00
❏ 27, May 87, SA 1.00		1.20	3.60	6.00
❏ 28, Jun 87, SA 1.00		1.20	3.60	6.00
❏ 29, Jul 87, SA 1.00		1.60	4.80	8.00
❏ 30, Aug 87, SA 1.00		1.40	4.20	7.00
❏ 31, Sep 87, SA 1.00		1.00	3.00	5.00
❏ 32, Oct 87, SA 1.00		1.00	3.00	5.00
❏ 33, Nov 87, SA 1.00		1.00	3.00	5.00
❏ 34, Dec 87, SA 1.00		1.00	3.00	5.00
❏ 35, Jan 88, SA 1.00		1.00	3.00	5.00
❏ 36, Feb 88, SA 1.00		1.00	3.00	5.00
❏ 37, Mar 88, SA 1.00		1.00	3.00	5.00
❏ 38, Apr 88, SA 1.00		1.00	3.00	5.00
❏ 39, May 88, SA 1.00		1.00	3.00	5.00
❏ 40, Jun 88, SA 1.00		1.00	3.00	5.00
❏ 41, Jul 88, SA 1.00		1.00	3.00	5.00
❏ 42, Aug 88, SA 1.00		1.00	3.00	5.00
❏ 43, Sep 88, SA 1.00		1.00	3.00	5.00
❏ 44, Oct 88, SA 1.00		1.00	3.00	5.00
❏ 45, Nov 88, SA 1.00		1.00	3.00	5.00
❏ 46, Dec 88, SA 1.00		1.00	3.00	5.00
❏ 47, Jan 89, SA 1.00		1.00	3.00	5.00
❏ 48, Feb 89, SA 1.00		1.00	3.00	5.00
❏ 49, Mar 89, SA A:Chakaal				
..................................1.00		1.00	3.00	5.00
❏ 50, Apr 89, SA A:Chakaal1.00		1.00	3.00	5.00
❏ 51, May 89, SA A:Chakaal				
..................................1.00		0.40	1.20	2.00
❏ 52, Jun 89, SA A:Chakaal1.00		0.40	1.20	2.00
❏ 53, Jul 89, SA A:Chakaal.1.00		0.40	1.20	2.00

	ORIG.	GOOD	FINE	N-MINT
❑ 54, Aug 89, SA.............. 1.00	0.40	1.20	2.00
❑ 55, Sep 89, SA.............. 1.00	0.40	1.20	2.00
❑ 56, Oct 89, SA.............. 1.00	0.40	1.20	2.00
❑ 57, Nov 89, SA.............. 1.00	0.40	1.20	2.00
❑ 58, Nov 89, SA.............. 1.00	0.40	1.20	2.00
❑ 59, Dec 89, SA.............. 1.00	0.40	1.20	2.00
❑ 60, Dec 89, SA.............. 1.00	0.40	1.20	2.00
❑ 61, Jan 90, SA.............. 1.00	0.40	1.20	2.00
❑ 62, Feb 90, SA.............. 1.00	0.40	1.20	2.00
❑ 63, Mar 90, SA.............. 1.00	0.40	1.20	2.00
❑ 64, Apr 90, SA.............. 1.00	0.20	0.60	1.00
❑ 65, May 90, SA.............. 1.00	0.20	0.60	1.00
❑ 66, Jun 90, SA.............. 1.00	0.20	0.60	1.00
❑ 67, Jul 90, SA 1.00	0.20	0.60	1.00
❑ 68, Aug 90, SA.............. 1.00	0.20	0.60	1.00
❑ 69, Sep 90, SA 1.00	0.20	0.60	1.00
❑ 70, Oct 90, SA.............. 1.00	0.20	0.60	1.00
❑ 71, Nov 90, SA.............. 1.00	0.20	0.60	1.00
❑ 72, Dec 90, SA.............. 1.00	0.20	0.60	1.00
❑ 73, Jan 91, SA.............. 1.00	0.20	0.60	1.00
❑ 74, Feb 91, SA.............. 1.00	0.20	0.60	1.00
❑ 75, Mar 91, SA.............. 1.00	0.20	0.60	1.00
❑ 76, Apr 91, SA.............. 1.00	0.20	0.60	1.00
❑ 77, May 91, SA 1.00	0.20	0.60	1.00
❑ 78, Jun 91, SAbookburners			
.... 1.00	0.20	0.60	1.00
❑ 79, Jul 91, SA 1.00	0.20	0.60	1.00
❑ 80, Aug 91, SA 1:Thaiis.. 1.00	0.20	0.60	1.00
❑ 81, Sep 91, SA Thaiis..... 1.00	0.20	0.60	1.00
❑ 82, Oct 91, SA Thaiis 1.00	0.20	0.60	1.00
❑ 83, Nov 91, SA Thaiis..... 1.00	0.20	0.60	1.00
❑ 84, Dec 91, SA.............. 1.00	0.20	0.60	1.00
❑ 85, Jan 92, SA.............. 1.00	0.20	0.60	1.00
❑ 86, Feb 92, SA.............. 1.00	0.25	0.75	1.25
❑ 87, Mar 92, SA direct sale			
.... 2.25	0.45	1.35	2.25
❑ 88, Apr 92, SA direct sale			
.... 2.25	0.45	1.35	2.25
❑ 89, May 92, SA direct sale			
.... 2.25	0.45	1.35	2.25
❑ 90, Jun 92.............. 2.25	0.45	1.35	2.25
❑ 91, Jul 92.............. 2.25	0.45	1.35	2.25
❑ 92, Aug 92 .... 2.25	0.45	1.35	2.25
❑ 93, Sep 92.............. 2.25	0.45	1.35	2.25
❑ 94, Oct 92 .... 2.25	0.45	1.35	2.25
❑ 95, Nov 92.............. 2.25	0.45	1.35	2.25
❑ 96, Dec 92.............. 2.25	0.45	1.35	2.25
❑ 97, Jan 93.............. 2.25	0.45	1.35	2.25
❑ 98, Feb 93 .... 2.25	0.45	1.35	2.25
❑ 99, Mar 93 .... 2.25	0.45	1.35	2.25
❑ 100, Apr 93,Groo learns to read			
.... 2.95	0.59	1.77	2.95
❑ 101, May 93, SA 2.25	0.45	1.35	2.25
❑ 102, Jun 93, SA 2.25	0.45	1.35	2.25
❑ 103, Jul 93, SA 2.25	0.45	1.35	2.25
❑ 104, Sep 93, SA 2.25	0.45	1.35	2.25
❑ 105, Oct 93, SA 2.25	0.45	1.35	2.25
❑ 106, Nov 93, SA 2.25	0.45	1.35	2.25
❑ 107, Dec 93, SA 2.25	0.45	1.35	2.25
❑ 108, Jan 94, SA 2.25	0.45	1.35	2.25
❑ 109, Feb 94, SA 2.25	0.45	1.35	2.25
❑ 110, Mar 94, SA 2.25	0.45	1.35	2.25
❑ 111, Apr 94, SA.............. 2.25	0.45	1.35	2.25
❑ 112, May 94, SA 2.25	0.45	1.35	2.25
❑ 113, Jun 94, SA 2.25	0.45	1.35	2.25
❑ 114, Jul 94, SA 2.25	0.45	1.35	2.25
❑ 115, Aug 94, SA 2.25	0.45	1.35	2.25
❑ 116, Sep 94, SA 2.25	0.45	1.35	2.25
❑ 117, Oct 94, SA.............. 2.25	0.45	1.35	2.25

	ORIG.	GOOD	FINE	N-MINT
❑ 118, Nov 94, SA............2.25	0.45	1.35	2.25
❑ 119, Dec 94, SA............2.25	0.45	1.35	2.25
❑ 120, Jan 95, SA,last Epic issue			
....................................2.25	0.45	1.35	2.25

SERIUS BOUNTY HUNTER
BLACKTHORNE

	GOOD	FINE	N-MINT
❑ 1, b&w....................................	0.35	1.05	1.75
❑ 2, b&w....................................	0.35	1.05	1.75
❑ 3, b&w....................................	0.35	1.05	1.75

SERPENTYNE
NIGHTWYND

	GOOD	FINE	N-MINT
❑ 1, b&w....................................	0.50	1.50	2.50
❑ 2, b&w....................................	0.50	1.50	2.50
❑ 3, b&w....................................	0.50	1.50	2.50

SETTEI
ANTARCTIC

	ORIG.	GOOD	FINE	N-MINT
❑ 1, Feb 93, b&w 7.95	1.59	4.77	7.95
❑ 2, Apr 93, b&w 7.95	1.59	4.77	7.95

SETTEI SUPER SPECIAL FEATURING:
PROJECT A-KO

	ORIG.	GOOD	FINE	N-MINT
❑ 1, Feb 94, color.............2.95	0.59	1.77	2.95

SEVEN MILES A SECOND
DC/VERTIGO

	ORIG.	GOOD	FINE	N-MINT
❑ 0, 96, nn;one-shot;prestige format			
....................................7.95	1.59	4.77	7.95

SEWAGE DRAGOON
PARODY PRESS

	ORIG.	GOOD	FINE	N-MINT
❑ 1, first printing.............2.50	0.50	1.50	2.50
❑ 1, second printing.........2.50	0.50	1.50	2.50

SEX AND DEATH
ACID RAIN

	GOOD	FINE	N-MINT
❑ 1, b&w....................................	0.50	1.50	2.50

SEX IN THE SINEMA
COMIC ZONE

	GOOD	FINE	N-MINT
❑ 1, adult, b&w..................	0.59	1.77	2.95
❑ 2, adult, b&w..................	0.59	1.77	2.95
❑ 3, adult, b&w..................	0.59	1.77	2.95
❑ 4, adult, b&w..................	0.59	1.77	2.95

SEX MACHINE, THE
EROS

	GOOD	FINE	N-MINT
❑ 1, adult, b&w..................	0.50	1.50	2.50

SEX WARRIOR
DARK HORSE

	ORIG.	GOOD	FINE	N-MINT
❑ 1 ....2.50	0.50	1.50	2.50
❑ 2 ....2.50	0.50	1.50	2.50

SEXECUTIONER
EROS COMIX

	GOOD	FINE	N-MINT
❑ 1, adult, b&w..................	0.50	1.50	2.50
❑ 2, adult, b&w..................	0.50	1.50	2.50
❑ 3, adult, b&w..................	0.50	1.50	2.50

SEXY SUPERSPY
FORBIDDEN FRUIT

	GOOD	FINE	N-MINT
❑ 1, adult, b&w..................	0.59	1.77	2.95
❑ 2, adult, b&w..................	0.59	1.77	2.95
❑ 3, adult, b&w..................	0.59	1.77	2.95
❑ 4, adult, b&w..................	0.59	1.77	2.95
❑ 5, adult, b&w..................	0.59	1.77	2.95
❑ 6, adult, b&w..................	0.59	1.77	2.95
❑ 7, adult, b&w..................	0.59	1.77	2.95

SEXY WOMEN
CELEBRITY

	GOOD	FINE	N-MINT
❑ 1	0.59	1.77	2.95
❑ 2	0.59	1.77	2.95

SGT. FURY AND HIS HOWLING COMMANDOS
MARVEL

	ORIG.	GOOD	FINE	N-MINT
❑ 1 ....0.12	100.00	300.00	500.00
❑ 2 ....0.12	48.00	144.00	240.00
❑ 3 ....0.12	30.00	90.00	150.00

	ORIG.	GOOD	FINE	N-MINT
❏ 4	0.12	30.00	90.00	150.00
❏ 5	0.12	30.00	90.00	150.00
❏ 6	0.12	12.00	36.00	60.00
❏ 7	0.12	12.00	36.00	60.00
❏ 8, Jul 64, DAy;V:Dr. Zemo (later Baron Zemo)				
	0.12	12.00	36.00	60.00
❏ 9, Aug 64, DAy	0.12	12.00	36.00	60.00
❏ 10	0.12	12.00	36.00	60.00
❏ 11	0.12	7.20	21.60	36.00
❏ 12	0.12	7.20	21.60	36.00
❏ 13, Dec 64, JK,SL,A:CaptainAmerica				
	0.12	45.00	135.00	225.00
❏ 13, JK,SL,A:Captain America;second printing				
❏ 14	0.12	7.20	21.60	36.00
❏ 15, Feb 65, DAy;1:Hans Rooten				
	0.12	7.20	21.60	36.00
❏ 16, Mar 65, DAy	0.12	7.20	21.60	36.00
❏ 17, Apr 65, DAy	0.12	7.20	21.60	36.00
❏ 18, May 65, DAy	0.12	7.20	21.60	36.00
❏ 19, Jun 65, DAy	0.12	7.20	21.60	36.00
❏ 20	0.12	7.20	21.60	36.00
❏ 21	0.12	4.00	12.00	20.00
❏ 22	0.12	4.00	12.00	20.00
❏ 23, Oct 65, DAy	0.12	4.00	12.00	20.00
❏ 24, Nov 65, DAy	0.12	4.00	12.00	20.00
❏ 25, Dec 65, DAy	0.12	4.00	12.00	20.00
❏ 26, Jan 66, DAy	0.12	4.00	12.00	20.00
❏ 27, Feb 66, DAy	0.12	4.00	12.00	20.00
❏ 28, Mar 66, DAy;V:Baron Strucker				
	0.12	4.00	12.00	20.00
❏ 29, Apr 66, DAy;V:Baron Strucker				
	0.12	4.00	12.00	20.00
❏ 30, May 66, DAy	0.12	4.00	12.00	20.00
❏ 31, Jun 66, DAy	0.12	4.00	12.00	20.00
❏ 32, Jul 66, DAy	0.12	4.00	12.00	20.00
❏ 33, Aug 66, DAy	0.12	4.00	12.00	20.00
❏ 34, Sep 66, DAy;O:Howlers				
	0.12	4.00	12.00	20.00
❏ 35, Oct 66, DAy;J:Eric Koenig				
	0.12	4.00	12.00	20.00
❏ 36, Nov 66, DAy	0.12	4.00	12.00	20.00
❏ 37	0.12	4.00	12.00	20.00
❏ 38	0.12	4.00	12.00	20.00
❏ 39	0.12	4.00	12.00	20.00
❏ 40, Mar 67, DAy	0.12	4.00	12.00	20.00
❏ 41	0.12	4.00	12.00	20.00
❏ 42	0.12	4.00	12.00	20.00
❏ 43	0.12	4.00	12.00	20.00
❏ 44	0.12	4.00	12.00	20.00
❏ 45	0.12	4.00	12.00	20.00
❏ 46	0.12	4.00	12.00	20.00
❏ 47	0.12	4.00	12.00	20.00
❏ 48	0.12	4.00	12.00	20.00
❏ 49	0.12	4.00	12.00	20.00
❏ 50	0.12	4.00	12.00	20.00
❏ 51	0.12	2.80	8.40	14.00
❏ 52	0.12	2.80	8.40	14.00
❏ 53	0.12	2.80	8.40	14.00
❏ 54	0.12	2.80	8.40	14.00
❏ 55	0.12	2.80	8.40	14.00
❏ 56	0.12	2.80	8.40	14.00
❏ 57	0.12	2.80	8.40	14.00
❏ 58, Sep 68, DAy	0.12	2.80	8.40	14.00
❏ 59	0.12	2.80	8.40	14.00
❏ 60	0.12	2.80	8.40	14.00
❏ 61	0.12	2.80	8.40	14.00
❏ 62	0.12	2.80	8.40	14.00
❏ 63	0.12	2.80	8.40	14.00
❏ 64	0.12	2.80	8.40	14.00
❏ 65	0.12	2.80	8.40	14.00
❏ 66	0.12	2.80	8.40	14.00
❏ 67, Jun 69, JSe(c);DAy	0.12	2.80	8.40	14.00

	ORIG.	GOOD	FINE	N-MINT
❏ 68, Jul 69, DAy;Fury goes home on leave				
	0.15	2.80	8.40	14.00
❏ 69, Aug 69, DAy	0.15	2.80	8.40	14.00
❏ 70, Sep 69, DAy;1:Missouri Marauders				
	0.15	2.80	8.40	14.00
❏ 71, Oct 69	0.15	2.40	7.20	12.00
❏ 72, Nov 69, DAy	0.15	2.40	7.20	12.00
❏ 73, Dec 69, DAy	0.15	2.40	7.20	12.00
❏ 74	0.15	2.40	7.20	12.00
❏ 75	0.15	2.40	7.20	12.00
❏ 76, Mar 70, DAy;Fury's father vs. The Red Baron				
	0.15	2.40	7.20	12.00
❏ 77, Apr 70, DAy	0.15	2.40	7.20	12.00
❏ 78, May 70, DAy	0.15	2.40	7.20	12.00
❏ 79, Jun 70, DAy	0.15	2.40	7.20	12.00
❏ 80	0.15	2.40	7.20	12.00
❏ 81	0.15	2.40	7.20	12.00
❏ 82	0.15	2.40	7.20	12.00
❏ 83, Jan 71, DAy;Dum-Dum Dugan vs. Man-Mountain				
McCoy	0.15	2.40	7.20	12.00
❏ 84, Feb 71, DAy	0.15	2.40	7.20	12.00
❏ 85, Mar 71, DAy	0.15	2.40	7.20	12.00
❏ 86, Apr 71, DAy	0.15	2.40	7.20	12.00
❏ 87, May 71, DAy	0.15	2.40	7.20	12.00
❏ 88, Jun 71, DAy;A:Patton				
	0.15	2.40	7.20	12.00
❏ 89, Jul 71, DAy	0.15	2.40	7.20	12.00
❏ 90, Aug 71, DAy	0.15	2.40	7.20	12.00
❏ 91, Sep 71, DAy	0.15	2.40	7.20	12.00
❏ 92, Oct 71	0.25	2.40	7.20	12.00
❏ 93, Dec 71	0.20	2.40	7.20	12.00
❏ 94, Jan 72, DAy	0.20	2.40	7.20	12.00
❏ 95, Feb 72, JK;reprint	0.20	2.40	7.20	12.00
❏ 96, Mar 72, DAy	0.20	2.40	7.20	12.00
❏ 97, Apr 72, DAy	0.20	2.40	7.20	12.00
❏ 98, May 72, DAy;1:Dugan's Deadly Dozen				
	0.20	2.40	7.20	12.00
❏ 99, Jun 72	0.20	2.40	7.20	12.00
❏ 100, Jul 72, DAy;A:Captain America, FF, Martin Goodman, Stan Lee, Dick Ayers, Gary Friedrich				
	0.20	3.60	10.80	18.00
❏ 101, Sep 72, DAy	0.20	0.80	2.40	4.00
❏ 102, Sep 72, DAy	0.20	0.80	2.40	4.00
❏ 103, Oct 72, DAy	0.20	0.80	2.40	4.00
❏ 104, Nov 72, DAy	0.20	0.80	2.40	4.00
❏ 105, Dec 72, DAy	0.20	0.80	2.40	4.00
❏ 106, Jan 73, DAy	0.20	0.80	2.40	4.00
❏ 107, Feb 73, DAy	0.20	0.80	2.40	4.00
❏ 108, Mar 73, DAy	0.20	0.80	2.40	4.00
❏ 109, Apr 73, DAy	0.20	0.80	2.40	4.00
❏ 110, May 73, DAy	0.20	0.80	2.40	4.00
❏ 111, Jun 73, DAy	0.20	0.80	2.40	4.00
❏ 112, Jul 73, DAy;V:Baron Strucker				
	0.20	0.80	2.40	4.00
❏ 113, Aug 73, DAy	0.20	0.80	2.40	4.00
❏ 114, Sep 73, DAy	0.20	0.80	2.40	4.00
❏ 115, Oct 73, DAy	0.20	0.80	2.40	4.00
❏ 116, Nov 73, DAy	0.20	0.80	2.40	4.00
❏ 117, Jan 74	0.20	0.80	2.40	4.00
❏ 118, Mar 74, DAy	0.20	0.80	2.40	4.00
❏ 119, May 74, DAy	0.20	0.80	2.40	4.00
❏ 120, Jul 74, DAy	0.20	0.80	2.40	4.00
❏ 121	0.25	0.80	2.40	4.00
❏ 122	0.25	0.80	2.40	4.00
❏ 123	0.25	0.80	2.40	4.00
❏ 124	0.25	0.80	2.40	4.00
❏ 125	0.25	0.80	2.40	4.00
❏ 126	0.25	0.80	2.40	4.00
❏ 127	0.25	0.80	2.40	4.00
❏ 128	0.25	0.80	2.40	4.00
❏ 129	0.25	0.80	2.40	4.00
❏ 130	0.25	0.80	2.40	4.00

	ORIG.	GOOD	FINE	N-MINT
131	0.25	0.80	2.40	4.00
132	0.25	0.80	2.40	4.00
133	0.25	0.80	2.40	4.00
134	0.25	0.80	2.40	4.00
135, Sep 76	0.30	0.80	2.40	4.00
136, Oct 76	0.30	0.80	2.40	4.00
137, Nov 76	0.30	0.80	2.40	4.00
138, Jan 77	0.30	0.80	2.40	4.00
139, Mar 77	0.30	0.80	2.40	4.00
140, May 77	0.30	0.80	2.40	4.00
141, Jul 77	0.30	0.60	1.80	3.00
142, Sep 77	0.30	0.60	1.80	3.00
143, Nov 77	0.30	0.60	1.80	3.00
144, Jan 78	0.30	0.60	1.80	3.00
145, Mar 78	0.30	0.60	1.80	3.00
146, May 78	0.30	0.60	1.80	3.00
147, Jul 78	0.30	0.60	1.80	3.00
148, Sep 78	0.30	0.60	1.80	3.00
149, Nov 78	0.30	0.60	1.80	3.00
150, Jan 79	0.30	0.60	1.80	3.00
151, Mar 79	0.30	0.60	1.80	3.00
152, Jun 79	0.30	0.60	1.80	3.00
153, Aug 79	0.30	0.60	1.80	3.00
154, Oct 79	0.30	0.60	1.80	3.00
155, Dec 79	0.30	0.60	1.80	3.00
156, Feb 80	0.30	0.60	1.80	3.00
157, Apr 80	0.30	0.60	1.80	3.00
158, Jun 80	0.30	0.60	1.80	3.00
159, Aug 80	0.30	0.60	1.80	3.00
160, Oct 80	0.30	0.60	1.80	3.00
161, Dec 80	0.30	0.60	1.80	3.00
162, Feb 81	0.30	0.60	1.80	3.00
163, Apr 81	0.30	0.60	1.80	3.00
164, Jun 81	0.30	0.60	1.80	3.00
165, Aug 81	0.30	0.60	1.80	3.00
166, Oct 81	0.30	0.60	1.80	3.00
167, Dec 81	0.30	0.60	1.80	3.00

SGT. FURY AND HIS HOWLING COMMANDOS ANNUAL

	ORIG.	GOOD	FINE	N-MINT
1, 65	0.25	5.00	15.00	25.00
2, 66, D-Day	0.25	1.00	3.00	5.00
3, 67	0.25	1.00	3.00	5.00
4, 68	0.25	1.00	3.00	5.00
5, 69	0.25	1.00	3.00	5.00
6, 70	0.25	1.00	3.00	5.00
7, 71	0.25	1.00	3.00	5.00

SGT. ROCK
DC

	GOOD	FINE	N-MINT
302, Mar 77	2.40	7.20	12.00
303, Apr 77	2.00	6.00	10.00
304, May 77	2.00	6.00	10.00
305, Jun 77	2.00	6.00	10.00
306, Jul 77	1.40	4.20	7.00
307, Aug 77	1.40	4.20	7.00
308, Sep 77	1.40	4.20	7.00
309, Oct 77	1.40	4.20	7.00
310, Nov 77	1.40	4.20	7.00
311, Dec 77	1.40	4.20	7.00
312, Jan 78	1.40	4.20	7.00
313, Feb 78	1.40	4.20	7.00
314, Mar 78	1.40	4.20	7.00
315, Apr 78	1.40	4.20	7.00
316, May 78	1.40	4.20	7.00
317, Jun 78	1.40	4.20	7.00
318, Jul 78	1.40	4.20	7.00
319, Aug 78	1.40	4.20	7.00
320, Sep 78	1.40	4.20	7.00
321, Oct 78	1.40	4.20	7.00
322, Nov 78	1.40	4.20	7.00
323, Dec 78	1.40	4.20	7.00
324, Jan 79	1.40	4.20	7.00

	ORIG.	GOOD	FINE	N-MINT
325, Feb 79		1.40	4.20	7.00
326, Mar 79		1.00	3.00	5.00
327, Apr 79		1.00	3.00	5.00
328, May 79		1.00	3.00	5.00
329, Jun 79		1.00	3.00	5.00
330, Jul 79		1.00	3.00	5.00
331, Aug 79		1.00	3.00	5.00
332, Sep 79		1.00	3.00	5.00
333, Oct 79		1.00	3.00	5.00
334, Nov 79		1.00	3.00	5.00
335, Dec 79		1.00	3.00	5.00
336, Jan 80		1.00	3.00	5.00
337, Feb 80		1.00	3.00	5.00
338, Mar 80		1.00	3.00	5.00
339, Apr 80		1.00	3.00	5.00
340, May 80		1.00	3.00	5.00
341, Jun 80		1.00	3.00	5.00
342, Jul 80		1.00	3.00	5.00
343, Aug 80		1.00	3.00	5.00
344, Sep 80		1.00	3.00	5.00
345, Oct 80		1.00	3.00	5.00
346, Nov 80		1.00	3.00	5.00
347, Dec 80		1.00	3.00	5.00
348, Jan 81		1.00	3.00	5.00
349, Feb 81		1.00	3.00	5.00
350, Mar 81		1.00	3.00	5.00
351, Apr 81		1.00	3.00	5.00
352, May 81		1.00	3.00	5.00
353, Jun 81		1.00	3.00	5.00
354, Jul 81		1.00	3.00	5.00
355, Aug 81		1.00	3.00	5.00
356, Sep 81		1.00	3.00	5.00
357, Oct 81		1.00	3.00	5.00
358, Nov 81		1.00	3.00	5.00
359, Dec 81		1.00	3.00	5.00
360, Jan 82		1.00	3.00	5.00
361, Feb 82		0.80	2.40	4.00
362, Mar 82		0.80	2.40	4.00
363, Apr 82		0.80	2.40	4.00
364, May 82		0.80	2.40	4.00
365, Jun 82		0.80	2.40	4.00
366, Jul 82		0.80	2.40	4.00
367, Aug 82		0.80	2.40	4.00
368, Sep 82		0.80	2.40	4.00
369, Oct 82		0.80	2.40	4.00
370, Nov 82		0.80	2.40	4.00
371, Dec 82		0.80	2.40	4.00
372, Jan 83		0.80	2.40	4.00
373, Feb 83		0.80	2.40	4.00
374, Mar 83		0.80	2.40	4.00
375, Apr 83		0.80	2.40	4.00
376, May 83		0.80	2.40	4.00
377, Jun 83		0.80	2.40	4.00
378, Jul 83		0.80	2.40	4.00
379, Aug 83		0.80	2.40	4.00
380, Sep 83		0.80	2.40	4.00
381, Oct 83		0.80	2.40	4.00
382, Nov 83		0.80	2.40	4.00
383, Dec 83		0.80	2.40	4.00
384, Jan 84		0.80	2.40	4.00
385, Feb 84		0.80	2.40	4.00
386, Mar 84		0.80	2.40	4.00
387, Apr 84		0.80	2.40	4.00
388, May 84		0.80	2.40	4.00
389, Jun 84		0.80	2.40	4.00
390, Jul 84		0.80	2.40	4.00
391, Aug 84		0.80	2.40	4.00
392, Sep 84		0.80	2.40	4.00
393, Oct 84		0.80	2.40	4.00
394, Nov 84		0.80	2.40	4.00
395, Dec 84		0.80	2.40	4.00
396, Jan 85		0.80	2.40	4.00

	ORIG.	GOOD	FINE	N-MINT
397, Feb 85	0.80	2.40	4.00
398, Mar 85	0.80	2.40	4.00
399, Apr 85	0.80	2.40	4.00
400, May 85	0.80	2.40	4.00
401, Jun 85	0.70	2.10	3.50
402, Jul 85	0.70	2.10	3.50
403, Aug 85	0.70	2.10	3.50
404, Sep 85	0.70	2.10	3.50
405, Oct 85	0.70	2.10	3.50
406, Nov 85	0.70	2.10	3.50
407, Dec 85	0.70	2.10	3.50
408, Feb 86	0.70	2.10	3.50
409, Apr 86	0.70	2.10	3.50
410, Jun 86	0.70	2.10	3.50
411, Aug 86	0.70	2.10	3.50
412, Oct 86	0.70	2.10	3.50
413, Dec 86	0.70	2.10	3.50
414, Feb 87	0.70	2.10	3.50
415, Apr 87	0.70	2.10	3.50
416, Jun 87	0.70	2.10	3.50
417, Aug 87	0.70	2.10	3.50
418, Oct 87	0.70	2.10	3.50
419, Dec 87	0.70	2.10	3.50
420, Feb 88	0.70	2.10	3.50
421, Apr 88	0.70	2.10	3.50
422, Jul 88, final issue	0.70	2.10	3.50

SGT. ROCK ANNUAL

		GOOD	FINE	N-MINT
1		1.00	3.00	5.00
2, Sep 82		0.80	2.40	4.00
3, Aug 83		0.60	1.80	3.00
4, Aug 84		0.60	1.80	3.00

SGT. ROCK SPECIAL

	ORIG.	GOOD	FINE	N-MINT
1, Oct 88, JKu, Viking Prince rep.	0.40	1.20	2.00
2, Jan 89, JKu, reprints	0.40	1.20	2.00
3, Mar 89, JKu, reprints	0.40	1.20	2.00
4, Jun 89, JKu, reprints	0.40	1.20	2.00
5, Sep 89, JKu, reprints	0.40	1.20	2.00
6, Dec 89, JKu, reprints	0.40	1.20	2.00
7, Mar 90, JKu, reprints	0.40	1.20	2.00
8, Jun 90, JKu, reprints	0.40	1.20	2.00
9, Sep 90, JKu, reprints	0.40	1.20	2.00
10, Dec 90, JKu, reprints	0.40	1.20	2.00
11, Mar 91, JKu, reprints	0.40	1.20	2.00
12, May 91, JKu, reprints	0.40	1.20	2.00
13, JKu, reprints	0.40	1.20	2.00
14, JKu, reprints	0.40	1.20	2.00
15, JKu, reprints	0.40	1.20	2.00
16, JKu, reprints	0.40	1.20	2.00
17, JKu, reprints	0.40	1.20	2.00
18, JKu, reprints	0.40	1.20	2.00
19, JKu, reprints	0.40	1.20	2.00
20, JKu, reprints	0.40	1.20	2.00
21, JKu, reprints	0.40	1.20	2.00

SGT. ROCK SPECIAL (1992)

		GOOD	FINE	N-MINT
1, WS(c), PCR, TT		0.59	1.77	2.95

SGT. ROCK SPECIAL (1994)

	ORIG.	GOOD	FINE	N-MINT
2, 94	2.95	0.59	1.77	2.95

SHADE SPECIAL
AC

		GOOD	FINE	N-MINT
1, Oct 84		0.30	0.90	1.50

SHADE THE CHANGING MAN (1977-1978 series)
DC

	ORIG.	GOOD	FINE	N-MINT
1, Jul 77, O:Shade, SD	0.35	1.20	3.60	6.00
2, Sep 77, SD	0.35	0.80	2.40	4.00
3, Nov 77, SD	0.35	0.80	2.40	4.00
4, Jan 78, SD	0.35	0.80	2.40	4.00
5, Mar 78, SD	0.35	0.80	2.40	4.00
6, May 78, SD	0.35	0.60	1.80	3.00
7, Jul 78, SD	0.35	0.60	1.80	3.00
8, Sep 78, SD	0.35	0.60	1.80	3.00

SHADE THE CHANGING MAN (beginning 1990)

	ORIG.	GOOD	FINE	N-MINT
1, Jul 90	2.50	1.60	4.80	8.00
2, Aug 90	1.50	1.00	3.00	5.00
3, Sep 90	1.50	0.80	2.40	4.00
4, Oct 90	1.50	0.80	2.40	4.00
5, Nov 90	1.50	0.80	2.40	4.00
6, Dec 90	1.50	0.60	1.80	3.00
7, Jan 91	1.50	0.60	1.80	3.00
8, Feb 91	1.50	0.60	1.80	3.00
9, Mar 91	1.50	0.60	1.80	3.00
10, Apr 91	1.50	0.60	1.80	3.00
11, May 91	1.50	0.50	1.50	2.50
12, Jun 91	1.50	0.50	1.50	2.50
13, Jul 91	1.50	0.50	1.50	2.50
14, Aug 91	1.50	0.50	1.50	2.50
15, Sep 91	1.50	0.50	1.50	2.50
16, Oct 91	1.50	0.50	1.50	2.50
17, Nov 91	1.75	0.50	1.50	2.50
18, Dec 91	1.75	0.50	1.50	2.50
19	1.75	0.50	1.50	2.50
20	1.75	0.50	1.50	2.50
21	1.75	0.45	1.35	2.25
22	1.75	0.45	1.35	2.25
23	1.75	0.45	1.35	2.25
24	1.75	0.45	1.35	2.25
25	1.75	0.45	1.35	2.25
26	1.75	0.45	1.35	2.25
27	1.75	0.45	1.35	2.25
28	1.75	0.45	1.35	2.25
29	1.75	0.45	1.35	2.25
30	1.75	0.45	1.35	2.25
31	1.75	0.35	1.05	1.75
32	1.75	0.35	1.05	1.75
33	1.75	0.35	1.05	1.75
34	1.75	0.35	1.05	1.75
35	1.75	0.35	1.05	1.75

DC/VERTIGO

	ORIG.	GOOD	FINE	N-MINT
36	1.95	0.39	1.17	1.95
37	1.95	0.39	1.17	1.95
38	1.95	0.39	1.17	1.95
39	1.95	0.39	1.17	1.95
40	1.95	0.39	1.17	1.95
41	1.95	0.39	1.17	1.95
42	1.95	0.39	1.17	1.95
43	1.95	0.39	1.17	1.95
44	1.95	0.39	1.17	1.95
45	1.95	0.39	1.17	1.95
46	1.95	0.39	1.17	1.95
47, May 94	1.95	0.39	1.17	1.95
48, Jun 94	1.95	0.39	1.17	1.95
49, Jul 94	1.95	0.39	1.17	1.95
50, Aug 94	2.95	0.59	1.77	2.95
51, Sep 94	1.95	0.39	1.17	1.95
52, Oct 94	1.95	0.39	1.17	1.95
53, Nov 94	1.95	0.39	1.17	1.95
54, Dec 94	1.95	0.39	1.17	1.95
55, Jan 95	1.95	0.39	1.17	1.95
56, Feb 95	1.95	0.39	1.17	1.95
57, Mar 95	1.95	0.39	1.17	1.95
58, Apr 95	1.95	0.39	1.17	1.95
59, May 95	2.25	0.45	1.35	2.25
60, Jun 95	2.25	0.45	1.35	2.25
61, Jul 95	2.25	0.45	1.35	2.25
62, Aug 95	2.25	0.45	1.35	2.25
63, Sep 95	2.25	0.45	1.35	2.25
64, Oct 95	2.25	0.45	1.35	2.25
65, Nov 95	2.25	0.45	1.35	2.25
66, Dec 95	2.25	0.45	1.35	2.25
67, Jan 96	2.25	0.45	1.35	2.25
68, Feb 96	2.25	0.45	1.35	2.25
69, Mar 96	2.25	0.45	1.35	2.25
70, Apr 96	2.25	0.45	1.35	2.25

	ORIG.	GOOD	FINE	N-MINT

SHADO: SONG OF THE DRAGON
DC

	ORIG.	GOOD	FINE	N-MINT
❏ 1		0.99	2.97	4.95
❏ 2		0.99	2.97	4.95
❏ 3		0.99	2.97	4.95

SHADOW AND THE MYSTERIOUS 3, THE
DARK HORSE

	ORIG.	GOOD	FINE	N-MINT
❏ 0, Sep 94, nn	2.95	0.59	1.77	2.95

SHADOW ANNUAL, THE
DC

	ORIG.	GOOD	FINE	N-MINT
❏ 1, 87, EC parody	2.25	0.45	1.35	2.25
❏ 2, 88		0.50	1.50	2.50

SHADOW CABINET
DC/MILESTONE

	ORIG.	GOOD	FINE	N-MINT
❏ 0, Jan 94	2.50	0.50	1.50	2.50
❏ 1, Jun 94	1.75	0.35	1.05	1.75
❏ 2, Jul 94	1.75	0.35	1.05	1.75
❏ 3, Aug 94	1.75	0.35	1.05	1.75
❏ 4, Sep 94	1.75	0.35	1.05	1.75
❏ 5, Oct 94	1.75	0.35	1.05	1.75
❏ 6, Nov 94	1.75	0.35	1.05	1.75
❏ 7, Dec 94	1.75	0.35	1.05	1.75
❏ 8, Jan 95	1.75	0.35	1.05	1.75
❏ 9, Feb 95	1.75	0.35	1.05	1.75
❏ 10, Mar 95	1.75	0.35	1.05	1.75
❏ 11, Apr 95	1.75	0.35	1.05	1.75
❏ 12, May 95	1.75	0.35	1.05	1.75
❏ 13, Jun 95	2.50	0.50	1.50	2.50
❏ 14, Jul 95	2.50	0.50	1.50	2.50
❏ 15, Aug 95	2.50	0.50	1.50	2.50
❏ 16, Sep 95	2.50	0.50	1.50	2.50
❏ 17, Oct 95, final issue	2.50	0.50	1.50	2.50

SHADOW EMPIRES: FAITH CONQUERS
(mini-series)
DARK HORSE

	ORIG.	GOOD	FINE	N-MINT
❏ 2, Sep 94	2.95	0.59	1.77	2.95
❏ 3, Oct 94	2.95	0.59	1.77	2.95
❏ 4, Nov 94	2.95	0.59	1.77	2.95

SHADOW OF THE BATMAN
DC

	ORIG.	GOOD	FINE	N-MINT
❏ 1, Dec 85		0.40	1.20	2.00
❏ 2, Jan 86		0.40	1.20	2.00
❏ 3, Feb 86		0.40	1.20	2.00
❏ 4, Mar 86		0.40	1.20	2.00
❏ 5, Apr 86		0.40	1.20	2.00

SHADOW OF THE TORTURER
INNOVATION

	ORIG.	GOOD	FINE	N-MINT
❏ 1, novel adaptation		0.50	1.50	2.50
❏ 2, novel adaptation		0.50	1.50	2.50
❏ 3, novel adaptation		0.50	1.50	2.50

SHADOW RAVEN
POC-IT

	ORIG.	GOOD	FINE	N-MINT
❏ 1, Jun 95	2.50	0.50	1.50	2.50

SHADOW RIDERS
MARVEL

	ORIG.	GOOD	FINE	N-MINT
❏ 1, embossed cover	2.50	0.50	1.50	2.50
❏ 2	1.75	0.35	1.05	1.75
❏ 3	1.75	0.35	1.05	1.75
❏ 4	1.75	0.35	1.05	1.75

SHADOW SLAYER
ETERNITY

	ORIG.	GOOD	FINE	N-MINT
❏ 1, #0 on cover		0.39	1.17	1.95

SHADOW STATE
BROADWAY

❏ 1, Sep 95, giveaway preview edition;Till Death Do Us Part/Fatale;b&w

---

	ORIG.	GOOD	FINE	N-MINT

❏ 1, Dec 95, BloodS.C.R.E.A.M., Fatale;enhanced cardstock

	ORIG.	GOOD	FINE	N-MINT
cover	2.50	0.50	1.50	2.50

❏ 2, Jan 96, Till Death Do Us Part; Fatale

	ORIG.	GOOD	FINE	N-MINT
	2.50	0.50	1.50	2.50

SHADOW STRIKES! ANNUAL, THE
DC

	ORIG.	GOOD	FINE	N-MINT
❏ 1, Dec 89, DS	3.50	0.70	2.10	3.50

SHADOW STRIKES!, THE

	ORIG.	GOOD	FINE	N-MINT
❏ 1, Sep 89	1.75	0.35	1.05	1.75
❏ 2, Oct 89	1.75	0.35	1.05	1.75
❏ 3, Nov 89	1.75	0.35	1.05	1.75
❏ 4, Dec 89	1.75	0.35	1.05	1.75
❏ 5, Jan 90, Doc Savage	1.75	0.35	1.05	1.75
❏ 6, Feb 90, Doc Savage	1.75	0.35	1.05	1.75
❏ 7, Mar 90		0.35	1.05	1.75
❏ 8, Apr 90, Shiwan Khan		0.35	1.05	1.75
❏ 9, May 90, Shiwan Khan		0.35	1.05	1.75
❏ 10, Jun 90, Shiwan Khan		0.35	1.05	1.75
❏ 11, Aug 90		0.35	1.05	1.75
❏ 12, Sep 90		0.35	1.05	1.75
❏ 13, Oct 90		0.35	1.05	1.75
❏ 14, Dec 90		0.35	1.05	1.75
❏ 15, Jan 91		0.35	1.05	1.75
❏ 16, Feb 91		0.35	1.05	1.75
❏ 17, Mar 91		0.35	1.05	1.75
❏ 18, Apr 91		0.35	1.05	1.75
❏ 19, May 91		0.40	1.20	2.00
❏ 20, Jun 91		0.40	1.20	2.00
❏ 21, Jul 91		0.40	1.20	2.00
❏ 22, Aug 91		0.40	1.20	2.00
❏ 23, Sep 91		0.40	1.20	2.00
❏ 24, Oct 91		0.40	1.20	2.00
❏ 25, Nov 91		0.40	1.20	2.00
❏ 26, Dec 91		0.40	1.20	2.00
❏ 27		0.40	1.20	2.00
❏ 28		0.40	1.20	2.00
❏ 29		0.40	1.20	2.00
❏ 30		0.40	1.20	2.00
❏ 31		0.40	1.20	2.00

SHADOW WAR OF HAWKMAN

	ORIG.	GOOD	FINE	N-MINT
❏ 1, May 85	0.75	0.25	0.75	1.25
❏ 2, Jun 85	0.75	0.20	0.60	1.00
❏ 3, Jul 85	0.75	0.20	0.60	1.00
❏ 4, Aug 85	0.75	0.20	0.60	1.00

SHADOW WARRIOR
GATEWAY

	ORIG.	GOOD	FINE	N-MINT
❏ 1, b&w		0.39	1.17	1.95

SHADOW'S EDGE, THE
LION

	ORIG.	GOOD	FINE	N-MINT
❏ 1		0.79	2.37	3.95

SHADOW, THE
ARCHIE

	ORIG.	GOOD	FINE	N-MINT
❏ 1, Aug 64	0.12	7.00	21.00	35.00
❏ 2	0.12	4.00	12.00	20.00
❏ 3	0.12	4.00	12.00	20.00
❏ 4	0.12	4.00	12.00	20.00
❏ 5	0.12	4.00	12.00	20.00
❏ 6	0.12	4.00	12.00	20.00
❏ 7	0.12	4.00	12.00	20.00
❏ 8	0.12	4.00	12.00	20.00

SHADOW, THE (1973-1975 series)
DC

	ORIG.	GOOD	FINE	N-MINT
❏ 1, Nov 73, MK	0.20	4.00	12.00	20.00
❏ 2, Jan 74, MK	0.20	3.00	9.00	15.00
❏ 3, Mar 74, MK/BWr	0.20	3.60	10.80	18.00
❏ 4, May 74, MK	0.20	2.40	7.20	12.00
❏ 5, Jul 74	0.20	1.20	3.60	6.00
❏ 6, Sep 74, MK	0.20	2.40	7.20	12.00
❏ 7, Nov 74	0.20	1.20	3.60	6.00
❏ 8, Jan 75	0.20	1.20	3.60	6.00

	ORIG.	GOOD	FINE	N-MINT
❑ 9, Mar 75 ....0.20		1.20	3.60	6.00
❑ 10, May 75.......................0.20		1.20	3.60	6.00
❑ 11, Jul 75.......................0.20		1.20	3.60	6.00
❑ 12, Sep 75.......................0.20		1.20	3.60	6.00

SHADOW, THE (1986 mini-series)

	ORIG.	GOOD	FINE	N-MINT
❑ 1, May 86, HC 1.50		2.00	6.00	10.00
❑ 2, Jun 86, HC 1.50		1.20	3.60	6.00
❑ 3, Jul 86, HC 1.50		1.00	3.00	5.00
❑ 4, Aug 86, HC.................1.50		1.00	3.00	5.00

SHADOW, THE (1987-1989 series)

	ORIG.	GOOD	FINE	N-MINT
❑ 1, Aug 87, BSz 1.50		0.30	0.90	1.50
❑ 2, Sep 87, BSz.................1.50		0.30	0.90	1.50
❑ 3, Oct 87, BSz 1.50		0.30	0.90	1.50
❑ 4, Nov 87, BSz 1.50		0.30	0.90	1.50
❑ 5, Dec 87, BSz 1.50		0.30	0.90	1.50
❑ 6, Jan 88, BSz 1.50		0.30	0.90	1.50
❑ 7, Feb 88 ....1.75		0.35	1.05	1.75
❑ 8, Mar 88 ....1.75		0.35	1.05	1.75
❑ 9, Apr 88 ....1.75		0.35	1.05	1.75
❑ 10, May 88.......................1.75		0.35	1.05	1.75
❑ 11, Jun 88 ....1.75		0.35	1.05	1.75
❑ 12, Jul 88 ....1.75		0.35	1.05	1.75
❑ 13, Aug 88, D:Shadow		0.35	1.05	1.75
❑ 14, Sep 88.......................		0.35	1.05	1.75
❑ 15, Oct 88		0.35	1.05	1.75
❑ 16, Nov 88		0.35	1.05	1.75
❑ 17, Dec 88, A:Avenger		0.35	1.05	1.75
❑ 18, Dec 88, A:Avenger		0.35	1.05	1.75
❑ 19, Jan 89, Shadow alive again		0.35	1.05	1.75

SHADOW, THE (mini-series)
DARK HORSE

	ORIG.	GOOD	FINE	N-MINT
❑ 1, Jun 94, movie adaptation				
.......................2.50		0.50	1.50	2.50
❑ 2, Jul 94,movie adaptation				
.......................2.50		0.50	1.50	2.50

SHADOW, THE AND DOC SAVAGE (mini-series)

	ORIG.	GOOD	FINE	N-MINT
❑ 1, Jul 95 ....2.95		0.59	1.77	2.95
❑ 2, Aug 95 ....2.95		0.59	1.77	2.95

SHADOW: IN THE COILS OF LEVIATHAN, THE (mini-series)

	ORIG.	GOOD	FINE	N-MINT
❑ 1 ....2.95		0.59	1.77	2.95
❑ 2 ....2.95		0.59	1.77	2.95
❑ 3, Feb 94 ....2.95		0.59	1.77	2.95
❑ 4, Apr 94 ....2.95		0.59	1.77	2.95

SHADOWALKER
AIRCEL

	ORIG.	GOOD	FINE	N-MINT
❑ 1, b&w		0.30	0.90	1.50

SHADOWBLADE
HOT

	ORIG.	GOOD	FINE	N-MINT
❑ 1		0.35	1.05	1.75

SHADOWDRAGON ANNUAL
DC

	ORIG.	GOOD	FINE	N-MINT
❑ 1, 95, "Year One";O:Shadowdragon				
.......................3.50		0.70	2.10	3.50

SHADOWHAWK
IMAGE

	ORIG.	GOOD	FINE	N-MINT
❑ 0, Oct 94, (coversays September)				
.......................1.95		0.39	1.17	1.95
❑ 1, Jim Valentino, foil cover		4.00	12.00	20.00
❑ 2, A:Spawn......................		1.00	3.00	5.00
❑ 3, glow cover		0.80	2.40	4.00
❑ 4, Savage Dragon...........1.95		0.39	1.17	1.95
❑ 13, Sep 94, A:WildC.A.T.s				
.......................1.95		0.39	1.17	1.95
❑ 15, Nov 94, A: The Others; The Monster Within part 4				
.......................2.50		0.50	1.50	2.50
❑ 16, Jan 95, A: Supreme..2.50		0.50	1.50	2.50
❑ 17, 95..............................2.50		0.50	1.50	2.50
❑ 18, May 95 ....2.50		0.50	1.50	2.50

SHADOWHAWK - VAMPIRELLA
IMAGE/HARRIS

	ORIG.	GOOD	FINE	N-MINT
❑ 2, Feb 95, crossover;continued from *Vampirella - Shadowhawk* #1 ....4.95		0.99	2.97	4.95

SHADOWHAWK GALLERY
IMAGE

	ORIG.	GOOD	FINE	N-MINT
❑ 1, Apr 94.......................1.95		0.39	1.17	1.95

SHADOWHAWK II

	ORIG.	GOOD	FINE	N-MINT
❑ 1, diecut foil cover 3.50		0.70	2.10	3.50
❑ 1, Gold..............................		8.00	24.00	40.00
❑ 2, Jul 93..............................1.95		0.39	1.17	1.95
❑ 3 ....1.95		0.39	1.17	1.95

SHADOWHAWK III

	ORIG.	GOOD	FINE	N-MINT
❑ 1 ....1.95		0.39	1.17	1.95

SHADOWHAWK SPECIAL

	ORIG.	GOOD	FINE	N-MINT
❑ 1, 94, KB.......................3.50		0.70	2.10	3.50

SHADOWHUNT SPECIAL

	ORIG.	GOOD	FINE	N-MINT
❑ 1, Apr 96.......................2.50		0.50	1.50	2.50
❑ 1, Apr 96, alternate cover				
.......................2.50		0.50	1.50	2.50

SHADOWLAND
FANTAGRAPHICS

	ORIG.	GOOD	FINE	N-MINT
❑ 1, b&w..............................		0.45	1.35	2.25
❑ 2, b&w..............................		0.45	1.35	2.25

SHADOWLORD/TRIUNE
JET CITY

	ORIG.	GOOD	FINE	N-MINT
❑ 1		0.30	0.90	1.50

SHADOWMAN
ACCLAIM/VALIANT

	ORIG.	GOOD	FINE	N-MINT
❑ 37, Jun 95, BH................2.50		0.50	1.50	2.50
❑ 38, Jul 95, BH................2.50		0.50	1.50	2.50
❑ 39, Aug 95, BH 2.50		0.50	1.50	2.50
❑ 40, Sep 95, BH................2.50		0.50	1.50	2.50
❑ 42, Nov 95, BH................2.50		0.50	1.50	2.50
❑ 43, Dec 95, BH................2.50		0.50	1.50	2.50

VALIANT

	ORIG.	GOOD	FINE	N-MINT
❑ 0, Apr 94.......................2.50		0.50	1.50	2.50
❑ 0, Apr 94, chromium cover				
.......................3.50		0.70	2.10	3.50
❑ 0, gold edition..................		2.00	6.00	10.00
❑ 1, May 92.......................2.50		1.50	4.50	7.50
❑ 2, Jun 92 ....2.50		1.00	3.00	5.00
❑ 3, Jul 92.......................2.50		1.00	3.00	5.00
❑ 4, Aug 92, FM(c) Unity ...2.50		0.80	2.40	4.00
❑ 5, Sep 92, WS(c) Unity ...2.50		0.80	2.40	4.00
❑ 6, Oct 92.......................2.50		0.70	2.10	3.50
❑ 7, Nov 92 ....2.50		0.70	2.10	3.50
❑ 8, Dec 92, V:Master Darque				
.......................2.50		0.70	2.10	3.50
❑ 9, Jan 93.......................2.50		0.70	2.10	3.50
❑ 10, Feb 93.......................2.50		0.70	2.10	3.50
❑ 11, Mar 93.......................2.50		0.60	1.80	3.00
❑ 12, Apr 93.......................2.50		0.60	1.80	3.00
❑ 13, May 93.......................2.50		0.60	1.80	3.00
❑ 14, Jun 93.......................2.50		0.60	1.80	3.00
❑ 15, Jul 93.......................2.50		0.60	1.80	3.00
❑ 16, Aug 93.......................2.50		0.60	1.80	3.00
❑ 17, Sep 93.......................2.50		0.60	1.80	3.00
❑ 18, Oct 93.......................2.50		0.60	1.80	3.00
❑ 19, Nov 93, Aerosmith....2.50		0.60	1.80	3.00
❑ 20, Dec 93.......................2.50		0.60	1.80	3.00
❑ 21, Jan 94.......................2.50		0.50	1.50	2.50
❑ 22, Feb 94.......................2.50		0.50	1.50	2.50
❑ 23, Mar 94.......................2.50		0.50	1.50	2.50
❑ 24, Apr 94.......................2.50		0.50	1.50	2.50
❑ 25, Apr 94, trading card..2.50		0.50	1.50	2.50
❑ 26, Jun 94 ....2.50		0.50	1.50	2.50
❑ 27, Aug 94.......................2.50		0.50	1.50	2.50
❑ 28, Sep 94 ....2.50		0.50	1.50	2.50
❑ 29, Oct 94, Chaos Effect .2.50		0.50	1.50	2.50

	ORIG.	GOOD	FINE	N-MINT
☐ 30, Nov 94 .... 2.50		0.50	1.50	2.50
☐ 35, Apr 95 .... 2.50		0.50	1.50	2.50
☐ 36, May 95 .... 2.50		0.50	1.50	2.50

SHADOWMASTERS
MARVEL

	ORIG.	GOOD	FINE	N-MINT
☐ 1, Oct 89, O:Shadowmasters				
.... 3.95		1.40	4.20	7.00
☐ 2, Nov 89 .... 3.95		1.00	3.00	5.00
☐ 3, Dec 89 .... 3.95		1.00	3.00	5.00
☐ 4, Jan 90 .... 3.95		1.00	3.00	5.00

SHADOWMEN
TRIDENT

	GOOD	FINE	N-MINT
☐ 1, b&w, adult	0.45	1.35	2.25
☐ 2, b&w, adult	0.45	1.35	2.25

SHADOWS FALL (mini-series)
DC/VERTIGO

	ORIG.	GOOD	FINE	N-MINT
☐ 1, Nov 94 .... 2.95		0.59	1.77	2.95
☐ 2, Dec 94 .... 2.95		0.59	1.77	2.95
☐ 3, Jan 95 .... 2.95		0.59	1.77	2.95
☐ 4, Feb 95 .... 2.95		0.59	1.77	2.95
☐ 5, Mar 95 .... 2.95		0.59	1.77	2.95
☐ 6, Apr 95 .... 2.95		0.59	1.77	2.95

SHADOWS FROM THE GRAVE
RENEGADE

	GOOD	FINE	N-MINT
☐ 1, b&w	0.40	1.20	2.00
☐ 2, b&w	0.40	1.20	2.00

SHADOWSTAR
SHADOWSTAR

	GOOD	FINE	N-MINT
☐ 1	0.30	0.90	1.50
☐ 2	0.30	0.90	1.50
☐ 3	0.30	0.90	1.50

SHADOWTOWN: BLACK FIST RISING
MADHEART

	ORIG.	GOOD	FINE	N-MINT
☐ 1, b&w 2.50		0.50	1.50	2.50

SHAIANA
EXPRESS/ENTITY

	ORIG.	GOOD	FINE	N-MINT
☐ 3, 96 .... 2.50		0.50	1.50	2.50

SHAIANA (mini-series)

	ORIG.	GOOD	FINE	N-MINT
☐ 1, 95, enhanced cover 3.75		0.75	2.25	3.75

SHALOMAN
MARK 1

	GOOD	FINE	N-MINT
☐ 1, b&w	0.35	1.05	1.75
☐ 2, b&w	0.35	1.05	1.75
☐ 3, b&w	0.35	1.05	1.75
☐ 4, b&w	0.35	1.05	1.75
☐ 5, b&w	0.35	1.05	1.75
☐ 6, b&w	0.35	1.05	1.75
☐ 7, b&w	0.35	1.05	1.75
☐ 8, b&w	0.35	1.05	1.75
☐ 9, b&w	0.35	1.05	1.75

SHAMAN'S TEARS
IMAGE

	ORIG.	GOOD	FINE	N-MINT
☐ 1, MGr 2.50		0.50	1.50	2.50
☐ 2, MGr,gatefold cover 2.50		0.50	1.50	2.50
☐ 3, MGr,ashcan		1.50	4.50	7.50
☐ 3, Nov 94, MGr 1.95		0.39	1.17	1.95
☐ 4, Dec 94, MGr 1.95		0.39	1.17	1.95
☐ 5, Jan 95, MGr 1.95		0.39	1.17	1.95
☐ 6, Feb 95, MGr 1.95		0.39	1.17	1.95
☐ 7, May 95, MGr 1.95		0.39	1.17	1.95
☐ 9, Jun 95, MGr 1.95		0.39	1.17	1.95
☐ 11, Aug 95, MGr 2.50		0.50	1.50	2.50

SHANDA THE PANDA (former MU Press title)
ANTARCTIC

	ORIG.	GOOD	FINE	N-MINT
☐ 1, Jun 93, b&w 2.50		0.50	1.50	2.50
☐ 2, Aug 93, b&w 2.50		0.50	1.50	2.50
☐ 3, Oct 93, b&w 2.75		0.55	1.65	2.75
☐ 4, Dec 93, b&w 2.75		0.55	1.65	2.75
☐ 5, Aug 94, b&w 2.75		0.55	1.65	2.75
☐ 6, Oct 94, b&w 2.75		0.55	1.65	2.75

	ORIG.	GOOD	FINE	N-MINT
☐ 7, Jan 95, b&w 2.75		0.55	1.65	2.75
☐ 8, Feb 95, b&w 2.75		0.55	1.65	2.75
☐ 9, Apr 95, b&w 2.75		0.55	1.65	2.75
☐ 10, Jul 95, b&w 2.75		0.55	1.65	2.75
☐ 12, Nov 95, b&w 2.75		0.55	1.65	2.75

SHANDA THE PANDA (Vol. 1)
MU PRESS

	ORIG.	GOOD	FINE	N-MINT
☐ 1, May 92 .... 2.50		0.50	1.50	2.50

SHANGHAIED
ETERNITY

	GOOD	FINE	N-MINT
☐ 1	0.36	1.08	1.80
☐ 2	0.39	1.17	1.95
☐ 3	0.39	1.17	1.95

SHANNA THE SHE-DEVIL
MARVEL

	ORIG.	GOOD	FINE	N-MINT
☐ 1 .... 0.20		0.20	0.60	1.00
☐ 2 .... 0.20		0.20	0.60	1.00
☐ 3 .... 0.20		0.20	0.60	1.00
☐ 4 .... 0.20		0.20	0.60	1.00
☐ 5 .... 0.20		0.20	0.60	1.00

SHATTER
FIRST

	ORIG.	GOOD	FINE	N-MINT
☐ 1, Dec 85 .... 1.75		0.60	1.80	3.00
☐ 2		0.50	1.50	2.50
☐ 3		0.50	1.50	2.50
☐ 4		0.35	1.05	1.75
☐ 5		0.35	1.05	1.75
☐ 6		0.35	1.05	1.75
☐ 7		0.35	1.05	1.75
☐ 8		0.35	1.05	1.75
☐ 9		0.35	1.05	1.75
☐ 10		0.35	1.05	1.75
☐ 11		0.35	1.05	1.75
☐ 12		0.35	1.05	1.75
☐ 13		0.35	1.05	1.75
☐ 14		0.35	1.05	1.75

SHATTER SPECIAL

	GOOD	FINE	N-MINT
☐ 1, 1:computer comic	0.60	1.80	3.00
☐ 1, 2nd printing	0.40	1.20	2.00

SHATTERED EARTH
ETERNITY

	GOOD	FINE	N-MINT
☐ 1, b&w, Ex-Mutants	0.39	1.17	1.95
☐ 2, b&w, Ex-Mutants	0.39	1.17	1.95
☐ 3, b&w, Ex-Mutants	0.39	1.17	1.95
☐ 4, b&w, Ex-Mutants	0.39	1.17	1.95
☐ 5, b&w, Ex-Mutants	0.39	1.17	1.95
☐ 6, b&w, Ex-Mutants	0.39	1.17	1.95
☐ 7, b&w, Ex-Mutants	0.39	1.17	1.95
☐ 8, b&w, Ex-Mutants	0.39	1.17	1.95
☐ 9, b&w, Ex-Mutants	0.39	1.17	1.95

SHATTERPOINT

	GOOD	FINE	N-MINT
☐ 1, Broid, b&w	0.45	1.35	2.25
☐ 2, Broid, b&w	0.45	1.35	2.25
☐ 3, Broid, b&w	0.45	1.35	2.25
☐ 4, Broid, b&w	0.45	1.35	2.25

SHAZAM!
DC

	ORIG.	GOOD	FINE	N-MINT
☐ 1, Feb 73, CCB,O:Capt. Marvel				
.... 0.20		0.30	0.90	1.50
☐ 2, Apr 73, CCB 0.20		0.20	0.60	1.00
☐ 3, Jun 73, CCB 0.20		0.20	0.60	1.00
☐ 4, Jul 73, CCB 0.20		0.20	0.60	1.00
☐ 5, Sep 73, CCB 0.20		0.20	0.60	1.00
☐ 6, Oct 73, CCB 0.20		0.20	0.60	1.00
☐ 7, Nov 73, CCB 0.20		0.20	0.60	1.00
☐ 8, Dec 73, CCB 0.20		0.20	0.60	1.00
☐ 9, Jan 74, CCB 0.20		0.20	0.60	1.00
☐ 10, Feb 74, CCB 0.20		0.20	0.60	1.00
☐ 11, Mar 74 .... 0.20		0.20	0.60	1.00
☐ 12, Jun 74 .... 0.60		0.20	0.60	1.00

	ORIG.	GOOD	FINE	N-MINT
☐ 13, Aug 74 .... 0.60		0.20	0.60	1.00
☐ 14, Oct 74, KS, A:Monster Society 100 pg.				
.... 0.60		0.20	0.60	1.00
☐ 15, Dec 74........................ 0.60		0.20	0.60	1.00
☐ 16, Feb 75 .... 0.60		0.20	0.60	1.00
☐ 17, Apr 75 .... 0.60		0.20	0.60	1.00
☐ 18, Jun 75 .... 0.25		0.20	0.60	1.00
☐ 19, Aug 75 .... 0.25		0.20	0.60	1.00
☐ 20, Oct 75 .... 0.25		0.20	0.60	1.00
☐ 21, Dec 75...................... 0.25		0.20	0.60	1.00
☐ 22, Feb 76 .... 0.25		0.20	0.60	1.00
☐ 23, Win 76 .... 0.30		0.20	0.60	1.00
☐ 24, Spr 76 .... 0.30		0.20	0.60	1.00
☐ 25, Oct 76 .... 0.30		0.20	0.60	1.00
☐ 26, Dec 76...................... 0.30		0.20	0.60	1.00
☐ 27, Feb 77 .... 0.30		0.20	0.60	1.00
☐ 28, Apr 77 .... 0.30		0.20	0.60	1.00
☐ 29, Jun 77 .... 0.30		0.20	0.60	1.00
☐ 30, Aug 77 .... 0.35		0.20	0.60	1.00
☐ 31, Oct 77 .... 0.35		0.20	0.60	1.00
☐ 32, Dec 77...................... 0.35		0.20	0.60	1.00
☐ 33, Feb 78 .... 0.35		0.20	0.60	1.00
☐ 34, Apr 78 .... 0.35		0.20	0.60	1.00
☐ 35, Jun 78 .... 0.35		0.20	0.60	1.00

SHAZAM! THE NEW BEGINNING

	ORIG.	GOOD	FINE	N-MINT
☐ 1, Apr 87, Legends......... 0.75		0.30	0.90	1.50
☐ 2, May 87 .... 0.75		0.20	0.60	1.00
☐ 3, Jun 87........................ 0.75		0.20	0.60	1.00
☐ 4, Jul 87 .... 0.75		0.20	0.60	1.00

SHE BUCCANEER
MONSTER

	GOOD	FINE	N-MINT
☐ 1, b&w	0.45	1.35	2.25
☐ 2, b&w	0.45	1.35	2.25

SHE'S JOSIE
ARCHIE

	GOOD	FINE	N-MINT
☐ 1, Feb 63	20.00	60.00	100.00
☐ 2	12.00	36.00	60.00
☐ 3	8.00	24.00	40.00
☐ 4	8.00	24.00	40.00
☐ 5	8.00	24.00	40.00
☐ 6	6.00	18.00	30.00
☐ 7	6.00	18.00	30.00
☐ 8	6.00	18.00	30.00
☐ 9	6.00	18.00	30.00
☐ 10	6.00	18.00	30.00
☐ 11	4.00	12.00	20.00
☐ 12	4.00	12.00	20.00
☐ 13	4.00	12.00	20.00
☐ 14	4.00	12.00	20.00
☐ 15	4.00	12.00	20.00
☐ 16, (becomes *Josie*)	4.00	12.00	20.00

SHE-CAT
AC

	GOOD	FINE	N-MINT
☐ 1, Jun 89, b&w................	0.50	1.50	2.50
☐ 2, Apr 90, b&w................	0.50	1.50	2.50
☐ 3, May 90, b&w...............	0.50	1.50	2.50
☐ 4, Jun 90, b&w	0.50	1.50	2.50

SHE-HULK: CEREMONY
MARVEL

	ORIG.	GOOD	FINE	N-MINT
☐ 1, leg shaving................. 3.95		0.79	2.37	3.95
☐ 2 .... 3.95		0.79	2.37	3.95

SHEEDEVA
FANTAGRAPHICS/EROS

	ORIG.	GOOD	FINE	N-MINT
☐ 1, Aug 94, adult;b&w 2.95		0.59	1.77	2.95

SHEENA
MARVEL

	ORIG.	GOOD	FINE	N-MINT
☐ 1, Dec 84, GM, movie 0.75		0.20	0.60	1.00
☐ 2, Feb 85, GM, movie 0.75		0.20	0.60	1.00

SHEENA, QUEEN OF THE JUNGLE 3-D
BLACKTHORNE

	ORIG.	GOOD	FINE	N-MINT
☐ 1, May 85, DSt................ 2.50		0.50	1.50	2.50

SHELL SHOCK
MIRAGE

	GOOD	FINE	N-MINT
☐ 1, anthology....................	2.59	7.77	12.95

SHERLOCK HOLMES
DC

	ORIG.	GOOD	FINE	N-MINT
☐ 1, Oct 75........................ 0.25		0.05	0.15	0.25

ETERNITY

	GOOD	FINE	N-MINT
☐ 1, b&w strip rep...............	0.39	1.17	1.95
☐ 2, b&w strip rep...............	0.39	1.17	1.95
☐ 3, b&w strip rep...............	0.39	1.17	1.95
☐ 4, b&w strip rep...............	0.39	1.17	1.95
☐ 5, b&w strip rep...............	0.39	1.17	1.95
☐ 6, b&w strip rep...............	0.39	1.17	1.95
☐ 7, b&w strip rep...............	0.39	1.17	1.95
☐ 8, b&w strip rep...............	0.39	1.17	1.95
☐ 9, b&w strip rep...............	0.39	1.17	1.95
☐ 10, b&w strip rep.............	0.39	1.17	1.95
☐ 11, b&w strip rep.............	0.39	1.17	1.95
☐ 12, b&w strip rep.............	0.39	1.17	1.95
☐ 13, b&w strip rep.............	0.39	1.17	1.95
☐ 14, b&w strip rep.............	0.39	1.17	1.95
☐ 15, b&w strip rep.............	0.39	1.17	1.95
☐ 16	0.45	1.35	2.25
☐ 17	0.45	1.35	2.25
☐ 18	0.45	1.35	2.25
☐ 19	0.45	1.35	2.25
☐ 20	0.45	1.35	2.25
☐ 21	0.50	1.50	2.50
☐ 22	0.50	1.50	2.50
☐ 23	0.55	1.65	2.75

SHERLOCK HOLMES CASEBOOK

	GOOD	FINE	N-MINT
☐ 1	0.45	1.35	2.25
☐ 2	0.45	1.35	2.25

SHERLOCK HOLMES IN THE CASE OF THE MISSING MARTIAN

	GOOD	FINE	N-MINT
☐ 1, b&w..............................	0.45	1.35	2.25
☐ 2, b&w..............................	0.45	1.35	2.25
☐ 3, b&w..............................	0.45	1.35	2.25
☐ 4, b&w..............................	0.45	1.35	2.25

SHERLOCK HOLMES IN THE CURIOUS CASE OF THE VANISHING VILLAIN
ATOMEKA

	GOOD	FINE	N-MINT
☐ 0, nn	0.90	2.70	4.50

SHERLOCK HOLMES OF THE '30S
ETERNITY

	GOOD	FINE	N-MINT
☐ 1, b&w;strip reprints.........	0.59	1.77	2.95
☐ 2, b&w;strip reprints.........	0.59	1.77	2.95
☐ 3, b&w;strip reprints.........	0.59	1.77	2.95
☐ 4, b&w;strip reprints.........	0.59	1.77	2.95
☐ 5, b&w;strip reprints.........	0.59	1.77	2.95
☐ 6, b&w;strip reprints.........	0.59	1.77	2.95
☐ 7, b&w;strip reprints.........	0.59	1.77	2.95

SHERLOCK HOLMES: RETURN OF THE DEVIL (mini-series)
ADVENTURE

	ORIG.	GOOD	FINE	N-MINT
☐ 1, Sep 92, b&w............... 2.50		0.50	1.50	2.50
☐ 2, 92, b&w...................... 2.50		0.50	1.50	2.50

SHERLOCK JR.
ETERNITY

	GOOD	FINE	N-MINT
☐ 1, strip reprints, b&w........	0.50	1.50	2.50
☐ 2, strip reprints, b&w........	0.50	1.50	2.50
☐ 3, strip reprints, b&w........	0.50	1.50	2.50

SHI
CRUSADE

	ORIG.	GOOD	FINE	N-MINT
☐ 1, Mar 94 .... 2.50		9.00	27.00	45.00
☐ 2		4.80	14.40	24.00
☐ 3		2.80	8.40	14.00

	ORIG.	GOOD	FINE	N-MINT
❏ 4		1.60	4.80	8.00
❏ 5		1.00	3.00	5.00
❏ 8, 96	2.95	0.59	1.77	2.95

SHI/CYBLADE: THE BATTLE FOR INDEPENDENTS
CRUSADE/IMAGE

❏ 1, Sep 95, crossover;concludesImage's *Cyblade/Shi: The Battlefor Independents* #1

	2.95	0.59	1.77	2.95

❏ 1, Sep 95, crossover;concludesImage's *Cyblade/Shi: The Battlefor Independents* #1;alternate cover

	2.95	0.59	1.77	2.95

SHIELD
ARCHIE

	ORIG.	GOOD	FINE	N-MINT
❏ 1		0.30	0.90	1.50
❏ 2, Aug 83	1.00	0.20	0.60	1.00
❏ 3, Dec 83, (becomes *Steel Sterling*)				
		0.15	0.45	0.75

SHIPWRECKED!
DISNEY

	ORIG.	GOOD	FINE	N-MINT
❏ 0, nn DS, movie adaptation	1.19	3.57	5.95	

SHOCK SUSPENSTORIES
EC/GEMSTONE

❏ 1, Ingels, Orlando, Kamen, Davis reprints

	GOOD	FINE	N-MINT
	0.30	0.90	1.50
❏ 2, reprints	0.30	0.90	1.50
❏ 3, reprints	0.30	0.90	1.50
❏ 4, reprints, WW,JO,JD,JKa			
2.00	0.40	1.20	2.00
❏ 5, reprints, WW,JK,JO,JD			
2.00	0.40	1.20	2.00
❏ 6, reprints, WW,JK,JO,GI			
2.00	0.40	1.20	2.00
❏ 7, reprints,AF(c),JK,WW,JO,GE			
2.00	0.40	1.20	2.00
❏ 8, Jun 94, r:AF(c),J,WW,AW,GE			
2.00	0.40	1.20	2.00
❏ 9, reprints	2.00	0.40	1.20	2.00
❏ 10, reprints	2.00	0.40	1.20	2.00
❏ 11, reprints	2.00	0.40	1.20	2.00
❏ 12, reprints	2.00	0.40	1.20	2.00
❏ 13, reprints	2.00	0.40	1.20	2.00

SHOCK THERAPY
HARRIER

	GOOD	FINE	N-MINT
❏ 1	0.39	1.17	1.95
❏ 2	0.39	1.17	1.95
❏ 3	0.39	1.17	1.95
❏ 4	0.39	1.17	1.95
❏ 5	0.39	1.17	1.95

SHOGUN WARRIORS
MARVEL

	ORIG.	GOOD	FINE	N-MINT
❏ 1, Feb 79	0.35	0.40	1.20	2.00
❏ 2, Mar 79	0.35	0.30	0.90	1.50
❏ 3, Apr 79	0.35	0.30	0.90	1.50
❏ 4, May 79	0.40	0.30	0.90	1.50
❏ 5, Jun 79	0.40	0.30	0.90	1.50
❏ 6, Jul 79	0.40	0.30	0.90	1.50
❏ 7, Aug 79	0.40	0.30	0.90	1.50
❏ 8, Sep 79	0.40	0.30	0.90	1.50
❏ 9, Oct 79	0.40	0.30	0.90	1.50
❏ 10, Nov 79	0.40	0.30	0.90	1.50
❏ 11, Dec 79	0.40	0.30	0.90	1.50
❏ 12, Jan 80	0.40	0.30	0.90	1.50
❏ 13, Feb 80	0.40	0.30	0.90	1.50
❏ 14, Mar 80	0.40	0.30	0.90	1.50
❏ 15, Apr 80	0.40	0.30	0.90	1.50
❏ 16, May 80	0.40	0.30	0.90	1.50
❏ 17, Jun 80	0.40	0.30	0.90	1.50
❏ 18, Jul 80	0.40	0.30	0.90	1.50
❏ 19, Aug 80	0.40	0.30	0.90	1.50
❏ 20, Sep 80	0.50	0.30	0.90	1.50

SHOOTY BEAGLE
EROS COMIX

	ORIG.	GOOD	FINE	N-MINT
❏ 1, adult, b&w		0.45	1.35	2.25
❏ 2, adult, b&w		0.45	1.35	2.25
❏ 3, adult, b&w		0.45	1.35	2.25

SHORT ON PLOT!
MU PRESS

	ORIG.	GOOD	FINE	N-MINT
❏ 0, nn b&w	2.50	0.50	1.50	2.50

SHOTGUN MARY (mini-series)
ANTARCTIC

	ORIG.	GOOD	FINE	N-MINT
❏ 1, Sep 95	2.95	0.59	1.77	2.95

SHOWCASE
DC

	ORIG.	GOOD	FINE	N-MINT
❏ 1, Apr 56, Fire Fighters	0.10	520.00	1560.00	2600.00
❏ 2, Jun 56, JKu, Kings of Wild				
	0.10	100.00	300.00	500.00
❏ 3, Aug 56, Frogmen	0.10	110.00	330.00	550.00
❏ 4, Oct 56, CI/JKu, O:Flash				
	0.10	5000.	15000.	25000.
❏ 5, Dec 56, Manhunters	0.10	140.00	420.00	700.00
❏ 6, Feb 57, JK(c), O:Challengers				
	0.10	550.00	1650.00	2750.00
❏ 7, Apr 57, JK(c), Challengers				
	0.10	280.00	840.00	1400.00
❏ 8, Jun 57, CI;Flash O:Capt. Cold				
	0.10	1240.00	3720.00	6200.00
❏ 9, Aug 57, Lois Lane	0.10	550.00	1650.00	2750.00
❏ 10, Oct 57, Lois Lane	0.10	330.00	990.00	1650.00
❏ 11, Dec 57, JK (c), Challengers				
	0.10	240.00	720.00	1200.00
❏ 12, Feb 58, JK (c),Challengers				
	0.10	240.00	720.00	1200.00
❏ 13, Apr 58, O:Mr. Element				
	0.10	550.00	1650.00	2750.00
❏ 14, Jun 58, O: Dr. Alchemy				
	0.10	520.00	1560.00	2600.00
❏ 15, Aug 58, Space Ranger				
	0.10	250.00	750.00	1250.00
❏ 16, Oct 58,Space Ranger				
	0.10	120.00	360.00	600.00
❏ 17, Dec 58, GK(c),O&1:Adam Strange				
	0.10	390.00	1170.00	1950.00
❏ 18, Feb 59, GK(c), Adam Strange				
	0.10	200.00	600.00	1000.00
❏ 19, Apr 59, GK(c), Adam Strange				
	0.10	200.00	600.00	1000.00
❏ 20, Jun 59, Rip Hunter	0.10	170.00	510.00	850.00
❏ 21, Aug 59, Rip Hunter	0.10	80.00	240.00	400.00
❏ 22, Oct 59, GK;O&1:Green Lantern				
	0.10	900.00	2700.00	4500.00
❏ 23, Dec 59, GK, Green Lantern				
	0.10	290.00	870.00	1450.00
❏ 24, Feb 60, GK, Green Lantern				
	0.10	290.00	870.00	1450.00
❏ 25, Apr 60, JKu,Rip Hunter				
	0.10	40.00	120.00	200.00
❏ 26, Jun 60, JKu, Rip Hunter				
	0.10	40.00	120.00	200.00
❏ 27, Aug 60, RH,I:Sea Devils				
	0.10	140.00	420.00	700.00
❏ 28, Oct 60, RH,Sea Devils				
	0.10	50.00	150.00	250.00
❏ 29, Dec 60, RH, Sea Devils				
	0.10	50.00	150.00	250.00
❏ 30, Feb 61, O:Aquaman	0.10	110.00	330.00	550.00
❏ 31, Apr 61, Aquaman	0.10	60.00	180.00	300.00
❏ 32, Jun 61, Aquaman	0.10	60.00	180.00	300.00
❏ 33, Aug 61, Aquaman	0.10	60.00	180.00	300.00
❏ 34, Oct 61, GK;O&1:Atom				
	0.10	280.00	840.00	1400.00
❏ 35, Dec 61, GK, Atom	0.10	140.00	420.00	700.00

	ORIG.	GOOD	FINE	N-MINT
36, Feb 62, GK, Atom	0.12	100.00	300.00	500.00
37, Apr 62, I:Metal Men	0.12	100.00	300.00	500.00
38, Jun 62, Metal Men	0.12	60.00	180.00	300.00
39, Aug 62, Metal Men	0.12	45.00	135.00	225.00
40, Oct 62, Metal Men	0.12	45.00	135.00	225.00
41, Dec 62, Tommy Tomorrow	0.12	20.00	60.00	100.00
42, Feb 63, Tommy Tomorrow	0.12	20.00	60.00	100.00
43, Apr 63, Dr. No/007	0.12	75.00	225.00	375.00
44, Jun 63, Tommy Tomorrow	0.12	18.00	54.00	90.00
45, Aug 63, JKu, Sgt. Rock	0.12	25.00	75.00	125.00
46, Oct 63,Tommy Tomorrow	0.12	14.00	42.00	70.00
47, Dec 63,Tommy Tomorrow	0.12	14.00	42.00	70.00
48, Feb 64, Cave Carson	0.12	7.20	21.60	36.00
49, Apr 64, Cave Carson	0.12	7.20	21.60	36.00
50, Jun 64, MA/CI, I Spy	0.12	7.20	21.60	36.00
51, Aug 64, MA/CI, I Spy	0.12	7.20	21.60	36.00
52, Oct 64, Cave Carson.	0.12	7.20	21.60	36.00
53, Dec 64, JKu, G.I. Joe	0.12	10.00	30.00	50.00
54, Feb 65, JKu, G.I. Joe	0.12	10.00	30.00	50.00
55, Apr 65, MA, Dr. Fate	0.12	35.00	105.00	175.00
56, Jun 65, MA, Dr. Fate	0.12	16.00	48.00	80.00
57, Aug 65, JKu,Enemy Ace	0.12	16.00	48.00	80.00
58, Oct 65, JKu, Enemy Ace	0.12	12.00	36.00	60.00
59, Dec 65, Teen Titans	0.12	13.00	39.00	65.00
60, Feb 66, MA, Spectre.	0.12	22.00	66.00	110.00
61, Apr 66, MA, Spectre.	0.12	8.40	25.20	42.00
62, Jun 66, JO, Inferior 5	0.12	7.20	21.60	36.00
63, Aug 66, JO, Inferior 5	0.12	3.60	10.80	18.00
64, Oct 66, MA, Spectre.	0.12	8.40	25.20	42.00
65, Dec 66, Inferior 5	0.12	3.60	10.80	18.00
66, Feb 67, B'wana Beast	0.12	1.20	3.60	6.00
67, Apr 67, B'wana Beast	0.12	1.20	3.60	6.00
68, Jun 67, Maniaks	0.12	1.20	3.60	6.00
69, Aug 67, Maniaks	0.12	1.20	3.60	6.00
70, Oct 67, Binky	0.12	1.20	3.60	6.00
71, Dec 67, Maniaks	0.12	1.20	3.60	6.00
72, Feb 68, JKu/ATh,Top Gun	0.12	1.20	3.60	6.00
73, Apr 68, SD, 1&O:Creeper	0.12	12.00	36.00	60.00
74, May 68, 1:Anthro	0.12	6.40	19.20	32.00
75, Jun 68, SD, 1:Hawk & Dove	0.12	13.00	39.00	65.00
76, Aug 68, 1:Bat Lash	0.12	6.00	18.00	30.00
77, Sep 68, 1:Angel & Ape	0.12	4.00	12.00	20.00
78, Nov 68, 1:Jonny Double	0.12	2.00	6.00	10.00
79, Dec 68, 1:Dolphin	0.12	3.00	9.00	15.00
80, Feb 69, NA(c), Phantom Stranger	0.12	2.00	6.00	10.00
81, Mar 69, Windy & Willy	0.12	1.20	3.60	6.00
82, May 69, 1:Nightmaster	0.12	6.00	18.00	30.00
83, Jun 69, BWr/MK,Nightmaster	0.12	7.20	21.60	36.00
84, Aug 69, BWr/MK, Nightmaster	0.15	7.20	21.60	36.00
85, Sep 69, JKu, Firehair	0.15	1.60	4.80	8.00
86, Nov 69, JKu, Firehair	0.15	1.60	4.80	8.00
87, Dec 69, JKu, Firehair	0.15	1.60	4.80	8.00

	ORIG.	GOOD	FINE	N-MINT
88, Feb 70,Jason's Quest	0.15	1.00	3.00	5.00
89, Mar 70,Jason's Quest	0.15	1.00	3.00	5.00
90, May 70, Manhunter 2070	0.15	1.00	3.00	5.00
91, Jun 70, Manhunter 2070	0.15	1.00	3.00	5.00
92, Aug 70, Manhunter 2070	0.15	1.00	3.00	5.00
93, Sep 70, Manhunter 2070	0.15	1.00	3.00	5.00
94, Aug 77, JA/JSA, 1&O:new Doom Patrol	0.35	1.40	4.20	7.00
95, Oct 77, JA/JSA, Doom Patrol	0.35	0.80	2.40	4.00
96, Dec 77, JA/JSA,Doom Patrol	0.35	0.80	2.40	4.00
97, Feb 78, Power Girl	0.35	0.80	2.40	4.00
98, Mar 78, Power Girl	0.35	0.80	2.40	4.00
99, Apr 78, Power Girl	0.35	0.80	2.40	4.00
100, May 78, JSA,all-star issue	0.60	0.80	2.40	4.00
101, Jun 78, MA,JK(c), Hawkman	0.35	0.80	2.40	4.00
102, Jul 78, MA,JK(c), Hawkman	0.35	0.80	2.40	4.00
103, Aug 78, MA,JK(c), Hawkman	0.35	0.80	2.40	4.00
104, Sep 78, OSS Spies	0.50	0.80	2.40	4.00

SHOWCASE '93

	ORIG.	GOOD	FINE	N-MINT
1, Jan 93, Catwoman	1.95	0.39	1.17	1.95
2, Feb 93	1.95	0.39	1.17	1.95
3, Mar 93	1.95	0.39	1.17	1.95
4, Apr 93, Catwoman	1.95	0.39	1.17	1.95
5, May 93, Robin	1.95	0.39	1.17	1.95
6, Jun 93, Robin	1.95	0.39	1.17	1.95
7, "Knightfall", Two-Face	1.95	0.80	2.40	4.00
8, "Knightfall", Two-Face	1.95	0.39	1.17	1.95
9, Huntress	1.95	0.39	1.17	1.95
10	1.95	0.39	1.17	1.95
11	1.95	0.80	2.40	4.00
12, Nightwing, Robin	1.95	0.60	1.80	3.00

SHOWCASE '94

	ORIG.	GOOD	FINE	N-MINT
1, Joker	1.95	0.39	1.17	1.95
2, Joker	1.95	0.39	1.17	1.95
3, Arkham Asylum	1.95	0.39	1.17	1.95
4, Arkham Asylum	1.95	0.39	1.17	1.95
5, May 94	1.95	0.39	1.17	1.95
6, Jun 94, Robin	1.95	0.39	1.17	1.95
7, Jul 94, Penguin	1.95	0.39	1.17	1.95
8, Aug 94	1.95	0.39	1.17	1.95
9, Sep 94	1.95	0.39	1.17	1.95
10, Oct 94	1.95	0.60	1.80	3.00
11, Nov 94	1.95	0.39	1.17	1.95
12, Dec 94	1.95	0.39	1.17	1.95

SHOWCASE '95

	ORIG.	GOOD	FINE	N-MINT
1, Jan 95	2.50	0.50	1.50	2.50
2, Feb 95	2.50	0.50	1.50	2.50
3, Mar 95	2.50	0.50	1.50	2.50
4, Apr 95	2.50	0.50	1.50	2.50
5, Jun 95	2.50	0.50	1.50	2.50
6, Jul 95	2.95	0.59	1.77	2.95
7, Aug 95, Mongul;Arion;New Gods	2.95	0.59	1.77	2.95
8, Sep 95, Mongul;Spectre;Arsenal	2.95	0.59	1.77	2.95
9, Oct 95, Lois Lane;Lobo;Martian Manhunter	2.95	0.59	1.77	2.95
10, Nov 95, Gangbuster;Ferrin Colos;Hi-Tech	2.95	0.59	1.77	2.95

	ORIG.	GOOD	FINE	N-MINT
☐ 11, Nov 95, Agent Liberty;Arkham Asylum;Hi-Tech 2.95		0.59	1.77	2.95
☐ 12, Dec 95, Supergirl;Maitresse;The Shade 2.95		0.59	1.77	2.95

SHOWCASE '96

	ORIG.	GOOD	FINE	N-MINT
☐ 1, Jan 96, Steel and Guy Gardner: Warrior; Aqualad; Metropolis S.C.U. 2.95		0.59	1.77	2.95
☐ 2, Steel and Guy Gardner: Warrior;Circe;Metallo 2.95		0.59	1.77	2.95
☐ 3, Mar 96, Lois Lane and Black Canary;Dr. Fate and The Shade;Lightray 2.95		0.59	1.77	2.95
☐ 4, Apr 96, Guardian and Firebrand;Dr. Fate and The Shade;The Demon.......... 2.95		0.59	1.77	2.95
☐ 5, Jun 96, Green Arrowand Thorn;Dr. Fate andThe Shade;New Gods........... 2.95		0.59	1.77	2.95

SHRED
CFW

	ORIG.	GOOD	FINE	N-MINT
☐ 1		0.45	1.35	2.25
☐ 2		0.45	1.35	2.25
☐ 3		0.45	1.35	2.25
☐ 4		0.45	1.35	2.25
☐ 5		0.45	1.35	2.25
☐ 6		0.45	1.35	2.25
☐ 7		0.45	1.35	2.25
☐ 8		0.45	1.35	2.25

SHRIEK
FANTACO

	ORIG.	GOOD	FINE	N-MINT
☐ 1, b&w		0.99	2.97	4.95
☐ 2, b&w 4.95		0.99	2.97	4.95

SHRIEK SPECIAL

	ORIG.	GOOD	FINE	N-MINT
☐ 1, b&w		0.70	2.10	3.50
☐ 2, Dangerbrain, b&w		0.70	2.10	3.50
☐ 3, b&w		0.70	2.10	3.50

SHRIKE
VICTORY

	ORIG.	GOOD	FINE	N-MINT
☐ 1		0.30	0.90	1.50
☐ 2		0.30	0.90	1.50

SHROUD, THE
MARVEL

	ORIG.	GOOD	FINE	N-MINT
☐ 1 .... 1.75		0.35	1.05	1.75
☐ 2 .... 1.75		0.35	1.05	1.75
☐ 3, May 94 .... 1.75		0.35	1.05	1.75
☐ 4, Jun 94 .... 1.75		0.35	1.05	1.75

SHUGGA
EROS COMIX

	ORIG.	GOOD	FINE	N-MINT
☐ 1, adult, b&w		0.50	1.50	2.50
☐ 2, adult, b&w		0.50	1.50	2.50

SHURIKEN
BLACKTHORNE

	ORIG.	GOOD	FINE	N-MINT
☐ 1, graphic novel	1.59	4.77	7.95	

ETERNITY

	ORIG.	GOOD	FINE	N-MINT
☐ 1, b&w		0.50	1.50	2.50
☐ 2, b&w		0.50	1.50	2.50
☐ 3, b&w		0.50	1.50	2.50
☐ 4, b&w		0.50	1.50	2.50
☐ 5, b&w		0.50	1.50	2.50
☐ 6, b&w		0.50	1.50	2.50

VICTORY

	ORIG.	GOOD	FINE	N-MINT
☐ 1, RBy	2.00	6.00	10.00	
☐ 2	1.60	4.80	8.00	
☐ 3		0.30	0.90	1.50
☐ 4		0.30	0.90	1.50
☐ 5		0.30	0.90	1.50
☐ 6		0.30	0.90	1.50
☐ 7		0.30	0.90	1.50
☐ 8		0.30	0.90	1.50

SHURIKEN TEAM-UP
ETERNITY

	ORIG.	GOOD	FINE	N-MINT
☐ 1, Shuriken, Libra, Kokutai b&w	0.39	1.17	1.95	

SHURIKEN: COLD STEEL

	ORIG.	GOOD	FINE	N-MINT
☐ 1, b&w, 16 pgs.		0.30	0.90	1.50
☐ 2		0.39	1.17	1.95
☐ 3		0.39	1.17	1.95
☐ 4		0.39	1.17	1.95
☐ 5		0.39	1.17	1.95
☐ 6		0.39	1.17	1.95

SICK SMILES
AIIIE!

	ORIG.	GOOD	FINE	N-MINT
☐ 1, Jun 94, b&w 2.50		0.50	1.50	2.50
☐ 2, Jul 94, b&w 2.50		0.50	1.50	2.50

SIDE SHOW
MATURE MAGIC

	ORIG.	GOOD	FINE	N-MINT
☐ 1		0.35	1.05	1.75

SIDESHOW COMICS
PAN GRAPHICS

	ORIG.	GOOD	FINE	N-MINT
☐ 1, b&w...........................		0.40	1.20	2.00
☐ 2, b&w...........................		0.40	1.20	2.00

SIDNEY MELLON'S THUNDERSKULL!
SLAVE LABOR

	ORIG.	GOOD	FINE	N-MINT
☐ 1, b&w...........................		0.39	1.17	1.95

SIEGE OF THE ALAMO
TOME PRESS

	ORIG.	GOOD	FINE	N-MINT
☐ 1, b&w...........................		0.50	1.50	2.50

SIEGEL & SHUSTER: DATELINE 1930'S
ECLIPSE

	ORIG.	GOOD	FINE	N-MINT
☐ 1, Nov 84, S&S...............		0.30	0.90	1.50
☐ 2, Sep 85, S&S...............		0.30	0.90	1.50

SIGMA
IMAGE

	ORIG.	GOOD	FINE	N-MINT
☐ 2, May 96, "Fire from Heaven" Part 6 .... 2.50		0.50	1.50	2.50

SILBUSTER
ANTARCTIC

	ORIG.	GOOD	FINE	N-MINT
☐ 1, Jan 94, b&w 2.95		0.80	2.40	4.00
☐ 2, Feb 94, b&w 2.95		0.59	1.77	2.95
☐ 3, Mar 94, b&w............... 2.95		0.59	1.77	2.95
☐ 4, Apr 94, b&w 2.95		0.59	1.77	2.95
☐ 5, Oct 94, b&w 2.95		0.59	1.77	2.95
☐ 6, Nov 94, b&w............... 2.95		0.59	1.77	2.95
☐ 7, Dec 94, b&w 2.95		0.59	1.77	2.95
☐ 8, Jan 95, b&w 2.95		0.59	1.77	2.95
☐ 9, Feb 95, b&w 2.95		0.59	1.77	2.95
☐ 10, Aug 95, b&w............... 2.95		0.59	1.77	2.95
☐ 11, Oct 95, b&w............... 2.95		0.59	1.77	2.95

SILENCERS
CALIBER

	ORIG.	GOOD	FINE	N-MINT
☐ 1, Jul 91, b&w 2.50		0.50	1.50	2.50
☐ 2, b&w........................... 2.50		0.50	1.50	2.50
☐ 3, b&w........................... 2.50		0.50	1.50	2.50
☐ 4, b&w........................... 2.50		0.50	1.50	2.50

SILENT INVASION, THE
RENEGADE

	ORIG.	GOOD	FINE	N-MINT
☐ 1, Apr 86, b&w............... 1.70		0.60	1.80	3.00
☐ 2, Jun 86, b&w............... 1.70		0.60	1.80	3.00
☐ 3, Aug 86, b&w............... 1.70		0.60	1.80	3.00
☐ 4, Oct 86, b&w............... 2.00		0.40	1.20	2.00
☐ 5, Dec 86, b&w............... 2.00		0.40	1.20	2.00
☐ 6, Feb 87, b&w............... 2.00		0.40	1.20	2.00
☐ 7, May 87, b&w............... 2.00		0.40	1.20	2.00
☐ 8, Jul 87, b&w............... 2.00		0.40	1.20	2.00
☐ 9, Sep 87, b&w............... 2.00		0.40	1.20	2.00
☐ 10, Nov 87, b&w............... 2.00		0.40	1.20	2.00
☐ 11, Jan 88, b&w 2.00		0.40	1.20	2.00
☐ 12, Mar 88, b&w............... 2.00		0.40	1.20	2.00

SILENT MOBIUS
VIZ

	ORIG.	GOOD	FINE	N-MINT
☐ 1, color		0.99	2.97	4.95
☐ 2, color		0.99	2.97	4.95

	ORIG.	GOOD	FINE	N-MINT
3, color		0.99	2.97	4.95
4, color		0.99	2.97	4.95
5, color		0.99	2.97	4.95
6, color		0.99	2.97	4.95

SILENT MOBIUS, PART 2

	ORIG.	GOOD	FINE	N-MINT
1		0.99	2.97	4.95
2		0.99	2.97	4.95
3		0.99	2.97	4.95
4		0.99	2.97	4.95
5		0.99	2.97	4.95

SILENT MOBIUS, PART 3

	ORIG.	GOOD	FINE	N-MINT
1		0.99	2.97	4.95
2		0.99	2.97	4.95
3		0.55	1.65	2.75
4		0.55	1.65	2.75
5		0.55	1.65	2.75

SILENT MOBIUS, PART 4

	ORIG.	GOOD	FINE	N-MINT
1	2.75	0.55	1.65	2.75
2	2.75	0.55	1.65	2.75
3	2.75	0.55	1.65	2.75
4	2.75	0.55	1.65	2.75
5	2.75	0.55	1.65	2.75

SILLY DADDY/KING CAT FLIP
JOE CHIAPPETTA

	ORIG.	GOOD	FINE	N-MINT
2, Sep 95, b&w;flipbook with King Cat back-up	2.75	0.55	1.65	2.75

SILVER HAWKS
STAR

	ORIG.	GOOD	FINE	N-MINT
1	1.00	0.20	0.60	1.00
2	1.00	0.20	0.60	1.00
3	1.00	0.20	0.60	1.00
4	1.00	0.20	0.60	1.00
5, (becomes Marvel comic)	1.00	0.20	0.60	1.00

SILVER HAWKS (was Star Comic)
MARVEL

	ORIG.	GOOD	FINE	N-MINT
6	1.00	0.20	0.60	1.00
7	1.00	0.20	0.60	1.00

SILVER SABLE AND THE WILD PACK

	ORIG.	GOOD	FINE	N-MINT
1, foil cover	2.00	0.80	2.40	4.00
2	1.25	0.25	0.75	1.25
3	1.25	0.25	0.75	1.25
4	1.25	0.25	0.75	1.25
5	1.25	0.25	0.75	1.25
6	1.25	0.25	0.75	1.25
7	1.25	0.25	0.75	1.25
8	1.25	0.25	0.75	1.25
9	1.25	0.25	0.75	1.25
10	1.25	0.25	0.75	1.25
11	1.25	0.25	0.75	1.25
12	1.25	0.25	0.75	1.25
13	1.25	0.25	0.75	1.25
14	1.25	0.25	0.75	1.25
15	1.25	0.25	0.75	1.25
16	1.25	0.25	0.75	1.25
17	1.25	0.25	0.75	1.25
18	1.25	0.25	0.75	1.25
19	1.25	0.25	0.75	1.25
20	1.25	0.25	0.75	1.25
21	1.25	0.25	0.75	1.25
22	1.25	0.25	0.75	1.25
23	1.25	0.25	0.75	1.25
24, May 94	1.50	0.30	0.90	1.50
25, Jun 94	2.00	0.40	1.20	2.00
26, Jul 94	1.50	0.30	0.90	1.50
27, Aug 94	1.50	0.30	0.90	1.50
28, Sep 94	1.50	0.30	0.90	1.50
29, Oct 94	1.50	0.30	0.90	1.50
30, Nov 94	1.50	0.30	0.90	1.50
31, Dec 94	1.50	0.30	0.90	1.50

	ORIG.	GOOD	FINE	N-MINT
32, Jan 95	1.50	0.30	0.90	1.50
33, Feb 95	1.50	0.30	0.90	1.50
34, Mar 95	1.50	0.30	0.90	1.50
35, Apr 95, final issue	1.50	0.30	0.90	1.50

SILVER SCREAM
RECOLLECTIONS

	ORIG.	GOOD	FINE	N-MINT
1, b&w reprints		0.40	1.20	2.00
2, b&w reprints		0.40	1.20	2.00
3, b&w reprints		0.40	1.20	2.00

SILVER STAR
PACIFIC

	ORIG.	GOOD	FINE	N-MINT
1, Feb 83, JK	1.00	0.30	0.90	1.50
2, Apr 83, JK		0.20	0.60	1.00
3, Jun 83, JK		0.20	0.60	1.00
4, Aug 83, JK		0.20	0.60	1.00
5, Nov 83, JK		0.20	0.60	1.00
6, Jan 84, JK		0.20	0.60	1.00

TOPPS

	ORIG.	GOOD	FINE	N-MINT
1, trading cards	2.95	0.59	1.77	2.95

SILVER SURFER (1968-1970)
MARVEL

	ORIG.	GOOD	FINE	N-MINT
1, Aug 68	0.25	88.00	264.00	440.00
2, Oct 68	0.25	25.00	75.00	125.00
3, Dec 68	0.25	32.00	96.00	160.00
4, Feb 69	0.25	72.00	216.00	360.00
5, Apr 69	0.25	15.00	45.00	75.00
6, Jun 69	0.25	13.00	39.00	65.00
7, Aug 69	0.25	13.00	39.00	65.00
8, Sep 69	0.15	13.00	39.00	65.00
9, Oct 69	0.15	13.00	39.00	65.00
10, Nov 69	0.15	13.00	39.00	65.00
11, Dec 69	0.15	8.00	24.00	40.00
12, Jan 70	0.15	8.00	24.00	40.00
13, Feb 70	0.15	8.00	24.00	40.00
14, Mar 70	0.15	9.60	28.80	48.00
15, Apr 70	0.15	8.00	24.00	40.00
16, May 70	0.15	8.00	24.00	40.00
17, Jun 70	0.15	8.00	24.00	40.00
18, Sep 70	0.15	8.00	24.00	40.00

SILVER SURFER (1982 one-shot)

	ORIG.	GOOD	FINE	N-MINT
1, Jun 82, JBy	1.00	2.00	6.00	10.00

SILVER SURFER (1987, Volume 3)

	ORIG.	GOOD	FINE	N-MINT
1, Jul 87, MR	1.25	2.40	7.20	12.00
2, Aug 87	0.75	1.60	4.80	8.00
3, Sep 87	0.75	1.00	3.00	5.00
4, Oct 87	0.75	1.00	3.00	5.00
5, Nov 87	0.75	1.00	3.00	5.00
6, Dec 87	0.75	0.80	2.40	4.00
7, Jan 88	0.75	0.80	2.40	4.00
8, Feb 88	0.75	0.80	2.40	4.00
9, Mar 88	0.75	0.80	2.40	4.00
10, Apr 88	0.75	0.80	2.40	4.00
11, May 88	1.00	0.80	2.40	4.00
12, Jun 88	1.00	0.80	2.40	4.00
13, Jul 88	1.00	0.80	2.40	4.00
14, Aug 88	1.00	0.80	2.40	4.00
15, Sep 88	1.00	1.60	4.80	8.00
16, Oct 88	1.00	0.80	2.40	4.00
17, Nov 88	1.00	0.80	2.40	4.00
18, Dec 88	1.00	0.80	2.40	4.00
19, Jan 89	1.00	0.80	2.40	4.00
20, Feb 89	1.00	0.80	2.40	4.00
21, Mar 89	1.00	0.80	2.40	4.00
22, Apr 89	1.00	0.80	2.40	4.00
23, May 89	1.00	0.80	2.40	4.00
24, Jun 89	1.00	0.80	2.40	4.00
25, Jul 89	1.50	0.80	2.40	4.00
26, Aug 89	1.00	0.80	2.40	4.00
27, Sep 89	1.00	0.80	2.40	4.00
28, Oct 89	1.00	0.80	2.40	4.00

Silver Surfer

One of Marvel's best-known heroes, the Silver Surfer, came about as an afterthought to the plotting of the first issue of what is, perhaps, Marvel's greatest super-hero story.

Stan Lee and Jack Kirby set out to devise a storyline in which The Fantastic Four would pit themselves against, in effect, a wrathful, all-powerful god, in the form of the world-devouring alien Galactus. Customarily, Lee and Kirby would discuss the general outline of the plot for a forthcoming issue, and then Kirby would draw the story, filling out the scenario as he went. To Lee's astonishment, when he received Kirby's pages, he saw a character they had not discussed: a heroic, seemingly impassive figure with glistening metallic skin riding through space atop what looked like a surfboard.

Kirby explained that a majestic being like Galactus would have a herald to precede him and announce his coming. Lee endowed the herald with a distinctive mode of speech that dramatically conveyed his innate nobility, and thus the Silver Surfer was born.

The Surfer's role was to find planets with "life energy" for Galactus to consume. In the course of the original Galactus trilogy, The Surfer met the blind sculptress Alicia Masters, who taught him the value of humanity and, just as importantly, led him to discover the humanity within himself. The Surfer then turned against his master, battling him until The Fantastic Four found the means to defeat Galactus. In retaliation, Galactus erected a barrier around the planet that The Surfer could not pass, condemning him to exile among the humans he had saved.

Through his further appearances in Fantastic Four, Lee and Kirby depicted the Surfer as a noble innocent, distressed by man's inhumanity to man. Kirby apparently intended The Surfer to be an alien, ignorant of the ways of humans, but when Stan Lee collaborated with John Buscema on The Surfer's first series, they revealed that he had once been a mortal like us.

Silver Surfer #1 ©1968 Marvel.

To save his idyllic world of Zenn-La from destruction, Norrin Radd had agreed to let Galactus transform him into The Silver Surfer. Trapped on Earth, he longed to return to Zenn-La and his true love, Shalla Bal.

Though The Surfer's first series ran only 18 issues, his idealism made him a pop-culture icon of the 1960s. In 1987, Marvel gave him a new regular series that endures to this day. The Surfer finally escaped the barrier in the first issue, and, since then, his adventures have principally been set in outer space and on distant worlds.

Big things are in the works for The Silver Surfer. Not only is his own comic book continuing, but he will appear in Jim Lee's revamped Fantastic Four. And, according to Variety, 20th Century Fox and Marvel have been discussing a Silver Surfer animated series to premiere in 1997 and a Silver Surfer live-action movie some time in the future.

Partial Checklist:

Fantastic Four #48-50 (Mar-May 66) ....Silver Surfer's first appearance (Galactus trilogy)
Fantastic Four #56-60 (Nov 66-Feb 67) ....Doctor Doom steals The Surfer's powers
Fantastic Four Annual #5 (Nov 67) ....First Surfer solo story
Silver Surfer Vol. 1 #1 (Aug 68) ....Silver Surfer's origin, Shalla Bal first appears
Silver Surfer Vol. 1 #3 (Dec 68) ....Surfer's first clashes with Mephisto
The Silver Surfer (1978) ....Graphic novel by Stan Lee and Jack Kirby
Silver Surfer Vol. 2 #1 (Jun 82) ....One-shot special written and drawn by John Byrne
Silver Surfer Vol. 3 #1 (Jul 1987) ....Current ongoing series begins
Silver Surfer: Judgment Day (1988) ....Graphic novel drawn by John Buscema
Silver Surfer: Parable #1-2 (1988) ....Stan Lee-Moebius collaboration
Silver Surfer/Warlock: Resurrection (Mar-Jun 93) ....Return of Shalla Bal

	ORIG.	GOOD	FINE	N-MINT
29, Nov 89 ....1.00	0.80	2.40	4.00
30, Nov 89 ....1.00	0.80	2.40	4.00
31, Dec 89....................1.50	0.80	2.40	4.00
32, Dec 89....................1.00	0.80	2.40	4.00
33, Jan 90 ....1.00	0.80	2.40	4.00
34, Feb 90, Thanos 1.00	3.60	10.80	18.00
35, Mar 90, Thanos........1.00	2.40	7.20	12.00
36, Apr 90, Thanos 1.00	1.20	3.60	6.00
37, May 90, Thanos 1.00	1.20	3.60	6.00
38, Jun 90, Thanos 1.00	1.20	3.60	6.00
39, Jul 90, Thanos 1.00	1.20	3.60	6.00
40, Aug 90 ....1.00	0.50	1.50	2.50
41, Sep 90.....................1.00	0.50	1.50	2.50
42, Oct 90 ....1.00	0.50	1.50	2.50
43, Nov 90 ....1.00	0.50	1.50	2.50
44, Dec 90.....................1.00	0.80	2.40	4.00
45, Jan 91 ....1.00	1.40	4.20	7.00
46, Feb 91, R: Adam Warlock			
...................................1.00	1.60	4.80	8.00
47, Mar 91 ....1.00	1.20	3.60	6.00
48, Apr 91 ....1.00	0.40	1.20	2.00
49, May 91 ....1.00	0.40	1.20	2.00
50, Jun 91, silver cover,1st printing			
...................................1.50	3.60	10.80	18.00
50, Jun 91, 2nd printing			
...................................1.50	1.20	3.60	6.00
51, Jul 91,Infinity Gauntlet			
...................................1.00	0.60	1.80	3.00
52, Aug 91,Infinity Gauntlet			
...................................1.00	0.60	1.80	3.00
53, Aug 91, Infinity Gauntlet			
...................................1.00	0.60	1.80	3.00
54, Sep 91,Infinity Gauntlet			
...................................1.00	0.60	1.80	3.00
55, Sep 91,Infinity Gauntlet			
...................................1.00	0.60	1.80	3.00
56, Oct 91, Infinity Gauntlet			
...................................1.00	0.60	1.80	3.00
57, Oct 91,Infinity Gauntlet			
...................................1.00	0.60	1.80	3.00
58, Nov 91,Infinity Gauntlet			
...................................1.00	0.60	1.80	3.00
59, Nov 91, Infinity Gauntlet			
...................................1.00	0.60	1.80	3.00
60, Dec 91.....................1.00	0.40	1.20	2.00
61 ....1.00	0.40	1.20	2.00
62 ....1.25	0.25	0.75	1.25
63 ....1.25	0.25	0.75	1.25
64 ....1.25	0.25	0.75	1.25
65 ....1.25	0.25	0.75	1.25
66 ....1.25	0.25	0.75	1.25
67 ....1.25	0.25	0.75	1.25
68 ....1.25	0.25	0.75	1.25
69 ....1.25	0.25	0.75	1.25
70 ....1.25	0.25	0.75	1.25
71 ....1.25	0.25	0.75	1.25
72 ....1.25	0.25	0.75	1.25
73 ....1.25	0.25	0.75	1.25
74 ....1.25	0.25	0.75	1.25
75, silver foil cover.........2.50	0.50	1.50	2.50
76 ....1.25	0.25	0.75	1.25
77 ....1.25	0.25	0.75	1.25
78 ....1.25	0.25	0.75	1.25
79 ....1.25	0.25	0.75	1.25
80 ....1.25	0.25	0.75	1.25
81 ....1.25	0.25	0.75	1.25
82 ....1.75	0.35	1.05	1.75
83 ....1.75	0.35	1.05	1.75
84 ....1.75	0.35	1.05	1.75
85 ....1.75	0.35	1.05	1.75
86 ....1.75	0.35	1.05	1.75
87 ....1.75	0.35	1.05	1.75

	ORIG.	GOOD	FINE	N-MINT
88 ....1.75	0.35	1.05	1.75
89 ....1.25	0.25	0.75	1.25
90 ....1.95	0.39	1.17	1.95
91 ....1.25	0.25	0.75	1.25
92, May 94.....................1.50	0.30	0.90	1.50
93, Jun 94......................1.50	0.30	0.90	1.50
94, Jul 94.......................1.50	0.30	0.90	1.50
95, Aug 94.....................1.50	0.30	0.90	1.50
96, Sep 94 ....1.50	0.30	0.90	1.50
97, Oct 94.......................1.50	0.30	0.90	1.50
98, Nov 94......................1.50	0.30	0.90	1.50
99, Dec 94......................1.50	0.30	0.90	1.50
100, Jan 95.....................2.25	0.45	1.35	2.25
100, Jan 95, enhanced cover			
...................................3.95	0.79	2.37	3.95
101, Feb 95....................1.50	0.30	0.90	1.50
102, Mar 95 ....1.50	0.30	0.90	1.50
103, Apr 95.....................1.50	0.30	0.90	1.50
104, May 95....................1.50	0.30	0.90	1.50
105, Jun 95, V:Super-Skrull			
...................................1.50	0.30	0.90	1.50
106, Jul 95, Relinquishes Power Cosmic			
...................................1.50	0.30	0.90	1.50
107, Aug 95 ....1.50	0.30	0.90	1.50
108, Sep 95, regains Power Cosmic			
...................................1.50	0.30	0.90	1.50
109, Oct 95.....................1.50	0.30	0.90	1.50
110, Nov 95.....................1.50	0.30	0.90	1.50
111, Dec 95.....................1.50	0.30	0.90	1.50
112, Jan 96.....................1.95	0.39	1.17	1.95
113, Feb 96....................1.95	0.30	0.90	1.50
114, Mar 96 ....1.95	0.39	1.17	1.95
115, Apr 96.....................1.95	0.39	1.17	1.95
116, May 96....................1.95	0.39	1.17	1.95

SILVER SURFER ANNUAL

	ORIG.	GOOD	FINE	N-MINT
1, 88, Evolutionary War ..1.75	1.60	4.80	8.00
2, 89, Atlantis Attacks.....2.00	1.00	3.00	5.00
3, 90, Lifeform.................2.00	0.40	1.20	2.00
4, 91 ....2.00	0.40	1.20	2.00
5, 92 ....2.25	0.45	1.35	2.25
6, 93, trading card 2.95	0.59	1.77	2.95
7, 94 ....2.95	0.59	1.77	2.95

SILVER SURFER VS. DRACULA

	ORIG.	GOOD	FINE	N-MINT
1, reprints 1.75	0.35	1.05	1.75

SILVER SURFER, THE (1988)
EPIC

	ORIG.	GOOD	FINE	N-MINT
1, Dec 88, Moebius.........1.00	0.60	1.80	3.00
2, Jan 89, Moebius 1.00	0.40	1.20	2.00

SILVER SURFER/WARLOCK: RESURRECTION
MARVEL

	ORIG.	GOOD	FINE	N-MINT
1 ....2.50	0.50	1.50	2.50
2 ....2.50	0.50	1.50	2.50
3 ....2.50	0.50	1.50	2.50
4 ....2.50	0.50	1.50	2.50

SILVER SWEETIE, THE
SPOOF

	ORIG.	GOOD	FINE	N-MINT
1, b&w...........................2.95	0.59	1.77	2.95

SILVERBACK
COMICO

	ORIG.	GOOD	FINE	N-MINT
1, O:Argent	0.50	1.50	2.50
2, O:Argent	0.50	1.50	2.50
3, O:Argent	0.50	1.50	2.50

SILVERBLADE
DC

	ORIG.	GOOD	FINE	N-MINT
1, Sep 87, GC..................	0.25	0.75	1.25
2, Oct 87, GC	0.25	0.75	1.25
3, Nov 87, GC	0.25	0.75	1.25
4, Dec 87, GC..................	0.25	0.75	1.25
5, Jan 88, GC..................	0.25	0.75	1.25
6, Feb 88, GC..................	0.25	0.75	1.25

	ORIG.	GOOD	FINE	N-MINT
❑ 7, Mar 88, GC..................	0.25	0.75	1.25
❑ 8, May 88, GC	0.25	0.75	1.25
❑ 9, Jun 88, GC	0.25	0.75	1.25
❑ 10, Jul 88, GC	0.25	0.75	1.25
❑ 11, Aug 88, GC................	0.25	0.75	1.25
❑ 12, Sep 88, GC................	0.25	0.75	1.25

SILVERHEELS
PACIFIC

❑ 1	0.30	0.90	1.50
❑ 2	0.30	0.90	1.50
❑ 3	0.30	0.90	1.50

SILVERSTORM
AIRCEL

❑ 1, b&w	0.45	1.35	2.25
❑ 2, b&w	0.45	1.35	2.25
❑ 3, b&w	0.45	1.35	2.25
❑ 4, b&w	0.45	1.35	2.25

SILVERWING SPECIAL
NOW

❑ 1, Jan 87 .... 0.95	0.19	0.57	0.95

SILVERWOLF COMIC BOOK TRIVIA COMIC BOOK
SILVERWOLF

❑ 1, b&w	0.30	0.90	1.50
❑ 2, b&w	0.30	0.90	1.50

SIMON AND KIRBY CLASSICS
PURE IMAGINATION

❑ 1, Nov 86	0.40	1.20	2.00

SIMPSONS COMICS
BONGO

❑ 1, 93............................ 2.25	1.00	3.00	5.00
❑ 2 .... 1.95	0.39	1.17	1.95
❑ 3, 94............................ 1.95	0.39	1.17	1.95
❑ 4, 94............................ 2.25	0.45	1.35	2.25
❑ 5, 94............................ 2.25	0.45	1.35	2.25
❑ 6, 94............................ 2.25	0.45	1.35	2.25
❑ 7, 94............................ 2.95	0.59	1.77	2.95
❑ 8, 95............................ 2.95	0.59	1.77	2.95
❑ 9, 95............................ 2.95	0.59	1.77	2.95
❑ 10, 95.......................... 2.95	0.59	1.77	2.95
❑ 11, 95.......................... 2.95	0.59	1.77	2.95
❑ 12, 95.......................... 2.95	0.59	1.77	2.95
❑ 13, 95.......................... 2.95	0.59	1.77	2.95
❑ 16, 96.......................... 2.25	0.45	1.35	2.25

SIMPSONS COMICS AND STORIES
WELSH

❑ 1, with poster.................	0.59	1.77	2.95

SIN
TRAGEDY STRIKES

❑ 1, b&w	0.59	1.77	2.95
❑ 2, b&w	0.59	1.77	2.95
❑ 3, b&w	0.59	1.77	2.95

SIN CITY: A DAME TO KILL FOR
DARK HORSE

❑ 1, FM, b&w 2.95	1.20	3.60	6.00
❑ 2, FM, b&w 2.95	1.00	3.00	5.00
❑ 3, FM, b&w 2.95	0.80	2.40	4.00
❑ 4, Mar 94, FM, b&w 2.95	0.59	1.77	2.95
❑ 5, Apr 94, FM, b&w 2.95	0.59	1.77	2.95
❑ 6, May 94, FM, b&w 2.95	0.59	1.77	2.95

SIN CITY: SILENT NIGHT
DARK HORSE/LEGEND

❑ 0, Nov 95, nn;one-shot;b&w;cardstock cover			
.... 2.95	0.59	1.77	2.95

SIN CITY: THAT YELLOW BASTARD
DARK HORSE

❑ 1, Feb 96, cardstock cover;b&w			
.... 2.95	0.59	1.77	2.95
❑ 3, Apr 96, cardstock cover;b&w			
.... 2.95	0.59	1.77	2.95
❑ 4, May 96, cardstock cover;b&w& yellow			
.... 2.95	0.59	1.77	2.95

SIN CITY: THE BABE WORE RED AND OTHER STORIES

❑ 0, Nov 94, b&w&red 2.95	0.59	1.77	2.95

SIN CITY: THE BIG FAT KILL (mini-series)

❑ 1, Nov 94, b&w............... 2.95	0.80	2.40	4.00
❑ 2, Dec 94, b&w;cardstock cover			
.... 2.95	0.59	1.77	2.95
❑ 3, Jan 95, b&w;cardstock cover			
.... 2.95	0.59	1.77	2.95
❑ 4, Feb 95, b&w, cardstock cover			
.... 2.95	0.59	1.77	2.95
❑ 5, Mar 95, b&w, cardstock cover			
.... 2.95	0.59	1.77	2.95

SIN OF THE MUMMY
EROS COMIX

❑ 1, adult, b&w	0.50	1.50	2.50

SINBAD (mini-series)
ADVENTURE

❑ 1, Nov 89, b&w;cardstock cover			
.... 2.25	0.45	1.35	2.25
❑ 2, Dec 89, b&w;cardstock cover			
.... 2.25	0.45	1.35	2.25
❑ 3, Jan 90, b&w;cardstock cover			
.... 2.25	0.45	1.35	2.25
❑ 4, Mar 90, b&w............... 2.25	0.45	1.35	2.25

SINBAD BOOK II (mini-series)

❑ 1, Mar 91, "House of God";b&w			
.... 2.50	0.50	1.50	2.50
❑ 2, Apr 91, "House of God";b&w			
.... 2.50	0.50	1.50	2.50
❑ 3, May 91, "House of God";b&w			
.... 2.50	0.50	1.50	2.50
❑ 4, Jun 91, "House of God";b&w			
.... 2.50	0.50	1.50	2.50

SINDY
FORBIDDEN FRUIT

❑ 1, adult, b&w	0.59	1.77	2.95
❑ 2, adult, b&w	0.59	1.77	2.95
❑ 3, adult, b&w	0.59	1.77	2.95
❑ 4, adult, b&w	0.59	1.77	2.95
❑ 5, adult, b&w	0.59	1.77	2.95

SINERGY
CALIBER

❑ 1, 94, b&w.................... 2.95	0.59	1.77	2.95
❑ 1, limited edition 5.95	1.19	3.57	5.95
❑ 2, 94, b&w.................... 2.95	0.59	1.77	2.95
❑ 2, limited edition 5.95	1.19	3.57	5.95
❑ 3, 94, b&w.................... 2.95	0.59	1.77	2.95
❑ 3, limited edition 5.95	1.19	3.57	5.95
❑ 4, 94, b&w.................... 2.95	0.59	1.77	2.95
❑ 4, limited edition 5.95	1.19	3.57	5.95
❑ 5, 94, b&w.................... 2.95	0.59	1.77	2.95
❑ 5, limited edition 5.95	1.19	3.57	5.95

SINISTER ROMANCE
HARRIER

❑ 1, b&w...........................	0.39	1.17	1.95
❑ 2, b&w...........................	0.39	1.17	1.95
❑ 3, b&w...........................	0.39	1.17	1.95
❑ 4, b&w...........................	0.39	1.17	1.95

	ORIG.	GOOD	FINE	N-MINT
SINNER				
FANTAGRAPHICS				
❏ 1		0.59	1.77	2.95
❏ 2		0.59	1.77	2.95
❏ 3		0.59	1.77	2.95
❏ 4		0.59	1.77	2.95
❏ 5		0.59	1.77	2.95
SINNIN!				
EROS COMIX				
❏ 1, adult, b&w		0.45	1.35	2.25
❏ 2, adult, b&w		0.45	1.35	2.25
SIREN				
MALIBU/ULTRAVERSE				
❏ 0, Sep 95, Infinity;alternate cover;"Black September"				
	1.50	0.70	2.10	3.50
❏ 0, Sep 95, Infinity;"Black September"				
	1.50	0.30	0.90	1.50
❏ 1, Oct 95, V:War Machine				
	1.50	0.30	0.90	1.50
❏ 2, Nov 95, V:War Machine;flipbook with "The Phoenix				
Resurrection" Pt. 3	1.50	0.30	0.90	1.50
❏ 3, Dec 95, final issue;continues in *Siren Special* #1				
	1.50	0.30	0.90	1.50
SIREN SPECIAL				
❏ 1, Feb 96, O:Siren	1.95	0.39	1.17	1.95
SIRENS OF THE LOST WORLD				
COMAX				
❏ 1, b&w, adult		0.59	1.77	2.95
SISTER ARMAGEDDON				
DRACULINA				
❏ 2, 95, b&w	2.50	0.50	1.50	2.50
SISTERHOOD OF STEEL				
EPIC				
❏ 1	1.50	0.30	0.90	1.50
❏ 2	1.50	0.30	0.90	1.50
❏ 3	1.50	0.30	0.90	1.50
❏ 4	1.50	0.30	0.90	1.50
❏ 5	1.50	0.30	0.90	1.50
❏ 6	1.50	0.30	0.90	1.50
❏ 7	1.50	0.30	0.90	1.50
❏ 8	1.50	0.30	0.90	1.50
SISTERS OF MERCY				
MAXIMUM				
❏ 1, Dec 95	2.50	0.50	1.50	2.50
❏ 1, Dec 95, alternate cover				
	2.50	0.50	1.50	2.50
SIX FROM SIRUS				
EPIC				
❏ 1, Jul 84, PG	1.50	0.40	1.20	2.00
❏ 2, Aug 84, PG	1.50	0.40	1.20	2.00
❏ 3, Sep 84, PG	1.50	0.40	1.20	2.00
❏ 4, Oct 84, PG	1.50	0.40	1.20	2.00
SIX FROM SIRUS II				
❏ 1	1.75	0.35	1.05	1.75
❏ 2	1.75	0.35	1.05	1.75
❏ 3	1.75	0.35	1.05	1.75
❏ 4	1.75	0.35	1.05	1.75
SIX-GUN HEROES				
A-PLUS				
❏ 1, b&w, reprints		0.50	1.50	2.50
SIZZLE THEATRE				
SLAVE LABOR				
❏ 1, adult, b&w		0.50	1.50	2.50
SKATEMAN				
PACIFIC				
❏ 1, Nov 83, NA	1.50	0.30	0.90	1.50
SKELETON KEY				
AMAZE INK				
❏ 1, b&w	1.50	0.30	0.90	1.50
❏ 2, b&w	1.50	0.30	0.90	1.50

	ORIG.	GOOD	FINE	N-MINT
❏ 3, Sep 95, b&w	1.50	0.30	0.90	1.50
❏ 7, Jan 96, b&w	1.50	0.30	0.90	1.50
❏ 8, Feb 96, b&w	1.50	0.30	0.90	1.50
SKELETON WARRIORS				
MARVEL				
❏ 1, Apr 95	1.50	0.30	0.90	1.50
❏ 2, May 95	1.50	0.30	0.90	1.50
❏ 3, Jun 95	1.50	0.30	0.90	1.50
❏ 4, Jul 95, final issue	1.50	0.30	0.90	1.50
SKETCHBOOK, THE				
TUNDRA				
❏ 1, Eastman, Melting Pot		0.79	2.37	3.95
❏ 2, Totleben		0.79	2.37	3.95
❏ 3, Zulli		0.79	2.37	3.95
❏ 4		0.79	2.37	3.95
❏ 5, CVess		0.79	2.37	3.95
❏ 6		0.79	2.37	3.95
❏ 7		0.79	2.37	3.95
❏ 8, Forg		0.79	2.37	3.95
❏ 9, MDooney		0.79	2.37	3.95
❏ 10, Paul Mavrides		0.99	2.97	4.95
SKIDMARKS				
❏ 1, b&w		0.59	1.77	2.95
❏ 2, b&w		0.59	1.77	2.95
❏ 3, b&w		0.59	1.77	2.95
SKIN GRAFT				
ICONOGRAFIX				
❏ 1, b&w	3.50	0.70	2.10	3.50
SKIN GRAFT: THE ADVENTURES				
OF A TATTOOED MAN				
DC/ VERTIGO				
❏ 1	2.50	0.50	1.50	2.50
❏ 2	2.50	0.50	1.50	2.50
❏ 3	2.50	0.50	1.50	2.50
❏ 4	2.50	0.50	1.50	2.50
SKIN13				
EXPRESS/PARODY				
❏ 1, 95, b&w	2.50	0.50	1.50	2.50
❏ 1, Oct 95, /2A;"Amazing SKIN Thir-Teen";reprints *Skin13*				
#1;b&w	2.50	0.50	1.50	2.50
❏ 1, Oct 95, /2B;"Barbari-SKIN";reprints *Skin13* #1;b&w				
	2.50	0.50	1.50	2.50
❏ 1, Oct 95, /2C;"SKIN-et Jackson";reprints *Skin13*				
#1;b&w	2.50	0.50	1.50	2.50
❏ 1, 95, /2A;"Amazing SKINThir-Teen";reprints *Skin13*				
#1;b&w;second printing	2.50	0.50	1.50	2.50
❏ 1, 95, /2B;"Barbari-SKIN";reprints *Skin13* #1;b&w;second				
printing	2.50	0.50	1.50	2.50
❏ 1, 95, /2C;"SKIN-etJackson";reprints *Skin13* #1;b&w;				
second printing	2.50	0.50	1.50	2.50
SKINHEADS IN LOVE				
EROS COMIX				
❏ 1, adult, b&w		0.45	1.35	2.25
SKIP WILLIAMSON'S GAG REFLEX				
WILLIAMSON				
❏ 1, Jan 94, b&w	2.95	0.59	1.77	2.95
SKIZZ: FIRST ENCOUNTER				
FLEETWAY/QUALITY				
❏ 1	1.95	0.39	1.17	1.95
❏ 2	1.95	0.39	1.17	1.95
❏ 3	1.95	0.39	1.17	1.95
SKREEMER				
DC				
❏ 1		0.40	1.20	2.00
❏ 2		0.40	1.20	2.00
❏ 3		0.40	1.20	2.00
❏ 4		0.40	1.20	2.00
❏ 5		0.40	1.20	2.00
❏ 6		0.40	1.20	2.00

	ORIG.	GOOD	FINE	N-MINT

SKROG
COMICO

	ORIG.	GOOD	FINE	N-MINT
❑ 1, b&w		0.70	2.10	3.50

SKROG (YIP, YIP, YAY) SPECIAL
CRYSTAL

	ORIG.	GOOD	FINE	N-MINT
❑ 1, b&w		0.50	1.50	2.50

SKRULL KILL KREW
MARVEL

	ORIG.	GOOD	FINE	N-MINT
❑ 1, Sep 95, cardstock cover	2.95	0.59	1.77	2.95
❑ 2, Oct 95, cardstock cover;A:Captain America	2.95	0.59	1.77	2.95
❑ 3, Nov 95, cardstock cover;A:Captain America	2.95	0.59	1.77	2.95
❑ 4, Dec 95	2.95	0.59	1.77	2.95
❑ 5, Jan 96, cardstock cover;final issue	2.95	0.59	1.77	2.95

SKULL AND BONES
DC

	ORIG.	GOOD	FINE	N-MINT
❑ 1		0.99	2.97	4.95
❑ 2		0.99	2.97	4.95

SKULL THE SLAYER
MARVEL

	ORIG.	GOOD	FINE	N-MINT
❑ 1	0.25	0.40	1.20	2.00
❑ 2	0.25	0.30	0.90	1.50
❑ 3	0.25	0.30	0.90	1.50
❑ 4	0.25	0.30	0.90	1.50
❑ 5	0.25	0.30	0.90	1.50
❑ 6	0.25	0.30	0.90	1.50
❑ 7, Sep 76	0.30	0.30	0.90	1.50
❑ 8, Nov 76	0.30	0.30	0.90	1.50

SKUNK
MU PRESS

	ORIG.	GOOD	FINE	N-MINT
❑ 0, nn adult, b&w	2.50	0.50	1.50	2.50

SKY COMICS PRESENTS MONTHLY
SKY COMICS

	ORIG.	GOOD	FINE	N-MINT
❑ 1, b&w		0.50	1.50	2.50

SKY GAL
AC

	ORIG.	GOOD	FINE	N-MINT
❑ 1, some MB reprint	3.95	0.79	2.37	3.95
❑ 2, 94, some color;some MB reprint	3.95	0.79	2.37	3.95
❑ 3, 94, some color;some MB reprint	3.95	0.79	2.37	3.95

SKY MASTERS
PURE IMAGINATION

	ORIG.	GOOD	FINE	N-MINT
❑ 1, JK, WW, strip reprints, b&w	1.59	4.77	7.95

SKY WOLF
ECLIPSE

	ORIG.	GOOD	FINE	N-MINT
❑ 1, Mar 88		0.35	1.05	1.75
❑ 2, May 88		0.35	1.05	1.75
❑ 3, Oct 88		0.39	1.17	1.95

SKYE BLUE
MU PRESS

	ORIG.	GOOD	FINE	N-MINT
❑ 1, b&w		0.50	1.50	2.50
❑ 2, b&w		0.50	1.50	2.50
❑ 3, b&w		0.50	1.50	2.50

SLAINE THE BERSERKER/SLAINE THE KING
FLEETWAY/QUALITY

	ORIG.	GOOD	FINE	N-MINT
❑ 1	1.25	0.25	0.75	1.25
❑ 2	1.25	0.25	0.75	1.25
❑ 3	1.25	0.25	0.75	1.25
❑ 4	1.25	0.25	0.75	1.25
❑ 5	1.25	0.25	0.75	1.25
❑ 6	1.25	0.25	0.75	1.25
❑ 7	1.25	0.25	0.75	1.25
❑ 8	1.25	0.25	0.75	1.25
❑ 9	1.25	0.25	0.75	1.25
❑ 10	1.25	0.25	0.75	1.25

	ORIG.	GOOD	FINE	N-MINT
❑ 11	1.25	0.25	0.75	1.25
❑ 12	1.25	0.25	0.75	1.25
❑ 13		0.30	0.90	1.50
❑ 14, 14 and 15 are one issue		0.30	0.90	1.50
❑ 16, 16 and 17 are one issue		0.30	0.90	1.50
❑ 18		0.30	0.90	1.50
❑ 19		0.30	0.90	1.50
❑ 20		0.30	0.90	1.50
❑ 21		0.30	0.90	1.50
❑ 22		0.30	0.90	1.50
❑ 23		0.30	0.90	1.50
❑ 24		0.30	0.90	1.50
❑ 25		0.30	0.90	1.50
❑ 26		0.30	0.90	1.50
❑ 27		0.30	0.90	1.50
❑ 28		0.30	0.90	1.50

SLAINE: THE HORNED GOD

	ORIG.	GOOD	FINE	N-MINT
❑ 1	2.95	0.59	1.77	2.95
❑ 2	2.95	0.59	1.77	2.95

SLAM DUNK KINGS
PERSONALITY

	ORIG.	GOOD	FINE	N-MINT
❑ 1, b&w		0.59	1.77	2.95
❑ 2, b&w		0.59	1.77	2.95
❑ 3, b&w		0.59	1.77	2.95
❑ 4, b&w		0.59	1.77	2.95

SLAPSTICK
MARVEL

	ORIG.	GOOD	FINE	N-MINT
❑ 1	1.25	0.25	0.75	1.25
❑ 2	1.25	0.25	0.75	1.25
❑ 3	1.25	0.25	0.75	1.25
❑ 4	1.25	0.25	0.75	1.25

SLASH
NORTHSTAR

	ORIG.	GOOD	FINE	N-MINT
❑ 1, adult, b&w	2.95	0.59	1.77	2.95
❑ 2, adult, b&w	2.95	0.59	1.77	2.95
❑ 3, adult, b&w	2.95	0.59	1.77	2.95
❑ 4, adult, b&w	2.95	0.59	1.77	2.95

SLASH MARAUD (mini-series)
DC

	ORIG.	GOOD	FINE	N-MINT
❑ 1, Nov 87, PG	1.75	0.35	1.05	1.75
❑ 2, Dec 87, PG	1.75	0.35	1.05	1.75
❑ 3, Jan 88, PG	1.75	0.35	1.05	1.75
❑ 4, Feb 88, PG	1.75	0.35	1.05	1.75
❑ 5, Mar 88, PG	1.75	0.35	1.05	1.75
❑ 6, Apr 88, PG	1.75	0.35	1.05	1.75

SLAUGHTERMAN
COMICO

	ORIG.	GOOD	FINE	N-MINT
❑ 1, b&w		0.70	2.10	3.50
❑ 2, b&w		0.70	2.10	3.50

SLAVE GIRL
ETERNITY

	ORIG.	GOOD	FINE	N-MINT
❑ 1, b&w rep		0.45	1.35	2.25

SLAVE LABOR STORIES
SLAVE LABOR

	ORIG.	GOOD	FINE	N-MINT
❑ 1, b&w		0.59	1.77	2.95
❑ 2, b&w		0.59	1.77	2.95
❑ 3, b&w		0.59	1.77	2.95

SLEDGE HAMMER
MARVEL

	ORIG.	GOOD	FINE	N-MINT
❑ 1, Feb 88, TV tie-in	1.00	0.20	0.60	1.00
❑ 2, Mar 88, TV tie-in	1.00	0.20	0.60	1.00

SLEEPWALKER

	ORIG.	GOOD	FINE	N-MINT
❑ 1, Jun 91, 1:Sleepwalker	1.00	0.70	2.10	3.50
❑ 2, Jul 91, 1:8-Ball	1.00	0.40	1.20	2.00
❑ 3, Aug 91	1.00	0.40	1.20	2.00
❑ 4, Sep 91	1.00	0.40	1.20	2.00
❑ 5, Oct 91, SpM	1.00	0.20	0.60	1.00
❑ 6, Nov 91	1.00	0.20	0.60	1.00

	ORIG.	GOOD	FINE	N-MINT
☐ 7, Dec 91,Infinity Gauntlet				
................................1.00	0.20	0.60	1.00
☐ 8, Deathlok....................1.25	0.25	0.75	1.25
☐ 9 ....1.25	0.25	0.75	1.25
☐ 10 ....1.25	0.25	0.75	1.25
☐ 11 ....1.25	0.25	0.75	1.25
☐ 12 ....1.25	0.25	0.75	1.25
☐ 13 ....1.25	0.25	0.75	1.25
☐ 14 ....1.25	0.25	0.75	1.25
☐ 15 ....1.25	0.25	0.75	1.25
☐ 16 ....1.25	0.25	0.75	1.25
☐ 17 ....1.25	0.25	0.75	1.25
☐ 18 ....1.25	0.25	0.75	1.25
☐ 19 ....2.00	0.40	1.20	2.00
☐ 20 ....1.25	0.25	0.75	1.25
☐ 21 ....1.25	0.25	0.75	1.25
☐ 22 ....1.25	0.25	0.75	1.25
☐ 23 ....1.25	0.25	0.75	1.25
☐ 24 ....1.25	0.25	0.75	1.25
☐ 25, foil cover 2.95	0.59	1.77	2.95
☐ 26 ....1.25	0.25	0.75	1.25
☐ 27 ....1.25	0.25	0.75	1.25
☐ 28 ....1.25	0.25	0.75	1.25
☐ 29 ....1.25	0.25	0.75	1.25
☐ 30 ....1.25	0.25	0.75	1.25
☐ 31 ....1.25	0.25	0.75	1.25
☐ 32 ....1.25	0.25	0.75	1.25
☐ 33 ....1.25	0.25	0.75	1.25

SLEEPWALKER HOLIDAY SPECIAL

☐ 1 ....2.00	0.40	1.20	2.00

SLEEZE BROTHERS, THE (1989-90)
EPIC

☐ 1 ....1.75	0.35	1.05	1.75
☐ 2 ....1.75	0.35	1.05	1.75
☐ 3 ....1.75	0.35	1.05	1.75
☐ 4 ....1.75	0.35	1.05	1.75
☐ 5 ....1.75	0.35	1.05	1.75
☐ 6 ....1.75	0.35	1.05	1.75

SLEEZE BROTHERS, THE (1991)

☐ 0, nn..............................3.95	0.79	2.37	3.95

SLIMER!
NOW

☐ 1, May 89.......................1.75	0.35	1.05	1.75
☐ 2, Jun 89........................1.75	0.35	1.05	1.75
☐ 3, Jul 89.........................1.75	0.35	1.05	1.75
☐ 4, Aug 89.......................1.75	0.35	1.05	1.75
☐ 5, Sep 89........................1.75	0.35	1.05	1.75
☐ 6, Oct 89........................1.75	0.35	1.05	1.75
☐ 7, Nov 89........................1.75	0.35	1.05	1.75
☐ 8, Dec 89........................1.75	0.35	1.05	1.75
☐ 9, Jan 90........................1.75	0.35	1.05	1.75
☐ 10, Feb 90......................1.75	0.35	1.05	1.75
☐ 11, Mar 90......................1.75	0.35	1.05	1.75
☐ 12, Apr 90.......................1.75	0.35	1.05	1.75
☐ 13, May 90......................1.75	0.35	1.05	1.75
☐ 14, Jun 90.......................1.75	0.35	1.05	1.75
☐ 15, Jul 90........................1.75	0.35	1.05	1.75
☐ 16, Aug 90 ....1.75	0.35	1.05	1.75
☐ 17, Sep 90......................1.75	0.35	1.05	1.75
☐ 18, Oct 90.......................1.75	0.35	1.05	1.75
☐ 19, Nov 90 ....1.75	0.35	1.05	1.75

SLUDGE
MALIBU/ULTRAVERSE

☐ 1, Oct 93, Rune, BWS 2.50	0.80	2.40	4.00
☐ 1, Ultra Ltd......................	8.00	24.00	40.00
☐ 2, Nov 93 ....1.95	0.39	1.17	1.95
☐ 3, Dec 93, Break-Thru...1.95	0.39	1.17	1.95
☐ 4, Jan 94 ....1.95	0.39	1.17	1.95
☐ 5, Feb 94 ....1.95	0.39	1.17	1.95
☐ 6, Mar 94 ....1.95	0.39	1.17	1.95

	ORIG.	GOOD	FINE	N-MINT
☐ 7, Jun 94 ....1.95	0.39	1.17	1.95
☐ 8, Jul 94.........................1.95	0.39	1.17	1.95
☐ 9, Sep 94.......................1.95	0.39	1.17	1.95
☐ 10, Oct 94......................1.95	0.39	1.17	1.95
☐ 11, Nov 94.....................1.95	0.39	1.17	1.95

SLUG 'N' GINGER
EROS COMIX

☐ 1, adult, b&w		0.45	1.35	2.25

SLUTBURGER STORIES
RIP OFF

☐ 1, Jul 90, b&w;adult 2.50	0.50	1.50	2.50
☐ 2, Jul 91, b&w;adult 2.50	0.50	1.50	2.50

SMALL PRESS SWIMSUIT SPECTACULAR
ALLIED

☐ 1, Jun 95, b&w;pin-ups;benefit comic for American

Cancer Society................2.95	0.59	1.77	2.95

SMILIN'ED
FANTACO

☐ 1, 80, R. Vezina;Hembeck				
................................1.25	0.25	0.75	1.25
☐ 2, 80, R. Vezina;Hembeck				
................................1.25	0.25	0.75	1.25
☐ 3, 80, R. Vezina;Hembeck				
................................1.25	0.25	0.75	1.25
☐ 4, 80, R. Vezina;Hembeck				
................................1.25	0.25	0.75	1.25

SMURFS TREASURY EDITION, THE
MARVEL

☐ 1 ....2.50	0.50	1.50	2.50

SMURFS, THE

☐ 1 ....0.60	0.12	0.36	0.60
☐ 2 ....0.60	0.12	0.36	0.60
☐ 3 ....0.60	0.12	0.36	0.60

SNAKE EYES
FANTAGRAPHICS

☐ 1, b&w..............................	1.59	4.77	7.95
☐ 2, b&w..............................	1.59	4.77	7.95
☐ 3, b&w..............................	1.59	4.77	7.95

SNAKE, THE
SPECIAL STUDIO

☐ 1, b&w..............................	0.70	2.10	3.50

SNARF (was underground)
KITCHEN SINK

☐ 10	0.40	1.20	2.00
☐ 11	0.40	1.20	2.00
☐ 12	0.40	1.20	2.00
☐ 13	0.40	1.20	2.00
☐ 14	0.40	1.20	2.00
☐ 15	0.50	1.50	2.50

SNARL
CALIBER

☐ 1, b&w............................2.50	0.50	1.50	2.50
☐ 2, b&w............................2.50	0.50	1.50	2.50
☐ 3, b&w............................2.50	0.50	1.50	2.50

SNOW WHITE
MARVEL

☐ 0, Jan 95, nn;movie adaptation;lead story is reprint of

Dell Four Color #49.........1.95	0.39	1.17	1.95

SNOW WHITE AND THE SEVEN DWARFS
GOLDEN ANNIVERSARY
GLADSTONE

☐ 1	3.00	9.00	15.00

SO DARK THE ROSE
CFD

☐ 0, 95, nn 2.95	0.59	1.77	2.95

SOB: SPECIAL OPERATIONS BRANCH
PROMETHEAN

☐ 1, May 94, b&w 2.25	0.45	1.35	2.25

	ORIG.	GOOD	FINE	N-MINT

SOCKETEER, THE
KARDIA

	ORIG.	GOOD	FINE	N-MINT
☐ 1, b&w parody		0.45	1.35	2.25

SOLAR: MAN OF THE ATOM
ACCLAIM/VALIANT

	ORIG.	GOOD	FINE	N-MINT
☐ 45, Jun 95	2.25	0.45	1.35	2.25
☐ 46, Jul 95, DJ;DG	2.50	0.50	1.50	2.50
☐ 47, Aug 95, DJ,DG	2.50	0.50	1.50	2.50
☐ 48, Sep 95, DJ,DG	2.50	0.50	1.50	2.50
☐ 49, Sep 95, DJ,DG	2.50	0.50	1.50	2.50
☐ 50, Oct 95, DJ,DG	2.50	0.50	1.50	2.50
☐ 51, Nov 95, DJ,DG	2.50	0.50	1.50	2.50
☐ 52, Nov 95, DJ,DG	2.50	0.50	1.50	2.50
☐ 53, Dec 95, DJ,DG	2.50	0.50	1.50	2.50
☐ 54, Dec 95, DJ,DG	2.50	0.50	1.50	2.50
☐ 55, Jan 96	2.50	0.50	1.50	2.50
☐ 56, Jan 96	2.50	0.50	1.50	2.50
☐ 57, Feb 96	2.50	0.50	1.50	2.50
☐ 58, Feb 96	2.50	0.50	1.50	2.50
☐ 59, Mar 96	2.50	0.50	1.50	2.50

VALIANT

	ORIG.	GOOD	FINE	N-MINT
☐ 1, Sep 91, BWS..............	1.75	2.00	6.00	10.00
☐ 2, Oct 91, BWS	1.75	1.40	4.20	7.00
☐ 3, Nov 91, BWS..............	1.75	1.60	4.80	8.00
☐ 4, Dec 91, BWS..............	1.75	1.40	4.20	7.00
☐ 5, Jan 92, BWS	1.95	1.00	3.00	5.00
☐ 6, Feb 92, BWS	1.95	1.00	3.00	5.00
☐ 7, Mar 92, BWS	1.95	1.00	3.00	5.00
☐ 8, Apr 92, BWS	2.25	1.00	3.00	5.00
☐ 9, May 92, BWS	2.25	1.00	3.00	5.00
☐ 10, Jun 92,black cover BWS				
....	3.95	3.00	9.00	15.00
☐ 10, second printing		1.60	4.80	8.00
☐ 11, Jul 92	2.25	0.80	2.40	4.00
☐ 12, Aug 92, FM(c) Unity.	2.25	0.80	2.40	4.00
☐ 13, Sep 92, WS(c) Unity	2.25	0.80	2.40	4.00
☐ 14, Oct 92	2.25	1.20	3.60	6.00
☐ 15, Nov 92	2.25	0.70	2.10	3.50
☐ 16, Dec 92	2.25	0.70	2.10	3.50
☐ 17, Jan 93	2.25	0.70	2.10	3.50
☐ 18, Feb 93	2.25	0.70	2.10	3.50
☐ 19, Mar 93	2.25	0.70	2.10	3.50
☐ 20, Apr 93	2.25	0.70	2.10	3.50
☐ 21, May 93	2.25	0.60	1.80	3.00
☐ 22, Jun 93	2.25	0.60	1.80	3.00
☐ 23, Jul 93	2.25	0.60	1.80	3.00
☐ 24, Aug 93	2.25	0.60	1.80	3.00
☐ 25, Sep 93	2.25	0.60	1.80	3.00
☐ 26, Oct 93	2.25	0.60	1.80	3.00
☐ 27, Nov 93	2.25	0.60	1.80	3.00
☐ 28, Dec 93	2.25	0.60	1.80	3.00
☐ 29, Jan 94, Valiant Vision				
....	2.25	0.60	1.80	3.00
☐ 30, Feb 94	2.25	0.60	1.80	3.00
☐ 31, Mar 94	2.25	0.45	1.35	2.25
☐ 32, Apr 94	2.25	0.45	1.35	2.25
☐ 33, May 94, Valiant Vision,trading card				
....	2.25	0.45	1.35	2.25
☐ 34, Jun 94, Valiant Vision				
....	2.25	0.45	1.35	2.25
☐ 35, Aug 94, Valiant Vision				
....	2.25	0.45	1.35	2.25
☐ 36, Sep 94	2.25	0.45	1.35	2.25
☐ 37, Oct 94	2.25	0.45	1.35	2.25
☐ 38, Nov 94, Chaos Effect				
....	2.25	0.45	1.35	2.25
☐ 40, Jan 95	2.25	0.45	1.35	2.25
☐ 41, Feb 95	2.25	0.45	1.35	2.25
☐ 43, Apr 95	2.25	0.45	1.35	2.25
☐ 44, May 95	2.25	0.45	1.35	2.25

SOLARMAN
MARVEL

	ORIG.	GOOD	FINE	N-MINT
☐ 1, Jan 89, O:Solarman	1.00	0.20	0.60	1.00
☐ 2, May 90......................	1.00	0.20	0.60	1.00

SOLD-OUT
FANTACO

	ORIG.	GOOD	FINE	N-MINT
☐ 1, 86	1.50	0.30	0.90	1.50
☐ 2, 87	1.50	0.30	0.90	1.50

SOLDIERS OF FREEDOM
AC

	ORIG.	GOOD	FINE	N-MINT
☐ 1, Jul 87......................		0.35	1.05	1.75
☐ 2, Aug 87		0.39	1.17	1.95

SOLITAIRE (mini-series)
MALIBU/ULTRAVERSE

	ORIG.	GOOD	FINE	N-MINT
☐ 1	1.95	0.39	1.17	1.95
☐ 1, trading card	2.50	0.50	1.50	2.50
☐ 2, Dec 93, Break-Thru.....	1.95	0.39	1.17	1.95
☐ 3, Feb 94	1.95	0.39	1.17	1.95
☐ 4, Mar 94	1.95	0.39	1.17	1.95
☐ 5, Apr 94	1.95	0.39	1.17	1.95
☐ 6, May 94	1.95	0.39	1.17	1.95
☐ 7, Sep 94	1.95	0.39	1.17	1.95
☐ 8, Sep 94	1.95	0.39	1.17	1.95
☐ 9, Sep 94	1.95	0.39	1.17	1.95
☐ 10, Oct 94......................	1.95	0.39	1.17	1.95
☐ 11, Nov 94	1.95	0.39	1.17	1.95

SOLO (mini-series)
MARVEL

	ORIG.	GOOD	FINE	N-MINT
☐ 1, Sep 94	1.75	0.35	1.05	1.75
☐ 2, Oct 94	1.75	0.35	1.05	1.75
☐ 3, Nov 94	1.75	0.35	1.05	1.75
☐ 4, Dec 94, final issue	1.75	0.35	1.05	1.75

SOLO AVENGERS

	ORIG.	GOOD	FINE	N-MINT
☐ 1, Dec 87	0.75	0.60	1.80	3.00
☐ 2, Jan 88......................	0.75	0.40	1.20	2.00
☐ 3, Feb 88......................	0.75	0.20	0.60	1.00
☐ 4, Mar 88......................	0.75	0.20	0.60	1.00
☐ 5, Apr 88......................	0.75	0.20	0.60	1.00
☐ 6, May 88......................	0.75	0.20	0.60	1.00
☐ 7, Jun 88......................	0.75	0.20	0.60	1.00
☐ 8, Jul 88......................	0.75	0.20	0.60	1.00
☐ 9, Aug 88......................	0.75	0.20	0.60	1.00
☐ 10, Sep 88	0.75	0.20	0.60	1.00
☐ 11, Oct 88	0.75	0.20	0.60	1.00
☐ 12, Nov 88	0.75	0.20	0.60	1.00
☐ 13, Dec 88	0.75	0.20	0.60	1.00
☐ 14, Jan 89	0.75	0.20	0.60	1.00
☐ 15, Feb 89	0.75	0.20	0.60	1.00
☐ 16, Mar 89	0.75	0.20	0.60	1.00
☐ 17, Apr 89	0.75	0.20	0.60	1.00
☐ 18, May 89	0.75	0.20	0.60	1.00
☐ 19, Jun 89	0.75	0.20	0.60	1.00
☐ 20, Jul 89, (becomes *Avengers Spotlight*)				
....	0.75	0.20	0.60	1.00

SOLO EX-MUTANTS
ETERNITY

	ORIG.	GOOD	FINE	N-MINT
☐ 1, b&w...........................		0.39	1.17	1.95
☐ 2, b&w...........................		0.39	1.17	1.95
☐ 3, b&w...........................		0.39	1.17	1.95
☐ 4, b&w...........................		0.39	1.17	1.95
☐ 5, b&w...........................		0.39	1.17	1.95
☐ 6, b&w...........................		0.39	1.17	1.95

SOLOMON KANE
MARVEL

	ORIG.	GOOD	FINE	N-MINT
☐ 1	1.25	0.25	0.75	1.25
☐ 2	0.65	0.20	0.60	1.00
☐ 3	0.65	0.20	0.60	1.00
☐ 4	0.75	0.20	0.60	1.00
☐ 5	0.75	0.20	0.60	1.00
☐ 6	0.75	0.20	0.60	1.00

	ORIG.	GOOD	FINE	N-MINT

SOLOMON KANE IN 3-D
BLACKTHORNE
	ORIG.	GOOD	FINE	N-MINT
❏ 1		0.50	1.50	2.50

SOLSON CHRISTMAS SPECIAL
SOLSON
	ORIG.	GOOD	FINE	N-MINT
❏ 1, Samurai Santa, first Jim Lee art				
	4.00	12.00	20.00	

SOLSON'S COMIC TALENT STAR SEARCH
	ORIG.	GOOD	FINE	N-MINT
❏ 1		0.30	0.90	1.50
❏ 2		0.30	0.90	1.50

SOLUTION
MALIBU/ULTRAVERSE
	ORIG.	GOOD	FINE	N-MINT
❏ 0, Jan 94, no cover price..				
❏ 1	1.95	0.39	1.17	1.95
❏ 2, Rune, BWS	2.50	0.50	1.50	2.50
❏ 3	1.95	0.39	1.17	1.95
❏ 4, Dec 93, Break-Thru	1.95	0.39	1.17	1.95
❏ 5, Jan 94	1.95	0.39	1.17	1.95
❏ 6, Feb 94, O:Tech	1.95	0.39	1.17	1.95
❏ 7, Mar 94	1.95	0.39	1.17	1.95
❏ 8, Apr 94	1.95	0.39	1.17	1.95
❏ 9, Jun 94	1.95	0.39	1.17	1.95
❏ 10, Jul 94	1.95	0.39	1.17	1.95
❏ 11, Aug 94	1.95	0.39	1.17	1.95
❏ 12, Oct 94	1.95	0.39	1.17	1.95
❏ 13, Oct 94	1.95	0.39	1.17	1.95

SOME TALES FROM GIMBLEY
HARRIER
	ORIG.	GOOD	FINE	N-MINT
❏ 1		0.39	1.17	1.95

SOMERSET HOLMES
PACIFIC
	ORIG.	GOOD	FINE	N-MINT
❏ 1, Sep 83, BA	1.50	0.30	0.90	1.50
❏ 2, Nov 83, BA		0.30	0.90	1.50
❏ 3, Feb 84, BA		0.30	0.90	1.50
❏ 4, Apr 84, BA (moves to Eclipse)	0.30	0.90	1.50	

SOMERSET HOLMES (former Pacific title)
ECLIPSE
	ORIG.	GOOD	FINE	N-MINT
❏ 5, Nov 84, BA		0.30	0.90	1.50
❏ 6, Dec 84, BA		0.30	0.90	1.50

SOMETHING DIFFERENT
WOOGA CENTRAL
	ORIG.	GOOD	FINE	N-MINT
❏ 1, b&w	2.00	0.40	1.20	2.00
❏ 2, Mark Twain's 1601, adult, flexidisc				
		0.40	1.20	2.00

SON OF AMBUSH BUG
DC
	ORIG.	GOOD	FINE	N-MINT
❏ 1, Jul 86, KG	0.75	0.20	0.60	1.00
❏ 2, Aug 86, KG	0.75	0.20	0.60	1.00
❏ 3, Sep 86, KG	0.75	0.20	0.60	1.00
❏ 4, Oct 86, KG	0.75	0.20	0.60	1.00
❏ 5, Nov 86, KG	0.75	0.20	0.60	1.00
❏ 6, Dec 86, KG	0.75	0.20	0.60	1.00

SON OF MUTANT WORLD
FANTAGOR
	ORIG.	GOOD	FINE	N-MINT
❏ 1, Corben, color		0.40	1.20	2.00
❏ 5, 90	1.75	0.35	1.05	1.75

SON OF SATAN
MARVEL
	ORIG.	GOOD	FINE	N-MINT
❏ 1	0.25	1.00	3.00	5.00
❏ 2	0.25	0.60	1.80	3.00
❏ 3	0.25	0.40	1.20	2.00
❏ 4	0.25	0.40	1.20	2.00
❏ 5	0.25	0.40	1.20	2.00
❏ 6, Oct 76	0.30	0.40	1.20	2.00
❏ 7, Dec 76	0.30	0.40	1.20	2.00
❏ 8, Feb 77	0.30	0.40	1.20	2.00

SONG OF THE CID
TOME PRESS
	ORIG.	GOOD	FINE	N-MINT
❏ 1, b&w	2.95	0.59	1.77	2.95
❏ 2, b&w	2.95	0.59	1.77	2.95

SONGS OF BASTARDS
CONQUEST
	ORIG.	GOOD	FINE	N-MINT
❏ 1, b&w		0.59	1.77	2.95

SONIC & KNUCKLES SPECIAL
ARCHIE
	ORIG.	GOOD	FINE	N-MINT
❏ 1, Aug 95	2.00	0.40	1.20	2.00

SONIC DISRUPTORS
DC
	ORIG.	GOOD	FINE	N-MINT
❏ 1		0.35	1.05	1.75
❏ 2		0.35	1.05	1.75
❏ 3		0.35	1.05	1.75
❏ 4		0.35	1.05	1.75
❏ 5		0.35	1.05	1.75
❏ 6		0.35	1.05	1.75
❏ 7, final issue;series unfinished	0.35	1.05	1.75	

SONIC THE HEDGEHOG
ARCHIE
	ORIG.	GOOD	FINE	N-MINT
❏ 1, Feb 93	1.25	0.25	0.75	1.25
❏ 2	1.25	0.25	0.75	1.25
❏ 3	1.25	0.25	0.75	1.25
❏ 4	1.25	0.25	0.75	1.25
❏ 5	1.25	0.25	0.75	1.25
❏ 6	1.25	0.25	0.75	1.25
❏ 7	1.25	0.25	0.75	1.25
❏ 8	1.25	0.25	0.75	1.25
❏ 9	1.25	0.25	0.75	1.25
❏ 10	1.25	0.25	0.75	1.25
❏ 11	1.25	0.25	0.75	1.25
❏ 12	1.25	0.25	0.75	1.25
❏ 13, Aug 94	1.50	0.30	0.90	1.50
❏ 14, Sep 94	1.50	0.30	0.90	1.50
❏ 15, Oct 94	1.50	0.30	0.90	1.50
❏ 16, Nov 94	1.50	0.30	0.90	1.50
❏ 17, Dec 94	1.50	0.30	0.90	1.50
❏ 18, Jan 95	1.50	0.30	0.90	1.50
❏ 20, Mar 95	1.50	0.30	0.90	1.50
❏ 21, Apr 95	1.50	0.30	0.90	1.50
❏ 22, May 95	1.50	0.30	0.90	1.50
❏ 23, Jun 95	1.50	0.30	0.90	1.50
❏ 24, Jul 95	1.50	0.30	0.90	1.50
❏ 25, Aug 95	1.50	0.30	0.90	1.50
❏ 26, Sep 95	1.50	0.30	0.90	1.50
❏ 27, Oct 95	1.50	0.30	0.90	1.50
❏ 28, Nov 95	1.50	0.30	0.90	1.50
❏ 29, Dec 95	1.50	0.30	0.90	1.50
❏ 30, Jan 96	1.50	0.30	0.90	1.50
❏ 32, Mar 96	1.50	0.30	0.90	1.50
❏ 34, May 96	1.50	0.30	0.90	1.50
❏ 36, Jul 96	1.50	0.30	0.90	1.50

SONIC THE HEDGEHOG IN YOUR FACE SPECIAL
	ORIG.	GOOD	FINE	N-MINT
❏ 1, 95	2.00	0.40	1.20	2.00

SONIC THE HEDGEHOG TRIPLE TROUBLE SPECIAL
	ORIG.	GOOD	FINE	N-MINT
❏ 1, Oct 95	2.00	0.40	1.20	2.00

SONIC'S FRIENDLY NEMESIS KNUCKLES
(mini-series)
	ORIG.	GOOD	FINE	N-MINT
❏ 1, Jul 96	1.50	0.30	0.90	1.50

SOUL
FLASHPOINT
	ORIG.	GOOD	FINE	N-MINT
❏ 1, Mar 94	2.50	0.50	1.50	2.50

SOUL TREK
SPOOF
	ORIG.	GOOD	FINE	N-MINT
❏ 1, b&w parody		0.59	1.77	2.95
❏ 2, b&w parody		0.59	1.77	2.95

	ORIG.	GOOD	FINE	N-MINT

SOULQUEST
INNOVATION
	ORIG.	GOOD	FINE	N-MINT
❑ 1		0.79	2.37	3.95

SOULSEARCHERS AND COMPANY
CLAYPOOL
	ORIG.	GOOD	FINE	N-MINT
❑ 1, b&w	2.50	0.50	1.50	2.50
❑ 2, b&w	2.50	0.50	1.50	2.50
❑ 3, Sandman parody	2.50	0.50	1.50	2.50
❑ 4	2.50	0.50	1.50	2.50
❑ 5, Oct 93	2.50	0.50	1.50	2.50
❑ 6, Feb 94	2.50	0.50	1.50	2.50
❑ 7, May 94, b&w	2.50	0.50	1.50	2.50
❑ 8, b&w	2.50	0.50	1.50	2.50
❑ 9, b&w	2.50	0.50	1.50	2.50
❑ 10, 94, b&w	2.50	0.50	1.50	2.50
❑ 11, Feb 95, b&w	2.50	0.50	1.50	2.50
❑ 12, May 95, b&w	2.50	0.50	1.50	2.50
❑ 13, Jul 95, b&w	2.50	0.50	1.50	2.50
❑ 14, Oct 95, b&w	2.50	0.50	1.50	2.50
❑ 15, Dec 95, b&w	2.50	0.50	1.50	2.50

SOUTHERN BLOOD
JM COMICS
	ORIG.	GOOD	FINE	N-MINT
❑ 1, b&w	2.50	0.50	1.50	2.50
❑ 2, b&w	2.50	0.50	1.50	2.50

SOUTHERN KNIGHTS (former Guild title)
COMICS INTERVIEW
	GOOD	FINE	N-MINT
❑ 8, Apr 85	0.40	1.20	2.00
❑ 9, Jun 85	0.40	1.20	2.00
❑ 10, Aug 85	0.40	1.20	2.00
❑ 11, Oct 85	0.40	1.20	2.00
❑ 12, Dec 85	0.40	1.20	2.00
❑ 13, Feb 86	0.40	1.20	2.00
❑ 14, Apr 86	0.40	1.20	2.00
❑ 15, Jun 86	0.40	1.20	2.00
❑ 16, Aug 86	0.35	1.05	1.75
❑ 17, Oct 86	0.35	1.05	1.75
❑ 18, Dec 86	0.35	1.05	1.75
❑ 19, Feb 87	0.35	1.05	1.75
❑ 20, Apr 87	0.35	1.05	1.75
❑ 21, Jun 87	0.35	1.05	1.75
❑ 22, Aug 87	0.35	1.05	1.75
❑ 23, Dec 87	0.35	1.05	1.75
❑ 24, Dec 87	0.35	1.05	1.75
❑ 25, Feb 88	0.35	1.05	1.75
❑ 26, Apr 88	0.35	1.05	1.75
❑ 27, Jun 88	0.35	1.05	1.75
❑ 28, Aug 88	0.39	1.17	1.95
❑ 29, Aug 88	0.39	1.17	1.95
❑ 30, Sep 88	0.39	1.17	1.95
❑ 31, Oct 88	0.39	1.17	1.95
❑ 32, Jan 89	0.39	1.17	1.95
❑ 33, Sep 89	0.39	1.17	1.95
❑ 34, 89	0.45	1.35	2.25

COMICS INTERVIEW/ HERO
	GOOD	FINE	N-MINT
❑ 35, b&w	0.70	2.10	3.50
❑ 36, b&w	0.70	2.10	3.50

SOUTHERN KNIGHTS (formerly Crusaders)
GUILD
	GOOD	FINE	N-MINT
❑ 2, 83	1.00	3.00	5.00
❑ 3	0.60	1.80	3.00
❑ 4	0.60	1.80	3.00
❑ 5	0.60	1.80	3.00
❑ 6, Jun 84	0.40	1.20	2.00
❑ 7, Sep 84, (moves to Comics Interview)			
	0.40	1.20	2.00

SOUTHERN KNIGHTS DREAD HALLOWEEN SPECIAL
COMICS INTERVIEW
	GOOD	FINE	N-MINT
❑ 1, Oct 88, b&w rep	0.45	1.35	2.25

SOUTHERN KNIGHTS PRIMER
	GOOD	FINE	N-MINT
❑ 1, rep, b&w	0.45	1.35	2.25

SOUTHERN KNIGHTS SPECIAL
	GOOD	FINE	N-MINT
❑ 1, Apr 89, rep, b&w	0.45	1.35	2.25

SOUTHERN SQUADRON
AIRCEL
	GOOD	FINE	N-MINT
❑ 1, MGr(c) b&w	0.45	1.35	2.25
❑ 2	0.45	1.35	2.25
❑ 3	0.45	1.35	2.25
❑ 4	0.45	1.35	2.25

ETERNITY
	GOOD	FINE	N-MINT
❑ 1, b&w	0.50	1.50	2.50
❑ 2, b&w	0.50	1.50	2.50
❑ 3, b&w	0.50	1.50	2.50
❑ 4, b&w	0.50	1.50	2.50

SOUTHERN SQUADRON: THE FREEDOM OF INFORMATION ACT
	GOOD	FINE	N-MINT
❑ 1, b&w	0.50	1.50	2.50
❑ 2, b&w	0.50	1.50	2.50
❑ 3, b&w	0.50	1.50	2.50

SOVEREIGN SEVEN
DC
	ORIG.	GOOD	FINE	N-MINT
❑ 1, Jul 95	1.95	0.39	1.17	1.95
❑ 1, Jul 95, foil edition;no cover price				
	2.00	6.00		10.00
❑ 2, Aug 95	1.95	0.39	1.17	1.95
❑ 3, Sep 95	1.95	0.39	1.17	1.95
❑ 4, Oct 95	1.95	0.39	1.17	1.95
❑ 5, Nov 95	1.95	0.39	1.17	1.95
❑ 6, Dec 95	1.95	0.39	1.17	1.95
❑ 7, Jan 96	1.95	0.39	1.17	1.95
❑ 8, Feb 96	1.95	0.39	1.17	1.95
❑ 9, Mar 96	1.95	0.39	1.17	1.95
❑ 10, Apr 96, "Road Trip" Part 1 of 3				
	1.95	0.39	1.17	1.95
❑ 11, Jun 96, "Road Trip"Part 2 of 3				
	1.95	0.39	1.17	1.95

SOVEREIGN SEVEN ANNUAL
	ORIG.	GOOD	FINE	N-MINT
❑ 1, 95, "Year One";A:Lobo,Big Barda				
	3.95	0.79	2.37	3.95

SOVIET SUPER SOLDIERS
MARVEL
	ORIG.	GOOD	FINE	N-MINT
❑ 1	2.00	0.40	1.20	2.00

SPACE ARK
AC
	GOOD	FINE	N-MINT
❑ 1	0.35	1.05	1.75
❑ 2, (moves to Apple)	0.35	1.05	1.75

SPACE ARK (former AC title)
APPLE
	GOOD	FINE	N-MINT
❑ 3, b&w	0.35	1.05	1.75
❑ 4, b&w	0.35	1.05	1.75
❑ 5, b&w	0.35	1.05	1.75

SPACE BANANAS
KARL ART
	ORIG.	GOOD	FINE	N-MINT
❑ 0, 95	1.95	0.39	1.17	1.95

SPACE BEAVER
TEN-BUCK
	GOOD	FINE	N-MINT
❑ 1	0.30	0.90	1.50
❑ 2	0.30	0.90	1.50
❑ 3	0.30	0.90	1.50
❑ 4	0.30	0.90	1.50
❑ 5	0.30	0.90	1.50
❑ 6	0.30	0.90	1.50
❑ 7	0.30	0.90	1.50
❑ 8	0.30	0.90	1.50
❑ 9	0.30	0.90	1.50
❑ 10	0.30	0.90	1.50
❑ 11	0.30	0.90	1.50

	ORIG.	GOOD	FINE	N-MINT

SPACE FUNNIES
ARCHIVAL
❏ 1, BW .... | | 1.19 | 3.57 | 5.95

SPACE GHOST
COMICO
❏ 1, Dec 87, SR .... 3.50 | | 0.90 | 2.70 | 4.50

SPACE PATROL
ADVENTURE
❏ 2, b&w .... 2.50 | | 0.50 | 1.50 | 2.50

SPACE SLUTZ
COMIC ZONE
❏ 1, adult, b&w .... | | 0.79 | 2.37 | 3.95

SPACE TIME SHUFFLE A TRILOGY
ALPHA PRODUCTIONS
❏ 1, b&w .... | | 0.39 | 1.17 | 1.95
❏ 2, b&w .... | | 0.39 | 1.17 | 1.95

SPACE USAGI
DARK HORSE
❏ 2, Feb 96, b&w .... 2.95 | | 0.59 | 1.77 | 2.95
MIRAGE
❏ 1, b&w .... 2.00 | | 0.40 | 1.20 | 2.00
❏ 2, b&w .... 2.00 | | 0.40 | 1.20 | 2.00
❏ 3, b&w .... | | 0.55 | 1.65 | 2.75

SPACE USAGI (Volume 2)
❏ 1 .... 2.75 | | 0.55 | 1.65 | 2.75
❏ 2 .... 2.75 | | 0.55 | 1.65 | 2.75
❏ 3, Mar 94 .... 2.75 | | 0.55 | 1.65 | 2.75

SPACE WOLF
ANTARCTIC
❏ 1, b&w .... 2.50 | | 0.50 | 1.50 | 2.50
❏ 2, b&w .... 2.50 | | 0.50 | 1.50 | 2.50

SPACE: 34-24-34
MN DESIGN
❏ 1, photos, b&w .... | | 0.90 | 2.70 | 4.50

SPACED
UNBRIDLED AMBITION
❏ 1 .... | | 0.60 | 1.80 | 3.00
❏ 2 .... | | 0.40 | 1.20 | 2.00
❏ 3 .... | | 0.40 | 1.20 | 2.00
❏ 4 .... | | 0.40 | 1.20 | 2.00
❏ 5 .... | | 0.40 | 1.20 | 2.00
❏ 6 .... | | 0.40 | 1.20 | 2.00
❏ 7 .... | | 0.32 | 0.96 | 1.60
❏ 8 .... | | 0.32 | 0.96 | 1.60
❏ 9, (moves to Eclipse) .... | | 0.32 | 0.96 | 1.60

SPACED (former Unbridled Ambition title)
ECLIPSE
❏ 10, b&w .... | | 0.30 | 0.90 | 1.50
❏ 11, b&w .... | | 0.30 | 0.90 | 1.50
❏ 12, b&w .... | | 0.30 | 0.90 | 1.50
❏ 13, b&w .... | | 0.30 | 0.90 | 1.50

SPACEGIRL COMICS
BILL JONES GRAPHICS
❏ 2, Nov 95, b&w .... 2.50 | | 0.50 | 1.50 | 2.50

SPACEHAWK
DARK HORSE
❏ 1, Wolverton .... | | 0.40 | 1.20 | 2.00
❏ 2, Wolverton .... | | 0.40 | 1.20 | 2.00
❏ 3, Wolverton .... | | 0.40 | 1.20 | 2.00
❏ 4 .... | | 0.45 | 1.35 | 2.25
❏ 5, BW reprints, b&w ...... 2.50 | | 0.50 | 1.50 | 2.50

SPAM
ALPHA PRODUCTIONS
❏ 1, b&w .... | | 0.30 | 0.90 | 1.50
❏ 2, b&w .... | | 0.30 | 0.90 | 1.50

SPANDEX TIGHTS
LOST CAUSE
❏ 1, Sep 94, b&w .... 1.95 | 0.39 | 1.17 | 1.95

	ORIG.	GOOD	FINE	N-MINT

❏ 2, Nov 94, b&w .... 2.25 | 0.45 | 1.35 | 2.25
❏ 3, b&w .... 2.25 | 0.45 | 1.35 | 2.25
❏ 4, Mar 95, b&w .... 2.25 | 0.45 | 1.35 | 2.25
❏ 6, Jul 95, V:Mighty Awful Sour Rangers;false cover
for *Mighty Awful Sour Rangers #1*;b&w
.... 2.50 | 0.50 | 1.50 | 2.50

SPANDEX TIGHTS SUMMER FUN
❏ 1, Sep 95, b&w .... 2.50 | 0.50 | 1.50 | 2.50

SPANK
EROS COMIX
❏ 1, adult, b&w .... | | 0.45 | 1.35 | 2.25
❏ 2, adult, b&w .... | | 0.45 | 1.35 | 2.25
❏ 3, adult, b&w .... | | 0.45 | 1.35 | 2.25
❏ 4, adult, b&w .... | | 0.45 | 1.35 | 2.25

SPANNER'S GALAXY
DC
❏ 1, mini-series.................. | | 0.40 | 1.20 | 2.00
❏ 2 .... | | 0.20 | 0.60 | 1.00
❏ 3 .... | | 0.20 | 0.60 | 1.00
❏ 4 .... | | 0.20 | 0.60 | 1.00
❏ 5 .... | | 0.20 | 0.60 | 1.00
❏ 6 .... | | 0.20 | 0.60 | 1.00

SPARKPLUG
HEROIC
❏ 1, b&w .... | | 0.59 | 1.77 | 2.95
❏ 2, b&w, trading card ...... 3.95 | 0.79 | 2.37 | 3.95

SPARROW
MILLENNIUM
❏ 1, 95, b&w .... 2.95 | 0.59 | 1.77 | 2.95
❏ 2, Apr 95, b&w .... 2.95 | 0.59 | 1.77 | 2.95
❏ 3, May 95, b&w .... 2.95 | 0.59 | 1.77 | 2.95
❏ 4, Jul 95, b&w .... 2.95 | 0.59 | 1.77 | 2.95

SPARTAN: WARRIOR SPIRIT
IMAGE
❏ 1, Jul 95 .... 2.50 | 0.50 | 1.50 | 2.50
❏ 2, Sep 95 .... 2.50 | 0.50 | 1.50 | 2.50
❏ 3, Oct 95 .... 2.50 | 0.50 | 1.50 | 2.50
❏ 4, Nov 95 .... 2.50 | 0.50 | 1.50 | 2.50

SPAWN
❏ 1, May 92, TMc.............. 1.95 | 4.00 | 12.00 | 20.00
❏ 2, Jul 92, TMc;cover says"Jun", indicia says "Jul"
.... 1.95 | 2.80 | 8.40 | 14.00
❏ 3, Aug 92, TMc .... 1.95 | 2.80 | 8.40 | 14.00
❏ 4, Sep 92, TMc, with coupon
.... 1.95 | 3.50 | 10.50 | 17.50
❏ 5, TMc .... 1.95 | 2.40 | 7.20 | 12.00
❏ 6, TMc .... 1.95 | 1.60 | 4.80 | 8.00
❏ 7, TMc .... 1.95 | 1.60 | 4.80 | 8.00
❏ 8, TMc, AMo script .... 1.95 | 2.00 | 6.00 | 10.00
❏ 9, TMc, NG script;1:Angela
.... 1.95 | 1.20 | 3.60 | 6.00
❏ 10, Dave Sim(story),TMc;A:Cerebus
.... 1.95 | 1.20 | 3.60 | 6.00
❏ 11, FM(story),TMc.......... 1.95 | 0.80 | 2.40 | 4.00
❏ 12, Jul 93, TMc.............. 1.95 | 0.80 | 2.40 | 4.00
❏ 13, TMc .... 1.95 | 0.80 | 2.40 | 4.00
❏ 14, TMc .... 1.95 | 0.80 | 2.40 | 4.00
❏ 15, TMc .... 1.95 | 0.80 | 2.40 | 4.00
❏ 16, TMc .... 1.95 | 0.80 | 2.40 | 4.00
❏ 17, TMc .... 1.95 | 0.80 | 2.40 | 4.00
❏ 18, TMc .... 1.95 | 0.80 | 2.40 | 4.00
❏ 19, TMc .... 1.95 | 0.80 | 2.40 | 4.00
❏ 20, TMc .... 1.95 | 0.80 | 2.40 | 4.00
❏ 21, May 94, TMc............ 1.95 | 0.70 | 2.10 | 3.50
❏ 22, Jun 94, TMc............. 1.95 | 0.70 | 2.10 | 3.50
❏ 23, Aug 94, TMc .... 1.95 | 0.70 | 2.10 | 3.50
❏ 24, Sep 94, TMc .... 1.95 | 0.70 | 2.10 | 3.50
❏ 25, 94, TMc .... 1.95 | 0.70 | 2.10 | 3.50
❏ 26, Dec 94, TMc .... 1.95 | 0.60 | 1.80 | 3.00
❏ 27, Jan 95, TMc............. 1.95 | 0.60 | 1.80 | 3.00

	ORIG.	GOOD	FINE	N-MINT
❑ 29, Mar 95, TMc 1.95		0.60	1.80	3.00
❑ 30, Apr 95, TMc 1.95		0.60	1.80	3.00
❑ 31, May 95, TMc 1.95		0.39	1.17	1.95
❑ 34, Aug 95 .... 1.95		0.39	1.17	1.95
❑ 35, Sep 95 .... 1.95		0.39	1.17	1.95
❑ 39, Dec 95, TMc;Christmas story				
.... 1.95		0.39	1.17	1.95
❑ 40, Jan 96 .... 1.95		0.39	1.17	1.95
❑ 41, Jan 96 .... 1.95		0.39	1.17	1.95
❑ 42, Feb 96 .... 1.95		0.39	1.17	1.95
❑ 43, Feb 96 .... 1.95		0.39	1.17	1.95
❑ 44, Mar 96 .... 1.95		0.39	1.17	1.95
❑ 45, Mar 96 .... 1.95		0.39	1.17	1.95
❑ 46, Apr 96 .... 1.95		0.39	1.17	1.95
❑ 47, Apr 96 .... 1.95		0.39	1.17	1.95
❑ 48, May 96 .... 1.95		0.39	1.17	1.95

SPAWN BLOOD FEUD

	ORIG.	GOOD	FINE	N-MINT
❑ 1, Jun 95, AMo(w) 2.25		1.00	3.00	5.00
❑ 2, 95, AMo(w) 2.25		0.80	2.40	4.00
❑ 3, Aug 95, AMo(w) 2.25		0.80	2.40	4.00

SPAWN/BATMAN

	ORIG.	GOOD	FINE	N-MINT
❑ 0, 94, nn FM(w),TMc 3.95		0.79	2.37	3.95

SPAWN/WILDC.A.T.S

	ORIG.	GOOD	FINE	N-MINT
❑ 1, Jan 96, "Devilday" Part 1 of 4				
.... 2.50		0.50	1.50	2.50
❑ 2, Feb 96, "Devilday" Part 2 of 4				
.... 2.50		0.50	1.50	2.50
❑ 3, Mar 96, "Devilday" Part 3 of 4				
.... 2.50		0.50	1.50	2.50
❑ 4, Apr 96, "Devilday" Part 4 of 4				
.... 2.50		0.50	1.50	2.50

SPECIAL COLLECTORS' EDITION
MARVEL

	ORIG.	GOOD	FINE	N-MINT
❑ 1, Kung Fu tabloid 1.00		0.20	0.60	1.00

SPECIAL HUGGING AND OTHER CHILDHOOD TALES
SLAVE LABOR

	ORIG.	GOOD	FINE	N-MINT
❑ 1, b&w		0.39	1.17	1.95

SPECIAL MARVEL EDITION
MARVEL

	ORIG.	GOOD	FINE	N-MINT
❑ 1 .... 0.25		0.60	1.80	3.00
❑ 2 .... 0.25		0.30	0.90	1.50
❑ 3 .... 0.25		0.30	0.90	1.50
❑ 4 .... 0.25		0.30	0.90	1.50
❑ 5 .... 0.20		0.40	1.20	2.00
❑ 6 .... 0.20		0.40	1.20	2.00
❑ 7 .... 0.20		0.40	1.20	2.00
❑ 8 .... 0.20		0.40	1.20	2.00
❑ 9 .... 0.20		0.40	1.20	2.00
❑ 10 .... 0.20		0.40	1.20	2.00
❑ 11 .... 0.20		0.40	1.20	2.00
❑ 12 .... 0.20		0.40	1.20	2.00
❑ 13 .... 0.20		0.40	1.20	2.00
❑ 14 .... 0.20		0.40	1.20	2.00
❑ 15, Dec 73, 1:Master of Kung Fu, JSn				
.... 0.20		4.00	12.00	20.00
❑ 16, Feb 74, JSn (becomes Master of Kung Fu)				
.... 0.20		2.00	6.00	10.00

SPECIES (mini-series)
DARK HORSE

	ORIG.	GOOD	FINE	N-MINT
❑ 1, Jun 95, movie adaptation				
.... 2.50		0.50	1.50	2.50
❑ 2, Jul 95, movie adaptation				
.... 2.50		0.50	1.50	2.50
❑ 3, Aug 95, movie adaptation				
.... 2.50		0.50	1.50	2.50
❑ 4, Sep 95,movie adaptation				
.... 2.50		0.50	1.50	2.50

SPECTACULAR SCARLET SPIDER
MARVEL

	ORIG.	GOOD	FINE	N-MINT
❑ 1, Nov 95, "Virtual Mortality"Part 4 of 4				
.... 1.95		0.39	1.17	1.95
❑ 2, Dec 95, "Cyberwar"Part 4 of 4				
.... 1.95		0.39	1.17	1.95

SPECTACULAR SPIDER-MAN

	ORIG.	GOOD	FINE	N-MINT
❑ 1, Jul 68, b&w mag;JR;1:Richard Raleigh, Man Monster				
.... 0.35		20.00	60.00	100.00
❑ 2, Nov 68, color mag;JR;V:Green Goblin				
.... 0.40		18.00	54.00	90.00

SPECTACULAR SPIDER-MAN ANNUAL

	ORIG.	GOOD	FINE	N-MINT
❑ 1, Dec 79, RB/JM, Dr. Octopus				
.... 0.75		0.80	2.40	4.00
❑ 2, Sep 80, JM, 1,O:Rapier				
.... 0.75		0.60	1.80	3.00
❑ 3, Nov 81, (becomes Peter Parker, The Spectacular Spider-Man Annual) 0.75		0.40	1.20	2.00

SPECTACULAR SPIDER-MAN ANNUAL (was Peter Parker, the Spectacular Spider-Man Annual)

	ORIG.	GOOD	FINE	N-MINT
❑ 7 .... 1.25		0.30	0.90	1.50
❑ 8, 88, Evolutionary War ..1.75		0.60	1.80	3.00
❑ 9, 89, Atlantis Attacks 2.00		0.60	1.80	3.00
❑ 10,90, tiny Spider-Man ...2.00		0.40	1.20	2.00
❑ 11, 91, Vibranium Vendetta				
.... 2.00		0.40	1.20	2.00
❑ 12, 92 .... 2.25		0.45	1.35	2.25
❑ 13,93, trading card 2.95		0.59	1.77	2.95
❑ 14, 94 .... 2.95		0.59	1.77	2.95

SPECTACULAR SPIDER-MAN SUPER SPECIAL, THE

	ORIG.	GOOD	FINE	N-MINT
❑ 1, Sep 95, flip-book;two of the stories conclude in Web of Spider-Man Super Special #1				
.... 3.95		0.79	2.37	3.95

SPECTACULAR SPIDER-MAN, THE

	ORIG.	GOOD	FINE	N-MINT
❑ 1, Dec 76, SB, Tarantula .0.30		8.80	26.40	44.00
❑ 2, Jan 77, SB, Kraven 0.30		4.00	12.00	20.00
❑ 3, Feb 77, SB 0.30		2.80	8.40	14.00
❑ 4, Mar 77, SB 0.30		2.80	8.40	14.00
❑ 5, Apr 77, SB 0.30		2.80	8.40	14.00
❑ 6, May 77 .... 0.30		3.00	9.00	15.00
❑ 7, Jun 77 .... 0.30		3.00	9.00	15.00
❑ 8, Jul 77 .... 0.30		3.00	9.00	15.00
❑ 9, Aug 77 .... 0.30		1.40	4.20	7.00
❑ 10, Sep 77 .... 0.30		1.40	4.20	7.00
❑ 11, Oct 77, SB 0.35		1.20	3.60	6.00
❑ 12, Nov 77, SB 0.35		1.20	3.60	6.00
❑ 13, Dec 77, SB 0.35		1.20	3.60	6.00
❑ 14, Jan 78, SB 0.35		1.20	3.60	6.00
❑ 15, Feb 78, SB 0.35		1.20	3.60	6.00
❑ 16, Mar 78, SB...............0.35		1.20	3.60	6.00
❑ 17, Apr 78, Angel/Iceman				
.... 0.35		1.20	3.60	6.00
❑ 18, May 78, Angel/Iceman				
.... 0.35		1.20	3.60	6.00
❑ 19, Jun 78 .... 0.35		1.00	3.00	5.00
❑ 20, Jul 78 .... 0.35		1.00	3.00	5.00
❑ 21, Aug 78 .... 0.35		1.00	3.00	5.00
❑ 22, Sep 78 .... 0.35		1.00	3.00	5.00
❑ 23, Oct 78 .... 0.35		1.00	3.00	5.00
❑ 24, Nov 78 .... 0.35		1.00	3.00	5.00
❑ 25, Dec 78 .... 0.35		1.00	3.00	5.00
❑ 26, Jan 79 .... 0.35		1.00	3.00	5.00
❑ 27, Feb 79, DC/FM 0.35		3.00	9.00	15.00
❑ 28, Mar 79, FM, DD 0.35		2.00	6.00	10.00
❑ 29, Apr 79 .... 0.35		0.80	2.40	4.00
❑ 30, May 79 .... 0.40		0.80	2.40	4.00
❑ 31, Jun 79 .... 0.40		0.80	2.40	4.00
❑ 32, Jul 79 .... 0.40		0.80	2.40	4.00
❑ 33, Aug 79 .... 0.40		0.80	2.40	4.00
❑ 34, Sep 79 .... 0.40		0.80	2.40	4.00

	ORIG.	GOOD	FINE	N-MINT
☐ 35, Oct 79	0.40	0.80	2.40	4.00
☐ 36, Nov 79	0.40	0.80	2.40	4.00
☐ 37, Dec 79	0.40	0.80	2.40	4.00
☐ 38, Jan 80	0.40	2.00	6.00	10.00
☐ 39, Feb 80	0.40	0.80	2.40	4.00
☐ 40, Mar 80	0.40	0.80	2.40	4.00
☐ 41, Apr 80	0.40	0.80	2.40	4.00
☐ 42, May 80	0.40	0.80	2.40	4.00
☐ 43, Jun 80	0.40	0.80	2.40	4.00
☐ 44, Jul 80	0.40	0.80	2.40	4.00
☐ 45, Aug 80, Vulture	0.40	0.80	2.40	4.00
☐ 46, Sep 80, FM(c), Cobra.	0.50	0.80	2.40	4.00
☐ 47, Oct 80	0.50	0.60	1.80	3.00
☐ 48, Nov 80, (becomes *Peter Parker, The Spectacular Spider-Man*)	0.50	0.60	1.80	3.00

SPECTACULAR SPIDER-MAN, THE
(was Peter Parker, The Spectacular Spider-Man)

	ORIG.	GOOD	FINE	N-MINT
☐ 133	0.75	0.40	1.20	2.00
☐ 134	0.75	0.40	1.20	2.00
☐ 135, Feb 88	0.75	0.40	1.20	2.00
☐ 136, Mar 88	0.75	0.40	1.20	2.00
☐ 137, Apr 88	0.75	0.40	1.20	2.00
☐ 138, May 88	1.00	0.40	1.20	2.00
☐ 139, Jun 88,O:Tombstone	1.00	0.40	1.20	2.00
☐ 140, Jul 88, C:Punisher	1.00	1.00	3.00	5.00
☐ 141, Aug 88, A:Punisher	1.00	1.60	4.80	8.00
☐ 142, Sep 88, A:Punisher	1.00	2.00	6.00	10.00
☐ 143, Oct 88, A:Punisher	1.00	1.60	4.80	8.00
☐ 144, Nov 88	1.00	0.40	1.20	2.00
☐ 145, Dec 88	1.00	0.40	1.20	2.00
☐ 146, Jan 89, Inferno	1.00	0.40	1.20	2.00
☐ 147, Feb 89, Inferno	1.00	0.40	1.20	2.00
☐ 148, Mar 89, Inferno	1.00	0.40	1.20	2.00
☐ 149, Apr 89	1.00	0.40	1.20	2.00
☐ 150, May 89	1.00	0.40	1.20	2.00
☐ 151, Jun 89	1.00	0.40	1.20	2.00
☐ 152, Jul 89	1.00	0.40	1.20	2.00
☐ 153, Aug 89	1.00	0.40	1.20	2.00
☐ 154, Sep 89	1.00	0.40	1.20	2.00
☐ 155, Oct 89	1.00	0.40	1.20	2.00
☐ 156, Nov 89	1.00	0.40	1.20	2.00
☐ 157, Nov 89	1.00	0.40	1.20	2.00
☐ 158, Dec 89, Acts of Vengeance, cosmic power	1.00	2.00	6.00	10.00
☐ 159, Dec 89, Acts of Vengeance, power	1.00	1.20	3.60	6.00
☐ 160, Jan 90, Acts of Vengeance, power	1.00	1.20	3.60	6.00
☐ 161, Feb 90	1.00	0.40	1.20	2.00
☐ 162, Mar 90	1.00	0.40	1.20	2.00
☐ 163, Apr 90, Hobgoblin	1.00	0.40	1.20	2.00
☐ 164, May 90	1.00	0.30	0.90	1.50
☐ 165, Jun 90, D:Arranger	1.00	0.30	0.90	1.50
☐ 166, Jul 90	1.00	0.30	0.90	1.50
☐ 167, Aug 90	1.00	0.30	0.90	1.50
☐ 168, Sep 90, Avengers	1.00	0.30	0.90	1.50
☐ 169, Oct 90, Avengers	1.00	0.30	0.90	1.50
☐ 170, Nov 90	1.00	0.30	0.90	1.50
☐ 171, Dec 90	1.00	0.30	0.90	1.50
☐ 172, Jan 91	1.00	0.30	0.90	1.50
☐ 173, Feb 91, Dr. Octopus	1.00	0.30	0.90	1.50
☐ 174, Mar 91, Dr. Octopus	1.00	0.30	0.90	1.50
☐ 175, AP 91, Dr. Octopus	1.00	0.30	0.90	1.50
☐ 176, May 91,O&1:Corona	1.00	0.30	0.90	1.50
☐ 177, Jun 91	1.00	0.30	0.90	1.50
☐ 178, Jul 91	1.00	0.30	0.90	1.50
☐ 179, Aug 91	1.00	0.30	0.90	1.50

	ORIG.	GOOD	FINE	N-MINT
☐ 180, Sep 91, Green Goblin	1.00	0.40	1.20	2.00
☐ 181, Oct 91, Green Goblin	1.00	0.40	1.20	2.00
☐ 182, Nov 91, Green Goblin	1.00	0.40	1.20	2.00
☐ 183, Dec 91, Green Goblin	1.00	0.40	1.20	2.00
☐ 184	1.00	0.20	0.60	1.00
☐ 185	1.25	0.25	0.75	1.25
☐ 186, Vulture	1.25	0.25	0.75	1.25
☐ 187, Vulture	1.25	0.25	0.75	1.25
☐ 188, Vulture	1.25	0.25	0.75	1.25
☐ 189, hologram cover	2.95	0.59	1.77	2.95
☐ 189, hologram cover, 2nd printing	2.95	0.59	1.77	2.95
☐ 190	1.25	0.25	0.75	1.25
☐ 191	1.25	0.25	0.75	1.25
☐ 192	1.25	0.25	0.75	1.25
☐ 193	1.25	0.25	0.75	1.25
☐ 194	1.25	0.25	0.75	1.25
☐ 195	1.25	0.25	0.75	1.25
☐ 196	1.25	0.25	0.75	1.25
☐ 197	1.25	0.25	0.75	1.25
☐ 198, X-Men	1.25	0.25	0.75	1.25
☐ 199, X-Men	1.25	0.25	0.75	1.25
☐ 200, foil cover	2.95	0.59	1.77	2.95
☐ 201, Maximum Carnage	1.25	0.50	1.50	2.50
☐ 202, Maximum Carnage	1.25	0.25	0.75	1.25
☐ 203, Maximum Carnage	1.25	0.25	0.75	1.25
☐ 204, SB	1.25	0.25	0.75	1.25
☐ 205	1.25	0.25	0.75	1.25
☐ 206	1.25	0.25	0.75	1.25
☐ 207	1.25	0.25	0.75	1.25
☐ 208, SB	1.25	0.25	0.75	1.25
☐ 209, SB	1.25	0.25	0.75	1.25
☐ 210, SB	1.25	0.25	0.75	1.25
☐ 211, Apr 94	1.25	0.25	0.75	1.25
☐ 212, May 94	1.25	0.25	0.75	1.25
☐ 213, Jun 94	1.50	0.30	0.90	1.50
☐ 213, Jun 94, TV preview,print	2.95	0.59	1.77	2.95
☐ 214, Jul 94	1.50	0.30	0.90	1.50
☐ 215, Aug 94	1.50	0.30	0.90	1.50
☐ 216, Sep 94	1.50	0.30	0.90	1.50
☐ 217, Oct 94, enhanced cover; flip-book with back-up story	2.95	0.59	1.77	2.95
☐ 217, Oct 94	2.95	0.59	1.77	2.95
☐ 218, Nov 94	1.50	0.30	0.90	1.50
☐ 219, Dec 94, "Back from the Edge" Part 4 of 4	1.50	0.30	0.90	1.50
☐ 220, Jan 95, flip bookwit illustrated story from *The Ultimate Spider-Man* back-up	2.25	0.50	1.50	2.50
☐ 221, Feb 95	1.50	0.80	2.40	4.00
☐ 222, Mar 95	1.50	0.30	0.90	1.50
☐ 223, Apr 95, enhanced cover	2.95	0.59	1.77	2.95
☐ 223, Apr 95	2.50	0.50	1.50	2.50
☐ 224, May 95	1.50	0.30	0.90	1.50
☐ 225, Jun 95, 1:Green Goblin; enhanced cover	3.95	0.79	2.37	3.95
☐ 225, Jun 95, 1:Green Goblin	2.95	0.59	1.77	2.95
☐ 226, Jul 95, "The Trial of Peter Parker" Part 4 of 4;identity of clone revealed	1.50	0.30	0.90	1.50
☐ 227, Aug 95	1.50	0.30	0.90	1.50
☐ 228, Sep 95, "Time Bomb" Part 1;continues in *Web of Spider-Man* #129	1.50	0.30	0.90	1.50
☐ 229, Oct 95, "The Greatest Responsibility" Part 3 of 3;the clone retires;enhanced acetate outer cover	3.95	0.79	2.37	3.95

	ORIG.	GOOD	FINE	N-MINT

☐ 229, Oct 95, "The Greatest Responsibility" Part 3 of 3;the clone retires;wraparound cover

		ORIG.	GOOD	FINE	N-MINT
	....................2.50	0.50	1.50	2.50
☐ 230, Jan 96............1.50	0.30	0.90	1.50

☐ 231, Feb 96, "The Return of Kaine" Part 1 of 4

	1.50	0.30	0.90	1.50

☐ 232, Mar 96, New Dr. Octopus returns

	1.50	0.30	0.90	1.50

☐ 233, Apr 96, "Web of Carnage" Part 4 of 4

	1.50	0.30	0.90	1.50

☐ 234, May 96, "Blood Brothers" Part 4 of 6

	1.50	0.30	0.90	1.50

☐ 235, Jun 96, return of Will o' the Wisp

	1.50	0.30	0.90	1.50

SPECTRE (1967-1969 series)
DC

	ORIG.	GOOD	FINE	N-MINT
☐ 1, Dec 67, MA 0.12	15.00	45.00	75.00
☐ 2, Feb 68, NA 0.12	10.00	30.00	50.00
☐ 3, Apr 68, NA 0.12	8.00	24.00	40.00
☐ 4, Jun 68, NA 0.12	8.00	24.00	40.00
☐ 5, Aug 68, NA..................0.12	8.00	24.00	40.00
☐ 6, Oct 68, MA 0.12	4.40	13.20	22.00
☐ 7, Dec 68, MA 0.12	4.40	13.20	22.00
☐ 8, Feb 69, MA...................0.12	4.40	13.20	22.00
☐ 9, Apr 69, BWr 0.12	6.00	18.00	30.00
☐ 10, Jun 69......................0.12	4.00	12.00	20.00

SPECTRE (1987 series)

	ORIG.	GOOD	FINE	N-MINT
☐ 1, Apr 87......................1.00	0.40	1.20	2.00
☐ 2, May 87......................1.00	0.30	0.90	1.50
☐ 3, Jun 87......................1.00	0.30	0.90	1.50
☐ 4, Jul 87 ....1.00	0.30	0.90	1.50
☐ 5, Aug 87 ....1.00	0.30	0.90	1.50
☐ 6, Sep 87......................1.00	0.20	0.60	1.00
☐ 7, Oct 87 ....1.00	0.20	0.60	1.00
☐ 8, Nov 87 ....1.00	0.20	0.60	1.00
☐ 9, Dec 87......................1.25	0.25	0.75	1.25
☐ 10, Jan 88, Millennium ..1.25	0.25	0.75	1.25
☐ 11, Feb 88, Millennium ..1.25	0.25	0.75	1.25
☐ 12, Mar 88 ....1.25	0.25	0.75	1.25
☐ 13, Apr 88......................1.25	0.25	0.75	1.25
☐ 14, May 88 ....1.25	0.25	0.75	1.25
☐ 15, Jun 88 ....1.25	0.25	0.75	1.25
☐ 16, Jul 88......................1.25	0.25	0.75	1.25
☐ 17, Aug 88 ....1.25	0.25	0.75	1.25
☐ 18, Sep 88......................1.25	0.25	0.75	1.25
☐ 19, Oct 88 ....1.25	0.25	0.75	1.25
☐ 20, Nov 88 ....1.25	0.25	0.75	1.25
☐ 21, Dec 88......................1.25	0.25	0.75	1.25
☐ 22, Dec 88......................1.25	0.25	0.75	1.25
☐ 23, Jan 89, Invasion! 1.25	0.25	0.75	1.25
☐ 24, Feb 89......................1.25	0.25	0.75	1.25
☐ 25, Apr 89......................1.50	0.30	0.90	1.50
☐ 26, May 89......................1.50	0.30	0.90	1.50
☐ 27, Jun 89......................1.50	0.30	0.90	1.50
☐ 28, Aug 89 ....1.50	0.30	0.90	1.50
☐ 29, Sep 89......................1.50	0.30	0.90	1.50
☐ 30, Oct 89 ....1.50	0.30	0.90	1.50
☐ 31, Nov 89......................1.50	0.30	0.90	1.50

SPECTRE ANNUAL, THE

	GOOD	FINE	N-MINT
☐ 1, Jul 88, A:Deadman.......	0.40	1.20	2.00

SPECTRE ANNUAL, THE (1992-)

☐ 1, 95, "Year One";A:Dr. Fate

	3.95	0.79	2.37	3.95

SPECTRE, THE (1992-)

	ORIG.	GOOD	FINE	N-MINT
☐ 0, Oct 94, (1994)............1.95	0.60	1.80	3.00
☐ 1, glow cover	1.60	4.80	8.00
☐ 2	1.75	1.40	4.20	7.00
☐ 3	1.75	1.00	3.00	5.00
☐ 4	1.75	0.80	2.40	4.00
☐ 5	1.75	0.80	2.40	4.00

	ORIG.	GOOD	FINE	N-MINT
☐ 6 ....1.75	0.60	1.80	3.00
☐ 7 ....1.75	0.60	1.80	3.00
☐ 8, glowing cover 2.50	1.20	3.60	6.00
☐ 9 ....1.75	0.50	1.50	2.50
☐ 10 ....1.75	0.50	1.50	2.50
☐ 11 ....1.75	0.50	1.50	2.50
☐ 12 ....1.75	0.50	1.50	2.50
☐ 13 ....1.75	1.00	3.00	5.00
☐ 14 ....1.75	0.35	1.05	1.75
☐ 15 ....1.75	0.35	1.05	1.75
☐ 16 ....1.75	0.35	1.05	1.75
☐ 17 ....1.75	0.35	1.05	1.75
☐ 18, May 94......................1.75	0.35	1.05	1.75
☐ 19, Jun 94......................1.75	0.35	1.05	1.75
☐ 20, Jul 94......................1.75	0.35	1.05	1.75
☐ 21, Aug 94 ....1.95	0.50	1.50	2.50
☐ 22, Sep 94......................1.95	0.50	1.50	2.50
☐ 23, Nov 94......................1.95	0.39	1.17	1.95
☐ 24, Dec 94......................1.95	0.39	1.17	1.95
☐ 25, Jan 95......................1.95	0.39	1.17	1.95
☐ 26, Feb 95......................1.95	0.39	1.17	1.95
☐ 27, Mar 95......................1.95	0.39	1.17	1.95
☐ 28, Apr 95......................1.95	0.39	1.17	1.95
☐ 29, May 95......................1.95	0.39	1.17	1.95
☐ 30, Jun 95......................2.25	0.45	1.35	2.25
☐ 31, Jul 95......................2.25	0.45	1.35	2.25
☐ 32, Aug 95......................2.25	0.45	1.35	2.25
☐ 33, Sep 95......................2.25	0.45	1.35	2.25
☐ 34, Oct 95......................2.25	0.45	1.35	2.25

☐ 35, Nov 95, "UnderworldUnleashed"

	2.25	0.45	1.35	2.25

☐ 36, Dec 95, "UnderworldUnleashed"

	2.25	0.45	1.35	2.25

☐ 37, Jan 96, "The Hauntingof America" Part 1

	2.25	0.45	1.35	2.25

☐ 38, Feb 96, "The Hauntingof America" Part 2;O:Uncle Sam

	2.25	0.45	1.35	2.25

☐ 39, Mar 96, "The Hauntingof America" Part 3;O:Shadrach

	2.25	0.45	1.35	2.25

☐ 40, Apr 96, "The Haunting of America" Part 4;O:Captain Fear

	2.25	0.45	1.35	2.25

☐ 41, May 96, "The Haunting of America" Part 5

	2.25	0.45	1.35	2.25

☐ 42, Jun 96, "The Haunting of America" Part 6

	2.25	0.45	1.35	2.25

SPECTRUM
NEW HORIZONS

	GOOD	FINE	N-MINT
☐ 1, b&w.............................	0.30	0.90	1.50

SPECTRUM COMICS PREVIEWS
SPECTRUM

	GOOD	FINE	N-MINT
☐ 1, 1:Survivors	0.60	1.80	3.00

SPEED DEMON
MARVEL/AMALGAM

	ORIG.	GOOD	FINE	N-MINT
☐ 1, Apr 96..............1.95	0.39	1.17	1.95

SPEED RACER
NOW

	ORIG.	GOOD	FINE	N-MINT
☐ 1, Jul 87......................1.50	0.60	1.80	3.00
☐ 2, Aug 87......................1.50	0.30	0.90	1.50
☐ 3, Oct 87......................1.50	0.30	0.90	1.50
☐ 4, Nov 87......................1.75	0.35	1.05	1.75
☐ 5, Dec 87 ....1.75	0.35	1.05	1.75
☐ 6, Jan 88......................1.75	0.35	1.05	1.75
☐ 7, Mar 88......................1.75	0.35	1.05	1.75
☐ 8, Apr 88......................1.75	0.35	1.05	1.75
☐ 9, May 88......................1.75	0.35	1.05	1.75
☐ 10, Jun 88 ....1.75	0.35	1.05	1.75
☐ 11, Jul 88......................1.75	0.35	1.05	1.75
☐ 12, Aug 88 ....1.75	0.35	1.05	1.75
☐ 13, Sep 88 ....1.75	0.35	1.05	1.75
☐ 14, Oct 88......................1.75	0.35	1.05	1.75
☐ 15, Nov 88......................1.75	0.35	1.05	1.75

	ORIG.	GOOD	FINE	N-MINT
☐ 16, Dec 88 .... 1.75	0.35	1.05	1.75
☐ 17, Jan 89 .... 1.75	0.35	1.05	1.75
☐ 18, Mar 89 .... 1.75	0.35	1.05	1.75
☐ 19, Apr 89 .... 1.75	0.35	1.05	1.75
☐ 20, May 89, Comics Code			
.... 1.75	0.35	1.05	1.75
☐ 21, Jun 89, Comics Code 1.75	0.35	1.05	1.75
☐ 22, Jul 89, Comics Code 1.75	0.35	1.05	1.75
☐ 23, Aug 89, Comics Code			
.... 1.75	0.35	1.05	1.75
☐ 24, Sep 89, Comics Code 1.75	0.35	1.05	1.75
☐ 25, Oct 89, Comics Code 1.75	0.35	1.05	1.75
☐ 26, Nov 89, Comics Code			
.... 1.75	0.35	1.05	1.75
☐ 27, Dec 89, Comics Code 1.75	0.35	1.05	1.75
☐ 28, Jan 90, Comics Code 1.75	0.35	1.05	1.75
☐ 29, Feb 90, Comics Code 1.75	0.35	1.05	1.75
☐ 30, Mar 90, Comics Code			
.... 1.75	0.35	1.05	1.75
☐ 31, Apr 90, Comics Code 1.75	0.35	1.05	1.75
☐ 32, May 90, Comics Code 1.75	0.35	1.05	1.75
☐ 33, Jun 90, Comics Code 1.75	0.35	1.05	1.75
☐ 34, Jul 90, Comics Code 1.75	0.35	1.05	1.75
☐ 35, Aug 90, Comics Code			
.... 1.75	0.35	1.05	1.75
☐ 36, Sep 90, Comics Code 1.75	0.35	1.05	1.75
☐ 37, Oct 90, Comics Code 1.75	0.35	1.05	1.75
☐ 38, Nov 90, Comics Code			
.... 1.75	0.35	1.05	1.75

SPEED RACER (Volume 2)

	ORIG.	GOOD	FINE	N-MINT
☐ 1, Jul 92, prestige format			
.... 3.95	0.79	2.37	3.95
☐ 1, Jul 92, direct version . 2.50	0.50	1.50	2.50
☐ 1, Jul 92, newsstand 2.50	0.50	1.50	2.50
☐ 2, Aug 92 .... 2.50	0.50	1.50	2.50
☐ 3, Sep 92 .... 2.50	0.50	1.50	2.50

SPEED RACER 3-D SPECIAL

	ORIG.	GOOD	FINE	N-MINT
☐ 1, Jan 93 .... 2.95	0.59	1.77	2.95

SPEED RACER CLASSICS

	ORIG.	GOOD	FINE	N-MINT
☐ 1, Oct 88, b&w 3.75	0.75	2.25	3.75
☐ 2, Feb 89, b&w 3.95	0.79	2.37	3.95

SPEED RACER FEATURING NINJA HIGH SCHOOL
NOW/ETERNITY

	ORIG.	GOOD	FINE	N-MINT
☐ 1, Aug 93, trading card .. 2.50	0.50	1.50	2.50
☐ 2, 93 .... 2.50	0.50	1.50	2.50

SPEED RACER SPECIAL
NOW

	ORIG.	GOOD	FINE	N-MINT
☐ 1, Mar 88, (Mach V) 2.00	0.40	1.20	2.00

SPEED RACER/NINJA HIGH SCHOOL
NOW/ETERNITY

	ORIG.	GOOD	FINE	N-MINT
☐ 2, Sep 93, 2 trading cards			
.... 2.50	0.50	1.50	2.50

SPEED RACER: RETURN OF THE GRX
NOW

	ORIG.	GOOD	FINE	N-MINT
☐ 1, Mar 94 .... 1.95	0.39	1.17	1.95
☐ 2, Apr 94 .... 1.95	0.39	1.17	1.95

SPEEDBALL
MARVEL

	ORIG.	GOOD	FINE	N-MINT
☐ 1, Sep 88, SD,O:Speedball			
.... 0.75	0.40	1.20	2.00
☐ 2, Oct 88, SD 0.75	0.30	0.90	1.50
☐ 3, Nov 88, SD 0.75	0.30	0.90	1.50
☐ 4, Dec 88, SD 0.75	0.30	0.90	1.50
☐ 5, Jan 89, SD 0.75	0.30	0.90	1.50
☐ 6, Feb 89, SD 0.75	0.30	0.90	1.50
☐ 7, Mar 89, SD 0.75	0.30	0.90	1.50
☐ 8, Apr 89, SD 0.75	0.30	0.90	1.50
☐ 9, May 89, SD 0.75	0.30	0.90	1.50
☐ 10, Jun 89, SD 0.75	0.30	0.90	1.50

SPELLBINDERS
FLEETWAY/QUALITY

	ORIG.	GOOD	FINE	N-MINT
☐ 1		0.25	0.75	1.25
☐ 2		0.25	0.75	1.25
☐ 3		0.25	0.75	1.25
☐ 4		0.25	0.75	1.25
☐ 5		0.25	0.75	1.25
☐ 6		0.25	0.75	1.25
☐ 7		0.25	0.75	1.25
☐ 8		0.25	0.75	1.25
☐ 9		0.25	0.75	1.25
☐ 10		0.25	0.75	1.25
☐ 11		0.25	0.75	1.25
☐ 12		0.25	0.75	1.25

SPELLBOUND
MARVEL

	ORIG.	GOOD	FINE	N-MINT
☐ 1, Jan 88, LS,CP 1.50	0.30	0.90	1.50
☐ 2, Feb 88, LS,CP 1.50	0.30	0.90	1.50
☐ 3, Feb 88, LS,CP 1.50	0.30	0.90	1.50
☐ 4, Mar 88, LS,CP 1.50	0.30	0.90	1.50
☐ 5, Apr 88, LS,CP 1.50	0.30	0.90	1.50
☐ 6, Apr 88, LS,CP 2.25	0.45	1.35	2.25

SPELLJAMMER
DC

	ORIG.	GOOD	FINE	N-MINT
☐ 1		1.00	3.00	5.00
☐ 2		0.60	1.80	3.00
☐ 3		0.40	1.20	2.00
☐ 4		0.40	1.20	2.00
☐ 5		0.40	1.20	2.00
☐ 6		0.35	1.05	1.75
☐ 7		0.35	1.05	1.75
☐ 8		0.35	1.05	1.75
☐ 9		0.35	1.05	1.75
☐ 10		0.35	1.05	1.75
☐ 11		0.35	1.05	1.75
☐ 12		0.35	1.05	1.75
☐ 13		0.35	1.05	1.75
☐ 14		0.35	1.05	1.75

SPEX-7
SHADOW SHOCK

	ORIG.	GOOD	FINE	N-MINT
☐ 1, Sum 94, b&w 1.50	0.30	0.90	1.50

SPICY ADULT STORIES
AIRCEL

	ORIG.	GOOD	FINE	N-MINT
☐ 1, pulp reprints		0.50	1.50	2.50
☐ 2, pulp reprints		0.50	1.50	2.50
☐ 3, pulp reprints		0.50	1.50	2.50
☐ 4, pulp reprints		0.50	1.50	2.50

SPICY TALES
ETERNITY

	ORIG.	GOOD	FINE	N-MINT
☐ 1, b&w reprints		0.39	1.17	1.95
☐ 2, b&w reprints		0.39	1.17	1.95
☐ 3, b&w reprints		0.39	1.17	1.95
☐ 4, b&w reprints		0.39	1.17	1.95
☐ 5, b&w reprints		0.39	1.17	1.95
☐ 6, b&w reprints		0.39	1.17	1.95
☐ 7, b&w reprints		0.39	1.17	1.95
☐ 8, b&w reprints		0.39	1.17	1.95
☐ 9, b&w reprints		0.39	1.17	1.95
☐ 10		0.45	1.35	2.25
☐ 11		0.45	1.35	2.25
☐ 12		0.45	1.35	2.25
☐ 13		0.45	1.35	2.25
☐ 14		0.45	1.35	2.25
☐ 15		0.45	1.35	2.25
☐ 16		0.50	1.50	2.50
☐ 17		0.50	1.50	2.50
☐ 18		0.59	1.77	2.95
☐ 19		0.59	1.77	2.95
☐ 20		0.59	1.77	2.95

	ORIG.	GOOD	FINE	N-MINT

SPICY TALES SPECIAL

	ORIG.	GOOD	FINE	N-MINT
1, b&w reprints...............		0.45	1.35	2.25
2, b&w reprints...............		0.45	1.35	2.25

SPIDER, THE
ECLIPSE

	ORIG.	GOOD	FINE	N-MINT
1, Jun 91, TT..................	1.20	3.60	6.00	
2, Aug 91, TT	1.19	3.57	5.95	
3, Oct 91, TT..................	0.99	2.97	4.95	

SPIDER-BOY
MARVEL/AMALGAM

	ORIG.	GOOD	FINE	N-MINT
1, Apr 96 .... 1.95	0.39	1.17	1.95	

SPIDER-FEMME
SPOOF

	ORIG.	GOOD	FINE	N-MINT
1, parody.........................	0.50	1.50	2.50	

SPIDER-MAN
MARVEL

	ORIG.	GOOD	FINE	N-MINT
0, 7-Eleven giveaway, child abuse, verbal				
1, Aug 90, TMc silver cover				
.... 1.75	1.60	4.80	8.00	
1, TMc bagged silver cover				
.... 2.00	2.40	7.20	12.00	
1, Aug 90, TMc newsstand cover				
.... 1.75	1.60	4.80	8.00	
1, TMc bagged newsstand				
.... 1.75	2.40	7.20	12.00	
1, Aug 90, TMc gold cover, 2nd printing, direct sale				
.... 1.75	1.20	3.60	6.00	
1, TMc gold cover, 2nd printing, UPC box				
.... 1.75	2.00	6.00	10.00	
1, Aug 90, TMc platinum cover, giveaway				
....	75.00	225.00	375.00	
2, Sep 90, TMc, Lizard ... 1.75	1.20	3.60	6.00	
3, Oct 90, TMc, Lizard.... 1.75	0.60	1.80	3.00	
4, Nov 90, TMc, Lizard ... 1.75	0.60	1.80	3.00	
5, Dec 90, TMc, Lizard ... 1.75	0.60	1.80	3.00	
6, Jan 91, TMc, Ghost Rider				
.... 1.75	1.20	3.60	6.00	
7, Feb 91, TMc, Ghost Rider				
.... 1.75	1.40	4.20	7.00	
8, Mar 91, TMc, Wolverine, Wendigo				
.... 1.75	0.60	1.80	3.00	
9, Apr 91, TMc, Wolverine, Wendigo				
.... 1.75	0.60	1.80	3.00	
10, May 91, TMc, Wolverine, Wendigo				
.... 1.75	0.60	1.80	3.00	
11, Jun 91, TMc, Wolverine, Wendigo				
.... 1.75	0.60	1.80	3.00	
12, Jul 91, TMc, Wolverine, Wendigo				
.... 1.75	0.60	1.80	3.00	
13, Aug 91, TMc 1.75	0.60	1.80	3.00	
14, Sep 91...................... 1.75	0.60	1.80	3.00	
15, Oct 91, Erik Larsen... 1.75	0.60	1.80	3.00	
16, Nov 91, TMc, X-Force				
.... 1.75	0.80	2.40	4.00	
17, Dec 91, AW 1.75	0.60	1.80	3.00	
18, Ghost Rider.............. 1.75	1.00	3.00	5.00	
19 .... 1.75	0.70	2.10	3.50	
20 .... 1.75	0.70	2.10	3.50	
21, Deathlok.................... 1.75	0.50	1.50	2.50	
22 .... 1.75	0.50	1.50	2.50	
23, Deathlok, Torch, Ghost Rider				
.... 1.75	0.35	1.05	1.75	
24 .... 1.75	0.35	1.05	1.75	
25 .... 1.75	0.35	1.05	1.75	
26, hologram cover......... 3.50	0.70	2.10	3.50	
27 .... 1.75	0.35	1.05	1.75	
28 .... 1.75	0.35	1.05	1.75	
29 .... 1.75	0.35	1.05	1.75	
30 .... 1.75	0.35	1.05	1.75	
31 .... 1.75	0.35	1.05	1.75	
32 .... 1.75	0.35	1.05	1.75	

	ORIG.	GOOD	FINE	N-MINT
33, Punisher 1.75	0.35	1.05	1.75	
34, Punisher 1.75	0.35	1.05	1.75	
35, Maximum Carnage.... 1.75	0.60	1.80	3.00	
36, Maximum Carnage.... 1.75	0.35	1.05	1.75	
37, Maximum Carnage.... 1.75	0.35	1.05	1.75	
38 .... 1.75	0.35	1.05	1.75	
39 .... 1.75	0.35	1.05	1.75	
40 .... 1.75	0.35	1.05	1.75	
41 .... 1.75	0.55	1.65	2.75	
42 .... 1.75	0.50	1.50	2.50	
43 .... 1.75	0.35	1.05	1.75	
44 .... 1.75	0.35	1.05	1.75	
45 .... 1.75	0.35	1.05	1.75	
46, May 94, w/print 2.75	0.55	1.65	2.75	
46, May 94...................... 1.95	0.39	1.17	1.95	
47, Jun 94 .... 1.95	0.39	1.17	1.95	
48, Jul 94........................ 1.95	0.39	1.17	1.95	
49, Aug 94 .... 1.95	0.39	1.17	1.95	
50, Sep 94 .... 2.50	0.50	1.50	2.50	
50, Sep 94, enhanced cover				
.... 3.95	0.79	2.37	3.95	
51, Oct 94........................ 1.95	0.39	1.17	1.95	
52, Nov 94....................... 1.95	0.39	1.17	1.95	
53, Dec 94....................... 1.95	0.39	1.17	1.95	
54, Jan 95, flip book with illustrated story from *The Ultimate Spider-Man* back-up				
.... 2.75	0.55	1.65	2.75	
55, Feb 95....................... 1.95	0.39	1.17	1.95	
56, Mar 95....................... 1.95	0.39	1.17	1.95	
57, Apr 95........................ 2.50	0.50	1.50	2.50	
57, Apr 95, enhanced cardstock cover				
.... 2.95	0.59	1.77	2.95	
58, May 95....................... 1.95	0.39	1.17	1.95	
59, Jun 95 .... 1.95	0.39	1.17	1.95	
60, Jul 95, "The Trial ofPeter Parker" Part 3 of 4;Kaine's identity revealed............. 1.95	0.39	1.17	1.95	
61, Aug 95, "MaximumClonage" Part 4 of 6				
.... 1.95	0.39	1.17	1.95	
62, Sep 95, "Exiled" Part 3 of 4				
.... 1.95	0.39	1.17	1.95	
63, Oct 95, "The Greatest Responsibility" Part 2 of 3; OverPower game cards bound-in				
.... 1.95	0.39	1.17	1.95	
64, Jan 96........................ 1.95	0.39	1.17	1.95	
65, Feb 96, "Media Blizzard" Part 3 of 3				
.... 1.95	0.39	1.17	1.95	
66, Mar 96, "The Return of Kaine" Part 4 of 4				
.... 1.95	0.39	1.17	1.95	
67, Apr 96, "Web of Carnage"Part 3 of 4				
.... 1.95		1.17	1.95	
68, May 96, "Blood Brothers"Part 3 of 6				
.... 1.95	0.39	1.17	1.95	
69, Jun 96 .... 1.95	0.39	1.17	1.95	
70, Jul 96......................... 1.95	0.39	1.17	1.95	

SPIDER-MAN & HIS AMAZING FRIENDS

	ORIG.	GOOD	FINE	N-MINT
1, Dec 81, A:Iceman;I:Firestar				
.... 0.50	0.20	0.60	1.00	

SPIDER-MAN & THE NEW MUTANTS

	ORIG.	GOOD	FINE	N-MINT
0, 83, nn giveaway, child abuse	1.00	3.00	5.00	

SPIDER-MAN 2099

	ORIG.	GOOD	FINE	N-MINT
1, O:Spider-Man 2099 .... 1.75	1.20	3.60	6.00	
1, autographed by Rick Leonardi & Al Williamson, with certificate of authenticity.1.75	2.00	6.00	10.00	
2 .... 1.25	0.80	2.40	4.00	
3 .... 1.25	0.60	1.80	3.00	
4 .... 1.25	0.60	1.80	3.00	
5 .... 1.25	0.25	0.75	1.25	
6 .... 1.25	0.25	0.75	1.25	
7 .... 1.25	0.25	0.75	1.25	
8 .... 1.25	0.25	0.75	1.25	
9 .... 1.25	0.25	0.75	1.25	

	ORIG.	GOOD	FINE	N-MINT
10 ....1.25	0.25	0.75	1.25
11 ....1.25	0.25	0.75	1.25
12 ....1.25	0.25	0.75	1.25
13 ....1.25	0.25	0.75	1.25
14 ....1.25	0.25	0.75	1.25
15 ....1.25	0.25	0.75	1.25
16 ....1.25	0.25	0.75	1.25
17 ....1.25	0.25	0.75	1.25
18 ....1.25	0.25	0.75	1.25
19, May 94......................1.50	0.30	0.90	1.50
20, Jun 94.......................1.50	0.30	0.90	1.50
21, Jul 94........................1.50	0.30	0.90	1.50
22, Aug 94 ....1.50	0.30	0.90	1.50
23, Sep 94.......................1.50	0.30	0.90	1.50
24, Oct 94 ....1.50	0.30	0.90	1.50
25, Nov 94, enhanced cover			
..................................2.95	0.59	1.77	2.95
25, Nov 94 ....2.25	0.45	1.35	2.25
26, Dec 94.......................1.50	0.30	0.90	1.50
27, Jan 95.......................1.50	0.30	0.90	1.50
28, Feb 95 ....1.50	0.30	0.90	1.50
29, Mar 95.......................1.50	0.30	0.90	1.50
30, Apr 95........................1.50	0.30	0.90	1.50
31, May 95.......................1.50	0.30	0.90	1.50
32, Jun 95.......................1.50	0.30	0.90	1.50
33, Jul 95........................1.95	0.39	1.17	1.95
34, Aug 95.......................1.95	0.39	1.17	1.95
35, Sep 95.......................1.95	0.39	1.17	1.95
35, Sep 95, alternate cover;says "Venom 2099" on cover			
..................................1.95	0.39	1.17	1.95
36, Oct 95, forms diptych with alternate cover			
..................................1.95	0.39	1.17	1.95
36, Oct 95, alternate cover;says "Venom 2099";forms			
diptych 1.95	0.39	1.17	1.95
37, Nov 95 ....1.95	0.39	1.17	1.95
37, Nov 95, alternate cover;says "Venom 2099"			
..................................1.95	0.39	1.17	1.95
38, Dec 95, forms diptychwith alternate cover			
..................................1.95	0.39	1.17	1.95
38, Dec 95, alternate cover;says "Venom 2099";forms			
diptych 1.95	0.39	1.17	1.95
39, Jan 96 ....1.95	0.39	1.17	1.95
40, Feb 96, V:Goblin 2099			
..................................1.95	0.39	1.17	1.95
41, Mar 96 ....1.95	0.39	1.17	1.95
42, Apr 96........................1.95	0.39	1.17	1.95
43, May 96.......................1.95	0.39	1.17	1.95
44, Jun 96.......................1.95	0.39	1.17	1.95
45, Jul 96........................1.95	0.39	1.17	1.95

SPIDER-MAN 2099 ANNUAL

	ORIG.	GOOD	FINE	N-MINT
1, 94...............................2.95	0.59	1.77	2.95

SPIDER-MAN 2099 SPECIAL

	ORIG.	GOOD	FINE	N-MINT
1, Nov 95 ....3.95	0.79	2.37	3.95

SPIDER-MAN ADVENTURES

	ORIG.	GOOD	FINE	N-MINT
1, Dec 94, enhanced cover; adapts animated series			
..................................2.95	0.59	1.77	2.95
1, Dec 94, adaptsanimated series			
..................................1.50	0.30	0.90	1.50
2, Jan 95, adaptsanimated series			
..................................1.50	0.30	0.90	1.50
3, Feb 95, adaptsanimated series			
..................................1.50	0.30	0.90	1.50
4, Mar 95, adaptsanimated series			
..................................1.50	0.30	0.90	1.50
5, Apr 95, adapts animated series;V:Mysterio			
..................................1.50	0.30	0.90	1.50
6, May 95, adaptsanimated series			
..................................1.50	0.30	0.90	1.50
7, Jun 95, adaptsanimated series			
..................................1.50	0.30	0.90	1.50
8, Jul 95 ....1.50	0.30	0.90	1.50

	ORIG.	GOOD	FINE	N-MINT
9, Aug 95, V:Shocker.......1.50	0.30	0.90	1.50
10, Sep 95, V:Venom.......1.50	0.30	0.90	1.50
11, Oct 95, V:Hobgoblin .1.50	0.30	0.90	1.50
12, Nov 95, V:Hobgoblin.1.50	0.30	0.90	1.50
13, Dec 95, V:Chameleon1.50	0.30	0.90	1.50
14, Jan 96, V:Doctor Octopus			
..................................1.50	0.30	0.90	1.50
15, Feb 96, V:Lizard;(becomes *Adventures of*			
Spider-Man) 1.50	0.30	0.90	1.50

SPIDER-MAN AND DAREDEVIL SPECIAL EDITION

	ORIG.	GOOD	FINE	N-MINT
1, Mar 84, (1983) 2.00	0.40	1.20	2.00

SPIDER-MAN AND THE DALLAS COWBOYS

	ORIG.	GOOD	FINE	N-MINT
0, Sep 83, nn, "Danger in Dallas" giveaway			
....	3.00	9.00	15.00

SPIDER-MAN AND THE INCREDIBLE HULK

	ORIG.	GOOD	FINE	N-MINT
0, Sep 81, nn, "Chaos in Kansas City" giveaway			
....	3.00	9.00	15.00

SPIDER-MAN AND X-FACTOR

	ORIG.	GOOD	FINE	N-MINT
1, May 94........................1.95	0.39	1.17	1.95
2, Jun 94.........................1.95	0.39	1.17	1.95

SPIDER-MAN AND X-FACTOR: SHADOWGAMES

	ORIG.	GOOD	FINE	N-MINT
2, Jun 94.........................1.95	0.39	1.17	1.95
3, Jul 94..........................1.95	0.39	1.17	1.95

SPIDER-MAN CLASSICS

	ORIG.	GOOD	FINE	N-MINT
1, reprints......................1.25	0.25	0.75	1.25
2, reprints......................1.25	0.25	0.75	1.25
3, reprints......................1.25	0.25	0.75	1.25
4, reprints......................1.25	0.25	0.75	1.25
5, reprints......................1.25	0.25	0.75	1.25
6, reprints......................1.25	0.25	0.75	1.25
7, reprints......................1.25	0.25	0.75	1.25
8, reprints......................1.25	0.25	0.75	1.25
9, reprints......................1.25	0.25	0.75	1.25
10, reprints.....................1.25	0.25	0.75	1.25
11, reprints 1.25	0.25	0.75	1.25
12, reprints.....................1.25	0.25	0.75	1.25
13, reprints.....................1.25	0.25	0.75	1.25
14, May 94......................1.25	0.25	0.75	1.25
15, Jun 94,r:l:Green Goblin			
..................................1.25	0.25	0.75	1.25
16, Jul 94........................1.25	0.25	0.75	1.25

SPIDER-MAN COLLECTORS' PREVIEW

	ORIG.	GOOD	FINE	N-MINT
1, Dec 94 ....1.50	0.30	0.90	1.50

SPIDER-MAN COMICS MAGAZINE

	ORIG.	GOOD	FINE	N-MINT
1, Jan 87, digest.............1.50	0.30	0.90	1.50
2, Mar 87, digest............1.50	0.30	0.90	1.50
3, May 87, digest............1.50	0.30	0.90	1.50
4, Jul 87, digest..............1.50	0.30	0.90	1.50
5, Sep 87, digest.............1.50	0.30	0.90	1.50
6, Nov 87, digest.............1.50	0.30	0.90	1.50
7, Jan 88, digest.............1.50	0.30	0.90	1.50
8, Mar 88, digest............1.50	0.30	0.90	1.50
9, May 88, digest............1.50	0.30	0.90	1.50
10, Jul 88, digest............1.50	0.30	0.90	1.50
11, Sep 88, digest...........1.50	0.30	0.90	1.50
12, Nov 88, SL;JR;JM;digest			
..................................1.50	0.30	0.90	1.50
13, Jan 89, digest...........1.50	0.30	0.90	1.50

SPIDER-MAN HOLIDAY SPECIAL 1995

	ORIG.	GOOD	FINE	N-MINT
0, 95, nn;one-shot 2.95	0.59	1.77	2.95

SPIDER-MAN MAGAZINE

	ORIG.	GOOD	FINE	N-MINT
0, Win 94, nn 1.95	0.39	1.17	1.95
0, Spr 95, nn...................2.50	0.50	1.50	2.50
1 ....1.95	0.39	1.17	1.95
2, Jun 94.........................1.95	0.39	1.17	1.95
3, Jul 94..........................1.95	0.39	1.17	1.95
4, Aug 94, X-Men............1.95	0.39	1.17	1.95
5, Sep 94 ....1.95	0.39	1.17	1.95
6, Oct 94, X-Men 1.95	0.39	1.17	1.95

	ORIG.	GOOD	FINE	N-MINT
❑ 7, Nov 94 ....1.95		0.39	1.17	1.95
❑ 8, Dec 94.........................1.95		0.39	1.17	1.95
❑ 9, Jan 95, flip book with Iron Man back-up				
......................................1.95		0.39	1.17	1.95
❑ 10, Feb 95, flip book with X-Men back-up				
......................................1.95		0.39	1.17	1.95

SPIDER-MAN MAXIMUM CLONAGE: ALPHA

	ORIG.	GOOD	FINE	N-MINT
❑ 1, Aug 95, Acetate wraparound cover overlay				
......................................4.95		0.99	2.97	4.95

SPIDER-MAN MAXIMUM CLONAGE: OMEGA

	ORIG.	GOOD	FINE	N-MINT
❑ 1, Aug 95, enhanced wraparound cover				
......................................4.95		0.99	2.97	4.95

SPIDER-MAN MEGAZINE

	ORIG.	GOOD	FINE	N-MINT
❑ 1, Oct 94 ....2.50		0.50	1.50	2.50
❑ 2, Nov 94 ....2.95		0.59	1.77	2.95
❑ 3, Dec 94.........................2.95		0.59	1.77	2.95
❑ 4, Jan 95 ....2.95		0.59	1.77	2.95
❑ 5, Feb 95 ....2.95		0.59	1.77	2.95
❑ 6, Mar 95, final issue 2.95		0.59	1.77	2.95

SPIDER-MAN SAGA

	ORIG.	GOOD	FINE	N-MINT
❑ 1, retelling 2.95		0.59	1.77	2.95
❑ 2, retelling 2.95		0.59	1.77	2.95
❑ 3, retelling 2.95		0.59	1.77	2.95
❑ 4, retelling 2.95		0.59	1.77	2.95

SPIDER-MAN SPECIAL EDITION

	ORIG.	GOOD	FINE	N-MINT
❑ 1, Venom, UNICEF tie-in, poster, donation				
....		1.00	3.00	5.00

SPIDER-MAN SUPER SPECIAL

	ORIG.	GOOD	FINE	N-MINT
❑ 1, Jul 95, flipbook;two of the stories continue in *Venom Super Special* #1 ....3.95		0.79	2.37	3.95

SPIDER-MAN TEAM-UP

	ORIG.	GOOD	FINE	N-MINT
❑ 1, Dec 95, A:X-Men 2.95		0.59	1.77	2.95
❑ 2, Mar 96, A:Silver Surfer				
......................................2.95		0.59	1.77	2.95

SPIDER-MAN UNLIMITED

	ORIG.	GOOD	FINE	N-MINT
❑ 1, Carnage......................3.95		0.79	2.37	3.95
❑ 2, Carnage......................3.95		0.79	2.37	3.95
❑ 3, Dr. Octopus................3.95		0.79	2.37	3.95
❑ 4, Mysterio.....................3.95		0.79	2.37	3.95
❑ 5, May 94 ....3.95		0.79	2.37	3.95
❑ 6, Aug 94 ....3.95		0.79	2.37	3.95
❑ 7, Nov 94 ....3.95		0.79	2.37	3.95
❑ 8, Feb 95 ....3.95		0.79	2.37	3.95
❑ 9, May 95 ....3.95		0.79	2.37	3.95
❑ 10, Sep 95, "Exiled" Part 4 of 4;V:Vulture				
......................................3.95		0.79	2.37	3.95
❑ 11, Jan 96 ....3.95		0.79	2.37	3.95
❑ 12, May 96, V:Boomerang, Jack O'Lantern, Beetle Shocker, Scorpia............3.95		0.79	2.37	3.95

SPIDER-MAN VS. DRACULA

	ORIG.	GOOD	FINE	N-MINT
❑ 1, RA, reprint 1.75		0.35	1.05	1.75

SPIDER-MAN VS. THE HULK

	ORIG.	GOOD	FINE	N-MINT
❑ 0, nn, giveaway		3.00	9.00	15.00

SPIDER-MAN VS. WOLVERINE

	ORIG.	GOOD	FINE	N-MINT
❑ 0, Aug 90, bookshelf 4.95		0.99	2.97	4.95
❑ 1, Feb 87 ....2.50		5.60	16.80	28.00

SPIDER-MAN, FIRE-STAR AND ICEMAN

	ORIG.	GOOD	FINE	N-MINT
❑ 0, 83, nn, "Danger in Denver" giveaway				
....		3.60	10.80	18.00

SPIDER-MAN, POWER PACK

❑ 1, Aug 84, giveaway, no cover price, 1984

SPIDER-MAN, STORM AND POWER MAN

	ORIG.	GOOD	FINE	N-MINT
❑ 0, Apr 82, nn, "Smokescreen" giveaway				
....		4.00	12.00	20.00

SPIDER-MAN/PUNISHER: FAMILY PLOT (mini-series)

	ORIG.	GOOD	FINE	N-MINT
❑ 1, Feb 96.........................2.95		0.59	1.77	2.95
❑ 2, Feb 96.........................2.95		0.59	1.77	2.95

SPIDER-MAN: "CHRISTMAS IN DALLAS"

❑ 0, Dec 83, nn, giveaway....

SPIDER-MAN: FRIENDS & ENEMIES (mini-series)

	ORIG.	GOOD	FINE	N-MINT
❑ 1, Jan 95......................1.95		0.39	1.17	1.95
❑ 2, Feb 95......................1.95		0.39	1.17	1.95
❑ 3, Mar 95 ....1.95		0.39	1.17	1.95
❑ 4, Apr 95......................1.95		0.39	1.17	1.95

SPIDER-MAN: FUNERAL FOR AN OCTOPUS (mini-series)

	ORIG.	GOOD	FINE	N-MINT
❑ 1, Mar 95......................1.50		0.30	0.90	1.50
❑ 2, Apr 95......................1.50		0.30	0.90	1.50
❑ 3, May 95......................1.50		0.30	0.90	1.50

SPIDER-MAN: MUTANT AGENDA

	ORIG.	GOOD	FINE	N-MINT
❑ 0, strip reprints...............1.25		0.25	0.75	1.25

SPIDER-MAN: POWER OF TERROR (mini-series)

	ORIG.	GOOD	FINE	N-MINT
❑ 1, Jan 95......................1.95		0.39	1.17	1.95
❑ 2, Feb 95......................1.95		0.39	1.17	1.95
❑ 3, Mar 95 ....1.95		0.39	1.17	1.95
❑ 4, Apr 95......................1.95		0.39	1.17	1.95

SPIDER-MAN: THE ARACHNIS PROJECT (mini-series)

	ORIG.	GOOD	FINE	N-MINT
❑ 1, Aug 94......................1.75		0.35	1.05	1.75
❑ 2, Sep 94 ....1.75		0.35	1.05	1.75
❑ 3, Oct 94......................1.75		0.35	1.05	1.75
❑ 4, Nov 94......................1.75		0.35	1.05	1.75
❑ 5, Dec 94......................1.75		0.35	1.05	1.75
❑ 6, Jan 95......................1.75		0.35	1.05	1.75

SPIDER-MAN: THE CLONE JOURNAL

	ORIG.	GOOD	FINE	N-MINT
❑ 1, Mar 95, one-shot........2.95		0.59	1.77	2.95

SPIDER-MAN: THE FINAL ADVENTURE (mini-series)

	ORIG.	GOOD	FINE	N-MINT
❑ 1, Dec 95, enhanced cardstock cover;clone returns to action one last time 2.95		0.59	1.77	2.95
❑ 2, Jan 96, enhanced cardstock cover				
......................................2.95		0.59	1.77	2.95
❑ 3, Feb 96, enhanced cardstock cover				
......................................2.95		0.59	1.77	2.95
❑ 4, Mar 96, enhanced cardstock cover;Peter loses his powers...........................2.95		0.59	1.77	2.95

SPIDER-MAN: THE JACKAL FILES

	ORIG.	GOOD	FINE	N-MINT
❑ 1, Aug 95, one-shot;files on main Spider-Man characters and equipment................1.95		0.39	1.17	1.95

SPIDER-MAN: THE LOST YEARS (mini-series)

	ORIG.	GOOD	FINE	N-MINT
❑ 0, Jan 96, collects clone origin back-up stories				
......................................3.95		0.79	2.37	3.95
❑ 1, Aug 95, enhanced cardstock cover				
......................................2.95		0.59	1.77	2.95
❑ 2, Sep 95, enhanced cardstock cover				
......................................2.95		0.59	1.77	2.95

SPIDER-MAN: THE MUTANT AGENDA

	ORIG.	GOOD	FINE	N-MINT
❑ 1 ....1.75		0.35	1.05	1.75
❑ 2 ....1.75		0.35	1.05	1.75
❑ 3, May 94......................1.75		0.35	1.05	1.75

SPIDER-MAN: THE PARKER YEARS

	ORIG.	GOOD	FINE	N-MINT
❑ 1, Nov 95, one-shot;retells events in the clone's life from *Amazing Spider-Man* #150 to the present				
......................................2.50		0.50	1.50	2.50

SPIDER-MAN: WEB OF DOOM

	ORIG.	GOOD	FINE	N-MINT
❑ 1, Aug 94......................1.75		0.35	1.05	1.75
❑ 2, Sep 94 ....1.75		0.35	1.05	1.75
❑ 3, Oct 94......................1.75		0.35	1.05	1.75

	ORIG.	GOOD	FINE	N-MINT

SPIDER-WOMAN

	ORIG.	GOOD	FINE	N-MINT
1, Apr 78, CI, O:	0.35	0.25	0.75	1.25
2, May 78	0.35	0.20	0.60	1.00
3, Jun 78	0.35	0.20	0.60	1.00
4, Jul 78	0.35	0.20	0.60	1.00
5, Aug 78	0.35	0.20	0.60	1.00
6, Sep 78	0.35	0.20	0.60	1.00
7, Oct 78	0.35	0.20	0.60	1.00
8, Nov 78	0.35	0.20	0.60	1.00
9, Dec 78	0.35	0.20	0.60	1.00
10, Jan 79	0.35	0.20	0.60	1.00
11, Feb 79	0.35	0.20	0.60	1.00
12, Mar 79	0.35	0.20	0.60	1.00
13, Apr 79	0.35	0.20	0.60	1.00
14, May 79	0.40	0.20	0.60	1.00
15, Jun 79	0.40	0.20	0.60	1.00
16, Jul 79	0.40	0.20	0.60	1.00
17, Aug 79	0.40	0.20	0.60	1.00
18, Sep 79	0.40	0.20	0.60	1.00
19, Oct 79	0.40	0.20	0.60	1.00
20, Nov 79	0.40	0.20	0.60	1.00
21, Dec 79	0.40	0.20	0.60	1.00
22, Jan 80	0.40	0.20	0.60	1.00
23, Feb 80	0.40	0.20	0.60	1.00
24, Mar 80	0.40	0.20	0.60	1.00
25, Apr 80	0.40	0.20	0.60	1.00
26, May 80, JBy(c)	0.40	0.20	0.60	1.00
27, Jun 80	0.40	0.20	0.60	1.00
28, Jul 80	0.40	0.20	0.60	1.00
29, Aug 80	0.40	0.20	0.60	1.00
30, Sep 80	0.50	0.20	0.60	1.00
31, Oct 80	0.50	0.20	0.60	1.00
32, Nov 80	0.50	0.20	0.60	1.00
33, Dec 80	0.50	0.20	0.60	1.00
34, Jan 81	0.50	0.20	0.60	1.00
35, Feb 81	0.50	0.20	0.60	1.00
36, Mar 81	0.50	0.20	0.60	1.00
37, Apr 81, TA: A: X-Men	0.50	0.50	1.50	2.50
38, May 81, A:X-Men	0.50	0.40	1.20	2.00
39, Jun 81	0.50	0.20	0.60	1.00
40, Jul 81	0.50	0.20	0.60	1.00
41, Aug 81	0.50	0.20	0.60	1.00
42, Sep 81	0.60	0.20	0.60	1.00
43, Oct 81	0.60	0.20	0.60	1.00
44, Nov 81	0.60	0.20	0.60	1.00
45, Dec 81	0.60	0.20	0.60	1.00
46, Jan 82	0.60	0.20	0.60	1.00
47, Feb 82	0.60	0.20	0.60	1.00
48, Mar 82	0.60	0.20	0.60	1.00
49, Apr 82	0.60	0.20	0.60	1.00
50, May 82, D:Spider-Woman	1.00	0.30	0.90	1.50

SPIDER-WOMAN (1993-)

	ORIG.	GOOD	FINE	N-MINT
1	1.75	0.35	1.05	1.75
2	1.75	0.35	1.05	1.75
3	1.75	0.35	1.05	1.75
4	1.75	0.35	1.05	1.75

SPIDERBABY
SPIDERBABY

	ORIG.	GOOD	FINE	N-MINT
1, signed, numbered		4.00	12.00	20.00

SPIDEY SUPER STORIES
MARVEL

	ORIG.	GOOD	FINE	N-MINT
1	0.35	0.40	1.20	2.00
2	0.35	0.30	0.90	1.50
3	0.35	0.30	0.90	1.50
4	0.35	0.30	0.90	1.50
5	0.35	0.30	0.90	1.50
6	0.35	0.20	0.60	1.00
7	0.35	0.20	0.60	1.00
8	0.35	0.20	0.60	1.00
9	0.35	0.20	0.60	1.00

	ORIG.	GOOD	FINE	N-MINT
10	0.35	0.20	0.60	1.00
11	0.35	0.20	0.60	1.00
12	0.35	0.20	0.60	1.00
13	0.35	0.20	0.60	1.00
14	0.35	0.20	0.60	1.00
15	0.35	0.20	0.60	1.00
16	0.35	0.20	0.60	1.00
17	0.35	0.20	0.60	1.00
18	0.35	0.20	0.60	1.00
19, Oct 76	0.35	0.20	0.60	1.00
20, Dec 76	0.35	0.20	0.60	1.00
21, Feb 77	0.35	0.20	0.60	1.00
22, Apr 77	0.35	0.20	0.60	1.00
23, Jun 77	0.35	0.20	0.60	1.00
24, Jul 77	0.35	0.20	0.60	1.00
25, Aug 77	0.35	0.20	0.60	1.00
26, Sep 77	0.35	0.20	0.60	1.00
27, Oct 77	0.35	0.20	0.60	1.00
28, Nov 77	0.35	0.20	0.60	1.00
29, Dec 77	0.35	0.20	0.60	1.00
30, JA 78	0.35	0.20	0.60	1.00
31, Feb 78	0.35	0.20	0.60	1.00
32, Mar 78	0.35	0.20	0.60	1.00
33, Apr 78	0.35	0.20	0.60	1.00
34, May 78	0.35	0.20	0.60	1.00
35, Jul 78	0.35	0.20	0.60	1.00
36, Sep 78	0.35	0.20	0.60	1.00
37, Nov 78	0.35	0.20	0.60	1.00
38, Jan 79	0.35	0.20	0.60	1.00
39, Mar 79	0.35	0.20	0.60	1.00
40, May 79	0.40	0.20	0.60	1.00
41, Jul 79	0.40	0.20	0.60	1.00
42, Sep 79	0.40	0.20	0.60	1.00
43, Nov 79	0.40	0.20	0.60	1.00
44, Jan 80	0.40	0.20	0.60	1.00
45, Mar 80	0.40	0.20	0.60	1.00
46, May 80	0.50	0.20	0.60	1.00
47, Jul 80	0.50	0.20	0.60	1.00
48, Sep 80	0.50	0.20	0.60	1.00
49, Nov 80	0.50	0.20	0.60	1.00
50, Jan 81	0.50	0.20	0.60	1.00
51, Mar 81	0.50	0.20	0.60	1.00
52, May 81	0.50	0.20	0.60	1.00
53, Jul 81	0.50	0.20	0.60	1.00
54, Sep 81	0.50	0.20	0.60	1.00
55, Nov 81	0.50	0.20	0.60	1.00
56, Jan 82	0.60	0.20	0.60	1.00
57, Mar 82	0.60	0.20	0.60	1.00

SPINELESS-MAN $2099
PARODY PRESS

	ORIG.	GOOD	FINE	N-MINT
1	2.50	0.50	1.50	2.50

SPIRAL PATH
ECLIPSE

	ORIG.	GOOD	FINE	N-MINT
1		0.30	0.90	1.50
2		0.30	0.90	1.50

SPIRAL ZONE
DC

	ORIG.	GOOD	FINE	N-MINT
1, CI/DG		0.20	0.60	1.00
2, CI/DG		0.20	0.60	1.00
3, CI/DG		0.20	0.60	1.00
4, CI/DG		0.20	0.60	1.00

SPIRIT OF THE WIND
CHOCOLATE MOUSE

	ORIG.	GOOD	FINE	N-MINT
1, b&w		0.40	1.20	2.00

SPIRIT OF WONDER (mini-series)
DARK HORSE/MANGA

	ORIG.	GOOD	FINE	N-MINT
1, Apr 96, b&w	2.95	0.59	1.77	2.95

	ORIG.	GOOD	FINE	N-MINT

SPIRIT, THE
KITCHEN SINK

	ORIG.	GOOD	FINE	N-MINT
1, Oct 83, WE rep.	1.75	1.00	3.00	5.00
2, Dec 83, WE rep.	1.75	0.80	2.40	4.00
3, Feb 84, WE rep.	1.75	0.80	2.40	4.00
4, Mar 84, WE rep.	2.00	0.80	2.40	4.00
5, Jun 84, WE rep.	2.00	0.80	2.40	4.00
6, Aug 84, WE rep.	2.00	0.80	2.40	4.00
7, Oct 84, WE rep.	2.95	0.59	1.77	2.95
8, Feb 85, WE rep.	2.95	0.59	1.77	2.95
9, Apr 85, WE rep.	2.95	0.59	1.77	2.95
10, Jun 85, WE rep.	2.95	0.59	1.77	2.95
11, Aug 85, WE rep.	2.95	0.59	1.77	2.95
12, Oct 85, WE rep.	1.95	0.59	1.77	2.95
13, Nov 85, WE rep.	1.95	0.59	1.77	2.95
14, Dec 85, WE rep.	1.95	0.59	1.77	2.95
15, Jan 86, WE rep.	1.95	0.59	1.77	2.95
16, Feb 86, WE rep.	1.95	0.59	1.77	2.95
17, Mar 86, WE b&w rep.	1.95	0.40	1.20	2.00
18, Apr 86, WE b&w rep.	1.95	0.40	1.20	2.00
19, May 86, WE b&w rep.	1.95	0.40	1.20	2.00
20, Jun 86, WE b&w rep.	1.95	0.40	1.20	2.00
21, Jul 86, WE b&w rep.	1.95	0.40	1.20	2.00
22, Aug 86, WE b&w rep.	1.95	0.40	1.20	2.00
23, Sep 86, WE b&w rep.	1.95	0.40	1.20	2.00
24, Oct 86, WE b&w rep.	1.95	0.40	1.20	2.00
25, Nov 86, WE b&w rep.	1.95	0.40	1.20	2.00
26, Dec 86, WE b&w rep.	1.95	0.40	1.20	2.00
27, Jan 87, WE b&w rep.	2.00	0.40	1.20	2.00
28, Feb 87, WE b&w rep.	2.00	0.40	1.20	2.00
29, Mar 87, WEb&w rep.	2.00	0.40	1.20	2.00
30, Apr 87, WE b&w rep.	2.00	0.40	1.20	2.00
31, May 87, WE b&w rep.	2.00	0.40	1.20	2.00
32, Jun 87, WE b&w rep.	2.00	0.50	1.50	2.50
33, Jul 87, WE b&w rep.	2.00	0.50	1.50	2.50
34, Aug 87, WE b&w rep.	2.00	0.50	1.50	2.50
35, Sep 87, WE b&w rep.	2.00	0.50	1.50	2.50
36, Oct 87, WE b&w rep.	2.00	0.50	1.50	2.50
37, Nov 87, WE b&w rep.	2.00	0.50	1.50	2.50
38, Dec 88, WE b&w rep..	2.00	0.50	1.50	2.50
39, Jan 88, WE b&w rep.	2.00	0.50	1.50	2.50
40, Feb 88, WE b&w rep.	2.00	0.50	1.50	2.50
41, Mar 88, WE, Wertham parody, b&w rep.	2.00	0.50	1.50	2.50
42, Apr 88, WE b&w rep.	2.00	0.40	1.20	2.00
43, May 88, WE b&w rep.	2.00	0.40	1.20	2.00
44, Jun 88, WE b&w rep.	2.00	0.40	1.20	2.00
45, Jul 88, WE b&w rep.	2.00	0.40	1.20	2.00
46, Aug 88, WE b&w rep.	2.00	0.40	1.20	2.00
47, Sep 88, WE b&w rep.	2.00	0.40	1.20	2.00
48, Oct 88, WE b&w rep.	2.00	0.40	1.20	2.00
49, Nov 88, WE b&w rep.	2.00	0.40	1.20	2.00
50, Dec 88, WE b&w rep.	2.00	0.40	1.20	2.00
51, Jan 89, WE b&w rep.	2.00	0.40	1.20	2.00
52, Feb 89, WE b&w rep.	2.00	0.40	1.20	2.00
53, Mar 89, WE b&w rep.	2.00	0.40	1.20	2.00
54, Apr 89, WE b&w rep.	2.00	0.40	1.20	2.00
55, May 89, WE b&w rep.	2.00	0.40	1.20	2.00
56, Jun 89, WE b&w rep.	2.00	0.40	1.20	2.00
57, Jul 89, WE b&w rep.	2.00	0.40	1.20	2.00
58, Aug 89, WE b&w rep.	2.00	0.40	1.20	2.00
59, Sep 89, WE b&w rep.	2.00	0.40	1.20	2.00
60, Oct 89, WE b&w rep.	2.00	0.40	1.20	2.00
61, Nov 89, WE b&w rep.	2.00	0.40	1.20	2.00
62, Dec 89, WE b&w rep.	2.00	0.40	1.20	2.00
63, Jan 90, WE b&w rep.	2.00	0.40	1.20	2.00
64, Feb 90, WE b&w rep.	2.00	0.40	1.20	2.00
65, Mar 90, WE b&w rep.	2.00	0.40	1.20	2.00
66, Apr 90, WE b&w rep.	2.00	0.40	1.20	2.00
67, May 90, WE b&w rep.	2.00	0.40	1.20	2.00
68, Jun 90, WE b&w rep.	2.00	0.40	1.20	2.00
69, Jul 90, WE b&w rep.	2.00	0.40	1.20	2.00
70, Aug 90, WE b&w rep.	2.00	0.40	1.20	2.00
71, Sep 90, WEb&w rep.	2.00	0.40	1.20	2.00
72, Oct 90, WE b&w rep.	2.00	0.40	1.20	2.00
73, Nov 90, WE(c) post-Eisner	2.00	0.40	1.20	2.00
74, Dec 90, WE(c) post-Eisner	2.00	0.40	1.20	2.00
75, Jan 91, WE(c) post-Eisner	2.00	0.40	1.20	2.00
76, Feb 91, WE(c) post-Eisner	2.00	0.40	1.20	2.00
77, Mar 91, WE(c) post-Eisner	2.00	0.40	1.20	2.00
78, Apr 91, WE(c) post-Eisner	2.00	0.40	1.20	2.00
79, May 91, WE(c) post-Eisner	2.00	0.40	1.20	2.00
80, Jun 91, WE(c) post-Eisner	2.00	0.40	1.20	2.00
81, Jul 91, WE(c) post-Eisner	2.00	0.40	1.20	2.00
82, Aug 91, WE(c) post-Eisner	2.00	0.40	1.20	2.00
83, Sep 91, WE(c) post-Eisner	2.00	0.40	1.20	2.00
84, Oct 91, WE(c) post-Eisner	2.00	0.40	1.20	2.00
85, Nov 91, WE(c) post-Eisner	2.00	0.40	1.20	2.00
86, Dec 91, WE(c) post-Eisner	2.00	0.40	1.20	2.00
87, Jan 92, WE(c), WW	2.00	0.40	1.20	2.00

SPIRIT, THE (1970-)

	ORIG.	GOOD	FINE	N-MINT
1, Jan 73, b&w	0.50	0.30	0.90	1.50
17, Nov 77	1.50	0.30	0.90	1.50
18, May 78	1.50	0.30	0.90	1.50
19, Oct 78	1.50	0.30	0.90	1.50
20, Mar 79	1.50	0.30	0.90	1.50
21, Jul 79	1.75	0.35	1.05	1.75
22, Dec 79	1.75	0.35	1.05	1.75
23, Feb 80	1.75	0.35	1.05	1.75
24, May 80	1.75	0.35	1.05	1.75
25, Aug 80	1.75	0.35	1.05	1.75
26, Dec 80	2.00	0.40	1.20	2.00
27, Feb 81	2.00	0.40	1.20	2.00
28, Apr 81	2.00	0.40	1.20	2.00
29, Jun 81	2.00	0.40	1.20	2.00
30, Jul 81	2.00	0.40	1.20	2.00
31, Oct 81	2.00	0.40	1.20	2.00
32, Dec 81	2.50	0.50	1.50	2.50
33, Feb 82	2.50	0.50	1.50	2.50

	ORIG.	GOOD	FINE	N-MINT
34, Apr 82	2.50	0.50	1.50	2.50
35, Jun 82	2.50	0.50	1.50	2.50
36, Aug 82	2.95	0.59	1.77	2.95
37, Oct 82	2.95	0.59	1.77	2.95
38, Dec 82	2.95	0.59	1.77	2.95
39, Feb 83	2.95	0.59	1.77	2.95
40, Apr 83	2.95	0.59	1.77	2.95
41, Jun 83	2.95	0.59	1.77	2.95

SPIRIT: THE ORIGIN YEARS

	ORIG.	GOOD	FINE	N-MINT
1, May 92, WE, b&w reprints	2.95	0.59	1.77	2.95
2, Jul 92, WE, b&w reprints	2.95	0.59	1.77	2.95
3, Sep 92, WE, b&w reprints	2.95	0.59	1.77	2.95
4, Nov 92, WE, b&w reprints	2.95	0.59	1.77	2.95
5, Jan 93, WE, b&w reprints	2.95	0.59	1.77	2.95
6, Mar 93, WE, b&w reprints	2.95	0.59	1.77	2.95
7, Mar 93, WE, b&w reprints	2.95	0.59	1.77	2.95
8, Mar 93, WE, b&w reprints	2.95	0.59	1.77	2.95
9, Mar 93, WE, b&w reprints	2.95	0.59	1.77	2.95
10, Dec 93, WE, b&w reprints	2.95	0.59	1.77	2.95

SPIRITS
MIND WALKER

	ORIG.	GOOD	FINE	N-MINT
3, Sep 95, b&w	2.95	0.59	1.77	2.95

SPIT WAD COMICS
SPIT WAD PRESS

	ORIG.	GOOD	FINE	N-MINT
1, b&w	2.50	0.50	1.50	2.50

SPITFIRE & THE TROUBLESHOOTERS
MARVEL

	ORIG.	GOOD	FINE	N-MINT
1, Oct 86	0.75	0.20	0.60	1.00
2, Nov 86	0.75	0.20	0.60	1.00
3, Dec 86	0.75	0.20	0.60	1.00
4, Jan 87	0.75	0.20	0.60	1.00
5, Feb 87	0.75	0.20	0.60	1.00
6, Mar 87	0.75	0.20	0.60	1.00
7, Apr 87	0.75	0.20	0.60	1.00
8, May 87	0.75	0.20	0.60	1.00
9, Jun 87, (becomes *Codename: Spitfire*)	0.75	0.20	0.60	1.00

SPITTIN' IMAGE
ECLIPSE

	ORIG.	GOOD	FINE	N-MINT
0, nn, b&w parody		0.50	1.50	2.50

SPLAT!
MAD DOG

	ORIG.	GOOD	FINE	N-MINT
1, b&w		0.50	1.50	2.50
2, Alan Moore		0.50	1.50	2.50
3, B.Kliban		0.50	1.50	2.50

SPLATTER
ARPAD

	ORIG.	GOOD	FINE	N-MINT
1, b&w		0.50	1.50	2.50

NORTHSTAR

	ORIG.	GOOD	FINE	N-MINT
1, adult, b&w	2.75	0.55	1.65	2.75
2, adult, b&w	2.75	0.55	1.65	2.75
3, adult, b&w	2.75	0.55	1.65	2.75
4, adult, b&w	2.75	0.55	1.65	2.75
5, adult, b&w	2.75	0.55	1.65	2.75
6, adult, b&w	2.75	0.55	1.65	2.75
7, adult, b&w	2.75	0.55	1.65	2.75

SPLITTING IMAGE
IMAGE

	ORIG.	GOOD	FINE	N-MINT
1, parody	1.95	0.39	1.17	1.95
2, parody	1.95	0.39	1.17	1.95

SPOOF
MARVEL

	ORIG.	GOOD	FINE	N-MINT
1	0.15	0.20	0.60	1.00
2	0.20	0.20	0.60	1.00
3	0.20	0.20	0.60	1.00
4	0.20	0.20	0.60	1.00
5	0.20	0.20	0.60	1.00

SPOOF COMICS
SPOOF

	ORIG.	GOOD	FINE	N-MINT
6, b&w		0.59	1.77	2.95
7, b&w		0.59	1.77	2.95
8, b&w		0.59	1.77	2.95
12, b&w	2.95	0.59	1.77	2.95

SPOOKY
HARVEY

	ORIG.	GOOD	FINE	N-MINT
1		0.25	0.75	1.25
2		0.25	0.75	1.25
3		0.25	0.75	1.25
4		0.25	0.75	1.25

SPOOKY DIGEST

	ORIG.	GOOD	FINE	N-MINT
1	1.75	0.35	1.05	1.75
2	1.75	0.35	1.05	1.75

SPOOKY THE DOG CATCHER
PAW PRINTS

	ORIG.	GOOD	FINE	N-MINT
1, Oct 94, b&w	2.50	0.50	1.50	2.50

SPORTS CLASSICS
PERSONALITY

	ORIG.	GOOD	FINE	N-MINT
1		0.59	1.77	2.95
2		0.59	1.77	2.95
3		0.59	1.77	2.95
4		0.59	1.77	2.95
5		0.59	1.77	2.95
1, limited edition		1.19	3.57	5.95

SPORTS COMICS

	ORIG.	GOOD	FINE	N-MINT
3		0.50	1.50	2.50
4		0.50	1.50	2.50

SPORTS HALL OF SHAME IN 3-D
BLACKTHORNE

	ORIG.	GOOD	FINE	N-MINT
1, baseball		0.50	1.50	2.50

SPORTS LEGENDS
REVOLUTIONARY

	ORIG.	GOOD	FINE	N-MINT
1, Sep 92, b&w, Joe Namath	2.50	0.50	1.50	2.50
2, Oct 92, b&w, Gordie Howe	2.50	0.50	1.50	2.50
3, Nov 92, b&w, Arthur Ashe	2.50	0.50	1.50	2.50
4, Dec 92, color, Muhammad Ali	2.50	0.50	1.50	2.50
5, Jan 93, color, O.J. Simpson	2.50	0.50	1.50	2.50
6, Feb 93, color, K.A. Jabbar	2.50	0.50	1.50	2.50
7, Mar 93, b&w, Walter Payton	2.95	0.59	1.77	2.95
8, Apr 93, b&w, Wilt Chamberlain	2.95	0.59	1.77	2.95
9, May 93, b&w, Joe Louis	2.95	0.59	1.77	2.95

SPORTS LEGENDS SPECIAL-BREAKING THE COLOR BARRIER

	ORIG.	GOOD	FINE	N-MINT
1, Oct 93, b&w	2.95	0.59	1.77	2.95

SPORTS PERSONALITIES
PERSONALITY

	ORIG.	GOOD	FINE	N-MINT
1, b&w		0.59	1.77	2.95
2, b&w		0.59	1.77	2.95
3, b&w		0.59	1.77	2.95
4, b&w		0.59	1.77	2.95
5, b&w		0.59	1.77	2.95

	ORIG.	GOOD	FINE	N-MINT
6, b&w		0.59	1.77	2.95
7, b&w		0.59	1.77	2.95
8, b&w		0.59	1.77	2.95
9, b&w		0.59	1.77	2.95
10, b&w		0.59	1.77	2.95
11, b&w		0.59	1.77	2.95
12, b&w		0.59	1.77	2.95
13, b&w		0.59	1.77	2.95

SPORTS SUPERSTARS
REVOLUTIONARY

	ORIG.	GOOD	FINE	N-MINT
1, Apr 92, b&w, Michael Jordan	2.50	0.50	1.50	2.50
2, May 92, b&w, Wayne Gretzsky	2.50	0.50	1.50	2.50
3, Jun 92, b&w, Magic Johnson	2.50	0.50	1.50	2.50
4, Jul 92, b&w, Joe Montana	2.50	0.50	1.50	2.50
5, Aug 92, b&w, Mike Tyson	2.50	0.50	1.50	2.50
6, Sep 92, b&w, Larry Bird	2.50	0.50	1.50	2.50
7, Oct 92, b&w, John Elway	2.50	0.50	1.50	2.50
8, Nov 92, b&w, Julius Erving	2.50	0.50	1.50	2.50
9, Dec 92, color, Barry Sanders	2.75	0.55	1.65	2.75
10, Jan 93, color, Isiah Thomas	2.75	0.55	1.65	2.75
11, Feb 92, color, Mario Lemieux	2.95	0.59	1.77	2.95
12, Mar 93, b&w, Dan Marino	2.95	0.59	1.77	2.95
13, Apr 93, b&w, Deion Sanders	2.95	0.59	1.77	2.95
14, May 93, b&w, Patrick Ewing	2.95	0.59	1.77	2.95
15, Jun 93, b&w, Charles Barkley	2.95	0.59	1.77	2.95
16, Aug 93, b&w, Shaq/Laettner	2.95	0.59	1.77	2.95

SPORTS SUPERSTARS ANNUAL

	ORIG.	GOOD	FINE	N-MINT
1, Feb 93, color, Michael Jordan II	2.75	0.55	1.65	2.75

SPOTLIGHT ON THE GENIUS THAT IS JOE SACCO
FANTAGRAPHICS

	ORIG.	GOOD	FINE	N-MINT
0, nn;b&w	4.95	0.99	2.97	4.95

SPRING BREAK COMICS
AC

	ORIG.	GOOD	FINE	N-MINT
1, Mar 87, b&w		0.20	0.60	1.00

SPRING-HEEL JACK
REBEL

	ORIG.	GOOD	FINE	N-MINT
1, b&w		0.45	1.35	2.25
2, b&w		0.45	1.35	2.25

SPUD
SPUD PRESS

	ORIG.	GOOD	FINE	N-MINT
1, Sum 96, b&w	3.50	0.70	2.10	3.50

SPUNKY TODD: THE PSYCHIC BOY
CALIBER

	ORIG.	GOOD	FINE	N-MINT
1, b&w	2.95	0.59	1.77	2.95

SPYKE
EPIC

	ORIG.	GOOD	FINE	N-MINT
1, embossed cover	2.50	0.50	1.50	2.50
2	1.95	0.39	1.17	1.95
3	1.95	0.39	1.17	1.95
4	1.95	0.39	1.17	1.95

SQUADRON SUPREME
MARVEL

	ORIG.	GOOD	FINE	N-MINT
1, Sep 85	1.25	0.25	0.75	1.25
2, Oct 85	0.75	0.20	0.60	1.00
3, Nov 85	0.75	0.20	0.60	1.00
4, Dec 85	0.75	0.20	0.60	1.00
5, Jan 86	0.75	0.20	0.60	1.00
6, Feb 86	0.75	0.20	0.60	1.00
7, Mar 86	0.75	0.20	0.60	1.00
8, Apr 86	0.75	0.20	0.60	1.00
9, May 86	0.75	0.20	0.60	1.00
10, Jun 86	0.75	0.20	0.60	1.00
11, Jul 86	0.75	0.20	0.60	1.00
12, Aug 86	1.25	0.25	0.75	1.25

SQUALOR
FIRST

	ORIG.	GOOD	FINE	N-MINT
1, Dec 89		0.55	1.65	2.75
2, Jan 90		0.55	1.65	2.75
3, Feb 90		0.55	1.65	2.75
4, Mar 90		0.55	1.65	2.75

SRI KRISHNA
CHAKRA

	ORIG.	GOOD	FINE	N-MINT
1, The Advent		0.70	2.10	3.50

ST. GEORGE
EPIC

	ORIG.	GOOD	FINE	N-MINT
1, Jun 88	1.25	0.25	0.75	1.25
2, Aug 88	1.25	0.25	0.75	1.25
3, Oct 88	1.50	0.30	0.90	1.50
4, Dec 88	1.50	0.30	0.90	1.50
5, Feb 89	1.50	0.30	0.90	1.50
6, Apr 89	1.50	0.30	0.90	1.50
7, Jun 89	1.50	0.30	0.90	1.50
8, Aug 89	1.50	0.30	0.90	1.50

ST. SWITHIN'S DAY
TRIDENT

	ORIG.	GOOD	FINE	N-MINT
0, one-shot b&w		0.50	1.50	2.50

STACIA STORIES
KITCHEN SINK PRESS

	ORIG.	GOOD	FINE	N-MINT
1, Jun 95, b&w	2.95	0.59	1.77	2.95

STAINLESS STEEL ARMADILLO
ANTARCTIC

	ORIG.	GOOD	FINE	N-MINT
1, Feb 95, b&w	2.95	0.59	1.77	2.95
2, Apr 95, b&w	2.95	0.59	1.77	2.95
3, Jun 95, b&w	2.95	0.59	1.77	2.95
4, Aug 95, b&w	2.95	0.59	1.77	2.95
5, Oct 95, b&w	2.95	0.59	1.77	2.95

STAINLESS STEEL RAT
EAGLE

	ORIG.	GOOD	FINE	N-MINT
1		0.40	1.20	2.00
2		0.40	1.20	2.00
3		0.40	1.20	2.00
4		0.40	1.20	2.00
5		0.40	1.20	2.00
6		0.40	1.20	2.00

STALKER
DC

	ORIG.	GOOD	FINE	N-MINT
1, Jul 75	0.25	0.50	1.50	2.50
2, Sep 75	0.25	0.30	0.90	1.50
3, Nov 75	0.25	0.30	0.90	1.50
4, Jan 76	0.25	0.30	0.90	1.50

STALKERS
EPIC

	ORIG.	GOOD	FINE	N-MINT
1	1.50	0.30	0.90	1.50
2	1.50	0.30	0.90	1.50
3	1.50	0.30	0.90	1.50
4	1.50	0.30	0.90	1.50
5	1.50	0.30	0.90	1.50
6	1.50	0.30	0.90	1.50
7	1.50	0.30	0.90	1.50
8	1.50	0.30	0.90	1.50

	ORIG.	GOOD	FINE	N-MINT
9 ....1.50	0.30	0.90	1.50
10 ....1.50	0.30	0.90	1.50
11 ....1.50	0.30	0.90	1.50
12 ....1.50	0.30	0.90	1.50

STALKING RALPH
AEON
	ORIG.	GOOD	FINE	N-MINT
0, Oct 95, nn;one-shot;cardstock cover			
...................................4.95	0.99	2.97	4.95

STAN SHAW'S BEAUTY AND THE BEAST
DARK HORSE
	ORIG.	GOOD	FINE	N-MINT
0, nn...............................4.95	0.99	2.97	4.95

STANLEY AND HIS MONSTER
DC
	ORIG.	GOOD	FINE	N-MINT
1, Feb 93, Phil Foglio 1.50	0.30	0.90	1.50
2, Mar 93, Phil Foglio 1.50	0.30	0.90	1.50
3, Apr 93 ....1.50	0.30	0.90	1.50
4, May 93, Phil Foglio 1.50	0.30	0.90	1.50

STANLEY THE SNAKE WITH THE OVERACTIVE IMMAGINATION
EMERALD
	ORIG.	GOOD	FINE	N-MINT
1, b&w	0.30	0.90	1.50
2, b&w	0.30	0.90	1.50

STAR (mini-series)
IMAGE
	ORIG.	GOOD	FINE	N-MINT
3, Aug 95 ....2.50	0.50	1.50	2.50

STAR BLAZERS
COMICO
	ORIG.	GOOD	FINE	N-MINT
1	0.35	1.05	1.75
2	0.35	1.05	1.75
3	0.35	1.05	1.75
4	0.35	1.05	1.75

STAR BLAZERS (Volume 2)
	ORIG.	GOOD	FINE	N-MINT
1	0.39	1.17	1.95
2	0.39	1.17	1.95
3	0.50	1.50	2.50
4	0.50	1.50	2.50
5	0.50	1.50	2.50

STAR BLAZERS: THE MAGAZINE OF SPACE BATTLESHIP YAMATO
ARGO
	ORIG.	GOOD	FINE	N-MINT
0, Mar 95 ....2.95	0.59	1.77	2.95

STAR BRAND
MARVEL
	ORIG.	GOOD	FINE	N-MINT
1 ....0.75	0.20	0.60	1.00
2 ....0.75	0.20	0.60	1.00
3 ....0.75	0.20	0.60	1.00
4 ....0.75	0.20	0.60	1.00
5 ....0.75	0.20	0.60	1.00
6 ....0.75	0.20	0.60	1.00
7 ....0.75	0.20	0.60	1.00
8 ....0.75	0.20	0.60	1.00
9 ....0.75	0.20	0.60	1.00
10, (becomes *The Star Brand*)			
....................................0.75	0.25	0.75	1.25

STAR BRAND ANNUAL
	ORIG.	GOOD	FINE	N-MINT
1, 87................................1.25	0.25	0.75	1.25

STAR BRAND, THE (was Star Brand)
	ORIG.	GOOD	FINE	N-MINT
11, Jan 88, JBy 0.75	0.20	0.60	1.00
12, Mar 88, JBy............ 0.75	0.20	0.60	1.00
13, May 88, JBy 1.25	0.25	0.75	1.25
14, Jul 88, JBy 1.25	0.25	0.75	1.25
15, Sep 88, JBy............. 1.25	0.25	0.75	1.25
16, Nov 88, JBy............. 1.25	0.25	0.75	1.25
17, Jan 89, JBy 1.50	0.30	0.90	1.50
18, Mar 89, JBy............. 1.50	0.30	0.90	1.50
19, May 89, JBy 1.50	0.30	0.90	1.50

STAR COMICS MAGAZINE (digest)
STAR
	ORIG.	GOOD	FINE	N-MINT
1, reprints 1.50	0.30	0.90	1.50

	ORIG.	GOOD	FINE	N-MINT
2, reprints 1.50	0.30	0.90	1.50
3, reprints 1.50	0.30	0.90	1.50
4, reprints 1.50	0.30	0.90	1.50
5, reprints 1.50	0.30	0.90	1.50
6, reprints 1.50	0.30	0.90	1.50
7, reprints 1.50	0.30	0.90	1.50
8, reprints 1.50	0.30	0.90	1.50
9, reprints 1.50	0.30	0.90	1.50
10, reprints 1.50	0.30	0.90	1.50
11, reprints 1.50	0.30	0.90	1.50
12, reprints 1.50	0.30	0.90	1.50
13, reprints 1.50	0.30	0.90	1.50

STAR HUNTERS
DC
	ORIG.	GOOD	FINE	N-MINT
1, Nov 77 ....0.35	0.40	1.20	2.00
2, Jan 78........................0.35	0.25	0.75	1.25
3, Mar 78 ....0.35	0.25	0.75	1.25
4, May 78 ....0.35	0.25	0.75	1.25
5, Jul 78..........................0.35	0.25	0.75	1.25
6, Sep 78........................0.35	0.25	0.75	1.25
7, Nov 78 ....0.35	0.25	0.75	1.25

STAR JACKS
ANTARCTIC
	ORIG.	GOOD	FINE	N-MINT
1, Jun 94, b&w 2.75	0.55	1.65	2.75

STAR JAM COMICS
REVOLUTIONARY
	ORIG.	GOOD	FINE	N-MINT
1, Apr 92, b&w, Hammer			
....2.50	0.50	1.50	2.50
2, Jun 92, b&w, Janet Jackson			
....2.50	0.50	1.50	2.50
3, Aug 92, b&w,90210....2.50	0.50	1.50	2.50
4, Sep 92, b&w, 90210....2.50	0.50	1.50	2.50
5, Oct 92, b&w, 90210....2.50	0.50	1.50	2.50
6, Nov 92, b&w, Kriss Kross			
....2.50	0.50	1.50	2.50
7, Dec 92, b&w, Marky Mark			
....2.50	0.50	1.50	2.50
8, Jan 93, b&w, Madonna			
....2.50	0.50	1.50	2.50
9, Feb 93, b&w, Jennie Garth			
....2.50	0.50	1.50	2.50
10, Mar 93, b&w, Melrose Place			
....2.50	0.50	1.50	2.50

STAR MASTERS
AC
	ORIG.	GOOD	FINE	N-MINT
1	0.30	0.90	1.50

STAR RANGERS
ADVENTURE
	ORIG.	GOOD	FINE	N-MINT
1	0.39	1.17	1.95
2	0.39	1.17	1.95
3	0.39	1.17	1.95

STAR ROVERS
COMAX
	ORIG.	GOOD	FINE	N-MINT
1, b&w, adult	0.59	1.77	2.95

STAR SLAMMERS (mini-series)
MALIBU/BRAVURA
	ORIG.	GOOD	FINE	N-MINT
1, May 94.......................2.50	0.50	1.50	2.50
2, Jun 94 ....2.50	0.50	1.50	2.50
3, Aug 94 ....2.50	0.50	1.50	2.50

STAR SPANGLED WAR STORIES
DC
	ORIG.	GOOD	FINE	N-MINT
90, May 60.......................	30.00	90.00	150.00
91	5.20	15.60	26.00
92	16.00	48.00	80.00
93	16.00	48.00	80.00
94	16.00	48.00	80.00
95	16.00	48.00	80.00
96	16.00	48.00	80.00
97	16.00	48.00	80.00
98	16.00	48.00	80.00

	ORIG.	GOOD	FINE	N-MINT
❏ 99		16.00	48.00	80.00
❏ 100		16.00	48.00	80.00
❏ 101		8.00	24.00	40.00
❏ 102		8.00	24.00	40.00
❏ 103		8.00	24.00	40.00
❏ 104, Sep 62	0.12	8.00	24.00	40.00
❏ 105		8.00	24.00	40.00
❏ 106		8.00	24.00	40.00
❏ 107		8.00	24.00	40.00
❏ 108		8.00	24.00	40.00
❏ 109		8.00	24.00	40.00
❏ 110		8.00	24.00	40.00
❏ 111, Nov 63, "War That Time Forgot"	0.12	8.00	24.00	40.00
❏ 112		8.00	24.00	40.00
❏ 113		8.00	24.00	40.00
❏ 114		8.00	24.00	40.00
❏ 115		8.00	24.00	40.00
❏ 116		8.00	24.00	40.00
❏ 117		8.00	24.00	40.00
❏ 118		8.00	24.00	40.00
❏ 119		8.00	24.00	40.00
❏ 120		8.00	24.00	40.00
❏ 121		6.40	19.20	32.00
❏ 122		6.40	19.20	32.00
❏ 123		6.40	19.20	32.00
❏ 124		6.40	19.20	32.00
❏ 125		6.40	19.20	32.00
❏ 126		6.40	19.20	32.00
❏ 127		6.40	19.20	32.00
❏ 128		6.40	19.20	32.00
❏ 129		6.40	19.20	32.00
❏ 130		6.40	19.20	32.00
❏ 131		6.40	19.20	32.00
❏ 132		6.40	19.20	32.00
❏ 133		6.40	19.20	32.00
❏ 134	0.12	8.00	24.00	40.00
❏ 135	0.12	6.40	19.20	32.00
❏ 136	0.12	6.40	19.20	32.00
❏ 137	0.12	6.40	19.20	32.00
❏ 138, May 68, Enemy Ace	0.12	7.00	21.00	35.00
❏ 139, Jul 68, Enemy Ace	0.12	4.80	14.40	24.00
❏ 140, Sep 68, Enemy Ace	0.12	4.80	14.40	24.00
❏ 141, Nov 68, Enemy Ace	0.12	3.00	9.00	15.00
❏ 142, Jan 69, Enemy Ace	0.12	3.00	9.00	15.00
❏ 143, Mar 69	0.12	3.00	9.00	15.00
❏ 144, May 69, Enemy Ace	0.12	4.00	12.00	20.00
❏ 145, Jul 69,Enemy Ace	0.12	3.00	9.00	15.00
❏ 146, Sep 69, Enemy Ace	0.15	2.00	6.00	10.00
❏ 147, Nov 69, Enemy Ace	0.15	2.00	6.00	10.00
❏ 148, Jan 70, Enemy Ace	0.15	2.00	6.00	10.00
❏ 149, Mar 70	0.15	2.00	6.00	10.00
❏ 150, May 70	0.15	2.00	6.00	10.00
❏ 151, Jul 70	0.15	3.60	10.80	18.00
❏ 152, Sep 70	0.15	2.00	6.00	10.00
❏ 153, Nov 70	0.15	2.00	6.00	10.00
❏ 154, Jan 71	0.15	3.00	9.00	15.00
❏ 155, Mar 71, reprints Enemy Ace story	0.15	2.00	6.00	10.00
❏ 156, May 71	0.15	2.00	6.00	10.00
❏ 157, Jul 71	0.25	2.00	6.00	10.00
❏ 158, Sep 71	0.25	2.00	6.00	10.00
❏ 159, Nov 71	0.25	2.00	6.00	10.00
❏ 160, Jan 72	0.25	2.00	6.00	10.00
❏ 161, Mar 72	0.25	2.00	6.00	10.00
❏ 162, May 72	0.25	0.50	1.50	2.50
❏ 163, Jul 72	0.25	0.50	1.50	2.50
❏ 164, Sep 72	0.20	0.50	1.50	2.50
❏ 165, Nov 72	0.20	0.50	1.50	2.50
❏ 166, Jan 73	0.20	0.50	1.50	2.50

	ORIG.	GOOD	FINE	N-MINT
❏ 167, Feb 73	0.20	0.50	1.50	2.50
❏ 168, Mar 73	0.20	0.50	1.50	2.50
❏ 169, Apr 73	0.20	0.50	1.50	2.50
❏ 170, Jun 73	0.20	0.50	1.50	2.50
❏ 171, Jul 73	0.20	0.50	1.50	2.50
❏ 172, Aug 73	0.20	0.50	1.50	2.50
❏ 173, Sep 73	0.20	0.50	1.50	2.50
❏ 174, Oct 73	0.20	0.50	1.50	2.50
❏ 175, Nov 73	0.20	0.50	1.50	2.50
❏ 176, Dec 73	0.20	0.50	1.50	2.50
❏ 177, Jan 74	0.20	0.50	1.50	2.50
❏ 178, Feb 74	0.20	0.50	1.50	2.50
❏ 179, Mar 74	0.20	0.50	1.50	2.50
❏ 180, Jun 74	0.20	0.50	1.50	2.50
❏ 181, Aug 74	0.20	0.50	1.50	2.50
❏ 182, Oct 74	0.20	0.50	1.50	2.50
❏ 183, Dec 74	0.25	0.50	1.50	2.50
❏ 184, Feb 75	0.25	0.50	1.50	2.50
❏ 185, Mar 75	0.25	0.50	1.50	2.50
❏ 186, Apr 75	0.25	0.50	1.50	2.50
❏ 187, May 75	0.25	0.50	1.50	2.50
❏ 188, Jun 75	0.25	0.50	1.50	2.50
❏ 189, Jul 75	0.25	0.50	1.50	2.50
❏ 190, Aug 75	0.25	0.50	1.50	2.50
❏ 191, Sep 75	0.25	0.50	1.50	2.50
❏ 192, Oct 75	0.25	0.50	1.50	2.50
❏ 193, Nov 75	0.25	0.50	1.50	2.50
❏ 194, Dec 75	0.25	0.50	1.50	2.50
❏ 195, Jan 76	0.25	0.50	1.50	2.50
❏ 196, Feb 76	0.25	0.50	1.50	2.50
❏ 197, Mar 76	0.25	0.50	1.50	2.50
❏ 198, Apr 76	0.30	0.50	1.50	2.50
❏ 199, May 76	0.30	0.50	1.50	2.50
❏ 200, Jul 76	0.30	0.50	1.50	2.50
❏ 201, Sep 76	0.30	0.50	1.50	2.50
❏ 202, Nov 76	0.30	0.50	1.50	2.50
❏ 203, Jan 77	0.30	0.50	1.50	2.50
❏ 204, Mar 77	0.30	0.50	1.50	2.50

STAR TREK
GOLD KEY

	ORIG.	GOOD	FINE	N-MINT
❏ 1, Oct 67, wraparound photo cover	0.12	60.00	180.00	300.00
❏ 2, Jun 68, photo cover	0.12	40.00	120.00	200.00
❏ 3, Dec 68, photo cover	0.15	30.00	90.00	150.00
❏ 4, photo cover	0.15	30.00	90.00	150.00
❏ 5, Sep 69, photo cover	0.15	30.00	90.00	150.00
❏ 6, Dec 69, photo cover	0.15	20.00	60.00	100.00
❏ 7, Mar 70, photo cover	0.15	20.00	60.00	100.00
❏ 8, Sep 70, photo cover	0.15	20.00	60.00	100.00
❏ 9, Feb 71, last photo cover	0.15	20.00	60.00	100.00
❏ 10	0.15	10.00	30.00	50.00
❏ 11, Aug 71	0.15	10.00	30.00	50.00
❏ 12, Nov 71	0.15	10.00	30.00	50.00
❏ 13, Feb 72	0.15	10.00	30.00	50.00
❏ 14, May 72	0.15	10.00	30.00	50.00
❏ 15, Aug 72	0.15	10.00	30.00	50.00
❏ 16, Nov 72	0.15	10.00	30.00	50.00
❏ 17		10.00	30.00	50.00
❏ 18		10.00	30.00	50.00
❏ 19		10.00	30.00	50.00
❏ 20, Sep 73	0.20	10.00	30.00	50.00
❏ 21	0.20	8.00	24.00	40.00
❏ 22, Jan 74	0.20	8.00	24.00	40.00
❏ 23, Mar 74	0.20	8.00	24.00	40.00
❏ 24, May 74	0.20	8.00	24.00	40.00
❏ 25, Jul 74	0.25	8.00	24.00	40.00
❏ 26	0.25	8.00	24.00	40.00
❏ 27	0.25	8.00	24.00	40.00
❏ 28, Jan 75	0.25	8.00	24.00	40.00
❏ 29, Mar 75	0.25	8.00	24.00	40.00

	ORIG.	GOOD	FINE	N-MINT
☐ 30, 75	0.25	8.00	24.00	40.00
☐ 31, Jul 75	0.25	8.00	24.00	40.00
☐ 32				
☐ 33				
☐ 34				
☐ 35				
☐ 36				
☐ 37				
☐ 38				
☐ 39				
☐ 40				
☐ 41				
☐ 42				
☐ 43				
☐ 44				
☐ 45				
☐ 46				
☐ 47				
☐ 48				
☐ 49				
☐ 50				
☐ 51, Mar 78	0.35	3.00	9.00	15.00
☐ 52				
☐ 53				
☐ 54				
☐ 55				
☐ 56				
☐ 57				
☐ 58				
☐ 59				
☐ 60				
☐ 61				

MARVEL

	ORIG.	GOOD	FINE	N-MINT
☐ 1, Apr 80	0.40	1.20	3.60	6.00
☐ 2, May 80	0.40	0.60	1.80	3.00
☐ 3, Jun 80	0.40	0.60	1.80	3.00
☐ 4, Jul 80	0.40	0.60	1.80	3.00
☐ 5, Aug 80	0.40	0.60	1.80	3.00
☐ 6, Sep 80	0.50	0.40	1.20	2.00
☐ 7, Oct 80	0.50	0.40	1.20	2.00
☐ 8, Nov 80	0.50	0.40	1.20	2.00
☐ 9, Dec 80	0.50	0.40	1.20	2.00
☐ 10, Jan 81	0.50	0.40	1.20	2.00
☐ 11, Feb 81	0.50	0.40	1.20	2.00
☐ 12, Mar 81	0.50	0.40	1.20	2.00
☐ 13, Apr 81	0.50	0.40	1.20	2.00
☐ 14, Jun 81	0.50	0.40	1.20	2.00
☐ 15, Aug 81	0.50	0.40	1.20	2.00
☐ 16, Oct 81	0.50	0.40	1.20	2.00
☐ 17, Dec 81	0.50	0.40	1.20	2.00
☐ 18, Feb 82	0.60	0.40	1.20	2.00

STAR TREK (1984-1988 series)
DC

	ORIG.	GOOD	FINE	N-MINT
☐ 1, Feb 84, TS	0.75	3.00	9.00	15.00
☐ 2, Mar 84, TS	0.75	2.00	6.00	10.00
☐ 3, Apr 84, TS	0.75	1.60	4.80	8.00
☐ 4, May 84, TS	0.75	1.60	4.80	8.00
☐ 5, Jun 84, TS	0.75	1.60	4.80	8.00
☐ 6, Jul 84, TS	0.75	1.00	3.00	5.00
☐ 7, Aug 84, TS	0.75	1.00	3.00	5.00
☐ 8, Nov 84, TS	0.75	1.00	3.00	5.00
☐ 9, Dec 84, TS;R:Mirror Universe				
	0.75	1.00	3.00	5.00
☐ 10, Jan 85, TS	0.75	1.00	3.00	5.00
☐ 11, Feb 85, TS;The two Spocks mind-meld				
	0.75	1.00	3.00	5.00
☐ 12, Mar 85, TS;Mirror Universe Enterprise's engineering				
hull destroyed	0.75	1.00	3.00	5.00
☐ 13, Apr 85, TS	0.75	1.00	3.00	5.00
☐ 14, May 85, TS	0.75	1.00	3.00	5.00
☐ 15, Jun 85, TS	0.75	1.00	3.00	5.00

	ORIG.	GOOD	FINE	N-MINT
☐ 16, Jul 85, TS;Kirk receives command of Excelsior				
	0.75	1.00	3.00	5.00
☐ 17, Aug 85, TS	0.75	1.00	3.00	5.00
☐ 18, Sep 85, TS	0.75	1.00	3.00	5.00
☐ 19, Oct 85, TS	0.75	1.00	3.00	5.00
☐ 20, Nov 85, TS	0.75	1.00	3.00	5.00
☐ 21, Dec 85, TS	0.75	1.00	3.00	5.00
☐ 22, Jan 86, TS;return of Redjac				
	0.75	1.00	3.00	5.00
☐ 23, Feb 86, TS;return of Redjac				
	0.75	1.00	3.00	5.00
☐ 24, Mar 86, TS	0.75	1.00	3.00	5.00
☐ 25, Apr 86, TS	0.75	1.00	3.00	5.00
☐ 26, May 86, TS	0.75	0.80	2.40	4.00
☐ 27, Jun 86, TS	0.75	0.80	2.40	4.00
☐ 28, Jul 86, TS	0.75	0.80	2.40	4.00
☐ 29, Aug 86, TS	0.75	0.80	2.40	4.00
☐ 30, Sep 86, TS	0.75	0.80	2.40	4.00
☐ 31, Oct 86, TS	0.75	0.80	2.40	4.00
☐ 32, Nov 86, TS	0.75	0.80	2.40	4.00
☐ 33, Dec 86, 20th Anniversary of Star Trek issue;original Enterprise meets Excelsior				
	1.25	0.80	2.40	4.00
☐ 34, Jan 87	0.75	0.80	2.40	4.00
☐ 35, Feb 87	0.75	0.80	2.40	4.00
☐ 36, Mar 87	0.75	0.80	2.40	4.00
☐ 37, Apr 87	0.75	0.80	2.40	4.00
☐ 38, May 87	0.75	0.80	2.40	4.00
☐ 39, Jun 87, return of Harry Mudd				
	0.75	0.80	2.40	4.00
☐ 40, Jul 87	0.75	0.80	2.40	4.00
☐ 41, Aug 87	0.75	0.80	2.40	4.00
☐ 42, Sep 87	0.75	0.80	2.40	4.00
☐ 43, Oct 87	0.75	0.80	2.40	4.00
☐ 44, Nov 87	0.75	0.80	2.40	4.00
☐ 45, Dec 87	0.75	0.80	2.40	4.00
☐ 46, Jan 88	0.75	0.80	2.40	4.00
☐ 47, Feb 88	0.75	0.80	2.40	4.00
☐ 48, Mar 88, first Peter David script				
	0.75	0.80	2.40	4.00
☐ 49, Apr 88, 1:Moron	1.00	0.80	2.40	4.00
☐ 50, May 88		0.80	2.40	4.00
☐ 51, Jun 88		0.80	2.40	4.00
☐ 52, Jul 88		0.80	2.40	4.00
☐ 53, Aug 88		0.80	2.40	4.00
☐ 54, Sep 88		0.80	2.40	4.00
☐ 55, Oct 88		0.80	2.40	4.00
☐ 56, Nov 88		0.80	2.40	4.00

STAR TREK (beginning 1989)

	ORIG.	GOOD	FINE	N-MINT
☐ 1		2.00	6.00	10.00
☐ 2		1.20	3.60	6.00
☐ 3		0.80	2.40	4.00
☐ 4		0.80	2.40	4.00
☐ 5		0.80	2.40	4.00
☐ 6		0.60	1.80	3.00
☐ 7		0.60	1.80	3.00
☐ 8		0.60	1.80	3.00
☐ 9		0.60	1.80	3.00
☐ 10, Kirk on trial		0.60	1.80	3.00
☐ 11, Kirk on trial		0.60	1.80	3.00
☐ 12, Kirk on trial		0.60	1.80	3.00
☐ 13, The Worthy		0.60	1.80	3.00
☐ 14, The Worthy		0.60	1.80	3.00
☐ 15, The Worthy		0.60	1.80	3.00
☐ 16		0.60	1.80	3.00
☐ 17		0.60	1.80	3.00
☐ 18		0.60	1.80	3.00
☐ 19		0.60	1.80	3.00
☐ 20		0.60	1.80	3.00
☐ 21		0.60	1.80	3.00
☐ 22		0.60	1.80	3.00

	ORIG.	GOOD	FINE	N-MINT
❑ 23, Harry Mudd..............		0.60	1.80	3.00
❑ 24, Harry Mudd..............		0.60	1.80	3.00
❑ 25	1.75	0.60	1.80	3.00
❑ 26	1.75	0.60	1.80	3.00
❑ 27	1.75	0.60	1.80	3.00
❑ 28	1.75	0.60	1.80	3.00
❑ 29	1.75	0.60	1.80	3.00
❑ 30	1.75	0.60	1.80	3.00
❑ 31	1.75	0.50	1.50	2.50
❑ 32	1.75	0.50	1.50	2.50
❑ 33	1.75	0.50	1.50	2.50
❑ 34	1.75	0.50	1.50	2.50
❑ 35	1.75	0.50	1.50	2.50
❑ 36	1.75	0.50	1.50	2.50
❑ 37	1.75	0.50	1.50	2.50
❑ 38	1.75	0.50	1.50	2.50
❑ 39	1.75	0.50	1.50	2.50
❑ 40	1.75	0.50	1.50	2.50
❑ 41	1.75	0.35	1.05	1.75
❑ 42	1.75	0.35	1.05	1.75
❑ 43	1.75	0.35	1.05	1.75
❑ 44	1.75	0.35	1.05	1.75
❑ 45	1.75	0.35	1.05	1.75
❑ 46	1.75	0.35	1.05	1.75
❑ 47	1.75	0.35	1.05	1.75
❑ 48	1.75	0.35	1.05	1.75
❑ 49	1.75	0.35	1.05	1.75
❑ 50, giant......................	3.50	0.70	2.10	3.50
❑ 51	1.75	0.35	1.05	1.75
❑ 52	1.75	0.35	1.05	1.75
❑ 53	1.75	0.35	1.05	1.75
❑ 54	1.75	0.35	1.05	1.75
❑ 55	1.75	0.35	1.05	1.75
❑ 56	1.75	0.35	1.05	1.75
❑ 57	1.75	0.35	1.05	1.75
❑ 58	1.75	0.35	1.05	1.75
❑ 59, Apr 94	1.75	0.35	1.05	1.75
❑ 60, Jun 94	1.75	0.35	1.05	1.75
❑ 61, Jul 94	1.95	0.39	1.17	1.95
❑ 62, Aug 94	1.95	0.39	1.17	1.95
❑ 63, Sep 94	1.95	0.39	1.17	1.95
❑ 64, Oct 94	1.95	0.39	1.17	1.95
❑ 65, Nov 94	1.95	0.39	1.17	1.95
❑ 66, Dec 94.....................	1.95	0.39	1.17	1.95
❑ 67, Jan 95	1.95	0.39	1.17	1.95
❑ 68, Feb 95	1.95	0.39	1.17	1.95
❑ 69, Mar 95	1.95	0.39	1.17	1.95
❑ 70, Apr 95	1.95	0.39	1.17	1.95
❑ 71, May 95	2.50	0.50	1.50	2.50
❑ 72, Jun 95.....................	2.50	0.50	1.50	2.50
❑ 73, Jul 95	2.50	0.50	1.50	2.50
❑ 74, Aug 95	2.50	0.50	1.50	2.50
❑ 75, Sep 95.....................	3.95	0.79	2.37	3.95
❑ 76, Oct 95	2.50	0.50	1.50	2.50
❑ 77, Nov 95	2.50	0.50	1.50	2.50
❑ 78, Dec 95.....................	2.50	0.50	1.50	2.50
❑ 79, Jan 96	2.50	0.50	1.50	2.50
❑ 80, Feb 96, final issue	2.50	0.50	1.50	2.50

STAR TREK ANNUAL (Series 1)

❑ 1, 85, Kirk's first mission on The Enterprise
.... 1.25 0.25 0.75 1.25
❑ 2, 86, The final mission of the first five-year
mission;A:Captain Pike .. 1.25 0.25 0.75 1.25
❑ 3, 88, Scotty's romances 1.25 0.25 0.75 1.25

STAR TREK ANNUAL (Series 2)

	ORIG.	GOOD	FINE	N-MINT
❑ 1, 90..............................		0.59	1.77	2.95
❑ 2, 91..............................		0.59	1.77	2.95
❑ 3, 92..............................		0.70	2.10	3.50

	ORIG.	GOOD	FINE	N-MINT
❑ 4, 93 ....3.50		0.70	2.10	3.50
❑ 5, 94 ....3.95		0.79	2.37	3.95

❑ 6, 95, "Convergence" Part 1;D:Gary Seven;continues in
Star Trek: TNG Annual #6
.... 3.95 0.79 2.37 3.95

STAR TREK GENERATIONS

❑ 0, 94, movie adaptation; prestige format one-shot
.... 5.95 1.19 3.57 5.95
❑ 0, 94, movie adaptation; one-shot
.... 3.95 0.79 2.37 3.95

STAR TREK MOVIE SPECIAL

	ORIG.	GOOD	FINE	N-MINT
❑ 1, 84, Star Trek III..........1.50		0.40	1.20	2.00
❑ 1, 89, Star Trek V...........2.00		0.40	1.20	2.00
❑ 2, 87, Star Trek IV..........2.00		0.40	1.20	2.00

STAR TREK SPECIAL

	ORIG.	GOOD	FINE	N-MINT
❑ 1, 94 ....3.50		0.70	2.10	3.50
❑ 2, Win 94 ....3.95		0.79	2.37	3.95
❑ 3, Win 95 ....3.95		0.79	2.37	3.95

STAR TREK VI: THE UNDISCOVERED COUNTRY

❑ 0, nn prestige format, movie 1.19 3.57 5.95
❑ 1, movie, newsstand........ 0.59 1.77 2.95

STAR TREK: DEEP SPACE NINE
MALIBU

❑ 0, limited edition ashcan... 5.00 15.00 25.00
❑ 0, premium limited edition, QVC offer
.................................28.00 5.60 16.80 28.00
❑ 1, Aug 93, photo cover (newsstand)
.................................2.50 0.80 2.40 4.00
❑ 1, Aug 93, line-drawing cover
.................................2.50 0.80 2.40 4.00
❑ 1, Aug 93, limited, black cover
.................................19.95 3.99 11.97 19.95
❑ 1, Aug 93, deluxe edition (black/foil)
.... 3.00 9.00 15.00
❑ 2, Sep 93, trading card ...2.50 0.50 1.50 2.50
❑ 3, Oct 93........................2.50 0.50 1.50 2.50
❑ 4, Nov 93.......................2.50 0.50 1.50 2.50
❑ 5, Dec 93.......................2.50 0.50 1.50 2.50
❑ 6, Jan 94........................2.50 0.50 1.50 2.50
❑ 7, Feb 94........................2.50 0.50 1.50 2.50
❑ 8, May 94, GPu................2.50 0.50 1.50 2.50
❑ 9, Jun 94 ....2.50 0.50 1.50 2.50
❑ 10, Jun 94 ....2.50 0.50 1.50 2.50
❑ 11, Jul 94.......................2.50 0.50 1.50 2.50
❑ 12, Jul 94.......................2.50 0.50 1.50 2.50
❑ 13, Aug 94.....................2.50 0.50 1.50 2.50
❑ 14, Sep 94.....................2.50 0.50 1.50 2.50
❑ 16, Nov 94.....................2.50 0.50 1.50 2.50

STAR TREK: DEEP SPACE NINE HEARTS AND MINDS (mini-series)

❑ 1, Jun 94 ....2.50 0.50 1.50 2.50
❑ 2, Jul 94.........................2.50 0.50 1.50 2.50
❑ 3, Aug 94 ....2.50 0.50 1.50 2.50
❑ 4, Sep 94 ....2.50 0.50 1.50 2.50

STAR TREK: DEEP SPACE NINE/STAR TREK: THE NEXT GENERATION (mini-series)

❑ 2, Nov 94, (part three of a four-part crossover with DC)
.................................2.50 0.50 1.50 2.50

STAR TREK: DEEP SPACE NINE/STAR TREK: THE NEXT GENERATION ASHCAN

❑ 0, no cover price; flip-book with DC's Star Trek: The Next
Generation/Star Trek: Deep Space Nine Ashcan

STAR TREK: THE MODALA IMPERATIVE
DC

❑ 1 .... 0.50 1.50 2.50
❑ 2 .... 0.50 1.50 2.50
❑ 3 .... 0.50 1.50 2.50
❑ 4 .... 0.50 1.50 2.50

	ORIG.	GOOD	FINE	N-MINT

STAR TREK: THE NEXT GENERATION
(1988 mini-series)

	ORIG.	GOOD	FINE	N-MINT
❑ 1		2.40	7.20	12.00
❑ 2		1.60	4.80	8.00
❑ 3		1.00	3.00	5.00
❑ 4		1.00	3.00	5.00
❑ 5		1.00	3.00	5.00
❑ 6		1.00	3.00	5.00

STAR TREK: THE NEXT GENERATION
(beginning 1989)

	ORIG.	GOOD	FINE	N-MINT
❑ 1		2.00	6.00	10.00
❑ 2		1.20	3.60	6.00
❑ 3		0.80	2.40	4.00
❑ 4		0.80	2.40	4.00
❑ 5		0.80	2.40	4.00
❑ 6	1.50	0.60	1.80	3.00
❑ 7	1.50	0.60	1.80	3.00
❑ 8	1.50	0.60	1.80	3.00
❑ 9	1.50	0.60	1.80	3.00
❑ 10	1.50	0.60	1.80	3.00
❑ 11	1.50	0.60	1.80	3.00
❑ 12	1.50	0.60	1.80	3.00
❑ 13	1.50	0.60	1.80	3.00
❑ 14	1.50	0.60	1.80	3.00
❑ 15	1.50	0.60	1.80	3.00
❑ 16	1.50	0.60	1.80	3.00
❑ 17	1.50	0.60	1.80	3.00
❑ 18	1.50	0.60	1.80	3.00
❑ 19	1.50	0.60	1.80	3.00
❑ 20	1.50	0.60	1.80	3.00
❑ 21	1.50	0.60	1.80	3.00
❑ 22	1.50	0.60	1.80	3.00
❑ 23	1.50	0.60	1.80	3.00
❑ 24	1.50	0.60	1.80	3.00
❑ 25	1.50	0.60	1.80	3.00
❑ 26	1.50	0.60	1.80	3.00
❑ 27	1.50	0.60	1.80	3.00
❑ 28	1.50	0.60	1.80	3.00
❑ 29	1.50	0.60	1.80	3.00
❑ 30	1.50	0.60	1.80	3.00
❑ 31		0.50	1.50	2.50
❑ 32		0.50	1.50	2.50
❑ 33		0.50	1.50	2.50
❑ 34		0.50	1.50	2.50
❑ 35		0.50	1.50	2.50
❑ 36		0.50	1.50	2.50
❑ 37		0.50	1.50	2.50
❑ 38		0.50	1.50	2.50
❑ 39		0.50	1.50	2.50
❑ 40		0.50	1.50	2.50
❑ 41	1.75	0.35	1.05	1.75
❑ 42	1.75	0.35	1.05	1.75
❑ 43	1.75	0.35	1.05	1.75
❑ 44	1.75	0.35	1.05	1.75
❑ 45	1.75	0.35	1.05	1.75
❑ 46	1.75	0.35	1.05	1.75
❑ 47	1.75	0.35	1.05	1.75
❑ 48	1.75	0.35	1.05	1.75
❑ 49	1.75	0.35	1.05	1.75
❑ 50	3.50	0.70	2.10	3.50
❑ 51	1.75	0.35	1.05	1.75
❑ 52	1.75	0.35	1.05	1.75
❑ 53	1.75	0.35	1.05	1.75
❑ 54	1.75	0.35	1.05	1.75
❑ 55	1.75	0.35	1.05	1.75
❑ 56	1.75	0.35	1.05	1.75
❑ 57	1.75	0.35	1.05	1.75
❑ 58, Apr 94	1.75	0.35	1.05	1.75
❑ 59, May 94	1.75	0.35	1.05	1.75
❑ 60, Jun 94	1.75	0.35	1.05	1.75
❑ 61, Jul 94	1.95	0.39	1.17	1.95
❑ 62, Aug 94	1.95	0.39	1.17	1.95
❑ 63, Sep 94	1.95	0.39	1.17	1.95
❑ 64, Oct 94	1.95	0.39	1.17	1.95
❑ 65, Nov 94	1.95	0.39	1.17	1.95
❑ 66, Dec 94	1.95	0.39	1.17	1.95
❑ 67, Jan 95	1.95	0.39	1.17	1.95
❑ 68, Feb 95	1.95	0.39	1.17	1.95
❑ 69, Mar 95	1.95	0.39	1.17	1.95
❑ 70, Apr 95	1.95	0.39	1.17	1.95
❑ 71, May 95		0.39	1.17	1.95
❑ 72, Jun 95	2.50	0.50	1.50	2.50
❑ 73, Jul 95	2.50	0.50	1.50	2.50
❑ 74, Aug 95	2.50	0.50	1.50	2.50
❑ 75, Sep 95	3.95	0.79	2.37	3.95
❑ 76, Oct 95	2.50	0.50	1.50	2.50
❑ 77, Nov 95	2.50	0.50	1.50	2.50
❑ 78, Dec 95	2.50	0.50	1.50	2.50
❑ 79, Jan 96, Q transforms the crew into androids				
	2.50	0.50	1.50	2.50
❑ 80, Feb 96, final issue	2.50	0.50	1.50	2.50

STAR TREK: THE NEXT GENERATION - ILL WIND
(mini-series)

	ORIG.	GOOD	FINE	N-MINT
❑ 1, Nov 95	2.50	0.50	1.50	2.50
❑ 2, Dec 95	2.50	0.50	1.50	2.50
❑ 3, Jan 96	2.50	0.50	1.50	2.50
❑ 4, Feb 96	2.50	0.50	1.50	2.50

STAR TREK: THE NEXT GENERATION ANNUAL

	ORIG.	GOOD	FINE	N-MINT
❑ 1		0.59	1.77	2.95
❑ 2	3.50	0.70	2.10	3.50
❑ 3	3.50	0.70	2.10	3.50
❑ 4	3.50	0.70	2.10	3.50
❑ 5, 94	3.95	0.79	2.37	3.95
❑ 6, 95, "Convergence" Part 2;continued from *Star Trek*				
Annual #6	3.95	0.79	2.37	3.95

STAR TREK: THE NEXT GENERATION SPECIAL

	ORIG.	GOOD	FINE	N-MINT
❑ 1	3.50	0.70	2.10	3.50
❑ 2, Sum 94	3.95	0.79	2.37	3.95
❑ 3, Win 95, "Pandora's Prodigy"				
	3.95	0.79	2.37	3.95

STAR TREK: THE NEXT GENERATION
THE MODALA IMPERATIVE

	ORIG.	GOOD	FINE	N-MINT
❑ 1		0.35	1.05	1.75
❑ 2		0.35	1.05	1.75
❑ 3		0.35	1.05	1.75
❑ 4		0.35	1.05	1.75

STAR TREK: THE NEXT GENERATION-
SHADOWHEART (mini-series)

	ORIG.	GOOD	FINE	N-MINT
❑ 1, Dec 94	1.95	0.39	1.17	1.95
❑ 2, Jan 95	1.95	0.39	1.17	1.95
❑ 3, Feb 95	1.95	0.39	1.17	1.95
❑ 4, Mar 95	1.95	0.39	1.17	1.95

STAR TREK: THE NEXT GENERATION-THE SERIES
FINALE

	ORIG.	GOOD	FINE	N-MINT
❑ 0, 94	3.95	0.79	2.37	3.95

STAR TREK: THE NEXT GENERATION/
STAR TREK: DEEP SPACE NINE

	ORIG.	GOOD	FINE	N-MINT
❑ 1, Dec 94, crossover with Malibu				
	2.50	0.50	1.50	2.50
❑ 2, Jan 95, crossover with Malibu				
	2.50	0.50	1.50	2.50

STAR TREK: THE NEXT GENERATION/STAR TREK:
DEEP SPACE NINE ASHCAN

❑ 0, 94, no cover price; flip-book with Malibu's *Deep Space Nine/Star Trek: The Next Generation* Ashcan

STAR TREKKER
ANTARCTIC

❑ 1, Dec 92, b&w, parody (never distributed)

	ORIG.	GOOD	FINE	N-MINT
	2.95	0.59	1.77	2.95

	ORIG.	GOOD	FINE	N-MINT

STAR WARS
MARVEL

	ORIG.	GOOD	FINE	N-MINT
❑ 1, Jul 77, HC;movie adaptation	0.30	7.00	21.00	35.00
❑ 1, Jul 77, HC;movie adaptation;35 cent variation	0.35	50.00	150.00	250.00
❑ 2, Aug 77, HC;movie adaptation	0.30	3.00	9.00	15.00
❑ 3, Sep 77, HC;movie adaptation	0.30	3.00	9.00	15.00
❑ 4, Oct 77, HC;low distribution;movie adaptation	0.30	2.00	6.00	10.00
❑ 5, Nov 77, HC;movie adaptation	0.35	1.40	4.20	7.00
❑ 6, Dec 77, HC;movie adaptation	0.35	1.40	4.20	7.00
❑ 7, Jan 78, HC	0.35	1.40	4.20	7.00
❑ 8, Feb 78, HC	0.35	1.40	4.20	7.00
❑ 9, Mar 78, HC	0.35	1.40	4.20	7.00
❑ 10, Apr 78, HC	0.35	1.40	4.20	7.00
❑ 11, May 78	0.35	1.20	3.60	6.00
❑ 12, Jun 78	0.35	1.20	3.60	6.00
❑ 13, Jul 78	0.35	1.20	3.60	6.00
❑ 14, Aug 78	0.35	1.20	3.60	6.00
❑ 15, Sep 78, D:Crimson Jack	0.35	1.20	3.60	6.00
❑ 16, Oct 78, I&1:Valance, the bounty hunter	0.35	1.20	3.60	6.00
❑ 17, Nov 78, low distribution;Tatooine adventure set before first movie	0.35	1.20	3.60	6.00
❑ 18, Dec 78, low distribution	0.35	1.20	3.60	6.00
❑ 19, Jan 79, low distribution	0.35	1.20	3.60	6.00
❑ 20, Feb 79	0.35	1.20	3.60	6.00
❑ 21, Mar 79	0.35	1.00	3.00	5.00
❑ 22, Apr 79	0.35	1.00	3.00	5.00
❑ 23, May 79	0.40	1.00	3.00	5.00
❑ 24, Jun 79, flashback to before first movie	0.40	1.00	3.00	5.00
❑ 25, Jul 79	0.40	1.00	3.00	5.00
❑ 26, Aug 79	0.40	1.00	3.00	5.00
❑ 27, Sep 79	0.40	1.00	3.00	5.00
❑ 28, Oct 79, A:Jabba the Hutt (not movie version)	0.40	1.00	3.00	5.00
❑ 29, Nov 79, A:Darth Vader	0.40	1.00	3.00	5.00
❑ 30, Dec 79	0.40	1.00	3.00	5.00
❑ 31, Jan 80, return to Tatooine	0.40	1.00	3.00	5.00
❑ 32, Feb 80	0.40	1.00	3.00	5.00
❑ 33, Mar 80	0.40	1.00	3.00	5.00
❑ 34, Apr 80, D:Baron Tagge	0.40	1.00	3.00	5.00
❑ 35, May 80, Vader, Luke meet	0.40	1.00	3.00	5.00
❑ 36, Jun 80	0.40	1.00	3.00	5.00
❑ 37, Jul 80, 1:Vader/Luke duel	0.40	1.00	3.00	5.00
❑ 38, Aug 80, TA/MG;living spaceship	0.40	1.00	3.00	5.00
❑ 39, Sep 80, AW;*Empire Strikes Back*	0.50	1.00	3.00	5.00
❑ 40, Oct 80, AW;*Empire Strikes Back*	0.50	1.00	3.00	5.00
❑ 41, Nov 80, AW;*Empire Strikes Back*	0.50	1.00	3.00	5.00
❑ 42, Dec 80, AW;*Empire Strikes Back*	0.50	1.00	3.00	5.00

	ORIG.	GOOD	FINE	N-MINT
❑ 43, Jan 81, AW;*Empire Strikes Back*	0.50	1.00	3.00	5.00
❑ 44, Feb 81, AW;*Empire Strikes Back*	0.50	1.00	3.00	5.00
❑ 45, Mar 81, first post-*Empire Strikes Back* story	0.50	1.00	3.00	5.00
❑ 46, Apr 81	0.50	1.00	3.00	5.00
❑ 47, May 81	0.50	1.00	3.00	5.00
❑ 48, Jun 81	0.50	1.00	3.00	5.00
❑ 49, Jul 81, low distribution	0.50	1.00	3.00	5.00
❑ 50, Aug 81, WS/AW;TP;double-sized;"Crimson Forever"	0.75	1.40	4.20	7.00
❑ 51, Sep 81, "Tarkin";Death Star successor	0.50	0.80	2.40	4.00
❑ 52, Oct 81, "Tarkin";Death Star successor	0.50	0.80	2.40	4.00
❑ 53, Nov 81	0.50	0.80	2.40	4.00
❑ 54, Dec 81	0.50	0.80	2.40	4.00
❑ 55, Jan 82	0.60	0.80	2.40	4.00
❑ 56, Feb 82	0.60	0.80	2.40	4.00
❑ 57, Mar 82	0.60	0.80	2.40	4.00
❑ 58, Apr 82, Return to Cloud City	0.60	0.80	2.40	4.00
❑ 59, May 82	0.60	0.80	2.40	4.00
❑ 60, Jun 82	0.60	0.80	2.40	4.00
❑ 61, Jul 82	0.60	0.80	2.40	4.00
❑ 62, Aug 82, Luke kicked out of Alliance	0.60	0.80	2.40	4.00
❑ 63, Sep 82	0.60	0.80	2.40	4.00
❑ 64, Oct 82	0.60	0.80	2.40	4.00
❑ 65, Nov 82	0.60	0.80	2.40	4.00
❑ 66, Dec 82	0.60	0.80	2.40	4.00
❑ 67, Jan 83	0.60	0.80	2.40	4.00
❑ 68, Feb 83	0.60	0.80	2.40	4.00
❑ 69, Mar 83	0.60	0.80	2.40	4.00
❑ 70, Apr 83	0.60	0.80	2.40	4.00
❑ 71	0.60	0.80	2.40	4.00
❑ 72	0.60	0.80	2.40	4.00
❑ 73	0.60	0.80	2.40	4.00
❑ 74	0.60	0.80	2.40	4.00
❑ 75	0.60	0.80	2.40	4.00
❑ 76	0.60	0.80	2.40	4.00
❑ 77	0.60	0.80	2.40	4.00
❑ 78	0.60	0.80	2.40	4.00
❑ 79	0.60	0.80	2.40	4.00
❑ 80	0.60	0.80	2.40	4.00
❑ 81, first post-*Return of the Jedi* story	0.60	0.80	2.40	4.00
❑ 82	0.60	0.80	2.40	4.00
❑ 83	0.60	0.80	2.40	4.00
❑ 84	0.60	0.80	2.40	4.00
❑ 85	0.60	0.80	2.40	4.00
❑ 86	0.60	0.80	2.40	4.00
❑ 87	0.60	0.80	2.40	4.00
❑ 88	0.60	0.80	2.40	4.00
❑ 89	0.60	0.80	2.40	4.00
❑ 90	0.60	0.80	2.40	4.00
❑ 91	0.60	0.80	2.40	4.00
❑ 92	1.00	0.80	2.40	4.00
❑ 93	0.60	0.80	2.40	4.00
❑ 94	0.65	0.80	2.40	4.00
❑ 95	0.65	0.80	2.40	4.00
❑ 96	0.65	0.80	2.40	4.00
❑ 97	0.65	0.80	2.40	4.00
❑ 98	0.65	0.80	2.40	4.00
❑ 99	0.65	0.80	2.40	4.00
❑ 100	1.25	1.20	3.60	6.00
❑ 101	0.65	0.80	2.40	4.00
❑ 102	0.65	0.80	2.40	4.00
❑ 103	0.65	0.80	2.40	4.00
❑ 104	0.75	0.80	2.40	4.00

	ORIG.	GOOD	FINE	N-MINT
❏ 105 ....0.75	0.80	2.40	4.00
❏ 106 ....0.75	0.80	2.40	4.00
❏ 107 ....0.75	0.80	2.40	4.00

STAR WARS ANNUAL

	ORIG.	GOOD	FINE	N-MINT
❏ 1, Dec 79, Chris Claremont (w)				
.................................0.75	2.00	6.00	10.00
❏ 2, 82.............................1.00	1.20	3.60	6.00
❏ 3, 83.............................1.00	1.20	3.60	6.00

STAR WARS IN 3-D
BLACKTHORNE

	ORIG.	GOOD	FINE	N-MINT
❏ 1, Dec 87......................2.50	0.50	1.50	2.50

STAR WARS: BOBA FETT
DARK HORSE

	ORIG.	GOOD	FINE	N-MINT
❏ 1, Dec 95, cardstock cover				
.................................3.95	0.79	2.37	3.95

STAR WARS: DARK EMPIRE

	ORIG.	GOOD	FINE	N-MINT
❏ 1, Dec 91......................2.95	6.00	18.00	30.00
❏ 1, Aug 92, second printing				
.................................2.95	0.59	1.77	2.95
❏ 2 ....2.95	7.20	21.60	36.00
❏ 3 ....2.95	3.00	9.00	15.00
❏ 4, Apr 92.......................2.95	2.40	7.20	12.00
❏ 5, Aug 92.......................2.95	2.40	7.20	12.00
❏ 6, Oct 92 ....2.95	2.00	6.00	10.00

STAR WARS: DARK EMPIRE -- PREVIEW

	ORIG.	GOOD	FINE	N-MINT
❏ 0, Mar 96, newsprint preview of trade paperback collection of mini-series;wraparound cover				
.................................0.99	0.20	0.59	0.99

STAR WARS: DARK EMPIRE II (mini-series)

	ORIG.	GOOD	FINE	N-MINT
❏ 1, Dec 94,cardstock cover				
.................................2.95	0.59	1.77	2.95
❏ 2, Jan 95, cardstock cover				
.................................2.95	0.59	1.77	2.95
❏ 3, Feb 95, cardstock cover				
.................................2.95	0.59	1.77	2.95
❏ 4, Mar 95, cardstock cover				
.................................2.95	0.59	1.77	2.95

STAR WARS: DROIDS (mini-series)

	ORIG.	GOOD	FINE	N-MINT
❏ 1, Apr 94, enhanced cover				
.................................2.95	0.59	1.77	2.95
❏ 2, May 94.......................2.50	0.50	1.50	2.50
❏ 3, Jun 94........................2.50	0.50	1.50	2.50
❏ 4, Jul 94.........................2.50	0.50	1.50	2.50
❏ 5, Aug 94.......................2.50	0.50	1.50	2.50
❏ 6, Sep 94.......................2.50	0.50	1.50	2.50

STAR WARS: DROIDS (Vol. 2)

	ORIG.	GOOD	FINE	N-MINT
❏ 3, Jun 95........................2.50	0.50	1.50	2.50
❏ 4, Jul 95.........................2.50	0.50	1.50	2.50
❏ 5, Sep 95.......................2.50	0.50	1.50	2.50
❏ 6, Oct 95........................2.50	0.50	1.50	2.50
❏ 7, Nov 95.......................2.50	0.50	1.50	2.50
❏ 8, Dec 95.......................2.50	0.50	1.50	2.50

STAR WARS: DROIDS SPECIAL

	ORIG.	GOOD	FINE	N-MINT
❏ 1, Jan 95........................2.50	0.50	1.50	2.50

STAR WARS: EMPIRE'S END (mini-series)

	ORIG.	GOOD	FINE	N-MINT
❏ 1, Oct 95, cardstock cover				
.................................2.95	0.59	1.77	2.95
❏ 2, Nov 95, cardstock cover				
.................................2.95	0.59	1.77	2.95

STAR WARS: HEIR TO THE EMPIRE (mini-series)

	ORIG.	GOOD	FINE	N-MINT
❏ 1, Oct 95, cardstock cover				
.................................2.95	0.59	1.77	2.95
❏ 2, Nov 95, cardstock cover				
.................................2.95	0.59	1.77	2.95
❏ 3, Dec 95, cardstock cover				
.................................2.95	0.59	1.77	2.95
❏ 4, Jan 96, cardstock cover				
.................................2.95	0.59	1.77	2.95

	ORIG.	GOOD	FINE	N-MINT
❏ 5, Mar 96, cardstock cover				
.................................2.95	0.59	1.77	2.95
❏ 6, Apr 96, cardstock cover;final issue				
.................................2.95	0.59	1.77	2.95

STAR WARS: JABBA THE HUTT

	ORIG.	GOOD	FINE	N-MINT
❏ 1, Apr 95.......................2.50	0.50	1.50	2.50

STAR WARS: JABBA THE HUTT - BETRAYAL

	ORIG.	GOOD	FINE	N-MINT
❏ 1, Feb 96.......................2.50	0.50	1.50	2.50

STAR WARS: JABBA THE HUTT - THE DYNASTY TRAP

	ORIG.	GOOD	FINE	N-MINT
❏ 0, Aug 95, nn;one-shot ...2.50	0.50	1.50	2.50

STAR WARS: JABBA THE HUTT - THE HUNGER OF PRINCESS NAMPI

	ORIG.	GOOD	FINE	N-MINT
❏ 0, Jun 95, nn;one-shot ...2.50	0.50	1.50	2.50

STAR WARS: RETURN OF THE JEDI (mini-series)
MARVEL

	ORIG.	GOOD	FINE	N-MINT
❏ 1, 83 ....0.60	0.40	1.20	2.00
❏ 2, 83 ....0.60	0.40	1.20	2.00
❏ 3, 83 ....0.60	0.40	1.20	2.00
❏ 4, Jan 84.......................0.60	0.40	1.20	2.00

STAR WARS: RIVER OF CHAOS (mini-series)
DARK HORSE

	ORIG.	GOOD	FINE	N-MINT
❏ 1, Jun 95 ....2.50	0.50	1.50	2.50
❏ 2, Jul 95 ....2.50	0.50	1.50	2.50
❏ 3, Sep 95 ....2.50	0.50	1.50	2.50
❏ 4, Nov 95 ....2.50	0.50	1.50	2.50

STAR WARS: SHADOWS OF THE EMPIRE

	ORIG.	GOOD	FINE	N-MINT
❏ 1, May 96, cardstock cover				
.................................2.95	0.59	1.77	2.95

STAR WARS: SPLINTER OF THE MIND'S EYE

	ORIG.	GOOD	FINE	N-MINT
❏ 1, Dec 95 ....2.50	0.50	1.50	2.50
❏ 2, Feb 96.......................2.50	0.50	1.50	2.50
❏ 3, Apr 96........................2.95	0.59	1.77	2.95

STAR WARS: TALES FROM MOS EISLEY

	ORIG.	GOOD	FINE	N-MINT
❏ 0, Mar 96, nn 2.95	0.59	1.77	2.95

STAR WARS: TALES OF THE JEDI

	ORIG.	GOOD	FINE	N-MINT
❏ 1 ....2.50	1.00	3.00	5.00
❏ 2 ....2.50	0.80	2.40	4.00
❏ 3 ....2.50	0.50	1.50	2.50
❏ 4 ....2.50	0.50	1.50	2.50
❏ 5, Feb 94.......................2.50	0.50	1.50	2.50

STAR WARS: TALES OF THE JEDI-DARK LORDS OF THE SITH (mini-series)

	ORIG.	GOOD	FINE	N-MINT
❏ 1, Oct 94........................2.50	0.50	1.50	2.50
❏ 2, Nov 94.......................2.50	0.50	1.50	2.50
❏ 3, Dec 94.......................2.50	0.50	1.50	2.50
❏ 4, Jan 95.......................2.50	0.50	1.50	2.50
❏ 5, Feb 95.......................2.50	0.50	1.50	2.50
❏ 6, Mar 95.......................2.50	0.50	1.50	2.50

STAR WARS: TALES OF THE JEDI-THE FREEDON NADD UPRISING (mini-series)

	ORIG.	GOOD	FINE	N-MINT
❏ 1, Aug 94.......................2.50	0.50	1.50	2.50
❏ 2, Sep 94, final issue 2.50	0.50	1.50	2.50

STAR WARS: TALES OF THE JEDI-THE SITH WAR (mini-series)

	ORIG.	GOOD	FINE	N-MINT
❏ 1, Aug 95.......................2.50	0.50	1.50	2.50
❏ 2, Sep 95.......................2.50	0.50	1.50	2.50
❏ 3, Oct 95 ....2.50	0.50	1.50	2.50
❏ 4, Nov 95.......................2.50	0.50	1.50	2.50
❏ 5, Dec 95 ....2.50	0.50	1.50	2.50
❏ 6, Jan 96........................2.50	0.50	1.50	2.50

STAR WARS: X-WING ROGUE SQUADRON

	ORIG.	GOOD	FINE	N-MINT
❏ 1, Jul 95.........................2.95	0.59	1.77	2.95
❏ 2, Aug 95 ....2.95	0.59	1.77	2.95
❏ 3, Sep 95 ....2.95	0.59	1.77	2.95
❏ 4, Oct 95 ....2.95	0.59	1.77	2.95
❏ 5, Feb 96, "The Phantom Affair" Part 1 of 4				
.................................2.95	0.59	1.77	2.95

	ORIG.	GOOD	FINE	N-MINT

☐ 6, Mar 96, "The Phantom Affair" Part 2 of 4

	2.95	0.59	1.77	2.95

☐ 7, Apr 96, "The Phantom Affair" Part 3 of 4

	2.95	0.59	1.77	2.95

STAR WARS: X-WING ROGUE SQUADRON SPECIAL
☐ 0, Aug 95, nn;promotional giveaway with Kellogg's Apple Jacks

STAR*REACH
STAR*REACH

		GOOD	FINE	N-MINT
☐ 1		0.40	1.20	2.00
☐ 2		0.40	1.20	2.00
☐ 3		0.40	1.20	2.00
☐ 4		0.40	1.20	2.00
☐ 5		0.40	1.20	2.00
☐ 6		0.40	1.20	2.00
☐ 7		0.40	1.20	2.00
☐ 8		0.40	1.20	2.00
☐ 9		0.40	1.20	2.00
☐ 10		0.40	1.20	2.00
☐ 11		0.40	1.20	2.00
☐ 12		0.40	1.20	2.00
☐ 13		0.40	1.20	2.00
☐ 14		0.40	1.20	2.00
☐ 15		0.40	1.20	2.00
☐ 16		0.40	1.20	2.00
☐ 17		0.40	1.20	2.00
☐ 18		0.40	1.20	2.00

STAR*REACH CLASSICS
ECLIPSE

		GOOD	FINE	N-MINT
☐ 1, DG		0.30	0.90	1.50
☐ 2		0.30	0.90	1.50
☐ 3		0.30	0.90	1.50
☐ 4		0.30	0.90	1.50
☐ 5, HC		0.30	0.90	1.50
☐ 6, CR		0.30	0.90	1.50

STAR*REACH GREATEST HITS
STAR*REACH

		GOOD	FINE	N-MINT
☐ 1, paperback reprints		1.39	4.17	6.95

STAR-LORD
MARVEL

	ORIG.	GOOD	FINE	N-MINT
☐ 1, Feb 82, JBy	1.50	0.30	0.90	1.50

STARBIKERS
RENEGADE

		GOOD	FINE	N-MINT
☐ 1, b&w		0.40	1.20	2.00

STARBLAST
MARVEL

	ORIG.	GOOD	FINE	N-MINT
☐ 1	2.00	0.40	1.20	2.00
☐ 2	1.75	0.35	1.05	1.75
☐ 3, Mar 94	1.75	0.35	1.05	1.75
☐ 4, Apr 94	1.75	0.35	1.05	1.75

STARCHILD
TALIESEN PRESS

	ORIG.	GOOD	FINE	N-MINT
☐ 0		1.00	3.00	5.00
☐ 1, b&w	2.25	1.20	3.60	6.00
☐ 2, b&w	2.25	0.60	1.80	3.00
☐ 3, b&w	2.50	0.80	2.40	4.00
☐ 4, b&w	2.50	0.60	1.80	3.00
☐ 5, b&w	2.50	0.50	1.50	2.50

STARDUSTERS
NIGHTWYND

		GOOD	FINE	N-MINT
☐ 1, b&w		0.50	1.50	2.50
☐ 2, b&w		0.50	1.50	2.50
☐ 3, b&w		0.50	1.50	2.50
☐ 4, b&w		0.50	1.50	2.50

STARFIRE
DC

	ORIG.	GOOD	FINE	N-MINT
☐ 1, Sep 76	0.30	0.40	1.20	2.00
☐ 2, Nov 76	0.30	0.30	0.90	1.50
☐ 3, Jan 77	0.30	0.30	0.90	1.50

	ORIG.	GOOD	FINE	N-MINT
☐ 4, Mar 77	0.30	0.30	0.90	1.50
☐ 5, May 77	0.30	0.30	0.90	1.50
☐ 6, Jul 77	0.30	0.30	0.90	1.50
☐ 7, Sep 77	0.30	0.30	0.90	1.50
☐ 8, Nov 77	0.30	0.30	0.90	1.50

STARFORCE SIX SPECIAL
AC

		GOOD	FINE	N-MINT
☐ 1, Nov 84		0.30	0.90	1.50

STARHEAD PRESENTS
STARHEAD

		GOOD	FINE	N-MINT
☐ 1		0.19	0.57	0.95
☐ 2		0.19	0.57	0.95

STARJAMMERS (mini-series)
MARVEL
☐ 1, Oct 95, enhanced cardstock cover;OverPower cards bound-in

	2.95	0.59	1.77	2.95

☐ 2, Nov 95, enhanced cardstock cover

	2.95	0.59	1.77	2.95

☐ 3, Dec 95, enhanced cardstock cover

	2.95	0.59	1.77	2.95

☐ 4, Jan 96, enhanced cardstock cover;final issue

	2.95	0.59	1.77	2.95

STARJONGLEUR, THE
TRYLVERTEL

	ORIG.	GOOD	FINE	N-MINT
☐ 1, b&w		0.40	1.20	2.00
☐ 2, Win 87, b&w	2.00	0.40	1.20	2.00

STARK: FUTURE
AIRCEL

		GOOD	FINE	N-MINT
☐ 1, b&w		0.40	1.20	2.00
☐ 2		0.34	1.02	1.70
☐ 3		0.34	1.02	1.70
☐ 4		0.34	1.02	1.70
☐ 5		0.34	1.02	1.70
☐ 6		0.34	1.02	1.70
☐ 7		0.34	1.02	1.70
☐ 8		0.34	1.02	1.70
☐ 9		0.34	1.02	1.70
☐ 10		0.34	1.02	1.70
☐ 11		0.34	1.02	1.70
☐ 12		0.34	1.02	1.70
☐ 13		0.34	1.02	1.70
☐ 14		0.34	1.02	1.70
☐ 15		0.34	1.02	1.70
☐ 16		0.34	1.02	1.70
☐ 17		0.34	1.02	1.70

STARLIGHT
ETERNITY

		GOOD	FINE	N-MINT
☐ 1		0.39	1.17	1.95

STARLIGHT AGENCY, THE
ANTARCTIC

	ORIG.	GOOD	FINE	N-MINT
☐ 1, Jun 91, b&w	1.95	0.50	1.50	2.50
☐ 2, Aug 91, b&w	1.95	0.50	1.50	2.50
☐ 3, Sep 91, b&w	1.95	0.50	1.50	2.50

STARLOVE
FORBIDDEN FRUIT

	ORIG.	GOOD	FINE	N-MINT
☐ 1, adult, b&w	2.95	0.59	1.77	2.95
☐ 2, adult, b&w		0.70	2.10	3.50

STARMAN
DC

	ORIG.	GOOD	FINE	N-MINT
☐ 1, Oct 88, O:Starman	1.00	0.60	1.80	3.00
☐ 2, Nov 88	1.00	0.40	1.20	2.00
☐ 3, Dec 88	1.00	0.40	1.20	2.00
☐ 4, Dec 88	1.00	0.40	1.20	2.00
☐ 5, Jan 89, Invasion!	1.00	0.30	0.90	1.50
☐ 6, Jan 89, Invasion!	1.00	0.30	0.90	1.50
☐ 7, Feb 89	1.00	0.30	0.90	1.50
☐ 8, Mar 89, A:Lady Quark	1.00	0.30	0.90	1.50

☐ 9, Apr 89, A:Batman,O:Blockbuster

	1.00	0.30	0.90	1.50

	ORIG.	GOOD	FINE	N-MINT
10, May 89, A:Batman, O:Blockbuster	1.00	0.30	0.90	1.50
11, Jun 89	1.00	0.30	0.90	1.50
12, Jul 89	1.00	0.30	0.90	1.50
13, Aug 89	1.00	0.30	0.90	1.50
14, Sep 89, Superman	1.00	0.30	0.90	1.50
15, Oct 89	1.00	0.30	0.90	1.50
16, Nov 89	1.00	0.30	0.90	1.50
17, Dec 89, Power Girl	1.00	0.30	0.90	1.50
18, Jan 90	1.00	0.20	0.60	1.00
19, Feb 90	1.00	0.20	0.60	1.00
20, Mar 90	1.00	0.20	0.60	1.00
21, Apr 90	1.00	0.20	0.60	1.00
22, May 90	1.00	0.20	0.60	1.00
23, Jun 90	1.00	0.20	0.60	1.00
24, Jul 90	1.00	0.20	0.60	1.00
25, Aug 90	1.00	0.20	0.60	1.00
26, Sep 90	1.00	0.20	0.60	1.00
27, Oct 90	1.00	0.20	0.60	1.00
28, Nov 90, Superman	1.00	0.20	0.60	1.00
29, Dec 90	1.00	0.20	0.60	1.00
30, Jan 91	1.00	0.20	0.60	1.00
31, Feb 91	1.00	0.20	0.60	1.00
32, Mar 91	1.00	0.20	0.60	1.00
33, Apr 91	1.00	0.20	0.60	1.00
34, May 91	1.00	0.20	0.60	1.00
35, Jun 91	1.00	0.20	0.60	1.00
36, Jul 91	1.00	0.20	0.60	1.00
37, Aug 91	1.00	0.20	0.60	1.00
38, Sep 91, War of Gods	1.00	0.20	0.60	1.00
39, Oct 91	1.00	0.20	0.60	1.00
40, Nov 91	1.00	0.20	0.60	1.00
41, Dec 91	1.00	0.20	0.60	1.00
42, Jan 92	1.00	0.20	0.60	1.00
43, Feb 92	1.00	0.20	0.60	1.00
44, Mar 92, Lobo	1.25	0.25	0.75	1.25
45, Apr 92, Lobo	1.25	0.25	0.75	1.25

STARMAN (1994-)

	ORIG.	GOOD	FINE	N-MINT
0, Oct 94	1.95	1.40	4.20	7.00
1, Nov 94	1.95	1.40	4.20	7.00
2, Dec 94	1.95	1.20	3.60	6.00
3, Jan 95	1.95	1.20	3.60	6.00
4, Feb 95	1.95	0.90	2.70	4.50
5, Mar 95	1.95	0.90	2.70	4.50
6, Apr 95	1.95	0.70	2.10	3.50
7, May 95	1.95	0.70	2.10	3.50
8, Jun 95	2.25	0.60	1.80	3.00
9, Jul 95	2.25	0.60	1.80	3.00
10, Aug 95, V:Solomon Grundy	2.25	0.60	1.80	3.00
11, Sep 95	2.25	0.50	1.50	2.50
12, Oct 95, "Sins of the Child" Part 1 of 5	2.25	0.45	1.35	2.25
13, Nov 95, "Sins of the Child" Part 2 of 5; "Underworld Unleashed"	2.25	0.45	1.35	2.25
14, Dec 95, "Sins of the Child" Part 3 of 5	2.25	0.45	1.35	2.25
15, Jan 96, "Sins of the Child" Part 4 of 5	2.25	0.45	1.35	2.25
16, Feb 96, "Sins of the Child" Part 5 of 5	2.25	0.45	1.35	2.25
17, Mar 96	2.25	0.45	1.35	2.25
18, Apr 96, Original Starman versus The Mist	2.25	0.45	1.35	2.25
19, Jun 96, "Talking with David '96"	2.25	0.45	1.35	2.25
20, Jul 96, "Sand of the Stars" Part 1 of 4;A:Wesley Dodds, Dian Belmont	2.25	0.45	1.35	2.25

STARMASTERS (mini-series)
MARVEL

	ORIG.	GOOD	FINE	N-MINT
1, Dec 95, Beta Ray Bill, The Silver Surfer, and Quasar team up	1.95	0.39	1.17	1.95
2, Jan 96	1.95	0.39	1.17	1.95
3, Feb 96, final issue;continues in *Cosmic Powers Unlimited* #4	1.95	0.39	1.17	1.95

STARRIORS

	ORIG.	GOOD	FINE	N-MINT
1	0.75	0.30	0.90	1.50
2	0.75	0.20	0.60	1.00
3	0.75	0.20	0.60	1.00
4	0.75	0.20	0.60	1.00

STARSLAYER
ACCLAIM/WINDJAMMER

	ORIG.	GOOD	FINE	N-MINT
5, Aug 95, MGr	2.50	0.50	1.50	2.50
6, Aug 95, MGr	2.50	0.50	1.50	2.50
7, Sep 95, MGr	2.50	0.50	1.50	2.50

PACIFIC

	ORIG.	GOOD	FINE	N-MINT
1, Feb 82, MGr	1.00	0.50	1.50	2.50
2, Apr 82, MGr, SA, DSt Groo, 1:Rocketeer	1.00	2.40	7.20	12.00
3, Jun 82, MGr, DSt Rocketeer	1.00	1.60	4.80	8.00
4, Aug 82, MGr	1.00	0.40	1.20	2.00
5, Nov 82, MGr, Groo	1.00	3.00	9.00	15.00
6, Apr 83, MGr (moves to First Comics)	1.00	0.40	1.20	2.00

STARSLAYER (former Pacific title)
FIRST

	ORIG.	GOOD	FINE	N-MINT
7, Aug 83	1.00	0.30	0.90	1.50
8, Sep 83	1.00	0.30	0.90	1.50
9, Oct 83	1.00	0.30	0.90	1.50
10, Nov 83	1.00	0.30	0.90	1.50
11, Dec 83	1.00	0.30	0.90	1.50
12, Jan 84	1.00	0.30	0.90	1.50
13, Feb 84	1.00	0.30	0.90	1.50
14, Mar 84	1.00	0.30	0.90	1.50
15, Apr 84	1.00	0.30	0.90	1.50
16, May 84	1.00	0.30	0.90	1.50
17, Jun 84		0.20	0.60	1.00
18, Jul 84		0.20	0.60	1.00
19, Aug 84		0.20	0.60	1.00
20, Sep 84		0.25	0.75	1.25
21, Oct 84		0.25	0.75	1.25
22, Nov 84		0.25	0.75	1.25
23, Dec 84		0.25	0.75	1.25
24, Jan 85		0.25	0.75	1.25
25, Feb 85		0.25	0.75	1.25
26, Mar 85		0.25	0.75	1.25
27, Apr 85		0.25	0.75	1.25
28, May 85		0.25	0.75	1.25
29, Jun 85		0.25	0.75	1.25
30, Jul 85		0.25	0.75	1.25
31, Aug 85		0.25	0.75	1.25
32, Sep 85		0.25	0.75	1.25
33, Oct 85		0.25	0.75	1.25
34, Nov 85		0.25	0.75	1.25

STARSTONE
AIRCEL

	ORIG.	GOOD	FINE	N-MINT
1, b&w		0.34	1.02	1.70
2, b&w		0.34	1.02	1.70
3, b&w		0.34	1.02	1.70

STARSTRUCK
EPIC

	ORIG.	GOOD	FINE	N-MINT
1, MK	1.50	0.30	0.90	1.50
2, MK	1.50	0.30	0.90	1.50
3, MK	1.50	0.30	0.90	1.50
4, MK	1.50	0.30	0.90	1.50
5, MK	1.50	0.30	0.90	1.50
6, MK	1.50	0.30	0.90	1.50

	ORIG.	GOOD	FINE	N-MINT

STARSTRUCK: THE EXPANDING UNIVERSE
DARK HORSE
	ORIG.	GOOD	FINE	N-MINT
❑ 1, MK b&w		0.59	1.77	2.95
❑ 2, MK b&w		0.59	1.77	2.95
❑ 3, MK b&w		0.59	1.77	2.95
❑ 4, MK trading cards		0.59	1.77	2.95

STARTLING CRIME ILLUSTRATED
CALIBER
	ORIG.	GOOD	FINE	N-MINT
❑ 1, b&w	2.95	0.59	1.77	2.95

STATIC
DC/MILESTONE
	ORIG.	GOOD	FINE	N-MINT
❑ 1, Jun 93	1.50	0.70	2.10	3.50
❑ 1, Jun 93, poster, trading card	2.95	0.59	1.77	2.95
❑ 2, Jul 93, O:Static	1.50	0.40	1.20	2.00
❑ 3, Aug 93	1.50	0.30	0.90	1.50
❑ 4, Sep 93	1.50	0.30	0.90	1.50
❑ 5, Oct 93	1.50	0.30	0.90	1.50
❑ 6, Nov 93	1.50	0.30	0.90	1.50
❑ 7, Dec 93	1.50	0.30	0.90	1.50
❑ 8, Jan 94, Shadow War	1.50	0.30	0.90	1.50
❑ 9, Feb 94	1.50	0.30	0.90	1.50
❑ 10, Mar 94	1.50	0.30	0.90	1.50
❑ 11, Apr 94	1.50	0.30	0.90	1.50
❑ 12, May 94	1.50	0.30	0.90	1.50
❑ 13, Jun 94	1.50	0.30	0.90	1.50
❑ 14, Aug 94	2.50	0.50	1.50	2.50
❑ 16, Oct 94	1.75	0.35	1.05	1.75
❑ 17, Nov 94	1.75	0.35	1.05	1.75
❑ 18, Dec 94	1.75	0.35	1.05	1.75
❑ 19, Jan 95	1.75	0.35	1.05	1.75
❑ 20, Feb 95	1.75	0.35	1.05	1.75
❑ 21, Mar 95	1.75	0.35	1.05	1.75
❑ 22, Apr 95	1.75	0.35	1.05	1.75
❑ 23, Jun 95	1.75	0.35	1.05	1.75
❑ 24, Jul 95	1.75	0.35	1.05	1.75
❑ 25, Jul 95, "Long, Hot Summer"	3.95	0.79	2.37	3.95
❑ 26, Aug 95, "Long, Hot Summer"	2.50	0.50	1.50	2.50
❑ 27, Sep 95, "Long, Hot Summer"	0.99	0.20	0.59	0.99
❑ 28, Oct 95	2.50	0.50	1.50	2.50
❑ 29, Nov 95	2.50	0.50	1.50	2.50
❑ 30, Dec 95, D:Larry	2.50	0.50	1.50	2.50
❑ 31, Jan 96	0.99	0.20	0.59	0.99
❑ 32, Feb 96	2.50	0.50	1.50	2.50
❑ 33, Mar 96	2.50	0.50	1.50	2.50
❑ 34, Apr 96	2.50	0.50	1.50	2.50
❑ 35, May 96	2.50	0.50	1.50	2.50
❑ 36, Jun 96	2.50	0.50	1.50	2.50

STEALTH FORCE
MALIBU
	ORIG.	GOOD	FINE	N-MINT
❑ 1		0.39	1.17	1.95
❑ 2		0.39	1.17	1.95
❑ 3		0.39	1.17	1.95
❑ 4		0.39	1.17	1.95
❑ 5		0.39	1.17	1.95
❑ 6		0.39	1.17	1.95
❑ 7, (becomes Eternity title)		0.39	1.17	1.95

STEALTH FORCE (was Malibu title)
ETERNITY
	ORIG.	GOOD	FINE	N-MINT
❑ 8		0.39	1.17	1.95

STECH
SILVERWOLF
	ORIG.	GOOD	FINE	N-MINT
❑ 1, b&w		0.30	0.90	1.50

STEED AND MRS. PEEL
ECLIPSE
	ORIG.	GOOD	FINE	N-MINT
❑ 1, Dec 90, Ian Gibson	4.95	0.99	2.97	4.95
❑ 2, May 91, Ian Gibson	4.95	0.99	2.97	4.95
❑ 3, 92, Ian Gibson	4.95	0.99	2.97	4.95

STEEL
DC
	ORIG.	GOOD	FINE	N-MINT
❑ 0, Oct 94	1.50	0.30	0.90	1.50
❑ 1	1.50	0.30	0.90	1.50
❑ 2	1.50	0.30	0.90	1.50
❑ 3	1.50	0.30	0.90	1.50
❑ 4, May 94	1.50	0.30	0.90	1.50
❑ 5, Jun 94	1.50	0.30	0.90	1.50
❑ 6, Jul 94	1.50	0.30	0.90	1.50
❑ 7, Aug 94	1.50	0.30	0.90	1.50
❑ 8, Sep 94	1.50	0.30	0.90	1.50
❑ 9, Nov 94	1.50	0.30	0.90	1.50
❑ 10, Dec 94	1.50	0.30	0.90	1.50
❑ 11, Jan 95	1.50	0.30	0.90	1.50
❑ 12, Feb 95	1.50	0.30	0.90	1.50
❑ 13, Mar 95	1.50	0.30	0.90	1.50
❑ 14, Apr 95	1.50	0.30	0.90	1.50
❑ 15, May 95	1.50	0.30	0.90	1.50
❑ 16, Jun 95	1.95	0.39	1.17	1.95
❑ 17, Jul 95	1.95	0.39	1.17	1.95
❑ 18, Aug 95	1.95	0.39	1.17	1.95
❑ 19, Sep 95	1.95	0.39	1.17	1.95
❑ 20, Oct 95	1.95	0.39	1.17	1.95
❑ 21, Nov 95, "Underworld Unleashed"	1.95	0.39	1.17	1.95
❑ 22, Dec 95	1.95	0.39	1.17	1.95
❑ 23, Jan 96	1.95	0.39	1.17	1.95
❑ 24, Feb 96	1.95	0.39	1.17	1.95
❑ 25, Mar 96	1.95	0.39	1.17	1.95
❑ 26, May 96	1.95	0.39	1.17	1.95
❑ 27, Jun 96	1.95	0.39	1.17	1.95
❑ 28, Jul 96, V:Plasmus	1.95	0.39	1.17	1.95

STEEL ANNUAL
	ORIG.	GOOD	FINE	N-MINT
❑ 1, 94, Elseworlds	2.95	0.59	1.77	2.95
❑ 2, 95, "Year One"	3.95	0.79	2.37	3.95

STEEL CLAW
FLEETWAY/QUALITY
	ORIG.	GOOD	FINE	N-MINT
❑ 1		0.15	0.45	0.75
❑ 2		0.15	0.45	0.75
❑ 3		0.15	0.45	0.75
❑ 4		0.25	0.75	1.25
❑ 5		0.25	0.75	1.25

STEEL PULSE
TRUE FICTION
	ORIG.	GOOD	FINE	N-MINT
❑ 1, b&w		0.40	1.20	2.00
❑ 2, b&w		0.40	1.20	2.00
❑ 3, b&w		0.40	1.20	2.00
❑ 4		0.70	2.10	3.50

STEEL STERLING (formerly Shield)
ARCHIE
	ORIG.	GOOD	FINE	N-MINT
❑ 4, Jan 84		0.15	0.45	0.75
❑ 5, Mar 84		0.15	0.45	0.75
❑ 6, May 84		0.15	0.45	0.75
❑ 7, Jul 84		0.15	0.45	0.75

STEELDRAGON STORIES
STEELDRAGON
	ORIG.	GOOD	FINE	N-MINT
❑ 1	1.50	0.30	0.90	1.50

STEELE DESTINIES
NIGHTSCAPES
	ORIG.	GOOD	FINE	N-MINT
❑ 1, Apr 95, b&w	2.95	0.59	1.77	2.95
❑ 2, Jun 95, b&w	2.95	0.59	1.77	2.95
❑ 3, Sep 95, b&w	2.95	0.59	1.77	2.95

	ORIG.	GOOD	FINE	N-MINT
STEELGRIP STARKEY				
EPIC				
☐ 1, Jun 86......................1.50	0.30	0.90	1.50
☐ 2, Aug 86 ....1.50	0.30	0.90	1.50
☐ 3, Nov 86 ....1.50	0.30	0.90	1.50
☐ 4, Dec 86......................1.50	0.30	0.90	1.50
☐ 5, Jan 87 ....1.50	0.30	0.90	1.50
☐ 6, May 87 ....1.75	0.35	1.05	1.75
STEELTOWN ROCKERS				
MARVEL				
☐ 1, Apr 90......................1.00	0.20	0.60	1.00
☐ 2, May 90 ....1.00	0.20	0.60	1.00
☐ 3, Jun 90......................1.00	0.20	0.60	1.00
☐ 4, Jul 90......................1.00	0.20	0.60	1.00
☐ 5, Aug 90......................1.00	0.20	0.60	1.00
☐ 6, Sep 90......................1.00	0.20	0.60	1.00
STELLAR LOSERS				
ANTARCTIC				
☐ 1, Feb 93, b&w..............2.50	0.50	1.50	2.50
☐ 2, Apr 93, b&w..............2.50	0.50	1.50	2.50
☐ 3, Jun 93, b&w..............2.50	0.50	1.50	2.50
STEPHEN DARKLORD				
RAK				
☐ 1, b&w	0.35	1.05	1.75
☐ 2, b&w	0.35	1.05	1.75
☐ 3, b&w	0.35	1.05	1.75
STERN WHEELER				
SPOTLIGHT				
☐ 1	0.35	1.05	1.75
STEVE CANYON 3-D				
KITCHEN SINK				
☐ 1, Jun 86.........................	0.40	1.20	2.00
STEVE ROGERS CAPTAIN AMERICA				
MARVEL				
☐ 444, Oct 95, (was *Captain America*)				
......................1.50	0.50	1.50	2.50
☐ 445, Nov 95, R:Sharon Carter;Cap revived				
......................1.50	0.30	0.90	1.50
☐ 446, Dec 95....................1.50	0.30	0.90	1.50
☐ 447, Jan 96 ....1.50	0.30	0.90	1.50
☐ 448, Feb 96 ....2.95	0.59	1.77	2.95
☐ 449, Mar 96, (returns to being *Captain America*)				
......................1.50	0.30	0.90	1.50
STEVEN				
KITCHEN SINK				
☐ 1, b&w	0.59	1.77	2.95
☐ 2, b&w	0.59	1.77	2.95
☐ 3, b&w	0.59	1.77	2.95
☐ 4, b&w	0.59	1.77	2.95
☐ 6, b&w 3.50	0.70	2.10	3.50
STEVEN'S COMICS				
DK PRESS/YELL COMICS				
☐ 3, 96, b&w 3.00	0.60	1.80	3.00
STICKBOY				
FANTAGRAPHICS				
☐ 1, 1st printing b&w	0.50	1.50	2.50
☐ 1, 2nd printing	0.55	1.65	2.75
☐ 2, b&w	0.50	1.50	2.50
☐ 3, b&w	0.50	1.50	2.50
REVOLUTIONARY				
☐ 4, Nov 90, b&w..............2.95	0.59	1.77	2.95
☐ 5, Feb 92, b&w..............2.50	0.50	1.50	2.50
STARHEAD				
☐ 1, b&w 2.50	0.50	1.50	2.50
☐ 2, b&w 2.50	0.50	1.50	2.50
☐ 3, b&w 2.50	0.50	1.50	2.50
☐ 4, b&w 2.50	0.50	1.50	2.50
☐ 5, b&w 2.50	0.50	1.50	2.50
☐ 6, b&w 2.50	0.50	1.50	2.50

	ORIG.	GOOD	FINE	N-MINT
STIG'S INFERNO				
VORTEX				
☐ 1, 84 ....1.95	1.00	3.00	5.00
☐ 1, b&w Book....................	1.39	4.17	6.95
☐ 2, 84 ....1.95	0.70	2.10	3.50
☐ 3	0.70	2.10	3.50
☐ 4	0.70	2.10	3.50
☐ 5, (moves to Eclipse)........	0.35	1.05	1.75
STIG'S INFERNO (was Vortex title)				
ECLIPSE				
☐ 6, b&w.............................	0.30	0.90	1.50
☐ 7, b&w.............................	0.30	0.90	1.50
STIMULATOR				
EROS COMIX				
☐ 1, adult, b&w...................	0.50	1.50	2.50
STING OF THE GREEN HORNET				
NOW				
☐ 1, Jun 92, bagged with poster				
............................2.50	0.55	1.65	2.75
☐ 2, Jul 92............................2.50	0.50	1.50	2.50
☐ 2, Jul 92, bagged with poster				
............................2.75	0.55	1.65	2.75
☐ 3, Aug 92 ....2.50	0.50	1.50	2.50
☐ 3, Aug 92, bagged with poster				
............................2.75	0.55	1.65	2.75
☐ 4, Sep 92 ....2.50	0.50	1.50	2.50
☐ 4, Sep 92, stitched with poster				
............................2.75	0.55	1.65	2.75
STINZ				
FANTAGRAPHICS				
☐ 1, b&w.............................	0.80	2.40	4.00
☐ 2, b&w.............................	0.60	1.80	3.00
☐ 3, b&w.............................	0.40	1.20	2.00
☐ 4, b&w.............................	0.40	1.20	2.00
STINZ (Volume two, was Fantagraphics title)				
BRAVE NEW WORDS				
☐ 1, b&w.............................	0.60	1.80	3.00
☐ 2, b&w.............................	0.50	1.50	2.50
STINZ: BUM STEER				
MU				
☐ 0, Oct 95, nn;one-shot;b&w				
............................2.95	0.59	1.77	2.95
STINZ: FAMILY VALUES				
☐ 0, nn, b&w....................2.50	0.50	1.50	2.50
STINZ: OLD MAN OUT				
MU PRESS				
☐ 0, Oct 94 ....2.95	0.59	1.77	2.95
STINZ: THE BOBWAR				
MU				
☐ 0, Feb 95, one-shot;b&w				
............................2.95	0.59	1.77	2.95
STINZ: WARHORSE				
MU PRESS				
☐ 0, Mar 93 ....9.95	1.99	5.97	9.95
STONE PROTECTORS				
HARVEY				
☐ 1 ....1.50	0.30	0.90	1.50
☐ 2 ....1.50	0.30	0.90	1.50
☐ 3, Sep 94 ....1.50	0.30	0.90	1.50
STORM (mini-series)				
MARVEL				
☐ 2, Mar 96, enhanced cardstock cover				
............................2.95	0.59	1.77	2.95
☐ 3, Apr 96, enhanced cardstock cover				
............................2.95	0.59	1.77	2.95
☐ 4, May 96, enhanced cardstock cover;final issue				
............................2.95	0.59	1.77	2.95

	ORIG.	GOOD	FINE	N-MINT

STORMQUEST
CALIBER/SKY

	ORIG.	GOOD	FINE	N-MINT
1, Nov 94	1.95	0.39	1.17	1.95
2, Dec 94	1.95	0.39	1.17	1.95
3, 95	1.95	0.39	1.17	1.95
4, 95	1.95	0.39	1.17	1.95
5, 95	1.95	0.39	1.17	1.95
6, 95	1.95	0.39	1.17	1.95

STORMWATCH
IMAGE

	ORIG.	GOOD	FINE	N-MINT
0	2.50	0.50	1.50	2.50
1	1.95	0.39	1.17	1.95
1, gold foil cover	1.95	0.39	1.17	1.95
2, May 93	1.95	0.39	1.17	1.95
3, Jul 93, A:Backlash	1.95	0.70	2.10	3.50
4, Aug 93,cover says Oct	1.95	0.39	1.17	1.95
5, Nov 93	1.95	0.39	1.17	1.95
6	1.95	0.39	1.17	1.95
9, Apr 94	2.50	0.50	1.50	2.50
10, 94, variant cover		1.00	3.00	5.00
10, Jun 94	1.95	0.39	1.17	1.95
11, Aug 94	1.95	0.39	1.17	1.95
12, Aug 94	1.95	0.39	1.17	1.95
13, Sep 94	1.95	0.39	1.17	1.95
14, Sep 94	1.95	0.39	1.17	1.95
15, Oct 94	1.95	0.39	1.17	1.95
17, Dec 94	2.50	0.50	1.50	2.50
18, Jan 95	2.50	0.50	1.50	2.50
20, Mar 95	2.50	0.50	1.50	2.50
21, Apr 95, cover says #1	2.50	0.50	1.50	2.50
22, May 95, "WildStorm Rising" Chapter 9;bound-in trading cards	2.50	0.50	1.50	2.50
23, Jun 95	2.50	0.50	1.50	2.50
24, Jul 95	2.50	0.50	1.50	2.50
25, May 94	2.50	0.50	1.50	2.50
25, Aug 95, second printing	2.50	0.50	1.50	2.50
26, Aug 95	2.50	0.50	1.50	2.50
28, Sep 95, cover forms right half of diptych with issue #29	2.50	0.50	1.50	2.50
29, Oct 95, cover forms left half of diptych with issue #28;cover says "Nov";indicia says "Oct"	2.50	0.50	1.50	2.50
31, Dec 95	2.50	0.50	1.50	2.50
32, Jan 96	2.50	0.50	1.50	2.50
33, Feb 96	2.50	0.50	1.50	2.50
35, Apr 96, "Fire from Heaven" Part 5	2.50	0.50	1.50	2.50

STORMWATCH SPECIAL

	ORIG.	GOOD	FINE	N-MINT
2, May 95	3.50	0.70	2.10	3.50

STORMWATCHER
ECLIPSE

	ORIG.	GOOD	FINE	N-MINT
1, b&w		0.40	1.20	2.00
2, b&w		0.40	1.20	2.00
3, b&w		0.40	1.20	2.00
4, b&w		0.40	1.20	2.00

STRAND
TRIDENT

	ORIG.	GOOD	FINE	N-MINT
1, b&w	2.50	0.50	1.50	2.50
2, b&w	2.50	0.50	1.50	2.50

STRANGE ADVENTURES
DC

	ORIG.	GOOD	FINE	N-MINT
136, Jan 62	0.12	5.00	15.00	25.00
137, Feb 62	0.12	5.00	15.00	25.00
138, Mar 62, Atomic Knights	0.12	10.00	30.00	50.00
141, Jun 62	0.12	5.00	15.00	25.00
142, Jul 62	0.12	5.00	15.00	25.00
143, Aug 62	0.12	5.00	15.00	25.00
144, Sep 62, Atomic Knights	0.12	8.00	24.00	40.00
145, Oct 62	0.12	5.00	15.00	25.00
146, Nov 62	0.12	5.00	15.00	25.00
147, Dec 62, Atomic Knights	0.12	8.00	24.00	40.00
148, Jan 63	0.12	4.00	12.00	20.00
149, Feb 63	0.12	4.00	12.00	20.00
150, Mar 63, Atomic Knights	0.12	6.00	18.00	30.00
151, Apr 63	0.12	4.00	12.00	20.00
152, May 63	0.12	4.00	12.00	20.00
153, Jun 63, Atomic Knights	0.12	6.00	18.00	30.00
154, Jul 63	0.12	4.00	12.00	20.00
155, Aug 63	0.12	4.00	12.00	20.00
156, Sep 63, Atomic Knights	0.12	6.00	18.00	30.00
157, Oct 63	0.12	4.00	12.00	20.00
158, Nov 63	0.12	4.00	12.00	20.00
159, Dec 63	0.12	4.00	12.00	20.00
160, Jan 64, Atomic Knights	0.12	6.00	18.00	30.00
161, Feb 64	0.12	3.00	9.00	15.00
162, Mar 64	0.12	3.00	9.00	15.00
163, Apr 64	0.12	3.00	9.00	15.00
164, May 64	0.12	3.00	9.00	15.00
165, Jun 64	0.12	3.00	9.00	15.00
166, Jul 64	0.12	3.00	9.00	15.00
167, Aug 64	0.12	3.00	9.00	15.00
169, Oct 64	0.12	3.00	9.00	15.00
170, Nov 64	0.12	3.00	9.00	15.00
171, Dec 64	0.12	3.00	9.00	15.00
172, Jan 65	0.12	3.00	9.00	15.00
173, Feb 65	0.12	3.00	9.00	15.00
174, Mar 65	0.12	3.00	9.00	15.00
176, May 65	0.12	3.00	9.00	15.00
178, Jul 65	0.12	3.00	9.00	15.00
179, Aug 65	0.12	3.00	9.00	15.00
180, Sep 65, Animal Man	0.12	40.00	120.00	200.00
181, Oct 65	0.12	2.00	6.00	10.00
182, Nov 65	0.12	2.00	6.00	10.00
183, Dec 65	0.12	2.00	6.00	10.00
184, Jan 66, Animal Man	0.12	24.00	72.00	120.00
185, Feb 66	0.12	2.00	6.00	10.00
186, Mar 66	0.12	2.00	6.00	10.00
188, May 66	0.12	2.00	6.00	10.00
189, Jun 66	0.12	2.00	6.00	10.00
190, Jul 66, Animal Man	0.12	24.00	72.00	120.00
191, Aug 66	0.12	1.60	4.80	8.00
192, Sep 66	0.12	1.60	4.80	8.00
193, Oct 66	0.12	1.60	4.80	8.00
194, Nov 66	0.12	1.60	4.80	8.00
195, Dec 66, Animal Man	0.12	15.00	45.00	75.00
197, Feb 67	0.12	1.60	4.80	8.00
198, Mar 67	0.12	1.60	4.80	8.00
199, Apr 67	0.12	1.60	4.80	8.00
200, May 67	0.12	1.60	4.80	8.00
201, Jun 67, Animal Man	0.12	10.00	30.00	50.00
202, Jul 67	0.12	1.60	4.80	8.00
203, Aug 67	0.12	1.60	4.80	8.00
204, Sep 67	0.12	1.60	4.80	8.00
205, Oct 67, Deadman	0.12	10.00	30.00	50.00
206, Nov 67, Deadman	0.12	8.00	24.00	40.00
207, Dec 67, Deadman	0.12	6.00	18.00	30.00
208, Jan 68, Deadman	0.12	6.00	18.00	30.00
209, Feb 68, Deadman	0.12	6.00	18.00	30.00
210, Mar 68, Deadman	0.12	6.00	18.00	30.00
211, Apr 68, Deadman	0.12	4.00	12.00	20.00
212, Jun 68, Deadman	0.12	4.00	12.00	20.00
213, Aug 68, Deadman	0.12	4.00	12.00	20.00
214, Oct 68, Deadman	0.12	4.00	12.00	20.00

	ORIG.	GOOD	FINE	N-MINT
❑ 215, Dec 68, Deadman...	0.12	4.00	12.00	20.00
❑ 216, Feb 69, Deadman ...	0.12	4.00	12.00	20.00
❑ 217, Apr 69	0.12	0.80	2.40	4.00
❑ 218, Jun 69.....................	0.12	0.80	2.40	4.00
❑ 219, Aug 69	0.15	0.80	2.40	4.00
❑ 220, Oct 69	0.15	0.80	2.40	4.00
❑ 221, Dec 69	0.15	0.80	2.40	4.00
❑ 222, Feb 70, Adam Strange;NA				
	0.15	2.00	6.00	10.00
❑ 223, Apr 70	0.15	0.80	2.40	4.00
❑ 224, Jun 70	0.15	0.80	2.40	4.00
❑ 225, Aug 70	0.15	0.80	2.40	4.00
❑ 226, Oct 70	0.25	0.80	2.40	4.00
❑ 227, Dec 70...................	0.25	0.80	2.40	4.00
❑ 228, Feb 71	0.25	0.80	2.40	4.00
❑ 229, Apr 71	0.25	0.80	2.40	4.00
❑ 230, Jun 71	0.25	0.80	2.40	4.00
❑ 231, Aug 71	0.25	0.80	2.40	4.00
❑ 232, Oct 71	0.25	0.60	1.80	3.00
❑ 233, Dec 71...................	0.25	0.60	1.80	3.00
❑ 234, Feb 72	0.25	0.60	1.80	3.00
❑ 235, Apr 72	0.25	0.60	1.80	3.00
❑ 236, Jun 72	0.25	0.60	1.80	3.00
❑ 237, Jun 72	0.20	0.60	1.80	3.00
❑ 238, Oct 72	0.20	0.60	1.80	3.00
❑ 239, Dec 72...................	0.20	0.60	1.80	3.00
❑ 240, Feb 73	0.20	0.60	1.80	3.00
❑ 241, Apr 73	0.20	0.60	1.80	3.00
❑ 242, Jul 73	0.20	0.60	1.80	3.00
❑ 243, Sep 73	0.20	0.60	1.80	3.00
❑ 244, Nov 73	0.20	0.60	1.80	3.00

STRANGE ATTRACTORS
RETROGRAFIX

	ORIG.	GOOD	FINE	N-MINT
❑ 1, May 93, b&w.............	2.50	0.70	2.10	3.50
❑ 2, Aug 93, b&w.............	2.50	0.50	1.50	2.50
❑ 3, Nov 93, b&w.............	2.50	0.50	1.50	2.50
❑ 4, Feb 94, b&w.............	2.50	0.50	1.50	2.50
❑ 5, May 94, b&w.............	2.50	0.50	1.50	2.50
❑ 6, b&w	2.50	0.50	1.50	2.50
❑ 7, b&w	2.50	0.50	1.50	2.50
❑ 8, Jan 95, b&w.............	2.50	0.50	1.50	2.50
❑ 9, b&w	2.50	0.50	1.50	2.50
❑ 10, b&w	2.50	0.50	1.50	2.50
❑ 11, Sep 95, b&w	2.50	0.50	1.50	2.50

STRANGE BREW
AARDVARK-VANAHEIM

	ORIG.	GOOD	FINE	N-MINT
❑ 1		0.60	1.80	3.00

STRANGE COMBAT TALES
EPIC

	ORIG.	GOOD	FINE	N-MINT
❑ 1	2.50	0.50	1.50	2.50
❑ 2	2.50	0.50	1.50	2.50
❑ 3	2.50	0.50	1.50	2.50
❑ 4	2.50	0.50	1.50	2.50

STRANGE DAYS
ECLIPSE

	ORIG.	GOOD	FINE	N-MINT
❑ 1		0.30	0.90	1.50
❑ 2		0.30	0.90	1.50
❑ 3		0.30	0.90	1.50

STRANGE EMBRACE
ATOMEKA

	ORIG.	GOOD	FINE	N-MINT
❑ 1, b&w..........................	3.95	0.79	2.37	3.95
❑ 2, b&w..........................	3.95	0.79	2.37	3.95
❑ 3, b&w..........................	3.95	0.79	2.37	3.95

STRANGE SPORTS STORIES
DC

	ORIG.	GOOD	FINE	N-MINT
❑ 1, Oct 73, b&w..............	0.20	0.50	1.50	2.50
❑ 2, Dec 73, trading cards.	0.20	0.50	1.50	2.50
❑ 3, Feb 74, trading cards .	0.20	0.50	1.50	2.50

	ORIG.	GOOD	FINE	N-MINT
❑ 4, Apr 74, trading cards..	0.20	0.50	1.50	2.50
❑ 5, Jun 74, trading cards..	0.20	0.50	1.50	2.50
❑ 6, Aug 74, trading cards .	0.20	0.50	1.50	2.50

STRANGE TALES
MARVEL

	ORIG.	GOOD	FINE	N-MINT
❑ 1	0.10	300.00	900.00	1500.00
❑ 2	0.10	120.00	360.00	600.00
❑ 3	0.10	80.00	240.00	400.00
❑ 4	0.10	70.00	210.00	350.00
❑ 5	0.10	70.00	210.00	350.00
❑ 6	0.10	45.00	135.00	225.00
❑ 7	0.10	45.00	135.00	225.00
❑ 8	0.10	45.00	135.00	225.00
❑ 9	0.10	45.00	135.00	225.00
❑ 10	0.10	45.00	135.00	225.00
❑ 11	0.10	35.00	105.00	175.00
❑ 12	0.10	35.00	105.00	175.00
❑ 13	0.10	35.00	105.00	175.00
❑ 14	0.10	35.00	105.00	175.00
❑ 15	0.10	35.00	105.00	175.00
❑ 16	0.10	35.00	105.00	175.00
❑ 17	0.10	35.00	105.00	175.00
❑ 18	0.10	35.00	105.00	175.00
❑ 19	0.10	35.00	105.00	175.00
❑ 20	0.10	35.00	105.00	175.00
❑ 21	0.10	24.00	72.00	120.00
❑ 22	0.10	24.00	72.00	120.00
❑ 23	0.10	24.00	72.00	120.00
❑ 24	0.10	24.00	72.00	120.00
❑ 25	0.10	24.00	72.00	120.00
❑ 26	0.10	24.00	72.00	120.00
❑ 27	0.10	24.00	72.00	120.00
❑ 28	0.10	24.00	72.00	120.00
❑ 29	0.10	24.00	72.00	120.00
❑ 30	0.10	24.00	72.00	120.00
❑ 31	0.10	24.00	72.00	120.00
❑ 32	0.10	24.00	72.00	120.00
❑ 33	0.10	24.00	72.00	120.00
❑ 34	0.10	24.00	72.00	120.00
❑ 35	0.10	20.00	60.00	100.00
❑ 36	0.10	20.00	60.00	100.00
❑ 37	0.10	20.00	60.00	100.00
❑ 38	0.10	20.00	60.00	100.00
❑ 39	0.10	20.00	60.00	100.00
❑ 40	0.10	20.00	60.00	100.00
❑ 41	0.10	20.00	60.00	100.00
❑ 42	0.10	20.00	60.00	100.00
❑ 43	0.10	20.00	60.00	100.00
❑ 44	0.10	20.00	60.00	100.00
❑ 45	0.10	20.00	60.00	100.00
❑ 46	0.10	20.00	60.00	100.00
❑ 47	0.10	20.00	60.00	100.00
❑ 48	0.10	20.00	60.00	100.00
❑ 49	0.10	20.00	60.00	100.00
❑ 50	0.10	20.00	60.00	100.00
❑ 51	0.10	20.00	60.00	100.00
❑ 52	0.10	20.00	60.00	100.00
❑ 53	0.10	20.00	60.00	100.00
❑ 54	0.10	20.00	60.00	100.00
❑ 55	0.10	20.00	60.00	100.00
❑ 56	0.10	20.00	60.00	100.00
❑ 57	0.10	20.00	60.00	100.00
❑ 58	0.10	20.00	60.00	100.00
❑ 59	0.10	20.00	60.00	100.00
❑ 60	0.10	20.00	60.00	100.00
❑ 61	0.10	14.00	42.00	70.00
❑ 62	0.10	14.00	42.00	70.00
❑ 63	0.10	14.00	42.00	70.00
❑ 64	0.10	14.00	42.00	70.00
❑ 65	0.10	14.00	42.00	70.00
❑ 66	0.10	14.00	42.00	70.00

	ORIG.	GOOD	FINE	N-MINT
❏ 67	0.10	14.00	42.00	70.00
❏ 68	0.10	14.00	42.00	70.00
❏ 69	0.10	14.00	42.00	70.00
❏ 70	0.10	14.00	42.00	70.00
❏ 71	0.10	12.00	36.00	60.00
❏ 72	0.10	12.00	36.00	60.00
❏ 73	0.10	12.00	36.00	60.00
❏ 74	0.10	12.00	36.00	60.00
❏ 75	0.10	12.00	36.00	60.00
❏ 76	0.10	12.00	36.00	60.00
❏ 77	0.10	12.00	36.00	60.00
❏ 78	0.10	12.00	36.00	60.00
❏ 79	0.10	16.00	48.00	80.00
❏ 80	0.10	10.00	30.00	50.00
❏ 81	0.10	10.00	30.00	50.00
❏ 82	0.10	10.00	30.00	50.00
❏ 83	0.10	10.00	30.00	50.00
❏ 84	0.10	10.00	30.00	50.00
❏ 85	0.10	10.00	30.00	50.00
❏ 86	0.10	10.00	30.00	50.00
❏ 87	0.10	10.00	30.00	50.00
❏ 88	0.10	10.00	30.00	50.00
❏ 89	0.10	10.00	30.00	50.00
❏ 90	0.10	10.00	30.00	50.00
❏ 91	0.10	10.00	30.00	50.00
❏ 92	0.10	10.00	30.00	50.00
❏ 93	0.10	10.00	30.00	50.00
❏ 94	0.10	10.00	30.00	50.00
❏ 95	0.10	10.00	30.00	50.00
❏ 96	0.10	10.00	30.00	50.00
❏ 97	0.10	10.00	30.00	50.00
❏ 98	0.10	10.00	30.00	50.00
❏ 99	0.10	10.00	30.00	50.00
❏ 100	0.12	16.00	48.00	80.00
❏ 101, SD/JK, Human Torch	0.12	160.00	480.00	800.00
❏ 102, SD/JK	0.12	80.00	240.00	400.00
❏ 103, SD/JK	0.12	70.00	210.00	350.00
❏ 104, SD/JK	0.12	70.00	210.00	350.00
❏ 105, SD/JK	0.12	70.00	210.00	350.00
❏ 106, SD, A:FF	0.12	32.00	96.00	160.00
❏ 107, SD, Torch V:Sub-Mariner	0.12	36.00	108.00	180.00
❏ 108, SD/JK	0.12	30.00	90.00	150.00
❏ 109, SD/JK	0.12	30.00	90.00	150.00
❏ 110, Jul 63, SD, 1:Dr. Strange	0.12	120.00	360.00	600.00
❏ 111, SD, 1:Asbestos	0.12	52.00	156.00	260.00
❏ 112, SD	0.12	18.00	54.00	90.00
❏ 113, SD	0.12	18.00	54.00	90.00
❏ 114, SD/JK, Capt. America	0.12	44.00	132.00	220.00
❏ 115, Dec 63, SD, O:Dr. Strange	0.12	60.00	180.00	300.00
❏ 116	0.12	12.00	36.00	60.00
❏ 117	0.12	12.00	36.00	60.00
❏ 118	0.12	12.00	36.00	60.00
❏ 119	0.12	12.00	36.00	60.00
❏ 120	0.12	12.00	36.00	60.00
❏ 121, SP	0.12	8.00	24.00	40.00
❏ 122, SP	0.12	8.00	24.00	40.00
❏ 123, SP	0.12	8.00	24.00	40.00
❏ 124, SP	0.12	8.00	24.00	40.00
❏ 125, SP	0.12	8.00	24.00	40.00
❏ 126, SP	0.12	8.00	24.00	40.00
❏ 127, SP	0.12	8.00	24.00	40.00
❏ 128, SP	0.12	8.00	24.00	40.00
❏ 129, SP	0.12	8.00	24.00	40.00
❏ 130, SD, C:Beatles	0.12	10.00	30.00	50.00
❏ 131, SD, Thing/Torch	0.12	6.40	19.20	32.00
❏ 132, SD, Thing/Torch	0.12	6.40	19.20	32.00
❏ 133, SD, Thing/Torch	0.12	6.40	19.20	32.00
❏ 134, SD, L:Torch, A:Watcher	0.12	6.40	19.20	32.00
❏ 135, SD/JK, 1:SHIELD	0.12	15.00	45.00	75.00
❏ 136, SD/JK, Dr. Strange	0.12	6.00	18.00	30.00
❏ 137	0.12	3.00	9.00	15.00
❏ 138	0.12	3.00	9.00	15.00
❏ 139	0.12	3.00	9.00	15.00
❏ 140	0.12	3.00	9.00	15.00
❏ 141	0.12	3.00	9.00	15.00
❏ 142	0.12	3.00	9.00	15.00
❏ 143	0.12	3.00	9.00	15.00
❏ 144	0.12	3.00	9.00	15.00
❏ 145	0.12	3.00	9.00	15.00
❏ 146	0.12	3.00	9.00	15.00
❏ 147	0.12	3.00	9.00	15.00
❏ 148, BEv/JK, O:Ancient One	0.12	3.20	9.60	16.00
❏ 149, BEv/JK	0.12	2.40	7.20	12.00
❏ 150, BEv/JK/JB, 1:Buscema	0.12	2.40	7.20	12.00
❏ 151, BEv/JK/JSo, 1:Steranko	0.12	4.00	12.00	20.00
❏ 152	0.12	2.40	7.20	12.00
❏ 153	0.12	2.40	7.20	12.00
❏ 154	0.12	2.40	7.20	12.00
❏ 155	0.12	2.40	7.20	12.00
❏ 156	0.12	2.40	7.20	12.00
❏ 157	0.12	2.40	7.20	12.00
❏ 158	0.12	2.40	7.20	12.00
❏ 159, JSo, O:Fury	0.12	3.00	9.00	15.00
❏ 160	0.12	2.40	7.20	12.00
❏ 161	0.12	2.40	7.20	12.00
❏ 162	0.12	2.40	7.20	12.00
❏ 163	0.12	2.40	7.20	12.00
❏ 164	0.12	2.40	7.20	12.00
❏ 165	0.12	2.40	7.20	12.00
❏ 166	0.12	2.40	7.20	12.00
❏ 167, JSo/DA	0.12	3.00	9.00	15.00
❏ 168, JSo/DA, O:Br. Voodoo (ends 1967 series)	0.12	2.40	7.20	12.00
❏ 169, Br. Voodoo (begins 1973 series)	0.20	0.40	1.20	2.00
❏ 170, Br. Voodoo	0.20	0.40	1.20	2.00
❏ 171, Br. Voodoo	0.20	0.40	1.20	2.00
❏ 172, Br. Voodoo	0.20	0.40	1.20	2.00
❏ 173, Br. Voodoo	0.20	0.40	1.20	2.00
❏ 174, JB/JM, O:Golem	0.25	0.20	0.60	1.00
❏ 175, SD, Rep-Torr	0.25	0.20	0.60	1.00
❏ 176, Golem	0.25	0.20	0.60	1.00
❏ 177, Golem	0.25	0.20	0.60	1.00
❏ 178, Feb 75, JSn, O:Warlock	0.25	1.20	3.60	6.00
❏ 179, Apr 75, JSn, Warlock	0.25	0.80	2.40	4.00
❏ 180, Jun 75, JSn, Warlock	0.25	0.80	2.40	4.00
❏ 181, Aug 75, JSn, Warlock	0.25	0.80	2.40	4.00
❏ 182, rep.	0.25	0.20	0.60	1.00
❏ 183, rep.	0.25	0.20	0.60	1.00
❏ 184, rep.	0.25	0.20	0.60	1.00
❏ 185, rep.	0.25	0.20	0.60	1.00
❏ 186, rep.	0.25	0.20	0.60	1.00
❏ 187, Sep 76, rep.	0.30	0.20	0.60	1.00
❏ 188, Oct 76, rep.	0.30	0.20	0.60	1.00

STRANGE TALES (1994)

❏ 1, Nov 94, prestige format, acetate overlay cover
......6.95 1.39 4.17 6.95

	ORIG.	GOOD	FINE	N-MINT

STRANGE TALES (Volume 2)

	ORIG.	GOOD	FINE	N-MINT
1, Apr 87, Dr. Strange, Cloak & Dagger	0.75	0.40	1.20	2.00
2, May 87	0.75	0.40	1.20	2.00
3, Jun 87	0.75	0.40	1.20	2.00
4, Jul 87	0.75	0.40	1.20	2.00
5, Aug 87	0.75	0.40	1.20	2.00
6, Sep 87	0.75	0.40	1.20	2.00
7, Oct 87	0.75	0.40	1.20	2.00
8, Nov 87	0.75	0.40	1.20	2.00
9, Dec 87	0.75	0.40	1.20	2.00
10, Jan 88	0.75	0.40	1.20	2.00
11, Feb 88	0.75	0.40	1.20	2.00
12, Mar 88	0.75	0.40	1.20	2.00
13, Apr 88	0.75	0.40	1.20	2.00
14, May 88	0.75	0.40	1.20	2.00
15, Jun 88	0.75	0.40	1.20	2.00
16, Jul 88	0.75	0.40	1.20	2.00
17, Aug 88	0.75	0.40	1.20	2.00
18, Sep 88, X-Factor	0.75	0.20	0.60	1.00
19, Oct 88, last	0.75	0.20	0.60	1.00

STRANGE TALES ANNUAL

	ORIG.	GOOD	FINE	N-MINT
1, 62, reprint	0.25	60.00	180.00	300.00
2, 63, SpM/Torch	0.25	80.00	240.00	400.00

STRANGE WORLDS
NORTH COAST STUDIOS

	ORIG.	GOOD	FINE	N-MINT
1, 95, magazine-size;cardstock cover;b&w	4.00	0.80	2.40	4.00

STRANGEHAVEN
ABIOGENESIS PRESS

	ORIG.	GOOD	FINE	N-MINT
1, Jun 95, b&w	2.95	0.59	1.77	2.95
3, Dec 95, b&w	2.95	0.59	1.77	2.95

STRANGELOVE
EXPRESS/ENTITY

	ORIG.	GOOD	FINE	N-MINT
1, 95, b&w	2.50	0.50	1.50	2.50
2, 95, b&w	2.50	0.50	1.50	2.50

STRANGER IN A STRANGE LAND
RIP OFF

	ORIG.	GOOD	FINE	N-MINT
1, Jun 89, adult;b&w	2.00	0.40	1.20	2.00
2, May 90, adult;b&w	2.00	0.40	1.20	2.00
3, Sep 91, adult;b&w	2.50	0.50	1.50	2.50

STRANGERS IN PARADISE
ABSTRACT

	ORIG.	GOOD	FINE	N-MINT
1, Sep 94, b&w	2.75	2.40	7.20	12.00
1, Apr 95, b&w;second printing	2.75	0.55	1.65	2.75
2, Nov 94, b&w	2.75	1.20	3.60	6.00
3, Jan 95, b&w	2.75	0.55	1.65	2.75
4, Mar 95, b&w	2.75	0.55	1.65	2.75

ANTARCTIC

	ORIG.	GOOD	FINE	N-MINT
1, Nov 93, first printing;b&w	2.75	9.60	28.80	48.00
1, Mar 94, second printing;b&w	2.75	1.00	3.00	5.00
1, Apr 94, third printing;b&w	2.75	0.55	1.65	2.75
2, Dec 93, b&w	2.75	6.00	18.00	30.00
3, Feb 94, b&w;(became Abstract Studio title)	2.75	4.80	14.40	24.00

STRANGERS, THE
MALIBU

	ORIG.	GOOD	FINE	N-MINT
1, Jun 93	1.95	1.20	3.60	6.00
1, hologram edition		6.00	18.00	30.00
1, Ultra Ltd. Edition	1.95	0.39	1.17	1.95
2, Jul 93, card	1.95	1.60	4.80	8.00
3, Aug 93	1.95	0.80	2.40	4.00
4, Sep 93	1.95	0.80	2.40	4.00
5, Oct 93, Rune, BWS	2.50	0.50	1.50	2.50
6, Nov 93	1.95	0.39	1.17	1.95
7, Dec 93, Break-Thru	1.95	0.39	1.17	1.95

	ORIG.	GOOD	FINE	N-MINT
8, Jan 94	1.95	0.39	1.17	1.95
9, Feb 94	1.95	0.39	1.17	1.95
10, Mar 94	1.95	0.39	1.17	1.95
11, Apr 94	1.95	0.39	1.17	1.95
12, May 94	1.95	0.39	1.17	1.95
13, Jun 94, contains Ultraverse Premiere #4	3.50	0.70	2.10	3.50
14, Jul 94	1.95	0.39	1.17	1.95
15, Aug 94	1.95	0.39	1.17	1.95
16, Sep 94	1.95	0.39	1.17	1.95

STRATA
RENEGADE

	ORIG.	GOOD	FINE	N-MINT
1, b&w		0.34	1.02	1.70
2, b&w		0.34	1.02	1.70
3		0.40	1.20	2.00
4		0.40	1.20	2.00
5		0.40	1.20	2.00

STRATONAUT
NIGHTWYND

	ORIG.	GOOD	FINE	N-MINT
1, b&w		0.50	1.50	2.50
2, b&w		0.50	1.50	2.50
3, b&w		0.50	1.50	2.50
4, b&w		0.50	1.50	2.50

STRAW MEN
ALL AMERICAN

	ORIG.	GOOD	FINE	N-MINT
1, b&w		0.39	1.17	1.95
2, b&w		0.39	1.17	1.95
3, b&w		0.39	1.17	1.95
4, b&w		0.39	1.17	1.95
5, b&w		0.39	1.17	1.95
6, b&w		0.39	1.17	1.95
7, b&w		0.39	1.17	1.95
8, b&w		0.39	1.17	1.95

STRAWBERRY SHORTCAKE
STAR

	ORIG.	GOOD	FINE	N-MINT
1	0.65	0.13	0.39	0.65
2	0.65	0.13	0.39	0.65
3	0.65	0.13	0.39	0.65
4	0.65	0.13	0.39	0.65
5	0.65	0.13	0.39	0.65
6	0.65	0.13	0.39	0.65

STRAY BULLETS
EL CAPITAN

	ORIG.	GOOD	FINE	N-MINT
1, b&w		1.20	3.60	6.00
2, Apr 95, b&w	2.95	0.80	2.40	4.00
3, b&w		0.70	2.10	3.50
4, Nov 95, b&w	3.50	0.70	2.10	3.50
5, 95, b&w;indicia contains information for issue #4	3.50	0.70	2.10	3.50

STRAY CATS
TWILIGHT TWINS

	ORIG.	GOOD	FINE	N-MINT
1, b&w		0.50	1.50	2.50

STRAY TOASTERS
EPIC

	ORIG.	GOOD	FINE	N-MINT
1, BSz	3.50	0.70	2.10	3.50
2, BSz	3.50	0.70	2.10	3.50
3, BSz	3.50	0.70	2.10	3.50
4, BSz	3.50	0.70	2.10	3.50

STREET FIGHTER
MALIBU

	ORIG.	GOOD	FINE	N-MINT
1	2.95	0.59	1.77	2.95
1, gold foil edition	15.00	3.00	9.00	15.00
2	2.95	0.59	1.77	2.95
2, gold foil edition	15.00	3.00	9.00	15.00
3	2.95	0.59	1.77	2.95
3, gold foil edition	15.00	3.00	9.00	15.00

STREET FIGHTER II
TOKUMA SHOTEN

	ORIG.	GOOD	FINE	N-MINT
1, Apr 94	2.95	1.00	3.00	5.00

	ORIG.	GOOD	FINE	N-MINT

STREET FIGHTER: THE BATTLE FOR SHADALOO
DC
❑ 0, 95, nn; movie adaptation, polybagged with trading card and temporary tattoos
.... 3.95 0.79 2.37 3.95

STREET HEROES 2005
ETERNITY
❑ 1, b&w 0.39 1.17 1.95
❑ 2, b&w 0.39 1.17 1.95
❑ 3, b&w 0.39 1.17 1.95

STREET MUSIC
FANTAGRAPHICS
❑ 1, b&w 0.59 1.77 2.95
❑ 2, b&w 0.59 1.77 2.95
❑ 3, b&w 0.59 1.77 2.95
❑ 4, b&w 0.59 1.77 2.95
❑ 5, b&w 0.59 1.77 2.95
❑ 6, b&w 0.59 1.77 2.95

STREET POET RAY
BLACKTHORNE
❑ 1, b&w 0.40 1.20 2.00
❑ 2, b&w 0.40 1.20 2.00

MARVEL
❑ 1, 90, b&w;cardstock cover
.... 2.95 0.59 1.77 2.95
❑ 2, 90, b&w;cardstock cover
.... 2.95 0.59 1.77 2.95
❑ 3, 90, b&w;cardstock cover
.... 2.95 0.59 1.77 2.95
❑ 4, 90, b&w;cardstock cover
.... 2.95 0.59 1.77 2.95

STREET SHARKS
ARCHIE
❑ 1, May 96 .... 1.50 0.30 0.90 1.50

STREET SHARKS (mini-series)
❑ 1, Jan 96, based on toy line and animated series
.... 1.50 0.30 0.90 1.50
❑ 2, Feb 96 .... 1.50 0.30 0.90 1.50
❑ 3, Mar 96 .... 1.50 0.30 0.90 1.50

STREET WOLF
BLACKTHORNE
❑ 1, b&w 0.40 1.20 2.00
❑ 2, b&w 0.40 1.20 2.00
❑ 3, b&w 0.40 1.20 2.00

STREETFIGHTER
OCEAN
❑ 1, Aug 86 .... 1.75 0.35 1.05 1.75
❑ 2, Nov 86 .... 1.75 0.35 1.05 1.75
❑ 3, Feb 87 .... 1.75 0.35 1.05 1.75
❑ 4, May 87 .... 1.75 0.35 1.05 1.75

STREETS
DC
❑ 1 .... 4.95 0.99 2.97 4.95
❑ 2 .... 4.95 0.99 2.97 4.95
❑ 3 .... 4.95 0.99 2.97 4.95

STRICTLY INDEPENDENT!
ONE SHOT PRESS
❑ 1, Jan 96, b&w 2.50 0.50 1.50 2.50

STRIKE FORCE AMERICA
COMICO
❑ 1 .... 0.50 1.50 2.50

STRIKE!
ECLIPSE
❑ 1, Aug 87, O:Sgt. Strike . 1.75 0.35 1.05 1.75
❑ 2, Sep 87, O:Sgt. Strike.. 1.75 0.35 1.05 1.75
❑ 3, Oct 87, O:Sgt. Strike .. 1.75 0.35 1.05 1.75
❑ 4, Nov 87, O:Sgt. Strike .. 1.75 0.35 1.05 1.75
❑ 5, Dec 87, O:Sgt. Strike.. 1.75 0.35 1.05 1.75
❑ 6, Feb 88, O:Sgt. Strike .. 1.75 0.35 1.05 1.75

STRIKE! VS. SGT. STRIKE SPECIAL
❑ 1, May 88 .... 1.95 0.39 1.17 1.95

STRIKEBACK! (mini-series)
IMAGE
❑ 1, Jan 96, reprints Malibu/Bravura first issue
.... 2.50 0.50 1.50 2.50
❑ 2, Feb 96, reprints Malibu/Bravura second issue
.... 2.50 0.50 1.50 2.50
❑ 3, Mar 96 .... 2.50 0.50 1.50 2.50
❑ 4, Apr 96 .... 2.50 0.50 1.50 2.50

MALIBU/BRAVURA
❑ 1, Oct 94 .... 2.95 0.59 1.77 2.95
❑ 2, Nov 94 .... 2.95 0.59 1.77 2.95

STRIKEFORCE: MORITURI
MARVEL
❑ 1, Dec 86 .... 0.75 0.40 1.20 2.00
❑ 2, Jan 87 .... 0.75 0.40 1.20 2.00
❑ 3, Feb 87 .... 0.75 0.40 1.20 2.00
❑ 4, Mar 87 .... 0.75 0.40 1.20 2.00
❑ 5, Apr 87 .... 0.75 0.40 1.20 2.00
❑ 6, May 87 .... 0.75 0.40 1.20 2.00
❑ 7, Jun 87 .... 0.75 0.40 1.20 2.00
❑ 8, Jul 87 .... 0.75 0.40 1.20 2.00
❑ 9, Aug 87 .... 0.75 0.40 1.20 2.00
❑ 10, Sep 87 .... 0.75 0.40 1.20 2.00
❑ 11, Oct 87 .... 0.75 0.40 1.20 2.00
❑ 12, Nov 87 .... 0.75 0.40 1.20 2.00
❑ 13, Dec 87 .... 1.25 0.40 1.20 2.00
❑ 14, Jan 88 .... 0.75 0.25 0.75 1.25
❑ 15, Feb 88 .... 1.00 0.25 0.75 1.25
❑ 16, Mar 88 .... 1.00 0.25 0.75 1.25
❑ 17, Apr 88 .... 1.00 0.25 0.75 1.25
❑ 18, May 88 .... 1.00 0.25 0.75 1.25
❑ 19, Jun 88 .... 1.00 0.25 0.75 1.25
❑ 20, Jul 88 .... 1.00 0.25 0.75 1.25
❑ 21, Sep 88 .... 1.25 0.25 0.75 1.25
❑ 22, Oct 88 .... 1.25 0.25 0.75 1.25
❑ 23, Nov 88 .... 1.25 0.25 0.75 1.25
❑ 24 .... 1.50 0.30 0.90 1.50
❑ 25 .... 1.25 0.30 0.90 1.50
❑ 26 .... 1.50 0.30 0.90 1.50
❑ 27 .... 1.50 0.30 0.90 1.50
❑ 28 .... 1.50 0.30 0.90 1.50
❑ 29 .... 1.50 0.30 0.90 1.50
❑ 30 .... 1.50 0.30 0.90 1.50
❑ 31 .... 1.50 0.30 0.90 1.50

STRIKER
VIZ
❑ 1, b&w 0.55 1.65 2.75

STRIKER: SECRET OF THE BERSERKER
❑ 1, 95, b&w 2.75 0.55 1.65 2.75

STRIKER: THE ARMORED WARRIOR
❑ 3 .... 0.55 1.65 2.75

STRIP (color magazine)
MARVEL UK
❑ 1 .... 2.50 0.50 1.50 2.50
❑ 2 .... 2.50 0.50 1.50 2.50
❑ 3 .... 2.50 0.50 1.50 2.50
❑ 4 .... 2.50 0.50 1.50 2.50
❑ 5 .... 2.50 0.50 1.50 2.50
❑ 6 .... 2.50 0.50 1.50 2.50
❑ 7 .... 2.50 0.50 1.50 2.50
❑ 8 .... 2.50 0.50 1.50 2.50
❑ 9 .... 2.50 0.50 1.50 2.50
❑ 10 .... 2.50 0.50 1.50 2.50
❑ 11 .... 2.50 0.50 1.50 2.50
❑ 12 .... 2.50 0.50 1.50 2.50
❑ 13 .... 2.50 0.50 1.50 2.50
❑ 14 .... 2.50 0.50 1.50 2.50
❑ 15 .... 2.50 0.50 1.50 2.50

	ORIG.	GOOD	FINE	N-MINT
❑ 16 ....2.50	0.50	1.50	2.50
❑ 17 ....2.50	0.50	1.50	2.50
❑ 18 ....2.50	0.50	1.50	2.50
❑ 19 ....2.50	0.50	1.50	2.50
❑ 20 ....2.50	0.50	1.50	2.50

STRIPPERS AND SEX QUEENS OF THE EXOTIC WORLD
FANTAGRAPHICS

	ORIG.	GOOD	FINE	N-MINT
❑ 3, Jun 94, adult; b&w; cardstock cover			
......................................3.95	0.79	2.37	3.95
❑ 4, Oct 94, b&w, final issue			
......................................3.95	0.79	2.37	3.95

STRIPS
RIP OFF

	ORIG.	GOOD	FINE	N-MINT
❑ 1, Dec 89, adult;b&w;multiple printings			
......................................2.50	0.50	1.50	2.50
❑ 2, Feb 90, adult;b&w 2.50	0.50	1.50	2.50
❑ 3, Apr 90, adult;b&w 2.50	0.50	1.50	2.50
❑ 4, Jun 90, adult;b&w 2.50	0.50	1.50	2.50
❑ 5, Nov 90, adult;b&w 2.50	0.50	1.50	2.50
❑ 6, Dec 90, adult;b&w 2.50	0.50	1.50	2.50
❑ 7, Feb 91, adult;b&w 2.50	0.50	1.50	2.50
❑ 8, Mar 91, adult;b&w 2.50	0.50	1.50	2.50
❑ 9, Jun 91, adult;b&w 2.50	0.50	1.50	2.50

STRONTIUM BITCH
FLEETWAY/QUALITY

	ORIG.	GOOD	FINE	N-MINT
❑ 1 ....2.95	0.59	1.77	2.95
❑ 2 ....2.95	0.59	1.77	2.95

STRONTIUM DOG
EAGLE

	GOOD	FINE	N-MINT
❑ 1	0.25	0.75	1.25
❑ 2	0.25	0.75	1.25
❑ 3	0.25	0.75	1.25
❑ 4	0.25	0.75	1.25

FLEETWAY/QUALITY

	GOOD	FINE	N-MINT
❑ 1	0.25	0.75	1.25
❑ 2	0.25	0.75	1.25
❑ 3	0.25	0.75	1.25
❑ 4	0.25	0.75	1.25
❑ 5	0.25	0.75	1.25
❑ 6	0.25	0.75	1.25
❑ 7	0.25	0.75	1.25
❑ 8	0.25	0.75	1.25
❑ 9	0.25	0.75	1.25
❑ 10	0.25	0.75	1.25
❑ 11	0.25	0.75	1.25
❑ 12	0.25	0.75	1.25
❑ 13	0.30	0.90	1.50
❑ 14, 14 and 15 are one issue	0.30	0.90	1.50
❑ 16, 16 and 17 are one issue	0.30	0.90	1.50
❑ 18	0.30	0.90	1.50
❑ 19	0.30	0.90	1.50
❑ 20	0.30	0.90	1.50
❑ 21	0.30	0.90	1.50
❑ 22	0.30	0.90	1.50
❑ 23	0.30	0.90	1.50
❑ 24	0.30	0.90	1.50
❑ 25	0.30	0.90	1.50
❑ 26	0.30	0.90	1.50
❑ 27	0.30	0.90	1.50
❑ 28	0.30	0.90	1.50
❑ 29	0.30	0.90	1.50

STRYFE'S STRIKE FILE
MARVEL

	ORIG.	GOOD	FINE	N-MINT
❑ 1 ....1.75	0.60	1.80	3.00

STUNT DAWGS
HARVEY

	GOOD	FINE	N-MINT
❑ 1	0.25	0.75	1.25

STUPID
IMAGE

	ORIG.	GOOD	FINE	N-MINT
❑ 1, parody 1.95	0.39	1.17	1.95

STUPID HEROES
MIRAGE/NEXT

	ORIG.	GOOD	FINE	N-MINT
❑ 1, Aug 94 ....2.75	0.55	1.65	2.75
❑ 2, Oct 94 ....2.75	0.55	1.65	2.75
❑ 3, Dec 94 ....2.75	0.55	1.65	2.75

STUPIDMAN
PARODY PRESS

	ORIG.	GOOD	FINE	N-MINT
❑ 1 ....2.50	0.50	1.50	2.50

STUPIDMAN: BURIAL FOR A BUDDY

	ORIG.	GOOD	FINE	N-MINT
❑ 1, A b&w.......................2.50	0.50	1.50	2.50

STUPIDMAN: RAIN ON THE STUPIDMAN
PARODY

	ORIG.	GOOD	FINE	N-MINT
❑ 1, A b&w.......................2.95	0.59	1.77	2.95

STYGMATA (mini-series)
EXPRESS/ENTITY

	ORIG.	GOOD	FINE	N-MINT
❑ 1, Jul 94, enhanced cover, b&w			
......................................2.95	0.59	1.77	2.95
❑ 3, Oct 94, b&w..............2.95	0.59	1.77	2.95

SUB-MARINER
MARVEL

	ORIG.	GOOD	FINE	N-MINT
❑ 1, JB, O:Sub-Mariner 0.12	28.00	84.00	140.00
❑ 2, JB, A:Triton................0.12	8.00	24.00	40.00
❑ 3, JB, A:Triton................0.12	4.00	12.00	20.00
❑ 4, JB 0.12	2.40	7.20	12.00
❑ 5, JB 0.12	2.40	7.20	12.00
❑ 6, JB 0.12	2.40	7.20	12.00
❑ 7, JB 0.12	2.40	7.20	12.00
❑ 8 ....0.12	2.40	7.20	12.00
❑ 9 ....0.12	1.60	4.80	8.00
❑ 10 ....0.12	1.60	4.80	8.00
❑ 11 ....0.12	1.40	4.20	7.00
❑ 12 ....0.12	1.40	4.20	7.00
❑ 13 ....0.12	1.40	4.20	7.00
❑ 14, Human Torch...........0.12	1.40	4.20	7.00
❑ 15 ....0.12	1.00	3.00	5.00
❑ 16 ....0.15	1.00	3.00	5.00
❑ 17 ....0.15	1.00	3.00	5.00
❑ 18 ....0.15	1.00	3.00	5.00
❑ 19 ....0.15	1.00	3.00	5.00
❑ 20 ....0.15	1.00	3.00	5.00
❑ 21 ....0.15	1.00	3.00	5.00
❑ 22, Dr. Strange 0.15	1.00	3.00	5.00
❑ 23 ....0.15	0.40	1.20	2.00
❑ 24 ....0.15	0.40	1.20	2.00
❑ 25 ....0.15	0.50	1.50	2.50
❑ 26 ....0.15	0.50	1.50	2.50
❑ 27, SB...........................0.15	1.00	3.00	5.00
❑ 28 ....0.15	0.50	1.50	2.50
❑ 29, SB, V:Hercules...........0.15	0.30	0.90	1.50
❑ 30, SB, A:Capt. Marvel....0.15	0.40	1.20	2.00
❑ 31 ....0.15	0.30	0.90	1.50
❑ 32 ....0.15	0.30	0.90	1.50
❑ 33, SB/JM, I:Namora 0.15	0.40	1.20	2.00
❑ 34, SB/JM, A:Surfer & Hulk			
......................................0.15	0.80	2.40	4.00
❑ 35, SB/JM, A:Surfer & Hulk			
......................................0.15	0.80	2.40	4.00
❑ 36, BWr/SB, M:Lady Dorma			
......................................0.15	0.50	1.50	2.50
❑ 37, RA, D:Lady Dorma....0.15	0.40	1.20	2.00
❑ 38 ....0.15	0.30	0.90	1.50
❑ 39 ....0.15	0.30	0.90	1.50
❑ 40 ....0.15	0.30	0.90	1.50
❑ 41, GT...........................0.15	0.25	0.75	1.25
❑ 42, GT...........................0.15	0.25	0.75	1.25
❑ 43 ....0.25	0.40	1.20	2.00
❑ 44 ....0.20	0.40	1.20	2.00

	ORIG.	GOOD	FINE	N-MINT
☐ 45	0.20	0.40	1.20	2.00
☐ 46, GC	0.20	0.25	0.75	1.25
☐ 47, GC	0.20	0.25	0.75	1.25
☐ 48, GC	0.20	0.25	0.75	1.25
☐ 49, GC	0.20	0.25	0.75	1.25
☐ 50, Jun 72, BEv, 1:Nita	0.20	0.35	1.05	1.75
☐ 51, Jul 72, BEv	0.20	0.30	0.90	1.50
☐ 52, Aug 72, BEv	0.20	0.30	0.90	1.50
☐ 53, Sep 72, BEv	0.20	0.30	0.90	1.50
☐ 54, Oct 72, BEv	0.20	0.30	0.90	1.50
☐ 55, Nov 72, BEv	0.20	0.30	0.90	1.50
☐ 56, Dec 72	0.20	0.25	0.75	1.25
☐ 57, Jan 73	0.20	0.25	0.75	1.25
☐ 58, Feb 73, BEv	0.20	0.30	0.90	1.50
☐ 59, BEv	0.20	0.30	0.90	1.50
☐ 60, BEv	0.20	0.30	0.90	1.50
☐ 61	0.20	0.25	0.75	1.25
☐ 62	0.20	0.25	0.75	1.25
☐ 63	0.20	0.25	0.75	1.25
☐ 64	0.20	0.25	0.75	1.25
☐ 65	0.20	0.25	0.75	1.25
☐ 66	0.20	0.25	0.75	1.25
☐ 67	0.20	0.25	0.75	1.25
☐ 68	0.20	0.25	0.75	1.25
☐ 69	0.20	0.25	0.75	1.25
☐ 70	0.25	0.25	0.75	1.25
☐ 71	0.25	0.25	0.75	1.25
☐ 72	0.25	0.25	0.75	1.25

SUB-MARINER ANNUAL

	ORIG.	GOOD	FINE	N-MINT
☐ 1, SB, rep.	0.25	0.40	1.20	2.00
☐ 2, BEv, rep.	0.25	0.35	1.05	1.75

SUBMISSIVE SUZANNE
EROS COMIX

	GOOD	FINE	N-MINT
☐ 1, adult, b&w	0.50	1.50	2.50
☐ 2, adult, b&w	0.50	1.50	2.50

SUBSPECIES
ETERNITY

	GOOD	FINE	N-MINT
☐ 1, color	0.50	1.50	2.50
☐ 2, color	0.50	1.50	2.50
☐ 3, color	0.50	1.50	2.50
☐ 4, color	0.50	1.50	2.50

SUBSTANCE QUARTERLY
SUBSTANCE

	ORIG.	GOOD	FINE	N-MINT
☐ 1, Spr 94, b&w	3.00	0.60	1.80	3.00
☐ 2, Sum 94, b&w	3.00	0.60	1.80	3.00

SUBTLE VIOLENTS
CRY FOR DAWN

	GOOD	FINE	N-MINT
☐ 1	5.00	15.00	25.00

SUBURBAN HIGH LIFE
SLAVE LABOR

	GOOD	FINE	N-MINT
☐ 1	0.35	1.05	1.75
☐ 1, (2nd printing)	0.35	1.05	1.75
☐ 2	0.35	1.05	1.75
☐ 3	0.35	1.05	1.75

SUBURBAN JERSEY NINJA SHE-DEVILS
MARVEL

	ORIG.	GOOD	FINE	N-MINT
☐ 1	1.50	0.30	0.90	1.50

SUBURBAN NIGHTMARES
RENEGADE

	ORIG.	GOOD	FINE	N-MINT
☐ 1, Jul 88, b&w	2.00	0.40	1.20	2.00
☐ 2, Jul 88, b&w	2.00	0.40	1.20	2.00
☐ 3, Aug 88, b&w	2.00	0.40	1.20	2.00
☐ 4, Aug 88, b&w	2.00	0.40	1.20	2.00

SUBURBAN VOODOO
FANTAGRAPHICS

	GOOD	FINE	N-MINT
☐ 1, b&w	0.50	1.50	2.50

SUCCUBUS
EROS COMIX

	GOOD	FINE	N-MINT
☐ 1, adult, b&w	0.50	1.50	2.50

SUGAR & SPIKE
DC

	GOOD	FINE	N-MINT
☐ 1	240.00	720.00	1200.00
☐ 2	120.00	360.00	600.00
☐ 3	80.00	240.00	400.00
☐ 4	80.00	240.00	400.00
☐ 5	80.00	240.00	400.00
☐ 6	60.00	180.00	300.00
☐ 7	60.00	180.00	300.00
☐ 8	60.00	180.00	300.00
☐ 9	60.00	180.00	300.00
☐ 10	60.00	180.00	300.00
☐ 11	50.00	150.00	250.00
☐ 12	50.00	150.00	250.00
☐ 13	50.00	150.00	250.00
☐ 14	50.00	150.00	250.00
☐ 15	50.00	150.00	250.00
☐ 16	50.00	150.00	250.00
☐ 17	50.00	150.00	250.00
☐ 18	50.00	150.00	250.00
☐ 19	50.00	150.00	250.00
☐ 20	50.00	150.00	250.00
☐ 21	40.00	120.00	200.00
☐ 22	40.00	120.00	200.00
☐ 23	40.00	120.00	200.00
☐ 24	40.00	120.00	200.00
☐ 25	40.00	120.00	200.00
☐ 26	40.00	120.00	200.00
☐ 27	40.00	120.00	200.00
☐ 28	40.00	120.00	200.00
☐ 29	40.00	120.00	200.00
☐ 30	40.00	120.00	200.00
☐ 31	32.00	96.00	160.00
☐ 32	32.00	96.00	160.00
☐ 33	32.00	96.00	160.00
☐ 34	32.00	96.00	160.00
☐ 35	32.00	96.00	160.00
☐ 36	32.00	96.00	160.00
☐ 37	32.00	96.00	160.00
☐ 38	32.00	96.00	160.00
☐ 39	32.00	96.00	160.00
☐ 40	32.00	96.00	160.00
☐ 41	25.00	75.00	125.00
☐ 42	25.00	75.00	125.00
☐ 43	25.00	75.00	125.00
☐ 44	25.00	75.00	125.00
☐ 45	25.00	75.00	125.00
☐ 46	25.00	75.00	125.00
☐ 47	25.00	75.00	125.00
☐ 48	25.00	75.00	125.00
☐ 49	25.00	75.00	125.00
☐ 50	25.00	75.00	125.00
☐ 51	18.00	54.00	90.00
☐ 52	18.00	54.00	90.00
☐ 53	18.00	54.00	90.00
☐ 54	18.00	54.00	90.00
☐ 55	18.00	54.00	90.00
☐ 56	18.00	54.00	90.00
☐ 57	18.00	54.00	90.00
☐ 58	18.00	54.00	90.00
☐ 59	18.00	54.00	90.00
☐ 60	18.00	54.00	90.00
☐ 61	15.00	45.00	75.00
☐ 62	15.00	45.00	75.00
☐ 63	15.00	45.00	75.00
☐ 64	15.00	45.00	75.00
☐ 65	15.00	45.00	75.00
☐ 66	15.00	45.00	75.00
☐ 67	15.00	45.00	75.00
☐ 68	15.00	45.00	75.00
☐ 69	15.00	45.00	75.00
☐ 70	15.00	45.00	75.00

	ORIG.	GOOD	FINE	N-MINT
71	12.00	36.00	60.00	
72	12.00	36.00	60.00	
73	12.00	36.00	60.00	
74	12.00	36.00	60.00	
75	12.00	36.00	60.00	
76	12.00	36.00	60.00	
77	12.00	36.00	60.00	
78	12.00	36.00	60.00	
79	12.00	36.00	60.00	
80	12.00	36.00	60.00	
81	9.60	28.80	48.00	
82	9.60	28.80	48.00	
83	9.60	28.80	48.00	
84	9.60	28.80	48.00	
85	9.60	28.80	48.00	
86	9.60	28.80	48.00	
87	9.60	28.80	48.00	
88	9.60	28.80	48.00	
89	9.60	28.80	48.00	
90	9.60	28.80	48.00	
91	9.60	28.80	48.00	
92	9.60	28.80	48.00	
93	9.60	28.80	48.00	
94	9.60	28.80	48.00	
95	9.60	28.80	48.00	
96	9.60	28.80	48.00	
97	9.60	28.80	48.00	
98	9.60	28.80	48.00	

SUGAR RAY FINHEAD
WOLF PRESS

	ORIG.	GOOD	FINE	N-MINT
1, b&w	2.50	0.50	1.50	2.50
2, b&w	2.95	0.59	1.77	2.95
3, b&w	2.95	0.59	1.77	2.95
4, b&w	2.95	0.59	1.77	2.95
5, b&w	2.95	0.59	1.77	2.95
6, Jul 94, b&w	2.95	0.59	1.77	2.95

SUGARVIRUS
ATOMEKA

	ORIG.	GOOD	FINE	N-MINT
0, nn, b&w	3.95	0.79	2.37	3.95

SUICIDE SQUAD
DC

	ORIG.	GOOD	FINE	N-MINT
1, May 87, HC(c)	0.75	0.40	1.20	2.00
2, Jun 87	0.75	0.30	0.90	1.50
3, Jul 87, D:Mindboggler	0.75	0.30	0.90	1.50
4, Aug 87	0.75	0.30	0.90	1.50
5, Sep 87	0.75	0.30	0.90	1.50
6, Oct 87	0.75	0.30	0.90	1.50
7, Nov 87	0.75	0.30	0.90	1.50
8, Dec 87	0.75	0.30	0.90	1.50
9, Jan 88, Millennium	0.75	0.30	0.90	1.50
10, Feb 88, A:Batman	0.75	0.40	1.20	2.00
11, Mar 88, A:Speedy,Vixen	0.75	0.30	0.90	1.50
12, Apr 88	0.75	0.30	0.90	1.50
13, May 88, A:JLI	0.75	0.30	0.90	1.50
14, Jun 88	0.75	0.30	0.90	1.50
15, Jul 88	0.75	0.30	0.90	1.50
16, Aug 88, A:Shade	1.00	0.35	1.05	1.75
17, Sep 88	1.00	0.30	0.90	1.50
18, Oct 88	1.00	0.30	0.90	1.50
19, Nov 88	1.00	0.30	0.90	1.50
20, Dec 88	1.00	0.30	0.90	1.50
21, Dec 88	1.00	0.30	0.90	1.50
22, Jan 89	1.00	0.30	0.90	1.50
23, Jan 89	1.00	0.30	0.90	1.50
24, Feb 89	1.00	0.30	0.90	1.50
25, Mar 89	1.00	0.30	0.90	1.50
26, Apr 89	1.00	0.30	0.90	1.50
27, May 89	1.00	0.30	0.90	1.50
28, May 89, Janus	1.00	0.30	0.90	1.50
29, Jun 89, Janus	1.00	0.30	0.90	1.50

	ORIG.	GOOD	FINE	N-MINT
30, Jun 89, Janus	1.00	0.30	0.90	1.50
31, Jul 89	1.00	0.30	0.90	1.50
32, Aug 89	1.00	0.30	0.90	1.50
33, Sep 89	1.00	0.30	0.90	1.50
34, Oct 89	1.00	0.30	0.90	1.50
35, Nov 89	1.00	0.30	0.90	1.50
36, Dec 89	1.00	0.30	0.90	1.50
37, Jan 90	1.00	0.30	0.90	1.50
38, Feb 90	1.00	0.30	0.90	1.50
39, Mar 90	1.00	0.30	0.90	1.50
40, Apr 90, Phoenix Gambit, poster	1.00	0.30	0.90	1.50
41, May 90, Phoenix Gambit	1.00	0.30	0.90	1.50
42, Jun 90, Phoenix Gambit	1.00	0.30	0.90	1.50
43, Jul 90, Phoenix Gambit	1.00	0.30	0.90	1.50
44, Aug 90, Flash	1.00	0.30	0.90	1.50
45, Sep 90	1.00	0.30	0.90	1.50
46, Oct 90	1.00	0.30	0.90	1.50
47, Nov 90	1.00	0.30	0.90	1.50
48, Dec 90, Joker	1.00	0.30	0.90	1.50
49, Jan 91	1.00	0.30	0.90	1.50
50, Feb 91		0.40	1.20	2.00
51, Mar 91	1.00	0.20	0.60	1.00
52, Apr 91	1.00	0.20	0.60	1.00
53, May 91	1.00	0.20	0.60	1.00
54, Jun 91	1.00	0.20	0.60	1.00
55, Jul 91	1.00	0.20	0.60	1.00
56, Aug 91	1.00	0.20	0.60	1.00
57, Sep 91	1.00	0.20	0.60	1.00
58, Oct 91, War of Gods	1.00	0.20	0.60	1.00
59, Nov 91	1.25	0.25	0.75	1.25
60, Dec 91	1.25	0.25	0.75	1.25
61	1.25	0.25	0.75	1.25
62	1.25	0.25	0.75	1.25
63	1.25	0.25	0.75	1.25
64	1.25	0.25	0.75	1.25
65	1.25	0.25	0.75	1.25
66, Jun 92	1.25	0.25	0.75	1.25

SUICIDE SQUAD ANNUAL

	ORIG.	GOOD	FINE	N-MINT
1, 88, A:Manhunter		0.30	0.90	1.50

SULTRY TEENAGE SUPER FOXES
SOLSON

	ORIG.	GOOD	FINE	N-MINT
1, 87, b&w	2.00	0.40	1.20	2.00
2, 87, b&w	2.00	0.40	1.20	2.00

SUN DEVILS
DC

	ORIG.	GOOD	FINE	N-MINT
1, Jul 84	1.25	0.40	1.20	2.00
2		0.30	0.90	1.50
3		0.30	0.90	1.50
4		0.30	0.90	1.50
5		0.30	0.90	1.50
6		0.30	0.90	1.50
7		0.30	0.90	1.50
8		0.30	0.90	1.50
9		0.30	0.90	1.50
10		0.30	0.90	1.50
11		0.30	0.90	1.50
12		0.30	0.90	1.50

SUN RUNNERS
PACIFIC

	ORIG.	GOOD	FINE	N-MINT
1, Feb 84, PB	1.50	0.30	0.90	1.50
2, Mar 84, PB	1.50	0.30	0.90	1.50
3, May 84, PB (moves to Eclipse)	1.50	0.30	0.90	1.50

	ORIG.	GOOD	FINE	N-MINT

SUN RUNNERS (former Pacific title)
ECLIPSE

	ORIG.	GOOD	FINE	N-MINT
4		0.35	1.05	1.75
5		0.35	1.05	1.75
6		0.35	1.05	1.75
7, (moves to Sirius)		0.35	1.05	1.75

SUN RUNNERS CHRISTMAS SPECIAL
AMAZING

	ORIG.	GOOD	FINE	N-MINT
1		0.39	1.17	1.95

SUNRISE
HARRIER

	ORIG.	GOOD	FINE	N-MINT
1		0.39	1.17	1.95
2		0.39	1.17	1.95

SUPER FRIENDS
DC

	ORIG.	GOOD	FINE	N-MINT
1, Nov 76	0.30	0.40	1.20	2.00
2, Dec 76	0.30	0.30	0.90	1.50
3, Feb 77	0.30	0.30	0.90	1.50
4, Apr 77	0.30	0.30	0.90	1.50
5, Jun 77	0.35	0.30	0.90	1.50
6, Aug 77	0.35	0.30	0.90	1.50
7, Oct 77	0.35	0.30	0.90	1.50
8, Nov 77	0.35	0.30	0.90	1.50
9, Dec 77	0.35	0.30	0.90	1.50
10, Mar 78	0.35	0.30	0.90	1.50
11, May 78	0.35	0.25	0.75	1.25
12, Jul 78	0.35	0.25	0.75	1.25
13, Sep 78	0.35	0.25	0.75	1.25
14, Nov 78	0.50	0.25	0.75	1.25
15, Dec 78	0.40	0.25	0.75	1.25
16, Jan 79	0.40	0.25	0.75	1.25
17, Feb 79	0.40	0.25	0.75	1.25
18, Mar 79	0.40	0.25	0.75	1.25
19, Apr 79	0.40	0.25	0.75	1.25
20, May 79	0.40	0.25	0.75	1.25
21, Jun 79	0.40	0.25	0.75	1.25
22, Jul 79	0.40	0.25	0.75	1.25
23, Aug 79	0.40	0.25	0.75	1.25
24, Sep 79	0.40	0.25	0.75	1.25
25, Oct 79	0.40	0.25	0.75	1.25
26, Nov 79	0.40	0.25	0.75	1.25
27, Dec 79	0.40	0.25	0.75	1.25
28, Jan 80	0.40	0.25	0.75	1.25
29, Feb 80	0.40	0.25	0.75	1.25
30, Mar 80	0.40	0.25	0.75	1.25
31, Apr 80	0.40	0.25	0.75	1.25
32, May 80	0.40	0.25	0.75	1.25
33, Jun 80	0.40	0.25	0.75	1.25
34, Jul 80	0.40	0.25	0.75	1.25
35, Aug 80	0.40	0.25	0.75	1.25
36, Sep 80	0.50	0.25	0.75	1.25
37, Oct 80	0.50	0.25	0.75	1.25
38, Nov 80	0.50	0.25	0.75	1.25
39, Dec 80	0.50	0.25	0.75	1.25
40, Jan 81	0.50	0.25	0.75	1.25
41, Feb 81	0.50	0.25	0.75	1.25
42, Mar 81	0.50	0.25	0.75	1.25
43, Apr 81	0.50	0.25	0.75	1.25
44, May 81	0.50	0.25	0.75	1.25
45, Jun 81	0.50	0.25	0.75	1.25
46, Jul 81	0.50	0.25	0.75	1.25
47, Aug 81	0.50	0.25	0.75	1.25

SUPER HEROES PUZZLES AND GAMES
MARVEL

	ORIG.	GOOD	FINE	N-MINT
0, Apr 80, giveaway, SpM,Hulk,Capt. America, Spider-Woman				

SUPER MARIO BROS.
VALIANT

	ORIG.	GOOD	FINE	N-MINT
1		0.39	1.17	1.95
2		0.39	1.17	1.95

	ORIG.	GOOD	FINE	N-MINT
3		0.39	1.17	1.95
4		0.39	1.17	1.95
5		0.39	1.17	1.95

SUPER MARIO BROS. (starting over, 1991)

	ORIG.	GOOD	FINE	N-MINT
1		0.30	0.90	1.50
2		0.30	0.90	1.50
3		0.30	0.90	1.50
4		0.30	0.90	1.50
5		0.30	0.90	1.50

SUPER MARIO BROS. SPECIAL EDITION

	ORIG.	GOOD	FINE	N-MINT
1		0.39	1.17	1.95

SUPER POWERS (1st series)
DC

	ORIG.	GOOD	FINE	N-MINT
1, Jul 84, JK(c)	0.75	0.30	0.90	1.50
2, Aug 84, JK(c)	0.75	0.20	0.60	1.00
3, Sep 84, JK(c)	0.75	0.20	0.60	1.00
4, Oct 84, JK(c)	0.75	0.20	0.60	1.00
5, Nov 84, JK(c)	0.75	0.20	0.60	1.00

SUPER POWERS (2nd series)

	ORIG.	GOOD	FINE	N-MINT
1, Sep 85, JK	0.75	0.20	0.60	1.00
2, Oct 85, JK	0.75	0.20	0.60	1.00
3, Nov 85, JK	0.75	0.20	0.60	1.00
4, Dec 85, JK	0.75	0.20	0.60	1.00
5, Jan 86, JK	0.75	0.20	0.60	1.00
6, Feb 86, JK	0.75	0.20	0.60	1.00

SUPER POWERS (3rd series)

	ORIG.	GOOD	FINE	N-MINT
1, Sep 86, CI	0.75	0.20	0.60	1.00
2, Oct 86, CI	0.75	0.20	0.60	1.00
3, Nov 86, CI	0.75	0.20	0.60	1.00
4, Dec 86, CI	0.75	0.20	0.60	1.00

SUPER SEXXX
EROS

	ORIG.	GOOD	FINE	N-MINT
1, adult, b&w	3.25	0.65	1.95	3.25

SUPER SOLDIER
DC/AMALGAM

	ORIG.	GOOD	FINE	N-MINT
1, Apr 96	1.95	0.39	1.17	1.95

SUPER SOLDIERS
MARVEL

	ORIG.	GOOD	FINE	N-MINT
1, foil cover	2.50	0.50	1.50	2.50
2	1.75	0.35	1.05	1.75
3	1.75	0.35	1.05	1.75
4	1.75	0.35	1.05	1.75
5	1.75	0.35	1.05	1.75
6	1.75	0.35	1.05	1.75
7	1.75	0.35	1.05	1.75
8	1.75	0.35	1.05	1.75

SUPER SONIC VS. HYPER KNUCKLES
ARCHIE

	ORIG.	GOOD	FINE	N-MINT
1, 96, one-shot	2.00	0.40	1.20	2.00

SUPER-TEAM FAMILY
DC

	ORIG.	GOOD	FINE	N-MINT
1, Nov 75	0.50	0.60	1.80	3.00
2, Jan 76	0.50	0.40	1.20	2.00
3, Mar 76	0.50	0.40	1.20	2.00
4, May 76	0.50	0.40	1.20	2.00
5, Jul 76	0.50	0.40	1.20	2.00
6, Sep 76	0.50	0.25	0.75	1.25
7, Nov 76	0.50	0.25	0.75	1.25
8, Jan 77	0.50	0.25	0.75	1.25
9, Mar 77	0.50	0.25	0.75	1.25
10, May 77	0.50	0.25	0.75	1.25
11, Jul 77	0.60	0.25	0.75	1.25
12, Sep 77	0.60	0.25	0.75	1.25
13, Nov 77	0.60	0.25	0.75	1.25
14, Jan 78	0.60	0.25	0.75	1.25
15, Apr 78	0.60	0.25	0.75	1.25

	ORIG.	GOOD	FINE	N-MINT

SUPER-VILLAIN CLASSICS
MARVEL

	ORIG.	GOOD	FINE	N-MINT
1, May 83, O:Galactus, reprint				
	0.60	0.12	0.36	0.60

SUPER-VILLAIN TEAM-UP

	ORIG.	GOOD	FINE	N-MINT
1	0.25	0.80	2.40	4.00
2	0.25	0.50	1.50	2.50
3	0.25	0.50	1.50	2.50
4	0.25	0.50	1.50	2.50
5	0.25	0.50	1.50	2.50
6	0.25	0.30	0.90	1.50
7	0.25	0.30	0.90	1.50
8, Oct 76	0.30	0.30	0.90	1.50
9, Dec 76	0.30	0.30	0.90	1.50
10, Feb 77	0.30	0.30	0.90	1.50
11, Apr 77	0.30	0.30	0.90	1.50
12, Jun 77	0.30	0.30	0.90	1.50
13, Aug 77	0.30	0.30	0.90	1.50
14, Oct 77	0.30	0.30	0.90	1.50
15, Nov 77	0.30	0.30	0.90	1.50
16, May 79	0.40	0.30	0.90	1.50
17, Jun 80	0.40	0.30	0.90	1.50

SUPERBOY
DC

	ORIG.	GOOD	FINE	N-MINT
67, Sep 58, O,1:Klax-Ar..	0.10	8.00	24.00	40.00
68, O&1:Bizarro		80.00	240.00	400.00
69, Dec 58	0.10	14.00	42.00	70.00
70		14.00	42.00	70.00
71	0.10	12.00	36.00	60.00
72, Apr 59	0.10	12.00	36.00	60.00
73		12.00	36.00	60.00
74		12.00	36.00	60.00
75		12.00	36.00	60.00
76		12.00	36.00	60.00
77		12.00	36.00	60.00
78, O:Mr. Mxyzptlk		18.00	54.00	90.00
79		12.00	36.00	60.00
80		12.00	36.00	60.00
81, Jun 60	0.10	8.40	25.20	42.00
82		8.40	25.20	42.00
83		8.40	25.20	42.00
84		8.40	25.20	42.00
85, Dec 60	0.10	8.40	25.20	42.00
86, 1:Pete Ross;A:Legion.		25.00	75.00	125.00
87		8.40	25.20	42.00
88, Apr 61	0.10	8.40	25.20	42.00
89, Jun 61, O&1:Mon-El ..		30.00	90.00	150.00
90, Jul 61	0.10	8.00	24.00	40.00
91, Sep 61	0.10	7.20	21.60	36.00
92		7.20	21.60	36.00
93, Dec 61, A:Legion	0.12	11.00	33.00	55.00
94, Jan 62	0.12	7.20	21.60	36.00
95, Mar 62	0.12	7.20	21.60	36.00
96		5.60	16.80	28.00
97		5.60	16.80	28.00
98, Jul 62, O&1:Ultra Boy;A:Legion				
	0.12	10.00	30.00	50.00
99, Sep 62	0.12	5.60	16.80	28.00
100, Oct 62, 1:Phantom Zone villains				
	0.12	36.00	108.00	180.00
101, Dec 62	0.12	3.60	10.80	18.00
102, Jan 63	0.12	3.60	10.80	18.00
103		3.60	10.80	18.00
104, Apr 63, O:Phantom Zone				
	0.12	4.80	14.40	24.00
105, Jun 63	0.12	3.60	10.80	18.00
106, Jul 63	0.12	2.00	6.00	10.00
107, Sep 63	0.12	2.00	6.00	10.00
108, Oct 63	0.12	2.00	6.00	10.00
109, Dec 63	0.12	2.00	6.00	10.00
110, Jan 64	0.12	2.00	6.00	10.00

	ORIG.	GOOD	FINE	N-MINT
111, Mar 64	0.12	2.00	6.00	10.00
112, Apr 64	0.12	2.00	6.00	10.00
113, Jun 64	0.12	2.00	6.00	10.00
114, Jul 64	0.12	2.00	6.00	10.00
115, Sep 64	0.12	2.00	6.00	10.00
116, Oct 64	0.12	2.00	6.00	10.00
117, Dec 64, A:Legion	0.12	2.40	7.20	12.00
118, Jan 65	0.12	1.40	4.20	7.00
119, Mar 65	0.12	1.40	4.20	7.00
120, Apr 65	0.12	1.40	4.20	7.00
121, Jun 65	0.12	1.40	4.20	7.00
122, Jul 65	0.12	1.40	4.20	7.00
123, Sep 65	0.12	1.40	4.20	7.00
124, Oct 65	0.12	1.40	4.20	7.00
125, Dec 65, O,1: Kid Psycho				
	0.12	1.40	4.20	7.00
126, Jan 66	0.12	1.40	4.20	7.00
127, Mar 66	0.12	1.40	4.20	7.00
128, Apr 66	0.12	1.40	4.20	7.00
129, May 66, giant	0.25	1.20	3.60	6.00
130, Jun 66	0.12	1.00	3.00	5.00
131, Jul 66	0.12	1.00	3.00	5.00
132, Sep 66	0.12	1.00	3.00	5.00
133, Oct 66	0.12	1.00	3.00	5.00
134, Dec 66	0.12	1.00	3.00	5.00
135, Jan 67	0.12	1.00	3.00	5.00
136, Mar 67	0.12	1.00	3.00	5.00
137, Apr 67	0.12	1.00	3.00	5.00
138, Jun 67, giant	0.25	1.20	3.60	6.00
139, Jun 67	0.12	0.80	2.40	4.00
140, Jul 67	0.12	0.80	2.40	4.00
141, Sep 67	0.12	0.80	2.40	4.00
142, Oct 67	0.12	0.80	2.40	4.00
143, Dec 67, NA (c)	0.12	0.80	2.40	4.00
144, Jan 68	0.12	0.80	2.40	4.00
145, Mar 68, NA(c)	0.12	0.80	2.40	4.00
146, Apr 68, NA(c)	0.12	0.80	2.40	4.00
147, Jun 68, giant O:Saturn Girl, Cosmic Boy				
	0.25	1.00	3.00	5.00
148, Jun 68, NA (c)	0.12	0.60	1.80	3.00
149, Jul 68, NA (c)	0.12	0.60	1.80	3.00
150, Sep 68, NA (c)	0.12	0.60	1.80	3.00
151, Oct 68, NA (c)	0.12	0.60	1.80	3.00
152, Dec 68, WW, NA (c)	0.12	0.60	1.80	3.00
153, Jan 69, WW, NA (c)	0.12	0.60	1.80	3.00
154, Mar 69, WW, NA (c)				
	0.12	0.60	1.80	3.00
155, Apr 69, WW, NA (c)	0.12	0.60	1.80	3.00
156, Jun 69, giant	0.25	0.60	1.80	3.00
157, Jun 69, WW	0.12	0.60	1.80	3.00
158, Jul 69, WW	0.15	0.60	1.80	3.00
159, Sep 69, WW	0.15	0.60	1.80	3.00
160, Oct 69, WW	0.15	0.60	1.80	3.00
161, Dec 69, WW	0.15	0.60	1.80	3.00
162, Jan 70	0.15	0.60	1.80	3.00
163, Mar 70, NA (c)	0.15	0.60	1.80	3.00
164, Apr 70, NA (c)	0.15	0.60	1.80	3.00
165, Jun 70, giant	0.25	0.60	1.80	3.00
166, Jun 70, NA(c)	0.15	0.45	1.35	2.25
167, Jul 70, NA(c)	0.15	0.45	1.35	2.25
168, Sep 70, NA(c)	0.15	0.45	1.35	2.25
169, Oct 70	0.15	0.40	1.20	2.00
170, Dec 70	0.15	0.40	1.20	2.00
171, Jan 71	0.15	0.40	1.20	2.00
172, Mar 71	0.15	0.40	1.20	2.00
173, Apr 71, GT, DG, NA (c) O:Cosmic Boy				
	0.15	0.50	1.50	2.50
174, Jun 71, giant	0.25	0.60	1.80	3.00
175, Jun 71, MA, NA (c)	0.15	0.45	1.35	2.25
176, Jul 71, MA, GT, WW, NA (c) A:Legion				
	0.15	0.60	1.80	3.00
177, Sep 71, MA	0.25	0.30	0.90	1.50

	ORIG.	GOOD	FINE	N-MINT
178, Oct 71, MA, NA (c) .	0.25	0.35	1.05	1.75
179, Nov 71	0.25	0.30	0.90	1.50
180, Dec 71..................	0.25	0.30	0.90	1.50
181, Jan 72	0.25	0.30	0.90	1.50
182, Feb 72	0.25	0.30	0.90	1.50
183, Mar 72	0.25	0.30	0.90	1.50
184, Apr 72	0.25	0.30	0.90	1.50
185, May 72, A:Legion ...	0.50	0.40	1.20	2.00
186, May 72	0.25	0.30	0.90	1.50
187, Jun 72	0.25	0.30	0.90	1.50
188, Jul 72	0.20	0.30	0.90	1.50
189, Aug 72	0.20	0.30	0.90	1.50
190, Sep 72	0.20	0.30	0.90	1.50
191, Oct 72	0.20	0.30	0.90	1.50
192, Dec 72.................	0.20	0.24	0.72	1.20
193, Feb 73	0.20	0.24	0.72	1.20
194, Apr 73	0.20	0.24	0.72	1.20
195, Jun 73, Legion;J:Wildfire				
....	0.20	0.24	0.72	1.20
196, Jul 73, last Superboy solo story				
....	0.20	0.25	0.75	1.25
197, Sep 73, MA, Legion begins				
....	0.20	1.00	3.00	5.00
198, Oct 73, V:Fatal Five	0.20	0.60	1.80	3.00
199, Nov 73	0.20	0.60	1.80	3.00
200, Feb 74, M:Bouncing Boy, Duo Damsel				
....	0.20	1.00	3.00	5.00
201, Apr 74	0.20	0.60	1.80	3.00
202, Jun 74.................	0.60	0.60	1.80	3.00
203, Aug 74, D: Invisible Kid				
....	0.20	0.60	1.80	3.00
204, Oct 74, 1:Anti Lad ..	0.20	0.60	1.80	3.00
205, Dec 74.................	0.20	0.60	1.80	3.00
206, Jan 75	0.25	0.60	1.80	3.00
207, Feb 75	0.25	0.60	1.80	3.00
208, Apr 75	0.50	0.60	1.80	3.00
209, Jun 75.................	0.25	0.60	1.80	3.00
210, Aug 75, O:Karate Kid				
....	0.25	0.60	1.80	3.00
211, Sep 75, A:Legion Subs				
....	0.25	0.50	1.50	2.50
212, Oct 75	0.25	0.50	1.50	2.50
213, Dec 75, A:Miracle Machine				
....	0.25	0.50	1.50	2.50
214, Jan 76	0.25	0.50	1.50	2.50
215, Mar 76	0.25	0.50	1.50	2.50
216, Apr 76, 1:Tyroc	0.30	0.50	1.50	2.50
217, Jun 76, 1:Laurel Kent				
....	0.30	0.50	1.50	2.50
218, Jul 76, J:Tyroc	0.30	0.50	1.50	2.50
219, Sep 76..................	0.30	0.50	1.50	2.50
220, Oct 76	0.30	0.50	1.50	2.50
221, Nov 76, O&1:Grimbor and Charma				
....	0.30	0.50	1.50	2.50
222, Dec 76.................	0.30	0.50	1.50	2.50
223, Jan 77, V:Time Trapper				
....	0.30	0.50	1.50	2.50
224, Feb 77, V:Stargrave	0.30	0.50	1.50	2.50
225, Mar 77	0.30	0.40	1.20	2.00
226, Apr 77, 1&J:Dawnstar;Stargrave's identity revealed				
....	0.30	0.40	1.20	2.00
227, May 77	0.30	0.40	1.20	2.00
228, Jun 77, D:Chemical King				
....	0.35	0.50	1.50	2.50
229, Jul 77	0.35	0.40	1.20	2.00
230, Aug 77, Bouncing Boy's powers restored;(becomes *Superboy & the Legion of Super-Heroes*)				
....	0.35	0.40	1.20	2.00

SUPERBOY (1994-)

	ORIG.	GOOD	FINE	N-MINT
0, Oct 94	1.50	0.30	0.90	1.50
1, Feb 94	1.50	0.30	0.90	1.50

	ORIG.	GOOD	FINE	N-MINT
2, Mar 94, 1:Knockout,Scavenger				
....	1.50	0.30	0.90	1.50
3, Apr 94........................	1.50	0.30	0.90	1.50
4, May 94........................	1.50	0.30	0.90	1.50
5, Jun 94	1.50	0.30	0.90	1.50
6, Jul 94, "Worlds Collide" Part 3;crossover with Milestone Media	1.50	0.30	0.90	1.50
7, Aug 94, "Worlds Collide" Part 8;crossover with Milestone Media	1.50	0.30	0.90	1.50
8, Sep 94, "Zero Hour";meets "original" Superboy				
....	1.50	0.30	0.90	1.50
9, Nov 94	1.50	0.30	0.90	1.50
10, Dec 94	1.50	0.30	0.90	1.50
11, Jan 95.......................	1.50	0.30	0.90	1.50
12, Feb 95.......................	1.50	0.30	0.90	1.50
13, Mar 95, "Watery Grave" Part 1 of 3				
....	1.50	0.30	0.90	1.50
14, Apr 95, "Watery Grave" Part 2 of 3				
....	1.50	0.30	0.90	1.50
15, May 95, "Watery Grave" Part 3 of 3				
....	1.50	0.30	0.90	1.50
16, Jun 95, V:Loose Cannon				
....	1.95	0.39	1.17	1.95
17, Jul 95........................	1.95	0.39	1.17	1.95
18, Aug 95, V:Valor........	1.95	0.39	1.17	1.95
19, Sep 95, Valor enters Phantom Zone				
....	1.95	0.39	1.17	1.95
20, Oct 95, A:Green Lantern				
....	1.95	0.39	1.17	1.95
21, Nov 95, "Future Tense" Part 1 of 3;continues in *Legion of Super-Heroes* #74	1.95	0.39	1.17	1.95
22, Dec 95, "Underworld Unleashed";A:Killer Frost				
....	1.95	0.39	1.17	1.95
23, Jan 96.......................	1.95	0.39	1.17	1.95
24, Feb 96, Knockout's past revealed				
....	1.95	0.39	1.17	1.95
25, Mar 96, "Losin' It" Part 1 of 6				
....	2.95	0.59	1.77	2.95
26, Apr 96, "Losin' It" Part 2 of 6				
....	1.95	0.39	1.17	1.95
27, May 96, "Losin' It" Part 3 of 6				
....	1.95	0.39	1.17	1.95
28, Jun 96, "Losin' It" Part 4 of 6;A:Supergirl				
....	1.95	0.39	1.17	1.95
29, Jul 96, "Losin' It" Part 5 of 6				
....	1.95	0.39	1.17	1.95

SUPERBOY (TV version)

	ORIG.	GOOD	FINE	N-MINT
1, Jan 90, photo cover....	1.00	0.20	0.60	1.00
2, Feb 90........................	1.00	0.20	0.60	1.00
3, Mar 90........................	1.00	0.20	0.60	1.00
4, Apr 90........................	1.00	0.20	0.60	1.00
5, May 90........................	1.00	0.20	0.60	1.00
6, Jun 90........................	1.00	0.20	0.60	1.00
7, Jul 90..........................	1.00	0.20	0.60	1.00
8, Aug 90, Bizarro...........	1.00	0.20	0.60	1.00
9, Sep 90, CS..................	1.00	0.20	0.60	1.00
10, Oct 90, CS	1.00	0.20	0.60	1.00
11, Nov 90, CS................	1.00	0.20	0.60	1.00
12, Dec 90, CS................	1.00	0.20	0.60	1.00
13, Jan 91, Mxyzptlk.......	1.00	0.20	0.60	1.00
14, Feb 91.......................	1.00	0.20	0.60	1.00
15, Mar 91.......................	1.00	0.20	0.60	1.00
16, Apr 91.......................	1.25	0.25	0.75	1.25
17, May 91.......................	1.25	0.25	0.75	1.25
18, Jun 91, (becomes *The Adventures of Superboy*)				
....	1.25	0.25	0.75	1.25

SUPERBOY AND THE LEGION OF SUPER-HEROES
(was Superboy)

	ORIG.	GOOD	FINE	N-MINT
231, Sep 77	0.60	0.40	1.20	2.00
232, Oct 77	0.60	0.40	1.20	2.00

	ORIG.	GOOD	FINE	N-MINT
❑ 233, Nov 77, O&1:Infinite Man				
....0.60	0.40	1.20	2.00
❑ 234, Dec 77....................0.60	0.40	1.20	2.00
❑ 235, Jan 78.....................0.60	0.40	1.20	2.00
❑ 236, Feb 78.....................0.60	0.40	1.20	2.00
❑ 237, Mar 78, WS;L:Saturn Girl, Lightning Lad				
....0.60	0.50	1.50	2.50
❑ 238, Apr 78, wraparound cover;reprints *Adventure*				
Comics #359 and 360....0.60	0.25	0.75	1.25
❑ 239, May 78.....................0.60	0.25	0.75	1.25
❑ 240, Jun 78, V:Grimbor;O:Dawnstar				
....0.60	0.25	0.75	1.25
❑ 241, Jul 78.......................0.60	0.25	0.75	1.25
❑ 242, Aug 78.....................0.60	0.25	0.75	1.25
❑ 243, Sep 78.....................0.50	0.25	0.75	1.25
❑ 244, Oct 78, Mordru returns				
....0.50	0.25	0.75	1.25
❑ 245, Nov 78, Lightning Lad and Saturn Girl rejoin				
....0.50	0.25	0.75	1.25
❑ 246, Dec 78.....................0.40	0.25	0.75	1.25
❑ 247, Jan 79.....................0.40	0.25	0.75	1.25
❑ 248, Feb 79.....................0.40	0.30	0.90	1.50
❑ 249, Mar 79 ....0.40	0.30	0.90	1.50
❑ 250, Apr 79......................0.40	0.30	0.90	1.50
❑ 251, May 79.....................0.40	0.30	0.90	1.50
❑ 252, Jun 79......................0.40	0.30	0.90	1.50
❑ 253, Jul 79, V:League of Super-Assassins;1:Blok				
....0.40	0.30	0.90	1.50
❑ 254, Aug 79 ....0.40	0.30	0.90	1.50
❑ 255, Sep 79, Legion visits Krypton before it's destroyed				
....0.40	0.30	0.90	1.50
❑ 256, Oct 79, O:Brainiac 5				
....0.40	0.30	0.90	1.50
❑ 257, Nov 79, SD.............0.40	0.30	0.90	1.50
❑ 258, Dec 79, V:Psycho Warrior;(becomes *Legion of*				
Super-Heroes) 0.40	0.30	0.90	1.50

SUPERBOY ANNUAL

	ORIG.	GOOD	FINE	N-MINT
❑ 1, Sum 64 ....0.25	20.00	60.00	100.00

SUPERBOY ANNUAL (1994-)

	ORIG.	GOOD	FINE	N-MINT
❑ 1, 94, "Elseworlds";concludes story from *Adventures of*				
Superman Annual #6 .....2.95	0.59	1.77	2.95
❑ 2, 95, "Year One";Identity of being who Superboy was				
cloned from is revealed.. 3.95	0.79	2.37	3.95

SUPERBOY SPECIAL

	ORIG.	GOOD	FINE	N-MINT
❑ 1, 92, TV tie-in 1.75	0.35	1.05	1.75

SUPERCOPS
NOW

	ORIG.	GOOD	FINE	N-MINT
❑ 1, Sep 90, double-sized.. 2.75	0.55	1.65	2.75
❑ 2, Oct 90 ....1.75	0.35	1.05	1.75
❑ 3, Nov 90 ....1.75	0.35	1.05	1.75
❑ 4, Feb 91 ....1.75	0.35	1.05	1.75

SUPERFAN
MARK 1

	ORIG.	GOOD	FINE	N-MINT
❑ 1, b&w	0.39	1.17	1.95

SUPERGIRL
DC

	ORIG.	GOOD	FINE	N-MINT
❑ 0, 84, 1984 Honda giveaway	0.40	1.20	2.00
❑ 1	0.40	1.20	2.00
❑ 2	0.30	0.90	1.50
❑ 3	0.30	0.90	1.50
❑ 4	0.30	0.90	1.50
❑ 5	0.30	0.90	1.50
❑ 6	0.30	0.90	1.50
❑ 7	0.20	0.60	1.00
❑ 8	0.20	0.60	1.00
❑ 9	0.20	0.60	1.00
❑ 10, Sep 74, A:Prez 0.20	0.20	0.60	1.00

SUPERGIRL (1994 mini-series)

	ORIG.	GOOD	FINE	N-MINT
❑ 1, Feb 94.......................1.50	0.30	0.90	1.50
❑ 2, Mar 94 ....1.50	0.30	0.90	1.50
❑ 3, Apr 94 ....1.50	0.30	0.90	1.50
❑ 4, May 94 ....1.50	0.30	0.90	1.50

SUPERGIRL (movie)

	ORIG.	GOOD	FINE	N-MINT
❑ 1, Feb 85, GM	0.25	0.75	1.25

SUPERGIRL
(was Daring New Adventures of Supergirl)

	ORIG.	GOOD	FINE	N-MINT
❑ 14, Dec 83	0.20	0.60	1.00
❑ 15, Jan 84......................	0.20	0.60	1.00
❑ 16, Feb 84......................	0.20	0.60	1.00
❑ 17, Mar 84......................	0.20	0.60	1.00
❑ 18, Apr 84.......................	0.20	0.60	1.00
❑ 19, May 84......................	0.20	0.60	1.00
❑ 20, Jun 84, C:JLA, Teen Titans	0.30	0.90	1.50
❑ 21, Jul 84, CI	0.20	0.60	1.00
❑ 22, Aug 84, CI.................	0.20	0.60	1.00
❑ 23, Sep 84, CI.................	0.20	0.60	1.00

SUPERGIRL ANNUAL

	ORIG.	GOOD	FINE	N-MINT
❑ 1, 96, "Legends of the Dead Earth"				
....2.95	0.59	1.77	2.95

SUPERGIRL MOVIE SPECIAL

	ORIG.	GOOD	FINE	N-MINT
❑ 1, 85, adapts movie 1.25	0.25	0.75	1.25

SUPERGIRL, DARING NEW ADVENTURES OF

	ORIG.	GOOD	FINE	N-MINT
❑ 1, Nov 82, CI...................	0.50	1.50	2.50
❑ 2, Dec 82	0.40	1.20	2.00
❑ 3, Jan 83.........................	0.40	1.20	2.00
❑ 4, Feb 83.........................	0.30	0.90	1.50
❑ 5, Mar 83.........................	0.20	0.60	1.00
❑ 6, Apr 83.........................	0.20	0.60	1.00
❑ 7, May 83.........................	0.20	0.60	1.00
❑ 8, Jun 83.........................	0.20	0.60	1.00
❑ 9, Jul 83..........................	0.20	0.60	1.00
❑ 10, Aug 83.......................	0.20	0.60	1.00
❑ 11, Sep 83.......................	0.20	0.60	1.00
❑ 12, Oct 83........................	0.20	0.60	1.00
❑ 13, Nov 83, (becomes *Supergirl*) 0.20	0.60	1.00

SUPERGIRL/LEX LUTHOR SPECIAL

	ORIG.	GOOD	FINE	N-MINT
❑ 1, 93, one-shot;cover says "Supergirl and Team Luthor"				
....2.50	0.80	2.40	4.00

SUPERMAN

	ORIG.	GOOD	FINE	N-MINT
❑ 100	200.00	600.00	1000.00
❑ 101	32.00	96.00	160.00
❑ 102	32.00	96.00	160.00
❑ 103	32.00	96.00	160.00
❑ 104	32.00	96.00	160.00
❑ 105	32.00	96.00	160.00
❑ 106	32.00	96.00	160.00
❑ 107	32.00	96.00	160.00
❑ 108	32.00	96.00	160.00
❑ 109	32.00	96.00	160.00
❑ 110	32.00	96.00	160.00
❑ 111	28.00	84.00	140.00
❑ 112	28.00	84.00	140.00
❑ 113	28.00	84.00	140.00
❑ 114	28.00	84.00	140.00
❑ 115	28.00	84.00	140.00
❑ 116	28.00	84.00	140.00
❑ 117	28.00	84.00	140.00
❑ 118	28.00	84.00	140.00
❑ 119	28.00	84.00	140.00
❑ 120	28.00	84.00	140.00
❑ 121	24.00	72.00	120.00
❑ 122	24.00	72.00	120.00
❑ 123	24.00	72.00	120.00
❑ 124	24.00	72.00	120.00
❑ 125	24.00	72.00	120.00
❑ 126	24.00	72.00	120.00
❑ 127	28.00	84.00	140.00

	ORIG.	GOOD	FINE	N-MINT
☐ 128		24.00	72.00	120.00
☐ 129		28.00	84.00	140.00
☐ 130		24.00	72.00	120.00
☐ 131		16.00	48.00	80.00
☐ 132		16.00	48.00	80.00
☐ 133		16.00	48.00	80.00
☐ 134		16.00	48.00	80.00
☐ 135		16.00	48.00	80.00
☐ 136		16.00	48.00	80.00
☐ 137		16.00	48.00	80.00
☐ 138		16.00	48.00	80.00
☐ 139		16.00	48.00	80.00
☐ 140, blue kryptonite		16.00	48.00	80.00
☐ 141		12.00	36.00	60.00
☐ 142, Jan 61	0.10	12.00	36.00	60.00
☐ 143, Feb 61	0.10	12.00	36.00	60.00
☐ 144, Apr 61	0.10	12.00	36.00	60.00
☐ 145, Apr 61	0.10	12.00	36.00	60.00
☐ 146, Superman's life		18.00	54.00	90.00
☐ 147, Aug 61, I:adult Legion	0.10	16.00	48.00	80.00
☐ 148		10.00	30.00	50.00
☐ 149, C:9th Legion		24.00	72.00	120.00
☐ 150, Jan 62	0.12	4.80	14.40	24.00
☐ 151, Feb 62	0.12	6.00	18.00	30.00
☐ 152, A:Legion		10.00	30.00	50.00
☐ 153		4.80	14.40	24.00
☐ 154, Jul 62	0.12	4.80	14.40	24.00
☐ 155, Aug 62	0.12	4.80	14.40	24.00
☐ 156, Oct 62	0.12	4.80	14.40	24.00
☐ 157, Nov 62	0.12	4.80	14.40	24.00
☐ 158, Jan 63	0.12	4.80	14.40	24.00
☐ 159, Feb 63	0.12	4.80	14.40	24.00
☐ 160, Apr 63	0.12	4.80	14.40	24.00
☐ 161, May 63	0.12	4.80	14.40	24.00
☐ 162, Jul 63	0.12	4.80	14.40	24.00
☐ 163, Aug 63	0.12	4.80	14.40	24.00
☐ 164, Oct 63	0.12	4.80	14.40	24.00
☐ 165, Nov 63	0.12	4.80	14.40	24.00
☐ 166, Nov 63	0.12	4.80	14.40	24.00
☐ 167, Feb 64, O:Brainiac	0.12	5.60	16.80	28.00
☐ 168, Apr 64	0.12	4.00	12.00	20.00
☐ 169, May 64	0.12	4.00	12.00	20.00
☐ 170, Jul 64	0.12	4.00	12.00	20.00
☐ 171, Aug 64	0.12	4.00	12.00	20.00
☐ 172, Oct 64	0.12	4.00	12.00	20.00
☐ 173, Nov 64	0.12	4.00	12.00	20.00
☐ 174, Jan 65	0.12	4.00	12.00	20.00
☐ 175, Feb 65	0.12	4.00	12.00	20.00
☐ 176, Apr 65	0.12	4.00	12.00	20.00
☐ 177, May 65	0.12	4.00	12.00	20.00
☐ 178, Jul 65	0.12	4.00	12.00	20.00
☐ 179, Aug 65	0.12	4.00	12.00	20.00
☐ 180, Oct 65	0.12	4.00	12.00	20.00
☐ 181, Nov 65	0.12	4.00	12.00	20.00
☐ 182, Jan 66	0.12	4.00	12.00	20.00
☐ 183, Jan 66, giant	0.25	4.00	12.00	20.00
☐ 184, Feb 66	0.12	4.00	12.00	20.00
☐ 185, Apr 66	0.12	4.00	12.00	20.00
☐ 186, May 66	0.12	4.00	12.00	20.00
☐ 187, Jun 66, giant	0.25	4.00	12.00	20.00
☐ 188, Jul 66	0.12	4.00	12.00	20.00
☐ 189, Aug 66	0.12	4.00	12.00	20.00
☐ 190, Oct 66	0.12	4.00	12.00	20.00
☐ 191, Nov 66	0.12	4.00	12.00	20.00
☐ 192, Jan 67	0.12	4.00	12.00	20.00
☐ 193, Feb 67, giant	0.25	4.00	12.00	20.00
☐ 194, Feb 67	0.12	4.00	12.00	20.00
☐ 195, Apr 67	0.12	13.00	39.00	65.00
☐ 196, May 67	0.12	4.00	12.00	20.00
☐ 197, Jul 67, giant	0.25	4.00	12.00	20.00
☐ 198, Jul 67	0.12	4.00	12.00	20.00

	ORIG.	GOOD	FINE	N-MINT
☐ 199, Aug 67	0.12	4.00	12.00	20.00
☐ 200, Oct 67	0.12	4.00	12.00	20.00
☐ 201, Nov 67	0.12	1.60	4.80	8.00
☐ 202, Jan 67, giant	0.25	1.60	4.80	8.00
☐ 203, Jan 67	0.12	1.60	4.80	8.00
☐ 204, Feb 68, 1:Q-energy	0.12	1.60	4.80	8.00
☐ 205, Apr 68	0.12	1.60	4.80	8.00
☐ 206, May 68	0.12	1.60	4.80	8.00
☐ 207, Jul 68, giant	0.25	1.80	5.40	9.00
☐ 208, Jul 68	0.12	1.60	4.80	8.00
☐ 209, Aug 68	0.12	1.60	4.80	8.00
☐ 210, Oct 68	0.12	1.60	4.80	8.00
☐ 211, Nov 68	0.12	1.60	4.80	8.00
☐ 212, Jan 69, giant	0.25	1.60	4.80	8.00
☐ 213, Jan 69	0.12	1.60	4.80	8.00
☐ 214, Feb 69	0.12	1.60	4.80	8.00
☐ 215, Apr 69	0.12	1.60	4.80	8.00
☐ 216, May 69	0.12	1.60	4.80	8.00
☐ 217, Jul 69, giant	0.25	1.80	5.40	9.00
☐ 218, Jul 69	0.15	1.60	4.80	8.00
☐ 219, Aug 69	0.15	1.60	4.80	8.00
☐ 220, Oct 69	0.15	1.60	4.80	8.00
☐ 221, Nov 69	0.15	1.60	4.80	8.00
☐ 222, Jan 70, giant	0.25	1.60	4.80	8.00
☐ 223, Jan 70	0.15	1.60	4.80	8.00
☐ 224, Feb 70	0.15	1.60	4.80	8.00
☐ 225, Apr 70	0.15	1.60	4.80	8.00
☐ 226, May 70	0.15	1.60	4.80	8.00
☐ 227, Jul 70, giant	0.25	1.60	4.80	8.00
☐ 228, Jul 70, CS/DA	0.15	1.60	4.80	8.00
☐ 229, Aug 70, CS/DA	0.15	1.60	4.80	8.00
☐ 230, Oct 70, CS/DA	0.15	1.60	4.80	8.00
☐ 231, Nov 70, CS/DA	0.15	1.60	4.80	8.00
☐ 232, Jan 71, giant	0.25	1.60	4.80	8.00
☐ 233, Jan 71	0.15	1.60	4.80	8.00
☐ 234, Feb 71	0.15	1.60	4.80	8.00
☐ 235, Mar 71	0.15	1.60	4.80	8.00
☐ 236, Apr 71	0.15	1.60	4.80	8.00
☐ 237, May 71	0.15	1.60	4.80	8.00
☐ 238, Jun 71	0.15	1.60	4.80	8.00
☐ 239, Jul 71, CS/MA, GM	0.25	1.60	4.80	8.00
☐ 240, Jul 71	0.15	1.60	4.80	8.00
☐ 241, Aug 71	0.15	1.60	4.80	8.00
☐ 242, Sep 71	0.15	1.60	4.80	8.00
☐ 243, Oct 71	0.25	1.60	4.80	8.00
☐ 244, Nov 71	0.25	1.60	4.80	8.00
☐ 245, Jan 72, CS, MR 100-pg. rep.	0.50	1.60	4.80	8.00
☐ 246, Dec 71	0.25	1.60	4.80	8.00
☐ 247, Jan 72	0.25	1.60	4.80	8.00
☐ 248, Feb 72	0.25	1.60	4.80	8.00
☐ 249, Mar 72, CS/NA	0.25	1.60	4.80	8.00
☐ 250, Apr 72	0.25	1.60	4.80	8.00
☐ 251, May 72	0.25	0.40	1.20	2.00
☐ 252, Jun 72, CS/MA	0.50	1.00	3.00	5.00
☐ 253, Jun 72, CS/MA, reprint	0.25	0.40	1.20	2.00
☐ 254, Jul 72, CS/NA	0.20	1.50	4.50	7.50
☐ 255, Aug 72	0.20	0.40	1.20	2.00
☐ 256, Sep 72	0.20	0.40	1.20	2.00
☐ 257, Oct 72	0.20	0.40	1.20	2.00
☐ 258, Nov 72	0.20	0.40	1.20	2.00
☐ 259, Dec 72	0.20	0.40	1.20	2.00
☐ 260, Jan 73	0.20	0.40	1.20	2.00
☐ 261, Feb 73	0.20	0.30	0.90	1.50
☐ 262, Mar 73	0.20	0.30	0.90	1.50
☐ 263, Apr 73	0.20	0.30	0.90	1.50
☐ 264, Jun 73	0.20	0.30	0.90	1.50
☐ 265, Jul 73	0.20	0.30	0.90	1.50
☐ 266, Aug 73	0.20	0.30	0.90	1.50
☐ 267, Sep 73	0.20	0.30	0.90	1.50

	ORIG.	GOOD	FINE	N-MINT
268, Oct 73 .... 0.20	0.30	0.90	1.50
269, Nov 73 .... 0.20	0.30	0.90	1.50
270, Dec 73...................... 0.20	0.30	0.90	1.50
271, Jan 74 .... 0.20	0.30	0.90	1.50
272, Feb 74, CS/BO, 100 pg.			
.... 0.50	0.60	1.80	3.00
273, Mar 74, CS/BO 0.20	0.30	0.90	1.50
274, Apr 74, CS/BO 0.20	0.30	0.90	1.50
275, May 74, CS/BO........ 0.20	0.30	0.90	1.50
276, Jun 74, CS/BO........ 0.20	0.30	0.90	1.50
277, Jul 74, CS/BO......... 0.20	0.30	0.90	1.50
278, Aug 74, CS/BO, 100-pg. rep.			
.... 0.60	0.60	1.80	3.00
279, Sep 74...................... 0.20	0.30	0.90	1.50
280, Oct 74 .... 0.20	0.30	0.90	1.50
281, Nov 74 .... 0.20	0.30	0.90	1.50
282, Dec 74...................... 0.20	0.30	0.90	1.50
283, Jan 75 .... 0.20	0.30	0.90	1.50
284, Feb 75, CS/BO, 100-pg. rep.			
.... 0.60	0.60	1.80	3.00
285, Mar 75 .... 0.25	0.30	0.90	1.50
286, Apr 75 .... 0.25	0.30	0.90	1.50
287, May 75 .... 0.25	0.30	0.90	1.50
288, Jun 75...................... 0.25	0.30	0.90	1.50
289, Jul 75 .... 0.25	0.30	0.90	1.50
290, Aug 75 .... 0.25	0.30	0.90	1.50
291, Sep 75...................... 0.25	0.30	0.90	1.50
292, Oct 75, CS/BO, O:Luthor			
.... 0.25	0.40	1.20	2.00
293, Nov 75...................... 0.25	0.30	0.90	1.50
294, Dec 75...................... 0.25	0.30	0.90	1.50
295, Jan 76 .... 0.25	0.30	0.90	1.50
296, Feb 76 .... 0.25	0.30	0.90	1.50
297, Mar 76 .... 0.25	0.30	0.90	1.50
298, Apr 76 .... 0.30	0.30	0.90	1.50
298, May 76...................... 0.30	0.30	0.90	1.50
299, May 76...................... 0.30	0.30	0.90	1.50
300, Jun 76, CS/BO, 2001, anniv.			
.... 0.30	0.40	1.20	2.00
301, Jul 76 .... 0.30	0.25	0.75	1.25
302, Aug 76 .... 0.30	0.25	0.75	1.25
303, Sep 76...................... 0.30	0.25	0.75	1.25
304, Oct 76 .... 0.30	0.25	0.75	1.25
305, Nov 76 .... 0.30	0.25	0.75	1.25
306, Dec 76...................... 0.30	0.25	0.75	1.25
307, Jan 77, JL/FS, NA(c)			
.... 0.30	0.30	0.90	1.50
308, Feb 77, JL/FS, NA(c)			
.... 0.30	0.30	0.90	1.50
309, Mar 77 .... 0.30	0.25	0.75	1.25
310, Apr 77 .... 0.30	0.25	0.75	1.25
311, May 77 .... 0.30	0.25	0.75	1.25
312, Jun 77...................... 0.35	0.25	0.75	1.25
313, Jul 77, CS/DA, NA(c)			
.... 0.35	0.30	0.90	1.50
314, Aug 77 .... 0.35	0.25	0.75	1.25
315, Sep 77...................... 0.35	0.25	0.75	1.25
316, Oct 77 .... 0.35	0.25	0.75	1.25
317, Nov 77, NA(c), R:Lana Lang			
.... 0.35	0.30	0.90	1.50
318, Dec 77, CS 0.35	0.25	0.75	1.25
319, Jan 78, CS............... 0.35	0.25	0.75	1.25
320, Feb 78, CS............... 0.35	0.25	0.75	1.25
321, Mar 78 .... 0.35	0.20	0.60	1.00
322, Apr 78 .... 0.35	0.20	0.60	1.00
323, May 78...................... 0.35	0.20	0.60	1.00
324, Jun 78...................... 0.35	0.20	0.60	1.00
325, Jul 78 .... 0.35	0.20	0.60	1.00
326, Aug 78 .... 0.35	0.20	0.60	1.00
327, Sep 78...................... 0.50	0.20	0.60	1.00
328, Oct 78 .... 0.50	0.20	0.60	1.00
329, Nov 78 .... 0.50	0.20	0.60	1.00

	ORIG.	GOOD	FINE	N-MINT
330, Dec 78 ....0.40	0.20	0.60	1.00
331, Jan 79......................0.40	0.20	0.60	1.00
332, Feb 79......................0.40	0.20	0.60	1.00
333, Mar 79......................0.40	0.20	0.60	1.00
334, Apr 79......................0.40	0.20	0.60	1.00
335, May 79......................0.40	0.20	0.60	1.00
336, Jun 79 ....0.40	0.20	0.60	1.00
337, Jul 79.......................0.40	0.20	0.60	1.00
338, Aug 79 ....0.40	0.20	0.60	1.00
339, Sep 79......................0.40	0.20	0.60	1.00
340, Oct 79......................0.40	0.20	0.60	1.00
341, Nov 79......................0.40	0.20	0.60	1.00
342, Dec 79......................0.40	0.20	0.60	1.00
343, Jan 80......................0.40	0.20	0.60	1.00
344, Feb 80......................0.40	0.20	0.60	1.00
345, Mar 80......................0.40	0.20	0.60	1.00
346, Apr 80......................0.40	0.20	0.60	1.00
347, May 80......................0.40	0.20	0.60	1.00
348, Jun 80 ....0.40	0.20	0.60	1.00
349, Jul 80.......................0.40	0.20	0.60	1.00
350, Aug 80 ....0.40	0.20	0.60	1.00
351, Sep 80......................0.50	0.20	0.60	1.00
352, Oct 80......................0.50	0.20	0.60	1.00
353, Nov 80......................0.50	0.20	0.60	1.00
354, Dec 80 ....0.50	0.20	0.60	1.00
355, Jan 81, JSn.............0.50	0.20	0.60	1.00
356, Feb 81......................0.50	0.20	0.60	1.00
357, Mar 81......................0.50	0.20	0.60	1.00
358, Apr 81......................0.50	0.20	0.60	1.00
359, May 81......................0.50	0.20	0.60	1.00
360, Jun 81 ....0.50	0.20	0.60	1.00
361, Jul 81.......................0.50	0.20	0.60	1.00
362, Aug 81 ....0.50	0.20	0.60	1.00
363, Sep 81......................0.50	0.20	0.60	1.00
364, Oct 81......................0.50	0.20	0.60	1.00
365, Nov 81......................0.50	0.20	0.60	1.00
366, Dec 81 ....0.50	0.20	0.60	1.00
367, Jan 82......................0.60	0.20	0.60	1.00
368, Feb 82......................0.60	0.20	0.60	1.00
369, Mar 82......................0.60	0.20	0.60	1.00
370, Apr 82......................0.60	0.20	0.60	1.00
371, May 82......................0.60	0.20	0.60	1.00
372, Jun 82 ....0.60	0.20	0.60	1.00
373, Jul 82.......................0.60	0.20	0.60	1.00
374, Aug 82 ....0.60	0.20	0.60	1.00
375, Sep 82......................0.60	0.20	0.60	1.00
376, Oct 82......................0.60	0.20	0.60	1.00
377, Nov 82......................0.60	0.20	0.60	1.00
378, Dec 82 ....0.60	0.20	0.60	1.00
379, Jan 83......................0.60	0.20	0.60	1.00
380, Feb 83......................0.60	0.20	0.60	1.00
381, Mar 83......................0.60	0.20	0.60	1.00
382, Apr 83......................0.60	0.20	0.60	1.00
383, May 83......................0.60	0.20	0.60	1.00
384, Jun 83 ....0.60	0.20	0.60	1.00
385, Jul 83.......................0.60	0.20	0.60	1.00
386, Aug 83 ....0.60	0.20	0.60	1.00
387, Sep 83......................0.60	0.20	0.60	1.00
388, Oct 83......................0.60	0.20	0.60	1.00
389, Nov 83......................0.60	0.20	0.60	1.00
390, Dec 83 ....0.75	0.20	0.60	1.00
391, Jan 84......................0.75	0.20	0.60	1.00
392, Feb 84......................0.75	0.20	0.60	1.00
393, Mar 84......................0.75	0.20	0.60	1.00
394, Apr 84......................0.75	0.20	0.60	1.00
395, May 84......................0.75	0.20	0.60	1.00
396, Jun 84 ....0.75	0.20	0.60	1.00
397, Jul 84.......................0.75	0.20	0.60	1.00
398, Aug 84......................0.75	0.20	0.60	1.00
399, Sep 84 ....0.75	0.20	0.60	1.00
400, Oct 84, FM, AW, JO, JK, SD, JD, MGr, WE, WS,			
giant 1.50	0.60	1.80	3.00

	ORIG.	GOOD	FINE	N-MINT
401, Nov 84 .... 0.75	0.30	0.90	1.50
402, Dec 84 .... 0.75	0.30	0.90	1.50
403, Jan 85 .... 0.75	0.30	0.90	1.50
404, Feb 85 .... 0.75	0.30	0.90	1.50
405, Mar 85 .... 0.75	0.30	0.90	1.50
406, Apr 85 .... 0.75	0.30	0.90	1.50
407, May 85, powers passed along			
.... 0.75	0.30	0.90	1.50
408, Jun 85 .... 0.75	0.30	0.90	1.50
409, Jul 85 .... 0.75	0.30	0.90	1.50
410, Aug 85 .... 0.75	0.30	0.90	1.50
411, Sep 85 .... 0.75	0.30	0.90	1.50
412, Oct 85 .... 0.75	0.30	0.90	1.50
413, Nov 85 .... 0.75	0.30	0.90	1.50
414, Dec 85, Crisis 0.75	0.20	0.60	1.00
415, Jan 86, Crisis 0.75	0.20	0.60	1.00
416, Feb 86, Superman learns Luthor's connection to			
Einstein 0.75	0.20	0.60	1.00
417, Mar 86, What if Kal-El's rocket landed on Mars?			
.... 0.75	0.20	0.60	1.00
418, Apr 86 .... 0.75	0.20	0.60	1.00
419, May 86 .... 0.75	0.20	0.60	1.00
420, Jun 86 .... 0.75	0.20	0.60	1.00
421, Jul 86 .... 0.75	0.20	0.60	1.00
422, Aug 86 .... 0.75	0.20	0.60	1.00
423, Sep 86, AMo(becomes *Adventures of Superman*)			
.... 0.75	0.20	0.60	1.00

SUPERMAN & BATMAN MAGAZINE
WELSH

	ORIG.	GOOD	FINE	N-MINT
5, Sum 94, magazine 1.95	0.39	1.17	1.95
7, Win 95, magazine 1.95	0.39	1.17	1.95
8, Spr 95, magazine 1.95	0.60	1.80	3.00

SUPERMAN (beginning 1987)
DC

	ORIG.	GOOD	FINE	N-MINT
0, Oct 94 .... 1.50	0.30	0.90	1.50
1, Jan 87, JBy,TA;R:Metallo			
.... 0.75	0.50	1.50	2.50
2, Feb 87, JBy,TA 0.75	0.40	1.20	2.00
3, Mar 87, JBy,TA Legends			
.... 0.75	0.40	1.20	2.00
4, Apr 87, JBy 0.75	0.20	0.60	1.00
5, May 87, JBy 0.75	0.20	0.60	1.00
6, Jun 87, JBy 0.75	0.20	0.60	1.00
7, Jul 87, JBy;O&1:Rampage			
.... 0.75	0.20	0.60	1.00
8, Aug 87, JBy A:Legion,Superboy			
.... 0.75	0.20	0.60	1.00
9, Sep 87, JBy V:Joker, Luthor			
.... 0.75	0.20	0.60	1.00
10, Oct 87, JBy 0.75	0.20	0.60	1.00
11, Nov 87, JBy,O:Mr. Mxyzptlk			
.... 0.75	0.20	0.60	1.00
12, Dec 87, JBy,O:Lori Lemaris			
.... 0.75	0.20	0.60	1.00
13, Jan 88, JBy,Millennium			
14, Feb 88, JBy,Millennium			
.... 0.75	0.20	0.60	1.00
15, Mar 88, JBy 0.75	0.20	0.60	1.00
16, Apr 88, JBy V:Prankster			
.... 0.75	0.20	0.60	1.00
17, May 88, JBy 0.75	0.20	0.60	1.00
18, Jun 88, JBy 0.75	0.20	0.60	1.00
19, Jul 88, JBy 0.75	0.20	0.60	1.00
20, Aug 88, JBy 0.75	0.20	0.60	1.00
21, Sep 88, JBy, Supergirl			
.... 0.75	0.20	0.60	1.00
22, Oct 88, JBy, Supergirl			
.... 0.75	0.20	0.60	1.00
23, Nov 88, A:Batman 0.75	0.20	0.60	1.00
24, Dec 88 .... 0.75	0.20	0.60	1.00

	ORIG.	GOOD	FINE	N-MINT
25, Dec 88 .... 0.75	0.20	0.60	1.00
26, Jan 89, Invasion! 0.75	0.20	0.60	1.00
27, Jan 89, Invasion! 0.75	0.20	0.60	1.00
28, Feb 89 .... 0.75	0.20	0.60	1.00
29, Mar 89 .... 0.75	0.20	0.60	1.00
30, Apr 89 .... 0.75	0.20	0.60	1.00
31, May 89 .... 0.75	0.20	0.60	1.00
32, Jun 89 .... 0.75	0.20	0.60	1.00
33, Jul 89 .... 0.75	0.20	0.60	1.00
34, Aug 89 .... 0.75	0.20	0.60	1.00
35, Sep 89 .... 0.75	0.20	0.60	1.00
36, Oct 89 .... 0.75	0.20	0.60	1.00
37, Nov 89 .... 0.75	0.20	0.60	1.00
38, Dec 89 .... 0.75	0.20	0.60	1.00
39, Jan 90 .... 0.75	0.20	0.60	1.00
40, Feb 90, Krypton Man 0.75	0.20	0.60	1.00
41, Mar 90, Krypton Man 0.75	0.20	0.60	1.00
42, Apr 90, Krypton Man 0.75	0.20	0.60	1.00
43, May 90 .... 0.75	0.15	0.45	0.75
44, Jun 90, Batman 0.75	0.15	0.45	0.75
45, Jul 90 .... 0.75	0.15	0.45	0.75
46, Aug 90 .... 0.75	0.15	0.45	0.75
47, Sep 90 .... 0.75	0.15	0.45	0.75
48, Oct 90 .... 0.75	0.15	0.45	0.75
49, Nov 90 .... 0.75	0.80	2.40	4.00
50, Dec 90, Clark proposes			
.... 1.50	2.00	6.00	10.00
50, Dec 90, 2nd printing ...	0.30	0.90	1.50
51, Jan 91 .... 1.00	0.20	0.60	1.00
52, Feb 91, 1st printing... 1.00	1.60	4.80	8.00
53, Mar 91, Lois knows (1st printing)			
.... 1.00	0.50	1.50	2.50
54, Apr 91 .... 1.00	0.20	0.60	1.00
55, May 91 .... 1.00	0.20	0.60	1.00
56, Jun 91, Red Glass..... 1.00	0.20	0.60	1.00
57, Jul 91, Krypton Man .1.75	1.00	3.00	5.00
58, Aug 91 .... 1.00	0.20	0.60	1.00
59, Sep 91 .... 1.00	0.20	0.60	1.00
60, Oct 91 .... 1.00	0.20	0.60	1.00
61, Nov 91 .... 1.00	0.20	0.60	1.00
62, Dec 91, Blackout #4.. 1.00	0.20	0.60	1.00
63, Jan 92, A:Aquaman... 1.00	0.20	0.60	1.00
64, Feb 92 .... 1.00	0.20	0.60	1.00
65, Mar 92, Capt. Marvel, Batman, Deathstroke, Guy			
Gardner, Aquaman.......... 1.00	0.20	0.60	1.00
66, Apr 92, Capt. Marvel, Batman, Deathstroke, Guy			
Gardner, Aquaman.......... 1.00	0.20	0.60	1.00
67, May 92 .... 1.00	0.20	0.60	1.00
68, Jun 92, Deathstroke.. 1.25	0.30	0.90	1.50
69, Jul 92 .... 1.25	0.25	0.75	1.25
70, Aug 92, Robin........... 1.25	0.25	0.75	1.25
71, Sep 92 .... 1.25	0.25	0.75	1.25
72, Oct 92 .... 1.25	0.25	0.75	1.25
73, Nov 92 .... 1.25	1.00	3.00	5.00
74, Dec 92, Doomsday ... 1.25	1.40	4.20	7.00
75, D: Superman; bagged, with armband, stamps, poster,			
card etc..........................	4.00	12.00	20.00
75, D: Superman, newsstand (unbagged)			
....	2.00	6.00	10.00
75, Jan 93, second printing			
.... 1.25	1.60	4.80	8.00
75, platinum edition..........	20.00	60.00	100.00
76, Feb 93, Funeral 1.25	2.00	6.00	10.00
77, Mar 93, Funeral 1.25	0.60	1.80	3.00
78, Jun 93, 1:cyborg Superman			
.... 1.50	0.60	1.80	3.00
78, 1:cyborg Superman, die-cut cover			
.... 1.95	0.60	1.80	3.00
79, Jul 93 .... 1.50	0.60	1.80	3.00
80, Aug 93 .... 1.50	0.60	1.80	3.00
81, Sep 93 .... 1.50	0.60	1.80	3.00

	ORIG.	GOOD	FINE	N-MINT
❑ 82, Oct 93, return of Superman				
....1.50	1.00	3.00	5.00
❑ 82, return of Superman,foil cover				
....3.50	0.70	2.10	3.50
❑ 82, return of Superman,with poster				
....2.00	0.40	1.20	2.00
❑ 83, Nov 93 ....1.50	0.30	0.90	1.50
❑ 84, Dec 93......................1.50	0.30	0.90	1.50
❑ 85, Jan 94 ....1.50	0.30	0.90	1.50
❑ 86, Feb 94 ....1.50	0.30	0.90	1.50
❑ 87, Mar 94, Bizarro 1.50	0.30	0.90	1.50
❑ 88, Apr 94, Bizarro.........1.50	0.30	0.90	1.50
❑ 89, May 94 ....1.50	0.30	0.90	1.50
❑ 90, Jun 94 ....1.50	0.30	0.90	1.50
❑ 91, Jul 94 ....1.50	0.30	0.90	1.50
❑ 92, Aug 94 ....1.50	0.30	0.90	1.50
❑ 93, Sep 94......................1.50	0.30	0.90	1.50
❑ 94, Nov 94 ....1.50	0.30	0.90	1.50
❑ 95, Dec 94......................1.50	0.30	0.90	1.50
❑ 96, Jan 95 ....1.50	0.30	0.90	1.50
❑ 97, Feb 95 ....1.50	0.30	0.90	1.50
❑ 98, Mar 95 ....1.50	0.30	0.90	1.50
❑ 99, Apr 95 ....1.50	0.30	0.90	1.50
❑ 100, May 95, "Death of Clark Kent" Part 1 of 7				
....2.95	0.59	1.77	2.95
❑ 100, May 95, "Death of Clark Kent" Part 1 of 7;enhanced cover 3.95	0.79	2.37	3.95
❑ 101, Jun 95....................1.95	0.39	1.17	1.95
❑ 102, Jul 95, V:Captain Marvel				
....1.95	0.39	1.17	1.95
❑ 103, Aug 95 ....1.95	0.39	1.17	1.95
❑ 104, Sep 95, Cyborg is released by Darkseid				
....1.95	0.39	1.17	1.95
❑ 105, Oct 95,A:Green Lantern				
....1.95	0.39	1.17	1.95
❑ 106, Nov 95, "Trial of Superman"				
....1.95	0.39	1.17	1.95
❑ 107, Dec 95, "Trial of Superman"				
....1.95	0.39	1.17	1.95
❑ 108, Jan 96, "Trial of Superman";D:Mope				
....1.95	0.39	1.17	1.95
❑ 109, Feb 96, Christmas story;return of Lori Lemaris				
....1.95	0.39	1.17	1.95
❑ 110, Mar 96, A:Plastic Man1.95	0.39	1.17	1.95
❑ 111, Apr 96 ....1.95	0.39	1.17	1.95
❑ 112, Jun 96....................1.95	0.39	1.17	1.95
❑ 113, Jul 96 ....1.95	0.39	1.17	1.95

SUPERMAN (miscellany)

	ORIG.	GOOD	FINE	N-MINT
❑ 0, 66, game giveaway	1.60	4.80	8.00
❑ 0, 77, Pizza Hut...............	0.30	0.90	1.50
❑ 0, 80, Radio Shack...........	0.30	0.90	1.50
❑ 0, 82, Radio Shack...........	0.20	0.60	1.00
❑ 0, 81, Radio Shack...........	0.30	0.90	1.50

SUPERMAN AND BATMAN MAGAZINE
WELSH

	ORIG.	GOOD	FINE	N-MINT
❑ 1, Sum 93, baggedwith poster				
....2.95	0.59	1.77	2.95
❑ 2 ....1.95	0.39	1.17	1.95
❑ 3, trading cards..............2.95	0.59	1.77	2.95
❑ 4, Spr 94 ....1.95	0.39	1.17	1.95

SUPERMAN ANNUAL
DC

	ORIG.	GOOD	FINE	N-MINT
❑ 1, 60, 1:Supergirl reprinted				
....0.25	60.00	180.00	300.00
❑ 2, 61, O:Titano	40.00	120.00	200.00
❑ 3, 61...............................	20.00	60.00	100.00
❑ 4, 62, Legion	16.00	48.00	80.00
❑ 5, 62, Krypton	14.00	42.00	70.00
❑ 6, 63, Legion...................	12.00	36.00	60.00
❑ 7, 63, O:Superman-Batman team				
....	6.00	18.00	30.00

	ORIG.	GOOD	FINE	N-MINT
❑ 8, 64	6.00	18.00	30.00
❑ 9, Sep 83 ....1.00	0.20	0.60	1.00
❑ 10, Nov 84, "Sword of Superman";CS				
....1.25	0.20	0.60	1.00
❑ 11, Sep 85 ....1.25	0.40	1.20	2.00
❑ 12, Jul 86, V:Luthor's Warsuit				
....1.25	0.25	0.75	1.25

SUPERMAN ANNUAL (beginning 1988)

	ORIG.	GOOD	FINE	N-MINT
❑ 1, Aug 87, O:Titano........1.25	0.25	0.75	1.25
❑ 2, Aug 88 ....1.50	0.30	0.90	1.50
❑ 3, Jun 91, Armageddon 2001				
....2.00	1.20	3.60	6.00
❑ 3, Jun 91, 2nd printing	0.40	1.20	2.00
❑ 3, 3rd printing, silver	0.40	1.20	2.00
❑ 4, 92, The Darkness Within				
....2.50	0.50	1.50	2.50
❑ 5, Bloodlines...................2.50	0.50	1.50	2.50
❑ 6, 94, Elseworlds 2.95	0.59	1.77	2.95
❑ 7, 95, "Year One";A:Dr. Occult				
....3.95	0.79	2.37	3.95

SUPERMAN FAMILY, THE
(was Superman's Pal Jimmy Olsen)

	ORIG.	GOOD	FINE	N-MINT
❑ 164		0.60	1.80	3.00
❑ 165		0.40	1.20	2.00
❑ 166		0.40	1.20	2.00
❑ 167		0.40	1.20	2.00
❑ 168		0.40	1.20	2.00
❑ 169		0.40	1.20	2.00
❑ 170		0.40	1.20	2.00
❑ 171		0.40	1.20	2.00
❑ 172		0.40	1.20	2.00
❑ 173		0.40	1.20	2.00
❑ 174		0.40	1.20	2.00
❑ 175		0.40	1.20	2.00
❑ 176		0.40	1.20	2.00
❑ 177		0.40	1.20	2.00
❑ 178		0.40	1.20	2.00
❑ 179		0.40	1.20	2.00
❑ 180		0.40	1.20	2.00
❑ 181		0.40	1.20	2.00
❑ 182, Apr 77.....................1.00	0.80	2.40	4.00
❑ 183, Jun 77 ....1.00	0.40	1.20	2.00
❑ 184, Aug 77 ....1.00	0.40	1.20	2.00
❑ 185, Oct 77 ....1.00	0.40	1.20	2.00
❑ 186, Dec 77 ....1.00	0.40	1.20	2.00
❑ 187, Feb 78.....................1.00	0.40	1.20	2.00
❑ 188, Apr 78.....................1.00	0.40	1.20	2.00
❑ 189, Jun 78 ....1.00	0.40	1.20	2.00
❑ 190, Aug 78 ....1.00	0.40	1.20	2.00
❑ 191, Oct 78 ....1.00	0.40	1.20	2.00
❑ 192, Dec 78 ....1.00	0.40	1.20	2.00
❑ 193, Feb 79.....................1.00	0.40	1.20	2.00
❑ 194, Apr 79.....................1.00	0.60	1.80	3.00
❑ 195, Jun 79 ....1.00	0.40	1.20	2.00
❑ 196, Aug 79 ....1.00	0.40	1.20	2.00
❑ 197, Oct 79 ....1.00	0.40	1.20	2.00
❑ 198, Dec 79 ....1.00	0.40	1.20	2.00
❑ 199, Feb 80.....................1.00	0.40	1.20	2.00
❑ 200, Apr 80.....................1.00	0.40	1.20	2.00
❑ 201, Jun 80 ....1.00	0.40	1.20	2.00
❑ 202, Aug 80.....................1.00	0.40	1.20	2.00
❑ 203		0.40	1.20	2.00
❑ 204		0.40	1.20	2.00
❑ 205		0.40	1.20	2.00
❑ 206		0.40	1.20	2.00
❑ 207		0.40	1.20	2.00
❑ 208		0.40	1.20	2.00
❑ 209		0.40	1.20	2.00
❑ 210		0.40	1.20	2.00
❑ 211		0.40	1.20	2.00
❑ 212		0.40	1.20	2.00

	ORIG.	GOOD	FINE	N-MINT
❑ 213		0.40	1.20	2.00
❑ 214		0.40	1.20	2.00
❑ 215		0.40	1.20	2.00
❑ 216		0.40	1.20	2.00
❑ 217		0.40	1.20	2.00
❑ 218		0.40	1.20	2.00
❑ 219		0.40	1.20	2.00
❑ 220		0.40	1.20	2.00
❑ 221		0.40	1.20	2.00
❑ 222		0.40	1.20	2.00

SUPERMAN FOR EARTH

	ORIG.	GOOD	FINE	N-MINT
❑ 0, Apr 91, nn 1991 JO(c)	4.95	0.99	2.97	4.95

SUPERMAN GALLERY, THE

	ORIG.	GOOD	FINE	N-MINT
❑ 1	2.95	0.59	1.77	2.95

SUPERMAN III

	ORIG.	GOOD	FINE	N-MINT
❑ 1, Sep 83, CS, movie adaptation	0.20	0.60	1.00

SUPERMAN IV MOVIE SPECIAL

	ORIG.	GOOD	FINE	N-MINT
❑ 1, Oct 87		0.40	1.20	2.00

SUPERMAN SPECIAL

	ORIG.	GOOD	FINE	N-MINT
❑ 1, Mar 83	1.00	0.20	0.60	1.00
❑ 1, 92, WS	3.50	0.70	2.10	3.50
❑ 2, Apr 84	1.25	0.20	0.60	1.00
❑ 3, Apr 85, V:Amazo	1.25	0.20	0.60	1.00

SUPERMAN VS. ALIENS (mini-series)
DC/DARK HORSE

	ORIG.	GOOD	FINE	N-MINT
❑ 1, Jul 95, prestige format;crossover with Dark Horse				
	4.95	0.99	2.97	4.95
❑ 2, Aug 95, prestige format;crossover with Dark Horse				
	4.95	0.99	2.97	4.95
❑ 3, Sep 95, prestige format;crossover with Dark Horse				
	4.95	0.99	2.97	4.95

SUPERMAN VS. SPIDER-MAN
DC

	ORIG.	GOOD	FINE	N-MINT
❑ 1, 76, RA/DG, oversized	2.00	5.00	15.00	25.00

SUPERMAN'S PAL, JIMMY OLSEN

	ORIG.	GOOD	FINE	N-MINT
❑ 133, Oct 70, JK;R:Newsboy Legion;1:Habitat				
	0.15	3.60	10.80	18.00
❑ 134, Dec 70	0.15	6.00	18.00	30.00
❑ 135, Jan 71	0.15	2.40	7.20	12.00
❑ 136, Mar 71	0.15	2.40	7.20	12.00
❑ 137, Apr 71	0.15	2.40	7.20	12.00
❑ 138, Jun 71	0.15	2.40	7.20	12.00
❑ 139, Jul 71	0.15	2.40	7.20	12.00
❑ 140, Jul 71	0.15	2.40	7.20	12.00
❑ 141, Sep 71	0.25	2.00	6.00	10.00
❑ 142, Oct 71	0.25	2.00	6.00	10.00
❑ 143, Nov 71	0.25	2.00	6.00	10.00
❑ 144, Dec 71	0.25	2.00	6.00	10.00
❑ 145, Jan 72	0.25	2.00	6.00	10.00
❑ 146, Feb 72	0.25	2.00	6.00	10.00
❑ 147, Mar 72	0.25	1.20	3.60	6.00
❑ 148, Apr 72	0.25	1.20	3.60	6.00
❑ 149, May 72	0.25	1.20	3.60	6.00
❑ 150, Jun 72	0.25	1.20	3.60	6.00
❑ 151		0.80	2.40	4.00
❑ 152		0.80	2.40	4.00
❑ 153		0.80	2.40	4.00
❑ 154		0.80	2.40	4.00
❑ 155		0.80	2.40	4.00
❑ 156		0.80	2.40	4.00
❑ 157		0.80	2.40	4.00
❑ 158		0.80	2.40	4.00
❑ 159		0.80	2.40	4.00
❑ 160		0.80	2.40	4.00
❑ 161		0.80	2.40	4.00
❑ 162		0.80	2.40	4.00
❑ 163, (becomes The Superman Family)				
		0.80	2.40	4.00

SUPERMAN, THE SECRET YEARS

	ORIG.	GOOD	FINE	N-MINT
❑ 1, Feb 85, CS mini-series	0.75	0.40	1.20	2.00
❑ 2, Mar 85, CS	0.75	0.20	0.60	1.00
❑ 3, Apr 85, CS	0.75	0.20	0.60	1.00
❑ 4, May 85, CS	0.75	0.20	0.60	1.00

SUPERMAN/DOOMSDAY: HUNTER/PREY

	ORIG.	GOOD	FINE	N-MINT
❑ 1, 94, prestige format	4.95	0.99	2.97	4.95
❑ 2, 94, prestige format	4.95	0.99	2.97	4.95
❑ 3, 94, prestige format	4.95	0.99	2.97	4.95

SUPERMAN/TOYMAN

	ORIG.	GOOD	FINE	N-MINT
❑ 1, 96, one-shot;promofor toy line				
	1.95	0.39	1.17	1.95

SUPERMAN: AT EARTH'S END

	ORIG.	GOOD	FINE	N-MINT
❑ 0, 95, Elseworlds;prestige format one-shot;D:Superman				
	4.95	0.99	2.97	4.95

SUPERMAN: KAL

	ORIG.	GOOD	FINE	N-MINT
❑ 0, 95, prestige format one-shot				
	5.95	1.19	3.57	5.95

SUPERMAN: THE EARTH STEALERS

	ORIG.	GOOD	FINE	N-MINT
❑ 0, May 88, JBy(w),CS,JOy				
	2.95	0.59	1.77	2.95

SUPERMAN: THE MAN OF STEEL

	ORIG.	GOOD	FINE	N-MINT
❑ 0, Oct 94, (1994)	1.50	0.30	0.90	1.50
❑ 1, Jul 91, JO,Bogdanove	1.75	0.35	1.05	1.75
❑ 2, Aug 91	1.00	0.20	0.60	1.00
❑ 3, Sep 91,War of the Gods				
	1.00	0.20	0.60	1.00
❑ 4, Oct 91	1.00	0.20	0.60	1.00
❑ 5, Nov 91	1.00	0.20	0.60	1.00
❑ 6, Dec 91, Blackout #3	1.00	0.20	0.60	1.00
❑ 7, Jan 92	1.00	0.20	0.60	1.00
❑ 8, Feb 92	1.00	0.20	0.60	1.00
❑ 9, Mar 92	1.00	0.20	0.60	1.00
❑ 10, Apr 92, Panic in Sky	1.00	0.20	0.60	1.00
❑ 11, May 92	1.25	0.25	0.75	1.25
❑ 12, Jun 92	1.25	0.25	0.75	1.25
❑ 13, Jul 92	1.25	0.25	0.75	1.25
❑ 14, Aug 92	1.25	0.25	0.75	1.25
❑ 15, Sep 92	1.25	0.25	0.75	1.25
❑ 16, Oct 92	1.25	0.25	0.75	1.25
❑ 17, Nov 92	1.25	1.00	3.00	5.00
❑ 18, Dec 92, 1:Doomsday	1.25	0.80	2.40	4.00
❑ 19, Jan 93, Doomsday	1.25	0.80	2.40	4.00
❑ 20, Feb 93, Funeral	1.25	0.25	0.75	1.25
❑ 21, Mar 93, Funeral	1.25	0.25	0.75	1.25
❑ 22, Jan 93, 1:Steel	1.50	0.30	0.90	1.50
❑ 22, 1:Steel, die-cut cover	1.95	0.39	1.17	1.95
❑ 23, Jul 93	1.50	0.30	0.90	1.50
❑ 24		0.30	0.90	1.50
❑ 25, Reign of Supermen	1.50	1.40	4.20	7.00
❑ 26		1.60	4.80	8.00
❑ 27	1.50	0.30	0.90	1.50
❑ 28	1.50	0.30	0.90	1.50
❑ 29, Jan 94	1.50	0.30	0.90	1.50
❑ 30, Lobo	1.50	0.30	0.90	1.50
❑ 30, vinyl clings cover, Lobo				
	2.50	0.50	1.50	2.50
❑ 31	1.50	0.30	0.90	1.50
❑ 32, Bizarro	1.50	0.30	0.90	1.50
❑ 33, May 94	1.50	0.30	0.90	1.50
❑ 34, Jun 94	1.50	0.30	0.90	1.50
❑ 35, Jul 94, Worlds Collide				
	1.50	0.30	0.90	1.50
❑ 36, Aug 94	1.50	0.30	0.90	1.50
❑ 37, Sep 94	1.50	0.30	0.90	1.50
❑ 38, Nov 94	1.50	0.30	0.90	1.50
❑ 39, Dec 94	1.50	0.30	0.90	1.50
❑ 40, Jan 95	1.50	0.30	0.90	1.50
❑ 41, Feb 95	1.50	0.30	0.90	1.50
❑ 42, Mar 95	1.50	0.30	0.90	1.50

	ORIG.	GOOD	FINE	N-MINT
43, Apr 95, A:Mr. Miracle1.50		0.30	0.90	1.50
44, May 95 ....1.50		0.30	0.90	1.50
45, Jun 95 ....1.95		0.39	1.17	1.95
46, Jul 95 ....1.95		0.39	1.17	1.95
47, Aug 95 ....1.95		0.39	1.17	1.95
48, Sep 95, A:Aquaman . 1.95		0.39	1.17	1.95
49, Oct 95 ....1.95		0.39	1.17	1.95
50, Nov 95, "Trial of Superman"				
......................................2.95		0.59	1.77	2.95
51, Dec 95, "Trial of Superman"				
......................................1.95		0.39	1.17	1.95
52, Jan 96,"Trial of Superman"				
......................................1.95		0.39	1.17	1.95
53, Feb 96 ....1.95		0.39	1.17	1.95
54, Mar 96, A:Spectre 1.95		0.39	1.17	1.95
55, Apr 96 ....1.95		0.39	1.17	1.95
56, May 96, V:Mxyzptlk.. 1.95		0.39	1.17	1.95
57, Jun 96, A:Golden Age Flash				
......................................1.95		0.39	1.17	1.95

SUPERMAN: THE MAN OF STEEL ANNUAL

1, 92, A: Eclipso 2.50		0.50	1.50	2.50
2, 93, Bloodlines; 1: Edge				
......................................2.50		0.50	1.50	2.50
3, 94, Elseworlds 2.95		0.59	1.77	2.95
4, 95, "Year One";A:Justice League				
......................................2.95		0.59	1.77	2.95

SUPERMAN: THE MAN OF STEEL GALLERY

1, Dec 95, pin-ups.......... 3.50		0.70	2.10	3.50

SUPERMAN: THE MAN OF TOMORROW

1, Sum 95 .... 1.95		0.39	1.17	1.95
2, Fal 95 .... 1.95		0.39	1.17	1.95
3, Win 95, "Trial of Superman/Underworld				
Unleashed";how Luthor regained strength and				
appearance.....................1.95		0.39	1.17	1.95
4, Spr 96, A:Captain Marvel				
......................................1.95		0.39	1.17	1.95

SUPERMAN: THE SECRET YEARS (mini-series)

1, Feb 85 .... 0.75		0.15	0.45	0.75
2, Mar 85, A:Lori Lemaris;Clark reveals his secret to Billy				
Cramer 0.75		0.15	0.45	0.75
3, Apr 85, D:Billy Cramer 0.75		0.15	0.45	0.75
4, May 85, Superboy becomes Superman; Clark Kent				
meets Perry White 0.75		0.15	0.45	0.75

SUPERMAN: UNDER A YELLOW SUN

0, nn............................... 5.95		1.19	3.57	5.95

SUPERNATURAL THRILLERS
MARVEL

1, Dec 72.........................0.20		0.20	0.60	1.00
2, Feb 73 ....0.20		0.20	0.60	1.00
3, Apr 73, REHoward story				
......................................0.20		0.20	0.60	1.00
4 ....0.20		0.20	0.60	1.00
5, I:Living Mummy.........0.20		0.20	0.60	1.00
6 ....0.20		0.20	0.60	1.00
7, Living Mummy...........0.25		0.20	0.60	1.00
8, Living Mummy...........0.25		0.20	0.60	1.00
9, Living Mummy...........0.25		0.20	0.60	1.00
10, Living Mummy 0.25		0.20	0.60	1.00
11, Living Mummy 0.25		0.20	0.60	1.00
12, Living Mummy 0.25		0.20	0.60	1.00
13, Living Mummy 0.25		0.20	0.60	1.00
14, Living Mummy 0.25		0.20	0.60	1.00
15, Living Mummy 0.25		0.20	0.60	1.00

SUPERPATRIOT
IMAGE

1, Jul 93 ....1.95		0.39	1.17	1.95
2, Sep 93.........................1.95		0.39	1.17	1.95
3, Oct 93 ....1.95		0.39	1.17	1.95
4 ....1.95		0.39	1.17	1.95

SUPERPATRIOT: LIBERTY & JUSTICE (mini-series)

1, Jun 95 ....2.50		0.50	1.50	2.50
2, Aug 95 ....2.50		0.50	1.50	2.50

SUPERSWINE
CALIBER

1, b&w............................2.50		0.50	1.50	2.50
2, b&w............................2.50		0.50	1.50	2.50

SUPPRESSED!
TOME PRESS

1, b&w............................2.95		0.59	1.77	2.95

SUPREME
IMAGE

1, silver foil cover 1.95		0.39	1.17	1.95
1, gold		12.00	36.00	60.00
2 ....1.95		0.39	1.17	1.95
3 ....1.95		0.39	1.17	1.95

SUPREME (Volume 2)

0, Aug 95 ....2.50		0.50	1.50	2.50
1, Nov 92 ....1.95		0.39	1.17	1.95
2 ....1.95		0.39	1.17	1.95
3 ....1.95		0.39	1.17	1.95
4, Jul 93..........................1.95		0.39	1.17	1.95
5, Aug 93 ....1.95		0.39	1.17	1.95
6, Oct 93 ....1.95		0.39	1.17	1.95
7, Nov 93 ....1.95		0.39	1.17	1.95
8, Dec 93 ....1.95		0.39	1.17	1.95
9, Jan 94..........................1.95		0.39	1.17	1.95
10, Feb 94.......................1.95		0.39	1.17	1.95
11, Mar 94 ....1.95		0.39	1.17	1.95
12, Apr 94........................1.95		0.39	1.17	1.95
14, Jun 94 ....2.50		0.50	1.50	2.50
15, Jul 94.........................2.50		0.50	1.50	2.50
16, Jul 94.........................2.50		0.50	1.50	2.50
17, Aug 94 ....2.50		0.50	1.50	2.50
18, Aug 94 ....2.50		0.50	1.50	2.50
20, Oct 94 ....2.50		0.50	1.50	2.50
21, Nov 94 ....2.50		0.50	1.50	2.50
22, Dec 94 ....2.50		0.50	1.50	2.50
23, Jan 95, polybaggedwith trading card; Extreme				
Sacrifice.........................2.50		0.50	1.50	2.50
24, Feb 95, Extreme Sacrifice Aftermath				
......................................2.50		0.50	1.50	2.50
25, May 94, Images of Tomorrow				
......................................1.95		0.39	1.17	1.95
26, Mar 95 ....2.50		0.50	1.50	2.50
27, Apr 95 ....2.50		0.50	1.50	2.50
28, May 95.......................2.50		0.50	1.50	2.50
29, Jun 95, "Supreme Apocalypse" Part 1 of 5;polybagged				
withPower Cardz............2.50		0.50	1.50	2.50
30, Jul 95, "SupremeApocalypse" Part 5 of 5;polybagged				
with PowerCardz.............2.50		0.50	1.50	2.50
31, Aug 95 ....2.50		0.50	1.50	2.50
32, Oct 95 ....2.50		0.50	1.50	2.50
33, Nov 95, "Babewatch".2.50		0.50	1.50	2.50
34, Dec 95 ....2.50		0.50	1.50	2.50
35, Jan 96, "Extreme Destroyer" Part 7 of 9;polybagged				
with Lady Supreme card.2.50		0.50	1.50	2.50
36, Feb 96 ....2.50		0.50	1.50	2.50
37, Mar 96 ....2.50		0.50	1.50	2.50
37, Mar 96, alternate cover				
......................................2.50		0.50	1.50	2.50
38, Apr 96........................2.50		0.50	1.50	2.50

SUPREME ANNUAL

1, May 95, A:The Allies ...2.95		0.59	1.77	2.95

SUPREME: GLORY DAYS (mini-series)

1, Oct 94..........................2.95		0.59	1.77	2.95
2, Dec 94, final issue 2.50		0.50	1.50	2.50

SUPREMIE
PARODY PRESS

1, b&w............................2.50		0.50	1.50	2.50

	ORIG.	GOOD	FINE	N-MINT
SURF CRAZED				
PACIFICA				
4		0.50	1.50	2.50
SURF-CRAZED				
3-D ZONE				
3, 3-D		0.79	2.37	3.95
SURFCRAZED COMICS				
PASKOWITZ				
1		0.50	1.50	2.50
SURGE				
ECLIPSE				
1, Jul 84		0.30	0.90	1.50
2, Aug 84		0.30	0.90	1.50
3, Oct 84		0.30	0.90	1.50
4, Jan 85		0.30	0.90	1.50
SURROGATE SAVIOUR				
HOT BRAZEN COMICS				
1, Sep 95, b&w	2.50	0.50	1.50	2.50
2, Nov 95, b&w	2.50	0.50	1.50	2.50
SURVIVE!				
APPLE				
1, b&w		0.55	1.65	2.75
SURVIVORS				
FANTAGRAPHICS				
1		0.50	1.50	2.50
2		0.50	1.50	2.50
PRELUDE				
1		0.39	1.17	1.95
2, (moves to Burnside)		0.39	1.17	1.95
SPECTRUM				
1		0.40	1.20	2.00
2		0.40	1.20	2.00
3		0.40	1.20	2.00
4		0.40	1.20	2.00
SURVIVORS, THE (was Prelude title)				
BURNSIDE				
1		0.39	1.17	1.95
SUSHI				
SHUNGA				
1, adult, b&w		0.50	1.50	2.50
2, adult, b&w		0.50	1.50	2.50
3, adult, b&w		0.50	1.50	2.50
4, adult, b&w		0.50	1.50	2.50
5, adult, b&w		0.50	1.50	2.50
6, adult, b&w		0.50	1.50	2.50
SUSTAH-GIRL: QUEEN OF THE BLACK AGE				
ONLI STUDIOS				
1, b&w	2.00	0.40	1.20	2.00
SWAMP THING (1972-1976 series)				
DC				
1, Nov 72, BWr, O:Swamp Thing	0.20	9.60	28.80	48.00
2, Jan 73, BWr	0.20	4.80	14.40	24.00
3, Mar 73, BWr	0.20	3.20	9.60	16.00
4, May 73, BWr	0.20	3.20	9.60	16.00
5, Aug 73, BWr	0.20	2.40	7.20	12.00
6, Oct 73, BWr	0.20	2.40	7.20	12.00
7, Dec 73, BWr, Batman	0.20	4.00	12.00	20.00
8, Feb 74, BWr	0.20	2.40	7.20	12.00
9, Apr 74, BWr	0.20	2.40	7.20	12.00
10, Jun 74, BWr	0.20	2.40	7.20	12.00
11, Aug 74, NR	0.20	0.60	1.80	3.00
12, Oct 74, NR	0.20	0.60	1.80	3.00
13, Dec 74, NR	0.20	0.60	1.80	3.00
14, Feb 75, NR	0.25	0.60	1.80	3.00
15, Apr 75, NR	0.25	0.60	1.80	3.00
16, May 75, NR	0.25	0.60	1.80	3.00
17, Jul 75, NR	0.25	0.60	1.80	3.00
18, Sep 75, NR	0.25	0.60	1.80	3.00
19, Oct 75, NR	0.25	0.60	1.80	3.00

	ORIG.	GOOD	FINE	N-MINT
20, Jan 76, NR	0.25	0.60	1.80	3.00
21, Mar 76, NR	0.25	0.40	1.20	2.00
22, May 76, NR	0.30	0.40	1.20	2.00
23, Jul 76, NR	0.30	0.40	1.20	2.00
24, Sep 76, NR	0.30	0.40	1.20	2.00
SWAMP THING				
(formerly Saga of the Swamp Thing)				
39		0.60	1.80	3.00
40		0.60	1.80	3.00
41		0.60	1.80	3.00
42		0.60	1.80	3.00
43		0.60	1.80	3.00
44		0.60	1.80	3.00
45		0.60	1.80	3.00
46, Mar 86, Crisis	0.75	0.60	1.80	3.00
47, Apr 86		0.60	1.80	3.00
48, May 86		0.60	1.80	3.00
49, Jun 86		0.60	1.80	3.00
50, Jul 86	1.25	0.60	1.80	3.00
51, Aug 86		0.60	1.80	3.00
52, Sep 86, Joker		1.20	3.60	6.00
53, Oct 86, Arkham Asylum		1.00	3.00	5.00
54, Nov 86		0.60	1.80	3.00
55, Dec 86		0.60	1.80	3.00
56, Jan 87		0.60	1.80	3.00
57, Feb 87	0.75	0.60	1.80	3.00
58, Mar 87, Spectre preview	0.75	1.20	3.60	6.00
59, Apr 87		0.60	1.80	3.00
60, May 87, new format		0.60	1.80	3.00
61, Jun 87		0.60	1.80	3.00
62, Jul 87		0.60	1.80	3.00
63, Aug 87		0.60	1.80	3.00
64, Sep 87, last with AMo.		0.60	1.80	3.00
65, Oct 87, Arkham Asylum		0.80	2.40	4.00
66, Nov 87, Arkham Asylum		0.80	2.40	4.00
67, Dec 87, I:Hellblazer		0.80	2.40	4.00
68, Jan 88		0.60	1.80	3.00
69, Feb 88		0.60	1.80	3.00
70, Mar 88		0.60	1.80	3.00
71, Apr 88		0.60	1.80	3.00
72, May 88		0.60	1.80	3.00
73, Jun 88		0.60	1.80	3.00
74, Jul 88		0.60	1.80	3.00
75, Aug 88		0.60	1.80	3.00
76, Sep 88		0.60	1.80	3.00
77, Oct 88		0.60	1.80	3.00
78, Nov 88		0.60	1.80	3.00
79, Dec 88, A:Superman	1.25	0.40	1.20	2.00
80, Dec 88		0.40	1.20	2.00
81, Jan 89, Invasion!		0.40	1.20	2.00
82, Jan 89, Sgt. Rock		0.40	1.20	2.00
83, Feb 89, Enemy Ace		0.40	1.20	2.00
84, Mar 89, Sandman		0.80	2.40	4.00
85, Apr 89, Jonah Hex, Bat Lash	0.40		1.20	2.00
86, May 89, Tomahawk, Rip Hunter, Demon		0.40	1.20	2.00
87, Jun 89, Shining Knight, Demon		0.40	1.20	2.00
88, Sep 89		0.30	0.90	1.50
89, Oct 89		0.30	0.90	1.50
90, Dec 89		0.30	0.90	1.50
91, Jan 90		0.30	0.90	1.50
92, Feb 90		0.30	0.90	1.50
93, Mar 90		0.30	0.90	1.50
94, Apr 90		0.30	0.90	1.50
95, May 90		0.30	0.90	1.50
96, Jun 90		0.30	0.90	1.50
97, Jul 90		0.30	0.90	1.50
98, Aug 90		0.30	0.90	1.50
99, Sep 90		0.30	0.90	1.50

	ORIG.	GOOD	FINE	N-MINT
100, Oct 90		0.50	1.50	2.50
101, Nov 90		0.30	0.90	1.50
102, Dec 90		0.30	0.90	1.50
103, Jan 91		0.30	0.90	1.50
104, Feb 91		0.30	0.90	1.50
105, Mar 91		0.30	0.90	1.50
106, Apr 91		0.30	0.90	1.50
107, May 91		0.30	0.90	1.50
108, Jun 91		0.30	0.90	1.50
109, Jul 91		0.30	0.90	1.50
110, Aug 91		0.30	0.90	1.50
111, Sep 91		0.30	0.90	1.50
112, Oct 91		0.30	0.90	1.50
113, Nov 91		0.30	0.90	1.50
114, Dec 91	1.75	0.35	1.05	1.75
115	1.75	0.35	1.05	1.75
116	1.75	0.35	1.05	1.75
117	1.75	0.35	1.05	1.75
118	1.75	0.35	1.05	1.75
119	1.75	0.35	1.05	1.75
120	1.75	0.35	1.05	1.75
121	1.75	0.35	1.05	1.75
122	1.75	0.35	1.05	1.75
123	1.75	0.35	1.05	1.75
124	1.75	0.35	1.05	1.75
125, Arcane		0.59	1.77	2.95

DC/VERTIGO

	ORIG.	GOOD	FINE	N-MINT
126	1.75	0.35	1.05	1.75
127	1.75	0.35	1.05	1.75
128	1.75	0.35	1.05	1.75
129	1.75	0.35	1.05	1.75
130	1.75	0.35	1.05	1.75
131	1.75	0.35	1.05	1.75
132	1.95	0.39	1.17	1.95
133	1.95	0.39	1.17	1.95
134	1.95	0.39	1.17	1.95
135	1.95	0.39	1.17	1.95
136	1.95	0.39	1.17	1.95
137	1.95	0.39	1.17	1.95
138	1.95	0.39	1.17	1.95
139	1.95	0.39	1.17	1.95
140	1.95	0.70	2.10	3.50
140, platinum		8.00	24.00	40.00
141	1.95	0.39	1.17	1.95
142, May 94	1.95	0.39	1.17	1.95
143, Jun 94	1.95	0.39	1.17	1.95
144, Jul 94	1.95	0.39	1.17	1.95
145, Aug 94	1.95	0.39	1.17	1.95
146, Sep 94	1.95	0.39	1.17	1.95
147, Oct 94	1.95	0.39	1.17	1.95
148, Oct 94	1.95	0.39	1.17	1.95
149, Dec 94	1.95	0.39	1.17	1.95
150, Jan 95	2.95	0.59	1.77	2.95
151, Feb 95	2.95	0.59	1.77	2.95
152, Mar 95	2.95	0.59	1.77	2.95
153, Apr 95	1.95	0.39	1.17	1.95
154, May 95	2.25	0.45	1.35	2.25
155, Jun 95	2.25	0.45	1.35	2.25
156, Jul 95	2.25	0.45	1.35	2.25
157, Aug 95	2.25	0.45	1.35	2.25
158, Sep 95	2.25	0.45	1.35	2.25
159, Oct 95, photo cover	2.25	0.45	1.35	2.25
160, Nov 95	2.25	0.45	1.35	2.25
161, Dec 95	2.25	0.45	1.35	2.25
162, Jan 96	2.25	0.45	1.35	2.25
163, Feb 96	2.25	0.45	1.35	2.25
164, Mar 96	2.25	0.45	1.35	2.25
165, Apr 96	2.25	0.45	1.35	2.25
166, May 96	2.25	0.45	1.35	2.25
167, Jun 96	2.25	0.45	1.35	2.25

SWAMP THING ANNUAL
DC

	ORIG.	GOOD	FINE	N-MINT
1, 82, movie	1.00	0.20	0.60	1.00
2, AMo		1.00	3.00	5.00
3, Nov 87		0.80	2.40	4.00
4, Oct 88, A:Batman		1.20	3.60	6.00
5, Sep 89, A:Brother Power		0.59	1.77	2.95
6, Aug 91		0.59	1.77	2.95

DC/VERTIGO

	ORIG.	GOOD	FINE	N-MINT
7, Children's Crusade	3.95	0.79	2.37	3.95

SWAN
LITTLE IDYLLS

	ORIG.	GOOD	FINE	N-MINT
2, Jun 95, b&w	2.95	0.59	1.77	2.95

SWEET LUCY
BRAINSTORM

	ORIG.	GOOD	FINE	N-MINT
1, Jun 93, b&w	2.95	0.59	1.77	2.95
2, b&w	2.95	0.59	1.77	2.95

SWEET XVI
MARVEL

	ORIG.	GOOD	FINE	N-MINT
1	1.00	0.20	0.60	1.00
2	1.00	0.20	0.60	1.00
3	1.00	0.20	0.60	1.00
4	1.00	0.20	0.60	1.00
5	1.00	0.20	0.60	1.00
6	1.00	0.20	0.60	1.00

SWEET XVI BACK TO SCHOOL SPECIAL

	ORIG.	GOOD	FINE	N-MINT
1	2.25	0.45	1.35	2.25

SWEETCHILDE
NEW MOON

	ORIG.	GOOD	FINE	N-MINT
1, adult, b&w	2.95	0.59	1.77	2.95

SWEETMEATS
ATOMEKA

	ORIG.	GOOD	FINE	N-MINT
0, nn, b&w one-shot		0.79	2.37	3.95

SWIFTSURE
HARRIER

	ORIG.	GOOD	FINE	N-MINT
1		0.35	1.05	1.75
2		0.35	1.05	1.75
3		0.35	1.05	1.75
4		0.35	1.05	1.75
5		0.35	1.05	1.75
6		0.35	1.05	1.75
7		0.35	1.05	1.75
8		0.35	1.05	1.75
9, Redfox		1.60	4.80	8.00
11		0.30	0.90	1.50
12		0.30	0.90	1.50
13		0.39	1.17	1.95
14		0.39	1.17	1.95
15		0.39	1.17	1.95
16		0.39	1.17	1.95
17		0.39	1.17	1.95
18		0.39	1.17	1.95

SWORD OF SORCERY
DC

	ORIG.	GOOD	FINE	N-MINT
1, Mar 73	0.20	1.60	4.80	8.00
2, May 73	0.20	0.80	2.40	4.00
3, Aug 73	0.20	0.40	1.20	2.00
4, Oct 73	0.20	0.40	1.20	2.00
5, Dec 73	0.20	0.40	1.20	2.00

SWORD OF THE ATOM

	ORIG.	GOOD	FINE	N-MINT
1, Sep 83, GK	0.60	0.30	0.90	1.50
2, Oct 83, GK	0.60	0.20	0.60	1.00
3, Nov 83, GK	0.60	0.20	0.60	1.00
4, Dec 83, GK	0.60	0.20	0.60	1.00

SWORD OF THE ATOM SPECIAL

	ORIG.	GOOD	FINE	N-MINT
1, Jul 84, GK	1.25	0.25	0.75	1.25
2, Jul 85, GK	1.25	0.25	0.75	1.25
3, Feb 88, PB	1.25	0.30	0.90	1.50

	ORIG.	GOOD	FINE	N-MINT
SWORDS OF CEREBUS				
AARDVARK-VANAHEIM				
1, (1st printing)	4.00	12.00	20.00	
1, (2nd printing)	3.00	9.00	15.00	
2, (1st printing)	3.00	9.00	15.00	
2, (2nd printing)	2.00	6.00	10.00	
3, (1st printing)	3.00	9.00	15.00	
3, (2nd printing)	2.00	6.00	10.00	
4, (1st printing)	3.00	9.00	15.00	
4, (2nd printing)	2.00	6.00	10.00	
5	3.00	9.00	15.00	
6	3.00	9.00	15.00	
SWORDS OF SHAR-PEI				
CALIBER				
1, b&w	0.50	1.50	2.50	
2, b&w	0.50	1.50	2.50	
SWORDS OF TEXAS				
ECLIPSE				
1	0.35	1.05	1.75	
2	0.35	1.05	1.75	
3	0.35	1.05	1.75	
4	0.35	1.05	1.75	
SWORDS OF THE SWASHBUCKLERS				
EPIC				
1	1.50	0.40	1.20	2.00
2	1.50	0.30	0.90	1.50
3	1.50	0.30	0.90	1.50
4	1.50	0.30	0.90	1.50
5	1.50	0.30	0.90	1.50
6	1.50	0.30	0.90	1.50
7	1.50	0.30	0.90	1.50
8	1.50	0.30	0.90	1.50
9	1.50	0.30	0.90	1.50
10	1.50	0.30	0.90	1.50
11	1.50	0.30	0.90	1.50
12	1.75	0.35	1.05	1.75

	ORIG.	GOOD	FINE	N-MINT
SWORDS OF VALOR				
A-PLUS				
1, b&w	0.50	1.50	2.50	
2, b&w	0.50	1.50	2.50	
3, b&w	0.50	1.50	2.50	
4, b&w	0.50	1.50	2.50	
SYNN, THE GIRL FROM LSD				
AC				
1, Aug 90, b&w	0.79	2.37	3.95	
SYNTHETIC ASSASSIN				
NIGHT REALM				
1	0.30	0.90	1.50	
SYPHONS (Volume 1)				
NOW				
1, Jul 86	1.50	0.30	0.90	1.50
2, Sep 86	1.50	0.30	0.90	1.50
3, Nov 86	1.50	0.30	0.90	1.50
4, Jan 87	1.50	0.30	0.90	1.50
5, Mar 87	1.50	0.30	0.90	1.50
6, Jul 87	1.50	0.30	0.90	1.50
7, Aug 87	1.50	0.30	0.90	1.50
SYPHONS (Volume 2)				
0, Dec 93, preview edition	2.00	6.00	10.00	
1, May 94	2.50	0.50	1.50	2.50
2, Jun 94	2.50	0.50	1.50	2.50
3, Jul 94	2.50	0.50	1.50	2.50
SYSTEM SEVEN				
ARROW				
1	0.30	0.90	1.50	
2	0.30	0.90	1.50	
3	0.30	0.90	1.50	
SYSTEM, THE (mini-series)				
DC/VERTIGO				
1, May 96	2.95	0.59	1.77	2.95
2, Jun 96	2.95	0.59	1.77	2.95

Shazam!

Following the success of Superman and other costumed super-heroes in the late 1930s and early 1940s, Fawcett Publications decided to get into the super-hero field. One of its earliest and best-known characters was Captain Marvel, a red-clad super-hero also known as "The World's Mightest Mortal."

In his origin story in *Whiz Comics #2*, orphaned newspaper peddler Billy Batson was taken into a subway tunnel by a shadowy figure and introduced to Shazam, an old wizard who ordered Billy to say his name. Lightning struck, thunder boomed, and Billy was transformed into Captain Marvel — who drew his powers from the six gods whose initials made up Shazam's name: Solomon, Hercules, Atlas, Zeus, Achilles, and Mercury.

The Shazam powers were later acquired by Billy's sister Mary (who shouted "Shazam!" to become Mary Marvel) and Freddy Freeman (who shouted "Captain Marvel" to become Captain Marvel, Jr., a super-hero who could not say his own name without losing his powers.) The trio became the principal members of The Marvel Family and were occasionally joined in their adventures by the three Lieutenants Marvel (Tall Billy, Fat Billy, and Hill Billy Batson), Uncle Marvel (who had no Shazam-based powers), and Freckles Marvel.

National Periodical Publications, as DC was known at the time, sued Fawcett for trademark infringement, claiming that Captain Marvel resembled Superman too closely. After dragging through the courts during the '40s and into the early '50s, the lawsuit was settled when Fawcett ceasing publication of all its Marvel Family-related titles.

In the early 1970s, DC acquired most of the Fawcett properties and revived the Marvel Family in a story that explained that the entire cast had been stuck in suspended animation for the intervening years. Due to Marvel Comics' claim to the Captain Marvel name (it began a title bearing the name in the late '60s), DC was forced to call the series *Shazam!*

The series folded after 35 issues, and Captain Marvel popped up only sporadically until late 1993, when *The Power of Shazam!* graphic novel was published, reviving the character and updating him and his supporting cast, while capturing the "feel" of the Golden Age series. The one-shot led to an ongoing series.

T

	ORIG.	GOOD	FINE	N-MINT

T-BIRD CHRONICLES
ME COMIX
	ORIG.	GOOD	FINE	N-MINT
☐ 1, b&w		0.30	0.90	1.50
☐ 2, b&w		0.30	0.90	1.50

T-MINUS-1
RENEGADE
☐ 1, b&w		0.40	1.20	2.00

T.H.U.N.D.E.R.
SOLSON
☐ 1		0.39	1.17	1.95

T.H.U.N.D.E.R. AGENTS
TOWER
☐ 1, Nov 65, WW;O:Dynamo, NoMan,Menthor	0.25	25.00	75.00	125.00
☐ 2, Jan 66, WW	0.25	15.00	45.00	75.00
☐ 3, Mar 66, WW	0.25	12.00	36.00	60.00
☐ 4, Apr 66, WW O:Lightning	0.25	10.00	30.00	50.00
☐ 5, Jun 66, WW	0.25	10.00	30.00	50.00
☐ 6, Jul 66, WW	0.25	8.00	24.00	40.00
☐ 7, Aug 66, WW;D:Menthor	0.25	8.80	26.40	44.00
☐ 8, Sep 66, WW;O:Raven.	0.25	8.00	24.00	40.00
☐ 9, Oct 66	0.25	7.20	21.60	36.00
☐ 10, Nov 66	0.25	7.20	21.60	36.00
☐ 11, Mar 67, WW	0.25	6.00	18.00	30.00
☐ 12, Apr 67, WW	0.25	6.00	18.00	30.00
☐ 13, Jun 67, WW;A:Undersea Agent	0.25	6.00	18.00	30.00
☐ 14, Jul 67, WW	0.25	6.00	18.00	30.00
☐ 15, Sep 67, WW	0.25	6.00	18.00	30.00
☐ 16, Oct 67, WW	0.25	4.80	14.40	24.00
☐ 17, Dec 67, WW	0.25	4.80	14.40	24.00
☐ 18, Sep 68, WW	0.25	4.80	14.40	24.00
☐ 19, Nov 68, WW	0.25	4.80	14.40	24.00
☐ 20, Jan 66, WW reprints	0.25	1.60	4.80	8.00

T2: CYBERNETIC DAWN (mini-series)
MALIBU
☐ 1, Nov 95, immediately follows events of *T2: Judgment Day*	2.50	0.50	1.50	2.50
☐ 2, Dec 95	2.50	0.50	1.50	2.50
☐ 3, Jan 96	2.50	0.50	1.50	2.50
☐ 4, Feb 96	2.50	0.50	1.50	2.50

T2: NUCLEAR TWILIGHT (mini-series)
☐ 1, Nov 95, prequel to first *Terminator* movie	2.50	0.50	1.50	2.50
☐ 2, Dec 95	2.50	0.50	1.50	2.50
☐ 3, Jan 96	2.50	0.50	1.50	2.50

TABOO
KITCHEN SINK PRESS
☐ 8, Jun 95, b&w;(was Spiderbaby/Tundra title)	14.95	2.99	8.97	14.95

SPIDERBABY/TUNDRA
☐ 1, 88, b&w	9.95	1.99	5.97	9.95
☐ 2, 89, b&w	9.95	1.99	5.97	9.95
☐ 3, 89, b&w	9.95	1.99	5.97	9.95
☐ 4, 90, b&w	14.95	1.99	5.97	9.95
☐ 5, 91	14.95	2.99	8.97	14.95
☐ 6, 92, with booklet	14.95	2.99	8.97	14.95
☐ 7, 92, with booklet;(moves to Kitchen Sink Press)	14.95	2.99	8.97	14.95

TAILGUNNER JO (mini-series)
DC
☐ 1, Sep 88	1.25	0.25	0.75	1.25
☐ 2, Oct 88	1.25	0.25	0.75	1.25
☐ 3, Nov 88	1.25	0.25	0.75	1.25
☐ 4, Dec 88	1.25	0.25	0.75	1.25

	ORIG.	GOOD	FINE	N-MINT
☐ 5, Wtr 88	1.25	0.25	0.75	1.25
☐ 6, Jan 89	1.25	0.25	0.75	1.25

TAILS (mini-series)
ARCHIE
☐ 1, Dec 95	1.50	0.30	0.90	1.50
☐ 2, Jan 96	1.50	0.30	0.90	1.50
☐ 3, Feb 96	1.50	0.30	0.90	1.50

TAINTED
DC/VERTIGO
☐ 1, Feb 95	4.95	0.99	2.97	4.95

TAKEN UNDER COMPENDIUM
CALIBER
☐ 0, nn b&w	2.95	0.59	1.77	2.95

TAKION
DC
☐ 1, Jun 96	1.75	0.35	1.05	1.75

TALE OF HALIMA, THE
EROS COMIX
☐ 1, adult, b&w		0.55	1.65	2.75
☐ 2, adult, b&w		0.55	1.65	2.75

TALE OF MYA ROM, THE
AIRCEL
☐ 1, b&w		0.34	1.02	1.70

TALE OF ONE BAD RAT, THE (mini-series)
DARK HORSE
☐ 1, Oct 94	2.95	0.80	2.40	4.00
☐ 2, Nov 94	2.95	0.59	1.77	2.95
☐ 3, Dec 94	2.95	0.59	1.77	2.95
☐ 4, Jan 95, final issue	2.95	0.59	1.77	2.95

TALE SPIN (beginning June '91)
DISNEY
☐ 1		0.30	0.90	1.50
☐ 2		0.30	0.90	1.50
☐ 3		0.30	0.90	1.50
☐ 4		0.30	0.90	1.50
☐ 5		0.30	0.90	1.50
☐ 6		0.30	0.90	1.50
☐ 7		0.30	0.90	1.50

TALE SPIN (mini-series)
☐ 1		0.30	0.90	1.50
☐ 2		0.30	0.90	1.50
☐ 3		0.30	0.90	1.50
☐ 4		0.30	0.90	1.50

TALENT SHOWCASE
(formerly New Talent Showcase)
DC
☐ 16, Apr 85		0.25	0.75	1.25
☐ 17, May 85		0.25	0.75	1.25
☐ 18, Jun 85		0.25	0.75	1.25
☐ 19, Jul 85		0.25	0.75	1.25

TALES FROM GROUND ZERO
EXCEL
☐ 1, b&w		0.99	2.97	4.95

TALES FROM THE ANIVERSE
ARROW
☐ 1		1.00	3.00	5.00
☐ 2		0.30	0.90	1.50
☐ 3		0.30	0.90	1.50
☐ 4		0.30	0.90	1.50
☐ 5		0.30	0.90	1.50
☐ 6		0.30	0.90	1.50

MASSIVE
☐ 1, b&w		0.45	1.35	2.25
☐ 2		0.55	1.65	2.75

	ORIG.	GOOD	FINE	N-MINT

TALES FROM THE CLONEZONE
DARK HORSE

	ORIG.	GOOD	FINE	N-MINT
❑ 1		0.35	1.05	1.75

TALES FROM THE CRYPT
COCHRAN

	ORIG.	GOOD	FINE	N-MINT
❑ 1, reprints, Davis, Ingels, Craig, Kamen, AW	2.00	0.40	1.20	2.00
❑ 2, reprints, Davis, Ingels, Craig, Kamen, AW	2.00	0.40	1.20	2.00
❑ 3, reprints, Davis, Ingels, Craig, Kamen, AW	2.00	0.40	1.20	2.00
❑ 4, reprints, Davis, Ingels, Craig, Kamen, AW	2.00	0.40	1.20	2.00
❑ 5, reprints, Davis, Ingels, Craig, Kamen, AW	2.00	0.40	1.20	2.00
❑ 6, reprints, Davis, Ingels, Craig, Kamen, AW	2.00	0.40	1.20	2.00
❑ 7, reprints, Davis, Ingels, Craig, Kamen, AW	2.00	0.40	1.20	2.00

EC/GEMSTONE

	ORIG.	GOOD	FINE	N-MINT
❑ 1, JC,AF reprints	1.50	0.30	0.90	1.50
❑ 2, reprints	1.50	0.30	0.90	1.50
❑ 3, reprints	1.50	0.30	0.90	1.50
❑ 4, reprints, JC,AF,JKa,GI	2.00	0.40	1.20	2.00
❑ 5, reprints, AF, WW,HK,GI	2.00	0.40	1.20	2.00
❑ 6, reprints, AF,GI,JK,JC..	2.00	0.40	1.20	2.00
❑ 7, reprints, AF,GI,JD,JC..	2.00	0.40	1.20	2.00
❑ 8, Jun 94, r:AF(c),JD, GI,JC,WW	2.00	0.40	1.20	2.00
❑ 9, reprints	2.00	0.40	1.20	2.00
❑ 10, reprints	2.00	0.40	1.20	2.00
❑ 11, reprints	2.00	0.40	1.20	2.00
❑ 12, reprints	2.00	0.40	1.20	2.00
❑ 13, reprints	2.00	0.40	1.20	2.00

GLADSTONE

	ORIG.	GOOD	FINE	N-MINT
❑ 1, Jul 90, reprint: Davis, Evans, Kamen, Ingels, Craig, Elder, Williamson, Frazetta;O:Crypt-Keeper	1.95	0.39	1.17	1.95
❑ 2, Sep 90, reprint: Davis, Orlando, Kamen, Ingels	1.95	0.39	1.17	1.95
❑ 3, Nov 90, reprint: Davis, Orlando, Kamen, Ingels, Craig, Wood, Kurtzman	1.95	0.39	1.17	1.95
❑ 4, Jan 91, reprint: Craig, Feldstein, Orlando, Kurtzman, AW, Kamen	2.00	0.40	1.20	2.00
❑ 5, Mar 91, reprint: Davis, Kamen, BKrigstein, Ingels, Craig	2.00	0.40	1.20	2.00
❑ 6, May 91, reprint: Davis, Kamen, Krigstein, Ingels, Evans	2.00	0.40	1.20	2.00

TALES FROM THE EDGE SUMMER SPECIAL
VANGUARD

	ORIG.	GOOD	FINE	N-MINT
❑ 1, Aug 94, b&w;cardstock cover	3.50	0.70	2.10	3.50

TALES FROM THE EDGE!

	ORIG.	GOOD	FINE	N-MINT
❑ 1, Jun 93, b&w	2.95	0.59	1.77	2.95
❑ 2, Sep 93, b&w	2.95	0.59	1.77	2.95
❑ 3, Dec 93, b&w	2.95	0.59	1.77	2.95
❑ 4, Jul 94, b&w	2.95	0.59	1.77	2.95
❑ 5	2.95	0.59	1.77	2.95
❑ 7, Jul 95, b&w	2.95	0.59	1.77	2.95

TALES FROM THE HEART
ENTROPY

	ORIG.	GOOD	FINE	N-MINT
❑ 1		0.30	0.90	1.50
❑ 2, (moves to Slave Labor)		0.30	0.90	1.50

TALES FROM THE HEART (was Entropy title)
SLAVE LABOR

	ORIG.	GOOD	FINE	N-MINT
❑ 3, b&w		0.35	1.05	1.75
❑ 4, b&w		0.35	1.05	1.75
❑ 5, b&w		0.35	1.05	1.75

	ORIG.	GOOD	FINE	N-MINT
❑ 6, b&w		0.35	1.05	1.75
❑ 7		0.59	1.77	2.95
❑ 8		0.50	1.50	2.50
❑ 10, b&w	2.95	0.59	1.77	2.95

TALES FROM THE OUTER BOROUGHS
FANTAGRAPHICS

	ORIG.	GOOD	FINE	N-MINT
❑ 1, b&w		0.45	1.35	2.25
❑ 2, b&w		0.45	1.35	2.25
❑ 3, b&w		0.45	1.35	2.25
❑ 4, b&w		0.50	1.50	2.50
❑ 5, b&w		0.50	1.50	2.50

TALES FROM THE RAVAGED LANDS
MAGI STUDIOS

	ORIG.	GOOD	FINE	N-MINT
❑ 1, 95, b&w;no indicia or cover date	2.50	0.50	1.50	2.50
❑ 2, b&w;no indicia or cover date	2.50	0.50	1.50	2.50
❑ 3, Jan 96, b&w	2.50	0.50	1.50	2.50
❑ 4, b&w;no indicia or cover date	2.50	0.50	1.50	2.50

TALES FROM THE STONE TROLL CAFE
PLANET X

	ORIG.	GOOD	FINE	N-MINT
❑ 1, 86	1.75	0.35	1.05	1.75

TALES OF ASGARD (1968)
MARVEL

	ORIG.	GOOD	FINE	N-MINT
❑ 1	0.25	6.00	18.00	30.00

TALES OF ASGARD (1984)

	ORIG.	GOOD	FINE	N-MINT
❑ 1, Feb 84	1.25	0.40	1.20	2.00

TALES OF EVIL
ATLAS/ SEABOARD

	ORIG.	GOOD	FINE	N-MINT
❑ 1, Feb 75	0.25	0.20	0.60	1.00
❑ 2, Apr 75	0.25	0.20	0.60	1.00
❑ 3, Jul 75	0.25	0.20	0.60	1.00

TALES OF G.I. JOE
MARVEL

	ORIG.	GOOD	FINE	N-MINT
❑ 1, Jan 88, rep.	2.25	0.45	1.35	2.25
❑ 2, Feb 88, rep.	1.50	0.45	1.35	2.25
❑ 3, Mar 88, rep.	1.50	0.45	1.35	2.25
❑ 4, Apr 88, rep.	1.50	0.45	1.35	2.25
❑ 5, May 88, rep.	1.50	0.45	1.35	2.25
❑ 6, Jun 88, rep.	1.50	0.30	0.90	1.50
❑ 7, Jul 88, rep.	1.50	0.30	0.90	1.50
❑ 8, Aug 88, rep.	1.50	0.30	0.90	1.50
❑ 9, Sep 88, rep.	1.50	0.30	0.90	1.50
❑ 10, Oct 88, rep.	1.50	0.30	0.90	1.50
❑ 11, Nov 88, rep.	1.50	0.30	0.90	1.50
❑ 12, Dec 88, rep.	1.50	0.30	0.90	1.50
❑ 13, Jan 89, rep.	1.50	0.30	0.90	1.50
❑ 14, Feb 89, rep.	1.50	0.30	0.90	1.50
❑ 15, Mar 89, rep.	1.50	0.30	0.90	1.50

TALES OF GHOST CASTLE
DC

	ORIG.	GOOD	FINE	N-MINT
❑ 1, May 75	0.25	0.05	0.15	0.25
❑ 2, Jul 75	0.25	0.05	0.15	0.25
❑ 3, Sep 75	0.25	0.05	0.15	0.25

TALES OF JERRY
HACIENDA

	ORIG.	GOOD	FINE	N-MINT
❑ 1, b&w		1.00	3.00	5.00
❑ 2		0.50	1.50	2.50
❑ 3		0.50	1.50	2.50
❑ 4		0.50	1.50	2.50
❑ 5		0.50	1.50	2.50
❑ 6		0.50	1.50	2.50
❑ 7		0.50	1.50	2.50
❑ 8		0.50	1.50	2.50
❑ 9		0.50	1.50	2.50
❑ 10		0.50	1.50	2.50

	ORIG.	GOOD	FINE	N-MINT

TALES OF LETHARGY
ALPHA

	ORIG.	GOOD	FINE	N-MINT
1, b&w	2.50	0.50	1.50	2.50
2, b&w	2.50	0.50	1.50	2.50
3, b&w	2.50	0.50	1.50	2.50

TALES OF NECROPOLIS
BRAINSTORM

	ORIG.	GOOD	FINE	N-MINT
1, b&w	2.95	0.59	1.77	2.95

TALES OF ORDINARY MADNESS
DARK HORSE

	GOOD	FINE	N-MINT
1, b&w	0.50	1.50	2.50
2, b&w	0.50	1.50	2.50
3, b&w	0.50	1.50	2.50

TALES OF SCREAMING HORROR
FANTACO

	ORIG.	GOOD	FINE	N-MINT
1, 92, b&w	3.50	0.70	2.10	3.50

TALES OF SUN RUNNERS
SIRIUS

	GOOD	FINE	N-MINT
1	0.30	0.90	1.50
2	0.30	0.90	1.50

TALES OF SUSPENSE
MARVEL

	ORIG.	GOOD	FINE	N-MINT
1	0.10	200.00	600.00	1000.00
2	0.10	100.00	300.00	500.00
3	0.10	65.00	195.00	325.00
4	0.10	80.00	240.00	400.00
5	0.10	48.00	144.00	240.00
6		40.00	120.00	200.00
7		40.00	120.00	200.00
8		40.00	120.00	200.00
9		40.00	120.00	200.00
10		40.00	120.00	200.00
11	0.10	30.00	90.00	150.00
12	0.10	30.00	90.00	150.00
13	0.10	30.00	90.00	150.00
14	0.10	30.00	90.00	150.00
15	0.10	30.00	90.00	150.00
16	0.10	30.00	90.00	150.00
17	0.10	30.00	90.00	150.00
18	0.10	30.00	90.00	150.00
19	0.10	30.00	90.00	150.00
20	0.10	30.00	90.00	150.00
21	0.10	30.00	90.00	150.00
22	0.10	30.00	90.00	150.00
23	0.10	30.00	90.00	150.00
24	0.10	30.00	90.00	150.00
25	0.10	30.00	90.00	150.00
26	0.12	25.00	75.00	125.00
27	0.12	25.00	75.00	125.00
28	0.12	20.00	60.00	100.00
29	0.12	20.00	60.00	100.00
30	0.12	20.00	60.00	100.00
31	0.12	20.00	60.00	100.00
32	0.12	20.00	60.00	100.00
33	0.12	20.00	60.00	100.00
34	0.12	20.00	60.00	100.00
35	0.12	20.00	60.00	100.00
36	0.12	20.00	60.00	100.00
37	0.12	20.00	60.00	100.00
38	0.12	20.00	60.00	100.00
39, Mar 63, JK, O&1:Iron Man	0.12	680.00	2040.00	3400.00
40, JK	0.12	200.00	600.00	1000.00
41, JK	0.12	120.00	360.00	600.00
42, DH/SD, I:Mad Pharoah	0.12	40.00	120.00	200.00
43	0.12	40.00	120.00	200.00
44	0.12	40.00	120.00	200.00
45	0.12	40.00	120.00	200.00
46	0.12	36.00	108.00	180.00
47	0.12	36.00	108.00	180.00

	ORIG.	GOOD	FINE	N-MINT
48, Dec 63, SD, new costume	0.12	40.00	120.00	200.00
49, SD, A:Angel	0.12	30.00	90.00	150.00
50, DH, 1:Mandarin	0.12	14.00	42.00	70.00
51, DH, Scarecrow	0.12	12.00	36.00	60.00
52, DH, 1:Black Widow	0.12	24.00	72.00	120.00
53, DH, O:Watcher	0.12	14.00	42.00	70.00
54, DH	0.12	12.00	36.00	60.00
55, DH	0.12	12.00	36.00	60.00
56, DH	0.12	12.00	36.00	60.00
57, DH, 1:Hawkeye	0.12	32.00	96.00	160.00
58, Oct 64, DH, Capt. America starts	0.12	44.00	132.00	220.00
59, DH/JK, I:Jarvis	0.12	52.00	156.00	260.00
60, DJ/JK, Assassins	0.12	25.00	75.00	125.00
61, DH/JK, Assassins	0.12	16.00	48.00	80.00
62, DH/JK, Assassins	0.12	16.00	48.00	80.00
63, O:Capt. America	0.12	36.00	108.00	180.00
64	0.12	14.00	42.00	70.00
65	0.12	20.00	60.00	100.00
66	0.12	20.00	60.00	100.00
67	0.12	10.00	30.00	50.00
68	0.12	10.00	30.00	50.00
69	0.12	10.00	30.00	50.00
70	0.12	10.00	30.00	50.00
71	0.12	10.00	30.00	50.00
72	0.12	10.00	30.00	50.00
73	0.12	6.00	18.00	30.00
74	0.12	6.00	18.00	30.00
75	0.12	6.00	18.00	30.00
76	0.12	6.00	18.00	30.00
77	0.12	6.00	18.00	30.00
78, A:Nick Fury	0.12	6.00	18.00	30.00
79	0.12	6.00	18.00	30.00
80, Cosmic Cube	0.12	6.00	18.00	30.00
83	0.12	6.00	18.00	30.00
84	0.12	6.00	18.00	30.00
85, GK/GC;V:Mandarin	0.12	6.00	18.00	30.00
86	0.12	6.00	18.00	30.00
87	0.12	6.00	18.00	30.00
88, GK/GC	0.12	6.00	18.00	30.00
89, GK/GC	0.12	6.00	18.00	30.00
90, GK/GC	0.12	6.00	18.00	30.00
91, GK/GC	0.12	6.00	18.00	30.00
92, GK/GC	0.12	6.00	18.00	30.00
93, GK/GC	0.12	6.00	18.00	30.00
94, GK/GC	0.12	6.00	18.00	30.00
95, GK/GC	0.12	6.00	18.00	30.00
96, GK/GC	0.12	6.00	18.00	30.00
97, GK/GC	0.12	6.00	18.00	30.00
98, GK/GC	0.12	6.00	18.00	30.00
99, GK/GC, Red Skull (becomes *Captain America*)	0.12	6.00	18.00	30.00

TALES OF SUSPENSE (Vol. 2)

	ORIG.	GOOD	FINE	N-MINT
1, Jan 95, prestige format one-shot;acetate outer cover	6.95	1.39	4.17	6.95

TALES OF TERROR
ECLIPSE

	GOOD	FINE	N-MINT
1	0.35	1.05	1.75
2	0.35	1.05	1.75
3	0.35	1.05	1.75
4	0.35	1.05	1.75
5	0.35	1.05	1.75
6	0.35	1.05	1.75
7	0.35	1.05	1.75
8	0.35	1.05	1.75
9	0.35	1.05	1.75
10	0.40	1.20	2.00
11	0.40	1.20	2.00
12	0.40	1.20	2.00
13	0.40	1.20	2.00

	ORIG.	GOOD	FINE	N-MINT

TALES OF THE BEANWORLD

	ORIG.	GOOD	FINE	N-MINT
☐ 1, 85, b&w 1.50		3.60	10.80	18.00
☐ 2		2.00	6.00	10.00
☐ 3		1.20	3.60	6.00
☐ 4		1.20	3.60	6.00
☐ 5		1.20	3.60	6.00
☐ 6		1.00	3.00	5.00
☐ 7		1.00	3.00	5.00
☐ 8		1.00	3.00	5.00
☐ 9, b&w		1.00	3.00	5.00
☐ 10, b&w		1.00	3.00	5.00
☐ 11, b&w		0.80	2.40	4.00
☐ 12, b&w		0.80	2.40	4.00
☐ 13, b&w		0.80	2.40	4.00
☐ 14, b&w		0.80	2.40	4.00
☐ 15, b&w		0.80	2.40	4.00
☐ 16, b&w		0.60	1.80	3.00
☐ 17, b&w		0.60	1.80	3.00
☐ 18, b&w		0.60	1.80	3.00
☐ 19, b&w		0.60	1.80	3.00
☐ 20, b&w 2.50		0.50	1.50	2.50

TALES OF THE CLOSET...
HETRICMARTIN

	ORIG.	GOOD	FINE	N-MINT
☐ 1, b&w		0.50	1.50	2.50
☐ 2, b&w		0.50	1.50	2.50
☐ 3, b&w		0.50	1.50	2.50
☐ 4, b&w		0.50	1.50	2.50
☐ 5, b&w		0.50	1.50	2.50
☐ 6, b&w		0.50	1.50	2.50

TALES OF THE CYBORG GERBILS
HARRIER

	ORIG.	GOOD	FINE	N-MINT
☐ 1		0.39	1.17	1.95

TALES OF THE FEHNNIK
ANTARCTIC

	ORIG.	GOOD	FINE	N-MINT
☐ 1, Aug 95, b&w 2.95		0.59	1.77	2.95

TALES OF THE GREEN HORNET
NOW

	ORIG.	GOOD	FINE	N-MINT
☐ 1, Sep 90, by Van Williams				
.... 1.75		0.35	1.05	1.75
☐ 2, Oct 90 .... 1.75		0.35	1.05	1.75

TALES OF THE GREEN HORNET (Volume 2)

	ORIG.	GOOD	FINE	N-MINT
☐ 1, Jan 92 .... 1.95		0.39	1.17	1.95
☐ 2, Feb 92 .... 1.95		0.39	1.17	1.95
☐ 3, Mar 92 .... 1.95		0.39	1.17	1.95
☐ 4, Apr 92 .... 1.95		0.39	1.17	1.95

TALES OF THE GREEN HORNET (Volume 3)

	ORIG.	GOOD	FINE	N-MINT
☐ 1, Sep 92, bagged with hologram card				
.... 2.75		0.55	1.65	2.75
☐ 2, Oct 92 .... 2.50		0.50	1.50	2.50
☐ 3, Nov 92 .... 2.50		0.50	1.50	2.50

TALES OF THE GREEN LANTERN CORPS
DC

	ORIG.	GOOD	FINE	N-MINT
☐ 1, May 81, JS/FMc, O:Green Lantern				
.... 0.50		0.25	0.75	1.25
☐ 2, Jun 81, JS/FMc 0.50		0.20	0.60	1.00
☐ 3, Jul 81, JS/FMc 0.50		0.20	0.60	1.00

TALES OF THE GREEN LANTERN CORPS ANNUAL

	ORIG.	GOOD	FINE	N-MINT
☐ 1, 85 .... 1.25		0.50	1.50	2.50
☐ 2, 86, AMo 1.25		0.40	1.20	2.00
☐ 3, 87, JBy,AMo 1.25		0.40	1.20	2.00

TALES OF THE JACKALOPE
BLACKTHORNE

	ORIG.	GOOD	FINE	N-MINT
☐ 1		0.40	1.20	2.00
☐ 2		0.40	1.20	2.00
☐ 3		0.40	1.20	2.00
☐ 4		0.40	1.20	2.00
☐ 5		0.40	1.20	2.00
☐ 6		0.40	1.20	2.00
☐ 7		0.40	1.20	2.00

TALES OF THE KUNG FU WARRIORS
CFW

	ORIG.	GOOD	FINE	N-MINT
☐ 1, 1: Ethereal Black, Squamous	0.39	1.17	1.95	
☐ 10		0.45	1.35	2.25
☐ 11		0.45	1.35	2.25
☐ 12		0.45	1.35	2.25
☐ 13		0.45	1.35	2.25
☐ 14, 1: Sumo		0.45	1.35	2.25

TALES OF THE LEGION OF SUPER-HEROES
(formerly Legion of Super-Heroes)
DC

	ORIG.	GOOD	FINE	N-MINT
☐ 314, Aug 84, O:White Witch				
.... 0.75		0.30	0.90	1.50
☐ 315, Sep 84 .... 0.75		0.25	0.75	1.25
☐ 316, Oct 84 .... 0.75		0.25	0.75	1.25
☐ 317, Nov 84 .... 0.75		0.25	0.75	1.25
☐ 318, Dec 84 .... 0.75		0.25	0.75	1.25
☐ 319, Jan 85 .... 0.75		0.25	0.75	1.25
☐ 320, Feb 85 .... 0.75		0.25	0.75	1.25
☐ 321, Mar 85 .... 0.75		0.25	0.75	1.25
☐ 322, Apr 85 .... 0.75		0.25	0.75	1.25
☐ 323, May 85 .... 0.75		0.25	0.75	1.25
☐ 324, Jun 85 .... 0.75		0.25	0.75	1.25
☐ 325, Jul 85 .... 0.75		0.25	0.75	1.25
☐ 326, Aug 85, begins reprints of *Legion of Super-Heroes* (1984-1989);V:Legion of Super-Villains				
.... 0.75		0.25	0.75	1.25
☐ 327, Sep 85 .... 0.75		0.25	0.75	1.25
☐ 328, Oct 85 .... 0.75		0.25	0.75	1.25
☐ 329, Nov 85 .... 0.75		0.25	0.75	1.25
☐ 330, Dec 85 .... 0.75		0.25	0.75	1.25
☐ 331, Jan 86 .... 0.75		0.25	0.75	1.25
☐ 332, Feb 86 .... 0.75		0.25	0.75	1.25
☐ 333, Mar 86 .... 0.75		0.25	0.75	1.25
☐ 334, Apr 86 .... 0.75		0.25	0.75	1.25
☐ 335, May 86 .... 0.75		0.25	0.75	1.25
☐ 336, Jun 86 .... 0.75		0.25	0.75	1.25
☐ 337, Jul 86 .... 0.75		0.25	0.75	1.25
☐ 338, Aug 86 .... 0.75		0.25	0.75	1.25
☐ 339, Sep 86, J:Magnetic Kid, Tellus, Polar Boy, Quislet, Sensor Girl ...0.75		0.25	0.75	1.25
☐ 340, Oct 86, V:Dr. Regulus				
.... 0.75		0.25	0.75	1.25
☐ 341, Nov 86 .... 0.75		0.25	0.75	1.25
☐ 342, Dec 86 .... 0.75		0.25	0.75	1.25
☐ 343, Jan 87, O:Wildfire ...0.75		0.25	0.75	1.25
☐ 344, Feb 87 .... 0.75		0.25	0.75	1.25
☐ 345, Mar 87 .... 0.75		0.25	0.75	1.25
☐ 346, Apr 87 .... 0.75		0.25	0.75	1.25
☐ 347, May 87 .... 0.75		0.25	0.75	1.25
☐ 348, Jun 87 .... 0.75		0.25	0.75	1.25
☐ 349, Jul 87 .... 0.75		0.25	0.75	1.25
☐ 350, Aug 87, Sensor Girl's identity revealed				
.... 0.75		0.25	0.75	1.25
☐ 351, Sep 87 .... 0.75		0.25	0.75	1.25
☐ 352, Oct 87 .... 0.75		0.25	0.75	1.25
☐ 353, Nov 87 .... 1.00		0.20	0.60	1.00
☐ 354, Dec 87, final issue ..1.00		0.20	0.60	1.00

TALES OF THE LEGION OF SUPER-HEROES ANNUAL

	ORIG.	GOOD	FINE	N-MINT
☐ 4, 86 .... 1.25		0.25	0.75	1.25
☐ 5, 87, O:Validus 1.25		0.25	0.75	1.25

TALES OF THE MARVELS: BLOCKBUSTER
MARVEL

	ORIG.	GOOD	FINE	N-MINT
☐ 1, Apr 95, one-shot;acetate overlay outer cover;prestige format 5.95		1.19	3.57	5.95

	ORIG.	GOOD	FINE	N-MINT

TALES OF THE MARVELS: WONDER YEARS
(mini-series)

	ORIG.	GOOD	FINE	N-MINT
1, Aug 95, wraparound acetate outer cover	4.95	0.99	2.97	4.95
2, Sep 95, wraparound acetate outer cover	4.95	0.99	2.97	4.95

TALES OF THE NEW TEEN TITANS (mini-series)
DC

	ORIG.	GOOD	FINE	N-MINT
1, Jun 82, GP;Cyborg	0.60	0.40	1.20	2.00
2, Jul 82, GP;Raven	0.60	0.30	0.90	1.50
3, Aug 82, GP/GD;Changeling	0.60	0.30	0.90	1.50
4, Sep 82, GP/EC;Starfire	0.60	0.30	0.90	1.50

TALES OF THE NINJA WARRIORS
CFW

	GOOD	FINE	N-MINT
1, b&w	0.45	1.35	2.25
2, b&w	0.45	1.35	2.25
3, b&w	0.45	1.35	2.25
4, b&w	0.45	1.35	2.25
5, b&w	0.45	1.35	2.25
6, b&w	0.45	1.35	2.25
7, b&w	0.45	1.35	2.25
8, b&w	0.45	1.35	2.25
9, b&w	0.45	1.35	2.25
10, b&w	0.45	1.35	2.25
11, b&w	0.45	1.35	2.25
12, b&w	0.45	1.35	2.25
13, b&w	0.45	1.35	2.25
14, b&w	0.45	1.35	2.25
15, b&w	0.45	1.35	2.25
16, b&w	0.45	1.35	2.25

TALES OF THE SUN RUNNERS (former Sirius title)
AMAZING

	GOOD	FINE	N-MINT
3	0.39	1.17	1.95

TALES OF THE TEEN TITANS
(formerly New Teen Titans)
DC

	ORIG.	GOOD	FINE	N-MINT
41, Apr 84, GP	0.75	0.25	0.75	1.25
42, May 84, GP, Judas Contract	0.75	0.40	1.20	2.00
43, Jun 84, GP, Judas Contract	0.75	0.40	1.20	2.00
44, Jul 84, GP, Judas Contract, 1:Nightwing	0.75	0.70	2.10	3.50
45, Aug 84, GP	0.75	0.25	0.75	1.25
46, Sep 84, GP	0.75	0.25	0.75	1.25
47, Oct 84, GP	0.75	0.25	0.75	1.25
48, Nov 84, GP	0.75	0.25	0.75	1.25
49, Dec 84, GP	0.75	0.25	0.75	1.25
50, Feb 85, GP/DG W:Wonder Girl	1.25	0.45	1.35	2.25
51, Mar 85	0.75	0.20	0.60	1.00
52, Apr 85	0.75	0.20	0.60	1.00
53, May 85	0.75	0.20	0.60	1.00
54, Jun 85	0.75	0.20	0.60	1.00
55, Jul 85	0.75	0.20	0.60	1.00
56, Aug 85	0.75	0.20	0.60	1.00
57, Sep 85	0.75	0.20	0.60	1.00
58, Oct 85	0.75	0.20	0.60	1.00
59, Nov 85	0.75	0.20	0.60	1.00
60, Dec 85	0.75	0.20	0.60	1.00
61, Jan 86	0.75	0.20	0.60	1.00
62, Feb 86	0.75	0.20	0.60	1.00
63, Mar 86	0.75	0.20	0.60	1.00
64, Apr 86	0.75	0.20	0.60	1.00
65, May 86	0.75	0.20	0.60	1.00
66, Jun 86	0.75	0.20	0.60	1.00
67, Jul 86	0.75	0.20	0.60	1.00
68, Aug 86	0.75	0.20	0.60	1.00
69, Sep 86	0.75	0.20	0.60	1.00
70, Oct 86	0.75	0.20	0.60	1.00
71, Nov 86	0.75	0.20	0.60	1.00
72, Dec 86	0.75	0.20	0.60	1.00
73, Jan 87	0.75	0.20	0.60	1.00
74, Feb 87	0.75	0.20	0.60	1.00
75, Mar 87	0.75	0.20	0.60	1.00
76, Apr 87	0.75	0.20	0.60	1.00
77, May 87	0.75	0.20	0.60	1.00
78, Jun 87	0.75	0.20	0.60	1.00
79, Jul 87	0.75	0.20	0.60	1.00
80, Aug 87	0.75	0.20	0.60	1.00
81, Sep 87	0.75	0.20	0.60	1.00
82, Oct 87	0.75	0.20	0.60	1.00
83, Nov 87	0.75	0.20	0.60	1.00
84, Dec 87	0.75	0.20	0.60	1.00
85, Jan 88	0.75	0.20	0.60	1.00
86, Feb 88	0.75	0.20	0.60	1.00
87, Mar 88	0.75	0.20	0.60	1.00
88, Apr 88	0.75	0.20	0.60	1.00
89, May 88	0.75	0.20	0.60	1.00
90, Jun 88	0.75	0.20	0.60	1.00
91, Jul 88	0.75	0.20	0.60	1.00

TALES OF THE TEEN TITANS ANNUAL

	ORIG.	GOOD	FINE	N-MINT
4, 86, reprints *New Teen Titans Annual* #1 (direct-sale series);A:Superman;V:Vanguard	1.25	0.25	0.75	1.25

TALES OF THE TEENAGE MUTANT NINJA TURTLES
MIRAGE

	GOOD	FINE	N-MINT
1	2.00	6.00	10.00
2	1.20	3.60	6.00
3	1.00	3.00	5.00
4	1.00	3.00	5.00
5	1.00	3.00	5.00
6	0.60	1.80	3.00
7	0.60	1.80	3.00

TALES OF THE ZOMBIE (b&w mag)
MARVEL

	ORIG.	GOOD	FINE	N-MINT
1, O:Zombie	0.75	0.15	0.45	0.75
2	0.75	0.15	0.45	0.75
3	0.75	0.15	0.45	0.75
4	0.75	0.15	0.45	0.75
5	0.75	0.15	0.45	0.75
6	0.75	0.15	0.45	0.75
7	0.75	0.15	0.45	0.75
8	0.75	0.15	0.45	0.75
9	0.75	0.15	0.45	0.75
10	0.75	0.15	0.45	0.75

TALES OF THE ZOMBIE ANNUAL

	ORIG.	GOOD	FINE	N-MINT
1, reprints	1.25	0.25	0.75	1.25

TALES TO ASTONISH

	ORIG.	GOOD	FINE	N-MINT
1	0.10	200.00	600.00	1000.00
2	0.10	80.00	240.00	400.00
3	0.10	50.00	150.00	250.00
4	0.10	50.00	150.00	250.00
5	0.10	50.00	150.00	250.00
6	0.10	40.00	120.00	200.00
7	0.10	40.00	120.00	200.00
8	0.10	40.00	120.00	200.00
9	0.10	40.00	120.00	200.00
10	0.10	40.00	120.00	200.00
11	0.10	30.00	90.00	150.00
12	0.10	30.00	90.00	150.00
13	0.10	30.00	90.00	150.00
14	0.10	30.00	90.00	150.00
15	0.10	30.00	90.00	150.00
16	0.10	30.00	90.00	150.00
17	0.10	30.00	90.00	150.00
18	0.10	30.00	90.00	150.00
19	0.10	30.00	90.00	150.00
20	0.10	30.00	90.00	150.00

	ORIG.	GOOD	FINE	N-MINT
21	0.10	24.00	72.00	120.00
22	0.10	24.00	72.00	120.00
23	0.10	24.00	72.00	120.00
24	0.10	24.00	72.00	120.00
25	0.10	24.00	72.00	120.00
26	0.10	24.00	72.00	120.00
27, SD/JK, 1:Ant-Man	0.10	520.00	1560.00	2600.00
28, SD/JK	0.12	20.00	60.00	100.00
29, SD/JK	0.12	20.00	60.00	100.00
30, SD/JK	0.12	20.00	60.00	100.00
31, SD/JK	0.12	20.00	60.00	100.00
32, SD/JK	0.12	20.00	60.00	100.00
33, SD/JK	0.12	20.00	60.00	100.00
34, SD/JK	0.12	20.00	60.00	100.00
35, Sep 62, SD/JK, 2:Ant-Man	0.12	250.00	750.00	1250.00
36, SD/JK	0.12	80.00	240.00	400.00
37, SD/JK	0.12	40.00	120.00	200.00
38	0.12	30.00	90.00	150.00
39	0.12	30.00	90.00	150.00
40	0.12	30.00	90.00	150.00
41, DH/SD	0.12	30.00	90.00	150.00
42, DH/SD	0.12	30.00	90.00	150.00
43, DH/SD	0.12	30.00	90.00	150.00
44, Jun 63, JK/SD, O:Wasp	0.12	50.00	150.00	250.00
45, DH/SD	0.12	18.00	54.00	90.00
46, DH/SD	0.12	18.00	54.00	90.00
47, DH/SD	0.12	18.00	54.00	90.00
48, DH/SD	0.12	18.00	54.00	90.00
49, JK/DH/AM, Giant Man	0.12	28.00	84.00	140.00
50, JK/SD, Human Top I	0.12	12.00	36.00	60.00
51, JK, Human Top II	0.12	12.00	36.00	60.00
52, 1:Black Knight	0.12	12.00	36.00	60.00
53	0.12	12.00	36.00	60.00
54	0.12	12.00	36.00	60.00
55	0.12	12.00	36.00	60.00
56	0.12	12.00	36.00	60.00
57	0.12	20.00	60.00	100.00
58	0.12	12.00	36.00	60.00
59, Giant-Man vs. Hulk	0.12	28.00	84.00	140.00
60, Oct 64, Hulk begins	0.12	34.00	102.00	170.00
61	0.12	11.00	33.00	55.00
62	0.12	11.00	33.00	55.00
63	0.12	11.00	33.00	55.00
64	0.12	11.00	33.00	55.00
65	0.12	11.00	33.00	55.00
66	0.12	11.00	33.00	55.00
67	0.12	11.00	33.00	55.00
68	0.12	11.00	33.00	55.00
69	0.12	11.00	33.00	55.00
70, Sub-Mariner begins	0.12	16.00	48.00	80.00
71	0.12	6.00	18.00	30.00
72	0.12	6.00	18.00	30.00
73	0.12	6.00	18.00	30.00
74	0.12	6.00	18.00	30.00
75	0.12	6.00	18.00	30.00
76	0.12	6.00	18.00	30.00
77	0.12	6.00	18.00	30.00
78	0.12	6.00	18.00	30.00
79	0.12	6.00	18.00	30.00
80, GC/JK	0.12	6.00	18.00	30.00
81, GC/JK	0.12	6.00	18.00	30.00
82, GC/JK	0.12	6.00	18.00	30.00
83	0.12	6.00	18.00	30.00
84	0.12	6.00	18.00	30.00
85	0.12	6.00	18.00	30.00
86	0.12	6.00	18.00	30.00
87	0.12	6.00	18.00	30.00
88	0.12	6.00	18.00	30.00
89	0.12	6.00	18.00	30.00

	ORIG.	GOOD	FINE	N-MINT
90	0.12	6.00	18.00	30.00
91	0.12	6.00	18.00	30.00
92, Silver Surfer	0.12	9.60	28.80	48.00
93, Silver Surfer	0.12	9.60	28.80	48.00
94	0.12	3.20	9.60	16.00
95	0.12	6.00	18.00	30.00
96	0.12	6.00	18.00	30.00
97	0.12	6.00	18.00	30.00
98	0.12	6.00	18.00	30.00
99	0.12	6.00	18.00	30.00
100, Hulk vs. Sub-Mariner	0.12	7.20	21.60	36.00
101, (becomes *The Incredible Hulk*)	0.12	6.00	18.00	30.00

TALES TO ASTONISH (2nd series)

	ORIG.	GOOD	FINE	N-MINT
1, Dec 79, JB, Sub-Mariner rep.		0.40	1.20	2.00
2, Jan 80, JB, Sub-Mariner rep.		0.30	0.90	1.50
3, Feb 80, JB, Sub-Mariner rep.		0.30	0.90	1.50
4, Mar 80, JB, Sub-Mariner rep.		0.30	0.90	1.50
5, Apr 80, JB, Sub-Mariner rep.		0.30	0.90	1.50
6, May 80, JB, Sub-Mariner rep.		0.30	0.90	1.50
7, Jun 80, JB, Sub-Mariner rep.		0.30	0.90	1.50
8, Jul 80, JB, Sub-Mariner rep.		0.30	0.90	1.50
9, Aug 80, JB, Sub-Mariner rep.		0.30	0.90	1.50
10, Sep 80, JB, Sub-Mariner rep.		0.30	0.90	1.50
11, Oct 80, JB, Sub-Mariner rep.		0.30	0.90	1.50
12, Nov 80, JB, Sub-Mariner rep		0.30	0.90	1.50
13, Dec 80, JB, Sub-Mariner rep.		0.30	0.90	1.50
14, Jan 81, JB, Sub-Mariner rep.		0.30	0.90	1.50

TALES TO ASTONISH (Vol. 3)

	ORIG.	GOOD	FINE	N-MINT
1, Dec 94, prestige format one-shot;acetate outer cover	6.95	1.39	4.17	6.95

TALES TOO TERRIBLE TO TELL
NEW ENGLAND

	ORIG.	GOOD	FINE	N-MINT
1, SRB(c) b&w reprints		0.59	1.77	2.95
2, b&w reprints	3.50	0.70	2.10	3.50
3, b&w reprints	3.50	0.70	2.10	3.50
4, b&w reprints	3.50	0.70	2.10	3.50
5, b&w reprints	3.50	0.70	2.10	3.50
6, b&w reprints	3.50	0.70	2.10	3.50
7, b&w reprints	3.50	0.70	2.10	3.50

TALK DIRTY
EROS COMIX

	ORIG.	GOOD	FINE	N-MINT
1, adult, b&w		0.50	1.50	2.50
2, adult, b&w		0.50	1.50	2.50
3, adult, b&w		0.59	1.77	2.95

TALL TAILS
GOLDEN REALM

	ORIG.	GOOD	FINE	N-MINT
1, 93, b&w	1.50	0.30	0.90	1.50

TALONZ
STOP DRAGON

	ORIG.	GOOD	FINE	N-MINT
1, b&w		0.30	0.90	1.50

TALOS OF THE WILDERNESS SEA
DC

	ORIG.	GOOD	FINE	N-MINT
1, 87, GK	2.00	0.40	1.20	2.00

	ORIG.	GOOD	FINE	N-MINT

TANK GIRL
DARK HORSE

	ORIG.	GOOD	FINE	N-MINT
❑ 1, trading cards, b&w, British	0.45	1.35	2.25	
❑ 2	0.45	1.35	2.25	
❑ 3	0.45	1.35	2.25	
❑ 4	0.45	1.35	2.25	

TANK GIRL 2

	ORIG.	GOOD	FINE	N-MINT
❑ 1	2.50	0.50	1.50	2.50
❑ 2	2.50	0.50	1.50	2.50
❑ 3, Aug 93	2.50	0.50	1.50	2.50
❑ 4	2.50	0.50	1.50	2.50

TANK GIRL MOVIE ADAPTATION
DC/VERTIGO

	ORIG.	GOOD	FINE	N-MINT
❑ 0, 95, prestige format one-shot	5.95	1.19	3.57	5.95

TANK GIRL: APOCALYPSE (mini-series)

	ORIG.	GOOD	FINE	N-MINT
❑ 1, Nov 95, Tank Girl becomes pregnant	2.25	0.45	1.35	2.25
❑ 2, Dec 95	2.25	0.45	1.35	2.25
❑ 3, Jan 96	2.25	0.45	1.35	2.25
❑ 4, Feb 96, Tank Girl gives birth	2.25	0.45	1.35	2.25

TANK GIRL: THE ODYSSEY (mini-series)

	ORIG.	GOOD	FINE	N-MINT
❑ 1, Jun 95	2.25	0.45	1.35	2.25
❑ 2, Jul 95	2.25	0.45	1.35	2.25
❑ 3, Aug 95	2.25	0.45	1.35	2.25
❑ 4, Oct 95	2.25	0.45	1.35	2.25

TANK VIXENS
ANTARCTIC

	ORIG.	GOOD	FINE	N-MINT
❑ 1, Jan 94, adult, b&w	2.95	0.59	1.77	2.95
❑ 2, Mar 94, adult, b&w	2.95	0.59	1.77	2.95

TANTALIZING STORIES
KITCHEN SINK

	ORIG.	GOOD	FINE	N-MINT
❑ 6, b&w	2.50	0.50	1.50	2.50

TUNDRA

	ORIG.	GOOD	FINE	N-MINT
❑ 1, b&w	2.25	0.45	1.35	2.25
❑ 2, b&w	2.25	0.45	1.35	2.25
❑ 3, b&w	2.25	0.45	1.35	2.25

TAOLAND
SUMITEK

	ORIG.	GOOD	FINE	N-MINT
❑ 4, Feb 96, b&w;continues numbering from mini-series	3.25	0.65	1.95	3.25

TAOLAND (mini-series)

	ORIG.	GOOD	FINE	N-MINT
❑ 1, Nov 94, b&w;cardstock cover	1.50	0.30	0.90	1.50
❑ 2, Aug 95, b&w;cardstock cover	2.95	0.59	1.77	2.95
❑ 3, Sep 95, b&w;cardstock cover	3.25	0.65	1.95	3.25

TAP (mini-series)
PROMETHEAN

	ORIG.	GOOD	FINE	N-MINT
❑ 1, Sep 94	2.95	0.59	1.77	2.95
❑ 2, Jan 95	2.95	0.59	1.77	2.95
❑ 3, Jan 95, indicia is for issue #2	2.95	0.59	1.77	2.95

TAPESTRY
SUPERIOR JUNK

	ORIG.	GOOD	FINE	N-MINT
❑ 1, Apr 95, b&w;second printing	1.50	0.30	0.90	1.50
❑ 1, 94, b&w	1.50	0.30	0.90	1.50
❑ 2, Apr 94, b&w	1.95	0.39	1.17	1.95
❑ 3, Jun 94, b&w	1.95	0.39	1.17	1.95
❑ 4, Oct 94, b&w	2.25	0.45	1.35	2.25
❑ 5, 95, b&w	2.25	0.45	1.35	2.25

TARGET: AIRBOY
ECLIPSE

	ORIG.	GOOD	FINE	N-MINT
❑ 1, Mar 88, hamsters		0.39	1.17	1.95

TARGITT
ATLAS/ SEABOARD

	ORIG.	GOOD	FINE	N-MINT
❑ 1, Mar 75	0.25	0.20	0.60	1.00
❑ 2, Jun 75	0.25	0.20	0.60	1.00
❑ 3, Jul 75	0.25	0.20	0.60	1.00

TARZAN
DC

	ORIG.	GOOD	FINE	N-MINT
❑ 207, Apr 72, (continues Gold Key series)	0.25	1.00	3.00	5.00
❑ 208, May 72	0.25	0.60	1.80	3.00
❑ 209, Jun 72	0.25	0.60	1.80	3.00
❑ 210, Jul 72	0.20	0.60	1.80	3.00
❑ 211, Aug 72	0.20	0.40	1.20	2.00
❑ 212, Sep 72	0.20	0.40	1.20	2.00
❑ 213, Oct 72	0.20	0.40	1.20	2.00
❑ 214, Nov 72	0.20	0.40	1.20	2.00
❑ 215, Dec 72	0.20	0.40	1.20	2.00
❑ 216, Jan 73	0.20	0.40	1.20	2.00
❑ 217, Feb 73	0.20	0.40	1.20	2.00
❑ 218, Mar 73	0.20	0.40	1.20	2.00
❑ 219, May 73	0.20	0.40	1.20	2.00
❑ 220, Jun 73	0.20	0.40	1.20	2.00
❑ 221, Jul 73	0.20	0.40	1.20	2.00
❑ 222, Aug 73	0.20	0.40	1.20	2.00
❑ 223, Sep 73	0.20	0.40	1.20	2.00
❑ 224, Oct 73	0.20	0.40	1.20	2.00
❑ 225, Nov 73	0.20	0.40	1.20	2.00
❑ 226, Dec 73	0.20	0.40	1.20	2.00
❑ 227, Jan 74	0.20	0.40	1.20	2.00
❑ 228, Feb 74	0.20	0.40	1.20	2.00
❑ 229, Mar 74	0.20	0.40	1.20	2.00
❑ 230, May 74	0.60	0.40	1.20	2.00
❑ 231, Jul 74	0.60	0.40	1.20	2.00
❑ 232, Sep 74	0.60	0.40	1.20	2.00
❑ 233, Nov 74	0.60	0.40	1.20	2.00
❑ 234, Jan 75	0.60	0.40	1.20	2.00
❑ 235, Mar 75	0.60	0.40	1.20	2.00
❑ 236, Apr 75	0.25	0.40	1.20	2.00
❑ 237, May 75	0.25	0.40	1.20	2.00
❑ 238, Jun 75	0.25	0.40	1.20	2.00
❑ 239, Jul 75	0.50	0.40	1.20	2.00
❑ 240, Aug 75	0.25	0.40	1.20	2.00
❑ 241, Sep 75	0.25	0.40	1.20	2.00
❑ 242, Oct 75	0.25	0.40	1.20	2.00
❑ 243, Nov 75	0.25	0.40	1.20	2.00
❑ 244, Dec 75	0.25	0.40	1.20	2.00
❑ 245, Jan 76	0.25	0.40	1.20	2.00
❑ 246, Feb 76	0.25	0.40	1.20	2.00
❑ 247, Mar 76	0.30	0.40	1.20	2.00
❑ 248, Apr 76	0.30	0.40	1.20	2.00
❑ 249, May 76	0.30	0.40	1.20	2.00
❑ 250, Jun 76	0.30	0.40	1.20	2.00
❑ 251, Jul 76	0.30	0.40	1.20	2.00
❑ 252, Aug 76	0.30	0.40	1.20	2.00
❑ 253, Sep 76	0.30	0.40	1.20	2.00
❑ 254, Oct 76	0.30	0.40	1.20	2.00
❑ 255, Nov 76	0.30	0.40	1.20	2.00
❑ 256, Dec 76	0.30	0.40	1.20	2.00
❑ 257, Jan 77	0.30	0.40	1.20	2.00
❑ 258, Feb 77	0.30	0.40	1.20	2.00

TARZAN DIGEST

	ORIG.	GOOD	FINE	N-MINT
❑ 1, Aut 72	0.50	0.40	1.20	2.00

TARZAN FAMILY, THE (was Korak, Son of Tarzan)

	ORIG.	GOOD	FINE	N-MINT
❑ 60, Dec 75	0.50	0.30	0.90	1.50
❑ 61, Feb 76	0.50	0.30	0.90	1.50
❑ 62, Apr 76	0.50	0.30	0.90	1.50
❑ 63, Jun 76	0.50	0.30	0.90	1.50
❑ 64, Aug 76	0.50	0.30	0.90	1.50
❑ 65, Sep 76	0.50	0.30	0.90	1.50
❑ 66, Nov 76	0.50	0.30	0.90	1.50

	ORIG.	GOOD	FINE	N-MINT

TARZAN OF THE APES
MARVEL

	ORIG.	GOOD	FINE	N-MINT
❑ 1, Jul 84, O:Tarzan	0.60	0.20	0.60	1.00
❑ 2, Aug 84, O:Tarzan	0.60	0.20	0.60	1.00

TARZAN THE WARRIOR
MALIBU

	GOOD	FINE	N-MINT
❑ 1	0.50	1.50	2.50
❑ 2	0.50	1.50	2.50
❑ 3	0.50	1.50	2.50
❑ 4	0.50	1.50	2.50
❑ 5	0.50	1.50	2.50

TARZAN VS. PREDATOR AT THE EARTH'S CORE
(mini-series)
DARK HORSE

	ORIG.	GOOD	FINE	N-MINT
❑ 1, Jan 96	2.50	0.50	1.50	2.50
❑ 2, Feb 96	2.50	0.50	1.50	2.50
❑ 3, Mar 96	2.50	0.50	1.50	2.50

TARZAN, LORD OF THE JUNGLE
MARVEL

	ORIG.	GOOD	FINE	N-MINT
❑ 1, Jun 77	0.30	0.50	1.50	2.50
❑ 2, Jul 77	0.30	0.30	0.90	1.50
❑ 3, Aug 77	0.30	0.30	0.90	1.50
❑ 4, Sep 77	0.30	0.30	0.90	1.50
❑ 5, Oct 77	0.30	0.30	0.90	1.50
❑ 6, Nov 77	0.35	0.20	0.60	1.00
❑ 7, Dec 77	0.35	0.20	0.60	1.00
❑ 8, Jan 78	0.35	0.20	0.60	1.00
❑ 9, Feb 78	0.35	0.20	0.60	1.00
❑ 10, Mar 78	0.35	0.20	0.60	1.00
❑ 11, Apr 78	0.35	0.20	0.60	1.00
❑ 12, May 78	0.35	0.20	0.60	1.00
❑ 13, Jun 78	0.35	0.20	0.60	1.00
❑ 14, Jul 78	0.35	0.20	0.60	1.00
❑ 15, Aug 78	0.35	0.20	0.60	1.00
❑ 16, Sep 78	0.35	0.20	0.60	1.00
❑ 17, Oct 78	0.35	0.20	0.60	1.00
❑ 18, Nov 78	0.35	0.20	0.60	1.00
❑ 19, Dec 78	0.35	0.20	0.60	1.00
❑ 20, Jan 79	0.35	0.20	0.60	1.00
❑ 21, Feb 79	0.35	0.20	0.60	1.00
❑ 22, Mar 79	0.35	0.20	0.60	1.00
❑ 23, Apr 79	0.35	0.20	0.60	1.00
❑ 24, May 79	0.40	0.20	0.60	1.00
❑ 25, Jun 79	0.40	0.20	0.60	1.00
❑ 26, Jul 79	0.40	0.20	0.60	1.00
❑ 27, Aug 79	0.40	0.20	0.60	1.00
❑ 28, Sep 79	0.40	0.20	0.60	1.00
❑ 29, Oct 79	0.40	0.20	0.60	1.00

TARZAN, LORD OF THE JUNGLE ANNUAL

	ORIG.	GOOD	FINE	N-MINT
❑ 1, 77	0.50	0.40	1.20	2.00
❑ 2, 79	0.60	0.40	1.20	2.00
❑ 3, 79	0.60	0.40	1.20	2.00

TARZAN/JOHN CARTER: WARLORDS OF MARS
DARK HORSE

	ORIG.	GOOD	FINE	N-MINT
❑ 1, Jan 96	2.50	0.50	1.50	2.50
❑ 2, Apr 96, A:Cathoris,Tars Tarkas, Dejah Thoris				
	2.50	0.50	1.50	2.50

TARZAN: LOVE, LIES AND THE LOST CITY
MALIBU

	GOOD	FINE	N-MINT
❑ 1, WS, MW	0.79	2.37	3.95
❑ 2	0.50	1.50	2.50
❑ 3	0.50	1.50	2.50

TARZAN: THE BECKONING

	ORIG.	GOOD	FINE	N-MINT
❑ 1	2.50	0.50	1.50	2.50
❑ 2	2.50	0.50	1.50	2.50
❑ 3	2.50	0.50	1.50	2.50
❑ 4	2.50	0.50	1.50	2.50
❑ 5	2.50	0.50	1.50	2.50
❑ 6	2.50	0.50	1.50	2.50
❑ 7	2.50	0.50	1.50	2.50

TATTOO MAN
FANTAGRAPHICS

	GOOD	FINE	N-MINT
❑ 1, b&w	0.55	1.65	2.75

TAXX, THE
EXPRESS/PARODY

	ORIG.	GOOD	FINE	N-MINT
❑ 1, 96, b&w	2.75	0.55	1.65	2.75

TEAM 7
IMAGE

	ORIG.	GOOD	FINE	N-MINT
❑ 1		1.00	3.00	5.00
❑ 1, Variant cover		2.00	6.00	10.00
❑ 2, Nov 94	2.50	0.80	2.40	4.00
❑ 3, Dec 94	2.50	0.50	1.50	2.50
❑ 4, Feb 95	2.50	0.50	1.50	2.50

TEAM 7-OBJECTIVE: HELL

	ORIG.	GOOD	FINE	N-MINT
❑ 1, May 95, with card	2.50	0.50	1.50	2.50
❑ 2, Jun 95	2.50	0.50	1.50	2.50

TEAM 7: DEAD RECKONING

	ORIG.	GOOD	FINE	N-MINT
❑ 1, Jan 96	2.50	0.50	1.50	2.50
❑ 2, Feb 96	2.50	0.50	1.50	2.50
❑ 3, Mar 96	2.50	0.50	1.50	2.50
❑ 4, Apr 96	2.50	0.50	1.50	2.50

TEAM AMERICA
MARVEL

	ORIG.	GOOD	FINE	N-MINT
❑ 1, Jun 82, O:Team America				
	0.60	0.30	0.90	1.50
❑ 2, Jul 82, LMc	0.60	0.20	0.60	1.00
❑ 3, Aug 82, LMc	0.60	0.20	0.60	1.00
❑ 4, Sep 82, LMc	0.60	0.20	0.60	1.00
❑ 5, Oct 82	0.60	0.20	0.60	1.00
❑ 6, Nov 82	0.60	0.20	0.60	1.00
❑ 7, Dec 82	0.60	0.20	0.60	1.00
❑ 8, Jan 83	0.60	0.20	0.60	1.00
❑ 9, Feb 83	0.60	0.20	0.60	1.00
❑ 10, Mar 83	0.60	0.20	0.60	1.00
❑ 11, Apr 83, Ghost Rider	0.60	0.60	1.80	3.00
❑ 12, May 83, DP, Marauder unmasked				
	1.00	0.20	0.60	1.00

TEAM ANARCHY
DAGGER

	ORIG.	GOOD	FINE	N-MINT
❑ 1	2.75	0.55	1.65	2.75
❑ 4	2.50	0.50	1.50	2.50

TEAM NIPPON
AIRCEL

	GOOD	FINE	N-MINT
❑ 1, b&w	0.39	1.17	1.95
❑ 2, b&w	0.39	1.17	1.95
❑ 3, b&w	0.39	1.17	1.95
❑ 4, b&w	0.39	1.17	1.95
❑ 5, b&w	0.39	1.17	1.95
❑ 6, b&w	0.39	1.17	1.95
❑ 7, b&w	0.39	1.17	1.95

TEAM ONE: STORMWATCH (mini-series)

	ORIG.	GOOD	FINE	N-MINT
❑ 1, Jun 95, cover says "Jul";indicia says "Jun"				
	2.50	0.50	1.50	2.50
❑ 2, Aug 95	2.50	0.50	1.50	2.50

TEAM TITANS
DC

	ORIG.	GOOD	FINE	N-MINT
❑ 1, Sep 92, O:Killowat	1.75	0.35	1.05	1.75
❑ 1, Sep 92, O:Mirage	1.75	0.35	1.05	1.75
❑ 1, Sep 92, O:Nightrider	1.75	0.35	1.05	1.75
❑ 1, Sep 92, O:Redwing	1.75	0.35	1.05	1.75
❑ 1, Sep 92, O:Terra	1.75	0.35	1.05	1.75
❑ 2, Oct 92	1.75	0.35	1.05	1.75
❑ 3, Nov 92, Total Chaos	1.75	0.35	1.05	1.75
❑ 4, Dec 92	1.75	0.35	1.05	1.75
❑ 5, Feb 93	1.75	0.35	1.05	1.75
❑ 6, Mar 93	1.75	0.35	1.05	1.75
❑ 7, Apr 93	1.75	0.35	1.05	1.75
❑ 8, May 93	1.75	0.35	1.05	1.75
❑ 9, Jun 93	1.75	0.35	1.05	1.75

	ORIG.	GOOD	FINE	N-MINT
❏ 10, Jul 93	1.75	0.35	1.05	1.75
❏ 11, Aug 93	1.75	0.35	1.05	1.75
❏ 12, Sep 93	1.75	0.35	1.05	1.75
❏ 13, Oct 93	1.75	0.35	1.05	1.75
❏ 14, Nov 93	1.75	0.35	1.05	1.75
❏ 15, Dec 93	1.75	0.35	1.05	1.75
❏ 16, Jan 94	1.75	0.35	1.05	1.75
❏ 17, Feb 94	1.75	0.35	1.05	1.75
❏ 18, Mar 94	1.75	0.35	1.05	1.75
❏ 19, Apr 94	1.75	0.35	1.05	1.75
❏ 20, May 94	1.75	0.35	1.05	1.75
❏ 21, Jun 94	1.75	0.35	1.05	1.75
❏ 22, Jul 94	1.75	0.35	1.05	1.75
❏ 23, Aug 94	1.95	0.39	1.17	1.95
❏ 24, Sep 94	1.95	0.39	1.17	1.95

TEAM TITANS ANNUAL

	ORIG.	GOOD	FINE	N-MINT
❏ 1, Bloodlines	3.50	0.70	2.10	3.50
❏ 2, 94	3.50	0.70	2.10	3.50

TEAM YANKEE
FIRST

	GOOD	FINE	N-MINT
❏ 1	0.39	1.17	1.95
❏ 2	0.39	1.17	1.95
❏ 3	0.39	1.17	1.95
❏ 4	0.39	1.17	1.95
❏ 5	0.39	1.17	1.95
❏ 6	0.39	1.17	1.95

TEAM YOUNGBLOOD
IMAGE

	ORIG.	GOOD	FINE	N-MINT
❏ 1	1.95	0.39	1.17	1.95
❏ 2, Oct 93	1.95	0.39	1.17	1.95
❏ 3, Nov 93	1.95	0.39	1.17	1.95
❏ 4, Dec 93	1.95	0.39	1.17	1.95
❏ 5, Jan 94	1.95	0.39	1.17	1.95
❏ 6, Feb 94	1.95	0.39	1.17	1.95
❏ 7, Mar 94, Extreme Prejudice	1.95	0.39	1.17	1.95
❏ 8, Apr 94, Extreme Prejudice	1.95	0.39	1.17	1.95
❏ 9, May 94	1.95	0.70	2.10	3.50
❏ 10, Jun 94	2.50	0.50	1.50	2.50
❏ 11, Jul 94	2.50	0.50	1.50	2.50
❏ 12, Aug 94	2.50	0.50	1.50	2.50
❏ 14, Oct 94	2.50	0.50	1.50	2.50
❏ 15, Nov 94, New Blood part 2	2.50	0.50	1.50	2.50
❏ 16, Dec 94, polybagged with trading card	2.50	0.50	1.50	2.50
❏ 17, Jan 95, polybagged with trading card	2.50	0.50	1.50	2.50
❏ 18, May 95, "Extreme 3000"	2.50	0.50	1.50	2.50
❏ 19, Jun 95	2.50	0.50	1.50	2.50
❏ 20, Jul 95	2.50	0.50	1.50	2.50
❏ 21, Mar 96, A:Angela and Glory	2.50	0.50	1.50	2.50
❏ 22, Apr 96, "Shadowhunt"	2.50	0.50	1.50	2.50

TEARS
BONEYARD PRESS

	GOOD	FINE	N-MINT
❏ 1, b&w	0.59	1.77	2.95
❏ 2, b&w	0.59	1.77	2.95

TEASER AND THE BLACKSMITH
FANTAGRAPHICS

	GOOD	FINE	N-MINT
❏ 1, b&w, adult	0.70	2.10	3.50

TECHNO MANIACS
INDEPENDENT

	ORIG.	GOOD	FINE	N-MINT
❏ 1, 94	1.95	0.39	1.17	1.95

TEEN COMICS
PERSONALITY

	GOOD	FINE	N-MINT
❏ 1	0.50	1.50	2.50

	GOOD	FINE	N-MINT
❏ 2	0.50	1.50	2.50
❏ 3	0.50	1.50	2.50
❏ 4	0.50	1.50	2.50

TEEN TITANS
DC

	ORIG.	GOOD	FINE	N-MINT
❏ 1, Feb 66, NC, Peace Corps	0.12	32.00	96.00	160.00
❏ 2, Apr 66, NC	0.12	15.00	45.00	75.00
❏ 3, Jun 66, NC	0.12	6.00	18.00	30.00
❏ 4, Aug 66, NC	0.12	6.00	18.00	30.00
❏ 5, Oct 66, NC	0.12	6.00	18.00	30.00
❏ 6, Dec 66	0.12	3.00	9.00	15.00
❏ 7, Feb 67	0.12	3.00	9.00	15.00
❏ 8, Apr 67	0.12	3.00	9.00	15.00
❏ 9, Jun 67	0.12	3.00	9.00	15.00
❏ 10, Aug 67	0.12	3.00	9.00	15.00
❏ 11, Oct 67	0.12	3.00	9.00	15.00
❏ 12, Dec 67	0.12	2.00	6.00	10.00
❏ 13, Feb 68	0.12	2.00	6.00	10.00
❏ 14, Apr 68	0.12	2.00	6.00	10.00
❏ 15, Jun 68	0.12	2.00	6.00	10.00
❏ 16, Aug 68	0.12	2.00	6.00	10.00
❏ 17, Oct 68	0.12	2.00	6.00	10.00
❏ 18, Dec 68	0.12	2.00	6.00	10.00
❏ 19, Feb 69	0.12	2.00	6.00	10.00
❏ 20, Apr 69, NA/NC	0.12	3.00	9.00	15.00
❏ 21, Jun 69, NA/NC	0.12	3.00	9.00	15.00
❏ 22, Aug 69, NA/NC	0.15	3.00	9.00	15.00
❏ 23, Oct 69	0.15	2.00	6.00	10.00
❏ 24, Dec 69	0.15	2.00	6.00	10.00
❏ 25, Feb 70	0.15	2.00	6.00	10.00
❏ 26, Apr 70	0.15	2.00	6.00	10.00
❏ 27, Jun 70	0.15	2.00	6.00	10.00
❏ 28, Aug 70	0.15	2.00	6.00	10.00
❏ 29, Oct 70	0.15	2.00	6.00	10.00
❏ 30, Dec 70	0.15	2.00	6.00	10.00
❏ 31, Feb 71	0.15	2.00	6.00	10.00
❏ 32, Apr 71	0.15	1.60	4.80	8.00
❏ 33, Jun 71	0.15	1.60	4.80	8.00
❏ 34, Aug 71	0.15	1.60	4.80	8.00
❏ 35, Oct 71	0.25	1.60	4.80	8.00
❏ 36, Dec 71	0.25	1.60	4.80	8.00
❏ 37, Feb 72	0.25	1.60	4.80	8.00
❏ 38, Apr 72	0.25	1.60	4.80	8.00
❏ 39, Jun 72	0.25	1.60	4.80	8.00
❏ 40, Aug 72	0.20	1.60	4.80	8.00
❏ 41, Oct 72	0.20	1.60	4.80	8.00
❏ 42, Dec 72	0.20	1.60	4.80	8.00
❏ 43, Feb 73	0.20	1.60	4.80	8.00
❏ 44, Nov 76	0.30	1.60	4.80	8.00
❏ 45, Dec 76	0.30	1.60	4.80	8.00
❏ 46, Feb 77	0.30	1.60	4.80	8.00
❏ 47, Apr 77	0.30	1.60	4.80	8.00
❏ 48, Jun 77	0.35	1.60	4.80	8.00
❏ 49, Aug 77	0.35	1.60	4.80	8.00
❏ 50, Oct 77	0.35	1.60	4.80	8.00
❏ 51, Nov 77	0.35	1.60	4.80	8.00
❏ 52, Dec 77	0.35	1.60	4.80	8.00
❏ 53, Feb 78	0.35	1.60	4.80	8.00

TEEN TITANS ANNUAL (1980-1984 series)

	ORIG.	GOOD	FINE	N-MINT
❏ 3, 84, (was New Teen Titans Annual, The (1980-1984 series);"The Judas Contract" Part 4;D:Terra	1.25	0.25	0.75	1.25

TEEN TITANS SPOTLIGHT

	ORIG.	GOOD	FINE	N-MINT
❏ 1, Aug 86	0.75	0.20	0.60	1.00
❏ 2, Sep 86	0.75	0.20	0.60	1.00
❏ 3, Oct 86	0.75	0.20	0.60	1.00
❏ 4, Nov 86	0.75	0.20	0.60	1.00
❏ 5, Dec 86	0.75	0.20	0.60	1.00
❏ 6, Jan 87	0.75	0.20	0.60	1.00
❏ 7, Feb 87	0.75	0.20	0.60	1.00

	ORIG.	GOOD	FINE	N-MINT
❏ 8, Mar 87	0.75	0.20	0.60	1.00
❏ 9, Apr 87	0.75	0.20	0.60	1.00
❏ 10, May 87	0.75	0.20	0.60	1.00
❏ 11, Jun 87	0.75	0.20	0.60	1.00
❏ 12, Jul 87	0.75	0.20	0.60	1.00
❏ 13, Aug 87	0.75	0.20	0.60	1.00
❏ 14, Sep 87, Nightwing,Batman	0.75	0.20	0.60	1.00
❏ 15, Oct 87, Omega Men	0.75	0.20	0.60	1.00
❏ 16, Nov 87	0.75	0.20	0.60	1.00
❏ 17, Dec 87	0.75	0.20	0.60	1.00
❏ 18, Jan 88, Millennium	0.75	0.20	0.60	1.00
❏ 19, Feb 88, Millennium	0.75	0.20	0.60	1.00
❏ 20, Mar 88	0.75	0.20	0.60	1.00
❏ 21, Apr 88	0.75	0.20	0.60	1.00

TEENAGE MUTANT NINJA TURTLES
MIRAGE

	ORIG.	GOOD	FINE	N-MINT
❏ 1, (1st printing) Beware of counterfeits		50.00	150.00	250.00
❏ 1, (2nd printing)		14.00	42.00	70.00
❏ 1, (3rd printing)		5.00	15.00	25.00
❏ 1, (4th printing)		3.00	9.00	15.00
❏ 1, (5th printing)		1.00	3.00	5.00
❏ 2, (1st printing) Beware of counterfeits		25.00	75.00	125.00
❏ 2, (3rd printing)		0.80	2.40	4.00
❏ 2, (2nd printing)		1.60	4.80	8.00
❏ 3, (1st printing, misprints)		12.00	36.00	60.00
❏ 3, (1st printing, correct)		8.00	24.00	40.00
❏ 3, (2nd printing)		1.60	4.80	8.00
❏ 4, (1st printing)		6.00	18.00	30.00
❏ 4, (2nd printing)		1.00	3.00	5.00
❏ 5, (1st printing)		6.00	18.00	30.00
❏ 5, (2nd printing)		0.60	1.80	3.00
❏ 6, (1st printing)		3.20	9.60	16.00
❏ 6, (2nd printing)		0.60	1.80	3.00
❏ 7, (1st printing)		3.20	9.60	16.00
❏ 7, (2nd printing)		0.30	0.90	1.50
❏ 8, Cerebus		2.40	7.20	12.00
❏ 9		1.40	4.20	7.00
❏ 10		1.40	4.20	7.00
❏ 11		1.40	4.20	7.00
❏ 12		1.40	4.20	7.00
❏ 13		1.40	4.20	7.00
❏ 14		1.20	3.60	6.00
❏ 15		1.20	3.60	6.00
❏ 16		1.20	3.60	6.00
❏ 17		1.20	3.60	6.00
❏ 18, 1st printing, b&w		1.20	3.60	6.00
❏ 18, 2nd printing, color		0.45	1.35	2.25
❏ 19, Return to NY		0.80	2.40	4.00
❏ 20, Return to NY		0.80	2.40	4.00
❏ 21, Return to NY		0.80	2.40	4.00
❏ 22, Mark Martin		0.80	2.40	4.00
❏ 23, Mark Martin		0.80	2.40	4.00
❏ 24, Rick Veitch		0.60	1.80	3.00
❏ 25, Rick Veitch		0.60	1.80	3.00
❏ 26, Rick Veitch		0.60	1.80	3.00
❏ 27		0.35	1.05	1.75
❏ 28		0.35	1.05	1.75
❏ 29		0.35	1.05	1.75
❏ 30		0.35	1.05	1.75
❏ 31		0.35	1.05	1.75
❏ 32		0.35	1.05	1.75
❏ 32, color reprint		0.55	1.65	2.75
❏ 33, Corben, color		0.39	1.17	1.95
❏ 34		0.35	1.05	1.75
❏ 36		0.40	1.20	2.00
❏ 37		0.40	1.20	2.00
❏ 38		0.40	1.20	2.00
❏ 39		0.40	1.20	2.00

	ORIG.	GOOD	FINE	N-MINT
❏ 40		0.40	1.20	2.00
❏ 41		0.40	1.20	2.00
❏ 42		0.40	1.20	2.00
❏ 43		0.40	1.20	2.00
❏ 44		0.40	1.20	2.00
❏ 45		0.40	1.20	2.00
❏ 46		0.40	1.20	2.00
❏ 47		0.40	1.20	2.00
❏ 48		0.40	1.20	2.00
❏ 49		0.40	1.20	2.00
❏ 50, Eastman & Laird b&w		0.40	1.20	2.00
❏ 51, b&w		0.40	1.20	2.00
❏ 52, b&w	2.25	0.45	1.35	2.25
❏ 53, b&w	2.25	0.45	1.35	2.25
❏ 54, b&w	2.25	0.45	1.35	2.25
❏ 55, b&w	2.25	0.45	1.35	2.25
❏ 56, b&w	2.25	0.45	1.35	2.25
❏ 57, b&w	2.25	0.45	1.35	2.25
❏ 58, b&w	2.25	0.45	1.35	2.25
❏ 59, b&w	2.25	0.45	1.35	2.25
❏ 60, b&w	2.25	0.45	1.35	2.25
❏ 61, b&w	2.25	0.45	1.35	2.25

TEENAGE MUTANT NINJA TURTLES (Volume 2)

	ORIG.	GOOD	FINE	N-MINT
❏ 1, color	2.75	0.55	1.65	2.75
❏ 2, color	2.75	0.55	1.65	2.75
❏ 3, color	2.75	0.55	1.65	2.75
❏ 4, Apr 94	2.75	0.55	1.65	2.75
❏ 5, Jun 94	2.75	0.55	1.65	2.75
❏ 6, Aug 94	2.75	0.55	1.65	2.75
❏ 7, Oct 94	2.75	0.55	1.65	2.75
❏ 9, Aug 95	2.75	0.55	1.65	2.75
❏ 10, Aug 95	2.75	0.55	1.65	2.75

TEENAGE MUTANT NINJA TURTLES -- SAVAGE DRAGON CROSSOVER

	ORIG.	GOOD	FINE	N-MINT
❏ 1, Aug 95	2.75	0.55	1.65	2.75

TEENAGE MUTANT NINJA TURTLES ADVENTURES (1996 mini-series)
ARCHIE

	ORIG.	GOOD	FINE	N-MINT
❏ 2, Feb 96	1.50	0.30	0.90	1.50
❏ 3, Mar 96	1.50	0.30	0.90	1.50

TEENAGE MUTANT NINJA TURTLES ADVENTURES (mini-series)

	ORIG.	GOOD	FINE	N-MINT
❏ 1, Aug 88	1.00	1.20	3.60	6.00
❏ 2, Oct 88	1.00	0.60	1.80	3.00
❏ 3, Dec 88	1.00	0.60	1.80	3.00

TEENAGE MUTANT NINJA TURTLES ADVENTURES (ongoing series)

	ORIG.	GOOD	FINE	N-MINT
❏ 1, Mar 89	1.00	0.80	2.40	4.00
❏ 2	1.00	0.50	1.50	2.50
❏ 3	1.00	0.50	1.50	2.50
❏ 4	1.00	0.50	1.50	2.50
❏ 5	1.00	0.50	1.50	2.50
❏ 6	1.00	0.50	1.50	2.50
❏ 7	1.00	0.50	1.50	2.50
❏ 8	1.00	0.50	1.50	2.50
❏ 9	1.00	0.50	1.50	2.50
❏ 10	1.00	0.20	0.60	1.00
❏ 11	1.00	0.20	0.60	1.00
❏ 12	1.00	0.20	0.60	1.00
❏ 13	1.00	0.20	0.60	1.00
❏ 14	1.00	0.20	0.60	1.00
❏ 15	1.00	0.20	0.60	1.00
❏ 16	1.00	0.20	0.60	1.00
❏ 17	1.00	0.20	0.60	1.00
❏ 18	1.00	0.20	0.60	1.00
❏ 19, I:Mighty Mutanimals	1.25	0.25	0.75	1.25
❏ 20	1.25	0.25	0.75	1.25
❏ 21	1.25	0.25	0.75	1.25
❏ 22	1.25	0.25	0.75	1.25
❏ 23	1.25	0.25	0.75	1.25
❏ 24	1.25	0.25	0.75	1.25

	ORIG.	GOOD	FINE	N-MINT
❑ 25	1.25	0.25	0.75	1.25
❑ 26	1.25	0.25	0.75	1.25
❑ 27	1.25	0.25	0.75	1.25
❑ 28	1.25	0.25	0.75	1.25
❑ 29	1.25	0.25	0.75	1.25
❑ 30	1.25	0.25	0.75	1.25
❑ 31	1.25	0.25	0.75	1.25
❑ 32	1.25	0.25	0.75	1.25
❑ 33	1.25	0.25	0.75	1.25
❑ 34	1.25	0.25	0.75	1.25
❑ 35	1.25	0.25	0.75	1.25
❑ 36	1.25	0.25	0.75	1.25
❑ 37	1.25	0.25	0.75	1.25
❑ 38	1.25	0.25	0.75	1.25
❑ 39	1.25	0.25	0.75	1.25
❑ 40	1.25	0.25	0.75	1.25
❑ 41	1.25	0.25	0.75	1.25
❑ 42	1.25	0.25	0.75	1.25
❑ 43	1.25	0.25	0.75	1.25
❑ 44	1.25	0.25	0.75	1.25
❑ 45	1.25	0.25	0.75	1.25
❑ 46	1.25	0.25	0.75	1.25
❑ 47	1.25	0.25	0.75	1.25
❑ 48	1.25	0.25	0.75	1.25
❑ 49	1.25	0.25	0.75	1.25
❑ 50	1.25	0.25	0.75	1.25
❑ 51	1.25	0.25	0.75	1.25
❑ 52	1.25	0.25	0.75	1.25
❑ 53	1.25	0.25	0.75	1.25
❑ 54	1.25	0.25	0.75	1.25
❑ 55	1.25	0.25	0.75	1.25
❑ 56	1.25	0.25	0.75	1.25
❑ 57	1.25	0.25	0.75	1.25
❑ 58	1.25	0.25	0.75	1.25
❑ 59, Aug 94	1.50	0.30	0.90	1.50
❑ 60, Sep 94	1.50	0.30	0.90	1.50
❑ 61, Oct 94	1.50	0.30	0.90	1.50
❑ 62, Nov 94	1.75	0.35	1.05	1.75
❑ 63, Dec 94	1.50	0.30	0.90	1.50
❑ 64, Jan 95	1.50	0.30	0.90	1.50
❑ 65, Feb 95	1.50	0.30	0.90	1.50
❑ 66, Mar 95	1.50	0.30	0.90	1.50
❑ 67, Apr 95	1.50	0.30	0.90	1.50
❑ 68, May 95	1.50	0.30	0.90	1.50
❑ 69, Jun 95	1.50	0.30	0.90	1.50
❑ 70, Jul 95	1.50	0.30	0.90	1.50
❑ 71, Sep 95, "The Early Years" Part 1	1.50	0.30	0.90	1.50
❑ 72, Oct 95, "The Early Years" Part 2 of 2	1.50	0.30	0.90	1.50

TEENAGE MUTANT NINJA TURTLES ADVENTURES SPECIAL

	ORIG.	GOOD	FINE	N-MINT
❑ 1	2.50	0.50	1.50	2.50
❑ 2	2.50	0.50	1.50	2.50
❑ 3	2.50	0.50	1.50	2.50
❑ 4	2.50	0.50	1.50	2.50
❑ 5	2.50	0.50	1.50	2.50

TEENAGE MUTANT NINJA TURTLES AUTHORIZED MARTIAL ARTS TRAINING MANUAL
SOLSON

	GOOD	FINE	N-MINT
❑ 1	0.80	2.40	4.00
❑ 2	0.80	2.40	4.00
❑ 3	0.80	2.40	4.00
❑ 4	0.80	2.40	4.00

TEENAGE MUTANT NINJA TURTLES CLASSICS DIGEST
ARCHIE

	ORIG.	GOOD	FINE	N-MINT
❑ 7, Dec 94, digest	1.75	0.35	1.05	1.75

TEENAGE MUTANT NINJA TURTLES GIANT SIZE SPECIAL

	ORIG.	GOOD	FINE	N-MINT
❑ 10, Fal 94	2.00	0.40	1.20	2.00

TEENAGE MUTANT NINJA TURTLES III: THE MOVIE

	ORIG.	GOOD	FINE	N-MINT
❑ 0, newsstand	2.50	0.50	1.50	2.50
❑ 0, prestige edition	4.95	0.99	2.97	4.95

TEENAGE MUTANT NINJA TURTLES MEET ARCHIE

	ORIG.	GOOD	FINE	N-MINT
❑ 0, Spr 91, nn	2.50	0.50	1.50	2.50

TEENAGE MUTANT NINJA TURTLES MEET THE CONSERVATION CORPS

	ORIG.	GOOD	FINE	N-MINT
❑ 1, 92	2.50	0.50	1.50	2.50

TEENAGE MUTANT NINJA TURTLES MOVIE II

	ORIG.	GOOD	FINE	N-MINT
❑ 0, nn	2.50	0.50	1.50	2.50

TEENAGE MUTANT NINJA TURTLES MUTANT UNIVERSE SOURCEBOOK

	ORIG.	GOOD	FINE	N-MINT
❑ 1, 92	1.95	0.39	1.17	1.95
❑ 2	1.95	0.39	1.17	1.95
❑ 3	1.95	0.39	1.17	1.95

TEENAGE MUTANT NINJA TURTLES PRESENT MIGHTY MUTANIMALS: INVASION FROM SPACE

	GOOD	FINE	N-MINT
❑ 0, nn reprints series	0.59	1.77	2.95

TEENAGE MUTANT NINJA TURTLES PRESENTS APRIL O'NEIL

	ORIG.	GOOD	FINE	N-MINT
❑ 1, 93, (May East Saga)	1.25	0.25	0.75	1.25
❑ 2, 93, (May East Saga)	1.25	0.25	0.75	1.25
❑ 3, 93, (May East Saga)	1.25	0.25	0.75	1.25

TEENAGE MUTANT NINJA TURTLES PRESENTS DONATELLO AND LEATHERHEAD

	ORIG.	GOOD	FINE	N-MINT
❑ 1, Jul 93	1.25	0.25	0.75	1.25
❑ 2, 93	1.25	0.25	0.75	1.25
❑ 3, Sep 93	1.25	0.25	0.75	1.25

TEENAGE MUTANT NINJA TURTLES PRESENTS MERDUDE AND MICHAELANGELO

	ORIG.	GOOD	FINE	N-MINT
❑ 1	1.25	0.25	0.75	1.25
❑ 2	1.25	0.25	0.75	1.25
❑ 3	1.25	0.25	0.75	1.25

TEENAGE MUTANT NINJA TURTLES SPECIAL

	ORIG.	GOOD	FINE	N-MINT
❑ 11, Win 94	2.00	0.40	1.20	2.00

TEENAGE MUTANT NINJA TURTLES SPECIAL: "TIME'S PIPELINE"
MIRAGE

	GOOD	FINE	N-MINT
❑ 0, color	0.59	1.77	2.95

TEENAGE MUTANT NINJA TURTLES SPECIAL: MALTESE TURTLE

	GOOD	FINE	N-MINT
❑ 0	0.59	1.77	2.95

TEENAGE MUTANT NINJA TURTLES SPECIAL: THE HAUNTED PIZZA

	GOOD	FINE	N-MINT
❑ 0, nn, b&w	0.45	1.35	2.25

TEENAGE MUTANT NINJA TURTLES/FLAMING CARROT CROSSOVER

	ORIG.	GOOD	FINE	N-MINT
❑ 1	2.75	0.55	1.65	2.75
❑ 2	2.75	0.55	1.65	2.75
❑ 3, Jan 94	2.75	0.55	1.65	2.75
❑ 4, Feb 94	2.75	0.55	1.65	2.75

TEENAGE MUTANT NINJA TURTLES: THE MOVIE
ARCHIE

	GOOD	FINE	N-MINT
❑ 1, newsstand	0.50	1.50	2.50
❑ 1, format	0.99	2.97	4.95

MIRAGE

	GOOD	FINE	N-MINT
❑ 0, nn b&w	1.19	3.57	5.95

TEK KNIGHTS
ARTLINE

	GOOD	FINE	N-MINT
❑ 1, b&w	0.59	1.77	2.95

TEKQ
GAUNTLET

	ORIG.	GOOD	FINE	N-MINT
❑ 1, 92, b&w	2.95	0.59	1.77	2.95
❑ 2, 92, b&w	2.95	0.59	1.77	2.95
❑ 3, 92, b&w	2.95	0.59	1.77	2.95
❑ 4, 92, b&w	2.95	0.59	1.77	2.95

	ORIG.	GOOD	FINE	N-MINT

TEKWORLD
EPIC

	ORIG.	GOOD	FINE	N-MINT
☐ 1	1.75	0.60	1.80	3.00
☐ 2	1.75	0.50	1.50	2.50
☐ 3	1.75	0.40	1.20	2.00
☐ 4	1.75	0.40	1.20	2.00
☐ 5	1.75	0.40	1.20	2.00
☐ 6	1.75	0.35	1.05	1.75
☐ 7	1.75	0.35	1.05	1.75
☐ 8	1.75	0.35	1.05	1.75
☐ 9	1.75	0.35	1.05	1.75
☐ 10	1.75	0.35	1.05	1.75
☐ 11	1.75	0.35	1.05	1.75
☐ 12	1.75	0.35	1.05	1.75
☐ 13	1.75	0.35	1.05	1.75
☐ 14	1.75	0.35	1.05	1.75
☐ 15	1.75	0.35	1.05	1.75
☐ 16	1.75	0.35	1.05	1.75
☐ 17	1.75	0.35	1.05	1.75
☐ 18	1.75	0.35	1.05	1.75
☐ 19	1.75	0.35	1.05	1.75
☐ 20	1.75	0.35	1.05	1.75
☐ 21, May 94	1.75	0.35	1.05	1.75
☐ 22, Jun 94	1.75	0.35	1.05	1.75
☐ 23, Jul 94	1.75	0.35	1.05	1.75
☐ 24, Aug 94	1.75	0.35	1.05	1.75

TELL TALE HEART AND OTHER STORIES
FANTAGRAPHICS

	ORIG.	GOOD	FINE	N-MINT
☐ 1, b&w		0.50	1.50	2.50

TELLTALE HEART, THE
MOJO PRESS

	ORIG.	GOOD	FINE	N-MINT
☐ 0, 95, nn;prestige format;adapts Poe stories;b&w	4.95	0.99	2.97	4.95

TELLURIA
ZUB

	ORIG.	GOOD	FINE	N-MINT
☐ 1, 94	2.50	0.50	1.50	2.50
☐ 2, 95	2.50	0.50	1.50	2.50

TEMPLATE
HEAD PRESS

	ORIG.	GOOD	FINE	N-MINT
☐ 1, Dec 95, b&w	2.50	0.50	1.50	2.50
☐ 2, Feb 96, b&w	2.50	0.50	1.50	2.50

TEMPLE SNARE
MU PRESS

	ORIG.	GOOD	FINE	N-MINT
☐ 0, nn b&w		0.45	1.35	2.25

TEMPUS FUGITIVE
DC

	ORIG.	GOOD	FINE	N-MINT
☐ 1, 90, Ken Steacy	4.95	0.99	2.97	4.95
☐ 2, 90, Ken Steacy	4.95	0.99	2.97	4.95
☐ 3, 91, Ken Steacy	5.95	0.99	2.97	4.95
☐ 4, 91, Ken Steacy	5.95	0.99	2.97	4.95

TEN YEARS OF LOVE AND ROCKETS
FANTAGRAPHICS

	ORIG.	GOOD	FINE	N-MINT
☐ 0, nn, b&w		0.30	0.90	1.50

TERMINAL CITY
DC/VERTIGO

	ORIG.	GOOD	FINE	N-MINT
☐ 1, Jul 96	2.50	0.50	1.50	2.50

TERMINAL POINT
DARK HORSE

	ORIG.	GOOD	FINE	N-MINT
☐ 2, b&w	2.50	0.50	1.50	2.50
☐ 3, b&w	2.50	0.50	1.50	2.50

TERMINATOR

	ORIG.	GOOD	FINE	N-MINT
☐ 1		1.20	3.60	6.00
☐ 2		0.80	2.40	4.00
☐ 3		0.80	2.40	4.00
☐ 4, Nov 90	2.50	0.50	1.50	2.50

TERMINATOR (mini-series)
NOW

	ORIG.	GOOD	FINE	N-MINT
☐ 1, Aug 90	1.75	0.35	1.05	1.75
☐ 2, Sep 90	1.75	0.35	1.05	1.75

TERMINATOR 2: JUDGMENT DAY
MARVEL

	ORIG.	GOOD	FINE	N-MINT
☐ 0, Sep 91, nn b&w reprint	2.25	0.45	1.35	2.25
☐ 1, Sep 91, movie	1.00	0.20	0.60	1.00
☐ 2, Oct 91, movie	1.00	0.20	0.60	1.00
☐ 3, Oct 91, movie	1.00	0.20	0.60	1.00

TERMINATOR ONE SHOT
DARK HORSE

	ORIG.	GOOD	FINE	N-MINT
☐ 0, nn MW, pop-up	1.19	3.57	5.95	

TERMINATOR, THE
NOW

	ORIG.	GOOD	FINE	N-MINT
☐ 1, Sep 88, movie tie-in	1.75	1.60	4.80	8.00
☐ 2, Oct 88	1.75	1.00	3.00	5.00
☐ 3, Nov 88	1.75	0.60	1.80	3.00
☐ 4, Jan 89	1.75	0.60	1.80	3.00
☐ 5, Feb 89	1.75	0.60	1.80	3.00
☐ 6, Mar 89	1.75	0.60	1.80	3.00
☐ 7, Apr 89	1.75	0.60	1.80	3.00
☐ 8, May 89, Comics Code	1.75	0.35	1.05	1.75
☐ 9, Jun 89, Comics Code	1.75	0.35	1.05	1.75
☐ 10, Jul 89, Comics Code	1.75	0.35	1.05	1.75
☐ 11, Aug 89, Comics Code	1.75	0.35	1.05	1.75
☐ 12, Sep 89, Comics Code	1.75	0.35	1.05	1.75
☐ 13, Oct 89, Comics Code	1.75	0.35	1.05	1.75
☐ 14, Nov 89, Comics Code	1.75	0.35	1.05	1.75
☐ 15, Dec 89, Comics Code	1.75	0.35	1.05	1.75
☐ 16, Jan 90, Comics Code	1.75	0.35	1.05	1.75
☐ 17, Feb 90, Comics Code	1.75	0.35	1.05	1.75

TERMINATOR: ENDGAME, THE
DARK HORSE

	ORIG.	GOOD	FINE	N-MINT
☐ 1		0.50	1.50	2.50
☐ 2		0.50	1.50	2.50
☐ 3		0.50	1.50	2.50

TERMINATOR: HUNTERS AND KILLERS

	ORIG.	GOOD	FINE	N-MINT
☐ 1		0.50	1.50	2.50
☐ 2		0.50	1.50	2.50
☐ 3		0.50	1.50	2.50

TERMINATOR: SECONDARY OBJECTIVES

	ORIG.	GOOD	FINE	N-MINT
☐ 1		0.50	1.50	2.50
☐ 2		0.50	1.50	2.50
☐ 3		0.50	1.50	2.50
☐ 4		0.50	1.50	2.50

TERMINATOR: THE BURNING EARTH
NOW

	ORIG.	GOOD	FINE	N-MINT
☐ 1, Mar 90		0.80	2.40	4.00
☐ 2, Apr 90		1.00	3.00	5.00
☐ 3, May 90	1.75	0.80	2.40	4.00
☐ 4, Jun 90	1.75	0.80	2.40	4.00
☐ 5, Jul 90	1.75	0.80	2.40	4.00

TERMINATOR: THE ENEMY WITHIN
DARK HORSE

	ORIG.	GOOD	FINE	N-MINT
☐ 1		0.50	1.50	2.50
☐ 2		0.50	1.50	2.50
☐ 3		0.50	1.50	2.50
☐ 4		0.50	1.50	2.50

TERRAFORMERS
WONDER COLOR

	ORIG.	GOOD	FINE	N-MINT
☐ 1		0.39	1.17	1.95
☐ 2		0.39	1.17	1.95

TERRANAUTS
FANTASY GENERAL

	ORIG.	GOOD	FINE	N-MINT
☐ 1, 86		0.35	1.05	1.75

TERRARISTS
EPIC

	ORIG.	GOOD	FINE	N-MINT
☐ 1	2.50	0.50	1.50	2.50
☐ 2	2.50	0.50	1.50	2.50

	ORIG.	GOOD	FINE	N-MINT
❏ 3	2.50	0.50	1.50	2.50
❏ 4	2.50	0.50	1.50	2.50

TERROR ON THE PLANET OF THE APES
ADVENTURE

		GOOD	FINE	N-MINT
❏ 1, b&w		0.50	1.50	2.50
❏ 2, b&w		0.50	1.50	2.50
❏ 3, b&w		0.50	1.50	2.50
❏ 4, b&w		0.50	1.50	2.50

TERROR TALES
ETERNITY

		GOOD	FINE	N-MINT
❏ 1, b&w		0.50	1.50	2.50

TERROR, INC.
MARVEL

	ORIG.	GOOD	FINE	N-MINT
❏ 1	1.75	0.35	1.05	1.75
❏ 2	1.75	0.35	1.05	1.75
❏ 3	1.75	0.35	1.05	1.75
❏ 4	1.75	0.35	1.05	1.75
❏ 5	1.75	0.35	1.05	1.75
❏ 6	1.75	0.35	1.05	1.75
❏ 7	1.75	0.35	1.05	1.75
❏ 8	1.75	0.35	1.05	1.75
❏ 9, Mar 93	1.75	0.35	1.05	1.75
❏ 10, Wolverine	1.75	0.35	1.05	1.75
❏ 10, Apr 93	1.75	0.35	1.05	1.75
❏ 11	1.75	0.35	1.05	1.75
❏ 12	1.75	0.35	1.05	1.75
❏ 13	1.75	0.35	1.05	1.75

TERROR, THE
LEADSLINGER

		GOOD	FINE	N-MINT
❏ 1, b&w		0.50	1.50	2.50

TERRORESS
HELPLESS ANGER

		GOOD	FINE	N-MINT
❏ 1, b&w, adult		0.50	1.50	2.50

TERRY BEATTY'S PHONY PAGES
RENEGADE

	ORIG.	GOOD	FINE	N-MINT
❏ 1, Apr 86	2.00	0.40	1.20	2.00
❏ 2, May 86	2.00	0.40	1.20	2.00

TEST DIRT
FANTAGRAPHICS

		GOOD	FINE	N-MINT
❏ 1, b&w		0.50	1.50	2.50

TEX BENSON
3-D ZONE

		GOOD	FINE	N-MINT
❏ 1, b&w (not 3-D)		0.50	1.50	2.50
❏ 2, b&w (not 3-D)		0.50	1.50	2.50

METRO

		GOOD	FINE	N-MINT
❏ 1		0.40	1.20	2.00
❏ 2		0.40	1.20	2.00
❏ 3		0.40	1.20	2.00
❏ 4		0.40	1.20	2.00

TEYKWA
GEMSTONE

		GOOD	FINE	N-MINT
❏ 1, b&w		0.35	1.05	1.75

THANOS QUEST, THE
MARVEL

	ORIG.	GOOD	FINE	N-MINT
❏ 1, Sep 90	4.95	3.00	9.00	15.00
❏ 2, Oct 90	4.95	2.00	6.00	10.00

THB
HORSE PRESS

	ORIG.	GOOD	FINE	N-MINT
❏ 1, 94, b&w	2.95	6.00	18.00	30.00
❏ 2, 94, b&w	2.95	4.00	12.00	20.00
❏ 3, Jan 95, b&w	2.95	1.60	4.80	8.00
❏ 4, Feb 95, b&w	2.95	1.20	3.60	6.00
❏ 5, Mar 95, b&w	2.95	1.00	3.00	5.00

THB (Vol. 2)

	ORIG.	GOOD	FINE	N-MINT
❏ 1, 95, reprints *THB* #1 with revised and additional material;b&w	5.50	1.10	3.30	5.50

THEOWN
PYRAMID

		GOOD	FINE	N-MINT
❏ 1, b&w		0.34	1.02	1.70

	ORIG.	GOOD	FINE	N-MINT
❏ 2, b&w		0.34	1.02	1.70
❏ 3, b&w		0.34	1.02	1.70

THESPIAN
DARK MOON

	ORIG.	GOOD	FINE	N-MINT
❏ 1, Apr 95	2.50	0.50	1.50	2.50

THEY WERE 11
VIZ

	ORIG.	GOOD	FINE	N-MINT
❏ 1, 95, b&w	2.75	0.55	1.65	2.75
❏ 3, 95, b&w	2.75	0.55	1.65	2.75
❏ 4, 95, b&w	2.75	0.55	1.65	2.75

THIEF OF SHERWOOD
A-PLUS

		GOOD	FINE	N-MINT
❏ 1, b&w reprints		0.45	1.35	2.25

THIEVES & KINGS
I BOX PUBLISHING

	ORIG.	GOOD	FINE	N-MINT
❏ 1, Sep 94, b&w	2.35	1.20	3.60	6.00
❏ 2, Nov 94, b&w	2.35	0.80	2.40	4.00
❏ 3, Jan 95, b&w	2.35	0.60	1.80	3.00
❏ 4, Mar 95, b&w	2.35	0.60	1.80	3.00
❏ 5, May 95, b&w	2.35	0.60	1.80	3.00
❏ 6, Jul 95, b&w	2.35	0.47	1.41	2.35
❏ 7, Sep 95, b&w	2.35	0.47	1.41	2.35

THING FROM ANOTHER WORLD, THE
DARK HORSE

		GOOD	FINE	N-MINT
❏ 1		0.59	1.77	2.95
❏ 2		0.59	1.77	2.95

THING FROM ANOTHER WORLD: CLIMATE OF FEAR, THE

		GOOD	FINE	N-MINT
❏ 1		0.50	1.50	2.50
❏ 2		0.50	1.50	2.50
❏ 3		0.50	1.50	2.50
❏ 4		0.50	1.50	2.50

THING FROM ANOTHER WORLD: ETERNAL VOWS

	ORIG.	GOOD	FINE	N-MINT
❏ 1	2.50	0.50	1.50	2.50
❏ 2	2.50	0.50	1.50	2.50
❏ 3	2.50	0.50	1.50	2.50
❏ 4, Mar 94	2.50	0.50	1.50	2.50

THING, THE
MARVEL

	ORIG.	GOOD	FINE	N-MINT
❏ 1, Jul 83, JBy, Origin	0.60	0.50	1.50	2.50
❏ 2, Aug 83, JBy	0.60	0.30	0.90	1.50
❏ 3, Sep 83	0.60	0.20	0.60	1.00
❏ 4, Oct 83	0.60	0.20	0.60	1.00
❏ 5, Nov 83	0.60	0.20	0.60	1.00
❏ 6, Dec 83	0.60	0.20	0.60	1.00
❏ 7, Jan 84	0.60	0.20	0.60	1.00
❏ 8, Feb 84	0.60	0.20	0.60	1.00
❏ 9, Mar 84	0.60	0.20	0.60	1.00
❏ 10, Apr 84	0.60	0.20	0.60	1.00
❏ 11, May 84	0.60	0.20	0.60	1.00
❏ 12, Jun 84	0.60	0.20	0.60	1.00
❏ 13, Jul 84	0.60	0.20	0.60	1.00
❏ 14, Aug 84	0.60	0.20	0.60	1.00
❏ 15, Sep 84	0.60	0.20	0.60	1.00
❏ 16, Oct 84	0.60	0.20	0.60	1.00
❏ 17, Nov 84	0.60	0.20	0.60	1.00
❏ 18, Dec 84	0.60	0.20	0.60	1.00
❏ 19, Jan 85	0.60	0.20	0.60	1.00
❏ 20, Feb 85	0.60	0.20	0.60	1.00
❏ 21, Mar 85	0.60	0.20	0.60	1.00
❏ 22, Apr 85	0.60	0.20	0.60	1.00
❏ 23, May 85	0.65	0.20	0.60	1.00
❏ 24, Jun 85	0.65	0.20	0.60	1.00
❏ 25, Jul 85	0.65	0.20	0.60	1.00
❏ 26, Aug 85	0.65	0.20	0.60	1.00
❏ 27, Sep 85	0.65	0.20	0.60	1.00
❏ 28, Oct 85	0.65	0.20	0.60	1.00
❏ 29, Nov 85	0.65	0.20	0.60	1.00
❏ 30, Dec 85, Secret Wars II	0.65	0.20	0.60	1.00

	ORIG.	GOOD	FINE	N-MINT
31, Jan 86	0.75	0.20	0.60	1.00
32, Feb 86	0.75	0.20	0.60	1.00
33, Mar 86	0.75	0.20	0.60	1.00
34, Apr 86	0.75	0.20	0.60	1.00
35, May 86	0.75	0.20	0.60	1.00
36, Jun 86	0.75	0.20	0.60	1.00

THIRD WORLD WAR
FLEETWAY/QUALITY

		GOOD	FINE	N-MINT
1		0.50	1.50	2.50
2		0.50	1.50	2.50
3		0.50	1.50	2.50
4		0.50	1.50	2.50
5		0.50	1.50	2.50
6		0.50	1.50	2.50

THIRTEEN O'CLOCK
DARK HORSE

	ORIG.	GOOD	FINE	N-MINT
0, nn, b&w	2.95	0.59	1.77	2.95

THIRTEEN SOMETHING!
GLOBAL

	ORIG.	GOOD	FINE	N-MINT
1	0.39		1.17	1.95

THIS IS HEAT
AEON

	ORIG.	GOOD	FINE	N-MINT
0, nn b&w	2.50	0.50	1.50	2.50

THIS IS SICK!
SILVER SKULL

	ORIG.	GOOD	FINE	N-MINT
1, foil cover, Zen, b&w	2.95	0.59	1.77	2.95
2	2.95	0.59	1.77	2.95

THOR (formerly Journey into Mystery)
MARVEL

	ORIG.	GOOD	FINE	N-MINT
126, JK, Hercules	0.12	16.00	48.00	80.00
127, JK	0.12	6.00	18.00	30.00
128, JK	0.12	6.00	18.00	30.00
129, JK	0.12	6.00	18.00	30.00
130, JK	0.12	6.00	18.00	30.00
131, JK	0.12	6.00	18.00	30.00
132, JK	0.12	6.00	18.00	30.00
133, JK	0.12	6.00	18.00	30.00
134, JK, I:High Evolutionary	0.12	9.60	28.80	48.00
135, JK	0.12	6.00	18.00	30.00
136, JK	0.12	6.00	18.00	30.00
137, JK	0.12	6.00	18.00	30.00
138, JK	0.12	6.00	18.00	30.00
139, JK	0.12	6.00	18.00	30.00
140, JK	0.12	6.00	18.00	30.00
141, JK	0.12	4.40	13.20	22.00
142, JK	0.12	4.40	13.20	22.00
143, JK	0.12	4.40	13.20	22.00
144, JK	0.12	4.40	13.20	22.00
145, JK	0.12	4.40	13.20	22.00
146, JK, O:Inhumans	0.12	4.40	13.20	22.00
147, JK	0.12	4.40	13.20	22.00
148, JK	0.12	4.40	13.20	22.00
149, JK	0.12	4.40	13.20	22.00
150, JK	0.12	4.40	13.20	22.00
151, JK	0.12	4.40	13.20	22.00
152, JK	0.12	4.40	13.20	22.00
153, JK	0.12	4.40	13.20	22.00
154, JK	0.12	4.40	13.20	22.00
155, JK	0.12	4.40	13.20	22.00
156, JK	0.12	4.40	13.20	22.00
157, JK	0.12	4.40	13.20	22.00
158, Nov 68, JK, O:Don Blake	0.12	10.00	30.00	50.00
159, JK	0.12	4.40	13.20	22.00
160, JK	0.12	4.40	13.20	22.00
161, JK	0.12	4.40	13.20	22.00
162, JK, O:Galactus	0.12	4.40	13.20	22.00
163, JK	0.12	4.40	13.20	22.00
164, JK	0.12	4.40	13.20	22.00

	ORIG.	GOOD	FINE	N-MINT
165, JK, Him/Warlock	0.15	8.00	24.00	40.00
166, JK, Him/Warlock	0.15	8.00	24.00	40.00
167, JK, Sif	0.15	4.40	13.20	22.00
168, JK, O:Galactus	0.15	8.00	24.00	40.00
169, JK, O:Galactus	0.15	8.00	24.00	40.00
170	0.15	3.60	10.80	18.00
171	0.15	3.60	10.80	18.00
172	0.15	3.60	10.80	18.00
173	0.15	3.60	10.80	18.00
174	0.15	3.60	10.80	18.00
175	0.15	3.60	10.80	18.00
176	0.15	3.60	10.80	18.00
177	0.15	3.60	10.80	18.00
178	0.15	3.60	10.80	18.00
179	0.15	3.60	10.80	18.00
180, NA	0.15	2.00	6.00	10.00
181, NA	0.15	2.00	6.00	10.00
182	0.15	1.00	3.00	5.00
183	0.15	1.00	3.00	5.00
184	0.15	1.00	3.00	5.00
185	0.15	1.00	3.00	5.00
186	0.15	1.00	3.00	5.00
187	0.15	1.00	3.00	5.00
188	0.15	1.00	3.00	5.00
189	0.15	1.00	3.00	5.00
190	0.15	1.00	3.00	5.00
191	0.15	1.00	3.00	5.00
192	0.15	1.00	3.00	5.00
193, JB/SB, Silver Surfer	0.25	2.40	7.20	12.00
194	0.20	1.00	3.00	5.00
195	0.20	1.00	3.00	5.00
196	0.20	1.00	3.00	5.00
197	0.20	1.00	3.00	5.00
198	0.20	1.00	3.00	5.00
199	0.20	1.00	3.00	5.00
200, JB, Ragnarok	0.20	1.20	3.60	6.00
201, JB	0.20	0.50	1.50	2.50
202, JB	0.20	0.50	1.50	2.50
203, JB	0.20	0.50	1.50	2.50
204, JB	0.20	0.50	1.50	2.50
205, JB	0.20	0.50	1.50	2.50
206, JB	0.20	0.50	1.50	2.50
207, JB	0.20	0.50	1.50	2.50
208, JB	0.20	0.50	1.50	2.50
209, JB	0.20	0.50	1.50	2.50
210, JB	0.20	0.50	1.50	2.50
211, JB	0.20	0.50	1.50	2.50
212, JB	0.20	0.50	1.50	2.50
213, JB	0.20	0.50	1.50	2.50
214	0.20	0.25	0.75	1.25
215	0.20	0.25	0.75	1.25
216	0.20	0.25	0.75	1.25
217	0.20	0.25	0.75	1.25
218	0.20	0.25	0.75	1.25
219	0.20	0.25	0.75	1.25
220	0.20	0.25	0.75	1.25
221	0.20	0.30	0.90	1.50
222	0.20	0.30	0.90	1.50
223	0.25	0.30	0.90	1.50
224	0.25	0.30	0.90	1.50
225	0.25	0.30	0.90	1.50
226	0.25	0.30	0.90	1.50
227	0.25	0.30	0.90	1.50
228	0.25	0.30	0.90	1.50
229	0.25	0.30	0.90	1.50
230	0.25	0.30	0.90	1.50
231	0.25	0.30	0.90	1.50
232	0.25	0.30	0.90	1.50
233	0.25	0.30	0.90	1.50
234	0.25	0.30	0.90	1.50
235	0.25	0.30	0.90	1.50

	ORIG.	GOOD	FINE	N-MINT		ORIG.	GOOD	FINE	N-MINT
☐ 236	0.25	0.30	0.90	1.50	☐ 308, Jun 81	0.50	0.20	0.60	1.00
☐ 237	0.25	0.30	0.90	1.50	☐ 309, Jul 81	0.50	0.20	0.60	1.00
☐ 238, JB,JSt	0.25	0.30	0.90	1.50	☐ 310, Aug 81	0.50	0.20	0.60	1.00
☐ 239	0.25	0.30	0.90	1.50	☐ 311, Sep 81	0.50	0.20	0.60	1.00
☐ 240	0.25	0.30	0.90	1.50	☐ 312, Oct 81	0.50	0.20	0.60	1.00
☐ 241, JB	0.25	0.30	0.90	1.50	☐ 313, Nov 81	0.50	0.20	0.60	1.00
☐ 242, JB	0.25	0.30	0.90	1.50	☐ 314, Dec 81	0.50	0.20	0.60	1.00
☐ 243, JB	0.25	0.30	0.90	1.50	☐ 315, Jan 82	0.60	0.20	0.60	1.00
☐ 244, JB	0.25	0.30	0.90	1.50	☐ 316, Feb 82	0.60	0.20	0.60	1.00
☐ 245, JB	0.25	0.30	0.90	1.50	☐ 317, Mar 82	0.60	0.20	0.60	1.00
☐ 246, JB	0.25	0.30	0.90	1.50	☐ 318, Apr 82	0.60	0.20	0.60	1.00
☐ 247, JB	0.25	0.30	0.90	1.50	☐ 319, May 82	0.60	0.20	0.60	1.00
☐ 248, JB	0.25	0.30	0.90	1.50	☐ 320, Jun 82	0.60	0.20	0.60	1.00
☐ 249, JB	0.25	0.30	0.90	1.50	☐ 321, Jul 82	0.60	0.20	0.60	1.00
☐ 250, JB	0.25	0.30	0.90	1.50	☐ 322, Aug 82	0.60	0.20	0.60	1.00
☐ 251, Sep 76	0.30	0.30	0.90	1.50	☐ 323, Sep 82	0.60	0.20	0.60	1.00
☐ 252, Oct 76	0.30	0.30	0.90	1.50	☐ 324, Oct 82	0.60	0.20	0.60	1.00
☐ 253, Nov 76	0.30	0.30	0.90	1.50	☐ 325, Nov 82	0.60	0.20	0.60	1.00
☐ 254, Dec 76	0.30	0.30	0.90	1.50	☐ 326, Dec 82	0.60	0.20	0.60	1.00
☐ 255, Jan 77	0.30	0.30	0.90	1.50	☐ 327, Jan 83	0.60	0.20	0.60	1.00
☐ 256, Feb 77	0.30	0.30	0.90	1.50	☐ 328, Feb 83	0.60	0.20	0.60	1.00
☐ 257, Mar 77	0.30	0.30	0.90	1.50	☐ 329, Mar 83	0.60	0.20	0.60	1.00
☐ 258, Apr 77	0.30	0.30	0.90	1.50	☐ 330, Apr 83	0.60	0.20	0.60	1.00
☐ 259, May 77	0.30	0.30	0.90	1.50	☐ 331, May 83	0.60	0.20	0.60	1.00
☐ 260, Jun 77, WS	0.30	0.80	2.40	4.00	☐ 332, Jun 83	0.60	0.20	0.60	1.00
☐ 261, Jul 77, WS	0.30	0.30	0.90	1.50	☐ 333, Jul 83	0.60	0.20	0.60	1.00
☐ 262, Aug 77, WS	0.30	0.30	0.90	1.50	☐ 334, Aug 83	0.60	0.20	0.60	1.00
☐ 263, Sep 77, WS	0.30	0.30	0.90	1.50	☐ 335, Sep 83	0.60	0.20	0.60	1.00
☐ 264, Oct 77, WS	0.30	0.30	0.90	1.50	☐ 336, Oct 83	0.60	0.20	0.60	1.00
☐ 265, Nov 77, WS	0.35	0.30	0.90	1.50	☐ 337, Nov 83, 1:Simonson Thor				
☐ 266, Dec 77, WS	0.35	0.30	0.90	1.50		0.60	1.20	3.60	6.00
☐ 267, Jan 78, WS	0.35	0.30	0.90	1.50	☐ 338, Dec 83, WS Beta Ray Bill				
☐ 268, Feb 78, WS	0.35	0.20	0.60	1.00		0.60	0.80	2.40	4.00
☐ 269, Mar 78, WS	0.35	0.20	0.60	1.00	☐ 339, Jan 84, WS, Beta Ray Bill				
☐ 270, Apr 78, WS	0.35	0.20	0.60	1.00		0.60	0.50	1.50	2.50
☐ 271, May 78, WS	0.35	0.20	0.60	1.00	☐ 340, Feb 84, WS Beta Ray Bill				
☐ 272, Jun 78	0.35	0.21	0.63	1.05		0.60	0.40	1.20	2.00
☐ 273, Jul 78	0.35	0.21	0.63	1.05	☐ 341, Mar 84, WS	0.60	0.30	0.90	1.50
☐ 274, Aug 78	0.35	0.21	0.63	1.05	☐ 342, Apr 84, WS	0.60	0.30	0.90	1.50
☐ 275, Sep 78	0.35	0.21	0.63	1.05	☐ 343, May 84, WS	0.60	0.30	0.90	1.50
☐ 276, Oct 78	0.35	0.21	0.63	1.05	☐ 344, Jun 84, WS	0.60	0.30	0.90	1.50
☐ 277, Nov 78	0.35	0.21	0.63	1.05	☐ 345, Jul 84, WS	0.60	0.30	0.90	1.50
☐ 278, Dec 78	0.35	0.21	0.63	1.05	☐ 346, Aug 84, WS	0.60	0.30	0.90	1.50
☐ 279, Jan 79	0.35	0.21	0.63	1.05	☐ 347, Sep 84, WS	0.60	0.30	0.90	1.50
☐ 280, Feb 79	0.35	0.21	0.63	1.05	☐ 348, Oct 84, WS	0.60	0.30	0.90	1.50
☐ 281, Mar 79	0.35	0.21	0.63	1.05	☐ 349, Nov 84, WS	0.60	0.30	0.90	1.50
☐ 282, Apr 79	0.35	0.21	0.63	1.05	☐ 350, Dec 84, WS	0.60	0.30	0.90	1.50
☐ 283, May 79	0.40	0.21	0.63	1.05	☐ 351, Jan 85, WS	0.60	0.30	0.90	1.50
☐ 284, Jun 79	0.40	0.21	0.63	1.05	☐ 352, Feb 85, WS	0.60	0.30	0.90	1.50
☐ 285, Jul 79	0.40	0.21	0.63	1.05	☐ 353, Mar 85, WS	0.60	0.30	0.90	1.50
☐ 286, Aug 79	0.40	0.21	0.63	1.05	☐ 354, Apr 85, WS	0.65	0.30	0.90	1.50
☐ 287, Sep 79	0.40	0.21	0.63	1.05	☐ 355, May 85, WS	0.65	0.30	0.90	1.50
☐ 288, Oct 79	0.40	0.21	0.63	1.05	☐ 356, Jun 85, WS	0.65	0.30	0.90	1.50
☐ 289, Nov 79	0.40	0.21	0.63	1.05	☐ 357, Jul 85, WS	0.65	0.30	0.90	1.50
☐ 290, Dec 79	0.40	0.21	0.63	1.05	☐ 358, Aug 85, WS	0.65	0.30	0.90	1.50
☐ 291, Jan 80	0.40	0.21	0.63	1.05	☐ 359, Sep 85, WS	0.65	0.30	0.90	1.50
☐ 292, Feb 80	0.40	0.21	0.63	1.05	☐ 360, Oct 85, WS	0.65	0.30	0.90	1.50
☐ 293, Mar 80	0.40	0.21	0.63	1.05	☐ 361, Nov 85, WS	0.65	0.30	0.90	1.50
☐ 294, Apr 80, KP, O:Odin	0.40	0.20	0.60	1.00	☐ 362, Dec 85, WS	0.65	0.30	0.90	1.50
☐ 295, May 80, KP	0.40	0.20	0.60	1.00	☐ 363, Jan 86, WS Secret Wars II				
☐ 296, Jun 80, KP	0.40	0.20	0.60	1.00		0.65	0.30	0.90	1.50
☐ 297, Jul 80, KP	0.40	0.20	0.60	1.00	☐ 364, Feb 86	0.75	0.30	0.90	1.50
☐ 298, Aug 80, KP	0.40	0.20	0.60	1.00	☐ 365, Mar 86	0.75	0.30	0.90	1.50
☐ 299, Sep 80, KP	0.50	0.20	0.60	1.00	☐ 366, Apr 86	0.75	0.30	0.90	1.50
☐ 300, Oct 80, KP, giant	0.75	0.30	0.90	1.50	☐ 367, May 86	0.75	0.30	0.90	1.50
☐ 301, Nov 80	0.50	0.20	0.60	1.00	☐ 368, Jun 86	0.75	0.30	0.90	1.50
☐ 302, Dec 80	0.50	0.20	0.60	1.00	☐ 369, Jul 86	0.75	0.30	0.90	1.50
☐ 303, Jan 81	0.50	0.20	0.60	1.00	☐ 370, Aug 86	0.75	0.30	0.90	1.50
☐ 304, Feb 81	0.50	0.20	0.60	1.00	☐ 371, Sep 86	0.75	0.30	0.90	1.50
☐ 305, Mar 81	0.50	0.20	0.60	1.00	☐ 372, Oct 86	0.75	0.30	0.90	1.50
☐ 306, Apr 81	0.50	0.20	0.60	1.00	☐ 373, Nov 86, Mutant Massacre				
☐ 307, May 81	0.50	0.20	0.60	1.00		0.75	0.60	1.80	3.00

	ORIG.	GOOD	FINE	N-MINT
374, Dec 86, Mutant Massacre				
........0.75		0.60	1.80	3.00
375, Jan 87 ....0.75		0.30	0.90	1.50
376, Feb 87 ....0.75		0.30	0.90	1.50
377, Mar 87 ....0.75		0.30	0.90	1.50
378, Apr 87 ....0.75		0.30	0.90	1.50
379, May 87 ....0.75		0.30	0.90	1.50
380, Jun 87 ....0.75		0.30	0.90	1.50
381, Jul 87 ....0.75		0.30	0.90	1.50
382, Aug 87 ....1.25		0.30	0.90	1.50
383, Sep 87, Secret Wars II				
........0.75		0.30	0.90	1.50
384, Oct 87, Thor of 2537				
........0.75		0.30	0.90	1.50
385, Nov 87, A:Hulk 0.75		0.40	1.20	2.00
386, Dec 87 ....0.75		0.30	0.90	1.50
387, Jan 88 ....0.75		0.30	0.90	1.50
388, Feb 88 ....0.75		0.30	0.90	1.50
389, Mar 88 ....0.75		0.30	0.90	1.50
390, Apr 88 ....0.75		0.20	0.60	1.00
391, May 88 ....0.75		0.20	0.60	1.00
392, Jun 88 ....0.75		0.20	0.60	1.00
393, Jul 88 ....0.75		0.20	0.60	1.00
394, Aug 88 ....0.75		0.20	0.60	1.00
395, Sep 88 ....0.75		0.20	0.60	1.00
396, Oct 88 ....0.75		0.20	0.60	1.00
397, Nov 88 ....0.75		0.20	0.60	1.00
398, Dec 88 ....0.75		0.20	0.60	1.00
399, Jan 89 ....0.75		0.20	0.60	1.00
400, Feb 89, anniversary 1.75		0.60	1.80	3.00
401, Mar 89 ....0.75		0.20	0.60	1.00
402, Apr 89 ....0.75		0.20	0.60	1.00
403, May 89 ....0.75		0.20	0.60	1.00
404, Jun 89 ....0.75		0.20	0.60	1.00
405, Jul 89 ....0.75		0.20	0.60	1.00
406, Aug 89 ....0.75		0.20	0.60	1.00
407, Sep 89 ....1.00		0.20	0.60	1.00
408, Oct 89 ....1.00		0.20	0.60	1.00
409, Nov 89 ....1.00		0.20	0.60	1.00
410, Nov 89 ....1.00		0.20	0.60	1.00
411, Dec 89, Acts of Vengeance, 1:New Warriors				
(becomes *The Mighty Thor*)				
........1.00		2.80	8.40	14.00

THOR (was Mighty Thor, The)

	ORIG.	GOOD	FINE	N-MINT
491, Oct 95 ....1.50		0.30	0.90	1.50
492, Nov 95 ....1.50		0.30	0.90	1.50
493, Dec 95 ....1.50		0.30	0.90	1.50
494, Jan 96 ....1.50		0.30	0.90	1.50
495, Feb 96 ....1.50		0.30	0.90	1.50
496, Mar 96 ....1.50		0.30	0.90	1.50
497, Apr 96 ....1.50		0.30	0.90	1.50
498, May 96 ....1.50		0.30	0.90	1.50
499, Jun 96 ....1.50		0.30	0.90	1.50

THOR ANNUAL (Was Journey into Mystery Annual)

	ORIG.	GOOD	FINE	N-MINT
2, 66, JK 0.25		8.00	24.00	40.00
3, JK, reprint 0.25		2.00	6.00	10.00
4, JK, reprint 0.25		2.00	6.00	10.00
5, Nov 76, JK/JB 0.50		1.00	3.00	5.00
6, Oct 77, JK/JB 0.50		1.00	3.00	5.00
7, Nov 78 ....0.60		0.60	1.80	3.00
8, Dec 79 ....0.75		0.60	1.80	3.00
9, Nov 81 ....0.75		0.60	1.80	3.00
10, Nov 82 ....1.00		0.60	1.80	3.00
11, Nov 83 ....1.00		0.60	1.80	3.00
12, Nov 84 ....1.00		0.60	1.80	3.00
13, Dec 85, (becomes *Mighty Thor Annual*)				
........1.25		0.60	1.80	3.00

THOR CORPS

	ORIG.	GOOD	FINE	N-MINT
1 ....1.75		0.35	1.05	1.75
2 ....1.75		0.35	1.05	1.75
3 ....1.75		0.35	1.05	1.75
4 ....1.75		0.35	1.05	1.75

THORR-SVERD
VINCENT

	ORIG.	GOOD	FINE	N-MINT
1, b&w		0.20	0.60	1.00
2, b&w		0.20	0.60	1.00
3, b&w		0.20	0.60	1.00

THOSE ANNOYING POST BROS.
AEON

	ORIG.	GOOD	FINE	N-MINT
39, Aug 94, b&w 2.50		0.50	1.50	2.50
40, Oct 94, b&w 2.50		0.50	1.50	2.50
41, Dec 94, b&w 2.50		0.50	1.50	2.50
42, Feb 95, b&w 2.50		0.50	1.50	2.50
43, Jun 95, b&w 2.50		0.50	1.50	2.50
44, Jul 95, b&w 2.50		0.50	1.50	2.50
45, Aug 95, b&w 2.95		0.59	1.77	2.95
46, Oct 95, b&w 2.95		0.59	1.77	2.95
47, Nov 95, b&w 2.95		0.59	1.77	2.95

THOSE ANNOYING POST BROS. ANNUAL

	ORIG.	GOOD	FINE	N-MINT
1, Aug 95, cardstock cover;b&w				
........4.95		0.99	2.97	4.95

THOSE ANNOYING POST BROTHERS
VORTEX

	ORIG.	GOOD	FINE	N-MINT
1		0.35	1.05	1.75
2		0.35	1.05	1.75
3		0.35	1.05	1.75
4		0.35	1.05	1.75
5		0.35	1.05	1.75
6		0.35	1.05	1.75
7		0.35	1.05	1.75
8		0.35	1.05	1.75
9		0.35	1.05	1.75
10		0.35	1.05	1.75
11		0.35	1.05	1.75
12		0.35	1.05	1.75
13		0.35	1.05	1.75
14		0.35	1.05	1.75
15		0.40	1.20	2.00
16		0.40	1.20	2.00
17		0.40	1.20	2.00
18, (becomes *Post Brothers*)		0.40	1.20	2.00

THOSE CRAZY PECKERS
U.S.COMICS

	ORIG.	GOOD	FINE	N-MINT
1		0.40	1.20	2.00

THREAT!
FANTAGRAPHICS

	ORIG.	GOOD	FINE	N-MINT
1, b&w		0.80	2.40	4.00
2		0.45	1.35	2.25
3		0.45	1.35	2.25
4		0.45	1.35	2.25
5		0.45	1.35	2.25
6		0.45	1.35	2.25
7		0.45	1.35	2.25
8		0.45	1.35	2.25
9		0.45	1.35	2.25
10		0.45	1.35	2.25

THREE MUSKETEERS
ETERNITY

	ORIG.	GOOD	FINE	N-MINT
1, b&w		0.39	1.17	1.95
2, b&w		0.39	1.17	1.95
3, b&w		0.39	1.17	1.95

MARVEL

	ORIG.	GOOD	FINE	N-MINT
1, movie adaptation 1.50		0.30	0.90	1.50
2, movie adaptation 1.50		0.30	0.90	1.50

THREE STOOGES IN 3-D
ETERNITY

	ORIG.	GOOD	FINE	N-MINT
1		0.79	2.37	3.95

THREE STOOGES IN FULL COLOR

	ORIG.	GOOD	FINE	N-MINT
1, reprints		1.19	3.57	5.95

	ORIG.	GOOD	FINE	N-MINT

THREE-DIMENSIONAL DNAGENTS
ECLIPSE
1, Jan 86		0.45	1.35	2.25

THRESHOLD OF REALITY
MAINTECH
1		0.20	0.60	1.00
2		0.20	0.60	1.00
3		0.20	0.60	1.00

THRILL KILL
CALIBER
1, b&w		0.50	1.50	2.50

THRILLER
DC
1, Nov 83, TVE(c)	1.25	0.40	1.20	2.00
2, Dec 83	1.25	0.30	0.90	1.50
3, Jan 84	1.25	0.30	0.90	1.50
4, Feb 84	1.25	0.30	0.90	1.50
5, Mar 84		0.25	0.75	1.25
6, Apr 84		0.25	0.75	1.25
7, May 84		0.25	0.75	1.25
8, Jun 84		0.25	0.75	1.25
9, Jul 84		0.25	0.75	1.25
10, Aug 84		0.25	0.75	1.25
11, Sep 84		0.25	0.75	1.25
12, Oct 84		0.25	0.75	1.25

THRILLING ADVENTURE STORIES
ATLAS/ SEABOARD
1, Feb 75, b&w mag	0.75	0.60	1.80	3.00
2, Aug 75	0.75	0.40	1.20	2.00

THRILLING ADVENTURE STRIPS
(formerly Best of Tribune Company)
DRAGON LADY
5		0.59	1.77	2.95
6		0.59	1.77	2.95
7		0.59	1.77	2.95
8		0.59	1.77	2.95
9		0.59	1.77	2.95
10		0.59	1.77	2.95

THRILLING SCIENCE TALES
AC
1, MK(c) reprints WW,AW,FF		0.70	2.10	3.50
2, reprints GE				

THRILLING WONDER TALES
0, nn pring '91 b&w, reprint: WW, JKu, Powell		0.59	1.77	2.95

THRILLOGY
PACIFIC
1		0.30	0.90	1.50

THUMB SCREW
CALIBER
1, b&w		0.70	2.10	3.50
2, b&w		0.70	2.10	3.50

THUMP'N GUTS
KITCHEN SINK
1	2.95	0.59	1.77	2.95

THUN'DA TALES
FANTAGRAPHICS
1, FF	2.00	0.40	1.20	2.00

THUN'DA, KING OF THE CONGO
AC
1, 89, b&w;Powell reprints		0.50	1.50	2.50

THUNDER AGENTS
J.C.
1, May 83		0.20	0.60	1.00
2, Jan 84		0.20	0.60	1.00

THUNDERBUNNY
ARCHIE
1, Jan 84		0.20	0.60	1.00

WARP
1, Jun 85, O:retold		0.30	0.90	1.50
2, Aug 85		0.30	0.90	1.50
3, Oct 85		0.30	0.90	1.50
4, Dec 85		0.30	0.90	1.50
5, Feb 86, (moves to Apple)		0.30	0.90	1.50

THUNDERBUNNY (former Warp title)
APPLE
6, 86, b&w		0.30	0.90	1.50
7, 86, b&w		0.30	0.90	1.50
8, 86		0.35	1.05	1.75
9, 87		0.35	1.05	1.75
10, Jul 87		0.35	1.05	1.75
11, Sep 87, A:THUNDER Agents	0.35	1.05	1.75
12, Nov 87, last		0.35	1.05	1.75

THUNDERCATS
STAR
1	0.65	1.20	3.60	6.00
2	0.65	0.60	1.80	3.00
3	0.75	0.20	0.60	1.00
4	0.75	0.15	0.45	0.75
5	0.75	0.15	0.45	0.75
6	0.75	0.15	0.45	0.75
7	0.75	0.15	0.45	0.75
8	0.75	0.15	0.45	0.75
9	0.75	0.15	0.45	0.75
10	0.75	0.15	0.45	0.75
11	1.00	0.20	0.60	1.00
12	1.00	0.20	0.60	1.00
13	1.00	0.20	0.60	1.00
14	1.00	0.20	0.60	1.00
15	1.00	0.20	0.60	1.00
16	1.00	0.20	0.60	1.00
17	1.00	0.20	0.60	1.00
18	1.00	0.20	0.60	1.00
19	1.00	0.20	0.60	1.00
20	1.00	0.20	0.60	1.00
21, (becomes Marvel comic)	1.00	0.20	0.60	1.00

THUNDERCATS (former Star Comic)
MARVEL
22	1.00	0.20	0.60	1.00
23	1.00	0.20	0.60	1.00
24	1.00	0.20	0.60	1.00

THUNDERMACE
RAK
1, b&w		0.30	0.90	1.50
2		0.35	1.05	1.75
3		0.35	1.05	1.75
4		0.35	1.05	1.75
5		0.40	1.20	2.00
6		0.40	1.20	2.00
7		0.40	1.20	2.00

THUNDERSAURS
INNOVATION
1, b&w		0.55	1.65	2.75

THUNDERSTRIKE
MARVEL
1, foil cover	2.95	0.59	1.77	2.95
2	1.25	0.25	0.75	1.25
3	1.25	0.25	0.75	1.25
4	1.25	0.25	0.75	1.25
5	1.25	0.25	0.75	1.25
6, Mar 94	1.25	0.25	0.75	1.25
7, Apr 94	1.25	0.25	0.75	1.25
8, May 94	1.50	0.30	0.90	1.50
9, Jun 94	1.50	0.30	0.90	1.50
10, Jul 94	1.50	0.30	0.90	1.50
11, Aug 94	1.50	0.30	0.90	1.50
12, Sep 94	1.50	0.30	0.90	1.50

Thor

The Mighty Thor #158 ©1968 Marvel.

It's easy to see how some heroes can be replaced. Slap on a suit of armor or a ring and most anybody could be Iron Man or Green Lantern. But Thor is a character from Norse mythology with a full history behind him. How do so many people get to be Thor? It must be that darned enchantment. Let's look at Marvel's Thunder Gods:

• Thor I: The Original. We thought Dr. Don Blake got lucky when he found the staff that turned into Thor's hammer. Could have been anybody, right? (After all, in an issue of *What If?*, Jane Foster found the hammer.) It turned out Blake wasn't just channeling the essence of Thor; Thor was real and Blake a phony identity created by Odin. He merged Thor with Blake to teach him humility. (See *Mighty Thor #415*.)

Ooops! Maybe there *was* a real Blake after all and Odin stole his life to set up Thor's cover. After he found the hammer, Odin separated Thor from the real Blake, whom he then imprisoned in stasis within Mount Wundagore (*Mighty Thor #479*). Oh, those wacky gods!

• Thor II: Beta Ray Bill. The enchantment on Mjolnir, Thor's mystical hammer, says that whoever holds it, if worthy, will possess the power of Thor. Odin didn't consider the possibility that anybody else could be worthy — least of all an alien champion with a face like an angry horse. But Bill (an alien named Bill?) bested Thor and earned the hammer. Odin couldn't have that, so he had a new hammer made for Bill, complete with enchantment enabling Bill to turn back into his long-lost, non-horse-faced self.

• Thor III: Dargo. In an oppressed future, Thor's hammer surfaced like a modern-day Excalibur. After rousting the oppressors, Dargo sent it back through time to its "rightful master." Why? If you found Excalibur, would you assume it was displaced in time and attempt to return it to King Arthur? But that darned hammer just came back, so Dargo served as the somewhat reluctant Thor of the future.

• Thor IV: Thunderstrike. Eric Masterson, a friend of Thor, was mortally wounded in *Mighty Thor #408*. To save his life, Odin merged Eric with the Thunder God. Eric could call upon Thor with a thump of the old enchanted cane. Eric himself was called upon to sub for Thor when Thor was imprisoned in an unknown location. Oops! Turned out Thor was hidden inside Eric. How ironic (not to mention crowded)!

"Here, Eric, you did such a good job, you keep the hammer. No, wait, I want it back. We'll make you a new one. OK, it's not exactly a hammer; it's more of a mace. How about we call you 'Thunderstrike'?" That's the short form. See *Mighty Thor #408-459* for the whole enchilada.

• Thor V: "Red" Norvell. Back in *Mighty Thor #276-278*, Roger Norvell obtained Thor's belt of strength, gloves of power, and hammer. He role-played Thor in a version of Ragnarok and fulfilled the prophecy of Thor's demise at the hands (coils?) of the Midgard Serpent. Ticked off at Thor, Odin retrieved Red from Valhalla; Thor the Blonde got banished again and Thor the Red set up shop in Asgard (*Mighty Thor #478*).

It should be noted that Beta Ray Bill, Dargo, and Thunderstrike are collectively referred to as the Thor Corps. They shared their own four-issue mini-series and fought "The Thor War" in *Mighty Thor #438-441*.

• Also-Rans: A number of beings presented themselves as additional aspects of Thor but turned out not to be. Donar (the Germanic name for Thor) appeared, with other gods, to trouble The Invaders in World War II. In *The Invaders #2*, he was revealed to be an alien. (The real thing showed up later, in issue #32.)

Thor 2099 appeared to be genuine at first. Like Donar, he had a whole entourage of gods, the "New Aesir." He turned out to be lowly Cecil McAdam, priest of a cult of Thor-worshippers. Technology had given him the power and made him believe himself to be the original. He appeared in the five-part "Fall of the Hammer" storyline that ran through the 2099 titles.

Because Thor is a mythological character, other companies have their own versions. DC has had one Thor in *Sandman* and another in *The Inferior Five*; Image's Thunderer is an enemy of Supreme. As with all myths, different legends arise in different cultures, usually mutually exclusive. What's unique about Marvel's Thors is they can all go out for coffee together.

	ORIG.	GOOD	FINE	N-MINT

13, Oct 94, flip-book with Code: Blue back-up
.... 2.50 — 0.50 — 1.50 — 2.50
13, Oct 94 .... 1.50 — 0.30 — 0.90 — 1.50
14, Nov 94 .... 1.50 — 0.30 — 0.90 — 1.50
15, Dec 94 .... 1.50 — 0.30 — 0.90 — 1.50
16, Jan 95 .... 1.50 — 0.30 — 0.90 — 1.50
17, Feb 95 .... 1.50 — 0.30 — 0.90 — 1.50
18, Mar 95 .... 1.50 — 0.30 — 0.90 — 1.50
19, Apr 95 .... 1.50 — 0.30 — 0.90 — 1.50
20, May 95 .... 1.50 — 0.30 — 0.90 — 1.50
21, Jun 95 .... 1.50 — 0.30 — 0.90 — 1.50
22, Jul 95, Identity of Bloodaxe revealed
.... 1.50 — 0.30 — 0.90 — 1.50
23, Aug 95, V:Seth;Avengers;Thor
.... 1.50 — 0.30 — 0.90 — 1.50
24, Sep 95, final issue;D:Eric Masterson
.... 1.50 — 0.30 — 0.90 — 1.50

TICK KARMA TORNADO, THE
NEC
1, Oct 93, b&w.............. 3.25 — 0.65 — 1.95 — 3.25
2, Jan 94, b&w.............. 2.75 — 0.55 — 1.65 — 2.75
3, May 94, b&w.............. 2.75 — 0.55 — 1.65 — 2.75
4, Jul 94, b&w .... 2.75 — 0.55 — 1.65 — 2.75
5, Aug 94, b&w .... 2.75 — 0.55 — 1.65 — 2.75
6, Oct 94, b&w.............. 2.75 — 0.55 — 1.65 — 2.75

TICK, THE
NEW ENGLAND
1, special edition .... — 10.00 — 30.00 — 50.00
1, Jun 88, b&w, 1st printing
.... 1.75 — 18.00 — 54.00 — 90.00
1, 2nd printing .... — 1.20 — 3.60 — 6.00
1, 3rd printing .... — 0.80 — 2.40 — 4.00
1, 4th printing .... — 0.45 — 1.35 — 2.25
2, special edition .... — 6.00 — 18.00 — 30.00
2, 1st printing .... — 12.00 — 36.00 — 60.00
2, 2nd printing .... — 1.00 — 3.00 — 5.00
2, 3rd printing .... — 0.70 — 2.10 — 3.50
2, 4th printing .... — 0.45 — 1.35 — 2.25
3, 1st printing .... — 5.00 — 15.00 — 25.00
3, 2nd printing .... — 0.45 — 1.35 — 2.25
4, 1st printing .... — 3.20 — 9.60 — 16.00
4, 2nd printing .... — 0.45 — 1.35 — 2.25
5, 1st printing .... — 2.40 — 7.20 — 12.00
6, 1st printing .... — 2.40 — 7.20 — 12.00
7, 1st printing .... — 1.60 — 4.80 — 8.00
8, 1st printing .... — 1.60 — 4.80 — 8.00
8, without logo .... — 1.00 — 3.00 — 5.00
9, 1st printing .... — 1.60 — 4.80 — 8.00
10, 1st printing .... — 1.60 — 4.80 — 8.00
11, b&w .... 2.75 — 1.00 — 3.00 — 5.00
12, b&w .... 2.75 — 1.00 — 3.00 — 5.00

TIGER-MAN
ATLAS/ SEABOARD
1, Sep 75, O:Tiger-Man.. 0.25 — 0.20 — 0.60 — 1.00
2, Jun 75, SD .... 0.25 — 0.20 — 0.60 — 1.00
3, Sep 75, SD .... 0.25 — 0.20 — 0.60 — 1.00

TIGER-X
ETERNITY
1, b&w .... — 0.39 — 1.17 — 1.95
2, b&w .... — 0.39 — 1.17 — 1.95
3, b&w .... — 0.39 — 1.17 — 1.95

TIGER-X BOOK II
1, b&w .... — 0.39 — 1.17 — 1.95
2, b&w .... — 0.39 — 1.17 — 1.95
3, b&w .... — 0.39 — 1.17 — 1.95
4, b&w .... — 0.39 — 1.17 — 1.95

TIGER-X SPECIAL
1, b&w (1st printing) .... — 0.45 — 1.35 — 2.25
1, (2nd printing) .... — 0.45 — 1.35 — 2.25

	ORIG.	GOOD	FINE	N-MINT

TIGER-X: THE ADVENTURE BEGINS
0, album, b&w, rep.......... 1.99 — — 5.97 — 9.95

TIGERS OF TERRA
MIND-VISIONS
1 .... — 0.60 — 1.80 — 3.00
2 .... — 0.60 — 1.80 — 3.00
3 .... — 0.60 — 1.80 — 3.00
4 ....
5 ....
6 ....
7 ....
8 ....
9, two covers: a and b .... 3.75 — 0.75 — 2.25 — 3.75

TIGERS OF TERRA (Vol. 2)
ANTARCTIC
0, Aug 93, b&w............. 2.95 — 0.59 — 1.77 — 2.95

TIGERS OF TERRA (VOL. 2)
1, Oct 93, b&w............. 2.75 — 0.55 — 1.65 — 2.75
2, Dec 93, b&w............. 2.75 — 0.55 — 1.65 — 2.75
3, Feb 94, b&w .... 2.75 — 0.55 — 1.65 — 2.75
4, Apr 94, b&w .... 2.75 — 0.55 — 1.65 — 2.75
5, Jul 94, b&w .... 2.75 — 0.55 — 1.65 — 2.75
6, Sep 94, b&w............. 2.75 — 0.55 — 1.65 — 2.75
7, Dec 94, b&w............. 2.75 — 0.55 — 1.65 — 2.75
8, Jan 95, b&w............. 2.75 — 0.55 — 1.65 — 2.75
9, Mar 95, b&w............. 2.75 — 0.55 — 1.65 — 2.75
10, Apr 95, b&w .... 2.75 — 0.55 — 1.65 — 2.75
11, May 95, b&w .... 2.75 — 0.55 — 1.65 — 2.75
12, Jun 95, b&w .... 2.75 — 0.55 — 1.65 — 2.75
13, Jul 95, b&w .... 2.75 — 0.55 — 1.65 — 2.75
14, Aug 95, b&w............. 2.75 — 0.55 — 1.65 — 2.75

TIGERS OF TERRA (was Mind-Visions title)
11, b&w .... 3.95 — 0.79 — 2.37 — 3.95
12, Jul 93, b&w .... 3.95 — 0.79 — 2.37 — 3.95

TIGRESS
HERO
1, b&w;A:Flare .... — 0.59 — 1.77 — 2.95
2, b&w, A:Flare .... — 0.59 — 1.77 — 2.95
3, b&w;1: Mudpie .... — 0.59 — 1.77 — 2.95
4, b&w............................ 2.95 — 0.59 — 1.77 — 2.95
5, b&w............................ 2.95 — 0.59 — 1.77 — 2.95
6, Jun 93 .... 3.95 — 0.79 — 2.37 — 3.95

TIJUANA BIBLE
STARHEAD
1, adult, b&w .... — 0.79 — 2.37 — 3.95
2, adult, b&w .... — 0.79 — 2.37 — 3.95
3, adult, b&w .... — 0.79 — 2.37 — 3.95
4, adult, b&w .... — 0.79 — 2.37 — 3.95

TIM HOLT WESTERN ANNUAL
AC
1, b&w reprints................ — 0.59 — 1.77 — 2.95

TIMBER WOLF
DC
1, Nov 92 .... 1.25 — 0.25 — 0.75 — 1.25
2, Dec 92 .... 1.25 — 0.25 — 0.75 — 1.25
3, Jan 93........................ 1.25 — 0.25 — 0.75 — 1.25
4, Feb 93........................ 1.25 — 0.25 — 0.75 — 1.25
5, Mar 93........................ 1.25 — 0.25 — 0.75 — 1.25

TIME BANDITS
MARVEL
1, Feb 82, movie .... 1.00 — 0.20 — 0.60 — 1.00

TIME GATES
DOUBLE EDGE
1 .... 1.95 — 0.39 — 1.17 — 1.95
2 .... 1.95 — 0.39 — 1.17 — 1.95
3 .... 1.95 — 0.39 — 1.17 — 1.95

TIME KILLERS
FLEETWAY/QUALITY
1 .... 2.95 — 0.59 — 1.77 — 2.95

	ORIG.	GOOD	FINE	N-MINT
❏ 2	2.95	0.59	1.77	2.95
❏ 3	2.95	0.59	1.77	2.95
❏ 4	2.95	0.59	1.77	2.95
❏ 5	2.95	0.59	1.77	2.95
❏ 6	2.95	0.59	1.77	2.95
❏ 7	2.95	0.59	1.77	2.95

TIME MACHINE, THE
ETERNITY

		GOOD	FINE	N-MINT
❏ 1, b&w		0.50	1.50	2.50
❏ 2, b&w		0.50	1.50	2.50
❏ 3, b&w		0.50	1.50	2.50

TIME MASTERS
DC

	ORIG.	GOOD	FINE	N-MINT
❏ 1, Feb 90	1.75	0.35	1.05	1.75
❏ 2, Mar 90	1.75	0.35	1.05	1.75
❏ 3, Apr 90	1.75	0.35	1.05	1.75
❏ 4, May 90	1.75	0.35	1.05	1.75
❏ 5, Jun 90	1.75	0.35	1.05	1.75
❏ 6, Jul 90	1.75	0.35	1.05	1.75
❏ 7, Aug 90	1.75	0.35	1.05	1.75
❏ 8, Sep 90	1.75	0.35	1.05	1.75

TIME OUT OF MIND
GRAPHIC SERIALS

	ORIG.	GOOD	FINE	N-MINT
❏ 1	1.85	0.35	1.05	1.75
❏ 2		0.35	1.05	1.75
❏ 3		0.35	1.05	1.75

TIME TWISTERS
FLEETWAY/QUALITY

		GOOD	FINE	N-MINT
❏ 1		0.25	0.75	1.25
❏ 2		0.25	0.75	1.25
❏ 3		0.25	0.75	1.25
❏ 4		0.25	0.75	1.25
❏ 5		0.25	0.75	1.25
❏ 6		0.25	0.75	1.25
❏ 7		0.25	0.75	1.25
❏ 8		0.25	0.75	1.25
❏ 9		0.25	0.75	1.25
❏ 10		0.25	0.75	1.25
❏ 11		0.30	0.90	1.50
❏ 12		0.30	0.90	1.50
❏ 13		0.30	0.90	1.50
❏ 14		0.30	0.90	1.50
❏ 15		0.30	0.90	1.50
❏ 16		0.30	0.90	1.50
❏ 17		0.30	0.90	1.50
❏ 18		0.30	0.90	1.50
❏ 19		0.30	0.90	1.50
❏ 20		0.30	0.90	1.50
❏ 21		0.30	0.90	1.50

TIME WANKERS
EROS COMIX

		GOOD	FINE	N-MINT
❏ 1, adult, b&w		0.45	1.35	2.25
❏ 2, adult, b&w		0.45	1.35	2.25
❏ 3, adult, b&w		0.45	1.35	2.25
❏ 4, adult, b&w		0.45	1.35	2.25
❏ 5, adult, b&w		0.45	1.35	2.25

TIME WARRIORS: THE BEGINNING
FANTASY GENERAL

		GOOD	FINE	N-MINT
❏ 1		0.30	0.90	1.50

TIMECOP (mini-series)
DARK HORSE

	ORIG.	GOOD	FINE	N-MINT
❏ 1, Sep 94, movie adaptation	2.50	0.50	1.50	2.50
❏ 2, Sep 94, movie adaptation	2.50	0.50	1.50	2.50

TIMEDRIFTER
INNOVATION

	ORIG.	GOOD	FINE	N-MINT
❏ 1, GJ, b&w	2.25	0.45	1.35	2.25
❏ 2, b&w		0.45	1.35	2.25
❏ 3, b&w		0.45	1.35	2.25

TIMEJUMP WAR, THE
APPLE

		GOOD	FINE	N-MINT
❏ 1, b&w		0.45	1.35	2.25
❏ 2, b&w		0.45	1.35	2.25
❏ 3, b&w		0.45	1.35	2.25

TIMESPIRITS
EPIC

	ORIG.	GOOD	FINE	N-MINT
❏ 1	1.50	0.30	0.90	1.50
❏ 2	1.50	0.30	0.90	1.50
❏ 3	1.50	0.30	0.90	1.50
❏ 4	1.50	0.30	0.90	1.50
❏ 5	1.50	0.30	0.90	1.50
❏ 6	1.50	0.30	0.90	1.50
❏ 7	1.50	0.30	0.90	1.50
❏ 8	1.50	0.30	0.90	1.50

TIMEWALKER
ACCLAIM/VALIANT

	ORIG.	GOOD	FINE	N-MINT
❏ 0, Mar 96, O:Ivar	2.50	0.50	1.50	2.50
❏ 7, Jun 95	2.50	0.50	1.50	2.50
❏ 8, Jul 95	2.50	0.50	1.50	2.50
❏ 9, Jul 95, DP	2.50	0.50	1.50	2.50
❏ 10, Aug 95	2.50	0.50	1.50	2.50
❏ 11, Aug 95	2.50	0.50	1.50	2.50
❏ 12, Sep 95, DP	2.50	0.50	1.50	2.50
❏ 13, Sep 95	2.50	0.50	1.50	2.50
❏ 14, Oct 95	2.50	0.50	1.50	2.50
❏ 15, Oct 95, final issue	2.50	0.50	1.50	2.50

VALIANT

	ORIG.	GOOD	FINE	N-MINT
❏ 1, Jan 95, cover has "Dec '94" coverdate	2.50	0.60	1.80	3.00
❏ 2, Feb 95, cover has "Jan" coverdate	2.50	0.50	1.50	2.50
❏ 3, Mar 95, cover has "Feb" coverdate	2.50	0.50	1.50	2.50
❏ 4, Apr 95, cover has "Mar" cover date	2.50	0.50	1.50	2.50
❏ 5, Apr 95	2.50	0.50	1.50	2.50
❏ 6, May 95	2.50	0.50	1.50	2.50

TIMEWARP
DC

	ORIG.	GOOD	FINE	N-MINT
❏ 1, Nov 79	1.00	0.20	0.60	1.00
❏ 2, Jan 80	1.00	0.20	0.60	1.00
❏ 3, Mar 80	1.00	0.20	0.60	1.00
❏ 4, May 80	1.00	0.20	0.60	1.00
❏ 5, Jul 80	1.00	0.20	0.60	1.00

TINY TOON ADVENTURES

		GOOD	FINE	N-MINT
❏ 1, magazine		0.39	1.17	1.95
❏ 2, magazine		0.39	1.17	1.95
❏ 3, magazine		0.39	1.17	1.95
❏ 4, magazine		0.39	1.17	1.95
❏ 5, magazine		0.39	1.17	1.95
❏ 6, magazine		0.39	1.17	1.95
❏ 7, magazine		0.39	1.17	1.95

TIPPER GORE'S COMICS AND STORIES
REVOLUTIONARY

	ORIG.	GOOD	FINE	N-MINT
❏ 1, Oct 89, b&w	1.95	0.39	1.17	1.95
❏ 2, Jan 90, b&w	1.95	0.39	1.17	1.95
❏ 3, Mar 90, b&w	1.95	0.39	1.17	1.95
❏ 4, May 90, b&w	1.95	0.39	1.17	1.95
❏ 5, Jul 90, b&w, (c)Robert Williams	1.95	0.39	1.17	1.95

TIPPY TEEN
TOWER

		GOOD	FINE	N-MINT
❏ 1		0.20	0.60	1.00
❏ 2		0.20	0.60	1.00
❏ 3		0.20	0.60	1.00
❏ 4		0.20	0.60	1.00
❏ 5		0.20	0.60	1.00
❏ 6		0.20	0.60	1.00
❏ 7		0.20	0.60	1.00
❏ 8		0.20	0.60	1.00

	ORIG.	GOOD	FINE	N-MINT
9		0.20	0.60	1.00
10		0.20	0.60	1.00
11		0.20	0.60	1.00
12		0.20	0.60	1.00
13		0.20	0.60	1.00
14		0.20	0.60	1.00
15		0.20	0.60	1.00
16		0.20	0.60	1.00
17		0.20	0.60	1.00
18		0.20	0.60	1.00
19		0.20	0.60	1.00
20		0.20	0.60	1.00
21		0.20	0.60	1.00
22		0.20	0.60	1.00
23		0.20	0.60	1.00
24		0.20	0.60	1.00
25		0.20	0.60	1.00
26		0.20	0.60	1.00
27		0.20	0.60	1.00

TITAN SPECIAL
DARK HORSE

	ORIG.	GOOD	FINE	N-MINT
1, Jun 94, one-shot	3.95	0.79	2.37	3.95

TITANS SELL-OUT!
DC

	ORIG.	GOOD	FINE	N-MINT
1, one-shot		0.70	2.10	3.50

TO BE ANNOUNCED
STRAWBERRY JAM

	ORIG.	GOOD	FINE	N-MINT
1	1.50	0.30	0.90	1.50
2	1.50	0.30	0.90	1.50
3	1.50	0.30	0.90	1.50
4	1.50	0.30	0.90	1.50
5	1.50	0.30	0.90	1.50
6	1.50	0.30	0.90	1.50
7	1.50	0.30	0.90	1.50

TO DIE FOR
BLACKTHORNE

	ORIG.	GOOD	FINE	N-MINT
1, b&w, movie		0.50	1.50	2.50

TO DIE FOR IN 3-D

	ORIG.	GOOD	FINE	N-MINT
1, movie		0.50	1.50	2.50

TO RIVERDALE AND BACK AGAIN
ARCHIE

	ORIG.	GOOD	FINE	N-MINT
0, 90, nn JBy(c),GC TV	2.50	0.50	1.50	2.50

TOM & JERRY
HARVEY

	ORIG.	GOOD	FINE	N-MINT
1, CB reprints	1.25	0.25	0.75	1.25
2, CB reprints	1.25	0.25	0.75	1.25
3, CB reprints	1.25	0.25	0.75	1.25
4, CB reprints	1.25	0.25	0.75	1.25
5, CB reprints	1.25	0.25	0.75	1.25
6, CB reprints	1.25	0.25	0.75	1.25
7, CB reprints	1.25	0.25	0.75	1.25
8, CB reprints	1.25	0.25	0.75	1.25
9	1.50	0.30	0.90	1.50
10	1.50	0.30	0.90	1.50
11	1.50	0.30	0.90	1.50
12	1.50	0.30	0.90	1.50
13	1.50	0.30	0.90	1.50
14	1.50	0.30	0.90	1.50
15	1.50	0.30	0.90	1.50
16	1.50	0.30	0.90	1.50
17, Jul 94	1.50	0.30	0.90	1.50
18, Aug 94	1.50	0.30	0.90	1.50

TOM & JERRY 50TH ANNIVERSARY SPECIAL

	ORIG.	GOOD	FINE	N-MINT
1, CB, reprints	2.50	0.50	1.50	2.50

TOM & JERRY ADVENTURES

	ORIG.	GOOD	FINE	N-MINT
1, reprints	1.25	0.25	0.75	1.25

TOM & JERRY AND FRIENDS

	ORIG.	GOOD	FINE	N-MINT
1, CB reprints	1.25	0.25	0.75	1.25
2, CB reprints	1.25	0.25	0.75	1.25

	ORIG.	GOOD	FINE	N-MINT
3, reprints	1.25	0.25	0.75	1.25
4, reprints	1.25	0.25	0.75	1.25

TOM & JERRY ANNUAL

	ORIG.	GOOD	FINE	N-MINT
1, Sep 94	2.25	0.45	1.35	2.25

TOM & JERRY BIG BOOK

	ORIG.	GOOD	FINE	N-MINT
1	1.95	0.39	1.17	1.95
2	1.95	0.39	1.17	1.95

TOM & JERRY DIGEST

	ORIG.	GOOD	FINE	N-MINT
1, CB reprints	1.75	0.35	1.05	1.75

TOM & JERRY GIANT SIZE

	ORIG.	GOOD	FINE	N-MINT
1, reprints	1.95	0.39	1.17	1.95
2	2.25	0.45	1.35	2.25

TOM CORBETT
ETERNITY

	ORIG.	GOOD	FINE	N-MINT
1, b&w		0.45	1.35	2.25
2, b&w		0.45	1.35	2.25
3, b&w		0.45	1.35	2.25
4, b&w		0.45	1.35	2.25

TOM CORBETT BOOK TWO

	ORIG.	GOOD	FINE	N-MINT
1		0.45	1.35	2.25
2		0.45	1.35	2.25
3		0.45	1.35	2.25
4		0.45	1.35	2.25

TOM MIX WESTERN
AC

	ORIG.	GOOD	FINE	N-MINT
1, reprint		0.59	1.77	2.95
2, b&w, reprint		0.50	1.50	2.50

TOMATO
STARHEAD

	ORIG.	GOOD	FINE	N-MINT
1, Apr 94, adult;b&w	2.75	0.55	1.65	2.75
2, Feb 95, adult;b&w	2.75	0.55	1.65	2.75

TOMB OF DARKNESS (was Beware)
MARVEL

	ORIG.	GOOD	FINE	N-MINT
9	0.25	0.20	0.60	1.00
10	0.25	0.20	0.60	1.00
11	0.25	0.20	0.60	1.00
12	0.25	0.20	0.60	1.00
13	0.25	0.20	0.60	1.00
14	0.25	0.20	0.60	1.00
15	0.25	0.20	0.60	1.00
16	0.25	0.20	0.60	1.00
17	0.25	0.20	0.60	1.00
18	0.25	0.20	0.60	1.00
19	0.25	0.20	0.60	1.00
20	0.25	0.20	0.60	1.00
21	0.25	0.20	0.60	1.00
22	0.25	0.20	0.60	1.00
23	0.25	0.20	0.60	1.00

TOMB OF DRACULA
EPIC

	ORIG.	GOOD	FINE	N-MINT
1, Nov 91, GC,AW	4.95	0.99	2.97	4.95
2, Dec 91, GC,AW	4.95	0.99	2.97	4.95
3, GC,AW	4.95	0.99	2.97	4.95
4, GC,AW	4.95	0.99	2.97	4.95

MARVEL

	ORIG.	GOOD	FINE	N-MINT
1, GC	0.20	16.00	48.00	80.00
2, GC	0.20	10.00	30.00	50.00
3, GC	0.20	5.00	15.00	25.00
4, GC	0.20	5.00	15.00	25.00
5, GC	0.20	5.00	15.00	25.00
6, GC	0.20	3.60	10.80	18.00
7, GC	0.20	3.60	10.80	18.00
8, GC	0.20	3.60	10.80	18.00
9, GC	0.20	3.60	10.80	18.00
10, GC	0.20	3.60	10.80	18.00
11, GC	0.20	2.40	7.20	12.00
12, GC	0.20	2.40	7.20	12.00
13, GC	0.20	2.40	7.20	12.00
14, GC	0.20	2.40	7.20	12.00
15, GC	0.20	2.40	7.20	12.00

	ORIG.	GOOD	FINE	N-MINT
☐ 16, GC	0.20	2.40	7.20	12.00
☐ 17, GC	0.20	2.40	7.20	12.00
☐ 18, GC	0.20	2.40	7.20	12.00
☐ 19, GC	0.20	2.40	7.20	12.00
☐ 20, GC	0.25	2.40	7.20	12.00
☐ 21, GC	0.25	1.60	4.80	8.00
☐ 22, GC	0.25	1.60	4.80	8.00
☐ 23, GC	0.25	1.60	4.80	8.00
☐ 24, GC	0.25	1.60	4.80	8.00
☐ 25, GC	0.25	1.60	4.80	8.00
☐ 26, GC	0.25	1.60	4.80	8.00
☐ 27, GC	0.25	1.60	4.80	8.00
☐ 28, GC	0.25	1.60	4.80	8.00
☐ 29, GC	0.25	1.60	4.80	8.00
☐ 30, GC	0.25	1.60	4.80	8.00
☐ 31, GC	0.25	1.60	4.80	8.00
☐ 32, GC	0.25	1.60	4.80	8.00
☐ 33, GC	0.25	1.60	4.80	8.00
☐ 34, GC	0.25	1.60	4.80	8.00
☐ 35, GC	0.25	1.60	4.80	8.00
☐ 36, GC	0.25	1.60	4.80	8.00
☐ 37, GC	0.25	1.60	4.80	8.00
☐ 38, GC	0.25	1.60	4.80	8.00
☐ 39, GC	0.25	1.60	4.80	8.00
☐ 40, GC	0.25	1.60	4.80	8.00
☐ 41, GC	0.25	1.40	4.20	7.00
☐ 42, GC	0.25	1.40	4.20	7.00
☐ 43, GC	0.25	1.40	4.20	7.00
☐ 44, GC	0.25	1.40	4.20	7.00
☐ 45, GC	0.25	1.40	4.20	7.00
☐ 46, GC	0.25	1.40	4.20	7.00
☐ 47, GC	0.25	1.40	4.20	7.00
☐ 48, Sep 76, GC	0.30	1.40	4.20	7.00
☐ 49, Oct 76, GC	0.30	1.40	4.20	7.00
☐ 50, Nov 76, GC	0.30	6.00	18.00	30.00
☐ 51, Dec 76, GC	0.30	1.20	3.60	6.00
☐ 52, Jan 77, GC	0.30	1.20	3.60	6.00
☐ 53, Feb 77, GC	0.30	1.20	3.60	6.00
☐ 54, Mar 77, GC	0.30	1.20	3.60	6.00
☐ 55, Apr 77, GC	0.30	1.20	3.60	6.00
☐ 56, May 77, GC	0.30	1.20	3.60	6.00
☐ 57, Jun 77, GC	0.30	1.20	3.60	6.00
☐ 58, Jul 77, GC	0.30	1.20	3.60	6.00
☐ 59, Aug 77, GC	0.30	1.20	3.60	6.00
☐ 60, Sep 77, GC	0.30	1.20	3.60	6.00
☐ 61, Nov 77, GC	0.35	1.20	3.60	6.00
☐ 62, Jan 78, GC	0.35	1.20	3.60	6.00
☐ 63, Mar 78, GC	0.35	1.20	3.60	6.00
☐ 64, May 78, GC	0.35	1.20	3.60	6.00
☐ 65, Jul 78, GC	0.35	1.20	3.60	6.00
☐ 66, Sep 78, GC	0.35	1.20	3.60	6.00
☐ 67, Nov 78, GC	0.35	1.20	3.60	6.00
☐ 68, Feb 79, GC	0.35	1.20	3.60	6.00
☐ 69, Apr 79, GC	0.35	1.20	3.60	6.00
☐ 70, Aug 79, D:Dracula	0.60	2.00	6.00	10.00

TOMB OF DRACULA (b&w mag)

	ORIG.	GOOD	FINE	N-MINT
☐ 1, Oct 79, MWo;GC	1.25	1.00	3.00	5.00
☐ 2, Dec 79, MWo;SD	1.25	0.80	2.40	4.00
☐ 3, Feb 80, MWo;GC;TP;FM	1.25	0.80	2.40	4.00
☐ 4, Apr 80, JB;GC;TP	1.25	0.80	2.40	4.00
☐ 5, Jun 80, GC;TP;JB	1.25	0.80	2.40	4.00
☐ 6, Aug 80, JSho;GC	1.25	0.80	2.40	4.00

TOMMY

	ORIG.	GOOD	FINE	N-MINT
☐ 0, (b&w mag;not comics) nn, filmbook	1.00	0.20	0.60	1.00

TOMMY AND THE MONSTERS
NEW COMICS

	ORIG.	GOOD	FINE	N-MINT
☐ 1, AAd(c) b&w		0.39	1.17	1.95

TOMOE
CRUSADE

	ORIG.	GOOD	FINE	N-MINT
☐ 0, Mar 96	2.95	0.59	1.77	2.95

	ORIG.	GOOD	FINE	N-MINT
☐ 0, Mar 96, alternate cover	2.95	0.59	1.77	2.95
☐ 1, Apr 96	2.95	0.59	1.77	2.95
☐ 2, May 96	2.95	0.59	1.77	2.95

TOMORROW KNIGHTS
EPIC

	ORIG.	GOOD	FINE	N-MINT
☐ 1	1.95	0.39	1.17	1.95
☐ 2	1.50	0.30	0.90	1.50
☐ 3	1.50	0.30	0.90	1.50
☐ 4	1.50	0.30	0.90	1.50
☐ 5	1.50	0.30	0.90	1.50
☐ 6	1.50	0.30	0.90	1.50

TOMORROW MAN
ANTARCTIC

	ORIG.	GOOD	FINE	N-MINT
☐ 1, Aug 93, foil cover, b&w	2.95	0.59	1.77	2.95

TOMORROW MAN & KNIGHT HUNTER: LAST RITES

	ORIG.	GOOD	FINE	N-MINT
☐ 1, Jul 94, b&w	2.75	0.55	1.65	2.75
☐ 2, Oct 94, b&w	2.75	0.55	1.65	2.75
☐ 3, Dec 94, b&w	2.75	0.55	1.65	2.75
☐ 4, Feb 95, b&w	2.75	0.55	1.65	2.75
☐ 5, Apr 95, b&w	2.75	0.55	1.65	2.75
☐ 6, Jun 95, b&w	2.75	0.55	1.65	2.75

TONY BRAVADO, TROUBLE-SHOOTER
RENEGADE

	ORIG.	GOOD	FINE	N-MINT
☐ 1, b&w		0.40	1.20	2.00
☐ 2, b&w (moves to Special Studio)		0.40	1.20	2.00

TONY BRAVADO: TROUBLE-SHOOTER
(was Renegade title)
SPECIAL STUDIO

	ORIG.	GOOD	FINE	N-MINT
☐ 3, b&w		0.50	1.50	2.50
☐ 4, b&w		0.50	1.50	2.50

TOO MUCH COFFEE MAN
ADHESIVE

	ORIG.	GOOD	FINE	N-MINT
☐ 1, b&w	2.50	1.50	4.50	7.50
☐ 2, b&w	2.50	1.00	3.00	5.00

TOOL & DIE
FLASHPOINT

	ORIG.	GOOD	FINE	N-MINT
☐ 1, Mar 94	2.50	0.50	1.50	2.50

TOP COW PRODUCTIONS INC./BALLISTIC STUDIOS SWIMSUIT SPECIAL
IMAGE

	ORIG.	GOOD	FINE	N-MINT
☐ 1, May 95	2.95	0.59	1.77	2.95

TOP DOG
STAR

	ORIG.	GOOD	FINE	N-MINT
☐ 1	0.65	0.13	0.39	0.65
☐ 2	0.65	0.13	0.39	0.65
☐ 3	0.65	0.13	0.39	0.65
☐ 4	0.65	0.13	0.39	0.65
☐ 5	0.65	0.13	0.39	0.65
☐ 6	0.65	0.13	0.39	0.65
☐ 7	0.75	0.15	0.45	0.75
☐ 8	0.75	0.15	0.45	0.75
☐ 9	0.75	0.15	0.45	0.75
☐ 10	0.75	0.15	0.45	0.75
☐ 11	0.75	0.15	0.45	0.75
☐ 12	0.75	0.15	0.45	0.75
☐ 13	0.75	0.15	0.45	0.75
☐ 14	1.00	0.20	0.60	1.00

TOP SHELF
PRIMAL GROOVE PRESS

	ORIG.	GOOD	FINE	N-MINT
☐ 1, Win 95, b&w anthology	5.00	1.00	3.00	5.00

TOPPS COMICS PRESENTS
TOPPS

	ORIG.	GOOD	FINE	N-MINT
☐ 1, 93, giveaway				

	ORIG.	GOOD	FINE	N-MINT

TOR
DC
	ORIG.	GOOD	FINE	N-MINT
1, Jun 75	0.25	0.30	0.90	1.50
2, Aug 75	0.25	0.25	0.75	1.25
3, Oct 75	0.25	0.25	0.75	1.25
4, Dec 75	0.25	0.25	0.75	1.25
5, Feb 76	0.25	0.25	0.75	1.25
6, Apr 76	0.25	0.25	0.75	1.25

TOR 3-D
ECLIPSE
	GOOD	FINE	N-MINT
1, JKu	0.30	0.90	1.50
2, JKu	0.30	0.90	1.50

TOR JOHNSON: HOLLYWOOD STAR
MONSTER
	GOOD	FINE	N-MINT
1, b&w	0.50	1.50	2.50

TOR LOVE BETTY
EROS COMIX
	GOOD	FINE	N-MINT
1, adult, b&w	0.55	1.65	2.75

TORCH OF LIBERTY SPECIAL
DARK HORSE
	ORIG.	GOOD	FINE	N-MINT
0, Jan 95, one-shot	2.50	0.50	1.50	2.50

TORCHY
INNOVATION
	GOOD	FINE	N-MINT
2, b&w reprints: Ward	0.50	1.50	2.50
3, b&w reprints: Ward	0.50	1.50	2.50
4, b&w reprints: Ward	0.50	1.50	2.50
5, b&w reprints: Ward	0.50	1.50	2.50
9, 1 Olivia(c), b&w reprints: Bill Ward	0.50	1.50	2.50

TORCHY SUMMER FUN SPECIAL
	GOOD	FINE	N-MINT
1, b&w reprints	0.50	1.50	2.50

TORG
ADVENTURE
	GOOD	FINE	N-MINT
1, b&w	0.50	1.50	2.50
2, b&w	0.50	1.50	2.50
3, b&w	0.50	1.50	2.50
4, b&w	0.50	1.50	2.50

TORMENT
AIRCEL
	GOOD	FINE	N-MINT
1, adult, b&w	0.59	1.77	2.95
2, adult, b&w	0.59	1.77	2.95
3, adult, b&w	0.59	1.77	2.95

TORPEDO
HARD BOILED
	ORIG.	GOOD	FINE	N-MINT
1, b&w reprint	2.95	0.59	1.77	2.95
2, b&w reprint	2.95	0.59	1.77	2.95
3, b&w reprint	2.95	0.59	1.77	2.95
4, b&w reprint	2.95	0.59	1.77	2.95

TORRID AFFAIRS
ETERNITY
	GOOD	FINE	N-MINT
1, b&w rep.	0.45	1.35	2.25
2, sexy cover	0.45	1.35	2.25
2, tame cover	0.45	1.35	2.25
3	0.59	1.77	2.95
4	0.59	1.77	2.95
5	0.59	1.77	2.95

TOTAL ECLIPSE
ECLIPSE
	ORIG.	GOOD	FINE	N-MINT
1, May 88, BSz(c) A:Airboy, Skywolf, Strike, Valkyrie, Sgt. Strike, Prowler, New Wave, Black Angel;V:Misery, Z	3.95	0.79	2.37	3.95
2, Aug 88, BSz(c) A:Airboy, Skywolf, Strike, Valkyrie, Sgt. Strike, Prowler, New Wave, Liberty Project, Miracle		0.79	2.37	3.95
3, Dec 88, BSz(c) A:Airboy, Beanish, Strike, Valkyrie, Sgt. Strike, Prowler, New Wave, Liberty Project		0.79	2.37	3.95
4, Jan 89, BSz(c) D:Strike! I:Dr. Eclipse A: Airboy, Beanish, Skywolf, Valkyrie, Sgt. Strike, Prowler, New Wave		0.79	2.37	3.95
5, Apr 89, BSz(c) A: Airboy, Beanish, Skywolf, Valkyrie, Sgt. Strike, Prowler, Heap, New Wave, Aztec Ace V:Mise		0.79	2.37	3.95

TOTAL ECLIPSE: THE SERAPHIM OBJECTIVE
	GOOD	FINE	N-MINT
1, Nov 88, Airboy, Heap, Liberty Project	0.39	1.17	1.95

TOTAL RECALL
DC
	GOOD	FINE	N-MINT
1, movie	0.59	1.77	2.95

TOTALLY ALIEN
TRIGON
	GOOD	FINE	N-MINT
1, b&w	0.50	1.50	2.50
2, b&w	0.50	1.50	2.50
3, b&w	0.50	1.50	2.50
4, b&w	0.50	1.50	2.50
5, b&w	0.50	1.50	2.50

TOTEM: SIGN OF THE WARDOG
ALPHA PRODUCTIONS
	GOOD	FINE	N-MINT
1, b&w	0.45	1.35	2.25
2, b&w	0.45	1.35	2.25

TOTEM: SIGN OF THE WARDOG (Volume 2)
	GOOD	FINE	N-MINT
1, b&w	0.50	1.50	2.50
2, b&w	0.50	1.50	2.50

TOUGH GUYS AND WILD WOMEN
ETERNITY
	GOOD	FINE	N-MINT
1, b&w Saint rep.	0.45	1.35	2.25
2, b&w Saint rep.	0.45	1.35	2.25

TOWER OF SHADOWS
MARVEL
	ORIG.	GOOD	FINE	N-MINT
1, Sep 69	0.15	0.80	2.40	4.00
2	0.15	0.60	1.80	3.00
3, Jan 70	0.15	0.60	1.80	3.00
4, Jan 70	0.15	0.60	1.80	3.00
5, May 70	0.15	0.40	1.20	2.00
6, Jul 70	0.15	0.40	1.20	2.00
7, Sep 70	0.15	0.40	1.20	2.00
8, Nov 70	0.15	0.40	1.20	2.00
9, Nov 70	0.15	0.40	1.20	2.00

TOXIC AVENGER
	ORIG.	GOOD	FINE	N-MINT
1, Apr 91, O:Toxic Avenger	1.50	0.30	0.90	1.50
2, May 91	1.50	0.30	0.90	1.50
3, Jun 91	1.50	0.30	0.90	1.50
4, Jul 91	1.50	0.30	0.90	1.50
5, Aug 91	1.50	0.30	0.90	1.50
6, Sep 91	1.50	0.30	0.90	1.50
7, Oct 91	1.50	0.30	0.90	1.50
8, Nov 91	1.50	0.30	0.90	1.50
9, Dec 91	1.50	0.30	0.90	1.50
10	1.50	0.30	0.90	1.50
11	1.50	0.30	0.90	1.50

TOXIC CRUSADERS
	ORIG.	GOOD	FINE	N-MINT
1	1.25	0.25	0.75	1.25
2	1.25	0.25	0.75	1.25
3	1.25	0.25	0.75	1.25
4	1.25	0.25	0.75	1.25
5	1.25	0.25	0.75	1.25
6	1.25	0.25	0.75	1.25
7	1.25	0.25	0.75	1.25
8	1.25	0.25	0.75	1.25

TOXIC!
APOCALYPSE
	GOOD	FINE	N-MINT
1, Marshal Law	0.50	1.50	2.50
2, Marshal Law	0.50	1.50	2.50
3, Marshal Law	0.50	1.50	2.50
4, Marshal Law	0.50	1.50	2.50
5, Marshal Law	0.50	1.50	2.50

	ORIG.	GOOD	FINE	N-MINT
❑ 6, Marshal Law		0.50	1.50	2.50
❑ 7, Marshal Law		0.50	1.50	2.50
❑ 8, Marshal Law		0.50	1.50	2.50
❑ 9, Marshal Law		0.50	1.50	2.50
❑ 10, Marshal Law		0.50	1.50	2.50
❑ 11, Marshal Law		0.50	1.50	2.50
❑ 12, Marshal Law		0.50	1.50	2.50
❑ 13, Marshal Law		0.50	1.50	2.50
❑ 14, Marshal Law		0.50	1.50	2.50
❑ 15, Marshal Law		0.50	1.50	2.50
❑ 16, Marshal Law		0.50	1.50	2.50
❑ 17, Marshal Law		0.50	1.50	2.50
❑ 18, Marshal Law		0.50	1.50	2.50
❑ 19, Marshal Law		0.50	1.50	2.50

TOYBOY
CONTINUITY

	ORIG.	GOOD	FINE	N-MINT
❑ 1, Oct 86, NA	2.00	0.40	1.20	2.00
❑ 2, Aug 87, NA	2.00	0.40	1.20	2.00
❑ 3, Nov 87, NA	2.00	0.40	1.20	2.00
❑ 4, Feb 88, NA	2.00	0.40	1.20	2.00
❑ 5, Jun 88, NA	2.00	0.40	1.20	2.00
❑ 6, NA	2.00	0.40	1.20	2.00
❑ 7, NA	2.00	0.40	1.20	2.00

TRACKER
BLACKTHORNE

	ORIG.	GOOD	FINE	N-MINT
❑ 1, b&w, WVH		0.40	1.20	2.00
❑ 2, b&w, WVH		0.40	1.20	2.00

TRAILER TRASH
TUNDRA

	ORIG.	GOOD	FINE	N-MINT
❑ 1, adult, b&w		0.40	1.20	2.00
❑ 4, b&w		0.59	1.77	2.95

TRANCERS
ETERNITY

	ORIG.	GOOD	FINE	N-MINT
❑ 1, movie, color		0.50	1.50	2.50
❑ 2, movie, color		0.50	1.50	2.50

TRANSFORMERS
MARVEL

	ORIG.	GOOD	FINE	N-MINT
❑ 1, Sep 84	0.75	0.80	2.40	4.00
❑ 2, Nov 84	0.75	0.60	1.80	3.00
❑ 3, Jan 85, SpM	0.75	0.40	1.20	2.00
❑ 4, Mar 85	0.75	0.40	1.20	2.00
❑ 5, Jun 85	0.75	0.40	1.20	2.00
❑ 6, Jul 85	0.75	0.40	1.20	2.00
❑ 7, Aug 85	0.75	0.40	1.20	2.00
❑ 8, Sep 85	0.75	0.40	1.20	2.00
❑ 9, Oct 85	0.75	0.40	1.20	2.00
❑ 10, Nov 85	0.75	0.40	1.20	2.00
❑ 11, Dec 85	0.75	0.30	0.90	1.50
❑ 12, Jan 86	0.75	0.30	0.90	1.50
❑ 13, Feb 86	0.75	0.30	0.90	1.50
❑ 14, Mar 86	0.75	0.30	0.90	1.50
❑ 15, Apr 86	0.75	0.20	0.60	1.00
❑ 16, May 86	0.75	0.20	0.60	1.00
❑ 17, Jun 86	0.75	0.20	0.60	1.00
❑ 18, Jul 86	0.75	0.20	0.60	1.00
❑ 19, Aug 86	0.75	0.20	0.60	1.00
❑ 20, Sep 86	0.75	0.20	0.60	1.00
❑ 21, Oct 86	0.75	0.20	0.60	1.00
❑ 22, Nov 86	0.75	0.20	0.60	1.00
❑ 23, Dec 86	0.75	0.20	0.60	1.00
❑ 24, Jan 87	0.75	0.20	0.60	1.00
❑ 25, Feb 87	0.75	0.20	0.60	1.00
❑ 26, Mar 87	0.75	0.20	0.60	1.00
❑ 27, Apr 87	0.75	0.20	0.60	1.00
❑ 28, May 87	1.00	0.20	0.60	1.00
❑ 29, Jun 87	1.00	0.20	0.60	1.00
❑ 30, Jul 87	1.00	0.20	0.60	1.00
❑ 31, Aug 87	1.00	0.20	0.60	1.00
❑ 32, Sep 87	1.00	0.20	0.60	1.00
❑ 33, Oct 87	1.00	0.20	0.60	1.00
❑ 34, Nov 87	1.00	0.20	0.60	1.00

	ORIG.	GOOD	FINE	N-MINT
❑ 35, Dec 87	1.00	0.20	0.60	1.00
❑ 36, Jan 88	1.00	0.20	0.60	1.00
❑ 37, Feb 88	1.00	0.20	0.60	1.00
❑ 38, Mar 88	1.00	0.20	0.60	1.00
❑ 39, Apr 88	1.00	0.20	0.60	1.00
❑ 40, May 88	1.00	0.20	0.60	1.00
❑ 41, Jun 88	1.00	0.20	0.60	1.00
❑ 42, Jul 88	1.00	0.20	0.60	1.00
❑ 43, Aug 88	1.00	0.20	0.60	1.00
❑ 44, Sep 88	1.00	0.20	0.60	1.00
❑ 45, Oct 88	1.00	0.20	0.60	1.00
❑ 46, Nov 88	1.00	0.20	0.60	1.00
❑ 47, Dec 88	1.00	0.20	0.60	1.00
❑ 48, Jan 89	1.00	0.20	0.60	1.00
❑ 49, Feb 89	1.00	0.20	0.60	1.00
❑ 50, Mar 89	1.50	0.30	0.90	1.50
❑ 51, Apr 89	1.00	0.20	0.60	1.00
❑ 52, May 89	1.00	0.20	0.60	1.00
❑ 53, Jun 89	1.00	0.20	0.60	1.00
❑ 54, Jul 89	1.00	0.20	0.60	1.00
❑ 55, Aug 89	1.00	0.20	0.60	1.00
❑ 56, Sep 89	1.00	0.20	0.60	1.00
❑ 57, Oct 89	1.00	0.20	0.60	1.00
❑ 58, Nov 89	1.00	0.20	0.60	1.00
❑ 59, Nov 89	1.00	0.20	0.60	1.00
❑ 60, Dec 89	1.00	0.20	0.60	1.00
❑ 61, Dec 89	1.00	0.20	0.60	1.00
❑ 62, Jan 90	1.00	0.20	0.60	1.00
❑ 63, Feb 90	1.00	0.20	0.60	1.00
❑ 64, Mar 90	1.00	0.20	0.60	1.00
❑ 65, Apr 90	1.00	0.20	0.60	1.00
❑ 66, May 90	1.00	0.20	0.60	1.00
❑ 67, Jun 90	1.00	0.20	0.60	1.00
❑ 69, Jul 90	1.00	0.20	0.60	1.00
❑ 69, Aug 90	1.00	0.20	0.60	1.00
❑ 70, Sep 90	1.00	0.20	0.60	1.00
❑ 71, Oct 90	1.00	0.20	0.60	1.00
❑ 72, Nov 90	1.00	0.20	0.60	1.00
❑ 73, Dec 90	1.00	0.20	0.60	1.00
❑ 74, Jan 91	1.00	0.20	0.60	1.00
❑ 75, Feb 91	1.50	0.30	0.90	1.50
❑ 76, Mar 91	1.00	0.20	0.60	1.00
❑ 77, Apr 91	1.00	0.20	0.60	1.00
❑ 78, May 91	1.00	0.20	0.60	1.00
❑ 79, Jun 91	1.00	0.20	0.60	1.00
❑ 80, Jul 91	1.00	0.20	0.60	1.00

TRANSFORMERS COMICS MAGAZINE

	ORIG.	GOOD	FINE	N-MINT
❑ 1, Jan 87, digest	1.50	0.30	0.90	1.50
❑ 2, Mar 87	1.50	0.30	0.90	1.50
❑ 3, May 87	1.50	0.30	0.90	1.50
❑ 4, Jul 87	1.50	0.30	0.90	1.50
❑ 5, Sep 87	1.50	0.30	0.90	1.50
❑ 6, Nov 87	1.50	0.30	0.90	1.50
❑ 7, Jan 88	1.50	0.30	0.90	1.50
❑ 8, Mar 88	1.50	0.30	0.90	1.50
❑ 9, May 88	1.50	0.30	0.90	1.50
❑ 10, Jul 88	1.50	0.30	0.90	1.50

TRANSFORMERS IN 3-D
BLACKTHORNE

	ORIG.	GOOD	FINE	N-MINT
❑ 1, 87		0.50	1.50	2.50
❑ 2, Dec 87		0.50	1.50	2.50
❑ 3, Apr 88		0.50	1.50	2.50

TRANSFORMERS MOVIE
MARVEL

	ORIG.	GOOD	FINE	N-MINT
❑ 1, Dec 86	0.75	0.20	0.60	1.00
❑ 2, Jan 87	0.75	0.20	0.60	1.00
❑ 3, Feb 87	0.75	0.20	0.60	1.00

TRANSFORMERS UNIVERSE

	ORIG.	GOOD	FINE	N-MINT
❑ 1, Dec 86	1.25	0.25	0.75	1.25
❑ 2, Jan 87	1.25	0.25	0.75	1.25
❑ 3, Feb 87	1.25	0.25	0.75	1.25
❑ 4, Mar 87	1.25	0.25	0.75	1.25

	ORIG.	GOOD	FINE	N-MINT

TRANSFORMERS: GENERATION 2

	ORIG.	GOOD	FINE	N-MINT
☐ 1, foil fold-out cover	2.95	0.59	1.77	2.95
☐ 1	1.75	0.35	1.05	1.75
☐ 2	1.75	0.35	1.05	1.75
☐ 3	1.75	0.35	1.05	1.75
☐ 4	1.75	0.35	1.05	1.75
☐ 5	1.75	0.35	1.05	1.75
☐ 6	1.75	0.35	1.05	1.75
☐ 7, May 94	1.75	0.35	1.05	1.75
☐ 8, Jun 94	1.75	0.35	1.05	1.75
☐ 9, Jul 94	1.75	0.35	1.05	1.75
☐ 10, Aug 94	1.75	0.35	1.05	1.75
☐ 11, Sep 94	1.75	0.35	1.05	1.75
☐ 12, Oct 94, final issue	2.25	0.45	1.35	2.25

TRANSFORMERS: HEADMASTERS, THE

	ORIG.	GOOD	FINE	N-MINT
☐ 1, Jul 87	1.00	0.20	0.60	1.00
☐ 2, Sep 87	1.00	0.20	0.60	1.00
☐ 3, Nov 87	1.00	0.20	0.60	1.00
☐ 4, Jan 88	0.75	0.15	0.45	0.75

TRANSIT
VORTEX

	GOOD	FINE	N-MINT
☐ 1	0.35	1.05	1.75
☐ 2	0.35	1.05	1.75
☐ 3	0.35	1.05	1.75
☐ 4	0.35	1.05	1.75
☐ 5	0.35	1.05	1.75

TRANSMUTATION OF IKE GARUDA, THE
EPIC

	ORIG.	GOOD	FINE	N-MINT
☐ 1	3.95	0.79	2.37	3.95
☐ 2	3.95	0.79	2.37	3.95

TRASH
FLEETWAY/QUALITY

	ORIG.	GOOD	FINE	N-MINT
☐ 1	2.95	0.59	1.77	2.95
☐ 2	2.95	0.59	1.77	2.95

TRAVELLER'S TALE, A
ANTARCTIC

	ORIG.	GOOD	FINE	N-MINT
☐ 1, b&w	2.50	0.50	1.50	2.50
☐ 2, Aug 92, b&w	2.50	0.50	1.50	2.50
☐ 3, Oct 92, b&w	2.50	0.50	1.50	2.50

TREK TEENS
PARODY PRESS

	ORIG.	GOOD	FINE	N-MINT
☐ 1, b&w, two different covers	2.50	0.50	1.50	2.50

TREKKER
DARK HORSE

	ORIG.	GOOD	FINE	N-MINT
☐ 1, May 87, b&w	1.50	0.30	0.90	1.50
☐ 2, Jul 87, b&w	1.50	0.30	0.90	1.50
☐ 3, Sep 87	1.75	0.35	1.05	1.75
☐ 4, Nov 87	1.75	0.35	1.05	1.75
☐ 5, Jan 88	1.75	0.35	1.05	1.75
☐ 6, Mar 88	1.50	0.35	1.05	1.75

TREKKER COLOR SPECIAL

	ORIG.	GOOD	FINE	N-MINT
☐ 1, 89	2.95	0.59	1.77	2.95

TRENCHER
IMAGE

	ORIG.	GOOD	FINE	N-MINT
☐ 1, KG	1.95	0.39	1.17	1.95
☐ 2, KG	1.95	0.39	1.17	1.95
☐ 3, Jul 93, KG	1.95	0.39	1.17	1.95
☐ 4, Oct 93, KG	1.95	0.39	1.17	1.95

TRENCHER X-MAS BITES HOLIDAY BLOW-OUT
BLACKBALL

	ORIG.	GOOD	FINE	N-MINT
☐ 1, Dec 93, KG	2.50	0.50	1.50	2.50

TREVOR - THE SAGA OF THE RED BOOTS
MCCLELLAN FALK

	ORIG.	GOOD	FINE	N-MINT
☐ 0, Dec 94, b&w tpb;collection of illustrated prose	8.99	1.80	5.39	8.99

TRIAD UNIVERSE
TRIAD

	ORIG.	GOOD	FINE	N-MINT
☐ 1, Jul 94	2.25	0.45	1.35	2.25
☐ 2, Aug 94, b&w	2.25	0.45	1.35	2.25

TRIAL RUN
MILLER

	ORIG.	GOOD	FINE	N-MINT
☐ 1, b&w		0.40	1.20	2.00
☐ 2, b&w		0.40	1.20	2.00
☐ 3, b&w		0.40	1.20	2.00
☐ 4, b&w		0.40	1.20	2.00
☐ 5, b&w		0.40	1.20	2.00
☐ 6, b&w		0.40	1.20	2.00
☐ 7, b&w		0.40	1.20	2.00
☐ 14		0.50	1.50	2.50
☐ 15		0.50	1.50	2.50

TRIARCH
CALIBER

	ORIG.	GOOD	FINE	N-MINT
☐ 1, b&w	2.50	0.40	1.20	2.00
☐ 2, b&w	2.50	0.40	1.20	2.00

TRIBE
IMAGE

	ORIG.	GOOD	FINE	N-MINT
☐ 1, Mar 93, foil cover	2.95	0.59	1.77	2.95
☐ 1, special edition		5.00	15.00	25.00

TRICKSTER KING MONKEY
EASTERN

	GOOD	FINE	N-MINT
☐ 1	0.35	1.05	1.75

TRIDENT
TRIDENT

	GOOD	FINE	N-MINT
☐ 1, b&w, adult	0.70	2.10	3.50
☐ 2, b&w, adult	0.70	2.10	3.50
☐ 3, b&w, adult	0.70	2.10	3.50
☐ 4, b&w, adult	0.70	2.10	3.50
☐ 5, b&w, adult	0.70	2.10	3.50
☐ 6, b&w, adult	0.70	2.10	3.50
☐ 7, b&w, adult	0.70	2.10	3.50
☐ 8, b&w, adult	0.70	2.10	3.50

TRIGGER TWINS
DC

	ORIG.	GOOD	FINE	N-MINT
☐ 1, Mar 73	0.20	0.04	0.12	0.20

TRINITY

	ORIG.	GOOD	FINE	N-MINT
☐ 1, foil cover,Green Lantern, L.E.G.I.O.N.,Darkstars	2.95	0.59	1.77	2.95
☐ 2, foil cover	2.95	0.59	1.77	2.95

TRIPLE-X (mini-series)
DARK HORSE

	ORIG.	GOOD	FINE	N-MINT
☐ 1, Dec 94, cardstock cover	3.95	0.79	2.37	3.95
☐ 2, Jan 95, cardstock cover	3.95	0.79	2.37	3.95
☐ 3, Feb 95, cardstock cover	3.95	0.79	2.37	3.95
☐ 4, Mar 95, cardstock cover	3.95	0.79	2.37	3.95
☐ 5, Apr 95, cardstock cover	3.95	0.79	2.37	3.95
☐ 7, Jul 95, cardstock cover;final issue;b&w	4.95	0.99	2.97	4.95

TRIUMPH (mini-series)
DC

	ORIG.	GOOD	FINE	N-MINT
☐ 1, Jun 95	1.75	0.35	1.05	1.75
☐ 2, Jul 95	1.75	0.35	1.05	1.75
☐ 3, Aug 95	1.75	0.35	1.05	1.75
☐ 4, Sep 95	1.75	0.35	1.05	1.75

TRIUMPHANT UNLEASHED!
TRIUMPHANT

	ORIG.	GOOD	FINE	N-MINT
☐ 0, free;Unleashed Prologue	1.00	3.00	5.00	
☐ 0, Unleashed Prologue	2.50	0.50	1.50	2.50
☐ 0, Unleashed Prologue;red logo;no cover price;mail-away version				

TROLL
IMAGE

	ORIG.	GOOD	FINE	N-MINT
☐ 1	2.50	0.60	1.80	3.00

	ORIG.	GOOD	FINE	N-MINT
TROLL II				
❏ 1, Jul 94	3.95	0.79	2.37	3.95
TROLL PATROL				
HARVEY				
❏ 1		0.39	1.17	1.95
TROLL: HALLOWEEN SPECIAL				
IMAGE				
❏ 1, Oct 94, A: The Maxx...	2.95	0.59	1.77	2.95
TROLL: ONCE A HERO				
❏ 1, Aug 94	2.50	0.50	1.50	2.50
TROLLORDS				
COMICO				
❏ 1		0.39	1.17	1.95
❏ 2		0.39	1.17	1.95
❏ 3		0.39	1.17	1.95
❏ 4		0.39	1.17	1.95
TRU STUDIOS				
❏ 1, b&w		1.60	4.80	8.00
❏ 1, 2nd printing		0.40	1.20	2.00
❏ 2		0.40	1.20	2.00
❏ 3		0.40	1.20	2.00
❏ 4		0.30	0.90	1.50
❏ 5		0.30	0.90	1.50
❏ 6		0.30	0.90	1.50
❏ 7		0.30	0.90	1.50
❏ 8		0.30	0.90	1.50
❏ 9		0.30	0.90	1.50
❏ 10		0.30	0.90	1.50
❏ 11		0.30	0.90	1.50
❏ 12		0.30	0.90	1.50
❏ 13		0.30	0.90	1.50
❏ 14		0.30	0.90	1.50
❏ 15		0.30	0.90	1.50
TROLLORDS SPECIAL				
❏ 1, color		0.35	1.05	1.75
TROLLORDS: DEATH AND KISSES				
APPLE				
❏ 1, b&w		0.45	1.35	2.25
❏ 2, b&w		0.45	1.35	2.25
❏ 3, b&w		0.45	1.35	2.25
❏ 4, b&w		0.45	1.35	2.25
❏ 5, b&w		0.45	1.35	2.25
❏ 6		0.50	1.50	2.50
TROMBONE				
KNOCKABOUT				
❏ 1, adult		0.50	1.50	2.50
TROPO				
BLACKBIRD				
❏ 1, b&w		0.55	1.65	2.75
❏ 2, b&w		0.55	1.65	2.75
❏ 3, b&w		0.55	1.65	2.75
❏ 4, b&w		0.55	1.65	2.75
❏ 5, b&w		0.55	1.65	2.75
TROUBLE WITH GIRLS				
COMICO				
❏ 1		0.39	1.17	1.95
❏ 2		0.39	1.17	1.95
❏ 3		0.39	1.17	1.95
❏ 4		0.39	1.17	1.95
EPIC				
❏ 1, embossed cover	2.50	0.50	1.50	2.50
❏ 2	1.95	0.39	1.17	1.95
❏ 3	1.95	0.39	1.17	1.95
❏ 4	1.95	0.39	1.17	1.95
MALIBU				
❏ 1, Aug 87, b&w	1.95	1.00	3.00	5.00
❏ 2		0.60	1.80	3.00
❏ 3		0.60	1.80	3.00
❏ 4		0.60	1.80	3.00
❏ 5		0.39	1.17	1.95
❏ 6, (becomes Eternity title)		0.39	1.17	1.95

	ORIG.	GOOD	FINE	N-MINT
TROUBLE WITH GIRLS (was Comico title)				
ETERNITY				
❏ 5, b&w		0.39	1.17	1.95
❏ 6, b&w		0.39	1.17	1.95
❏ 7, b&w		0.39	1.17	1.95
❏ 8, b&w		0.39	1.17	1.95
❏ 9, b&w		0.39	1.17	1.95
❏ 10, b&w		0.39	1.17	1.95
❏ 11, b&w		0.39	1.17	1.95
❏ 12, b&w		0.39	1.17	1.95
❏ 13, b&w		0.39	1.17	1.95
❏ 14, b&w		0.39	1.17	1.95
❏ 15, b&w		0.39	1.17	1.95
❏ 16		0.45	1.35	2.25
❏ 17		0.45	1.35	2.25
❏ 18		0.45	1.35	2.25
❏ 19		0.45	1.35	2.25
❏ 20		0.45	1.35	2.25
❏ 21		0.45	1.35	2.25
❏ 22		0.45	1.35	2.25
❏ 23		0.45	1.35	2.25
TROUBLE WITH GIRLS (was Malibu title)				
❏ 7, b&w		0.39	1.17	1.95
❏ 8, b&w		0.39	1.17	1.95
❏ 9, b&w		0.39	1.17	1.95
❏ 10, b&w		0.39	1.17	1.95
❏ 11, b&w		0.39	1.17	1.95
❏ 12, b&w		0.39	1.17	1.95
❏ 13, b&w		0.39	1.17	1.95
❏ 14, b&w (becomes Comico title)		0.39	1.17	1.95
TROUBLE WITH GIRLS ANNUAL				
❏ 1, b&w		0.59	1.77	2.95
TROUBLE WITH GIRLS CHRISTMAS SPECIAL				
❏ 1, b&w		0.59	1.77	2.95
TROUBLE WITH TIGERS				
ANTARCTIC				
❏ 1, Jan 92, b&w	2.50	0.50	1.50	2.50
❏ 2, Feb 92, b&w	2.50	0.50	1.50	2.50
TROUBLEMAN				
IMAGE/MOTOWN				
❏ 2, Jul 96	2.25	0.45	1.35	2.25
TROUBLESHOOTERS INC.				
NIGHTWOLF GRAPHICS				
❏ 1, Win 95, b&w	2.50	0.50	1.50	2.50
❏ 2, Spr 95, b&w	2.50	0.50	1.50	2.50
TRUE CONFUSIONS				
FANTAGRAPHICS				
❏ 1, b&w		0.50	1.50	2.50
TRUE CRIME COMICS SPECIAL				
ECLIPSE				
❏ 1, b&w	2.95	0.59	1.77	2.95
❏ 2, b&w	2.95	0.59	1.77	2.95
TRUE LOVE				
❏ 1, DSt(c)		0.60	1.80	3.00
❏ 2		0.30	0.90	1.50
TRUE NORTH, THE				
COMIC LEGENDS DEFENSE FUND				
❏ 0, 88, nn;b&w;benefit comic;cardstock cover				
	3.50	1.00	3.00	5.00
❏ 0, 91, nn;II;cardstock foldout cover				
	4.50	0.90	2.70	4.50
TRUE SWAMP				
PERISTALTIC PRESS				
❏ 1, b&w	2.50	0.50	1.50	2.50
TRUFAN ADVENTURES THEATRE				
PARAGRAPHICS				
❏ 1		0.60	1.80	3.00
❏ 2, 3-D		0.40	1.20	2.00

	ORIG.	GOOD	FINE	N-MINT

TRULY TASTELESS AND TACKY
CALIBER

	ORIG.	GOOD	FINE	N-MINT
❑ 1, b&w 2.50		0.50	1.50	2.50

TRYPTO THE ACID DOG
RENEGADE

	ORIG.	GOOD	FINE	N-MINT
❑ 1, 88, b&w 2.00		0.40	1.20	2.00

TSC JAMS
TSC

	ORIG.	GOOD	FINE	N-MINT
❑ 0, 94 .... 3.95		0.79	2.37	3.95

TSR WORLDS ANNUAL
DC

	GOOD	FINE	N-MINT
❑ 1	0.79	2.37	3.95

TUG & BUSTER
ART & SOUL

	GOOD	FINE	N-MINT
❑ 1, Nov 95, b&w 2.95	0.59	1.77	2.95

TUROK THE HUNTED (mini-series)
ACCLAIM/VALIANT

	GOOD	FINE	N-MINT
❑ 1, Mar 96 .... 2.50	0.50	1.50	2.50
❑ 2, Mar 96 .... 2.50	0.50	1.50	2.50

TUROK YEARBOOK
VALIANT

	GOOD	FINE	N-MINT
❑ 1, 94 .... 3.95	0.79	2.37	3.95

TUROK, DINOSAUR HUNTER
ACCLAIM/VALIANT

	GOOD	FINE	N-MINT
❑ 0, Nov 95, ro:Turok, Andar, Lost Land			
.... 2.50	0.50	1.50	2.50
❑ 24, Jun 95, TT 2.50	0.50	1.50	2.50
❑ 25, Jul 95, TT 2.50	0.50	1.50	2.50
❑ 26, Jul 95, TT 2.50	0.50	1.50	2.50
❑ 27, Aug 95, TT 2.50	0.50	1.50	2.50
❑ 28, Aug 95 .... 2.50	0.50	1.50	2.50
❑ 29, Sep 95 .... 2.50	0.50	1.50	2.50
❑ 30, Sep 95 .... 2.50	0.50	1.50	2.50
❑ 31, Oct 95, TT,PG 2.50	0.50	1.50	2.50
❑ 32, Oct 95, TT,PG 2.50	0.50	1.50	2.50
❑ 34, Nov 95 .... 2.50	0.50	1.50	2.50
❑ 35, Dec 95 .... 2.50	0.50	1.50	2.50
❑ 36, Dec 95 .... 2.50	0.50	1.50	2.50
❑ 37, Jan 96, TT 2.50	0.50	1.50	2.50
❑ 38, Jan 96, TT 2.50	0.50	1.50	2.50
❑ 39, Feb 96 .... 2.50	0.50	1.50	2.50
❑ 40, Mar 96 .... 2.50	0.50	1.50	2.50
❑ 41, Apr 96 .... 2.50	0.50	1.50	2.50
❑ 42, Apr 96 .... 2.50	0.50	1.50	2.50
❑ 43, May 96 .... 2.50	0.50	1.50	2.50
❑ 45, Jun 96 .... 2.50	0.50	1.50	2.50
❑ 46, Jul 96 .... 2.50	0.50	1.50	2.50
❑ 47, Aug 96 .... 2.50	0.50	1.50	2.50

VALIANT

	GOOD	FINE	N-MINT
❑ 1, Jul 93, chromium cover			
.... 3.50	0.70	2.10	3.50
❑ 1, Gold edition	4.40	13.20	22.00
❑ 2, Aug 93 .... 2.50	0.50	1.50	2.50
❑ 3, Sep 93 .... 2.50	0.50	1.50	2.50
❑ 4, Oct 93 .... 2.50	0.50	1.50	2.50
❑ 5, Nov 93 .... 2.50	0.50	1.50	2.50
❑ 6, Dec 93 .... 2.50	0.50	1.50	2.50
❑ 7, Jan 94, TT 2.50	0.50	1.50	2.50
❑ 8, Feb 94, TT 2.50	0.50	1.50	2.50
❑ 9, Mar 94 .... 2.50	0.50	1.50	2.50
❑ 10, Apr 94 .... 2.50	0.50	1.50	2.50
❑ 11, May 94, trading card			
.... 2.50	0.50	1.50	2.50
❑ 12, Jun 94 .... 2.50	0.50	1.50	2.50
❑ 13, Aug 94, Captain Red 2.50	0.50	1.50	2.50
❑ 14, Sep 94, Captain Red. 2.50	0.50	1.50	2.50
❑ 15, Oct 94 .... 2.50	0.50	1.50	2.50
❑ 16, Oct 94, Chaos Effect. 2.50	0.50	1.50	2.50
❑ 17, Nov 94 .... 2.50	0.50	1.50	2.50
❑ 22, Apr 95 .... 2.50	0.50	1.50	2.50
❑ 23, May 95 .... 2.50	0.50	1.50	2.50

TURTLE SOUP (1991)
MIRAGE

	ORIG.	GOOD	FINE	N-MINT
❑ 1, color		0.50	1.50	2.50
❑ 2, color		0.50	1.50	2.50
❑ 3, color		0.50	1.50	2.50

TWICE-TOLD TALES
OF UNSUPERVISED EXISTENCE
RIP OFF

	GOOD	FINE	N-MINT
❑ 1, Apr 89, b&w 2.00	0.40	1.20	2.00

TWILIGHT (mini-series)
DC

	GOOD	FINE	N-MINT
❑ 1, 91, prestige format 4.95	0.99	2.97	4.95
❑ 2, 91, prestige format 4.95	0.99	2.97	4.95
❑ 3, 91, prestige format 4.95	0.99	2.97	4.95

TWILIGHT AVENGER
ELITE

	GOOD	FINE	N-MINT
❑ 1, Jul 86	0.35	1.05	1.75
❑ 2, Oct 86	0.35	1.05	1.75

TWILIGHT AVENGER, THE
ETERNITY

	GOOD	FINE	N-MINT
❑ 1, Jul 88, b&w	0.39	1.17	1.95
❑ 2, Aug 88, b&w	0.39	1.17	1.95
❑ 3, Sep 88, b&w	0.39	1.17	1.95
❑ 4, Nov 88, b&w	0.39	1.17	1.95
❑ 5, Feb 89, b&w	0.39	1.17	1.95
❑ 6, May 89, b&w	0.39	1.17	1.95
❑ 7, Aug 89, b&w	0.39	1.17	1.95
❑ 8, Feb 90, b&w	0.39	1.17	1.95

TWILIGHT MAN
FIRST

	GOOD	FINE	N-MINT
❑ 1, Jun 89	0.55	1.65	2.75
❑ 2, Jul 89	0.55	1.65	2.75
❑ 3, Aug 89	0.55	1.65	2.75
❑ 4, Sep 89	0.55	1.65	2.75

TWILIGHT PEOPLE
CALIBER

	ORIG.	GOOD	FINE	N-MINT
❑ 1, b&w 2.95		0.59	1.77	2.95
❑ 2, b&w 2.95		0.59	1.77	2.95

TWILIGHT X
PORK CHOP PRESS

❑ 1, b&w			
❑ 2, b&w			
❑ 3, b&w			

TWILIGHT X (VOL. 2)
ANTARCTIC

	ORIG.	GOOD	FINE	N-MINT
❑ 1, b&w 2.50		0.50	1.50	2.50
❑ 2, b&w 2.50		0.50	1.50	2.50
❑ 3, b&w 2.50		0.50	1.50	2.50
❑ 4, Sep 93, b&w 2.50		0.50	1.50	2.50
❑ 5, Feb 94, b&w 2.75		0.55	1.65	2.75

TWILIGHT X QUARTERLY

	ORIG.	GOOD	FINE	N-MINT
❑ 1, Sep 94, b&w 2.95		0.59	1.77	2.95
❑ 2, Nov 94, b&w 2.95		0.59	1.77	2.95
❑ 3, Feb 95, b&w 2.95		0.59	1.77	2.95

TWILIGHT ZONE 1993 ANNUAL
NOW

	ORIG.	GOOD	FINE	N-MINT
❑ 1, Apr 93 .... 2.50		0.50	1.50	2.50

TWILIGHT ZONE 3-D SPECIAL, THE

	ORIG.	GOOD	FINE	N-MINT
❑ 1, Apr 93, glasses 2.95		0.59	1.77	2.95

TWILIGHT ZONE SCIENCE FICTION SPECIAL

	ORIG.	GOOD	FINE	N-MINT
❑ 1, Mar 93, hologram button				
.... 3.50		0.70	2.10	3.50

TWILIGHT ZONE, THE

	ORIG.	GOOD	FINE	N-MINT
❑ 1, Nov 90, BSz(c), NA, HE				
.... 2.95		1.00	3.00	5.00

	ORIG.	GOOD	FINE	N-MINT
❏ 1, Oct 91, collector's edition, gold cover, polybagged, NA, HE ... 2.50	2.00	6.00	10.00
❏ 1, Oct 91, squarebound, prestige ed., NA, HE 4.95	0.99	2.97	4.95

TWILIGHT ZONE, THE (Volume 2)

	ORIG.	GOOD	FINE	N-MINT
❏ 1, Nov 91, (two covers)	1.95	0.39	1.17	1.95
❏ 2, Dec 91	1.95	0.39	1.17	1.95
❏ 3, Jan 92	1.95	0.39	1.17	1.95
❏ 4, Feb 92	1.95	0.39	1.17	1.95
❏ 5, Mar 92	1.95	0.39	1.17	1.95
❏ 6, Apr 92	1.95	0.39	1.17	1.95
❏ 7, May 92	1.95	0.39	1.17	1.95
❏ 8, Jun 92	1.95	0.39	1.17	1.95
❏ 9, Jul 92, Prestige, 3-D, with glasses, hologram 4.95	0.99	2.97	4.95
❏ 9, Jul 92, bagged, 3-D, hologram 2.95	0.59	1.77	2.95
❏ 10, Aug 92	1.95	0.39	1.17	1.95
❏ 11, Sep 92	1.95	0.39	1.17	1.95

TWILIGHT ZONE, THE (Volume 3)

	ORIG.	GOOD	FINE	N-MINT
❏ 1, May 93	2.50	0.50	1.50	2.50
❏ 2, Jun 93, computer special, 2 diff. covers	2.50	0.50	1.50	2.50
❏ 3, Jul 93	2.50	0.50	1.50	2.50
❏ 4, Aug 93	2.50	0.50	1.50	2.50

TWILIGHT-X: INTERLUDE
ANTARCTIC

	ORIG.	GOOD	FINE	N-MINT
❏ 1, Jul 92, b&w	2.50	0.50	1.50	2.50
❏ 2, Sep 92, b&w	2.50	0.50	1.50	2.50
❏ 3, Nov 92, b&w	2.50	0.50	1.50	2.50
❏ 4, Jan 93, b&w	2.50	0.50	1.50	2.50
❏ 5, Mar 93, b&w	2.50	0.50	1.50	2.50
❏ 6, May 93, b&w	2.50	0.50	1.50	2.50

TWILIGHT-X: INTERLUDE (Volume 2)

	ORIG.	GOOD	FINE	N-MINT
❏ 1, Jun 93, b&w	2.50	0.50	1.50	2.50
❏ 2, Jul 93, b&w	2.50	0.50	1.50	2.50
❏ 3, Aug 93, b&w	2.50	0.50	1.50	2.50
❏ 4, Sep 93, b&w	2.50	0.50	1.50	2.50
❏ 5, Oct 93, b&w	2.75	0.55	1.65	2.75

TWIN EARTHS
R.SUSOR

	GOOD	FINE	N-MINT
❏ 1, b&w strip reprints	1.19	3.57	5.95
❏ 2, b&w strip reprints	1.19	3.57	5.95

TWIST
KITCHEN SINK

	GOOD	FINE	N-MINT
❏ 1, BW,b&w	0.40	1.20	2.00
❏ 2	0.40	1.20	2.00
❏ 3	0.40	1.20	2.00

TWISTED
ALCHEMY

	GOOD	FINE	N-MINT
❏ 1, b&w	0.79	2.37	3.95

TWISTED 3-D TALES
BLACKTHORNE

	GOOD	FINE	N-MINT
❏ 1	0.50	1.50	2.50

TWISTED SISTERS COMICS
KITCHEN SINK

	ORIG.	GOOD	FINE	N-MINT
❏ 1, 94, b&w	3.50	0.70	2.10	3.50

TWISTED TALES
PACIFIC

	ORIG.	GOOD	FINE	N-MINT
❏ 1, Nov 82	1.50	0.30	0.90	1.50
❏ 2, Apr 83	1.50	0.30	0.90	1.50
❏ 3, Jun 83	1.50	0.30	0.90	1.50
❏ 4	1.50	0.30	0.90	1.50
❏ 5	1.50	0.30	0.90	1.50
❏ 6	1.50	0.30	0.90	1.50
❏ 7	1.50	0.30	0.90	1.50
❏ 8, (moves to Eclipse)	1.50	0.30	0.90	1.50

TWISTED TALES (former Pacific title)
ECLIPSE

	GOOD	FINE	N-MINT
❏ 9	0.30	0.90	1.50
❏ 10	0.30	0.90	1.50

TWISTED TALES OF BRUCE JONES

	GOOD	FINE	N-MINT
❏ 1	0.30	0.90	1.50
❏ 2	0.30	0.90	1.50
❏ 3	0.30	0.90	1.50
❏ 4	0.30	0.90	1.50

TWISTED TANTRUMS OF THE PURPLE SNIT
BLACKTHORNE

	GOOD	FINE	N-MINT
❏ 1	0.35	1.05	1.75
❏ 2	0.35	1.05	1.75

TWISTER
HARRIS

	ORIG.	GOOD	FINE	N-MINT
❏ 1, 93, trading card	2.95	0.59	1.77	2.95

TWO HOT GIRLS ON A HOT SUMMER NIGHT
EROS COMIX

	GOOD	FINE	N-MINT
❏ 1, adult, b&w	0.45	1.35	2.25
❏ 2, adult, b&w	0.45	1.35	2.25
❏ 3, adult, b&w	0.45	1.35	2.25
❏ 4, adult, b&w	0.45	1.35	2.25

TWO-FISTED TALES
EC/GEMSTONE

	ORIG.	GOOD	FINE	N-MINT
❏ 1, Oct 92, reprints;HK;AF;WW;JCr 2.00	0.40	1.20	2.00
❏ 2, JS/WE,HK, JC,WW reprints 1.50	0.30	0.90	1.50
❏ 3, HK,WW,JD, JS/WE reprints 1.50	0.30	0.90	1.50
❏ 4, Jul 93, HK,WW,Jack Davis, JS,WE reprints 2.00	0.40	1.20	2.00
❏ 5, HK,JD,AT,WW, S&E reprints 2.00	0.40	1.20	2.00
❏ 6, HK,JD,WW, JS/BE reprints 2.00	0.40	1.20	2.00
❏ 7, HK,JD,WW, JS/WE reprints 2.00	0.40	1.20	2.00
❏ 8, reprints	2.00	0.40	1.20	2.00
❏ 9, reprints	2.00	0.40	1.20	2.00
❏ 10, reprints	2.00	0.40	1.20	2.00
❏ 11, reprints	2.00	0.40	1.20	2.00
❏ 12, reprints	2.00	0.40	1.20	2.00
❏ 13, reprints	2.00	0.40	1.20	2.00

TYPHOID (mini-series)
MARVEL

	ORIG.	GOOD	FINE	N-MINT
❏ 1, Nov 95, wraparound cardstock cover 3.95	0.79	2.37	3.95
❏ 2, Dec 95, wraparound cardstock cover 3.95	0.79	2.37	3.95
❏ 3, Jan 96, wraparound cardstock cover 3.95	0.79	2.37	3.95
❏ 4, Feb 96, wraparound cardstock cover 3.95	0.79	2.37	3.95

TYRANNOSAURUS TEX
MONSTER

	GOOD	FINE	N-MINT
❏ 1, b&w	0.50	1.50	2.50
❏ 2, b&w	0.50	1.50	2.50

U

	ORIG.	GOOD	FINE	N-MINT

U.N. FORCE
GAUNTLET

	ORIG.	GOOD	FINE	N-MINT
❏ 1, color	2.95	0.59	1.77	2.95
❏ 2, color	2.95	0.59	1.77	2.95
❏ 3, color	2.95	0.59	1.77	2.95
❏ 4, color	2.95	0.59	1.77	2.95
❏ 5, color	2.95	0.59	1.77	2.95

U.S. 1
MARVEL

	ORIG.	GOOD	FINE	N-MINT
❏ 1, May 83, HT, origin	0.60	0.40	1.20	2.00
❏ 2, Jun 83, HT	0.60	0.20	0.60	1.00
❏ 3, Jul 83, FS	0.60	0.20	0.60	1.00
❏ 4, Aug 83, FS	0.60	0.20	0.60	1.00
❏ 5, Sep 83, FS	0.60	0.20	0.60	1.00
❏ 6, Oct 83, FS	0.60	0.20	0.60	1.00
❏ 7, Dec 83, FS	0.60	0.20	0.60	1.00
❏ 8, Feb 84, FS	0.60	0.20	0.60	1.00
❏ 9, Apr 84	0.60	0.20	0.60	1.00
❏ 10, Jun 84, FS	0.60	0.20	0.60	1.00
❏ 11, Aug 84, FS	0.60	0.20	0.60	1.00
❏ 12, Oct 84, SD	0.60	0.20	0.60	1.00

U.S.AGENT

	ORIG.	GOOD	FINE	N-MINT
❏ 1	1.75	0.35	1.05	1.75
❏ 2	1.75	0.35	1.05	1.75
❏ 3	1.75	0.35	1.05	1.75
❏ 4	1.75	0.35	1.05	1.75

ULTRA KLUTZ
ONWARD

	GOOD	FINE	N-MINT
❏ 1	1.00	3.00	5.00
❏ 2	0.60	1.80	3.00
❏ 3	0.50	1.50	2.50
❏ 4	0.50	1.50	2.50
❏ 5	0.50	1.50	2.50
❏ 6	0.50	1.50	2.50
❏ 7	0.50	1.50	2.50
❏ 8	0.50	1.50	2.50
❏ 9	0.50	1.50	2.50
❏ 10	0.50	1.50	2.50
❏ 11	0.50	1.50	2.50
❏ 12	0.50	1.50	2.50
❏ 13	0.50	1.50	2.50
❏ 14	0.50	1.50	2.50
❏ 15	0.50	1.50	2.50
❏ 16	0.30	0.90	1.50
❏ 17	0.30	0.90	1.50
❏ 18	0.35	1.05	1.75
❏ 19	0.35	1.05	1.75
❏ 20	0.35	1.05	1.75
❏ 21	0.35	1.05	1.75
❏ 22	0.35	1.05	1.75
❏ 23	0.40	1.20	2.00
❏ 24	0.40	1.20	2.00
❏ 25	0.40	1.20	2.00
❏ 26	0.40	1.20	2.00
❏ 27	0.40	1.20	2.00
❏ 28	0.40	1.20	2.00
❏ 29	0.40	1.20	2.00
❏ 30	0.40	1.20	2.00
❏ 31	0.40	1.20	2.00

ULTRA KLUTZ '81

	GOOD	FINE	N-MINT
❏ 1	0.30	0.90	1.50

ULTRA MONTHLY
MALIBU

	ORIG.	GOOD	FINE	N-MINT
❏ 1, actually giveaway	0.50	0.10	0.30	0.50
❏ 2, actually giveaway	0.50	0.10	0.30	0.50
❏ 3, actually giveaway	0.50	0.10	0.30	0.50
❏ 4	0.50	0.10	0.30	0.50
❏ 5	0.50	0.10	0.30	0.50
❏ 6	0.50	0.10	0.30	0.50

ULTRAFORCE
MALIBU/ULTRAVERSE

	ORIG.	GOOD	FINE	N-MINT
❏ 0, Sep 94	2.50	0.50	1.50	2.50
❏ 1, Aug 94	2.50	0.50	1.50	2.50
❏ 2, Oct 94	1.95	0.39	1.17	1.95

ULTRAFORCE (Vol. 2)

	ORIG.	GOOD	FINE	N-MINT
❏ 0, Sep 95, Infinity;alternate cover;"Black September"				
	1.50	0.70	2.10	3.50
❏ 0, Sep 95, Infinity;"Black September"				
	1.50	0.30	0.90	1.50
❏ 1, Oct 95	1.50	0.30	0.90	1.50
❏ 2, Nov 95, contains reprint of *UltraForce* #1;flipbook with "The Phoenix Resurrection" Pt. 7				
	1.50	0.30	0.90	1.50
❏ 3, Dec 95	1.50	0.30	0.90	1.50
❏ 4, Jan 96	1.50	0.30	0.90	1.50
❏ 5, Feb 96	1.50	0.30	0.90	1.50
❏ 6, Mar 96	1.50	0.30	0.90	1.50

ULTRAFORCE/SPIDER-MAN

	ORIG.	GOOD	FINE	N-MINT
❏ 1, Jan 96, alternate covers denoted by "1A" and "1B"				
	3.95	0.79	2.37	3.95

ULTRAMAN
HARVEY/ULTRACOMICS

	ORIG.	GOOD	FINE	N-MINT
❏ 1, newsstand, O:Ultraman				
	1.75	0.35	1.05	1.75
❏ 1, no type on cover, trading card				
	2.50	0.70	2.10	3.50
❏ 1	2.25	0.45	1.35	2.25
❏ 2, newsstand	1.75	0.35	1.05	1.75
❏ 2, direct sale, no cover type, trading card				
	2.50	0.50	1.50	2.50
❏ 3, newsstand	1.75	0.35	1.05	1.75
❏ 3, trading cards	2.50	0.50	1.50	2.50

NEMESIS

	ORIG.	GOOD	FINE	N-MINT
❏ 1	1.75	0.35	1.05	1.75
❏ 2	1.75	0.35	1.05	1.75
❏ 3, Aug 94	1.95	0.39	1.17	1.95
❏ 4, Sep 94	1.95	0.39	1.17	1.95

ULTRAMAN CLASSIC:
BATTLE OF THE ULTRA-BROTHERS
VIZ

	ORIG.	GOOD	FINE	N-MINT
❏ 1, b&w	4.95	0.99	2.97	4.95
❏ 2, b&w	4.95	0.99	2.97	4.95
❏ 3, 94, b&w	4.95	0.99	2.97	4.95
❏ 4, 94, b&w	4.95	0.99	2.97	4.95
❏ 5, 94, b&w	4.95	0.99	2.97	4.95

ULTRAVERSE ORIGINS
MALIBU

	ORIG.	GOOD	FINE	N-MINT
❏ 1, Jan 94	0.99	0.20	0.59	0.99

ULTRAVERSE YEAR ONE
MALIBU/ULTRAVERSE

	ORIG.	GOOD	FINE	N-MINT
❏ 1, Sep 94	4.95	0.99	2.97	4.95

UNCANNY X-MEN '95
MARVEL

	ORIG.	GOOD	FINE	N-MINT
❏ 1, Nov 95, wraparound cover				
	3.95	0.79	2.37	3.95

UNCANNY X-MEN (formerly X-Men)

	ORIG.	GOOD	FINE	N-MINT
❏ 142, Feb 81, JBy/TA	0.50	4.80	14.40	24.00
❏ 143, Mar 81, JBy/TA	0.50	2.00	6.00	10.00
❏ 144, Apr 81, BA	0.50	2.00	6.00	10.00
❏ 145, May 81	0.50	2.00	6.00	10.00
❏ 146, Jun 81	0.50	2.00	6.00	10.00
❏ 147, Jul 81	0.50	2.00	6.00	10.00
❏ 148, Aug 81	0.50	2.00	6.00	10.00
❏ 149, Sep 81	0.50	2.00	6.00	10.00
❏ 150, Oct 81, V:Magneto	0.75	2.00	6.00	10.00
❏ 151, Nov 81	0.50	1.60	4.80	8.00
❏ 152, Dec 81	0.50	1.60	4.80	8.00

	ORIG.	GOOD	FINE	N-MINT
153, Jan 82	0.60	1.60	4.80	8.00
154, Feb 82	0.60	1.60	4.80	8.00
155, Mar 82	0.60	1.60	4.80	8.00
156, Apr 82, DC	0.60	1.60	4.80	8.00
157, May 82, DC;Phoenix				
	0.60	1.60	4.80	8.00
158, Jun 82, DC;Rogue	0.60	1.60	4.80	8.00
159, Jul 82, BSz, A:Dracula				
	0.60	1.60	4.80	8.00
160, Aug 82	0.60	1.60	4.80	8.00
161, Sep 82	0.60	1.60	4.80	8.00
162, Oct 82	0.60	2.80	8.40	14.00
163, Nov 82	0.60	1.40	4.20	7.00
164, Dec 82, DC, I:Binary				
	0.60	1.40	4.20	7.00
165, Jan 83	0.60	1.40	4.20	7.00
166, Feb 83, PS	1.00	1.40	4.20	7.00
167, Mar 83, PS	0.60	1.40	4.20	7.00
168, Apr 83, PS	0.60	1.40	4.20	7.00
169, May 83, PS;1:Morlocks				
	0.60	1.40	4.20	7.00
170, Jun 83	0.60	1.40	4.20	7.00
171, Jul 83, J:Rogue	0.60	2.00	6.00	10.00
172, Aug 83	0.60	1.60	4.80	8.00
173, Sep 83	0.60	1.20	3.60	6.00
174, Oct 83	0.60	1.20	3.60	6.00
175, Nov 83	1.00	1.20	3.60	6.00
176, Dec 83	0.60	1.20	3.60	6.00
177, Jan 84	0.60	1.20	3.60	6.00
178, Feb 84	0.60	1.20	3.60	6.00
179, Mar 84	0.60	1.20	3.60	6.00
180, Apr 84	0.60	1.20	3.60	6.00
181, May 84	0.60	1.20	3.60	6.00
182, Jun 84	0.60	1.20	3.60	6.00
183, Jul 84	0.60	1.20	3.60	6.00
184, Aug 84	0.60	1.20	3.60	6.00
185, Sep 84	0.60	1.20	3.60	6.00
186, Oct 84, BS/TA, Storm				
	1.00	1.20	3.60	6.00
187, Nov 84, JR2	0.60	1.20	3.60	6.00
188, Dec 84, JR2	0.60	1.20	3.60	6.00
189, Jan 85, JR2	0.60	1.20	3.60	6.00
190, Feb 85, JR2	0.60	1.20	3.60	6.00
191, Mar 85, JR2;A:SpM, Captain America				
	0.60	1.20	3.60	6.00
192, Apr 85, JR2;Magus	0.60	1.20	3.60	6.00
193, May 85, JR2, 20th anniv.				
	1.25	1.20	3.60	6.00
194, Jun 85, JR2;V:Juggernaut				
	0.65	1.20	3.60	6.00
195, Jul 85, JR2;A:Power Pack				
	0.65	1.20	3.60	6.00
196, Aug 85, JR2 Secret Wars II				
	0.65	1.20	3.60	6.00
197, Sep 85, JR2	0.65	1.20	3.60	6.00
198, Oct 85	0.65	1.20	3.60	6.00
199, Nov 85, Phoenix	0.65	1.20	3.60	6.00
200, Dec 85, Trial of Magneto				
	1.25	2.00	6.00	10.00
201, Jan 86	0.65	3.60	10.80	18.00
202, Feb 86, Secret Wars II				
	0.75	1.40	4.20	7.00
203, Mar 86, Secret Wars II				
	0.75	1.40	4.20	7.00
204, Apr 86	0.75	1.40	4.20	7.00
205, May 86, A:Power Pack				
	0.75	4.00	12.00	20.00
206, Jun 86, V:Freedom Force				
	0.75	1.00	3.00	5.00
207, Jul 86, Wolverine vs. Phoenix				
	0.75	1.00	3.00	5.00
208, Aug 86	0.75	1.00	3.00	5.00

	ORIG.	GOOD	FINE	N-MINT
209, Sep 86	0.75	1.00	3.00	5.00
210, Oct 86, Mutant Massacre				
	0.75	3.20	9.60	16.00
211, Nov 86, Mutant Massacre				
	0.75	3.20	9.60	16.00
212, Dec 86, Mutant Massacre;Alan Davis;A:Sabretooth				
	0.75	7.60	22.80	38.00
213, Jan 87, V:Sabretooth				
	0.75	6.40	19.20	32.00
214, Feb 87, BWS	0.75	1.20	3.60	6.00
215, Mar 87, Alan Davis	0.75	1.20	3.60	6.00
216, Apr 87, Jackson Guice				
	0.75	1.20	3.60	6.00
217, May 87, Jackson Guice				
	0.75	1.20	3.60	6.00
218, Jun 87, MS;V:Juggernaut				
	0.75	1.20	3.60	6.00
219, Jul 87, Bret Blevins	0.75	1.20	3.60	6.00
220, Aug 87, MS	0.75	1.20	3.60	6.00
221, Sep 87, MS;V:Mr. Sinister				
	0.75	3.60	10.80	18.00
222, Oct 87, MS;V:Sabretooth				
	0.75	3.00	9.00	15.00
223, Nov 87	0.75	1.20	3.60	6.00
224, Dec 87, registration card				
	0.75	0.80	2.40	4.00
225, Jan 88, Fall of Mutants				
	0.75	1.60	4.80	8.00
226, Feb 88, Fall of Mutants				
	1.25	1.20	3.60	6.00
227, Mar 88, Fall of Mutants				
	0.75	1.20	3.60	6.00
228, Apr 88	0.75	0.70	2.10	3.50
229, May 88	1.00	0.70	2.10	3.50
230, Jun 88	1.00	0.70	2.10	3.50
231, Jul 88	1.00	0.70	2.10	3.50
232, Aug 88	1.00	0.70	2.10	3.50
233, Sep 88	1.00	0.70	2.10	3.50
234, Sep 88	1.00	0.70	2.10	3.50
235, Oct 88	1.00	0.70	2.10	3.50
236, Oct 88	1.00	0.70	2.10	3.50
237, Nov 88	1.00	0.70	2.10	3.50
238, Nov 88	1.00	0.70	2.10	3.50
239, Dec 88, Inferno	1.00	0.70	2.10	3.50
240, Jan 89, Inferno	1.00	0.70	2.10	3.50
241, Feb 89, Inferno	1.00	0.70	2.10	3.50
242, Mar 89, Inferno	1.00	0.70	2.10	3.50
243, Apr 89, Inferno	1.00	0.70	2.10	3.50
244, May 89	1.00	4.00	12.00	20.00
245, Jun 89	1.00	0.70	2.10	3.50
246, Jul 89	1.00	0.70	2.10	3.50
247, Aug 89	1.00	0.70	2.10	3.50
248, Sep 89, JLee art	1.00	5.00	15.00	25.00
248, reprint	1.25	0.25	0.75	1.25
249, Oct 89	1.00	1.00	3.00	5.00
250, Oct 89	1.00	1.00	3.00	5.00
251, Nov 89	1.00	1.00	3.00	5.00
252, Nov 89	1.00	1.00	3.00	5.00
252, Nov 89	1.00	1.00	3.00	5.00
254, Dec 89	1.00	1.00	3.00	5.00
255, Dec 89	1.00	1.00	3.00	5.00
256, Dec 89, Acts of Vengeance				
	1.00	2.40	7.20	12.00
257, Jan 90, Acts of Vengeance				
	1.00	2.40	7.20	12.00
258, Feb 90, Acts of Vengeance				
	1.00	2.40	7.20	12.00
259, Mar 90	1.00	0.80	2.40	4.00
260, Apr 90	1.00	0.80	2.40	4.00
261, May 90	1.00	0.80	2.40	4.00
262, Jun 90	1.00	0.80	2.40	4.00
263, Jul 90	1.00	0.80	2.40	4.00

	ORIG.	GOOD	FINE	N-MINT
264, Jul 90	1.00	0.80	2.40	4.00
265, Aug 90	1.00	0.80	2.40	4.00
266, Aug 90	1.00	8.00	24.00	40.00
267, Sep 90	1.00	4.00	12.00	20.00
268, Sep 90	1.00	5.60	16.80	28.00
269, Oct 90	1.00	2.00	6.00	10.00
270, Nov 90, X-Tinction	1.00	2.40	7.20	12.00
271, Dec 90, X-Tinction	1.00	1.40	4.20	7.00
272, Jan 91, X-Tinction	1.00	1.40	4.20	7.00
273, Feb 91, JBy, MG	1.00	1.40	4.20	7.00
274, Mar 91, Magneto, Nick Fury, Ka-Zar				
	1.00	1.20	3.60	6.00
275, Apr 91	1.50	2.00	6.00	10.00
276, May 91	1.00	0.80	2.40	4.00
277, Jun 91	1.00	0.80	2.40	4.00
278, Jul 91	1.00	0.80	2.40	4.00
279, Aug 91	1.00	0.80	2.40	4.00
280, Sep 91	1.00	0.80	2.40	4.00
281, Oct 91, WPo;wraparond cover;first printing;new team				
	1.00	2.00	6.00	10.00
281, Oct 91, WPo;wraparound cover;second printing;new team	1.00	0.20	0.60	1.00
282, Oct 91	1.00	1.60	4.80	8.00
283, Dec 91	1.00	2.00	6.00	10.00
284, Jan 92	1.00	0.50	1.50	2.50
285	1.25	0.80	2.40	4.00
286	1.25	0.80	2.40	4.00
287	1.25	0.80	2.40	4.00
288	1.25	0.80	2.40	4.00
289	1.25	0.50	1.50	2.50
290	1.25	0.50	1.50	2.50
291	1.25	0.50	1.50	2.50
292	1.25	0.50	1.50	2.50
293	1.25	0.50	1.50	2.50
294, X-cutioner's song;with card				
	1.50	0.50	1.50	2.50
295, with card	1.50	0.50	1.50	2.50
296, with card	1.50	0.50	1.50	2.50
297	1.25	0.50	1.50	2.50
298	1.25	0.50	1.50	2.50
299	1.25	0.50	1.50	2.50
300, shiny cover	3.95	1.60	4.80	8.00
301	1.25	0.40	1.20	2.00
302	1.25	0.40	1.20	2.00
303	1.25	0.40	1.20	2.00
304, hologram	3.95	1.00	3.00	5.00
305	1.25	0.40	1.20	2.00
306	1.25	0.40	1.20	2.00
307	1.25	0.40	1.20	2.00
308	1.25	0.70	2.10	3.50
309	1.25	0.40	1.20	2.00
310	1.95	0.40	1.20	2.00
311	1.25	0.25	0.75	1.25
313, Jun 94	1.50	0.30	0.90	1.50
314, Jul 94	1.50	0.30	0.90	1.50
315, Aug 94	1.50	0.30	0.90	1.50
316, Sep 94, enhanced cover				
	2.95	0.59	1.77	2.95
316, Sep 94	1.50	0.30	0.90	1.50
317, Oct 94	1.50	0.30	0.90	1.50
317, Oct 94, enhanced cover				
	2.95	0.59	1.77	2.95
318, Nov 94, deluxe	1.95	0.39	1.17	1.95
318, Nov 94	1.50	0.30	0.90	1.50
319, Dec 94, deluxe	1.95	0.39	1.17	1.95
319, Dec 94	1.50	0.30	0.90	1.50
320, Jan 95, deluxe	1.95	0.39	1.17	1.95
320, Jan 95	1.50	0.30	0.90	1.50
321, Feb 95, deluxe	1.95	0.39	1.17	1.95
321, Feb 95	1.50	0.30	0.90	1.50
322, Jul 95, V:Juggernaut				
	1.95	0.39	1.17	1.95

	ORIG.	GOOD	FINE	N-MINT
323, Aug 95, I and 1:Sack and Vessel				
	1.95	0.39	1.17	1.95
324, Sep 95	1.95	0.39	1.17	1.95
325, Oct 95, enhanced gatefold cardstock cover				
	3.95	0.90	2.70	4.50
326, Nov 95	1.95	0.39	1.17	1.95
327, Dec 95	1.95	0.39	1.17	1.95
328, Jan 96	1.95	0.39	1.17	1.95
329, Feb 96	1.95	0.39	1.17	1.95
330, Mar 96	1.95	0.39	1.17	1.95
332, May 96	1.95	0.39	1.17	1.95
333, Jun 96	1.95	0.39	1.17	1.95
334, Jul 96, A:Juggernaut				
	1.95	0.39	1.17	1.95

UNCANNY X-MEN ANNUAL (was X-Men Annual)

	ORIG.	GOOD	FINE	N-MINT
5, 81, BA/BMc, A:FF	0.75	2.00	6.00	10.00
6, 82, BSz, A:Dracula	1.00	2.00	6.00	10.00
7, 83, MG	1.00	1.60	4.80	8.00
8, 84, Kitty	1.00	1.60	4.80	8.00
9, 85, AAd	1.25	2.40	7.20	12.00
10, 86, AAd	1.25	2.40	7.20	12.00
11, 87	1.25	1.20	3.60	6.00
12, 88, AAd Evolutionary War				
	1.75	0.80	2.40	4.00
13, 89, Atlantis Attacks	2.00	0.80	2.40	4.00
14, 90, Future Present	2.00	1.20	3.60	6.00
15, 91, Kings of Pain	2.00	0.80	2.40	4.00
16, 92, Shattershot	2.25	0.60	1.80	3.00
17, 93, trading card	2.95	0.59	1.77	2.95
18, 94	2.95	0.59	1.77	2.95

UNCENSORED MOUSE
ETERNITY

	ORIG.	GOOD	FINE	N-MINT
1, Mickey Mouse		3.00	9.00	15.00
2, Mickey Mouse		3.00	9.00	15.00

UNCLE SCROOGE
GLADSTONE

	ORIG.	GOOD	FINE	N-MINT
210, Oct 86, CB	0.75	1.60	4.80	8.00
211, Nov 86, CB		1.50	4.50	7.50
212, Dec 86, CB	0.75	1.50	4.50	7.50
213, Jan 86		1.50	4.50	7.50
214, Feb 87, CB	0.75	1.50	4.50	7.50
215, Mar 87	0.75	1.50	4.50	7.50
216, Apr 87, CB	0.75	0.80	2.40	4.00
217, May 87		0.80	2.40	4.00
218, Jun 87, CB	0.95	0.80	2.40	4.00
219, Jul 87, DR;1st Rosa Disney story				
	0.95	4.00	12.00	20.00
220, Aug 87, DR, CB	0.95	1.60	4.80	8.00
221, Sep 87, CB	0.95	0.40	1.20	2.00
222, CB	0.95	0.40	1.20	2.00
223, Nov 87, CB	0.95	0.40	1.20	2.00
224, Dec 87, Don Rosa, CB				
	0.95	1.60	4.80	8.00
225, Feb 87, CB	0.95	0.40	1.20	2.00
226, Don Rosa, CB		0.80	2.40	4.00
227, Jul 87, CB	0.95	0.40	1.20	2.00
228, Aug 87, CB	0.95	0.40	1.20	2.00
229, Aug 87, CB	0.95	0.40	1.20	2.00
230, Oct 87, CB	0.95	1.00	3.00	5.00
231, Don Rosa (c), CB		0.40	1.20	2.00
232, CB		0.40	1.20	2.00
233, CB		0.40	1.20	2.00
234, CB		0.40	1.20	2.00
235, Jul 89, Rosa	0.95	1.20	3.60	6.00
236, CB		0.40	1.20	2.00
237, CB		0.40	1.20	2.00
238, CB		0.40	1.20	2.00
239, CB		0.40	1.20	2.00
240, CB		0.40	1.20	2.00
241, CB, Don Rosa		1.00	3.00	5.00
242, CB (moves to Disney)		0.40	1.20	2.00

	ORIG.	GOOD	FINE	N-MINT

UNCLE SCROOGE (former Gladstone title)
DISNEY

	ORIG.	GOOD	FINE	N-MINT
☐ 243		0.50	1.50	2.50
☐ 244		0.40	1.20	2.00
☐ 245	1.50	0.30	0.90	1.50
☐ 246	1.50	0.30	0.90	1.50
☐ 247	1.50	0.30	0.90	1.50
☐ 248	1.50	0.30	0.90	1.50
☐ 249	1.50	0.30	0.90	1.50
☐ 250, CB		0.45	1.35	2.25
☐ 251, CB	1.50	0.30	0.90	1.50
☐ 252, Van Horn	1.50	0.30	0.90	1.50
☐ 253, CB		0.30	0.90	1.50
☐ 254, CB		0.30	0.90	1.50
☐ 255, CB		0.30	0.90	1.50
☐ 256, CB		0.30	0.90	1.50
☐ 257		0.30	0.90	1.50
☐ 258, CB		0.30	0.90	1.50
☐ 259		0.30	0.90	1.50
☐ 260		0.30	0.90	1.50
☐ 261, Don Rosa		0.60	1.80	3.00
☐ 262, Don Rosa		0.60	1.80	3.00
☐ 263, Feb 92, Don Rosa	1.50	0.60	1.80	3.00
☐ 264		0.30	0.90	1.50
☐ 265, CB		0.30	0.90	1.50
☐ 266, CB		0.30	0.90	1.50
☐ 267, CB		0.30	0.90	1.50
☐ 268, Jul 92, CB;contains Duckburg map piece 6 of 9				
	1.50	0.30	0.90	1.50
☐ 269, CB reprints		0.30	0.90	1.50
☐ 270, CB reprints		0.30	0.90	1.50
☐ 271, CB reprints		0.30	0.90	1.50
☐ 272, CB reprints		0.30	0.90	1.50
☐ 273, CB reprints		0.30	0.90	1.50
☐ 274, CB reprints		0.30	0.90	1.50
☐ 275, CB reprints		0.30	0.90	1.50
☐ 276, Mar 93, Rosa	1.50	0.60	1.80	3.00
☐ 277, CB reprints	1.50	0.30	0.90	1.50
☐ 278, CB reprints	1.50	0.30	0.90	1.50
☐ 279	1.50	0.30	0.90	1.50
☐ 280, (returns to Gladstone)				
	1.50	0.30	0.90	1.50

UNCLE SCROOGE (was Disney title)
GLADSTONE

	ORIG.	GOOD	FINE	N-MINT
☐ 281, Aug 93, DR(c), CB reprint				
	1.50	0.30	0.90	1.50
☐ 282, Oct 93, CB reprint	1.50	0.30	0.90	1.50
☐ 283, Dec 93, CB reprint	1.50	0.30	0.90	1.50
☐ 284, Feb 94, CB reprint	1.50	0.30	0.90	1.50
☐ 285, Apr 94, DR;"Life and Times of Scrooge McDuck" Pt. 1	1.50	3.60	10.80	18.00
☐ 286, Jun 94, DR;"Life and Times of Scrooge McDuck" Pt. 2	1.50	2.80	8.40	14.00
☐ 287, Aug 94, DR;"Life and Times of Scrooge McDuck" Pt. 3	1.50	2.00	6.00	10.00
☐ 288, Oct 94, DR;"Life and Times of Scrooge McDuck" Pt. 4	1.50	1.00	3.00	5.00
☐ 289, Dec 94, DR;"Life and Times of Scrooge McDuck" Pt. 5	1.50	1.00	3.00	5.00
☐ 290, Feb 95, DR;"Life and Times of Scrooge McDuck" Pt. 6	1.50	0.30	0.90	1.50
☐ 291, Apr 95, DR;"Life and Times of Scrooge McDuck" Pt. 7	1.50	0.30	0.90	1.50
☐ 292, Jun 95, DR;"Life and Times of Scrooge McDuck" Pt. 8	1.50	0.30	0.90	1.50
☐ 293, Aug 95, DR;"Life and Times of Scrooge McDuck" Pt. 9	1.50	0.30	0.90	1.50
☐ 294, Oct 95, DR;"Life and Times of Scrooge McDuck" Pt. 10	1.50	0.30	0.90	1.50
☐ 295, Dec 95, DR;"Life and Times of Scrooge McDuck" Pt. 11	1.50	0.30	0.90	1.50

UNCLE SCROOGE ADVENTURES

	ORIG.	GOOD	FINE	N-MINT
☐ 1, CB		1.00	3.00	5.00
☐ 2, Dec 87, CB	0.95	0.60	1.80	3.00
☐ 3, Jan 88, CB	0.95	0.40	1.20	2.00
☐ 4, Jan 88, CB	0.95	0.40	1.20	2.00
☐ 5, Jun 88, Don Rosa	0.95	1.20	3.60	6.00
☐ 6, Sep 88, CB	0.95	0.40	1.20	2.00
☐ 7, Sep 88, CB	0.95	0.40	1.20	2.00
☐ 8, Sep 88, CB	0.95	0.40	1.20	2.00
☐ 9, Nov 88, Don Rosa	0.95	1.00	3.00	5.00
☐ 10, CB		0.40	1.20	2.00
☐ 11, CB		0.40	1.20	2.00
☐ 12, CB		0.40	1.20	2.00
☐ 13, CB		0.40	1.20	2.00
☐ 14, Aug 89, Don Rosa	0.95	1.00	3.00	5.00
☐ 15, CB		0.40	1.20	2.00
☐ 16, CB		0.40	1.20	2.00
☐ 17, CB		0.40	1.20	2.00
☐ 18, CB		0.40	1.20	2.00
☐ 19, Rosa(c), CB		0.40	1.20	2.00
☐ 20, CB, Don Rosa		1.00	3.00	5.00
☐ 21, CB, Don Rosa		1.00	3.00	5.00
☐ 22, Sep 93, CB reprint	1.50	0.30	0.90	1.50
☐ 23, Nov 93, CB reprint	1.50	0.30	0.90	1.50
☐ 24, Jan 94, CB reprint	1.50	0.30	0.90	1.50
☐ 25, Mar 94, DR(c);CB reprint				
	1.50	0.30	0.90	1.50
☐ 26, May 94, CB (c) and reprint;"Back to the Klondike"				
	2.95	0.59	1.77	2.95
☐ 27, Jul 94, DR;O:Junior Woodchucks Handbook				
	1.50	0.30	0.90	1.50
☐ 28, Sep 94, CB reprint;A:Terries and Fermies;64 pages				
	2.95	0.59	1.77	2.95
☐ 29, Nov 94, newsstand distribution by Marvel				
	1.50	0.30	0.90	1.50
☐ 30, Jan 95, 64 pages	2.95	0.59	1.77	2.95
☐ 31, Mar 95	1.50	0.30	0.90	1.50
☐ 32, May 95	1.50	0.30	0.90	1.50
☐ 33, Jul 95	1.50	0.30	0.90	1.50
☐ 34, Sep 95	1.95	0.39	1.17	1.95
☐ 35, Nov 95	1.95	0.39	1.17	1.95
☐ 36, Jan 96	1.95	0.39	1.17	1.95

UNCLE SCROOGE DIGEST

	ORIG.	GOOD	FINE	N-MINT
☐ 1, CB		1.00	3.00	5.00
☐ 2, CB		0.60	1.80	3.00
☐ 3, CB		0.60	1.80	3.00
☐ 4, CB		0.40	1.20	2.00
☐ 5, CB		1.00	3.00	5.00

UNCLE SCROOGE GOES TO DISNEYLAND

	ORIG.	GOOD	FINE	N-MINT
☐ 1, CB		1.00	3.00	5.00
☐ 1, (digest)		3.00	9.00	15.00

UNDER TERRA
PREDAWN

	ORIG.	GOOD	FINE	N-MINT
☐ 2, b&w	2.45	0.49	1.47	2.45
☐ 3, b&w	2.45	0.49	1.47	2.45

UNDERDOG
HARVEY

	ORIG.	GOOD	FINE	N-MINT
☐ 1	1.50	0.30	0.90	1.50
☐ 2	1.50	0.30	0.90	1.50
☐ 3	1.50	0.30	0.90	1.50
☐ 4	1.50	0.30	0.90	1.50
☐ 5, Jul 94	1.50	0.30	0.90	1.50

SPOTLIGHT

	ORIG.	GOOD	FINE	N-MINT
☐ 1		0.30	0.90	1.50
☐ 2		0.30	0.90	1.50

UNDERDOG 3-D
BLACKTHORNE

	ORIG.	GOOD	FINE	N-MINT
☐ 1		0.50	1.50	2.50

	ORIG.	GOOD	FINE	N-MINT

UNDERDOG SUMMER SPECIAL
HARVEY
	ORIG.	GOOD	FINE	N-MINT
❑ 1 ....2.25		0.45	1.35	2.25

UNDERGROUND
AIRCEL
❑ 0, nn b&w		0.34	1.02	1.70

DARK HORSE
❑ 1, b&w 4.95		0.99	2.97	4.95

UNDERGROUND CLASSICS
RIP OFF
❑ 1, Dec 85, b&w;adult;multiple printings				
...............1.50		0.50	1.50	2.50
❑ 2, Feb 86, b&w;adult;first printing				
...............2.00		0.50	1.50	2.50
❑ 2, b&w;adult;second printing				
...............2.00		0.50	1.50	2.50
❑ 3, Mar 86, b&w;adult;first printing				
...............2.00		0.50	1.50	2.50
❑ 3, b&w;adult;second printing				
...............2.00		0.50	1.50	2.50
❑ 4, Sep 87, b&w;adult 2.50		0.50	1.50	2.50
❑ 5, Nov 87, b&w;adult 2.00		0.50	1.50	2.50
❑ 6, Feb 88, b&w;adult...... 2.00		0.50	1.50	2.50
❑ 7, Apr 88, b&w;adult....... 2.50		0.50	1.50	2.50
❑ 8, Jun 88, b&w;adult.......		0.50	1.50	2.50
❑ 9, Feb 89, b&w;adult........		0.50	1.50	2.50
❑ 10, b&w;Jesus		0.50	1.50	2.50
❑ 11, b&w;Jesus		0.50	1.50	2.50
❑ 12, Jul 90, Shelton 3-D;first printing				
....	0.59	1.77	2.95	
❑ 12, Shelton 3-D;second printing	0.59	1.77	2.95	
❑ 13, b&w;Jesus		0.50	1.50	2.50
❑ 14, b&w;Jesus		0.50	1.50	2.50
❑ 15, b&w;Rudahl		0.50	1.50	2.50

UNDERSEA AGENT
TOWER
❑ 1, Jan 66 ....0.25		2.40	7.20	12.00
❑ 2, Apr 66 ....0.25		1.60	4.80	8.00
❑ 3, Jun 66 ....0.25		1.60	4.80	8.00
❑ 4, Aug 66 ....0.25		1.60	4.80	8.00
❑ 5, Oct 66 ....0.25		1.60	4.80	8.00
❑ 6, Mar 67 ....0.25		1.60	4.80	8.00

UNDERWORLD
DC
❑ 1, Dec 87..........		0.25	0.75	1.25
❑ 2, Jan 88		0.20	0.60	1.00
❑ 3, Feb 88		0.20	0.60	1.00
❑ 4, Mar 88		0.20	0.60	1.00

UNDERWORLD UNLEASHED (mini-series)
❑ 1, Nov 95, D:Boomerang, Captain Cold,Heat Wave, Mirror Master,Weather Wizard,Mongul				
...............2.95		0.59	1.77	2.95
❑ 2, Dec 95.............2.95		0.59	1.77	2.95
❑ 3, Dec 95.............2.95		0.59	1.77	2.95

UNDERWORLD UNLEASHED: ABYSS - HELL'S SENTINEL
❑ 1, Dec 95, one-shot....... 2.95		0.59	1.77	2.95

UNDERWORLD UNLEASHED: APOKOLIPS - DARK UPRISING
❑ 1, Nov 95, one-shot 1.95		0.39	1.17	1.95

UNDERWORLD UNLEASHED: BATMAN - DEVIL'S ASYLUM
❑ 1, 95, one-shot....... 2.95		0.59	1.77	2.95

UNDERWORLD UNLEASHED: PATTERNS OF FEAR
❑ 1, Dec 95, one-shot;A:Oracle				
...............2.95		0.59	1.77	2.95

UNDIE DOG
HALLEY'S
❑ 1, b&w		0.20	0.60	1.00

UNFUNNY X-CONS
PARODY PRESS
❑ 1, first printing...............2.50		0.50	1.50	2.50
❑ 1, second printing with trading card				
...............2.50		0.50	1.50	2.50

UNICORN ISLE
APPLE
❑ 1, b&w...............		0.30	0.90	1.50
❑ 2, b&w...............		0.30	0.90	1.50
❑ 3, b&w...............		0.30	0.90	1.50
❑ 4		0.35	1.05	1.75
❑ 5		0.35	1.05	1.75

UNICORN KINGS, THE
KZ COMICS
❑ 1, b&w...............		0.19	0.57	0.95

UNION (1993-94 mini-series)
IMAGE
❑ 0, Jul 94.........................2.50		0.50	1.50	2.50
❑ 1, foil-embossed cover ...2.95		0.59	1.77	2.95
❑ 2, Oct 93 ....1.95		0.39	1.17	1.95
❑ 3, Dec 93 ....1.95		0.39	1.17	1.95
❑ 4, Mar 94 ....1.95		0.39	1.17	1.95

UNION (1995-)
❑ 1, Feb 95.........................2.50		0.50	1.50	2.50
❑ 3, Apr 95.........................2.50		0.50	1.50	2.50
❑ 4, May 95, with cards 2.50		0.50	1.50	2.50
❑ 5, Jun 95 ....2.50		0.50	1.50	2.50
❑ 7, Aug 95 ....2.50		0.50	1.50	2.50
❑ 8, Oct 95 ....2.50		0.50	1.50	2.50
❑ 9, Feb 96, covers says "Dec", indicia says "Feb"				
...............2.50		0.50	1.50	2.50

UNION JACKS
ANACOM
❑ 1, b&w...............		0.40	1.20	2.00

UNITY
VALIANT
❑ 0, Aug 92, giveaway..........		0.80	2.40	4.00
❑ 1, Oct 92 ....1.50		1.60	4.80	8.00

UNITY YEARBOOK
❑ 1, 94, A:X-O Manowar, 1994				
...............3.95		0.79	2.37	3.95

UNIVERSAL MONSTERS: DRACULA
DARK HORSE
❑ 0, nn 4.95		0.99	2.97	4.95

UNIVERSAL MONSTERS: FRANKENSTEIN
❑ 0, nn 3.95		0.79	2.37	3.95

UNIVERSAL MONSTERS: THE CREATURE FROM THE BLACK LAGOON
❑ 0, nn movie adaptation, AAd				
...............4.95		0.99	2.97	4.95

UNIVERSAL MONSTERS: THE MUMMY
❑ 0, nn movie.....................4.95		0.99	2.97	4.95

UNIVERSAL SOLDIER
FLEETWAY/QUALITY
❑ 1 ....2.95		0.59	1.77	2.95
❑ 2 ....2.95		0.59	1.77	2.95
❑ 3 ....2.95		0.59	1.77	2.95

NOW
❑ 1, Sep 92, newsstand 1.95		0.39	1.17	1.95
❑ 1, Sep 92, direct-sale, hologram cover				
...............2.50		0.50	1.50	2.50
❑ 1, Sep 92, Waldenbooks, has UPC box and hologram				
...............2.50		0.50	1.50	2.50
❑ 2, Oct 92, direct-sale 2.50		0.50	1.50	2.50
❑ 2, Oct 92, newsstand 1.95		0.39	1.17	1.95
❑ 3, Nov 92, newsstand 1.95		0.39	1.17	1.95
❑ 3, Nov 92, uncensored....2.50		0.50	1.50	2.50

	ORIG.	GOOD	FINE	N-MINT

UNKNOWN SOLDIER (mini-series)
DC

	ORIG.	GOOD	FINE	N-MINT
☐ 1, O:Unknown Soldier		0.30	0.90	1.50
☐ 2		0.30	0.90	1.50
☐ 3		0.30	0.90	1.50
☐ 4		0.30	0.90	1.50
☐ 5		0.30	0.90	1.50
☐ 6		0.30	0.90	1.50
☐ 7		0.30	0.90	1.50
☐ 8		0.35	1.05	1.75
☐ 9		0.35	1.05	1.75
☐ 10		0.35	1.05	1.75
☐ 11		0.35	1.05	1.75
☐ 12		0.35	1.05	1.75

UNKNOWN SOLDIER (1977-)

	ORIG.	GOOD	FINE	N-MINT
☐ 205, May 77	0.30	0.20	0.60	1.00
☐ 206, Jul 77	0.35	0.20	0.60	1.00
☐ 207, Sep 77	0.35	0.20	0.60	1.00
☐ 208, Oct 77	0.35	0.20	0.60	1.00
☐ 209, Nov 77	0.35	0.20	0.60	1.00
☐ 210, Dec 77	0.35	0.20	0.60	1.00
☐ 211, Jan 78	0.35	0.20	0.60	1.00
☐ 212, Feb 78	0.35	0.20	0.60	1.00
☐ 213, Mar 78	0.35	0.20	0.60	1.00
☐ 214, Apr 78	0.35	0.20	0.60	1.00
☐ 215, May 78	0.35	0.20	0.60	1.00
☐ 216, Jun 78	0.35	0.20	0.60	1.00
☐ 217, Jul 78	0.35	0.20	0.60	1.00
☐ 218, Aug 78	0.35	0.20	0.60	1.00
☐ 219, Sep 78	0.50	0.20	0.60	1.00
☐ 220, Oct 78	0.50	0.20	0.60	1.00
☐ 221, Nov 78	0.50	0.20	0.60	1.00
☐ 222, Dec 78	0.40	0.20	0.60	1.00
☐ 223, Jan 79	0.40	0.20	0.60	1.00
☐ 224, Feb 79	0.40	0.20	0.60	1.00
☐ 225, Mar 79	0.40	0.20	0.60	1.00
☐ 226, Apr 79	0.40	0.20	0.60	1.00
☐ 227, May 79	0.40	0.20	0.60	1.00
☐ 228, Jun 79	0.40	0.20	0.60	1.00
☐ 229, Jul 79	0.40	0.20	0.60	1.00
☐ 230, Aug 79	0.40	0.20	0.60	1.00
☐ 231, Sep 79	0.40	0.20	0.60	1.00
☐ 232, Oct 79	0.40	0.20	0.60	1.00
☐ 233, Nov 79	0.40	0.20	0.60	1.00
☐ 234, Dec 79	0.40	0.20	0.60	1.00
☐ 235, Jan 80	0.40	0.20	0.60	1.00
☐ 236, Feb 80	0.40	0.20	0.60	1.00
☐ 237, Mar 80	0.40	0.20	0.60	1.00
☐ 238, Apr 80	0.40	0.20	0.60	1.00
☐ 239, May 80	0.40	0.20	0.60	1.00
☐ 240, Jun 80	0.40	0.20	0.60	1.00
☐ 241, Jul 80	0.40	0.20	0.60	1.00
☐ 242, Aug 80	0.40	0.20	0.60	1.00
☐ 243, Sep 80	0.50	0.20	0.60	1.00
☐ 244, Oct 80	0.50	0.20	0.60	1.00
☐ 245, Nov 80	0.50	0.20	0.60	1.00
☐ 246, Dec 80	0.50	0.20	0.60	1.00
☐ 247, Jan 81	0.50	0.20	0.60	1.00
☐ 248, Feb 81	0.50	0.20	0.60	1.00
☐ 249, Mar 81	0.50	0.20	0.60	1.00
☐ 250, Apr 81	0.50	0.20	0.60	1.00
☐ 251, May 81	0.50	0.20	0.60	1.00
☐ 252, Jun 81	0.50	0.20	0.60	1.00
☐ 253, Jul 81	0.50	0.20	0.60	1.00
☐ 254, Aug 81	0.50	0.20	0.60	1.00
☐ 255, Sep 81	0.50	0.20	0.60	1.00
☐ 256, Oct 81	0.60	0.20	0.60	1.00
☐ 257, Nov 81	0.60	0.20	0.60	1.00
☐ 258, Dec 81	0.60	0.20	0.60	1.00

UNKNOWN WORLDS OF FRANK BRUNNER
ECLIPSE

	ORIG.	GOOD	FINE	N-MINT
☐ 1, FB		0.35	1.05	1.75
☐ 2, FB		0.35	1.05	1.75

UNKNOWN WORLDS OF SCIENCE FICTION
(b&w mag)
MARVEL

	ORIG.	GOOD	FINE	N-MINT
☐ 1, Jan 75	1.00	0.25	0.75	1.25
☐ 2, Mar 75	1.00	0.20	0.60	1.00
☐ 3, May 75	1.00	0.20	0.60	1.00
☐ 4, Jul 75	1.00	0.20	0.60	1.00
☐ 5, Sep 75	1.00	0.20	0.60	1.00
☐ 6, Nov 75	1.00	0.20	0.60	1.00

UNKNOWN WORLDS OF SCIENCE FICTION
SPECIAL

	ORIG.	GOOD	FINE	N-MINT
☐ 1, 76, reprints	1.25	0.25	0.75	1.25

UNLEASHED!
TRIUMPHANT

	ORIG.	GOOD	FINE	N-MINT
☐ 1	2.50	0.50	1.50	2.50

UNSUPERVISED EXISTENCE
FANTAGRAPHICS

	ORIG.	GOOD	FINE	N-MINT
☐ 1, b&w		0.40	1.20	2.00
☐ 2, b&w		0.40	1.20	2.00
☐ 3		0.50	1.50	2.50
☐ 4		0.50	1.50	2.50
☐ 5		0.40	1.20	2.00
☐ 6		0.45	1.35	2.25
☐ 7		0.45	1.35	2.25

UNTAMED
EPIC

	ORIG.	GOOD	FINE	N-MINT
☐ 1, embossed cover	2.50	0.50	1.50	2.50
☐ 2	1.95	0.39	1.17	1.95
☐ 3	1.95	0.39	1.17	1.95

UNTAMED LOVE
FANTAGRAPHICS

	ORIG.	GOOD	FINE	N-MINT
☐ 1, 87, FF	2.00	0.40	1.20	2.00

UNTOLD LEGEND OF BATMAN
DC

	ORIG.	GOOD	FINE	N-MINT
☐ 1, Jul 80, JBy/JA, O:Batman	0.40	1.40	4.20	7.00
☐ 2, Aug 80, JA	0.40	1.00	3.00	5.00
☐ 3, Sep 80, JA	0.50	1.00	3.00	5.00

UNTOLD ORIGIN OF FEMFORCE
AC

	ORIG.	GOOD	FINE	N-MINT
☐ 1, 89, O:Femforce		0.99	2.97	4.95

UNTOLD ORIGIN OF MS. VICTORY

	ORIG.	GOOD	FINE	N-MINT
☐ 1, Dec 89, b&w O:Ms. Victory		0.50	1.50	2.50

UNTOLD TALES OF SPIDER-MAN
MARVEL

	ORIG.	GOOD	FINE	N-MINT
☐ 1, Sep 95	0.99	0.20	0.59	0.99
☐ 2, Oct 95	0.99	0.20	0.59	0.99
☐ 3, Nov 95, V:Sandman	0.99	0.20	0.59	0.99
☐ 4, Dec 95	0.99	0.20	0.59	0.99
☐ 5, Jan 96	0.99	0.20	0.59	0.99
☐ 6, Feb 96, A:Human Torch	0.99	0.20	0.59	0.99
☐ 7, Mar 96	0.99	0.20	0.59	0.99
☐ 8, Apr 96	0.99	0.20	0.59	0.99
☐ 9, May 96	0.99	0.20	0.59	0.99
☐ 10, Jun 96	0.99	0.20	0.59	0.99

UP FROM BONDAGE
EROS COMIX

	ORIG.	GOOD	FINE	N-MINT
☐ 1, adult, b&w		0.59	1.77	2.95

URBAN LEGENDS
DARK HORSE

	ORIG.	GOOD	FINE	N-MINT
☐ 1, b&w	2.95	0.59	1.77	2.95

URTH 4
CONTINUITY

	ORIG.	GOOD	FINE	N-MINT
☐ 1, May 89		0.40	1.20	2.00

	ORIG.	GOOD	FINE	N-MINT
2, Apr 90		0.40	1.20	2.00
3, Oct 90		0.40	1.20	2.00
4, 91		0.40	1.20	2.00

USAGI YOJIMBO
FANTAGRAPHICS

	ORIG.	GOOD	FINE	N-MINT
1, 1st printing		2.80	8.40	14.00
1, 2nd printing		0.40	1.20	2.00
2		2.00	6.00	10.00
3		1.20	3.60	6.00
4		1.20	3.60	6.00
5		1.20	3.60	6.00
6, b&w		0.80	2.40	4.00
7, b&w		0.80	2.40	4.00
8, b&w		0.80	2.40	4.00
9, b&w		0.80	2.40	4.00
10, A:TMNT		2.00	6.00	10.00
10, 2nd printing		0.40	1.20	2.00
11, SA		0.60	1.80	3.00
12, b&w		0.60	1.80	3.00
13, b&w		0.60	1.80	3.00
14, b&w		0.60	1.80	3.00
15, b&w		0.60	1.80	3.00
16, b&w		0.60	1.80	3.00
17, b&w		0.60	1.80	3.00
18, Oct 89, b&w	2.00	0.60	1.80	3.00
21		0.60	1.80	3.00
22		0.60	1.80	3.00
23		0.60	1.80	3.00
24, Lone Goat & Kid		0.60	1.80	3.00
25		0.50	1.50	2.50
26		0.50	1.50	2.50
27		0.50	1.50	2.50
28		0.50	1.50	2.50
29		0.50	1.50	2.50
30		0.50	1.50	2.50
31		0.50	1.50	2.50
32		0.50	1.50	2.50
33		0.50	1.50	2.50
34		0.50	1.50	2.50

	ORIG.	GOOD	FINE	N-MINT
35		0.50	1.50	2.50
36		0.50	1.50	2.50
37		0.50	1.50	2.50
38		0.50	1.50	2.50

USAGI YOJIMBO (Vol. 3, mini-series)
DARK HORSE

	ORIG.	GOOD	FINE	N-MINT
1, Apr 96, b&w	2.95	0.59	1.77	2.95
2, May 96, b&w	2.95	0.59	1.77	2.95

USAGI YOJIMBO (Volume 2)
MIRAGE

	ORIG.	GOOD	FINE	N-MINT
1, color	2.75	0.55	1.65	2.75
2, TMNT	2.75	0.55	1.65	2.75
3	2.75	0.55	1.65	2.75
4	2.75	0.55	1.65	2.75
5	2.75	0.55	1.65	2.75
6, Jan 94	2.75	0.55	1.65	2.75
7, Apr 94	2.75	0.55	1.65	2.75
8, Jun 94	2.75	0.55	1.65	2.75
9, Aug 94	2.75	0.55	1.65	2.75
10, Oct 94	2.75	0.55	1.65	2.75
11, Dec 94	2.75	0.55	1.65	2.75
12, Feb 95	2.75	0.55	1.65	2.75
13, Apr 95	2.75	0.55	1.65	2.75
14, Jun 95	2.75	0.55	1.65	2.75
15, Aug 95	2.75	0.55	1.65	2.75
16, Oct 95, (moves to Dark Horse Comics)	2.75	0.55	1.65	2.75

USAGI YOJIMBO COLOR SPECIAL
FANTAGRAPHICS

	ORIG.	GOOD	FINE	N-MINT
1		1.00	3.00	5.00
1, 2nd edition		0.70	2.10	3.50
2		0.70	2.10	3.50

USAGI YOJIMBO SUMMER SPECIAL

	ORIG.	GOOD	FINE	N-MINT
1		2.00	6.00	10.00

Undersea Agent

First Appearance: *Undersea Agent* #1 (January 1966)

Undersea Agent, Tower Comics' companion comic book to *T.H.U.N.D.E.R. Agents,* ran for six 68-page issues (Jan 66-Mar 67). The "undersea" of the title was both descriptive of the protagonist's field of operations and an acronym for United Nations Department of Experiment and Research Systems Established at Atlantis. Although ostensibly engaged in peaceful research projects, U.N.D.E.R.S.E.A. managed to produce a lot of weaponry and had more than its share of run-ins with world-conquering villains.

The cast of characters included Lt. Davy Jones, the agent of the title; Prof. Weston, the gray-bearded, pipe-smoking scientist at the head of U.N.D.E.R.SE.A.; Skooby Doolittle, Jones' young sidekick; and Renaca Del Mar, who joined U.N.D.E.R.S.E.A. to avenge the death of her father at the hands of the evil Dr. Fang. Dr. Fang was a typical oriental villain in the tradition of Ming and Fu Manchu, complete with financial backing by "Red China." As U.N.D.E.R.S.E.A. was based in the undersea ruins of Atlantis, Fang ruled sunken Lemuria and its sea-dwelling inhabitants.

Initially a non-super hero, Jones gained the power of electromagnetism as a result of an encounter with an eel and an atomic sub in issue #2. Issue #5 introduced Merman, an amphibious agent with surgically implanted gills.

Each issue featured multiple stories with uncredited scripts and art. Art by Mike Sekowsky appeared in issues #2 and #3. Art by Gil Kane began in issue #3 and continued until the end of the series. Issues #4 and #5 featured Kane covers.

Although periodic efforts have been made to revive *T.H.U.N.D.E.R. Agents, Undersea Agent* was a Tower title that never surfaced again.

V

	ORIG.	GOOD	FINE	N-MINT
V				
DC				
❑ 1, Feb 85 ....0.75	0.15	0.45	0.75
❑ 2, Mar 85 ....0.75	0.15	0.45	0.75
❑ 3, Apr 85.......................0.75	0.15	0.45	0.75
❑ 4, May 85 ....0.75	0.15	0.45	0.75
❑ 5	0.25	0.75	1.25
❑ 6	0.25	0.75	1.25
❑ 7	0.25	0.75	1.25
❑ 8	0.25	0.75	1.25
❑ 9	0.25	0.75	1.25
❑ 10	0.25	0.75	1.25
❑ 11	0.25	0.75	1.25
❑ 12	0.25	0.75	1.25
❑ 13	0.25	0.75	1.25
❑ 14	0.25	0.75	1.25
❑ 15	0.25	0.75	1.25
❑ 16	0.25	0.75	1.25
❑ 17	0.25	0.75	1.25
❑ 18	0.25	0.75	1.25
❑ 19	0.25	0.75	1.25
❑ 20	0.25	0.75	1.25
❑ 21	0.25	0.75	1.25
❑ 22	0.25	0.75	1.25
❑ 23	0.25	0.75	1.25
❑ 24	0.25	0.75	1.25
❑ 25	0.25	0.75	1.25
❑ 26	0.25	0.75	1.25
❑ 27, Sep 91 .... 1.25	0.25	0.75	1.25
V (TV adaptation)				
❑ 1, Feb 85, CI................... 0.75	0.35	1.05	1.75
❑ 2, Mar 85, CI................... 0.75	0.30	0.90	1.50
❑ 3, Apr 85, CI................... 0.75	0.30	0.90	1.50
❑ 4, May 85, CI................... 0.75	0.30	0.90	1.50
❑ 5, Jun 85 ....0.75	0.20	0.60	1.00
❑ 6, Jul 85, CI................... 0.75	0.20	0.60	1.00
❑ 7, Aug 85, CI 0.75	0.20	0.60	1.00
❑ 8, Sep 85, CI 0.75	0.20	0.60	1.00
❑ 9, Oct 85, CI 0.75	0.20	0.60	1.00
❑ 10, Nov 85, CI................. 0.75	0.20	0.60	1.00
❑ 11, Dec 85, CI................. 0.75	0.20	0.60	1.00
❑ 12, Jan 86, CI................. 0.75	0.20	0.60	1.00
❑ 13, Feb 86, CI................. 0.75	0.20	0.60	1.00
❑ 14, Mar 86, CI................. 0.75	0.20	0.60	1.00
❑ 15, Apr 86, CI................. 0.75	0.20	0.60	1.00
❑ 16, May 86, CI................. 0.75	0.20	0.60	1.00
❑ 17, Jun 86, DG............... 0.75	0.20	0.60	1.00
❑ 18, Jul 86, DG............... 0.75	0.20	0.60	1.00
V FOR VENDETTA				
❑ 1, Sep 88, AMo 2.00	1.00	3.00	5.00
❑ 2, Oct 88 .... 2.00	0.60	1.80	3.00
❑ 3, Nov 88 .... 2.00	0.60	1.80	3.00
❑ 4, Dec 88....................... 2.00	0.60	1.80	3.00
❑ 5, 88................................ 2.00	0.60	1.80	3.00
❑ 6, 88................................ 2.00	0.60	1.80	3.00
❑ 7, Jan 89 .... 2.00	0.60	1.80	3.00
❑ 8, Feb 89 .... 2.00	0.60	1.80	3.00
❑ 9, Mar 89 .... 2.00	0.60	1.80	3.00
❑ 10, May 89 .... 2.00	0.60	1.80	3.00
VALENTINO				
RENEGADE				
❑ 0, nn;b&w 1.70	0.34	1.02	1.70
VALENTINO THE 3RD				
❑ 0, nn;b&w 2.00	0.40	1.20	2.00
VALENTINO TOO				
❑ 0, nn;b&w 1.70	0.34	1.02	1.70

	ORIG.	GOOD	FINE	N-MINT
VALERIA THE SHE-BAT				
ACCLAIM/WINDJAMMER				
❑ 1, Sep 95 ....2.50	0.50	1.50	2.50
CONTINUITY				
❑ 1	1.00	3.00	5.00
❑ 5 ....2.50	0.50	1.50	2.50
VALIANT READER				
VALIANT				
❑ 1, background.................0.75	0.15	0.45	0.75
VALIANT VISIONS STARTER KIT				
❑ 1, comic book, glasses, poster				
.....................................2.95	0.59	1.77	2.95
VALKYRIE! (1987 mini-series)				
ECLIPSE				
❑ 1, May 87, PG.................1.75	0.35	1.05	1.75
❑ 2, Jun 87, PG.................1.75	0.35	1.05	1.75
❑ 3, Aug 87, PG 1.75	0.35	1.05	1.75
VALKYRIE! (1988 mini-series)				
❑ 1, Jul 88, BA 1.75	0.35	1.05	1.75
❑ 2, Aug 88, BA................. 1.75	0.35	1.05	1.75
❑ 3, Sep 88, BA................. 1.75	0.35	1.05	1.75
VALLEY OF THE DINOSAURS				
HARVEY				
❑ 1, Oct 93.......................2.25	0.45	1.35	2.25
VALOR				
DC				
❑ 1, Nov 92 ....1.25	0.25	0.75	1.25
❑ 2, Dec 92 ....1.25	0.25	0.75	1.25
❑ 3, Jan 93.......................1.25	0.25	0.75	1.25
❑ 4, Feb 93, Lobo.............1.25	0.25	0.75	1.25
❑ 5, Mar 93.......................1.25	0.25	0.75	1.25
❑ 6, Apr 93.......................1.25	0.25	0.75	1.25
❑ 7, May 93.......................1.25	0.25	0.75	1.25
❑ 8, Jun 93 ....1.25	0.25	0.75	1.25
❑ 9, Jul 93.......................1.25	0.25	0.75	1.25
❑ 10, Aug 93 ....1.25	0.25	0.75	1.25
❑ 11, Sep 93 ....1.25	0.25	0.75	1.25
❑ 12, Oct 93 ....1.25	0.25	0.75	1.25
❑ 13, Nov 93 ....1.50	0.30	0.90	1.50
❑ 14, Dec 93 ....1.50	0.30	0.90	1.50
❑ 15, Jan 94 ....1.50	0.30	0.90	1.50
❑ 16, Feb 94.....................1.50	0.30	0.90	1.50
❑ 17, Mar 94 ....1.50	0.30	0.90	1.50
❑ 18, Apr 94 ....1.50	0.30	0.90	1.50
❑ 19, May 94.....................1.50	0.30	0.90	1.50
❑ 20, Jun 94, KB 1.50	0.30	0.90	1.50
❑ 21, Jul 94.......................1.50	0.30	0.90	1.50
❑ 22, Aug 94 ....1.50	0.30	0.90	1.50
❑ 23, Sep 94 ....1.50	0.30	0.90	1.50
VALOR THUNDERSTAR AND HIS FIREFLIES				
NOW				
❑ 1, Dec 86 ....1.50	0.30	0.90	1.50
VAMPEROTICA				
BRAINSTORM				
❑ 1, 93, adult, b&w 2.95	0.59	1.77	2.95
❑ 1, Sep 94, adult, b&w (second printing)				
.....................................2.95	0.59	1.77	2.95
❑ 12, Feb 96, adult, b&w.....2.95	0.59	1.77	2.95
VAMPIRE COMPANION, THE				
INNOVATION				
❑ 1, 91, Cardstock cover....2.50	1.00	3.00	5.00
❑ 2, 91, Cardstock cover....2.50	0.50	1.50	2.50
❑ 3 ....2.50	0.50	1.50	2.50

	ORIG.	GOOD	FINE	N-MINT

VAMPIRE LESTAT, THE
(see Anne Rice's The Vampire Lestat)

VAMPIRE TALES (b&w mag)
MARVEL
	ORIG.	GOOD	FINE	N-MINT
1	0.75	0.15	0.45	0.75
2	0.75	0.15	0.45	0.75
3	0.75	0.15	0.45	0.75
4	0.75	0.15	0.45	0.75
5	0.75	0.15	0.45	0.75
6	0.75	0.15	0.45	0.75
7	0.75	0.15	0.45	0.75
8	0.75	0.15	0.45	0.75
9	0.75	0.15	0.45	0.75
10	0.75	0.15	0.45	0.75
11	0.75	0.15	0.45	0.75

VAMPIRE TALES ANNUAL
	ORIG.	GOOD	FINE	N-MINT
1, reprints	1.25	0.25	0.75	1.25

VAMPIRE VERSES, THE
CFD/VISUAL ANARCHY
	ORIG.	GOOD	FINE	N-MINT
1, Aug 95, b&w	2.95	0.59	1.77	2.95

VAMPIRELLA
HARRIS
	ORIG.	GOOD	FINE	N-MINT
0, Dec 94, enhanced cover; contains Vampirella timeline	2.95	0.59	1.77	2.95
1, Nov 92, color	2.95	0.59	1.77	2.95
2, 93, color	2.95	0.59	1.77	2.95
3, 93, color	2.95	0.59	1.77	2.95
4, 93, color	2.95	0.59	1.77	2.95
5, 93, color	2.95	0.59	1.77	2.95

VAMPIRELLA (Morning in America)
	ORIG.	GOOD	FINE	N-MINT
1, 91	3.95	9.60	28.80	48.00
2, 91	3.95	6.00	18.00	30.00
3, 92	3.95	4.00	12.00	20.00
4, 92	3.95	4.00	12.00	20.00

VAMPIRELLA - SHADOWHAWK
HARRIS/IMAGE
	ORIG.	GOOD	FINE	N-MINT
1, Feb 95, crossover; concludes in *Shadowhawk - Vampirella #2*	4.95	0.99	2.97	4.95

VAMPIRELLA CLASSIC
HARRIS
	ORIG.	GOOD	FINE	N-MINT
1, Feb 95	2.95	0.59	1.77	2.95
3, Jun 95	2.95	0.59	1.77	2.95

VAMPIRELLA STRIKES
	ORIG.	GOOD	FINE	N-MINT
3, Feb 96	2.95	0.59	1.77	2.95

VAMPIRELLA ZERO
	ORIG.	GOOD	FINE	N-MINT
0, Dec 94, JQ(c)	2.95	0.80	2.40	4.00

VAMPIRELLA'S SUMMER NIGHTS
	ORIG.	GOOD	FINE	N-MINT
0, 92, nn b&w	3.95	1.20	3.60	6.00

VAMPIRELLA/SHADOWHAWK:
CREATURES OF THE NIGHT (mini-series)
	ORIG.	GOOD	FINE	N-MINT
1, Feb 95, Joe Jusko(c)	4.95	0.99	2.97	4.95

VAMPIRIC JIHAD
APPLE
	ORIG.	GOOD	FINE	N-MINT
0, 91, nn;b&w;cardstock cover;reprints material from *Blood of Dracula* #14-19	4.95	0.99	2.97	4.95

VAMPRESS LUXURA, THE
BRAINSTORM
	ORIG.	GOOD	FINE	N-MINT
1, 96	2.95	0.59	1.77	2.95

VAMPS (mini-series)
DC/VERTIGO
	ORIG.	GOOD	FINE	N-MINT
1, Aug 94	1.95	0.39	1.17	1.95
2, Sep 94	1.95	0.39	1.17	1.95
3, Oct 94	1.95	0.39	1.17	1.95
4, Nov 94	1.95	0.39	1.17	1.95
5, Dec 94	1.95	0.39	1.17	1.95
6, Jan 95	1.95	0.39	1.17	1.95

VAMPS: HOLLYWOOD & VEIN (mini-series)
DC
	ORIG.	GOOD	FINE	N-MINT
1, Feb 96	2.25	0.45	1.35	2.25
2, Mar 96	2.25	0.45	1.35	2.25
3, Apr 96	2.25	0.45	1.35	2.25
4, May 96	2.25	0.45	1.35	2.25
5, Jun 96	2.25	0.45	1.35	2.25
6, Jul 96, final issue	2.25	0.45	1.35	2.25

VAMPYRE'S KISS
AIRCEL
	ORIG.	GOOD	FINE	N-MINT
1, adult, b&w		0.50	1.50	2.50
2, adult, b&w		0.50	1.50	2.50
3, adult, b&w		0.50	1.50	2.50
4, Sep 90, adult, b&w	2.50	0.50	1.50	2.50

VAMPYRE'S KISS, BOOK II
	ORIG.	GOOD	FINE	N-MINT
1, adult, b&w		0.50	1.50	2.50
2, adult, b&w		0.50	1.50	2.50
3, adult, b&w		0.50	1.50	2.50
4, adult, b&w		0.50	1.50	2.50

VAMPYRE'S KISS, BOOK III
	ORIG.	GOOD	FINE	N-MINT
1, adult, b&w		0.50	1.50	2.50
2, adult, b&w		0.50	1.50	2.50
3, adult, b&w		0.50	1.50	2.50
4, adult, b&w		0.50	1.50	2.50

VAMPYRES
ETERNITY
	ORIG.	GOOD	FINE	N-MINT
1, b&w rep.		0.45	1.35	2.25
2, b&w rep.		0.45	1.35	2.25
3, b&w rep.		0.45	1.35	2.25
4, b&w rep.		0.45	1.35	2.25

VANGUARD
IMAGE
	ORIG.	GOOD	FINE	N-MINT
1	1.95	0.80	2.40	4.00
2	1.95	0.60	1.80	3.00
3	1.95	0.39	1.17	1.95
4, Feb 94	1.95	0.39	1.17	1.95
5, Apr 94	1.95	0.39	1.17	1.95
6, May 94	1.95	0.39	1.17	1.95

VANGUARD ILLUSTRATED
PACIFIC
	ORIG.	GOOD	FINE	N-MINT
1		0.30	0.90	1.50
2, DSt		0.60	1.80	3.00
3		0.30	0.90	1.50
4		0.30	0.90	1.50
5		0.30	0.90	1.50
6		0.30	0.90	1.50
7, 1:Mr. Monster		0.60	1.80	3.00

VANITY
	ORIG.	GOOD	FINE	N-MINT
1, Jun 84, Will Meugniot	1.50	0.30	0.90	1.50
2, Aug 84, Will Meugniot	1.50	0.30	0.90	1.50

VANITY ANGEL
ANTARCTIC
	ORIG.	GOOD	FINE	N-MINT
1, Sep 94, adult;b&w	3.50	0.70	2.10	3.50
1, May 95, adult;b&w; second printing	3.50	0.70	2.10	3.50
2, Oct 94, adult;b&w	3.50	0.70	2.10	3.50
2, Jun 95, adult;b&w ;second printing	3.50	0.70	2.10	3.50
3, Nov 94, b&w	2.95	0.59	1.77	2.95
4, Dec 94, b&w	2.95	0.59	1.77	2.95
5, Jan 95, b&w	2.95	0.59	1.77	2.95
6, Feb 95, b&w	2.95	0.59	1.77	2.95

VARCEL'S VIXENS
CALIBER
	ORIG.	GOOD	FINE	N-MINT
1, b&w	2.50	0.50	1.50	2.50
2, b&w	2.50	0.50	1.50	2.50
3, b&w	2.50	0.50	1.50	2.50

	ORIG.	GOOD	FINE	N-MINT

VARMINTS
BLUE COMET
	ORIG.	GOOD	FINE	N-MINT
❑ 1		0.36	1.08	1.80

VARMINTS SPECIAL
	ORIG.	GOOD	FINE	N-MINT
❑ 1, Panda Khan		0.50	1.50	2.50

VAST KNOWLEDGE OF GENERAL SUBJECTS, A
FANTAGRAPHICS
	ORIG.	GOOD	FINE	N-MINT
❑ 1, Sep 94, b&w	4.95	0.99	2.97	4.95

VAULT OF DOOMNATION
B-MOVIE
	ORIG.	GOOD	FINE	N-MINT
❑ 1, b&w		0.34	1.02	1.70

VAULT OF HORROR
COCHRAN
	ORIG.	GOOD	FINE	N-MINT
❑ 1, reprints	2.00	0.40	1.20	2.00
❑ 2, reprints	2.00	0.40	1.20	2.00
❑ 3, reprints	2.00	0.40	1.20	2.00
❑ 4, reprints	2.00	0.40	1.20	2.00
❑ 5, reprints	2.00	0.40	1.20	2.00

EC/GEMSTONE
	ORIG.	GOOD	FINE	N-MINT
❑ 1, reprints, Craig, Davis, Evans, Ingels, WW, AW, Kamen, JO		0.40	1.20	2.00
❑ 2, reprints, Craig, Davis, Evans, Ingels, WW, AW, Kamen, JO		0.40	1.20	2.00
❑ 3, reprints, Craig, Davis, Evans, Ingels, WW, AW, Kamen, JO		0.40	1.20	2.00
❑ 4, reprints, Craig, Davis, Evans, Ingels, WW, AW, Kamen, JO	2.00	0.40	1.20	2.00
❑ 5, JC,GI,AF,JK, reprints	2.00	0.40	1.20	2.00
❑ 6, reprints	2.00	0.40	1.20	2.00
❑ 7, JC,JD,JK,GI reprints	2.00	0.40	1.20	2.00
❑ 8, reprints	2.00	0.40	1.20	2.00
❑ 9, reprints	2.00	0.40	1.20	2.00
❑ 10, reprints	2.00	0.40	1.20	2.00
❑ 11, reprints	2.00	0.40	1.20	2.00
❑ 12, reprints	2.00	0.40	1.20	2.00
❑ 13, reprints	2.00	0.40	1.20	2.00

GLADSTONE
	ORIG.	GOOD	FINE	N-MINT
❑ 1, Aug 90, reprints, Craig, Davis, Ingels, Kamen	1.95	0.39	1.17	1.95
❑ 2, Oct 90, Craig, Davis, Ingels, Evans, Kamen, Ray Bradbury	1.95	0.39	1.17	1.95
❑ 3, Dec 90, reprints: Ingels, Evans, Kamen, Davis, Craig, Feldstein, WW, Kurtzman	1.95	0.39	1.17	1.95
❑ 4, Feb 91, reprints: Ingels, Craig, Davis, Kamen	2.00	0.40	1.20	2.00
❑ 5, Apr 91, reprints: Craig, Davis, Kamen, Ingels, Feldstein, Roussos, Wood	2.00	0.40	1.20	2.00
❑ 6, Jun 91, reprints: Craig, Davis, Evans, Ingels, Feldstein, Kurtzman, Kamen, Wood	2.00	0.40	1.20	2.00

VAULT OF SCREAMING HORROR
FANTACO
	ORIG.	GOOD	FINE	N-MINT
❑ 0	3.50	0.70	2.10	3.50

VC'S, THE
FLEETWAY/QUALITY
	ORIG.	GOOD	FINE	N-MINT
❑ 1, b&w		0.39	1.17	1.95
❑ 2, b&w		0.39	1.17	1.95
❑ 3, b&w		0.39	1.17	1.95
❑ 4, b&w		0.39	1.17	1.95
❑ 5, b&w		0.39	1.17	1.95

VECTOR
NOW
	ORIG.	GOOD	FINE	N-MINT
❑ 1, Jul 86	1.50	0.30	0.90	1.50
❑ 2, Sep 86	1.50	0.30	0.90	1.50
❑ 3, Nov 86	1.50	0.30	0.90	1.50
❑ 4, Jan 87	1.75	0.35	1.05	1.75

VEGAS KNIGHTS
PIONEER
	ORIG.	GOOD	FINE	N-MINT
❑ 1, MGr(c)		0.39	1.17	1.95

VEGETABLE LOVER
EROS COMIX
	ORIG.	GOOD	FINE	N-MINT
❑ 1, adult, b&w		0.55	1.65	2.75

VELOCITY
ECLIPSE
	ORIG.	GOOD	FINE	N-MINT
❑ 5, b&w		0.59	1.77	2.95
IMAGE
	ORIG.	GOOD	FINE	N-MINT
❑ 3, Jan 96	2.50	0.50	1.50	2.50

VELVET
ADVENTURE
	ORIG.	GOOD	FINE	N-MINT
❑ 1, b&w	2.50	0.50	1.50	2.50
❑ 2, b&w	2.50	0.50	1.50	2.50
❑ 3, b&w	2.50	0.50	1.50	2.50
❑ 4, b&w	2.50	0.50	1.50	2.50

VELVET TOUCH
ANTARCTIC
	ORIG.	GOOD	FINE	N-MINT
❑ 1, Oct 93, adult	3.95	0.79	2.37	3.95
❑ 1, Oct 93, color, adult only, platinum				
❑ 1, Apr 95, adult; second printing	3.95	0.79	2.37	3.95
❑ 2, Jan 94, adult	2.95	0.59	1.77	2.95
❑ 3, Jul 94, adult	2.95	0.59	1.77	2.95
❑ 4, Aug 94, adult	2.95	0.59	1.77	2.95
❑ 5, Oct 94, adult	2.95	0.59	1.77	2.95
❑ 6, Jan 95, adult	2.95	0.59	1.77	2.95

VENDETTA: HOLY VINDICATOR (mini-series)
RED BULLET
	ORIG.	GOOD	FINE	N-MINT
❑ 1, 93, b&w;first printing limited to 500 copies	2.50	0.50	1.50	2.50
❑ 2, 94, b&w;first printing limited to 500 copies	2.50	0.50	1.50	2.50
❑ 3, 94, b&w;first printing limited to 3000 copies	2.50	0.50	1.50	2.50
❑ 4, 95, b&w; final issue	2.50	0.50	1.50	2.50

VENGEANCE OF THE AZTECS (mini-series)
CALIBER
	ORIG.	GOOD	FINE	N-MINT
❑ 1, b&w	2.95	0.59	1.77	2.95
❑ 2, b&w	2.95	0.59	1.77	2.95
❑ 3, 94, b&w	2.50	0.50	1.50	2.50

VENGEANCE OF VAMPIRELLA
HARRIS
	ORIG.	GOOD	FINE	N-MINT
❑ 1, 94, red foil cover, Quesada/Palmiotti(c)	2.95	6.00	18.00	30.00
❑ 1, 94, second printing, blue foil cover, Quesada/Palmiotti(c)	2.95	1.40	4.20	7.00
❑ 2, 94, color	2.95	3.20	9.60	16.00
❑ 3, 94		1.20	3.60	6.00
❑ 4, 94		0.80	2.40	4.00
❑ 5, Aug 94, 1: The Undead	2.95	0.80	2.40	4.00
❑ 6	2.95	0.59	1.77	2.95
❑ 7	2.95	0.59	1.77	2.95
❑ 8	2.95	0.59	1.77	2.95
❑ 9	2.95	0.59	1.77	2.95
❑ 10	2.95	0.59	1.77	2.95
❑ 11, Feb 95, polybagged with trading card	2.95	0.59	1.77	2.95
❑ 12, Mar 95, 1: Passion; cover has a "Feb '95" date		0.59	1.77	2.95
❑ 13, Apr 95	2.95	0.59	1.77	2.95
❑ 15, Jun 95	2.95	0.59	1.77	2.95

VENGER ROBO
VIZ
	ORIG.	GOOD	FINE	N-MINT
❑ 1	2.75	0.55	1.65	2.75
❑ 2	2.75	0.55	1.65	2.75
❑ 3, 94	2.75	0.55	1.65	2.75
❑ 4, 94	2.75	0.55	1.65	2.75

	ORIG.	GOOD	FINE	N-MINT
❏ 5, 94	2.75	0.55	1.65	2.75
❏ 6, 94	2.75	0.55	1.65	2.75
❏ 7, 94	2.75	0.55	1.65	2.75

VENOM SUPER SPECIAL
MARVEL

	ORIG.	GOOD	FINE	N-MINT
❏ 1, Aug 95, flipbook;two of the stories continue in *Spectacular Spider-Man Super Special #1*	3.95	0.79	2.37	3.95

VENOM: ALONG CAME A SPIDER (mini-series)

	ORIG.	GOOD	FINE	N-MINT
❏ 1, Jan 96	2.95	0.59	1.77	2.95
❏ 2, Feb 96	2.95	0.59	1.77	2.95
❏ 3, Mar 96	2.95	0.59	1.77	2.95
❏ 4, Apr 96	2.95	0.59	1.77	2.95

VENOM: CARNAGE UNLEASHED (mini-series)

	ORIG.	GOOD	FINE	N-MINT
❏ 1, Apr 95, cardstock cover	2.95	0.59	1.77	2.95
❏ 2, May 95, cardstock cover	2.95	0.59	1.77	2.95
❏ 3, Jun 95, cardstock cover	2.95	0.59	1.77	2.95
❏ 4, Jul 95, cardstock cover	2.95	0.59	1.77	2.95

VENOM: FUNERAL PYRE (mini-series)

	ORIG.	GOOD	FINE	N-MINT
❏ 1, foil cover, Punisher	2.95	0.59	1.77	2.95
❏ 2	2.95	0.59	1.77	2.95
❏ 3	2.95	0.59	1.77	2.95

VENOM: LETHAL PROTECTOR (mini-series)

	ORIG.	GOOD	FINE	N-MINT
❏ 1, foil cover	2.95	2.00	6.00	10.00
❏ 1, gold edition		15.00	45.00	75.00
❏ 1, black cover	2.95	25.00	75.00	125.00
❏ 2	2.95	0.80	2.40	4.00
❏ 3	2.95	0.70	2.10	3.50
❏ 4	2.95	0.59	1.77	2.95
❏ 5	2.95	0.59	1.77	2.95
❏ 6	2.95	0.59	1.77	2.95

VENOM: NIGHTS OF VENGEANCE (mini-series)

	ORIG.	GOOD	FINE	N-MINT
❏ 1, Aug 94, red foil cover	2.95	0.59	1.77	2.95
❏ 2, Sep 94, cardstock cover	2.95	0.59	1.77	2.95
❏ 3, Oct 94	2.95	0.59	1.77	2.95
❏ 4, Nov 94, cardstock cover	2.95	0.59	1.77	2.95

VENOM: SEPARATION ANXIETY (mini-series)

	ORIG.	GOOD	FINE	N-MINT
❏ 1, Dec 94, enhanced cover	2.95	0.59	1.77	2.95
❏ 3, Feb 95	2.95	0.59	1.77	2.95
❏ 4, Mar 95	2.95	0.59	1.77	2.95

VENOM: SINNER TAKES ALL (mini-series)

	ORIG.	GOOD	FINE	N-MINT
❏ 1, Aug 95	2.95	0.59	1.77	2.95
❏ 2, Sep 95	2.95	0.59	1.77	2.95
❏ 3, Oct 95	2.95	0.59	1.77	2.95
❏ 4, Nov 95	2.95	0.59	1.77	2.95
❏ 5, Dec 95	2.95	0.59	1.77	2.95

VENOM: THE ENEMY WITHIN (mini-series)

	ORIG.	GOOD	FINE	N-MINT
❏ 1, glow cover	2.95	0.59	1.77	2.95
❏ 2	2.95	0.59	1.77	2.95
❏ 3	2.95	0.59	1.77	2.95

VENOM: THE HUNTED (mini-series)

	ORIG.	GOOD	FINE	N-MINT
❏ 1, May 96	2.95	0.59	1.77	2.95

VENOM: THE MACE (mini-series)

	ORIG.	GOOD	FINE	N-MINT
❏ 1, May 94	2.95	0.59	1.77	2.95
❏ 2, Jun 94	2.95	0.59	1.77	2.95
❏ 3, Jul 94	2.95	0.59	1.77	2.95

VENOM: THE MADNESS (mini-series)

	ORIG.	GOOD	FINE	N-MINT
❏ 1, embossed cover	2.95	0.80	2.40	4.00
❏ 2	2.95	0.59	1.77	2.95
❏ 3	2.95	0.59	1.77	2.95

VENTURE
AC

	ORIG.	GOOD	FINE	N-MINT
❏ 1, 86		0.35	1.05	1.75
❏ 2, 86		0.35	1.05	1.75
❏ 3, 87		0.35	1.05	1.75

VENTURE SAN DIEGO COMIC-CON SPECIAL EDITION
VENTURE

	ORIG.	GOOD	FINE	N-MINT
❏ 1, Jul 94, b&w	2.50	0.50	1.50	2.50

VENUMB
PARODY PRESS

	ORIG.	GOOD	FINE	N-MINT
❏ 1, b&w	2.50	0.50	1.50	2.50

VENUS WARS
DARK HORSE

	ORIG.	GOOD	FINE	N-MINT
❏ 1, Apr 91, Japanese, b&w, trading cards	2.25	0.45	1.35	2.25
❏ 2, 91, Japanese, b&w, trading cards	2.25	0.45	1.35	2.25
❏ 3, 91, Japanese, b&w, trading cards	2.25	0.45	1.35	2.25
❏ 4		0.45	1.35	2.25
❏ 5		0.45	1.35	2.25
❏ 6		0.45	1.35	2.25
❏ 7		0.50	1.50	2.50
❏ 8		0.45	1.35	2.25
❏ 9		0.45	1.35	2.25
❏ 10		0.50	1.50	2.50
❏ 11		0.50	1.50	2.50
❏ 12		0.55	1.65	2.75

VENUS WARS II, THE

	ORIG.	GOOD	FINE	N-MINT
❏ 4		0.50	1.50	2.50
❏ 5, b&w	2.25	0.45	1.35	2.25
❏ 6, b&w	2.25	0.45	1.35	2.25
❏ 7, b&w	2.25	0.45	1.35	2.25
❏ 8, b&w	2.75	0.55	1.65	2.75
❏ 9, b&w	2.95	0.59	1.77	2.95
❏ 10, b&w	2.95	0.59	1.77	2.95
❏ 11, b&w	2.95	0.59	1.77	2.95
❏ 12, b&w	2.95	0.59	1.77	2.95
❏ 13	2.50	0.50	1.50	2.50
❏ 14, Jul 93	2.50	0.50	1.50	2.50
❏ 15, Aug 93	2.50	0.50	1.50	2.50

VERBATIM
FANTAGRAPHICS

	ORIG.	GOOD	FINE	N-MINT
❏ 1, b&w	2.75	0.55	1.65	2.75
❏ 2, b&w	2.75	0.55	1.65	2.75

VERDICT, THE
ETERNITY

	ORIG.	GOOD	FINE	N-MINT
❏ 1, HC(c)		0.39	1.17	1.95
❏ 2		0.39	1.17	1.95
❏ 3		0.39	1.17	1.95
❏ 4		0.39	1.17	1.95

VERONICA
ARCHIE

	ORIG.	GOOD	FINE	N-MINT
❏ 1, Apr 89	0.75	0.40	1.20	2.00
❏ 2		0.30	0.90	1.50
❏ 3		0.30	0.90	1.50
❏ 4		0.30	0.90	1.50
❏ 5		0.30	0.90	1.50
❏ 6		0.30	0.90	1.50
❏ 7		0.30	0.90	1.50
❏ 8		0.30	0.90	1.50
❏ 9		0.30	0.90	1.50
❏ 10		0.30	0.90	1.50
❏ 11		0.30	0.90	1.50
❏ 12		0.30	0.90	1.50
❏ 13		0.30	0.90	1.50
❏ 14		0.30	0.90	1.50
❏ 15		0.30	0.90	1.50
❏ 16		0.30	0.90	1.50

	ORIG.	GOOD	FINE	N-MINT
17		0.30	0.90	1.50
18		0.30	0.90	1.50
19		0.30	0.90	1.50
20		0.30	0.90	1.50
21		0.30	0.90	1.50
22		0.30	0.90	1.50
23		0.30	0.90	1.50
24		0.30	0.90	1.50
25		0.30	0.90	1.50
26		0.30	0.90	1.50
27		0.30	0.90	1.50
28		0.30	0.90	1.50
29		0.30	0.90	1.50
30		0.30	0.90	1.50
31		0.30	0.90	1.50
32		0.30	0.90	1.50
33		0.30	0.90	1.50
34		0.30	0.90	1.50
35		0.30	0.90	1.50
36, Aug 94	1.50	0.30	0.90	1.50
37, Sep 94	1.50	0.30	0.90	1.50
38, Oct 94	1.50	0.30	0.90	1.50
39, Dec 94, "Love Showdown"	1.50	0.30	0.90	1.50
41, Mar 95	1.50	0.30	0.90	1.50
42, Apr 95	1.50	0.30	0.90	1.50
43, Jun 95	1.50	0.30	0.90	1.50
44, Jul 95	1.50	0.30	0.90	1.50
45, Aug 95	1.50	0.30	0.90	1.50
46, Sep 95	1.50	0.30	0.90	1.50
47, Oct 95	1.50	0.30	0.90	1.50
48, Nov 95	1.50	0.30	0.90	1.50
49, Jan 96	1.50	0.30	0.90	1.50
50, Feb 96	1.50	0.30	0.90	1.50
51, Apr 96	1.50	0.30	0.90	1.50
53, Jul 96	1.50	0.30	0.90	1.50

VERONICA'S DIGEST MAGAZINE

	ORIG.	GOOD	FINE	N-MINT
4, Sep 95, digest	1.75	0.35	1.05	1.75

VEROTIKA
VEROTIK

	ORIG.	GOOD	FINE	N-MINT
1	2.95	2.00	6.00	10.00
2, Jan 95	2.95	1.20	3.60	6.00
3	2.95	0.80	2.40	4.00

VERSION
DARK HORSE

	ORIG.	GOOD	FINE	N-MINT
1, b&w, Japanese	2.50	0.50	1.50	2.50
2, b&w, Japanese	2.50	0.50	1.50	2.50
3, b&w, Japanese	2.50	0.50	1.50	2.50
4, b&w, Japanese	2.50	0.50	1.50	2.50
5, b&w, Japanese	2.50	0.50	1.50	2.50
6, b&w, Japanese	2.50	0.50	1.50	2.50
7, b&w, Japanese	2.50	0.50	1.50	2.50
8, b&w, Japanese	2.50	0.50	1.50	2.50

VERSION 2

	ORIG.	GOOD	FINE	N-MINT
1, b&w	2.95	0.59	1.77	2.95
2, b&w	2.95	0.59	1.77	2.95
3, b&w	2.95	0.59	1.77	2.95
4, b&w	2.95	0.59	1.77	2.95
6	2.50	0.50	1.50	2.50

VERTIGO
DC

	ORIG.	GOOD	FINE	N-MINT
1, previews, Sandman story	0.15	0.45	0.75

VERTIGO GALLERY, THE: DREAMS AND NIGHTMARES
DC/VERTIGO

	ORIG.	GOOD	FINE	N-MINT
1, 95	3.50	0.70	2.10	3.50

VERTIGO JAM

	ORIG.	GOOD	FINE	N-MINT
1	3.95	1.00	3.00	5.00

VERTIGO RAVE

	ORIG.	GOOD	FINE	N-MINT
1, Aut 94	0.99	0.40	1.20	2.00

VERTIGO VISIONS: DR. OCCULT

	ORIG.	GOOD	FINE	N-MINT
1, Jul 94, one-shot	3.95	0.79	2.37	3.95

VERTIGO VISIONS: PREZ

	ORIG.	GOOD	FINE	N-MINT
1, 95, one-shot	3.95	0.79	2.37	3.95

VERTIGO VISIONS: THE GEEK

	ORIG.	GOOD	FINE	N-MINT
1	3.95	0.79	2.37	3.95

VERTIGO VISIONS: THE PHANTOM STRANGER

	ORIG.	GOOD	FINE	N-MINT
1	3.50	0.70	2.10	3.50

VERY VICKY
ICONOGRAFIX

	ORIG.	GOOD	FINE	N-MINT
1, b&w	2.95	0.59	1.77	2.95

MEET DANNY OCEAN

	ORIG.	GOOD	FINE	N-MINT
1, b&w, second printing	2.50	0.50	1.50	2.50
2, 93, b&w	2.50	0.50	1.50	2.50
3, 94, b&w	2.50	0.50	1.50	2.50
4, 94, b&w	2.50	0.50	1.50	2.50
5, 94, b&w	2.50	0.50	1.50	2.50
7, 95, b&w	2.50	0.50	1.50	2.50
8, 95, b&w	2.50	0.50	1.50	2.50

VIC AND BLOOD
MAD DOG

	ORIG.	GOOD	FINE	N-MINT
1, Oct 87, Corben, b&w	2.00	0.40	1.20	2.00
2, Feb 88, Corben, b&w	2.00	0.40	1.20	2.00

VIC BRIDGES FAZERS SKETCHBOOK
AC

	ORIG.	GOOD	FINE	N-MINT
1, 86		0.35	1.05	1.75

VICIOUS
BRAINSTORM

	ORIG.	GOOD	FINE	N-MINT
1, adult, b&w	2.95	0.59	1.77	2.95

VICKI
ATLAS/ SEABOARD

	ORIG.	GOOD	FINE	N-MINT
1, reprints Tippy Teen		0.20	0.60	1.00
2, reprints Tippy Teen		0.20	0.60	1.00
3, reprints Tippy Teen		0.20	0.60	1.00
4, reprints Tippy Teen		0.20	0.60	1.00

VICKI VALENTINE
RENEGADE

	ORIG.	GOOD	FINE	N-MINT
1, b&w		0.34	1.02	1.70
2, b&w		0.34	1.02	1.70
3, b&w		0.34	1.02	1.70
4, b&w		0.34	1.02	1.70

VICTIMS, THE
ETERNITY

	ORIG.	GOOD	FINE	N-MINT
1, b&w rep		0.39	1.17	1.95
2, b&w rep		0.39	1.17	1.95
3, b&w rep		0.39	1.17	1.95
4, b&w rep		0.39	1.17	1.95
5, b&w rep		0.39	1.17	1.95

VIDEO CLASSICS

	ORIG.	GOOD	FINE	N-MINT
1, Mighty Mouse, b&w		0.70	2.10	3.50
2, Mighty Mouse, b&w		0.70	2.10	3.50

VIDEO HIROSHIMA
AEON

	ORIG.	GOOD	FINE	N-MINT
0, Aug 95, nn; b&w;one-shot	2.50	0.50	1.50	2.50

VIDEO JACK
EPIC

	ORIG.	GOOD	FINE	N-MINT
1, Sep 87, KG	1.25	0.25	0.75	1.25
2, Nov 87, KG	1.25	0.25	0.75	1.25
3, Mar 88, KG	1.25	0.25	0.75	1.25
4, May 88, KG	1.25	0.25	0.75	1.25
5, Jul 88, KG	1.25	0.25	0.75	1.25
6, Sep 88, KG, FH,JS,WS	1.25	0.25	0.75	1.25

VIETNAM JOURNAL
APPLE

	ORIG.	GOOD	FINE	N-MINT
1, Nov 87, b&w	1.75	1.20	3.60	6.00
1, 2nd printing		0.60	1.80	3.00
2, Jan 88	1.75	0.80	2.40	4.00

	ORIG.	GOOD	FINE	N-MINT
❏ 3		0.60	1.80	3.00
❏ 4		0.60	1.80	3.00
❏ 5		0.60	1.80	3.00
❏ 6		0.39	1.17	1.95
❏ 7		0.39	1.17	1.95
❏ 8		0.39	1.17	1.95
❏ 9		0.39	1.17	1.95
❏ 10		0.39	1.17	1.95
❏ 11		0.45	1.35	2.25
❏ 12		0.45	1.35	2.25
❏ 13		0.45	1.35	2.25
❏ 14		0.45	1.35	2.25
❏ 15		0.45	1.35	2.25
❏ 16		0.45	1.35	2.25

VIETNAM JOURNAL: BLOODBATH AT KHE SANH

	ORIG.	GOOD	FINE	N-MINT
❏ 1, b&w	2.75	0.55	1.65	2.75
❏ 2, b&w	2.75	0.55	1.65	2.75
❏ 3, b&w	2.75	0.55	1.65	2.75
❏ 4, b&w	2.75	0.55	1.65	2.75

VIETNAM JOURNAL: TET '68

	GOOD	FINE	N-MINT
❏ 1, b&w	0.55	1.65	2.75
❏ 2, b&w	0.55	1.65	2.75
❏ 3, b&w	0.55	1.65	2.75
❏ 4, b&w	0.55	1.65	2.75
❏ 5, b&w	0.55	1.65	2.75
❏ 6, b&w	0.55	1.65	2.75

VIETNAM JOURNAL: VALLEY OF DEATH

	ORIG.	GOOD	FINE	N-MINT
❏ 1, Jun 94, b&w	2.75	0.55	1.65	2.75

VIGIL: DESERT FOXES II
MILLENNIUM

	ORIG.	GOOD	FINE	N-MINT
❏ 0, Aug 95, nn;b&w	3.95	0.79	2.37	3.95

VIGIL: FALL FROM GRACE
INNOVATION

	GOOD	FINE	N-MINT
❏ 1, b&w	0.80	2.40	4.00
❏ 2, b&w	0.60	1.80	3.00

VIGIL: KUKULKAN

	ORIG.	GOOD	FINE	N-MINT
❏ 1	2.95	0.80	2.40	4.00

VIGIL: THE GOLDEN PARTS

	GOOD	FINE	N-MINT
❏ 1, b&w	0.80	2.40	4.00

VIGIL: VAMPORUM ANIMATURI
MILLENNIUM

	ORIG.	GOOD	FINE	N-MINT
❏ 0, May 94, nn, b&w	3.95	0.79	2.37	3.95

VIGILANTE
DC

	ORIG.	GOOD	FINE	N-MINT
❏ 1, Nov 83, KP/DG	1.25	1.00	3.00	5.00
❏ 2, Jan 84, KP	1.25	0.60	1.80	3.00
❏ 3, Feb 84	1.25	0.50	1.50	2.50
❏ 4, Mar 84	1.25	0.50	1.50	2.50
❏ 5, Apr 84	1.25	0.50	1.50	2.50
❏ 6, May 84	1.25	0.50	1.50	2.50
❏ 7, Jun 84, O:Vigilante	1.25	0.60	1.80	3.00
❏ 8, Jul 84	1.25	0.50	1.50	2.50
❏ 9, Aug 84	1.25	0.50	1.50	2.50
❏ 10, Sep 84	1.25	0.50	1.50	2.50
❏ 11, Oct 84	1.25	0.30	0.90	1.50
❏ 12, Nov 84	1.25	0.30	0.90	1.50
❏ 13, Dec 84	1.25	0.30	0.90	1.50
❏ 14, Feb 85	1.25	0.30	0.90	1.50
❏ 15, Mar 85	1.25	0.30	0.90	1.50
❏ 16, Apr 85	1.25	0.30	0.90	1.50
❏ 17, May 85, Alan Moore	1.25	0.60	1.80	3.00
❏ 18, Jun 85, Alan Moore	1.25	0.60	1.80	3.00
❏ 19, Jul 85	1.25	0.50	1.50	2.50
❏ 20, Aug 85	1.25	0.50	1.50	2.50
❏ 21, Sep 85	1.25	0.30	0.90	1.50
❏ 22, Oct 85, Crisis	1.25	0.30	0.90	1.50
❏ 23, Nov 85	1.25	0.30	0.90	1.50
❏ 24, Dec 85	1.50	0.30	0.90	1.50
❏ 25, Jan 86	1.50	0.30	0.90	1.50
❏ 26, Feb 86	1.50	0.30	0.90	1.50
❏ 27, Mar 86	1.50	0.30	0.90	1.50
❏ 28, Apr 86	1.50	0.30	0.90	1.50
❏ 29, May 86	1.50	0.30	0.90	1.50
❏ 30, Jun 86	1.50	0.30	0.90	1.50
❏ 31, Jul 86	1.50	0.30	0.90	1.50
❏ 32, Aug 86	1.50	0.30	0.90	1.50
❏ 33, Sep 86	1.50	0.30	0.90	1.50
❏ 34, Oct 86	1.50	0.30	0.90	1.50
❏ 35, Nov 86	1.50	0.30	0.90	1.50
❏ 36, Dec 86, A:Peacemaker	1.50	0.40	1.20	2.00
❏ 37, Jan 87	1.50	0.30	0.90	1.50
❏ 38, Feb 87	1.50	0.30	0.90	1.50
❏ 39, Mar 87	1.50	0.30	0.90	1.50
❏ 40, Apr 87	1.50	0.30	0.90	1.50
❏ 41, May 87	1.50	0.30	0.90	1.50
❏ 42, Jun 87	1.50	0.30	0.90	1.50
❏ 43, Jul 87	1.50	0.30	0.90	1.50
❏ 44, Aug 87	1.50	0.30	0.90	1.50
❏ 45, Sep 87, 1:Blackthorn	1.50	0.30	0.90	1.50
❏ 46, Oct 87	1.50	0.30	0.90	1.50
❏ 47, Nov 87, A:Batman	1.50	0.60	1.80	3.00
❏ 48, Dec 87	1.50	0.30	0.90	1.50
❏ 49, Jan 88	1.50	0.30	0.90	1.50
❏ 50, Feb 88, D:Vigilante	1.50	0.60	1.80	3.00

VIGILANTE ANNUAL

	ORIG.	GOOD	FINE	N-MINT
❏ 1, 85	2.00	0.40	1.20	2.00
❏ 2, 86	2.00	0.40	1.20	2.00

VIGILANTE: CITY LIGHTS, PRAIRIE JUSTICE (mini-series)

	ORIG.	GOOD	FINE	N-MINT
❏ 1, Nov 95	2.50	0.50	1.50	2.50
❏ 2, Dec 95	2.50	0.50	1.50	2.50
❏ 3, Jan 96	2.50	0.50	1.50	2.50
❏ 4, Feb 96	2.50	0.50	1.50	2.50

VIGNETTE COMICS
HARRIER

	GOOD	FINE	N-MINT
❏ 1, b&w	0.39	1.17	1.95

VILE
RAGING RHINO

	ORIG.	GOOD	FINE	N-MINT
❏ 1, 94	2.95	0.59	1.77	2.95

VILLAINS & VIGILANTES
ECLIPSE

	GOOD	FINE	N-MINT
❏ 1, Dec 86	0.30	0.90	1.50
❏ 2, Mar 87	0.30	0.90	1.50
❏ 3, Apr 87	0.30	0.90	1.50
❏ 4, Apr 87	0.30	0.90	1.50

VINCENT J. MIELCAREK JR. MEMORIAL COMIC
COOPER UNION

	ORIG.	GOOD	FINE	N-MINT
❏ 0, nn b&w	3.00	0.60	1.80	3.00

VINTAGE COMIC CLASSICS
RECOLLECTIONS

	GOOD	FINE	N-MINT
❏ 1, Feb 90, Red Demon reprints	0.40	1.20	2.00

VINTAGE MAGNUS ROBOT FIGHTER
VALIANT

	GOOD	FINE	N-MINT
❏ 1, Russ Manning reprints	0.80	2.40	4.00
❏ 2, Russ Manning reprints	0.60	1.80	3.00
❏ 3, Russ Manning reprints	0.60	1.80	3.00
❏ 4, Russ Manning reprints	0.60	1.80	3.00

VINTAGE PACK
MARVEL

	ORIG.	GOOD	FINE	N-MINT
❏ 0, 20 Marvel comic-book reprints	19.95	3.99	11.97	19.95

VIOLATOR
IMAGE

	ORIG.	GOOD	FINE	N-MINT
❏ 1, May 94	1.95	0.90	2.70	4.50
❏ 2, Jun 94	1.95	0.70	2.10	3.50
❏ 3, Jul 94	1.95	0.39	1.17	1.95

	ORIG.	GOOD	FINE	N-MINT

VIOLATOR VS. BADROCK

	ORIG.	GOOD	FINE	N-MINT
❏ 1, May 95, AMo(w)	2.50	0.50	1.50	2.50
❏ 2, Jun 95, AMo(w)	2.50	0.50	1.50	2.50
❏ 3, Jul 95, AMo(w)	2.50	0.50	1.50	2.50
❏ 4, Aug 95, AMo(w).........	2.50	0.50	1.50	2.50

VIPER (mini-series)
DC

	ORIG.	GOOD	FINE	N-MINT
❏ 1, Aug 94	1.95	0.39	1.17	1.95
❏ 2, Sep 94.......................	1.95	0.39	1.17	1.95
❏ 3, Oct 94	1.95	0.39	1.17	1.95
❏ 4, Nov 94	1.95	0.39	1.17	1.95

VIRUS
DARK HORSE

	ORIG.	GOOD	FINE	N-MINT
❏ 1	2.50	0.50	1.50	2.50
❏ 2	2.50	0.50	1.50	2.50
❏ 3	2.50	0.50	1.50	2.50
❏ 4	2.50	0.50	1.50	2.50

VISION & SCARLET WITCH
MARVEL

	ORIG.	GOOD	FINE	N-MINT
❏ 1, Nov 82	0.60	0.35	1.05	1.75
❏ 2, Dec 82.......................	0.60	0.25	0.75	1.25
❏ 3, Jan 83	0.60	0.25	0.75	1.25
❏ 4, Feb 83.......................	0.60	0.25	0.75	1.25

VISION & SCARLET WITCH (2nd series)

	ORIG.	GOOD	FINE	N-MINT
❏ 1, Oct 85	1.25	0.25	0.75	1.25
❏ 2, Nov 85	0.75	0.20	0.60	1.00
❏ 3, Dec 85.......................	0.75	0.20	0.60	1.00
❏ 4, Jan 86	0.75	0.20	0.60	1.00
❏ 5, Feb 86	0.75	0.20	0.60	1.00
❏ 6, Mar 86	0.75	0.20	0.60	1.00
❏ 7, Apr 86	0.75	0.20	0.60	1.00
❏ 8, May 86	0.75	0.20	0.60	1.00
❏ 9, Jun 86	0.75	0.20	0.60	1.00
❏ 10, Jul 86	0.75	0.20	0.60	1.00
❏ 11, Aug 86				
❏ 12, Sep 86......................	1.25	0.25	0.75	1.25

VISION, THE (mini-series)

	ORIG.	GOOD	FINE	N-MINT
❏ 1, Nov 94	1.75	0.35	1.05	1.75
❏ 2, Dec 94.......................	1.75	0.35	1.05	1.75
❏ 3, Jan 95	1.75	0.35	1.05	1.75
❏ 4, Feb 95	1.75	0.35	1.05	1.75

VISIONARIES
STAR

	ORIG.	GOOD	FINE	N-MINT
❏ 1	1.50	0.30	0.90	1.50
❏ 2, (becomes Marvel comic)				
....	1.00	0.20	0.60	1.00

VISIONARIES (was Star Comic)
MARVEL

	ORIG.	GOOD	FINE	N-MINT
❏ 3	1.00	0.20	0.60	1.00
❏ 4	1.00	0.20	0.60	1.00
❏ 5	1.00	0.20	0.60	1.00
❏ 6	1.00	0.20	0.60	1.00

VISIONS OF CURVES
EROS

	ORIG.	GOOD	FINE	N-MINT
❏ 1, Apr 94, b&w...............	4.95	0.99	2.97	4.95

VISIONS: R.G. TAYLOR
CALIBER

	ORIG.	GOOD	FINE	N-MINT
❏ 0, 94, nn;b&w	2.50	0.50	1.50	2.50

VISITOR VS. THE VALIANT UNIVERSE (mini-series)
VALIANT

	ORIG.	GOOD	FINE	N-MINT
❏ 1, Feb 95, cardstock cover				
....	2.95	0.59	1.77	2.95
❏ 2, Feb 95, cardstock cover				
....	2.95	0.59	1.77	2.95

VISITOR, THE
ACCLAIM/VALIANT

	ORIG.	GOOD	FINE	N-MINT
❏ 3, Jun 95.......................	2.50	0.50	1.50	2.50
❏ 4, Jul 95........................	2.50	0.50	1.50	2.50
❏ 5, Jul 95........................	2.50	0.50	1.50	2.50
❏ 6, Aug 95.......................	2.50	0.50	1.50	2.50
❏ 7, Aug 95.......................	2.50	0.50	1.50	2.50
❏ 8, Sep 95, The Harbinger's identity is revealed				
....	2.50	0.50	1.50	2.50
❏ 9, Sep 95.......................	2.50	0.50	1.50	2.50
❏ 10, Oct 95......................	2.50	0.50	1.50	2.50
❏ 11, Oct 95......................	2.50	0.50	1.50	2.50
❏ 12, Nov 95......................	2.50	0.50	1.50	2.50

VALIANT

	ORIG.	GOOD	FINE	N-MINT
❏ 1, Apr 95.......................	2.50	0.50	1.50	2.50
❏ 2, May 95......................	2.50	0.50	1.50	2.50

VISUAL ASSAULT OMNIBUS
VISUAL ASSAULT

	ORIG.	GOOD	FINE	N-MINT
❏ 1, 93, b&w.....................	2.50	0.50	1.50	2.50
❏ 2, 94, b&w.....................	2.50	0.50	1.50	2.50
❏ 3, 94, b&w.....................	3.00	0.60	1.80	3.00

VIXEN WARRIOR DIARIES
RAGING RHINO

	ORIG.	GOOD	FINE	N-MINT
❏ 1, adult, b&w	2.95	0.59	1.77	2.95

VIXEN WARS: VENGEANCE MANIFESTO

	ORIG.	GOOD	FINE	N-MINT
❏ 1, adult, b&w	2.95	0.59	1.77	2.95
❏ 2, adult, b&w	2.95	0.59	1.77	2.95
❏ 3, adult, b&w	2.95	0.59	1.77	2.95
❏ 4, adult, b&w	2.95	0.59	1.77	2.95
❏ 5, adult, b&w	2.95	0.59	1.77	2.95

VLAD THE IMPALER
TOPPS

	ORIG.	GOOD	FINE	N-MINT
❏ 3	2.95	0.59	1.77	2.95

VOGUE (mini-series)
IMAGE

	ORIG.	GOOD	FINE	N-MINT
❏ 1, Oct 95........................	2.50	0.50	1.50	2.50
❏ 1, Oct 95, alternate cover	2.50	0.50	1.50	2.50
❏ 2, Nov 95.......................	2.50	0.50	1.50	2.50
❏ 3, Dec 95	2.50	0.50	1.50	2.50

VOID INDIGO
EPIC

	ORIG.	GOOD	FINE	N-MINT
❏ 1, VM.............................	1.50	0.70	2.10	3.50
❏ 2, VM.............................	1.50	0.70	2.10	3.50

VOLCANIC NIGHTS
PALLIARD

	ORIG.	GOOD	FINE	N-MINT
❏ 1, adult, b&w		0.59	1.77	2.95

VOLTRON
SOLSON

	ORIG.	GOOD	FINE	N-MINT
❏ 1		0.15	0.45	0.75
❏ 2		0.15	0.45	0.75
❏ 3		0.15	0.45	0.75

VOLUNTEERS QUEST FOR DREAMS LOST
LITERACY

	ORIG.	GOOD	FINE	N-MINT
❏ 1, Turtles, Trollords, b&w.		0.40	1.20	2.00

VOODOO INK
DEJA-VU

	ORIG.	GOOD	FINE	N-MINT
❏ 0, b&w...........................	1.95	0.39	1.17	1.95

	ORIG.	GOOD	FINE	N-MINT
ESTUDIOS DEJA-VU				
☐ 1, b&w	1.95	0.39	1.17	1.95
☐ 2, b&w	1.95	0.39	1.17	1.95
☐ 3, b&w	1.95	0.39	1.17	1.95
☐ 4, b&w	1.95	0.39	1.17	1.95
☐ 5, b&w	1.95	0.39	1.17	1.95
VOODOO-ZEALOT: SKIN TRADE				
IMAGE				
☐ 0, Aug 95, nn;one-shot	4.95	0.99	2.97	4.95
VORTEX				
COMICO				
☐ 1		0.50	1.50	2.50
☐ 2		0.50	1.50	2.50
HALL OF HEROES				
☐ 1, b&w	2.50	0.50	1.50	2.50
VORTEX				
☐ 1		0.35	1.05	1.75
☐ 2		0.35	1.05	1.75
☐ 3		0.35	1.05	1.75
☐ 4		0.35	1.05	1.75
☐ 5		0.35	1.05	1.75
☐ 6		0.35	1.05	1.75
☐ 7		0.35	1.05	1.75
☐ 8		0.35	1.05	1.75
☐ 9		0.35	1.05	1.75
☐ 10		0.35	1.05	1.75

	ORIG.	GOOD	FINE	N-MINT
☐ 11		0.35	1.05	1.75
☐ 12		0.35	1.05	1.75
☐ 13		0.35	1.05	1.75
☐ 14		0.35	1.05	1.75
☐ 15		0.35	1.05	1.75
VORTEX THE WONDER MULE				
CUTTING EDGE				
☐ 1, b&w		0.59	1.77	2.95
☐ 2, b&w		0.59	1.77	2.95
VOX				
APPLE				
☐ 1, JBy(c) b&w		0.39	1.17	1.95
☐ 2		0.45	1.35	2.25
☐ 3		0.45	1.35	2.25
☐ 4		0.45	1.35	2.25
☐ 5		0.45	1.35	2.25
☐ 6		0.45	1.35	2.25
VOYEUR, THE				
AIRCEL				
☐ 1, adult, b&w		0.50	1.50	2.50
☐ 2, adult, b&w		0.50	1.50	2.50
☐ 3, adult, b&w		0.50	1.50	2.50
☐ 4		0.59	1.77	2.95
VULTURES OF WHAPETON				
CONQUEST				
☐ 1, b&w		0.59	1.77	2.95

Vampirella

First appearance: *Vampirella* #1 (September 1969)

Not a traditional vampire, Vampirella doesn't avoid sunlight, sleep in a coffin, or create other vampires. She is a refugee from the planet Drakulon which flows with literal rivers of blood. As the series began, only a serum, which had to be taken every 24 hours, prevented her from being overtaken by a thirst for human blood. A "Bad Girl" with a heart of gold, Vampirella is in constant battle with the sinister Cult of Chaos. She has been assisted by her lover Adam Van Helsing (yes, a descendant of *that* Van Helsing) and an alcoholic ex-stage magician named Pendragon.

Vampirella originally appeared in a black-and-white magazine from Warren Publishing which ran through 1983, to issue #112. The character's first story was written by Forrest Ackerman and her look was established by Frank Frazetta's painting for issue #1. Her principle artists during the Warren years were Tom Sutton and José Gonzales, with Archie Goodman and later Flaxman Loew writing most of the stories.

Harris Comics printed issue #113 in 1988 and, in 1991, published a four-issue black-and-white comic-book mini-series, *Vampirella: Morning in America*, in conjunction with Dark Horse Comics. Harris published its first color *Vampirella* series in 1992 and began the ongoing series *Vengeance of*

Vampirella in 1994. In addition to the ongoing series, Harris has printed several Vampirella mini-series and specials, including reprints of the original Warren material. Vampirella has also appeared in an inter-company crossover, *Vampirella/Shadowhawk: Creatures of the Night*, co-starring with Jim Valentino's vigilante character published by Image Comics.

Partial Checklist:

Vampirella #1 (Sep 69)	First Warren issue
Vampirella: Morning in America #1 (1991)	Harris/Dark Horse series reintroducing Vampirella
Vampirella #1 (Nov 92)	Color Vampirella series
Vengeance of Vampirella #1 (Apr 94)	First issue of ongoing series

W

	ORIG.	GOOD	FINE	N-MINT

W.O.W. THE WORLD OF WARD
ALLIED AMERICAN ARTISTS
☐ 1, b&w, Bill Ward, Jack Cole reprints

		0.79	2.37	3.95

WABBIT WAMPAGE
AMAZING

		ORIG.	GOOD	FINE	N-MINT
☐ 1		0.39	1.17	1.95	

WACKY SQUIRREL
DARK HORSE

☐ 1, b&w	0.40	1.20	2.00
☐ 2	0.35	1.05	1.75
☐ 3	0.35	1.05	1.75
☐ 4	0.35	1.05	1.75

WACKY SQUIRREL
HALLOWEEN ADVENTURE SPECIAL

☐ 1, A:Mr. Monster	0.35	1.05	1.75

WACKY SQUIRREL SUMMER FUN SPECIAL

☐ 1, Jul 87	0.35	1.05	1.75

WALDO WORLD
FANTAGRAPHICS

☐ 1, b&w	2.50	0.50	1.50	2.50
☐ 2, b&w	2.50	0.50	1.50	2.50

WALK THROUGH OCTOBER
CALIBER

☐ 1, 95, b&w	2.95	0.59	1.77	2.95

WALKING DEAD ZOMBIE SPECIAL, THE
AIRCEL

☐ 1, b&w	0.45	1.35	2.25

WALKING DEAD, THE

☐ 1, b&w	0.45	1.35	2.25
☐ 2, b&w	0.45	1.35	2.25
☐ 3, b&w	0.45	1.35	2.25
☐ 4, b&w	0.45	1.35	2.25

WALL OF FLESH
AC

☐ 1, b&w, reprints	0.59	1.77	2.95

WALLACE WOOD'S HORNY TOADS
EROS

☐ 1, adult, b&w	2.95	0.59	1.77	2.95

WALLACE WOOD'S PIPSQUEAK PAPERS

☐ 1, adult, b&w	2.75	0.55	1.65	2.75

WALLY THE WIZARD
STAR

☐ 1	0.65	0.13	0.39	0.65
☐ 2	0.65	0.13	0.39	0.65
☐ 3	0.65	0.13	0.39	0.65
☐ 4	0.65	0.13	0.39	0.65
☐ 5	0.65	0.13	0.39	0.65
☐ 6	0.65	0.13	0.39	0.65
☐ 7	0.65	0.13	0.39	0.65
☐ 8	0.65	0.13	0.39	0.65
☐ 9	0.65	0.13	0.39	0.65
☐ 10	0.65	0.13	0.39	0.65
☐ 11	0.65	0.13	0.39	0.65
☐ 12	0.65	0.13	0.39	0.65

WALLY WOOD'S THUNDER AGENTS
DELUXE

☐ 1, Nov 84, GP,KG,DC	2.00	0.40	1.20	2.00
☐ 2, Jan 85, GP,KG,DC	2.00	0.40	1.20	2.00
☐ 3, Nov 85, GP,KG,DC	2.00	0.40	1.20	2.00
☐ 4, Feb 86, GP,KG,DC	2.00	0.40	1.20	2.00
☐ 5, Oct 86, JOy,KG	2.00	0.40	1.20	2.00

WALT DISNEY GIANT
GLADSTONE
☐ 1, Sep 95, newprint cover;DR;"Hearts of the Yukon"

	2.25	0.45	1.35	2.25

	ORIG.	GOOD	FINE	N-MINT
☐ 2, Nov 95	2.25	0.45	1.35	2.25
☐ 3, Jan 96	2.25	0.45	1.35	2.25

WALT DISNEY'S AUTUMN ADVENTURES
DISNEY

☐ 1, CB	0.59	1.77	2.95
☐ 2, CB	0.59	1.77	2.95

WALT DISNEY'S CHRISTMAS PARADE
GLADSTONE
☐ 1, Win 88, CB reprints;100 pages;cardstock cover

	2.95	0.80	2.40	4.00
☐ 2, CB reprints		0.80	2.40	4.00

WALT DISNEY'S COMICS & STORIES

☐ 511, Oct 86, CB	0.75	1.00	3.00	5.00
☐ 512, Nov 86	0.75	0.80	2.40	4.00
☐ 513, Dec 86	0.75	0.80	2.40	4.00
☐ 514, Jan 87	0.75	0.60	1.80	3.00
☐ 515, Feb 87	0.75	0.60	1.80	3.00
☐ 516, Mar 87, CB	0.75	0.60	1.80	3.00
☐ 517, Apr 87	0.75	0.60	1.80	3.00
☐ 518, May 87	0.75	0.60	1.80	3.00
☐ 519, Jun 87	0.75	0.60	1.80	3.00
☐ 520, Jul 87, CB	0.95	0.60	1.80	3.00
☐ 521, Aug 87, CB, Walt Kelly				
	0.95	0.40	1.20	2.00
☐ 522, CB, Walt Kelly O:Huey, Dewey, Louie				
		0.40	1.20	2.00
☐ 523, Oct 87, CB;1st Rosa 10-page story				
	0.95	1.00	3.00	5.00
☐ 524, Nov 87, CB	0.95	0.40	1.20	2.00
☐ 525, Dec 87, CB	0.95	0.40	1.20	2.00
☐ 526, Jan 88, CB	0.95	0.40	1.20	2.00
☐ 527, Mar 88, CB	0.95	0.40	1.20	2.00
☐ 528, Mar 88, CB	0.95	0.40	1.20	2.00
☐ 529, Jun 88, CB	0.95	0.40	1.20	2.00
☐ 530, Aug 88, CB	0.95	0.40	1.20	2.00
☐ 531, WK(c),Don Rosa,CB		0.60	1.80	3.00
☐ 532, CB, Don Rosa		0.60	1.80	3.00
☐ 533, CB		0.40	1.20	2.00
☐ 534, CB		0.40	1.20	2.00
☐ 535, CB		0.40	1.20	2.00
☐ 536, CB		0.40	1.20	2.00
☐ 537, CB;1st Wm. Van Horn 10-page story				
		0.40	1.20	2.00
☐ 538, WK(c), CB		0.40	1.20	2.00
☐ 539, CB		0.40	1.20	2.00
☐ 540, CB		0.40	1.20	2.00
☐ 541, WK(c),CB 48 pgs.		0.40	1.20	2.00
☐ 542, CB		0.40	1.20	2.00
☐ 543, WK(c), CB		0.40	1.20	2.00
☐ 544, WK(c), CB		0.40	1.20	2.00
☐ 545, CB		0.40	1.20	2.00
☐ 546, CB, WK		0.40	1.20	2.00
☐ 547, CB, Don Rosa (moves to Disney)				
		0.60	1.80	3.00

WALT DISNEY'S COMICS AND STORIES
DISNEY

☐ 548		0.30	0.90	1.50
☐ 549, CB		0.30	0.90	1.50
☐ 550, CB:Milkman story		0.45	1.35	2.25
☐ 551, CB		0.30	0.90	1.50
☐ 552, CB		0.30	0.90	1.50
☐ 553, CB		0.30	0.90	1.50
☐ 554, CB		0.30	0.90	1.50
☐ 555		0.30	0.90	1.50
☐ 556		0.30	0.90	1.50
☐ 557, CB		0.30	0.90	1.50
☐ 558, CB		0.30	0.90	1.50
☐ 559, CB		0.30	0.90	1.50
☐ 560, CB		0.30	0.90	1.50

	ORIG.	GOOD	FINE	N-MINT
561, CB		0.30	0.90	1.50
562, CB		0.30	0.90	1.50
563, CB		0.30	0.90	1.50
564	1.50	0.30	0.90	1.50
565, CB		0.30	0.90	1.50
566, CB		0.30	0.90	1.50
567, CB		0.30	0.90	1.50
568, CB		0.30	0.90	1.50
569, CB		0.30	0.90	1.50
570, CB		0.30	0.90	1.50
571, CB		0.59	1.77	2.95
572, map piece, CB		0.30	0.90	1.50
573, map piece, CB		0.30	0.90	1.50
574, map piece, CB		0.59	1.77	2.95
576, CB		0.59	1.77	2.95
577, CB reprint		0.30	0.90	1.50
578, CB reprint		0.30	0.90	1.50
580, strip reprints		0.59	1.77	2.95
581, CB reprint		0.30	0.90	1.50
582, WK, FG Sky Island		0.59	1.77	2.95
583, WK, FG Sky Island		0.59	1.77	2.95
584, CB reprint	1.50	0.30	0.90	1.50
585, CB,FG reprint (returns to Gladstone)				
	2.50	0.50	1.50	2.50

WALT DISNEY'S COMICS AND STORIES
(was Disney title)
GLADSTONE

	ORIG.	GOOD	FINE	N-MINT
586, Aug 93	1.50	0.30	0.90	1.50
587, Oct 93, Van Horn	1.50	0.30	0.90	1.50
588, Dec 93, Van Horn	1.50	0.30	0.90	1.50
589, Feb 94	1.50	0.30	0.90	1.50
590, Apr 94	1.50	0.30	0.90	1.50
591, Jun 94, WVH	1.50	0.30	0.90	1.50
592, Aug 94	1.50	0.30	0.90	1.50
593, Oct 94	1.50	0.30	0.90	1.50
594, Dec 94	1.50	0.30	0.90	1.50
595, Feb 95, WVH	1.50	0.30	0.90	1.50
596, Apr 95	1.50	0.30	0.90	1.50
597, Jun 95	1.50	0.30	0.90	1.50
598, Aug 95	1.50	0.30	0.90	1.50
599, Oct 95	1.95	0.39	1.17	1.95
600, Dec 95, reprints first Barks, Rosa, and Van Horn Donald Duck stories	2.95	0.59	1.77	2.95

WALT DISNEY'S HOLIDAY PARADE
DISNEY

	ORIG.	GOOD	FINE	N-MINT
1, CB		0.59	1.77	2.95
2, CB		0.59	1.77	2.95

WALT DISNEY'S ONE HUNDRED AND ONE DALMATIONS

	ORIG.	GOOD	FINE	N-MINT
1, 91	2.50	0.50	1.50	2.50

WALT DISNEY'S PINOCCHIO SPECIAL
GLADSTONE

	ORIG.	GOOD	FINE	N-MINT
1, 90, WK	1.00	0.40	1.20	2.00

WALT DISNEY'S SPRING FEVER
DISNEY

	ORIG.	GOOD	FINE	N-MINT
1, CB		0.59	1.77	2.95

WALT DISNEY'S SUMMER FUN

	ORIG.	GOOD	FINE	N-MINT
1		0.59	1.77	2.95

WALT DISNEY'S UNCLE SCROOGE
GOES TO DISNEYLAND
GLADSTONE

	ORIG.	GOOD	FINE	N-MINT
1, 85	2.50	0.50	1.50	2.50

WALT DISNEY'S COMICS DIGEST

	ORIG.	GOOD	FINE	N-MINT
1, WK, CB		1.00	3.00	5.00
2, CB		0.80	2.40	4.00
3, CB		0.60	1.80	3.00
4, CB		0.40	1.20	2.00
5, CB		0.60	1.80	3.00
6, CB		0.40	1.20	2.00
7, CB		0.40	1.20	2.00

WALT KELLY'S CHRISTMAS CLASSICS
ECLIPSE

	ORIG.	GOOD	FINE	N-MINT
1, WK, Peter Wheat		0.35	1.05	1.75

WALT KELLY'S SANTA CLAUS ADVENTURES
INNOVATION

	ORIG.	GOOD	FINE	N-MINT
0, pb WK reprints		1.39	4.17	6.95

WALT KELLY'S SPRINGTIME TALES
ECLIPSE

	ORIG.	GOOD	FINE	N-MINT
1, WK, Peter Wheat		0.50	1.50	2.50

WALTER (mini-series)
DARK HORSE

	ORIG.	GOOD	FINE	N-MINT
1, Feb 96	2.50	0.50	1.50	2.50
2, Mar 96	2.50	0.50	1.50	2.50
3, Apr 96	2.50	0.50	1.50	2.50
4, May 96, final issue	2.50	0.50	1.50	2.50

WANDA LUWAND & THE PIRATE GIRLS
EROS COMIX

	ORIG.	GOOD	FINE	N-MINT
1, adult, b&w		0.50	1.50	2.50

WANDERERS, THE
DC

	ORIG.	GOOD	FINE	N-MINT
1, Jun 88	1.25	0.25	0.75	1.25
2, Jul 88	1.25	0.25	0.75	1.25
3, Aug 88	1.25	0.25	0.75	1.25
4, Sep 88	1.25	0.25	0.75	1.25
5, Oct 88	1.25	0.25	0.75	1.25
6, Nov 88	1.25	0.25	0.75	1.25
7, Dec 88	1.25	0.25	0.75	1.25
8, Dec 88	1.25	0.25	0.75	1.25
9, Jan 89	1.25	0.25	0.75	1.25
10, Jan 89	1.25	0.25	0.75	1.25
11, Feb 89	1.25	0.25	0.75	1.25
12, Mar 89	1.25	0.25	0.75	1.25
13, Apr 89	1.25	0.25	0.75	1.25

WANDERING STAR
PEN AND INK

	ORIG.	GOOD	FINE	N-MINT
1	2.00	2.00	6.00	10.00
2	2.00	1.20	3.60	6.00
3	2.00	0.80	2.40	4.00
4	2.00	0.80	2.40	4.00
5	2.00	0.60	1.80	3.00
6, Mar 94, b&w	2.00	0.40	1.20	2.00
9, Aug 95, b&w	2.50	0.50	1.50	2.50
10, Oct 95, b&w	2.50	0.50	1.50	2.50

WANDERING STARS
FANTAGRAPHICS

	ORIG.	GOOD	FINE	N-MINT
1		0.40	1.20	2.00

WANTED, THE WORLD'S
MOST DANGEROUS VILLAINS
DC

	ORIG.	GOOD	FINE	N-MINT
1, Aug 72	0.20	1.20	3.60	6.00
2, Oct 72	0.20	1.60	4.80	8.00
3, Nov 72	0.20	0.70	2.10	3.50
4, Dec 72	0.20	0.70	2.10	3.50
5, Jan 73	0.20	0.70	2.10	3.50
6, Feb 73	0.20	0.70	2.10	3.50
7, Apr 73	0.20	0.70	2.10	3.50
8, Jul 73	0.20	0.70	2.10	3.50
9, Sep 73	0.20	0.70	2.10	3.50

WAR
A-PLUS

	ORIG.	GOOD	FINE	N-MINT
1, WW, b&w reprints		0.50	1.50	2.50

WAR CRIMINALS
COMIC ZONE

	ORIG.	GOOD	FINE	N-MINT
1, b&w		0.59	1.77	2.95

WAR DANCER
DEFIANT

	ORIG.	GOOD	FINE	N-MINT
1, Feb 94	2.50	0.50	1.50	2.50
2, Mar 94	2.50	0.50	1.50	2.50
3, Apr 94	2.50	0.50	1.50	2.50
5, Jun 94	2.50	0.50	1.50	2.50

	ORIG.	GOOD	FINE	N-MINT

WAR GAMES
BISHOP PRESS
	ORIG.	GOOD	FINE	N-MINT
☐ 1, b&w	2.50	0.50	1.50	2.50

WAR HEROES CLASSICS
RECOLLECTIONS
	ORIG.	GOOD	FINE	N-MINT
☐ 1, b&w reprints		0.40	1.20	2.00

WAR IS HELL
MARVEL
	ORIG.	GOOD	FINE	N-MINT
☐ 1, Jan 73, reprints	0.20	0.30	0.90	1.50
☐ 2, reprints	0.20	0.20	0.60	1.00
☐ 3, reprints	0.20	0.20	0.60	1.00
☐ 4, reprints	0.20	0.20	0.60	1.00
☐ 5, reprints	0.20	0.20	0.60	1.00
☐ 6, reprints	0.20	0.20	0.60	1.00
☐ 7, reprints	0.25	0.20	0.60	1.00
☐ 8, reprints	0.25	0.20	0.60	1.00
☐ 9	0.25	0.40	1.20	2.00
☐ 10, Dec 74	0.25	0.40	1.20	2.00
☐ 11	0.25	0.40	1.20	2.00
☐ 12	0.25	0.40	1.20	2.00
☐ 13, Jun 75	0.25	0.40	1.20	2.00
☐ 14, Aug 75	0.25	0.40	1.20	2.00
☐ 15, Oct 75, final issue	0.25	0.40	1.20	2.00

WAR MACHINE
	ORIG.	GOOD	FINE	N-MINT
☐ 1, ashcan edition	0.75	0.15	0.45	0.75
☐ 1, foil cover	2.95	0.59	1.77	2.95
☐ 1, newsstand	2.00	0.40	1.20	2.00
☐ 2, May 94	1.50	0.30	0.90	1.50
☐ 3, Jun 94	1.50	0.30	0.90	1.50
☐ 4, Jul 94	1.50	0.30	0.90	1.50
☐ 5, Aug 94	1.50	0.30	0.90	1.50
☐ 6, Sep 94	1.50	0.30	0.90	1.50
☐ 7, Oct 94	1.50	0.30	0.90	1.50
☐ 8, Nov 94, polybagged with 16-page Marvel Action Hour preview, acetate print, coupon, sweepstakes entry form	2.95	0.59	1.77	2.95
☐ 8, Nov 94	1.50	0.30	0.90	1.50
☐ 9, Dec 94	1.50	0.30	0.90	1.50
☐ 10, Jan 95	1.50	0.30	0.90	1.50
☐ 11, Feb 95	1.50	0.30	0.90	1.50
☐ 12, Mar 95	1.50	0.30	0.90	1.50
☐ 13, Apr 95	1.50	0.30	0.90	1.50
☐ 14, May 95	1.50	0.30	0.90	1.50
☐ 15, Jun 95, flip book with War Machine: Brothers in Arms part 2	2.50	0.50	1.50	2.50
☐ 16, Jul 95	1.50	0.30	0.90	1.50
☐ 17, Aug 95	1.50	0.30	0.90	1.50
☐ 18, Sep 95	1.50	0.30	0.90	1.50
☐ 19, Oct 95	1.50	0.30	0.90	1.50
☐ 20, Nov 95	1.50	0.30	0.90	1.50
☐ 21, Dec 95	1.50	0.30	0.90	1.50
☐ 22, Jan 96	1.50	0.30	0.90	1.50
☐ 23, Feb 96	1.50	0.30	0.90	1.50
☐ 24, Mar 96	1.50	0.30	0.90	1.50
☐ 25, Apr 96, final issue	1.50	0.30	0.90	1.50

WAR MAN
EPIC
	ORIG.	GOOD	FINE	N-MINT
☐ 1	2.50	0.50	1.50	2.50
☐ 2	2.50	0.50	1.50	2.50

WAR OF THE GODS
DC
	ORIG.	GOOD	FINE	N-MINT
☐ 1, Sep 91, GP	1.75	0.35	1.05	1.75
☐ 2, Oct 91, GP direct sale cover	1.75	0.35	1.05	1.75
☐ 2, Oct 91, GP newsstand cover		0.35	1.05	1.75
☐ 3, Nov 91, GP direct sale cover	1.75	0.35	1.05	1.75
☐ 3, Nov 91, GP newsstand cover		0.35	1.05	1.75
☐ 4, Dec 91, GP direct sale cover	1.75	0.35	1.05	1.75
☐ 4, Dec 91, GP newsstand cover		0.35	1.05	1.75

WAR OF THE WORLDS
ETERNITY
	ORIG.	GOOD	FINE	N-MINT
☐ 1, b&w		0.39	1.17	1.95
☐ 2, b&w		0.39	1.17	1.95
☐ 3, b&w		0.39	1.17	1.95
☐ 4, b&w		0.39	1.17	1.95
☐ 5, b&w		0.39	1.17	1.95
☐ 6, b&w		0.39	1.17	1.95

WAR PARTY
LIGHTNING
	ORIG.	GOOD	FINE	N-MINT
☐ 1, Oct 94	2.95	0.59	1.77	2.95

WAR SIRENS AND LIBERTY BELLES
RECOLLECTIONS
	ORIG.	GOOD	FINE	N-MINT
☐ 1, b&w reprints		0.99	2.97	4.95

WAR SLUTS
PRETTY GRAPHIC
	ORIG.	GOOD	FINE	N-MINT
☐ 1, 93, b&w	3.95	0.79	2.37	3.95
☐ 2, 94, adult;b&w;cardstock cover	3.95	0.79	2.37	3.95

WAR, THE
MARVEL
	ORIG.	GOOD	FINE	N-MINT
☐ 1, Jun 89	3.50	0.70	2.10	3.50
☐ 2, Jul 89	3.50	0.70	2.10	3.50
☐ 3, Aug 89	3.50	0.70	2.10	3.50
☐ 4, Feb 90	3.50	0.70	2.10	3.50

WARBLADE: ENDANGERED SPECIES
IMAGE
	ORIG.	GOOD	FINE	N-MINT
☐ 1, Jan 95	2.50	0.50	1.50	2.50
☐ 3, Mar 95	2.50	0.50	1.50	2.50
☐ 4, Apr 95	2.50	0.50	1.50	2.50

WARCAT SPECIAL
EXPRESS/ENTITY
	ORIG.	GOOD	FINE	N-MINT
☐ 1, 95	2.95	0.59	1.77	2.95

WARCHILD
MAXIMUM PRESS
	ORIG.	GOOD	FINE	N-MINT
☐ 1, Dec 94	2.50	0.50	1.50	2.50
☐ 2, Jan 95	2.50	0.50	1.50	2.50
☐ 2, Jan 95, alternate cover	2.50	0.50	1.50	2.50
☐ 3, Jun 95	2.50	0.50	1.50	2.50
☐ 3, Jun 95, alternate cover	2.50	0.50	1.50	2.50
☐ 4, Aug 95	2.50	0.50	1.50	2.50

WARHAWKS COMICS MODULE
TSR INC.
	ORIG.	GOOD	FINE	N-MINT
☐ 1		0.59	1.77	2.95
☐ 2		0.59	1.77	2.95
☐ 3		0.59	1.77	2.95
☐ 4		0.59	1.77	2.95
☐ 5, Warhawks 2050		0.59	1.77	2.95
☐ 6, Warhawks 2050		0.59	1.77	2.95
☐ 7, Warhawks 2050		0.59	1.77	2.95
☐ 8, Warhawks 2050		0.59	1.77	2.95
☐ 9, Warhawks 2050		0.59	1.77	2.95

WARHEADS
MARVEL
	ORIG.	GOOD	FINE	N-MINT
☐ 1, Wolverine	1.75	0.35	1.05	1.75
☐ 2	1.75	0.35	1.05	1.75
☐ 3	1.75	0.35	1.05	1.75
☐ 4	1.75	0.35	1.05	1.75
☐ 5	1.75	0.35	1.05	1.75
☐ 6	1.75	0.35	1.05	1.75
☐ 7	1.75	0.35	1.05	1.75
☐ 8	1.75	0.35	1.05	1.75
☐ 9	1.75	0.35	1.05	1.75
☐ 10	1.75	0.35	1.05	1.75
☐ 11	1.75	0.35	1.05	1.75
☐ 12	1.75	0.35	1.05	1.75
☐ 13	1.75	0.35	1.05	1.75
☐ 14	1.75	0.35	1.05	1.75

	ORIG.	GOOD	FINE	N-MINT

WARHEADS: BLACK DAWN

	ORIG.	GOOD	FINE	N-MINT
❑ 1, foil cover	2.95	0.59	1.77	2.95
❑ 2	1.75	0.35	1.05	1.75

WARLASH
CFD

	ORIG.	GOOD	FINE	N-MINT
❑ 1, Apr 95	2.95	0.59	1.77	2.95

WARLOCK (1972-)
MARVEL

	ORIG.	GOOD	FINE	N-MINT
❑ 1, Aug 72, GK Origin	0.20	8.00	24.00	40.00
❑ 2, Oct 72	0.20	3.20	9.60	16.00
❑ 3, Dec 72	0.20	3.20	9.60	16.00
❑ 4, Feb 73, GK	0.20	2.00	6.00	10.00
❑ 5, Apr 73	0.20	2.00	6.00	10.00
❑ 6, Jun 73	0.20	2.00	6.00	10.00
❑ 7, Aug 73	0.20	2.00	6.00	10.00
❑ 8, Oct 73	0.20	2.00	6.00	10.00
❑ 9, Oct 75, JSn	0.25	2.80	8.40	14.00
❑ 10, Dec 75, JSn	0.25	6.40	19.20	32.00
❑ 11, Feb 76, JSn	0.25	3.20	9.60	16.00
❑ 12, Apr 76, JSn	0.25	2.40	7.20	12.00
❑ 13, Jun 76, JSn	0.25	2.40	7.20	12.00
❑ 14, Aug 76, JSn	0.25	2.40	7.20	12.00
❑ 15, Nov 76, JSn	0.30	5.20	15.60	26.00

WARLOCK (1982-1983)

	ORIG.	GOOD	FINE	N-MINT
❑ 1, Dec 82, JSn, rep.	2.00	0.80	2.40	4.00
❑ 2, Jan 83, JSn, rep.	2.00	0.60	1.80	3.00
❑ 3, Feb 83, JSn, rep.	2.00	0.60	1.80	3.00
❑ 4, Mar 83, JSn, rep.	2.00	0.60	1.80	3.00
❑ 5, Apr 83, JSn, rep.	2.00	0.60	1.80	3.00
❑ 6, May 83, JSn, rep.	2.00	0.60	1.80	3.00

WARLOCK (1992)

	ORIG.	GOOD	FINE	N-MINT
❑ 1, reprints	2.50	0.50	1.50	2.50
❑ 2, reprints	2.50	0.50	1.50	2.50
❑ 3, reprints	2.50	0.50	1.50	2.50
❑ 4, reprints	2.50	0.50	1.50	2.50
❑ 5, reprints	2.50	0.50	1.50	2.50
❑ 6, reprints	2.50	0.50	1.50	2.50

WARLOCK 5
AIRCEL

	ORIG.	GOOD	FINE	N-MINT
❑ 1, b&w		1.00	3.00	5.00
❑ 2, b&w		1.00	3.00	5.00
❑ 3, b&w		1.00	3.00	5.00
❑ 4, b&w		1.00	3.00	5.00
❑ 5, robot skull cover		0.80	2.40	4.00
❑ 6, misnumbered #5, woman's face on cover		0.80	2.40	4.00
❑ 7		0.34	1.02	1.70
❑ 8		0.34	1.02	1.70
❑ 9		0.34	1.02	1.70
❑ 10		0.34	1.02	1.70
❑ 11		0.34	1.02	1.70
❑ 12		0.34	1.02	1.70
❑ 13		0.34	1.02	1.70
❑ 14		0.34	1.02	1.70
❑ 15		0.34	1.02	1.70
❑ 16		0.39	1.17	1.95
❑ 17		0.39	1.17	1.95
❑ 18		0.39	1.17	1.95
❑ 19		0.39	1.17	1.95
❑ 20		0.39	1.17	1.95
❑ 21		0.39	1.17	1.95
❑ 22		0.39	1.17	1.95

WARLOCK 5 BOOK II

	ORIG.	GOOD	FINE	N-MINT
❑ 1, b&w		0.40	1.20	2.00
❑ 2, b&w		0.40	1.20	2.00
❑ 3, b&w		0.40	1.20	2.00
❑ 4, b&w		0.40	1.20	2.00
❑ 5, b&w		0.40	1.20	2.00
❑ 6, b&w		0.40	1.20	2.00
❑ 7, b&w		0.40	1.20	2.00

WARLOCK AND THE INFINITY WATCH
MARVEL

	ORIG.	GOOD	FINE	N-MINT
❑ 1	1.75	1.20	3.60	6.00
❑ 2	1.75	0.80	2.40	4.00
❑ 3	1.75	0.60	1.80	3.00
❑ 4	1.75	0.60	1.80	3.00
❑ 5	1.75	0.60	1.80	3.00
❑ 6	1.75	0.60	1.80	3.00
❑ 7	1.75	0.60	1.80	3.00
❑ 8	1.75	0.60	1.80	3.00
❑ 9, Infinity war	1.75	0.35	1.05	1.75
❑ 10	1.75	0.35	1.05	1.75
❑ 11	1.75	0.35	1.05	1.75
❑ 12	1.75	0.35	1.05	1.75
❑ 13	1.75	0.35	1.05	1.75
❑ 14	1.75	0.35	1.05	1.75
❑ 15	1.75	0.35	1.05	1.75
❑ 16	1.75	0.35	1.05	1.75
❑ 17	1.75	0.35	1.05	1.75
❑ 18	1.75	0.35	1.05	1.75
❑ 19	1.75	0.35	1.05	1.75
❑ 20	1.75	0.35	1.05	1.75
❑ 21	1.75	0.35	1.05	1.75
❑ 22	1.75	0.35	1.05	1.75
❑ 23	1.75	0.35	1.05	1.75
❑ 24	1.75	0.35	1.05	1.75
❑ 25, diecut cover	2.95	0.59	1.77	2.95
❑ 27	1.75	0.35	1.05	1.75
❑ 28	1.95	0.39	1.17	1.95
❑ 29, Jun 94	1.95	0.39	1.17	1.95
❑ 30, Jul 94	1.95	0.39	1.17	1.95
❑ 31, Aug 94	1.95	0.39	1.17	1.95
❑ 32, Sep 94	1.95	0.39	1.17	1.95
❑ 33, Oct 94	1.95	0.39	1.17	1.95
❑ 34, Nov 94	1.95	0.39	1.17	1.95
❑ 35, Dec 94	1.95	0.39	1.17	1.95
❑ 36, Jan 95	1.95	0.39	1.17	1.95
❑ 37, Feb 95	1.95	0.39	1.17	1.95
❑ 38, Mar 95	1.95	0.39	1.17	1.95
❑ 39, Apr 95	1.95	0.39	1.17	1.95
❑ 40, May 95	1.95	0.39	1.17	1.95
❑ 41, Jun 95	1.95	0.39	1.17	1.95
❑ 42, Jul 95, final issue	1.95	0.39	1.17	1.95

WARLOCK CHRONICLES, THE

	ORIG.	GOOD	FINE	N-MINT
❑ 1, foil embossed cover	2.95	0.59	1.77	2.95
❑ 2	2.00	0.40	1.20	2.00
❑ 3	2.00	0.40	1.20	2.00
❑ 4	2.00	0.40	1.20	2.00
❑ 5	2.00	0.40	1.20	2.00
❑ 6	2.00	0.40	1.20	2.00
❑ 7	2.00	0.40	1.20	2.00
❑ 8	2.00	0.40	1.20	2.00

WARLOCKS
AIRCEL

	ORIG.	GOOD	FINE	N-MINT
❑ 1, b&w		0.39	1.17	1.95
❑ 2, b&w		0.39	1.17	1.95
❑ 3, b&w		0.39	1.17	1.95
❑ 4, b&w		0.39	1.17	1.95
❑ 5, b&w		0.39	1.17	1.95
❑ 6, b&w		0.39	1.17	1.95
❑ 7, b&w		0.39	1.17	1.95
❑ 8, b&w		0.39	1.17	1.95
❑ 9, b&w		0.39	1.17	1.95
❑ 10, b&w		0.39	1.17	1.95
❑ 11, b&w		0.39	1.17	1.95
❑ 12, b&w		0.39	1.17	1.95

WARLOCKS: THE SPECIAL EDITION

	ORIG.	GOOD	FINE	N-MINT
❑ 1, b&w		0.45	1.35	2.25

WARLORD
DC

	ORIG.	GOOD	FINE	N-MINT
❑ 1, Feb 76, MGr	0.25	2.80	8.40	14.00
❑ 2, Apr 76, MGr, I:Machiste	0.25	1.60	4.80	8.00

	ORIG.	GOOD	FINE	N-MINT
❏ 3, Nov 76, MGr	0.30	1.60	4.80	8.00
❏ 4, Jan 77, MGr	0.30	1.50	4.50	7.50
❏ 5, Mar 77, MGr	0.30	1.50	4.50	7.50
❏ 6, May 77, MGr, I:Mariah Romanola				
	0.30	1.20	3.60	6.00
❏ 7, Jul 77, MGr	0.35	1.00	3.00	5.00
❏ 8, Sep 77, MGr	0.35	1.00	3.00	5.00
❏ 9, Nov 77, MGr	0.35	1.00	3.00	5.00
❏ 10, Jan 78, MGr, Deimos				
	0.35	1.20	3.60	6.00
❏ 11, Mar 78, MGr, r: 1st Issue Special				
	0.35	1.00	3.00	5.00
❏ 12, May 78, MGr	0.35	1.00	3.00	5.00
❏ 13, Jul 78, MGr	0.35	1.00	3.00	5.00
❏ 14, Sep 78, MGr	0.35	1.00	3.00	5.00
❏ 15, Nov 78, MGr	0.50	1.00	3.00	5.00
❏ 16, Dec 78, MGr	0.40	1.00	3.00	5.00
❏ 17, Jan 79, MGr	0.40	1.00	3.00	5.00
❏ 18, Feb 79, MGr	0.40	1.00	3.00	5.00
❏ 19, Mar 79, MGr	0.40	1.00	3.00	5.00
❏ 20, Apr 79, MGr	0.40	1.00	3.00	5.00
❏ 21, May 79, MGr	0.40	0.55	1.65	2.75
❏ 22, Jun 79, MGr	0.40	0.55	1.65	2.75
❏ 23, Jul 79, MGr	0.40	0.55	1.65	2.75
❏ 24, Aug 79, MGr	0.40	0.55	1.65	2.75
❏ 25, Sep 79, MGr	0.40	0.55	1.65	2.75
❏ 26, Oct 79, MGr	0.40	0.55	1.65	2.75
❏ 27, Nov 79, MGr	0.40	0.55	1.65	2.75
❏ 28, Dec 79, MGr	0.40	0.55	1.65	2.75
❏ 29, Jan 80, MGr	0.40	0.55	1.65	2.75
❏ 30, Feb 80, MGr	0.40	0.55	1.65	2.75
❏ 31, Mar 80, MGr	0.40	0.55	1.65	2.75
❏ 32, Apr 80, MGr	0.40	0.55	1.65	2.75
❏ 33, May 80, MGr	0.40	0.55	1.65	2.75
❏ 34, Jun 80, MGr	0.40	0.55	1.65	2.75
❏ 35, Jul 80, MGr	0.40	0.55	1.65	2.75
❏ 36, Aug 80, MGr	0.40	0.55	1.65	2.75
❏ 37, Sep 80, MGr	0.50	0.55	1.65	2.75
❏ 38, Oct 80, MGr	0.50	0.55	1.65	2.75
❏ 39, Nov 80, MGr	0.50	0.55	1.65	2.75
❏ 40, Dec 80, MGr	0.50	0.55	1.65	2.75
❏ 41, Jan 81, MGr	0.50	0.40	1.20	2.00
❏ 42, Feb 81, MGr	0.50	0.40	1.20	2.00
❏ 43, Mar 81, MGr	0.50	0.40	1.20	2.00
❏ 44, Apr 81, MGr	0.50	0.40	1.20	2.00
❏ 45, May 81, MGr	0.50	0.40	1.20	2.00
❏ 46, Jun 81, MGr	0.50	0.40	1.20	2.00
❏ 47, Jul 81, MGr	0.50	0.40	1.20	2.00
❏ 48, Aug 81, MGr, EC I:Arak				
	0.50	0.50	1.50	2.50
❏ 49, Sep 81, MGr	0.50	0.40	1.20	2.00
❏ 50, Oct 81, MGr	0.60	0.40	1.20	2.00
❏ 51, Nov 81	0.60	0.30	0.90	1.50
❏ 52, Dec 81, MGr	0.60	0.40	1.20	2.00
❏ 53, Jan 82	0.60	0.30	0.90	1.50
❏ 54, Feb 82	0.60	0.30	0.90	1.50
❏ 55, Mar 82	0.60	0.30	0.90	1.50
❏ 56, Apr 82	0.60	0.30	0.90	1.50
❏ 57, May 82	0.60	0.30	0.90	1.50
❏ 58, Jun 82	0.60	0.30	0.90	1.50
❏ 59, Jul 82	0.60	0.30	0.90	1.50
❏ 60, Aug 82	0.60	0.30	0.90	1.50
❏ 61, Sep 82	0.60	0.30	0.90	1.50
❏ 62, Oct 82	0.60	0.30	0.90	1.50
❏ 63, Nov 82	0.60	0.30	0.90	1.50
❏ 64, Dec 82	0.60	0.30	0.90	1.50
❏ 65, Jan 83	0.60	0.30	0.90	1.50
❏ 66, Feb 83	0.60	0.30	0.90	1.50
❏ 67, Mar 83	0.60	0.30	0.90	1.50
❏ 68, Apr 83	0.60	0.30	0.90	1.50
❏ 69, May 83	0.60	0.30	0.90	1.50
❏ 70, Jun 83	0.60	0.30	0.90	1.50

	ORIG.	GOOD	FINE	N-MINT
❏ 71, Jul 83	0.60	0.30	0.90	1.50
❏ 72, Aug 83	0.60	0.30	0.90	1.50
❏ 73, Sep 83	0.60	0.30	0.90	1.50
❏ 74, Oct 83	0.60	0.30	0.90	1.50
❏ 75, Nov 83	0.60	0.30	0.90	1.50
❏ 76, Dec 83	0.75	0.30	0.90	1.50
❏ 77, Jan 84	0.75	0.30	0.90	1.50
❏ 78, Feb 84	0.75	0.30	0.90	1.50
❏ 79, Mar 84	0.75	0.30	0.90	1.50
❏ 80, Apr 84	0.75	0.30	0.90	1.50
❏ 81, May 84	0.75	0.30	0.90	1.50
❏ 82, Jun 84	0.75	0.30	0.90	1.50
❏ 83, Jul 84	0.75	0.30	0.90	1.50
❏ 84, Aug 84	0.75	0.30	0.90	1.50
❏ 85, Sep 84	0.75	0.30	0.90	1.50
❏ 86, Oct 84	0.75	0.30	0.90	1.50
❏ 87, Nov 84	0.75	0.30	0.90	1.50
❏ 88, Dec 84	0.75	0.30	0.90	1.50
❏ 89, Jan 85	0.75	0.30	0.90	1.50
❏ 90, Feb 85	0.75	0.30	0.90	1.50
❏ 91, Mar 85	0.75	0.30	0.90	1.50
❏ 92, Apr 85	0.75	0.30	0.90	1.50
❏ 93, May 85	0.75	0.30	0.90	1.50
❏ 94, Jun 85	0.75	0.30	0.90	1.50
❏ 95, Jul 85	0.75	0.30	0.90	1.50
❏ 96, Aug 85	0.75	0.30	0.90	1.50
❏ 97, Sep 85	0.75	0.30	0.90	1.50
❏ 98, Oct 85	0.75	0.30	0.90	1.50
❏ 99, Nov 85	0.75	0.30	0.90	1.50
❏ 100, Dec 85, MGr(c)	1.25	0.30	0.90	1.50
❏ 101, Jan 86	0.75	0.30	0.90	1.50
❏ 102, Feb 86	0.75	0.30	0.90	1.50
❏ 103, Mar 86	0.75	0.30	0.90	1.50
❏ 104, Apr 86	0.75	0.30	0.90	1.50
❏ 105, May 86	0.75	0.30	0.90	1.50
❏ 106, Jun 86	0.75	0.30	0.90	1.50
❏ 107, Jul 86	0.75	0.30	0.90	1.50
❏ 108, Aug 86	0.75	0.30	0.90	1.50
❏ 109, Sep 86	0.75	0.30	0.90	1.50
❏ 110, Oct 86	0.75	0.30	0.90	1.50
❏ 111, Nov 86	0.75	0.30	0.90	1.50
❏ 112, Dec 86	0.75	0.30	0.90	1.50
❏ 113, Jan 87	0.75	0.30	0.90	1.50
❏ 114, Feb 87, Legends	0.75	0.30	0.90	1.50
❏ 115, Mar 87, Legends	0.75	0.30	0.90	1.50
❏ 116, Apr 87	0.75	0.30	0.90	1.50
❏ 117, May 87	0.75	0.30	0.90	1.50
❏ 118, Jun 87	0.75	0.30	0.90	1.50
❏ 119, Jul 87	0.75	0.30	0.90	1.50
❏ 120, Aug 87	0.75	0.30	0.90	1.50
❏ 121, Sep 87	0.75	0.30	0.90	1.50
❏ 122, Oct 87	0.75	0.30	0.90	1.50
❏ 123, Nov 87	1.00	0.30	0.90	1.50
❏ 124, Dec 87	1.00	0.30	0.90	1.50
❏ 125, Jan 88	1.00	0.30	0.90	1.50
❏ 126, Feb 88	1.00	0.30	0.90	1.50
❏ 127, Mar 88	1.00	0.30	0.90	1.50
❏ 128, Apr 88	1.00	0.30	0.90	1.50
❏ 129, May 88	1.00	0.30	0.90	1.50
❏ 130, Jul 88	1.00	0.30	0.90	1.50
❏ 131, Sep 88, Bonus Book #6				
	1.00	0.30	0.90	1.50
❏ 132, Nov 88	1.00	0.30	0.90	1.50
❏ 133, Dec 88, JDu	1.50	0.30	0.90	1.50

WARLORD (1992 mini-series)

	ORIG.	GOOD	FINE	N-MINT
❏ 1, Jan 92, MGr(c)	1.75	0.35	1.05	1.75
❏ 2, Feb 92, MGr(c)	1.75	0.35	1.05	1.75
❏ 3, Mar 92, MGr(c)	1.75	0.35	1.05	1.75
❏ 4, Apr 92, MGr(c)	1.75	0.35	1.05	1.75
❏ 5, May 92, MGr(c)	1.75	0.35	1.05	1.75
❏ 6, Jun 92, MGr(c)	1.75	0.35	1.05	1.75

	ORIG.	GOOD	FINE	N-MINT

WARLORD ANNUAL

	ORIG.	GOOD	FINE	N-MINT
1, 82, MGr	1.00	0.60	1.80	3.00
2, 83	1.00	0.25	0.75	1.25
3, 84	1.25	0.25	0.75	1.25
4, 85	1.25	0.25	0.75	1.25
5, 86	1.25	0.25	0.75	1.25
6, 87	1.25	0.25	0.75	1.25

WARNER BROS. PRESENTS BUGS BUNNY & THE LOONEY TUNES MAGAZINE
WELSH

	ORIG.	GOOD	FINE	N-MINT
19, Fal 94, magazine	1.50	0.30	0.90	1.50
20, Win 95, magazine	1.95	0.39	1.17	1.95

WARP
FIRST

	GOOD	FINE	N-MINT
1, Mar 83, FB	0.40	1.20	2.00
2, Apr 83, FB	0.30	0.90	1.50
3, May 83, FB	0.30	0.90	1.50
4, Jun 83, FB	0.30	0.90	1.50
5, Aug 83, FB	0.30	0.90	1.50
6, Sep 83, FB	0.30	0.90	1.50
7, Oct 83, FB	0.30	0.90	1.50
8, Nov 83	0.25	0.75	1.25
9, Dec 83	0.25	0.75	1.25
10, Feb 84	0.25	0.75	1.25
11, Mar 84	0.25	0.75	1.25
12, Apr 84	0.25	0.75	1.25
13, May 84	0.25	0.75	1.25
14, Jul 84	0.25	0.75	1.25
15, Aug 84	0.25	0.75	1.25
16, Sep 84	0.25	0.75	1.25
17, Oct 84	0.25	0.75	1.25
18, Dec 84	0.25	0.75	1.25
19, Feb 85	0.25	0.75	1.25

WARP GRAPHICS ANNUAL
WARP

	GOOD	FINE	N-MINT
1	0.80	2.40	4.00

WARP SPECIAL
FIRST

	GOOD	FINE	N-MINT
1, Jul 83	0.30	0.90	1.50
2, Jan 84	0.20	0.60	1.00
3, Jun 84	0.20	0.60	1.00

WARP-3
EQUINOX

	GOOD	FINE	N-MINT
1, b&w	0.30	0.90	1.50

WARPWALKING
CALIBER

	ORIG.	GOOD	FINE	N-MINT
1, b&w	2.50	0.50	1.50	2.50
2, b&w	2.50	0.50	1.50	2.50
3, b&w	2.50	0.50	1.50	2.50
4, b&w	2.50	0.50	1.50	2.50

WARRIOR
QUALITY (BRITISH)

	GOOD	FINE	N-MINT
1, b&w mag	0.60	1.80	3.00
2, b&w mag	0.60	1.80	3.00
3, b&w mag	0.60	1.80	3.00
4, b&w mag	0.60	1.80	3.00
5, b&w mag	0.60	1.80	3.00
6, b&w mag	0.60	1.80	3.00
7, b&w mag	0.60	1.80	3.00
8, b&w mag	0.60	1.80	3.00
9, b&w mag	0.60	1.80	3.00
10, b&w mag	0.60	1.80	3.00
11, b&w mag	0.60	1.80	3.00
12, b&w mag	0.60	1.80	3.00
13, b&w mag	0.60	1.80	3.00
14, b&w mag	0.60	1.80	3.00
15, b&w mag	0.60	1.80	3.00
16, b&w mag	0.60	1.80	3.00
17, b&w mag	0.60	1.80	3.00
18, b&w mag	0.60	1.80	3.00

	ORIG.	GOOD	FINE	N-MINT
19, b&w mag		0.60	1.80	3.00
20, b&w mag		0.60	1.80	3.00
21, b&w mag		0.60	1.80	3.00
22, b&w mag		0.60	1.80	3.00
23, b&w mag		0.60	1.80	3.00
24, b&w mag		0.60	1.80	3.00
25, b&w mag		0.60	1.80	3.00
26, b&w mag		0.60	1.80	3.00

WARRIOR NUN AREALA
ANTARCTIC

	ORIG.	GOOD	FINE	N-MINT
1, Dec 94	2.95	1.20	3.60	6.00
1, Dec 94, no cover price;collector's edition (5000 made)	4.00	12.00	20.00
1, Mar 95, second printing	2.95	0.59	1.77	2.95
2		1.00	3.00	5.00
3, Apr 95	2.95	0.59	1.77	2.95
3, Apr 95, silver foil cover edition (1000 made)				

WARRIOR NUN AREALA, RITUALS

	ORIG.	GOOD	FINE	N-MINT
1, Aug 95	2.95	0.59	1.77	2.95
2, Oct 95	2.95	0.59	1.77	2.95

WARRIORS
ADVENTURE

	GOOD	FINE	N-MINT
1	0.39	1.17	1.95
2	0.39	1.17	1.95
3	0.39	1.17	1.95

WARRIORS OF PLASM
DEFIANT

	ORIG.	GOOD	FINE	N-MINT
1, Aug 93	2.95	0.59	1.77	2.95
2	2.95	0.59	1.77	2.95
3	2.95	0.59	1.77	2.95
4	2.95	0.59	1.77	2.95
5, Dec 93	2.50	0.50	1.50	2.50
6, Jan 94	2.50	0.50	1.50	2.50
7, Feb 94	2.50	0.50	1.50	2.50
8, Mar 94	2.75	0.55	1.65	2.75
9, Apr 94	2.50	0.50	1.50	2.50
10, May 94	2.50	0.50	1.50	2.50
11, Jun 94	2.50	0.50	1.50	2.50

WARRIORS OF PLASM: HOME FOR THE HOLIDAYS

	ORIG.	GOOD	FINE	N-MINT
0, nn	5.95	1.19	3.57	5.95

WARSTRIKE
MALIBU/ULTRAVERSE

	ORIG.	GOOD	FINE	N-MINT
2, Jun 94	1.95	0.39	1.17	1.95
3, Jul 94	1.95	0.39	1.17	1.95
4, Aug 94	1.95	0.39	1.17	1.95
5, Sep 94	1.95	0.39	1.17	1.95
6, Oct 94	1.95	0.39	1.17	1.95

WARWORLD!
DARK HORSE

	GOOD	FINE	N-MINT
1, b&w	0.35	1.05	1.75

WARZONE
EXPRESS/ENTITY

	ORIG.	GOOD	FINE	N-MINT
1, 95, b&w;enhanced cardstock cover	2.95	0.59	1.77	2.95
2, 95, b&w;enhanced cardstock cover	2.95	0.59	1.77	2.95
3, 95, b&w;enhanced cardstock cover	2.95	0.59	1.77	2.95

WASH TUBBS QUARTERLY
DRAGON LADY

	GOOD	FINE	N-MINT
1	0.99	2.97	4.95
2	1.19	3.57	5.95
3	1.19	3.57	5.95
4	1.19	3.57	5.95
5	1.19	3.57	5.95

WASHMEN
NEW YORK

	ORIG.	GOOD	FINE	N-MINT
1	1.70	0.34	1.02	1.70

Wonder Woman

First appearance: *All-Star Comics* #8, Winter, 1941, DC.

Psychologist William Moulton Marston created Wonder Woman under the pseudonym Charles Moulton. Wonder Woman's creation is grounded in the Greek legend of the Amazon women.

In Marston's story, the modern-day Amazons lived on Paradise Island, hidden from the rest of the world, until American pilot Steve Trevor crashed offshore and was rescued by Diana, the daughter of Queen Hippolyte. Learning that war threatened the outside world, the Amazons and their patron goddesses, Aphrodite and Athena, decided to send one Amazon back with Trevor to help fight the forces of evil. The Amazons held a competition with several tests of strength and skill to select their representative.

Diana, who was attracted to Trevor, won the competition and assumed the identity of Wonder Woman. In addition to her great strength and athletic ability, she had bracelets that could deflect bullets, a golden lasso that could compel people to speak the truth, and an invisible robotic plane. Diana also assumed the name Diana Prince to pass as an ordinary mortal and to stay near Trevor.

In Wonder Woman's early adventures, the ancient Greek gods and goddesses often meddled in human affairs. This has continued, to a limited extent, in the more recent comics.

In 1959, Wonder Woman's world underwent a startling alteration — the creative team introduced younger versions of Diana's heroic identity: the teenage Wonder Girl and the toddler Wonder Tot. As the "Wonder Family," all three occasionally teamed up for "imaginary" adventures, which don't fit into regular Wonder Woman continuity. While Wonder Girl appeared as a member of The Teen Titans in *The Brave and the Bold* #60, she was eventually transmuted into a completely different person: Donna Troy, an orphan who had been raised by the Amazons.

Wonder Woman substituted a jumpsuit for her colorful costume from 1968 to 1973. Early in that period, Steve Trevor died, although he was revived, killed again, and revived again, after Wonder Woman resumed wearing her costume. The first Wonder Woman series ended in 1986, although Wonder Woman still made appearances in other DC comics and starred in her own mini-

series, *Legend of Wonder Woman*, afterwards.

Wonder Woman began again in 1987, with yet another take on the Diana's origin story, this one by artist George Prez. Prez went back to the original story (which meant that Diana's younger incarnations went by the wayside), putting greater emphasis on the mythological underpinnings of Paradise Island and its inhabitants. Steve Trevor's role was greatly reduced; Trevor's mother, Diana, became Paradise Island's first visitor from "Man's World" and introduced the Amazons to the concepts and technology of modern society. Steve Trevor did not remain as a supporting character in the second series.

Wonder Woman was a charter member of the Golden Age Justice Society of America and the Silver Age Justice League of America; she now has a leadership role in the JLA.

Recent developments in Wonder Woman include a brief period where Diana lost the right to wear the Wonder Woman costume. The role was assumed by another Amazon, while Diana simply continued battling evil wearing a different costume. Diana regained her title in the 100th issue of the series.

While Wonder Woman was created in the Golden Age of comics, this guide covers only appearances from the Silver Age to the present, including the following (listed chronologically):

	ORIG.	GOOD	FINE	N-MINT

WASTELAND
DC

	ORIG.	GOOD	FINE	N-MINT
1		0.35	1.05	1.75
2		0.35	1.05	1.75
3		0.35	1.05	1.75
4		0.35	1.05	1.75
5, cover of #6		0.35	1.05	1.75
5, right cover		0.35	1.05	1.75
6, blank cover		0.35	1.05	1.75
7		0.35	1.05	1.75
8		0.35	1.05	1.75
9		0.35	1.05	1.75
10		0.35	1.05	1.75
11		0.35	1.05	1.75
12		0.35	1.05	1.75
13		0.35	1.05	1.75
14		0.35	1.05	1.75
15		0.35	1.05	1.75
16		0.35	1.05	1.75
17		0.40	1.20	2.00
18		0.40	1.20	2.00

WATCHCATS
HARRIER

	ORIG.	GOOD	FINE	N-MINT
1		0.39	1.17	1.95

WATCHMEN
DC

	ORIG.	GOOD	FINE	N-MINT
1, Sep 86, D:Comedian	1.50	2.00	6.00	10.00
2, Oct 86	1.50	1.20	3.60	6.00
3, Nov 86	1.50	1.00	3.00	5.00
4, Dec 86	1.50	1.00	3.00	5.00
5, Jan 87	1.50	1.00	3.00	5.00
6, Feb 87	1.50	1.00	3.00	5.00
7, Mar 87	1.50	1.00	3.00	5.00
8, Apr 87	1.50	1.00	3.00	5.00
9, May 87	1.50	1.00	3.00	5.00
10, Jul 87	1.50	1.00	3.00	5.00
11, Aug 87	1.50	1.00	3.00	5.00
12, Oct 87	1.50	1.00	3.00	5.00

WAVE WARRIORS
ASTROBOYS

	ORIG.	GOOD	FINE	N-MINT
1, color		0.20	0.60	1.00

WAVEMAKERS
BLIND BAT

	ORIG.	GOOD	FINE	N-MINT
1	3.00	0.60	1.80	3.00

WAXWORK
BLACKTHORNE

	ORIG.	GOOD	FINE	N-MINT
1, movie, b&w		0.40	1.20	2.00

WAXWORK IN 3-D

	ORIG.	GOOD	FINE	N-MINT
1, movie		0.50	1.50	2.50

WAY OUT STRIPS
FANTAGRAPHICS

	ORIG.	GOOD	FINE	N-MINT
1, b&w	2.50	0.50	1.50	2.50
3, Aug 94, b&w	2.75	0.55	1.65	2.75

TRAGEDY STRIKES

	ORIG.	GOOD	FINE	N-MINT
1, b&w		0.59	1.77	2.95
2, b&w		0.59	1.77	2.95
3, b&w		0.59	1.77	2.95

WAY OUT STRIPS VOL. 3
FANTAGRAPHICS

	ORIG.	GOOD	FINE	N-MINT
2, May 94, b&w	2.75	0.55	1.65	2.75

WAYWARD WARRIOR
ALPHA PRODUCTIONS

	ORIG.	GOOD	FINE	N-MINT
1, b&w		0.39	1.17	1.95
2, b&w		0.39	1.17	1.95
3, b&w		0.39	1.17	1.95

WCW: WORLD CHAMPIONSHIP WRESTLING
MARVEL

	ORIG.	GOOD	FINE	N-MINT
1	1.25	0.25	0.75	1.25
2	1.25	0.25	0.75	1.25

	ORIG.	GOOD	FINE	N-MINT
3	1.25	0.25	0.75	1.25
4	1.25	0.25	0.75	1.25
5	1.25	0.25	0.75	1.25
6	1.25	0.25	0.75	1.25
7	1.25	0.25	0.75	1.25
8	1.25	0.25	0.75	1.25
9	1.25	0.25	0.75	1.25
10	1.25	0.25	0.75	1.25
11	1.25	0.25	0.75	1.25
12	1.25	0.25	0.75	1.25

WEAPON X (mini-series)

	ORIG.	GOOD	FINE	N-MINT
1, Mar 95	1.95	0.39	1.17	1.95
2, Apr 95	1.95	0.39	1.17	1.95
3, May 95	1.95	0.39	1.17	1.95
4, Jun 95	1.95	0.39	1.17	1.95

WEAPON ZERO
IMAGE

	ORIG.	GOOD	FINE	N-MINT
0, Jun 95, T-4;(first issue of series)				
	2.50	0.50	1.50	2.50
0, Aug 95, T-3;(second issue of series)				
	2.50	0.50	1.50	2.50
0, Sep 95, T-2;(third issue of series)				
	2.50	0.50	1.50	2.50
0, Oct 95, T-1;(fourth issue of series)				
	2.50	0.50	1.50	2.50

WEAPON ZERO (Vol. 2)

	ORIG.	GOOD	FINE	N-MINT
1, Mar 96, indicia gives year of publication as 1995				
	2.50	0.50	1.50	2.50
2, Apr 96, indicia gives year of publication as 1995				
	2.50	0.50	1.50	2.50
3, May 96, indicia has correct year of publication				
	2.50	0.50	1.50	2.50
4, Jun 96, indicia gives year of publication as 1995				
	2.50	0.50	1.50	2.50

WEASEL PATROL, THE
ECLIPSE

	ORIG.	GOOD	FINE	N-MINT
1, b&w		0.40	1.20	2.00

WEAVEWORLD
EPIC

	ORIG.	GOOD	FINE	N-MINT
1, Clive Barker;squarebound				
	4.95	0.99	2.97	4.95
2, Clive Barker;squarebound				
	4.95	0.99	2.97	4.95
3, Clive Barker;squarebound				
	4.95	0.99	2.97	4.95

WEB ANNUAL
IMPACT

	ORIG.	GOOD	FINE	N-MINT
1, 92, trading card	2.50	0.50	1.50	2.50

WEB OF SCARLET SPIDER
MARVEL

	ORIG.	GOOD	FINE	N-MINT
1, Nov 95, "Virtual Mortality" Part 1 of 4				
	1.95	0.39	1.17	1.95
2, Dec 95, "Cyberwar" Part 1 of 4				
	1.95	0.39	1.17	1.95
3, Jan 96, "Nightmare in Scarlet" Part 1 of 3				
	1.95	0.39	1.17	1.95
4, Feb 96, "Nightmare in Scarlet" Part 3 of 3;final issue				
	1.95	0.39	1.17	1.95

WEB OF SPIDER-MAN

	ORIG.	GOOD	FINE	N-MINT
1, Apr 85	0.65	5.00	15.00	25.00
2, May 85	0.65	2.00	6.00	10.00
3, Jun 85	0.65	2.00	6.00	10.00
4, Jul 85	0.65	2.00	6.00	10.00
5, Aug 85	0.65	2.00	6.00	10.00
6, Sep 85, Secret Wars II				
	0.65	1.40	4.20	7.00
7, Oct 85	0.65	1.60	4.80	8.00
8, Nov 85	0.65	1.20	3.60	6.00
9, Dec 85	0.65	1.20	3.60	6.00
10, Jan 86	0.65	1.20	3.60	6.00

	ORIG.	GOOD	FINE	N-MINT
11, Feb 86	0.75	0.80	2.40	4.00
12, Mar 86	0.75	0.80	2.40	4.00
13, Apr 86	0.75	0.80	2.40	4.00
14, May 86	0.75	0.80	2.40	4.00
15, Jun 86	0.75	0.80	2.40	4.00
16, Jul 86	0.75	0.70	2.10	3.50
17, Aug 86	0.75	0.70	2.10	3.50
18, Sep 86	0.75	0.70	2.10	3.50
19, Oct 86	0.75	0.70	2.10	3.50
20, Nov 86	0.75	0.70	2.10	3.50
21, Dec 86	0.75	0.70	2.10	3.50
22, Jan 87	0.75	0.70	2.10	3.50
23, Feb 87	0.75	0.70	2.10	3.50
24, Mar 87	0.75	0.70	2.10	3.50
25, Apr 87	0.75	0.70	2.10	3.50
26, May 87	0.75	0.70	2.10	3.50
27, Jun 87	0.75	0.70	2.10	3.50
28, Jul 87	0.75	0.70	2.10	3.50
29, Aug 87, A:Wolverine	0.75	4.80	14.40	24.00
30, Sep 87	0.75	2.40	7.20	12.00
31, Oct 87, V:Kraven	0.75	2.00	6.00	10.00
32, Nov 87, V:Kraven	0.75	2.00	6.00	10.00
33, Dec 87, BSz(c)	0.75	0.40	1.20	2.00
34, Jan 88	0.75	0.35	1.05	1.75
35, Feb 88	0.75	0.35	1.05	1.75
36, Mar 88	0.75	0.35	1.05	1.75
37, Apr 88	0.75	0.35	1.05	1.75
38, May 88,V:Hobgoblin	1.00	0.80	2.40	4.00
39, Jun 88, Cult of Love	1.00	0.40	1.20	2.00
40, Jul 88, Cult of Love	1.00	0.40	1.20	2.00
41, Aug 88, Cult of Love	1.00	0.40	1.20	2.00
42, Sep 88, Cult of Love	1.00	0.40	1.20	2.00
43, Oct 88, Cult of Love	1.00	0.40	1.20	2.00
44, Nov 88, A:Hulk	1.00	0.40	1.20	2.00
45, Dec 88, V:Vulture	1.00	0.40	1.20	2.00
46, Jan 89	1.00	0.40	1.20	2.00
47, Feb 89, Hobgoblin, Inferno	1.00	1.20	3.60	6.00
48, Mar 89, Hobgoblin, Inferno	1.00	2.40	7.20	12.00
49, Apr 89	1.00	0.40	1.20	2.00
50, May 89	1.50	0.40	1.20	2.00
51, Jun 89	1.00	0.40	1.20	2.00
52, Jul 89	1.00	0.40	1.20	2.00
53, Aug 89	1.00	0.40	1.20	2.00
54, Sep 89	1.00	0.40	1.20	2.00
55, Oct 89	1.00	0.40	1.20	2.00
56, Nov 89	1.00	0.40	1.20	2.00
57, Nov 89	1.00	0.40	1.20	2.00
58, Dec 89, Acts of Vengeance	1.00	0.40	1.20	2.00
59, Dec 89, Acts of Vengeance	1.00	0.40	1.20	2.00
60, Jan 90, Acts of Vengeance	1.00	0.40	1.20	2.00
61, Feb 90, Acts of Vengeance	1.00	0.40	1.20	2.00
62, Mar 90	1.00	0.40	1.20	2.00
63, Apr 90	1.00	0.40	1.20	2.00
64, May 90, Acts of Vengeance	1.00	0.20	0.60	1.00
65, Jun 90, Acts of Vengeance	1.00	0.20	0.60	1.00
66, Jul 90	1.00	0.20	0.60	1.00
67, Aug 90	1.00	0.20	0.60	1.00
68, Sep 90	1.00	0.20	0.60	1.00
69, Oct 90	1.00	0.20	0.60	1.00
70, Nov 90	1.00	0.20	0.60	1.00
71, Dec 90	1.00	0.20	0.60	1.00
72, Jan 91	1.00	0.20	0.60	1.00
73, Feb 91	1.00	0.20	0.60	1.00
74, Mar 91	1.00	0.20	0.60	1.00
75, Apr 91	1.00	0.20	0.60	1.00

	ORIG.	GOOD	FINE	N-MINT
76, May 91, Fantastic Four	1.00	0.20	0.60	1.00
77, Jun 91	1.00	0.20	0.60	1.00
78, Jul 91, Cloak & Dagger	1.00	0.20	0.60	1.00
79, Aug 91	1.00	0.20	0.60	1.00
80, Sep 91	1.00	0.20	0.60	1.00
81, Oct 91	1.00	0.20	0.60	1.00
82, Nov 91	1.00	0.20	0.60	1.00
83, Dec 91	1.00	0.20	0.60	1.00
84	1.00	0.20	0.60	1.00
85	1.25	0.25	0.75	1.25
86	1.25	0.25	0.75	1.25
87	1.25	0.25	0.75	1.25
88	1.25	0.25	0.75	1.25
89	1.25	0.25	0.75	1.25
90, hologram	2.95	0.59	1.77	2.95
90, hologram, 2nd printing	1.25	0.25	0.75	1.25
91	1.25	0.25	0.75	1.25
92	1.25	0.25	0.75	1.25
93	1.25	0.25	0.75	1.25
94	1.25	0.25	0.75	1.25
95	1.25	0.25	0.75	1.25
96	1.25	0.25	0.75	1.25
97	1.25	0.25	0.75	1.25
98	1.25	0.25	0.75	1.25
99	1.25	0.25	0.75	1.25
100, foil cover	2.95	0.59	1.77	2.95
101	1.25	0.50	1.50	2.50
102, Maximum Carnage	1.25	0.25	0.75	1.25
103	1.25	0.25	0.75	1.25
104	1.25	0.25	0.75	1.25
105	1.25	0.25	0.75	1.25
106	1.25	0.25	0.75	1.25
107	1.25	0.25	0.75	1.25
108	1.25	0.25	0.75	1.25
109	1.25	0.25	0.75	1.25
110	1.25	0.25	0.75	1.25
111	1.25	0.25	0.75	1.25
112, May 94	1.50	0.30	0.90	1.50
113, Jun 94	1.50	0.30	0.90	1.50
113, Jun 94, TV preview, print	2.95	0.59	1.77	2.95
114, Jul 94	1.50	0.30	0.90	1.50
115, Aug 94	1.50	0.30	0.90	1.50
116, Sep 94	1.50	0.30	0.90	1.50
117, Oct 94, enhanced cover	2.95	1.00	3.00	5.00
117, Oct 94	1.50	0.30	0.90	1.50
118, Nov 94	1.50	0.30	0.90	1.50
119, Dec 94, polybagged with *Marvel Milestone Edition: Amaz S-M* 150 and POP card for *A S-M* 396, *S-M* 53, *SS-M* 219	6.45	1.29	3.87	6.45
119, Dec 94	1.50	0.30	0.90	1.50
120, Jan 95	2.25	0.45	1.35	2.25
121, Feb 95	1.50	0.30	0.90	1.50
122, Mar 95	1.50	0.30	0.90	1.50
123, Apr 95	1.50	0.30	0.90	1.50
124, May 95, "The Mark of Kaine" Part 1 of 5	1.50	0.30	0.90	1.50
125, Jun 95, enhanced cover	3.95	0.79	2.37	3.95
125, Jun 95	2.95	0.59	1.77	2.95
126, Jul 95, "The Trial of Peter Parker" Part 1 of 4	1.50	0.30	0.90	1.50
127, Aug 95, "Maximum Clonage" Part 2 of 6	1.50	0.30	0.90	1.50
128, Sep 95, "Exiled" Part 1 of 4	1.50	0.30	0.90	1.50
129, Oct 95, "Time Bomb" Part 2;A:New Warriors	1.50	0.30	0.90	1.50

	ORIG.	GOOD	FINE	N-MINT

WEB OF SPIDER-MAN ANNUAL

	ORIG.	GOOD	FINE	N-MINT
❑ 1, 85	1.25	1.00	3.00	5.00
❑ 2, 86	1.25	0.80	2.40	4.00
❑ 3, 87, pin-ups	1.25	0.45	1.35	2.25
❑ 4, 88, Evolutionary War;1:Poison				
	1.75	0.40	1.20	2.00
❑ 5, 89, Atlantis Attacks	2.00	0.40	1.20	2.00
❑ 6, 90, Tiny Spidey	2.00	0.40	1.20	2.00
❑ 7, 91, Vibranium Vendetta				
	2.00	0.40	1.20	2.00
❑ 8, 92	2.25	0.45	1.35	2.25
❑ 9, 93, trading card	2.95	0.59	1.77	2.95
❑ 10, 94	2.95	0.59	1.77	2.95

WEB OF SPIDER-MAN SUPER SPECIAL

	ORIG.	GOOD	FINE	N-MINT
❑ 1, 95, flip book	3.95	0.79	2.37	3.95

WEB, THE
IMPACT

	ORIG.	GOOD	FINE	N-MINT
❑ 1, Sep 91	1.00	0.20	0.60	1.00
❑ 2, Oct 91	1.00	0.20	0.60	1.00
❑ 3, Nov 91	1.00	0.20	0.60	1.00
❑ 4, Dec 91	1.00	0.20	0.60	1.00
❑ 5, Jan 92	1.00	0.20	0.60	1.00
❑ 6, Feb 92	1.00	0.20	0.60	1.00
❑ 7, Apr 92	1.00	0.20	0.60	1.00
❑ 8, Apr 92	1.00	0.20	0.60	1.00
❑ 9, May 92, trading card	1.00	0.20	0.60	1.00
❑ 10, Jun 92	1.25	0.20	0.60	1.00
❑ 11, Jul 92	1.25	0.25	0.75	1.25
❑ 12, Aug 92	1.25	0.25	0.75	1.25
❑ 13, Sep 92	1.25	0.25	0.75	1.25
❑ 14, Oct 92	1.25	0.25	0.75	1.25

WEB-MAN
ARGOSY

	ORIG.	GOOD	FINE	N-MINT
❑ 1, gatefold cover	2.50	0.50	1.50	2.50

WEDDING OF DRACULA
MARVEL

	ORIG.	GOOD	FINE	N-MINT
❑ 1, reprints	2.00	0.40	1.20	2.00

WEIRD FANTASY
EC/GEMSTONE

	ORIG.	GOOD	FINE	N-MINT
❑ 1, Oct 92, reprints;AF;WW;JKa;HK				
	2.00	0.40	1.20	2.00
❑ 2, reprints, AF,WW,JK,HK				
	1.50	0.30	0.90	1.50
❑ 3, reprints, AF,WW,JK,HK				
	1.50	0.30	0.90	1.50
❑ 4, reprints, AF,WW,JK,HK				
	1.50	0.30	0.90	1.50
❑ 5, reprints, AF,WW,JK,HK				
	1.50	0.30	0.90	1.50
❑ 6, reprints, AF,WW,JK,HK				
	1.50	0.30	0.90	1.50
❑ 7, reprints, AF,WW,JK	2.00	0.40	1.20	2.00
❑ 8, reprints	2.00	0.40	1.20	2.00
❑ 9, reprints	2.00	0.40	1.20	2.00
❑ 10, reprints	2.00	0.40	1.20	2.00
❑ 11, reprints	2.00	0.40	1.20	2.00
❑ 12, reprints	2.00	0.40	1.20	2.00
❑ 13, reprints	2.00	0.40	1.20	2.00

WEIRD MELVIN
MARC HANSEN STUFF!

	ORIG.	GOOD	FINE	N-MINT
❑ 1, 95, b&w	2.95	0.59	1.77	2.95
❑ 2, 95, b&w	2.95	0.59	1.77	2.95
❑ 3, Jun 95, b&w	2.95	0.59	1.77	2.95
❑ 4, 95, b&w	2.95	0.59	1.77	2.95
❑ 5, Oct 95, b&w	2.95	0.59	1.77	2.95

WEIRD MYSTERY TALES
DC

	ORIG.	GOOD	FINE	N-MINT
❑ 1, Jul 72	0.20	0.04	0.12	0.20
❑ 2	0.20	0.04	0.12	0.20
❑ 3	0.20	0.04	0.12	0.20
❑ 4	0.20	0.04	0.12	0.20
❑ 5	0.20	0.04	0.12	0.20
❑ 6	0.20	0.04	0.12	0.20
❑ 7	0.20	0.04	0.12	0.20
❑ 8	0.20	0.04	0.12	0.20
❑ 9	0.20	0.04	0.12	0.20
❑ 10	0.20	0.04	0.12	0.20
❑ 11	0.20	0.04	0.12	0.20
❑ 12	0.20	0.04	0.12	0.20
❑ 13	0.20	0.04	0.12	0.20
❑ 14	0.20	0.04	0.12	0.20
❑ 15	0.20	0.04	0.12	0.20
❑ 16	0.20	0.04	0.12	0.20
❑ 17	0.20	0.04	0.12	0.20
❑ 18	0.20	0.04	0.12	0.20
❑ 19	0.20	0.04	0.12	0.20
❑ 20	0.20	0.04	0.12	0.20
❑ 21	0.20	0.04	0.12	0.20
❑ 22	0.20	0.04	0.12	0.20
❑ 23	0.20	0.04	0.12	0.20
❑ 24, Nov 75	0.25	0.05	0.15	0.25

WEIRD ROMANCE
ECLIPSE

	ORIG.	GOOD	FINE	N-MINT
❑ 1, b&w		0.40	1.20	2.00

WEIRD SCIENCE
EC/GEMSTONE

	ORIG.	GOOD	FINE	N-MINT
❑ 1, Kurtzman, Wood, Kamen, Feldstein reprints				
	1.50	0.30	0.90	1.50
❑ 2, reprints	1.50	0.30	0.90	1.50
❑ 3, reprints	1.50	0.30	0.90	1.50
❑ 4, reprints, AF,HK,GI,JKa				
	2.00	0.40	1.20	2.00
❑ 5, reprints, AF,WW,HK,JK				
	2.00	0.40	1.20	2.00
❑ 6, reprints, AF,WW,HK,JK				
	2.00	0.40	1.20	2.00
❑ 7, reprints, AF,WW,HK,JK				
	2.00	0.40	1.20	2.00
❑ 8, Jun 94, r:AF,JK,WW	2.00	0.40	1.20	2.00
❑ 9, reprints	2.00	0.40	1.20	2.00
❑ 10, reprints	2.00	0.40	1.20	2.00
❑ 11, reprints	2.00	0.40	1.20	2.00
❑ 12, reprints	2.00	0.40	1.20	2.00
❑ 13, reprints	2.00	0.40	1.20	2.00

GLADSTONE

	ORIG.	GOOD	FINE	N-MINT
❑ 1, Sep 90, reprint: AW, GEvans, WW, JO, HK, JKamen				
	1.95	0.39	1.17	1.95
❑ 2, Nov 90, reprint: WW, AW, JKamen, JO, Elder, Ray Bradbury	1.95	0.39	1.17	1.95
❑ 3, Jan 91, reprint: WW, Feldstein, JKamen, Kurtzman				
	2.00	0.40	1.20	2.00
❑ 4, Mar 91, reprint: WW, RCrandall, JKamen, JO, Feldstein	2.00	0.40	1.20	2.00

WEIRD SCIENCE-FANTASY
EC/GEMSTONE

	ORIG.	GOOD	FINE	N-MINT
❑ 1, reprints	1.50	0.30	0.90	1.50
❑ 2, reprints, AF(c),WW,JO,BK,AW				
	1.50	0.30	0.90	1.50
❑ 3, reprints, AF(c),WW,JO,BK,AW				
	1.50	0.30	0.90	1.50
❑ 4, reprints: UFO issue	1.50	0.30	0.90	1.50
❑ 5, reprints: WW,RCrandall,JK,JO				
	2.00	0.40	1.20	2.00
❑ 6, reprints: AF(c),WW,AW,JK,JO				
	2.00	0.40	1.20	2.00
❑ 7, May 94, reprints: WW,AW,RC,JO				
	2.00	0.40	1.20	2.00
❑ 8, reprints	2.00	0.40	1.20	2.00
❑ 9, reprints	2.00	0.40	1.20	2.00
❑ 10, reprints	2.00	0.40	1.20	2.00
❑ 11, reprints	2.00	0.40	1.20	2.00

	ORIG.	GOOD	FINE	N-MINT
WEIRD SUSPENSE				
ATLAS/ SEABOARD				
☐ 1, Feb 75	0.25	0.20	0.60	1.00
☐ 2, Feb 75	0.25	0.20	0.60	1.00
☐ 3, Mar 75	0.25	0.20	0.60	1.00
WEIRD TALES ILLUSTRATED				
MILLENNIUM				
☐ 1, color		0.59	1.77	2.95
WEIRD TALES OF THE MACABRE				
ATLAS/SEABOARD				
☐ 1, Apr 75	0.75	0.40	1.20	2.00
☐ 2, Apr 75	0.75	0.40	1.20	2.00
WEIRD WAR TALES				
DC				
☐ 1, Sep 71	0.20	1.00	3.00	5.00
☐ 2		0.60	1.80	3.00
☐ 3		0.40	1.20	2.00
☐ 4		0.40	1.20	2.00
☐ 5		0.40	1.20	2.00
☐ 6		0.40	1.20	2.00
☐ 7		0.40	1.20	2.00
☐ 8		0.40	1.20	2.00
☐ 9		0.40	1.20	2.00
☐ 10		0.40	1.20	2.00
☐ 11		0.30	0.90	1.50
☐ 12		0.30	0.90	1.50
☐ 13		0.30	0.90	1.50
☐ 14		0.30	0.90	1.50
☐ 15		0.30	0.90	1.50
☐ 16		0.30	0.90	1.50
☐ 17		0.30	0.90	1.50
☐ 18		0.30	0.90	1.50
☐ 19		0.30	0.90	1.50
☐ 20		0.30	0.90	1.50
☐ 21		0.30	0.90	1.50
☐ 22		0.30	0.90	1.50
☐ 23		0.30	0.90	1.50
☐ 24		0.30	0.90	1.50
☐ 25		0.30	0.90	1.50
☐ 26		0.30	0.90	1.50
☐ 27		0.30	0.90	1.50
☐ 28		0.30	0.90	1.50
☐ 29		0.30	0.90	1.50
☐ 30		0.30	0.90	1.50
☐ 31		0.30	0.90	1.50
☐ 32		0.30	0.90	1.50
☐ 33		0.30	0.90	1.50
☐ 34		0.30	0.90	1.50
☐ 35		0.30	0.90	1.50
☐ 36		0.30	0.90	1.50
☐ 37		0.30	0.90	1.50
☐ 38		0.30	0.90	1.50
☐ 39		0.30	0.90	1.50
☐ 40		0.30	0.90	1.50
☐ 41		0.30	0.90	1.50
☐ 42		0.30	0.90	1.50
☐ 43		0.30	0.90	1.50
☐ 44		0.30	0.90	1.50
☐ 45		0.30	0.90	1.50
☐ 46		0.30	0.90	1.50
☐ 47		0.30	0.90	1.50
☐ 48		0.30	0.90	1.50
☐ 49		0.30	0.90	1.50
☐ 50		0.30	0.90	1.50
☐ 51		0.30	0.90	1.50
☐ 52		0.30	0.90	1.50
☐ 53		0.30	0.90	1.50
☐ 54		0.30	0.90	1.50
☐ 55		0.30	0.90	1.50
☐ 56		0.30	0.90	1.50
☐ 57		0.30	0.90	1.50
☐ 58		0.30	0.90	1.50
☐ 59		0.30	0.90	1.50
☐ 60		0.30	0.90	1.50
☐ 61		0.30	0.90	1.50
☐ 62		0.30	0.90	1.50
☐ 63		0.30	0.90	1.50
☐ 64		0.30	0.90	1.50
☐ 65		0.30	0.90	1.50
☐ 66		0.30	0.90	1.50
☐ 67		0.30	0.90	1.50
☐ 68		0.30	0.90	1.50
☐ 69		0.30	0.90	1.50
☐ 70		0.30	0.90	1.50
☐ 71		0.30	0.90	1.50
☐ 72		0.30	0.90	1.50
☐ 73		0.30	0.90	1.50
☐ 74		0.30	0.90	1.50
☐ 75		0.30	0.90	1.50
☐ 76		0.30	0.90	1.50
☐ 77		0.30	0.90	1.50
☐ 78		0.30	0.90	1.50
☐ 79		0.30	0.90	1.50
☐ 80		0.30	0.90	1.50
☐ 81		0.30	0.90	1.50
☐ 82		0.30	0.90	1.50
☐ 83		0.30	0.90	1.50
☐ 84		0.30	0.90	1.50
☐ 85		0.30	0.90	1.50
☐ 86		0.30	0.90	1.50
☐ 87		0.30	0.90	1.50
☐ 88		0.30	0.90	1.50
☐ 89		0.30	0.90	1.50
☐ 90		0.30	0.90	1.50
☐ 91		0.30	0.90	1.50
☐ 92		0.30	0.90	1.50
☐ 93		0.30	0.90	1.50
☐ 94		0.30	0.90	1.50
☐ 95		0.30	0.90	1.50
☐ 96		0.30	0.90	1.50
☐ 97		0.30	0.90	1.50
☐ 98		0.30	0.90	1.50
☐ 99		0.30	0.90	1.50
☐ 100		0.30	0.90	1.50
☐ 101		0.30	0.90	1.50
☐ 102		0.30	0.90	1.50
☐ 103		0.30	0.90	1.50
☐ 104		0.30	0.90	1.50
☐ 105		0.30	0.90	1.50
☐ 106		0.30	0.90	1.50
☐ 107		0.30	0.90	1.50
☐ 108		0.30	0.90	1.50
☐ 109		0.30	0.90	1.50
☐ 110		0.30	0.90	1.50
☐ 111		0.30	0.90	1.50
☐ 112		0.30	0.90	1.50
☐ 113		0.30	0.90	1.50
☐ 114		0.30	0.90	1.50
☐ 115		0.30	0.90	1.50
☐ 116		0.30	0.90	1.50
☐ 117		0.30	0.90	1.50
☐ 118		0.30	0.90	1.50
☐ 119		0.30	0.90	1.50
☐ 120		0.30	0.90	1.50
☐ 121		0.30	0.90	1.50
☐ 122		0.30	0.90	1.50
☐ 123		0.30	0.90	1.50
☐ 124, Jun 83		0.30	0.90	1.50
WEIRD WEST				
FANTACO				
☐ 1	2.95	0.59	1.77	2.95
☐ 2	2.95	0.59	1.77	2.95
☐ 3	2.95	0.59	1.77	2.95

	ORIG.	GOOD	FINE	N-MINT

WEIRD WESTERN TALES
DC

	ORIG.	GOOD	FINE	N-MINT
☐ 12, Jul 72, (was *All-Star Western*)	0.25	1.00	3.00	5.00
☐ 13, Sep 72	0.20	1.00	3.00	5.00
☐ 14, Nov 72	0.20	1.00	3.00	5.00
☐ 15, Jan 73	0.20	1.00	3.00	5.00
☐ 16, Mar 73	0.20	1.00	3.00	5.00
☐ 17, May 73	0.20	1.00	3.00	5.00
☐ 18, Aug 73	0.20	1.00	3.00	5.00
☐ 19, Oct 73	0.20	1.00	3.00	5.00
☐ 20, Dec 73	0.20	1.00	3.00	5.00
☐ 21, Feb 74	0.20	1.00	3.00	5.00
☐ 22, Jun 74	0.20	1.00	3.00	5.00
☐ 23, Aug 74	0.20	1.00	3.00	5.00
☐ 24, Oct 74	0.20	1.00	3.00	5.00
☐ 25, Dec 74	0.20	1.00	3.00	5.00
☐ 26, Feb 75	0.20	1.00	3.00	5.00
☐ 27, Apr 75	0.20	1.00	3.00	5.00
☐ 28, Jun 75	0.20	1.00	3.00	5.00
☐ 29, Aug 75	0.25	2.40	7.20	12.00
☐ 30, Oct 75	0.25	0.30	0.90	1.50
☐ 31, Dec 75	0.25	0.30	0.90	1.50
☐ 32, Feb 76	0.25	0.30	0.90	1.50
☐ 33, Apr 76	0.25	0.30	0.90	1.50
☐ 34, Jun 76	0.30	0.30	0.90	1.50
☐ 35, Aug 76	0.30	0.30	0.90	1.50
☐ 36, Oct 76	0.30	0.30	0.90	1.50
☐ 37, Dec 76	0.30	0.30	0.90	1.50
☐ 38, Feb 77	0.30	0.30	0.90	1.50
☐ 39, Apr 77	0.30	0.30	0.90	1.50
☐ 40	0.30	0.30	0.90	1.50
☐ 41	0.30	0.30	0.90	1.50
☐ 42	0.30	0.30	0.90	1.50
☐ 43	0.30	0.30	0.90	1.50
☐ 44	0.30	0.30	0.90	1.50
☐ 45	0.30	0.30	0.90	1.50
☐ 46	0.30	0.30	0.90	1.50
☐ 47	0.30	0.30	0.90	1.50
☐ 48	0.30	0.30	0.90	1.50
☐ 49	0.30	0.30	0.90	1.50
☐ 50	0.30	0.30	0.90	1.50
☐ 51	0.30	0.30	0.90	1.50
☐ 52	0.30	0.30	0.90	1.50
☐ 53	0.30	0.30	0.90	1.50
☐ 54	0.30	0.30	0.90	1.50
☐ 55	0.30	0.30	0.90	1.50
☐ 56	0.30	0.30	0.90	1.50
☐ 57	0.30	0.30	0.90	1.50
☐ 58	0.30	0.30	0.90	1.50
☐ 59	0.30	0.30	0.90	1.50
☐ 60	0.30	0.30	0.90	1.50
☐ 61	0.30	0.30	0.90	1.50
☐ 62	0.30	0.30	0.90	1.50
☐ 63	0.30	0.30	0.90	1.50
☐ 64	0.30	0.30	0.90	1.50
☐ 65	0.30	0.30	0.90	1.50
☐ 66	0.30	0.30	0.90	1.50
☐ 67	0.30	0.30	0.90	1.50
☐ 68	0.30	0.30	0.90	1.50
☐ 69	0.30	0.30	0.90	1.50
☐ 70	0.30	0.30	0.90	1.50

WEIRD WONDER TALES (1973-1977)
MARVEL

	ORIG.	GOOD	FINE	N-MINT
☐ 1, reprints	0.20	0.30	0.90	1.50
☐ 2, reprints	0.20	0.20	0.60	1.00
☐ 3, reprints	0.20	0.20	0.60	1.00
☐ 4	0.25	0.20	0.60	1.00
☐ 5	0.25	0.20	0.60	1.00
☐ 6	0.25	0.20	0.60	1.00
☐ 7	0.25	0.20	0.60	1.00
☐ 8	0.25	0.20	0.60	1.00
☐ 9	0.25	0.20	0.60	1.00

	ORIG.	GOOD	FINE	N-MINT
☐ 10	0.25	0.20	0.60	1.00
☐ 11	0.25	0.20	0.60	1.00
☐ 12	0.25	0.20	0.60	1.00
☐ 13	0.25	0.20	0.60	1.00
☐ 14	0.25	0.20	0.60	1.00
☐ 15	0.25	0.20	0.60	1.00
☐ 16	0.25	0.20	0.60	1.00
☐ 17	0.25	0.20	0.60	1.00
☐ 18	0.30	0.20	0.60	1.00
☐ 19, Dr. Druid	0.30	0.20	0.60	1.00
☐ 20, Dr. Druid	0.30	0.20	0.60	1.00
☐ 21, Dr. Druid	0.30	0.20	0.60	1.00
☐ 22, Dr. Druid	0.30	0.20	0.60	1.00

WEIRD WORLDS
DC

	ORIG.	GOOD	FINE	N-MINT
☐ 1, Sep 72	0.20	0.70	2.10	3.50
☐ 2, Nov 72	0.20	0.40	1.20	2.00
☐ 3, Jan 73	0.20	0.40	1.20	2.00
☐ 4, Mar 73	0.20	0.40	1.20	2.00
☐ 5, May 73	0.20	0.40	1.20	2.00
☐ 6, Aug 73	0.20	0.30	0.90	1.50
☐ 7, Oct 73	0.20	0.30	0.90	1.50
☐ 8, Dec 73	0.20	0.30	0.90	1.50
☐ 9, Feb 74	0.20	0.30	0.90	1.50
☐ 10, Nov 74	0.20	0.30	0.90	1.50

WEIRD, THE (mini-series)

	ORIG.	GOOD	FINE	N-MINT
☐ 1, Apr 88, BWr;A:JLI	1.50	0.60	1.80	3.00
☐ 2, May 88, BWr;A:JLI	1.50	0.60	1.80	3.00
☐ 3, Jun 88, BWr;A:JLI	1.50	0.60	1.80	3.00
☐ 4, Jul 88, BWr;A:JLI	1.50	0.60	1.80	3.00

WEIRDFALL
ANTARCTIC

	ORIG.	GOOD	FINE	N-MINT
☐ 1, Jul 95, b&w	2.75	0.55	1.65	2.75
☐ 2, Sep 95, b&w	2.75	0.55	1.65	2.75
☐ 3, Nov 95, b&w	2.75	0.55	1.65	2.75

WENDEL COMIX
KITCHEN SINK

	ORIG.	GOOD	FINE	N-MINT
☐ 1, b&w, adult		0.59	1.77	2.95

WENDY IN 3-D
BLACKTHORNE

	ORIG.	GOOD	FINE	N-MINT
☐ 1		0.50	1.50	2.50

WENDY THE GOOD LITTLE WITCH
HARVEY

	ORIG.	GOOD	FINE	N-MINT
☐ 1	1.25	0.25	0.75	1.25
☐ 2	1.25	0.25	0.75	1.25
☐ 3	1.25	0.25	0.75	1.25
☐ 4	1.25	0.25	0.75	1.25
☐ 5	1.25	0.25	0.75	1.25
☐ 6	1.25	0.25	0.75	1.25
☐ 7	1.25	0.25	0.75	1.25
☐ 8	1.25	0.25	0.75	1.25
☐ 9	1.25	0.25	0.75	1.25
☐ 10	1.25	0.25	0.75	1.25
☐ 11	1.25	0.25	0.75	1.25
☐ 12	1.50	0.30	0.90	1.50
☐ 13	1.50	0.30	0.90	1.50
☐ 14	1.50	0.30	0.90	1.50
☐ 15, Aug 94	1.50	0.30	0.90	1.50

WENDY WHITEBREAD, UNDERCOVER SLUT
EROS COMIX

	ORIG.	GOOD	FINE	N-MINT
☐ 1, adult, b&w		0.50	1.50	2.50
☐ 2, adult, b&w		0.50	1.50	2.50

WEREWOLF
BLACKTHORNE

	ORIG.	GOOD	FINE	N-MINT
☐ 1, b&w, TV show	2.00	0.40	1.20	2.00
☐ 2, b&w, TV show	2.00	0.40	1.20	2.00
☐ 3, b&w, TV show	2.00	0.40	1.20	2.00
☐ 4, b&w, TV show	2.00	0.40	1.20	2.00
☐ 5, b&w, TV show	2.00	0.40	1.20	2.00

	ORIG.	GOOD	FINE	N-MINT
WEREWOLF AT LARGE				
ETERNITY				
1, b&w		0.45	1.35	2.25
2, b&w		0.45	1.35	2.25
3, b&w		0.45	1.35	2.25
WEREWOLF BY NIGHT				
MARVEL				
1, MP	0.20	2.00	6.00	10.00
2, MP	0.20	0.80	2.40	4.00
3, MP	0.20	0.60	1.80	3.00
4, MP	0.20	0.60	1.80	3.00
5, MP	0.20	0.60	1.80	3.00
6, MP	0.20	0.60	1.80	3.00
7, MP	0.20	0.60	1.80	3.00
8	0.20	0.40	1.20	2.00
9	0.20	0.40	1.20	2.00
10	0.20	0.40	1.20	2.00
11	0.20	0.40	1.20	2.00
12	0.20	0.40	1.20	2.00
13	0.20	0.40	1.20	2.00
14	0.20	0.40	1.20	2.00
15	0.20	0.40	1.20	2.00
16	0.20	0.40	1.20	2.00
17	0.25	0.40	1.20	2.00
18	0.25	0.40	1.20	2.00
19	0.25	0.40	1.20	2.00
20	0.25	0.40	1.20	2.00
21	0.25	0.40	1.20	2.00
22	0.25	0.40	1.20	2.00
23	0.25	0.40	1.20	2.00
24	0.25	0.40	1.20	2.00
25	0.25	0.40	1.20	2.00
26	0.25	0.40	1.20	2.00
27	0.25	0.40	1.20	2.00
28	0.25	0.40	1.20	2.00
29	0.25	0.40	1.20	2.00
30	0.25	0.40	1.20	2.00
31	0.25	0.40	1.20	2.00
32, O&1:Moon Knight	0.25	5.00	15.00	25.00
33, Moon Knight	0.25	2.40	7.20	12.00
34	0.25	0.40	1.20	2.00
35	0.25	0.40	1.20	2.00
36	0.25	0.40	1.20	2.00
37, BWr, A:Moon Knight	0.25	1.40	4.20	7.00
38	0.25	0.40	1.20	2.00
39	0.25	0.40	1.20	2.00
40	0.30	0.40	1.20	2.00
41	0.30	0.40	1.20	2.00
42	0.30	0.40	1.20	2.00
43	0.30	0.40	1.20	2.00
WEREWOLF IN 3-D				
BLACKTHORNE				
1, 88	2.50	0.50	1.50	2.50
WEST COAST AVENGERS				
MARVEL				
1, Sep 84, BH	0.75	1.00	3.00	5.00
2, Oct 84, BH	0.75	0.40	1.20	2.00
3, Nov 84, BH	0.75	0.40	1.20	2.00
4, Dec 84, BH	0.75	0.40	1.20	2.00
WEST COAST AVENGERS (2nd series)				
1, Oct 85	1.25	1.20	3.60	6.00
2, Nov 85	0.65	0.80	2.40	4.00
3, Dec 85	0.65	0.60	1.80	3.00
4, Jan 86	0.65	0.60	1.80	3.00
5, Feb 86	0.75	0.60	1.80	3.00
6, Mar 86	0.75	0.60	1.80	3.00
7, Apr 86	0.75	0.60	1.80	3.00
8, May 86	0.75	0.60	1.80	3.00
9, Jun 86	0.75	0.60	1.80	3.00
10, Jul 86	0.75	0.60	1.80	3.00

	ORIG.	GOOD	FINE	N-MINT
11, Aug 86	0.75	0.40	1.20	2.00
12, Sep 86	0.75	0.40	1.20	2.00
13, Oct 86	0.75	0.40	1.20	2.00
14, Nov 86	0.75	0.40	1.20	2.00
15, Dec 86	0.75	0.40	1.20	2.00
16, Jan 87	0.75	0.40	1.20	2.00
17, Feb 87	0.75	0.40	1.20	2.00
18, Mar 87	0.75	0.40	1.20	2.00
19, Apr 87	0.75	0.40	1.20	2.00
20, May 87	0.75	0.40	1.20	2.00
21, Jun 87	0.75	0.35	1.05	1.75
22, Jul 87	0.75	0.35	1.05	1.75
23, Aug 87	0.75	0.35	1.05	1.75
24, Sep 87	0.75	0.35	1.05	1.75
25, Oct 87	0.75	0.35	1.05	1.75
26, Nov 87	0.75	0.35	1.05	1.75
27, Dec 87	0.75	0.35	1.05	1.75
28, Jan 88	0.75	0.35	1.05	1.75
29, Feb 88	0.75	0.35	1.05	1.75
30, Mar 88	0.75	0.35	1.05	1.75
31, Apr 88	0.75	0.35	1.05	1.75
32, May 88	0.75	0.35	1.05	1.75
33, Jun 88	0.75	0.35	1.05	1.75
34, Jul 88	0.75	0.35	1.05	1.75
35, Aug 88	0.75	0.35	1.05	1.75
36, Sep 88	0.75	0.35	1.05	1.75
37, Oct 88	0.75	0.35	1.05	1.75
38, Nov 88	0.75	0.35	1.05	1.75
39, Dec 88	0.75	0.35	1.05	1.75
40, Jan 89	0.75	0.35	1.05	1.75
41, Feb 89	0.75	0.35	1.05	1.75
42, Mar 89, JBy	0.75	0.20	0.60	1.00
43, Apr 89, JBy	0.75	0.20	0.60	1.00
44, May 89, JBy	0.75	0.20	0.60	1.00
45, Jun 89, JBy	0.75	0.20	0.60	1.00
46, Jul 89, 1:Great Lakes Avengers	0.75	0.20	0.60	1.00
47, Aug 89, (becomes *Avengers West Coast*)	0.75	0.20	0.60	1.00
WEST COAST AVENGERS ANNUAL				
1, 86	1.25	0.40	1.20	2.00
2, 87	1.25	0.40	1.20	2.00
3, 88, Evolutionary War (becomes *Avengers West Coast Annual*)	1.75	0.60	1.80	3.00
WESTERN ACTION				
ATLAS/SEABOARD				
1, Jun 75	0.25	0.20	0.60	1.00
WESTERN GUNFIGHTERS (1970-1972)				
MARVEL				
1	0.25	0.60	1.80	3.00
2	0.25	0.40	1.20	2.00
3	0.25	0.40	1.20	2.00
4	0.25	0.40	1.20	2.00
5	0.25	0.40	1.20	2.00
6	0.25	0.40	1.20	2.00
7	0.25	0.20	0.60	1.00
8	0.25	0.20	0.60	1.00
9	0.25	0.20	0.60	1.00
10	0.25	0.20	0.60	1.00
11	0.25	0.20	0.60	1.00
12	0.25	0.20	0.60	1.00
13	0.25	0.20	0.60	1.00
14	0.25	0.20	0.60	1.00
15	0.25	0.20	0.60	1.00
16	0.25	0.20	0.60	1.00
17	0.25	0.20	0.60	1.00
18	0.25	0.20	0.60	1.00
19	0.25	0.20	0.60	1.00
20	0.25	0.20	0.60	1.00
21	0.25	0.20	0.60	1.00
22	0.25	0.20	0.60	1.00

	ORIG.	GOOD	FINE	N-MINT
☐ 23 ....0.25		0.20	0.60	1.00
☐ 24 ....0.25		0.20	0.60	1.00
☐ 25 ....0.25		0.20	0.60	1.00
☐ 26 ....0.25		0.20	0.60	1.00
☐ 27 ....0.25		0.20	0.60	1.00
☐ 28 ....0.25		0.20	0.60	1.00
☐ 29 ....0.25		0.20	0.60	1.00
☐ 30 ....0.25		0.20	0.60	1.00
☐ 31 ....0.25		0.20	0.60	1.00
☐ 32 ....0.25		0.20	0.60	1.00
☐ 33 ....0.25		0.20	0.60	1.00

WESTERN TEAM-UP

	ORIG.	GOOD	FINE	N-MINT
☐ 1 ....0.20		0.20	0.60	1.00

WETWORKS
IMAGE

	ORIG.	GOOD	FINE	N-MINT
☐ 1, Jun 94 ....1.95		1.00	3.00	5.00
☐ 2, Aug 94, alternate cover		0.80	2.40	4.00
☐ 2, Aug 94 ....1.95		0.39	1.17	1.95
☐ 3, Sep 94 ....1.95		0.39	1.17	1.95
☐ 4, Nov 94 ....2.50		0.50	1.50	2.50
☐ 6, Mar 95 ....2.50		0.50	1.50	2.50
☐ 7, Apr 95 ....2.50		0.50	1.50	2.50
☐ 8, May 95, "WildStorm Rising" Part 7;bound-in trading cards 2.50		0.50	1.50	2.50
☐ 9, Aug 95 ....2.50		0.50	1.50	2.50
☐ 10, Aug 95 ....2.50		0.50	1.50	2.50
☐ 11, Sep 95........................2.50		0.50	1.50	2.50
☐ 12, Nov 95, indicia says "Nov";cover says "Dec" 2.50		0.50	1.50	2.50
☐ 13, Jan 96 ....2.50		0.50	1.50	2.50
☐ 14, Feb 96 ....2.50		0.50	1.50	2.50
☐ 16, Apr 96, "Fire from Heaven" Part 4 ....2.50		0.50	1.50	2.50

WETWORKS SOURCEBOOK

	ORIG.	GOOD	FINE	N-MINT
☐ 1, Oct 94 ....2.50		0.50	1.50	2.50

WHACKED!
RIVER GROUP

	ORIG.	GOOD	FINE	N-MINT
☐ 0, nn.................................2.50		0.50	1.50	2.50

WHAT IF? (Volume 1, 1977-1988)
MARVEL

	ORIG.	GOOD	FINE	N-MINT
☐ 1, Feb 77, SpM................0.50		4.00	12.00	20.00
☐ 2, Apr 77, GK(c), Hulk.. 0.50		1.60	4.80	8.00
☐ 3, Jun 77, GK/KJ, Avengers 0.50		0.80	2.40	4.00
☐ 4, Aug 77, GK(c) 0.50		0.80	2.40	4.00
☐ 5, Oct 77, Capt. America 0.50		0.80	2.40	4.00
☐ 6, Dec 77, Fantastic Four 0.60		0.70	2.10	3.50
☐ 7, Feb 78, GK(c), SpM.... 0.60		1.20	3.60	6.00
☐ 8, Apr 78, GK(c), Daredevil 0.60		0.80	2.40	4.00
☐ 9, Jun 78, JK(c), O:Marvel Boy 0.60		0.60	1.80	3.00
☐ 10, Aug 78, JB, Thor 0.60		0.50	1.50	2.50
☐ 11, Oct 78, JK, Fantastic Four 0.60		0.40	1.20	2.00
☐ 12, Dec 78, Hulk 0.60		0.40	1.20	2.00
☐ 13, Feb 79, JB, Conan 0.60		0.80	2.40	4.00
☐ 14, Apr 79, Sgt. Fury 0.60		0.40	1.20	2.00
☐ 15, Jun 79, CI, Nova 0.60		0.40	1.20	2.00
☐ 16, Aug 79, Fu Manchu.. 0.60		0.40	1.20	2.00
☐ 17, Oct 79, CI, Ghost Rider 0.60		1.00	3.00	5.00
☐ 18, Dec 79, TS,Dr. Strange 0.60		0.40	1.20	2.00
☐ 19, Feb 80, PB, SpM 0.75		0.60	1.80	3.00
☐ 20, Apr 80, Avengers 0.75		0.40	1.20	2.00
☐ 21, Jun 80, GC, Sub-Mariner 0.75		0.40	1.20	2.00

	ORIG.	GOOD	FINE	N-MINT
☐ 22, Aug 80, Dr. Doom.....0.75		0.40	1.20	2.00
☐ 23, Oct 80, JB, Hulk........0.75		0.40	1.20	2.00
☐ 24, Dec 80, GK/RB, SpM 0.75		0.60	1.80	3.00
☐ 25, Feb 81, Thor, Avengers 0.75		0.40	1.20	2.00
☐ 26, Apr 81, JBy(c), Capt. America 0.75		0.40	1.20	2.00
☐ 27, Jul 81, FM(c), X-Men 0.75		1.80	5.40	9.00
☐ 28, Aug 81, FM, Daredevil 0.75		1.80	5.40	9.00
☐ 29, Oct 81, MG(c), Avengers 0.75		0.30	0.90	1.50
☐ 30, Dec 81, RB, SpM 0.75		1.60	4.80	8.00
☐ 31, Feb 82, Wolverine.....1.00		3.20	9.60	16.00
☐ 32, Apr 82, Avengers 1.00		0.40	1.20	2.00
☐ 33, Jun 82, BL, Dazzler ...1.00		0.40	1.20	2.00
☐ 34, Aug 82, FH/FM/JBy/BSz 1.00		0.40	1.20	2.00
☐ 35, Oct 82, FM, Elektra ...1.00		0.50	1.50	2.50
☐ 36, Dec 82, JBy, Fantastic Four 1.00		0.40	1.20	2.00
☐ 37, Feb 83, Beast............1.00		0.40	1.20	2.00
☐ 38, Apr 83, Daredevil 1.00		0.40	1.20	2.00
☐ 39, Jun 83, Thor, Conan .1.00		0.40	1.20	2.00
☐ 40, Aug 83, Dr. Strange ..1.00		0.40	1.20	2.00
☐ 41, Oct 83, Sub-Mariner .1.00		0.40	1.20	2.00
☐ 42, Dec 83, Fantastic Four 1.00		0.40	1.20	2.00
☐ 43, Feb 84, Conan...........1.00		0.40	1.20	2.00
☐ 44, Apr 84, Captain America 1.00		0.40	1.20	2.00
☐ 45, Jun 84, Hulk 1.00		0.40	1.20	2.00
☐ 46, Aug 84, SpM.............1.00		0.40	1.20	2.00
☐ 47, Oct 84, Thor, Loki.....1.00		0.40	1.20	2.00

WHAT IF? (Volume 2, 1989)

	ORIG.	GOOD	FINE	N-MINT
☐ 1, Jul 89, Avengers..........1.25		1.00	3.00	5.00
☐ 2, Aug 89, Daredevil 1.25		0.80	2.40	4.00
☐ 3, Sep 89, Capt. America 1.25		0.80	2.40	4.00
☐ 4, Oct 89, SpM................1.25		0.80	2.40	4.00
☐ 5, Nov 89, Avengers 1.25		0.40	1.20	2.00
☐ 6, Nov 89, X-Men 1.25		1.60	4.80	8.00
☐ 7, Dec 89, Wolverine 1.25		1.60	4.80	8.00
☐ 8, Dec 89, Iron Man.........1.25		0.60	1.80	3.00
☐ 9, Jan 90, X-Men 1.25		0.60	1.80	3.00
☐ 10, Feb 90, Punisher.......1.25		0.60	1.80	3.00
☐ 11, Mar 90, Fantastic Four 1.25		0.25	0.75	1.25
☐ 12, Apr 90, X-Men 1.25		0.40	1.20	2.00
☐ 13, May 90, X-Men 1.25		0.40	1.20	2.00
☐ 14, Jun 90, Capt. Marvel.1.25		0.25	0.75	1.25
☐ 15, Jul 90, F4, Galactus ..1.25		0.25	0.75	1.25
☐ 16, Aug 90, Wolverine, Conan 1.25		0.80	2.40	4.00
☐ 17, Sep 90, D:SpM 1.25		0.25	0.75	1.25
☐ 18, Oct 90, FF, Dr. Doom 1.25		0.25	0.75	1.25
☐ 19, Nov 90 ....1.25		0.25	0.75	1.25
☐ 20, Dec 90, SpM.............1.25		0.25	0.75	1.25
☐ 21, Jan 91, SpM, D:Black Cat 1.25		0.25	0.75	1.25
☐ 22, Feb 91, Silver Surfer.1.25		0.60	1.80	3.00
☐ 23, Mar 91, X-Men..........1.25		0.60	1.80	3.00
☐ 24, Apr 91, vampire Wolverine 1.25		0.25	0.75	1.25
☐ 25, May 91, Atlantis Attacks 1.25		0.60	1.80	3.00
☐ 26, Jun 91, Punisher 1.25		0.60	1.80	3.00
☐ 27, Jul 91, Namor, F4.....1.25		0.25	0.75	1.25
☐ 28, Aug 91, Captain America 1.25		0.25	0.75	1.25

	ORIG.	GOOD	FINE	N-MINT
29, Sep 91, Captain America, Avengers				
.... 1.25		0.25	0.75	1.25
30, Oct 91 .... 1.25		0.25	0.75	1.25
31, Nov 91 .... 1.25		0.25	0.75	1.25
32, Dec 91, Phoenix 1.25		0.25	0.75	1.25
33, Phoenix 1.25		0.25	0.75	1.25
34, humor 1.25		0.25	0.75	1.25
35, F4, SpM, Dr. Doom .. 1.25		0.25	0.75	1.25
36 .... 1.25		0.25	0.75	1.25
37, Wolverine 1.25		0.40	1.20	2.00
38, Thor 1.25		0.25	0.75	1.25
41, Avengers vs. Galactus				
.... 1.75		0.35	1.05	1.75
42, SpM 1.25		0.25	0.75	1.25
43, Wolverine 1.25		0.25	0.75	1.25
44, Venom, Punisher 1.25		0.25	0.75	1.25
45, Ghost Rider 1.25		0.25	0.75	1.25
46, Cable 1.25		0.25	0.75	1.25
47, Magneto 1.25		0.25	0.75	1.25
48, Daredevil 1.25		0.25	0.75	1.25
49, Silver Surfer 1.25		0.25	0.75	1.25
50, Hulk/Wolverine, silver sculpted cover				
.... 2.95		0.59	1.77	2.95
51, Punisher/Capt. America				
.... 1.25		0.25	0.75	1.25
52, Dr. Doom 1.25		0.40	1.20	2.00
53, SpM,Hulk,Iron Man 2020				
.... 1.25		0.25	0.75	1.25
54, Oct 93, Death's Head 1.25		0.25	0.75	1.25
55, Nov 93, Avengers 1.25		0.25	0.75	1.25
56, Dec 93, Avengers 1.25		0.25	0.75	1.25
57, Jan 94, Punisher 1.25		0.25	0.75	1.25
58, Feb 94, Punisher/SpM				
.... 1.25		0.25	0.75	1.25
59, Mar 94, Wolverine/Alpha Flight				
.... 1.25		0.25	0.75	1.25
60, Apr 94, X-Men wedding				
.... 1.25		0.25	0.75	1.25
61, May 94, SpM 1.50		0.30	0.90	1.50
62, Jun 94, Wolverine 1.50		0.30	0.90	1.50
63, Jul 94, War Machine 1.50		0.30	0.90	1.50
64, Aug 94 .... 2.00		0.40	1.20	2.00
65, Sep 94 .... 1.50		0.30	0.90	1.50
66, Oct 94 .... 1.50		0.30	0.90	1.50
67, Nov 94 .... 1.50		0.30	0.90	1.50
68, Dec 94 .... 1.50		0.30	0.90	1.50
69, Jan 95 .... 1.50		0.30	0.90	1.50
70, Feb 95 .... 1.50		0.30	0.90	1.50
71, Mar 95 .... 1.50		0.30	0.90	1.50
72, Apr 95 .... 1.50		0.30	0.90	1.50
73, May 95 .... 1.50		0.30	0.90	1.50
74, Jun 95, Mr. Sinister forms The X-Men				
....		0.30	0.90	1.50
75, Jul 95 .... 1.50		0.30	0.90	1.50
76, Aug 95, Flash Thompson as Spider-Man				
.... 1.50		0.30	0.90	1.50
77, Sep 95 .... 1.50		0.30	0.90	1.50
78, Oct 95, New Fantastic Four remains a team				
.... 1.50		0.30	0.90	1.50
79, Nov 95, Storm becomes Phoenix				
.... 1.50		0.30	0.90	1.50
80, Dec 95, Hulk becomes The Maestro				
.... 1.50		0.30	0.90	1.50
81, Jan 96, "Age of Apocalypse" didn't end				
.... 1.50		0.30	0.90	1.50
82, Feb 96, J.Jonah Jamesonadopts Peter Parker				
.... 1.50		0.30	0.90	1.50
83, Mar 96, Daredevil was the disciple of Doctor Strange				
.... 1.50		0.30	0.90	1.50
84, Apr 96, Shard lived instead of Bishop				
.... 1.50		0.30	0.90	1.50
85, May 96, Magneto ruledall mutants				
.... 1.50		0.30	0.90	1.50
86, Jun 96, Scarlet Spider kills Spider-Man				
.... 1.50		0.30	0.90	1.50
87, Jul 96, Sabretooth 1.50		0.30	0.90	1.50

WHAT IF? SPECIAL

	ORIG.	GOOD	FINE	N-MINT
1, Jun 88, Iron Man 1.50		0.30	0.90	1.50

WHAT IS...THE FACE?
ACE

	GOOD	FINE	N-MINT
1, Dec 86, SD.................	0.35	1.05	1.75
2, May 87, SD.................	0.35	1.05	1.75
3, Aug 87, SD	0.35	1.05	1.75

WHAT THE--?!
MARVEL

	ORIG.	GOOD	FINE	N-MINT
1, Aug 88 .... 1.25		0.25	0.75	1.25
2, Sep 88 .... 1.25		0.25	0.75	1.25
3, Oct 88 .... 1.25		0.25	0.75	1.25
4, Nov 88 .... 1.25		0.25	0.75	1.25
5, Jul 89 .... 1.50		0.30	0.90	1.50
6, Jan 90, JBy/TA........... 1.00		0.30	0.90	1.50
7, Apr 90, JBy(c) 1.25		0.25	0.75	1.25
8, Jul 90, JBy(c) 1.25		0.25	0.75	1.25
9, Oct 90, JBy(c)............ 1.25		0.25	0.75	1.25
10, Jan 91, JBy(c) 1.25		0.25	0.75	1.25
11, Mar 91, JBy(c).......... 1.25		0.25	0.75	1.25
12, May 91, JBy(c) 1.25		0.25	0.75	1.25
13, Jul 91, JBy(c) 1.25		0.25	0.75	1.25
14, Sep 91, JBy(c) 1.25		0.25	0.75	1.25
15, Nov 91 .... 1.25		0.25	0.75	1.25
16, EC parody 1.25		0.25	0.75	1.25
17 .... 1.25		0.25	0.75	1.25
18 .... 1.25		0.25	0.75	1.25
19 .... 1.25		0.25	0.75	1.25
20 .... 1.25		0.25	0.75	1.25
21 .... 1.25		0.25	0.75	1.25
22 .... 1.25		0.25	0.75	1.25
23 .... 1.25		0.25	0.75	1.25
24 .... 1.25		0.25	0.75	1.25
25 .... 2.50		0.50	1.50	2.50
26 .... 2.50		0.50	1.50	2.50
27 .... 2.50		0.50	1.50	2.50

WHAT'S NEW?
PALLIARD

	GOOD	FINE	N-MINT
1, color & b&w	1.19	3.57	5.95

WHERE IN THE WORLD IS CARMEN SANDIEGO?
DC

	ORIG.	GOOD	FINE	N-MINT
1, Jun 96, based on computer game series				
.... 1.75		0.35	1.05	1.75

WHILE FIFTY MILLION DIED
TOME PRESS

	ORIG.	GOOD	FINE	N-MINT
1, b&w........................... 2.95		0.59	1.77	2.95

WHISPER
CAPITAL

	GOOD	FINE	N-MINT
1, Dec 83	0.80	2.40	4.00
2, Mar 84, (moves to First)	0.40	1.20	2.00

FIRST

	GOOD	FINE	N-MINT
1, Jun 86	0.25	0.75	1.25
2, Aug 86	0.25	0.75	1.25
3, Oct 86	0.25	0.75	1.25
4, Dec 86	0.25	0.75	1.25
5, Feb 87	0.25	0.75	1.25
6, Apr 87	0.25	0.75	1.25
7, Jun 87	0.25	0.75	1.25
8, Aug 87	0.35	1.05	1.75
9, Oct 87	0.25	0.75	1.25
10, Dec 87			
11, Feb 88			
12, Apr 88			
13, Jun 88	0.35	1.05	1.75
14, Jul 88	0.35	1.05	1.75

	ORIG.	GOOD	FINE	N-MINT
15, Aug 88		0.35	1.05	1.75
16, Sep 88		0.35	1.05	1.75
17, Oct 88		0.35	1.05	1.75
18, Nov 88		0.39	1.17	1.95
19, Dec 88		0.39	1.17	1.95
20, Jan 89		0.39	1.17	1.95
21, Feb 89		0.39	1.17	1.95
22, Mar 89		0.39	1.17	1.95
23, Apr 89		0.39	1.17	1.95
24, May 89		0.39	1.17	1.95
25, Jun 89		0.39	1.17	1.95
26, Jul 89		0.39	1.17	1.95
27, Aug 89		0.39	1.17	1.95
28, Sep 89		0.39	1.17	1.95
29, Oct 89		0.39	1.17	1.95
30, Nov 89		0.39	1.17	1.95
31, Dec 89		0.39	1.17	1.95
32, Jan 90		0.39	1.17	1.95
33, Feb 90		0.39	1.17	1.95
34, Mar 90		0.39	1.17	1.95
35, Apr 90		0.39	1.17	1.95
36, May 90		0.39	1.17	1.95
37, Jun 90		0.39	1.17	1.95

WHISPER SPECIAL (former Capital title)

	ORIG.	GOOD	FINE	N-MINT
1, Nov 85		0.50	1.50	2.50

WHISPERS AND SHADOWS
OASIS

	GOOD	FINE	N-MINT
1, b&w	0.30	0.90	1.50
2, b&w	0.30	0.90	1.50
3, b&w	0.30	0.90	1.50
4, b&w	0.30	0.90	1.50
5, b&w	0.30	0.90	1.50
6, b&w	0.30	0.90	1.50
7, b&w	0.30	0.90	1.50
8, b&w	0.30	0.90	1.50

WHITE DEVIL
ETERNITY

	GOOD	FINE	N-MINT
1, adult, b&w	0.50	1.50	2.50
2, adult, b&w	0.50	1.50	2.50
3, adult, b&w	0.50	1.50	2.50
4, adult, b&w	0.50	1.50	2.50
5, adult, b&w	0.50	1.50	2.50
6, adult, b&w	0.50	1.50	2.50
7, adult, b&w	0.50	1.50	2.50
8, adult, b&w	0.50	1.50	2.50

WHITE FANG
DISNEY

	ORIG.	GOOD	FINE	N-MINT
0, nn movie adaptation		1.19	3.57	5.95
0, nn newsstand version		0.59	1.77	2.95

WHITE LIKE SHE (mini-series)
DARK HORSE

	ORIG.	GOOD	FINE	N-MINT
1, May 94, b&w	2.95	0.59	1.77	2.95
2, Jun 94, b&w	2.95	0.59	1.77	2.95
3, Jul 94, b&w	2.95	0.59	1.77	2.95
4, Aug 94, b&w	2.95	0.59	1.77	2.95

WHITE TRASH
TUNDRA

	GOOD	FINE	N-MINT
0, nn	0.50	1.50	2.50
1	0.79	2.37	3.95

WHO REALLY KILLED JFK?
REVOLUTIONARY

	ORIG.	GOOD	FINE	N-MINT
1, Oct 93, b&w	2.50	0.50	1.50	2.50

WHO'S WHO IN STAR TREK
DC

	GOOD	FINE	N-MINT
1, HC,GP,JBy	0.30	0.90	1.50
2, HC,GP,JBy	0.30	0.90	1.50

WHO'S WHO IN THE DC UNIVERSE

	ORIG.	GOOD	FINE	N-MINT
1, Aug 90, looseleaf	4.95	0.99	2.97	4.95
2, Sep 90, looseleaf	4.95	0.99	2.97	4.95
3, Oct 90, looseleaf	4.95	0.99	2.97	4.95
4, Nov 90, looseleaf	4.95	0.99	2.97	4.95
5, Dec 90, looseleaf	4.95	0.99	2.97	4.95
6, Jan 91, looseleaf	4.95	0.99	2.97	4.95
7, Feb 91, looseleaf	4.95	0.99	2.97	4.95
8, Apr 91, looseleaf	4.95	0.99	2.97	4.95
9, May 91, looseleaf	4.95	0.99	2.97	4.95
10, Jun 91, looseleaf	4.95	0.99	2.97	4.95
11, Jul 91, looseleaf	4.95	0.99	2.97	4.95
12, Aug 91, looseleaf	4.95	0.99	2.97	4.95
13, Oct 91, looseleaf	4.95	0.99	2.97	4.95
14, Nov 91, looseleaf	4.95	0.99	2.97	4.95
15, Jan 92, looseleaf	4.95	0.99	2.97	4.95
16, Feb 92, looseleaf	4.95	0.99	2.97	4.95

WHO'S WHO IN THE DC UNIVERSE UPDATE 1993

	GOOD	FINE	N-MINT
1, looseleaf	1.19	3.57	5.95
2, looseleaf	1.19	3.57	5.95

WHO'S WHO IN THE IMPACT UNIVERSE
IMPACT

	ORIG.	GOOD	FINE	N-MINT
1, Sep 91	4.95	0.99	2.97	4.95
2, Dec 91	4.95	0.99	2.97	4.95
3, May 92	4.95	0.99	2.97	4.95

WHO'S WHO IN THE LEGION OF SUPER-HEROES
DC

	ORIG.	GOOD	FINE	N-MINT
1, Apr 88	1.25	0.25	0.75	1.25
2, Jun 88	1.25	0.25	0.75	1.25
3, Jul 88	1.25	0.25	0.75	1.25
4, Aug 88	1.25	0.25	0.75	1.25
5, Sep 88	1.25	0.25	0.75	1.25
6, Oct 88	1.25	0.25	0.75	1.25
7, Nov 88	1.25	0.25	0.75	1.25

WHO'S WHO UPDATE '87

	ORIG.	GOOD	FINE	N-MINT
1, Aug 87	1.25	0.25	0.75	1.25
2, Sep 87	1.25	0.25	0.75	1.25
3, Oct 87	1.25	0.25	0.75	1.25
4, Nov 87	1.25	0.25	0.75	1.25
5, Dec 87	1.25	0.25	0.75	1.25

WHO'S WHO UPDATE '88

	ORIG.	GOOD	FINE	N-MINT
1, Aug 88	1.25	0.25	0.75	1.25
2, Sep 88	1.25	0.25	0.75	1.25
3, Oct 88	1.25	0.25	0.75	1.25
4, Nov 88	1.25	0.25	0.75	1.25

WHO'S WHO: THE DEFINITIVE DIRECTORY OF THE DC UNIVERSE

	ORIG.	GOOD	FINE	N-MINT
1, Mar 85, GP,GK,JOy,MR	1.00	0.20	0.60	1.00
2, Apr 85, GP,TA,GK,JK,JL,JOy,MR	1.00	0.20	0.60	1.00
3, May 85, GP,TA,GK,JK,JOy,BSz,SR	1.00	0.20	0.60	1.00
4, Jun 85, GP,AAd,JBy,GK,JK,WS,DSt	1.00	0.20	0.60	1.00
5, Jul 85, GP,TA,GK,JK,JOy,MR	1.00	0.20	0.60	1.00
6, Aug 85, GK,JK,JL,JOy,MR,WS,MW	1.00	0.20	0.60	1.00
7, Sep 85, TA,JBy,GK,MR,BSz,DSt	1.00	0.20	0.60	1.00
8, Oct 85, TA,GK,JK,JOy,GP	1.00	0.20	0.60	1.00
9, Nov 85, GK,JK,GP,BSz	1.00	0.20	0.60	1.00
10, Dec 85, GK,JK,JOy,GP,SR,WS	1.00	0.20	0.60	1.00
11, Jan 86, AAd,JC,GK,JK,JOy,GP,MR	1.00	0.20	0.60	1.00
12, Feb 86, JK,JL,JOy,GP,MR	1.00	0.20	0.60	1.00
13, Mar 86, GP,GK,JK,JSn	1.00	0.20	0.60	1.00
14, Apr 86, GP,JBy,MK,JK,BSz,WS,JSn	1.00	0.20	0.60	1.00

	ORIG.	GOOD	FINE	N-MINT
15, May 86, GP,TA,JK,GP,MR,BSz 1.00		0.20	0.60	1.00
16, Jun 86, GP,TA,JBy,GK,JK,BSz,JSn 1.00		0.20	0.60	1.00
17, Jul 86, GP,JK,JOy,GP 1.00		0.20	0.60	1.00
18, Aug 86, GP,AAd,JBy,JK,JOy,SR,DSt 1.00		0.20	0.60	1.00
19, Sep 86, JBy,SD,GK,JL,GP 1.00		0.20	0.60	1.00
20, Oct 86, AAd,SD,JK,JL 1.00		0.20	0.60	1.00
21, Nov 86, SD,MK,GK,JOy,BSz 1.00		0.20	0.60	1.00
22, Dec 86, JGy,TA,SD,GK,JK,JL,JOy,GP 1.00		0.20	0.60	1.00
23, Jan 87 ...... 1.00		0.20	0.60	1.00
24, Feb 87 ...... 1.00		0.20	0.60	1.00
25, Mar 87 ...... 1.00		0.20	0.60	1.00
26, Apr 87 ...... 1.00		0.20	0.60	1.00

WHODUNNIT?
ECLIPSE

	ORIG.	GOOD	FINE	N-MINT
1, Jun 86, DS		0.40	1.20	2.00
2, Nov 86, DS		0.40	1.20	2.00
3, Apr 87, DS		0.40	1.20	2.00

WHOT NOT!
FANTAGRAPHICS

	ORIG.	GOOD	FINE	N-MINT
1, b&w 2.50		0.50	1.50	2.50
2, b&w 2.50		0.50	1.50	2.50
3, b&w 2.50		0.50	1.50	2.50

WICKED
MILLENNIUM

	ORIG.	GOOD	FINE	N-MINT
3, Apr 95, b&w;cover has a "Mar" date 2.50		0.50	1.50	2.50

WIINDOWS
CULT

	ORIG.	GOOD	FINE	N-MINT
1, b&w 2.50		0.50	1.50	2.50
2, b&w 2.50		0.50	1.50	2.50
3, b&w 2.50		0.50	1.50	2.50
4, b&w 2.50		0.50	1.50	2.50
5, b&w 2.50		0.50	1.50	2.50
6, b&w 2.50		0.50	1.50	2.50
7, b&w 2.50		0.50	1.50	2.50
8, b&w 2.50		0.50	1.50	2.50
9, Nov 93, b&w 2.50		0.50	1.50	2.50
10, Dec 93, b&w 2.50		0.50	1.50	2.50
11, Jan 94, b&w 2.50		0.50	1.50	2.50
12, Feb 94, b&w 2.50		0.50	1.50	2.50
13, Mar 94, b&w 2.50		0.50	1.50	2.50
14, Apr 94, b&w 2.50		0.50	1.50	2.50
15, May 94, b&w 2.50		0.50	1.50	2.50
16, Jun 94, b&w 2.50		0.50	1.50	2.50
17, Jun 94, b&w 2.50		0.50	1.50	2.50

WILD ANIMALS
PACIFIC

	ORIG.	GOOD	FINE	N-MINT
1		0.30	0.90	1.50

WILD BILL PECOS
AC

	ORIG.	GOOD	FINE	N-MINT
1		0.70	2.10	3.50

WILD CARDS
EPIC

	ORIG.	GOOD	FINE	N-MINT
1 ...... 4.50		1.50	4.50	7.50
2 ...... 4.50		1.00	3.00	5.00
3 ...... 4.50		1.00	3.00	5.00
4 ...... 4.50		0.90	2.70	4.50

WILD DOG
DC

	ORIG.	GOOD	FINE	N-MINT
1, Sep 87 ...... 0.75		0.20	0.60	1.00
2, Oct 87 ...... 0.75		0.20	0.60	1.00
3, Nov 87 ...... 0.75		0.20	0.60	1.00
4, Dec 87 ...... 0.75		0.20	0.60	1.00

WILD DOG SPECIAL

	ORIG.	GOOD	FINE	N-MINT
1, Nov 89 ...... 2.50		0.50	1.50	2.50

WILD KINGDOM
MU

	ORIG.	GOOD	FINE	N-MINT
1, Oct 91, adult;b&w 2.50		0.50	1.50	2.50
2, May 93, adult;b&w 2.95		0.59	1.77	2.95
3, Jan 95, adult;b&w 2.95		0.59	1.77	2.95
4, Apr 95, adult;b&w 2.95		0.59	1.77	2.95
5, Aug 95, adult;b&w 2.95		0.59	1.77	2.95
6, Dec 95, adult;b&w 2.95		0.59	1.77	2.95

WILD KNIGHTS
ETERNITY

	ORIG.	GOOD	FINE	N-MINT
1		0.39	1.17	1.95
2		0.39	1.17	1.95
3		0.39	1.17	1.95
4		0.39	1.17	1.95
5		0.39	1.17	1.95
6		0.39	1.17	1.95
7		0.39	1.17	1.95
8		0.39	1.17	1.95
9		0.39	1.17	1.95
10		0.39	1.17	1.95

WILD LIFE
ANTARCTIC

	ORIG.	GOOD	FINE	N-MINT
1, Feb 93, b&w 2.50		0.50	1.50	2.50
2, May 93, b&w 2.50		0.50	1.50	2.50
3, Jul 93, b&w 2.50		0.50	1.50	2.50
4, Nov 93, b&w 2.75		0.55	1.65	2.75
5, Feb 94, b&w 2.75		0.55	1.65	2.75
6, Apr 94, b&w 2.75		0.55	1.65	2.75
7, Jun 94, b&w 2.75		0.55	1.65	2.75
8, Aug 94, b&w 2.75		0.55	1.65	2.75
9, Oct 94, b&w 2.75		0.55	1.65	2.75
10, Dec 94, b&w 2.75		0.55	1.65	2.75
11, Feb 95, b&w 2.75		0.55	1.65	2.75
12, Apr 95, b&w;final issue 2.75		0.55	1.65	2.75

FANTAGRAPHICS

	ORIG.	GOOD	FINE	N-MINT
2, Aug 94, b&w 2.75		0.55	1.65	2.75

WILD STARS
COLLECTOR'S

	ORIG.	GOOD	FINE	N-MINT
1, b&w		0.20	0.60	1.00

WILD THING
MARVEL

	ORIG.	GOOD	FINE	N-MINT
1, embossed cover 2.50		0.50	1.50	2.50
2 ...... 1.75		0.35	1.05	1.75
3 ...... 1.75		0.35	1.05	1.75
4 ...... 1.75		0.35	1.05	1.75
5 ...... 1.75		0.35	1.05	1.75
6 ...... 1.75		0.35	1.05	1.75
7 ...... 1.75		0.35	1.05	1.75

WILD THINGS
METRO

	ORIG.	GOOD	FINE	N-MINT
1		0.40	1.20	2.00
2		0.40	1.20	2.00
3		0.40	1.20	2.00

WILD WEST C.O.W.-BOYS OF MOO MESA
ARCHIE

	ORIG.	GOOD	FINE	N-MINT
1 ...... 1.25		0.25	0.75	1.25
2 ...... 1.25		0.25	0.75	1.25
3 ...... 1.25		0.25	0.75	1.25

WILD WILD WEST, THE
MILLENNIUM

	ORIG.	GOOD	FINE	N-MINT
1, 90, TV		0.59	1.77	2.95
2, 90, TV		0.59	1.77	2.95
3, 90, TV		0.59	1.77	2.95
4, 90, TV		0.59	1.77	2.95

	ORIG.	GOOD	FINE	N-MINT

WILD, WILD WEST, THE
GOLD KEY

	ORIG.	GOOD	FINE	N-MINT
1, Jun 66, photo cover	0.12	20.00	60.00	100.00
2, Nov 66, photo cover	0.12	14.00	42.00	70.00
3, Jun 68, photo cover	0.12	10.00	30.00	50.00
4, Dec 68, photo cover	0.12	10.00	30.00	50.00
5, Apr 69, photo cover	0.12	10.00	30.00	50.00
6, Jul 69, photo cover	0.15	10.00	30.00	50.00
7, Oct 69, photo cover	0.15	10.00	30.00	50.00

WILDC.A.T.S ADVENTURES
IMAGE

	ORIG.	GOOD	FINE	N-MINT
1, Sep 94	1.95	0.39	1.17	1.95
2, Nov 94	1.95	0.39	1.17	1.95
3, Nov 94	1.95	0.39	1.17	1.95
4, Dec 94	2.50	0.50	1.50	2.50
5, Jan 95	2.50	0.50	1.50	2.50
7, Mar 95	2.50	0.50	1.50	2.50
8, Apr 95	2.50	0.50	1.50	2.50
9, May 95	2.50	0.50	1.50	2.50
10, Jun 95	2.50	0.50	1.50	2.50

WILDC.A.T.S ADVENTURES SOURCEBOOK

	ORIG.	GOOD	FINE	N-MINT
1, Jan 95	2.95	0.59	1.77	2.95

WILDC.A.T.S SOURCEBOOK

	ORIG.	GOOD	FINE	N-MINT
1, Sep 93	2.50	0.50	1.50	2.50
2, Nov 94	2.50	0.50	1.50	2.50

WILDC.A.T.S SPECIAL

	ORIG.	GOOD	FINE	N-MINT
1	3.50	0.70	2.10	3.50

WILDC.A.T.S TRILOGY

	ORIG.	GOOD	FINE	N-MINT
1, Jun 93, enhanced cover	2.50	0.50	1.50	2.50
2	1.95	0.39	1.17	1.95
3, Nov 93	1.95	0.39	1.17	1.95

WILDC.A.T.S: COVERT ACTION TEAMS

	ORIG.	GOOD	FINE	N-MINT
1, Aug 92, JLee	1.95	2.00	6.00	10.00
1, gold		9.00	27.00	45.00
1, gold signed		15.00	45.00	75.00
2, JLee, shiny cover	2.50	1.60	4.80	8.00
3, JLee	1.95	1.00	3.00	5.00
4, JLee, bagged, red trading card	2.50	2.40	7.20	12.00
4	1.95	0.80	2.40	4.00
5, Nov 93, JLee	1.95	0.80	2.40	4.00
6, JLee	1.95	0.39	1.17	1.95
9, Mar 94	2.50	0.50	1.50	2.50
10, Apr 94	2.50	0.50	1.50	2.50
11, Jun 94	2.50	0.50	1.50	2.50
11, Jun 94, Variant cover	2.50	2.00	6.00	10.00
12, Aug 94	2.50	0.50	1.50	2.50
13, Sep 94	2.50	0.50	1.50	2.50
14, Sep 94	2.50	0.50	1.50	2.50
15, Nov 94	1.95	0.39	1.17	1.95
16, Dec 94	2.50	0.50	1.50	2.50
17, Jan 95	2.50	0.50	1.50	2.50
18, Mar 95	2.50	0.50	1.50	2.50
19, Apr 95	2.50	0.50	1.50	2.50
20, May 95, with cards	2.50	0.50	1.50	2.50
22, Aug 95	2.50	0.50	1.50	2.50
23, Sep 95	2.50	0.50	1.50	2.50
24, Nov 95	2.50	0.50	1.50	2.50
25, Dec 95, enhanced wraparound cover	4.95	0.99	2.97	4.95
26, Feb 96	2.50	0.50	1.50	2.50
27, Mar 96	2.50	0.50	1.50	2.50
28, Apr 96	2.50	0.50	1.50	2.50
29, May 96, "Fire from Heaven" Part 7;cover says "Apr", indicia says "May"	2.50	0.50	1.50	2.50

WILDMAN (former Megaton title)
MILLER

	ORIG.	GOOD	FINE	N-MINT
3, b&w		0.37	1.11	1.85

	ORIG.	GOOD	FINE	N-MINT
4, b&w		0.37	1.11	1.85
5, b&w		0.37	1.11	1.85
6, b&w		0.37	1.11	1.85
7, b&w		0.37	1.11	1.85
8, b&w		0.37	1.11	1.85
9		0.40	1.20	2.00
10		0.40	1.20	2.00
11		0.40	1.20	2.00

WILDSTAR (mini-series)
IMAGE

	ORIG.	GOOD	FINE	N-MINT
1, Sep 95	2.50	0.50	1.50	2.50
3, Jan 96	2.50	0.50	1.50	2.50

WILDSTAR: SKY ZERO

	ORIG.	GOOD	FINE	N-MINT
1, JOy silver foil	2.50	0.50	1.50	2.50
1, JOy gold	2.50	4.80	14.40	24.00
2, JOy,AG	1.95	0.39	1.17	1.95
3, JOy	1.95	0.39	1.17	1.95
4, Nov 93, JOy	1.95	0.39	1.17	1.95

WILDSTORM CHAMBER OF HORRORS

	ORIG.	GOOD	FINE	N-MINT
1, Oct 95, anthology	3.50	0.70	2.10	3.50

WILDSTORM RARITIES

	ORIG.	GOOD	FINE	N-MINT
1, Dec 94	4.95	0.99	2.97	4.95

WILDSTORM RISING

	ORIG.	GOOD	FINE	N-MINT
1, May 95, with cards	2.50	0.50	1.50	2.50
2, Jun 95, bound-in trading cards	2.50	0.50	1.50	2.50

WILDSTORM SWIMSUIT SPECIAL

	ORIG.	GOOD	FINE	N-MINT
1, Dec 94	2.95	0.59	1.77	2.95
2, Aug 95, pin-ups	2.50	0.50	1.50	2.50

WILDSTORM UNIVERSE SOURCEBOOK

	ORIG.	GOOD	FINE	N-MINT
1, May 95	2.50	0.50	1.50	2.50

WILDSTORM!

	ORIG.	GOOD	FINE	N-MINT
1, Aug 95, anthology;color and b&w	2.50	0.50	1.50	2.50
2, Oct 95, anthology;color and b&w;cover says "Sep"; indicia says "Oct"	2.50	0.50	1.50	2.50
3, Nov 95, anthology	2.50	0.50	1.50	2.50
4, Dec 95, anthology	2.50	0.50	1.50	2.50

WILDSTORMS PLAYER'S GUIDE

	ORIG.	GOOD	FINE	N-MINT
1, Mar 96, tips on WildStorms card game	1.95	0.39	1.17	1.95

WILL EISNER PRESENTS:
ECLIPSE

	ORIG.	GOOD	FINE	N-MINT
1, Dec 90, Bob Powell, Mr. Mystic, b&w		0.50	1.50	2.50

WILL EISNER'S 3-D CLASSICS: SPIRIT
KITCHEN SINK

	ORIG.	GOOD	FINE	N-MINT
1, Dec 85	2.00	0.40	1.20	2.00

WILL EISNER'S QUARTERLY

	ORIG.	GOOD	FINE	N-MINT
1, Nov 83		0.40	1.20	2.00
2, Feb 84		0.40	1.20	2.00
3, Aug 84		0.40	1.20	2.00
4		0.40	1.20	2.00
5		0.40	1.20	2.00
6		0.40	1.20	2.00
7		0.40	1.20	2.00
8, Mar 86		0.40	1.20	2.00

WILL TO POWER
DARK HORSE

	ORIG.	GOOD	FINE	N-MINT
1, Jun 94	1.00	0.20	0.60	1.00
2, Jun 94	1.00	0.20	0.60	1.00
3, Jun 94	1.00	0.20	0.60	1.00
4, Jul 94	1.00	0.20	0.60	1.00
5, Jul 94	1.00	0.20	0.60	1.00
6, Jul 94	1.00	0.20	0.60	1.00
7, Jul 94	1.00	0.20	0.60	1.00
8, Aug 94	1.00	0.20	0.60	1.00
9, Aug 94	1.00	0.20	0.60	1.00

	ORIG.	GOOD	FINE	N-MINT
❑ 10, Aug 94 ..... 1.00		0.20	0.60	1.00
❑ 11, Aug 94 ..... 1.00		0.20	0.60	1.00
❑ 12, Aug 94 ..... 1.00		0.20	0.60	1.00

WILLIAM SHATNER
CELEBRITY

❑ 1		1.19	3.57	5.95

WILLOW
MARVEL

❑ 1, movie 1.00		0.20	0.60	1.00
❑ 2, movie 1.00		0.20	0.60	1.00
❑ 3, movie 1.00		0.20	0.60	1.00

WIMMEN'S COMIX
(former Rip Off Press underground)
RENEGADE

❑ 11, b&w		0.40	1.20	2.00
❑ 12, 3-D		0.50	1.50	2.50
❑ 13, (returns to Rip Off Press)		0.40	1.20	2.00

WIMMEN'S COMIX (was Renegade title)
RIP OFF

❑ 14, Feb 89, b&w;adult.... 2.50		0.50	1.50	2.50
❑ 15, Aug 89, b&w;adult ...2.50		0.50	1.50	2.50
❑ 16, Nov 90, b&w;adult ...2.50		0.50	1.50	2.50

WIMMIN'S COMIX

❑ 17, Aug 92, b&w;adult ...2.50		0.50	1.50	2.50

WINDRAVEN
HEROIC/ BLUE COMET

❑ 1, b&w		0.59	1.77	2.95

WINGING IT
SOLO

❑ 1		0.40	1.20	2.00

WINGS
MU PRESS

❑ 1, Sep 92 ..... 2.50		0.50	1.50	2.50

WINTERWORLD
ECLIPSE

❑ 1		0.35	1.05	1.75
❑ 2		0.35	1.05	1.75
❑ 3		0.35	1.05	1.75

WISH UPON A STAR
WARP

❑ 1, May 94, no price, giveaway				

WITCH
ETERNITY

❑ 1, b&w rep.		0.39	1.17	1.95

WITCH HUNTER
MALIBU/ULTRAVERSE

❑ 1, Apr 96, O&1:Witch Hunter				
.... 2.50		0.50	1.50	2.50

WITCHBLADE
IMAGE

❑ 1, Nov 95 ..... 2.50		1.40	4.20	7.00
❑ 2, Jan 96 ..... 2.50		1.00	3.00	5.00
❑ 3, Mar 96 ..... 2.50		0.80	2.40	4.00
❑ 4, Apr 96 ..... 2.50		0.50	1.50	2.50
❑ 5, May 96 ..... 2.50		0.50	1.50	2.50
❑ 6, Jun 96 ..... 2.50		0.50	1.50	2.50

WITCHCRAFT (mini-series)
DC/VERTIGO

❑ 1, Jun 94 ..... 2.95		0.59	1.77	2.95
❑ 2, Jul 94 ..... 2.95		0.59	1.77	2.95
❑ 3, Aug 94 ..... 2.95		0.59	1.77	2.95

WITCHING HOUR
DC

❑ 1, Mar 69 ..... 0.12		2.40	7.20	12.00
❑ 2		1.60	4.80	8.00
❑ 3		1.20	3.60	6.00
❑ 4		1.20	3.60	6.00
❑ 5, Nov 69 ..... 0.15		1.20	3.60	6.00

	ORIG.	GOOD	FINE	N-MINT
❑ 6		1.00	3.00	5.00
❑ 7		1.00	3.00	5.00
❑ 8, May 70	0.15	1.00	3.00	5.00
❑ 9	0.15	1.00	3.00	5.00
❑ 10, Sep 70	0.15	1.00	3.00	5.00
❑ 11, Nov 70	0.15	0.60	1.80	3.00
❑ 12, Jan 71	0.15	0.60	1.80	3.00
❑ 13, Mar 71	0.15	0.60	1.80	3.00
❑ 14, May 71	0.15	0.60	1.80	3.00
❑ 15, Jul 71	0.15	0.60	1.80	3.00
❑ 16, Sep 71	0.25	0.40	1.20	2.00
❑ 17		0.40	1.20	2.00
❑ 18		0.40	1.20	2.00
❑ 19		0.40	1.20	2.00
❑ 20		0.40	1.20	2.00
❑ 21		0.25	0.75	1.25
❑ 22		0.25	0.75	1.25
❑ 23		0.25	0.75	1.25
❑ 24		0.25	0.75	1.25
❑ 25		0.25	0.75	1.25
❑ 26		0.25	0.75	1.25
❑ 27		0.25	0.75	1.25
❑ 28		0.25	0.75	1.25
❑ 29		0.25	0.75	1.25
❑ 30		0.25	0.75	1.25
❑ 31		0.25	0.75	1.25
❑ 32		0.25	0.75	1.25
❑ 33		0.25	0.75	1.25
❑ 34		0.25	0.75	1.25
❑ 35		0.25	0.75	1.25
❑ 36		0.25	0.75	1.25
❑ 37		0.25	0.75	1.25
❑ 38		0.25	0.75	1.25
❑ 39		0.25	0.75	1.25
❑ 40		0.25	0.75	1.25
❑ 41		0.25	0.75	1.25
❑ 42		0.25	0.75	1.25
❑ 43		0.25	0.75	1.25
❑ 44		0.25	0.75	1.25
❑ 45		0.25	0.75	1.25
❑ 46		0.25	0.75	1.25
❑ 47		0.25	0.75	1.25
❑ 48		0.25	0.75	1.25
❑ 49		0.25	0.75	1.25
❑ 50		0.25	0.75	1.25
❑ 51		0.25	0.75	1.25
❑ 52		0.25	0.75	1.25
❑ 53		0.25	0.75	1.25
❑ 54		0.25	0.75	1.25
❑ 55		0.25	0.75	1.25
❑ 56		0.25	0.75	1.25
❑ 57		0.25	0.75	1.25
❑ 58		0.25	0.75	1.25
❑ 59		0.25	0.75	1.25
❑ 60		0.25	0.75	1.25
❑ 61		0.25	0.75	1.25
❑ 62		0.25	0.75	1.25
❑ 63		0.25	0.75	1.25
❑ 64		0.25	0.75	1.25
❑ 65		0.25	0.75	1.25
❑ 66		0.25	0.75	1.25
❑ 67		0.25	0.75	1.25
❑ 68		0.25	0.75	1.25
❑ 69		0.25	0.75	1.25
❑ 70		0.25	0.75	1.25
❑ 71		0.25	0.75	1.25
❑ 72		0.25	0.75	1.25
❑ 73		0.25	0.75	1.25
❑ 74		0.25	0.75	1.25
❑ 75		0.25	0.75	1.25
❑ 76		0.25	0.75	1.25
❑ 77		0.25	0.75	1.25

	ORIG.	GOOD	FINE	N-MINT
❏ 78		0.25	0.75	1.25
❏ 79		0.25	0.75	1.25
❏ 80		0.25	0.75	1.25
❏ 81		0.25	0.75	1.25
❏ 82		0.25	0.75	1.25
❏ 83		0.25	0.75	1.25
❏ 84		0.25	0.75	1.25
❏ 85		0.25	0.75	1.25

WITCHING HOUR, THE
MILLENNIUM/COMICO

	ORIG.	GOOD	FINE	N-MINT
❏ 1	2.50	0.50	1.50	2.50
❏ 2	2.50	0.50	1.50	2.50
❏ 3	2.50	0.50	1.50	2.50
❏ 4	2.50	0.50	1.50	2.50

WITHIN OUR REACH
STAR*REACH

	GOOD	FINE	N-MINT
❏ 0, nn SpM, Concrete	1.59	4.77	7.95

WIZARD OF 4TH STREET
DARK HORSE

	ORIG.	GOOD	FINE	N-MINT
❏ 1, b&w	1.75	0.35	1.05	1.75
❏ 2, b&w	1.75	0.35	1.05	1.75

WIZARD OF TIME, THE
DAVID P. HOUSE

	GOOD	FINE	N-MINT
❏ 1	0.30	0.90	1.50
❏ 2	0.30	0.90	1.50
❏ 3	0.30	0.90	1.50

WIZARDS OF THE LAST RESORT
BLACKTHORNE

	GOOD	FINE	N-MINT
❏ 1	0.35	1.05	1.75
❏ 2	0.35	1.05	1.75
❏ 3	0.35	1.05	1.75
❏ 4	0.35	1.05	1.75

WOLFF & BYRD, COUNSELORS OF THE MACABRE
EXHIBIT A PRESS

	ORIG.	GOOD	FINE	N-MINT
❏ 1, b&w	2.50	0.50	1.50	2.50
❏ 2, b&w	2.50	0.50	1.50	2.50
❏ 3, Sep 94, b&w	2.50	0.50	1.50	2.50
❏ 4, b&w	2.50	0.50	1.50	2.50
❏ 5, Feb 95, b&w	2.50	0.50	1.50	2.50
❏ 6, Apr 95, b&w	2.50	0.50	1.50	2.50
❏ 7, Jun 95, b&w	2.50	0.50	1.50	2.50
❏ 8, Sep 95, b&w	2.50	0.50	1.50	2.50
❏ 9, Nov 95, b&w	2.50	0.50	1.50	2.50
❏ 10, Feb 96, b&w	2.50	0.50	1.50	2.50

WOLFPACK
MARVEL

	ORIG.	GOOD	FINE	N-MINT
❏ 1, Aug 88	0.75	0.20	0.60	1.00
❏ 2, Sep 88	0.75	0.20	0.60	1.00
❏ 3, Oct 88	0.75	0.20	0.60	1.00
❏ 4, Nov 88	0.75	0.20	0.60	1.00
❏ 5, Dec 88	0.75	0.20	0.60	1.00
❏ 6, Jan 89	0.75	0.20	0.60	1.00
❏ 7, Feb 89	0.75	0.20	0.60	1.00
❏ 8, Mar 89	0.75	0.20	0.60	1.00
❏ 9, Apr 89	0.75	0.20	0.60	1.00
❏ 10, May 89	0.75	0.20	0.60	1.00
❏ 11, Jun 89	0.75	0.20	0.60	1.00
❏ 12, Jul 89	0.75	0.20	0.60	1.00

WOLPH
BLACKTHORNE

	GOOD	FINE	N-MINT
❏ 1	0.40	1.20	2.00

WOLVERBROAD VS. HOBO
SPOOF

	GOOD	FINE	N-MINT
❏ 1, b&w parody	0.59	1.77	2.95

WOLVERINE '95
MARVEL

	ORIG.	GOOD	FINE	N-MINT
❏ 1, Sep 95	3.95	0.79	2.37	3.95

WOLVERINE (mini-series)

	ORIG.	GOOD	FINE	N-MINT
❏ 1, Sep 82, FM, A:Mariko	0.60	8.40	25.20	42.00
❏ 2, Oct 82, FM	0.60	6.00	18.00	30.00
❏ 3, Nov 82, FM	0.60	6.00	18.00	30.00
❏ 4, Dec 82, FM	0.60	6.00	18.00	30.00

WOLVERINE (ongoing series)

	ORIG.	GOOD	FINE	N-MINT
❏ 1, Nov 88	1.50	8.80	26.40	44.00
❏ 2, Dec 88	1.50	4.00	12.00	20.00
❏ 3, Jan 89	1.50	2.80	8.40	14.00
❏ 4, Feb 89	1.50	2.80	8.40	14.00
❏ 5, Mar 89	1.50	2.80	8.40	14.00
❏ 6, Apr 89	1.50	2.00	6.00	10.00
❏ 7, May 89	1.50	2.00	6.00	10.00
❏ 8, Jun 89, Hulk	1.50	2.00	6.00	10.00
❏ 9, Jul 89	1.50	2.00	6.00	10.00
❏ 10, Aug 89, BSz	1.50	7.60	22.80	38.00
❏ 11, Sep 89	1.50	1.60	4.80	8.00
❏ 12, Sep 89	1.50	1.60	4.80	8.00
❏ 13, Oct 89	1.50	1.60	4.80	8.00
❏ 14, Oct 89	1.50	1.60	4.80	8.00
❏ 15, Nov 89	1.50	1.60	4.80	8.00
❏ 16, Nov 89	1.50	1.60	4.80	8.00
❏ 17, Nov 89	1.50	1.60	4.80	8.00
❏ 18, Dec 89	1.50	1.60	4.80	8.00
❏ 19, Dec 89, JBy, Acts of Vengeance	1.50	1.60	4.80	8.00
❏ 20, Jan 90, JBy, Acts of Vengeance	1.50	1.60	4.80	8.00
❏ 21, Feb 90, JBy/KJ	1.50	0.80	2.40	4.00
❏ 22, Mar 90, JBy	1.50	0.80	2.40	4.00
❏ 23, Apr 90, JBy	1.50	0.80	2.40	4.00
❏ 24, May 90	1.50	0.80	2.40	4.00
❏ 25, Jun 90	1.50	0.80	2.40	4.00
❏ 26, Jul 90	1.75	0.80	2.40	4.00
❏ 27, Jul 90, Lazarus Project	1.75	1.20	3.60	6.00
❏ 28, Aug 90, Lazarus Project	1.75	1.20	3.60	6.00
❏ 29, Aug 90, Lazarus Project	1.75	1.20	3.60	6.00
❏ 30, Sep 90, Lazarus Project	1.75	1.20	3.60	6.00
❏ 31, Sep 90	1.75	1.00	3.00	5.00
❏ 32, Oct 90	1.75	1.00	3.00	5.00
❏ 33, Nov 90	1.75	1.00	3.00	5.00
❏ 34, Dec 90	1.75	1.00	3.00	5.00
❏ 35, Jan 91	1.75	1.00	3.00	5.00
❏ 36, Feb 91	1.75	1.00	3.00	5.00
❏ 37, Mar 91	1.75	1.00	3.00	5.00
❏ 38, Apr 91	1.75	1.00	3.00	5.00
❏ 39, May 91	1.75	1.00	3.00	5.00
❏ 40, Jun 91	1.75	1.00	3.00	5.00
❏ 41, Jul 91	1.75	2.00	6.00	10.00
❏ 42, Jul 91	1.75	1.20	3.60	6.00
❏ 43, Aug 91	1.75	1.00	3.00	5.00
❏ 44, Aug 91	1.75	0.50	1.50	2.50
❏ 45, Sep 91	1.75	0.80	2.40	4.00
❏ 46, Sep 91	1.75	0.80	2.40	4.00
❏ 47, Oct 91	1.75	0.50	1.50	2.50
❏ 48, Nov 91, Logan's past	1.75	0.50	1.50	2.50
❏ 49, Dec 91, Logan's past	1.75	0.50	1.50	2.50
❏ 50, diecut cover	2.50	1.60	4.80	8.00
❏ 51	1.75	0.40	1.20	2.00
❏ 52	1.75	0.40	1.20	2.00
❏ 53	1.75	0.35	1.05	1.75
❏ 54	1.75	0.35	1.05	1.75
❏ 55	1.75	0.35	1.05	1.75
❏ 56	1.75	0.35	1.05	1.75
❏ 57	1.75	0.35	1.05	1.75
❏ 58	1.75	0.35	1.05	1.75
❏ 59	1.75	0.35	1.05	1.75

	ORIG.	GOOD	FINE	N-MINT
❏ 60	1.75	0.80	2.40	4.00
❏ 61	1.75	0.80	2.40	4.00
❏ 62	1.75	0.80	2.40	4.00
❏ 63	1.75	0.80	2.40	4.00
❏ 64	1.75	0.80	2.40	4.00
❏ 65	1.75	0.35	1.05	1.75
❏ 66	1.75	0.35	1.05	1.75
❏ 67	1.75	0.35	1.05	1.75
❏ 68	1.75	0.35	1.05	1.75
❏ 69	1.75	0.35	1.05	1.75
❏ 70	1.75	0.35	1.05	1.75
❏ 71	1.75	0.35	1.05	1.75
❏ 72	1.75	0.35	1.05	1.75
❏ 73	1.75	0.35	1.05	1.75
❏ 74	1.75	0.35	1.05	1.75
❏ 75, hologram	3.95	2.50	7.50	12.50
❏ 76	1.75	0.50	1.50	2.50
❏ 77	1.75	0.35	1.05	1.75
❏ 78	1.75	0.35	1.05	1.75
❏ 79	1.75	0.35	1.05	1.75
❏ 80	1.75	0.35	1.05	1.75
❏ 81, May 94	1.95	0.39	1.17	1.95
❏ 82, Jun 94	1.95	0.39	1.17	1.95
❏ 83, Jul 94	1.95	0.39	1.17	1.95
❏ 84, Aug 94	1.95	0.39	1.17	1.95
❏ 85, Sep 94, Final Sanction	1.95	0.80	2.40	4.00
❏ 85, Sep 94, Final Sanction;enhanced cover	3.50	0.70	2.10	3.50
❏ 86, Oct 94	1.95	0.39	1.17	1.95
❏ 87, Nov 94, deluxe edition	1.95	0.39	1.17	1.95
❏ 87, Nov 94	1.50	0.30	0.90	1.50
❏ 88, Dec 94, deluxe edition	1.95	0.39	1.17	1.95
❏ 88, Dec 94	1.50	0.30	0.90	1.50
❏ 89, Jan 95, deluxe edition	1.95	0.39	1.17	1.95
❏ 89, Jan 95	1.50	0.30	0.90	1.50
❏ 90, Feb 95	1.50	0.30	0.90	1.50
❏ 90, Feb 95, deluxe edition	1.95	0.39	1.17	1.95
❏ 91, Jul 95	1.95	0.39	1.17	1.95
❏ 92, Aug 95	1.95	0.39	1.17	1.95
❏ 93, Sep 95, V:Juggernaut	1.95	0.39	1.17	1.95
❏ 94, Oct 95, A:Generation X	1.95	0.39	1.17	1.95
❏ 95, Nov 95, A:Vindicator	1.95	0.39	1.17	1.95
❏ 96, Dec 95	1.95	0.39	1.17	1.95
❏ 97, Jan 96	1.95	0.39	1.17	1.95
❏ 98, Feb 96	1.95	0.39	1.17	1.95
❏ 99, Mar 96	1.95	0.39	1.17	1.95
❏ 100, Apr 96, enhanced cardstock cover	3.95	1.50	4.50	7.50
❏ 100, Apr 96	2.95	0.59	1.77	2.95

WOLVERINE AND THE PUNISHER: DAMAGING EVIDENCE

	ORIG.	GOOD	FINE	N-MINT
❏ 1	2.00	0.40	1.20	2.00
❏ 2	2.00	0.40	1.20	2.00
❏ 3	2.00	0.40	1.20	2.00

WOLVERINE IN GLOBAL JEOPARDY

	ORIG.	GOOD	FINE	N-MINT
❏ 1, embossed cover	2.95	0.59	1.77	2.95

WOLVERINE POSTER MAGAZINE

	ORIG.	GOOD	FINE	N-MINT
❏ 1, 95, pin-ups	4.95	0.99	2.97	4.95

WOLVERINE SAGA, THE

	ORIG.	GOOD	FINE	N-MINT
❏ 1, Sep 89, O:Wolverine	3.95	1.40	4.20	7.00
❏ 2, Nov 89	3.95	1.40	4.20	7.00
❏ 3, Dec 89	3.95	1.40	4.20	7.00
❏ 4, Dec 89	3.95	1.40	4.20	7.00

WOLVERINE VS. SPIDER-MAN

	ORIG.	GOOD	FINE	N-MINT
❏ 0, Mar 95, one-shot;cardstock cover;collects story arc from *Marvel Comics Presents* #48-50	2.50	0.50	1.50	2.50

WOLVERINE/GAMBIT: VICTIMS (mini-series)

	ORIG.	GOOD	FINE	N-MINT
❏ 1, Sep 95, Cardstock enhanced cover	2.95	0.59	1.77	2.95
❏ 2, Oct 95, enhanced cardstock cover	2.95	0.59	1.77	2.95
❏ 3, Nov 95, enhanced cardstock cover	2.95	0.59	1.77	2.95
❏ 4, Dec 95, enhanced cardstock cover	2.95	0.59	1.77	2.95

WOMEN IN ROCK SPECIAL
REVOLUTIONARY

	ORIG.	GOOD	FINE	N-MINT
❏ 1, Dec 93, b&w	2.50	0.50	1.50	2.50

WOMEN ON TOP
EROS COMIX

	ORIG.	GOOD	FINE	N-MINT
❏ 1, adult, b&w		0.45	1.35	2.25

WONDER MAN (1986 one-shot)
MARVEL

	ORIG.	GOOD	FINE	N-MINT
❏ 1	1.25	0.80	2.40	4.00

WONDER MAN (beginning 1991)

	ORIG.	GOOD	FINE	N-MINT
❏ 1, Sep 91, poster	1.00	0.50	1.50	2.50
❏ 2, Oct 91	1.00	0.40	1.20	2.00
❏ 3, Nov 91, 1:Splice	1.00	0.40	1.20	2.00
❏ 4, Dec 91	1.00	0.28	0.84	1.40
❏ 5	1.00	0.28	0.84	1.40
❏ 6	1.25	0.28	0.84	1.40
❏ 7	1.25	0.30	0.90	1.50
❏ 8, Galactic Storm	1.25	0.25	0.75	1.25
❏ 9, Galactic Storm	1.25	0.25	0.75	1.25
❏ 10	1.25	0.25	0.75	1.25
❏ 11	1.25	0.25	0.75	1.25
❏ 12	1.25	0.25	0.75	1.25
❏ 13	1.25	0.25	0.75	1.25
❏ 14	1.25	0.25	0.75	1.25
❏ 15	1.25	0.25	0.75	1.25
❏ 16	1.25	0.25	0.75	1.25
❏ 17	1.25	0.25	0.75	1.25
❏ 18	1.25	0.25	0.75	1.25
❏ 19	1.25	0.25	0.75	1.25
❏ 20	1.25	0.25	0.75	1.25
❏ 21	1.25	0.25	0.75	1.25
❏ 22	1.25	0.25	0.75	1.25
❏ 23	1.25	0.25	0.75	1.25
❏ 24	1.25	0.25	0.75	1.25
❏ 25, embossed cover	2.95	0.59	1.77	2.95
❏ 26	1.25	0.25	0.75	1.25
❏ 27	1.25	0.25	0.75	1.25
❏ 28	1.25	0.25	0.75	1.25
❏ 29	1.25	0.25	0.75	1.25

WONDER MAN ANNUAL

	ORIG.	GOOD	FINE	N-MINT
❏ 1 92	2.25	0.45	1.35	2.25
❏ 2, 93, trading card	2.95	0.59	1.77	2.95

WONDER WART-HOG, HOG OF STEEL (mini-series)
RIP OFF PRESS

	ORIG.	GOOD	FINE	N-MINT
❏ 1, 95, b&w reprints	2.50	0.50	1.50	2.50
❏ 2, 95, b&w reprints	2.50	0.50	1.50	2.50
❏ 3, 95, b&w reprints	2.50	0.50	1.50	2.50

WONDER WOMAN
DC

	ORIG.	GOOD	FINE	N-MINT
❏ 100		15.00	45.00	75.00
❏ 101		5.00	15.00	25.00
❏ 102		5.00	15.00	25.00
❏ 103		5.00	15.00	25.00
❏ 104		5.00	15.00	25.00
❏ 105, O:1st Wonder Girl		12.00	36.00	60.00
❏ 106		5.00	15.00	25.00

	ORIG.	GOOD	FINE	N-MINT		ORIG.	GOOD	FINE	N-MINT
❏ 107		5.00	15.00	25.00	❏ 179		0.60	1.80	3.00
❏ 108		5.00	15.00	25.00	❏ 180		0.60	1.80	3.00
❏ 109		5.00	15.00	25.00	❏ 181		0.60	1.80	3.00
❏ 110		5.00	15.00	25.00	❏ 182		0.60	1.80	3.00
❏ 111		4.00	12.00	20.00	❏ 183		0.60	1.80	3.00
❏ 112		4.00	12.00	20.00	❏ 184		0.60	1.80	3.00
❏ 113		4.00	12.00	20.00	❏ 185		0.60	1.80	3.00
❏ 114		4.00	12.00	20.00	❏ 186		0.60	1.80	3.00
❏ 115		4.00	12.00	20.00	❏ 187		0.60	1.80	3.00
❏ 116		4.00	12.00	20.00	❏ 188		0.60	1.80	3.00
❏ 117		4.00	12.00	20.00	❏ 189		0.60	1.80	3.00
❏ 118		4.00	12.00	20.00	❏ 190		0.60	1.80	3.00
❏ 119		4.00	12.00	20.00	❏ 191		0.60	1.80	3.00
❏ 120		4.00	12.00	20.00	❏ 192		0.60	1.80	3.00
❏ 121		2.40	7.20	12.00	❏ 193		0.60	1.80	3.00
❏ 122		2.40	7.20	12.00	❏ 194		0.60	1.80	3.00
❏ 123		2.40	7.20	12.00	❏ 195		0.60	1.80	3.00
❏ 124		2.40	7.20	12.00	❏ 196, DG		0.60	1.80	3.00
❏ 125		2.40	7.20	12.00	❏ 197, DG		0.60	1.80	3.00
❏ 126		2.40	7.20	12.00	❏ 198, DG		0.60	1.80	3.00
❏ 127		2.40	7.20	12.00	❏ 199, Apr 72, DG	0.25	1.20	3.60	6.00
❏ 128		2.40	7.20	12.00	❏ 200, Jun 72, DG	0.25	1.20	3.60	6.00
❏ 129		2.40	7.20	12.00	❏ 201, Aug 72, DG	0.20	0.25	0.75	1.25
❏ 130		2.40	7.20	12.00	❏ 202, Oct 72, DG	0.20	0.40	1.20	2.00
❏ 131		2.40	7.20	12.00	❏ 203, Dec 72, DG	0.20	0.40	1.20	2.00
❏ 132		2.40	7.20	12.00	❏ 204		0.25	0.75	1.25
❏ 133		2.40	7.20	12.00	❏ 205		0.25	0.75	1.25
❏ 134		2.40	7.20	12.00	❏ 206		0.25	0.75	1.25
❏ 135		2.40	7.20	12.00	❏ 207		0.25	0.75	1.25
❏ 136		2.40	7.20	12.00	❏ 208		0.25	0.75	1.25
❏ 137		2.40	7.20	12.00	❏ 209		0.25	0.75	1.25
❏ 138		2.40	7.20	12.00	❏ 210		0.25	0.75	1.25
❏ 139		2.40	7.20	12.00	❏ 211		0.25	0.75	1.25
❏ 140		2.40	7.20	12.00	❏ 212, Jul 73	0.20	0.25	0.75	1.25
❏ 141		2.40	7.20	12.00	❏ 213, Sep 73	0.20	0.25	0.75	1.25
❏ 142		2.40	7.20	12.00	❏ 214, Nov 73	0.60	0.25	0.75	1.25
❏ 143		2.40	7.20	12.00	❏ 215, Jan 74	0.20	0.25	0.75	1.25
❏ 144		2.40	7.20	12.00	❏ 216, Mar 74	0.25	0.25	0.75	1.25
❏ 145		2.40	7.20	12.00	❏ 217, May 74, JL	0.50	0.25	0.75	1.25
❏ 146		2.40	7.20	12.00	❏ 218, Jul 74	0.25	0.25	0.75	1.25
❏ 147		2.40	7.20	12.00	❏ 219, Sep 74	0.25	0.25	0.75	1.25
❏ 148		2.40	7.20	12.00	❏ 220, Nov 74	0.25	0.25	0.75	1.25
❏ 149		2.40	7.20	12.00	❏ 221, Jan 75	0.25	0.20	0.60	1.00
❏ 150		2.40	7.20	12.00	❏ 222, Mar 75	0.25	0.20	0.60	1.00
❏ 151		1.20	3.60	6.00	❏ 223	0.25	0.20	0.60	1.00
❏ 152		1.20	3.60	6.00	❏ 224	0.25	0.20	0.60	1.00
❏ 153		1.20	3.60	6.00	❏ 225	0.25	0.20	0.60	1.00
❏ 154		1.20	3.60	6.00	❏ 226, Oct 76	0.25	0.20	0.60	1.00
❏ 155		1.20	3.60	6.00	❏ 227, Dec 76	0.25	0.20	0.60	1.00
❏ 156		1.20	3.60	6.00	❏ 228, Feb 77	0.25	0.20	0.60	1.00
❏ 157		1.20	3.60	6.00	❏ 229, Mar 77	0.25	0.20	0.60	1.00
❏ 158		1.20	3.60	6.00	❏ 230, Apr 77	0.25	0.20	0.60	1.00
❏ 159		1.20	3.60	6.00	❏ 231, May 77	0.25	0.20	0.60	1.00
❏ 160		1.20	3.60	6.00	❏ 232, Jun 77	0.25	0.20	0.60	1.00
❏ 161		1.20	3.60	6.00	❏ 233, Jul 77	0.25	0.20	0.60	1.00
❏ 162		1.20	3.60	6.00	❏ 234, Aug 77	0.25	0.20	0.60	1.00
❏ 163		1.20	3.60	6.00	❏ 235, Sep 77	0.25	0.20	0.60	1.00
❏ 164		1.20	3.60	6.00	❏ 236, Oct 77	0.25	0.20	0.60	1.00
❏ 165		1.20	3.60	6.00	❏ 237, Nov 77	0.25	0.20	0.60	1.00
❏ 166		1.20	3.60	6.00	❏ 238, Dec 77	0.25	0.20	0.60	1.00
❏ 167		1.20	3.60	6.00	❏ 239, Jan 78	0.25	0.20	0.60	1.00
❏ 168		1.20	3.60	6.00	❏ 240, Feb 78	0.25	0.20	0.60	1.00
❏ 169		1.20	3.60	6.00	❏ 241, Mar 78	0.25	0.20	0.60	1.00
❏ 170		1.20	3.60	6.00	❏ 242, Apr 78	0.25	0.20	0.60	1.00
❏ 171		1.00	3.00	5.00	❏ 243, May 78	0.25	0.20	0.60	1.00
❏ 172		1.00	3.00	5.00	❏ 244, Jun 78	0.25	0.20	0.60	1.00
❏ 173		1.00	3.00	5.00	❏ 245, Jul 78	0.25	0.20	0.60	1.00
❏ 174		1.00	3.00	5.00	❏ 246, Aug 78	0.25	0.20	0.60	1.00
❏ 175		1.00	3.00	5.00	❏ 247, Sep 78	0.25	0.20	0.60	1.00
❏ 176		1.00	3.00	5.00	❏ 248, Oct 78, JL		0.25	0.75	1.25
❏ 177		1.00	3.00	5.00	❏ 249, Nov 78, A:Hawkgirl		0.20	0.60	1.00
❏ 178		1.00	3.00	5.00	❏ 250, Dec 78		0.25	0.75	1.25

	ORIG.	GOOD	FINE	N-MINT
251, Jan 79		0.25	0.75	1.25
252, Feb 79		0.20	0.60	1.00
253, Mar 79		0.20	0.60	1.00
254, Apr 79		0.20	0.60	1.00
255, May 79		0.20	0.60	1.00
256, Jun 79		0.20	0.60	1.00
257, Jul 79		0.20	0.60	1.00
258, Aug 79		0.20	0.60	1.00
259, Sep 79		0.20	0.60	1.00
260, Oct 79		0.20	0.60	1.00
261, Nov 79		0.20	0.60	1.00
262, Dec 79		0.20	0.60	1.00
263, Jan 80		0.20	0.60	1.00
264, Feb 80		0.20	0.60	1.00
265, Mar 80		0.20	0.60	1.00
266, Apr 80		0.20	0.60	1.00
267, May 80, A:Animal Man		2.00	6.00	10.00
268, Jun 80, A:Animal Man		2.00	6.00	10.00
269, Jul 80		0.20	0.60	1.00
270, Aug 80		0.20	0.60	1.00
271, Sep 80, JSa, Huntress	0.50	0.25	0.75	1.25
271, Sep 80		0.20	0.60	1.00
272, Oct 80, JSa, Huntress	0.50	0.25	0.75	1.25
273, Nov 80	0.50	0.20	0.60	1.00
274, Dec 80	0.50	0.20	0.60	1.00
275, Jan 81	0.50	0.20	0.60	1.00
276, Feb 81	0.50	0.20	0.60	1.00
277, Mar 81	0.50	0.20	0.60	1.00
278, Apr 81	0.50	0.20	0.60	1.00
279, May 81	0.50	0.20	0.60	1.00
280, Jun 81	0.50	0.20	0.60	1.00
281, Jul 81, Joker	0.50	0.50	1.50	2.50
282, Aug 81, Joker	0.50	0.50	1.50	2.50
283, Sep 81, Joker	0.50	0.50	1.50	2.50
284, Oct 81	0.60	0.20	0.60	1.00
285, Nov 81	0.60	0.20	0.60	1.00
286, Dec 81	0.60	0.20	0.60	1.00
287, Jan 82, DH/RT, A:New Teen Titans	0.60	0.45	1.35	2.25
288, Feb 82	0.60	0.20	0.60	1.00
289, Mar 82	0.60	0.20	0.60	1.00
290, Apr 82	0.60	0.20	0.60	1.00
291, May 82	0.60	0.20	0.60	1.00
292, Jun 82	0.60	0.20	0.60	1.00
293, Jul 82, GC/FMc, A:Starfire, Raven	0.60	0.25	0.75	1.25
294, Aug 82	0.60	0.20	0.60	1.00
295, Sep 82	0.60	0.20	0.60	1.00
296, Oct 82	0.60	0.20	0.60	1.00
297, Nov 82	0.60	0.20	0.60	1.00
298, Dec 82	0.60	0.20	0.60	1.00
299, Jan 83	0.60	0.20	0.60	1.00
300, Feb 83, 9 artists, C:New Teen Titans	1.50	0.55	1.65	2.75
301, Mar 83	0.60	0.20	0.60	1.00
302, Apr 83		0.20	0.60	1.00
303, Apr 83		0.20	0.60	1.00
304, Jun 83		0.20	0.60	1.00
305, Jul 83		0.20	0.60	1.00
306, Aug 83		0.20	0.60	1.00
307, Sep 83		0.20	0.60	1.00
308, Oct 83		0.20	0.60	1.00
309, Nov 83		0.20	0.60	1.00
310, Dec 83		0.20	0.60	1.00
311, Jan 84, DH		0.20	0.60	1.00
312, Feb 84, DH		0.20	0.60	1.00
313, Mar 84, DH		0.20	0.60	1.00
314, Apr 84, DH		0.20	0.60	1.00
315, May 84, DH		0.20	0.60	1.00
316, Jun 84, DH		0.20	0.60	1.00

	ORIG.	GOOD	FINE	N-MINT
317, Jul 84, DH		0.20	0.60	1.00
318, Aug 84, DH		0.20	0.60	1.00
319, Sep 84, DH		0.20	0.60	1.00
320, Oct 84, DH		0.20	0.60	1.00
321, Nov 84, DH		0.20	0.60	1.00
322, Dec 84, DH		0.20	0.60	1.00
323, Feb 85, DH		0.20	0.60	1.00
324, Apr 85, DH		0.20	0.60	1.00
325, May 85, DH		0.20	0.60	1.00
326, Jul 85, DH		0.20	0.60	1.00
327, Sep 85, DH		0.20	0.60	1.00
328, Nov 85, Crisis		0.20	0.60	1.00
329, Feb 86, Crisis		0.25	0.75	1.25

WONDER WOMAN (Beginning 1987)

	ORIG.	GOOD	FINE	N-MINT
0, Oct 94, (1994)	1.50	1.00	3.00	5.00
1, Feb 87, GP O:WW	0.75	0.60	1.80	3.00
2, Mar 87, GP	0.75	0.40	1.20	2.00
3, Apr 87, GP	0.75	0.40	1.20	2.00
4, May 87, GP	0.75	0.40	1.20	2.00
5, Jun 87, GP	0.75	0.40	1.20	2.00
6, Jul 87, GP	0.75	0.40	1.20	2.00
7, Aug 87, GP	0.75	0.40	1.20	2.00
8, Sep 87, GP	0.75	0.40	1.20	2.00
9, Oct 87, GP	0.75	0.40	1.20	2.00
10, Nov 87, GP,gatefold	0.75	0.30	0.90	1.50
10, Nov 87, GP,no gatefold		0.30	0.90	1.50
11, Dec 87, GP	0.75	0.30	0.90	1.50
12, Jan 88, GP Millennium	0.75	0.30	0.90	1.50
13, Feb 88, GP Millennium	0.75	0.30	0.90	1.50
14, Mar 88, GP	0.75	0.30	0.90	1.50
15, Apr 88, GP	0.75	0.30	0.90	1.50
16, May 88, GP	0.75	0.30	0.90	1.50
17, Jun 88, GP	0.75	0.30	0.90	1.50
18, Jul 88, GP, Bonus Book	0.75	0.30	0.90	1.50
19, Aug 88, GP	0.75	0.30	0.90	1.50
20, Sep 88, GP	0.75	0.30	0.90	1.50
21, Oct 88, GP	1.00	0.30	0.90	1.50
22, Nov 88, GP	1.00	0.30	0.90	1.50
23, Dec 88, GP	1.00	0.30	0.90	1.50
24, GP	1.00	0.30	0.90	1.50
25, Jan 89, GP(c) Invasion!	1.00	0.30	0.90	1.50
26, Jan 89, GP(c) Invasion!	1.00	0.30	0.90	1.50
27, Feb 89, GP(c)	1.00	0.30	0.90	1.50
28, Mar 89, GP(c)	1.00	0.30	0.90	1.50
29, Apr 89, GP(c)	1.00	0.30	0.90	1.50
30, May 89, GP(c)	1.00	0.30	0.90	1.50
31, Jun 89, GP(c)	1.00	0.30	0.90	1.50
32, Jul 89, GP(c)	1.00	0.30	0.90	1.50
33, Aug 89	1.00	0.30	0.90	1.50
34, Sep 89	1.00	0.30	0.90	1.50
35, Oct 89	1.00	0.30	0.90	1.50
36, Nov 89	1.00	0.30	0.90	1.50
37, Dec 89	1.00	0.30	0.90	1.50
38, Jan 90	1.00	0.30	0.90	1.50
39, Feb 90	1.00	0.30	0.90	1.50
40, Mar 90		0.20	0.60	1.00
41, Apr 90		0.20	0.60	1.00
42, May 90		0.20	0.60	1.00
43, Jun 90		0.20	0.60	1.00
44, Jul 90		0.20	0.60	1.00
45, Aug 90		0.20	0.60	1.00
46, Sep 90		0.20	0.60	1.00
47, Oct 90, A:Troia		0.20	0.60	1.00
48, Nov 90		0.20	0.60	1.00
49, Dec 90		0.20	0.60	1.00

	ORIG.	GOOD	FINE	N-MINT
❑ 50, Jan 91, GP(c), SA, BB, PCR, MW				
		0.30	0.90	1.50
❑ 51, Feb 91		0.20	0.60	1.00
❑ 52, Mar 91		0.20	0.60	1.00
❑ 53, Apr 91		0.20	0.60	1.00
❑ 54, May 91		0.20	0.60	1.00
❑ 55, Jun 91		0.20	0.60	1.00
❑ 56, Jul 91		0.20	0.60	1.00
❑ 57, Aug 91		0.20	0.60	1.00
❑ 58, Sep 91, War of Gods				
	1.00	0.20	0.60	1.00
❑ 59, Oct 91, War of Gods ..		0.50	1.50	2.50
❑ 60, Nov 91, War of Gods..		0.50	1.50	2.50
❑ 61, War of Gods		0.20	0.60	1.00
❑ 62		0.20	0.60	1.00
❑ 63, BB(c)		0.25	0.75	1.25
❑ 64, BB(c)		0.25	0.75	1.25
❑ 65		0.25	0.75	1.25
❑ 66		0.25	0.75	1.25
❑ 67, BB(c)		0.25	0.75	1.25
❑ 68		0.25	0.75	1.25
❑ 69		0.25	0.75	1.25
❑ 70		0.25	0.75	1.25
❑ 71		0.25	0.75	1.25
❑ 72		0.25	0.75	1.25
❑ 73, BB(c)	1.25	0.25	0.75	1.25
❑ 74	1.25	0.25	0.75	1.25
❑ 75	1.25	0.25	0.75	1.25
❑ 76	1.25	0.25	0.75	1.25
❑ 77	1.25	0.25	0.75	1.25
❑ 78	1.25	0.40	1.20	2.00
❑ 79	1.25	0.25	0.75	1.25
❑ 80	1.25	0.25	0.75	1.25
❑ 81	1.25	0.25	0.75	1.25
❑ 82	1.25	0.25	0.75	1.25
❑ 83, BB(c)	1.50	0.30	0.90	1.50
❑ 84, BB(c)	1.50	0.30	0.90	1.50
❑ 85, BB(c)	1.50	0.45	1.35	2.25
❑ 86, May 94	1.50	0.45	1.35	2.25
❑ 87, Jun 94	1.50	0.45	1.35	2.25
❑ 88, Jul 94	1.50	1.50	4.50	7.50
❑ 89, Aug 94	1.50	0.80	2.40	4.00
❑ 90, Sep 94	1.50	2.40	7.20	12.00
❑ 91, Nov 94	1.50	0.60	1.80	3.00
❑ 92, Dec 94	1.50	0.60	1.80	3.00
❑ 93, Jan 95	1.50	0.60	1.80	3.00
❑ 94, Feb 95	1.50	0.50	1.50	2.50
❑ 95, Mar 95	1.50	0.50	1.50	2.50
❑ 96, Apr 95	1.50	0.50	1.50	2.50
❑ 97, May 95, V:Joker	1.50	0.50	1.50	2.50
❑ 98, Jun 95	1.75	0.35	1.05	1.75
❑ 99, Jul 95	1.75	0.35	1.05	1.75
❑ 100, Jul 95, "Fall of an Amazon";enhanced cover				
	3.95	1.40	4.20	7.00
❑ 100, Jul 95, "Fall of an Amazon"				
	2.95	1.40	4.20	7.00
❑ 101, Sep 95, JBy	1.95	0.50	1.50	2.50
❑ 102, Oct 95, JBy	1.95	0.40	1.20	2.00
❑ 103, Nov 95, JBy	1.95	0.39	1.17	1.95
❑ 104, Dec 95, JBy	1.95	0.39	1.17	1.95
❑ 105, Jan 96, JBy	1.95	0.39	1.17	1.95
❑ 106, Feb 96, JBy	1.95	0.39	1.17	1.95
❑ 107, Mar 96, JBy;A:Demon				
	1.95	0.39	1.17	1.95
❑ 108, Apr 96, JBy	1.95	0.39	1.17	1.95
❑ 109, May 96, JBy;V:Flash?				
	1.95	0.39	1.17	1.95
❑ 110, Jun 96, JBy;V:Sinestro?				
	1.95	0.39	1.17	1.95

	ORIG.	GOOD	FINE	N-MINT
WONDER WOMAN ANNUAL				
❑ 1, 88, GP,AAd,BB,RA,CS				
	1.50	0.30	0.90	1.50
❑ 2, 89, JDu	2.00	0.40	1.20	2.00
❑ 3, Eclipso		0.50	1.50	2.50
❑ 4, 95, "Year One"	3.50	0.70	2.10	3.50
WONDER WOMAN SPECIAL				
❑ 1, Deathstroke		0.35	1.05	1.75
WONDERWORLD EXPRESS				
THAT OTHER COMIX CO.				
❑ 1		0.20	0.60	1.00
WONDERWORLDS				
INNOVATION				
❑ 1, reprints		0.70	2.10	3.50
WOODY WOODPECKER				
HARVEY				
❑ 1	1.25	0.25	0.75	1.25
❑ 2	1.25	0.25	0.75	1.25
❑ 3	1.25	0.25	0.75	1.25
❑ 4	1.25	0.25	0.75	1.25
❑ 5	1.25	0.25	0.75	1.25
❑ 6	1.25	0.25	0.75	1.25
❑ 7	1.25	0.25	0.75	1.25
❑ 8	1.25	0.25	0.75	1.25
❑ 9	1.50	0.30	0.90	1.50
❑ 10	1.50	0.30	0.90	1.50
❑ 11	1.50	0.30	0.90	1.50
❑ 12	1.50	0.30	0.90	1.50
WOODY WOODPECKER				
50TH ANNIVERSARY SPECIAL				
❑ 1, reprints	2.50	0.50	1.50	2.50
WOODY WOODPECKER ADVENTURES				
❑ 1, reprints	1.25	0.25	0.75	1.25
WOODY WOODPECKER AND FRIENDS				
❑ 1, reprints	1.25	0.25	0.75	1.25
❑ 2, reprints	1.25	0.25	0.75	1.25
❑ 3, reprints	1.25	0.25	0.75	1.25
❑ 4, reprints	1.25	0.25	0.75	1.25
WOODY WOODPECKER DIGEST				
❑ 1, reprints	1.75	0.35	1.05	1.75
WOODY WOODPECKER GIANT SIZE				
❑ 1	2.25	0.45	1.35	2.25
WOODY WOODPECKER SUMMER SPECIAL				
❑ 1	1.95	0.39	1.17	1.95
WOOFERS AND HOOTERS				
EROS COMIX				
❑ 1, adult, b&w		0.50	1.50	2.50
WORD WARRIORS				
LITERACY VOLUNTEERS				
❑ 1, 87, HC(c) Ms. Tree, Jon Sable, b&w				
	1.50	0.40	1.20	2.00
WORDS & PICTURES				
MAVERICK STUDIOS				
❑ 1, Fal 94, b&w	3.95	0.79	2.37	3.95
❑ 2, Spr 95, b&w	3.95	0.79	2.37	3.95
WORDSMITH				
RENEGADE				
❑ 1, Aug 85, b&w	1.70	0.34	1.02	1.70
❑ 2, Oct 85, b&w	1.70	0.34	1.02	1.70
❑ 3, Dec 85, b&w	1.70	0.34	1.02	1.70
❑ 4, Dec 85, b&w	1.70	0.34	1.02	1.70
❑ 5, May 86, b&w	1.70	0.34	1.02	1.70
❑ 6, Aug 86	1.70	0.40	1.20	2.00
❑ 7, Nov 86	2.00	0.40	1.20	2.00
❑ 8, Nov 86	2.00	0.40	1.20	2.00
❑ 9, May 87	2.00	0.40	1.20	2.00
❑ 10, Aug 87	2.00	0.40	1.20	2.00
❑ 11, Nov 87	2.00	0.40	1.20	2.00
❑ 12, Jan 88	2.00	0.40	1.20	2.00

	ORIG.	GOOD	FINE	N-MINT

WORLD BANK, THE
PUBLIC SERVICES INTERNATIONAL
☐ 1, 95, educational comic;no indicia
.... 2.95   0.59   1.77   2.95

WORLD HARDBALL LEAGUE
TITUS
☐ 1, Aug 94, b&w 2.75   0.55   1.65   2.75
☐ 2, Jan 95, b&w 2.95   0.59   1.77   2.95

WORLD OF ARCHIE
ARCHIE
☐ 11, Sep 94 .... 1.50   0.30   0.90   1.50
☐ 12, Nov 94 .... 1.50   0.30   0.90   1.50
☐ 13, Jan 95 .... 1.50   0.30   0.90   1.50
☐ 14, Mar 95 .... 1.50   0.30   0.90   1.50
☐ 15, Jun 95 .... 1.50   0.30   0.90   1.50
☐ 16, Sep 95 .... 1.50   0.30   0.90   1.50
☐ 17, Dec 95 .... 1.50   0.30   0.90   1.50
☐ 18, Mar 96 .... 1.50   0.30   0.90   1.50
☐ 19, Jun 96 .... 1.50   0.30   0.90   1.50

WORLD OF GINGER FOX
COMICO
☐ 1 .... 5.59   16.77   27.95

WORLD OF KRYPTON (1979 mini-series)
DC
☐ 1, Jul 79, HC/MA, O:Jor-El
.... 0.40   0.30   0.90   1.50
☐ 2, Aug 79, HC 0.40   0.20   0.60   1.00
☐ 3, Sep 79, HC 0.40   0.20   0.60   1.00

WORLD OF KRYPTON (1987-88 mini-series)
☐ 1, Dec 87, JBy(c) 0.75   0.40   1.20   2.00
☐ 2, Jan 88, WS(c) 0.75   0.20   0.60   1.00
☐ 3, Feb 88, JBy/WS(c) 0.75   0.20   0.60   1.00
☐ 4, Mar 88, JBy/WS(c) 0.75   0.20   0.60   1.00

WORLD OF METROPOLIS
☐ 1, Aug 88 .... 1.00   0.20   0.60   1.00
☐ 2, Sep 88 .... 1.00   0.20   0.60   1.00
☐ 3, Oct 88 .... 1.00   0.20   0.60   1.00
☐ 4, Nov 88 .... 1.00   0.20   0.60   1.00

WORLD OF SMALLVILLE
☐ 1, Apr 88 .... 0.75   0.20   0.60   1.00
☐ 2, May 88 .... 0.75   0.20   0.60   1.00
☐ 3, Jun 88 .... 0.75   0.20   0.60   1.00
☐ 4, Jul 88 .... 0.75   0.20   0.60   1.00

WORLD OF WOOD
ECLIPSE
☐ 1, WW 0.35   1.05   1.75
☐ 2, WW 0.35   1.05   1.75
☐ 3, WW 0.35   1.05   1.75
☐ 4, WW 0.35   1.05   1.75
☐ 5, WW 0.35   1.05   1.75

WORLD OF X-RAY, THE
PYRAMID
☐ 1, b&w 0.36   1.08   1.80

WORLD OF YOUNG MASTER
NEW COMICS
☐ 1, Demonblade 0.39   1.17   1.95

WORLD WITHOUT END
DC
☐ 1 .... 0.50   1.50   2.50
☐ 2 .... 0.50   1.50   2.50
☐ 3 .... 0.50   1.50   2.50
☐ 4 .... 0.50   1.50   2.50
☐ 5 .... 0.50   1.50   2.50
☐ 6 .... 0.50   1.50   2.50

WORLD'S FINEST (mini-series)
☐ 1, 90, Dave Gibbons (writer), SR Superman, Batman,
Luthor, Joker 3.95   1.20   3.60   6.00

☐ 2, 90, Dave Gibbons(w), SR Superman, Batman, Luthor,
Joker 3.95   0.79   2.37   3.95
☐ 3, 90, Dave Gibbons(w), SR Superman, Batman, Luthor,
Joker 3.95   0.79   2.37   3.95

WORLD'S FINEST COMICS
☐ 71 .... 150.00   450.00   750.00
☐ 72 .... 95.00   285.00   475.00
☐ 73 .... 95.00   285.00   475.00
☐ 74 .... 95.00   285.00   475.00
☐ 75 .... 95.00   285.00   475.00
☐ 76 .... 56.00   168.00   280.00
☐ 77 .... 56.00   168.00   280.00
☐ 78 .... 56.00   168.00   280.00
☐ 79 .... 56.00   168.00   280.00
☐ 80 .... 56.00   168.00   280.00
☐ 81 .... 45.00   135.00   225.00
☐ 82 .... 45.00   135.00   225.00
☐ 83 .... 45.00   135.00   225.00
☐ 84 .... 45.00   135.00   225.00
☐ 85 .... 45.00   135.00   225.00
☐ 86 .... 45.00   135.00   225.00
☐ 87 .... 45.00   135.00   225.00
☐ 88 .... 50.00   150.00   250.00
☐ 89 .... 45.00   135.00   225.00
☐ 90 .... 45.00   135.00   225.00
☐ 91 .... 30.00   90.00   150.00
☐ 92 .... 30.00   90.00   150.00
☐ 93 .... 30.00   90.00   150.00
☐ 94 .... 88.00   264.00   440.00
☐ 95 .... 30.00   90.00   150.00
☐ 96 .... 30.00   90.00   150.00
☐ 97 .... 30.00   90.00   150.00
☐ 98 .... 30.00   90.00   150.00
☐ 99 .... 30.00   90.00   150.00
☐ 100 .... 53.00   159.00   265.00
☐ 101 .... 20.00   60.00   100.00
☐ 102 .... 20.00   60.00   100.00
☐ 103 .... 20.00   60.00   100.00
☐ 104 .... 20.00   60.00   '100.00
☐ 105 .... 20.00   60.00   100.00
☐ 106 .... 20.00   60.00   100.00
☐ 107 .... 20.00   60.00   100.00
☐ 108 .... 20.00   60.00   100.00
☐ 109 .... 20.00   60.00   100.00
☐ 110 .... 20.00   60.00   100.00
☐ 111 .... 16.00   48.00   80.00
☐ 112 .... 16.00   48.00   80.00
☐ 113 .... 16.00   48.00   80.00
☐ 114 .... 16.00   48.00   80.00
☐ 115, Feb 61 .... 0.10   16.00   48.00   80.00
☐ 116, Mar 61 .... 0.10   16.00   48.00   80.00
☐ 117, May 61 .... 0.10   16.00   48.00   80.00
☐ 118, Jun 61 .... 0.10   16.00   48.00   80.00
☐ 119, Aug 61 .... 0.10   16.00   48.00   80.00
☐ 120, Sep 61 .... 0.10   16.00   48.00   80.00
☐ 121, Nov 61 .... 0.10   12.00   36.00   60.00
☐ 122, Dec 61 .... 0.10   12.00   36.00   60.00
☐ 123, Feb 62 .... 0.12   12.00   36.00   60.00
☐ 124, Mar 62 .... 0.12   12.00   36.00   60.00
☐ 125 .... 7.20   21.60   36.00
☐ 126, Jun 62 .... 0.12   7.20   21.60   36.00
☐ 127, Aug 62 .... 0.12   7.20   21.60   36.00
☐ 128, Sep 62 .... 0.12   7.20   21.60   36.00
☐ 129, Nov 62, A:Joker 0.12   9.60   28.80   48.00
☐ 130, Dec 62 .... 0.12   7.20   21.60   36.00
☐ 131, Feb 63 .... 0.12   6.40   19.20   32.00
☐ 132, Mar 63 .... 0.12   6.40   19.20   32.00
☐ 133, May 63 .... 0.12   6.40   19.20   32.00
☐ 134, Jun 63 .... 0.12   6.40   19.20   32.00
☐ 135, Aug 63 .... 0.12   6.40   19.20   32.00
☐ 136, Sep 63 .... 0.12   6.40   19.20   32.00

	ORIG.	GOOD	FINE	N-MINT
❑ 137, Nov 63	0.12	6.40	19.20	32.00
❑ 138, Dec 63	0.12	6.40	19.20	32.00
❑ 139, Feb 64	0.12	6.40	19.20	32.00
❑ 140, Mar 64	0.12	6.40	19.20	32.00
❑ 141, May 64	0.12	6.40	19.20	32.00
❑ 142, Jun 64	0.12	7.20	21.60	36.00
❑ 143, Aug 64, CS	0.12	4.40	13.20	22.00
❑ 144, Sep 64, CS	0.12	4.40	13.20	22.00
❑ 145, Nov 64, CS	0.12	4.40	13.20	22.00
❑ 146, Dec 64, CS	0.12	4.40	13.20	22.00
❑ 147, Feb 65, CS	0.12	4.40	13.20	22.00
❑ 148, Mar 65, CS	0.12	4.40	13.20	22.00
❑ 149, May 65, CS	0.12	4.40	13.20	22.00
❑ 150, Jun 65, CS	0.12	4.40	13.20	22.00
❑ 151, Aug 65	0.12	3.60	10.80	18.00
❑ 152, Sep 65	0.12	3.60	10.80	18.00
❑ 153, Nov 65	0.12	3.60	10.80	18.00
❑ 154, Dec 65	0.12	3.60	10.80	18.00
❑ 155, Feb 66	0.12	3.60	10.80	18.00
❑ 156, Mar 66, 1:Bizarro Batman;A:Joker,Bizarro Superman	0.12	14.00	42.00	70.00
❑ 157, May 66	0.12	3.60	10.80	18.00
❑ 158, Jun 66	0.12	3.60	10.80	18.00
❑ 159, Aug 66	0.12	3.60	10.80	18.00
❑ 160, Sep 66, reprint	0.12	3.60	10.80	18.00
❑ 161, Nov 66, giant	0.25	1.60	4.80	8.00
❑ 162, Nov 66	0.12	1.00	3.00	5.00
❑ 163, Dec 66	0.12	1.00	3.00	5.00
❑ 164, Feb 67	0.12	1.00	3.00	5.00
❑ 165, Mar 67	0.12	1.00	3.00	5.00
❑ 166, May 67, Joker	0.12	3.20	9.60	16.00
❑ 167, Jun 67	0.12	1.00	3.00	5.00
❑ 168, Aug 67	0.12	1.00	3.00	5.00
❑ 169, Sep 67	0.12	1.00	3.00	5.00
❑ 170, Nov 67, giant reprint	0.25	1.20	3.60	6.00
❑ 171, Nov 67	0.12	0.80	2.40	4.00
❑ 172, Dec 67	0.12	0.80	2.40	4.00
❑ 173, Feb 68	0.12	0.80	2.40	4.00
❑ 174, Mar 68	0.12	0.80	2.40	4.00
❑ 175, May 68, NA	0.12	1.20	3.60	6.00
❑ 176, Jun 68, NA	0.12	1.20	3.60	6.00
❑ 177, Aug 68	0.12	0.60	1.80	3.00
❑ 178, Sep 68	0.12	0.60	1.80	3.00
❑ 179, Nov 68	0.25	0.60	1.80	3.00
❑ 180, Nov 68	0.12	0.60	1.80	3.00
❑ 181, Dec 68	0.12	0.60	1.80	3.00
❑ 182, Feb 69	0.12	0.60	1.80	3.00
❑ 183, Mar 69	0.12	0.60	1.80	3.00
❑ 184, May 69	0.12	0.60	1.80	3.00
❑ 185, Jun 69	0.12	0.60	1.80	3.00
❑ 186, Aug 69	0.12	0.60	1.80	3.00
❑ 187, Sep 69	0.12	0.60	1.80	3.00
❑ 188, Nov 69	0.15	0.60	1.80	3.00
❑ 189, Nov 69, giant	0.25	0.40	1.20	2.00
❑ 190, Dec 69	0.15	0.60	1.80	3.00
❑ 191, Feb 70	0.15	0.60	1.80	3.00
❑ 192, Mar 70	0.15	0.60	1.80	3.00
❑ 193, May 70	0.15	0.60	1.80	3.00
❑ 194, Jun 70	0.15	0.60	1.80	3.00
❑ 195, Aug 70	0.15	0.60	1.80	3.00
❑ 196, Sep 70	0.15	0.60	1.80	3.00
❑ 197, Nov 70, giant	0.25	0.40	1.20	2.00
❑ 198, Nov 70	0.15	0.40	1.20	2.00
❑ 199, Dec 70	0.15	0.40	1.20	2.00
❑ 200, Feb 71	0.15	0.40	1.20	2.00
❑ 201, Mar 71	0.15	0.40	1.20	2.00
❑ 202, May 71	0.15	0.40	1.20	2.00
❑ 203, Jun 71	0.15	0.40	1.20	2.00
❑ 204, Aug 71	0.25	0.40	1.20	2.00
❑ 205, Sep 71, Frazetta ad, Titans	0.25	0.50	1.50	2.50

	ORIG.	GOOD	FINE	N-MINT
❑ 206, Nov 71, giant reprint	0.35	0.40	1.20	2.00
❑ 207, Nov 71	0.25	0.25	0.75	1.25
❑ 208, Dec 71	0.25	0.25	0.75	1.25
❑ 209, Feb 72	0.25	0.25	0.75	1.25
❑ 210, Mar 72	0.25	0.25	0.75	1.25
❑ 211, May 72	0.25	0.25	0.75	1.25
❑ 212, Jun 72	0.25	0.25	0.75	1.25
❑ 213, Sep 72	0.20	0.25	0.75	1.25
❑ 214, Nov 72	0.20	0.25	0.75	1.25
❑ 215, Jan 73	0.20	0.25	0.75	1.25
❑ 216, Mar 73	0.20	0.25	0.75	1.25
❑ 217, May 73	0.20	0.25	0.75	1.25
❑ 218, Aug 73	0.20	0.25	0.75	1.25
❑ 219, Oct 73	0.20	0.25	0.75	1.25
❑ 220, Dec 73	0.20	0.25	0.75	1.25
❑ 221, Feb 74	0.20	0.25	0.75	1.25
❑ 222, Apr 74	0.20	0.25	0.75	1.25
❑ 223, Jun 74, NA, giant	0.60	0.60	1.80	3.00
❑ 224, Aug 74, giant	0.60	0.40	1.20	2.00
❑ 225, Oct 74, giant	0.60	0.40	1.20	2.00
❑ 226, Dec 74, NA, giant	0.60	0.60	1.80	3.00
❑ 227, Feb 75, giant	0.60	0.40	1.20	2.00
❑ 228, Mar 75, giant	0.60	0.40	1.20	2.00
❑ 229, Apr 75	0.25	0.20	0.60	1.00
❑ 230, May 75, giant	0.50	0.40	1.20	2.00
❑ 231, Jul 75	0.25	0.20	0.60	1.00
❑ 232, Sep 75	0.25	0.20	0.60	1.00
❑ 233, Oct 75	0.25	0.20	0.60	1.00
❑ 234, Dec 75	0.25	0.20	0.60	1.00
❑ 235, Jan 76	0.30	0.20	0.60	1.00
❑ 236, Mar 76	0.30	0.20	0.60	1.00
❑ 237, Apr 76	0.30	0.20	0.60	1.00
❑ 238, Jun 76	0.30	0.20	0.60	1.00
❑ 239, Jul 76	0.30	0.20	0.60	1.00
❑ 240, Sep 76	0.30	0.20	0.60	1.00
❑ 241, Oct 76	0.30	0.20	0.60	1.00
❑ 242, Dec 76	0.30	0.20	0.60	1.00
❑ 243, Feb 77	0.30	0.20	0.60	1.00
❑ 244, May 77, giant	1.00	0.25	0.75	1.25
❑ 245, Jul 77, giant	1.00	0.25	0.75	1.25
❑ 246, Sep 77, KS/MA/MN/TA/GM, A:JLA	1.00	0.25	0.75	1.25
❑ 247, Nov 77, KS, giant	1.00	0.25	0.75	1.25
❑ 248, Jan 78, KS, giant	1.00	0.25	0.75	1.25
❑ 249, Mar 78, KS, giant	1.00	0.25	0.75	1.25
❑ 250, May 78, KS, giant	1.00	0.25	0.75	1.25
❑ 251, Jul 78, KS, giant	1.00	0.25	0.75	1.25
❑ 252, Sep 78, KS, giant	1.00	0.25	0.75	1.25
❑ 253, Nov 78, KS, giant	1.00	0.25	0.75	1.25
❑ 254, Jan 79, KS, giant	1.00	0.25	0.75	1.25
❑ 255, Mar 79, JL/DA/SD	1.00	0.30	0.90	1.50
❑ 256, May 79, giant	1.00	0.25	0.75	1.25
❑ 257, Jul 79, giant	1.00	0.25	0.75	1.25
❑ 258, Sep 79, giant	1.00	0.25	0.75	1.25
❑ 259, Nov 79, RB/DG/MR/MN/DN/KS	1.00	0.40	1.20	2.00
❑ 260, Jan 80	1.00	0.25	0.75	1.25
❑ 261, Mar 80	1.00	0.25	0.75	1.25
❑ 262, May 80	1.00	0.25	0.75	1.25
❑ 263, Jul 80	1.00	0.25	0.75	1.25
❑ 264, Sep 80	1.00	0.25	0.75	1.25
❑ 265, Nov 80	1.00	0.25	0.75	1.25
❑ 266, Jan 81	1.00	0.25	0.75	1.25
❑ 267, Mar 81	1.00	0.25	0.75	1.25
❑ 268, May 81	1.00	0.25	0.75	1.25
❑ 269, Jul 81	1.00	0.25	0.75	1.25
❑ 270, Aug 81	1.00	0.25	0.75	1.25
❑ 271, Sep 81	1.00	0.25	0.75	1.25
❑ 272, Oct 81	1.00	0.25	0.75	1.25
❑ 273, Nov 81	1.00	0.25	0.75	1.25
❑ 274, Dec 81	1.00	0.25	0.75	1.25

	ORIG.	GOOD	FINE	N-MINT
☐ 275, Jan 82	1.00	0.25	0.75	1.25
☐ 276, Feb 82	1.00	0.25	0.75	1.25
☐ 277, Mar 82	1.00	0.25	0.75	1.25
☐ 278, Apr 82	1.00	0.25	0.75	1.25
☐ 279, May 82	1.00	0.25	0.75	1.25
☐ 280, Jun 82	1.00	0.25	0.75	1.25
☐ 281, Jul 82	1.00	0.25	0.75	1.25
☐ 282, Aug 82	1.00	0.25	0.75	1.25
☐ 283, Sep 82, GT/FMc/GK	0.60	0.20	0.60	1.00
☐ 284, Oct 82, GT, DS, A:Legion	0.60	0.30	0.90	1.50
☐ 285, Nov 82	0.60	0.25	0.75	1.25
☐ 286, Dec 82	0.60	0.25	0.75	1.25
☐ 287, Jan 83	0.60	0.20	0.60	1.00
☐ 288, Feb 83	0.60	0.20	0.60	1.00
☐ 289, Mar 83	0.60	0.20	0.60	1.00
☐ 290, Apr 83	0.60	0.20	0.60	1.00
☐ 291, May 83	0.60	0.20	0.60	1.00
☐ 292, Jun 83	0.60	0.20	0.60	1.00
☐ 293, Jul 83	0.60	0.20	0.60	1.00
☐ 294, Aug 83	0.60	0.20	0.60	1.00
☐ 295, Sep 83	0.60	0.20	0.60	1.00
☐ 296, Oct 83	0.60	0.20	0.60	1.00
☐ 297, Nov 83	0.60	0.20	0.60	1.00
☐ 298, Dec 83	0.75	0.20	0.60	1.00
☐ 299, Jan 84, GC	0.75	0.25	0.75	1.25
☐ 300, Feb 84, RA A:JLA, Outsiders, Titans	1.25	0.20	0.60	1.00
☐ 301, Mar 84	0.75	0.20	0.60	1.00
☐ 302, Apr 84	0.75	0.20	0.60	1.00
☐ 303, May 84	0.75	0.20	0.60	1.00
☐ 304, Jun 84	0.75	0.20	0.60	1.00
☐ 305, Jul 84	0.75	0.20	0.60	1.00
☐ 306, Aug 84	0.75	0.20	0.60	1.00
☐ 307, Sep 84	0.75	0.20	0.60	1.00
☐ 308, Oct 84	0.75	0.20	0.60	1.00
☐ 309, Nov 84	0.75	0.20	0.60	1.00
☐ 310, Dec 84	0.75	0.20	0.60	1.00
☐ 311, Jan 85	0.75	0.20	0.60	1.00
☐ 312, Feb 85	0.75	0.20	0.60	1.00
☐ 313, Mar 85	0.75	0.20	0.60	1.00
☐ 314, Apr 85	0.75	0.20	0.60	1.00
☐ 315, May 85	0.75	0.20	0.60	1.00
☐ 316, Jun 85	0.75	0.20	0.60	1.00
☐ 317, Jul 85	0.75	0.20	0.60	1.00
☐ 318, Aug 85	0.75	0.20	0.60	1.00
☐ 319, Sep 85	0.75	0.20	0.60	1.00
☐ 320, Oct 85	0.75	0.20	0.60	1.00
☐ 321, Nov 85	0.75	0.20	0.60	1.00
☐ 322, Dec 85	0.75	0.20	0.60	1.00
☐ 323, Jan 86	0.75	0.20	0.60	1.00

WORLD'S WORST COMICS AWARDS
KITCHEN SINK

	ORIG.	GOOD	FINE	N-MINT
☐ 1, 90, b&w	2.50	0.50	1.50	2.50
☐ 2, Jan 91, b&w	2.50	0.50	1.50	2.50

WORLDS COLLIDE
DC/MILESTONE

	ORIG.	GOOD	FINE	N-MINT
☐ 1, Jul 94, enhanced cover	3.95	1.00	3.00	5.00
☐ 1, Jul 94	2.50	0.50	1.50	2.50
☐ 1, Jul 94, premium edition				

WORLDS OF H.P. LOVECRAFT: DAGON, THE
CALIBER

	ORIG.	GOOD	FINE	N-MINT
☐ 1, b&w	2.95	0.59	1.77	2.95

WORLDS OF H.P. LOVECRAFT: THE MUSIC OF ERICH ZANN

	ORIG.	GOOD	FINE	N-MINT
☐ 0, nn, b&w	2.95	0.59	1.77	2.95

WORLDS OF H.P. LOVECRAFT: THE PICTURE IN THE HOUSE, THE

	ORIG.	GOOD	FINE	N-MINT
☐ 0, nn, b&w	2.95	0.59	1.77	2.95

WORLDS UNKNOWN
MARVEL

	ORIG.	GOOD	FINE	N-MINT
☐ 1, May 73	0.20	0.20	0.60	1.00
☐ 2, Jul 73	0.20	0.20	0.60	1.00
☐ 3, Sep 73	0.20	0.20	0.60	1.00
☐ 4, Nov 73	0.20	0.20	0.60	1.00
☐ 5, Feb 74	0.20	0.20	0.60	1.00
☐ 6, Apr 74	0.20	0.20	0.60	1.00
☐ 7	0.25	0.20	0.60	1.00
☐ 8	0.25	0.20	0.60	1.00

WRATH
MALIBU/ULTRAVERSE

	ORIG.	GOOD	FINE	N-MINT
☐ 1	1.95	0.39	1.17	1.95
☐ 2, Feb 94	1.95	0.39	1.17	1.95
☐ 3, Mar 94	1.95	0.39	1.17	1.95
☐ 4, Apr 94	1.95	0.39	1.17	1.95
☐ 5, May 94	1.95	0.39	1.17	1.95
☐ 6, Jun 94	1.95	0.39	1.17	1.95
☐ 7, Jul 94	1.95	0.39	1.17	1.95
☐ 8, Oct 94	1.95	0.39	1.17	1.95

WRATH GIANT SIZE

	ORIG.	GOOD	FINE	N-MINT
☐ 1, Aug 94	2.50	0.50	1.50	2.50

WRATH OF THE SPECTRE
DC

	ORIG.	GOOD	FINE	N-MINT
☐ 1, May 88, JA rep.	2.50	0.50	1.50	2.50
☐ 2, Jun 88, JA rep.	2.50	0.50	1.50	2.50
☐ 3, Jul 88, JA rep.	2.50	0.50	1.50	2.50
☐ 4, Aug 88, JA new stories	2.50	0.70	2.10	3.50

WULF THE BARBARIAN
ATLAS/ SEABOARD

	ORIG.	GOOD	FINE	N-MINT
☐ 1, O:Wulf		0.20	0.60	1.00
☐ 2		0.20	0.60	1.00
☐ 3		0.20	0.60	1.00
☐ 4		0.20	0.60	1.00

WWF: WORLD WRESTLING FOUNDATION
VALIANT

	ORIG.	GOOD	FINE	N-MINT
☐ 21841, Ultimate Warrior's Workout		0.59	1.77	2.95
☐ 21842, Lifestyles of the Brutal & Infamous		0.59	1.77	2.95
☐ 21843, Out-of-the-Ring Challenges		0.59	1.77	2.95
☐ 21844, Wait Till I Get My Hands on		0.59	1.77	2.95

WYATT EARP (1960-1961, revival of old title)
MARVEL

	ORIG.	GOOD	FINE	N-MINT
☐ 30	0.20	0.20	0.60	1.00
☐ 31	0.20	0.20	0.60	1.00
☐ 32	0.20	0.20	0.60	1.00
☐ 33	0.20	0.20	0.60	1.00
☐ 34	0.20	0.20	0.60	1.00

WYOMING TERRITORY
ARK

	ORIG.	GOOD	FINE	N-MINT
☐ 1, b&w		0.39	1.17	1.95

How's That Again?

"Amazon training has made my fingernails stronger than steel!"

Wonder Woman #120

X

	ORIG.	GOOD	FINE	N-MINT
X				
DARK HORSE				
❑ 1 ....2.00	0.40	1.20	2.00
❑ 2, Mar 94 ....2.00	0.40	1.20	2.00
❑ 3, Apr 94 ....2.00	0.40	1.20	2.00
❑ 4, May 94 ....2.00	0.40	1.20	2.00
❑ 5, Jun 94 ....2.00	0.40	1.20	2.00
❑ 6, Aug 94 ....2.00	0.40	1.20	2.00
❑ 7, Sep 94 ....2.00	0.40	1.20	2.00
❑ 8, Oct 94 ....2.50	0.50	1.50	2.50
❑ 9, Nov 94 ....2.50	0.50	1.50	2.50
❑ 10, Dec 94 ....2.50	0.50	1.50	2.50
❑ 11, Jan 95 ....2.50	0.50	1.50	2.50
❑ 12, Mar 95 ....2.50	0.50	1.50	2.50
❑ 13, Apr 95 ....2.50	0.50	1.50	2.50
❑ 18, Sep 95, V:Predator;FM(c)			
.....................................2.50	0.50	1.50	2.50
❑ 19, Oct 95, FM (c) 2.50	0.50	1.50	2.50
❑ 20, Nov 95, FM (c) 2.50	0.50	1.50	2.50
❑ 21, Dec 95, FM (c) 2.50	0.50	1.50	2.50
❑ 22, Jan 96, FM (c)..........2.50	0.50	1.50	2.50
❑ 23, Feb 96 ....2.50	0.50	1.50	2.50
❑ 24, Mar 96 ....2.50	0.50	1.50	2.50
X 1999				
VIZ				
❑ 1, 95, b&w 2.75	0.55	1.65	2.75
X-CALIBRE (mini-series)				
MARVEL				
❑ 1, Mar 95 ....1.95	1.00	3.00	5.00
❑ 2, Apr 95, cover says "Jun"			
.....................................1.95	0.70	2.10	3.50
❑ 3, May 95 ....1.95	0.50	1.50	2.50
❑ 4, Jun 95.......................1.95	0.50	1.50	2.50
X-FACTOR				
❑ 1, Feb 86 ....1.25	2.40	7.20	12.00
❑ 2, Mar 86 ....0.75	1.00	3.00	5.00
❑ 3, Apr 86 ....0.75	1.00	3.00	5.00
❑ 4, May 86 ....0.75	1.00	3.00	5.00
❑ 5, Jun 86 ....0.75	1.00	3.00	5.00
❑ 6, Jul 86.........................0.75	0.80	2.40	4.00
❑ 7, Aug 86 ....0.75	0.80	2.40	4.00
❑ 8, Sep 86.......................0.75	0.80	2.40	4.00
❑ 9, Oct 89, Mutant Massacre			
.....................................0.75	0.80	2.40	4.00
❑ 10, Nov 89, Mutant Massacre			
.....................................0.75	0.80	2.40	4.00
❑ 11, Dec 89, Mutant Massacre			
.....................................0.75	0.80	2.40	4.00
❑ 12, Jan 87 ....0.75	0.60	1.80	3.00
❑ 13, Feb 87 ....0.75	0.60	1.80	3.00
❑ 14, Mar 87 ....0.75	0.60	1.80	3.00
❑ 15, Apr 87 ....0.75	0.60	1.80	3.00
❑ 16, May 87 ....0.75	0.60	1.80	3.00
❑ 17, Jun 87 ....0.75	0.60	1.80	3.00
❑ 18, Jul 87.......................0.75	0.60	1.80	3.00
❑ 19, Aug 87 ....0.75	0.60	1.80	3.00
❑ 20, Sep 87.....................0.75	0.60	1.80	3.00
❑ 21, Oct 87 ....0.75	0.60	1.80	3.00
❑ 22, Nov 87 ....0.75	0.60	1.80	3.00
❑ 23, Dec 87, registration card			
.....................................0.75	2.00	6.00	10.00
❑ 24, Jan 88, Fall of Mutants			
.....................................0.75	2.00	6.00	10.00
❑ 25, Feb 88, Fall of Mutants			
.....................................0.75	2.00	6.00	10.00
❑ 26, Mar 88,Fall of Mutants			
.....................................0.75	2.00	6.00	10.00
❑ 27, Apr 88 ....0.75	0.40	1.20	2.00
❑ 28, May 88 ....1.00	0.40	1.20	2.00

	ORIG.	GOOD	FINE	N-MINT
❑ 29, Jun 88 ....1.00	0.40	1.20	2.00
❑ 30, Jul 88.......................1.00	0.40	1.20	2.00
❑ 31, Aug 88 ....1.00	0.40	1.20	2.00
❑ 32, Sep 88, A:Avengers ..1.00	0.40	1.20	2.00
❑ 33, Oct 88 ....1.00	0.40	1.20	2.00
❑ 34, Nov 88 ....1.00	0.40	1.20	2.00
❑ 35, Dec 88, Inferno.........1.00	0.40	1.20	2.00
❑ 36, Jan 89, Inferno..........1.00	0.40	1.20	2.00
❑ 37, Feb 89, Inferno 1.00	0.40	1.20	2.00
❑ 38, Mar 89, Inferno.........1.50	0.50	1.50	2.50
❑ 39, Apr 89, Inferno 1.00	0.50	1.50	2.50
❑ 40, May 89, RL 1.00	1.60	4.80	8.00
❑ 41, Jun 89 ....1.00	0.40	1.20	2.00
❑ 42, Jul 89.......................1.00	0.40	1.20	2.00
❑ 43, Aug 89 ....1.00	0.40	1.20	2.00
❑ 44, Sep 89 ....1.00	0.40	1.20	2.00
❑ 45, Oct 89 ....1.00	0.40	1.20	2.00
❑ 46, Nov 89 ....1.00	0.40	1.20	2.00
❑ 47, Nov 89 ....1.00	0.40	1.20	2.00
❑ 48, Dec 89 ....1.00	0.40	1.20	2.00
❑ 49, Dec 89 ....1.00	0.40	1.20	2.00
❑ 50, Jan 90, TMc(c) Acts of Vengeance			
.....................................1.50	0.40	1.20	2.00
❑ 51, Feb 90......................1.00	1.20	3.60	6.00
❑ 52, Mar 90.....................1.00	1.20	3.60	6.00
❑ 53, Apr 90......................1.00	1.20	3.60	6.00
❑ 54, May 90.....................1.00	0.40	1.20	2.00
❑ 55, Jun 90 ....1.00	0.40	1.20	2.00
❑ 56, Jul 90.......................1.00	0.40	1.20	2.00
❑ 57, Aug 90.....................1.00	0.40	1.20	2.00
❑ 58, Sep 90 ....1.00	0.40	1.20	2.00
❑ 59, Oct 90 ....1.00	0.40	1.20	2.00
❑ 60, Nov 90, X-Tinction 1.00	1.60	4.80	8.00
❑ 61, Dec 90, X-Tinction 1.00	1.20	3.60	6.00
❑ 62, Jan 91......................1.00	1.20	3.60	6.00
❑ 63, Feb 91......................1.00	1.60	4.80	8.00
❑ 64, Mar 91.....................1.00	1.20	3.60	6.00
❑ 65, Apr 91......................1.00	1.20	3.60	6.00
❑ 66, May 91.....................1.00	0.40	1.20	2.00
❑ 67, Jun 91 ....1.00	0.40	1.20	2.00
❑ 68, Jul 91.......................1.00	0.40	1.20	2.00
❑ 69, Aug 91.....................1.00	0.40	1.20	2.00
❑ 70, Sep 91 ....1.00	0.40	1.20	2.00
❑ 71, Oct 91, new team......1.00	1.40	4.20	7.00
❑ 71, 2nd printing 1.00	0.40	1.20	2.00
❑ 72, Nov 91 ....1.00	0.60	1.80	3.00
❑ 73, Dec 91 ....1.00	0.60	1.80	3.00
❑ 74 ....1.00	0.60	1.80	3.00
❑ 75 ....1.75	0.50	1.50	2.50
❑ 76 ....1.25	0.40	1.20	2.00
❑ 77 ....1.25	0.40	1.20	2.00
❑ 78 ....1.25	0.40	1.20	2.00
❑ 79 ....1.25	0.40	1.20	2.00
❑ 80 ....1.25	0.40	1.20	2.00
❑ 81 ....1.25	0.40	1.20	2.00
❑ 82 ....1.25	0.40	1.20	2.00
❑ 83 ....1.25	0.40	1.20	2.00
❑ 84, bagged, with card, X-Cutioner's Song			
.....................................1.50	1.20	3.60	6.00
❑ 85, bagged, with card 1.50	0.30	0.90	1.50
❑ 86, bagged, with card 1.50	0.30	0.90	1.50
❑ 87 ....1.25	0.25	0.75	1.25
❑ 88 ....1.25	0.25	0.75	1.25
❑ 89 ....1.25	0.25	0.75	1.25
❑ 90 ....1.25	0.25	0.75	1.25
❑ 91 ....1.25	0.25	0.75	1.25
❑ 92, hologram cover 3.50	0.70	2.10	3.50
❑ 93 ....1.25	0.25	0.75	1.25
❑ 94 ....1.25	0.25	0.75	1.25
❑ 95 ....1.25	0.25	0.75	1.25

Note: For #24, the price line reads: 0.75 2.00 6.00 10.00

	ORIG.	GOOD	FINE	N-MINT
96	1.25	0.25	0.75	1.25
97	1.25	0.25	0.75	1.25
98	1.25	0.25	0.75	1.25
99	1.25	0.25	0.75	1.25
100, foil cover	2.95	0.59	1.77	2.95
100	1.75	0.35	1.05	1.75
101	1.25	0.25	0.75	1.25
102, May 94	1.50	0.30	0.90	1.50
103, Jun 94	1.50	0.30	0.90	1.50
104, Jul 94	1.50	0.30	0.90	1.50
105, Aug 94	1.50	0.30	0.90	1.50
106, Sep 94, Life Signs	2.00	0.40	1.20	2.00
106, Sep 94, Life Signs; enhanced cover	2.95	0.59	1.77	2.95
107, Oct 94	1.50	0.30	0.90	1.50
108, Nov 94, deluxe	1.95	0.39	1.17	1.95
108, Nov 94	1.50	0.30	0.90	1.50
109, Dec 94, deluxe	1.95	0.39	1.17	1.95
109, Dec 94	1.50	0.30	0.90	1.50
110, Jan 95, deluxe	1.95	0.39	1.17	1.95
110, Jan 95	1.50	0.30	0.90	1.50
111, Feb 95	1.50	0.30	0.90	1.50
111, Feb 95, deluxe	1.95	0.39	1.17	1.95
112, Jul 95	1.95	0.39	1.17	1.95
113, Aug 95	1.95	0.39	1.17	1.95
114, Sep 95	1.95	0.39	1.17	1.95
115, Oct 95	1.95	0.39	1.17	1.95
116, Nov 95	1.95	0.39	1.17	1.95
117, Dec 95	1.95	0.39	1.17	1.95
118, Jan 96	1.95	0.39	1.17	1.95
119, Feb 96	1.95	0.39	1.17	1.95
120, Mar 96	1.95	0.39	1.17	1.95
121, Apr 96	1.95	0.39	1.17	1.95
122, May 96	1.95	0.39	1.17	1.95
123, Jun 96	1.95	0.39	1.17	1.95

X-FACTOR ANNUAL

	ORIG.	GOOD	FINE	N-MINT
1, 86	1.25	1.00	3.00	5.00
2, 87	1.25	0.60	1.80	3.00
3, 88, Evolutionary War	1.75	0.40	1.20	2.00
4, 89, Atlantis Attacks	2.00	0.40	1.20	2.00
5, 90, Future Present	2.00	0.40	1.20	2.00
6, 91, Kings of Pain	2.00	0.40	1.20	2.00
7, 92, Shattershot	2.25	0.45	1.35	2.25
8, 93, trading card	2.95	0.59	1.77	2.95
9, 94	2.95	0.59	1.77	2.95

X-FARCE
ECLIPSE

	ORIG.	GOOD	FINE	N-MINT
1, b&w parody	2.50	0.50	1.50	2.50

X-FILES ANNUAL
TOPPS

	ORIG.	GOOD	FINE	N-MINT
1, Aug 95	3.95	0.79	2.37	3.95

X-FILES COMICS DIGEST, THE

	ORIG.	GOOD	FINE	N-MINT
1, Dec 95, digest;Ray Bradbury back-up stories	3.50	1.00	3.00	5.00

X-FILES SPECIAL EDITION

	ORIG.	GOOD	FINE	N-MINT
1, Jun 95, reprints issues #1 and 2	3.95	0.79	2.37	3.95

X-FILES, THE

	ORIG.	GOOD	FINE	N-MINT
1		10.00	30.00	50.00
2		6.00	18.00	30.00
3		3.20	9.60	16.00
4		2.40	7.20	12.00
5	2.95	1.60	4.80	8.00
6, Jun 95	2.95	1.00	3.00	5.00
7, Jul 95	2.95	0.80	2.40	4.00
8, Aug 95	2.95	0.80	2.40	4.00
9, Sep 95	2.95	0.80	2.40	4.00
10, Oct 95	2.95	0.80	2.40	4.00
11, Nov 95	2.95	0.59	1.77	2.95
16, May 96	2.95	0.59	1.77	2.95

X-FORCE
MARVEL

	ORIG.	GOOD	FINE	N-MINT
1, with Cable card	1.50	2.00	6.00	10.00
1, with Deadpool card	1.50	1.20	3.60	6.00
1, with Shatterstar card	1.50	1.20	3.60	6.00
1, with Sunspot & Gideon card	1.50	1.20	3.60	6.00
1, with X-Force group card	1.50	1.50	4.50	7.50
1, 2nd printing	1.50	0.30	0.90	1.50
2, Sep 91, RL	1.00	0.60	1.80	3.00
3, Oct 91, RL	1.00	0.60	1.80	3.00
4, Nov 91, SpM	1.00	0.80	2.40	4.00
5, Dec 91, R:Brotherhood of Evil Mutants	1.00	0.60	1.80	3.00
6	1.00	0.60	1.80	3.00
7	1.25	0.40	1.20	2.00
8	1.25	0.40	1.20	2.00
9	1.25	0.40	1.20	2.00
10	1.25	0.40	1.20	2.00
11	1.25	0.40	1.20	2.00
12	1.25	0.40	1.20	2.00
13	1.25	0.40	1.20	2.00
14	1.25	0.40	1.20	2.00
15	1.25	0.40	1.20	2.00
16, w/card, X-Cutioner's Song	1.50	0.40	1.20	2.00
17, with card	1.50	0.40	1.20	2.00
18, with card	1.50	0.40	1.20	2.00
19	1.25	0.40	1.20	2.00
20	1.25	0.40	1.20	2.00
21	1.25	0.25	0.75	1.25
22	1.25	0.25	0.75	1.25
23	1.25	0.25	0.75	1.25
24	1.25	0.25	0.75	1.25
25, hologram cover	3.50	1.00	3.00	5.00
26	1.25	0.25	0.75	1.25
27	1.25	0.25	0.75	1.25
28	1.25	0.25	0.75	1.25
29	1.25	0.25	0.75	1.25
30	1.25	0.25	0.75	1.25
31	1.25	0.25	0.75	1.25
32	1.25	0.25	0.75	1.25
33, Apr 94	1.25	0.25	0.75	1.25
34, May 94	1.50	0.30	0.90	1.50
35, Jun 94	1.50	0.30	0.90	1.50
36, Jul 94	1.50	0.30	0.90	1.50
37, Aug 94	1.50	0.30	0.90	1.50
38, Sep 94, enhanced cover	2.95	0.59	1.77	2.95
38, Sep 94	2.00	0.40	1.20	2.00
39, Oct 94	1.50	0.30	0.90	1.50
40, Nov 94	1.50	0.30	0.90	1.50
40, Nov 94, deluxe	1.95	0.39	1.17	1.95
41, Dec 94	1.50	0.30	0.90	1.50
41, Dec 94, deluxe	1.95	0.39	1.17	1.95
42, Jan 95, deluxe	1.95	0.39	1.17	1.95
42, Jan 95	1.50	0.30	0.90	1.50
43, Feb 95, deluxe	1.95	0.39	1.17	1.95
44, Jul 95, L:Cannonball to join X-Men	1.95	0.39	1.17	1.95
45, Aug 95	1.95	0.39	1.17	1.95
46, Sep 95, V:Mimic	1.95	0.39	1.17	1.95
47, Oct 95	1.95	0.39	1.17	1.95
48, Nov 95	1.95	0.39	1.17	1.95
49, Dec 95, direct edition	1.95	0.39	1.17	1.95
49, Dec 95	1.50	0.30	0.90	1.50
50, Jan 96, enhanced wraparound fold-out cardstock cover	3.95	0.79	2.37	3.95
50, Jan 96, wraparound fold-out cover	2.95	0.59	1.77	2.95
51, Feb 96	1.95	0.39	1.17	1.95

	ORIG.	GOOD	FINE	N-MINT
☐ 52, Mar 96, V:Blob	1.95	0.39	1.17	1.95
☐ 53, Apr 96	1.95	0.39	1.17	1.95
☐ 54, May 96	1.95	0.39	1.17	1.95

X-FORCE AND CABLE '95

☐ 1, Dec 95, one-shot;wraparound cover

	ORIG.	GOOD	FINE	N-MINT
.... 23.95		0.79	2.37	3.95

X-FORCE ANNUAL

	ORIG.	GOOD	FINE	N-MINT
☐ 1, 92, Shattershot	2.25	0.45	1.35	2.25
☐ 2, trading card..............	2.95	0.59	1.77	2.95
☐ 3, 94...............................	2.95	0.59	1.77	2.95

X-MAN

	ORIG.	GOOD	FINE	N-MINT
☐ 1, Mar 95	1.95	1.20	3.60	6.00
☐ 2, Apr 95	1.95	0.70	2.10	3.50
☐ 3, May 95	1.95	0.50	1.50	2.50
☐ 4, Jun 95	1.95	0.50	1.50	2.50
☐ 5, Jul 95	1.95	0.39	1.17	1.95
☐ 6, Aug 95......................	1.95	0.39	1.17	1.95
☐ 7, Sep 95.......................	1.95	0.39	1.17	1.95
☐ 8, Oct 95	1.95	0.39	1.17	1.95
☐ 9, Nov 95	1.95	0.39	1.17	1.95
☐ 10, Dec 95.....................	1.95	0.39	1.17	1.95
☐ 11, Jan 96, A:Rogue.......	1.95	0.39	1.17	1.95
☐ 12, Feb 96	1.95	0.39	1.17	1.95
☐ 13, Mar 96	1.95	0.39	1.17	1.95
☐ 14, Apr 96	1.95	0.39	1.17	1.95
☐ 15, May 96	1.95	0.39	1.17	1.95
☐ 16, Jun 96, V:Holocaust.	1.95	0.39	1.17	1.95
☐ 17, Jul 96, V:Holocaust..	1.95	0.39	1.17	1.95

X-MEN '95

	ORIG.	GOOD	FINE	N-MINT
☐ 1, Oct 95	3.95	0.79	2.37	3.95

X-MEN (1963-)

☐ 1, Sep 63, JK;O:X-Men;1:Magneto

	ORIG.	GOOD	FINE	N-MINT
....	0.12	1050.00	3150.00	5250.00

☐ 2, Nov 63, JK;1:Vanisher

	ORIG.	GOOD	FINE	N-MINT
....	0.12	290.00	870.00	1450.00

☐ 3, Jan 64, JK;1:Blob	0.12	130.00	390.00	650.00

☐ 4, Mar 64, JK;1:Brotherhood of Evil Mutants

	ORIG.	GOOD	FINE	N-MINT
....	0.12	140.00	420.00	700.00

☐ 5, May 64, JK;A:Evil Mutants

	0.12	60.00	180.00	300.00

☐ 6, Jul 64, JK;A:Evil Mutants, Sub-Mariner

	0.12	30.00	90.00	150.00

☐ 7, Sep 64, JK;A:Evil Mutants, Blob

	0.12	30.00	90.00	150.00

☐ 8, Nov 64, JK;1:Unus, the Untouchable

	0.12	30.00	90.00	150.00

☐ 9, Jan 65, JK;1:Lucifer ...	0.12	30.00	90.00	150.00
☐ 10, Mar 65, JK;A:Ka-Zar.	0.12	30.00	90.00	150.00
☐ 11, May 65, JK;1:Stranger				
....	0.12	20.00	60.00	100.00

☐ 12, Jul 65, JK;1&O:Juggernaut

	0.12	20.00	60.00	100.00

☐ 13, Sep 65, JK;V:Juggernaut

	0.12	20.00	60.00	100.00

☐ 14, Nov 65, JK;O&1:Sentinels

	0.12	20.00	60.00	100.00

☐ 15, Dec 65, JK;O:Beast ..	0.12	20.00	60.00	100.00
☐ 16, Jan 66, JK	0.12	20.00	60.00	100.00

☐ 17, Feb 66, JK;V:Magneto

	0.12	15.00	45.00	75.00

☐ 18, Mar 66, JK(c);V:Magneto;A:Stranger

	0.12	15.00	45.00	75.00

☐ 19, Apr 66, JK(c);O&1:Mimic

	0.12	15.00	45.00	75.00

☐ 20, May 66, JK(c);V:Lucifer; Unus

	0.12	15.00	45.00	75.00

☐ 21, Jun 66, JK(c);V:Lucifer

	0.12	11.00	33.00	55.00

☐ 22, Jul 66, JK(c);V:Count Nefaria

	0.12	11.00	33.00	55.00

☐ 23, Aug 66, V:Count Nefaria

	ORIG.	GOOD	FINE	N-MINT
....	0.12	11.00	33.00	55.00

☐ 24, Sep 66, JK(c)	0.12	11.00	33.00	55.00
☐ 25, Oct 66, JK(c)	0.12	11.00	33.00	55.00
☐ 26, Nov 66, JK(c)............	0.12	11.00	33.00	55.00

☐ 27, Dec 66, JK(c);Mimic returns;V:Puppet Master

	0.12	11.00	33.00	55.00

☐ 28, Jan 67, JK(c);1:Banshee

	0.12	20.00	60.00	100.00

☐ 29, Feb 67, JK(c);V:Super-Adaptoid

	0.12	10.00	30.00	50.00

☐ 30, Mar 67, JK(c)............	0.12	10.00	30.00	50.00

☐ 31, Apr 67, JK(c);1:Cobalt Man

	0.12	8.00	24.00	40.00

☐ 32, May 67, JK(c);V:Juggernaut

	0.12	8.00	24.00	40.00

☐ 33, Jun 67, GK(c);V:Juggernaut

	0.12	8.00	24.00	40.00

☐ 34, Jul 67, DA;V:Mole Man, Tyrannus

	0.12	8.00	24.00	40.00

☐ 35, Aug 67, JK(c);A:SpM, Banshee

	0.12	10.00	30.00	50.00

☐ 36, Sep 67, RA;1:Mekano

	0.12	8.00	24.00	40.00

☐ 37, Oct 67, JK/DH(c);RA

	0.12	8.00	24.00	40.00

☐ 38, Nov 67, DA(c);DH;V:Blob, Vanisher;"The Origins of the X-Men" back-ups begin

	0.12	10.00	30.00	50.00

☐ 39, Dec 67, GT(c);DH;D:Mutant-Master

	0.12	8.00	24.00	40.00

☐ 40, Jan 68, GT(c);DH;V:Frankenstein

	0.12	8.00	24.00	40.00

☐ 41, Feb 68, DH;1:Grotesk the Sub-Human

	0.12	8.00	24.00	40.00

☐ 42, Mar 68, JB(c);DH;V:Grotesk

	0.12	8.00	24.00	40.00

☐ 43, Apr 68, JB(c);GT;V:Brotherhood of Evil Mutants

	0.12	8.00	24.00	40.00

☐ 44, May 68, DH;A:Magneto;R:Red Raven

	0.12	8.00	24.00	40.00

☐ 45, Jun 68, JB/GT(c);DH;V:Evil Mutants

	0.12	8.00	24.00	40.00

☐ 46, Jul 68, DH;V:Juggernaut

	0.12	8.00	24.00	40.00

☐ 47, Aug 68, DH;V:Maha Yogi

	0.12	8.00	24.00	40.00

☐ 48, Sep 68, SB(c);DH;V:Quasimodo

	0.12	8.00	24.00	40.00

☐ 49, Oct 68, JSo/DH;1:Mesmero, Lorna Dane

	0.12	8.00	24.00	40.00

☐ 50, Nov 68, JSo;V:Mesmero

	0.12	7.00	21.00	35.00

☐ 51, Dec 68, JSo;V:Mesmero

	0.12	7.00	21.00	35.00

☐ 52, Jan 69, DH/MSe/JSt, O:Lorna Dane

	0.12	4.80	14.40	24.00

☐ 53, Feb 69, BS, Smith's 1st

	0.12	7.00	21.00	35.00

☐ 54, Mar 69, BS/DH, O:Havok

	0.12	5.00	15.00	25.00

☐ 55, Apr 69, BS/DH, O:Havok

	0.12	5.00	15.00	25.00

☐ 56, May 69, NA..............	0.12	7.00	21.00	35.00
☐ 57, Jun 69, NA...............	0.12	7.00	21.00	35.00
☐ 58, Jul 69, NA................	0.15	7.00	21.00	35.00
☐ 59, Jul 69, NA................	0.15	7.00	21.00	35.00
☐ 60, Sep 69, NA..............	0.15	7.00	21.00	35.00
☐ 61, Oct 69, NA...............	0.15	7.00	21.00	35.00
☐ 62, Nov 69, NA..............	0.15	7.00	21.00	35.00
☐ 63, Dec 69, NA...............	0.15	7.00	21.00	35.00

	ORIG.	GOOD	FINE	N-MINT
❏ 64, Jan 70, DH, O:Sunfire				
......................0.15		4.00	12.00	20.00
❏ 65, Feb 70, NA, A:Havok, SHIELD				
......................0.15		6.40	19.20	32.00
❏ 66, Mar 70, SB, A:Hulk, Havok				
......................0.15		2.00	6.00	10.00
❏ 67, reprint 0.25		2.00	6.00	10.00
❏ 68, reprint 0.25		2.00	6.00	10.00
❏ 69, reprint 0.25		2.00	6.00	10.00
❏ 70, reprint 0.25		2.00	6.00	10.00
❏ 71, reprint 0.25		2.00	6.00	10.00
❏ 72, reprint 0.25		2.00	6.00	10.00
❏ 73, reprint 0.25		2.00	6.00	10.00
❏ 74, reprint 0.25		2.00	6.00	10.00
❏ 75, reprint 0.25		2.00	6.00	10.00
❏ 76, reprint 0.25		2.00	6.00	10.00
❏ 77, reprint 0.25		2.00	6.00	10.00
❏ 78, reprint 0.25		2.00	6.00	10.00
❏ 79, reprint 0.25		2.00	6.00	10.00
❏ 80, reprint 0.25		2.00	6.00	10.00
❏ 81, reprint 0.25		2.00	6.00	10.00
❏ 82, reprint 0.25		2.00	6.00	10.00
❏ 83, reprint 0.25		2.00	6.00	10.00
❏ 84, reprint 0.25		2.00	6.00	10.00
❏ 85, reprint 0.25		2.00	6.00	10.00
❏ 86, reprint 0.25		2.00	6.00	10.00
❏ 87, reprint 0.25		2.00	6.00	10.00
❏ 88, reprint 0.25		2.00	6.00	10.00
❏ 89, reprint 0.25		2.00	6.00	10.00
❏ 90, reprint 0.25		2.00	6.00	10.00
❏ 91, reprint 0.25		2.00	6.00	10.00
❏ 92, reprint 0.25		2.00	6.00	10.00
❏ 93, reprint 0.25		2.00	6.00	10.00
❏ 94, Aug 75, GK/DC/BMc, I:New X-Men				
......................0.25		56.00	168.00	280.00
❏ 95, Oct 75, GK/DC, D:Thunderbird				
......................0.25		15.00	45.00	75.00
❏ 96, Dec 75......................0.25		9.00	27.00	45.00
❏ 97, Feb 76......................0.25		9.00	27.00	45.00
❏ 98, Apr 76......................0.25		9.00	27.00	45.00
❏ 99, Jun 76......................0.25		9.00	27.00	45.00
❏ 100, Aug 76, DC............0.25		14.00	42.00	70.00
❏ 101, Oct 76, DC, I:Phoenix, A:Juggernaut				
......................0.30		9.60	28.80	48.00
❏ 102, Dec 76, DC, O:Storm				
......................0.30		6.00	18.00	30.00
❏ 103, Feb 77......................0.30		4.80	14.40	24.00
❏ 104, Apr 77......................0.30		4.80	14.40	24.00
❏ 105, Jun 77......................0.30		4.80	14.40	24.00
❏ 106, Aug 77......................0.30		4.80	14.40	24.00
❏ 107, Oct 77......................0.30		6.00	18.00	30.00
❏ 108, Dec 77, DC/JBy/TA, A:FF				
......................0.35		11.00	33.00	55.00
❏ 109, Feb 78, DC/JBy/TA, I:Weapon Alpha				
......................0.35		7.20	21.60	36.00
❏ 110, Apr 78, DC/TA, A:Warhawk				
......................0.35		4.80	14.40	24.00
❏ 111, Jun 78, DC/JBy/TA, A:Beast, Magneto				
......................0.35		4.80	14.40	24.00
❏ 112, Aug 78 ....0.35		4.80	14.40	24.00
❏ 113, Sep 78......................0.35		4.80	14.40	24.00
❏ 114, Oct 78......................0.35		4.80	14.40	24.00
❏ 115, Nov 78......................0.35		4.80	14.40	24.00
❏ 116, Dec 78......................0.35		4.80	14.40	24.00
❏ 117, Jan 79......................0.35		4.80	14.40	24.00
❏ 118, Feb 79......................0.35		4.80	14.40	24.00
❏ 119, Mar 79 ....0.35		4.80	14.40	24.00
❏ 120, Apr 79, JBy/TA I:Alpha Flight				
......................0.35		6.00	18.00	30.00
❏ 121, May 79, DC/JBy/TA, A:Alpha Flight, Mastermind				
......................0.35		7.20	21.60	36.00

	ORIG.	GOOD	FINE	N-MINT
❏ 122, Jun 79, DC/JBy/TA, I:Hellfire Club;V:Arcade				
......................0.40		4.40	13.20	22.00
❏ 123, Jul 79, V:Arcade 0.40		4.40	13.20	22.00
❏ 124, Aug 79, Phoenix cover				
......................0.40		4.40	13.20	22.00
❏ 125, Sep 79 ....0.40		4.40	13.20	22.00
❏ 126, Oct 79......................0.40		4.40	13.20	22.00
❏ 127, Nov 79......................0.40		4.40	13.20	22.00
❏ 128, Dec 79 ....0.40		4.40	13.20	22.00
❏ 129, Jan 80, JBy/TA, I:Kitty Pryde				
......................0.40		7.60	22.80	38.00
❏ 130, Feb 80, JR2/JBy/TA, I:Dazzler				
......................0.40		4.40	13.20	22.00
❏ 131, Mar 80, JBy/TA, A:Angel, White Queen				
......................0.40		4.40	13.20	22.00
❏ 132, Apr 80, JBy/TA, A:Angel				
......................0.40		4.40	13.20	22.00
❏ 133, May 80, JBy/TA, A:Angel;1:Dark Phoenix				
......................0.40		4.40	13.20	22.00
❏ 134, Jun 80, JBy/TA, A:Angel, Dark Phoenix				
......................0.40		4.40	13.20	22.00
❏ 135, Jul 80, JBy/TA, A:Angel, Dark Phoenix				
......................0.40		4.40	13.20	22.00
❏ 136, Aug 80, JBy/TA, A:Angel				
......................0.40		4.40	13.20	22.00
❏ 137, Sep 80, JBy/TA, A:Angel				
......................0.75		7.00	21.00	35.00
❏ 138, Oct 80, JBy/TA, A:Angel				
......................0.50		4.40	13.20	22.00
❏ 139, Nov 80, JBy/TA.......0.50		6.40	19.20	32.00
❏ 140, Dec 80, JBy/TA 0.50		4.80	14.40	24.00
❏ 141, Jan 81, JBy/TA (becomes Uncanny X-Men)				
......................0.50		5.60	16.80	28.00

X-MEN (1991-)

	ORIG.	GOOD	FINE	N-MINT
❏ 1, Oct 91, cover A: Storm				
......................1.50		0.40	1.20	2.00
❏ 1, Oct 91, cover B: Colossus				
......................1.50		0.40	1.20	2.00
❏ 1, Oct 91, cover C: Wolverine				
......................1.50		0.40	1.20	2.00
❏ 1, Oct 91, cover D: Magneto				
......................1.50		0.40	1.20	2.00
❏ 1, Oct 91, cover E: double gatefold				
......................3.95		1.00	3.00	5.00
❏ 2, Nov 91 ....1.00		0.40	1.20	2.00
❏ 3, Dec 91 ....1.00		0.40	1.20	2.00
❏ 4 ....1.00		1.00	3.00	5.00
❏ 5 ....1.25		0.40	1.20	2.00
❏ 6 ....1.25		1.00	3.00	5.00
❏ 7 ....1.25		0.80	2.40	4.00
❏ 8 ....1.25		0.40	1.20	2.00
❏ 9 ....1.25		0.40	1.20	2.00
❏ 10 ....1.25		0.40	1.20	2.00
❏ 11 ....1.25		0.40	1.20	2.00
❏ 12 ....1.25		0.40	1.20	2.00
❏ 13 ....1.25		0.40	1.20	2.00
❏ 14, X-Cutioner's Song, trading card				
......................1.50		0.40	1.20	2.00
❏ 15, bagged, with card 1.50		0.40	1.20	2.00
❏ 16, bagged, with card 1.50		0.40	1.20	2.00
❏ 17 ....1.25		0.40	1.20	2.00
❏ 18 ....1.25		0.40	1.20	2.00
❏ 19 ....1.25		0.40	1.20	2.00
❏ 20 ....1.25		0.40	1.20	2.00
❏ 21 ....1.25		0.40	1.20	2.00
❏ 22 ....1.25		0.40	1.20	2.00
❏ 23 ....1.25		0.40	1.20	2.00
❏ 24 ....1.25		0.40	1.20	2.00
❏ 25, hologram 3.50		1.60	4.80	8.00
❏ 26 ....1.25		0.25	0.75	1.25
❏ 27 ....1.25		0.25	0.75	1.25

	ORIG.	GOOD	FINE	N-MINT
❏ 28 .... 1.25		0.25	0.75	1.25
❏ 29 .... 1.25		0.25	0.75	1.25
❏ 30, W: Jean & Scott 1.95		0.39	1.17	1.95
❏ 31 .... 1.25		0.25	0.75	1.25
❏ 32, May 94 .... 1.50		0.30	0.90	1.50
❏ 33, Jun 94 .... 1.50		0.30	0.90	1.50
❏ 34, Jul 94 .... 1.50		0.30	0.90	1.50
❏ 35, Aug 94, Generation Next 1.50		0.30	0.90	1.50
❏ 36, Sep 94, Generation Next 1.50		0.30	0.90	1.50
❏ 37, Oct 94 .... 1.50		0.30	0.90	1.50
❏ 37, Oct 94, enhanced cover 2.95		0.59	1.77	2.95
❏ 38, Nov 94, deluxe edition 1.95		0.39	1.17	1.95
❏ 39, Dec 94 .... 1.50		0.30	0.90	1.50
❏ 39, Dec 94, deluxe edition 1.95		0.39	1.17	1.95
❏ 40, Jan 95, deluxe edition 1.95		0.39	1.17	1.95
❏ 41, Feb 95, deluxe edition 1.95		0.39	1.17	1.95
❏ 41, Feb 95 .... 1.50		0.30	0.90	1.50
❏ 42, Jul 95 .... 1.95		0.39	1.17	1.95
❏ 43, Aug 95 .... 1.95		0.39	1.17	1.95
❏ 44, Sep 95 .... 1.95		0.39	1.17	1.95
❏ 45, Oct 95, enhanced wraparound gatefold cardstock cover 3.95		0.79	2.37	3.95
❏ 46, Nov 95, R:X-Babies .. 1.95		0.39	1.17	1.95
❏ 47, Dec 95 .... 1.95		0.39	1.17	1.95
❏ 48, Jan 96 .... 1.95		0.39	1.17	1.95
❏ 49, Feb 96 .... 1.95		0.39	1.17	1.95
❏ 50, Mar 96, enhanced wraparound cardstock cover 3.95		0.79	2.37	3.95
❏ 51, Apr 96 .... 1.95		0.39	1.17	1.95
❏ 52, May 96 .... 1.95		0.39	1.17	1.95
❏ 54, Jul 96, Identity of Onslaught revealed 1.95		0.39	1.17	1.95

X-MEN 2099

	ORIG.	GOOD	FINE	N-MINT
❏ 1, foil cover 1.75		0.35	1.05	1.75
❏ 1, gold edition		5.00	15.00	25.00
❏ 2 .... 1.25		0.25	0.75	1.25
❏ 3 .... 1.25		0.25	0.75	1.25
❏ 4 .... 1.25		0.25	0.75	1.25
❏ 5 .... 1.25		0.25	0.75	1.25
❏ 6 .... 1.25		0.25	0.75	1.25
❏ 7 .... 1.25		0.25	0.75	1.25
❏ 8, May 94 .... 1.50		0.30	0.90	1.50
❏ 9, Jun 94 .... 1.50		0.30	0.90	1.50
❏ 10, Jul 94 .... 1.50		0.30	0.90	1.50
❏ 11, Aug 94 .... 1.50		0.30	0.90	1.50
❏ 12, Sep 94 .... 1.50		0.30	0.90	1.50
❏ 13, Oct 94 .... 1.50		0.30	0.90	1.50
❏ 14, Nov 94 .... 1.50		0.30	0.90	1.50
❏ 15, Dec 94 .... 1.50		0.30	0.90	1.50
❏ 16, Jan 95 .... 1.50		0.30	0.90	1.50
❏ 17, Feb 95 .... 1.50		0.30	0.90	1.50
❏ 18, Mar 95 .... 1.50		0.30	0.90	1.50
❏ 19, Apr 95 .... 1.50		0.30	0.90	1.50
❏ 20, May 95 .... 1.50		0.30	0.90	1.50
❏ 21, Jun 95 .... 1.95		0.39	1.17	1.95
❏ 22, Jul 95 .... 1.95		0.39	1.17	1.95
❏ 23, Aug 95 .... 1.95		0.39	1.17	1.95
❏ 24, Sep 95 .... 1.95		0.39	1.17	1.95
❏ 25, Oct 95, enhanced wraparound cardstock cover 3.95		0.79	2.37	3.95
❏ 26, Nov 95 .... 1.50		0.30	0.90	1.50
❏ 27, Dec 95 .... 1.95		0.39	1.17	1.95
❏ 28, Jan 96 .... 1.95		0.39	1.17	1.95
❏ 29, Feb 96 .... 1.95		0.39	1.17	1.95

	ORIG.	GOOD	FINE	N-MINT
❏ 30, Mar 96 .... 1.95		0.39	1.17	1.95
❏ 31, Apr 96 .... 1.95		0.39	1.17	1.95
❏ 32, May 96 .... 1.95		0.39	1.17	1.95
❏ 33, Jun 96 .... 1.95		0.39	1.17	1.95

X-MEN 2099 SPECIAL

	ORIG.	GOOD	FINE	N-MINT
❏ 1, Oct 95 .... 3.95		0.79	2.37	3.95

X-MEN ADVENTURES

	ORIG.	GOOD	FINE	N-MINT
❏ 1, TV cartoon version 1.25		0.50	1.50	2.50
❏ 2 .... 1.25		0.25	0.75	1.25
❏ 3 .... 1.25		0.25	0.75	1.25
❏ 4 .... 1.25		0.25	0.75	1.25
❏ 5 .... 1.25		0.25	0.75	1.25
❏ 6 .... 1.25		0.25	0.75	1.25
❏ 7 .... 1.25		0.25	0.75	1.25
❏ 8 .... 1.25		0.25	0.75	1.25
❏ 9 .... 1.25		0.25	0.75	1.25
❏ 10 .... 1.25		0.25	0.75	1.25
❏ 11 .... 1.25		0.25	0.75	1.25
❏ 12 .... 1.25		0.25	0.75	1.25
❏ 13 .... 1.25		0.25	0.75	1.25
❏ 14 .... 1.25		0.25	0.75	1.25
❏ 15 .... 1.75		0.35	1.05	1.75

X-MEN ADVENTURES (Volume 2)

	ORIG.	GOOD	FINE	N-MINT
❏ 1 .... 1.25		0.25	0.75	1.25
❏ 2 .... 1.25		0.25	0.75	1.25
❏ 3 .... 1.25		0.25	0.75	1.25
❏ 4, May 94 .... 1.25		0.25	0.75	1.25
❏ 5, Jun 94 .... 1.25		0.25	0.75	1.25
❏ 6, Jul 94 .... 1.25		0.25	0.75	1.25
❏ 7, Aug 94 .... 1.25		0.25	0.75	1.25
❏ 8, Sep 94, (second season adaptation) 1.25		0.25	0.75	1.25
❏ 9, Oct 94, (second season adaptation) 1.50		0.30	0.90	1.50
❏ 10, Nov 94, (second season adaptation) 1.50		0.30	0.90	1.50
❏ 11, Dec 94, (second season adaptation) 1.50		0.30	0.90	1.50
❏ 12, Jan 95, (second season adaptation) 1.50		0.30	0.90	1.50
❏ 13, Feb 95, (second season adaptation) 1.50		0.30	0.90	1.50

X-MEN ADVENTURES (Volume 3)

	ORIG.	GOOD	FINE	N-MINT
❏ 1, Mar 95, (third season adaptation) 1.50		0.30	0.90	1.50
❏ 2, Apr 95, (third season adaptation) 1.50		0.30	0.90	1.50
❏ 3, May 95, (third season adaptation) 1.50		0.30	0.90	1.50
❏ 4, Jun 95, (third season adaptation) 1.50		0.30	0.90	1.50
❏ 5, Jul 95, (third season adaptation) 1.50		0.30	0.90	1.50
❏ 6, Aug 95, (third season adaptation) 1.50		0.30	0.90	1.50
❏ 7, Sep 95, (third season adaptation) 1.50		0.30	0.90	1.50
❏ 8, Oct 95, (third season adaptation) 1.50		0.30	0.90	1.50
❏ 9, Nov 95, (third season adaptation) 1.50		0.30	0.90	1.50
❏ 10, Dec 95, (third season adaptation) 1.50		0.30	0.90	1.50
❏ 11, Jan 96 .... 1.50		0.30	0.90	1.50
❏ 12, Feb 96 .... 1.50		0.30	0.90	1.50
❏ 13, Mar 96 .... 1.50		0.30	0.90	1.50

X-MEN ALPHA

	ORIG.	GOOD	FINE	N-MINT
❏ 1, Feb 95, enhanced cover, one-shot 3.95		2.00	6.00	10.00
❏ 1, gold edition		8.00	24.00	40.00

	ORIG.	GOOD	FINE	N-MINT

X-MEN ANNIVERSARY MAGAZINE
❏ 1 ....3.95 0.79 2.37 3.95

X-MEN ANNUAL (second series, '92-on)
❏ 1, 92..............................2.25 0.45 1.35 2.25
❏ 2, 93, trading card..........2.95 0.59 1.77 2.95
❏ 3, 94..............................2.95 0.59 1.77 2.95

X-MEN ANNUAL/SPECIAL
❏ 1, Dec 70, reprint;listed as "X-Men" in indicia; "X-Men
Special" on cover............0.25 6.00 18.00 30.00
❏ 2, reprint........................0.12 4.00 12.00 20.00
❏ 3, Jan 80, FM/GP/TA, I:Arkon
....0.75 1.60 4.80 8.00
❏ 4, Nov 80, JR2, A:Dr. Strange (becomes *Uncanny X-Men
Annual*) 0.75 1.60 4.80 8.00
❏ 5, Nov 81 ....0.75 1.60 4.80 8.00
❏ 6, Nov 82 ....1.00 1.60 4.80 8.00

X-MEN ARCHIVES
❏ 2, 95, cardstock cover....2.25 0.45 1.35 2.25
❏ 3, 95, cardstock cover....2.25 0.45 1.35 2.25
❏ 4, 95, cardstock cover....2.25 0.45 1.35 2.25

X-MEN ARCHIVES FEATURING CAPTAIN BRITAIN
(mini-series)
❏ 1, Jul 95, reprints Captain Britain stories from British
Marvel Super Heroes #377-383;wraparound cover
....2.95 0.59 1.77 2.95
❏ 2, Aug 95, reprints Captain Britain stories from British
Marvel Super Heroes #384-88 and *The Daredevils* #1
....2.95 0.59 1.77 2.95
❏ 3, Sep 95, reprints stories from *The Daredevils* #2-5
....2.95 0.59 1.77 2.95
❏ 4, Oct 95, reprints stories from *The Daredevils* #6-8
....2.95 0.59 1.77 2.95
❏ 5, Nov 95, reprints stories from *The Daredevils* #9-11
....2.95 0.59 1.77 2.95
❏ 6, Dec 95, reprints stories from *The Mighty World of
Marvel* #7-10.................2.95 0.59 1.77 2.95
❏ 7, Jan 96, reprints stories from *The Mighty World of
Marvel* #11-13;final issue
....2.95 0.59 1.77 2.95

X-MEN ASHCAN
❏ 0, 94..............................0.75 0.15 0.45 0.75

X-MEN AT THE STATE FAIR
❏ 1, Dallas Times-Herald 6.00 18.00 30.00

X-MEN CHRONICLES
❏ 1, Mar 95 ....3.95 0.79 2.37 3.95
❏ 2, Jun 95.........................3.95 0.79 2.37 3.95

X-MEN CLASSIC (was Classic X-Men)
❏ 46, Apr 90, reprints........1.25 0.25 0.75 1.25
❏ 47, May 90, reprints........1.25 0.25 0.75 1.25
❏ 48, Jun 90, reprints........1.25 0.25 0.75 1.25
❏ 49, Jul 90, reprints.........1.25 0.25 0.75 1.25
❏ 50, Aug 90, reprints 1.25 0.25 0.75 1.25
❏ 51, Sep 90, reprints........1.25 0.25 0.75 1.25
❏ 52, Oct 90, reprints.........1.25 0.25 0.75 1.25
❏ 53, Nov 90, reprints 1.25 0.25 0.75 1.25
❏ 54, Dec 90, reprints 1.25 0.25 0.75 1.25
❏ 55, Jan 91, reprints........1.25 0.25 0.75 1.25
❏ 56, Feb 91, reprints........1.25 0.25 0.75 1.25
❏ 57, Mar 91, reprints 1.25 0.25 0.75 1.25
❏ 58, Apr 91, reprints........1.25 0.25 0.75 1.25
❏ 59, May 91, reprints........1.25 0.25 0.75 1.25
❏ 60, Jun 91, reprints........1.25 0.25 0.75 1.25
❏ 61, Jul 91, reprints.........1.25 0.25 0.75 1.25
❏ 62, Aug 91, reprints........1.25 0.25 0.75 1.25
❏ 63, Sep 91, reprints........1.25 0.25 0.75 1.25
❏ 64, Oct 91, reprints 1.25 0.25 0.75 1.25
❏ 65, Nov 91, reprints 1.25 0.25 0.75 1.25
❏ 66, Dec 91, reprints 1.25 0.25 0.75 1.25
❏ 67, reprints 1.25 0.25 0.75 1.25

❏ 68, reprints 1.25 0.25 0.75 1.25
❏ 69, reprints 1.25 0.25 0.75 1.25
❏ 70, reprints 1.25 0.25 0.75 1.25
❏ 71, reprints 1.25 0.25 0.75 1.25
❏ 72, reprints 1.25 0.25 0.75 1.25
❏ 73, reprints 1.25 0.25 0.75 1.25
❏ 74, reprints 1.25 0.25 0.75 1.25
❏ 75, reprints 1.25 0.25 0.75 1.25
❏ 76, reprints 1.25 0.25 0.75 1.25
❏ 77, reprints 1.25 0.25 0.75 1.25
❏ 78, reprints 1.25 0.25 0.75 1.25
❏ 79, reprints 1.75 0.35 1.05 1.75
❏ 80, reprints 1.25 0.25 0.75 1.25
❏ 81, reprints 1.25 0.25 0.75 1.25
❏ 82, reprints 1.25 0.25 0.75 1.25
❏ 83, reprints 1.25 0.25 0.75 1.25
❏ 84, reprints 1.25 0.25 0.75 1.25
❏ 85, reprints 1.25 0.25 0.75 1.25
❏ 86, reprints 1.25 0.25 0.75 1.25
❏ 87, reprints 1.25 0.25 0.75 1.25
❏ 88, reprints 1.25 0.25 0.75 1.25
❏ 89, reprints 1.25 0.25 0.75 1.25
❏ 90, reprints 1.75 0.35 1.05 1.75
❏ 91, reprints 1.25 0.25 0.75 1.25
❏ 92, reprints 1.25 0.25 0.75 1.25
❏ 93, reprints 1.25 0.25 0.75 1.25
❏ 94, Apr 94, reprints 1.25 0.25 0.75 1.25
❏ 95, May 94, reprints 1.25 0.25 0.75 1.25
❏ 96, Jun 94, reprints 1.25 0.25 0.75 1.25
❏ 97, Jul 94, reprints 1.25 0.25 0.75 1.25
❏ 98, Aug 94, reprints........1.25 0.25 0.75 1.25
❏ 99, Sep 94 ....1.25 0.25 0.75 1.25
❏ 100, Oct 94, reprints.......1.50 0.30 0.90 1.50
❏ 101, Nov 94, reprints *Uncanny X-Men* #197
....1.50 0.30 0.90 1.50
❏ 102, Dec 94, reprints *Uncanny X-Men* #198
....1.50 0.30 0.90 1.50
❏ 103, Jan 95, reprints *Uncanny X-Men* #199
....1.50 0.30 0.90 1.50
❏ 104, Feb 95, reprints *Uncanny X-Men* #200
....1.95 0.39 1.17 1.95
❏ 105, Mar 95, reprints *Uncanny X-Men* #201
....1.50 0.30 0.90 1.50
❏ 106, Apr 95, reprints *Uncanny X-Men* #202
....1.50 0.30 0.90 1.50
❏ 107, May 95, reprints *Uncanny X-Men* #203
....1.50 0.30 0.90 1.50
❏ 108, Jun 95, reprints *Uncanny X-Men* #204
....1.50 0.30 0.90 1.50
❏ 109, Jul 95, reprints *Uncanny X-Men* #205
....1.50 0.30 0.90 1.50
❏ 110, Aug 95, reprints *Uncanny X-Men* #206;final issue
....1.50 0.30 0.90 1.50

X-MEN CLASSICS
❏ 1, Dec 83, reprint............2.00 0.50 1.50 2.50
❏ 2, Jan 84, reprint 2.00 0.50 1.50 2.50
❏ 3, Feb 84, reprint 2.00 0.50 1.50 2.50

X-MEN COLLECTOR'S EDITION
❏ 2, Pizza Hut giveaway in 1993; contains fold-out poster
cover................................. 0.30 0.90 1.50

X-MEN FIRSTS
❏ 1, Feb 96, reprints *Avengers Annual* #10, *Uncanny X-Men*
#221 and 266, and *Incredible Hulk* #181
......................................4.95 0.99 2.97 4.95

X-MEN OMEGA
❏ 0, Jun 95, enhanced wraparound cover
....3.95 1.50 4.50 7.50
❏ 0, gold edition.................. 8.00 24.00 40.00

X-MEN POSTER MAGAZINE
❏ 1, 92 ....4.95 0.99 2.97 4.95

	ORIG.	GOOD	FINE	N-MINT
2, 93	4.95	0.99	2.97	4.95
3, 94	4.95	0.99	2.97	4.95
4, 95, wraparound cover	4.95	0.99	2.97	4.95

X-MEN PRIME

	ORIG.	GOOD	FINE	N-MINT
0, Jul 95, enhanced wraparound cover with acetate overlay	4.95	1.20	3.60	6.00

X-MEN SPECIAL EDITION (1982)

	ORIG.	GOOD	FINE	N-MINT
1, reprint	2.00	0.40	1.20	2.00

X-MEN SPOTLIGHT ON THE STARJAMMERS

	ORIG.	GOOD	FINE	N-MINT
1, May 90, DC	2.50	0.90	2.70	4.50
2, Jun 90, DC	2.50	0.90	2.70	4.50

X-MEN ULTRA III PREVIEW

	ORIG.	GOOD	FINE	N-MINT
0, Nov 95, nn;enhanced cardstock cover;previews Fleer card art	2.95	0.59	1.77	2.95

X-MEN UNLIMITED

	ORIG.	GOOD	FINE	N-MINT
1	3.95	2.00	6.00	10.00
2	3.95	0.79	2.37	3.95
3	3.95	0.79	2.37	3.95
4	3.95	0.79	2.37	3.95
5, Jun 94	3.95	0.79	2.37	3.95
6, Sep 94	3.95	0.79	2.37	3.95
7, Dec 94	3.95	0.79	2.37	3.95
8, Oct 95	3.95	0.79	2.37	3.95
9, Dec 95	3.95	0.79	2.37	3.95
10, Mar 96, "Age of Apocalypse" Beast imprisons and replaces "real" Beast	3.95	0.79	2.37	3.95

X-MEN VS. DRACULA

	ORIG.	GOOD	FINE	N-MINT
1, reprint	1.75	0.35	1.05	1.75

X-MEN VS. THE AVENGERS

	ORIG.	GOOD	FINE	N-MINT
1, Apr 87	1.50	0.30	0.90	1.50
2, May 87	1.50	0.30	0.90	1.50
3, Jun 87	1.50	0.30	0.90	1.50
4, Jul 87	1.50	0.30	0.90	1.50

X-MEN/ALPHA FLIGHT

	ORIG.	GOOD	FINE	N-MINT
1, Dec 85	1.50	0.80	2.40	4.00
2, Feb 86	1.50	0.80	2.40	4.00

X-MEN/MICRONAUTS

	ORIG.	GOOD	FINE	N-MINT
1, Jan 84, BG, Limited Series	0.60	0.60	1.80	3.00
2, Feb 84	0.60	0.40	1.20	2.00
3, Mar 84	0.60	0.40	1.20	2.00
4, Apr 84	0.60	0.40	1.20	2.00

X-MEN: BOOKS OF ASKANI

	ORIG.	GOOD	FINE	N-MINT
1, 95, wraparound cardstock cover	2.95	0.59	1.77	2.95

X-MEN: SURVIVAL GUIDE TO THE MANSION

	ORIG.	GOOD	FINE	N-MINT
0		2.00	6.00	10.00

X-MEN: THE EARLY YEARS

	ORIG.	GOOD	FINE	N-MINT
1, May 94, reprints X-Men (1st series) #1;O:X-Men	1.50	0.30	0.90	1.50
2, Jun 94, reprints X-Men (1st series) #2	1.50	0.30	0.90	1.50
3, Jul 94, reprints X-Men (1st series) #3	1.50	0.30	0.90	1.50
4, Aug 94, reprints X-Men (1st series) #4	1.50	0.30	0.90	1.50
5, Sep 94, reprints X-Men (1st series) #5	1.50	0.30	0.90	1.50
6, Oct 94, reprints X-Men (1st series) #6	1.50	0.30	0.90	1.50
7, Nov 94, reprints X-Men (1st series) #7	1.50	0.30	0.90	1.50
8, Dec 94, reprints X-Men (1st series) #8	1.50	0.30	0.90	1.50
9, Jan 95, reprints X-Men (1st series) #9	1.50	0.30	0.90	1.50
10, Feb 95, reprints X-Men (1st series) #10	1.50	0.30	0.90	1.50
11, Mar 95, reprints X-Men (1st series) #11	1.50	0.30	0.90	1.50
12, Apr 95, reprints X-Men (1st series) #12	1.50	0.30	0.90	1.50
13, May 95, reprints X-Men (1st series) #13	1.50	0.30	0.90	1.50
14, Jun 95, reprints X-Men (1st series) #14	1.50	0.30	0.90	1.50
15, Jul 95, reprints X-Men (1st series) #15	1.50	0.30	0.90	1.50
16, Aug 95, reprints X-Men (1st series) #16	1.50	0.30	0.90	1.50
17, Sep 95, reprints X-Men (1st series) #17 and 18;final issue	2.50	0.50	1.50	2.50

X-MEN: THE ULTRA COLLECTION (mini-series)

	ORIG.	GOOD	FINE	N-MINT
1, Dec 94, reprints card art	2.95	0.59	1.77	2.95
2, Jan 95, reprints card art	2.95	0.59	1.77	2.95
3, Feb 95, reprints card art	2.95	0.59	1.77	2.95
4, Mar 95, reprints card art	2.95	0.59	1.77	2.95
5, Apr 95, reprints card art	2.95	0.59	1.77	2.95

X-MEN: THE WEDDING ALBUM

	ORIG.	GOOD	FINE	N-MINT
0	2.95	0.59	1.77	2.95

X-MEN: WRATH OF APOCALYPSE

	ORIG.	GOOD	FINE	N-MINT
1, Feb 96, reprints X-Factor #65-68	4.95	0.99	2.97	4.95

X-MEN: YEAR OF THE MUTANTS COLLECTOR'S PREVIEW

	ORIG.	GOOD	FINE	N-MINT
1, Feb 95, one-shot	1.95	0.39	1.17	1.95

X-NATION 2099

	ORIG.	GOOD	FINE	N-MINT
1, Mar 96, enhanced wraparound cardstock cover	3.95	0.79	2.37	3.95
2, Apr 96	1.95	0.39	1.17	1.95
3, May 96	1.95	0.39	1.17	1.95
4, Jun 96	1.95	0.39	1.17	1.95

X-O MANOWAR
ACCLAIM/VALIANT

	ORIG.	GOOD	FINE	N-MINT
43, Jun 95	2.25	0.45	1.35	2.25
44, Jul 95	2.50	0.50	1.50	2.50
45, Jul 95	2.50	0.50	1.50	2.50
46, Aug 95	2.50	0.50	1.50	2.50
47, Aug 95, D:Ken Clarkson	2.50	0.50	1.50	2.50
48, Sep 95	2.50	0.50	1.50	2.50
49, Sep 95	2.50	0.50	1.50	2.50
50, Oct 95, -X; cover forms diptych with X-O Manowar #50-O	2.50	0.50	1.50	2.50
50, Oct 95, -O; cover forms diptych with X-O Manowar #50-X	2.50	0.50	1.50	2.50
51, Nov 95	2.50	0.50	1.50	2.50
52, Nov 95	2.50	0.50	1.50	2.50
53, Dec 95	2.50	0.50	1.50	2.50
54, Dec 95	2.50	0.50	1.50	2.50
55, Jan 96	2.50	0.50	1.50	2.50
56, Jan 96	2.50	0.50	1.50	2.50
57, Feb 96	2.50	0.50	1.50	2.50
58, Feb 96	2.50	0.50	1.50	2.50
59, Mar 96	2.50	0.50	1.50	2.50
61, Apr 96	2.50	0.50	1.50	2.50
63, May 96, Master Darque acquires X-O armor	2.50	0.50	1.50	2.50
64, May 96, D:Master Darque	2.50	0.50	1.50	2.50
65, Jun 96	2.50	0.50	1.50	2.50
66, Jul 96, D:Ax, Gamin;Aric's armor rebels	2.50	0.50	1.50	2.50

	ORIG.	GOOD	FINE	N-MINT

VALIANT

	ORIG.	GOOD	FINE	N-MINT
☐ 0, Aug 93, chromium cover 3.50		0.70	2.10	3.50
☐ 0, chromium cover, gold logo edition	3.00	9.00	15.00
☐ 1, Feb 92 .... 1.95		1.60	4.80	8.00
☐ 2, Mar 92 .... 1.95		1.20	3.60	6.00
☐ 3, Apr 92 .... 1.95		1.20	3.60	6.00
☐ 4, May 92 .... 1.95		1.00	3.00	5.00
☐ 5, Jun 92 .... 1.95		1.00	3.00	5.00
☐ 6, Jul 92 .... 2.25		0.80	2.40	4.00
☐ 7, Aug 92, FM(c) Unity ... 2.25		0.80	2.40	4.00
☐ 8, Sep 92, WS(c) Unity .. 2.25		0.80	2.40	4.00
☐ 9, Oct 92 .... 2.25		0.80	2.40	4.00
☐ 10, Nov 92 .... 2.25		0.80	2.40	4.00
☐ 11, Dec 92 .... 2.25		0.60	1.80	3.00
☐ 12, Jan 93 .... 2.25		0.60	1.80	3.00
☐ 13, Feb 93 .... 2.25		0.60	1.80	3.00
☐ 14, Mar 93, Turok 2.25		0.60	1.80	3.00
☐ 15, Apr 93 .... 2.25		0.60	1.80	3.00
☐ 16, May 93 .... 2.25		0.60	1.80	3.00
☐ 17, Jun 93 .... 2.25		0.60	1.80	3.00
☐ 18, Jul 93 .... 2.25		0.60	1.80	3.00
☐ 19, Aug 93 .... 2.25		0.60	1.80	3.00
☐ 20, Sep 93 .... 2.25		0.60	1.80	3.00
☐ 21, Oct 93 .... 2.25		0.45	1.35	2.25
☐ 22, Nov 93 .... 2.25		0.45	1.35	2.25
☐ 23, Dec 93 .... 2.25		0.45	1.35	2.25
☐ 24, Jan 94 .... 2.25		0.45	1.35	2.25
☐ 25, Feb 94, with *Armorines* #0 .... 3.50		0.70	2.10	3.50
☐ 26, Mar 94 .... 2.25		0.45	1.35	2.25
☐ 27, Apr 94, C:Turok 2.25		0.45	1.35	2.25
☐ 28, May 94, trading card 2.25		0.45	1.35	2.25
☐ 29, Jun 94, C:Turok ... 2.25		0.45	1.35	2.25
☐ 30, Aug 94, A:Solar 2.25		0.45	1.35	2.25
☐ 31, Sep 94 .... 2.25		0.45	1.35	2.25
☐ 33, Nov 94 .... 2.25		0.45	1.35	2.25
☐ 34, Dec 94 .... 2.25		0.45	1.35	2.25
☐ 35, Jan 95 .... 2.25		0.45	1.35	2.25
☐ 36, Feb 95 .... 2.25		0.45	1.35	2.25
☐ 37, Mar 95 .... 2.25		0.45	1.35	2.25
☐ 38, Mar 95 .... 2.25		0.45	1.35	2.25
☐ 39, Mar 95 .... 2.25		0.45	1.35	2.25
☐ 40, Mar 95 .... 2.25		0.45	1.35	2.25
☐ 41, Apr 95 .... 2.25		0.45	1.35	2.25
☐ 42, May 95, contains Birthquake preview 2.25		0.45	1.35	2.25
☐ 51, Nov 95 .... 2.50		0.50	1.50	2.50

X-O MANOWAR YEARBOOK

	ORIG.	GOOD	FINE	N-MINT
☐ 1, Apr 95 .... 2.95		0.59	1.77	2.95

X-PATROL
MARVEL/AMALGAM

	ORIG.	GOOD	FINE	N-MINT
☐ 1, Apr 96 .... 1.95		0.39	1.17	1.95

X-TERMINATORS
MARVEL

	ORIG.	GOOD	FINE	N-MINT
☐ 1, Oct 88, Inferno 1.00		0.80	2.40	4.00
☐ 2, Nov 88, Inferno 1.00		0.50	1.50	2.50
☐ 3, Dec 88, Inferno 1.00		0.50	1.50	2.50
☐ 4, Jan 89, Inferno 1.00		0.50	1.50	2.50

X-THIEVES GRAPHIC ALBUM
COMICS INTERVIEW

	ORIG.	GOOD	FINE	N-MINT
☐ 3, b&w rep.		1.39	4.17	6.95
☐ 4, b&w rep.		1.39	4.17	6.95

X-TV
COMIC ZONE

	ORIG.	GOOD	FINE	N-MINT
☐ 1, adult, b&w		0.59	1.77	2.95
☐ 2, adult, b&w		0.59	1.77	2.95

X-UNIVERSE
MARVEL

	ORIG.	GOOD	FINE	N-MINT
☐ 1, May 95, enhanced cardstock cover 3.50		1.40	4.20	7.00
☐ 2, Jun 95, enhanced cover 3.50		1.20	3.60	6.00

X: ONE SHOT TO THE HEAD
DARK HORSE

	ORIG.	GOOD	FINE	N-MINT
☐ 0, Aug 94, one-shot 2.50		0.50	1.50	2.50

XANADU
3-D ZONE

	ORIG.	GOOD	FINE	N-MINT
☐ 1, b&w		0.40	1.20	2.00
☐ 2, b&w		0.40	1.20	2.00
☐ 3, b&w		0.40	1.20	2.00
☐ 4, b&w		0.40	1.20	2.00

XANADU COLOR SPECIAL
ECLIPSE

	ORIG.	GOOD	FINE	N-MINT
☐ 1, rep.		0.40	1.20	2.00

XANADU: ACROSS DIAMOND SEAS
MU PRESS

	ORIG.	GOOD	FINE	N-MINT
☐ 1, b&w 2.50		0.50	1.50	2.50
☐ 2, Feb 94, b&w 2.50		0.50	1.50	2.50
☐ 3, Mar 94, b&w 2.50		0.50	1.50	2.50
☐ 4, Apr 94, b&w 2.50		0.50	1.50	2.50
☐ 5, May 94, b&w 2.95		0.59	1.77	2.95

XENO-MEN
BLACKTHORNE

	ORIG.	GOOD	FINE	N-MINT
☐ 1, 89, I:Xeno-Men		0.35	1.05	1.75

XENOBROOD
DC

	ORIG.	GOOD	FINE	N-MINT
☐ 0, Oct 94 .... 1.50		0.30	0.90	1.50
☐ 1, Nov 94 .... 1.50		0.30	0.90	1.50
☐ 2, Dec 94 .... 1.50		0.30	0.90	1.50
☐ 3, Jan 95 .... 1.50		0.30	0.90	1.50
☐ 4, Feb 95 .... 1.50		0.30	0.90	1.50
☐ 5, Mar 95 .... 1.50		0.30	0.90	1.50
☐ 6, Apr 95 .... 1.50		0.30	0.90	1.50

XENON
ECLIPSE

	ORIG.	GOOD	FINE	N-MINT
☐ 1, Japanese b&w		0.30	0.90	1.50
☐ 2, Japanese b&w		0.30	0.90	1.50
☐ 3, Japanese b&w		0.30	0.90	1.50
☐ 4, Japanese b&w		0.30	0.90	1.50
☐ 5, Japanese b&w		0.30	0.90	1.50
☐ 6, Japanese b&w		0.30	0.90	1.50
☐ 7, Japanese b&w		0.30	0.90	1.50
☐ 8, Japanese b&w		0.30	0.90	1.50
☐ 9, Japanese b&w		0.30	0.90	1.50
☐ 10, Japanese b&w		0.30	0.90	1.50
☐ 11, Japanese b&w		0.30	0.90	1.50
☐ 12, Japanese b&w		0.30	0.90	1.50
☐ 13, Japanese b&w		0.30	0.90	1.50
☐ 14, Japanese b&w		0.30	0.90	1.50
☐ 15, Japanese b&w		0.30	0.90	1.50
☐ 16, Japanese b&w		0.30	0.90	1.50
☐ 17, Japanese b&w		0.30	0.90	1.50
☐ 18, Japanese b&w		0.30	0.90	1.50
☐ 19, Japanese b&w		0.30	0.90	1.50
☐ 20, Japanese b&w		0.30	0.90	1.50
☐ 21, Japanese b&w		0.30	0.90	1.50
☐ 22, Japanese b&w		0.30	0.90	1.50
☐ 23, Japanese b&w		0.30	0.90	1.50

XENOTECH
MIRAGE

	ORIG.	GOOD	FINE	N-MINT
☐ 1, Aug 94 .... 2.75		0.55	1.65	2.75

MIRAGE/NEXT

	ORIG.	GOOD	FINE	N-MINT
☐ 1 .... 2.75		0.55	1.65	2.75
☐ 2, Oct 94 .... 2.75		0.55	1.65	2.75

	ORIG.	GOOD	FINE	N-MINT
XENOZOIC TALES				
KITCHEN SINK				
☐ 1, Feb 87, (1st printing)	2.00	1.00	3.00	5.00
☐ 1, (2nd printing)	2.00	0.40	1.20	2.00
☐ 2		0.60	1.80	3.00
☐ 3		0.60	1.80	3.00
☐ 4		0.60	1.80	3.00
☐ 5		0.40	1.20	2.00
☐ 6		0.40	1.20	2.00
☐ 7		0.40	1.20	2.00
☐ 8		0.40	1.20	2.00
☐ 9		0.40	1.20	2.00
☐ 10		0.40	1.20	2.00
☐ 11		0.40	1.20	2.00
XENYA				
SANCTUARY				
☐ 1	2.95	0.59	1.77	2.95
XIMOS: VIOLENT PAST				
TRIUMPHANT				
☐ 1, Mar 94	2.50	0.50	1.50	2.50
☐ 2, Mar 94	2.50	0.50	1.50	2.50
XIOLA				
XERO				
☐ 1, b&w	1.95	0.39	1.17	1.95
☐ 2, b&w	1.95	0.39	1.17	1.95
XIOLA PREVIEW EDITION				
☐ 0, 94, b&w, no cover price				
XL				
BLACKTHORNE				
☐ 1, 89, b&w		0.70	2.10	3.50
XOMBI				
DC/MILESTONE				
☐ 0, Jan 94, Shadow War	1.95	0.39	1.17	1.95
☐ 1, Jun 94	1.75	0.35	1.05	1.75
☐ 1, platinum cover		3.00	9.00	15.00
☐ 2, Jul 94	1.75	0.35	1.05	1.75
☐ 3, Aug 94	1.75	0.35	1.05	1.75
☐ 4, Sep 94	1.75	0.35	1.05	1.75
☐ 5, Oct 94	1.75	0.35	1.05	1.75
☐ 6, Nov 94	1.75	0.35	1.05	1.75
☐ 7, Dec 94	1.75	0.35	1.05	1.75

	ORIG.	GOOD	FINE	N-MINT
☐ 8, Jan 95	1.75	0.35	1.05	1.75
☐ 9, Feb 95	1.75	0.35	1.05	1.75
☐ 10, Mar 95	1.75	0.35	1.05	1.75
☐ 11, Apr 95	1.75	0.35	1.05	1.75
☐ 12, May 95	1.75	0.35	1.05	1.75
☐ 13, Jun 95	1.75	0.35	1.05	1.75
☐ 14, Jul 95	2.50	0.50	1.50	2.50
☐ 15, Aug 95	2.50	0.50	1.50	2.50
☐ 16, Sep 95	2.50	0.50	1.50	2.50
☐ 17, Oct 95	0.99	0.20	0.59	0.99
☐ 18, Nov 95	2.50	0.50	1.50	2.50
☐ 19, Dec 95	2.50	0.50	1.50	2.50
☐ 20, Jan 96	2.50	0.50	1.50	2.50
☐ 21, Feb 96, final issue	3.50	0.70	2.10	3.50
XXX WOMEN				
EROS				
☐ 1, adult, b&w	2.95	0.59	1.77	2.95
☐ 2, adult, b&w	2.95	0.59	1.77	2.95
☐ 3, adult, b&w	2.95	0.59	1.77	2.95
☐ 4, adult, b&w	2.95	0.59	1.77	2.95
XXXENOPHILE				
PALLIARD				
☐ 1, 1st printing, adult, b&w	1.60	4.80	8.00	
☐ 2, 2nd printing, adult		0.50	1.50	2.50
☐ 2, b&w, adult		1.00	3.00	5.00
☐ 3, b&w, adult		0.60	1.80	3.00
☐ 4, b&w, adult		0.60	1.80	3.00
☐ 5	2.95	0.59	1.77	2.95
☐ 6, adult, b&w	2.95	0.59	1.77	2.95
☐ 7, adult, b&w	2.95	0.59	1.77	2.95
☐ 8, adult, b&w	2.95	0.59	1.77	2.95
☐ 9, adult, b&w	2.95	0.59	1.77	2.95
XXXENOPHILE PRESENTS				
☐ 3, Aug 94, adults;b&w;"Utopia Unlimited" Part 1				
	2.95	0.59	1.77	2.95
☐ 4, Jul 95, adults;b&w;"Incubus" Part 2				
	2.95	0.59	1.77	2.95
XYZ COMICS				
KITCHEN SINK				
☐ 0, nn;sixth printing;b&w;adults;R. Crumb				
	2.95	0.59	1.77	2.95

X-O Manowar

In one of Valiant's earliest comics series, Aric Dacia, a Visigoth, was kidnapped by spider-like aliens and taken aboard their spaceship as a slave in an early century A.D. He eventually managed to escape from his alien captors when their ship returned to our solar system and stole their most advanced class of combat armor in the process.

The X-O Manowar class armor formed a psychic bond with its user. Dacia called it "good skin" and eventually it taught him much of what he needed to know about 20th-century Earth, such as language and customs. It also enabled him, through the use of its sophisticated weaponry and computer-hacking skills, to take over Orb Industries, a front corporation the spider-aliens were using to take over Earth.

Dacia was assisted in his battle against the aliens by Solar and Harbinger. He later met the other Valiant heroes during Unity, the company's first crossover.

Dacia was severely injured during one of the battles of Unity to such an extent that he had to remain in the X-O armor for a number of years to allow it to repair all the damage.

Due to the temporal displacement following Unity, Dacia found himself back among his own tribe of Visigoths. Unfortunately, he found that his 20th-century experiences has altered his perceptions to the point at which he no longer agreed with his tribe's viewpoints. Eventually, he put himself into a state of suspended animation to return to the 20th century.

After his return to the 20th century, Dacia found that he was losing control of both Orb Industries and the X-O armor itself. The armor had been infected by the spider aliens with a virus that finally destroyed it. Solar then flew to another planet to retrieve a seed that the X-O armor had laid before its demise and used the seed to create a new suit of armor for Dacia. The new suit eventually rebelled and took on a life of its own, as the first series ended.

Acclaim is in the process of revamping the series as this book goes to press.

Y

	ORIG.	GOOD	FINE	N-MINT
YAHOO				
FANTAGRAPHICS				
❏ 1, b&w		0.40	1.20	2.00
❏ 2		0.45	1.35	2.25
❏ 3		0.40	1.20	2.00
❏ 4		0.50	1.50	2.50
❏ 5		0.50	1.50	2.50
❏ 6		0.50	1.50	2.50
YAKUZA				
ETERNITY				
❏ 1		0.39	1.17	1.95
❏ 2		0.39	1.17	1.95
❏ 3		0.39	1.17	1.95
❏ 4		0.39	1.17	1.95
YARN MAN				
KITCHEN SINK				
❏ 1, Oct 89, b&w.............		0.40	1.20	2.00
YAWN				
PARODY				
❏ 1, b&w, Spawn parody, first printing				
...........................2.50		0.50	1.50	2.50
❏ 1, b&w, Spawn parody,second printing				
...........................2.50		0.50	1.50	2.50
YIN FEI THE CHINESE NINJA				
DR. LEUNG'S				
❏ 1		0.36	1.08	1.80
❏ 2		0.36	1.08	1.80
❏ 3		0.36	1.08	1.80
❏ 4		0.36	1.08	1.80
❏ 5		0.36	1.08	1.80
❏ 6		0.36	1.08	1.80
YOGI BEAR				
HARVEY				
❏ 1 ....1.25		0.25	0.75	1.25
❏ 2 ....1.25		0.25	0.75	1.25
❏ 3 ....1.25		0.25	0.75	1.25
❏ 4 ....1.25		0.25	0.75	1.25
❏ 5 ....1.50		0.30	0.90	1.50
❏ 6 ....1.50		0.30	0.90	1.50
YOGI BEAR BIG BOOK				
❏ 1		0.39	1.17	1.95
❏ 2		0.39	1.17	1.95
YOGI BEAR GIANT SIZE				
❏ 2		0.45	1.35	2.25
YOU AND YOUR BIG MOUTH				
FANTAGRAPHICS				
❏ 4, Aug 94,b&w anthology				
...........................2.50		0.50	1.50	2.50
YOU'RE UNDER ARREST! (mini-series)				
DARK HORSE/MANGA				
❏ 1, Dec 95, b&w 2.95		0.59	1.77	2.95
❏ 3, Feb 96, b&w 2.95		0.59	1.77	2.95
❏ 5, Apr 96, b&w 2.95		0.59	1.77	2.95
❏ 6, May 96, b&w 2.95		0.59	1.77	2.95
YOUNG ALL-STARS				
DC				
❏ 1, Jun 87 ....1.00		0.20	0.60	1.00
❏ 2, Jul 87 ....1.00		0.20	0.60	1.00
❏ 3, Aug 87 ....1.00		0.20	0.60	1.00
❏ 4, Sep 87 ....1.00		0.20	0.60	1.00
❏ 5, Oct 87 ....1.00		0.20	0.60	1.00
❏ 6, Nov 87 ....1.00		0.20	0.60	1.00
❏ 7, Dec 87 ....1.25		0.25	0.75	1.25
❏ 8, Jan 88, Millennium ...1.25		0.25	0.75	1.25
❏ 9, Feb 88, Millennium 1.25		0.25	0.75	1.25
❏ 10, Mar 88,O:Iron Munro.				
...........................1.25		0.25	0.75	1.25

	ORIG.	GOOD	FINE	N-MINT
❏ 11, Apr 88, O:Iron Munro				
...........................1.25		0.25	0.75	1.25
❏ 12, May 88...............1.25		0.25	0.75	1.25
❏ 13, Jun 88...............1.25		0.25	0.75	1.25
❏ 14, Jul 88...............1.25		0.25	0.75	1.25
❏ 15, Aug 88...............1.25		0.25	0.75	1.25
❏ 16, Sep 88, Dzyan Inheritance				
...........................1.25		0.25	0.75	1.25
❏ 17, Oct 88, Dzyan Inheritance				
...........................1.25		0.25	0.75	1.25
❏ 18, Nov 88, Dzyan Inheritance				
...........................1.25		0.25	0.75	1.25
❏ 19, Dec 88, Dzyan...........1.50		0.30	0.90	1.50
❏ 20, Dec 88, O:Flying Fox.1.50		0.30	0.90	1.50
❏ 21, Jan 88, Atom & Evil..1.50		0.30	0.90	1.50
❏ 22, Jan 89, Atom & Evil..1.50		0.30	0.90	1.50
❏ 23, Mar 89, Atom & Evil.1.50		0.30	0.90	1.50
❏ 24, Apr 89, Atom & Evil..1.50		0.30	0.90	1.50
❏ 25, May 89, Atom & Evil.1.50		0.30	0.90	1.50
❏ 26, Jun 89 ....1.75		0.35	1.05	1.75
❏ 27, Jul 89...............1.75		0.35	1.05	1.75
❏ 28, Aug 89...............1.75		0.35	1.05	1.75
❏ 29, Sep 89...............1.75		0.35	1.05	1.75
❏ 30, Oct 89...............1.75		0.35	1.05	1.75
❏ 31, Nov 89...............1.75		0.35	1.05	1.75
YOUNG ALL-STARS ANNUAL				
❏ 1, 88, A:Infinity, Inc. 2.00		0.40	1.20	2.00
YOUNG CYNICS CLUB, THE				
DARK HORSE				
❏ 0, nn, b&w...............2.50		0.50	1.50	2.50
YOUNG DEATH				
FLEETWAY/QUALITY				
❏ 1 ....2.95		0.59	1.77	2.95
❏ 2 ....2.95		0.59	1.77	2.95
❏ 3 ....2.95		0.59	1.77	2.95
YOUNG DRACULA				
CALIBER				
❏ 1, 92, b&w...............3.50		0.70	2.10	3.50
❏ 2, 93, b&w...............3.50		0.70	2.10	3.50
❏ 3, 93, b&w;indicia says #2				
...........................3.50		0.70	2.10	3.50
YOUNG GUN				
AC				
❏ 1, 92, b&w...............2.95		0.59	1.77	2.95
YOUNG HERO				
❏ 1, Dec 89, b&w rep.......2.50		0.50	1.50	2.50
❏ 2, Aug 90, b&w reprint ...2.75		0.55	1.65	2.75
YOUNG INDIANA JONES CHRONICLES				
DARK HORSE				
❏ 1 ....2.50		0.50	1.50	2.50
❏ 2 ....2.50		0.50	1.50	2.50
❏ 3 ....2.50		0.50	1.50	2.50
❏ 4 ....2.50		0.50	1.50	2.50
❏ 5 ....2.50		0.50	1.50	2.50
❏ 6 ....2.50		0.50	1.50	2.50
❏ 7 ....2.50		0.50	1.50	2.50
❏ 8 ....2.50		0.50	1.50	2.50
❏ 9 ....2.50		0.50	1.50	2.50
❏ 10 ....2.50		0.50	1.50	2.50
❏ 11 ....2.50		0.50	1.50	2.50
❏ 12 ....2.50		0.50	1.50	2.50
YOUNG INDIANA JONES CHRONICLES, THE				
HOLLYWOOD				
❏ 1, reprints		0.79	2.37	3.95
❏ 2, reprints		0.79	2.37	3.95
❏ 3, reprints		0.79	2.37	3.95

	ORIG.	GOOD	FINE	N-MINT

YOUNG MASTER
NEW COMICS

	ORIG.	GOOD	FINE	N-MINT
☐ 1, b&w		0.35	1.05	1.75
☐ 2, b&w		0.35	1.05	1.75
☐ 3, b&w		0.35	1.05	1.75
☐ 4, b&w		0.35	1.05	1.75
☐ 5, b&w		0.35	1.05	1.75
☐ 6, b&w		0.35	1.05	1.75
☐ 7		0.39	1.17	1.95
☐ 8		0.39	1.17	1.95

YOUNG WITCHES, THE
EROS COMIX

	ORIG.	GOOD	FINE	N-MINT
☐ 1, adult, b&w		0.45	1.35	2.25
☐ 2, adult, b&w		0.45	1.35	2.25
☐ 3, adult, b&w		0.45	1.35	2.25
☐ 4		0.55	1.65	2.75

YOUNG ZEN INTERGALACTIC NINJA
EXPRESS/ENTITY

	ORIG.	GOOD	FINE	N-MINT
☐ 1, b&w, trading card	3.50	0.70	2.10	3.50
☐ 2, b&w	2.95	0.59	1.77	2.95

YOUNG ZEN: CITY OF DEATH

	ORIG.	GOOD	FINE	N-MINT
☐ 1, 94, b&w, cardstock cover				
	3.25	0.65	1.95	3.25

YOUNGBLOOD
IMAGE

	ORIG.	GOOD	FINE	N-MINT
☐ 0, RL		1.00	3.00	5.00
☐ 0, RL, gold		13.00	39.00	65.00
☐ 0, RL, gold signed		19.00	57.00	95.00
☐ 1, RL, trading card		1.60	4.80	8.00
☐ 1, (second printing)		0.80	2.40	4.00
☐ 2, RL		1.20	3.60	6.00
☐ 3, RL		0.80	2.40	4.00
☐ 4, RL	2.50	0.50	1.50	2.50
☐ 5, backed with *Brigade* #4				
	2.50	0.80	2.40	4.00
☐ 6, Jun 94	1.95	0.39	1.17	1.95
☐ 7, Jul 94	2.50	0.50	1.50	2.50
☐ 8, Sep 94	2.50	0.50	1.50	2.50
☐ 9, Sep 94	2.50	0.50	1.50	2.50
☐ 10, Dec 94, D:Chapel	2.50	0.70	2.10	3.50

YOUNGBLOOD (Vol. 2)

	ORIG.	GOOD	FINE	N-MINT
☐ 1, Sep 95	2.50	0.50	1.50	2.50
☐ 2, Oct 95	2.50	0.50	1.50	2.50
☐ 2, Oct 95,alternate cover				
	2.50	0.50	1.50	2.50
☐ 3, Nov 95, "Babewatch"	2.50	0.50	1.50	2.50
☐ 3, Nov 95, "Babewatch";alternate cover				
	2.50	0.50	1.50	2.50
☐ 4, Jan 96, "Extreme Destroyer" Part 4 of 9;polybagged				
with Riptide card	2.50	0.50	1.50	2.50
☐ 5, Feb 96, A:Jeriko	2.50	0.50	1.50	2.50
☐ 5, Feb 96, A:Jeriko;alternate cover				
	2.50	0.50	1.50	2.50
☐ 6, Mar 96,A:Angela and Glory				
	2.50	0.50	1.50	2.50
☐ 7, Apr 96, "Shadowhunt"				
	2.50	0.50	1.50	2.50

YOUNGBLOOD BATTLEZONE

	ORIG.	GOOD	FINE	N-MINT
☐ 1	1.95	0.39	1.17	1.95
☐ 2, Jul 94	2.95	0.59	1.77	2.95

YOUNGBLOOD STRIKEFILE

	ORIG.	GOOD	FINE	N-MINT
☐ 1, Apr 93, RL	2.50	0.50	1.50	2.50
☐ 1, RL, gold edition		5.00	15.00	25.00
☐ 2, RL, gold edition		5.00	15.00	25.00
☐ 2, Jul 93, RL	2.50	0.50	1.50	2.50
☐ 3, Sep 93	2.50	0.50	1.50	2.50
☐ 4, Oct 93	2.50	0.50	1.50	2.50
☐ 5, Jul 94	2.95	0.59	1.77	2.95
☐ 6, Aug 94	2.95	0.59	1.77	2.95
☐ 8, Nov 94, (cover says October)				
	2.95	0.59	1.77	2.95
☐ 9, Nov 94	2.50	0.50	1.50	2.50
☐ 10, Dec 94	2.50	0.50	1.50	2.50
☐ 11, Feb 95, Extreme Sacrifice;polybagged with card				
	2.50	0.50	1.50	2.50

YOUNGBLOOD YEARBOOK

	ORIG.	GOOD	FINE	N-MINT
☐ 1, Jul 93	2.50	0.50	1.50	2.50

YUMMY FUR
VORTEX

	ORIG.	GOOD	FINE	N-MINT
☐ 1, b&w		4.40	13.20	22.00
☐ 2, b&w		2.80	8.40	14.00
☐ 3, b&w		2.00	6.00	10.00
☐ 4, b&w		2.00	6.00	10.00
☐ 5, b&w		2.00	6.00	10.00
☐ 6, b&w		1.60	4.80	8.00
☐ 7, b&w		1.60	4.80	8.00
☐ 8, b&w		1.60	4.80	8.00
☐ 9, b&w		1.60	4.80	8.00
☐ 10, b&w		1.60	4.80	8.00
☐ 11, b&w		0.80	2.40	4.00
☐ 12, b&w		0.80	2.40	4.00
☐ 13, b&w		0.80	2.40	4.00
☐ 14, b&w		0.80	2.40	4.00
☐ 15, b&w		0.60	1.80	3.00
☐ 16		0.40	1.20	2.00
☐ 17		0.40	1.20	2.00
☐ 18		0.40	1.20	2.00
☐ 19		0.40	1.20	2.00
☐ 20		0.40	1.20	2.00
☐ 21		0.40	1.20	2.00
☐ 22		0.40	1.20	2.00
☐ 23, (moves to Drawn & Quarterly)				
		0.40	1.20	2.00

YUMMY FUR (was Vortex title)
DRAWN & QUARTERLY

	ORIG.	GOOD	FINE	N-MINT
☐ 25, adult, b&w	2.50	0.50	1.50	2.50
☐ 26, adult, b&w	2.50	0.50	1.50	2.50
☐ 27, adult, b&w	2.50	0.50	1.50	2.50
☐ 28, adult, b&w	2.50	0.50	1.50	2.50
☐ 29, adult, b&w	2.50	0.50	1.50	2.50
☐ 30, adult, b&w	2.50	0.50	1.50	2.50

YUPPIES FROM HELL
MARVEL

	ORIG.	GOOD	FINE	N-MINT
☐ 1, b&w	2.95	0.59	1.77	2.95
☐ 2, b&w, Son of...	2.95	0.59	1.77	2.95
☐ 3, b&w, Sex, Lies	2.95	0.59	1.77	2.95

Didja know?

Writer Roy Thomas reworked DC's *Superman vs. Wonder Woman* treasury-sized one-shot story to reflect post-Crisis changes to the DC universe (mainly the non-existence of a Golden Age Superman or Wonder Woman) as "Atom and Evil," a five-part storyline in *Young All-Stars* #21-25.

Young All-Stars was a 31-issue series that focused on the 1942 adventures of a group of young heroes who were introduced following events in *Crisis on Infinite Earths*. *Superman vs. Wonder Woman* had the duo attempting to protect the men responsible for building the atomic bomb during World War II.

Z

	ORIG.	GOOD	FINE	N-MINT
Z (mini-series)				
KEYSTONE GRAPHICS				
☐ 1, Nov 94, b&w	2.75	0.55	1.65	2.75
☐ 2, Jul 95, b&w	2.75	0.55	1.65	2.75
☐ 3, Nov 95, b&w	2.75	0.55	1.65	2.75
ZATANNA				
DC				
☐ 1	1.95	0.39	1.17	1.95
☐ 2	1.95	0.39	1.17	1.95
☐ 3	1.95	0.39	1.17	1.95
☐ 4	1.95	0.39	1.17	1.95
ZATANNA SPECIAL				
☐ 1, Apr 87, GM	2.00	0.40	1.20	2.00
ZEALOT				
IMAGE				
☐ 1, Aug 95	2.50	0.50	1.50	2.50
ZEALOT (mini-series)				
☐ 1, Aug 95	2.50	0.50	1.50	2.50
☐ 2, Oct 95	2.50	0.50	1.50	2.50
ZELL SWORDDANCER				
3-D ZONE				
☐ 1, b&w		0.40	1.20	2.00
THOUGHTS & IMAGES				
☐ 1, b&w		0.40	1.20	2.00
ZEN INTERGALACTIC NINJA				
EXPRESS/ENTITY				
☐ 0, 93, b&w, foil cover	2.95	0.59	1.77	2.95
☐ 0, 93, b&w, chromium cover	3.50	0.70	2.10	3.50
☐ 1, 93, b&w	2.95	0.59	1.77	2.95
☐ 2, 93, b&w	2.95	0.59	1.77	2.95
☐ 3, 93, b&w	2.95	0.59	1.77	2.95
ZEN INTERGALACTIC NINJA (mini-series)				
ARCHIE				
☐ 1, 92, Defend the Earth;color	1.25	0.25	0.75	1.25
☐ 2, 92, Defend the Earth;color	1.25	0.25	0.75	1.25
☐ 3, 92, Defend the Earth;color	1.25	0.25	0.75	1.25
ZEN INTERGALACTIC NINJA (regular series)				
☐ 1, Sep 92, color	1.25	0.25	0.75	1.25
☐ 2, Oct 92, color	1.25	0.25	0.75	1.25
☐ 3, Dec 92, color	1.25	0.25	0.75	1.25
ZEN INTERGALACTIC NINJA ASHCAN EDITION				
EXPRESS/ENTITY				
☐ 0, 94, b&w; no cover price; contains previews of *Zen: Hazardous Duty* and *Zen: Tour of the Universe*				
ZEN INTERGALACTIC NINJA COLOR				
☐ 1, 94, diecut foil cover	3.95	0.79	2.37	3.95
☐ 4, 94	2.50	0.50	1.50	2.50
☐ 5, 94	2.50	0.50	1.50	2.50
☐ 7, 95, enhanced cardstock cover; says #6a on cover, but #7 in indicia	2.95	0.59	1.77	2.95
ZEN INTERGALACTIC NINJA MILESTONE				
☐ 1, 94	2.95	0.59	1.77	2.95
ZEN INTERGALACTIC NINJA STARQUEST				
EXPRESS				
☐ 1, 94, b&w	2.95	0.59	1.77	2.95
☐ 2, 94, b&w	2.95	0.59	1.77	2.95
☐ 4, 94, b&w, cardstock cover	2.95	0.59	1.77	2.95
ZEN INTERGALACTIC NINJA SUMMER SPECIAL: VIDEO WARRIOR				
☐ 1, 94, b&w	2.95	0.59	1.77	2.95

	ORIG.	GOOD	FINE	N-MINT
ZEN INTERGALACTIC NINJA: TOUR OF THE UNIVERSE SPECIAL, THE AIRBRUSH ART OF DAN COTE				
EXPRESS/ENTITY				
☐ 1, 95, enhanced cardstock cover	3.95	0.79	2.37	3.95
ZEN INTERGALATIC NINJA COLOR (2nd series)				
☐ 2, 95	2.50	0.50	1.50	2.50
ZEN, INTERGALACTIC NINJA				
ZEN				
☐ 1, Nov 87, 1st printing, b&w	1.75	0.35	1.05	1.75
☐ 1, 2nd printing		0.40	1.20	2.00
☐ 2, 88, b&w	1.75	0.35	1.05	1.75
☐ 3, 88, b&w;1st printing	1.75	0.35	1.05	1.75
☐ 3, 2nd printing		0.40	1.20	2.00
☐ 4, 88, b&w	1.75	0.35	1.05	1.75
☐ 5, 88, b&w	1.75	0.35	1.05	1.75
☐ 6, 89, b&w	2.00	0.40	1.20	2.00
ZEN, INTERGALACTIC NINJA (Volume 2)				
☐ 1, 89, b&w	2.00	0.40	1.20	2.00
☐ 2, 89, b&w	2.00	0.40	1.20	2.00
☐ 3, 90, b&w	2.00	0.40	1.20	2.00
☐ 4, 90, b&w	2.00	0.40	1.20	2.00
ZEN, INTERGALACTIC NINJA (Volume 3)				
☐ 1, 91, b&w	2.25	0.45	1.35	2.25
☐ 2, 91, b&w	2.25	0.45	1.35	2.25
☐ 3, 91, b&w	2.25	0.45	1.35	2.25
☐ 4, 92, b&w	2.25	0.45	1.35	2.25
☐ 5, 92, b&w	2.25	0.45	1.35	2.25
ZEN, INTERGALACTIC NINJA CHRISTMAS SPECIAL				
☐ 1, 92, b&w	2.95	0.59	1.77	2.95
ZEN, INTERGALACTIC NINJA EARTH DAY ANNUAL				
☐ 0, 93, b&w	2.95	0.59	1.77	2.95
ZENITH: PHASE 1				
FLEETWAY/QUALITY				
☐ 1	1.95	0.39	1.17	1.95
☐ 2	1.95	0.39	1.17	1.95
☐ 3	1.95	0.39	1.17	1.95
ZENITH: PHASE II				
☐ 1	1.95	0.39	1.17	1.95
ZERO HOUR: CRISIS IN TIME (mini-series)				
DC				
☐ 0, (#5 of 5)	1.50	0.80	2.40	4.00
☐ 1, Sep 94, (#4 of 5)	1.50	0.60	1.80	3.00
☐ 2, Sep 94, (#3 of 5)	1.50	0.70	2.10	3.50
☐ 3, Sep 94, (#2 of 5)	1.50	0.70	2.10	3.50
☐ 4, Sep 94, (#1 of 5)	1.50	0.80	2.40	4.00
ZERO PATROL				
CONTINUITY				
☐ 1, NA		0.30	0.90	1.50
☐ 2, NA		0.30	0.90	1.50
ZERO PATROL (1987-)				
☐ 1, NA		0.40	1.20	2.00
☐ 2, NA		0.40	1.20	2.00
☐ 3, NA		0.40	1.20	2.00
☐ 4, NA		0.40	1.20	2.00
☐ 5, NA		0.40	1.20	2.00
ZERO TOLERANCE				
FIRST				
☐ 1, Tim Vigil		0.60	1.80	3.00
☐ 2, Tim Vigil		0.60	1.80	3.00
☐ 3, Vigil		0.45	1.35	2.25
☐ 4, Vigil		0.45	1.35	2.25

	ORIG.	GOOD	FINE	N-MINT

ZERO ZERO
FANTAGRAPHICS
☐ 4, Aug 95, nn in indicia or on cover, issue number determined by back cover cartoon;b&w anthology 3.95 0.79 2.37 3.95
☐ 5, Sep 95, nn in indicia or on cover, issue number determined by back cover cartoon;b&w anthology 3.95 0.79 2.37 3.95
☐ 8, Mar 96, nn in indicia or on cover, issue number determined by back cover cartoon;b&w anthology 5.95 1.19 3.57 5.95

ZETRAMAN
ANTARCTIC
☐ 1, Sep 91, b&w 1.95 0.39 1.17 1.95
☐ 2, Oct 91, b&w 1.95 0.39 1.17 1.95
☐ 3, Feb 92, b&w 1.95 0.39 1.17 1.95

ZETRAMAN 2: REVIVAL!
☐ 1, Oct 93 ...... 2.75 0.55 1.65 2.75
☐ 2, Dec 93 ...... 2.75 0.55 1.65 2.75
☐ 3, Aug 95 ...... 2.75 0.55 1.65 2.75

ZILLION
ETERNITY
☐ 1, b&w 2.50 0.50 1.50 2.50
☐ 2, b&w 2.50 0.50 1.50 2.50
☐ 3, b&w 2.50 0.50 1.50 2.50
☐ 4, b&w 2.50 0.50 1.50 2.50

ZIPPY QUARTERLY
FANTAGRAPHICS
☐ 1, b&w 4.95 0.99 2.97 4.95
☐ 2, b&w 4.95 0.99 2.97 4.95
☐ 3, strip reprints 3.50 0.70 2.10 3.50
☐ 4, strip reprints 3.50 0.70 2.10 3.50
☐ 5, strip reprints 3.50 0.70 2.10 3.50
☐ 7, Aug 94, b&w, strip reprints 3.50 0.70 2.10 3.50
☐ 8, Nov 94, b&w, strip reprints 3.50 0.70 2.10 3.50
☐ 12, Dec 95, b&w, strip reprints 3.95 0.79 2.37 3.95

ZOLASTRAYA AND THE BARD
TWILIGHT TWINS
☐ 1, b&w 0.34 1.02 1.70
☐ 2, b&w 0.34 1.02 1.70
☐ 3, b&w 0.34 1.02 1.70
☐ 4, b&w 0.34 1.02 1.70
☐ 5, b&w 0.34 1.02 1.70

ZOMBIE 3-D
3-D ZONE
☐ 0, nn 0.79 2.37 3.95

ZOMBIE BOY
TIMBUKTU
☐ 1 ...... 0.30 0.90 1.50

ZOMBIE BOY RISES AGAIN
☐ 1, Jan 94, b&w 2.50 0.50 1.50 2.50

ZOMBIE WAR
TUNDRA
☐ 1 ...... 0.70 2.10 3.50

ZOMBIE WAR (mini-series)
FANTACO
☐ 1, KEastman 3.50 0.70 2.10 3.50
☐ 2, KEastman 3.50 0.70 2.10 3.50

ZOMBIE WAR: EARTH MUST BE DESTROYED
☐ 1, b&w 2.95 0.59 1.77 2.95
☐ 1, trading card 3.95 0.79 2.37 3.95

☐ 2, b&w 2.95 0.59 1.77 2.95
☐ 3, 93, b&w 2.95 0.59 1.77 2.95
☐ 4, 94, b&w 2.95 0.59 1.77 2.95

ZOMOID ILLUSTORIES
3-D ZONE
☐ 1, b&w, not 3-D 0.50 1.50 2.50

ZONE
DARK HORSE
☐ 1, b&w 0.39 1.17 1.95

ZONE CONTINUUM (VOL. 1)
CALIBER
☐ 1, b&w 2.95 0.59 1.77 2.95
☐ 2, b&w 2.95 0.59 1.77 2.95

ZONE CONTINUUM (VOL. 2)
☐ 1, b&w 2.95 0.59 1.77 2.95
☐ 2, b&w 2.95 0.59 1.77 2.95

ZONE ZERO
PLANET BOY
☐ 1, b&w 2.95 0.59 1.77 2.95

ZOONIVERSE
ECLIPSE
☐ 1 ...... 0.25 0.75 1.25
☐ 2 ...... 0.25 0.75 1.25
☐ 3 ...... 0.25 0.75 1.25
☐ 4 ...... 0.25 0.75 1.25
☐ 5 ...... 0.35 1.05 1.75
☐ 6 ...... 0.35 1.05 1.75

ZOOT!
FANTAGRAPHICS
☐ 1, b&w 2.50 0.50 1.50 2.50
☐ 2, b&w 2.50 0.50 1.50 2.50
☐ 3, b&w 2.50 0.50 1.50 2.50
☐ 4, b&w 2.50 0.50 1.50 2.50
☐ 5, b&w 2.50 0.50 1.50 2.50
☐ 6, b&w 2.50 0.50 1.50 2.50

ZORANN: STAR WARRIOR
BLUE COMET
☐ 1, b&w 0.40 1.20 2.00

ZORI J'S 3-D BUBBLE BATH
3-D ZONE
☐ 0, nn b&w 3.95 0.79 2.37 3.95

ZORI J'S SUPER-SWELL BUBBLE BATH
ADVENTURE-OH BOY!
☐ 0, nn b&w 2.95 0.59 1.77 2.95

ZORRO
MARVEL
☐ 1 ...... 1.00 0.20 0.60 1.00
☐ 2 ...... 1.00 0.20 0.60 1.00
☐ 3 ...... 1.00 0.20 0.60 1.00
☐ 4 ...... 1.00 0.20 0.60 1.00
☐ 5 ...... 1.00 0.20 0.60 1.00
☐ 6 ...... 1.00 0.20 0.60 1.00
☐ 7 ...... 1.00 0.20 0.60 1.00
☐ 8 ...... 1.00 0.20 0.60 1.00
☐ 9 ...... 1.00 0.20 0.60 1.00
☐ 10, ATh(c) 1.00 0.20 0.60 1.00
☐ 11, ATh(c) 1.00 0.20 0.60 1.00
☐ 12, ATh(c) 1.00 0.20 0.60 1.00

TOPPS
☐ 0 ...... 1.00 1.50 4.50 7.50
☐ 1 ...... 2.50 0.50 1.50 2.50
☐ 2 ...... 2.50 1.00 3.00 5.00
☐ 3, Mar 94 ...... 2.50 4.40 13.20 22.00
☐ 4, Apr 94 ...... 2.50 0.60 1.80 3.00
☐ 5, May 94 ...... 2.50 0.60 1.80 3.00
☐ 6 ...... 2.50 1.60 4.80 8.00
☐ 7 ...... 2.50 1.20 3.60 6.00
☐ 8 ...... 2.50 0.50 1.50 2.50

	ORIG.	GOOD	FINE	N-MINT
9 .... 2.50		1.00	3.00	5.00
10 .... 2.50		1.00	3.00	5.00
11 .... 2.50		1.00	3.00	5.00

ZOT!
ECLIPSE

	ORIG.	GOOD	FINE	N-MINT
1, Apr 84, color 1.50		1.60	4.80	8.00
2, May 84 .... 1.50		1.00	3.00	5.00
3, Jun 84 .... 1.50		0.80	2.40	4.00
4, Jul 84 .... 1.50		0.80	2.40	4.00
5, Aug 84 .... 1.50		0.80	2.40	4.00
6, Nov 84 .... 1.50		0.80	2.40	4.00
7, Dec 84 .... 1.50		0.80	2.40	4.00
8, Mar 85 .... 1.50		0.80	2.40	4.00
9, May 85 .... 1.50		0.80	2.40	4.00
10, Jul 85, 1st printing... 1.50		2.00	6.00	10.00
10, 2nd printing		0.05	0.15	0.25
11, Jan 87 .... 2.00		0.40	1.20	2.00
12, Mar 87 .... 2.00		0.40	1.20	2.00
13, May 87 .... 2.00		0.40	1.20	2.00
14, Jul 87 .... 2.00		0.40	1.20	2.00
15, Oct 87 .... 2.00		0.40	1.20	2.00
16, Dec 87 .... 2.00		0.40	1.20	2.00
17, Feb 88 .... 2.00		0.40	1.20	2.00
18, Apr 88 .... 2.00		0.40	1.20	2.00
19, Jun 88 .... 2.00		0.40	1.20	2.00
20, Jun 88 .... 2.00		0.40	1.20	2.00
21, Aug 88 .... 2.00		0.40	1.20	2.00
22, Oct 88 .... 2.00		0.40	1.20	2.00
23, Nov 88 .... 2.00		0.40	1.20	2.00
24, Dec 88 .... 2.00		0.40	1.20	2.00

	ORIG.	GOOD	FINE	N-MINT
25, Feb 89 .... 2.00		0.40	1.20	2.00
26, Apr 89 .... 2.00		0.40	1.20	2.00
27, Jun 89 .... 2.00		0.40	1.20	2.00
28, Sep 89 .... 2.00		0.40	1.20	2.00
29, Dec 89 .... 2.00		0.40	1.20	2.00
30, Mar 90 .... 2.00		0.40	1.20	2.00
31, May 90 .... 2.00		0.40	1.20	2.00
32, Jul 90 .... 2.00		0.40	1.20	2.00
33, Oct 90 .... 2.00		0.40	1.20	2.00
34, Dec 90 .... 2.00		0.40	1.20	2.00
35, Mar 91 .... 2.00		0.40	1.20	2.00
36, Jul 91 .... 2.95		0.59	1.77	2.95

ZU
MU PRESS

	ORIG.	GOOD	FINE	N-MINT
0, Feb 92, nn;one-shot....3.95		0.79	2.37	3.95
1, Jan 95, b&w 2.95		0.59	1.77	2.95
2, Mar 95, b&w 2.95		0.59	1.77	2.95
3, May 95, b&w 2.95		0.59	1.77	2.95
4, Jul 95, b&w 2.95		0.59	1.77	2.95
5, Sep 95, b&w 2.95		0.59	1.77	2.95
7, Jan 96, b&w 2.95		0.59	1.77	2.95

ZULUNATION
TOME PRESS

	ORIG.	GOOD	FINE	N-MINT
1, b&w 2.95		0.59	1.77	2.95
2, b&w 2.95		0.59	1.77	2.95
3, b&w 2.95		0.59	1.77	2.95

ZWANNA, SON OF ZULU
DARK ZULU LIES

	ORIG.	GOOD	FINE	N-MINT
1 .... 1.95		0.39	1.17	1.95

Zot!

First appearance: *Zot!* #1, April 1984, Eclipse.

Creator Scott McCloud's 36-issue series chronicled the adventures of Jenny Weaver, a 13-year-old who longs to escape her boring, ordinary life, and Zachary T. Paleozogt, aka Zot, teen super-hero from another dimension.

The two met when Jenny witnessed Zot's arrival in the "real" world, in pursuit of destructive robots that were sent to our dimension in search of a stolen relic. After the robots were destroyed (with a life-saving assist from Jenny), Jenny and her brother, Butch, found the relic and followed Zot through the dimensional warp to his world — the far-flung future of 1965 (Jenny's from the '80s).

Zot's home is a near-utopian setting where the grand, optimistic predictions of the future have come true. Many of the villains Zot confronts are comic figures, like the Devolutionaries — although the group did succeed in turning Butch into a chimp, the effect goes away when he returns to his world). The tragic villain Artie Dekko and the sinister assassin 9-Jack-9, who killed Zot's parents, were darker elements within Zot's apparently perfect world.

The series struck a balance between lighthearted, action-filled adventures, in both Zot's world and Jenny's, and serious explorations of the characters' lives and the challenges and choices they face as they near adulthood. One run of issues, toward the end of the series, focused on the personal lives of several supporting characters,

Zot! #1 ©1984 Silver Linings (Eclipse)

Jenny's circle of friends at school.

The first 10 issues were published in color, the rest of the series in black and white. The series ended with unanswered questions — most notably, why is it *always* 1965 in Zot's dimension, and why is Jenny the only person who realizes this after attending New Year's celebrations there? However, McCloud has not ruled out returning to the series in the future, so the answers may yet be revealed.

After *Zot!*, McCloud went on to produce *Understanding Comics*, a volume which set out to define and explain comics and how they work, done in comics format.

Eclipse released a trade paperback collecting the early issues of *Zot!* in 1990, but a planned second volume was never released. In 1996, Kitchen Sink Press announced plans to collect the entire series in four volumes.